A MOMENT IN TIME
1995

Caroline Sullivan, Editor
Joy L. Esterby, Associate Editor

THE NATIONAL LIBRARY OF POETRY

A Moment in Time

Library of Congress
Cataloging in Publication Data

ISBN 1-56167-266-1

Proudly manufactured in the United States of America by
Watermark Press
11419 Cronridge Dr., Suite 10
Owings Mills, MD 21117

Editor's Note

It has been said that "to experience a poem fully, one must respond to it both emotionally and intellectually." Perhaps it is because of this ever-important interplay between writer and reader that poetry remains the most enigmatic of literary art forms. And though two readers may experience the same work with varying attitudes, it is the responsibility of the poet to evoke similar emotions from both, and in doing so, ensure these elicited emotions are consistent with the complexity of ideas portrayed. Although quite a formidable task, this feat was accomplished by many of the poets featured here in **A Moment in Time**.

Within these pages is a collection of poetry selected for publication through our North American Open Poetry Contest. The poems are so resplendent with ideas, images, and language that one will not merely read the words, but rather experience the works on aesthetic, literal, and emotional levels. The submission of so many fine works rendered the judges' endeavor almost impossible, but there were some poems which caught their attention and merit special recognition.

"Dorothy," by John Martin, is unique in this volume in that the poet uses terza rima to display his strong command of the English language. At first glance this form may not seem very difficult (*aba bcb cdc*...), but one soon realizes that to continue the pattern without stilting syntax and losing meaning to trite words is very difficult indeed.

The life she lived was like some gentle air
That rose like goldfinch from her violin.
She treated folk, like tunes, with tender care

Responded to with love by kith and kin;
Not only by her clan, but luckless those
For whom her touch went deeper than the skin.

Another example of a skillful use of poetic form is George Braman's English sonnet, "Orion Rising." The rhyming and use of iambic pentameter appear effortless, but like the terza rima, require a strong command of language.

In "Solace Unfathomed," Simon Legge culminates alliteration, assonance, internal rhyme, and end rhyme into a masterfully written poem:

Sweet solace, my solace, in bathos and bores,
sweep me to heavenly roars in my snores:
-- off to an elevatorial realm --
roundabout people asleep at the helm;
portulaca, pansies with primrose and greens:
Sweet solace, my solace, such picturesque dreams.

Ultimately, however, it was Scott Clair's submission of "Ode to John Keats" which was awarded the grand prize. This meditative piece, inspired by "Ode on a Grecian Urn," questions

Keats' ideas of truth and beauty. While Keats apostrophized the Grecian urn to conclude that "Beauty is truth, truth beauty, -- that is all / Ye know on earth, and all ye need to know," Clair apostrophizes Keats himself:

> *... But you have passed*
> *and leaving your song you have left those chaste,*
> *the critics, pursuing backward through your letters*
> *and terms in their breathless search, till at last*
>
> *One comes to hear you touch that ancient urn.*
> *Keats: Beauty, truth, are not for man.*

This work is remarkable both in its ideas and subtlety of rhyme.

I do wish I could comment on all the fine poems published here -- there are so many that, like the aforementioned, are unique, fresh, and skillfully crafted works. I congratulate all of you featured here and truly hope you enjoy reading **A Moment in Time**.

Caroline Sullivan, Senior Editor

Acknowledgements

The publication **A Moment in Time** is a culmination of the efforts of many individuals. Judges, editors, assistant editors, customer service representatives, typesetters, graphic artists, layout artists, and office administrators have all brought their respective talents to bear on this project. The editors are grateful for the contributions of these fine people:

Kim Albert, Elizabeth Barnes, Thomas C. Bussey, Amy Dezseran, Chrystal Eldridge, Joy Esterby, Andrea Felder, Jeffrey Franz, Ardie L. Freeman, Hope Goodwin Freeman, Kathryn Hudson-Frey, Paula Jones, John McDonough, Steve Miksek, Diane Mills, Eric Mueck, John J. Purcell III, Lamont A. Robinson, Rick Schaub, Michelle Shavitz, Jacqueline Spiwak, Cynthia Stevens, Nicole Walstrum, Ira Westreich, Tiffany Wilson, and Diana Zeiger.

Howard Ely, Managing Editor

Grand Prize

Scott Clair / Chicago, IL

Second Prize:

Robert W. Bates / Jersey City, NJ
George N. Braman / Bronx, NY
Ione T. Damasco / Dublin, OH
Monika Dykes / Folsom, CA
Kate Lowenstein / Boston, MA
Simon Alexander Legge / Toronto Ont. Canada
Kevin B. O'Connell / East Patchogue, NY
Vivienne Rowe / San Francisco, CA
R. Smith / Charlottetown PE. Canada
Molly Tennyson / Upper Darby, PA

Third Prize:

Elizabeth Andrews / Brooklyn, NY
Caitlin Barrett / Cambridge, MA
Paul C. Brodeur / Edmonton AB. Canada
Jennifer Bull / River Falls, WI
Kalyn Carjan / South Euclid, OH
Christopher H. Carlberg / Omaha, NE
Steven A. Coach / El Cajon, CA
Gesso Cocteau / Indian Wells, CA
James A. Donaldson / Albuquerque, NM
Lillian Donaldson / Casselberry, FL
Kevin T. Durkin / Oak Park, IL
Dorothy Fairweather / Tustin, CA
Joseph Grom Feinberg / Ravenna, OH
Rashbehari Ghosh / Dhanbad Bihar, India
Amy Goodrich / Laramie, WY
Sithy Hamid / Glendale, CA
Bernard Hardy / Weston Canberra, Australia
Catina Hatgipetros / Brooklyn, NY
Pendleton Herring / Princeton, NJ
Krista Hogg / College Station, TX
Karen E. Hughes / Adrian, PA
Marilyn Jackson / Niagara-On-The-Lake Ont. Canada
Penelope Jacques / Walnut Creek, CA
Duane F. Johnson / Fullerton, CA
Mark Francisco Jones / Berkeley, CA
Patricia Kelly / Linden Hill, NY
Roger O. Kent / Colgate, WI
John King-Farlow / Edmonton AB. Canada
Kenneth J. Lamberson / Bayside, NY
George B. Markle / Carlsbad, NM
Bruno Almaviva Marte / Paris, France
John Martin / Epsom Auckland, New Zealand
Patrick McNelly / Fullerton, CA
W. Scott Mishley / New York, NY
Douglas McLean Morrison / Sudbury Ont. Canada
Frank R. Nardone / Magnolia, NJ
Richard D. Newquist / Magnolia, NJ
Robert Norwood Jr. / Tacoma, WA
Raymond O'Connor / Miami, FL
Norma K. Pattavina / Omaha, NE
Bart Ezra Plaskoff / Dayton, NV
George Guntur A. Pajalta / Manila, Philippines
Barnabas J. Ramon-Fortune / Trinidad, West Indies
Bill C. Rogers / Carlsbad, CA
Leena Ronalds / Negara, Brunei
Ivan Roussetzki / Brooklyn, NY
John G. Royal / Tulsa, OK
David P. Ryan / Austin, TX
C. Samsel / Flushing, NY
Byron Shewman / San Diego, CA
Marie Shimane / Hikari-machi Sosa-gun Chiba, Japan
Edward S. Smith / Birmingham, AL
Gregory A. Smith / Nanaimo BC. Canada
Richard Smith / Beaumont, CA
Judi Billings Sparagna / Morgan Hill, CA
Patricia J. Tury / Henderson, NV
Peter F. Vaira / Newtown Square, PA
David Weldon / Charlottetown PE. Canada
David H. Wilson / Ada, MI

Grand Prize Winner

Ode To John Keats

In what silent land are you this pious morn
John Keats? Your silent tongue now speaks
to the sensual ear for ever, but your
burning forehead and heart high-sorrowful below
leave these two late lines for me to complete.

Why must I look at one quotation to know
all I need? Why is beauty first?
That still salvation has moved you to show
me this? O, that Bold Lover who can never taste
his lover's lips can never still your thirst!

"When old age shall this generation waste"
it is unchanged. But you have passed
and leaving your song you have left those chaste,
the critics, pursuing backward through your letters
and terms in their breathless search, till at last

One comes to hear you touch that ancient urn.
Keats: Beauty, truth, are not for man.
I come here young, and want to hear you turn
that attic shape, that cold pastoral with those shaped
men and maidens always breathing in your hands.

—Scott Clair

What Value Life

What value life, ferment from a gooey, primordial concoction
From the kindling of stars 12 billion years ago; this genetic mutation,
This conscious oddity of time, beating a zillion odds, O, gee!
This so called life has become ultimately ME.

At whose behest these births bring forth ancestral links of DNA,
These fleeting trials of organic existence come to play
Arrogant, callous and privileged; oppressed, resigned and poor;
Than perceived values of class, than vested attributes, life is more.

This conscious world of hopeless infirmity, of suffering, of pain
Makes abortionists, kevorkians among us seem compassionate
and sane;
But the innocent succumbs to judgment expedient, selfish, primitive,
Who must decide which death is impartial, which life is fit to live.

If the Universe we know in billions of years were to implode
Losing all civilization's gains, ending all evil and all good;
Why must man turn against brother, what intransigence so profound,
Let's waste no time to coexist in peace and face destiny we're all
bound.

When this freak sprout of time wilts, I should reflect
Have I helped other lives live as I did mine with dignity and respect;
Only then to those million other seeds and lost chances, could I
Be proud and say: Thank you. Life was worth a try!

Wilmo C. Orejola

A Moment In Tonga

What have we when a moment sings?
A delicate frangipani
wilts fragrantly
in the foreground
of a million different blues
overlaying a distant reef below.

And above,
wild hibiscus frame
a cloud-pinned sun
soon setting behind
a distant still dewy mountain
of a million textured greens.

And all the while
the coco-palms sway
to the lilting lullabies
of far off schoolgirls
and the southeast Trades
gently embracing

Now as before and forever
The Friendly Isles.

Richard T. Rauch

Mental Pictures

Letter box man bringing news of dread
A fragile psycho hangs by a thread
Full moon mourning greets the day
Hop scotch pavement wash away
Black cloud rain pouring down
A neurotic clock is tightly wound
The tic carries a deadly germ
A fish is fooled by a rubber worm
Oil covered gulls lay dead on the shore
Precious creatures will fly no more
Some are born with a silver spoon
Everything 'cept the sun and moon
A votive candle flickers a plea
Is any one up there listening to me?
A thousand birds take off in fear
Why they fly is not really clear
It must be something only they can hear
Could the enemy be near?

Michael Fossell

Madretsma

Get a little playful sometimes
a little time to myself, tickle
my bones till they grin and
grind together and
the whole loving world
laughs itself right into my soul,
turns it all a
wonderful silly

Jennifer Arcuni

Reflection

What willow's sinewy branch does cast
A shadow o so dark and thick
Across my spirit across my soul
It's for my heart the bell does toll
What segments of sun's fiery light
Do trickle 'tween these burly boughs
Beneath this tree I sit alone
And for this moment call it home
For 'till the hour my arms do drape
About the shoulders of my love
I'll hearken as the lonely drake
Calls his mate at evening's break
And reflect upon these waters still

Frank R. Nardone

Portals

The door quivers slightly at my touch,
A tall wooden barrier (keeping me in
Or keeping me out?) of solid, rich oak
Leading to the parlor (said the spider
To the fly) but shall I open it?
Shall I grasp the tarnished handle
To free the woman within? No, for
'Tis only mother on the other side
Slumbering peacefully, her lips sewn shut
As the watchers in black look on.

So I shall stand here, and stare at the
Door, and lose myself in the swirls of
The grain of the wood, and look for
Animals in the patterns, like the
Lions in the clouds (do I see a Serpent,
Slithering away from the Lamb, resting
On the hill?) while my hand falls
Away from the handle, slack and lifeless,
For mother will soon sleep below, the pine
Door to her airless room nailed shut.

Ione T. Damasco

My Friend Draco

As did
Akkadian, Greek, Goth, Sir Francis Drake
And settler on the prairie, I trace tonight
Old Draco, the friendly dragon.

Rejoice!
To hear that this clear night each shining joint
Is in its place. From tip of tail to heedful
Head he soars entire.

Alert
That head, in faithful hope that once again
From Lyra's string will ring a clean true note
By Vega's bright light struck.

Be neck
All tail or tail all neck is all the same
To stately timeless purple-floated Draco,
Whose friendliness we lend from here.

Maxwell Kirkpatrick

A Poem

A poem is a fragile thing:
A verbal flare, bright shimmering
With ardent thoughts, new taught to sing,
Both joy and sorrow commingling.

Some trumpet like a tyrant king,
Or winter storm forgathering;
Some tell of zephyrs of the spring
When lover's vows start flowering,
And rhythmic melodies take wing,
All alien discords silencing.

A missile from high Fortune's sling
That sends a message shattering,
Sharp poisoned with a nettling sting;
Or gift of light that's comforting
And hands of faith with which to cling
To hope that soothes our whimpering.

Its words we may not idly fling
But treasure, full reverencing.
A poem as a fragile thing
That can with might of thunder ring!

Pendleton Herring

Vision Quest

Totems at Ninstints
A village of graves
Stumps from that forest
are ancient extincts
In a still spirit chant

Moresby Island and
the Eagle crest tribe
I paddle in your wake
and rest upon forgotten beach
With cedars writ in ruin
Through my trespass of time
your song is heard
About these misty shores

Totems at Ninstints
Long house middens
One century lost
To moss and brush
And the blankets from Europe
On the tall sailing ships

David Landrum

Reflections

The sun has laid a golden path
Across the gulf to me
And, down the path come rolling waves
From far out on the sea

I wonder now where they have been
What shores they've swirled around
Far Afric's coast or near Murmansk
Or closer Puget sound

Perhaps they stilled', round arctic shoals
Till spring sun set them free
Or did they rampage down some coast
Despite the sea folk's plea

They roll on down the seas of time
A sobering thought to me
Those waves will surge on, through the years
When I am history!

James W. Beetham

Bizarre

But your life is drenched with sand in a trench
Already for orange skies to change to purple haze
Zig- zagging your emotions thru the tempestuous maze
And touching the smell of the "Temple Bar" stench
All at the same time you want your life to remain
Revolving thru the door of your own freeze frame

You know that there's times that you've gone too far
Times that you wonder if that's really who you are
Red faces glowing fiery like a star
Minds linger to fathom it's actually that bizarre

Beginning exploits of an entirely new life
Azure skies can determine your trail
Zelus that you have for life will never allow you to fail
Allowing illusions of grandure to continue your strife
And never ending the sands of time
Reality will allow you to seek and secure what you will find

Times when you know that you've gone too far
Times when you know who you really are
Times when you know you want to be the star
The illusions to be abstract - the illusions to be bizarre!!!

Richard D. Newquist

The Blue Hour

Between the long shadows of the day
Amongst the myridal tones
That change in blue array
Before it heralds the night
It reckons with the soft hour,
The long blue twilight;
Made more arable still
By fortuitous dreamers
Upon their castellated hill
Striving to keep the time between
Day ending and ebon dark
A lengthening sunset scene,
And warding off the lonely night
Bargaining for time
To gain the eventide of light.

Patricia J. Tury

Desolation

The wintry Nun of the night goes out of her temples
And slowly steps down under comets and stars.
She has held an holly vespers in the Helios' altar
And her robe flourishes now above my sleeping town.
As a dog of devotion my emptiness squats on the doorsteps,
And I see it to lick lonely memories left by occasional guests.
As besotted my home spins his roof over near black squares,
And a cold gloomy wind is just kissing his windows tonight.
And the doorbell keeps his silence
As a shell thrown out by the Ocean.
And the watch moans his dreams
Crucified on the wall.
If you come towards me
As a moon full of a love and emotion,
Show me only an hint,
I will be happy to open
Every gate of my soul.

Ivan Roussetzki

Epitaph For A Traveller Still Unknown

You cannot be like Houseman's friend
And wear the globe you've left behind.
Flotsam in gravity's ocean, you drift forever free,
Having cast aside forever, all earth and wind and sea.

Your body won't to earth return
But to transcendent cosmic dust,
Eaten not by brother worms,
But by the energetic rust
Of fundamental particles
Spinning in frantic, Brownian race
Beyond the reaches of perception,
Into the kaleidoscopic space
Where isolated atoms dance
And to fusion do aspire,
To set free at last in radiance,
The scintillations of the soul,
The luminescence of the heart.

Patrick McNelly

The Challenger Lament

Lift off! Suddenly no retreat! instincts raising hackles,
Are we equal to this feat? feeling maniac chemicals,
Impulsing us to greet yet unimagined worlds.

Of metal bones, ceramic skin, excreting oxy-hydrogen
From icy bladders deep within.
This screaming booster blows, in frightful, rampant pose.
Now stately, pausing, rising; roiling, wasted clouds disguising,
Redundant warnings gone unheeded, tragedy unfolding.

What specter drove this NASA thing,
Wrote monstrous rhyme to "thee we sing",
Purred corrupted creed once more,
To soothe our weary, stricken shore?

Epitaph
Nations heard their jaunty talk,
Looked upon that short, short walk,
Loved them that faith and expectation,
Knowing not the implication,
Of officialdom unled,
And tears a bureau cannot shed.

John G. Royal

A Sonnet From Life To A Child

The dear beautiful things of life astound me——
Aren't they wonderful; but I must tell you,
Care deeply now, these summer days are few
And autumn strips the tired tree or every leaf.
The magic cycle breaks and all we see
Is left behind, a kiss a wave still due;
We'd like to keep the beautifulness of youth
But memory's children must one by one go free.
For the littlest while in the world we trust
The dear, the beautiful is really ours
But mystery, to remain, vanishes as it comes—-
So we must part from them, and them from us
And each to each in time is little more
Than memory, calling her children home.

Beverly Brian

Rocks Worn Smooth

Between bank and sand,
Armies of rocks and pebbles stand.
Along the shores of restless seas,
Water, malcontent, grinds endlessly.
Grinding and shaping its innocent toll.
The rocks ground to an ever shapeless mass,
Fill and flow into every crevice.

Pity the rocks and pebbles as they lie free,
Infinite in variety, along the sea.
Transformed from individuals jagged, rough hewn,
To shapes worn, polished and smooth.

Thus in meeting their ignoble demise,
Might we say freedom is only premise?
Or might we solve this mental thorn...
Saying, no!!! It is just variety of form.

Roger O. Kent

9 To 5

The wind licks lazily through my hair, like fire
As I sit watching the silent world of the tadpoles.
The trees sway in the blue, blue sky,
Lackadaisically.
Thinking how maybe I'll be professional when I grow older,
If maybe, just maybe, they let me go barefoot to work.
So that during lunch break when all the tick-tock accountants
And secretaries maybe,
Go to their fast-food dream worlds to pay $1.99 for a meal...
And heartburn,
I can go to the pond and watch the tadpoles,
Back and Forth.
Like a tick-tock accountant,
And let my tired feet sink lazy-like in the water
And have the mud squish up between my toes,
Like Old Faithful to a tadpole,
And then at 1:00 I can go back to my tick-tock
Job and type a dictation from my tick-tock
Tadpole.
I mean, boss.

Krista Hogg

Far Behind, You Stand

There you are, in the back,
behind the roses, bleeding from the thorns,
tasting the hazy light that shines off each bitter petal.
I know you aren't hiding.
Far behind, you stand.

You feel I'm watching,
A grin stretches, as your teethe grind in satisfaction.
Proud and sober, arms tucked under each other,
I know you aren't hiding.
Far behind, you stand.

The stinging of my eyes lands on the pit of your back,
I know pain, I own pain.
My strength, in all of its purity, can't tame you.
I know you aren't hiding.
Far behind, you stand.

The light is burning you,
landing on the tip of your scull, a fire ignites.
And you melt, along with the roses and petals,
My eyes are shut.

Catina Hatgipetros

Harper's-Harp

Wiser than vain
    bettors to editors
A silent moment
    of game - ah !
    with
the light of a cat.

Wilder refrain
    beams of misreckoners - nay -
    when
A candle's aflame
        is
Truer than that ?

Lie 'ere and drain
    off
  ha ! the greedy begetters
    hm ! in the fire'
s Claim to eternal sap - zap

ZAP!

Likewise
peel your fingers
Wiselike
    plucking
    the

GAP!

Bruno Almaviva Marte

The Passing Of An Era

In that era long forgotten with the coming of the rail,
bringing markets to the heartland, where the six-gun did prevail.
Came a hardy breed of person from the stark southwestern plain,
bringing herds of longhorn cattle, the market there to gain.

With his wagon and his horses and his rangy longhorned beef.
His only law the six-gun, so beware oh cattle thief.
To the railheads in Kansas where the buyers could be found.
Where the whiskey, painted ladies, and the gamblers did abound.

To Waterville and to Abilene, to Fort Dodge and Wichita.
Driving herds of Texas cattle, while enforcing his own law.
Men like Jesse Chisholm who with sweat and blood and tears,
built themselves a reputation that has lived down through the years

'Til at last it all was over with the rails spreading course.
The mustang and the cowboy replaced by the iron horse.
So as we look back in history to those romantic days of yore.
It leaves a somewhat hollow feeling that those days will be no more.

So we glory in the stories of the men who rode the trails.
Bringing beeves up from the southland to connect them with the rails.
It was the passing of an era of the taming of the wild west,
by the drover and the buyer, mustangs, cows, and all the rest.

Dwight Burgess

Requiem For An Unborn Child

Now I am old and life has passed me by
and there is mockery in the winds of age:
O, I am cold; am cold: to whom shall I
bequeath the dregs of my love's heritage?
O, barren is my womb; my withered heart
is like a dried fruit hanging from its stem;
soon shall arrive the moment to depart;
soon I shall go and not a requiem
of my loins' voices chant me to my grave.
I huddled in a handful of young years
quicksilver joy, believing I could keep
this joy forever: but it ran like tears
out of my porous hands. I could not save
one drop of it. Now I am bound for sleep.

Barnabas J. Ramon-Fortune

Sixteen Year Old Maid

Evicted at 16
By an enraged mother estranged from life and herself
I unwillingly sought refuge
As an illegal maid
For a blase, wealthy couple
Concerned with their careers and luxurious lives.
During the day,
I metamorphosed into the idealized robot:
Obeisant-obedient, and efficient
Gladly receiving my wages and tiny room in the basement
But within:
My thoughts and I remained stubbornly apart
Awaiting the night when I retired downstairs
Free to envision another life
To study and attain my high school and college diplomas —
Such superficial requisites serving as
Watchdogs sheltering its civilized members
Until - at last! - I was able to leave
And seek my destiny!

Susan Fischer

Ghosts Of Steeltown

At night Mr. Frick and Mr. Carnegie walk their mill in swallow tail coats; once again
great furnaces burn with a fire that outshines the moon and turns the sky deep red.
Flashes of light flare in buildings while shadows dance across yards;
Steel wheels scream against rails, steam hisses as it escapes;
The air is thick with coal dust, sulfur, and coke fumes.

At midnight a whistle blows and tough men in rough clothes stream through the gates with dinner pails to tend the bubbling heat;
while others leave to visit tiny bars that never close,
or return to square houses on steep streets to sleep with weary women with clorox hands.
The town slumbers against the constant rumble of great machines.

In the morning Mr Frick and Mr. Carnegie are gone; and
All that remains in the feeble light are rustling beams and patchy weeds.
Shabby stores line lonely streets, and quiet men stand on broken corners, and talk of baseball scores.

Peter F. Vaira

Christian Ascending The Staircase

All men step lively down the stairs to ruin.
Despair, and death seem not unwilling dread
To fractured lives in darkness, sin mislead.
It's I, who like all men, go down therein.
The man is dead! Humanity seems gone — had been;
A very complex machine, absurd machine.
Descending nude kneels down to pray for clean
White garments that are made to fit, blood kin
With Jesus Christ thru His forgiving grace.
Now turn from sin to holiness — arise,
To walk in newness! Clothed, we receive
A blessing given each upward embrace
  Of God, to keep our nakedness not perceived.
  Reborn, we live! New birth, we are baptized.

Bill C. Rogers

Haiku

Mystic stamp, glue!
Elvis and Prissy - flowers
Massive spots Kurl
as frogs jump!

Echo prayers-ways? Means?
Pliable mind froth plastic breath.

Emily McKown

Bumper Sticker Lingo

Take a trip and sanctify your memory
Do a flip and memorize vitality
Make a joke and vitalize rigidity
Take a toke and rectify reality
Hum a tune and realize fragility
Climb a dune and fortify integrity
Take a chance and integrate ethnicity
Do a dance and emulate mobility
Shed a tear and recognize mortality
Shed your fear and paralyze uncertainty
Take a stand, immobilize brutality
Be a ham and socialize absurdity
Make a friend and harmonize humanity
Make amends and humanize hostility
Make a love and exercise fertility
Look ahead and visualize longevity
State your mind and emphasize validity
Build a shrine and sacrifice a deity
Rhyme a line and clarify what's hazy
Take your time to stop and smell a daisy.

Caitlin Sidlo

The Circular Path

There is a time within the mind that follows he who hesitates.
Each empty scheme inside the dream becomes the key that segregates.
The teachings flow and later grow around the seed that deviates.
The soul expands in foreign lands but close to home it enervates.

The crime endures and passions soar for those who cannot see the sun.
The truth proclaims the bitter rain to be the source from whence we come.
Each poet dreams and later schemes to find the end to nature's sum.
But each endures the endless chores and leaves the race to those who run.

The wind blows free above the sea but cannot find the promised land.
The echo sounds and later drowns the prophet's cry on desert sand.
The flowers bloom beside the tomb so no one's left to take a stand.
And each regrets what time forgets within the soul that is not planned.

Kenneth J. Lamberson

At The Year's End

Today, light snow has fallen on the village,
Each ephemeral flake screaming for identity,
Then bonding softly with the thin, white crust
Upon the sweet-mince of our Christmas countryside.
Snow into snow, as dust into dust. Just like us.

Suspended coldly in the eastern sky,
An old hydrogen holocaust, oven eye agape,
Beams down a texturing on fields and hills.
The trees are ready, snowballs in their palms, for play
But human heads are safely tucked away.

Seen from the kitchen window,
Between the burst of birdsong and the school bell chime,
The garden is a pool of still, bright silence
Where a lingering strawberry hangs its flushed, late head;
A tear-filled Ruth amid the alien corn;
An Alice, gauche, among the playing cards;
A red lamp, glowing in the daytime;
An August, stranded in December.

Now, August I do remember.

James A. Donaldson

Shy Moon

The moon is full above the trees
embraced by a dark grey sky
and clouds around - like little bees
covet nightfall's only light

And as I look from down below
at that illuminated sphere
I often wish that I could know
if anyone can hear

It seems as if I'm meant to stay
in obscurity-unclear
without a chance to run away
the darkness I must fear

In sombre hours of the night
The clouds may leave the moon
a stretch of heaven left and right
so to escape her doom

And as she scintillates above-
Her mystic brilliance so divine
rays penetrate my saddened soul
and tears turn into wine

Lourdes V. Arrata

The Woman You Imagine

The woman you imagine does not bleed for five days out of thirty, she fills your sheet with long bronzed thighs just glistening from sleep. Her hair fans out across your pillow, the air between her fingers dense with mystery. She lies as still as water reflecting your image in perfect symmetry. She brings you thick skinned oranges and blossoms, fragile as a whisper that open only for one night. She hums a sweet adagio and melts into the morning leaving no question in her wake. She is a woman only man can make, I lay beside her, swollen with your secrets, my belly talcum-white my wound still open waiting, to be filled. Your face distorted in my turbulence, your fingers sticky with my blood. I come to you with seeds that will survive you. I bring you doubts no sunrise will erase; the shadows that I cast will form the contours of your face. The woman you imagine has never placed her feet in stirrups, seen a life scraped from her womb. She dilates only to receive you. Her tongue caresses without threatening. She swallows, but will never taste your salt. Your juice burns initials in my throat, a white froth bubbles, curdling on my lips; it drips like tears. I take the hard shaft of your anger, rub the foreskin clean against my teeth; I force you to admit my pain, pulling you beyond my death, I make you glimpse your own. The woman you imagine holds no terror like the woman that you've known.

Patricia Kelly

Seismic Certitude

Small freckled hands
Finger keys on black batteried box
Fragmented forms fill the tiny screen
Grandson's pink tongue and wrinkled brow
Coax answers from flashing columns:
4 + 4   6 - 3   2 x 7   10 / 5
Concentration focused on content,
Numbered certainties.

And what of the mathematics of grief?
Two minus one equals nothing
Three divided by death equals despair
Loss multiplied by anguish equals numbness
Sum of one plus some perhaps equals hope.
An infinitude of numbers: ideas: things
Equals black-hole calculus;
I'm still working on fractions.

Barbara F. Kovner

Home

She stands unwavering, her black eyes
gazing upon a time long gone,
and still she mourns
as she stands longing for the kiss of
morning across softly sighing
mountains of home.
Evening sun's turning the tamaracks
to a burning yellow, then brown
in the cool air,
while winds wafting colder and the night
ever bolder weave moonlight through
ebony hair.
These images haunt her memory
like an ancient melody from
an unknown past
causing her to wonder if dreams of
homes of others are also so
easily cast
aside as holy sacrifices in the name
of logic, or love, or fame.

Jennifer Bull

"The Willow"

Gently bent, the willow sways,
gives way in breeze a blowing
O'er wispy grass that softly waves
round banks with brook aflowing.

Ennobled she, in graceful dance,
bonded at her birth
To nature: mute of question
tied by covenant with the earth.

Her fancy flight casts shadows bright
and stretches nimble limbs
To catch at darting butterflies
caressed on subtle winds.

Embracing glints of sunlight,
filtered cloud, thru fingered jade
Abiding the breath of emerald scent
her dance of fate is made.

She shares her whispered secret
out brief silence of my day
When willows soul, with spirit freed
enjoin' with me in play.

Pat Reynolds

A Sip Of Brugge

Quixotic winds
glide
through white, waffled blades.

Don's monsters
capture
Belgian mounds, then

Surrender

To barley fermented
waterways,
lacing Flemish walls and bridges.

Drink the Bruggian
silence
which trickles

Across

Yellow, dew-filled cups
inviting
two messengers of Peace,

To preach,
perch;
roost upon this convent wall.

Bart Ezra Plaskoff

The Lord Of Love

Long counts and plucked days
grab magi of the Lord
stretching a long shadow as twilight in the east
when the first sun kisses darkness
to hail love in a mute heart.
Here He comes at midnight
with a lamb in sight
bleating master's day, a Good Friday
for resting in delight at heaven's lawn
till faith, hope and love can find a new dawn.
He appears in dream - a voiceless spirit
at sumptuous alter of the holy mark
streaming His agony at supper.
He visits at Easter - morn alone
in flesh and blood
still pouring wine of love
to flood devil's mass
eating Easter-eggs for dance
with crooked lot on the Christmas.

Rashbehari Ghosh

The Big Bully Boy

Tiny pieces of his pitifully broken heart
had lodged in his bowels and he was
unable to run in the Boston Marathon
because of the bleeding

Conceding to that he sat thoughtfully
by the fire conspiring with his Sicilian
friend to put an end to her and
her damned disposition-in this position
he stayed till the pains stopped.

His fair hair was falling fast in the past
he had hidden the fact by wearing hats
these days he also shaved more often
he was plainly aging away from pain
his brain was becoming butter-another
love would have done nothing.

An inborn heir with an ingrown hair somewhere
where the corner couldn't find it he died of
mysterious causes.

Norma K. Pattavina

When Rainbows Explode

When the corpses of wise-men
Have filled up the graves,
And the souls of the true-men
Become freedom's slaves;

When the river of genius
Is damned up in chains,
And the fire of passion
Is drowned in its flames;

When the cups of the poor-men
Are overflowing with greed,
And the flowers of inspiration
Are subdued by the weeds;

When compassion is imprisoned
By paranoid screams,
And political theories have
Destroyed all the dreams;

When the glasses are all empty
And the nights are too cold,
We'll take shelter in rainbows
'Til the rainbows explode.

Michael Drummond

Last Time I Saw Jesus

Last time I saw Jesus,
he was standing in aisle 24 at a local supermarket
handing out recipes on how to save your soul.
Then he gave out coupons.
"Redeemable for a free of bread"
A lady pushing a cart loaded with Ding Dongs
asked if it was white or wheat,

and Jesus said, "It doesn't matter, it's free".

Diana Chang

My Typical Day

Fleeing phantoms of imaginary boys,
head swimming on deluge laneways
tailed by boners on empty bicycles!
Screaming about injustices with paper scissors,
being hammed-handed and double-fisted by ink blotches
and fiery-eyed, mealy-mouthed, mass-beloved,
big-boy-hate-machine warrior airwaves!
Tossing pitiable sobbing flowers in file cabinets
whilst wrenching bony hands about gore-myths!
Cruising black sedans down fear thoroughfares
across the nether regions of scab-town,
filled with angst-ridden, broken-winged faeries,
bitch-mimicking about too tight shackled lip-zippers!
Storming cubicle pads in darkness clutching dope-threads,
binocular-eyeing sweet street visions
and riding memories of celluloid keepsakes on punk notes,
with exploding mind-guts across the skull stratosphere!
Vainly grasping at airy sun-ladders
through ponderous ideal-fissures,
sinking starry-eyed in the mire of acceptance!

Octaevius Altair

Time of Weeds

These weeds in wild profusion
here at the station
bobbing in the wind
I remember from another time,
here again now years later
standing tall like sentinels,
surrounding the once-esteemed,
now-crumbling station:
bobbing heads like pompous clones
of soft fur, flailed
in the fierce wind,
yielding only their seeds,
blown along the tracks,
taken by the wind
or some unsuspecting carrier
to another place and time
where apathy dwells
and hope also lies
covered with weeds.

C. Samsel

The Mystery Of Life

Are we alone in the Universe
Human beings with beating hearts
The only ones with blood that flows
The only ones who think and act
Who procreate, who speak, who die
Creative beings who walk upright?

How sad, since all is made to end.
Will we return to cosmic dust
To fall upon some wet and distant world
Endowed with warmth and light
To form again, to live again
Perhaps ten trillion years away?

Adolph R. Lugo

Wall Of Death

Blue explodes white as
hereditary sovereigns
of the deep - caught in
the seine set for yellow fin -
throng to free blow holes for breath.

Cries climb to a range
inaudible as the red
curtain of death is
brailled, leaving fewer in the
native realm than they once were.

By fits and starts the
spool of the power block turns
pulling mammal and
mesh through its tight opening.
Emerging, the crushed descend.

Flukes flutter as arms
- bloody to the elbows - slide
the disentangled
to the top of a sluice way.
An ocean coffin awaits.

Kalyn Carjan

Abreit Macht Frei

Rusted nazi iron gate,
How many soulful eyes
Have passed beneath
Your cold sardonic welcome,
Wallpapered with
The blood of innocence?
"Work will make
You free" you tell me.
Your kind of freedom
I do not want.
The type you offer
Is cold and deadly,
Appealing only
To the monsters
Who placed me here.
For the dead will remember,
In there restless bones,
That which you have promised them.

Chris Bodanza

Snapshots

Imagining my daughter,
I always saw her skin too white, pale like ash.
Her hair, I thought, would be longer, blonder,
And herself not at all as long.
Nor did I think she would laugh so much —
It runs like water from a spring.
And her eyes dart like an animal's, and take in everything.
(Yet sometimes, I know, she cries softly at night,
And dreams of flying, arms spread wide, over barn and rooftop.)
Now she, gruffly tries to make me mind, because there was a time I didn't.
There was a garden there. We talked between tomato plants and moss rose.
She asked me why I wouldn't stay. And then there was really no good reason,
Except that I would be a fish in farm-land.
But I might have sailed on boats in summer,
Rolled over Superior and down St. Mary's, heard woodmen chop a few feet away from breakfast,
Run off boats in winter, and come home to lambs and snow and to her.

But, as it was, I saw her only in between—summers and Christmas,
Saw her change like a series of snapshots.
I sit here with these snapshots, wondering which is the real girl,
And whether I have lost or captured her in these years' remembered essences.

Robert W. Bates

More Beautiful Than Nature's Best

In comparing the beauties of the earth,
I believe I've found the best of them all.
Greater than the sight of a waterfall
Is my true love, my destiny from birth,
The beauties of nature can't show her worth.
The oceans are deep, the trees grow tall,
The sunset glistens and the birds do call,
But only she can fill my heart with mirth.
How can my feelings be said in just words
When earth's wonders can't even describe her,
For me to try would simply be a jest.
The sights that I've seen, the sounds that I've heard
In my love's presence they become a blur.
Just the thought of her exceeds nature's best.

Benjamin J. A. DeLoach

To The Native American

Dark clouds and purple mountains
I borrowed time
To feel this country,
Content to love
Among the whispers of the past.

I intrude
Where majestic sights hold secrets
To me unknown.
Your land
Where once was silence
With nature calling.

I respect the haunted wildness,
The simplicity of a people
Long gone.

I'm glad I listened;
Iheard—
A people too strong
To let go.

Hazel Mulcahy

Tongue In Check

Desirous of erudite linguistic competency,
I consulted an unabridged English dictionary.
Recompensed with many a recondite expression,
I attained beatitude far beyond expectation.

Ah! How great, how supple, the word "infinituple"!
And "refulgent" and "lambent," for another couple!
Ah! How paradisiacal the evocation
of "flocci-nauci-nihili-pili-fication"!

Finally cognizant of "obdiplostemonous,"
I am zenithally amorous of "siphonostomatous."
"Hypaethral" is my desiderated diabolifuge
When against parvanimity I require refuge.

"Epitome" and "pterygostome" are Greek to me,
But are "puranic" and "pundit" from Latin or Sanskrit?
To our subitaneous succour, etymology!
- or is it entomology? Quick, look up it!

Paul C. Brodeur

Untitled

'Baker rises through the eerie opaqueness
of the cool coast mist.
I know what it's like to live in the
shadow of a volcanic dream.
And I wonder how I came to be
here in this place.
On an island
in the ocean,
paradise.

Kathy Peddlesden

Give Me Something

Give me something to hang onto
I have staggered high
on a rickety bridge for so long
I am becoming deaf to the
wood-crack-warning of the fall

Give me your outstretched arms
for support
alone, I cannot balance

I could lunge at you
but you may back away
and lose my life

Give me something to hang onto!
What is it with you?
Is it the fear of falling
off sanity's banister
or, do you,
sense
my gentle
push?

Marilyn Jackson

Untitled

I haven't won a medal in a track and field event.
I haven't penned a published work. I barely earn the rent.
I haven't towed the social line or been father to a kid.
But, I wouldn't trade the lot of these for what it was I did.

I've loved you in the fiercest way my being knew to do.
I risked myself to love you in the only way I knew.
I hurt myself. I caused you pain. And as time went on I lost
The only thing whose price I'd pay no matter what the cost.

Eventually I'll wonder what I ever saw in you.
Or so some friends assure me if I knew what they all knew.
Somehow it doesn't matter what these people say is so—
They didn't see the secret seed or stay to watch it grow.

So excuse me if I haven't given up my love for you;
But, I haven't built a bridge as yet or likely will get to.
My love is one accomplishment whose light cannot be hid—
And I'll never shed a sorry tear for what it was I did.

Kevin T. Durkin

Wolf Is Me

Some idiot boy shouted wolf once too often
I never understood myself
why mothers and lovers seem to come
yes come, whenever wolf is mentioned
left to the world one would begin to think it wise to stop
to stop
responding to the wolf cries
the whistles
the sheared paining hearts
clawed by life and bleating blood
throbbing lives
beseeching smiles
whining Edwinas
the growing recession and its children
or the unending hands stretched out
Pardon my stupidity if every time I hear the word wolf
I drop my pen and pick up my axe and come
running running running
into laughter.

Mark Francisco Jones

The Interview

The interview went well
  I went into the jungle
Went to learn about myself

Cowards stood amazed and gazed
Upon the carnivores at feast
Talking up a storm and clashing horns
In the heartland of the beast

"Hello?" I called
From the trophy stand.
In the den, my head upon the mantle.
Jackals wine and wait to dine
As the killers set examples

The thought is reign and to parade
In the outland we call home.
Here the land has open hands,
And so free we are to roam.

Yes, the interview went well
  I went into the jungle
With the devil, with myself.

Robert Norwood Jr.

Spirit Skin

I'm screaming suns out -
I'm melting down to the vines and the dew,
down into the huddled visions.
You join me and we are quiet and shapeless.

  We've all been there in the dirt.
  All melting, pooling, gathering the mud of ages -
  the elk spinnings of day into night,
  the circus of the spirit world.
  Heavenly jaguars -
    their stolen eyes in the night.
    We can slide through their pupils
    and live where we can only touch.

  Night comes and I'm upside down,
  breathing backwards and dancing on the dark earth.

Come — dance hands in hands upon hands:
we will burn our circle in the earth
we will spiral deeper into worlds
we will each stand naked and take new shape
and we will widen.

David Weldon

Autumn On Cape Cod

The bogs are red with ruby fruit now
in abundant measure
The bees are ever busy there
filling up their hives
as pickers hasten to the bogs
to scoop their tasty treasure
before the frost arrives.

The frost -
that harbinger of winter's cold
who throws a party for the trees.
They come resplendent (if somewhat arty)
in coats of orange, red and gold.

At eventide I bundle up,
walk the beach with rapid gait,
and then
sit atop a dune
to muse and wait
to watch the sun give up the day
in deference to her errant mate
the bold and blushing harvest moon.

Dorothy Fairweather

playground

beneath the clouds
in concrete shadows
of afternoon city
the sign reads
NO REALISM OR PROPAGANDA ALLOWED

between the skyscrapers
you are so old
watching
this metal
tangle with little hands

the sand begins at your feet
where she is a girl
with a black hand holding yours
as you forget this contrast
and take your first step

Raymond O'Connor

Empty Eyes

Love's left wanting
in empty eyes.
Little boy brave heart,
alone, afraid, never cries.

Wasted effort
on a hopeless fight.
Father in prison; poverty births
the child of night.

Death hungers,
hunting the dark.
Tempers flare, back alley dare,
knees buckle, dogs bark!

Shots fired!
She catches her breath?
Mother, welfare, ghetto trap;
blind reporters script a death.

Heavy headlines:
"Wealthy citizens public outcries!"
Over the lost boy,
with empty eyes.

Ira Lee Williams

"Buttercups" (The Gutter Primrose)

My favorite flower is seldom seen
In formal gardens hands have preened;
It flourishes best in heat and dust
And on the fringe of clay and crust,
Where unremembered sorrow shows
Within the glow of sweet primrose.

When spring is at its flowering best,
And crocus blooms have gone to rest;
When daffodils' brief moments fade,
Impatiens brightens only shade;
When dogwood sheds its pastel bows,
The gutter glows with sweet primrose.

When I have passed my final mark
And reach a country churchyard park
God grant that some remain who care,
Whose love for that dear spot we share.
Please seed the gentle breeze that blows,
So my space glows with sweet primrose.

Edward S. Smith

Plumage

Dress up your mediocrity
In peacock-feathered finery.
Like iridescence each doth shine
When humble words in verse align.
Embellished intermittently
With borrowed plumes of novelty,
Use peacocks' eyes to titillate
The sparrows' ordinary fate.

Conceal your blatant wretchedness
With burlap sack or silken dress;
'Less man or beast your shame may see,
Decrying your iniquity.
The Master paints the peacock's eyes
And robes the sparrow as is wise.
To you is given sense to use;
So, mensch, with wit your plumage choose!

Monika Dykes

Warfare

Clamming for peanuts
In the hunter's green jungle
makes a man marvel and wonder,
But a bone-ravished hand
Gripped deep in the dirt
Makes a man wish for the tomb.

A mountain zephyr streaks overhead
As talk of death continues
By one too fresh from the womb.
He shudders like an alley cat
In the dank, night air
Too dense to know the truth.

So run those phalanges
Through the black, sanded chasm,
Those fingers still tepid with life;
And run that ass
Through the jungle depths
Away from all this strife.

David H. Wilson

Untitled

There was talk this morning
in the park
earth's way with her children
favoritism
the peacock's head and tail
the swan's neck
royalty
grace
no crown for us, they, no train for us
never gliding over water, always hopping over ground
they had never heard a peacock sing
nor seen a swan walk

S. Franes Jacob

...Driven To Perform

Don't feed me your life, death, and after-life
my mouth is already full of my own misconceptions
seeping down
drenching me

Reeking myths keep my life
Oh
So
Interesting

Anthony Metivier

Passage

My dreams are dreaming me
In the shadows of my mind
As consciousness eats away
At the sharp rocky shores of time
Like eternity held glistening
In the flicker of an eye
So the cries so innocent
Shall ever die
Like ripples on the water
You can only see
These are the depths of eternity
Past words or thought
That take shape in the night
Past emotions or flesh
That take to wings of flight
Or the call of a bird
Echoing through valley's of wonder
Like the purest of light
For shadowing thunder

Jason Lau

Cliff

You stand at the cliff edge, your gaze drawn down
into eddies of restless, rock-spined foam,
as if, an archetype, you might symbolize
the difference between the formless and what we realize.

But it's a troubled contrast, poised between
the day's bright sunlight on your shoulders,
And the drowning surge below that sucks
all detail into its churning depths.

Yours was a suicide of the mind
as you stood against the gusting sky.
Then you made your decision not to die
into nature's will, to live beyond
the screams of gulls circling round your head.

Even now, the tanker against the horizon's flare
still marks for me your choice of fate,
as it holds its navigator's course to score
his intention on that waste of salt.

Bernard Hardy

Untitled

I close the shoji window:
it was never kept opened anyway
before you came and
they built you that
huge kennel because
you would grow so
big.

You did.
You were big for all your three months to the day you
were carried out of there
and now I don't want to see it from the second-floor
window
and remember how you played with my old slipper...
The emptiness of it is
still so painful
but a kennel built
into the ground and rising on strong beams is
hard to tear down.

It's so much easier to
close the window.

Marie Shimane

Views From A Window In Cheshire, CT

January: the rhododendron bush is braced against the cold.
Its olive leaves stand stiff and straight like
Roman mercenaries poised for war.
Its yellowed buds like helmets entrap
The faces of those blossoms that will open
Warm and flushed and soft against the leaves
That like green fingers will embrace them in the spring.

March: snowdrops appear before the crocuses arrive.
Fragile and white like melancholy angels
They withstand rain and sleet and cold
Until the bolder flowers in their Lenten purple
Emerge to join them in "the cruellest month,"
Reminding us that Paradise was always fragile
And that suffering is never delicate.

May: such a small but a necessary act
That these narcissi among the gray and pitted rocks
Return each spring and claim their right
To move in the wind and frame in palest white
The crimson red and yellow at their core.

Mary O'Brien Fox

Ode To John Keats

In what silent land are you this pious morn
John Keats? Your silent tongue now speaks
to the sensual ear for ever, but your
burning forehead and heart high-sorrowful below
leave these two late lines for me to complete.

Why must I look at one quotation to know
all I need? Why is beauty first?
That still salvation has moved you to show
me this? O, that Bold Lover who can never taste
his lover's lips can never still your thirst!

"When old age shall this generation waste"
it is unchanged. But you have passed
and leaving your song you have left those chaste,
the critics, pursuing backward through your letters
and terms in their breathless search, till at last

One comes to hear you touch that ancient urn.
Keats: Beauty, truth, are not for man.
I come here young, and want to hear you turn
that attic shape, that cold pastoral with those shaped
men and maidens always breathing in your hands.

Scott Clair

Untitled

Let me tell you about it all; all.
Let me sum it up again with an awkward, imprecise cascade.
... Truth is a mighty volume of epigrams and paradoxes.
... Real truth is caught in a single word.
... And the ultimate truth bleeds even now in a
wretched mess of skinless time. Time.

The last living poet just crossed the fence and told all his secrets.
So, now I can't even try to script bad poetry anymore.
So, now I can no longer try to sound like an eclectic
little son of a bitch.
Now, I'm gonna hafta wait for the next last living poet.
The last living magician sold all his tricks and then he disappeared.
So, now I can't even try to fool my friends at all their so-called
parties.
So, now the illusions are less than fodder for fools - and even
so called wisemen - and maybe poets too.
The last living politician is about to ...

W. Scott Mishley

The Woods At Night

On the outskirts of our village
Lie the woods in creepy plight.
And all the elders say to us;
You must not go to the woods at night.

Wide-eyed monsters say "Tu-whit,"
And little ones shine in eerie light.
Ghosts in trees keep rustling leaves.
You must not go to the woods at night.

Woodchucks chuck with a creepy noise,
Painfully, large mosquitoes bite.
Tree roots grow upward to trip you down.
You must not go to the woods at night

Once I ventured into these woods.
Not a soul I perceived in sight.
Frightened, I recalled the elders' words,
You must not go to the woods at night

Was it a ghost I saw on that tree?
I heard a howl and nigh died of fright.
It seemed the leaves were counselling me
You must not go to the woods at night.

Cherian Eapen

Elizabeth At The Test On Saint Valentine's Day

For just a dragon's breath, I dangled on the platform sky,
Like Daedalus's son, the feather-ticklish Icarus,
I watched crazed boulders nip my ankles by their heels:
In toe-green times I found fog's voids within the sea -
And void on void, stacked each upon each me.

The humpbacked world came back to prove a trend in jokes
Kicked off the seaweed strings, to drowse in more jailed Fury
Then most half-needed answers rose to turn geese paranoid
Those answers made me feel too fat and sleekly justified for ships
Feel vindicated all bloody soon for guiltless dreams
Ride, ride, ride, all you gulls! Go chase the plump sea fowl!!
For Icarus has saved us from aquatic wombats
And cleaned us with a salt, drip-plopp'gous tow'l.

So, Liz be nimble, Liz be quick,
Liz, jump across the Valentine stick!
All the Kings' horses, and all Kings' farces
Could not stop my Liz from making passes!
All Kings' voices and all Kings' forces
Could not stop Liz from trading kisses!!

John King-Farlow

Dance

Suspended between earth and sky,
motion itself motionless,
the dancer's impudence in the face of gravity
insults the deity who pouts in his chamber.
What has he to do with this wild thing
suspended between the earth and sky,
motion itself, motionless
on music's sensuous string?
Unconscious of the stars and deities,
the dancer pirouettes
or churns up dust beneath his feet
to the beat of native drums
as natural to him as body heat.
The dancer is the spirit's astronaut.
Flightless, he flies; wingless, he rises
with me at his side weightless with joy.

Barbara Gene Fisher

Stone Images

Moist music around my neck,
My eyes glistening to
Stringed tears.
Choking pearls listening to
An incautious night.
A narrow turn on backstreets
Poisoned by phantoms
With tainted tins.
Memory blurs a reckless spirit behind
A rotting mulch.
Masked in mellow yoga
Yawning a frontier to kneel before time.
Stone images,
Trading intensity for indifference.
Knocking at the door begging for alms,
Just to sway in the breeze of stormy palms.
For whose art can remain pure in
The presence of vipers? Dealers of our beliefs.
In this desert of dying dreams
Ours prayers have turned to dust.

Gesso Cocteau

Enmeshed

I took the fabric of my love, and in
My innocence I thought that if I placed
A pattern, made of pearls and diamonds traced
With subtle charm and wit, that I would win
Your praise, then like a spider, I would spin
A web, with warp and woof of moonbeams laced
With guile. And when you paused, then I with haste
Would hold you fast, entangling you therein.

But you were not a novice at this game,
For other snares were set before I came,
And while I sat there dreaming at your knee,
I never saw the web you wove for me,
And now, in retrospect, I know that I
Who meant to be the spider, was the fly.

Molly Tennyson

Whispers Of Death

This road leads on, never to end,
My wounds with your help will not mend.
I feel like I'm going to fall,
Whispers of death flow through the hall.

Down a valley to lead the way,
Never to see another day.
He is out there making his call,
Whispers of death flow through the hall.

Please don't climb the stairway to hell,
Stay inside your protected shell.
Death isn't for one, it's for all,
Whispers of death flow through the hall.

Death will go on never to cease,
None is left not even a piece.
No longer a road, just a wall,
Whispers of death flow through the hall.

No person would ever believe,
How much these whispers can achieve.
Look up and see how very tall,
Whispers of death flow through the hall.

Jessica M. Brown

The Keepers Of The Night

These things that scare you in the dread of night?
N'er fear them for your dreams are their plight.
To writhe inside your mind's most secret place,
frightening you with each ugly self-conjured face.

They are your friends though they seethingly creep,
inside dark corridors of your mind, life, and sleep.
Allotting within them come such pleasures and pain,
undeniably your fears brood 'round your slumb'ring brain.

Their journeys have taken them beyond these realms,
inside of darkened dream scapes, into themselves.
Always knowing your soul's darkest fears
in constant unity with your subconscious years.

Keeper's of the night are within another dream.
Thriving on the fear whilst awaiting the scream.
For in these realms all that is secretly dreamt
is merely their dominion and seldom unkempt.

Soon you will wake and you pray it is so
for in your sleep their love for you grows.
In rising you fight these fears to recede
for in your reality true fear doth breed.

Helen Hamar

Untitled

We stand o'erwhelmed at magnificence here
Now ours from ages of creativeness.
The wars depressions, pestilence ungear
But fail to check its penetrativeness!

They're ours - the galleries of treasured art,
Vast science, music, poetry and prose,
Philosophies from ancients still impart
Their observations on our present woes!

Religions with their mysticness and truths
Told through their beauteous symbols courting awe
Have been purveyors to our Sacred booths
Of wonderments of grace on which we draw!

We stand intoxicated by this fair
To which mankind's commission air!

As I contemplate the Universe —
The length of time; the breadth of space,
The anxieties of life disperse,
Unmask and take their rightful place!

Pauline M. Fox

The Bitter Fare

We dined in splendid elegance
On lace with silver bright,
We drank from crystal goblets
That caught the candle light.

And I remember that I wore
Gardenias in my hair,
I didn't know I was to dine
On such a bitter fare.

But when the candle glow had died
With shadows in its stead,
He found the words to tell me then
That he was soon to wed.

He scarcely saw my grief at all
And keeping tears deferred,
I tried to say the proper things
But choked - on every word....

Rosemary Muntz Yasparro

My Season

A wave, a rush
of green gold scent
rolls through and by
and over me.

I feel the rusty
burnished brown
to come; the air is redolent.

With kiss of this,
in air, on ground, my senses reel
with call of Fall.

Most sensuous of all the year,
this season lures with velvetness.

There is no richer panoply
of tints or tones or scents, to me.

A little girl, I loved it then
and chased brown leaves in balmy breeze.

And now, as Fall first touches me,
in hair, on skin and innerly,

I greet the meeting of the two;
within, without, a shimmer through.

Cheryl Peoples Perez

Blackest Of Pearls

On December 7, 1941, the sun beat down
on a red convertible speeding along
a hot graveled Hawaiian path.

The sexy blonde driver didn't care
that her tires kicked dirt
into the quiet waters of the harbor.

She cared only about the wind, the sun,
and her picnic with Jack.
His white teeth would match his uniform
and he'd smile when he saw pickles
in the chicken salad.

She'd planned for this alright.
Hard boiled eggs, crackers and cheese - the works.
She'd even managed a bottle of chilled wine.

She swung her car off the path
and stopped abruptly. Jumping
from the car she chose the picnic site.

It was perfect. The sun was dazzling.

"Where is he?" she thought.

And suddenly looked skyward.

Rebecca A. Lowery

Decision

In the rawness of that night the silence roared.
Inside moaned the wide-eyed woman breaking
The sacred nothing. Small was she and aching.
Life, loneness and love — her only chord.

Another carried the child warily toward
Her and placed him close to love, making
An effort not to care and quickly taking
Leave for now; to be was to be ignored.
He nestled as if to make himself lost
Giggling and giving a "Don't forget me" stare.
She felt that perfect face and strong — until
The one-legged body understood and tossed.
Her thoughts of the then, now and when — despair.
But she, needing him, whispered, "I will."

Madelynn Miezio

Poof!

A cat perfectly named.
One eye gone in a brutal fight
the other left to melt,
broken lip to drool
and gasp

Half blind,
an asian warrior of fallen stature
safest now in cupboards
in the quiet and the dark
where the strong are more or less equal

Mary's friend
when she slept in Sweet Alyssum
the summer she disappeared,
loneliness sewn-up in his face
in this festal and frightening place

Where joy
has a half-life of its presence
and sadnesses are cumulative,
where we leave our blood
and lose our warrior ways.

Richard Smith

Elusion

Ah sweet despairing interval
Pass on,
Yet stay one moment
Where you may not bide;
So does the poet
Rest his little pain,
Upon a little part
Of restless time.

G. Young

Untitled

Once there was a plant in an untouched part of the woods.
People loved the forest but to this part brought no goods.
It was quiet and didn't bloom as its neighboring parts.
Change wasn't as evident, in sporadic starts.
Asleep one night the plant awoke to a strange sensation.
A caterpillar was struggling up his stem with great determination.
They became dependant on each other as friends often do,
for companionship that both new was true.
One day the movement stopped upon the plant's stem.
No leaf of his revealed the presence of his friend.
"Here I am" said a voice but the plant failed to see
Anywhere that his friend might be.
"Look up and before you question why,
look how beautiful I am as a butterfly."
The butterfly explained how this came to be
In order for the plant to be able to see.
"I'll still be here and rest on your leaves,"
and with this the plant was glad
"I know you don't bloom flowers, but I'll be the one you never had."

Lorelei Ann Pearce

Lost Soul

The mirror was dirty behind the bath -
room door. I took a wet cloth to the
dirty mirror and was swallowed. I had
fallen into a boxed mirror. I stood up to
find three of me standing but one
sitting with his head in his hands. I
looked down at him, get up, get up.
I bent to my knees to reach for his
hands. I felt his cold tears
harden onto my skin. I was a ghost
that had relived a failure.

Jim Seifert

CX 880

Airport lounge;
plush and exclusive;
quiet and restrained
beckons seductively.
Only Business or First Class Ma'am
the snotty voice said to me
clad in my scruffy heather grey sweats.
Expensive embossed manila card
waved in her disappointed plastic face
lets me sail through.
I scrutinize the faces of privilege.
Blank and impersonal identities
tied to lap top computers and
top grain leather briefcases.
Male's the word, in this world,
A Good-bye gift from an estranged husband
brings me briefly
to this once familiar life.
I take stock of oozing wealth and prepare to
step gingerly into the world of have-nots.

Sithy Hamid

Marlfield House

All night the window was open
propped by a book: Five thousand
Years of Irish Art and Architecture
bedded beneath sheets. A seep
of cold air carved a cheek. Sleep
settled smooth as a column.

In the morning cows compress
to an inch and low
across the carpet. Birdsong wells
in liquid detonation. Sheep baa
miraculously. A shower
spurts next door. Above
floorboards creak. Rain drips.

Yesterday gleamed, driving to Wexford
the harbor in bright snarls
the grass so green it seemed
to fission. Dublin to Gorey to Mallow
Cork and Kerry and a ring
of painfully blue sea.

Kate Lowenstein

$5,000

$5,000 could change it all
pull a fast one on despair
get me running more, another plate on the weight machines
fill my gas tank and enfranchise me
Highway 15 would be the glorious road to the Holy Land
I could pay myself for a few poems and careful prose
buy me love in Boulder, Colorado and self-esteem
with pin money in an oversized paper clip, blessed portion riding
on my thigh.
tote up the attributes of your God and divide that number into $5,000
I could sell you any single virtue, at fair market value
and still no one I know would buy
no one knows what bargains there are
in $5,000

Byron Shewman

Homage To Monet On Lake Nipissing

Shock of brush strokes
purple, blue
red and yellow
- they glide
vibrate into whirls
of magic,
circles of gold.

What crowded presence shines
in these colours?

Miraculous rings of lotus
ensnare the water currents.

Light - is the only memory.

Monet's "Impression"
has come to visit

A northerly lake
in Ontario.

Katarina Kostic

Trout Fishing in Northern Idaho - 1959

or

Reflections of a Father's Final Breath - 1987

Moments lost
revealed as Memories
that flash in the Soul
Past and Present
arrive at a crook in unison
Rivers and Streams
fishhooks and woods
Father and Son
The scent of pine
and galactic billowing clouds
that surrender to the Divine blue sky

an old Soul
Gently Molds the contours of life's fragments
into the Perfect Prayer
slowly transforming like snow crystals into ice
like cindering coals into a Single Flame
Gathering life
melting and simmering into the baptismal Harvest

Christopher H. Carlberg

"End Of August"

Don't try to end this time in repetition of the others that have so
rotted myself that I aim to be
I belong to be better than in the middle of what I think I should be
After all the thoughts that I've had about being together with myself
Don't let this black colored month belong to anyone else but me
I am the August that nobody else wanted
I am the little child that wanted to run out and play with his friends
Between the outside and the in of me, don't let the way I was back
to the way I am now
Walk down to the park and let fury pine leaves brush my gentle face
and hands... the gentle inside of me and the gentle end of August
Under the message of alphabet letters I will assure that I completely
spell out the end of August
Not overly being bothered by being changed I correctly concern only
myself from that I want now
Light rain to have my mind not break or enough
I lay down and soak the wet into my body and let it touch me in
some sort of way
I'm keeping awake to hear every word that's moving me from fading
away

Bret T. Jenny

The Gears Of Night

So complex they are — teeth, pivots,
screws coiled
in their own gangrenes.

The syntax in their blockades
and the semantics (in their mouths
the weight of asphyxia)
dream of mornings without manacles.
The gears model
the timbres and intonations
and the jagged shape of the verb.

(The gears of night
cannot catch the dreams
of the chained faces.

The dreams pierce the sleeps
and will open eyes at seeing
the death of the gears
and the verbs of captivity
blossoming in the streets.

The gears of night,
no one will weep for them.)

Joanyr De Oliveira

The Piano Player

Within a familiar frame
she exists
jowls sagging - eyes vacant.

Her pendulous breasts
sway in tempo to the honkytonk tunes
she hammers out on the aged upright.

Frayed curtains fail to filter the shafts of sunlight
that scorch the brittle white roots
which strangle the last vestiges of titian curls.

Rotted stumps envelop
a final acerbic sucker
causing her pale crinkled lips to pucker.

Oh, ancient one—
age has robbed your beauty
and left a shell which belies your youth.

Long gone the speak-easy queen—
only at those hoary 88's are you truly alive;
may you never know the cruel trick
life has schemed against you

Play on, Gram, play on...

Margaret O'Farrell

Sonnet To My Lady

That thou again with bleeding, bruised heart
Should seek once more for friendship's healing balm,
Did'st touch my empathy and made a start,
Towards love that could not ever do you wrong;
But I am settled in my willful ways,
As you are, too, though never mean and crude
Like I, whose dress has seen such better days,
And snatches morsels of his lady's food,
It was good cause to turn rejection's cheek,
And to decide alone to wend your way,
Or else to find a husband mild and meek
Who'll acquiesce to everything you say,
I think this thing of love we can not fix;
I am too old a dog to learn new tricks.

George B. Markle

"First Born"

The light has gone, it's midnight now, beside me lies my love, in slumber wrapped.
Suddenly I feel—what is it? Like a flutter 'neath my breast.
A bubble maybe, just of gas—Wait, what do I feel?
A finger crooked, a little heel?
Again, it moved! It really did! A lump now, in my throat, so very big. A tear forms. In darkness, yet I see the sparkle of it light my heart. Again! It did! Oh, Lord above, it really lives! My heart fills and as it does, my eyes flow over with my tears. "Honey?" I call softly, but he sleeps on with just a murmur. "Honey," again I cry, "It moved, it did! It moved! Oh, please wake up before it stops. Honey, Wake up, it moved!"
And then he wakes and feels a thump, and even then I can't believe!
He grins so big and kisses me, then quickly turns.
"Okay, it moved, now go to sleep!" and thought I didn't see the sparkle of his own pride's tear.
For who'd believe a man full grown, would shed a tear,
the first time he felt his first son's life, so dear?

Nora Lee Brown-Dawson

Dream Of Andros Island

Sleep comes like a cat in autumn
soft in the night on silent feet
betraying the secrecy of overlooked memories,
calling back the sands and sky and blurred waters...
Thoughts of returning are like leaves in the wind
-passing with a rattle -...and without difference.
The advancing clouds of winter cast shadows like bricks to the Earth
while a once-clear image bends under the load
of knowing there will not be a second time.
Slowly fading laughter burns on bitter lips
sinking away beneath the subconscious blackness
(A guard receding in the fog
leaving the dying in the open)
So alone with frozen fingers and slowed heartbeats
a fallen angel
a missing scar
a fleeting rerun of peace left behind... Awake with a new loss.
Everything else slides so far away
-Sometimes all that matters
Has already slipped through your hands.-

Amy Goodrich

Harvest

Now are gathered fruits of labor
summer's lushest bounty reaped
from browning vines once laden
prepare their limbs for winter's sleep

The slanting light more precious now
its warmth elusive quick escaped
strange nights rimed with harvest chill
bare fields in pumpkin moonlight draped

Sleepy sunflowers hang their heads
exhausted by the summer's glory
and roses shed their ballroom gowns
for the telling of the autumn story

Cascades of leaves with withered sighs
loose their hold on tired bough
indignant swirls like broken wings
on russet knee surrender now

All nature drawn within herself
prepares to weather harshest storm
surrounded by her harvest bounty
golden autumn memories keep her warm

Karen E. Hughes

Chapters of Life

Treat your life like an open book
Take time to read it and take a good look
There are some chapters that close but stay
In our thoughts and our memories stored away
Some we take down and reuse to grow
To strengthen our lives in meaning as we go
Take the bad with its sadness and take time to weep
Look deeply and find there is goodness to keep
We tend to dwell on the chapters of sadness
When in reality we should dwell on the gladness
These three chapters I send to you today
Love, peace and happiness important chapters to play
Take time to smell the roses a part of each day
Remember the saying all work and no play
So take a few moments for yourself if you can
Life is too short and I'm sure it's God's plan
Your chapters of life are important to all concerned
All you experience you pass down and they learn
So take this poem and store it away
Take it down and read it on a rainy day

Debbie Perkins

Because Of You — A Love Poem

I thought you were a summer breeze
That echoes softly through the trees
And sings the lovers' lovely song
But alas! I discovered I was wrong!
A tornado is what you truly are
A whirlwind blowing fierce and hard
Pain and confusion is your wrath
Destroying all that's in your path
And like the twister, you don't care
You just move on when you've taken your share
I thought you were the fruits and flowers
But the fruit's now rancid and the milk is sour!
All from your lips is so untrue!
Even kisses lie for you!
Because of you, I have no heart
You robbed it of its vital parts
The part that loves, the part that feels
The part that helps the soul to heal
Because of you, I write with strength
For that one reason, I give you thanks!

Jody Kopit

Dorothy

The life she lived was like some gentle air
That rose like goldfinch from her violin.
She treated folk, like tunes, with tender care

Responded to with love by kith and kin;
Not only by her clan, but luckless those
For whom her touch went deeper than the skin.

In answer to their need, when need arose,
She'd never hesitate to give her all
To thawing hearts, dead-cold as winter snows.

She'd visit the distressed without a call,
Bring converse, smiles and laughter and the treat
That for a time sun-stripped their gloomy pall.

Her soul was finely tuned to youth's heartbeat.
She mothered one and all and ever drew
On plume-light tact to guide unsettled feet.

She'd beam the empathy that mothers knew
Went hand in hand with action. Not a few
Recall her life as melody, played true.

John Martin

Green Meadows

And if you heard it says the girl
the birds chirped in the green meadows
the magenta shadows spanning noon and dawn
she says to him I wish you were there
and there was so much left unsaid
the blowing wind and spring leaves fall
boy waits hoping while purple mountains fill his mind
but rears the wall of brick and stone to cover him
no laughing sweet with birds will call, the playing child
sad are the colors of magnolia and rose
meadows and day's bloom on the flowers
oh how I wish that you were there but still you weren't
you never come and I was alone
lonely and all the bright noises, the dark cloud shadow
on and on the day will come, is rising
but hopes like wares and dreams dash on the gritty beach
and splinter on the rocks and sink below
and by the broken winds that sweep the waters
the seashore blue and someone's crying
you're never never coming here

Caitlin Barrett

A Stone Circle In Ireland

Morning
the circle of stones obtrude
upon the grassy hilltop bestrewn
with ruminant cattle, indifferent
to the stony hallowed silence
reigning mystical in morning mist.

Afternoon
the sun's warm aura pervades
the hilltop where children invade
a sacred ground, indifferent
to the murmurings of chanted litanies
as they laugh and tumble down the lush slope.

Evening
In the moonlight lies the blanched trace
of weather-beaten monuments where lovers embrace
with passionate sighs under starry skies, indifferent
to its mystery of spiraling galaxies and woolly nebulae
that inspired this temple of heavenly communion.

Timothy Taggart

The World We Would Not See

One-eyed man, his face creased with pain,
The dirt-grayish cloth upon his eye oozing blood;
He, upon ember asphalt pavement lain,
Sane, but barely, blaming all but God.

Woman with painful smile, gazing at a malicious grin,
Her neck gripped by pervert fingers,
Her body weaving through libidal stares, inviting sin,
A part of her nocturnal curse.

A figure cast in black upon the gray walk way,
Hands outstretched to the world he bears upon his shoulders;
"See, I ask for alms as I have nothing," as if to say
His face upon the mud as a storm above him thunders.

Through blind eyes do we see
That such pain, though drawn so explicitly,
Evokes not so much action, if it does, pity.
It is from seeing pain suffered daily
In the first place, that we learn to not even see
How we are living in a world so callous, so unashamed of its apathy.

George Guntur A. Pujalte

The Sandman - A Fantasy

Through drowsy lanes at twilight time
The dusky Sandman tiptoes by:
His head is bent, his hair is white,
But laughter twinkles in his eye.

Down from the starry hills of sleep
He comes with steps that none may stay,
To scatter dream-dust in the eyes
Of little children there at play.
He does not linger anywhere
But what a change his coming brings;
The children, with their toys aside,
Think wistfully of other things.

A cot that's waiting, warm and soft,
A pillow for a little head,
All ready at the Gate of Dreams,
When prayers and soft good-nights are said.

And when at last each little one
Is tucked in slumber, still and deep,
The Sandman's off to other lands,
The children there to put to sleep.

Mary E. Lawrence

Memo

on the edge of sAnity
the fields of flowers
beckon me,
fragrant rainBows of color
so enticing; allUring;
inviting me.

on the edge of reality
charred embers
still Smoking
bare; stark; Empty
fields of black,
rancid oDors permeaTing
my senses.
gO now!

broken mOments
pieces of time
fragMents of thoUght
shattered dreams
wind blown. sCattering
tHrough space.

Judy M. Grotsky

On Leaving

'Journeys end to begin anew.'
The flowing stream is never still.
The roving wind; beaming light—
This is the way of Nature.

The tiny shoot becomes the tree;
The number of generations grows.
Beating heart; enlightened thought;
The quest of one's Spirit.

Behind me now the city gate,
The swaying tree, the river's song.
Old friends lower the stirrup cup;
The rising sun beckons.

Before me, tomorrow's mystic lure.
The Silk Road calls; the Tao moves.
My house remains—my home is in me.
A history of footprints greets my face.

Huangshan before—Huangshan behind.
A single footfall has started my journey.
I tread a carpet of bright tomorrows.
Now I have no past.

Paul T. N. Chapman

The Immigrant's Tale

Foreigners, aliens, immigrants—yes, but we have been
the genes and hormones of this country since the first Thanksgiving.
For some of us the barriers were slight, acceptance easy—especially
for those of us whose ancestors had driven the dissenters of the day
from their own then-arrogant country, super-power, Empire,
and watched them recreate a home across the grim Atlantic.

We were fortunate; no need to penetrate the border in a sweltering truck,
to creep across the desert in the star-dark and find ourselves next day
hunted down by the ruthless sun, by dogs and guards. We didn't crowd
on leaky rafts or boats in desperate struggle to reach these shores.
We signed, took blood tests, cruised to the land we knew from the movies.

What have I contributed? A few poems, gardens grown, scientific papers,
by fellow foreigners edited. But thousands of others from Europe or
warmer continents, have mated, created, and latticed burgeoning roots
from coast to coast. They don't look back, except when the scent
of flowering privet, or mimosa, or fresh-turned earth in spring rain
plays a poignant note from the past. For passion, fear and danger,
boredom, anger, venture and adventure brought them here, to glean
among the alien sheaves and earn their share, and in return,
give all their skills and talents, all they are.

Vivienne Rowe

The Trap

He is gone but his essence lingers.
The senses are alerted to his absence.
A hint of damp earthy sweat emerges from the rumpled
shroud that held us when
our passion died.

I try to erase all evidence from our trysting place
but to no avail.
The trap reveals a tapestry of hair and lint woven with
love and lust.

The trap is clean now.
All visible evidence of our encounter gone -
but how do I cleanse my heart?

Anne Huddleston Dean

Calgary Badlands

Above the desert horizon
the still-warm disc of doubt rises
and cool hopes turn to dust,
bound to the searing torment
of the sun's lost kindness.

The furnace, now naked and full-grown
rains seemingly gently deceit,
and tenderness is frozen,
polished by the cool light of indifference,
to a bronzed memento of things past.

Where before the shadows of twilight
hid the moist benefits of uncertainty,
now the fierce and voiceless thirst
creates its own mind-display
of invented accidents and made-up excuses.

Without a flash-flood of desire,
love withers in this callous wilderness,
and slowly, with no swift, kind death
nor any shrub or friendly shisham to provide the merest shade
from the remorseless, pounding, glare of heart break.

Douglas McLean Morrison

The Man On His Old John Deere

There's a new straw hat on the table, it's firm and just brand new
There's a woman making the coffee and pouring a cup or two
He's twenty-four and she's twenty and he holds her with hard, calloused hands
He's making a life for his pretty, young wife on ninety acres of land

Through the dust bowl and the Great Depression they weathered the plight of the years
Fighting the forces of nature, fighting back floods of tears
But he drove his mighty chariot, his John Deere tractor ne'r let him down
His wife looked on full-well knowing they'd bring life to the barren ground

Now there's an old straw hat on the table with a hole that shows clean through
There's a woman making the coffee and pouring a cup or two
And the crowd out in the pasture is looking for a bargain to find
The two sit back and watch 50 years of hard work reduced to a bottom line

Together they walk to the corn crib as he holds her with hard, calloused hands
For a last look at the tractor that worked their ninety acres of land

And they climb one last time on the tractor, on the cracked leather seat at the wheel
He drives his once-mighty chariot through the barren snow-covered field
They remember the sound of corn rustling as he steers down the last head row
The auctioneer motions for him to come in and they know it's time to let go

He drops the throttle slow to neutral and then he pulls his graying wife near
And a feeling of peace subsides in her and the man on his old John Deere.

Michael D. Hastie

Orion Rising

With grace did I, Poseidon's son, bestride the earth
Till felled by fair Artemis' arrow's shaft,
I learned to pace the night (for all I'm worth)
And clear the stars from frosty Winter's path;
And here I chase the seven Pleiades
Across the sky, and wonder what's the use
Of my exalted birth; I pledge to please
The Gods, and flaunt my bright star Betelgeuse;
I strive to hold my sagging shoulders high,
Keep my Sirius-minded dog at bay,
And on cold nights I heave a hunter's sigh
And make a pillow of the Milky Way -
Belted giant with a heart of iron,
Hunter in the quilted sky, Orion.

George N. Braman

A Sonnet To My Wife

When winter cold conspires with angry rain
To bring on misery to heart and limb,
And nagging ague joins with bitter pain,
Increasing endless woe and vision dim;
When all the joys of nature seem but dreams
Of one fair day with sun and flowers dressed
In April's ancient time by laughing streams,
And singing birds against the sky up pressed;
Faint memory and hope combine to bring
New dreams of summer days and spring delights,
With gentle breeze and joyful birds that sing
In merry chorus. Now, with these sounds and sights,
I look upon your lovely face, and then
I touch your cheek, and I am young again.

Duane F. Johnson

D'une Optimiste

Were life
to come up and stare you in the face
you'd have forgotten your glasses.
Were the sun
to shine right into your eyes
the shade would be in your way.
Were the wind.
to blow fresh,
igniting new fires
stirring life's ashes
you'd have been numbed by its coldness.
I don't understand you Sir,
viewing the world through opaqued lenses;
dark overpowering shadow
negating whatever bit of light there is
whatever bit of sight you have;
have you ever thought of getting glasses?

Sherry Sosis

At Waves' Edge

Don't change your rhythm
to conform to me.
Never recede without coming again
in your own established time.
For I lie affected, responding
to the stages of your advance,
while recovering from the motion
of your retreat.

Vary your force if you will, but come.
Pound me into the hard sand.
Imprint my form on its smooth face.
Dash my being
into its own myriad parts
and with the dislodged grains
drag us with you to your source.

As the sand slips away
I yet remain,
not united with the mighty one,
but bruised and content
awaiting his return.

Bliss Safford

How To Sculpt A Frog

Oh, how I wish
to peer down upon the earth.
To climb the highest tree and
to rise above it all.
To watch over the world and
to reach down
to find our souls and
to crush the death from them.
To hunt through the forests and
to search through the weeds and
to scour the dirt and
to unearth an ounce of dignity and
to toss about that dignity and
to drown the world with it.
To take the sphere in my palm and
to wring it through my fingers and
to hurl it against the unforgiving wall and
to pick up the pieces and
to sculpt
a frog from them.

Joseph Grim Feinberg

October Days

September drops her vixen veil
to reveal her fiery fashion
A green August canvas pales into a
burst of autumn passion.

From golden rod and orchid asters
to pink clouds against azure skies,
a warmth and gentle ending
this kaleidoscope implies.

There are yellow splashes on crimson purple
to shades of red and orange-amber;
the royal dress a rich display
of color to remember.

Then the flaming palette fades
within its glory and its splendor
to shadows of gray and cold steel days,
...the nakedness of November.

Phyllis O. Phillips

"Can't Steal My Song"

I've never thought it wrong before
to whistle sing or hum,
And put to music metaphors
in beat without a drum.
's okay to blast profanity
and curse 'til air turns blue,
But, question they my sanity
if whistling a tune!
I never dreamed I'd see the time
offensive it would be
to hum a tune or sing a rhyme
express a melody.
I see, for now, that Satan's won
this battle - not the war.
But, keep in mind this battle's one
and far from being o'er.
Don't hold your breath 'ole Satan boy
within my heart's a tune.
Try as you may to stifle joy
will whistle, hum or croon!

James A. McClelland

The Amperage Of The Heart In Passion

Two crows
  Two squirrels
And a bee

One field
  One sky, one earth
One sea

One He
  One us
One you, one me

Two squirrels
  Their home
A hollowed tree

Two crows
  Weary from the flight of days
And nights that fool in countless ways
  The polarity of my heart
And the amperage of its passion.

  A witness to all this am I
And thus thank the forces that created me.

Alexis A. Alvarez

Emergence

The glorious unspread wings
Upon the backs of the human beings
Lay curled and unseen...
Changed now upon the clay
Fluttering in the need to play...
How came we upon this land,
The precious few, to change the plan
Lain so blindly in great parts
By still-yet wildly beating hearts
Of Heavens young...
Lift up your feet, my dear
And spread those wings that you so fear.
For on that lifted wind you'll fly
God's own, the perfect butterfly...

Doreen Dunn

Waiting For That Bump In The Night

Thump, thump, bump bump bump - BUMPF!
We hear it, both at once, he and I
And we fly out of our bedroom
He with his hair standing on end, his body still erect and warm
Forced to stop mid-way in the act
Me with my robe half-open
The damp, draughty air grazing my calves
As sharply as the thump and the bumpf grazed my mind
And we see her sitting at the bottom of the steps
Sitting up straight, her back ramrod straight
And looking as slender as a lotus
I crouch in front of her, peering through myopic eyes
At the dark red smudge that has clotted, is clotting, above her eyes
And is trickling, wet and slick, down her haggard and unfeeling cheek
Her eyes are vacuous, seeing nothing
Not even me, not feeling me who is shaking her out of her stupor.
"I am sick of this!" he spits through clenched teeth
"Sick of it." But nonetheless I dress her, wash her wound
And bundle her into the car

Just like before.

Leena Ronalds

Bonds

"We always were," he whispered, "a timeless memory"
"We soar above convention, on winged affinity"

"Together...more than two," she mused, their uncapped alchemy
Billowing beyond rapport, in singularity

Echoes from the Pantheon, deific euphony
Proclaimed their bonding preordained, recorded destiny

"Life's a quest for complement, a rapt congruity
"Your union rides the fulcrum of a rare fortuity"

"Unfettered by the ligatures of custom's sophistry
"A wealth eclipsing 'virtuous', your serendipity"

"You see," he said, enfolding her, "set obligation free
"I'll lead the way to Camelot to live our 'meant-to-be'"

But habit held her hostage, and he wooed uncertainty
Wrapped around the words he spoke in timid prophecy

A flight to the familiar, to home and family
He lives with how it might have been....she lives in reverie

Judi Billings Sparagna

Star Dust

Suppose you are outside of it,
what, then, do you see?

Well, she said,
there's a fiery point,
but mostly nothing ness.

When she looked around again,
godly creatures did appear.
Blazing yellow.
Blinding brightness.
Swirling at the speed of light.

What, then, is this business,
the business of the universe?
Why making stars, I see.

And we?
Oh, just the dust left over.
And me?
So happy just to be.

Nancy Kieffer

Useless Sighs

This is the street I walked along many years ago
When I was young and beautiful, invincible and free.
I saw this tree, that window there, its curving arch and bow
From deep within some people smiled admiringly at me.

I walked along this street quite proud still thinking homage due
When I was careless, strong and sure and scornful too I think.
So though their gaze was warm and bright and meant to show its hue
I hurried on and turned my head and felt their kindness shrink.

I'd no need of such a glow to light my wayward stride
No needs at all I could not fill myself it seemed to me.
For if I wanted company or love, a place to hide
Why then I'd stop and take the nearest hand that I could see.

Swift my steps, I tarried not nor paused nor thought nor cared
That surging life might flow too fast for me to keep the pace.
How I yearned then for might, for aid, a strength that could be shared
But youth and beauty too had fled and age had slowed my race.

There had been a hidden force that coloured all my days
I thought it mine to keep, to use but I was wrong I fear.
That dazzling girl is gone and with her all her merry ways,
In vain I call "It's I" if they don't see me am I here?

Penelope Jacques

The Tumble And Toss

The wind and waves, forever rift,
Though kinsfolk ever one;
They tumble and toss, and churn, and sift
To every form but calm.

The plainness of his dry-weeds way
That stirs inside the wind
Is stranger not, nor far away,
From waves that splash and swim.

Entreats again her surging sea
To stir his sleepiness;
Her secret hidden mystery
Has woke him with a kiss;

And out he steps upon the sea,
The foolish thought to dare,
Or courage take, whatever it be,
He sets his foot out there.

Now, falling through the failing wave
Is not the major thing,
But that one has set out at all
Invites the victor's ring.—

Steven A. Coach

Day Breaker

In the early hours of morning, when shadows' soldiers fight,
When the lords of darkness take a stand in their feud against the light,
It is you I can depend upon as so many times before,
I have watched your journey's end unwind on your way towards the shore.

What message do you bring with you? What gifts have you to bare?
What secret tales from far-off lands have you the right to share?
Has your passage been a pleasant one or have storms been bad at sea?
Are the stars as bright at sea night? What do you have for me?

In your ever changing, supple form are you really what you seem?
Could it be that you're what stirs my soul, the center of my dreams?
Have you captured what within me lies, my castle in the sky?
Or is it merely wishful thoughts I keep as time goes fleeting by?

Then, as if you sense my gnawing plight, you are lapping at my feet,
And in your foam the questions asked are now one by one complete,
As I watch you neap upon the sand and slowly ebb away,
I realize I have the will to see through another day.

For when dawn appears upon the sea so I'll return once more,
As if as planned your foam I'll see as you make your way to shore,
We'll be as one for a little while, brothers of the morn,
For each day seems to be a time when we both are thus reborn.

Gregory A. Smith

The Bather

I do not know
where the light comes from.
I never wanted to be this
beautiful and faceless I
will never fail you. Before me
the tub slants footless, flat,
a carpet forever apricot and jade.
Walls of silk surround me;
aniline dyes in folds I press
this whiteness to my side I ache against,
my back an arch, a question mark;
my hair upswept, combed back,
shall not darken, or come undone down.
I will never leave this moment.
I am what time has done
when time has done with me.

Elizabeth Andrews

Solace Unfathomed

O Bard, my bard, what hast thou writ?
Wherefore and when in time does it fit?
What is the verse and for whom is it sung?
Why's of the meter that matters when rung?
How, but indeed, didst get thou its theme?
O Bard, my bard, what does it mean?

Sweet solace, my solace, in bathos and bores,
sweep me to heavenly roars in my snores:
—off to an elevatorial realm—
roundabout people asleep at the helm;
portulaca pansies with primrose and greens:
Sweet solace, my solace, such picturesque dreams.

Sweet solace, my solace in legions of smoke,
as phantoms fantastic afloat with their folk:
drifting and twisting and lifting the soul;
—without and within quaft brimming the bowl—
many the few and the far-off betweens:
Sweet solace, my solace in fathomless reams.

Such fairy-like fancies too fabulous seem:
O Bard, My Bard, what does it mean?

Simon Alexander Legge

Solitude

My geography and noiseless friend is sweet solitude
Which ever so scarcely will my fortune allow,
Until the day is spent and I can disavow,
And close my ringing ears to seek brief interlude,
Before my world and all its wailing woes again intrude.
Oh! Sweet eternal whisperings of solitude, how
You soft my madness with your gentle kiss upon my brow
And save my dizzy, spinning conscience with your quietude.
Not alone in madness, but by myself when griefs do dress
Themselves in dreams, and by those dreams absolve
My soul and transient pleasures with mournful resolve
To rid my melancholy and damnation from daily consciousness.
Let mankind sing of Heaven's gate and in that ecstasy dissolve,
But shed no tears for solitude - only for its loneliness.

David P. Ryan

A Scent Of Spring

A scent of Spring rides airborne wave-crests
Which only the living-Mother-Earth affords.
She bears her fruit-forms:
In entities that shoot towards the sky
Like giant beanstalks.
Other entities.....
Wintertime cocoons of constricted confinement,
Now stretch loosed, untested wings of freedom,
Wind-drying in sunlight of metamorphosed birth,
Spray-perfuming the atmosphere
For all to revel in,
With their sex-scent,
Most of all....for each other,
Asking their mate,
In humble interrogation,
To join them.

Michael W. Miller

Drowned

Is it the labor of a love lost if the ship,
while in the midst of sinking,
seeks the ivory lips of a casually breasted mermaid?
'Tis the angst of an old salt that within the confines of
Jones' locker
that a pillow of pearl and unkempt kelp wave him home:
wherein the windows now octupi
dances the warm glow of an unlit flame,
wafts the aroma of unground coffee,
swings pendulum the pumpkin buttocks of an aproned wife; her
eyes too blue to be the sky,
the ocean must be!

Kevin B. O'Connell

Il Pleut, Encore

How you can laugh, and careless do
While rain and rain still falls
And falls, in falling through
This life, in supplication calls
To you, in leaving left me blind
To stumble in each darkened day
This pain and pride my spirit bind
Like wolves in wilderness they bay
But all this was my own device
A chain that I have welded tight
And you to stay could not entice
Though try I did with fire and fight
And now I fall so, with the rain
That gathers puddles in the street
That drowns the world, my pallid bane
And seems to seal my death complete.

R. Smith

A Writer's Gift

His snake eyes glow with silent rage
While words from him spill on the page;
Writing quick and violently,
He screams his craft, but silently.

In insane bliss he finds his zone,
His comfort's found in all alone;
No one is there to taint his mind
With normal thoughts of any kind.

So writing, he goes on to tell
Of something someone knows quite well,
But never knew just how to say
This something in a moving way.

When thoughts escape his stranger mind
His zone has found its end of time;
His madness left, and finally gone;
He had a work to look upon.

Clay Lewis Roan

To My Son On His Wedding Day

I dream of winter days gone by.
window panes, crisscross scripts,
written images of frost and snow.
Life searching out in all directions,
I held you, mothered your diminutive ears,
with melodies of life,
Enabling you to understand
that frost was cold and why your hands,
entwined in mine,
were warm like the bread I baked.

You thought that snow was winter's food,
wrapped up in a ball,
gradually melting in a large pot,
crimson lights filtered through the window pane,
casting a dancing reflection on your cherubic face.
My lap was full. My lap is empty now.
Window pictures cease to be.

Love holds your hand now,
and that love will give me the gift of life,
one again there will be frosted pictures on my window pane.

Rosemary Clarkin

Lonely Miller's Wail

The sun hid behind the lonely hills,
Yonder in the west
As I retreat from the mills
Tired, exhausted, towards my lonely seat of rest.

I stumbled over a stone,
As I have often done in life's dusky journey,
And often in pain did I moan,
But there was nobody around to hear me.

The moon behind the clouded skies mocked as I did fall
As fate grinned behind my dusky life,
When I did call,
For a mate to help in my strife.

None answered my painful cries,
Nothing did I hear
But the silent sighs of the vast emptiness of the
land and the skies,
And, echoes of my own pains and fears.

Like a foundling of this world,
Deserted even by fate,
Darkness around me curls
Endearing me to my fallen state.

Kanchan

Untitled

It won't be long maybe an hour or two
A baby will be born given life by you
You lie in your bed you wait and you pray
Please be with me Lord all the way.

You try to forget the stinging pain
By thinking of what you are going to gain
A tiny bundle helpless and warm
You soon will cradle in your loving arms

From far away a voice you hear
Wake up wake up it is all over dear
You open your eyes and you can not believe
The reward for your pains you will now receive.

The nurse brings the baby and you watch with pride
As she carefully puts it by your side
Your heart fills with love and with tears in your eyes
You have forgotten the pains you are nursing the prize.

Erik Petersen

Lover Of Mine

An empty space in my heart,
A feeling of loneliness that never departs.
Longing for the warmth of love,
So wonderful it fits like a glove.
Knowing that my one true love will never be,
His love has been sent out to the sea,
If only he could share the love I feel in my heart,
A feeling that sets him apart from the rest,
Even though I feel like I am being put through
a certain test.
I wish I could finish this test of time,
When he will finally be a true lover of mine!

Paula McCoy

Did They Ever Think?

The closet door closes, I feel tight all within
A long narrow hallway scares me half to death
Dark dampen basements, I can no long breathe
Why? Why have they done this to me?
A childhood should be happy, full of laughter, love
My childhood was full of tears, not laughter, but fear
So scared to go home, not sure what I've done
Afraid of the black belt that hits you one on one.

The back of a hand or a piece of wood
Anything handy would be good
I'd cry and cry through my blacken eyes
to sore to sleep, the welts they were to deep
To pick and choose, and to know I'd lose
So on - my own I go, eleven years old
Don't have a home,
Just run and run your free
No more locked in child you'll be
But never did I know, the scars would never go,
"Did they ever stop to think of what they've done to me!"

Kim Lemke

Coming Out Of The Fog

It shocks to wake up from a happy dream,
And find the one you love has told you lies.
I never really knew he was so bad,
I rose today and then found out he was.
He use to say keep smiling to stay young,
I have no smiles, no joy no laughter left,
A sense of loss is all my heart can hold.
I now can see he thought I was a fool
My love for him has truly reached its end.

Shaketra Clarke

2050

The purple haze of a bygone sky, no rolling silken cloud
a lunar landscape shrouds the Earth, no skylarks break the silence.
The sea is sad, with waves of woe, no dolphins frolic here
no whales to sing their haunting songs, where are the shrieking gulls.
No fishermen for nets have perished, no herring shoals we should
have cherished.
No fish can live in this domain, but no one should blame me.

Farmers till what soil remains with ploughs that groan with haste,
our legacy is to suffer now from all that toxic waste.
I dine upon synthetic fare, how it's made I do not care,
no apples, plums and orchard fruits, please tell, what was a tree?
Our children born, some with three toes, others born without a nose,
genetic games they try to play, cloning babies in a tray.

Blinkered eyes that could not see, blinded with technology,
factories that belched with fury, sewers spewed their stomachs slurry,
poison dumps of modern faeces, mass internment of the races,
God, please forgive, for they went wrong, but no one should
blame me.

David Morgan

Sonnet

Thou art more beautiful that peace
A man who'll hot judge nor condemn
but love and cherish
Thou art more gentle that a child's heart
touching my soul to leave it warm
and secure by your hand
Thou art the light that lives inside
flowing outward to
guide me through
when darkness comes
My sweet inspiration
your eyes feed me color
your lips the reddest wine
Your body is my blanket soft and secure
when I lay down at midnight
Thou art time to love
and linger in heaven

Nicole D. Myers

Reel Of The Ravens

Flying in tandem,
a pair of resident ravens
rise above the river flats, over corrals...
to reach the garden heights.

Now, flying always abreast,
they dip and dive...
mount higher ... ride thermals.
Wings held steady ... tip to tip...
they flash with reflected light.

As they make the graceful curves
of squares and figures,
swoops and climbs,
a rusty voice calls, "Swing your partner!"

No square dance caller more precise;
no brightly costumed
nimble-footed dancing pair
executes the figures with more grace
than these iridescent aerialists,
voicing and winging spontaneous joy!

Ruth R. Ford

An Impressionist's Dream

If only I had possessed a clue,
a sea of light that shown into your heart
With the softness of Cezanne's brush the portrait I drew
would have brought us together, in a world
that tears us apart

If only I could have touched you
with the powerful hands of radin
I would never forget the lines of your beautiful face
perfection, time and time again
would shape the bronze statue my fingertips trace

If only I could have remembered the sweat whisper of your voice
I'd repeat these lonely words in my head
You were my choice, you were my choice
only to have forgotten when the record stopped turning
no one was dancing, you were gone, the music was dead

If only our inspiration had been one in the same,
Moliere would smile down at me from above
and say, "Patience is the virtue with which to catch you dame"
but I've been struck blind, deaf, and mute
in my breathless "impressionist's dream"

Jim Levering

Behind The Glass

As the darkness settles and the children are asleep,
A wind may softly blow your mind, making you jump to your feet,
You know she's never far away, but not one by your side,
Although you'd like to tell someone, you hide it all inside.

You find yourself beside a window, yet gazing into space,
Your realize another presence and turn to meet her face,
She smiles at you and softly says, "I guess it's just the heat,
But you have a long day tomorrow, so try to get some sleep."

You now phase back to reality, and your madness blows away,
You think about how short the night, and how long the day,
Yet just outside your window, it seems another world,
A young girl waits there for your call, receiving not a word.

She'll always be there waiting to hear, the thoughts you keep inside,
Again tonight there are no words, again tonight she cries.

Diane Louise Stirling

Window...

(To My New Found Friend)
Look at my heart, my mind, through the window...
a window I have constructed soundly
from transparent words and fragile feelings...
A window unhampered by curtain,
unafraid of scrutiny.

Please don't break it - it was hard to make,
and oft' times foggy,
dirty with outside grime...
I'll wipe it clean for you to see
this time.

Richard Blair Hughes

She Wrote

She wrote a poem a time ago
About what others wanted to know.
She sat at night
When silence was right
Creating the poem she thought to write.
Listening to her inner self
She thought about a little elf.
The magic of the moment
Brought a twinkle to her eye.
Gazing out the window to the early morning sky
The words began to flow just right;
And then she wrote with all her might.

Carole Ann Wood

Just Remember

I can't believe it, I'm leaving home
all on my own and I'm going to make it stick.
I might not be of age but I know
the world isn't a stage.

All of it will be new but I know I'll get through.
Things ain't going to be the same and
I know life isn't a game.
There might be hard times but I'll
work them out 'cause their mine.
What I'm leaving behind
is warm loving and kind
Something I know I'll miss
so let's say goodbye with a kiss.
Just remember I'm leaving a part of me
behind, so please don't cry.
Just remember I love you all?
and I know you'll be close if I fall.

Pamela Cyr

Soldier

In silence I cry.
Alone I will die.
Dreams become dear.
Reality is fear.

Boys we are no more.
Death is at our door.
Buddy. Dear Buddy. Get up. Please try.
Such sights for my virgin eyes.

The smell of death I can't escape.
The wounded, the dying have been raped
Of youth, of life, of growing old.
Of wife, of mother, of daughter to hold.

My enemy is less than a mile away.
Does he think of me where he lays?
I cannot see him in this sea of dark.
Am I in his sights? Am I his mark?

There is no pain while I rest.
Something warm running from chest.
I heard the knock. I opened the door.
God. Dear God. This is war.

Rhonda Lippert

Without You

I will always wish that we're together
Although it's true that I should know better
The whispers I hear from far above
Keep telling me that I am in love
In love with you, although I can't see
Your beautiful eyes looking right at me
The feeling of your sweet palm's touch
It's obvious why I miss you so much
Your face, your lips, your soothing kiss
They're the things I truly miss
I miss your voice, your feel, your inside
All that I feel when you're near beside
I just can't change what's so very true
Hell's on earth when I'm without you.

Franz Archibald

First Thought

First thought never comes alone,
Always more... legions of memories
or wishes or sad feelings
all wrapped into a shell.
Never comes sweetly into view,
pronounced as some grand mountain...
But hazy, foggy realness stealing pictures,
stealing sounds of life, and fear.

First thought, never joyous in awakening
Always low and dark... intruding,
Casting sadness into shadows,
Forcing saneness into view.
First thought, negative emotion, pain
or guilt or fear,
A longing for some peace, some laughter,
For the music to return within my soul again,
And leave me full and happy,
As the sunlight on my morning wall...

Wendy D. Zilke

Untitled

A piercing scream lost in the wind
An innocent child a victim of crime
A plea for help left unanswered
A needy person denied the necessities
Her cries ring through the empty house
His footsteps echo through the desolate halls
Darkness consumes them both
Her soul is yearning for an escape
His body is asking for more
She turns him away as she feels him close
And shudders at the sound of his voice
She tries to touch him deep inside
But she can find nothing within him
And so she asks why
Please tell me why
Daddy

Andrea Wolf

Just Another Dream

Somewhere a bird sings a sweet melody
And a curled up cat purrs quietly
A sailboat heads south to the open sea
And my lover lies sleeping so close to me

Somewhere in a forest thick with tall trees
When danger approaches the animals flee
The quiet of nature brings a feeling of peace
And my lover lies sleeping so close to me

Somewhere there's bridge that crosses a stream
Where the fishing is good or so it would seem
The water so cold, to ice it will freeze
And my lover lies sleeping so close to me

Somewhere in a valley the tall grass grows green
Where butterflies dance and the air is so clean
A hawk soars above and little lambs run free
And my lover lies sleeping so close to me

Somewhere there's a small child who is but three
Her innocence and smile warm you heart tenderly
She is the hope for our future, our prayers she will need
And my lover lies sleeping or is that just another dream

Lin Dressler

All Through The Night

Walking breathless down the silent shore
And by my side the guy I adore
Whispers in the wind, as the trees sway
I knew today would be my day

As the waves quietly made little sound
And the sun was no longer round
The layers of colours across the sky
Feeling of freedom, I thought, I could fly

The cold but refreshing waters of the sea
I could feel his love burning for me
The stars up ahead, like rain in a puddle
We lay there, silent, but still as we cuddle

The comfort and support of his arm around me
And the moon's reflection shining on the sea
Like crushed velvet blowing smooth
And the rubbing sensation that tends to sooth

His heart filled with passionate heat
And the water's waves moistening our feet
The moon in the darkness, made the light
And the smell of freshness in the night

I felt his heartbeat, pounding like a hand
As we lay there, arm in arm, on the sand
Then he grabbed me and held me tight
We kissed and made love all through the night

Shelley Ruiz

If You Care...

Before you hope, you first must care
and feel the earth and breathe the air.
Then realize you're worth much more
than anyone has told you, ever before.

Before you dream, you first must hope;
hope for the future, grab hold of that hope!
You'll climb and climb, and blister and burn
but soon you'll see, you get what you earn.

Before you love, you first must dream;
dreams of tomorrow, of what you have seen.
Be sure for yourself you want only the best,
and caring and hope will take care of the rest.

Before you live, you first must love;
love all that's around you, especially above.
Then suddenly the earth full of clouds and thunder
will unfold and you'll see all the beauty and wonder.

And, before you die, you first must live
love all those around you, and always forgive.
Your hopes and your dreams will always come true
if you care for the future, and believe in you!

Debbie Hodl

Sonnet On Life

To live each day as if it were the last.
To think, to say, to live, to be, to do
The things you want to, ought to, as if you knew
That when the day is over- Life is "past"
And all your deeds, both good and evil, ask
To have their say before the Great One, who
Through love and understanding learns if you
Have faltered, failed, or won in your life's task.

How great would all of man's achievements be!
What strife we'd see to conquer and to win
True friends, peace, memories - happiness.
When life grew old - then man would feel that he
Could go - not weary that it had to end -
For life was full and he need die - there rest.

Lillian Donaldson

Precluding Creation

Our world was created to house the wonders of life,
and God's immaculate juices quenched the thirst for
this, his dream, and slowly it began turning into reality.

So life evolved before the watchful eyes of God,
and nature's distinction glorified his moral, so
he found his dream to have been fulfilled.

Dreams can change, however, as God found,
for he realized that life simply wasn't enough,
he wished to grant more than life to a worthy
being, and this was cogitated on for a time.

God experimented at first with clumsy beasts, they failed,
and he reluctantly destroyed them; after, he allowed time to
pass as his genius derived his greatest creation yet.

It was at this period in which God created man;
they were unique in that God had reflected on his
own image for their development, they seemed promising.

God was mistaken, however, and he was struck by confusion
as he watched man perform their own genocide,
his dream was gone and all hope was lost; God's dreams were
never fulfilled the same again. . . in the Darkness Lucifer
chuckled.

Robert Duhaime

Three Cheers

Here's to the people that govern our land
And here's to those that get out of hand.
Without people doing things wrong
This mess of a world would be getting along.
Here's to the people who love and are loved
And cheers to the shover as well as the shoved:
Because without them our world is dead
And everything right would go to our head.
Here's to the geniuses who make all the plans,
And cheers to the losers and also-rans:
For in a lifetime, more likely than not
There's half a genius for every crack-pot.
Here's to inventors of all fine inventions
And cheers to the people with reckless intentions:
Because in this era of learning and schools
We all start out as blossoming fools.
Here's to the writers, their stories and prose
And cheers to the man with the curious nose:
For when no one bothers to get in our hair
It's time to quit... there's nothing there.

Neal McCord

My Son

So many nights you've woken me,
And I have dragged my tired body
from my bed,
Believing, I couldn't possibly
take another step,
Then I see your face,
I feel your little arms wrap around my neck,
As your body melts into mine so trustingly,
My nostrils are filled with the sweet baby scent of you,
And I know, if need be,
I could move mountains or swim seas,
For the love of you,
My son.

Violet Styfunyk

My Philosophy On Life

I've thought about life
And I want to say,
That while you have it
You've got to enjoy each day.
Listen to the birds' song, chase butterflies,
Smell the sweet roses, watch the stars in the skies.
Be a good person, be a good friend,
And your life will be worthwhile
Until it comes to an end.
Look for the rainbows and the pot of gold,
Fill your heart with all the love it can hold.
Believe in yourself, be ready to smile,
And don't be afraid to go the extra mile.
Take pride in your work,
Make the best of each day,
Try to be cheerful all along the way.

Brenda Pilling Mapes

Things Will Only Get Better

The joy doesn't remain in what you do,
and it doesn't remain in where you go,
but it remains in your heart, in your mind,
in your life, and in who you really are.
Because I know that deep down inside of you,
with every beat of your heart
there is a little voice whispering to you,
things will only get better
I believe in my heart that is true.
Let our world's nature guide you too.
Like a rainbow after the rain,
like a sunshine after the dark.
Like a moonlight in the night
your days will become bright
your ways will surely be right
don't surrender before a fight.
Embrace your dreams and hope both,
hold on and believe in your life,
believe in your mind that thing -
will only get better.

Hana Al Youssef

Second Wind

Just when I think I've been at this for so long
And it's driving me 'round the bend
When they say - "a change is as good as a holiday..."
Along comes my second wind.

Just when I think I'm all alone
And I indulge in foolish pride
The words come loud and clear
Get your sorry self 'outta' here;
Along comes my second wind

My second wind, He made me into who I am today
He knows me better than I know myself.
He's the truth, the life, the way.

My second mind He saved me from who I am today.
He loves me even when I hate myself.
Ask Him to take your sins away

My second wind - closer than a friend
The bottom line - He rose again!

My second wind is as refreshing as a cold drink on a hot day.
Dig deep and take a sip. Until you want to say...

My second wind.

Ian Boyd

Refuge

I will go up to the woods again
and let me in through a vaulted door
to the sunlit nave, for there
nothing will matter anymore.

Here is a passive priestess done
with love and laughter and strife and stir
she kindles her candles one by one
and does not dwell on the things that were.

Walling her spirit with sky and earth
she does her penance to sky and trees
she sweeps the floor with a holy mirth
and joins in the birds' bright melodies.

But if ever a footfall wake the calm
till the tall ferns tremble and draw apart
she will snuff the taper and still the psalm
and bar the door with a beating heart.

Anne Sutherland Brooks

Remember

You've got to forget the past,
And live in the present,
And when the present,
Turns into the past,
Think about the future,

Remember the love forget the pain,
Go for peace not war,
Remember your friends,
Love your enemies,
Don't be afraid to show your true feelings.

Elizabeth Pinkney

Thinking Of You

I think of you as I lay down for bed
And once again when I raise my head
When I need to be picked up for a little while
I think of your face and your loving smile
I see things as the day goes on
that reminds me of you
Small things like a light snowfall
or a sky of blue
The thought of you comes during late hours of the night
A simple blessing toward off any fright
On my mind the thought of you is always on top
For when it comes to thinking of you
I'll never stop

Marc McNay

Busy Man

Golden Sunshine on blue waters-reflects
and shimmers on silver sand,
a lone white swan wings there onwards -
on its way to far off land, this
lovely picture tells a story if you're
not too busy-man!
Great green mountains tower high above
The fair fresh fields of summer-time,
small birds sing out in chorus tender
and in your heart sweet peace could linger
if you are not, too busy- man!
The scents and sounds of soft winds blowing
could lead you to a restful state,
Trees, and leaves and creatures crawling
some to love - some to hate,
all these things - have you forgotten?
since you became the busy man.

Norla-E Tormey

Retrospection

A man sits on a worn wooden stage,
and stares at the blackness before him.
He remembers his life,
memories, dark and cold
and silent screams in pain.

He accepts no judgments,
no judgement is given.
But the dead sound of silence is deafening.

He wants to kneel
and beg for forgiveness.
But can only replace the mask,
hear the sounds of applause
and fade away.

Lisa Boniface

The Gift Of Opportunity

They asked me to canvass for a disease,
And the soft wind whispered to me,
"Unto the least of these, my child,
Is also unto Me."

They asked me for money, time and again,
And I flinched and I frowned, in shame;
But the soft wind whispered again to me,
"Be merciful — in My name."

They asked my opinion on immoral shows;
"Oh, I never watch," I replied;
But the soft wind whispered again to me,
"Is that any reason to hide?"

When He saw the rascals cheating the poor
In the temple one day, long ago,
HE cried out the shame; HE stood for the right,
HE wasn't afraid to say NO.

So, the soft wind whispers each day to me,
As I look at God's sky so blue;
"Give back to the lonely and weak, my child,
As the Master has given to you."

Mildred Gomoll

The Seasons

As the month of March approaches,
And the Spring brings the birth of new buds,
The rain that pours falls steady,
Causing all small brooks to flood.

June brings the summer season,
As the young leaves frolic in the air,
You could smell the salt in the ocean,
And see people barbecuing everywhere.

In September the leaves change their colour,
It's the most beautiful season of all,
As you walk down a path and gaze at the view,
Oh that magical essence of fall.

The cold winter is in the month of December,
The old leaves fall gracefully to the ground,
The people look out their windows anxiously,
For the first snowfall to come around.

The seasons make changes in us also,
In our health and in the way we feel,
For the work of such powerful people,
Is so creative and miraculously real.

Brenda St. Coeur

My Need

My need for honesty, sincerity
and truth is so great.

Someone to be with when it is
comfortable in silence or in laughter.
Someone who is understanding of my need
for solitude and individuality.
And will allow me my time to be alone.

Someone who can offer an enlightening solution
for my problem but understands when I solve
it in my own way.
Someone who is willing to listen when I'm expressing
my excitement of a new challenge as well as when
I'm expressing my disappointments.

I have a need to feel that closeness and security
of a relationship that is centered around the
search for understanding and acceptance of the inner being.
The very center of the being which can not be seen
or touched but is yearning to be understood.

Understand and accept me for what I am, not for
what you see or what you want me to be.

Lana Hartmann

Untitled

It's been several years now,
And vivid memories still enter her mind.
Naivete, misplaced trust, even stupidity played a role.
And she once again feels vulnerable.

A secret, kept well hidden, deep in her soul,
letting them think untrue things about her.
The look of disappointment in her father's eyes,
And she once again feels shame.

Then the truth began to unfold.
Shock surprise, even pity, enveloped those close to her.
And so she began to deal with the pain,
And she once again feels anger.

Now, she has become a good actress.
Letting them believe she has overcome tragedy.
Little do they know the extent of the damage done.
And she once again feels alone.

It's been several years now
And vivid memories still enter her mind.....

Lynette Boehr

Stormy

It was a cold bleak night,
As the poor old man continued to fight
Against the raging wind and snow,
Where he was heading he did not know.

A small run-down shack, he sighted ahead,
So on through the drifts he speedily tread.
Not knowing how far or how long it would take,
He prayed to the Lord, not far for his sake.

A few hours passed but he didn't give in,
For he knew that the Lord would help him to win.
The struggle continued throughout that dark night,
But with sun in the morning, his eyes opened bright.
For just a few paces off to the right,
This little old shack stood out like a light.

He ran to the door and pushed this way through,
At last he found shelter from out of the blue.
He lay on the floor with eyes that were closed.
And where he is now, nobody knows.

Gale Rivers

Holocaust Day

Today we remembered the holocaust hell - and our own six
million dead.
And we promised ourselves that we'd never forget -
and would never again be afraid.

We say this today in our own promised land -
a people fearless and free.
So why do we continue to crawl and to flinch - and who is our enemy?

We watch over factories and farms -
our view scans each road and each tree.
So what makes the stones fly into our eyes -
to blind us to what we should see?

We have our religion, culture and law, our music, song and prayer.
So why do our ears catch the terror and hate -
and fear is the sound that we hear?

We are proud of our children, our joy and hope, in each town,
field and home.
So why are we fenced in, wired and barbed -
and where has that freedom flown?

We learned to be quick, brave and strong we left our enemies behind us
So who is the friend who attacks all the time -
do we carry him around inside us?

Today is the day we swore to recall - our memory guards its own hell.
But somehow our senses became so confused - we are not using
our memory well!

Rachel Klein

React!

People are killing, the results are chilling,
Animals are dying 'cause hunters are lying.
Forests are burning and no one is learning,
Everyone's sighing, the world is crying.

If no one dares to show they care,
The world will die, no one will be left to cry.
Somewhere, someplace there must be a trace,
Of a cure, to make the world pure.

There must be a clue, for a place that is blue,
A place where people share and care.
Where people smile, mile by mile,
And show they love by a kiss and a hug!

A place where people like to prance,
Like to laugh, and like to dance!
A place where people aren't afraid,
To walk outside whether night or day!

Listen to me and do what's right,
Help the earth and make it bright!
We must hurry to stop the fury,
Don't waste our earth, give it rebirth!

Rita Louise Vincent

Indigo Moment

My life was touched by an angel tonight,
as I rejoiced in the magnificence
of the burnished twilight.

The enchanted air wrapped me in a cloak
of gossamer wings, that led me gently
through cool forests that spoke:

"Seek and find the one who honours the needs
of your spirit", whispered quietly in
breaths of frangipani.

With bewitching fascination I knew
in that indigo moment - the angel
had guided my soul, to you.

Claire Bruce

Gifts

God quietly, gently speaks to me
as in the whispering lone pine tree.
The birds soar gracefully in the blue sky
as slowly the day drifts by.
The bright sun tells of the life he brings,
to every creature and living thing.
The aroma of field flowers fill the air,
reminding me how much God cares.
The rolling fields of tall wild grass
remind me of his love so strong,
that continues on and on and on...
Glistening water, dancing all day
reminds me there is time to play.
The children's laughter, oh so near...
remind me of the gift of tears.
So many gifts we are sent each day;
if we only a little attention do pay.

Marilyn Allanson

When The Clock Strikes Twelve

A strange face glared at me from amongst the trees
As it began to die, away blew all their leaves.
Shadows of the past were everywhere to be seen
How rapturous it is to be a part of this dream.
Voices of ghosts heard through blowing wind that is crisp
Burning wood creates little streaks of wisp.
All of this is said to be in the past
Yet, upon me a curiosity spell has been cast,
I notice the things, not many see.
I love entering the darkness from which most people flee.
We cannot live without fear until we've conquered all gloom
If you do not conquer fear, your fate shall be the worst of all doom.
Study the stars, gaze upon the face of the moon
Watch, as all around you slowly goes to ruin.
Am I the only one who can sense the scorning?
Won't anyone else heed mother nature's warning?
One day our sad, lonely lives will come to an end
Can't we live in peace until then, so we can all gain a friend?
I'll tell you once, fulfill all you desire and lust,
Before the time comes when you return unto the earth and again
become dust.

Gus McFadden

September Noctourne

There's a plaintive sigh in the wind tonight
As it rustles the Birches high
And croons a tune to the harvest moon
That rides a dappled sky.
I hear it moaning along the shore
And shaking the dry marsh grasses,
Caressing the rows of golden swath
In the stubble fields, as it passes.
Now here, now here, it dies, it cries;
As the Autumn night dreams on,
Mourning the loss of the golden days
Of another summer gone.

Elspeth Fitzmaurice

My Obsession

I thought, I let you go, my obsession.
But I saved a special spot for you.
No more are you an obsession.
Reality is such.
Just a special place in my heart, a special hope I cling to.
You are with me, whenever I need you.
Your strength has become my will.
Or will I be tormented to death, by my obsession?

Janet Hassefras

"To Those We Remember"

It all began in thirty-nine,
As they stood waiting in the line.
Off they went on their own,
Never knowing if they'd ever come home.
They hit the fields, with guns in hand,
Prepared to act on the command.
As shots fired and hit the ground,
The bombs made a frightening sound.
Soldiers travelled through harsh, cold winds,
As they prayed for God to forgive their sins.
Maybe He could carry them through,
For failing they could never do.
The soldiers fought and lost their lives,
Never last seeing their loving wives.
In the eleventh month, the eleventh day,
The whole world would change in a different way.
It was eleven a.m, there was nothing but silence,
Gratefully, there was an end to the violence.
These who died will be forgotten never,
For they we remember for ever and ever.

Jeffrey R. White

Sleep

Dear Lord I lie here in my bed
At dead of night
And long for peace and quiet to round me fold,
My mind is still as busy as the day,
When thoughts and happenings within it play.
This bed is sweet,
The room around it neat —
The pillow 'neath my head is soft and clean.
It's that elusive butterfly within
Which holds me from that calm and soothing rest,
Some know so well, and others less than best.
The clock and hours slowly tick away
While the butterfly, my nerves begins to fray,
Dear Lord, let pollen dust my eyes with sleep,
And wipe away the tears that they would weep,
And let this bed and room become my fortress for the night
Until my mind awakes again to morning light.

Olive Parsons

Away

I am a scared turtle, hiding in my shell
Away from love
Away from hell.

I hold my tears back from dripping down.
Away from people
Away from town.
I think about running away
Away from tomorrow
Away from today

I keep my thoughts out of my head
Away from sorrow
Away from dread.

But now it's time to fill my life with gladness
Away from cries
Away from sadness

Though it was hard, I changed very fast
Away from my pain
Away from my past.

And now I fly through the sky as a dove.
Away from my shell, away to find love.

Shannon Graham

My Black Joseph

I am back with you again today,
back each Friday morning, eternal optimist I am,
back to have you fix the thing, that thing
that's wrong with me. I hope you get your way.

You are sartorial, you are a dream, you are my Joseph,
my reader of dreams.
A splendid man I'd say, with faith in me,
the faith of Peter in his Lord, more faith than I have ever seen
in the eyes of others.
The others are all Thomases, Thomases and Pharisees.

Defective I came, I slid, rolling off the assembly line,
onto the gurney in a pool of afterbirth. A chip was missing,
a screw was loose. There was no sign of that back then
however. Only later did my worth come into question.

You are not the first who has come to my succor.
There have been many others, some bullies,
some lovers and now I have found, perhaps it's dumb luck or
my own crazy luck or just fate. But I have found you my black man,
my dark man who lifts the bushel, who helps me uncover the light.

Rondi Adamson

Remember The Blue Poppy

In a far off land
beauty grows, on a hillside, in a forest.
A sea of azure blue
Delights all who wander by.

And close at hand,
A million miles from home,
A poppy grows, beside a fence.

In the dark of night
A miracle bursts forth,
From bud to bloom, to begin anew,
The cycle, of life.

Leaves, soft, fuzzy, as green as a woodland glade,
Climb upon a stem of sturdy strength,
To a pinnacle
Of petals, crinkly, delicate,
As blue as the morning sky
Surrounding a heart of sunrise yellow.

A symbol, of possibilities, of renewal, of hopes and dreams,
Fulfilled.

Remember always, the blue poppy.

Pauline Reaburn

An Ode To E

Sad eyed hound dog waits an endless wait.
Beneath the white marble columns,
That adorn the graceful mansion.
It's been many years now.
Since I last heard his song.
Little sister asks me where he is,
But I know he will never return.
For I've seen his blue suede shoes.
Walking on the moody blue clouds,
With blue eyed angels singing by his side.
Now all the children who mourn,
By the gates of Graceland,
Will leave with suspicious minds,
And wonder why he did it his way.
When the rains fall in Kentucky,
We will know, old blue eyes is crying from above,
Many will drown their sorrows, at the Heartbreak Hotel,
Amongst the lonely soldiers who sing the G.I. Blues.
And a lonely child. Will be crying in the ghetto.
For they all know, the King is lonesome tonight.

Bill Fontaine

Autumn Moon

Raging rivers rushing past
Birds migrating flying fast
Leaves are falling to the ground
Drifting soaring tumbling down
October nights are crisp and cool
And the moonlight shimmers in a midnight pool
Fall is here winter on its way
You can see the autumn moon shining far away.

Victoria Johnston

Cold War In A New Garment

On a dusty windy day a small segment of a torn page
blinded me on my face.
Natural reaction. My hand flew, removed the veil, put
my vision back but in a maze.
'His God abandons his perverted mind'.
A single line, the rest is missing from the page.

Autumn storms, falling leaves are the sounds of time.
Silence follows the whirlpool whoop. Moments ago,
They were there, now they are not.
But I hold on with all my strength,
the torn page which blinded me.

Dear Poet, tell me whose mind you see, why it is so.
Whose presence is everywhere, how He cannot be here!
Has the rage of a new sonnet grounded thee?

Sujit Chakrabartty

The Duck That Could Not Swim or The Feline

The Duck could not swim and he detested water
bring him near the lake and his fur would stand on end
his nails dug into you
This was a special kind of duck
because really it was a cat
Kids called him Duck or Ducky
since his feet were webbed
and his nose so big it looked like
—A Bill—not a twenty dollar bill
A Bill of a Duck
And so you see how this story came about
A cat like that was pretty Ducky indeed.

Sharon L. Scully

Bonjour Tristesse

I walked along the lonely paths of life,
But blindness hurt, and pain was every strife,
For where to go I did not know,
Nor how to live through every blow!

I turned and searched, and searched and turned,
I found no help, no voice I heard.
Yet, then I saw the light of love
Had come to me. You were my love.

Our destinies together went,
And mine was love, and only love.
How could I doubt my happiness?

And now it's dark, and now it's sad.
Where went the light of love I had?
Where went our love? Bonjour tristesse...

Michael Eckhoff

Feelings And Thoughts

Some say I'm a lucky man
but do I really think so.
My life has had a lot of rough roads
and I just don't know where to go.
So I sometimes talk to the boss upstairs
because he knows what I'm going through.
I was taught to think of positive things
but sometimes it's hard to do.

Maybe someday I will have the strength
of standing up against my fears,
the fears of negative thoughts
and the pain that draws so many tears.
Starting from now on, I will try to learn
to walk where there is light,
there's no more standing in the dark
it's time to face the facts of life.

Ross Connell

Tears Of Blood

I have tried to forget you
but it's a hard sacrifice for me to do
You left a gap that in my soul remains
When remembering you it fills my heart with pain
cause your love from me was hidden,
cause your love to me was forbidden
placing me into this state where I happen to be.
When I think of you, yesterday comes back to me.
I try to ignore you,
but it hurts like an edged dagger
cutting deep inside my heart.
Yet, I have not cried for you
and if I ever do
tears of blood my eyes may cry
cause my love for you will never die

L'Amonté

An Unanswered Question

I am no man's master,
but master to myself
as is everyone.
If I feel something is proper, and good and right,
and all others feel it is wrong,
is it wrong?
And who would punish me?
Not, God, for God made me feel it was right.
Then man? Perhaps a man of God?
But I am a man of God!

Eve Church

Far Far Away

He was alive
But now he's dead
I wish he was home
Awake in his bed
I loved him so
But he had to go
Far far away
As I waved goodbye
I started to cry
As my eye got a tear
It struck me with fear
I knew he'd never come home
For now I'm all alone
Far far away
Now as I look at his bright star in the sky
I always whimper and start to cry
God knew it was meant to be
But I don't understand why this happened to me?

Lori Makarowski

Untitled

Being sober isn't easy, it's quite a difficult task,
But now I know there's help for me, all I need do is ask,
I know it's gonna be hard and I may stumble or fall,
But I've made up my mind that I don't want to drink I plan on giving my all.

So don't condemn me for who I am, or what I have done in my past,
Simply remember I'm trying my best to clean up my act at last.
I know it won't make me perfect, in fact none of us are,
but I'm one step farther from being a drunk, and happiness isn't as far.

I drank for many reasons, I can't blame a certain one,
but after repeating the same mistakes, it certainly wasn't for fun.
I didn't enjoy the end results, not in the least little bit,
that's when I finally realized, "maybe it's time to quit."

So the next time that I feel worthless, or angry or sad or alone,
instead of grabbing a bottle, I believe I'll pick up the phone,
There are lots of people to help me, they've travelled this way before,
they can give me directions, but I have to open the door.

Duane R. Hiltz

Natural Instinct

I get up in the morning and lay down at night
But the day is void without a child by my side.

I don't remember the date or weeks passing by
I am only existing I don't even try.

Til the end of December nineteen seventy-one
I adopted you and my living began.

You came and turned my despair into victory
Miracles do happen you bonded with me.
You came and turned my hours into happiness
Miracles do happen with you I feel blessed.

I get up in the morning and lay down at night
but the day now is happy with you by my side.

The weeks and the years are rushing too fast by
I am growing weary but for you I will try.

Til the end of my life and eternity too
My love will enfold and always be with you.

You came and turned my despair into victory
Miracles do happen you bonded with me.
You came and turned my hours into happiness
Miracles do happen with you I feel blessed.

Elsbeth Richards

For You

Pain that lies intensely is sometimes quite a scare.
But the evilness I grew to know
Can't make me try to care.

I know the evil eyes that watch me through the night.
I've heard the deadly screaming
It gives me quite a fright.

I see the blood dropping down so true,
I know the pain she's feeling, now
I have been there too.

The moon will soon turn hollow,
But I can't keep the light.
I shall turn it back to you.
And stay here in the night.

I will turn away now,
Go back to where I came.

Then you can go on living
In your deathly evil game.

Raven B. Payne

Memories

I've nothing left to remember you by
But the songs you sang to me,
A smile and a tear and a memory dear
Of a haunting melody
The red rose seemed to be more red,
The forget-me-nots more blue,
When you and I were sweethearts,
For then our love was new.

You're nothing left to remember me by
And the days that used to be
But a ribbon of blue and a snapshot or two
And a lovely melody.
The red rose seemed to be more red
The forget-me-nots more blue
When you and I were sweethearts
For then I thought you true.

A. Gertrude Davies

My World, Our World

In the world there may seven wonders be
But the wonders in my life are as endless as the sea.
The mysteries of life and death and even in between
Broken hearts and tragedies are all my life has seen.
I marvel at the ways people seem to live their lives
Children crying in the streets, husbands beat their wives.
Coping is a tricky thing though I really don't know why
Everyone seems to hang their heads and heave a heavy sigh.
Why must the world be so deceitful, mean and cruel?
These, to me, resemble the behavior of a fool.
If life's a rose - the essence of beauty all
Then I was pricked too many times before I let it fall.
When Shakespeare wrote his piece on life, he must have felt its sting,
He said, "A tale full of sound and fury, signifying nothing."

Darlene Cox

Justice

Justice is blind, so you must see for her,
But you cannot see with your eyes
For they will judge unfairly, you must see with your heart.
Even though it can sometimes be mislead,
It judges by the only way it knows: fairly.
For the heart sees what the eyes cannot reveal
The heart knows what the mind does not begin to understand
Justice must be fair, it should not discriminate,
Through justice we have happiness,
Through justice we have hope.
A hope that shall never die, a hope that lies within us
wishing for a better tomorrow.

Lily Gulcev

Untitled

Alone, it seems,
with blood-stained dreams
and nights of fear
with teary streams that leave
my soul secluded—
No assistance comes to me
to ease this heart, deluded—
Blood fills my throat and
takes my breath,
I cannot look to see
the angels calling out to me,
as Satan's crimson victory
takes all in precious Death

Sheila M. Cogan

Listen To Our Mother Earth

Put your ear to the ground,
can't you hear her scream in pain?
It is our doing, we've hurt her yet again.

Place your hand upon this tree,
can't you feel, it's growing weary?
It is us, who have killed the ones she loves dearly.

Cast your eyes unto the sky.
The stars once lit up the sky.
This we will never see again.

Smell the air that surrounds you,
can't you sense the sourness,
of something that was once pure?

Dip your hands into this spring and drink,
don't you know it was once pure?
It is our waste that spoils it.

Now, what our bodies need to
survive, maybe the very thing
that kills our species.

Heather Moorhead

One Way Street

Should of turned right maybe moved left
Cats in a cradle I'm pushing straight ahead
On a one way street with No stop sign
Leave all memories past behind

Wipe a last tear from your eye, on a one way
Street man no longer cries
Howl if you can? Bark at the moon
One way street
I'm living by my own tune
Emptiness up above, cold
down below, hold my
hand down the street we go.

Rene Clements

"Rainbow Poem"

A cool breeze! BABY BLUE bubbles in a bathtub!
Cherries, roses, RED our heart!
The sun in the sky, YELLOW daisies, bananas
It is like melted chocolate BROWN in my mouth
It is like roses blooming PINK in the autumn
It is like pumpkin ORANGE pie in the sky
Smoke night, BLACK cats, tarantula

Sheena Kailik

Bibble Brew for an Evil Stew

Bibble, bobble, little one,
Come here and let's have some fun.
See this head, let's chop it up.
See that snake, pierce it with a
stake.
Mix it together and what do you get?
You think that's weird, that's nothing yet!
Cat whisker, rabbit ears, puppy tails.
Yes! And maybe even squished up snails.
Add some water, add some blood,
Make sure it doesn't overflood!

Bibble, bobble, little one,
Come here and let's have some fun.
See this knife? Isn't it sharp?
Let me stick it through your heart!
Lion hair, hippo teeth, frog legs,
Lamb chops, monkey brains, and fly eyes too.
Eagle beaks, pony tail, moose horns, rose thorns!
Mix it into a creamy stew!
Now we have something good to chew!

Nicole Lavergne

Little Jimmy

Way down in dee valley where
dee grass is fresh and green,
'Der was dee big — gest
watermelon patch you ever seen.
Wid pride aw watched 'dem grow each day.
Soon 'dey will be ready to haul away.
'Den wid' dee biggest smile on ma face
Aw'l take dem down to dee ma'ket place.
But one night w'en ma boy Jimmy should be in his bed,
An 'aw looks for him all over dee ol' homestead.
'Den dee bright idea comes to me
Down in dee watermelon patch is he.
So down dee hill aw goes
Soft an' quiet so nobody knows.
An' den it sure did break ma heart
To see all doze watermelon bust apart.
Der 'dey lay all nice and red
An Jimmy looked at me an' said
"Aw had ta taste dem all you see
to know which taste dee best to me."

Dora Morasch

Untitled

My thoughts are nuzzled
deep inside, tucked far away.
They are safe there
they will never be found
in the bottomless pit, of my stomach.

People say it's not right to keep feelings
of bought emotion bottled up
fermenting painfully within.

But I say, nobody understands me
nobody feels my pain
nobody tries to either.

Hopefully one day
I will swallow my pride,
get over my fears,
and spill my guts - completely
that is the day
when I will be finally able
to live again.

Andrea Ravensdale

Ada

Ada, Ada I love you deeper than the clouds in the sky
Deeper than the waves in the ocean I'll love you till the day I die.

Ada, Ada I love you my love is deeper than you understand
My love is as wide as this world I love you like no other man.

Ada, Ada I love you tho sometimes we are far apart
Distance seems to draw us together and puts you deeper into my heart.

Ada, Ada I love you our disagreements are few
And our love keeps on growing for I can love no one but you.

Ada, Ada I love you sometimes you ask me why
I can only say that I love you probably I'll find out by and by.

Ada, Ada I love you forever for that is the case
I'll keep on loving you, my darling until time itself wins the race.

Ada, Ada I love you deeper than the clouds in the sky
Deeper than the waves in the ocean I'll love you till the day I die.

Claude Barefoot

A Woman's Tear

There she stands shaken by her man.
Did she know such a man could ruin her life?
He sits and demands am I not a man?
She sighs and laughs you have no command.
For I am a woman, not a man!
He raises his hand then gently brushes her cheek,
for I was a fool to be so cruel.
My wife so sweet, you are worth more to me than jewels.
In my life of pain, there are rules.
For I shall never love again.
As I can not hide a woman's tear.

Zorica Jergovic

A Blood Red Rose

A blood red rose I remain,
Distinctive from all others,
Pride and strength coursing through my veins,
My petals feel renewed,
In the rain and morning dew.

Each year you cut me and place me onto your table,
You make me feel proud,
I am your way of admiring nature,
With beauty that I inspire,
Others pale in comparison.

Time is not kind for I begin to wilt,
It doesn't matter to you,
Although lifeless and brittle,
You place me towards the tip of your nose,
Trying to inhale the last of my fragrant scent.

As I am the only blood red rose,
That blossoms each year and doesn't change colour,
You gently place me into a book,
The sight of my petals warms your heart,
Cherishing the memories of past summer months.

Svetlana Konstantinov

The Splendor Of Darkness

Can you improve upon the splendor of darkness?
Don't you know that darkness has a beauty of its own?
Can't you realize that Elsewhere
Darkness becomes powerless and light unnecessary?
Is it not so that it is when your eyes are shut
That you see much more clearly
The face of your beloved:
Her smile flash like moonbeams on waves' crests
The sparkle in her eyes newly bedewed with tears
Her hilariously undisciplined eyebrows
The shapeliness of her lips and forehead
And the gentle lines of her chin?

Ladé Wosornu

Soul Riding

Caught in the tide,
engulfed and overwhelmed.
Only human, you cannot fly,
or touch stars and ride on clouds.
Leaping and stretching, gliding over the beach.
Water and land mixing,
moving billions of sand particles with
the sun overlooking the situation.
Whish, it is but a dream, but where have I been?

Jim Watts

Untitled

Dream not of today. Think of it as one day closer, another day gone by
Dream not of yesterday. Thinking of broken promises, always hurting, always asking why.
Dream only of tomorrow. About the dreams that will come true.
Remember who you are. It is time to dream for you.

Think only of the good times. Little things, memories you hold so dear
Put away the bad times. No more wishing away the pain, no more of those feelings, no more of that fear.
Your heart is your special gift, look towards yourself, start looking in
Stop letting them take. Don't let them win.

Wish those special wishes. All of your fondest hopes, your most precious dreams.
Reach out for them. They are waiting for you. Not as far away as they way seem.
Begin your journey through those doors. The doors holding you back, those doors of doubt.
Show the world what you are made of. Let that person out.

Dream not of today. Another step closer, nearer to who you long to be
Dream not of yesterday. Your heart has no more room, hide those feelings, let them go, set them free.
Dream only of tomorrow. It will happen, your dreams will come true.
Let yourself believe, as I have always believed in you.

Chris Harris

The Rain

It's late at night and I'm all alone
Driving down the road
The rain beats down on the windshield
Pitter-patter, pitter-patter
Windshield wipers swishing back and forth
Symmetrical and rhythmatic
I reach forward and flip on the radio
They are playing our song
I hum a few bars as I round the corner
Gradually I slow down
It appears the rain is speeding up
Or maybe it's just the tears in my eyes.

C. Ferguson

The End

Lost in the river of unforseen quarrels
drowning below some untold dream
Feeling within, the heartache of sorrows
Searching for meaning in holding back screams

Using as weapons, the renegade stories
holding for ransom, a love of deceit
Unspoken forgiveness, false passion is borrowed
sharing alone, a slow dying heart beat

Julie Epp

The Feeling

When I look into your eyes, I know who I am
Each and everyday, I feel more like a man
I love your soft skin and your soft touch
I guess this is why my heart pounds for you so much
When I'm with you, I feel so free
Just like the fish, swimming in the sea
You're in my dreams when it is night
You'll always be there from dawn to light
You're always able to light my heart on fire
Just like the burning blue in a sweet sapphire
You mean so very much to me
Just like a door that needs its key
There are loves that do come and go
I hope for ours, it's forever so.

Paul Matthews

Meus Convictio

Belief: The conviction that something is true.

I believe in mystery, majesty and mercy, all people are equal, that no one person is less then any other.
I believe in freedom, will and preference, we can choose, our choices are infinite and inexhaustible.
I believe that Christ suffered under Pilate, that Jews suffered under Hitler, and that we suffer under each other.
I believe wholly in the Spirit, strong, individualistic and pure.
I believe we should listen more and speak less.
I believe that love is an undying force that may be ignored, but not dismissed or distorted.
I believe that I was told that the Pope is the head of the Catholic Church, I also believe I have been told other things men decided were my beliefs.
I believe in an open mind, forgiveness and life.
I believe in death.
I believe in art.
I believe in the power of moonlight, naps, imagination and innocence.
I believe in you and most of all, I do believe in me!

Michael S. W. Moriarty

Never Complete

Have you ever watched flowers in a meadow,
Everywhere you look there seems no sorrow,
When I'm with you I feel no pain,
Even if it where to snow, thunder and rain.

My love for you I cannot measure,
Your love for me gives me to much pleasure,
Your love for me seems to surround,
For everywhere I look, your all around,

The scent of your cologne lingers in our room,
I see your smiling face in the moon,
I see your handsome face when flowers bloom,
Together we have a special song, a special tune,

One day our children will be grown and gone,
Together we will dance to their wedding song,
One day they will find a love to treasure,
A love that will give them so much pleasure.

You've helped me along through good times and bad,
When I'm with you it's hard to be sad,
Our love for each other will never be complete,
For it grows every day, it grows much to deep.

Simone Schwaier

Song At Dawn

Words conspiring to form lines of verse
Exquisite verse
Are a songbird's line of duty
Are a songbird's dream
And a ballad
Like unto the way of a man with a maiden

Linking their arms like children at moonlight play
The conspirators whisper their plot one to the other
The conspirators whisper their plot stanza to stanza
Giving it the beauty of flowers and the sound of music
They play till dawn
And end the play with a song

Words at moonlight play tintinabulate with a lyre
Birds at moonlight play
Sing a love poem
And say
Will mother tell a bedtime story at dawn

Emeka Asuzu

Painted Faces

Cruelty starts in the morning,
fallen through cactus.
Torrent rivers run down streets,
everyone screams like fresh cut flowers.
In the air, nowhere.

Inside out, inside her lips,
unbearable chills, feedback so close from a mouth.
Vocal cords, crossed into knots,
a desert land unlocked.
Everywhere is nowhere.

Papa's gold is whiskey,
tears down a child's face to the floor.
Heavy feet come and fetch,
traffic lights flash anger.
Flash red.
Evil is everywhere.

Empty boats float today, sails torn, ragged, ripped.
Away in the distance, where oceans fall away,
People drown.
Voices scream like cut flowers, for everyone is no one.

Mike Hardy

The Beginning

I walk alone on this earthly trail,
Feeling so cold, as a baby so frail.
Ahead in the darkness, the stillness of the night,
A vision of perfection, silhouette in the light.
The moon ponders over this shadow of a man,
Laughing at the success of his plan.
Being unknowing pawns in the game,
I confront this stranger and ask his name.
To look into his eyes embraces my speech,
Our lips meet, our hearts both reach.
Standing together at dawns first light,
He whispers my name, my heart takes flight.
For the first time in centuries of war,
Someone has entered and unlocked the door.
The chains fall silent, at last I'm free,
He speaks of love, of a life with me.
The sun rises, glowing its brightest hue,
To signify the re-birth, my life anew.
I have found my God, and my heaven with you.

Nancy Bennett

True Love

It's been two months, to the day, since our lips
first met.
The tingling thrill of that first kiss, lingers
with me yet.
I don't know why, I don't know how, it ever came to be.
On that night, my heart was lost, I wanted you for me.
As the days went by, they seemed so short, I lived in ecstasy.
One night you blew my mind, and said
"I love you."
My days are spent in thoughts of you, my nights in dreams so sweet.
Always wishing you were here, dying for our lips to meet.
When you smile that special smile, your eyes do twinkle so;
The beauty of your inner self, is revealed in their glow.
Your scent drives me so crazy.
I want to hold you tight, to feel your
body pressed to mine, throughout the lonely night.
The gentle caress of your soft hands, make my knees go weak
I get all shivery deep inside and find it hard to speak.
All my life I've waited for, a special girl like you
I will never let you go, now that I found you, I am complete.

Walter McCallum

"Hope The Graveyard Of The First"

Autumn comes again —
Fish come in to lie, and die in shallow waters,
where their graves are found.
Without a sound, they come and go to where?
We do not know?! —
All Kinds —
Red, Purple flesh, falling from their bodies —,
So, so many—.
Small — large —
The river is so shallow, so small when they come in —.
After they depart,
the rain pours and pours —.
The river tries to drown the land —.
Bridges nearly fall,
after the fish have gone.

Marilyn Rutter

The Storm

Please remember me for who I was
For I was all I wanted to be
Overwhelmed with love for the storm of life
Forever happy and free

My storm on earth has been short
For God has planned it this way
Now is my time to move on
Allow me...if I may

I know it hurts to say "Good-bye"
So final... So complete
But storms go by fast, so please do not cry
For someday again we will meet

Your heartache and teardrops are part of your storm
Which brings much sorrow and pain
Your heartache pounding like thunder
Your teardrops falling like rain

But storms fade away as time moves on
Though clouds may still come around
But I want you to see the rainbow again
For it is happiness I have found

Glenna Pearson-Bell

Untitled

Alone in the world I shall forever be.
For no one will ever understand me.
No one can make it no one will try.
To get past the wall for which I am inside.
Sadness and darkness take over
inside, for the wall closes in and
leaves all light behind.

A force takes my hand and I
follow in fright.
I don't try to fight for it knows
and it see's the pain inside me.
The happiness, the love, and laughters, all gone.
The place I end up, I look at in shame.
All I can see is rows upon rows
of people standing right before me.
Quickly I turn trying to run, trying
to get out, but the door closes
quickly right before me.

I fall in despair and cry endlessly,
As I turn unwilling to see the life left upon me.

Cyndy Hughes

"A Prayer"

O' give thanks for years gone by
For puppy dogs and birds that fly
For music gold and ringing bells
For fairy tales and wishing wells

Thank you, Lord, for answered prayer
For strength and wisdom through lifelong dares
For sunny days and peaceful nights
For crystal hopes and guiding lights

And thank you, too, for pains and sores
That teach us of life and love and more
And, dear Lord, and for this mostly
Thank you for a memory.

Victoria Lynn Hill

"Their Golden Star"

She walked along the moonlit beach, always trying to reach,
For that one golden star, to make a wish upon that silvery night.

Her long, gorgeous auburn hair blowing, around the breeze which flew,
Over the midnight shivering sea.

She knew she was the only one around as she soaked her feet in the warm sand, upon the tender ground. Her hazel-green eyes gazed down the Coast line, Until her eyes met a sight from the Heaven above.

He stood there, gazing at the same distant star. She knew he was the one right away, because he had shared the same star and the same wish.

It happened. He noticed her and came closer. She smiled shyly, as she noticed, his handsome eyes, almost as grey, as the sky on a breezy winter day.

His eyes had a hint of mint-green in them, yes, she knew, her wish had come true as they both gazed over the sky of that distant midnight blue.

His smile was so attracting, that a milk-white dove flew by,
and started to sweetly sing, and then swifted up high.

He then opened his lips, to reveal beautiful ivory, he whispered to her with a gentle tone, he asked her if she was all alone. She then explained gently back, that she wasn't alone, she and he, had that same distant star.

Melanie Steele

Memories Forever

Dedicated to my husband Michael Acadia and my children and grandchildren: Michael, Cathy, David & Stacey, Michelle, Michael & Ashley.

Forever, we said I do
Forever, a love so true
Together, we are so strong
Together, we've shared our joys and
disappointments too.
Together where we belong
Forever, you're closer to me my love
Together, forever (with you)
On this our Thirtieth Fifth Anniversary
We're getting closer, closer to a dream
and countless blessings remain you must remember
I love you just the same, just the same.
Our crosses have weighed us done
Our teenager's time was a chaotic state
We were here or there to listen, pickup
and willing to do till death, they were our life
Yet blessings remain so strong
I love you, I love you, just the same
Forever, forever, you'll remain my love
Together, forever. Our memories forever.

Helen Accadia

Reflections

Sat atop this rock formed ledge looking out to sea
Freeing my mind of problems with a sense of tranquility
The sunlight on the water reflecting the rolling waves
Save for a passing distant ship I could be in a by gone age
The haunting sound of water echoed from the rocks below
As it has for countless centuries in times past long ago
My thoughts are suddenly distracted by the cries of terns in flight
I look to their direction as they glide upon the breeze so light
Their eager eyes constantly scan the cold dark murky water
Hoping the sun will reflect some silvery fish to satisfy their hunger
I will remember this day tomorrow when I'm back in the urban city
Where time waits for no one and time shows so little pity
In the hustle and bustle of city life with its hectic speed and pace
Of trying to live but being part of running with the human race
In contrast to this tranquil place with its miles of endless sea
An atmosphere so serene and timeless with spirit that is forever free
These sounds of August travel like whispers in the wind
My thoughts reflect a vision of what the seasons change will bring

Bill Rogerson

Life In A VCR

Push pause on the VCR,
Freezing the liquid moment
For endless pleasure.
Savour the taste of yesterday's tomorrow.
In suspended animation,
Existence becomes bearable.
Rewind -
To obscured memories;
Ancient days of yore.
Edit regrettable mistakes enhancing one's today.
Fast forward -
To the unseen future.
Obtain the knowledge of humanity's fate.
Satisfy the curiosity of questioning minds:
Is there a God?
Or do U.F.O.s save us from ourselves?
Only the weak-minded,
Who play simple parts in this film,
Are fool enough to hit the stop button,
Terminating the show......

Matt Comiskey

Hold My Hand

When the time comes to an end, you'll depend on us to be your friend. But when the time comes, don't treat us like we misunderstand, and if it comes, to an end, we'll always be there to hold your hand. When you go up on the stand, don't just think of three acres of land, because there's two little girls in your hands. What ever you both decide, to keep one or put the other aside, won't keep me from crying or saying goodbye. I know it's hard to make a decision but you got to do what parents got to do. Your thoughts and wishes shine deeply in my heart, sun and clouds we'll never be apart, for the love we have, it will never end, but I will always send, no matter when, so don't forget I'll always be here to hold your hands.

Jennie-Lee Kluke

THE LAD FROM THE CREWE

He wooed her he won her he said 'Love is True'
He promised to wed her THE LAD FROM THE CREWE
Like a fool she believed him then what did he do
He up and he left her alone on the Crewe
And so now my daughter my secret I tell
To protect you from heartache perhaps shame as well
When a lad comes acourtin' take care what you do
In case he's a son of the LAD FROM THE CREWE.

Elizabeth Quinn

Saved By Grace

One day a preacher came
From a far off place,
To tell our people
That Jesus loves them.
That Jesus wants to save them.

So one night, as the preacher
Preached the wonderful gift of Jesus,
I heed to his words;
As it touched the very end of my soul.

There that night, I repented of all my sins
Before the mighty King of Kings,
And He washed them all away,
By His precious blood
That was shed for me.

I know He has touched and cleansed my soul.
I know He has come to dwell within.
I know now I am His child,
And He is my coming King.
Now I know I was saved by grace!

Elizabeth Lord-Ottereyes

Sounds Of The Country (West Wales)

Sweet is the chorus at early dawn,
Gentle the breeze that fans the trees;
The lowing of cows on the way to the dairy
Awakens the farmer, - his work starts early!

The plaintive cries of wean-ed lambs,
The call of ewes, still heavy with milk.
Buzzards soar, mewing, in lazy flight
And above them the rare and majestic kite.

Wild are the storms and heavy the rain
But after the land is washed fresh again;
Peace is restored, with a rainbow so proud
And the sun peeps out shyly, through mists and cloud.

Rude is the roar of jets above,
Drowning the call of the gentle dove;
But safe are the people that cringe from the noise,
Because of the valour that's shown by these boys.

Joan E. Clark

Oh Precious Lord

Oh precious Lord come unto thy little children,
Give them faith, hope, charity and put an end to their suffering;
Their swollen bodies wracked in pain and agony,
Heed not your words, "Little children come unto me."

Are they to enter your Kingdom a wretched Race,
An agonizing sight to see the pain on their face;
Please give them a chance to live with dignity not humility,
Oh precious Lord, are they to suffer through eternity.

They have wronged no one to deserve such a fate,
Lend a helping hand before it's too late;
Thousands die yearly of disease and malnutrition,
Isn't there a way to remedy the situation.

Let there be peace and tranquility in the World once more,
Put an end to all the strife and War;
For Guns have taken the place of the Garden tools,
How long will it take them to realize, that they are fools;

For it's the young who have no future and the most to lose in War,
Put an end to the drought and let the Fields be Green once more;
For generations have sung the praises of you dear "Champion of
the Poor,"
In God we Trust, and it's you and only you we adore.

Lloyd Jones

Be Good To Your Manners

Be good to your manners,
Give them something to do.
Don't go to your glass,
Make it come to you.
Whenever it gets there,
Don't slurp it down,
Be hospitable, and don't act like a clown

Chew your food twenty-two times
Don't take too much,
Take what you can eat,
Sit up straight
And don't reach.

Thank your mom,
say grace.
Use your napkin to wipe your face.
Don't lick your fingers,
Don't put up a fuss.
Give your manners something to do,
Or you won't be eating with us!

Gabrielle Freedom

The Enderby Cliffs

The magnificent splendor of Enderby cliffs,
Gives the heart and soul a tremendous lift.
Watch the sun as it goes to its resting place.
It leaves a pink glow on their craggy face.

On some early mornings, the mist hangs so low,
Concealing their face, — but soon it will go.
The mist and fog lift, the view to surrender
Revealing cliffs, in unchallenged splendor.

The majestic view of Enderby's Cliffs.
Pictures of which, would make loveliest gifts.
Ah! By pictures, there beauty can never be told.
So, come see the Cliffs, their Beauty behold.

Destiny Quzoel Brightstar

Kinetic Battle Cry

Sentimental claptrap yapping 'gainst war,
Gotta fight back with a gung ho corps.

Ain't gonna think like an egghead dummy,
Gonna go to war and do somethin' crummy.

Can't let motherhood go down the drain,
Gotta let loose and raise some cain.

What if a thousand, a million people die?
That's what it takes to be a patriotic guy.

Gotta get the enemy, gotta get him good!
Kill him in a jiffy, he's nut 'n but a hood.

Freedom, goodness and hot apple pie,
Gotta get the enemy to give up or die.

I'm no enemy, I'm a good guy.
That's why I'm willin' to fight and die.

Michael Driver

The Bird

Love is like a beautiful bird.
Hang on to it, or it will fly away.
Nourish it, or it will starve.
Keep it warm, or it will freeze,
But most of all cherish it.
For that beautiful bird comes only once in a lifetime.

Glory Przekop

Conflict

Conflict is the opposite of harmony.
Harmony is the way of nature.
Conflict means fight, clash, collision.
May it be of bodies, groups or opinions.
Harmony is getting along well together.
Conflict is all strife and contention.
Conflict is something which should be abhorred.
Harmony, favorite of mother nature be adored.

Aisha Mir

The Farmer's Life

The farmer's life, some people say,
Has long since gone by the way.
A person's skill, their sweat and pain,
Can make you wonder if you're really sane.
To keep on struggling, to keep on going,
Season after season, not ever knowing.
If nature's weather, her many pests,
Will eat your profits, drained at best.
But for the future, your loved one's claim,
It makes you strive to win the game.
To know when all is done and said,
True feelings from the heart and head,
Will state the struggle, the act indeed,
Was one of love, not just of need.
Not for a way of life long gone,
But for one that will carry on.

Gloria L. Lundago

The Invitation

The last dreary days of winter,
Have silently slipped away,
And "Spring" sends out invitations,
For all to come to the play.

The stage is a lawn of green velvet,
Curtains, are soft willows swaying.
The spot light, the warm summer seen,
The actors are young children playing.

The birds are the band,
They strike up a note.
Little flowers come forth so excited
As we watch the birth of another spring
I'm so glad that I was invited

Joan N. Lawler

Game From The Beginning Lost

Can you believe without seeing
Have you learned to dream beyond hope
Don't you know yourself is a stranger
And your life is not your own

Well, Big talking, small lies
I can't follow your path into the light
You think you know but what you know is all wrong
And we're just fooling each other, fooling each other

Can you give without first asking
Will you let go and not cry
I know you're scared to seek truth in my dark waters
But I wish that you would try

well, clear thoughts in crystal lights
I have no colours left to paint up your life
You feel your way through me, but your touch
Burns my soul
And we're just hurting each other, hurting each other.

Eftihia Mentzelopoulou

The Board Member

We see it one day, he seems much more bald,
He doesn't hear well when his name's being called.
We've seen him each day, but our busy routine
Forbade us from seeing what others had seen.

For he's growing older, he's even less tall -
The man who for years didn't falter at all.
We see him, head bowed, as we stand at the door
And know that his briefcase is near on the floor.

His heart and his mind on church business affairs;
The boards and committees are part of his prayers.
It's humbling to watch him so lost in that prayer
Keeping his place in the pew that we share.

A man of conviction, admired by his peers,
He's taken that place every week through the years,
So who could imagine what we dare not say,
That place will be empty some future Sunday.

And all of his papers and notes laid aside,
The tasks all completed with care and with pride,
To meet with the Chairman, his Friend and his Lord,
To serve for all time on that Heavenly Board.

Carol Christensen

To Search For A Trace

It's April and ugly, the students are cranky -
He goes for a walk... he's long lean and lanky...
An old bum approaches, these two stand alone.
A brief conversation: a small hint of home?

But homeless persists, demands some small change -
The college hero's eyes flash red...black...mange!
A roar in his throat, punch puckers mouth...
Broken nose...broken jaw...serves him right, the uncouth!

R. Crummey

My Farmer

He quietly wakes while asleep most still stay,
He makes his own breakfast and prepares for the day.
Then the sun rises.

To the barn he goes — the animals must be fed,
Then to fix this, that, or the other machine at the shed.
The sun is bright and high.

Now he is hungry — he's worked hard and steady,
It's time for a break — the noon meal is ready.
The blue sky smiles.

He gobbles up lunch — there's more work to do,
It seems never ending — free days? he has but few.
A cloud floats by.

The neighbor comes over needing a hand,
His own work will wait — he must help his friend.
The sun gets warmer.

He looks out to the fields — so much of him is there,
Then goes in for supper, the evening meal to share. The sun sets.

He doesn't stop to think about how much he does,
His family knows and is grateful for this symbol of his love.
The sun rises and sets. On him.

Elizabeth Jean Godkin

Have Mercy Sarajevo

The bombs exploding sound so distant,
He tries to move, but he can't,
He wants to block his ears from the sound,
But his bloody arms are lying on the ground,
A great slab of concrete pins his legs,
Please stop this pain he begs,
Tears form as he starts to cry,
How long will he wait to die,
The loss of blood takes its toll,
And his pain filled eyes start to roll,
His head falls to one side,
Another innocent child has just died.

Ronnie S. Thoresson

Adam And Eve

In the garden of Eden God placed Adam and Eve
He warned them of satan - do not be deceived
Eat from every tree except that one in the middle
It's the tree of the knowledge of good and evil

Eve was so curious she went to the tree
As she looked up the serpent she see
Come! taste of the fruit he said to her
It is the best - she did not deter

She ate of the fruit and thought it was good
So she took it to Adam he ate it for food
Suddenly the eyes of them both were open
Satan had deceived them - they hid in the garden

God strolled to meet Adam for His usual talk
He couldn't find Adam so He walked and walked
Then He shout aloud - Adam! where are thou?
Here am I Lord, Adam replied

What have you done my dear son?
We ate of the fruit he went on and on
By the sweat of thy brow thou shall eat bread
You shall till the ground until you are dead

Sheila Mark

The Return

He will come God's beloved Son
He will come when we don't think
He will be our friend and our king
All trouble and sorrow will ease
Nations will live together in peace
The earth will tremble
The wicked will fear
Realizing the end is near
The Lord will reach out His loving
Hand and take the righteous to a better land.

Elisabeth Couper

The Silent Tears Of A Beautiful Girl

A beautiful girl stands alone,
Her heart is now marked with dark scars.
Words sting her pride.
But words are not her only sorrow,
Her father's hands have bruised her flesh.
Threats keep her silent,
She lives in constant fear.
A sharp blade offers escape.
A drop of blood stains the blade,
It will forever remind.

She is like a crimson rose.
It opens its petals to the summer sun,
But soon the cruel winds of winter blow.
To end its short life.

Christine Robitaille

Mother

She left when I was young.
Her life was nothing but disgrace.
She loved me so very much,
but she couldn't make me live in this place.

Someone else came into my life,
and helped me through my bad times.
All she needed was some space,
to think about the things done wrong.
How could she make me live in this fear?

I tried to be strong,
but she never left my mind.
Now I start my life again,
hoping I will find,
the one and only,
one of a kind,
Mother.

Trisha Flannery

How Can Our Love Grow?

I felt her body, beneath my own,
Her warmth, her charm, her grace.
She stands for all the love I know-
The love I give her-no haste.

Her innocent look at me-she gave,
Her words quiet, precise-yet unknown.
Like in the sea, deep in a wave
..."How can our love grow"?...

While being caught, deep in love,
My mind at labour to think.
Like an ant being caught by a hungry bug,
My thoughts were perilous, confused and weak.

"Like a tree"..., I spoke-
Not knowing what she's say.
To rise, to grow, to dance about-like smoke,
To branch out, and point every way.

Like a trickling stream in spring,
Which never stops flowing-or still,
will be ours, to dance, to fling,
I will love you forever... to die if it-you will-

Leslie Chortos

The Hired Hand

He rises with the break of day
He's in the field 'til dark
He lives and breathes the working of the land
But his mind is in a turmoil
And his heart is torn in two
Because you see, he's just the hired hand

His yesterdays he now regrets
Today won't meet his needs
His future holds no promise as he'd planned
His summer nights he spends alone
And lives in fantasy
He tells himself he's owner of the land

I've watched him drown his sorrows
When he comes in from the field
His eyes betray the hurt his voice commands
But he'll go right on pretending
Thinking no one else can see
The tired, worn, and bitter hired hand.

Terry Benson

My Music Teacher

I hate my music teacher very much.
His name is David Dutch.
He is hard upon everyone.
He looks at me as if he will shoot me with a gun.
He is always carrying a fat stick and he hates it
if someone plays on him a trick
He has a bald head,
And whenever angry he goes red.
He wears a large ear ring in one of his ear,
and I think he looks more like a bear.
He tries to show our parents that he is very kind,
but I think he is a real fiend.

Kiran Riaz

Ship Of Ruin

Oh, ship of ruin upon your lonely shore
How bleak your shape, how black your form.
Long ago how mighty your splendour did soar.
From skilled hands and seaman's love, you were born.
Your glory once mocked the chanting gull's cry.
You gleamed and you thrived on the sailor's song.
Now yesterday is just more than a word.
You are filled with the youth of men now gone.
Just bare hollow echoes of sounds once heard.
Yes, dead but not your downfall in their sighs.
Oh mournful ship, misshapen by the empty thuds of fickle waves.
Oh forsaken ship, abandoned by those who love and gaze.

Nancy Jane Edey

Constance-Feeding Dish

My name is Constance-Feeding Dish.
I am but a plain pink bowl.
No bears or bunnies or flowers on me,
But I have so much love to show.

My name is Constance-Feeding Dish.
I hold a tasty treat.
Every morning, Baby Jenny
Has something good to eat.
Maybe this morning it will be pancakes,
Or maybe a soft boiled egg.
Sometimes a sausage, or maybe a waffle,
Or perhaps porridge with nutmeg.

I watch with pride as a plump, dimpled hand,
Grasps her tiny spoon, and tries so hard to land
That last precious morsel
That tastes, "Oh, so good, Mommy! May I have more for my little tummy?"

My name is Constance-Feeding Dish.
My job may not be a feat,
But my heart is aglow every morning
As I watch Baby Jenny eat.

Janis L. Parr

"Dreams"

I could be your worst nightmare;
I could be all your hopes and aspirations;
I could be anything that you want me to be...
And all you have to do is just dream about it.

I could let you fly up in the sky...
I could let you dive in the deepest oceans...
I could let you go in to the centre of the earth...
I could let you soar in space and visit distant planets...

But I'm only a dream,
It's only you who could make me real.
It's only you who could fulfill all of this...
Only you.

Daniel Lim

Faith

Is it of my faith unbroken
I am one of Your chosen
To do Your work
Believing all the words
You write in white letters
When asking about matters
I cannot answer nor solve
Frustration and revolt
In the hearts of friends
Who came for the touch of a curing hand

Lord, they believe
Through my hands You give relief
You guide me night and day
What more can I say
I climbed mountains, walked valleys and forests
Slipped, crawled, but did my best
Though wounded, hurt, cried
I got up and kept the tears inside
Lord, I bow in humble obedience
For Your Love - Your Guidance.

Soemarweni Ismet

Don't Mind Me

Don't mind me as you walk on by.
I can lie back, catch diamonds in my mouth from the sky.
Don't mind me, I don't exist.
Nobody important, not high on your list.
Just someone who loved you when you were in deep despair.
Grieved right along with you and I'll always care.
Don't mind me as I have a lot to give.
Have feelings inside, I know how to live.
I love the given things like Earth, wind and sky.
My friends are the butterflies.
Ever really watched a bird fly?
Don't mind me, I see your indifferent smile.
I'm just a little speck.
Are you greater than I?
Leaves flitting in the breeze are the tears that I've cried.
I clutch to the rainbow I hold deep inside.
Stand tall, I'm beside you every step of the way.
And thanks for the music you perform each day.

Yvonne Preston

A Transsexual In Search Of Herself

My friends don't know me they don't know what I am,
I can't admit to them that I am not a man.

Born a boy to this world my life is in a whirl,
because as a teenager I became a girl.

I first saw the image that I wanted to be,
when puberty came to change me.

The image was everywhere the female form,
to be wanted by others that was the norm.

I've given up praying for God to change me,
I'm unable to purchase the female me.

I took my chances to borrow and steal,
moments in time to help me heal.

Outside alone I wander in search of myself,
lost in a dream of richness and wealth.

Wrapped in my clothes I was wanted by all,
That's what I imagined as I saw no one at all.

Oh! time runs out I might get caught
the repercussions are a terrible thought.

My world collapses I'm alone in distress
lost in this life's wilderness.

Hilary Cooke

The Farmer Dell

The farmer in the Dell, didn't look well;
I could tell, cause he looked like hell.
Things were not well, down there in the dell.

He told me how he was at the end of his rope;
He couldn't take any more, just couldn't cope!
I remember clearly in my head just exactly what the old farmer said...

"Oh, how I hate that ugly old duck, and all those little pigs that suck,
I'm fed up with all this barnyard muck -
There's gotta be a better way to make a buck!!"

I heard him scream as he ran for his truck;
Poor Farmer Dell was down on his luck!
So he drove through the swamp in his dirty old truck...but YUCK!!
Poor Farmer Dell got stuck, there in the muck and all that guck.

As the truck started sinking, the farmer started thinking...

Maybe the duck wasn't really that bad;
The pigs are all healthy so I should be glad,
And as for all that barnyard muck, why, I can haul it away in my truck
And I can make some money by getting bees and selling the honey!
I'm gonna go back and try to cope, cause now I see there is some hope!

But...the CROCS in the swamp went CHOMP, CHOMP!!
That's where it ended for Farmer Dell - He never even had a chance to yell,
He ran out of luck and died in his truck!

Faye Keller

The Land Of The Bare Trees

Oh, yes
I do so clearly remember
It was winter, of the month December
A sight not easily forgotten
The sense of hopelessness still burns within

It was in the leaves' nature
They had no other choice
So they abandoned their position
And fell to the ground

The emptiness before me
Scarred me ever so deeply
And the gray-coloured sky
Provoked fear within me

I walked away slowly-
For my feet could hardly support me-
Never to look back again

But the memory still haunts me
And I shall forever wake in the night
Remembering that so dark sight.

Elizabeth Agiantritis

Under And Over

I'm no longer the reflection he's looking for.
I don't remember the nervous excitement.
Or that I would call it love.
Although I have confused orgasms before.

Something about sex makes me vulnerable.
I remember watching us in a mirror one time.
I don't know what I had seen but I had started to cry.
Once when eating between my legs he said, "Beautiful."
I can't describe what that did to me. Inside.

Sex takes me to the loneliest space I've been.
Despite the body beside me.

No one ever says the plateau is a lonely place to be.

Destiny Bedwell

My Darling Sis

As she reaches for my hand,
I feel a sense of fear.

I touch her face;
I feel great heartache.

She calls me "Sweetheart"
And there is great warmth.

She smiles as she sleeps,
For she knows, she finally at peace within.

Her body quivers, as the night draw's closer.
She closes her eyes with tears of what maybe!

Her heart with enough strength to smile at
me yet another day.

Her soft voice as she speaks;
Good Night, my dear.

Her eyes of endless questions, yet to be answered.
Her quietness; for she'll have her answer's soon.

S. McGahan

Depression

Knowing what I have lost
I feel as though I can not move
my eyes are red as I weep out my pain
why is it I live?
For he was all I lived for.
Remembering the way his arms embraced me
How he touched me
and the love I felt when his lips touched mine
was it love? I thought it was Destiny
Is it over or yet to begin
my stomach aches, my head throbs
I feel so very weak
How can I possibly love another
after I have given him all the
love I will ever have.
Our love was not to be broken.
He has taken my heart and soul
therefore I can love no other
And until my dying day
I will always love him

Tanya Rempel

Moody

When I set by my window and I look out,
I feel so lonely, I think I'll pout
But a bird in the tree, by my window I see,
Singing a love song, just for me
His song in my heart, yes, he did stir
And my cat on the hearth, began to purr
God had a reason, I'm sure of that
For why did He bring me that stray cat
Yes, in His wisdom, God above
Sends to you and me all His love.
Yes, I should do unto others, what He has done for me
Having that cat and a bird in the tree.

Ella Rumble

The Face In The Mirror

Penetrating the mirrored visage
I see a sick child
Cutting clouding bonds with a golden knife
Isolated, starving in captivity
Nursed by an overbearing visage
Bleeding from the cuts of the rusting blade
Dying

Nova Hamilton

The Little Girl Inside Of Me

I saw his face in my dreams,
I felt his sadness or though it seems.
How could I have done this to someone so true,
I would have stopped if I only knew.
He was there when I needed him most,
He stood over me with the Holy Ghost.
But I was too concerned with living free,
That I didn't stop to hear his plea.
I had always loved from the heart,
Yet, no matter what I did my life fell apart.
Finally, I saw what was inside of me,
A little girl crying endlessly.
Where was the love that I thought I knew?
Where was my heart that was once so true?
Now it wouldn't be easy to change my ways,
But it was better than living in a daze.
Now I live my life differently,
And I've stopped and listened to his plea.
That little girl doesn't cry anymore,
And she found the love that she knew once before.

Monica O'Gorman

My Little Brother

I get up in the morning to go to school,
I got to get ready to look real cool.
I put on my make-up and fix up my hair,
When the boys get fresh, I growl like a bear.

I leave for school in a real big rush,
Get halfway there and forget my brush.
I ran back home to get it right,
And I almost got into a real big fight.

My little brother wouldn't give it to me,
Unless I gave him a great big fee!
So I gave him what he wanted - a great big fee,
It was a knuckle sandwich delivered by me,

My mother, as usual, as before,
Sent me to my room and locked up the door.
When I didn't show up for my classes in school,
My teachers were wondering why I was fool.

But if they had a brother as ornery as mine,
They'd know I'd have to do something to keep him in line.
but I'll tell you a secret that nobody would know,
I love my little brother even though it doesn't show!

Lee-Anne Woods

Untitled

"And this is how I whispered good-bye.
I have stared it in the eye and have it in the dark;
but now it lurks in sleep, silent and peaceful in
the night, like a mother's child; a gleam of light
at sunrise. I have the memory in my palm,
the image of a lost being in my eyes. And I
see a road, a long road, rigid as a mountain
peak and coloured like the sky. A shadow in the
distance, and I turn and walk away, struggling
to find a way in the starlight, and suddenly
a drop of rain, a small and salted drop with
the company of others, seeps away - the first
sign of truth. That, I can never forget. It was
devastating and incurable, like a lie, like a
memory of the past."

Tracy Davidson

Childhood

In the river of time,
I hear lilting strains
of gentle chimes and drifting refrain,
of childhood spent
in happiness, with no intent;
And I seek the tinder-box of youth's flame;
And as life goes on, (this tedious game),
I know the tide will never be the same,
Yet, I go on and on from canoe to canoe,
Hoping some day I'll confront
the familiar port again,
and sight an innocence with no stain,
meeting many a song of my heart
and thoughts in my brain
of laughter and smiles and childhood fun;
Where each day's bright and brown sun
is joyfully met and tunefully sent
to a shelter without shame,
Where I feel love with no thoughts of gain,
Unwakened by the enchantments of wealth and fame.

K. Eswaran

Homestead

The walls vibrated with energy.
I laid in bed watching shadows dance in the darkness.
Sparks flashing here, there, everywhere before my eyes.
I asked myself, "is this real?"
I smiled knowing
Better to have asked such a question.
I closed my eyes even though shadows continued to perform.
Unable to fall into a deep slumber because of excited spirits.
The floor creaked on and
Something periodically banged in the hallway.
I got up to see if one of my toddlers was awake wandering.
Everyone was fast asleep
With only pita-patter of a light rain hitting the hip-roof.
I climbed back in bed and shut my eyes.
Again the creaking of footsteps.
Again the unidentified banging.
There was not even a breeze outside.
The house went quiet, I fell asleep.
And then the spirits would
Start all over again.

Susan George

Untitled

Every inch a Lady, and some to spare
I like the way you talk, I like the way you walk.
It seems nice to be near you, it's something
special you give me.
How can I say your wonderful, it's been said
before and we say it again.
The way your nose wiggles when you smile and
the colour in your eyes seem to shine just for me.
Never an angry word was ever spoken for us to hear.
Yes, you kissed me many times with warmth and
tenderness and love, it seemed that I could
not have lived without you.
We like the way you talk, we like the way you
walk, we will always love you.
As you are very special to me, you are My Mother

R. Lloyd Smith

A Poem For Children

To Remind Them How Important Our Environment Is

Hi Kids! My name is planet earth!
I live in the universe.
I shine like a jewel in space.
I'm home to the human race.

You can run through my grass, play in my sand,
Sail my blue seas and plant food on my land.

You may climb up my trees and swing from a tire,
Try not to fall — that would be dire!

When people make me dirty
And throw trash on my ground,
I want to hide and never ever be found.
Throwing junk on my ground,
That's what's called "Litter",
When it goes in my mouth,
It really tastes bitter!

I want to cry out! I want to kick!
All this pollution is making me sick!

So wherever you go, enjoy all my wealth.
Remember, don't litter,
You'll enjoy better health!

Marcia Allen

Our Guiding Light

As we drove through the night...
I looked at you with great delight!
There must have been a million stars out that night....
But only one caught our sight!
Then I turned and said to you with great delight...
Did you see thy light?
You replied with a sparkle of delight...
Did you wish upon thy sight?
There in a flash we saw the light...
And this is what guided us through the night!

Cynthia Trylinski

Depths Of Disaster

Helplessly I float, noticing my separateness.
I observe only infinity, a constant roar of conceptions.
Now I debate a God, caring and loving.
Curiosity presently aids in my insanity, and
Shadows lurk in the Depths of Disaster with the help
of my on-going imagination.

My life depends on a piece of driftwood, now cold and wrinkled clean.
The peers of mine, I have none, for the waves are my only friends.
Sickness lingers around me, but my supreme terror is the frigid water.
Life is now just a hope to ponder and cherish for it is limited.

Why do they leave me here? Have I done any harm?
They mustn't have noticed my small, tired body being swept away
from the blazes.
Their faces disappear, new ones emerge of hurt, loneliness and despair

If I only could see my hated enemies, or hard days of work.
Things I once detested, now ones I'd love to have again.
The darkness now surrounds me, and I feel no fear but a
sense of peace.
In order to escape from the Depths of Disaster, I must travel
further on its pathway until I reach———paradise.

Amanda M. Pilgrim

'An Endless Search'

In the stillness of night
I search for my heart
And in the pitch darkness
I search for myself,

Who I am?
A human body
consisting of five elements
- fire, air, water, earth and cosmos
with abode of the deathless
omniscient, omnipotent, ever-glorious Soul.

I watch my reflected image
in the Mirror of relationships
to analyse my mysterious Self
I search endlessly for
my own BUDDHA
to seek self-knowledge.

Arun K. Seam

Ropes That Bind

I look beneath your disguise,
I see deep within your eyes,
A web of lies which you have spun,
But you are not the only one.
For I too, wear a mask,
And try desperately to cover up my past.

We are so different...
And yet so much the same.
I'm tired of playing life's sick, twisted games.
I want you to see me;
For I've become blind.
Touch my heart,
Clear my mind.
Free my soul,
For all are tied...
With unseen ropes that bind.

Laura Aube

Wasted Years And Wasted Time

Wasted years and wasted time.
I sit here alone and ask why.
Twenty-nine years of wasted time;
I go back through the years and cry.
Wasted years and wasted time.

Wasted years and wasted time.
My first love said;
Forever, we shall never part.
He gave me three girls and broke my heart.
Wasted years and wasted time.

Wasted years and wasted time.
My second love said till death, we will not part.
A family we will be; you wait and see.
My girls he destroyed, and he broke my heart.
Wasted years and wasted time.

Wasted years and wasted time,
Is all I see as I sit here and cry.
Anger and sadness is all I see;
Twenty-nine years of wasted time. I ask why, as I sit here and cry.
No more happiness that I can see wasted years and wasted time.

Doris Lambert

Trial And Error

One threw me into the waters of life
I still was so young, could swim not nor strive,
And fighting awoke my pride - that was good
"I can swim, I can, I am wood, I am wood!"
And out into storms of life I was hurled
Was, before I perceived it, in fight with the world.
The storms, so I thought, will tear me apart
But I learned to fight back and made it an art.
The storms should not fell me, have reason to mock
And I said to myself, "I am stone, I am rock."
The fire of life also I got to know
Without knowing I stirred around in the glow.
Warnings mean not much when life still's a riddle
I must have sprung daring right into the middle.
The fire was hot - I fast became wise,
I made myself free — became ice, cold, cold ice.
But this is just figuratively spoken,
Had I not thought this way I would've been broken.
All mankind must struggle, life's not always good
And I know I'm woman - not ice, stone or wood.

Liselotte Reich

When Daddy Is Away

I'm happy to go, but I want to stay.
I want to take you with me when I go away.
The thrill of adventure, the mystery of new places,
the curiosity to learn, to encounter new faces,
the thoughts of fun and the play,
but the sadness of leaving you
is more than I wish to pay.
You, who hold their hands in mine,
who snuggle up to me, day or night, anytime,
you who make me laugh and smile,
you who make my days worthwhile,
whose smiles can melt any ice,
warms me from the inside thrice
whose happiness makes me forget all worries.
It's no wonder it's your pleasure I curry.
This is what makes me say,
you should come with me when I go away.

Michael W. Farmer

Believe Me

I was not going to choose you,
I was away from you.
But it was an affair of my heart,
that chose you, not I.
I didn't want to think about you,
it was my heart, that started to admire you.
I couldn't change its way
because it isn't a slave.

It's you, that changed my style of life
yes, indeed, I am a master of love
but I'm afraid that love means more
not only suffering for lack,
the lack I feel every way,
the lack of not touching you,
but I'm an optimist
and I don't like my verse, I love you.....

Jolita Borkowska

Lost Love

My love for you is so strong
I wonder what did I do wrong
To make it disappear in the air
Now my happiness has turned into despair

I lay in bed at night
Dreaming of making love to you in the daylight
Your breath on my face was like a caress
Your touch left me breathless

I can see you smile at me
I think of happiness that will never be
I can see your eyes
Eyes so blue as the skies

I wonder why we didn't last
Those memories will have to stay in the past
I've done all that I can do
Now I have to forget you

Angele Basque

Soaring Lightness

If we lived in the sky
I would ride on the white caps of the blue ocean clouds
or make blueberry mousse with the colour of sunset

From above the world is solid the sky is the one with the power
crying with rain arguing with clouds
or just sleeping in deep deep blue
the sky soothes the weight of the world

I float from the cloud and rise
to the surface of the unending well of blue
I look up to the sky, the sky has nothing on his mind
nothing to remember
nothing to forget
nothing to regret

Then it teases my senses
It changes to a striking pink and orange mellowness
Oh it absorbs what it sees
The ocean, the flowers, the stone

A puzzle of blue fits around me
feeling dappled and drowsy I sleep
under the starry starry night

Joanna de Haan

If I Were Little Again

If I were little I'd jump so high
  I'd land on the black-birds drifting by,
And fly with them to the bye and bye,
  If I were little again.

If I were little, I'd dig so deep
  I'd waken the China-boy from his sleep
And giggle out loud as back up I'd creep,
  If I were little again.

For being small was such jolly fun,
  When I could pretend I was anyone,
And do all the things that couldn't be done
  Unless I were little just then.

But I can still dream as I rock and rock
  And follow the hands of the pokey clock,
Though it's just only me, to whom I can talk
  About being little again.

Louise A. J. Friesen

The Fighter

If I wanted to cry... I could cry all day
If I wanted to die... no one could stand in my way.

I won't shed more tears... what's the sense anymore
It's gotten me nowhere... just made my eyes sore.

I have so much to live for... that's not a lie
I refuse to surrender... I'll not lay down and die.

I'll face all life throws me... I'll stand my ground
No matter what's in store for me... I'll not be brought down.

I'll continue to give of myself... give till life drains me dry
For then and only then... will my heart falter and die.

I'm a fighter... I'll fight all the way
Just to hold on to my dreams... and keep the nightmares at bay.

Maria Bavaro

"If"

If someone came up to you and said,
"I'm sorry about your friend, but he's dead."
I would say, "It's okay to hurt, it's okay to have pain,"
"Because if I were you, I'd feel the same"
If someone stole your life away,
I would walk up to you and say.
"Trust me, my friend I really do care"
"Here's my soul for us to share"
If the sky up above should be covered in grey,
That terrible incident will not affect my day.
If you came up to me and told me that you loved me,
All I had to do was look into your eyes to see
That your love for me was true.
So I would say, "I love you too!"

Tracy Anderson

Early Morning Pink

The sun rises over the pineforest
in east, color heavens light sky pink.
To sleep is impossible the glowing
cannonball spins fast in the stomach
Taking the scorch on.
Out in the mild calm air.
Start to run infuriated on unknown
tracks.
Known and unknown plants becomes
in the increasing light mighty beautiful almost
divine.
The track suddenly divide. Choose
the one that seem most exciting.
Over me comes an inexplicable peace.
Choosing another way homewards.
The cannonball falls into oblivion.
Falling asleep unrock.

Per-Ove Lofdahl

A Friend In Need

A friend in need -
Is a friend in deed.

Old age is like a disease,
Takes away most of the ease,
Of bending backs and knees,
The pain in them is the disease.

Nobody can sit back and boast,
As sooner or later we're all in the same boat,

But, old friend here's my hand,
The least I can do in help you stand.

Joan Bosse'

Alpha and Omega

Born first, sensitive and wise and full of strength, was Alpha.
In his eyes shone passion, and in his soul burned the need to love,
the need to give and the need for her.

Born after, as every Beginning has an End, was Omega.
Bright in mind and beautiful in spirit, she knew no greater desire
than to be complete.

But TIME is as mischievous as the ancient EROS, and a lover of games.
And as the unfaithful manipulator kept them separate and
unknowing of each other, the games turned cruel.

But as TIME sped on, sweet FATE intervened, as the gentle
mediator so often does when TIME treads on the heels of lovers.

So with FATE's gentle guidance they stood close together, face
to face, with recognition in their eyes and relief in their hearts.

And lifting his strong capable hands, palms up, Alpha smiled and
softly said: "the Beginning."

And placing her delicate hands on his, palms down, Omega
smiled and whispered: "the End."

So hand-in-hand, two becomes one as they recognized the truth
their hearts had always known: Every Beginning has and End,
and the joining of the two brings forth Forever.

And TIME turned slow in defeat as FATE clapped her hands in
delight.

Cathy Carter

The Sea Of Life

He stood alone atop the rocky impregnable cliffs and gazed in rapture across the swirling mass of blues, greens and greys of the shimmering seas below.

He watched in fascinated spell-bound silence as the magnificent enormous waves crested in powerfully towering white-foamed sweeps only to crash down upon the pristine virgin sands of the lonely uninhabited shore.

Drawn by their magnetism and mesmerized by their sun-split spray, he held his breath in awe as the turbulent waters spewed upward in a glorious fountain and then just as quickly, descended in cascading splendor.

Entranced, he watched as his ocean surrendered itself to the impervious rocks and finally, be consumed by the following seas.

The steady unrelenting rhythmic pounding of the waves as their vast undulations thundered in his ears, was a poignant reminder of his own mortality.

How like life, with its plateaus and crisis and inevitable ending, he thought to himself. Then he sighed, shrugged his shoulders, turned and slowly made his way back down the rugged path, to ponder and perhaps, to dream.

Norma Dunbar-Skillen

In Search

I left my homeland, far away,
in search of happiness, a life,
where no-one knew me, or judged
according to that which I'd been before.

I searched and travelled, looked and saw.
Not finding my happiness, or life,
hidden in a desert canyon, rocky alp,
or amongst new summer friends.

I went home, looked within, and found,
that which I felt in my heart, the ache,
was not one of loss, or emptiness,
but the sprouting seed of new life, of happiness.

Alison Trebilco

Love Not Meant To Be

Everywhere I turn - you're there,
In spirit, heart and mind.
So as the rain falls, so do my tears,
So let the rain remind you of me my dear!

For every tear drop of mine,
Is like a thunderstorm in my heart.
As each time tears come to my eyes,
Memories of you keep passing by and I die.

Gifts you gave, things you said,
Things we did and places we went,
I'm reminded of these everywhere I go,
But at nights I lay in my bed, cold and alone.

Let the rain remind you of me,
For everywhere I go, or things I see,
Will remind me of a love
"Not meant to Be"

Ena Mirella Ortiz

Darkness

The air is still, the water calm
In the growing shadows the trees have arms, the benches feet
I can't help but imagine what I might meet

As I walk alone it seems that there is no others,
Only me
I feel alone as dark descends
Then I walk away, again,

It's all too strange to understand
So I hide away, again,
I know it's wrong for me to do,
But I can't face it,
I must talk to you
You can help I know you can
But if you can't I'll just pretend

Pretending isn't helping, but that I know by now
So let the darkness find me

Now it's like an old friend
In many ways but one,
It is never welcome
For the darkness stops all fun

Lindsay Unger

Our Not So Beautiful Earth

I was sitting on a city bench
In the middle of the country
In the middle of nowhere
Staring at the midnight sky.

The sky was close that night
As I stretched the essence of my being, my imagination
Into that low sky.

My being stretched past thousands of light years
As though they were merely inches
Encasing the brightest jewel
And dragging it from the sky
Back to the black abyss of the Earth.

When the night time sky's jewel reached the Earth
It no longer shone, it appeared dull and tarnished
On the Earth among the heaps of trash where no jewel can shine.

Undecided for but a moment I released my grip
Not on the jewel but on your garbage ridden Earth
And I flew off into the night time sky with the jewel
Leaving our not so beautiful Earth behind
Where no jewel could shine brightly.

J. B. Gauthier

The Night

The night is filled with dreams
In the night I'm feeling free
The night is healing me
It's all so still and the silence is for me

The night is a time to feel
In the night I rest in peace
The night surrounds me
It's all so still and the silence is for me

Time's slowing down and it's talking to me
Hands coming out of the dark caressing me
The night's for the lovers and dreamers
And for me

The night is when lovers meet
In the night the children sleep
The night is soothing me
It's all so still and the silence is for me

Andreas Ahlenius

The Apple

Imagine one apple
in the store keeper's barrel
berating the selling qualities
of another apple
grown from the same seed
and lying in the same barrel.

"It's the red color I don't care for
and the crunchy sound
and the shine that gleams on the outside."

"The best looking apples, after all
might be rotten to the core"
said the crunchy, shiny, red apple.

Why are we so quick
to count our brothers out-
So quick to be an authority.
Can it be we fear too much
to ripen on the same branch
and produce the same seed?

Karen Hoover

Life

A man tries to make his own path
In the world as he travels
Most of the time that path
Has already been worn and beaten for him
But the man who goes his own way and starts a new path
Others will eventually follow
His path will become worn and beaten too

Keith Carew

In Your Garden, Francis

Oh Francis! Let me linger here, awhile longer
In your Garden; and forget the pain we'll know,
When we're left to walk alone, again;
For soon we must part, and far I shall go.
Let us treasure these precious memories, Dear,
When you and I in Scotland walked,
Just you and I, that blossoming year;
And I, who loves you so......
Shall always hold these golden memories
Of our happiness, where-ever I may go.
And let's not shed another tear,
To mar the loveliness of our Castle scene,
Where we've learned to smile, and not to fear.
Oh, Francis! When we walk together, again,
We'll remember, and our dearest thoughts
Shall also cancel all our pain.

Diane S. Rutledge

Givingness

Omnipresent life - never ending -
Infinite abundance - always giving itself -
Splendor of life - pressing forward - pushing through earthly ground -
Stony soil has become heavenly ground!

Life - know yourself as life -
Not you here - and life there - you are life in expression -
Neither negative life - nor positive life -
But the Isness of life - abundant!

It will express itself through you -
Stand still - and let it come through -
Like the sunbeam - it shines in every garden -
It does not ask if one is good or bad -

Its function is to shine - just to shine!
Life's splendor is in bestowing - in blessing - in outpouring -
In giving of the Infinite Storehouse of God —
Is this - what the world is longing for? - The price is high!

Whomever it touches - they will never be the same -
they have given up personal claim -
And giving themselves - to build a consciousness of love
around the world -
That will stand - and shine into dark places -
that the darkness is no more -
They are fulfilling the promise: "Love is the Fulfilling of the Law"!

Ingeborg Heitmann

Pain

The pain that is stabbing at my heart
Is a mountain whose core is exploding
And an ocean wishing to drown me.
It's the end of the world for my being.

My partner in life, my companion, best friend,
The sole purpose of my being
I held him dying in my arms.
While I whispered farewell to his leaving.

Where did he go, what did he do.
Why am I not with him.
It's the end of our road.
Faith had decided to part us.
It was time that I learned
What real living meant,
With its pain and sorrow and parting.
Maybe some day, as I follow my way
There is a soul that is close to drowning.
I will hold out my hand
For I understand
The power that hides in hurting.

Hannelore M. Gluklev

"Frost"

I awoke this morning to frost on the ground.
It lay on the roof tops and came without sound.
The leaves on the bushes were shrinking in fear,
Their season was over and death was now near.
The hot sun rose with its rays so deep.
The wind blew the leaves in a rustling heap.
Red ones, pink ones and yellow ones too.
Danced in the air as they picked up the dew.
The smothering frost soon melted away.
Waiting to come another fall day.
The leaves on the bushes relaxed with a smile,
Their life would continue another short while!

Muriel E. Dundass

Saying Good-Bye

To say good-bye to the one you love
is like saying good-bye to your whole life.
What we had, could have stayed longer
but instead it has to end.
You haven't phoned, you haven't written.
What's there to do when the one you loved
for oh, so long, turns his back towards you.
It might have been different, if things
weren't as they were. If only there was a sign,
that you truly did care.
But there wasn't.
A long time ago, you showed you cared.
You held me close, with tears in your eyes.
I'm sorry to say, but things have changed and
now it's time to go our own ways.
It's time to let go, forget the past,
keep your dreams, but don't look back.
I'll remember you always, I truly will.
And remember,
I truly do care.

Melanie Klassen

My Poem

What is love
Is love, believing, your Mom is always right,
Is love, finding a love so great everything is sunshine,
Then telling your Mom, who replies,
Your love is the boy you grew up with,
Is love, crying on your wedding day,
For the boy you couldn't have
Is love, like my Dad
Who loved his country and went away to war,
But came back a different man.
Is love, to find a granddaughter ring you
To put a hand out for her father
She hasn't seen for many years
I know I have the love of my
Children, grandchildren, and great grandchildren,
But me, where is my great love.
I turned away from because I couldn't
tell my Mom she was wrong I need my great loves arms around me
To heal the hurt, I have had for many years
Because the word love, can't turn back the clock
to give you a second chance

Esther Clark Davison

We Cannot Waste....

A vision of my hopes and dreams
is not possible.
With the thousands of men brutally killed
all is lost through their eyes.

Why see into the future
if tomorrow will be like today?
A place filled with wonders,
but never the right path.

Visions through a lens of red
the pictures through human blood,
A sign of the times.
Nothing left,
but what we don't call life.

Why force myself to see
what won't come true?
I only see what I have seen before -
a place where no one says
HELLO.

And over and over in the lens of red
GOODBYE.

Nancy Quedado

Belief Is Religion Is Belief

If having a belief in something, anything,
is religion,
Then are we all not religious?
Some may say they have no belief,
Yet that is a belief in itself.

Derrick Logan

Untitled

The vast crowd seems so empty....

The beauty of one
is tied to that of another.

Memories taunting from the past
one feels alone without love
searching, seeking until at last
joy stems from within, a tightened soul
is set loose.

We are all one in a vast space of which we call our own.

The power to begin is far greater than
that to continue and much less than that to end.

Trap one single fly in a glass and watch it die
Yet place two and capture the birth of life.

Sing to the voice of coming thunder yet cry with the rain.

I now pronounce you man and wife
said once, only once
married for life.

Inspired by the likes of Floyd
and the dreams of Marley sets one
adrift into a life of confusion hate and desire.

Simon McIntosh

The Joy Of Laughter And Humor

Good Humor dispels anything that does not bring us delight
It casts out the gloom and miseries of life
And it's an attitude that many people to-day should have
Because of it being around, no one need to be sad.

It lightens the every day cares we do have
Good Humor and Laughter makes us all feel glad
People that have Laughter and Humor we should never reject
For they help us our problems and stress to forget

A good sense of Humor we all should enjoy
It casts out the gloom and sorrow that did us annoy
Therefore people with a sense of Humor we should not cast aside
For they bring us happiness and we are glad their at our side

Because of the cares in this life when it does matter
They are the ones that gloom and doom do scatter
For in the end we all know that they brought us laughter.

Sylvester Snoes

The Rapid Advance Of A Violent Thunderstorm

A blast of thunder was heard to the east
It sounded like the roar of a hideous beast
The sky drew dark as the clouds stole the sun
The winds were whispering "a storm has begun"
The sky looked as if it were covered in ashes
And thundered loudly between lightning flashes
The rain that was falling felt as cold as ice
It started off lightly like the footsteps of mice
Then a bold of lightning pierced through the sky
And the winds started twirling, tossing dirt high
The rain now fell viciously, washing everything away
And the storm took over the rest of the day

Nicole Kaiser

Such Is The Rain

Rain is an integral part of human existence;
it droppeth where it will: on streets and
sidewalks of great cities washing away the day's
accumulation of dirt and grime; it is seen over
harbors and airport hangars; it loiters around bus
terminals and rain stations, reminding commuters
of its whereabouts; it is intimate with factories
and warehouses and huge skyscrapers reaching up
into the night. It pounds on the rooftops of
houses in quiet neighborhoods and then moves away
— out of the city into far off places: visiting
lonely country roads, and cutting across fields
and ditches, only to expend itself beside an old,
abandoned farmhouse. Here it must face
dissolution, its work completed. It will leave
behind a benediction, an ablution of water to
revive the human spirit and make the earth a fairer
place. Such is the rain that droppeth where it will.
For this inestimable gift, Great Overseer, we
tender our profound thanks.

L. H. Collins

A Lifetime Friendship

A marriage is a very important part of your life
It is a commitment to both the husband and the wife
May you be best friends your whole life through
Have a lot of fun times and just sharing time too
Remembering to always communicate and say I love you
Especially if your buddy is sad or feeling blue
May your home be blessed with bundles of joy
Whether it be a sweet little girl or a jolly boy
To create a beautiful family to learn and grow
To teach each other all the wisdom you know
And when your children grow up and away from home
And it's just the two of you once again alone
May you dance to an old tune and hold each other tight
And to love one another all through the night
To still have the commitment and friendship to share
To still be best of friends and know each of you still cares
For being together through all of life's ways
Can be very tiresome some of the days
So keep the twinkle in your eyes and the fire within your hearts
And have the greatest feelings inside that your love together shall
never part

Dara Jeffery

Seeing You

Upon coming here, I had many hopes and fears.
Just by glancing at you made the fears dissolve.
To much has changed, yet something's remain the same.
I found myself really laughing and smiling, because of you.

Seeing you made things more clear,
maybe a little too clearly.
For I feel my heart starting all over again.
How I'll miss you when I leave.

How to explain this, I'll never know.
While we were together, my heart soared.
But when I leave, I know we will carry on as we did before.
Yet there will always be a space in my heart
that will never be filled, unless I'm with you.

As I sit on the plane, I'm torn.
As I walked through the gate, I turned
to watch you go and you were watching me.
The closer I get to the gate,
I start to fill the emptiness fill my heart.
Tears begin to swell in my eyes, but they can never fall.

I guess what I'm trying to say is, I've fallen in love with you.

Tara C. Townend

The Love Of God

My children, you do not need to search for My love, open your eyes, it is all around you.
Do not try to understand it, do not try to fathom its concept,
It is a unique love beyond your understanding,
It is a mystery to you, you must simply accept it.

My love is evident all around you.
It is the sun in all its brilliance, shining upon you, bringing blessing, can you see it?
My love calls to you, it whispers your name, it beckons you and draws you to me, can you hear it?
My love is the air that you breathe, you cannot escape it, you need it to live,
And yet - it is not forceful, it gently breathes with you, can you feel it?
My love is My spirit living inside you, engulfing you, guiding you, protecting you,
It fills your whole being, can you sense it?

But My love is also the storms, yes, it is the thunder and the lightening, the strong winds and the hail.
For how could I be a true Father if I did not bring discipline?
And how could there be growth without the rain?
But then My love becomes the calm after the storm,
It is tranquility and perfect stillness, it is restoration and the soft breeze on your face.

My love is strong and powerful, for what man can control the thunder and what man can withstand the sun?
It is a love with subtle strength.
My love is a mist covering you, a veil enveloping you, but most of all, it is a gift set before you.
Take it - step into the mist, and lose yourself in My love.

G. Johnston

Essence Of Life

There is nothing so precious as time,
It is neither yours nor mine,
To use it well, we have to learn,
For yesterday's time will never return.

Time and tide will wait for no man,
It can't be bought, bottled or put in a can,
It can't be seen or even heard,
It has no wings but flies as a bird.

It can be use by Rich or Poor,
And quite often used for a definite cure,
It is always at hand, but for no one to hold,
It can't be bought nor can it be sold.

When you're a little Child,
You learn to tell time,
It's time for school, It's time for bed,
It's time for this, It's time for that, It's time....

And when you grow much older still,
And you've almost reached your goal,
Your memory is there to recapture the time,
That no person has yet been able to control. God bless.

Roger "Ted" Cleroux

The Library

Oh how I love the peace and quiet of this special room I'm in,
it's free from noise and confusion, crowds and loud shouting.
It holds hundreds of other worlds and journeys to explore,
and everyone is quiet as they enter through the door.

I come here many days, in order to find rest.
This special place is always meeting my divine request.
A place that blocks out a bustling world outside,
and in me, creative thoughts would abide.

Yes the library is a friend indeed,
Your very good pal, once you've learned to read.

Julie Wade

Memories

When we look back on the passing of time,
It passes so quickly it may leave us behind,
But when we look back on the road we have passed,
We cannot but wonder about the up hill task,
The things left unfinished, the dreams unfulfilled,
Then we are standing at the top of a hill,

Wondering, time! Oh time! Where did you go?

The climb up the hill was exhausting and slow,
But with patience and dedication confidence grow,
We all have memories deep inside,
Which we will cherish in the eventide,
Some may be happy, some may be sad,
But these are memories we have had.

We pause - to remember.

The joys and laughter of childhood,
The heartaches and tears of youth,
Silences shared with a loved one,
The peaceful glow of a sunset,
A quiet time for prayer, at the end of day.

We cherish these memories in the Golden Years.

Yvonne Cecily Brathwaite

Half A Century Of Love

You suddenly meet that Special One.
It seems Lightning Strikes you from Above
No matter what comes to block the way.
She's the Only One you'll ever Love.

Then our children each are born.
A girl, a boy, another girl.
It's feeding time, and changing time.
From day to night, night to morn.

The years go by with ups, and downs.
With good and bad entwined.
Hardships, and the need to fight.
Makes love grow stronger you will find.

I've loved my girl nearly fifty years.
Through the good, and through the bad.
The most Beautiful Woman I've ever met.
And the Best Friend I've ever had.

Together we have done our best.
We've nothing to defend.
I've loved her for near fifty years.
I'll love her till the end.

Robert V. Griffin

First Love

The fireplace is going, we're drinking your wine,
It's getting colder, shall we get out of line?
We could waltz the night away just you and me
We could get closer like you touching me.
Listening to love songs while the fire burns out
Having you near me, is that what loves about?
Touching you, caressing you making you feel no pain.
Touching me, kissing me, you're using your vain
Don't stop it now, I'm feeling so good
Touching me, holding me, forget the firewood.
I'm right here with you, just like I should.
The times gone so fast, we had a great time
Call me tomorrow, and here's a dime
Will he still need me, does he still care?
I hope he didn't use me, it just wouldn't be fair.

Debbie Dale

But What Of The Children

That night of the year is here again
It's Christmas Eve you know
That night of the year is here again
And we have lots of snow

Little children are asleep this night
All ready for Santa Claus
Dreaming of the gifts he will bring
For all the girls and boys

But what of the children
Who have nothing at all
For we are those children - the victims of war
There's no - one to love us and no - one to care
Is there no-one out there who will say us a prayer

The winter winds are blowing
The war torn trees are kissed with snow
There's people out there dying
And we have no where to go

So come on all you grown ups' who wage all these wars
End all this fighting and stop all this pain
And make no more children Orphans' again

Michael J. Regan

"Seduction"

It's my eyes, liquid pools of moonlight
It's my lips, dew kissed and soft
It's my smile, warming you with sun rays
It's my tongue, honey sweet and enticing
It's my voice, mesmerizing music on -
your ear waves

It's my breasts, mounds of quivering ecstasy
It's my hips, girting in slow tantalizing tempo
It's my arms and legs entwined like creeping vines
It's all of me, sensuality immortalized
passion emblazoned

Charisma crystallized
Alluring grace
PROVOCATIVE
That's why you return
It's why you can't leave
Run, flee, I will not hold you
I'll be there waiting round the corner
Like tomorrow....
YOU MUST COME!!

Jocelyne Fletcher

Too Hard

Just a taste
Just a taste of something wonderful
Is too hard
Letting go is not as easy as it should be
Not when you are thinking of what could be

Just a sign
A sign of something you may want
There but not
It's such a sad and melancholy thing
Waiting to see what new days will bring

And hope
Hope and fear are what remain
Releasing dreams
Of a lover who was wonderful but too much
With the moment as it was, both were out of touch

Too hard
Too hard to let go of what couldn't be
To know that
Tomorrow may bring what you both may need
Separately.

Claudia Fenton Wicki

"Kiss Of Inspiration"

The dawn sun called out to the rose
kiss me, my love and I shall
drive away the mist that stops
my rays from gleaming thro' tree-tops.

The cloud paused over the mountain
kiss me, my love, and I shall
rain honey onto this barren earth,
and all shall drown in love's mirth.

The moon rose over the ocean
kiss me, my love, and I shall
flood this earth, steeped in darkness,
in light, and love upon all I shall bless.

The star made haste to darkness
kiss me, that I shall
start twinkling excited by your kiss
that no man ever to wonder shall miss.

Time, the Hunter, beheld space
kiss my arrow, and I shall
take you to love's deeper dimensions
that hold the universe in delicate suspensions.

S. Raghotham

Peace

When I find myself in times of trouble, hurt and pain
knowing I am not alone, seeing the hurt with knowing disdain.
Oh, you so young that was once so full and ripe,
Weep no more alone, in this your troubled life.

We have taken this our very first step, to life anew, we all now
peek, like that butterfly free from the cocoon, free to fly ne'er
again be weak.
To unfurl our wings reach up to the sun,
for our life a new beginning begun.

As we were once so captive, tied and bound,
now we search together, life's treasures to be found.
For is it not so that life once begun has but a short time to be spun.
Like a spiders web glistening with dew,
so shall we shine, both me and you.

Glisten and shine to a fruitful life serene
after such a deadly beginning, a frightening, harrowing scene.
Guilt, pain and hurt once the backcloth to our life
will glow from a cold, white, winter sun
to one with depth warmth and love, Gods natural gift of life.

Dee Wilson

Now I Know

I just don't know what to do, what to say, where to head,
knowing that if I make the wrong move, I can end up with a heart
full of lead

I read, I watch the T.V., I look outside the window,
....and what do you know

Now I know what to do, change the cruelty around,
(the system) put in all that I can, into what should:

My people suffer oppression of color, of culture, of land,
a magic wand won't change that but something real will

Now I know what to say, speak the truth, for my people, for
those that can't, now along with some others I have to make a
true chant... you may call it all a dream but it's not to me

Now I know where to head, go where innocent blood is being
shed... it may be down the road, it may be down south where I'm
from, I will go, where many are afraid to, where the sun don't
shine, where the border line is a dangerous one, to make the land
not ones' but alls'

I may or may not know the risk, so what!
I want to see a change for the better, a change for all.

Mauricio Rodas

The Kiss

As darkness fell like a black velvet curtain across the land, he leaned over and took my hand. Our fingers entwined like the gnarled branches of the apple tree, as he whispered, "I love you" to me.

He said not a word as we rose from the hill, just pulled me close as the wind gently blew across us. We swayed back and forth, and the night world was our band.

The bullfrogs, the crickets, the bubbling spring, gushing over the rocks in a haunting melody. The rustling leaves kept time as we waltzed across the hill into the moons' shining light.

The trees cast a dramatic shadow across his face as he leaned toward me, and our lips met in a bitter-sweet kiss. The feeling was beyond explanation.

My face was flushed as I slid my arms around his neck, my fingers caressed the hair that was brushing against them. His hands slid up and down my back, making me shiver.

Then, just as quietly as the kiss came, it was over. Breathless, he gazed into my eyes not saying a word for what seemed like eternity.
Then he held me close, whispered, "I'm sorry", and disappeared into the night.

Valerie Cole

Masks

You sit there, at the checkered table,
Legs crossed, confident smile.
Talking.
People surround you, talking about a party they went to,
Or what their boyfriends said about you.
An annoying giggle escapes your lips -
The ones who already have a reputation of their own.
What did you have to do to become what you are?
My ears know, but my mind doesn't.
Outside, you look happy, self-assured.
But I know the truth.
I know that you're scared.
That you secretly want to be lying in your bed,
Reading Anne Frank, knowing how smart you really are.
Do you really like who you are - on the outside?
People like you don't talk to people like me.
To someone you used to be.
To tell you the truth,
I wish I were you.

Patricia McFarlane

"Let Me Go Back"

Let me go back to a child again, to a house on a dusty road.
Let me sit by the river where the green fields in the valley fold.
Let me walk down the lane again, where the Golden Rod grows high,
Where wild geese call and evening falls
O'er the land with a gentle sigh.

Let me see the Kind faces I knew when I was young,
Seems the world was new then, everything just begun.
Let me go back just for a day, just for one day's rest.
To that place that's warm in the Summer's Sun,
That place I remember best.

Let my mind go back in time to when I was a child.
Where summer sun shone bright and hot, and breezes were so mild.
Where roses grew wild along the ditch and lilacs filled the lane,
Where crows called loudly in the morn,
And farmers prayed for rain.

I want to go back to yesterday to fields so wide and green.
To a place that has the bluest skies that I have ever seen.
So you'll find me down in Spring Brook,
I'm going there for a day, to stroll around the Old Churchyard
And dream my cares away.

Thelma Sanderson

The Open Door

The Open Door leads into a place that was once a busy haven of life's emotions, complete with passion, laughter, and tears. This claimed by a typical family through their daily but significant adversities.

Now the wind has taken over those passages that at one time anchored those within. The walls, now faded and peeling, have forgotten the warmth of a lighted fire as shadows flirted and danced to the rhythm of voices now silenced by the past. And as the rain falls, unmercifully upon crumbling panes, the house resigns itself to the cruelty of nature's powers upon its battered remains.

But now, the sunlight streams through the chasms of its time-worn frame, and the door unlocks its past, and a new energy takes over, and filters onto the snow covered floorboards — creating warmth, and awakening the new life within. Although forgotten, abandoned, and silent, the small creatures have found shelter amidst the ruins, and made it their refuge.

So, once again the house is a busy haven in which these humble spirits struggle, in their own ways, to survive.

And the Door, as long as it stands, will remain, and always be, Open.

Karen E. Baudais

Untitled

What keeps our lives always intertwined
Like a spiders web, so delicate and defined
There has to be a reason for all of this
Was the answer in our first kiss

The feelings we have are they real
Of how our lips and bodies could feel
Pressed gently together to satisfy our crave
Or are they only years of fantasies we have created and made

When our eyes meet in that hypnotic stare
The feelings we once shared are still there
We want each other now, like we wanted then
Will our obsession ever come to an end

Someone or something always keeps us apart
But, we still hold each other close to our hearts
Our time together will eventually arrive
Only then will our true passions come alive

Laura D. Podzorski

An Angel Used To Love Me

Once upon a time, an angel was sent to me. He brought a smile that, like the sun, announced the dawning of a glorious new day. He brought the two brightest stars, that shone in his soft brown eyes. And he brought a heart full of love ... enough to last forever. My Angel taught me how to live again... in a world of happiness and laughter. The gentle touch of heaven that he held, kissed my lips with everlasting sweetness. Alone he made my heart soar, like a shooting star through the night sky. Not knowing limitations; Not realizing it could end. For a moment I held paradise, but I let it slip away. I let my fear pry open my hand; loosen my grip. Through a rainstorm of tears I saw my one piece of heaven, fly away on golden wings. The sweetness that turned bitter as my heart began to question, was all that remained. A blanket of guilt now keeps me warm, instead of the loving arms that once did. I have one wish, yet nothing to wish on, for the radiant glow from the stars cannot be seen any more. I'll never be able to forget how the sun rose, every morning right on cue. Or how beautiful it was, even when I saw it set for the last time. I'll never enjoy the sound of soft music in the distance; knowing only that it's a choir of lost angels. And I'll never forgive myself for being so weak; when my angel needed me to be so strong.

Laura Hubbard

To Feed The Power

It's hard.
Liking a person this much.
It's a nice feeling in a way,
To always have someone to think about.
It hurts, almost, being around her,
And not being able to wrap your arms around her.
But you have to be around her,
Because you have to feed this power.
You can't just stop liking her.
The feelings run a lot deeper than your thoughts.
Deeper than your heart.
You are always looking for her, watching her.
Always tense.

This is a power that cannot be controlled.
A power that can be felt by everyone,
But only one person has it.
This power is Love.

It's just as nice a feeling to love someone
As to be loved by someone.

Jeff M. Perry

Cat Sam Blues

A jolly jumpin' fish named Sam
lived in the bottom of a garbage can.
He never took no for an answer
And was never much of a belly dancer.
But he did lead a life of luxury and fun,
His shoes never came undone.
Generally speaking, fish don't wear shoes,
But Sam was a funky little fish
Who liked to sing the blues.
Then one day a cat came prowling
And poor little Sam could be heard howling
Singing his last blues.
No more fish,
No more blues.

Mark Austin

Tumblin' Down

I wrestle in the darkness of a lonely land
Living in the fortress that I alone command
My future, all of my hopes and my dreams
Everything my heart desires is in my hands

My castles, temporary foundations on sand
Tumbling down around me as I surrender all
I lay down my arms and give up the fight
I give up all the glory, for praise is yours alone

For the life I now live is no longer my own
For I have surrendered it all, given it to you
Everything that my human soul desires
Is in your hands now as my kingdom falls

Pam S. Clarke

A Wedding Wish

Your two lives are now entwined,
Love eternal may you find.

My wishes for you are oh so beautiful,
May they be for you oh so bountiful.

Love and health, compassion and sharing,
Friendship, consideration, laughter and caring.

With these your marriage will have meaning,
God will have bestowed on you a blessing!

Lois Barlow

What The Ocean Brings

Before my eyes in lapping jade
lolling spectre glide, and fade
o'er hungry stars who slowly graze
on boulders dark, and eerie.

And out beyond the inbound waves
life goes on in times deep haze,
where storms are born to want, and rage,
till mellow age does spend them.

There's something about a ship at sea
brought to cruel fangs by squalls, and shrieks
with timber's roar, and sailor's screams
hushed by kisses briny.

Then all join in the spectral dance,
where some men's eyes do stare askance,
and bits of wood do swirl and prance
like stars before my eyes.

William A. Salmon

Losing My Grandad

I never thought It would happen to me,
Losing my grandad to a horrible disease.
He'll never tell jokes that make me laugh,
He won't ever take another photograph.

To me he was the number one,
We always had so much fun.
We always went to the candy store,
Whenever we visited him he was never a bore.

But I ask, "Why did you have to go?"
If there's a reason I'll never know.
Right now his ashes cover the largest pine tree,
I'm happy to know he's where he wants to be.

I wish it was all just a bad nightmare,
Leaving us all heartbroken, it really isn't fair.

Michelle Oswald

Alone

I am too weak to listen and too strong to hear
Losing my wisdom, for death holds me near
Turning my bright days now to a dark
My soul now dying, I leave you my mark
A piece of my knowledge, a trace of my figure
Up in the heavens I roam and I linger
Misty the wind is, it dusts my heart
Life- vs.-death and now we must part
Up by my lonesome I hug myself
I am the only, there is no one else
Alone in the darkness, I sing a song
Wondering if I'm where I belong
Being afraid, this I know
Is the only emotion that I show
A lone tear streams from my eye
I'm all alone there's no need to cry
A heavenly host along my side
It's my time to go, for now, I abide.

Mandi Fletcher

Loves Flight

Be quick my love and entwine thy arms with mine but let not thy moist lips be chaste, but impart thine love with eternal passion. Be careful my paramour I beg thou must divulge thy secrets with unhurried pace, lest I awake and find it's but a fevered dream and you were never by my side.

Veronica A. Denyer

Love

Love is beautiful,
Love is kind,
Love is not something that comes from the mind.

Love is understanding,
Love is unique,
Love that is true is not something weak.

Love is what comes from the heart,
Love grows stronger in many ways,
Love is something you give,
To your loved ones each passing day.

Kelly Lawryniw

Wild Thing

He dances in the sky,
Mane and tail flaming,
Flashing hooves cutting the air.
His once gentle eyes, burning with anger
As he neighs his challenge to the world.
He comes down from his great height,
To take off like a black shadow
Flying low across the earth.
So wonderful, exciting, so beautiful!
His pounding hooves echoing through the silence,
Rebounding off the cliffs around him.

With the lead rope hanging broken from the halter,
He is a picture of freedom, an unbridled spirit.
He is the most magnificent animal living.
He is high spirited, wild, fearless, and wonderful!
He is a horse, a wild stallion!

Mindy Wilkinson

Good Night, Sleep Tight

Good night, sleep tight, my little one,
May all your dreams come true.
May you not know what a nightmare is,
Just the dreams that are good.
With the teddy bear in your arms, 'n' the cat by your feet,
May you dream of golden sunsets upon the silver beach.
With the birds of a rainbow flying without a care.
Good night, sleep tight, sleep tight my dear,
Let all your worries go away.
Don't you worry 'bout mom and dad, or what you'll be doing tomorrow.
Just think 'bout waterfalls, and how the waters flow,
Think 'bout the mammals and how they might look.
The lion with his mane, the coon with its mask.
And the Children of the world sleeping with their nighties on.
Good night, good night, sleep tight my dear,
May all your dreams come true.
May you not know what a nightmare is,
Just the dreams that are good.
Just the dreams that are good.

Marjua Nadeau

Love

What is love?
Must it be between a couple.
Or can you just be friends and still love.
I have once loved and been loved,
Now I don't remember how.
Why must love be broken,
Like a shattered piece of glass.
Why can we not feel love all the time,
Other than just feeling a piece of the happiness.
So you tell me,
What is love?

Joni Ronaldson

Beginnings

Evening mist has left its signature,
Milky colored grass, dew upon the rose.
Daylight struggles with the darkness,
Until at last it goes.

A silent breeze slithers across the land,
Leaves dance to its silent tune.
Flowers also bend and sway,
As if saying good-bye to the moon.

Far off in the distance a rumble is heard,
Flashes of light bolt across the sky.
Grey-green mountains move closer,
Droplets fall as they begin to cry.

The muggy odour of the earth sweeps upward,
Mother robin snuggles in her nest.
Tiny rivers are formed in the soil,
As the greyish-green mountains move west.

Oh now the mighty wind does scream,
Causing the storm to fade away.
Rays of light begin to warm,
This earth for another day.

Monica S. Kehler

The Seeker

In a world so full of greed, how much is enough?
Millionaires desiring, yet surrounded by the impoverished.
All their fortunes fall short in supplying happiness.
In the end they wander eternity with hollow memories.
Was happiness and satisfaction over the next hill?
They will never know.
There was always one more hill to climb.

They loved the taste of the fruit they wed.
Yet pursued others in the search of one that was sweeter.
Hearts like balloons filled once with joy.
Could something else expand them further?

I sit and look at the last mountain before me.
Yet make no effort to surmount it.
I am content to admire it from afar.

Other fruits offer me no curiosity.
I have found the sweetness I enjoy.
I need not worry of the expansion of my heart.
It has no boundaries as it is infinite.

I understand what enough is,
And I am happy.

T. Moore

Scattering

The words are breaking
Moss from time decayed
left abandoned.
There, where the voice is lost
the wind deepens
empties the eternity with a pass key
orphans the drowned.
The tree at the seashore died yesterday
giving its roots to the last hung man
simple continuity
simple journey.
You hope but, something in your expression
is constantly getting further away.....

Georgia Daliana

My Beloved

His bounty of beauty
Must be something unimaginable

His frightful eyes ask the question
Nobody else would want to know
Stretching inward I am froze
For no one knows what he is thinking
No one wants to know

And as he walks through endless, narrow halls,
He wonders something
And he stops. Still.
I can only imagine deep inside what he is thinking
Because nobody else would want to know

Look at me, see my face
Hear my voice say things my heart will regret
You will never be my beloved
Because nobody else should know
What we are thinking
What a shame

Shannon Lee Tully

Feelings

I must shake the strands that bind me to the people that I love, I must move away from them gently at firth, both to free them and myself from our mutual dependence.

I must distance my self from the birds, the trees, my garden my animals, MY PEOPLE, IN FACT, THE WORLD, for they were never mine anyway. I must be gentle with them and myself, but even my, (I) will have to go, for this also binds me to the earth. This essence I call me must be free to face whatever dispersion brings, and yet stay alert!

I have preconceived ideas about that state that waits for us all, yet I must be open, for it suspect that we make our own state of being, here and there, but especially there.

Will the essence of my thoughts and tenuous beliefs find the right way forward, will I meld into the melody of others and make a song of my life?, in my deep feelings I know that many parts of me have been left behind, and many parts wait for me again, so it goes on throughout eternity.

Breaking the threads that tie us to Earth, and all that it entails is so difficult, and maybe even more so if we have to meet the earth life again, to die in reverse, to life on Earth if this is so it should not be so difficult for we should not feel threatened, but only to be able to quiet my mind, yet be conscious, for a brief moment, then in that span I might truly see, to find the one temple of bright light inside me, every atom, every electron, every nucleus, that makes me, has a life of its own, they connect me to everything and everyone, why cannot I see? although I know, but knowing deeply is not enough. I need to see the purpose of it all.

Doreen Challis

Lament

No one shall remember me after my death
None shall give me a wreath.
No epitaph be written in my memory
As I produced nothing bright and glory,
Me neither a Hero nor a Writer or a Scientist
My name is not engraved with the Greatmen's list.
Mother only shall weep for a few days
'A man were', my relatives would say
Quick they forget, for good, my heirs
Used to divide themselves their shares.
I, like all those common remain unknown
As I came silent so silent gone.

Manash Mazumder

The Dinner Party

Running around all in a dither
My, all my flowers are going to whither
The guests are arriving in all their wealth
Oh, God, I need a drink for my health
The table's not set
And I am not dressed, but
Hubby is out there doing his best
Drink here, appetizer there
While I am deciding what to wear
The black, red, green or gold
Maybe nothing
If I could be so bold
Finally, ready to face the crowd
Drinks flowing, voices loud
No one notices, I see them ahead
Maybe I'll just turn around
And go to bed.

June Hole

My Sweet Child

My child will be full of comfort and everlasting love.
  My child will be dearest to heaven up above.
My child will have no evil, just happy thoughts of me.
  My child will be thankful for the sky and the sea.
My child will have no problems with understanding God.
  My child will be a fish swimming in a pond.
  My child will be learning how to live a life.
My child will have happiness to his family and his wife.
  My child will be a man, for me to let him go.
  He will always be my child, that I truly know.

Lani Miller

In The Dark

There is nothing in the dark that isn't in the light.
My dad told me this, most every night.
"What about the goblins," I would say.
His reply, "Well look for those during the day."
Just believe there is nothing in the dark that isn't in the light.
So long ago, so many years.
School, marriage, children, his death and tears.
I walked my grandchildren home last night.
It's dark, a noise a small child's fright.
A wee voice piped, "It's alright" —
There is nothing in the dark that isn't in the light.
Last night I had a terrible dream
A tunnel black no lights, no beam.
I tried to turn and run and hide.
You must enter to get to the other side
Once again I heard him say.
There is nothing in the dark that isn't in the night
It was then I saw "God's Perfect Light."

Jeanne Roberts

The Tale Of A Masterpiece

The devouring fire - stopped and pondered
  "My food fret!
  My wood's wet!?"
The dwarf in the wood trembled and grew
  "My home dies;
  my mind cries"
The soul in the dwarf yawned and got worried
  "My body's sad;
  it can't be that bad!"
The God in the soul woke up and danced
  "My babes are playing;
  I feel like staying!"

Maggie Rouki

Untitled

I sit here, feeling quite useless actually,
My head throbs to the beat of the music.
Amidst the crush of hot, sweaty bodies on the dance floor
I feel pretty much alone
There are others who, very much like me
Bob and weave with the crowd
They fit in about as well as I do
We are commonly referred to as "Outsiders"
Those who, on the outside appear perfectly normal
However we are viewed as "unacceptable"
There really are no reasons for why we are this way.
Outside of the group we come with we are very social creatures,
But, put us along side a familiar element
We become mentally angular and socially awkward
Seldom do we smile under the strain of obligation,
We are too honest and often forgo the pressure to: Smile
  a little wider and laugh a little more
We are highly vulnerable on a social degree
We do not thrive to socialize, only to crawl up to the surface
Every now and then, to see what's going on.

Cassandra King

When Blows The Wind

When blows the wind,
My heart does follow.
And like in some trance,
In a sleepy hollow,
I am transformed.

And my mind blows with it,
wild and free.
My thoughts are echoes of what used to be;
What my ears have not heard.
But all is familiar somehow.

Answers are everywhere,
Questions abounding.
The whispers are louder.
My heart sets a pounding.

My soul is uplifted
By God's great grace.
For a moment I'm sure
There's a glimpse of his face.

Ravishing, rigid, crisp... ultimate sincerity.
Blessed be the Wind!

Jody Kathleen Adair

Sleepless Nights

I toss, turn and toss again
My heart yearns to be free and escape
I fly high, up in the sky, fancy free spirit
Know no boundaries, feel no chains, no barriers
My mind, body and soul tuned into you
Sweat spreads over my body
My arms long to hold, heart longs to keep and cherish
Your voice, whispers in my ears
Your soft hands explore, lips caress
My heart misses a beat, throat all dry
"Water, water", I call as I awake
Morning dawns, heart weeps, hopes sink
If only the sun never rose, nights went on
Separation could then never occur, as you would still be with me
throughout my sleepless nights in thought.

Rahima Kassam

Pen Pal

Pen Pals are people you meet from other places
  My pen pal is someone I wrote to
I found her name in an ad in a national fan club
  I noticed we had a lot in common
We both liked the same TV shows, soap opera,
  She's from the United States, I'm from Canada
Discussing our favorite soap is great fun
  We have a great time talking or writing to each other
Discussing story plots and twists, joking about scenes
  Having fun telling each other what we would do
Talking about families and our hobbies
  Trusting each other with secrets
Describing your country or province to one another
  I know she enjoys the stories I send her in the mail
She likes receiving them and I like sending them
  She does the same for me
Family is important to her and to me
  Having a Pen Pal means you get to see other states
Viewed from another person's eyes
  A Pen Pal is someone other than your family
Someone to write to when you need time to yourself

Darlene McKay

Clouded Eyes

If I could show you the world through my eyes,
My tears would paint you
a picture with a whirlwind of blue.
If, for a day, you could see life
through my blurred vision,
your black and white world would cry in radiant hues.
If only I could open your eyes to the world I live in,
you would no longer be blinded by false dreams.
If you saw the world through me,
there would be no more
fairytales, rainbows, and magical golden sunbeams.
If only I could show you what it's like to be chained
to endless fears and pain.
If, just once, you could know,
what it's like to never hold sunshine,
to only catch rain.
But, instead, you look through ignorant eyes,
and wonder why I lay in silence,
with tears pouring from my
clouded eyes.

Denise L. Greene

Summer's End

When I stand above that grave,
my tired soul becomes a slave.
A huge price to pay, for the
God above we must not disobey.
The price was dear, her cheerful
voice we no longer hear.
Gone to a place absent of time,
their innocence's, is that a crime.
We cannot bring back the dead you know,
let always the cold, forbidding truth show.
The shocking news affects us all,
some are sure to fall.
Remember of all fun things,
be wary of summer flings.
Just one last thing I want to know,
why God did they have to go?

Brent Noiles

Little By Little

As you sit by your piano, you notice the silence of the keys.
Naked white, naked black.
Your heavy heart reaches to your fingertips that warm the keys
and heat the soul.
A teardrop falls and mixes with the chords.
Your eyes close.
Your eyebrows crinkle, your forehead wrinkles.
The weight seems unbearable, then...
You open your eyes.
A blade of sunlight touches your hand.
It doesn't surprise you.
You understand.
Little by little the tears will be less.
Little by little you'll smile a bit more.
Little by little you'll find the right one.
Understanding all too well.
Your music has only
just begun.

Rosemarie Horner

Dreams

Dreams are so precious
Never give them up
Always dream of tomorrow
And remember, don't give up.

Go out and make your dreams come true
Don't let them slip away
Always believe in yourself
And you'll never loose your way.

Broken dreams stay broken
Unless they are rectified
Then the dreams you dream will never come true
And never will you be satisfied.

So grasp your dreams with both hands
And never let them go
Take them and nurture them
So they will grow for tomorrow.

Only you can do it
Take one step at a time.
Stick-to-itiveness is all it takes
And you'll be proud of yourself your whole lifetime.

Brenda Brewer

No One Like You

There is no one like you.
No one else can do the things you do.
There will never be anyone else for me.
It's you I always hope to see.
Some people can fall in love time and again,
But without you I feel only pain.
If you would forgive me, it would ease this pain in my heart,
For I realize that it was fate that forced us to part.
I want to show you my pain,
But which one of us would gain?
You would only laugh at me.
This is the worst pain you will ever see.
It's the kind that won't go away.
I miss you with all my heart, but maybe it is best this way.
The fact that we are through is one I'll have to face.
For, even as we speak, I can't help staring into space.
The past holds sweet memories of you and me,
But fate has decided, so I guess this is how it must be.

Wendy J. Finlay

For You

On this Father's Day of ninety-four,
No one will love you any more.
All the love you showed me through the years,
Will not go unforgotten and lost in tears.
Today I hope that you will see,
My love for you is an open sea.
Although at times it's hard to say,
I'll say I love you on Father's Day.
You will find enclosed no gifts, nor shade
Because things bought with money often fade.
I give you this from deep inside,
And may you read it with lots of pride,
For you and only you,
Are a father so true.

Happy Father's Day

George El-Koura

The Enemy

He rides not upon a charger
Nor sails upon a stormy sea
I need not look any farther
The enemy...is me

His edge cuts deeper than any sword
His aim is always true
Against him there is no ward
For those who must pay their due

His armour glitters brilliant light
That reveals more than it shields
All of this he brings to the fight
Upon this mortal field

His onslaught there is no resistance
In succumbing can one be free
For he brings to battle the sharpest lance
The enemy...is me

Wilfred J. Walker

Storm Before the Calm

It was a dark and windy night
Not even stars were shinning bright
The moon was lost behind the clouds
And all the trees wore great black shrouds.

But with the dawn the skies were bright
No sign of any stormy night
There was no rain, no shrouded trees
Just the songs of the birds and a gentle breeze

Lesley Maudsley

Crime In Everywhere

We read in the papers, we hear on the air,
Of gambling and stealing, crime everywhere
Of poor children encouraged to roam
But too many parents who won't stay at home,
They don't make the gangsters or make the crooks
For what they don't see they read in books
As Mother's old Bible is used as a souvenir
If they would take in down from the shelf and say
a small prayer
You wouldn't read so much in papers hear on the air
If their parents would of told the truth and the right
Their son daughter wouldn't be in a prison cell
perhaps tonight

Doris Cummings

The Eyes

He steps into the dark of the night,
Not knowing what is out there.
He hears the sounds of footsteps.
Is it friend; or foe? He looks up, into the distance,
And sees a pair of eyes. Who do they belong too?
The footsteps sounds are coming closer.
The eyes are doing the same.
Should he stay there and see the eyes bring out.
Or should he run? He tries to take off, but he can't.
The eyes have him glue to the spot.
He stares into them.
They keep coming closer, and closer.
The closer they got the more scared he was.
Suddenly, she came into the light.
Was it true? Was it the love of his life?
The one that he lost years ago?
Her embrace was with warmth.
Their kiss locked their lips together, as
a bolt of lightning strike them,
making them lovers through all... eternity.

Karen L. Daniels

Meditation

As I sit watching this great body of water as far as the eye can see
Not knowing where the ocean ends and the sky begins
It is beyond my comprehension
Then I watch the small waves become larger and larger as they come
Rushing, turning, swirling, churning up sand, debris
Dashing it up on the shore as the waves are foaming,
Bursting relentlessly back and forth.
Then gently and silently the ocean takes them back again

Like a mother, loving takes back her wandering hurt and bruised child,
To love and hold and forgiving and forgetting
All the restlessness that was, longing to give peace and comfort.

The restless ocean forever bringing such peace, quiet, relaxation
to some, destruction, grief, sadness to others.
The restless ocean forever on the move is encircled with mountains,
Like guarding arms saying, all is well.
God is still on his throne.
He created the world and the oceans and all that is in them,
He created!
How great thou art.

Katharina Dyck-Wiebe

Perhaps A Dream

I watch the dusk fade to night,
Observing the stars appear in the vast sky.

Beginning to dream, as I drift away,
Reality becomes aloof to my senses.

I'm with you and you're holding me,
A circle of love entangles us,
We kiss - this feeling is forever.

You, are my prince, my lover, my best friend,
I'd give my life for yours.

Our photograph symbolizes love,
Until it totters, smashing to he floor,
Bringing with it my future and our love.

I awaken to discover sleep was haunting me,
The stars remind me; I'm alone and we're distant.

Once again, as many nights before,
I lock the book of memories,
But never throwing away the key,
In hopes that someday my novel will be completed.

And so, as I drift away again,
My last thoughts are of a broken heart, a tear, a key
and perhaps.....a dream.

Dayna Morrow

At The Doorstep Of My Tower

I hear the rumbling off in the distance
Of a storm that threatens to break these walls
I am alone, a stone pillar amongst a field
Encased and engulfed as harsh winds attempt to throw me
I stand and closing my eyes
I wait
Cracking, thrashing, screaming the thunder pushes into my brain
Which is a feeble escape
A tiny utopia rendered useless in such a large space
Scratching at my cells, incoherent sounds of angry wind fronts
Reveal that you are there swirling around me
Enveloping me in a hurricane of thoughts
That flow as easily as leaves carried on the wind
Of words that pass as quickly and silently and smoothly
As an eruption of electric fire
Surround me, suffocate me, entangle me
Because when morning comes and calm remains
I will be standing
And you
Will be gone

Tanya Galtress

"Races"

We all are different races,
of all nationalities,
speaking different languages,
with different accounts,
of different skin colors,
in different countries.

We all are different races,
facing racial inferiority and discrimination,
which tears people and countries apart.
For all of us are human beings,
created in the image of God,
for we all breathe, bleed and die.

We all are different races,
reflecting and procrastinating,
whether black, white, yellow or brown.
For the way forward,
is to learn, teach and educate,
our children and families racial harmony.

David A. Carmichael

A Lonely Night In The City

No sounds but wilderness!
Of nothing I can see.
No sounds just the rare urban tranquility.

Nothing to see but who we are.
Nothing to see but the great aged stars.

No where to go but back inside.
No where to go but in to hide.

No where to play but adulterate cement.
And nothing to feel but total lament.

Lionel Brouillard

'Knowing'

Rain caresses her face as she walks down the dim lit alley,
Night creatures scurry past her feet as they stare with fright.
As she approaches the building she stops and turns
around to see a woman standing behind her.
A bridge of knowing is formed and she turns around;
She continues to walk but this time towards a
brightly lit tunnel with no end and no beginning.

Tina Quade

Childhood Memories

As I sit by my window and gaze on the scene
Of that far reaching wild-wood, and meadows so green,
It reverts to my vision fond memories beguiled,
When I think of those places I loved as a child.

I could name them as long as my pen could hold ink
And the more that I name, they are dearer I think.
Oh how dear they seem now since my memory's compiled
All those phantom like places I loved as a child.

Just to quote you a few of the dearest I might-
And yet are they not all as dear to my sight,
As they were in those days of my infancy wild
All those wonderful places I loved as a child.

There's the old swimming hole that sure ranks with the best
That Elm - branch teeter stands out with the rest,
And those bon-fires at night, that with branches we filed
Holds a mark mid those places I loved as a child.

This is only a sample of fond memories charm
As back in my childhood I romped on the farm;
Yet now when my memory reverts to that time
It holds me in ecstasy, childish sublime.

Suzanne McGugan

Listen To The Silence

Listen to the silence;
Of the busy, bustling chapel on a Monday morning, bleak.
Of the midnight in the country when there 're only stars to speak
Of the lonely prairie wheat field after harvesting is through.
Of the bedroom, after door is slammed, as he walks out on you.

Listen to the silence;
Of the trees that stand so still after raging, roaring, winds.
Of the court room after months of thought, death sentence judge rescinds.
Of the nursery where the new born breathes its shallow breath.
Of the moment, pushing up through grief, you accept a loved ones' death.

Listen to the silence;
Of the feeling of elation when you know a test you've won.
Of the golden dawn of morning as you watch the rising sun.
Of the opening of young heart to tender stirring of first love.
Of the echo of the answer to your prayer to God above.

Listen to the silence.

Dorothy Warwick

A Poetic Attempt

I wish that we humans, had been designed, with the stomach
Of the camel, or the cow.
With a hump on our back, not one stomach, but two,
Just imagine the things, that we'd be able to do!

We could go off for days, or weeks at a time:
Without food, or water, beer, rum or wine.
We could save all that cooking, and washing up too;
By eating, in one meal, a weeks helping of stew.

There would be no leftovers, to be eaten next day,
Because we would fill up our stomachs, or hump.
I'm not talking about eating grass, corn, or hay
But a delicious meal, of vegetables and rump.

It would save on gas and electrical bills.
On our good china, pots, pans, and table top frills.
We could do without freezer and less cupboards and things.
It's easy to see, the savings that brings.

We would save lots of time, 'cause we'd not have to dine,
In a restaurant, and very seldom at home.
We would not need plastic plates or utensils,
Or those coffee cups, made out of foam.

Michael A. Halsall

God's Evening Bird

The shrill chirping
Of the evening bird,
Bathed
In dusk's soft, golden hued light
As if in worship of
The orange-yellow orb dipping
And bobbing at horizon's edge.

But no;
Her song, so adoring, so wondrous
Seems to spread,
So much wider
Than this pin-prick of fire in the distance,
Traversing the ends of the firmament,
Beyond,
To touch the very heart of love
That loves me.

Mark Gacii

"I Was There"

When the shadow
Of the Mountain
Glooms my soul—
And I say "There is no way to reach my goal!"
I hear Him say:
"I was there! I knew Gethsemane!
Be with Me."
And the shadow of the Mountain turns to day.

When the fires of hell
Like lightning
Rage my soul—
And I say "I am not fit to reach my goal!"
I hear Him say:
"I was there! I knew Calvary!
Be with Me!"
Death and hell were both defeated long ago!

Ah, the blessing of His Presence
Glows my soul!

B. A. Bailey

Ode To A Cricket

Little creature thou art pure;
Of thine own essence thou be.
And yet thou be one of us
In the essence of all.
Your little chirp sings out.
Your little body vibrates with life.
In tune we are.
And you, by rubbing your feet against your wings,
Make music;
And we, by touching our fingers to the piano keys,
Make music.
But the Creator, it is as if the Creator flies on angel wings
That flutter like the butterfly in the blush of dawn
E'er floating higher and higher,
As if to gain from the sun
More golden in his wings,
The phosphors of which
Touch like circles and kiss upon black velvet
Of the etheric being which he is."

Helen Engel

Grandma's Love

To my special granddaughter as you now turn two
Oh how I treasure the moments with you.
Looking like mommy in her early years
Sometimes just watching, my eyes fill with tears

Just listen your chatter, just watching you smile
I turn to my life, you've made it worthwhile
I'll try to give you whatever you need
I'll try to help you to write and to read
I'll try as a grandma to give you my best
I know that I'll try till they lay me to rest.

For thinking of angels I think of you
I know you can't read this cause your only two
But when you grow up, I know you'll read this
As I sign off with love, and leave with a kiss.

Margaret W. Gill (Rye)

The Raven

Black beast! Black bird, what words describe?
Oh how shine thee!
Blue black the flanks upon your back,
That sharp quick eye, and wings to fly
So proud, so large, larger than life
No fear, but sheer with boasting pride.
That boot black beak, plucked out the eye,
of many a dead spike impaled head
when London was a poets place,
and blackness swept to wipe a race.
The Raven aloft the London streets,
scattered black watchmen, about their beats.
They mused, they flapped - ruffled their coat
when perched on rails would korr and gloat,
outstared who dared look in their eyes,
yet who would pause to observe such spies?
Glide over Thames with rot delight
and merge as one with London's night.
Through London's mist and fog filled days,
would gleam - black lanterns, seen through the haze.

Rebecca Blackhurst

I Told You Not To Leave

Cold and grey, I remember your eyes
On the day you left
fierce pride surging in your veins
Brought between us a searing cleft

"Your country needs you"
I hate those words, so false
I need you Dad,
You came back a broken man.

I saw you crumble before my eyes
Come back to summer breeze
Let's laugh, go fishing and swap some jokes
Don't leave me Dad

Now you lie before me.
Cold grey eyes, as cold as
the trenches in which you slept
Your lips, bluer than the sky under which you killed

I told you not to leave.

S. Du Plooy Jr.

Ode To Autumn

The year is dying
On the earth are lying
Leaves where once bloomed flowers
Daylight is shorter, and the hours
Of darkness longer than at Summer's height
When morning's sunshine Heralds day's delight
Scattered blossoms, summer's dying flowers
Wounded driven by autumnal showers
Autumn Herald the dying year
Warning Winter's birth is near

Edward Keogh

Mystery Untold

A slender thread through a needle's eye
One moment's touch, an instant past,
to live a life that cannot last
We thread our way till life's goodbye.

The meaning lost, the severed thread
Hold true these words, they come to say,
The time is now, the last today,
Our life is lost, among the dead.

Can it be, this life that is
Be nothing more than just a dream
A distant rainbow, an endless seam,

Or does it hold a deeper quiz?
Is it more than it may seem?
Life and Death, the winning team.

Wayne A. McDonald

An Ode To The Morning Paper

Silently and punctually you wait for me
Orderly, last day's history you display
To some you are the perfect combination to coffee
To dogs you are the paper stick to fetch
To birds you are the perfect target
To flies you are the cylinder of death
To newspaper boys you are a job
To children you are the sunday cartoons
To me you bring the gray topics of life
In black and white.

Evandro Lopes

Untitled

We watched each other, only with a sideways glance
Our emotions played tug of war, as we denied the strength of our trust in each other
But the pull was consistent and even enough to coax our hands to meet in the middle, away from our beaten hearts
Now we tie a knot in the middle of our rope where our hands finally met, and bound together it will remain, through sun showers, and through storms until it appears weather and tried
The small frays it will suffer through time are necessary to create the friction against the natural forces that may challenge the strength of our knot
And even though there may come times when the elements seem harsh enough to pull our knot apart, a timely, gentle chinook wind will come upon us and whisper a song in our ears to remind us of a time when all we knew was each other and we will each take one end of the rope and pull with all our might to restrengthen the familiar knot we have cherished
Then we will look up at one another with a sideways glance and smile at each other as we reach forward through the wind to grasp securely onto each other's hands and renew our promise to never let go

Danielle Christie

Indian Sorrow

Who were they so long ago?
Our pride, our religion, where did it go?
They came and slaughtered, wanting our land
Now all we can do is join a religious band
Invading Mother Natures peaceful earth
We shall not mirth
For we fought for tomorrow
And lost in sorrow
We shall not cry
Though we question why
How could people be so cruel?
If all they wanted was to rule
They shattered a world of peaceful dreams
So many threads ripped at the seams
Though I hope one day we can relive
A path of dreams that lies on our grave

Erin Burke

Can There Be Peace On Earth?

Peace is tenderness
Peace is gentleness
Peace is solitude
Peace is unconditional love
And understanding.
Can there be peace on earth?

Peace cannot be legislated
Nor can it be bought
Peace is patience
Peace replaces anger and heartache
Peace is triumph over death.
Can there be peace on earth?

Peace is attitude exuded from within
Each human soul.
Peace is love unending, unconditional, unsolicited.
Peace is contentment in any situation.
The pathway to peace is in poverty and in plenty.

CAN THERE BE PEACE ON EARTH?

Dahlia Campbell

The Unyielding Dome

The sun shone down on the unyielding dome
People went about in their usual way
Not thinking twice about the safety of their home
The thought of death far from their minds that day

Then the earth erupted in a shattering instant
Nobody had time to wonder what had occurred
Not one knew about the plane, so high, so distant
It was too late; the burning city was obscured

By the searing dust, smoke and rubble
All that was left were graveyards of steel and brick
The few survivors gathered together to huddle
Their memories of that day would forever stick

That day is a memory of the past
The memory of a belligerent time, over at last.

Rein Cummins

"The Hunter"

The hunter moves with purpose and grace
pounding heart and piercing gaze,
No reason is found to comfort his lust
but excepts in doing in what he must,
The urge is strong the adrenaline is pumping
muscles are tightening and his senses are one,
With perfection he handles his tools
for the time is right, it's now his rules!

His breath shallows, his eyes narrow, beads
of sweat have effects like arrows,
He watches his prey and studies its nature
admiring its grace and its proud stature,
With stealth he positions and skill he selects
bullet away as the cartridge ejects,
The shot is true it has found its mark
and in his remorse he can't even remark.

Lech Kwasiborski

Old Fort Erie

At old Fort Erie, a battle took place, from across the river attackers raced. With guns in their hands and boots on their feet, The British hoped they weren't close to defeat.

The struggle went on, for some days on end, and the much needed help, no one would send. Under the command of Colonel Drummond, Courage from within the men, was summoned.

Drummond claimed victory, in that small fight. But sometime later, in the dark of night. He and his men left for Fort Chippawa and a few Americans, Drummond saw.

Commodore Yeo to Fort Erie went, and with all of his men also were sent. All of the buildings were put on fire, The rooms, the kitchens, the whole entire.

Not a thing remained, but ashes and dust. About the old ruins, some people fussed. Then in 1930, bodies were found, In many large trenches and all around.

In honour of the long-forgotten dead, Let's rebuild this old fort, some people said. And now Fort Erie stands upright again, a tourist attraction it will end.

Michelle Walker

Remember Me

When the world is all but against you
Remember my love
When things go wrong and the pressure is on
Remember my healing hand
When time is frozen still, you are lost
Remember my friendship
When you are alone in the dark, in need of a friend
Remember my smile
If you remember these things about me
And our friendship... I will never disappear
In those times of despair or need
I will be there beside you

Amber Teclaw

The Rain

Can you hear it falling. Outside the window sill
The trees and leaves are drinking. And everything
is still. In the night the rain is creeping, down the
outside wall. And as you lay awake you can hear it in
the hall. All the animals are hiding in their
little holes, waiting for the rain to stop thumping
on their burrows and homes. Inside the house the
dogs and cats are sleeping. And you can hear your child
weeping. You hope that soon you will be sleeping.
So that you can leave the rain in your dreaming.

Tamara Bailey

And The Butterfly Said To Me

Set me free Set me free Set me free
Said the butterfly to me
Let the wind once again flow beneath my wings
Let me once again soar into the heavens into the Hall of Kings
May I taste again the fragrance of the flowers
May I once more delight in the blossoms where they lie sweetest
beneath the Castles Towers

For my life is short but the journey long
The miles must pass like hours
before I reach the shores of where I belong
So set me free young man of mystery
Let me again sing my song of worlds a you long to see
Your wish I'll grant but one no more
on my journey to the shore
For who knows my love that cannot be
when I am changed and again fly free
If not again we may shall meet
then my dearest love whom I adore
it may be me who captures thee to carry to my home
on yonder distant shore.

P. Longden

The Man In My Head

You know, I used to hear the moon
screaming in my ear, "Where did it go?
Where did it go?". To tell you the truth,
I really don't know. I can't find something
if I don't know what it is. I tried to help him,
I honestly did, but whatever he was looking for
was very well hid. He continued to scream and
the pitch increased. After two years, the screaming
had ceased. I never heard from him again but I heard
a story told. "The man in the moon has gotten old".
I learned some time ago that the man is a tale, it was
all in my head, but I heard him calling to me, I heard
every word he said. I've been made to deny the voices,
to forget they were ever there. They all
think I'm crazy and I'm sure none of them care.
When the moon gets full, I listen for him still.
I want to know why he called, but somehow,
I don't think I will. He doesn't cry out any more,
not one single word. The man in the moon has gotten old
...at least that's what I've heard.

Jessie Roberts

Who Will Guide Me

God I am so tired of climbing this hill
See how steep it is
My feet and my heart
Find it very hard
Yes I am tired of climbing up
'Cause I never reach the top
When I almost make it
I lose faith

Because I keep falling down over and over again
All I do is climb and climb but there is no end
What should I do
Oh God I ask you
'Cause my fingers nails are all broken can you see
And I have such a hard time to find thee
So I hate to cry
But please come back by my side

'Cause Oh God this hill
See how steep it is
Oh God don't let me stop
Please God give me strength to reach the top.

Mary Garden

On Holding A Bronze-Age Skull: Orkney

Cupping a bronze-age skull in my hands is a most extraordinary
sensation, its rounded smoothness the shade of burnished sand,
yet hard as marble and as cold. This fragment of humanity,
this other woman, binding us down the centuries. What did she
see and do, all those years ago? How feel? She lived, she died,
maybe welcomed rest eternal in some long-forgotten grave.
In death itself her rest was not forever, nor in peace. One
day a farmer turning the furrow, made a find: Now her 'coffin'
is of glass. What would she think, could she but see her
sightless skull, on view for all who come to stare at and touch
should they so wish? Some shudder, and turn reviled at so
crass a spectacle. I, too, at first drew back, afraid to
touch, but then could not resist the lure of feeling death-
that great taboo, which never yet has quelled the curiosity
of man. Feeling the weight of that skull in my hands I count
this moment as a rare and privileged experience. Carefully
I place her back beneath the glass, wishing she might return to
the Orkney soil where she more properly belongs. Cupping a
bronze-age skull in my hands truly links life to death.

Elspeth Wallington

When She Was Born

When she was born they sung in the sunshine
She grew up happy and sound
With determination, vigour and obedience
She achieved what many have and will fail

She the village beauty and mirror
But you merciless beast...
A gift, a curse? From God? Satan

She, a reflection of my idea of humanity
Much affection bestowed on her
Born the other day many morning ago
She was no more when I saw her.

Then from nowhere you came
Your work now is a common sight
As common as oxygen
You're a thorn in our emotions

Down by the river when collecting firewood
She used to sing me nice song
Then we could listen to the bird sing in peace
Then life was so good
But now...

Jane N. Bosire

Seasons

She's innocent, breathtaking, eager to trust—unconditionally!
She knows not of perils so cleverly disguised.
She is mischievously pretty thus, she is pretty.
She's a symbol of angelic purity.

She's vibrant, care-free, intriguingly witty!
She knows not of limits that inhibit fulfillment.
She's magical, mystical, spiritual—bound not by mortal boundaries.
She manipulates the very fibre of being!

She has prospered; she has aged; she is consumed with wisdom.
She has flourished beyond appeal to wither with the passing of time.
Graced is her era with such beauty; she gracefully bows to fate.
Thus, she remains a mystic of prophecy in her time.

She embraces death as a mother embraces her child.
She will leave behind wisdom bestowed onto such a child.
She knows departure is near—she knows in sleep there is light.
She will not again exist for time cannot replace her roots.

Julien Bain

A Higher Call

In profound submission to a higher call
She turns her silver form in the direction of her birth
Considering not at all the miles ahead, the rocks,
The rapids, or the "Final End."

She does not in her secret mind's desire
Seek to fall back into the ocean's mire
But steadfastly and in obedience pursues
A charted course which from her instincts grew.

She faces not alone the rushing currents
For others weave about her on the way
But each alone must choose to take the journey
Instinctively prepared the price to pay.

She thinks not of the sacrifice required
To birth new life now nestled in her flesh
But rather presses forward in anticipation
Of her home - the Final Rest!

Beverly

Lady

She comes alone in solitude and goes with others.
She visits graveyards, cemeteries, morgues and funerals.
Her skin is pale against her black robes,
She is beautiful, yet do not stare into her eyes,
her eyes are like an abyss of darkness that draw you in.
She commands the cold, the kind that creeps up your skin,
the cold the kind that chills your heart and seeps into your bones.
She commands the darkness,
the kind that clouds your still chilled heart,
darkness that clouds the mind,
darkness that creates nightmares.
She controls pestiferous insects and parasites
that create pestilence which sweeps nations like plagues.
She rides a horse, pale as she named Pestilence,
her name is Death,
Lady Death.

Jackie Overton

Grey Power

If we caused a fire I framed you
she'll slip through your teeth my friend
don't have to take another opinion
don't have to break the glass inside my shell

don't have to be the cause of a failure
though I live for second best
made an underline in the theory of changes
what to say when your grey power to all the rest

listen to the sound of a facet mime
blistered by the threat of run down undermined
your florid walls around me all the time
eye walls penetrate the crumbling sky

wet my bed for a faith healer
I had to cry but I laughed instead
no one has ever brought you to meet her
wandering eye passing through your head

she doesn't know where she came from
so tired of the temperate life she lead
she's got tonight to think about tomorrow
saves a prayer for the thankless silhouette

J. Bayer

Killarneys Lakes

They lie beneath the azure skies,
Shimmering in the golden sun.
Their peaceful lapping waters now grey,
Now silver, now blue-green,
Rest amid the purple heathered hills
That tower to the skies, cloud dappled.
Upon the still blue waters the white swans rest,
Serenely silent.
Beneath the waves their webbed feet paddle
Gently, but strongly,
Bearing the white birds, Lir's fabled children,
Upon their stately way.
Far out on the horizon the red sun sets
In a blaze of golden glory,
Lighting upon the still waters.
Athwart the blazing skies the swallows fly,
Swift winged.
The fading sunlight lights their feathers and soft heads
With gold and orange tints.
While, flying westward, the black crow seeks its rest.

Marianne Kelly

"Evening In A Monastry Garden"

Softly whispers the gentle evening breeze,
Silently the noon has crept away.
On the elm branch doves fold their silver
Wings, as monks they droop their
heads to pray.

Beneath the twilight lilac glow,
The Angelus bell peels soft and low,
The Virgins prayer at parting day,
When friars chant their sweet ave.

A crescent moon behind the hill,
With inner calm I stand alone,
To breathe this holy solitude
Where peace has found a home.

Leona Gabriella

Birthday Child

Eighteen years have come and gone,
Since my only son was born.
An eighteenth birthday is a time of love
For some...for me, well I can only look above,
And pray he's happy,
And send my love.
Love I've held for all these years,
Close inside with all my tears.
For five short months I was blessed.
My faith was then put to the test.
God claimed back his precious gift,
And I was left alone to drift.
Oh! Dear God, I loved that boy,
Always good...a joy to hold.
He should have grown tall and bold.
I know he would have turned out fine.
Happy birthday man of mine.

Joan K. Walker

To My Companion

Tears of compassion, memories and love
Slide down my cheeks,
As I watch my best friend fade away.
The words "I love you" just aren't good enough,
For all the love you brought into my life.
All the memories of us playing,
Thirteen years of memories.
This poem is for you my friend,
You will always be in my heart.

It's over now and you are asleep,
Your pain and suffering is over.
I would not let you suffer at all if I had my way.
Life isn't fair, but at least I know you are at peace.
I hope to see you again someday,
I'll miss you, for you will always be in my heart.
You will always be my best friend.
My companion, My K-9 Bandit.

Christine Brown

Time Is Short

The time for living is now.
So cast off your gloom and doom.
Love today, laugh tomorrow.
Live fully, vivaciously!

The radiant beauty of a sunrise.
We've been given yet another day.
Ripples of time rolling forward.
Quickly, merrily, hopefully!

Time moves on, like hands on a clock.
Grains of sand on a beach.
All washing away one by one.
Just as the minutes of each day, month, year
drift by so does time.

Doria Arthur

Deadly Enemies

A tribe, a nation
So full of life
No one could take it away
So they thought

The White man made his way
Through the dark, rough world
Of the Red skin, buffalo hunter
In search of new territory, new soil

He stole the pride of this glorious tribe
They fought back
But in their primitive nature
Couldn't hold back the futuristic White man

They cracked under the amazing blow
Of the White man's rifle
Blood pouring down
Coloring the ground, the leaves
And leaving a deadly mark
Of violence for a few acres of soil
In which the blood of the Indian now flows

Marelda Oosthuizen

"Autumn Leaves"

Autumn leaves of golden brown,
so gently falling to the ground.
Leaving the trees so stark and bare,
just like skeletons, standing there.

"Ho", it seems like yesterday,
when Spring we thought, was here to stay.
But in a moment past, Spring's gone.
Now, only the cold and dreary winter, beckons.

Autumn leaves, like the time of day,
quickly came, but did not stay.
Like another life, just passing through,
reminiscent, to the morning dew.

P. H. Cameron

"Tales"

Tales are stories of old,
Some are exaggerated or bold.
Yarns are oft passed down from father to son,
There are strains, never just one.

As a child I heard of strange odes,
I heard miners speak of the "Motherlode".
Grandpa spealed at length of his hunting chase,
Many a strange pursuit he faced.

Grandma talked softly in hushed tones,
She spoke of legends etched in stone.
I was told of traits passed down,
Family history was very profound.

Now, I reflect on those tales of old,
In my mind they never run cold.
I remember always the past,
Cherished memories that will forever last.

Suzanne C. Sanford

You Became My Love

You became my love, for a time somehow.
Some days felt so good, I would like that now.
Many times has passed, since we've had to part.
Lonely nights grew long, with my lonely heart.

I will never love someone, the way that I love you.
Everyone around me happy, making me more blue.
Darkness here, and darkness there, not being able to run.
Friends taking you places, trying to make you have some fun.

Finding someone else, to match your perfect love.
One seems to be close, and fits like a glove.
Finding out about that person, in a spying sense.
To see if that person wants what your first love wanted,
a white picked fence.

The person seems to be opposite, and you feel real down.
Your eyes start to water, and your face starts to frown.
Knowing you can't get someone, exactly the same.
All you can think of, is the lost love's first name.

You became my love, for a time somehow,
Someday felt so good, I would like that now.
Many time has passed, since we've had to part.
Lonely nights grew long, with my broken heart.

Glady Reta Fisher

Friends

As ours lives go by, there are people we meet,
Some forgotten, some remembered ever so sweet,
Things that are in common become part of your day,
No matter what happens, someone has something to say.

You party, drink, sing or act like a fool,
Some think your weird, but your friends think your cool.
Your friends are there with you in good times and bad,
For they're the ones you lean on when your feeling sad.

The jokes, the kidding, the pranks we may play,
It's all in fun and helps the time pass away.
To understand why we do the things we do,
It's friends that cheer you up when you feeling blue.

Some days are frustrating and crazy but in any case,
It's friends who come along with that happy face.
If that don't work and you still feel like a slug,
One thing for sure that works, it's a great big hug.

This time together has gone by quickly you see,
After a few months, heading home, happy we'll be.
Some will be leaving us and one thing for sure is this,
They can't always go with you, friends you'll miss.

Mike B. Palka

Our Best Friend

Life brings us many surprises,
Some happy, some sad, some good, some bad,
We each must evaluate life,
In every situation, that is dropped upon us;
No one is ever alone or unloved
And should never feel this way;
Because, in our lives,
We all have the one, very special friend above,
That does not care, who or what we are.
To help us all, with his unconditional care;
We all seem to call on him, only when in despair,
But his love is all around,
Even though, we can't see him, and he doesn't make a sound,
To talk to him, fulfills our souls,
As he listens quietly, to our prayers,
When we have spoken, and our hearts have been poured,
This very special spirit, who always helps us;
Is no one else, but the Ever Loving Lord!

Manuela Klohs

The Fork in the Road

There's a time in one's life, when you come to the fork in the road
Sometimes we don't notice, if our life's on an even keel
We carry on doing what we normally do
Not even paying attention, that we've taken the wrong road.
The little things that happen, we don't notice at all.
But a bystander sees them, and is watching us go.
There's potholes, and cracks, and corners and curves,
We step around many, stumble into a few.
We blame it on life, taking it all in stride
Thinking this is the way, there's nothing we can do.
If we were the ones on the sidelines, looking in
We'd have taken, the other, fork in the road.

Linda Irene Upton

I Amn't "I", Nor You Are "You"

I amn't "I", nor you are "you"
Sounds rather odd, but it is true.
We live by the "image" we happen to form
Or by the one which is created by others.
We are always desperate in order to conform
Our life to it, while the "self" smothers.
The "self" is unique and hasn't a norm,
It conceives its own life that it mothers.
Though known to most it's practised by few.
In the heart of hearts we want to be free
To express the uniqueness of our own soul
But lacking courage we stunt this tree
For, we all have fears
Of others' jeers
Sounds rather odd, but it is true!

S. S. Bhatti

Voice Of Apartheid

I cry, I weep blood
Spilt on the parched earth
I am absorbed, to nurture our children
I grow hope.

I cry, I weep from gaping sores
My soul runs free from cages
I flee, the cinder tiger, the cage of law
Unjust justice.

I cry, I weep flames
Fueled by ignorance, fanned by misunderstanding
Fires of the soul in the night
Ashen silhouettes

I quench the fires of hatred
Smother the fuel, the renewable resource
I open wire doors, broken by the light
I dissolve pain.

I open, I nudge
Keys to cages that turn with words
Hold with music bridges that lead to the winds of hope
The language of power.

Vera Havard

Spring

Again proud youth flutters upon the earth,
Spreading its glory throughout this land,
Revealing ancient youth of distant birth,
Dotted hills and burning sands.
Time steals on, and the silent screen of light advances slowly
To cover the shade of bleak, blinding night.
Yet, I defy thee, spring, for by thee only
Do my years travel in full flight.
"Father Time waits for no man",
Thus, old man winter sleeps, and, waking,
Finds Autumn dead, lying in its faded corpse, and,
Though spring lies afar off, it now is beauty making.
Hear the birds, their songs they all sing.
Oh, well I remember. It's a sign of Spring.

Brian George Ward

A Stranger's Eyes

Watching the world through a stranger's eyes
Spying upon a thousand skies
Beyond the world that we all know
Lies a treasure of silver and gold

A glittery past, a silent future
The clock of time keeps moving faster
Sending us farther and farther away
Far from home and silence stays

Deep in the conscience of unknown thoughts
Lies a trail to follow, it may be the last
Lost in the world that we once knew
Deeper and deeper, and out of the blue

Still, watching the world through a stranger's eyes
Spying upon a thousand skies
Beyond the world that we all knew
Lies a treasure lost in thoughts

Michelle Wicks

"Tree In The Forest"

That mighty tree in the forest
Stands so straight and tall;
In summer, it wears a cover of green,
But turns a colorful sight in fall.
We see God's hand in its making,
Of beauty, a sight to behold;
It houses the birds in their glory
Chirping songs for the young and the old.
Like an arm the branches are waving.
Come here, stay awhile and ponder.
The soft cool breeze that is blowing.
Give your thoughts sometime to wonder
Over the dense and quiet forest
Where the tree stands not alone;
In all its greatness and splendor.
Where the work of God's hand is shown.

Clara J. Mitchell

Saturday Morning Kids

Saturday morning kids
staring at the TV screen,
What's the latest pimple cream,
keep up with the action figure scene.

Saturday morning kids
eating sugar-coated plastic toys,
change the channel for another joy,
watch a baby pig or a super hero boy.

Saturday morning kids
know who's the ghost with the most,
know Care Bears and Sugar Cinnamon Toast,
know Bo Jackson and every wrestlers boast.

Saturday morning kids
don't care if the sky is blue.
On Sunday they know there's nothing to do,
so they watch TV till Saturday morning's through.

Garry Welshman

The Child

The fog is caught in the trees, like a young child hiding.
The water is washing up onto the shore, it is getting closer.
The mountains are in the background, her mother's arms are trying to reach her.
The sun is towering above, burning the peaceful landscape.
The albatross soars bravely with the small hands of an offspring clutched at its neck.
The giant creature glides into the fog, which slowly disappears, like the child.

Catherine McClarty

Skier's Dream

Poling, gliding, shushing, striding,
Telemark turn, quick turn and step,
A new dance, or a new craze?
Not really - just skier's language used on winters beautiful days.
Preparation of gear; waxing skies satisfaction,
anticipation,
Companionship,
Fresh air, surge of energy, endless action.
Emotionally on the highest peak.
Fantastic scenery, leaves one speechless.
Ski—ing into the bottomless gully of flat light,
Then shushing the hill; once more into the sunshine, awe
inspiring
sights,
The sunburned face of the leader breaking trail,
If the tracker has not invaded the virgin snow.
Enjoyment,
The homeward glide,
Experience, which can be repeated as long as
There are skiers ready to go
as long as there is snow.

Madeline Joyce Pegg

With Dignity

A fall, and soon the pain begins.
tests and even more tests
And grave faces telling the facts as they are.
and anger and tears.
Therapy and bile,
Then blessed relief
And too soon again pain.
Welcomed liquid gulped from plastic cups.
A glassy stare; occasionally a smile;
Some tears, some laughter.
It has all been said:
"I love you - I always have - only you."
Daffodils on a window ledge because it is April,
And warm sun shining through the cold to cheer the room.
Concerned eyes begging - "Please, with dignity."
Lift up this head, this body, this spirit....
Stand there, be brave... this is dignity.
Through faraway thoughts a bell rings, "I'm sorry"....
A kiss - a touch - goodbye - I love you.
Final relief - with dignity.

Lorraine Naster

Memories

There are many things in life
That bring a bittersweet pain.
The sight of a butterfly,
The feel of soft spring rain.

These things never last
But impressions of them we keep:
To guide our lives through depths of despair,
And bring awareness to its peak.

But
Expressions of beauty
could never be
As important as memories
of them to me.

For these memories warm our hearts
when cold
They reach into
our very souls.

The flames from some
may flicker and wane.

But the brightness of yours
will be eternally the same!

P. Brenda Drover-Vardy

Black Rain

Black is the rain
that falls outside my window
as I cry from the pain,
as I suffer from my sorrow.

I stare at the rain drops
that splash on the ground.
They're like the tears that my eyes have found.
They're black and sour and they're letting me lose all my power.

The glow from the moon is blinding my eyes,
as I am left hypnotized.
I fight to escape this transe,
but I don't seem to have a chance.
I'm trapped in your world;
I'm imprisoned in your hands.

I'm trying to fight it;
for I know this is only a dream
that is created from my pain.
For when I wake, you will be gone,
and I will continue to stare at the black rain.

Sabrina Gentile

I Wish I Would Have Never Known

I picked up a flower
That flower was a rose
And brought it close to my face
And held it under my nose
I savored a deep breath
And was taken in by the power
For the fragrance I engulfed
From that beautiful flower
Brought me the dream
The dream to fly up past the clouds
High in the sky
Then I opened my eyes and looked in dismay
For the walls began to crumble
And people turned away
My rose began to wilt
And fade in my hand
And slowly crumbled
Into tiny pieces of sand and there I stood
I stood all alone in the world of reality
I wish I would have never known

Keri Chrystian

Untitled

May the rose of life bloom in your heart,
that it may bring peace and joy into your being.
May the sun's rays light up your heart and soul
so others may see the beauty in life and serenity
in your words of wisdom.
Let love grow deep in your heart for it is the fruit of life.
Let the generosity and kindness reach out beyond your finger tips
to others so they to can feel your love pouring out to another
human being.
But most of all, let love, generosity
and kindness light your way in life for it is the food of
eternal life.

Robert J. Swartz

The Light

At first I saw Him in the dimness
Then in a glimmering glow
The glow turned into a flaming brightness
The brightness into a transilluminating brilliance
And truly at last I am in his radiant light

Luciene Azique

Walking

I strolled down the winding path
that makes for what some would call life.

My hands in my pockets of my well worn suit
thread bare and worn by the passage of time

Jingling the couple of coins I'd found along the way
in tune to some half-forgotten song of inspiration

My eyes stared down at the hard stony ground
while my feet kicked over stones of discontent.

Hoping against hope I might find some treasure
hidden by one of these rocks only to find dust
where a shadow had once been.

Silence prevailed as echoes of hopelessness
bounced off the walls of my quiescent mind

My shoulders slumped from the weight
of the burden imagined or real

I watch the horizon for some relief or rest
but I can't see that far through the smear
the tears have left in my eyes.

My body aches and my spirit wanes but I can't give up
as I day dream it can't be that far ahead.

Owen Wagg

Nineteen Ninety-Four

The wintry wind beat against the weary trees
That stood naked, yet firm, in the frozen breeze;
Drenched in the tears of the distressed dawn
They wept in the bosom of the winter morn.

Half dead leaves twitched on the ground
Writhed in pain but made no sound,
Lest they disturb the springtime flowers
That slept blissfully under the mound.

Amidst the trees, where I stood, I heard
A melancholy dirge of some lonely bird,
Whose friends to warmer skies had fled
And at its feet its love lay dead.

There, beside the brook, beneath a barren tree,
Suddenly I saw a chrysanthemum solitary;
Dressed in gold and decked with dew
It stood there smiling in all its glory.

Sheena Singadi

Man's Storm

The heavens opened with a thunderous blow
That trembled to the midst of our vast estate
Bright flashes bewitched our eyes aglow
The haunting face was our only fate.

Amidst the presence of our Almighty Lord
The rumbling breathed the wind that rose
Wisdom rays of life shot down like a sword
'Mid boughs of evergreens that was to close.

From the ocean's roar of bidding mystery
The Earth's cry to shake down despair
Shrieks like death for all man to see
To ease the load for us many must bear.

Isabella Wehner

Former Prostitute

The air was deafening with silence.
The buzz of human voices went unrecognizable.

Staring out the uniform rectangular window,
I found myself thinking thoughts which had no connection to the grey,
Stormy wall of clouds I was engulfed in.

Searching for answers in God's playground, I found none.
A tear of light in the horizon offered hope but,
the questions filling my head remained.

An elderly gentleman across the aisle offered conversation;
I refused knowing too well my questions and answers would be hollow.

A young misfit sat along side of me. Her fingers nervously playing
with her shirt sleeves, her eyes finding her mother's two rows
behind offering her all the reassurance needed.

My flight was coming to its conclusion, returning me to a part
of my past but, only for a night. This offered hope......

Judy Filonov

My Little Partner

I watched as tears ran down my face,
the end of sadness, sickness and disgrace.
Although I knew he could not hold on
I made him struggle all night, through dawn.
As the pain grew through limb by limb
Death arose and was coming for him.
His heart beat fast whenever I'd come
The great love for him was like mother and son.
All I needed to say was said then and there
I showed my young brother how much I cared
Tiny tears ran down his chubby cheeks
And at that moment a happy face I couldn't keep.
As I gazed in his eyes, sapphire blue.
His grip on my hand grew weak then I knew.
His eyes grew together, his lips lay still.
As the room grew silent, I was living against will
My little partner, my young brother.
I loved him dearly like no other.

Christina Abbott

"The Enchanted Flute"

The littlest shepherd that first Christmas day gave a gift to the Christ Child but who is to say, since no one made mention of that which he did; of the present he gave to the Babe in the crib.

He had a flute which he carved out of wood. He played it so sweetly that surely he could make the coldest of hearts beat purely for joy, as they listened enchanted to this shepherd boy.

This winter evening was different than most, for with it came choirs of a Heavenly Host singing "Glory to God. Glory to God. Peace to men of good will."

"Ye shall follow the Star from the meadow until to an inn, in a manager, in Bethlehem town, ye shall find the new King wrapped in swaddling-down, with none but the beasts of the field all around."

The littlest shepherd his eyes shining bright, gazed in wonder at Angels who sang in the night. This Babe he must see and a present to bring. He would play on his flute for this new Baby King...

With eyes on the Babe, he picked up his reed and he blew such sweet notes, as ever he did, and the Baby cooed softly and nestled in bed, and smiling so sweetly, lay down His sweet head.

The gift of the flute and the music it made has endeared the wee lad to the Heart of the Babe.

T. Anne Marvel

This Is The Place Called Hell

In the fiery pit where the Devil lurks,
the evil souls descend from bodies,
a pitchfork welcomes the new arrivals,
even the souls can feel the heat.
This is the place called Hell.

Fangs of Satan will close on you,
the blood type of evil will run in your veins,
your heart be ripped out with a swipe of his hand,
he shows no mercy for now you are damned.
This is the place called Hell.

Demons of Darkness will call your name,
the flames of Ghenna engulf your flesh,
your bones be crushed with a single breath,
Lucifer's fortress has no escape.
This is the place called Hell.

The virginal mist of Heaven above,
will swirl and sway with gentle ease,
it protects the Good from the Evil below,
the Father of Darkness won't let you go.
You're in the place called Hell.

Damian S. Fischer

Marilyn

My life is like a makeup table.
The Craft of Illusion.
Tilted mirrors, makeup brushes and bright light bulbs
are a part of my labyrinth.

As I paint over my impediments, I think about my fans.
They want me to be glamorous and I
can't let them down.
Layer upon layer I create that 'someone' everyone
else wants me to be.

When the curtains go down and the light bulbs have
dimmed, I see
a skinless peach in the tilted mirror.
Another pretty dope trying to impress.

But then, that's my life.
It is more than an act,
it is happening.

Anne Quinn

Within

Remember the warmth she felt inside as she lay there unaware
The feeling so secure without any despair
She wept as her small fingers found that special place
To her was the brightness of your smiling face
Through the years she found the need to stray
Hoping that your proud smile would help her on her way
One day her family fell apart
Leaving behind a child's broken heart
Needing the most attention she became proud
Looking for the affection that has yet to be found
Vulnerable and innocent she became the prey
All the while wishing she could be happy and gay
Survival has become her most difficult mission
With the hope that "LOVE" is her final admission

Michelle Connolly

To Beauty

Thee I beheld: Ah! memory sweet, subtle such as spell
The future visions, my clouded present fled
Like morning mists before the rising sun dispels;
Eternity was life, time and space were sped!

My heart stood still, and blinded were my eyes
With tears; that blended light as dawn
That both day and night denies;
Ah Mortal maid immortalized by beauty's might!

Vision divine, was human form created to they mould?
Thy oval face and raven hair Madonna's envy dare!
That beauteous look Mona Lisa's smile unfolds;
Thy eyes, the stars alone their mystery share!

The music of your footsteps in rhapsody did pass
Reality fetters fastened as storms do darkness brew;
My tears ceased, my heart was filled with sighs
For truth Eternal; Beauty I visioned in you.

James Gideon

Untitled

Yesterday's fallen rain has vanished
the glowing sun rays are now appearing.
During all that time,
our Lord watches eternally.

Our feelings to implore him are within.
Our soul is the reward of our questioning.
To us it is given by the One,
who's eyes forever endure earth.

Mysteries unsolved.
Miseries forever existent.
Ever-present crime, hatred and jealousy.
All but eternal love and happiness found the key to Him.

One day, judgment will come.
Some will face it fearlessly and honestly,
Others will be inevitably confronted,
While some and others live on earth, only some will live.

Normand Laniel

Twenty-Nine

Burnt, and browned by the warmth's age,
the leaf falls, and the wind tastes;
and the sun, as heading low,
with beams on other half-globes,
finds a broader crevice
to pause,
as thought on a second thought
to shine
lighter through the leaf's absence:
Here the leaf falls and the wind hast't.
Here the rain sang, and the sun shone
On every pulse, and a beat tasted.
Here the fall falls with dazzling colours.
Here the sun leaves till a time later
When boughs are again shaped as honours.
Here the line gets doubled
And the words follow.
Here comes an old rite
And comes this hollow.

Behrouz Fallahi

Wesley Hjelmeland - My Son

I remember when I held you, so tiny and so pink
the love I felt right then nothing could compare
Blond, blond hair and ice blue eyes, was a dream come true,
God gave us a special gift, when He created you
a special little boy we called "Wesley",
I remember, when I held you in my arms, I felt so close to you
You were so tiny in my arms I loved you all the more.
where have all the years gone? You're such a handsome boy
I haven't always been there with you, I hope you'll understand,
your sixteen now, still growing and soon to be a man,
when you "sign" "I love you mom", I feel so proud inside
It doesn't matter how far apart we are, just as long
as you know, I love you, wherever I will go, with in me
in my heart, it doesn't matter how big you grow,
I'll always remember that tiny little baby boy I loved is you!

Lauralynn Hankins

Great Fish River At Dubbeldrif

Solemn and sluggish, broad and brown
the pace and colour of Africa
Fringed with scrub and wicked thorn,
the face and mood of Africa.

No other waters of the earth
could claim such sheer indifference
to man's mighty toil or climate's curse,
or any other influence.

Shouldering its way through hard dry land,
forging a highway of danger.
Careless of everything in its path -
And why not, you ignorant stranger?

Well, mighty you are, you wild wide river,
as cruel and as careless as man.
Enjoy your freedom, you wild wide river -
while you can - while you can!

For just as forests and all wild life
are bowing to man's insatiable lust
Your powers will fade, your aims will die
and God's good earth be turned to dust.

Cicely Langston

The Search

To seek and find within one's self,
The peace of mind that brings good health,
To find the happiness in life,
Good fellowship without strife.

No need for wealth, power or fame,
This should not be man's goal of the game,
For no one may own the sky and the sea,
Or the trees and flowers that all may see.

For these are God's own gifts to man,
Regardless of race, color or clan.

Robert Jones

My Best Friend

We will always be the best of Pals
There is no other like us two Gals.

Remembering our shopping and trips together
Will be locked within my heart forever.

The laughter and tears we have shared
You let me know who really cared.

No matter what life deals us to cast
My friendship for you will always last.

Hazel Hartman

A Dieter

Is this a cake which I see before me,
The plate toward my mouth? Come, let me cut you!
I haven't tasted you yet, but I can smell you.
Are you, fattening vision, sensible
To taste as to smell? Or are you but
A cake of the mind, a false creation,
Coming from my hunger-oppressed stomach?
I can still see you, as obvious
As this celery stick that I am holding.
You point me toward the bakery
And such food I was going to eat.
My eyes deceive me,
Or else my other senses are wrong. I can still see you;
And on the top and sides mounds of icing,
Which were not there before. There is no cake.
It is the Weight Watchers diet which makes
This seem real.

Valerie Reid

On The Love Of A Bird

Beyond...
The shape of your arms
The swelling curves of your ample bosom,
Your water your scent, your blood, your tears,
The compelling softness of your cheek,
All humming gently of the purpose
Of the unconditioned and our shared destiny.
Beyond...
Verse after verse sung silently though the clear blue grey
Burning of your eyes and the gracious mournful splendor of your
uncelebrated form.
More than grace, more than beauty, more than ecstasy...
Beyond joy, beyond pleasure...through any morbid agony,
any sadness and pain, beyond time itself and through all space,
I bathe with desire still, in the blossoming light of a thousand
petaled lotus aflame in my chest.
Our love is the calm ocean caressing a round pebble beach.
It is deer leap/crashing through the forest in the cool half moon
light of October.
How can it not be eternal?

Jim Phillipoff

Simple Pleasures

Have you opened your door in the early morn as the sun first kissed
the skies
And glistened on the dew-dropped leaves like an ocean of tear-filled
eyes
Or heard the birds proclaim the dawn in unison of song
The cattle lowing on the lea-or streams that go gurgling on
Have you breathed the perfume of a rose-from the heavenly
rain-washed store
Of fragrance from a garden that loving hands adore
Or watched the clouds go scudding by like galleons from the past
The swirling winds in boisterous mood astride their wispy masts
Sat quietly in transient pose as gentle breezes play
A lullaby on the dancing reeds in the moonlights silvery rays
Or strolled along a sandy shore - with windswept spray-flecked hair
While salt-filled ripples soothe a mind preoccupied with care
P'raps wandered over craggy hills with distant views enchanted
Intoxicated by the scent of heather no ones planted
Heard the nightingale in leafy lane - full throated in its praise
Of the creators orchestration of natures wondrous ways
These are the wonders of the world - among its greatest treasures
For once experienced - then you've scaled the heights of simple
pleasures
No sculptors chisel, artists brush could reproduce for me
The glory in the beauty of natures panoply.

Phillip David

Knowing You're All Right

Another day comes to an end
the sun starts to fade down in the sky again.

As the moon appears in the sky
So bright that it lights my way
I follow the path that's laid before me,
And it leads to a place that seems to be at peace...

A little lake that still in the night
The moon shines in and I swear
I see your face staring up at me
from the water in the dim light

I look at your smile in the reflection
of the water and I feel at ease with
the peace you show me. I now know
I can move on as you are content
in your new place.

I'm grateful you're taken care of and
my life feels lifted knowing you
rest in peace at last.

Carla-Marie Roach

Armageddon

The man stands at the bottom of the wall.
The wall he was once one with,
A seemingly unassailable fortress.

Then, starting at the bottom,
He slowly begins to work his way up;
Using the wall,
And tools fabricated of the wall to aid him in his crusade.
And by cutting away the vegetation which grows there,
He fashions ladders with which to attain the power
He is so sure lay on the other side.

And when the wall cracks and splits,
And the great gusts of wind seek to sweep him off,
These, the walls only defenses, merely slow him;
Knock him down.
With new devices so carefully fashioned
He is able to avoid even these.

And continually he struggles against the wall,
Or now is it the wall who struggles against him?
With the top now so close at hand, he contemplates the
Wisdom of his journey, yet still proceeds.

Jeffrey Leggo

The Dive

She steps up to the edge
the water's a terrifying, dizzying speck of blue below.
Backwards now, her body
tensed in anticipation
then she plunges
hurtling through the air
twisting
tumbling
turning
then
slicing cleanly into the water
leaving only a few bubbles behind
to show a moment of precision,
of perfection
ever existed in this world.

Brandi Durda

Love

Childhood memories bring often to me,
The way our life used to be.
Sharing our time and lives so much,
Needing each other's love and such.
How is it that our lives have changed so and grown,
No more a child, not living at home?
Our families have spread across the globe,
Adding more children and space from the fold.
How is it that in our quest for the rest,
We leave behind us a love that is best?
More loving and giving than we can understand,
Until we're grown up and our kids are in hand.
All the time thinking, that we knew it all,
And finding out we knew nothing at all.

Betty Pastir

Silent Cries

I stand in this unsheltered place;
The wretched jackel commands his space
Love has gone somewhere unclear
Instead lies emptiness and fear
I hear cries from far away
This is unreal - I pray
Stripped of my dignity for reasons unknown
I can't find my way home
My warm tears fall to a distant thunder
As I feel myself over, then under
My silent cries try to change his mind
But he is so deaf and blind
I can't begin to understand
The power he holds in his hand
My freedom he will deny
Yet this creature still seems high
As I am frightened;
He is enlightened
I fear the memory
I can't let go.

Shanty Royce Deriger

All That I Am

If you look up at the night sky and only see the stars,
then you have not seen the sky.
If you look at the ocean and only see calm,
then you have not seen the ocean.
If you look at the wizard and only see magic,
then you have not seen the wizard.

If you look at my race and only see white,
then you have not seen me.
If you look at my speech and only see English,
then you have not seen me.
If you look at my gender and only see female,
then you have not seen me.

The sky is more than stars, it is planets, air and the sun.
The ocean is more than calm, it roars and whips a hurricane.
The wizard is more than magic, or do you see him at all?
I am more than a white, English, female,
I am much more than that indeed,
But you will have to get to know me,
To find out all that I am.

Lisa Budney

Out Of The Ordinary

Until now I had no faith to lose.
Then your belief taught me it is
Ordinary things that speak the language
I once thought only God would use.
Chaos still rolls beyond our little fences,
And the wrong place is always only
A split second away. The cell can mutate,
Brakes fail, and we must take our chances.

You hold off fear with small certainties,
And rhythmical days where each minute
Flows easy to the next, and in to sleep.
Wakening with you I am at ease.
Few declarations, more steadfastness,
Little considerations I so nearly missed.

Moyra Donaldson

Vietnam's Children

My mind hurts.
These children smiled once
Old women laughed, men worked.
I didn't know what they were saying as I killed them.

Johnny's right arm is missing, Ted is blind in one eye
Danny only talks to his gun.
Kevin can't walk or have children anymore
If I'm lucky I'll only be killed.

The helicopters came today
At our request: black, sleek dragonflies
Beating their soft thumping pattern, coming out of the dawn
Their bullets — so fast, so fast — cut down trees
and children

I don't cry here
It's easier to stop thinking.
Morning coffee and napalm; it all smells so sweet.

Half of me pulls the trigger.
My mind hurts.
These children have grenades.

Joel Semchuk

The Spring Clouds

They are soft as your bedtime pillow.
They are white as winter's snow.
They can always change their color,
and shed tears to the ground below.
They can hide the daily light,
but still manage to stay up all night.
They will be wherever you are,
but follow you wherever you go;
through rain, hail, or snow.
But wherever you both end up,
you may get lucky and see a beautiful rainbow!

Pamela Dawn Erickson

My Love

Home is where the heart is, so they say,
Thus, my home is where you are any day.
For you hold my heart now and for evermore,
you are my friend, my lover and my mentor.
My strength when life becomes too heavy to hold,
and warmth when the long night becomes cold.
Your arms are always open to hold me or dry my tears,
your courage is my courage, and banishes my fears.
Stay always beside me through life, my love,
though oft times it is hard, yet still we share
a love so warm, so gentle and so rare.

J. G. Shinn

Bad Dreams

Dreams aren't always happy ones.
They could scare you so much you'll cry.
You'll never know what will happen next.
You'll never know when it's going to end.

Your worst dream of all could be the one,
that comes true.
Just the thought of that happening scares you,
so much that you don't want to sleep.
You try so much to stay up,
but your eyes won't stay open.

Before you know it your asleep, and you have
the worst nightmare you ever had.
Then it happens the dream came true.
You scream for help but no one answers.
You run but there's no place to hide.
You give up, and it catches you.

At least you won't be having anymore
BAD DREAMS

Melanie Serroul

The Promise

The old lady and her husband sat on their couch,
They had been sitting there a very long time.
Their son was gone, taken away from them,
Though he had committed no crime.

He was fighting for his country,
The 'ol red, blue and white.
What he thought was a country of peace
Was really a country of strife.

They were sure he'd come back
Alive and well.
There was no way his great country
Would put him through hell.

He was captured by the enemy,
They beat him 'till he couldn't sleep.
Yet he remained strong,
Remembering the promise he wanted to keep.

They remembered the last time they saw him.
They made him promise, as they wept,
They made him promise to come back.

A promise they will never know he kept.

Melinda Lontoc-Roy

Grandparents

Grandparents are fragile and old.
They tell us wise tales of old.

Grandparents care about what you say.
They always try to help in a special way.

Grandparents have strong religious beliefs.
That stay in my mind through life's roughest times.

They have a smile so sweet and kind.
It always stays in my mind.

Grandparents are kind and caring you see.
That's why I'm glad I have grandparents for me.

January Martin

"The Essence Of Life"

Having been born with limited capacity
Thinking of what kind of life it would be,
—full of love, joy and happiness?
or a life filled with emptiness, sufferings and sorrow?

As we journey through life,
Walking alone or holding someone's hand
This is the real thing, this is life.

Each day we open a door,
a new chapter, that door is closed.
Another one has to be opened
To overcome grief, a triumph of human soul
To live another day...
....A gift from God.

Maria Dolores T. Aguirre

The Wedding

Here on the threshold of wonder we stand
This moment, a wedding, and us hand in hand

Love tiptoe softly between us, we two
Alight in our eyes and our hearts, always new

Gently persuade us your worth to hold dear
Each day and each month and each 'wakening year

Love, be thou eager, be certain, be swift
Pour out your balm on each hurt, heal each rift

When anger is sudden, forgiveness is sweet
Let not sun set in its wrath or its heat

But let love beget love, in wonder be lost
O great Love eternal, be ours what e'er cost

For human love's precious, a blessing beside
But only God's love is poured out like a tide

So help us reach out to receive what He gives
Then love cannot die, but forever will live

Daphne Jackson

This Old Tractor

There it sits, in a corner.
This old tractor.
Rusted and ruined, never to work again.
Dreaming of working, but only sitting.
Waiting to pull the plow again.

Looking at the other tractors working.
Wanting to show them how it's done.
Now an eye sore.
To be sold as a project.
Now in a shop, with other tractors.

It is tore apart, from top to bottom.
Everything is cleaned and fixed.
Feeling good about being together again.
This old tractor, can pull again.
To show how to pull the plow.

Alec Steiert

An Old Time Morning

The old man awakes at six
With youth in his heart, age in his bones
Springs out of bed imaginarily.
He's ready, like the train
To run his runs like old time.
For those were the day's he made his way.
But, now, retirement forces his day
Into peace, quiet and relaxation with no pay.
Finally, asleep he falls, with many a dream fulfilled

Wayne Farish

"Listen"

It's growing stronger from day to day. I never thought I'd feel this way all I think about is you wishing you were mine.
No matter where I run too you're always here.
In my mind, in my heart, your always near.
I cannot stay away, loving you could be wrong
I don't care, my feelings are too strong
Sometimes I wonder if this were meant to be? Was it meant that I should cry for your love? Should I fear my love for you?
When I talk to you, I wish I were kissing you.
When I look at you, I wish I were "loving" you.
First time I saw you my heart skipped a beat.......
Since that day on your absence despairs me.
Not to see your gentle face, or your foolish eyes...,
Maybe time from now, I'll find another lover, so will you.
But you'll always be my only true love.
Hope your listening, I'm not whispering.
I'm letting you know how I feel.
Take these words and cherish them.
They are no lie. Just my feelings.!?

Priscilla Pacheco

Wake Up

Shadows lurk in every corner
Thoughts lurk in every mind
Words sometimes unspoken, hearts forever broken
Wind sometimes turning, fire forever burning

Shadows lurk in every mind
Thoughts lurk in every corner
Hands for holding, hands for scolding
Body dances, body prances

Corners are filled with shadows
Minds are filled with thoughts
Of a life in a cloud, cars so loud
Of a life in a castle, without a hassle

Minds are filled with thoughts
Corners are filled with shadows
Wake up from your dreams of a bed full of roses
This world of dreams is not what it poses
See the shadows of a true life unwind
Hear the thoughts of a true life, be kind

Lorraine Lacroix

The Meaning Of Life

Through the years,
Through the happiness, sorrow and tears
Even when close to death,
You stood by my side.
You gave me children that I love,
More than anything on earth or above.
We have had more than our share,
Of hard times to bare.
You have always been there for me,
It's taken a lot of years for me to finally see.
That you'll be with me till the end of my life,
You are not just my best friend,
You are my wife,
THE MEANING OF MY LIFE.

Barry Wirchenko

State Of Confusion

The black clouds surround my eyes
Time does not exist where my mind now lives
There is a small light of passion deep within my heart
I am trying with all my strength to grab onto that light
For I feel that it is my only chance for survival in this world which others can find success in.

When I look in the mirror, at times I'm not quite sure who's face it is staring back at me
This is a question I find I am asking myself more and more each day
I also find myself wondering why do I get up each morning
Then I look to my side and see him lying there so peacefully and my question is answered.

When I am in his world all is safe and I feel so free
His love, confidence in me and friendship take my doubts for away from me
But reality hits hard when it is time to face all the pressures, stresses and problems of our real world
While he lies a sleep each night the creatures of my mind are very much awake
Roaming the walls of my brain, going through the tunnels of my thoughts, fears, hopes and dreams
Words running through my eyes; sounds dwelling in my ears
While the world rests I roam

Why is it that someone who has so much love and happiness can be in a world of such confusion
So many questions unanswered, so many fears, so many worries, so much hope and so much love to give
But how to balance it all to make it work, when you live in a State of Confusion?

Carly DeMille

Reality

Time to face reality things change people change

No more princes and princesses
time to face reality
Brutal stabbings Murders assassinations
that our way of life

No more Romeo and Juliette
time to face reality
Pornography Prostitution Rape
that's our way of life

No more green grass, clean air
time to face reality
Pollution extinction global warning
that's our way of life

No more believing in peace
time to face reality
Destroy the enemy we most rule
that's our way of life

The world has prospered for centuries time to face reality

Kalyn Hale

Dreams

To look at a flame and see piles of gold.
To look at a photo and remember days of old.
To wish for eternity and fly high on the wings of imagination.
Is to like what you have and let dreams make the
best of all situations.

For a dream is like the medicine that heals you from
your ill.
It gives you a chance to be what you only hope you will.
If only for a moment, there's tranquility and peace.
That's why a dream will always be my freedom,
my release!

Heidi Slack

Humble Submission

Nobody is perfect in this world
Time you make mistake, time you make good
People criticize you, some defend you
Some dishonor you
Accept whatever comes
God always defend an honest man.

Admit your fault and reconcile
For God delivers, comfort you with love
He even open the secret of His heart
A love for a humble man.

Make humility your strength
Struggle can be more light to bear
Submit yourselves whatever comes
With God on your side, Virtues will win and shine.

A humble man is always at peace
He endures what ever put on him
Even do the world consider him low
For trust in God is more than wealth to come.

Socorro V. Tinidad

Haiti

Genetic line, black and defiant, transplant from Africa
to an alien shore
Yours the ignominy of a french colonial shame.
Fair sister of the emperor, languishing in gardens
of tropical repose
Silent your cry of pity for tormented flesh.

Toussaint, self-freed liberator of the tortured masses
Rip apart the system of depravity and pain
Oblivious to the awesome portent of a lingering death
Duped and decaying in a European Dungeon.

Born the Republic, feet, hands and eyes intact
To run towards the centuries beyond
Yet hindered in your growing by false fathers
Who ruled with hate and deep demonic dread.

Towering above the cape, a testament of countless
labouring hands.
Stout walls and cannon of the citadel remain as sentinel
But whence the guard and sentinel of human frailty
and despair
Against this modern slavery of a military arrogance?

Denise Nelson

A Prayer On Highway 12

Thank you, Great Spirit, for the opportunity to walk with you,
To be with those who have great knowledge
And for the privilege of glimpsing that knowledge.
Allow me to be the Warrior I was meant to be,
Let me have the wisdom to be wise.

I am here, Great Spirit, take me home, back to the beginning,
Show me the rudiments of life, and of love.
Teach me the elements of nature, pure and simple.
Give me understanding, to give it to others.
Let me be as you, I am part of you.

Peace and harmony, oneness, togetherness, a natural order.
This is the path which was intended for us.
Guide me, Great Spirit, I give my life to you alone,
Take it, and give my spirit to the people.
We all need you... and each other.

Alexander Lich

Falling World

The world is falling and no one
to catch it before it falls completely
down.
It's a shame to see it go but no
one cares how it will be for the future.

People insist on having it destroyed
but we will be there to stop it one
day from falling

My children and I will not allow
the world to fall down.
There is so much we need to know
before we go with it.

The world is a mystery to us and
we will see what it is to the end.
What it is we need to complete it
by saving the world by the end of
time is over.

Loretta Fraser

Fort York

We left our school and were on our way,
To Old Fort York where we would stay.
The Fort was such a lovely sight,
I couldn't wait to see it at night.

We learned where the families of 1812 grew,
And of all the troubles that they went through.
Later, we got to the real deal,
We had to make part of an historical meal.

Following that we got into a line,
For it was already, marching drill time.
Then, we left our marching drill line,
For it was already time to dine.

Next, Wayne was ready to teach us a game,
It was from the old time, that's from where it came.
Then it was time to get into our beds,
Good night, sleep tight, you sleepy heads.

We awoke bright and early the very next day,
All praying and wishing that we could all stay.
The rest of the day went by really fast.
We were all hoping, it would always last.

Stephanie Hensen

My Fallen Comrades

The quiet of dawn is breaking,
To sleep - is now only a dream,
We marched through the endless night,
To yet another battlefield of bloodshed.

The soles of our boots are worn bare,
The wicked cold has crippled many,
We find the strength to march again,
To yet another battlefield of bloodshed.

Young lads have lost their precious youth,
They cry in darkness for their mothers,
Their innocent eyes have seen the horrors,
To yet another battlefield of bloodshed.

Our provisions have been gone for days,
The pain in our bellies grows deeper,
Each tormented day rolls into another,
To yet another battlefield of bloodshed.

Our vast numbers have dwindled to few,
Lifeless all around me - lay fathers and sons,
When will this hellish dream end,
To yet another battlefield of bloodshed.

Renate Buxton

My Daddy

When I was small you were away at work,
to support your wife and children.
Jobs were rough so you went away,
and it was refineries you were building.

This went on for quite a few years,
you'd come home for a couple of days.
Then you'd leave for another month or so,
it was the only way to get your pay.

Until that terrible telephone call,
when I was only seven.
I knew before my Mommy told me,
my Daddy may be in heaven.

You were taken to the hospital,
the doctors put you back together.
Your guardian angel helped you that night,
so you could be with us forever.

I really don't remember very much,
because I was just so small.
I remember I almost lost my Daddy,
and I remember that terrible call.

Michele Viveiros

The Wind Of Change

Is tapping at doors, rattling windows, opening eyes, ears, minds,
To the possibility of an idea gathering
Momentum to create a monumental miracle.

But is it more than in a flight of fancy, we hear a roll
Of gigantic drums awakening humankind to feel
The universal pulse giving birth to a renewal
Of tenderness; arousing us to view hate and revenge
As a false tracery to be chased time out of time beyond mind's sight
Until, our tread mill memory is stilled.

Even the birds seem to be chirruping feel the warm glow
Spreading through the people of the land.

But the warm, gentle breeze changed to a cold, strong wind,
Denuding trees while dry leaves seemed to sigh - if only -

And in the crisp morning light, with a hunger for peace,
Myriads of people all races and creeds joined in the refrain - if only

As a strong wind picks up the voices, carrying them over
Land and sea; and as it softens to a gentle breeze
People from many lands sing - in harmony - we
Celebrate our diversity.

Suzie Cooper

Sally's Mind

You, with your mocking grin and evil mind,
To think I am that naive or just blind;
Not to notice how cruel you are,
Not until you have gone too far.
I hear you laughing at me, I see you pointing at me,
I feel you staring at me, I know you all hate me.
And because you make me scream and cry from frustration,
They treat me as if I am the devil's creation.
In this padded cell the doctors watch me,
And they always ask, "What do we do with Sally?"
I faintly whisper that Sally is still here,
But your ignorance to my needs is my only fear.
The bullet in this gun is my only way out,
My trembling finger and frail mind are in a bout;
For now I hear the shoes of nurses in the hall,
And with a violent blast, to my knees I fall.
My life is still dangling when the nurses run in,
I pray to God not to treat this as a great sin.
After my last breath I am ready to die,
Good-bye cruel world, good-bye.

Darlene Brown

Risk It!!

To laugh is to risk appearing the fool.
To wee is to risk appearing sentimental .
To reach out to another is to risk involvement.
To express feelings is to risk exposing your true
self to place your ideas.

Your dreams before the crowd, is to risk their loss.
To love is to risk not being loved in return.
To live is to risk dying.
To hope is to risk despair.
To try is to risk failure.

Risks must be taken,
Because the greatest hazard in life is to risk nothing
The person who risks nothing does nothing.
He nothing send me nothing
He may avoid suffering and sorrow
He simply cannot learn, feel, change, grow
love or really live.
Only a person who risks is really free!!

Jocelyn Trepanier

The Memories I Make

Each day I live I make another memory:
Today's words, thoughts and deeds are tomorrow's history.
Lord help me please to "seize the day" while I have life —
May I bring harmony and peace where there is strife;
Where there is anger, hate or pain, give me the grace
To bring forgiveness, love and comfort in their place;
Where there is heartache, may I bring your healing to a soul;
Through me, may broken hearts and spirits be made whole.

Tomorrow, what I've done today will all be past:
Just the memories of my words and deeds and thoughts will last.
Help me to make those memories golden ones for those
Who'll cross my path today — for soon my book will close,
And each page and chapter stand as a memorial to me —
Help me to live, dear Lord, as I'd want that book to be!

Margaret B. Osborne

Only One

Once strangers, oceans apart,
Together, a feeling of warmth, secure and freedom,
Walking along the shore,
Sighting a body of sparkling water,
Listening to the sound of waves,
Sailing, so relaxing,
Soothed by the cool ocean breeze,
Watching the radiance of sunset,
So peaceful, so beautiful, and so warm.

Once never known, then met and fell in love.
With you, I experienced the true meaning of life,
In love; now apart is ...
Devastating, heart-breaking, overwhelmingly painful.
Forever and ever you'll be in my mind,
Feeling your presence no matter where you are,
Your warmth surrounding me wherever I go,
Your existence is worth more than life itself,
Do you realize how much . . . I love you.

Diana Lee

True Or Not..? It Is The Story Of Nightingale Bird

The nightingale bird sings both day and night, and its lovely liquid tone is a delight to all birds lovers..
There is a lovely story that the purity of its song was a gift from MARY Mother of JESUS ... When Mary was sitting nursing her baby, she sang quietly to lull Him to sleep....A nightingale sitting nearby was so enchanted with the sweet music that it flew into the barn and perched on MARY's shoulder, joining on her song... When the baby JESUS had fallen asleep. MARY turned to the nightingale to thank it... "In recognition of your help" She said... "You shall have my voice. And for ever more people will stop and listen to its beauty.

Alice Tester

Dreams of You

I saw you once again last night, you tiptoed softly through my tranquil sleep.
I felt your breath upon my skin whispering quietly to my broken dreams
I know not how you came to me. A million moments passed since first you came,
And yet last night, you came to me again, gently whispering my name.

You took my hand and willingly I went back with you to a time since gone
You smiled when our eyes met and time stood still for me to gaze upon
The wonders of your gentle face, so full of love and quiet mystery
You touched my hand, then when I thought you gone, still you were there in memory.

Was this our love, so powerful in its might, that it would span the outstretched hands of time
And cross all barriers ever known to man to touch again in slumbers restless night
The part of me which held you for all time.
As daybreak steals across the morning sky to rouse me from those images sublime
You came to me last night again, and touched my mind.

Wilma Rae

drowning...

Raindrops
Trickle through endless puddles
In haunted laughter
The children splash and
I tickle their faces, eyelashes, cheeks
With bones that melted long ago
That night when HOPE forgot to win
The ice slowly dissolved my dreams
And icy fire dripped, pierced through my veins
And I, subdued by the screams
Of tomorrow's ghosts
And angels hovering just above
I focused on the brightest star and hoped,
Wished it might be mine
And every time a star dies (someone falls...)
I lost the moon, her smiling glow
She hid behind clouds of agony, ashamed
Twinkle, twinkle tiny star
Dancing with death, melody of despair... spin, spin
The bright star smiled, and slowly It died.

Joanne Gauthier

Flight! As If In A Summer Storm

Swiftly as a summer storm your life on earth was ended.
Until we meet again my friend, our friendship lies suspended.

In all your friends will do and say, you'll not be very far away.
The laughter and the tears we share, enhanced will be,
for you'll be there.

The memories of the years gone by, will cause each one
of us to sigh. Deep within our hearts so warm, we'll remember
you left, as if in a summer storm.

I touched your brow and it was cold, as if you had
just stepped in from the icy blast of a winter wind.
Yet you were in the warmth of our Master's fold.

Farewell my true and trusted friend, until the road of my life ends.
Life's road of living and those unborn,
remembering you left, as if in a summer storm.

Remembering too, the clouds do clear. The skies turn blue,
the rain a tear. Life goes on
with friendships warm. Yes, we'll remember you left,
as if in a summer storm.

Joy Stonelake

Untitled

The beaches of my mind are in solitude
waiting life to free them
waiting to acknowledge
waiting to live
waiting...

The mind wanders to depths unknown
only to which is one
knows where it goes.

God gave me hope from the sky
He gave me faith in my heart
Most of all he gave me courage to go on.....

Monique Laroche

"A Child's View"

The air raids are warning the people tonight,
Warnings of dangers of killing and fright.
Where do I run where can I hide
or will the soldiers come through for me tonight.
The soldiers so brave who fight
for us tonight, where do they run,
where do they hide and who will
come through for the soldiers tonight.
Bombs are flying, people are dying,
Why does this have to go on.
I remember when my grandfather held
me tight and rocked me on his knee saying
he would be safe and be home soon and
a gift he shall bring me, grandfather gave
me a special gift that day he won the fight
he gave me freedom, life and so much more.

Mandy Miles

Who Knows The Answer?

Years and days run on rule - everywhere.
We try to find steps in time.
To keep the day - to find in our life the right way!
But water and Earth run forever - decades
and one each of way included are our
uncounted days!
We try to fight.
To change the life,
To know the way.
How can we stop
Our last days?

Ghita Malvina

Sitting By Myself

I sit here alone,
watching the sunset.
With pink and blue clouds,
the sun reflecting across the river.
Each day it's more beautiful than ever,
I wouldn't let anybody change it if they could.
Early in the morning,
you wake to birds singing.
I could sit here rest of my life,
not letting anything bother me.
The days turn into weeks,
the weeks turn into months.
Then one day it's all over,
winter has come and taken it all away.
The only thing that is beautiful,
is the northern lights.
As they dance, you see the colors change,
purple, red, blue.
My life is so great,
I wouldn't want to change it at all.

Amanda C. K. Edgi

Friendship

Our friendship meant so much to me
We've known each other since we were three,
We always did everything together,
And said that it would last forever.

Together, we always had fun,
Laughing and playing in the hot sun.
Then our friendship had to die,
And since that day I wanted to cry.

I always told my troubles to you,
Whenever I was feeling blue.
You always seemed to listen to me.
Like a true friend should always be.

Our memories will never leave.
That's what I will always believe.
I'm sorry that our friendship ended,
I wish it was something that could be mended.

Sorry for what we did!

Krystal Andrusyk

Your Sheep Am I

You, Lord, are my shepherd!
What could I want?
Your green pastures harbour nettles,
the still waters run deep and deadly.
Your sheep am I.

The paths of righteousness are rough,
the valley of death frightens me,
evil tries to devour me,
others beat me with sticks and stones.
Your sheep am I.

I feast on the sacrificial bread and wine.
Those who would harm me
see my head anointed with oil.
You fill my life with blessings.
Your sheep am I.

Surely you will not desert me
in my hours of need.
I pray that I might live in you
all the days of my life.
Your sheep am I.

Heather Vis

Water

What glistens in the sun at high noon?
What sparkles in the night under the moon?
What rages with the wind of an almighty force?
What lies subdued when winds change their course?

What sustains life and quenches thirst?
What creates silver rings when coerced?
What adopts marine blue from the open sky?
What is clear in a glass to the naked eye?

What can bear tons of steel upon its breast?
What can coddle a sea gull when at rest?
Who knows what this wondrous phenomenon might be?
Water...so mysterious and free!

Gina D. Stass

There Were No Words...

There were no words,
What there was, spoke of an eternity.
There was only silence,
But the world moved between him and me.

There was no greater power,
Than the force that made us see.
There was only love,
Which I knew could never be.

Then there were tears,
So pure and holy, the heart was stained.
There was something,
Yet I knew nothing could be gained

There were no thoughts,
As we begun to drift and roam.
Then there was a caress,
Which turned our tears to stone.

There was nothing so pure,
As the simple touch I gave from the heart.
There is nothing so together,
As two lonely souls torn apart.

Debbie Thompson

Done

Our land, our trees, our ocean
What's they potion
Thy desire of passion
Let be an anxious emotion
They felt for my nation

How fast the flitting figures come!
The mild, the fierce, the stoney face,
Some bright with thoughtless smiles, and some,
Where secret tears have left their trace,

Thy ploughed the black and fertile plain,
Sowed the waiting soil,
Harvested the yellow grain,
And spent my days in toil,

Struggling tides of life that seem
In wayward, aimless course to tend,
Are eddied of thy mighty stream,
That rolls to its appointed end.

.Louise Banette

Believe In Your Dreams

In times of a troubled mind,
When everything seems lost,
When deep within, you feel an empty feeling
For the dreams you've dreamed
always seem to get shattered,
Don't be defeated.

Believe in your dreams,
For there is nothing wrong with dreams,
When there is hope for materialization
into reality,
And yes, there is always hope.

Keep believing in your dreams,
Keep working towards them, telling yourself
Yes it can, yes it will.
For it is not only those who succeed
from the start that are winners,
But those, who have held the patience of Job,
Who have had the courage and faith to keep on
working towards those dreams,
Yes! they too are winners.

Patricia J. Whittingham

Untitled

This is a poem that I wrote shortly after the death of my friend and former classmate, Joan Heinbecker. On March 30, 1994, Joan was brutally murdered in her McMaster University dormitory by an ex-boyfriend.

Who decides,
   when it's over?
Who takes away,
   and leaves others behind?
The tears come to us,
   but for whom do we cry?
The soul that is taken
   or the empty space left.
We search in our hearts,
   for some reason why,
To try to understand
   the cruelty of our world.
We need to make sense,
   of a life cut too short
To find some meaning,
   an answer to why.

Michelle Burlock

A Seasonal Lament

Where are the springs that once we knew?
When the days grow warm, and the skies turn blue,
And the last snows melting on the hills,
Feed the swollen streams and rills.

When the morning chorus shrilled at five,
And bees prepared to leave the hive,
And flowers wakening one by one, turn to face the rising sun.

Then will we once again behold, cherry pink and laburnum gold,
Blossoms of each shade and hue, contrasted with a sky of blue.

But now these skies stay cold and grey,
The wind blows from the north each day,
If the sun shines, it's a nine days wonder,
To be followed by a week of thunder.

Tulips and daffodils bent in pain,
Lashed by constant wind and rain,
The fields are squelching seas of mud,
And rivers burst their banks in flood.

Each year we hope for better things, for earlier and warmer springs,
And while we shiver with the cold,
We dream once more of the springs of old.

Barrie Cooke

Beauty

Why must it stare us in the face,
When we know we can't compete.
How can such beauty,
Be so cruel?
You think wisdom and beauty go hand in hand.
And why shouldn't such grace and elegance
Have intelligence.
It is an inevitable pair.
But maybe it was meant
Not to have anything to do with her.
Maybe beauty can be cruel
When you have no soul.
It's just what everyone expects,
And it is so hard to reach
You know it can't be true.

Alissa Lysack

You Were There

You were there as the first ones I laid eyes on
when you brought me into this world
to have to hold onto when I wasn't strong.

And you were there when I took my first steps
and said my first words; always watching over me
to teach me right from wrong.

And you were there as I began to learn things of new and old
with an outstretched hand of aid
when I didn't know what to do.

And you were there when I began to change
from youth to adulthood always looking over my shoulder
to make sure my head was still there.

And you were there through the fights of my independence
knowing full well that you always knew best.

And you were there through my final year
of which I spend at home
hoping you've prepared me for life out on my own.

Yet I know from the start of my life
until the bitter sweet end I'll look in my heart
and you will always be there!

Simon M. Sorensen

The White Garden

Summer days are put aside, for nature's law it must abide.
Where a garden once did reign, its beauty white brought much acclaim.
Embraced by frost and fraught with chill, all stand together,
   tranquil, still.
As I watched their naked plight, heaven kissed them all good night.

A thought arose within my heart, and a lesson made its mark.
Crushed and broken life can make us, fragility like blossoms shake us.
Nature says, "I have a plan, bring love to all - my first command."

My garden white gave such delight, glimmering through long summer
   nights.
We'll rise with them just wait our time, for winter's whiteness also
   shines.
While winds and rains caress our cheeks God's love is all around to
   seek.
We must reach out like flowering branches, be brave, take risks,
   don't miss life's chances.
And when we feel some sweet emotion, we raise our minds with clear
   devotion.

My garden tells me many stories, such enchantment of its glories.
Children come, enjoy the berries. Pick the flowers, make life merry.
When the snow flakes start to fall, the magic of the stars enthrall.
Glistening shimmering shed their light on this heavenly blanket white.
As winter's coat lays on the ground, my white garden still abounds.

Corinne Boyd

"Forever Love"

Your heart is my haven
Where I hide when I'm weak and emerge strong
Each rainy day it's your love I'm saving
I know this is where I belong

In your eyes I see a dream come true
In your arms I feel complete and whole
We began as friends and as lovers we grew
Sharing moments of desire where passions unfold

Another breath I take another minute has past
And the days and the years quickly go by
Our time together I wish forever will last
Like the ageless beauty of a sunset in the sky

You've taken my hand and led the way
To faraway places where only the heart can go
Sometimes it's easier to leave than to stay
You've been there always and this I know

I'll never leave a word of faith unspoken
I'll never turn away from your good heart
I'll always cherish our love as a precious token
And in my life you'll always be the most important part

Diane Radcliffe

Peace

Where is peace?
Where is peace in the haunting
mask of suffering of Somali child?
Where is peace in the muzzle of the smoking gun?
Where is peace in the dark depths of the warlord hearts?
Where is peace in Somalia?

Where is peace in cholera racked body
where is peace in the hordes crossing in the half
submerged canoe to'safety'
Where is peace in Rwanda?

There is peace in love
"Love your neighbour as you love yourself"
The peace we want is everywhere, hidden
from selfish human eyes.
Me, My, Mine, never 'Ours', never 'theirs'
Let peace flow from our hearts
Carry your message of peace to
your neighbour, to the world.
Here is Peace!

Anne O. Olewe

The Rebirth Of Adonis

Oh, 'Um Qais, "Gadara" of the Decapolis
Where once "Adonis", roamed thy hills

Thus the Myth was told,
Centuries back before the Lord
Though archery and hunting his skill and fond,
Adonis was killed, a Boar did the slain
In the land of Cana'an.

"Astarte", tore her dress
Bewailed and mourned, nights and days,
And hills and valleys roves,
Thy beloved consort seeks.

Rancorous "Persephone" of "Hades"
Tore "Adonis" to pieces
And over the land dispersed his limbs,
So as not he returns.
But "Adonis" did return.

His blood, Red Anemons His arms, Tulips
And in the land of Cana'an chanted the Shepherds,
Back you came, Oh "Adonis",
In a thousand and a thousand "Adonis".

Asem Barghouti

Beyond...?

Beyond my life lies the endless light,
Where stars and myriads of crystal sprites
Beam forth their love,
Within my sight...

Beyond my life lies the endless song,
Within the lute, that is its home,
Between the chords of timeless tune,
Before the bell, within the thong...

Beyond my life lies the endless breath,
Vibration from the love of love,
No rise, no fall, just ease such rest,
Peace all known within my chest...

Beyond my life lies the endless taste
Of love, more sweet than any rose,
All beauty, honey, precious dew,
Beyond my life, there is just you...

Diane Mary Gregory

A Family Affair

It began as a brief encounter
which evolved into an affair
Missy knew it shouldn't have happened
but the temptation was too much to bare

With sparkling eyes of azure blue
and a one hundred watt heart-stopping smile
Andy was one of life's winners
who always did things with style

All too soon it was over
Missy had to get on their her life
Andy went home to the city
back to his kids and his wife

It was an affair to remember
despite all the heartbreak and pain
but a poignant and lasting reminder
with Missy will always remain

A little girl with sparkling blue eyes
blessed with beauty and style
from her mother she's inherited courage
and from her father, a heart-stopping smile

Joanne Smith

Untitled

Here is that kind of love
  which floweth from deep within
  blowing as a gentle breeze
  in the cool of the day
Hers is that kind of love
  silky smooth and soft as butter
  yet with a strength
  which beneath not from this day's heat
And her's that kind of love
  an enduring growing light
  a stern, strong hand
  beaming thru a darkened heart
  squeezing strong; clutching hard
For her's that kind of love
  not hers alone nor finite
  but stemming from her God
  complete, infinite, and ultimate.

Nathan Nyabam

Time

Time is something never-ending, though never seems to last,
Which races towards the future, leaving memories in the past.
It changes all our lives, sometimes not letting us ever know...
Like leaves washing down a river in a rapid flow.

It drains away our youth and who we use to be,
It locks the door of our childhood, throwing away the key.
Time takes us through our life never stopping along the way,
As everything grows older as it quickly ticks away.

Never knowing where time will lead us or what it will ever hold,
As if our life is clay that we must carefully mould.
Time will spin on forever like a shining, silver dime,
Leading you on a path to fulfil your own lifetime.

Selena MacPherson

"Lonely, But Not Alone"

Her cheeks are stained with tears
While across the bed she lies;
Now subdued she wears,
A forced smile of disguise.

Hear voices close by
But remain attentive to her sigh
As desolation's picture shouts
A lullaby of loneliness and doubt.

She remembers harsh words spoken
Until her fragile heart was broken;
With only a burdened soul left to show
And a life with no aims and nowhere to go;

Not even time, with its mercy and consolation
Can erase a well-carved memory of pain;
No long periods of duration can soothe the rage within.

Though life must go on, she keeps looking back
To the restless nights that are now past and gone.

Then she raises her head and gathers her strength
Cursing silently the thoughts of torment,
As she smoothens her bed.

Taryn Jacobs

City Poem (Dehli - Poem India)

The morning air blowing,
While the little children in uniform are walking to school.
Baggers on the street picking up grimy leftovers,
That the wealthy people have thrown away.
The afternoon monsoon rain,
Making it humid and muddy.
Annoying salesmen with their wooden tables,
Shouting out with loud rough voices come and get your fresh fruits and vegetables.
Lonely animals walking on the streets,
With no idea of where to go.
The polluted air making it hard to breathe,
As working people are rushing through heavy traffic.
The housewives walking through the crowded streets
Shopping for the latest fashions of today.
Young teenager's going out with their friendly best friends,
Enjoying the taste of cool vanilla ice cream.
And then again the morning air blowing,
While the little children in uniform are walking to school

Shaloo Gupta

Like Roses

Children are lovely and beautiful
White, Black, Indian and Chinese
They all represent humanity
And share one common destiny

They are like roses soft and gentle
They must be watered and not be tortured
Feed them well and they will grow
Give them a hug and they will love

Teach the children to pray and to share
Guide them along the right way
Give them hope for tomorrow
Tell them dope brings sorrow

Give the children the right toys
And they will find joy
And one day, they will say
We are glad to be here!

I can imagine the question arising
As to who am I, and why?
And with a smile, I hasten to reply
I am just a child!

Leonard Clark

Kitante Primary School

On the edge of Kampala City lies a school
Whose atmosphere has always been cool,
And will always remain the more,
Even in times of war.

At the age of six years
I joined Kitante full of fears
Equipped with a mind which was bare
Thanks to the teachers who handled me with care.

The name Kitante makes my pulse react.
At first I thought I was just sentimental,
But my days in Kitante have been instrumental
In forging my personality,
Which has made my life a reality.

Luyiga Irene

In Time

The pain you feel now,
Will be gone tomorrow
So there's no need for tears
Or sorrow

The wounds of hurt you wear today
Will slowly heal as time goes by
You may hurt inside, but it will soon go away
So there's no need to cry

All the feelings that are now
In time will pass away
So always remember whenever your hurt
That it never always stays.

Leora Shammas

Suffered Are The Children

Heart felt tears, a message lies.
Youth forgotten years, a soul that cries.
Touches so soft, a child in pain.
Blackened caresses, a love lost and slain.
Voices from beyond, a memory wakes.
Dancers of Evil, an innocence takes.
Days of darkness, a child lost.
Nights of loneliness, an endless frost.
Those less believing, a prayer ignored.
Colors of pain in the eyes that implore.
Slash of a blade, the nightmare awakes.
Dancers of Eden, a spirit takes.

Lalania L. Laybourne

Canary Face

Last night I went to sleep
With a cat that swallowed the canary face.
And an I feel I've been through the war body.
My head hit the pillow
Like a ton of bricks hitting qualofil,
And my mind and my eyes closed like a book.
I dreamed the strangest things
Like your face close to mine, in a room.
And the sky is around us swallowing our hunger.
I awoke with your eyes
Floating in my subconscious soul, how provocative,
And the need to forget a lion's roar strong.
My mind reeled with speculation
And with an I dream to remember face
I reached for the clouds and found your arms.

Stephanie Cronk

Precious Memories

The mysteries of our lives unfold,
with each passing day.
The days are forever changing,
but precious memories with forever remain.

Memories of good and bad,
days never forgotten.
Flashbacks and faint recollections,
cloud our perceptions and tell us stories.
Reflections, and emotions
stir from within our souls.

Pangs of loss and sorrow,
the ache to go back in time.
Returning to those moments,
days forever trapped within our minds.

Memories that warm the heart,
special reflections of the past.
A guiding light that paves the future,
and keeps the candles of our hearts burning.

Precious memories are forever,
something that will always warm our hearts.

Tara Stephens

A Lost Soul Remembering His Love

Was there ever anyone as lovely as you
with eyes so bright and delightfully blue
Your beauty is like something that reaches the heart
and I pray constantly to God that we won't forever be apart
Every time I remember those eyes, it's sheer nostalgic
and I can't help but feel lonely and terribly sick
Being away from you is like my worst nightmare coming to past
and I can't help but wonder how long it will last
I stare constantly at your picture as if I am hoping for it to come to life
and I hope and pray for the day to come when you'll say yes, you'll be my wife
It's only you in my thoughts that keeps me alive
the memories of those wonderful days together that helps me to survive
How much longer must I live without you
How much longer must I go on feeling lonely and blue
These are questions I keep asking myself
only you can answer, no one else.

Earl Thompson

The Letter

The postman brought a letter to his mama yesterday;
With shaking hands she reached for it in dread.
It was from her darling son and, until this very day,
She had almost given him up for dead.

Dear Mama: I'm in prison so very far from you.
And I couldn't write you sooner, you see,
I'm so ashamed, dear mama, because you've always taught me right
And your love still means so very much to me.

Now, please don't cry, dear mama, because I'm locked up doing time
To pay for all the wrong that I have done.
But I promise you I'll come home and make it up to you somehow.
Just remember that I love you and that I'll always be your loving son.

She thought of all the nights she'd cried thinking that her son had died;
Then her old, white head fell down upon her breast.
The pages drifted to the floor; she'd never read them anymore.
She had passed on to her final rest.

They never told him she had died; he never knew of the times she'd cried;
Or that he'd always be her loving son.
He never saw her again; he died alone in prison,
At the tender age of only twenty-one.

Lillian Morrison

Somalia Woman

You travelled far on fested feet
Woman of sorrow and child of grief
Your scorched sun body so frail and weak
Here take this scepter and go in peace.

The time will come, when battle will cease
When famine, starvation and hunger will end
When mortal man must take a stand
Life has no guarantee, survival is the key.

O world untouched by mortal hand
Bend close rescue your child from harm
Hear ye the voice of anguish and pain
Go quench and free her from her pain.

Oh world untouched, oh world untouched
Bend close and rescue your child from harm.

Cynthia Poitier

My Journey

I sit here contemplating
Wondering where I have come from
Where I am going
I have brought myself to new heights
And these heights have brought their own depths

To go forward means new explanations
To stay limits emotions and learning
To go backwards means anguish and pain

The logic is evident and I should push on
And yet the fear of the unknown
The wondering of what will happen holds me back

To remain stagnant would be so simple
Attempt to do nothing important
And still I know the boredom is suicidal

The anguish of attempting to go back is unfathomable
I cannot change what is past
I can only revive old memories and pain

The evolution of logic pushes me on
The fear attempts to hold me
And the memories want to be re-written

I have risen above myself and must now go on
Only the knowledge will quell the fear
And the pain will pass with the growth of myself.

Geoffrey M. Coombs

The Cane Cutters

Early in the morning they start,
Working until dark,
Working in the hot, hot sun,
No time for pleasure or fun.

They live a very hard life,
Both the cane farmer and his wife,
Even the children who are younger than you,
Help their parents in the fields too.

Some of the canefarmers are not very strong,
And work in the fields all day long,
They have very little education,
And cane-cutting is their only occupation,
So next time you eat a cake or drink your tea,
Please say a prayer for the cane-cutter and his family.

Ria Grace Seeperad

The Little Girl In Me

How old would a man be if he didn't know his age,
Would it bring contentment to his life; would he live it differently,
There's a need to grow up quickly - there's a longing to be grown,
And the one thing left neglected is the child in you and me.

We relive those childhood moments each and every Xmas eve,
The world is filled with wonder as the lights blink on the tree,
In the air there's an excitement that extends to every age,
And I feel a new connection with the little girl in me.

The innocence and joy we feel - we bury in the past,
Too soon replaced by burdens of responsibility,
Lives of never ending trials make you old before your time,
And it leaves behind the feelings of the little girl in me.

Tiny baby kittens, little puppies with huge paws,
Sleeping in the pet shop - just as cute as they can be,
I long to buy each one of them and give them a good home
And make another wish come true for the little girl in me.

Brenda M. Vaudry

Worry Is Like A Rocking Chair Something To Do But It Get's You...

If we truly believed in God,
Would we worry so?
If we really thought He cared,
Would we hurry so?

It doesn't solve the problem
Or make a burden light,
But only adds more wrinkles,
And dark hairs turn to white.

It's something to do when idle
Or even when busy we are;
But it really gets you nowhere,
Except worse off by far.

We need to get right busy,
Get going and get things done,
As battles of life and war
By worry were never won.

So let's try trusting our Father,
And try not to worry so,
Because worry all day you can
But like the chair you never go.

Vivian Barnett

My World

A world so strange to me,
yet so close and familiar.
I can feel the warm and muggy scent,
and almost taste the sweet, bitter taste.
This world is beautiful and special
and is perfect in every way.
It has a peacefulness and relaxing atmosphere
that brings forth the good qualities
instead of the bad qualities in the world.
I want to stay there and never return.
Everyone is so happy and rejoiceful.
But all of a sudden!
It vanished!
I think will it ever be like that again
and now realize that this world only exists in my mind.
All I must do to make it reappear,
is close my eyes and use my imagination.
But I can't help but wonder,
If I will ever see this world with my eyes open?

Shefalee Shukla

My World

Society our foundation and our loyalty
Yet where are our morals;
Forgotten?

Children our future and our hope
Yet where is their pride;
Unfound?

Environment our salvation and our freedom
Yet who are the polluters;
Ourselves?

Corruption our undoing and our downfall
Yet how can we overcome this;
With sympathy?

My world we all corrupt, pollute and victimize;
Lets stop!

Paula Demill

Israel's Independence Day 1994

This country glows with illuminating lights
yet why does darkness creep in so thick
and gush through the hearts of our people.
They say that Peace is on her way
that sunshine will forever shine soon.
I think she may have gotten lost
perhaps bleed to death with our brothers
or burnt in the terror of our children.
The world waits and watches
as we breathe and live
trying to filter through
the darkness focusing on the
light of hope.
Worlds dying every day
Jewish souls soaring
Peace will find her way home
to her temple soon
But for now we are left
with forsaken eyes
and blood stained tears.

Ardith Paige Henoch

Broken Dreams

I'm the boy you left on welfare, remember me your only child
You left me about four years ago, in your ways you were so wild
I couldn't understand your logic, of what you were trying to do
But did you ever think of me, if I was eating or wearing shoes

See, you ran out for unknown reasons, and left me all alone
No father son relationship, Dad, you never even phoned
You broke my heart and hurt me dad, more than you'll ever know
But I'll grow up and do just fine, the scars will never show

You never thought of helping out, you were too busy with your friends
Always out carousing, while we had nothing left to spend
One day you'll want back in my life, when I become a man
But if I turn and walk away, I hope you'll understand.

When I have a son, he'll know that I care
Cause I'll show him the love, that you would not share
But just remember this, through all your guilty thoughts
That now and in the years to come, my love cannot be bought.

Loni Keall

Unannounced Visitor

"It's watching me! Get it out!"
You scream, you point and in panic shout.
With irresistible motivation to surprise
Comes advancing quickly a giant miniature prize.
For there standing with multi all seeing eyes,
Is the reason for those desperate cries.
All at once your body begins to climb,
Directing tingling messages up the spine.
Eyes open wide, hands begin to sweat,
Ears begin to ring and the body feels wet.
It scares the wits of the two legged kind,
Drives them crazy out of their mind.
For it's very common to display fear,
Whenever such and unexpected visitor comes near.
Legs, webs, feelers to poke,
I just can't treat spider as a joke.

J. H. Mathew

An Angel Above Us

You walk into class with that beautiful smile,
You walk down the halls always in style.

I walk into class and I see an empty desk,
At least I know you're safe at rest.

Life goes on and you're not there,
You chose to die and that's not fair.

I miss you more and more each day,
Each night I look up and silently pray.

My tears have slowly stopped since you went away,
I think to myself how different it
would be if you were to stay.

Time passes by and each day goes on,
I wish you would of told me what was wrong.

I talk to you through the clouds in the
sky, thinking to myself the reasons why!

Now you've chose to die and it's for good,
If I could bring you back, believe me I would.

Korie Kinsella

To Kurt

Through great musical creation
You were our angry voice
There's a spokesman for every generation
And Kurt, you were our choice.
We know you didn't want money, glory or fame
All you wanted was to release your anger and pain.
Kurt, when you were doing those drugs
Didn't you know you were digging your grave
Burying all your hopes and dreams
And sadly, any chance to be saved.
Although your death wasn't a total surprise
We all agree it's a very tragic demise.
Even though you didn't mean to
You've caused lots of sadness and grief
You'll be forever missed by your wife and daughter
And all of us in a state of disbelief.
There will never be another like you
To us you were the best
We pray you are eternally blessed in your place of rest.
Love forever, from your fans everywhere.

Shawn Zwikstra

The Scar Of A Tear

You feel the pain,
Your body trembles with fear.
You try not to cry,
But down your cheek rolls a tear.

Why is this happening to me?
What did I do wrong?
This goes through your mind,
As well as happiness, for which you long.

You're only so little,
You have your whole life yet to live.
You wish it was not a hit,
Your father had to give.

You try to fight back,
But what's the use.
A person can only take,
So much abuse.

Cuts and bruises fade away...
...But the scar of a tear is here to stay.

Stacie VanKralingen

Just A Dream

You caress my face and I feel shivers up and down my spine.
Your fingers delicately go over my lips and all the while
we are locked in a gaze filled with unspoken passion.
Your strong arms gently go around my waist
and bring me closer to you, we are a perfect fit.
I see your face moving towards my own.
My heart is beating quickly as I wait for our lips to meet.
Finally your tender lips touch mine and all control is gone.
I slip my arms around your neck and let all my feelings
be shown to you through this one kiss.
As I inhale your intoxicating scent, you stop kissing me
and hold me tight.
And then as if reading my thoughts you softly whisper
the words I have been longing to hear, "I love you" you tell me.
A tear of happiness falls down my cheek and as you kiss it away
while I tell you that I feel the same, I wake up.
Sadly realizing it wasn't happening, I wipe away my own tears,
close my eyes and keep telling myself, it was just a dream.

Chantelle Arruda

You

Time was when you did bestow,
Your smile at me and first hello;
Stranger indeed you touched me too,
With willing hands, to hold on you.

We played the game of discovering,
Sown friendship seed, and now it's growing.
Soaring to the sky with song to sing,
Melodious purport that friendship brings.

Yet, there are times, game's hard to play,
You're there for me, to show the way.
In laughters, in tears or in every way,
You imbue my life with reasons to stay.

In this mercurial world, friends come and go
And life seems so ephemeral, too!
In the bivouac of life, there's chagrin and incognito,
But you're always there, candidly true.

Oh! for the days to see us through,
Conquering time, distance, status, too!
To love and trust, I'll always do,
So long as there'll always be you....

Virgilio M. Panapanaan

Into The Frame

I respect your pride not letting the pain come through
Your sweet, tender face - I believe in you
But if, in the dead of night, the veneer should burn in flame
My darling you're not alone, I'll step into the frame

The joy deep inside when I think of your gentle heart
The heaven's light you gave to heal my own wounds and scars
If your tower of strength should fall there is no shame
Just reach out for me and I'll step into the frame

Maybe I'm not the vision of a perfect dream
But I'd lay down my life when I hear your cry of need
For Oh, my love, you're all that I can think of
Sweetheart let me bring you home to me

Inspiration you provide, so glorious and divine
You gave me the belief to walk the long thin line
It's my turn now to be there, honey just cry my name
Over your heart I'll cross and step into the frame

It's my turn now, just cry my name
I'll be there, I'll be there
To step into the frame

Christopher Goodyear

To You

You chase the language
with light and lantern
which can lighten up your darkness
and your emptiness
the precise word
which fall well on lip and tongue
the word which rings of music and cymbals
word with content and meaning
which not is thrown on the rubbish-heap
when you turn your back
You want to be read, understood and loved
It is not easy
to be a poet today

Jan Idlinge

"Valued"

Dear Mom And Dad,
You've seen the stamp on the merchandise,
The symbol of its quality,
The influence on its price.

A toy car is stamped, "made in Hong Kong",
"Made in Canada, marks a doll,
that sold for a song.

A product is known by the stamp that it bears,
and the price on the tag,
says it's cheap or it's rare.

A stamp was placed on me at birth,
it's a priceless signature,
it tells of my worth.

"Made in the Image of God", is the sign,
that put a price so high,
on this life of mine....

Only the Son of God could afford,
to pay the expense,
for the one He adored.

Love, Your Daughter, Becky

Becky Olver

"Fly Away"

As the sun dies,
And the moon is born,
I lay awakened by the grasp of reality.
My only escape
Is offered by the open arms of fantasy
Ready to caress my soul.
When the arms curl around my shoulders,
The embrace is strong.
I don't try to break free,
It's the last fight for sanity.
I let myself be guided to a new place.
A world of birds
Swooshing back and forth
With stories of happiness and freedom.
The realms of melancholy bliss
Is left for those who tread insanity.
But as the sun blooms again,
And the moon is drowned,
A vulture clings to my chains and leads me back to insanity
I'm still searching for a way to escape the vulture.

Erin Fox

Journey

The winds are blowing
time is changing
night to day and day to night,
as evening shade vanishes
everything changes in shape and color,
oh, the spirit of the night is upon us,
you have the key of light with inside,
for the road is long
and hard to make it to morning light,
with the risk of life thee fears are shown
next to return in vain
but to prevail in victory over darkness,
for to find thy way into thee heart
thy will risk all,
to see thee at the end of the road,
open hand,
ready to greet thee with all.

Jamie Orlando Matthews

deception

the whole of life
is lived
inside the mind's
incessant voices
never stilled
deciding each emotion
whether conscious
or unwilled
stretching all our senses
screaming do
and then
begone
the faces in the voices
dusk and dawn
like darkness
shading slowly into light
we charm the demons
into thinking
we are right

Rose-Marie Lohnes-Hirtle

The Evils Of Caring

"Trust Me!
I'm your doctor."

"Help me to die,
Please."

"I can't."

The End of

John O'Connor

Little Butterfly

Mona's Cafe
poetry reading
poets, laughing, talking, discussing
coffee machine hissing
cups and saucers moving in motion
drowned by the noise of traffic

He held my hands
amid this madness
so gentle and warm
over a cup of steaming short black
'la mio piccolo farfalla!'
(my little butterfly)
wide mischievous grin
illuminating his soft gentle face.

Dona Samson

Memories Of Children

Laughter, crying, playing and fights.
A big hug and kiss,
And a story at night.

Playdoh, crayons, paper and pens.
A cuddle, a tickle,
The fun never ends.

A scrape on the knee,
A bump on the head
Mommy kisses it better,
There's nothing to dread.

All of these memories,
I hold locked in my heart.
I've loved you my darlings,
Right from the start!

Lorrie Brooks

A Baby's Smile

A smile must be a natural act,
A baby's smile makes that a fact;
We buy things we think worthwhile
But there's no charge for a baby's smile.

A baby comes from head to feet,
Then the smile makes it all complete;
So innocent, so genuine
Could we see a thing more fine?

But alas, as we grow old
And acts of woe, we do behold
Life could somehow change our style,
We may lose our natural smile.

But if the right moment comes along,
A happy time or a favorite song,
We may find that still on file
Is our easy baby smile.

A Maker we must know we had,
And that Maker wasn't bad
Or mean to worry us a pile
If He could make a Baby's Smile.

Edward W. Britt

The Story Of My Life

Before me
A blank page.
Waiting....
Receptive......
Accepting of what I have
Before I even put forth my offer.
And as I attempt to share
it gently gathers as I surrender,
it softly envelops my every attempt,
it quietly shapes my words,
it lovingly glimpses inside,
Until my page is full
And I have seen my soul.

Julie Parr

Empathy

Once, long ago,
A child looked
Into the heart of a buttercup.
It looked and looked,
Until it fell,
Into the heart of the golden bell.

Completely immersed,
It rested there,
Spell-bound, enchanted in a golden glow.
No longer child -
Only buttercup wild,
Drowsing
In the richness of Summer's air.

Jennifer C. Zini

Previously Green

A song
a sound
is coming
down on me

Previously
green the trees
in front of my house
windows painted black

Who is to preen my garden?

Christian T. Schön

Steel Bubble

Soft and fluffy,
A childhood image,
Playing games,
Escaping reality.

As friends grew older
They floated downwards,
To plant both feet
Firmly on the ground
And wither.

The clouds felt safe,
My cozy crows nest.
Above reality;
But not humanity.

Occasionally I look downwards,
On ironic fields of green and yellow,
Knowing I should be there,
But buoyed by my steel bubble.

Chris Edwards

Memories

A memory is a special gift
A gift from God above
And in our precious memories
We find a thing called love

Looking back throughout the years
We remember good and bad
And in our minds, stand out the times
The happy and the sad

So if you have a memory
Of something that you've lived
Share your thought with someone else
For it is a special gift

Cheryl MacKinnon

Sadness

A hole,
a hole filled with
happiness, love, and joy.
A hole,
a hole emptying slowly,
leaking all its contents
freeing all in it.
A tear falls as everything
slips away so quickly that
nobody notices.
The hole,
the hole is empty.
No, no, no.
It's full,
full of sadness.

Divya Chatani

Like Father Like Son

Same eyes, ears, nose
and mouth.
Ideas, fears, beliefs
and doubts.
Everything the same
right down to the toes,
an impersonator, a couple
of clones.
So similar, but yet...
(would you believe)
These twins have never met.

Jill-Ann Storey

Our Hummingbirds

I just heard
a hummingbird;
I had my back to him
And because I moved,
It was like I shooed
It quickly back to a limb.

The feeder quietly
lures them shyly
Just outside my door.
The wings twir
Just a blur
With me holding my breath for more!

If I sit long enough,
and that's rather tough,
I'm rewarded with great satisfaction,
That rarely granted nature's gift
Of a beautiful, iridescent sight so swift,
It's become our summer's main attraction.

Judy Hicken

The Wretched And Woeful Child

I saw her sitting there
a lonely, wretched little soul.
Like the marks upon her tender cheeks
the scars inside were not so bold.

Inside she feels all broken
her heart breaking, full of fear.
She yearns to cry out help me'
to anyone who will care.

People ask her of the bruises
and the marks her body bears.
Remembering how it is each day
her eyes fill up with tears.

She told how she had tripped,
and fallen, while she was out to play.
How she'd tumbled of her bicycle
just the other day.

She cannot understand it
why her worlds tumultuous and so cold.
Though she longs to let someone in
her story will never be told.

Loretta Lockyer

The Bud

The bud glistens, dew on its lips
A new life is beginning,
Continuing to flourish with
Nature's love and tenderness.

It will open as if yawning
Fresh, new and unsuspecting,
But with time it will become wise
Knowing only four seasons.

Mother Nature and Father Time
Will have their way as they turn
The leaf fragile, and golden brown
Letting it fall to the ground.

Discovered between two pages
Preserved, safe and undisturbed,
It is considered a treasure
And we remember the bud.

Connie Christenson

Growing

Like a bloom opening up,
A new stage has begun,
Like the petals of a rose
Opening up to the sun.

Though the rain sometimes falls,
With no sun there to glow,
There must be the rain
For the flower to grow.

And the rose is always reaching,
Aiming high in the sky,
With only one way to get there,
A determination to try.

The rose's reward,
For this never-ending duty,
Is to achieve in its lifetime
The greatest of beauty.

You cannot help but grow,
And to always try to,
Is proof of the beauty
That is found throughout you.

Gregg Clark

A Great Passion

There is this passion between us
a passion greater than love
more incomprehensible than love
but also more intense than love.

At first it was unknown to us
but as you held my hand
we looked into each other's eyes
and found this incredible passion.

It is an unbelievable passion
never thought you could be mine
didn't believe you were mine
but now I know you are mine.

The passion flies in the air
it sings like the birds
our hearts sing like the birds
and melt together in the moonlight.

Lene Kottal

A Special Love

Hark! I say, what is this
A smile, a hug, a gentle kiss
From someone who is sweet and true
With all the love, from me to you

Now, with this gentle kiss it seems
You've placed yourself into my dreams
Your vision is before my eyes
My love for you, I cannot hide

The memory of your fond embrace
The beauty of your lovely face
Within my memory, they are burned
It is forever, this love I've earned

Now, with these thoughts of love I see
This love is only meant for me
Which I shall cherish, evermore
Remembering the one, that I adore

Hark! I say, now what is this
I'm captivated by a kiss
From someone who is sweet and true
With all your love, to me from you

Don Simpson

Suicide

By candle light and motives dark
A thief slips through the empty halls
His passage known to none who sleep
Secure within these hollowed walls.

His stealth betrays a planned deceit,
His heel leaves naught on dusted floor
The night's long shadows guide his eye
To note with care each numbered door.

No siren's scream, no buying hounds
This thief will meet no prison fold.
Behind his chosen's sightless eyes,
Forever stays the tale, untold.

And now he stands outside my door
Sound not the warning bell my friend
The thieving Reaper wants my soul,
And offers me a timely end.

Christie Koehler

Hometown

We come from a world
A world that your kind
Could not possibly fathom
An incredible maze of light,
Energy, and union
Music that teases and fulfills
Expanses of information
Skies, flowing like crimson rivers
And a love, a love that cures
Home is too far
So far it can never again be reached
Don't give up hope just yet
We may be able to adjust
To the hate, fighting, and war

Martin Gilson

No Escape

Loneliness to cure the pain,
Alone I sit to watch the rain,
Angriness, suppress the fear,
A cry for help, but no one near.
Solitude for peace of mind,
There's nothing left to tell your kind.
People talk but no one knows,
The kind of feelings I do not show.
Describe the void, I cannot do.
It's like the world's forgotten you.
To "let it go" is really rough,
'Cause second best is not enough.
Spare me thoughts of days abroad,
A twist of fate I laugh and nod.
The hope of death to come to me,
My one true break to set me free.
Toss aside the things I feel,
I may be young, but my thoughts are real.

Shawn W. Ferris

Animals

Humans think they are supreme
But animals are the extreme
They bark or purr
Pedigree or cur
Their love 'tho
Humans can never know
For tho' their speech
Is not like ours
Our children
They can help to grow.

Gina Perrin

Shadows

There this part of me that wishes,
And a part of me that dreams.
But no matter what I do,
The nightmares will not end.

Until the end of time,
I think I will not know.
So forever I will sit here,
Swaying to and fro.

Some people often wonder,
But others surely know,
The water has its currents,
While mountains have its snow.

Lying in pools and wonder,
And often in the dark.
Alone and very scared,
Waiting to see the light.

Shadows of hope and faith,
Lie right before our eyes.
But we often cannot see these things,
For we're buried beyond all fright.

Kristine Woods

Take This Head

Take this head
And all its suffering
I want to see you live through
These black nightmares
Like I have done.

These cold walls which surround me
Are the prison these thoughts
Have built
They are with me
Like my mind's own leprosy
Tearing at my very soul.

The tears of my confusion
Burn through the hands
I put up for protection
Against the words and hatred
Of the world against me.

John Savage

They Who Hesitate

They who hesitate, procrastinate
And always wait for the right
Moment, for the right time,
For the right circumstance,

Before they boldly venture to take
A brave chance whenever opportunity
Makes its fleeting appearance

Will forever be left sitting
On the sidelines, outside and away
From the entrance

Which is on the pathway to the
Gateway leading to success

They who hesitates on success forever
they will continue to wait...

Anthony Shurland Phillander

O Christmas Tree Fine

It's tall and imposing,
And its lights blink and shine,
It's always sparkling and glittering,
O Christmas tree fine.

Under the tree
Lie presents galore,
O wonderful tree,
Shed your magic once more.

For now is the time
When love gathers near
When everyone is happy and fine
And full of good cheer.

For now is the time
When people admire,
And drink a glass of wine,
And sit around the fire.

Its green sprucy smells
Are heavenly it seems,
And the ringing of the bells,
Touch everyone's dreams.

Gul Choudhry

Eternity

The snow falls silently
And my sadness deepens
As I watch the tiny snowflakes
Fall quietly to the ground
My love continues and grows
For even though we are apart,
We are still together.
I love you, dearest,
And although you can not feel
This love for me, or can you?
You will be forever in my heart.
So, I will give you a gift
One which no one else has had.
My tears, which are silent.
And like the snowflake
Which falls alone,
So will I be the same.
Only to be united with you
Someday.

Deborah Talbot

Which Once I Felt

I think the words which once I felt
And now remain unsaid
I feel the fear which once I thought
And love has left unbled

I hear the words which once I said
And echo in my mind
I see the sights that once I saw
And now I can not find

I touch his lips which once I kissed
And once again I long
I sense the moon which once was dim
And bath inside its song

I dreamt the dream which once I had
And yet I have not slept
I taste the heart which once was full
And hold what can't be kept.

Carissa Gibbs

In Sorrow

What twisted fate
and ravages of hate
compelled you and me
to part our ways.
We watched you
so close and yet so far,
and the tears I shed
from the anguish of my heart,
I shed not only for me,
but for the pain and despair
that gripped our children.
Long have I known their laughter,
and I see now their tears.
Their pain is my pain
and their despair is mine too.
Your eyes misty, you walk away.
We too stumble into the unknown
no consolation could I offer.
When will we see you again
or will we ever?

Bernedette Weerasinghe

Precious Time

If you possessed the power
And the willingness too,
Would you turn back the clock
And start anew?

A place only dreamt about
A book never read
So little time with the family
Things left unsaid.

Words spewed in anger
Actions that were mean
You could right all the wrongs
If the slate were wiped clean

But it is from our past
Important lessons are learned
So start right now
Leave no stone unturned.

Live out your dreams
Find happiness within
We have only one chance
It can't be done over again.

Gaylene Lazar

"Heaven's Promise"

Although the hand of God does bend
And time on this earth comes to an end
Remember always it's only the start.
And not forever of being apart.

Love and kindness in times of need
For an eternity helps plant the seed.

On earth we are put
But for a short time
Until the bell of God does chime.

Then we are called unto His care
And life everlasting
Are promised to share.

Coleen Grace Meldrum

Thank You, Lord

I thank Him for the mountains
and valleys of life;
For illness, tension and strife.
For it's times like these,
if we allow it to be,
That we can draw closer
and closer to Thee.

I thank Him for all blessings
He has given to me,
For ears, health and eyes to see,
For energy to serve Him,
however it may be,
Could be by helping and sharing His love
at any opportunity.

My heart is full of joy,
My lips are full of praise
For my Savior, who died for me.
Because of His shed blood,
I am set free
To live with Him throughout all eternity.

Ruth Murdoch

My Wishing Star

I held a star upon my palm
And watched its five-pronged light.
It bathed my face in its Silver Sheen,
And chased away all fright.
Gently, I held it near,
And it turned into a dream:
Alone I stood, by a babbling brook,
And held out my empty arms,
When all around me stardust fell
Like shiny magic charms.
I shook my head, to clear my mind,
And wonder what they are...
The dream had flown,
And in my heart, was, my Wishing Star

Lauretta Anamta

"Grandpa, I'll Try, I'll Try"

Mama said, "Son, he's just sleeping
And we've come to say goodbye,"
There are some things I don't understand
But Grandpa, "I'll try, I'll try."

I remember so well one summer
It wasn't that long ago,
We watched the boats on the river
And Grandpa said, "I love you so."

You walk was a little slower,
But your smile was still there,
As we sat in the park together
You whispered this very prayer.

You said, "Son, always remember
To hold your head up high,
Keep your dreams before you —
Be the best in whatever you try."

It's going to be lonely without you
As time it passes by,
I'll keep my dreams before me
And Grandpa, "I'll try, I'll try."

Jannette Neal

Ode To Bandit

As I look toward the heavens, the gray and white fluffiness float by a pale blue background. For a moment the cold window pane reflects the colors of fall and my mind lets go of the gripping sadness within me; I hear the sound of the rolling waves when we played and splashed in the cool water as he ran by my side. Tears pouring down my cheeks suddenly brings me back to the reality that death claims us all, needlessly, carelessly, with no thought of such pain it causes. He was my best friend, my happiness, my protector, my beautiful black dog - my Bandit.

Elva P. Black

What Does It Mean

The love of art, it's in all of us,
Around we go and make a fuss,
Not understanding what is seen,
Only the Artist knows what it means,

How the Artist talks in slang,
In a gallery, his paintings hang,
In his heart, such gladness and sorrow,
Will there be a new tomorrow,

All his paintings bright and dull,
Hang in gallery, on sober walls,
There they'll hang, until there sold,
Or until they become quiet old,

The love of art, it's in all of us,
Around we go and make a fuss,
Not understanding what is seen,
Only the Artist knows what it means.

Donelda Smith

Our World

Think about our world
As a huge revolving ball,
An airport, a highway
Many crowded shopping malls.

Horrendous pollution
Deadly wars causing despair,
Increasing extinction
We are so cruel, don't we care?

Intense propaganda
Causing indoctrination,
People being brain washed
With no justification.

Rain forests being burned
Killing our fresh air each day,
Animals are destroyed
Lets find joy another way.

We must look at the trees
Baby blue hypnotic skies,
Amazing animals
This is the time to be wise.

Jennifer Woods

A Journey

Deep in the mist, I fell within
As I follow the stream
Never to find an end

Beyond the horizon, I have reached
As I gaze to the heavens
To find a sign of peace

A breeze of warmth, fills my soul
A new essence appears
But what will unfold

Darkness I fear, to which I linger
So I keep a flame
To take away evil

As I walk along, it's a dusty path
But what I've discovered
Will never turn me back.

Arlene Rout

The Departing Train

Tender tears trickled down her face,
As the departing train won the race.
She waved till it was out of sight,
Prayed her father would be alright.
Reached home and faked a smile,
Thought of dad all the while.
Dreamt of him through the night,
Lost his presence in broad daylight.
Came his call the following eve,
She heard his voice and longed to weep.
She arrested her tears for a cause,
She didn't want daddy's eyes to gloss.

Ruqya Begum

Ski Time

Fast asleep, wrapped in warmth,
as the silence screams his name.
He rises with patience,
and fights for energy.

Into the cold and onto the lake.
A moment of silence,
for he plans his attack.

In a second he's up
with the water at his feet
and the world in his palm.
Grace and beauty fight the cold.
With his mind on a single task
nothing can stop him but fear.

The set is done and success is obvious.
As the boats return
a silence is heard, but nothing is done.
Not a word is spoken.
Not a step is taken.

A moment of contempt
then back to the water, for **Champions**
Never Rest!

Paul Macdonald

Untitled

spinning, weaving
creating
in your absence
the genesis of Our life

Colleen E. Donovan

Lost Child

The candle breaks the midnight hour,
As thoughts disrupt the night,
Alone I sit and contemplate,
In search of inner sight.

Tormented moments long ago,
Exist within the mind,
They fester in a hollow place,
The spirit left behind.

The child has lost her childhood.
The woman has evolved.
The darkened places I have been,
Will never be resolved.

Alanna Higgins

Stormy Sunset

Customary retirement
at 60 or thereafter.
I should have entered a peaceful time
enjoying leisurely things:
should travel and visit,
go to hit shows,
play euchre, cribbage or bingo.
No worries, no hurries.
But what do I do?
I strive to hold the day.
Too many questions unanswered,
too many little things bypassed before.
My heart is tumbling,
lost in unexpected storm
at Life's only sunset.

Anna Plesums

At The Restaurant

Sitting across from you
At the restaurant
I felt your eyes
Searching mine...
...What was it?
Curiosity or
The silent cry
Of a heart
Starving for love?...

In a hurry
Without finding the answer
My heart followed
Into the unknown...
Will the broken hopes
Be put together?
Or, will another link be attached
To the chain?

Lisa DeBozy

First Snow

Last night it came as silently
As dreams come in the night;
Concealing drab and ugly things,
And hiding ground from sight.

And all is white and silent now,
As one in slumber sweet!
White velvet drapes the rolling hills,
And beautifies the street.

How strange that only yesterday
The world seemed dark and sad;
Yet now my soul rejoices
To see the hills snowclad!

Evelyn Madden Tracy

Violence

What Future can there
Be for me
Amongst these pots and
Dishes
Aimed mercilessly with
Anger's wrath
They lie motionless upon
The floor
As flour and sugar hurled
Endlessly
Waits in silence
To my beck and call
To clean the mess of
Shattered dreams
With whitewashed hands
Oh little child
Sweet innocence of life
That you should have
To bear this thing called
VIOLENCE.

Avaleen McIntosh

I Swear

I have nothing to say to you
Because I have nothing to say
Not that I'm swayed
By your eyes
By your smile
By the fact that you can make me laugh
And that I like that in a man
Not that I'm influenced
Bowled over
By your little ways of doing things
Your clothes
Your walk
Your all together put together air
I swear
I'm simply blanked
By the panic
In my own mind
By the fear of hurt
In my heart...

Jean Elizabeth Eugene

Just Imagine

Your dreams coming true
Being on top of the world
For a minute or two

For once my thoughts
That were written

Got published and
Established my way
To a bright, big beautiful day

Now that the pavement was paved
Opportunities cascaded my way

Just imagine
Your dreams coming true
If only for a minute or two

Being on top of the world
Living your dream

Just imagine
How true it can be

Just Imagine

Yvonne Olofsson

Fifty Nine Plus One

A gentle breeze
bent the summer grass
and ruffled the leaves;
the afternoon sun
smiled upon us,
as we said goodbye.
We wept.
We heard her voice,
reminding us,
that she had gone ahead,
and that today
she was free.
She was fifty nine plus one.

Jim Hill

From A Travelling Poet

From one womb of a mother
born the twenty-two of us
and we survives
the rugs and blues.

Still we shares the joy of life
with the fourteen of us
left behind
by beloveds laid in tomb.

In the land of maple leaf
I saw my little sister
Walking fast thou she was
Stranger in the snow
crying out silently.

Winter, Spring, Summer and Fall
as you come and go
I see again my dear sister
no more tears in her eyes
but the joy of being
a Canadian forever.

Darius Alc. Evangelista

Why?

A baby. His tiny buttocks
burned and scarred by cigarettes.
Abused; unloved; unwanted;

Too small to hurt!

Snatched from his teenage mother,
and taken to live with strangers.
Alone; Afraid; and Helpless;

A child. At nine he took
a gun and shot a girl.
She was no threat
to him; but she was
Loved; Secure; and sheltered;

Too young to kill!

A victim. Lying on his belly
in an alley;
his small head smashed
and silenced by a bullet.
At peace at last.

Too young to die!

Carole Pizzolante

Candles

Love is like two candles
burning side by side.

Full of flame and beauty
with nothing left to hide.

One is burning brightly
while the other waits to die.

So never fall in love
for you'll feel
the happiness I felt.

Then one day before your eyes
you'll see the candles melt.

Tracy Goudreault

Young Love

I was told by a younger,
but some what a man
to not do what he did
he betrayed and he ran

He went on for hours
of dreams left behind
then stopped rather suddenly
and asked if I'd mind.

He told me to never stop
dreaming of love,
that someday I'd find
my free flying dove.

When that thunder rolls
and the lightening strikes
hold on to your dreams
'cause you'll all be all right.

So if I was ever told
to stop dreaming of love
I'd simply reply,
"It's an honour I dream not of."

Heather Donaldson

Life

Life is strange in so many ways,
But to live life to the fullest.
You must learn to face many things,
Also learn to except reality.
No matter what the turn,
If you or someone else has wronged.
Then we should admit our mistakes,
Instead of blaming others.
And thinking we're so great,
Life is strange in so many ways.
It deals you a good hand,
And maybe a bad one to.
But face what life hands out,
And learn to give and not
always take.

Theresa A. Cormier

Emotions

Should I be sad,
Could it be mad?
I'm so mad
Of being sad;
Or because of sad
to get mad.
I don't know that
But... I do know
... that I'm going crazy!!!

Khoa Nguyen

This Rose

He put the rose
By her side,
The way she laughed
Still in his mind.

He had placed a rose
Each time she slept,
And she pressed
Each one he left.

Then one night
She went to sleep
And never awoke,
This rose ... he'd keep.

Desi Harcourt

Our Hazelnut Tree

Our tree was shared
by the steller's jay,
Who has so brilliant plumage
blue in every way,
And screeched his song
through out the day,
As it picked the hazelnut
and peeled the husk,
Like an apple corer,
Then thumping away
at the shell in his way,
Extracting the nut on his way,
swallowing it
as much to say,
Thank you for sharing
the hazelnut tree,
And I will sing another
song for thee,
Flying off into the sunset
as happy as can be.

G. Misewich

Ways Of Looking At The Same

English men
Call it love making
Suggesting
Achievement through effort;

Baganda children
Refer to it as sex playing
Expressing
Pleasure through sport;

Take the Gujarati when
They talk of time-wasting
Signifying
Something to which to resort;

So one in some den
Might name it something - doing
Meaning
Enjoyment of some sort.

Gerald M. M. Matovu

The Power And The Glory

Presuming I was God
I raised my potent rod
And summoned up my might
To change each wrong to right
And Lo! A white dove lit
Upon my rod - and s
h
i
t
.

Jim Reid

Childhood Anxiety

Awake! Look around you,
Can you hear the children
Crying out from hunger?

Ribs sticking out,
Faces drawn and sad,
Eyes sunken with despair.
Stomachs so distended
Bodies frail and weak.

Can you see the children
Suffering from abuse?

Orphaned, destitute, despised
Locked away, forgotten!
Their rights violated
Their helplessness ignored!

Can you feel the plight
Of those children left to die?

They are frightened, scared and lonely,
Unable to smile or laugh.
Lives devoid of meaning,
Beings deprived of love!

Etty A. Cameron

She is different
Certainly not everyone else
I've burned away the plastic
over my eyes
I know what beats
Beats in her heart

You're not everyone else
That thing that is everything
only walks city streets
But you lie with me on the sand

That makes you different
So different you're real
But mostly you're real
because you're not me

And I see more clearly who it
is that I am
When I see you're not me and
certainly not everyone else

John McCurdy

Winter

She, like Midas
Changes with a touch
The once warm surroundings
Turn cold in her clutch.

The once fertile lands
now reject vegetation
The trees so grand
Disrobe in humiliation.

The sun seemingly supreme
Retreats behind clouds
Under her regime;
Wearing a shroud.

Even the mighty sea
Feels her icy grip
Unable to flow free
A large frozen strip.

Marion MacDonald

A Poem Story Of Jesus

About two thousand years ago,
CHRIST our Lord and Savior was born,
In a lowly manger in Bethlehem.
He was the poorest of the poor,
But 3 Magi Kings went to worship Him,
Whose LIFE left to us a legacy,
Far greater than the pomp and power,
Of potentates and kings.
He lived and preached by example,
The Gospel of Christianity:
Love, Faith, Hope and Penitence.
He loved all men and proved it by
His Crucifixion in Calvary!
Yes He DIED, but in all history,
Only HE ALONE ROSE FROM THE DEAD,
Affirming His DIVINITY!
Empires and kingdoms have been
Crushed to earth since then;
But until now and forevermore,
CHRIST our Lord reigns supreme!

Filomeno L. Pacis

The Dream

Color of the earth
Color of the skies
Color of my dreams
Color of your eyes

Love in moonlit calm
Time ... and no end
Sleepy tenderness
Softness of your hands

Wind across the streets
You, and me, and night
Whispers of the trees
Shadows outside ...

Sound of broken glass
Something very new
Sudden morning light—
Life without you.

Olga M. Verbovskaya

Think

Think about a rainbow
Colours girdling the sky
Think of how a garden
Delights both nose and eye
Think about Australia
Ayers Rock, Emu, Kangaroo
Think about America
Niagara, New York, Angelou
Think about South Africa
Tutu, Mandela and De Klerk
Think of peace and harmony
As the end result of work
Think about all nations
Rich in different shades of skin
Think about our children
And the world they're growing in
Think of Yugoslavia and Rwanda too
Think about it please,
Please think

Alwyn Lewis

The Walk

I could hear my feet
crunching the leaves.
A cold wind was blowing,
but I didn't care.
I saw a squirrel run up
a big oak tree.
Fall was here,
it was easy to tell.
Red, yellow, orange,
the leaves were the color
of fire.
Geese above me formed
a V to prove that
winter was close.
As I reached home
I heard summer say
goodbye.

Serena Kolida

"Daddy, Who Is God?"

My little girl asks of me,
"Daddy, who is God?"
And I answer, faithfully,
As off she starts to nod.

He's the Father of us all,
He lives up in the sky,
And He makes the raindrops fall,
His wind shakes trees so high.

He wakes the sun to rise at morn,
He takes the moon out at night,
When you and your sister were born
He helped you through, all right.

Those big blue eyes listen well
But, gently, start to close...
Another time, the rest I'll tell;
I smile and kiss her nose.

Goodnight, my little bunny,
Sleep tight, one day you'll know,
You are such a little honey,
He and I both love you so.

Douglas Peters

The Terrorist

HATE is my Master
Despair is my Hero
Love is but a shadow
WANT is the ghost who knocks at my door

Decay is my future, for no reason do
I possess, lost in the midst of chaos
and misunderstanding;
GREATNESS but for a fleeting moment;
The pen that lays asleep
never to move again
dried ink and paper abound,
no hand to move the pen in the hope of
things that could be;
the Beast is born to lay the land awaste
no drop of reason to quell
its consuming appetite of decay...

Tom Hennessey

Progress

I watched six men
Dig a trench today
With pick and shovel
Quietly, with steady pace
Carefully, placing the earth
In a neat pile beside the hole
Ready to fill again.

I couldn't help but compare
Two, maybe three men
A jack hammer, loader, truck
Traffic blocked
Noise, dust flying
Diesel emissions
Job done quickly.

Three times the cost
Less men employed
Progress?

Marilyn Spilchen

The Vicissitudes Of Life

Wedding bells ring in array,
Divorce suit filed in sorrow:
A hero today,
A prisoner tomorrow.

Discords unpleasant in strife,
Concords applauded in life:
Fading health there,
Absolute joy here.

Neither brag of your position,
Nor brood over your plight:
Remembering the vicissitudes of life,
Only pray for His will.

John M. Mensah

Let There Be Peace

Let there be peace in this world
Don't turn your back right now,
We have to make a better place
So our children will know how.

Let there be peace in this world
No more war in the country side,
We have to stand up strong and tall
Our strengths we cannot hide.

Let there be peace in this world
No more hate between race and creed,
Let's join each other, hand in hand
The friendships, we all need.

Let there be peace in this world
Let's one and all unite,
Save our world for our little ones
Then they won't have to fight.

Let there be peace in this world
Is there such a thing,
Cause if there is, let's do it now
What beauty peace can bring.

Norma Kopp

A Rose

A single rose spells LOVE
From the heart of God
It falls from heaven
Into your hands
And makes you smile.

Alacia Star Holdershaw

The Foothold

She's fed-up already with D-day
down at the rumour-mill
names and pictures
the cynical edge
of newspapering
over the gaps
which are the dead.

Across the beaches
Normandy that morning
might have seemed like hell
at least no breeze
or the dreaded Nazis
like giants astride
the raped land of France.

Alan C. Kerse

Amoureux

The family leaves,
drift past my window.
The raindrops fall,
on you below.

I hear your voice,
Whisper my name.
My heart cries out,
I turn away.

The cold, harsh winds,
bring winter's snow.
I see your face,
of long ago.

The sun-burned hands,
I used to hold.
Now far away,
feelings untold.

Julie Binet

A Cry For Help

The pain is more than I can
endure
It's stabbing, piercing
through my skin
Gnawing at my soul
My heart aches
I plead for help, though
My cries are silent and left
unheard
I am trapped and saddened -
Saddened by what has been
and what has come to be
When will the agony end
Who is it who will set me free-
free from this chamber of mercy
I cannot hold on much —
I am falling

Please... somebody.
Anybody!
Please save me.

Tracey Connors

Love

I love you so much,
even more than life itself.
I wish I possessed your picture,
and had it lain upon my shelf.
For I'd climb the highest mountain,
or swim the deepest sea.
If only you could be here,
next to me.

J. Michael Francis

Lust Of Love

Alone in a dark, stormy night,
Ever ready for the losing fight.
Cold and hungry, struggling for leaven,
Finally faced the absence of heaven.

The sweet tone and angelic face,
Long gone, still full of grace.
To the open arms of the sky,
Something is missing and I can't fly.

Tired and spent from all walks of life,
Yet eager to see the distant light.
There, reached a hand, a hand so sure,
Cherished me with love so pure.

Full of hopes and dreams to be free,
Kaleidoscope of colors sparkling spree.
A friendly toast to my lonely heart,
Never again we'll be apart.

The hollow emptiness from above,
Still seeking for the burden of love.
I bid hatred a last goodbye,
I'm strong, I'm a survivor, I will not cry.

Jennifer So

Eternally

The years roll on
Every second, minute and hour
Will pass on into the future
The future for every mortal being
For you, for me
Through the ages of eternity
The rain will fall in showers
Or in sprinkles
The sun will blaze and burn
Making the earth brown and dry
The seasons will change each year
Spring, Summer, Autumn, Winter
Covering the land with their cloaks of
Green, Gold, bronze and soft snow
Through the years in all these changes
I will be there by your side
Reaching out, feeling for your hand
To hold in mine
Eternally.

Yolanda Marie Nienhaus

Alone

Lost is how you are feeling
Facing the world alone
You think you can't go on
Can't survive

But dreams are hard to follow
You do all that you can
Even when the world is too much to take
You finally realize
You can make it on your own

Your sorrow melts away
And you finally see the truth
There is always tomorrow
Where you can face the world
Alone

Carla Cormack

"Self Turmoil"

There are times in our lives when we
feel good about decisions we make.

As time creeps on we sometimes realize
our earlier decisions we'll break.

People change, feeling are not as strong.
What was so right before is now so wrong
We must go ahead and alter the course
Before we die inside from remorse.
Our feelings to others can change.
So our lives we should rearrange
To feel a empty inside
Because you have denied,
To take and follow your heart.
This will someday tear you apart.

Cecelia A. Patry

Peace

People here, people there,
Fight for peace everywhere.
To see the world clear and free,
To see the world filled with glee.

To fight, to win strong and tall,
To see an ending once and for all.
And what shall we fight about,
Colour, people and all and out.

Stop the war, start the peace,
To find our people finally at ease.
For now happy, peace began.
Not to long it will have ran

Anastasia-Maria Aravantinos

Untitled

Insects that crawl,
Flowers that grow,
Grass that tickles,
and cold, bright snow;

Trees so tremendous,
Water that's wet,
Jello that jiggles,
and that's not all yet;

Stars that twinkle,
The sun that's so bright,
The moon's out of reach,
but wish hard and you might...

Bubbles that pop!
What a surprise,
It's a wondrous world,
through a child's eyes.

Lee-Ann Mascis

Inspiration

Looking for inspiration.
For words of meaning that would rhyme.
Reading books of poetry,
that's how I'll spend my time.

Searching high and searching low,
searching everywhere I went,
But inspiration could not be found,
to think the hours that I've spent.

And then I said; "Oh, I give up,
forget it, let it be."
When the search was over,
Wouldn't you know.
Inspiration came to me.

Lucy De Groot

Mother

A mother is someone
For a child to look up to
And someone to be proud of
Their whole life through

And as life goes on
We know you will do your best
And there will be times
When your patience
Will be put to the test

So remember the word mother
And what it is meant to be
And in closing I will tell you
What it means to me

M is for much
O is for love
T is for them
H is for her or him
E is for everyone
R is for ever

Doug Tremblay

Thank You God

Thank you God ....
For giving me the eyes to see
The hands to feel
The tongue so that I can taste
And a mind to think

Thank you God
For giving me the mouth to speak
Ears to hear
Fear to walk and run
Lungs to breathe

And thank you God ...
For giving me a heart so that I
can LOVE and FORGIVE

Carmel B. Celosia

Recall Me,

Recall me,
For I will not speak nor walk no more,
I was swept away by the winds of war.
I was washed away by the tide,
Of cold and merciless pride.

Recall me,
For I have fought the enemy within,
Wrestled with the Emperor of Sin.
But during the battle I lost,
And paid the morbid cost.

Recall me,
For I am an image that's old and rotten,
A burden that's better forgotten.
One can never lose my pain,
An eternal, loathsome stain.

Recall me,
For my sacrifice was not in vain,
An act of honour it shall remain.
All of my joys given up for thee,
Remember my sorrow, recall me.

George Turchanyi

Untitled

There's no future in the past
Freedom will never last
Environment is so vast
Have we achieved this huge task?
Love being no. 1 priority
Voting gets the majority
Who has the authority
To believe in all that jazz.
Man must learn to smell the flowers
Have patience for many hours
Knowing well the chore ahead
Maybe being environmentally dead
Seeking sweet tranquility
Peace of mind within thyself
Acknowledge the wanting one by one
And knowing the difference
When it is done

Edwin Koch

Dawsyn

She is a bundle of joy
fun and full of life;
maybe someday,
she will be somebody's wife.

Right now she had no worries
no aches, or pains;
But further in life
there will be much to gain.

About life's trials
and temptations,
But she will have
a firm foundation.

She'll always have a home,
when the going gets tough;
And when things
just seem a little too rough.

But she's so cuddly and cute
and that's a long time away,
Just thank God
and remember to pray.

Tanya Penner

Breath

Breath - given freely
gently; easy, requiring little effort,
of, or bearing little weight

Breath - fills, occupies completely
supply; as much as desired,
full, containing as much
as possible.

Breath - exhale
Breathe out; give, pass off as vapor
complete, perfect, finished, ended.

Breath - life
time of it's lasting, history of such
existence,
way of living, vigor, vivacity.

Breath - mine, belonging to me,
force, strength; energy,
lively, gay, sprightly,
me - and my breath.

Beverley A. Matchett

Scented Candles

Scented candles
glow aromatic mirages

Fire Goddess grows wild
above the wick-an coven

A new religion burns
in the darkness
roars meaning that makes
scents to me

brought to the lilac bush
during a Canadian February
or to Gramm's kitchen
where she made vanilla ice cream
in July
to blueberry fields behind Gramp's shed

but the cinnamon in my apple cider
sitting around the Christmas tree
with you
-my mantra

Brenda Biron

Kismet

To Earth we come,
God's gift of joy...
for Mum and Dad,
a girl or boy.

We tread the path,
whe'r near or far,
discovering
life's shining star.

But when time stills
in sorrow's wake,
we must return...
for Heaven's sake!

Bryan Moore

Pollution Of The Land

God gave us the birds and the bees
He blessed us with beautiful trees
With land so rich and grass to green
A beautiful sight indeed
But as decades and years went by
Our land began to die
With chemical abuse we did pollute
The rivers and the sky
Our sun is now hot and dry
And its rays are harmful to our eyes
And not to speak of the cancers we treat
Because of our beautiful sky

Debbie Thibeault Proulx

Two Minutes Silence

And we around the cenotaph,
Honouring one and all,
Hang our heads respectfully
And unashamedly cry;
while they who paid the price
For peace, whose courage we recall,
In wreathes symbolic circle
Entwined forever lie;
Their spirits ever warmed by flame,
And those of us who mourn;
A silent tribute to the men
We dare to call unknown.

Selina Pimblett

'Gentle Soldier'

The first time I saw him
he was shy and tender,
like a gentle breeze of summer,
so young, so tall, so beautiful,
this soldier boy.
The next time I saw him
gone was all the tenderness,
his eyes were full of bitterness,
scars of war upon his face,
he hated war and what he'd done,
wasn't meant to fire a gun
this gentle boy.
The last time I saw him
his face was quiet in its peace,
a medal pinned upon his breast
for killing someone else's son,
this boy who couldn't fire a gun
was laid to rest.

Anne W. Robertson

Untitled

lovely house neglected
head is of the water sprite
it comes to life at night

the next door neighbor
hears her cry comes to the rescue
nearly dies two bright eyes
in her head

She looks like some one
who came back from the dead

he flies home and takes a jar
and crawls

Into bed once more
draws his bed clothes
up to his chin
half sodden on the bottle of gin.

Anne Crehan

Punctuations:

A fly cleaning
his wings,
A cat preening
and things
Like that,

Are drawing strings
and repeating,
Are bearing rings
and discreting
Our chat,
And dust flies revealing meaning.

D. Kenning

Say It!

Say what you have to say
(I could never stand not knowing);
Better words than silence
(Even if it means you're going);
So say it, say it, say it
(Better I know that not know);
Say what you have to say -
(Please God, don't let him go).

Patricia Hughes Scott

My Mother's Love

Strong, gentle arms,
holding me close.
Comforting me,
where I need her love the most.
My beautiful eyes,
she would say,
need no tears.
Telling me,
she would help me battle,
all my fears.
Her contagious laughter,
and beautiful ways,
in my heart,
I know,
my mother's precious love,
will always stay.

Sara Devecseri

The Journey

O Moon
how bright you are tonight
casting sparkles
in my lady's eyes.
We lie entranced,
Roses gleam
beneath your light.

Whispers sweetly
swim ashore,
o night
how dark you could have been
if love
had passed us by
again.

Sail on
the compass is set
your heart is at the helm
tonight
may the stars lead you
into day.

Gerald J. LaTouche

To Tony (My First Grandson)

You came we saw, you conquered,
How can I explain,
Among the joy and happiness,
I felt a little pain,
No one knew what I was thinking,
Or how I felt inside,
I felt my heart was breaking,
Tho it was filled with pride,
I just wish your other grandmother,
Could have seen your lovely face,
And now and then held you in her arms,
In a warm loving embrace,
But she will be watching over you.
She will keep you from all harm,
As you make your way through life,
May you inherit all her charm,
Tony when you read this poem,
Here is my one piece of advice,
It's nice to be important,
But it's more important to be nice,

From you loving granddad.

W. R. Skidmore

"Wind"

Hear the wind blowing and
howling
Trees swaying and bowing
Dancing to the minuet of the
wind
Yet, I do not hear the birds
sing
See the sky dull and grey
Looks like snow or rain is on
the way
Still the wind has its
say

Irene Edstrom

Purity

Please don't turn your face away,
I am a child of God,
My face is hideous, but, inside,
I'm not so very odd.
My sisters and my brothers,
They all love me from the heart
Knowing I won't be here that long,
And then we'll have to part.
I see your cringe and turn away
Whenever they take me out to play,
It really hurts me deep inside
But it's impossible to confide,
My lips can form a letter round,
But nothing else, I have no sound,
My legs no pain, for they are dead,
My father lifts me into bed,
I lay my twisted face to sleep
To dream, a beautiful dream so deep.
When my face untwisted, I'll walk
straight,
My soul clean, shining, to the heavenly
gate.

Margaret Laws

"Continuity - I"

People move around me
I am alone

People laughed beside me
I am in tears

People shouted cried out loud
I was whispering

People talking - voices heard
I was silent

People come to and fro
I was gone...

Ethelrida Zabala-Laxa

Live On

Do not stand at my grave and weep;
I am not there. I do not sleep.
I am a thousand winds that blow.
I am the diamond glints on snow.
I am the sunlight on ripened grain.
I am the gentle Autumn's rain.
When you awaken in the morning's hush;
I am the swift uplifting rush
Of quiet birds in circled flight.
I am the soft stars that shine at night.
Do not stand at my grave and cry;
I am not there. I did not die.

Susan Welch

The Glories Of Nature

Early on a summer's eve,
I did gaze on distant hills
Watching shades of different hues,
Enough to make your heart stand still,

First the rosy sunset shone,
And the hills did softer glow,
Yellow, orange, purple, black,
And they then did darker glow,

Twilight was soon drawing nigh,
And the panorama changed,
For it was then I did see,
Shades from blue to purple range,

When as even tide drew nigh,
The hills turned to a shaded black,
The sun had set on glory fair.
As it travelled on its endless track,

Even as I still did gaze
Everything was hushed and still,
And it seemed a silent prayer,
Issued from the darkened hills.

Gladys Kadatz

Untitled

There's a face in the mirror
I don't recognize.
She looks familiar,
but who can she possibly be?

Is this a reflection of who
I am, or what I have become?
Who can she be, this face
staring back at me?

Do I like her? I'm not sure.
The smile still seems clean and pure.
But the eyes; they're not the same,
Do they hide some kind of pain?

It seems that not so long ago
life was easy, simple, fun.
Now there are so many complications
I'm not sure what I've done.

The easy decisions, all the blacks and whites
have become one large shade of grey.
And the decisions, my God! Who needs
them anyway?!

Who is this face staring back at me?

Terri-Lyn Love

Untitled

Hey Carrie, my lovely wife
I dream of you all on through the night
and when I wake and you're not here
I close my eyes to wish you near
I walk all day, all alone
passing by thee only phone
I wait all day for the night
So I could hear you say goodnight
As the days are passing by
I always keep you in my mind.
I wish I could see your lovely smile,
even if it's for only a while.
I hope that now you can see,
How great my love is for you, CARRIE.
No matter when or where I go
I'll always love you with my heart and soul.

Craig Rubletz

The Serpent

The morbid pleasures of life excite me
I drown in self-content
I bleed happiness
I crave misery
such confusion
yesterday I was thunder,
today I am a tree
maybe tomorrow I'll be nothing
perhaps I'll cease to live
One day, I hope to fly
One day, I hope to meet the sun
Other days, I wish to end,
everything I know

What I know is nothing
What I've learnt, I don't remember
Significance has no meaning
when meaning is not important
Next week, I think I'll have
Saturday over for tea.

Shawna Clark

Simply Me

Just a speck in the universe
I feel it is a must
To try and do much better,
And become a particle of dust.

And if I could graduate to that
I would like to see
If I could at least attain
The status of a flea.

Maybe some day per chance
If I could get it right,
I would become a shining star
You look up to every night.

But if I could reach my highest goal
How perfect it would be,
To have a second chance
At simply being me.....

Lynn Barany

Treasures

Once I found a buried treasure,
I found it in the sand,
And when I brought it to my family,
They all cried out, "It's grand!"

Treasures are also other things,
Not just buried chests;
To little boys - a cowboy hat,
To little girls - a dress.

To men, treasures are other things, still,
Like women, money and cars;
To women - children and diamond rings;
To grandfathers - big cigars.

To me, some treasures are part of nature,
Like grass, sparkling with dew,
But my greatest treasure of them all,
Is being loved by you.

Carol McCleary

Love To Love

'I love to love lovers of love
I hate to hate haters of hate
Haters of hate loves to love
Lovers of love loves haters of hate
Lover of hater of hate loves love
Hater of hate loves lovers of love
Hater hates haters of love
Lover hates haters of love
Lover loves haters of hate
Hater of hate loves lovers of love
Love hates hater of love
Love loves hater of hate
Hate loves lovers of hate
Love loves lover of love
Hate hates hater of hate
Hate hater hates hate
Love lover loves love
Lover of love loves love
Hater of hate hates hate
Love loves lovers, Hate hates haters'.

U. N. Fabian

Why

Ever since the divorce,
I have felt so much force.
He used to be so nice,
now he is as cold as ice.
I haven't heard from him for so long,
it seems to me he lives in Hong Kong.
Why doesn't he love me any more,
am I really that much of a chore.
He would rather be playing ball,
than catching me when I fall.
What did I ever do to my Dad,
Could I have ever done anything that bad.
He has never ever been there,
and to me that is not very fair.
The thing most important to me,
is that at least I know my Mom loves me.
My Mom has always been there,
and I know that she will always care.

Janet Peterson

I'm The Victim

I'm the victim of such a thing,
I hear the word, singing in my head,
bullying, bullying.
As I walk to school each-day,
I wonder what words the Bully will say,
Or how much money I'll have to pay.
No-one's my friend,
It's as if I'm on my own, in a dead end.
If I don't bring the money,
He won't think it's funny.
A punch here, a punch there,
He doesn't care,
He's a Bully.

Satveer Nijjar

A Second Grader's Hit List

That boy bugs me.
I hope he falls out of a tree.

That girl hates me.
I hope *she* falls out of a tree.

Those kids are laughing at me.
I hope *they* fall out of a tree.

Gee. I hope I don't run out of trees.

Lindsey Carmichael

When I Think About You

When I think about you,
I know we are right,
to be with each other,
every day
every night,
I will always love you,
but will you love me,
only time will tell,
I'll wait and see,
When we find each other,
we'll know there's no other,
For you and me,
were meant to be,
When I think about you,
I know it's true,
but this is only
When I think about you.

Tannis Barnes

Realization

As you gently weep,
I know you hurt within,
You say not a peep,
My mistakes are classed as sin,

I want all you forgiveness,
And all your gentleness,
But I am afraid to ask,
Due to my great mask,

Your love is always here,
Asking for it is up to me,
I want to feel you near,
I love you can't you see.

To me, you are what I need,
You are with me, I asked you to lead.

Amen

Wesley Trenholm

A Second Glance

Now that I am an adult
I look back at all the years
Those times we really struggled
yet you still hid all your fears
We had so much fun together
even though some times were hard
You always showed those smiles
You always played the right card

Now that I am a mother
your loving ways show through
The way I care for my son
is the way you cared for me too
You always have been there for me
and now that we are apart
A part of you is always there
And I love you with all my heart

Rhonda Bailey

Best Friends

Dedicated to Lori and Cheryl

Best of friends, side by side;
Inseparable in death as in life.
But, oh how this loss scars our hearts
Cutting deep and twists the knife.

So keep each other safe and warm
As you travel the great beyond.
Remember us as we remember you
And keep safe the spiritual bond.

Suzanne Sarty

Nana And Grandpa

Nana and Grandpa
I miss you so much
The sound of your voices
The warmth of your touch.

I can still hear your laughter
When I'm reminiscing
I can still taste your short bread
that we're all dearly missing.

Nana and Grandpa
My heart is still aching
Each day that goes by
My heart keeps on breaking

I know there'll come a day
When we're all reunited
When the tears are all gone
And the pain has subsided
But until that day comes
You'll be in our prayers,
And just know that we love you,
And a loved one still cares.

Dedicated to John and Theresa Thomson

Kathleen Clowe

"A Sister's Love"

When I look in the mirror
I see her face
When I am happy
I see her smile
When I cry
I see her tears
She is my inspiration
My life
The armour in my deepest fears
She is the light that show's me the way
To live my life with a new golden day
Together or apart
We are joined heart to heart
A bond even death couldn't break
As a reminder, God created the sky,
So as I look up I see the reflection of her
deep blue eyes.

Johanne Beaudry

The Queen Of Rain

If you're the queen of sunshine,
I shall be the queen of rain.
You bring joy and happiness,
I shall bring the pain.

I'll take it upon myself,
To make all people hurt.
I cannot stop now.
It will only get worse.

So close your windows,
And lock your doors,
Before the queen of rain,
Chooses on you to pour.

Don't let her get inside,
And tear your heart to pieces.
Stay away from the queen of rain,
And hope that she soon ceases.

Wait until the queen of sunshine,
Is shining in the sky.
Then you can come out,
For the queen of rain will die.

Deirdre Main

Shelf Memories

As I took the Photo Album out
I studied the pictures so
I took a look back down memory lane
Oh so many years ago

How time passes by so quickly
Without even giving it a thought
A picture of me as a child
clutching a teddy bear
The next picture a child I am not

The next picture reveals my wedding Day
Oh what a dream come true
The day I expressed my love for you
The day I said I do

I turn the pages of my book
to see a beautiful babe in blue
But don't stop there,
we have more love to share
three girls come into view

A family portrait to end it all
and I close my book up tight
Back on the shelf, I rest it there, the
memories of my life.

Jane Bible

Petals On A Rose

When I need someone to talk to
I turn and you are there,
When I need someone to listen,
You understand and care.

When I need someone to laugh with
Your laughter warms me through,
When I need someone to love
There isn't anyone but you.

Our love is shared through feelings
Although no - one really knows,
It's like we've grown together
Just like petals on a rose.

Tammy Lynn Gallant

'Search'

Over green mountains
  I walk,
Seeking the trace of
  your feet;
In the beautiful woods
  I wander,
Straining to glimpse
  your face;
In the blue waters
  of the lake I wade,
Hoping to see at least
  your image;
My pursuit, an
  endless penance,
Like seeking a mirage
  in a desert;
You, always just
  beyond reach,
And yet there is no respite for me...;
But to continue with this endless quest...

Niti Chopra

The Day I Lost My Smile

I watched you laugh
I watched you cry
But when I said goodbye something
Inside me died. This was
The day I lost my smile.
When ever I think of you I cry
for it makes me want to lay
down and die.
The years I spent with you
Our love grew. I'll miss you so
It hurt to let go.
The pain it hurts so much
I miss your smile and warmth
of your touch.
Someday we may meet again
this is when my crying will end.

Richard D. Kosinski

Untitled

When I was a young child,
I wondered what would be;
and as I grow to a young dame,
I know I will never see.

What I have looked for, all of my life
is what I will not find,
and the day I let my eyes rest
I'll get my piece of mind.

No one can force an outcome;
what will be, will be.
If you do not trust in that;
Oh! What a fool we'll see.

Regan Forsyth

House Of Cards

This is where I live:
In a house of cards.
Intrigued by the wisdom,
The Jacks are my guards.

My only obsession:
To turn up an Ace.
The dealer can shuffle
An incredible pace.

The chips they do fly;
The money does flow.
I sit in my courts;
The ante is low.

My foes they do lance me
With stern face of poker.
Life is a gamble,
And I am the Joker.

Wilma Pidhayny

Untitled

The under dog never loses
In his own way
He always wins
He can not be taken lightly
He disarms
With his all covering laugh
He'll make it in the world
Because
He has nothing to lose
And everything to gain

Mike Hanna

I Do

Do you see the hurt,
in my eyes, in my heart
in my soul, in my mind,
I do.

Do you share the fear,
of the daytime hours
of the people you love
of future encounters
of giving up,
I do.

Do you know the welcoming,
of the night
of the loneliness
of the world in your mind
of a corner
of wanting death's door to open,
I do.

To think, never turned into doing.

I live, I endure, I survive,
I am alive.

Mel Moser

Every Way

She was with me last night
in my heart
my love
in my head
my thoughts
in my fingers
my touch
in my mouth
my taste
in my ears
my hearing
in my eyes
my sight
in all my body
my very existence.

Adrian Bolsmann

Poems

I love to tell my stories
In the form of poems
I love to tell of glories
In every shape or form...

Poems are things of beauty
When expressed sincerely
Poems are very poignant
When every word is meant...

One must delve inside his heart
And also inside his mind
The words do come in fits and starts
And rhymes may be hard to find...

But no matter as one must try
To find the words that are hid inside
It takes some time but the words do come
One need not follow the "rules of
thumb"...

I try to write, I try to rhyme
But they don't come out every time
But no matter, at least I try
As the words come... by and by...

Suzanne Morin

Tragedy Of Innocence

She creeps into the bedroom,
In the middle of the night.
Her footsteps barely audible,
She's unseen in the soft moonlight.
A grimace is upon her face.
Her brow, with sweat is drenched.
Her heart pounds loudly in her ears.
In her fist the knife is clenched.
She gazes at the beauty
Of the child as he sleeps,
And hopes that he will feel no pain
As around the bed she creeps.
She hesitates a second
As she ponders her regrets.
And the loss of her own childhood,
When the baby she begets.
Children playing grown-ups;
Trying to find their own self-worth.
What tragedy of innocence,
A child giving birth.

Debbie Benninger

Broken Vows

Here I sit all alone —
In the shadows, of a broken home.
While I worked with horse and plow.
You chose to break our wedding vows.

For nineteen years, we n'er did part
Now! you have chosen to break my heart.
I live alone each day somehow —
Facing all of our broken vows.

You threw away your wedding ring —
And ruined the songs, I used to sing.
But! I hum a tune somehow,
Facing each day of broken vows.

For seven years, I laid alone
In the shadows, of our broken home.
Did I throw a stone, somehow —
That helped to break our wedding vows?

William J. Lambert

"Be True To Yourself"

Be true to yourself.
In whatever you feel,
And whatever you say and do.

Be true to yourself,
And you will find
Your friends will believe in you.

Be true to yourself,
And pursue your dream.
No matter how hard it may seem.

Try not to worry about anyone else.
Just live your own life,
And be true to yourself.

Candise-lynn Smith

To A Child

In the darkness
  of a sky without stars
morning light came
  and once more
I can see
  springtime
    in you eyes.

Franco Crivelli

Tears Of Darkness

I pray for the night,
in which I may hide
my tears, my sorrow,
and my despair.

I yearn for the night,
for the touch that will
soothe my weary soul.

I ache for the night,
so that I may hide from others
tears which are
angry, desperate,
and afraid.

I call for the night,
for it is then I feel alive,
awakened from the deadness
that seeps into my heart.

I accept the night,
for it is without prejudice
my confidante, my lover,
and my friend.

Juliet Allen

A Winter's Pause

The sun was shining brilliantly,
Inveigling me to taste its splendour.
I was charmed, so I accepted.
Departing from a cosy home
I entered a cold and frosty winter day.
Crunch, Crunch, Crunch,
My footsteps echoed from the ground.
I paused and listened for living sounds.
The silence was profound.
I wallowed in the bliss of it,
Inhabiting a world comprised of one.
The newly fallen snow dazzled,
Glittering like millions of diamonds
Piled along the roadway for the taking.
A stunning fairyland for me alone.
Oh! Blissful silence to last for so few moments.
The approaching sound of airborne
engines broke the spell.
So I moved on to add to the cacophony.
Crunch, Crunch, Crunch.

Brenda Letts

Shower Curtain Innocence

You know something
is behind, beyond
You sense it is there
but can't understand

Once the curtain
is drawn, lifted
You still can't see
through steamy haze

Only after the mask
is dropped, moved
You sense and see
something there and not.

Bugsy Dawn

The Gift Of Mankind

The mystery of all mankind,
Is hidden inside one's self.
Many do not know it.
It's left laying on a shelf.

It is hard to discover.
And may never be found.
It can be overlooked
And thrown to the ground.

For many it is different.
Love, hate, life, death.
Some may even ponder
Over a mere little myth.

For me it is a dream
A dream only I know.
One to help me live and learn
But most of all to grow.

Once it is discovered,
It's there all the days you live.
It will help you to remember,
All the things that life will give.

Andrea Merrick

Unknown Emotion

Fear
Is merely an emotion
A simple state of mind
And yet,
It grabs hold of us and
Takes control

Fear
Will make a gentle man,
aggressive
A rational man,
irrational
And the strongest man,
weak

Fear
Is caused by life's dilemmas
And problems we encounter
It comes and goes
With quickness and ease
And takes away our laughter.

R. J. Kosan

Yellow

This yellow dyed scarf
is the only color I wear
I can't taste anything
except for my salty tears
that have traced their way to
my lips that still burn
with the harsh words I've spoken
to you when I was out of turn

This yellow rose wilted
in my shaky hand hold
from standing too long
in this winter of mine so cold
if I could breathe back
these words that I've spoken
I know I'd inhale so hard
my lungs would be broken

But I can't reverse the things I've said
wish I could exchange my yellow rose for red

Jonathan Dam

Explosion

Do you hear the vibrations?
It is part of the earth;
part of choice.

The howling
the wimpering
the voiceless.

All the oboes and violas.
All the blue-black and virulent purple,
and the ultimate white.

All the smashing, the ripping,
the burning of pulsating nerve-ends.
The shuddering convulsive fear
entombed in grey,
between void and being.

The need to escape, chilling the need
to cling to that once-known crust of self.

The bitter thirst.
Sound turned inward,
focussed on the erratic rhythm
of choice.

Edith Helen Papert

Untitled

The pain - so unbelievable
It thrives and rides on
the crest of the torrent
and burnished the
fire of sorrow
screaming like molten lava
from the arid crevassed lips
of the tumultuous cavern
which resides in the unfathomable
depths of my heart.

Rana Barwood

The Rose [Love]

Through time eternal
Its beauty lives
Its tiny petals spring forth.
A sea of life, a beacon so bright
A gazed on it a long lost light.
A tiny moment in an expanse of time
That gives life's blood, fresh wine.
A crystal spring, in the desert sands
I held it close in my hands.
This living thing,
Oh, so rare
What in life can compare.
Its sensuous fragrance
Fills my soul
And though in time
I grow old,
A glorious splendor, I shall remember,
Of a once blooming flower
I held in my hour.

Sean Kavanagh

One Day

Perhaps one summer's afternoon,
Perhaps one winter's day.
You might remember me,
In some kind of way.

Although we two parted,
And took a different way.
Perhaps in fate, we two,
Might meet again, some day.

Kathy Hanford

Friends

When the evening greets the sunset.
Its shadow filters through.
And caresses every living thing
including me and you.
The serenity lies waiting
it gives to us, with care.
And silence comes, in passing
we sigh and know it's there
We look upon the darkness
with aw! We mesmerize
the peacefulness we feel
with affect... We close...
our eyes.

Brenda Hanna

Prayer

Broken, angry and upset
Left alone again
To cope with life's unveiling trials
Without support or love
Where will I go, where will I turn
I feel so all alone
No one to talk to, no one to run to
No home to call my own
Oh Lord, I'm lost or am I
Have I no friend at all
Do I not have just one good thing
To make my life worthwhile
Yes I do, I have a friend
He's been there all along
I speak to him most every night
When no one is around
He answers prayers to those in need
So I say a prayer for me
Thank you Lord, oh thank you
For this opportunity.

Elaine Dawson

Pitter Patter

Pitter Patter
Let's get at 'er
The people sit and stop to chatter.

The work is waiting to be done.

Pitter Patter
Let's get at 'er
Now I see it doesn't matter.

The work's still waiting to be done.

Julie Walker

The Garden Of Childhood

Broken seed
Licking the air
and breathing
The soil's heat missing

Bright leaf
Touching the rain
and wetting
The earth's tears dressing

Breeding flower
Painting the field
and feeling
The world's forest bereaving

Beatriz Helena De Assis Pereira

Freedom

When you lose the one you love
Life is over
It's ended
You want to die
And part of you does
Life is empty inside
But the birds still sing
Although you are sad and numb
They remind you that life goes on
You will sing again
That after death of life and limb
Spring comes again to flourish and bloom
Like nature, Spring is reborn within you
The jigsaw of life falls into place
Piece by piece until it's complete again
A new life begins.

Marion Chornobrywy

Dying Young

At one time
life was so carefree
without any worries
now, as I lie in bed
my life is
as precious as gold
I don't want
my life to end so young
so soon
I don't know
if I'll be here tomorrow
I'm afraid to close
my swollen eyes
for fear they won't see
the light of day again
I wish I could
relive my life
without any worries and
without worrying about
dying so young, so soon

Stephanie Fedorkiw

Anonymous

I am the freeborn of an osu
Like odagu my anger is relentless
And it makes me restless
But I am not listless

I ask
if I am free
why this sacrifice?
If I am a slave
why this service?

They tell me it doesn't matter
but there is a dozen matter.
Tell me, tell me my birthday
now that I know my deathday
Why this task
I ask.

Austin Chiazor Onuoha

Someone Like You

A long long time ago, what seems
like only yesterday to me, I went out
walking on a cool summer's night.
As I walked, I wished with all my heart
that someone like you would come into
my life.

Someone who's bright and sparkles
like the moon and the stars in the
sky, as they show me the way and
protect me from the shadows of the
night, just as you do.

Someone who's cool, but gentle like
the breeze that blew in my hair, like
a soft touch, just as you touch me.

Someone who's warm, and giving, and
caring, and sweet — and everything
I've ever dreamed of. Someone like you,
that I now have and will hold forever
and ever.

Robyn Ings

Untitled

Tears fall from my eyes
like rain from the sky.
In a puddle I see
a reflection of you.
The tears come harder
and faster and then there's
a storm.
Soon I am left
with just a memory of you.

Janel Wiebe

"Rain"

Rain,
like the showers of pebbles
that stream through the fingers of gods,
is pelting the tin roofs.

Later to rust and be ruined
as caskets are ruined with mud
tossed by mourners at funerals.

Pity is madness
too readily manifest.

Felicia Mohammed

Suckle My Soul

Drink my pale clear sweetened sweat,
Matured within my paper heart.
Be also reborn to burst this net,
And together help my toil depart.

Eat my thoughts of black, blue, red.
Ungarnished, unseasoned, underdone.
Let me rest inside your head,
To devour your love, become one.

Sleep my love upon my warming breast.
Banish unrest, suckle my soul.
Gather your amorance to fleece the nest.
Now so pure, so white, we can enrol.

George Henderson Baxter

A Holiday Wish

To most of us, the holidays
Mean laughter and good cheer,
A christmas tree with sparkling lights
A loving family near.

The tree is set with lights and balls
And tinsel placed just right,
With gifts around the branchless base
It's such a lovely sight.

To help us with the holidays
Our friends and family,
Will show up here or have us there
Together we will be.

On Christmas morn, we see in fact
That Santa Claus has come,
And left that special wanted gift
For each and everyone.

The children and the grandchildren
Of course take center stage,
But Christmas day is meant for all
People of every age.

Donald Head

Cold

Might call its midnight gale,
Might call it disastrous air;
Far north at sea waves struck,
Ship with anchor, since, 1850.

In darkness, cold, freezing -
In early hours destroyed vessel;
Rough sea, made list and sank,
Regular passengers Ferry - ESTONIA.

Baltic sea has surprised folks,
Neptune fork hit skies in dark;
Destroyed people confidence,
Based on number of ill death.

Sacramental magic could not help,
Navigation lost course as well;
Living human lost its price,
Swallowed sea, without surprise.

Who thought kind of weather,
Ever innocent has punished all;
Ship as wood shoe turned over,
Introduce vacuum news as will.

S. West

Silent Soldiers Of Christ

Soldiers are sometimes silent carriers
Moving gently in the spirit
and carrying love.

They speak softly and know
that the war has only just begun

In their hearts they carry a light
and it shines on you.
If your eyes are open
this light pierces all darkness
warms any doubt and
shadows any fear.
Lucky is the lost soul
who has a silent soldier near

Mary Broadhead

Goodbye

Here I sit I think of you.
My eyes they shed a tear or two.
My heart it cries out loud in fear.
I'm longing just to hold you near.
Daddy
Oh Daddy, please don't go
So many times we've said goodbye
Daddy
Oh, Daddy, please don't die
Tears and sorrow joy and pain.
Here I sit I'm thinking again.
Three years later, the pain is strong
This has not left, as you have gone
So here I sit I think of you.
My eyes they shed a tear or two.
My heart it cries out loud in fear.
For, I still long to hold you near.
Daddy
Oh, Daddy, I love you so...

Goodbye.

Crystal Vanduzee

Our Love

I love you, without conditions,
My feelings, my own admission,
Why not accept the love I give?
Let our lives begin to live -
The wonders- of a love so true -
The wonders - of love with you.

Love, you and I, no conditions,
Forever love, no remission.
Nothing to loose, no repentance
Loving me, your life sentence.
Loving you, no regrets,
An ecstasy we won't forget.

Love me now, no conditions,
Now, and always, your admission.
I accept the love you give,
That day, is when our lives will live -
The wonders - of love, a love so true -
The wonders, together, me and you.

Let those wonders soar with splendour,
Love always, forever tender - OUR
LOVE.

Jane E. Christensen

Everlasting

Where can I go,
My legs just sit beneath me.
Silence is my world,
What do I hear.
How can I tell you,
Words, I cannot talk.
My eyes are open,
I only sense your near

Your arms embracing,
Feel your heart beat I love you.
Tears they fall,
Feel your touch, see your comfort.
Share my silence,
Know you understand.
Walk for me.
Always by my side.

Carolyn Neufeld

A Little One's Thank You

With dancing eyes of sparkling blue
my smiles' as bright as sunshine.
I have hair just a few.

Ten tiny fingers and ten tiny toes
And a cute little button nose.

Crawling on my hands and knees
I look up to see you are pleased.

So much to learn and so much to see
In my new world exploring I will be.

With every new step and each passing day.
I will have come a long way

With the warmth of your love
And the kindness of your heart
I'm off to a great start.

But there will come a day when
your help I'll need no more.
For your love and guidance has
prepared me for what's in store.

Kim Soubliere

Decisions, Decisions

Like a dandelion blowing in the wind,
  my thoughts are scattered.
Afraid that with the decision I make
  my dreams will be shattered.
I feel divided, torn between two
  forces.
As if I were tied to two moving
  horses.
Why is decision making so hard
  for me?
Is it a sign of immaturity?
When I outgrow my fear of mistakes,
  I know that I will have what
    it takes
To be a success at the things
  I do.
When that day comes, all of my dreams
  will come true.

Cynthia Hamilton

Broken Glass

Broken glass hiding in
my windows
is beautiful when the sun
runs through it and
sticks to the wall

But

Broken glass pieces
then cries remorse
Doesn't forget you with blood
on the edges

Broken glass lets the wind
tickles its legs.

Jason Gennaro

Heroin

Reality slips under my brain
She moves viciously through my veins

Ecstasy is in with the comfort of a lover
She grabs me, caresses me, lets me down
In sexual agony, I dream
She hurts me, I need her

My brain turn over
Life slips under me

Christopher-Robin Chouinard

Field Of Dreams

No more war,
No more hate,
No more religion,
Tacked to a state.

One united world,
One united nation,
One united people,
Without segregation.

All people different,
All morally sane,
All accept love,
Nothing to be slain.

Living together,
Living in succession,
Living in comfort,
Never facing depression.

Is this peace among the people?
Is this peace found in a wall?
Is peace just a dream?
Is peace possible at all?

Kevin P. Jones

Our Pike Lake Bide-A-Wee

A cottage out beside the lake
No sign of grand array,
We love each nook and corner
And long to go and stay.
The peace we find along the shore
At the setting of the sun
Is broken by familiar sounds
And we welcome every one.

A jumping fish or a gliding crow
With wings so big and strong
A muskrat for his evening swim
or a beaver comes along.
A barberque or a weinner roast
And maybe a sing song too
or even a trip in the motor boat
Or maybe the canoe.
The season is too short we know
But we love our bide-a-wee.
Late fall we go and close it up
And wait for spring you see...

Margaret C. Acton

Who But The Poet

Often wonder disappears in crevices
of
silence

But a poem is a singing chord flying
a colored symphony,
remembering all the beauty in itself and
the shattering truth of love,
listening to the secret darkness,
speaking for the light in ringing tones:

Oh, who but the poet will write a tree
and flowers free from
a speechless page, and wrought
a mountain in the setting sun
in one contrapunctual thought?

Marguerite Enslin

Will You Still Love Me

You said I'm your rose petal,
Of each day in a row.
One you'll love forever,
And more as I grow.

Yet, with the autumn's fall-in,
Heart's clouded with distress.
As I'm growin' older wanderin'
Will you love me less?

As the pendulum clock swings,
Each day ticks fast, and flows
Leavin' eyeballs tired,
From the wind that blows.

With each passin' year,
The wind pulls hair wisps slow.
Leavin' what's left,
Whiter than snow.

Your rose petal will wither, then,
Limpin' through forests, half bold.
Will you still love me then?
When I grow old.

Nevenka Simunic

Summer Cumlaude

Treasure filled rock pools
of emerald and ruby
anemone studded and musseled
within.

Anxious small bodies
salt prone on black boulders,
waiting for bull-cat with baited
bent pin.

Water washed shingle
sieved fine through small fingers,
pebble sea dashed and sucked clean by
the sea.

Grandfathers salty
and sequined with fish-scales
watching white surf sugar coating
the quay.

Sharon Tregenza

Memories

Today is a day of memories
of happy times
carefree youth, security
Family, home and growing up
Changes, new faces.
Today is a day of memories
Of sadness, shock and disbelief
Of tears and sorrow
Of things unsaid, wishfulness
Grief and mourning
A circle broken
But deep inside
Faith and knowing
We will meet again!

Dorothy Sewell

Time Is Running Out

I hear the ticking
of my little clock
As I drift off
into a restless sleep
Oh to sleep without
the coming nightmare
Of a time I will
have to keep.

I awaken to the sound
of ringing in my ears
From my clock
and from my ancient age
As I arise to face
the coming of this day
My fears are stilled
by God's words - JUST PRAISE.

Barbara E. Stewart

The Agreement

This is my second day
Of not thinking about you

Not thinking about
how the breeze stirs your hair
like sand in the long grass

Not thinking about
how softly you lie among pillows
with eyes pulling me closer

Not thinking about
how your arms, even now,
enfold me

Not thinking about
how, because I love you,
I am not thinking about you

Graham Guest

A Compact With The Wind

I run into the stillness
of time crying a frenzied
wish - it's a fervent prayer
from within to hold me whole.

I wish there would be a friend
to every heart that breaks down
when lives are pulled apart, wrecked
by destinies uncertain.

I wish there would be no minds
that would kill, hold back the dreams
of youth flowing in a stream
when rainbows promise no wrong.

I wish there would be no might
Hurled against the weak and meek
exchanging valor for grief
in a rugged toil for peace.

I wish there would be just love
strewn on the highway of life
that for me, the wind could pluck
in remembrance of our pact.

Remedios Nalundasan-Abijan

Wishes

I wish I had the purity
Of white.
I wish I had the sweet soul
Of my youth.
I wish I could sing, or dance, or jump
In freedom.

All that I wish is in my heart,
Caught there
In the cage of my adulthood.
I am what I am,
Sensible and mature,
Because I am grown.

I wish I wasn't.

Mary Gillanders

Only One Wish

I have but one wish;
One dream;
One goal to achieve.
Only one thing stands in my way.

I know one day;
All my wishes will come true,
But until that time comes,
I shall continue to dream.

And when my wishes come true,
I shall never look back,
Only forward
To enjoy life to the fullest.

Hailey Harfman

Innocent Man

On
One fine chilly winter evening
I saw -
On the white tiled slippery floor
Of our lavatory -
A cockroach, upside down
Trying hard to turn round
Unsuccessful attempts, painful groans
A pitiable urge to survive
But failed at every time, it tried

In
Materialistic society of all times
An innocent, being compelled
For what not to,
Helpless endeavors, to be true

When I threw some water
To give a jerk, to set right
It went straight into the hole
Never to return, never to return

K. Rajkumar

Revelation

Sweet light of thine oh Lord to see,
Revealed through all eternity,
The empathy of human tears
To gently sooth life's daunting fears;
Your love our spirit freed, to be
released in joy, renewed in thee.
To touch the hurt in tortured eyes,
To know the heart where sorrow lies,
To feel the pulse of nature bound
by love, in selfless giving found.
Christ's law to heal, to grow, to be-
His gift for all humanity.

Margaret Page-Purser

Untitled

One flower, amidst a field.
One heartbeat, refusing to yield.
No more questions in my mind,
serenity slides in line.
The heart, the flower, pictured there,
both of these now so rare.
Wandering around,
stumbling, blind,
knowing not what I'll find.
Trapped, alone, no defenses,
smells and sounds cloud my senses.
Exploding from a tangled maze.
Running from a thickened haze.
My heart on fire,
my soul ablaze.
Wander back through a dream.
Someone tell me what it means.

Tammy Wubs

Carpediem

Life comes only once.
Opportunities come and go.
Only in living can life be found.

Time flies and passes us by,
And often times we miss the chance.
Always afraid and unwilling to try.
So dreams slip through our hands.

Life is but blessing in disguise,
But unless we make a move to unfold
The beauty hidden from the eyes,
Then life remains barren and cold.

Each one is unique in his own way,
With goals and ideals, each one can stand.
Do and be, seize the day.
Make the most while we still can.

Learn to live for what is right,
Though foolish minds block our way
Go on, believe; learn to fight.
Don't be misled, seize the day!

Maria Cielo G. Cueto

Where Do I Stand?

Are we friends,
Or a little bit more?
Does he like me,
Or am I a horror?
I think he's sweet,
But he does not know,
That I like him that way,
But how to show?
Maybe it's my secret,
Something he doesn't want to learn.
Maybe someday,
The tables will turn.
I hope someday he tells me,
So I know where I stand.
That day that we,
Are hand in hand.

Rejane D. Herzog

The Mona Madonna

A life of depletion
Or so she says
She's withering away
Yet is incased and framed

She sets a cool white
Against the black
A pretty painted picture
For others to admire.

She knows this isn't her
That isn't her shade
Her colours seem to clash
Taking away attention...
From her own convictions.

She blends and paints to cover up
The immortal picture that's
never been seen...
Or so she convinces of her critics.
This picture is titled "center stage"
Yet is reknown as self pity.

Meggan Nanton

Untitled

We are but a speck in the universe.
Our existence, a mere episode
in the grand ebbing flow of time.
Life begins to seem
so trivial,
each individual seems
absolutely insignificant,
and saving the environment
seems so futile.
Our planet is simply
one of millions
and when we are gone
the universe will know no difference.

Sean Welling

Your Fist

When your fist would shake
Our happiness would brake
Shattered dreams,
Laying on the ground
Never to be found
Your fist would fly
All I could do is cry
They say I was too young
But I remember
You tried to buy me love
Love is what you never got
At least from me
I watched your fist fly
Over and over
Until there were no more tears to cry
The tears in my eyes
As I watch,
How your fist flies.

Tammy Chaykoski

The Weaker Vessel

No one noted the only drop
That fell from her brimming eyes
As she stood
Alone
Empty hands folded
Beneath her swollen belly
While with glasses raised
They toasted his heir-to-be.

Donna J. Richards

Forever

With a Queenly posture she stood
Over looking the valley below
Protecting all that was in sight
She ruled over high and low

Her doors were solid oak
Her strong stone pillars stood tall
Her foundation was rock solid
She could not be budged at all

Her Crown was made of stone
Cut and placed so perfect
It rested on the highest tower
Where nothing could get to it

As the years came and went
Many things faded away
But her Majesty above the valley
Forever she would stay

Kelley Galloway

Untitled

Rain....
Peace... a new beginning...
A fresh world...
Nature at its best.

Heavy drops
Connecting
To become
One...

Water pooled,
Chilled by night,
Open to the sun
New life...

A cycle begins
Each new day,
Each new rain...

Zonnie Smith

Plays In Emotion

Entities trapped in undreamt dreams
Proceeds away from enchantment it seems
Dallies in thoughts of fantasy
Plays in emotions of ecstasy
Dwarfs in life's material means

Misunderstood and taken apart
Brings the child back to the start
Nurture the existence
Pronounces the resistance
Delicate energies touch the heart

Thus, time to point to a clue
For I'm sure, tis long over due
Dreams, Elegance and thoughts of things
Emotional memories for which it brings
Enlightenment of knowledge, tis for you

Patricia Nesbitt

Honey-Mane

Honey-mane falls her fleece;
Sleid skein in the aurum trees.

Honey-mane falls here fleece
To the half-faced finch,
A'lie of brittle leaves.

In mosses yellow,
Through verdant gold.

Honey-mane threads roping fire
In the greenwood fold.

Jason Lonnquist

Life

We are puzzles of life
Putting together our lives
Piece by piece
Day by day
With every new piece of knowledge
With every loss or gain
It helps us grow
With all life's ups and downs
We continue to put it together
Piece by piece
Day by day
And when life seems to fall apart
We take those pieces out
And begin to build again
So that maybe one day
We can be whole
And finally when we have fulfilled
Our life's dreams, hopes and prayers
Our puzzle of life is complete.

Marguerite Touzeau

Charter Flight

Drone, drone, drone
rattle, rattle, rattle
Squeak, squeak, squeak
"Coffee or tea?"

Rattle, rattle, rattle
Squeak, squeak, squeak
"Excuse me, Sir
Would you like some duty free?"

Drone, drone, drone
rattle, rattle, rattle
squeak, squeak, squeak
Wish I could get some sleep!

Flying over islands in the sky.

E. A. Cooke

My Song

My soul is in the clouds
Reaching out across time...
"Floating overhead"
As if to hide my reason,
"Waiting for a place to be"

My freedom is in the water
Up and down...sometimes almost drowning,
In its transparency
I see myself...as I am and should be

My laughter is in the wind.
Soaring away above the cloud's
Where behind a cool mask
I hide and spread myself too thin.

But my heart is in the sun
Smiling down on me
Knowing of my mistakes and waste,
That I'm growing in reality
And I am
still
free

Frank Wilson

The Machine

The machine
Remains serene.
Dispassionately
It performs its programmed norms.
Unaware,
It never chooses;
Unconcerned
Who wins or loses:
Fried or foe,
Causes,
Just or otherwise.
The machine does not philosophize,
It works for them as well as us.
Whether safe or
Dangerous
Depends perforce, not on the goals,
But merely who's at the
Controls.

Ida Myers

Lake Nagagami Bald Eagles

Saw them fly, I've heard their cry,
Saw them hatch, I've seen them die,
Eaglets small, matures proud and tall,
Young and old, curious and bold,
At the surface, or fifteen hundred feet,
Wings of power, never miss a beat,
Catching fish, catching dinner,
Always losses, in the life of a winner,
Looking down with engine noise,
They look up with silence and poise,
Bold and free, will I ever be?
Bold and free, why not me?
What if? Next time around,
I'll grow wings, get off the ground
Maybe someday, I'll be their way
Soaring above with young at play
Dive with my mate, follow her dive
Wind rushing past, we're really alive
I'll look at her, she'll look at me,
Flying high, forever free!

John R. Stell

Sarah

Sarah's room is empty
She doesn't live there anymore
Sunday afternoon, a beautiful day
When she walked out that door.
Now Sarah's gone forever
He took her away
No one can ever know the horror
She went through on that day.
Sarah's horror ended
As she was laid to rest
But her family cries every day
As they're put to the test.
Can justice be served?
Sarah will never laugh again
Her family is forever lost
Ease their pain, nothing can.
It seems justice is in his favor,
He may only serve ten years
Memories of Sarah linger in our hearts
Her laugh, her smile, our fears.

Holly Thrones

My Very Special Grandma

I see my Grandma in the garden
She hums a special song
the way she plants. works and digs
it seems to take so long.

No time to play laugh or sing
the works must be done,
and after that it's time to bake
why can't she have some fun.

But there are times
she spends with me,
times of happiness
that will always be.

She teaches me how to speak
the language of her past,
she says I'm good, I make her her laugh
and that I learn real fast.

I love my Grandma very much,
She's the one that has a special touch.
She understands the way I feel
and makes me better with a delicious meal.

Kendra Kovitch

Popcorn

A group of seeds
small and light
motionless in prison
clinging together
suddenly one by one
bursting
full of life
flying on their own
each taking a different path
a few escape
but most are pushed back down
to live out their short existence
behind the walls
the walls of the unescapable bowl

Carol Sedgwick

Grandmother's House

Grandmother's house,
So close to the beach,

Grandmother's house,
Always in reach,
Grandmother's house,
Protects how I feel,
Grandmother's house,
Tasty nourishing meals,
Grandmother's house,
I'm never a burden,
Grandmother's house,
Fire's always a burnin',
Grandmother's house,
My first, second home,
Grandmother's house,
My thoughts always roam,
Grandmother's house,
Contains my grandmother,

No other way,
To express how I love her.

Jodi Jane Longley

Peace

A child's slumber
so deep in sleep
not a stroke of hand
or kiss of cheek
will he awaken
Life flows through
so strong and free
desires, challenges, dreams
yet to unfold
When morning warmth
shines through
His soul and heart will stir
to a yearning for excitement
yet to come.

Susan Peebles

The Breath Crash

Her tangled Posterior with a sight,
So gracefully turned way upright,
The pain that bares the eye so wistful
Brings strength in her heart,
That is mighty and true,
until her forever depart.

She is flying in the night
On her soon to be grave,
The disease shall take her life,
Like a huge tidal wave.
Then we shall see finally last
The death of her
and facing the past.

Her breath almost gone,
in one sweeping slash,
Her eyes fade away,
Drawing us to the past.

Gino Olvera

Friends

Friends are like flowers
So lovely and sweet;
They brighten each moment
Whenever we meet.

No two are alike,
Yet we love each and all,
The wee and the modest,
The sturdy and tall.

Like flowers we cherish
The dear friends we gain,
With sunshine of kindness,
With good deeds like rain.

Friends are like flowers,
And happy are they
Who have many blossoms
In friendship's bouquet.

Bonnie Lee Morris

The Difference

Black, white, yellow, red;
we're all the same in the dark.

Christian, Jew, Catholic, none;
inside we're as free as a lark.

Boy, girl, lady, man;
they are all as equal as me.

How do they feel when they are hurt?
Friendship is the key.

Sarah E. Leidy

Forever Is My Love

Forever is my love
So strong we'll never part,
Forever we will share our love
From deep within our heart.

Forever I am yours
Whatever we may do,
I'll keep my love in store
For - my love, I give to you.

Forever me and you
Whatever we may do,
Through day and night
We share - our love and light.

Forever is my love——-

Elizabeth Wolfe Dyck

I Need

I need someone to be my friend
Someone I can rely on
Even my worst problems, I can depend
She'll understand me for whatever reason

A person who will be there to
comfort me
Who will keep me company when I'm
alone
I need her to advice me
And will cheer me up even if it's dawn

Someone whom I'll be sharing secrets
And someone I can share my ambitions
and dreams
Not just my loneliness but as well
as my happiness
She's there to hear with no regrets.

Elaine Ruth S. Reyes

Someday

All my life I've thought about,
Someone sweet, loving and kind,
For I knew that he would be,
The best gift I would ever find,

Then my thoughts came together,
And I realized all along,
I'd gotten all I'd hoped for,
In a love shared for so long,

For Daddy you mean more to me,
Than my words could ever express,
I knew I had something special,
For in you I'd found the best

Even though you're here no longer,
My love for you grows even stronger,
I feel your presence is with me today,
And I know in my heart I'll see you again

...Someday.

Amanda Lambert

Always

Even though we're far apart,
we're close together,
I always have you with me,
you're by my side forever.

Every choice I make,
Every step I take,
Every tear I cry,
you're there,
By my side,
always

Gloria Leney

A Quite Moment

Cherished by many
Sought out by a few
But seen by others
Only a void to elude.

For it might seem a blessing
But also a pain
What you make of the moment
Only you are the blame.

Left only to wonder
By those not too sad.
What a moment of peace would mean
In a day that's gone bad.

Many hold it so dearly
Few would let it slip by
Others fear its presence
Afraid to give it a try

Reflect to something peaceful
Relax your body, mind and soul
Knit together your self being
To where you are in control.

Larry Watters

The Naughty Rain

After a long thought
Soul rised in the nature
Since the evolution kept growing
Escaping itself from its prime goal

What instructions did God give me
Before He left me going free
On the roads of my imagination
Waiting for the truth

Doubting of my convictions
Wasting my springs be questioning
Answers don't come easily
God so far away

I left God behind me
Then how may He hurt my pride
Spirituality has been buried while alive
Its gravestone has gotten bigger

Life went through
The naughty rain showered down
Soul gave away
God sighed

Diane Cote

Sunrise

the rays
spill red over the golden wheat
shoot yellow straight up
and orange to the side

blue is the background
with fluffy distractions
tinted red
yellow
and orange

its cheerfulness
its confidence
brightens my world
starts my day out right

Holly Lacelle

The Celestial Staircase

The Celestial Staircase is on the anvil
stair after stair we have to recede
crawling/walking/galloping/eloping with
Childhood dream of fantasies.

Hope/despair in beloved's lips
Nectar we have to search once more.
Affixed, suffixed with one word
Each lip now/ life, life, life',/
Affixed/suffixed with one World
Each lives now, peace, peace, peace!
Like morning new/ Like morning dew
A living life / flower from pensies,
A living sun!
Whereabouts of death long lost
A living anguish!
Fallen flowers, petals, trunk, trees,
Soil - A root!
Few drops of blood oozing - A war!
Vein / lungs / air / your name's sky,
A Heart! All that we aspire......

Prahallad Kumar Satpathy

Night Of The Hunter

Creeping
stalking
in shadows
gun aimed
ready,
looking out the window
I see him
watching me
wanting me
everything
everyone I have,
silently
closer and closer
he comes,
I'm the game,
the hunted,
the screams
the shots,
Beware,
it's the night of the hunter.

Ruthanne Monahan

Wind

Gentle the feel of tiny leaves;
Still the sound of shattered dreams;
Violent the beat of running feet;
Fiery the warmth of intense heat;

Below the sea of blue and green
Behold a light to be seen;
Arise the light, awaken the sky;
Create a bird, make it fly;

Let the ball of light be seen;
Tell the future, part the seas;
Hum a song, sing to please;
Feel the touch, the gentle breeze,

Dim the color that guides the day;
Watch it sink, deep, deep;
Quiet is the setting of the morning sky;
Await the dark to arise;

A speck of light in the sky;
Then comes a wind, flickers and dies;
Darkness awakes,
And silence roams the night;

Taniele Tucker

Night Answers

'Tis an awesome night we have,
 Stillness looming through the skies.
Rhythmed breathing whispers here,
 Have to sleep, will not fear.

Hours pass so we can rest,
 Collecting thoughts of what is best.
Look into the night and see,
 Answers scattered, though sparingly.

For what may seem a time to come,
 We quickly store what we've begun,
To understand and recognize,
 As bits of knowledge for our minds.

We must be quick, absorb it all,
 The moments now are fleeting past.
Then the puzzle is pieced together,
 As the sun comes shining brightly.

Fading fast the insights before us,
 Losing sight, if only slightly.
Return it will, as night befalls us,
 To leave us again, with new knowledge.

Elisabeth Engelen

The Mystery Of The Sea

Listen to the waves
Striking the shore,

A beautiful sound
You should not ignore.

The ocean mist in the wind,
Gently falling upon your skin.

Smell the seaweed
Slicing the air,

The sun shimmering in a glare.

You're stunned by the beauty
All around,

Just yesterday
Unaware of this place you found.

Now, open your eyes
And take it all in,

Feel the energy build within.

If you express how you feel
It will mean a great deal
And capture the creativity in me.

For I am, the Sea.

Ray Mutter

Nature Of Love

Rivers run,
Sun shines,
Wind blows,
Clouds move,
Rain falls,
Thunder rolls,
Lightening strikes,
You leave,
My heart breaks,
I cry,
You're gone,
I'm alone,
It's over.

Michelle Mowbray

Sailing

Hove to
Sure God
To belly up
Sails blown out
Taut lines shrieking
Nerves, too
My lips shrill
Against the tumult's rise
Yet I am whole
A man still
My last breath
Swept by this gale
Will warm the gentle gust
That interrupts
Your reverie.

Sanford M. Russell

For Always

Loves happiness
Surrendering to the sweet innocence
of youth.
With tender sighs
calling out to mother spring.
Creating an emotion that can overcome all.
For always
Without the darkness of hurt
shadowing its growth.
Promises of forever kept close
to the heart that beats
for the other.
Living solely on a breathe
and a kiss.
For always

Amanda Di Michele

Happiness Is.....

There are many forms of happiness
That come to me and you.
And in this poem I have tried
To mention just a few.

Happiness is a real good book
And a chair beside the fire.
Especially when it's cold outside
And you are very tired.

And what a special feeling
To take a small surprise
To someone old and lonely
And see happiness in their eyes.

And how about a letter
That you really don't expect.
Especially when you open it
And find a nice fat cheque.

Most people will find happiness
In fact it's quite a thrill
When the dentist says "no cavities"
And you escape the drill.

Eileen Walt

The Holocaust

Some scholar said, "That God is dead.
That we alone are left."
Who'd close his eyes to children cries?
If God's not dead—He's deaf.

William Douglas Hart

These Tears

Behind these tears are loving eyes
That know you had to go.
In this chest, an aching heart
Loves you more than you can know.
In my head, a tiny spark
That lights a memory.
In these arms, a warm embrace
That never lets you free.
In these lips, a gentle kiss
To send you on your way.
In my voice, a whispered prayer
That in heaven you will stay.
Behind these tears are loving eyes
And you again they'll see.
In heaven or atop a star,
Together we will be.

Tara-Lynn Colbow

An Inspiration

If ever there was something
That meant a lot to you
I say go after it
Or forever feel blue

For me, I have a dream
I long to fulfill
And I know that with practice
Someday, I will

I've always wanted to write
A story of love and hate
Where good will always triumph
Before it's too late

I started that book long ago
But I laid it down to rest
I needed more inspiration
Something, like this contest

Donna L. Hudson

The Shedding

A last look,
The end of today.
Of love,
Of brotherhood,
Of crimson leaves in Autumn.

A first glance,
The beginning of tomorrow.
Of trials,
Of triumph,
Of green leaves in Summer.

A return home,
The realization of change.
Of passion reborn,
Of loyalty,
Of Life.

Josh Newton

Forever

Children-
The very apples of the earth.
Apples-
Fruit of Eden, forbidden.
Eden-
The beginning of time.
Time-
Going on forever.
Forever-
Will there be children?

Laura Huston

The Changes

I look out my window
The leaves are nearly gone
There's two deer in the garden spot
And four more on the lawn

The wonderful days of summer
Are now all in the past
And the golden glory of Autumn
I knew it wouldn't last

The haying job is long over
And the wood is all put in
The nights are getting colder
In the mornings the pond is skimmed

The songbirds have all left us
And the gray jays took their place
And overhead the wild geese
Are honking on their way.

Naked limbs reach to the sky
It's that time of the year
Hunting season is upon us
And the gray days are here.

Isabell Clark

Endless Search

I think I'm going to lose my mind
The man I love I cannot find
He's lost in darkness for the time
For what he does...no reason; rhyme.

His heart is good but aching so
He's trapped inside of this I know
The fight to find his inner soul
To be exposed the ultimate goal.

A cry for help is what I hear
Whenever we're apart or near
I want him back to stay with me
And pray to God to set him free.

He needs to know real inner peace
And desperately searches for release
But nothing worldly will suffice
He truly needs to heed advice...

From one who loves him from the heart
And offers him a fresh new start
To stand beside and coax him on
And believe in him until he's gone.

D. J. Babs

Enough

Forever isn't long enough,
The strongest isn't strong enough.
In a satisfied world.
In a perfect world.
The bravest isn't brave enough
Killers haven't killed enough.
Survivors haven't survived enough,
In a world of hurt,
In a world of dreams,
The dreamers haven't dreamt enough
Blind ones haven't seen enough.
Deaf ones haven't heard enough,
In a world to forgive.
In a world to forget.
This poem hasn't explained enough.

Amanda Sulymka

Where A Mind Roams Free

In spring like air,
the summer sun delights us with its kiss.
And in the trees the dryads play,
throughout the autumn bliss.

You are there in summer's day
surrounded by your glory.
In fields of gold where angels lay,
with beauty never sorry.

Show again your shining face,
where winter never lies.
And take me to that wondrous place,
in which my spirit flies.

Matt Defouw

Reflections

A reflection is seeing yourself,
the way others do,
memories of the past,
regrets, successes, victories, failures,
gains, losses, joy and pain.
A reflection is a way,
of seeing the world differently
then you do regularly, it is a way
to reflect on your life or your self.
A reflection is a flickering image,
that can be with you one minute,
and gone forever the next.

Twyla LeClerc

Horizon Hunter

White shines on the horizon
Then blue shines on the horizon
Then light purple
Then dark purple
Somewhere in between a
brilliant red
Wicker chair watching
wickedness
Then grey shines on the horizon
It is getting dark and
no one can see me
naked in the
darkness.

Jason Gennaro

Gentle Light

You say you can't accept me,
Then you shall never know
The bonding of my heart and mind,
With the kinship of my soul.
I cry for thee my solemn friend
That you visualize only an act.
That you cannot see the love within
Only society's moral fact.
No. You dare not understand me,
Now that my heart is open wide,
Do you fear what you don't know,
Or is it what you see inside?
Could it be there is a reflection
In the gentle light you see?
Or is it a vivid image,
Of what you might like to be?
You have your reasons to turn away
From the friend you thought you knew.
Just remember if you need comfort,
I can still be there for you.

Linda Shirley

Must Be Love

There's someone special I'm thinking of,
There's so much care it must be love.
If I could see him one more night,
Oh he's such a perfect sight!
It wouldn't hurt him if I cried,
It hurts me so that he has lied.
The choice was ours to make,
Though I'll never be able to take.
The words he used to say to me,
He's the only one I wish to see.
I guess it's time for us to part,
I'll try again to make a new start.
In my mind I can hear him say,
God shall guide us on our way.

Sherri Shaver

The Vanquished

Life is really hard for me
These doctors say I've lost my mind
I'm in this room without a key
Why are these people so unkind?

Where has Peter Rabbit gone
And dear Jemimah Puddleduck
And Bambi, quite my favorite faun?
Being grown-up's nothing but bad luck.

I thought I was a special boy
That Life would be a merry-go-round
With kindly friends and lots of joy
But it's a cell without a sound.

Man's inhumanity to Man
Makes thousands mourn the Poet says
Where those you love do all they can
To hurt you in a million ways.

So I've decided to return
To childhood's fantasies and dreams
Frozen upon my Grecian Urn
Where everything is as it seems.

Henry M. Reddin

The Writing Of Poems

The writing of poems
They come from the head,
The best ones created,
When lying in bed.

A sudden thought,
To put pencil to pad,
Before you forget
Whatever you had.

To leave it til morn,
Could be gone from the skull,
And trying to remember,
Make Brain go all dull.

Some poems, are intense,
Out of the norm,
They rattle your feelings
And take you by storm.

Yet others, are mild,
Soft and smooth.
Caress your mind
Becalm and sooth.

Brian Thompson

The Show Kittens

Two kittens came for the north
They lost their way of course,
I seen them in Eden,
On bugs they were feeding,
On a rather hot day,

They played and purred for hours,
Around purple blueish Iris flowers.
The monarchs came in pairs,
As one kitten stares,
And wonders "Is that good to eat"?

Jennifer Hollett

Racism

People gaze upon you
think of you as nothing
nothing compared to them

You are something else
a something with no meaning

You look around
feeling abandoned, alone.
You notice people looking at you

Your dark skin begins to crawl
you don't know how to feel
you don't know how to be

Nobody knows why they are there
Why they are staring
people....
who can understand them?

Marsha Bruneau

A Slow Death

As tears come to my eyes
Thoughts go flying by,
Of the way you used to hold me
And say our love would never die.

As tears come to my eyes
I just now realize,
That it's you I'll always love
And for you I would die.

As tears come to my eyes
I wish you were so near,
To whisper gentle loving thoughts
And help me chase my fears.

As tears come to my eyes
My heart is slowly torn,
For you have walked all over it
And now it's weak and worn.

As tears come to my eyes
I brush them all aside,
For you have taken all my love
And with that my soul has died.

Caren McPherson

Father Time

You are old - so many things to do yet
Too bad -
So leave things half undone
And go at his command
Not a day - nor yet a minute longer
Can you stay -
Like a father to a child
It's bedtime now
So - put your toys away
And dream of bye - gone days
Reluctantly - accept the fact
We go - It's "father time" who stays!

Molly Lippert

Back To The Beginning

Back to the beginning
Throughout each passing day
In search of love around us
We give ourselves away

Don't give yourself away to soon
Look for strength within
It's never wrong to share your heart
That's where love begins

Life is like a marathon
From beginning till the end
It's the good we leave behind us
On that our life depends

Don't give yourself away to soon
Look for strength within
It's never wrong to share your heart
That's where love begins

Back to the beginning
Throughout each passing day
In search of love around us
We give ourselves away.

David Young

Lost Soul

Wandering aimlessly
throughout life,
he continues his
ever important journey
after death.

Lost to those
whom he once loved,
yet ever present
amongst the living.

He sees their lives
sift and change
like the sand
on some hot desert
in a summer storm.

Yet, he is powerless
to help them
and cries his weakness
to other lost souls.

Kim Hornby

Birthday

There's nothing like a birthday
To bring the family home,
Whether grandchild, niece or nephew,
Cousin, daughter, son or whom.

To-night 'tis a granddaughter,
The oldest girl of all.
She starts the birthday season
As we enter into fall.

If we're spared from now 'til Christmas
There'll be several more we know,
And we sense anticipation
As the birthdays come and go.

Harry B. Dulmage

Expert Destruction

It takes but an hour
to destroy a whale.
Gut it,
slice it,
boil the blubber down for oil.
Gone a majesty and grace
from the freedom of the seas.

It takes but an hour
to destroy a tree.
Lop it,
fell it,
mince it into wood-chip.
Gone a rhythm of leaves and light
from the symphony of the forest.

Huldah M. Turner

D-Day

D-Day had finally come,
to do what had not been done,
why did the Germans have to kill,
what were they trying to fulfill.

When a soldier comes to fight,
the circle around him gets too tight,
he will fight until he dies,
and where he falls he just lies.

Tanks shooting from the ground,
planes flying all around,
soldiers shooting at each other,
a German just shot my brother.

Explosions, craters, people dead,
soldiers lying in their coffin bed,
they fought for freedom without regret,
that's something we will never forget.

John Cherwinski

A Song Of Love To Nature

Maybe I'll awake in early morn,
to find my room with sun adorn.
My heart will sing a song of love,
to the sky above.

For you my love, I'll sing of Spring,
the stream of golden lilies bring.
A song of love a song of cheer,
For you my love who is so dear.

Summer bright as early morn,
Daffodils, morning-glories born.
Illustrious trees of green,
So majestic to be seen.

Autumn with its colours changing,
far and near birds are singing
The glory of God in its nature bright,
to us oh! Lord it's pure delight.

Winter with its coat of white,
Looks like ermine in the night.
Christmas is near, a child is born,
to save the world from its thorns.

Alexina Laviolette

Little Someone

A new little someone
to have and to hold,
To love and to cherish
through the days when I'm old.

A new little someone
whom I've still yet to meet,
To look in your eyes
and your face, oh so sweet.

A new little someone,
you've so much to learn.
There's a whole new adventure
around every turn.

A new little someone
to make my life complete.
Your life will have purpose
with no need to compete.

A new little someone
to hold dear to my heart.
My love will be with you
as it has from the start.

Lori Hegarty

Silence

Now and then I rest
to live through the day.
With all the thoughts of a restless mind
I try to find a way out.

Tearful shadows filled with regret,
where are they going,
what can't I forget?

Dwelling in sorrow,
in that kind of pain
that leads towards growing
when the sun breaks through rain.

Renata Wirkner Lyall

Who Will Notice

I can't hear but I can see
To read your lips
And watch your hands speak
To see shadows move when
You are coming and going

I can't hear but I can feel
Music's vibration to dance
And a partner's body movement
Left to right, back and forth

I can't hear but I can play
Cards, chess, bowling and baseball
And with my little one with gladness
Knees stained with grasses and
Eyes filled with tears for me to comfort

I can't hear but I am loved
By family, friends and Heaven above
Everyone is a chosen treasure of a human
heart
For me to know that they are there for me
to love

I can't hear but who will notice

Barbara Anne Pealow

Living With Chronic Pain

Our family members would do well
To remember the four C's
They did not cause the illness
They cannot control the disease.

They also cannot cure it
Oh, but there is hope
They cannot control or cure it
But they can learn to cope.

We must develop a program
And follow it all our lives through
Develop a wellness program
And that's up to me and to you.

We've got to develop daily
A balance between leisure and sleep
Between exercise, food and, if needed,
Professional counseling seek.

We know that what really is needed
Is to slow down and try to unwind
To take special care of our bodies
And to live just one day at a time.

Norma Jean Smith

Folklore

As our ship glides up the rocky coast,
To the ever changing scene
Among the rocks and trees and shore
Was a ghost of what has been.
You can almost hear the Indians,
Calling to their own
Their fishing boats put out to sea
You can hear them creak and groan.
They soon return with their large catch,
To feed them winter long,
They work together to get it done
It's borne in their song.
The children run down to the shore
To greet the boats return
Excited chatter does abound
As they crowd around the stern.
Our ship moves further up the coast
In the fading light, the erie ghost
Waves farewell to us from land
We hear the clap of its silent hand.

Doreane Bothwell

Best Of Friends

Friends
together
Friends
apart
Friends
forever
Friends
at heart.
You
and
Me
will
always
be
Best
of
Friends
'til
Eternity.

Gilda L. Shirahada

Hear Me

There is a wall
Too high to climb
No one speaks
No one listens

Are they deaf
Or are they not listening
I feel lost
I feel lonely
The love is there
But just ignored
Speak to me
Listen to me

I'm all I have
Although their here
I will talk
I will listen

Christine Mackenzie

The Wedding Dew

To thou and thee,
Tranquillity,
And comfort in each other's arms.
Emotion-reciprocity, and still you
Retain your sense of self,
Your individuality.
May let this be
A marriage notation,
To dangle above
The mantle-Peace,
While in and out
Your private Haven.
In the morning
You will see,
Upon the lawn
And gardenry,
The Wedding Dew,
Made just for you,
True love is beauty,
Point and view.

Peter J. Dutton

A New Season

Leaves are falling!
Trees are getting bare,
Harvest is here,
Now, there is no stalling

A change of season,
Is upon us,
Birds will migrate,
For whatever reason

Just as a new season,
We accept change,
It's a part of life,
For whatever reason.

This change of season,
earth accepts,
It's called new life
That's the reason.

Annette Boutin

Unable

Imagine never seeing the light of day
Unborn, living in a dark place
Feeding upon the remorse and pain
Never able to see your mother's face.
Being locked up inside
Away from the world
Being torn apart
Stolen from the heart
Taken away.
Unable to decide your life
Alone, helpless,
Not capable of fighting the fight.
Made...not breathing
Born living impaired
Gone as fast as you came
Murdered
Mom feeling shame
Unable to grow to the size of a pin
A life never was that could have been.

Stephanie Trudel

Untitled

The last day of March
was a sorrow-filled day
The one that you love
was taken away

Through sadness and grief
The sorrow and tears
Think back on the laughter
Remember those years

We'll never know why
We'll always know where
In Heaven above
He lives peacefully there

With the Almighty Father
New seeds he will sow
Peace and happiness
Is all he will know

The pain that you feel
Seems to great to bear
But remember he's happy
In Gods loving care.

Stephanie Prins

View From A Lonely Child's Eyes

A long time ago,
Was short lived for me,
I remember her face,
So big and always so happy.
She was my beloved grammie

And before I could say I love you,
God took her away,
Leaving me to this lonely day.
Every night I spend praying to her
To say I love you,
I miss you
And I always will.

She raised me as a youth
Teaching me all the right values,
To care
To love
To love always my beloved Mother.

Christopher Edward William Pratt

Height Of Hope

I sit here,
watching helplessly
As the dying embers fade
Knowing nothing I could do
Would make it blaze into
fire again...
Then I saw a spark
I thought it was just
my imagination
But there it was again
As clear as daylight
then I thought
Maybe there's still a chance
For the fire to go a-blaze again
Maybe not with the embers
But maybe with us
And that at least made
me smile
Knowing somehow it's
not over yet

Liza Patricia B. Driz

Untitled

A sandy beach,
waves slapping against rocks,
pushing, hard enough to kill,
I am the waves,
killing all I touch,
yet, I am the rocks,
waiting, hoping when the tide comes in,
being broken,
yet only one
I am me

Brenda Tocp

Untitled

We are innocent,
We are pure,
We pray to God,
And he says, "Yeah, right. Sure."

It comes to me
in the peak of the night
playing with my head,
and leaving me dreading
the inevitable fright.

I may be innocent,
I could be pure,
But if I ever prayed to God,
He'd say, "Yeah, right. Sure."

Charlene McPherson

Ode In Memory

Oh Soldier boy,
We give you praise;
With pen and quill;
Faith for these days;

With uniform
and marching feet;
You faced the foe;
Training complete;

God bless you all;
In memory
We write these lines;
For you to see.

Oh soldier boy;
Your life you gave;
In flander's field,
There is a grave!

Mable Boucher

To Love And Not To Look For Faults

Where do we go from here?
We have undressed our minds
there is nothing new to wear
but feelings still appear
from out of the clouds of despair.
Hindering the state of unity
within our hope of reunion.

I have loved you with all my heart,
but my intellect has questioned
the reason for this form of art
and entangled itself within
the shelf of dust and rust,
trying to find fault
within the nest of love
that has settled in accord
hovering overhead like a dove.

Dominick Browne

In Memory Of

Here's to the sacrifice.
We made as a youth.
Here's to the punishment.
For being uncouth.

Uncouth and undisciplined.
Growing up as a child.
Then you became violent.
Outrageous and wild.

So wild and so frantic.
That you reached out for more.
You collected their hatred.
Then closed up your door.

You locked it with anger.
Then told them your sin.
You showed them the fire.
That burned from within.

So here's to your world.
And what you call truth.
Here's to the memory.
Of a past with know youth.

Mike Demchuk

Ode To Ferdie

Ferdie is a King Charles spaniel
We saved him from the final needle
He was sad and flea ridden and underfed
And at every chance he cocked his leg
After a while he was perfect
We really thought it was all worth it
Then alas, he started stealing
His escapades they send us reeling
He takes it all into his bed
Crutch and hearth brush, shovel and bread
Toys and books we haven't read
He eats the books from cover to cover
He really gives us so much bother
But when he's good he is so nice
We forget about his awful vice
It's ten years now and we've learnt to cope
For his redemption there is no hope
But when he finally steals his last
We know that we'll be so downcast
'COS WE LOVE HIM!

C. Reed

From Outer Space

From dark, outer space
We see the planet of our birth,
A planet very blue
Is our lovely planet Earth.

Blue is the colour of harmony,
Of peace and balance
That's how it should be.
But what have we done to our Earth?

From dark, outer space
We see patches of dull red and brown,
It is the human race
That has let our planet down.

For greed and power have grown and grown,
Ruining this planet of our own.
Blue is the colour that Earth should be,
Only peace and balance and harmony.

So let us heal our planet Earth,
Do not let our planet die.
Let's save the planet of our birth,
We can do it if we try, we can do it if we try.

Adelaide Rhead

The Pit Trader

What's going on in my mind?
What did I see or hear?
Only for a moment
There was no fear.

I opened my mouth to do the trade.
Buy, sell, I forget which.
I'm right, I'm right.
C'mon, you son of a bitch.

It doesn't matter
if it's slower or faster
just go my way
your dirty rotten bastard.

Well, here I stand, hoping again.
Why am I just staring at this loss?
Do you really know what you are doing?
Open your mouth, get out, you're the boss.

Of all life's occupations and careers
is trading the road to riches and fame?
Solid accounts and lives turn to dust.
I thought love was a fools game.

Louis Madzo

Question Of Living

When you open your eyes
what do you see?
A crystal blue sky
or a raging sea?
In the horizon above
do you see love?
Underneath the deep sea
do you see a corpse resembling me
if it's the sky
do you ask why?
If it's the sea
do you say, how could this be?
These are all questions we ask
when pondering the task
just before it is done
ask yourself, was your life fun?
For one minute go back to your past,
seconds later make the slash.
Congratulations, your end has come at last.

Thomas James Fleming

Sleepless Nights

I often sit and wonder
What things are best to do.
In my time of wondering
I thought I loved you.

You were the one that kept me up.
You were the one that always hung around
You were very sweet then
But now you're the one who has
My face all in a big frown.

I cannot describe what I feel for you.
All I know is that my words
Are not too many, just a few.

I cannot forget the times we shared
You were my pillar then
I really thought you cared

I was the one who was the fool.
I wish with all my strength and might
That we were together,
Whenever I spend those sleepless nights.

Doreen Rienzi

Soul In The Dark

A fear beyond
what you can see.
A scared child
wanting to be free.

To be itself
to wander free.
Its soul free to be.

The pain is no longer
the fear is gone too.
But how can we do this
to a person so true.

The soul would be gone
the mind would be too.
The person would be unable to do.

The things she loved
the things she liked.
But her soul would be free
to roam in the night.

Under the sky into the dark.
No one can see soul in the dark.

Lisa Kleinsteuber

Older Women, Younger Men

Be careful, older women,
When handsome younger men
Pay too much attention,
Get too close now and then.

I once knew a young Frenchman
Whose heart was full of lies.
He captured my attention
With long-lashed, flashing eyes.

His mind was on the money
That he thought I had.
Although he tried to trap me,
I soon tripped up the cad.

"I live with my poor mother,
Who can't be left at home,"
I told my would-be lover,
And he left me alone.

Joyce M. Gogain

"To All My Children"

Should God decide to call me home
When it is least expected,
As hard as it may seem to be
Please try hard to accept it.

So many things have gone unsaid
I wish now I had spoken.
Like how much you all mean to me
Each one a special token.

I always had a hard time
Expressing how I felt.
The things I'd mean would come out wrong
And another heart would melt.

Please don't mourn tears of sadness
Just live from day to day
And if things get too unbearable
Kneel down "Loved ones" and pray.

So if God calls me suddenly
Remember "He knows best"
Live on the way we always have
Until your turn to rest.

Alberta Hutchins

Untitled

Why, oh why do we smoke?
When it makes us all cough and choke.
It's bad for our health,
it's worse for our wealth,
yet still we insist on a smoke.

Why, oh why do we smoke?
In the mornings we wheeze and we croak.
Our pockets are empty
save a packet of twenty,
so we can be sure of a smoke.

Why, oh why do we smoke?
We're going to give up, that's a joke.
We kick up a racket
when there's none in the packet,
and search the whole place for a smoke.

Why, oh why do we smoke?
We'll all end up poorly AND broke.
The habits a curse,
but cancer is worse,
so why on earth DO we smoke?

J. A. Browne

The Beginning Of The End

My heart was breaking
When you said we were through—
I thought I'd never find someone,
As charming and sweet as you.

But life went on
And you didn't seem to care.
You had someone else,
Yet I thought it wasn't fair.

And then one day I met someone
I'd known for quite awhile.
I hope your as happy as I am,
'Cause I'd walk a country mile—

Only to see you happy
Only to see you smile.
The laughter in your face
Will settle the pain for awhile.

Diane Smith

What If?

There are times of silent contemplation
when your desires or tribulations secede
and a curious what if
sparks in the essence of your soul
wishing to let go
you share not the moment
for the moment is almost gone

Having taken a journey of resilience
you have caressed and wooed
your wondering soul
to wherever your hearts' content may lie
and you have forgotten
its naked thoughts
only to be intruded on again
in a time of turbulence or peace
by a passing
what if.

Ronen S. Levin

Untitled

Do you know how you make me feel,
Whenever you're with me?
My lonely heart you dare to steal,
And hold so tenderly.

I know no tears but those of joy,
When I'm alone with you.
You bring a smile to this poor boy,
With everything you do.

It seems as if you've always been,
The one I'd someday hold.
The one with whom I will be seen,
Loving till I grow old.

So share your future and your heart,
And I'll teach you to fly.
Never shall we be torn apart;
Forever just you and I.

David Loermans

My Garden

I was awakened, by the sunlight,
Which danced upon my face,
Little birds were singing,
How wonderful this place

I stood by my window,
Entranced with what I saw,
Of course it was my garden,
In all its summer show

It looked just like a picture,
Mother Nature's best,
The colours were so warming,
As if they had been blessed,

I knew that I had captured
In that very hour,
A beauty so enraptured,
Of each and every flower,

I really was so thankful
For such a lovely place,
How I wished forever,
It would never change its face

David Bowman

The Rose

The rose of beauty,
Which its petals possess,
The rose of death,
Which evil withholds,
The rose of life,
Which reveals happiness,
The rose of love,
Which creates joy,
But when the winds;
Of sorrow blow,
And the petals have fallen,
The Rose is just another memory,
And a forgotten emotion.

Glenda Leahey

To You, My Song

My voice has a million voices
Which only I can sing.
While others turn to shouting
I dare to make worlds sing.

And though I'm just a peapod
Too small for any soul to see—
And though, perhaps, you are
The secrets of my being.

The bursting bubble inside o'me
Is something growing big
That no mortal has yet heard of
Nor wise men ever seen.
Yet, you my love have.

Karin M. Moltz

I Love You

The snowflakes fall upon my head,
While the clouds drift slowly by,
I stare upon the icy lake
As I dream in my mind's eye.
That I am as a snowflake,
Drifting slowly to the ground
Landing on the frozen hill.
In silence .... not a sound.
I dream that I am light as air,
My troubles they are few,
And as I dream,
I see your face, within my distant view,
You came to watch the snowflakes,
And think of love so true,
And as I fell I touched your cheek,
And whispered - I love you.

Mirella Sarrapochiello

The Mysteries Of Life

Don't ask, I can not answer.
Who on Earth can say?
The past and future
Are far away.

The past and future
Are both combined,
Locked in the part,
Of the unborn mind.

The human mind is sleeping,
Just waiting for the key,
To answer all those questions,
Asked by you, and me.

Gloria Crowe

My Hands Touch

I once met a girl
who was dumb and blind.
She taught me to see
and know, the lines and
...the leaves on a tree.

She was homely as mud.
Not a face you would find
in a picture book.
But, the beauty I saw in her
...was beyond the look.

And though I forgot her face
in my life's design,
I would never forget
the tender embrace
...of her hand on mine.

I will always remember those hands
that could see and speak so well.
And my hands, as they reach
and they seek, and they touch,
....have much to tell.

V. Lee Barnett

Serenity Within The Blues

Time spent alone
wishing down by the sea.
Waves from the ocean
wash over me.

And I see your face
in a sunrise just for me.
It steals my heart
And reminds me

that I view the world
different than you.
I'd swim the ocean
to drown my blues

Cause I've not forgotten
our place in time.
The face in the mirror
commits all my crimes.

So I'll sail away
with no set course,
I'll chart these oceans
to find your shores.

John Wick

Wistful Soul

Looking wistfully out the window,
with eyes as blue as
only a lake can be,
she longs to get out in the world.
All by herself there is nothing to do.
No toys to play with,
not even a book to read.
How has she made it through
all these years, without anyone,
since people come and go.
There are animals to see,
but often she can't touch them.
Some have drank part of her soul,
though they did not know this.
Since she can only utter faint whispers,
few people hear her.
While most people would have given up,
she is brave and strong
so she keeps trying to get out,
out in the world.

Belinda Dengler

Hate

Menacing mood
with eyes like an eagle,
Piercing..
Pulling me a part
dragging me down deeper
into a place where I've been
but don't belong,
forcing me to feel
what I want to forget.

The faking, the taking
the biting blows that often grows,
if you don't close the doors,
... and walk away.

Karen Ann Phillips

A Thousand People

A thousand people passed by
with eyes low
A thousand people passed by
without saying hello

A thousand people passed by
with a child at their side

A tug on the arm,
"don't look at him" they said,

It makes me sad

A thousand people passed by
going places,
with wax smiles on their faces

A thousand people passed by me
like an unseen object

God help them understand
the real person that I am

J. R. Paterson

Spring

I walked the forest lush and green
With flowers blooming beside a stream
My heart was aching, my grief was new
And I looked up and the sky was blue.

I had suffered long so full of pain
I wondered if I would laugh again.
My love had been so deep and true
Was there a chance I could start anew!

Breathing in the soft spring air,
Gathering flowers without a care,
Pausing to listen to a bird that sings,
I was thankful for these simple things.

In every life some rain must fall
But surely God's love surrounds us all,
And as the winding path I trod
At long last I felt close to God.

Among nature's beauty I could hear the
angel's sing,
God has given me another chance with spring

Edna Cromack

Lucy

Here comes Lucy down the street
With her pretty little dancing feet
She's so pretty she's so sweet
When she is dancing down the street
Eyes so blue hair like gold
She is the cutest five year old
She is my baby she is my love
She is my little turtle dove
She is the sunshine of my day
She gives me love in every way
This little girl with golden curls
Is just the sweetest in the world.

Anne Wilkinson

Wind, Rain And Ice

Fall is hard upon us
With it, wind
heavy with icy freshness

Waning Sunbeams watch leaves
float and flirt
as they dance to their bitter end

Rain comes as a warning
to the expected snow

Raindrops fall in calculated rhythm
beating upon the
dead carcass of summer

The frosty irreverence of winter
casts its evil hand upon the land

Painting trees
with its white death

Threatening to let loose the burden
within near bursting clouds
cached up - waiting

Laurie Walker

A Child

What is a child?
With its aches and pains,
With love and hurt
Where no one's to blame.

Yet in your hearts
You both endure,
The love and laughter,
Each child brings.

There's hurt and sorrow,
That's hard to forecome.
But the love they all give us
Makes it worth a run.

Happiness is all we ask
For God is whom we trust.
Give us that Perfect child
With whom our love we will entrust.

Roselin

Being Young

Too often we expect to receive
with no giving at all
demands far too bold
wanting and not receiving
in a while of time

Too early to expect affection
the time of being together
slowly it will come
as far away as it is
a waiting of patience

Claudette Schmidtke

Lost Child

A child is hurt and so alone
with no one around to care, she
keeps her dog close to her heart
to share the joys and fears.

She wonders why nobody
cares if she is alone and sad,
why can't they love her as God
did when he sent her to be born.

She feels the hurts others
put on her and all the pain
they cause, but there is never
anyone to listen only her
friend dog.

Her dog is there when she
is sad, when she is happy
too, to love her all the time
even when she's blue.

Mary Violet Mills

I Promise

Stand still in the breeze
With the assurance of love
That you'll always receive
From me
Stay dry in the rain
I'll protect you from pain
I'll love you so much
You'll see
Stay strong when they're weak
For nothing will keep
You and I
Apart
Stand up when they fall
I'll be there through it all
With nothing but love
In my heart

Angela Brockett

Spirit Of Dreams

Born in the spirit of dreams
with the need of freedom
to run the streams
of time and life.

In my heart and soul
you live as a symbol
of my love and my strength
through the ancient eyes
of a sightless child.

Living in a dream world
where you run free and proud
to the power of grace
caught in a timeless race.

Born in the spirit of dreams
with the need of freedom
to live the way I desire
with the greatest of pride.

Susan Lomonte

reality

two sons sometimes play crazy
with their dad
virtually left behind by their reality

like
racing through a biker chip
to the thunder drum of
a horny harley song

one falls rolling in the vision
skidding across the creation spinning

oh wow he says grinning
in the middle of a barren room

lets go daddy o
and i did

i end alone in a desert unknown
and i am dead it seems
then they laugh out loud out of the dust
and sun
and take me home

i think

bruce busby

Fall

Fall is a time,
with wind and with rain.
Blowing against the trees
and on the window pane.

The leaves will fall,
upon the grass so green.
And they are different colors,
Like none I've ever seen.

Have you ever captured the beauty,
when fall has just begun.
But mostly best of all,
Fall is very fun.

Tomorrow will still be fall,
And the leaves will still be falling.
The grass will still be green.
The trees will still be blowing.

Terri Needle

Balance

Within me is my greatness,
Within me is my smallness,
I balance each with the other,
I need each and its brother,
So's not to tilt to one side,
So's not from myself to hide.

I am greater than I can contain.
I am smaller than I can maintain.
Yet each dwells within me,
To sing and dance in me,
To move me as the light guides,
To grow and not to hide,
To love and not be shamed,
To accept and not to blame,
To soar on eagle wings,
To stoop and see the little things.
Let me always know that in me
My smallness and my greatness set me
free.

Kay Finner

A Child Running

If I wasn't a child running ...
Would you sweep me off my feet?
Hold me tenderly
so gently
so close?
Would we laugh
and cry
together, forever?
But I am running ...
I've been running forever
I'll run away from you
Just turn your head once
And I'm gone
I know no other way
Goodbye
Forgive me
I could never learn to stay

Sue Kerek

"Quiet Waters"

Through the early morning sun-ray
You could see around the bay
Where silent waters in the night
Busy tearing wearing with a might
As sifting sands along the shore
Quiet waters without a roar
Never cease to ebb and wear
These quiet waters nature share
Always flowing to the sea
With rainbow colours magnificently

Above the rocks into the sky
With black-tip sea-gulls when they fly,
Dipping diving into the waves
Nature always on the move
Certainly has its wonder days
Nudging, nudging along the shore,
These quiet waters forever more.

Jenny Broadway

Desertion

Sipping the fever of virginity,
You grip the manifestation of the
weaver of self.

Through decaying sins
let me help you witness
the hour of my birth, and
through living words let
me help you die.

Such is the way of
my existence to the
serpent of Eden...
With severed hands
let me whisper
the apple to death.

And with each
gasp of air,
I calm you
to dream in
the garden of
sinners.

Przemek Pietucha

Lost And Alone

Feeling lost and alone,
you're here but where?
In bed you're so close,
yet so far away.
Do you really care.

Feeling lost and alone
You promise words,
That never come true!
You tell me lies,
That I can't prove!

Feeling lost and alone,
You say "I love you",
but is it true.
Are they just words,
that you hope will come true.

Christine A. Wilson

My Son The Graduate

From crayons to computers
You've grown up through the years
My son you're now a graduate
Who leaves behind his peers

Those school days are no longer
But your learning has just begun
For life is a learning process
That can't be taught my son

You may be faced with failure
In your efforts to succeed
But learn from every challenge
And in life you will proceed

My faith is in your future
It reflects in all you've done
I'm proud of you a graduate
A man and more my son

Verna A. Gionet

An Angel's Sight

Pure and white,
A beautiful sight.
Wings of glory,
Heart of gold;
Soft and gentle,
Sweet and bold.
Singing softly,
Pure in tone;
Harps are playing,
Lullaby songs.
Pure and white,
Is an angel's sight.

Jennifer Carlile

"My Love"

My love for you is an endless road,
A black hole,
A lonesome home.
My love for you is unexplainable,
Too hard to see,
Too much to hide.
My love is held within my soul,
within my heart,
within my mind.
My love is felt too strongly to let go,
too tight to let fly,
but too loose to not let you know.
My love is your love,
So let your love be mine.

Jennifer Cox

Untitled

I would like to see the day
A day none too far
A day when races come together
prejudice dissolved
A day when religions decide
they are no better than another
A day when world leaders speak
of nothing but peace.

Christina Hensley

"Myself"

Stars above shine down below
a fever you hold of silent cold
I feel you from this side, the
caress of unearthly glow
The moon is full and stars
are bright, the sky a hidden
garden of delight
and I've the ways and means
going to the river warm and green
To be so quiet, not so loud
Have a lot to think about...
Myself

Crystal Collier

Untitled

If I was a dog and you was
a flower I would lift
my leg and give you a shower

Carroll Jr
blue and gold
let me see
you shoot
that goal

Carroll Jr
blue and God
let me see
that tootsie roll

When I want it
I want it bad
When I get it
makes me frisky
I'm not talking
What you thinking about
I am talking about whisky

Deesha Thomas

Beckoning Wind

Poets never mind
a foolish kind
Working, breathing
their frustration is mine.
Talking, living
I'm asking why
they still gently pass me by.
Going on to different things
becoming lonely memories
sprouting wings.
Laughing in distant motion,
beyond my quest
with words as their potion.
Making something
from your bitter toil
from the earth's leather-like wisdom.
I tried to reach them
Seeing only their coattails in the breeze,
I missed their brilliance
but caught their disease.

Jacob D. Maguire

Sounds Of L.A.

The breaking of glass
And ear shattering blast from gunshots...
Zzzzppp..Bullets pass;
Pounding feet terrified to be caught.
Piercing screams of those afraid
After a muggers swish of his blade.
Drums beat as fists fly
As metal hits metal sparks fly! (People die!)
Echoes of the screeching tires
Ricochet off alley walls as fires
Crackle and burn.
And then you turn,
You turn around
To escape the sounds;
Into your car with the radio blaring
Get on the freeway without caring
HONK, HONK! BEEP, BEEP!
Rush hour traffic-stuck in your jeep—
Then as you leave L.A. behind
All of the confusion leaves your mind.

Alison Owens

Happy Father's Day

To the man who said he would always stay
But instead went along his merry way
Happy Father's Day

To the man who said he wanted to be a father
Now he doesn't even know his daughter
Happy Father's Day

To the man who thought love was just a game
All he knows about me is my name
Happy Father's Day

As the years pass and I grow older
For my crying I will not have your shoulder
Happy Father's Day

You will always miss my springs
And all the wonderful joy I bring
Happy Father's Day

But don't dismay
Because some day
You might have a Happy Father's Day
The choice is yours

Amanda H. Beihl

Lofty Ideas

Ride high the wild whirling winds
Move up and down rugged basins
Search around and over mystical mountains
Find the ever presence of the omnipresent mind.

Clever was our creator
Not to leave behind this thought to us mortals
To show us our humanity that apparitions come by illusion
And great is our world of delusion
For we strive to die, to live or to become
What lofty ideas we have had for something so simple as life's love.

Forget not our love to life with its true friend — Unconditional Love
Without this love we are companionless moving helplessly backwards
Creating misery with our every thought and desiring what we least want
Destroying the very life within by thinking selfishly of our own world.

Discover the universe by seeking love in the heart's inner recesses
So we can live the present, see the future
and take part in life's majesty
See with eyes that see this love, hear with ears that hear this love
Deeply feel this life's love in all things
and we will have lofty ideas to guide us.

Bruce J. Moran

Forever In My Heart

Oh, what a discovery we made when we saw you both in the womb that day.
It was such a wonderful and special surprise that put a twinkle in your Mommy's eyes.
As time went on and I learned of a boy and a girl, I was so excited with a thought that came to mind,
A boy, Jonathan, a perfect playmate for Ben; a girl, Amber Marie, to dress up now and then.
You were so healthy and playful inside of me, I would never have thought it would end in tragedy.
Oh, how hard I fought to keep you safe within me, but much to
my despair it was not meant to be, for within a few short hours
you were thrust from my womb and, oh, how sad I am, as it was
three months too soon.
Even though you were too young to live, in those short precious
moments I gave you all the love I could give.
Though I can never hold you close in my arms, I will always
hold you ever so close in my heart, for you are my children, no
matter how small, and both of your names I so often will call:
I love you, Jonathan; I love you, Amber Marie
Forever in my heart,
Mommy

Christy Harnden

Chance Meeting

I've loved you all my life; I've needed you life long.

We've shared walks together; hand in hand, through rain of heaven born.
I've often dreamed of how it feels; to run my fingers through your hair.
Many a time, I've held you tight; dusk til night, night til the dawn.
Our loving is the coming together of two great nations;
Joined by the power of a passion to be one.

Loved you all my life; I've needed you life long.

Your slender frame, has the sculptors envy.
Skin soft and smooth, tightened in its effort to keep the woman within.
Eyes so bewitching, enchanting and engulfing; mirrors to a soul, so vulnerable to love.
Arms of a mother with infant newly born; enfolding with warmth, compassion and adorn.
The shoulder, that can not be matched; to sustain the burden of my despairs.

I've loved you all my life; needed you life long.

Short hair streaming of arrogance and confidence;
Covering the crest of a statue of beauty.
Sparkling eyes illuminating every encounter; filling the room with a brilliance of joy.
Head rolls back, releasing your laughter; commanding smiles from all who's eyes behold.
You danced, with a ballerinas grace...The "EYE DANCE" of first face to face.

I've loved you life long; I've needed you all my life.
Only by chance...Tonight I meet my Wife.

Glen M. Weathers

Soul Masters

Souls...spirits...the essence of truth.
Once vibrant and passionate...now, without luster...bound by deception.

Wreathed in tendrils...suffocating...subduing life in talons-grip.
Living ceases...life endures...clenched to submission...truth abandoned.

Pervading tentacles seeking avenue of mastery...digits probing at unwary prey...embraced in deceit.

The catacombs of the soul submit...sanctuary defiled...tranquility lost...souls of tyranny.

Not to yield to boas zeal...spirit crown...will regained...soul master demise.

Andrea Nelin-Roth

The Unfamiliar Face

Transformed
Standing by the pond wondering what happened to the sweet
child within.
Did she slip away, or was she being replaced by the Unfamiliar Face staring back at her?

Thinking once more, how life changes so much. The past she remembered so well has vanished, but the flood of childhood memories return.
The Unfamiliar Face,
quavering in the water, takes on the appearance of a child; full of life, her smile so bright, her face beaming with pride, but that is nothing but an image. It shall be eventually replaced by the Unfamiliar Face.

The vows she had made to regain her childhood are having no effect.
A single tear sliding down her cheek, the rippling water, distorting the reflection of the Unfamiliar Face.

The present is here, the future lies ahead, but the past has gone, she realizes now: the Unfamiliar Face is but that of her own. It sickens her to see it piled high with dressing. Dunking her head in the water, she begins to feel the fear, sorrow, and depression, drain slowly away.

The present is here, the past remains unchanged, but the future lies ahead: time to redeem herself from the Unfamiliar Face.

Heather Schnee

Fate

I see it all shiny and silver, the edge coming nearer and nearer.
The blade of death chasing us all, the turmoil we feel inside is small.
We are not afraid, only sad, if life were any better,
we'd know what we had.
The ridges are itching its way up and down, but what can we say.
Closer and closer, inch by inch, death is upon us like a mighty pinch.
Can we not stop this ugly fate, or are we only able to hate.
No, I say not of a knife to slice our throat, but of an enemy
that is afloat.
Not on water or in the air, but in our hearts and minds to wear.
The one I speak of is very near. If we look into ourselves we will see the nasty destruction ahead, for it is planned, just as I am standing here.

Christina M. Bettale

Club Fed

There's a ranch out West that borders on a place they call "Club Fed",
where criminals are kept in style. They're clothed, and clean, and fed.

The recreation room they have boasts large, new, TV sets.
why—anything an inmate wants—that's just what he will get.

With visitors and gifts and all, the time they serve goes fast,
and even when their time is up, they want the stay to last.

Well, anyway, this ranch out West that borders on "The Club"
is cared for by an old cowboy who never asked for much.

He's worked hard all his life, from early dawn, to late at night, but,
sometimes he can't help but think that things just aren't quite right.

When days are long, and dust is thick, and water tanks go dry,
and things just keep on going wrong no matter how he tries.

Yup, fifty years of riding can sure make a man's bones ache,
so sometimes he'll just stop his horse, to take a little break,

And look at where the prison sits—he'll squint his eyes and stare,
then mutter, "Wonder what a man'd have to do to get in there."

Carolyn Carver

"Woe To This Child"

This constant haranguing reminds me of children
A banging their heads on the floor
For they"must" have "their way", though
they ruin the day, for a dozen people or more.
It would have been better if fathers and mothers
had taught their kids to obey,
and not let them"Rant"
when they're told that they can't
by a tantrum their temper display.
It makes life so hard for a child not corrected
to handle his life when he's grown.
This trait is reflected and all souls dejected,
as they reap from the seeds that were sown.
And what a sad plight when he
"Must" have"His Right."
All others are just disregarded
There is no Fair Play in having "His Way"
All notions but his are discarded.

Helen E. Baird

"Once Again My Own"

Girl, I walked the Ohio River wit
a banjo on my knee:
A headin' for Johns Hopkins for a
banjoectomy?
God no Hosanna: No orisons for
me...
I got to get a no fault dee-vorce from
reality!
So I slog through the fog like a
broken dick dog.!
I'll fish for pork brains in rain!
Puttin' locks on my clocks, I'll blow
up my block:
Some Golden Moment to retain...
Bolster palisades 'gainst mad
salty cascades:
Pressing my lips to my own!
Till a time and place; In a clime,
and a space;
When my mind is one more my own....

Billy Christian

Most Wanted

A world full of peace, love and harmony
A beautiful place for you and for me
People of all races getting along
Being able to distinguish right from wrong

Caring, sharing and lending a helping hand
Giving that little extra whenever you can
Showing our youth the right way to go
Imparting knowledge, teaching respect are just a few things they need to know

Uplifting and applauding our seniors and thanking God for them
Constantly making them feel special—never letting their lights go dim
Feeding the hungry with our abundance of food
And helping the homeless will surely brighten their moods

Enjoying the beauty of places far and near
Counting our many blessing throughout the year
Recognizing just how precious life is
Honoring and glorifying the Supreme Being — for all of this is his

These are all the things that I want most
All things are possible — Let's try a dose!

Jonnie Elam

Matthew A Gift From God

Your prayers have been answered from above
A beautiful son to enjoy and love.

It took two weeks for Matthew to find his way
Into your hearts and lives, he's home to stay.

So bright and alert he seems to be,
Mommy and Daddy and baby make three

Forever it seemed for Matthew to come to you
God checking his list for someone special, took a long time to do

Such a wonderful family to love and enjoy,
No better place could have been chosen for this baby boy.

His name was decided especially for him,
A gift from God, it really has been

Beverly Sinak

A Birthday Message

On a cold November day in nineteen thirty seven
A bouncing blue-eyed baby boy was sent to me from heaven.

You've done a lot of bouncing since, sometimes up and some-
times down
But through the years it's been sheer joy just having you around.

I wouldn't change you for the world, you're grand the way you are
And in the years ahead of you, I know you will go far.

It's been rough and it's been fun, watching you mature
Wondering if you'd become a gentleman or a boor.

The days of wondering have ceased and I can proudly say
You are still the finest son of all, in every kind of way.

Frank E. Rytell

"A Mother's Cry"

A child was born only 15 years ago
A child died just 14 years ago
The child's smile laugh and cry are still heard
The child's memory is brought back by a tiny bird
The echo of the child still melting my mind
The sight of the child is making me blind
The pictures on the wall are of my child
The bags under my eyes are driving me wild
I cant eat I cant sleep I'm dying inside
I cant help my feelings my child has died
Days go by and by as I sit to ponder and cry
2 Years ago I passed away the cause was starvation and dehydration
I'm with my child now laughing and playing
I'm ready for my body to start decaying
My soul is gone I've left my shell
I've taken the turn away from hell
I'm here to stay with my son
My life on earth is done

Jennifer J. Stewart

Our Distant Neighbor

Walking down the street
A cold wind at my back
I see this homeless man on the ground
All covered in black
I first experience a feeling a sadness
He lives in a world of his own
To society he is not alive and is considered unknown
His spirit have been broken not to mention his heart
Everyday he wakes up its gloomy and dark
He travels the earth with no shoes on his feet
Spends half of the day looking for something to eat
His body has become fragile from the weather outside
He spends the second half of the day looking for his bedside
And when the day is over and night has finally arrived
He braces himself for the cold
But when the morning comes, our distant neighbor is not alive

Clarence E. Jones Jr.

Untitled

Dark clouds, hushed wind
A command performance this summer night.

She looked down into a sea of nameless faces...and saw HIM.
Anonymous, yet special.

Summer rain and fresh cut grass.
Overhead lights luminated a certain sort of magic there,
A magic she knew was hers.
Eyes met; searching, questioning with looks, not words.

The crack of the bat, roar of the crowd, silence for the pair.
The air crackled when those fingers met in a life-long bond.

Years later, entwined by twin gold loops... A sunny summer day;

The crack of the bat... Twinkle-like laughter of a child.
Older, yet just as young.

The magic of the ballpark never fades away.

Jennifer Church

"Our Country"

Our country's not like it used to be,
A country safe for you and me,
A country honest, good and strong.
Now we wonder what went wrong?
Once we had leaders, honest and trustful.
Now they are greedy, something awful
Spending our money on everything
Counting on it more votes to bring.
No matter if it's good or right
They don't have the guts to stand up and fight.
But for something silly or something wrong
That's where we see them come out strong!
Instead of things moral and good
Upon which our nation always stood
They are leading us away from God
So we must go after them roughshod!
Just who are they trying to fool,
We can't mention God or Pray in school?
If we don't do something and do it fast
I'm afraid our country will not last.

Edgar Lorain Grapes

Life

A Birth A Laughter
A Death A Scream

A Fear A Cry
A Regret A Why?

A Joy A Hello
A Pain A Good-bye

The situations change but the words remain the same.

Jennifer Lynn McKay

Donegal Dignity

In mountains mellow made by mists,
a festal folk abides.
The family of man finds intercourse,
for here a ritual discourse strives.
Pleasure mixes mirthily at the
harvest hearth's night cellarside.
Work, a benison rises in votive
candles burning bright.
Sunday sees a regal reverence
raised on an altar ornate, while
wood kneelers knowingly recall the rocky road.
Pilgrim's progressing life's journey
find a stony path made stately
by a jocund jar of joint humanity.

John Barry Kelly

Thanksgiving

A time to be thankful for all good things that we possess,
A difficult task when faced with great duress.

To have health and wealth without peace and contentment,
Might well create pain and resentment.

To exist in a limbo that is so unkind,
Is unjust and torturous to the mind.

The only great gifts which we can count on are with us each day.
We can say what we want to say, be who we want to be,
And enjoy our thoughts that are free.

We can battle adversaries with all our might,
And be grateful that we put up a good fight.

To feel and express anger, joy, love and sorrow,
And always hope for a better tomorrow.

To have fire in the soul with a great passion,
Is a way to live in an admirable fashion.

To blend it altogether in just the right measure,
Is quite an undertaking.
But isn't it wonderful that it's always in the making?

Diana Sutcliffe

Whispering Love

Softly it lies all about us
A fair land, and heavenly
One sweet day the veil shall rift and
Gently bring us there to be.

If we quiet our hearts and listen
When in moments of despair,
We'll hear its voices whisper love
And mingle with our prayers.

whispering love, O how sweet is thy voice
Making my heart in its sorrow rejoice.
Whispering love, O how sweet is thy voice
Making ny heart in its sorrow rejoice.

"Nearer are we than e'er before,
Our hands still clasp yours," they say,
"We have not gone anywhere at all
We'er just a loving thought away."

"So carry on till we meet again
In our fair land, and heavenly,
Where no parting nor tears shall make
Our bliss for all eternity."

Alda Eldora Underwood

For God Be The Glory

Because of you, Mother's Day should be everyday.

I am grateful that God sent you to be a Mother not for
a few but for many. If all mothers were like you what a
beautiful world it would be, for the love you show for all
the people you know—your family, friends and others too.
Through the laughter and pain, sorrow and rain you are so
kind and sweet you are one Mother, one friend, that can't be
beat, you are special in every way, you are special to me every day.

You put the (M) in Mother and the (O) because there is no other
the (T) because of the togetherness that we share.
the (H) that stands for her and that is you.
the (E) is for every day God sends to let you know
that He is blessing you and He
will always be there beside you.
the (R) is for that real love and rough times in
your life.

I want you to know whether you're up or whether you're
down there is still no other Mother I rather be around
and it's no wonder, because you are one of the "sweetest,
sweetest" Mothers in town.

Audrey M. Wise

A Friend

A friend is one who cares about you,
A friend is one who you know will ALWAYS
Be there when things get tough and the
Road gets rough, that's when friend comes
Through strong and tough.

A friend is one who's there when good
Times aren't, a friend is one who knows you
Can trust to tell your most deepest and
Darkest secret to, that's the kind of friend
I've found in YOU!

Dawn Lorenson

Be True

Don't ever play games with your true love.
A game can be won or lost
When the stakes are happiness, like heaven above.
If you lose, can you afford the cost?

Be honest and follow your heart,
for with lies, if you win, you lose.
Stay true to each other, and you'll never be apart.
Be on each other's side, the only sure team to choose.

Each day give your love a brand new start.
Don't ever lose it, never let it die,
Or you'll end with a broken heart.
Finders keep, and losers cry.

Joseph R. La Grasso

Autumn

The warm breeze penetrates my soul,
a glowing light, a soft dewy scent.
The autumn leaves swiftly flow,
into a watery bliss where time is spent.

The sky is a careful watcher of mine
as the dusky damp air drifts away.
Taking with it all reality and time,
making new thoughts form and stay.

I can see the powerful change take place,
a symbolic peace which few can possess.
Sending me into a distant daze,
wondering which course my life may arrest.

Surely this everlasting change
could only mean a drifting chance,
Of the peaceful times that must arrange,
in a wonderful passing, this new and seasonal dance.

Heidi Eckhardt

Alone

As the water flows, it speaks to me,
A quiet voice it seems to be
Alone, but not alone.

You're far away, yet you seem so near,
It's your voice in the waterfall I hear.
Alone, but not alone.

Your voice is so soft, yet I hear my name,
And the words 'I love you' again and again.
Alone, but not alone.

Speak to me so I know you're here,
Then being alone I will never fear.
Alone, but not alone.

Dianne Lewis

Autumn's Gift

As in the last quiet days of any life,
A golden light is shed as if for comfort
in the waning hours.
One last array of brilliant dress
displayed in ambered color by the flowers.

How grateful are the trees for each prized leaf and bloom;
For now they make an offering of each
to mother earth;
For she had given them the strength
for these to whom they'd given birth.

Soon death will come with icy wind its herald;
The golden light turned gray
will make the Winter seem eternal and unended.
The limbs clothed now in frost
that seems somehow suspended.

Ah, but for now this glorious reward is savored!
The life is lived;
The fruit is gathered from the bough;
A quiet time 'til life shall be renewed
The golden Autumn gives us now.

Gloria Cox

"A Precious Gift To Me"

Nine long months of nurturing inside a new found home,
A life begins to breathe and think in a womb of his own.
Carefully you care for him to ensure a healthy path,
To a lifelong journey of wonderment by which God will draft.

As time rolls on the miracle of life comes too pass,
Unknowing of the dangers that may be in his grasp,
You lie awake at night to pray, to keep your son alive,
For with experience, you know with life, at times you must survive.

Take away the love you gave, I wonder where I'd be,
Cause I often think the care you gave, was surely the key,
To keep me off the streets at night and find another way,
For surviving in this crazy world in which we live today.

On Mother's Day I pray for you in return for all you've done,
Not just for me or the one's you Love, but for everyone.
Cause you see Mom, their are few today, who deserve the little Mother,
For the Love you give unselfishly, makes you like no other.

November Twenty Second Nineteen Sixty Three,
Too many this means nothing, but surely not to me.
For this is the day that through God's Love A miracle was to be,
That miracle on that day was you, "A PRECIOUS GIFT TO ME."

John Kennedy Wedge

Stale Innocence

At first there is not a drop of light
A heaping innocent darkness protects the land
Only the deep darkness that holds within a dignified mystery of its own
A peace, an untouched indulgence naive to hurt.

Through the pure womb a speck of golden evil is born
Piercing and ripping like a demented soul
Another follows, and another.

Agony is felt as the sinful inbreeds keep stabbing and clawing
To reach within, to break the lowly silence, to destroy the peace.
The silent innocence is at once bright with the screaming light.

Forced upon and violated
Till left to whimper in mourning, till left to whither and cease
Existence.
Now exists a golden pollution that chokes out all else.
Sameness throughout the land, as the last shreds of dignity are gone.

All is bright now, all is naked
There is no more shy, lonesome darkness
Just the light, the overrated light.

Christina Nikolai Sintihakis

Telephones

In our house there's a little box, sitting on a table.
A little handle on its top, with a funny twisted cable.
Sometimes this crazy little box, goes ring-a-ling-a-ling,
Mom picks up the handle, and starts talking to the thing.
She talks, and then she listens, it's such a mystery,
Why she is talking to that box, when she could talk to me.

This didn't happen only once, it goes on all day long.
Why is she talking to that box, did I do something wrong?
Once Mom was in the kitchen, when the box went ring-a-ling,
I picked up the handle, and said something to the thing.
Then I heard a voice inside, I couldn't believe my ear,
The voice inside, I recognized, it was so loud and clear.

"Well, Hello, This is Grandpa, how is my little man?"
What's Grandpa doing in that box? I didn't understand.
Then I heard another voice, "Hi baby, how are you?"
Goodness sakes! What's going on? Grandma was in there too!
Then Mommy took the handle, and talked in it again,
And I knew they were okay, 'cause she would laugh, and grin.
It was Grandpa and Grandma, I knew without a doubt;
But how they both got in that box, I'll never figure out!

Carl W. Burns

Clown

A shy look to the young lady,
A leer to the one with the frown.
Does your wonderment never cease?
Never— if you are a clown.
Show me the marshmallow cake to tease.
Taste it and offer to give me a piece
(Not in the face?)—Oh, no, no please!
Bring a smile to the face of the littlest boy
Make him roll 'round in belly-laugh joy
Of seeing you up, then down.
Should one only fall
On your backside or face
To be remembered as the clown???

Harvey Sapot-Ferer

Just A Bad Feeling

Emptiness in my heart and Emptiness in my head.
A longing with this strong feeling. That just won't go away.
Can't get you out of my head it's a heartache everyday.
An aching pain that doesn't hurt. You just won't go away
Just a bad feeling, it's just a bad feeling
Pressures in my heart, over you!
A longing for a friend that's gone I can't change the past
The feelings that are in my mind, hit me
hard and fast. If I only this or if I only that can't
change the time that's gone and my memory is
strong over who? Just a bad feeling it's just
a bad feeling over who?
Spring time is gone summer and fall
winter is here for now and empty feeling
strong at hand
over you

Joette Vargo

Lullaby

The nightly wind is singing a lullaby,
a lullaby of good-byes,
As it passes by my ears,
my eyes can't help but fill with tears,
thinking so fondly of the past years,
The lullaby is whispering sounds of good-byes,
sounds that were never heard,
dreams never came to be,
The sound is fading fast,
it soon will be in the past,
but the last of the lullaby describes a place,
a place were he has gone to be,
a place were his spirit is peacefully free.

E. K. Brown

Untitled

A master piece of art, a fine mold of clay, a hollow inside,
A mind of her own and a life no other can share.
Pure utter bliss of sheer loneliness.
A sense of emptiness filled to capacity.
Belonging with no where to go.
All alone in a crowd.
Change your image, your very way of thinking.
Only to fall down again, over and over.
Be someone else as long as you promise never to look back.
It's only reality. What's the difference?
If you wrap yourself up real tight, and squeeze your eyes shut,
there's only darkness anyway.
Solitude without regret.
No one but me is all I need.
I will not have anyone else, under no circumstances.
You'd only hit the hollowness anyway.
Be your own.
Love yourself.
Others hurt too much.

Abby Mazer

Blakey's Garden

A shady place in shallow soil,
A myriad of seed, spinach, squash, and something else,
Gentle hands digging, patting, watering,
Oblivious to Grandmommy, Neil, and almanac,
Incessant explanations of worms and other wondrous things -
These will make his garden grow.
Perchance like the "flower in the crannied wall,"
And help us "know what God and man is."

Jake N. Veal

Homeless Man

I'm a homeless man
A poor man
I don't want much
People walk by me everyday
Some give me a penny
Some give me a dime
Some people give me nothing
Can you please
Can you please
Spare a dollar
Maybe two or three, it won't hurt you, please.

Allison Andrade

Confusion

As I sit and contemplate my mere existence
A question pops up and is quite persistent.
I wonder and think, I think and wonder
I think to see if life is a blunder.
If so, would it matter if my life I take
A quick bullet and I could let my soul escape.
If I'm wrong my soul would be forever damned
Is it worth it to find out who I am?
So I sit back and try to give my brain a break
Just be here and be in my confused state.

Lxander Willyums

Closet Doors

It's so dark where I stand.
A quick light for a moment, then it ends.
With my eyes close it seems even darker.
No matter how wide I open them it's still dark
from where I stand.

In the closet, is where I am.
Standing on the other side is my plan.
I got there once, to find myself in a jam.
A jammed door is where I was.
Open say me, open says you.
In another closet is where I am.

Deitra Dinkie Foster

The Graveyard Path

Tall and dark stood the castle drear,
A river flowed along quite near.
A lady fair stood by the bank,
Staring in, her reflection sank.
She walked along the graveyard path,
A mother's soft cry, her angry wrath.
And from behind the large oak tree,
Stood another lady as fair as thee.
Silently the moonlight crept,
Together the ladies softly wept.
For each had buried a child there,
Amid the graves that each did fear.
Together the lonely mothers mourned,
By the pale moonlight were their faces adorned.
Weep, weep! Oh mothers dear!
These whispers soft, yet both could hear.
And each one softly said good-bye.
To the place where forever their children must lie.

Alicia Lentricchia

A Strange Demise

It is a death to fall asleep,
A short mild ceasing to exist
When eyes have closed from counting sheep.

Across the eves to dawn we leap
Unknowing of what nights consist,
It is a death to fall asleep.

Unknowing of the rise and sweep
Of moons that bathe in halo-mist,
Our eyes have closed from counting sheep.

The consciousness of mind dives deep,
While only fragment-dreams persist,
It is a death to fall asleep.

There is no hope that life will keep,
Death comes disguised to shake his fist
When eyes have closed from counting sheep.

Thank God the rims of suns will creep
Into the sky; wake and be kissed.
It is a death to fall asleep
When eyes have closed from counting sheep.

Arthur J. Luchan

A Touch Of Fall

A touch of fall is in the air.
A sprinkle of autumn colors can be seen everywhere.
Even the breeze whispers promises of things to come,
like trees with golden leaves glowing in the autumn sun.
Relief from summers' awesome heat may be near,
along with autumn skies we hold so dear.
Skies filled with purple Martins on their southern flight,
Canadian geese silhouetted against the moon on a starry night.
So hurry on dear planet, in your heavenly flight,
onward in your solar journey that will bring us such delight.

Darrel K. Douglas

"Sugar Cookies, Bread Pudding, And Cakes"

Down home, by the Chesapeake Bay,
a sweet old lady, baked cookies and cakes
all the towns people come by everyday.
The old lady bakes sugar cookies everyday.
The sweet old lady, baking cookies
bread pudding and cakes. The sweet smell,
of maple, ginger and butter. Spices
so good to taste. Little children would
gather by the window, staring at the
cookies all day. Sugar cookies, bread pudding
and cake.

Earlean Doty

The Creator Of The Rose

As a dew drop falls from a new spring rose,
A teardrop trickles down a little girl's nose.
As a fresh bloom pure and bright,
She cries for hers, "What happened last night?"
Like a stem strong and tall,
She sits by weak from yet another fall.
Like a thorn green and fresh,
It seems to harden in her flesh.
As the rose dances in the morning sun,
She fears the day that has just begun.
When it sways in the breeze,
You can see her fall to her knees.
As the rose starts to die, in weather cold and bleak,
She knows an answer she must seek.
Sure enough as the rose was gentle and sweet,
A special friend did the little girl meet.
The rose very soon faded away,
As the little girl promised to see it on a new spring day.
But when the last blow caused her eyes to close,
She was soon with the Creator of her rose.

Christy Abbott

Love Returned

A touch of the lips, love is revealed,
A touch of a hand, worries healed.
From touch to touch the feeling expands,
A touch of love with each stroke of your hand.
I want this feeling again, but we've lost sight,
Of the love that used to go with us at the end of the night.
Smiling faces have seemed to fade,
Replaced by the fights for continuing days.
I love you, I want this love to be returned,
I love you, over the passing months, this I learned.
A touch of the lips, love is revealed,
I want our relationship to mend and heal.

Julie Chambers

Keeper Of My Dreams

A moon that hasn't rays nor light in the night
A wandering soul in the sands
Of times, a dove that hasn't flight

Sands that shift...Pyramid of never quest....Who then,
Will ever be my guide?
I was lost, no love to behold, is my fortune told?

Comfort in solace a sad virtue to enstow
a light, a sign from the very temple
an ember to grow
warmth indeed

My eye turned to the skies for life anew
bluing heavens in your eyes.....and then I knew
it seems oddly, it seems that you are the keeper of my soul
mind and spirit you are the keeper of my dreams

Bodet Morales Licea

One Moonlit Night

On the second night of the full moon
a wish was granted, the inner feeling
of isolation and grief was banished
by a single touch of tenderness.
The thought of searching was no longer present.
Love, acceptance, and truth
were no longer a confusion.
A single gentle touch of soft lips was the
answer at the end of my search.
Someone kinder than nature and filled with
more beauty than that of the moonlit
night caressed and eased away my grief.
One moonlit night was granted by nature,
but the moon had deceived me.
With the promise of content I stood.
But just as the moon came, it went,
and with it, its blasphemous promise.

Jose Cardenas

Worm

After a heavy long rain,
A worm could easily drown.
This is why above all,
We must stay above ground.

Now, let me make this clear,
A worm lives in constant fear.
We are always in danger it's true,
Seen some crushed by a walking shoe.

We must hide from all the birds,
Watch for hunting bugs, and stomping herds.
Avoid that man made traffic,
Keep our head, and don't panic.

We can't afford to be bold,
Or ever should a worm roam.
I admit we live in a hole,
But to us, "It's Home Sweet Home."

Harry De Marzi

A Little Piece Of Death

A little piece of death would now do me just fine.
A little piece of death to sooth my restless mind.
A little piece of death, something we all crave
No one can resist it, not the strong, nor the brave.
A little piece of death, a venture into the unknown
Which if ventured too far, one may never return home.
It may seem to you that I am one obsessed with death,
but it is quite the opposite, for I love every breath.
You see a little piece of death, which is oh so hard to keep
is just a little piece of death, the way that I define sleep.

Jeremiah Dotson

Clydesdale

In total obscureness next to the
age of ignorance. A shadow that beheld
exquisiteness and Irenicism rode through
the field of snow against the wind flaunting
its pallid flesh.

I hear his cry like the banshee shatter
dismalness lividly indicating eccentricity
with profound sadness. Its wandering soul,
looking for Azrael discovered Serendipitously
the garden of sorrow.

Its Enrapturing beauty enthralled my soul
then I watched his deadening strength reach
its vulnerable point and collapse leaving
me to watch the soft color of blood soften
the snow and blend with his flesh mortally gold.

Diminishing his thoughts and held before the
lamb of God his weakened eyes rest eternal
and the Clydesdale became lost to sight.

Blanca Puente

Missing You

All alone, I see myself
All alone I feel.
Thinking about what we once had,
Just doesn't seem real.
Where did all that time go
The happiness I once knew?
Away with you, away with you,
Away your love flew.
Was your love a dream, or perhaps a fantasy?
Do I want to know the truth, or shall I leave it be?
Despite how hard I try,
No matter what I do
The bottom line of all is -
I am missing you!

Alicia Gonchar

Sand Castles

The seaside abounds with sand castles
All constructed as the owner fancies them,
And as time and talent permit.
The tide will exact its price,
But each will have its day in the sun.
There are onlookers to enjoy and appreciate
What has been loved and labored for.
Others are indifferent to the array.
Some would gladly kick them over,
Just for the momentary pleasure of it.
But the builder is intent on his project,
Scarcely aware of anything around him.
Totally oblivious that he is captive.
We builders of sand castles like to forget,
That we are vulnerable by our works.

John J. Mangano

Fall

Leaves are falling red, orange, and gold,
all of them I want to hold. Where is all
that corn going? Those squirrels eat till
they are over flowing. Is that a spider
that I see? No, it looks more like a rock
to me. The birds are happy because they
have food, but it's going to get cold out,
and that makes them in a bad mood. I see
a purple flower blooming, I wonder what it
thinks it's still doing? Sometimes I get
peeved from raking up all the leaves.

Heather Dwyer

Roosevelt

I've seen some changes taking place.
All for the better I might add.
Where there were rocks and broken glass,
There's now in all that space,
Beautiful green grass.
When once we had a lake in our backyard.
Then people spoke and got it fixed.
Now it rains and that space is no longer in disregard.
We have a fence, when there was none.
Thus, games can be worry free and fun.
Our playing and other activities were limited.
Now, with a gym there are more activities for those interested.
Teachers, students and parents we can only go one way,
forward, with pride and intelligence.
Let's show them all just how much we are
A breed of excellence!

Alfredo Luna Sr.

Silent Night, Lonely Night

Silent night, lonely night
All is wrong, nothing's right.
My Dad passed away in nineteen sixty-seven,
But my Mother said that he went up to heaven.

I was already disabled when Dad left this universe,
And from that day on Satan has gave me a curse,
Because I can't forget that time when Dad passed away,
But I still love him every night, every day.

His body was buried in the cemetery ground,
But this soul went up high cause he was heavenly bound.
But one of these days we will both meet again,
In that beautiful land where there is never a sin.

When I leave this earth where there is human and humane,
I will leave every trouble and leave every pain.
And when he sees me coming I know he will run,
Like the Father did for the prodigal son.

Joe Dunkin

Untitled

Mr King was number one in this Land.
All over the world, He was King of man
Remembering his words one will always Preach.
To the mountain top he finally reached
In every sermon, He would always say.
Non violence is the only way.

Let us now do what he has preached.
Until our mountain top has been reached.
There could be no other joy in this land.
Having a dream come true for such a wonderful man.
Each and every hour of the day.
Remember, He was King in every way.

King now sits on his throne on High.
In His Fathers house beyond the sky.
Now, knowing how our King left this Land.
Gives us pride to Honor this Man.

Charles L. Winslow

God Waits

The night clouds gather and the watchman waits
And waits for man to decide his fate;
Voices whisper in the air with shadows dancing everywhere
God looks down from his lofty height
And waits for man to decide the night.

Burton H. Boroff

The Naive Believe

The Naive Believe
All that glitters in these lands
Should be ensconced in their buttered hands
The Naive Believe This —

The Naive Believe
Theirs is the force that earns the buck
That raises them above and beyond the muck
The Naive Believe This —

The Naive Believe
That when the reaper grim
Comes to seek his pay, he'll heed their pleas
And wend his way —
The Naive Believe This —

The Naive Believe
In Thy Kingdom Come
This, that and everything can be done — Yes
The Naive Believe This

Bert Patrick

Soul

Swaying and swishing through the sound of serenity
Allusions of illusions not so carefully designed
Turning inside out of the raindrops
falling on the roof of the mind
Forgetful fascinations of facts
So blind yet still seeing the birds of prophecies
yearning to find the branches of evergreens
Climbing with the ascending notes
yet can never go higher than the hawk
or the flight from the earth's boundaries
and oceans of thoughts
Dancing around the flickering fire in the dimness of the stars
Hearing the silence in the sounds of singing
Free to fly higher
than the boundaries of nothingness to revival
Talking out loud inside
and running through the spokes of the wheels
rolling through the trees on the paths of paved perceptions
Flying now without ever taking off
Disconnecting from body but soul conversing with the wind

Jean Elisabeth Kiene

Surreal Diversity

Across the Great Beautiful of God's construction.
Along a dark moon of wicked design.
I soar on the brink of immortality,
Whether it be evil or brightly divine.
If I should drink the tear of cherub.
Shall I absorb the eyes of a demon?
Injection of my soul is truly sublime
Into a power of any kind.
The hate that burns, the love that drives.
Shall both keep my spirit alive?
This, tis truly inevitable
Both thrive and radiate from my love, surreal.

Graham Hackney

"Rainbow"

A rainbow painted in the sky reflects colorful hues,
Appearing as ribbons flowing delicately to the earth,
Captured only by the beholders eye, that's true,
A beauty, as a precious gem having great worth.

You are visible, but not concrete, an elusion I know,
Discreet, showing your lovely presence now and then,
As an orchestra in harmony, gently you do flow,
Majestic, awesome, revealing a little of heaven.

Carol J. Lyons

Pictures Of Time

Through the many years
Along with a few tears
Turning pages for happy hours
Looking from faces to colorful flowers
The pleasures and joy appears
With the coming of the little dears
Adding new pages for our picture book
Time now to have a second look
Watching changes in their stages grow
With each holiday more memories to show -
One day for their smaller eyes to see
The love and fun married life can be
And knowing they shared a large part
Of life we lived turning pages in their heart.

Dorothy I. Brown

My Mother

Sweet as the gentle falling rain,
 Always there to share my pain.
Gives warmth and shelter from the storm,
 Willing to protect me from all harm.
Will put all my fears to rest,
 Will stay up late, and help me study for my test.
Gives all her love, faith and trust, and ask nothing in return,
 will always be by my side when others are on the run.
When times are hard, and my endurance low,
 I call her up, and to her I can always go.
In our lives we will have others,
 BUT, never forget there's none like Mother.
Therefore, when clouds are dark, and you can't find any trusting other
 Lift up your head and call your dear Mother!

Annette Wallace

Blue Bottle

I was sittin' right there in my big easy chair
Amindin' my stuff like I oughta
When out of the air with no visible flair
Came this fly that is known as blue bottle.

Straight at me he came and he took deadly aim
At a place where he sure shouldn't oughta.
Now that place I'll admit is the place where
I sit and there's little room left for blue bottle.

While I sat there on high with no room for
The fly I was sure that at last I had got 'I'm.
But that pesky old fly just as quick as an
Eye dove down and came up from the bottom.

I'm a flier, my self, and that ploy by the
Fly took courage and knowledge of combat.
He was small, even so he knew right where
To go to arrive at the scene where the fight was at.

Blue bottle's now gone but his fame will live on
Wherever the news will be practical; on trains
Or on planes or on Spain's lovely plains.
I sure hope this poem's syntaxical.

John Milton Foster

Nature

The wind whispered through the field as the grasses talked
 among themselves.
The rain jumped from the sky with the earth sleeping below.
The trees reached out their arms to console the frightened
 baby flowers.
The sitting moon waited for the resting sun.
The soil battled with the humble water for leadership.

Gregory DeLong

Renascence

There is a satisfaction in aloneness.
An adventure in survival.
A refreshing oneness with myself
That demands occasional revival.

When cobwebbed fancies torn free
Dangle in my mind's eye
As multihued memory-bubbles
Without design, proceed to stream on by.

That effervesce from an indelible well
Sometimes latent, steadfastly never dry!
I've gathered and preserved and treasured
The moments of my life—in not so short supply.

Embellished dreams and blighted hopes
Fashion the mosaic of my being.
I define myself by what's perceived
And the rainbowed gossamer I'm seeing.

I haven't the capacity to organize
Nor edit the patchwork I beget.
Thusly resigned, I can only conclude
A pregnant awareness defies regret!

Hank Lowenstein

"Moon Venture"

Landing on the moon was simply fantastic,
An ancient dream of all mankind.
Which has always been there for yours and mine.

A rare desolation, but no longer a revelation
The moon is powerful, but was unknown to us,
Until three brave men probed its outer crust
Being a goal man has always wanted to achieve.
So landing there, as they stare, the world is pleased.

To them we are grateful
In this month of July
And know there are others on whom we can rely.

These brave men left "old glory there" for America and
All the world to share.

May our flag forever stand for the good of man.
For it is only the beginning in outer space.
As America and all the world strive onward to
Win the race.

So as we go forward in this magnificent adventure,
Lord lead and guide us through this alien venture.

Clara Stephens La Comb

Whispers of Love

In the light of day warm rays beat upon us,
An earthly shadow befalls.
Like children we dance till the suns end,
Then fall into an earthen blanket of love.
You caress and shield me from the howling wind,
The sting of air is no more.
You enter me with your heart,
To see me light up the stars.
Then we unite,
Like the fold of night to day.
What do I say to an earthly form
That holds me with a kiss.
The same words used every day
by poets,
The words eternal to me,
With all my heart I love thee.

Joseph Constable

Untitled

Forever dark,
An endless sea,
silhouettes against the sun.
Beneath her majestic beauty
the love of night will come,
wash away, time and day.
Come and feel the ambiance.

As stars begin to play a song for me,
I feel I do belong, running free upon her stage,
an endless dream, I want to stay.

In this night, I close my eyes and open up my heart.
Hold my hand and walk with me,
and we will never apart.

Utter softly the words I seek,
and I will follow you.
By my side, an endless tide,
my dreams of love come true.

Joe Dooley

"God's Handiwork"

O what infinite greatness in God's spacious skies —-
An ever changing scene, that meets the eyes.
The moon and stars shine brightly at night,
And those sunrises and sunsets — what a majestic sight!
The cotton-like clouds midst the heavenly blues.
Praise be unto God, for these spectacular views.

For this Planet Earth, and the fullness thereof,
All glory is given to our Maker above.
The seeds that are planted spring upward to yield.
There are cattle which graze, and beasts of the field.
Look unto the hills, mountains, and birds of the air —
O God, your finger-prints are everywhere.
Flowers of beauty, fruits of the trees, and fish of the seas, too. —
Praise be unto God, for the Earth so beautifully dressed by you.

Great is our Creator of all mankind,
And by Him, we are so miraculously designed.
The heavens, and the earth, declare the glory of the Lord.
Praise and thanks unto God, adored.

Ethel L. Voelker

Optical Illusion (The Migraine)

It's an optical illusion, or is it delusion
An infinite pattern and a false conclusion
Selective perception without exception
We see what we want and believe deception

Fire pounding in my temples, anger lashing out like flames
Suddenly my eyes can't focus, in my ears the sound of hurricanes
Nerve ends getting tight and dense and the signal transmits pain
I hope this time it's over soon I can't stand the growing pain

It's an optical illusion, or is it delusion
An infinite pattern and a false conclusion
It's a new sensation of pain and frustration
Mental resistance and isolation

The pattern swirls into illusion with colors streaming in my head
Red of anger, white of love, my sanity hanging by a thread

Flashes of lightning around me fly
Pressure is building behind my eyes

It's an optical illusion, or is it delusion
An infinite pattern and a false conclusion
Perpetual charade of light and shade
Ghosts in the dark I'm so afraid

Brian R. Morrow

Tragedy Or Hope?

A stolen car, a police chasing scene
an innocent girl, caught in between.
Some are angry and some still cry,
Some have hope and others ask why,
Some say unlucky, while others say fate,
Either way, life we must not hate.
Five years in a hospital she stays
A girl that loved life's ways.
Five years now, not able to talk,
Not only that, but not able to walk.
For now her recovery is not yet clear
But her faithful family is always near.
Her life is on hold for a while
But soon, soon, everyone will smile.
For this girl's new life will start,
Making hope a reality in her family's heart.

Edward Morrison

From A Distance

I saw him from a distance
And at that point I knew
He would be my love.

So I used my intuition
And worked my way around
To meeting him, this man
I saw from a distance.

When I met him our eyes
Locked and smiles came from
The heart, I knew then I cared
For this person with out ever knowing him.

So if you ever have feelings for
A man from a distance, take some
Time to meet him he could be your love.

Carla L. Davenport

Sister Mary Silent

Graveler crawl
and attract your slime.
Dear, you're no mother
but to petty words.
Foreign thank you's may gesture the time.
Homer takes my heart
flying away with righteous birds.

Clergical separation
sits under my habit
with the sweat
and the goblet undeserved.
Out in the fields
we continue to mouth it,
but the place on the grass next to you is reserved.

Horses with fire
seem to sense that you're higher,
while I drop below when they joust.
It's a moment uncertain
if I am your window,
or if you are with me under clouds.

Jennifer Gray

Empty Nest

My Babe has finally left the nest,
And did not even leave a feather behind
To show that she was here.
Of all my treasures, she was most dear.
She will not see the tears I shed,
It was time for her to go.
She's grown now-has other roads to travel,
Life's mysteries to unravel,
Her own nest to build.
I could not hug her, kiss her, say "Goodbye."
She had to spread her wings and fly
On her own.

Alison Blomgren

To Julie

I can sit in repose and gaze upon the starry curtain of night
And dream with the forever men of what might be;
Or I can stand and witness the ascent of the sanguine fire
that colors the sky
And embrace the glorious nascency of the awakening dawn;
Or I can sing the heroic words of the poets of yesterday
As I drown in a painted sea upon the descent of the sweet star;
Yet,
I cannot be enfranchised from this pernicious entombment
Of my abysmal loneliness
Without you.

Jeff Schieder

Twilight Whispers

As twilight falls
and evening settles over valley and meadow
I think I hear you call.
Shall I listen, shall I come
to reach the voice I think I hear?
It sounds familiar, from my past.
But this cannot be you,
for you left without good-bye
and broke my heart in two.
I think that I shall listen
and hear what whispers call me.
I wait not long and understand,
Longing soon is with me.
In the misty twilight hours
I turn and you are there,
We reach to touch each other's hands
and slowly we embrace
This time we speak no words
for we both know that together
we will always be and quiet these twilight whispers.

Frances J. Robinson

Cowboy And His Horse

A mighty things is the bond between a cowboy
and his horse.

This bond is tall and strong and keeps with a
special force.

There customary dwelling place is the dusty
trail.

There honorary pride is often pleased by a long
long ride.

Erin Clancy

I'm Thankful

I'm thankful for our home so dear
And for the one who shares it with me
For the many friends so far and near
They make the time pass happily.

I'm thankful for our sons and daughter
And their sons and daughters too
Their blessed love so warms my heart
They spur me on and life stirs anew.

I am thankful for the life I've had
For the many things I've seen and known
For times of joy, for strength when sad
For the years granted me so swiftly flown.

So thankful for the miles I've been
The chance to see the beauties of this earth
Unfold like a panoramic screen
Thankful for stored memories from my birth!

I'M THANKFUL!

Dorothy Harrison

Of Purest Love

How beautiful you are from without,
and from within.

Whenever I depart from you, that is my
greatest sin.

Your very glance warms my heart,
your touch, my soul.
Your loveliness free's me,
from the cares of this world.

You have given so much, yet are so humble
and pure.

It is true what I say, this I can reassure.
Your love is like a diamond. It glows right
on through, giving me peace and calm, that
is true.

Please do not change from this perfect
rapport, you will shine like a beacon, for
ever more.

Alexander Presniakov

The Rarest Flower

You gathered all Heaven's joy
And gave it to my heart
Destroying all the emptiness
Filling light in place of dark
No one else could do this
Only you with the sweetest power
Any other rose would whither
You are truly the rarest flower
All the astral points glow in honor of this love
No more need for wishing
The seraphs are now dishing out
Heaps of rapture from above
You and me together
Will find our ways as one
When it is hard we'll make it better
On our journey now begun
From my soul of passion
For your sole possession
My devotion is whole and true
The only channel for my affection flows to you and only you

Amanda Lee Wilson

"Rise"

Our ancestor rise up from slavery
And get freedom and pass it on to us
now it's our turn to rise....
Now we rise, rise from the dead
Rise from our ancestor soul
Which they use to betrayed for Gold.
Rise for our education for tomorrow
We will swims in fortune, rise for
freedom of speech freedom of religion
And God bless our nation

So we rise like a flying bird
So there he guide us with words
So we rise yes we rise, we rise
With prides so together well make it better

We came from the darkness
Now we rise up with lightness
When rising let no shadow tells you wrong

So rise yes rise, "rise" rise with
prides and bless our ancestor who
was mighty and wise. So we rise

Ermide Fieneant

A Poem

But if a poem I could write
And have it full of bright delight
Where the sun shines all the day
This is where I'd like to play

Where the birds are singing in the trees
And the flowers make nectar for the bees
Where God's wonders are all around
I'll never feel I'm earthly bound

For if upon a cloud I could ride
I'd fly high above the drifting tide
Out Or seas and oceans blue
And see beautiful things where I flue

I'd soar high above the valleys green
And look for things I've never seen
For many wonders out there lay
I hope some day to see I pray

Ellery E. Inman

To My Daughter

I believe in you
And have seen
Your dreams come true.

You have been blessed with talents to spare
And you must know that this is very rare.

Your life has been so full
Not a moment has been dull.

I'm so proud of you
And everything you can do.

To me you are a bright shining star
And I know your desires will take you far.

I wish for you a good life
And that doesn't meant just being someone's wife.

You deserve to be a princess
And experience a greater happiness.

Barbara Lewallen

The Awakening

He took my hand
  and held it long
As though he had always
  meant to do so
The fingers, strong and sure I came to know
  as they remained
  with mine
No urgency to disentangle
  no regret did I sense
  in the blood
  that flowed beneath his skin
The moments stark and passionate
  then imprinted a pain
  as I felt his flesh move from me
  in a cruel and swift way
For with the dawn through my window
  so rudely rushed in a sound
The command of the canine out there
  did cause my rapture to fold
  and opened my eyes to the empty light

Elizabeth Niziolek

Lefty

I've got one more hole in my latigo
  and he's puffed up full of air.
His white eyes shine, and his old hide
  quivers beneath his hair.

He's as snuffy a colt, as I've ever seen
  built long and lanky, you can't call him mean.
Just spooky, cold backed, and cinchy at times
  but, he can turn the crank if you let him unwind.

When the storm is over, if you're still in the seat
  why he'll jog so pretty, and lope so neat.
And I'll boast and brag as he handles so fine
  Boy's, I believe I've got him this time.

But along comes morning, and it could all be the same
  and I have to wonder just what's to blame
for the scars in his mind
  and the fury that will not be tamed.

I guess he's just a little like me:
  He don't care much for rules, he would rather be free.
So around here when things don't seem quite western enough.
  I can saddle old Lefty and cowboy up.

Billy Ward Savage

Grandma

Thinking of a woman who's bold
And how her story should be told
Of one who gave to us her all
And always seemed to stand so tall

The one who gave unconditional love
And always believed in the power from above
The one who'd listen to all your loss
No matter how much it seemed to cost

She's the one who seemed so strong
Even when things were going so wrong
She could show you the beauty of a simple tree
And you can always tell she means so much to me

The beauty of her heart isn't skin deep
And the love she has isn't hers to keep
For she gives it away to those who care
And isn't afraid to praise those who share

I guess it's the same in every home
When a grandma you love is never alone
And I guess it's as simple as can be
When the love is there and easy to see

Janese Rogers

"My Dearest Son's And Daughter"

"I am very, very proud of you,
and how well you're doing.
I'm glad you have such wonderful people
to take care of you, since I can't.
I want you to know that even
though we can't be together,
I will always, always love you very much."
"You will always be with me in my heart.
I love you dearly.
Mom."

Janie S. Hacker

To Lilo

I came to her and my heart was cold
and I vowed never to love again
full of self pity.

A crazy time, misery and pain and anger
Over and over the confrontation scene
Was I to blame

Did I bother her because she would not love me
Asking more than she could give
Since I loved her, could she not love me back
If I asked for less.

Purple dusk, loneliness, ambivalent dreams
A suicidal thought - It scared me
Iris dead 5 years
Reach deep inside for strength
Live for work, for your daughters.

Then Lilo, gentle Lilo, sensitive, she knew my hurt
In my arms, my life, softness, elegance, warmth, joy
Optimism, magic, femininity, perfume
Whatever happens, even if I fail -
She gave me back my life.

Jerome Rothman

Diminished

I waited in the jet black night
  And I watched in the cold dark silence
But the sunshine never came
  And the dewdrops fell
So I blinked my eyes
  As I gazed into the wishing well
The days passed slowing
  But I could wait no longer
Because my body was weak
  And my mind no stronger
I tried to pull out of darkness
  I didn't want to be diminished
But I found I could not prolong
  What had long been finished.

Cheri S. Finley

Eventide

The coolness of the evening makes it worth the wait.
  And thru our busy schedules we learn to recreate,
    The sounds and smells for a Summers Eve.

Oh eyes, we love the evening and the glorious setting sun.
  But sights of the morning can be just as fun
    As we long for a life to live
      And a song to sing.

So lets us grow and be happy thru these eventides,
  And live for the mornings as well as the nights.

Cindy K. Doyle

His List Of Beautiful People

There was an old man who lived near the courtyard,
And I'd stop to talk as I walked by.
He told me of the beautiful people,
Who brought so much joy to his life.

His smile concealed his deep sorrow,
For he lived in sheer loneliness.
Still he spoke of the beautiful people,
And he had them all down on his list.

But today as I walked through the courtyard,
The old man was no where in sight.
As I knocked on his door, it came open,
And I saw that he had died in the night.

As I said my goodbyes to my old friend,
The tears from my eyes fell so free.
I saw his list of beautiful people,
And the only one on it was me!

He had a list of beautiful people,
Who brought so much joy to his life.
All we wanted was someone to talk to,
Thank God, I had taken the time! Thanks God!

Eileen Pruyne

Living

My life is not worth living unless He's by my side,
And if I stray from Him, there is no place I can hide.

His Holy Spirit calls me and draws me ever near,
Then His love caresses me, vanquishing all my fears,
And if I but stumble, He takes me by the hand,
And leads me over the rough spots to a smoother land.

Then I saw His footsteps, they were so big and wide.
I tried to step within them, but could not match the stride.

But I know I can follow Him with His love and care, for He
will always stop and listen when I go to prayer,
And He never fails to answer me in spite of my erroring
ways of pride, I just want to be with Him on the other side.

Etta R. Bottazzo

His Presence

In the still of the night I feel His presence
And, it fills my soul with peace and hope,
Not anxiety like I've known for so long,
I wonder at what I'm feeling
For I've made so many mistakes.

Day by day, I'll get over my fears,
With God's help, I'm sure of it,
I'll keep my husband
And, make my family proud,
But, I can't do it without my Lord.

In the still of the night,
All is asleep as I talk with Him,
I know He understands my fears,
And, the peace I'm feeling now
Lets me know He's there.

I love my Father in Heaven,
Though I wonder how He
Can love one such as me,
But, I feel it in my heart,
As He smiles down on me.

Danee M. Redd

To My Friend

When you're feeling so low and have thoughts of self doubt,
And it seems as though nobody cares,
friend is someone you can't live without,
Someone who'll always be there.

Just remember the laughter, the sorrow, the tears,
And the pain that we've shared with each other,
Forgive and let go of all of your fears,
For I promise I'll be here tomorrow.

If I should go before you do my friend,
I'll send down an angel with love.
I promise she'll stay and be with you forever,
As I watch with my heart from above.

So don't be afraid to take the next step,
For you know that I'll always be there,
As you've been there for me, I'll be there for you,
Because a friend - is someone who cares.

Christine Herrick

Walking The Beaches Of Michigan

Well, it's nice to see something besides stalks of corn.
And it's nice to see something besides pick-up trucks.
Pack my bags, on my way, I've got to go
To the mountain top of this world that I know.

Walking the beaches of Michigan
Is about as close as I'll ever get to heaven.
Walking the beaches of Michigan
Is about as close as I'll ever get to heaven.

Now, if I were ever to make it to heaven,
It would be as an extra fielder to make teams even.
And until that times comes
I'll more than gladly spend
My days
Walking the beaches of Michigan.

Daniel H. Holden

True Exposure

Darkness falls, once around me here
And like a blanket, I wrap myself inside
And play hide and seek with time.

The last lamplight fades away
And I am prepared for journey into myself
When a kaleidoscope of what I hope and fear most
Appear before me in rotating images and intervals
And I will never be more aware than I am now..and I think
Where is my place in the passing show of my dreams?

I want to suspend myself—in the pulse
Long enough, to have who I am, and who I could be,
Snapped—in one true exposure
Ahh—a righteous unconscious, a savory existence
I become what I already am— Dawn.

Instead, a strong sense of destiny reaches out
And touches my soul
Lifting me back to surface of life.

As I approach the light, again I think
Morning is a rude awakening... and the feeling remains
I want to write my name across time.

Bevin S. Rolfs

My Thoughts of You

If dreams were given to lonely men
And lonely men's dreams came true,
I'd force myself to sleep each night
So that I'd dream of you

If wishes were given to lonely men
And lonely men's wishes came true
I'd only wish to be your husband
So I can spend my life with you

If tears could write love songs
Before these love songs were through,
You would know just how I feel
And how much I care for you

But dreams are just for dreamers
And wishes don't always come true,
Although my tears cannot write love songs
My thoughts are always of you.

David Avitia

Wind

I went walking this evening, down by the sea.
And met my lover there, who enfolded me.

The moonlight was like magic as he softly touched my hair.

Oh, how beautiful, just like velvet; he caressed my
body everywhere.

He made my body bubble like champagne in a lovely
crystal glass.

The warmth of him made my inner-soul soar so high, I
felt like the moon. All aglow in the sky.

And just as my joy and passion soared, my lover, the
wind, embraced me once more.

My desire was to hold onto my lover I met by the sea.

But, I knew in my heart, he could never just belong to me.

So, my lovely, warm and gentle wind, that my lover be;
flowed ever so gently out to sea.

Blow my sweet lover. Blow warm and free.

Blow my lover. From sea to sea.

Joan Adams-Byers

Little Prayers

From hand to hand
and mouth to ear
I bring you tidings
of good life and cheer.
Now prayers being spoken then prayers being done
The prayer you said was just for one.
The one being me, a prayer of concern
For life and healing I now return.
To a soldier of Christ
a prayer warrior for life.
Thank you for the trouble of remembering me,
when your day got busy
and on your knees.
Thank God for little prayers like these.

Jeni Roberts

Where Did You Put My Dignity?!!

Prison is an attempt to get into our brain
and muscle. It's a crazy mixture of boredom
and terror, boredom because nothing happens,
terror because anything could happen -
anytime. They don't just strip off your
clothes; they go deeper than that. They take
off any little dignity you have. They make
you live, eat, sleep and shit close to other
men. And when they dress you up again, you
can't separate yourself from the others. You
can't even wear a scrape or pin a note on
your chest saying "This is me, I am separate
from the rest." We are like a herd of animals.
Think of me and all those here with me, as
you go on your way, while your brothers and
sisters rot in these concrete and steel
tombs, where the society that you are a part
of, hides their mistakes and creates new ones.

The question is, when will you become a
mistake like me?

John Estes

The Seeker's Tree

When around you creeps insanity
And no one hears your prayers but me
I'm here to help - to set you free.
Find me, find me, I'm the Seeker's Tree.

Find the valley of Old Gooseberry's nest
Then ask of me your secret request.
I'll do for you when you do for me,
Trust me, trust me, I'm the Seeker's Tree.

Adoration or greed either will do
Sacrifices to me will return to you.
The touch of my branches holds the key
Want me, need me, I'm the Seeker's Tree.

If truth you seek, then you shall hear it
Don't come too close, he'll steal your spirit;
A word of warning to those who plea
Stay away, stay away, from the Seeker's Tree.

Take care dear one or you might find
You'll loose your heart, your soul, your mind.
The tree is wicked as you will see,
No one escapes from the Seeker's Tree.

Gregory G. Capistrant

My Darling

My darling I know-that you love me true,
And oh, my darling-I do love you too.
And I wanted you to know- on this special day-
The things in my heart- I could never say.
You've always been there- when I needed you,
Even at death's door-you prayers pulled me through.
You've always had- the right things to say,
And tender love-that made the hurts go away.
A shoulder to cry on-both tender and warm,
Strong and determined-to keep me from harm.
With love and adoration-you've always seen,
That you put me on a pedestal-just like a queen.
You've never been able to give me-the riches of this life,
But, darling, I'm contented-just to be your wife.
One day we may-have to say goodbye
But, my sweet darling-please don't you cry.
We've been together-thru thick and thru thin,
And my darling, in heaven-we'll be together again-
To walk those streets-both you and me,
Together with Jesus-throughout all Eternity.

Dorothy Jean Lolley

Untitled

A gray mist blankets the streets and alleys,
and old familiar sights
become far away places.

David E. Jones

Heaven

I sometimes wonder what happens to us when we die,
And our soul rises up to be with God in the sky.
Everything must be beautiful in heaven up above,
Angels are probably singing and the whole place is filled with love.
Pain and sadness are gone way up there,
It all gets left behind for the people we love yet to bear.
Just happiness and joy all around,
And not a worry to be found.

Christine Mattson

She Can't Breathe

She opened up the table draw,
And placed the baby inside.
She took the sheet right off the bed,
And covered the baby right up.

Sweetie she can't breathe like that
Here tuck her in right here.
Don't worry Grandma
She's already used to it.

She proceeded to close the baby up,
Inside the table draw.
Sweetie, I don't think that's a good idea,
Well she can't sleep with us.

Why sweetheart there's plenty of space
In this Queen size bed we have.
The baby she can't breathe
If you put her down like that.

Grandma I understand the stance,
That you have taken here.
But even I know two is company
And three is only a pain!

Janette Anderson

My Little Gold Mine

She's a joy to me, like summer days where children laugh
and puppy dogs play.

What riches she has given to me in time. You know, she's my
little gold mine.

Her laughter is far finer than the onyx stone. Her smile
much brighter than a diamond throne;

And life with her is pure gold refined. To me there's no
doubt, she's my little gold mine.

When I talk to her it's time well spent, more valuable
than all the money in a mint.

Oh, you say you have money stacked high to the sky. Well
let me just say that is just fine. However; I tell you,
she's my little gold mine.

Happiness and joy explode from her soul like rivers of
silver and jewels untold.

She's certainly not difficult to define. She's just simply,
my little gold mine.

Freeman Grant Chambers

Autumn Leaves

The season of Summer says farewell,
And really, it's not hard to tell.

Just look upon the trees, both short and tall,
For you'll see the most beautiful sight of all.

The leaves are changing day by day,
Into what will be a most colorful array.

Behold their magnificent colors galore,
For in a little while they will be no more.

Their colors of red, yellow, orange, and brown,
Fill the air as they fall to the ground.

They lay on the ground so lifeless and thin,
Until they are ruffled by a swift wind.

Many things are beautiful, but don't be deceived,
Because nothing is as beautiful as Autumn Leaves.

Albert G. Colbert, Sr.

Homeless

When I drive by on those damp and chilly days
and see you lying there,
I try my best to ignore your plight. But deep
in my soul - I care.
I wish that I could wrap you and baby up
in blankets pink and blue
and tuck you in a safe place so that I could
watch over you two.
I want a chance to guide you awhile - so that
you can sing a happier song.
Without food, without hope, without a home you
cannot exist for long.
Please! Come in from out of the rain - you need
to find out what our system will do.
Have a little faith in yourself and the system will
find a warm place for you.
Then, if I drive by tomorrow and see you - I'll
ask "Are you being fair?"
YES, why should you and baby be homeless; is it I
or is it YOU who don't care?

Faye Flanagan

Yesteryear

The good ole days are often observed
And seemingly longed for by all
Were thought to be days when all was well and good
But what made them great was nothing small

Coke, Ice Cream cones, gum and candy bars were a nickel
Penny candy was easy to obtain
But to gain the money wasn't easy or funny
And the laborer worked often in pain

Wages were low but the cost of living was too
If your shoesole wore out cardboard would do
Clothes with patches were popular and worn by all
Catalogs took the place of supermarkets and malls

Neighbors were close and all seemed to care
In a small town all liked to share
Churches were full on Sunday and never bare
There was a sense of oneness in the air

When hard times come today, violence or crime
It seems many look back in memory of time
And pause to think of yesteryear
When times were good and little to fear

Ira William Moots

"Sweet Papa"

Sometimes, when angels are in flight
And sounds become so dim,
A tired, restless soul can relax
To silently wait, for Him.

The life we led on earth
Is never over because one's gone.
But, will live forever, through the love,
From generation to generation on.

Sweet papa, rest your head now,
Dream of happier times that were.
Your love and devotion has taught us,
That your memories, will keep the mind pure.

I could never say good-bye to you.
Nor tell you I'll miss your touch.
For, up there, in Heaven's arms and care,
Is what you've needed so much.

If I promise to close my eyes at night
And look for you to be near;
Will you promise, to always open your arms,
And with a big smile, appear?

Julia Tuttle

The Sights And Sounds Of Somewhere Someone Has Never Seen

The crying earth in which I dwell sobs,
and squeezes out tears of hate;
The dying people of which I am,
flowers that have been plucked from the ground;
The echoing cries of screaming children linger;
The writhing, teeming crowds that roam the land
searching for a home;
The reeking air flowing and swishing like a whirlpool of death
The persecuting powers overwhelm a younger, more naive nation;
The alternating flashes of bright light with the complete darkness
of the night sky;
The plaguing presence of a greater being, all to realistic;
The erasing of a standard that has long since been forgotten;
The contrasting of black and white, yellow on blue, orange on green-
all in a gray world;
The revolving of this fiery world has ceased;
The upturning of an empire whose roots have not yet grown into
the ground;
The massacring of innocent people for the wealth of others;
Their unceasing screams reverberate throughout the rotten walls;
The horrifying sights and sounds of somewhere someone has never seen.

Cammi McCormick

If I Could Only Be With You

If I could only be with you, I'd take your hand in mine
And tell you it will get better
Just to give it time

If I could only be with you, I'd hold you close and tight
And help you bare this cross
That keeps you awake at night

If I could only be with you, I'd wipe away your tears
Guide you through your sorrow
And help you calm your fears

If I could only be with you, I'd stand right by your side
Lend you the shoulder that you need
On your long and difficult ride

If I could only be with you, I'd take you in my arms
I'd tell you that I love you
And I'd keep you from all harms

So think of me in spirit, know that I really care
And If I could only be with you
You know I would be there.

Cheryl Slifka

Season's End

The paths are strewn with the colors of fall leaves all around
and the happy noises of summer in the park no longer sound.

The damp leaves deaden the sound of the striding walker's feet,
creating a pall where once was the sound of a much faster beat.

It's a rather lonely time of the year with the dark, cloudy skies,
the rain in the air and a brisk wind blowing the mist in your eyes.

The beauty and sunshine of the summer gone for another year
and there are only memories of the wildlife playing so near.

It makes one think of burning leaves, October fest and German lieder,
football games and rallies with red-cheek sweatered cheerleaders.

And who can forget all those wonderful dances after the game
when you danced with your football hero, that is, if he came.

In those days parents never got older; they would live forever;
we never disobeyed them (at least overtly), we were too clever.

Oh, those were the halcyon days of so little responsibility,
but we matured like the oaks and accepted aging's inevitability.

Constance M. Delman

The Other Child Of The Sixties

Between the youth of yesterday
And the menopausal relic of today
lies our passion,
Its powder, triggered into explosive force,
Leaves behind an empty casing
etched by right of passage
through the barrel of a gun;
Or maybe it is just a trickle of black dust
Lit by a blue-tipped-cardboard match
That starts with a fizzle of fire
and ends with a dud,
its brass shell battered and bent,
Ground deep into the barren sod
beneath the hobnailed heel of God.

Gay E. Tanner

Prelude

The silver thread of the thermometer
and the silver needle of the barometer
drop together.

Swaying erratically as the short
gusts of wind play with it, the rooster weather vane
sends its signals.

Above, clouds are like a human pyramid,
built one on two on three on four on five on six
to endless heights.

The telephone wires are a music staff,
the sitting birds are notes scattered in six/eight time,
arpeggio.

A sudden lightning bolt is the baton,
giving the downbeat, while thunder plays staccato
percussion.

With the opening crescendo, the birds fly.
From the bottom of the pyramid a cloud falls,
and rain begins.

Barbara Quackenbush

Together

I remember our love towards each other.
And the way you've changed me,
You will always be in my heart,
No matter how many hours we're apart.

Not knowing where true love begins,
Outside I haven't learned to just be good friends,
If only love could find us,
That way we wouldn't have to fuss!

Then we'd be together forever.
Some where out there,
There is a black pot of gold,
At the end is a colorful rainbow!

We used to share our dreams,
But now it's going down stream,

There's something missing in my life,
All I want is to be with you,
To put your arms around me again,
Like we used to do back then.
So that we can still be together
And start something brand new!

Connie White

The Price Of Life

When all seems irreversibly confused and lost
And there appears to be no hope
Have you really reached deep and paid the cost
That's due on your life to cope?

Inner strength is what you must find
You need only search your soul
The tools are there, in your mind
Are you willing to pay the toll?

The debt that you owe is quite small
And sadly for some goes unpaid
Hold your chin up and stand tall
For payment on your life must be made!

LOVE will lift your spirits high
And FAITH will end your strife
HOPE will give you a relieving sigh
So AFFORDABLE is THE PRICE OF LIFE.

Clifford W. Campbell

A Thought of You

Today I sat and thought of you
And things we used to do
I cried a little, I guess you know
Why did you have to go
The space you filled, once in my heart
Is now tearing me apart
Why you...I hate it so
Why did you have to go
For only memories now take its place
Where once you held and filled that space
I can't help loving you so
Why did you have to go
I never thought that it would be you
And I often wondered what would I do
It's not that I'm letting go
Why - why did you have to go

Jame DeStefano

Dreams

Sometimes at night I lie in bed,
And think of all the things he's said.
I conjure up a dream or two,
And child-like hope they will come true.

But when the morning starts to dawn,
My dreams like darkness soon are gone,
And woman-like I face the truth.
And laugh to scorn my foolish youth.

For night's soft blackness seems to hold
A thousand castles made of gold,
But morning sees them fade away,
In stern reality of day.

Abby Westenberg

My Father's Chair

I had a talk with Dad tonight, I sat down on his chair
And thought about the days before when he was sitting there.

I squeezed my eyes shut very tight and hoped that I could see.
A picture of my little Brandon sitting on his knee.

He loved my little boy so much, if only for a while.
I surely knew that for a fact, the way he made him smile.

Each night that little boy of mine would kneel down and he'd pray.
For Jesus to make Papa well, so both of them could play.

And all the things he'd pray for just before he went to bed.
Were such amazing things to be in such a little head.

He has a special angel now to watch him from above.
An angel we call Papa who surrounds him with his love.

Now I can spend my time with him and I don't have to cry.
I feel him with me everywhere, I almost hear him sigh.

I always did appreciate just how much he was worth.
More than silver, more than gold or treasures of this earth.

The lessons that I learned from him no school could ever teach.
Treat others as you would yourself and stay within God's reach.

I know for sure that when I need him, Dad is always there.
He told me that tonight while I was sitting on his chair.

Elayna O'Neil

Sunshine And Moonbeams

When the sun is raining tears, the moon clears the sky.
And through all of life's darkness, the sun will sometimes cry.
So, when cold, cold tears come falling, from high up above,
the sun will find warmth and shelter in Moon's friendship and it's love.

Their friendship will always be, because strong is the bind.
The sun and moon are siblings, two of a kind.
Throughout life's experiences, they will sometimes stray.
But support and love will never be too far away.

The sun and moon have too many years in between.
But without the sun's light, the moon will never gleam.
They are content to let the other shine, without them in their days.
So everyone receives their love in bright and shining rays.

Becca Martin

As Each Day Passes

As each day passes I think of you.
As each month passes I think of you.
I feel so lonely without you in my life.
I can't help but think of you.
Every breaking moment of my heart yearns for you.
Your soft touch, your whispering word.
As your soft touch tenderly touches mine.
I think of you.

Deborah Heaton

Love

Love is like a garden in the spring.
And to make it grow you've gotta have a lot of rain.
Then with tender loving care,
Love will grow most anywhere.
Cause love is like a garden in the spring.
You can see new flowers blooming every day.
in a little kiss or a thank you along the way.
The trick, is don't be blind.
Cause their blooming all the time
And love is like a garden in the spring,
Me and my lady never fuss or fight.
We talk it through and find out what is right.
This might take a day or two,
Cause I'm so in love with you.
Our love is like a garden in the spring.

Darl L. Haines

A Place For Seeking

Leaves fall like tiny rocks,
And too fast to ever belong.
And so, to print a page of forgotten,
And think it wise and full of reason -
Never feeling the pleasure of this journey
Or making the future a bearable past -
This for apathy seasons,
Living off blood indifferent.
Where do swans mate?
Where do birds nest?
Where does snow tickle like tiny laughs?
First - a place from which to start -
Knowing the importance of such an art.

Chris Moya

Pictures In The Sky

As I sit here on a slightly windy afternoon
and watch the pictures in the sky
you can glance up into the foreverness of the
mighty blue sky and watch the floating angel hair
drift by
One minute you may see a person's face and with
the next gust of wind she is gone
You just float with the calmness of the soft white
cotton and you can escape to your own fantasy
in the sky
The most beautiful scenery and art is there only long
enough to remember the creativity of that moment
and then it's gone
To let your mind wander to the heights of the flawless
shapes of nothing and everything in the blue and white puzzle
As I sit here on a slightly windy afternoon
and watch the pictures in the sky.

Andy Reed

Take Time For Right Living

take time for right living, while rushing along,
And lighten the load with a lilt of a song.
From learning and living, in wisdom we grow,
And come to full stature while onward we go.
Take time for right living, in habits of thought,
Remember the errors that brought you to naught.
The truth has a sound like the peal of a bell,
Right thinking brings water up from a deep well.
Take time for right living, in all that you do,
In planting and tending and harvesting, too.
In gaining contentment, your greatest reward,
And finding that sorrows are not in life's chord.
Take time for right living, bring joy to each day,
To live in the sunshine that brightens your way.
And search for the power faith only can give.
I knowing what glory there is just to live.

Gladys Tyler

That's When I Write

In tender hours when babies sleep
And waves run quiet through the moon-drenched deep
And sounds of waking have no voice at all
To call
Interrupting my silent dreams
That's when I rise

These are the hours my heart loves best
Quixotic hours when day-folk take their rest
And stars come out each one a point of light
And gentle winds drift questing through the night
That's when I take my pen

Deep calls to deep
And in the still recesses of my soul
Mind patterns stir and come alive and breathe
And each emotion these late hours bring
Lives in a chapter of my yet unfinished book

Thoughts unwanted can't intrude the solitude
That draws me here

That's when I write

Bethell Whitley Hice

My Love

Days have gone when we were young
And we are past our prime
Now we live from day to day
Try not to notice time

Only seasons do we see, and fast
they come and go
The warm gentle rains of spring
Then soon cold winter snow

You are the beating in my heart
The courage in my soul
You lifted me when I was down
Your love has made me whole

As we join hands and walk thru life
It's certain in my heart
That, though we've started past our prime
We shall never never part.

So when I close my eyes in death
Do not weep for me
For we shall walk, hand in hand
Throughout eternity

Dorothy Evans

Cleaning Out The Garage

I help her roll back the door
And we step into the cool relief of the car cave.
No Chinese horses decorate these walls,
Yet still a sanctuary.
Piled up against our cracked plaster pictures
Reminders of some summer rituals:
Rusty crab cage; crinkled rubber quoits,
once red, now the color of burned wine.
An aroma of Good Gulf still lingers,
after-shave of a '49 Chevy.

Mother reaches down to lift the heavy box,
his shirts, ties, pants, shoes...
I move to help,
And as I look into this casket in this place,
I find him.
I see him "warming up the car", "taking out
the trash", cleaning out the garage".
Gently I lift the box and carry it into the sunlight,
The two of us stretch to reach and pull, rolling thunder.
A whispered prayer..."Dad's home, go down and let him in."

Judith M. Shannon

Black and White

When night arrives, the day is gone.
And what isn't right, can only be wrong.
What is ours, that cannot be taken?
And what good is a heart, at the time when it's breaking?
Being without you is being alone.
And nothing is written, even in stone.
Without the sky, there is no ground.
And what is silence, if there is no sound?
Without the darkness, where is the light?
And what we can be seen by those without sight?
What is now, is already then.
And what never was, can never be again.

Jennifer Campbell

Which Way

I sometimes feel like trying
And when I mean to do right
I always come out wrong
Because the difference between them
I can never really understand
And when the time comes for me
To make the right choices
The weight of the world
Comes heavily upon me
And I will be ready to be buried
Beneath the deep dark dirt
I have lost my soul in this world
Confusion and hate dominate here
I can feel it coming down - it's all around now
There so many people out there
Can you hear me? I'm sinking in here
Can you close in on my fear?
I want to disappear
Lose myself - over and over
Until my spirit comes full circle again

Aaron C. Harding

The Day Mam Died From A Broken Toe

Mam tell down and broke her toe
And why it killed her I guess I'll never know.
She died a horrible death with a frown on her face,
Saying all the time she was going to a better place.
At last the frown was gone and replaced with a smile
I knew then she had walked her last mile.
She left us all behind with a heart full of woe
But at least I was sure she hadn't gone down below.
When she fell down the steps she also hurt her knee
And I just knew she would blame it on me.
She said "I fell down the steps and I think my toe is broke"
Then she closed her eyes and not another word she spoke.
She lay right down upon the ground
And when she quit moaning she didn't make another sound.
I knew right away she must be dead
And I thought "I wish she had died in bed."
She just lay there on the ground still holding her toe,
I tried to move her hand but she wouldn't let go.
There's lots of things in life I'll never know
But the one most puzzling is why she died from a broken toe.

Henry Durham

Dear Allan

You will be unfocused for a while
And wish the world to stop

He's not here

You will need to talk about him all the time
And call upon his name

He's not here

You will see a show, a book, an outfit
And know he would have loved that

He's not here

You will remember a better person than he was
And learn to even love his faults

He's not here

You will be brave to face tomorrow
And say I will recover but he is always in your thoughts

He's not here

You will keep him in your heart, in you
And see, feel and smell him in your child

He is still here

Diana M. R. Frazier

In Your Hands

The Master Potter knows well His craft
And with Precision and Skill derives His design
Artfully..he sees..the inherent potential
And endeavor with patience to sculpt and refine.

Pliant and fluid must be this matter
And is crucial to the exactness for what He has in mind,
For involved..is the process..of transfigured development
Which takes time..to unearth He will find.

Without His touch this lump of clay is naught
But a muddle of messiness one must endure
But to the Potters Keen Eye He piercingly sees
The underlying promise of such refined contour.

In the same manner, within a being lies dormant
The intrinsic elegance that constitutes ones soul
And if you give your heart unto the Masters hands
Loveliness shall fashion Thee..and grace shall make Thee whole.

A vessel so blessed ... forged by might and mercy
Hammered, caressed, and smoothed to His will
Glazed to perfection in the fires of devotion
Empty and ready for Himself to instill.

Jan Buchalter

For Mother

For the battles were many,
and the war were never won.
For we chased her up the walls,
and ran across the floors that were just done.

For all the pain and torment,
and the hell we put her through.
For all the crying in the night,
and the floors she paced too.

For there is no one like her,
and there will never be another.
For that crazy nerve racked women,
we all called Mother.

Deborah Hehnly

Untitled

You lied, you cheated, you deceived,
And you know
That I was Vulnerable
And I needed someone
But that person wasn't you,
I played it cool,
For as long as I could stand,
But you came at me with your hand in a fist,
And I came back twice as hard,
With words, they cut like a knife,
You flinched, I smiled,
I'd won this fight,
But my smile slowly faded,
As I realized what I'd said,
I'd just sunk as low
As I could have,
For you hurt me bad
And I think you knew,
I was a hurting soul
Trying to get back at you.

Jennifer J. Mott

Transition

When you are feeling quite depressed
And, your world is a scrambled mess;
PLEASE, put it on hold - let it rest.
Get out of the world of mental stress
And, overcome your loneliness by looking at nature.

Open your mind to see what goes on
Of insects and birds of the feathery kind-
Like a hummingbird busily plying its trade
By sipping nectar of flowers, so pretty, so many.

I marvel at this tiny bird, so quickly it moved about
Backward and forward and sideways it went
And, I marvelled how fast it maneuvered its wings
So its needle like beak gained the nectar it needs.

With iridescent colors that seemed to change
From red, blue and gold-yet silvery green,
Well, I have decided I won't try to analyze
This tiny bird more but just to enjoy it as part of nature.
So, PLEASE, you do the same and you will gain pleasure
And, gone is the strain!

Floyd G. Hair

The Pugilist

I saw him come down through the long, dusty lane,
angry, disheveled, and tired,
and I knew at a glance of the monstrous pain
in which his worn soul was mired.

A cut on his lip, and a nose pouring blood,
and I though, as he turned at the gate,
he's defended his honor again with his fists,
but he's finally accepted his fate.

He's a kid on a monstrously large ego-trip
and he won't stop to count up the cost,
the many black eyes and the bruises and such,
and the numerous teeth that he's lost.

They called him a coward, when first he came here,
a thing that he could not contend,
so faced with a fight, he'll throw down his gear,
and double his fists to defend.

Someday he will learn, as he moves through this life,
that fighting's not always so grand.
Face up to your problems and rein them about.
That's the way of becoming a man.

Ceil Whitley

Life's little Mountain

I have built a mountain for all to climb; not wanting to leave
anyone behind.
I surrounded the mountain with gates so wide and paved a narrow
path leading high on the side.
Sitting on the right being watchful everyday; I sent my Spirit
to lead the way.

Somewhere around the bottom all desire the light and wonder if they
should take a climb or flight.
Sooner or later someone comes along to say, "Get on that road-it's
the easy way".
Not by power nor by might, but let my Spirit be your sight.

This journey calls for nourishment of all kind, ingredients of
wisdom, knowledge and grace to keep piece of mind.
You should be clothed in glory with feet strapped in peace-it's
the outfit to be worn that keep you free.

All Saints warn, "Stay strong everyday, because there will always
be more souls to pull on the way".
There will come a time to sit for a while, rejoice, dance and
enjoy the fruit of your labor, that has grown to a pile.
It must be nice to have so much to give-since the only requirements
were to keep my commandments and live.

The same words are uttered as Saints run out of time, "What a
joyful endurance-it was worth the climb".
Response from the GREAT ONE so full of faith, "My precious
child-it was well worth the wait".

Fidel May

Sentimental Journey

Such a long road to travel.

The gateway to the past swung open with a few gentle creaks that
appeared to be warm and embracing.

Floating snowflakes tantalized me to dance with the memories
memories that filled a life time - Joyful, destructive, infatuating,
crippling, inflating...

Luminating amber leaves danced and crackled like burning
torches as
they guided and hastened my footsteps toward my
destination...The
black marble Norwegian headstone bearing my family name.
RIVETING;
jolting my pain, anger and longing...

The stones were cold. I had yearned for a sign of warmth to
nurture
and comfort me. Unrealistic expectations...They were not
there!!!

MOTHER NATURE attempted to soothe my sorrow with her
concert of peak
solace...The explosion of colors so rarely seen.

However, her wand lacked the necessary magic to meet my
standard of
living, loving and loss.

Constance F. Knutson

Destined Memories

Time stands still
And is looked away in the souls of the lovers
Minutes and seconds freeze
As new horizons are reached and new territory explored
The face of the clock is painted red
And shaped into a heart
That is carelessly tossed around by those in love.
But then the minutes and seconds melt into hours
Time skips ahead to make up for the steps lost.
The lovers part as the red paint cracks
And only memories are left in the souls of the lovers.

Jenn Raskayskas

Them Wind I see

Them wind I see
Are forever mind blowing

Them wind I see
Leaped through my soul at time-

Them wind I see
Will fill my expression in life

Them wind I see
Assure all my love to carry me "O" so deeply

Rest assure I will seek
Life through innocent wisdom

Them wind I see
Will carry me to the end of time
—and time thereafter

Them I wind I see
With every energy of passion mind.

Them wind I see
Are forever chasing me.

Let's seek them wind—

Elaine Copeland

God's Blessings

God's greatest blessings before me I see
Are in my children count them 1, 2, 3.
All bundles of life, happiness and joy
Nine months of waiting to hear "It's a Boy."
We heard those three words with each pregnancy
My husband's ecstatic this I can see.
The greatest challenge for us now to bear
Is to teach God's children love is to share.
We promise to raise them with loving hands
God's in their hearts and over them he stands
I vow to be patient, loving and kind
Doing my best as long as they are mine.
We need to be good parents everyday
For God's greatest gift we cannot repay.

Andrea M. Szala

An Invitation

Our passions and emotions raging
Are not meant for repressive caging.
For without them, life is incomplete;
And, our time for living knows no retreat.

Pretty girl with the golden hair,
It is you with whom my bed I wish to share.
Hold me in your warm embrace,
Let me feel your ardent breath upon my face.

Put aside your fears and foolish pride,
And together we will glide
Upon the petal of a flower,
As each other with love we shower.

And then, lying closely in a drowsy after-hush,
Covered with that rose-red lovers' flush,
We can plan, and dream, and dare
About the future we seem to want to share.

John S. Brookes

Of Lesser Service To All

Ambiguous statements and non-definitive solutions
Are offered by our politicians seeking their "own" resolutions.
None really solving our socio-economic woes;
They resort to evasive distractions, and place the former on hold.
They claim our problems are based on punishment and crime
As fear, bigotry, and crime are not products of socio-economic decline

To admit the truth is to surrender power positions
That we all become victims to by electing these officials.
Elect me and I will institute the death penalty
Is the hue and cry among the political mediocrity.
Our nation is becoming number one in the world;
As the bell tolls ominously, it's our nation's death knell.

Anthony Torres

"Winter Enchantment"

Swirling snow and gusty winds
Are raging from the sky,
And shifting lots of frigid air
On the masses scurrying by

Falling branches make a snapping sound
As they quickly sprawl on the snow,
Creating a dazzling artistic design
While the sunlight provides a soft glow

Tall furry cattails shiver in the snow
As the birds seize food for survival,
The neighborhood's tomcat is battle-fatigued
From fighting snow-wars and survival

The sidewalks are carpeted with blankets of snow
No artist can match such true beauty,
As snowflakes are falling like feathers of down
Upon the vast earth's splendid beauty

The storm has now subsided, it's tranquil and calm
The earth is disguised as a dream-land
With layers of glistening fluffy white snow
In a scene that you'd never believe-land

Florencen E. Ross

It's Harvest Time

There's a cold wind blowing up north and the apple trees are yielding their fruit, the nut trees such as the pecan tree are springing forth with the fruit of its long Summer labor. The birds are preparing to fly South, oh yes you see they know it's that time of the year. The squirrels are scurrying to store their nuts for safe keeping. The big Black bears are preparing themselves for a long winters nap, yes you see they know it's time to hibernate. The sweet potatoes are ready for hoeing up and the peanuts are ready for pulling up, yes you see it's that time of the year. The harvest Moon is shining bright as we all gather around the camp fire singing Harvest Home. Gone are the long hot days of summer replaced by the world engulfed in a glorious array of rich fall beauty. The leaves are dancing around our feet to the whistle of the cool fall breeze. The world is making a great transformation, it's a time of gladness and sadness all wrapped up together, but I thank God almighty it's finally here, yes it's finally Harvest Time.

Anna J. Slaughter

Last Rose

Last Rose of Summer, why are you the prettiest,
biggest of the year.
Is it to try and hide the fact that winter, will soon be here.
Or don't you know Jack Frost, is near.
Till then we will hold you warm and dear.
Next year hoping from your bush other Red Roses, will appear.
But they will not seem quite as big or as Red, I fear.
As the last Rose, we had this year.

Carolee Smith

To My Friend

My friend I thank you for being there, for caring, for opening up your arms and loving me even though you know my deepest darkest secrets, my pain. You have loved me when I couldn't even love myself. You have accepted me when I had no tolerance of myself. Thank you friend for your warm words, your kind hand, and your loving touch. Thank you for listening your kindness has meant so much. My friend I have many flaws, many defects of character, and you love me anyway. Your love is unconditional, in your eyes my flaws one day will become my strengths, there's no limit to your encouragement. Thank you for not judging me when it is so easy for me to condemn myself. The future looks bright in your eyes even through my tears. Your smile, your love, you, you friend are a blessing a star sent down to me. Your power, your strength, and kindness has helped me. Thank you for understanding why I have walls, and for giving me space and time to take them down. Thank you for loving me at a distance when I'm too afraid to be close, and for hugging me when I feel lovable. Friend when I feel ugly you always see my beauty. When I feel scared you lend a hand. Friend there are many reasons why your here and I thank you for them all. Your a blessing, your an angel, I thank God your here. Thank you friend, I love you, please always stay near!

Ginny Cerar

Autumn Portraited

There is a lovely golden view.
Around each and everyone of you.
Sparkling high from the sunset
Overlooking where we met.

There is a special brilliant glow like flame.
Staring at us from the sand.
We admired it across the meadow.
Assembling colors as they glow.

As we gaze at it late in the evening.
Till we realize it's the season.
What picturesque sights are on the ground!
Portraiting colors orange, green, yellow, and brown!

Temporarily they'll soon be out of sight.
Ah! when we close our eyes real tight!
Now we know it's time for night fall.
As we revolve around on earth-ball.

Then slowly we drifted away in sweet slumber.
Dreaming how these colorful leaves did tumble.
We talked and toss, but slept very sound.
Still wondering, how autumn brings mums and pumpkins all in a mound?

Julia E. Key

The Farmer

T'was a cold winter day, with overcast skies,
As Daddy stood back, with tear in his eyes.

The auctioneer's voice, was loud and clear,
As he sold off that farm, and the very last steer.

Daddy's dreams were shattered, all broken apart,
I knew how it hurt, as they tore out his heart.

Now when I drive to the country, I drive by the farm,
Where there's memories of Daddy, and my dear old Mom.

Memories of hardships, memories of strife,
But Daddy loved farming, it was his way of life.

He always worked hard, and so did Mom,
Trying to make a living on that blasted old farm.

Is it Reagan economics, who's to say?
Why the farmer goes broke, and his hair turns gray.

I'll always have visions, of overcast skies,
And when Daddy stood back, with tears in his eyes.

Duane Murphy

As He Walked Away

I watched in flooded vision,
as he slowly walked away,
never to look back.

He became numb to my love,
mute to my cry,
and blind to my need
for his love.

I begged silently,
that he would turn back,
plead my forgiveness,
and all would be,
as before the harsh words of the end.

I realized at length,
as the cold silence closed in around me,
as I listened to his foot steps grow fainter,
that he will never love me or hold me,
ever again.

Courtney C. Krallman

Poetry Of Lies

As I look out of my window
As I look far as I can see there is a shadow.
Shadow of Lies

As I go out side there I see a maze.
As I try to find my shadow I can no
longer find the days a dead white
Rose all alone yes, there it lays.
A maze of Lies

Soft but not far cries of a baby
Soft but not far cries of a lady
Would I see them? Whispers of voices say someday maybe.
Cries of Lies

Read this and believe not but of lies,
shadows, a maze, and babies cries that
someday we all will read poetry of lies.

Dawn Jackson

The Window Of Life

The rain falls down with a melancholy sound
as I peer through the window of life.

No space untouched on a surface once smooth
as tears streak the face of a child.

Youth dissipates like clouds in the sky
as the secrets of the world unfold.

No candle alight in the depths of the dark
as the heartbeat we love drives us home.

A life born to live in the shadow of pain
as we struggle with hope and despair.

No future ahead of a past that's behind
as the wind whips the petals from a rose.

Janice Spallin

Testaceous

My virtued years I never spent
Anyways they came and went
I don't want them back I never did
They say I must and I say they don't exist
But who are they and who are you
The telltale flies say you're one too
A whisper can get you as much as a sigh
On each side is an evil to regret or deny
This isn't the end but the eye of the storm
And here I am not cold inside just nauseatingly warm

Amber Cooper

Autumn

It's a warm, breezy, beautiful autumn day,
As I watch the trees swing and sway
The leaves float down to the ground swirling at a pace,
Then the wind comes and put them in a different place

I look up and see the clouds moving in slow motion,
Just like the waves you see upon the ocean
The birds with fluttering wings soaring on high,
I just close my eyes, and with them I to can fly

Its beauty starts my heart to really palpitate,
And my whole being begin to exhilarate
Now the sun is about to go down for the evening,
I can't wait to see what tomorrow will bring

Henrietta Smith

A Life Of Your Own

Sometimes don't you feel trapped
As if people have your life planned out on a map

You aren't allowed to think the way you think
It's like your thoughts are slowly draining down the sink

It feels like you are locked up in a cage
Because your body is filled with so much rage

But soon you will get it through their minds
You will then release your thoughts and it you will find

A life of your own

Denise Michelle Rascon

To Mom, With Love

You gave me life, you gave me love,
As pure and innocent as a snow-white dove.
You gave me guidance and a strong will,
But this emptiness, when you left, can never be filled.

The gentleness of your voice, the warmth of your embrace,
I carry with me, each night and each day.
And all the sweet memories we made together,
Will be in my heart, forever and ever.

You touched so many hearts in your journeys here,
And we all miss your physical presence, so dear.
I visit you often in my dreams,
And it helps me to go on, it seems.

As you watch us from heaven, with God at your side,
I pray for your wisdom, and unconditional pride.
If only I could hold you, one more time,
I'd tell you, I love you, and you will always be special,
and always mine.

You gave me so much, and in your own gentle way,
I know you are listening to me today.
So Mom, may you hear my cries of joy,
To this life you gave me, I rejoice!

Dana Alligood

Untitled

You can't be happy all the time
because the sun doesn't always shine
sometimes the clouds rest over your head
and you feel the doom and dread
but than another day comes
and the sun creeps out from behind the gloom
you realize that your life is good
besides the rough and jagged edges

Heather Emerson

The Power

The thunder is softly rolling in the middle of the night
as the rain begins to fall washing everything in sight
In this quietness I contemplate the celestial wonder
of this power so immense from above called thunder

Periodically it mightily crashes and lightning flashes
caused by the negative and the positive power clashes
The wind begins to blow with such strength and power
as the rain pours in sheets, this is no mere shower

I do not think it's a mere confrontation of minds
rather a struggle which more oft than not blinds
Is this God's reminder of the futility of confrontation
or an attempt to make a point beyond our comprehension

I bask in the beauty of the power, whatever it may be
as I absorb the nurturing shower within, I begin to see
Heart and mind empowered, my soul joyously sings
for I am thankful for the enrichment to life it brings.

Harry N. Roso

An Impassioned Plea

I do not know, much less conceive, of the joy those must have as their destiny, to have someone with whom they can share, the abundant love God placed in their care.

He gave to us all of his own divine love, to share with others and that one special love. True love, He knew, once received cannot stay, but must return to the giver in a most pleasing way.

Such mutual giving cannot long remain stagnant, but increases with use, growing yet more abundant. It was never my fate to be so blessed, but mine, kept bottled up and my soul much depressed.

My one consolation has been my love for Him, while my human demands another more akin. Such terrible loneliness is most bitter indeed, for my flesh ever craves one to fulfill its need.

But the hour is spent, my time's running lean. The odds ever greater as few know that love means. They believe love is taking all they can while living, unaware that love lives, only in giving.

Love is the total surrender of one's self to another, both with mind, will and body, of each to the other. Love never demands or seeks its own pleasure, for this it finds in pleasing its treasure.

Within is the hope I may yet find, a loving mate with compatible mind. If given reprieve, then can I say, "I've found my Eve."

Charles E. Watson

Sea Of Beauty

On the shore I stood watching the waves,
As they rolled in from the magic of the sea,
the colors it changed from gold to blue-green
I wondered what kind of secrets it kept beneath.

The waves broke against the mound of rocks,
sending up sprays of glorious gold in the glittering
rays of the sun, which contrasted beautifully
with the turquoise blue-green water.
The beauty across the waves as the sun
shone down on the sea, made the water
look like silver-gold weaves, that shimmered
like diamonds in the sea.

I was often curious about the depths unknown to me,
I wanted to see the bottomless paradise,
to explore the sea bed of wonders and delight,
to find hidden treasures and old ship wreck sights
of those who once sailed during the night,
But till then the sea and I shall meet.

Aimee Wisk

A Special Mother

I often wonder how I ever became so fortunate
as to have a mother like you, you give so much
of yourself to helping others, yet you don't
always receive much in return. Through the years,
your patience and understanding have
become very comforting in a time of need.

When I think of you, I think of all the things
you've taught me, the many values in which
I am so grateful to have learned. You have
always accepted me not, for someone whom
you wished I could be...but for who I am.

Your love is one that will always be cherished,
and a very important part of our family.
You are someone who is quite special,
And truly an inspiration to all mothers.

Diane Punchard

"Twenty Years Ago Today"

"Just two crazy kids in love," so many of them say,
As we walked the aisle arm in arm, Twenty Years Ago Today.

"It won't last" so many scoffed; "The bills, how will they pay?
They don't know how hard life is, "Twenty Years Ago Today.

"Just wait till they start having kids, then they'll have hell to pay!
They're just two crazy kids in love," Twenty Years Ago Today.

We told them then; we'll tell them now: "You watch, we'll make
our way."
And it just so happens, that it's been, Twenty Years Ago Today!

Through fears and tears, the kids, the years, we've had to fight
our way.
But we pulled through, with love somehow, for Twenty Years Today!

So as the doubters see us now, I wonder if they say:
They're still two crazy kids in love, with Twenty more years on
the way!!!

David G. Spurrier

Woman

A woman's love bears down to the depths of her soul,
as wide as the width of her might,
as high as the height of her passion.
Free yet trapped.
Yearning to be matched or challenged.
Reaching out to receive
To retrieve from
To be united in oneness
she awaits
Trapped yet free
A tantalizing appetite dominates her.
Her emptiness reveals pain.
Pain converts change.
Change bestows truth.
And behold -
truth sets her free.

Irene L. Carter

Blind Faith

They asked me to believe how my parents tried to mold me
Blind faith
They asked me to believe what the churches sold me
Blind faith
They asked me to believe all that AA told me
Blind faith
You ask me to believe what you say when you hold me
Well, I'm all outta blind faith,
You're gonna have to proof it.

Claudia Hazard

River Of Tears

Allow the tears, flowing gently,
As you release the pain of millenniums.
The river of tears is the greatest gift of love,
Moving serenely across generations and irrigating the barrenness.

The dry land, parched and undernourished,
Receives the water graciously and forgets not its indebtedness.
There is no dishonor or embarrassment in the river of tears;
It is only our souls releasing
And crying out in joyful exaltation!

It is the nourishment, feeding the roughness,
Softening the fertile land, long held tight and unproductive.
It is the banner of truth, waving contentedly,
Always willing to release much more,
If only its message is received.

Why the tears in the barren land?
It is prophesied that what one sows, so shall one reap.
The river of tears nourished what has been sown,
And the fruit will be born as it has been foretold.

This we know, all plants need water and fertile soil to grow;
Now you have created your promised land.

Jan Knight

No Time (For Us)

Honey said she missed me when I got home yesterday
askin' if this time around I really meant to stay
As I took her in my arms and promised heaven I would try
Honey kissed me softly and I asked her not to cry
So young at heart I had to have more time to find my space
And honey looked away to hide a sad and empty face

Remember love it never hurts forever
Maybe next year you could find somebody new
But a place inside my heart will still be empty
and that's the place I'll always keep for you

Honey watched and waited for the things I couldn't say
Words that would so easily make everything okay
As I looked outside the window through a cloud of silent tears
remembering the rainy nights she helped to calm my fears
I thought about the day we met, a time I called her friend
Wondering why the life we knew had somehow reached its end

Chuck Dowling Jr.

Remembering Mama!

I still remember when I was a small child, about four or five.
I fell asleep on my bed, sakes alive! I remember my darling
Mama undressing me there, thinking I was sound asleep; but I
was actually fuzzily awake, not a sound was I to make! Just too
lazy in sleep to want myself to undress, but a moment to remember
so long ago to this day, on my memory to impress!
I will always remember what she did say, that day.
"My little darling is so tired 'tis true, so I will undress you, your
clothes to undo!" I can still remember the feeling of pleasure, of
lying there, being undone, a feeling of well-being for she was
always the one, always there to make it all seem like fun; and as
she gowned me and lifted me up to blanket me, she laid me
gently down for the night to be and whispered softly, with nary a
gruff, my pillow she did lift to fluff,
"Sleep well my sweet baby, Mama loves you so!"
Suddenly, I awoke and reached for her for I didn't want her to go!

Clotilda C. Booth

Our View - Past - Present - Future

Most of us at our VFW Post are "over the hill",
At that age when we must rely on youngsters our needs to fulfill.
Transportation needs arise, prescriptions need filling,
appointments to keep,
Post functions to attend so the oldster can meet.
Our quartermaster works all day at the VA Clinic his fellow Vets
to serve, then off the our Post and more requests, enough to unnerve.
Through all of this there is a smile on his face, Ready to assist,
prepare, listen, no task too large that smile to erase. Not only
has he served our country long and with zest, He is not yet fifty
and at his best. On and on I could go about this man's grace.
He is our future, this man with the smile on his face.
He needs help, his duties to perform,
For in his job there is no norm. We need younger
blood for our post to survive, So where are more men with similar
drive? Volunteers under fifty to join so our post is not forsaken,
To pickup the yoke of those the grim reaper has taken.
Those of Viet Nam, Granada, the Gulf, Haiti and?
The VFW needs you to continue our chores and assist the man
with the smile on his face, "STAN".

Janice Rhoades-McDonald

My Loves Cold Winter

I jumped in fright
At the ring of the phone,
For all was silent,
In this cozy little home.

But soon my fright was over,
For on the other line,
'Twas the man in which I longed for,
The one who made mine eyes shine.

He seemed so silent, I soon found out why.
As he ripped my heart straight from my chest.
For this cruel punishment was his way,
Of saying goodbye

"My Heart?" you ask, it feels so bare and empty,
Like a thornfull stem of a rose
"The Rose?" you ask, it is not but a splinter.
For the rose was killed,
By my loves cold winter.

Amanda L. Freeman

The Silence Of An Angel

Lies voiced by a fool,
attempting to disgrace
the innocence of an angel.
Slander may be spoken,
but foolish ears
do not bother to hear
the just words.
For the fool is always right
and never wrong.

Silence is best
when arguing with a fool.
Its sonance
may shower him with confidence,
for his lies are not defied,
therefore, stand as words of an honest man.
But for those who listen to the silence,
they find the truth.
And for those who do not bother to hear...
Are the fools.
For they find the truth within their lies.

Ben Korzec

"Dark"

The rain pours slowly down through the night,
awry sight.
Smile upon my face,
hidden disgrace.
A reason for your plotted schemes,
shattered dreams.
Revenge you seek in the worst way,
fears allay.
Into the night I slowly become,
turning white, my end arrives.
Begging for life, the death man calls.
Broken sunshine, left in the dark.

Jennifer Gockley

Cleansing Agents Say Come To Church

DUZ you DREFT with the TIDE?
Be BOLD, this is the DAWN of a new ERA.
Now is the time to CHEER up if you want to gain
more JOY and SUNLIGHT in your life.
The TREND is to BREEZE or COAST to church on Sunday.
Yet too many people SNUGGLE their heads in a DOWNY pillow,
Or work until 409 to make their cars SPIC & SPAN, forgetting
that the Lord's day was made for LESTOIL.
When you put GOD first, you will have a SHIELD and a DOVE
will never be sent with an S.O.S. from you.
Maybe we ought to DIAL you to remind you of
the IVORY palaces beyond the SUN.
Worship can be a LEVER or a LIFEBUOY, so WISK yourself
out of bed on Sunday, put on CARESS, dress up in your
CLINGFREE hose, make a FRESHSTART, set the TONE for the
day, catch the SPIRIT and DASH like a COMET to Sunday
School and church. As you sing PRAISE to GOD, SHOUT, and
say YES to His word, You will get a BOUNCE in your step, a
wonderful CLEANSER for your soul, feel FANTASTIK and you
will be full of ZEST ALL week long.

Hermione Dockett-Randle

The Alpha and The Omega

Who can light up a dark room,
Be it in the world or in the heart?
Who can lift up the deepest sorrow,
Keep Faith and Fear apart?
The Alpha and The Omega

Who forgives the unforgivable,
No matter how bad it may be?
Who can create a new life,
Before birth, and from sin's grasp make us free?
The Alpha and The Omega

Who was born with farm animals,
And makes the righteous flourish like the Palm Tree?
Who accepted dozens of slashes and holes in His body,
Bled and died for you and me?
The Alpha and The Omega

Who is coming back one day,
To bring His children Home?
Who from The Beginning to The End,
Lets us know we are "never" alone!
The Alpha and The Omega!

Cherice R. DuMond

The Prophesy

One day long ago, I received a prophesy in which I still believe to be true.

A prophesy in which the beauty of a certain woman would shine through.

I believed and received the words that the Lord had spoken to me, concerning my future bride to be.

And on that certain day, even as a sinner, the Lord quickened within me the spirit to know, as my eyes beheld the appearance of your beautiful glow.

Since then my love has grown to an overwhelming height, crying out to the heavens, asking God to help me win this fight.

I was told of the beauty of your soul, but I was not told of the pains and the hurts that it holds.

I think back over the years when our laughter seemed real and our joy seemed true, enjoying one another in all things being new.

But somewhere during our up and downs the joy and laughter seems to have gotten lost and knowing not how to be refound.

Your faith in our future has been constantly up and down, wearying my heart of the truth that God said will abound.

Alphonso Green

A Blissful Night

The sun's white heat scorches the cracked dirt.
Beads of sweat run down his back and dampens his shirt.
His muscles tighten as he forces the hoe in the ground.
Over and over with a thumping sound,
Hours and hours yet hardly the day passes.
Slowly oh so slowly just like molasses.
The sun goes down the stars come out,
In the distance far away you can
Hear slaves holler and shout,
Night has come; work comes to an end.
The lights in the main house go out as he rounds the bend.
The night is blissful for him and for me.
The only thing he dreams about is to be free.

Charly Michelle Adkinson

Gone

Gone are the new spring leaves who budded last spring and beautified my world.

Gone are all the truly honest men who would rather die than steal.

Gone are last fall's wonderful colors who fell from the sky and covered the ground like a blanket made by a loving hand.

Gone are the blue eggs that sat in a nest over my garage.

Gone are the fuzzy balls who used to play around my feet, and are now grown-up cats.

Gone is my playful filly who roamed the pasture and tripped on her own long legs.

Gone are the waves that knocked me over when I met the ocean for the first time.

Gone are the clouds that were in the sky on the day of my birth.

Gone are the tennis shoes who took me everywhere for almost a year.

Gone are the things I remember and have heard of, but yet they live on in my heart and my mind.

Jessica Snodgrass

Untitled

While driving down a highway, you see tall and towering trees
Beautiful and green and you see clumped with these,
An extra tall and brown one whose leaves have long been shed
And weathered through the winter months, staying brown instead.
You think of this old broken tree as an elder in the clump
Soon to be cut down to leave, just a broken stump.
But at one time he stood tall and green and swayed within the wind,
All the other trees then small, all looked up at him.
He sheltered them from sun and rain and snow that blew about
So they could grow up tall and straight, something he was really proud
He knew these young and restless trees first started from his seed
From sprout to sampling they now have grown, his shelter they no more need.
For now it is their turn sway and spread their seed
And shelter their sprouting offspring as they grow up with speed.
The time has come to leave your spot and make room for another sprout,
With purpose served, your time has come, that's what life is all about.

Iona M. Reynolds

Gazing At The Lady

I sit and gaze upon a body,
Beautifully smooth.
A shiny mirror of glass.
Ripples roll across in melodic vibrations
Calming the innermost being.
Playfully she advances and retreats,
Flirting with the thought of being contained.
A light appears from above-
Her face shines.
Her womb hides a diverse kingdom.
Flow on precious lady-
Explored and walked upon
But never are your treasures discovered.
Soothing, Peaceful,
Robed in emeralds,
Your eyes-glittering sapphires
With dashes of white.
May you glide into eternity.

Aubrey Hull

The Mountains Beauty

The beauty of the mountains are endless
Beauty is the gift of God that is upon the mountains
Hand in hand mountains and beauty come to us
In forms that are easily seen from a glorious trail
For nothing can stand before it
Nor thy try to stop its wondrous beauty.

The mountains beauty is a wonder less passage
None has passed such beauty except the wild ones
Thy travel far for rich goods and loveliness
Who shall tell anything but the wonders
Of nothing but the beauty of new land
For no one is as wonderful as the beauty of the mountains.

The beauty is spread everywhere in the day time
For sunset is over the endless mountains
The moon is more wondrous for there is no mistake
For thy dances for there is no resistance
The mountains a low there to be free in day and night.

Charity Hope Akers

"Ode To An Odor"

Whenever I open my refridge, I nearly go out of my mind
Because it is such a mysterious place, I never know what I will find.
I'm sure when the fabled Pandora opened her infamous box
She didn't find a whole half pound of month old Novie Lox.
She must have been a lady who showed much bravado
But didn't find a package of cheese the color of avocado.
How about that blob in my veggie bin that looks like a potato
I surmise, 'cause it doesn't have eyes, it must be a rotten tomato.
Now, let us consider the lettuce, a head that's supposed to be firm
The one lying limp in my GE looks like it needs a new perm.
And one thing I know very well:
Throw cold cuts away when they start to smell.
When seltzer begins to lose its fizz
Just plain water is what it is!
It's not that I really do not care
That my bread and cake start to grow green hair
So I start throwing things away
That I dare not keep for another day.
Now my fridge is all cleaned out, I'll keep it that way, I vow
But time elapses, my vow collapses, it's messy again somehow!

Doris Fisher

Our Favorite Seasons

MOMMY LOVES SPRING THE BEST
because it's warm and pretty,
Birds are chirping and flowers are blooming
It makes you have a pretty feeling.

My sister loves winter the best
because it's cold and snowy,
She loves to skate and have some fun
while drinking her hot cocoa,
But most of all, she loves to feel
the snowflakes on her eyes.

But I love summer the best
because it's hot and boiling,
I love to swim and jump the waves
the sandy beach twinkling my toes.
But the best of all, to end a warm summer day
is to be strolling the boardwalk
with a big ice cream cone in my hand.

Alyson Salonger

"Because Of Him"

Because of him we were brought to existence and born
Because of his Holly will, power and love,
We can see all his wonders
And enjoy his blessings from above.

Because of him we can see in the early spring
In meadows and prairies the flowers bloom,
With fragrant aromas and multiple colors that bring
The greatness and power owned, just by him.

Because of him daily we see the sun shine
And share the silver moonlight almost every night,
But when the moon is hidden of our constant glance
We see gleaming like diamonds, the miraculous stars.

Because of him we are rich in spirit and believe,
We are alike and have the opportunity to be with him
Because of him you better be, no not to be
Because of him we all really know "know he is".

Arquelio Caraffa

The Broken Heart

Have you ever had a broken heart
because the one you love says you have to part
He says that you'll be real good friends
but then you think well why will it end
He says he has to leave you now
but I don't know why, I don't know how
You close your eyes as you think of the past
the times we had, will this be the last
You see a tear fall down his cheek as he begins to cry
but all you can do is keep asking why
Why did this happen
why must we part
The last thing you gave me
was a broken heart.

Cynthia Sams

"Time Is Of The Essence"

Why should our children pay?
Because we have nothing to say.
So what if we are only common folk
With the taxes we pay why is it
We are told that our cities are broke.
Yes! Time is of the essence
All it needs is our presence.

Our elderly told they aren't needed anymore.
And yet their wisdom is the key to open the door.
Schools closing, libraries and museums, too.
While we citizens play the character part of a fool.
We have to get together right now.
Because it's time for us to take a bow.
Yes! Time is of the essence
All it needs is our presence.

Johnathan Rella

In Flight

When the struggle at home seems to be lost and direction
becomes obsolete and cloudy, then you know the gong has
just ignited flight. You fulfill all the requirements,
play by the rules, yet success eludes you. Joy remains
dim in you countenance, happiness takes a back seat in
your innermost heart and just before the sky darkens up
escape stares in your eyes.
In confusion you run to a strange land where everything
you have learned before has to be relearned albeit in a far
different tune. So you begin to master the norms of the
place, but you still cannot understand why your home is so
different in many ways. Defeat here cannot be pardoned
much less tolerated by the folks across the Atlantic.
In desperation and zeal to succeed,
you labor, toil and sweat all in one huge effort to justify
your flight and give meaning to your earlier confusion.

Ise Osayimwen

Home

There she was standing at the door;
at a place she had never been before.
She knocked at the door breath by breath;
hoping that her baby could find a place to rest.
She laid the baby at the door,
for she did not want him anymore.
They opened the door with great surprise;
saw a baby boy with big blue eyes.
His hair was brown shaded,
and his little blue shoes were slightly faded.
But as he got older, he could not remember,
but his mother's sweet fragrance still lingered.
For all we know, his mother might still roam,
but at least her baby boy has found a home.

Hayley Markham

Unforgetful Memories

I despise the awful enormous fear of a special loved one's death becoming near. I have so many things to say to her and I don't know where to start, but one thing that's important is that she'll always be in my heart.

Ever since the day that I was born, she's been there by my side. No matter if I was happy, or if on someone's shoulder I needed to cry.

She's made me laugh, she's made me cry.
She taught me right from wrong and to never lie.

She taught me how to bake cookies and made me
my own apron. I enjoyed that special
memory, because it forever gave me a great sensation

She's taken me to the movies, she's taken me to the park.
She lightened up a part of my life that could never ever be dark.

She's made me healthy. She's made me strong.
She's given me wonderful framed memories and
in my heart they'll always be hung.

She's taught me how to play many games.
She helped me put puzzles together.
Those are just a few portions of my memories
that will stick with me forever.

Crystal Orth

"Cherish"

Cherish all the memories in your mind,
Before they fade away,
Love those that bring such joy in your life,
Before they fade away,
Embrace tightly to what is in your heart,
Before they fade away,
Share with those all your triumphs,
Before they fade away,
Tell the one who earns your love,
That you love them again and again,
Lest they forget,
And it all fades away!

I will always love you dearly,

Bernard Didier Akle

How Many Dreams

How many dreams do we let go by
before they live, before they die
before they have a chance to live
we see them suddenly sometimes, in a conceive
and then they disappear, unless we believe
the little idea, the little dream, such a small thing
but it deserves a believe, it deserves love, it deserves to
be thought upon
and more than thinking on, it needs to be dreamed upon
and more than dreaming on, it needs to be acted upon
the dream, to live before it dies
the little dream we saw and loved
and what if it was never moved to real and fulfillment
for sometimes a little dream can become, a big dream and more
more of dreams of commitment and contentment
so don't let a little dream go by, for
too often things we love, just leave, and go and pass away,
goodbye
for, thoughts have wings, beauteous things, sudden things
and too soon, too fast, they fly away, in just a moment
goodbye

Eileen B. Ciuccarelli

Our Destiny

Looking back in time,
Before you were mine,
I realize that when we met,
Our destiny was already set.

I was hurt and confused,
There was someone else whose love I didn't want to lose.
But then we started dating,
And little by little I stopped waiting.

So as time passed on and the story ends,
We became more than just friends.
And although my feelings were slow to arrive,
I finally realized that my love was alive.

Then came that time in front of the sea,
When you confessed your love for me.
You asked me to be your wife,
And I said yes for the rest of my life...

Denise Fink

"I Wish You Peace"

No more than the power of light rising
behind the spread of oak trees against the sky

No more than the installation of the moon
in the darkness of a shadowed mind

No more than the song of a sparrow or
the declaration of prayer
did you enter into my life
with a soft profusion of a holy impact

There's no sadness in your absence...
Only a breeze against my cheek
only a current of ionized atoms
that tried to fill the outer shell
where completeness creates a noble element

I wish you peace

Aileen Lassiter

The Disturbed Soul

Smeared with blood, I came to the worlds' end.
Below me a storm swept out over the sea.
Losing flight, bird's wings drooped and drooped,
As crests of the waves sank them.

I threw myself onto the shore, an ugly tenant seeking shelter.
Tracts of wood, houses like traprock lay in ancient shade.
Voices in death moaned without bodies.
Nailed in my unmade bed, I listened.

Off in the distance, I could see a hill steep as the side of a silo;
Smooth as glass windowpanes, slippery as ice.
On the top a figure sat, clothed in a sanguinary gown
Of plaited bird's wings.

Around his fingers, the jowls of spiders crowned the ribs of insects.
Holding a golden bridle, a golden bird, a gilded tree,
He dribbled flesh, falling on the tolling bell.
I moved upwards grubbing amongst the ashes.

Eggshell, bits and scraps; such as rats eat... I ate.
A series of shadows fell across my sagging arms.
Legs bent taut in the reflections,
One bears life worse than death.

Dolores V. Gardella

Christmas Tree

Seeing Jesus through a Christmas Tree
Bethlehem's star atop the tree proclaims where the baby lay
Angels adorn announcing "Glory to God, peace on earth and good will toward men"
The ornaments sparkle of his love for all tribes of people, each unusual and different adding a touch of mystery

Red for the blood Jesus shed at Calvary for mankind
Blue for majesty and splendor
Gold for a crown of righteousness for a crown of thorns
Purple for a royal robe torn, tattered, and gambled for
White for purity and holiness
Green for everlasting life

Garland wrapped around the limbs giving hugs of warmth and love as Jesus wraps his children in warmth and love

Presents beneath the tree remind us of three wise men who traveled far to present gifts to a newborn king

Tinsel and glitter burst forth with an awareness that God is the one who bring meaning to the lives of men

O Christmas tree, O Christmas tree, O Christmas tree, what a story you tell of peace, love and hope for all mankind.

Elizabeth Gail Sewell

Life's Awakening Touch

From the womb of a woman unknown I came
blinded to the world and still without a name,
and, yet, even then through my mind's eyes I saw,
people in black shadows with images flaw
of life's distortions, and of people being,
there in my mind a reality unseen.

Silence was there too with his new rubber shoe,
and stagnance was asleep, but everyone knew
of his habit. But I couldn't help but hear
noise walking around in his clamorous wear
of rusty suit, as he fights with silence
while pain slowly hid in his shady presence.

The world, my spectator, was turned upside down
and life hung helplessly above the ground
and then all around, suspense filled the air
playing hide and go seek with everyone there
I wanted to scream, but life held my breath
I wanted to run — I couldn't walk as yet.

Chaz Bover

My Room

Here in my room I sit alone,
blocking out the sound of everyone's drone.
Any word said is always a nag,
but here in my room nothing's a drag.
Here in my room my own design,
I could sit here for days and be just fine.
Having fun 'till someone dare disturb I,
but here in my room it's as peaceful as the sky.
Here in my room, my music, my phone, all the gab,
while my family on the couch, whoever could be so drab.
Here in my room, my palace, I rule,
Now just try and get in — ha
What a fool!

Jamie Gilbert

Neo-Ankh

Cradle the flickering blade;
blow out the sanguine flame and keep teary wax from dripping;
and blue smoke from sinking, so tomorrow it may be relit.
roll your paisleyandcalico marbles behind; click cat's eyes out of the circle;
stare into a clear mountain spring: your mind's eye and find new understanding. Pry your sticky fingers apart, little child, free the stale rubber air from a green balloon. It drops in your palm again.
stop this dizzy lacquered carousel and let me off.
I've been spinning in circles forever.
yellow popcorn and pink cotton candy will still be here tomorrow.
finite grains of sand, cupped in dove-like hands
let them crawl through your fingers, back onto the beach.
listen to living waves glide out into aureate eyes of setting suns
only to return once more. Look at your placid reflection under whispery grass; above in the kaleidoscopic sky.
Gaze deeply at heaven's constellations
projected on the backs of your eyelids. Can you see them?
fiery golden pyramids have grown wild in the desolate desert for all eternity and you'll return to see them later.

Ethan Alan Pang

Dreams

There are no more dreams, they are nothing must a mist
Blown and scattered in the cool gentle breeze

You live without dreams as a dark empty shell
Where there is no hope, no feeling, no tears

It's a lonely place to be, but you can't come near
For then you would see there is nothing there

Nothing but sadness, for all the pain and hurt
Which has becomes unbearable, it drives you insane

Your heart is used to keep you alive
Not to love or hope, but living to die

You keep breathing to know that you live
Until you breath no more and the gentle breeze takes you away

Elizabeth Ann Perez

Yet Love For You Flows On

Love this America, U.S.A.
Bold of courageous stance along the years' way.
Disappointed in the bending to greet and dishonesty's sway
Worried of the violence and hatred at bay.

Yet love for you flows on.

Tradition of family near to the heart,
Many think wanting and unwanted, depart.
Relationship sought fast fall apart.
When will they come back to the place of the heart?

Yet love for you flows on.

In our children we've placed hopes and dreams.
They are caught, however, in the world's dread schemes.
Become angry, hurt; we cry, sometimes scream.
Languish to see faces with smiles and eyes agleam.

Yet love for you flows on.

In God we trust, foundation of our building.
Our guide to freedom and liberty wielding.
We've distanced ourselves from these principles, unyielding
Waiting our bowing, offering shieldings.

Yet love for you flows on.

Eloise Murphy

Windows

A window can be looked through
both inward and outward,
Sometimes as clearly as a spring morning,
Sometimes not so clearly, like a foggy fall morning.

It's said to be a window to your soul,
For anyone to dwell in intimacy,
To gaze and see who you really are,
The emotions stirring within.

As you look to the world around you,
Every scene is recorded,
whether good or bad,
Pondered upon with the stillness of a starry night or
glanced at with the speed of a rushing river.

Wondering if all see what you interpret,
Colors, shapes, sizes,
Impressions becoming the reality,
A window that is vital to us all,
These windows are your eyes.

D. Black

Untitled

Indians, free people, free in a way whites were never.
Bound only by the ancient traditions of their fathers,
not by rules and regulations of civilization.
Courageous warriors, who fought for the precious
land they have lived.
Mother nature their provider.
Their many Gods watching over them from every direction.
Women who carry the seed of their men,
bringing young ones into the tribe.
Young girls, helping Mothers, and learning to be fit wives.
Young boys, playing games, and becoming proper warriors
to help fight for land that's rightfully theirs.
Dancing around fires to the story of the beating drums.
Beating freely, like the beat of your own heart.

Reservations, jails that held Indians
back from their dreams, their freedom.
The love they gave the land, taken
by whites who didn't give a damn.

Joy M. Berry

Beauty Complete, Lost Through Haste

It's cold and with hurried steps and
Bowed heads against the howling wind,
We enter in, seeking warmth and a
Happy welcome from a friend.

In our haste we fail to observe the
Sturdy, reaching arms of a naked tree;
The beauty of its gnarled branches,
Standing magnificent, for all to see.

A squirrel far up on a limb
Twitching its bushy tail, watching anxiously
As we hurriedly trample the terrain,
Guarding, fearfully its lofty domain.

A cardinal balancing so gracefully,
Fearless, and beautiful on a tiny twig,
Filling the air with its happy song,
Feels safe and secure from the passing throng.

Now from inside where it's cheerful and warm
We look out and observe what was there all along,
Too bad we hurried in and can only see
But not hear, the cardinal's joyous song.

Dorothy Lea Talbot

The Growth of Love

Moon, stars, sunsets in the sky, I sit here
broken hearted and watch them all go by.

Oceans meet the sea, the flatlands open up, wide
sunsets rise and fall as time proceeds to pass.

It is only true to say that what is meant to be,
is meant to be. The greatest future awaits. Time will
give power and time will give security: A lock on
life itself, and a grasp on you from the beginning

So, as the moon rise and fall, your name is what
I call. I'll love you till the day I die, and love you
more as time goes by. Hugs and kisses and words
I give, forever and ever as long as I live.

I close this with a caring phrase (over a
deep, black night and a thick haze).

Our life together has just begun, full of love,
laughter, and lots of fun.
So hold on tight and keep it strong, knowing one day
that this pain was not wrong.

Moon, stars, sunsets in the sky, I sit here pondering and
wanting to cry. Instinct tells me though, that time will fly.

Chad R. Davidson

God's Paint Brush

Autumn, falling leaves, orange, purple,
brown red and green.
Multiple colors from straight broad trees.
Looks as though God's hand itself
has touched the forests and the earth.
As though a paint brush be twirled around
in water colors and dabbed,
Going from loud, bright, to soft colors,
mixing with the blue sky and undertones of earth.
A spectacular event that happens once a year.
Some people call it fall, others autumn.
I call it God's paint brush, and as the
artist steps back to look at his work
he smiles in great delight.

Bobby Glenn Conley

City Of Angels

Dirty alleys, poverty, madness amongst the people.
Brutality rampid. The city of many faces.
I am told of your beauty but I hear screams from alleys as I pass
them by,
Buildings loom into the sky, staring down in an ominous way,
Beauty gives way to terror as the sun fades from the sky,
The pavement becomes littered with those who have no beds,
How you rave of your accomplishments, vast territory you cover.
The light hides your shame, darkness allows sin,
You have crushed many spirits, they hunger for life without you.
You laugh at them, there is no escape,
They are trapped as are the rats in your sewers,
They eat from the trash cans, and praise their concrete God for
his goodness.
As you tower overhead, decay eats at your feet,
You are too foolish to notice, vanity is sin.
You are the great jester, hiding behind a sinister vail.
How you crumble as the earth moves beneath your feet.
God feels his revenge and laughs at your weakness.
The mighty city topples and begs for mercy.

Joyce Bishop

The Stream Of Love

Days slip by like water in a
Bubbling stream, nice things pass and
So do bad.

Let us build a dam so we may pause, drink
And let our fingers, toes and souls be
Refreshed in our stream of love.

You ask what will the dam be made?
Loving looks, tender words, kisses, sharing work
And thoughts of joy, all of these little
Rocks calm the waters and make them stay.

Jean Saake

Need An Overhaul

I look in the mirror and what do I see,
But a wrinkled old face looking back at me!
With big brown blotches and hair of white,
I swear it happened over night.

I slowly inventory the rest of me,
And find fat pads where none should be.
Arthritic knuckles and flabby arms,
Whatever happened to all my charms?

Who's that old gal who got inside my skin,
And crawled to where I should have been?
Could it be someone from outer space,
Who wants to be some other place?

But I can still walk and talk and see,
And drive to places I must be.
I look again and suddenly,
There's the same old smile, so it must be me.

Erva Ande Anderson

The Killer Within

There is a killer within all of us,
But controlling this killer we all must.
When your anger turns to rage, the killer within
Us released from his cage.

The killer within may not kill or cause physical
Harm, but it will cause heat of the moment
Words to form. The killer within may never
Arise, but it is present even if sleeping it lies.

Whether the killer is a friend or a foe,
That is what each of us must know.
There is a killer within,
Each of us has to choose whether it is a enemy
Or a friend.

Edward Ellis

Just One Chance

I watch where he walks and I see where he goes,
but I keep myself hidden where nobody knows.
It's a true love that's secret, and I can't seem to find,
the words which to say so that he will be mine.

How does he feel, does he care about me?
Will it ever be real, or will it stay just a dream?
Can there ever be hope, will he make the first move?
Does he see me as nice, or think that I'm rude?

I don't mean to rush, or jump in it too soon,
but all that I ask is just one chance with you.
A chance in your life when you'll call me your girl
it's the one wish I have and it's the best in the world.

But if things don't work out, and if it comes to an end,
just remember I said that we'll always be friends.

Jacqueline Clinger

Roses In The Sand

You say roses can't survive in sand,
but I know for a fact there are some who can:
for freedom and love of country they stand
with just as much courage as any man.

They're someone's daughter, wife, or mother.
Who has gone to stand beside her brother
for the liberation of a strange land,
and to take power from a tyrant's hand.

In a crowd, they wear a tough disguise,
but when alone, dew fills their eyes
as memories of home overwhelm their souls.
Their love for their country can't be bought with gold.

They ponder the fallen, the wounded, the dead,
and pray over sacrificial stains of red.
They pray for the battle to come to an end,
and listen for cease-fire in the wind.

God bless and comfort the roses who stand
for the peace and good of their fellow man,
and give them the strength needed for each new day;
'til they will be free to come home to stay.

Esteene Isbell

Final Farewell

I'll take of times fond my friend, forgotten moments pass and end.
But I still stand for what I said, that's what I feel that's what I meant.
We've cried for things we couldn't change, hearts can often swell
in pain.
Eternity can never fade a memory which time has made.

Sad this time that we live in, a world which slaves to weaker men.
Dedication to a slower pace, killing off the thoughtful race.
And never will I claim to know, the ignorance which sets them so.
Eternity can never fade a memory which time has made.

Now take a walk into the clouds, a journey with the other gods.
They wander to a different place, completely void of time and space.
Where dreams are what they seem to be, eyes are lost so minds can see.
Eternity can never fade a memory which time has made.

Corey Weinfurt

Longful Wishes

I wish I were a fish; In all the oceans I'd be heard
But if I were a fish; I'd fall in love with a bird
Deep green would be my world
Bright blue would be her eyes
Though it's her that I would love
I could never hear her sighs
She would grace the clouds and winds
I would swim the oceans deep
Her love would go unspoken
My heart I would have to keep
Thru the depths I would admire
Thru the clouds she would soar
My heart would reach to her
But could not transverse the door
Our worlds are so much different
Our paths would never cross
The joining of our souls would forever be a loss
I wish I were a bird and the clouds my domain
I'd fall in love with a fish and my heart would feel the same

Helmuth Aukes

Untitled

Are you ready, well this one's just for you
But in all actuality this one's just for me too.
So let's see what I can do with 20 lines or less
What I'll write about, even I can't guess.
Should I write about the weather, how beautiful it's been
Or about how life's so much better then, way back when.
Shall I write about the world and all the problems that there are
Or shall I write about my dreams for which I dream upon a star.
Whatever I write about I hope you'll enjoy
For my talent I believe in and wish to employ.
Anyway, it's late afternoon, as we're relaxing with a friend
Everything's great, with no need for any of us to pretend.
The day has been wonderful the sun's shone all day
It's been very wonderful in every way.
I've accomplished some things that I've needed to do
And also found time to write for you too.
So how many lines are we up to so far
And what do you think - am I up to par.
Well I guess I should get this ready to send
For we've reached 20 lines, so this must be "the end".

Evelyn M. Carter

Why He Came

No room in the inn, the innkeeper said,
But in the stable, you can make a bed,
He told Joseph and Mary... so tired and worn.
On that bright starry night. Christ Jesus was born.
Angels told the shepherds, where He could be found.
The little babe in a manger...with cloth He was bound.
He came for one purpose. It had to be.
Christ came to die for you and me.
He lived His life without sin...and yet
Jesus died on the cross to pay our debt.

Geraldine Latham

Untitled

My name is George, I'm past seventy six
but just like a dog, in a terrible fix,
it's hard to teach me, a new bag of tricks.
I am fully aware that my youth has been spent,
that my get up and go, has got up and went,
but I really don't mind when I think with a grin,
of all the grand places my get up has been.
I could ramble on with big tales I say,
having and hearing other things of the day,
so just a few words of wisdom to you,
why worry? "be happy, with nothing to do".
I know I am old, "cause" my eye sight is spent
even my glasses, have got up and went.
So much for my grumbling, but I'm not alone,
there are others, sick and staying at home,
Yes, quite a few, without much to do, only
wishing for the best happy Thanksgiving to YOU.

George R. Baker

Prejudice

The cruel act of prejudice
brings a feeling of pain
like the emptiness
when you're left out of a game.
Like the music of
a sea shell; hollow and distant.
The prejudice you feel
when you never reach the front door,
always being turned away
before you ever reach the first step.
Prejudice, the heartless judgement
that turns you away without even a chance.

Becky Reedy

Hands Of A Pianist

When he was born, Daddy said he had the hands of a pianist -
but never made sure the boy got lessons.
He would've loved to play, but never got the chance.
Mama made him read, and he learned a new music.
Books became his piano,
using empty notebook pages as blank music sheets
at the desk he did his playing - on words.
Between blue lines were his unspoken notes:
Letters - eighths and quarters
words were halves and whole
sentences - full measures of sound
Stirring hymns within his soul.
The first page on which he placed his feelings,
would probably be his first song -
Making his first novel,
nothing short of a symphony.
At his desk he continues to play,
simply making music with his words.
Rehearsing all of his compositions,
because opening night is just around the corner.

Jason G. Morrow

Memories Of You

When we were together, I thought it would've last,
but now we're not together, I think it went too fast,
you said you loved me but you lied,
cause if it was love you'd be by my side,
holding me and kissing me with those tender lips
and like always just watching you would make my
heart do flips

When our relationship was fading away,
I pleaded and begged just for you to stay
To stay in my arms forever more
cause it is you and only you I adore;
you were the sun rising everyday,
you were my hero here to stay

You stood by my side for a very long time
but you recently left me without a clue or sign
the only sign you left that tells you don't want
me no more
Is the thought of you saying, "being with me is
like doing an despicable chore".

Dana Philogene

Colors

I stagger not in a world of black
but one of too many colors
Where red is not just red
And blue could be purple
they rush at me
hitting me and screaming.
I try to put red with Red
and green with Green
But that does not work.
"Who are you to judge me?"
they shout "Look at us as unique!"
So I try to look as they bombard me,
at each individual color.
Soon they cry "You stare because we are different."
Confused, I stop. What is right or wrong?
So I hold up my hands
and part the colors
and one color shines on the world.
I see only white,
but close my eyes to the Truth

Jerelyn N. Parker

Misery

"I love you, baby" that's what you say
but only after you'd beat me that day
bruises and scratches are all over me
but you're so high you can't even see
on Mondays you're sweet, Tuesdays you're not
Wednesdays you're half sober, Thursdays you're high
Weekends with you weren't so swell
frankly weekends with you were a living Hell
I never see the out doors unless you're gone
I can't even sleep in my own home
you treat me as if I'm only a child
or someone you can win with just a hug and a smile
when we first met I thought there was love
I even thought you were sent from above
you beat me in front of my kids without the slightest thought
now all they talk about is when mommy and daddy fought
I can't and I will not take this another day
I refuse to let my life go to waste
I really thought you'd make my life complete
But you only kept me in misery!

Halaveshia Hall

My Miracle

My miracle is a lady who is common by most
But she walks in beauty like our heavenly host
A smile on her face
Never a frown
Light in her eyes when she's around
A touch of her hand and warmth in our hearts
Knowing her love will never depart
Love love is her answer to all
Trust in our hearts for she will not fall.
My miracle
My lady
My love

Deborah Adams

Silence

The silence is almost deafening
but such a pleasure to the ears
It's such a good sensation
one I haven't felt in years.

I found the nerve to turn it off
the T.V. set I mean
I discovered all the shows
are the same ones I have seen.

And now I find that I still can read
though I thought I'd forgotten how
So I discovered an old pastime
that I can get back to now.

Though the children's books I used to read
are far too young for me
I still remember "Tom Sawyer"
which I read before T.V.

I hope now, I can find to read
a mature story as good as that
So at least I might get smarter
as I sit reading and getting fat.

Jack Campbell

The Midnight Oil

You lie there sound asleep, and somewhat tousled is your hair,
But the beauty never leaves you, and it's all that I can bear
To sit immersed in study of purely scientific fact,
When my heart within me swells, 'bout to burst from being attacked
By an emotion, a sensation, which slowly turns to pain,
And which no man of science could ever venture to explain.

Love is not hypothesis, nor theory for experiment,
But love's a feeling deep within, like God omnipotent.
Never shall it truly in concrete detail be explained,
But by wordless words that swell the heart, no cage of ribs restrains.
O science - against you I rebel - for me you hold no intrigue.
Countless data, theory, fact lead only to fatigue.
But nature, beauty, that which only He alone creates,
Solely is responsible for love - that forever permeates.

Irwin Jacovsky

The Ocean Is Alive

I try to sleep
But the waves lapping at the shore
Keep me awake.
The sound is soothing
But oddly scary
Like moaning ghosts drowning in the waters.
Screaming, wailing, the spirits cry,
Sea people that talk in the language of the sea.
The animals that own the ocean
Make the ocean come alive,
Whispering deep, dark secrets
To the ears of the cool night air.
The sea growls and breathes
in a foreign breath.
Waterfowl call a warning
Of the power of the moving, living sea.
I steal a glance
And almost BLIND myself.
The ocean is alive.
The ocean is alive!

Joshua Clay Phillips

Sadness

Immortality reigns in the mind of an ignorant five-year old,
But the years quickly go racing by and the real world takes its toll,
He realizes his imaginative dreams become shattered by reality,
And as if his childhood never mattered; maturity he now sees,
Memories of his "good ole years" are drowned out by present times,
And recollecting on his long lost youth is like hearing distant chimes,
Thinking of how the care-free life is lost and forever gone,
Tears of nostalgia roll down his cheeks and he hears an ancient song,
And the past comes flooding back like a wild, mindless deluge,
Remembering old times and friends as they creep from subterfuge,
Tears of happiness now flow from his sobbing eyes,
While smiling is a rarity one forms as he cries,
In time the weeping stops and he clears his present mind,
Carrying on with his adult life, leaving the past behind.

Eric White

Thinking Of You

I said I'd always be with you and would never stand alone.
But to walk away and leave today made my heart drop like a stone.
It took everything I had to lock and hide my tears of pain.
The thought of being without you is driving me insane.
Tonight, I'll lay awake in bed with thoughts of you in mind.
My love for you is tender and sweet but your love is one of a kind.
My emotions are crashing in although my heart is standing strong.
But I'll wait was long as it takes, I would never do you wrong.
So we have to hold onto memories cause it will be a while.
What ever you do, when you are blue, just think of me and smile.

Colleen L. Brown

This Old Train

This old train just huffs and puffs
But this old train still knows its stuff.
The track has been long, up and down hill,
But this old train can still fill the bill.

There may be a creak here and there.
The whistle may be weaker
But who cares?
Times have really changed as the story goes,
But if this old train could talk
What a story to behold.

So just look out and stand back,
Here comes the old train down the track!
It still has steam to go and go.
So what if it is eighty years old!

Barbara Sue Barnett

Revolution

A change in life
But we still have strife
We struggle and struggle,
He gave us a dream but we still feign
And feign to see the
Promised land we have never seen.

Revolution a change, freedom
No more evil rule, but equal rule
We jump for joy,
We scream and scream freedom has come
To see the promised land we have never seen.

Revolution a change in life
Are we going back to the struggle and strife
In which we sleep at night and
Hear shots that make you fright.
Revolution we need a solution
To stop this destruction
That causes corruption
In this trial of tribulation

Revolution! Revolution!

Ahmed Yilla

Glistering Waters

I looked into the glistering waters and saw my reflection
But what I saw was a state of flawlessness and perfection
You have a sparkle about you, which shines so bright
I want to reach out to grab you but, I am spattered by the light;

What radiance you have and a deep inner glow
Your movement is smooth from the path that you flow
The surface is wet, with a mild luster within
My mind becomes a glow, I soon becomes frighten;

What I saw was an object of my reflection
It's not the waters I saw but, my own imperfection
I realize what was lacking when I started to gaze
Then suddenly it hit me I was so amazed;

The answer came to me in the glistering waters,
I started out life without thanking my heavenly father
The shine I saw here, I could have it too
I'm glad I stumbled upon the glistering waters for life I'll start anew.

Jacqueline Williams

That Voice

That voice I heard before—
But where—?
In some past incarnation, or in a fleeting dream.
But how can I remember — that voice
And yet my heart and soul knows —

My heart quickens, my being is intoxicated with
vibrations of his nearness,
It denotes love and tenderness,
His eyes show the ebbing of passion —
And his hand on mine is —
Like the tide that takes hold of the land
Fiercely, and then — slowly lets go —

That voice—
When spoken in tendertones
Wears a million notes of melody —
All reflecting, the perfection, of a melodious symphony —
And yet I go on wondering —
That voice I heard before —
But where—but where—

Ann Manganaro

Towards Home... Gotta' Stay

Slanting rain on asphalt hard last fall's tawny leaves
By round evergreen like whispers in the breeze
Towards home, ... Gotta' Stay
Someday ..... Someway
Evergreens sitting high!
on a half hill whispering back to all
The tiny daffodils ...
Towards home, ... Gotta' Stay
Someday, Someway travel on up the hill
East on the Adamsville
Dark rain ..... Slanting rain
Towards home ..... Gotta' Stay!
Someday ..... Someway
One day Someway ...
Dark rain, slanting rain .....
Black night ..... insane,
With fear ..... no one knows
On your face ..... why the tear
Towards home ..... Gotta' stay
Someday. Someway!

Barbara Falcone

My Wooded Path

I walked along a wooded path, a path that was forgotten by time.
It was a path traveled often in my youth, in a happier time.
With a heavy heart I stop by a bubbling brook and let my tears
join in racing waters in search for a place of content.
I sat there on a rock next to the hickory tree and listen as
the wind in the tree tops played a song just for me.
My path takes me to the old rotten boards of the home place
back up in the mountains where I had spent my youth
and in the old yard long emptied of us all I could see the
ghost of my brother and me as we played barefoot beneath
the old oak tree.
There is the old well, the logs from the old barn and
what is that I see a carving that my dad had made and
hung from the old tree "Be still and let Peace come to thee"

Carolyn Suggs

Love

Love is a wonderful emotion that's shared,
By two wonderful people that have been paired.
It's an intense liking that goes;
Just beyond "like," it's a seed that's been sown.

It says in the Word, the Lord Jesus who said:
"Greater love hath no man than who'd die for a friend."
The Lord's utter love (and love never lies)
Was the same utter love that compelled Him to die.

The love that consumes you, and burns in a flame;
That love's filled with passion, and has no other name.
The drive to please your partner and to want to fill their needs,
To make them always happy and to give them trifle things.

A soft and coddling motherly love that swirls around her children
The fierce and rushing general's pride for the soldiers that
fought until the end.

Though many names are given to the melody of love's song,
Through the eyes of love that see, there can be no wrong.

Brandie J. Britt

Between The Lilac And The Pine

Between the lilac and the pine I sit on wood worn bare
By wind and rain and careless feet not going anywhere

But in and out from life to death I hear them laugh and cry
Another step-another breath they live and then they die

I sit here now where they once stood between the lilac and the pine
I rub my hand across the wood and pray I won't run out of time

If I don't move-go in or out perhaps the clock will stop
I'll whisper only to myself and learn to dream a lot

But then I wouldn't live at all so how could I fear death
With thoughts forever growing small a statue made of flesh

Between the lilac and the pine life will simply pass me
I'll climb the stair and jump the stair
And dare old death to catch me

Dianne Baumgartner

Gallant Confusion

Define the divine infant one.
Call it a sacred soul of love, and happiness
shall envelop its timid mind.
Without disgrace shall it grow in peace.
In disguise shall it embrace the indo.
It's in sceptical piece and every everlasting
mellow time.
Recognition of style and race.
Summon my soul and steal his face.
Indeed a life of depending synchronity.
I have risen to bleed.
A firm and just intention to feed.
To have to with hold
And everything.
For it is not an outrage, but a clear devotion
for yet a life's destination.
I feel the world will terror my quick fixed human
being, and every thing.
Shadows dance, circling my soul.
I crawl to my door step of darkness.

Heidi M. Stanat

Why Must It Be Me?

Why must it be me, who is the center of attention? Everyone calls my name when my back is to them and smiles in my face when I am before them. Why must it be my business that everyone consider their own? Just because I do things differently and live my life for me instead of society's chosen standards. Why must it be me who everyone wants to succeed in what they've chosen for me to do? When I have to make my own decisions and be happy in the end. Why must I be happy all the time, when I don't feel that way? To put up a front for everyone else who doesn't care about me. Why must it be me on which loneliness falls? When there's plenty of love in my heart and a lot of care in my eyes. Why must it be me who settles for second best? When I know I deserve better. Why must it be my life that follows trails of rugged paths lined with malignate fields? When I haven't hurt a soul or done anything wrong. Why must it be me who questions everything in my life? Every twist, every turn, every rise, every drop. I think I know why it must be me; to be strong and to make a difference. No one could show it better, no one could work any harder; It had to be me.

Eugenia Webb

A Poem About The Sioux

In our state a long time ago,
came the Sioux Indians in search of buffalo.
Their lives depended on the herd,
which the buffalo thought was quite absurd.
For from this mighty, shaggy beast
they got lots of food, enough for a feast!
From its hides they made their homes,
and tools were made from the buffalo's bones.
To prepare for the hunt which they did not fear
they held the Sundance, the most important ceremony of the year.

Along about 1742 a wonderful thing happened to the Sioux.
The "sacred dog" came along, and the Indians sang a different song.
For here was an animal that could do the work of more than one
big dog
and could pull loads heavier that a great big log!

In battle the Sioux were very brave,
they were taught at a young age how to behave.
Sitting Bull and Crazy Horse were among the great chiefs,
and of the Great Spirit, they had strong beliefs.
One of the greatest tribes of all times,
was the mighty Sioux, and this ends my rhyme!

Danielle Nielsen

Silent Scream

When a baby is not yet a baby,
Can he not still scream like a man?
For no one knows his motives for screaming.
When is it that his life began?

By the slightest twitch of tiny toes,
Did he suddenly spring into being?
Maybe with first sign of sentience
By a pain that he may have been feeling?

Was it by a dull beat to the ear
That alive he then became?
Or from the beginning, when meeting occurred
And the two became one in the same?

'Tis a question that all may argue-
Without resolution, may always be torn.
For the answer lies in the mind of a child
Who's not near the time to be born.

Jonathan W. Munden

Truth

Truth is an abstract thing.
Can you show it to me, or at least tell me what it means?
Truth to some is a banner
Worn so proudly for all to see
Yet, secretly they hid the fact that their truth may not reach to me.
The boss expects the truth from me at all times.
Yet, from him the truth is hard to find.
You say, "tell me the truth, I need to know!"
But when I do it hurts you so
and our friendship is under a strain.
It seems telling the truth gives me nothing to gain.
I've heard it said, "The truth shall set you free."
But tell that to the innocent under lock and key,
Who told the truth but none could see.
Truth is an abstract thing.
I try to catch hold but it alludes me.

Donna Christenberry

Little Man

Dreams appear, oh times so near, some not so clear.
Can you understand what I'm saying little man?
See if you can, in the place where I stand.
Not so near.
Not so far.
Just beyond the dreams I dare.
Can you see the places I fear? Can you feel the feelings I feel?
Do they seem so unreal?
Or is it only my mind in a fog, fading into problems beyond its control.
Beyond my dreams, there is something there, for me to seek and for me to find.
Am I right little man?
Do I feel the truth?
Tell me little man, I ask you please.
Will I find what I need?
A dream somewhere there ... in time I will find.
Tell me little man, how far do I go, how far do I look?
Help me little man, I ask you please, to help me to find
what I seek.

Brenna A. Cole

"Thoughts From Afar"

Darling can't you just hear me calling,
Can't you hear me say your name!
Darling nothing at all has happened,
Everything is just the same!
All the loneliness I've been feeling.
Equals up to all the pain!
For I just can't keep from crying
or holding back my tears like rain!
All our dreams and hopes have vanished
like a passing hurricane, just leaving bits of nothing,
Washed away by the fallowing rain.
Please understand my darling, what I'm about to do!
I'm sending all my thoughts Dear for across the sea to you!
Please understand the feelings and the loss I feel tonight!
As I see your face appearing and then fade out of sight;
Does this mean that it's all over? Is there any hope at all?
I'm not just going to give up! I'll fight until I fall!
But, please, send me some answers even though your far away!
Better yet send me your thoughts.
Dear I'll get them in just a day!

Jean Gasper

Iowa Winter On The Farm

Black cattle, white snow.
Car and tractors, got no go!
Paths icy, winds chill—
Freeze a little if you stand still.

Winds howl, dogs bark,
Went to city, no place to park!
Grimy windows, snow in crack.
Hold together, please, old shack!

Long cold nights and lonely days,
Time to ponder and change our ways;
Why do we stay in this frigid clime?
Why don't we go to a place sublime?

Guess we don't want to change our way.
Remember, dear friends, there is always MAY!

Iowa L. Honn

The Sea

The air chilled them like two homeless people in a cardboard box,
on a cold winter's night
The night closely gathered them like two scared children wrapped in a blanket,
as they flushed the sea's water with sadness
The waves were slashing against the walls of terror,
as the sea gulls filled the sky
The ship off the coast sailed quietly in,
as the fish splashed against the clear blue surface,
of the deep,
dark sea to their arrival
The two who were walking finally came upon a cliff
They looked over the sea,
saw that there was love to thee;
and jumped to their death's in the dangerous,
blue sea

Dennale Jehoich

Sabbath

Ivory crosses dangle from
chains of false gold. Eyes,
once proud, submit now to
their pale savior. Modern
Nubian queens, with feet
swollen and raw, give rent as tithe, while the
man from the corner clasps shaky hands in a
prayer of repentance. Preacher Tom urges
patience in this earthly fight, and timid voices
find thunder in amen and hallelujah. King James
gives his own kind of message—Love thy enemy,
and Jesus. A stick-figured mother grieves the
death of her murdered
child. The congregation cries
and sings the day's hymn
to the glory of God. They end
with prayer, then file out
slowly—offering smiles of
faith to the blue - eyed
Messiah over the exit door.

Adrienne Maxwell

Pivot

Crystalline, minute, the sand stings on the wind.
Could the sand that bombards me have risen from the earth's convulsions?

The sea that enfolds me rises on the wind
and returns again.
Could that be the same water that created me?

It is said that the earth's gold has been recycled over millennia.
Am I wearing the necklace of a Queen?

Betty Ann Zeoli

Beyond Time And Hope

The shadows slowly hide behind the sky
Changes come as the sky darkens up high
The clouds are showing signs of wonder
Drifting slowly as raindrops fall
Each drop bringing vast changes in the sky
Falling toward a point of happiness
Smiles come out and magic enters the sky as
Beauty moves the flow of silent clouds
Changing movements into lovely strange shapes
High above the tone of mind action drifts
It's now beyond time and hope

JoAnn White

Untitled

Let's pretend that...
Chicago is the New Jerusalem,
Lake Michigan, The Sea Of Galilee.
Cook Country is The Modern Palestine
and the Chicago River (north and south
branches) is the current River Jordan.

Let us enjoy the good old U.S.A.
and from all foreign cities stay away,
ignoring London, Paris, Berlin, Rome.
Let's close our airports and all stay at home.
We need not live in total isolation
to make United States a famous nation.
So, let us solve our local problems first,
before conditions here get any worse.
Let us make up and put The First Things First.

David P. Boyd

Alexa

Pacing, muscles tense, bated breath,
Childbirth's moans, cries
pierce the night.
A child's birth is imminent,
my child's child!
Where have the years gone
that bring us to this time, this place?

Black, shiny wet hair
glistening red face.
Emerging from the womb
with a whimper.
My child hands me the shears -
To set his child free!

My heart, my soul
pulsating with love
For this newborn, precious
baby granddaughter.
Life's purpose now to keep her safe.
And guide her thought life's
journey!

Eileen Hirschhorn

Untitled

We lay together on the floor of nature
Close together, yet so far apart
Your body fits next to the curve of my own
Our hands entwine much like the clouds
Where does one end and the other begin?
Our souls connected, as did our emotions
I turn my head to look at you
Only to see you already looking back
And I see peace and love in your blue eyes
What are your thoughts
As we lay so close together, yet far apart?

Ayra D. Mathis

Meditation You And I

Meditation
Clouds drifting in an azure sky
Reaching their branches way up high, you and I
Cascading waters down a mountainside
Screech of an eagle with wings
spread wide, the trill of a bird
as we stroll down a country lane, the gentle rain
All these wonders that I embrace
I find reflected on thy sweet face.
You and I.

Helen N. Sousa

Voices Of Roses

Roses, revealing of one's emotions;
colors speaking for themselves

White, innocence, purities, spiritualities
and beauty within our own beings

Yellow, strength of respect, sensations
of affection and the zeal of friendship

Pink, serene but painful for it can
bring about beauty, but put an end to
one's time

Roses, revealing of one's emotions;
colors speaking for themselves

Violet, rages of passion, vibrant intensity
to love, the decline of longing

Black, the deepest of all affording protection
and security from outside forces;
prone to damage one

Red, the King of all roses, a Knight in
shining armor bowing his love; to
the honorable lady of his worthiness.

Irene G. Bender

The First Spring Rain

Rain; warm, refreshing, renewing
Come and cleanse the dirt of winter
Give drink to the thirsty earth
Replenish the babbling brooks
Dance on my face and renew my spirit
Be a friend to the first blades of grass
Whisper a soft melody to the deary
Bringing restful peace to the weary

Raindrops are liquid sunshine, precious as pure gold
Treasure each drop, they refresh your very soul
rain brings life, rain brings joy
Rain is our assurance that God Loves us,
Blesses us with comfort filled kisses from above — RAIN!

Felicia J. Walker-Wilson

Turtle

Little green tortoise scrunched inside your shell;
Conjuring up memories of a life you knew so well.
Ageless and wandering, plucked from your home; in the
hot desert sands where you happily roamed.
Unjustly transported to a house in the city; to live in
a cage, how said! what a pity!
Confined to a box filled with gravel and grit, to live out
your days to just crawl or sit.
No longer to roam over wide open spaces; now you are cared
for by children with braces.
Confined to a cage and no longer free; to bask in the sun, or
swim in the sea; to roam in the desert or just calmly be.
In your memories I'm sure you're still back in the sun;
where you're peacefully sleeping when the long day is done.

Judith Heller

Little Black Boys, Little Black Girls

Little black boys, little black girls
Come out, Come out
From the alley ways, the back streets
And run-down apartment buildings
From the Crack House
From the gangs, pushers, and pimps

Little black boys, little black girls
We need you to come out
And help your generation to grow
We need you to become the next generation's
Doctors, Lawyers, Scientists, Nurses, Teachers
Professors, Dentists, and Discoverers
Our Stars of Tomorrow

So come out, come out and let us live as we are
supposed to live
Proud and free as our ancestors lived
Stop the killing and let's come together as a family
Because we all need each other to survive
So come, come little black boys, and little black girls
Let's live together, and never separate again.

Ella Louise Bailey

The Climb

Amid the swell and heave of a falter
comes the incline and fortune of the altar
paying the respects of a sacrifice
we climb the heights of the mountain peak's ice
Slowly we creep
Until we stand very steep
with every step
the noises echo the depth
On high we prepare
for the last breath of thin air
and atop the precipice
is the pinnacle of success
How the earth melts away
as we wend down the way
coming back to the foot
of once was solitude
in our souls we carried the mission
and in our spirit remains the mountain

Bradley Glazer

The Wolf

Through the swirling mists of time,
Comes the mysteries of the past.
Haunting the future and calling the wolf,
Who roams our minds so vast.

In the darkness, howls the wolf,
Prowling in the outskirts of our minds,
Stealing our hopes and dreams,
Destroying our will to keep our lives in rhyme.

The wolf devours our reason,
Tramples our self-respect,
Destroys our sense of justice,
And sheds not a tear of regret.

A beam of light interrupts the darkness,
Showing us what hope is,
Chasing away the wolf of the dark,
And bringing life back into focus.

Ginny Retzner

Only A Dad

Only a dad with a tired face,
Coming home from the daily race;
Bringing little of gold and fame
To show how well he has played the game
But glad in his heart that's his own rejoice
To see him come and to hear his voice.
Only a dad of a brood of six; one of ten million
Men or more. Plodding along in the daily strife
Bearing the whips and scorns of life; with never
A whimper of pain or hate, for the sake of those
Who at home await. Only a dad neither rich nor poor
Merely one of the surging crowd; toiling striving
From day to day; facing whatever may come his way;
Silent whenever the harsh condemn and bearing it all
For the love of them. Only a dad but he gives it his all;
To smooth the way for his children; doing with courage stern
And grim the deeds that his father did for him; these are the
Lines that for him I pen; only a dad but the best of all men

Elizabeth G. Thomas

A Friend Until The End

A friend is a person or animal. If they
console your heart. A loving soul or little dog.
With feeling to impart. A friend is tenderness
and hope. A word of kindness too. Or anything
that tends to make. The sun come smiling
through. A friend is faith and understanding.
Expressed by those who care. Dependability
and trust. Which form a friendship rare. A friend
is sweet companionship. Woven from sacrifice.
A person with a helping hand. Who gives
sincere advice. A friend is kindness without
stain. And goodness wrapped into a smile. The
mate that you have chosen will see you through
the bad and the good. Through trials and tribulation.
Across the weary miles. Will I have
made more than just one friend? My definition
is for real. I hope you recognize your friend?
By virtues they reveal. From one friend
to another. A friend until the end.

Jackie Savage

How Do I Know?

Maybe I have what I don't really need.
Could it be I'm lacking what I do?
Maybe I want what I shouldn't have.
Help me to make it through.
Show me what it is I need in life.
Keep far from me that which I don't.
or in this reach, is it my test, to learn that
I have hope?
To show I'm worthy of your love, I don't
want to stumble.
Walking backward instead of forward is
bound to give me trouble.
Erase from me desires of the flesh.
Build me strong to know what's best.
You've already done so much it's true.
I know my life's meaningless without you.
Thank you for putting up with me.

Candy May Webb

Violence

The world is full of violence today.
Could it be the TV or the toy guns
that makes the world this way.

As days, months and even years pass by
is there a true answer to determine why.

In the meantime the hearts of families and
friends are hurting sincerely.
Can God intervene to strengthen the hearts
and souls of those who suffer dearly.

Shall the families lift their heads up high
and bare the pain.
Or maybe lower their heads in shame.

Life must go on in hopes to free this world
from some of this terrifying violence.
Oh! Dear Lord will there ever be any silence.

Bonnie Kapral

Lonely Night

Walking slowly along the beach,
Crashing waves fill the still night air.
The cool water softens the sand,
Washes away the sand castle built during the day.
The full moon shines a glowing path
To the endless waters.
Yet it doesn't brighten the surrounding
Darkness.
The tiny lights twinkle above.
Trying to speak.
But they are not seen.
There is only darkness.
Then, a stream of fire flies by
Breaking the darkness.
With its trace of faint light, a wish is made
For a special someone to share the beauty of the night.
But he left.
He walked away from something beautiful.
And now
There is only darkness.

Julie Dioguardi

Morning Rose

The intricate drops of dew glisten upon each petal as the morning sun creeps over the horizon and yawns the light of day upon the sleepy world. Wearily each leaf groans while stretching and groping for a place to rest on the stem of life in the early morning breeze and bask in dawn's crimson light. The dew becomes restless: pushing, shoving, shouting. Each drop scurries in a fitful attempt to become one with the drop ahead leaving behind only a hint of its existence in a trail of dampness. Each thorn in nature's perfect interval forces its ugly face out along the smooth and winding road crying a story of pain, hate, and anger...stealthfully hiding in wait, planning spiked revenge upon those foolish enough to swiftly grab for life's best. Yet, through all the bleakness and pain lies a vision of perfect beauty...each petal expands in an array of splendid color; opening up as if to say, I am here. One day I will die but I will leave behind a legacy of silent beauty and graceful charm.

Amber Marie Baker

Sparrow

O little bird do not take fright,
Cruel, vicious, taunting, stoning,
Thrown from your nest without flight,
O City Angel of Warm Mother Spring
Come to my house.

This Sanctuary is yours, you will be fed
Good things to eat, drink and a safe bed
All these are yours and as for me
Grow strong of Heart and Wing- Fly free.

It will be sad, that I know,
To see you grow Strong and then to go,
But in Truth, you were born to be free
And to be part of God's Plan will suffice for me.

Irwin H. Pantell

The River Of Dreams

Deep in a dark forest, there flows a small stream. It yields to the currents of the River of Dreams. It flows from the mountain of hope and despair and ends in the valley where the dreams are left there.

The dreams, they are many and all scattered about. They were thrown in the river for the sake of their doubt. They were made to be silent by the ones who believe that a dream is just something that can not be achieved.

It is seen in the faces of the dreams that are there, that the cost of their dying was tragically clear. For a man builds a castle made of marble and stone. When inspired by dreaming, he had built him a home.

A man's great ambitions are hindered by fear. It strides to compel us to hold nothing dear. It is known in the valley by the dreams of the shame. Though the fear was a factor, still the man is to blame.

With each day that passes, the dreams all grow old. They will fold like a flower left out in the cold. A hand full of wishes show nothing to bare. But a dream is made living by the dreamer who dares.

So run to the river and cast in your line. And get back the dreams that you once left behind. For the valley grows wider and deeper it seems. And it waits for the dying in the River of Dreams.

Remember, that the origin of all things created by mankind, began with a dream.

C. J. Clayton

The Noble Strain

'Twas a quarter century past since the crimson Eve
danced down pulpit's aisle for Adam's wait.
Two perishable hearts met to consume their adoration
and become one, together forever.
Fall's blooming buds witness their kiss to seal the
inauguration, while throws of Uncle Ben's raw profits
blind them to leave their deity house.
The start of a dynasty was on course.
With rights there but spirit not, they wait with
open fisted cycles to bear a son.
With their mind and hearts full, but pockets empty
they seek shelter.
Five barren winters past to find labor on the bed
once again, a girl.
A societal dream.
All that an utopist could find fault could be a four
spoked mongrel of dusty color to fulfill the fantasy.
Hence they lived together, in unison, careless of
what was to come.
No love has been so true since the rose hit the morning dew.

Brandon Robert Barlieb

Chicago Winter Show

Winter comes but once a year
dark and dreary and certainly not clear.
Days are short with the wind blowing strong
Nights are long with heart fire a glowing.
Snow falling at a steady pace
People trying to keep up with the constant rat race.
Expressways are kept as clean as a whistle
Side streets are headache and are very miserable.
O'Hare kept open regardless of the snow
People flying to and fro.
With the temperature at 23 below
It take some serious consideration before going out the door.
People do and button up from head to toe
Because they know this is just a Chicago winter show

Dan Wesley Smith

Emissary Of Love And Salvation

Within her loving presence she brings light, to an otherwise, dark and lifeless world.

With the presence of this warmth and love, even the furniture seems to take on a personality, the dogs more playful, the children gravitate to her like flowers seeking the sun.

Like a flower without sun, like furniture without a home, like a stone, lifeless in a dark place. Thus is how she found me.

She prodded me into living, she goaded me into life, she teased me into smiling, and with each event she seemed to act as if the world was born anew.

Thus, is how God brought life into my world, by virtue of this Emissary of love and salvation. She is not a blockhead like me full of facts, and knowledge to impress the teachers and professors. She is full of simple unquestionable, unconfused love, she loves in her all. Thus, her faith laid in the hands of her love, and if that be true, then her love would move mountains.

Thus, is what it took for her to bring me from that dark and lifeless place of self hate. Thus, is how I can say to my wife today if it were not for you I would not be.

Clifford J. Bodiford

The Soul Of A Man

Dark Woman
dark woman, won't you stay away from me
You know you broke my heart, and ran away with my soul too
Dark woman won't you let me be
caus' just being around you makes me so blue.

Bluesman sits in his cold empty life
he sings his song to himself
He sings the blue song to be happy
if he is happy he can't sing his song
Did his father know she would kill him?

Weak is the soul that can conquer pain
Empty is the heart that can conquer pain
Cold is the life that can conquer pain
But painful is the body with a soul
He can't get dark woman out of his head.

Bluesman knows his pain is his life
His rhyme has no rhythm
His life has no reason but his song
dark woman knows he is not a bluesman
And the man can be happy.

David Jay Goren

Seasons Of Life

Before God created light to give us day and night
Darkness prevailed the earth and nothing was in sight
Now as the days and months and years go by and by
The seasons will affect everyone who walk and fly

Moments of our life is filled with joy and pain
Feeling like the summer days of sunshine and rain
We're warm, happy and will also sing and shout
But when it gets cloudy, we are looking to get out

It's dark, you're running, trying not to get wet
But you come across a wind that you never before met
And like the leaves on trees you will experience a fall
On the ground getting trampled, like you're nothing at all

The coldness of our trials has gotten us numbed and grieved
Struggling hard to figure out a way to get relieved
To escape before all our hope is winterkilled by fear
Having us believe in no help or happiness near

You fall asleep, awaken by the warming of the sun
Realizing that your day of spring has finally begun
For God has melted every hurt which only caused you gloom
And now you're free as a bird, and like a flower in bloom

Andrea Barlow

In Memory of Sixty-Five Years

Sixty-five years ago, I met you at a party in an old country home
Days past by and our friendship turned into a love that had grown.

You came to see me often, you proved to me you cared
Pleasant days we spent together and with our lives we shared.

Walking down a pathway we stopped under a big oak tree
You put your arm around me and said "Will you marry me"

In an old country home we were married just as the clock struck twelve noon.
We made our vows together with family and friends in the room.

The ring you put on my finger has remained on it all this time
And sixty five years later, I remember you said.
You wear this as long as your mine.

The white roses on your casket is a flower that you loved too
I put them there in memory of sixty five years with you.
The ring will stay on my finger, as I go my way alone.
For I know that you will be waiting at the gate to our heavenly home.

Amalia M. Helms

What Is Love?

Love is a feeling,
Deep within your heart,
Caring sharing, trusting
Knowing you can count on one another,
Love is like a dream,
The impossible can happen, and will,
Love, is magical, feeling like walking on air.
Love is the willingness to do anything,
Willing to die for each other,
Willing to show your true self,
Love may hurt, but it's always worth it.
Love is a feeling deep within your
Heart that will never go away.
So now I ask once more,
What is Love?

Angela Downs

Canvas Of One

Two Artists.

Our canvas of one:
delicate brush strokes,
bold, rhythmic splashes;
saffron spiced with cinnamon and nutmeg;
lightning sky-blue flash
   nursing a rose gone purple.

Giant bird twinning a mate, spinning.
Feathers like silver scales,
feathers like aeolian harps,
   whistling Nepalese Wind Songs.

Fingertip caresses of face, of hair,
of everywhere as instrument can be strummed.
savoring nectar like tiny hummingbirds Now,
remembering our ancient Vow of Together.

Two Artists in love,
both partaking of Hawk and Dove.
   Your brush on my lips,
      My soul kissing your hips.

Jess Barillaro

When We Make Love

When you kiss me your sensuous lips remind me of how
deliciously they trail feathery kisses from my lips
to the tips of my toes and tease that tiny core of
femininity that trigger explosion after explosion
of ecstasy within my body.

When we make love it is indescribable. In your arms
it's as if time stands still, as if the years that
I didn't know you never existed.

When I feel your probing hardness and feel the warm
moistness of your mouth against that most secret
part of me I open to you taking you inside me
momentarily forgetting how completely you fill
me up, then remembering with a joyous cry of
satisfaction.

When that sudden, desperate climatic victory begins
rushing over me, I fight it with all my might till
I can pull you to the summit with me. Then we are
completely one for a brief moment, lost in a world
where thought is impossible - where emotions are
near delirium.

Geridell A. Reeves

A Credo For Modern Times

The world keeps on tuning, despite you and me,
Despite our dismay over what shouldn't be.
"I want mine now!" is the constant refrain,
All rules are abandoned, all rulers insane,
So keeping the faith now is no easy task,
Refilling the cup of truth from your flask,
And seeping it down over dry barren minds,
Would vex even job or the keepers of time.
But we are the faithful few locked in a battle,
one mind to convert, one conscience to rattle,
turning each head towards the mission of man-
God's work is our work, placed in our hands.

Gerard F. Keogh Jr.

Those Three

Father once wondered why mother was so tired,
Didn't seem to him that her work was so hard.
Only six rooms and three kids to keep clean,
Wondered why mother felt grouchy and mean.

Couldn't understand when he'd worked the day thru',
Why she didn't greet him with a kiss, maybe two.
Wondered if she thought it had gone out of style,
To welcome him home with a kiss or a smile.

Sorta' perturbed him to come home and see
The toys and books strewn about by those three.
Thought it not too much for him to demand,
The house be more clean and those three kept in hand.

'Til mother one time was called quickly away,
Left him and the kiddies for just a short stay.
Now he's secretly hoping and praying that she
Will not leave him alone anymore with those three.

He understands now why mother's so tired,
And why she complains that her work is so hard.
Now father is thankful he doesn't have to stay
At home and ride herd on those three every day.

Isabelle Barton

Inner Peace, Inner Power

At dawn, we live to see,
Disarray, disaster since the world began
Is our fighting plan. If mankind at any condition
Agony, poverty, struggles to be free.
We have been lonely inside ourselves.
But never want it that way.

Try to make obvious differences
Try to love, share, give compassion and understanding.
There is always tomorrow
In the renaissance of human spirit.

Thus, the awakening reflections, of who we are to be.
We must relinquish our selfish interests,
And lift our hearts into true love.
Let our feelings grow, for passion makes us love.
To share the courage of our transformation.

Once our vision and soul has not yet died.
The strength, the variety, the richness of our words
   and ideas must prevail.
In the atmosphere of hope, pride, strength and respect for
humanity.

Bernard Bangura

Reflections

Lost in jumbled dreams,
Discovering everything isn't what it seems.
Emotions sweep in and out like an angry tide,
Drawing me into a strange, turbulent ride.

Wandering through a web of lies,
My soul descends and flies.
Reality is always just beyond my hold,
The deception is not what I been told.

Clinging to an anchor in this sea of sad blue,
Finding that now my refuge is vanished too.
All I trust has traveled far away,
Only shattered dreams and confusion will stay.

Many the storms I've been through,
Learning the hard way all might not be true.
But still I will try,
Reflecting and wandering, here am I.

Dawn Alldridge

Confusion

People
do they understand what I am thinking?
do they ever feel the way I feel?
do they think about their future?
is the life we're all living really real?

People
there is so much sadness in this place.
always hurting all the time.
we all try to bring great joy and laughter.
is showing your tears of pain such a crime?

People
I'll never know how we survive,
or why we sometimes try to go on.
no more laughing for this child,
for now my hope hath gone

Jessica Hanwacker

Numb

Are we always lost,
Do we sometimes not know it?
I feel like the winds of time keep me tossed,
back and forth through life's shit.
Where are my life's companions,
Will I know them in years to come?
Damn, I feel like a broke down engine,
craving for my old home comfort.
Miles and miles away, I'm losing myself,
though I keep myself numb most of the time.
Take me home, I'll cry myself to sleep,
Give me my time, I have committed no crime!
My baby cries, my friends ask why,
is there no answer for this feeling?
What of my bloodshot eyes?!
Old times make my bones creek weary,
hold me, I'm gonna fall, my love is left to only a theory.
Brake my walls of anger, or I'll brake my back!
Am I lost, I'll never know,
A soft extensive tear.......CRACK!!

Ivan Clymer

What Is Beautiful?

Do you see the dirt and grime - that covers things around?
Do you smell the smog and dust - from the sky down to the ground?
Do you feel the pain that someone gives by being so unkind?
And are you angry at the deeds done toward you and your mind?
Yet all these things are coverings - removed by a steady deed
Like dusting and like scrubbing to reveal the beauty - freed!
The beauty that was always there was hidden to your sight
All you ever needed was to give it - its true light,
To work through all you see with diligence and persevere
As things are really beautiful not always as they appear.
For people are not really bad and they do not mean to hurt
We all must do our house cleaning eliminating life's pain and dirt.

Barbara Floyd

Harvest Time

Sometimes I wonder if everything is under a plan for us all.
Doesn't it seem that we follow our dreams, and by luck we are called!
Just think of the times that were best.
Don't you find that the happiness came from the days you were here?
Love is the key. It will open you'll see
All life's pleasures. Harvest time.
Look at the sky. Its expense fills our eyes.
How to tell impossible wonders the earth.
Mountains peaks, thunderous serfs!
Babies born-happy times-countless joys for mankind.
Love is the key. It will open our dreams; all live treasures.
Harvest Time!

Alfie Fester-Student

Love

What is love?
Does love differ between woman and man,
Do we all get what we can?
Is love thought everyday through,
Or is it just me...or maybe you?
Is it a material thing or something we can't see,
Is it shared between you and me?
Does it stay with us night and day,
Or at times do we put it away?
What is love?
Is love here today and gone tomorrow,
Or is it something we think we can borrow?
Is it a cat in the box,
Or is it sly as a fox?
What is love?
Well from what I know it doesn't come
Around every day, but when it does between
Two people it should stay and that's what I
Think love is!

Jeffrey M. Spring

Sleepless

This bunch of feathers
doesn't comfort my head.
The thoughts
of tomorrow
rush through my mind.
Instead of counting sheep,
I'm counting the number of checks
I must write,
the errands that I must finish,
and the people that I must present myself to.
Lending a helping hand
means a lot to others,
but barely anything to me.
Can't anyone see that I need help?
I am left alone to wonder
for what tomorrow will bring me.

Heather Granelli

Speak Out For What You Believe In

Speak out for what you believe in, always say what you think
Don't be discouraged by anyone who says your ideas stink.

Speak out for what you believe in, for life is very short
Keep those ideas flowing, make your mark don't fall short.

Speak out for what you believe in, there's strength in your every word
Hold on tight for the stronger you get, no one will say you're a nerd.

Speak out for what you believe in, stand tall and be very proud
Be a teller of your great story, don't be afraid say it loud.

Speak out for what you believe in, later in life you'll see
If you become real silent, no one will listen believe me.

Speak out for what you believe in, it's coming from the soul
The ones who came before us, should make us proud and bold.

I will speak out and I will shout about whatever fills me with pride
No one can stop me from being, a young man with a big stride.

Herman McLean

My Ex Boyfriend

You and me, me and you belong together as two.
Don't you know Kenny you are like a penny,
I picked you up when you were down,
you helped me when my life was on the ground.
I just wish that we would have stayed found all time around.
Just like kissing in the sand holding hand and hand.
I never would want another man.
I loved you and you loved me why cant it still be.

Billie Jo Young

"The Emancipation"

I just want to have fun in all seasons,
Don't have to prove any damn reason.

Don't f*!@ with my life,
"Cause you'll never be my wife.
What! With all the strife?
It will feel like getting sliced with a knife.

You are not going to be with me anymore.
We cannot rack up any score.

Ingredients themselves are what makes good stew.
Amazing how this turned out to be such a bad brew.
I scream and I yell, till my face turns blue.
All the reasons being, the person is you.

No rhyme, nor reason I can find,
What the hell goes on in your fuseblown mind!

You say my life is in disarray,
When who are you who is in decay.
The confusion and frustration even makes me pray,
that God willing soon, it will be my day.

Tomorrow is the day you pack your bags,
My life turns to riches and yours to rags.

John Joyce

Tomorrow Is Another Day

Live for today! You know not what tomorrow brings.
Don't procrastinate! Take care of all those little things.
Things you often put aside until another day,
With a gesture of impatience that they could surely stay,
Until you feel you have a little time to spare,
But moments of free time you find are few and rare.
Don't put off that phone call to someone far away,
Or the visit to your friend that you promised you would pay.
The letter to a friend or relative that you promised you would send.
The function or event that you were planning to attend.
An act of kindness to a neighbor who can use some love or aid.
The trip that you desire to make but plans aside are laid.
These things mean more than you can possibly perceive,
So do yourself a favor, give yourself a leave.
Do these most important things, take care of them today.
For now is here, life is short, tomorrow's just
another day.

Anne Bartunek

Don't Ask

Don't ask me the questions for answers unknown.
Don't tell me to smile for you silent alone.
Don't ask me what's wrong if you don't want to know.
Don't ponder the mysteries of worlds that aren't shown.

Welcome the warmth of love's constant embrace.
Welcome the beauty of white wedding gown lace.
Welcome the swiftness of the world's hectic pace.
Welcome the vastness, the silence of space.

I weep for the martyrs, I weep for the damned.
I weep out of joy for the salvation of man.
I weep while I scrub to make my life "spic and span".
I weep as I watch God unfold His great plan.

Smile as you see the brightness of the sun.
Smile as you watch the old world come undone.
Smile as you witness the control of the gun.
Smile as you notice what's still to be done.

Halima Amira Fahtima Horton

Peace

Hello! My name is Peace;
Don't you want to know me?
You should know me already;
I was here before the world;
They call me God;
Yet they call me Peace also;
Because I'll give you peace in your mind;
And I'll give you peace in your heart;
And I'll also give you peace in your soul;
Oh! Don't you even want to know?
I'll wipe away your tears;
And I'll take away your sorrows;
Because my name is Peace;
And that's all I give'
I give peace;
So if you need a good friend;
Just call on Peace;
I'm always there when you need Me;
Peace

Gerald Wilson

Our World

Sometimes we look at the beautiful blue sky
Dreaming about growing wings and fly
God has made this a wonderful pretty world
Just think about the oyster that makes the pearl
Then there is the cocoon that holds the butterfly
When it comes out in the most splendid colors to fly.
On a perfect day you can see God in everything, even
little honey bees.
A waterfall, Great big green trees that
are gently swaying in the breeze
Then there are the many different colored birds
They are so beautiful you almost have no words
Sometimes you see the rainbow way up high
There are so many colors they make you sigh
Big soft white clouds slowing gliding by
Wild flowers everywhere that stretch there petals
toward the sky.
If you pray and ask God and really believe, you
can have anything you want to receive

Evelyn J. Campbell

Green Manifesto

Unfold your leaves and lay your heart bare
Drink in the sun's golden light
Sigh in the embrace of soft silky air
Stretch out in sensuous delight

Entangle your roots in the dark secret deep
Suckle her bittersweet bust
Up through your stem the life juices seep
Swelling your leaflets with lust

Live while you can the passionate life
The night will come too soon.
Roots in the ground with limbs reaching high
Dance for your lover the sun!

Jonathan Nagel

"The Pain You Cause"

The pain you cause
drives deep into my heart.
I feel that I am falling or just
coming apart.
Tears roll down my face
and burn like acid on my cheeks.
Each one holding a piece of my soul,
that you carry around and forever behold.
The pain you cause
is like something I've never known.
To hold my trust is to
never be told.
You hold the key to my every
emotion.
Opening each one with a
Heart filled commotion.
I want to lock each one and
throw away the key.
So you will never know
the pain you cause me.

AnnaMarie A. Caulo

The Sunny Side Of The Street

Head bowed, I walked briskly down the avenue,
Dwarfed by skyscrapers, propelled by the wind.
Everything around me
Distorted my point of view.

I kept my stride straight ahead
Trying with all my might,
To keep from veering from my path
And to still the wind's cold bite.

But my sense of purpose, nerve, and sinew
Were no match for the wind and cold.
They quickly numbed by body's sense,
And even chilled my soul.

I glanced to my right, and the sun beamed brightly,
Belying this early cold hour.
And there forcing its way through a sidewalk crack,
Sprouted a tiny sun flower!

The sun beckoned me to its warmth and light,
With a call so gentle and sweet,
That I quickly ran from the dark, cold, and wind
To the sunny side of the street.

Carolyn Allen Lovett

Untitled

I felt - and counted - every heartbeat this morning
each beat....

A labour of love
as I lay there....
unable to move.

Take this Weight - this pain - from
me!

How can a burden so heavy dwell in a body this
frail?

My mind is powerless over this physical assault,
.... yet, assists it....

Why?
I thought we received only

WHAT?
we could handle,
and nothing...
more....

Deborah Stambaugh

I Have To Have A Dream

Each day I walk down the same street.
Each day I think the same ideas.
A dream is something I need.
Something I can desire and look forward to.
When I look in the future I need to see something there,
Something to keep me going.
Maybe I will only see something small.
Maybe I will see something too large to imagine.
What ever I see I must go after,
Do what ever I can to achieve it.
If I never achieve my dream,
Maybe in reality my dream is out of reach.
If I stop going after the desire to achieve,
I will lose my dream.
Life without a dream is walking down the same street,
And thinking the same ideas.

David L. Coleman Jr.

Je Suis La Petite Etoile ("I Am The Little Star")

Each star a light among lights,
Each light a herald in the darkness,
A million holes in the sky
allow my sanity to die...
The star, alone amongst kin
I the Star.
Fearing Day, I run for cover,
little star.
Shunning sunlight I hide my face,
little star.
No longer shall I turn my back to the Sun.
Face it I will.
Overcome it I shall.
I the Star.
Shall I break free of the night,
and invade the realm of Helios?
Who shall stop the star!
No one can hold me back!
Little is my light,
Strong is my might.

Dean Berlin

Depression

Now I live where the North Wind blows.
Don't come to me. The cold seeps through
And permeates each thing I touch.

Keep spring alive in other realms
Where dogwoods bloom and turtles breed.
These things must still be there if I return.

God knows when that will be.
The North Wind has strong arms. I can
Not tell when he will let me go.

Jean S. Taylor

A March Morning

Coming out of the house on a fresh March morning,
A butterfly,
of the most splendid colors greets me,
The flowers,
Gently sway in the clean breeze,
The sun,
Soothes my skin with its soft rays,
The grass,
Glistening with early morning dew,
The birds,
Sing the spring melody,
Coming out of the house on a fresh March morning.

Stacey Paulhus

Christmas In The Country

Christmas in the country is a beautiful thing to see,
with snow upon the rolling hills, it's breathtaking to me.

You can look up in the sky night,
to see the stars all shining bright.
Even with the lights up in the sky,
the Christmas Star stands out on high.

It's the true spirit of Christmas,
where God's love comes shining through,
and the miracle of baby Jesus birth
is celebrated with great joy and mirth.

I love living in the country,
there's no place I'd rather be,
the beauty and peace and quiet here,
are definitely the life for me!

In a world that's full of stress and strife,
it's good to live the country life,
where friends in your community,
are like one great big family.

My Christmas wish to you this year,
I hope will be evidently clear,
for I send to you the gift I've found,
where peace and joy and love abound!

Patti Sadler

Ah Love!

Ah love!
How I thought it was mine to keep
I thought it was mine to hold

Lost love
I did not know it was holding me
The strength that gave me Joy
The Joy that gave me Laughter
The Laughter that made me free

So much love, I felt so very full
Only a little left now, I am nearly empty

But the years of loving formed me
The me that can now hold on
I cannot hold on to the love
But the love taught me to hold fast the day

Though the love is no longer here
I "remember" and gain strength from the memories
Memories that hold me like the love
I'll remember the laughter, the joy and the love

One day God will take the memory
But that day he will give me back the love

Margaret Huffman

Untitled

Love.
A word without definition. For how can you define
a word so powerful as it stands. Still I wonder
what it means, for people say it every day.
But do they mean it? And what does meaning it mean?
I guess the only way to define love is to look
inside and define it yourself.
All I know is if you truly and honestly
believe you are in love, if you care about
the life, happiness, and being
of another more than your own, then
follow that road and never give up your dream.
But keep in mind love is not always
as bright as a sunny Spring day,
for love can hurt far more than any pain
inflicted upon. By letting love grow,
a dream to love free.

Pete Schneider

A Cry Of Loneliness

When you lose something close to you it hurts my mind is blank
I feel like my life is gone everything is different people act different
Around me loneliness hurts when you no longer have that special bond.
Everything around me reminds me of him. I wait desperately for
A call of freedom from the pain. I miss him dearly and I have nothing
From this tragedy that is there for me to gain.
I wonder if he's feeling the way I do, all sad and alone. I wish I
Could take his pain away. I never thought it would end this way, all I
Hear in my mind is a silent cry...
Of Loneliness

Karen Kuntz

Suppression Unleashed

Death, rampage, fires burn;
17 years unleash to yearn.
Suppress, bury, hide all fears;
Unleash the Dam, let out the tears.
The Ignorant and two-faced deserve to die;
Unleash your will, the primal cry.
The tale is true, of Jekyll and Hyde;
Hang on folks, for the killer ride.
Hate and love, one in the same;
Emotions flooding are never tame.
Your heart is pounding, unending pain;
No one is deserving, the answer: More slain.
Total carnage is to come;
Kill the world! Who stands?

-But One.

Shaun Young

The Angel

One day a wagon pulled up the drive,
A beautiful woman stepped slowly outside.

She took us all into her arms,
Out of the reach of others harms.

She grew up fast, with this new man,
She held the grips of a new child's hand

She learned to love those not her own,
At last they cried, "we're not alone!"

She did her best, she showed them love,
She made them safe from all that was.

As time pass on, the peace subsides,
The day the angel says good-bye.

As years passed by, we remember the past.
The tears are shed but the memories last.

But through the years a bond remains,
Sometimes unspoken, but just the same.

A reunion is called and the children unite.
They've all grown up, but still, all is right.

And then comes an evening of laughs, thoughts and tears,
And finally, at last, my Mom reappears.

Lisa Groden

One Perfect Day

Father grant me one perfect day.
A day when I can cast my will away.
Show me how this can be
When I can live for you, not me.

May I not complain this day,
Or criticize what one may say.
And then Father, when this day is through
Give me another to live for you.

Mary Sue Zeiger

A Beautiful Day

Sitting at the breakfast nook — chose to pick up
a book to look — look at things so I
could imagine, imagine how small — imagine how
tall, I realized — it's the first day of
fall. The beauty before me, my eyes
do see, my heart's full of glee —
what a beautiful tree, a beautiful tree
down by the sea — I see before
me a shinny sea with sun shine
on it — what a beautiful tree — down
by the sea — waves pounding the
shore — bits of shell and moss to feed
the flocks — hear ringing bells —
I'll pick me some shells — the sound
it makes lulls me to sleep —
In my dream world so far away —
I pray for another
Beautiful, Beautiful day.

Mary McCarthy

When I'm All Alone

A cloud in the sky
A bug on the ground
When I wonder why
When I make a sound
It turns into song
But who is around?
To hear any tone
When I'm all alone

Of course I have friends
I won't make a list
But nothing depends
On those I have missed

When I'm all alone
I think about God and ways to a tone
For a world that is sad I know I could sing
The songs from the heart
Then people would sing
And wars wouldn't start
But I'm all alone
When I'm all alone

Michael D. Forsman

Building I

Up up up and away
A building is built every day.

Story by story they go
How high; I don't know

From out of the ground it starts
While I sit here eating my tarts

One floor, two floor, three floor, four
When it's done I'll go thru its door

Up as high as the elevator takes me
When I get to the top I'll be about a tree

On my way down to the ground
How many floors, I will have found

Ah ha there starts another
With its contractors acting as its mother

Up up up and away
A building is being built every day

Michael E. Compton

Answer

Love, an escape
A escape from reality
A reality of pain and suffering
Thou the conditions of love are different
having true love is the best of all
that I have haven't experienced
the supreme feeling,

The hole in the heart
The needing of love and affection
It can last forever
Is it strong enough?
have I found it or is it a false answer
Wanting to believe, believe in hope
love is hope what will one find
Will the answer be there hopefully yes
Then excepting ones self and other problems
the answer to more than one question
then almost all problems will be solved or will it?

Shawn Troyer

Wings Beyond A Dream

Gazing into the stars on a moonlit night,
A feeling of peace I have, no longer uptight
As I looked around, I felt a touch
This feeling of serenity, I had never felt so much
Closing my eyes, to dream my dream
The wings of an angel, caressed my esteem
Oh! Guardian Angel, please stay by my side
I need your love to protect me and be my guide
As I walk the path of life, sharing my dreams
My heart beats faster, the unknown, the unforeseen
The passion caresses me, all over, all around
Attaching the wings of the dream beyond
Immediately I open the door to my heart
Allowing angelic forces to start
To feel the wings beyond a dream
Foretell a life-style so beautiful and serene
Please take a moment, to gaze at the stars
While feeling the wings of your angel afar
Be a vessel of spiritual love, while living on earth
And reap the benefits for all they are worth.

Romain Ann Deevers

"Reality"

It was a hot sunny day
a gentle breeze blew my way
I sat on the sand, opened a book called "me".
I cried out in pain, this can't be!
I began to dread
with each page I read
this hard backed book
made me take a good look.
I gazed out across the sea
this really "is" me.
I've struggled so hard in this life of mine
to make others lives so divine.
It's taken many years
to see through my tears.
To care, to love for others is fine
but I've forgotten about this life called "mine".

Rebecca L. Troutman

Into The Green

He stands before me,
A handsome man,
framed by the shadows of early evening,
fanned by a soft autumn breeze.
I move closer. He turns to me...
the reflection of my face drifting slowly over the surface of his eyes...
submerging, spiraling, descending...
from the surface of light, where mortal thought conforms,
to the depths of his soul,
where form has no thought, and thought has no form...
Where all that I know is suspended, upended...
simultaneously separate, yet together, whole...
I surrender my being...
I get lost in the pull
of his eyes...
those deep clear pools of evolving emotion...
ebb and flow enveloping me...gently and rhythmically as the ocean tide,
and if I should drown in the course of my lifetime,
it will be in the green of this man's eyes.

Susan Roller

Untitled

In Memory of Mary Louise Fournier
"A Heart of Gold"
Who passed away 5 years ago on November 3rd

The leaves have fallen it's that time of the year
Your voice is callin we feel your spirit near

Times have been hard but, we've made it through
Keeping our hearts on guard it hasn't been easy without you

Your absence has made us stronger we just don't understand
Why you couldn't stay longer

You were the glue to this puzzle of life
Being a friend, an ear, a mother and wife

Now after 5 years, our puzzle has come apart
It's amazing what can happen.
When your missing one heart

We just wanted to say how important you are
And we hope you stay near us
And never go far

We love you and miss you
More than words can ever say
There's never an end to memories
We have a new one every day!

Lisa Fournier

The Nightmare

Walking through the nightmare
a horror in itself.
Seeing you lying there
so content, so still.
I can't believe it's over
I don't believe your gone.
I see all the good and fun times
yet bad ones haunt me now that your gone.
The guilt never leaves
The nightmare never ends.
I can't believe your never coming back
I can't believe we were only ever friends.

Tammi Sliker

A Letter From Uncle Sam

It was the summer of sixty-eight,
A letter came issuing me a date.
I was to be a member of the U.S. team,
Uncle Sam said "Buddy this isn't a dream."
I told my girl I would be home soon;
Kiss me good-bye, I am leaving at noon.
Running, shooting, and taking orders,
Making my home in canvas quarters.
One year in Vietnam packing a gun,
Drinking beer, smoking pot, and having fun.
An experience I'll always remember,
Long after my return home in December.
I served my country and I'm feeling well,
Because I already spent my time in hell.

Robert Wagens

No one knows what all happened that day.
A life is such a high price to pay.
Tortured and murdered - there he lay;
Involved in a War - This is not play!
Once they took his life away,
None of the people knew what to say.
All their sorrow and dismay
Left them with a message to relay.

Red is the color chosen for
Enrique "Kiki" Camerena's honor;
DEA member who lives no more.

Regret in his loss —
Initiated by children with cause;
Believing in his efforts to stop the Drug Boss.
Bereaved by this unjust cost;
Overwhelmed with sadness, they paused;
National Drug Awareness Week to remember who he was.

Won't you please join in - Let's make a fuss
Everyone unite like a gust.
Education's the key - Your support a must! And remember.....
"**K**iki" put his life on the line for us.

Katherine Sanchez

The Death Of A Dream

A young boy, Nahshon Waxman
A little younger than my annoying old brother
But now I realize that if my sibling had died
Just how much pain would be eating away at my heart.

I cry for a total stranger; how bewildered he must have felt at his last moments
That his betrayer was getting a reward for his suffering
But his friend was also getting the prize;
A betrayer his friend became; he let his follower rot away.

The juvenile shivers while the coldness sweeps over his body
The coldness of a starved blood-thirsty alien entering the room.
The teenager's pleas are recorded on tape
His cries will echo forever through the darkness.

So in a little town called Bir Nabala
A stream of blood gushes from a gunshot wound to the neck
His rescuers come, killing the evil ones;

But too late, too late; his dreams and soul are gone.

Only a corpse, the young man is dead;
Just one being in the vast percentage of death taking place each day
You would think a 12 year-old child wouldn't care; but I do.

Michelle Rueda

When You Believed In Me...

When you believed in me, it only took awhile
A living memory snapped to attention, hidden beneath a
lifetime of repression
Your affirmation reached out, extinguishing my fear,
allowing me to hear

I stepped out from the dark facing that time and tension
After losing the fight year after year
Words I couldn't remember, oh! the apprehension
Not by default, but an allegiance to fear

Overwhelmed by the clarity, I did nothing wrong
A restoration of balance, a sparkling exuberant light
I defined myself achieving insight
Relinquishing the seat of the victim, I'm free to be me

Patricia A. Gottlieb

Final Exit

D usk lights up the sky,
A lthough his day has just begun.
V acant eyes can not see,
I nfinity that came to rest.
D aring all to accept and believe,
A lthough the pain tortures the heart.
C ardinal virtues can not stem, the
E mptiness of his unfinished work, for the
L amb was called home too soon, to complete.
L ament though we must, remember
O utstanding was his dawn.

Walter Shea

Whispering Secrets

A whisper tamed by the night
A pillow to soften the tears
The wind, silently blows,
Whispering secrets, no one will know
A chill, runs down your spine
A fear, creeps in your heart
The sounds, coming towards you,
Whispering thoughts, you don't want to hear
A hand, brushes your shoulder,
A scream, doesn't exist
The wind, silently blows,
Whispering secrets, you don't want to know.

Tiffany A. Whitten

Untitled

As I sit back and recall a day,
A place in time where things were fine.
My mind starts to wander, and it leads the way
to that elusive land of pleasure.

We will travel together, but in separate directions
Through time and space, from place to place.
Searching to find what once had flourished
But lost in a world that's foreign to both.

There is no light to guide by
Only instinct, and the help of others.
In which to set the course, and continue the journey
to that land where peace and love,
sit side by side as king and queen.
Keeping a close watch and giving guidance to
those who would risk to dream.

Rob Sullivan

Fear Of Introspection

Inside my mind there is a place where all my secrets hide.
A place so dark and filled with pain I dare not go inside.

For close examination might reveal some hidden truth
Locked away with agony while suffering in my youth.

My mind recorded memories, then for my sanity
It shrouded them with vagueness, then threw away the key.

Like a black and growing cancer deep within my soul
These best forgotten moments wait to take their toll.

I'm scared to face the darkness. I'm scared to feel the pain.
For if I swim in that dark sea, I'll surely go insane.

Michelle Barefoot

A Small Blessing

I've been given a blessing from above,
a precious little baby to give all my love.
I know I've got a lot of learning to do
but with God on my side I will see it
through.
There's no better feeling than a little
one's touch;
the laughter, the smiles, and to be needed
so much.
A new mother is what I am
but to my small blessing I'm also his friend.

Veronica Salisbury

Puzzled?

Life is like
a puzzle.
Lots of pieces,
colors,
patterns.
United when worked together.

Broken and sorry when not!
Selfishness causes people to take pieces out.

We must work it together.
If we don't
it won't be a pretty picture.

Shawn Scott

Sand Dollar

I wish I could find a sand dollar,
A sand dollar in the sea,
I wish I could find a sand dollar for me,
A sand dollar nice and round,
A sand dollar on the ground,
A sand dollar is what I wish,
If I had a sand dollar I'd put it in a dish.

Mariah Porta

Twilight

When Twilight is fading and night has not set in
A hush falls unnoticed and everything is still
This is the time of day I love so well,
as the dusky twilight weaves its spell.
The crickets are chirping and a locust sings
a bird flies by on silent wings
Then I see a firefly flashing his light
Twilight has faded and now falls the night.

Nada Harris

Tunnel Vision

When I first saw my boy hanging from those ties
A scream came out of me, I couldn't believe my eyes

Tears of desperation ran down my cheek
I couldn't control my feelings, I felt so sick and weak

There wasn't much to say and there wasn't much to do
I told my little Anthony I want to go with you

Why have you done this? Why didn't you tell?
What was your reason? I wanted to yell

My mind was gone, my heart was dying
My insides were empty, my eyes were crying
If you had only spoke and broke down our division
You wouldn't have gone into that dark tunnel vision

Rosa Flores

"The Struggle"

To me, you are a book of mystery
a shell within a shell
A creation, God made to reach
the heights of man made acclaim.
Obstacles will never be too
great to stop thy mighty desire
to prove your worth.
I need but find the right clue
to unfold thy tender true self
Tell me, tell me it is not so,
that you are two persons.
The first, trying to achieve in life the heart's desires.
The second, plotting against
the aims of the first.
It is a defeated cause that you are seeking.
Let not the second rob you.
Seize it, cast it away forever and ever.
It is not beautiful yet, you let it possess you.
It is a vicious robber. Imprison it before it is too late.
Do not become an aid to your own robbery.

Nancy L. Parker

Unicorn

Innocent, pure, a secret untold.
A shimmering white with
a heart made of gold.
Wild and free from the day it was born,
It has no weapons except for a horn.

The horn holds magic forever flaring,
The magic is of love, life and caring

Heart filled with joy, knows nothing but love,
happy and wild was sent from above.
No more of this horse has yet born,
one day it shall roam again; the magical unicorn

Tamara Rasheed

Postscript To Jessie

My letter wasn't long, but it would be
A thousand pages if I were to write
The things I think of when I speak your name:
Like soft rain falling, or sunrise at sea,
A dreamy symphony, fantastic, light,
A chapel bathed in flickering candle-flame.
But most of all, I think that this is true:
such precious love could only come from you!

Lloyd E. Wing

Ascension

That the flame through two ignites and incites,
a spark in its rights satisfies cycle ninth.
Out of tender entrails, the wails bring in sight
animal wonder, conqueror, to doom and shine star bright.

Time flies. Innocence outshines.
On four holds, exposed, wonder kind strives,
bows to words and kinds.
In time, life will worth the fights early on one survives.

Nature provides. The obscene multiplies.
Vertical, the fine kind born to image
divine, spreads through deeds and gospel of lies
that it is fine all else lives in bondage.

Fauna cries out foul in howls, growls and mighty roars,
the frail mammal on a quest, with stealth and distant bangs ends
beastly prowess. Flora whips and twists, drilled to its core,
the breed supreme scars more to fuel the tools of trade and chance.

Fauna, flora, waves blue: all of creation reels and strains.
A kind tames not its own instincts, marshals its kind in chains.
Then... all sparks light out, brilliance gone like tears in rain.
It stinks to think you shine so bright and vain: son of man.

Kernst Volmar

"Life"

I have a story to tell you that most of the time is true.
A story about the life of love and the things we are brought into.

A mother's heart so tender and real,
The barrier of love around her you can reach out and feel.

But one day that mother's heart will be torn with heartache,
Sorrow, and be battle worn.

From the phone call she'll one day receive,
she will for days to come weep and grieve.

They told her that her son's life is gone,
no more sunshine but slow sad songs.

Someone said they saw how he said goodbye with the look in his face and the innocence in his eyes.

Hurtful hearts and sorrowful days are all around where her child lays. Where she said her last goodbye. Where her heart goes to cry.

The tears in her eyes could not explain the difference between her joy and pain.

I have a story to tell you that most of the time is true.
A story about the life of love and the things we are brought into.

Shakimbra A. Young

A Streams Journey

From the tree studded mountains to the lush valley below.
A stream on its wandering path continues to flows.
Wondering where it is going, where will it end?
You look upward to the mountains where it began.
Seeing the beautiful cascading waterfall,
Passing between the many pines standing so tall.
The water from the mountains comes boldly rushing,
Over the boulders and rocks as it is awashing.
The white water seems to boil and thrash with rage,
Then the anger and fury starts to abate as with age.
Suddenly the stream becomes calming and serene.
Flowing ever so gentle through the valley was the scene.
Others with whom this stream you know you have to share,
You wonder as it flows by will they lavish it with care.
Treating it kindly as it continues to wind and weave,
Reaching the river which within it will flow with ease.
For that little stream, like everything else has a destiny,
Like you and I taking a winding path, the stream
will reach the sea.

Lela Mae Burnette

Wintermist

This time of year, I love so much,
A time for celebration and caring touch,
Even the morning beckons winter's arrival
With flowing silver tresses and such.

What is it that we can barely resist
About the morning fog I call wintermist?
It does seem to hide a mystery, a secret,
Veiled in an ethereal embrace as one who is kissed.

What different feelings are evoked
As winter lumbers on, unprovoked?
A feeling of warmth, of comfort, of yearning,
Which is encapsulated in the mist that is cloaked.

Do we long for the unattainable, unreachable star
That daily disappointments cannot mar?
The mist is a symbol for our grandest desires,
A haven, a refuge for all our tomorrows.

Perhaps the beauty of wintermist will pass some by,
Those who sadly are unwilling to try
To find loveliness and contentment
In the not too distant sky.

Lynn Jones

The Sands Of Time

Closing my eyes that night I saw
a time that I thought grand
and a place I could sit and bury my fears
on the soft and silvery sand

Daylight thrills and midnight chills
showing life's delight
I was walking along the beach that day
when all was turned to night

That was my time and place of joy
my life was in its prime
when all was well, no sickness lie
that was my moment in time

For now I am old and crippled with fear
it's gotten the best of me
my sickness is mounting with perilous rage
I have lived my destiny

I open my eyes, extend my hand
I look up toward the sky
now is the end, the time to pass
goodbye my life, goodbye

Marlene K. Peplinski

"Who Needs Wheel's?"

Some view a car as a ticket to freedom
a vehicle for adventure,
an omega to boredom,
though it may simply detour them back to the alpha of ennui.

Not I,
I see them trapped in their own mind cage.

Adventure has only one ticket.
Some try to buy it -
it can not be bought,
yet is given to all.

The few who know adventure -
well,
they know the secret -

How the soul perceives life.

Laura Beth Taken

Poverty

Poverty etched its brand upon her life.
A vassal whom he claimed all for his own,
Caged with his iron bars and fettered chains;
Her life seemed crushed as by a torturous stone.

A youth to education and its claims—
A wretched sickness was her constant lot.
Couldn't there a drop of joy now flow
Into this suffering one, with trouble wrought?

Flowers—oh how greatly were they loved
By this one whose hands dug in the soil—
A gardener so accomplished in the art
Of making her yard glow 'midst burning toil.

To speak with her, no one would ever know
That hers had been a painful lot to bear;
For she was always cheerful, and bestowed
On others her warm love, and hid her cares.

She learned the secret of a life of joy:
To think of others and forget one's self;
And in the process, life more sweetly grows,
And, even more, she found a life of wealth.

Maxine Trigleth

The Beating

A slap and a punch, a fist of hair pulled out.
A wall appears in time for you to crash to the ground.
Another blow and the darkness begins.
It creeps in from both sides.
I can hear but not see the next blow.
Oh God! I can feel the fear and taste the terror.
I know if I can't distract the pain I won't survive.
I give myself to the blackness and I feel nothing!
The silence is peaceful.
The pain is gone along with the fear and terror.
Light appears and I'm alive I survived the pain,
till the next blow that's sure to come again.

Tammy Mendoza Luntsford

Brothers

At daylight he can hardly wait,
a whole day's action he anticipates,
some time for work, some time for fate,
yet his life partner, upon him waits.

Once in a while, loving brother number one,
to number two provides safe laughs for fun,
he's the best, a pain sometimes,
yet they are one and walk in rhyme.

Around the corner, and up the stairs,
they play the game as at everywhere
isn't it great, a time so fair,
time for brothers, that today has no tear.

Boy! it's great to see,
the you in him, and the I in he!
Growing together buying tomorrow you see,
tomorrow's the brothers, some you, some me!

Michael R. Stover

Halloween

The moon so full and full with light,
a witch that rides upon the night,
with goons and goblins that haunt with fright,
and all that means it's hollow night.
While you take an apple here and there
you may not know what's bound to scare,
so please be careful on that night,
and don't forget to scare with dread and fright.

Valerio Martino

Silence Is Not Always Golden

There she sits, silently
A wife, mother, and grandmother.

She has seen so much in her 89 years.
The history she has lived!
From horse and buggies to space shuttles,
Woodburning stoves to microwave ovens.
The rise and fall of the Berlin wall.

She can no longer tell stories to the children.
No, silence is not always golden.

She saw light and good in everyone and everything she touched.
Her world is different now, dark and foreign.
The very essence of her that nurtured us, we can no longer reach.
God, please let there be children, animals and gardens
where she is now.

No, silence is not always golden,
When that silence is the silence of Alzheimer's.

Peggy Blanford

Eternal Love

It all started a long time ago in the Blue Grass State of Kentucky-
A wonderful woman was born, and wow were we Lucky!
She graced this world with spirit and love-with the strength of an eagle, the softness of a dove.
She enjoyed Billy Graham and Lawrence Welk too-Always patriotic,
standing behind the red white and blue.
We could count on Grace to remember us in prayer-We always teased her about having a direct line up there.
When you were around you always brighten up the place-It's no wonder Martha called you "Amazing Grace."
Humming birds, butterflies, horses, bird of paradise-When we see Grace's favorite things our thoughts can only be nice.
We know you physically gone but you will always stay-close in our hearts, missing you everyday.
With all our love to you our friend, Mother, Gram and Great Gramma Grace-You will be in our hearts forever filling that one special place.
Our hearts are full of all your love-Peace be with you on your journey above.

Susan Gilbert

Me And My Bird

I am a captive in this unimaginative world,
A world where my freedom of mind has no place.
Man cannot be free without a release from reality.
As a child we are free, free to feel, to live.
But as an adult you're forced to bury and murder that which
Makes you most free, your imagination.
I don't want to become a robot in which reality molds me
A captive slave to the world of work and the hostile surroundings
Of seriousness, where the grass is no longer green and the
Bird no longer sings to me accept from a cage next to mine.
Me and the bird, we become cellmates, to sing in toneless
Harmony to an unimaginative world.
I seem to find some wildness left in me, some freedom
Left unburied. It will just take a light rain to uncover
The tips of the remains, just enough to set me and my caged
Bird free. Free to fly away, far far away from captivity.

Kimberly Johnson

The Gift

On a warm spring day in the month of May
A young boy touched my soul
With straw blonde hair and big blue eyes
And a smile of solid gold.

He needed care and tenderness
to ease his troubled heart
A friendly smile - a gentle touch
I loved him from the start

The months have passed from then 'til now
and so my love has grown
He gave to me the greatest gift
my heart has ever known

The greatest feeling ever felt
above all - like no other
Is the pride and joy that I have known
in being Joshua's mother

Michelle D. Carlson

Dream Of The Return

Another cold moon mocks the midnight sky,
Above my weary craft, which drifts upon this open sea.
He holds no light for me—no word of peace,
Save for his dim which tells the naked truth
Of how this barren womb in which I float
Is empty: Less your brimming form,
To capture darkness from my gaze,
And drown it in your flowing love,
Where flames of passion forcefully burn,
Yet now I may only dream of the return.
The willful waves pound like my heart against this crusted frame,
And toss my spirit to the depths of this abyssal main;
For here your presence is a wish that wildly runs between the
deep and stars,
Chasing wind and mist, upon this steely blue expanse.
Your image blends my wake with sleep,
And fades beyond the water's edge.
The wrinkles on Poseidon's face express no hope to leave this place.
Each slapping spray against my cheeks forbids the tears to dry;
Yet all the while my sighs confirm
Such love for you that I may only dream of the return.

Vincent G. Novo

The Music Of the Spheres

The moon sings softly in the night
Accompanied by soprano of stars,
Hark! Shooting star glissando
A distant storm adds tympani.
Daybreak bring trumpet of sun
Birds make morning music
Joyful cardinals sand soon a chorus
of bird song. Rollicking robin
Chickadee in minor key Robins rejoice at rain
and swallows twitter and curvette.
Night and crickets sing, soon buzz of locust.
Dove mourn sadly and owl raise announcement
We are here dawn to dark and new dawn breaks
with chorus. Let is sing too.

Stanley K. Jensen

God's Hands

Sometimes God gives gifts, which He must take away,
And in our grief we fail to see that this is just His way.
God has chosen your precious child for tasks that we can't see,
And as you cry and as you grieve, in heaven he will be.
He may not grow to be a man, he won't grow old and gray,
But as sure as the sun will rise tomorrow,
In God's loving hands he'll stay.

Theresa A. Hugel

Pain...

Sometimes I hurt so very deep inside.
Aching ... Breaking... Shaking
I hurt so very, very deeply

Sometimes my mind is so painful weary
Teary... Bleary... So very weary
I hurt so very, very deeply

Sometimes my physical body is so painfully tired
Afired... Mired... So very tired
I hurt so very, very deeply

Sometimes my heart is so painfully breaking
Unheeding... Quietly pleading... Always painfully bleeding
I hurt so very, very deeply

Inside me aching, breaking and shaking
Mind painfully teary, bleary and so very weary
Body afired, mired and so very tired
Heart unheeding, quietly pleading and always bleeding

Did you know I hurt so deeply inside?
No! I guess you didn't see the pain...

Melisha Clark-Gold

"My Mother"

You might have been an Empress queen of the Orient.
Adorned in silks and satins, for beauty truly meant.
You could have been a flower or a garden better yet.
Surrounding your heart with growing things,
You leave small room for regret.

The earth holds life for you, warm when the season's right.
Unfolding bits of happiness in seeds of delight.
As the fruit tree unyielding, you know not defeat
Strengthened by firm independence, tempered by blossoms sweet.

In such a fragile world, you were not meant to be.
Chained to duty and tradition that won't set your spirit free.
Kindness, love and tenderness others find hard to see.
But I see them deep within, for mother-daughter are we.

Kathleen Cornwell Gary

Through My Eyes (A Granddaughter's Tale)

There she goes, she's never late;
Age hasn't taken a beat from her gait;

She comes from a very special era;
When life was slower, families nearer;

She looks at you, eyes sparkle and wink;
What's behind them? She makes me think...

My mind wanders to special times;
When she first shared her lyrical rhymes;

She had such presence, charm, and grace;
And Oh! She took me everyplace!

She shared her tales about days of yore;
In all her expression, she was ne'er a bore;

Always a kindred heart-in-tow;
I enjoyed each precious moment and lo;

Now this face that once held such expression;
Has wrinkled and softened with time's transgressions;

But, if you look deep in those eyes;
I wouldn't doubt that somewhere lies;

The fire, sparkle, passion, and grace;
That carved a story in this dear face.

Laurie McIntosh-Kerans

Another Chance

It's morning! Another day - another year.
Alarm clock ringing; I pretend not to hear.
Today will be like yesterday and like the day before.
The days will change a little - but little and no more.
I see things from these eyes from many years gone by.
Memories come to visit me; lurking like a spy.
They'll creep into my life on my brightest days,
To prove they haven't left me and that they're here to stay.
Good memories can be beautiful but are often hard to find.
The bad ones find their way up front and leave the good ones in behind.
There've been times I thought to beat this I would have to be no more.
But when the cold steel touched my temple, I thought about the Lord.
HE gave HIS only Begotten SON for people just like me,
So I thought that I would talk to HIM to tell HIM I believe.
Every night you can find me with my knees upon the floor.
I feel I was given another chance by talking to the LORD.

Leslie H. Powell

The Creatures Of The Land

A multitude of creatures inhabit our land
All created by God's hand
Some fly, some walk or swim
All creatures have a beginning and an end.

A creature may be a pet or a wild beast
All have food on which they must feast
If a species dies out it is Providence's decree
If destroyed by man's carelessness, a tragedy.

For those of us who preserve the past of man
Let us preserve nature's present
From the largest whale to the smallest pheasant
For man needs to consume only a certain amount of nature
Let nature, like the past, be preserved for the future.

William E. Plants

Two Lovers In A Garden

The rosebuds, the daffodils,
All flowers lovely as they are,
Bring beauties scent amongst this trail,
To wander slowly, touch each nerve.

Sunlight shines in lovebird's eyes,
One blue, one red, undying love,
Drenched with dew, two teardrops fall,
Sweet mist from heavens rain.

Floating seedlings gently caress the soil.
For beauty to begin again,
Again begin beauty as it was.

Two lovers in a garden,
Seldom seen, these whispered secrets,
Like rosebuds and daffodils,
All flowers lovely, become one.

Robert S. Whitehair

Dare To Discover

Dare to discover the love that runs so deep inside and all your worries and fears subside. Take a moment to remember the love you gave to me. That I will save close to me.

Love is something so beautiful that you spend most of your life searching deep with in and then finding that certain someone that you want your life to begin. Then years go by and you can't help, but hope your love never dies, but soon every thing comes down with a big crash. And then you find out that your love was never meant to last. But take some time and your heart will mend. And you'll begin your search once again.

Starla McCranie

Eat Cake

It came to me one day, in the form of a piece of cake.
All fluffy, white, and shiny. My desire to taste it was greater
than my will.
The pain and sorrow made it even easier still.
I stuffed myself full, of the idea, that I could have my cake and eat
it too.
I forgot that, for every thing, there is a price to pay.
The price was almost a gift, a precious and sad gift.
I wanted to show the world my expression, my pain.
The avenue to destruction so tempting and disguised.
A young women's perception influenced by a nation. The cake seemed so inviting at first, then it changed, like the wind in a firestorm. The frosting turned black, and its insides to mush. The outside turned to stone, though still pretty to the eye, the cake destroyed me. I could not stop wanting the cake, it consumes my life, and goes with me wherever I go. Like cancer, I cannot get rid of it. I hate the cake! It sits at the bottom of my stomach waiting to be purged. If only I could go back in time, and change that day I ate the first piece. It wouldn't matter though, because it was the days proceeding, that led me straight to the cake.

Mary E. Klante

Holly And Molly And Folly By Golly

There was underneath my tree, in the tall grass, a rustling.
All I could see was a dimpled knee and a pink ear, no, two.
It was Molly by golly!
Bustling.

"What have you got there, you seem so busy,"
I asked, as she pulled and tugged about.
"I haven't got anything!" Molly replied.
"The thing's got me! I'm fit to be tied!"
And all 'round about from her tail to her snout
Was Holly on Molly by golly.
I hung down from my branch to see them more clearly
I had no idea I'd pay so dearly for wanting to help a good friend.
And as I got there I got my full share
Of Holly and Molly and folly by golly!

We thrashed about till we flattened the grass
The all of us weakened and ran out of gas
Holly unwound, laying limp on the ground
And Molly collapsed on her tummy.
I think it was fun. Although over done.
And so do Holly and Molly, by golly!

Louise Bray

S.O.S. Soul In Distress

When we set out upon life's sea
All is calm, or, so it seems
Not a cloud seen in the sky
And we wave to other ships as we pass by.

Then, suddenly storms come upon us
With out warning, winds start blowing
Dark clouds, now on our horizon
With thunder and lightening, we are surrounded

Then, icy rain comes pouring down
Angry waves swell and capsize us
Who, will see us out so far?
Who, will hear us when we call?

S.O.S. S.O.S. SOMEONE COME AND RESCUE US
Fearful and desperate, we drift further away
But, JESUS is listening, He hears us when we pray
Our Savior is on call, 24 hours a day

CHRIST is our beacon light, and shows us the way
OUR MASTER OF THE SEA, will guide us night and day.
He, will never leave nor forsake us, but will take us all the way
In JESUS WE ARE ANCHORED at SAFE HARBOR BAY

Nancy R. Binder

Our Love

What more could be said, about the situation at hand,
All so very strange and hard to understand,
We want each other so badly, and yet we shy away,
Because of the others we've had,
Will we turn out that way,
What more could we do or say?
We've both said it before, just when we think it's over,
I hear your voice once more,
There are no easy answers to the feelings we both share,
The feeling of love; hate; anger and despair,
Should we keep trying?
This pitiful...pain or give up on a love so beautiful and so rare,
I'm crying inside...I'm crying again,
and not of my own will,
just as I sit here thinking, on paper my tears do spill,
I know this is crazy and all so very sad,
Because we're both trying not to lose
the best love ever had.

Tricia Porrazzo

Memories Of The Fourth Of July

The fresh, mowed grass provides a carpet.
All the family gathers 'round
Telling jokes, laughing, eating,
Watching the night sky
For that first glimpse of shooting stars
Sunbursts of glory...

The children, caught up
in the wonder of fireworks and family,
grow quiet
And those now absent from the beloved clan,
Look down
and rejoice in the living.
Not really gone from us,
Their spirits brush close,
gently whispering
And we are all one again,
forever

Sue Lancaster

The Ghosts Of Halloween

'Twas the halloween eve and all through the cave,
All the witches were dancing and practicing to be brave.

The black cats and the ghosts, they came with a howl,
It was so very dark, you couldn't even see the owl.

When up on their brooms, they arose with a flutter,
I jumped out of bed and slammed down the shutter.

I didn't stick around to get a trick or a treat,
I bolted out the back door, in utter defeat.

I fell on my knee and skinned my big nose,
I lay there exhausted with all my torn clothes.

The witches few over while I lay under the oak,
They were only big puffs of black, yellow and green smoke.

I laughed at myself for being so scared,
'Twas nothing at all, when their secret was bared.

Loren A. Johnson

Friendship

Talk about it, don't be worried, believe in yourself and it will be alright.
Talk to me you know I'll listen.
Tell me all your problems good or bad.
Give it some time and I'm sure you'll find the answer.
But then again you always do.
Think good thoughts and I'm sure they'll come true.
Before you know it you'll find all the answers.
You know you can talk to me whenever you have a problem.
I never denied you and I never will.
Sit down and we'll discuss it.
No matter what happens you can always count on me.
Together we can lean on each other.

Roseann Acosta

You Are There

You are there when I have hurt feelings,
Always there to comfort me.
You are there with just the right touch,
I can tell that you care so very much.
You are there to wipe away my tears,
There to calm my fears.
You are there to understand,
There to lend a helping hand.
I know raising me is tough,
And after all you've done for me,
I could never thank you enough.
To me, you are a gift from God above,
A wonderful angel giving me all of your love.
You are my guardian angel here on earth,
Watching over me since birth.
I love you, Mom.

Liliana M. Cabrera

Untitled

You always seem to understand
Always wanting to lend a hand
Our age difference doesn't seem to bother you
Now that's a friend who's really true

The first time I laid eyes on you
I thought it was a dream come true
Your face I'll never forget
Was it fate that we met?

You're so perfect in every way
Too bad you weren't here to stay
Let's not ever say good-bye
Or let our friendship die

All I have is a faded memory
Close to my heart you will always be
Here's to our friendship, newly found
Without you I'm lost, please stick around

Sara Cereno

An Angels Words

When times get rough, when times get hard, when I am lost, when I am low, God only knows which way to go. But when God can't hear, and I start to fear, you are there, yes you hear me loud and clear. But why can't I see you? And that's when you answered, "I am your angel to guide and protect you. You can not see me for your mind is to young and your soul not yet free. But you need not to worry, when you come to heaven then will you see me. For now you must go on living on earth until God has called you onto his planet. Be patient and wise and I will help you, but you must help others to be patient like you. For the earth is a blessing from God unto you where you must decide whether to love or to hate." And that's when I realized that as long as I love and Believe God and all others, heaven awaits me and so does my angel. And now you can see that loving God is the key!

Kimberley Marie Castleton

People?

People are the special breed,
Among all life that walks and breathes.

In every person the "Core" is the soul,
Be it spiritual or be it one's goals.

They have good sense to be decisive,
But never learn what should entice them.

While claiming the title of intelligent life,
People stand idle, not seeing the light.

The selfish desires? There's no way to stop them.
But what about brotherhood, has this been forgotten?

Wealth is a need, they say, to be free,
But more often than not, wealth creates greed.

To rob from one's brother causes no second thoughts.
It may not be right, but he suffers the loss.

Yes, people are clever but can "Out-Fox" themselves,
When wants above morals expose their own separate hells.

The worst thought of all is of human destruction,
Caused only by those who live lives of corruption.

With "Peace On This Earth" as their greatest motto,
Why does killing continue, keeping lives from tomorrow?

Karl Katzmarek

Mr. J. Daniels

Sometimes I wonder about the main abstract thing;
An anger with unconcerning rage,
Nothing like the humming bird singing.

And then I look at you, and what is in your heart.
I wonder if the thing you want
Will give you a brand new start.

I know the frustration and even better the low;
Constantly asking how and why;
Feeling that there is no place to go.

Then comes the emotional pain,
Too big to grin and bear.
So you reach for that which soothes the hurt;
Yet it never seems fair.
The great toughness on that outer shell.
But no one ever knows of the danger of the inner hell.

Lisa McClennon

Depressed

A blended twist of emotions flow through
an empty mind
The mind going nowhere while the body
double times
Pain and heartache, confusion and lose,
does hurt know no bounds.
A frown where once a smile was on this
lonely clown.
Once there was some laughter, a feeling of
hope and joy.
Now the man you used to know is
shadowed by a frightened boy.
Where the road of life may take me
only time will tell.
Until the angel of death comes stalking
and rings the ending bell.

Steve Petrone

Willis

Passing by that big old house, I recall
An old lady with a wave and a smile,
Moving slowly for fear that she might fall.
She seemed to say, "Please stop and chat awhile."
When springtime came and storms brewed up quickly,
The fearful old lady was gone away
To the hospital. She was not sickly.
Just seeking refuge from a storm that day.
Body, old and frail, mind, young and alert,
Due to glaucoma, she had poor eyesight:
She never complained, even when she hurt,
Such an inspiration and a delight.
Thankful for knowing her, she was so dear,
And walked "The Last Mile of the Way" last year.

Peggy A. Bareford

"Birthday Wishes"

Birthday greetings to you today.....
And a heart full of wishes I send your way.....

Wishes for answers, to questions unasked
Wishes for acceptance, of feelings still masked
Wishes for peace, for that active mind
Wishes for joy, to a heart that's so kind
Wishes for courage, to face each new day
Wishes for patience, to help guide the way
Wishes for vision, for things yet to be
Wishes for wings, to set your soul free
Wishes for success, in all that you do
Wishes that all of your dreams come to you

If I had the power to make wishes come true
These are the gifts I'd give to you.....

Sharon L. Bobula

My Parents, My Friends

There were so many times when the road seemed too long
And all of the obstacles prevented me from going on
Yet through all of this darkness there was a light that shone through
It was the light of love reflecting from the two of you
You may be unaware of how much you have influenced me
But without you as parents, who knows where I would be
You were my constant companions in good times and in bad
And yours were the smiles that dried the tears when I was sad
Whenever I felt pain without or within
Yours were the healing touches of an unending friend
You were the two most precious gifts I had ever possessed
And how I thank God that He gave me only the best
For both of you are truly the best parents ever made
And there is nothing in the world that would make me want to trade
All of the joys that were ours throughout time
For they are sweet, precious memories that remain in my mind
If I could wish for one thing in my life it would be
To be even half the parent that you have been to me
So know one thing is as sure as the heavens above
Both of you shall always have my undying love.

Terri Tolliver

A Dream Of True Love

There they lay, quiescent and serene,
An aura of death surrounds these once living things.

True love never dies, I've heard them all say.
They carried it with them, along their way.

There was something between them, gentle and sweet,
The thing that is shared when two lovers meet.

Now they are gone, but they left us one thing,
A dream of true love, of this we can sing.

Sarah M. Swindle

This Is The Moody Blues

The days of future passed are gone,
and as strange as it may seem,
we've been in search of the lost chord,
and on a threshold of a dream.

It's a question of balance,
that keeps us alive,
But it's our children's, children's, children,
in a seventh sojourn strive.

It's our prelude of the future,
as we look up and cry,
at the long distance voyager,
and those voices in the sky.

We've seen the other side of life,
and watched hearts turn to sand,
We've learned the keys of the kingdom
from this legend of a band.
Now it's Sur la Mere,
with knowledge you can use,
this was and will be forever,
The Moody Blues.

Michelle Morgan

What Love Is There?

Sometimes people look at themselves,
And ask what have I become,
I hate looking at myself,
There's to much pain, no love.
God said be kind to others,
Is that so easy to do,
I try, try, and try,
But I just can't seem to be able to.
Sometimes my friends are loyal,
But other times there just not there,
I feel like a little lost girl in the dark,
I feel like they just don't care.
They'll never know the real me,
Or see the person I want to become,
Or ever have that feeling,
She is just so fun.
So now as I write this poem,
Tears swelled up in my eyes,
I know I don't deserve them,
I finally learned inside.

Suzanne Outman

Wishes

For Carl... If I could have three wishes
And be sure they'd all come true
The first thing that I'd wish for
Would be happiness for you!

The second wish I'd ponder
To make sure I got it right
I'd close my eyes and hold my breathe
Then I'd wish with all my might...

That you and I together
For a long, long time to come
Would always feel that "Magic"
That's so often lost to some.

Included in my final wish
Is a closeness shared by few
A gift so rare and precious
To be shared with only you!

Two hearts that beat together
At the end of every day
And a look that tells the other
What mere words could never say.

Sharyn Perron

When I Cross Over

When one day I cross over Jordan,
And beams of mercy lead me home,
Just know that I love you,
Left behind, more than ever,
And will wait for you,
Where we'll never more roam.

I will meet my Savior in that Homeland,
And God's blessing all around will flow,
And then I will go to greet loved ones,
That on earth I used to know.

What a happy day that will be,
And you left on earth, just trust your Savior.
And in God's spirit abide,
One by one, we will greet you,
Over on the other side.

Wynell Bryant

Bessie

Bessie went to bank school at night
And brought home books with her name in rounded letters.
Her family would be proud
When she no longer needed X's to sign her checks.
Yet, she still preferred to keep her 'bitela' or Yiddish purse
Tucked against her breast to be removed in shops' hidden corners.

Bessie never did learn English. She left that to her children,
To her children's children, and to her husband of 50 years.
Abraham carried the news in the browned-page Daily Forward.

Still, she could tell her tales in broken Yiddish,
Salted with the language of the Czar,
His horses trampled Vilna's peasants; his army froze her tears.

Others learned to read and write; Bessie rolled cigars and sang,
Marrying Abraham, mothering his children,
And waiting two full years in Vilna for her paid reunion
On the gold-paved streets of New York.

He tailored his English as his clothes.
Her words flowed with tears and laughter over hot brewed tea.
In struts and slouches, faithful to words and accents,
She breathed new life into those she met in a legacy of laughter.

Marlene M. Pomper

A Mother To Be

Thinking of you who is so small
and building you something like a cradle,
Getting around to doing it, you'll be able to crawl
or be walking very unstable,
So I'm glad that you are still attached to my cord
I thought that I had felt a movement,
Well I would just like to say welcome aboard
and to get use to the environment,
I had felt you burping
and moving very violently,
You must have been slurping
there was no way you were going to move around gently,
I guess it's because you don't have too much room
in my little womb.

Rebecca Mensch

Margi

When you are feeling down
And burdened with a pain,
Remember...
In life a little water must fall,
Because...
Even Roses need the rain.
You've cried in desperation
When you think you've tried in vain,
Believing you have failed with exasperation
Because you fail to see what you have gained.
Then you find yourself wondering
If you could really be going insane.
Only to finally give up pondering
On whether success can come from shame.
When you are feeling down
And burdened with a pain,
Remember...
In life a little water must fall,
Because...
Even Roses need the rain.

Timothy Scott Krell

My Home Sweet Home

As I turned
And cast a look at it one more time
I knew in my heart
This was going to be the last time
I was leaving home.

Suddenly, every memory I ever had
Of childhood, of Papa and my Mama
Came hugging my whole heart
And then I struggled to remember
Everything, everything I ever had.

Oh, my home, sweet home
Whose grounds, as a child
I ran, played and trodded
And as youth came close by
Filled laughter and sentiments at its very air.

Must, I ever go?
Leave you behind buried in my past
If perchance time should ever stood still.
Let it be now
Here in this old heart, at home, sweetest home.

Melodie B. Ocampo

"The Meeting"

I looked across the crowded room
and caught your eye.
Are you looking at me, too?
Do you feel what I am feeling now?
Do you want to meet me as much as I want to meet you?

I approach hesitantly at a complete loss of words.
And, then you smile, so warm
I return your smile immediately
At that moment, I know the attraction
I feel for you is shared.

Don't move too fast, slow down and pace yourself,
We must not ruin this moment.
Timing, and the right words are important.
Friendships can begin and end in
a few short minutes,

We share a short conversation trying
not to ask too much
It's obvious we are drawn to each other
I'm the mother you've always wanted
You're the little girl I need and want so much.

Patricia King

"Affirmations Of Autumn"

As summer fades away
and fall draws nigh,
our Creator paints yet another
precious season in which our
senses awaken and our hearts
fill with delight.

Autumn involves brilliant beautiful changes,
warm promises of comfort,
cool crisp reminders
that it is the hand of the Almighty
sweeping the brush across the canvas,
decorating our lives.

At this harvest time,
may we display Allah's artistry
with all the uniqueness, love and splendor
in which we were created.

ALLAH, bless our families and our community
as we expand to adapt for each and every
masterpiece of beauty you have designed
specifically for your earthly gallery.

Fountain of Life

Somewhere Is Utopia

Somewhere outside democracy or socialism
And far beyond the realm of dictatorship
Is the land of everyone's hopes and dreams.
It is the destination of explorers' treks across the globe.
A place that exists in philosophers' minds
 And where they go to die.
It is the Promised Land to the mass migration of spiritual refugees.
This *best of all possible worlds.*
The paradise thought lost.
The island of fantasy,
The region at journey's end of one's life.
Alas, — not Heaven,
But a divine landscape given human form.
Only to be recognized by those whose hearts are pure and with peace in mind.

Sheldon M. Ross

A Walk

Today,
And for years past,
I have walked on my favorite path,
Across the bridge,
Along the creek,
Past its rippling flows and quiet deep pools,
Up through the forest road of cool green arches,
To the top where the sky opens out
To spreading fields and rising hills,
A red barn
And fences
Holding in spun rolls of hay,
With wildflowers everywhere,
Purple spiked loose-strife,
Mauve tufted joe-pye weed,
Yellow goldenrod.

I took pictures.
Everything seems the same each year
And yet different
As I am different.

Ralphine Gross

Pastime

On the heavenly grass glistens the hot summer sun,
And from that grass shines an invisible light
That shines on those who seem like us.
But when their game starts they transform
And transcend impossibility;
Soaring to the unknown and unreachable,
Becoming heroes and legends and immortals.

As the countless multitude watches in awe,
Dreaming that for one moment
The impossible becomes possible
And the unreachable is in our grasp firmly.
It is the dreams that bring them here;
It is this game that touches their hearts;
It is in these men that they see heaven.

The thrill of victory brings them together;
Grueling defeat brings them even closer.
But it is the dreams that drive them.
The wonder of the age-old game lives on
To grow in the hearts of all;
It is the pastime where dreams are kept.

Paul Danifo

Anger, Heartbeats and Dreams

In my heart when I speak to him, he stops
and hears what I say.
In reality when I speak to him, he turns
and walks away.

In his heart does he hear my solace?
Or, as in reality, push me aside?
Will he fall victim to his anger
when there's no place left to hide?

In my minds' eye I see him running,
in an effort to elude,
all the secrets that chain and bind him
to his mental solitude.

I worry for his sanity, the fragileness
of his soul,
and mourn the anger hidden within, so
deftly under control.

In my dreams I see his chains broken,
his anger in the past.
No longer a threat to himself
behind that eloquently worn mask.

Valjean Xaiz

The Long Night

The night has been long - and lonely,
 And here in the dark I've lain,
Seeing the years pass by in review,
 Wakefully living them all again.

I remember you putting your hair up,
 The magic wrought by your fingertips,
How you lifted your face at my touch,
 And how warmly responsive your lips.

I remember you tranquil in sleep,
 The moonlight accenting your charm,
And the feeling of absolute peace
 With your head in the curve of my arm.

And then - like a spectre arising
 From recesses deeply hidden,
The sharply etched hour of parting,
 Always returning, always unbidden.

Then I long for the respite of daybreak,
 For a rift in my life's overcast,
To roll back the curtain of gloom,
 Until night again beckons the past.

Richard Anglin

Only God Can Send

I travel down road long
And I grow tired as I journey on
In search of a special friend
One that only God can send

A friend who's there to lend a hand
Or just to talk and maybe understand
With a caring heart and a smile that tends
As one that only God can send

Well God heard a prayer that day
For you, with your smile and cheerful way
Came along and soon a friendship begins
With one that only God can send

And now there's someone who seems to care
Someone who's kind with the time to share
Until they are such special friends
One that only God can send

Now as I travel I'm not alone, you see
For my best friend walks with me
And I'm thankful for such a special friend
One that only God can send

S. L. Reynolds

The Rain Symphony

The rains came today
and I know not how to feel
sad, somber, cleansed, or healed.

The rains came today
and that means the paths will be filled with
wandering dreamers who only come out when the
rains are over and mother nature lets out her silent cry.

The rains came
and I laid down upon the wet grass
and let its moist fingers find their way to my soul.

The rains came
and I dreamed of the star filled Virginia nights of my youth.

It rained today
and I shook the branches of a dogwood tree
and let it play God once again
as its leaves let loose the rain down upon me.

The rains have come
and as God raised his arms
to his magnificent world symphony,
I could only wonder to myself what instrument I should play.

Todd A. Bailey

Memories

There are times I think of you,
and I thought our love, our love was true.
As I cried all night long,
Just thinking of our favorite song.
Remembering the good times and the bad,
How it sometimes made me sad.
Thinking of how we shared our thoughts.

Remembering how it was so right,
As you held me oh so tight.
As I sat there watching the wall,
Just waiting for you to call.
As I lie there in the bed,
With the memories going through my head.
As I gave a little sigh,
Oh, how I hate to say goodbye.

Traci Butts

"The Passing"

What was once is now no more, I must accept my fate,
And just beyond the gathering storms I think I see the gate.

It beckons me to please abide,
That I may glimpse the other side.

The mysterious gate we all pass through at our appointed hour.
Just as the rain must surely fall to make the rosebush flower.

So many years, so many days, and what lies in between,
Determines all our destinies, unknown and unseen.

Persevering through the years, generations yet to be born,
Who are we to question fate, or take the time to mourn.

Yes, what was once is now no more, yet wonders never cease,
I've found what I was looking for, my moment of lasting peace.

Ruth V. Shafer

I'd Like to Get Inside Your Head

I'd like to get inside your head
And know what you are feeling.
Perhaps there is a sadness
or a pain you're not revealing.

If I could get inside you and be there for just a day,
Perhaps I'd understand your fears
And could wipe your tears away.

The face we show the outside world
isn't always what we feel.
We cover our inadequacies in a desire to conceal.

We sometimes withhold love
if we've a reason not to show it,
thinking we're one ones who suffer
And we want the world to know it.

We're all the same, and it's hard to know
what makes another tick.
We hardly even know ourselves
and that's the worst of it.

But if we always talk things out with those who love and care,
We'll find that life is easier with no need to despair.

Phyllis S. Howard

Untitled

I have a dream that one day we'll look beyond color
and learn to love each other a just sisters and brothers.
There'll be no more bigots and no more racists,
we'll live together with just our smiling faces.
I feel violence in our world would just disappear
if we learn to love each other with our hearts so dear.
Nobody is the better because we all our family,
the Lord has created us and this is a plan, see
you and I are one as it's seen through his eyes
it's time for us to stop, take a moment, and realize...
the last thing, on earth, we need right now
is to hate one another, we need to take time and bow
to the Lord Almighty, let him hear our prayers
"I want to treat all of my brothers and sisters with care."
No matter what your race and no matter what your creed
love, peace, and unity is what we need.

Kenneth Gilbert

Closed Inner Doors

Give me your heart and your soul,
And I give you my sex life secrets
What really happens behind closed doors of my life.
As a whore master of kindness,
Life is a bowl of jelly,
But the cherries are inside.
Do you eat them out?

Robert Stanley

If I Could Be An Eagle

If I could be an eagle, I'd soar up, up away,
And leave below the troubles that beset me day by day.

If I could be a river, I'd rush out to the sea,
And deposit there the problems that perplex and bother me.

If I could be a mountain spring from which cool waters flow,
I'd wash away my own sins, and no one would ever know.

But I can't be an eagle, a river or a spring,
I'm just a common person, a mortal human being.

Oh, I don't need to be an eagle, a river or a spring.
You see, I have a Saviour who takes care of everything.

When I come in faith believing and leave my cares with Him,
He'll renew my strength, restore my joy and refresh me once again.
He'll give me wings as eagles, I shall run and never fall.
But I must learn to trust and wait and give to Him my all.

Shirley Russell

Racism

Racism has caused problems throughout our nation.
And leaving us without anymore patience.
It has taught us to hate others because of their race.
But we have to get to know each other in a more positive way.
We have to become color blind.
And not use violence but to use our minds.
We must join hands and make reality out of Dr. King's dream.
And all become one big team.
A team of all races.
And different faces.
We should do it for those who died trying to make peace.
And those who tried to make all other evil cease.
Let's try and make racism disappear.
So in the eyes of our future generation it won't reappear.

Odelia Pyron

A Letter To My Love

When death intrudes its presence
And love is parted
Is it condemned to wander without hope,
In a world of thought that has no
further purpose
Can love endure as it steps through
Death's door.
From where will faith come for the rejoining
For which a forlorn love blindly searches
Is oblivion the only gain - or
Does she wait for me, a shadow in
another time
Waiting patiently for a message
Written in ink dipped from my heart
Words that float on a timeless sea
Horizonless yet with gentle winds,
Has she the net in which my heart is snared
To find the ceaseless longing in my
Words of love.

Ken Goodman

Substitution, No Resolution

Kind hearts and warm thoughts
Are these things that now belong to the past?
Taking chances, and getting cold glances,
Are these things that now belong to the present?
Why the substitution?
Kind thoughts cast away for angry threats.
Love cast away for hatred.
Joy cast away for sorrow.
Is this our new tomorrow?

Katherine Anderson

Untitled

Look inside for one sweet breath
and love will overcome the hardships
No longer see the pain
but walk in the light
We shall not be brought down
for his memory will remain in our hearts

What lies ahead for us may not be certain,
but it will eventually get easier
Go on and live with the memories
that shall remain forever
They shall fill the emptiness in our hearts
we should never let them leave

It is in this which we will find strength
for not have I lost a friend - but found one
eternally in my heart.

Thomas McCabe

Our Love Forever

Sometimes there are tough times.
And maybe I am the reason. There are all the love signs.
And I will love you through all seasons

You are the reason, I fell in love.
You are everything I could ever ask for.
You're always there when push comes to shove.

With you I've got everything.
I couldn't ever ask for more.
I don't want anyone else.

My love for you is so strong.
Sometimes maybe I do just think of myself
I don't want to make everything go wrong.

If it wasn't for you.
My life would be a living hell.
you're the one who I belong to.
I don't know what I'd do.
If I were to lose you.

My love for you is the strongest in the world
Honey, promise you'll love me
Forever and always

Sky Thompson

Life's Way

Thoughts start out so innocent and pure, we were all guided and most were sincere. Sometimes you must look on as a child first walks away, have the confidence you guided the best you could each day.

Knowing now that you have a mind of your own, listen to your conscience now that your grown. It may not always agree with what you have learned, listen to it anyway, make your own decision, on which way to turn.

If life gets so bad and your looking for someone to blame, look hard at your problem and not at the shame. This is when it really comes to your heart, that your mind and your soul plays a very big part.

We all can say we love in our special way, yet most of us can hate that very same day. If only we would take the time to listen to our mind and our soul, in the end there would be no question, which way we would go.

Each one of us has ideas of what lies ahead,they may not be the same, but just a little different instead. The beauty of it all is We didn't have to be the same and in the end be glad you took the time to listen, then realized, life wasn't a game.

Lorraine Butler

Untitled

There's nothing more to live for and no one else to love
And no one really cares about what I've been dreaming of
I have a feeling of desertion and loneliness in my heart
And when I speak to anyone I feel we're worlds apart
I haven't got a life and I haven't got a friend
Oh how I wish and pray that today it would all end
I'm tired of getting hurt my future has been crushed
I long for this crying in my head to slowly become hushed
I'm so tired of trying I don't even know what I've been trying for
I cannot make my dreams come true, I just don't care anymore.
I cannot just forget so please don't ask me to
I could never leave behind the things that I've been through
My world is so confusing which way do I turn
I don't know how to deal with him I guess it's something I must learn,
I don't know when and I'm not sure just why,
But somehow I get hurt and it gets worse
Nothing I care to see because time's too much to handle
It's just too hard for me.

Misty Simon

The Oak

Protecting from the harshness of the day
and obscuring the darkness of the night.
You are always there for me without fail
with a complimentary opposing breath for each of mine.

Content to listen without a response
with neither argument nor agreement.
Nevertheless impartial when I speak,
you are firm in your position with a tendency to sway.

You need not me as I strongly need you
however I am forever welcome.
Reaching up and out to better yourself,
I seek refuge and hiding in your arms without objection.

You are desired both dead or alive,
I much rather desire the latter.
Unfairly taken for granted by most
but nothing beautifies a walk in the park as much as you.

Michael A. Fernandez

Prisms

The sun shines through and paints the peach
and opal blush upon the twigs;

Soft they glisten, while the breeze
gently blows on whipped cream cheese;

Slow their motion, almost nil,
as they stand tall on the hill.

While below bowed threads remain:
noodle bits of cellophane.

Were they drawn by fairy hand?
Shaped by alkali and sand?

I dare not hear a tinkling sound,
or watch clear dirks drop on the ground.

Though beautiful the music be
I'd rather see ice grass, ice tree.

Ruby L. Agnir

In August

Gentle breeze turns leaves aflutter
As trees glance upward to majestic mountains,
Aspen quaking in the Sierra.

Nancy Kelly-Smith

Caged

When Freedom's lost.
And Open Space we do not have, any more.
What thoughts...run thro' the mind?
When small space cramps your style.
And confinement...is all you know!

How does the spirit...run Free?
When your nostrils flare...longing for, that breath of Freedom.
And staleness...is all you smell!
When...pacing in small space, makes You crazy!

With...what was...and what could be!
Is this...how the caged animal feels?
As he moves to and fro?
Eagle...eagles flying high.
On the wings of the wind...
Flying up so high...
Beyond the reach of man.
My God...my God...how I, wish I could be free!
Blue sky...blue sky...oh, cover me...
With endless freedom...
To be free!

Remick

In The Middle Of Rage

Here I stand, cowardly fool, forever in rage
And pains like winds blow me over, securing me in fear
I understand nothing, yet everything in my heart
There is no solace in man's unyielding mind or soul
He is not, nor can he ever be content.

Here we stand within and amongst our selves
Some born to be free in their hearts, others encaged
Each one hoping to escape the prison of their self
Preferably to unknown and unseen places,
Where no other man dares to follow.

They leave the rest of us, in the midst of life
In the arms of God, between the forces of time and age
Looking toward the sky, eyes up, heads lowered
Shoulders once again, dropping pitifully to the ground
As we stand, all of us, cowardly fools, full of our rage.

Keena S. Neal

Untitled

Make unto thyself a tiny enclosed
And place a moat deeply and well posed
To keep away the commoness of life
The dreadful boors and their companion - strife
Adore the blooms that grow within thy space
Caress the flowers and hold them to thy face
For short the day, then gone the merry song
And seconds fly until the final gong,
When the fluttering of angel's wings awaken thee
To ask what was so lovely - (quite mistakenly)
That ye detained arrival to thy heaven,
And dallied so for four scale years and seven,
Regale them with beauties of the earth,
Of songs and wine and flowers and mirth
And dear ones who have been with thee since birth.

Robert MacIntosh

Untitled

I'd give you the moon... as I know it.
As the flowers, I'd give you the stars that I pick.

As if my world would have no ending
Then the tender love yet lies till you might see.

For ever those cunning eyes can't see the wind
And only in the minds will is there an end.

Latricia Turpin

'Sarah'

Sarah Faby had a baby at 15 years of age
And she had to get on welfare and work at minimum wage.
Drop out of school she did and when she did she was sad,
Because of all she had said or done and could never ever turn back.
Sarah sat with her infant one night, caressing and holding the young suckling tight,
She thought of all the things she did wrong and wished she had done them right.
Going with every Tom, Dick and Larry, until one of their babies she did carry,
She felt bad that she was a young mother and to the baby's daddy she was not married.
Smoking crack at the age of 10 she stopped and now she's at it again
Forgetting every single thing she'd been taught in school,
Sarah sat her infant in a play pin and started sniffing cocaine like a fool.
Sarah Faby died last year and her daughter was only two, so please to all the teens out there
Don't let this happen to YOU!

Virginia Charles

My Friend

She was nice, she was kind,
and she will never leave my mind.
She was my friend, she was yours,
and now she is with the Lord.
She didn't live to see what life was like,
so, now we live it for her,
and we'll try to keep it right.

She is in my heart,
she is in my soul,
and I will never let her go.
She was nice, she was kind,
and she will never, ever leave my mind.

Penelope Jean McKeever

This Is The World Where You Belong

We've all thought about it
And some have even tried
To enter the unknown
To step into the other side.
Some believe it'll be paradise
Some believe it'll be hell
But only at our given time
Should we be able to tell.
I know at times life is hard
And you can't find a reason to stay
But no matter what the cost
Don't let your life be the pay.
Who knows, once you got there
That world could be freezing and black
And you would wish for your previous world
And would not be granted it back.
So please, do your best
And really try to hang on
Although you may feel out of place,
This is the world where you belong.

Rachel J. Bowlby

Christmas Thought

I waited a long time to pick up a pen
Asking myself, how does it go again?
It's all in there, it should come out
In a well-spring of gushes or in a small spout
The thoughts are there, but like shadows in sunlight they disappear
Oh, Holy night, now it's all come right
Merry Christmas to all and Happy New Year
Blessings of the season, may your hearts be light

Susan Connell

A Voice From Above

I'm here, not far away
And soon we'll be together to stay
But, for now, you're always in my heart
So we're never far apart

And here I'm never alone
I'm with the friends and family I've known
And the Lord is here with us now
To Him we all humbly bow

Your name is in the Book of the Lamb
And soon we'll be joined again where I am
But, for now, just know there's no need to fear
And let me hear laughter not tears

Phillip Wheless

For Angie

I will wrap my memories carefully
And store them in a special place...

Bare summer feet racing along a dirt path,
Stormy clouds sprinting across a winter sky.

Memories of a friend's embrace, a loved one's caress.
Memories of a child's first giggle and trusting hug.

When my feet can no longer dance
And my eyes are blurred by pain,

I will take my memories out, one by one,
And play them over like well-loved melodies.

When I stand before the throne of God,
I will proudly lay my treasure out

And say:
This,
My God,
My friend,
is me.

Loretta Calfee

Memories Of You

I can remember sitting together laughing, and talking in the yard. I see spring flowers budding; they make me remember. I feel the cool wind on my face, and I remember. You are gone now, yet everything is you.

I can remember him, how he loved you so dearly. We would sit, and talk; we talked always of you. Now he too has gone, and I am alone. What now can I do but mourn the death of you, and the friendship we once knew.

Rachel E. Werner

A Prophecy

Today, Jupiter's bird unfolds his wings
And the benevolent Christ child is born
upon the golden dawn of a new Jerusalem.
Weep not for me or yourselves;
Whatever will be will be. . .
I forgive myself and return to myself,
And return to myself a thousand cries of emotion.
The great wild spirit is our friend,
Three Magi become one star,
which is the Universe. . .
Bethlehem. O Bethlehem.
How I long to awake in that holy manger
by your side, and the brotherhood of man
see its final fruition. . .

Martin Dies

Because You Love Me

You've seen me when my sadness reigned
and tears poured from my eyes.
When the world seemed hopeless - you've seen me.

You've laughed with me at jokes you knew were dumb
but that tickled me anyhow.
When the world was without humor - you've laughed with me.

You've held me close when anger rose
and hate and spite became me.
When the world was out to get me - you've held me close.

You've been a friend to me at times
I didn't deserve to have one.
When I was lonely, you were there - you've been a friend.

You've loved me each and everyday
We've shared each passing hour.
You've been with me through good and bad - because you love me.

Linda Santee

Friends

We're great friends right now
And that's a matter of fact.
We'd do anything that could be done
To help one another.
But how do I tell him I love him so?

His personality is great, his looks are terrific,
And a heart as big as the moon,
But soon he'll depart for some far off part,
And love someone else by June.
But how can I tell him I love him so, and no other?

I don't want him to ever change,
For our lifestyles were not by choice,
Just knowing that he is there, and that we care,
Makes life bearable, even if not fair.
But how can I tell him I love him so?

There is someone out there for each of us,
But today I know not who,
But God knows, and will give me a guy to love,
And guess, it's going to be like guess who!

Robert J. Sakowski

Yesterday

I believe our deepest thoughts and fears are held in yesterday
and the dreams that never came true, and as for tomorrow
what will it bring, as I spend my today's with you.

Should I not look too far behind, nor search ahead too soon
For today can be so much more, than to remember yesterday's wounds.

Though we all wish and hold our hopes so high, it's ok to dream
But always remember to believe in yourself, as hard as it may seem.

Grab on to your rainbows, which come and go, and reach for every one
If you find the sun, it may rain, but believe and you may find love.

All the memories tomorrow will bring, as yesterday's seem too slowly die
And as for the pain, try to forget old memories left behind.

True thoughts and feelings, always hold them near your heart each day
I believe our deepest thoughts and fears are held in yesterday.

Lisa Roesner

Ode To A Trash Basket

We've heard your office can get full of trash
And the mess you make is quite a bash.
Wads against the ceiling and bounced off the door
With it all winding up in the middle of the floor.

We looked and we looked for something to assist
And this little gadget we couldn't resist.
And you can bet your very best hat
This'll prevent such a mess as that.

What'll worry us most from day to day,
If you use it in the usual way,
Trying to be so neat, so prim, so prissit
Sure as hell you're gonna miss it!

Then there it'll be back on the floor
And to quote the maid. "NEVERMORE"!
So, look and watch before you throw
And your neatness will grow and grow and grow.

Wilna Keith

Remembering Way Back When

The trains came puffin' down the track
And the telegraph keys went clickety clack.

Back in the year nineteen forty-three
A bunch of girls worked for the old U.P.
From town and country they came in a group
To learn all about the whistle and hoot.

They braved the weather day and night
Trying to do everything just right.
Taking the place of the men in the station
Who were at the front defending our nation.

Folks called them brave - a few found fault
But to praise they often called a halt.
"We're not here for self-esteem —
Just backing up the old home team."

With a "Keep em Rollin'" and a wave of the hand
They went back to homes all over the land.
The war was over - the fighting was done -
"Now how about those weddin' bells, hon'?"

The trains came puffin' down the track,
And the telegraph keys went clickety clack.

Marjorie Stelter

The Gift

I walked to the top of the hill one day,
And there was this beautiful patch of flowers
This was in the month of May.
The flowers were red, lavender and white
All growing together in a circle,
My what a wonderful sight!

The sky was blue, the valley green
Warm breezes blowing by
Then I began to softly cry - how man to man
can be so mean.

What a wondrous planet this is - with deserts and
forests, waterfalls - glorious nature at its best,
the greatest gift to man it is
From God.

Sylvia Wright

A Mother's Love

Tatyana, I love you
And there's no one in this world
More precious to me
Than my little girl

Golden round face
Radiant smiling teeth
Jet black wavy hair
Bright eyes chubby cheeks

You bring a smile upon my face
Even when I'm feeling down
It's such a joy and will always be
Having you around

Blessed the day I gave birth to you
God blessed me with someone to love
You give me bear hugs and sweet candy kisses
You're all I'm thinking of

Vanessa Y. Small

Self Love

When you love some whole
And they love you half
You feel like you're going down separate paths
You know he loves you, but only a little
Nothing to compare to how you feel
You say to yourself it's no big deal
You go on with life accepting a piece
But deep down in side you feel cheated
Hoping that, that someday comes and you will be needed
But maybe when that someday comes
You'll say to yourself it doesn't matter
Because now you love yourself and feel whole
Right where it counts, deep in your soul.

Sharon Gambatese

A Soul Misunderstood

When your family doesn't care
And they're never hardly there
Their shallow looks and hollow glares
Still haunts my very soul

When bad vibes are very thick
That you can't break it with a brick
They'll tell you that you're very sick
And mentally insane

It cuts so deep
This morbid pain
I feel as though I'd been slain
The good I'd done, I've done in vain
So tell me, good friend, please

I've tried so hard, to the point of strain
But always still, that morbid pain
You'd think, by now, that I'd be trained
To hold this hurt within

But all I can see
Is that my family
A different heart, they'll never see

Suzette M. Adams

Momma's Love

Momma's love was all so hard to obtain
and to sustain, never forgiving always severe.
A single compliment she could not
seem to give, only
Criticism and double-edged truth;
Pain is synonymous to love in her eyes
to hurt you enough to force your
tears to spill down your cheeks was
to love you more than any warm
embrace could convey.
Cry child, speak child give in to
the pain, admit momma's right and
turn over your life, then momma
will take away the pain, don't try to
fight it girl, rebellion is useless.
She cackles like a witch, her steel blue
eyes ablaze with ice as her talons
dig deep into your heart, binding your
will, making it hers, until you see only
Momma's Love....

Tracy M. Roy

The mighty sir Gable

I am the mighty sir Gable
and upon my steed do I ride
faithful and true through forest and brush
to fight the evil dragon on the hillside

There a pretty lady pleads
for her life the serpent's to take
she calls me by name
and to her rescue I rush, headlong, without break

I fight with the monster
and viciously swing at its head
I hack it and slash it
then stab it until dead, dead, dead

The lady mounts up
and soon she is safely home
then me and my steed
off we ride; alone

I retire for the night
with my mount in the stable
there's a monster at my bedpost;
who will save me, the mighty sir Gable...

Thomas Alan Greve

The Key To My Heart

I closed the door that led to my heart,
and vowed to let no one in.
I've loved and trusted and then I got hurt,
but it would never happen again.

I locked that door and threw the key
as far and as hard as I could.
Love would never enter again;
my heart was closed for good.

Then you came into my life,
and made me change my mind;
just when I thought that tiny key
was impossible to find.

That's when you held your hand to me,
and showed me I was wrong;
inside it was the key to my heart...
you had it all along.

Lanie Ermitanio

My World

Come inside my heart and see the world I live in I'll welcome you
And walk you through and share with you my thoughts

My world may not be real as others they may see it, but to myself
My world is real and allows me to be taught

It has a softness all its own, a glow that soothes my mind, there
Are no mysteries in this world there's only endless time

It's full of creatures big and small that to the eyes delight
Its heavens are filled with dazzling stars that light the moonlit night
They're butterflies and flowers and birds, rabbits that can't be counted
There's fog that lights the webs with jewels as spiders go undaunted

The hummingbird that comes each morn to sing his single song
Who dashes by across the sky and just as fast is gone

My hand is very careful as it lovingly does reach to gather from
The flowers taking only one of each

The days are like a dream and the dreams seem real indeed
Perhaps, you see, if my world was gone
Then I just would not be

Susan K. Gumm

'Remember'

Remember when I met you and I became your friend
And we would share our troubles, until the very end
Remember when we gathered and laughed our cares away
And sat around together, until the break of day
And when your hand I needed, and when you needed
mine, working hard together helping yours and mine
Remember all the fun, and all the things we shared
And the tears and sorrow, of the one we loved
and cared.
All these things remembered deep inside my heart,
And now it all has ended for we are now
apart.
And if someday you need me, for anything you do,
I sit around and wait because,
I'm a friend of yours.

Sheryl Lucas

Politicians

The environment is in trouble,
And we'd better do something on the double.
Global warming is an issue,
Which can't be resolved by a politician with a tissue.
Rain forests, plants, and animals are routinely destroyed,
But the politicians aren't even annoyed.
Their fixation is not the nation,
But merely a connection to the next election.
Politicians won't act in haste
Until the special interests are mired in toxic waste.
By then it will be too late,
Because the politicians, will have sealed our fate.

Simeon Lakritz

Soul Love

He left me when I was quite young
And with him went my beautiful sun
The years to follow were filled with pain
Without my sun ... there was always rain

I searched through men that I might find
Those eyes I remember so well in my mind
They came to me from across the seas
As God had heard my unspoken pleas

The rain is gone ... there are no clouds
What I thought was lost ... I finally found
For the soul who had given my life its sun
Has returned to me in this special one.

Pamela McClellan

Friend Owl

I looked out my window,
and what did I see?
An owl perched in my old oak tree.
Sitting on an limb looking back at me,
just as proud as he could be.

Feathers all ruffled,
brown, black and white.
That owl was quite a sight,
with round, wide eyes and a beak of yellow,
he seemed quite an elegant fellow.

I will miss friend owl in my old oak tree,
and hope that some day I'll see
that same owl looking back at me.
Just as wise as he can be,
sitting on a limb in my old oak tree.

Marlys Kuehne

Untitled

God took the sunshine from the skies,
And with his love, made your eyes.
From the sun he took the light,
And with his touch, granted you sight.
A kiss upon your lips he did leave,
In order that you would breathe.
Two ears he gave, so you could hear,
His words to trust him, he'll always be near.
Then from an angel, he took the arm,
To wrap around you, safe from harm.
With every beat your heart does take,
A new day begins as you awake.
Most precious of gifts, is that of his love,
With ever lasting life, in his kingdom above.

Paulette Johnson

Love Will Grow

A beautiful day, a lovely bride, a groom standing straight and tall.
And with nervous anticipation, the relatives start to fill the hall.
Tis the day of all days for this couple in love, a day for the rest
of their life. In just a short time they will be entwined, to be
known as husband and wife.

Friends that are close have set the stage, working hard to make
everything just right. The chapel is set with flowers and plants,
as the bride stays well out of sight. Last minute changes and
rearranges, that magical time is drawing near. The bride and
groom are now apart, possibly starting to have a touch of fear.

But at last the moment has come, a flute softly begins to play.
The groom and the best man stand arm to arm, all agree this is a
glorious day. As the bride starts to enter the chapel, a hush
quickly fills the air. Her beauty is so radiant, everyone there can
not help but to stare.

She slowly walks with a special friend, arm in arm up the bridal walk.
He will give her away on this glorious day, a special bond will
be shared without talk. The groom stands ready to except her
hand, and share the rest of his life. The bride smiles lovingly
through the veil, knowing she soon will be his wife.

The ceremony has finally started, each holding the others left hand.
Their vows are shared at this time, that will stand through out the
land. The Bishop shares with a special spirit, what the Lord
would have them hear. He tells them that their love will grow,
and to always call each other dear.

Terry Arrow

Words Can't Express

Words can't express how much you mean to me,
And words can't express what we could be.
Words can't express the sunshine in the sky,
And words could never explain the sparkle in your eye.
Words can't express your ever so tender touch,
And words can't express your warm embrace that I need so much.
Words can't express your soothing voice,
And words could never explain why you were my choice.
Words can't express your chilling kiss,
And words could never explain why it's you I miss.
Words can't express the songs that the birds sing,
And words can't begin to express the joy you bring.
Words can't express the calmness in the wind,
And words could never explain the cards you send.
Words can't express the sadness I feel when we are apart,
And words could never express the happiness in my heart.
Words can't explain the things that you do,
And words would never express the way I love you!

Mark Cannady

Peace Poem Love Poem

When I lay me down
and you pick me up
telling me a bedtime story
that's peaceful love

when I hurt myself with nasty tools
and you bandage me up
telling me not to do it again
that's peaceful love

when I think evil thoughts
and you console me with hugs and kisses
telling me there's goodness in the world that's peaceful love

when I am lonely and in need of companionship
and you willingly volunteer to be my friend
telling me that you will always be there that's peaceful love

when I am dead and gone
and you bury me with a biblical verse and a piece of your heart
telling me that you will see me later that's peaceful love

peace and love, love and peace, hand in hand, toe to toe, down the road up the hill, always side by side, never so far apart, togetherness
oneness

Son B. Nguyen

Idling

I get up in the morning, thanking God for awakening me to see another beautiful day-
I think of what needs to be done today, of what I want to do today-
And in the process of my assessing and doing,
I begin to think again of just doing nothing-
To let things go for today-
To take the day for whatever it brings-
To just do simply **nothing**.
And so the day is gone, and the night creeps in with its stillness, darkness, and starry sky, lit with a full bright moon
I began to recant the day's memories;
A day which will never come exactly the same again **ever**.
This day of simply doing nothing-
A day of idling.

Sheila P. Perry

Time

Here I sit with clouds of cotton; where times old times are not forgotten.
Thing can start to poppern; where the clouds of gray/white are filling the sky just right.

Things just might flow; here I sit with the creek.
Where the trees will shriek as, winds tickle the top with light breezes. Thing of tropical breezes, can cause you some sneezes.

Here where I sit next creek, with clouds of cotton that won't be forgotten.
Where a day of quiet becomes a moment of time, that will become treasure.

Things that will be come measures of time, in place of clouds of grey/white, that fill with rain that needed to water the earth of this place where time is not forgotten.
Memories of time of old seem to come, to reach out to let us search, for the ideas of breeze with whispers that talk as you sit in the place, of clouds of cotton where time of old is not forgotten.

Marie E. McKerlie

For Your Eyes Only

Those eyes that glitter in perfect green —
Are the dew on the flower, I have just seen...
Those gentle waves of the sea on the earth's face ...
Are you that flow and my head embrace ...
This hair in blond that streams like rays ...
Is the silk with which I weave my days ...
You are my love and fire ...
You are my spring of wine and desire ...
On the turn roads of my life, you are the voice of time...
That fills me with wonder and inspires my rhyme...
A mermaid that's born in the depth of pure water ...
Aging through, I proudly dive through each layer ...
Time carves you on my face as wrinkles and lines ...
Writing my legend in eternal signs ...
Telling the story of a passing star ...
Of a hand of sand that lighted far...

So you stay my only sun!
My future that my past has done!
And my flute stay singing in loud murmur...
And I stay sailing into you, until no more, forever ...

Mike Fayad

A Gift From God

And then there was Robin a true
artist in every way a soul of pure
sensitivity who sculptured the sensitivity
into every sculpture he created.
He worked among other great ones whose
work blinded with his beliefs and ideas
there was no jealousy of his fellow
artists only deep appreciation of their
work and suggestions which opened his
mind to help him find his way in what
he was trying to convey.
Art is a true sharing of the soul only
God can give this gift to man.
Treasure it with deep gladness and
waste it not the precious sweetness
of God gift to humanity is to share
the beauty in our souls.

Rita E. Feuer

"God For Tom"

Yesterday was a day of great and dreadful sadness
As a mother, I witnessed on the television set
An agonizing display of my son's body, racked with pain
Not to mention the emotional distress that he met

I often said to this brave mature son of mine
"When I am witness to any of your pain
It becomes nearly more than I can bear
And the will to endure it for you, is always in vain"

God, I've learned throughout the years
Your will is always as it should be
Needless to say, my son Tom is in grief
I for one, am calling for you to see

From all of the trials he has had to endure
It's obvious, that he will pull through this
But to have you lighten his load a little now
Would help me, his giver of life, to find some bliss

The time has come with this troubled situation
He may need some comfort to regain his focus
Please, guide my heart and soul and then maybe
You and I, can give him strength, the both of us

C. C. Kay

Untitled

The concept of expectation flows through us
as a wave forced against our beings.
A conflict deep within us, repeatedly brushed aside,
as a gentle hand to a wisp of hair,
ignoring the force of the wind that blows it astray.
Reminders of love and universal law
toil with the earthly variations.
The answers that lie in the child's eyes
sanction our belief in Angels.
And the existence of bewilderment lies dormant once again,
as the fulfillment of peace is acknowledged
with the presence of karmic resolution.

Sandra P. Holton

"Alaska"

The mountains here move my soul,
as eagles glide on drafts from low.

The forest sings of life year round,
through rain and snow it still abounds.

The clouds do cling to all the things,
that stand or stood for life to bring.

The ghostly clouds drift and glide
from valley floors up mountainsides.

The misty spirits that bring all life,
ebb through the forest with little strife.

And when the rains come to an end,
the sun is greeted, a sure old friend.

The waters perk down mountainsides,
to form the rivers where life abides.

The land's still wind, the sea's still free,
This is where I must always be.

I think I've finally found my home,
this place where there's still room to roam.
From Sitka to Nome I call her home.
This grand land: "Alaska"

Shawn Nolan

Wistful

Close the windows draw the blinds.
As from the corner of the glass
Cobwebs spread, staring down the rain
Within the thoughts that I contain...
Remove the stilled and painful
Strands of memories I'd not tell
Sadness falls between the drops
On the other side of life
Mockingly they land on the pane before my hand.
The world it seeps not through
And as through the spiders eye
I'm incapable of flight.
Marked my path in life no side roads will I follow.
I am captured like the fly
Unlike the rain I will not flow.
Like the spider I'm aware of my faith unto the web.
No world do I belong but on tattered strands I am
Hopelessly forever clung. Remove the stilled and painful
Strands of memories and the hold ov'r me...
Chances are, however, I'll cease to ever be!

Linda S. Atkins

I Would Liked To Have Been With Jesus

I would liked to have been with Jesus,
as he walked by the sea of Galilee.
Seen him quiet the roaring tempest
and calm the raging sea.

Been there when he fed the multitudes
made the lame to walk and the blind to see.
Healing the sick and cleansing the Leper,
tired and weary yet uncomplaining was he

Yet he must go on, he had a job to do,
with stripes he was beaten and spit upon too.
He carried his own cross, and hung on the tree,
forsaken by God, that we might be free.

Willingly he went to the cross to die,
suffered and bled for you and I.
We can never, no never, such a debt repay,
but our love and devotion at his feet we can lay.

Dear Christians wake up! Our redemption draws nigh.
Our Savior is soon coming in clouds from on high.
Are we watching and praying for others to win?
There are souls that are lost, let's garner them in.

Ora Sell

"The Chicken"

The chicken walked as proud.
As I can see, onto the lake and over the sea,
He puffed out his chest, and grinned his teeth,
He walked up to the butcher and bit him with glee,
The butcher looked down and gave him a slap.
The chicken looked up and started to quack,
The butcher knew this couldn't be,
A chicken that quacked as far as the eye could see..
was wrong,
Something ticked and then he heard a sound,
It was the chicken that had started to sing,
The butcher had an idea, a mean one of course,
He would sell the chicken and then buy a horse,
After all these terribly things,
The chicken ended up, nothing more than a tiny string.
He was not proud at all for all his pride was gone,
The poor thing was sold and resold all over town,
Which made him very thin.
And being thin is not a nice thing,
When you were once a proud big "little" thing, like a chicken.

Sharifa Jarrett

Photograph

One thing reminds me of you
as I look across the nightstand to your photograph

One thing reminds me of you only
it cannot help me feel your touch
those hands so big and strong
yet so gentle

it cannot help me kiss your perfect
mouth
so sweet to taste
so tender to touch

it cannot help me remember the
warmth of your body
making love to me in passion
curling with me in sleep

One thing reminds me of you only
it cannot bring you back to me
where I need you to be
It can only remind

Your photograph gets me through the days
It cannot fill my nights.

Regina Mae Haun

A New Day

As I awaken at break of a new day,
As I look to the land so tranquil,
And the beckoning light of the sun so still,
A dark cloud darkens my way.

I see a child living in fear and pathos;
I see a youth wasted by drug misuse;
I see elderly languishing in abuse
I see people succumb in world ghettos.

Is there a meaning to life?
Can the beast of hatred be tamed?
Can the pervaders be maimed?
Can the raiders of peace be put to strife?

I must not despair.
I must give of my strength and goodness
With one little gesture of kindness
And one moment of care.

This can vanquish dismay.
Can slay the untamed beast,
Can strengthen the very least
So, all awaken at the break of a new day!

Mary A. Tummillo

"The Rough Path"

Trapped in a box with no way out...
As she knocks on the wall she falls into a deep trance...
Dreaming of ways she could make the world a better place...
Hoping that she would be given a chance.

Then she awakes and realizes what lies ahead on the
dark and unpaved road...
She does have a life ahead and she realizes that she
does have the potential to go farther than the farthest.
There is a light at the end of this dark, unpaved road
that grabs her attention and hypnotizes her to
get to the end of the path...
As she goes along the rough path she faces problems;
both good and bad...
As she grows more and more mature she learns her nature.
Making the decision to follow the rough, unpaved road
she leads a long successful life in which she makes
choices that will control the way her life will ensue.

Samantha Cohea

A Sailor's Night Prayer

Oh Lord, I know your magnificence
As I see; the heavens, the moon, the stars, the sea.

As my spirit moves me
To the moonlit sea,
I feel your presence in the salt sprinkled breeze.

I can read your message
In the stars above,
They tell me the answer to my prayers, and your unselfish love.

And now, as I lay myself down to rest,
In my seaward vessel that the ocean has caressed

I dream of sharing with
All my loved ones and friends
All the new adventures
That lie all the ports,
Full of countries and peoples all sizes and sorts.

But I can never forget
As I dose off to sleep
Those things that tell me most of your magnificence;

The heavens, the moon,
The stars, the sea

Stephen R. Schuer

Father Of The Bride

My lips won't utter what I feel inside,
As I stand before you, O lovely bride,
There's unspoken poems, songs yet to be sung,
Angelic choirs, bells yet to be rung.

Is it accidental or by design,
That I'm silent now like a pantomime?
'Tis an infant I see in her mother's embrace,
Where was I during her growing-up race?

But you're just a babe, my little girl,
And I'm speechless now, my mind's a-whirl,
No longer a child, but a woman I see,
O God, let my eyes now speak for me.

Let me hold you a moment, in silence convey
All my hopes for your future on your wedding day,
Take my arm precious daughter, I'll walk by your side,
While my heart whispers softly, O beautiful bride.

Ruth Peters

Le Poeme

I like the feel of earth under my feet
as I walk through the fields.....
The willow tree is my living cathedral
more majestic, more beautiful than
any artifice man could ever make with his hands....
All of the truly great works of art
are made by the world's of nature...
The red and yellow tulips in spring,
A summer thunderstorm, the blaze of colors
vivace of autumn leaves over the forests
and mountains, and the dancing white snow
on a winter crystal garden that decorates
all the trees for the dance...

Robert Lee Greystone

Untitled

The wind touched me softly
As if you were dancing through the air
And in the morning dew that surrounded me
I could feel you everywhere

And strangely I kept hearing your whisper
Brush gently upon the trees
So I tried to paint your picture, on every falling leaf

But when the rain washed the earth
all the colors began to fade
So I reached for you in prayer, feeling lonely and afraid

Then suddenly a rainbow, fell quietly from the sky
And with the light that shined before it
There God stood before my eyes

He assured me of your happiness
In eternal life that had begun
And then he dried my tears, with the warmth of the rising sun

But before God disappeared
Into the sky of shades of blue
He said, "Your mother is a part of me
But she'll always be a part of you."

Regina Ponzi

Black Swelling Surf

I stare at the black water under the pounding surf
As it roars toward the shore.

It slows and trickles aimlessly at my feet,
Slowly, softly, caressingly
with peace and contentment surrounding it.

In one brief moment it is gone, returning to the sea,
Only to be replaced by another.

Life, as we perceive it is a series of black swells,
followed by soft, loving foam covering our feet.

Time when peacefulness surrounds us,
however fleeting.

The time we must cherish this awareness of peace.
As it is written -
The Black Swells will again appear.

The time we will need all of our strength and faith,
to withstand the recurring pounding on our very being.

Rita Rollins

"I Wear A Guitar"

There stood a man, with guitar in hand —
as music flowed from his fingers and soul.

The guitar appeared as part of his body
from the way the two formed a whole.

He played with pride, he played with feeling...

He didn't utter a word, and yet through
the playing I heard, a message so revealing.

When he was done, like an inquisitive son
I asked him, "Do you know how good you are?"

He just shrugged his shoulders
with a humble grin and said
kid
"I just wear guitar".

Michael L. Damico

Torn Away

And as the Clouds now follow Close, Her back is to the Wind.
As tears flow slowly down her Face, She still tries to Pretend.

She now imagines Happiness, To cover up the Pain.
To somehow ease away the tears, Before it starts to Rain.
She Dwells on what is Missing, Although she doesn't know.
She reaches deep inside her Heart, To let her feelings Go.

But still inside she's Troubled, She just can't understand.
What it is she needs so Bad, And what her Heart Demands.

To walk up and to meet Her, You'd think her life was Fine.
So full of Love and Happiness, Of roses and red wine.

But still her Soul is searching, No Peace is to be found.
And still this girl sits all alone, While thoughts go Round and Round.

So Sad to watch a young girls Life, Be torn away at Birth.
For the Only Peace that She will Find, Will not be on this Earth.

Sharon Lynne Markle

"You're Just Not Thinking"

My ice creamed snot stuck to the bottom of my eyelid
as the frozen tongues drank off another slice of dust.
While down in the valley of chewed light bulbs
ariptituded ascending aardvarks united for
the enslaved blind armpits,
to trip the light fantastic on a horny
eaglet's ass hair.
So I write with 10 dimensional monkey balls
While the big frothy milk cake took
an enormous little flying jumping galloping
trip off the hallway inside the canister
outside the middle of my mind
And then on some sunny night the darkened
noontime moon will pant lustingly at the
barking rocks, below the upside
up of the twenty ten psycho cat rats
of the concrete wood ninnies

Lalena Freeman

The Panther's Coat

The chilling winds go rushing by,
As the panther stalks its prey,
Its thick, black coat swishes back and forth,
As the mountains behind are grey.

Its thin, sleek paws crush twigs below,
Its senses, sharp and keen,
It sees its prey - a rabbit - in front,
Though the panther is never seen.

As swift as the day passes by a fool,
The panther gets its wish,
With rabbit in mouth, it heads back to its cave,
And its black coat goes swish, swish.

Shasta Lyn

Angels

They always seem to love me, no matter what I do,
Angels to me, how 'bout you?

I've tried to be there in their time of need.
When they laugh, cry, and even when they bleed.

They never judge me like some people do,
Angels to me, how 'bout you?

God sent them to me from the skies so blue,
Angels to me, how 'bout you?

There's nothing as precious as a baby brand new,
Angels to me, how 'bout you?

Tammy Cosby

Reins Of Metal

My world shatters while the chains that bind me fuse and collide.
As the sound of their clanking and grinding rises in fury, I call out in agony, "God save me! Save me my God, bring me home!"
But the chains are drawn tighter and tighter, each pull tearing into me more intensely than that which precedes it.
My antagonists smile ferociously and knowingly as each holds unrelentingly upon the reins of metal which bind me.
One by one, the antagonists pull viciously on the chains, contributing their own doses of pain and torment.
And suddenly the chains are pulled simultaneously and I feel my heart collapsing in on itself.
I hear the shrieking, burning, grating sound of metal cutting metal.
"Oh God!" I cry out. "Where does this nightmare end and reality begin? How long must I suppress the churning and grinding of the chains I feel within me?"
But I know there will be no peace for me. For I remain certain the antagonists will yank a second time on the reins and send me flying in anguish calling out for God.

Lisa Melton

Eternity

Eternity is that what love is,
As the sun rises and the dew parts from the grass,
The day anew, I can't help but think
Eternity, is that what love is?
Eternity is an endless flow of water in a river,
But love, a delicate thing, like a dove on a flight,
Or a nightingale's feather,
As endless as the sky, love is a storm,
On a stormy night a dove has no flight,
As rare as a nightingales feather does that storm occur.
Without love is eternity.
Without love is like light peering into an empty room.
Now the sun is setting, an ending to the day, now it's night
the crickets are in their sweet cheep, but I can't help but wonder,
Eternity, is that what love is?
Another morning starts, as son many have before I've seen,
I peer out the window and find a rose,
Each petal delicate and brittle, love is brittle, love is strong,
Love is never wrong, never, as I peer out of the glass,
I look at the sun and I now know what love is. Do you?

B. J. Smith

Brother And Baseball

Brother's watching from the stands,
As the umpire yelled strike and threw up his hands.

Brother said, "If that's a strike the ump is blind,"
And proceeded to yell from behind.

The fans want the umpire's head to roll, fourth bad call,
They want to send him back to T-Ball

The umpire swung around as swift as a deer,
Pointed at brother and said, "You're out of here!"

Another fan shocked at this power crazed punk,
Said brother was right, "You're call stunk!"

Again this Hitler of an umpire did bark,
"Man you too, you're out of this park."

The coach walked over to ask about the fans,
The umpire so rudely from this game had banned.

He yelled at the coach like a hoarse lark,
"Out of this park or this game will not again start."

Three men left the field in order not to duel,
Because a temperamental umpire lost his cool.

Little brother talked to and fired up his mates
They won this game for coaches, fans and big brother who rates.

Peggy Curtis Capouano

Reflections

I saw you last night in a dream,
As you walked with the moon along by the sea.
Your hair was golden by the glistening light,
I was amazed at your beauty and your hazel eyes.
You walked as though not a care in the world,
for all those who remember you as a little girl.
The one who was so quiet, so content, and so free,
for everyone would ask, "for who is she"?
And as time passed you faded away,
Many remember that saddened day.
It's now long passed since you're been gone,
but your memory lasts and lingers on.
Now as the picture comes clearer in my dream,
I see a face, a face you see,
of that once little girl, that face is me.

Michelle J. Leaser

Serenity

Looking from my window
At the moon's reflection on the lake
And listening to the night sounds
To the songs that crickets make,

Or the golden rays of sunshine
Of early mornings dawn
And the sleepy peaceful innocence
Of a newborn fawn,

Our love has the same peace
And is as strong as can be
As far as it can reach inside you and me
This is God given love filled with serenity.

Mary Rose

In Exchange For My Heart

He made his move the moment we met
Attraction so strong, emotions are set
Can't show my excitement
Hard to get I must play
If I make this look easy
I'll look the same way

'Cause I know just how this story will end
Felling used and alone, disappointment sets in
So tonight I'll be writing a brand new book
He'll know I deserved more than a second look
Another notch on his belt is what I won't be
No more casual flings for the brand new me

I need to feel appreciated
Not torn apart
I won't accept promises
In exchange for my heart

Kristin Walker

I'll Hurt More

Don't look back when you head for the door
Because if you do It will only hurt more
Don't stop to explain, don't tell me why
If your going to leave just say good-bye
I love you, I'll miss you but I can make it alone
I want you, I need you, But, I will hold my own
because I can't tie you down you will be free
I can't make you love only me
So don't look back, I'll tell you again just
kiss me good-bye if this is the end

Renae Danielson

Love's Life Cycle

Winter: Buried beneath the cold, cold snow
Away from winter wind's chilly blow
Within the banked fire's glow
The sparks of love lay low, lay low.

Spring: Warmed by the soft southern winds
The snow banks crusty melt begins
Flames of love stirred from within
Spring forth slowly as smoke rings spin.

Summer: Love bursts forth in blossom's glory
Thrusts aside its blanket hoary
Shouts to all its old, old story
I love you, I love you, I love you - surely.

Fall: Time moves on with love in tow
Love grows warmer in summer sun's glow
It reaches its peak in a colorful tableau
Then starts to fade like fall leaves, slow.

Winter: Life takes its toll, love drifts down
To form a carpet of gold and brown
To rest and sleep against earth's ground
To await renewal of love's next round.

H. Johnson Roberts

Love At 80 Years

When I was young, I never even dreamed of a love like this.
Back then, it seemed, every love story ended with a wedding
vow, and was never extended. But I know now,
That connubial bliss is strengthened, enhanced,
By shared tribulations, as well as romance.
And now that we're old, who would ever have thought
I'd still love you like this?
Besides, I like you a lot!

Louise Price Davenport

My Fantasy

I fantasize walking beside our Lord-
Barefoot, up and down the hills....
Oh, that would-be my reward...
Down dusty roads, through tiny rills.
His voice like a steady rain-
Softly marked as echoes of muted thunder,
Like you want to hear again and again.
Your spirit's awed into complete wonder.
Suddenly-the Lord has disappeared- gone!
Alone! I'm frightened- what'll I do?
Dry throated, I try a song. Words seem to die.
Seems I hear the master speak: In revue-

Ramon Adkins

"Halloween"

On this night as the moon hangs low
barren trees stand in an eerie glow,
Leaves have fallen Autumn's carpet is laid
Pumpkins are carved decorations are made,
Candles are lit while the fog still lingers
chilling our bones all the way to our fingers.
Soon will come a knocking for I hear their feet,
with bags full of candy they call TRICK OR TREAT!
They're off in a hurry Halloween can't wait,
running house to house before it's too late.
And at the end of the evening
all our goblins tucked in,
I'll keep for a memory
each sugar coated grin.

Vicki Vilsmeyer

Untitled

Every time you are near me my heart
beat out your name. Your sweet gentle
voice is the sound that I hear every
night before I go to bed. Your passionate
kisses send me to ecstasy and the stroke
of your gentle hands carry me into heaven.
My dream is loving you for eternity
and having you by my side. Life is
nothing without you. You are my soul mate
and there could be no-one to replace you.
My joy is your joy, and my sorrow is
life without you, and to me there would be no life.

Rotha Haynes

Waves

The water rushes in
beating itself against the rocks.
When will this insanity end?
When the world itself ends.

The waves are created by
the push and pull of the water.
As the ripples in people's personalities
are caused by past and present experiences.

We are all affected by outside forces.
no matter what we do.
We must try to be like the waves
and take things as they come.

Paula Fenton

Mirror Upon Life

Arrive in the East
Beautiful as a new bloomed flower
Not knowing deceit lays upon the land
Fresh meat for the political animals to devour

Clouds wanderers of the vast sky's
looking upon with my jealous eyes
tears descent from unfulfilled wishes of being as
free as they
then the clouds just drift away

Moon sits upon its heavenly throne
Now angels come to people near and afar
the door to our world a distant shining star
they come in a dream and give a message from the
heavens, how we translate them is for they to decide

Someday we must beckon to the bells ringing call
so like the tides we rise we fall
when will I join the angels in their flight
when will I penetrate the golden abysses of night

Sean Kelly

The Beach

Who knows why God put forth this natural
beauty and splendor,
Was this meant as an admirable treat or
an item to be treasured?
The sand beneath your feet, the water
crashing against the rocks,
This is truly a marvelous and wonderful thing,
There's so much to do there and so much
to name,
I wish that I could live there forever.

Steven Cernak

A Grown-Up Christmas

All you little boys enjoy your Christmas while you can,
because a Christmas ain't the same when you've become a man.

When I was small I got swell stuff, a train, a drum, and blocks.
But now I'm older all I get is handkerchiefs and sox.

But every little now and then I get a big surprise,
when with my handkerchiefs and sox some kind friend gives me ties.

But then I guess I can't complain, because poor St. Nick tries,
and it's really not his fault the best I get is ties.

'Cause when you come to think of it, St. Nick that jolly elf
doesn't get much more than sox and handkerchiefs himself.

Of course I'm old enough to know who's really Santa Claus.
I know that jolly jovial face of Santa's is just Pa's.

And as I come to sum it up and think about it now
the gifts I get are pretty good, I need sox anyhow.

R. William West

Reflections

You told me just to let you go, that is was time to say goodbye
Because there was nothing left for you, and you told me not to cry

But instead I held on tighter, and in a selfish plea,
I prayed "Dear God don't take her now, don't take my mom from me"

But as I watched you struggle, and suffer more each day,
I felt such overwhelming guilt, I can't ask for you to stay

And God gave me strength that I can't explain,
A strength unlike no other
Because I turned to Him this time and prayed,
"Please come and take my mother"

And when He finally came for you, I sat down by your side,
I held your hand and from your face, I dried the tears I'd cried
I told you that I loved you, and how much you would be missed,
I held you in one last embrace and gave you one last kiss

I still think about you everyday, I still see you in my dreams
I still can't believe you're really gone,
And how unfair that it all seems

And I wished that I could see you, if only for a while
And God lets me see so much of you,
In my reflection when I smile

Leslie B. Schaper

Feelings

Family I know we fuss and fight
because we do it with all our might.
But there is a time to let the anger fade away
and there is a time to let it stay.
There's many times when it stays
and it will not go away.
I know you don't believe that I care
because my feelings I do not share.
Late at night I feel no fame
but dream of me on the wall of shame.
Early in the morning a black cat crosses my path
and in the distance I hear a strange laugh.
I look around and no one is there
and all I do is laugh and stare.
All my feelings are left bottled inside
and I feel sick like I'm on a roller coaster ride.
I close my eyes and look deep inside
to find my family right by my side.
I wrote this so you know I have an opened hand
And hope and pray you all understand.

Kelly Classen

The Day My Mother Passed Away

Today my family was sad
Because we had been acting bad.
My mother is gone with my Lord.
We felt he stabbed us with a sword.

Because I was wrong, I have sinned.
Her ashes blowing in the wind.
I guess I was put to the test.
I failed because I could not rest.

My mother is in heaven now.
My heart has been hit by a plow.
I will remember mother's smiles.
Her memories will stack in piles.

Dear God, please take care of my mom.
Like those who fought in Vietnam.
Now she is gone, and I still care
But in my heart I'm feeling bare.

Today she's gone but in my heart,
There's no time we will spend apart.
I always will remember her.
Why did you have to take her Sir?

Tonya Rohn

Ellen

The intense blue sky, mountains, valleys and patched fields stretch out before me in an uplifting expanse of peace and solitude.
Nature's pristine surroundings in perfect harmony create an inner serenity.
Yet here I sit bereaved, for she'll leave my intimate and caring world.
Tears will not subside; love will die, and the pain of love lost runs through my brain.
Soon to be toppled from life's pinnacle, and knowing it is not a dream.
Lines of reality are smudged into a world of pure emotion — reasoning ceases.
She cries in sorrow for me yet the words that will set me free are not decreed.
Love's more essential than life itself.
Death in life is a reality — yet only death could efface the immeasurable loss.
Instincts, memories, children and hope carry me forth knowing
life has changed and will never be the same.
A king's ransom for a simple - I love you.
Joy limitless, smiles endless, life's *raison d'etre* resurrected.
Yet the words will not come, and I'll weep for the morning
in my seasonless world.

Todd M. Tadkowski

"Come In Before The Nightfall"

Come in before the nightfall, child,
Before the darkness surrounds you,
Ere the nocturnal animals wake.
Come in before the nightfall.

Don't you know that the darkness that appears
Will leave you sad and grieving,
Feeling lost and alone?
Come in before the nightfall.

You may go out and play right now,
With your other friends,
But don't forget what I have said:
Come in before the nightfall.

Please child, do come early,
I fear that you will wait
For that last glimpse of light
That lingers before the nightfall.

For when you return, I'll be joyous
And all my fears forgotten.
Then together and safe, we will watch
The sunset before the night falls.

Tania A. Vikki

The Tin Man

Tick-toc-tick, talked the Tin Man of the time when the torture first began when tarnish-free tools did twist, to turn, to tear the Body's Meat, the stuff of his flesh undone. Scrupulous scalpels skulked his skin scrawling scurrilous little scars on what had been once a man, now gaunted and thinned; paled and worn by a life far beyond mend. On the wicked bench, lights were brilliant white, objects intruded from left to right faces masked danced silhouettes 'cross the ceiling amidst a room, painted in Babel and Clamour. Aware of his thoughts, he looked out to sight hypocrites hurrying about to help a Life that had yet been lived,
Virgin Bones did crackle, red fluid did spew.
'Till the scarlet brush of pandemonium dulled; leaving its stroke, a vast emptiness lulled His monitors soon found silence, his passage began; heart to air, more Dead than Dead my brother lay.
Where were the whores and prostitutes of destiny calling themselves, 'Surgeons of Society' such a vulgar mockery, this travesty to Pass Degrees for the pilferage of Humanity. O' my Matteo cries the cryless cry; desiccated tears, they all fall dry on his cheeks that merely lie his visage, parched and mummified.
For a Tin-Man now treads his walk with a tin heart to tick his toe while that tiresome tag-a-long, who trespassed my teens talk to me only in timeless memories.

Mark Robert Pannek

"Creation Of Life"

Creation of life, so beautiful in sight,
Beginning a childhood of dreams.

Blanket of warmth for the quiet sleep,
In tears of glittering streams.

No understanding, but soon to be, the child-
will begin to grow.

A maturing apple in the family tree,
From the first strand of hair, to the babies toes.

Troy B. Schuuring

Protect You Heart

My heart has been broken bad two times,
behind my wounded heart I now tend to hide.
With a new relationship I hold much fear,
because my eyes have seen too many tears.
A heart broken twice is quite enough,
because wounded hearts are not very tough.
My emotions have now been locked up tight,
hidden away from any human's sight.
For emotions that are locked inside your heart,
are guarded from people who tear them apart.
People who neglect to guard their emotions,
end up like blind fish lost in the ocean...

William J. Kuyawa

"Roses Blooming In The Snow"

When ever he first saw her standing there —
Behold her youth so soft and fair
Her enchantment stood elusively calling
Adorned in deep dark red, so rich and rare
Her voice made sounds of soft petals falling.
Born a tender bud, bursting into open bloom
Gently caressed in the early morning's dew
Swayed in the warm gentle winds of June
Her fragrance traveled across the open miles
Her beauty was so hard to hold and believe
Fading in the sunset, are her kiss, her touch, her smile
Awakening to the cool air of a chilled Autumn's eve
Her beauty is burned into his brain, whenever he may go
But, was it just a dream like roses blooming in the snow?

Rosanna Fisher-Prowant

"The Storm"

Along a narrow roadway
Beneath a shadowed tree
Lies the daylights remains of spectrum
On a cliff above the sea

The ocean stirs immensely
As the night creeps up the coast
An osprey flies above the waves
Stalking his unexpecting prey
He senses the storm and for his last meal
He tries to get the most

It will come and go as most storms do
Leaving some traces behind
Of fallen nests and broken branches
And shattered rays of sunshine

Laurie Purnell Smocovich

The Life Line

As I travel to the left
beneath but still beside.
A person waits for everyone
bringing joy and modest pride.
You are taken to a place
full of wander, joy, and magic grace.
We are taken up by one great hand,
we listen to one great command.
Our love, our life, what drives each on,
is prettier than a picture drawn.
It's almost done, my closing line,
life's much too short, it's much too fine.

Whitney Dees

Name Of The Game

Pride, Integrity, and Patriotism inherent from birth
Bequeathed to us by our forefathers who lived on this earth,
America the land of freedom and sought by all,
Is now perched precariously awaiting its fall;

The root of all evil, money no less
Responsible for leading us into this mess,
Our elected leaders full of corruption and greed,
Have surrendered to immorality and follows its lead;

To the honest and sincere certainly a shame
To those in office "THE NAME OF THE GAME",
No longer the style to get out and work,
It's how much of my duties can I possibly shirk;

No wonder today's youth displays apathy
When our leaders creed is "How much is in it for me",
Lord help those sinners who determine our fate,
Let's hope God can save them before it's too late;

To all loyal Americans "LET US STAND STRONG"
And help our leaders determine "WHAT'S RIGHT AND WHAT'S WRONG".

Victor C. Hicks

Landmarks Of Time

Lazy waves of a tired sea
Break forever in eternity
Time which heals all mortal wounds
Also blows the dust off ancient dunes.
And shifting sands on cliffs of lime
Are naught but seconds in the hands of Time.
Trees will grow up, and trees will fall down
Even after all civilizations are drowned
Beneath the weight of all the years
When at last the sounds fall upon no human ears.

Megan Covert

Sometimes/Devotion

Sometimes I wonder why you had to go away,
Beyond a land so distant,
that I sometimes know you'd say,
that you'd always treasure our unconditional love,

But life circumstances doesn't always fit
like the proverbial glove.

Sometimes I truly miss you,
more than you'd ever dreamt I could,
although, as destiny played its part,
I sensed you knew I would,
always love you deeply, more than words
can ever say,

Yet, still, sometimes I wonder,
why you had to go away.

Phyllis Carole Bruce

To Grandpa, With Love

He always rose before the dawn,
black coffee in hand, and he was gone.

Feed those chickens, milk those cows,
never ask why, only wonder how.

With God's help, his garden grew,
fed his young 'uns and neighbors too.

I loved him; he was my childhood world,
he even dubbed me his "Tater Girl".

The cancer took over, he never complained.
I never knew my hugs had caused him pain.

Memories are now all that I hold.
Grandpa, to me, you will never be old.

Melissa Beers

Racism

Racism,
black, red, white,
Africa, Mexico, England.
Who are you and what do you represent?
Me, what am I you ask,
African - American
Yes, I know some people do not like this,
yes, I know what my ancestors went through,
I refuse to be put into slavery,
I can still feel their pain,
The suffering that they went through,
Racism,
What are you?

Michaela Turner

The Game

The cards have all been dealt since birth.
But how they're played determines their worth.
Each shuffle brings new beginnings and ends;
Sometimes we find lovers, and sometimes friends.

Each and every second, with each passing day,
Lives change direction as cards come into play.
Our dreams can take us as high as the sky,
Or we can stand still and watch life pass by.

Living is like gambling for unknown treasure,
And the wins and losses are tough to measure.
So, ante up and place your bets,
And never look back with regrets.

Virginia Allen

Forever Real, As If Sane

A loving heart so full of pain, frightening reality never gains,
Bleeding truth as if like rain,
Loneliness remains in side a shattered window,
An empty cry, feeling death with a life,
Change in need, a twist in time.

Unanswered questions proven true.
Without the answer told to you, the truth will surface undenied,
Like a feeling deep inside, constant ripples in the tide.

No one to turn to when in need, dishonest people filled with greed,
I trust myself a soul to lead, protect the children as a seed,
It's time to fill our world with care,
Heal the damage of poisoned air.

Our world is full of black delight,
Make strong the children of the light,
A journey conquered by the sight comfort love as if it's night.
A soaring eagle plans his flight,
Break not you will or think you might
A rushing future, hate and spite

Chase not their madness or their buck
In the fight they self destruct.

Tina Louise Clark

One Special Star

Together; we were like the colors of the rainbow, our personalities blended just right. How different the world becomes, when viewed through misty eyes.

In the state of Love, I left the Castle-of-Happiness to view the Valley alone. In the heart of the City-of-Dreams, stands the star-laden tree of Wishes-Come-True.

From the world of fantasy to the world of reality; I moved to the Sunshine State. In the City of Inverness, I spend my free-time swimming in the pool of memories.
Its waters kept warm by the sun of promises and rays of hope.

When the moon is full, I visit the Graveyard-of-Love.
I am a Lady with Willpower, determined to retrieve my heart from him.
To shatter, irrevocably, the seal we placed upon the vow we made.

No more swimming in the pool of memories; I'll pull its plug and throw it far into infinity. I'll watch with impish glee as each memory struggles to remain; Every last one will be gone forever more!!

It will no longer matter that, somewhere far away, there's another world and in that world; a City where a star-laden tree still hold One-Special-Star. A star that the Sea-of-Tears; Sands-of-Time, have erased our names from upon it.

And I...I shall place my heart under lock and key. Such a remarkable recovery should be where all the world can see, in a museum of oddities; a place Mr. Ripley holds very dear..."Believe it or not!"..

Linda Lukehart

Two Birds

I wondered, as I gazed into the bright
blue sky, if birds ever fall in love. If I
was a bird I'd fly far away from
from all of this pain and anger.
In a far off place I'd meet you
and together we'd fly, side by side, never
looking each other's way but knowing
we'd never leave each other's side. As I
began to drift back into my own world,
you were there. I took your outstretched hand
and we both spread our wings and flew,
never looking back or at each other.
Then everybody and everything disappeared,
but we knew we had each other
and that was all we needed.

Marlene Tilton

Love Forever

'Forever love', inscribed on tree,
Bold letters carved painstakenly,
By one who's feelings touched the highest note
Of heart felt symphony.

The aspen shared the secret of a tender love,
And swayed the love song whispers from its boughs,
Then broadcast from its bark
That all might see,
The magic of a lovers vows.

Forever love, not just today,
Though ravages imposed by time,
Corrode and warp away,
The etchings on the whittled bark,
Wiped free from sight.

Yet, time does not erase the mark.
A passion love placed on the heart.
'Forever love' marks permanently.

How precious life and love can be...
For love inscribed deep in the heart,
Will last eternally.

Toma Waldbeiser

You Can Do It!

Do you feel fettered, enslaved and
bound?
And you long to be joyous and free;
Do you think of yourself as a worm of
the dust,
Living in fear, vain regrets and distrust?
O have courage dear heart, there's good
news for you!
You can lose those chains that bind,
Fear not those who would scorn and the
scoffers too;
They'll do all in their power to
discourage you;
Have courage, dear heart, to make that
new start
And the door will open for you.

Marie Gray

The Night Walker's Kiss

Feeling something, I cannot explain, the night is black and cold.
Breeze gently tosses my hair, as I look upon the land and stare.
Looking up to endless skies, stars shine bright and bold.
Power sting in the wind, the electricity pulsates through the air.

Walking down the stone covered path to the river,
I watch the trees, across the bank, light up with fire flies.
Feeling the magic covering me, it makes me shiver.
Sudden turning, I stare into a pair of ghostly black eyes.

Unable to move, to breathe, heart pounding, I gasp for air.
Chest tightens, I start to speak, my voice catches in my throat.
I cannot look away, nor can I break his piercing-icy stare.
I began to shake. Slowly, calmly, he removes his coat.

Draping the coat about me, pulls me close to him, I felt everything.
My eyes shut tightly, in fear, for a moment his lips touch mine.
I open my eyes, he is gone, I cannot find him. Is it a dream?
I look up to the heavens, for anything, a clue, evidence, or a sign.

As my weak knees carry me back up the misty solemn trail,
Am I crazy, I must have been in a trance, or I was dreaming,
The night is so cold, I am warm, yet I feel so pale.
Touching my arms, I feel his coat, no I was not dreaming!

Natalie Canary

Sanguine Moments Of Dawn

Scarlet suns in silent peace shatter into gold
Bringing forth a day of light seconds more to hold
A piece of blue shades a cloud crystals flash our hair
Sudden hours come to life time erupts a flair
Till it's gone...
Sanguine moments of dawn
Here we are in the eyes of dusk just above the sea
Stars of midnight move along somehow magically
Passive swans of newborn grace climb the hidden winds
Darkened colors turning space the birth of wonder begins
Till it's gone...
Sanguine moments dawn
Breathing love like Sunday rain never touching land
A state of bliss a granted kiss are shells in neptune's hand
Until the black has come again with twinkled specks of white
A twilight place of mystery that God has named the night
Till it's gone...
Sanguine moments of dawn...

Reno West

Always There

Learning a new sense of freedom,
Bringing it out from my innerself,
Letting God create a new spirit within me
Humbling my heart, setting my soul free,
Giving in to the will of God,
Knowing he knows what's best for me.
Teaching me to see past all understanding
Learning more than I thought I could
About his love,
Righteous and pure
Unconditional and sure,
About myself once again,
Knowing he is my trusted friend.

Finding a new path to take,
Through all my mistakes,
He is always there.

Lisa Marie Hock

Stars

The stars in the night shine ever so bright,
bringing light to make things right. Glittering in
the heaven above all, twinkling and sparkling in awe.

The white light that falls to earth causes me
to think of their births. Not knowing where they
are from or what they shall become.

The first star of the night comes out with
such might. I look upon it with delight knowing
that it is a special night.

Then I look upon another evening star and
I wonder where it shall fall. As it shoots
through the sky I look towards where it might lie.

I close my eyes in bliss remembering to make
a wish. Hoping that my dream to be will
be able to come to me.

Stephanie Jackson

Black

Black is what keeps me awake at night
Black is what keeps me ready for a fight
Black is the color of fear in my eyes
Black is the color of my tears when I cry
Black is the hostility in my might
Black is always in my sight.

Misty K. Sargeant

Untitled

The deceit of a loyal friend,
Brings forth revenge 'till no end.
Pain and anguish stand in my way,
For my friend betrayed me,
I can't forgive today.
Sunk in my sorrow,
Engulfed in rage,
Madness has abducted me; a beast out of its cage.
Today brings forth feelings of hate,
Deceit was wrong; an enormous mistake,
Trust I seek and I find in my friend,
Trust demolished; not able to mend.
An emptiness inside me,
A hole was left behind,
The friendship I gave; shriveled up in my mind.
For my friend betrayed me,
But now, no more,
For my friend is no longer with us,
Revenge took its score.

Tara Kolinsky

Reflections In An Autumn Leaf

Have you ever seen the reflections in an autumn leaf,
bronzed at the end of a life all too brief?
Such beauty from its past when first it did grow,
awakened to life at the end of snow.
The green bud sprang forth, to take hold and live,
passive and indifferent to the pleasure it would give.
Drawing nourishment from the roots
to a hundred feet in the air,
to give off a fragrance, delicate and fair.
Facing the sun from morning to night,
or drinking in the rain with an amused delight.
To dance on the wind and laugh at the squirrel,
glad to be part of nature's wonderful world!
To give shade to others from its part of the tree,
its soft verdant hue to please you and me.
The autumn brings scarlet, red, yellow, or gold,
to mantle its shoulders and to honor the old.
Magnificent colors, what pleasure they give;
reflecting the good and full life it has lived.

Richard Anderson Love

Thank You

It's almost time for me to go,
but before I do, I want you to know
that sometimes the only thing that kept me going,
was the strength that you kept on showing.
Through the hard times, the fear, and all the tears,
I was content just knowing you were near.
You never let me down,
and you always stood your ground.
You have taught me a lot about being strong
trying to do right, and avoiding the wrong.
It must have been tough not to just give up,
but you had finally been through enough.
I look up to you for all you've been through
I know now you were scared, but then I had no clue.
I know you sacrificed a lot for me,
and it's time that I let you see
just how much you've done for me.
I want you to know that I will always love you
and I'm taking this chance to say "Thank you!"

LezLee Janelle Agee

Anne Boleyn

Of Death I have been shown and told again and yet again,
But do I listen? Nay, not I,
I whose stubborn independence brought about the sorrow of my years,
Left me helpless,
All my hopes and wishes turned to tears,
For in my heart I know my time has come,
Time to face the enemy; Death!
The word portrays a towering shadow,
Lurking around every corner,
Watching and waiting until I am alone at last.
So be it! Go! Leave, me alone with the Devil,
For I know my destiny now.
Oh, how the hatred, love, jealousy and anger have built in me!
Oh, how the emotions which I mocked others for have suddenly
turned upon me
And seen me crying at the mercy of fear!
I meet him now with still a hint of pride,
And mask my terror with braveness,
For what is said will be, will be,
And only Death knows why.

Lucinda Griffin

Dawes And Me

I'm Paul Revier as you see, I'm sure you have heard of me.
But do you know my friend? He is William Dawes.

I'm sure you'll ask, "William Dawes who is he?"
Well he is the one that rode with me,
We rode to tell the people
The British are a coming.

We met the enemy,
I got captured and wasn't free
only he got away, and lived to say
The British are a coming.

Only he rang out, only he did shout
The British are a coming.

Now who is William Dawes?
He's the one who told the people
The British are a coming.

It's not me, it's really he
Don't you see it's William Dawes.
Now people won't you pause.
Now he rang out with a mighty shout
THE BRITISH ARE A COMING!

Timothy M. Borrego

The Book

My brand new computer was a wonderful sight
But for goodness sakes - it just wouldn't work right
I checked out the socket - the machine was plugged in
So then I sat down to try it again.

When all of a sudden what did I see
A computer manual just staring at me
So I said to myself "Why not open the book"
It really won't hurt if you take just one look.

So I picked up the manual and started to read
The instructions were there - I just had to heed
So I read for a while - then went back to work
And the computer performed - I just had to smirk!
For not taking the time to read the directions
I sure was one who needed correction.

Margaret Kay Lilly

Vietnam

Vietnam was not just a word, but a place
But, for many people, they just turned their face
Young men, both black and white
Were doing, what they were told, was right
They all had guts, but got no glory
Because nobody, wanted to hear their story
Moms and Dads prayed for their sons
And hoped that theirs, would not be the one
You could hear the noise, from the choppers overhead
This meant, they brought the wounded, and the dead
Doctors and nurses, helped saved their lives
So, they could go home, to their friends and wives
Protesters cussed and called them names
Some would die, others come home lame
Over the years, stress and emotion held within
Proved too much for some, and did them in
So remember these brave lads of war
So we never, have to fight no more
Over twenty years, has passed
But their names on the wall, will forever last

Michael K. Bauer

Heidi

Loved so well
But here so briefly.
No reason or rhyme
For this season and time.

Life was green with promise,
But the leaves fell, the sky burned black.
Unfeeling cold—death's shroud.
Tears rained, nature wept.

Unthinking, unfeeling, automaton.
Anxiety, depression, panic, desperation.
Clouds pressing down, noises grating.
Nighttime flight to the light, sleepless exhaustion.

Holiday pain thresholds,
Yearly milestones awaken you again.
Peace at last,
Until I think of you.

I cope,
But I do not forget.

Linda K. Lilienthal

My Mountain

Uncle would visit and say "That mountain is North,"
But I knew better.
Gold diggers said "Pikes Peak or Bust,"
And they were going West.

Comanches hunted beside it;
Utes lived on its slopes;
Zebulon Pike named it.
Kathryn Lee Bates looked down on the "amber waves of grain"
And knew America was beautiful.
Will Rogers never met a mountain he didn't like;
Old Louie and the Unser nephews started racing up those hairpin curves;
And we always stayed up to watch the fireworks exploding from the Summit on New Year's Eve.

All my days of growing,
Each morning it brought me up,
At night it took the sun down.
And it stood and watched me,
Always there - keeping my West in place.

Margaret McFadden

Halloween

Halloween is the scary day of the year
but I personally do not fear.
Trick or treaters wear their costumes,
but rarely get some prunes.
Treaters have sweet tooth I bet
from all the candy they get.
Halloween can be spooky, and the Addams
family is cooky.
When vampires eat food blood is what they include.
Vampires are certainly Halloween creatures.
They are part of many sci-fi features.
Elvira is scary in a way,
but she shoots commercial in a beer display.
Yes, it's that time of the year again where kids
get to dress up like their favorite people.
And kids get as much as they please.
They're lucky they don't have to pay fees.
Halloween is fun and to houses kids run.

Marvin Ryan B. Bairan

In Your Life Again

It sure has been a long time,
But I still count the days slowly passing by.

I've long forgotten why, you meant this much to me.
Could it be, I'm still in love with you.

Many nights I spend just thinking,
About the love you tried to find.

And I cannot stop believing,
It was right here all the time.

And if it was here all along, then what went wrong.
Why did you have to go.

Now only you can tell me.
I really need to know.

So if ever you discover,
When you take a look behind.

That everything you hoped for,
Like the love you tried to find.

Was right here all along, it won't be wrong,
To come back home again.

You know I'll be here waiting, not knowing if or when.
Your search for love may find me, in your life again.

Skip M. Plonka

A Man Called Freedom

Freedom is something we all seem to want.
But it's also something we can't seem to handle.
When we get it we find ourselves caught in another scandal.
When I was young I thought freedom was all I needed,
by any means necessary I was going to achieve it.
I said to myself, when I become a man, I'll make my own decision.
Little did I know drugs would put me in a mental prison.
A prisoner to my own addiction suffering all kinds of afflictions.
But now I'm free of that drug called crack and I say to myself.
there is no looking back.
As I'm doing this time I lay on my rack...
And I'm asking God when will I meet him,
that very elusive man called freedom.

Orlando Creswell

"L"

These hands have held gold, diamonds and pearls,
But I've never felt like a wealthy man.
These hands have held ice and fire,
But I've never burned or grown cold.
These hands have held the sands of time, the waters that
were Poseidon's and the winds that were Gaoh's,
But I have never felt myself invincible or almighty.
These hands have held life and death, glory and defeat,
But I never shook in fear or reveled in victory.

But now you see,
I have been the richest Pharaoh in all of Egypt,
I have froze to death and burned back to life,
The sands of time have slipped through my hands as
Poseidon laughs and Gaoh howls at me.
I have been scared of holding on and terrified of ever letting go,
For in my trembling hands, she rests her beautiful delicate face,
The most precious and breathtaking treasure that these hands
have held
or will ever hold.

Patrick Clemens

Life

Eyes that cannot see,
but know that you are there.
Arms that cannot touch you,
but move continuously around.
Legs that long to walk,
but cannot support the weight.
The life inside that you nurture now,
will one day understand that gift you gave.

Pamela K. Flores

The Pearl Divers

Rarely does the oyster produce a natural pearl
But knowing that if we force the issue
The seed may slip away
And leave us empty-handed
Once again we take the plunge
In search of the real thing

Once again we dive into the sea of love
Where we've been trounced before
By the enemies of happily-ever-after

Once again we try
To change our luck
Or learn to swim with the tide.

Rosalie Calabrese

Ghosts

People believe that they are not real
But listen when the house is cold and still.
The creaking of that attic floor,
and the sound of the banging doors.
Who says Ghosts are not real?

The moaning and groaning on the stairs,
The scuffling of the feet across the floor.
The eyes that follow you in the night,
The silent breathing of the intruders delight,
Who says Ghosts are not real?

Mary Lou Plotts

"The Forgotten Ones"

You hear their cries in the night;
but no once will come.

They ache to be held, and loved;
but no one wants them.

No one cares about the forgotten ones;
they are left to die.

They sit in a corner, because they are scared;
but no one will comfort them.

They cry for someone to help them;
but no one will answer.

For they are the forgotten ones.

Kathryn Johnston

Forgiveness

Forgiveness is Divine,
But Pain of Sorrow of
Decision is hard to overcome!

Forgiveness is Divine,
But possible humiliation, questions
that he can't answer are hard to pass by!

Forgiveness is Divine,
And you should always forgive
And never forget that
Love is a variable!

Forgiveness is Divine.
He never wanted
To Hurt or Sorrow you.
He still loves you.

Forgiveness is Divine.
Give him a chance, he tries to
see the best, and will do his best.

If you cannot forgive, remember
he still is your friend, and he will ALWAYS
Have a place in his heart for YOU!!

Megan J Stillwell

A Friend With A Pen

I know a woman, who has been hurt many times before.
But she is strong, and goes through life searching for something more.

Tho not a virgin she has an innocence about her that's gentle almost
pure.
For her broken heart, I wish I had a cure.

When I am feeling down, angry, hurt, or sad.
She sends me cards and letters, to tell me things ain't so bad.

I hope to one day meet her, this woman so loving, and kind.
But for now it's only through letters we speak, as I am doing time.

Well I must be off, it's time to write her once again.
I think every lonely heart, needs a friend with a pen.

Michael Smith

Together

I wake to hear your heart deep inside my soul
but then it's just a dream and I'm the only one
who knows. When I look into your eye's I'll tell
you what I see, you and me together always' faithfully.
I can't live without you. I've told you that before,
I want' you in my world your the one that I adore. I
will truly love you always and forever it's destiny
you know the two of us together. Is it just a dream
or is it paradise having you beside me feels so out of
sight. I want to promise you we'll always be together
all you have to promise is that you'll stay forever.

Mary Ellen Thistlewood

"The Cry Of Loneliness"

I stepped outside today, like every other day.
But something in the air cried out to me.
The gentle breeze clasped its unseen arms around me.
There's something so frightening in the breeze, what could it be?

Barefoot each step I take, echoed in the late afternoon.
For the lawn full of dead and dying leaves before me,
Like a carpet had been laid,
Cried out for life, but knew they could not be saved.

Once the meadow's tall green grass being swayed in the wind,
Now fallen, brown, and lifeless, waits for winters call again.
And as I stand in the mist of Autumn I wonder, "Where are you?"
As I walk away the breeze caresses me once more.

With each step I take the leaves cry out for life.
The trees whisper, and the meadows lay still.
I hear the cry of Autumn's Loneliness, and with it a sudden chill.
For without you in my life, my life's like Autumn too.

I walk away with the breeze, and the afternoon shadows,
And still I wonder, "Where are you?"
Orange, red, yellow, and gold,
Life fades like Autumn's colors, so I've been told.

Rosanne Roehrick

"My Winter Dreamland"

My opening into the world is foggy with a coating of frost
but still I peer out to My Winter Dreamland.
The shield that is spread out over the land is beautifully
done it must have been done so dreamful it creates an
atmosphere for one to dream.
The birds are singing a song of "Sweet Winter Dreams"; it
creates a pleasant feeling for all to embellish in.
The hollyberries add a touch of color to the winter season.
The little tots are spreading their laughter and joy around
the area for all to be entertained by.
What a dreamland to have in wintertime —
White to take away the blues.
Song to create a feeling of harmony.
Color to bring a bit of hope.
Laughter and joy of children to bring a sense of happiness.
It takes away the dreariness of winter ever so cleverly.

Mari S. Wilpiszewski

Untitled

Eyes so blue and beautiful at first glance.
But the coldness seeps into the soul when looking deeper
to find death and misunderstanding.
Abused so young, never grasped the idea that the little boy
was the victim, not the one at fault.
Colored the world in frightful tones of black that never let
the little boy grow up.
Trying to find comfort in the arms of those who did not care
until one person broke through the hardened shell.
The shell destroyed, how could anyone love you knowing the truth?
Scared you ran and destroyed the one thing you secretly
craved above all else.
Disappearing, was happiness to be found?
Holidays brought thoughts of misery and all that was lost,
so no one could smile.
Taking pieces from everyone you met to make a whole new child
that lives and breathes with no knowledge of your soul.
Wanting to die, terrified to live, you worked to destroy
those parts that were not pure.
We pray for you so that one day you'll be able to see the sun.

Sara Horwath

Untitled

Oops, she made a mistake today.
But, then she's made them along the way.
So, once again she stops to pray.
Dear God reach out to me and hold me close
For this is when I need you most.
And now her load seems very light
For now she has Gods love in sight.

Patricia A. O'Malley

Children

Children are small - and they may be young:
But they are still people and their song is still sung.

So they may look at the grass and say "why is it green?"
Or they may look in the sky and see bright moonbeams.

Or look up in a tree and see branches of life:
They wee what it might be like to be a husband or wife.

Their minds travel far - high up in the sky:
They plan out each day - each day until they die.

So they may be young and don't really understand;
But they could make a difference in this place we call our land.

Kristi Hammel

Too Late

You can't hurt me, I have walls surrounding my heart.
But when you come around, they fall apart.
You know you rule me; my thoughts, my visions, my life.
You have me on a leash that I'd never betray.
You had the key to my heart, that lightened up the dark.
It was for you I rose everyday.
You had my life in the palm of your hands.
But, no, you had to go look for others.
Now, you know, your lesson is learned.
It's too late; my heart is burned.
And this time I've learned.

Renae A. Wood

Loneliness

Covers can fold, covers can keep you warm
But, when you need someone to talk to you're all alone.

Needing someone to say - "I love you" in a special way.
For that's one thing covers can not say.

You look upon it as a substitute,
Wishing you were a classy prostitute.
To have someone hold you all times of the night.

Not care what cruel game the "JOHN" wants to play.
You pretend he loves you in a special way.

But, deep in your heart you know it isn't true.
So, you lie to yourself time and time again that your
Cameo is yet to come.

For a long journey filled with loneliness has just begun...

Valentina D. Barnes

Secrets And Memories

With all secrets, there's painful memories.
But with all memories, there's thoughtful
secrets - that I will cherish forever.

Ralph Peterson

Dear God

My Great Grandmother is alive
But yet in a way she's actually dead.

Her life consists of tubes, machines, and a bed.
Day after day and night after night, the only thought
That runs through her mind is "Why can't I die?"

I could give her many different reasons, but they'd all be a lie.
I myself, don't know why.

Each day is a nightmare for her.
She has nothing left to live for.
A lot of the time she's not sure where she's at or
Even if I'm who I am.

So God, please give my dear grandmother what she wants;
To be at peace with no more pain.

Sarah J. Weaver

To All Those Struggling Out There...

Your mom always said that life is tough,
But you never imagined it was all that rough,
Next thing you know your 14 years old,
You think your grown, all-that, and bold.
Now here you are with 9 months bound,
Having no idea where money is found.
You've been sentenced with 18 years or maybe more,
Others are saying "Oh! She's just a whore!",
You are the one with problems to bare,
There is no one else who wants to share.
All alone you sit and cry,
All you want to do is die.
How can you support a child?
She'll probably be a hellion and grow up wild,
Your child is the one that's gonna need you,
You can't just say "Hey I'm through!",
Your not gonna quit, give every little bit,
Hold her tight, with all your might,
You have to try and try and try, listen can't you hear her cry.
DON'T GIVE UP YOUR GONNA TRY!!

Tracey Sheetz

Dirge For Summer

When lacy oaks turn brown and skies turn grey,
butterflies give their two weeks' notice. I missed
the last mushroom hunt — something summer had to say
about life. Is it a secret ... a mystery ... the gist?
Autumn can't begin to know how a warm breeze
can stir the soul and sing the sweetest melody.
But at what other time and space could these
colors unite and paint a fire in a tree?
It's dark and cold as night falls without sound.
Soon the sun will rise, busy with fears to dispel;
cautiously glancing over rooftops. Igniting. Profound.
Are the answers to life's riddles difficult to foretell?
I sense the absence of those sultry days, pale blue skies.
Sighs for Autumn: summer in a bleak disguise.

Mary Jo McIntire

What Was Once

What was once an endless road has now come to an end. The time spent, the memories made, with friends never to be forgotten. The memories made will always live forever as long as they remain in our hearts. Now we take this final step, the step that takes us from the world we once knew, and into a world much different than the one we grew up in. What was once an endless road isn't the end after all, it's the beginning; the beginning of our adulthood.

Valerie R. Green

A Woman In Waiting

A woman in waiting is something to treasure
By far her patience you cannot measure

She waits for her man in shining armour
Even though their living together is a dishonor

Her heart pounds for him, her love is true
Hoping that he won't walk out on what they
Have and leave her blue

Leaving together can be such joy
Hoping he doesn't toss her aside like a toy

A woman in waiting is full of hopes and prayer's
Hoping that her virtue will not be in despair

A woman in waiting, oh the agony and pain,
When her man walk's out and say's,
Oh by the way, I found another dame....

Theresa A. Wilson

I Never Thought

I never thought that it would be you
Calling to me with none else to turn to.
Not knowing the answers, but listening the same,
Hoping that somehow I'd ease your pain.

I never thought I could take it away,
But yet made a promise that I surely would pray.
It's always when we're at the end of our rope-
Through supplications to heaven we can find hope.

I never thought we'd lean on each other -
And find that friend "closer than a brother".
The one that's beside you through thick and thin,
Cries when you lose and laughs when you win.

I never thought it would take us this long
To finally realize with whom we belonged.
And as always, not in the storybook way,
We lose what we could have had yesterday.

I never thought we'd want the past back,
Then young and proud, from wisdom we lacked.
Experience shows us what we could have caught
If we'd only known then, but we never thought.

Lisa Shoemaker

Big Bang (As Explained To My 8yr Old Grandson)

All you can see and even more,
Came from a speck, a spot, a spore.
When it exploded, it became atoms
Blasted from this primal flame.
They formed the stars, the sun, the earth of course,
The still expanding universe.
Combined, some came to life and grew
Into a tree, a dog, and you.
Now here is something really odd
That tiny speck was really God
But, James, as I look at the night sky,
It isn't how it's only why
You look to prospects yet unknown,
I slip toward nothing - both alone.

Robert G. Schumm

Hold On

When the world seems dark and you
can't find your way, "hold on"

When tears wet your pillow and you
spend sleepless nights, "hold on"

When your friends let you down and
you feel all alone, "hold on"

When you give and don't receive and
you feel let down, "hold on"

When you feel like a failure and trouble
seems to find you, "hold on"

When you feel that you can't make
it and you feel like giving up, "hold on"

Stand still, time will heal, "hold on"

Shirlene Bryant

"Love"

Love's a blessing from above,
Carried down from heaven on the wings of a dove;
So like a child's favorite toy on a shelf,
Love's no good inside oneself.
It's something one feels, instead of hears,
Like a wee one's smile or one's tears.
God showed us what love can do,
So then shouldn't we show it to?
Instead of keeping it bound,
Give it to the people around;
Be like a child who shares his things,
And see what true love can bring.
What a happier world this would be,
For people like you and me!

Martha Sue Downs

Viva Las Vegas!

Show girls in glittering gowns
Cars and tourists pack the bustling strip.
Hotels and casinos,
   Which will you pick?
People come and people go,
Yet they gamble their money away.
If the casinos don't get it,
   The pickpockets will.
At night the people see the neon lights.
And the cowboy greets everyone with a wave
As he smiles a
   Neon smile to those below.
A pirate ship is sinking in the desert sand.
Save she crew if you can.
Did you see the Sphinx
   And the MGM so Grand?
People come and people go,
Yet the memories last forever
Where a lone volcano explodes
   And white tigers vanish into the night.

Melanie R. Boone

Progress

The impure haze painting a bleak impressionist mural
concealing the refinery from the depths of the murky sea
the low crimson moon's balmy radiance diverging, diffusing its aura
throwing shadows on this dichotomy of nature and anomaly
forlorn baying of forgotten malnutritioned hounds
resonating sluggishly through the rusting carcass of industry
and the grey, unctuous mist turns to rain
washing, wafting down in torrents earthbound

Michael Mackenzie

Me, And My Shadows

Shadow within a shadow
Caught within a shadow.
Nothing best darkness surrounds me
Caught in the darkness, as I walk along.
And out of the darkness I walk.
The high steps near and for on the other side.
What danger there was, I know cause I've been there before.
Nothing but attack dogs. Slowly and slowly walking
backwards and running down the hill to the bottom.
A shadow within a shadow
Caught within a shadow
A shadow on each side of me.
One in front, one in back
My own shadows, I walk here and there, go places
then the shadows disappears then come back in
different parts of the City.
Then their back with me again,
Me, and my shadows.

Theresa Ann Snider

To The Reaper

The Countryside you travel round,
causing pain with gruesome sound.
My time will come, please go away,
upon this earth I want to stay.

I'll cheat you once, I'll cheat you twice,
you give to me such sad advice.
Claim your dead on other heads,
my life to you hangs on a thread.

In flowing gown and hood of black,
sickle in hand you've got the knack.
The souls in which you try and reap,
you lull them in and endless sleep.

Go away old friend I know you well,
with scent of death of which you smell.
Go away old friend you've missed your mark,
I've known your game right from the start.

My life's worth living, can't you see,
go away I tell you, let me be.
Come again one gloomy day,
perhaps by then I'll want to play.

E.D.S.

Child Of Mine

Eyes that are searching - searching for a reason
Chest heaving, struggling for every breath.
Skin so pale, so cold, so near death
Hold on, Child of Mine
Don't let go.

Doctors, nurses, long, cold corridors
Child of Mine, do you see my reflection in the glass
Windows that separates us?
Do you see the tears rolling down my cheeks from
All the pain I feel for you?

My son, my son - you will live. You will survive,
For there are many years ahead, Child of Mine.
At last there is a response - there is a sign
That the life I brought forth *is* the child of mine.

Mike R. Markoff

A Cry Unspoken

Abandonment, Abuse, Tears...
Children crying and howling for their parents to stop,
and nothing, nothing does the cop,
Troubles, Problems, Fears...
A baby trapped in a corner being beaten with a mop,
wondering, wondering, wondering when will it stop,
Drugs, Drinks, Beers...
Children crying please, please, please stop,
wondering maybe there's a cop,
Days, Months, Years...
A child growing up thinking the pain will never, ever stop,
this child thinking I will never succeed to the top,
Tears, Beers, Fears...
And finally, finally there shows up the cop,
and no more mop, and no more wondering
when the pain will stop.

Stephanie Aurora Santini

Memories

Within these walls and rooms and hall
Children laughter echoes still
Footsteps running through it all
I remember now, and always will

Even though my kids are gone, their lives here linger on
Dogs and cats and old straw hats, fishing nets and baseball bats

I have pictures as they all grew up, from day one to their thirty's
Dressed in Jammies with a sipping cup, and making mud pies
and so dirty

Graduations, proms and their first dates
Parties, friends and birthday cakes
Xmas's and all their gifts
And showing how much they could lift

Some things they loved and their new cars
My girls who looked like movie stars
In gowns and pageants they made me proud
Or in sloppy clothes with colors loud

Ones they grew to love who loved them too
My grandkids, who are all to few
Dinners when they all were home
Yes their still here even though their gone

Nancy Taylor Robertson

"Memories Of Hope"

As the gas filled the room,
children's heart filled with gloom.
They did not know what was going on.
They did not know their parents were dead and gone.
Their clothes were old and torn, just like everything they had worn.
Their faces looked down, and they wore a sad frown.
They lived inside a camp
where hope burned like a small lamp.
The walls were all cold showing
absolutely no bold.
At night when they were all
alone, the children knew they
were surely not at home.
The bodies were stacked ever
so high, children learning Hitler
was so cruel and sly.
But, all the children did was
suffer and mope, not knowing if
there would ever be hope.
"Memories of the holocaust"

Tanja Gullestrup

Involuntary Decadence

We laugh like wind among
chips of crystal, until it
stole our identity away.

We sit alone in a world full of
evils and beyond the reach of decay.

Just bury me softly in a grave,
where I will stand forsaken.
I will speak no more of my feeling to end today.

Our hopes and dreams
have boiled in our brains,
only to understand reality,
and to be betrayed.

All I want to do is play,
but I get on my knees
for it is time to pray.

Gaily colored masks can hide the past,
but never the feelings within.

The pain moves on and swells in my heart.
The agony starts all over again,
will it ever end??.....

Shannon Beth Richardson

Merry Christmas

It's that time of year when memory recalls the
Christmas days of yesteryear by one and by all
Of frosted windowpanes and cold winter morns
Of turkeys baking and pastries galore
The awareness "It's Christmas" when eyes see the dawn
An old fashion tree and real snow on the lawn
Shirley Temple dolls and Mickey Mouse watches
Riding shiny new bicycles in floppy galoshes
Visiting dear friends after big family dinners
Building the block's first snowman as the cold grew grimmer
Happily singing carols at fireside hearth
Thinking you were the luckiest kid on earth
Climbing the stairs as Christmas day ends
Tucked under the quilts, what a day it had been
So for all of our children and grand kids if any
Look deep in your heart and bestow memories aplenty
For someday they too will smile and remember
The magic you gave them on the 25th of December

P. J. Vitruk

Choke On This

I would swim the oily depths of the ocean black,
Climb the highest mountain of chemical waste;
Cut my way through the receding forest
To get your love, my dear. . .
I need your Love, my dear

I'm not angry with you
But I'll be happy when you're dead
You are a curse upon my soul
My water and my bread

No, I am not crying
Smoke is in my eyes
Life cannot be cost effective
Until another dies

Salt is in my lungs
I've been breathing peanuts
Rain is burning up my skin
With Iif's and And's and But's.

Nick Harris

I Live

Dedicated to Moses Ignasius Kingston
This dry and arid land
cold and odorous
is moistened by my spirit

The Crouched silhouette
took aim at my dream
stamped upon my shadow
and punctured the Barren
land upon which my shadow lay

Indeed the mind is bridled
by the master it serves...
Inevitably my spirit lives
it lives within and beyond
The confines of these boundaries

For while you can puncture the barren Land
you cannot Quell my Indomitable spirit
or Quench my love for life

Noel Moses

Midwest Seasons

Do you like the springtime when all the trees
Come forth with new and delicate leaves

And when the creek is swollen so
That it bathes the rocks with its gentle flow

The tulips and daffodils arise from their beds
To wink at the sun and bow their sweet heads

Or is it the summer with the trees in full bloom
Changing the earth into a great, giant greenroom.

A frog sings his song in a deep and cool pond
While the ducks create circles on a lake and beyond.

Yet the Autumn has a beauty that is great to behold.
The frost tips the oak leaves with bright red and gold.

The air smells of cleanness, so crisp and quite cool
Creating dim ghosts at the side of a pool.

Now the starkness of winter has a peace of its own
A contrast of shadows with origins unknown.

Snowflakes altering dark objects to light
Making the dead winter somehow seem bright.

So if you travel the midwest, whatever the reason
Be assured you will enjoy a beautiful season.

Luella A. Thise

Untitled

Childhood has hidden behind this bride and vail.
Commitment to love forever is now left to tell its tale.
Young lovers watch in a wide eyed desire, love
forever, they want that eternal fire.
Mother cries tears of a woman on her own,
that she has created and now it's time to let her go.
She will never forget the innocent smile of her newborn baby,
but now it seems that her baby has grown into a lady.
Cover her no more, it's time to close this heartbreaking door.
She cries tears, not of loss, but of love as God
casts down his blessings from above.
Nervous anticipation burns inside this bride and groom.
Forever - is so long to venture together through joy and gloom.
Forever they commit to each other.
A wanton stare of what now seems to just
past oblivion is exchanged between the two.
Eyes of blazing love rise to hover above any sorrow they ever knew.
And these vows are exchanged, just a few menial words,
and they scream it with their hearts,
"I will always love you."

Lillian Pierson

Lost Forever

I gaze through the tender eyes of youth,
Contemplating whether or not the term is now relative.
My body and soul feel fountains of my age,
But my mind is plagued
By the desperation of what my eyes see.
They see the innocence of youth stripped away from frail fingers;
The virtues of childhood pillaged by unmerciful hands;
Fiery spirits once raging as an unleased river,
Forced back into a teardrop of sadness.
And when I look further, into the eyes of my aggressor,
I see not a monster, not a demon -
I find instead, the eyes of another child.
What does a child lose at the hand of another?

Everything...

For it takes a kindred soul to unleash that spirit, virtue and innocence.
God help us if only one child loses their soul or life to the violence.
For when one life is taken, two lives are lost.

Lost forever.

Rebecca M. Bustamante

Untitled

Here lying awake
Couldn't sleep
Thinking about you
But that's nothing new
Although I haven't seen you in a while
I know every angle and every inch from your scent
To the curve of your smile
Am I just wasting my time, believing I'll see you again
Or should I stop nursing this bottle of gin
I do whatever I can to get me by
From sleeping to getting high
Sometimes I wonder am I really getting through
Do you think of me the way I think of you
Gotta stop playing with time
But eventually I'll be on cloud nine
It's been so long
I realize what I did wrong
Seems like I've fallen in love with the waiting in vain
More than with you coming back to me again.

Mark Carrillo

Sometimes At Night

Sometimes at night I sit alone
Counting the stars that glow
Sometimes at night I sit and stare
At clouds floating in the air
Sometimes at night I wonder what if?
What if dreams could come true
And I was with you
Sometimes at night when the silence is all you hear
I wonder if sometimes at night you wish you were here

Tammy Loughry

Untitled

I was born in sin and cleansed in the waters of an ancient civilization.
I was born of pain as the last wave flowed to the beach, and
receded to death.
I was born of thought, to reach into the cosmos and question
mortal insight, no matter how great the prophecy.
I was born of heart, to grieve when all the answers had been found.
I was born of soul, to share with creation the beauty of my words.
Now I stand in turmoil, between the dust covers of fact and fiction.
Between a dead God's thunderous parable, and a new risen
phoenix-child; called melancholy.

Matthew Allen Garrison

Untitled

Hide the tears my child
Cover up the pain
They look and point
Look and laugh
I look at myself
Ain't I doing a good job of hiding my sadness?
My mask is melting away
Dripping down my face
Only to reveal my true self
Only people are scared of my true self
Run child far, far, away
Hold on to what hope you've got
Look deep and find the real you
Not in friends and family
But yourself
Reach deep down
Past the sewage and there it lies

Maria Ford

Untitled

To be blanketed in,
covered up in gray flat clouds
Cool morning, all snuggled in, expectant
for that precious, refreshing rain, God's grace.
The yesterdays, hot, dry, crackling yesterdays,
even man withered beneath its rays.
Afternoons draped in the song of cicadas
and 4:00 eking toward dusk. Nightfall.

But this morning is different.
Nothing but God's mercy makes it different.
Awake, alert, I sense the faint smell in the air.
Autumn hidden somewhere within the coming days.

Rain, like music,
I feel the drops of melody on my uplifted face.
Rain, splashing all around,
music to my soul.
As rain to parched ground, turn me upward to
from where it comes.

Marjel Barnes Jones

None Sweeter Than You

You chocolate, honeyish,
cranberry-flavored
woman I love.
You are better for me than those vegetable people
and that skinny fish.
You're sweet and sugary,
and I like that
because
I become rebellious
in your company
and allow myself to eat
the things others avoid, to have
the joy I've always denied myself, to think
in a way that would raise rigid people's blood pressure.
My blood pressure?
Low as it should be, because of you,
You wry, original, flexible,
sweet
woman I love.

Patrick Monteleone

White Demons

Harbingers of doom encased in wood and cloth
crossing ocean to spread the havoc which they control.

Landing on the virgin soil,
plants die underneath their leather feet.

Mother earth reels in pain at their countenances,
which hide behind looks of greed and want.

They rip up the land with their homes and their tobacco
and their entrepreneurship.

Rape and steal and hunt and kill and soil and destroy
the leave behind them in pursuing their "destiny."

We came from a world we made into hell,
in hopes of regaining divinity.

In vain was our effort,
for all we did was expand the kingdom
of the one who set us into motion.

Perry Horton

A Peace Of Life

I cry for death it awaits me, I cry for love it escaped me
Crying long, crying hard all my emotions in a jar.

Through a sea of tranquility, I cry for love, gone
Carried away in her song
The laud of painless tragedy.

The breath of life is passed by all, I grasp tight for my sweet life
carrying me high, I fear I might fall.
It heals my pain, hate and deadening strife.
Peace brushes past my shoulder, a look at the Promised land.
Drawn away, I go flying older
Seeking a safe place to stand.

I have drunk the froth of pure peace, left dripping down
Another's plain glass but constricted by my self-imposed police
I can't drink freely from the flask.

But I stretch my mind to its edge, I cry for love lost and shaded black
Through the memories of life I dredge
To the puppet I was, never turn back.

Floating over the mountain I see, I wander at lifestyles, everyone
diverse I will choose and thus forever be free,
To behold the entire universe.

Scott W. Beach

Always Remember

Football games, basketball games, and school dances,
Best friends, boyfriends, and long term romances.

Staying up for a midterm until three,
Memories and sadness,
Soon high school will be just a memory.

Always remember the good and the bad,
And all the fun we all once had.

Michelle Bowles

Seasons Change

Sky's sullen, the coming of winter, leaves floating to the ground.
Days are shorter, nights longer, soon, soon cold to be found.

Fires are burning, keeping us warm, knowing soon, winters wrath.
So clean, fresh, this time of year, new foot prints of the deer.

They, like us, aware of change, two and four footer, follow the path.
The cold, the snow, lead to brighter times, warmth ahead, you'll see.

Spring awaiting us, out there, ready to be freed, as too, honey bees.
The fires won't burn as oft, more sun, rain, and growth of new leaves.

Marjorie J. Dugan

Fragrance

I have the fragrance from your perfume
Dancing in my room
It has me fantasizing of the day
I will become your bridegroom.
As I close my eyes
I realize how much I really want you near
For it comes as no surprise that
I see you as a prize
That I wish to endure
For you are the queen that means everything
Yes, you are the woman who makes my heart sing
For it is the fragrance from your perfume
That sends my thoughts to the moon
Also causing my heart to swoon
Oh I wish I had you here within this room
Just from the fragrance of your perfume.

Michael C. May

The Essence Of Jasmine

Once impressive images of joyous rain,
dancing to the thundering rhythm of
Mother Nature's heartbeat,
Now inconceivable with an ever-leadened soul,
and a deceived heart.
A mind unfruitful of glorious thoughts...
of golden meadows of sunflowers,
of countless dazzling stars quilting
the Earth with love,
of transformative dreams that would just touch
the beginning of forever.
Every minute filled with doubt... and of pain,
of unbearable memories of an unborn child,
Jasmine.
A child called upon to create...
the marvelous, breath-taking stars for the Mother,
the goldenest-golds in meadows,
the greatest roars of thunder,
those unrelenting hopes
and dreams of forever.

Shana Kanaswood

My Early Prayer

Night's blackness leaves the quiet and peaceful skies,
Dawn's radiating brightness brings the purest light to my eyes;
As I awake, gathering myself, this innermost thought took hold,
Appreciation of God's Love should be our real treasure, not gold;
Looking skyward, I begin my early prayer to the Creator,
I ask, Dear Lord, look down on your children's misdeeds with favor,
I humbly ask, Dear Father, for your divine forgiveness,
To a world that's gone mad because of its own wretchedness;
Mankind needs your perfect will to enhance its spiritual awareness,
Your immortal wisdom will lead us to understand strength from
weakness;
How wondrous it is for mankind to be part of your divine creation,
Our various ways of worship attempt to show our sincere appreciation;
As this day begins, Lord, we are your daughters and sons,
We are mortal souls, waking up from the light of your Heavenly Sun.

Timothy L. Carter and Salome G. Fierros

Are World Is Crying With Joy

Are world is crying with joy it's crying o boy!
Days and days past it keeps filling up with trash
we should put up a fine that would be so kind
time by time past it still kept filling up with trash
we should put up another sign that would by so kind
years and years past it kept filling up with trash
"Stop polluting" are world is crying with joy

Kristy Bowman

The Linen Closet

Let me crawl into your linen closet,
dear Grandma,
and rest my smile on your musty woolen blankets.
Closing the door,
lost to the world,
yet content with no identity.
I will frolic in the finely embroidered,
lavender scented, quilts of childhood.
The world I live in isn't safe,
dear Grandma,
not at all like your linen closet
where only you knew my giggling presence.
There is no one here to trust,
dear Grandma,
there is no one here to trust.

Sylvia Storm Cloninger

Untitled

Death for you,
Death for me,
For the world around us.
Our lives are dim,
But the sun shines brightly.

Sad, yet true; Death,
The part we hate to see.
We cry forever; our tears infinite.

Cry for your loved ones and for
Those who cried when they died.
Burning sorrow, sadness, and madness.

OUR LIVES ARE SHORT, AS LONG AS THEY MAY SEEM.

Michael Akapnitis

Death

Death is not a bad thing;
Death is a beautiful thing.
You think of all the good things
That you did with the person
Who has passed away.

The person is happy
Up there
Doing his most favorite things,
Whether they be fishing,
Working, or playing in the snow.

You will be sad
When you have to let him go.
But always remember, you must never forget
The good times with him,
And he will never forget you, as long as you live.

You will never forget him,
Whoever he may be.
He will never let you stumble or fall;
He will always be looking out for you
Because of your great love for him.

Stephen Michael Aldenderfer

Afternoon In Valhalla

Winding up, up, up, our rented Silver Shadow
dodged crevasses, curves, bends to Kilauea.
My second grandson drove from Lihue.
To visit three sisters, married daughters
of a dearly remembered brother-in-law.
The changeling sea stretched purple, green, opal
below the ranch where palms and fruit trees
waves aloha. Sixty-nine years of reminiscence
from an operatic stage-set.

Virginia E. Smith

Little Voice

Softly speaking. Sometimes screaming.
Deep inside myself it says,

"Things are changing. Rearranging.
Choose a different path instead.
Look between the black and white to see
the grayness you are in.
Weigh the circumstances wisely.
What are the chances you will win?

Always thinking of the other. Considering your
feelings last. Start to look toward the future.
Leave all that's painful in the past.

You have a brightness like a candle. And such
a glow should not be hid. Use the gift that you
were given. Like once upon a time you did.

I feel the sadness in your tear drops and hear
the echoes of your cries. But I can see that you
are rising, for I am looking through your eyes.

Remember, it is me who's talking. In the stillness
of the night. It is me, your little voice and all I
ask is that you write."

Patricia Phillips

God Sent The White Egrets Today

The storm clouds were swirling around me.
Deep was my soul lost in pain —
Then Jesus came by, and spoke to me —
He sent the white egrets from the sky.
To be with me today!
Now, I can smile again!
Now, I can smile again in Jesus —
Oh, Precious Jesus you always are there, and you care.
When all the world seems in darkness and chaos, despair.
His white egrets come to me from the sky!
A catalyst to be with me this day —
To love me, to tell me, to bring me, to give me a message —
"God loves me - and that God, He really cares!"

Rose B. Stevens

An Acrostic

E'er we appreciate the flight of time,
Deeply absorbed in daily toil and care,
We hear again the Merry Christmas chime
And songs of children floating through the air.
Rejoicingly we join their glad refrain.
Dismissing sordid thoughts of trade and gain.

A happy Christmas may this be to you,
Crowned by a bright and prosperous New Year.
Rich may you be in friendships staunch and true
And family ties unbroken, fond and dear,
In retrospect, though sundered far by space,
Good friends at Yule - tide are as face to face.

Kathie Craig

Memories Of A Lifetime

Two rows of framed photographs on the bookcase
Denote the passages of my life.
The key figures, some now gone
Captured in squares of silver or gold.
Never a day passes that I will not reflect on my photographs
And miss those who are absent now.
The influences that they had, or do have on me.
How lucky I have been to have these memories.
Will I someday be a photograph on someone's shelf?
An inspiration, a source of comfort.
An image that they may know I'll always be there for them.

Wendy Deleo

"A Child"

A child of mother and father,
Dependent of nurturing shows no bother.
Their selfishness is undenying,
The love and honesty is never dying.

Respect as shown always to their elders,
Honestly, the mouth of babes are always tellers.
Parents bring the love of life, a child,
Upbringing can never be measured as mild.

A child, the product of love,
As pure and clean as a dove.
Soaring in laughter high above the clouds,
Determination comes in leaps and bounds.

Their love is unmeasurable and non-prejudice,
The coming into being a genesis.
From my mind and heart you've read awhile,
These are the things that go into a child.

Sherry Moton

The Call Of The Wild

I heard it call me yesterday; also the day before. I acted as if I did not hear, but it's a voice I can't ignore. I close my ears, squint my eyes and think of other thoughts. Somehow the fluid taunting voice seeps in and throws me off. "Young child, young heart come soar with me. I know you want to go, I know your deepest fantasies, the secrets of your soul. Release your heart, release your mind, come with me and you'll see for life is one big bowl of bliss and I posses the key. If you should come, I promise you no reasons to look back. I promise you love, peace and joy no-one else can give you that." I open my eyes, sit up in my bed and wish for the voice to leave. Deep inside I long for this my soul wants to be freed. It is the call of the wild that is calling me, but my heart begs me to stay. It aches with fear and swollen pride that will not go away. The voice returns and this time says: "You must make up your mind. You haven't long to make your choice, you're running out of time." I've made my choice although unsure. I whisper "what must I do?" There's a wicked laugh and then the voice answers; "I knew I'd capture you." The voice replies "Please close your eyes," and sweet music softly flows. It's the end of my innocence, but I can still fight. Too late, my eyes have closed.

Monique S. Wallace

The Game

In this world of our there's a wicked game
Differently played, but the rules are the same,
The consequences for losing goes beyond shame
Because beside myself, there's no one to blame.

When I used drugs, how good I would feel
I always thought I was behind the wheel,
But I was just a passenger, destination unknown
The end of the line was when my money was gone.

I let my addiction take me for a ride
When I wanted to get off, I was denied,
Until my addiction felt I had enough aches
Only then did it decide to step on the brakes.

Since my well has now gone dry
I search for answers to find out why,
In the game of survival, I suffered defeat
I had plenty of chances, I just couldn't compete.

Yes, once upon a time I had it made
But now I'm living on Public aid,
Now all I have left is wishful thinking
The end result of drugs and drinking.

Larry D. Dukes

And There He Stood

And there he stood before my eyes. Standing before me with dignity and pride. Just to say he is fine. And everything will workout in time. Although he hated to leave my side, he will await me in the sweet bye and bye. And we will only be separated for an earthly time.

With amazement in my eyes. And chills running through my spine. I wondered, if it really was him. This man I watched grow so very, thin. Struggling, struggling so hard to breathe. Desperately trying to stay alive and remain with me. But, with each passing day, he seemed to physically, wither away. A result of Lung Cancer, Doctor's would say.

But, there he stood in his old, healthy, form. For he had conquered that horrible, storm. And as he passed into God's heavenly, light. I knew everything would be all right.

Linda K. Coleman

He's Always There For Me!!

How does it feel when you know you are being selfish?
Do you think our God will forever heal that blemish?

He knows our every move, we feel that awesome greatness,
He's with us daily by our side, but yet we want more riches.

He continually blesses me and my family with riches beyond measure.
He watches over me in everything I do, and brings me so much pleasure.

He's always, always, there for me, and I know his strength and power,
But even when the times are good, I don't even stop to smell the flowers.

And even when I forget to pray, he's always still there for me.
So when I thank him for the things he does, it's right there for me to see.

Now, when I go to bed at night, I thank my God above,
That I will live the kind of life, that he will be so proud of.

Lorie A. Watson

Freedom To Be Me

Don't want to follow in the footsteps of my mother
Don't want to live in the shadow of my father
Don't want to act like my sister or my brother
Just let me live with the freedom to be me

To live a lie is as bad as being faithless
Don't want to hurt anyone especially me
I won't turn my back on all of my feelings
I won't sacrifice my whole attitude

Don't want to follow in the footsteps of my mother
Don't want to live in the shadow of my father
Don't expect me to act like my sister or my brother
Just let me live with the freedom to be me

We all have our lives to live
No matter how we live it
Good or bad that one life
Is surely ours to live

Don't expect me to follow in the footsteps of my father
Don't expect me to live in the shadow of my father
Don't even think I'm going to act like my sister or my brother
Just let me live with the freedom to be me

Lisa Lorence

The Beauty

your full-kiss mouth beckons me
don't you realize
caress my heart with your eyes
voice tastes like honey to my ears
confidence of your stride
smells like clean mountain air
the purity of your soul
reflects in this physicalness
no affectations
this is your beauty - The Beauty

my mind's eye drawing your form
too limited
then exploding like a kaleidoscope
blossoming again and again into itself
this is your truth - The Beauty

your life - my life - life
no parameters
connected to your very essence
shine The Beauty through my life
forever please

Philip Guy Parks

What To Do

Birds in the cage.
Doves laying dead.
Cars passing by.
No one sees you there.

Many buildings have taken you away.
Me, I don't do anything. I just see you flying away.
Me, I am content.
It seems I don't care.
I am driving to the city. You, you are going away.

I see your eyes through the cage and I wonder if you are safe.
Are you happy or do you want to be the dove laying there?
I see your eyes and I feel sad but I keep walking away.
It seem I don't care. I keep walking, walking away.

I see you every morning on my way to work and you are still for sale.
What to do to make you safe.

Birds in the cage I want you to sing every day.
I will plant flowers and trees in your little cage.
I will give you water so you don't die of thirst.
No, I better not, I rather see you fly away.

Maria Elena Bejarano

Death

Death wears a human face,
Dresses in clothes lined with lace,
It comes and tears you apart,
Then leaves you to hold your bleeding heart,
Death may win you over with deadly charm,
But it brings you no good, only harm,
If you look close you will probably see,
Through its mask-but don't you flee,
Face death and be very bold,
And if you run you'll surely turn cold,
Fear it not, because it will bring you only pain,
Welcome it and maybe you won't be slain,
Show it that you have the strength of will,
Will to live, make sure it's real,
Then it will fade - fade away,
And you will to but in a beautiful way.

Nicole A. Mount

Scorpio

By the milky way's — misty, wisp of fate, I,
dropped into...scorpio, by a weird...blunder of
blundering, and desire!!!

Werewolves of Armenia: Play
only on the...oceans's bottoms!!!.

Richard C. Miller

Scarecrow

Drippings from the faucet
echo hollow through the room.
Memories of a face
I cannot make a connection
I hear the jackal in the distance,
I hear his cry to the night
My lips are damp and weeping
under a glowing lantern light.
My thoughts, misunderstood
Confused about it all
I lie among the deadwood, and the trees with evil faces
their many branches like wicked decrepid fingers
their mouths moan in agony
knowing they will never blurt a sound.
I feel my body breathing, I feel my body rise
Insomnia and the nightmare await
my heavy blackened eyes
the crow and the vultures smile sick, beyond their peer
then scatter clumsy as I frighten them
From my post here, in the garden.

Stacy Lass

Feeling low

When you feel you should have said something
else, or when your actions seem wrong,
you feel low
When you feel you should have handled that
situation better,
you feel low
When your friends or family are mad at you, or
people make fun of you,
you feel low
When you just want to dig a hole and lie in it,
you feel low
When you did something bad, and you
know you shouldn't have
you feel low
When I feel low, I think of happy times
and wait till the day is over.

Michelle Materko

Beauty

Everyone needs to look deep down into themselves before we
can look at someone else.
We look at beauty before we look at the person.
Beauty is extra by God. But it can also hurt you.
If you have beauty without a heart of gold no one can find
you beautiful cause your cold heart makes you ugly.
Where as if God has blessed you with both beauty and heart
of gold. You'll have every for chance on a good life.
Because it makes you beautiful and special.
Beauty can be made not only by faculty looks so don't judge on it.
Beauty can be deserving, so look deep down to the soul of the
person.
Beauty is not all glory.

Myra Istre Crochet

Dishearten

Searching for someone to be sought
Endlessly repressing once devout thoughts
Not quite past tense and shamefully immense
Love, there's no defense
I dream of her smile
The scent of her fragrance ever so vile
She cast a spell upon my dream
Raped me naked of self esteem
Depression has lead to decay
My once intense passion has perpetually faded away
She says, "I love you" and there's no guarantee
I stand in quicksand with a shallow minded pat on the back
"There's other fish in the sea"
Sinking, I remember the wicked one who smiled as she left me behind
Shattered promises
I now define love as crucifixion of the mind
Her beautiful eyes served as a remarkable disguise
She slashed my throat with her lies
There will never be another candle to burn by my bedside

Phil P. Testa

Alone Again

I stood on the craggy cliff. The sun glistened golden beams of energy. I wanted to be rooted there. My thoughts began exploring. The cliff was worn with years of erosion and decay, it was something of a marvel. A crystal waterfall was running wild with beauty. A mist of coolness refreshed me as water trickled into a shallow cove. As I stood there for hours, looking down, I caught a reflection of myself in the water. My starry brown eyes changed into a empty stare. I wiped my face as a few teardrops fell to the rocks. What I didn't want to happen, happened; I was without emotion. As I walked away, I left something behind that I didn't need anymore. I stood there; a field of wild flowers with tall sharp blades of grass surrounding them, browned from the sun, rose before me. I was going to pick a few of the flowers but suddenly, I felt an emptiness. They were beautiful sun flowers with shades of passion, love and self. I stepped back and reflected on my loneliness and my life. I took a deep long breath and I gave a silent stare. As I walked away, I knew the flowers could enrich more than one person. I turned and saw the sunset a soft orange and yellow glow. I was alone with my thoughts once again.

Tamitha Dawn Wahlstrom

The Returning

Windy... spooky... scary night....
Enough ghosties and ghoulies to give me a fright!!
Bedroom windows resound with a rat-a-tat-tat.
Could it be a demon, a branch, or perhaps the neighbors' cat?
I retreat to my covers 'cause I cannot look.
The house creaks and groans as I turn back to my book.
I try hard, and harder still, to absorb the words written there;
but find it impossible
for the prickling and tingling of my skin and hair!
Oh, no — now what is **that**?
Strange sounds, yells, and screams that I hear,
getting louder... stronger... coming ever so near.
Summoning up my last ounce of courage,
I look out the door...
Ah, ha, ha, ha, haaa - sweet relief!
Only "trick-or-treaters"
It's Halloween once more.

Sharon Kohlmeier

Stagnant Waters

Our once pure mountain snow waters are changing,
Entering now and polluting the air and streams,
Are myriads of poisonous chemicals everywhere
Creating stagnant waters and impure dreams.

Our forest and meadows must perfume our air
The birds and bees, and bald eagles too,
Must have their habitat as God gave them,
An Eco-system untampered through and through.

Why has our environment been so devastated
And sold to the greed of a powerful few,
Our national parks are in danger folk,
Surely there's something we each can do?

Stagnant waters from atomic fallout is shameful
Our ozone layer of protection is wearing thin,
What will it take, for us to awake?
Before our whole world caves in?

Thomas D. Glenn

Journey's End

On life journeys, I have never travelled alone.
Even at life's start I was accompanied by my twin.
Now 'tis said on my last journey, I must go alone.
Die alone? Never, that I will not do.
When I hear that final call, I'll summon my Alter
Egos from the computer bites of my mind and soul...
All who shared my life from birth to old age...
The Babe, Child, spiritually awakening youth,
The Bride, the Wife, the Mother and Grandmother,
Myriads of experience all shared with me, but
We really lived, loved and were loved.
I'll join hands with all in prayer and then,
Tearfully, fearfully, hopefully but joyfully,
Face this final challenge, the last journey into
The unknown...to the journey's end...to the
Source of all life and love...to God and eternity.

Maude I. Ponticello

Not One Earthly Friend

I have traveled many miles
Each one I delivered a smile,
Those that did accept me
turned around and rejected me,
my salty tears I've tasted many days
trying to understand people and their ways,
After giving all that I had away
they laughed in my face and walked away
I've been told not to speak the truth
it makes people not love you.
As I walk this earth plane
I find no two people the same,
But through my eyes they all look
the same, people only want friends
that tell them what they want
to hear, they don't seem to care
about why we are here,
They love lies, games and gossip
and these things I stay clear
So you see I have not one earthly friend.

Darlene Dearing Rhodes

The Mountains

A peaceful spring rain, water trickling over rocks
Deer drinking, a bird sounds
The deer run gracefully, land after land in peace
The stream flows on continuing in a silver mist
A murmur from the stream answered by the wind
A squirrel gathers seeds in silent peace.

Matt Gugel

Earth Child

EARTH, a liquid blue ball in the glimmer of the planets
EARTH, elegantly revolving around the fiery sun
EARTH, blossoms with wise foliage
EARTH, water trickles my delicate skin
EARTH, the cross of changes
EARTH, she cries of pain and agony
EARTH, returns to its innocence
EARTH, the forms of land are delicately threaded on her chest
EARTH, the wise animals and birds bellow and chirp for her praise
EARTH, she feels her skin fading away
EARTH, she falls down but the EARTHCHILD catches her in his arms

Jay S. Shetty

For Love Nor Money

On tepid wings I traveled to the ends of
earth for only you.
My love and heart beat out the cry, no more
am I to die.
For what of life and what of death, two
friends though they not be,
cry, cry, cry oh mournful soul within my
sorrow, I die.
This talk of death, is it an omen? Can't
you see me frown? This smile of mine is real
I say, this smile is what you see.
But love is what you see and don't see, one
side smiles and the other frowns.
It's hard to die, easy to love, why must they
be together? Love, life, love death,
I've died so hard a million times.
The release is fine but bitter, both tastes are
better if not familiar,
no one can shout "I've Lived" unless you've
died for love - once.

August VanDeVoorde

"Power"

Power is so corrupting, as it
Eats the integrity and glow of the
Soul,
Bringing people under the eternal
Shadow of the gargoyle of
Order,
Crushing heart and minds in its
Quest to feed.

Butcher the buzzard;
Feed its entrails to the fires of past
Genocide, and see how the
Truth
Stirs the ghost of the murdered, to
The vengeance against the princes of
Power and Glory, for which their
Blood
Was spilled.

Anarchy is the rule of law for the dead.

James Hershiser Jr.

An Acrostic For Poetry

Poetry is imagery at its best,
enticing the mind's eye to attest
Opening of vistas of life's joys and sorrows,
Evidencing their shortcomings and powers.
The poet writes a dirge or a psalm,
or with pithy words and no qualm
Revelatory insights to help the reader to understand
Youthful passions, and feelings of:
"Life is really so grand!"

Joyce S. Field

A Friend

What is a friend you ask?
A friend is someone to have fun with,
to talk to,
to go shopping with.
They're weird, funny,
shy, quiet,
They share,
They care,
They're always there when you need them
Through the good
Through the bad
When you need a shoulder to lean on
or
When you're bouncing off the walls
From all the pop you drank
A friend is always there
Till the very end.
And that my friend is what is what
a friend is all about.

Amanda Euriech

Untitled

Two bodies alone in the night
...a gentle breeze
...a moonlit sky
...stars glistering overhead.
Two bodies alone in the night
...a word is whispered
...a heart is touched
...the bodies become one.

Chelby Schoppa

Forever!

The unforgettable day is forever,
A gift invariably mysterious,
Removing thoughts already clever,
A day expectant to one so serious!
Winds blow and rain proceeds
Our hearts bleed in sorrow,
Someone cares for our needs,
For there arrives No Tomorrow!
Clear the path for others,
Show kindness toward the past,
Somewhere we hear our mothers,
There will be many brothers.

Eunice S. Jenkins

Loneliness

A man
A hopeless man
A man without anything
Nothing to live for
No one who cares
No one who loves him.

Like a mouse running from a cat
Like a wilting flower
Like a dance without music
A mountain without a peak.

He has nothing to eat
He mopes all day
He waits to die
To drift away
Into the heavens
In the sky.

Donald F. Law Jr.

The Child

There comes a time upon -
a human heart.
We look darkly into -
a mirrored pond.
Awakened by a start;
we feel through
The rippled image be -
yond all reason.
Falling for life's child;
sweet mystery
Beyond living's treason;
knowing not guile.
We feel ourselves between;
heartbeats...sublime.
Knowing not innocence;
from elves unseen.
Only laughter's divine -
joyous incense.
When we see the child;
life with a smile.

Joseph Anthony Ortiz Noriega

Inheritance

A life of woe,
A life of fears,
gave birth to life,
raised pretense and tears.
A heart unsung,
a soul weighed heavy,
gave birth to life,
gave not to many.
A being so plagued
can not instill,
life giving joy,
a desire, a will.
A creature so torn,
unable to share,
gave birth to another
who can not dare.
To live life fully
without the qualms,
bred in the weary womb
from whence she comes.

Amelia Spencer

Forget Me Not

Strange how in battle
a man can die,
Without hesitation,
in the blink of an eye.

He is gone, nevermore
to walk among men,
Another fatality in
a war based on sin.

He had no face or name
as he died for God and country,
No body for burial
his mourners cry for mercy.

He gave his life and
his family got his medal,
Time passes on and yet,
an empty space remains at the table.

Chris Cloke

Nights Without You

When you're away and I'm alone
a part of me is missing
I wonder off into my thoughts
and bring you back to me
We touch, we hold and kiss endlessly
It makes me warm inside
But nothing compares to having you
Here, leaving those nights without you
Behind

Gerald R. Jackson

Homeless

An empty space filled with a home.
A place to feel safe and
to call your own.
Flowers grow below the kitchen window.
my, how the trees have grown.
Birds singing high above sweet,
sweet songs of love.
My front door always open
for everyone to greet.
A smile on my face
and arms stretched out
to each person I'll meet.
This home is a space
filled with my heart
in hopes that we will never part.

Dena C. Gregor

Love Poem

I would like to write
a poem for you
lines bloated with sugar
lamentations
bursting at each seam
with bloody passion
And fiery bits of my desire.
But the truth is:
I don't even really like
you much!

Cynthia Libbee

Untitled

Beyond coral reefs
a porpoise carves the water
as summer arrives

Greg Sakamoto

Earthquake

In the morning...
A red rose bends
With quivering leaves
As the earth moves
Under them to test
Their grace!

In the afternoon...
Chatty crows in love
Bathed in a puddle,
Gathered cat's fuzz
And left, leaving
A patio still.

In the evening...
Fire, earthquake,
Mudslide and more;
Mercifully my man
Missed them all
By a sleep!

Betty O'Meara

Fantasy

A stolen moment
A silent stare
It is a secret
one we share
A sexy smile
A seductive look
you read me like an open book
A kiss good night
or maybe two
all I want is to make love to you
I'll dream tonight
of you and me
Together
in my fantasy

Dana M. Sanchez

Revealing Light

Somewhere in the darkness
A strange kind of light
Believe in it and seek it
It's the guidance of insight.

This light opposes darkness
In the soul of man
revealing all God's wisdom
as only light can.

Some will sense its presence
be guided through peril and shame
living in faith and obedience
assuring the absence of blame.

The soul forever protected
will find its commanded way
having been supplied with eternal light
forever will remain, if you pray.

Glorify the name of God
be pleasing in his sight
trust in him and serve him
you too, will see the light.

Ann Austin Der Kacy

The Call Of Compassion

Deep calls unto Deep

Loneliness dwells within
a well of emptiness
where the depths don't meet

A reach across the chasm
seeks to touch and invite
the lonely, aching, alienated one

Compassion meets grey emptiness

Who is she
the one who weeps with longing pain
then shrinks and hides
when beckoning love invites
with a will to embrace?

Deep Loneliness   Deep Compassion
Can they meet and wed?

What is this uninvited hollow, aching emptiness
which has intruded so boldly
weeping lonely grey tears
into bottomless depths?

Deep waits as Deep weeps

Audrey Doetzel

The Verdict

While sitting in the courtroom
About to do my job,
I felt a wet drop on my cheek;
I had begun to sob

I thought for just moment;
Just what had made me cry?
I knew that my decision
Could mean that one might die

And as I pondered through my mind;
Just what gave me the right?
To make one's verdict heavy
Or to make one's verdict light

The decisions were not easy
In fact, they were very hard
because I'm merely human
Indeed, I am not God

So is he guilty? or is he not?
How cruel to judge a man
But since it's my civic duty
I'll just do the best I can

Betty J. McAdams Ellis

Cousin

A cousin is a gift from
above, on loan to his
family, friends, and mate
A memory of delight, a
love held tight
once alive, dancing
teasing, carousing
seeking his place after
birth - nothing
matters now that he
has left this earth.

Barbara Sparks

Seasons Of Love

As the winter wind blows
Across my face
I think of the feelings
We chase
When spring comes around
And birds sound
Like the whispers of your
Thoughts
Summer rings in with the
Ocean breeze
And you are sure to please
The corners of my mind
Autumn sneaks in with
Falling leaves
The way I feel in love
With you

Alberta Thomas

Today

Today stretched
across the sky,
Kissed awake by sunlight
and the breeze of a sigh.

Dressed in colored garments
Today came into view,
Symbol of God's Grace that
greets each day anew.

Jean Jumara

Seasons

Faint sound of leaves falling
Across the forest path
Light dims, the wind blows cold
Leading the way for winter

Wind blows the barren trees
I see the cold clear skies
Night falls, the stars show through
The deer bed down in the brush
Early morning dawns with frost
Reaching the end, a new season turns

Sun shines down across the horizon
Ponds begin to thaw
Rains bring life to a thriving earth
In harmony, birds begin to sing
Now the days are warm and bright
Great nature sings its song

Billy Jones

From The Strings Of The Violin

As the bow glides
across the strings of the violin
with notes so sweet
like a meadow lark
sitting on a distant limb
singing mournfully,
and begging for spring to arrive.
Clear cool water comes from clouds above
with the promise of the season
That takes hunger away
the violin seems to say
stay and listen
and let it be
music for your soul to hear
lifts your heart beat from despair
to bring you happiness
instead of tears

Geneva Laura T. Spencer

Afire With Fall

So startled was I by the bush
Afire with fall,
Nestled in the dark green bed
Of ever-grove,
I took off my shoes and bowed.
Like Elijah still drowsy from some dream
I heard the wind of Yahweh's voice,
A tiny, whispering sound:
This is a holy ground.

Charles Patrick Mudd

Rainbow

When I look up in the sky
After it rains.
I see the most beautiful creation
Ever made.
With red, yellow,
And blue.
Then I wonder?
What's on the other side,
GOLD,
Or a broken heart.
Full of sorrow,
For all it cared for was riches,
But know it yearns for love.

Brandi Jenkins

I Found Love

I still remember...
All that we've been through.
Love was right before my eyes...
It showed above in the stars and skies.
But deep inside I know...
This time it's truly right.
When I look into your eyes.
I see forever...

When I hold your hand.
I hear a whisper...
The search is over.
It all comes down to me and you..
I guess it's got to be
Me - You - Forever

Danielle Tocci

"Memories"

All the memories we have had,
All the good, yet the bad,
I love you so much
more than you can ever see
can't you see
won't you please, forgive me?
I understand if you don't
want me back,
but my dreams,
and, ambitions will never lack;
I will look to the future
and remember the past,
Oh how I wish
those memories would last.

Hope Yarrington

Instead Of Wine

Instead of wine,
All the time,
I'll sit and sip my tea
My son is gone,
I'm all alone,
But that's okay
With me!

Instead of wine
All the time,
I'll sit and sip my tea!
I don't care what people say,
I will have a good day!
Instead of wine,
All the time,
I'll sing my troubles away!

Elisabeth Funderburk

A Feeling

I have a feeling within me-
an unexplainable cry of ecstasy-
a dizziness of disbelief.

I have a groping within me
for unattainable sharing-
in vain, for others to keep.

I have a confidence about me
that a precise emulation of perfection
surrounds my brightest dreams.

I have a daughter-you see
a gem of grace never known
a hollow universe is filled-
and spills-with infinite love I've grown

Gioacchino LaGreca

Untitled

The mirror reflects
all things seen;
from people to places
making all gleam.

The mirror, it feels
what all is felt;
from hunger to heartache
and all is dealt.

The mirror, it hears
every little sound;
chirps of birds and barks of dogs
even rain—hits the ground.

The mirror, it speaks
when all is heard;
thunder and lightning
and the flight of a bird.

The mirror I talk about
is no lie;
it's me and you
and you and I.

Brooke A. Moore

Jesus

Have you taken them to Jesus?
All your troubles and your cares?
If you'll let Him, He will help you,
All your burdens He will bear.
He will walk the way beside you,
And He'll never, never leave,
Everything you need He's promised,
If on Him you will believe.

Put your trust alone in Jesus,
All He's promised He will do,
There's no other friend so loving,
There's no other one so true.
Jesus wants to walk beside you.
Lead you, help you, come what may,
Oh, if only you will let Him
He'll be with you all the way.

Charles A. Walker Jr.

Princess Star

Here she comes
Along her way
To light the room
And bring the day

The peace and warmth
That floods my heart
And in my dreams
We shall never part

For I truly love
This shining star
Who keeps me smiling
Even from afar

But shadows bring
The DEMONS of Despair
As the Princess moves
To her cloud for care

And the tears will fall
Like the rain will pour
Until that tender moment
When I can see her once more

Glenn Alan Parker

Searching

Everyone is always searching for love,
Although some people never find it,
And some never find it to be true.

Jessica Ann Richter

Untitled

First a boy, now a man.
Always a good friend to me.
I wish I could hold his hand.
That he'd let me see.

It's by his side I'd love to stand.
He's so sweet and fun.
Not at all what I had planned.
But in him I can see the sun.

All these feelings, I keep inside
Never thinking they'd grow,
So far from him, at times I've cried
Hoping somehow He'd just know.

Good to him I'll always be
If my feelings I never show
I guess to blame, can only be me
Because I never let him know.

I care for him so
He could be more than a friend
Never will I be able to let go
Not even at the very end.

Carol J. Polzin

Babes

Now that I
am past my prime;
It's: "Darling"—"Honey"
all the time!

The babes are cute
and cuddly too!
But how are they
at pitching woo?

Now that I
am getting old,
does that mean
I should be less bold?

It is not age
that makes me Mellow,
for I can whip
that other Fellow?

It is just that time
brings caution.
What do I do
ifIcatch—em?

Donald K. McCarty

Untitled

With silver light a candle burned,
And cast its hungry shadows.
Your marble hands have gently learned
The sweetness of the meadows.

The silk and satin of your skin,
The spiral of your story
Are burning holes, so sad, so mean,
In essence of my glory.

You look and sigh, your brown eyes,
Exquisitely reserving,
Draw pictures, that no longer lie.
So tender. Candle. Burning.

Boris Evelson

Strong

For I am a flower
Among a group of weeds
They are too strong
So they take all my needs
I am too weak
So I cannot stay
I wished I had legs
So I could walk away
I am still here
But not for long
I have no water
So this means I'll be gone
Can you help me?
Can you see my despair
But you cannot hear me
And all you do is stare
I must leave now
For my roots are dry
But their is still time
Time for one more cry

Jason A. Zaremba

The Week Before State

It was the week before State
and all through the school
everyone was talking about just one rule

Loving was champs in '93
But State champions this year
we would soon be

The posters were hung
on the walls with care
soon the smell of victory
would be in the air

The players were focused
with their heads in the game
all anticipating their well earned fame

Coaches Davis, Ventura and Montes
had drilled them all week
for State champs was the title that we
would soon seek

The game Saturday is to be shown on the news
as the whole State watches the Jal Panthers
loose

This is almost the end with only one task more
becoming the champions of 1994

Angie Hutchison

The Clown

My painted face
and baggy clothes;
spirited eyes and
red-ass nose;
making people laugh
at the sight of me.
Children, they point
and jeer and scream.
I trip and I fall
and I tumble around;
how well I can play
the funny ol' clown.
But always the act
comes to an end,
I wipe away the paint
the grease and the friends.
I sit and I stare
in endless ridicule
at the naked face
of the real-life fool.

Domonic J. Delrose

Forever Defeated

I glanced across the way,
And caught you watching me.
So much I wanted to say,
As you walked over to me.
When our eyes met,
Something happened inside.
I wasn't aware yet,
But all my fears died.
The pain of the past,
The hurt of yesterday,
It didn't last,
It all went away,
Your love is all,
I ever needed.
I still fall,
Forever defeated.

Holly M. Thomas

Being Awakened

I saw rainbows
And chased them to their ends
I saw dandelions in my salad
And called them my friends
I heard sparrows
Singing in nonsense
While obnoxious children
Pretended innocence
I can smell air
From the distance
And I see eagles
Killing prey in a glance
But I feel you
In all your pretence
Filling my soul.
With happiness

James McKernan

"Skyler"

With wispy lashes, rosebud lips
and cheeks aglow
such delicate features
framed in hair which could be
made of spun gold

Oh for the eyes
to be hold.

Such radiance and beauty
many have fallen silent
as she sauntered by
with poise and assurance

That only she
could carry

Like the feel of velvet
her voice, spread upon thee
To be treasured, cherished
and loved

Till the last breath
has been drawn
from your lips

Cecilia Garcia

Which

Psyche and dear Cupid sat
And "chewed the fat,"
Concerning life, and this and that;
Each in their separate way,
Passing the time of day;

One thought of man as mostly bad,
As clod or fool, as crumb or cad;
One saw a knight, a shining light,
Of hope eternal in the night;
I wonder which envisioned right?

Edward E. Crawford

Old And Alone

I had a house to clean
And children to raise
And I did it all
Without any praise

But now I'm old
And all alone
I wish they'd take time
And visit their home

Knock on the door
And give me a smile
And say, "Mom, I love you"
Just once in awhile.

Fanny Lee Baker Shaw

Untitled

Rose are red
And did you know?
Violets are blue
Know what else is blue?
The sky,
And yes, I am too.
Why? Why am I that way?
Not because the grass is green
Not because your eyes are too
Not because you left
Not because you took my heart with you
Not because it's cloudy
or rainy
or storming
Not because you made my life that way
Not because saw HER with you
And she smiled at me...
But because you didn't smile too.

Crystal Day

Rumors

Started by one
and dispersed amongst others,

Like a fire it grows and consumes
what little truth it may hold.

Causing damage in its course to others,
as the truth regains controls.

Out is the fire finally put.
as the truth roams free.

Leaving the carnage of the fire
For everyone involved to see!

Eric H. Adeleye

Loneliness

I heard it lurking
And droning in the darkness
As I lay awake in my bed.
My heart was thundering, and
My eyelids refused to fall.
The morning after, I lay unmoved
And hoped that it was Saturday.
It was then that I realized
During my sleep it had come,
Stolen my feelings,
Burned them,
And enveloped itself within me.

Carole Ann Hamer

Sure Sign

The sky is sorta grey outside
And everything is still
I hear a whippoorwill's call
On yonder wooded hill.

I feel the touch of dampness
Floating in the air
And know that Mother Nature
Has something hidden there.

Maybe we'll get a snow storm
Or just some winter rains
My bones are giving signals
With a little jagged pains.

The old folks can tell it
If the weather's gonna differ
Their rhuematiz has a fit
And they don't feel so chipper.

Edith M. Baker

The Loneliness

When dark overcome you
And fills you with despair,
The loneliness of waiting
Is often hard to bear.

The feeling is everlasting
As the moon and stars above,
And neither night nor shadows
Separate us from the sorrow.

I have done with foolish yearning
For the things I cannot keep.
No more of years of searching,
No more crying in my sleep.

To everything is a reason
And a time for every season,
A time to weep and laugh,
A time to mourn and dance.

An when my days are over
And all the shadows dim,
There is always someone near,
That bears a love to you.

Eva E. Lembo

Untitled

Morality is a dead god.
And, like Apollo of the poets,
Whose gifts are no longer sacred,
We, the lost, stand forsaken in
The midst of translated icons.

Jeff Brockway

Nothing But Love

"The days have come
and gone"-
"Leaving behind many
great moments"

"I will carry on here,
in my heart"...
"As well as the bad ones"...

"I can just learn from them,
and try to make
the best, of what I can
give"....

"And what I have here
in my Heart is nothing
but love"....

Dolores Arredondo

You're Gone

You're gone now
And I don't know what to do
There's a hole in my heart
Pierced all the way through
My emotions have vanished
I've become a black hole
I still walk the earth
Forever now with no soul
As I hold a gun
Firmly pressed to my head
I'll bravely squeeze the trigger
Soon to be dead
To continue my life
I could not see
To live without you
Would be eternal misery

Jason Pummill

Grandpa

Grandpa I miss you,
and I have for many years.
I was six when you died,
and eleven years have passed.

Grandpa we were close,
as close as two could be.
Even though I was young,
and you were old to me.

Grandpa I miss you,
and I wanted you to know.
I'm proud to be your granddaughter,
even more as I grow.

Grandpa I wish you could be there,
as I graduate next year.
But even though you can't,
I'll remember your face quite clear.

Grandpa I miss you,
and I have for many years.
I was six when you died,
and eleven years have passed.

Casandra M. Young

Behind The Times

Great-grandson eyed his new-patched jeans
And moaned a string of "Gees!"
"I'm doomed! I'm doomed!" he cried.
"You cannot see my knees!"

Ella Black

Suddenly, I Remember Her

When my whole existence shatters
and I know I must be strong,
when I cannot seem to find the strength
but I know I must go on,
who do I think of?
Suddenly, I remember her.

When I reflect on meaningful moments
about things that matter to me,
I dream of a shining star
a vision I wish you could see,
Who do I think of?
Suddenly, I remember her.

I am reminded of a spiritual soul
Who thrives on peace and love,
I'm thinking of a friend of mine
a special delivery sent from above,
Who do I think of?
My dear Mother
Suddenly, I remember her.

Jennifer J. Brown

"Silly Little Things In Life"

I like the flowers
And I like the spring
I like all the silly
Little birds that sing.

I like the summer
And I like the trees
I like all the silly
Little things like these.

I like the moon
And the stars above
I like a mild June breeze
And some one to love.

I like the sunshine
And a car to drive
I like all the silly
Little things in life.

Joseph H. Berkman

A Baseball Dream Through A Child's Eyes

I dreamed a baseball dream
And I was on the greatest team
Was it real I asked myself
It seemed that way I really felt

Then I dreamed I was a pitcher
Was it possible I might get richer
If only in my dream as I sleep
Someday not to worry nor to weep

To dream a dream so wonderful
And then to my surprise
I awoke from my dream
To find I was rubbing my eyes

I yawned and sighed after all
It was just a dream about baseball
Or could it be that I
Might have that dream come true someday

Cynthia Romeo

Cycles Of Expression

With each new leaf bud of Spring
and its lifetime of greenery,
Lies the potential of the glorious
coloration of fall.

The babe-in-arms has the potential
in its lifetime of service,
To display a life force radiance
as brilliant as the leaf.

The leaf flutters to the Earth and lands
with stem pointing Heavenward,
And while resting in repose,
evolves to nurture its source.

In his way, man looks to heaven
holding fast to life's ideals,
Knowing that in his quiet time
he will add to the source of his beingness.

Leaf and man experience a time of being,
a burst of glory, a quiet retreat.
Rising refreshed, each resumes, in its own
way,
a never ending expression of God.

Eleanor L. Williams

"The National Library Of Poetry"

"The heights of great men, reached
and kept, were not attained by
a sudden flight, but, they, whilst
their companions slept, they were
toiling upwards in the night"

Charles Agbenyega

A Tree Is Gone

I heard the ominous buzz.
And knew exactly what it meant.
A squirrel is now homeless.
The birds will not return to nest.

No leafy kisses to cool the brow.
Or sturdy trunk to lean against.
Where once leafy patterns danced.
And soothing, rustling sounds were heard.

Grotesque poles are standing bare.
And concrete sizzles in the sun.
The eye at night glares balefully.
No shadow softens evening's glow.

A setting, unyielding, unfeeling.
Will we with constant vision
Become the same?
Another tree was felled today.

Barbara McQuown

Ode To My Love

Gloom rolled in on quiet feet
and misery kept up the pace;
despair the drum did constant beat,
the day I didn't see your face.

No happy thought or smile did pass;
the river Styx rose at my place
and ghosts and ghouls marched in en masse
the day I didn't see your face.

The day I didn't see your face
they might as well have buried me
and left my grave without a trace,
The day I didn't see your face.

Eugene Silver

House Talk

I sometimes lie awake at night
And listen to our house -
It seems to have a lot to say
While I lie as a mouse
And wait for pipes to lose their heat
And so contract with cold
When we have turned the thermo' down
For that's what I've been told.
We're gone a lot, but when were back
I do my "sillies" - these -
I like to give the walls a pat
Or give the couch a squeeze -
And so these noises that I hear
Are really music rare
That this old house puts into words
I'm really glad to share -
And best of all it seems to say
"I love you all you see -
I'm glad that you did make the choice
To come and dwell in me."

Elvera Trana

Untitled

Love lingers
And looks through
Laughter and tears
To the heart

It waits for a sign
Then passes boundaries
Through wide open gates
To share the secrets inside

Barbara Kern

Untitled

Dine and dance, rekindle romance
and misty remembrances.
Was then the dream? Or now?
The past fast becomes future
the present fleeing to eternity;
immediacy disappearing, evanescing
into existential nothingness.
Or something?
Hope Belief and Prayer
conspire the future in our favor,
filtering such unhappiness as was;
saving the best to be repeated
in other forms;
recognizable as the echoes
of songs begun
but unfinished.
We grow older.

Arnold Neustadter

Rest In Peace...

Death awaits in many ways
and no one knows just why.
It doesn't matter black or white
or the voice of which pain cries.
Although you may be gone,
My grampa you will always be.
Always in my heart,
of which only you shall have a key.
But now the battle's over.
The fighting now may cease.
So from me to you my grandfather.
May you "REST IN PEACE."

Julie Christine

Into White

Awakening -

The Snow Falls Gently
And Never stops.

My eyes are open
And, (once more),
I am engulfed in Virgin Frost.

The Wind Echoes my thoughts
As Icicles Cling
and never let go.

I see a pearl
Lost and Alone
Untouched, Yet beautiful.

My mind wanders, but
Thoughts go nowhere.
Only I can distinguish
The hidden treasure.

The snow falls gently
And never stops.

My mind still wanders, but
It always helps me find my pearl.

Jane Compere

Woman

Alone she stands...

When rains fall hard
And nights grow cold

Alone she must be aware

Of danger and suffering
Knocking at her door.

Like a lonesome pine
Shaggy but glittering
She attracts and repels men

Protecting herself
With dignity

Because she is
The daughter of earth
And the queen of fertility
She is a woman!

Clara Lefler

What Is Pink?

Pink is the color of sticky ink.
And pretty girls on a large skating rink.
Pink is the color of a sunset in the sky
Or a kite flying way up high.
Pink is the color of a bunny's nose
Or the color of a nice pretty rose.
Pink is a beautiful carnation
Or the color of a child's imagination.

Jennifer Higgins

Untitled

To see the sparrow fly so
delicately into the sky, no reason to
ever die so free never has to sigh.
The little feather slowly drops forever
flowing in the breeze like a whisper
with such ease, fly little bird live
this day to the fullest, you've made
me smile my special little high...

Tiffany Krache

Reflections

I look into the mirror round,
and see a person, sane and sound
Bound together by a dream,
relatively churlish it may seem
Ready for the pain-filled world,
tangled within a web of pearl
Broad horizons, dreams of gold,
reflections of myself so bold
Outward appearance has no meaning,
that is why I'll keep on dreaming
A river of endless fear,
a drop of light, a single tear
Endless love, a caring source,
reflections of my life so course

Justin Stadler

On Growing Old

If I could live my life again
And shape it to my heart's desire,
How would I ease the pain
Of memories which oft transpire
To enter in the twilight zone
Where dreams and reality co-exist,
But are for my thoughts alone
Willing my being not to resist
The panoramic view unfolding
Of my journey from the day of birth
Like a kaleidoscope ever-changing
Giving glimpses of my life on earth.
No change in this fabric would be gain
For the Rites of Passage herald pain.

Joan F. Girvan

A Dolphin's Life

Up with the sunrise ready to jump
and sing, as we greet the day with
a friendly grin.

We swim and jump until it's lunch time
then it's little fishies for us to find.

See us jump and play among the giant
waves. You can see us racing down the
waves, if you were to come out and play.

We swim and jump and sing all day
until it's time to say good day.

Amy Shimerman

Walk Lightly

Walk lightly. Time flies on golden wing
and so must you.
Don't plod or trudge or sink too firmly
into mother soil.
Instead tread softly, barely there
as children do at play.
For days and hours fly by as fleet
as infant steps
And soon
you too will trip silently away.

Georgia Payne Pinkston

Boundaries Of Being

Reality conquers a dream with ease,
And the dream disappears,
Hurt, bewildered, without any credence,
Unaware that reality also disappears,
Hurt, bewildered, without any credence,
An easy victim of death.

George Malhame

Your Leaving

I'm going to miss those blue eyes
And that unique laugh of yours,
But over a period of time
My heart will slowly cure.

I'll still think of your words
That tried to help me out.
You wanted nothing but the best
And never had a doubt.

I'll miss your warm smile
Because your not with me.
I'll miss the times we should've had
But will never come to be.

I know I'll miss picking up the phone
And hearing your voice.
I was so happy you thought of me.
It was then I would rejoice.

But I'll mostly miss my feelings for you
Because they can't stay forever.
After this last good bye
I won't see you again, never.

Amanda Fae Burk

Serenade Of Oblivion

The archaic way of the one
And the consequences, well that depends,
After all, you'll never know,
You'll never know.
Where everything encloses
When everything touches,
For there can be no other
You'll never know.
Up above the line
Visions pass like waves,
Never staying, but constantly there
Agitating your mind in cascading motions,
In the cynical manner which you prefer
Amiable, but not aesthetic;
Putting together in soul and mind
Curiosity that sets in perpetuity
Hunger that needs to be assuaged.
To be in silence and constancy
Let it be eternally unknown.

Jeanne Cho

The Seasons

When there is no longer snow,
And the flowers begin to grow.
When the true are wearing green
And no icicles can be seen.
Spring is here.

When the grass is very green
And the roses are in bloom,
When in the swimming pool is seen,
That there is very little room.
Springtime is here.

When the leaves begin to fade,
And no longer give us shade
Then comes the coolness of the breeze,
And the flowers begin to breeze
Fall is here.

When the cold winds begin to blow,
And the raindrops turn to snow,
Children don sweat suits and mittens,
Appearing warm as tiny kittens
Winter is here.

Eva R. Lee

Untitled

On a bright clear day
and the sun shining on
the bay, as the clouds roll
by, the birds are soaring
high above the sky, I
think of you as time goes
by, wondering why we
did not say goodbye.
When knowing we
should have tried, but the
tears came to our eyes
in our hearts and in
our minds there will
never be any good byes.

Cheryl Lynn Fresquez

There's A Time

There's a time to try.
And there's a time to cry.
There is a time to go through.
And there's a time to be blue.
There's a time to clown.
And there's a time to go to town.
There's a time to fall.
And there a time to have a ball.
There is a time to sing.
And there a time to bring.
There's a time to so some where.
And there a time to beware
There a time to rise above.
And there a time to love
There is a time to see
And there is a time to be free.

Earl Ruger

Grandma's Apron

Grandma always wore an apron,
And tied her hair back in a bun;
And when the house was still
I could hear her softly hum.

She was quite a lovely lady,
With character in her face;
She cast a spell on Grandpa
That kept him in his place.

Grandma had seven children in all,
Three girls and four boys;
Raised them in the country
On rag doll dreams and hand made toys.

Grandma's world was her home,
Her family was her life;
She was happy to be a Mother
And proud to be a wife.

She's up in heaven now,
I guess she's resting awhile;
And I'm putting on my apron
Remembering with a smile.

Charlotte McPhail

The Whale

Have you ever seen a whale
As it jumps its magic spreads throughout
So graceful so sleek
When you see it, it makes you wonder how
It also seems to fly
And when you see it you'll wander how

Justin Morgan

Most Valuable Player

Dads tell them to play baseball
and to hit a homerun.
You'll see them all bragging
"Hey, that one's my son."

Dads tell them to play football
and make a touchdown for me.
Someday you're gonna be a pro
and I'll watch you on a T.V.

Dads tell them go play soccer
and kick the goal to win.
One day you're gonna grow
to be the best you've ever been.

Dads tell them to take wrestling
and pin them to the mat.
You're gonna rise above the rest
there's no doubt about that.

Dads tell them "just be my son"
and the winner that you are
because in all the games of life,
you're the best to me by far!

Billie McIntyre

My Mother

Proudly she stands,
and very tall,
Harsh fears, she has many,
But can conquer them all.

Helpful she is,
it's just her way,
If you need something done,
She will work all the day.

Loving she is,
yes, that's mother,
I'll love her for always,
There would be no other.

Debora Bundage

Doing What Comes Naturally

The caterpillar did his thing
And walked as proudly as a king
Until a frog croaked from the ditch,
"Do tell, which leg comes after which?"
Confused and flustered by the thought,
He analyzed until distraught.
Then lay transfixed with legs all locked,
Wondering how it was he walked.

Edith Reed

Clouds

I sit here staring at the sky,
And watch the clouds go passing by.
Like beautiful birds they drift and float.
The sky's the water,
The cloud's the boat.

Courtney Yates

I'm Not Alone

I look at the sky
And what do I see?
The stars are starring at me.
What shall I do?
Shall I run,
Shall I hide,
Or shall I blow them a kiss
And wave good-bye.

Brisa Mar Rodriguez

Untitled

Look in your heart
and you can see
this picture I tell you,
of a cabin nestled
deep in the woods,
With trees so green and tall
that reach beyond
the clouds adrift
And touch the sky so blue.

The picture you see
Hangs in my house
A gift of love to me
From my friend
Who's talents flow
From her heart - to her
hands
And then to thee

Dorothy Pierce

Untitled

A tragic chapter in history
Annihilation

A power hungry soul
Sadistic

The extermination of those unworthy
Genocide

Death, starvation, torture
Suffering

The rape of the soul
Emptiness

The loss of love, hope, and happiness
Loneliness

A haunting of horrific memories
Eternally

Carlos Davis

Homeward Bound

Oh, if there ever was
any other girl
anymore confused,
Quite a lonely feeling,
being lost and abused.
If only I could stop the world
from spinning round and round,
I could collect my thoughts
and being homeward bound.
Oh,Lord, I can see you
now hazy in my mind,
"Hard to reach yet easy to find."
Come and comfort me
and send me homeward bound.

Debra Starr Travers

Impetus

Haunting the soul,
aspirations of one's dreams.
Though having no solid form,
are the foundation on which
life is built.
Without mobility, moving
us to higher achievements.
Not uttering a sound,
yet screaming.

Bill Fannin

Anyone

Pray for me someone
anyone
I've left faith behind
Take my hand someone
anyone
I'm reaching for you
Light the way for someone
anyone
I'm walking in darkness
Fight my battles someone
anyone
I've lost all my strength
Kiss my lips someone
anyone
I need to be loved
Speak to me someone
anyone
I'm losing control

Alexa Edick

Rainbows

I love to see the rainbows
arching thru the sky.
They are put there for their beauty
while a storm is passing by.

They tell us that what happens,
if the sun is shining thru,
It shines down on those raindrops
just like it hits the morning dew.

And reflects all of the colors
from purple down to red
And hangs them in the sky
like a giant silken thread.

That's the thing about a rainbow
that I don't understand.
How it always lays its beauty
in a spectrum colored band.

Maybe why I like it
is the story I am told.
Once you find a rainbow's end
sure you'll find a pot of gold.

Harold A. Reed

Teddy Bears

The fur is soft the eyes
are bold you can't compete
with this fantastic mold
It's rough and tough through
out the years but still dries
little children tears you
can not through this rag
away it brings cheer on
the way and when you
squeeze it tight at night
it snuggles back just right

Amber Pullen

Untitled

The wooden plow
at the end of the row
waiting for
hands that come no more

Helene Heuvel

Apology

Many words worth the time to say
Are filled with thoughts of you;
Spoken under shades of doubt
For who is sure what's true?
Reach out into this darkness,
But return with blind words cast,
Concealed within a promise,
Revealed when days had passed,
And remember how it hurts to feel;
The truth at last!

But freedom sits beside them,
And reminds us fate is free,
And beware of false relations,
Long commitments; obligations,
Promises and strangers,
Harbingers of dangers,
They leave no space to fill in when
they've gone.
But forgive and forget,
Still with regret,
All the many words....

Christine T. LeDoux

Mother

Her tears
are razor blades
in my eyes—
Every word
was a pierce
in my heart,
Each look
caused lesions
in my soul—
My thoughts
were nothing
to her.

Christi Lewinski

Divine Captives

Smouldering deep within us
Are restless captive forces
All-knowing and all-seeing—
A secret core of being.
Veiled elusive shadows,
Distant muted echoes,
Mysterious semblance
Of Mystical expectance
Plaintively calling,
Rippling and falling
From some sequestered stream
Of unremembered dream
Slowly emerging,
Then vibrantly surging
Till freely they pour
And upward they soar
To wake within our hearts
Their reigning Captive Sparks.

Clara Bowie

"To Deem Necessary"

We do as we deem,
As we deem necessary,
Necessary to be stationary..
Stationary seems stable,
Stable until we are able,
Able to understand,
To understand what is really necessary,
Necessary to be stationarily
Stable—stable, as
we do deem...

Eileen Smith

Soldiers Of Fortune

The soldiers of fortune
Are walking off to war
Through the valleys they go
Marching to the battles
They listen to the trumpets sound

The soldiers of fortune
Are walking off to war
Through the valleys they go
Do they march to victory
Or do they march to their graves

The soldiers of fortune
Can never forget
Through the jungles they go
They fight for their lives
But no one wins the game

The soldiers of fortune
Can never forget
Over the mountains they go
Is this just a dream
Or am I still there

Andrea S. Page

Untitled

Ruby fires glow
Arrows pointing toward the sky
Burning through the night

Heather Vander Zwaag

Never

I've never seen a flower,
as beautiful as an hour,
spent with you.

I've never had a day,
long enough to stay,
forever with you.

I've never heard a song,
as sad and as long,
as time away from you.

I never thought I'd roam,
to the end of this poem
without a kiss from you.

Alexander Ewart Peter

And Then There Were None

Four friends.
As close as can be.
One was shot dead.
And then there were three.

Three were left.
It seemed like the flu.
The diseased progressed.
And then there were two.

Two, only two.
Alone with a gun.
A bullet was fired.
And then there was one.

One lonely boy.
Nowhere to run.
Thoughts turned to suicide.
And then there were none.

Chris Sollecito

Barber Benny's Blues

He's feeling terrible today
As he begins to play
With the scissor's in hand
They move as fast as a fan
You sit down and look
At his hair styling book
As you turn each page
You seem to sense his rage
It's time for your cut
So get ready with a buck
But you ran out of luck
Cause he's gonna cut up your butt
I guess your head was one too many
For that barber benny

James Patrick McGowan

Ode To White Watergate (The Arkansas Traveler)

Bubba J. Clinton campaigned
As honest and hicksey,
While spouting artful words
From slick to tricksey,
Carried to victory by Liberal
Promises and media guile,
Billy and Hillary stuck together
In regal and royal style,
As sounds of white water
From yonder dixie,
Echoed in Washington and warned
Of their fixie.

Don Vanderboegh

Crying

my face burns
as i feel the hot tears
streaming down my face
soaking me

and my entire body shakes
violently
with uncontrollable sobs
and terror of this world around me

but i know that
when the tears
and the shaking
finally end,
like the sun
breaking through after the storm,
the horrible agony
and the pain
will evaporate with my salty tears
leaving only the faint, sticky residue
to remind me of the past.

Alissa Abbey

Doing It Right

You can rely on your dream
As your destination and guide
To succeeding.
Erasing and demolishing your wrong
doings,
And immediately setting them right.
Contributing to the future is our
obligation.
Making us the role models of the
future.
And never getting discouraged.

Crystal Luong

Crimson Dawn

My heart nearly skipped a beat
As I gazed upon the sight
Of a gold and crimson sunrise
Dawns first shred of light
I could hear the whispered song
Of a soft and gentle sea
Whose harmony and verse
Brought life back into me
If ever a man need to find
His place upon this Earth
Step out amidst the humbling sea
And witness a new days birth
For men too low in spirit
And those riding high on pride
There lies a gentle asylum
Within the quiet tide
My eyes nearly shed a tear
As I watched the sun resign
But the promise of the crimson dawn
Gave me comfort 'til that time

Joseph S Mannino II

"Rebirth"

Lights are out
as I lie awake,
listening.
Thunder rumbles
and crashes, breaking
the steady rhythm
of falling rain,
sinking deep down
into the earth
awakening a dormant power.
Sounds of fury
unleashed
and of soothing gentleness.

Donna Shockley

Untitled

I live each day
as if it were my last.
So if it don't kiss you today,
I'll surely die tomorrow
with a tear in my eye.

The seeds I sow
are ripened by your eyes
and nourished by your soft breath.
Your gentle touch softens
the petals of my life.

The shoes I walk in
were made for me and you.
The footsteps we take today
lead us down a path that
we didn't have yesterday.

The keys I hold
unlock the mysteries of your heart.
The pen I use to write with
unveils the words I long to say
but say to late.

Daniel P. Dugan

What's In A Fantasy?

I watch the eagle spread its wings—
As it begins to soar the mountain high,
I watch the unicorns dance about—
Their horns reaching for the sky.

Gnomes and trolls running about—
in and out of the forest near,
mermaids and maidens joining hands—
Becoming friends secretly here.

I see the good over the evil—
And there's no one to fight or fret,
I see only happiness here—
And no love's been lost yet.

The trees blow the leaves so quietly—
Like they're singing their own song,
The world here is so perfectly built—
And it seems nothing could ever go wrong.

Only one problem ever exists—
And it dwells inside of me,
All of these beautiful things—
Can only be seen in a fantasy!

Alicia Cortes

The Nineth Hour

The Hour of Nine is past and gone
As now his dreams unfold.
Since I've said my last good-bye
To another dear soaring soul.

The scene changes as years roll by.
The old arm chair unoccupied.
It stands alone against the wall
With cords a hand has tied.

The Bible lies surrounded with dust
On the cobwebbed, covered stand.
The one that Father had read
Was untouched by human hand.

Each of us must face that hour
When the clock of time chimes nine.
"Come my child, it is time to go,"
So many now form the line.

The Nineth Hour soon will be,
When before the King we stand.
How will it be with you, dear friend,
Since you have reached that Land?

Clinton E. Riddle

Time

"Time is of the essence"
As poets used to say

Never look back
Always know the way

Time will never leave
Time will never die

You can never out run it
It's always by your side

Live your life by the rules of time
And in the end you'll be just fine

"Time is of the essence"
As poets used to say

Never look back
Always know the way

Amber Rodgers

Remember

He was as strong as steel,
As tall as the trees,
And as soft as the wind.
I called him "Pappa",
He called me "Shorty".
He was my grandfather,
And now I dearly miss him.
He saw me off to school,
And greeted me as I came home.
He helped me through the thick and thin,
But now I can only remember him.
As I gaze at the world
He stares with me.
As I stand on this earth
He guides me.
He watches me
With the greatest of care,
But now,
All I can do,
Is remember the times we shared.

Bonnie Dulaney

Memories Of A Day

All things come to pass
As the day goes by.
The memories forever last
As each minute ticks its cry.

This dance to cherish
Is a million in one —
Holding to the memories
Like the morning sun.

A day never to forget
Like the birth of light,
As I recollect the emotions
Before the day turns to night.

Ida Barbee

Ode To A Sister

Sister, mentor, protector, friend,
Assisting siblings, it matters not when.
Walking to school in first grade,
teaching reading till sunlight fade.

Washing faces and combing hair,
tending siblings each moment spare.
Wiping noses and tying shoes,
counting and multiplying by twos.

Helping with reading and penmanship,
mending and sewing seams that rip.
Washing and ironing all the clothes,
All dressed up the handiwork shows.

Giving answers the teacher can't hear,
minus grades points held secretly, dear
Knowing you are the head of the class,
notwithstanding who's acclaimed alas.

Tending, giving, loving, providing,
teaching siblings, always guiding,
A selfless sister, it's quite clear
thanks many million, Lena dear.

Hazel B. Franklin

"Cocaine Hell"

His life it did not matter
at least that's what he said
As he smoked up some cocaine
And laid upon his bed.

He smoked cocaine every day
To calm his nerves he said
As his heart begin to hurt
So he laid upon his bed

When he drove his car
he handed in a jail
his mind was confused and worn
When he landed in the pits of hell.

To me, his life mattered
as I held his shaking head
Then he drew his last breath.
And I laid him upon his bed.

Donna V. Beck

To A Praying Mantis

This morning you left us
at the first light of dawn.
Softly you spread your wings
and flew, who knows where.
We, who challenged your environment
and brought you in to save you
for we thought that you would die.
We mourn, for we will miss you.
You, an insect, that we came to love.
Wondering to what strange god you
prayed.
We promise we will care for, nourish
The amazing legacy you bequeathed
your young, safely cocooned
waiting to be born
to bring the joy of you again.

Gillian M. Stone

So Much Love

Country music
At the Yucatan Liquor Stand.
Remember the
Laughter, the
Loyalty, the

Very beginning of;
I love you
Now and forever.
Compatible,
Easy going,
Noble,
The man that holds my heart.

Just you and I in
Unison, day and
Night.
I
Only need your love for the
Rest of my life.

Gina L. Hadley

Array Of Kisses

Before conception was creation
Before desire was motion
Trembling with tenderness
an idea became an act
descending the notion
Thought became the morning
Morning moved with the sun
Angels kissed the galaxies
and the earth was born.

Doris Hartsell Brewer

Crawling Into The Wooden Box

I stared into the wooden box
At your silent little face
Trying to grasp
Some understanding
Of a fate which would make you come
And go so soon

It seemed impossible to bear
Standing there much longer
So I crawled into the box with you
Drawing up my knees to my chin,
Hoping that someone would close the lid
Before they noticed
That I was still alive

It was only when I heard
Them say
Silly grown woman
Get out of there
And behave normally
That I began to cry
And cry, And cry

Christa G. Long

Our Freedom Is Our Aim

One day we will be free
away from lock and key
away from heavy chains
Our freedom is our aim.

No-one will put us down
nor hold us to the ground,
no-more hurt or pain
Our freedom is our aim.

But they all come at night
to late for us to fight,
and stay till it was day
Not a thing that we could say.

They would hit us with their bats
and make us sleep like rats,
but they couldn't feel our pain
To them it was just a game.

During the day our heads held high
but by night you will hear our cry,
they beat us till we're bruised and red
They wont stop till we're all dead.

Chayneen Strachen

Warriors Of The Night

Wingtipped warriors of the night
barbarians, social blight
redefining wrong and right
warriors of the night

Corporation, mother's scum
sit lizard like neath plastic suns
they bob and weave
yet bow to none
warriors of the night

Harlotry, sister dear
all understand and draw her near
they'll sell their souls
to eat it whole
warriors of the night

Vampirism, they embrace
draining you to win the race
they'll bleed you dead
to get ahead
warriors of the night

Bob Culbertson

Wondering

I wonder what it would
be like to live in a world unaccustomed
to pollution.
I wonder what it would
be like to drink fresh, clear water
from a crystal clear lake.
I wonder what it would
be like to walk through
one of many rain forests.
I wonder what it would
be like to know instead of
wonder.

Angie N. Davis

Different

They say I'm strange,
because my actions and thoughts
differ from theirs.
They care not to listen
or understand the inner me,
for if they would,
they fear to find themselves in me,
so judge not, cause others may act
or think different from thee.

Betty Hough

Sad People In The World

Sad people in the world are sad.
Because people in there family get
kill or hurt. People are sad. Because
they have no money no food for
there kids or they got put out of
there home. Or they got fired. The
kids out side are sad. Because they
have no food to eat or no clothes
to wear everyday. They get food
for the store. But they steal from
the people that work there. They
get sent to jail or get kill.

Cliffanee Page

Will You Be There For Me?

Dedicated to Steven Forshey

Will you be there for me
before I even call,
Will you be there for me
to hold me all night long,
Will you be there for me
to ease my pain,
Will you be there for me
to dry my eye's
Will you be there for me
So I won't have to cry,
Will you be there for me
my whole life through
Will you be there for me
If so: I know your love is true
because I feel that no one can
love me the way you do!

Becky DePoty

As I Dream

I often ponder,
Does anyone want to share them with me?
I wonder if I will grow old alone.
Maybe, maybe not.
I think of this,
As I dream.

Danny Ohman

Win Me A Prize

Win me a prize
Before the storm do rise
Do win me a prize
Give me a big surprise
Win me a prize
That really shock my eyes
Do win me a prize
One that satisfies
I want a big prize
Not a tiny one
One with many colors
That will bring me fun
Win me a prize
Before the storm do rise
Oh win me a prize
That's what my heart cries.

Frances Minor Trotter

In And Out

Behind the sun I faced the day
Behind the moon I felt this sway
Behind the stars I found the night
Behind the night I vanished from sight

Inside the colors there were shades
Inside the shades there were shapes
Inside the shapes, there was form
Inside the form, I found the function

Behind the door I found the opening
Inside the opening I noticed the shift
Inside the shift I found my memory
Inside my memory I found myself

Facing forward I noticed space
Noticing space I found the negative
Finding the negative I found the positive
Finding the positive I found proportion

Seeing light I saw the edge
On the edge I saw dimensions
Seeing the dimensions, I found you
Finding you I complete the cycle

David Timothy Ferrell

The Beauty Of A Rose

As I was walking through the park
Beside an old stone wall
I saw a little rose bud
In withered grass so tall.

It look so very out of place
For something Oh! so fair
I wondered quietly to myself
Why God paced it there.

There was a crevice in the wall,
A gleam of light shone through,
The rose bud lifted its sleepy head
And to a lofty height it grew.

As it grew up the old stone wall
And through the crevice came,
It became a beautiful rose
And its fragrance was the same.

Bonnie Snively

"Thorns Of Love"

Love is like a Rose
but the thorns of jealousy
cut just like a knife.

Gardner John Clark IV

Stormy Day In Arizona

One stormy day in Arizona I saw
Black dark clouds with a
Beautiful rainbow, which hovered the
Sky like a shooting star.

When I stood there and watched
The clouds move swiftly, I noticed
Something was weird, the sky was
Dark and ground was light as day.

I wondered how that could be,
Till I noticed the sun was
out in an opening where the
clouds were spread wide apart.

Jason Niedermaier

The Pale

Cracks run deeper with the day
Black springs left to flood
Some icy seaweed bay
Whispers from the outside
Nestled in the curl of a sullen tide
Spiral flight from the shore
Meant to stay nevermore

I've come to the chasm
Below where bright eyes laugh
The Pale scuttle in spasm
Driftwood the mossy chaff
The dead dying still
Out of the light
They shiver but rejoice in the chill
For they breathe better in the night
And I've come to breathe with them

Andrew M. Claps

Underground

Young white woman on the "F" train
bound for who knows where...
Reading a book called "Celestial
Navigation"
Does anyone really care?
A black woman sittin' opposite her reads
her red lettered Bible and purses
her lips...
Looks up now and then to glance at
the scholar -
Who's dreaming about gypsy pirate ships
- Sail on into the quiet -
- Sail on into the night -
Both children of the darkness
And children of the light. . .

Charlene F. Hoffmann

She And He

Craving and anxious to get,
but deranged about her feelings.
Wondering if an immense family
is right for her. A house of
minute size crowed, with lots.
Thinking, is he unison with
kids. What if mishap should
happen while she was absent,
would he be present. Asking
herself will he be there to
promote me or pull me down.
Pondering about the questions
that face her, she determines
unwed is wright for her

Grace Williams

Passion

Passion makes you and
breaks you.
It soars you to
the highest mountain
It,
makes you sweat
or
brings the coldest chill,
Passion
Gives you aches
that no one but
no one understands
like you
Passion is
The deepest expression
of
One's innermost desires
Passion is
The climax of
Body and soul and mind.

Cynthia Blount

Four Seasons

Spring is here, this we see
Breezes so mellow drift with glee
Wild flowers too, all over the place
Glorious feeling, look at our face!

Now summer has come bye
Sun shining bright, blue is the sky
These happy days are for all living
Nights are for our love giving.

Brilliant autumn is now here
All of us are of good cheer
Leaf colors so very bright
Are indeed a beauteous sight.

Our winter has finally come
With snow and wind, and for some
Awareness of all these seasons four
Let us be thankful; who could ask for
more?

Frances Lewis

Lady Autumn

The coming of autumn
brings sadness
to the heart of some
who cherish Summer's warmth
and penetrating sun.

But as for me
I welcome
Lady Autumn
with her leaves of red and gold
my curtains dance above the sill
within her wind so bold.

Lady Autumn
a frisky one is she!
Nobody's sleepy fool
her tempo bold and free

I welcome her with excitement
and energy to spare
brisk winds speak of the Holidays
and the goodwill that we'll share
Welcome back most beautiful Lady

Joan E. Stanley

To The West

It is written on children's faces
But I remember not that tongue
A silent void has replaced
The angels that once sung.

It has been long since I have spoken
To the wind on a summer's day
And in the time I have forgotten
What it means to laugh and play

Dreams that once were held so dearly
Fill me only with empty sorrow
At memories I forgot to make
And lost chances I can not borrow

In a field of dandelions
I sat and watched my life gone by
And wasted still the rest of it
Because all I could do was weep and sigh

I should have looked toward the east
Taken my life anew with the rising sun
Instead I looked only to the west
And waited 'til my life was done.

Cheryl Thayer

I'm The One Called "Doc"

I shall not walk in your footsteps,
but I will walk by your side.
I shall not walk in your image,
I've earned my own title of pride.

We've answered the call together,
on sea and foreign land.
When the cry for help was given,
I've been there, right at hand.

Whether I am on the ocean,
or in the jungle wearing "greens".
Giving aid to my fellow man,
be it Sailors or Marines.

So the next time you see a corpsman,
and you think of calling him "squid",
Think of the job he's doing,
as those before him did.

And, if you ever have to go out there
and your life is on the block,
look at the one right next to you.
I'm the one called "Doc".

Harry D. Penny Jr.

Why?

You said it be forever,
but then I knew you lied.
You said you loved me,
but then one day it died.
You said it was over.
But I was just a friend.
You said this all to me,
but how could it end?

Tell me how it went so good,
but then how fast it went?
Tell me how you said you loved me,
but how much I really meant?
Tell me how I went so wrong,
but what I did so bad?
Tell me how we don't belong,
but what we could have had?

Gina Taormina

"Dripping Moon"

I started to walk so all alone
But in a short distance
My heart screamed
And my mind moaned.

The thickness of the forest
Etched in my aching soul
To get out was my only goal.

Darkness of the day
Lightness by the night
Evil spirits dance about
Wearing lustful smiles of delight

The moon dripped its last tear
Near the flames below
The sizzle did nothing
But make the winds blow bitter cold.

Which way to go
Up or left, down or right
It doesn't matter
It's all a guess
On these strange nights

John David Correa

The October Breeze

Autumn leaves and chilling breeze,
but in between, a summer breeze,
that keeps us going all around;
To work or school, or even play,
it's all in the October breeze.

Cool nights and refreshing days
That bring us all to a start,
hustling off or taking it cool, or
Just drifting in the blues,
It's all in the October breeze.

Passing by the falling leaves
for so much is seen in them,
An ending tide, a new beginning
for this is the course of nature
In the October breeze.

A little here, a little there, it's some
celebration
Columbus day, some affair, it's also
Halloween,
Happy faces, sad faces and those in
between,
View the changes all around us
In the October breeze.

Icilma Thorpe

Untitled

The past is gone, or so they say
But it has a part, in your lives today
we remember. The good, to cover the bad
but it makes us believe, these days
are the best, we have. Ever had
the right over wrong, has served us well
our belief in God, gives us a story
to tell.

So as we strive, to do our best,
and life puts us to the test,
we can leave, a path that others
will seek
which will serve the great,
as well as the meek.

Edna B. Knose

"Long Live"

It lives forever,
But never breathes.
It's extremely clever,
Almost a dream.

It never cries,
But often one will weep.
It chills the spine,
But can generate heat.

It can give love,
And take it away.
It generates faith,
But cannot pray.

Thy see it undying.
It never is lying.
It needs no chiding,
For it's heart is a writing.

So live forever!
Never breath!
Be extremely clever!
Become a dream!

Gregory James Rinaldi

To Each One A Home

The earth God gave to man
But not to man alone
Animals and birds both small and great
To each one He gave a home.

All of these creatures are our neighbors,
Homes of every kind and size we see,
They like us... strive to live
As a result of all their labor.

Their life and home means all to them
Then a family all their own
God watches over all their needs
And to each one He gives a home.

On earth all have one life to live
It's part of God's great plan
As neighbors we all should be
On this earth God gave to man.

We all belong to God
He left not man or beast alone
We should work and try to live in peace
Until God shall call us home.

John Beckstead

The Letter

When a letter from home,
Came in the mail,
I was no longer alone,
Hearing from the place I had hailed.

The letter brought a smile,
But only for a while,
I then thought of the days,
While thinking in a gaze,
About when I was alive.
It came too late, I failed to survive.

How I wish I could answer,
But had died of cancer.
Only from above,
Could I send my love.

Carla M. Roccapriore

Love By Reflection

I know of no greater beauty
but that which my eyes do behold
Nor do I know a greater desire
for the one I wish to enfold

I know of no sweeter nectar
but the moment your lips touch mine
Nor do I know another heartbeat
to share my walk through time

I know of no greater sadness
than the moments we are apart
And together there is no greater joy
but the love which lies in my heart

I know of no greater feelings
but those which are shared by two
Or those which come from deep within
from the one who cares for you

I know of no greater ecstasy
but the warmth of your sensual dew
There is nothing more magnificent
than the total magnificence of you

James B. Edwards

Elusive Path

I am ready
But where are the roads
Wait listen
Sardonic whispers
They've all gathered for my show

Will I recognize the audience
of vast uncertainty

Ironic delight
They reek of
status quo
Who were those strangers
Masked in placid faces
Deaf
silent
Must walk through that door
O beautiful solitude

Juan Fernandez

The Criminal

There is a man, that is truly cursed,
By his own and bitter shame,
And there is a hatred, and a fear,
At the mention of his name!

What are his thoughts,
As he sits in his cell?
Has he ever a thought
Of God's Heaven or Hell?

Is he to be forever outcast
Even to the end of his days?
And must his sad, old parents
Take blame for his murderous ways?

What help is there to ever be,
For this doomed and troubled man?
Hasn't there always been his kind
Ever since the world began?

Now his life is behind barred doors.
For him, it's the only way.
And for all of his crimes, a wasted life,
Is the price that he has to pay!

Alice DeBow Krohne

Sappling

The little tree
by itself
in the field

How did I get here
How come I'm
all alone

I have some leaves
but just a few
life is essentially meaningless
what should I do

The other day
A little bird
came and sat on my branch
but didn't build a nest

He had a lot of feathered friends
and they took him away
but that's ok

The wind sings to me
and the dew embraces me
mother earth is so polite

Damien Cavicchi

Tap! Tap! At The Door!

There's a sound in the darkness
By the door as the morning rooster crows
Tap! Tap! At the door!
My dozing mind speaks
Are you a friend? Are you a foe?
Are you evil at the door?
Silence it is, just
Tap! Tap! At the door!
What is it that's tapping?
No! Don't open the door!
In my frenzy
I fear not the foe
For what is there
Is just a tap at the door
I shut my eyes
Delirious for sleep . . .
When terror strikes!
Eeeeeeee-ow-wow! wow! wow!
The screams of the cats unbelievable in heat
Shrieks with painful savor

Benjamin Diama

Jesse

In the dark, you sit and wait
By the door, I stand and state
I need time, to think and find
one bright star and peace of mind,
Let this soul, run free and tall
Let the past, leave me and fall
Only to make a new start,
And have your smile in my heart.
The wind blows, I turn away
By my side, you stand and say,
Love is hard, all this I know,
But it's cold out, please don't go

Arlene Guzman

Earth And Sky

Bound to flight
By two, wide spread wings
Spawn of Father Sky
'Tis where she belongs

Tied to the land
With four. Sturdy paws
Born of Mother Earth
'Tis where he belongs

Yet, earth and sky,
The two torn lovers
Find a way to keep
Their beautiful love whole

Both torn by boundaries of spirit
Love finds a way
Where wings and paws can meld
And lovers can love

Far as the eye can see
Impossible to reach
Where earth and sky make love
There lies the horizon

Dina Rivera

Shadows

Quiet,
calm,
deadly fright,
weeping winds in the moon light.
Walking darkness,
creaking stairs,
shadows dancing without cares.
Feelings cry in the dark,
shadows have fallen
and made their mark.

Jocelyn Dunn

Two Girls Sitting In The Dark

Sitting, smiling in the dark,
Can you hear my beating heart?
Staring deep at your sweet face,
Cannot blink; no better place.
Laughing, giggling nervously.
Thinking back; sweet memory.
Coming close,in front of me,
Heart is beating rapidly.
Close your eyes, you start again.
Then we laugh and turn away.
Close your eyes, you start to say
I am kissing my best friend.
Too late now; we can't go back,
Feel a sudden heart attack.
I love you, but in what way?
World keeps turning every day
There is no one, only you.
Oh, tell me, what did we do?
Two girls sitting in the dark,
Can you see my broken heart?

Dawn Marie

The New Slaves

No-face bodies, soulless forms,
Corridors of buildings, fog, cold rain,
Nimble fingers well trained,
From the vines trim the thorns
For the Master's climb rung by rung,
And in the evening
All the children's songs unsung.

June Warrington Williams

The Smell

The smell
Can you smell it?
I can
The name I can't tell you
But the girl
I always remember the girl
Just a fading scent
Just a whiff of the perfume
Sometimes a smile
Sometimes a shiver
The name I can't tell you
But the girl
I always remember the girl.

Claude Rayfield

Arise, Young Ishmael!

Abandoned by my mother!
"Cast from him" by my Dad!
The food and waters used up
There's nothing now but bad!
So weakened — days of hunger!
So famished for a drink!
I just can't keep from wailing!
I care not! E'en to think!
I know that Sarai Hates me —
She's jealous of my mom!
By mocking her (my "fun-time") —
DEATH I've brought upon!
I guess it'll soon be over
A boy — thirteen, to cry!
No! I'll not let death take me!
Not 'til there's ONE MORE TRY
What? Do I hear Mom — coming!
That's Mother-Love no doubt
She's lifting up my head now!
Cool water's pouring out!

Florence I. Frazee

Ode To The Cat

Our love and pleasure's a red striped
Cat.

He's recognized by every bird, mouse and
Rat.

Here and there in our garden—smooth
Stalker,

In our family room, he's one big
Talker.

Under trees and flowers, he traps his
Prey,

Then displays catch in dining room, same
Day.

He doesn't question that he is our
Pet:

He decided when at animal shelter we
Met.

Carl Schaefer

The Water People

We glide along, effortless, soundless,
drifting through shadows and sun,
As if our lives could intermingle
with the infinity of the world...

Helen Ganger

Pure Flight

Shrouded in a cloak of flesh
Certain to abscond its cocoon
one day
Whence I do not know
Nor in what way?

Invisible as the wind
And silent as the night
Like a metamorphosis—
Changing into flight

When the transformation occurs
Gracefully, as a white dove
To the GREAT BEYOND
Soaring to the Heavens above

Seeking my reward
Eternity is my goal
For with this passing
I speak of my SOUL!

Evelyn Hilpp Heslin

Time

Time has endless flight
Changes Spring to Fall
Day to night
Birthdays come and go
Time is a great healer
God helps us, he is a fair dealer

Time is an essence in our life
Accomplishment is our strife,
Time is enclosed in our living soul
And heaven is our spirits goal

Ethel Hansen

Summer Is Best Of All

Summer now has gone away,
children rarely go to play.
Falling leaves are not a boon,
winter winds will be here soon.

Falling leaves are fun to see,
but in summer you'd rather be.
December seems to hold some fun,
yet still depressed that summers done.

In spring the buds begin to grow,
getting ready for the summers show.
Summer is the best of all,
not spring, nor winter, not even fall.

Eric K. Hoover

Lost In The Blaze

I see her figure in the way:
Clothes tossed in a daze,
Cuteness fading.
Of a stream thrown West,
Nightmare is habit,
A silent rage,
Mind blowing views;
My position fading,
Lost in the blaze.
Coma returns now,
Again in a daze.

David Davare

What Is The Matter?

I am the quiet,
closed books stacked in the stillness;
the calm,
colored carpet
laid to rest; the living
room television set lit
with sounds;
the radio singing
everyone's favorite
song; the coffee perking
in the pot;
the child;
the air;
the sun;
the seas.
"I am
all
this," Atom
said
spinning.

Dana Knudson

So The Song Ends

Empty,
Cold and confused,
Sorrow felt,
For a man I never knew.

But his words, so strong,
They cut and heal,
He grips my soul,
While I listen and feel.

Life can be black,
His pain I have known,
But when he spoke in his songs,
I knew his dreams were my own.

Yesterday we were lovers,
Tomorrow we'll be brothers.
Today he sings while I cry,
Today he died while I asked why.

Brilliance wasted,
Still so much to give,
Too tired to see,
Just what it's worth to live

David C. Hurne

Wandering

Wandering together through the
cold sand at night
Together, we walked completely
out of sight
The moonlight gleamed
upon the lake
Was it special or
was it just fate
Together forever and
never apart
We promised each other
by crossing our heart
The cool night breeze
brought us closer together
We promised that our love
will last forever

Edwin Santiago

The Tide

Peacefully lapping onto the sloped shore,
Coming and going like a pendulum...
Never ending,
But watch for El Nino to kick in...

Crash! The sea is a beast,
Roaring and raging without calming,
Not even caring about how much
Destruction is being done.

It floods everything
That doesn't keep its distance,
Going in the water would be suicide,
Virtually a liquid guillotine.

The storm has moved away,
Leaving complete and utter devastation
In its path.
The tide is once again a pendulum,
Swaying with the peacefulness
Of a daisy in the breeze.

Eric Oberschmidt

The Desirous Kill

The Tyger and the Lamb,
Compared and contrast.
With his experience
death is in sight;
To stalk and to hunt
naturally comes to claws.
Ripping and tearing the flesh
until the urge,
the hunger, is gone.

The tiger's instincts
are to survive-
to multiply.
So, tiger meets tyger
and the hunt goes around, again.
Today not to kill,
but always to instill.

Jennifer Richards

Concert

I hear the electricity,
Conducted through the strings.
The sound of thunder,
A drumset brings.
The rain falls,
Through a piano's keys.
The words of a song,
How a singer sees.
The roar of the crowd,
The sound of applause.
The lights go out, a sudden pause.
A scream cries out,
From the darkened sky.
An encore begins, the final good-bye.
The stage lights up, one last time.
The shadows dance,
And sing the rhyme.
The music fades into the lights.
The faces become shallow,
And escape in the night.

JoAnna Stramel

Fears

Everybody has fears but
Cry with tears
Too much pain can't take away
Your fears
But understand, having tears is
Washing away your fears
There will always be a tomorrow
For your tears but
Try to understand your fears
These fears will not stay forever

Andrea Ozenna

"In My Mind's Eye"

In my minds eye came a vision of
dancing and laughter, of love and,
of such heated passion. I wanted
to forever embrace this magnificent
vision and never let go. Suddenly!
to my disbelief I realized this
vision was the life I had yearned
for mine to be, but time has passed
and much to late for me, so I will
keep this vision in my minds eye
for only me to see.

Donna Tygh

Enchanted Love

Enchanted love
Dancing under the pale moon light,
Embracing hearts,
Visions of delight.
A chemistry flow,
So few do know,
This life,
This love,
So true we show.
Like a view of the stars,
Shining diamonds in the night,
This call of serenity,
Fulfillment taking flight,
Soaring higher, and higher,
Each day so new
Enchanted love,
I hold this for you.

Christopher K. Miller

Thorns For Sleeping Beauty

My heart is hidden, like a cove
Dark shaded by a thickset grove;
My heart is dormant, like a seed
That none will cultivate or weed.

Deep is my heart, like mountain lakes,
Reflecting all the light it takes;
Heavy my heart, and like a stone
That broods upon the hill alone.

Find the science or the spell
To reach the heart unreachable;
Speak what magic can be spoken
To restore the heart that's broken.

Will some hero, late and panting,
Bring the remedy that's wanting —
Or must I, as it now appears,
Sleep for another hundred years?

Joanne Ramey Cage

A Broken Heart Cry

As I sit in the
darkness all alone in
think of what I should do
what I should say how can
I hate someone I love.
The more I think about
us the more it hurts
the more I picture us
together the more I see
you with her. You have
left, I have started to
except maybe it's better
that way.
We are apart, you
are together will you always
remember.

Christine Patricia Helbig

Please

Into my soul the night slides
darkness seeps where light abides
shadows creep across my thoughts
memories wane, goodness rots
skewed and bent, oblong and hazed
logic, coherence stand dazed
silent wishes, evil dreams
ominous clouds, blood red streams
those suppressed, held back so long
now are ready, firm, and strong
currents course within my veins
Its power over me reigns
mindless slave, a helpless pawn
inward further I am drawn
ruin and desecration
atrocious consummation

Chris Lincoln

Untitled

Clear blue water
Deep and yet so shallow
Like the sun's bright beam
And the touch of winter's first snow

The secret of insanity
So fresh upon the grave
Leave it- let it be
Soon returns the old darkness
We've known for so long

The hate that dwells upon a corps
So thick in the midnight air
Trying to be released
Yet learning to be held

The cries of fear
The tears of joy
The laugh of hate
Destroys us all in a single moment
Insanity- the key that unlocks it all

Ann Conner

Salvation

This weariness is all consuming -
Driving me down
Into depths of deep despair.

But, "This too will pass," was written -
To keep hope burning -
I remember - and once more -
Start to care.

Anne Underwood

Searching

I've always been searching
deep in thought
For oh, so many, many years,
wondering what I ever did
To cause your painful tears.
Now I know they had nothing at all,
to do with me,
And all to do, with your own
inner, hurting plea.
A plea for loving acceptance of
your own true self.
The precious self that you never
were able to reveal to me.

Helena M. Roessler

Untitled

Burning, churning
Depression's pain
Lurid, twisting
I have no name
Looking, looking
I can not see for the rain
There are red marks on my window pane
Now I live on madhouse Lane.

Erica Himes

Untitled

Did you hear the people crying?
Did you hear them just the same?
Did you see the children dying?
Did you hear me call your name?

Yes. But you just kept on walking,
You didn't even look back.
You just kept on running,
You and your knapsack.

Did you hear the people screaming?
Did you hear me cry 'Come back'?
Did you hear the sirens blaring?
I know there's something that you lack.

Angela Battisti

Wishing Well

If you let go of pain,
do you think it will leave?

If you kick your feelings out,
would you then never grieve?

If you drain all your fears,
will no hurt come about?

If you bottle up your tears,
could you live through a drought?

If you told your hate
it's not welcome here,
would you then see purity
when you look in a mirror?

If you drop a coin
in a wishing well,
will it be listening
as you humbly dwell?

Would it all be gone
and life begin new
just as the sky
always returns blue?

Judith Lynne Todd

God's Precious Gift

Lying so peaceful,
does she ever dream?
She's the most beautiful
person I've ever seen.
Her ivory white skin,
her subtle, but clear smile;
I think I'll just sit here
and watch her awhile.
Her sweet, pink lips,
her soft, gentle smell;
why God gave her to me.
I'll never be able to tell.
Will I be good enough for her?
Will she come to me when in pain?
Since she entered my life,
I haven't been the same.
I know I owe God
for putting you in my world,
my beautiful, beautiful,
Sweet baby girl.

Amanda Davies

Please Don't

Don't tell me, you're surprised,
Don't tell me, you have realized
Don't tell me more lies
Don't tell me you'll cry,
Don't tell me you're sorry,
Don't tell me, you're sad
Don't tell me, you regret:
Don't tell me, you still care,
Don't tell me, to forget,
Don't, don't it's too late
Don't you see, you had your fun
Don't you know, now is my turn
Don't be sorry, be glad.
Don't regret, the past is gone
Don't, please don't tell me.
more lies.

Anita M. Mill

Nature

Rustling leaves, beautiful trees.
Don't you love nature?
Foxes leaping, squirrels sleeping.
Don't you love nature?
Coyote's moaning, stream's flowing.
Don't you love nature?
I always did I opened a lid into
a beautiful world God made.
Don't you love nature?

Heather Holding

Love Cycle

You live, you die
Every time you love you live
You find, you love
You feel, you give
You do, you know -
Every time you love, you die
You want, you will
You hurt, you cry
Every time you love, you live
You need, you believe
You try, you smile
You seek, you find
You love, you live
Every time.

Delores Redd

One Immortal Soul

One immortal soul
drifting through space and time
searching...searching...searching

For a home in the arms
of a woman!

One immortal soul
drifting from shell to shell
it has occupied the shells
of those whose hands are torn
From serving and the shells
of those they have served.
Searching...searching...searching

For a home
in the arms
of a
woman.

for Ann Doyle

Brian J. Murray
(11/5/67 - 12/23/94)

Ashes To Ashes

Ashes to ashes
Dust to Dust
What ever happened to simple trust?
Has it suffered the final fate of death?
Perhaps in some dreamless state it lies,
A most appropriate disguise,
For simple trust,
Within the heart it hides,
And only will awaken,
When openly is broken,
Then in the offended heart
Is oft times put to death.

Charlie London

"A Moment In Time"

I watched in patience this little bud
Each morning a marvel, a little more
Until in its fourth day, an unfurling
dewy radiance
I cupped it in my hands a tear fell.
I think of God, kissed its sweet petals
and walked away.
In my heart a moment of eternity will
forever stay.

Ann Conway

The Spree

Cheeky shopper rose
early on Sunday
to gather the stock
of imagination
- any loose toy
her imprecise tongue
clucking
grocery store brogue
and the rules
as we go,
her tiny hands
pass goods to
her elder-checker
over a makeshift counter,
tipped red cooler,
and she thanks him
properly for the
priceless memory

David C. Scruggs

Your Smile

Your smile won me over
Even though I once feared,
Your eyes make me blush
Whenever you're near.

Where are you going
And where have you been?
I long for the day
To be more than a friend.

I know what we can have is
limited as such,
Still my heart keeps on yearning
While I hope for too much.

So please don't run away
And leave me behind,
I won't give you trouble
of any kind.

I just want to see you
and hold your strong hand,
Stoke your face, kiss your lips
for as long as I can...

Donna Wright Stofer

"Finding Love"

I want to be near you
  Every hour of the day-
I now have a clear view
  Of the real you, I'd say!

You came into my life
  Slowly, but quite sure,
I forgot all strife
  And now I can endure!

You make me feel like somebody!
  I'm up on "cloud nine,"
Like I just had a "hot toddy,"
  And like I've found a gold mine!

Don't ever let me down
  Just keep my spirits high,
And keep on hanging around
  And I'll love you till I die!

I love everything about you
  You're such a dear!
I'll try to never doubt you,
  If you'll just stay near!

Ella Mae Vogt

Spring

Spring is a beautiful time of the year,
Everything is in bloom.
For here and there and everywhere,
Birds sing a happy tune.

Animals are happily prancing around.
The meadows are gleaming and bright.
The air is full of pleasant sounds.
Oh what a beautiful sight.

Baby animals are being born
On many days in spring.
We love to wake up every morn
To hear all the wonderful things.

We love spring, yes we do,
When all the snow melts away.
We love spring, yes we do,
So let's all say hip hip hooray.

Deana Lyann Smith Asbury

Ashes

I belong in the air
Everywhere
From there you can see
You can see far and clear
Where there is no fear
There's no need to hide
Up and away far and wide
Up in the air
Where everything's clear
At times you can hear
A voice that is dark
Darkness can hide
All that is
All that is you
All that is me
Far and away, where
There is no need
No need to be seen
No need to be heard
All that is you, all that is me.

A. J. Diaz

Stress

Fingers thumping,
Eyelids jumping,
Heartbeat pounding,
Siren sounding,
  Breathing racing,
  Sleepless pacing,
  Headache screaming,
  Moonless dreaming,
    Shelter fading,
    Friendships trading,
    Stomach wrenching,
    Thin lips clenching,
      Thoughts all scattered,
      Nothing matters,
      Numbness calling,
      Teardrops falling,
      God, I need a break.

Debora Ledford

A Single Tear

A single tear falls from the
  Eyes of a child,
A child so tender, and yet so
  mild.

The child sits in a corner all
  alone,
For knowing that no one is
  at home.

For sitting and hearing the
  sounds of the night,
Trying to live with his terror
  and fright.

In the corner he tries to
  hide,
For no one is there by his
  side.

Torn apart by his family
  so dear,
All his emotions in A Single
  Tear.

Christina L. Brittingham

Untitled

Slipping away,
Eyes open, eyes closed.
Orange light. Beautiful.
Breathe, yes, deep breaths.
Life is so hard sometimes.
I should be afraid
But I'm not.
Breathe, deep breaths.
What?
All is one.
I get it,
Now.

Chappy Morris

Untitled

The sky
face of Moons
and Suns
Emotions, colors of chaos
Dripping
Tinted mixtures of Love

SPACE STORM
Dark waters of the Universe
Rain falls
over moons, city's of Golds
thunder rocks planets
snow frozen
cave of blackness
stars swim through summer satellites

Christine Braeuner

The Rain

I stood in the glistening street
face upturned towards the darkened sky
letting the rain mingle with my tears
wishing the raindrops could wash away
this feeling of despair

Erin McElroy

"I Love A Storm"

As I sat in my living room
facing the open door,
The lightening flashed
and the thunder rolled,
While the Lord washed
the world once more.

Next morning, how clean
the world did look.
So fresh from its bath
of the night before.
All the flowers and even
the weeds looked up.
In praise to God
who had blessed them once more.

I love a storm, in it I see
the power of God, and His love for me.
His protecting hand
yet His mighty power.
And His great love
when He sends the shower.

Edith Barnes Rader

Wonderful Winter

Snowflakes falling...
Falling softly to the ground
Step outside
Winter's all around

The rumble of snowplows
Clearing off the streets
The crying of children
With frost-bitten feet

The snowmobiles sailing
Across the frozen lake
The cars that fish-tail
When they try to use their brakes

This is the time of year
When many men wish
They didn't have to use a chisel
Just to catch a fish

The weatherman predict a thirty below day
With Great Frustration
So the family embarks
On a Tropical Vacation.

Amy L. Cicchese

Hospice

He entered our doors
fear on his face,
All staff within
gave love to his case.
His family, his friends
all gathered round,
Helping this patient
so peace could be found.
Handling the anger
denial and pain,
Pleading and bargaining
for time gain.
Finally acceptance
from patient and all.
There is a smile
He's received his call.
A hospice has
so much to give
A place not to die
But rather to live.

Gail A. Isaac

Eternal Love

Living our lives as one,
Feeling each other's joys,
While sharing our memories of youth,
Feeling each other's pain,
While wiping each other's tears.

Knowing apart we our weak,
Caring together we our strong,
Our minds are intertwined as one,
Learning with each new day we seek,
Our love for life is growing.

Even through unknown dimensions in time,
We are as one with our hearts,
Now with God's good grace,
From this day forth,
We will always have eternal love.

Gabrielle Foster

Untitled

Chasing after dreams sometimes
feels like chasing the end of the
rainbow. Sometimes it seems like
there's never an end to success.
At a moments chance there comes
a time when life begins to become
full but reality can sometimes be
harsh. When the luck of the draw
is down never give in because it
can turn around. All it takes
is a little time and effort within yourself.

Donna Cox

"The Rain"

The sky is black,
filled with clouds and rain.
Life it is showing us,
grief without any pain.
The clouds are a symbol,
of the sorrow built inside.
The rain symbolizes tears,
as we feel them collide.
Puddles forming there,
upon the brownish grass.
Often wondering when,
this will finally pass.
Just like the grief,
and someone full of doubt.
Sorrow is like the rain,
you just have to wait it out.

Christopher Hunter

Life

I'm lost in my words, I can't
find my way. What does this
life really portray?
The loneliness of a fallen
bird or the happiness of a
rising sun?
Life, is a wonderful thing
Not just for me, for everyone.

Elizabeth Tarin

On Leonard - My Friend

A man's passing should not go unheralded.
Fires should light the skies,
As when a worrier dies
For has he not died in true battle?

There should be a great display
To brightly portray
His transition from life
Hasta La Vista Leonardo.

Francis J. Pogan

Falling Stars

Falling Stars, lights of shear
first time ever I see them hear
someone special by my side
my hopes and dreams still alive.

Romance there I hear the
cheers of sound full people with no fears.

Lights are dimmed, people
shouting all along there is no crowding
he and I sit alone watching falling
stars shown.

Jodi-Anne Simeone

The Boxer

Punching, pummeling, pounding
Fists with a fury fly.
Jabbing, jostling, jolting
Gladiators at war.
Struggling, stiffly, stumbling
The canvas breaks his fall.
Dazed, delirious, defeated
He struggles with his all.
Like a new born fawn he stands on legs
It seems for the very first time.
For the fawn life has just begun
For the boxer he's past his prime.

Brian M. Curtin

Hallucinations

A purple valentine
Floating on the wind.
Is it in my imagination?
Am I in a dream?
Are you here with me, wherever I am?

I am dreaming of you now.
You are holding a yellow flower.
As real as we are,
Drifting by are the hours.

A rhyme is a rhyme is a rhyme
They say.
Are we real?
Or hallucinations.

Julia S. Hudgens

The Scented Garden

How many of us recall the past with a
flower's sweet perfume?
Out of the mists of memory it plays
its lovely tune.
We can build our future daydreams in
our gardens today
By planting scented flowers to liven
up our days.
Tobacco plant and scented stocks, and
rosemary and thyme,
Lavender and hyacinths, all have their
slot in time.

And when the eyes are failing, as they
tend to do with age,
The gentle scent of flowers can recall
the happier days.

Joyce L. Peters

An Angel

An angel is what I'd like to be
Flying high and feeling free
No cares or worries about tomorrow
Only joy and feeling no sorrow

We all have a chance to be that way
If by God we live and pray
Trusting and believing never asking why
Just living each day
By and by

Christine Pyles

"Without Butterflies"

Beautiful butterfly
Flying in the sky
So gently in the sky
How their wings
Flutter in the wind
How those wonderful designs
Like diamonds and circles
An a pair of eyes
Just how beautiful they are
How marvelous, how God
Made this creatures
How they drift in the wind
How they land in the flowers
So peacefully how gentle it is
Just imagine without butterflies?

Jessika L. Lopez

Untitled

I been married to Marvin Gaye
fo' at least 17 years
it's hard to remember
I was underage at the time of our union
and changed my birth date so
much I can't count the years
only the gratification.
Marvin Gaye is my husband
but whether our marriage is legal
has to do with where you live

Jill Robinson

Herr

I hunger
For
Give me
What I
Need
Less is
More
All
Is nothing too
Ward
Off
Herr
Me
To be
Have
Is everything too
Ward
Off
End.

Jenny Lee

A Poem For Martin

Everyday I look up I thank God
for Martin Luther King
A man that He sent down
to show the world a dream
A dream of black man and white man
working hand in hand
A dream to say we all shed blood
to make this a great land
But now Martin we all know
you're somewhere around God's throne
And we thank you for what you did for us
and we'll, see that your dream
lives on.

Calvin L. Penny

Light Of Lights

Great Point Light stood faithful
For a hundred years or more.
A beacon through the long dark nights
Shining tall above the shore.

Great Point Light sent warnings
Of the shifting shoals and tides
Watching brave men heave their oars
On fearful whale 'sleigh rides'.

Great Point Light stood faithful
Tall and proud above the sound
The first glimpse of Nantucket
For the sailor, homeward bound.

Great Point Light stood faithful
'till the storm of `eighty four'
When mighty ocean waves and wind
Sent her crashing to the shore.

Great Point Light is standing now
Tall against the sky...
Captured hues on canvas
By an artist...such as I.

Hilda Cook

My Poetry's Reasons

God, I like to say thank you,
For making me feel proud
And giving me the power
To become a writer.

I like to keep writing
For whoever's crying
Because of their suffering
Thinking they're perishing.

I want to keep writing,
For all the sick people,
Who think they're dying
Even though they're not old.

I will always write
Not because of my soul
But to tell my people,
Children, youngsters, and old
That I will love them like Jesus
Even if they nail me to a cross.

Guillaume Louitus

Falter Not

Falter not for it is worth fighting
for the hope of a new day. God has not
given us over to failure. There is
joy in striving for a brighter day
that the Lord has promised. If God said
it, believe it, there is no faltering in
the Master.

If you receive a faith that's strong,
hold fast to God's unfaltering hand,
for He is able to keep you in perfect
peace if you keep your heart and mind
stayed on Him.

When the struggle is hard, falter not,
hold out for just a little while. You
will know it was worth the fight.
When things seem to go wrong in your
life that is when you must falter not.
FALTER NOT! FALTER NOT! FAL-
TER NOT!

Cardell Clinkscales

Homeward

I am homeward bound today
For too far have I roamed
To lose at last
The cares amassed
And rest on your sweet ground

I'll reach into a memory
To wrap myself in you
And suddenly
The many miles
Become but just a few

I'll walk again, as I did then
Along your placid shore
And quietly
Become again
The child I was before

Yes, I am homeward bound today
For too far have I roamed
I'll reach into a memory
And find my way
Back home

Diane L. Bixler

Autumn Leaves

Be good but not very bold.
For when the summer fold,
The leaves will turn to gold,
For it's a sign of the cold.

As the sun shines bright,
As the leaves fall light,
Yes! Study them what a sight,
While dropping there's no fight.

Yet as they hit the ground,
They weigh less then a pound.
There is hardly any sound,
As special ones are rarely found.

Together like pigs in a pen,
Together like chicks with a hen,
Together like lions in a den,
You can not count them by ten.

David C. Paca

A Poet's Mind

A poet looks for little things
for which we must take time
to put them down on paper
and try to make them rhyme.
Just like a spider's silken web
our very souls unwind
and flow through pen to paper
not from our mouth, but mind
Our words are fairly simple
the meaning very deep
Our minds are always seeing
even while we sleep

Irene Gliem

We Are the Ghosts of the Future

We are the ghosts of the
future for we are yet to be.
Someday when we fade away
What will we be? A ghost
People can see, a fading memory
We are the ghost's of the future
When the time comes to be.

Amber Thompson

Beauty Is

Beauty is - not just skin deep,
For which you'll find out.
'Tis the rhythm of your heart,
that beats far beyond a doubt.

Beauty is - an inner glow,
that radiates your very soul.
For someone who loves you,
far beyond your control.

Beauty is - every line 'N Curve,
front to back 'N Tip to Toes.
With a frown or a smile,
for a loved one who knows.

Beauty it - many, many things,
for people who wish to love.
From fantasy to glorious reality,
stimulated by a tender love.

Elmer A. Rasmussen II

Arizona Tattoo

I've always wanted you
for you bring freedom no remorse
You make me smile
when I look at you
The shattered skin and nails dug
in were worth
the dream come true
Hours spent pondering
conversations
not worth having
Desire, fear, a curse
and a tear brought a piece
of the peace I once knew
in the form of a tattoo
Mts. high, White winds
Red sky
Summer souls all days old
Valleys, Canyons
Youth and decisions
are with me now from these incisions

Alexis Erica Eldridge

Anniversary

Forty years to journey life together,
forty years of up and down
so I give you rubies,
rubies for your crown.

Forty years of joy and laughter
Forty years of love we've sown,
So I give you rubies
A jewel of your very own.

Forty years of love that binds
Forty years a love knot bow.
So I give you rubies, red rubies
While we love and grow.

Forty years seems so few
When we were young and life was new.
Rubies I give you for inside
You are always young as love abides.

Forty more would not be too many,
If God would grant us time,
So rubies I give you till death do us part
A promise we made right from the start.

Grace Spiker

Faith

The first step taken
Forward...
Must be one of your own making;
The faith that moves mountains
Must also spring up fountains.

Believe in yourself
If in no one else.
Your perseverance
Must be in abundance!
Be not discouraged
Even when not encouraged
You may step out on your own
But you're not really all alone.

So believe in yourself
If in no one else
Your perseverance
Must be in abundance

If you step by faith
Your life won't be a myth
Just believe in yourself
If in no one else.

Aissa Bright

Prove Nothing Accept Yourself

I wanted to prove to my
friends that there are
some things I can do
But whenever I come
around them they treat
me like a fly and say
shew fly, shew
I wanted to show them some
sports they can do, I can do
myself
But you know what I
learned?
You don't have to prove
Nothing accept yourself

Dorthia Martin

Fools Gold

Friendship: A precious gift
From Jehova...
Based on all the qualities of
His spirit...
Offered whole hearted and
true...
Never to be taken for granted
nor treated as worthless
fools gold...
True friendship is tested like
purest gold...
Refined by the fire of patience
and love
Until it is precious
beyond compare

Elizabeth A. Rickert

March

Bees awake
from their winter slumber.

Birds sing
God's wonderful song
as days get warmer
and warmer.

Rain pours as flowers bloom
a sweet treat for the bees.

Ian Michael McNulty

A Snowflake Ballad

North winds swirl round and round
frost forming on windows
air so cold it freezes ground
this is when it snows.

Howling winds into the night
trees begin to quake
clouds give way to no moonlight
this is when they wake.

Drifting down from up above
gently the snowflakes fall
each design is filled with love
this is what they call.

"Carried by winds of fate
the journey begins here
but no snowflake can have a mate"
this said with a tear.

Coming closer to the end
their song must close
for now they've something to attend
this is when it snows.

Audrey Warrenfeltz

The Garden

Once there was a garden,
full of flowers and green.

When spring come,
it was a beautiful thing to be seen.

Birds chirping, children playing,
flowers seem to bloom;

And the sun would be shining,
on the children in the afternoon.

Yes, there was garden
where the flowers would bloom.

And the sun would shine,
on the children,

On a spring afternoon.

Ilona Albino-Pogan

Dreams Of A Teen

You're finally out of school,
Full of life and freedom,
So full of dreams of the future,
Thinking nothing can ever hurt you,
One careless accident of a drunk
Smashed your hopes and dreams
Of a future so bright,
Now you sit and dream and wonder
Of what should have been,
You can take another path,
make a new life and new dreams
God gave you another chance.

Barbara Kelley

Sentinels Of The Desert

Out on the desert all alone
Giant soldiers stand;
Guarding the hills and desert flowers
And the desert sand.

Standing up tall in solitude
Arms extended high;
Thorny and gaunt is their outline
'Gainst the desert sky.

Ernest Moretti

Wanted To Be Needed

Give me love
give me peace
give me affection
to help me ease

Give me praise
on my lonely days
and forever I'll be rewarded
with your sincere praise.

Julian Menon

Perennial Music

The music plays
Give praise my soul
Be still my mind
Imbibe its whole

Desire its cadence
Rejoice in its light
Find strength in its power
Conceptualize its sight

Celebrate its glory
Be enraptured by its fire
Be inebriated by its spirit
Be illuminated by its desire

Live your life like the music
Never compromise your mind
Let your ideas never cease to flow
Let your passions never die.

Let your spirit live in harmony
Let your soul radiate peace
Let your life reflect glory
Let the music never cease

Cindy T. Sutherland

Love's Pinnacle

What causes one to faulter;
Give up let go the rope...
Destroy years of building,
Crushing every hope?

Made to be companion -
Help meet for man...
Mother of his children,
Lover to the end.

I've taken God's great pattern,
His design for the human race;
And built a coffin for my soul
Then lined it with disgrace!

Loving you so completely,
Though you to another belong...
I won't let go; I can't let go-
Yet, I know that I am wrong.

Standing a top love's pinnacle-
Lost forever in your kiss;
I freely cast my soul -
Into eternity's dark abyss.

Connie Mull Stewart

Untitled

Upon retirement
I can tell,
Life is going
To be pure hell!

Frank V. Palmisano

Moonlight's Glow

Moonlight on the fresh fallen snow
Giving off its bright white glow.
Shadows standing out so dark,
Silence shattered by dog's bark.
Frost growing on the panes of glass.
Now waiting for the cloud to pass.
Here inside the house I stand,
Staring out at winter's grand.
Night is looking so crisp and clear.
Pond reflects just like a mirror.
Accidentally I fall asleep
No more looking, taking a peep.
In the morning when I rise
No more moon up in the skies.

Elizabeth Allen

A Writer's Dream

Blood flows in rivulets of ink
Gleaming upon the pages of life
The scars of powerful magic
Of love and loss
Of beauty and sorrow
Of the glories of living
And the agonized passions
Tendrils of a life in words
All trapped enchanting upon the page
This paper, these words
That run like a river of blood
Give life to the gods
To hopes and dreams
To memorial scenes
Within their patterns hold
The lives of all humanity.

Dwayne Tharpe

Early Morn

A field of diamonds
glistening in the morning sun,
An illusion of color
brought forth by the gentle wind.
It is the dew
upon the tips of grass,
its brief moment before cloaking
itself in the mist.
Must beauty always be so fleeting,
once savored and then no more.
Returning to what is,
and the cruel what is not.
Remember the frailty,
it is the true life of all.

Charles A. Matza

Blessed Event

When your precious heir descends
Gloriously from heaven
Like a shooting star
Sow your joy upon the earth
Shout to loved-ones near and far
Come, celebrate his birth!
When your sterling traits are etched
Brilliantly upon his face
Deep within your soul reflect
All is gift - all is grace.

Cecelia H. Greco

My Imaginary Friend

Flowing in the breeze with glee,
Going with the flow,
Someone only I would see,
Someone only I would know.

Is this someone really here,
Or is it something I just feel,
Warmth surrounds me everywhere,
This feeling is so real.

Jillian Contey

Fade

Going, going
Gone away
Slowly, slowly
I fade away
Some place far
High away
sorry, sorry
I could not
stay

Brandy K. Eberhardt

"Of Times Gone Past"

Many's the time "of times gone past"
Good books, fine food
Friends and the rest.
Talking at length 'bout
things here and then.
Laughter charged with the
current of friends.
Food that would make us
"The Envy of Gods;"
But yet always knowing
we're "Ashes of Sod."
Hoping tomorrow produces
what things that last—
from all our efforts
among the mass;
Careful Planning "Of times gone Past."

Adrienne D. Buck Jr.

"Communion"

A quiet place, amid enfolding hills,
Green grass beneath my feet
And overhead, blue sky
With in between long, distances
To dream about;

Within a green-roofed house,
Sweet memories blessing every room;
Across the road, a small white church
Whose open door invites to prayer;

And, just around the turn,
On yonder hill, God's plot
Where sleep His dead-and mine-
Beneath two guardian pines;

So dear a place on earth,
So near the home called heaven;

And yet, the unwise ask,
Where is thy God.

Grace Goodhue Coolidge (1929)

"Ode To A Troubled Man"

Cast over us like a milky shade of
grey he indulged in his music like
a mask of certain decay. A stain on
the landscape or just an ink spot in
your head his steely message runs
true far and ahead. I knew only his
voice but the tremors released by
his soul captured my world with a new
rejoice. A sad exit, let it be said but
one's departure can be more than pure
dread. The message is there for all
to see; the crimson serpent is running
free in the land of Nirvana and me.

Bob Schumacher

Coyote

Brown, silver greens and
Greys of the desert,
Almost gone, hidden away
By winter's cold light and snow.
Coyote trembles.

Sky still blue,
Air crystal, cold.
Stern winter descends on
The desert world.
Coyote Watches.

Moon circled by halo
Purple and gold and away on the rim
Of that silent world,
Coyote sits.

Coyote looks
Beyond the rim to
City lights, far and dim,
Looking warm with
Heatless fires,
Coyote cries.

Dee Bartels

Bug Recipe

Gooey gum and green grass,
Grimy grasshoppers frying fast.
Big brown beetles,
Brought to a broil,
Crispy and crunchy in sesame oil.

Spiders and flies,
Sweet centipede pies.
Mix all the above
For a dinner you'll love.

Dena Ventrudo

Looking Away

I look away
Holding back these tears of sadness
Not knowing how to control the madness
I look away
Holding back these tears of pain.
Lost, with nothing left to gain.
I look away
Holding back these tears of fear
Afraid of the words I hear
I look away
Holding back these tears so deep
Knowing the promise you could not keep.

Deirdre A. Cavano

Angel On My Shoulder

There's an Angel on my shoulder
guiding me to light
taking all the wrongs
and making them all right

There's an Angel in my day
showing me the way
to take the dark and lonely
and send it on its way

This life has been so full of pain
I risk it all to say
that the Angel on my shoulder
is what makes it all okay

Yes the Angel on my shoulder
guides me to my light
so I can take what seems so wrong
and change it to be right

Yes I can take what seems so wrong
and change it to be right

Jana D. McKinley

Generation Love

Generation Love and its seeds
has ladened a society
with after shocks and
changes for a lifetime

The message of Love so powerful
confusion of people's minds
starved for direction, cries
to save the world...grows louder

Protest from angry bearers of Life
whose children are sent to die
for unknown causes in the name
of Justice and Liberty

The fruits of the Love Generation
blooms, prepared to pave pathways
of Love, Peace, and Happiness

It will never be the same
yesterday and tomorrow
but for now, we will recognize them
The Love Generation.

Duncan W. Haylock

Lover

I'm in love with a lover who
has loved many
Does he love me or is it just a phase?
Does he love me or just treat me
Good for no apparent reason?
I'm a lover not of many
Just of a few
I know how it feels to feel wanted
Amazed and also excited and amused
Lover do you love
Me or am I just
One of your many?
Could I be one of your
Few?

Gina Giorgi

You

Is it daytime already?
Has the night gone so soon...
Your arms wrapped around me
felt safe and warm,
your body touched mine...
I listened to your breathing
wondered where your thoughts were,
dreaming of me?

Yes, you must be, there's a faint smile
Your face looks so serene,
perfectly suspended in a peaceful sleep.
If I cried, you would not here me
your dreams have carried you far from me.

Where...
Where have you gone...
take me there, share with me
what you have so much of.
I want to be in your space, always.

Deborah Guin

Yes! I Feel The Pain

No cry for pain and a sudden death
he is gone just like that.
Sitting at home
watching the game by myself
Yes! I feel the pain.

Everyday I think about him
and that tragic play.
The first son, he taught
to run, speak and play.
Yes! I feel the pain.

I wish he was still here, my dad, I miss.
It makes me mad that he is not here.
He is with me in heart
but not here in body.
Yes! I feel the pain.

No, I won't stop feeling the pain
because it's my dad that won't be at my games.
Yes, I will always feel the pain of my father
who is in the sky when I cry and
I'll see him again when I die.

Fred Longar

The Turtle

The turtle is a wondrous beast,
He rides his house from within,
Of speed he has the very least;
But Hare; how did he win?

He's small and meek, but very wise,
He knows and loves his shell,
And when it's danger that he spies;
His armor serves him well.

So proud, secure inside that shell;
There; nothing brings him pain.
It quickly blocks out every hell,
Until it's calm again.

And once the turtle feels its safe,
To venture forth once more,
He'll slowly glide his head and face,
Just past his secret door.

He can't help feeling so afraid,
Of things he can't control,
That's why his shell was custom made,
A million years ago.

Christopher W. Boyden

Listen

She stood and SHOUTED!
He stood and SHOUTED!
She SCREAMED!
He SCREAMED!
She YELLED!
He YELLED!
She HOLLERED...
He HOLLERED...
Was anyone really listening?
YES... The Children...

Dave Treadwell

"Remembering Uncle Bud"

To the Greatest Uncle who ever did live
He was smart, he was funny
Always willing to give.
He's remembered this day
and everyday after
For all his stories and jokes
His love and laughter.
On this day, two years ago
He was taken from us
and why we don't know.
While our hearts still weigh heavy
and our tears still fall.
We can remember the joy
he bought to us all.

Julie E. VanDurmen

Father Reach Down

Touch me with your hand
Heal my wounds
Where even I may stand
I'm begging for you help
Way down her is where I've knelt
I'm waiting for you
Please stop making me feel so blue
I believe in you
I know you're true
Why am I hurting?
I haven't a clue
Father give me strength to carry on
This road looks way to long
Father give me hope
I can be strong
Let me know where I went wrong.
Amen.

Elaine K. Dormer

Keepers Of The Light

I was drawn to your rugged beauty,
held by your silent strength.
You shined through my darkest moment,
flooding my fear away.
Now I bask in your glow,
united we grow brighter.
We are the keepers of the light,
guardians in the night.
While the world sleeps,
the moon will rest on calm waters.
Our golden light shall dance in the wake,
playful in the mist.
Shining with undying faith,
lasting to the end of time.
Forever guarding the night,
together as keepers of the light.

Jodi Alaspa

A Reflection Of You

A reflection of you, dear Lord,
help me to be
just like your spirit, Lord,
so others will see
the image of your glory
so authentic and true.
Help me to be Lord, a reflection of you.

Brenda Weygandt

Mom

It's her
Her figure
Her face
Her smile
Her eyes
Her heart
Her touch ...
... touch of love.

Bozena Dushek

The Camp

The year is 1943.
He's a little Jewish boy.
His name is Thomas.

He and his family are sent off,
off to a dingy camp.

His parent died of starvation.
Thomas's harmonica is singing,
it sings of a life the boy
wishes he could live again.

Thomas and his sister are weakening.
The next morning his sister doesn't wake.
His harmonica is heard once more.

He works on and on,
and plays his harmonica.

Finally, the harmonica
sings no more.

Amie Hull

Hand Over Hand

He touches me
His hand over mine
I'm scared, I tremble
My hands turns cold
Freezing in place
His eyes look into mine, I'm scared
Scared of love, scared of getting hurt
Thinking he'll look away before me
I turn away
Pretending I didn't notice
But I feel his eyes upon me
Remembering his touch
Remembering that feeling
Suddenly his hand is near mine
Touching mine
Searching his eyes I find love and care
Our eyes never leave each other
My hand stays with his
My fear is gone
We walk together; hand and hand forever.

Gina Fedock

Loving Portal

His love is deep
His love is wise
His love can fill a country side
You can feel it like a wave of bells
For in your heart is where
He dwells.
So if you're feeling sad or blue
It's alright, he'll comfort you.

Justine Bacon

Emotive

Love left lying
holding forbidden pleasures
bringing desires
in the greatest measures
envelopes a mind
with emotional stress
captures a heart
an affectionate pest
it comes to you
maybe by choice, maybe fate
some say it is given
on a silvery plate
and like silver
not cared for will tarnish
love can leave scars
that only time will polish
in essence of this
true love fills a being
it is the secret for life
that gives it its meaning

Carole Nichols

Honey Do Hat

Honey could you,
Honey would you,
Honey I hope you remembered...

Honey do this,
Honey do that,
Today I'm wearing my Honey do hat.

Jessica Smith

"The Attack"

Where would I be without you?
How could I sleep at night?
No one can take you away,
without a major fight.

He came along one evening,
and threatened us with a gun.
He wanted all our money,
and to have a little fun.

I yelled and screamed for help,
but nowhere was I heard.
Not by a passing car,
not even a lonely bird.

I kicked him in the back,
the gun flew in the air.
Then, away he ran,
like a hunted grizzly bear.

Now you are in my arms,
safe as safe can be.
Once again I'll sleep tonight,
with you next to me.

Jason Cain

A Lifetime Guarantee

Today, tomorrow or next year
How long on earth will I be here
There is no guarantee you see
Of where tomorrow I will be
A breath of air, a gift from God
To be taken back with just a nod
So I enjoy life to the fullest each day
Giving of myself in every way
Someday in heaven there might be
A better life with a guarantee.

Jane Fake

Moments

How many moments are in forever
How many stars light the sky

Why look for tomorrow
While there is today.

Moments are in the present,
And in it...

Forever lies.

Donna Dixson

Fall Night

The chill November wind
howled outside.
The thick arms
of the great oak
moaned at its icy touch.
The swing out front
creaked violently
as it thrashed about
hitting the porch rail
with an occasional thud.
The shadows flitted slowly
with taloned hands,
as all outside
was silently murdered
with one last scream.
My breath the only comfort,
as I hid tensely
under my covers
and tried to sleep.

Jamie Washrock

Our Children, Our Hope

Our Children should be Treasured,
Hugged every night and day,
And made to feel so special,
In every possible way.

Since little ones are open,
And are honest through and through,
Let's follow their example,
Put some love in what we do.

Girls and boys do not see faults,
And love each other blindly,
A smile, a hug, or a kiss,
To treat each other kindly.

So hold on to our children,
So they can spread all their love,
To make our world the best place,
With some guidance from above.

Helen Boyer Bryla

Love Still Grew

You never noticed I was there.
I always did really care.
I already new I was in love.
I always gave a loving shove.
You just gave me a dirty look.
I thought you were going to
throw the book.
After a while I gave up hope.
I felt like such a dope.
But when you smiled,
and looked my way.
I knew that was the day,
that love still grew,
For me and you.

Danielle Magdziarz

I Am

I am Song.
I am Light.
I am Beauty.
I am Bright.
I am Needful
  of thy wondrous Light.

I am Thankful.
I am Kind.
I am Joyous.
I am Soulful.
I am Wishful
  of thy wondrous Light.

I am Smiling.
I am Laughing.
I am Crying.
I am Mournful.
I am Consoled
  with thy wondrous Light.

Carol A. Vliet

Untitled

I am the power that you fear
I am your dreams and your nightmares
I can give you life or take it away
Through the fear you possess
I am forever strong
As long as you exist
I shall be the shadow in your soul,
The darkness in your mind and
the pain in your heart.
You have no choice but to embrace me
For as much as you fear me,
you need me.

Cheryl Crouse

Ode To My Runt

Well! Well here we are.
I do declare what day it wear.
I thought and thought
about what we bought.

To wish you well
or what the e'll
But here it is
and here we is
To wish you something
on this your day of nothing.

Eilleen Bradley Hall

Glory

When you see me coming, be aware!
I bring along a haven of grace.
A tower of strength.
Music and songs of triumph,
A heart of rejoicing, dancing feet,
I bring glory.

There is therefore no more shame,
For as the sun shines, and the
  mountains stand strong.
And the oceans roar, so founds
  my soul, in honor of a
  memory of my fathers victory.

So when you see me coming,
I walk with pride.
Squaring my shoulders,
  with head held high,
A heart of rejoicing,
Dancing feet.
I bring glory!

June Arlene Brown

Livid

You stomp around,
I can hear you.
I can see your tears
and your electrifying
rage.

Your eyes and clouded
over,
dark and dank.

I can't wait to hear,
your sigh,
and see you bright and alive,
again,
my,
sky.

Heather E. Jones

Why Do I Love You

Why do I love you?
I can't be specific
You're witty and charming
And simply terrific!

I just can't explain
Why I love you so much
Being held in your arms
Or the warmth of your touch

Your kindhearted nature
So simple and giving
Makes my world so special
Gives me reason for living

So don't ask me
I love you - I DO
I love you, I love you
I ONLY LOVE YOU!

Joanna Steves-Kennedy

The Last Dying Day

On this last dying day
I do so pray
That my life will begin
At morn.
And on that morn
May I forget the hell
That has driven me
Quite insane,
It has reaped my harvest
It has done me wrong
Now how shall I
Pay it back?
By ending this day
As I always do pray
And begin my life at morn.

Julie Wood

From The Sky

When I look into the sky
I find a sea of endless dreams
Rivers lakes
Babbling brooks and streams.
The stars are as they always are
Small, shiny, and bright
They give me energy
As if I'm on an eagle's flight.
And suddenly I see
What others don't
Maybe I should tell,
But I won't.
Why?
Because the man in the moon
Tells me that what I see
Shall be me very very soon.
I am frightened and scared
But excited and willing
For I am certain that I
Shall make it ever so fulfilling.

Alyson Genean McKay

I Forgot

I forgot his voice,
I forgot his face,
I forgot his touch,
his warm embrace.

I forgot his laughter,
I forgot his smile,
I forgot the way
he went the extra mile.

I forgot the way his
hair was curled,
I forgot the fact that
he was my whole world.

His death was sudden,
it came so fast.
Now that he's gone,
I think of the past.

Danielle Rodriguez

Coup d'Etat

Death is proud, he brags:
"I hold every living soul
Under my sway."

To death, sing this ode:
(Death, We have this
Word to say:)

"Yes, you are killer,
Taking people's lives;
Some long to live forever,
Yet, you cut them down to size.
No, they won't cry at
your funeral;
This fact we know;
Therefore, in the End
Remember:
You, too, will "Reap
What you sow!"

Jon Ragsdale

Untitled

Hey mom I'm so lonely
I hurt like hell inside
Mom did you know
I think reality really blows
Hey mom
Tell me it's just
A phase I'm going
Through cause mom
I don't want to live
Cause I see too much hell
I know mom
You don't understand
But that's ok mom
Someday you will
Hey mom
I love you anyway
For giving birth to me
Even though
You don't know me
Remember me
I'm your bridge

Bridget Flannery

Revival

Where are my damn metaphors?
I kept them with me
Before you—
I kept them watered
And they grew
Before you—
Now,
I dig and scrape the bottom
Of used cliches
Hoping to find them
Buried
Beneath your rubbish—
You know,
That pile of crap
You buried me under,
So now,
As I struggle for air
I search for my metaphors—
The ones I kept with me
Before you.

Diedre L. Badejo

Little Boy Mine

Little boy mine.
I left you behind.
That was not my intention.

They hurt and abused me.
Solely for pleasure.
As though I were their own invention.

I grew up fast.
Left you in the past.
With no one to love or guide you.

Now I've returned.
To help you, I yearn.
For I know the turmoil inside you.

Little boy mine.
I won't leave you this time.
I promise to protect and nurture.

Come take my hand.
Together we'll stand.
And no one will hurt us in the future.

Clifford Rodgers

Sign Of The Times

Times are hard, or so they say
I lost my job, the other day

I worked full time, hardly a break
So much free time, I just can't take

Take my job away from me
You also take my dignity

I pound the streets and answer ads
They want dim-wits or college grads

I've lost my sight, my hearing too
But always seemed to make it through

On freeway off ramps now I stand
No self esteem, my sign in hand

I used to yell out "get a job"!
Now when I see them, I just sob

Could you be just one check away?
Please think of that next time, O.K.?

So when you see someone in need
Give from your heart, and you'll succeed

Holly Telford

Dear Lord

I lost my little yellow bird
I loved her oh so much
She'd look at me so lovingly
I'd tremble at her touch

Her little leg was oh so lame
She tried so hard to walk
She flapped her wings so joyfully
It seemed she tried to talk

I cannot rest my heavy heart
To know that she is gone
Since first I knew her helplessness
My love by her was won

Such sadness I have never known
and many pets I've had
It's cause she needed me so much
Dear God, I feel so bad

Please comfort my ole lonely heart
For it is full of pain
and let me spread my love around
to share it once again

Adeline Paulos

I Love You

When I said "I love you"
I meant it in every way
When I said "I love you"
I thought you understood
When I said "I love you"
I thought we'd be together
When I said "I love you"
I didn't mean it to be the end
When I said "I love you"
I thought you felt the same
But after all the "I love you's"
In the world
You still didn't care
All you could do was play along
Then eventually just walk away
And leave me standing and crying
To say to myself over and over again
"I still love you, and always will!"

Jill Kerrigan

Missing You

I miss your love,
I miss your care,
I miss your touch
not being there.
I miss your smile,
I miss your face,
I miss your lust,
your warm embrace.
I miss your lies,
I miss your excuses,
I miss your eyes,
they were so abusive.
I'll miss you always,
and forever,
you'll stay in my heart,
and leave never.

Antonia Martinez

Memories

Though we go through hard times.
I often think about you especially
When I am down and in trouble
That I cannot overcome.

You mean so much to me boy
That most of the time all I think
About all nights is you
I always want to be with you,
And to share everything I have.

Sometimes we feel so right together
And then again there is sometime
I feel you don't want me around
For you would leave without a trace
A word or kiss as if you were in a race.

We may not have said those three
Powerful words to each other
But someday we'll say them forever
Not just because we know how to
Say them but because it's for keeps.
I Love You!

Ardell McKenzie

Transformed

I am a leaf;
I once was green,
But life has changed me:
I may now seem...
Somewhat discolored,
A little bit worn,
A tad bit wrinkled,
And just a bit torn...
Although I am not
Who I used to be,
I possess a new beauty:
If you look,
It's still me...
The colors I've had
Deep inside have shown thru...
Life's elements have changed me
To more beautiful hues.

Jennifer Emery

I'm Sorry That You Died

Yesterday in my heavens
I saw you
Yesterday in my thoughts
I saw you
Yesterday in my daydreams
I saw you
Yesterday in my memories
I saw you
Yesterday only yesterday
There was you
How come Today
Will never be Yesterday

Dave Douglas

Untitled

As I look upon that cross
I see a Soul at Rest.
And while he walked this earth
His life was put to a Test.
In the Bible it is written,
All the things he did so much.
With each Faith he Healed...
without a single touch.
Yes he knew he died that day
For each one of you and me
He looked to the Heavens
For Peace and Serenity.
After he did die...
And three days came to pass.
He arose Alive to show us...
His Love would always last.

Brenda Lange

In The Still Of The Night

In the still of the night,
I see your every move,
Think your every thought,
Feel your every breath,
And hear your every heart beat.
In the still of the night,
You're in my thoughts,
My dreams, my heart,
And soul, so in the still of the night
let me in your thoughts,
Your dreams, your heart, and soul.

Elizabeth A. Nace

Untitled

My Ma, what made little sister die?
I loved her when we play.
You told me if I would not cry
You would show me where she lay.

Here my child sweet sister lies
Down in this cold ground.
No light can come to her little eyes
And she can hear no sound.

My Ma take little sister up
And put her on my little bed.
Feed her from my little cup
And then she won't be dead.

Irene Pafford

Can't See

Lonely, is when you can't see a star,
In the universe.
Or feel the warmth of the sun
At noon.
Lonely is when your body aches,
For, no one.
Lonely is when your pain is so great,
You can't cry.
And,
Hurt and lonely is
No anger, no tears,
But so many feelings,
You can't even express,
Just one.

C. C. Teague

Leaves In Autumn

liquid gold flowing down,
shafts of sunlight streaming off
bouncing and winking at me
twisting and shimmering like a
chandelier
marking like Rubies, Autunite,
Rhodochrosite spilling across the land
Mimetite dancing in the wind
Masuyite upon Uranotile
covering the world.

Rhonda J. Borland

The bass

A
fish is
a wonderful
thing to be. It
swims through a lake,
a stream or even the sea.
This fish we refer to is the
bass. It moves through the water
oh so fast. The fisher man is
the evil one. He thinks that
fishing is all in fun.
But when he throws
that lure so
fast, he
tries to
catch us fish
we bass. So if you
catch us please release.
Then we could live in harmony
and peace.

Rylee Inman

The Dream

I know the face coming quietly through the shadows.
Emerging again and again, when the need arises.

With your arms around me, me tears flow freely, as I speak.
Pain, sorrow, anguish burst forth as I look into eyes,
that are the color of mine.
My emptiness and desperation are soothed,
by your kind words, your gentle presence.

You comprehend my thoughts and feelings,
for it too, happened to you.

The day will come when you will tread no longer.
When the darkness has gone, and I have healed.
You will disappear knowing none of this,
for we have never met.

You will not know, for in my sleep, you came,
and in my sleep, you will vanish.

Pity, isn't it.

Irene F. Marotta

Mother Goin' Home, November 27, 1993

The shadow's long that walks before us
End of day
Heal to toe and foot by foot
We wend our way.

As servant coupled with the task at hand
Takes light to lamp
And lamp to room; skimmering cobwebs
Chase to corners damp.

And from the yard the gate is heard, creaking wide
Husband calls
The dog is spent, he's run the day
As shadow falls.

Wife's fingers smile across his chest embracing night
Does settle down
Kitchens warmed, and all the while we've known
Been goin' home.

Flo Lawrence

Retirement

Remember us while you relax
Enjoys being your friend, you always
Treat people with love and respect.
Instant friendship you have always given.
Relax and visit with Family and Friends,
Enjoy it while you can
Memories are many and good.
Early to rise no more, hurry!
Never fuss or argue.
Travel with your husband, we'll be hearing from you.

Dora Campos

On Call

Silence..I take my leave.
Entering the world inside my head.
Thoughts and Plans travel at the speed of light.
All within reach, but untouchable.
Only a brief interlude with de'ja'vou focuses them to reality.
A flash of light I don't see.
Sounds heard in the unconscious transmit to the conscious.
2:45 A.M.
I leave the world inside my head at your request.
The sound of your voice awakens me.
I take in all you have to say.
Your day relived to me in 20 minutes.
A high pitched beep.
'Til tomorrow...Kisses.

Alicia M. Denley

"The Shield"

O Lord, what precious creation
Enthralls my eyes and quivers the
Beating heart within?
Lay thee in peace, O gentle creature,
Hear not the Turbulent Winds that
Carry the Icy Daggers which
Blow from hell itself.
Sorely 'tis wounded, the spirit
Within; the piercing Daggers
Are delivered with no remorse.
Great God! Is not the shield of
Light mightier than the Dagger-
Or is it written the Tunic of Life
Thereon shall the Dagger harry?
With trembling hands stretched forth,
O gentle creature fret not for
The Shield has won this Day.

Jeffrey R. Miner

Democracy And Apartheid

Democracy is to achieve peace for the entire world
Equality is the purpose of a better life for all
Nations will unite in one voice and sing its praise
You cannot survive by trampling on freedom at any price

The olive branch of Democracy was offered to the world
But, the destructive hands rejected it and were buried in the soil
Democracy triumphed and restored values that remained
From Anarchy and despotism to freedom and justice was the aim

The bloody hands that hoist their flag to the sky fell and died
Their life span was written on the wall, but they did not comply
And so they lost their glory and sovereignty, no one could deny, and
pride all the warning signals were arrogantly despised and laid aside

Democracy broke down the wall of Apartheid that was feared
Lift your hands high in the air, dance and sign loud and clear
Freedom to walk, freedom to speak and freedom from tyranny,
let the world hear that bloody hands cannot deprive a Nation of
its RIGHTS for years.

Freedom to live, freedom without fear, and to worship GOD
But the heart of stone, and the ear were closed, and we shed blood
Planes roared overhead to bring GOODWILL AND GREETINGS
TO THE NATION
THIS IS THE DAY OF VICTORY, JUBILATION AND THE
FAMOUS CELEBRATION.

Eustace G. Brewster

Alone

There were times in my life all silent and gray,
Erasing the thoughts of memories to stay.

I felt all cold and deep inside,
The fading heart so memorized.

The familiar faces disappear.
As the loneliness for me draws near.

I become a strange to myself and
especially to others.

Alone is a word that kills the soul,
Alone for the world and I to be whole.

Jennifer Tantoco

"Away From You"

Being lonely is the worst thing of all.
Especially when phoning home and no one answers the call.
You wonder where everyone's at.
When you dial several times and get no contact.
My mind begins to think weirdly as I worry about you.
So I dial once again and still can't get through.
I begin to tire as my eyelids fall.
So I try one final time, just be home when I call.
Having fun has its limits.
Trouble somehow find its way in it.
Your kinda fun you may consider right.
But think how I feel when I can't
get through to you all night.
Having fun tends to get people pissed.
Especially your husband you claim to miss.
I don't expect for you to stay home all day.
But during the time that you're out
you're safety I pray.
Remember one thing while you're on the run.
That trouble tends to find those having fun.

Betty Bender

His Eyes

He has deep deep brown eyes that,
even though he won't admit it,
are scared.

When he looks into my eyes it seems as
if he's reading my mind and sometimes his
gaze makes me cry.

For in his eye I see years of
pain and suffering.
Years of hate and disbelief
And years of tears after being beat.

In his eyes I see him trying not to love me
for every time he learns to love
the pain and suffering comes
the hate and disbelief comes
And the tears come.

And then nothing is the same
And it seems like it was all a game
But what he doesn't know is I love him
And in his eyes our love will grow.

Desirae Whitfeldt

Nature

Timeless, endless, Nature
Ever changing, ever beautiful, ever strong;
Toss your pretty head in the wind;
The meadows sing your song.

Drink in the rain, collect the sun;
Guide your rivers to the sea;
Command me and mine and all that's here;
It was meant to be.

Fling the willing birds into the sky
And let them float so free;
Paint your sunsets and your dawns
So each and all can see.

Hang your head in guilty shame
When your storms have injured thee;
Find your own forgiveness
And let us mortals be.

Leave your mountains standing guard
As you quietly usher in the night;
You are creation's finest hour
As the dawning turns to light.

George Hoag

Love Without End

The differences between us seem smaller with
every affectionate glance.
Later only to find out fate left us little chance.

We had moments that would quickly fade directly to
the past.
We had moments we wanted to always last.

We both had a gift to give one another.
A gift that would only benefit the other.
This gift would eventually make each one a whole.
A gift to be carried throughout our soul.

Many people ask how we can stand seeing only one;
holding only one hand.
And to these people we cannot lie.
For we have a love that will never die.

Heather Hedge

Tarin's Love

I love him can't you see?
Every day I beg, a not-so-silent plea.

I say let me go back don't keep me here.
Then I shed the saddest tear.
For I am afraid of what awaits me.

What awaits me is your anger and rage,
which has grown bitter and stronger with age.
You didn't want me to love.

Just because you wanted me to love you.
Don't you see, for me to love you the love has to be true?
You don't care about my happiness.

When I'm with him my heart's filled with love,
joy, and pride.
When you stole me my heart just died.
Will you ever let me go?

Chrissie May

Everything

Everything in the world is sad.
Everything in the world is mad.
Why must our lives be this way?
It will be this way until the very last day.
Everything in the world is crying.
Everything in the world is crying, over the dying.
Everyone hates their lives.
Every man hates their wives.
Every rose has a thorn.
Every devil has a horn.
Every little baby is helpless.
Every waterfall is tall.
Every brick can make a wall.
It is getting late, and I must go to sleep.
I must climb the stairs that are steep.

David Brown

Pangaea

Winter approaches, there's holiday cheer,
expect for Sally; she lives over there:
On that cold corner is her dwelling place,
Shunned by society—what a disgrace:
Sally's days are free; she punches no clock,
her only shelter is that cardboard box:
She wears a sign that reads, "will work for food;"
the Yuppies pass by and exclaim, "how crude!"
She begs and pleads to people who pass by,
but they walk right by her and close their eyes:
She won't vanish, despite how hard we wish;
Sally's just one of the many homeless.

Francine Pensabene

Black And White

In a rainbow I see colors
except black and white.
I ask myself why are
Blacks and Whites so uptight?
God must have made a reason
not to have these colors in the sky.
Again, I ask beyond
the surface - why?
As I look at the
situation Blacks and Whites are in,
I wonder if there is a possibility
that it is ever going to end.
Blacks and Whites sometimes
judge according to skin.
But deep down inside, beyond the surface,
we are all some kin.

Diane Watts

The Parade

What is this sound within my breast
Exhilarating to explode my chest?

From marching feet and beating drum
of cymbals clash make percussions hum.

Of flags that wave and voices cheer
this parade of youth, that's coming near.

I hear before I see,
I feel before I view,
The sound grows louder still
reflects my body through

I am the sound and glory in it!
I join the throng in cheering it.

My shout releases from within
a flow of emotion, a spiritual din.

I stand in wonder and hold it near
this passionate feeling, the radiance here.

The moment passes, my parade is gone-
while others revel as the sound moves on.

Joyce E. Bunker

Vacation

Shopping returning Christmas presents, the joy of the holiday still exists.
Winds strengthen and the dark clouds cover and absorb the sun.
A voice is heard screaming commands and an object is buried in one man's back.
Two hearts beat with fear, the other with...?
They drive, their destination is unknown.
The voice speaks reassuringly, with a calm coolness.
"Don't worry I won't hurt you"
The snow feels warm to the face on this day.
A shot rings out, soon there will be peace.
However only anger exists now
Questions of why and how flash through an innocent mind
The snow, red with death frightens one man, and pushes the other.
Another shot, another death is presumed.
The object of desire was already his but not enough.
Summers is insatiable.
These two lives will earn him money, perhaps to furnish a career.
A future doctor, his role to save lives, has not lost a life
But taken two.

J. Michael Hull

Desert Life

The sun, energy core of the universe
expels one tiny ray
to move downward, ever downward
a tiny thread in a blanket of heat
wrapped around a scorched earth
baking, boiling all life below, until it disappears
leaving a desert like landscape, seemingly lifeless

A dark pocket of moisture, pushed by storm winds
races across the desert sky
releasing a single droplet of water to move
downward, ever downward, straight to
the hard baked earth
there to splash. A seed is moistened,
a flower springs to life! the desert lives!

Gene W. Carrington

Untitled

The growing brightness of the freshly fallen snow burned deep into my eyes.
Winter's ghost slowly push its long thin hand through my chest to wrap its cold bony fingers around my heart.
Harsh winds ate away at my mind decaying the precious heat of my soul into an icy mist.
Chills hit me in the pit of my stomach knocking me to my knees.
Drifting souls flow through my body in memory of lost loves.
A single tear slides down my face as the dying sun falls into the shadows of the distant hills.
Looking to the moon for the kingdom of the night, my life is consumed
by the darkness. Upon his throne, the Lord of night peers into
the blackness of my soul. Death takes my hand. A sweet dream
delicately kisses my mind to slowly close the eyes of a child
crying alone in the dark. Sitting in the loneliness and sorrow of
a child's mind. The sun rises over the mountain of chaos,
brightening everything by bringing life and love the countryside.
Flowers bloom like the yearly fireworks on the Fourth of July.
Colors danced around on the waking morning dew drops.
Thin blades of grass sway to the misty song of the cool breeze.

Francix Xavier Parker

sEaSCAPE

Bright fire, cloud concealed, spy from above;
Eyes focus all yours save a single white dove.
Graceful, majestic, on wind currents fly,
Whispering hope to the gray empty sky.
Waves meet dark sculptures in conflict below
With open contempt for the menacing foe.
Crash of white water, battle rage on!
Fury breeds victor when times' wounds are gone.
At a distance, a man makes to his feet
Cursing the horizon, his life incomplete.
"Don't let me drown in the endless sea,"
He cries to the dove. "Let me be free."
Lead me back to the path I began
When I was a young and simple man."
Motionless he waits on dove's reply.
Time passes on to moving sky.
Clouds vacate and ocean grows calm,
Flat stones spring from clasping palm.
The seascape mystically soothed his soul;
Heavy heart lifted - sorrows toll.
Troubles diminished and now he'll cope
Smiling, grateful to his dove of hope.

Jeffrey W. Gase

Fill My Void

I'm in my own world, loneliness
Family wanted, friends are as one
With no friends were alone.
Very alone, I need you
Be one with me

In the sky - birds are as one
I'm flying, I am alone
Clouds all around us are as one
Loneliness - friends wanted
We need them to be as one
You have needs
Please be one with me

Widely crushing ocean - schools are as one
Am I that lone fish?
Don't be hurt, be careful
With me we will be as one
No loneliness
You are half, let me be half of you
Us two - together as one
Thank you for filling my void.

Donna Jo Mersch

Untitled

I really do not know how to say
Farewell to you, my very dear friend
Having lived in our world where both of us
Wished it would never end
Hard to believe that you have departed
To the great beyond
However I am filled with a great deal
Of sadness and tears, immersed in
Memories for together we played a great love song
Strong is what I hope I will be
Remembering our caring relationship
Between you and me

Beatrice Aarons

Family Portrait

The old family picture hangs on the wall
Father, mother, and eight children in all,
They are looking at me and I at them—
What memories from that portrait stem.
Some of the number have passed away,
But they look from that portrait
As if to say—
We are still united, the same as of old
Though our bodies lie buried
In a grassy mold.
But we are the same identity
The same forever, throughout eternity.
For God in His infinite and merciful plan
Said, that there should be no end to man
No permanent peril or jeopardy
To dissolve the unit of the family tree.

Ida Arnold Isaacson

"Spring"

As spring comes the leaves turn green
flowers bloom and birds sing
pounds fill with water from the winter past
brown bare spots green with grass

The sun shines ever so high
with its light we see the sky
and the colors so bright and blue
brings the spring morning to
me and You.

Connie S. Peters

A Progression To Love

I want to feel life!
Feel love; sunsets and sunrises
The sun on my face
A woman's hand through my hair.

I want to smell life!
Old scents of childhood spent;
The subtle narcotic of my woman.

Life is a game, the end for all the same.
But joy is at hand, if we would just
Keep breathing, keep hoping.

It is not the other one, or the next time, or the past times.
It is now with one's own love intact.

But it seems so shallow without someone to share.
Without that special person to care.

But, alas, we are all special.
Stay the course, lean well on the tiller.

Head her to the sun; watch the sunsets together.
Hold hands and hold hearts.

If not flesh to flesh, then spake three thine
In the utterances that know no bounds.

Dallas E. Butler

Looking In The Mirror

Looking in the mirror
Feeling ugly
Wishing pretty
Depressed as the sun when it don't shine
The moon when it don't glisten
Ya know, like a bee when it can't sting

Looking in the mirror
I realize, a mirror must be lonely to
When it has no one to flash back
An image of what is really you

Now by looking in the mirror, I realized
That it's looking in me to, trying to find
Itself respect, but it can't, cause it see's
No reflection, and that's when I realized
That I am thee one who is something, and
The mirror is the one who is nothing

The mirror is the one who made me feel
Ugly, wishing pretty, someone new,
It's all jealously, you see, cause in reality
All the mirror wanted was to be me

April Adams

Return

I slipped, did miss a step,
fell to the rocky ground -
and my soul shattered,
its million fragments
clink-clonceting down - down - down...
Where does the abyss end?
Where is its beginning?
Without resistance down I whirled,
hauled ever closer unto the core of gravity.
'My God!' - a flash passed through my unravelled mind,
'for sure I can't be lost enough
that it be unbeknown to you where in thy All I am...'
And at that very instant
a spark,
a single point of light much like a fire-fly,
moved gently upward,
and my scattered being rose with it, now gathering, as one.
My soul was coming home.

Elisha Southworth

Sides

This half of my heart is sad
Filled with loneliness, grief and anger
It trusts no one, feels love for no one
Has lost all faith in people,
love and friendship
This half is the one that will
keep me lonely, sad and filled
with grief as long as I let it

This side of my heart has faith
in all people, it feels that God
will send someone good for it at
the right time this side loves everyone
it doesn't hate, it even
forgives sometimes. This side
of my heart wants Everyone to be
happy someday and Eventually
This side of my heart will
Dominate the other and I will be
Vulnerable once AGAIN!

Which side WOULD YOU side WITH

Angela Prater

A Robin In The Spring

Our winters are drab and dreary,
Filled with snow and sleet and rain.
Few things make the world seem brighter,
Than a robin in the spring.

For days one's cooped up in the house,
T'aint fit to do a thing.
But, our spirits are heightened when appears
The first robin in the spring.

There's times our soul gets weary,
And our hearts refuse to sing.
That's one more reason Mother Nature sends
The first robin in the spring.

Bob Walter

The Golden Years

I once was young and full of pep.
Finally reached the Golden Years, you bet!
They call me Pop and say, "Hi, Old Timer"—
It's true I'm no longer a mountain climber.
I try to walk erect with a smile on my face
So they won't think I 'm a total disgrace.
Don't know who coined the phrase
Golden years. Golden Years—these are the days—
I hate that phrase! It makes me sad
When I reminisce the good times I've had.
So listen up young folk to what I say.
We've learned many lessons on life's roadway.
Vision us lonesome, tired, racked in pain,
Wishing we were back on our feet again.
Getting old is no bed of roses—it stinks!
It won't be long until you join our ranks;
So lend an ear when we try to advise
We've learned from hard knocks that haven't been nice.
Do, please, abolish that old cliche'
And offer a little kindness to help us on our way.

Delmar F. Dennison

"Gunshots"

Gunshots
Fired into the alley from the boom-boom car.
A young girl slips away into the dark
Unnoticed for eternity.
Obliterated. Anger.
For what they've become is who they are.
Freedom from choice,
A futile liberation in denial seeking retribution.
Fear. Annihilated.
Too young to die, nothing to live for.
Save brotherhood,
Where loyalty proven is too soon forgotten.
Abandoned. Lost.
Belonging not even to themselves.
A mother's hope turned shattered dreams.
Kill or be killed no in between.
Endlessness.

Cameron James

Top Of A Tree

I wonder how it is to be, A top of a tree
First to feel a summers breeze,
first to feel the deep freeze.

It appears to be so peaceful and serene,
To stand alone, powerful, tenacious and green.

Many don't take the time to look, listen and feel,
The benevolent existence, through time so still.

So, its tranquility, permeates our soul,
And allows us to be.
I wonder how it is to be A top of a tree.

Charles A. Grimes Jr.

The Master Poet

A poet is a builder whose workshop is the mind.
Fitting the words to phrases, each one of a kind.
Master craftsman, is he, shaping a written masterpiece.
Bonding and polishing ideas into text piece by piece.
Creating works of arts, packaged as a kit.
Easy to carry, to place, and to sit.
A poet is a builder whose workshop is the mind.
Fitting the words to phrases, each one of a kind.
Shaping the tool to pry loose wit and emotion
A wedge of laughter, more soothing than a rare potion.
Drafting with his pen vivid pictures of the mind.
Drawings, worthy to become fixtures, ever you'll find.
Poetic heirlooms, handed down friend to friend.
Chiseling away line after line, end upon end.
A poet is a builder whose workshop is the mind.
Fitting the words to phrases, each one of a kind.

Garry L. Dalton

"Death Of A Leaf"

Leaves aglow with color
Flashing in the rays of sunlight
A vibrant, bold, spectacular display
Carried through the air by a fall breeze
Twisting, turning, fluttering downward,
Ever downward, laying one on another
In a brief moment of fleeting beauty,
A mosaic of shapes, wilted leaves forever
Now in a radiant bed of color
This beautiful event is the recognition
Of the process of a dying leaf
In the eyes of the beholder!

Betty Van Hook

Yellowstone

Ripe colors
flow down across the fire
swept hills, renewed out of the
ashes of death,
resurrected by the spark of
the life giving sun.
Sweeping breathlessly, their
hands of flowers
season the land with a magical touch;
painting with the brush of creativity
transforming in fertile simplicity.
The sprouting rainbow meadows
unspoiled gardens of richness
laugh in joy, merry of the wondrous spring.
Their voices singing
in celebration;
God's symphony, synthesizing
in nature's glory

Garin Samuelsen

Grandfather

Soar like the eagle that rides the wind.
Fly like the bird in circled flight.
The time has come for you to part,
And the only thing left will be your heart.

The time in passing will always remind me,
But the soul that once cared so much will always stay.
The pain will not control me,
But at one time I felt nothing but.

Now that you have gone,
There is no reason to grieve,
For you love me just as before.
And there will come a day,
When we can join as Grandfather, Granddaughter once again.

Joanna Darlington

The Geese

The geese are flocking overhead.
Flying from a land that will soon look dead.
They are not fooled by its sight.
Colors they have found are bright.
Red, orange, yellow, and brown
Are slowly floating to the ground.
From the dark depths of Hudson Bay
Is where they chose not to stay.
They will journey far, far and away.
Searching! Searching! for a place to stay.

Heather Boggs

Flight Of A Caged Eagle

She's like a Eagle
Flying in and out of the cages of my heart and head
Flying to the freedom she longs for

Leaving behind sorrows and pains
of being caged and hurt
Hoping one day this beautiful Eagle
will return home to settle in the beautiful
skies of love

Not only to fly free, but have a companion
to share the beautiful landscapes and rolling plains
As I watch the Eagle spread her beautiful wings
to fly, there's a somewhat relief, knowing
that she will never be unhappy or caged again

Someday, I hope to see this beautiful Eagle
Return to the first companion that set her free
And realize the love for the Eagle will remain the same...

Darren Gray

The Ethnic Slaughter

He looks up with thankful eyes and a pleading look on his face.
Food and medicine come floating down, gifts of love and grace.
Vicious sniper fire takes the life of this young child;
As he recovers a package with a thankful smile.
What chance did he have to bind up his wounds or his soul to heal?
Death came all too quickly, so very soon, and all too real.
No more birthdays will he ever see, or walks along a creek bank
where boys like to be.
His future has been snuffed out like a snap of a twig it could
have been you or it could have been me.
How can this ethnic hate run so very deep?
My GOD, how can they ever lie down and sleep?
Destroying innocent lives with little or no whim.
Oh I'd hate to be that person, when the time comes to stand before HIM
No justification regardless of how strong;
Can ever validate the death of these innocents who've done no wrong.
How long will this carnage be permitted to last?
Some effort of the free world must intervene and fast.
Stop it now with justifiable force.
Fight this genocide the way we know how and without any remorse.
Silence the guns and bring those who hate,
To a resolving peace table before it's too late.

James Milton Lea

November

The Hell's Angels lived
for a while in
a ramshackle gray house by
the highway.
One day I looked while
passing by and
saw that they were gone-
no motorcycles on the front lawn or
hefty bearded men in Grateful Dead T-shirts
sleeping on a couch on the porch or
empty crumpled beer cans scattered everywhere like fallen leaves
or anything.
Even the faded Rebel flag had disappeared.
Maybe they went on a vacation-20 big mean guys
playing in the ocean and buying things made of shells
at Virginia Beach.
Or maybe they all had jury duty that day.
While they're gone, the ghosts of pirates live in
their house.

Christie Chapman

I Can Not Wait

I can not wait on Judean hill
For angels song my soul to thrill.
I cannot go to a manger bare,
To see the Christ Child lying there.

I cannot travel as eastern kings
Who followed the star to stranger things.
No myrrh have I, no gold or frankincense
To kneel and offer in His Presence.

But I can go to the good Old Book,
And turn its pages for serious look
At the marvelous story it tells inside,
How God came down with man to abide.

I can with serious heart and mind
Begin to search, to seek, to find
The peace and good will of angel's song...
The peace He brings lasts all life long!!!

Herbert Bulkley

You I Think

You, I think are nearer to my heart
For I feel the confusion that is there
To think of you I feel my senses
Reeling from the chaos you build within.
I dream of you. I think of you.
You, I think are too near my heart
For the pain that I taste on my mind's eye
Burns the dreams I have to naught.
Will you hold me when I ask?
Will you need me when I ask?
Will you love me when I ask?
I think you are nearer to my heart
Than I dare to believe,
You will never be.

Hasina Jahan Hai

When I Die

When I die I don't want anyone to cry
for I want my memories to fly,
think of the good times and not the bad
just be glad that I'm somewhere away
from all the gangs and violence.

When I die it's ok to be sad but someday
hope and pray that up here our paths may cross.
That's all I have to say because it's time
for me to go, just remember what I said and
I'll always be with you.

Joanna Corona

To Be With You

To be with you, or not to be with you that I cannot do
For if you had to be surely I would have died
You came from heaven to be my savior
You helped me to be free, my soul was free
I was no longer in that burden where I was held prisoner
I was free, free as a bird, and when I left I was in harmony,
with myself, and everyone, and everything around me
The world was in peace, I was in peace
The world was like a world I never knew before
I never want to forget, nor leave this wonderful place and
it was all because of you
You, and your magical angels brought me here to this place
that is called heaven
Here you say that no one can hurt you, no one can take me
away from you.

Hilario M. Taveras

Mississippi

I remember Mississippi for the state where I was born,
for its beauty, the people with their southern charm,
their expressions that reflected a certain kind of grace,
and for a lifestyle that took on a different pace.

I remember moss hanging from the trees, the cotton fields,
the countryside with sunflowers and wagonwheels,
and watching ferryboats cross the Mississippi River
that seemed to flow on and on forever and forever.

I remember southern style houses, yards with Magnolia trees,
grown-ups sitting on verandas in the summer breeze,
church bells, Sunday School, and church on Sunday morn,
the wooden pews, and the hymns that were always sung.

I remember winter school days and then the summertime,
skipping rope, playing barefoot in the warm sunshine,
and happy childhood days that have long since been gone,
but most of all I remember it because it was home.

Edna Orr Crone

Transplant Me, Please!

I'm alive — even though I will die;
For my organs donated will be —
And I hope that my eyes that I leave behind
Will help a poor little blind child to see!

And my kidneys and liver and tissues
Which has helped me in my life so much,
And my skin — to relieve all the burning and pain
Of a suffering victim and such!

And my heart will be thumping in somebody else—
A thumping and pumping away—
I hope it will hold a lifetime of love
For otherwise it would decay!

And last, but not least—
A truly good brain
To think thoughts of beauty
Within God's terrain.

My frailties will go with me
But I will go in peace -
Because I know I did some good —
To be alive — though I cease!

Harriet Gordon

Guess Who Taught Me To Ski!

I'd say my teacher was the very best
for on the slopes she passed every test,
Remembering when she taught me to ski,
I knew she'd instilled the challenge in me.

She admonished me, "keep those boards together!"
as I followed her in the chilliest weather,
She patted my cheek and led the way
teaching me skis were like runners on a sleigh.

When I'd come to a stop at the bottom of the hill,
I'd sigh with relief for not taking a spill,
I knew that I'd made it all the way from the top
just like a snowball rolling non-stop.

Many winters have passed since she taught me to ski,
and white snowy mountains still beckon to me,
But none can compare to those days that are o'er,
when she made me feel like a champ who could soar.

First falling snowflakes as I look to the sky
remind me of her and those days gone by,
For I was really good you see,
because my Grandmother taught me to ski!

June H. Garrity

"Life"

The life you live can treat you well
For some it's heaven and for others it's hell
As the homeless sleep on the streets of the city
People pass by and think what a pity
Murders go on, and so does the crime
They said they'd help, but they can't find the time
Men and women laid off from their work
Through garbage and rubbish is where they lurk
And the children who live without love, without care
There are many few people who have just that to share.
But the world is not all a horrible place,
Not everyone judges by color and race
Birds soar high in the glorious sky
For the freedom they show is not a lie
And the breathtaking colors that trees turn in the Fall
The cold winter comes but they still stand tall
The fresh smell of flowers makes you glad you're alive
So will many others things in the future that arrive
Your life is what you make of it, weak or strong
Only you can decide what to do, right or wrong

Estela Lugo

Relationship

Relationships sometimes are very hardcore, and coleus.
For some reason this is why, I have no mercy upon guys.
I enjoy their company, but despise their actions in the
Way they present things to me.

So when you see me on the street guys, don't approach me,
Like I'm some piece of meat, in a corner market waiting
To be nod on. Speak to me with respect and dignity.

For when you come up to me with a sorry line, I reject you
Like ice rejects heat. I won't melt in your arms with any
Old line, it can't be anything that comes to mind.

To win me over you better have a plan or be ready to be
Rejected. And please take it like a man. I don't think
I'm to good so don't get me wrong, I'm just a girl who
Knows what she wants, and how she wants it.

It's not all about looks and attitude it is about respect,
I want you to respect me and I'll respect you.

Crystal M. Collier

For My Parents

It grieves me so to see them go
for they are little children still
who trod the road of love until
the world did tear them all apart
and back they came for a fresh start

But Eden's closed
the door is guarded by a dragon fiery
with a tail, that lashes those who cry and wail

"Oh take me back I didn't know
I never had a chance to grow
Oh take me back, I don't have wings
or understand or anything
and to the feet of God I'll bring
a basket of forbidden fruit."

"Then to the devil you must go
the door is shut, the answer's 'no'!"

It grieves me so to see them go
for they were little children still
and trod the road of love.

Elizabeth K. Perry

The Words Of Helen

Strangeness, what are the causes?
For those of us locked into our own worlds,
where words nor kindness can penetrate; please,
read of me.

My past is vivid; the present void,
I call out, but you don't hear;
I cry, and you don't see; please,
think of me.

For I am locked within a living death,
for no apparent reason or cause to explain;
my love is there and always will be; please,
cope with me.

As time finally goes on and eternal glory found,
I am finally at peace with myself and my Lord;
one day we will be together in heaven; please,
weep no more.

For I am whole and at peace in my world
where all pain and suffering have disappeared;
in my world of eternal glory; please,
always remember me.

Dedicated to my Nana who passed away on October 7, 1994 of Alzheimer's Disease

Erin Browning

The Sun Never Really Sets

The sun never really sets it only seems that way,
For when the skies are dark for you, for someone else it's day.

The stars may disappear each day without a single trace,
But when the sun goes down at night the stars are in their place.

Our life is like the sun and stars that light the wondrous sky
We only go to another place, we never really die.

Doris Kirk

Willie The Kid

Elfin you are a varmint you had better watch out,
For Willie The Kid and his horse named Mount.
What ever you do never make him mad
He will look you up and stare you down,
For you know what hit you are on the ground.
His horse is quicker than lightening
And Willie is twice as fast,
If he draws on you, your future is your past.
When Willie was little his gun was fun,
He shot all the bandits, the cattle rustlers he hung.
As he got older he just got meaner
Long and lanky he just spelled danger.
You don't want to know him better to keep him a stranger.
He keeps law and order wherever he goes
He is the last of the good guys as everyone knows.
So Effin you are a bad guy, what ever you do
Stay clear of Willie The Kid and everything will be cool.

Iva Lee Bohanan

"Time"

If you want me to love you give me a time. Time to
forget the pains of growing in a world that has been
hard and lonely, time to forget the friends who have
stabbed me in the back, time to forget when my life
was dominated by failure. If you want me to love
you, give me time to forget these things and more.
Time to forget when my identity was unknown to
others and myself, time to forget when I had chosen
to live my life alone, because it was safer, time to
forget the days of depression when I often ended it
with a bottle, time to forget the long walks into
oblivion never caring if I made it back, time to
forget when I couldn't be my own best friend.
If you want me to love you please, give me time!

Dennis L. Cotton

Imprisoned Love

In the chastening chambers of my heart,
Fortressed as the petals on a rose unbloomed,
Imprisoned here, shall your love be;
In the chilling chasms of time entombed.

Centaurian calvaries,
Wielding brazen bows,
And mighty Mermen,
Bracing fathomed fury of the sea waves plumed,
Shall never rescue this love from me;
This faithless love of thine,
Which I've consumed.

Should I accede to Death's righteous hand,
The bitter verdict of which I'm doomed;
Only then shall I take the key,
Release the chains that have shackled thee,
And bid thy lonely love abandon me....
A love, I so long ago assumed.

David W. Gordon

Four Covered Bridges

Looking out my window, what do I see?
Four covered bridges staring at me
As I crossed the first covered bridge - there
were flowers as pretty as can be

As I crossed the second covered bridge - there
were animals as tall as me

As I crossed the third covered bridge - there
was water as blue as the sea

As I crossed the fourth covered bridge - there
was a field to be whatever I wanted it to be

Allison E. Hines

Upon This Wall

Your parents or grand parents come to this country
from across the sea
and you say, through them is me
There is an island that they came to, it's called Ellis
you ask them, what did you first see, what did
you first feel, please could you tell us
You hear they are building a wall
and you wonder will this be small
To your amazement many have said,
upon this wall lies my family name
a few have even reached a certain fame
As you bear your name, these words come forth
upon this wall lies my family name
for you now have little to hide
To all it's a matter of pride
And as you trace your name, with tears
all around you doing the same, are your peers
So we will end with this refrain
Upon this wall lies my family name

Gary Maxwell

War

Behold the monster man has cast,
from all the lessons of the past.
In every age — in every clime,
each history's page - all down through time.
Must still remind that mankind takes,
the same blind path to his mistakes.
Must the meager peace, man sought to gain
be bought with blood, and paid with pain?
Is this the answer GOD receives,
that man repents - that man believes?
So peel away the mask of hate,
of vanity, pain and pride.
Reveal the cruel insanity,
the curse of Cain can hide.
Until he prays unto the Lord,
endeavor man to see,
Unless he lays away the sword,
he never can be free.

Carl L. Breson

Untitled

As another door closes I began to take flight,
for out there is waiting a whole new life.
But when the path splits which road do I take?
They are not marked, which is love, which is hate?
Is there hope if I choose the wrong one?
Or is it a rule, that what's done is done?
The road you choose I cannot follow,
For me it may lead to a life that is hollow.
So please let me find the right way for me
I need to know, so please, leave me be.

Jana K. Little

Mt Helix

They've taken down the cross, my Lord,
From off the mountain top.
And the people cry their loss, my Lord.
With a yearning that cannot stop.
No more your name is spoken
In the schooling of the young,
So they removed your holy token.
For your gentle words are not the fashion.
Nor your lovely songs are sung.
It is the age of mind less passion,
And the self-indulgent brute.
A time of greed and bloody violence,
For man is at the Zenith, so the law presumes.
But your name is all the sweeter
By being made forbidden fruit,
And we will defeat the "Age Old Cheater".
For 'tis this very silence, where the
Spirit best communes.

Helen M. O'Connor

Salt The Spice

The days grow shorter and colder of feelings,
from sad eyes saltless tears spurt.
I cry out to God, and ask: did time lose its saltiness?

How much longer must I suffer hard slings from
mortal hearts of stone?

Whatever happened to the singing voices whose celestial
melodies so compassionately embraced?

No longer red is my heart. It is blue and saltless.
Oh, Lord infuse me with Your salty fire.

Ethan Courtney

Foreboding

The evilest and most deadly thoughts
from the blackest of hell's rots.
Creeping unnoticeably into your minds
leaving cold and twisted binds.
After destroying your mind it drives you insane
slowing the body and corrupting the brain.
Away from the brain it moves toward the heart
waiting for the destruction that will soon start.
Boxing in the feelings and not letting them free
hiding their meanings so they are hard to see.
A power struggle that depletes the soul
it takes over the mind and deepens the hole.
The eternal pain that will be found here
is filled with broken dreams and deathly fear.

Donovan Cortney

My Child's Lesson

I watched my child, small and wee, play with the cat,
gaze at a tree.
He did not understand nor care just why those things
are sweet and rare.
He did not question, doubt or hate, he merely did
appreciate.

Hold on, dear one, to simple joys. For soon you'll
learn from older boys:
That big folks lose their looks of peace and do not
have that sweet release.
Because of knowledge gained and learned our simple joys
we all have spurned.

Big folks need to watch and learn what small ones see
in that old tree.
That life is nice and sweet and kind if only we can
look behind;
And remember lessons long ago before we all began to grow.

Joi Bouwman

My Search

Once the world was a wholesome place,
Generosity and kindness in every face.

You were there at every turn,
Easy to see and full of concern.

Today, I look though never seeing,
It seems not worth believing.

In the soul of my very being, I begin to cry.
I search and search and know not why.

I now know You are always there,
Able to comfort and truly care.

Cry no more for You are here,
Holding me close and holding me dear.

Elizabeth Schmidt Bingham

"Gene Shining Through"

Your love breezes through my soul, as warm winds gently blow giving life to leaves of ever growing trees. Your love does feed me gently.

As each petal opens to flower, so does my soul never to expire from your love of which I must devour.
As I bud to growth such delicacy of beauties of flower and flowers of any name.

Inspired by your roots of spring from light. A love as one with ability to adventure, laugh and cry will never die.
Just keep shining through.

Alicia Rettinger

Our Angel

Angel of heaven, sent down from above,
God gave you to us with all his love.
Always you'll be our greatest pleasure,
Ten years of waiting has shown its treasure.
Immaculate in every feature we see,
Namesake of both your Nani's are thee.
Abide in our hearts till our time is due,

Lil
Madonna we're both so in love with you.
Aflame with pride we'll walk hand in hand,
Receiving more happiness each day on this land.
Image of God, always stay as you are,
Answer to him as bright as a Star.

Doretta Torrisi

Untitled

No I softly replied. It wasn't me who scuffed into green and red grasses. It was not me who jumbled up the skies into camps of tears.
Yes, I quaintly spoke. It was me who arose from tufted white linen sheets to stare at you...A hopeless child crouched on the gnarled floor of a doorless room. It was me, who kneeled on the water and accepted the wounds to your heart.
Why did I reply that way? Why did I loose all that I had to say?
Rumors of you and your mangled glances; and your raging liquor filled fists, those rumors all spread before I could speak.
How could I have let you appear as only a lonely stranger?
Who, but you, would listen if I boasted selfishly and momentarily thought of only me?
Who, but you, my screeching angel, would be with me in candlelight and find the strength to only listen?
So, I loudly replied, to me you lied. Deep in your soul you died.
Yes, I regretfully spoke, to you I too lied. I horridly cried...
I desperately cried! When their rumors killed you inside.

Connie Smith

A Mothers Cry For Help

I remember the day, my bundle of joy
God had sent us from heaven a beautiful boy

We loved him, we nurtured, we gave from the heart
He grew strong, he grew athletic, he pierced like a dart

We became proud of all his accomplishments
The trophies, the future, the times of enjoyments

I can't recall when darkness fell
Somewhere between being caught up in life, on your way to hell

The shock, the denial, God had let us astray
What became of? What happened? It was time to pray

Our beautiful son had fallen from life
Into a world of drugs - it cuts like a knife

Four years have past now, we became united and strong
We still love, we still nurture, we still see right in what's wrong

No person is ever given up on, let down or cast away
We are here for a purpose, we are watched everyday

The memories are so alive of all his goodness and joy
That God has no other choice than to bring back our boy

Barbara Rack

Exhausting Day

Do you always find yourself,
Going from morning till night.

No relaxation time or, a minute of respite.

Each morning getting up early,
To send the children off to school.

With so much going on you mix-up the,
Days, time and activities then feel like a fool.

Finally it's quiet except for your,
4 year old who is home still.

He's a little imp so your patience wears thin,
He is stubborn and known for his strong will.

The morning is finally over,
Your lunch is through.

You settle your son with a movie,
Then start to feel blue.

You have to make dinner for your family,
Before your off to work by three.

Being manager your tired at 10:00 p.m.
Then it's home bound for a cup of herb tea.

Diane L. Provost

A Special Song

There is nothing like a special song,
to fix whatever has gone wrong.
It mends a broken heart,
or brings together those apart.
It can bring the world together
or stay in your heart and last forever.
It can remind you of a special place
or put a smile on someone's face.
A special song can remind you of
a special person whom you love.
A special song can give you hope,
it can even make it easier to cope.
As time goes by you can get a new one.
Having a special song can be fun.
Just listen to it and you can not go wrong.
Everyone needs a "SPECIAL SONG".

Heather Elledge

Was There Ever A Time...

We learned to laugh, we learned to dance, then we learned to say good-bye
But didn't we just say hello, and who is left questioning why?
Darting in and out of happiness, a revolving door that we can't close
Reaching for the highest of highs, falling to the lowest of lows...
And still, life goes on, we go on, acting out our chosen roles
Pretending all is perfect, hiding the essence of our souls.
From time to time we take a chance, behind forbidden doors
Just enough to ease our minds, in times of needing more.
If not me, then some else would carry you away
If not you, then another would have the time to play.
I see the picture, but it isn't always black and white
I hear the words, but something's not quite right...
Inside a voice is calling me, begging me to find
A mate of long ago, another place, another time.
And each step I take, my journey leads me away from you
Each time I stumble, I wonder just what it is I stand to lose.
My memories deceive me, we were never what we wanted to be
And I'm more determined than ever to set my heart free.
My senses are awakened. My life is terribly shaken...
Was there ever a time, when your love was mine?

Janine Marie Sly

When I Dream A Dream, I Dream

When I dream a dream, I dream of many things
Good things and bad things but mostly good.
When I dream a dream, I dream of our world
And what it would be like if everybody
Would understand everybody and wouldn't
Kill them because they're not alike.
It's time to wake up so my dream is over.

Donielle L. Berry

Tough Tow

A car passed a red light
Got smashed... what a sight
It should have been going slow
Not it is a car in tow.

The tow truck was moving much too fast
With car in tow, it should not have passed
It too should have been going slow
Now car and truck are both in tow.

Tow truck pulling tow truck pulling car
Of course, that isn't regular
If they continue at that speed
Another tow truck they will need.

Tow truck pulling tow truck pulling tow truck
pulling car.

Racing on the road won't get them very far
If they don't slow down from lane to lane
Soon they'll be a tow truck chain.

Tow truck pulling tow truck pulling tow truck pulling
tow truck pulling car
Did you see that? WOW! That's bizarre.

James Allen Giampa

Daring To Cross

Daring to cross boundaries of immense proportions slipping into forms of an uncontrollable manner grasping at hands I can never hold speaking of visions that still to this day and time can't be told people anger my throbbing middle ground for no reason at all they rattle my unstable foundation to the point of blood curdling madness give me a moment and I'll take your visions and thoughts turn them against you they shall become your own living, breathing nightmare before there done with you, you'll wish you were dead 12 days dead, 12 days dead leave me be I can't be the one to set you free...

Andrew J. Zeutzius

What Is Green?

Green is the wind, rustling the leaves
Green is an elf, something not to believe
Green is a lime, wet and sour
Green is the stem of a bright, healthy flower
Green is calm, cool, and bright
Green will shine in the sunlight
Green whistles, green blows
Green dies, green grows
Green is life, green is death
Green is the touch of an angel's breath
Green is happiness which we feel
Green is love, green is real

Jamie Costello

40th Birthday Ode

To the feistiest, funniest '40' I know,
Greetings, salutations and a big HO HO!
For it's here at last, the BIG FOUR-O
And "life begins at 40", don't you know!

So commiserate, commemorate and celebrate
The milestones and mishaps of fickle fate
Spanning four decades of life's colorful freight
In which Motion and Progress sometimes did equate!

Clinically dubbed "Mid-Life Crisis" time,
It conjures up scenes as from a weird pantomime;
Of one missing from the belfry, some critical chimes
Which lock life's work into rhythm and rhyme.

I do believe, though, that you're doing fine
With your sense of humor and touch of star shine!
There are roads still to travel on down the line
Love, laughter, rainbows, toasts with old wine!

So on this momentous occasion, my friend
Savor the memories wherever they may wend
And know in your heart that you are loved blessed
And that "yet to be" may indeed be life's best!

Elizabeth Frazier Ledoux

Indian Summer Harvest

Now...finally, I am reaping the rewards of so many years of hard work.

For so long, I've been healing, learning, planting, nurturing, tending, grooming;
"in the process" but with little rewards.

I've conditioned and prepared once parched and neglected ground
until now, at last, it is the sweet fertile earth I've needed
to create what I want.

I relied on my tenacity and strong will, when my faith and belief faltered.

Then when I realized I didn't believe my dreams could come true,
you gently soared into my life;
the Dove bringing me a promise of hope.

Our Great Spirit sent you to me,
to rekindle my belief, and restore my faith.

Now, it's harvest time and I am having a bumper crop!

My harvest is sweet, ripe, overflowing; it is good -
an extraordinary demonstration of life's abundance.

Yes, it is harvest time, and I want to share it all with you.

Without you even knowing it,
you're the inspiration that gave my vision wings.

April Rieck

The Life Of Our Flowers

Wild flowers in a field —-
Growing helplessly by themselves.
Many with bountiful yield,
Will they end up on a shelf?

Velvet like petals; their crown —-
Proudly the stem lifts its head tall.
Tempting the elements to knock them down,
Knowing full-well, soon will come fall.

Beautiful heads are their glory —-
Many are cut and put on a shelf.
It seems such a sad story,
Others are left to fend for their self.

So helpless in wilderness - alone —-
No matter how hard they try.
In all their splendor - at last full grown!
Soon — too soon, you all shall die.

Barbara J. Lach

A Quiet Moment In Hell

I never owned a cottage right on the beach,
Had cocktails in crystal with "right" people
Or being "politically" correct quite in my reach.

I have walked barefoot at the shore in wet sand,
Shared cheap wine in even cheaper paper cups
And laughed with friends about life being bland.

Before I leave this quiet little contemplation
I have to adjust my mind to life's deceptions
And fight the terrible, but real temptation,

To believe that reality is only an accepted dream
That separates people all over the known world
Because we each see only our own little scheme.

Andrew Paul Stark

The Void In The Soul

He spent his life gathering worldly treasure,
Had no time to stop and smell a rose.
The storehouse of gain gave no pleasure,
It did not fill the void in his soul.
At life's end his blind eyes were opened,
He possessed treasure greater than gold.
He had owned it before his search began,
But its value to him was unknown.
And when he opened its pages and its
Treasures began to unfold,
He knew the book of eternal life was the
Treasure that could fill the void in the soul.

Ada S. McCoy

So Much To Be Thankful For

I find myself I hate to admit
Have times that I sometimes forget

That I have so much to be thankful for
I feel so ashamed when I want more

For I have my life and my family
And so many things for all to see

I have friends that support me, who really care
With an overwhelming willingness to give and to share

I know I'm a very lucky person to have such precious things
That I look forward each morning to see what the new day brings.

Judy Brown

Wades O' Wandering

Beyond the wades o' wandering dire
happened per chance that I did sight bye a fire
a man appearing ancient as life
bringing forth song upon a golden life
And long through the night the fire there swayed
casting about shadows which danced to the serenade.
Out then the forest night from deep within the wild
timid creatures wooed he this man with tune so mild
that too I ventured another step near
perhaps to see him or his song to hear
His tune was mellow seeming even sadly sweet
yet I feared that somehow our eyes would meet.
And as echoed across the night a whisper list of names
blue then arose from the fire's mystic flames
too I then discovered that this sage with fife in hand
did stir by his song life from the depths of sand
The air then became suddenly chilled and I shivered
but not from cold more the knowledge that
in that moment souls from their tombs were being delivered.

Gerard J. Paulauskas

Fingerprints Of The Soul

I hear you calling, whispering my name.
Have we met before?
You are pleasant, charming, seductive.
You are violent, destructive, powerful.
What more can I do but love you?
I yearn to see you-always calling, clashing, whispering.
You are beautiful, wonderful, majestic.
You bring life and you bring death....
you have no mercy....
You are mysterious, wandering,...
What more can I do but love you?
You are the inspiration, the life-giver...
You make me see my abilities...and humilities.
What more can I do but love you?
Some see you only as a body of nothing...always filled with danger-
some only use you.
I see you as the fingerprint of my soul.
...You are the Sea.
What more can I do but love you?

Anna W. Slaven

A Breath Not Taken

He lost his life before it began.
He didn't get the experience to become a man.

It was almost as if he wasn't even there;
He didn't even get to take his first
Breath of air.

The small memory he left imprinted in our brain
Will be there until we are united again.
United in a place where there is no hurt
and no sorrow.

A place where we can roam free;
A place where we can cry as long
As should be.
A place where we won't be locked in;
A place where we can talk until the end.

Charla Ubersox

"Love"

He want's us to pray for peace and unity, everywhere and everyday.
For our Brother's and Sister's to show them the right way.
To get out of the darkness and into the light, to take a turn around.
And make all our wrongs. Into right.
To make good goals for a better and healthy life.
"Love"

Carol Celli

Good-Bye

Tears ran down my face and into my lips
He gently wiped them away with his finger tips.
I looked up sadly into his dark blue eyes.
I tried really hard to muffle my cries.
He held me tight in a strong embrace
I rested my head on his chest and buried my face
Our last embrace ended with a sweet kiss
There was so much about him I knew I would miss.

Carla Radsick

The Man

As he stumbles along the streets of Allentown,
he is stared at and reminded of his life.
What it was like before,
what it is like now,
and how he got to where he is.

You can see the pain in his eyes
just like the sorrow in his soul,
for he never got to say his goodbyes
to the friends he has lost to the cold.

Like a lost dog, he moves from place to place
trying to find a place to stay,
whether it be a box or a park bench,
he always finds somewhere, somehow, someway.

I know now that I should never complain
of what I have or did not get.
For he has nothing but a box for a home
which does not help him when it is wet.

Hope McDonald

Thank You

Why is it he had to die
He never did wrong or told a lie
He's the man that gives us our air
Everyone takes it in, but doesn't care to hear
The words that are spoken of this man
He gave us life and he gave us death
But best of all he gave us love
Which comes from the heavens so high above
To what do we call this man who gave
us his time and air
I know I'm not the only one who really cares
So I say once again what is his name
I tell you, say it loud, because this is no game
Now all together we will say,
"Thank you Jesus for giving us birth
Because without you, we wouldn't be on this earth."

Jovon Renee Dixon

Family Gathering

Family gathering, last minute or planned.
Head filled with tumbling thoughts,
excitement, warmth from the past, and now.
At last we gather again, searching
for sameness, the familiar, and changes.
Much said, shallow, deep, brilliant,
mundane, earthy, our history.
Later to ponder things, that shouldn't
have been said, by familiar lips.
And yes, things unsaid that should
have been, as we take the familiar for granted.
But above all else, the gladness
in knowing, that I was there to
partake in the family gathering.

Elizabeth Emberson

The Dancing Butterfly

The Dancing Butterfly gave a big sigh
He seemed to say, come and play
We'll dance the day away
Then I'll fly high, in the sky
For I'm the Dancing Butterfly.

The Butterfly shimmered thru the sky
He said, "I'm free, and happy I'll be
If you'll come and dance with me
I'll fly high, in the sky
For I'm the Dancing Butterfly."

I jumped high and caught the Butterfly
He seemed to say, I don't want to stay
I let him go merrily on his way
He flew high, in the sky
For he was the Dancing Butterfly.

The Dancing Butterfly gave another sigh
He didn't want to wait, he had a date
He was lonesome for his mate
So he flew high, in the sky
For he was Dancing Butterfly.

Dottie Clancy Kerbow

To A Very Special Nephew And Person That I Love

On a very blessed day, a special child was born..
He showed us how to love and pray, he gave us joy
and peace...he bought us all together as one...
before he had to leave

He was ours for only a little while, because there
was more for him to do...he had to join our heavenly
Father....in helping to see us through.

We miss his love, warmth and caring, we miss his sunny
smile...we know that he is safe and warm, because he is
God's child.

We thank God for this precious child, who showed us
joy and love...we will always remember him, with Praise
to God above...for sending us this gift of love, that
truly gave us peace.... and on that day when Jesus comes,
we will be re-united for e-ter-nity.

Irma D. James

The Dishwasher

His apron tied with swollen hand
He stands beneath the growing mound
Of plates and pots and silverware
That threatens to entomb him there.
But deftly then he frees a few,
And scrapes and scours and rinses through,
And china rattles on the racks
And knives and forks are neatly stacked -
One by one, and on and on
Until the job is all but done.
Then, drowned in sweat, with forearm bare
He frees his brow of matted hair,
And with pounding head and aching knee
Dives one last time in frothy sea
To stalk those that to flee their fate
Had crept in corners to escape.
Triumphant then he looks around,
And with sinking heart does eye the mound
Of plates and pots and silverware
The threatens to entomb him there.

Judy Zaragoza

It's Starting To Rain, Outside The Diner

At two in the morning
he waits for her outside the diner
because she knew someone inside.

He smokes a cigarette
and watches her through
the neon lit window.

He imagines bed covers draped over her legs.
The rise of her hip
and a man's hand, palm up, laying across it.

He stares at the oil rainbow of a dirty puddle.
It's starting to rain and to him
it looks like drops of black ink
on the pavement.

She's going to the clinic next week.
She said that it's time for her to go.

Yeah, he says.
She's leaving him.
Fresh rain is like black ink
on pavement to him.

Jeff Iacovelli

The Unseen Power

Silent whispers
Heard only in stillness,
Gentle forces
Whose power weakens the strong,
How complex its character,
Yet how simple its beauty.

For hours it moves on,
Unobserved to the busy crowds,
But the green giants appreciate its gentle care,
Their bodies laugh at its humor,
The weeping willow cries for its joy.

The racing cages cut its freedom,
Its only wish is safety,
Safety from wheels and engines,
And objects that want a part of its independence.

Its beauty can not be captured,
Its freedom can not be grasped.

It eagerly bestows youth to the old,
It cheerfully gives joy to the mourning,
It lovingly brings out the beauty in the ordinary.

Caryn Neiswender

Emily

The news that God was adding a baby to our family filled our hearts with great joy.
We cared not if it was girl or boy.

When the time came for you to be born.
It's important for you to know, that your life, our world would adorn.

As a flower in His Garden, you were nourished and loved by God and all, about.
Like the beautiful flower, you have each day unfurled yourself to expose beauty inside and out.

You have reached out with your life, like the flowers scent,
to engulf and show the people around and you how full and
beautiful life can be lived, without a doubt.

Seventeen, you have accomplished, conquering your goods thusfar.
We who love you know that you are our Shining Star.

Jannie Davis

Untitled

She greets me with a smile, warm like a Summer's day,
Her big brown eyes they sparkle, her hair flows in the wind.

A gentle touch she shows me, as she extends to me her hand;
I am transported off to somewhere else; a far and distant land.

As she laughs it is so soothing; I am reminisce of time gone by,
When I was young and so care-free, with my playmates by my side.

Leaning now I kiss her; the feelings rush inside, her lips as soft
As petals, leave me captive—suspended, somewhere in time.

The hugs I love, she offers, as she slips her arms around my neck,
We two are one as I hold her; like puzzle pieces, a perfect fit.

Our ages are so different, "too great" she does believe, yet, I
Don't see it matter, when you are happy and at ease.

I wish I could convince her, to give it one more try, to care; and
Want to, deeply—that "age" is a state of mind.

"Life's too short," I've heard it said, that when the "right one"
Comes along, to sweep her up, adore her, that is what must be done.

That day I fear, may never come, already, attitudes have
changed; I had come too soon, and she too late, our "union",
destined like ships in the night just to pass. Still, she does effect
me in some special kind of way, makes me feel that I and love
are not too far to stay.

Bruce S. Beran

Lost And Found

Adrift in seas of loneliness and hurt,
her coat of armor shone like a flare
as she glided through the maze of nameless,
inquiring faces, body feeling bare.
Emerging out of smoky shadows,
he approached with words of admiration,
unmercifully chipping grooves in her
steely flesh with every declaration.
Intense and knowing eyes invaded her soul,
acknowledging the beauty dwelling within.
His gentle hands, outstretched and pleading,
were taken gratefully to hungry skin.
A melted pool of misery lay drowned
where she had been lost and finally found.

Donna M. Horn

Untitled

She was a social worker. That's what they were told.
Her face looked honest and bold.
Everyone knew her as a true friend.
If anyone needed an ear, hers they would bend.
A few years back she had adopted to become a mom.
She seemed the type to make cookies, and not worry about the crumbs.
An outsider would see nothing but unconditional love.
Her daughter seemed to be as happy as a snow-white dove.
But as outsiders took a look inside and saw horror was there.
Now that daughter's friends could see the act behind the mother's stare.
Few thought it would ever get really bad.
Months passed and the mother suddenly became extremely mad.
The daughter came home with fear in her eyes.
She could not talk at school because her mother had spies.
Friends told the daughter to talk to her mother and maybe work something out.
Wherever they would talk, the neighborhood could hear them shout.
One day she worked up the nerve to tell the terror that lived in her heart.
When she arrived home her mother told her to pack her things and part.

Jodi Lambert

She Had Seen

She's laid back in a field of grass
her wind swept hair turned to dust,
with eyes wide open appearing as glass
and all left unto the color of rust.

She had seen the trees an ugly brown
and felt summers day a chilling cold,
all from a darkened space beneath the ground
untouched by time yet not so old.

Now to bear upon her virgin head
a crown of stone worn only by the dead,
can that which goes untouched by time
be touched again not so unkind.

Again the sun does shine once more
upon the earth her warmth does spread,
for that which is living and will always grow
and that which is dead for those who know.

Ernest Serna

Danielle

A child of five so sweet and so dear,
her young life so full of cheer.
Danielle, my daughter, so bright and sunny,
her every word, her actions so funny.

Joy is all she brings to me,
for this I live my life to see.
I love her now and I shall love her forever,
on this I know I will never waiver.

Jamie Stockdale

The Midnight Night!

"Here I am, oh! all alone to sit right
here down on my throne, to hear the fish
swimming by, and the birds flying high,
to see the frogs go leaping by, the sound of
the wind rustling through my eyes,
the smell of the sea breeze air just
make my nose twizzel here and
there, to hear the birds go tweap,
tweap, tweap, just makes my
heart go ba-beep-ba beep,
I think tonight I'll take myself,
flying through the midnight, night".

Ashaki E. R. Gaines

The True Potter

God is the only true potter
He's still molding, he still making me
He's still shaping me.
God is sovereign and he can do whatever he wants to
God is still molding, making me

God is still molding, making me
He's still washing, he's still cleaning
He wants to use and send me
Now my peace I leave
See to it you cleave
God is still molding, making me

Seems when I accepted his calling
The storms began to rage
The sun won't shine
It rains all the time
And it seems my God is not there
But he told me he'd never forsake me
Nor my seed would beg for bread
God is still molding, making me

Janice K. Garland

Drunk Driving

Close by the door he pauses to stand as he slips
his class ring off of her hand.
All those who watch do not care to speak as a
single tear rolls down his cheek.
All though his mind memories ran of all the fun
times they had once had.
He held his class ring and began to cry.

He kissed her cheek and wanted to die!

As the wind began to blow they lowered her
casket down below.
This is what happens to many alive when
friends let friends DRINK AND DRIVE!!!!!

Amanda Ruth Petersen

Wonders Of God

Who can know the wonders of God
His deep and mysterious ways,
Whoever could measure the mighty power
That silently turns nights into days?

Who understands how great ocean waves
Come singing in endless refrain,
Who can look up at the sky in the night
And count how many stars it contains?

Who can define just what makes their breath
Through waking and sleeping repeat,
Or circulates blood and digests their food
Or causes each heart to beat?

How foolish a person, would ever deny
What keeps planets and suns on their course,
And not bow their heads, and humbly adore,
This mysterious, wonderful source.

Jane Rose Hoffman

"Silent Anger"

Mad and frustrated, he runs to the woods once again.
His face is full of cuts and bruises.
His father, in a drunken rage, had beaten him for just being.
For each blow, the more of himself he loses.

He comes to this silent place to calm himself, but every soon he fears
he will lose control. He can't take much more of the constant abuse;
He has come here once again to find his soul.

Each time it becomes harder to lose the anger, to find the peace
he is looking for. His hate for his father is boiling up inside of
him. In his mind, there is constant war.

He looks up at the quiet flora around him and is filled with an
instant want to kill. The rage in his mind blocks out all else;
He has a lust for blood that he must fill

He walks inside to find his father; He has no idea left of wrong
and right. His father looks up with blood-shot, drunken eyes;
He sees the gun, and his eyes give away his fright.

The boy presses the trigger, but cannot shoot. He slowly moves
the gun to his head. He says his last words, "I Love You, Dad."
Then pulls the trigger and falls over dead

Bridget Vetterkind

Faith

He's the only one I'd give my life, my everything for.
He's my role model, my counselor, the one that I adore.
Sometimes the trials seem too much and I may not comprehend
But I know he's there, he's watching me, this heart he'll
surely mend.
His plan is beyond anything these human eyes can perceive
And one day I'll realize through all this, he taught and
strengthened me.

cristal bell

A Comrade

His name was Joe, a loyal friend,
His hearty hello's a welcomed trend.
Often he seemed a brother, often a young son
But, he was something other
And a tremendous amount of fun.
He seldom spoke but always his feelings,
Never a hoax, just his simple dealings.
A quick study and always alert,
He was a buddy who tried to eliminate all hurt.

Then on one sunny autumn day
A speeding car and Joe went away.
As we rushed to the scene, it was too late
For the father above had opened the gate.
There by a sugar maple he lay,
Leaving friends and family all in array!

The grave was dug,
One last hug;
But my dog Joe
Would never again know.

Dwight Larue Brown

Kismet

A child is born,
His name shall be called alpha and
Omega, the true light out of darkness
and desolation. Come, let us reap
his crucifixion, then rape his people
of their true knowledge; Go destroy
the lands with hunger and disease;
Smite his children with bullets of division
And deceit. His mighty nations shall
bathe lifelessly in the stench of lustful
greed, adultery, fornication and death.
Relish hatred and bitterness upon
the seed of his fore barriers, causing
them to bear fruit of the same. Tears
of the angles cry out in heavenly
rain drops upon the earth to wash
Away blood stained concrete........
Father forgive them, for they
Know not, what they do.

Alicia Denise Skipper

Last Breath

I know it's time for me to go now
Hold me gently, I'm filled with pain.
I never thought this day would come
Life is too fragile, unpredictable as rain.

Don't bother to wipe away my tears
They are only cries, from inside my heart.
Everything I have ever felt within
Is leaving me now, and tearing apart.

Looking back on who I am
I can see clearly, all I have done.
Some things I wish that I could change
But now it's too late, someone else has won.

Love and memories are sheltering me
Pulling me close, filling me up.
Please don't be afraid to leave my side
Remembering me always, will be enough.

Don't bother to wipe away my tears,
Don't be afraid to leave my side.
I know it's time for me to go now,
There's nothing left for me to hide.

Carolyn Nieman

My Winter Place

In the winter I have my
home, and go to a place no one knows.
It's not in Russia, it's not in
space, it's not like a genie's place.
It's not for away, it's not next door
but my winter place is in the
beautiful outdoors.
It is so quiet, it is so peaceful,
it is so cold you have to ware wool.
The mountains are high, so high in the
sky, when you are on them you wish
you could fly. Mountains have white
caps like waves in the ocean, when
I'm at my winter place I'm full
of emotion. I love my winter place.

Ed Plazek

Las Vegas

As I look out the window, the lights shine on the casinos and hotels. The cars move swiftly far below. Beyond the city, I see mountains. The mountains are faint, but luminous against the moonlit sky.

Christine Gould

Why?

Why is bigger better?
How come slim is in?
What does it matter where we come from,
We are all the same within.

We are all born with loving hearts, a gift at birth,
But we don't always remember how our loving
hearts should work.
We question color, height and face,
And forget one's worth.

Maybe my brother who is blind is better off than us,
He's never had to ask the question
Why? are people different from us?

Jessica Broadbent

Steal Away

My cry is grief, rage, anger, and pain.
How could you? What did you have to gain?
Leave someone who loved you so.
The Gods called and you had to go.
What whisper did you hear?
Was it muffled or loud and clear?
Where are you? You're not here,
In this quiet place where I go to weep.
What unknown appointment did you keep?
I feel your presence on the winds in my hair.
It's your touch, and I know you still care.
In Rage I beat my fists on your chest.
Why did you leave? How can you lie at rest?
When I'm still here with problems I can't solve.
I try and try but in tears dissolve.
My anger consumes me, I shake like a leaf.
Your soul left in the night like a thief.
Taking my reason for living away.
Where are you? Call, and I too will steal away.

Betty Dupuy

The Hospice Nurse

You care for the dying? What a terrible job.
How do you stand it? They say with a sob.
Making each moment count here and now,
I care for the living, and that dear, is how!

I've learned more of living than ever before
With each new patient I learn more and more.
Some have lived long and are ready to go,
Some of the young are the bravest to know.

I let them talk, or just hold their hand,
I make them as comfortable as I can.
You care for the dying? What a terrible task.
How do you stand it? They often ask.

I look at the questioner and state with glee,
I'm as close to the Angels as I can be!
To ease someone's troubles, pain and strife,
To help shepherd them to a better life.

My job is full of rewards for me!
I'm as close to the Angels as I can be!

Judi Landry

Play Dead On My Life

I couldn't have helped the way I washed away;
How I floated and rose like the break of day.
You left me with a reflection so cracked;
I always thought I could glue it back.
Pictures of you in my head;
Heavy feelings hang like lead.
Your words carved into a steel knife;
Playing dead on my life.
I suppose if I cut the support of your idols and superficial intelligence;
Your mind wouldn't be flashing vacancy, dripping in negligence.
Ghosts of you hovering over my bed;
Visions of words that we never said.
All of the expressions were hard to deciphe;
While you were playing dead on my life.

Catherine Ann Roden

The Diary

Oh, little green book full of tales,
How I wonder the stories you tell.
Are they real? Are they lies?
Why are they hidden from prying eyes?
From cover to cover, your tales they spin:
Like weavings of ropes of love and life.
Do you know the boundaries to which they extend?
Ah, little book. Do you hear the whispers or feel the tears?
Do you understand the words 'neath your covers?
Tales told of life and its lovers.
Do you, little book, know the mysteries inside?
Do you know the secrets that you yourself hide?
So tell me, do you know?
Will you ever realize?
The dark riddles of these pages
And of mine own life?

Jill MacMillan

Untitled

When something bad happens,
I always tell him about it.
No matter how bad it makes either of us feel.
He gets mad and threatens to hurt
the persons who did it.
I just feel so guilty about it and so I cry a lot.
To him, nothing matters anymore.
Everything matters to me
I feel our relationships slipping through my fingers.
It's very obvious he doesn't want me anymore.

Chrissy Hester

Job, Money, Career

The alarm goes off like a siren.
How many times does this make today?
I throw the covers back and curse the day light.
My feet find their way to the shower.
Warm water rains on my head,
and I fumble for the shampoo.
The gray lifts and I remember why I'm up.
Job, Money, Career.

I get dressed, do my hair,
look in the mirror. Oh, hel.........p.
Where's Mr. Max Factor?
Find my shoes - where's my keys?
Darn does the sun have to be so bright?
The key turns, the engine starts -
I guess I have to go to work.
Job, Money, Career.

Judy Bechtle

"From Within"

Day by day I sit and wonder,
how our world came to such blunder.

Drugs and crime run rampant in our streets,
children are crying out from pain and deceit.

Is it because we've forgotten to love our brother,
caring only for ourselves; leaving room for no other.

From stories I have overheard,
it has not always been this absurd.

Years ago neighborly kindness was done by choice,
when people spoke, it was of one voice.

Pay close attention the signs are plain to see,
we need to make a stand, you and me.

Yes - we are all responsible, we are all to blame,
but - it's not too late to go back from which we came.

Together in harmony the change will begin,
but for today - I will start from within.

Gail A. Sullivan

Within You

My feelings for you lay buried under my hidden tears.
How sad that time descended to entomb our silent fears.
At last my old tired memories have begun their gradual fade,
Replaced by regained dreams of peace with no will to be afraid.

You are not my childhood memory of anger, fear and shame.
Instead, you are a harbor for other's loss and pain.
You see into the very soul of those who are so longing
And lend your strength and courage to those who are alone.

By coming to know you, I have come to know myself.
To know that living in the past is like being on a shelf.
And how holding on to pain is like a hole inside your soul,
Where feelings that want to dwell there can't find a place to grow.

Inside you is the wisdom of the lifetimes you have known.
You have gained a sense of honesty that cannot be disowned.
You give of you so freely that your beauty shines around you,
There is no need to look outside to find the you inside you.

How often I give thanks that we have sought our healing,
Knowing we stand as one makes the future more appealing.
Our love which once donned its mask of hate and fury,
Soars now on its gentle wings without need for strain or hurry.

Janna S. Sipes

A Tribute To A Worthy Man

On farm in childhood this boy knew
How to ride horse named Sue,
Had orchards and gardens where fruit and vegetables grew,
Gave friends pecans, plums, peaches, pears, corn,
   peas, beans, and squash, too.
He shared his whole life through.
After retiring from Dow Chem, on Board of Aldermen,
His judge duties were settling disputes of quarreling men.
He collected traffic citation fees from speeding men.
His village was better then.
He used fast, top efficiency.
He did work completely.
He gave double measure, told the truth, and displayed honesty.
His humor and quick wit were filled with originality.
He spoke words sincerely:
"I'm glad I chose to live here and
Enjoy favorite land.
I consider my town life's quality worthwhile and grand.
I just want to help community as long as I planned.
Then bury me in its sand."

Gwendolyn Bryant Grossman

Silence Heard

Listen to the silence in the air
However far, strangely enough, never too near
Continuously flowing euphoric and cold
This before my eyes never to hold
Silent whispers equally knowing
Siren to the ear, yet, constantly soaring

As bright and lustrous as a brisk morning dew
The thoughts of silence come forth slightly askew
Unknown to us all we share this touch
A feeling too few and none too much

It is with the faint of a sigh
That such quietness may pass along
The tone, solemnly low or exquisitely high
Which may never be seen, so much for the naked eye
From within one may hear its song
Only to itself are the words condoned
Thus we hear, a silence, in the air

Bobby Brown

Untitled

Scold me with your dreadful words. Words that
hurt my ears when I hear them. Drive that
knife in my back further in my back. Listen to
my cries. Tears of pain and suffering. Smell the
fear, the pain, the agony that's in me. Feel
the hell I go thru. Feel the aches I have.
Understand my emotions, my stress, myself.
Bring me sanity, back to Earth, bring me new
blood. Wanted by me yourself, sense of
humanity, a pepsi. Tell me my thoughts, your
thoughts, what my thoughts should be. Look at
my inner being, my expression, the Earth. Wish of
peace, togetherness, devotion. Touch the beautiful,
loveliness of the soul within. Proved the soul
with liveliness, courage, awareness. Give me a
state of mind, a new soul, a mind of good thoughts.

Holly Kranz

Hush Little Baby

Shots fire into the daylight hour.
   Hush little baby don't say a word.

On the ground lies nine years of life dead.
   Momma's gonna buy you a mockingbird,

Mother holds her child's lifeless body in her arms.
   And if that mockingbirds don't sing,

Mother covers her child's body like a blanket.
   Momma's gonna buy you a diamond ring,

Mother kisses her child one last time.
   And if that diamond ring turns to brass,

Darkness falls over the child's pale face.
   Momma's gonna buy you a looking glass.

Nine years of life is lowered into the earth.
   And if that looking glass gets broke,

The earth covers the child's flesh and blood.
   Momma's gonna buy you a billy goat,
Mother walks into her child's room holding her child's first
home run ball.
   And if that billy goat runs away,

Mother listens as another shot is fired - and another mother cries.
   Hush little baby don't you cry.

Ashley Greer

Across The Street

Across the street
I always see the dog up on the roof
It's flat, the roof, around the chimney pots
   and pipes and tumbled piles of brick
He strolls and peers and
Unafraid
He stands at unprotected edge
   high above the street
Looking down
A proud and guileless silhouette
   against the morning sky
   against the evening sky
Always unconfined in California's winter air
Free to roam about
Free to sleep...to trot,
To lap his water
   anytime...
To go wherever he might want to go
On the flat roof across the street...
A prisoner after all.

Betty Fairchild

I AM

I AM but a tool to be used by thee;
I AM a mountain to be climbed;
I AM a book to be read, educate and understand;
I AM a child to be nurtured for the future;
I AM a vessel to be filled with His love;
I AM a valley to be explored slowly, but totally;
I AM freshness to vaporize your mind;
I AM His for He is mine;
I AM young in age but full of knowledge;
I AM beginning a new journey but never forgetting the old one;
For without it, I AM would not be;
I AM strong in might because I have the spiritual tools of
knowledge;
I AM going on but, I will return more brighten than before, more
loving, caring, understanding than the last time.

So don't forget ME because... I AM your own.

Betty R. Jones

She Sleeps

Silence stares uninhibitedly through my eyes
I am but a wanderer through the barren, lifeless streets
Only the fog hanging from the piercing black sky greets me
My eyes travel in one house and out another
Bewildered in repetition, I lower my eyes to the ground
Crouching I find a woman wrapped in infinite blankets
I shake her soiled face, her lifeless limbs
She does not arise
Nor does her body shiver as each bitter wind passes
Slowly through her pores
A traveler through the gates of hell and beyond
I stare at the randomly scattered nickels lying beside her
The old stained coffee cup rests at the edge of evenly cut blades of grass
My eyes are blinded by the approaching light
As the radiance of dawn approachers, her soul fades away
I never saw what surrounded me

Ashley Ciment

White Tree Run

White is wonderful. It is pure and soft. It enchants me. When I am filled with unrest and turmoil, I sometimes close my eyes and envision total whiteness. Even though my eyes are closed and it is truly dark, my imagination creates my peace.
The most wonderful entities in this world need my time. Trees represent time perfectly. As trees grow they mature and need space to enrapture themselves in. This space becomes their own. Trees need the thoughts and careful insight of others to survive. The thought of only one tree can assure the survival of many. When troubles become heavy and seeing clearly is too difficult, the only thing to wish for is distance from the bothersome spirits. To gain that distance, one might start to run. Running to find some security and some sort of peace, one tries to hide. Hiding becomes tiresome and does not guarantee that the troubles are going to remain in the distance.
I just close my eyes and imagine whiteness. I create a small tree. I picture its growth. I can then picture the entire world white and filled with trees that have their own space. I am at ease. Picture your life in whiteness. Picture yourself as a tree.

Elizabeth Jo Skrzypczak

The Heart Of The Year

I am soft rain and blue skies.
I am melting snow and warm breezes.
I am "freedom".
I see children with smiles,
as they pour onto the fields of green.
For they know...
The sun, a friend of mine, is here to stay for many days.
The buzz of bees signifies a new life.
A life for a flower, who needs a friend.
My water sparkles like a diamond,
anxiously waiting for an engagement.
I not only warm the skin with heat,
but warm the soul with my beauty.
I am proud of my ways.
For I never end hope, I always promise new beginnings.
I am spring, the heart of the year!

Janet Vizina

Death

Death is so real and so true,
I bet you wonder where the after life will lead to
One day you will die,
People might angrily cry,
Why? Why? People may say,
What kind of price to pay,
Death is so horrifying sad,
That's what makes everyone mad,
There may be no heaven or hell,
But with death know one can tell

Jenny Orlando

I Am Never Alone

Each time I take a walk
I am never alone
Because I have a friend
Who walks beside me
His footprints I can not see
But he is there to guide me

I look at the world around me
And see all the beauty that surrounds me
Between the evergreens and pines
A fresh smell of God's woods-lands
That relaxes me and make me feel good inside

I stand and watch a mother deer and her baby fawn
Stop for just a refreshing drink
And in my mind it gave me time to think
God made everything beautiful
He said, "I am with you always
And everywhere you go I am your shadow
And in all the beauty that you see
When you look at all the beautiful things around you
It is me."

Judy Ann Brown

Self Validation

I love myself, M. S. and all.
I am not a disease
I am healthy, I am alive!
A victim I am not.
Despite limitations, I am still Me
Multiple Sclerosis is not me
I embrace my humanness
It is not for me to understand all the whys
Because I accept, I can go on
Feel my spirit soar in the triumph of being me again
Enjoying divine's blessings of fun and pleasure
Exploding in the kind of laughter that bubbles up and out
From deep within.
The mischievous elf that giggles in sheer delight and pleasure,
Has returned.
This "Me Again" gives freely to others
Willingly helps and shares with others.
I can love again
Like the God-child that I am!

Barbara Welch

Why

Fields of golden wheat so fine,
I am so glad you are mine.
We swing on a swing so high up above,
Like the white, satined feather of a newly wed dove.

Why is the sky so very blue?
It seems to be looking right at you.
A smile so great, a smile so powerful,
You look up and say. "It is so wonderful."
Why are the flowers so beautifully bright?
Why is the sky as dark as the night?
"Why?" is the question we all ask,
It seems as if were a task.

Ivory McAlister

I Am...

I am the person dancing alone in a club.
I am the person silently picking at his meal at a restaurant counter.
I am the person on the couch at a party,
nursing a beer, speaking to no one,
laughing at the jokes of other people's conversations.
I am the person who sits in the corner,
leans against the wall, intently smoking a cigarette,
then lighting one off of the other.
I am the person alone on the bus,
solemnly staring through the window,
backpack in my lap,
hoping anyone will fill the emptiness beside me.
I am the person who smiles a hello,
hanging my head when introduced,
answering questions with awkward affirmation,
asking them with hesitant uninterest.
I am the person whose name you can never remember,
the familiar face, the expected presence, I occupy the empty space.
I am the person standing alone at a club.
I am the person slouching at a restaurant counter...

John Abele

The Dark Side Of Liberty

Cold is the wind the immortal breeze of insanity
I am walking like a ghostly gust realizing there is no relief
The greatest grief is that I no more feel what I once called belief...
The air is fire the earth is free there is no voice to my humanity
Death is not, not life do I sense, just the sigh of eternity
Just the cry for a reverie from the demon inside my ache
He, the demon, the shriek, Wake! Wake!
And a promethean shake pulls me out into the blaze of liberty
I surrender to the sigh of the new birth found
Now my soul is left facing her self in my obscurity
What am I going to be? Not the slave to a system sound
Not the one that in a smile hides the wound
But the youth who will scream: creative reality!
The warrior with dragon on the ground.

Enzo Danielle Finore

My Thoughts In Dedication To Lance

The feelings I have I thought would never come true.
I ask myself why it had to happen to you.
As we all sit here and cry.
We reminisce of the good times.
I sit and wonder why it had to be.
Maybe it's true what they say
"Only the good die young."
I wish I could take your place.
Only if everyone knew how you were.
(Funny, Caring, and Very Sweet)
I wish I could have said good-bye.
But now I can only write thoughts of you
as we sit here and cry.
We'll miss you so
But as we all know
Someday we will see you again.
Until that day
We will just sit and pray
That you know that love that's shared because of you.

Beverly A. Roy

The Greatest Love

As I sit and ponder the meaning of life,
I become overwhelmed with emotion, pride and serenity.
I reflect without hesitation toward my family -
The greatest love of life.

They nurture me with pure strength, ambition and joy.
They are a treasured, irreplaceable gift....
An unconditional gift.

It is one to exemplify deep genuine concern and love for.
To emit respect as equally as believing it be received.
And by far, a gift, in which never taken for granted.

As I sit and ponder the meaning of life,
My family is the essence of my being.
We are each other's guardian, ally and confidant,
Blessed with the eternal spirit of togetherness.

Jennifer O'Loughlin

In His Garden

One day I was sitting singing praises to my Lord,
I closed my eyes, such a magnificent garden I saw.
Flowers were everywhere, in every color of the rainbow.
I saw a path extending further than I could see.
On the path two people were walking hand in hand.
The closer they came, the clearer their faces became,
One was me, and the other was JESUS!!
He was smiling at me.
We walked together, His arm protectively around me.
He listened to my praise, and asked about my prayers.
We talked, it seemed for hours, there in His garden.
My tears and fears would come, ever so gently He would wipe them away.
"You have all eternity to discover my love, never will I turn away."
He said this to me there in His garden.
I will sing Him songs of praise and thanksgiving.
Daily I will pray.
To Him these things are like the sweet fragrance of the flowers.
In my faith He delights, He loves me like I am.
Take me back to your garden time and time again.

Deanya Mendoza

Separation Divorce

A spark took place the first time we met.
I could not let it flame because of my marriage.
I tried to shut the damper, it always flew open.
Each time spark flared brighter, for eighteen years.
Your wife died, my husband passed away
The spark was still there, now it had a chance to burn,
It flamed high with your kindling for the world to see,
Bright and hot, delightful traveling for two months.
Eleven months of marriage you stop kindling fire.
Your spark burned out, I could not keep flame alive,
My kisses and hugs didn't set off a flame in you.
I'd walk past you hoping your arm would catch me.
Why did you ask to marry me? People hurt the ones they love.
The money was not hot- or was it? I could not feel its warmth.
You're nobody until someone loves you, I needed your love.
I loved how you called me Hon until you said Hon to others.
Now that we have drifted apart, are you happy in your own home?
I've found someone new, so I'm washing you out of my hair,
Don't come crawling back to tear my world apart.

Josephine Weathers

The Cockfighter

The feathers from your head are standing up
I could see the intensity of your emotions to fight
Your enemy comes charging - ready to hit you first with
its own claws and bills.
You stood your ground and let your strength envelop
your total being to win this game.
Suddenly the whole crowd applauded - you have won this
cruel game
I wish common sense would be instilled
In everyone's head
That if only you could speak
You would have said, "it hurts when I do this fight."

Eleanor O. Clemente

The Dream

There were velvet capes, coats, frocks everywhere that night,
I could see them all gleaming as they danced, all circling
Around and around the dance floor, as if in a slow
Motion, twirling, gliding, laughing, laughter echoing
Throughout the halls, the ceiling, the balcony.
Ladies white skin glowing, dark eyes closing and opening.
Sweet voices singing soft melodies. Violins playing
Haunting chords, wind blowing through every door.
Lovers embracing in the garden, with moonlight on
their faces. And then the dawn. Each moment that passed
Was the sunlight burning through each window every
Curtain seemed to crumble to dust, every face fading away,
Laughing then crying.
Then the quiet embraced every room and dust clouded
Each corner until all lay still.
Then my eyes opened with a suddenness and fear.
It was all a dream, just a dream so real that throughout
The day I heard laughter and saw white faces and dark
Eyes until I slept again that evening.
Such sweet slumber, lying so still, in the dark,
Waiting for the dance to begin...

Judith Myers

An Artist's Song

When I see the blue in your wonderful eyes
I darken the oceans and brighten the skies,
Give the lakes and rivers a more vivid hue
Improving my talent with lovable you

Your lovely hair with its soft mellow glow
Make sunsets more brilliant from my brushes flow,
You are my inspiration whatever I do
Improving my talent with lovable you.

When I have the thrill of your lips so divine
From roses I'm painting more beauty I find,
Making an artist's work easier too!
Improving my talent with lovable you.

And now dear, I ask you to give me your heart
Remember my talent, remember my art,
All work and no play forever adieu
Improving my talent with lovable you.

Hillyard A. Wittenmyer

Left Behind

After I wondered where everyone's gone
I decided to write a song
When the lyrics were written and the music was done
I realized I couldn't sing with anyone
Then after that, I wrote a book
But onto the pages, no one could look
My heart pounded out a nice clear rhythm
But the beats of my heart, no one could hear them
Time has passed, like a turtle walking slow
And I still wonder, "Where did everyone go?"

Andrea Wells

Genesis

I can feel it welling up inside me
I do not know what it is
it is crying to get out
To release it is to release salvation, or insanity

I yearn to release it, but yet I am afraid
Afraid of losing the comfort
Afraid of losing all I know
Will I lose it, or will it just become another intricate part of
myself

I can feel my mind reaching out
but always it is drawn back again
hidden within the depths of my soul
covered in the blackness of fear

Every thing is so obscure
I fear the haze will never dissipate
I fear the truth will never be known
I fear my life will be lost, or just never found

Edward M. J. Krynak

God Cry

In my dream I see a million children die everyday
I don't know why.
I cry a lot watching my face in the mirror get more and more old.
I pray to God to do something for the world.
I don't get an answer.
Maybe he's busy like me to cry all the time.
I wish to be somebody.
But it's only a dream that can never come true.
In the meantime a million children die everyday.
If we don't do anything one day it will be too late.
Only for us do we do something.
Maybe it's a part of life.
One day it could happen to my grandson or your grandson.
One day they could wake up and not see the sun.
I pray to God again
But he still doesn't answer.
I believe he's still crying.
In the meantime millions of children are dying.
I don't know why.

Antonio Bittarelli

When I Was Three - And Twenty

[With Apology to A.E. Hausman]

Way back - when I was twenty-three,
I envisioned the "Perfect He."
Tall, dark and handsome he must be
A man of perfect Pedigree-
Preferably with a Ph. D in physics, math, or history.
A perfect build, and perfect health
And, of course, possessing enormous wealth!

Now, that I am forty -five
And grateful to be well and alive-
And both my waist and hips have spread,
The sort of man I want instead:
Is one who's thoughtful, sweet and kind.
Who's interested in what's on my mind -
Such a man, to me, is a real find!

Today, in my maturity,
It's easy to look back and see -
The banal triviality
Of my "Perfect Man" - at twenty - three!

Audrey M. Juresic

"One So Small"

Here alone in my mommy's womb,
I fear the day that is coming soon.
The day when I will be no more,
And mommy can live her life just
like before.

I will never hear the sound of laughter,
or see the sight of joy.
And I will never be able to play
cowboys and Indians with
all the other little boys.
But that's okay, for I am one so small,
And maybe it would be better if I never
saw the world at all.
Please don't be sad because of the choice
my mommy wanted to choose.
Besides one so small is what she wanted to lose.

Now the day is already here,
And in an hour or so, there will be no more fear.

April Daigle

60

What a beautiful experience!
I feel f-r-e-e,
I feel wise,
I feel intelligent,
I feel very important.
There is nothing I cannot accomplish
Right now, except of course, having another beautiful child,
Can you imagine just driving to a friend,
doing unplanned activities?
Like shopping for shoes, but buying none.
Picking up three loaves of bread,
Laughing, l-a-u-g-h-i-n-g and laughing some more,
then say, "It sure is good to laugh and take a walk."
It really is your exercise to help reduce blood pressure
But you laugh some more. You can go over the hill gracefully.
Oh! Look at that beautiful flower, you stop and admire the
colors of
deep blue, "that sure looks like black,"
But you know what! The sight is really going, you don't see well
But that's OK
Life is still beautiful at 60.

Doslyn E. Gordon

I Am Of A Different Race

Undeserved loneliness has stationed itself within my mind.
I feel out of place.
Where is the right place for me to dwell?
Among the hot pits of Hell?

I am of a different race.
Surrounded by aliens.
All of unusual faces.

Silently, my orbit swells.
But only my soul remains.
On this unaccepting land of God's puppets.
While on the inside I am dying in vain.

Jennifer Todd

Desire

A touch, a shiver. Desire inside feelings
I have for you too long denied. Needs,
wants, quiet desires, love and passion burning
like fire. Love so strong, needs so great.
When you leave, the passion abates. How
can this work, when will I know, whose
gonna love me when you go.

Becky Shepherd

A Young Widow's Lament

As dawn breaks and I go about my daily chores,
I feel the silent rage:
The grief, the pain, the anger, the abuse,
The humiliation, the desolation of my loneliness;
So I fall to my knees and pray.

The sorrow I feel is too much to explain,
I withdraw,
Thinking I can protect myself
From it all, but yet I am alone and it never stops.
So I fall to my knees and pray.

At times rage enters my privateness and
Takes without even knocking at my door, unwelcome.
It fills my mind as I try to find peace,
Each night before I fall asleep.
So I fall to my knees and pray.

Why must the tears fall? How can this be?
When will the smile not hide the deceit or
The helping hand not reach out with malice?
When will it end? So I'll fall to my knees and pray
Until the answers can be found, in my lifetime.

Alaina M. Fulks

To My 16 Year Old Daughter

I wonder as I sit here why I don't know what to do,
I feel very old and weary, as I worry over you.
We've always had our problems and they've tripled as of late,
I want so many things for you, but we can't communicate.

I wish that I could tell you all the things that I went through,
Not to make myself feel better, but to help in what you do.
Every time I mention about "well when I was young",
You either say "not that again" or yawn or "that is dumb".

I'm 37 years old and the way you look at me,
You make me feel like I was born in total stupidity.
I know you hate to hear it and you think that I'm a fool,
But my greatest wish and prayer is that you finish school.

It isn't always easy and school work is no whiz,
But nothing in life worth having every really is.
You've said some awful things to me and I never will forget them,
What I want you to know is I certainly do forgive them.

I am aware of the tears you've shed and the loneliness you know,
Some of this is a fault of mine ...... a love I cannot show.
Whatever you have done or ever plan to do,
Remember dear, I love you now and always will love you.

Bunky Doherty

Through the Darkness

As I hide in the shadows,
I find safety in the darkness.
But in the darkness
I lose myself.
I cannot see who I am,
Or who I want to be.
And than he comes looking for me,
Searching through the darkness
With his torch of love, light, warmth, and freedom.
He shows me who I am as he brings me into his light
And illuminates me.
He will not let me slip into the darkness,
And I won't let myself be lost.
He taught me not to be afraid of myself
And who I am.
Never again will I need the solace of darkness,
For I have his light to guide my way.
I will never be lost again.

Elly Carifio

My Brethen

"Once again we reap, what we weep"
I find this earthly world confusing,
but I keep myself abreast through
Prayer, and love for one another.

In the mist of anger, and a point
of guilt. We find ourselves at each
other throat, my brethen we not
responsible for our fleshly sins.

So let us come together, to cherish
our love for each other from within. Brethen
be strong, and try not to stand along.
For without one another our brotherly
love will go no farther.

Give not into sin, for without it
we will not no how to win, Brethen
Let all mankind come together by the
Grace of God love for each other.

Brethen keep your heart with all
diligence for out of it are the issues
of life.

Henry J. Watson

The Red Leaf

A red leaf, that once was of a luscious green,
I found it under a tree amongst many dead leaves.
As it was in the month of May, it was not an autumn leaf.
I did not take it from the woodsy mother tree.
You need to have the heart of a heartless beast
To take even a leaf from a mother tree.
I picked it up before the approaching stormy winds
Would blow away the lovely lonely leaf.
To try to understand why the lonely red leaf
Was amongst myriads of dead leaves,
Oh, how difficult a thing it is.
From the shady foliage, was it an unwanted leaf?
Is it the blood of a wounded heart the red color of the leaf?
And so, I took the red leaf before the stormy winds
Would blow it away and next to my heart I put it
To join the gifts reserved in a voyage of dreams
That only a fool, a worthy fool! dares to compete
Against those smart enough to have the hearts of beasts.

Gelasio A. Saumell

"Madly In Love"

When you look at me the way you do
I get a beautiful feeling
When you touch me, tease me and kiss me
I get a beautiful feeling

That must be the reason
The you make me feel in heaven
This is my confession
That I am madly in love with you

And you surrender my heart
With so many beautiful actions
Your smile looks of your eyes
Give me feeling that your love for me is True

That must be the reason
That you make me feel in heaven
This is my confession
That I am madly in love with you

That I am madly in love with you

Jesse Govea

Clay Dreams

I am like a lump of clay.
   I get molded every way.
Just when I know what I'm about
   someone flattens me right out.

How can I take so much abuse
   for someone else's selfish use?
I wish they knew how bad I feel.
   Don't they know that I am real?

I'm waiting for that special day
   when they roll me up and throw me away.
So someone nice will find me there
   and pick me up with tender care.

I would feel his gentle hand.
   and at last I'd understand.
He'd mold me into something good
   and treat me like I know he would.

Florence Magnin

Life

My name is Emily.
I hate life.
I want to die bungee jumping over a helicopter.
I hate school.
I want to move as far away as I can.
I hate English.
I like to write long meaningless poems.
I like baseball.
I want to play ball for hours and never stop.
I hate parents.
I want to live my life the way I want to.
I hate being a twin.
I want to throw her off a bridge
And see how big a splash she'll make.

Emily Cornet

A Friend From The Sea

Amidst the confusion of the sea in which we swim,
I have found serenity.
The loneliness has faded behind the sun,
For my soul has estranged the darkness.
Only far beyond the surface wake though, did I discover the depths.

I have not voyaged alone, for
an unknown force has freed the shadow.
This gift has now come and gone - like the tide,
only to return by fate.
For if destiny permits, the power of their souls
will be bound once again.
If not, sadness will prevail, but there shall be no regret,
because the storm is finally over, the gift has been given.
The door once closed has now been opened,
and I'm longer afraid to enter.

You have taught me to fly, and
together hope to seek the heights, and soar with the wind.
For you, my friend, are my gift.
My rare and special gift
My gift from the sea.

Heather Panzella

Untitled

I never got to say goodbye
I hope you hear me although you up so high.
I never got to say goodbye
Why did you have to go I miss you so.
I never got to say goodbye
I hope you're happy up there you know I still care.

Fawn M. Wiitala

The Beach Is My Golden Answer

By many waters and on many ways
I have known golden instants and bright days

When I walk to the beach on the beautiful sands
I think to myself, was her life in my hands

Everyone tells me her life was not
But could I have stopped that terrible gun shot

I wonder to this day is she in heaven or hell
Then I look at the sand and see a beautiful sea shell

It's a sign from the Lord saying in heaven is she
Deep down in my heart I knew that's where she would be.

Brandy Jackson

The Strength Of You

Of all the friends I've made over the years,
I have to say you're one of the best.
When they left me standing there in the cold,
With tears in my eyes
And salt in my wounds,
You seemed to know just what to say
To make all of the hurt and pain
Just float away.
I've got a good feeling
It will always be that way.
When the going got tough,
You were the one with the strength enough
To stick by my side,
Telling me everything would be fine
Even when you didn't know the answers
To all of my painful questions.
You helped me through it all,
And I guess it was all the strength of you.

Jesi Haynes

Broken Hearted

I'm sorry to do this to you, but
I have to think about my happiness, too.
Awhile back I told you to shield your heart,
otherwise it would probably be torn apart.
I can't find love no matter how hard I try,
I just keep pushing it away — I wonder why?
Actually, I know why I wouldn't love you,
it's because I don't want to endure what you are going through.
I'm sorry because I know your heart is aching.
I'm sorry because your heart I know I'm breaking.
This will probably be hard for you, but
you have to understand that to hurt you is to hurt me, too.

Heather Stockdale

I Am...

I am a sympathetic person with lots of hopes and dreams.
I hear my hopes calling to me, so loud they often scream.
I want to achieve the goals so carefully set by me!
I am a sympathetic person with lots of hopes and dreams.

I pretend, sometimes, that I've already reached my goal.
I feel that I can make it! I feel so able and bold!
I touch my dreams with hands outstretched,
I worry that I'll become perplexed.
I cry out when I feel that I'm precariously perched upon a
balance beam.
I am a sympathetic person with lots of hopes and dreams.

I understand that there will be obstacles along the way.
I say, "My Lord, God, will protect me and lead dangers away."
I dream that I will be successful, but always remember my friends.
I try to think of them often, so our friendships will never end.
I hope that to the world joy I can bring
Because,
I am a sympathetic person with lots of hopes and dreams.

Angela M. Jones

Oh What A Day........

I open my eyes each morning and say....
I hope it's gonna be an easy day...

I try to get up...then my mind fills with dread...
How the heck do I get out of this bed???

One leg at a time...now I'm up and I'm ready....
Oh no! Where's my cane that I need to keep steady???

I put on my shoes which is really hard work...
But they're on the wrong feet, no wonder they hurt!

I start to get dressed...Oh I'm really a pip...
I put on a dress that I just cannot zip!

I finally sit down to knit if I'm able...
Then I look and the yarn is on the kitchen table!

A nice summer nap while my bird sweetly sings...
But just as I doze the telephone rings...

I'm tired...I'm hungry...I'm only half dressed..
I hope no one comes...'cause I'm really a mess!!!

This day was the pits...then I laugh for a minute..
This is life...and it's hard...
But I'm glad that I'm in it!

Diane Zizzo

I'm Sorry

I've called to say I'm sorry.
I hope you can forget and forgive.
Because if I don't have your friendship,
how am I post a live.
Friendship is like a flower and a bee.
If I didn't have your friendship,
I don't know where I'd be.
You're so important in my eyes.
If one of us hurts the other one dies.
If I were to die right now, I'd be thinking of you.
Wishing and hoping all your dreams would come true.
If you have doubt about this poem.
Just pay attention because it's all shown.
Because I need and want your support and love.
Even that big guy believes me who's above.
Friendship is like a rock and a stone.
If I didn't have you I'd be all alone.
Now can you see why you're so important to me.
Our friendship was meant to last, future and past.

Eva Garcia

I Imagine

I take flight and I take dimensions of another element.
I, human body and universal spirit.
I imagine if I was the sun, I would shine my light so intensely
upon your desires until you would erupt and offer me energy to burn.
Oh lady, if I was the sun, I would hug you so gently as I rise and
passionately between my desires I would set.
Oh lady, if I was the sun.
There would be holidays because of my intense heat. I would turn
all of the bodies of this earth brown and world would get around
that the sun is shining the vibration of love.
Oh lady, oh lady, if I was the sun.
I would reflect through you. Oh, if I was the sun, Lady, I would
make you new. If I was the sun. I would rise and I would bring
forth a day of radiance. Oh lady, oh lady, if I was the sun.
There would be no rain. Oh lady, oh lady, if I was the sun.
There would be sunshine every day and there would be medicine for
health in my rays.
Oh lady, if I was the sun. I would rise and I would set
and I would be a reflection of daily activities of love.
Oh, if I was the sun.

B'nai Faulkner

Miscarriage

M is for my memories that never fade away
I is for the idea that God's with him everyday
S is for my sadness because God took my son
C is for my crying for which I'm never done
A is for my anger for having to part with you
R is for my rage because there's nothing I can do
R is for the relationship between a mother and her son
I is for my inability to have this battle won
A is for my angel who's always by my side
G is for his grave to which his spirit lies
E is for my emptiness to which I'll always feel
For the loss of a child bears grief that never heals.

Gina J. Shears

Bound By An Oath

Love enfolds two people as one.
"I, John, take you, Susan, to have and to hold..."
A thunderbolt in the torrid air
Love resounds for all to hear.

Love wounds with utter abandon.
A streak of lightning in the evening sky
Love retreats, then hastens to make amends.

Love is the vow that stays the course.
"I, Susan, take you, John, from this day forth..."
A steady wind before the setting sun
Love recedes to rise again.

Love plants the seeds of new life.
A friendship forged in ever-changing seas
Love harbors the spirit of unity.

Love is holy and profound.
Sealing the promise spoken in the vow
Love ensures the oath will always survive.

Like God who became the Son
Love enfolds two people as one.

Jane Newbury Feore

The Surrender

So long life - I am tired of giving
I just lost my only reason for living.

So long world - it's time for me to go
Why I was put here I will never know.

Good-bye to all of my family
From your shame and hatred, I am finally free.

Good-bye to all of my many friends, too
Every word ever spoken to me was untrue.

I've spent my whole life trying desperately to please
With friends and family like you, who needs enemies?

There is no more hope, only pain and despair
I loved all of you, but not one of you care.

If only they knew how hard I have tried
My faith has been shattered and my heart has died.

I may be confused, but of this I am sure
the more love that I give, the more pain I endure.

To all of the people who thought I was strong
You must now face the fact you were terribly wrong.

To all of the people who crushed me for fun
I raise my white flag, I have lost and you won.

Denice Peterson

My Spring

When I walk in the woods;
  I just might see
A chipmunk running 'round a tree.
  I listen and I hear
A hoot-owl, whippoorwill or woodpecker
  hammering in a tree.
The Jack in the pulpit are most
  amazing to see;
With Jack shouting his sermon to
  you and me.
The trail by the lake, is a beauty to see,
  With all its green finery and
even a frog jumped out in front of me.
  What made the ripple over yonder?
Could it be a busy beaver, or a
  fish playing tag with me?
Just you wait and we shall see!

Hazel A. Weld

"The Angels Say"

Pretty, pretty, little baby, sleeping in your bed;
I just want to come near you;
To see what a pretty, pretty little baby you are.
Don't touch, no you can't touch, the angels say.
Just to get closer,.. closer.
To see my pretty, pretty little baby.
Can't see me, mustn't see me, the angels say.

Whoops!! eyes opened, she sees me.
The pretty, pretty little baby, sees her angel;
Not startled, but surprised.
Who is this pretty, pretty, young lady
by my bedside?
Who covers her face, only to run;
Not to be seen, not to return.

Only the innocents see the angels;
The pretty, pretty little baby had become wise.
You can only see the angels in her eyes.

Annette Tiseo

Hey Brother, What's Happening

  Hey Brother, what's happening? The man is on my ass.
I keep trying to get it together, to maintain some class.
  Hey Brother, did you go vote to help yourself pass?
I see you with your wine bottle in your hand...class?

  Hey Brother, what's happening? You take your kid to church?
Brother, did you send your kid to church?
  Brother, your kid just doesn't go to church?
You don't take, you don't send, he doesn't go...what's happening?

  Hey Brother, how is your kid in school?
Man he got suspended for acting a fool.
  Ain't got time to see about the boy, gotta stay cool.
Hey Brother, no vote, no church, no school...

  Hey Fool! What The Hell Is Happening?

Donald R. Richardson

Hidden Hell

I was born here, it's where I dwell.
I hide the cuts, so you can't tell.
Each day is lived, up on a stage.
Not among the cast, are sorrow and rage.
No one's to know, how much I've cried.
They'll never see, that my spirit has died.

Janice Sugita

What Is Your Name

The first time I saw you,
I knew not what to say
But something inside of me
just wouldn't go away.
I had to walk across the room
to introduce myself to you;
It was what I felt,
all so different and new.
Not a feeling of holding you near
But yet to ask, "How are you dear?"
As if I'd known you forever.
With those thoughts moving through my head,
I just passed you by instead.
You smelt of fresh air on a beautiful day
But I couldn't bring myself to say,
"How are you" and What is your name?

Georgia F. Stokes

A Mother Is Forever

As my son turns twenty-one
I know his life has just begun
No more toy cars, no skinned knees
"I'm a big boy now mom, No help please"
His life's his own with lots come
Schools, travel, excitement he'll sample each one
He'll find a love to make his wife
Then it's wife not mom who'll share his life
But I'll always be there for you are My Son
To hug you, to love you, to baby-sit some
Our time together has flown by so fast
My little boy is a glimpse of the past
From a child to a man, I'm so very Proud too
Now and forever Your Mother Loves You.

Jane Pedersen

The Night After Christmas

T'was the night after Christmas and, as I went to bed,
I know how a pig felt that had been overfed.
I tossed and I tumbled to get myself right
When a pain hit my belly and put me to flight.

I jerked open the door and stumbled into the night,
For there wasn't enough time to fetch me a light.
When I approached the outhouse, I went quickly inside.
I sat down over that cold hole, though it sure hurt my pride.

I desired as I sat there to finish the matter,
For only a country boy knows, how my teeth they did chatter.
As I reached for the paper, I found only a book,
So I flipped the thing open and some paper I took.

Of the paper that I tore from the book on my right,
First I used colored and then I used white.
The reason being simply to use red and then white -
I wanted to make sure that I did the thing right.

As I came in from the cold how my teeth they did chatter,
So I slowly sat down to consider the matter.
So next night after Christmas, instead of running the path,
You can bet your fat fanny I use my new heated bath!!

Delbert Carraway

My Love

I love you for the tenderness in your heart,
I love the way you say, "I'll miss you," when we part,
I love the way you cheer me up when I'm sad,
I love all those little things you make me glad,
I love you for the faith and strength you give me,
I love you for all the beauty you help me see,
I love the way you love me so faithful and true,
But most of all Babe I love you cause your you.

Dorothy P. Ryan

What Can I do?

How can I get out of this place
I know so much about?
The walls keep coming closer,
but yet they are so far away.
The sounds I hear around me,
are so full of silence.
I see so many faces,
yet I am alone.
The light that comes through the ceiling
is so dark and cold.
I sense coldness around me,
yet when I reach out, I burn myself.
I feel as if I can fly away,
yet I feel so much pressure holding me down.
I feel free in this place I am in,
though there is no way out.
So now I will close my eyes,
to go back to the dream
from which I awoke so long ago.

Eric Barragan

Nature's Enchantment

I decided to go fishing,
I left at the crack of dawn;
I took some worms and minnows
Also, took my lunch along.

The wind was calm as could be
And the sun was shining bright,
Nature was dressed in her finest
It was truly a glorious sight.

I saw a pheasant across the bay
He would crow and really strut his stuff,
There was an echo in the distance
Then his feathers he did fluff.

A deer was grazing by the shore
He's look up—then graze some more.
He didn't mind my being there,
He'd wag his tail and not flick a hair.

When I went home,
I thought I had such a good time;
What a beautiful day! so
I'll but it into rhyme.

Blanche Phifer

Surviving Soldier!

War - and all the friends
I left behind
some survived
many died -
I pledged - my life
to this war - how I survived
this hell - the gunfire - the mine - my mind
how I survived — this hell
on this earth -
the bomb - the explosion -
all the noise - I left behind
the Fighter in the sky
the fight on the ground
and how I survived - this darn war
enemy at times.

Ingeborg Strausbaugh

Eternally

A wide open field full of wildflowers,
I lie in the tall grass gazing at the sky.
The clouds seem to brush against one another
and then slowly move away.
I wonder if they are really moving or if my eyes make
them appear to separate. The
air smells sweet as if every
breath I take is fresh and new.
I feel so at peace with the everchanging world.
If only I could freeze that moment in time so
that I could breathe that air, see that sky,
and feel that warmth eternally.
It seems so perfect, like innocence and security is preserved.
Every thing else is forgotten for the moment
and everything is o.k. I can keep that vision with
me and revert back to it. The
field is a part of me and I
in turn am apart of it too.
For when I am surrounded by
its aura of life is when I am truly living!

Amanda McGee

Kathy

The days have come, the days have passed
I lie in this cell, my heart runs fast.
I met this lady whose sweet as can be
She talked with me and helped me see.

The pain I felt the first day I came
She helped me deal and believe again.
A heart of gold, a smile so bright,
And eyes that promise care and delight.

No matter where life may take me
Memories of her will stay with me.
The time has come to say goodbye,
Circumstances make me feel sad inside.

You are someone I will certainly miss
I wish I could give you a big hug and kiss.
I come to you with one more saying,
For you my heart and soul will be praying.

Andre Sewell

Untitled

I live inside a deep dark hole that no one else can see
I like to go and see my friends that live inside of me

It's my own world that I've made myself
I worked to make it just right for me

No one can enter except for one person and
That is the builder, creator, that's me

I locked the door and I'm inside, but I'm never coming out
For I will never be apart of the world outside,
since I am inside out

Jillian Middleton

Why???

I looked into his eyes, they were so full of life.
I listened to his words, he spoke of only bravery,
and strength.
I saw into his soul, a beautiful bowl of laughter,
dreams, and love.
I felt his heart beat, so strong, and so loud.
But in his mind he knew, life would be short lived.
For laughter stopped all to soon,
and his dreams only live in the next persons fight.
For now his heart beat is silent,
but his soul is still searching for the answer.
To why he had to die ????

Brandi Lee Royer

Cora's Song

Where'd she go?
I long to pinch those chipmunk cheeks and wipe that runny nose.
Where's she now?
Locked inside a big girl's heart in a place where I can't go.
I toss, and turn, and wonder what it is my dream has said.
Then a vision of a little girl awakes within my head.
She's not the one who sees me now, as her mother's former man,
But the one who'd try to please me in any way she can.
Where'd she go?
Why does she think that I don't need her love, and feel no pain?
Is it because her daddy always left the dragon slain?
That sword that made me famous has now become a cross.
And I kneel and pray before it for the daughter that I've lost.
Where'd she go?
When will we fly that kite again? When will we run so free?
When will I hold her tight again? Is it too late for me?
Will she walk—that field—above me, and place flowers in the grass?
Before she can feel she loves me, and be with me at last?
Where'd she go?

Bob Bruneau

A Wish In The Sky

As I walk out into the cool night air,
I look above into the skies of wishes and dreams.
I feel a sense of wonder in a world far away,
A world untouched, as my mind falls astray.

As I watch the moon cast its shadows around,
I remember the time that we felt its presence.
As the light shone in your delicate eyes,
My heart it spoke, but only in silence.

With the refreshing waters down below,
A smile is uplifted that is yet untold.
As the lights dance upon the waves,
Your face enlightens, my eyes catch hold.

Though the clouds so often change their pace,
My thoughts they always come back to you.
To your laughter and smiles, and simple peace,
Like the warmth from the sun that is so true.

And though I am alone tonight,
I wish my dreams upon the sky.
With memories of you close in heart,
I realize I need you here by my side.

April Dickinson

My Friend Me

Alone as we often are
I look inside myself
I find the only friend I will have forever—ME
This friend I call me is with me always
Me hears my thoughts
Me feels my feelings
Me knows me like no one else can
Inside my mind me talks to me about what it's like to be me
Me is my eternal friend
The one I can always trust to be with me
Me has and will travel lifetimes with me
Me teaches me about who I am
I am lucky to have the special friend I call me
Because I have me as a friend I am never really alone.

Debrah J. Englert-Jackels

Wishful Thinking

I thought of you this morning as I do everyday
I looked out of the window to watch the bluebirds at play

How beautiful the springtime with blossoms everywhere
And then I saw you running the wind blowing thru your hair

How beautiful you were with arms spread open wide
A priceless expression you could no longer hide

Then I ran to greet you could not wait to squeeze you tight
To hold you in my arms with all my earthly might

Then the vision vanished just as quickly as it came
I looked up towards heaven and thought that I saw rain

It was not rain my darling it was tears pouring down
Because my wishful thinking brought sadness and a frown

Reluctantly I wiped the warm tears away
And continued to watch the bluebirds at play

Jacquelyn Estopinal Franklin

Through The Eyes Of A Child

A streak of light crossed the endless black sky.
I looked over and saw the fright in my sister's eye.
Alone by the fire, no one around,
We huddled together to try and cheer up our frown.
I tried to stand up,
My sister gave a jolt,
I looked outside and saw another bolt.
Big and fast
The bolt soared through the sky.
The scorching light pierced my eye.

After the storm my parents came home.
Then I realized the fright of being alone.
They made us feel safe and sound.
I knew then and there I needed someone around.
When my mom came home she put up some beef.
I knew that smell,
It was RELIEF.
I went up to bed tucked my self in
and gave my mom a kiss on the chin

Austin Myerson

I Go To See Liberty

I go to see the liberty,
I lost all things, but I am very happy!!!
I go to find the freedom,
It's very terrible, but I am still joyful!!!

Oh! My liberty...
I lost it under the V. C.* regime,
Oh! my freedom...
I don't find it in Vietnam.

My country now is the hell of men,
And babies can't smile,
Now my country is the big prison,
Plants can't grow, and the people,
Suffer, and suffer again...

I go to seek humanity,
I left my country, but I am very optimistic!!!
I go to look for human rights,
It's very dangerous, but I am still hopeful!!!

Viva Freedom!!!
Viva Liberty!!!

*Vietnamese Communist

Huan Do

So Much In Love That It Hurts

Every time I look at him my heart melts,
I love him, so, can't seem to forget about him.
I'm in a battle that I can't seem to win,
Oh how I wish I knew how he felt.
SO MUCH IN LOVE THAT IT HURTS.....

The little things that he does,
makes me want to melt away,
but I'm scared to tell him,
that i'll never stray.
SO MUCH IN LOVE THAT IT HURTS.....

I want to be with him so much,
but I'm afraid to say, that I have a hunch,
that I'm only in his way.
SO MUCH IN LOVE THAT IT HURTS...

He treats me like a friend, a buddy or a pal,
I want it to be so much more.
I can only wish though, cause I know it
can't be that way. A girl's gotta have wishes though,
cause wishes can come true.
SO MUCH IN LOVE THAT IT HURTS....

Cindy Zapata

Love Is Lost

There once was someone that I loved so much,
I never loved a one like this before.
He did so much, I need not ask for more.
Now what I'll miss the most is his sweet touch.
I tried to do all things that he could love, but
The day he left my heart was feeling sore.
Our love was rich, but now left for this poor
child, just pain to feel, no help above.

Now I'm left with no one by my side.
Why does this love have to end this way?
Without him here I wish I could just die.
I wish our love could be the way it was.
I wonder why he acts the way he does,
My love is lost. This is what's left to say.

Dori Gray

The End Of Time.....

In loving memory of my cousin, Paul Fusco

So many people die, each and every day
I never thought you'd be one, I can honestly say.
I loved you so much, it just isn't fair
Your death, Paulie, is something I cannot bear.
There's been so many bad times, we've always
Stuck together
But losing you so soon is a pain that will last
Forever.
I hope you can see me from where you are above,
And think of all the memories that are so full of love.
Maybe someday I can think of you and smile
Instead of cry
But I wish someone could tell me, why it was
you who had to die.
You are in my thoughts, all day through
I hope somehow you know how much I miss you.
It's just hard to believe that you've died
When you were the one who was always so alive.
I will never forget you, the special cousin of mine,
I will always remember your smile until the end of time....

Jeni McArthur

Snow Blind

You thought I was your friend when we first met.
I offered you fancy cars, money, and things you couldn't get.
I waited patiently for an opportunity to catch you down and out.
To relieve your stress and pain while fighting all your bouts.
So I finally got you, again, again, and again.
I made you steal from your mother and lose your best friend.
You were out of control and had no place to hide.
You looked as if death had struck you and stripped away your pride.
Yes indeed I had won, I most certainly got you hooked.
You dropped out of school, had no job, and couldn't read a book.
Life had dealt you a very bad hand so it would seem.
I came like a thief in the night and took away your dreams.
Fall to your knees son and pray, it's never ever too late.
Rise up, you can redeem yourself from such an awful fate.
One lesson your mother should have taught you long time ago.
Son, if someone offers you drugs please, please, say no!

Evette M. Figgs

Untitled

Looking out the window I see the moon.
I pray to the heavens for my nightmare's doom.
I'm afraid to go to sleep, afraid to close my eyes.
Afraid of what everyone close will someday realize.
That I am covered with dirt, can be looked at but never touched.
just to think of it is too painful, to bare it is too much.
It's something I must come to terms with,
the memories won't leave me in peace.
I look in the mirror and wonder.
Who could ever love this beast?

Angeles M. Vazquez

The Mask

To hide my feelings away,
I put on a mask.
Why does it have to be that way?
Please don't ask.
Whenever I'm sad,
my mask shows I'm glad.
Whenever I'm happy,
of course my mask shows I am happy.
But whenever I'm hurt,
my mask shows I'm alert,
so people don't hear all that dirt.
Only the people close, know me the most.
I try to act tough, through the rough,
but it's hard putting up with all that stuff.
I wish I could rest,
but my mask has to look best.
So you say,
why does it have to be that way?
Please don't ask.
Remember, that is the way of the mask.

Geneva A. McIntosh

Falling Leaves

I look out my window
I see the leaves falling off the trees
People say that death is ugly
They have not seen the leaves fall
So beautiful as they lightly fall from their mother
Not one that follows the path as the one before
I want to be a leaf and float freely
To follow my own path
To go my own direction
When I die I will let my body be free
My ashes will fly across the world
Never to the same place
Never landing for long
When I die I will become a falling leaf

Jami Honeyman

I Remember

I remember the day you asked me
I remember the day clear; the sky was light
blue and pink almost like we were
meant to be. I remember the first time I saw
you, I remember the blue shirt and jeans.
I remember thinking that you
were the one for me. I remember the pink flowers
you picked for me, I remember the lollypop
you gave me in Spring. I remember you taking
off your shirt for me so that I could
be warm. I remember. I remember the times
we had together the laughter we shared.
The jokes you told me, the times we were mad
and the times we were sad. I remember
those days clear. I remember you as a gentle
and harmless dove that seemed to
know everything, I remember. Yes I remember
more.
You were the only dove I ever really loved!

Jessica Denise Matelski

Untitled

I sometimes look, not sure I see, a tiger out behind that tree.
I rode that tiger once before but I won't ride him anymore
His eyes so golden shining bright I see to them in my dreams at
night, come ride with me "they seem to say and urge me on as
I start to sway. "Come dance" the eyes say, burning gold, I'll
tell you story's never told! I'll show you things that were
never seen just come to my Jungle, burning green"
Come to my jungle burning bright I'll ride you there this very night!"

The golden Moon in a silver sky shone down as the jungle birds
flew by the tiger's lair could not be seen in the tangled
Jungle's boiling green. We rode so fast and raced so far tree
tops blocked out every star all I could see from every rise
was coldly watching tiger's eyes. The howling wind sang a
sirens song and the tiger's breath smelled very strong then I woke
and saw a patch of light the sun was shining very bright
The birds were singing as if to say, now that you see the
light of the day I think it would be very wise, never to look
into a tiger's eyes!

Jacqueline Vogelsang

What's The Use Of The Sky

I saw the angels falling down from the highest heights
I saw myself falling in love for the first time
What's the use of falling in love
What's the use of falling

I looked around and I saw no one
I closed my eyes and I saw the sunshine on you
What's the use of seeing no one
What's the use of shining

There was an apple-pie in the sky
Once it was yours and now it's mine
What's the use of making apple-pies
What's the use of the skyline

I saw the angels falling down from the highest heights
I saw myself falling in love for the last time
What's the use of falling in love
What's the use of falling
What's the use of flying too high
What's the use of the sky
What's the use of the sky
What's the use of the sky

Guennadi Slasten

"Would You Die For Him?"

The window of my soul brings this vision into view—
I saw myself weeping inside, carrying the pain, isolated, no one to blame—
As I looked up, there he was, standing alone to my dismay—
And he said unto me, "Come my child, for I will love you"—
With his outreached arms, he gentle took me by the hand—
To let me know he'd understand—
He looked at me with the gentleness of eyes—
And I wondered how he had touched other lives?
Was it me, he was thinking of?
As he revealed with the greatest of love—
Who was this man with the deepest compassion?
That saw the tears, knew the pain, felt the hurt I couldn't explain—
How did he know me?
When did he see me?
Where did I know him from?
Then I remembered from where he came—
The price he paid for carrying my name—
I just kept thinking again and again—
But, would you die for him?
Would you die for him?

Betty J. Ritchey

"I Know Without Wondering, There's A God Somewhere"

I rode through the country in the time of spring
I saw the trees budding I heard the birds sing
I saw the flowers blooming in their beauty so rare
And I know without wondering there's a God somewhere.

I saw a tree weeping, a willow it's called
I heard a breeze whisper I didn't see it at all
I felt it caress me as it tangled my hair
And I know without wondering there's a God Somewhere.

I looked in wonder at a sparrow so small
And I said Lord you feed them they don't worry at all
If they fall from their nest you said you care
And I know without wondering there's a God somewhere.

Now the flowers bloom and the birds sweetly sing
The people say it's a sure sign of spring
But if we knew the language of the lilies so fair
They would say man repent for there's a God somewhere.

Fannie Lee Parrott

To Uncle Jim

Dear Uncle Jim:
I saw you once again at a table
in the back of the tobacco shop,
far away look in those dreamy blue eyes.
What were you remembering?

Cheers, when you were the star
of the high school football team?
Fear, as you piloted the bomber
over the churches of Cologne?
Anticipation on your wedding night?
The feel of your new born baby in your arms?

Are you remembering aching muscles
after a long day on the job,
or the evening warmth of a home,
supper on the stove?

Are you content as you sit there
with that quiet smile,
nothing to do but pilot checkers
over other old men's kings?

Geneva Werfal

Homeless Man Pleads Case In Santa Monica Court

I stand here unrepentant and alone.
I scrounge for food and call these mean streets my home.
I'm charged with sleeping in the parks at night.
A crime is thus created by my plight.

I once was charged with a most heinous crime
and thought the court would surely give me time.
The judge deciding that I was insane
committed me to ne'er be free again.

For thirty years my keepers were the guards
at state hospital psychiatric wards.
Now that has changed due to state budget cuts.
Am I now sane or has the state gone nuts?

'Twould serve no public good to have me jailed
to enforce policies so flawed and failed.

Joseph R. Millner

My Lord Looks Down On Me

As I look about the starry skies,
I see God's wondrous eyes
Looking everywhere.

So when I say my prayers,
Does God really care?

When I look about the starry skies,
What should I see but God's glistening eyes
Looking down on me.

I have no doubt what He will see-
A lonely soul in need of Thee.

To teach and guide and comfort me.
What He must think of me.

I know no one is perfect, you see,
But Jesus gave Him life for me.

To wash away my many sins:
So I will give my soul to Him.

So if you're ever in despair,
Know Jesus really cares.

Janice K. Ross

True Love

When I look into your eyes
I see no hate, you don't despise.
And when I am feeling down
You always seem to come around.
You hug me in your own special way
It's the highlight of both our day.
You kiss me gently on the cheek,
I feel a bit better and we didn't even speak.
At night you sleep next to me,
Protective and caringly.
You do all of this out of love,
You certainly are blessed from above.
I'll love you till the very end,
It's true what they say,
You are Man's Best Friend.

Carrie Barber

Sisters

Flowers, diamonds, gold and bangles,
I think it's great to be one of "Charlie's Angels",
I'm glad you're my sister and friend as well,
Being a part of your life makes my heart swell,

Today, tomorrow and forever we'll be,
A continuing closeness so happy and free,
I'm glad you are my sister and wouldn't have it no other way,
So I'm taking this time to wish you a happy, happy day.

Joyce Turner

Nothing

I have nothing.
I see nothing.
I hear nothing.
Why I have nothing?
Why I see nothing?
Why I hear nothing?
If only once I can grab hold of something.
Then and only then can I see and hear something.
For so long I disbelieved.
But now learned to say please.
Nothing begins to leave my way of life.
I smile, say hi and don't wonder why.
Now I have something.
Now I hear something.
Now I see something.
But-in the end we all still have nothing.

Johnathan Marshall

Prayer Of Desolation

Oh GOD Hear my cry! Help me to fight despair and desolation. I see the black clouds above my head and I weep in sorrow for I can no longer see the sun. Thy children have deserted me and I know not why.

What was my crime GOD? What was my sin that they would turn against me and cast me out? Why do they blindly follow where you do not lead? Oh GOD I look into their eyes and I see hatred where once there was love and friendship.

GOD I cry out to you in my anguish! Am I so low that they would treat me so? They accuse me of the sins they commit. They lie and thy Servant believes them. He does not see the truth that is in my heart. Their voices are the one voice. Their leader is thy enemy and they would tear me apart for that one voice.

I pity them in their blindness and cowardness GOD for they know not what they do. They would not willingly turn from you. Help me to forgive them GOD. Help me to be strong in my love for you. Let the river of my tears run dry, my bones stop shaking. Let my Soul sing again GOD. Let thy people be free of the Darkness that overcomes.

Hear My Prayer GOD

Barbara B. Fredericks

Predestination

As I sit upon this throne
I see the people that are my own.
As I forgive forever more
I know that many will knock some more.

I will open this door so very wide.
So I can have as many people to be by my side.
In all of time and all of day
I can truly say, walk my way
For on the sand my foot prints were seen.

Even today I am seen.
I am a friend
An ear I will lend
A hand I will give
But you must live
In my light
Be good and Righteous.

Dianne O'Bray

See And Love Again

I look in your eyes and I see the whole world ahead of me
I see us together, forever, sailing out on the sea
Our love for each other shines across the sky
There will never be a day when we say good-bye
We laugh, we sing, we love each other through the years
We share our feelings, our thoughts, and our fears
The day comes when we make our vows to each other
Soon you become a father, and I, a proud mother
Our baby looks just like you, with those eyes shining bright
An end to our devotion is no where in sight
Through the years our love is better than before
You have been the biggest part of me, then, now, forever and more
You've made my life so full of fun, so full of your endless
love for me
Another love like ours in this world could never, ever be
I look in your eyes and see the whole world behind me
Your love for me, your precious, precious love is all I see
I lay in your arms, where I kiss you and say I love you, my love
No good-byes, for I will see and love you again in the heavens above.

Debra J. Hastee-Dixon

For Awhile You Loved Me

I thank God each and every night,
I sit here and pray in the pale moonlight,
I thank him for everything we've done,
All the good time and all the fun.

We had good times none were bad,
'Til all the sudden bad times were all we had,
Now we don't laugh, we don't even speak,
It tears at my heart making we weak.

In the future I hope you find love,
'Cause that's what real happiness is made of,
I hope you don't forget me and what we shared,
For awhile you loved me, for awhile you cared.

Angel D. Archie

Loving A Friend

We were best friends no secrets to hide
I stood next to you, you stood by my side
Whenever I needed someone you were there
I'll be there when your feeling down
I'll make you smile, get ride of your frown
We shared a friendship I never knew
Then there was that moment of magic
one second in time
I can still feel you with me no matter where I go
I close my eyes and you will always be there
I love you and will always care
loving a friend is the hardest thing to do
But I can't help, loving you

Anita Trejo

Little Jimmy, My Darling Son

Go to sleep Jimmy, my darling son
I stroke his hair,
Oh but none can compare
to my little darling son.

His little hands are clutched on my breast
It doesn't seem minutes ago
I called him a pest.

Now to tiptoe out and close the door.
His little toys all over the floor.
I'll open the door in just a little while
And receive a big beautiful smile
From my little one, my darling son.

Joann Ebel

Assured Of God's Love

As I walked down by a quiet little brook;
I stopped for a while just to take a better look.
I saw God's handi-work so grand,
And I knew he must really love this great land.

And then I walked in a meadow so green,
There never before such beauty had I seen.
I saw the wild flowers, the birds and the bees.
Yes, God is ever mindful of all of these.

So when I feel sad or lonely or low,
Back down by the brook or the meadow I go.
Then I feel a tear as it slips from my eye;
For I feel God's presence and I know he's nearby.

It's there I hear him whisper in a voice kind and low,
My child I'm mindful of all things below.
So I lifted my eye and my heart up above,
And I know that it is me that God really loves.

Doris Baughn

The Struggle

I long ago ceased being amazed at the way life's events unfold;
I take what comes, give as good as I get, and place no worth in rumors told.

There is no pot of gold, no pie in the sky, no cloud with a silver lining;
Life is, however—they say, if you're clever—rewarding and most benigning.

Many lives have been spent on decaying hopes, and others on broken dreams;
But the distance runner, like the lonely hunter, has the best idea, it seems:

Depend on self—this is all you have. Do with it what you will.
This may seem strange, but dependence on others, I swear, is stranger still.

Go out into the world, meet life head-on. Don't surrender in utter disgust;
Confront trial face-to-face, don't back down—but be nimble when you must.

For yours is the right, the right to fight—the right to have what you've earned;
And in the end they will know, by your eyes that glow—that you fought, though you must have been burned.

Eddie Thomas

Mom And Dad

With the light of each day I drop to my knees and pray,
I thank God for all He has given me, and opening my eyes to see
All the blessing that I have had a loving family and mom and dad

Sometimes it's hard to say what is the best blessing of each day,
To wake to see the bright sunlight
Knowing those love are alright

I don't ask for much, the blessing I count on one hand
Like pebbles in a river or grains of sand
Mom and Dad were always there to talk to, and guides us, they always Cared.

You raised seven children and did your best
Though at times we put your patience to the test

As loving parents you stayed in there through thick and thin
Giving us all the love and confidence and support you could lend
Sometimes we didn't listen it's sad to say
And some of us regret it to this day
It was hard at times but you rose above
To show us that anything is possible if you have family to love

Now I know that all you have taught me is true
For not a day goes by when I don't miss you.

Crystal Lynn Thomas

From The Window

I look in wonder to the outside,
I think and imagine of all that have cried.
I see the birds, I see the trees.
I see a world that's no longer free.
People are in chains, becoming a slave.
They are possessed by what they crave.
More and more is what they need.
You get your way by being a fiend,
People hurt others to have their way,
Not caring what they do not caring what they say.
From the window I sit and stare.
I'm glad I'm in here instead of out there.

Jessica Davis

Earth's Lament

I'm scared, said the earth to the moon,
I think I'm going to die very soon.
There's a constant haze in my blue sky,
And that's what happens before you die.

The air has become so stale
That it's difficult to inhale.
The pollution makes it heavy and thick,
And I'm beginning to feel quite sick.

They're razing the forests, hundreds a day,
And the rivers and seas are full of decay.
How can they expect their children to endure
When they've sentenced me to a death, so premature.

Suffocation is imminent, I'm afraid,
The oxygen supply is going to fade.
Without the trees to replenish the air,
My demise is certain, does no one care?

How sad, never again will I feel the breeze,
Or watch the rain, or touch the cool seas,
Or smell a flower, or welcome a new spring,
Or see a green field, or hear a human being.

Gordi Turnbull

Dear Doc

We have a serious problem
I think maybe a family brake
Please come do our rescue
It may already be to take

We have developed Some Timers
It spreading really quick please find a cure
The minds are getting sick

You didn't respond soon enough often timer's has set in
We go about our daily lives
and wonder where we've been

In your busy bury schedule
Could you please check this out
It's leading on to all timers I haven't any doubt

If you find a remedy send it air express
It's really much needed
afore we all become a mess

Please, please here our cry
respond quickly to our call
before this things called all timers

Gets us all sometimes and often timers sisters

Florence Rutherford and Anita C. Newbold

Yellow And Orange

What is yellow and orange to you?
I think of Autumn.
Autumn leaves piled in a stack,
But before you play someone steals the pack.
When I think of flowers
I think of a bouquet of yellow roses
and orange wildflowers.
For mother, teacher or you.
Who knew?
A yellow and orange fire to warm your love,
On a cold day in December.
Wrapping paper of orange with yellow flowers
For Christmas or someone's birthday.
A part of life?
A part of you?
Yellow and orange,
Who knew?

Emily A. McCormick

Memories

At times when I am feeling down and sad,
I think of old relations from my past.
Recalling all the great friends I have had,
I ponder joyful times I thought would last.

In the midst of childhood we were so free,
The world was still something to be explored.
We laughed and played, and dreamed of what would be;
All obstacles before us we ignored.

We talked of what the future had in store,
And told of the grand way we would succeed;
Our tales of wealth and fame never did bore...
How ever-pleasant, the lives we'd soon lead!

Although my childhood has passed me by,
Fond memories, treasured, will never die.

Anthony A. Antaki

My Kingdom

To far away lands I wanted to go,
I thought I would like to roam,
But instead I'm content to stay right here
In this my own little home.

I'll visit far away lands in a book
About them I'll get enthused,
Until a curly head climbs on my knee,
Or a baby unties my shoes.

Perhaps the next time I'm reading my book
on sunkissed shores I will be
When I hear someone call out "Oh mother,
have you any cake for me?"

I'll put my book down till some other time,
I'll wait for I do not care.
When I've boys to ask for cake and baby
Fingers that rumple my hair.

Childhood days pass quickly by, so before
Another chapter I start,
I'll be thankful for home, It's my Kingdom
And in this Kingdom my heart.

Carrie E. Parton

No Turning Back

My life is meaningless, it just seems so small,
I try to walk straight, but all I do is fall,
Suicide, death, my vocabulary,
The older I get, the better I see.

I take out the bullets, they are silver and shine,
I load them slowly into the gun that is mine,
Up against my head, the cold of the steel,
Russian roulette, let's make a deal.

The hammer's pulled back, there's a sound of a click,
Think of my life, it just makes me sick,
Pull down the trigger, it starts with a spark,
One minute there's light, the next there is dark.

Cameron Gaston

Amanda's Choice

Fall comes and it's time to pick my steer.
I walk through the cow herd with a little bit of fear.
I finally pick my steer out, I really think he's best.
I guess we really won't know, the fair will be our test.
The cold winter days while caring for my steer,
only to hope someone will appear.
I quiet him down with some frustration.
But only keep dreaming with big expectations.
My hands get all rope burned, my feet are all mud.
My steer just looks at me as he chews on his cud.
I pull on his halter to teach him to lead,
when all of a sudden he runs to his feed.
It's funny some days I can't keep him from stalling.
This summer I work him daily and think of the fair.
Hoping somehow that we'll make a wonderful pair.
The time will soon come when the work will be done.
Then the fair will be here for us to have fun.
I'll walk in the show ring so proud to be there.
As the buyers bid with their hands in the air.

Amanda Leonard

I Am A Proud Breastfeeding Mother

I am a proud breastfeeding mother
I want everyone to know
I breastfeed my baby where ever I go.

In the beginning of my pregnancy, I was very shy -
wasn't sure if I wanted to breastfeed.
Then I come to WIC and received the
encouragement we all sometimes need.

The WIC staff was so patient
using their infant doll models and breast model for demonstrations
and if that wasn't enough, they used flipcharts, videos, guest
speakers or private consultation.

They convinced me without a doubt, formula is something my
baby can do without.

Yes, I am a proud breastfeeding mother.
It's such a healthy thing to do,
so beneficial in every way
It means so much more then words can ever say.

Delores B. Johnson

If You Could...

If you could feel the pain I'm in,
If you could see the tears I cry,
If you could taste the tears I cry while I
cry myself to sleep at night.
If you could only understand the pain I'm in,
then you would feel the pain,
See the tears
And taste the tears that I cry!

Amanda Bowers

Creation

In the beginning there was me and before me there was only me
I was in the beginning and I was all there ever was or had been
You did not exist neither did anyone else or anything else
There was only me and life was almost perfect
Then my life turned upside down I suffered a great shock
There seemed to be more than me after all
Something or someone else did exist DRAT!!!
Why oh why was it necessary I was quite happy when there was just me
But then there was you and them and all the others
I hated it I kicked and screamed and carried on so
But then I found alcohol and drugs
And there was just me again all alone at the center of creation
To float and fly and sing in the illusion of control
Until I fell exhausted from the dance desperate I asked for help
And you touched me and from then on you existed
As you directed the building of my relationship with you and others
You came to be immense in my life growing bigger every day
I saw you in others first in the stars in the earth
In myself in all of art and science too and now oh yes now
There is only you and you have always been and you will always be
And everything else in creation fades into you and I thank you

Joseph B. Kelly

Untitled

Through years of systematic and calculated torture
I was taught to trust no one, young or old
learning to use the world inside me. I lived
yet still I called his name

Locked away in a personal cell
one in a million a million more
alone from the word with only one guest
I still call his name

When past history becomes present life
And the world is in total chaos
one thing will remain true, only him
I'll still call his name.

Jodie Gonzalez

Tennis Match

Our tennis match was tied,
I was the last one to play.
I walked on the court as nervous as can be.
We hit for a little bit, it seemed like an hour.
I warmed up my serve,
It was a slow as a turtle,
But on the other side it was blazing fast.
It was a long first game but I stayed tough.
My opponent got tired but I still played strongly.
Mario, my tennis coach was watching,
He said I was playing fine.
My hands started sweating all over my racket,
My white shirt was wet from all the sweat.
The people on my team where cheering me on.
As I walked off the court my smile began to grow,
I had done it. I finally won!!!

Ali Goldberg

"A Poet's Prayer"

Send me a vision.
I want a blinding, throbbing vision.
I want a ball of light to descend upon me and
burn my eyeballs to their very core.
I want to know, I want to really know.

Tear me down
And rebuild me from the soul out.
Raise me up
And let me soar through the ages.
I'm ready for my journey.
Let's begin.

Alice Sarti

Hold Me

I am so alone, scared, and blue,
I wish I knew what to do
All these weird things are happening to me
I wish someone would hold me.
Most people have turned on me,
Cause they think I'm crazy.
I'm just trying to be me.
I'm always sad,
But I don't show it,
But nobody cares anyway.
If people only knew my pain
But nobody cares enough to ask,
I don't understand why,
And all I do is cry, deep down inside
All I really want and need is
Someone to hold me,
So if anyone does care then please
Hear my plead and hold me!

Jennifer Phillips

I'm A Seed — I'm A Rose

It all started when I was given birth,
I wish it never happened, now I'm stuck on this earth.
I feel like a plant that has never been grown,
Never had much of anything or did I own,
I feel small about everything like a piece of grain,
Can't get a grasp to start my life, depression in my brain,
With a final cry and a final yelp,
I can't take it no more I need some help.

Everyday I feel I grow little bit more,
I think bigger, I'm feeling different, I'm really not sure,
My wish to God has been granted,
I'm not that flower I thought was planted.

I'm starting to feel as rich as a gem,
I broke through that seed and grew a stem,
I feel like winning, my goals turn to medals,
My life is getting better, I'm growing some pedals.
I'm still confused, as I start spinning,
But I just learned that losing is a part of winning.
I feel fresher, cleaner, I can smell it in my nose,
I'm not that plant, ...I'm a rose.

Gary Akins

Positive

As I sit and hold back tears,
I wonder about future years.
How many will there be,
How much longer will there be me?
The push of pain has come to shove,
Now I pray to you above.
Give me new strength, make me strong,
Keep me alive, it's where I belong.
My life is being stripped away,
Getting shorter, day by day.
My future cut short with a single sign,
Of all the lives, why pick mine?
All this agony from one mistake,
One I thought I would never make.
I wish I could go back and set things right,
When I shot up my first time, that fateful night.

Jennifer Sullivan

I Am

I am an individual with deep thoughts who listens to the rain
I wonder if racism will ever be a thing of the past
I hear the thunder tells us beings that we do not walk alone
I see a Native American showing me his people's purity
I want all ignorance to step off and go plummeting to Hell!
I am an individual with deep thoughts who listens to the rain
I pretend not to let my dark secret bother my soul
I feel my guardian angel touch me with the hand of serenity (at times)
I touch my god with my pulsating heart
I worry about ignorant people's reaction toward my sister's
beautiful self
I cry for the lonely
I am an individual with deep thoughts who listens to the rain
I understand other's pain and lost souls
I say that other's pain is not someone else's gain
I dream of going off into another universe to be alone
I try not to be shy and timid
I hope to one day be out amongst the star's secrets
I am an individual with deep thoughts who listens to the rain

Elizabeth (Loneseek) Castañeda

"Leaving"

As I walk out this door tonight
I wonder if you'll be all right
I might regret this someday
But it's a price I'm just gonna have to pay

There is another I care about too
But I'm leaving him behind the same as I am you
Trying to choose between you two is tearing me apart
So I'm leaving to save the rest of my heart

I wish I knew who I loved more
I wouldn't be spending all this time walking the floor
Leaving isn't going to help much
But I can't stay here wanting both's touch

I know I shouldn't run from my troubles
But the longer I stay the more the hurt doubles
I can't stay here feeling blue
So leaving is all I know to do.

Amanda Cook

"Red"

I see red all around
I wonder where this red is bound
and if I give chase
will I catch this storm of red,
this crimson tide?
Or maybe all this is just a dream
no matter what it is, this red is my pride
the pain, the gushing, the red is streaming
out of its system, on to the ground.
Now I know where this red and I are bound
and I can see the eyes of death, their gleaming.
I never should off, I know that know.
How I ever thought I could change my fortune
through a gun.
The life I've lived flashes through my mind
and all the things I should have done
now I know, I have no more time to find.
I guess that's what happens when life is lived
with no remorse and a gun.

"MORE PEACE, MORE LIFE."

Eugene Hong

Daddy Came Through The Door No More

I remember at the age of two, that Daddy was gone, gone, gone!
I wondered what had gone wrong, wrong, wrong!
Daddy came through the door no more.
I'll play until the sun would go down.
For I knew it was time for Daddy to come around.
Daddy come through the door no more.
I'll sit and wait for that door to open.
Sit and wait and keep hoping, hoping, hoping!
Daddy came through the door no more.
He would come through the door each day.
Come over, me waiting for him to play.
I would give him the biggest smile, smile, smile!
My tiny hands would clap for him awhile, while, while!
Daddy came through the door no more.
I only sit and feel sad, sad, sad!
Mom only looks mad, mad, mad!
For she lost someone we both once had, had, had!
Daddy came through the door no more.
I sit each day and watch that door, door, door!
Hoping that Daddy comes through the door once more, more more!

Denise Williams

Four Quartets

I would I could levitate as Saint John;
I would I could meditate mystery's bond:
I would lose myself as old Tom Browne;
I would leave my pelf upon the ground;

I would feel like upending mortality's car;
I would feel like ascending Orion's star.
I would I were shattered, blown to bits
Beyond Plato's ladder minus wits:

I would suspend my soul on a stasis wire,
Afflatus to control the Yeatsean gyre;
I would no longer seek an identity;
I would have reached the peak in a unity;

I would have laid the splay of soul on rocks,
Danced antic hay to Einstein's' clocks;
For there where somewhere unification is,
Clang-bang-cymballed air ends symphonic fizz.

John J. Murray

Homeless

Sensation comes and with it a blast of frigid air.
Ice melting, dripping down my neck, encasing strands of hair.
My mind does swirl and I can feel the pain that grows within.
Come sweet darkness, it does not stop, awareness marches in.

The more I struggle to disappear, the more conscious I become.
And in my desperation I pray that I may die, frozen, numb.
Oh God please help me not to feel the icy cold that's burning me,
the pain that's growing with every nerve that is screaming out to me.

I dare not move, lying still within my tattered home of wool.
I peer through my wretchedness, into a world that is so cold,
and watch the shoes go passing by, running by, and wonder if
they notice me.
Dying here in full sight of those who look, but can not see.

Oh for a pint or two to ease the pain, to take me home again,
back beyond the numbing cold, back to where there is no ice or rain,
back to where this grief and misery can not follow me.
Oh God, just a sip or two to take me where I want to be.

Wretched life I live in pain, less than human in much despair.
Toss me a coin, throw me a crumb, and look if you dare.
For I am you, and you can't run or turn your head in shame.
I lost my world and you can to, for we are both the same.

Barbara A. Santos

If I Were An Eagle

If I were an eagle, I'd fly away.
I'd fly away almost every day.
To a place that was far, out by the sea.
And there would be nobody there but me.
I'd sit in the trees and rest my feathers.
And watch the wind blow on the heathers.

If I were an eagle, I'd fly away.
I'd fly away almost every day.
But then one day as I sat alone,
I would begin to want - a friend of my own.
And maybe another, to make us three.
Two friends - to give me company.

If I were an eagle, I'd fly away.
I'd fly away almost every day.
And while in my tree, out by the sea
I'd realize that it was O.K. to be,
Alone, or in the company of three.

Dahlia Bell-Allen

If I

If I were a bird under the clear blue sky
I'd travel far and travel wide
To distant place, to distant field
The breeze and wind for me to feel

Across the seas and isles of Spain
Spreading my wings through the driving rain
To a place where all is calm
Beyond the volcano and the storm

Where the birds of heaven do fly, for the grace of God go I
To peer upon the crystal sea, to catch a glimpse of eternity

But suddenly a distant call, from out of the clouds a restless thrall
To bring me back from whence I came, to crush my spirit, to make me tame

To fight this force that pulls me down
That forces me upon the ground
That shuts my eyes so I can't dream, and never reach the golden stream

But out of the clouds I hear a voice
Telling me I have a choice
To fly and reach the greater day, across the rivers and the bay

Until I find my final place
Where I can see God face to face

Gene Evers

Please Don't Cry

You tell me all of the things you would do
If a second chance were to come to you
You cry your tears and I try to comfort you
The Lord know what all you have been going through
All your life you never knew a real love
That special gift sent from heaven above
Now that you have and you have lost it too
You know that no one else could ever do
Your tears flow down your tired sad face
No one else could in your heart replace
That special guy you truly love so
Oh, now how you wish he did not go
But I say all hope is not lost
If you will but pay the high cost
Perhaps you will win him back with care
If you are still strong enough to dare
Being gay is not for the weak
For true love is what we all seek
So give your best shot while you may
It is worth what ever cost you pay

Alexander Martin

Beauty In Exile

Let me be the wind
If I but care,
To seize ones Dream
Would be unfair.
For I am but a face,
Where beauty resides.
That brings happiness and grace to another eye
But where darkness reigns I can never be,
So onward and upward
To my destiny.
Worn a bit, from the trial.
Tears but amble for a while
But then subside by Gods grace
For in a Garden is my Place.....

Ira Lazarowitz

Good Morning Sunshine

Good morning sunshine, you are so beautiful today
If I had a playmate I'd go out and play,
We were so young and gay just yesterday
But when I awaken this morning that world had gone away.

Want it be wonderful when we meet again
A brand new ball game without any sin,
You will be as handsome as you were before
We just want have those needs and desires any more.

I'm not as sad as others think, neither do I sigh
I'm putting on buds right now for meeting in the sky
I could write a book of our yesteryear
But a book of pages can't tell how I miss you dear

Arra A. Chipman

"Touch Me When I Am Old"

Please touch me when I am old.
If I should lie dying in a white
Hospital fold...
Curled up in a fetal pose,
Read to me.
Talk to me while I can still listen.
If in my sleep my rest seems deep.
Remember to hold my hand.
Don't sit quietly by my bed
Come close....
Lay your hand on my weary head.
If I seem lonesome and cold.
Please touch me when I am old.
I loved and touched you for all of your days...
So do this for me when I reach the
ends of life's way.
Before the angels claim my soul.
Please touch me when I am old.

Carrie Maxine Estill

Reflections

Did you ever wonder, when your children are full grown...
If there might have been more time to share, if you had only known..
That years go by so quickly..
The boys are shaving now.
My daughter's wearing lipstick.
In her gown she'll take a bow.
Rewards will be forth coming though...
For soon right at your door,
Your grandchildren will smile and say..
"Grandma, I love you more!!"

Betty Ann Bonnis

"The Loud Silence"

In the middle of a forest, a tree falls to the ground,
If no one is there ... does it make a sound?

Is that tree important ... or, should it die?
If other trees follow ... does it matter why?

Young trees, old trees, start to silently fall,
The oak and elm ... and giant redwoods, so tall ...

The leaves no longer rustle, as, the fall winds blow,
The birds no longer sing ... it begins to snow.

The sun beats down, on the forest floor.
The shade is gone now ... for ever-more!

All Gods creatures ... have gone away.
There's no reason ... for them to stay!

The forest is gone now, and left death all around,
the silence -
is everywhere!
it makes a deafening sound!

Daryl Gaertner

A Year For Us

A couple years have come and gone, I'm so glad you came along.
If not for you I wouldn't see, what a love could mean to me.

A year of love, patience and hope, how did we manage to ever cope!
Through love, caring, friendship and trust, we only did
what we knew we must.

Another life we share so dear, our path seems so very clear.
To nurture, protect and defend, this small miracle until the end.

Treasure the moments when he's small, until he
hears that loving call.
When he finds that love so true, she will also cherish him to.

Our life revolves around our son, now I know we are as one.
Without you dear I couldn't see, just how much love means to me.

The child we share I hope will recall, the times we
had through it all.
His memories shall be good and long, of the love that is so strong.

I hope our grandkids will recall, of our love that weathered all.
To you my dear when said and done, I hope you recall you're
my only one

Eve C. Dunnihoo-Schumacher

Hold On

Climb the rainbow, reaching toward your heart;
If you slide down begin from a new start.
When your feelings are hurt and you can't really understand why;
Do your best not the break down and cry.
If a touch of someone's hand will guide you along;
Don't go on believing whatever you do is wrong.
Give me a smile, wipe away that tear;
Sit down with me, and tell me what you fear.
If your life there will be many loves and many hates;
Many laughs and of course heart breaks.
Keeping holding on, don't let go;
Give yourself a chance to grow.
Keep that smile upon your face;
Leaving this sadness without a trace.
Follow your heart into the sky;
Show the world how hard you've tried.
Lie down, and close your eyes;
Let memories drift slowly into your mind.
Give your heart a chance to mend;
And remember me, I am your friend.

Jayme Moulton

Wearing Mother's Hat

What a daily occurrence
I'll always remember that
Do not forget to wear my hat child!
Every time you go outside
You're not too old to catch a cold
Me! Wear that stupid looking old felt hat!
I'd madly ask, What are you staring at?
Oh! Please let me go bear-headed
To breathe the hot fumes of my hair in the air
Blowing wind, brim down, flopping eyelids
I couldn't see where I was heading
A fit for two heads, hers and mine, but so what
It's the only hat that she has got
Shrinks to fit on a rainy day
I have to wear that hat today
I want to taste the raindrops from my face
I tried to fix it properly you see
While all the time she was watching me
Securely pressed the old brown felt
Wearing mother's old felt hat

Barbara Christobel DeMoura

"Spring"

Spring is hear, and I have a fear
I'll have to sneak away,
The soft wind blows the scent of the rose
As the budding branch's sway.

My soul yearns release
To fly as the wild geese
Be free of my daily care,
Soar over yonder hill, where meadow larks twill
Find peace and solitude there.

Though my soul longs to flee
The pines I may never see
Or follow just where the rivers goes
There's a secluded part, hid within my heart
Where I sometimes dreamily go

So if you ever see, when you look at me
A far-away gaze in my eyes
I'll be twiddling my toes
As the clear water flows
Way out where the lone eagle flies.

Hazel A. Hickman

Next Time It Rains

I'll see colors through prisms in the droplets
I'll see diamonds of rare price clinging
to the boughs.
I'll remember when last the sun
was shining.
Next time it rains.

I'll remember when my heart was lighter.
I'll remember when my eyes were brighter
and everything was going my way -
Next times it rains.

I'll hear trickling brooks and bees buzzing
in meadow grasses.
I'll see rainbow's - and thank the Lord
for my mind's eye.
Next time it rains.

Juanita Thompson

(Hi)

I'm a solar eclipse.
I'm a photo of a starving child.
I'm the bill.

I'm what's under the band-aid.
I'm a losing score.
I'm the split-second you realize the killer is behind the door.

I'm a bad grade.
I'm the draw on an inside straight.
I'm a surgical procedure.

I'm Medusa.
I'm what you just put your hand in.
I'm his thingy.

I'm a gift horse's mouth.
I'm the other passengers in a car accident.
I'm what's under the bed.

I'm your seventh grade school picture.
I'm the price of the dress that makes you look so angelic.
I'm a needle piercing your beautiful skin.

I'm standing right in front of you.

Damian Fraticelli

Untitled

Little boy blue.
I'm lost inside you.
I don't know where I'm going or where I've been.
Don't keep yourself locked up inside
That attic dungeon of a mind.
The pain you are feeling is true,
But I've been there, that I know.
This world isn't as easy as it sounds,
Please come down.
You may say no one understands,
But I am pleading with you,
There may be someone who does,
An ear, a shoulder,
An arm, a sleeve,
That's all I can offer, except,
My love.

Gehlen Exum

A Letter To Santa

Dear Santa,
I'm writing to tell you
What I want for Christmas this year
Don't worry about the stain on the paper
Because, Santa, it's just a tear.
And the reason that I'm so sad is because things
Around here are bad Daddy got laid-off from work at the factory
So bring him a job instead of me some toys.
And Mama works all day standing on her feet
So please bring her new shoes instead of candy for me.
If you want to stuff my stocking
Fill it with baby food for my little brother
And I promise I'll be good.
And, if you want to, please bring me a coat
For I don't have one and outside it's cool
And I'm afraid I'll get sick
While walking to school.
If you bring all these things
I'll be a good little girl and one more thing, Santa
Please bring peace to the world.

Frankie Annette Woods

"My Daughter"

When you gain a daughter, she need not be of blood. What is most
Important is the element of love. It makes no difference how she
came, adoptive, step, or birth, she can be a daughter with all
the love on earth.

You came to me a young girl. At the time it did not show,
That you would give me so much more, then I could ever know.
You gave me love and kindness and tried so hard to show, that I
was part of your family. Just like I was your own.

You grew to be a beauty, with eyes of candle glow. And even
more Important, is the beauty of your soul. Then you had a
family, Wonderful to behold, that added something to my life.
Much more then you could know.

So if there is something I have learned, through all the years gone
Past, is that a family need not be of blood, for love to ever last.

Frank Ponticello

The Seed Of A Poem

As a tear trickles down my face or as I envelope my self
in a turban of quilts,
Something happens inside of me as if a cool splash of
fragrant light is slung upon my mind.
I sit and ponder of the words to express my emotions-
fear, defeat, loss, or losing, but none of them fit.
Because I'm like a central station of thought.
All the information is raked into my brain but when I
think about it, it all comes out raw and crumpled.
Then the raw thoughts are all weaved into poetry and
then on paper. As that tear hits the floor the thought
ends and another enters my mind.
So grab that thought before it blends into eternity.
It's like trying to grab that last ray of sun light before
it's enveloped in the clouds.
For a poem is a way to cry without tears or to sing
with out song. A poem is like therapy to the mind so
hold onto one and it will never let you down.

Austin B. Cummings

Now And Then

We all live
In a world we make
A land of memories and wishes
Of dreams and fantasy
For each moment we live in the present
We live a lifetime in the past
Forever reaching back in time
We try to snatch what we have left behind
Handfuls at time, at time just pinches
So we spice our life
Every now and then
With faded colors
Sometime melancholy
The sound of laughter and taste of tears
So they linger and mingle
Until we can't tell them apart

Aitzaz Ahmed

The Promise

The promise you gave me on our wedding day has scattered
in the Wind like the Ashes of a Corpse from an Empty urn.
Floating aimlessly caught by breezes here, then there
not knowing where to land.
The promise I gave you on our wedding day was kept
like a Shrine for all to see, blazing in the sun, circle of Life
steadfast, born of Love from deep within, a Treasure unto myself.
It seems the only Promises we keep are those we make unto Ourselves.

Diana Carmack Storhoff

A Touching Of Spirits

In another time
In another dimension
In another world
A soul touched the depths of my essence
So deep — this soul became part of mine
So intense — my soul was set afire
With a blaze that will last
An eternity of eternities
Where is this spirit
I will search for you wherever I am
To find the soul that touched my spirit
Who left me so quickly and so far behind
Now — while I'm in this body
Come — join me in the flesh
To quench the desires of this fire.

Deloris Kennedy

Midwife-Grandmother

By the dark of the moon,
In Kershaw County, South Carolina,
Midst corn ready for harvest,
And other things awaiting a dawning,
There came a lone horseman at two in the morning.

"Mrs. Miller," he called, breathless,
"Her time is soon."

Hitch up the buggy.
Where's my black bag?
I left it here in the parlor before retiring.
It's my grandchildren, playing doctor again,
I'll blister their britches.

Boil water, bring clean white cloths,
To bandage a heart, and bundle the loss.

We're taught not to ask, WHY?
Because there's a time to live, and a time to die.
But for now there's only emptiness for the horseman,
As he gazes upon the ash of an ember,
That for a moment was his son.

Anne H. Rando

Bond Of Love

One individual and one individual, comes together in love.
In love a bond is formed, an intertwining of blood, sweat, tears,
Odor, hair and underwear meshes together, flesh upon flesh is molded-
like clay to unite two individuals into one, one flesh, one blood
drops - the same essence.

The essence of love combines into an exotic fragrance
that only those two individuals together can make-
When one fails, the other is there for support.
When both fail, they fall twice as hard.
When both succeed, their success is unlimited.

Two heads is better than one - likeminded -
When two comes together
the rain can't penetrate
the cold can't separate
Man and woman,
Husband and Wife
forever!

Charles De Jesus

God, Where Are You?

God is mysterious places
in many cases.
It was a beautiful clear day
and the child heard a voice say,
"Hello, this is God,"
and the child's head bent to a nod!
Every time he went back to playing
he heard, "Are you a good boy?" someone was saying.
With bewildering eyes
This child searched the skies.
Again the voice came thru!!
Now, "What am I supposed to do! I can't see you!"
The blonde headed boy went to the house
which was a short walk.
Mother, "God was talking to me
and I promised to be as good as He,"
It was a game of hide and seek -
but God, where are you?"

Hilda Sumwalt

Choices

There are choices we make
In our lives every day.
Will we give or will we take
And will we be true or stray?

Some choices to be made are small
And some are big indeed.
But we should scrutinize them all
With the very fabric of our creed.

A choice size is not its true grit
Because we view it thru a veil.
For sometimes we choose a "nit"
And get a tiger by its tail.

Little choices made over the years
Is the rudder for our ship of fate.
They set the heading our "lifeboat" steers
As we navigate life's storm tossed strait.

Really big choices are but a few
And here is one I say.
The one whom I choose to love is you
And it's forever and a day.

John D. Cameron

The "Cut"

Listening to rolling waves,
In the distance a sea gull raves,
I plop down to feel warm sand
Cutting on a shell, my hand.

Dripping blood, deep and red,
I feel some water hit my head.
I turn around to see what's new,
A crashing wave was coming, true blue.

I ran until I could no more,
And fell flat on the ocean floor.
The giant wave swept me up without warming, And
I was knocked senseless, not knowing if it was
morning.

I woke and to my surprise
I thought I was dead, but I was alive.
I was lying in the sand,
No longer bleeding, the cut on my hand.

Jennifer Fischer

Hope

My eyes have seen the struggle on the faces of one so young and innocent. The depth of their soul is mirrored through their eyes, the yearning, the longing, the bewildered. One so young and precious has face so many challenges, yet their heart sings with music, their heart shines aglow. They are uplifted to a high, a high filled with hope. Each day is savored and held in the palm of their hands. With such embracement brings forth new light, that brightens a way to the future. As each passage clears, the warmth that circles and touches their very being, engulf into flames that flickers and gleams. The screech of laughter echo their enchantment, because tomorrow will bring new triumphs. The cloud that threatens to damper their spirits, is mystified by the shower of serenity, the peace and tranquility bestowed upon them, in the name of hope.

Beverley Davis

Anger justifies no means,
Inside the minds of youthful teens,
Bitter words and destructive minds,
Ticking time bombs locked in mental confines,
Soothing sounds leave a hole in his chest,
One foolish soul is laid to rest,
Flowers mark an early grave,
The loss of innocence in a world unbathed,
Tempers rise as many will fall,
The death of civilization once and for all,
This is a life of what might be,
If I do not stop killing you
And you killing me.

Bryant C. Smith

My Flight

Flying in a cloud unable to see,
instruments say everything is "normal."

Long awaiting my destination
I begin to lose sight.
Feeling nervous and afraid, thinking...

My heart and instinct
tell me I am falling;
not rapidly, but enough to raise question.

Time begins moving slowly;
when in reality, it remains the same.
I look around and still am sightless,
again I check, everything reads fine.

I want to run with the feeling
to grab the stick and pull up fast;
only to realize I must trust.

Flying in a cloud unable to see,
instruments say, everything is normal.

For Melita, my inspiration, and love of my life.

Charles A. McAninch

Be Not Alone

It is not good to be alone for any length of time,
It does not give us confidence or help our spirits climb,
Of course there are some periods our neighbors should not share,
Including special study and the time for silent prayer.
But in the normal passing of the hours of the day,
We ought to have companionship in labor and in play.
Too often we become inclined to worry or to brood,
When we withdraw into a shell of utter solitude.
God filled the world with souls for us to love and call our own,
And He did not intend that we should wander off alone.

Donald Hall

A Seed

From a seed doth one grow, as any seed from the earth
Into a tender innocent fresh growth.
Where at which time beauty abounds, sunshine surrounds
And youth seems everlasting .
But alas, a season passes were time has no value,
And without a single word, this young seed has withered much
And has fallen to the ground with society as such
But with the right inspiration and support from those who care
A young seed can prosper when true love is there
Its form will be proud and sturdy
Its eagerness in learning for the mind
Heart of toleration, a personality sublime
And whence such time emerges when the sun is not as warm
And our eyes are not as brilliant and all our time is dusk and dawn
And a lot of other senses we must wake up to though we mourn
For all is disappearing, we cherished in our need
And return from whence we came from
Thee earth this wonderful seed.

Aileen McSweeney

As Evening Falls

Blue sky melts
Into grey, into black.
Claustrophobic people take to bed
Waiting for the day, neglecting the night.
But she is awake
Soaking in the stars and the shadows
She, the nocturnal one,
Swims in the Pleiades and Orion.
She walks amongst the darkness, the dew,
Looks up at the burnt, blackened leaves
And smiles.
She is among the electric insects
And the midnight animals who prey on the tired
She is not afraid of the blanketed above
She is not afraid of the naked sky,
Nor the brilliant azure.
She is not afraid of difference.
She fears loss...
So she walks and swims in the night
as the ignorant sleep.

Emily A. Kane

"Who Are You"

The seconds and minutes continue to mount
Into hours and days I'm unable to count
And for each precious moment, a memory is stored
Of a person so special, so completely adored
But now I'm finding, the space isn't there
To store all the memories, I want to share
I've sorted and shaped, to make them all fit
My candle's of memory, I've kept them all lit
The weeks and the months have turned into years
And some of the laughter has turned into tears
But still you are there, in my memory
So I must find a place, cause you're so dear to me
Now I've discarded here, reduced some from there
To eliminate any is so hard to bear
But do it I must, I must have the space
To store one more memory, that I can't erase
There, I've pushed and I've squeezed 'til it is in place
I've finally made room to remember your face
It's right here before me, but oh! what a shame
I can see your face but I've forgotten your name

Hal Whaley

Infinity

I watched the sea gull launch himself
into the beckoning sky and,
in a moment, was in spirit with him there,
owning all that vast expanse
my eager eyes could view:
the scope of earth,
the patchwork quilt of colors every hue,
uniting earth, white-crested waves
and sky of azure blue.

Such wonder filled me at the
Love that caused all this to be,
and I could know that when I die
my spirit will still be free to fly,
and my body, wherever it may lie,
will be as one
with earth
the sea
and the sky.

Alice E. Ross

Incest

Beauty, its skin unmarred
Is but a crimson letter of olden days.
Whether it be beauty of mind,
Spirit, heart or body,
It quickly turns to black ash
When with malice my child embrace is answered..

My soul hides within the ashes
No one knows I'm here
No one cares
I am safe.

Decades later, smoke from the ashes
Sculpts my soul.
Fear, pain, illness follow.
Mountains, obstacles, roads and bridges interfere.
To become, begin, endure.
I am again

Barbara J. Weber

Earth Mother

The Earth - our mother
Is crying out

Why must the greedy destroy me?
Why do they close their eyes in unfelt rage and pain?

I am here to provide your needs if only you would let me

I am the Earth
Your mother
The mother of all

Without me you are no more

So open your eyes and embrace your unfelt rage and pain

Let me hold you with my arms of earth
And bathe you in my perfumed air

Let my energy come alive within your heart

For without me
You are no more

I am the Earth
Your mother

Judy Hayes

What Is It Like

WHAT IS IT LIKE TO BE A BLACK BOY?
Is it growing up in poverty, or just being coy
When you're around white people that point and make fun?
Most of the time you want to hit them, but instead you run.
When you're behind their back, you laugh, snicker and swear,
But if you're face to face with them, oh no, you won't dare.

WHAT IS IT LIKE TO BE A BLACK BOY?
Do you laugh with white kids and play with their toy?
Do you even go to the same school to which they go?
Well I'll tell you, you don't, because of the laws of Jim Crow.
These laws were of the past, but now we're in the present,
Being Black is beautiful, being Black is pleasant.

WHAT IS IT LIKE TO BE A BLACK BOY?
There's nothing better in the world, there's no greater joy.
Blacks are different, but yet we're all the same,
We have different ways of talking; we call it slang.
Blacks are unique, we were the first on this land;
Now tell me, "WHAT IS IT LIKE TO BE A <u>BLACK MAN</u>?"

Frederick T. Shelton

My Place

My place is somewhere
Is it here? Is it there?
My place is where I'm going.
Where is that?

My place is somewhere,
I am on my way.
Do you know where it is?
I don't want to stray.

I've been heading to my place
for such a long time.
I'm moving at a steady pace,
Because I want to win this race.

How long does it take to find your niche?
How do you know when it comes your way?

For I've been heading to my place for so long,
I don't want anything to go wrong.

Cynthia Sapp

Justice

How did I enter this war
  Is it not enough - I've lived thus far
Why is my struggle always in vain
  Must each generation feel the pain
You say my every statement must be validated
  Are my sentences and words so complicated
Is it because of the pitch of my voice
  Or because my preferences are a different choice
When you see the shade of my skin
  Do you choose not to comprehend
Will justice allude me as the wind
  Or will it come at Armageddon's end
Do you not know who and what I am
  I am female. I am human.

Esther F. Buggs

Tolerance

Anger, Death, and violence is what's going on these days
Is it becoming a well known phrase?
Peace, love, and Harmony makes a world of difference.
What's the difference?
Tolerance
Learning to live and except each other for two we are.
It's like wishing on a star
Do we take heed?
There's too much greed.

Fawna Finnell

Bowhunters Day

Why do we do it? It's beyond me,
Is it so exciting to sit in a tree?
Patiently waiting for one stroke of luck,
that one chance to arrow a record book buck.
Watch and listen, don't make a sound
you can hear the wind blow, you can hear your heart pound.
Soon from behind you, you hear a rustle,
but you don't see him yet, so you don't move a muscle.
Finally you see what it is that you hear,
but how can a chipmunk sound like a deer?
It gets disappointing, but still you stay.
The big buck could come any time today.
But it's getting late, and it's time to go
and bring to an end today's nature show.
So you hit the trail, and head for your truck
Then off in the distance, you see the big buck.
And you feel like a fool, because you know down deep,
you guarded his territory while he was asleep.
Seems he wants to thank you for being so kind,
Since he got a good day of sleep, with peace of mind.

Jeff Elliott

Love...

Love;
Is like a dove

It's free;
That's the way love should be

If you find that special someone;
Then you won;
But sometimes it is no fun

I think people are lucky if they find that special someone;
Because then they will not run

Is it worth all the pain you go through?
Only if the love is true

True love lasts forever;
Because you will do what it takes to stay together

And, it's a chance of a life time;
So do not let the chance go by;
Because then your heart will die!

Hollie L. Clark

The Song Of The Greys Of A Bluebird

The song of the greys of a bluebird,
is never seen and never heard,
only the sightless of the seeing can find it,
only they can find what can't be found,
the song of there greys of a bluebird.

A silver sheen of light did I see upon the greys of a bluebird,
upon seeing the song my loneliness was torn from me,
for I was the greys of a bluebird.

The light goes out,
and I'm gone too.

To the greys of a bluebird I must sing,
but who will see my song,
now that I'm gone.

For I'm the greys of a bluebird.

Andrew K. Meikle

Owl Nature

One solemn polished drop of water
is plucked from her brittle
balsam hand of pine.
A hardened, crusted beak
consumes the transparent jewel,
leaving a parched and lonely branch of fir.
It is prey that the owl seeks tonight,
as the moon wanes,
and the leaves of Autumn
curl to the mercy of an intense wind.
Prey, which scatters and whimpers about,
squeaking and crawling on the ground,
detected with ease by bold
and blackened eyes, set deadlocked,
to move only as a unit
with the feathered head itself.
A thousand nights have passed with fury,
in these green and dampened woods.
Yet the owl remains perched upon hardwood
secured by everlasting sharpened claws.

Heather Wilkinson

The Wings Of An Angel

To ride upon the wings of an angel
Is something that would set most peoples' heart and soul aglow
But to ride upon the wings of an angel
We should live a good life in the world below.

Most people are sure they have a guardian angel
Watching over them from up in the sky
Because we have lived through so many sicknesses and injuries
There seems to be no other reason why.

When we have crossed that shining water
And our time on earth shall be no more
There we will meet our guardian angel
Waiting for us on the other shore.

Maybe then we will be a guardian angel
And watch over someone from up in the sky
Always ready to reach out and help them
And never letting then know the reason why.

Herbert H. Smith

Today Is Ours

Today
is yesterday's tomorrow.
Filled with hope, dreams, joy and sorrow.
A new sunrise, a new beginning.
An empty page, waiting to be written.
With the wind in our wings and the sun on our faces
We are challenged with the opportunity to explore many places.

Today
is a gift with anticipation and surprise,
Opened with our hearts, hands, thoughts and bright eyes.
It is through us, that this day gets its purpose.
The direction, energy and goals are driven by us.
We are the gatekeepers of today with all its bliss.
Dance with the wind, shine with the sun - for today is all that
is promised.

Cheri Plyler

"Friendship"

As we walk the path, of life's long road,
It always helps, if we can share the load;

To have a friend, who's loyal and true,
Someone you know, that's always there for you;

A shoulder to lean on, a smile when you're sad,
Steadfast and solid, through good and bad;

A hand to grab, should you stumble and fall,
A door to open, if backed against the wall;

Consideration and acceptance, to be who you are,
Support and encouragement, to reach for your star;

In order to achieve, this special kind of sharing,
You must return, a sincere sense of caring;

But it's a peaceful bond, between you and me,
Quiet and serene, and forever free!

Christine Ely-Spence

Imaginary Things

When I close my eyes I see a place,
it appears right in front of my face.
There is a person standing on a lot of money,
and he looks pretty funny.

Bats and owls have dollar bills for wings,
I wonder if they can sing?
When I look to the right I see a lot of fire,
it's so hot it could burn a tire!

There is a man with a dinosaur neck and head,
I wonder if it's been fed?
Then I see water all around,
and a strange horse not making a sound.

Just then I saw a strange sight,
an insect with a helmet on floating in the air like a kite.
Suddenly I heard a great big boom.
and appeared in my own bedroom.

David Cho

Cage

A cage can be many things,
It can be stone and wire, and it can be metal and plaster
A cage is a hateful, a cruel filled thing
It holds animals, and barbarians.
A cage is not a cell it is a live thing, it holds an animal.
It is no place for a human like you or me,
It stinks and reeks and holds you in,
It growls, it bites, its claws sink in.
It holds you down till you can't move.
It holds you down till you don't want to move.
You twist and scream yet it don't care, you see the light yet
it's a bear, sitting on your shoulders. Your soul shrinks
from the yearning for freedom, it screams to God, why?
And then you hear a whisper, no a scream so loud it becomes a shriek!
Your soul's agony fills with a crescendo for the answer!
And the whisper comes back, it was right in your face the whole time,
How simple it all seems now. You now know the name of your jailor,
You have the key to your cage, it all comes in one big whisper
that only the deaf can hear, the name of your jailor is you.
And the key to the cage is love.

Alonso Velez

What Is It?

Extra! Extra! Read all about the panacea that cures all ills!
It comes in every form: syrup, gel-caps, cream, shots, and pills.
It redeems your sanity when on the brink of losing it.
It cheers your friends and dear family when you are using it.
It lingers in your memory of loved ones no longer near.
It pacifies and halts your cry; it calms your greatest fear.
It melts a cold heart of stone into a warm heart laced with gold.
It allows the elderly to forget that they have grown old.
It prevents prejudice and changes strangers into your friends.
It finds a broken heart that it carefully begins to mend.
It repairs your looks on even your worst bad hair day.
It sounds like a great discovery! How much does one pay?
It costs nothing my dear friend — you have had "it" all the while...
Instead of coming in different forms, it comes with special style...
Whether it be toothless, mustached, lipsticked, or as long as a mile..
"It" inevitably is...
A SMILE.

Jill Sunshine Watson

Perseverance

How I invite pain into my life
It declares my strife for perfection
It declares my pursuit for the truth
I cherish the suffering, the agony
They stand as trophies

I must set my limits
A lifetime of anguish shall bring forth my true disposition
A lifetime in pursuit

Death shall be the time to rest
Until then, and only until then,
I will stop feeling
Now I welcome the plight of society
My friend Misery

David Koo

What Is Love?

Love is a priceless gift of life. It is great!
It embraces all and eliminates hate.
Love is much needed, and it should come to all.
For without it everything in life would fall.

Love is beyond compare because it is life.
It is something special between man and wife.
Love flowers, and it grows - it reproduces
New life, and new hope. Love never abuses!

Love is our dear families and dear friends
Who've become part of our lives. For God sends
Them to us to share our joys together -
To help ease the pains which we all must weather.

Love is God's gift to all who will follow Him.
They'll preach His words of love with vigor and vim -
Without prejudice or discrimination -
For they know true love without reservation!

Love is caring about others. It's sharing
Both good and bad. It's endless and fulfilling -
For the essence of life is unselfish love
In one for another and in God above!

Barbara Cammarata

Souls Apart

The love we have has its ways in depth.
It gives us safety combined with longing.
Yes, the longing one has so deep that needs to be shared,
with one believed to be complete.
In many ways this love will be,
the fighting strength to bring the world its holding peace.
This peace we crave, but never have.
As if we starve to eat, but have no food.
In either way we seem to lose,
which shows to be life's wholesome truth.
Our honest love we hold inside,
as if it forgets to come out by our side.
Without its help all may be lost,
in shattered dreams and broken hearts.
Our lives will live to wonder in full regret,
with hope of dying to soothe the deaths.

Gabriela Steuer

Seventeen

Senseless memories fill my mind of childhood laughter I never knew
Even though my memory is blocked in some paths, like dead end streets, I remember some

Virtually everything I remember is fogged, as if the wind blew a cloud into my head

Eventually I can pull and pick at my brain as if I were searching for something lost, but
Never can be found

Through the years my mind has lost pictures of faces and voices I once knew
Every memory I now have I keep and cherish as if it were gold
Every time I forget I create a scene of seventeen
Now that I am old and can not see or hear, my mind creeks back to scenes of seventeen

Rachel Buckheit

The Wager

He walks through the night as if in a summer's fog.
Events and occurrences surround him in shadow as well as mist.
He perceives them as does the professional gambler —
before making his bet.

So soft, so soft and Easy
The toss from money pile to gaming table.
And when the chip lands all eyes are upon it
For they now know it's out in the open and up for grabs.
Ravenous are the vultures of business and politics
Oh, how they want his dream - to pick clean
In their gruesome beaks and not spare the bones!

The warm heated air surrounds him in the mist everything is still now,
His hand reaches out to turn the cards to see
He does not touch them - He draws back
He hears the inaudible intake of breath around him
His hands folded he waits.
It won't be long before the sun rises
And dispels this summer's fog around me
He wagers.

Scott Bennett

A Forever Memory

So many of my days are filled with
faded blue jeans, scuffed boots and spurs,
strands of windblown hair sticking to a sweaty neck
and too many broken fingernails.

In a breath I remember an evening of
silk stockings, black lace and velvet,
ballet slippers and a little girl's dreams;
an evening when you made me feel like Cinderella.

Noel Visor

Greed

You can live your life on a wire
everyday a boss fires.
Life is harder than we thought and
dreamed, it's tough being a human being,
it's harder living in a world of greed.
Employees over working and getting under-
paid, it's all neglect, they get a small
amount while the CEO gotta billion dollar
bank account. You should help those who
are in of need, but it's cold living in a
world of greed. Corruption people say they
know of it let me see some hands for a
show of it. If you wake up one day and
there's mass hysteria those greed investors
we ought a bury 'em.

Omar Stroman

"Beyond The Darkest Cloud There Lies A Rainbow"

Beyond the darkest cloud there lies a rainbow following
Existing sunshine belonging to all of mankind. If we only open up
Our eyes and be willing to see, open up our hearts and
Wholeheartedly believe, beyond negativity we can succeed the test
Of time.

So strive to keep your faith alive, never let it die. Let your
Tears flow, it's okay to cry. When it rains it pours.
So weather the storm through perseverance and you can endure.
Breath, breathe, believe in yourself. Never forget that you are
The owner of your hope and dreams. Be willing to succeed.

Rely not on man, confidently throw your burdens up above for
There resides a true god of love who knows beyond the darkest
Cloud there lies a rainbow, following existing sunshine.

Yvette Means

A Girls Life

Even me, a girl of high potential.
Faces many hardships in life.
I always have bad hair days.
My blush is up too high.
My lipstick is never the right shade.
My earrings don't match
My chapstick is in clumps.
I can't find my other sock.
None of my clothes fit together.
But hay, you got to admit...
...It's hard to be a fourteen year old girl!

Marjorie Samagaio

Reflections On Some African Artifacts

Your smile upon the window pane today,
Faint like the hint of mink oil in the hall
With rich runners and far sounds of déjeuner,
Speaks volumes, and his silence is a wall.

What is the price of green globes or black thongs
Brought from the shades that close as ages do—
Whether, as she says, vestiges of wrongs
Brook no excuse, or he, to see time through?

Here in the cave of glass and cinnamon
She lifts her cup and as her eyes the shades,
"What though we sin? Perhaps we also send
An image that preserves the light that fades."

Her hair against the mask is like pale fire
In his still heart, the nail god's holy pyre.

Wilson F. Engel III

Alone

As a single leaf blew gently to the ground,
far off in the distance the thunder yelled loudly,
the rain screamed as it fell.

A rumbling noise came from behind
and blackness filled the view.

For a moment is was dead silent,
as the leaf crumbled
and the breeze carried it away.

Torri S. Craig

Helikion

You have come back to haunt my faltering mind
Fast snippets of a long forgotten past
Like charred autumn leaves from hopeful springs
Burned by a summer something I half knew
For I have scoffed in years of proud repose
Among the labyrinthine ways of undirected dreams
Chasing circles in the ebb and flow of fitful tides
Seeing faces in the waves all pearled by the sun
A lycanthropic libertine I ask for one more grace
Heli-ki-on

Michael Malone

Life's Alterations

There are times of limitation of halting one's desire of tension
Festering on endless cloudy visions with
dreams of gaiety and splendor

Lurking through devastation amid memories
gesturing ways of continuous passion
and hovering over repetitive fantasies

Domineering by pressures in the pattern of life
thy thirst that yearns and quenches the inner soul

Splendid cries of hopelessness and frustration
decking of humiliation and sadness

Scorned and cuddled with nestled life lines
beckoning to retrieve the beginning of birth

....The vision is clear as a brisk sunny morning
thy purpose that was once smothered

What manifests to thy end result
is to eliminate one chain of direction

Survival is the ultimate destiny of learning and growing and
blossoming to a new person

Then sharing with mankind...and laughter...which can't be
limited for it's the true source of infinitive life.....

Maria Barr

Textures

Textures of humanity — Godhood touching man fused
Finite with Infinity — Earth hosting Heaven's plan.

The vulnerable velvet of babe-soft scented skin
Teased by dusty manger straw that prickled Him within.

Joseph's wiry curling bread as his rough lips kissed
The miracle of newborn Son — and contemplated bliss.

The Child fussed and felt the gentle flow of Mary's hands;
Incarnate Grace in Earth's embrace of clothy swaddling bands.

The huffing warmth of oxen breath and glint of frosty star.
The wet caress of lambkin tongue mid singing from afar.

Textures of Divinity were touching humankind —
Such sweet bonded affinity, when mortal met Divine.

Kay Trudell

We Never Have Time

Time goes so swiftly, like birds in their flight.
First it's the morning, then comes the night.
If our intentions are good and we don't have a care,
There seems never a moment we have, we can spare.
Problems seem to arise, from out of nowhere,
And again we put off, what we expected to share.
"Why let things stop us?", sometimes we ask,
When something so simple we make a big task.
A smile, a short call, a small friendly letter
Could make someone happy, feeling much better.
As loving care and brief showers help flowers to grow,
So small deeds of kindness speak; we reap what we sow.
Let's take a few moments from our brief busy day
To remember the lonely, forgotten, and pray
That life can be better because we will share,
And take time to remember and show that we care.
There will be a reward for the people who give.
Yes, a real purpose in life, and a reason to live.

Priscilla C. Pyfrom

Hello Lord!

Hello Jesus, I miss you today
First thing this morning, I kneel down to pray
Thanks for helping me be the person I am
The gift of the Holy Spirit, the guide of your hand
Makes me joyous and happy, for I know you're true
I've Gone through the valleys, but you've carried me through
The tug in my heart told me you were always there
I'm your vessel for others Lord, they need not despair
Take my hand and guide me, as you've always done before
For you alone are the only God, the one I adore
I love you Jesus, I'm yours and you're mine
From this day forward, till the end of time.

Maydelle Greig

Heaven

As I think...my mind wonders
first to reality...then to fantasy...
I ponder deep in thought...
Heaven comes to focus...
If Heaven is on Earth...you certainly created it...
Without you...life has little meaning.
I feel warmth...I feel sincerity...
Little things you do...you say...mean so much to me.
I love you for that.
It is difficult for me to put into words...
How much you inspire me and bring out the
qualities that are shaded in my inner soul.
I pray for you...to know...
How much you mean to me.
I love you... I love you...
As my mind drifts from now to then...
It's destined... it's inevitable... that I and Heaven will be as one.

Rich Deirocini

The Ocean

Ocean tides were smashing against rocks, mist sprayed up
into my face.
Surfers at the horizon were getting rides on the waves,
And you could hear the churning of the sea monsters below.

Mermaids lounged on rocks as the sun tanned their shoulders,
Kids ran on the sand enjoying the evening.
Whales surfaced for air as a fountain of mist sprayed
into the heavens.
As the sun set, I heard captains yelling orders to their crews.

As the moon rose, it spread a shadow over the water,
The sea monsters calmed down and the mermaids swam back to sea.
Lighthouses shined their lights onto the ocean,
And all was calm once again...

Annie Moranski

Fishing Town

Along the coast cypress laced with fog point the winds' direction
Fishing town a place I'm looking for
Boats at anchor bob among the waves
Smell of salt and fresh caught fish fill the air
I see a fishing town
An old man with a long gray beard sits on a pier
Telling stories with no one to hear
Sea gulls circle waiting for a meal
Fishing town
Bleached wood of an old cannery give a feeling of age
Mountains of oyster shells glisten pearl essence in the sun
Fishing town
An old decaying motel has no vacancy displayed
A pelican makes it his home
Sounds of a buoy bell Low blast of a fog horn
Signal a safe harbour
A fishing town

Michael Mainini

The Unfortunate

From afar I came
Flew across oceans and mountains
Navigated all the four corners of the earth

Seeking greener pastures
Striving for survival
Searching for fortunes and wealth
Looking for peace of mind

In remote and distance countries
But all my dreams shattered away
For never did I find wealth
Bliss and peace eluded me

Troubles and woes became my constant companions
Poverty and misfortunes my daily existence
I gave up giving thought for the 'morrow

There was no way going back to the cradle
For what shall I recount my folks
In joy and cheerful mood
They bade me farewell
With tears and saddened hearts
My kinsmen will welcome me.

Tamimou Ouro-Agouda

In My Father's House

My Father lived with my Mother
for 19 years
In my Father's house he lived
and drempt of a better life
In my Father's house he worked
in a room in the back on works of art
that he sold and trinkets
that he gave away to the kids in
the neighborhood
In my Father's House he grew sick in
the month of March 1994 and died
In my Father's house my Mother still lives
alone and whispers to my Father's spirit
at night.

Rick Weaver

My Little Leprechaun

He is not a Irish Folklore,
He can't reveal a crock of gold.
But catch him if you can,
For my little leprechaun has a heart of gold.
Hold on tight and don't let go,
For my little leprechaun will love you so.

Patricia Kingsbury

The Birthday Gift

It's very hard to choose a gift
for a friend on his birthday, to find something
that will give him a lift and something very nice to say.

A present that transmits respect
and says what I want to say, but nothing I'd want to bet
he wouldn't have a nice day.

So I'm running up and down the aisle wondering what to buy,
a key chain holder, a TV set, or maybe a cabinet file,
Or should I buy a plastic fly?

He doesn't like to be tidy so a cleaning set is out.
But if I get him something mighty
I'm very sure he's going to pout.

Last year I gave him a Sega game that I stole from him a year
before, my mother sent him a fat Great-Dane
that got smashed behind a door.

But, wait. I've got the very thing that he's going to like and love
forever. I'll get him something that will really sting.
So, will I get him something? Never!

Nathan Kelmes

Conditional

O mind keep alive your Aesculapian-healing-dream
For a world more than just body and of earth
more than just soil;
For in our cat-calls of song and our heart-beat
of error
Your people are re-awakening to the great call
for change
And for a new world which already is out of the body
Ever since the eyes of old lovers began re-addressing
the earth.

Would that our evolvement be as a psalming of
psalter..
For the labor of creation needs a solace to soften
The blow and the wound to the head of the whole...
So let the issue of offspring be as the rising
of the phoenix
With the world's face of all people lighted up
by its role
In a world day of renewal with a watchword called
"good".

E. Manuel Huber

The Angst

To the rocket generation, this is for you
For all that I say now is true.
I speak softly, not a voice for all,
Yet what I say is important, so you too don't take the fall.

Why, oh why, can't we be seen and heard.
Instead of a bullet being the final word!
And why, oh why does no one try
To figure out why minors die.

In a world where separations are the ties that bind
And addiction takes over any mind
I just don't know why they don't try
To figure out what makes us cry.

So, to the dreamers of the future, this is for you-
From one statistic who sees things true.
Please, oh please, I hope you try
From just one who doesn't want to die.

Lauren Terilli

Let's Write A Lyric Poem

Let's write a lyric poem
For autumn, spring and summer
For wealthless people who sleep on street at winter
Rivers flow, who come from thousand miles
Distance to ocean
And she sacrifice her life for him!

Let's write a lyric poem
For beauty of all creature and creative
The sun winked from behind a cloud
Birds have sweet song, flower have scent,
And a whole field of plantain.

Let's write a lyric poem
For life is truth, graceful and benefactor
Freedom of humanity
Hearsay noble soul of national prosperity.

Let's write a lyric poem
For peace, a new world where no more war
For feelings of human heart
Let's write a lyric poem
For love.

Nazim Uddin Nazim

Untitled

Do not forsake me nor pass me by
for God watches over me there's no need to cry
I will obey the Lord and do as he says to
Knowing that in this life his love will shine through

For into each life some rain may fall
Yet God's light will shine through
Never leaving us by ourselves
As others often do

I will trust in the Lord with all my heart
Knowing we will never part
Keeping him close near me
For his love will not depart

Roberta Rogers

Little Bird Of My Heart

Fly back to me, my little bird of my heart,
For I can no longer bear for us to be apart.
The sunshine has been stolen from my day,
Never again, to return, to shine the way.
The days grow dark, and long,
And I so do wish, that you were back where you belong.
I want to be able to see my shining light,
And never again, let her out of my precious sight.
How can I ever endure such a terrible fate?,
For the need to see the little bird of my heart is great.
Oh, how I shall miss her sweet, musical, laughter,
Each, and every-day, here-after.
I'm drowning in a whirlpool of raging emotion,
Only seeking my little bird's undying, devotion.
Why do they seek to steal my little bird away,
When I only wish my little bird to stay?
My heart grows sadder, with each passing day.
I no longer have the desire to pray.
Come back to me, my little bird of my heart,
For I will surely die, if we are kept apart.

Karen L. Carron

Untitled

To all who've died, I bid farewell
  For I will miss you all.
To those who live, live on, find truth and fade.
  For "soon" I'll miss you all
But I pray that soon time's toll will take
  And then you'll all miss me.

Mimi Amor Amburgy

Thoughts

Sit, and listen to the wind,
  for it carries souls of foe or friend.

And like the leaves high in the trees,
  We too, must fall upon his call.

For it does not matter whether we love or hate,
  There's no control of one's own fate.

As each mornings dawn is bright,
  It's just too hard to keep up life's fight.

Then look upon the days quiet, inevitable
  end and retire,
With sole thoughts and feelings of being tired,
  just so tired.

Patricia Brummer

Daddy

Daddy was here for me-
For me to sit upon his knee,

For me to get a good education,
To dance with me at my graduation,

To walk me down the aisle when I wed,
To tuck me tight into bed,

To watch me walk, to watch me crawl,
To watch me throw my first ball

When I am confused, to help me,
To pick me up when I can't see,

When I am stuck on hard questions,
To keep me moving in the right directions

All this does is make me blue.
For he was not here long enough to see it all come true.

Kristy Thomas

The Word Of God

Extraordinary is the word God
For not only does your mind give
A meaning but so does your heart

The meaning of it, is up to the giver
The reward in it, is up to the receiver
But the punishment in it, is the deceiver

For some of the people that word is a provider
That word is their answer

For some of the people the world is a fear
And that word is their cancer

And for me, the word is a creation
And that word is my salvation

The word is not of God, but it is of you

Katalin Bloodgood

Holidays

The turkey is here, Hooray! Hooray!
For now we can tell it's Thanksgiving day.
The table is set with flare and precision.
The men are all watching television.
The turkey is dressed on a huge silver platter.
Just one look and I know I will get fatter.
My daughter is crying, for what I know not,
maybe for the deer that had been shot.
The dishes of course are never ending
my back really hurts from all of the bending.
The children are screaming and are running a maze
Now where would we be without holidays!

Thelma Ryan

No More

Dear old friend, remember the things we've done
For our memories together are all but gone.
Save them in time and don't let them go
Don't pause to question, go on with the show.
Destiny turns, but the wheels of time don't stop
The waters will run down to the last drop.
Dangling it hesitates, unsure about the fall
So long my friend, the time has come to call.

Free wheeling wanderer, he wanders no more
His destiny determined as he walks through the door.
Hearing the ocean breeze, sounds of a distant shore
Free wheeling wanderer, he wanders no more.

Speak swiftly friend for the time is creeping near
Be strong my request and please do not fear.
Constant hope and faith will always see you through
Shed few a tear and celebrate the life that he knew.
In sound and silence we proclaim a life that has end
Speaking volumes by simply saying farewell my friend.

May a thousand voices unite for a friend we all adore
Free wheeling wanderer, he wanders no more.

Richard A. Gramlich

Yesterday Child

The days has turn lone and cold for the child of yesterday
for she is a child of gold and is pure as the first snow.
Now she just don't know where to go for she took the final bow.
And she said I must go.
Go to bring back the gold and the pure snow.
That is the only thing that will let this child of yesterday to grow.
For the snow is gone and there is no gold no more
For the land I look upon is so dark and cold as if this land
has no soul
And won't let the child of yesterday grow.
So go my child of yesterday go find that gold and that first
pure snow.
So the shine of the gold can return to your soul.

Mark A. Brown

Ashes To Sea...

I look toward the sea
for some sort of answer in me
Past the boats in the harbor
I look for a shadow of my father
In the water all blue and gray
does his soul swim my way...
With flowers and tears
his ashes were thrown...
Into the ocean forever... to remain not at home.
He left no goodbye
not a hug but a why?
The Angels are saying, with them he is staying
to guide him and take him to a more peaceful place.
Where with warm light and grace time will erase,
all the pain and sorrow he could not bear for tomorrow.
The Angels will shield him in their wings of love
'till the day we all see him in heaven above...

A. R. Koszeghy

"Searching For Love"

As each day goes by, I'm searching for you,
For something to hold on to:
A gentle smile, or kind word would do,
Yet, time seems to pass me by.

Then, as I ponder and think awhile; as I look up to the sky.
I hear the birds as they flutter by,
Sending me a message of Love as they fly.

Then I know that only God could bring;
Such beauty as this up in the sky
For Love can be found in everything
If only we listen and give it a try.

Then while pausing my heart yearns for more.
As the clock ticks the minutes and hours away.
Time quickly flies by - As I pause to sigh, or maybe even cry-

For now, my soul, my body be; a temple of love, right here in me.
If God can put up with thee, I'm sure we'll meet in eternity.
Then my search for Love will no longer be,
For I found Love when I found thee.

Rosalie T. Beiermann

Untitled

Forgotten loves rise again in the present.
For the future is uncertain but the past is forever
sealed in the vault that is my mind.
Fond but distant memories stir a feeling within me
That only a single person shall know to the full extent.
The present is life, the future is a different day
that will pass like most things thus continuing the
circle of events that we call life.
The feeling is love, not a bad feeling but it is not
completely a good one in its entirety, shrouded mist,
it often confuses us making our thoughts retreat
into the inner most depths of the brain.
These loves dwell in a beautiful world that has
yet to be discovered. The last frontier is in ourselves,
thoughts wait to be made into feelings and actions.
Sadly they wait in despair, until we learn
to release them we shall never know true happiness.

Kevin W. Jones

"When A Mother Goes"

When a mother is gone it hurts the heart,
For this is the one person who took part,
in all our losses and all our gains,
in all our hurts and all our pains, and
we feel hurt...when a mother goes.

Whether they are sick or they are well,
Or when they were hurt or when they fell,
a great part of our heart feels hurt,
When a mother goes.

We have the comfort of our memories of our
own dear mother in our hearts and we hold that
memory dear, and heaven knows, our mother really
isn't gone, when a mother goes.

Loretta A. Fivizzani

Angels

Now look around you, and what do you see everything God has created, for you and me. He created His angels, for His glory, and to watch over us. So what ever we do, where ever we go, There's an angel watching over us, I want you to know. Their messengers, swift as the wind. And an army of angels blowing in the wind. They are protecting us, and spreading the truth, and watching over us, from our youth. They keep us from falling, whether we know it or not. They speak to us, whether we listen or not. So open your ears and you may hear, an angel speaking to you. Now if you don't know the reason why, things happen the way they do. Just ask your guardian angel, he may talk to you. Now if you ever feel all alone. No matter where you are or if you are at home. There is always an angel right next to you, watching over you. So you will never really be, all alone. Now you may hear an angel playing a trumpet or singing a song, as they shout for joy praising the Lord all day long. So open your heart, and you will hear, their song. Now look up at the sky one night and try to count the many stars that are so bright. There are just too many to number. So are the angels too many to number, So always remember this, where ever you go, what ever you do. There is a special angel, watching over you.

Robert V. Brown

Untitled

The sound of the crashing waves
forever pounding the shore
as the rocks take their mark
so the mists can fly
to touch the hawk poised overhead
watching the sound of the crashing waves
the clouds have parted and quickly fleet
to reveal the painted heights
where wings of vision oversee
and backdrop the realm of the pelicans
while the sound of the crashing waves
lull to simplicity, all of me
and the great rocks, a catalyst for the dance
as the water breaks to greet their stand
and swirls and flies in celebration
as the rocks are content to be
a part of the sound of the crashing waves...

valerie wilhelm

My Love

Sometimes you make me cry
Forgive me when I'm wrong
I can't always be that strong
Through good and bad you've always been there for me.
I'm always here for you
I'll do anything you want me to.
Whenever you need me I'll be there.
Everything I say is sincere
You may have hurt me in the past
But I knew that the hurt wouldn't last.
Our love would soon be shining through
Again I would be sitting next to you.
Now you say that the other is only a friend in your life
I trust in you once again.
We've already been through bumps and bends.
I love you more than anything in this world
But I want you to know that my love is real
I'll love you until the end of time
And hope that you will always be mine

Sara Barnard

Winter

The brave birds of the south have
found their winter homes.

Red, brown, and orange leaves curl
up near the trees, where they carelessly were blown.
The algae-filled creeks are still quite froze.

While all the hibernating animals
stayed fitted in their holes.

The grass on the wild-looking
plains is still waiting to turn its shade of green.

The mid-morning fog has not yet
lifted, to show off its grayish steam.

The snow on the mountain top
is colored frostiest white.

The evergreen trees stand so
proudly seeping in the light.

The wilderness flowers have folded
their hands and their head.
The sweet-smelling roses are brown, where once they were red.
The busy-bodied squirrels have stored enough to eat.
The labor has all ended, God's creatures now can sleep.

Patricia A. Liles

A Box Of Treasure

My memory of life is held within
Four small boxes made of tin.
These boxes have many items to hold
My favorite possessions both new and old.

They're special because of what they hold within,
They are the soul of my existence from beginning to end.
I love looking through them when I feel down,
For they bring joy to my face with each thought and sound.

They hold both sorrow and victory
And mean everything in the world to me.
Others think they should be sold
But to me they're a treasure of gold.

Kristal Stovall

Finis

I was born, Black and beautiful, in a strange, hostile land.
Free but outcast, by our forefather's, diabolical plan.

"Low IQ, over sexed". Centuries old lies, still prevailed.
Our leaders, oblivious to education, "too costly," they railed.
Humanity, most precious, natural resource, born to be jailed.

For me, love was elusive, dreams exclusive, work intrusive.
Naive, my hopes and spirits soared, fragile but inclusive.
My fantasies were a blue print, for my reality, all conducive.

I held the spotlight, briefly, relishing the exalted applause.
Submerged in adulation, passion and betrayals; without pause.
My tan, exotic, mirrored image, belied the ugly fear, the cause.

Love found me; joyous mother-hood, grand-parenting; I took root.
Enjoyed the wealth of happiness, gleaned from prejudicial soot.

I have sown seeds of love, tolerance and compassion, to sustain.
Triumphant, over the scourge of hate and violence, I remain.
I face my demise, resolute, confident; final judgement will reign.
The text evolves, I am content. My many heirs will proclaim.

Soon, mother earth will restore sanity and harmony to her land.
Destroying the arrogant, power hungry, war mongering, of man.
Love will embrace the world. The fulfillment of God's plan.

Marion H. Everett

Man-The Beguiled

What makes the day seem far away yet basks the smell of a fresh bouquet.
What taunts ones thoughts to drift a-stray in search of food (forbidden) one could say.
What tastes like nectar from potion nine, to drive one foolish or insanely blind.
What has the will to lure one on, yet has the power to subdue ones mind.
What aspiring force abounds so strong to distort ones dreams by the wake of dawn.
So for a time one may taste the lust?
From the sultry prey that could steel ones trust.
Now if by chance one fails to see?
It's a female, being the life man breathes;

William T. Gorrecht

Weeping Widow

My weeping widow with tears of sadness
Fret not, cry not

For the days of your sorrow shall be multiplied to greatness
I pledge for you

Let not your shame be displayed like a self-portrait
Nor your great worthiness be withered
My love, still loved

Blanket yourself with the joy I shall bring
Remember me as you are
Hence my return

For the love that guided me with everlasting promise
Was a kiss, an embrace, a parent

For the caring is always remembered
And thy loneliness shall my memory not.

Mitchell D. Pugh

Forgiving A True Friend

I remember when we started becoming
friends about a month ago.

Time past by like a crystal clear
river constantly going slow.

Right now I know times are hard and
what your going through.

But if you need a shoulder to lean
on I'm here for you.

I would give all the riches in the world
and all I want is you to be with me.

I would give my heart to you
till eternity.

I think of us walking thru the park
seeing the flight of a white dove.

I can't spend my life without
your eternal love.

Keith Perez

Untitled

He appeared one night in my doorway.
He looked just like my father.
Once he came closer I knew it wasn't.
He said he loved me and always had.
He started to cry and said what a beautiful
woman I turned out to be.
He added you look just like your grandmother
did when we first met.
Then he was gone.
Was he real or a figment of my imagination.
I'll never know.

Melisa Cate

Untitled

The sweetest day was your date of birth,
from amidst the essence you appeared on
this earth, no dictionary can define
the beauty within your heart divine.

The warmth I receive from your radiant smile,
makes me hope and pray that I may bask awhile,
your eyes...they pierce my very soul.

When you're around love is in the air,
beyond comparison are the feelings we share,
like the desire in every line of your poetry
intertwined in those verses, long to be.

And so without any further ado
I must say the sweetest day is,
everyday I see you!

Winter Perkins

Stonewall [1969-1994] 25 Amber Fiery Years

Stonewall is 25 years past
From beyond fiery flames lit that stormy June battle night
Our fight so long for liberty finally won us our gay-lesbian rights
A legacy arose across Europe and our the USA out of that New York City weekend
On those Greenwich Village Streets that crest tidal wave hard on hit
The NYC police again raided 53-55 Christopher St. — the Stonewall Inn
Fires of war burned over the horizons high all that night long
Drag queens and boy hunks in leather and curbside roller skate pixies
For three endless blazin' muggy june nights rapid wilde we gays ran
Light tonight a candle — burn that fire bright 'til the a.m. dawn
For we here at Sheridan square this night united hath as one proudly stood
Ever again be thou free in keepin' no hidden gays and lesbians secrets
With lovin' hearts heavy we shout: out of the closets—into the streets
Give we a rainbow of thanks rememberin' Judy Garland and the Stonewall Inn
Now 25 years later in these 1994 times as we all battle H.I.V./AIDS
Dim all the lights all -/- ever in our solitude of rage and of remembrance
This 1994 24th-26th June this silver [25th] jubilee we in unity celebrate
In shadow of dark not over amber skies fly high forever our rainbow flags
No victory, no dryin' of our tears over our lost unforgotten friends,
No riots, no shadows of dark in unity and joy we the dawn of the 21st century await

Michael Aronson

"A Cry For Help"

There are people in this world who will turn
from you and walk away. They could care less
if your hungry, or need a place to stay.

Although you after all that you got, you struggle
using the skills you were taught.

It's a lonely cruel place out on the street, trying to
hide all of the pain. Keeping on your tired feet.
There are times when your ready to give up...
"Actually stop living", because your hungry, tired
and cold, and cannot stop shivering.

Keeping a smile on your face, hiding all of the
hurt, as you sit under a tree on the cold damp dirt.

Looking at the sky, dreaming of a happy home,
tears dwell in your eyes, and still very alone.
You want to sleep, but you don't close your eyes,
You scream and scream, unfortunately no one hears you cry.

Wendy Jean Areeda

The Yellow Crow

I would scan the scare crow
From its paunchy belly and ruffled shirt
Down to its mighty, reaffirming legs.
Its horrid body would halt me in my path.

And when I saw what great treasures
Lay about the vile guardian,
Eternal hope filled my small mind,
But my heart panged full of despair.

For I'd be stopped by the scarecrow
And would remain with the others,
Yearning for everlasting corn,
Controlled by the horrid scarecrow.

But now, upon looking on the scarecrow,
Tassels of corn distort its fat and crooked legs,
Its orange nose and transfixed eyes now clearly seen,
I can gallantly walk towards my desires.

For I know that it is nothing.
And many of life's dreams are barred,
And many of life's troubles made,
By a mere scarecrow in the way.

Rafael Verduzco

Guardian Angels

Some people believe in a special gift from God
from the day we're born, they say it's there.
The gift is an angel, to guide, guard and direct us.
Through the trials of life, that we must bear.

Though invisible, (most of the time), to the mortal
eyes of mankind.
But if we look for them with our heart,
We can then hear them with our mind.

If you've ever had plans of flying somewhere
but for some reason, you NEVER went.
Only to find out later, that the plane crashed.
Then you understand that they're "HEAVEN SENT!"

But then that's a guardians job, most
would agree, to guard, protect and defend.
So we must learn to listen to our angels voice.
And thus, we'd be much better off, in the end.

Tracy S. Jackson

A Day In A Mother's Life

Sometimes I wish I could go and hide,
From two kids, a husband, and a house besides.
The work is never ending, jobs never get done,
Toys all around, and there is a ton!
I pick things up and it's just a start,
For the floor, I can see only a little part.
The kids again want something to eat,
Just after I vacuumed around their seat.
So the vacuum comes out once more for the floor,
Oh no! What do you want another cracker for?
After dishes, laundry, and cleaning child's room,
I have to get back in the kitchen and zoom.
Dinner will never defrost at this rate,
Each child wants something and just can't wait.
Husband home soon, just look at this place!
Where I cleaned, there's not a trace.
I gotta get it all done as soon as can be,
So maybe I can find a little time for me.
For in a short time, I know it will begin,
And this day will start all over again.

Karen McLeod

Neptune

Crystal me than mountain's
Frozen frigid fountains
Blue - green orb so distant
Calls to the imagination this instant.

Violet lakes and secret caves
Deserts of ice and frozen waves
Lavender skies with brilliant stars
Crosses by Aurora's Viridean Bars.

Neptunes! last planet in the void
Pluto nipping at your herds

With Nereid and Triton for your missions
You only share imaginative open-ions.
The ancient race inside the giant crystals
The rose of women with laser pistols

The spaceship lands from earth
Imagination has formed its rebirth.
Distant turquoise disk so far
Closer than the closest star so far.

Van Newcomb

"Kickin The Can"

A long time ago, when we were kids
full of energy, force and might,
I remember one way we released our vim,
Was kickin' the can - day or night

I'm happy to note that even today,
The kids kick the can in a vigorous way,
When I take a nap, or just close my eyes,
I'm awakened by the can, kicked by the guys

A feeling of nostalgia comes over me now,
As I think of my youth once more,
And hope that the day will never come
When it will be a thing of yore.

I pray when I die, to heaven I'll go,
And when I'm napping amid the clouds,
That the kids will be kickin' the can again,
Soft pedalled and not quite so loud.

Marie Enenbach

Nature, the Gift of my Journey

A step into the sunlight, where peace lies.
Gathering my thoughts, my heart is broken.
Swaying trees, falling leaves, teary green eyes.
Dazed and confused, why the harsh words spoken.
Knowing that for me he hasn't a care.
Remembering all the times in the past
Therefore I walk leading myself nowhere.
Looking down upon the flowing green grass.
White clouds, blue skies, I'm sensing a laughter,
Determination enters my body.
Nature so beautiful, I find my cure,
I realize the loss has come to he.
All of my thoughts, I have to comprehend.
My journey will end just beyond the bend.

Valerie Bailey

Fright

Dancing in the night's light
gave me such a fright,
for as the song went on
I danced until dawn.

I feel like I could dance on and on,
but I don't think I would live that long.
For I dance with feeling in the night's light
because it rids me of all my fright.

I'm scared of a frog
For I might not see it in the fog.
The fog is very light
but just that, might, be my fright.

The fright that comes at night
might just be the moonlight,
for the sight of the light
might give me that fright.

For my fright is within the night.
It might be the moonlight.
It might be the fog,
or maybe just a frog on a log.

Pam Watters

Good Morning

People sit by the meadow
gazing at the hummingbirds
Enchanted by the waterfalls beauty
moonlight shines along the pond
Such a sight for sore eyes
an image of a ballerina
dancing in the trees
Sparkles of the stars shine
across the sky glittering silver
of a flame of fire.
Surprised by the sunrise that brings out light
flowers, I say flowers
wake-up, wake-up for a brand new day.

Lisa M. Chavez

A Vision

I lay in a lush, moist blanket of grass,
gazing at the stars, realizing this my
only way to cope.
While specks of light that shine through
the darkness bellow a call of hope.
My heart shattered. The fiery pain immense
Though the stream I bare possesses light
to a new life within
My mind, my body quiver for rest
For the one I showered, has flown my nest.
A free spirit in his soul, is why he
claims no settle
I loved him and at his departing
he saw a piece of metal.
Appearance of strength, not able to crack
My feelings real are now being lacked.
This unending love a roaring fire.
His silhouette burns, it's my passionate desire.

Shannon Hodous

Tribute To My Dad

My Dad is a kind man gentle and warm

No wonder to him, little children swarm

He is a man of great strength and power

A man you can rely on at any hour

He's a man of great patience, whose
gentle and kind

Someone who has always brought me peace of mind

You have led me through dark
and very troubled waters

And has shown nothing but Love
and care to my two daughters

Just knowing your there through thick and thin

There's nothing I can't
get through - conquer and win

I love you Dad with all
my heart - I always have right from the start

Thank you Dad for all you do and say,

God Love and keep you well, for this I pray.

Your a wonderful father
of whom I couldn't be prouder!

Margaret Del Vecchio

Stardust And Streamers

Stardust and streamers, jesters and dreamers,
Glittering like diamonds in the sky —
Handsome romancers, ladies and dancers,
How lost in enchantment am I!

This symphony of color, this rainbow of music,
Swirling, twirling, turning 'round the guests,
The satins of the harlequin performing his tricks,
Laughing, crooning, crying, at every girl's behest...

Champagne and crystal, descants and minstrels,
Whirling as the hours pass them by —
A la mode dresses, curled, braided tresses,
Singing like birds, and soaring as high...

My very first real party - how incredible it is!
The moonlight reflecting off the emeralds in the trees —
What magical enchanter has turned me into this?
A burning bright comet, a flirtatious little tease...

Hurry and hustle, fur coats and bustles,
Oh, the morning draws too quickly nigh!
Dark, silent hallways — I'll remember it always —
And in a whisper, in a blink, it disappears...and leaves behind
only a sigh....

Vanessa Wright

Having To Say Good Bye Is So Hard

Having to say good-bye is so hard.
I cannot get you out of my mind.
You are here with me always
Every minute of everyday.
Although you are gone physically
You are always here mentally.
You have been gone for six years now
And everyday I grieve more and more.
I cannot wait to be with you again.
It may be days, weeks, months, or years.
One day we will be together again,
But until then I will always think of you.

Tammy Cox

Another Year

Another year, another dream come true.
God gave us life that we may bring joy to others.
That in our lives, each day to give
Of our lives to our brothers.
In love of life, in illness too,
The strength of our prayers, do.

So each year, when we add to the count
Our good deeds, will ever mount.
The repeating our prayers of the Rosary to Mary,
To the Queen of Heaven, or prayers may vary.

While our Lord, Jesus Christ has honored His Mother,
And empowered Her grants of intercessions,
We receive Her love and loyal inspirations
As our prayers - requests, have made impressions

So on this day, that we add one more year
Knowing God will protect us from all fear,
Let us give thanks, that we are still here
To enjoy the life, that is oh - so dear!

A. E. Wixon

All Things Happen For A Reason

All things happen for a reason we don't quite understand,
God knows best, so hold on to His unchanging hand.
There's no need to wonder why things happen the way they do,
things happen the same way for me, as they do for you.
If we could have only made a difference yesterday,
maybe things wouldn't be the same today.
If we could have made a difference yesterday, there are
some things we just wouldn't change today.
Always be thankful for one more day with the one's you love,
remember, if the flower is plucked, it will continue to
grow in the heavens above.
God's tomorrow is just another yesterday held in his hand,
that's why all things
happen for a reason we don't quite understand.

Priscilla A. Valet

Worry

It's night time outside; I am lying on pure green
grass...
Looking up at stars and the silver moon.
I feel a cold breeze go past me and I wonder
every second if that is God's wind. Telling me not to worry
and to brush everything off my shoulders.
Then again another cold breeze blows harder.
I think again - is that God blowing on me?
"Yes, it's me and don't let yourself worry.
I am the man to worry for everyone on my
earth!"
I sit for a few minutes and say to myself;
That was God speaking to me by wind. I was right.
You and I should not let ourselves worry.
Let God take care of your...
WORRIES!

Traci Fabac

"Autumn"

The evening dusk on winged flight,
Hastens to embrace the sunlight;
Bronzed leaves torn from their mother's arms,
Lie as a rustling carpet disturbing the calms;
Barren stalks of trees lose beauty and grace,
While birdlings strive to cover them with a nest's lace;
The winds wail and lament the loss of the soft summer air,
When they had nought to do but lie lazily when days were fair;
Rivers rise to challenge the winds,
And throb against the lands bends;
The earth's surface lies all exposed to the autumn's crest;
Until the first snow gently mantles her breast.

Muriel D. Cook

Innocent Enchantment

Brown, cloudy lake water beats against earthen banks and
green pastures.
Boy and grandfather float on a glassy surface.
Bamboo poles bob up and down
to rhythmic motions.

Summer sun beats down on a metal john boat,
which is actually a cruise ship.
There is no difference between big and small, old and young,
lake and ocean.

A gray-headed man heaves a slippery fish into the cruise ship.
Something new and exciting enchants the boy's world.

He rubs the silver stomach,
pushes the glassy eyes.
Mystic beauty in its simplest form.

A far away cow lows,
and bamboo poles bend to rhythmic motions
on a farmside pond.

—G. Todd Smith

Grief And Joy

Grief and joy, strange companions these two,
Grief; that her beloved face I'll no longer see.
Joy: that she is with the father for all eternity.
Grief; that her companionship is no longer shared.
Joy; for all the pain she has been spared.
Grief; that we may no longer share that simple cup of tea.
Joy; and thanks to Oh Lord, you have taken her to be with thee.
Grief; that we may no longer sit together and share wine and bread.
Joy; that as she went down that "valley of the shadow", Lord, you led.
Grief; as I watch the dawn of spring alone with no loved one
one by my side.
Joy; and praise too, Oh Blessed King, that thou art on the throne,
and faith, hope, love, these abide, and one day with my beloved
we will both be by your side.

Nigel Ivan Stone

Loss

At night you walk in my dreams
grieving
woman who was
my mother. You didn't know
he'd died, your husband.
Now you've gone too, and come back
in my darkhours dreams
searching
crying
like a cat
trills and mournful calls, I explain
once more (like I did when I was ten and he
moved out)
"Surely Mama, surely
He is somewhere
you can find him."

Mary Carol Randall

Mary-Mary

It must have been in the month of May
I can't recall it was late in the day
She said her name was Mary in a very extraordinary way
I said have a nice day and went on my way
Finally one day I decided to make a play
I tried I cried I must have even lied
This love will have to be true cause no one else will do
I lost he won the race is done but I'm not sad I'm kind of glad
And he will be sorry too when she is all through
And then he will regret the day they met and tell me I was no fool

Richard Burkes

The Grindstone

Faster turned the grindstone: grinding, grinding, turning, turning
Grinding all to dust!
Like the grindstone of swords, like the grindstone that sharpens all
To the keenest blade, to cut, sever, and destroy.
Such as the winds that howl and moan high into the clouds and utmost mountain peaks
So desolate, so isolated, so alone.
Such as the winds, cold, bitter and keen that cut deep into the mighty mountains
That seemingly would stand forever and reduces every mountain
To dust!

Such as the wheel that turns and grinds in spinning monotony
Hypnotically turning, hypnotically spinning for eternity.
Forever grinding, grinding—forever spinning, spinning in hypnotic monotony.

Turn the wheel once more, grind that dull blade edge till it's keen, till it's sharp,
Till it glitters bright amid the burning sparks that fly off the grindstone wheel!
Watch it grind, watch it turn, watch the burning sparks fly in that dark, dark night!
And how the blade shall destroy as the grindstone forever grinds, grinds
Forever turns, turns in spinning monotony—and continues on:
Like the ever-grinding wheel of Time.

Kimberly Schure

"Mom"

Through the years I've learned a lot, I've
grown to an adult from just a tot.
When I was little, I could do no wrong,
Now that I'm grown, I have to be strong.
You told me one day that I would grow up,
and I thought to myself, it's not soon enough.
When you're young, you want to be grown,
and when you are, you're on your own.
No Mom to tell you what to do,
No Mom is there to see you through.
Now that I'm here and you are gone,
I sometimes feel I can't be strong.
Then I remember what you used to say,
"Don't wait for tomorrow, live for today."
All I have now are the memories,
of how things were and used to be.
Now I'm grown up, and it plain to see,
Mom, you were always there for me.
"I miss you!"

In loving memory of Billie Schuette.

Kelene Mendoza

Photo's, Memories And Our Love

Look at the photo's then memories will start
Happiness held forever, treasured deep in our hearts.

We were so young, our love so new
The glow on our faces, our love so true.

Look at the photos, they won't tell lies
The truth in the pictures, the love in our eyes.

You're still the angel I thought of you then
The warmth of your heart still soothes me within.

Look at the photos, they'll age with time
Our love is still holding, I'm yours forever and you are mine.

As years go by, and our children grow older
The one thing for sure, we are meant for each other.

Look at the photos, true love for each other
God chose this time and brought us together.

Lisha Jaramillo

"Happiness"

Happiness comes from being content deep within yourself
Happiness means more to life than houses, fame, or wealth
Happiness is the joy that you feel after helping a loved one out
Happiness is knowing you treated everyone right and what
joy that brings about
Happiness is waking up to see each blessed day
Happiness is knowing that it was God who started you on your way
Happiness has a way of making each of us smile
Happiness comes from knowing our troubles will be over after while
Happiness won't make you worry, nor will it make you sad
Happiness is a great feeling, the best I've ever had.

Tara B. Magee

Feelings

When something happens
Happy or sad
Feelings are there snappen
Whether it's good or bad
They pop up everywhere
There inside you.
Fellings feel the air
If you give your feelings
It fills the other person with thought
Good feelings come with love
Bad feelings come with hate
Feelings come in all sizes and shapes
Feelings can burst
Feelings can hurt when they are sad or bad
Feelings are everywhere
That's what keeps the world up and aware.

Tania Marie Viramontes

The Wall

Silence - it is an enemy.
Harbored thoughts, feelings and emotions refusing to reveal themselves
A wall is slowly being built.
They destroy you from the inside out.
The feeling of being choked between everything is great.
Knowledge of how to stop this is not abundant, but the pain is-
The wall continues to be built.
Does anyone see you?
Does anyone hear your silent cries?
Loneliness - it is a companion.
An unwanted friend.
The wall has been built.
It is higher and wider then you expected.
You can't get out,
No one can get in.
The wall is there.
Any will you had is gone,
Your passion has faded away.
No one tries to get in, you don't care to get out.
It's too late - you're in forever.

Robyn O'Brien

Brother

His chest rises and falls rhythmically
He is sleeping peacefully for once.
Suddenly, his chest stops moving.
My heart begins to pound. Please, please keep breathing!
Oh, god, this can't be happening. He moves again.
Silently, I watch him. Yes, he's breathing again. Then,
he stops and time stands still. Tears well up in my eyes.
No! Breathe, damn it! Why don't you breathe?

The tears are flowing freely as they lower a tiny casket into the earth. I lean over and look in the hole. I toss a handful of dirt on top. Goodbye, baby brother. I love you and I'll never forget you.

Shanna H. Sissel

"Replenishing The Sand"

Faith
has slowly passed
like sand through an hour-glass.
Once the top is empty, only Power remains.
Alone, Power destroys my soul and my life.
I may persevere, but only after a self-induced beating.
Alas, a granule of hope lingers like
my favorite love song.
With all my God-given
strength, I turn the glass.
Together, Power and Faith begin to heal my soul and my life.
Although the precious sand continues to
flow, I shall closely monitor its descent.
Now, I frequently turn the glass and,
once again, eagerly await my
tomorrow.

Sheila Powell

"We Movin On"

Well, as we look on the past, life for the Benjamin-Rogers family
haven't been no crystal ball.
It's had nails in it, and fragments, and walls torn up, and
places with NO HEAT, COLD!
But at the same time, we been moving on, and stretching, landing,
and turning corners - looking to move on!
Where there was no light - sometimes we would stumble through
the dark - we kept moving on! So, don't you turn back!
We can't sit down, now!
Cause we will find it kind of hard.
We can't fall now - for we have seen the light!
We kept moving on! And life for the Benjamin-Rogers family
haven't been no crystal ball.

Sandra Jones

Lonely Heart

Feeling lonely and feeling sad
Having no one to share a thought
Crying yourself to sleep at night
Wondering why you were put on earth.
Feeling down and feeling out
Having no reasons for being happy.
Thoughts of the future and thoughts of the past
Remembering the days of your young youth.
Playing with friends having fun
Wondering where you'd gone wrong.
But what happens know shall I perish with my lonely heart
Or shall I go on with life as it shall be.
Everyone seems happy and everyone seems proud
Enjoying themselves and going on with life.
Sitting at my window looking at them
Wishing some day that I might join them.
Walking by them being ignored, feeling stupid for what I am.
"Being a lonely person" my heart cries out.
Is not a joy nor a prize. Wanting to be what you are not.
Isn't a cure for a lonely heart.

Shondel Roach

"Waiting To Die"

She holds up the mirror to him;
He peers in at himself proclaiming
"Here I am, and I cannot turn back!"
There's heartache and dismay for both.
Was it by chance, or by fate deemed just
By a higher power, one who knows
All, sees all, and judges by his own model?

Painful hacking, racking coughs make him wish
For peace as she wails, "I will never
See you again, I will always see your
Face, your face in everything I do."

Sandra D. Gallo

"Cocaine" The Fool's Gold

In the "underground world" it's more precious than gold;
Having the instincts of a 49'er, we can find where it's sold.
Like the "Golden State Rushers" of 1849,
We sell all we own hoping to find,
The equivalence of "Fool's Gold," in a Christian's mind.
From the shores of California to the Hudson Bay;
It's the "Puff" we crave, both night and day.
We're pan-handlers by day and bandits by night,
And all is fair prey if within our sight.
From P.C.H. to Atlantic City's Boardwalk,
It's fluent in all languages, but money makes it talk!
From the nation's largest states to its smallest towns,
There are very few places "Puff" can't be found.
Throughout Alaska, Texas, and Californ I-A,
"Puffs" are purchased from January 2, 'til New Year's Day.
Philadelphia, Chicago, L.A., New York; four major cities where "Puffs" can be bought.
Clarksville, Port Gibson, & Avon Park are small towns where "Puffs" are found after dark.
On Interstates, Hwys, Streets, & roads, "Puffs" are found in grams, ounces & much "Kilos."
I-10 east, I-10 west, HWY 27N and S bound, at any Rest Area exit a "Puff" can be found.
"Puff" keeps its user in a constant haze; keeping mankind in a quagmire state.

Paul Turnipseed

The Phantom

He is from my imagination
He is my own creation
I wonder why I am so scared
My heart is pounding deeply for he is near

I do not understand why he is following me
Why couldn't he haunt someone else you see
I feel his hand on my shoulder
His hand is cold, yet not real

I am so confused, for I feel his presence everywhere
I turn around but he is not there
He is only an image of my mind
And yet why do I feel him here

He will always be a figment of my imagination
He will always be my creation
I wish this phantom of mine would just go away
He is just a subject of my mind,
An image of my imagination

Morgan Calloway

Martin Luther King, Jr. - A Black Man

Martin Luther King to the world peace tried to bring.
He marched across the Jim Crow South for victory he had no doubt
He was a giant of a man and his voice was heard throughout the land
He prayed that one day his brother would be free
and no more hangings from a tree
He was so noble and so grand he taught us to walk a hand in hand.
He also taught us not to be violent just walk in peace and be silent
He left us at an early age and thousands come to visit your grave.
You've reached the promise land and have joined the heavenly band
One day we shall overcome and look back from where we started from
The Lord was walking by your side and you footsteps he did guide
We mourn your passing when you died we work to keep your dream alive
Martin Luther King, a brave and courageous man
Martin Luther King, a Black man

Rosa Vessels

The Stray Dog

We found a dog. Lost his home or was he kicked out?
He never told us. Looked kind of gray but looked proud.
It's easy for a dog to be pretty proud.
They are loved, never feel to be left out.

We walked down to the river where a little willow tree
Was chewed up by the beavers late fall last year.
Would it still grow this spring, would be for my cheer,
But when spring comes, I will not be any more here.

I shall not see the birds we fed, not the old deer.
I am no dog, I am only an American Engineer...
The phone rings again: "Sir, we got your resume.
But I have some questions. First: Will you relocate?"

Sure, why not? "I am not a dog with a steady place.
I am handled by most people with much more disgrace.
I am an item in their books. A screw, a bolt.
Decisions about me are quick, final and cold.

Looking for new jobs, always for new homes...
Chased out as soon a few years are gone...
I am no gypsy. There is no ring in my ear.
But I know my score: I am only an American Engineer...

Dr. Laszlo Javorik

"If"

He said it broke his heart to see her cry.
He said his love for her would never die.
She looked back upon these thoughts,
And to hold back her tears she fought,
Now she tries hard to avoid his mean stares.
It tears her apart to see his cold glares.
If only again they were together,
She would promise to love him forever.
He was the one for which she devoted her life,
And yet it all had to end in such a terrible strife.
He was her world,
All that she had,
And thoughts of him make her so sad,
And for him she will always have love in her heart,
Always wishing that they were never apart.

Lisa Kyes

The Cook Out

My neighbor went fishing, got the catch of the day,
He said to all, now it's time to play.
We built a fire, down on the beach,
There was plenty of fish for all to eat.

The wood burned quickly, the coals got bright,
It's time for cooking, the heat is just right.
They added the sauce and lemon you see,
All wrapped in the leaf, of a banana tree.

In less than a hour, the fish was done,
I hurried to the fire to get me some.
The fish was so good, with food all about,
Its taste was superb, and melted in your mouth.

The day was ended, the night was clear,
We sat on the beach, with the fire so near.
So this is the life, way down by the sea,
It's not for everyone, but it is for me.

William R. Balling

Untitled

There is no selfishness in our Lord Jesus Christ
he sees clearly what we cannot see
simply trust in the thee and let it be

Your troubles will not become more than you can bear
that's the Father's promise, that is how much he does care

Trials and tribulations, afflictions to your heart
are not brought on from above, Jesus is peace and full of love

Pour out your inner most heart
Jesus loves you and will never depart

Lean on me whispers softly
I'll take you by the hand and help you to understand

better things are yet to come and blessings to be given
remember child you came to me and your sins have been forgiven

Hold fast unto the garment of my cloth
when you're down of feeling lost

I'll pick you up and carry you on
like a mother or father would their tiny little son

For in this world you are my child and heaven holds a place for you
that I have created; take not heed to mankind, through me you
will have peace of mind

Tonya Randazzio

Untitled

In darkness his black, sleek body blends well.
He stalks in the shadows, following his
Prey. Those he catches are doomed to Hell.
His eyes flash red. All evil in him is.
Do not cross the line and join him in flames.
His followers pay for all they receive.
They burn in eternity. What? His names?
You know them already if you believe.
God's people have thought them to you: Envy,
Sloth, Greed, Gluttony, Drunkenness, and Lust.
They are the seven deadly sins, you see.
You must avoid them. At all costs stay just!
The Devil takes forms appealing to us,
Accepting them is very dangerous.

Katherine Ressman

"Kiss An Angel"

A star falls from heaven and drifts on a cloud
Heading for earth to make any parent proud.
A house now a home with a new cause for delight
A star to an angel Laura was born that night.
With velvet skin, golden hair and eyes so blue
We knew she was from heaven an angel through and through.
I'm the grandfather and proud to say
I was there when Laura was born that day.
Did I say she was beautiful and smart as can be
She get's all A's and sometimes a B.
Some days when things don't go as they should
I look at her pictures and start to feel good.
As the grass grows greener and the trees grow tall
So does this fair-haired beauty she is a doll.
For an angel that God sent from heaven above
All I can give her is my undying love.
As I sit here alone trying to find words to say
I think of how lucky I am to be just a few miles away.
So let me close and ponder while I am able
Just to say in the next life ""I Kissed An Angel"".

Robert L. Coleman

"I Was Naked..."

The old man crawled across the road at a snail's pace.
He stopped only to rest his bandage hands and tired knees he leaned upon.

Passing cars ignored him, like a dead eat or fallen tree limb.

I stopped. And thankfully, so did two others,
We all stood over the old man in the road. Two men, and me,
I touched him first.

He had to be eighty. His pants, saturated with rain and mud, had fallen to his uncles.
Sores on his legs oozed with puss. He could not stand. He had no shoes.

We carried him to his home—a soaked blanket under a tree with no leaves. We wanted to take him to a hospital or a shelter. I pleaded, but he said no, content to die.

The sun set enveloping us in an eire blackness. It started to rain again. No one came. We were on our own. His gnarled fingers began the crawl again.

He wanted to eat and his dinner was in the garbage can across the road. Our hearts wrenched. And so we began. One man save him sweatpants, the other man, a blanket. I offered my letterman's jacket. I wanted to take him home. What right did I have to leave the old man this way? But he looked up at me, put his crumpled hand on mine and whispered "thank you." I stopped by the nest day with lunch, and the next. And the next day he was gone. I don't know where the letterman's jacket, the sweatpants, or the blanket went. I do know he died. we cared, and we learned. I know his life had meaning.

Malia M. Zimmerman

Momentary Reflection

He stares with an unseeing gaze.
He thinks with a mind in a maze.
Fingers appear to unclutch an imaginary ball.
He does not respond when you call.
His body has become a victim of his mind,
as you tuck in the restraint to gently bind.
Time has etched deep lines in his gaunt face.
His weakened legs are covered with a quilt of lace.
Alzheimer's disease has become his prison each day.
Oh just to turn back time, and hear him speak,
what would he say?

Marsha Peters

A Tribute To John Wayne

In 1906 in Winterset, Iowa, was born Marion Michael Morrison;
He was active as any boy, energetic, loving, clean, fun.
His stature was tall, his physical features handsome;
He dressed for the part always attractive in each costume.
A kerchief was usually an article of his attire;
He favored it and wore it for others to admire.
He became John Wayne, actor, legend, hard working man;
He had a specific goal and a definite plan.
His action spoke louder than his word;
Yet, his speech was natural, distinct, easily heard.
He knew what needed to be done, he lead;
He was famous, loved, respected, yet fame went not to his lead.
In 1965, his first battle with cancer was fought to remain alive;
His determination, will, faith helped him over this ordeal strive.
He didn't give up, he didn't remain silent, hope he gave;
He continued to work playing the hero both tough and brave.
True Grit, one of twenty more movies, won Academy Award, 1969;
Death in 1979 ended his life of many facets hard to define.
His legacy is family, cancer research/insurance, and films that live;
His life gave hope, inspiration, and assurance it's more blessed to give!

Lera Bailey Hamilton

Martha

"Who is the woman that I love?" I ask the Wind.
He whispers, "Martha," in my ear and touches my face with his cool hand.
"Who is the woman that I adore?" I ask the Sea.
She shows me your reflection in Nature's Mirror and washes my feet of the golden sand.
"Who is the most beautiful woman in all the World?" I ask the Moon.
He smiles, writing Martha in stars across the Black Sky.
"Who is the woman that holds my heart?" I ask the Sun.
He fills my heart with warmth as warm as your Love, it makes me cry.
So when we are in each other's arms and you ask, "Who is the woman that you love-is it me?"
I will pull you close to me, kiss you firmly on the lips and answer
"Martha, ask the Sun, the Moon, the Wind or ask the Sea."

Randy L. Williams

Untitled

I have walked here before,
Heard joyous birdsongs,
Seen the bouncing, inquisitive butterfly
Approach from somewhere, and disappear.
I open my hand and think,
Butterflies are not friendly at all.
I am wrong, for she lands on my hand!
I feel the gentle pressure of her grasp -
Note the shining light in her eyes.
Resting wings move slowly in flight pattern,
Sunlight glistens on iridescent wing powder.

I have known the exquisite pleasure of
Having a bouncing, inquisitive butterfly
Land on my hand!
In my mind I feel her soft hand on my face,
Her warm lips caressing mine.
I press her lithe body closer
And we are showered by iridescent wing powder!

Richard T. Smith

Untitled

I lay here listening as scared as can be,
Hearing something I don't want to see.

As the feeling get's strong, I try to
curl up thinking it will be gone.

But when it's inside, there's no running away;
because the fear always stays the same.

Waiting and wondering what will be,
makes me want to leave.

But believing in faith and having strength
will allow me to see, that fear; is what
you make it to be.

Rosemary Amaral

Nightime

Sometimes it draws me to it, like a mother
her babe to her breast
At other times I fear what the darkness
will bring.
When twilight is gone, and darkness
begins, then I begin my test.
To spend more time with my soul
alone to remember sadness makes my
eyes sting.
Where once it was filled with love and trust
it's now empty, tell me Lord,
can a heart rust?

Liz Roberts

The Witch

The witch lived on the sandy beach.
Her eyes were alert like a guard on watch at Buckingham Palace.
Her nose was long, resembling a torn and corroded carrot.
Her mouth was as withered as three-year-old raisins deposited in a sewer.
Her hair was straggly, like seaweed, partly brown,
partly black, partly pink and partly red.

The witch couldn't fly.
She was too poor to own a broomstick.
She had no aptitude in demonic arts, voodoo, chanting or casting spells.
Her one ability in life was to fix toilets.
This activity was done with her long straggly hair which
was used as a sort of sponge, washing away debris.
Later after fixing toilets all day on the beach the witch
would come home and lather her hair in Breck shampoo.
Even then her shining glory never looked good.
Ah, what a pitiful creature, that witch.

Linda Berg

The Witness

The old tree gazed out upon a deserted land.
Her gray, sun bleached roots bare with gnarled
twisted knees lay spread wide, like those of
an old harlot, holding onto the land.
She too had been raped by man.

The earth that once had covered her now traveled
on the wind, with the leaves of green velveteen,
from the crown of her willowy head.
Warmed now only by a weakened sun shining through
her thinning leaves of red.

She sighed. The dark wind whispered in her limbs,
"The time is now."
Mingled with the thunderclap her loud cries echoed
round, as her shallow roots were ripped and torn
and she fell across the barren land.
And the ground trembled.
And the wind moaned.
But none was there to hear the sound.

Marion Alderson

Old Woman In A Chair

There was an old woman whose heart was forlorn.
Her hair was all tattered, her clothes were all torn.
Her bones seemed so fragile, her grey arms were bare.
In silence she shivered and sat in a chair.
There was rot on the wood of this old rocking chair,
But it held up the woman — it was no worse for wear.
The old woman cherished it. She saw in it rest
And the happier days of an age-tarnished past.
She rocked back and forth at a slow, rhythmic pace
With the patience and torment of Job on her face,
And those who rushed by her all headed somewhere
Where they could rest their tired hearts and tired heads without care.
Then they'd see the old woman, turn their eyes to their feet,
And forget she was there
In her chair
On the street.

Tracy A. Evans

Ocean Thinker

She sits with her knees drawn up beneath her chin;
her hands clasped at her ankles.
The wind coming up from the sea plays with her
long skirt and loose curly hair.
Before her eyes, a single killer whale arcs over the
water, the black streamlined body gleaming in the
dying light of the sunlight.
As she sits on the cliff, overlooking the ocean,
she stares at the ocean, but, not giving her attention.
She thinks hard, about a decision that would
alter her life forever.
As the sunlight fades, she stands, hoping she made
the right decision, for she has made up her mind.
He waits for her, behind the rock.
She holds him close, hesitating to answer.
He dreads the word, "nay," hoping she believes in
his love. His heart soars as she whispers "yes."
They walk away from the rock and the sea,
their backs to the deepening twilight sky.

Sarah Lynn Kelley

Who Am I

Who am I she asks her reflection.
Her reflection just stares back with no answer to
help her solve her question.
Where's the little girl that was there eight years ago?
Then she remembers that little girl lost her childhood
on one cold winter night. Why did she have to go away?
Then it hits her, that little girl couldn't understand
what was happening and the only way she thought she
would be able to understand would be to grow up as
quickly as she could.
But now she's all grown up and all she can think about is going back
to that lost little girl, she wants her childhood back.

Who am I she questions her reflection.
Her reflection changes to the image of a frightened girl.
Why has her reflection changed?
She realizes that inside her grown up body is that little
girl wandering alone and terrified of something she
can't ever explain.

Who am I she screams at her reflection.
But only the silence is her answer.

Katrina Taft

Midnight Crossing

The night lay heavy, like an ebony curtain.
Her silhouette moved on a path that was certain.
Alone she traveled in black velvet shroud.
She silently tread, the crickets more loud.
A small rise she sought, different from none.
Except there were visitors tonight on this one.
Soon she drew near a clearing of wood.
And on a mound, dark figures there stood.
All shapes and all sizes there seemed to be.
Waiting for her in night's reverie.
As she approached, lovely music she heard.
And she was greeted by a man sized bird.
Or so it seemed, for on second glance.
It was a winged man that asked her to dance.
It was faery dancing in which she involved.
While all around her the world dissolved.
In a new realm she found herself.
She'd never return, she now was an elf.
She was quickly caught up in more festivities.
And was happily joined with night's mysteries.

Robert Andrew Kramer

"She"

She, is my best friend, and my love for
her will never end.

She, has helped me in so many ways,
So believe me when I say,
"I am grateful everyday."

She, has given unto other's more than
money could ever buy, and that's no lie.

In what ever she does, she will do her
best, even when she is put to the test.

She, well always tell you the truth; never lie,
that's until the day she die.

She, is hold and strong, and
will never led you wrong.

She, will make you laugh when you
are mad, and make you smile
when you are sad.

She, will talk to you and uplift your sorrows,
and replace your sorrows with hope for tomorrow.

That's why I can say, "I love you"
mommy each and every day

Talesia E. Smallcomb

Untitled

For you my love with teardrops in my soul...
Here I am crying and sighing for you.
Here I am before you, the one that had what always pretended
not to have.

Now is my time to tell you I don't care about your confusion
because confusion is very mine.

You already know, because I have said thousands of times, that
everything is written and engraved in an eternal rock, a divine rock.

You see the proof because star dust is here all over around us
and will remain forever.

Don't you see beloved woman what I see? do not distract yourself,
feel the light,
you are with me!

Pay attention to my sighing, not being with you makes me
exclaim out
of my mind with anxiety, exasperated:
Come to me my love, don't ever tell me you are not mine!...

The fluttering of many ideas from my feelings like white doves
toward the arcanum in direct flight, they find
you quickly, they identify with your desires of being with me!

You can feel, you know what has been known, don't doubt anymore,
come to me my soul is waiting. I am telling you sweet love.

Lewis H. Trogler

Time Is Of The Essence

My, my, my, where does time go?
How can I catch him, or is he out of my reach.
How can I hold on to him? Or, does he want to be held?
I need time to think
I need to reminiscence.
I think there's time for a change.
Do you think I have a chance?..
A chance to have time to think,
Reminiscence and change?
Time is so, of the essence.

Katie Flowers

"My Dad"

My Dad is a clever old man,-
He's been around for a long time.
But he loves me and I love him,-
That is why I am writing this rhyme.

Maybe he is big and weighs a ton,-
But he is my Dad and that is good.
Because he doesn't beat me at all,-
And tries to treat me as he should.

My Dad doesn't jump around too much,-
You have to watch close to see him move.
Except when he's doing things he likes,-
Then my old dad is really in the groove.

He likes all my friends that he meets,-
And they think he is funny in a way.
No matter how he looks I love him,-
And he loves me a little more everyday.

Kathi Lee Liller

"God's Blossoms Of Spring"

God's "Breath of springtime", are we.
His "Creations of Beauty", each unique!
With His care, we grow strong,
Never to wither beneath "The Weeds".
Stand tall, "Beauty" to be seen.
Our colors are bright and bold,
Our "Touch and Smell",
Should be Gentle and Sweet!

God had planted our beginning, our seed.
He nurtured us,
Giving us the love and care that we would need.
In the Darkness, our Petals will close,
To open, it is "His Light" we must seek.
Quenching our thirst from "His showers of rain",
We feed.
Then, under his "Rainbow",
We BURST forth,
"BLOSSOM'S OF SPRINGTIME",
In "Fields of Green"!

Melody Godines

Warrior's Heart

The Warrior stares off into the distance,
his mind is taken away.
Finding peace in thoughts of a better time,
when his Nation was not astray.
A time of honor, deep respect, all creation
immeasurably holy.
The well being and safety of his people came first,
not thoughts of him and him only.
To sacrifice his life young while protecting his people,
was far better than death at old age.
His unselfish heart he purified, with sweet grass,
cedar, and sage.
No greater, stronger, more loving heart,
has the Creator ever made.
Than the impassioned heart of a Warrior,
his life for his people he gave.
Not forgetting his deeds of unselfish love,
they'll sing songs of admiration.
He'll live on forever through stories and songs,
that give hope and strength to his Nation.

Ricky Chavis

The Second Commandment

The man was an alcoholic. Life's agonies had overwhelmed him!
His young children were "legally" seized - never seen again;
Voluntary return from AWOL was finalized in Leavenworth;
Unproven charges of arson resulted in jail time.

As in baseball, life throws fast-balls, hard-balls and curves.
Being highly sensitive, and with minimal coping skills,
Leon deeply buried his agonies, drowning his pain in liquor -
His life resembled a small barque on a stormy sea...

Alone and ill, in the final hours of his anguished journey
Came his pencilled confession: For a lifetime
He could achieve emotional feeling only by
Hurting himself and those he loved.

With the burden lifted came unconditional recognition
Of a Higher Power and his surrender to it.
The power of AA's Step I and step II
Had brilliantly illumined his path.

Surrender completed, he shaved and dressed for departure;
When found, serenity and peace attested to the gentle terminus.
How like the Christ's last minute forgiveness of the thief!
LOVE THY NEIGHBOR AS THYSELF!!

G. Calvin Tooker

Coaster D'Amour

From this day forward,
hold unto you the love that surrounds us all,
emitting brightly from your gaze as you stare into each other's passion blazed eyes.
Do not waste or make haste of what are today's possibilities.
For tomorrow holds the key to the rest of your lives together
use it to unlock the golden door
and hold on forever more
sometimes the ride will be rocky,
and sometimes the ride will be smooth
for most the ride seems endless
Don't fall prey, for that day will come
but you can change that fate it's never too late,
true love and true friendship will last a lifetime
in your mind,
is where the work takes place.
It's not a race, my friend, for good thing come to those who wait
and like I said, hold on tight and ride the coaster d'amour.
Keep your minds and hearts open
and you shall share the days together for ever more.

Michelle Dirat

Prisoner

My heart is empty
Hollow from the loss of love.
Empty from the lost promises,
Promises shattered by lies.
An emotion such as this
Is hidden away, away from the world.
My eyelids are heavy and swollen,
Cursed from the deluge of tears.
Tears wash away some pain, but do not be fooled
The pain will linger on
Until someone heals your broken heart.
My smile has faded.
The smile that used to be loved is lost.
The happiness has been murdered,
The longing look of another is the criminal.
But, I feel as if I am in jail.
You stole my heart.
You stole my smile.
You stole my happiness.
Who do you think should be in jail?

Melissa I. Weiss

Dream Or Reality?

The winds blew through your hair with such grace. I'm freezing hot. Elemental magic maker, spin your web of mystery.
My barriers are rotting. The decay of my sanctuary makes me ill.
Disturbed and bewildered, I venture out beyond the safety of light. Night sands whisper between my digits. I'm falling below the line. There's no way back for me now. So serene and terrifying. Vast clouds of impenetrable brilliance swarm in circles around my being. I have stepped through the threshold.
It's too late to resist. I have succumbed to the fury of the beast. Disconnected from mind and body. I am now a particle within the tide. The abyss is near. Swallow.
The pull is irresistible. I need this. It's my only choice.
I've hit the bottom, but I'm still sinking. I hear your tears.
They speak to me in a tongue so foreign, yet so relative. The distance is incomprehensible. Fight. Scream. Panic. I can't.
I've lost all control. No longer do I exist as a whole.
Scattered about like broken glass, I lay quietly.
The agony. How sweet.
Goodbye.

Tim Brummett

One

Look at me now.
How can you be so bold, yet so unsure?
Your eyes shine like sparkling diamonds
And your face betrays...
Your secret love for me.

Kiss me softly, like the morning rain
Silvery, Golden, all of your rainbow colors.

Your soulful glances,
And a face touched by feathery angels' wings.

Beneath the stars at night
Your sweet love transforms me

I tremble from our combined emotions...
So strong,
So real.

One. That's what we've become.

Tiffany A. Taylor

Death Be Not Proud

I ask God
How could death overcome my brother?
Look up in the heavens, He answered;

I look up into the heavens
There a new star appears
A glistening light that shines other stars

I ask as to the origin of that star
It is the light of your brother
That shines ever so brightly

I ask God
Why was he taken away, so young?
Death had smile upon him, he answered;

Be not with sorrow
For his light shine in my presence
He no longer has pain nor sorrow

My brother shines in the heavens
Death be not proud
Death be not proud

Ron Beauvais

Awakening

Somehow I lost you. Why did you go?
How could you leave me when I loved you so?
Was it something I said or something I did?
Was it something I showed you or something I hid?
Somehow I lost you. I don't understand why
Our love was so strong, so how could it die?
If ever you needed me, was I ever not there?
If there were such times were they not rare?
I did what you wanted. I never said no
We only went places where you wanted to go
Yet, somehow I lost you, the reason, I guess
I didn't value myself, so you valued me less

Ruth Olefsky

"He Is Deaf"

How does he know when the school bell rings?
How does he know anything?
How come he is by himself?
Can he help it that he is deaf?

How does he know when the fire truck sounds?
How come he doesn't smile, but frowns?
How come he is always left?
Is it his fault that he is deaf?

How does he know when tractors roar?
How does he know there's a knock at the door?
How does he know when there's burglary or theft?
How come it was he who was born deaf?

How does he feel not to hear any noise?
Why wasn't he like the other boys?
Just think of worse, like crippled or blind
He ought to be glad he can see the sun shine.

Laura Whiteley

The Vow

How many times can a vow be taken,
how many times be respoken?
Which time will the brittle syllables break
on temptation and have to be swept up broken?

None of the many times, of course.
China cement, or flour and water will do.
Leave over night under constant force.
Hope springs eternal at the sight of glue.

How do vows spring? Do Phoenixes fly?
Does the jig-saw puzzle put perfectly together
convey even what the poor print did
of Constable's sky? Do Phoenixes sing?
Can these questions excuse me now
from picking up the pieces of my vow?

Wendel Agne

Missing You

As I sit here and the days pass by
I always ask myself the question why.
Wishing I was at that place
Where it doesn't matter what's your race.

Here the grass is greener and the sky more blue
But God knows I've been missing you.
This poem is not to entice a tear
But since day one I wish you were here.

Love is something found deep in the heart
I always ask why did we part.
I love you more than a solid gold charm
That's why I shed this tear as I say "I Miss You Mom".

Ken Lackey

A Message To Gabrielle

Just 19 days is all you spent
However brief it was
Although the time was very short
You brought us lots of love

We didn't understand it then
Nor claim that we do now
Forever we will wonder why, the what for and the how?

You have a little brother now
And he is quite divine
And though his life does not replace
The place you hold within
The happiness that he has brought
Reminds us all again...

That when we flew those pink balloons
On upwards way up high
That you had felt the love we sent
And kissed us through the sky
For every thorn, there is a rose
Its petal we embrace
And when your brother smiles at us, our God extends His grace...

Phyllis Ferraro

Through The Eyes Of A Boy

A tidal wave crashes like a 747 airplane crashing into a mine field.
Huge waves break on each other like boys playing football.
Rain pounding on mad water like marbles on a cement walkway.
Wind blowing like large horns in the air. Thunder booming like a ghost's deep voice.
As far as the eye can see, it looks like a furious fire jumping on a deck of a pirate ship with music playing from a fiddle.
Then ends as if you were floating to a promised land, away from the treacherous storm.

Nathan Raher

The Snail

Slithering slimy sentient on a silver trail-
hurrying slowly down life's time-tunnel to tomorrow.
Purposeful advance that defies distraction:
Eventual arrival, without question -
at a snail's pace.

Patricia Landis

A Summer Day

Hush! Hush winds ....
Hush everything ... Hush!
A grey light enters the eastern horizon
Soon a joyful bright face climbs over the shoulders of hills
First one cheep .... then another
A chorus of birds sing a morning melody
The golden sun plays peak-a-boo with dancing leaves
And tosses dapples of sunlight on a green lawn
The garden awakens and refreshes with morning dew
Each little glistening drop holds a happy rainbow
The world is abuzz with fluttering butterflies
Nectar laden bees and hi-fi insect song
White clouds sail in a sea of blue sky
While the summer sun drums up heat and humidity
Sunflowers follow the suns crossing to the western horizon
Where it slips quietly behind tall mountains
Purple fingers reach across a crimson sky
And pull the blanket of night over a tired land.

Loraine Gayle Schwarz

Prince, My Cat

On a warm sunny day.
I acquired a little gold cat.
When Prince arrived he was a bundle of joy,
Our bundle of joy was a wholly terror.
On his first night home he played hide and seek on us.
My little cat walks on a leash.
Prince sometimes thinks he is a dog.
Our little cat runs and plays,
Which is a little child at play.
Bill and I have hours of fun playing with our precious one.
Prince purrs like a little baby when he wants his way,
To play in the autumn leaves our cat takes his
early morning walks.
Prince is a lovely and affectionate cat to our neighbors.
Our Prince is only three years old.
He has a little mind of his own.
When he is sleeping, and he is cute as a bug.
Our cat is a little devil at times.
But I love my cat.
Prince is our pride and joy.

Mary L. Forney

The Way

I discover a cave in the forest, I am mysteriously drawn to it.
I am afraid, but enter the cave alone.
It is dark, I cry out for help. I never find my way.

I discover a cave in the forest, I am mysteriously drawn to it.
I am afraid, but enter it with my family.
It is dark, our differences paralyze us. I never find my way.

I discover a cave in the forest, I am mysteriously drawn to it.
I am afraid, for I too, am hollow.
A light beyond dispels the darkness, accepting its guidance,
I find my way.

I discover a cave in the forest, I am mysteriously drawn to it.
I am filled with excitement.
The light is within me, I explore the cave, I find my way.

I am a cave in the forest, the light within mysteriously draws
others to my entrance.
I hide it, afraid it will go out.
It goes out. Others never find their way.

I am a cave in the forest, the light within mysteriously draws others
to my entrance.
Thankful for illumination, I share the light.
It shines brighter. Others find their way.

Michael G. Semon

C.P.R.

I am qualified for C.P.R. for two years now
I am asked to be a teacher; Yes I'll accept
I pray to God that I never have the opportunity to
use this skill, but how will ever know that I have
mastered the course and can save a life unless
there is a victim.
But can only one victim conclude that I
am successful, will I need two, or maybe three.
What if I try and the attempt still leads to death.
What if I saved one and another dies, am I successful or does
that make me a failure?
What if I
fall to the floor and stop breathing and my heart stops cold
I have my C.P.R., why don't I save myself...then death.....
Was I successful or am I a failure?

Perin D. Tinsley Jr.

Moving

The movers are here, and as I feared it is me they have come for.
I am off the ground and in the air and slowly rocking to and fro
as on a flatbed truck I go.

Through trees and things that poke my blinds.
Past powerlines that hum and whine.
Snaking down the road so slow as on and on and on I go.
I am finally here my new plot of land.
A new foundation is where I am planned.
It is good to feel the sun on my roof and moonlight rays in every nook
To have it rain and cool me down and have the wind come
whistling round.
To feel the footsteps once again of women, children and of men.
To be filled with laughter, love and joy is what makes this house
a home.

Karen L. Bauer

The Grass

In the limitless valleys,
I am there.
I am a single blade
in the monotonous color of green.

People look past my individuality
and only realize the similar traits
between me and my brothers and sisters.
Although I am surrounded by people of my kind,
I feel lonely.

As people walk by and trample on me,
they don't care that I'm hurt.
When they stand on me
for minutes on end
and I'm suffocated from the beloved air,
I pray for the wind to blow
a breeze so hard
that the human topples over
and relieves me of
death.

Kristie Briggs

'Am I A Nubian Princess'

Am I a Nubian Princess?
I ask myself time after time again.
Is it the shape of my face
Is it the color of my skin
Or is it the way I hold my head, so high, so proud.

Am I a Nubian Princess?
The assertive but yet shy
Am I a Nubian Princess?
Is it the twinkle of my dark eyes.
My sunny disposition or the way I stare,
but sometimes hide.

Am I a Nubian Princess?
The tall one, but with much grace,
The one who's always smiling and greeting all the human race.
Am I a Nubian Princess?
Proud of my ancestral heritage, not afraid to stand
For freedom or beliefs, no price, no fame.
I am a Nubian Princess, beauty from within,
Not ashamed of who I am and loved just the same.

Zina Cason Broxton

Miracles

I believe in miracles; do you?
I believe some things will be,
Things I cannot understand,
Sometimes can't even see.
But I believe in miracles; do you?
I believe that five thousand people
Were fed beside a sea,
Fed with five small barley loaves
Andfishes—three.
I believe the dumb were made to talk,
And that the lame were made to walk.
I know that water was turned to fine wine
By the self-same one who changed this life of mine.
I must believe in miracles; do you?

Mary Waye Baker

Can You Hear Me Mister

Can you hear me mister,
I can only whisper.
I don't know your name,
but may I tell you my pain.
It started many years ago,
'till finally I cried out no.
How could this be happening to me,
but it must be.
He replied and said, please don't cry,
I once also felt like I should die.
I know one day you will find,
that one that will be kind.
I asked why he was alone,
he told me, that way back then I found the one.
But the pain inside of me fought like a burning sin,
and the sad part is I did not win.
So, sonny go get that little gal,
because she is your future pal.
I then left in a hurry,
for that old, bitter man solved my worries.

Sean Gustatson

Eternal Memories

I can still see you laughing, playing and crying,
I can still see your warmth, your love for self,
I can still see you, in your children and your siblings,
I can especially see you as I look at Mom and Dad.
The lasting love emanating from their eyes:
The loss of such a beautiful and giving son.
I can still hear you saying to me "I Love You" with no
provocations.
I can still hear me saying to you, "I Love You," feeling,
meaning and missing it.
I can still see in all of whom you've touched,
the loss they are enduring.
As you look upon us, I know you see our "errs,"
but, with understanding.
Now it is our turn to come to you for guidance we crave,
to overcome our trials and tribulations,
I can still see your searching eyes, trying to make
sense of the ways of the world.
I will remember you always, because in that I
will know love, and feel you in my heart forever.

Susanne "Steward" Taylor

The Thread

I tried to love someone new but all
I could do is think of you, your
tender touch your warm embrace that
devilish smile that lights up your face.

My heart is so bruised and still so
tender from past years of pain that others
have rendered. I'm so afraid to let you see
the love that I feel when your next to me.

When we first met my heart was in
shreds but your love has stitched it
together just like a thread. All the
hurt and all the pain has disappeared
and I'm whole again.

If you take your love and leave me now,
I couldn't go on I wouldn't know how.
Open your eyes and see who I am, love
me forever and please be my friend.

Robyn Quarnberg

Choices

As I looked at him
I could see the emptiness behind his eyes
And although he said not a word
I could hear his silent cries

Oh, how I wanted to reach out and hold his hand
But, he turned his back on me
Because he didn't understand

I had to make a choice
between two
The choice was either a friend
or it was YOU

I know we all have choices we must make
And I hate to make the choice that was right for my sake

For after a while, he'll be able to see
That the choice I made, wasn't only, to benefit me

I hope he uses our time apart
to seek, search and find
To experience Real Love, that is truly divine

I know one day he'll have to make a choice TOO
Lord, I just pray, that he chooses YOU!

Monique Jewell Hillman

To Robbie

For lending me a shoulder, when I needed to cry
I cross my heart and hope to die,
That our love will last forever, through good and bad times,
And I promise I'll always be there, even when the stars don't shine.
I was kind of disappointed, when you told me how you felt,
But if I could never see you again, my heart would just melt.
So friends is better than nothing, I found out the hard way,
So I'll ask you only once...
Will you please stay?
Don't leave me in the dust, don't forget about me,
I still want to be part of your life,
So let's go back to how it used to be.
Let's talk about our personal lives, and share all of our stories.
Let's talk about our problems, and sometimes our glories.
Let's be the best of friends, that anyone's ever found.
We can't wait forever, so let's start right now!

Nichole Y. Wallace

Friends Gone Before Us

He was my best friend.
I do not say that I was his best friend, but I know he was mine.

There are times when I am in the shade, when I had my fill of stars,
And throw my gaze up with such forces to extinguish
those burned planets.
The wolf is outside the door, and I wince with the pull of years,
Afraid of this kind of growing old.

Perhaps I have outlived myself. Hunched against some cold inner wind,
I pass others; convicts of a separate grief.

But for a time, I walked with him, my friend, and learned
To match my stride with his. With him I learned to sculpt
sorrow and beauty
Into coherence, provided myself with the purity of his grace.
I knew that as long as he lived and spoke to me,
I would not be ushered into an eternity
Of anonymity.

Now, in his death, I find the best and worst of myself,
That rare distillation of dust that makes up a man.

I miss him. I shall always miss him.

Penelope Leavitt

What Joey Found Out About Santa After Losing His Faith

I had to write this letter to misses Santa Claus
I don't want to snitch on Santa but it's really just because
He promised me a stereo and a bike if I'd be good
Three Christmas's I waited—each year he said he would
Oh I remember all good children is all he always says
But he really don't mean it—it's just a second guess
I know it's not the right thing—to snitch on Santa Claus
But when he breaks a promise I really got a cause
I talked to dad about this—he said he had a way
Just do your homework every night—be extra good all day

Joey's writes a second letter the following year

Tell Santa I'm sorry and now I'm really sad
For now I know that Santa's helpers are really Mom and Dad
I was hit while riding on the road—and then my helpers cried
When the doctor came and told them that I really could have died
Tell Santa I learned myself a lesson—a lesson about our toys
For Santa and his helpers know what's best for girls and boys
Our Moms and Dads are Gods gifts to little kids like me
And I pray to Jesus every night—please don't take my helpers
away from me

Theodore G. Malecki

How Can It Be?

I ask why I no longer can see the blue of the sky
I ask why I no longer can see the golden rays of the sun
Yet I remember the times shared with each other
But now it seems that these days are done. . . .

HOW CAN IT BE?
HOW CAN IT BE?

We do not know the answer of time nor love, but
Now I must walk alone as our rapture has parted
And our ecstasy is gone. I reach for your hand
And realize that we are no longer just one. . . .

HOW CAN IT BE?
HOW CAN IT BE?

Virginia Newsom

Cleaning My Master's House

With broom and mop and dust cloth
I dust each and every pew
Joyfully, I sweep and mop my Lord's house
But, tomorrow, I'll be sitting there by you

For a man to sweep and mop, some may say
Would eternally damage his pride
But, first being saved, then baptized
Makes me a part of Christ's bride

And like a new bride
Who cares for her husband's own
So shall I take care
Of my heavenly Father's home

For when we get to Heaven
We'll have no spouse
But all be one in Christ
So today, I joyfully clean my Master's house

In Heaven we'll all be equal to the angels
Down here, I'll work with all due prowess
Humming a most joyful tune
While cleaning my Master's house

Terry Coston Wallace

Thoughts On A Young Poet Of 14

What silent pain and desperate hope
I feel, confronted by an eager mind
expressed through poetry and prose,
waxing eloquent with words not yet
fully understood but pressed to the
surface through expression's need.
This same voice, fraught with anger and despair,
stifled in its infancy — like a delicate flower
blasted by the exhaust fumes of urban blight.

The suppressed anger of a generation, raised
and nurtured on violence, in a society
that supports the arming of the populace —
a society that feeds self-interest with fear
and reasons that, to save itself, all must be armed.
This anger, dormant until now, without
lyrical release — where will it spend itself?
Will poetry prevail?

Ruth Nagenda

By The Great Big Tree And On The Hilltops

By the great big tree
I feel free
By the great big tree
All the leaves fall on me.
Under the great big tree
I look at the sun
Under the great big tree
I know I'll always have fun.

When I look down from the hilltops
I can see the world below
When I look down from the hilltops
I can feel the cool wind blow.

I sit here under the great big tree
I sit here all afternoon
And when it's dark I stand on the hilltops
And I can almost touch the moon!

Under the tree
Under the sun
I'll always know a place
where to have fun.

Sunny Lee

The Cool Wind

The cool wind blows through the trees,
I feel only a cool breeze.
Everything that had happened before,
wouldn't happen forever more.
It all changed in a blink of an eye,
it all ended when my grandma died.
I don't feel a warm kiss good-night,
there isn't a gentle hug to hold me tight.
No family dinner on Sunday afternoon.
no children's laughter in the other room.
No more fireworks on the fourth of July.
no more family - and I know why.
The only thing that lingers of that time,
are the memories that remain in my mind.
The cool wind still remains there,
but nothing else - and no one to care.

Michael J. Young

My Life

As I remember my childhood cast
I felt a need as sharp as glass

Time was forever, heaven is high
Questions of self, who am I?

A soul was given, melted inside out
A fire created, love was about

The need was lost in limbo years
Pain, growing, time and some tears

Emotions blended and thoughts provoked
My life savored seed, a soul and an oath

In my mind and soul an image was set
A mirror of what I wanted, but not yet

I searched for years along with this oath
But I soon then realized, I've felt a stroke

My mirror deceived me, love at last?
No you child, that layer was glass

I feel out loud, how many layers for it, I pray to God,
my mirror won't split, remember your mirror created by you?
Yes I know, your glass was cracked too. Hold your soul open,
it's time for you too, our glass is all gone, my mirror's in you

E. Robert Polins

Waiting Is Worth It

What a change from the past,
I finally have him back at last,
I've waited and waited for so long,
when people were doubtful I still remained strong;
I am so very happy that he chose me,
I'm no longer trapped in my anger since I've been set free;
When I heard the answer joy suddenly filled my mind,
I can once and for all leave my sadness behind;
although I'm risking a lot, to open my heart and let him in,
I'm definitely ready for our new relationship to begin;
It takes a lot to trust someone with your heart,
but it's time to forget the past and have a new start;
May be our relationship started as fate,
but good things do come to those who wait!

Karen Arnold

Gone By

My kindness and love led you to success.
I gave all I had because to me you were the best.
Being innocent my body was drained with emotions
for no one but you, and now that you're gone
my feelings are still on our past.

I want to go on with my life and perhaps
forget you ever existed but, every time I try;
I seem to get stuck into something that has gone by.

Linda Hurdle

Three Days

Think about this carefully...I am sure you'll see
I got quite a jolt from it, when it came to me.
There are three days known to man; count them one, two, three
But, fact is, of all of them, only one can be!
"Yesterday" is never here...just a memory
Whether good, whether bad, it's in the past, you see.
"Tomorrow's" really something...hoped by you and me
Future bright, a shining light: that day just won't "be"!
We've got but one single day...make it good, I plea.
"Today" is here, it is now... face it cheerfully.
"Yesterday" is old news; "tomorrow's" never free
Make "today" more special...to life...that is the key!

Narda Curlee

I'm Blessed

I'm not the greatest of writers and my punctuation isn't the best.
I have some trouble with spelling but what I am is truly blessed.

My sentence structure may be wrong and some words may be misplaced.
But, I thank my Father, God above, for His mercy and His grace.

I'm not sure of what to say at times, and with some thoughts I wrestle.
But once again I humble myself, and allow God to use this vessel.

Sometimes I feel my poems aren't good enough for saints of the church.
Then God sets me straight, and lets me know that it's not of me but His work.

I often wonder why I was chosen to be a child of the King of Kings
To have the honor of being a princess, and covered in the blood of royalty.
With a worth that is far beyond rubies, and a value equivalent to wisdom
With my head held high and my nose turned up as I strut my walk of freedom,
And why I have the privilege to be entitled to nothing but the very best;
But, I don't wonder for long for it is because I'm truly blessed.

Stephanie R. Joyner

Thoughts From A Hunter's Wife And Mother

Lying in bed this Sunday morning, awakened, by familiar sounds that I hear.
It's a drama repeated, unequaled, when the first days of autumn draws near.
The drama unfolds about five, the clock has been checked to make sure,
That he, whose hearts are pounding, are found, awake, ready and allure.
The coffee's rich aroma, the murmuring of voices low,
The constant bark of DOC, the dog, reminds the guys, LET'S GO!
So off in the autumns still, the hunters pace their steps,
And a smile of joy and gratitude, moves across my lips.
For GOD has heard my prayer this morning, and in my heart has spliced,
An overwhelming sense of LOVE, unending, for the HUNTERS OF MY LIFE!

Karen Lindstrom

Echoes

While walking to my bedroom, down the dark and narrow hall,
I hear faint echoes calling, from the lonely barren walls.
The walls that once were laden with pictures of a life
A house, three dogs, two children; a husband and a wife.

I hear the children laughing; who knows what they're about?
The slamming of the screen door, as they scamper in and out.
"Stop running through the house!" I hear their mother call.
Pups growling at each other, over a tattered rubber ball.

The echoes of a family, once heard most every day;
Now locked inside these lonely walls, slowly fade away.
What happened to this family that once appeared to all who passed
Something to be proud of, something that would last?
Were they lost in some great tragedy? My mind just can't recall.
The only things remaining - are the echoes in these walls.

William L. Condra

From Inner Growth To Harvest

As I sit here alone remembering past years,
I hear the sounds of laughter and the silence of tears.

I feel hate and love, courage and fear,
And great lose for loved ones no longer here.

I've known people who made it easy, and those who made it rough,
A few left too early, some not soon enough.

One thing all had in common, either in a big or small way,
They each had a hand in making me the person I am today.

Some left me thinking, "I'll do enough to just get by",
While others have said to be a success, "You must continue to try".

I have heard the saying, "You reap what you sow",
My possessions are many, but to deserve them? I really don't know.

In the fields of the world, I have plowed a few rows,
Raked, seeded and watered, and watched myself grow.

But the two people that have brought a rich harvest to my life,
Are a wonderful son, and a beautiful, understanding wife.

Paul Kubaszak

"Once More"

I just want to see you once more.
I just want to hold you once more.
I just want to kiss you once more.

But I can't.

To see your face.
To hold your hand.
To kiss your lips.
Once more-
That's all I want.

But I won't.

I want to call and hear your voice.
I want to hear you say you love me.
Once more.

But I don't.

The pain of remembrance grows in my heart,
every time I hear your name.
I want you back to be with me.
I just want to cry.

But I can't. I won't. I don't.
And I never will again - Once more.

Tiffany M. L. Bogue

My Granddaughter

Before she was even born
I knew it was going to be a girl.
My daughter gave birth to her
And brought her into this complex of a world.
Tiarie, is the name they've given
To this precious human being
She means the whole world to us
Watching her grow everyday, I'm seeing
She's always alert of things
Going on around her and also curious
and if she can't get what she wants
She gets very frustrated and furious.
We give her a lot of love and attention
She's such a happy baby
I always wonder later on in life
when she's grown up a lady
That we'll always be here for her
Through the good times and bad
Life today is never easy
but there's Tiarie, she makes grandma glad.

Roxanne F. Thurston

Old Maid Washes Feet

Whenever I see a Marlboro man go strutting by,
I let out a great big old maid sigh.
Ooohhh, those big bulging muscles makes me swoon,
Whenever I can lure a Marlboro man into my room.
I kneel down and take off his old worn boots,
Who cares if people think I'm an old mixed up coot.
I'll first rub his feet and make him purr,
Ooohhh, just being with this hunk makes my head whirl.
I love to soap his calloused, manly feet,
As he looks down upon me, so burly and ruggedly sweet.
He knows I love him dearly when I wash his smelly feet,
I think this humble feet washing is really quite neat.
The Marlboro man leans over and kisses my old maid lips,
That's all I can write, as I faint to the floor.

Terry Lee Pieszchala

Freedom

Here I am, alone at last
I lie in bed, my mind so fast
My lawyer came, and said to me.
On this day, you will be free
About the day, that is so near
No longer will, I live in fear
This nightmare is about to end
I'll go home, to be with friends
How will I act, when I get out
I'll breathe the air, and I will shout
I'll run and laugh, and how I'll talk
I'll kiss the ground, that I do walk
I'll hug my children, and kiss their face
And never again, will I think of this place
For now this part, of life is past
My future ahead, so very vast
I thank you man from up above
For giving me back, the ones I love

Lynn Whitesel

Untitled

I awake with the sound of thunder in my head;
I remember what they said.

I feel alone with no one to help me
I scream aloud, I hear them again

They tell me things that no one know;
In the corner something glows

As I approach this strange secret;
It grabs me and sucks me into its mighty grasp

Kelly Scobie

A Walk In The Forest

I walk along in the forest so green,
I look at all that can be seen,
The pretty blue sky,
The birds that fly by,
The swaying trees,
Blowing in the breeze,
Oops! I fell in the brook,
How funny I must look!
Oh-no! A bear is eating my lunch,
It's a good thing I have a bunch!
And that, my friend, was a day in the forest,
And, Oh, it was the dearest!

Shawna R. Kingsley

How Do I Feel

I sit in my dorm room all alone,
I look at the lights which shine so bright.
Wondering, thinking, will anyone phone,
I listen to the silence of the night.

I gaze at the stars in the pitch black sky,
I begin to feel sad as I remember.
I think of my family who wants to know why,
I won't be home 'til the month of December.

Tears fall down my eyes as I begin to cry,
My heart feels alone way deep down inside.
I pray to God, please let me try,
To keep my dignity, honor, and pride.

As I look outside the window of my room,
I begin to think, is college life for me.
I look away and clean with a broom
I think, what do I really want to be.

Nicole Law

I Want To Be Free

I look back on my life and wonder what went wrong,
I look back and write this song.

I look back to see who loves me,
I look back and want to be free.

I wonder if anyone sees what I'm going through,
I wonder if anyone wants to.

I feel forgotten, I feel not loved I wonder if anyone sees,
That I've longing to be free.

I wonder if anyone cares,
I wonder if I really want to share.

I wonder if it's just me,
Who is longing to be free.

Maybe I'll never know,
Maybe it'll never show.

But I hope you can see,
That I'm longing to be free.

Molly McDaniel

Ever Since Your Heart Melted Mine

Ever since your heart melted mine away,
I look up to cogitate.
What was the reason, I do not know.
What am I to do, where am I to go.
I am like a soldier, on a mission untold.
I am confused and don't know where to go.
But every night I look up to God with all my trust,
I am confident that someday,
He will bring you back, my love.

Regulo Renden

Open Minded

My mind is open. Once it was not.
I once had it closed to unordinary beings until I looked at my warped reflection in the wading pond yet recognized it as being myself.
I once closed my mind to unordinary places, until I walked through rough, unfamiliar terrain down a new, narrow path and at the end of the road I recognized it as being home.
I once closed my mind to unordinary feelings until I felt I could no longer watch men being belittled, women harassed and children tortured.
I felt this as an anger. I hated my teachers and I loved those who were hated.
I once closed my mind. It is now open and I am scared.

Laura J. Larck

Looking For Love

I feel so alone. Will you ever care?
I reach out to you but you aren't there.
What shall I do? Where shall I go?
My heart wants to stop, but God says no!
The hurt is so deep and I don't know why.
The pain is so painful all I can do is cry.
Since I cannot find you, do you still have
to hide?
Your name I call and no response at all.
I want you to pick me up every time I fall.
So many days I wait for you. I ask again,
what shall I do?
Will I always weep and lose my sleep?
Please send me one that I can keep!
Will you come to me on the wings
of a dove?
Can't someone tell me, will I ever
find love?

Lucille J. Tyndall

Lost And Gone

Lonely and sad on a cold winter night,
I recalled my memories of a boy,
And mourned for the past in the opaque night
For our love began with kisses and joy.
Then visions began to form in my eyes,
And suddenly I remembered us there,
When he was my sweetheart who never lied,
And was holding me with comfort and care.
But soon my visions were shattered and gone,
Just like my sweetheart-lost and never found;
Even though I searched, prayed, and called till dawn,
I had no luck for he was in the ground.
Now, with flowers blooming and birds singing,
I could still hear my sweetheart's bells ringing.

Nancy Chan

"Was It"

I smile with a tear down my face.
I remember a slight trace
Of all the things that took place.

"Was It" reality or pure insanity.
It seemed like a game, so hard to explain,
It sounds as if to complain
When I try to tell of the pain.

"Was It" reality or pure insanity.

Lillian Figeac

The Winds Of Time

When I pause and consider the winds of time;
I remember the mountains I have failed to climb
And the valleys of death I have left behind;
But along the way there has been joy that has been mine.

The winds of time makes me think much of my past
And how my memories of sad times seem to ever last;
Still I know I can not change things gone by
Even though at times I can't help but wonder why.

The winds of time brings many thoughts of yesterday;
While it also brings thoughts of a home far away
Where the streets are purest gold they say,
And now I begin to long for my appointed day.

But when I think of God and His precious Son,
The winds of time makes me realize my work isn't done;
For He has commanded that I must witness and teach
And for the present, lost souls I must continue to reach.

Matt Smallwood

Texian Woods

In Texian woods, hot and still,
I sat upon an old stone mill, and felt,
quietly, softly,
the presence of that time, long ago,
which lingering real, shadowed me.
It was the history of my people,
proud, tough and true,
whose mark on life and land, so premium priced,
by generations sacrificed, lay,
traced and tempered, in that place.
And, which now, mine possessed, was secreted
in my bones, and in my breath,
and within and without my Texian self,
and had become a hallowed and eternal part,
of me.

L. D. Vance

"It's Not So Much What You Say As How You Say It"

It's not so much what you say as how you say it,
I say I love you, you say, I love you, too.
I know you do, but don't you think,
I'd feel much better with a hug from you, loving words and a wink.

It's not so much what you say as how you say it,
Your tone of voice scares me to tears.
You raise your voice and shout like no one else was ever about,
If you could only talk to me softly,
It would take away all my fears.

It's not so much what you say as how you say it,
You come home and tell me your day was bad.
And change my mood from glad to sad.
It's not my fault you're hurting inside.
Your anger shows what your words can't hide.

It's not so much what you say as how you say it,
I hear it in your tone of voice, I read between the lines.
I remember all the times, I never knew what I had done,
And all the fights I thought I had won.
But I was wrong, I didn't win, 'til you give in and learn,
It's not so much what you say as how you say it.

Lee Irwin Morrow

When I look At You

I see love and all that it should be
I see a perfect picture of you and me
I see all the things that make life complete
When I look at you

I feel so alive every time I look in your eyes
Brings out a special something from deep inside
You make me notice things I've never realized
When I look at you

When I look at you
You turn my gray skies blue
You're everything,
And I thank God for you
All that I have, I see....
When I look at you

Lawrence Kizzee Jr.

On Top Of The World

On top of the world what do I see?
I see hunger, confusion, and no philosophy.
On top of a mountain what do I see?
I see an eagle staring at me.
On top of rainbow what do I see?
I see a little green man with buckled shoes who is he?
On top of a cloud what do I taste?
I taste a misty rainy paste.
On top of a city what do I smell?
I smell pollution who cares who could tell.

On top of a building what do I hear?
I hear a child crying I know there is a tear.
On top of my bed what do I see?
I see an angel watching over me.
On top of the world what do I see?
I see no hunger, no confusion, and philosophy and it's my friend to be!

Kristin Lea Tidaback

Shadows Of My Past

A candle slowly burning, casting shadows from my past
I see the images of what was and what could have been.

Was I really there, a part of all that was so shell like
empty nights filled with regrets of not seeing the inside,
only the deception of the surface

I cry out for the shadows to stop
they consume my dreams,
some cry out from the pain I sent their way
while others, faceless images haunt my thoughts

Thoughts of what I left behind,
what I should have taken with me
from that past with no rhyme or reason
leaving me here with no clue

I search for the answer to an unknown question
following me here and staying, unwanted

The question of me,
who I was, and why
looking down on those images
forming the shadows of my past.

Sandra Strejcek

Untitled

Scarred and aged tree, I dream your history in my reverent gaze.
I see the slender legs of children twining round...
small feet clinging to your hardness.
I hear their shouts and chuckles and small gasps of struggle.
There are lovers who carved their future dreams and on your
flesh tattooed their hope, their oneness.
And birds who used you as their viewpoint and their shelter
and brought new life to you in peeps and chirps of hunger.
A horse tethered long ago, and, in some dark and horrid hour
a man swung from your high branch...losing his
life in your arms.
A happy family sprawled beneath your awning telling stories
and spreading butter on aromatic bread.
I dream of what you were in vision clouded by the cruel rain
we make...
praying that when you fall there is a tear to mourn for you.
Old tree you've taught me my humanity, displayed without
your leaves life's dignity...
And I have wept your history.

Renee B. Rayel

My Feelings

When I look out on the ocean,
I see waves wanting to soar high like the birds.
I see all kinds of feelings trapped inside,
Wishing and wanting to get out.
When I look deep down in me,
I see the same feelings.
I feel like a wild animal wanting to be freed,
like a bear living in a tiny box.
I feel that if I don't watch out,
My feelings are going to erupt like a volcano.
I don't know what makes me feel this way,
Maybe it's my family, my friends.
Maybe it's me,
trying to be my own person.
I don't know,
don't know if I'll ever know.
All I know is I feel like an ocean,
the waves waiting to soar as high as the birds.

Sheri Gregory

Today

When ever troubles fill me with gloom,
I shudder and cry alone in my room,
but I don't want to cry:
I don't want to be sad.
These thoughts just confuse me
and make me more mad!
But before I give in and become more depressed,
I get up from bed, wash my face and get dressed,
and take a long hike in the outdoor wilderness.

Where all of Gods great work is at its best,
Where the birds sing their song,
in the fields and the trees
all around you are the sounds
of the squirrels and the bees.

This is the place that makes me feel,
Oh, so good
I'd stay here forever if I knew that I could.

Marlene Da Silva

Dreams Of Rough Kindness

When I am feeling low and sad and blue,
I sit alone and think of you.
And I can't hear your voice with my futile climbs,
and I look in the mirror and cry until nighttime,
Wanting to be the one who's full of dreams of you,
Wishing like someone would, like others do for clues,
Desiring your love and knowledge of your feeling for me,
I am contented least with my sadness to be-
Yet in my heart I defy sad contests,
Suddenly I think of you, and see the truth best,
Then to the bird that chirps your name at daybreak,
Like a sinner receives forgiveness for being pity's sake,
For remembering the love and bitterness of rough kindness,
That then I lull to sleep from your innermost senses.

Raymond J. Monhart

Passing Thoughts

It has been a bright and lovely autumn day
I sit in my garden, musing, absorbing all around
The sky, the breeze, the sinking sun and every subtle sound
All blend in a sort of interplay inside my mind.
I watch great puffs of cotton cloud
Slowly drift across the sky's expanse of crystal blue:
Bluer than spring; autumn's own singular hue.
I watch the changing shapes as I have from childhood on.
I think-nothing is as certain as is change.
I ask myself why should I think it strange. I change.

A monarch alights on a cluster of purple asters near the gate
It sways and bends slightly with the weight.
The afternoon sun paints leaves green-gold;
Tree-tops move in the wind. The air grows cold.
The clouds gather, darken; a few drops fall.
I must go in. Time has passed, and much else will surely pass.

More drops fall soundlessly in the grass.
I hurry; but I think I have spent an hour I will long remember.
I look back and feel a touch of sadness as I see
The heavens weeping for the passing of September.

Reba Gibson

As I...

As I cover my eyes, but not in shame,
I still see the one who was chosen to blame.
As I cover my mouth, no words shall I speak;
Holding so much in eventually becomes deep....
As I cover my ears, no disgrace will I hear,
As I run in the shadow of darkness then disappear.
I hold my nose, no scent of a smell,
As my brothers and sisters survive in a place of hell....
My hands I keep free as I stare at the color,
I know now, I was born a child of a
"Negro Mother"....

Lorraine Simons

Your Mountain My Mountain

You see the world as a mountain to climb,
I see the world from the mountain side

You have dreadful steps and adventurous
paths to overcome,
I have the surroundings wilderness and
trees to dream of

Your vision of the world is less confident,
but then again I haven't met the world yet.

Lana Rachele Moore

Happily Ever After

Where did you go? Looking in your eyes
I take what I cannot find there
and try to pretend I know you, like you pretend to be known
but no one ever said I was an actress...
So the game goes on
And we smile while we spit knives
and everyone says we are beautiful together
and why disillusion them
when we can pretend to be perfect?
Strange to think you made me laugh
strange to think I made you... happy
strange to think that we were us
fools who actually believed the world was round
when all along anyone could have sailed right off the edge...
but you would have caught me before it was too late
wouldn't you?
All that was once upon a time, though
when we lived in a world where fairytales were gospel
And I knew what I saw in your eyes
was not an academy award-winning performance

Kirsten B. Alford

Untitled

I talked to my father today,
I talked to my father on the telephone.
I talked to my father for the first time in a hundred million
thousand
years.

Well, let's not exaggerate too much.
But his voice came through like a silver bell
filled with love and care for me.
Now there can be no doubt.
Why did it takes so long for me to hear?

Perhaps my brother has never heard our Dad like this.
That is why he is a cowboy,
and a sailor,
and a ninja.
It is not easy to find crystalline facts,
So he wanders the bayous and the highways.

But sometimes jewels come from unexpected places.
Even from the telephone.

Peter Bokor

Nobody Believes Me

Nobody believes when
I tell the story,
I think I am not self-explanatory.
So I just go on about it everyday saying
"This is what I am going to say."
"I am going to make you notice me,
I'm gonna make you believe me Guaranteed!"

Pamela Johnson

"Lee"

I want to share my life with you,
I want to be part of all you do.
I want you to know how I feel,
And, please know, my feeling's real.
I want to be there by your side,
And I know I can stand there, tall with pride.

I want us to tell our hopes and fears,
And support each other through smiles and tears.

I want you to be forever mine,
As we love each other until the end of time.

Sharon Waltman

When I Think Of You, Arthur Ashe

When I think of you, Arthur Ashe,
I think of the great tennis player and man that you were
You on the tennis court, playing
because you were a winner, a survivor, a champion, and a legend.
I think of the style and elegance
which you possessed, and maybe something more
of character and the person each of us should be.
I think of balls whizzing by, people cheering,
the world standing in ovation.
And when I think of you, Arthur Ashe,
I think of AIDS and how we have to stop it,
I think about that blood transfusion
that caused you to get AIDS,
and wonder why?
I think of you, Arthur,
so calm, graceful, and eloquent.
I think of February 6, and wonder why
you had to die.

Narishia Singh

On Rainbow Ranch

As I look out my window
I think to myself, "my, what a beautiful day".
I whisper, "Thank-you", to God 'cause I know,
in my heart that He is who made it
that way.

When the wind blows you always know
by the leaves that are flying by,
and the trees are swaying back and fourth
as if they were waving good-bye.
I look up above and pray to our father
As I sip my hot cup of tea.
Thanking Him that in a world of turmoil
He makes beautiful mornings like these.

Kelli J. Polack

Letting Go

You came into my life,
I thought I had it all.
Then I saw the way that you looked at her,
And my dreams began to fall.

I'd call you every night,
Just to hear you say, "Hello".
Then I'd remember the way you touched her face,
And I knew that I had to let you go.

When I see you in the halls with her,
I keep thinking that it should still be me.
People keep asking me why I let you go,
And I knew that we weren't meant to be.

Now I finally think that I'm over you,
But the road to this point wasn't easy.
I can't believe that you chose her over me,
Because you said that you would never leave me.

Now every time that I go to sleep,
I see dreams of you and me together.
I just thought that I should let you know,
That I'll love you forever and ever.

Linda Jandrokovic

"While Walking Guard"

While walking guard one rainy night
I thought of you and things seemed bright
I thought of times when we had fun
And secretly knew that you were the one

And as I walked my lonely post
I thought of things which I liked most
Of Mom and Dad and friends back home
And places where I liked to roam

And as the rain poured steadily down
I heard a distant but familiar sound
The blowing of taps to my buddies at rest
And I felt proud, for they were the best

And when this war does finally end
And I am a civilian once again
I will think back times when I walked the most
As a rain soaked guard on some lonely post

Robert Liptak Sr.

"Today I Lost A Friend"

Today I lost a friend, we had a friendship,
I thought, would never end.
So suddenly you went away, to be with
the Lord, I pray.
Friends and family you left behind.
For them, I pray, the world will be kind.
We didn't get a chance to say good-bye.
But somehow, I hope your hear my cry.
Something will be missing in my heart.
Now that you are not a apart.
I pray your finding peace at lost, now
that your life is a thing of the past.
Yes! Today I lost another friend, and
it's going to take time for my heart to mend.
I pray to the Lord up above, that you
somehow feel all of my love.

Marilyn L. Gorman

God's Creative Hand

'Twas the year of nineteen-hundred & ninety-two
I took my diesel truck of blue.
I went to travel this great land,
I wanted to see it first hand.
I headed west to see the ocean
That was my first notion,
I went south, I went North,
I traveled back and forth.
I went from the East to the West
I saw some of the worst, & some of the best
I saw the mountains and seas
Checking out the rocks and trees.
This is a really great land
So lets be thankful for God's creative hand.

William Warrick

"Shame"

Why is it a shame for me to like someone
I try so hard for people to like me
why can't they see that I'm a person
that has feelings and need someone to
I'm not pretty,
I'm not a genius,
I'm not perfect either
all I'm trying to do is be ME!!
Instead of laughing, teasing, and hurting my feeling
Why don't you try to find out who I am
not who you want me to be!!!!

Tona Rae Meints

Blue Monday

Sometimes on Monday I feel so blue
I try to shake it but I don't know how to.
Where did my weekend go?
How come the weekdays go by so slow?

Feels like a dark cloud
Dangling over my head
It makes me want to crawl back into bed.
Yes, Monday is the one day that I truly dread.

I'm feeling an indigo blue
For those of you who don't know that hue,
Give me a minute and I'll try to explain it to you.
Dark blue like the sky at half past two.
Or your favorite blue jeans when they were brand new.

I attempted several times but, I can't alter my mood.
So I will just continue to brood.
My mind is roaming
I can't comprehend
Oh! When, Oh! When is this blue Monday going to end!!!

Kelli L. Woodard-Carter

Thanks Giving

I smell the herbs in the kitchen air
I turn around and stare!
I see a big brown thing on the counter
I hear mom say, it will be done in an hour.

I come to sit down to say the grace
And when I'm done, I look at every face.

I start to eat and then I say, thank you
God for this THANKS GIVING Day.

Valonda Green

Majesty

When my morning chores are done,
I turn to greet the rising sun.
Its golden rays fill all the East,
bursting forth love for man and beast.

I stand enthralled by what I see,
asking myself, "Can this be?".
Then its grandeur fades away,
bringing forth still another day.

Toward home I start, hope and joy fill my heart.
Ever thankful I shall be,
God gave me eyes to see,
all his wondrous Majesty.

William F. Kelly

"It Was Only Yesterday"

It was only yesterday, when you were small,
I used to hold you in my arms.
Now you're older and out of school!
Yes, it was only yesterday,
When I clothed you and fed you.
It was a joy watching you play.
I hope yesterday I was a good Mother,
So when yesterday passes and in the future
you'll be a good Father.
May yesterday have good memories
of how we played and did things together.
And the little talks that made things brighter.
Of course yesterday was hard and enduring.
The pains of growing up
and the joys of our love we gave yesterday.
Happy graduation my son.
It was only yesterday.

Sanda May Benlien

"Doll Of My Dreams Come True"

When I was a little girl, I never owned a doll
I vowed someday, I'd buy me one, the fairest of them all
With flaxen hair and rosy cheeks, and eyes of clearest blue
A walking doll, one that could talk and call me "mama", too
As I grew up my dream slipped away
It was almost forgotten, but came true one day
Now a little blue-eyed baby calls me "mama"
As she softly whispers "I Love You"
She's my doll to caress, my darling to dress
And tuck in bed when the day is through
Angels look down from above, guard this little girl I love
She's the doll of my dreams come true

Mary Tackett Beaver

Theater

All around me I hear the crowd roaring,
I walk out on stage and stand beside the piano,
I want to go back but I can't; it's too late now.

I sit on the hard oak piano bench,
So cool and smooth under my hot, sweaty body,
And I force my clammy fingers to play.

Suddenly I am swept into another world,
the beautiful world of music has entered my soul,
I am aware only of the music around me.

Unaware of the crowd held in suspense,
I continue to play my favorite song,
Surrounded by the precious music.

I concentrate on how it sounds and feels,
Almost automatically the keys come down,
Under my swiftly flowing fingers.

The music flows rapidly, pounding loudly in my head,
The beat continues louder, then softer,
Then it is over and I am standing beside the piano,
I no longer want to go back.

Laura Dettloff

Searching

Putting limitations within human bounds,
I was always searching, but never found.
Wanting acceptance and love from all,
Trying to catch myself when I fall.

Going through life without a clue,
Looking for someone to pull me through.
Kicking up dirt beneath my feet,
Running in circles that never meet.

Lack of direction from morning till night,
Never giving up without a fight.
Hoping not praying that all will be fine,
Not knowing what day, not knowing what time.

I knew someone was helping me through,
Guiding and telling me what to do.
I felt it within, but I did not know,
Who it was that was helping me so.

When I opened the bible, I opened the door,
The light shined down from ceiling to floor.
I suddenly saw who was there all along,
It was God in heaven rejoicing in song!

Larry J. Medved

"A Day I Will Never Forget!"

Early in the morning June twenty-six
I was in a terrible fix,
A day to remember, a blessed event
A baby girl from Heaven was sent.

A little later that same Morn
To a Gypsy mother, a son was born,
He had already four other brother
A girl this time was the wish of the Mother.

As the story goes, it has often been told
A gypsy's wish makes them very bold.
In a language I could not understand,
They talked and motioned with their hand.

Imagination and fright took hold of me,
So glad my baby was in the nursery.
Their stay was short, no harm was done,
They left that morn with their fifth Son.

Veloice Skinner

Untitled

I was born on the night of the Harvest Moon,
I was raised in The Fields of Gold.
Set loose within my boundaries,
My imagination's hand to hold.

I was Queen of My Castle,
I was the Light in His Eyes.
I was anything I wanted to be,
In a world where nothing dies.

Sitting by myself,
There was always someone with me.
Talking to no one,
With people as far as ones eye wants to see.

Those born on the night of The Harvest Moon,
Those raised in The Field of Gold,
Who were set loose within their boundaries,
Will always have memories to hold.

Shannon Sando

Sonnet For The Lost

I stand in the living, looming soul pit.
I watch as, before me, thousands of youths
Writhe and twist like people's spirits, all damned.

It is too crowded here for us to sit.
We stand and listen to so many truths
Screamed from main stage without musical plan.

Super heated power burns away flesh.
Society destroys so many souls.
The future citizens screw their own minds.

Pois'nous smoke is pulled through filters of mesh.
On bodies, alcohol will take its toll.
Their important message is lost in time.

They strive for permanent absence of lies,
But they do not hear their own bodies' cries.

Paul T. de Barros

Our Environment

A clean environment we all must strive
If we want to stay alive.
Let's think of ways to keep it clean
Including adults, children and teens.
We must be positive and think alike
So we can make this world a beautiful sight.

Tia Hansen

So Wounded

I wail tonight like a wounded coyote
I weep for my love who's gone
buried beneath the soil far, far, away from me, and yet so near
a strength I have I did not want, or relish now
The wound not so raw anymore
but so deep, it pulls me inside myself with such force
it rips apart my soul
the tears come not so often now
but sting my face - they will not stop

I grieve tonight
from inside out
and outside in

death—so final
I hurt everywhere
my love protected me from the pain of the world
we curled inside each other and shut out any threat of darkness
I face it alone now
now wailing can not be heard by anyone but me
so wounded

Sharon Reardon

Remorseful Repose

On a sunny Saturday after cleaning the yard,
I went to the dump for a load to discard;

While unloading the truck in a hurried manner,
My eyes were averted by a crimson banner;

As I walked towards this heap of vile debris,
A feeling of heartache swept over me;

Crumpled and torn in this unworthy grave,
Our symbol of freedom lay unable to wave;

The people around worked at a feverish pace,
Ignoring this symbol of beauty and grace;

How ignorant and callous some people can be,
To a country that gave them the right to be free;

I thought to myself what's happened to us,
Is this what the absence of conscious does;

What does one see when they look at our flag,
The millions who've died, or a red, white and blue rag;

I gathered the flag up and headed for home,
For a dignified end to the life it had shone.

Robert A. Sandoval

Like Me

I am stray and meaningless.
I wonder about our system of communication.
I hear the footsteps coming closer.
I see the insanity in the world of wars.
I want this pain to come to an end.
I am stray and meaningless.

I pretend the suffering doesn't hurt.
I feel the blood rushing to my head.
I touch the mount hung above.
I worry if I need another chance.
I cry to fade away.
I am stray and meaningless.

I understand the hurt people face.
I say that I will die for you, but will I?
I dream about a sword that lies next to me.
I try to understand the first time.
I hope to encounter a being of another kind.
I am stray and meaningless.

Kelly Saggio

In Memory Of Me

Hello there, you big old pine tree.
I wonder... do you remember me?
Back when Dad planted you, I was but three.
You were so small, you didn't even reach my knee.
Now years have gone and my how you've grown,
but we had some great times, didn't we?
I've climbed your limbs, scraped both my shins.
Remember... how I hid from my friends?
When I was ten, the ice made you bend.
Oh! You were a beauty to see.....
I was afraid they would cut you away, but
you were so strong, you proved them all wrong!
You still stand so proud, almost to the clouds.
To look up at thee, makes me, feel so very wee.
For you have certainly out-grown me!
I guess what I really mean to say —
very soon, will come my day, and all that I ask —
is when they put me away...
My final resting place will be,
at the base of my old pine tree!

Sue Ann Thompson

I Am

I am a playful and funny girl.
I wonder what it's like playing in the ocean.
I hear the fishes laughing at my jokes.
I see the mermaids swim beautifully.
I want to be there with them.
I am a playful and funny girl.

I pretend to be a mermaid in the pool.
I feel the water on my fin.
I touch the life of other beings.
I worry about the whales that die.
I cry when they do.
I am a playful and funny girl.

I understand it will never be that way.
I say it never hurts to dream.
I dream about hearing the waves under water.
I try to be the best I can be.
I hope that no more whales die.
I am a playful and funny girl.

Mandy R. Silcock

The Loneliest Of Times

As I watch my children grow
I wonder where did the time go
When they were little they needed me
But now they have more important places to be
While I sit here waiting for them to come home
I remember the times I left my mom all alone
Now I hear myself pleading with them to stay
Just hoping they would give me some of their time today
Before I know it they will be grown
With families of their very own
Then I will see my mom in me
Wishing one of my children I could see

Karen Jones

Untitled

Whispered voices of leaves joined
in chorus with wind sighs.
Dappled shadows dance with birds in flight,
Insistent calls of winged lovers
in heated anticipation.
Beckoned to quarters of drapery green
halls of white-lined birches and
delicate promises of blossoms on
transparent jade pillows.

Karen Abston

I Am

I am a fourteen year old girl who loves to dance.
I wonder why the sky is so blue and why we all are so different.
I hear a sound that is not there.
I see imaginary sights.
I want to become someone special.
I am a fourteen year old girl who loves to dance.

I pretend to be something I'm not.
I feel feelings that aren't there.
I touch things that I make up.
I worry about things that will make life for all worse.
I cry about the things in the world that are bad,
I pretend to be something I'm not.

I understand that the world is round.
I say things that aren't always true.
I dream about people who aren't there.
I try hard; but sometimes can't succeed.
I hope for great new beginnings and the world to be at peace.
I am a fourteen year old girl who loves to dance.

Kaila Klein

My Old Piano And Me

I was four years old. The piano was a toy. It was my entertainer,
I would sit down with legs dangling - too short to reach the pedals,
and I would plunk and plunk away, tickling the ivories,
trying to make a beautiful song. It sounded wonderful to me.
But that was not true music - it was nothing.

I was seven years old. The piano began to make sense.
It was not a toy - it was an instrument. The sound was not just
plunking, it was notes. The songs I played became familiar.
Mary had a little lamb was now played with ease.
But that was not true music - it was nothing.

I was ten years old. The piano was nice. It seemed a past time -
something to do. The sound was not a plunk nor a note, it was
now a beat in time, a rhythm to follow.
But that was not true music - it was nothing.

I am fifteen years old. The piano is a beautiful work of art.
It is my life, a friend - not just a past time. The sound is not a
plunk not a note, nor a beat in time, it is an expression of feelings,
a cry to be heard. Bach, Beethoven, and Mozart are now the
familiar sound.
This is true music, this is everything.

Lisa Baker

If I Could Write A Poem

If I could write a poem
I'd write it to you not them
I'd write of the flowers, the birds
I'd write such beautiful words

And in the poem I'd write to you
I'd write my heart to make sure it's true
I'd write of how sweet to me your lips are
I'd write about wanting you near not far

If I could write at all
I'd write large words not small
I'd write about the things you do
I'd write about the beauty in you

But that is only if I could write
If I could write of poem.

Virginia Francois Davo

Kiss The Hurt Away

When I was a little bitty child a growing up,
If I feel down and hurt myself, Mama'd pick me up,
Hold me on her knee, hug me tenderly and kiss the hurt away,
Saying, "That will make it better, Honey.
That will make it better, Babe."

Depression came; Daddy lost his job and things got bad,
I went to school in hand-me-downs 'cause that's all I had.
Daddy'd pick me up, hug me tenderly and kiss the hurt away,
Saying, "Things will get better, Honey.
Things will get better, Babe,"

I was born with love and pride,
Leaned on no one to survive,
Thankful just to be alive,
Believing that God would provide.

The years have passed and this old world has changed a lot,
It's not what you do or what you say - it's what you've got,
It's just push and shove, with no time for love
or to kiss the hurt away,
Saying, "That will make it better, Honey.
That will make it better, Babe."

LaVon Anderson

"How Far Is Far Enough?"

So green is the grass, as far as my eye can see,
If I move far enough, nothing will touch me.
I will live in my fine house surrounded by my worldly goods.
I will live happily and contented, just like I believe that I should.
I will sit on my big porch and hear the stillness as
the night passes by.
If I move far enough, I won't hear that hungry child cry.
I will raise my children, and keep them safely unto myself,
Never will they endure danger, or be faced with some violent death.
I will walk through my garden, and feel the morning dew
tickle my feet.
If I move far enough, I'll be free from the violence of the street.
But how far is far enough? Is there really a place?
How far must I move to escape the human race.
For as long as there are babies crying and young people dying.
Drug dealers dealing and law officers killing.
Families without bonds, living in homes where all hope is gone.
As long as these things shall continue to be, I know
in my heart that I am not completely free,
Because no matter how far I move, something will always touch me.

Pearlie Wallace

Answered Prayers

Although I did not know if prayer could somehow be the way,
If wishes, hopes and fervent pleas could brighten up her day.
I prayed and wished and hoped that answers would appear
To help my friend who so despaired return from there to here!

Those many days and many weeks were gray inside my mind
Continued hope and daily prayers and writings did remind
Of how the sunshine of the years would put the past behind.

Then slowly through the darkened clouds a ray of light appeared
To bring her back from darkness that hovered very near.

As many factors then combined the threads were slowly sewn
Affecting healing powers before which were unknown.
Constant prayer and meditation became my daily passion
I wondered how could God abandon that which he so finely fashioned.

Who knows exactly what divine or spiritual request
Was answered by these prayers and hopes
But no one will be pressed except to offer gratitude,
For all that was expressed.

D. E. Shanfeld

RECIPE FOR HEALING

CLING TO YOUR GOD WITHIN YOUR HEART!

If you are in trouble and know not what to do,
If you have a heavy heart that's far too much for you,
If you not find your path of life which you have to tread,
Cling to your GOD WITHIN YOUR HEART, and GOD WILL DO THE REST!

If fear comes along and blinding you with hate,
If you stumble back and forth NOT knowing what to make;
If your friend become your foe then bless him in despair,
Cling to your GOD WITHIN YOUR HEART as GOD for you doth care!

If you have spilled your loving cup and lost your precious friend,
If you have lost your dearest thing and feel you cannot mend,
It there's NO WAY to turn, be Silent and be Still,
For GOD WITHIN WILL FILL YOUR CUP AND LIFT YOUR HEART, GOD WILL!

Phirozie P. Nazir

Ode To Our Daughter Nikole; A New Life

A child is living proof that there's a God amongst us.
Ignore the doubters, for they do not understand divine purpose.
Creation is by design, heralded by an infant's cry.
A sweet sound that ushers in the melodic innocence of a lullaby.

The heavens filled with cherubs, the earth bowed to a lone dove.
For you were the answer to prayers, conceived out of love.
Embraced by Mom and Dad, we did not cradle scientific fact,
Rather a gift of life, from the passions of a Godly act.

In a galaxy of brilliant stars, you are the essence.
A predestined dream guided your deliverance.
Therefore sweet Nikole, celebrate life as testament,
To a miracle ordained by the highest form of sacrament.

William S. Lonardo

"My Babe"

You ask me babe if I love you so
I'll write a poem to let you know

My love for you is so great
That being apart is what I hate
My love for you is so strong
That our future together would never be wrong

My love for you is so dear
That I want nothing but to have you near

Stay with me my beautiful woman
and my love for you will never be ruined

A little reminder to let you know
'my babe', 'my babe' I love you so...

Sharon Caparino

Temper

When I have lost my temper, and I lost my reason too.
I'm never proud of anything, that angrily I do.
When I have talked in anger, and my cheeks are flaming red,
I always say something that I wish I hadn't said.
In anger I have never done a kindly deed or wise.
But many things for which I felt, I should apologize.
In looking back across my life, and all I've lost or made,
I don't recall a single time when fury ever paid.
So I struggle to be patient for I've reached a wiser age;
I do not want to do a thing or speak a word in rage.
I've learned by sad experience that when my temper flies,
I never do a worthy thing, a decent deed or wise.

Viola Mendicki

Author Un-Known

One of these days, when I'm grown-up and smart
I'll write beautiful poems and songs
I'll make the world notice - I'm here I'm alive
And I'll know I really belong.

That's how it began thru my childhood and teen's
the vision of fortune and fame
The thought ever with me. That one of these days
Though, none of these days ever came

So I worked to survive, with life's up's and downs.
At job's I frightfully hated and the dreams came
And went and got deeply submerged
In a now empty heart, while I waited.

So much for a name-maybe that's my false pride
Rejection is hard on the soul
It's a sad thing to fail, and watch time running out
And see your getting too old!

So you look for a spark of a candle within
Where once, a bright light had shown.
And you write, and you write,
But now carefully sign - everything - Author Unknown.

Pauli Knight

Untitled

As I sit in this empty home,
I'm lonely but I'm not alone.
No one else around here to see,
But the comforter dwell within me.
He reminds me of life and its strife,
As He reveals to me, the life of Christ.
How God sent from Heaven above His Son,
The Christ, full of Love
All though the night, and during the day,
Jesus will lead you, and show you the way.
When it's time for me to bid this world good-bye
I'll raise up from my knees,
And take my journey though the skies,
Jesus as I look up to thee,
Receive me in your arms and cradle me.
All the love ones, gone on before
I want to be there to meet them once more
Beside the river of life, that flow
I will give praise and glory to Jesus
For saving my Soul.

Marion Stewart

Above And Beyond

You can't hurt me unless I let you.
I'm past taking the scorching blame.
You can't bruise this heart anymore.
I'm above and beyond anything you can name.

The fault was mine it was said.
Being a child I took your blame.
Well no more I tell you now.
That child and I are not the same.

Too many people like you destroy the innocent.
My self-worth I have restored.
You won't ever hurt this heart again.
From now on your taunts will be ignored.

K. Lucille Woods

"As A New Life Begins"

Walking down the isle hand in hand,
I'm proud to be your husband and man.
And yes my darling, so am I,
Proud to be yours - to do or die.

As we walk through life's winding paths,
We'll explore together what we have.
Each day growing stronger deep inside,
We have begun in our new married life.

We'll walk together planting new seeds,
Stopping only to pull out old weeds.
Starting out fresh and shining like new,
Sharing always in the things that we do.

Hardships we will - come to know,
But almost always, they'll come and go.
Together we can conquer them all,
The good, the bad, the short or tall.

And later on in our older life,
I'll forever be your loving wife.
When rocking softly hand in hand,
I'll always be your loving man.

Vicki Bolduc

My Grandson And Me

Beautiful day, my grandson and me!
I'm sixty-six, he's almost three.

I danced today with my grandson,
Dancing, laughing and having fun.

He danced a circle, we clap, clap, clapped.
We danced a circle and laugh, laugh, laughed.

'Twas so much fun, we did it again.
We jumped, and hopped, and did some spins.

Anyone can dance a dance that's done,
But grandson dances are original ones.

We danced our best, 'twas harder for me,
I'm sixty-six, he's almost three.

He's taking his nap. I need one too!
To dream of things that grampas do,

When grandsons come and want to play,
And jump and dance, as we did today!

My prayer for him, for all girls and boys,
My prayer for them, to give them joys,

In equal amounts to the love they bring
When with their grampas they dance and sing.

Marne Meyer

Friends

When times are rough and seem so sad
I'm sorry things aren't great and life just seems real bad,
But keep a look for tomorrow when there may be joy again,
If you need someone to open a door, to give you a shoulder to cry on, or to make you laugh once more
You will always have me here for you,
No matter what you say or do
I love you, now, I always will,
So tomorrow if you need me still,
My hand, my shoulder, or my heart I will lend,
Isn't that what it means to be a bestfriend?

Michelle Ballard

They

Why do they have to question me and my existence? Why do they butt in?
Why, I can't help it anymore, I have to leave or change something.

But I can't leave or change it. How they see me. Life is life.
It is bad and good, in my case Bad.

They always limit me and what I need is not boundaries but freedom and room.
Room to grow. To live, to let me have a life but enjoy it too.

Why do they have to ruin everything that is Good and meaningful to me.
I did not ask to be born. Did not ask for this heavy burden on my shoulders.

All I need is to live like I want to. Not how they all want to see me. To know myself in a different light, time, and space.

Melanie Ferreira

Promises To A Child

Hence forth this world I shall one day depart
In a casket - my body they will cart
To a resting place not far away
Where others as myself do lay
Though we can no longer walk hand in hand
Nor play together in the sand
Though my lips can no longer touch your cheeks
nor play with you hide and seek
Though I can no longer protect you from your fears
Nor wipe away your little tears
I will be as near to you
As the sky is always blue
Therefore I have not deserted you
Just gone ahead as we all must do

Theresa E. Felder

Memories

A hand cranked victrola
In a room with a pot-bellied stove
Are memories of a childhood that last
Even though 6 decades have past.

We later listened to a radio,
Only two stations, though;
Then television became a need
Black and white, of course, yes indeed.

These inventions proliferate!
And now the computer comes along to complicate.
We go to school to learn and know
How to make the information flow.

Being old in a modern world
Ain't all that mean
But the thing that drives me nuts
Is the telephone answering matching!!

"If you want your bank balance, press 1"
"If you want current interest rates, press 2"
"If you want safety deposit box info, press 3"
"If you want to talk to a real person, press 4"

Lewis A. Ketring

Betty Never Had A Poem

No birthday bash or shopping spree on me
In February. Candy hearts are out
This year as there is something different we
Should air before you start to stomp and pout.
Reaching sixty-five, still in overdrive,
With children raised who stay in touch and care,
That's what makes you thrive, glad to be alive.
So enjoy your fair entitlement share.
Well-trained, underpaid, self-sacrifice now
Creates new causes fraught with fun and you.
On this day let these lines, though few, allow
A special valentine of words quite true.
Instead of birthday cake, take this sonnet
As our love compete with frosting on it.

Mahlon S. Hunt

Racism

As I sit and think as the word sinks
in my head
Racism
How people can choose black over blue
or blue over red
Racism
And how people can choose white
over black
Racism
But it's not just a color issue
it's also a people issue
Racism
Blacks, whites, latinos, etc are
all part of this disease that could
be and should be stopped.
Racism

Raphaela Hodges

My Memories

The river carves its memories
In the banks along the way
Then the wind and rain they come along and
To take it all away.

The shifting desert sand dunes
The white caps on the sea
We cannot capture in our minds
They're gone so fleetingly.

But all my memories are etched
Forever in my mind
And they'll remain there always
For only me to find.

It makes me stop and wonder
Why my memories linger on
No matter whether good or bad
They're never really gone.

Some memories fade as time goes by
Like tides gone out to sea
But none are ever gone for good
They'll soon come back to me.

Richard C. Poff

We Got The Gospel

voices shouting and wailing; choir robes swinging and sailing
in the Baptist...Holiness...Sanctified...Pentecostal...Methodist
Churches and storefront meeting places.
Crying, laughing and smiling faces. We got the gospel!

The sermon..the fervent prayer, stirring us, moving us, taking us
"There!" the scripture, the naked truth, the joyous song.
Giving praises to the Lord...all night...all night long. Patting a
foot in response to the rhythm..Let us pray..Let us pray...the
Reverend hums. We go the gospel!

Preacher, Soloist, Piano and Organ contributing to the Jesus
beat...Glory Hallelujah! Let's get on our feet. Glorious singers
and ardent shouters; emotional responses...amen...amen...Amen!
Praise the Lord...Yes, Lord, Yes, Lord! We got the gospel!

Drums and Horns, Guitars and Tambourines. Lord, You sho' is felt
but not seen! Emotional fervor...talkin' in
tongues...handclappin'...
sweatin' and prayin'...Makin' a joyful noise unto the Lord.
We got the gospel! Gabriel...Gabriel! Blow your horn. Voices
shoutin' and wailin', choir robes swingin' and sailin'...Renewed
Inspiration...Divination...Amens...Praise the Lord...We Got the
Gospel! We Under God's Spell! PASS THE PLATE!

Seirgaster Spells

"OneDay"

And there was those gypsies that I met yesterday
In the big green grass field with their instruments lying
Though it was hard to find my way
It was sure worth the trying

The first was a show in all sitting alone
Upon his guitar strumming show
On this day of tremendous glow
No one else could have known

There I sat by that gypsy and we sang for a while
Singing and laughing and wondering why this isn't real life

And so it was known the gypsies won and I flew away
Wondering when we would meet again
So I could sing with the gypsies' caravan

Mark Johnson

Make Believe

The richness of a child's laughter
In the golden summer sun,
Is only surpassed by the tyke's endeavor
To show "making believe" is such fun!

A box and a tin can become a castle
On the beautiful river Rhine.
A bit of paper and ribbon from the mantle
Become an expensive, inexpensive Valentine.

The little white pearl-like rock,
Found beneath the garden wall,
Is carefully washed, painted and buffed,
To be presented as a bejeweled ball.

Weeds with tops of white, purple and gold,
Are lovingly offered in a little dirty fist.
Envisioned as beautiful orchids, in numbers untold,
Are placed then, in a priceless crystal dish.

Child fantasy makes the gift that is given,
A most precious and irreplaceable one.
As it is given honestly, with love unmeasurable,
By that dear little, your little one!

Martha E. Robinson

You

Since I can remember, I have wished for someone like you...
In the shadows of my life... I have felt your presence
I have been told that the "knight in shining armor" is just a fairy tale story
When I met you, I realized you were the one I had waited for all my life
My wish and story became a reality
Now that you are here... we must part...
Reasons that add up to the answer of why... yet my heart cries out... no
Though I am sad... I am so grateful that you crossed my path in this life
Chasing the clouds of loneliness away...
to bring in the rays of sunshine
lighting my way in a world that was dark till you
When trust made no sense...
I looked in your eyes and found the reason to trust
finding joy through my tears because of you...
Though we go our separate ways...
embedded in my spirit will be the love, joy and life... from you
I will remember we parted because of love.

Mona Vidales

Natural Selection

Though I know I am not included
in the tender term "People of Color,"
neither am I transparent.
I feel for the controversy
of Crayola "flesh", but find
my face most matching "pink."
Why do we find attraction
for what we are most not?
Dark finds in light an appealing affection,
and light to dark attracts,
while some of similar hue
shine in their self-selection.
If ethnicity could prove to improve,
I'd ask for a more noticeable nose,
while those with what I want
might wish to be me.

Kent Wells

Rejected

It was a cold gray night,
In the tiny, little town, as two people of middle age
Hurriedly scurried around

From Inn to inn, they knocked, they inquired.
But nowhere could they find rest,
For their bodies which were tired.

The first keeper said,
"I'm sorry no room.
But you better find shelter,
It's gonna be cold real soon."

They kept on going
With results still the same.
And all the while their donkey
Was becoming quite lame.

Finally the last one said,
"I have a cave out back where you can sleep
There's nothing out there
But some cows and some sheep.

And in this humble place, a place quite neglected.
A savior was born, a savior rejected

Ted F. Mendoza, Jr.

The Soul And The Sea

How the sea renews the body, mind and soul.
In the vastness of this spectacular view
We are reminded of the eternal width
Depth and breadth of life,
There are no beginnings, no endings, no boundaries
Only the eternal ebb and flow that no human can control.
Many have tried and many more will try until the end of time.
Men rise up and seek control
Control over life, control over lands and dominions
Even control over the heavens and earth.
Men seek control through acquisitions, aggression and anger.
They seek control through baseness, belittlement and bribery
Through chastisement, confrontation and criticism
Through denial, delegation and despotism.
The list goes from A to Z on ways men have tried to control.
But the human spirit is much like the sea..
The more one tries to control it
The more it seeks to be free...

Nina Spearman Reese

The Writer's Gift

I've caught them now!
In this very moment,
the Essential Emotions to reproduce.

My r i s i n g heroes,
They've just appeared!
Their souls longing to let loose.
Wait,

I feel a
moral thought
making its way...

ALL of these things I must rush to convey!
These thoughts can't be predicted, they flee
asquicklyastheycome.

Yet, I know if I don't record them
they'd be shared with no one.

For if we grasp a writer's Message,
Hear the Voice
Feel the Tone

None of us would ever
have to be alone.

Marisa R. Santoro

Days Gift

TODAY, this moment,
Is called the PRESENT
Because it is a GIFT
Remember when you were a child
And that brightly wrapped present demanded.
YELLED for your attention
You shook it turned it
Smelled it...
Expectantly, curiously
Waiting anxiously to rip open the wrappings
To see what was inside

TODAY is the PRESENT
Unwrap it
RIP the wrappings off
JUMP into it
Eagerly, curiously
Revel in each breath
Thank the GIVER
For today is your GIFT

Rose Anna Hines

Unformed Tears

(For My Mother)
White sheets surround her body
in this white room
while wise men and women
walk the halls in their white coats and uniforms.

Her face deep with concern,
she rests, twitching and tapping
her foot to an unknown rhythm,
content, or nervous.

She adjusts, struggles.
I offer my aid
but "it just hurts."
There is no comfortable place.

We sit, talk, stare.
Strong. Emotionless.
O to know her thoughts,
connect with her soul.

Cancerous fears realized
her strength fights
the forming tears
Truth lies in her unformed tears.

Steven Schueler

After The Storm

I step out the door,
inhale the air deeply,
and I smile,
my face brightens,
and my eyes take on a dreamy quality
as I glance around me and allow my
eyes to take in the sights,
the damp sidewalks,
the rain glistening on the bright green grass,
I love the air,
after a long, sweet rain,
so crisp, so clean,
I love to breathe it in,
a rainbow starts to form,
the colors bright against the dark sky,
the only thing better than being out
in the storm,
is being out,
after the storm

Laura Burcham

Dedicated To Me

Yes I'm worth it, this I know
Inside me there is a thin soul
It's dying to come out and to see the world
But then there is food and I get discouraged
I want to exercise and feel energy rise within
But then there is TV and there I sit
I'm only 28, almost 29
I want to live, I don't want to die
I need positive reinforcement and feel it within
But then I get up and it's gone again
I look in the mirror and think, oh not so bad
But then I turn sideways and then I get mad
Food covers almost every waking thought
How please tell me, do I get out of this whirlwind knot
I know what to do deep down inside
I have to eat less and to exercise
It sounds so simple and easy to do
But try being an addict to food
This is not an excuse, but a cry from within
I want to be **healthy** and I want to be **thin**!

Karen Stypa

"The Love Of A Friend"

When I look at you I do not see the person seen by all.
Instead I see a small child afraid to fall.
Holding on to the one characteristic which separates him from
the rest, as slowly emerges into the next, to make him seem less.
By doing so he has temporarily cushioned his fall.
But nothing truly protects the heart when love calls.
I myself have heard the cry.
and ran to the child before he could die.
I approached the child with open arms
and allowed my love to heal the pain.
I gave him my hand for his support and soon became his cane.
I taught him love.
I taught him trust.
I allowed him to be all he can.
I gave him the chance to believe again
and become once more the man.
All this was done with no repay.
No owing in the end.
All except one special gift.
The love of a friend.

Katherine Maria Perino

Fading Love

Our love is fading away, like the night
into day. Please don't leave don't ever go,
don't you know I love you so?
The laughs we've shared, the pain we
bore, the fun we've had, times
good or bad. Sweet kisses in the
wind, does it all have to end?
Oh what shall I do, I only want you.
In the still of the night
I cry, I find myself asking why.
The questions in my mind, are the
answers there to find? The pain
that fills my heart, to think we
had to part. Memories shattered
like bits of glass, do you think this
feeling will ever pass. To feel that
you came from heaven above, and
now to think of our fading love.

Trina Bowman

The Firefighter

From a soft cozy bed with warmth aglow
Into the dark, cold night and the blowing snow

We make it to the station with utmost haste
For there's not one precious moment to waste

We start our motors and don our gear
For the thought at the fire is "Why aren't they here?"

We arrive at the scene with a nagging fear,
And give a silent prayer to God for no life lost here.

And when the danger's over, and the fire is out
The feeling inside makes you want to shout.

Then a warm handshake and misty eye, indeed
That is all the thanks we will ever need.

We don't do this job for money or fame,
And we sure don't do it to enhance our name,

It's our community, too, and we love it so
Now that's the force that makes us go.

So support your department with 911 on the doors
For their very next fire could indeed be <u>yours</u>!

Vern Marlow

Untitled

May the flowers fade
Into the darkness of reality
Only to bloom again in the
Light of fantasy,
And when they bloom
May they show only their true colors
As an illusion,
So that only those who look may find them
Not as a flower, but as an example of
LOVE.

Tiffany A. Southern

The Flight Of Song

When my spirits sink low,
Into the painful depths of depression,
I reach for the sweet balm
That is sure to soften the blow.
Rather than wallow in a pool of self-pity,
I soar on high with a song of joy.
A slow, gentle ballad or a fast, happy refrain,
Either way, singing brings the endorphins that remove the pain.
The emotional release is flight in music;
The eagle has burst the bonds of his captivity,
He has paid his dues,
Like the singer who ascends into the blues.
May the flight be long, and never part,
From the joy of song that dwells in my heart.

Mark Stuart Ellison

Spirits

His spirit will find it way
into the spirit world, the wind
will blow the spirit above the earth.
The earth is full of beauty.

The star sings with the light.
The birds are the fire. The light is
a voice from above the mountain.

God will look upon all the children from above.
Our hearts are full of piece throughout the soul.

Let us work together when dawn comes,
let it be a peaceful time for all of us.
Let's not think of our troubles, think of the good
times in your life.

The sun is red as a nice rose, like
blushing bright as ever. I found my spirits while
looking at the mountain, looking peacefully at the
blue sky, I feel the gentle breeze, in my soul.

Valentina Rabbitt

You With The Charm

A rainbow aura from you
Is a scenery of a little pond
A fairy lotus swims by
In crystals water at dawn—
Whose ballet's spread is chanting;
My spirit floats to fly.

As our mirror mind keeps in tune,
The man made time passes by.

When you are feeble of flowery charms
Do remember, you shield me from harm.
You're in my world through the fights you fought;
Now, hand me a flower
That says, forget-you-not.

Kady Krouch

Spring Is So Special

The beauty of God's earth,
Is fairest in the spring,
The flowers bloom, the trees turn green,
Hear the birds chatter and sing.

There are patches of green and blossoms of white,
Spring is such a wondrous sight,
Fluffy white clouds in the skies above.
A world filled with beauty, a heart filled with love.

Spring is truly the season, of renewal and rebirth,
When winter time is past and gone,
And all is new upon God's earth.

The beautiful days of spring are here,
A season so precious, each hour is dear,
Spring is so special, it makes my heart sing,
Yes, now it's the season of beautiful spring.

Sylvia M. Duris

Diamonds In The Dirt

It appears that everyday a new trial is born.
Is God testing the spirit of the people
  or is the soul of the person blackening?
Life, so easily snuffed, is a precious gift,
  a jewel muddied by the feet of man.
Often a body lives in fear and insecurities
  ruining his little time on earth with superficial worries.
Take your Life, mind, heart, and soul,
  and live and rise and fly to soar through the sky!
Fear not, for fearing is fear itself,
  and courage is living in spite of fear,
And happiness is conquering the fear in order to live.
Take hold,
  feel,
    live, love,
      and learn.

Stacy Slaten

"What Is Love?"

Is love a look between a mother and her baby?
Is love a touch of passion that sparks two lovers flames?
Is love the scent of fresh cut flowers, on a misty springtime morn?
Is love the sound of vows exchanged, when one takes one for life?

Or is love something more than this?
Something we don't know
Love can make us feel emotions
That are not too hard to show
Oh, love is present
All around
I tell you it is here
For love is something in your heart
You share with those that you hold dear

There really isn't one right answer
To the question that's at hand
For love means something different
To every woman, child and man

Michael Thomas Tiedemann

Untitled

His lips delivered a hint of a smile,
Jilted promises upon a lying tongue.
Eyes dancing, cunning and guile;
Neck stretched, head high-held, hung.

His fingers curling like twisted snakes
With destruction in the palm of his hands.
His nails extending out like stakes,
Nothing with a heart can understand.

Yuo-Fong Chang

Anticipation

Like a moth drawn to a flame
Is my desire to see him again.
Five decades, a lifetime, have elapsed
Since I last saw his youthful form;
Yet, now I long to hear the voice
and touch the hand
Of one, whose once familiar countenance,
I probably wouldn't recognize.

How devastating to greet a stranger,
one once loved,
Whose former self is just as lost
As other comrades long since gone;
But he still lives and breathes,
And memory draws me to him
Who might look on me with an indifferent eye,
And I would rue the moment 'til I die.

Sylvia K. Dreyfus

The Very Young And The Very Old

The very young and the very old, know the truth many times told,
Is not heard nor understood, by me, by you, they wish we could
Listen, look and really believe; they cry for help,
They beseech in need we smile, we tolerate, pay no heed,
The very young, what do they know? we teach, we judge, we crow,
Faded mind — slow — left behind
And so the very young and the very old,
Join hands and take time, to hear a bird, to see a flower,
Each in the other, feel magic in their hour,
In our neglect, they cling to each other, keep hope bright,
Find delight, in lending courage for tomorrow.
Our blindness, they will not borrow.
Hurry! Catch the door before it closes, on childhood,
And what it imposes, the aged too, have much to give,
Listen-watch-while they still live! Rip off your veneer,
Stop! Deplore! Get down to the real core, wonder offers one
Wisdom-holds forth the other, add their views to your knowledge.
A many-sided prism life holds, balance, true balance we gain,
When we really look at each other,
And realize each has their own domain.

A. J. Higgins

The City Engulfed In The Sea

Beneath the world's low coastline regions
Is the deep, blue, silent renaissance row....
A hidden space of mirror and magical legions
Showing calm crescents coaxing Merlin's grass to grow!
Now coral-gabled mansions with cockle shelled gleams
Influenced surely by King Neptune's dominion....
T'was instances of starfish replete in streams
Within ships; and yesteryear's' bones are in pinion
On this crystal floor guarding sunken treasure:
Myriads of diamonds, rubies, pearls and gold
Surely the aquatic pleasure-seeker's vast measure
Yet, he grabbed neither of them nor gave away nor sold;
To be relinquished to solace, leaving this city behind
Joining powers of extension.
merchants of the mind.

R. K. Bittle

Only Yesterday

It seems like it was only yesterday when you held me in your arms.
It seems like it was only yesterday when I felt your tender touch.
Your arms around me, made me so secure and afraid of nothing but of losing you.
It seems like only yesterday when I had no doubts of our love.
It seems like only yesterday when I knew I was yours and you were mine, sharing one love, one heart.
It seems like only yesterday when you were all I lived for... but yesterday is now gone.

Kenia DeLos Santos

"Train"

The purpose of my whistle.
Is to keep you alive
If you get caught on my tracks you may even die.
I am built for power and some speed to.
I have schedules to meet and a job to do.
Don't estimate me at the crossings.
I may be traveling faster than you.
I travel on my tracks by night and day.
Please please stay out my way.
For my hours may be different night or day.
For I have no conscious.
I am just a train.

Vernie Almus Glidewell

"Love, Hate, Fear"

Love, hate, fear, it's all part of life. You may take or handle it in different ways. I know I do. Why is it so wrong to be different? You can get hurt by being different.

A tear is nearly a drop of sadness. Never a happy one to someone who doesn't have anyone to look up to. Why is it so hard? Nobody knows, but I do. Too much hate, too many tears. How can we love, when love is not out there.

They don't understand how not being "in", can kill you. They have never been there, when someone gets murdered.

How did this happen? A seventeen year old boy gets shot. Not because he was committing a crime, but because he was in the wrong place at the wrong time.

What should a child know about death? You're probably thinking now, "it's a shame they even have to know about it all." Well, it is a shame that as a teenager, I can't even walk down a street, without some fear of something happening.

A baby was born today. A life that wants to love, that wants to accept all, everyone, and everything around it. It's a life that won't judge by skin, but by personality.

We can make a difference, just love and not hate.

Kristin Eder

Evil

Evil is not a fire as we were taught,
It is a well of cold, hard and distraught.
Though we fight it and break it down,
It builds stronger with an everlasting frown.
And as we look down to the depths of hell,
We wonder if we can ever drain this well.
Where time is dead and also eternal,
and the devil is the malicious, silent colonel,
that commands who shall brutally die,
and who will suffer in pain and cry,
and eventually fall into his black sea,
where everyone cries, even you and me,
and someday we'll hit the well's hard base,
and be forced to see the devil's face.

Tanya J. Evans

Untitled

When I look into your eyes, I see a distant light.
I'm not going to let you do this without a fight.
How could you ever consider something so cruel?
The beginning of a new life should be your tool.
To end such a beautiful creation is simply insane.
How could you ever want to play that game?

I never knew you to do such an evil thing.
When we were younger, we would always cling.
My feeling on this did not mean anything.
Now you've crossed the road and the light is dimming,
You've destroyed the life that was just beginning.

Kimberly Palasik

Inter Self

Sitting on my bike waiting to die,
It is dark as I cry, the tears hit the ground as my soul runs away,
The wind and the coldness take away a heart,
My nose is stuffed I need to take a breath,
My eyes are watery I can not see they can not see I ask the
skies why me,
Then I ask them to stop and look for I am the only soul that loves,
And now it is time for me to say good-bye to eternity,
Going to see the light of the moon as I die,
I might go to a far-side were life is great and I can't die,
The sun crush the earth with the sky,
Are will it end like suicide,
One small way to die on a one-way road to the sky,
Cause I am a human a mortal soul, take my mind and my unborn soul,
Take me to a place were it all begins, my breath into the wind,
My eyes into the sun, my mind into the moon,
My hearing into the heaven above, my body into the earth,
My soul into space, my hair into the trees,
My blood and semen into the water,
That is when I become a GOD and find my peace.

Sean Gipti

Spring

After the cold and darkness,
it is good to sense the light,
to visualize the precious new beginning,
as souls marching to heavens gate.
However, momentary anew,
vibrant and potent,
seen only without despair,
colors without prejudice or hate.
Only to wither with the heat of humanity,
this passion of spirit,
returns, to the mundane.

Paul Cornell

A World Full Of Dirt

The world is full of dirt. Can you see it?
It is on the faces in the street.
It is on the tables of Congress.
The junkie pushes dirt through his veins.
It resides in the hearts of world leaders.
I want to be a scrubwoman for life.
I want to put the colors back into the crayon box.
I want to put the handicaps back into golf.
The world is full of dirt.
Homeless people live in it.
Reporters crave it.
Bigots manufacture it.
Wherever I go, I shall bring my bucket and sponge.
After all is said and done, I hope my hands are clean.

Mary Cahoj

Imagine

Imagine a daisy sprinkled in morning dew;
its fallen petals saying I love you.
Imagine sunlight glistening on a window pane;
forming constant beadlets from the warm rain.
Imagine the soft breeze making it's way through a field of wheat;
and the rustle of sound made by bare feet.
Imagine your reflection in a crystal clear pool;
the splendor of blue eyes; a reminder of jewels.
Imagine a child running barefoot through the sand;
searching aimlessly for his mother's hand.
Imagine, if you can, a love so brand new.
Imagine, my dear, my love for you.

Lynette Wensing

"It"

It has left me many memories-all good.
It is something I wouldn't have missed-if it never started.
But "It" did.

It has taught me a new way to look at life-openly.
It has given me greater hope-for the future.
But "It" left.

It can't stay in one spot-to accomplish the task.
It had to move on-to show that growth is good.
But "It" hurt.

It didn't leave me empty-I feel fulfilled.
It may decide to appear again-I will be there.
For "It" remains in me.

It has been two years-since I've felt the excitement.
It appeared softly, gently-then grew intense.
And I welcomed "It".

It started with small sparks-that became a flame.
It offered no excuses, no lies-as I bathed in its warmth.
And I accepted "It".

It gave out a long, even sigh-as it covered me.
It held me in a trance-as it offered me passion.
And I loved "It".

It will never leave-the feeling is too strong.
It will simply appear-whenever needed.
And I need "It".

Susan M. Hendrickson

The Faces Of Love

Love is a smile on his face when I walk through the door;
it is the touch of his hand on mine.
On a cold day in winter, it is his arms that wrap around
me to share the warmth from his body.
Love is the happiness we give to each other and it is the
joy we receive back.
Love that is real can be seen, touched, and above all, felt.
Pain and hurt from the past make him unsure whether to say
the words but his eyes and his heart reveal their well kept secret.
The faces of love are many—yet—they are the same; tender
and wonderful feelings that are only waiting to be discovered.

Nancy Moss

Lapse In Time

To many of us, time is a curious thing;
It measures our lives while Life it also brings;
It forever escapes from our very grasps;
Yet it can linger long and wide in a lapse;
A Lapse in Time can have real significance
For one, between two, or among many, for instance;
It marks a time for people, places, and things,
And the relationships that these three bring;
Within that time, friendships bloom and events sprout
From the seeds of circumstance without a doubt;
As events pass, Time does, too,
But friendships last even if only a few,
For that period of time also acts as a bond
To hold together the memories that are so fond;
It doesn't matter the length of this time
As long as these memories are easy to find
And the friendship that has grown will continue to flourish
With the passing of more time, from which it will nourish;
Time can make the friendship strong and last
Even after that period of time has passed...

Sharon Ahat McGee

"No Strength"

I have no strength...not since his last breath
It slowly withered away along with him
I feel like collapsing, I have no strength to hold myself up
Tears fall down my cheeks to my chin
I have no strength to hold them back
I had a lot of strength in the beginning
But at the end it died along with him
I lost a bit of my strength with every passing day
He was my strength, but now he's gone, so now I have none
I fear soon I won't be able to cope
My body will become numb, enabling me to move
Without strength I'll become a jellyfish
Only able to move by the ocean's waves
My strength faded away with every second
He was my strength, without him my strength fades
I have no strength now
Will I ever get it back?
I haven't the strength to even hope for that

Mary-Anne Bowen

Cousin Louisa

Louisa, my dear
It was so good to hear
From my childhood friend,
A letter she did send,
She wrote a cute poem on how she did feel
I told her, we all for get, what's the big deal?
Write yourself a note to remember
That Santa comes again in December
A gift of love, I'm sure you will get
Or old pussyfoot will lose her one bet.

Memories of squam lake come to mind
Walks down schoolhouse road were one of a kind
Catching fire-flies in a jar
Beats watching T.V. by far,
Burying little dead birds in a box
Or looking out to the field and see a red fox,
Jumping from the rafters into the hay
Always thinking we'd come again, the next day

Priscilla Sadler

Silence

Silence will never be the answer
It will always be the problem
Silence can never help you
It can always hurt you
Silence can kill
And it did.
If you have problems and need to talk to someone, do;
don't take the easy way out, because it's actually
hard on everyone else. Suicide is not a game, it's very real.
Just ask Kurt.
Kurt Cobain 1967-1994

Laura Schweigman

To Emily

Upon rising and feeling low
In the mornings we do the puzzles
Afternoons we watch O.J.'s troubles
Evenings are spent with TV's "Come what mays"
But never missing the mystery plays
No need to leave wealthy
As long as we're both healthy
Lets continue to live this day here
In this seniors rare atmosphere
Where the air is so free and clear
And I'll always love you my dear.

William D. Dashe

The Compassion

How can I compete with something I can't beat?
It's a liquid gold that entices your soul.
It's your answer to the hurt and misdoings
It feeds you liquid strengths
It's your answer to a rainy day
It's there when you play
It's there 24/7
It's there today
Was there yesterday
And you'll grasp out for it tomorrow
The tears I cry are transparent
It's the color of fools gold that you grasp for.
The empty excuses
The long justifications
They all fit in one small bottle or glass
"I'm sorry" said so often that means have no more.
Broken promises, shattered dreams
Falling tears, eternal fears
How can I compete with something I can't beat?
To all those fighters, never give up hope.

Kimberly Griffith

"Tears Of Death"

I hear a cry, a moan, out yonder
It's a plea of a soul that it's cold out yonder
I'll be there, I do care, I shout with thunder,
But he died as I wait and despair in slumber.

I hear rumbles, and shoving out yonder
It's the fight by the weak to be free out yonder
I'll be there, I do care, I shout with thunder,
But they died in despair as I look and wonder.

I hear a voice like my sons' out yonder
It's a call for his dad to be here out yonder
I'll be there, I do care, I shout with thunder.
But he is gone, never to be seen as I ponder.

I hear a voice from whence I know not where
'Tis the voice of a child from out there yonder,
A voice of pain, of grief of want
That chills my soul and beats my ears
Dear Lord above why do men suffer
From greed that chokes and blinds us ever.

Samuel Bowlay-Williams

"The Vine Of Love"

I can't imagine my life without you:
it's all that you are, and all that you do.
we're like two vines;
entangled around a tree
I can't imagine you without me.

Our time together is cherished forever.
Forget about you; how could I ever?
loving you is like, a warm summer breeze.
You holding me, kissing me, loving with ease.

The passion we share, makes me drunker than wine;
come tangle around me, my loving vine.
As long as I live, that vine will remain:
to tangle around you whenever I can

Your sweet, pure love, is surely the best
that's why I've forgotten all the rest:
to my grave, I will carry, this
tough, uncut vine
and remember that your love
will always be mine.

Rhonda B. Stone

The American Heritage

The bald eagle, big and strong, nests high upon lofty clefts.
Its magnanimous wings spread out and sours throughout the skies.

With watchful eyes and keen insight it dominates the skies.
With firm authority and dignity it governs those in sight.

Esprit of the bald eagle, an emblem of our American Heritage,
Directs and shields her in her beliefs and binds all nations on
land and sea.

Symbolism represents in her flag — the red, white and blue — her
Vigilance,
Perseverance and Justice; Purity and Innocence; and Hardness
and Valor.

These signify the strength and greatness of america
The Liberty Enlightening World stands high on broken chains -
unbound!
She extends her torch up high so men may see the light.

And in our coins it is inscribed, "In God We Trust,"
It bears our faith in God to restore and regain our resources,

And to live in peace and harmony.

M. G. Carraseo

"Hi, God"

Hi, God
It's me - I mean Maria -
Daughter of Sue, and aunt of Lucia
And adopted aunt of little Kyle
Who's just so sweet he makes everyone smile.
Anyway, how are things up there?
Down here they are, well, good to fair.
Thanks for giving me breath to be alive
And, oh, another one of my poems
Will be published in the Spring of '95.
I think it was a sign from you
That you have faith, and believe in me, too.
Watch over and protect all those who are in my heart
And will always be a special part of me.
And guide me in all that I do
For all that is good and loving comes from You.
So help me, God, through another day
Let me always walk in Your Light, in Your Way.

Maria Facchini

My Weeping Willow Tree

Why are you so low?
"It's raining, and I weep getting all wet,
That can make me so upset."

You are my tree, weeping willow.
Weeping in the rain.
Just to relieve, of such sorrow
And plaguing pain.

My weeping willow, sees the rainbow.
Green, Pink, Blue, Red, and Yellow.
And the breeeeeezes.
Blows sof—tly.

It begin to smile.
Eyes so wide and mild.
With a sign of reli——ef.
"Beautiful" (sighing). It said to me,
"I like you, `and I like you too." '

Come shower and the breezing.
Through the clouds, the sun is peeping.

And all at the same time,
Just bring joy to my mind.

William C. Walker Jr.

God's Blood

God's blood is wonderful
It's so precious to me
Jesus shed His blood to cover our sins
When He was nailed to the tree.

Jesus is so wonderful
He is the blood of Calvary's Lamb
He will call and I will answer
Send me, send me, here I am.

Jesus is wonderful
He is my blessed Lord
Many new promises I will find
As I keep reading and trusting His word.

Jesus is my wonderful Savior
He is God's only Son
As I trust in thee
He gives me answers one by one.

Mary E. Riggle

Jasmine

Joy or happiness, it's one of the same,
it's taken to long, I can't play this game.
Aspirations of people my heart is a mist
the time has wound down this game is dismissed
Some people might say I'm a Fool to have tried.
but I did cause I cared, there was no way to hide
My feelings were surfaced, the heart makes no mistakes
I'd climb the highest mountain and do whatever it takes.
I wouldn't feel your a prize to be won,
yet a goodness on a pedestal of time.
No one can compare to your own sense of style,
your beauty and intelligence if Refine.
Emotion is the least of my trouble cause the words
come to me with ease; I can honestly sat there
is "on one" in the world like thee, enchanting
Jasmine Ortiz!

Micheal Boyd

A New Born Baby Girl

A new born baby child is so very sweet,
it's the beginning of a brand new life.
The love for a child that comes from within,
which is shared between a man and his wife.

Congratulations to the both of you,
on your brand new baby girl.
The bundle of joy that you have created,
in this great and wonderful world.

I hope you both are very happy,
with your new God created gift.
When they look up at you, and they give you a grin,
it will give your heart a lift.

I guarantee you'll feel their love,
when they look at you and smile.
It's a feeling that lasts within your heart,
for a very wonderful long while.

I guess what I want to say here,
is that I hope your lives are great.
With your brand new baby girl,
that with your love you did create.

Kristene Diaz

Rush Lake - October 11, 1991

Words can't begin to tell you what today is like at all -
It's the greatest of creation, a Minnesota fall.

The maple leaves are yellow with just a tinge of red.
The North wind dances them around and drops them in a bed.

The air is clean and vibrant, the sky the brightest blue
And here and there's a puffy cloud with sunshine peeping through.

Our lake is like a sparkling gem, its ripples catch the sun
Two ducks are paddling round and round, escaping hunter's gun

Outside we go to catch the leaves falling through the air
Tomorrow they might all be gone, or we're no longer here.

Myrtle E. Telstad

The Invention

There's one invention I can do without
It's the remote control, without a doubt.
From channel to channel all night long,
One second of a movie, two of a song,
With forty plus channels, each gone is a wink;
The only way to end it is to hide it, I think.
I curse the day I got him that toy;
He treats it like it's his pride and joy.
There ought to be a law to govern its use
Husbands should not be allowed to commit remote control abuse.

Vicki Sullivan

AIDS Doesn't Discriminate

Folks listen up, that's right before it's too late,
It's time to practice safe sex, because AIDS doesn't discriminate.
Even you can catch it, as well as the next ten,
Showing love and affection comes with, using protection.
Don't be a fool, because there's no excuse,
Think about it for a minute before you produce.
That's right, you gotta use protection, cause who can you trust,
Don't become another one, dying from lust.
Because anyone can catch it, any race color or creed,
The safe sex relationships, folks that's what we need.
There's no need for being careless, playing Russian Roulette,
Being sure of yourself, that's the meaning of sex.
And if you're not sure about one, why consider the price,
When you can just say no, and move forward to a healthy life.
Why take the risk, when we can all take a stand,
To fight against AIDS, and give the next one a helping hand.
Make the right decision folks, before it's too late,
Because time is running out, and AIDS doesn't discriminate...

Robert L. Wright

"A Poem For My Lost Love"

Even though I'm not in your life
I've always longed to be your wife
We were so good together at one time
I'd given my life and last dime
You were my world night and day
I still love you to this day
You made me sad and happy too
I always wished it would be me and you
It's been many a years since we part
But you still hold the key to my heart
I'm married with children it's true
But Jay it will always be you
Your the one that consumes my thoughts and my soul
For I long to have you part or whole
I'll always love you forever I will
You'll always be the one for me still
I have always hoped and prayed Jay
That it would be me and you one day

Wendi Jandle

Waiting

Since you've been gone dear
I've found myself alone
Not unlike a ship afloat
Without a keel, a rod without a reel

I'm like a cork bobbing aimlessly
upon the waters of the sea of loneliness
Even though, here on earth, we are
apart, you still live on within
my heart.

And in my memories I recall
your loving face so clear, so near
as everyday I miss you more
my husband dear.

The only hope that holds me steady
is in the thought that when God's ready
on that wonderful day, he'll clear the way
When once again we'll be together.

M. Alice Cooper

My Secret Love — Ever More Near!

The lock to my heart, my soul, can be reopened again — who knew?
I've given out special keys but no one yet knows to use them.
Funny how easy it will be, with your key, to get inside the real me.
Joy with caring, laughter, passion sharing, and hugs—like no other.

They had taken our hearts; cruelly tried to abuse and misuse—them. Though to hurt us. Truth is they all but destroyed themselves. Gave up on our passions' too early. Worse, they are lost even to themselves. Yet together, our souls' spark anew, each ones' past lost — soon forgotten. No baggage left to scare you away now; even less — so I'll care for you now? No strings or things needed just knowing that you're on your way to me. A little love now? No! No time to compromise for our passion's this life now. Souls' stronger, richer, deeper, magnified in continuity together — than whenever apart. Pillow talk and smiled knowing in each others arms holding — your in my mind dear. An intensity neither imagined nor dreamed of, just joy in the soon sharing of you. How could this happen, already knowing infinite fulfillment in each others' secret heart. Love so strong neither can control it, too valuable for either to hold it — back. You will know me—you will behold me! You're the key that will instantly free me. Someone, spiritually guided, says it's our turn. Yes, and we know it's our time, too. Together in contentment; happier yet for the prime of each other's contentment. You're so close and near now that all I know I feel now — is this secret love just for you.

Ron Manclaw

I'm Not Dead

Don't weep for me for I'm not dead.
I've gone on my journey up ahead.

I've made reservations a long time ago.
To live in a mansion, oh don't you know.

If you trust in Jesus and you saved,
You'll have reservations like I've made.

To walk downtown on streets of gold,
Just like in Bible stories we are told.

Trust in Jesus, oh don't delay,
Then you will be on your way

To live in a mansion upon high,
With our Heavenly Father up in the sky.

Marilyn Street

For Martha Graham, A Thank you Poem

Thank you for calling me to your home.
I've held the joy of dancing in my heart as a seed.
I've been one with God when I danced and tasted
the freedom and upliftment.

But a hard journey was set for me this time
And dance was not often there to sustain me,
And often I did not want to be here.

Now I've come home and I'm glad.
There are challenges to this art.
I face the mirror; I face myself who cannot articulate ever
the deep wound which has begun unwinding in myself.
Much to my dismay I must face the myriad feelings,
memories, longing and awkwardness
that my body has contained for so long.

And some deep longing, some longing for something so deep
has taken me. I long to find my voice,
To give statement to the deepest part of me.

Thank you for guiding me to your home
Where I can heal my heart and soul and body
and dance and dance and dance.

Patricia Ripin

Charlie

My heart is breaking, it's heavy laden
I've lost a friend today
It might not have been his fleshly wish
But God Called him away
He was a child of God, his soul was ready
It's not my will, it's too soon
I say with my heart heavy
As his body's put to rest, his spirit soars above
And even though I miss him so, I'm glad he's up above
Now a better friend besides the
Lord, I'll never ever have
But the day will come very soon and
I'll meet them in the clouds
He's in a better place I know
He's happy as can be
He's standing there on heavens shore
He's waiting there for me.

Priscilla McGill

Premenstrual Syndrome

Antique lamp shattered against living room panel plated walls
James and John scurry under their sergeant inspected race car
bunk beds

In post labor tones mother screams "Clean this pig sty of a room"

The boys pass silent glances questioning how could
washed baseboards,
perfectly arranged closets,
and lint free floors,
be a "pig sty"?

Others might observe
abuse, anal retention, and scared children,
but James and John see
just another week to weather
in an otherwise calm month.

Lacy Finn

AIDS In My Life

Relentless panther stalking, sneering, sweeping
jewels off life's shelf
world rushing, spinning, passing by now
left to just myself

Life flooded with bewilderment, fear and
loathing taking hold
stripping purpose, endless questioning, losing
vibrance, endless cold

Pain, despair, uncertainty, ravaged frail
too many gone
terror gripping, realizing, even comforted
I'm alone

Inner strength, outer dignity sustain
brief, waning days
turn to beauty, peace, serenity, cherished
moments, sunlit haze

Life lived now! Panther circling, taunting
never old, always ill
sly, terrible, tolerable Panther knowing,
waiting for the kill

Tom Marshall

On The Loss Of A Faithful Friend, Penny

A guard unequalled; a tug at a leash on a five mile
jog; a gentle walk and wag at a scent; a bark at
the head of a strange neighbor to retrieve
a steak surprise; watchful eyes on little girls and
dolls at play, but never to bother those most cherished delights;
unbounded love for love returned, or even not returned;
Penny was this and more, but now is history.

A bolt of lightening and clap of thunder, a firecracker discharged;
a light dimmed by eyes of waning years;
all these and more to frighten, but no more.
Pulled and twisted plants; soiled spaces; ripped screens; and,
mournful yelps; these and more remembered, but now forgotten.
Weren't these all trivial in the grand scheme of things?
But what does it matter now? Penny is history.

Twisted legs and longstanding pain but a love to transcend all;
nothing in return but adoration and service; never an ill
refrain. Now to sleep while loving eyes are here to peer on.
Now to sleep where all pain is no more. Now sleep while
those you served are heavy in heart and will remember well.
Yes, Penny is history but will never be forgotten!

Michael R. Pent

God's Heart

Puppy's breath, infant's coo.
Jumping, tumbling, gnawing and drooling.
All is new.

School-books, games and pretending.
Secrets, moaning, groaning and best friends.
Seems never-ending.

Hair, smell, clothes and complexion.
Music, proms, pictures and self awareness.
Working to-ward perfection.

Cars, college, work and sharing.
Marriage, mortgage, guilt and grit.
All about caring.

Sunsets, birds, sea-breeze and pine trees.
Reverence, forgiveness, remembrance and creating.
A time to seize.

God's heart is life's heart,
Where it pauses momentarily.

Rae Clark

Beginnings

In the quietness of the morning
Just before the break of dawn
is when I commune with my spirit
and talk to God alone.

It is so peaceful then like the
world is standing still; then the
tweet of the birds, the appearance of
the sun and life begins all over again.

How great it is to arise each day
and face the challenges that come your way;
some are small, others are big,
some make you angry, with others you cry.

But then you think as you begin your day,
this is a part of life;
And so, in the quietness of the morning
You thank God for the night.

Susan R. Jones

"Anguish"

From innocents playing in the yard so near
Just fun and frolic, no sign of fear
As life seems simple, problems aside
Games to be played and bikes to ride
The sudden sound disbursed with such speed
Respect for life has no place in this deed
A piercing ring, silencing all other sound
Then suddenly, screams of anguish all around
Blood begins to pour from his chest
A horrified playmate is put to the test
An innocent child in the wrong place
Now has such pain engraved on his face
In just a few seconds his mother appears
The shock and torment turn into tears
Her cries so intense they cut straight to the soul
Another shooting has taken its toll

Diane Compagno

Innocent Eyes

A little girl with a smile so bright
Just turned three on a March spring night
That's when I met her
So small and shy
Big and brown were her innocent eyes
Now a young woman
And still a beautiful smile
She had to grow up fast
A lot of pain in her past
Not so shy anymore
More worldly and wise
And now I see sadness
In those big brown eyes

Paula Alcaraz

"Little Bird"

Little bird up in the tree;
Just what is it you happen to see?
Way up high perched with a branch for a seat
You sit, and twitter, and chirp, and tweet.
Here I lie beneath the towering tree,
Wondering what kind of life a bird's could be.
You flit, and fly, and flutter about;
Sometimes you stop and listen as if in doubt.
Little bird I surmise maybe it would be nice
To sit in a shrouded tree just once or twice.
You watch the world from your little branch.
Yes I'd do it, if I had a chance.

Lauren Shumbat

"Growing Old"

Lord Thou Knowest I am growing older.
Keep me from becoming talkative and possessed
with the idea that I must express myself on
every subject.
Release me from the craving to straighten out
everyone affairs. Keep me from the recital of
endless detail. Give me wings to get to the point.
Seal my lips when I am inclined to tell of my
aches and pains. They are increasing with the
years and my love to speak of them grows sweeter
as time goes by.
Teach Me the glorious lesson that occasionally I
may be wrong. Make me thoughtful, but not nosey,
helpful but not bossy. With my vast store of
knowledge and wisdom, including experience it does
seem a pity not to use it all. But I ask the Lord,
I want a few friends at the end. AMEN.

William J. Simonini

Kidnapped

Oh! I've been kidnapped, taken from my home.
Kidnapped, kidnapped, now I'm on my own.
There's a struggle, in my native land
And I have got, to take a stand
I'm gonna break free, high jacked,
You won't break me, who skowed,
I've got to wake up, shanghaied,
Then we can make love, side tracked.
Kidnapped, I've been kidnapped!
You and me baby, we got to think about,
What's in the future; and taking a new route.
All our dreams; seem to be going up in smoke.
I know what they say, but life is no joke.
Kidnapped, I've been kidnapped!
I've been kidnapped, taken from my home,
Kidnapped, now I'm on my own.
There's a struggle, in my native land.
And I have got to take a stand.
Now I found my friends.
And I swear by God, I'll never lose you again.

Kenzie Heard-McCormick

"Beauty Of Christmas"

"A mother puts her kids downs for the night
Kissing them and saying it will be alright
Her kids talking of happiness and good things
And all the goodies that Santa brings,

"The kids wondered did Ms. Claus take care of him
For this Christmas he was coming to visit them
The Mother choked to fight back the tears
This Christmas would be the same as past years,

"The mother said, Goodnight with tears in her Eyes
Knowing she soon had to make them realize
Santa would have to pass them again this year
For Santa just can not make it by here,

"The kids said, Mommy put our list under the tree
So Santa will know what our presents will be
Tears blurred her vision, feeling as she was dead
She open the list to read what it said,

"Mommy, tells us things will be alright
Yet! We hear her in the dark crying late at night
Santa! This Christmas don't leave us a toy
instead give Mommy back her smiles of joy.

Linda Coots

Night Person

I can make it through the day,
knowing night will come eventually
with all its velvet promise, its mystery
the wonder of the galaxy of stars,
  the milky way,
and all the soft small murmurings
of little things too shy
to brave the day.

I can watch the shadows on the wall;
tears can flow, no one to see or ask me why.
I can hear with heart-tuned ear
the night bird's call
or dream that I am following
the moon path in the sky.

Leah Rothrock

Thinking

I awoke this morning, just thinking of you
  knowing that Nothing could make me feel blue

But I wake up every morning with you on my mind
  In the middle of the day—and at bedtime
    My thoughts are of you— you are my thoughts.

You make me feel so happy, before I know it, I smile
  I go to walk a block and end up walking a mile

You make me feel secure—Yet like a bird I fly free
  How could anyone do for anyone —what you do for me

Thanks my love for being the way you are
And , for when I need you—not being too far

Whenever you need me just call out my name
But most of all, my love, I hope that you can feel the same.

Margaret M. Parker

My Abortion

Blinded with ignorance and innocence as well, not
knowing the power of control; I allowed myself not
to feel what I would have to live with; my experience
was very real. I went against my own natural
will, for wanting so to please, those final words
of others, and hoping that I'd fine some peace.
What a price to pay, to abort my child that day.
I'd like to send a message, "ABORTION IS NOT THE WAY",
for one will pay a heavy price you see, it never
goes away, Further in my journey, came a time of
making my own way, in having my own say so, came
the realization of that day. An awakening answer to
myself of all that I had lost. My confession came
much later from knowledge of THE TRUTH, that a life
is so precious and a woman is one who gives it root.
I know, I've been forgiven, starting with myself,
but my wondering years will wonder always, wondering
all by myself.

Sofia Lamb Coronado

A Beautiful Angel

Heaven holds dear to a beautiful angel,
Keeping him safe with a love so rare.
This precious treasure, surely he will be waiting.
Your time will come, somehow, somewhere.

I know your hearts are so heavily burdened,
And your sorrow seems never to fail.
But again you'll meet your beautiful angel,
Where only joy and peace prevail.

Shari A. Sarazin

The Artist

It calls to me, it is my every breath
It is every part of my existence, it is who I am
I feel because of its presence, I think because it is my mind
When I laugh it is because of its hold on me
When I cry it is because it has moved my being in such a
way tears have no choice but to fall
I am powerless against its grip
And yet because of its gentle hold I am full of enthusiasm and passion
To it I owe my ability to see as most do not, and to feel
what many never will
It has always been part of me
It will always be
It is a gift beyond all gifts
This person - the artist

Brenda Lee C. Trumpold

Moonlight

My night light is like a spotlight in the night sky.
It is like a beacon that leads me on my way through a long journey.
It gives me the guidance that I need after my day has led me astray.
The blackness of the night is an easel for my imagination.
The stars are the beginnings of ideas and dreams.
They are pinpoints of my imagination waiting for me to peek through.
The moon guides me to another place where I am safe.
Here I can go and create.
There are no boundaries like in daylight; the night is endless.
My dreams will never end.
They will be here when my mind falls into darkness once again.
With the moon as my guide, and the stars the destinations,
  my dreams can become reality.
The moon is my night light, and it takes me to where I need to be.

Atina M. Davis

Peaceful Moments

How can I define the feelings when I think of you?
It is like a rainbow reaching to the sky and illuminating
If only for a little while.

It is like a flower filling my senses with fragrance and delight
If only for a fleeting flight.

It is like a dream a treasure to keep
If only to draw upon in time of need.

When you can recall only the pleasant times you enjoyed
And be thankful for the moment given
Only then can you truly understand the nature of loving and living.

Irma B. Marroquin

One's Night Stand

This is meant to put a smile on your face.
It is not a competition, a rhyme or a race.

It is a guessing game, where you may win...
a prize, that is me, to do with at your whim.

I am your secret admirer, and hope you see,
that if you guess well, you can have one night with me.

I will fulfill your needs, wants and desires,
to hear you crescendo to the tops of spires.

So guess my name and come to my door.
Leave me a note or, if need be, more.

So choose well and choose fast,
because I wish to make this prize last and last.

Whatever you want is what you'll receive.
This is totally sincere. Please believe.

So, until then, I bid you farewell,
until that special night, who can tell.

Bruce D. Wienckowski

Rhyme & Reason (The Poet's Poem)

I have with me an active mind,
some paper, pen, and ink.
I place this sheet beneath my hand,
and with my pen can think.

I write things that I cannot say,
draw feelings with the words.
Once on paper, thus thought out,
they often can be heard.

I only ask you understand,
and leave my pen to write.
If I can see what's inside me,
perhaps, in time, you might.

Ren Marie Cherry

On Meeting God

At the end of whatever time it takes
For a newborn's eyes to clear,
That's the time it took till I met Him,
And felt His love so near.

I was only days old when first I viewed
All that was good to see.
I saw love — complete and infinite,
When my Mother smiled down at me.

That very first view of life for me
Was to be unlike any other.
I opened my eyes and saw God Himself,
In those soft brown eyes of my Mother.

Kathy Taylor Slack

In the Eagle's Eye

I see the eagle soaring
in the sky
gracefully flying through
the clouds,
clouds that seem to say
goodbye.

The eagle looks down
into the valley,
his eyes piercing the layers
of mist.
What he sees is dirty
and frightening.

So he soars higher
and higher,
until he can touch
the sky,
forgetting the specks of
dust below.

Manuela Lehti

The Troll Within

Within me hides a troll,
A contradictory force
That, like a camera,
Turns my life
Into a negative,
Black to white and white to black.

Instead of building
Castles in the air,
I find myself hopelessly
Building dungeons.

Letitia Scott

My Earthly Delight

Your smile affects me like
A bright sunny day
The feel of your touch
Is like a warm rain in May

When I admire your beauty
You remind me of a sunset
On the ocean waves

There is never a day
That I want you too far away
The only thing I know
Is that you make my love grow
Just as you are my sunrise
Just as you make the stars shine
It's all because of you
Every day is brand new

As days turn unto months
And months unto years
You keep getting younger and make my
love hunger
Even tho the words are never uttered
It's your spell that I am under

Ron Bumgardner

Love Is

Love is...
a feeling between two people
an emotion that bonds you together
an unexplainable attraction

Love is...
the greatest gift you can give
the prize of all prizes
the one thing that is only found in you

Love is...
freely given with no questions asked
non exchangeable and non refundable

Love is...
always there for you
between you and that special someone

Love is...
that something special between you and me

Sherry Heidkamp

Commandments Of Peace

A tear for the crying
A flower for the dying
feathers for the bird
peace on this earth
A leaf for the tree
A little love for the peace

A prayer for the asking
A song for the dying
A voice for the unspoken
pride as my token
freedom for the free
A picture for the blind
A river of dream
Knowledge for the mind
My Commandments of Peace.

Maria Salas

For My Sister

I will give you the Sea.
A form without form
to nurture fair life.

By preserving with salt
So that you'll persevere,
I will give you the Sea.

To moisten soft cheeks
When our tears have gone dry
And the earth has become hard,
I will give you the Sea.

Paul Stuart

"Summer Wonders"

Leaving the sky I saw,
A golden glow afar.

The ocean water down below,
Reflecting it with stars

Dancing diamonds on the blue
I found amidst my gaze

A sweet, soft breeze touching me
The reeds bow down, amazed

Cool white sand beneath my feet
The tide afraid to come

I shut my eyes and wonder not
For, God is near and one.

Kathryn Elizabeth Vickers

Perilous Journey

A trip thru a revolving door
A journey I detest-abhor!
A whirling dervish spinning trap
Designed for fools like me who nap.

I've cycled over rough terrain
Cross countried on decrepit trains
And blithely stepped into the maws
Of eerie metros on the bourse.

Yet this I must with fear declare
Where doors revolve? I won't be there!

Sonia P. Alloy

Miracle

When a little baby is born,
a large miracle takes place.
A unique responsibility
the parents are soon to face.

This tiny bundle of joy
will be for you to love
As the Lord Christ Almighty
watches adoringly from above.

You will begin to experience parenthood,
an adventurous stage of life,
United together as parents,
a loving husband and wife.

Tanya Feszchak

A Modern Fairy Tale

Once upon a time
a long long
time ago
a man **hit**!
his wife
Society recoiled in
HORROR
"This is intolerable" they said
"We won't stand for this" they cried
then *they*
all went home
and left the wife
standing
alone
unprotected
with their support
lying
in tatters
at her feet

Sheri Donovan

"Prisoner Of Love"

There lives within my heart this day
A love beyond compare
Of sweet and tender memories
Those dreams I could not share
For visions of a life so sweet
Meant not, for such as me
Yet, loving you so tenderly
By measures thus conceive
Thy truth beyond me still shines
The misery of my usefulness
A love that was my crime

There are special times
That we have shared
That gave my heart such a joy
Then yet, a pain returned to me
Thy love but did destroy
Still my heart adore thee so
My body crave thy touch
And my minds obsessiveness
I love you, oh so much

Patricia A. Reed

Wrong Mr. Right

A day that never starts,
A night that never ends.
Time heals all wounds,
But when does that begin.

You were here today,
but gone tomorrow.
I've never felt so much pain,
And tried to cope with so much sorrow.

Everyday filled with sadness,
Every night the same.
To bring a little calmness,
I whisper your name.

I listen for a reply,
not a sound do I hear.
Then I ask myself why,
is your voice in my ear.

Where are you lover,
in what kind of place.
Only in my sleep,
do I see your face.

Sherry Sherry

A Prisoner's Dreams

Jail's a place of heartache,
A place of steel and stone.
Of dirty cells-my home in hell,
Where I sit alone.

They came today and took away,
The man who lived next door.
To end his strife he took his life.
Cause he could take no more.

Now it's quiet here upon this tier,
Since death has claimed another.
The lost seems small, but to us all
It's like we lost a brother.

My only dreams, or so it seems,
Is to leave this place some day.
For my crime, I paid with time,
Then go my merry way.

But if I die, please don't cry
Or shed a tear for me.
Just take my kids in your arms
And say," He's finally free."

Sean Taylor

The Traveler

The sun melts away.
A queer shadow looms.
The travel begins.
His fate he assumes.

His footsteps echo,
and tear through the night.
His thoughts are unspoken,
as he moves out of sight.

This man I once knew,
just as everyone did.
He would stand, proud,
when the others hid.

He's a traveler, true,
and he seeks without sound.
He seeks not like the world.
He seeks to be found.

So on this still night,
at this time before dawn.
The travel continues,
the traveler moves on.

Zachary J. Novak

Hide

When I look in the mirror, I see
a redness in my eye. Than as I look
deep inside, I see a little girl
trying to hide. While I stand looking
in the mirror I see another tear
slip out my eye and then I start
to cry because I am just a little
girl trying to hide, my feelings
for him that I hold deep inside
where my heart lies.

Melissa Ann Bradt

A Poem

A poem is a pretty girl
A rhapsody in verse
A poem is a catchy smile
And lipstick in a purse

A poem is a low lit room
Perhaps after a dance
A poem is a stolen kiss
The prelude to romance.

William J. Schereck

Home

A beautiful sapphire throne,
A river crystal clear,
Streets of gold and gates of pearl,
With walls of precious stones
Where all Christians,
will call home.

We will sit on the bank
of that sparkling river,
on grass so soft and green,
Greeting our love ones.
Oh, what a glorious scene.

Then all will sing songs
of joy and praise,
to our Glorious God,
Saviour and King.

How grateful we will be,
At last to see our Saviour
face to face,
In that grand and glorious place.

Pauline C. Lasher

"Heaven"

A single word of kindness.
A smile upon a face.
A gentle touch of the heart.
A happy warm embrace.
A special kind of love.
Surrounded by satin and lace,
A warm and meaningful place.

Tonya Zeallor

Your Eyes

Your eyes are like a song
A song I choose to sing
Though I do not know the melody
on the rhyme

your rhythm is unique - I've seen -
I haven't got it yet
I've been trying hard
to learn your song
But, I still my need more time

I tap, I hum, I know your song
It's at the tip of my tongue
The tune won't come...

It just could be that once you've learned
and sung the song of another
If your song was wrong
It could be hard to sing the song
Of a new lover

Margaret V. Foss-Neilson

The Richest Of Friendships

A gift of self, and a time to just be.
A special friend to set me free.

A time for love, a time for caring.
A magic moment, a special sharing.

A sparkle of hope in the distance.

It's soothing.

Whispering,

Go forward, keep moving.

Pamela S. Brogla

Life's Just A Seasons

Life's just a Season — a Winter or Fall
A Spring or Summer to live — that's all

Would we enter into this world
if we had a choice
To say we'd be a boy or girl
we had no voice
Where is my niche my solid reason
For being here for just a Season

By choice I'd have taken another path
to escape all the sorrows
The pain and the wrath and
never plan tomorrows
For Season's end will come much too soon
Like a flower dies—after it blooms

Life's just a Season a Winter or Fall
A Spring or Summer to live—that's all.

Loretta Sweeden

Abortion

It was the seventeenth of September,
A star fallen in the sea.
It was the seventeenth of September,
when the white wolves
burned my soul in cage of pain.
I still remember the smell
that will never cease to exist.
It was the seventeenth of September,
Where my tears taste like the sea
and warmer than the sun.
It was the seventeenth of September,
When we lost our child.
a child that we never saw
only in our dream
only in our pain.
It was the seventeenth of September,
that I asked:
What it must be like
to go to haven.

Maati E. Faris

To Be

A tree a flower what should I be
A tree a flower could this be me
I think I'll be a big oak tree
Standing tall yes that is me
As a tree I'll live so long
I'll see the birds I'll hear their songs
Wait a minute stoop right here
To be a flower would be so dear
Out of the ground I would grow
Little white petals you would know
A round little center nice and bright
Looks like yellow in the light
If I had a choice of what to be
I'd be a daisy not a tree

Rick Jacobs

Expressions

Love is a flower,
a sweet young flower
still moist from the morning's dew.
And love is a shower,
a summer shower
bringing dawn and a day that's new.
Love is an ocean,
a deep, strong ocean
with a breeze and a storm and a tide.
And love is devotion, a pure devotion
from which nothing can ever hide.
Love is a blessing,
a wonderful blessing
from God in the Heavens above.
And love is expressing,
yes, always expressing
that all of these things are love.

Karen Lisa

Benjamin's Bank

Ere adam saw what eve had done,
A tick tock cadence had
begun;
Though, truly a fraudulent
thing;
Our late deposits in the
spring;
And early withdrawals in the
fall,
Are all required by the
law.

Matt Walls

Life

I pluck a rose,
A vision's beauty I behold.
Each petal like a day of gold.

And then alas,
The petals drop now one by one,
Life fails me in the race I run.

But hopes renewed,
The seeds remain to bring new life,
And joy to know above the strife.

Renelda A. Frazee

I've Always Loved The Wind

You came into my life like
A whisper on the wind,
Not really with a beginning
And seemingly without an end.

You blew across my face with
A coolness in your touch.
There was no concept then that
I'd savor you so much!

Your breeze gained momentum as
With heat from desert sands;
I felt in your kisses and the
Journeys of your hands.

Your warm air is flowing now
Over this body of mine,
Preparing all my places for
Unity with thine.

When the tempest is finally over
It will bring a blessed calm.
I will remember you, my wind,
And all your wondrous balm.

Mary B. Pepper

A Time For Us

Will there ever be a time for us,
A year, a month, a day?
Will there ever be a time for us,
Or have we given it away?

When we were young, we gave our hours
To friends and family.
We didn't save much for ourselves
Because our time was free.

In later years, we had our work,
Careers took all our days.
We had to help our children, too,
Through each financial maze.

If I have a dream to dream,
I know what it will be,
I'll dream of carefree, happy hours,
Just for you and me.

But now we have to pay our debts.
They keep us working night and day.
Will there ever be a time for us,
Or have we given it away?

Robert R. Roberts

Desire

A desire I've been wanting
A yearning, a burning
Deep inside
I feel much pride
On the outside
I'm very shy
For the desire is willing
In my heart
But for me is far apart
From my soul and from my mind
That it could never be mine
A true desire is painful
For it pulls and nags
Until we take control
We have to play the role
That we do not mind
For someday it will be mine
A desire is a wanting
That's just waiting for the taking
For what is rightfully mine

Susan Zembo

Running From The Boars Of War 1946

Out of Frisco...
Across Bay...
To art school each day
On our C train you sea
You sea should wee stay
Is our poem bee'gining to Rhyme?
Ass we unvail as a bust
O'Sublime...
Gunners' creed & VMSB133
If the japs. bad weather or our
Dauntless doesn't
make the kill
You may bet
Your asp...that
Leo J. Will (Leo J.'s Will)?

Wesley James Watson

Messy Myrtle's First Love

I looked at him
across the room
he looked at me
I know he likes me
he smiled at me
I know he likes me
he came over
and touched me
Wow! I know he loves me

Otella Waller

Again

For here I go again,
after promising I wouldn't do this.
Now I sit alone in my den,
mesmerized by your kiss.
I'm so afraid of being hurt,
knowing I can't take it again.
I couldn't help it, I had to flirt,
I never want this feeling to end.
Please be able to tell me,
this relationship will last.
You now hold the key...
if only I could ask.
Only once have I been in love,
I felt like I was soaring so high...
Just like a new mother dove.
Please don't tell me goodbye.

Kristi Minckler

Have You Ever Wondered

Have you ever wondered
After you've prayed, it's me Lord.
I'm your child Lord, and he still
Haven't answered your prayers.
You say to yourself, let me go to the
Bible and see if I can find the answer
There.
But still no success.
Then as you are walking around feeling
Sorry for yourself, you look and see a
Lady with her child begging for a meal.
Then you walk a little further and see a
Blind man with a cane.
You think for a moment and then
You look up and say, "Never mind Lord,
You've already
Answered my prayers."

Patricia Jones

A Dream

I am a tiny star
Against a vast velvet night.
I am a golden ray
From dawn's awakening light.
I am a crystal dewdrop
On the petal of a budding rose.
I am a special gift
Wrapped in bright red bows.
I am the glowing reflection
Of the moon's silvery beam.
I am what you would hope,
For I am all and but a dream.

Raquel Chandler

Mama's House

Empty house
All alone
After all these years
No one home

Worn step patched door
Squeaky hinge
Tile floor
Windows that look only in

Who will come?
Who will stay?
Sort the things
To throw away?

Will strangers come
And light our fire
Hold the keys
To our empire

Cut & chop break and bend
The House
That the windows
Only look In?

Terryl Esther Jensen

October Miracles

Not a breath, no movement.
All is dark, where is this place?
It's quiet here, nobody is laughing,
or crying.
Just one breath, one chance,
laugh, cry, please breath!
One movement, one more breath.
They laugh, they cry, they breath.
It's warm, and bright, my glass
little house.
I laugh, I cry, I breath and I live.

Vickie Boyer

God's Surprise

You arrived at the hospital
All the tests had been run.
Your baby girl is soon coming,
Her little nursery is done.

The delivery went well,
And the baby is fine.
The doctor calls "It's a boy!"
You think, "Can this baby be mine?"

Modern science had failed you.
Mother nature had won.
All the test showed it's a girl,
But God blessed you with a son!

So you'll take back the dresses
With all the ruffles and lace.
And you'll think of a name
For this handsome new face.

And you'll soon come to realize
That life's mysteries are grand.
Along with the memories he'll bring you
As your son grows into a man!

Patty Steinshouer

The Flu Bug

The flu bug has bitten
Already this year
I'm as weak as a kitten
Oh! that pain in my ear!
My appetite's low
My temperature's high
It's a 103°, Oh I'm too sick to die!
But with bedrest and juice
And good care it's true
I'll be back on my feet
Then I'll take care of you,
For if you tend me today
My dear to your sorrow,
the flu bug, I fear
Will bite you tomorrow!

Ramona Heller

A Casualty Of War

I love you right on
Although your being is gone.
And though God has seemed unfair
He's our all.
I will wait for you.
You will wait for me.
Then someday
We shall be
together
In eternity.

Sara Carolyn Davis

Truth

I have seen the truth
Amid its truthfulness
Bound in the chains of time
Lost all its toughness
They said, 'truth be told'
Lo and behold
Though it's often cold
Integrity must be bold
Isn't that, what we have already sold.

Mohammad Afzal Khan

Untitled

I slept the sound of water laps
amidst the doldrums
of life's abundant traps.
Out of nowhere
you came to see,
and woke me
from despondence' nap.
Breathing hope in the cloth you kiss
I found direction,
escape from all of this.
Without you there
on my side,
I would have died
drifting in that loneliness.

Rob Carlton

A Soldier Of God

I'm a soldier of God,
An ambassador I claim.
I put on my armor,
I was chose by name.
To do His commission,
His words I proclaim.
To spread His salvation,
That is my aim.

Robert L. Hernandez

From A Window Pane

Verdant leaves swaying crisp,
An arid afternoon.
Vague breezes singing secret,
Saturating my mood.
Racing to catch the feeling of this-
Sometimes it is you,
From ancient laughter
Breeding frowns.

Sunless sounds
In still instant.
Gray the day,
And yet it is nothing-

And with certain crystal vision,
Clouds veil my unconscious view.

Kerry Heuer

Morning Greeting

From translucent blue infinity
An unnamed melody trembles on my lips.

It is as warm, as the Earth's kiss,
It is fresh as the morning due,
It has fragrance, color and sound,
It is harmonious, peaceful and found.
It was weaved by the sun's ray,
It is born this glorious day
Reminding salute from interspace

On his wings
I am an atom unweighed,
A sound
Which came from boundless far,
A little ring of endless chain,
Unfinished song, a dream, a pain
A transitive minute
In inconceivable space.

An unnamed melody
Sent by astral infinity
Trembles on my lips as a kiss.

Sonya Mkryan

Death Stopped By Yesterday!

I was in such a hurry yesterday,
And ...

Death stopped for me!

How could it have been so unkind
So untimely ...

To stop by just for me.

It knew that I was not finished yet and
Had so much more to do.

And still...

Death stopped by...

I was in the autumn of my years —
With no particular ills to speak of

A good job - paid my taxes and went
To church from time to time...

Oh! Why oh why did death stopped
By for me yesterday.

It must have been in error.

How can it be corrected?
The computer made a mistake!

What did you say — I cannot hear you.....

Yvonne A. McCoy

"A Portrait Of Paulene"

A good looking gal,
and a sweet kid too.

Her eyes are blue,
and her smile is golden too.

With her long brown hair,
and her loving soul too.

So, when you look into her,
what do you see, a portrait

Of a loving soul, were dreams
can come true too.

Paul Wayne Hamp

The Whole

All the drops of all the showers,
And all the petals of all the flowers,
All the strata of all the layers,
Plus all the thoughts of all the prayers,
All the purrs of all the kitties,
And all the folks of all the cities,
Are just a part,
Of all the living and giving of one big
Heart.

Mary Lou Garrett

My God

Where came the wonders of this world,
And all the universe!
Where came the beast of every field
That treads upon the earth!
Who timed the moon!
Who set the sun!
Where came the night and day
How can a man beget a son,
Without a woman's way!
Then was the earth its only cause.
A seed without a pod -
SURELY, all of nature's laws do GLO-
RIFY -
MY GOD.

Walter M. Horton

Search For My Love

If everyday I could hear your laugh
And also see your face
It would make my heart burn with joy
Taking me to a happy, loving place.

It would give my mind such peace
To know you are here
and give my heart such content
To feel you are near.

If you were not close
Or right by my side
I would search all the lands
I would look far and wide.

I would swim the vast oceans
And tackle the highest mountains
I would wish for luck
By throwing pennies in fountains.

I love you, my darling,
This you know is true
So no matter where you go
I will always find you.

Nicole Emde

Untitled

Today is a new day from yesterday,
and an old day for tomorrow.
So live today to the fullest
because you can't relive yesterday,
and you can't see tomorrow.

Tony Gene Broxton Jr.

A Tribute To Venus

With eyes that were expressive
And beauty to behold
A creature full of trust
To love for all my own
Oh, how I miss dear Venus
She made my life complete
Some said "Just find another"
It would not be the same
There could not be another
The loss is just too great
Now, memories are all I have
Of a cat that is no more

Natalie Lizanich

Holding On

The harsh voices
and breaking plates
are a cacophony
of misunderstanding and pain
but the girl no longer hears them
She is busy painting rainbows
and clouds with silver linings
in the corner of her mind
that refuses to believe
that love can fade
as simply as the stars appear to
in the light of day

Kari Feldman

"Jamie"

Deep blue eyes
And curly black hair -
"Mama," he cried,
Seeking her care.

"Yes my darling"
Her loving reply,
While comforting Jamie
With tears in her eyes.

Don't cry my baby,
Please don't weep -
Tender words of love
Put Jamie to sleep?

P. B. Van Campen

Untitled

Time is our enemy
And death is our friend
The reaper walks slowly seeking within.
Picking the soul's who are next to go
Black on black no smile to show
Without a sound the fates decide
Who will be the next to die.
Slowly the reaper responds to his call
And multitudes run, but many fall
Who is to say; you will escape
No one, no where, knows their fate.

Sandy Tripp

Proof For Our Eyes,
Truth To Our Minds

No more happiness, just new fears
And eternal sadness for coming years.
Away he is, his act was last,
With no goodbyes, his life has past.
Reaching for that answer
But, we know we'll never find it.
Searching for a prayer
Dedication towards our friend.
Emotions quickly screamingly,
For comfort and relief.
But now it's time to realize
His soul has been released.
His pain has been devoured
by all the peacefulness.
No longer shall he cry
Though, he shall be missed.

In memory of Mike Farrell 1992

Peter J. Monaster

It's All In The Mind

If I close my eyes real tight,
and feel the wind blow by,
and smell the rains drop down,
It could be spring again!
If I look up; not left or right,
and see the clear blue sky,
and hear the birds talk on,
It could be spring again!

If I feel the warmth of sun,
and recall the cricket's hum,
and breathe the coolish air,
It could be spring again!
If I taste some fresh fruit gum,
and hear the children's fun,
and hours pass without a care,
It could be spring again!!

Marjorie L. Steptoe

The Couple

I looked into his eyes
and found pain
He didn't need it
but had it
a damned shame

I looked at her face
and found fear
she always had it
never lost it
the poor dear

At this time; they should know
joy and peace
they don't have it
they miss it
Their lives decrease

I looked across the diner
at mirrors of Mom and Dad
I felt sorry
I felt guilty
I felt bad

R. William Hughes

If There Is No God

How in the world did I arrive,
And furthermore did survive,
If there is no God?

How does the sun in the sky,
Shine and pretty birds fly,
If there is no God?

How do the flood waters rise,
And wise men become wise,
If there is no God?

How do we believers have hope,
and manage to always cope,
If there is no God?

How did the trees get here,
The rabbit, the squirrel and deer,
If there is no God?

Could man make the grass so green,
And paint these realistic scenes?
Not at all! There is God!

Sue M. Hedden

To My Beloved Father

Tell a child about heaven
And he looks up to the stars
But when I gaze at my dad
I know how close I am to God.

He's got a twinkle in his eye
And a kind word for a friend
You never see him scowling
Lest injustice has set in.

His favorite pastime is telling stories
To children small and large,
But his love of other people
Is what gives him such a charge.

His life's been spent working
All the long day through
To bring joy to all he knows
While serving his Master too.

What more could one ask for
Than to be loved by this man
Who gives all God's creatures
A kind and loving hand.

Winifred Green Cheney

To My Family...Here And There

Family, I love you,
and I need you to know,
I miss you and am angry
that some of us let go.

We all grow up,
none of our lives are the same.
Are we a family,
or is it just in name?

We know more about the president,
and I wish there could a change.
Family....our priorities
We need to rearrange.

Neighbors come and go,
but family we'll always stay.
Together again someday,
I Pray!

Kelly Elgin

Poetry

I used to think poetry was boring,
and I would do a lot of snoring

My teacher said a poetry folder,
It made me feel a lot older

But poetry is fun,
and now my folder is done

I guess I was wrong
Now I want to sing a song

Lisa Andrews

Transformation

It feels like fullness
and it feels like emptiness
It feels like awareness
and it feels like
"I don't want to know"
It feels like peace
and it feels like disquietude
It feels like a search has ended
and it feels like, if this is so,
where do I go from here?

It feels like I somehow
need a shoehorn
to slip more easily into
whatever comes next.

I. Duane Goochey

"Always There"

When we are at the end of our rope
And it seems we can no longer cope
With our problems so many
There is someone who at any

Time will be there to
Help us through
Any problem great or small
For He knows them all

He promises never to leave us alone
For He is like a great stone
He will stand firm and not lean
For in all His wisdom He has seen

All the ages come and go
And He will always know
Each one of His sheep
For like a good shepherd He never sleeps

Jesus is someone everyone should know
And with Him in one's life they will show
How caring a person can be
And the fact Jesus will never leave.

Thomas E. Van Vleet

Opening Night

A baton waves
And music doeth flow,
Over voices hushed,
As the lights grow low,
Entrancing the night
with their magic,
Conveying to us their arts,
Enfolding the night with their music,
Blending their songs, to the strings
of our hearts.

Rudy M. Wieland

Double Time Of Life

When I hit the Razor's edge
And I've been split in two
Let me separate to meet
Myself up in the blue

And then rejoin as one
To fly around the earth
Let me become one again
Like a baby born at birth

Then let me start over
As I fly in the wind
Let me remember my mistakes
So I don't make them again

Let me walk much slower
As my life starts brand new
Let me become much better
At everything that I do

Then my knowledge will grow
Twice as fast as before
Life will be so easy
When I greet myself once more

Monte R. Shockley

Set Me Free

Set me free. Don't clip my wings
and make me stay here. Allow me
to fly free. Release me into the blue
sky and allow me to love. To keep me
here will be to kill me. So, set me
free into the clear blue sky. Oh! how
I long to be free. I long to spread my
wings and fly again. I long to live
free as free as I once did. But, still
you keep me here. Even knowing my
longings you keep me here. Please set
me free to live again. Set me free so
that I do not die. To set me free,
to see me fly will open your heart
to new love. So, set me free so that
I can fly.

The Raven

Racing Thru...

Here's to us
And may we see
We all were formed
Imperfectly.
Here's to us
And may we know
That winners come
Win, place and show.

So many races
We all must enter
So what.. if our place
Is near the center?

We did..and do
Participate...
And so deserve to
Celebrate
Each stage that we
Negotiate.

Mae Burnham Carson

Missing You

When we're apart I have my thoughts
and memories to keep you close, but
thoughts can't take the place of being
with you, hearing your laughter, seeing
your happy smile. All the things that
distance takes away are the things
I miss the most. I can't wait to
see you again. So often I find myself
wishing I could be with you, I want
to see you, I want to talk to you, I
wonder what you might be doing and if
everything okay. When I start feeling
sad because I miss you, I remind
myself how lucky I am to have you
to miss, to have been with you
through so many close and happy days.
They say it's a small world, and maybe
they're right,
but it doesn't seem that way when I'm
apart from you.

Sandy McClurg

Untitled

When friends' ties are broken
and my loved one had to part,
it left a wound that never healed
and also a broken heart.
We cannot bring the old days back
when we were both together.
But secret tears and longing thoughts
will live with me FOREVER!!!!

Stephanie Furtado

Thoughts On A Rainy Night

The rain falls heavy on the rooftop,
And now comes the sound of wind;
Restlessly, the mind keeps thinking
Of where I'm going and where I've been.

The clock moves slowly forward,
As if the dawn to win;
And thoughts emerge like phantoms,
Of where I'm going and where I've been.

Then memory keeps on working,
And sleep eludes again,
As I muse about life's highway,
Of where I'm going and where I've been.

William J. O'Brien Jr.

Winter Magic

I looked outside my window
And saw a world of white.
The snow was gently falling
Against the darkened night.

Snow flurried past my window
And fell without a sound
To the soft and fleecy blanket
That lay upon the ground.

The trees were dark and shiny,
Outlined in frosty white
Making graceful, lacy branches
For shadows in the night.

Then the wind began to howl
As faster fell the snow.
I pressed my nose against the pane
And watched the blanket grow.

Rachel Sebastian

Vampires Night

No more light, the sun is gone,
And now I must awake.
The sun's too bright for my eyes,
Much more than I can take.
So sleep here in my cellar,
Is what I'm doomed to do.
If God gave me a choice,
I'd rather be like you.
As I dress I wonder,
Who my prey will be.
Why in God's name,
Did the dark choose me?
As I walk this stone road,
The trees all seem to bow.
It's as if they remember
About that night somehow.
For it was this same place,
That witnessed late one night,
The taking of my soul,
The torment of my fright.

Rebecca Painter

Miss Pansy

In her haste she forgot
And rushed from her house
Thinking about the day
Miss pansy
No panty
Bare fanny

Out into the world
She hurried
Thinking about the day
Miss Pansy
No panty
Bare fanny

A puff of wind
Came along
And blew her dress up
Thinking about the day
Miss pansy
No panty
Bare fanny

Mary Wandler

Come Sing Softly To Me

Come sing softly to me.
And tell me tales of awe.
Paint a rainbow for my eyes.
Please tell me who we are.
Leave not a tale untold.
Talk on through the night.
Speak of life as true.
With beauty and the fright.
Take my mind to far off places,
Where Kings and Queens do roam.
Tell me of the Eagle's flight,
And where the stars call home.
To my ears be not false.
Speak the tales of truth.
Of my trust that's placed in you,
Need you not the proof.
All the wondrous things there are,
But never mine to see.
So come sing softly now,
And tell the things that be.

Robert Andrews

Just A Question

You say that we take
And the government gives;
You say God is dead
And that Elvis lives.

Of course I agree, dear-
I don't disagree, dear-
But, how can you say that you're right?

You say that there's no
longer poverty here
As you sit in your trailer
and finish your beer.

So I just say nothing-
How could I say something?
But, "How can you say that you're right?"

Patrice Bartell

You Forever Me

When the sun rises tomorrow
and the morning light wakes me up
I'll say a prayer to heaven
and thank the Lord for your love

I'll whisper to you good morning
and gently kiss your lips
and smile to myself knowing
that the world is now at our fingertips

The oceans for us to sail
the mountains for us to climb
and all the stars to wish upon
until the end of time

I wish the end of time
was a day we'd never see
so I could forever love you
and you forever me

But if the world should end tomorrow
in peace how I'd sleep tonight
knowing the woman I hold in my arms
is the woman I've loved for all my life

Robert Kumbatovic

Mamaw's Kitchen

From the garden to the cellar
And then into Mamaw's kitchen
Why does every meal taste so good?
I'll tell you if you'll listen

Every seed is planted
And raised with special care
Then picked at just the right time
With a pride that's very rare

It is then brought to the kitchen
Here's the most important part
This is where she adds the love
That comes straight from the heart

So if your meals aren't quite this good
Now you know what's missin'
The care, the pride and special love
Found here in Mamaw's Kitchen.

Kelley D. Maynard

Guiding Light

For the light once was blinding
and then the darkness came
after it all settled. Come the
tears with all the pain.
Then in time the clouds
of darkness, a light come
shining through.
And there with-in the
midst, I saw the one I
love, that's you...

Paula L. Cox

Untitled

As sleep takes one into its arms
and they fall within its charms.
Nought but silence to which to succumb.
All around is black and numb.
Not a care or troubled sigh
and the world passes by.
Then visions, sometimes wise
well before our eyes.
While others are those to fear
until we wake up here.

Seth Wilder

Can She

Can she walk a mile in me
And trace the footsteps
As far as her eye can see

Can she confront
The pain and fear
To find the well of a single tear

To walk along
Is to walk within
The door is not open
Will you come in?

Are you able to confront the past
And see the lurking dreams of last
Of laughter and cries
that we all try to hide

Will she walk a mile with me
And embrace the footsteps that we leave

Michael Lyons

Rio Grande Sunset - 1938

The day is falling to its end
And vagrant breezes gently bend
A rose against the wall.
The palms awaken to the night
And in the slowly failing light,
Stardust falls on the huisache bloom.
And shadows silhouette quiet fields.
The shadow of the earth consumes
The shadows in the fields.
An arch of light holds back the night
And slowly settles out of sight;
Then shatters in a golden haze,
That scatters on tomorrow's wind.
A cool breeze springs up from the sea
And fireflies pulse their tracery
Upon the evening air.
A crescent moon and evening star
Adorn the western sky;
Then like a dry and weightless tide
Night comes, engulfing everything.

A. R. Davis Jr.

My Place

Where is my place;
And when will I know?

And when I know where my place is;
Will you be there too?

And if you are, will you say:
This is your place.
If so, then I can say:
As long as there is a space next to me,
There will always be a place for you.

W. W. Young

Behind All Boulders

What is it that makes you trudge?
And when will they know your triumph?
You hush the rain
Set all afire

Your head is bent for now
But you can fly
If you pull away
If I demand
You to pull back
and watch if fall behind
You'd trudge to die
Is it better than running there now?
I couldn't capture your unicorn...
when misery
Is all you sought.....

Natalie Ikhlassi

Alone

I sat alone
and wondered why
people must
grow old and die,
and, why it's said that
"Men don't cry"
And then the child
within me wept
loosing all the sorrow
it had kept
and gently turned its head.
and slept.
But I, I sit alone
and wonder why
people must grow old
and die.

Robert Ruiz

Gracie Lou

I know that I should
And would if I could
do an itty-bitti
witty ditty for pretty
Gracie Lou

I'd be so proud
to shout out loud
an itty-bitti
witty ditty for pretty
Gracie Lou

As the days fly by
I'm sure to try
an itty-bitti
witty ditty for pretty
Gracie Lou

Robert J. Klein

Innocence Unveiled

Can it be, you're only three?
And yet, so much to do.
Are you sure, that just last year,
You turned a tender two?

Close your eyes, remembering,
Tell me what you see.
A lonely child so misunderstood
Trying to be ever so good.

Your eyes are dry.
You cannot cry.
No one must hear,
or see a tear.

Can you feel the sorrow now,
And know that it was real?
Awareness gives us power.
In knowing, we can heal.

Kay F. Skinner

Fear Again

An old cliche
and yet, surprisingly still true,
Fear clutches at my heart
like fingers grasping
fruitlessly for air.

Will I learn in time
or will I endlessly struggle
against the inevitable?

I cannot trust my love
I will not trust my heart.

THERE IS NOTHING ELSE!

Sing and dance
tiny falling leaves
this is your only day of flight.
Savor every moment
there is no tomorrow
Only
FOREVER.

Sandra Cathleen Christopher

Our Lost Love

You walked into my life
and you took away my soul,
You made me love you oh
so much and left my heart
to roll.
You gave all your love and
then took it all away,
and I want you just
to know, that my love is
here to stay.
Just because we're not
going out doesn't mean it
has to end.
So let's talk to each other,
and work things, and
hopefully be friends.

Terry Joven

Child's Prayer Upon Awakening

Now I find myself awake
Another day The Lord did make.
Help me, God, Your Word to keep
Ere again I go to sleep.
— Amen

Robert B. Martin

Portrait

I went to paint this morning.
Any color - but not blue.
Tried to think of what to paint.
Kept getting images of you.

I mixed red and yellow sunshine.
Bright to hide the pain
Painted fields of summer flowers.
Somehow my sunshine looked like rain.

I painted crowds of happy people.
Each face was filled with cheer.
Every single mouth was smiling.
Yet each eye held back a tear.

Unbidden on my canvas.
A portrait came to be.
A woman — drenched in sadness.
Stared back — and it was me.

Mary Janet Bionde

Spring In Wisconsin

Tapping maples and boiling sap,
Are in this Springtime Ritual.
Stately trees come out of nap,
To yield this table victual.

Pussy-willows first to spring,
With others soon to follow,
Canadian geese now on the wing,
And frogs sing in the hollow.

Flowering trees in full array,
With fragrance most appealing.
The cold, cold, winter blues allay,
The change now most revealing.

The birds do chirp in melody sweet,
The flowers in gorgeous spread.
All are witness that spring complete,
Has risen from winters bed.

The robin's busy with her nest,
The swallows all are back.
The bear comes forth from den of rest,
And campers now can pack.

Ralph M. McGuire

Silent Hero

He never thought of himself
as a hero of war.
When airplanes like eagles
screamed with an earth trembling roar.
Shells awakening the darkness
bombarding the ground.
Volcanic oil wells
erupt sparks of flames heaven bound.
Desert Storm is only distant,
faded memories now.
Victory is forgotten
by the welcoming home crowds.
"What is left," said Michael,
"after devastation of war?
The belated illness produced
from chemicals of horror!
As the horrendous bombs exploded.
Was I shielded from the storm?
From my bedside I'm now wondering,
Without strength to carry on."

Tamara L. Wireman

"Spring Time Morn"

The fog does lift
As falls the dew
The sun does shine
On morn' a new

A loft the trees
The birds do sing
The bees do buzz
Blooms of spring

The beauty abounds
From here to there
And can be found
On earth-in air

A loft the trees
The birds do sing
The sights and sounds
Of morn' in spring

A. K. Steele

Symbol Of Love

You stood there
as I gazed upon
your menacing body.
My heart is a symbol of love.

I gape at the
way you move,
the way you speak.
You are my symbol of love.

You make my body
shiver then melt a mile away.
As we stand hand in hand,
swaying back and forth,
your kiss is a symbol of love.

Nancy Vang

Words

Words tumble inside my head,
As I lay upon my bed.
Words of life, death, and sorrow.
Words today and of tomorrow.
Words of laughter, health and seeking.
Steal my sleep, as I lay weeping.
Words of children, hunger, crying
Parents tired working trying.
Words tumble inside my head.
As I lay upon my bed.

Sharon A. Winters

"Sadness"

raindrops fall
as i sit and write
my hands are numb
without feeling
like the raindrops
that fall on my head

Wayne Yuen

Reflection

In the purple haze of Twilight
As I sit to reflect upon the day
Images of past Moments
Come to play.
Running and dancing before my mind's eye
How lucky I sigh - - -
To be here and there and alive.

Veronica Gardner

Soliloquy

We celebrate his life, my friends;
As life continues, it never ends.
As promised by our Lord, most high;
He "Graduates," but does not die.

His memories most fondly shared
This day by many will be bared.
Be very careful what you say
He watches over us this day.

Our brother was a man who cared
You're here as testimony to this part
His presence with us still is felt
He's here with us in every heart.

His suffering is over now
Be happy for this man at peace
He left with us his greatest gift
His love for us, which will not cease.

It grows within us like a seed.
Remaining in each heart and head
Remember always this kind soul
Go now, and let his seed be spread.

Stephen L. Birks

To One

To one,
As one tear shed.
When we let cry.
As inconsonant to our souls.
All are left to sigh.

Have the sun burn a new fire.
Let it flame to the angels higher.

To one,
As one bloodshed.
When we let die.
As in our world,
Conscience contorts the lie.

Allow the earth evil and hate.
Let it rage to die by fate.

To one,
As one life shed.
when we let live.
As righteousness is deemed,
For others, as pure, to give.

To one, as one, can only be immortal

Travis Skillings

Street Boy

The city boy learns cement,
As the country child does grass,
The sight and smell and
Feel of it does surpass by far
The earliest lessons of living and
being, and knowing;
Stenciled and inked and repeated by rote
On a sensitive lining that's growing.

Nature's child learns early
The world is underfoot,
Summer sun can bake a slab
And sizzle a tender sole,
But gutter water cools the heels
And waters the dream of relief
From artificial turf and auto droppings,
To an honest-to-goodness dirt street.

Marie N. Hatfield

"Sunset"

The feet of God are on fire -
As the sun does now retire.
A golden glow above us all -
Surrenders sadly to night's call.
Daily rite of cyclical turns -
Becomes the joy each one yearns.
Life itself is no disgrace -
We leave the world a better place!

Ron Fournier

Birthdays

Each birthday is a new beginning.
As your birthday is ending, a
new birthday is beginning. Birthdays
Are a blessing from one year to
another, to be living to be with
family and others. Forget the
old birthday, leave the bad and
hurt behind. Began this birthday
with hope, love and forgiveness blended
with time. To live to see your
children's, children is a blessing so
special. To be fruitful, and multiply,
with God's blessings. Help when possible
to those in need. With Gods blessings
you will succeed. Take each day with
time and love, spread it all
over with strength from above.
Try to live right whatever you do,
and always, do unto others as
You would want them to do to you.

Lucy Y. Harrell

Unspoken

There she lies silently
Asleep in gesture...
But her vibrance reaches out to me
Like a mother for her child.
Her eyes, they are closed...
But I know she sees me.
Like a magician in the night,
Her beauty is her wand.
She wades through my heart, each step
A little faster, searching for an end...
She knows does not exist.

Timothy L. Koester

Once More

The sun set and we gazed
at the orange and red
spread between the hues
of the sky

One more time
we walked
and in the night
we became as the
sun blending with the
earth as it sets

Laurina Marnie Kusell

Untitled

A colorful Heart
and unending beauty
Contained in every being
Waiting for a reason to shine
is a friendly smile

Tina M. Bridges

For You, Mother

Mother, it seems that when I look
at you I see the sun
if there's a picture in my mind
it's colored with this one

Mother, it seems that when I laugh
I hear your voice in mine
tones filled with beauty to be heard
with eyes that brightly shine

Mother, it seems that when I cry
I cry the way you do
a quivering lip, tear stained cheeks
yet pain burns something new

Mother, it seems that when I help
a stranger or a friend
I see the light which you have been
with love that has no end

Mother, these words are for your heart
to hear and claim each day
and they are for the world to know
the beauty you display

Lace Marie Williams

Time Is Precious

Time is most precious. It should
be valued in a very special way.
It's a gift we sometimes take
for granted as we got through
Life each day-
As I look to this day with
gladness-
I feel comfort in my heart-
It will be a day of pleasure-
A day to a bright new start-
It will be a good beginning-
For the tomorrows that have
yet to come
And I'll strive to do the best
I can till my goal is won

Ruth Cot'e Brown

Reflections

Laying by the fire on a thick
bear rug with a smile on
your face and a halo up above.
You told me there's a way
through a shining golden gate
where happiness shines through
with thoughts of me and you.

Nicole Nikniai Ozaeta

Skeleton

Kings and queens are rulers
Beggars wearing next to nothing
People wearing next to nothing
Women selling babies buttons
Babies giving their own milk
Many men not minding
Morons
Supreme fights for equilibrium
Red and black and yellow and white
Men and women making skeletons
Skeletons creating more skeletons
Rape and reign and rain
Reality
We all turn to dust.

Sara Silberger

Eliza

She walks in the
beauty of sunset
wind blowing her
golden hair.
He looks at her with
sparkling eyes
and takes the cloud
off her bad day.

He moves closer
her body trembles
as he runs fingers
through her hair.

With love and laughter
thru whisper of the wind
they walk down
the rolling hills
down by the shore.

Marcia Skow

Doors

A door open
beckoning beyond
The steps I stand
upon.

A shell a key -
a call beyond
The voice I hear
within.

The door closed
to those not privy
to my thoughts.

But like my thoughts
the door opens easily
to those who take
the time to care.

Tish Redden

A Natural Wonder Land

On an early Saturday morning
Before the world was awake,
I walked through the meadows
And down a hill to a lake.
The grass was wet with dew
And cold on my bare feet.
I reflected upon this day
That I had yet to meet.
Cautiously I stepped upon the dock,
And settled myself where it was dry.
I lowered my feet to the water
As I gazed upon the sky.
I reveled in the trees' divinity
As they sheltered me with their arms.
As I flew myself up the hill,
The wind frolicked with my tresses.
The green carpet below nursed my feet.
The sun painted me with kisses.
I wished the day would never end,
Even though, it had just begun.

Tammy K. Stevenson

Untitled

The edge so close I must be.
Behind all shadows lurk
The unknown misery.
Try to keep away
Unaware a perpetual magnet
Draws you near.
Sometimes conceivable
Yet
Uncomprehending
Understanding obscurities
Of the
Deep dark edge of sanity...

Pamela GaLán

Best Friends

We are friends, very good friends,
best friends to be exact.
No, it's not a rumor or a joke,
It's plain to see, it's just a fact.
Yes, we love each other,
but not in a boyfriend, girlfriend way;
We respect and trust one another,
and that's more than anyone can say.

Meghan Moquin

Patience

I hear my children cry to me
Beyond their birthed Fate,
"Oh Father shall you bring to us
Our life which cannot wait?"
I've seen their eyes in many more
I know a love exists,
But know upon the destined strife
which painfully persists.
"My children how I long for you
To hold you in my arms
And feel of this great sorrow
which derives the searching charm.
For soon shall I to find her
Now I promise this to thee;
You must now always realize
of the Destiny to be.
We'll meet upon the lighted wheel
And greatest music hall,
With but to find our happiness
Upon the Fated call."

Scott A. Osborn

The Mall

The mall is tall
big and small so
many stores, you
can see. When you
go to the mall there
are stores like The Limited,
Rainbow Gate, and more
just don't forget so
many stores. The
mall is tall big and
small just go to the
mall that's all!

Lauren Caswell

Mi Tesoro

Pelo guero, piel blanca
Big gray eyes looking up at me,
Her mother of 18.

Tears in my eyes.
We will be ok.

A stamp on her nose
Chocolate pudding everywhere
Chee-tos her favorite

We will grow-up together

Long blonde hair, big hazel eyes
Looking at me while she boards the plane

Tears in my eyes.
She will be ok.

We will grow-up some more

Roberta Bolanos

Life Cycle

Pain
Birth
Hunger
Knowledge
Education
Religion
Salvation
Hypocrisy
Politicians
Promises
Lies
Corruption
Police
Oppression
Rebellion
Wiser
Older
Disease
Pain
Death

Thomas L. Whisenhunt

"Blackness"

Blackness isn't a color
Blackness isn't derogatory
Blackness is of a people's
struggles and hardships
It tells of their proud, rich
and elegant past; of their
triumphs and misfortunes; of their
will to sustain and be heard.
Blackness is the depth of our souls
Blackness is our being
Blackness is humility, that has
been endured in the past, present and
future.
Blackness is my man's strength and
his willingness to stand for what
he believes
Blackness is our love
Blackness is ME!

Nadine Y. Holliman

Autumn Savors

The Canada Goose arrows south...
Bohemians gulp Mountain Ash berries...
Pheasants feast in shelter belt...
Bunnies nibble windfall fruit.

Cattle trail to winter range...
Culls trucked to packers...
Cacophony of weaner calves...
Stockliner string at scales.

"Mackerel" sky - unstable weather?
Garden spaded for holding snow...
Logs split and stacked in row...
Root crops stored for winter.

Round bales resemble jelly rolls...
Hen house cleaned and "strawed"...
New gate latch on the cattle pen...
Fence repaired on old hay lot.

Wooly worm shows a wide belt...
Washed windows sparkle in the sun...
Wind chills and gathers strength...
Autumn's work is nearly done.

Merilyn J. Hall

The Maker

When the wind blows the trees
bow, because it knows who
its maker is.

In a clear field the grass
is as tall as you are,
when the wind blows softly, the
grass bows, because it knows
who its maker is.

When the wind blows
I bow willingly, because I
know who my maker is.

When the wind blows on
his side he refuses to bow
and he knows who his
maker is, therefore we know
where he's bound to spend
Eternity.

Monica Spangler

Untitled

For the love of GOD
bring our soldiers back
None of us could bare
if there were an attack

We don't want a war
for fear we may lose
So let them come home
or at least let them choose

If war does arise
before the days out
Watch over our loved ones
and don't yell if they shout

If the war is to take
one soldier or more
Bring the rest back home
to our front door

But for the time being
don't let them forget
All of the good times
they'll never regret

Penny M. Seel

Problems

Sometimes someone
brings up old memories
and it makes you
want to drop to your knees.

Stop it! Stop it!
Is all you scream
and it feels like
your in a never-ending dream.

The problem is yours
not theirs
You wish there was someone
who really cares.

Then you see
A big smile and bright eyes
Someone who doesn't
believe all the lies.

It's just a storm
go on, go on
for there's a rainbow
shortly beyond.

Sara Martin

Madrigal

Hesitant and with guile
Brocade dips on the stair
And lies inert at last
By candlelight and shadow.
The gray falcon on its perch
Sees it fall and lie as dead.
Breathing gold on those wet stones
The long folds are whispering musk
Going tediously about the room.

Brocade full of sounds
Fair smiling in the candlelight
Slithering full of fine folly -
Fall gently in the darkening hall!
Glint of shadows, hint of fire
Creeping in the regal wake.

The touch of seas in shells
Translucent on a scan of silk
So full of roses and leafing -
A finished dream half told.

Mary Kellerman

Maybe Tomorrow

Day is cold, prediction is snow,
Bundled people hurriedly go.
Trees are bare, Sun found hiding,
Traces of Summer, dead or dying.
A long time since we saw the beach,
Warmth and joy seem out of reach.
Children playing their games inside,
Mother's eyes show they have cried.
Season's clothed in dismal blue,
Passing thoughts, and some of you.
So long ago, another season,
We all could smile without a reason.
Remember back when we were new?
We never felt the color blue.
But past is past and done is done,
Maybe tomorrow will bring some Sun..

Lou Addimando

Reflection

The touch
Burns, festers
Stone, dead, emotionless
The hate she feels
For war
Down he fell
Tasting his metallic essence
Tears loitering in his eyes
Mother laments
Her infant gone
Ghastly the colour
Tears, blood
She dies holding
Her still one
The world falls
Rushing, colliding
The fluid face
Goes black again
She turns, paces away
Lonely and lost

—Julian Dean

Untitled

It's easy to love you,
But harder to lie.
I'm caught in a trap,
And yet I must try
To keep what I'm feeling
From harming what's real.
We're the best of friends,
But that's less than I feel.
I pray for the time
Your love for me stirs,
But until that day
Your heart is still hers.

Nicole Brunet

The Sleepy Colors

Indigo and red,
But I don't want to go to bed.
Orange and yellow,
Oh how mommy yelled when I told her so.
Blue and green,
Green and blue,
She made my cry-boo hoo!
Purple and Pink
Daddy just winked
and told me not to worry.
White and black,
can you picture that.
a nice little present,
All for me?
Oh wow!
All mine!

Wendy-Nicole Lane

Souls

The sun lights the sky
But there is no one to see it
The wind blows hard
But there is no one to feel it
The world is empty
But there is no one to notice it
Our souls are empty
But there is no one to fill it
We are a world of dead souls
With no way of living

Kristi Kirwin

Taking Leave

I now take leave of you
But I'll see you again
Oh do not be discouraged
For sunshine follows rain.

And when I leave you here
You won't be here alone
Remember God is with you
And sees you from His throne

Look up to God dear one
You know he cares for you
Just trust the Heavenly Father
Cheer up and don't be blue

These word I give to you
To comfort and to cheer
Be thankful for God's presence
For he is with you here.

Mary L. Davis

Whither The Wind

You can not see the wind in Spring,
But it is everywhere,
In lilting bird songs wafted
On blossom scented air.

You can not see the wind in Summer,
But it is every place,
Shifting sands at seashores
And breathing hotly in your face.

You can not see the wind in fall,
But its benediction earth receives,
In amber, red and golden,
Downward drifting leaves.

But in winter,
When it swirls the snow,
And molds it into designs
Of its own artistic notion-
Ah, then you see the wind,
In graceful, frozen motion.

Winifred N. Caterson

The Wanderer

Once, I lived in Principalia,
But left there for Episcopalia;
Living there was truly hard, indeed.

In time, I ailed with echolalia,
And as sure as my name is Ukelelia,
High-strung, I simply went to seed.

But fair winds carried me to Hegelia
And on from there to Bacchanalia;
Oh, happy, happy days of honey and mead.

They wait for me in Mesmeralia,
With a final stop in Euthanalia,
But that is JUST NOT yet decreed.

And that's my story, Urbanalia —
I smell the rose and stroke the dahlia;
I ponder hopes and faiths and creeds,
Thinking lofty thoughts of noble deeds.

Ralph E. Bodfish

First Hunt

A snowy winter morning
Cold steel in my hand
rustling in the bushes
I aim and shoot
One less animal in the forest
I shall never kill again.

Timothy Arnold Waller

A Day Of You

I spoke to you on the phone.
But, still I felt all alone.

Your voice was a gift of love.
You are the girl that came from above.

Talking to you was like a wish come true.

I dialed your number.
But, still I slept with no slumber.

I tossed and turned.
And my hart still yearned.

I spoke to you clearly.
But, still felt weary.

Then I did something wrong.
And I know it true and strong.

Knowing you touch is so far away.
I lost it in one short day.

Micah Johnson

Here I Sit ...

Here I sit married and all,
But, still so very lonely,
Not, knowing why!
Why it wont go away.

We go places together,
but it seems like
were so far apart.
Where-ever I go I see
people like us,
but they're not really like us.
They're not feeling lonely.

It's rather weird but here I sit still
feeling as lonely as ever.

Wendy Burlee

Strangers!

You say you love me
  but you don't even know me
I'm flattered by what you say
But I know the feelings is
  gonna go away
You don't know me from
  the inside
You just like what you see
  from the outside
You tell me everything I
  want to hear
You even say it with sincere
  but I'm afraid to get to near
I tell you were just friends
  and that's where we stand
I'm watching over myself to
  keep me from danger
So the next time I see you,
  you'll be nothing
    but a stranger...

Renea Burg

Deep

Deep as the sea,
Deep as its darkest point.
Let it all swallow me up.
Deep,
Deep,
Deep.

Kristen Smith

i cried today

i cried today—
but you held me close
and dried my tears
and eased my pain
and calmed my fears
you stopped the rain
and understood
the anguish
that no other could
and you loved me
  until
i smiled today

Monica E. Smith

A Woman's Cry For Help

She said she was car jacked
by a blackman, who's taken her
children without leaving a
demand.

Their ages were fourteen months;
and three years old, not old enough
to be in controlled.

For money and jewels, or any other
contraband, and now she's left crying
and asking everyone to lend a
helping hand, to find her
children as soon as they can.

Peoples came from all over the
world to help on the hunt, to
find out it was a stunt.

Her confession was very upsetting
she had driven her children into
the lake, now she must face the
deadly intake.

Mattie Polk

Staring

I was caught quickly,
By a cold, hard glance,
Staring into cloudy eyes,
As they were staring back.

Kristi Steffy

"Emily" A Precious Moment

A precious moment
Came into our lives
With the sweetest grin
And the devil in her eyes
So loving and caring
As she grew
A beautiful smile
And eyes of blue
But as she reached the age of eleven
An angel was sent
To take her to heaven
Sweet precious moment
You touched our lives
We'll love you forever
And never forget
How precious your moment was

Marie Sciacchitano

Learn To Live

The soul that is afraid to die
can never learn to live
Hiding from the world
not learning to fly
Sitting in its nest
as life passes him by
Making his world as small
as a seed of a tree
A vision of the world is all he'll ever see
Without a sight of the beauty of the earth
He'll never know what living is worth

Kia Shanic Scott

"We Are One"

We have started our life together.
Caring, sharing, giving to each other.
As time passes, our love grows.
Treasuring our love as we go.

After our vows we became one.
To have and to hold as life goes on.
To share all our hopes and our dreams.
To know what love really means.

Love like this is a blessing we share.
Our chance to have someone to care.
As our lives pass I will give to you.
This love I have, so very true.

Kathy Snipes

Lament

Where did I put that dream!
Caught in the lace of my wedding veil -
Tucked in a baby's shoe?
Apron pocket - button box -
Lost in a field of rue?

Where did I put that dream!
Modest it was - more gingham than gold,
Filled with a child's delight,
Heroes of passion engaging the foe,
Galloping into the night.

Where did I put that dream!
More enamored with living than dreaming,
I deemed dreaming the lot of the old.
Spun in the web of the cunning years
Daring was left to the bold.

Where did I put that dream!
Not lost - nor yet quite found
A wraith to mourn at even song
"Madam, my friend, how sad for you -
Delaying your search so long!"

Maxine F. Prehler

First Words

I am a lucky person
cause I am free
Free from all old addictions
Free from all old pain

Today is different from yesterday
and my mind will never change.
God has rescued me from all my shame.

Thank you Lord for me
for you created me long ago
and it will be a long hard Road
but... I am stronger now
and I just can be me.

Teresa Stouffer

Damaging Entities

Death of stonealm is set by a figure,
Causing war wage the white figure.
Doom until Amaranthine cure,
Cease pain the magical lure.

The member of Amarantines,
  Warrior of 4,000 years,
The amber among thanes,
  Withholds the magical spears.

As the war lasts for on,
  The white figure's work is done—
As the old world recovers,
  The black figure's fate suffers.

Entity is stopped by white breath,
  The Figure—
Eternity is sentenced by black death,
  The Figure—

In the figure's quick demise,
It shall create a fresh sunrise—
The Amaranthine watch and fend,
The genesis of a world-without-end.

Peter K. Peers Jr.

The Lovely Birches

So majestically you withstand
  challenge upon challenge
    from acquaintance and stranger.

So steadily you repel
  attack upon attack
    from nature and beast.

So arrogantly you stand
  onslaught upon onslaught
    from wind and rain.

Oh, lovely birches
  what is your secret
Or is the naturally divine
  unable to reveal
    their immortality?

Ralph L. Lundberg

Peacefulness

People in their suits and hats,
Children with their little rafts,
Colors here of every hue,
All the boys are cuties too.

People walking hand in hand,
Lovers rolling in the sand,
Babies in the water cry,
Others shaking themselves dry.

Strangers wander to the sea,
Fishing boats that sail free,
Joggers run all aimlessly,
That boy I wish he sat with me.

What is it that I come here for,
The sunshine?
No it's much much more.

It's peacefulness I feel inside,
Here you have no need to hide.

Mindy Hughes Cannon

The Hand

Icy winter hand of death
cold embracing every breath

Evening shadows frozen still
leafless gallows on every hill

Pale members grasping every shape
skimming over field and lake

Hollow, empty, lifeless ground
devoid of movement, warmth, or sound

Tender is the hand
that melts the snow and warms the land

Soft the hand must be
that sets the waters free

Life must flow within its veins
to stop the cold and cease the rains

Love must flow within its tips
to soften Lady Winter's lips

MarDee J. Haring

Arms Of Love

Need my restful arms of love to sleep
Come, thou restless wondering sheep,
So weak and lonesome, cold and sad
So awful looking, tattered clad.

Tus for refuge, from thy tyrant flee
In no other arms thou could be?
If in faith has come, not in hate
Come in the house of my estate.

Delay thee not, oh, wondering sheep,
Come within where no one shall weep,
Take off thy clothing, tattered worn
In Love, to wear my crowing own.

All thy sorrows, I've made to freeze
Thy griefs no more thy feeding trees,
Shall tire no more in want of love
That of house of heaven above.

Oh, now within thy hundred fold
No more art lonesome sad and cold,
To be thy soul, in my sweet rain
In arms of love, in sweet refrain.

Osbourne Blake

Jesus Said

Jesus said oh come you sinners
Come to me I'll guide you home
No more sorrow will be there for you
When your sins you have atoned

Jesus said I hear you calling
But you haven't took the step
My friend I know you need me
But you haven't asked me yet

To forgive your sins and lead you
Straight toward heavens shore
Where you'll want to meet your family
And be happy for evermore

Jesus said you need his help
But you won't give the final word
His arms are open wide to help you
And in heaven you will be heard

I know you need him and you're lonely
Walking around so all alone
Jesus said just give the signal
And he'll be there to guide you home

Ruth Shelton

Thoughts, Sitting By The Sea

Inner peace, serenity, cool breezes,
Comforting warm sun.
Sounds, the wind unique like a
conch shell.
Really alone
Sea gulls pumping and soaring by.
Reflection is the glassy ripples
Far off sails and ships
A broken pier and pilings
People, quiet muffled voices
Seven rows of white caps ever moving
Shadows of sea gulls on the shallow water.
Bubbles bursting, miniature tides, sands
shifting
My hat blew off on to three shells
A hint of pink clouds
Sea gulls again on pilings, landing,
hopeful, hungry
Jetties reaching out into the sea
toward the endless horizon

Patricia Galloway

Thoughts Of Johnny

Reflections of/the way life used to be
consumes me totally with morning tea

I try hard to hide, my hurt inside
say I'm happy, then know I lied

Emotions are = all of life
each must learn to handle

to take the good
to take the bad
to take, to take, is really sad
Giving is getting/so there's my setting

The power of love is like no other
it can move you, it can stall you
it can and will control you

So when your times reflect
take caution/don't neglect
Remember all remember well
you'll be released from your prison cell

Veronica Mulligan

Crying Heart

I hear your heart
Crying out in pain,
Among the wind
Or the slow pouring rain.
I can hear the cry
Because I've heard it before,
Locked in my heart
Behind a closed door.
The more I hear it
The more I fear,
That this love
I have found,
Will never
Be near.

Michelle Balstad

The Pearl

Formed inside the shells of oysters
Deep beneath the watery world.
Sand forms into lovely pearls
Desert life just seems to cruel
Oceans of dried up wanna be pearls

Raymond L. Welch

Veteran's Day/Washington/1994

A black stone wall
Cuts the earth
With a procession of names
Set in dying order.
The sun makes somber
Reflections on the dark granite.
Carved names are alive in memory
Only.
Candles, trinkets, and flowers
Mark
Remembering visits
And beginnings ended.
No patriotic songs will
Raise these dead.
The ended lives here are
Jagged.
The edges still
Cut the living.

Michael Itomlenskis

The Dancers

Come,
dance with me.
Let
us feel
the rhythms in our souls
as we move as one.

Come,
glide with me
over earth and radiant sky.
The passion in our steps
connects our forms.

Come,
join with me.
Drink the music of the universe,
as we spin and dip,
balancing
life and love,
freeing our spirits
to soar in heavenly harmony.

Roberta Leffler

A Single Rose

A single rose alone in the day
Dances in the breeze
A single rose alone in the day
Not having anyone to please.

A single rose alone in the day
Sways beautifully in the sun
A single rose alone in the day
Its dancing is now done.

A single rose alone in the day
No more dancing it will do
A single rose alone in the day
Was given from me to you!

Nicole Mercier

Nightingale

On the shores of the
deep blue sea,
a nightingale sings
for thee.

O, how it sings
so beautifully,
on the shores of
the deep blue sea

Tallie Ben Daniel

Two North

Wings of shadow,
dark-furled around my heart.
No life-joy sparkle
lighting blackened days.
Dreams dead aborning;
endless night - no morning.
Anger, rage, injustice - uncried
for who will listen
Or listening - care
or caring
resurrect the dreams
in ashes scattered at my feet?

Susan Ann Lawrence

Today

Today I watched a butterfly
Dart quickly through the flowers;
And then I saw a child at play
I could have watched for hours.

Today I wondered here and there
Without a thought or reason;
Taking in the joy and beauty
Displayed through Nature's season.

Today I called a special friend
And took the time to chat;
It was so good to hear her voice
As we talked of this and that.

Today I took the time to do
Just simple things — none trying;
I'd like to spend more days like this
. . . Today I learned I'm dying!

Minnie C. Batting

The Seed To The Future

The future begins from a seed
deep within

If you follow your heart it will
never grow dim

It grows thru a process we call
give and take

And it learns to bend but never
to break

One day you will wake and find
that the seed

Has grown to a tree that you
can call home

Mary Didszun

Thoughts Of Boredom

Blissful days of wishful thinking
Delightful calmness, mellow dreams
Pleasant people, solemn people
People solely dolls of you
Extreme uniqueness judged from those
Who only judge themselves
Anger tries to rumble from
Within the freshened wounds
Gulping hard to keep in tears
The ignorance is gone
You realize what your life's become
You wonder where your youth has
Gone

Sarah Cadman

Madman Lost

A silhouette of a different kind
Depicted rays from the morning sun.
They burned away this complex mind
And caused a man to come undone.

Alone he sits and retracks time
Of days gone by when love was lost.
If being different is such a crime
Then this young man must pay the cost.

His mind is now a spinning wheel
Caught in the pages of his dreams.
With nightmares that will not reveal
The chapters of archaic schemes.

The room grew dark, his eyes turned cold
And soon his message would be clear.
He knew his story would be told
Of what had happened here.

His train of thought was struck by rain
As if the clouds began to cry.
He knew that he had gone insane
And that he had to die.

Kathleen Johnston

"Mountains"

From the Ark on Mount Ararat,
did we all descend,
To go and conquer earth and then,
wait until the end!
Mountains hold a majesty,
to let us view our land,
In helping learn how small we are,
they give us quite a hand!
On every mass of land they range,
giving up their water,
Nourishing the earth below
and giving us our larder!
Wondrous though they rise and fall,
creating quite a show.
Reminds one of man's history,
THAT - we all should know!
Descending on the Mount of Olives soon,
from two millenniums past,
One will come in glory,
redressing things at last!

Philip T. Kachmarek

Encourage Me Not

Encourage me not too much, I ask
don't make a big deal
of my every task

Give me not words, just ideas, please
keep words in your mouth
leave my mind at ease

Build me not dreams up to the sky
it's not what it seems
my actions can lie.

Just give me time; room to improve
give to me hope
something I can use

Throw me a rope, made up of love
let me hang on
its length from above

With it bind me, all parts shall be one
without it my mind
shall all come undone

Theresa E. Meyers

A Tribute To My Mother

She was an angel
Down here on earth.
She is an angel
Up there in Heaven.

So kind and loving
So patient and understanding
So gentle and forgiving
Her friends were many
Who mourned her passing.
For over ninety-two years
She lived here an earth.
October 23, 1983 she left
To live with her maker
In heaven so bright.
The angels are rejoicing
And she is at peace
While God she is praising
And jubilantly singing.

Virginia B. Guthrie

Sleepwalker

Cold winter's night,
Dreamt I was a sleepwalker,
Waging through a barren land,
Void of love, life.

Felt the eyes of truth,
Watching my every move.
My heart has turned to stone.
Voice whispers,
In every stone lies a crystal.

Destiny is a chance,
I must take in my hands.
I am chained to the floor,
Staring hatred in the face.

As a sleepwalker,
I feel no danger,
Only obsession.
My soul a mirror,
To passion in an evil place.

Cry, laugh, scream.
I am who I am... a sleepwalker.

Warren K. Todd

A Bronx State Of Affairs

She stoops to sweep the street
Dressed in the same old coat,
No matter what the weather
She mumbles to herself
As her eyes dart about
For the coins some throw at her.
But most walk quickly away
From the odor of unwashed clothes.

Her daughter waits by the store
To help you load your car,
And adds to their meager income.
They live in a vacant building.

What's happened in their lives?
What's happened in our world
To allow this state of affairs?

S. Barbara Lenniger

Desire

A leaf
Drifting down a river bed
Reminds me of a loved one
Who once loved then fled.
It drifts so far
As though never to return
But I have hopes
Though my heart will burn
For that leaf
To change its way
And come back to me
To stay.

Rachela Pranzo

Among Those Hardest Hit

Among the hardest hit
During the endless increase
of confusion,
Among the greatest
Who made their stand throughout,
Conquering, pushing on,
was the signal that among
Those were those who shared
Many of his views about
The complexities of new blood.
The age of ignorance,
Lost some in between.
Re-creating the past, melting
Away what should be our future,
Desperate circumstances that place
One in that other one's shoes.
The shoes that have been
Owned by many,
And walked across the earth.

Shasta A. Amiss

Forget Me Nots

Each day we awake
Each breath we take
Our blood that flows
Our strength that grows.

The common sense to think
The water we drink
The food we eat
The loved one's we meet
And the unforgettable memories we keep.

Eyes that see, ears to hear
The fragrance's we smell
And the stories we tell

The will to live
The generosity to give
The faith to hope
And the strength to cope

Happiness that make us smile
Tears that let us cry
The grace to say hello
And the courage to say goodbye.

Nellie M. Hayes

"Wings"

A soul's silent rapture
eludes the restless heart.
But...
even a wanderer's restless
heart must rest,
and so then the soul breaks
free from its shadow, in a burst
of brilliant light,
its wings unfurled,
fairy body quivering,
to release the unborn side
of yourself,
So that you may fly and breathe,
and be free.
In this you will find, yourself.
Now test out your wings.

Kela Jolene Cady

Time

Twisting, turning, swirling.
Endlessly, continuously, unfurling.

Flowing, rolling, going.
Forever, dutifully, sowing.

Time moving, time standing.
Time soothing, time demanding.

With every moment, every breath.
With every heartbeat, closer to death.

Time to live, time to die.
Time to laugh, time to cry.

Twisting, turning, swirling.
Endlessly, continuously, unfurling.

Flowing, rolling, going.
Forever, dutifully, sowing... Time.

Lisa Carol Andes

The Model

She is like a flower
enticing men with her beauty
put on display for all to see
her beauty slowly fading away

Hidden from sight
she withers with age
hoping to be remembered
as she used to be
beauty....

Robin L. Sullivan

I Want You Forever

I want you forever
even though forever doesn't exist

I want your lips touching my lips
and your lips in my ear
whispering sweet nothings

I want your arms around me
and your hands caressing me

I want your body touching
my body and creating magic

I want you forever
Even though forever doesn't exist

Empress

Untitled

Captures Me
Entrances me
Every time
You look at me
Beautiful
So beautiful
Every time
I look at you
It makes me think
It makes me dream
How much I
Want to love you
Someday
A blessed day
Our lips
Will softly touch
Your hand in mine
Our lives entwined
There's nothing else
That I could want

Randy Rush

Untitled

Strike the match and lead me away
Envelop me in the solitude of night
and blind me so as not to see the hurt
in the eyes of the reflection
Numb me so I can't feel my heart pumping
out blood so cold that it freezes my
brittle veins
Take my love away for not even death
could equal its pain
When all is done leave me alone to revel
in the divine torture of inner sanctum.

Kimberley Boyd

Carousel

'Round and 'round we go
Even though we never know
How long the dream will spin
Or if the fantasy should end,
Will a better one begin?
Hold on my friends.

I'll ride the blue horse
With the gold and diamond reins.
Things will never be the same
Once the music starts to play.
We could ride our troubles away,
If only we could stay.

There's a reindeer with a sleigh
To pull us happily on our way
Past the clowns with painted tears.
Do they realize our fears?
Will we have this through the years?

Will you hold on my friends?
Hold on until the end?
Is that where life begins?
Does it seem so out of place
That there should be tears on my face?
Only the rats can run this race.

Sylvia A. Peters

Shiloh Is Coming

Alleluia, Alleluia, Shiloh is coming.
Every knee will bow to Him,
He will be our only King,
Alleluia, Alleluia, Shiloh is coming.

He will come to mount Zion when He comes,
When the devil see Him coming
Like a rabbit he'll be running,
Alleluia, Alleluia, Shiloh is coming.

He will have an iron rod when He comes,
He'll be ruling all the nations
From mount Zion to New Orleans,
Alleluia, Alleluia, Shiloh is coming.

He'll destroy Lucifer when he comes,
There will be no more tear,
There will be no more fear,
Alleluia, Alleluia, Shiloh is coming.

Earth will be a paradise when He comes,
And the righteous will live forever
In the kingdom here on earth
But the devil and the wicked they will perish.

Santos Camacho

Mother's Soup

Mother soup is special,
Everyone has a claim,
Tasting others on the way,
None is just the same.

What is it that she uses?
Where is that special jar?
The cupboards I've climbed endlessly,
Her secret can't be far.

Mother's soup a mystery,
No bowl tastes alike,
My only samplings are granted,
On a could winter's night.

A warm blanket it is,
To my body, my soul and my mind,
My mother's soup I'll tell you,
Is truly one of a kind.

Stephanie Howe

"Reasoning"

Why do some things happen?
Everything happens for a reason
like the changing of the weather
and the changing of the season.

It's time to think it over
and make your own decision
Don't allow a new thing
to blur up your clear vision

Fate could play a part
in the changing of your mind
Why are hearts left broken
and the pieces left behind

Everyone will hurt sometime
We all must feel the pain
and learn from our mistakes
so we don't make them again

We've been together briefly
and I Love you so
and if you choose to be with me
I will never let you go

Michael T. Oakes

In Searching

If you are tired of
everything your tried

Have you tried Jesus?
He'll be all you will ever need.
Also peace within besides.

Shirley Henry

For Her

Have you ever asked yourself
exactly what is love,
Have you searched deep inside
or asked up above.

Have you found it in her eyes
or felt it in her kiss,
Is it when you are apart
that it is her touch that you'll miss.

Well I have the answer
and I believe it is true,
The love that we feel
Comes from the hearts of me and you.

Socratis Sarras

My World

The world I see
Exists in me.

The people I meet
In my heart they beat.

The places I go
Exists in my soul.

The things I feel
My mind will reveal.

For everything out
Must come in.
And what I sense not,
Exists not within.

For I created
The world I see.
And when I die
It dies in me.

Lyle A. Feigenbaum

Life

The joy of birth
Experienced by our mother,
As painful as can be, yet
As wonderful as one can see,
A new piece to the puzzle
Where one carries no more
Weight than his brother,
Stimulated by faith
Love and energy,
Each piece shall have
Its place in this world,
Not to get lost in confusion
For life was meant
To be more simple.

Lisa Garcia Mikailian

Another Chance

A rose gleaming,
  facing the world.
Now suddenly wilted,
  isn't gleaming,
  but is still there.
Just a spark
  waiting to shine again.
It will be given
  another chance
  to gleam,
  facing the world
  once more.

Rita Szablewski

Shadows

Faded memories like
Faded photographs
Pasted in my mind.

Yellowed dreams
Of days gone by
Found in the shadows of my mind.

Stained and aged
They begin to fade -
Those memories I once made.

Now I am old and
My hair is grey
But I won't let
Those memories fade away.

Katt Miller

Confusing Intimacy

Looks that blind an innocent soul,
falling in the tramp
of the confusing intimacy.

Touch that burns,
living a footprint
that could never be replaced.

Taste that challenges
to fulfill ones dreams,
leaving aside those memories
dominating ones thoughts.

Sounds that affirm
the intensity that rouses,
penetrating, in each pore of the skin,
the humidity produced touch to touch.

Smell that bares that silhouette,
the truth of an adulteress
loving is secrecy.

Past time of great memories
leaving awake,
deep inside the heart.

Maria F. Perez-Grau

To My Love

Searching for tomorrow
Feeling for today
Thoughts that none can borrow
Emotions you must obey
Lest time takes them away
Where there is no feeling to say
I miss you.

Thelma R. Catalani

Life's Banquet

Art! Music! Dance!
Feasts for the senses...
Our lenses open wide,
Picturing sumptuous colors-
Carrot orange,
Lemon yellow,
Beet burgundies-
Served on blue, amid red roses...

An orchestral menu
Entering hungry ears-
Singing along agile arteries.
Nourishing, soothing,
Harmonizing our existence...

Dancing desserts venting vibrations.
Saucy little tarts in can can costumes.
Rich creamy chocolates waltz in
Seduction...
Indulge art, music and dance-
Life's banquet to pleasurable
Passion...

Martha Skinner Blackman

Insanity

The golden rays of the
fiery sun keep my body warm as I lay
on the side of this hill.
From my eyes the tears will spill.
One by one roll down my face.
Land on the earth cold
and fresh. Pink and frail
was my flesh. A bird sang
its song of freedom and
pain. I might be mistaking,
but am I insane? The world spins
round, the clouds roll by. If the
moon's so full why doesn't
it fall from the sky? A
strong wind blows. In the
breeze the bare branches sway.
Silence fills an empty
room. Pharaohs lay in their forgotten
tombs.
But I just sit here on this hill.
Am I insane I wonder still.

Krista Sciotto

Scared Of........

Away with the world.
Fighting the truth of nature,
with-in itself.
Wrinkled old and red,
falling into the world
of death.
Beneath the surface
It rises again.
The flower of your life.
For the next time it is spring!
To feel happy!!
That it has been reborn
In spirit, color and all.
Many wonder what to say,
and what to do.
To face the real way of dying
Is a way of dying in itself.
Are you scared of dying?

Melanie Nelson

My Example

One day when heaven was
filled with God's praises,
One day when sin was
black as could be,
Jesus, came forth to be
born of a virgin.
Dwelt among men my
example is he.
Living, he loved me.
Dying, he saved me.
Buried he carried my
sins far away;
risen, he would never
hurt again;
one day he is coming!
Oh, what a wonderful day.

Matthew Tehonica

Untitled

Second Best...
First Class,
A Patient Fool,
Silence is the Rule.

Never First, Not Last,
Never as Important
Only when Convenient,
Only when Needed.

Second Best...
Has no Voice,
Answers if Spoken to,
Ask not, for it Matters Not.

Second Best...
Not the Chosen one,
Easily Replaced,
Easily Forgotten.

Second Best...
When will You Learn,
Those who Rate you Less
Lose the Best.

Patricia L. Del Vecchio

Bouquet Of Imagery

Behold beauty;
Flora of fragrance.
Pleasant thoughts;
Sweet dreams.

Victor Volpe

Untitled

Mr Creator says He always gives thanks
For the Love we return to Him
Highest among the things He ranks
Is the joy in our hearts therein

For what He does in every way
To make our days worthwhile
Thanks He says everyday
For each and every smile

My creators touch is so very sweet
I often feel He is kissing us too
For His Love's so great it can't be beat
It shows in the good we do

Think of a God as great as that
No jealousy in His heart
Because He always made His beings
Beautiful from the start

Polly Streiff

Imagine That

The lost hurt feelings of a human being
Flows back and forth. I try to imagine.
What it was like for him to be around.
I miss something maybe everything
about him as time is seen
to drift by I feel a lot of
pain and hurt

That
Something I feel will
never be the same like
something was being
taken for all of the
wrong or right reasons

Today I'm turning
bends of depression
What happens when the
next corner isn't being
with you. How will
I feel and when Do I
begin to know you again

Tonya Kessler

"Birds"

Birds can fly -
fly sky high.
Up in the breeze -
then, the trees.
Some robins so fair -
I see them there.
Some making a nest -
just to rest.
Guess a Whippoorwill -
can really shrill.
In flight -
they seem so light.
As they look for seed -
some people take heed.
Birds often gather -
any kind of matter.
To make a house -
anywhere from a mouse.
So listen for a bird -
it's something to be heard.

Paulena R. Cucchetti

River Of Love

Love runs wild on water's edge.
Foam of seduction
On a lily pad pledge.
Turbulent waves that beat against
Tides crossing;
Heart of many seasons, sends dew drop
Waves a tossing.

Blue waters on the banks,
Washed up by nature's force,
Sought after many times,
As if love was cohearsed.

Traveling on a cycle
In water built for two
A systematic splash.
Fantastic dajavou.

Disturbances of undertow
Never to be regained,
Memories on rivers of love
Watery
Mysteries still remain.

Monica Leach Tate

My Love

My love is like the air,
For I cannot live with out it;
My love is like a revolution,
For I feel that I must shout it.

My love is like a river,
For it flows and flows;
My love is a vine of ivy,
For it knows not where it goes.

Regina Yvette Wise

"Your Love Shows All The Way"

You're love is magic pure and sweet
for it is the magic that makes my
life complete
Love is given freely and never bought
Love is the gift mankind has always
sought.

Love is eternal through the years
Love stands strong through joy and tears.
Love never changes it self.
But it works wonders large and small.

Love turns all of the common places
to matchless beauty, joy and graces
Love makes happiness, its specialty
and gives it self unselfishly.

Love is a mystery that is age old
It's impossible to see to hold
But there's something that hearts
would say...
You're Love is magic and it
shows all the way.

Suzyelle Rodrigues

Your Body - Your Self

Your body your self you must take care
For other people are unaware

It needs food and sleep and work and fun
In order no, there is none.

Hours of each is a major requirement
for a body to function before retirement.

Karen McQueary

Greatest Upon Great

The greatest is the dreamer
For their visions never die
In their hearts there is a candle
And the light caught in their eye

Not knowing all the boundaries
Not a care to take along
Going on towards tomorrow
With a poem or a song

With words that tell a story
They can lead us to a place
Where only dreamers dream
And poets join the chase

All that is around them
Has a beauty all its own
Their eyes always seeking
To others must be shown

The greatest is the dreamer
Getting lost inside the thought
The mind is always seeking
What others must be taught

Susan Gibson

Solace

To provide the smiles
For those who frown
To supply the hugs
For those who are down
To find the lost
And fix what's wrong
To share the dreams
With those with none
To have the shoulders
For all the tears
To soothe the mind
From all the fears
To mend the heart
When shattered and torn
To comfort and care
When it's time to morn
To all the times
When you need someone
Remember I'm here
Come rain or sun.

Stacy Ferguson

The Two Young Boys

The nation cries
for two young boys.
They'll never again laugh,
or receive new toys.

Together we joined
as one to search.
Already knowing their fate,
the mother sits perched.

The nation feels
pain and grief.
We all listen
and cry in disbelief.

How could someone
harm their own kid?
She hides from the world
as they close each coffin lid.

Those two young boys
only one and three,
alone in the cold ground,
forever they'll be.

Tammy Bauguess

Thanksgiving

Thank you God,
for what you've done,
for the sacrifice
of your precious Son.

He died on the cross
that we might live.
Our thanks, Dear God,
to you we give.

We owe our lives,
our souls to you,
for you cleansed our hearts
and made them new.

When our lives are over
and the victory's won,
we'll see you in heaven
because of your Son.

We thank you now
for your gift we pray
as we pause to celebrate
Thanksgiving Day.

Susan D. Rudd

"Thank You, Dear Lord"

Thank you, dear Lord
For your loving ways...
For the warm sunshine
That brightens up my days

For the song of the robin
That wakes me at early dawn...
The beauty of the flowers
And the smell of a fresh cut lawn

Thank you, dear Lord
For the peace that fills my soul
And the strength to help me
Reach my lofty goals

Thank you, dear Lord
For what you've given me...
Your gospel...family...friends
For all eternity

Thank you, dear Lord
For loving me like no one ever can...
Wishing I was an angel
But..for now..taking me as I am

Laurel Lee Holmes

Untitled

I can run among them now
free
and gypsy wild
in the scarlet morning rains
We are dew kissed and sodden
rearing high against Western winds
the thunder in our hooves
We bolt, crashing and rumbling
over blue grasslands
wet whipping manes like
lightening fire, crack and lash
muscles quiver and bunch
contract and explode
brilliantly hued in the birth of day
And in great heated puffs
We breath out
phantoms of ancestrial pride
galloping still
across mountain top clouds.

Marlailene A. Masino

The Bird Of Prey

The Baseball-like a shot
From a cannon-left the pitcher's hand.
Toward home plate-it streaked
Like an eager bird of prey.

The Catcher's mitt-the beacon,
Sent a signal. Like radar
It tracked the Baseball
Toward its target.

I crouch in position-waiting
For the elusive bit of leather and twine
Bound together to make it
The Object of every hitter's affection.

It crosses the plate-This commanding
Bird of prey-In search of
Its next victim. I must not
Falter under his eagle eye.

In a split second-I swing
With great force-and meet
This hungry Predator-My bat connects,
I send him back to the skies.

Tereasa J. Cool

Untitled

No rose shall have a fallen bud
From frost and cold
Nor shall she become withered
From common blight
She shall rise above all tragedies
That threaten her life
For eternity will be hers
When her soul takes flight.

Sharon Wavrunek

Angels Near

I heard the flutter of the wings,
From the darkness where I slept.
I felt the peace wash over me,
and in my sleep I wept.

My despair was gone, my heart was light,
for the first time my eyes could see.
I felt the love take over me,
at last my soul was free.

They are always near, and walk with me,
though I stumble on my path.
They pick me up, and love me still,
and taught my heart to laugh.

When I hear the flutter of their wings,
I smile, for now I know.
Upon this earth the Angels walk,
the seeds of Love they sow.

Marsha F. Perge

Grandpa's Girl

You and I have been friends
From the day I came home
We would be until the end
Now you're gone and I'm alone

Outside, you took me by the hand
When I was older and not so frail
We went to explore the land
Excitedly, we headed for the trail

We explored so many treasures
Too many to recall
You and I shared many pleasures
I can't believe I'd forgotten them all

I was out on my own
When you got older and frail
Wishing time could turn around
Taking my hand, we'd head for the trail

I was deeply hurt when you died
Feeling lost, like I was in a whirl
Needing the trail, I went outside
To remember when I was Grandpa's girl.

Kelly Lafferty

Perspective

My open eyes can only seem to lend
greater hunger to the ever insatiate,
wonderful and mysterious beast we
call, "perspective".
Unrelenting, it demands of all our
senses, while always as fragile
and dependent as newborn life, to
not only survive, but grow.
Unlimited in potential, and virtually
abstract in parameter, this gift of
perspective simply gives my open
eyes... more sight.

Richard Allen Olmsted

Autumn's Gift To Winter

Autumn brings the walnuts falling
from their husks and lofty height
Brings them to the earth for resting
on the leaves turned yellow bright.

As warnings of impending storms
they do not cease their dropping.
Warning us to dress up warm
or suffer colds and coughing.

My wife and I in coat and hat
gather them from leafy beds
For future use in winter treats
Like cookies, cakes, and buttered
breads.

Our task before the baking starts
is cracking one by one
These little gifts that Autumn brings
Till each is shelled and done.

We sit and crack and talk and laugh
these hours are precious time
for winter will be over soon
and warm the sun will shine.

Kendrick T. Scott

Love Awakens

A gentle breeze awakens
from within my soul
three soft pedals
alighting softly
upon my lips

Satiny Silky Velvety
just as your embrace

In the early morns dew
of a newborn day
Whispering
I place them tenderly upon your heart
Those fragrant blossoms
of I love you

Mitch Gurney

Untitled

The pain I see, as I
get older.
The pain from knowing,
I may never live to see
tomorrow.
The pain of seeing my
friends lying dead.
The pain from the tears
that fall.

The pain from the world,
The pain from inside
Is life really worth living?

Stephanie Cooney

Lone Tree

Lone tree standing there in majesty
Glorified by winters tapestry
Adorned with jewels of the night
Sparkling diamonds in magical light.
A gift of an artistic scene
Glistening in mid winters dream
Lone tree standing there in majesty
A glorious sight thou art to see.

Rae Ann Theobold

I'm Outta Here

Get outta
get outta
this town
they say
get outta
I'm outta
this town outta here

Tiny town
small town
watchin me
watchin you
eyes tiny eyes
watch
their own
frightened own

Spooky places
boxy lives
no more chikenshit

Steve Erwin

Fog

Emerging from the wood,
ghostly goliaths glide
across the west field
trailing lesser wraiths
in their wake,
all hooded against the rain.

Where are they going?
Is there a coven
in session to the east?
Or do these ethereal beings
anticipate another Woodstock,
ignoring the persistent rain?

Shrouded in voluminous veils,
the procession rolls on
past my back door,
through the hedges
toward their rendezvous,
and the downpour continues.

Miriam Selb Roberts

Journey

For what I have I,
give freely-
For what I gave I am,
now blest-
Living cool water,
to save you-
Holy love,
to stand the test-

I walk along beside you,
as we journey down the trail-
Speaking of a savior,
drinking from the grail-
Helping you understand,
the Love of the tail-

For what I had I,
gave freely-
For what I gave,
May you be blest!

Blackfeather

Untitled

Angels of morning, angels of light
Give me the strength
to see past the night
Shadows may come
shadows may fall
Help me to stand
though, first I must crawl

Angels of wisdom, angels of love
Whisper your softness
to me... from above
Lead in the search
for love that is lost
trust gone array
through paths that have crossed

Angels of sunshine, angels of rain
Teach me the lessons
through joy, not in pain
Help me to give as well as receive
Open my heart so I can believe...

Timi Anne Carl

"Angel By My Side"

One cold morning
Got in my car for a ride
I thank God everyday
For the angel by my side

Sudden turns
In a motion so fast
In front of my eyes
My life flew past

A pole struck the side
I was thrown to the floor
A man came to my rescue
"Jaws of life" opened the door

My father was on the hood
Blood was on the sheet
"Get up!" he screamed
To his daughter so sweet

When the shock faded
I sat down to pray
Thank God for that angel
She rode all the way

Stacy Adkins

Slaves-To-Heroes

Their eyes are fearless
Hands were very strong,
The heart is very kind
And, still, they do wrong.
Many centuries they fought.
For freedom, strength and pride.
Brought here from hatred.
Some even tried to hide.
Now a days we fear them,
For they have gotten power,
Ancestors of these people,
Tell us to beware,
That now times have changed,
We have been slaves to heroes.

NicholeMcNeese

Dear Daughter

Every time I see your picture
Hanging upon my wall
It brings me back to a happier time
And I cry about it all.

I miss you running to me
When I came home from work
The stories you told about your day
Gave me a sense of worth.

You filled my life with so much love
I thought my heart would burst
You were always so very happy
And made me smile when I was at my worst.

If you only knew how my heart aches,
And how lonely that I've been
Maybe someday you'll understand
About what happened way back when.

I'll always love you my little one
It never seems quite fair
That you should live with our mistakes
Just know how much I care.
Love, Daddy.

Robert Dee Barrett

Rainbows

My crystalline self
has many flaws.

Every time one is
struck,
Shards go flying.

The smallest fragments
Can get into your soul.

Taking root to grow.

They will give you
Rainbows
Inside your eyes.

Lynda Ferrell

Ode To Someone

You can't say anything that
hasn't already been said.
Not your ugly, or stupid,
or you ought to be dead.
Immune to it all,
It doesn't hurt anymore.
The only problem is,
I can't open the door.
It seems to be stuck,
I'm alone in this room,
I guess it's the trade off,
for being immune.

Mark Kramer

"Questions In Love"

She had problems
He was her salvation
And after a year, her problems
diminished with his love and compassion

Now he has chosen his path
without her but yet she loves him

How can she save the love
that was once there?
She has no answer,
but she is waiting.....

Mhalou Durano

"Still In Love"

When you refused me, and lied I could have cried. When none of my glances were returned I could have died. But then once in a while you almost give me a smile and I don't know what to think. Deep inside I still love you even though I know, I deny it so. I feel I can never open my heart again unless you give me a "sign" just to be able to start again. Sometimes it seems you still care, but then why aren't you here with me sharing my loving stare? Any day, anytime in anyway if you ever came back to me I know I'd give in. It may be foolish to keep holding on but you are the one that makes me strong. Please stop playing games and show me the way, because if you can't love me please at least help me love someone again.

Stefanie Haid

Getting Together

A blue woolen sock on the discard pile,
having lost its mate,
nestles next to one red mitten,
also useless in a world
of two-handed people.
Each sensing the other's need,
they wriggle free of the stuff and junk
before being carted away in a truck;
slip and slide down a laundry chute,
escaping out the cellar door
into the night.
I see them in the moonlight
dancing a disjointed jig,
heroically holding each other up,
oblivious to style and form,
so puppy-love happy
they seem to be waving farewell
to all the fingers and toes
they helped to keep warm.

Thomas L. Harris

"Maybe In Time"

Forgive me for not
having noticed the
tear drops

Left solemnly on your
pillow
For your kindness
I always will
think of you...

As my unspoken
willow

But when I saw
the sorrow that
came across
your face

I knew there was
nothing but memories and sadness
that you had to
erase

Kathy Ayers

Why Me Lord?

Christ died on the cross, for me.
He died in torment and shame, for me.
Why me, Lord?
I am not worthy to touch the hem
of your garment.
Not worthy to kiss your dusty feet.
And yet, you died for me.
Why me, Lord?

Martha Corlett

Trying Makes You A Winner

My son plays baseball
He is having a blast
But, he gets upset if
His pitches aren't fast
"It's OK son," I tell
Him and smile
Your speed will pick-up
After a while.
Keep trying hard
And let the ball sail.
Your mother will love you
Triumph or fail

Sheila Moon

Grandpa's Teeth

He was always rather common,
he lived quite modestly.
He never climbed the highest mount,
he never went to sea.
But he made a sharp impression
at little Stevie's house
the day he left the dentist shop
with gold caps in his mouth.
His guns, and cars, and saddle horse
the other kids could own.
Steve said, I want those golden teeth
when you are dead, and gone."
So Grandpa fixed it in his will
so every one would know
that Stevie got his bright gold caps
when Grandad had to go

Now since he's gone up glory road,
that luscious fruit to eat;
the old boy has to gum it
cause Stevie's got his teeth.

Keith Blauvelt

The-Land

The man in the house had a plan.
He would give all mankind a hand.
His plan was to rebuild the land.

To plant seed's that would remain.
For no one to see his pain.
He then planted, his seed's in
the rain. He now is gone.

But his plan will always remain.
For that no man can complain.
The seed's of truth remain.
No man can stop the plan.
May we all remain at hand.
Forever to see the land.

No man can ever erase his plan,
to rebuild the land.
We all must take care of the land.
It was placed in our hand.

Patricia Ann Perkins

Cat

My Cat's eyes are green and fiery.
Her coat is black and a glow.
She likes to prowl the neighborhood
and watch the shadows grow.
When the sun comes up, she hurry's
home for food and a long nap.
Then it's night again and time for
another prowl and a new friend.

Mabel Lesch

Aborted

She was made with dangling arms,
her eyes were made to see.
She could cry and she could laugh,
the same as you and me.
But there is a difference,
in her and all the others
the only one who knew of her
was her young and guilty mother.
She will not experience the joys,
yet to come
because her childhood is already lost.
As the mother wonders why she did it,
her conscience pays the cost.

Mandi Milam

A Lifelong Blessing

Beautiful.
Her face is hidden in mystery
Haloed by sparks of red
Eyes of peacock blue watch softly

Intellect echoes in all of her words
Surrounding her like feathers of a bird
All of the labyrinths I tread
She has already explored

My mistakes are my own
And I see all the while
She is right in her wisdom
Still I find my own way

Many say I am like her,
I took no time to notice.
But I am blessed.

Nicole Maria Skorka

Strength Within

As I looked upon her weathered face,
her sparkling green eyes show not
a trace of the hardship she left
behind she had to work hard for
every dime. Nine children she bore,
to the family tree. She did what she
could to fill their needs. She chopped
wood to keep them warm for another
child had just been born. She
worked everyday, at night
she ironed clothes for little pay.
No matter how tired at the end
of the day, she never forgot to
kneel down and pray. To look at
her so little and weak, she's the
strongest person you'd hope to meet.

Rhonda Henderson

Rest Now

The sky is crying
here at the end of the day.
Nature is weeping
because you are passing away.

A mighty warrior you are
but your battles are done.
All the others think you finally lost,
a few know that you finally won.

The battles you fought
were never physical ones.
They were what had to be done
for the lives of your loved ones.

Rest peacefully now,
your have won what you sought.
Your children shall carry on
with their own battles to be fought.

Stanley Thomas Evans

In The Shadows

Running down paths,
hidden from view,
I stumbled, in the dark,
not knowing who.

I met you there searching
in the shadows,
far from the mainstream,
awake in your dreams.

We touched, removing the facade,
clinging to the truth,
crying from inside
a nightmare.

You took my hand with hesitation,
waiting for the night.
And in your sleep we touched again,
holding on so tight.

Lorraine Kay

Untitled

This mask I wear before me
Hides these tears I cry
This shell around my heart
Holds out the reason why
This smile I show to you
Shows how hard I try
These fears I hide within me
Says it's much too hard to survive
My soul is held forgotten
For the pain would make me blind
Money don't make you happy
For happiness you I cannot buy
Forgive me for this deceit I do
I've learned so well to lie
To tell the truth I can not do
No one must get inside
I hope someday you'll understand
And I won't need to hide
Maybe someday I can show my love
Instead of the tears I cry!

Sarah E. Beaird

Human Metamorphis

To all the lonely people
Hiding out in reachless places.
Try to remember traces of the faces
Of your youth,
It's all still you.
Life cannot change the truth.
If your sun isn't shining
You should be mining
for a full moon,
Never give up too soon.
Then you realize your cocoon is
For changing and not for aging.
Let the moon turn the tide,
Butterfly ride,
Let the sunshine release your wings
In full color.

Robert Treglio

His Eyes

When I look up into
his eyes, I see a man
of questions.
It looks as if he is
hated, but is really loved.
When people love so
short, and forget so long,
he is not one of them.
He lives life the way
it comes, and doesn't mind
the past.
His eyes are filled
with wonder. People love
him, but he won't reach.
Once he knows, it will
stop.
He will never question
someone, they will
question him, with looks
of wonder from his answer.

Leann Jaskulsky

The Frost Of Jack

Jack Frost had come,
His icy work was done,
The pictures were all in white.
The light would show,
The windows would glow,
Giving off a beautiful sight.

No etchings were lost,
In his fingers of frost,
His mystical paintings were true.
The figures in ice,
A glassy glaze so nice,
Some appeared to be almost blue.

I have tried so hard,
To draw a copy on card,
All this strange and whimsical etchings.
As of this moment now,
I still don't know how,
He produces all his sketchings.

Royce D. Wellman

Thinking Of You

Compromising and Coping
Honest and True
Sitting and waiting
Thinking of you...

....Thinking of you
Alone not lonely
Sad not blue
Quiet not silent
Thinking of you...

...Thinking of you
Lies and secrets
Deceiving and wrong
Hurt and pain
Now you're gone...

...Thinking of you

Miriam Green

Mona's Song

Alone at last
How could the time
Go so fast!
The earth forever turns
Making my heart,
Endless to burn!
For days gone by
To memories so sweet
Will love ever; I chance to meet.
Sorrow and sadness
I lay to rest
As I try to do my best.
So bird in the sky,
Sing me a song
Wake me in the early morning dawn,
To fly with you to blue skies above
Onward and homeward
To My Only True Love.

Mona Adams

My Pain

Who are they to say,
how I feel inside?
What gives them the right today,
to evaluate and decide?

I'm so tired of only being,
a number in their books.
It's so frustrating knowing,
they can decide just by a look.

How can my pain be measured,
by those outside of my skin?
Do they have a magic method,
to say when it ends and begins?

I am the only keeper,
of my body and my mind.
I know my pain is deeper,
than what the naked eye can find.

I am a true believer,
in fighting for my rights.
I am a truth seeker,
that's why I say my prayers at night.

Sunny Dawn Cooper

The Sprinter

She crouches
Hunched in the blocks
Every muscle tensed
Boom
She flies out of the blocks
Sprinting
Flashes of color around her
A girl in blue catches up
She hurls herself across the finish line
Shakes hands with the girl in blue
And graciously accepts
Second place

Karen Sander

Kitchen

When
I
turned off
the
coffee pot
..bubbling,

It
kept
right
on
..bubbling

Like
your
spirit
when
   you
     died.

Mildred Swan

I Am For Them What They Aren't For Me

People say I am different
I am not like another
I am just someone to pick on like
their little brother
People say I am sweet but that is
All they seem to say
when their problems are solved I
Just seem to fade away
I am always there for them
I always hear them through
But they always seem to use me
Like it is nothing new
They say they understand and
They will always be around but
When I have a problem they are
No where to be found

Patricia Blevins

A Strong Foreboding

Like an evil jester being absurd
He's grotesquely gadding about
   like a total nerd
It's an erie dream
I have awakened and can't see a thing
Going to the back door softly
   quickly
As I opened it for a split second
   choking,
And immediately I
   Called 9-1-1

Kathleen Menken

Why?

Why do you hurt me?
I am your child,
meek and mild.

Why do you hurt me?
I came to stay,
to laugh and play.

Why do you hurt me?

Was I in a fall?
Was I playing ball?

Why do you hurt me?
Doctors say;
I'll no longer play.

Why do you hurt me?
My casket made,
to rest I'm laid.

Why did you hurt me?
Mom and Dad;
too late to be sad.

Laura M. Chavez

The Wind And The Sea

Thou art the wind.
I be the sea.
You ruffle my waves
As I reach out for thee.

And when I catch thee
Whispering sounds,
All is drowned out
By the surf as it pounds.

Paul G. Phillips

A Glance Within

Your sheltered soul
   I can see;
Rigid, assured, obstinate
   Yet fragile.
Your voice silently echoes
   bearing your heart;
As your iron chiseled features
   start to liquefy;
Yielding they become;
   malleable - angelic.
Concealing yourself, and its burden
   are no longer essential.
No motive to lie,
   for as human as you am I.
Covered equally are we,
   with smile and laughter;
Beneath my smile and laughter;
   like you;
I am in sadness, delight,
   amazement, fright.

Robert P. Gorsuch Jr.

Mother

The warm womb — whence I came —
   I can't conceive of now —
Yet, when enwombed in your embrace
   It takes me back — somehow.

And when I lie — a broken frame —
   Shattered on life's cold stone —
You warm me in a womb of grace
   And heal me — bone to bone.

Robert L. Manecke

Untitled

Is she real or just a memory,
I can see her in my dreams,
she seems so kind and loving,
she satisfy's my needs,
I can't think of life without her,
she's everything to me,
when I close my eyes to every thing,
she's always there you see,

Is she real or just a memory,
I can't say if it's true,
but I know I'll keep on dreaming,
until my love for her comes true,
And I hope that she can see me,
In her own special way,
As the clouds of love surround us,
and takes us far away.

Tye Galloway

"Ever Present Tendency"

Throughout our world of life,
I cannot help but think freely.
Perceptions and feelings are boundless,
giving birth to the signs of life.

Throughout our world of life,
truth and lies are still revealed.
Yet I can know and not deny,
that I am part of the signs of life.

Throughout our world of life,
poor to rich walk the line.
With my possessions I stake a claim,
and delight for the signs of life.

Throughout our world of life,
good and evil mesh tenaciously.
I am not alone to be right or wrong,
but behavior dictates the signs of life.

Throughout our world of life,
there is that tie that binds.
A magnificent force touching all beings,
the tendency for the love of life.

G. Freeman Gibson

The Accident

The sorrow felt
I can't explain.
For this lost son
Was not born of my pain.

In my heart,
The tragedy I know.
It could be me,
Letting the tears flow.

Tormented eyes
Peer from his mother's face.
A piece of her gone
Ravaged at a swift pace.

A smile, a tear;
One in the same.
For then in life,
And the now that came.

Let me hold you my son,
Blessed be this day.
For now as you are with me
Time, dear time, keeps ticking away.

Peggy Lynch

Time

I never knew how,
I could love someone so much
I guess it is possible
I love him a bunch.

We grew up together,
Fighting and all
I never realized that,
Soon he'd be gone.

Soon the day came,
We said our goodbyes
Little did he know,
I had tears in my eyes.

Where did the time go,
What happened to us
I always ask myself,
Why my big brother — Josh?

Toni L. Gunnells

I Cry Because...

I cry because my mother cries,
I cry because of pain.
I cry because it's dark outside,
I cry because it rains.
I cry because my fathers left,
I cry because of loss.
I cry because the Lord is sad,
I cry because the cost.
I cry because no others knows,
I cry because lost trust.
I cry because it's over now,
I cry because of dust.

Rachel Kruse

Sea Of Despair

Caught up in fantasy,
I find visions of reality;
Hunting me like a rabbit
To reform my old habits.

Reaching into the fathoms of my debts
I find I have no regrets.
Trying to treat myself right;
I have to put up with this fight.

Love of another kind,
I long to find.
Or have I found
What makes me drown?

No longer, shall I be,
Struggling to the top of this sea
Of despair designed for me.
For now, I must set me free.

Lynda Yvonne Waller Diemont

Infinity

As I gently caress her in my arms,
I know our love is forever...
When I kiss her tender lips,
I know our love is forever...
Running my tongue up and down
every curve of her luscious body,
I know our love is forever...
Being with her every second of the day,
And expressing my overflowing love,
I know our love is forever...
Infinity.

Nicholas Chumbley

Fort Mifflin Soldier

As fate would have it
I found you here
amongst the dead and wounded
now found in time

Your uniform of wool
a buckle of gold
wounds oozing
your grandfathers blood

The smell of gunpowder
fills your nostrils
the stench of death
stirs your soul

So tall you stand
scars of centuries
children not yet born
voices no longer silent

Son of the son of your grandfather
music of the dead
your wounds are now open
no more silence to be heard

Sami Buisson-Daniel

Untitled

I've sunk into the Abyss
I go alone, alone, alone
A sorrowful kiss
I send to you, to everything
Off to nothingness I sway
Dark and cold freedom
You know I could not stay
I smile my sick, faceless smile
A sorrowful kiss
I stare for a while
Everything fades, always fades
Now it's my turn
To taste the black arrow
It burns, burns
The hands close around me, take hold
My forever is alone
The numb of the cold
The silent blindness of Death
I leave with nothing
I close my eyes

Sara Wherley

Sigma Pi Theta

Though others have gone astray
I have vowed to stay.
Whenever there is something you need
Come to me...do not heed.
In each of you I've placed my trust
Which will never rust.
Friends come and friends go,
A sisters love however, can only grow.
Day by day; year by year,
For you, I will always be here.
Now and until the sweet bitter end
Sisterhood, Unity and Discipline.
I love each and every one of you—
Love,
Turquoise, Gamma Pledge of Spring 1992.

Michelle Y. Roseberry

The World

I wonder about the world.....
I hear someone calling for help.
I see someone needing help.
I want to help.
I pretend to help.
I try to help as much as I can.
I understand that not
everything can be helped.
But, I say you have to try.
I touch the needing world....

Rebecca Spindler

Reflections After Forty

I toppled a mountain and swam in the sky;
I kissed the moon and swallowed the sea.
A planet whirled on the lid of my eye;
I broke a star across my knee.

I ran the maze of a flake of snow;
I dodged a microbe's hungry hand.
I crawled around and dug below
The continents of a grain of sand.

I lived forever and died each day
I was the best; I was the worst.
I stood, a God; I knelt to pray-
By angels blessed, with devils cursed.

Lou Guttman

When We Were One

My heart still aches from when
I knew you, when you would hold
Me close into your arms and
embrace my love into your heart.
When you would sing sweet melodies
into my ear, when you would shower
me with affection. When it didn't
matter about tomorrow, if there was
only us. When time meant
Nothing as it passed us by. When
eternity was forever. When
love really meant love, and when
bye really meant bye.
When we were one, so very long ago.

Misty Sheppard

Ferris Wheel

I was scared once
I know how you feel
It was at a carnival
On a ferris wheel

It took me to heights
That I'd rather not see
In a cage I sat
In hopes to be freed

Around in circles
And up and down
Never know
If I'd hit the ground

Pray beginning to end
That I'd make it alive
Now that it's over
It was only a ride

Tonya M. Frost

Lonely Road

As I walk down this lonely road
I know that I can see
Just another lonely road
Waiting there for me.

As I walk down this lonely road
I know there will always be
Heartache and loneliness
Reaching out to me.

As I walk down this lonely road
I know it won't be easy
Only time will heal the pain
That's slowly killing me.

As I walk down this lonely road
I know deep inside of me
I will love you forever
For all eternity.

Missy Weber

Company

I love company
I love guests
When I'm entertaining, I'm at my best!
But, If you drop-in un-announced
And I-m 'Rarin' to go
I'll feel free
To be me
And continue with
My original frivolity!
Please call first ***

Marian B. Gow

Untitled

W ith a helmet of resolution
I n your dream I was a mighty warrior
L eaving home to make me grow
L isten to my heart
I t beats like celestial drums
A mber skies on a summer day
M arita writes to you.

Marita Baldemor

Forgotten World

I can not find a word
I need so much to say
And like a blinded bird
This word has flown away

In dark unconsciousness
It sings somewhere alone
I always knew this sound
I always knew this song

From very far away
I recognize this place
A lonely sailing boat
It waits on limpid waves
It needs just me to start
To sail and anything
Can happen to my soul
Which makes my boat swing.

Vera Nova

Kevin, My Son

I never saw your smile,
I never heard you giggle.
I wonder
what your voice would sound like.
I don't know what your
favorite color would be.
But I expect it would be purple.
I don't know what your
favorite food would be,
Maybe pizza
or spaghetti
Peas, a dislike?
Would these make you say "yuck!"?
I wonder for sure if I'm right.
I'll always wonder the answers,
ponder what you'd be like.
One thing I'm sure of,
My son,
I will love you forever.

Theresa Barnouski Parks

No Way

She said: Hemingway.
I said: Yeah!

She said: Gay.
I said: No way!

She began to laugh.
I reached for the carafe.
It couldn't be true.
She: I know people who knew.

Who?
Two who knew
him in Paris with Stein.
I began to whine.

No! It just can't be
he'd fondle another's wee-wee.

She: Now you can understand
why he's called a man's man.

Ralph Gaby Wilson

I Know Jesus

I know Jesus,
I saw him in
Sunday school.
I know Jesus, Mama said junior
put that thirsty-five cent in the plate.
I look up and he was watching,
the nickel and five pennies
fell and I know Jesus,
he said boy what did ya Mammy say,
with ya big buck teeth (smile)
Yes Sir, Mr Jesus, I just
Ya quarter in the plate.
I told you I know Jesus

Walter Johnson

Punishment

As the waves come over my
head. I feel terror and fright.
The cries and pledging of help.
A life taken and survived before
me. There was nothing I could
do. So fore then I have taken a life.

Sarah LaPare

In Her Shadow

I love you, you say.
I say, who is you?

No answer

A song on the radio takes you away.
Shhh, you say. I say, who are you
thinking of?

No answer

A smell from a towel you carry
To take in a scent.
You sigh. I say what's that?

No answer

I sleep alone. You embrace another.
Yet you say it's over. I say, why then?

No answer

I say, I love you. You say, I wondered
When you would say those words?

But for me there was

No answer

Mary E. Griffin

In Your Eyes

In your eyes
I see the mystery of love
And friendship and fantasy
Between you and me.

In your face
I feel the glow and radiance
Of beauty that shines
Above all others.

In your lips
I taste the sweet wine of desire
That flows so deeply
In your soul.

In your embrace
I feel the comfort of the earth
And touch the passion
Of the stars.

In your eyes
I see the union of our souls
United in love
Forever.

Paul F. Noerenberg

Untitled

Reaching to me
I see your smile
courageous and sweet
what but love could I feel
your arms ready for my embrace
time couldn't fade this feeling
nothing could
I run to you when I need someone
always there
always smiling
you are there
mine to hold
mine alone!!

Lizz Murphy

Finale

When I am old
I shall have beautiful gray hair
And bushes of roses the
the color of pink wine...
And I shall have purple socks
and blue shoes
The color of sky and sunsets.

When I am old
I shall be wise and calm
Knowledgeable of the soul and self...
Content to wear the shawl of time,
As I plant daffodils and pumpkins.
To fill my house of love and flowers.

When I am old
I shall love what I have loved
Cherish my past and present
Laugh and embrace each new morning
While gathering bouquets of stars
for the final night...
When I am old.

Margaret M. Hamann

Questions

Sometimes in the darkness
I sit and wonder why the
ocean's blue the night is black
the clouds are very high, and
thus I figure things are things
they're just the way they are,
but questions come and as they
do the answer seems so far.

Lauren Clancey

Teacher

I stand and hope it's not in vain
I speak and pray you hear
Is there something I might do for you
To bring your conscience near

What I teach perhaps you will learn
And so remember me
Could it be my gift of knowledge
Is but a grasp at immortality?

No! I say stimulated growth
Is a priceless act to witness
To activate a human heart
That once was grey and listless

A fragile process is my duty
To help a seed grow to a tree
And my reward for task well done
Is continued growth in me

Stephanie Y. Evans

Old Friends

Although we've only met
I stand in awe
For as I glanced, I saw
The depth of ages
A day gone by, from the pages
Another era, another time
Then I wonder how you relate to mine

Wanda A. Higgins

True Love

I think about the future
I think about the past
I think about my love for you
And how long it will last

True love is forever
At least that's what they say
So true love is what I search for
Each and everyday.

I thought that I had found it
But it turned out it wasn't true
So now I look for true love
In someone much like you

So if this was meant to be
And we just pass it by
How will we ever know
If we don't even try.

Scott R. Butler

Each Time That A Leaf Falls

Each time that a leaf falls
I think of you
Each time that a baby cries
Or I see the sky, I think of you.
Each time that the sun comes out
Or I feel the raindrops upon my face;
I think of you
Each time that I see lover's
strolling and holding hands;
I think of you
Each time that the aged, the sickly
and the poor are AGAIN ABLE TO SMILE:
I think of you
As birds are flying I think of you!
And newborn babies, are being born;
I think of you
In autumn as the leaves are falling
I think of you.

Olivia D. Lawe

If I Had Three Wishes

If I had three wishes
I think that they would be
For things that will help others
And not things just for me.

The first would be for peace,
The second would be for wealth,
The third would be for everyone
to be in perfect health.

I know these things are asking a lot
but they would be worth while
There would be laughter and happiness
for mile after mile.

I know that these three wishes
probably would not come true
But a big difference could be made
by people like me and you.

Tona Jones

Life Goes On

I thought ours was a true love,
I thought it was for real.
And it has taken some time
for my broken heart to heal.

All along I really thought
our love was based on trust.
Little did I know
that you had fallen in lust.

You could have just told me
instead of telling me lies
that you loved someone else.
Now my nights are filled with cries.

My body you had used,
my love you have betrayed.
My mind has been abused,
but no longer do I walk astray.

There's a new man in my life
who knows how to treat me right.
Pretty soon I will be his wife.
No longer will I have another sleepless night.

Melissa Pagan

"The Kingdom Of God"

As I lay in bed at night,
I try to grasp a clearer sight
Of reaching the end of my race;
And meeting God face to face.
I dream of the heavenly place
Which needs no glitter or fancy lace.
No sun, no moon, to make it bright:
The glory of God gives it light.
I dream of gates - standing tall,
Streets of gold, an emerald wall.
The River of Life - crystal clear;
Then His voice I start to hear.
I see the Lord on the Throne,
I'm in our eternal home.
No more tears, no more pain;
To live is Christ, to die is gain.

Melanie Coffaro

The Couch

You came
I unlocked
We walked
the couch seemed
heavy
Moving it to
your truck
I grasped
the nubby fabric
of one cushion
The couch smelled like me
you said
It will fade
I thought
as another sits on its cushions
shares a kiss
feels its texture
It will be yours again

Sarah Irvin Connolly

Control

I want to be free.
I want to fly high.
I want just to be,
Like a bird in the sky.

I want to take charge.
I want to be known.
I want to be larger
Than any star shown.

I want my own way,
I want it right now.
I want just to say,
"Stand up and bow!"

Stop!
What are you saying,
You're only a child.
Such wishful thinking,
So let it be mild.

Sarah Ezell

Dearest Patricia,

Ever since I could remember
I wanted to be with you. I have
loved you for so long. I never could
go up to you and ask you for a
date. I was so afraid you
would say no and laugh in my face.
I want to hold you in my
arms and kiss your perfect red
lips. I want to get lost in your
big brown eyes. I would love
to gaze into your beautiful face
all day long.
You could be my perfect
angel or you could be my
Juliet while I can be your Romeo.
I love you! Please give me a
chance. I won't hurt you, I swear!
Love always,
Scott Mason

Suzanna Boyle

"Like Dinosaurs"

Coons... Spooks... Blacks...
Black Americans...
And now... We're
African Americans.
Soon to be extinct!
like DINOSAURS!
Dying in Prisons...
Or on Drugs. Or dead already
From Drugs or AIDS.
Or another Brother's knife blade.
Or shot down in the streets
By Racist Police.
Or shot down for fun
By another Brother's gun.
One Day we may be gone.
like DINOSAURS...
Our stories will be told and
Movies made about
The Ex-slaves who tried to rise
But fell so deep into their graves.

Marvin Mays

My Lady

My lady is beautiful and sweet.
I will sweep the ground that she
walks on.
I will dress her up with gold
and silver.
I will feed her with diamonds
and pearls.
I will carry her in my heart.
I will lay her down in the mass
of flowers.
I will keep her warm with white
feathers.
I will admire her but not touch.
I will set her free because she
is too beautiful to be my lady.

Domenico Longo

One Day

One day, after the war
I will take you in my arms
And we'll make love.
If after the war there's a day.
If after the war there's love

George Schneider

Together Forever

They say the charm is three,
I will wait for you my dear.
When you realize we're meant to be
Don't hide behind your fear.
My heart I give to you,
For my love is never leaving.
Forget the past and the other two,
In our love you will be believing.
Look inside your heart and you will see,
You found the true love of your life.
Now you know that it is me,
One day soon you will be my wife.
It will be so grand,
Our love and life together.
Just take hold of my hand,
In love we'll be forever.
Till death do us part,
You will forever be in my heart.

Joseph R. Cerny

My Yellow Rose Of Peace

When I give you a yellow rose
I wish you the peace
That only heaven knows
As you look upon its beauty
and feel the love
Know that our relationship
Is blessed from above.

Accept my yellow rose
With love and peace
I pray that your joy in land
will never cease
When He comes to take you
From this land
May He walk with you in eternity
Hand in hand.

David Fallis

Without Her Words

There is a song I know I am supposed to feel.
It is something some people say they knew upon first touch.
Some have,
Most were wrong.

It is something Life has taught me,
Living has taught me.
It is something she has taught me.

I would say it was something in her eyes,
I imagine I see it there.
I would say it was in her touch,
I have felt it there.
But most of all it is in the way she tells me
Without her words.

I do not know what forever is.
Maybe she will choose to teach me that too.
But I now know what Pure is,
And as forever
Maybe that is soon

Dan O'Toole

Pilgrim's Sonnet

The wisdom of the ages lies in the silent wood
It is to a man to dwell among
But here are all things good
For in the noise of man, visions may be lost
So here I learn to see again amongst the crystal frost
Where deer know naught of nothing
And, perhaps, I know much less
And all is pure and lovely within the moon's caress
To preserve a boundless beauty
These holds of mystery
Is, perhaps, the noblest hunt of all
The why of bended knee
What I learn is that of pensive peace
from answers in the brook
And leave a part behind as marching on I look
come away aloft to do
A better man for been
Having found a brother in the wood
And forever forged a kin....

Greg Halvorson

Untitled

Love is like, a ship that puts to sea.
It leaves gently on the out going tide.
For days the weather is good, and all is well.
Then storms move in, the ship struggles
Agents the sea, and wind. The sails become strained.
When the storm subsides, the ship is still intact.
The calm that follows brings renewed faith.
So it is with love, through many storms,
The ship and sea have forged an everlasting bind.
And so like the ship and sea, love survives
all, and like the depth of the sea, love can not be measured.

James P. Whipple

The Wait Is Over

When I hear your voice,
I want to listen to you for hours.

When I see your face,
I want to gaze into your eyes forever.

When you caress me,
My whole body shudders in response.

You are the man I've waited for
all of my life.

Marcelle Maggio

Be Proud

I sit and stare at the clear blue sky.
it makes me stop and wonder why.
New life begins as other ones die,
a baby always starts life with a cry.
Life can be happy sad fantasy or real,
you have the power in your mind to control how you feel.
So the next time your feeling all sad and blue,
just think happy thoughts that's what I do.
As we plan our life and set our goals our time we do bide,
we seem to set our goals so high our quest is never satisfied.
As you look at the past and plan your future keep one thing on your mind, be happy who and what you are cause someone like you is had to find.

Joseph R. Monthony Sr.

The Painter's Psalm

Painting is my hobby, I shall want no other.
It maketh me to lay down my mop and broom,
Walk by my dirty dishes to my studio room.
It restoreth my pieces of mind
And leadeth me into strange places, subjects to find.
Yea, tho, I am alone with brushes and paints,
I feel no loneliness.
The sight of colors and odor of oils, they comfort me.
I prepare a canvas on my easel and paint
While my dishpan runneth over...
Surely, I will have a rainbow in the gravy at dinner,
And I will dwell in a state of confusion forever.

Julia Anne Bierbaum

"SUCCESS"

What is success? Do you really know?
It means live life to the fullest
and let yourself grow.
Don't let other people inhibit your plans
and chain down your spirits
with unfair demands.
Develop your talents.
Share your strengths with your friends.
If you've done something wrong,
always please make amends.
Look for beauty in others, and don't criticize
or join in on gossip...
and never tell lies.
If you do what feels natural
and say what's in your heart,
you'll have peace of mind
as each new day you start.

Joan F. Holdman

The Magic Show

Taking your hands off with the greatest of ease,
it must be fun since you are doing this for free.
You entertain us for hours on end,
you can't really do this,
it's all just pretend.
It's in your pocket the audience does know,
but isn't that really just for the show.
It comes out of your head taking a peek,
everyone laughs you look like a geek.
Off comes the hat, the star of the show,
what will come from it no one will know.
With a swipe of the hand and a mystical word,
out pops a dove a most magnificent bird.
Don't tell me how you did it I don't want to know,
for knowing the answer would ruin the show.
Now it's all over we go home at last,
taking the memories of the spells you have cast.
We lay down to sleep, not saying a word,
for we don't want to turn into that sweet little bird.

Brian Greer

To My Son Victor

I really never knew you, although you were my son,
It seems like only yesterday, that you were the only one.
The years went by, you went away
I never knew just where
You kept in touch, and now and then you'd
suddenly appear.
You finally came home to stay
I didn't know then, why -
Then I had to let you go again,
'Cause you came home to Die -
I finally got to know you, during the sickness
that took your life.
We shared a lot of happiness and bitterness
and strife.
But that is all behind us now,
My son, you're truly free
Into the arms of the loving God -
for all eternity.

Jeannette Annunziato

A Long Walk

As I walk thru this life
It seems to get harder each day
The walk seems longer
And my legs get weary with each step

The work seems endless
And the pressures of the day weigh heavy on my shoulders
My mind never gets enough rest
My eyes burn before the day is half gone

I hope before this walk is done
That my body will be rested
And my mind clear of all the pressures that I seem to encounter
Thru the day

And the marks that I have made
Will be noticed by my peers

And I can be proud of this walk that I made

Glen Ficklin

"Today I Made A Rainbow"

Today I made a rainbow, I'm telling you no lie.
It shined in seven colors, but not up in the sky.
Today I made a rainbow without a cloud in sight.
In fact the sun was shining and all the world was bright...
The lilacs bloomed profusely perfuming all the air...
And there were birds aflutter, singing everywhere.
Today I made a rainbow, in such a splendid way.
I fashioned it from sunbeams and water I could spray.
For as I washed my old back porch. A humble, homely chore.
I made the lovely sign of Noah Arch over my back door.
Today I made a rainbow, while watering my rose...
I didn't have a magic wand, but just a garden hose...

Alfred P. Rea

Mind Over Matter

No one is born with mind over matter.
It should be acquired as you grow taller.
A mind being wasted, what could be sadder?
This is why our world is so torn and tattered.
With heavy hearts our world leaders gather,
to ask each other what is the matter.
Why do we kill, destroy and batter?
More laws and more rules is not the answer.
The answer lies with Jesus; King of all matter.
He gives his solution to the mind of the listener.
Always remember it's truly mind over matter,
if you do not mind nothing will matter.

Carlton Bridges

I Know You Won't

A hot cup of coffee gets cold,
It sits and waits for you to return,
But, I know you won't.

Your chair by the window gets dusty,
It is waiting for you to sit in it again.
But, I know you won't.

As I sit here by your grave I wish you would return.
But, I know you won't.

I wonder, why did you have to leave us behind.
Bringing so much sadness into our hearts.

I wonder, will I ever see you again?
And now I know that someday,
Yes, I will.

Amber George

"To My Angel"

I saw an angel,
it took me a moment,
only a moment and:
I smiled toward my heaven.

All of sadden it appeared before me,
it all appeared like a dream; briefly;
through wonderfully intimate.

No air exists as transparent as my angel.

I saw the angel fly away,
disappear among the immense clouds,
expansive and enormous as my sadness.

I had seen that angel who brought me up;
from the abyss of the oceans,
where the currents brought me far:
far form reality, dark and without meaning.

I allow the waves to drive me away.....
To determine my destiny.

Gior Gio Sortino

"After Thoughts"

I had a dream the other night -
It was one of horrible fright,
As visions raced throughout my head -
I saw myself laying dead.

Laying there, I could see - people looking down at me,
Some I knew, some I did not -
Some faces familiar, but names forgot.

I never realized so many cared -
So many came, some hadn't dared.
They all talked as they mingled around -
So often I heard a familiar sound.

I thought, "Why so many tears over me?
I haven't set any records or made history."
They spoke of me as a saint, but the Lord knows, I ain't.

I lived a half way decent life -
In this world of toil and strife.
Good God, man, what's that you say?
You're glad I passed away!

Well, I guess to each his own -
Some want me to stay, some glad I'm gone.

Donald D. Willis

Imageless Mirror

In the ancient of days there existed a pattern worthy of imitation,
it was this very quality that caused the beginning of time,
a Grand Master at his craft
set in motion from himself something that we
remotely know the meaning of.

Being far more than a Grand Artist he also being a Grand Teacher,
through his invention of time
he has educated the lowly into his very being
and as history has proven
those who possess wisdom in action have been few.

As for the few they became many yet never to become the populous,
the populous possess knowledge but it does not dwell with wisdom,
this wisdom proved true by its works even when there was a minority.

This minor given the instinct to love
yet needing insight as to where, how and should,
succeeded through his physical being
failing miserably in his pattern of imitation.

What he has given as his progeny
bears no reflection to the Ancient of Days.

Joe Young

"The Christmas Tree"

The christmas tree stood quite alone in the corner of a room
It was very gaily decorated, yet it wore a touch of gloom.
There were garlands of shiny gold, some tinsel and ornaments galore.
Yet none of these bright trimmings helped the sadness that it bore.
What more is needed here as the answer still it sought
Something, indeed, was missing and the tree was deep in thought.
Now high upon the topmost branch a lovely angel perched
her smile, too, was sad as though she also searched;
For that extra bit of something that would finish up the tree
and then a thought occurred to her and she shouted out with glee.
Oh Christmas tree oh Christmas Tree, tis love and brotherhood we lack
I'll whisper to old Santa when he gets here to unpack.
So when the joyous evening came, the angel kept her word
and Santa listened very hard and a thought to him occurred.
He reached within his bag and brought forth a snow white dove
the very purest symbol of brother hood and love.
Santa stood silent for a minute, then placed the dove up high
and the angel spread her tiny wings and caroled to the sky.
Oh Holy Night, oh joyous night, oh Blessed Mary's son
bring Peace on Earth, and please, oh Lord, love to everyone!

Gene Olcott

The Coming Night

I long to embrace the coming night
Its chilling breeze caresses my skin
Alone and together with the desolate sky
It empties my soul, devours all thought

A taunting dawn disguises the rage
Of tired dreams and numbered days
Aging leaves fall, while children weep
Silent rakes gather the fallen gold

The human pain that sunlight brings
Invades my comfort, exposes my home
Blinded by faith and led to the slaughter
Corrupting pressure destroys simple pleasure

I long to embrace the coming night
Winter's dream is summer's plight
A tear for humanity, from my eye was stole
As the coming night envelops my soul

Chris Layman

No One Like You

In your pond of problems; someone cast yet another stone,
Its form so different, it's never been known.
I salute the wisdom and courage you were able to find,
Kept healthy always, your body and mind.
You have a gracefulness for living free,
Making known your own personal liberty.
Warmth to ones' heart your happiness fills,
Brighter than a field full of daffodils.
You have a heart made of pure gold,
Anger and hatred to you have gotten way too old.
Love and caring was never left unspoken,
Because of your strength, it seems your heart is not one to be broken.
Is there a special class that teaches how to be so clever,
Cause I never met anyone like you ever.

Jaime Anderson

"The Love For My Children"

The love for my children is so strange;
It's like a stormy day without rain.

This love will make me smile,
When I sometimes need to cry.

It makes me want to live -
when the world pressures say die.

This love makes me comfort them,
at times when it's me who needs comforting.

It made me hurry on into adulthood,
at a time in my life when I felt a bit childish.

It made me settle myself down, and it has
turned my whole life around.

At times in my life when I've gotten tired,
It has given me the strength to go on.

It has made me stop, and hold my tongue,
when I have had so much to say.

It has made the burden light—
While trying hard to raise them right.

This love has made me fall to my knees and pray.
For God to watch over them while I'm away.

Joyce A. Bailey

A Mother's Love

A mother's love is different from any love on earth,
It's not a love that must be won, it starts before your birth;
At the moment of conception, God installs a special part,
That connects the child inside her to a mainline from her heart.

You belong to her, (through the Grace of God)
For nine months hers alone!
Her body nourishes, her love unfolds,
Unconditionally, from deep within her soul.

And then you make your "Grand Debut,"
No longer hers alone,
She must cut the cord and proudly watch
As you set out on your own.

New people, places, so many things,
Start filling up your life,
Then one day you're all grown up,
And some young man's new wife!

So, now life's cycle starts a new,
But this time you're the mother,
You've now been blessed with that Special Love,
God gives to only mothers.

Barrie P. Maddox

Soul

My soul is not brand new,
It's older than you and you and you.
Was a slave and a fighter, maybe even a famous writer.
I lived through time, explored reason,
been through every changing season.
I've seen days of strange belief.
And I've seen days of horrible grief.
When I pass from life to life,
I face death like my loving wife.
This is the strangest life I've ever known,
On this feeling I'm not alone.

Daniel P. Barletta

Rosemarie's Paper Flower

My friend Payton made me a flower of finest silk and tissue.
It's pink, blue and alabaster hue,
Oh, dear one how I miss you.
She was my friend for neigh a year,
Though I feel I know her well.
She met a boy who stole her heart,
It's love, you know; I can tell
I wait for school to end for her, to come back home and play,
But she is with the other one,
I know she'd rather stay.
His name is Teddy Bear you see,
a handsome chap for sure.
He dries her tears and calms her fears,
he's good and true and pure.
He fights the demons, to keep her safe, and never tells her lies.
I once was her only one, but now my love it dies.
My friend made me this flower,
of finest silk and tissue.
It's pink and blue and fading too,
oh, dear one how I miss you.

Anthony Wilkins

Always And Forever

Time and time goes by and I begin to realize,
It's quite simple really to say I love you.
Thinking about you night and day,
Wondering when the next time I'll see you and what I'll say.
I wish there was something I could do,
to stop thinking about you.
You say you don't care,
and the pain for me is to hard to bare.
I loved you for so long that you were like a key to
my heart that couldn't be unlocked, and
that you were the only one right for me.
I really never stopped to think about us being
together, but only if we could, that probably
won't be ever.
Everyone said we would look good together,
All I can do for now is wish we
could be together always and forever.

Candi Jones

Dream

Dream any dream,
It's yours until it comes true,
Nothing can stop it from being except you.

Believe in your heart,
Believe in your soul,
Because one day you'll find it to be so,
That all you had -
Was all it took
And that was enough to make it reality.

Charlta King

"Who Is He"

The power to hypnotize is definitely there,
It's something so mystical and so vastly rare
Imagine the sea gulls, the ocean and sand,
From feeling a voice like the touch of a hand
Who is that grants me the power to possess
All that I require of love and nothing less

The mind is relaxed and taken through age,
Where Utopia exists and the world's a stage
Engulfed in a trance of this ebony space,
Enhances my yearn for a divine, tranquil place
Who is he that grants me the power to possess
All that I require of love and nothing less

Of nature's surroundings, disclosures of grace,
Invites my whole being in mental embrace
As time lingers by and love's gone on a spell,
The imprint that's left will forever dwell
Who is he that granted me the power to possess
All that I required of love and nothing less

Who is He

Ada Manning

Free

Free is unentangled, loose and open.
It's the air of openness and relaxation.
Free is peacefulness as the waters of the spring.
It's the crystal clear and refreshing movement, the
water makes as it exits the earth.

Free is walking on the beach.
Feeling the warmth of the sand beneath your barefeet.
It's the roar of the Ocean.
It's the whispering motion of comfort as the water moves.
It's the song of rolling freedom as it bounces gradually to shore.

Free is the dawn breaking cool and calm.
It's the first chirp of the birds singing and fluttering.
It is the dew upon the fresh cut grass.
It is the sun gradually rising to begin a beautiful day.

Free is the dusk the ending of a well worn day.
Free is recognizing the beauty and the colors of an ending day.
It is the preparing for rest and the beginning of a new dawn.

Free is the opportunity to see what is free.
It is the ability to appreciate the real meaning of free.
Free......................

Caroline LaShare

Feelings

I've been hurt I know how it feels to be betrayed
I've been friends with someone that was taken away from me.
This person was my next door neighbor.
The people that took one of my other friends.
The first day of school is when it happened I was
with her. Then She walked away.
The next day I was all alone. I wanted to have a friend.
I cried when I was on the playground. I was sitting all alone
watching everyone so happy when I was so sad and lonely.
The days past on still sitting alone. Waiting for someone to care
and brighten my spirit. No one came. No one at all. I learned
to fight back the tears. But I still cry for help. I still cry for
another friend. Someone to tell how I feel. How I want to feel.
To be free and do as I please. Not worrying about my shyness,
afraid to open myself up. Afraid of what others would think.
Feelings are so hard to get over on a sadness moment. But soon
I won't worry about what others think. I just know God is
waiting for me to come. My feelings for God will be mine all
mine. God is the only one that really knows about my feelings.
And I would like it to be like that until it comes for a special
friend to know.

Brandi Leigh Warnhoff

Guy Friends

For those of you who'd like to know, I'll tell you what
I've been through.
A good friendship that ended 'cause I told what was true.
My close friend...my guy friend, that's who we're talking about.
My special feelings towards him weren't there from
the beginning, no doubt.
But when he found out about how I felt, the phone stopped ringing.
Tears then rolled down my cheek, remembering that it was okay
to cry, I learned that in my upbringing.
I remember our good times, and now our bad.
A descriptive word that describes my days without
his friendship is sad.
What have I learned from all this you ask?
Not to get too close to your guy friends, in order to make it last
Of course that that's not true in every situation, but
unfortunately it was in mine.
Hopefully, I'll learn to take my own advice next time.

Jocelyn Tumacder

That Special One

There's someone out there for everyone
I've heard this so many times
I didn't believe it until I met you
Now you've gone but the memories live on.

The man of my dreams that's what I used to call you
I felt like I was dreaming every time I was near you.

You made me so happy
You made me feel it was great to be alive
Before I met you I was sad and lonely
You won my heart and my soul.

We had some great times together
At least they were great for me
I won't let you go, I'll put you back
in my dreams where you belong,

And maybe someday we'll meet again
And take up where we left off.
I'll not say good-bye just so long
Until our paths cross again
And they will.

Debbie Ray Gulley

Friendship

Good luck Jackie, I'll miss you so much.
I've known you over half my life,
My heart you'll always touch.

Thru grade school and high school,
Our first apartment we shared
The good times and bad times, you know we always cared.

The boyfriends and breakups, the happy times and tears
All the plans we made together
All our hopes and fears.

But time goes on and now we part,
Your moving far away
Wherever you go, whatever you do, friendship doesn't stray.

So long for now Dear, I will see you one day
Take care of yourself, your husband,
Rick, Michael and Ray.

Christine M. Smith

When Have I Seen Too Much

I've seen a lot as I've grown to understand.
I've seen the power of dope kill a man.
I've seen the value of money rise and take
Innocent minds in control, dominate the mind
Of a child who has yet more time to grow.

I've seen the law be broken into bits and pieces
At a time, purposely replacing the meaning of
Justice only to commit more crime.

I've seen prejudice be define more each day
I've seen people kill people without reason
Just passing time away,

I've seen life become a hustle and dope become
A dangerous game. I've seen money become a
Murderer and people go insane. I've seen love
Become a gamble and destroy by its touch. I've
Seen people go so easy simple because they've
Seen too much.

Then I look at what I've seen and tremble to
Think of such, that I could someday be one of
Those people that have seen too much.....

Juliette Terrell

City Symphony

Windowpanes blink on here—there—then—here,
Just as glittering stars of evening when they appear.

Baton rays of sun part the curtain of the dark
Far off in the distance, a dog begins to bark.

Now, a sweetly warbled prelude by waking birds of night,
An occasional staccato note by sparrows taking flight.

The trash truck's chugging bassoon chugging drowns
our prelude oh so sweet.
Then, the keepers of the city start to sweep the city street.

Blinding noontime sunlight illuminates the stage!
The vehicular crescendo swells with mighty rage!

Softly diminishes the tempo as night's curtains slowly close,
Once more metropolis musicians curl up and take a doze.

Elizabeth Gury

"Theresa, Wherever You Are"

Death is but an interlude, a twilight sleep,
Just before the dawn tiptoes across the sky
And the sun stretches from its weariness brilliantly
Calling upon the universe to rise.

Theresa, it is true life is but a fleeting moment,
A twinkle in the eye of the Almighty, a sigh
From the heavens releasing the burden of time,

But surely one's existence is never without
Purpose for those we touch become the
Reflection of our own souls and like a mirror,
One cannot be seen without the other

A consciousness cast unbridled into the
Star-speckled universe to forever yield to
Nothing but its own cosmic state of
Ultimate tranquility fills every corner of
infinity; and therefore is
"with us always."

Denise Grajales

Each Day

As each day passes into the night
Just close your eyes real tight.
And think of me holding you right
remembering one day your eyes will open
and I'll be in sight.

As each day passes.....

As the sun falls and the sky turns into purple hue
relax and make your thought new.
And think of me being true
remembering one day our days
apart will be very few.

As each day passes....

As the morning comes and the darkness fades
into a beautiful sky
Go ahead sweetheart it is alright to cry
and think of me as your man who won't say goodbye
remembering I'll keep every promise
if you allow me to try.

Ian D. Clark

Tough Guy

I'm a tough guy, I'm lean and mean,
Just look at me, I'm in my teens.
I know the language of the streets,
I hang out with the guys I meet.
If there is trouble brewing anywhere,
You can bet, I'll be the first one there.
My name is known all over town,
This tough guy ain't nobody's clown.
The example I set before my brother's eyes,
Who cares... I'm just being one of the guys.
To lie and cheat, and steal now and then,
It's no big deal, I'm cool with my friends.
To be part of the gang, and accepted you see,
Is the only thing that really matters to me.
I know I've hurt others, by things that I've done,
My parents no longer consider me their son.
Life does involve choices, that much I can see,
The choices I make now, determine who I'll be
I should leave the gang, and a life filled with crime,
Or I'll spend my life, behind bars doing time.

Delene Collins

Why?

If you want to see how much I hurt inside,
just look into my eyes.
The smile on my face is a little too wide,
just a mask of my pride.
The laugh is a part of the act,
it's not real and that's a fact.
No one hears me cry,
no one asks me, why?
Will no one hear,
do they fall on a deaf ear?
Tell me I'm not alone in this place,
tell me someone else runs this race.
Let it be, let it go,
just don't say I told you so.

Annastasia McDonald

Just Me

Sitting, waiting in the dark,
Just me wanting, needing to see
Things happen before your eyes
May someday bring you a big surprise

Looking, searching, just me
Finding things from where I was three
No information was found
Except sad pictures that I left on the ground

Laughing, crying, just me
Wondering what I should be
Every one is different I finally see
I know now what I should be...

Angela Caddy

Untitled

Winter's fury, snow so blurry
Just no sense, to get in a hurry.
As icy snow, pelts down hard
And just a walk, has made him tired.
All at rest, except a man
Staying warm, the best he can
Snuggling down, in pelts of fur
The snow continues, in a blur
Still hoping for, a touch of spring
with toes and nose, froze in numbing sting
Little warmth, received from the fire
He adds a log, to build it higher.
At rest finally, he is taken
In blinding light, to awaken
To snowy ground, all around
Still no stir, nor a sound.

Johan C. Alberts

Untitled

So many people got hurt today
just simply because we don't want to
hear what the next person has to say
not because who we are but because we're set in our own way.

I've been to heaven and I've been
to hell but I'm glad I lived so
I would have a story to tell.

I'm gonna take your hand you see
because some how you understand me
it's weird to know someone believes in me.

As I walk along this street alone
I know you're home waiting by the phone,
but I can't call just because
of what I saw. I could take your
heart into my hand because you
seem to understand where I've been
yet whenever I think of you I have to grin.

People do many things to hurt you
but never worry I will never desert you.

Don Jones Snowden

Commitment

When the sadness overwhelms you and brings with it despair,
Know that I am with you, that always I'll be there.
When the demons rear their heads and make you feel afraid,
Know that I watch over you; feel the strength of which I'm made.
Do not turn away from me; do not go forth alone.
Come to me for shelter within our happy home.
Nestle deep within my arms; bow your head and cry.
I'll be with you forever until the day I die.

Carolyn R. Tompkins

Life

Sometimes life seems so dull and dreary,
Just the thought of it leaves you worn out and weary.
Daily frustrations as you journey along your way,
Momental happiness you wish were here to stay.

Violent eruptions in countries far and near,
Thousands dying, many living in fear.
Underground terrorists, planned explosions,
Brutal assassinations, internal erosions.

Countries wrangling over foreign policy,
Some in chaos, others arguing about fallacy.
Floods, Volcanoes and sometimes Drought,
Disease and starvation must come about.

Gross unemployment, growing inflation,
Too many financially embarrassed Nations.
Border disputes are on the increase,
The cry of territorial integrity will never cease.

People being suppressed in their own land,
Numberless, but too weak to stand. However,
despite the constant turmoil and tension,
I hope to be around to receive my pension.

Barbara Ramsay

How Great Thou Are

Let Jesus visit you tonight.
Keep the faith.
Our Jesus, He is great.
Keep love going, it's so right.
Let Jesus visit you tonight.
Tell Him all that's in your heart.
Somehow you will see the light.
The gift of life and love will show you the way.
Keep the light shining in your life today.
For today is all you got.
Tomorrow I don't know.
God will guide me and you to the gift of life and love.
It's the only way.
God's will be done.
Be prepared to let Jesus visit you tonight.
The gift of life and love will be yours forever more.
Seek and you will find Jesus standing at your door.

Jean Ferris

My Prayer

Dear Lord, every day through each year to come,
Keep their love growing and keep them young.
To ride their bikes over many a hill,
And never ever losing that special thrill.

"Shutterbur" and "Sunshine" always together,
Riding along in all sorts of weather.
Just so long as they are side by side,
Keep an eye on them, Lord, while they ride.

Sometimes thinking back when there were four,
Something that can't ever be anymore.
the "Over-the-Hill Gang" is down to three,
Just Bub and Jean, and of course me.

This being your anniversary, I want to say,
I hope it will be a most special day.
Five years ago now, we lost number four,
Please dear Lord, we don't want to lose any more.

Lord, bless these people that I love,
And keep them safe from up above.
I am going to stop now, before I cry,
But I know God loves you, and so do I.

Bill F. King

Jennie Moves To L.A.

Jennie. My muse. My delight.
Keep your hair long. Wild. Unrefrained. The classic ideal of rebellion. How I adore that in you.
Liberated. Not by man but self. A deity trait, you know. Stay and grow the Goddess you are. And maybe. Someday. Human kind will catch up. With you.
To Earth herself. I will think you in all the galleries.
See you in the untamed, savage, and gentle.
Embrace the you within myself. The stroke of genius.
The sensitive curve. My definition of woman. Redefinition (challenge) of beauty. Go further and call yourself exquisite.
Larger than life. At least this one. And when this one splits at the seams, when the skies possess an orangy hue, come looking. Beth and I will be waiting. For your glorious self.

Amanda Love

Let The Running Game Begin

Quietly slipping
knowingly blind
future unknown
running is peace
feelings all numb
into the darkness
far far away—
No one will notice
the quiet escape
the pain is all over
the running is peace
this game is over
I never was—
I slipped into darkness and ran into space
The feeling of running into unknown time
Will anyone notice or is there no trace
The game has begun
don't look back
just run—

Denise Marie Sobel

"What About Me"

I tried ballet, it was magnificent,
Ladies on pointe and men in tights.
I tried reading and writing, they surprised me,
They brought me to a new place.
My life is in my words alone,
So what about me.

Erin Straubinger

Depth

God bless America, home of the brave,
Land of the free, a melted mix of water color
Where blunt colored butterflies
Wearing clipped wings upon manicured lawns
Believe they can fly away from immaculate cages.

Lost souls skim the bottom of the ocean
Searching for their welfare checks.
Glass figures leagues above the fall
Struggle not to drown, heads above water
Challenged and threatened by angry tow and current;
Desperately gripping Mercedes autos and majestic castles
With every perking bubble of their pale life blood.

In another class whitened, brightened toothpaste smiles
Compliment designer luggage as the happy couple
Locks their doors and their minds, blinking infection
Acute suburban apathy manifested in a twisted serendipity;
Faucets left dripping and a rebel gas knob in half rotation.
Now is their chosen time to run off and dig a well abroad
To water renegade soil that is but dust and desert.

Ann L. Jordan

Marker In Time

A flower to lay at the foot of a marker to life's times.

A plaque to which a name rest with date of birth and death
lays atop a place you rest in peace.

A tree laid in seed many years before sprays a sweet breeze
above your peaceful rest.

The sounds of nature and man-made rush by with all
commotion in your place of rest.

A marker kept by plot keepers and thieves that disturbs
your solitude.

What sort of person lays to rest beneath my feet?

A family comes and lays tokens of affection long since
past, but of memories still alive and thriving.

This marker to someone's life is little to the unknown,
but a great richness to those who remember this person who once
crossed their path.

A time I wish we could all share of markers across America
that represents common to rich folks; what lives did they bear?

What stories are untold beneath those markers that I care.

Julie L. Turner

A Daughter's Words To Her Mom

If you leave tonight
Leave knowing that I care
And know that I am sorry for everything you've feared.

If you go tomorrow
Please go without a frown
And try your hardest to forget the times I've let you down.

If you part from me next week
Let's part together as one
And forget what's happened in the past because what's done is
done.

If you fall asleep in a month
May you drift into a dream
And never relive the nightmares
When I was cold and mean.

If you pass away next year
Please leave me with your love
Help me make decisions and guide me from above.

I do not know when you'll leave me
Now that my arms are opened wide
I wish you could stay forever
And never leave my side.

Becky Talarico

Storm Of Pain

Leave me now, all alone, to drown in my tears.
Leave me now, all alone, to confront my fears.
The thought of your breath and your kisses on my
neck remain.
Memories of you are holding me down like chains.
Thunder rumbles above me and lightning strikes.
Insecurely I lay there, an open wound I am like.
Circling like a vulture you pick at my flesh, taunting me.
Your cold hands, cold words, uttered lies haunting me.
So cruel with a heart of stone.
If only sooner I could have known.
I hope you're delighted for the sweltering pain you
made me feel.
So leave me now in peace, for I need time to heal.

Dawn McMullin

Ask Me Not

Ask me not why the night crawls across the sky
Leaving little space for stars to dart about.
Ask me not why, with darkness, comes a peace
That eludes the length of light that pours
Through the window invading the need for rest.
Ask me not why, but send the clouds with rain
That dulls the day and drenches the body and soul,
Pouring love as liquid, bathing the heart,
Reviving a lost past like arms enfolding the flesh.
Ask me not why thoughts continue the invasions,
As nature's beauty runs rampant along the way.

Sure, tis' known that love has long since gone,
And need for conversion wanes as the sun sinks.
Ask me not why thunderstorms are peaceful.
Dark clouds with fingers of sparkling light
Brings glorious rain to wash away the pain
From loneliness suffered in a hole of despair.
Ask me not why time is endless, when love.
Once as bright as the sun, now awaits the clouds
to uplift the ponderous heart.

Annie L. McClure

Fragments

Empty hours of days longer than the years,
Leaving more to forget than remembered.
Memories, like yellowed leaves, flutter against
The mind's gossamer webs, delicately clinging
Until wisped away in a sigh.
All the fragile yesterdays don't come flooding anymore.
A laugh, a face, a kiss, a baby's moist breath
Are bitter - sweet drops briefly traced
On the worn cheeks of time.
Is this the solace?
Cushioned grayness in the stead of vibrant color,
Pianissimos replacing passion's great, crashing chords,
Delicate petals of thought flitting across faded eyes?
Oh, to once more grasp pain, laughter, love.
To feel the rough tweed instead of rustling silk.
When young, how eagerly we turn ahead life's pages
Not knowing how brittle they soon become,
Too delicate to be turned back again at will,
Obscured forever in the lavender of old age.

Geraldine Bauer

True Feelings

Lonely....
Left in a sea of tears
Heart Broken...
To think it is over after all these years
Saddened...
By the thought of what will never be
Lost...
Is the love for you and me
Hate...
Is a feeling deep inside
Angry...
Because of a love that has died
Ashamed...
To have believed everything you said
Scared...
To think my heart is dangling on a thread

Angela Hubbs

Rebecca's Prayer

Lord shine on me, let your light penetrate my soul.
Let me absorb your blessings
and let me reap them unto others I love.
Let your beauty be known;
despite the world and its impurities.
Be my guide and my inspiration.
My hope and faith will be in you,
Always and forever.

Joyce Robertson

The Artwork Of God

Let me witness the mastery of his art
Let me be awed by its wonder

He beckons the sun and orders it to rise
And makes wonderful magic before our eyes.

He colors the sunset and paints it with ease
And blows down from heaven and creates the breeze

He commands the rainbow at one corner to stand
And throws the stars in place with a wave of his hand

The clouds he gives a silver lining
And makes the sun obey by shining

He anchors the moon on the darkness of night
And commands it to shine, to make night and bright

The masterful art of this master at work
Is a great phenomenon we can observe from
Down here earth

Barbara Spencer

Song And Ceremony

Oh, old and feeble heart!
Let not the flame die out!
All heard, seen, felt and shared,
In this and previous lives,
By the flowers of the human race.
Guard in your bosom, therefore, this secret;
Let not the hope die out!
And cherish in memory, but cherish
That which is decent and good in all forces,
From the stars to the pebble.
For only when all is uplifted in Nature
Will you apprehend the Ways of Heaven,
Follow on the same Path,
And hear the Song of the Morning Stars!

Barbra Ammon

Prayer

Light, drag from me the signs of sleep
Let the cudgels of hate and fear
Prod me through the long nights. Let me leap
Into the words, and let me shape,
Avoiding all that makes me weep
For lost hours. Fill me with the drive
The seize and pillage the people—sheep
Dissected and devoured through
My fountain pen — and let me reap
Success in all I undertake.
Help me endure my foes and keep
Me safe from faltering and death.

Brendan McEntee

Expressions

Dance—as free as the wind.
Let the spirit of your movements release you,
Such as the mighty Eagle soaring high above.

Dance—with the passion of love that is within your heart.
Unleash your inner feelings.
Color each vein of your imagination like the rainbow after a storm.

Dance—as smooth and softly as the white silence of clouds on a summer's day.
Allow yourself to be captured amidst the gentle breezes that fill the air with the scent of life.

And when the lightening strikes, my friend,
You will dance—with the power and the ferocity of the sparks and fires,
That will have awakened the stage.

Donna L. Murphy

"Fly Away"

With the faith to move a mountain, in the spirit of your flight,
let your heart grow wings and fly to new horizons - - - - - -
see the world in a different light.

I'd love to see you in your glory, like a hero on parade,
with all your girls, Julie, Jamie, Beth and Tori - - - - - - -
oh how I'd love to see that day.

If there be a cool breeze, upon your lovely face,
it's my spirit passing by - - - - I know one day girl,
our two hearts will embrace, and together we will fly - - - - -

To rise above the rain and thunder, to get to see the clear
blue sky, all it takes my love, is a little awesome wonder - - - - -
then tears of joy will fill your eyes!

We know that love can last forever, and dreams are meant to
all come true, so spread your wings now girl, let's find our dreams
together - - - - And follow love to where they flew - - - - -

Fly away, we will fly away, on wings of love against the wind - - -
Fly away, we will fly away, it's time we learn to live again - - - - -

Gregory Alexander Demeter

Life

In our youth we wanted so many, many things.
Life was rich with challenges
That came to stretch our wings.
We felt that we could reach the stars,
Could overcome all odds.
We needed only our own strength
To make us be like gods.
The years have passed, our dreams have changed,
We're more content to be
Just ordinary people
And no celebrity.
We find delight in simple things,
In flow'rs, and all the seasons.
We do not question everything
And look always for reasons
For everything we cannot know,
But trust in God above
For patience and for tolerance,
And most of all, for love.

Evelyn L. Harris

Dreams

A dream is a vision of life to be
Made up in the mind by you and me.

Dreamt by night, dreamt by day
Just taken every step of the way.

Some may come true, some may fade away,
But often thought of every minute of the day.

Janice Smith

A Rose In Time

So here I am, another space in time.
Light years away, from an earlier day.
When the first rose blossomed,
Into its earthly prime.
It knew well the sun,
And the moon on the run.
And how the night's always laid it to sleep.
Cradled by morning dew,
Its petals would weep.
It cried for the rain,
And it longed for the sun.
And waited for the winter,
When its work would be done.

Jackie Klonsky

The Blind Man's Wife

The blind man's wife, a shining star!
Like a non-vanishing light in the darkest infinity,
You guide the blind man to his destiny.

Through your words of supreme good,
The unfortunate blind man sees
The sun, the moon, and the stars;
The mountains, the forests, and the seas,
And God's gracious faces.

You are the truth, the way to your man,
He follows you all along with attention.
You need no cosmetics and no fashion,
Your beauty is beyond his imagination.

Lifetime's selfless sacrifice,
Rewarded only with sightless eyes.
Though happiness may have gone afar,
Yet no mortal is ever as you are:
Overpowering the soul of a man
With love's power mighty-
The Truth, the Good, and the Beauty!

Chauncey Chen

Pass And Review

We stand in columns, stiff,
Like marble, weapons in hand. Minds
Reverberating essences of thieves in the
Night. Crash, clump, and sighs as
The weak fall to the ground.
The agony of it all is unending. The time
comes, we move as one to break
Apart and run away. Grins
Of delight splashed on our faces.
Screams of fright hanging in
The heavy air. A wild
Orgy of sorts, the sounds of
The sexually oppressed.
Ding dong ding.
Ding dong ding.
The bugle calls, and all
Is silent. Bodies lie in the
Field, deprived, weak, panting for life
In this rainbow world
Of monotony.

Aimee Buchanan

Untitled

You are my Brother, that will always be
Like the stars, the sun and the endless sea

And like the sea we will never part
For our minds and souls are joined at the heart

We've laughed, we've cried - we've seen it all
So this crazy thing won't make us fall-

We'll fight, we'll pray and we'll even cry
But damnit Brother, we'll never say die!

I know you are tired and often cry
Why Dear Lord must it be I?

I don't know the answer, I do not know why
Some people keep smiling and others must cry

I do know for certain this is not the end
For with prayers and love you'll soon start to mend

So let us join hands so all can see
YOU ARE MY BROTHER - THAT WILL ALWAYS BE

Anna Marie Speruta

The Other Side Of The Rain

Staring out the window, trying to break the spell
Lines of falling rain form the grey bars of my cell
The loneliness I'm feeling never seems to wane,
I wonder what you're doing on the other side of the rain

A painter with no canvas knows no happiness
Tormented by the visions she cannot express
So I suffer with this love, that seeks for you in vain
Since you have gone your own way on the other side of the rain

As gentle as the loving, the pain you leave is cruel
Still from coal's dark blackness is formed the brightest jewel
Passion passes, sorrow's spent, a purer strength remains
Ascending like a rainbow on the other side of the rain

Debra A. K. Collins

Tapestry

She's lost in a world of feldspar and quartz
listening to mandolins and violins
while she weaves a tapestry
that unravels at her feet

Silken threads tangle in her fingers
and then she'll bend in concentration
until the violins capture her ears
and the sparkle of the quartz traps her eyes
Then the woof and the warp of the weave make
their own meaning. The tapestry struggles
beneath her numb fingers.

The blood of her pricked and numb fingers,
bits of dreams and laughter, disappointments and lust
find their way into the tapestry of her soul

A chorus of children sing her lullabies
but she dare not sleep for her work's not done
and endlessly the pattern moves randomly
as though lost in her lost world

She's lost in a world of gossamer and mercury
weaving her life into meaning that unravels at her feet.

Connie Augustine

Stranded In Oblivion

Sitting in my dark, murky room
Listening to music preaching doom.
I sometimes wonder how my life will end
Wishing somehow, something would make sense.
My life is just one big bore
Nothing to do, just a snore.
I wonder if life's any fun at all
I wonder if life is just a ball.
But, it's not for me
It's not full of glee.
Sometimes, it makes me feel so small
It sometimes makes me want to end it all.

Effath Choudhury

Two Beady Eyes

Walking in the woods,
Listening with every step you take.
No moon or stars, and hopefully no cars.
Clouds cover the Earth like a huge blanket.
Darkness that splashes across the edge of the grassy field,
Quietness, stillness and there it is,
You hear the chop and bark,
Skillfully trying to distinguish the leader of the pack.
It is time to pick up the pace.
The dogs are jumped, chasing and leaping, the coon is on the run.
Tapping trees, dodging leaves, and running for his life,
All you can see is the glimmering pathway of light streaming from your forehead as you run through the woods.
You can hear the leaves crackle as you run,
The incessant beat of your heart pushes faster and faster.
Finally you reach the tree and look up. You see those two beady eyes.
You have chased them for a seemingly endless, short time.

Eric Evenstad

The Little Girl From Galilee

The little girl from Galilee was not there that day when He took little children on His knee and loved and blessed them tenderly.

But she had heard about the Stranger her folks told her about the manager the night the angels sang of glory... O peace, 'twas such a thrilling story. How He had made the blind to see; the lame to walk... how happy she Would be if she could run like others And be a playmate to her brothers.

Now that could never be, for they had crucified Him yesterday. The earth in anger had been shaken and He, like she, had felt forsaken.

The next morn early in still grey hours she choose her favorite friends, the flowers and with them limped through cold dank gloom to where they laid him in a tomb.

The strangeman seated on the rock said, "Little girl, don't limp, dear, WALK! In years to come your love will be a symbol of our victory."

Cosette G. Vreeland

"Dying Is Special"

The rose petals have surrendered for today!
Make record of the death coming
Take breath, rejoice - the rose labors forth many buds

Comfort then in the reflection of our labors
The mirror reflects what has been and what is-COMPLETION
We shall always be!
Once captured, the image evokes yesterday's strengths

Today's friendship has been born of many deaths
Take then the hand of tomorrow's bud
The blossoming reaches out touching, caring, experiencing, dying!

Craig R. Frost

What It's Like To Be Young

Deep inside the heart of every person
Lives a child who longs to hurt them.
Yet never again will they understand.
They say they remember when they were young.

When they were young, they were free.
When they were young, pain could never be.
But I don't see the world that way.
They don't remember how it is to be young.

Soon the time will come to be
They will feel the pain and misery
Of youth, no way to deny it!
But they still say they remember when they were young.

When they were young, people never lied.
When they were young, the good never died.
How can they see it all that way?
They don't remember how it is to be young.

No pain, yesterday to far away, no youth remains.

Heather Oswald

Paradoxical Irony

Love is a game and I'm not a player
Lonely tears mix with rain
So young to feel so old
Lightning dies to be mourned by thunder

Only closed doors around me
Heartbeats are lost in the rhythm of rain
Extinguished candles lead the way
Loud lightning and bright thunder mix

My special self reflects on images
Cool rain burns gentle souls
Lonely heart dies amid screams
Light is created - sound initiated - both die

A phoenix rises from my ashes
The rain falls upward to the sky
Being love - I no longer need it
Intertwined - the lightning and thunder - live forever

Bobbie Ann Ford

Daily Constitutional

Walking the streets of my city - in sneakers.
Looking down at sidewalks polka-dotted with gum,
swirling candy wrappers, recyclable cans,
Passing stores boarded up or staring out - hollowed eyed
as spectre,
then
Remembering - walking in Sunday shoes,
Seeing clean pavements - defined cracks.
Jumping over so not to break my mother's back.
Staring in store windows spot-lighting new fashions and toys,
Pausing
now
to wonder what happened?
am I to blame?
Should I now look only UP
and pray?

Jeanne Andrews

What Is A Puppy?

Did you ever wonder as you passed the shop,
Just what it was that made you stop?
A ball of fur with needle teeth,
And stubby legs stuck out beneath,

He's black and fat with floppy ears,
with two small eyes at you he peers,
He may not be much from either end,
But in between, he's man's best friend.

Caryn M. Wagner

Wasteland Of My Soul

Searching through the stygian depths of my being
Looking for an angelic soul to join with and take me from this
limbo of existence
When I'm alone this chaotic plane is a desolate wasteland without
another to guide me
Starless nights greet every feature in this personal Hades
Broken dreams manifest their sorrow into demons that feed on my soul
Tears flow freely to fill the River Styx.

A beacon illuminates the area and I race to hug its warm light,
caress its pure soul, and love its very being
The beacon flitters as I come near and despair nearly overwhelms me
The hellspawned memories come for me again to drag me back
to the Styx
The beacon sees my peril and comes to my aid, melting the
hounds of despondency into pools of steaming ichor
The beacon burns brighter than ever touching my shapeless soul
and giving me a new light
Now two beacons show over this once ravaged land making everything
we touch live in brilliance in this mighty Utopia.

Josh Rudelbach

Alone In My World

Here I stand in the shadows of the night,
Looking for the good and searching for the light.
I stare at the people in the open having a good time,
Searching for a Savior so I can be fine.
Alone in the world, away from all others,
I trusted one too many, I'll never trust another.
I'll make it-I'll make it! I know I can.
I'll make it to be an adult, yeah a maturing young man.
Standing in the shadows trying to conceal my face.
Searching across the land, trying to find my place.
So much love and yet no one to take it.
I say to myself, I know I can make it.
Alone in this world, looking for a friend.
To bring my sorrows, my fears, to an end.
I travel through this world never being accepted.
All my time and money has never been invested!
In the shadows I step out. Must move on
Because all that I've hoped for is gone.
Alone, here, yes my friend- all by myself.
All in this world without anyone else.

Frank Crawford

"The Fortress"

Sitting here in morning's silence
Looking through the window, inside
I can feel my self defiance
Relent to tears I've longed to cry.

For years I've tried to touch your heart to
open places in need of light.
Finding the darkness better suits you...
A haven for your fears and spite.

Closing doors and never trusting.
Leaving me love so bitter not sweet.
You tell me you're happy, but you're forever lusting....
Believing in those who breed deceit.

Preferring to be solitary, yet wondering why
you're left alone.
The excess baggage that you carry, has
turned your heart to one of stone.

I can't reach you. Your wall's too high!
A fortress you won't let nobody in.
Can't understand your reasons why,
I've scaled your walls but never win.

Gillian P. Cook

A Son's Love For His Father

My father is gone! I feel so sad I never thought I
loose him he was the dearest Dad. I still can't believe it
I just don't understand the thought of loosing him
just drives me mad. The love I've shared with my father
with all of my heart as is only son I thought we would
never part. The unforgettable times were shared he always
showed me how much he cared, now that he's gone I
must carry on for I know in my heart he would want
me to go on. I try to be strong in every way but then I
break down and I know it's ok! Sometimes I can't hide the tears
because I just wish he was here. God took my father
home to a place called heaven you have a new life Dad.
God gave to you the garden of happiness full of love
Because He Close You!

Dawn M. Lilley

Deliverance

Here lies the soul of silent mask,
Lost in thoughtful wake.
No more tears to cry from drying eyes;
No more strength this world can take.

A maze of black and seething red,
Beyond the realm of sane;
No more wrath to slay my soul,
In these fields of precious pain.

I flee from all indifference-
Rebuke all that I am taught to know.
No more can earthly desires bind this mind;
No more can this world be my home.

Normal no longer suites this soul-
Reality no longer touches this heart.
What used to be the descent of man,
No longer may play its part.

For within this vessel of savage flame, wherein all sense is lost;
The beat of flesh slowly fades, and temptation sings its cost.

And standing here above the black, above the valley of fear;
I drift among the stars that call my name, and forever await you here.

Dawn Smith

"Transient"

A man stood alone in the cool evening fog
lost within his thoughts of his life and his God
It was unknown to him where he should begin
and the alcohol he drank kept his senses quite dim.
The smoke from his cigarette lingered in the air
he had lost everything and he didn't really care
He wondered with desperation why he was still here
The evening's coolness bit at him as he began facing his fear
"God, forgive me for things I've done,
especially denying love to my only son!"
"I've never found a place I felt at home, but please
don't let me die alone!"
He felt an aura of death surround him and it brought a tear to his
eyes
he had wasted away his life and couldn't understand why
"God, give me one more chance" he shouted towards the sky
but it only got him odd stares from some people passing by
He walked on until he saw his reflection, he looked thin and old
shivering, he ducked into a doorway to escape the bitter cold.
He curled up in a corner, praying that tomorrow wouldn't be the same,
Then he fell asleep and was granted his wish,
for his tomorrow never came.....

Donna Hornak

Love Is Like A Child's New Toy

Love can make you sad.
Love can make you mad.
Love can make your heart fill up with joy.
Love can make you happy like a child getting a new toy.

The child loves to have this new toy around.
For it brings the child up whenever they are down.

But soon that toy falls apart.
And so does a lover's heart.
Then the child feels sad, because they have lost their toy.
Just like a lover when they lose their only pride and joy.

It is easy to fix a broken toy that has been torn apart,
Or just replace the batteries,
But it isn't as easy to replace happy memories
With thoughts that are sad from a lover's heart.

If there is someone out there
And you really give a care.
Then you'll never hurt them, even if you're mad,
Because that would only make them sad.
You'll love them with all your heart,
Like you did in the start.

Bobby V. D. E.

"Black Roses"

Darkness and silence and endless cold
madness and violence and terrors unfold
Back breaking, bone crushing pressure
punishment too great to measure

Numbing depression and senseless pain
chaotic aggression with nothing to gain
Hope of salvation is so long past
then comes a desperate submission at last

You've taken my soul and left me to die
bound by the chains of your terrible lie
Heartbroken, torn, and forsaken
cause you'll never give back what you've taken

Still, you're precious to me, lovely flower
and when Death frees me from your power
Your fragrance and softness still will thrill me
it's your thorns of vengeance that will kill me

Oh, pretty petals are falling
see me bleed - bleeding for you
When the end is finally here
cover me with black roses

Jason Khasey Fint

Thank You For Nothing

I continue to live on even though your
love is gone. I was left alone and lonely
without anyone's shoulder to cry on.
You showed me just how much you cared
when you left me on a truth or dare.
I thought that you cared for me, but I guess
this was a love that wasn't meant to be.
To you I must say goodbye for you gave me
all the right reasons to cry. You had no
sensitivity within your heart, by your actions
you tore mine all apart.
Many questions I need to endure my love
I had for you was all good that's for sure.
Answers to why you left me I seek to find
many doubts you put into my mind.
When you left me without a goodbye,
you left me with just plenty of tears to cry.
To me that was so ignorant and thank
you for nothing cause that's something I'll
never forget.

Carlier L. Floyd

Heavenly Father

"Oh" Heavenly Father, Thou art love and divine
Make our hearts like unto Thine
Love and guide us day and night
Help us walk through the shinning light.

Keep us in Your heart of love
With rays of calling from above
If we grow weak, make us strong
So that nothing can go wrong.

In times of trouble and despair
Give us strength to know You're there
"Lord," You are the way, You are the sun
You are the word for everyone.

"Oh" Heavenly Father, please hear our prayer
Let us know You truly care
For we love You, so very much
Bless us Father, with Your Heavenly touch.

Grace Sardisco

Set Free

I was the fool to think that you ever could
love me as long as you said you would.
There once was a time, not so very long ago
you said "be my wife, and I'll never let you go"
I suggested we wait until you are a little older
now your heart has grown so much colder
Now I'm left alone, all by myself
to bad my heart fell off that shelf
It's not the first and won't be the last
at least I learned something from the past
Friends is what we'll always be
financially combined, well that's not for me
I gave you it all, my heart and soul
for what? we never hit our goal
Married is what I someday want to be
but all you want is to be set free.

Ester Ruth Salziger

The Falling Of The Raindrops

The Pitter-Patter of the rain
Makes me wonder and think again
Why is life the way it is?
Tell me, tell me answer me please!

Little children jumping in puddles
While others inside gather in cuddles
The pitter-patter of the rain
Makes life seem so peaceful again

While I lay in bed at night
The pit-pit patter of the raindrops fall light
Giving me hope that was gone long ago
They give me strength to carry on

I hear the pitter-patter - as I walk
down life's long road - I have my
blankets wrapped around me
so that the journey won't seem as cold
I keep on walking forward - Each
little drop helps me onward.

Johncy Sara George

Mother Earth

Oh Mother Earth, I marvel at how you
manage to sustain each living thing.
Oh Mother Earth, with your ruins of old
I wonder at your stories untold.
Oh Mother Earth, how fine you are for us
to behold with your graceful valleys and towering mountains.
Flawless are your colors of life,
a breathless beauty for wanders delight.
May your mysteries always exist for us to unfold.

Judith Patterson

A Lesson Learned

What I feel in my heart cannot be denied,
Many things happened, before the sign.
What I could not see in your face,
Now appears on your hand.
It will be this day, that I understand.
So much love you expressed to me.
Only now I know, you are not free.
It is said that, "love is blind"
A meaning in this, I could not find.
Lonesome and alone, I look at days gone by.
This life of mine has been such a lie.
Your sweet words are forever in my mind.
Yet, no meaning in them can I now find.
Why couldn't I see what was happening to me?
A harder lesson learned, there will never be
What I feel in my heart has been set free.

Juli Adams

Serenity of Morning

Bring back the solitude of the night.
March on to the beat of all that troubles
The fragile state of tranquility.
For it is tranquility which shields the silent
truth of morning's caress.
Awake, awake, awake
Awake and know no more of that silent, cautious slumber.
That cautious slumber which masks the feelings of all that needs to be.
Fear not the sharp reality of all you feel, all that you need.
In the harshness of the morning,
Know that you are alone no longer.

Julie M. Stone

Marriage

Marriage is not for today.
Marriage was blessed in God's own way,
He gave you a companion to love and cherish.
Hold on to each other and don't make a blemish.
Marriage is not just for today,
You both have to plan life your own way,
Please take good care in all your plan,
For Satan is there to cause a confusion.
Join hands together and pray to God,
To keep you both in one accord.
And do the things you know best,
For God is there to do the rest.
God will bless the things you do,
For he's watching over you,
He will provide the things you need,
To give to those you have to feed.
God the father of divine.
Bless these two children who seek and find,
Keep them safely in your arms,
And shelter them from temptation and wrong.

Egbert Grosvenor

A Day At The Fair

Oh!... A land of candy, cookies, popcorn and pop!
Marshmallows and ice cream with cherries on top
Rides, games, prizes and toys
No work at all — just these joys!

At the fair all day,
Daddy, Mommy and me
Rode ride after ride
Bought treat after treat

Then as playing so hard did its take,
I went home with a bellyache

But when I woke up the very next day
We went back to the fair to have fun and play!

Aleasha Wales

Trust

Trust is just not a word to
me, it's based upon reality.
Right and wrong is what it's
about, be true to the word without any doubt.
Use common sense with what you
do, because you will answer to you know who
some people don't know it, but
will learn, it's better to be honest then to burn
take the time to check what you
do, have trust and faith and always be true.

Gabriel Ramirez

Thrown In A Garbage Can

My 12 year old frightened mother was raped. She tried to carry
me to the expected date.

I'm a cute little girl, 5 pounds that's all. I must be very special
I survived the fall.

I was thrown in a garbage can, broken bottles, wasted food,
hypodermic needles, and another new born, but he didn't make it.

She wrapped me tenderly with love in her eyes but to me that
was a terrible disguise. She opened the chute from the 15th floor
and threw me down the garbage can door.

I fell and fell and screamed and cried, Dear Jesus save me before
I die and fortunately the garbage can man heard my new born cry -
He picked me up with tears in his eyes and I knew ma ma I knew
the sorrow was no disguise.

So tell my 12 year old mother that I'm a lovely bundle of joy to
a newly wed couple
but I'd prefer so much the tender touch of my mother
cause I was thrown in a garbage can!

Berrinda Jean Evans

Parents Of Boys

Three boys were born over thirty years ago,
Michael, Timothy, Darren because no girls showed.

One day they are small,
Little bundles to hold
You turn around
Suddenly they are tall and bold.

They go to work get a place of their own
Now this is called their home.

Although they are grown
Let it be known
We'll always be Mom and Dad

Jean Brandt

Untitled

Once again, you have captured my heart,
Mind, body, and soul;
My whole self; and every part,
You have in your control.

I love every part of you,
There is nothing I would rather you be;
Your heart is with everything I do,
You are a special part of me.

Every time you laugh, I laugh too,
Every time you cry, I have to wipe my eyes;
Every time you're happy, I am happy too,
Every time you leave me, a part of me dies.

You are perfect in every way,
Your eyes, hair, and smile;
My heart can only say,
Stay with me all the while.

So if this is a dream,
My love, my best friend;
Do not let me wake;
And my heart is what I will send.

Jennifer M. Bergmann

An Indian Summer Day

For Lisa

The breath of spring arrived, again I dreamed.
Missed colors dyed a dull, brown countryside.
Immersed in a bright May sun, my hopes redeemed.
The love of life I could not seem to hide.
The summer solstice, I was now robust,
Nurtured by nature, I could not foretell.
The tempest, raging gale descended just
when winter mem'ries seemed a scene from hell.
The fall... it came before I was prepared.
Soon cold, long nights befell my weary bones.
Destruction from the storm, still unrepaired.
I fought to reap from seeds in spring I'd sown.
An Indian Summer day, reprieve from work.
Bright hues, warm breeze, and I think not what lurks.

Gregg Greene

Poetic Verses

The human being.
Mixed with emotions.
Each human is unique.
Fate leading the way.

Emotions live life.
Guide you as a human.
Help create a personality.
Make a human as a whole.

Hatred a fierce emotion.
Must be in control.
Guide your mind to better things. Focus yourself.

To live, to create, to heal, is life.

To write, to express,
To appreciate, write the mind.

Forgive the past, look to the future,
Find the unknown, live from the future.

Hidden within yourself, personality is not known.
Find it in your heart, become what you are.

The world hurts worse. The pain strikes everything.
No one listening. The world it cries.

David J. Ross

Eternal Is Love

Patience and time, faith and strength,
moments together sharing.
Loving for life, and not taking for granted,
holding and feeling and caring.
I love you so now, I love you for always,
heart and soul and mind.
Let us look to each other,
respecting the other.
For our bond, will hold steadfast in time.

Colleen C. Holle

"My Memories Are Young As Yesterday"

My autumn years are falling 'round me,
More and more my hair turns grey,
But dear you're in my every memory,
And each memory young as yesterday,

As years go by, my memory wanders,
Wanders back to when you were here,
We loved and, laughed and had our good times,
Not dreaming once your time was near.

The few short years we had together,
Are much more precious than I can say,
Each year is burned upon my memory,
And each memory young as yesterday.

But now I walk alone my darling,
Just drifting with my autumn years,
But in my memory you walk beside me,
That's why I can smile through all my tears.

And when my autumn years are over,

And I've been gently laid to rest,
I'll thank God for the years he gave us,
Of all my years I love ours best.

Andrea Blizzard

A Place Not So Far Off

Faced with IT everyday, we hurry through traffic of a normal American morning.
As we go, we think not of those who hurt, but only of what we could have to make our own life better.
Most are even scared to face this unknown place and force.
From day one, it is said that we are put on this planet for a reason and only of HIS choice.
They say THERE you feel no pain.
They say there are no winners nor losers, and they say there are no doctors or hospitals because nobody hurts.
They also say that going THERE is not so hard, but what is being left behind is the tough job.
Through teardrops and anger they show their emotions.
Some are quiet, some are angry, and some don't even know what to think
But every time you have a little guy on your shoulders telling you there are MIRACLES, so DON'T GIVE UP!

But when our time comes, everybody has to let go, and watch them go away; not in pain this time, but in peace.

Now they know I'm in peace.

I always try and remember that they love me, I love them, and I'm going to A PLACE NOT SO FAR OFF!

Jim Osborne

Minnesota And Her Boom

The fall of autumn releases her hue
Morning sun light revealing her dew
Reluctant now of chill in the air
Spiteful is she to create such despair

Winds howling and broad oaks bent
One feels her approach hardly spent
Coercing hibernation to take on its course
Knowing clear well she will debut with force

Her first deed controlling, no place to flee
Hopeful it's over she thrust a new plea
Blinding white flakes plunging a blow
When does it stop, this blanket of snow

Dismiss her and spring ceases to occur
Cardinals won't whisper their musical words
Rivers won't flow past the great divide
Who would abandon her sensational ride

Carrie E. Boyce

"To You, My Friend"

Never was there orange behind the rest,
Mounted like an atlas full of sermons,
Full of bones. The professors proved otherwise,
That steeples were built since volcanoes erupted,
That the carpenters were also great frogs.
Fires carve the sky better than blades do,
An untimely invention like a time machine
Whose destiny predicts the future. They were sculptors
Like us, with failing livers and arthritis,
But the powerful wind went with them
And the watchtowers went up with them, for better vision,
Better reaching. Here we are now, all of us,
Three of us in line for ice cream sundaes with things that go
up close to our noses, with the orange in the distance.

It ripens and decays, and this is common,
And the bearer does so too, ripens and decays and ripens
Until it's stripped of juice, then it folds hands
And takes a step forward in the long line. To you, my friend,
And to you, too, my friend: The orange was never there before,
But it's been proved otherwise.

Brian Wolak

A River of Life

Inside the center of my inner self my soul swirls, and
moves in a circular pattern. Parts of my life rise to the top.

This fantastic splendor of movements is explained in
dramatic force. I rush and emit my power in prelude. I
thrust myself against the problems. They are easily
overcome. I move and go in a never ending amazement.

After time my body begins to become angular. All my
force died. The life I had in me vanished. I am just a
useless life. I will just thin out to nothing
and let the sun dry me out to sand.

Craig Kaelin

Jacky Frost

Jacky Frost, Jacky Frost come in the night
Left the meadows that he crossed all gleaming white
Painted with his silver brush every window pane
Kissed the leaves and make them blush, blush and blush again.

Jackie Frost, Jackie Frost drift around the house
Sly as a silver fox still as a mouse.
Out our little Rhonda came, blushing like a rose
Up jumped Jacky Frost and perched her little nose.

Grayce E. Kuhn

In A Single Drop Of Water

In a single drop of water there is much life
Much of that life is not visible to the naked eye
There are: smilbys and shnoodles, billbys and more
Not to mention things that really are
Not things that have been, will be
Or never will occur.
Anything you cannot see in a drop of water,
You can with a microscope
A microscope that can help one to see
Into new worlds, ideas, fantasies, and even more.
Look through your window and see
A growing lake with many drops of water
Close your eyes and think how much life
Lives in that lake. One day if the lake dries up
Still the life lives on in fantasy.
Fantasy can preserve anything, real, fake.
A human living in the worst circumstances
Can be happy thinking of fantasy
Fantasy a necessity a desire of life
Fantasy that can preserve a drop of water.

Caroline Hagood

Stepping On Air

Stepping on air I fly into
my dream in the middle of the
earth to find you sitting
legs up, tv on, almost reading your
Popular Mechanics, one eye open.
I try to reach for you, but snow
showers blow my arms sideways and
the air moves left as my steps fall
and glide on escalator-like sidewalks.
I pass by the university where Jung
waves and tells me it's ok.
With his approval I fall backward and jump
down to reach for you.
This time you are there.

Christine Colaiacovo

Untitled

As I look at my mother, so childlike yet so old
My eyes, heart and soul, grieves for tales yet untold

I feel that someday, I too will be
A legend of my own, for my children to see

From all my mother's loving good, I follow her example
For all her teachings were so wise and ample

A legend she is and will always be
She's an inspiration for all to see

Now as she slows, no longer in prime
Teaching her wisdom and knowledge, the privilege becomes mine

Beverly Faulkner

Together Again

As the sun goes down and turns to night
My mind just can't seem to set things right

While I lie awake at night in bed
Thoughts of you always return to my head

And when sleep arrives a simple dream I dream
Of you and I walking across a moonlit beam

You come to me to my waiting arms
together we fall to watch the stars

They streak across the blackened sky
Where there are no questions of why

So we follow them hand in hand
For our love will take us to the promised land

Carlos Ramirez

What Might Have Been

I know in my heart without any doubt,
My feelings for you are what love is about.

That I've loved more than once I will not deny,
But until I loved you I never knew why;

One person, just one, could make such a difference to me
That the way I had lived could no longer be.

Each day is so special when love fills your heart
Nothing or no one can keep you apart.

Through all of the good times and even some bad
When the depth of my feelings is all that I had;

I remember your smile, the feel of your kiss,
And the warmth of your arms are the things I will miss.

I know that my feelings are ones you don't share
I know you don't love me; you say that you care.

How can I keep going when I know it is true,
That no matter what happens, I'll always love you.

Andrea Hilger

Battered

Help me dear Lord, I'm begging you.
My heart is so heavy, I don't know what to do.

This hold he has so tight on me,
I cannot explain, I need to get free.

He constantly hurts me, and calls me bad names,
He always keeps telling me I am to blame.

I ask you tonight, to show me the way,
Help me to leave, I know I can't stay.

I want to walk out, but I don't know how,
I'll fear for my life, if he finds out now.

Again I'll forgive until the next time,
I pray for your strength, to change my mind.

It happened again but this time I am strong,
I'm leaving today, for I will be gone.

You answered my prayers and for this I give grace
I have lost all my fear, I put you in his place.

Deborah Jordan

Dangerous Game

It's dangerous, yes. The game we play.
My heart's at stake, I fear.
Despite my flirting ways, you'll find,
I long to hold you near.
I see much more than a handsome face,
much more than your deep dark eyes.
I see much more than the
ready smile on the mouth that tells me lies.
I see the you that stays in mind,
a thought that makes me smile.
I wish to make this game be real.
But, I wonder all the while,
I wonder how you'd take all this,
have you guessed? Or would you be surprised
I wonder how it would feel to look
and find love there in you lips.
Our playful words come all the time.
But, I beg of you, look beyond
see the meaning behind the
actions and then my dear respond?

Christine Anderson

The Fabric Of Life

My feelings are scrambled and my thoughts are scattered.
My heart's in pieces and my whole world has shattered.
I don't understand my feelings today
So much has happened along the way.

I must face what has happened in the past.
I can't take it back and a new mold recast.
I must face the feelings that have brought me here
To this fork in the road that I can see so clear.

A new stitch is added without delay
As the fabric of life takes shape today.
A pattern is made for the living to share
But sometimes the fabric may weave a tear.

Within this tear, a new pattern takes hold.
Two separate worlds; mine is warm and yours cold.
To feel your presence, if only I would,
To see your fabric, if only I could.

My thoughts may scatter to the days now gone.
As feelings unscramble as I move on.
One step at a time with each moment I face.
I weave a new pattern in my time and space.

Dana Holloran

Alcohol

Long ago, faraway,.....yesterday,
my life was in total disarray.
I played by the devil's rules.
My, how I must have made him drool!
He had a grip. I had his vice.
His fire can be misconstrued as glacier ice;
covered and frozen as was my heart.
His light is nothing more then living in the dark.
I cowered behind my very breath,
and yet, I bullied the Angel of Death.
He provides the courage you lack.
He pushed and shoved me forward,
and then he bullishly pushed and shoved me back. I feel.
You can't see the sights or hear the sounds,
when your face is touching the ground. Alcohol!
Watch your step, if you trip, it's quite a fall.
I got up, climbed back to the top.
Today, I walk with pride.
By simple rules I abide.
You see, I had the Angel of Life by my side.

Ben Davila

Memories

I look back on myself, and I see from afar,
My memories like light from a glittering star.
They're there for the time, real and new,
Yet bringing them back I never can do.

I glance at my life, on all that has passed,
It's etched in my mind, in iron it's cast.
But the star is now dead, and all of my tears,
Can bring but some light from millions of years.

Our memories are such, such as we have them made,
But can never be reached, can never be saved.
Though our memories may be, as our memories remain,
The future's to come — we'll have nothing shame.

But the day that I reach the hour of decline,
All I ask are some of those memories of mine;
To hold up my head, to hold onto my life,
Some memories of mountains on crystalline nights.

So we must keep these memories, keep track of our past,
For our next recollection may well be our last.
And the day that I die, and some memory I mar,
May I be but the light of some glittering star.

Amanda G. Mabey

Through The Smoke

Like the cigar I smoke,
my mind twists and turns.
Evaporating into thin air.
I sit and wonder,
is it wrong to hate, hate?
I see the world with different eyes,
eyes the are not blinded by hostility.
The cold feeling, abundant on the streets.
Look at yourself,
don't blame YOUR problems on someone else.
Take a breath of fresh air!
Don't choke,
see through the smoke.
As I sit back and puff on my cigar,
and dream of a new tomorrow.

James Robert Johnson

Untitled

It seems like just yesterday when I was a little girl
My mommy and daddy were my whole world
Then I grew up and was soon on my own
They never deserted me or left me alone
I wanted to believe they would live forever
When reality is, everyone has to go sooner or later
I never thought it would happen this way
Now daddy you are gone to stay
All they ever wanted was for me to do good
Only I did not do a lot of the things that I should
It's always when someone passes away
We think we should have done things a different way
They never put me down for the things I had done
If anyone understood, daddy you were the one
I will always thank God that he was my dad
He was the best anyone could have
He will always be in my heart and mind
He will remain there until the end of time
Daddy I know you will be watching over me
I love you so much may you forever rest in peace.

Julie Madrigal

"Homeless"

No time to rest, must keep walking,
My only asset is my expendable talking.
I sleep in an alley, behind a tall building,
To look up at the sky for my only ceiling.

I patch up my shoes that cover my feet,
Then set out on a journey for something to eat.
I sit and watch, people in such a hurry,
To get to their homes, they need not worry.

I wait and I wonder for some place to stay,
But why should it be different than any other day.
My hopes and dreams have all been shattered,
But to people, though few, what should this matter.

In this horrible life of living on the street,
I must hope and pray for the generous I may meet,
For I am a person, a person no less,
For I am a person, a person who is Homeless,

Cynthia S. Tussing

My Love

I see you once again...
My lips ache to meet yours
I feel your caress once again...
My body aches to meet yours
I hear your sweet nothings once again...
My ears search to catch your voice
There's undenying torment..
When I see you once again.

Bansari Patel

Child

So long I have waited for you
My perfect joy
You are my inspiration for a thousand daydreams
Always catching up with me
Stealing a moment
Taking hold of my heart
I wake
Only to find myself
Gently slipping back to you
Your love is the sweetest peace I have ever known
Never will I leave you
Forever you are my gold

Deanna Delgado

Paul Revere

Listen my children and you shall hear,
my side of the story I'm Paul Revere.
On the 18 of April in 75,
I scaled up a horse that was twelve times my size.
And I said to my friend now you listen to me,
it's not one lamp if by land and two if by sea.
I got a new pager I simply must try it,
now off to the belfry and remember be quiet.
Then I mounted my steed and took off like a storm,
like a hound on a fox, towards the opposite shore.
But I had a delay, it was a ticket to pay,
though I said, Hey I'm fighting a war.
But the constable clocked me, he said he was sure,
that I rode past his speed trap at one-hundred-four.
I'd tell you the rest,
but it's quite a long story.
And I'm late for my date,
with my girlfriend named Lorrie.

David Conrad

Elements Of My Love

Iron to your arms, but you are not there
My tears Argon from you pain and despair.

Fluoride need you love to smooth my fear.

You were the only one who Xenon past my flaws
With your Neon the ground you pledged your love.

You Krypton to my life, but you left in a flash
I Zinc I know why you didn't last.

My love I shall Sulfur no longer
I am over you and now I am stronger.

Amanda N. Mayberry

Your Ladyship

You are the waters to my thirst the feelings to my needs an answer to a prayer. The woman you will find will be royal and silk and sweeter than honey in a vine. If money has kissed your lips and made you happy just wait until you kiss mine.

If you have been loved by many lovers then you can compare how sweet and tender. The grass might be greener on the other side but it's only a reflection of what you'll be leaving behind. This crown that I have has been passed down from ancient time through a royal blood line. I fought many battles and came out on top just like David and his Sling Shot.

There are not many women that have walked in my shoes put to a test, tried and true. Like an ant to a colony you can come and sit by my side we'll leave this chapter open for the next one to succeed down the line.

Brena Otekpen

Trust

I knew that if I were still and could hear my silence,
my vessel would be filled with knowledge to know what is.
I knew that if I quit fighting and bent my knees to the ground
and touched my chin to my chest and opened my hands,
my burdens would release and seep out of my fingertips.

I knew that if I cried hard enough my pain would have a voice
and it would sing a song of freedom
to let me know that it didn't own me.

I knew that if I said, "God, you know what I need,"
that that would suffice and set me free;
that if I only asked for truth,
everything else would follow in the order of my needs.

I knew that if I said, "I love you,"
I would be giving my love away;
and the more I give, the more I have,
and my saying I love you,
my love is put into action and it is made known.

And I know that if I love with no
want of return,
I will be blessed by being loved by you.

Alma Villanueva

Sunrise

I arise,
Naked,
From my bed when all
The city lies in sleep and
I am freed
From the anguished mental onslaught
Of its din.
I pass through my prison's diaphanous door
Into the mists,
And barely breathe, into the longing night.

I listen,
Transported,
By the soothing heart beat of
The world soul lying
Peacefully dreaming in her bed
Until
The God of the cosmos awakens his lover
And takes her in his warm embrace.

Edgar Wyatt Stephens

Recipe For Life

There is no mercy in selfishness
Neither doth true love abide there in
But giving our self freely in service to others
The battle of life is fought and won.

Life is never thorns without roses
Neither the beauty of the rose with out thorns
But by holding the hands clasp tightly
We can find our path of love - for this we were born.

Ada Kuipers

New Beginning

Wild and free, wild and free
Never again will chains bind me.
Flash of delight, crowned Queen of the Night
Ruler of daytime and dawn's blinding light.
Sky at my hands, mountains at my feet
I stand at the gates where the two meet.
Wild and free, wild and free
I have broken the chains which bound me.

Jennifer Bond

Letting Go

The times that we had spent, the memories that we had shared,
Never came to an end because I loved and I really cared.

Letting go of you that day, wasn't hard at the time,
My heart has filled with regret, still wishing you remained mine.

Yet I was prepared to give you up, at any given hour,
I thought I was strong and had enough will power.

The one thing I had hoped for, was to say our last good-byes,
To embrace you for one final moment and look into your brown,
warm-filled eyes.

A day doesn't conclude, without me reminiscing your name,
Picturing you in my mind, that my life will never be the same.

I hope through this poem, I'll be able to put you to rest,
You'll always be in my heart, and my feelings will always
be expressed.

Remembrance will always be there, in my soul and in my mind,
This is my final goodbye to you, Rudy . . .I love you,
and you'll always be my special find!

Abby Archer

The Dark Angels

The Dark Angels never smile
Never speak, never feel
But they maw they are bound to earth in the
most undesirable fashion
not to be freed tormenting Blinding
Seeking misfortune Seething Breathing, Breeding, Infesting
In the deepest hollows of your black soul
Screaming in silence that is to loud to be heard
Drowning in your melting mind
Thoughts a vicious cycle of continue
The dark angels watching waiting
Waiting with an almost intolerable patience
Never deviating never ceasing always deceiving
Thin line to be walked if strayed
There will be pray for the dark
Angels to feed on
Enhancing their eternal life.

Diana D'Arconte

Nuclear Defence

Back in the year of 1932, a couple of Englishmen, created something
new.
They took a little Lithium, and a bit of Hydrogen too, and pasted
them together, with Elmer's glue.
Now I know, to you, this makes no sense, but this is how Russia,
started, its Nuclear defence.
They took this formula, and encased it in Lead, and then exploded it,
in a Polar Bear's Bed.
Now this old Bear got up, lame, and sore, and shook his fist in
the air, yelling, don't try that anymore.
Ever since then, no one has ever Nuked, the Arctic again.

Charles A. Fabian

Day By Day

The earth was created for all of us to live,
Not for us to take and none of us to give.
People are living their lives each and every day,
They're not realizing the pain they cause simply by words they say.
Life is not perfect and no one says it is,
But people should take pride in the world in which they live.
There are so many problems that none of us can mend,
So let's stop fighting among ourselves and all try to be friends.

Cheryl Goeser

Rose Of Inner Beauty

There was a rose that grew alone
Next to a great wall of stone.
Hidden from everything but rain and sunlight
For no eye had seen this sight.
Such beauty so concealed for no one to touch
And no one to steal.

To often like the rose, we keep our inner beauty inside;
We use the wall for us to hide.
To show this beauty, we think is wrong
Until eventually it is gone.

So tear down your wall, and let your inner beauty out.
And maybe a new rose will begin to sprout.
There was a rose that grew alone.

Johnny Edward Schmitt

The North

Just the words, "Jean Sibelius," are carved on black polished stone;
no dates, places, or epitaph on that marble slab implies
any horizon other than vast and immovable ice.
There's a pedal point in our winter, a solid sadness there,
where the moon-spun madness found at a conjugal peak decries
a fearsome and dark solemnity brooded over alone.

There lays the trap in a polar cap of our mind's Helsinki:
No sun, no new thaw, no more songs in which hearty voice ascends
on wordless choir of wind up into our escaping souls;
Now we're blanketed in our cozy room by the warming hearth,
Where touching hands weave comfort on which our happiness depends
before we're taken away and know the truth to tell: Think, be.

Daniel Reaver

A Degree for Living

Do I intend to earn a degree? I was asked
No I replied... unless it's one for just being
plain me--
A spokesperson for other folks like me, that might
have something to say about life and crisis that be;
Maybe my thoughts will touch a few, and start
them to thinking about life's ugly view, from
where I stand only a few are really thinking,
most are lost and know nothing to do, or even want to.
I'm just me doing what I feel I got to do, "Who
knows" what I have to say might count in the
history books too!

Jai De Smith

Patterns Broken, Wishes Made

Patterns of lonely existence
No longer made, now broken
Wishes sent for things
Things unknown but loved
Answers come in forms bestowed
Warmth, love, security, peace
Treasures donated to inner places
Rest is reached, no longer worried
Temporary acts of intimacy
Nothing large, yet quietly big
No harm is brought, at least not now
Only serenity and love, not war and hate
Overpower my body, by God
Wishes answered, gifts bestowed
Patterns of lonely existence, no longer made

Heather Davison

Words

Words are but words,
No matter how soft or loud.
Their meaning is oft times misunderstood
By blocked or closed minds.

Time passes with each painful tick.
The distance grows within the mind's images
Of shattered memories and unfulfilled dreams,
Between reality and fantasy.

Father and Son
Love or Hate? Is it too late?

They're drowning in an undertow.
They've been there before.
Escaping each time to come back for more.

Suppressed emotions surface again,
Among little boys or grown men?
Love or Hate? The great debate.

The flame, tho flickering, still burns
With hope and trust.
Hope and trust the foundation was strong.
It must.

Judi Douglass

What Is A Mother?

A mother is someone who is patient and so kind;
No matter what she's doing, for you she always has the time.

A mother is someone who always puts herself in second place;
Always there to see you smile or wipe the tears off from your face.

A mother is someone who's love can be put to any test;
No matter if you pass or fail, in her eyes you've done you best.

A mother is someone unselfish and whom you can count on to be true;
When no one else is there for you she will always see you through.

A mother is someone special who's role in life means so much;
She can heal you with kind words, she just has that special touch.

A mother is someone God has given to you, she's not someone you can choose;
I'm so glad God gave you to me Mom, but if I had to choose it would be you!

Barbara J. Bodfield

The Arc

Upon stopping to review the cycle of Human Life,
No one can tell you anything about Your precious Life.
Start from Natural Conception- through Final Death,
Nothing human wise will change from first to Final Breath,
No matter roles you-play You're ,no real Hero,
From your start-beginning at the number Zero,
Be you whomever-by what name you choose to be called,
From your six-sides Prison-Your stay is still walled,
Oh! Soulful you,
No more Human values, that the "Chosen Few",
The only prize is the knowledge of your Creator.
And what knowledge could you find that would be any Greater,
When (HE, SHE, IT, THEY, THEM,)—really Finally comes to be Known.....to you.

Ismail Abdus Shaheed

Love

L earning in depth about one another.
O pen, honest communication.
V alue the feelings and views of your lover
E merging in life with elation!!

Debi Craig

Voice Of Our Country!

I am not a big country anymore.
No one seems to agree.

When there is so much giving..
without time to rest between.
So much giving....

Countries just show more greed.
What have they done with all
the help that's given?
It's time to check for me.

Who are the men who make me weak
Don't they have a love for me?
I must have some strong to hear my plea..
It's time for others to stop, before
they ask help from me.

I have little left to help my own.
Because, my wealth was given..
More than I could spare.
The little left is for them to share..
maybe then.. with time.. I will
grows strong once more...

Dorothy Peterson

The Land Where No One Wanders

It is the land of my mind.
No open doors only little cracks, slivers of light
A peek, an elusive sight
No more. No less.
A tantalizing glance
Not shared; fought to gain more.
Then suddenly, an uneasy hidden thought.
The reality will present itself,
Something learned; not of happiness, only disappointment.
The mystery is no more.
A beautiful bubble has burst.

Dorothy D. Longfoot

Little Babe

Little Babe, where is your cradle?
No silk and satin cover you.
Or laces fine and rare.
The sun sweetened straw will be your bed.

Little Child, are you cold?
No marble palace to shelter you.
But breath from the cattle warms the stall
Of the small, snug stable where you lie.

Little One, where are the velvet hangings
For a royal prince?
Only the velvet muzzles of oxen
To brush your cheek.

Little Babe, are you crying?
If your mother's lay soothes you not,
You may call on a chorus of angels
To sing you to sleep.

Little King, where is your court?
No pages and lackeys
To care for you.
But wise men and shepherds kneel at your feet.

Jo Moore

Just An Ordinary Day

Hark! Is that the morning birds that I hear singing?
No? Then it must be our telephone ringing.
Let me put you on hold; someone is at the door;
"Honey, did you say, `I need coffee - come pour me some more'?"

Oh, No! The dog is loose; his chain is broken.
The baby is gasping; I'm afraid she is choking.
The washing machine is too full; it's overflowing to the floor;
My mop has disappeared; I'll have to get one at the store.

Did I hear you say that the battery's dead, and the car will not
crank?
If we fix it, we'll need some money from the bank!
Well, I'll just have to stay home this entire weekend.
I'll just polish, vacuum, do dishes, and hunt clothes I need to mend.

All is now finished; I'll get in my recliner and lie very still;
I'll read a good book and not worry about the late income tax bill.
Oh no, what was that noise that I just heard in the driveway!
The car will need a new fender! Here goes just another ordinary day!!

Frances D. McCloud

Him!

Nobody knows the pain she feels
Nobody even cares
Nobody sees the tears she hides
When he is close and near
To be loved by him just one time
To be held close and in his arms.
These are her only wishes
These are her only dreams
She awakes at night just to cry.
She bury's here face and then sighs
What has she done to make him feel this way
What has she done to make him hate her this day.
He loves another so why does she bother?
To win his love that is what she lives for
To win his love forever more

Brooke Thomas

Unconditionally

I don't know the reason you came into my life
Nor do I question it
Words could not describe the happiness I finally feel
Having you by my side in these hard times
Feels like being reborn
Lifting my spirits
Helping me understand the reason I was put on this earth

Filling my soul with eternal happiness
Showing me how to be strong for myself
Knowing it's okay to cry
Loving unconditionally
Showing me the good and the bad within me
Facing the demons inside
Facing the angles inside
Understanding without judgement
I finally see what life means to me
Now I can finally say the words "I LOVE YOU" with my heart and soul
UNCONDITIONALLY

Carmen Sandoval

"Mamma's Crying"

I hear you mamma, you're in the other room, you sound so full of gloom. What can I do, mamma, you're crying all alone, I want you to hold on, mamma. I want to say I love you, I want to hold you while you're blue. I want to go into your room, I want to know what you're dreamin', mamma. My eyes are wet from yours, I want to hold you till I'm sure you're alright, mamma. I love you from the other room, I can't wait to see you at noon, then I'll know you're o'kay, and some bloom will be put back into day. Hold on, mamma. Please hold on.

Edward J. Taylor

I Hear Not

I hear not the sound of bells that ring
Nor the chatter of people;
The only sound I hear are the echoing
Of my own feet as they carry me through
The empty halls of school.

No more will I see my friends
Nor feel the bumping of people
From the crowded sea of unknown faces;
It's time to say goodbye to the only life I've known
It's graduation time, so long friends, so long school...

Esther R. Pazos

Southland Phenomenon

T'was still and silent on the lawn,
Not a living creature stirred.
With awe, I looked about me,
A miracle had occurred!

The sunshine bright, above green trees,
A certainty of spring
But its rays reached down and touched a freeze,
And made a shimmering dream.

The sparkling ice, like diamonds,
Flashing round the lovely blooms
Of azaleas and the dog woods,
Making rainbows in the pool.

Icicles hanging from the roof,
Looked like a fairy's wand -
An april revelation,
Of a rare, celestial bond.

This brilliant scene touched my soul,
As my eyes, beheld the glory-
Of dancing lights, entwined with flowers,
Whispering nature's wondrous story.

Emily Addison Edgeworth

"A Summer Place"

Oh, what is so lonely as a summer place
Not for months on end to see a human face
But winter will go and spring will appear
And families and those they hold so dear
Will once again begin to arrive
And once more the place is alive
With mother and dad serving meals galore
To children and guests enticed ashore
From lakeside fun with many a thrill
And very often a watery spill
From boat and float and wayward skis
The exuberant fun-loving he's and she's
But fall steals the heal from waning day.
And it's time inevitably to go away
Alas, some fall when years have flown
And girl and boy are fully grown
To seek new lives at some distant place,
Oh, what then, is so lonely as our summer place?

Evelyn L. Baker

"One Lonely Soul"

Though misty are the skies, and dark shadows all around,
One lonely soul, wanders endlessly and abound.
What sadness flourishes through this soul,
As the hours slowly pass, and the minutes take their toll.
Only clouds away's, a new dawn is breaking,
As the darkness turns to light, will the sun taking.
With that alone, a new day shall arise.
Then one lonely soul can close his eyes.

Benny Vanderpool

My Son

My son is a special child through everyone's eyes, not just mine,
He's a precious gift to society, he really walks the line.
He tries so hard to please, and please is what he does best,
With a special child like this I really get my rest.
He has a sunny disposition, it's composed of several things,
It's as if love and laughter were riding on his wings.
I don't know what I've done to deserve a child like him,
But I think whatever it was must have been a gem.
This special child of mine is sensitive, kind and sweet,
and down the road of life I'm sure some malice he will meet.
I just pray it will never change him, seeing all the
heartaches and pain,
For we've kept him very sheltered,
oh by the way, his name is SHANE!!

Janet Lea Rohlf

She's Not Gone

She's not there beneath the ground
not laid to rest in death's cold gown,
but rather flown to heights unknown
where other angles before have flown.
No not deep beneath the clay
but rather with her God to stay,
so I'll not think of her as gone
but in that mansion all her own.
And when at last I climb death's stair
we shall be united there,
hand in hand we'll walk those streets
as friends and loved ones we shall greet.
And sitting in the heavenly seat
at last my savior I shall meet,
Yes all of this awaits my soul
when Mother's hand again I hold.

Doris Selhorst

Years Of Life

One day I know I'll go away
not now, I know but someday
until that time whenever it comes
I hope to achieve what I can become.
To have lots of memories and things to acquire
with love and happiness hour by hour.
To raise my children the best I can
and play with the grandkids now and then.
To be able to look back at all the years
to remember the memories with very few tears
and when I know my time has come
I'll go to heaven and relax some.

Janet K. Daniel

Untitled

Love is such a wonderful feeling
Nothing could possibly match its beauty
Until it is broken in two halves,
It savagely tears your soul away
Until you've nothing to live for
Like ripping your heart out ruthlessly
You can feel the scratching and burning
As a death dark hand reaches down your throat
Just then it grasps what is left
And with a scornful smile on its face
Tears it apart - piece by painful piece
Pain - love is really other than.
You wait for death to come - you cry
But not tears of sadness - oh no
You cry tears of pain, agonizing pain
If you still think love is wonderful
Wait until you're left with nothing too.

James Fuger

"Vows"

Together with time grows heart and mind.
Now here we are as one foe the very first time.

Two bodies and souls walking one long road,
Understanding the obstacles and sharing the loads.

Never wanting to stray or turn away,
We stand together now to begin a new day.

Looking in your eyes I see it's no surprise
I found the love in you, I know you feel it too.

We've waited here so long and always been so strong,
And now we've found the key and set our hearts so free.

Aime B. Charlebois

Dream In Time

T he sun will wander up as it has everyday
O nly it will be brighter with no trace of gray
M emories like raindrops return to the skies
O vercast feelings disappear from the eyes
R aise now your new vision to hopes now less cold
R each, restless spirit for dreams you can hold
O ur dreams are never left lying to rust
W hen friends, faith, and future absorb all our trust
I ntentions long languishing deep in our heart
S omehow survive, sweetly surging for the start
T he journey they have been planning since birth
H appiness, joy, and a soul with some worth
E ach step into future one further from pain
A gate gently closed never closing again
N ext day the next life and it's almost here
S cenes from our hearts and our eyes will be clear
W ait not for tomorrow for it waits for you
E ngage your future with spirit anew
R evel in revealing what is really you

Bruce D. Bissmeyer

My Vampire

O' you look handsome and so divine,
O' you act sweet and so kind;
Though I am frightened of the beast beneath,
Your seduction just makes me more weak.

Your eyes are so clear,
Your compassion is so dear,
A weapon of teeth
For blood from beneath.

So in the words of my vampire,
"I will give you desire;
When touched by my kiss,
You can not resist."

Jennifer L. Wilder

My Child

How wonderful it is to know you my child,
Observing how intricately
You were made to be;
Every facet of your youthful life
Designed to awaken my joy.
This joy surrenders my selfish ways,
Strengthening my love for you,
Pointing my attention to discovering your essence.
For you have captured my heart,
Allowing me to be grateful again.
For that, I express to you my child
My undivided devotion.

France Marie Casey

Legend Of The Rose

In the eternity of legends lives a story told and true
Of a woman from the first days when life was bright and new
The woman was but young then with beauty dark and bold
Her laughter like a river no course could ever hold
Green eyes were hers like emeralds, the deepest oceans hue
Her movement like a dancer, a grace possessed by few
Her hair the flame of sunset burning red across the sky
Her smile a flight of sparrows who've heard the eagles cry
She was envied by so many but spoken to by few
Her lips a fragrant promise that no man ever knew
In passing time she faded like colors in the fall
For the promise of her beauty had heard no lovers call
When bitter winter took her and her lonely heart was still
A gentle magic touched her, the promise then fulfilled
In the garden when you see her fear not her sharpest thorn
From the gentle woman's beauty, the magic rose was born

Janice K. White

Sailor Bids "Goodbye Mom"

I will always regret something I do, but worst
of all is saying goodbye to you. You picked me
up when I was down, and made me smile instead
of frown. You were always by my side, and
willing to help me with all your pride.

You took my hand and led the way, and in
my heart you'll always stay. You showed
me how it should be, but then you left it
up to me. On me you never made a demand,
and all my decisions you'd understand.

When I was young you set the pace, now you
I could never replace. Although from me
you had to part, I still hold you close in
my heart. Another like you I'll never
know, but I am sorry you had to go.

It still doesn't matter what I try, for of
my lose I'll always cry. The pain I feel
will never disappear, but I'll always wish
that you were here. Now it's you I'll
always miss, and I give to you a final kiss.

John Ormsby

Uncommon Values

This troubled world is full
Of common men and women
Who crossed the frontier
Dividing personal security from risk,
And returned to sanctuary with their prize.
Heroes all in their own right.
Yet for most their glory is short lived,
The result of a singular excursion
Along the path beyond their familiar horizons.
True heroes revisit that frontier
Time and time again;
There for the cause, chasing an ideal.
Glory, as it were, confounds them, perplexes them;
As it comes for doing that
Which they felt was right and worthy all the while.
History will not long recall their deeds,
Yet is will enshrine their ideals.
For from the outset it is the hero's values,
Not his valor, that earn him honor,
And that perpetuate honor.

James A. Grace

Home Again

It wasn't just a night in the backseat
of Daddy's Cadillac,
but going on from the trees in the park,
from the quiet guitar and soft voice
to the close breath and tightening jeans,
from the hair in the eyes
to the hair on the chest.

Your spoken names of the Savior
completed the cycle of beginnings
and I was introduced to the light of the world
in darkness.

What you began in shyness you carried
forward with one and then another touch
of frantic shame, until this dark, back seat,
alley, home, prison freed your soul of me.

It wasn't just a night in the backseat
of Daddy's Cadillac
but going on from the life between your eyes
to the death between your legs.

Billy Woodward

My Dear Old Town

I often dream of days gone by;
Of falling leaves in an Autumn sky.
With old folks scurrying through the streets while children
played hopscotch with their nimble feet.
Yes, these are some sights that did abound on an Autumn day
in my dear old town.
And all too soon the seasons changed, for we left the fall
for the snow and rain.
And in the homes of so many a few loomed large kettle pots
filled with homemade stew.
The soul-piercing scent would fill the air as it traveled from
the kitchen to the top of the stairs.
Yes, these are the moments so precious to me that I'll always
remember
for eternity.
For this was indeed a privilege so rare
where everyone loved and everyone cared; for this was
My Dear Old Town.

Cemille Parker

Our Garden

I walked into the garden for more soul satisfying views
of flowers of every description and many colors and hues.
Enormous full blown roses with buds and even thorns,
orchidaceous blooms of white and purple with centers like
holiday horns.

Rose Begonias and rose geraniums blossomed profusely red and pink,
tiny rose bushes with enormous flowers which caused you to think
that the roses would weigh too much for the little plant to stand
up straight and tall.
But the dewdrenched white roses I thought were the most beautiful of all.

God created flowers for us to love, care for and enjoy.
We use them for many reasons be we adult, girl or boy.
For parades, they become parts of costumes and decorate the floats,
that cause us to marvel at their beauty and cause cheers to emit
from our throats.
We hear they are even used for food in the mysterious far east.
One way or another they have always delighted man and beast.

Fortunate Fuller

Inner Reflections

If I should paint a picture
Of how you look inside,
Would I paint scenes of calm and rest
And a great peace that abides?

Or would I paint a picture
Of dark clouds rolling o'er;
With trees bent low in swirling winds,
As waves crash against the shore?

What's down inside will always show
In the countenance that we wear,
No matter how we groom our face
Or how we fix our hair - -

For the inner man will show right through,
And the lines upon our face
Will show if we have love inside,
Or if there's bitterness, and hate.

So the heart is what we must keep right
If we would look our best;
And the smile we wear that others see
Will show inner peace, and rest.

Beatrice Northcutt

The Journey

Her caress filled the void
of loneliness that once enveloped his path.
Her compassion soothed the pain
of longing during their passage.

They were two souls whose spirits
linked on the path of life.
Yet all too suddenly the crossroad came,
it was time for each to take a separate road.

He watched as she gathered her pride and courage
knowing her course he could not follow.
As she faded from his view a tear moistened his cheek
and a smile brightened his face.

A smile wrought by the memories of
secrets shared, friendship found and trust rekindled.
It was she who had returned to him this smile,
a joy he would keep until journey's end.

Armando V. Galella Jr.

Treasures

Our attic holds many treasures
of our life from long ago,
It has sleds and winter coats
from the deep white winter snows.

There's tables and there's tricycles
from when I was three years old,
And there's furniture from our old house
which we sold.

Memories come and memories go,
But when I'm in the attic,
The memories just start to flow.

Caroline Pintner

Sparkle In God's Eye

I am a light for all those who cannot see
Only because I strive to be the best that I can be.
I might not do everything with peace and grace,
But I always try to keep a smile on my face.
When there are times that I am feeling bad,
I always turn to my mom and dad.
I can be sure that they will never tell me a lie,
Because they always say that I put the sparkle in God's eye!

Jina Ahern

When I Was Young

I used to dream of dancing in the fields,
of running through the grass
and kicking up my heels.

I used to dream a little girl's dream,
of being free and safe, of never ending happy,
a small child's blissful place.

I used to dream of a country barn
white curtains blowing in the breeze,
to have a mama, not a mother, who would rock me on her knees.

I used to dream of a place in time
where siblings would abound,
and always there to help me when I needed them around.

Now I watch my daughter dance to tunes I never heard,
to the angels in her tiny head
the love of her mother's word.

And when I feel empty from dreams gone by,
from days that were never sweet,
I watch my daughter dance those steps,
and I can feel the beat.

Joyce Gerber

Today I Watched The Roses Die

There was a time when roses reminded me
of the love I had for you.
Yet, like a rose our life had thorns too.
They seemed to grow much stronger than the rose itself.
Then the seasons began to change,
and all that was left were stems of thorns.
In the past months, I have watched our roses die.
But now spring is upon me, and a new hope has rescued me.
So today is the last day I will watch our roses die.
I will rip these thorned stems from the earth,
like you from my heart, and plant new ones.
And when they begin to bloom,
my heart will begin to heal.
You know, I still love roses, but no longer
will they remind me of you.
They will remind me of the strength I have to start again.

Heather R. Elliott

"I Thank You"

I thank you for the story that's told
of the love you hold, is all in your eyes,
some how I'm not surprise.

Being captivated by your smile
The gentleness in your eyes...
Will never show lies.

Allowing me to feel,
The love in your heart, The peace in your soul,
The warmth in your touch,
It sounds like too much!

The control in your voice.
The power felt from your concern.
The listening to your God.
The way it's confirmed.

Your beauty inside, manifest outside.
If you walk with a glow... Then people will know..
your way of love, comes from heaven above.

All these things that describes you,
are my wishes that has come true.
Thank You

Deborah A. Harris-Williams

Sunset

The gentle whisper,
Of the soft sunset rays,
The nightly wonder,
That the sundown portrays.
Velvety reds and blues meet horizon,
Pink laced skies, somewhat violet,
To the eyes seems surprising.
Precision so fine, to nature's tune,
The settling of shine,
And the rise of the moon.
A panorama of heavenliness,
In spacious skies surrounding,
Atmospheric changes not unusual,
Just simply astounding. Sunset so elegant,
Decorating blue filled billowy skies,
Toppled with fluffy white peaks,
Edged in soft delicate strides.
Shades so precious, to the sight of what's known,
Contentment in God's world,
The beauty that is shown.

Chris Termini

Endless Love

We've grown together, we've grown apart
Of this I have a heavy heart,
Though the years have quickly past
This bond we've formed will ever last.

We've shown our success in that we sing
Of cars, house, boats and material things,
But our precious daughter is by far the best
Our creation of love, above the rest.

Whatever the direction we pursue
I'll always have tremendous love for you,
Bound by love and bound by time
Comfort in you, I will always find.

Debra Conway

The Market At Sarejvo

Igor dreamed of American pie,
of Torvil and Dean-faint strains of Bolero,
of hamburgers, coke, an order of fries,
of a time when Olympians hailed Sarejvo.

A decade passed-the greed of man.
Destroyed the village where children once played,
Raped helpless women who screamed and ran,
left starving widows alone and afraid.

Igor dreamed of a time long since gone,
When his skis lifted him to the Bosnian sky,
Now he saw children beg to go home,
He quietly watched Sarejvo die.

The ice rink collapsed as rocket shells screamed,
Igor's scrapbook reflected his plan,
In spite of the horrors he worked and dreamed,
Selling coffee at market-a gentle young man.

A mortar shell hit the market that day,
Blood flowed through the streets as Igor lay dying,
His grief stricken father took his body away,
Some said it was raining, it was really God crying.

Jimmie Page Gunter

The Night

I remember being afraid
of what I can not recall
only that the terror was true
and was coming for me as it will for you,
I remember hearing a growling
I remember hearing a sound
I even saw blood on the ground,
But I did not see a trace of the beast
or the monster rip off his face,
What I tell you is no lie
So I suggest you take note
For what I say is no joke,
For I have heard the beat of its heart
And the cry of its prey
And I can ensure you it's coming today,
Oh by the way I remember what I was afraid of
but I'll tell you this way,
When your walking through the dark
always go with a group, carry a light
for it's hell to get caught in the night.

John Adam

Untitled

The darkness of my soul
often chills me to the bone.
The evil in my heart awakening every nerve.
The monster inside, clawing its way through.
And it will not rest.
No, it cannot rest.

I struggle with myself.
This demon I must shun.
Keeping below the surface, emotions that wage war.
Erupting in a battle
that can never be won, that can never end.
Death could be the Victor.
No, death will be the Victor.

Life is just outside my grasp.
but to far for me to reach.
Lessons of pain and suffering,
blood and fear, too late to teach.
Engulfed in self hatred, my heart slowly stills.
To sleep forever in peace.
No, to be forever in peace.

Barbara Batson Passos

"I Never Shell Forget"

Oh! I never shell forget, how Jesus died on calvary.
Oh! I never shell forget, how my soul from
sin be set free, and now he's up in
heaven to prepare a place for me, and
someday I'm going to meet him, and his
blessed face I'll see.

Oh! I never shell forget how he wore
the crown of thorns,
Oh! I never shell forget, how the blood
came streaming down, but I know that
Jesus love me for he died to set me free,
and some day I'm going to see
him in that land of eternity.

Oh! I never shell forget how they laid
him in the tomb, oh! I never shell
forget of the solicitude and gloom,
But the angel came from heaven
and rolled the stone away, and I know
I'll see my savior on that great judgment day.

Anna Morrow

Caught Up Between A Smile, Laughter, And A Tear

Times and things, certainly aren't what they once were-
Oh' to just be able to brings back those Young Times of Joy.
Or maybe to stop time, as things now, stand.

The good times, the bad times, uncompleted adventures, gestures that
were in vain. Changes, romances, and all that were mine.
Now gone to history, and some way back in passed time.

As I recall, some of those Sweet Young things, my hearts Joys,
still vibrate and sing. So many memories, all so dear to me.
At times, I find time to smile, and cry...

What is passed is did and done, all in the key of life. I was hoping
to just live a little, hurt no one. A young fellow having some,
innocent fun. All in growing up. What is to come, will come.
There is a good life for each and everyone.

Life can be beautiful, life can be anything you choose to make of it.
Life sometimes comes about when you are planning something else.
Life is one of the Greatest Gifts, that was granted to Man...

Try to live a good life. De what you have to. Make a honest decent
livin' go for the gust. In your Golden Diamond years, you will
perhaps live with your memories, reminisce, smile, laugh,
then just you try to hold back - the tears...

Archie Walker

Untitled

Down went another tree in the woods today.
Oh, to some it looked unimpressive but beneath it was the best place
to play.
Near its trunk I learned about nature, and the sounds of life.
Among its covering branches I was protected from pain and strife.
Lying beneath it, I would fall asleep using leaves as a pillow for my
head.
Dreams aplenty were spawned beneath its leafy spread.

Limbs told of survival from many a weathered storm, but somehow it
it managed to thrive and grow up norm.

Crowned in autumn splendor - my lifelong friend.
Reds, greens, and yellows came a colorful season's end.
Eventually nature took its course, and I lost that wonderful tree.
Every time I see that woods it seems somewhat smaller without
that one particular Cree.

Donald W. Cree

Gift of Life

Ten little fingers, ten little toes, and
oh what a perfect little nose.
Two little eyes full of Sunshine and gold.
Two little arms reaching out to be-hold
Two little ears to hear lullabies of Love,
a song from your Ma-Ma, sing a song of Love.
Ah-Ah I love you.
A smile that is as precious and perfect as
a rose.
This little child so perfect and rare, is
yours to protect, love, cherish and care.
Life is a gift from the Lord above,
as the flowers in springtime as the sun shines
above.
Look at the stars that shine so bright, then
look at Erin and hold her tight. And Thank God
for giving you this gift of life.

Joan Driscoll

Shut In

Sometimes she cries in her weary sleep.
Oh why my child must you weep,
is it because you just don't understand.

I can't explain but instead I'll take your pain.
A whole world of pain people drink their drugs so smooth,
as they run away to die. A liquid forms below my eye,
and the child will always question why, why must we die?

Is this the end when I become shut in
will I see all that is true, will I believe in you.
Is this the end when I become shut in?

Open it to me. Show this thing, set me free. Forever is too long, and I can't go on. Sometimes she cries in her corner of fading light, too blind to see in a world of simplicity. You wrought yourself this way, now suffer through my eternal day. Hung on this cross for all to see, and you still don't believe.

Is this the end when I become shut in. Will I see all that is true, will I believe in you. Is this the end when I become shut in.
A world that is untrue, and they're so easily convinced. Followers' eyes closed tight only to be burned of false light. Sinners' fire burns the night, and the fools will become shut in

Jerry L. Brooks

A Walk In The Woods Behind My House

A vast, picturesque forest full of life
On a cool, bright summer's day
In early morn-
A shallow, free flowing stream
A woodpecker's insistent tapping
A tiny squirrel scurrying up a tree
A faun nervously nibbling my father's flowers
A rabbit hopping on the soft ground
The trees softly swaying to the tune of the wind
The soft scent of the dewy grass and wildflowers
Millions of colors spread out around me, enveloping me
No other sounds of everyday life
No cars, no people, no pollution
None of the chaotic traffic of the people in a big city
Absolutely serene and peaceful,
Time is at a complete standstill,
As I lay here gazing at the clouds floating in the sky
Listening to the sounds of God's creations rise around me
Feeling the soft breeze glide against my skin
Calm and at peace.

Caroline Pinder

The Farmer's Field

I gaze across the farmer's field
On a crisp and cool October morning.
Beyond the mist patches of rose peek out
From behind the tall willow trees.
Soon the sun will slowly rise,
Its rays stretching forth
Across the farmer's field.

Now the sun in all its brilliance appears
Its warmth and splendor gently fading the mist
Across the farmer's field.

Blazing hues of red, orange, yellow and green
Reach up and greet the cornflower blue of
The morning sky and dance in the delicate breeze.

Crows in their lustrous black plumage together fly
Mingling sounds of blue jays and wrens round out the scene.

Sunrise, a new day dawns across the farmer's field.

Jean Piacentini

Autumn

I watched the leaves upon the tree, break loose and drift on down, riding the wind rolling tumbling on. The beauty of the gold and red was thee for all to see, but long it took for me. A half a century to understand Gods artistry. I pray someday my children will feel this special kind of excitement, and realize there's so much life in these golden Autumns. As I sit and watch the scene unfold of Gods creations the beauty of his work, we pass so lightly of it. A picture that cannot be bought or sold, a priceless jewel our very own. No frame to hide the edges, no nail to hang it by it just appears each day as if an act it plays. The curtain rises on it, no price our we to pay. God has put no price upon it, just comes with the day. Surely we should realize this part of life is free, or will it take so long for you as it did for me. Oh God I pray for it to come this very special day, so you may know and realize in this world of grief and pain a mother passed on, a child not born a lonesome struggling pain. But God is near and with his brush will paint it all away.

Anna P. Kozar

God Cares

Today I'll take a moment to reflect
On how I've been wonderfully blessed

Sometime I think I have more than my
share of problems
But somehow the Lord always resolve them

Friends, loved ones and accusers -
God is our judge and jury
We may say what we think but God knows
And if we truly love Jesus it shows

A pure heart, a clean mind, an upright walk
Mean more to the world than a lot of talk.

Alease S. Alston

"I Remember"

I know the sun still shines and gleams,
On shaded woods and glistening streams,
But nothing is the same it seems,
Since you have gone.

I wonder if the wild flowers still grow,
Where you and I would love to go,
And if the soft Spring breezes blow,
On our beloved hills.

Do you still think the moon shines bright;
And makes so beautiful the night,
And brings the bottom lands its light,
For our moonlight hikes?

I wonder if the apple and the plum will bloom,
And fill the air with sweet perfume,
And bring the winter air its doom,
And make the world seem young.

We know the wonder of nature will never cease,
And when the world has found its peace,
The happiness of my life will then increase,
When you come home.

Dell L. Harris

God's Love

Have you ever smiled, and you don't know why?
Or looked to the heavens with tears in your eyes?
Have you ever held a little baby, and sensed something heavenly?
Or felt that angels were surrounding you in times of uncertainty?
There are times in our lives when we need a helping hand.
Or maybe just a friend who we know will understand.
During these times when we feel a touch of heaven up above.
We have a link with God who is always there to love.

Joanna N. Neyman

Memories

1908 - 1994 forever etched in my mind.
On the gray stone,
by the small church,
where she cherished time after time.

This woman walked through life with me.
She stood by me
all the way
to guide, love and protect me every single day.

I know that we will never again meet.
Yet I know,
that she is near,
for the love that she has given me grows stronger year after year.

As I leave this little church fond memories flood my mind.
Memories of a woman
so giving, so kind.
These memories I will cherish time after time.

Diana Nason

You Are At Peace

You are still present in you home
On this first anniversary of your passing away.
When enduring the loss of our loves one.
It's people that makes it easier to bear.

One year ago left us, you are at peace.
Our souls will always be with you
Forever in our thoughts.
We love and miss you after the year.

There will never be another person.
That will take the place of father
You are in our hearts and prayers.
We remember the happiness you brought us.

God Bless you all!
Words cannot express how your caring,
And love has meant for the loss of my friend.
This does not stop the tears falling.

Loving memories never fade.
As years roll on and days pass by.
In our hearts a memory is kept.
Of one we loved and will never forget.

Evelyn T. Tallman

Life's Game

Please God, just give me a level playing field
On which to play life's solemn and worthwhile game,
One on which I can share my part of the honors.
And on which I can share my part of the blame.

As the clock of life is slowly ticking away,
God keep the playing field level, and the players within thy sway.
For the game of life is fragile and so precious
We must give our all to protect it in every way.

Then when life's fragile game is over,
In fame and blame I may have lost, won or tied.
Anyway I can say I had a level field to play on
And regardless of the score I tried.

Now, if I tried in all honesty and sincerity,
And played by the rules the Divine Refree set.
I want inscribed on my final marker -
"I have many wonderful memories, but no regrets."

Burris O. Smith

The Odyssey Of A Tree

The tree will always embark on its lonely journey
once again

A summer tree of beauty
Gives shelter from the sun
But how can we destroy them
And then have none

As fall comes upon us
We wait for change
As the falling leaves of autumn shades
Will once be on the ground again

As the winter months arrive
The tree will stand alone
Again undressed by mother nature
Her bountiful leaves have gone

Then once again spring has arrived
With the budding of the leaves
Will once again see the sign of life
In the nature of a tree

Claire J. Dimascolo

"The Loss Of One"

All my favorite things are gone
One by one they all disappeared
It started so very long ago
It's almost like a familiar game
One you never really wanted to play
The rules are never clear, or the same
All my favorite people are gone
You know, the ones you loved the most, that were so close
So why am I still here?
No one knows who comes or goes, or so they say
I keep the memories vivid and clear, always near
They seem so rich, full of laughter and cheer
So why the tears?
I start each day looking forward
I end each night in quiet reflection
Most of the time I'm OK
Sometimes I'm an empty shell
Loss is hell
All my favorite things are gone

Janet Z. Wingfield

Me

I know who I am
Only a few people know too
Most others want to put me in their set
...doesn't fit
I don't talk, act, walk, play, work, sleep, eat, enjoy life
the right way they say
Re-ject, dismissed, out-cast
Who are you?
Lonesome, sometimes I conform
but only for awhile, I like ME
I need to love ME more
The FEW let me just be ME
They ask not that I change
I'm just ME
I give to their life and they to mine
I grow and they grow
Do you know who I am?
I was a humanoid female
Now an entity therein

Debora F. Hurst

Awareness...

Early this January morn the silence was broken
   only by the crunch of my feet against the virgin snow,
The moonlight glistened almost electrically as the beams
   cascaded across the drifts in a heavenly light show,
Twinkling like a million stars in a universe of white,
The moonlight covered the ground, alas, awakening the night,
In a glimpse past the horizon and down the street,
I saw a solo set of foot prints indicating life beyond my feet,
The large lacy snowflakes gracefully began to fall,
As I stood by the road in amazement and awe,
In the wintry wilderness as the day came to pass,
I felt, I'd been touched by the icy intricacies
   of nature's beauty at last!

Janet M. Dalrymple

Your Soul Is Of Earth

Yearning for an answer as to why you are here
Open to teachings from those who cannot steer
Until you feel empty and hopeless inside
Reaping the values that nurture your pride

Set your heart flowing like the rivers of earth
Open the mind to accept your beauty and worth
Under the skin lies a world of great places
Like mountains and canyons and oceans of vast spaces

Inhale the air that comes from the trees
Smell the flowers that blow in the breeze
Observe the surroundings that bring you peace
Forget not the sun for warmth will not cease

Enjoy what is here and from where it comes from
All that is given is not for just some
Realize that you are a being with need
Then use what is here to strive and succeed
Here comes the soul from which earth will breed

John W. Lippelt

Morning Glory

Did one awaken to a glorious day of sunshine
or a morning filled with clouds and gloom?
Were the birds singing in the trees
or the frightening sounds of a storm?

Did the joyous sound of children at play
fill the air with moments so gay?

Look around you and begin to think,
I must appreciate the most simple
But precious things life has to offer.

I can see! I can hear!
I can touch! I can feel!
I can laugh! I can cry!
And oh yes I can be thankful!
And I can love!

Dorothea Poulson

Love Unactualized

A light is extinguished if love is not acknowledged,
Or done justice for.

Can we deny its birth?
If love is true, its pages are already written.
Do you not then end its truth, its voice,
Even before the book has been opened?

That love we conspire to create, left unrealized,
Is part of the soul left unknown.
A secret never to be told or to be felt.
A death before birth and after conception.

Cynthia Macias

What Is Beauty?

Is beauty observed from the look of the face
Or is beauty the inward feeling that takes place

Is beauty lip stick, powder and paint on the face and mouth
Is beauty in the smile you give when you are socially out

Is beauty in the roses that appears in colors of the rainbow
Is beauty in the kindness you say about folks

Is there beauty in the sun, moon and stars that glow
Is there beauty in money, silver and gold

Is there beauty in being fair and loving one another
Is there beauty in the way we treat our sisters and brothers

Is there beauty in this world that never changes
Is there beauty in peoples' lives that causes danger

If we stop and think is there beauty in good health
Is there beauty in material things or wealth

So in conclusion is beauty the inner parts of a being
Or is beauty the out portion of nature and things

If beauty means all these things in the world is beauty our
desire for one's self

I say you be the judge of what beauty is
I cannot judge for anyone else

Charles E. McClain

Dance

Life is a dance, by chance?
Or planned? - a pattern in the sand.
This bird, this flower, this word,
these sounds that I hear
make me dance, make me dance!

Life is a sport, too short! - romance,
and I've come to court life,
and I dance!

Life is a top, - will it stop? It twirls,
the water whirls as I dive
into the depths for pearls.

Life is a thought, untaught,
the open air, to each his share.
It's love, a gift, a burden, a lift,
a prayer and a puzzle, a question of whether - ?
a taking apart and a putting together.

Life is a dance, by chance,
or planned? - a pattern in the sand.
I take my place and to the music's pace
I dance, Ah - I dance!

Diana Fabiani Suplee

Loved Psalm

Yellow, rust and brown leaves in irregular piles
Punctuate the sidewalk and scream: hide!
   If I tiptoe around them
   I will not disturb their winter sleep.

I look in the pond and see sludge and silt and algae.
But, where is the reassurance I need,
   The comforting Narcissus-smile,
   That tells me I will win the day?

In the gloomy, gray mist of early morning,
I stumble along the cobble stones
   Of life and love and nevermore.
   I hug the cold, hard earth,
Caress and kiss it, call it, "My love."
   And, die.

Jason Grant

Untitled

I once was happy
or so I thought...
This life I see,
What change has brought.
Vain glory once I guess I sought,
To fill my emptiness took
Time to be taught.

Broken dreams you might say are bought,
The price sometimes... Wrong things
Are sought.

The greatest joy I've found within,
Arrived on wings only truth can send.

To mend the soul and dry ones tears,
You first must search within your fears.

Though hand the task and narrow the path,
You'll not regret this courageous task.

For one day soon you'll find, at last,
There's no more need for the mask...

That held you captive alone in the dark,
You need only find the place to start.

Brenda J. Beal

Me, Myself, And I

To reveal my secrets from my innermost self?
Or to place them in hiding on the upper most shelf?

To accept what has happened and make a fresh start,
Or to wallow in sorrow and let it tear me apart?

To forgive all the mishaps and try to forget?
Or to let them take over and live in regret?

Do we kill birds of prey to right what is wrong?
Or accept what they do, and love them for their song?

Should it matter to others the things in my past?
Those that are close will forget oh so fast!

Should I care what is seen through the eyes of another?
Or make peace with myself, for my soul, is my brother?

I step outside and look within, I don't know where I should begin.
I see this child standing there, I think to judge, but am I fair?

Should I see him for the wrong he's done?
Or remember the smile, the laughter, and fun?
Should I condemn him for the things he'll do?
Or pity Him for what he's been through.
For me to guess would be insane for I hath felt none of his pain!

Who am I to judge His thoughts
It's His own battles that he has fought!

James Allara

Taking Too Long

You have finally opened your eyes to the differences.
Our friendship has flipped one way to another with no temptation
Influenced by the tree growing in our so called
world and divided among statues we struggle for popularity
Lifting my spirit after a slow unkind crash into the concrete
The others blinded by their bones can not
See what we have found
These things called friendships I deeply cherish in my divine mind
Chalked up memories ruin the undertaken heritage of the heart
Forgiveness of the pain can only shut the window to
the field and make your insides fry like the french fries
you earlier ate
Take me away into the fishing pond enjoy the
fresh drops of dew on the bottom of our feet
close by my side their you stand my friend.

Dawn Marie Doud

If

If I promised you forever would you stop the hands of time?
Or would you wind the clock each hour, count the bells each
time they chime.

If I poured my love into a glass, would you drink until your fill?
Or would you pour it into my hands, through my fingers watch it spill.

If I told you that I'd die for you, would you stop me at the wall?
Or would you build the bridge for me and watch me as I fall.

If I needed your arms around me would you hold tight, never letting
go?
Or would you pull away from me, afraid to let you feelings show.

If tears upon my face did fall, would you kiss each one away?
Or would you cause one more to fall and step out of the way.

If I told you that I loved you, would you hear each cherished word?
Or would you turn away from me and pretend you never heard.

If, by chance, someday you found someone to take my place,
Would you say good-bye to me, or just leave without a trace.

The answers are trapped within your soul, you alone can set them free.
But the only ones I'll know for certain are the ones that come from me.

You stopped the clock at midnight, you left the glass half full.
You built the bridge to challenge me, away you chose to pull.
You stepped out of the way, closing your eyes to the tears I cry.
You never heard the words "I love you", because you never said
good-bye.

Jolie Nourse

Colors

Red is anger the way we feel when things don't go our way
orange is warm like the sun on a beautiful spring day
yellow is happy the way we feel when we look at children play
green is life so precious and gay
blue is sadness when we don't succeed
pink is love which we all need
purple is royalty like throne of king
black is death the end of everything!

Bambi Michel

Memories Of Mother

Though the years may swiftly pass
Our love and sweet memories of you will always last;
Memories of a precious Mother
Whose love and kindness were like no other.

In autumn we miss you from watching the blue skies
And at Thanksgiving your special sweet potato pies,
Mostly we miss your loving smile
That made life so worthwhile.

In winter we miss you at Christmas time
This is the holiday that you stay on our minds,
Especially when we decorate the tree
And your face we cannot see.

In the Spring we think of your flowers
And how you sat on the porch, watching them for hours.
In Summer your gathering of butter beans
And our visits to Aunt Dean's.

You are missed through all the seasons
For many memorable reasons,
And though the years swiftly go by
We still often sit and cry.

Beverly M. Riley

We Have Overcome

Yes, we have overcome,
Out of the cruelty of ancient sins
And in the deep depths of bondage;
Out of the chains that bound our forefathers, we, have overcome.

From royalty and kingship we were torn apart,
From names that defined us, we were demolished;
But yet like steel, we surely overcame.

Tis not what other men might say that will break us,
Nor evil that will harm us, for we like ancient pyramids,
Will never be destroyed.

We are chosen, and we are blessed;
No force is too great to destroy our spirits of steel
Not even death will wash us away, for after us, will come many
And like us, they too will survive.
In the days to come the worse will come
Like the rock of ages and the spirits of our ancestors,
We will survive; when we look at our hardships we'll remember
our people
Fighting in chains, bleeding for a cause, dying to free their souls
From bondage; and through it all, each of us will then say,
I HAVE OVERCOME!!!!!

Genevieve Nimako

The Honkers

The geese are flying everywhere
Over here and over there
The sky is covered with beautiful birds
All talking in a language I've never heard.

They are black and white and gorgeous to see
Whenever I see them it amazes me
That they know how to fly and when and where
It seems their voices just fill the air.

They flew low today-so close to see
I like to think it was just for me
They are low enough to see facial features
Another of God's most beautiful creatures.

Sometimes they're in formation
Sometimes single file
And sometimes from a distance
They appear they're in a pile!

The sound is indescribable
The voices-the wings
But I guess we're not to understand
For we're only human beings.

Darlene Richardson

Humanity, What?

The door unseen,
passed by long and long
Conditioned blindness are we,
but for undisguised descryers
Which we shun and lock away,
whom hold the key to the secret, the passage
Magic pills to hide the truth before us
Shock their heroic quests into oblivion
Gone from sight our saviors,
willing ignorance we embrace
Until destruction steps into our space
will we writhe and wither to such as we've delivered
To the seers
And watch our children, slaves to the terror,
accusations become their eyes, their hearts
"You knew, and chose not!
But, what for us now?"
What, indeed

J. D. Warner

"Pacifist Aggression"

River of mercy fills my veins
Peace comes again
Maybe I dread the fight
but I know my choice is right

I live with pacifist aggression
Detour your quilted possession
I live, and you say it's odd
Passive and aggressive, a messenger from God.

Lifted up, a starry sky
Who are the fascists to ask why
My tolerance is a banner
a sight of a dreamful planner.

Sometimes I feel like my message won't get across
Because people say they understand and they don't
Let me say it for you to hear
With passive aggression that unpaved road can be clear.

To be realistic and straightforward
Can be hard to do
But to be passive and aggressive
can live only if it's true.

Heath Greenbaum

The Beginning?

Have you ever stopped and wondered why
People are—then apologize?
Do you often criticize what you see,
Then think for awhile and say, "Hey, they're just like me."

Have you often felt that peace was right
Then go out for fun and get into a fight.

Do you often try to make ends meet,
Then find out soon it can't be beat.
Have problem one day with a friend
Try to solve the problem, and someone says, "Do it again!"

Sit around and stare at the walls
And feel yourself beginning to dissolve,
So I ask you, "Is there an end?
An end to where it must begin..."

Ernest Cleveland Taylor

The God's Tree

They sat there, those three, the triumvirate of the majesties.
Perfect in form, width, and make—with wrath second to none but
their king.
The perfect grapes hung from the tree—
Perfect in its beauty.
They sat there leisurely and plucked those grapes one by one.
All day long they plucked that tree—
Delighting in its treasures.
Happy and joyful were they.
They sat there all day until the sun went down;
Then, as with the sun—
They too went away.
Alone by itself,
Stood the tree,
Silent
And
Happy.

Jonathan W. Spaeth

"Total Love"

My need for you my Lord is great my Savior
Perhaps the actions of this day to you finds favor
Condemn me not, for past or present actions
Let me atone to you without retractions
My love for you knows no bounds or reservations
You, O Lord, the core of my very existence
To you O Lord myself I give without resistance

Elvera Flores

Hallow's Eve

Oh Hallow's eve, oh blackest night,
perhaps the moon will be a light.
Goblins, and witches, werewolves a fright,
ring door bells with delight.
Eerie winds that whine and blow,
Splashing dark black shadows to and fro.
Scatting and scurrying black cats of the night.
Whispering and wondering what a gruesome sight.
Jack-o-lanterns grinning with fright, just to
say trick or treat on sight.
Oh Hallow's eve what a night

Joan DragoNette

Only Mothers

With empty hands and heart full,
poetry is the only gift I bring
To the mother of the girl moving to Summer, late of Spring.

With empty arms and worried heart,
you watch your full grown little girl depart
To a world with someone else, and you are wondering

What will tomorrow bring
now that she's gone, flown away?
To guide her there, what is left to say?

The path she follows you too have seen,
regrets and joys like an endless stream.
With guidance gone will the flower go on,

The beauty to blossom into joy
with this young man, too recently a boy?
I cannot say; nor do I know.

But this is true, into what and who,
children are meant to grow
Silently dreaming, only our mothers know.

Diane Stuart

The Garden Of Life

At hush of eve in the garden I sit,
Pondering there in the quiet and still,
Where birds that chattered through sunlight's glow
Now sleep in the trees on the hill.
And I sense a wealth of glory there
At the edge of the day time hours,
And I know the Master Gardener is there
Tending His precious flowers.
I feel Him there in the fragrant breath
Of each blossoming plant that grows —
The daisies, the violets, the pansies and pinks,
The myrtle, the lilac, the rose.
Each of them speak of His unending love
For all that is growing there;
And I muse, "Are humans not also His plants
That He blesses with love and care?
He gives us the food our bodies need,
Gives sleep for the long night hours;
He tends and guards, and loves us all —
Are we, too, not one breed of His flowers?"

Exa Wall Timm

Autumn

This is the time of new crop apples and amber afternoons,
Quiet that listens, sound that travels far,
Cirrus clouds, lace thrown across the sky,
The stain of walnut hulls on schoolboy's hands,
And under the aging autumn's lingering warmth, a whispered chill
That tells the coming of the frost.

James D. Weakley

HIGHER POWER

While listening to a message at a meeting, my HIGHER POWER spoke to me — saying, "write this down."
The Joy of this Life, Sober and Clean, stretches on down the way; no twists, no turns, no bends, no hills, but just chock full of frills.

"It's my life," some may exclaim. The truth is that it's GOD'S Temple, and I have to fill it up with what HE wants it to hold.
Yesterday, I lived for greed and gain—leading always to great pain; today, I strive to give back to GOD what things I can—according to HIS Plan; tomorrow, I reach for that which HE holds before me—things I now cannot see.

Time and space for me to learn all I can, and peace and serenity allow me to learn to love the human race, each and every woman and man.

Yesterday, today, and tomorrow, with my hand in GOD'S I'll not know sorrow.

Gary R. Elbert

What Joy In Heaven Awaits Me

Walking with Jesus is such a pleasure,
Praising his name is such a thrill;
Trusting in his precious promises,
Joyfully striving to do his will.

What joy I find in serving Jesus;
Since from sin I have been set free,
My heart goes on happily rejoicing,
Having the assurance that he walks with me.

Lord, let me daily feel thy presences,
Safely guide me every day.
When the enemy comes to hinder,
Your tender voice I will obey.

When the journey here is finished,
When life here on earth is o'er
Oh' what joy awaits me in glory,
I will dwell with Jesus forever more.

There I will have no pain or sorrow,
No sadness or grief I will have to bear;
For the Saints will be always rejoicing,
There will be a home-coming welcome for me there.

Flora J. Taylor Evans

A Heart "N" Love

You're beautiful as a blooming rose
Pretty as a summer breeze
You will always be there...
In my heart and dreams

I see you there waiting...
With your glittering eyes
And breezy hair of rainbow shine...
My only wish is for you to be mine

My body, my mind, my soul won't let go
Because of the way you show you...
This kind of love can't be wrong...
Because this kind of desire is far too deep and strong...

Benny Innamorato

"God's Miracles"

A beautiful rainbow so bright,
Pristine snow so pure and white,
A glowing red sunset at eventide,
A tiger swallowtail with wings so wide,
Busy ants going up and down a hill,
Buzzing bees getting their fill
of nectar flowing so sweet,
For each of them a treat.
But the greatest miracle is you and I,
Made like God's image on high.
Let's be still and see
God's world made for you and me.

June W. Hunter

I Need You

I'll never know you like I should
Probably because I never could
We're so many miles apart
It really hurts down in my heart

You found someone else to take my place
My reaction couldn't be seen on my face
You were never there to help me out
When all those guys made me pout

I cried myself to sleep at night
You weren't there, you were so out of sight
I need your arms to hold me tight
Until the come of morning's first light

Your words I really need to here
To tell me, "I'm really sorry dear".
But no, you are miles away
You say next year, I need you Today

She found someone else to take your place
He's definitely not that king or that ace
I want to see you, but I don't know how
I need you dad, I need you now.

Debra Maurer

My My My...

I try hard not to think about you
Push thoughts of you aside
With other matters of the moment
My book, my boys, my work, my letters, my my my...

So busy. So busy? During the day it's easy.
Preoccupations and occupations keep those gray cells in line
Like a caterpillar climbing up a pole

But at night when I close my eyes
And lose control of that beast
My gray cells start jumping around
And the caterpillar falls off the pole.

Whether he loses his balance
Or finds it on the way down
Is difficult to know

I guess I'll find out
If I wait at the bottom of the pole
And watch him land with a thump.
Or look up and wave goodbye
As he discovers his transparent wings
And flies away. Then I think of you...

Cheri Papier

Anger

Rain drips and falls off the rocks.
Quiet fire glow in the cave,
A cold drip down my neck;
'Light, I need the flashlight' I hear.
Swearing, angry words follow.
YOU....Call Me! These nasty things?
When you are the one who has failed?
Why? Why destroy my calm?
Do you like to fight and cause a problem?
Stay on your side and fight,
I will not argue any longer.
It is cold, it is wet.
 I am going back,
 Breath slowly,
 RESTORE CALM.

Christyne Stackhouse

"Drifted Dreams"

Many, many, were my dreams, when I was yet
Quite young and gay; Many, many were the
Days - when, boarding my dream boat, I sailed
 Away -
Into the far-off lands of make believe, I
Steered my tiny shiff. There in dreamy
Dreamland, I knew every mountain, dell and
 Cliff.
Life was pleasant in those dreams. For
Mine was a world of bliss and joy. I
Cherish those dreams - I did, for mine
Was the ideal world of a boy.

I hitched my wagon to a star and
Began reaching for the distant moon. But
When it was within my grasp, like a
Bubble, my dream burst too soon.

Oh, if I were still a simple child, How
Happy I would be! The world and all
That's in it, would sooth and comfort
 Me.

Ann E. Garman

Untitled

Lift your head and face to the morning sun,
 Raise your hands in praise to the Only One.
Thank Him for bringing you thru the dark night,
 And giving you a new day -fair and bright!
Ask Him to direct your footsteps this day,
 And maybe to someone you will get to say-
"Do you know Jesus? God's only Son?
 He gave His Life for you" Now our work has begun-
To tell all we meet about our blessed Saviour;
 So they won't go to hell by their behavior.
Proclaim His Love so that they may live-
 A brand new life and then they may give,
Someone else the blessed news of Life-
 To help them get thru the hurting strife.
And when the day has ended and we kneel to pray-
 May we lift our hands to Him and say-
"I did my best today, Lord, hopefully they heard Thy Word-
 May the seeds that were planted grow in their heart,
That they may reach heaven and from you never depart."

Georgia Anne Gray

Behold, A Prayer Of David:

Shout without shame, that we love the Lord.
Raise your hands in praises - love God with all your heart.
Feel His holy presence, come and be sanctified.
Sing loving words of praises: Let the Lord Be Magnified.
Oh, let the Lord be magnified.
Exalt yourself in God, praise His holy name.
Dance and sing what love He brings and how He never changes.
Bring the love, spread the joy - give grace and testify.
Proclaim the word of God and let my Lord be magnified.
Oh, let the Lord be magnified.
Praise God Almighty - let's always keep Him first.
Let go of self-indulgence, pride and sinful work.
Give your time to Jesus, in Him we shall abide.
Holler, scream, shout, sing: Let my Lord be magnified.
Oh, let the Lord be magnified.
Triumph in His name, seek and become holy.
Rejoice in His salvation, teach of all His glory.
Fellowship together, worship God on high.
Behold, a prayer of David: Let the Lord be magnified.
Oh, let the Lord be magnified.

Edward L. Ellis

New York, New York

Sleaze Capital of the Western World
Rancid with the Stench of Corruptions
Where pushers and Prostitutes solicit Connections
While Thousands of Homeless Sleep on the Streets

Millions pay Billions in tribute to crack
While one Tenth of its families exist on the Dole
And Half of its Youngsters drop out of School

Spring shuddering pot holes Moonscape the Streets
Gridlocked Cacophony Curses each crossing
Pavements are Eyesores with Dirt and Debris
Subway are Riddled with Crime and Graffiti

Darkness bring fear, Shuts Tight Every Door
As aimless violence adds one victim more.

Ed Burnett

Rage

The age of rage began over a decade ago. I was not encouraged while reading the times, from the Big Apple to the Minne-apple. It was the first unfortunate page.

Then Ricky died in Salt Lake City. After several years of missing him, I listened to his incoherent, courageous babbling about beating "it"; I said good-by over the phone.

Former lover Michael phoned from New York to let me know he was positive. Three months later he was dead. The outrageous disease had ravaged my neat world.

"Buddy" Dana died in San Francisco shortly after my week-long stay arranging his dying business.

It's been two years since the death of forever best friend Charley. Finally I was privileged to be at someone's bedside.

This range of death robbed me of hundreds of friends and lovers. I am not assuaged, still here, feeling aged and lonely, albeit healthy, at forty-five.

Absent a gauge of rationality, rejecting my safe conventional life as a school principal, I sold everything but my soul.

I am now engaged in buying a barraca on a beach in Brazil, where I first fled after Michael's death, to try to remove the salt from these wounds.

I want so to place peace, and a bit of sage in this soul of rage.

Gary Sticha

Reality

On the day of awakening I slumbered in truth
Reality was but an illusion, or so it seemed.
My life until now, I saw as a dream.
In reality there are true feelings of love or
This is at least what I'm taught to believe.
My reality is mine-yours is yours-
To all is there truth of falsity?
It's in what we may choose to believe.

Corey McKethan

The Silent Inner Cry

People walking pass me by; they can't hear my silent cry. They can't really understand that I am not like them. Some will judge by what they see; but they're not looking inside of me. I have a beauty not exposed to all who are not me. I have felt the sting of pain, over and over, and over again. Some was caused from trusted ones. They caused my pain time and again. My inner child reaches out to win. The inner woman wants to be whole again. Together they long to find peace and reach out to others who are like them. I long to be free from the prison of pain. I long to run free and not stay inside. I long to fly high up in the sky and enjoy the flight of a butterfly. I was a cocoon just existing inside a protective coating to curl up and hide, but now I have emerged and dried out my wings, no one will keep me from doing anything! No matter the pain I have endured, my Lord and Savior suffered more. And for His sufferings, I am free, Free for all Eternity. My physical pain may never be gone, it may just be my earthly thorn, but I know that my Lord is by my side and He can hear my silent cries. The scars from the mental pain may never leave, but it's the promise of God to which I will cleave. I am not alone and I feel His love, and I can take flight like a beautiful white dove.

Hope Anne Radley

Untitled

The sun shines on your lively face,
Reflecting all your warmth, your grace.
You smile at me, what do you think,
As I wave from our kitchen sink?

Do you hope I'll come out soon
To tell you 'bout the trees, the moon?
A stick for me? A stone, too?
What a surprise, how nice of you!

You're gone again, a bird flew by,
There'll be more, my son, don't cry.
Our world will never seem too cold
With smiles like yours, my three year old.

Jeanne M. Rock

Unbroken Spirit

A crystallized limb hangs low on a barren tree, yet the moonlight reflects a glow of beauty. The ever present wind now becomes the enemy. The limb cries of itself not to weaken or to become anxious. Yet the challenge itself seems unjust. How can one so fragile withstand such opposition.

I must hold on to hope, for the darkness will pass, and the morning sun will provide me strength. Be patient, and the clouds will make way to a new tomorrow. The limb continues to sway, only now notices the warmth of its enemy. Its weight has lessened, its spirit never broke, and the limb hangs high again, against the sunlight, reflecting a glow of beauty.

Connie Hubbell Carter

A Summer Song

Oh gentle summer breeze, always remain
Refreshing as the early morning rain
Swaying the buttercups and rustling the leaves,
Breathing a song through the trees.

Jerome Nadel

The Alien

...must I walk with aimless feet,
remain unknown to all I meet...?
Is there no place in this land
where I can touch another's hand...?

...thoughts and dreams, ideas all sublime
tip-toe yet into my unresisting mind
like nuns with little candles,
leaving blue and aching tracts of brain-sparks
with their rough, unfinished sandals...

...I am all the poets and musicians
to whom no one ever stops and listens...
am a multitude of balladeers
singing songs that no one hears...
I'm an artist's subtle charcoal line
destroyed by an unperceptive Time...

...but still I walk with aimless feet,
remain unknown to all I meet,
for there *is* no place within this land
where I can touch another's hand...

Judith L. Hemphill

Captured My Heart

I'll never forget holding you tight—-
Remembering those romantic dinners we had over candlelight.

You gave me memories that will last forever—-
My heart keeps telling me I'll never find anyone better.

Knowing we we're together was good for my heart—-
Now that were separated I'm falling apart.

So I'm asking you to hear my cry—-
Let's get together and give it one last try.

It's important to me that you're back in my life—-
Because one day I know you'll make a wonderful wife.

David Olhoeft

"Ready Or Not"

Inside...silent movement
rolling, kicking, nudging
feelings well up
the unknown comes closer, so vague yet scary
can she truly hear me?

Days pass, growth evident
so far so good, yet...what if?
Mustn't think that way
told all is fine

Time creeps, no, no please,
not yet, wait...

Outside...jerky movement
crying, kicking, hiccoughs
new feelings well up
disbelief, relief, wonder
is she real?

Yes, ten here and ten here
she hears me now
cuddling, nudging, contentment.

Janet De Stefano

The Four Seasons

Spring is the dawn of life. Birds build homes for new additions. Roses, daffodils, and tulips blossom beautifully as the gray slush slowly disappears. Gentle breezes blow through trees as they start to show their green leaves in the warm bath of the bright sunlight. People start to bring out lawn mowers as others put away their shovels and snow blowers, while children ride their bicycles through the plentiful life around them.

Summer is full of activity. Children spray each other with water as the sizzling sun overlooks them. Birds dance in peoples' lush, green lawns searching for large, tasty snacks. Thunderstorms many times rule the skies, bringing relief to otherwise unbearably hot temperatures. As a summer's day ends, swarms of mosquitoes patrol the streets, biting anyone who dares come out at night.

Autumn is the preparation time for winter. Trees shed their leaves creating deep, beautiful seas of orange, red, and yellow. Bushy, brown-tailed squirrels gather mammoth acorns, digging a hole for each and every one. Large, noisy flocks of birds head to Florida for long winter vacations. Beautiful orange-red sunsets are the entry to cool, quiet nights.

Winter is the harshest time of the year. Blizzards bring freezing, coat-slicing winds and blinding white snow, making it feel like thirty below when temperatures hover around zero degrees. Children get frostbitten while creating snowmen to withstand the cold. The cool, white light of the sun brings no help to the frozen lands. In winter, only the strong survive the harsh, but sometimes soft peacefulness.

Garry Ng

Untitled

Foredoom walked cobbled streets;
rubbing off on passers spreading ill blood.
Locking arms with old Nick, their Hymn
of Hate faintly creeps through Chaple doors,
melting the noble priests golden crucifix;
closing the innocent child's eyes to the
drops of blood spilt.
Even song falls making no sound-
young maiden doest thou shudder;
Belle tournure unadorned with spite.
Passion fills thy veins!
"Impunity?!" Laughs carnage; none is
there here. Saints lose faith, shrink from hope.
Compassion an enchantment of misdoubt,
carried in letters of relic engravers.
Old hag doest thou cry out!?
Death fills thy veins;
Relic is thy hope.

Hailey Barber

Who Am I?

Who are you? A friend once asked.
Sad as it was, I had no reply,
Because the ME in me was afraid to
discover the ME in me that refused
to be.

Who am I? Ask the ones who probably know best—
Mom, because she "raised" me; dad, because he
"made" me; husband, because he "changed" me.

I am mother — yes — absolutely, all-consuming,
unequivocally so, fulfilled, but incomplete in that
role alone.

Who am I? As sad as it is, I have
no reply, because the ME in me is still
afraid to discover the ME in me that
doesn't know how to be free.

Audrey Forrest-Carter

Love, Locked Away

Happy thoughts of you, takes away the
Sadness that crosses my heart
I look to heaven in prayer, and pray that
Our love remains strong, while were apart

So many nights, I lay awake and think of
How it should be
At home, lost in your arms, me loving you,
You loving me

Never, have I felt like this before, for anyone,
I've ever known
When I first met you, I understand, for the
First time in my life
What it felt like to be home

It may seem like an eternity, while I'm away
But listen, closely to the night, and you'll
Hear me say

Sleep softly, and wipe away that tear
Because there's nothing in this world, that
Could ever stop me, from forever and always
Loving you, Dear

Donald R. Bartram Sr.

Mystic Night

Bright salt sky
sails the rooftops of
shops and cars and fluorescent ice cream.

In and out and in they mill;
the keepers are quiet
yet respondent to vacant,
smiling wanderers.

Photos and frames, watercolors,
bleeding oil pine shingles,
glass ball floats attract, but do not connect.

The rigging titters.

Elizabeth E. Hurt

Who Is Santa Claus?

It's Christmas now, and you will hear people say,
"Santa Claus is on his way."

Oh, I'm not talking about the man in the red suit,
Who comes once a year and brings us some loot.

I'm talking about the one I see all year,
Who brings joy to my house and lots of good cheer.

It could be someone I don't even know;
Someone with a smile and a cheery hello.

Could be the doctor, lawyer, teacher
Or even our parish preacher.

But we know in our hearts and throughout this land,
Whatever is done is too big for man.

So we kneel and pray, and for a moment we pause,
We know, JESUS,........YOU ARE Santa Claus.

Edward J. Struck

Christina at Midnight

There she stands on burning sands, staring across an endless sea,
satin nights and velvet dreams surround her like a mystery.
Walking towards you on the water with a smile so sweet and rare,
she lets you touch her silky skin and smell the lilacs in her hair.
She's warm and bright as summer sunshine following the rain,
look in her eyes and hear her sighs of pleasure with no pain.

Even as you caress her, you know you can't possess her. One last
kiss, a promise whispered in your ear.
Then like the mist that is gone by morning, she too, will disappear.

Bill Huttunen

Passion

It jumped out at me.
Scared me half to death.
My heart was in my throat.
Yet, it was familiar.
I knew I'd felt it before a long time ago.
But I couldn't figure out what it was.
It intrigued me.
I started to like it.
I began to crave it.
I wanted more of it.
It didn't go away - as if it decided to stay with me.
It refused to leave me - it was here to stay.
For now.

Janet K. Strupp

"Summer"

Summer time is finally here,
School is out and fishing time near.
Barefooted boys and fishing poles,
Down to the creek, to the ole swimming hole.
Running through the woods, along the river bank,
That old boat they used went and sank.
A can of worms, a hook and line,
Looking for a fishing pole, if they can find
Two good friends who share their fun,
They run and jump and chase the sun.
Running here, and running there,
Not any worries, not a care.
But too soon, it must all end
for these two that were good friends.
Summer comes and summer moves on,
A few summers in your life, then you're grown.
But there are days we can recall
When we were friends, we had it all.

Doug Beggs

Untitled

We had our differences,
Screamed and bitched,
I cried and hoped,
That you would come back to me
Now, that is all in the past,
We've went our separate ways
But sometimes I just can't help thinking,
Of how it would be,
How it would be if it was still you and me.

Julie Race

Saying Alive

Dive too deep, to sudden, to reach the
sea pearls. The beauty of something quite
priceless. Leaving now fear, fear in me.
Who me? Put so high a price on
My life. Who would fear me, who
not take a liking to I.
Thou, I'm now only minutes to
darkness, I have no defense against.
the sea. With seconds of air, it is
I, and only I, whom hear my despair.
Soul weeps for a world it don't
know. Time passes, the river ceases to flow.
Visions of the raven, now meets the crow.
Tainted soul, gestures an internal farewell.
So silent, who can hear me, my confession.
For it is saying alive, what
we need not have time to say
when we die.

Eddie Harden

What Is Love?

I've pondered the meaning of this word,
Searching near and far -
To find an explanation
Of the way things really are.

Is it something you see or touch,
A word, a phrase or two -
The things we did, the time we've shared,
The memories we knew?

Is love the union of our souls,
When hearts shall intertwine -
Or, it is just a dream to find,
Until the end of time?

The masters and the poets,
Have written thought and verse-
Still none have found the meaning,
Not one has been the first.

A mystical word, known near and far,
Whispered, throughout the land -
What is love I ask you,
Please help me understand.

Judith A. Manco

A Halloween Spook In The Delivery Room

October 24th, one week to go
Searching the night for a good place to spook
What's this big building all aglow
I'm here for a reason, or is it a fluke.

Fly in a window drawn by the screams
There is someone there, a women in bed
She's being tortured or so it seems
The spirits are early for the night of the dead.

I'll sit on this shelf and watch the scene
There is something inside her beating her walls
She's attached to electrics, who is this fiend
He is so low, I'll bet you he crawls.

A machine is there that measures her yell
It spits out paper and prints a graph
Oh this devil he must be from hell
What a strong woman, she manages a laugh

People in white rush in, they must be demons too
Being a spook, this scene I'll enjoy
I've made a mistake, it's a hospital crew
The spirit inside is a beautiful baby boy.

Joseph Thomas Joyce

Befriending The Grandfather Clock

Birth rejoice, death mourn, every home, every land
Seconds, hours, months, seasons, years
Time continues without emotion, relentless, determined
A fallen leaf, a grain of sand, can the earth distinguish

Moments seized, perhaps days
The storms will pass, the floods, the quakes, the flames
An hour or two, serene, taken from the clock
Joy, pleasure, peace and understanding

Clocks will stop, but the Grandfather Clock chimes on
A flash or an ancient soul, the tone the pitch indifferent
Moments seized, perhaps days
A smile, a laugh, a good day, time a friend?

John Achoukian

Old Age - Tomorrow

"Walking makes you do all the things you want to do
See all the things you want to see
Because it's your feet that have to take you there."

I want to walk the paths I used to walk
To have the life that too soon has passed too fast,
I reminisce with all my heart and mind,
To be young again and think about what the future might well bring.
In my heart memories will last and dreams each night will make me agile again to jump, to climb the roads ahead, over the detours that life submits.

Tomorrow, I'll powder my face, and comb my hair, put my make up on to change what the mirror reflects because your reflection can do great things, so that a good reflection for you and for others will make you limber again.

Gloria Unger

Little Child

Little child please forget the past,
See the future forever at last.
Let go of the hurt and the lies,
Only keep inside the lullabies.

Little child please don't hide,
Trust yourself to be your own guide.
Always walk with your head held high,
Keep moving on remembering the sky.

Little child please keep seeing,
Start to forgive, stop your fleeing,
Memories will always be hard,
But your heart you cannot forever guard.

Little child please stop your tears,
Soon will come when you'll have no fears,
Knowing then you'll have reached your goal,
When finally, for eternity, you release your soul.

Caralee C. Fields

Hide And Seek

Two little squirrels were having fun,
Seeking acorns in the morning sun.
Digging here and burying there
Storing nuts for the winter, everywhere.
But lookout now, for here comes trouble,
A fat cat sneaking at the double,
Hoping to catch them by surprise
But the two little squirrels, are really wise,
Scampering up the nearest tree
They disappear - the cat can't see
Them, looking warily through the branches
They're not taking any chances,
Part way down the tree they run
Chasing each other, and still having fun
Then up again, well out of sight.
While the cat decides, this isn't right
He prowled around, but the squirrels were gone
High up above him, teasing him on
So the baffled cat, went off on his way
While the squirrels ran down to seek acorns and play.

Joan M. Laube

Untitled

One little kiss, a peck on the cheek,
seems to be small payment from mother to son.
But without these affections the son does wither,
away from the love given non other.
And into his life he takes this reminder,
of the love that was lost in his life.
He takes it to heart, to body and soul
and teaches his own sons to be more like him.
But of the love that he lost, how can it be replaced
now that he is out of the shadows
of his mother's dark shadow that dances above him.
He learns to love again, but this time different,
it is a much deeper love that he's looking for —
the kind of love he feels that was missed,
a peck on the cheek and one small kiss.

Greg Young

Racism And Tears

Why oh why can't people be blind, and be
seen for their soul or mind?
To be looked at and be called a name, or
to be looked at and be treated the same.
Would you like to see a tear running down
a child's face, and to know it's because they're a
different race?
To see a man walking down the street, and
watch him get harassed or beat.
Or to look at someone deep down inside
and to know that they have nothing to hide.
And if they're hurt and shed a tear,
reassure them to have no fear.
So don't judge someone from what you see,
cause they're no different from you or me.
Look behind this world of racism and tears,
and you'll enjoy life for many more years.

Athena Avalos

A Serious World

Look into the mirror; see the reflection of one's
self. Look out the window; see society's fails.
There's a long way to go; it's still a serious world.

Guns, drugs on every corner. Kids going down under.
There's a long way to go, it's still a serious world.

Save the water, save the Rain Forest,
if all else fail, save one's self.
There's a long way to go; it's still a serious world.

Welfare, politics, everything's for sell.
Justice, what is it? There's a long way to go; it's still
a serious world.

War, hungry, for me, it's insane. Homeless, crime, gangs;
it is insane. There's a long way to go; it's still a serious world.
What unbearable weight this world must feel, for death and
despair had become entertainment. Charity acts by many, has
become wealth for few. There's still along way to go; it's still a
serious world!

Dwight J. Underwood

I Cry

As we lie silently I am lulled by the repetition of your breathing. Sensing the warmth of your body, I embrace it, grasping the huddled mass as a child would a cherished blanket. I pull your body even closer to mine, making sure you can't escape from this temporary paradise.

I feel the rhythmic beating of your heart as your sides expand and collapse with every breath taken. I brush the hair from your forehead, your supple skin tender to my touch. Your face seems to glow with light, chasing the darkness from the room. I stare, hoping maybe your light will fill the dark corners of my heart. Quickly, I turn away. Fear suddenly swells within my body. My heartbeat quickens as I recall the anguish and betrayal of a previous relationship. Like drunken Vikings plundering an unprotected village, emotions run rampant, terrorizing my soul.

I want to wake you, talk to you, anything to stop this perpetual bombardment of insecurity. Cowardly, I don't; too afraid you won't understand that what I so desperately want to hear are the three words I am terrified to say: I love you. Quietly, as I hold this sleeping beauty, I cry.

Bryan E. Johnson

Fire

I build a fire.
Shades of orange, yellow, blue, and white flashing in chaotic beauty;
A gleaming warmth, flowing upward reaching for the sky,
Bring hope, courage, and nourishment when tame.

I see a fire in the distance.
A devastating monster,
Destroying all when one can only watch in awe;
Taker of life,
Murderer of many;
Fast and Fierce, leaping from tree to tree, destroying homes and hopes.

I study the dying embers.
With fuel and oxygen diminishing;
Like humans, it too dies.

I stare at the ashes.
A blaze of light and glory shrunken into black coals;
These remnants of its short life are the basis for life
In the future generations.

The heroes of history are fire.
After a short blaze of light and glory called life,
They leave something for future generations.

Daniel Abraham Handwerker

The Walker

It's always just before the sun goes down,
She comes walking with her slow graceful stroll.
Always smiling, with never the sign of a frown.
The walker who shows she has peace in her soul.

She goes strolling by, never in a hurry,
Sometimes stopping, to have a few words if cheer.
Sometimes stopping to watch the nature she holds so dear.

I watch her till she finally disappears over the hill,
Playfully kicking stones, picking some dainty wild flower.
And enjoying each and every breath of air, with its chill.
She seems to enjoy her walk, even when there is a shower.

Then I must watch the hill for her to reappear;
And the waiting is what makes her walks seem so long.
Her walks are sometimes far, but she need never fear,
For her heart is surly pure, and always full of song.

On her return, she always pauses, to chat with me,
Telling me of what she has seem, just like a happy child.
She is one, who wants only Nature's beauty, to see
I say as she departs, may all your walks be mild.

Joseph B. Myers

'The Girl Next Door'

All it took was one look at her and my heart beat faster.
She has the face of a angle green eyes that sparkle and glow.
And long blonde hair that shines like gold.
She is perfect in every way but to me she is out of reach.
My heart breaks at the cruel reality of the fact that she
doesn't know me at all, if only I could tell her how I feel.
That just seeing her fills me with joy. That before she came
along I was dead inside my heart had fallen a sleep.
But she came and changed all that now I can feel again.
And what I feel is the deepest love for her. She has cast a
magic spell on me I would do anything for her. To show
her how much I care all she has to do is ask. I would
give her the moon sun and stars if I could and yet that
would not be enough. For her she deserves all there is
in the world to give all the purity and beauty to match her.
Without her there is nothing for me my life would be over.
When she is not around time drags on slowly and lonely.
One day I will Tell how I feel may be she will see me
for who I am a person loves her with my entire being.

Jacqueline Flores

My Mother

My mother is not only mother,
she is a friend to me, my sisters and my brother.

Not only is she my friend, but my very best friend,
and it is so even when taking care of others' needs.

No matter what I tell her she will listen,
and with joyful pride glisten.

The whole time waiting to say something helpful,
and she is most definitely not spiteful.

There have been many times I know,
that she didn't even bother to show.

That she had burdens of her own,
and that she has needs to be sewn.

She is now 80 years old,
and doesn't like to be told.

That she gets more beautiful every year,
and if you attempt, it will usually bring a tear.

I thank God for her health and wisdom,
and I know one day she will be in His Kingdom.

I also thank God for the blessings of this time,
and for the opportunity to have this wonderful mother of mine.

Eleanor Jo Miller

The Green Psychiatrist

My office door opened my patient walked in
She looked at me her face in a grin
She said Doctor why are you dressed in green
That's my favorite color even for jeans
I told her I used to dress in red
But for some reason my patients tried to get me in bed

Your switch to green was clever and smart
In your profession it gives you a head start
Green is the color which typifies balance and rest
If people can't get that they are a mess

I looked at my patient as she gave me a wink
She was dressed in soft green and she made me think
Why are you here you don't need me
But she read my mind and was quick to disagree

Doctor, you're tall and blond and built divine
I checked your credentials and you'll do just fine
You dress in green though it's a different shade
We'll do great together, we have it made
I want you for my partner you are my dream
I too am a psychiatrist who dresses in green.

Elva Blair

The Girl In The Glass Box

You have this little girl in your glass box,
she never tries to escape, because of society's locks.

She just sits in a corner and silently cries,
she did nothing but trust you, you and your lies.

You said you would take care of her...truth it was not,
the box you have left her, alone there to rot.

As she was developing you left her inside,
the women she was becoming you closed and denied.

As she was growing, the box too cramped to contain,
the tighter you squeezed ignoring her pain.

She just kept growing, was nothing you could do,
she grew out of your box and became someone new.

She was still the same little girl only by heart,
you reached in her soul and ripped it apart.

Now she is gone, to far from your grip,
protected by strength, used as a whip.

The sting of emancipation she has left you behind,
tormented by your own box is what you will find.

The only way out is for you also to grow,
but remember where you are, since you reap what you sow.

Cynthia M. Totman

Old Sneakers

On a bed I lay waiting, hope will find you soon,
she says, I'm still waiting.

Laughter lies beside me, she's dying too,
being plagued by a disease, sun shines no longer.

Dark images squeeze me tightly, I touch my
Mother's hand tenderly, scared, she pulls away.

Slipping, I fall down through the gates of death,
while smothering my cries with the torn hankie of my life.

Nothing can cure my pain I know, my blood is infected,
contaminated, black and unpure.

Evening shadows hang from my eyes
like curtains soon to be shut, I lay waiting.

All my friends have left, gone with the wind,
too scared to fall into my black hole.

Kicking me, I fall deeper into my pit,
this time not able to stop.

Ending props have been set and staged,
only I am not acting this time.
Relying on services, I lay crippled in a bed by a disease that
I can not help. Sustained to a web of misery, I lie dying.

I exist, waiting to be murdered by a ruthless killer,
waiting to be murdered by AIDS.

Erin Beth Metnick

My Sister The Land Lover

My sister, the one who Loves Land
She'd rather kiss the dirt
than have a hook for a hand
No sea legs she has, brings me head to a sigh
No captain's hat she wears
No patch on her eye
She eats no trout or fish steaks
Not any swabby or cabin boy she makes
A chipped tooth she has
that's all she be
My land loves sister and a sailor like me

Jessica Golick

"Comeuppance"

He's home
She stands, innocent, smiling
He stood as he had endless times
Drunk, coming toward her

Full of unnamed hate, his hair disheveled
A button torn from his ragged tee shirt
He weaves, To-and-fro
Says she is worthless, calls her a bitch!

A numbing chill fills his heart
He cannot put his finger on why
How white her skin
How strange the expression in her eyes

Suddenly his mouth opens in a silent scream
She literally dissolves!
The doctors called it heart-failure
Those who had known her, a stressed out heart

They had tried to reach him earlier
Lost in the shadowy, impersonal
bar scene
No prior notification possible

Carol Pritt

Special Memories

It's early in the morning - she hears her baby weep,
She stumbles in to comfort her - aware but half asleep.

And as she holds her closely - she's filled with so much pleasure,
A memory she will always have - and one she'll always treasure.

As she rocks the baby slowly - she reflects upon her life,
So proud to have the title of a mother and a wife.

The baby softly sleeping now - she feels two tiny hands,
Her little boy can't sleep so good - but mommy understands.

She helps him crawl onto her lap - and holds her children near,
She couldn't bear to move just yet - the moment was so dear.

She tucked the children snugly - returning back to bed,
She saw a light upon his face - her husband and her friend.

She didn't want to wake him - he worked so hard all day,
She closed her eyes and promised God that she would never stray.

Her family meant the world to her - their future was so bright,
And she'll always be as close to them as she was that special night.

Carol A. Borden

Los Ángeles, Los Angeles

On a far away distant snow covered land, freezing and
shivering, all alone I stand. I look at the clouds and
start pondering where can the good old sun be wandering,
I could clearly almost hear him, say, if you want to find
me come home to L.A. Los Ángeles, Los Angeles, your
warm days I do miss. Los Ángeles, Los Angeles, to be there
I do wish surrounded by beaches that were made for kings
surrounded by mountains with magic things, near-by is
a fantasy land where there's a prince and a sleeping
beauty waiting for his kiss. There are movie stars, good
music, beats and great performing top athletes.
Los Ángeles, Los Angeles, your entertainment I do miss.
Los Ángeles, Los Angeles, to be there I do wish,
architecturally designed by people from many a land
with various structures built by many a hand skyscrapers
adorn the earth where they were carved upon, glitter like
diamonds underneath the sun with its multi-cultural
atmosphere, all kinds of flavors you'll find here.
Los Ángeles, Los Angeles, your great people I do miss.
Los Ángeles, Los Angeles, to be there I do wish.

Carlos Lizarraga

Beneath A Shower Of Meteors

Who would hold one night in deep regard;
Should climb a balsam scented trail
And make a bed of pine boughs at its ending,
And watch the curling of the campfire smoke
Straight up in the traffic of stars;
Should know the ageless stillness of a mountain night;
To feel a oneness with the furry things
That roam soft footed close beside;
To watch a swift light cloud so close above
We reach to touch it with our finger tips.
To scan a sky inhabited by stars
With the mind's conjecturing.
A star falls here, another there...
We lose the counting of them finally.
To watch and wait for what time's calendar will stage this night.
For learned men, this frenzied game
Of searching out the stuff of stars...
How many million light years from the sun?
For us it is enough... just now...
To feel included in this magnificent panoply.

Catherine Edwards Speer

The Invitation

High above stillness of vast earthly night
Shown a star glittering heaven's pure light.
In the far east promised region Judea
Shepherds watched over their flocks vast arena.

Lo, when the eastern star gently lit down,
Sighted and travelled to the holy town.
In the mean streets of dear Bethlehem lay
Jesus the Savior in manager of hay.

One of Whom all prophets past did proclaim,
Christ and Emmanuel is His Sweet Name.
God's Only Son Who had died for all our sin,
Only One Way to God, enter by Him in.

He is the Shepherd Who is the True Way.
He is the gate which sheep enter alway.
He is the Savior, Messiah, we say.
He is the narrow way, come in today.

Shepherds did follow the star with great joy,
Having told by the angelic envoy.
Wise men who found Him did worship and sing.
You can find Life through Christ Jesus the King.

Doreen Marie Hoge

Yellow Bird

Her footsteps whisper across the sand
Silently she steps to the beat
The drummer pats quickly, eyes are closed
Oblivious to the heat

She sings and it echoes on desert land
Pounding rhythm connects with the heart
The eagle screams as he takes his stand
He does what he can to take part

Like the ocean who rushes to shore at night
Black hair waves on her forehead and mouth
The daughter of Iroquois and Apache moves
A blend of the North and South

Her grace and her beauty capture the eye
Her arms wave like wings of birds
She listens and sings and dances alone
To the pounding of drums voiceless words

Cynthia A. Schreyer

He

Congealed autumn air in a sunken park,
Silhouettes emerge under a silent speckled sky.

Cigarette smoke and rebel youth souls
Searching for inspiration, they assemble
Birthing profound redundancies.

Hatched of the Night he emerges.
Tanglèd mass over glazed eyes
Intoxicated with knowledge,
He is Sage of the dew-kissed grass.

Ceded kindness beckons a visit from an
Unwanted stranger.
Fleeting fear replaced by melody of wisdom,
Slurred verses from Catcher in the Rye,
Intimate words seduce the soul.

'All killers know poetry.'
Then let us fall victim.
Thriving on each drunken revelation,
Share your fancies. Ignite our dreams.

Out of one shadow and into another
The Phantom is gone, but the spirit remains.

Julie Ezelle and Julie Goodson

Memories Of A Hobo During The Great Depression

I've done a lot of travelin'
Since the day I lost my home;
Tossed a knapsack o'er my shoulder
And started out to roam.

It takes a lot of courage
Hanging on an old freight train,
As the cinders get into your eyes,
And the tears, they fall like rain.

A-walkin' down a countryside,
Or a lonesome railroad track,
Your only possessions in the world
In that knapsack on your back.

And when you're hungry late at night,
Boiling coffee in an old tin can;
Stuffing cardboard in your worn-out shoes;
Just a raggedy, flea-bit man.

As I come shuffling to your door,
I think, "God bless you, Mum,"
As you give some soup or sandwich
To a harmless, homeless bum.

Gertrude Warner Frederick

"Loren - My Best Friend"

It's been a long time
since we've seen each other.
Things have changed,
with me and my brother.
I don't even bother that much with my friends,
and the crew,
cause I know I'd have more fun,
hanging with you.
It's been about 2 or 3 years since my depart.
Everyday I go thinking,
Why me? Why us?
Even though we've been apart,
We are still friends,
two souls and two hearts.

Jessica Fox

Patriots

Flag wavin' patriots dancing in their Hawaiian shirts.
Singin' the praises of old glory, but not knowin'
  What she's all about.
Bible thumpin',
Pistol packin',
Foot stompin',
Beer guzzlin',
Bellies hanging over black leather belts,
With red necks flaming at the local veterans' hall.
White stocking, hairless poles supporting rotund globs
  Of triple by-passes.
Nigger hatin',
Narrow minded',
Hymn singin',
Double chinned patriots in polyester leisure suits.
Shootin' pool,
Bowlin' strikes,
Telling jokes about pollacks, whops and kikes,
Singin' the praises of old glory, but not knowin'
  What she's all about.

Frank Macchione

"Here I'll Stay"

I'm not an Angel; I'm a woman;
  Take my hand...
We laughed and played at first, like a game;
  And then into my Heart you came...
Here I'll stay until it's time for me to go!

Yes, we've seen different worlds'
  We're not always the same...
You could of stayed outside my Heart;
  But, in you came...
Here I'll stay until it's time for me to go!

My love has no beginning;
  My love has no end...
And tho I won't ask for forever;
  I'll just ask your heart for now...
Here I'll stay until it's time for me to go!

The future is, just that;
  How long we have is uncertain...
Even tho behind a curtain...
  But Still;
Here I'll stay until it's time for me to go!

Pamela Hunnicutt

To Say I Love You

Without thought it's so easy.
Single syllable words-three of them.
Like a nuclear meltdown, my brain ceases to function.
Feelings alien in nature consume my being throwing me into cosmic space.
This unnatural blend of excitement and fear leaves me with a melancholy sadness.
What dreadful meaning lurks behind these words?
Causing this menacing havoc within me. Leaving my very existence threatened.
In calm, I let my mind wander to the images of your face.
Our eyes lock fusing us together as one.
Flesh awakening with a touch-electrifying. Senses take over where words are forgotten.
Now, while we're apart and I try to command my lips to say the words,
I am mute.
Why?
Do I fear the words will tumble clumsily from my mouth. That I will be scorned for my lack of eloquence.
Or, perhaps words will erase the luminance of this force between us?
Dare I chance?

Diane R. Tuttle

A Look Into Loneliness

Someday we will all be there -
sitting alone, by a closed window,
in a stuffy room watching children
play outside
We will feel alone; though some of us need
not be.
That is all our choosing.

A place where all forms of tenderness and
compassion seems patronizing
A place where time creases our skin as if it
was paper.

This is inevitable, burdensome, wretched, decrepit
and wicked are what we have become.
So we sit patiently by the closed window waiting
to die.
As we see the children playing we remember that
we were once that young.

Gina Marie Scialla

I Don't Understand Why

I'm sitting here thinking of you
Sitting here feeling so blue.

Thinking of all the times we shared.
All the times we acted, we didn't care.

All the risks we had taken.
All the things we went around breakin'.

Even though a lot of time has gone by.
It doesn't matter, it still makes me cry.

I don't remember anything from day to day.
I don't understand why you couldn't stay.

When I think about you it makes me sad
I don't understand why it makes me so mad.

Everything around me makes me want to cry
But all I can say is "I don't understand why."

Jane Huston

"Dusk, 'til Forever"

Nightfall now, on my horse
Skimming the sphere of the moors...
Years of fields to deflect
Nothing wished there was possible
scattered about, not to forget...
turning... turning...
This eventide, the sky merle
And over the turns... the cape leaves my soul
Time to close, love.
Offer no more...
Immerse in solitude...
...Dusk, 'til Forever...

Do not pass under the Dark Trees
Their mosses descend to sweep the ground
Writhing with more motive than the healthiest kudzu
Long hair sighted - dripping through their tops
And six foot copperblue wingspans fan their branches
Their sordid screams
A Mockery...
of long gone mornings.

Carl Floyd

Silent Sounds

I shall not build towers
Skyward to the sun
Lest, in climbing I be blinded by the light,
And stumbling fall, to see
My broken dreams scattered
On desert sands to parch and die.

Instead, when skies are gray
On an autumn late day,
I would plant soil, patting it firmer
Into its soon seasonal slumber.

And when they will have said -
"The snowdrifts seemed the highest
That long winter was even the worst"
There, bravely flowering in wonder,
Jewelled snowdrops in white radiance,
Silently awakening my heart
To sounds of the unseen vibrant earth.

Gladys D. Craft

Our Seasons

Winter is our chilly season.
Sleet, snow and ice are the reason.

Spring melts all that ice and snow.
Then the grass and plants begin to grow.

Summer has hot winds and cooling showers.
Then swimming, picnics and lots of fun are ours.

Autumn is when leaves of red, gold and yellow are falling.
"Time to gather nuts," the squirrels are calling.

Bertie P. Welborn

Metamorphosis

A caterpillar single-mindedly weaves,
Slowly, methodically winding a cocoon.
Protection from the elements and prey.
So did I
Feeling safe at last, he sleeps
stirring not, feeling nothing.
The seasons pass, and the caterpillar,
not realizing, grows in its cocoon.
Metamorphosing.
So am I
Spring arrives!
The cocoon slowly breaks revealing.....
the butterfly
His wings unfold, and he takes to flight.
Finally feeling freedom and the joy of life.
So shall I

Debbie Hammond

Good News

My sister just told me the most wonderful thing.
She's trying to have a new human being!
To bring a life to this earth,
oh what a miracle to give birth!
First child's there, and she's so excited.
Has all kinds of questions, like how soon united?
Whether it's a boy or a girl, I know it won't matter.
Baby will be loved and Grandmas will chatter.
This news is the best, it's made my day.
I can't wait till the baby's old enough to play.
They're so little, but they grow up so fast.
I only hope this one's not the last.

Ellen Blum

Ode To SPA Dining Room

Everything and everybody in place?
Smile on the face, ready for the race.
"Pour me some coffee, pour me some tea."
"I want soup and salad, so does she."
The food must be served just right.
As we work far into the night.
Changed orders, trying to cope.
"Diet jello? Strawberry yogurt? Cantaloupe?"
It's almost time to go home,
The late stragglers always come.
They eat and eat more and more.
They can hardly get through the door.
They mustn't gain weight, if we get tips,
Or, add any more inches to those hips.
Our feet are hurting, our backs are breaking.
And they just sit there yakkity, yakking.
"Lord, have mercy," we are praying.
"How long are these people staying?"
Gone at last, "Clean up the table,
We're going home if we're able."

Dorothy Bell Harris

Untitled

As I sit engulfed by many "friends," I feel tension in the air.
Smiling faces and girlish laughter, can't hide the silent stare.

No words can express the feelings, that only eyes can bring across,
A feeling of complete and utter despair, of something that was lost.

Yet as I look around the room, and join in all their fun,
I feel their eyes shoot through me, like the bullets of a gun.

They smile, and laugh, and pretend to care, but never truly listen.
And the tears forming in my eyes, against the light they glisten.

I send a silent cry for help, through this silent stare of mine,
And though engulfed by many "friends," they all seem to be blind.

If only they'd all take the time, to look around and see,
The pain in each other's eyes, the pain in you, and in me.

No one seems to know the meaning of a friend, or importance of a friendship,
Or even the need of a shoulder to cry on, in times of hurt and hardship.

As it turns out, what I thought was lost, was never lost at all,
But instead it was never there, it was just a dream that I saw.

This dream that I have dreamed so long, I thought it had turned real,
But now I know I was just overwhelmed by what I long to feel.

Jennifer L. Fort

Untitled

The wind carries our destiny
Smoke from factories pollutes our destiny
Trees carry our souls forgotten
Men destroy trees souls become rotten
Dolphins carry our health and our
Dreams so real
In a trash filled ocean
Our fate has been sealed
The animals of our forest harbor our
Innocence
Men destroy our forest as our innocence
Burns away
We should get to our knees and pray
Pray that our earth will still be here
But our future seems so dismal
With destruction so near

Darbie Husted

Beautiful

Beautiful? What is beautiful? Why is beautiful,
so beautiful? Would you be so beautiful if I
had not noticed you? Standing in this world of
hate, fear, bricks and steel? Would you still
be beautiful if your eyes were not as blue
as the ocean? Would you still be beautiful if
your skin was not as soft as it is? Well how
soft is that? How soft can someone's skin
be in this world of toughness? Would you be
so beautiful if your hair was not so soft
and silky? How silky you ask! As silky
as a web of dreams, spun by the spider
of life. Well I know how beautiful you are.
Even if I had no eyes, blind to the world,
would you be so beautiful. But how do
you judge beautiful??? — From the inside out!

John Mobley

Happy Birthday My Friend

On this day God gave us a gift
So blow out the candles and make a wish
If I had a wish that wish would be
That this friendship would last between you and me
This friendship is treasured within my heart
After all we've been through we haven't been apart
Our friendship is caring, kind, and unique
I know there are times I'm very oblique
We've come along way...The road in which we traveled
The problems we've faced as it seemed the world unraveled
We've been through so much...The things we have faced
Made our friendship so strong....It kept us in place
I love you so much for being my friend
The laughter..The joy...The heartache will mend
I thank you for supporting...And being at my side
For helping me with the problems I myself prescribed
I hold this friendship dear to my heart
Always hoping the problems never tear it apart
I thank God for blessing me with you
And also my friend a very Happy Birthday to you.

Jo Ann Wisniewski

The Face In The Rainbow

Breathtakingly beautiful
So close I could almost touch it
yet just out of my reach
The colors so vivid so alive
Not a flaw in this piece of God's work

The face within has pastel pink cheeks
sparkling eyes so dark they are almost black
skin as smooth as a newborn baby
not weathered with time
nor wrinkled from worry

The face within smiling content at peace
in this astonishingly colorful
creation by God

The face is not that of God
but a gift from Him
The face within looking so serene
is my Father

Betty R. Pike

"Empty"

As I look in that dark, deep, empty hole,
So dark,
So empty,
As I sat at the top looking down at the bottom,
So dark,
So empty,
but yet so familiar.
After sitting at the top of that dark, deep, empty hole,
I finally figured out why it seemed so familiar,
I was looking at the same dark, deep, empty hole,
you made in my heart when you left me!

Arron Brumfield

Untitled

The leaves are falling, sun is setting, the air is cool and brisk.
So full of life, energy, so full of love, all flowing tremendously through her veins.
Silence. Tears come. No it's not supposed to end this way. She's just a little girl. PLEASE!
She's supposed to grow up, boyfriends, dances, graduate, fall in love, start a family of her own.
It's not supposed to be like this. Stillness. Quiet. Where's that smiling face? Where's that laughter?
Nothing. The tears fall harder, will they ever stop? The hurt. Oh, how it hurts.
There is so much that wasn't said. I love you. Did she know? Yes, she knew. So much love.
The anger comes. So much anger. Why? There's never an answer.
No one knows. Tears fade. Numb.
No feelings, only wonderful memories. Have to hold on to those memories. We have to be strong.
Strong for each other. God is in control now. No more suffering, no more pain. There is peace.
She's is in His care. He needed her now. She's special. She always will be special. Take care of her.
We love her. We'll miss her. We'll be with her again someday. God Bless Her.

Becky Kay Flanagan

"I Can Stay No Longer"

Sitting in silence,
So many thoughts, so many emotions
Still nothing comes accept
The blank stare
Why can't you see?
Why are you hurting me?
Please, stop the pain.

An empty silence, a broken heart
present is gone, only future remains.
Why must we go on like this?
Why the emotional future?
Why don't you see?
Please understand what you're doing to me.

Tears build up, but never fall
Is it lack of love?
Did we lose the bond?
Why is this happening?
Why do our memories only bring us together
Why can't we get off this path?
Please let me go, I can stay no longer.

Elizabeth Hyland

Flowers

Flowers are found most everywhere
so pretty in the ladies hair.

In a yard, pot or a vase
a smile found on every face.

Wild flowers don't care where they grow
enjoyed by all, young and old.

Texas state flower, Blue bonnets you know
do not pick, we are told.

Tulips represent spring
roses your love one brings.

Daisies are so nice and bright
Poinsettia's are a beautiful sight.

Flowers are given for many a reason
there are some for every season.

In many colors, sizes and shapes
flowers are for all, to appreciate.

Edith R. Eichmann

From The Back Seat

From the back seat, my father's neck, my mother's gaze we see;
So we sit quietly, my brother and me.

We just sit and fight the urge to break this quiet peace;
Two little boys' aggressiveness hovers near the point of release.

Frustration at first, then initiative takes charge as our eyes meet;
We play a game called "Look at That!" from the comfort of the back seat.

Other cars, churches and bars, city lights and Christmas nights;
Steel mill stacks and railroad tracks, crowded downtown and amusement park grounds;
Oh, we've seen it before, but please Dad! Once more!

Our mother turns her lovely head;
A pretty smile gives way.
Our father knows, so on he goes;
It's time to go home today.

And visiting another world,
Where angels and baseball bats meet;
The boys do sleep, their joys they keep,
From the wonder of the back seat.

Clarence F. White

The Wake-Up Call

She pretends
Learned this while still young, won't let her world collapse
The sun came up even though angry words were spoken
He's still not gone, new day begun
This is good, so...
She pretends
To stay the course
The course of course means accepting the one who's supposed to love her doesn't
He utters the word D I V O R C E
This is bad, so...
She pretends
She doesn't mind the silence
That she understands
Then suddenly it all makes sense in the wee hours of the morning
This is God's wake-up call
The Lord says be comforted for I will always love you and never leave
So he gently whispers to her soul it's time to rise and shine so
The act ends

Karen S. Johnson

Earth's Cry

Can you feel the pain while watching the rain, knowing the world has gone insane, all of mans' work has been in vain, losing all we have tried to gain, today our thoughts are all profane, selling the earth for personal gain, raped, wounded, and full of shame, soon we will look to her and to us she will do the same.

Michael Stiers

The Smelly Gurg

In the faraway land of weirdos and things,
Known as "The Land Of Shnurg".
There are Goblins and Ghosts and other Ghouls,
But there's one called "The Smelly Gurg".

The Smelly Gurg is big and fat,
And he can eat the most fattening thing.
He slurps the lard and sips the grease,
And snacks all day like a king.

The Smelly Gurg looks like a whale,
With arms and legs and a head.
His nose sticks in and his eyes bulge out
And his cheeks are always red.

The Smelly Gurg has an awful stench,
Like a skunk that was flattened by a car.
He also smells like Doggie poop
And sometimes like an old Cigar.

I've always hated the Smelly Gurg,
"Don't hate him," says my mother.
The Smelly Gurg is related to me:
He's my stinkin' older brother.

Mykie Pidor

Bring The Children

Take the children before the throne.
Lay them before the Father's feet...
The broken hearts, the mending bones;
the questioning souls, emotions confused.
Searching for answers...
How do I find you?
How do I get it out?
How do I remember?
I question myself.
Kneel beside the unspoken prayers.
Release the power, the might, the wisdom of old.
Prayerfully utter for the release of oppression.
Witness the seeds planted for a bountiful harvest.
A burden of the conscience is no mistake.
You are my earthly angel.
Draw near to me son...
And bring the children.

Lynn Smythe

My Leadership

To solve many problems there is one device. My leadership is represented by the name of Christ.

Many innocent people have cried out for help. But the pain of their hearts has not been felt.

There's a culture that creates wars and pains. But my leadership had stayed the same.

We must hear the poor and the wealthy,
only a fool will believe a sabotaged world is healthy.

It's time to shape the future and to forgive the past, and the memories that had travel very fast.

Even though my leadership may deal with sorrow, therefore it may continue tomorrow.

Tina Jones

Our Dear Mother

In the fall, when leaves turn to gold.
Leaves let go and no longer hold.
The night air chills, the days are short, so are our lives...

Life is so short, so live for today.
Like spring into fall, we have no say.
Cherish your love, and keep it so strong.
There may come a day...and life will be gone.

Winter will come and nights will grow cold.
We will miss our dear Mother, with no one to hold.
Having her with us for so many years.
We've come to depend...But now...Only tears.

In the spring when the sun warms the earth.
The flowers will bloom, divide and given birth.
The tears will be gone...Our memories forever.
Our love will be strong forever and ever.

So Mom... While you're away, and we are still here.
Watch for us coming - we will be there.
Know that we're waiting, while we are apart.
And know that we love you with all of our hearts.

Until we meet again... We love you...

Kathy Blanton and Toni Aguila

Ode To Spring

Old man winter has retired at last
Leaving in his wake a riotous Spring
Such beauty!
The grass so green the forsythia so yellow
The lovely scent of buds bursting into bloom.

The Weeping Willow wearing a lace mantilla
Of soft Chartreuse
The myriad tiny leaves of the maple tree
Shimmering and whispering in the breeze
seem to join the chorus of the birds
in their canticle to the Lord.

The sun peeping in the through the windows
enhancing all colors chasing the gloom
uplifts the heart and the mind
Awakening in the depths of the soul
A thrill of unity
A stirring desire to meet the artist.

Marion Mann

"Free"

Let me free myself from the pouring rain
Let me free myself from the relentless pain
Take me away to the nearest oblivion
Let me free, let me run

I see myself in everybody's shadow
I see myself screaming from below
Close my eyes from this relentless dream
I see myself, but you cannot hear my scream

It is time now escape from life
It time now to embrace my knife
It will soon be over without a cry
It is time now for me to die

But now I come to sleep for good
But now I hide from the place I stood
I lie six feet under, unable to breathe
But now I'm free, I can no longer grieve

Rochelle Messmer

Master Of The Universe

Hear me when I cry, Oh master of the universe.
Let not my tears be in vain, Nor my sorry be in
Shame, restore my soul, and let joy and please abide.

Oh Master, of the universe my soul longeth for
your touch, and my heart morn for your love.
My days or empty and my nights or lonely, my
mornings or filled with despair for ever more
you make, my heart cries for your love.

For in your eyes, I see truth, wisdom, honesty,
Peace, and forgiveness and with in your smile
I see Understanding, joy and love, your ever move
awoke me and your tender voice restore me

Oh master, let not my soul perish for your love.
Redeem my wounded heart, from dying,
and restore my body, with your blessing.
For my strength lies with in you soul
and my prayers with in your trust
Hear me, oh master and set me free.

Mitsie Hines

"If You Love Someone, Let Them Go. If They Return, Love Them Forever"

If you love someone
Let them go
Because in time you will know

Just how much love
Is really there
And just much they really care

They will find their way back
It is meant to be
Just hold on and believe in destiny

Be sure that it's right
Forever is a long time
If it is true love God will be kind

He'll grant you the strength
To carry on
And help the two of you
To press on

If the love returns
Never say never
Hold it close
And love it forever

Lauren Edwards

"Let Us Go"

Daddy turn us loose, set us free,
Let us be where we want to be.
We love you, but we're not happy,
Please Daddy, can't you see?

We know you think your doing what's right,
By putting up this nasty fight.
This fight has gone on long enough,
Do you really think we're all that tough?

Daddy, we're not confused anymore,
We can see right through your door.
It took a while to realize,
We're just prisoners in your eyes.

Sometimes we get hurt and want to cry,
But we can tell by that look in your eye.
The tears swell inside, they mustn't come out,
Because Daddy says it's wrong, for boys to pout.

But one day Daddy, you will see,
That the way we are- is what you made us to be.

Nancy E. Sexton

Reflections

I rested my eyes upon the land and thought
Life is an endless ray of possibilities -
Possibilities that come with the rising of the sun
Or flow within the current of our veins.

My focus drifted to a pool of water where reflections
Reveal the image of ourselves
And I realized our self perceptions are distorted -
An imagined charade of our destined reality.

I raised my eyes to the beauty of leaves billowing, yet attached, to trees
A solitary leaf lingering amidst its friends:
As we dance in another's presence
But glow in the light of ourselves.

I viewed the rolling hills that crest the valleys low
An illumination of life's highs and lows
As we rise in joy and fall with sorrow
Sometimes our only hope is tomorrow

I sat here upon this earth and characterized the way we live
Our faults, hopes, and loves
I realized my reminiscences are weak
For they shall never contain the courage and strength of human passion

Sarah Mardon

Life Is

Life is not for the individual
Life is for the world together, everyone.
We are a part of each other
You are me as I am you
We needed each other as we need ourselves.
Life is light
Life is love
But most of all
Life is

William A. Smith

In Loving Memory Of Our Grandpa

Grandpa,
Life may bring sorrow and tears but one day all disappears. To be carried to heaven where all comes success, we all know our grandpa's the best. Mellow sorrow, mellow sorrow, alive today and gone tomorrow. Pond and streams all filled with water, this man would give his one last quarter. Happiness brought, happiness taken we'll never again see our grandpa awaken. Not able to see, not able to talk, just one last whisper, we will never part. I'm sorry I never said the words, "I care, I love you gramps, I'll always be there." Like all rocks and grass disappears, no more tears in heaven Sal Palma appears. Full of life and joy no doubt be was, why did he die? Because.
Because. Nobody knows what they took from my mom, please don't cry he is in no pain but within God's hands and no one to blame. To be able to reach in a river and pick up a rock, we all know life's on a clock. Day's shattered and broken without a doubt, grandpa don't cry, your time has just run out. God has called on his mighty fellow friend, Sal Palma hangs strong to the end. Miles walked and miles ran, torn up feet upon the sand. To be there for the family we combined like a knot, now we lost that one special spot. Children he had, grandsons
too, Grandpa good-bye, we all love you.

Sal LoPiccolo

As Shadows Fall

Somewhere between the end of summer and the holidays,
life seems somehow simpler.
Summer's haze, hot and dry, is but a memory,
and the hustle bustle of the holidays has not yet taken hold.

Change is all around us as winds blow,
warm at first,
to stir the imagination.
With dawn's first light,
the frost begins to melt from the roof tops,
and as days grow shorter afternoon shadows,
like long slender fingers,
seem to stretch out endlessly.
Fall is in the air as evenings cool,
the air becoming crisp and sweet.
This is the season where witches and goblins rule the night.

As leaves float slowly ever downward,
Mother Nature prepares for her long winter nap,
and for a brief moment it's as if the world is at peace,
before spinning off in search of a new year.

Larry Watson

To Gary Forever

When we met we were so young we hadn't reached our twenties
Life was like a candy store replete with Good and Plenties
You will find some cynics who deny love at first sight
We are living proof to show that they are just not right

With your guidance I explored my sexuality
Tender hands began to mold a woman out of me
Entering my world I realized I found a treasure
And I ached to cherish all the days and nights of pleasure

For a decade I existed just to have you near
Needing you so much I planned a future rich and clear
But my love was not enough to penetrate your heart
Finally I recognized that we would have to part

Twenty years have passed since then and you've made a new life
There's another woman somewhere whom you call your wife
Many years before we spoke of babies I would carry
But these dreams were buried when we didn't come to marry

I've known other men, affairs begin and then they finish
Yet my feelings for you I fear never will diminish
So I pray that somehow I will have another chance
And you'll come and once again rekindle our romance

Vivian Natah Degani

"His Love Is The Strongest"

His love is stronger than
life's worst pains;
His love is stronger than
the thickest chains;
His love is best of them all.

His love is stronger than
the biggest bull;
His love is stronger than
the gravitational pull;
His love is the greatest of them all.
His love is the strongest, and the greatest.
But best of all it is free, and it lasts forever.
You be the judge,
How many people do you know who love you enough
to be humiliated, tortured, and hung naked on a
cross while people laugh and mock them, just so
you would not die?
The answer is one just one,
Jesus Christ my Lord and risen Savior.
His love is the strongest!

Nicole Lynette Allen

Above All

Children
Lift up your heads
It's not so bad
You have a friend
that you can depend
I understand you because I was once you
I understand where you're coming from because I have been there
I see where you are heading but please don't go
Life seems not to bring much promise or hope
But I believe you can cope
Life is meant for you to enjoy, grasp, to hold
Only you can mold it
Your future and destiny is in your hands
So my children
Listen, learn, and obey
it is the only right way
You are a star in your own right
Shine for your parents
for you are their Diamonds
Over come those obstacles of peer pressure
be your own best friend
and above all always be yourself.

LaSheila Anderson

"If Only We Knew"

You came to us as a special child, so very meek and mild. To be our light in this dark wilderness, and guide us out of this madness into your tenderness.

If only we knew.

As a child you grew in wisdom and stature, in favor with God and man. If only we knew we were supposed to do this too.

If only we knew.

As the only perfect man you did only the will of God not the will of man. It was in God's plan that we should follow you.

If only we knew.

This was God's plan that you would come and die, and then by His hand be raised again, so that we could be redeemed by the blood of the Lamb, born again and sanctified too, as part of the plan.

If only we knew.

Now as the Light has shown us, or someone has told us, we, the new redeemed, are to share your purpose.

Now we know.

Sharon Ware

"As I Am Resilient"

As I am resilient, I feel more brilliant
like a dark shadow has lifted.
Over the years, I shed so many tears,
I got so sick of my child-like fears.
I learned not to worry, to get over it in a hurry.
So, they would not linger in my brain,
for I would have nothing to complain.
I am resilient, my spirit is much more brilliant.
I live without strain, I suffer from no pain.
Misfortune is long gone by now,
for I get over it quickly, I do know how.
resilient is the way to be, to recover quickly
from illness you see.
So if you are suffering long and hard, you'd
be resilient if I sent you a card.

Susan Lowerre

"Just The Beginning"

The leaves blew across the yard,
like a dog chasing a cat.
The wind ran through my hair,
like fingers.

The sun upon my face,
like a warm wool blanket over my head.
The sound of leaves crunching,
as if someone was walking on them.

The distant sound of dogs barking,
like a soft humming.
And the smell of hot chocolate,
As the families gather around the fireplace.

I knew this was just the beginning of
Autumn.

Kami Marie Kaufman

"What I Found In You"

The love I found with you is like no other.
Like a flower in winter,
Like a snowflake in fall
It's rare, but special.

And the trust I have in you is everlasting.
Like the love we share
Like the way we care for one another.

And our hearts together are forever entwined
As our love grows deeper
As the days roll by
And I love you more.

Lisa Bailey

Perfect Morning

Fresh dew glistens on the ground,
Like a nearby star scintillating on a clear night.
Bright leaves dwindle slowly to the welcoming ground,
As if they knew their place and took it.
Rays of sunlight creep up through the trees,
Like a newborn child learning its environment.
The transparent rays of light are now seen in the misty air,
Swirling fog reveals brilliant illuminated shafts that warm the
frigid ground.
The cool air tickles with every breath,
And warm moist air is put in its place.
The subtle breeze passes by,
Like a stranger in the dark.
The wind seems to play a beat,
As leaves dance to its soothing music.
The morning passes by with every astounding breeze,
And soon is no more.
But it will endure in my mind as the loved,
Perfect morning.

Keith Glass

Cajun Girl

I am a Cajun girl
Living my life on the bayou
Everything so simple
Everything so beautiful
My Grandmere's gumbo
always so good
Money may be tight
But for the life of the richest girl
I would never give up my life or my heritage
as the poor little Cajun Girl I am.

Kelly Rainey

Nature Baby

You were implanted in my womb,
like a seedling in the ground.
You made me see the beauty of life,
like a rainbow after a storm.
You were growing everyday,
like a flower blooms in spring.
You fluttered around inside of me,
like a butterfly dancing round and round.
You moved about every now and then,
like a fish jumping out of the sea.
You let me hear your tiny heart beat,
like droplets of rain falling on a tree.
You were not given the chance to live,
like a cancer without hope.
You were my nature baby,
the child I never knew,
If I had the chance to,
I would give your breath back to you.

Wendy Labigan

The Mist

You slip softly thru my mind
like a spirit in the mist.
I hardly know at times you are there
But when I become still
I see you clearly
Standing boldly, real, alive and forever with me
In the mist of my mind

Such are the soft lights of memory
Always present, yet always elusive
The mist swirls and moves
And for a brief instant
I see clearly
Then suddenly, you are gone

I miss you yet at times
You are more real in my mist
Than you were in my life

The mystery of the midst holds the answers
To all that we seek
And the mystery floats
Gently thru the mist of my mind

Nancy Bright

A Rush Of Raindrops

A rush of raindrops:
like angel tears from up above
the sound of a heart breaking
a dream shattering and a hint of hope slowly
fading away.

A rush of raindrops:
like the sound of a river
flowing over green hills
and through lush valleys
only to end at the beginning.

A rush of raindrops:
like the silent hush of a newborn child
breathing freely with no worries
dreaming of things
to come.

A rush of raindrops:
slowly disappearing into only a mist
leaving the imagination to wonder...
if rainbows
are to follow.

KayeLynn Bivins

Teach My Love

When my soul frays so,
Like fields of grain in the torrential rain,
You soothe me, comfort me.
You envelop me in your warm-light glow of love.

I say "I don't know, I don't understand."
You say "It's OK, just let it be"
"But there's no reason! It frustrates me!"
"You're doing what you need to do"
"But I don't see, it's just not there!"
"And that is because you are looking"
"But I'm numb, like I'm in a coffin"
"That scares me, for I see you withdraw from me.
But I will love you, for that is all I can do"

And when my soul frays so,
Like the stricken vessel in storm-tossed sea,
You love me, simple love me (unconditional)
And with this given love,
The sea is calmed.

Rudy Smith

Ghost

Light is radiating from the morning sun
Like my bed I unravel coming undone
There are memories of whispers now silent
A lost murmuring of laughing sentiment
Your eyes sparkle in the dewy rose
The spirit of the mountain misty and flows
They like you still hover around
Calling your name without a sound
There is a part of me you stole
Your smile bright, glowing like coal
You have left but you are still hounding
You're in my head painful and pounding
Your footsteps still walk in my room
False promises just add to the gloom
Blinded by a mass of brilliant sunlight
I see you evaporate into the night
A ghost of love with secrets concealed
What you really thought is never revealed
So many dreams of you are taking their toll
Old lovers never die, they just haunt your soul.

Shirley Bolstok

Love Lost And Locked

Listen close my weary friend to a tale both sad and old.
Listen not with your ears
but with your heart
or better, old friend, with your soul.

For there once was a love that had no strings
that was free as the wind and sea;
A love that was strong, deep and unwavering —
a love that just wanted to be.

And there once was a heart that beat with such passion,
listen close for its echo remains.
It was pure as a child and as bright as the sunrise
and as warm a clear summer day.

But that love was rejected—it took more than one blow
and at first it was bent but not broken;
And the heart made a case to try—try again—
but that love was now shy and unspoken.

So, now only those that know just where to look
can glimpse it but not set it free;
it is locked in a place that is dark but is safe
and no longer wanting to be.

Mary Jo Shotting

The Storm

I lay on my bed
Listening to the rain tapping on my window
Watching the rain soak the ground
Listening to the thunder
Watching the storm

The rain is my tears soaking the pillow
The thunder is my heart pounding
The storm is my feelings for you.

Sarah Johnson

"Drugs"

Drugs are greatly amongst us today,
Literally killing our youth, making their minds go astray.

Eating them up, from the inside out,
Putting deadly chemicals in their bodies without knowing
what they're about.

Rolling a joint, taking a hit,
Not even caring if they burn their lip.

Tapping their arms trying to produce a vein,
Not realizing that what they're doing is inflicting
mental and physical pain.

Buying some coke, cutting a couple lines,
Just like that commercial... your brain is frying.

Cooking up That crack, making a rock,
Wake up people...this nonsense has to "STOP".

Make a change now for it's never too late
Throw away those quills, needles and pipes and just go straight!

Shamada Reed

"Reflection"

The leaves in autumn, arrayed in all their "Golden-Glory",
looking as tho each were touched but the "Master's Hand"
"Blessed" for all their labors done, "under the sun"...
"Seasoned" from all their long-hot-days and cold-damp nights;
giving shade-and-shelter, to all-God's-creatures...
reflections-of-the-days-gone-by:

Once, the green leaves of spring, budding out their wing-shaped bodies;
"like angles" providing protection to all who came under their boughs...
now weathered-and-wind-blown, clinging to their last days as
part of a living tree...

Time-worn and withered, soon returning to the earth; "as weary-souls
resting upon the mother's breast that sustained them during their -
Year-long life...

"Pausing" for a season to "GIVE-GLORY", before passing on, to
make way for the leaves that will bloom again, next spring.

Ecclesiastes 3-1:
To every thing there is a season and a time to every purpose done;
"under-the-heaven".

Karen Haymaker

Matches

Love's eye scans the horizon
Looking for compassion,
incongruities and intensity.
Matches are quick and satisfying
Mismatches can wrench the soul for generations!

Sheila Baylis

Looking Over the World

Looking over the world, I see so many sad faces
Looking over the world, I see so many happy faces
I see tears of joy, I see tears of sadness
Tears flowing like the rivers and lakes...
It's not the world, but the people in the world,
We must rebuild, we must reach out to one another,
Where has compassion gone? We must find it and bring
it back... Where is the respect gone? We must learn
to respect one another, then when we are looking
over the World, we will see that all of God's people
are beautiful.

Myrtle Allen

Mother On Welfare

I wake up each morning, to two beautiful sweet faces
Looking up at me waiting for love.
My heart filled with fears, doesn't understand,
Why these two beautiful faces will never taste the
love of someone who's left them behind
The struggle of our everyday existence, to
supply my children with love, food, clothing, and
space for them to grow, is left for me alone.
If not for help from cold and faceless strangers,
There would be no hope for us to breathe
If not for these beautiful, sweet faces
There would not be love, there would not be hope.
If not for the help of cold faceless strangers
there would not be "us"
If not for my children, there would not be me.

Monica Payne

To My Mother

Dearest Mother of my love, whom I ask the
Lord to keep safe and sound and full of love.
I remember what father said to me,
A mother is a treasure that God gave
To you
Don't forget her and always love her for the life
She gave to you
Dear Mami I sure love you in my mind you always are.
When I hear of your prayers to my mind
You come to me.

Rosie Bowman

Love Be

Love be a mystical world where life and happiness are our
hosts,
Love be unlimited and everlasting; a fearless immortal ghost.
Love be a bridge that leads to heaven and
sadness never lead us back.
Love be a sacred jewel, and diamonds would never lack.
Love be a gift of friendship that would never go to waste,
Love be a tasteful passion, that time would never haste.
Love be not a sadness or loneliness that would cause us pain,
Love be a crystal sky, and sun to chase away the rain.
Love be a medieval castle and a fortress made of gold,
Love be a priceless gift; too important to ever be sold.
Love be a lending hand that would never expect return,
Love be a necessity of life, and a lesson we all should learn.

Lydia C. Siciliano

Angels That Fly

Oh angel of my heart why do you fly and fly beyond the tears of my heart. The height of your flying lifts my spirits beyond the rivers of my tears of sorrow. The breeze of your wings comforts the fire of my burning desires. Angels that fly never die in a pure heart wings.

Rambha B. Chappell

True Romance

True romance is the only form of life,
Love for one, that comes from the wife.
True romance is the kisses in the dead of night,
Love for one, or a friend and a fight.
True romance is the power of forgiveness,
Love for one, after seeing your mistress.
True romance is the final plea for chance,
Love for one, and that saved last dance.
True romance is the dying breath of fear,
Love for one, that ends with a tear.
True romance is the bite of dust,
Love for one, with a heart of rust.
True romance is the cry of fate,
Love for one, until the next date.
True romance is a way of life,
Love for one, and their suicide knife.
True romance is the end of all,
Love for one, then your heart takes a fall.
True romance is the purest form of love,
Love for one, that comes from above.

Michael Denning

What Is Love

Love is a river that winds to the sea
Love is a field between you and me
Love is a mountain we cannot climb
Love is a boat on an ocean of time.

Some people say Love is only a thought or a word
Some people say Love is really a bird
Some people say Love is not really there
That it's just a fancy, a thing of thin air.

But love is hope and showing you care
Love is for those who will always be there
Love is not just a word or a thought
Love is something won, not something bought.

Love is to be cherished, not thrown away through the years
Love is something that lasts through all of our tears
Love is something to keep really close to your heart
Love is something that lasts till death do you part.

Rowena Lorraine Taylor

What Is Love?

Love is being happy, love is having fun.
Love is like playing outside, when there is sun.

Love comes from one's own heart.
It gives and receives but seldom falls apart.

Love is tenderness and being very kind
Yet it's from our heart and also in our mind.

We should all possess love and offer it to
family and friends.
But here on earth it's not likely, as we know,
hatred never ends.

Loving and caring for each other, is what
we need to do.
God bless those who are doing this
to me and all of you.

Victor Daniel Gallegos

Love

Do not feel alone
Love surrounds us through our journeys
It's always there watching and waiting
Laughing with a sweet soul and warm guiding thoughts
Someday we will embrace this love
The day we understand more than we know

Tanya Kracinski

Fields Of Angels:

There are fields of angels growing in small towns everywhere
Loved ones taken from us before we were aware
Amidst the floral tributes, echo anguished voices crying
Please take care..... Please take care....
Each has left an imprint of laughter, love and tears
Permanent and lasting in parents everywhere

Long ago there was a mother, who reluctantly gave her son
To a world full of hatred and corruption, so God's master plan
might get done
He sits now by the Father, His arms are open wide
To welcome fields of angels, and keep them by His side.

He offers this same solace to those they left behind
His comforting Holy Spirit will with each of us abide

Just ask and He will answer, He'll help relieve the pain
He'll fill your heart with memories, He'll help you smile again.

Stand silently in fields of angels, when overcome with grief
And surely you will hear, the whisper of the Master calling
I am here.... I am here....

Nancy J. Thorndyke

A Wife Is

A wife is caring and compassionate
loving and giving
sincere and honest
Someone who is there day and night
A warm hand and heart at all times
good and bad
A shoulder to lean on when
nobody else cares
A warm partner who listens to problems
The person that you respect and trust
Someone who will sacrifice her limited time
to give unconditionally for her man
To have and to hold
To protect and provide for
The sunlight in a man's life
One of God's greater gift in a lifetime
A wonderful woman who holds the heart
of her husband close to hers
This wife is my Kathy
I love you my wife

Ron Chandler

When The Green Lights All Turn Blue

When the green lights all turn blue, cross the street to
luck's there's just you.
You were in chains to the comestibles
All imposed morsels were detestibles
Now no worldly vexations and demanding clamor, seek out the
hunger pangs hammer
See the fine wine with the transparent lies
The sandman's gone no varietal disguise
The check out stand is out of date
The new order rules on fate
When the green lights all turn blue
There goes a new and sagious you.

D. W. Hayden

Star Light Star Bright

While I sit with the sky as dark as night.
My heart just glows while wondering does your do the same.
Or am I the only one who's feelings just glow as bright as a
star that lights up the sky like a light. Are your feelings
as near and dear as mine for you? Is love dark like the sky
or as bright as a star that glows like a light in the darkness
of the black sky?

Melissa Spears

Freedom

Look at that bright light in my eyes
Ma'am it is pretty
Ain't it freedom?

It's love in a gentle bit,
Not master throwing his whip
Ain't it freedom?

Running through streams, meadow and mottons
Not in the hot fields picking cotton
Ain't it freedom?

Moses is coming soon tonight then everything
gonna be alright

The star from the north is going to take
us home
With God help we'll never be alone
That Freedom!

Natalie R. Arnold

Portrait Of A Woman

To paint a portrait of a woman.
Made to be: protected, provided for, and cultivated.
Called along side to help.
A gracious woman, girded with strength and strength in her arms.
She fears the Lord, and for this, she shall be praised.
Harvest in life depends entirely on what is sown.
Her diligence to sit at the feet of Jesus allows her to see:
her worth as a woman through God's eyes.
Complete stability in Christ, that's her goal.
And on this, she will remain focused.
It's not where she stands, but the direction in which she is moving.
A loser, that she most certainly is not!
She knows that she is what God says she is,
And that she can do what He says she can do.
Strength and honor are her clothing that's why:
Her worth is far above rubies.
A woman of this rare beauty, is a joy forever.

Kandie Lundy

Untitled

The past makes its way to the present
Making it hard to forget what you don't wish to remember
Your past is a part of my past
Now that you are a part of my life

You have been hurt so many times
Your heart reaching out, but reluctant to take hold
You've seen how much I do care for you
Without asking for a return
Feel the comfort of not being alone, and never shall be again

To know that you are missed, and loved by one
I'm here for you
Every time you need me.

D. J. Smith

Jeanne

Her eyes, the color of emeralds,
mesmerizing at a glance.
Hair the color of gold,
long and beautiful.
Her smile, brilliant and breathtaking.
A heart full of love and care,
with a fire never to be extinguished.
A body smooth and voluptuous,
electrifying to the touch.
The most sensual woman I've ever met.
A love that you would do anything to keep.

Robert M. Elliott II

A Christmas To Remember

T'was a Christmas Eve long ago,
Mary's face was all aglow.
For unto this virgin maid was born,
Baby Jesus, God's Son to adore.
Joseph was filled with wonder,
Mary had much to ponder.
He lay in a manger of straw,
As foretold in God's holy law.
No room in the inn, born in a stable,
In a manger not a cradle.
Angels sang praise to the most High,
As shepherds and wise men all drew nigh.
They followed a bright and shining star,
And traveled so very far.
They brought gifts - gold, frankincense, myrrh,
Baby Jesus caused their hearts to stir.
Long they waited for their King,
For salvation He would bring.
May the Christ Child born long ago, I pray,
Fill your hearts full of love on this Christmas Day.

Susan K. Arnold

God Is Watching You And Me

Stature of steel, heart of stone
merciless man of the deep
He's dwarfed and sometimes lost
when the decks are pitching steep.

Mighty and intimidating,
though the galleon be;
'Tis dwarfed and sometimes lost,
beneath the angry sea.

Still the sea with all its force,
though alarming to the eye;
'Tis dwarfed and sometimes lost,
beneath the stormy sky.

Still that sky, with all its dreadfulness,
that drives us to our knee;
'Tis dwarfed and sometimes lost from sight
for God's watching you and me!

Oh, Lord My God, How Great Thou Art!

Michael T. Laramore

Fifty-Four Years On A Bottle

Fifty-four years on a bottle —
Milk, oatmeal and soy bean gruel,
Grandma said, "Give that baby a bottle,
To starve little tykes would be cruel."

The bottles he took soon were larger,
Cokes, Fizzes, and Strawberry pop,
Lemonade, tea—all confections—
Each consumed in its time and its place.

There is soup from a thermos for lunches,
Steak, sauces and condiments more
Come onto the table each setting,
From out of the cupboard's good store.

Fifty-four years on a bottle —
The journey must be half way o'er,
But he'll keep using straws in the bottles
And trying for Fifty-four more.

Lawrence H. Lancaster

A Sunday In The Park

Jugglers on the grass, balancing balls of color,
Mimes in the meadow, moving melodically.
Kites flying child-tied, bouncing in the breeze,
Mothers talking measuredly—stroller hawks.

Lovers linked hand-to-hand, basking in their blissfulness,
Families gather at their tables, eating mother's gifts.
Floating butterflies breeze-borne sailing away—-
From snapping dog jaws, salivating sunshine.

Laughter-laced air joyously laps the ear,
The happy universe surrounds with beauty.
Busy chores of living, forgotten in peaceful noise.
.... Simply, Sunday in the park.

Steven J. Schimmel

Minute Men

Life is but a moment, a flicker of brilliant light.
Minute men who race against the tide of time.
Lighting across the earth, the senses barely receive.
Each mission but a breath too mysterious to perceive.

Minute men who race, the goal in visions mind.
Striving forward, slipping back, straining against the wind.
Mighty marching minute men, thunder rolling across the sky,
Death the unescapable victor, revelation beyond the eye.

Past the portals of the moment one can never know.
Death keels the hour, nameless minute soldiers fall.
Minute men rush on pausing at fate but to gaze.
Life is for the present, the light to swiftly fades.

Listen, a flutes sweet melody dances upon the breeze.
Amidst the clamor of marching feet the harmony stirs the soul.
Pause and contemplate, feast upon notes uttered so elusively.
The song upon the wind, an invoking invitation, to immortality.

Tomorrow holds nothing, the cup is full today.
Attend to the sweet melody, listen to the piper play.
Life is but a moment, lightening across the sky.
Man a lonely soldier who knows that he must die.

Valoree Hickman

The King Of Thieves

Princes inherit a name of great respect, but Kings
Mold from ambitions and conquering great kingdoms
That thrive within the world which they have created.

Nymphs, with sweet smiles and hearts that burn
With the fires of a fierce passion, unlock their
Souls to roguish Kings.

Feelings of untapped tenderness run through the
Veins of those seeking their links of fulfillment.

The moon looks over the world and spots us,
Mingled within our captured souls.

Chance brings together two persons with raw
Passion and eternally entwined existences.

Experiences unimagined, deep labyrinths that have yet to
Be discovered. Time is thus given to those of curiosity
Who will explore the sea of life to its fullest extreme.

There are always possibilities which, in time, become reality.
With this nymph there is a possibility that her King of thieves
Will take hostage her most valuable possession.

Kim Campbell

If Only For A Moment

If only for a moment I could put you in my place. If only for a moment I could have you feel my pain. If only for a moment I could have you shed my tears. If only for a moment.

Everybody has their own individual way of dealing with pain and healing and, if only for a moment people thought before they spoke, then maybe only for a moment it might be understood what I am feeling.
If only for a moment.

We all take too many things for granted in life and, if only for a moment you thought about what it would be like not to be able to do the things you enjoy and look forward to doing, then maybe only for a moment it might be understood what I am feeling.
If only for a moment.

If only for a moment you thought about what it would be like not to able to laugh and smile, then maybe only for a moment it might be understood what I am feeling. If only for a moment.

If only for a moment you thought about what it would be like to fight a battle you thought was never going to end, then maybe only for a moment it might be understood what I am feeling.
If only for a moment.

If only for a moment you thought about your worst nightmare coming true, then maybe only for a moment it might be understood what I am feeling. Because, only for a moment I thought of mine and now, I alone, am living it.

And now, because of only for a moments thought, each night as I lay myself down to sleep I pray that my family be kept safe and never have to feel this pain, and that they only have to feel this pain, only for a moment.

Susan Sutula

Memories

Memories are made of things that happen everyday
Moments as we've lived them, things we do or say
Little bits and pieces of laughter mixed with tears
Paragraphs and pages we've written through the years
The carefree days of childhood, the growing pains of youth
A few illusions shattered by the endless search for truth
The friendships we remember, mistakes that we regret
The times with someone that we loved we never could forget
Yes, memories keep happening, each one a different kind
Each one a separate chapter that is printed in the mind
We can't erase the sadness, or edit out the tears
We can't undo the wrong we've done, we can't relive the years
But since memories keep building, each day can be the start
Of making new and happy ones to store within the heart

Michele Lombardi

Moments

There have been many moments of sadness in my life.
Moments I remember that were painful.
Moments such as loneliness.
Moments I've been teased.
Moments I felt like no one cared.
Moments I felt like no one was there.
Moments I wish I was not there.
Moments people have said they hate me.
Moments people said they don't care.
Moments I feel it would be better if I wasn't there.
Moments I've been laughed at.
Moments I wish I had not experienced.
Moments I've been yelled at.
Moments I wish I could get away from.
Moments I wish I could forget.

Leah Marie McNally

Ashley's 1st Halloween

It's my first Halloween ever
mommy was going to be clever.
As she cut and sewed to make it just right
we heard a scary noise! "Oh, it's Midnight".

As I got dressed and all snapped in
daddy smiled and said "I love my pumpkin".

Off we go to trick or treat
to get lots of candy for us to eat.
Knock, knock, on the door as I wait for my candy
what a surprise, it was Raggady Andy.
I looked at him and gave a big smile
then we walked around for over a mile.

The sun is going down and it will get dark
I knew I was close to home, I heard Midnights bark.

All undressed and out of my costume
I looked out my window to see the full moon.
Good night for now, it's time for bed
what a wonderful Halloween fresh in my head.

Susan E. Derby

San Felipe

A white narrow strip, ribboning its way by
Moonlight to a remote village steeped in loneliness
Surrounded by pulsating tides drawing in and out
The life line of the people.

Here the twin barren mountain points converge
In brilliant, blue bay, prominence showing off
The tiny fishing vessels, bobbing cork-like on
Fickle, fecundate waters.

Little dark faces, drawn by meager existence
Appear with wares, sea shell woven
Lightened by purchase, gleefully off nickel in hand.

No laws here, existence unhampered
Moves on in simple servitude and self-preservation.

Moonlight bathes the silvery white sand
The glistening water, shimmers as I lying
On my back gaze, in silent wonder, at the cosmos.

Cosmos shot with fantastic lights deep-basined canopy
Of moon, stars, planets. Light years, did you say?
Fathomless, spaceless, shooting into nowhere
Timeless, existenceless.

Patricia Ahrens Stewart

Los Angeles

City of Angels, by an ocean great
Mountains and desert surround the throng
Of people, hurrying, scurrying,
To points known only to them.

Sea Port, Movies, TV, Aircraft
All support the great hoards
While sunshine smiles upon all
Who venture herein.

Earthquake, fire, mud and flood
Challenge serenity
Of those within and around the spreading masses
Of people and cars.

This city beckons many
And more have come
To share its warmth and scenic views
And ethnic ways—of colors aplenty.

Some will stay and some will go
Children born and families spread
Some are buried, some are fed
But the city remains and calls once more.

R. G. Lestak

A New Beginning

You came as a caterpillar,
moving slow.
Weighed down with an aching heart and frozen tears,
yearning for a new day.

Then you learned the truth.
You were not alone.
Tears fell as secrets were revealed,
together you wove your cocoon.

A time of work and struggle,
you accepted the challenge.
Building accomplishments with tools of change,
reaching and growing to help each other.

A new day is dawning.
Here is a different creature,
with wings of beauty.
Free to choose where she will fly.
With joy and wonder,
Ready to begin a new beginning.

Sarah Altman

What Happened?

Blue eyes, brown hair,
muscular build, not too big though.
Nice car, great personality.
Thought you'd never lie to me.

What happened? What'd I do wrong?
What did I do to lose you?
I don't know, can you tell me?

Why'd you lie? Why'd you say one thing and
do just the opposite? Why did you leave me?
Will you take me back?

I don't want to go through any more, pain.
I just want to know...what happened?

We had a good relationship. It was strong, full of love.
Then the flame went out without a warning
and you were gone.

I miss you.
I still need you.
I just have to know.
What happened?

Melissa Fazio

Celestial Rhythms

Droplets of thought enter my mind like a procession of
musical notes. Spiraling and never ending, the melody
awakens a part of me that I somehow , and somewhere, lost
along the way.

I am resurrected; alive from the swirling cosmic streams of
emotions and feelings that radiate from her heart. The
baptism is total.

Engulfed by the randomness of the of universe, I find center with
her. She cloak me with the primordial dust of the beginning
and I start to spin in synchrony with stars.

I reach out and pull her into me, and am overwhelmed by her
rhythm of life. I am forever lost in her spirit only to find
myself.

The blending of our fluids; the spark of life, takes me on a
trajectory out from this mortality. I see glimpses of her in
their smiles. I hold their tiny hands only to feel her
gentle presence.

I sway in concert to her songs that cross the night sky and
quietly hum the gift of love she has given me.

Rocco J. Verducci

Untitled

The story of love and dreams
Must now come to a close;
What the future has in store for us
God only knows.

In the beginning of it all
Love swept us away;
We cherished every moment
And pledged our love would never stray.

I thought that you and I
Were going to always be together;
I thought you were the one
Who was going to be in my life forever.

As time has drifted by
We have learned what we are all about;
We are two different people
With different outlooks, without a doubt.

Only time will be able to tell
If we were meant to be together or apart;
But no matter what happens
I will love you forever with all my heart.

Krista Ann Marven

Maybe

My nerves are dead so I can't feel,
My brains so warped, I don't know what's real
I only know I love you.

My arms don't move so I can't write
My legs are stiff, I can't take flight
I only feel I love you.

You're all I see when you are near
When you speak, you're all I hear
But you don't know I love you.

My heart just dies when another's ring you wear
My soul begins to cry when he plays with your soft hair
And you don't care I love you.

Mark Francis

Message From A Black Man

I am growing old, I fear that I have failed my people.
My children have outraged me so that I don't care for them no more.
I feel sorry for others like me, the sick and the dying, who are being
disrespected by two bit hoods that I call my own.
This is a message from a black man who can't remember much,
but what I do makes me horrified for the future.
I thought we had overcome the wars, but in my attempt to find
happiness, left me to find that my own destroyed my home.
This is a message from a black man, a fool and his dreams.
Yes, this is a message from a foolish old man, a fool for a better
place for the good.
This has been the last message from a black man.

Robert Greenwood

Gizmo, My Friend

Gizmo was a friend of mine
My mother sold him for a dime
I cried all day I cried all night
Then I thought I lost my sight
I said, "Mommy please don't take him no!"
Sorry honey he has to go
So that's the story of my pet
I will get him back, but just not yet.

Kyla Yvette White

Of Soldiers Past

I lay beneath the earth at the mercy of sin
my country made true
Of unwritten blood in written stone
I still remember you
Access to hell with pennies of passions led
treacherous lies of truth
Admirably graced danced our hopes of compassion
Admirably graced danced was I as two
You cheered me away and away stood I still
Alone bye the memory of you
Real might be the answer to the question
that is
Favors of wonder
Will you remember this?

Linda Force

The Panther And The Butterfly

Be still, my love, and let my hungry eyes devour you.
My eyes that never blink can't follow your titillations.
Can't fathom your incessant flitting, flirting, fluttering,
Your incandescent light is like a candle glowing from within
Drawing me into your circle.

Be still, my love, and let these giant black paws cuff, cup, maul
and use all means to quell your capricious, tantalizing moves.
If this is war, can I use my array of weapons too?
Then I will still you with a swift jab through the heart.

But what can I do to erase the dust of your wings from my
paws, how can I rid myself of it,
so that I can live to play the game again?.
Be still my love.

Sarah Baker

Precious Moments

Our baby girl, a new life;
My family became more than just husband and wife.

A bundle so warm, as I gazed into her eyes;
A feeling more wondrous than I could surmise.

We were a family and read "The Cat in the Hat",
A kingdom of riches, in the chair where we sat.

A giggle on the rug, a kiss goodnight;
A healing hug just felt so right.

But life goes on, through years of school;
And sharing warmth was no longer "cool".

The kingdom faded; no kiss, no hug.
So I sit by myself, in the chair, on the rug.

For precious moments, we share what we feel;
A glimpse of the warmth that was so real.

It's not too late, to listen and share;
A kiss and a hug need not be so rare.

Lewis Cotton

To The Guy I Like

The moment I saw you walk down the hall.
My heart skipped a beat.
Ever since then my feelings for you grew stronger and stronger.
I can't imagine a day without you.
Knowing that you are somewhere with someone else just breaks
my heart.
I sit in bed at night and wonder "Do you feel the same for me?"
"Would we ever be together?"
"Would our friendship get in the way of thing?"
Please let me know how you feel!

Nicole Newberg

My Family

My family is special, my family is great
My family is full of different people
And one of them is Kate!!!!

Some people have short relatives
Some people's relatives are tall
Some families are big, and some are small!

My relatives are Filipino, Italian, and French
Some of them do their nails and some work with a wrench!

Uncle Jim is fun and he's really really nice,
Aunt Lou and Gram make great black beans and rice!

Abu's really great and he's also very tall
He's married to Beba and she's very small!

I have a lot of cousins, and step cousins too
Specific numbers - ten cousins and out of step
Cousins - Michael and Gregory, who's new!!!!

Kate Bastida

Gizmo, My Friend

Gizmo was a friend of mine
My mother sold him for a dime
I cried all day I cried all night
Then I thought I lost my sight
I said, "Mommy please don't take him no!"
Sorry honey he has to go
So that's the story of my pet
I will get him back, but just not yet.

Kyla Yvette Whitetep

My Side Of The Wall

If I could go back in time, I'd know how hard to fall
My feelings I would keep inside; brick by brick I'd build a wall
From my side of the wall, I'd tell you that I cared
From your side of the wall, you might not think that's fair
From my side of the wall, I'd hold your hand in mine
I'd say how much I loved you, keep my love forever blind

If I could stop the hands of time, before one moment I recall
When I felt your love was safe and climbed upon the wall
Declaring my love to you and the world, no shame had I to hide
The feelings I had poured out my heart, the ones I'd kept inside
You helped me down to your side, put loving treasures in my hand
But then our time was over, like an hourglass out of sand

If I could see the future, I'd see a bigger wall
One too tall to climb upon if I felt the need to fall
A wall so high and mighty, no voice could penetrate
My shattered heart surrounds the key, to the long and rusty gate
With stones so thick and heavy, I would never hear the call
Of any other love to be-on my side of the wall...

Shandi Lynne Murdoch

I Called

Leave a message after the beep...(BEEP)
My love, I thought you were
My life, I thought you'd be
My feelings for you deeply, Came out for you to see
You didn't show affection, You didn't seem to care
You don't want my presence, But ache when I'm not there
You always say you love me, You never show me how
You say you're thinking of me, But say it's not right now
I want you in my life, I need you with my soul
Your love would build my faith up, And make my body whole
To you I send this message, So please don't be appalled
To you I send this message, To let you know I called.(CLICK!)

Tameka Norton

Friendship

Do you have a friendship that never ends?
My friendships always bend.
Everyday I go to school,
And everyone says I act like a fool.
Everybody laughs at me,
And I feel I want to flee.
I ask a girl if she like me so,
As most girls say, she said no.
I try to do something to take my mind off it,
But it's stuck in me bit by bit.
I try to concentrate on what I need to do,
But my mind wonders off in the clear blue.
Why do people dislike me so?
I don't think I ever will know.
I close this poem saying why,
If there's a girl without a guy,
Hey at least it's a try,
I know when pigs fly.

Ronald J. Deifer

In His Eyes

As I walk in the spirit of the Lord
My heart focuses on the things that pleases him
My deeds of faith cometh from love and my service
looks not for any reward
For my reward awaits me in heaven
I was once in the darkness of evil
But now I dwelleth in the light of peace
I feel the warmth as I carry the light
And I mourn to share with those in need
As my faith grows stronger
I praise and worship him
I rejoice and give thanksgiving for I suffer no longer
I must set aside thine past
For I am renewed with a spirit that will last
I must strive forward towards the goal
And serve and love Him with all my soul
For when the final day arrives
There I will be In His Eyes

Troy P. Gacayan

Tears That Burn

I'm feeling lost and don't know which way to turn,
My heart that makes my eyes shed tears, my face they burn.
Someone tell me do I turn left or do I turn right?
Which way is darkness and which way is the sun that shines so bright.

Lord please tell me why my tears burn my face?
Am I going to be lost forever or am I going to find a place?
Lord please tell me why my heart from inside wants to burst?
Will the pain feel less or will the pain feel worst?

Lord when I smile I'm really crying to cover my pain.
I want to cry more so when I smile I feel something I've gain.
Lord I wish I could pretend that there is nothing wrong,
That's when I need you most; I need for you to make me strong.

My tears they burn my face but, Lord you wipe them away.
As each day passes by they burn less than they did yesterday.
I know I'm going to make it, I have you by my side
One day to my burning tears I be able to say good-bye.

Maria Gonzalez

Untitled

He loves me, he loves me not — as the last petal falls to the ground
My heart grows heavy and I look around

I start to cry - I'll always be alone - that's the way it must be
Because no one could ever really fully understand me

I don't know what will happen or what I'm here to do
But I know I'll never hear him say - I love You.

Mónica Cedeño

Love And War

I met you on a party night
my heart was pounding and I was full fright
we were all chillin and had no place to go
you looked to me like every other john doe

There was something special in the way you smiled
it had me hypnotized on you for a while
I wanted to say something but I didn't have a clue
if you would try to clown like some boys do

At first I was a bit afraid
my courage is no way comparable to superdave
I did not know what to say
you probably had a girlfriend anyway

Your smile so pretty and so nice
every time I saw you I needed some ice
to cool me down from head to toe
I found you weren't the average tom dick or moe

Your timberlands and you karl kani's
those sleeting looks and your round black eyes
it took all the courage to come your way
and then you smiled at me and that made my day

Ngwebifor M. Fobi

Two Roads

External religion, or living God, that is
my hearts choice
To follow men, or to follow Christ and hear
my shepherd's voice
Law of rules, or Law of Love, which one
shall I chose?
A life of failure, or a life of glory in which
I cannot lose
To save my life in reputation, or Lose it to
gain "His life"
To live in harmony with my maker or live
in constant strife
the decision is mine, the choice is not hard
- He's the better part
O' precious Light of Israel has become a flame
inside my heart

Kim Rees

My Uncle Lamar

My dear Uncle,
My hopes, my dreams,
My everything a little girl could ask for and more.
I remember all our good times spent,
Every waking moment with you was heaven sent.
I came to see you as often as I could,
But we still never got to do the things that Uncle and niece should.
The holidays when you would come home I stayed by you tight,
Wondering if you had to leave again or could you spend the night.
Your artistic talent and ability to live,
I wonder why no one seen the love in you like I did.
You are a uncle I would of really liked to have known and now that
You've left me,
A part of me feels empty and now I don't know which way to go.

In loving memory of: Uncle Lamar Toledo
The one I love and the one I lost.
May you rest in peace and carry my heart and soul with you always
Forever in my thoughts,

Nerissa Sherrod

"The Ticking Of The Clock"

Tick, Tock, Tick, Tock
my hours, minutes in this world are short
I feel death as it is knocking on my door
The time is coming when he will burst in
Now I know what is the truth of battle
as I see many of my buddies, dying on the battle field.

I hear the machinery sounding in the air
I hear a soldier screaming with pain
a bullet is piercing, pounding, penetrating through his flesh
I see the tears in his eyes as he says:
'Oh God, I want to stay alive.'

I am shooting the enemy like all others who are fighting for the old U.S.A. I am proud to be an American and defend our country but I am desperate to get home from this dry and desolate desert
when all of a sudden I feel as if my insides are going to explode.
Oh no! I'm shot!
I feel something spooky entering me
Oh god! I feel cold and weak
the ticking of the clock has stopped
death is no longer near, it's h...e...r...r...

Veronica Marie Dominguez

Love Messages

Glorious sunlight sink into the sea
My love is so far across the land from me
Two hearts wanting to be close, now sigh
For their wanting could well cause them to die
They send messages on white clouds
And on cool moonlight nights where shadows linger
Remembering lovers arms like boughs
Reaching out for each other across the space
Two beings wanting to join the race
Of bringing souls together at long last
A loving dream of love two from the past,
Those sweet times together lived so many times
Recalled so vivid in both their minds
Both look forward to when time will depart
When sweet joy both will not again be apart.

Sanford W. Brown

The Seduction Of Love

As I gaze into the enchanting colors of fall,
my mind and soul are overwhelmed with desires

My passion for him is mesmerizing;
his silhouette so alluring

I am seduced by his every word;
aroused by his every gesture

Oh how I wish our lives weren't so feverish;
the pleasures so entrancing

I long for his tenderness and sensitivity;
I need his everlasting love to breath

I want his presence close by my side;
I need him to love me similarly

Though love is a miraculous feeling
its effects can be poisonous to one's self.

Letitia Pagano

An Ode To Dad And My Pipe

T'is a special occasion, the birthday:
My mind is always going back to childhood.
I sit in warm wonder, cobwebs form around the hearth,
I've learned EVERYTHING and NOTHING, the SHOULD.
The WOULD and the COULD.

Life is a moment, an ever ending moment.
A man is held tightly as air in a brown paper bag.
A child is an emotion lying dormant,
To grow cold as a tombstone, only to bloom then sag
Like flowers watered, fed, cherished, then discarded onto a coiling heap of placid worms, gorging on the decay of flesh and its bone and its spirit; a meal, delicious with vibrant EXISTENCE.

CHILDHOOD, a luxury of the past
Yearning for its libertine, free flowing magic.
A whimsical splash of fresh exhilaration.
The young man and the old man yearn for their joy-past;
They will obtain it,
They must gain it.
Time, only a memory, fleet, and filled with meaningless ablution.
Let childish time be a merry journey betwixt birth and death.

Michael Loring

"And When The Morning Comes"

As I toss and turn, hoping and praying for sleep
My mind is filled with burdensome problems that pile in a heap
Yet I know, God takes care of me, all during the night
And when the morning comes, everything seems alright.

Life seem some what chaotic when sleep won't come
My body and mind feels like an exploding atomic bomb
Yet I know, God takes care of me, all during the night.
And when the morning comes, everything seems alright.

As yesterday's today's and tomorrow's problems arise and repeat
Some people tell me "exercise, drink warm milk or count sheep"
Yet I know, God takes care of me, all during the night
And when the morning comes, everything seems alright.

With an overwhelmed heart and mind, I cannot let go
Yes, I have this awesome feeling that my mind will blow
Yet I know, God takes care of me, all during the night
And when the morning comes, everything seems alright.

Lucille Foster-Fitzpatrick

Why

At times I sit alone and ask myself why?
My mind races with thoughts and my eyes cry.
People are suffering from disease and pain.
Babies are born addicted to cocaine.
Kids killing kids to gain respect.
Drug dealers are collecting welfare checks.
Children being molested; the elderly are beat and robbed.
A father with a wife and children is without a job.
People are mistreated because of the color of their skin.
Is the world really near the end?
Wars started over religious belief.
Blood and oil being spilled in the Middle East.
Children over the world without food to eat.
People everywhere are living on the street.
At times I sit alone and ask myself ... Why!
Life is unfair and then we die..... Why!

Robert Dillard

Sunday

When I was a little girl
My mother would clean me up
And make my hair into curls

My socks were white
And I had to sit still
Till it was time to walk up the hill
To the church painted grey steel
Where the children sat in the back
and old ladies were decorated with
multicolored hats.

The preacher would swoon, scream and cry.
The old ladies would "Praise the Lord" and sigh.
The old men pretended to be awake
For the Lord's sake.

The children would squirm and yawn
Wishing it was time to go home.

And there we sat,
Children, old ladies and old men,
Til the sermon's end.

Mendall Kaye Rogers

Nightmare

I wake up! My hand plastered to the bed,
My nails trying to tear through the sheets,
My eyes like a hawk's wide with fear,
Glued to the ceiling like wallpaper on a wall.
Suddenly a black panther jumps out and vanishes into me.
Unexpectedly my body cools like sand and lies in a pool on the bed.

I dream I'm in a jungle running for my life.
The trees reaching out trying entangle me in their branches.
The leaves are suffocating me. Broken twigs scratch my legs.
I come to a dead end a black panther awaits me with grace in his eyes.

I wake up in a cold sweat, moisture dripping from my face like
water from a faucet I'm finding it hard to breathe,
My pillow clings to my face from the sweat,
My legs are knotted in my blanket,
The animal's hair sticking up straight jabbing me.
My curtains are blowing wildly from the wind.

I get up and grab for the door but find myself
holding on to a panther's paw its nails are digging into me.
I collapse with fear, terror and horror I'm clueless when I wake up.
I don't remember a thing but I have claw marks on my hand.

Kim Smith

The Pond Road

There are yellow violets
  Near the moss beneath the tree,
For it's springtime along the Pond Road
  And a special day for Grandpa and for me.

Over in the meadow it's all white;
  Wild strawberries are in bloom,
Beside an old log, daffodils
  Stand in yellow uniform.

As we slowly make our way
  Back to Grandpa's Model A
It seems like it's been
  Such a special kind of day.

Oh Grandpa, what a legacy you left me.
  For fifty springtimes I've traveled,
Down the Pond Road in memory,
  As we did so long ago,
I often pause to wonder, if you know!

Marjorie K. Legters

Thank You Lord For Johnny

Thank you Lord for Johnny and his special love for me,
My only son, and what a joy, dear Lord, you gave to me.

I know you're first and foremost; that you watch and care for me,
But just for added love, Lord, you gave me J-O-H-N-N-Y.

He puts me on a pedestal, where no one e'er belongs,
Surrounds me with flowers, fills my heart with song.
It seems so many years ago, I cared for him each day,
Never one time dreaming he'd return that love one day.

His heart is oh, so big, Lord, and made of purest gold,
He ne'er forgets or ceases his undying love to show.

His life is very busy there in the business world,
But somehow, he finds time for his very special GIRL.

When death came for a visit, as it eventually does,
Right beside me, all the way, my special Johnny stood.

He sees my every worry, each heartache and each care,
Within the twinkling of an eye, there is no problem there.

Though miles may separate us, and have for many years,
He makes the time, he takes the time, for all a heart holds dear.

Again, Dear Lord, I thank you, for this special son of mine,
For deep inside I realize it is Thy Love Divine!

Mary Evelyn Edmundson

God Made Me Too!

When you look at me, look deep inside
My outer appearance has much to hide!

My face is different, that is a fact
I can't speak like you do, but that is no act!

My looks to you may appear strange
My body may have been slightly rearranged!

I have to work harder to reach all my goals
But I do have feelings, emotions and a soul!

When I try to speak I make funny sounds
Sometimes others resent my being around!

Some people accept me, some people don't
But those of the latter, can't try, or just won't!

If you're in this group, for you I will pray
Cause like it or not, I'm here to stay!

So don't look at me like I belong in a zoo
After all ... GOD MADE ME TOO!

Scherri L. Douthit

I Love You

How do I say good-bye?, when I hate to cry.
My pain, is no game.
To you, what shall I do?
I love you, more than the God above you.
it hurts to see you with another, why I can't
seem to find a new lover.
The passion I feel, is so alive and real.
Your touch allows me to live in this dream, as
though it seems.
I love you more than the devil below you.
For a moment you give me a touch, a kiss or a bunch.
This feeling shall end, only you can let it begin again.
A few years ago, untouched we were alone.
My only wish is that I can live again, until then
this is the end.

Ronald Rovinski

"Hymn"

I would like the sea to carry
My song of happiness -
For the waves to scream!
With every pounding of their waters,
What is love and sorrow,
What is joy and pain...

I would tell the lonely beaches
And whisper to my stars in the night,
That I'm not alone any more,
That I can reach for the skies...

I would make the wind jealous of my soul,
Because, in this precious moment that I know
He loves me,
I cry and laugh;
And my happiness carries me away
In freedom with the sea...

I'm part of the ocean now,
And I'll be forever singing
This song without words,
This song, as old as the world...

Sonia M. Neil

Gentle Winds

Last night as I stood beneath your sky,
my soul thrilled at your revelation.

So great and so distant was your expanse,
yet so near that I could feel your gentle caress.

Distant rumblings of a storm brewing to the west,
soothing night sounds to the east.

So different, so separate, like two worlds,
and yet here was an oneness, a completion.

My soul expanded to a new level of awareness,
humility was mine as I felt but a part of the whole.

My heart is akin to your midnight sky,
as your gentle breeze guides the clouds of my life.

Your earth beneath my feet, your sky a canopy above,
and my soul is the doorway for your gentle winds of love.

Lisa Knight

My Teddybear

All soft and furry,
My Teddy is magic.
It has the powers to put me to sleep.

A farmer's straw hat,
Small enough for Teddy,
Sits on its fuzzy, brown head.
A ragged cloth, many years of age,
Covers the length of its small body.
She is only five inches in height.
She is as chubby as bears come,
Around the middle.

Even though she is a worn out, old, stuffed teddybear,
Her dress torn, a button eye missing,
To me she is beautiful.
In my imagination, she is fairy,
A radiant creature of protection.
Who can control my ability to sleep at night.
Who every night I pull into my arms,
Gently pushing all thought away.
I believe my Teddy is...magic.

Mary A. Horsey

Moving On

I have walked along a course unknown.
My thoughts and my wishes, were never my own.
For years I knew that something's been wrong,
but I knew what I felt and I could not move on.
As years past I kept hoping for change,
but instead I found myself feeling enraged.
Since time does heal all wounds, I found
myself discovering something new. My
feelings changed and strength I grew.
My dependence vanished and my independence bloomed.
I started to focus on myself for a change.
The blinders came off to clear the haze.
I always thought it was something I had done,
to later realize it was a woman I had become.
My mind is getting clearer and my hopes are alive,
I could only hope this anger subsides.
I am beginning to love myself and my life.
I am finally moving on to live my own life.

Michael Schena

An Ode To Life

As I look at life today at sixty-three
My thoughts meander back through time to see
The generations of family that belonged to me.

Oh, what a beautiful life unfolds on the tree of life
As we see the elders of yesteryear and the babes born of a recent wife
One can only say that God has blessed us all in spite of strife.

We count our blessings every day as we toil and work
And marvel at the sky, the stars, the beauty that surrounds
our every perk
Of health, happiness, ability to smile and cry and look at life
without a smirk.

We cannot turn back the clock of time to yesteryear
When drugs and crime were not as rampant, and whole family
values were held dear
Foul language, child abuse, lack of respect for the elderly were
loathe to hear.

But today we marvel at the technology of telephone, TV and the video
Add to that the sophistication of the jet plane, computer and Hi-Fi radio
And as we approach the 21st century new wonders of development
become just so...so

Dear God above, we thank you for allowing us to share in some
of nature's beauty
And though we now approach the twilight of our life becalmed
and not moody
We want to live out our life the fullest, and share with our
children life's boundless booty.

Robert W. Cameron

Drugs

Blinded by my illusive appearance, controlled by
My uncanny powers. I'll take your money, mind, and
Your life.

Those who place their trust in me are disillusioned
By my cleverness. I am superior to those poor
Insecure souls.

I shake my head and laugh even at their torment. I
Grow stronger by preying on their pain and weakness.

Sooner or later I will be the victor causing total
Destruction, which will end their plight and mine to.

Until another victim shall surely succumb to my
Wishes..but I can not understand why?

Linda M. Rankin

Why?

I sit in the empty theatre by myself, starring at the black screen,
My whole life is like a big picture window.
I see my family, my friends, good times, tough times,
and relationships with ones loved and hated.
A light blared out from the screen,
and a hand reached out to my face.
I felt no fear, just peace.
But I don't understand, why do I feel hate inside my heart?
The hand read to me that hate was only in my mind,
but loved filled my heart for myself and others.
I can't let my guard down to anyone.
I will get hurt, or hurt others. Every time!
Why? Why do I do this? They were so kind and loving to me
and I just shunned them away. Help me... please. "You can't
know the answer to every question Natasha,
you're only human. Keep peace with yourself and God.
Give others a chance to let down their guard, and both of you
will come together as one,
lovingly and soulfully." Silence filled the theatre, it was dark.
Mind clear. Break down the walls.....

Natasha Ro Mell Adkins

Twelveth Avenue Terrace

Like a peaceful Resort, quiet on kind
Near a busy city caught up in time
As we get older it's time to rest
To enjoy our life, reflect on the past
The twelveth avenue terrace a nice place to be
We have earned the solitude on security.

Ron Wyman

Girl From Milk

Men want to taste her like bees
need their honey

But she's not letting anyone in
'cause she is waiting

For the one who can see that she's walking
with the seasons

Changing colour everyday
Girl from milk, girl of ivory

She's collecting petals in her pockets
of all sizes

The stem inside her is growing the more
she wishes to be happy

Growing right out of her mouth when she
opens for another tongue

She will never forget the taste of corn flower
here bell, blue anemone

Come drink my milk
Come touch my ivory

Changes colour every day
Today she is blue

Katja Zaraste

Just A Moment In Time

Just a moment in time. Just a moment of sorrow.
Nowhere to turn. No chance of a better tomorrow.
Many lives have faded away, because they had no reason
to stay. A fire is burning deep within the soul of man.
All creatures are walking around with their hearts in
their hands. No passion for life, many lives full of
passion, and love is just a natural reaction.
Just a moment in time. Just a moment of sorrow.
Nowhere to turn. No chance of a better tomorrow.

Marcie Buckingham

Coronation

To everyone it is weal, to Seneca it could heal
Newton thought it was a plan, for power, speed, and weight
He thought it beyond mere man and always akin to fate
Kant, when in the depth of mind, feeling its chronic limits reign
Knew men had bought themselves in kind, a strange serpent,
a crazy train
Einstein doubted the pallor of power, trusted God's judgement revealed
Remained faith-ful to the cosmic tower and unified the field
For Will Rogers it was perdition, to Cervantes it ripened all things
For the soul it was the mission, for the musician it's color rings
For Goethe it was abundance, to the poet a storm and a winged car
To Gandhi it was thank-less, to the astronomer a whirling star!

Ralph M. Gulbrandsen

The Sweet Asylum Flower

No happy voices calling outward,
no happy faces to look toward.
No happy songs, no paradise,
no one to hold you, to share your life.

Darkened voices of anger and untrust,
a thousand souls die and rust.
Voices calling forever confused,
receiving no answer, forever used.

Cold concrete walls fill your head,
empty darkened halls haunt your heart.
Left to die in this eternal hell,
your soul slowly drifts down this darkened well.

And, within these walls of hate and madness,
through a window, shines a light of forgiveness.
In a darkened room where no one goes,
you silently watch the sweet asylum flower grow.

Korey Snyder

In God We Trust: Truth

One Nation under God
no jurisdiction on the truth
we pledge allegiance to the flag
an idea or an image
freedom, equality, bondaged dreams
we hold these truths to be
confirmed Gospel, dictated verity
that all men are created equal
Stars and Stripes your sign
mottoed come one, come all
declaration independent
entitled and endowed
foundation by their Creator
unalienable rights: life, liberty, happiness
oh beautiful spacious skies
His grace from sea to shinning sea
reliance on sacred honor
protection of Divine Providence
we, the people, on bended knees
plea healing in the land.

LaVerne Harvey

An Old Man

An old man sitting all alone,
No life, no friends, nowhere to go,
Unhappy in his loneliness,
Left all alone just to rest.

An old man chatting with himself,
His heart is screaming out for help,
No one listens to his cries,
In silence and seclusion, an old man dies.

Kyle Ickes

Children Are Tops

Your faces always carry a glow,
No matter how sad, love must show.
You are always eager to read,
Listen to the teacher and please take heed.
Reading will get you through this world
Wherever you go.
Your teacher taught you well so let it show.

Stars shine brightly in the sky at night,
Learn your lesson, so you will be alright.
Obedience pays off in the by and by,
Love your self and hold your head high.
You are so special and your teachers are too.
Education is precious and so are you.

Vel Captain

When You Fall In Love With Your Dreams They Will All Come True

I say dream till your dreams come true
No matter what others may say to you
It appears that some have let their dreams
been washed away by the rain
And now it seems the only thing they can feel is the pain
So I still say, dream my friend
Dream till it comes to a good end
But please don't fret
Because you can bet
That there are some poor souls that never dream at all
And before you know it the sandman will call
But sleep these don't know how to do
So they not only never dream
But what dreams they would have, will now never come true
Most dreams are only good
Give them a chance if you only would
Then I know that someday all your wishes will come true
Because dreams were meant for people like you

Robert Lee Elliott II

Love Always.....

A day of joy, a day of pain, a day of tears that's been kept away.
No more waiting for this day to come, a time to leave that special someone.

Telling them you'll miss them so, feeling the pain of having to go.
Wishing them joy in all that they do, hoping that they'll never forget you.

Yes, the time has come and this is our last, for your future will endure a special past.

Never to forget the things that you've done, leaving time and change for things to come.

Holding a special place in the heart, for the things you'll remember from ending to start.

Now wipe your eyes, it's a time to be glad, rejoicing, exciting, the things that you had.

I will miss you dearly, your heart knows I will.
You'll always be special to me.

Selena Walden

Black Moon

No cries of praise to Mother Earth
No Mother to soothe the papoose cry
The cradle boards, they rock no more

The blue haze of pipe smoke... No longer lingers
Black moon in the sky
The communal fire no longer burns
And the tribal chant can't be heard

No feathers and no war paint
Just like brave and courageous warriors
These have perished and are long since dead
Black moon in the sky

But on the trail of tears
I've heard the weeping
And the many secrets they were keeping
And for them I've mourned

Scarlett A. Smith

Please...

Don't buy me diamonds, ermine, or sable,
No, not even mink, though your budget were able.
I don't crave a caddy, a penthouse, or yacht,
For, I'm afraid, a gold-digger I'm not!!!!

But there's one thing I NEED, beyond any doubt,
Like the air and the sunshine, I can't live without;
It costs not a penny or nickel or dime—
Not even a dollar - just a bit of your time.

A glance, a touch, a kiss, a caress,
A whisper of love, and tenderness.
Give me these, my beloved, and I will possess,
Riches beyond measure, and deep happiness!

Marguerite M. Badour

My Beautiful Hero

The most beautiful person,
No one can see.
The most beautiful person,
Lies inside of me.
No one knows it,
But she's always there.
No one sees it,
But she does not care.
She goes from place to place,
Always left to roam.
She has never had that special place
That all others may call home.
She cries herself to sleep at night,
Works herself into a fright,
Because she lives out on the streets.
This beautiful person, that no one sees,
Sleeps with the grungy and the sleeze.
This beautiful person no one will ever know.
This beautiful person, she is my hero.

Shellie R. Taylor

The Little Bird Who Couldn't Sing

Wasn't that a terrible thing?
No sound was made on sunny mornings.

She dug her worms in silence.
Her belly full of thistle seed,
She couldn't express her joy.

Not even a peep to express her thanks
with rapturous glad tidings.
Instead, in muted silence she had to cling
and listen to her neighbor's song
and wonder at the voice of spring.

Ralph Martell

Images

I went on a boat ride, to another land
Nobody there to lend me a helping hand
I see a creature far away
One that wouldn't be seen in my day
The creature moves up to me
Then jumps into the distant sea
I jump into the sea and to my surprise
As soon as I jumped in, the water began to rise
I started to swim round and round
Until I came upon a coral reef ground
It was colors of pink and red
Then I saw a shark's head
I started to swim and came upon a wave
I decided to hide in a small cave
I looked out and saw a blue whale
It's the largest animal on everyone's scale
I closed my eyes and shut them tight
And tried to think with all my might
I opened my eyes and I was in my bed
For all these things were images in my head!

Samantha Kelly

Sitting here in this darkness of mine
Not knowing what to expect
Not knowing if things will ever be fine
All due to this neglect

I feel inside so alone and misunderstood
I don't think anyone would understand
Even if they said they could

I felt like I had to let someone know
My hidden tears were beginning to show
To him molesting showed acts to "affection"
My anguish all along his horrid intention

To think that this could be happening to someone else
Was in itself enough to drive me insane
I could not ignore it
Because my reality could also be their pain

Silent I no longer choose to be
Now your faced with my childhood tragedy
Secrets I unchained from me
The darkness released and the pain set free

Lisa Marie Geinosky

Nightmares Do Come True

She came to me when we were small to comfort - no, that was not to be. She came to me when she was sad. She came to me when she was mad, now we are so very bad.

She came to me and gave us pain before we even knew his name. Then there he was to ease his own, and she came to give us more.

Then all was quiet, 'cept for fights and we would hide - stay out of sight.

Tug-of-war was their game; now she was theirs, the child with no name.

Their all gone - buried deep, but we're not yet free for we cannot weep. Her reality is false, only fantasies exist. Our realities are the nightmares which will persist.

Tina S. Klein

Untitled

I know I put them somewhere, my memories,
notes scratched on scraps of paper, unformed
thoughts that had not the time to evolve,
pictures I meant to draw,
the crooked tree branch,
twisted mouth,
the line that never found its end.
I know I put them somewhere,
would never have discarded them,
could not have erased all those moments of
spontaneous enlightenment,
visitations of clarity,
buried in all the other stuff,
the bits and pieces of me.
I know I put them somewhere
to finish at some later time.

Kim A. Watanabe

Pretty Pictures

Pretty pictures is what you've painted,
nothing more and nothing less.
Painted a picture of what you wanted the world to see,
to think, to feel -
complete with pretentious purpose and belief.
Hiding behind a mask,
truth is foreign to your kind.

Empty words spilled freely and thoughtlessly from your lips,
day in and day out, year after year.
Pretty pictures is what they painted,
nothing more and nothing less.

It is no surprise that the colors have faded,
revealing selfish, shallow desires-
the extent of your vanity.
Such a shame,
life was only pretty pictures,
painted by your own hand,
nothing more and nothing less.

Marie Hurt

Distant Love

When you're not around and I'm all alone,
  Nothing seems the same.
I have to wonder if you love me,
  Or was this all a game.

You've been gone so long without a word,
  My heart is more than confused.
I sit and think about what we've shared,
  Was it love, or have I been used.

I've always been there by your side,
  To lend a helping hand.
We've strived through so much to stay together,
  That's why I don't understand.

Not knowing is the hardest part,
  Of how you really feel.
It seems unfair to put me through
  This emotional ordeal.

I can't handle your distant behavior,
  I don't know what to do.
But in my heart I know I'll always,
  be in love with you.

Robin Rutkosky

Suffering

Born with innate sadness,
Now I'm afraid of madness.
Machiavellian fingers daub and desecrate,
And shuffle through the fibers of my fate.

The comfort of a coffin is what I'd choose:
A respite from this barbaric bite and bruise,
Fire to light the way home is cold,
Never to rekindle, or so I'm told.

Could they be so dogmatic?
Even Aristotle would think it enigmatic.
Their hands command imperially, and body appears sane.
But Hades conducts that apathetic head, which carries a moldy brain.

I'm fettered with tethers of a single race might,
Dousing the flame that once glowed so bright.

Fallacies are harvested every season.
And every death comes without reason.
I wish I were deaf to unjust screams,
Or sick in bed, blind to the scenes.
But without my family I could not be,
Without my brother next to me.

Kevin Crocker

Uncle Jimmy

God....be hospitable to him
now in his death days
Hospitality will be my remembrance of him.
She served him well and still....he was -
is - a lonely, lonely man. Her children
always came first. Oh how he needed her
to be his love thru their years. And, now,
on his deathbed, unable to speak, to have
eye contact,

His visitors are afraid to touch him - touch
the death of this lonely man. He lay there
empty of love.

I will not be among them. Yes, Uncle Jimmy,
I will whisper in your ear, pray into you,
beg you to know of love in your dying breaths.
I will hold your hand, say yes to the response
I'm not imagining. Hold on sweet uncle.....
receive love from our God - as you have given
to me as a little child over a glass of
anisette and many Christmas cookies.

MarieElena Sarnicola

Looking Back

Looking back at it
Now, it was all
for the best we said
our last goodbye
With anguish and unrest.
How could we let
it happen?
How did we let it end?
When all our hearts
were looking for was a way to let
love in.
Instead of seeing the future, we look back
on the past and our hearts still ask
the question,
Why love didn't last?

Stacey Fawley

Little Girl Doe

Found in the fields was little girl Doe
Now lying silent with tags on her toes
Who is this girl, everyone wonders
And where is she from all sit and ponder

She could be no more than eighteen years old
Her heart may of been black or of solid gold
She had dark brown hair and eyes the same
Do you know her, can you tell me her name

She cannot answer where she is from
And cannot talk she's forever dumb
No help or claim has come to show
For the years ahead she'll be little girl Doe

Killers have taken her will to live
Her alias they're unable to give
No one to give her identity
And we're forever puzzled as to who she may be

Michael Britt

"Wake Up America"

Over two centuries ago we were blessed with the constitution
Now our forefathers must be restless in their graves
With the events unfolding today damaging the very foundation
It is making their great.... grandchildren slaves
The society of today has no moral obligations
Hideous are the means justifying expedient enclaves
Those were the puritans and the pioneers for pro-creation
Here are the politicians surfing on immoral waves
Everything is saleable in the name of civilization
Jingoism is the motto of self-declared braves
On and on we can continue until the crucifixion
But brethren, is the constitution for the people living in caves?

Mohammed K. Mohiuddin

Years Narrowed Once More

For years they had done the routine together
now they disclose assets of another kind
for this is the day of truth..........
Their minds melt together: Washed in dwindling light.
Things not known of one another come to them
as naturally as breathing itself.
Two minds, two bodies..........
Filling the air with their cries and laughter.

For what they wanted was to become their mutual reward.....

No longer are they separate:, and never again
would it be an individual desire..........
But what burned between them was only the
beginning of a new entry into life's on going saga.
Never to let sunshine be spent waiting for darkness,
to hide what their eyes would not accept in sunlight.....

Because this day a child was born and the gap
of years is narrowed once more..........

William Epperson

Nothing Dark Will Come

My mother used to tell me,
Nothing dark will come.
At first I believed her,
Then, I discovered the truth.
Nothing dark will come,
For darkness is already here.
You and I both know it's true.
We can see it everywhere.
Darkness must have come some time,
Or was it darkness that created the earth?
From every view it seems to make sense,
Except from the view of light.

Sarah Nelson

"My Eyes Are Blue"

Hello Mother, Hello Father,
Now to you I am no bother.
Don't feel guilty, don't be sad -
I want you to know, I'm not mad.

You didn't let me be born on Earth,
Someone told you I had no worth.
Mommy, you thought I was just some tissue,
But if I'd been born, I'd want to kiss you.

Jesus loves me, He loves you too -
Accept Him as Lord and you'll know it's true!
I love you now more than ever -
Please accept Jesus, so we can be together.

I'm up in Heaven, it's wonderful here;
There is no sorrow, nor any fear.
I'm waiting for you, I miss you so;
God wrote this poem so you would know.

I'm up above, I'm waiting for you -
And, by the way, Mommy,
My eyes are blue.

Tom Doscher

Untitled

Best friends we once were
Now we stand together no more.
Something happened that got out of hand,
I'm not sure what, I don't understand.
I remember how we were inseparable.
Now were separated and I'm miserable
Whenever I needed a friend you were there,
You were the only one who seemed to care
Now your gone and I'm alone,
I wish that you could hear my silent moan
But every time I try to call my words seem to die and fall
And now I'm writing this to you
Because I wanted to make sure you knew
How much our friendship meant to me
And friends again I hope we'll be.

Katie Curry

Time Flies

When I was young, the days dragged by:
Now when I'm older, time surely does fly.
If only there was some happy medium,
Not so slow as to cause tedium,
Just slow enough for me to do
All the things I'd like to.

I'd like to chase a rainbow or two,
Gaze a while at a sky of blue;
Walk the beach through the gentle surf;
Spend some time on my own turf.
I'd try to count the stars at night:
I'd like to live, and do it right.

I guess I'll accept time flying fast;
I'll run toward the future, learning from the past.
I'll take each day as it comes to me;
I'll be thankful for each sunset I see.
I hope time slows down a bit,
Someday soon, I'd like to just sit.

Mary S. Erickson

In Memory

It seems like yesterday, you were here with me
Now your picture is all I see
I want so much to hear your voice, to touch your face or see your
smile
But, I'd have to travel a million miles
I know you're safe in Heaven above
But I still need your undying love
I hope one day we'll meet again
So I can thank you for being a great friend
I have your picture in a frame
I only wish it could be the same
As it was yesterday when, it seemed, you were here to stay
Sometimes I pick up the phone
Only to realize you're not going to be home
I guess you never really know
How much each other means to you until they go
I loved you dearly and now you're gone
I hope you know, my love for you lives on
In my heart you'll never die but when I think of you I will cry
Only because I miss you so and I didn't want to see you go.

Paula C. Felder

Foster Grandparenting

F rail in physique, but staunch in spirit,
O nward moves this segment of humanity in their 60's, 70's or 80s.
S teadfast in the performance of their daily duties,
T racing their oft trodden routes.
E eagerly looking forward to embrace their responsibilities.
R eading, talking, or dancing with their individuals.

G oing there or coming here as they fill the Rapaport corridors,
R ound and round their wheelchairs go,
A bly steering them around the Agnews premises.
N either wintry chill nor summery heat could
D eter their spirit from their job performance.
P atiently wiping mouths and running noses,
A lways caring and foreseeing their wards every need;
R eady to lend a helping hand to give them comfort,
E ver alert to keep open channels of communication and love between
them,
N urses and hospital staff nod approvingly as
T enderly and lovingly they care for these hapless beings,
I nstead of loneliness, they make the blind see and the deaf hear,
N amed aptly Foster Grandparents and Senior Companions,
G od-sent are these volunteers to our special children.

Lilia L. Evaristo

Extinction Of The Whales

A long time ago on a brisk
October day,
Sat on a dock a young fishers
daughter
Whom everyone called Sarah May,
She sat and she listened, she
watched for the whales,
She had heard of their beauty, their
power from the old fishers tales,
She sat and she waited for those
beautiful whales,
She sat and she waited on those rusty metal nails,
Everyday she hopes to see them rise,
Who knows what beneath the sea lies,
The whales haven't come, they won't still,
We all know they never will,
The girl still sits there to wait,
But, we all know she's just a day
too late.

Rosa Lynn Hagedorn

Shadow

I feel that I only stand in the shadow
Of a presence
Too superior
To withhold

I feel that I only stand in the shadow
Of a life so great
And a passion
So bold

And I often sit and envy this presence,
This potential, so beautiful
Yet so hard
To attain.

What if the sun sneaks away
From this presence?
The shadow is gone
And I am left in pain.

I feel that I only stand in the shadow
Of a presence so near
Yet so far,
But at least I stand

Vanessa Anne Turner

"The Silence Of Success"

Unless human beings
of all ages put-away their
conspiratary plots to reach
goals the world among us has no future.
But there is hope if everybody binds together.
Strong words will do nothing.
Action, without violence
will help people who feel
inferior to others, understand
and accept other people.
In order to live in a
world that "works," everybody
has to learn to live with each other.
How else can people live
and get along in a world
That "wall" has to be
broken into, and then its
inhabitants can start
"opening up" to each other's feelings.
Then there will be a "silence of success..."

Larry Bruce Rubin

That's Life

Life is just a dream unspoken
Of many thoughts that are provoking
Moments of bliss, sorrow and sunshine
Elations, depression, recession
Runs with the time
If we could wish our life away
With complete joy and happiness every day
We would become bored, stagnated and stale
Enough to destroy all talents
In every child, female or male
So lets enjoy the moment for the day
Look at moment nature and see the sky
Enjoy the birds flying by
Restore your soul with greater goals
Capture the moment and make it pay
Help your fellowman along the way
With this you will receive
All your blessings forever and a day.

Lucille J. Fritcher

Untitled

Reality falls far short
of the world of my imaginings
Who would not choose, if not prefer,
at least on occasion,
A place suspending time
A garden of love everlasting
and light never-ending
No clouds gathering
No rain ever falling
Soft music and the songs of birds filling the air
Flowers, fields, and trees surrounding me
And those I've ever loved walking beside me
No quarrels subdividing our souls
No conflicts tearing our hearts apart
Peace ruling
-Not by the blood of battle
-Or as the fruit of strife
Would it be heaven I yearn for?

Zena C. Gedz

Faith

Painted rose,
Of your memories.
Holding the candle,
Until it burns your hand.
Seeing,
Until you go blind.
Hearing the sounds that drum away your life.
Inside of you; bitterness,
And on the outside; your fate.
The choice you'll never forget,
To stay,
Just one more breath longer.

Tyler Ugolyn

Immortality

If we seek, we shall find there is no dearth
Of youth who left their mark upon this earth.

Joan of Arc, the sainted Maid of Orleans,
Was burned at the stake when only nineteen.

Patriot Nathan Hale, his life was done
When hanged by the British at twenty-one.

Poets Keats and Shelley, those immortals,
Though not yet thirty, passed heaven's portals.

Alexander the Great, it's verified,
Before thirty-three, had conquered and died.

Schubert and Mozart, by age thirty-five,
Were famous composers, but not alive.

And Vincent Van Gogh, at thirty-seven,
He might have been painting up in heaven.

So many achieved fame before their prime;
Would that I could before age ninety-nine.

Sherry Levy

Nature

Nature is such a beautiful thing!
Oh how I love to sit and listen to the birds sing.
Or to see the animals playing merrily with one another.
Or to see a baby deer running to its mother.
Or seeing the flowers bloom in the spring,
And smelling the wondrous scent that they bring.
Or to see the majestic mountains rising high into the sky,
Or to sit beside a lovely pond and watch the fish swim by.
Or running down a hill of nothing but green,
Or swimming in the ocean with no islands to be seen.
Oh, nature is such a beautiful thing.

Misty Olivia Chapman

Unlike

Unlike the stars above,
Often covered by clouds that fills the sky.

Unlike the leaf of a tree,
that has its season to die.

Unlike the shores of the sea,
that often meet with sand and stone.

Unlike the beauty of a Queen, as she sit upon her throne,
Now you see it perhaps later it's gone.

But how to explain my love for you
These words will never do.

For it's like the skies.
But only when they're blue.

Filled with the warmth of sunshine
knowing of a heaven above
Built on a foundation
of nothing less than love.

Raymel Everett

Dreams

Yesterday I moved into the old house Grandma used to live in.
Oh Grandpa used to live there to.
They have been gone for sometime now.

Last night when I laid down to sleep,
dreams of them crept into the shadows of my mind.
They were sitting on the old porch swing telling stories to their
Grandchildren. Of days gone by, of times gone by,
of people gone to other places.

As the stories unfolded before me, they looked out
across the fields to a place that they could only
see in their minds. Of green fields and white fences,
of towering steeples and of God.

They are up there now. Up there with people who had
moved to other places, of friends gone before them.
Up there where JOY is their future, of LOVE

Kathy Amoureux

Oh My Little Precious One

Oh my little precious one, a gift from the angels above.
Oh my little precious one with your smile just as bright as the sun,
and your squeals of laughter that delight every me.
Oh my little precious one, all through the day you like to sing
songs and play with the ball and I can see your love for me
without one word at all.
Oh my little precious one, then you got a new hat, we look at you
and see that it doesn't get more precious than that.
Oh my little precious one everything you do is taken in and cherished
throughout my heart and I've watched every second right from the
start.
Oh my little precious one and pray with all my might that you will
be safe throughout the might.
Oh my little precious one, what did and ever do to deserve this
love from you?

Kimberly Carter Beal

Wicked Game

The cloak of darkness brings a
peculiarity about this juxtaposition.
Their affinity, with bated breath, sums the climate.
Why this wicked game to make them feel this way?
Significant other's hearts are hardened.
But, there is beauty in passion, it burns
like Christmas embers.
Forget not of pain in this wicked game.

Mike Russell

Mamie B. Anthony

Seems like she's been around for years
Old enough to predict our own fears
Saw a lot come and go
My great-grannie, I love her so,
Born in the first state of flight
Born not to slavery
She is free by right
Black coffee and toast
Which is chosen as everyday fare
For a 97 years old woman,
very, very rare
But who is to tell her so?
not me indeed
For she, in so many words, would tell you,
"Don't tell me what I need!!"
Mamie B., Mamie B.,
Four generations, she has lived to see
Saw many moons come and go,
My great-grannie, how I love her so.

Victoria Robinson

Change

Sitting on the roof of my barn;
On an old quilt from long ago.
The wind blowing the hair off my face;
To the North, the South, the West, but not to the East.
I wish upon a star, I feel my eyes squint from the grin
on my face as I think about my faith in such things.
Leaves blow all around me;
yellow, brown, red, and orange, but not green.
The crickets play a familiar song.
The song on mind, so long ago.
Memories of younger times spring through my mind;
Oh how I ache to go back but instead I'm faced
with one option: To go forward.
I walk home, grass under my feet;
Hard from the kiss of fall.
And the crickets change their song.
This song is new and unfamiliar.
I think I like this song. I do.

Whitney Hooper

In The Dusk Of Life

As time goes by and we look back
On talks and accomplishments attained
We see more clearly the abundance and the lack
The ingredients needed in all we've been trained.

Through these many years of labor and love
We find a great measure of peace and joy
In sharing our faith in the God above
With man and woman, girl and boy

The tasks have changed through the years of time
Those illnesses, accidents, pains of all sort
The stress and the strain beyond reason or rhyme
The choice is ours, to rejoice or retort.

It's so encouraging to see as years go by
Those many ways our children express
Concern and strength for a will to try
And show to others His will to bless.

Though many of our goals we had to change
The years of experience give us the plan
In spite of needs, circumstances or range
With God's help, we do the best we can.

Louis Reincke

Lake Storm

I think Lake Michigan is "getting it" today.
On the horizon lightening is slashing in jagged lines
Straight down to where I know the water is.
The way the wind is tossing the tree leaves
I know the waves on the lake are whipped into a frenzy,
The water dark and threatening,
The whitecaps fleeing in fear to the shelter of the shore.
The fish must be descending at rocket speed
To the safety of the deep.
This lake and I have an affinity
For storms like this affect the ebb and flow
Of my own blood.
That's how I know
My lake is "getting it" today.

Viv Latus

Night Cry

As the afternoon puts its faded laughter
on the shelf of time,
the night sneaks in with a spell-binding blackness.
The moon soon comes into view,
and giggles with a shiny cast of delight.
However, the stars cry soft tears,
for the beloved sun is not there to shine with them.
The creatures of the night scamper from their hiding places,
as God watches over His restless creation.
Later, when the night grows old, in the distance,
a wolf howls with a painful agony,
and whimpers his sad song; to his only friend, the moon.
The moon looks down in sympathy, He can only shine brighter,
for the wolf's pain has touched the deepest depths of his heart.
The echoes of his cries and oh, the sadness of his song!
The stars show they care by inviting their friends to listen.
God watches down from heaven and hushes all creatures,
as He puts his little ones to sleep and brings the happy morning
to start a new day.

A. R. Muntz

Those Special People We Call "Dad"

If you are a father
On this special day
You will surely understand
What I am about to say
So listen very closely
With your eyes and ears
Allow my words to touch you
Allow your heart to hear
My father was a special man
Who always gave a helping hand
A man who was gentle, kind, and caring
A man who never took, but was always sharing
A man who worked hard and never complained
A man who was happy whether sunshine or rain
A man who watched his children play
A man who guided us every step of the way
A man who gave his heart and soul
To his wife and children who made him whole
This was a man I once had
A man I was proud to call "My Dad"

Sherry Lynn Dailey

The Moon

What if the moon could be the Lord's eye,
On which of the world he could spy
Watching over us every day,
As we speak, as we talk, and as we pray,
Seeing everything we do and say,
Learning more each and every day,
Guiding us along the way,
So if you see the moon tonight,
Remember the Lord's eye is still shining bright,
Showing us his eternal love through bright beams of light,
Keeping us always in his sight,
Bringing us his goodness and might.

Nicole Samons

"Soul-Talk"

We don't "fit" anymore. . .
Once we were so close
That our souls intertwined
In a oneness that ruled
The itinerary of each day:
"I thought about you all day, today."

A visible oneness
Oftouching—
Hands, fingers, arms
Magnetically drawn together
Whenwalking—
Shoulders, nudges whenever seated side by side
Be it on a church pew
Or in the awkwardness of a bucket-seated sports car.

But one of us did not want this unique togetherness
— Was drawn away by foreign magnetic forces
— Other glances, other gazes, other intimacies —
While the other half, left alone,
Wept.

G. Martha Jones

Your Majesty, Sire, Your Highness

(To Johnny Carson - March 20, 1992, the last show)

JOY is leaving the Screen
Once You decide to retire
HUNDREDS of US hurt the spleen
Not by Hope....but You Sire.

CARSON Show is the Cradle of Laugh
And We are left with the Sorrow
Really sad that won't be a TOMORROW
Since we learn that without You is rough....
Only You Are the KING and in spite
Nonsense foes, You forever will Light......
The TONIGHT.
May I bid NOW GOOD LUCK and Farewell
Condescendently and Sincere Vi(e)orel

Viorel Berezowski

Gifts

I woke with the dawn, the world filled with song,
Only the birds can sing.
They spread their wings and soared, then sang some more,
Their beautiful melodies rang.
As the dew glistened, I thought as I listened,
They have gifts I cannot claim.
Can they sing because they fly, I asked with a sigh,
Or can they fly because they can sing?
Then a still small voice said you have a choice,
You can do both you know.
If you soar to great heights, with no wings for your flight,
Your heart will learn to sing.
If you sing with your heart, it's really no art,
You can fly though you have no wings.

Virginia Hunt

Images

Images. I assemble the images.
One after another, the essence flows from
one to other. I assemble images.

On a huge canvas, a picture of a catholic
church to the right, a weasel right after,
an adobe stock piled up, a pineapple,
a crescent moon, a hungry Somalian child
with his mouth agape.
And finally the metamorphosis of an evening owl.

I assemble my images.
Images that are sewed in a torturous way,
splattered on the huge canvas.

Oh! I forgot to collect another one!
That is the benign light from the morning sun.
I assembled my images on a huge canvas.

Sobhan Mukhopadhyay

Only A Memory

He's "only a memory"
One day he was a reality but now he's "only a memory"

I hear something in the night so I go to tell him, but I remember
He's "only a memory"

good news about something trivial so I go to tell him, but I remember
He's "only a memory"

I feel lonely, needing to be held so I go to him, but I remember
He's "only a memory"

When I'm scared and need reassurance I go to him, but I remember
He's "only a memory"

As I sleep in my bed I reach for him, but I remember
He's "only a memory"

He calls, comes over and for awhile I have reality, but still I
remember, He's "only a memory"

The love is there always had been, but I must remember
He's "only a memory"

There's been another but he couldn't live up to him even though
He's "only a memory"

One day he might be a reality again, but for now I have to remember
He's still "only a memory"

Nancy Gingrich

Why Me Lord?

Did you ever retreat from every one; thinking you wanted no
One near?
Did you ever secretly cry out for help; knowing no one could hear?
Did you ever reach out for affection; not expecting it al all?
Did you ever refuse and offer of help; thinking it would make
You feel small?
Did you ever strike an inanimate object; then think you were
Losing your mind?
Did you ever speak, and there was no one to listen; to share
Your thoughts, and be kind?
Did you ever stroll through the woods alone; and enjoy the sound
Of peace?
Did you ever immerse yourself in a through of people; seeking
Emotional release?
Did you ever turn your face to heaven; and say, "why me Lord"?
Did you ever think, even in his omnipotence, his scope was not
That broad?
Well, if you have ever had these thoughts; no matter when or
Where. Just remember, what he said in his word;
He knows how much you can bear.

Shirley J. Parker-McCoy

In An Artist's Studio

One face looks out from all his canvasses
One self same figure sits or walks or leans.
We saw her hidden first behind those screens
That mirror gave back all her loveliness.
A queen in opal or in ruby dress.
A nameless girl in all her freshness.
Summer greens, a saint, an angel every canvas means
The same one meaning neither more or less.
He feeds upon her by day and night.
And she with true kind eyes looks back on him
Fair as the moon and joyful as the night.
Not with waiting, not with sorrow dim.
Not as she is, but full of dreams of him.

Robert Lee

"Second Chance"

Nature holds a beauty we should not overlook,
One that is basic and all too real.
If we could do more than to read a book,
We might understand and begin to feel.

Man is the most primitive creature on Earth,
It is doubtful God meant that to be.
From the time we die, all the way back to our birth,
It is highly unlikely that we truly see.

If we were to be given a second chance,
Many would take it, most would not.
But those that did would be able to enhance,
A lifetime of dreams that had been forgot.

Vicky L. Neal

The Wounded Soul

They say that time heals all wounds, but who's to know better than
oneself: the agonized, the loner, the solitude self, whose suffering
is thoroughly felt by the individual soul.

Why is it that emotion, so easy a victim of love and hate's constant
path, is easily snared, until time's solutions come to pass?

The bitter outer wounds of war, baffling to human eyes, yet
wordless to the victim's lips, with soundless inner cries, that fade
into the depths of the soldier's wounded soul.

The helpless cries of hunger, with skeletal wounds unmending,
scarcely leave room, so scars be seen, but vast within the painful
self, with eyes that cry with tear-ducts dry of famine's waste.

Of prisons filled by victims of chances run out, where instead of
feeling self-pity and being down and out, silent prayers prevail
and faith endures of hope for another chance at freedom even
after years.

The homeless, weary of footsteps lost - in search of security in a
rich man's land - to find but cardboard strength and warmth, and
disappear into the night without a helping hand.

Addictions polluting once healthy forms - like beautiful scenery
gone to waste, till sober mind from black-out's nightmare search
- to put events together like jig-saw puzzle to find there's a
missing piece.

So who's to judge better than oneself - of life's trials and paths
well trodden, who's time-given wisdom and experiences never
forgotten, that live forever captured, in the depths of the
wounded soul.

Robert L. Fransua

In My Heart

What's in my heart that you cannot see?
Only I know what He means to me.

He nurtures and comforts thru my darkest days.
He's loving and gentle in all of His ways.

I envision His touch, a dream from above,
reaching out of my hand in unconditional love.

He makes my heart soar; my spirit, it flies;
how I yearn again to look into His eyes.

I pray that He knows with love I adore
each moment He gives me; His blessing endure

His pray foundation is steady.
His promise is sure.
I had but to answer His knock at my door.

What's in my heart that you cannot see?
Only I know what He means to me.

Susan A. Theobald-Harless

The Aged Path

The forest is still and quiet now.
Only the cold wind passes through the trees,
And the grass below grows wild and undisturbed.

But there was a man who passed so often
that the grass remembered his path;
Just as the tree branches grew to allow him passage.
He would walk from the golden field to the dark lake and back again.
Other men had passed before but never returned or stayed long.

One day, the man stopped coming.
His absence was not so evident at first
As the grass and branches still held his path.
But the more time passed, the less the forest remembered.

His path no longer exist now; the grass is overgrown
and the branches intertwined.
The path is now void to the passers glance.

Yet one tree will never forget his passing;
For she wears his name on her trunk.
On his last journey through the forest,
The man etched his love for an unknown girl in the trees bark
and never returned.

Though the forest and the man have forgotten the aged path,
the tree cannot.

Mary Arreola

Little Bird

Release yourself, fly long and free.
Open up to all the new things that surround you.
Taste the best, for the best will
slowly come to you.
Savor the possibilities, for they are
endless - and unknown.
The laws will only be the ground that
you walk on for the journey, put there
to make you appreciate the bluest of skies.
Spread your wings and those skies will
be on your tips, there to grab hold of
when you need its calm the most.
Be the person inside - open, caring, full of
the eagerness for this walk that you embark upon.
Respect and love who you are as well as
those you encounter along your way.
These words I say come not with enormous wisdom,
for my path is still before me. These words
come only from the heart of someone who
loves you for everything you are now... and ever will be.

Lynette Danz

Love Is The Way

Listen to my words I have something to say
Open your hearts and hear my call
Hate is growing everyday
It's a problem far from small

Hate makes us feel pain
It causes much sorrow
Hate brings clouds and rain
Yet, love brings a sunny tomorrow

When it seems there is no hope
Keep on loving and you'll find a brighter day
When hate brings problems and you think you can't cope
Remember, those who choose hate will soon have to pay

Still, maybe people will learn
Hate isn't what we should preach
Away from it we should turn
Letting love be what we teach

All the Earth should become aware
Everyone needs to hear this voice
Hate is waiting for you everywhere
Let love instead be your choice

Sarah Stancato

My Garden - A Refuge

A rose of Sharon pure and white
Opens its petals at morning's light.
A special cardinal without fear
Feeds at my feet while I'm quite near.
Radiant roses deserve their praises.
In my heart, there's room for daisies.
Morning glories called heavenly blue,
Clinging to a rickety fence, are kissed by dew.
Tree stumps stand so straight and tall,
Look like sentinels on a castle wall.
In early spring there are daffodils.
And wild flowers that bloom at will.
A few vegetables have their place.
Best of all is the open space-
That allows me to lift my eyes
And feast on the beauty of the boundless skies.
Whether in the evening, so serene,
Or in the morning's golden sunbeam,
My garden is my refuge - a treasure,
That keeps me in tune with pleasure.

Opal L. Nankivell

A Different World

Have you seen someone running gleely?
Or an animal running freely?
Someone who has the heart to love?
A white turtle dove?
People walking around, on a clean ground?
Enemy's that love one another?
The rich helping the poor, at a door.
Kids who learn, a little red fern?
Blue fresh water, an awful slaughter?
Someone taking a life?
Someone with an enjoying life?
Someone saying "Please don't fight!"
A person with a tear, that just recovered fear?
Some of this all happened, but some is to come.

Katie Collins

"Words"

If words could express the glory of sunrise
or define the beauty that I see
Then we could speak those eloquent phrases
and explain it all indeed-

If there were words to describe what my
ears hear, the sounds of the early morning,
the song of a bird so near.

If words could expound upon all I
know and feel, about the God I love
who holds me so dear.

To see to hear and understand how he
made this earth abound with radiant colors
and beauty in splendor.
He my mind astounds-

He must have taken sometime to make the flowers
and trees, to change their dress from green to red,
and lose all their leaves.
Oh how wonderful his thoughts must be, who made
the earth, sky, and sea, and with patience
still he is making me.

Nina Godsey

Here To Stay

Did you need a way to hurt me too?
Or did you want me to just forget
that I ever fell in love with you?
Well if it's that simple for you then fine
but for me I just can't find it in my
soul to leave this pain behind
Yes I realize I must and someday I will
so go ahead and laugh because if you
were out to get me, then realize that
you left upon my heart a hole that's too
big to fill
You just left and didn't care about the pain,
the pain I hold deep inside
Nor this love I hold for you which you denied
You leave me to drown in all my tears
for it's the only place I've been all these years
As you wash all our memories away
Just remember the hurt you caused me
looks like it's here to stay.

Kirsten Keiser

October In Ohio

Have you ever seen the maple when the leaves are brilliant red,
Or the orange, brown or hues of yellow with a blue sky overhead,
Or the mighty oak that stands so firm, hanging on until the end,
Have you ever seen October in Ohio?
Have you ever seen the harvest moon lighting up the sky,
Or the field of golden pumpkins for that very special pie,
Or watched the leaves come floating down or heard the children's
laughter,
Have you ever seen October in Ohio?
Have you ever seen the woolie bear whose lineage will never die,
As you keep in mind the miracle of the future Butterfly,
While old jack frost is dusting off his brushes long at rest,
Have you ever seen October in Ohio?
Have you ever seen the silhouette of trees against the sky,
As you dream of a newborn season and to autumn say goodbye,
Oh, that glorious vivid picture to carry thru 'till spring,
Have you ever seen October in Ohio?

Vivian Moses

Do You Know?

Do you know the worries of my mind?
or the pounding of my heart?
Do you know how much I think of you
when the days are cold and blue?
Who? Who?
Echoes through my mind
Who? Who?
beats my heart when I am down
Down, down
are my days when I am without you.
But as I lie here drying the tears that are tearing at my soul
And quieting my heart with mellow vibes of reality
I wonder: Who you are that I should always think of you?
And I remember.

Terri Jo Branham

I Speak Of A Goddess

When I think of you I see a brilliant flow of elegance that no other being could ever portray.
Of all the others in between, it's you, and only you with such dignity and grace.

Don't even think you're disrespected by me, or any others of my kind.
Indeed, your status is uplifted, and honored, for you are the first and last of your time.

Yet sometimes you feel neglected and scorned, by those who are immature and simply too blind to see.
But come in agreement with yourself that these are only boys, as compared to men - like me.

Society contempts my love for you, feeling threatened when we're together.
For they know that Nubian love is the ultimate love, and that's why we must be, and will be - forever.

You wonder, "Who is this great goddess?" whom I speak of through and through.
Well, Black Woman, when I speak phenomenally,
Yes! Black Woman, I speak of you.

Kenneth Jones

While Our Souls Sleep

While our souls sleep in Blake's "beams of light"
Others rest on park benches, under bridges and subways
Hidden from dignity, worth and hope
In the subterfuge of their lonely silent subsistence

Scrounging to survive in tattered threads
With holes in their soles and without bread
Spirits broken like brittle bones
Crushed by the weight of a careless world

With pomades and hand grenades we strive
To restore ourselves and to rescue our neighbors
Yet fail to recognize the face of our brother
On our own doorstep

My heart cries out from the graves of my ancestors
From Auswitz, Treblinka and Buchenwald
From Angola, Bosnia, and the Beaches at Normandy
Have we learned nothing from those scarred and sacred grounds

How can we live with our own spirit
And ignore our brothers like unseen ghosts
When will we awaken from our somnolence
And smite this sinister silence of our souls.

William Warren Wolf

Our Love

I once fell in love, with a guy, I thought a lot about. At first our love was strong. As time went by our love was gone. I can't understand what happened, all of a sudden our love and trust was gone. He came back and said that he loved me. I believed it, until I saw what he had done. I told him it was over this time. And that I would never take him back. He told me that he wouldn't hurt me anymore. But the love and trust was gone. The hurt and pain is hard to get over. I sometimes wonder what went wrong. My love for him, I will never forget. Each night sometimes, I think about him. And realize the good times are over. And now I sit back and realize that I was a fool. When we made love it felt that you didn't care. Then I knew then, that love and trust was gone. So many times I wondered, where did it go wrong. But not a day passes by, that I don't think of you. But I know that I will find another love, and someone new. And someone to love me, more than you ever said you did. Now I can say farewell to you and the love that was really never there. Do You really care? So now, I have to go on with my life, with someone new.

Sharon Youtsey

Take My Hand

Take my hand and we'll sail through the seas of ecstasy.
Our love will gently push us into the tides of desire
We will bask in the rays of our dedication.
Take my hand and we'll soar among the clouds of heaven,
where the angels sing of our love.
The winds of true love will gently blow through our hair
as we caress each other in passion.
Take my hand and we'll run through meadow of longing.
We'll run hand in hand as our love fills the air.
The flowers will bloom in lust with our sensuality nurturing them.
Take my hand and I will love you for all eternity.
Take my hand and I will treasure you for all time.

Maria Chantell Partee

Time For The Dancers

Time for the dancers and all the romancers, the time of the reality of our oblivion. The time of age when our whole life is driven, by reflection in our mirror of forever.

Never a glimpse of romance growing dimmer as the dances-romancers float blissfully by. The floating are descending from their place way up high, as the clock inside each of us winds down with a sigh.

Each clock is different and some may re-wind, but sometimes the key is lost for the moment of forever, totally helpless of human endeavor. Now I have said about all there is to say that leads us to that fateful day, When the dancers-romancers float through the sky, and away, and away.

We're living with memories and things that are past and facing reality of how long we'll last. That's the mistake that most of us make when we mix reality with our ultimate fate - too late.

Dancers-romancers have never been real, but all of us cling to this romantic ideal. If we let go for an instant and we're both still up there floating, we'll surely float by. That will be the end of the dancers-romancers, for both you and I.

Though most of us struggle with tubes and pumps that hopefully may get us over the humps, when if we only knew what so few of us seem to comprehend, that no one has told us or even can say exactly the end, so keep all your romancers and dancers and this is the reason why.

We may float away but no one can tell us that we all really die. mystery is with us all as long as we're living, who can say? May never be known. So accept this as the great unknown, don't even try or ask to be shown.

Martin Duane Grady

An Eagle In Chain

Though missing in action, in our hearts remain,
Our prisoners of war, our eagles in chain.

In our daily dedications, we kneel and then pray,
Oh! You are not forgotten, in the heart of every day.

We send you love across the air, the air you can not fly!
Every day that you are chained, we hear an eagle spirit cry!

I see an eagle tied to iron, I see him in tortured pain!
There is no mercy granted to , an eagle that is chained!

Oh God! forgive us what we do! Lead us from human wastelands!
It is so hard to understand, the treachery of warring man.

Though missing in action, though prisoners of war,
We love you brave soldiers, as we will forevermore!

And there are scores more to follow, to fly at your wing!
They will take to the skies, SO THAT FREEDOM CAN SING!

Forever missing in action, forever then you will remain,
The very best on this planet...an eagle in chain!

No sky shall be empty, not ever again...
With every flag that waves freedom, YOU WILL FLY WITH US
THEN!

Patricia L. Lindsay

Surfer In The Sky

As the sun crosses the horizon, its light reflects upon the waves
out there upon his surfboard, is our brother Dave.
The ocean is mysterious, its waves harmful yet fun
this young man's ride is quickly over, before it has begun.
Yet he rides the waves to their fullest, each and every one
as if he knows they'll quickly fade, like the setting sun.
He seems to know this ocean, ahead of every bend
his mind continuously creative, until the very end.
Never satisfied with the current, always looking for the new
as if to say never blend, let them blend with you.
Seemingly very modest, everything he does with style
all of his features are highlighted, by a crooked smile.
The waves prove very difficult, still they do not harm
they too are quickly captured, by his wit and charm.
His will is very strong but his body grows very weak
these waves of life win only because his heart fails to beat.
This was our brother, David, like the waves he'll never die
for out upon the horizon is the Surfer in the Sky.

Thomas E. Moser, Jr.

Save The Earth

Above the sky and blue atmosphere
Overlooking this great planet.
Man so cruel, how you have abused.
All these things God had created

Golden sunshine that warms everyone
Free oxygen that we breathe around
And all the plants that are from the ground.
These are all free to everyone.

Listen fellowmen.
It's high time to conserve
Let us not all pollute, beautiful planet earth.
Preserve beauty, cultivate harmony
That all men in this world
Will be happy.

Hatred let's forget
Love let us cultivate
Harmony will prevail, in this beautiful Earth.

Lolita B. Dacanay

"When Children Are Born"

When children are born,
parents rejoice
when children are born, heard is a voice
when children are born, life is celebrated
when children are born,
a child's life is fated
when children are born,
they are born into hell
when children are born,
their souls they would sell
when children are born,
it's the beginning of their end
when children are born,
the truth they shall bend
when children are born,
they are rarely born true
when children are born,
they are deceitful when new
when children are born,
people should care
when children are born,
now life they must bare...

Tristan Phillips

What Christmas Means To Me

I look at Christmas beyond the snow,
past the gifts and candles glow.
What I see strikes the ear before the eye,
and it shouldn't be a child's cry.
For all those kids who Santa missed,
For all those parents on life's hard list.
Don't fret if you can't have some pleasures,
Each others love is life's real treasures.
It's the businessmen who buy and sell,
While another's love can stay so well.
There are few true gifts we have in life,
The best being love 'tween man and wife.
Take time to reflect on one's friends and kin,
For Christmas is the love within.

Lenny Augello

Tribute

When I grow old I'm going to sit on your
patio and sip brandy,
And watch the sunset and the sky change colors and smile...

Share with you the dreams we've
had and the dreams we've lost,
And the loves we've had and the loves
we've lost and cry....

When I grow old I'll take time to sit on
your patio and sip brandy
And wish I'd done it sooner!

I'll be joyful for the time we took to
laugh out loud like children,
And sad for the days we lived through
pain and heartbreak like women.

To think about our lives and how we lived them,
or didn't live them and be proud...

That you are my sister, confidant, best
friend and vibrant younger self,
Who taught me to share my life and heart,
and love others confidently, especially me.

Kenlyn Kay Kiener

Silly's Hunt

Animal creeps
Paws silent on the ground
Tail twitching
Eyes steady on the prey
Muscles tightening
Ears carefully checking for others
Legs exploding
Belly softly rumbling from hunger
Body flying
Mouth watering with desire
Paws swiping
Heart yearning for adventure
Target escaping.
Silly waddles to the ever present food bowl.

Simon Z. Jameson

A Day In The Life

She climbs out of bed with half-closed lids,
Peeps through the blinds at the still gray morning.
Hmm, sweater, jacket or blouse day?
She sips her coffee and stares listlessly at the T.V.
Two more gang members shot last night.
After the weather report she makes her way upstairs.

The commute to work is always the same.
Why don't those idiots ever signal before changing lanes?
Oh no! They're re-surfacing the parking lot.
She parks on the roadside and struggles upstairs
With her backpack, jacket and purse.
The phone is ringing as she struggles with the door.
Flinging her bags on the desk she reaches for the phone,
But gets the dialing tone.
The day goes, by work, lunch, work, till the clock hits five.

The drive back home is the same every day,
With the traffic back-ups in the usual places.
She picks up the mail and starts on dinner.
Two more days to go till the weekend.

It's just a day in the life of all of us!

Yasmin S. Kocur

Poetry

The feelings rise to the surface, with
pen in hand and thought in mind.
Twisting fate brought me here again.
Drunk with thought the pen begins
a path yet uncarved. A whirlwind
of emotions, built up, tearing to get
out. Innocent no more than a sinner.
The thoughts are raw, their meaning
unknown. So eloquently they flow, pausing
only to breathe. Belief brought these
words here. Created and destroyed, their
life is short. Long enough, though, to capture
life's true meaning, unmutalated and untouched.
Beauty becomes the result, found within
the words and hidden between the lines.

Kari Pechous

Winter's Lullaby

Stark bare trees, like bony fingers,
Reach toward foreboding gray heavens.
The awesome winter sky ensconces the earth
And bides on forever and ever.

Winter lulls the earth with her slumberous song
Into a still deep rest;
As the fading earth embraces winter
And surrenders to a peaceful death.

W. G. Blackmon

Tears That Last Forever

I feel like someone who has lost their best friend.
People are knocking on the door, but I won't let anyone in.
Holding back the tears though I know I could cry for days.
Trying to hide the pain inside, but everyone sees it in my face.
Sitting on my bed wishing things were different,
but knowing that they'll never change.
The hardest thing I ever did was say goodbye to my best friend.
Years may go by, but a part of my heart will always be tired,
weary, cracked, and rundown.
But I guess someday I'll smile instead of frown.
As I get older and the days go by,
I might be smiling but a part of my heart will always cry.

Katy Reynolds

Life

Life is a glorious thing
people go and do what ever they want
know matter how much it hurts.

Life is a wonderful thing
it has its ups and downs
good and bad feelings.

Life is a splendid thing
know matter how polluted this world is
no matter how much pain.

Life is a great thing
since your alive
and happy and healthy.

Life is a glorious, wonderful, splendid, great thing
and we made it that way. But man had to
mess it up with pain, bad feelings, and so much
hurt, hopefully there is a cure for life.

Meleisa Dixon

I'm The Door!

I'm the door
People open me and close me
They slam me.
I'm the door!
They twist me and turn my knob each day
I'm the door!
They stick and pull things on and off of me
They decorate me
They even sometimes leave me with no clothes on.
I'm the door!
When they get mad, they kick me and
punch me and slam me and open me and shut me
I'm the door!

Matthew Selman

"Life"

Life, what is it all about?
People rant and rave and shout,
I've got rights don't you see
You can't do that to me!
Certain rights we have 'tis true,
But sometimes what's good for me
is not good for you.
And so the age old story goes
Our fight for survival brings many woes
However, there is a cure that can be found
It's tried and true and very sound,
'Tis the golden rule, do unto others
Then in harmony all can live as brothers.

Lillian M. Kiefer

Petals, Bows, And Crystals

Within a bundle of enchantment,
Petals, bows, and crystals
Pulled tight by the strength of yarn
Securely gathered; the essence of love
Its mystery released with but a tender tug

Fragrant roses which grew passionately upon their vine,
Remain unfolded blossoms, seasoned with time
Antiqued pink petals, a foliage reaped potpourri...
Bouquets and tiny bows, silky bows
Arched delicately, bend to submission
Taut love knots, unbound by loops,
Yet tied by pure chastity...

Like pureness of cleansing rain,
Where clusters of crystals radiate....Divine... prisms magnify
Golden light through the faceted crystalline
Spectrums shine curving bows... rainbows
Colorful octaves, shields of glowing auras some of vibrant rose
At one point transparent, are but perceptual windows

And unraveling this, I have found,
These interlaced strings weave magic abound

Tina M. Sanders

Untitled

Blackberries, kissed by the rain,
Picked one by one as down the
Lane I walked, with no one.

Blackberries, eaten one by one,
Succulent, juice rolls over my tongue,
Blackberries seductive, no thoughts of pies or jam
making.
Only being kissed by my loved one.
My thoughts go back to when I ran
along a similar lane to meet my love,
the only one.
We met by the sea, wind and rain in my face, caressed by
him, insenced by the waves, which wrapped around
naked thighs.
The blackberry was given from his lips to mine,
Blackberry and tongue as one.

Shirley Gardener

Untitled

Blue sky across the water
Pink color mixes so pretty
Cool breezes blowing through our hair

The water splashes along the lake shore
Birds singing their evening songs

We stand holding each other
Warm and tenderly together

As you gaze into my eyes
I can feel your love for me
Your eyes are so soft, patient, caring

You bring so much warmth to a cold life
Once known
Your love surrounds my every thought as my
Day goes on

The sun is going towards the land now
It brighten our day and kept us warm

Now we have each other to hold and love
forever.

Maureen Jean Taggart

Ode To A Double Reed

Willowy, graceful reed bending with each phrase
Player and Instrument blending together in one
intricately sounding maze.
Who could have thought this slender wisp of
girl and cane
Could produce such haunting, melancholy refrain?

Caught in a web of incredible beauty; unable to breathe
lest spell be broken
We are lifted up into realms of divine melody
drinking in each seductive note poured out in breathless token.
True art in purest form touches then transforms
Player into Instrument, creating artistry as it performs.

If this moment captured in time could so remain-
With notes suspended like ebony beads on delicate chain
Then with such music, death might summon to eternal rest
And I would gladly go, lost in the mystical wonderment
of music truly blessed.

Kaaren J. Hill

Unwed, Unwanted Plea From Within

Give me this life, and let me live
Please Lord, don't let them in.
Give me the chance and I can show
The love I hold within.
Mommy, if you could just look in my eyes,
I'm sure you will easily see,
Holding me in your arms couldn't do you much harm,
And I know you'll decide to keep me.
If you make this decision to give me my life,
I can be the best baby, you'll see
And you won't have to worry if your never a wife,
Cause you'll always be mommy to me.

Richard E. Longo Sr.

My Own Private Africa

In Africa, on the serengetti plains
post colonial dreams
hold hands
with bloody dictatorships
colonels in Raybans
their faces lined deep with
ruthless aging
ageless cruelty
terror

In Africa, on the veldt
golden as wheat
weary as motherhood, dry as death
beauty is stark
in the curve of a woman's breast
or her tattooed forearm, a shiny silver bracelet on
her slender wrist

In Africa, svengalis and sorcerers
march across the jungle of my fears
hot like anxiety, wasted as my breath,
puerile as my dreams.

Melissa DeLa Cruz

Summer Storms

Thunderstorms, nature's fury at her best.
She wakes the earth from its summer's rest,
and with her winds she brings the rest.
With a roar of thunder, her rains begin.
As earth opens its arms to let her in,
Her lightning bolts light the sky,
to remind us all, how little am I?

Theresa Edwards

Vague Destination

Division is knocking, subtly
pounding
Division's resounding
I'm torn apart
Out warm my heart
It's you and it's you and
It's me and it's you
Everything, everything
Swept into a twisting and mixing and
speeding distraction
Don't rationalize, it's you and it's you
in my head
in my bed
in my everything
I can't get away from your face in my head
in my brain
in my bed
in my head
you are there
I'm insane don't you care?

Pamela Primi

Games

The sound of a toxic stream,
Product of a deadly scheme.

The stench of acidic rain,
Endless tears of nature's pain.

Decomposing flesh on the sand,
What suicidal whales demand.

Ancient predators of the sea endangered,
Thousands and thousands of families they've angered.

The games of humanity shall one of these days,
Kill Mother Earth, then the innocent pays.

Valerie Resor

The Living

And the dead, who are also living,
prowl my house unbidden

Tinkling holiday silver, murmured conversations, fade
revealing luminous shapes
Mad yellow eyes stare through powder pink smiles
and old ladies sweat sweet perfume,

Invisible beasts in chiaroscuro pace the room,
the stinging scent of pungent, wet fur
relentless claws scrape and clack
on the hardwood floor,

Dry, cracked men who cut the golden wheat,
rode the rocking, clanging, reaper
and laughed in their whiskey
in the dusty sun of South Dakota

Matriarchs of another age, my grandmother's torment
a weeping woman, fists clenched, rips at bloodstained
white gauze a granite voice rasps through the night
grease-soaked skillets clang,

I close my eyes, try to turn away,
laughter quivers the pack.

Stephen Mark Bartell

"Day Dreamer"

Fantasies in frenze as they race through the temples of my imagination.
Quickly moving like in desperation.
Escaping reality, dreams thought out with great care
Never knowing how distant for only a blank stare.
A world I create what I wish it to be.
Where all my troubles surrender and my soul could rome free.
All noise deafened by the humming of my own voice.
Who will I become today? My dream, my choice.
Slowly I focus as noises become more distinct.
My dream as ended as soon as I blinked.
No reason to worry I can return whenever I desire.
I can wish, hope and always admire.
Believe in your dreams for they can come true.
But most important of all believe in you.

Melissa Raymond

Brooke Shields

Blue Lagoon girl of my dream,
Radiantly smiling sweeter than cream,
Over and over I pray that you're real;
Outwardly no one knows how I feel.
Kisses so warm and so tender,
Endless Love - oh the joy! oh the splendor!

Sahara sunsets I wish we could share,
Holding you close and caressing your hair.
Irresistible woman just a little bit tall,
Excitement grips me each time I recall
Lovely young eyes that sparkle and gleam.
Do tell me now you're not just a dream.
Sexy lady, you truly thrill me, Brooke Shields!

Raymond Olvera

"A-Cooing"

Sitting in the room doors opened wide,
Rain pours on the outside,
Birds a-cooing in the shelter without a care
Seeing now from within the air
How I dare trade them for a ride
While they chose to hide
Birds sitting in my chair watching ginger
dance with Fred Astaire
My wings pull me oh so high directing
me from side to side
Little marks in the sand show excellent
two-step stance
Such awesome wonder what a sigh
I shall wish that I reach this level before I die
Eating marshmallows roasted by the flames
Singing songs full of earthly shames
What these two spirits have to share
Is they will meet in a place beyond the sky
God touches all who are alive then some shall die
Forgive them and I for never seeking or asking why.

Teri J. Marquard

Lost Soul

I looked in the mirror and found a
person whom I did not know.
Could this be the person I've become?
My spirit, lost. My self esteem, gone.
I found I had no reason to live. I
also found my being was like a
white ghost, floating around, not knowing
which road to take in life.
Then quickly I thought, "No, my life is too
precious to the people around me,
I could never hurt them that much.
So as I continued to look at the
person in the mirror I realized, I
found the person I was looking for.

Nycki Roberts

Untitled

I dream of someone at night. I dream that he is holding me tight. Real tight in his arms. I feel so secure, my love for him is so pure.

My dreams of you are so clear. To me you are always near. Near my heart, loving you is no problem, but people say don't trust him. They say he'll do me wrong, but our love is so strong.

This one person I dream of is very special to me. Everyone can see. See how much I care and see how much I can love. It feels like the heavens above. I think of you everyday and night. Hoping to see you next to me in the morning light. Holding me tenderly and caressing me with your soft touch. Kissing me with passion, and with no hesitation. We gave our love a chance to enhance our romance. I thank you for loving me, and treating me kind, and not making me blind. Blinded by your love.

My world of reality would be happy, if this wasn't just a dream. You giving your love to me would mean the world, but I heard that you can ever love another but yourself. My one wish would be that you realize and admit that you can give your heart and not tear mine apart.

Rowena Puno

My Memories

I do look back these past few years
Recalling memories, wiping tears.
Try to recall the smallest sound
My babies made when they were around.

Days have gone by for several years
The laughter of the past, not here!
My days of hurrying - gone with the past,
Their needs as children, gone at last!

My children grown - their lives to build
With children of their own, they feel -
No need to call - no need to write.
Mom and Dad are over fifty-five.

This house that once was a family home,
The sound of children gone - alone.
The need to see our loved ones near
Denied - refused - rejected - tears!

Mary K. Willey

Untitled

Walking along the beach watching sea gulls fly
Recapturing those old memories of all the days gone by.
Smiling from some, crying for others, feeling so alone
I stop, take a deep breath and wonder where time has gone.

All those yesterdays, things I'd like to change
All those tomorrows and things I'd rearrange.
Life is just a mystery one we live with fear
But, holding all those memories in our hearts so dear.

Life is like the sand slipping with the tide
With no where to go and no where to hide
Take another deep breath, continue with my walk
Hoping to come across someone to sit awhile and talk.

But, as I continue walking, I see no one in sight
Only the sea gulls at their daily flight.
But, as I look, I notice the heavens above
And what's most often forgotten.
My heavenly fathers love.

Mittie Nash

An Autumn Poem

Glowing coals in the trees,
Red hot embers of crimson,
Goldenrod yellows, fiery orange, and once radiant greens
melting into brightly burning coppers and smoldering browns.

The wind scatters the leaves into a frenzy
Forming restless dance troupes on funnels of air
Doing pirouettes in the haunted, smoky atmosphere.

Autumn, elegant heiress, has arrived.
Overseer, to Summer's surprise,
Letting her hair down, slowly,
so that her crown of all season's jewels would not be disturbed...
To shine as brightly in Fall's wine colored reflection
As in a thousand sunlit white dawns-
As Summer before her.

Susan M. Calabrese

Sleepless Night

I couldn't sleep, tossed and turned all night
Relived the pain of our bitter fight
Regretted nasty words I said
Didn't mean to wish you dead
Spoke not from my heart/out of spite

Didn't mean to ban you from sight
Never wanted you to take flight
Dejected prisoner in my bed
I couldn't sleep

Yearned to escape in morning light
Longed for your loving arms to hold me tight
Losing you I most dread
Rehearsed sweet lines in my head
Wanted to talk and make things right
I couldn't sleep

Vera L. Turner

Lola 1994

Lola, gentle spirit, playmate to my kids
Reluctantly accepted by a promise of perpetual care
Became the responsibility of a harried woman
Who took on your physical care but not your heart
Until years of your love bore pink grooves in my soul

Lola, my running partner, when we both could run
Coincidence that we stopped together-you aged, me infirmed
Your daily innocent joy demonstrated my goal
To approach each dawn with love, happiness and freedom
Regardless of past disappointments, ignorant of future dreads

Lola, my sweet, after seventeen years of loyalty
You are slipping out of your beautiful beagle body
To run again in the breeze, pee on every tree
Conscious of the love you have co-created
With humans here who will always miss you.

Shelley Sparks

Love

Love is an amazing wondrous thing of which grace and beauty are revealed in their most high and truest meaning.
It separates the fact of true physical desire to the understanding of true feelings and absolute and uncontrollable passion that invades the mind throwing out all reasonable thoughts.
Creating images of a perfect world were everything is in total perfection consisting only in the one true person that you have uncontrollable feelings for.
That's my Idea of love but you must understand that it is only an Idea, my Idea, you yourself have to form that perfect Idea of love.

Sasa Vasic

Embracement

There came a wind of change
Remarkably noticeable in range

Whispering! What's happening to my children?
I wrote the whispering thought down with my Pen

Capture the call...Embrace the life!
Sharpen the edges of your knife

Our children once so proud and pristine
Tall and willowy as a forest pine

We must look forever windward
Continue moving forever forward

A child represents the many faces that will Restore the Earth
The first step representing a third and fourth.

Robert G. English

"Remember Me"

Remember me, as the sun peeps over the hilltop and begins a new day,
Remember me, when a soft gentle breeze blows thru the trees and whisper softly.
Or as the bright flash of lightening sweeps across the sky and the clap of thunder roars as you shudder with fear, remember me,
Remember me, as you smell the sweet fragrance of the yellow daffodils or the lavender in the lilacs.
Remember me, as a new born baby cries softly and brings a mist of joy to your eyes,
Remember me, when the summer moon glistens on the warm waters
Remember me, as you hear children's laughter while playing,
Remember me, as you sit quietly in the early evening light recalling the words I have spoken.
Remember me, for I have not gone far away,
For each new day, new adventure, and every soft raindrop will be me
there with you to help you get through times of sorrow as well as
all the happy times......
Remember me, remember me.

Margaret J. Woodall

Untitled

Remembering the smiles you "brang"
Remembering the songs that were sang
Remembering the love that would never go away
Remembering how I thought you would always stay
Remembering the touch and soft caress
Remembering your love the best
Remembering how much you cared and wanted the best
Remembering how I sat there amazed and impressed
Remembering the times we would sometimes fight
Remembering how we would make up during the night
Remembering the night how I noticed you started to change
Remembering if this would be a loss or a gain
Remembering how you talked over the phone
Remembering then how I knew I would be alone
Remembering how it was over but not the end
Remembering the best how we would always stay friends.

Marianne Farr

Equality

Within the scope of each one's mind and heart
Resides the seed of all that Man has shown.
In some the seed has blossomed into art,
In some the seed has spoiled and weeds have grown.

And oh what richness each should have at birth,
Like buds by being born the right to sun;
So each a share to all the gifts of earth
Has right as every bud has right, not one.

All things that breathe when given proper care
Will show the beauty held in every seed.
There's none with special right to air
And none with right to claim a special breed.

Sam Robert

Within A Distant Pine

Gazing through the pane glassed door
resting my eyes on a distant pine. Majestically
tall, figuratively shaped, stands out upon the
landscape. Evergreen bows heavily laden
by a snow storm long since gone. Between
these white patched limbs, shows river and
distant shore like a frame with picture
within. This view between caressing limbs
changes with the wind. Sometimes widens
to include a farm or cause some
clinging snow to fall, creating there upon
a wintry storm.

There are so many scenes within this
one pine tree, as endless as man's
imaginative creative dreams.

Robert M. Green

A Biker's Prayer

May the good Lord,
Ride before me,
Anywhere I choose to go,
Cause the highway's not always smooth or dry,
And there's many dangerous back roads.

In the heavy city traffic,
May "He" see before I can,
All the "left turning" "cagers",
And my "best friend", the man,

May "He" find good motels, cheap and empty,
With guards to protect my ride,
Or nice, level camp grounds,
with girls camping on all four sides.

Hope "He" helps keep the Ol' bike running,
Till I'm safely home again,
I promise to have it fixed
For my next road trip begins.

I knew it'd make it! Amen!
Thanks again Lord!

Ron C. Allen "Bigun"

The Pond

The reflection of the sky, with its butterflies and birds,
Ripplings upon its waters, caused by deer that come in herds.
With white and yellow lily pads, that float atop its glass,
To the splashing wings of landing geese, to sleep before they pass.
The beaver that come to build their homes, their tails they splash
in fear,
They always know when man is close, they protect their young so dear.
The dragon flies that skim the pond, don't seem to have a care,
The water spiders that glide along, looking for bugs to snare.
And when I cast my lures and flies, and await for my fish to strike,
I can only hope, it will be a trout, a pickerel, bass or pike.
But in the end, does it really matter, if we catch a fish or not,
This gift from God, with its beauty and grace, again Lord,
thanks a lot.

Mark V. Marino

Sandals

I wanted a new pair of sandals I knew my mom would say no,
so I asked my sister what to do, but all she said was so!
My old ones, well, first I fell in the lakes. Second of all they were
fake! My sister melted them in the microwave, also my dog threw up
steak. I would never handle those sandals again!
Finally I visited my dad, he said you need a new pair of sandals,
I said, "Do you really think so?"

Whitney Holden

Mother's Day

Oh be nice to your Daddy on Mother's Day when that time
rolls 'round in May, cause if it wasn't for what your Daddy did
There'd be nothing to celebrate for a little kid
So be nice to Daddy on Mother's Day

Oh be nice to your Daddy on Mother's Day
When that time rolls 'round in May
Though your mommie calls him a little louse
Remember he is the head of the house
So be nice to your Daddy on Mother's Day

Oh be nice to your Daddy on Mother's Day
When that time rolls 'round in May
He slaves in the office and does his chores
And then come, home and shines the floors
So be nice to your Daddy on Mother's Day

Each Mothers Day through out the land
Gifts galore to each mother from her band
Poor Dad in his corner broke and bent
Wasting away without a cent
So be nice to your Daddy on Mother's Day

Richard P. McGann

The Doors Are Locked But Open

"All that activity and no movement"
Said the visitor-
"All those dreams and little vision"
He muttered to himself
Standing on an avenue of ghostly lives-
"All that hope and little freedom"
He reflected to a door-keeper-
"All those chances and little motivation"
Before he was stopped
At the doors to his accommodations-
"All that survival but little life"
He tried to reevaluate the direction of
"All those footsteps leading to nowhere"
As the doors were opened for his acceptance-
"All those smiles but little love"
He lamented as he passed the locked doors
Leading to the opening of his heart.

Robert Jude Forese

A Near-Death Experience

I stand outside my body, looking from above,
See my still of figure, feel a drawing shove.
The brightest light, in long of tunnel,
Is drawing me near, to the top of the funnel.

Peace warmly robes me, a dispelling of all fear;
As love fills me, viewing relatives, friends so near.
They speak to me of promise and fulfillment,
Calm and tranquil, alive my wonderment!

Strong desire covers me to leave forever body of pain,
Never to return, as all beauty before me to gain.
Voices all around me, make welcome my presence,
All seems so urgent, time is of the essence.

Alas! words are related to my visiting form,
"The hour has not come yet," for me to stay, conform.
At that moment, suddenly, I precisely descend,
And step inside myself, my breath again defend.

As I stir, awake to all around me,
I vision life so differently, dawn proper way to see!
My inner-self is as a stranger; someone new,
I bear the mark of the hereafter, penetrating view!

Patricia J. Skufca

"Tell It To Him In Prayer"

When the world and things around you
Seem dark and cold and blue,
Just remember our heavenly Father
And how He died for you.

Was for you He bled and suffered
On the cross of calvary,
Was for your sins and transgressions
He died to set you free.

Though the cross He bore was heavy
Yet He bore it with a smile,
Hoping that someday someone along the way
Would realize the worthwhile.

So when your burdens grow heavy
And everything seems hard to bear,
Just remember the Lord up in heaven
And tell it to Him in prayer.

Verna M. Weaver Ernst

L.A. Panic

Remembering when
seems distanced by planes separating skies from cities glowing
When eyes shone sun brightly back
Savoring beauty, hope
Dream when
Girls become ladies in white dresses
why some stay in black fantasy
Riding with the unicorns
Why's sleep on the pillow
Greeting tears in the night
Once when a heart is opened and then closed shut
Seeking God when dancing on the souls of a madman
Breaking rules of voices screaming to get out
Listening now to a voice calling from my mothers grave
Be still my child.

Luellen Smiley

A Dream

Darkness, velvet smooth, all encompassing.
Settling softly, a warm blanket of blackness.
Quiet, softly soothing, peaceful with its unvoiced words.
Filling the air with thoughts yet unknown.

Floating, feather light, on a sea of air.
Body weightless, drifting gently.
Light, faintly shining then brightening slowly.
Warm, gently illuminating.

Shadows, flickering images, dancing obscurely against the minds wall.
Hazy, features yet unclear.
Love, flowing strongly, senses tingling.
Boldly shown, yet shyly held.

Emotions, raging rampant, fully felt. Fiery red, warming the soul.
Realization, sparkling clear, refreshingly sweet.
Knowing, yet unsure of what it knows.

Shadows, swiftly fading, images yet unseen.
Darkness creeping in, light melting away.
Unknown loves, dreams not yet dreamed.
Unfelt emotions, lives not yet lived.

Fading, wafting away, back into the future.

Kristi L. Axelson

- My Sister Is....

We grew up close
sharing everything.
My sister is
my best friend.

When we couldn't
talk to mother,
my sister knew we could talk
because we had each other.

My sister grew up
and began to have her own friends.
She stopped talking to me
I didn't understand, I thought we were friends.

My sister came to me
one day.
She told me I may not understand,
she opened up and told me she was gay.

She was right
I didn't understand.
As she opened my eyes to her world,
she held tight to my hand.

Victoria A. Jackson

Ode To A Lost Love

I miss the days I've spent with her.
Sharing stories from her past.
My friend, mentor, and my love.
She's now passed on and I'm alone.

I miss her kiss and warm embrace.
I miss the essence of her place.
I miss the kindness in her heart.
I loathe the days we spend apart.

I know someday again I'll see her soon.
When heaven calls me to my tomb.
I see her standing in that great white light.
To embrace, love, and guide me to the place that's right.

For now I know I must go on.
And live life to my fullest of dreams.
In spirit and soul she's here with me.
I love you much my dearest G.G.

D. L. Hapgood

For My Dearest Carla

She is the girl, the lady, that I loved from the start
She appears to me night and day, but what can I say?
When I see her everywhere, all that I can do is glare.
For she is the stars up above and the one that I do love.
She lights up the path of the night with her eyes,
Never to be led or driven from disguise
And that enterprising smile, which startles me so, but lets me know .....
She is not just a figure of impression,
But a person of great expression.
Yet I stand far from her complexion
Afraid am I of pure rejection.
Not a twinkle in her eye or a glitter from the sky
She sees me as a person, yet undesirable
Though I hold her with a passion,
She is a pearl of power, a gem of stone
Her thoughts are yet not my own.
Will I take the fall to be with her and at last be free of all complexities of the thoughts I have of this day?
But will I ever be so free? Well no .....

Michael J. Newman

A Mother's Hand

There is nothing like a Mother's hand,
She can heal, just about anything.
There is nothing like a Mother's ear,
Who will listen to you no matter
What you have to say, and take
your hand in hers with a smile on her face
And, say my child I understand
It happens every day.

There is nothing like a Mother's feet
She will walk a mile just to
Be with thee or pick you up off
the street.
When you have no food to eat
Her house is open for all of
Thee.

There is nothing like a Mother's hand
Because she can heal
With God's help just about
Anything.

Shirley Collins

Untitled

Grasping for something...
She feels only air,
Suddenly bolting upright in her bed,
She attempts to catch her breath.
What was it she was reaching for?
She only wishes for the knowledge.
Noticing her goose bump-covered body,
She lays her head amongst the pillows once again
Only to discover she'd sweat all over them,
Sleep overtakes her regardless.
She is standing alone
In an empty world
With the exception of one door
Which leads to a world full of people and things;
Loneliness overcomes her.
She longs to go through the door
But she can't.

Sarah Sommerville

The Good Husband

Day in and day out,
She greets him with a smile and a kiss.
He greets her with his hat and coat.

Night after night,
He takes her in his arms and makes fiery love.
Whether she wants to or not.

Month by month,
She sheds a shadowed smile
At the knowledge of not bringing another into his world.

Month by month,
He supplies her with food, money, and clothes.
She is to blame for all his bills,

Night after night,
His palm touches her rosy cheek.
As lightening caresses the Earth,

Day in and day out,
She should be thankful for the good husband.
So why does she grasp the blankets and weep?

Peter A. Ceresa

Mother

A mother is born as a frail baby girl.
She grow into a pretty girl.
Then she matures into womanhood.
As she grows to woman she becomes a mother.
A mother is something all young
And middle aged women want to be
As they grow older.
A mother is so sweet and special to have,
Without mother we have nothing.
There is nothing we can have better
Than a mother's love, and love again.
Thank God for the love of mothers
And understanding of all the mothers
In the world, thank God.

Mary L. Freeman Jones

"College"

Almost wanting to cry out,
She looks up and about,
Fifteen more minutes till she can scream,
This class she realized has turn into a bad dream,
So many notes and so little time,
She tries so hard to take notes like a mime,
Slowly she looks up to the clock on the wall,
She has two minutes before she can escape to the hall,
With a slow breath she raises her head,
She notices her pencil she was grasping has lost its lead,
The teacher with a smile says class is over,
The girl jumps up and rushes out to the grass covered in clover,
And with a deep, slow breath of melancholy,
Realizes another day at college is gone.

Susann Whitehead

A Mother's Heart

For nine months, a woman carries a soft, living being.
She loves it before it's even born,
Because her heart won't comprehend anything else.

She's born, and she's beautiful, just like she
Knew she would be.
She promises her the best life she can possibly give her,
Because her heart won't comprehend anything else.

The years begin to pass by.
There are a lot of rocky roads.
She continues to nurture and protect her,
Because her heart won't comprehend anything else.

She watches this child grow into a beautiful young lady.
The pride and love she feels at that moment is overwhelming,
Because her heart won't comprehend anything else.

Wendy Symons

Bittersweet Collected

Her colours blend. The orange. The red.
Significant of the alive — and the dead.
As, thru happiness and sorrow, we all are lead.

Life's brilliance is pictured, in the colours of fall;
Yet death, with winter-white stillness, comes to all;
Sometimes so blended, we even listen-await his call.

'Tis only, as we learn to let go of our lives,
Just as amongst weeds, the bittersweet thrives,
It is only Jesus, that the weakest survives.

Bittersweet has a beauty which calls to us all;
A picture of summer orange becoming the red of fall,
Armloads we gather, in to dry. Ready for winter.
Ready to die.

Kat Abner

Nouveau Ms. Muffet

Like her own nouveau Ms. Muffet
she tuffet sits next to her roaring fire.

Consuming warming evening spirit
she rolls and rolls her aging clay...

Her favorite toy lies briefly idle —
while Muffet Ms. clay caresses...

She molds and molds and molds
— creating new family out of family.

Her baby-boy cat, the man of men,
becomes lover/husband/father/son.

Her wondrous girl of ashen fur
recreates as daughter — and/mother.

Baby bear her boy of joy transforms
into new visions of herself —

Mother will just have to stay herself
— The Empress of All Bitches!

Susan Aven Delaplane

Big And Little Winner

We play games every night, my daughter and I
She wants so badly to win.
I tell her it's simply a matter of chance
The right card or a lucky spin.

Winning does something to make her feel good;
To be better than mom or her friends.
While losing reminds her she's still a small girl
Feeling helpless and needy again.

She'll move ahead three when she only got two
Or insist she spin one or more time.
Where the spinner stopped clearly said, "Move back one space"
Yet she's sure it was right on the line.

When I get near the finish and she weeps in despair
I'll give up saying "O.K. You've won."
She'll wipe her tears back and cry, "Mommy, no fair.
To win that way just isn't much fun."

My little girl helps me when I play my games,
I enter each sweepstakes I see.
I too dream of winning—instant wealth and success
Am I different or better than she?

Nancy G. Bernstein

A Dear, Sweet Mother-In-Law

Mom may be leaving us tonight,
she's tired and wants to slip away.
She'll be passing over to the purest light,
There's no pain there, she'll want to stay!

She lived her life, and lived it well
and did the things she had to,
Parts of her life were a living hell,
leaving now? I think she's glad to.

She was an artist who could no longer paint,
she was weak and tired and so very faint.
A poetess whose hands wouldn't let her write,
so she's trying to slip away tonight.

My thoughts keep going to her now,
Saying, "Mom, let go, you're free to leave."
That's all I can give you and all I'll allow,
We'll miss you dear, but we will not grieve.

Soon your pain will all be gone,
your sadness and your sorrow.
We'll meet again some happy day,
and share a new and bright tomorrow.

Robert Kent

Mother's Day

It is fitting that a person like you
should receive accolades at least once a year.
Although we try to remember to do it often,
sometimes we forget just how lucky we are.

How many people can rejoice in having a Mother
who is a Mother, confidant and friend?
Someone who is always there for you, no matter what.
This is a treasure to cherish to the end.

Few have a relationship that stands the test of time,
through thick, thin and all the middle ground.
But, you are there whenever we call,
to counsel, comfort and lend a hand.

Although sometimes we have caused you grief,
I hope we have never been a disappointment.
We are what we are in large part due to you;
so you must have been heaven sent.

Take care of you and keep up the good work,
because it will take a very big slate
to tell and show you just how much you mean
in ways that are too many to enumerate.

Roberta L. Stevenson

The Life Of The Saplings

Years ago, there stood two saplings in a pasture.
Side by side they did grow.
The cold frosted, the rain pelted, the wind came to tow.
Yet the saplings continued to grow.
The parasites came to infect,
But no flaws could anyone detect.

Through time, the saplings became trees.
With their branches interlocked, and their
leaves blowing in the breeze.
Such an intriguing sight, that bird came to rest and
to build their nest.
Other plants grew amid them, flourishing in their shade.
Knowingly hiding from the sun, so not lose their color or to fade.

Now as I look into that pasture, I no longer see those two trees,
For they have closed the distance as two, to become as one.
Stronger are the branches that touch the sky, and the roots
that embed the earth.
A refuge for the weak, a cradle for the young.
So serene, so secure, giving each bird their own berth.
To open their hearts below the heavens and bless the world
with a song.

Kenneth Miran McGee

The Place

Amazingly a lily of the valley clings to the shear
side of the cliff face looking out over horsetailed surf.
The light drizzle driven by the wind strikes
a young man's face as he watches the clouds race by.
Droplets soothe his weary brow as rivulets of tears
find their source in reddened eyes.
This always was a lonely place.
A place where a young man could come,
To sit surrounded by the wildness of nature;
To dream of what future lies beyond the horizon;
To dream of what might have been.
A place where he felt instinctively that absent
friends weren't really gone;
Forever spirits soaring with the clouds.
An intrinsic part of the wind, surf and bejewelled
dewdrops on the harsh spines of the Marram grass.

Mark Anderson

I Wonder

I sometimes wonder
Sifting through my human colander
What the world would be like
If we all were alike
Would we have the same features
Pleasures, desires and signatures
Identical mannerisms and tastes
And countless other distastes.

Then I wake up and I wonder
Why people want to follow another
Who is completely different in looks and character
Which only makes them into a prisoner
In a life of unaccomplishment
With a painful feeling of imprisonment
We should learn from other but be an individual
Because our strengths and mentality is not equal

Petra Johnson

Death of a Hilldweller

I watch him
Silently...
Clinging to his almost lifeless body
I notice the clouds above us
They are slowly gathering, turning grey
As if the Gods were preparing a ceremony for him
Taking his very life's last breath
I watched him, skin like cream pale, soothing
As if freshly awaken from a dream, yet, I watched him
In his dying face I saw a hidden sorrow, a hidden pain
It frightened me
And seared my soul with one-thousand swords
A pain I prayed I would never have to know 'tis too late...
Rain falls like memories forgotten
Suddenly rushing back to you
Pouring down over your brow, then your body
As if purifying you like a first fallen snow, pure...
Untouched by evil
Giving back things which you thought were lost forever
I will not forget you...

In Memory of Matt Hoy (1974-1994)

Mandie Brassington

Untitled

Anxiety, tension, so many people in fear
Since Adam and Eve, the very first pair.
Prevalent violence in all cities and towns
Public safety is now nowhere to be found.
Innocent children, while still in their prime
Losing their lives long before their time.
Sad, grieving parents, oh how the cry
Since illegal weapons are so easy to buy.
Most assailants are young and riddled with fears
They are coaxed and coerced by their own peers.
Human life is not worth much any more
As street gangs have to even the score.
Many elderly people who must live alone
Live in constant fear in their very own home.
We must all teach our children no matter how small
To love one another and respect one and all.
We must turn things around and this is the time
The next young victim may be your child or mine.

Peggy DiVenuti

For the Sake of Love and Peace!

"We know the truth, we know the way, all of us are here to stay!"
"Since the beginning of time and space,
The good and evil continue to race!"
"The force, as a shield of beauty in the good,
Makes evil and weakness feel in no mood!"
"Our founding fathers gave us the lights,
The constitution, the bill of rights!"
"To believe in fairness and tolerance,
To run with the force in long distance!"
"We are in front, feeling so glad, seeing that evil becoming mad!"
"Through infinity, to finish line,
Evil and weakness are in decline!"
"It's history telling these things,
For good and bad leaders, good and bad kings?!"
"Some lived, we saw the evil empires,
People in chains, nations in fires!"
"Some lived ethnic cleansing, starvation and holocaust,
Genocide-exodus, towns turning into ghosts!"
"Our founding fathers gave us the lights,
Civilization, not to pick fights!"

Ndoc T. Kacaj

Something, Someone

I see something old, a brass cup
sitting, waiting peacefully
for someone to come for it.

I see someone old, a grandmother
sitting, rocking back and forth, back and forth
swaying to the sweet sound of rain.

I see something new, a brand new doll
in a little girls arm staying close
to its new found owner.

I see someone new, a baby just born
in its mother's arms, waiting to grow-up.

I see something young, a fawn
running, playing, walking in the woods
smelling the flowers.

I see someone young, me
lying in the tall grass, looking at the stars
in the midnight sky, wondering
what life will bring.

Leslie Allen

"A Whisper In The Dark, A Cry In The Night"

I didn't think I could cry in my
sleep and actually know the feeling
of hurt against me in my dreams.
But I did.

I craved your love when you first
left, but the wonderful memories
are all I kept.

I don't know if what they say is
true, and I don't want to believe
it unless I hear it from you,
because I know you loved me,
And I think you still do

It's just a whisper in the dark,
And a cry in the night that keeps
you wondering in fright, for it is
not you who died with an unhealed
heart and an untamed cry,
For it is I! My love, you ruined my
life!

Melissa Mann

Untitled

The long, bone fingers of November
slowly reach out to wrap around the core.
Closing its grasp, grasping for life.
Dark, hidden notions of grandeur
taking their toll on each blade of grass.
Swaying left and then to the right, to choose but one.
Black, tar whirlpools gently, patiently pulling at us.

Explosions of fear tear the sun from its sleep.
Clashing castes with dire needs,
to and fro,
till one,
or some,
succeeds.

The sweet, spring showers of April cleanse the grime from the air
Springs forth anew, time without end, life inspired, a leader
perhaps. The eyes of future gaze into past to see November slowly,
creeping to its conclusion at last, shedding its seed.

Rosalind C. Kleinberg

Ryan

Just yesterday, you were here
smiling, laughing, being obnoxious, your usual self
Now you are gone, just like the minutes of yesterday.
Nothing can bring your or those memories back
The memories that I am talking about are
seeing you smile, laugh, tease, and talk.
All of those are gone and so are you.
We feel your presence, but it's still not enough.
We want to hear you laugh, hear your voice and see your smile.

Just yesterday you were here,
now you are gone.

Leeann Laylon

"A Night In September"

Sad, lonely, feeling blue,
so depressed, you don't know what to do.

Hunger, tears, and many,
many beers, every night you live
in fear.

Sick, always living
in pain, it's like being crushed by a crane.

Thoughts, memories, to
much to remember, on a
very rainy night in September.

So gather around so that
the body can be crown, everyone's
quiet, there's no sound.

After the quiet emotions
you and yourself walk on the
ocean. The ocean is so
high she wants to die.

Her footsteps are
all the remember the night
She died in late September.

Melissa Ann Stilley

Roses

Today I'm so weary and blue
So I came by for awhile.
Just to sit and talk to you.

I brought some roses by:
They're red; your favorite,
And so pretty they make me cry.

Well, the old house is still standing,
I go by now and then.
Just being there makes you seem close by again;
And I recall all the things we shared:
The love and strength you gave me cannot be compared.
So as I look back through the years and start to cry,
I know you understand and will pardon my tears.

It's so peaceful here: all quiet and still,
The breezes dart and sigh. Listen!
I just heard your voice whispering in the pine.
Oh yes, you live forever on, in these memories of mine.

It's growing late now,
The stars are starting to shine; the moon is on the way.
Enjoy you roses Mom, we'll talk again another day.

Roberta Williams

Back

I don't have any words to use.
So I'll make this short, but sweet.
Try not to get confused,
Because I just can't take the heat.

If I told you that I loved you,
And I told you that I cared.
Would it be enough to keep you,
Through the distance of the air?

I sit by your granite roof,
Each and everyday;
Wondering without proof,
Who did this to you and who should pay?

But, my searching and my looking seem to come to no avail,
So I'll just go back, back into my cell.

Michael Weldon Tackett

Untitled

I never realized...
so many people,
they wish nothing more than to be dead.
They feel life has no more to offer.
Life has more offer, other than death.
Maybe they wish to rest in peace, in solitude.

They have every right, to wish for
peace and
solitude.
But they don't see,
Suicide is not going to make
the world
peaceful and solitary
Look at all the broken hearts,
the sad memories.
The gap between your friends,
the tissue boxes continuously emptying.
Then again, maybe no one will mourn for you.
Someone always cares.
If no one does, I do.

Rita Erickson

Look Again

So much can be seen, in just one glance-
So much, to be seen —
Should he give you the chance.

A man of wisdom, strength, and courage —
Thoughtful and caring,
Though, easily discouraged.

He's a friendly soul-
a man you can trust.
But, he's paying his toll- his feelings; not discussed.

My eyes see a man, destined to achieve,
"great power, and wealth"...
But, his eyes, reflect a man, deceived...
One, trapped within himself.

A victim of society — though, not faceless in a crowd...
Embracing life with such propriety —
He's compassionate, yet, proud.

His heart reveals feelings, expressioned in ways,
not easily gauged-

But, his eyes are those, of a bird; extinct...
Doomed, forever... among the caged.

Tina Oliva

A Special Journey

God has handed you the reins to take hold of your life
So ride it right into the earth
For many good things will rise up to you
To show your potential worth

If there was any one more proud of you
That person would have to be me
You're growing into that special someone
That I always knew you could be

I never lost the faith from the very first time we met
The wishes that I had for you that never happened
Was really my only regret

We've walked down this road of life together
Just a short part of the way
But my hopes were for you to do something for yourself
And for this each night I prayed

God speed my son, and don't look back
Keep striving for your special goal
I'm betting on you and I know you'll come thru
With all my heart and soul...

Mary Czolno

Wishing For The Day

Wishing upon a star seems so far I wish for
something that isn't so far.
I wish for the day to come
when I get to see you right then.
Wishing and wishing for that day
I hope I'll just what to say.
Everyday that we're apart it breaks my heart. I feel as
if my heart has been stuck with a dart.
We've built a friendship that is worth more than gold.
I know that because gold is so cold.
Having you for a friend I know that you will always
have an ear to lend.
I hope your ear will be here forever because
I'll need it forever and ever.
Life without you now wouldn't be worth a dime
because I would be lost in time.
With each passing day I'll keep counting till
the day when you come my way.

Kylie Miner

Memories

The wondrous days of innocence
so softly amble on
As the wind that rustles through the trees
so suddenly they are gone

Carefree days and carefree ways
lie beside the road of time
The hills where youth coasted down
now must begin to climb

As a chameleon on a rainbow walks
so life is ever changing
Passing through the prism of life
with spectrum re-arranging

The waves that roll upon the shore
will surely roll away
As the sand that rides upon the tide
dreams often swept astray

The lights of home glow brightly
as our steps grow short and slow
And we wonder at the innocence
of those days so long ago

Ronald E. Donaldson

Adam

Momma's favorite name was Adam.
So that's what she called him
As she carried him into his new room
In the house on the corner.

And he grew amongst the sights and smells
Of perspiration, and marijuana, and Momma's cooking.
And the blood that splattered the night
The shots rang out and they took
Daddy away in a body bag.

Nothing would ever be the same.
Momma cried all the time
And the boys down the street
Became Adam's new Family.

He remembered now the sights and smells
Of perspiration, and whiskey,
And Lydia's sweet perfume.
And the blood that splattered the night
The shots rang out and they took Him away in handcuffs.

She swore he wouldn't be like Adam. As she took the baby
To see his Daddy for the first time On Death Row.

Susan White

Omnipotent Love

Emotions, so deeply hidden within fine lines,
Sometimes make life seem so unkind.

It is said one's fear is all in one's
Mind, I wonder my dear if that's why
You're not here.

No, I think strife put an end to the life
That I knew, and starting over is so hard
To do when my heart and soul still cries
Out for you.

True love is omnipotent, yet gentle and
Kind, it can conquer all fear, both
Yours and mine.

Darling remember I'll always be here.
And from the bottom of my heart, I
Vanquish all that tore us apart!

Kevin Allen Plumstead

Poodle White

People say that colors I do not see
So when I begot a litter of three
They said that it could not be
Not even one resembles me

They only spoke of what they saw
One pup had a speckled paw
The large one had too big a jaw
And the runt they chose to ignore

They all loved me a Poodle white
But those other three were just a blight
To be cared for and kept well out of sight
It made me very sad all thru that night

Cuddling close was sheer delight
To me life could not be more bright
Love did not rely on my dim sight
It was not only for Poodles white

This love overcame my sadness
What I saw brought only gladness
Color is not what causes badness
Hate is the catalyst of madness.

Olga Wakal

Seasons Of Love

His fingers wrapped around my bare shoulders
softly as flames cover a burning log.
The intense, comforting sense of touch,
so loving and gentle quickly penetrated my skin.

In this season of winter I had found
the light and pleasure of summer.
The cold, harsh air left my heart and body
as a warm, soft blanket of love surrounded me.

Pain ceased to exist as ecstasy filled my body
like water soaks into a dry sponge.
I cried from my soul the bitterness
and heartbreak of hours with silent, tender tears.

To know the healing power of love
and experience the grace of another human being
so forgiving. I safely surrendered
the entirety of myself to him forever.

This is life in the season of love.

Marie J. Balonis

The News in Brief

News from Rwanda:
Some are fleeing.
Some have fled.
Many are already dead.

News from Korea:
North Korea is making bombs.
South Korea is preparing for war.
Will a nuclear bomb even the score?
Spare the (fuel) rod and save the children.

News from Sarajevo:
Some are fleeing.
Some have fled.
Many are already dead.

News from L.A.:
A drug lab explodes, burning acres of land.
The race for governor is out of hand.
A Northridge aftershock measures 3.7.
More news at 11.

E. D'Annunzio

The Way

I hear people talking about you.
Some believe that you are a living spirit
in their lives
and you perform miracles.

Others, don't care who you are,
why are they here for, and still you
perform miracles...
for so immense is your love.

When the night comes slowly
it brings us light,
because it is your spirit that brightness
every soul, every mind.

It is you, the one who watches
over us, over me, over everything you
have created.

Please,
show me the way.
Don't ever let me fall into the darkness
of my incredulity.

Magdalena Marines

Cut Off

They totter in or walk briskly,
Some led by another's hand.
They pause, for the step they are taking
Is a big one and they should understand.

They are laden with the fruit of their body.
It is growing, sheltered from strife.
But they've chosen to refuse to birth it.
They've rejected its right to a life.

So they enter to shed blood of their children,
To kill the fruit of their womb,
To stop a heart from its beating,
To ruin a rug yet in its loom.

Do they know when they leave what they've done?
Do they realize the end that they've made
To our playmates and spouses denied us,
Does it not make you, the living, afraid?

For if Mothers who should love their children
Choose to bear them no more,
What hope have we for the quality
Of love left us, who were born before?

Ulena Robinson

A Special Friend

Sometimes in life, you find a special friend.
Someone who changes your life
Someone who makes you laugh
Someone who makes you believe that there is
  really good in the world
When you're down and the world seems
  dark and empty
Your forever friend lifts you right up
And if you find such a friend you feel
  happy and complete
You have a forever friend for life.

LaTrena Pixley

Unfaithful Love

How could you hurt a heart that's true
Someone who will love and care for you.
I can't understand what went wrong.
Did I push you away?
Was our love not strong?
Apparently, because you went astray
Leaving me lonely, feeling betrayed
Of course I forgive you and tried to forget.
That what stays in my mind I often regret
The pain in my heart, the tears that fall
Can't you understand me at all
I pray everyday to the stars up above.
That there will be an end
To this unfaithful love.

Kelli McReynolds

So Long Until We Meet Again

Just as when life is at the new
Something can happen to remove it from view
When God has called an angel home
We can be left to feel so all alone.

Messages from God we can really hear
If we open our hearts and let him appear
Some prayers we pray seem to fall on open spaces
But he has heard and puts this in his perfect places.

We're often left to ask him why
then he will say, dear child don't cry
His work on earth has been well done with love
Now he's at home with me singing with the dove.

He looks down with a watchful eye
Saying I'm in perfect peace please don't cry
Some day soon you too will be here
He will open the gates and you will appear.

Live each day
Giving praise and thanks to him along the way
Dear love there has been only one soul mate for me
So I say so long until the day you again I see

Zetta Hardin

The Vietnam Soldiers

As north invaded south near a place called Saigon,
Something in America went terribly wrong.

It was called a conflict; a term politically correct;
But such terms treated our warriors with disgrace and reject.

America sent, some of its most valiant men,
But our government, would not allow them to win.

And only after 58,000 took a fall;
Were they remembered, by their names on a wall.

They went to fight, "A noble cause",
To keep a free people, from communist claws.

But from war protesters, to those refusing to fight,
America was no longer, a country of might.

Hippies hated, and spit on our men;
As the morals of america, were lost in sin.

Some taunted marines; calling them vicious fighting machines,
But they were just men, with our same hopes and dreams.

Now let those who served in the "conflict" gone wrong,
Be not ashamed but stand proud and stand strong.

It is time for America to repent from her past,
And call the Vietnam soldiers, heroes, at last.

Timothy A. Hunt

"Take A Good Look At Me"

You take my love for granted with each passing day,
Sometimes I really feel like , I'm only in your way,
We're still good friends as close as friends can be,
But what hurt's so bad is you never stop,
And take a good look at me,
It's not funny that your so blind and cannot see,
The pain in my eyes, my broken heart, of what your doing to me,
I listen to you talk of other loves in your life,
But you never will know, in my heart you're stabbing a knife,
If you can't take my hand and walk with me,
Please for my sake, say good bye, and set me free.

Ruby Darlene Williams

"Crying Whippoorwill"

A whippoorwill is calling to his mate,
Somewhere in the night.
The sound I hear clearly from far away,
Somewhere in the night.

I hear the silence of a whisper,
Someone is calling my name.
The sound I hear clearly, maybe the whippoorwill,
But the cry isn't the same.

Sounds like someone hurting,
Crying all alone.
The sound I hear clearly; like a wolf howling,
And it chills me to the bone.

Who could be out there so full of sorrow,
And crying in the dark.
The sound I hear clearly, someone I know,
But I can't see in the dark.

The sun is rising now, over a moon
That's still up late.
I can still hear the crying,
But in the light I can see it was only me,
Missing my mate.

Wayne Woody Curtis

Beauty Is Only Tongue Deep

The Beautiful noise she made,
Sounded like a mellow blues group.
The gentle clicking of her teeth,
Like the soft touch of an experienced drummer,
Blended with various notes issuing
From her throat which softly
Lulled the listener into believing
Her lyrics had meaning.

Richard E. Potter

For Sale Again

On a high sand hill north of the county line,
soybeans planted in June are still in the bud six inches high.
Sloughs are choked with brome.
Cinquefoil and mountain mint are in bloom
while mullein is a dry torch.

Empty foundations gape and totter,
pried apart by saplings,
A for sale sign by the gate.

You can see everything from here.
The two river valleys converge in a land diked and drained.
The corduroy fields spread valvate, swell, and lift up the horizon.
A water tower is on the rim.

Karolyn Ramnani

Untitled

Honey golden hair, shining in the sun
Sparkling pools of blue tell me I'm the only one
He flashes me a bright smile
And within I see a child
His heart is tender, actions brave
Easily broken, needing to be saved
He fills my life with so much love
If I could, I'd give him the stars above.
He deserves the world, something
I can't give.
But I can love him as long as
I live.
I gaze at him with my big browns
He reaches for my hand, not making a sound
Our hands meet, and hold on tight.
I'm never going to let him out of my sight.
I see in him his love for me
I know forever, it will be.

Penny Sayre

Looking Over The Shard Fence

The trolls dance through crimson paths
Speaking of unspeakable things.
The shadows laugh through the forgotten past
Colliding with ancient myths.
The cathartic creatures with frightening features
Slither into the night.
The long ago leaches and those who burned witches
Sneak in through the times.

The trolls dance as if in a trance
Eating each others flesh.
The metal lance with a graceful stance
Pierce the night in jest.
The centuries pass without backward glance
Breaking fragile ties.
The demons band to tango on the grass
Trampling on leaves that die.

Thushari Jayasekara

What Is Laughter?

Laughter is a smile that bubbles over,
Spilling drops of happiness around;
A frown turned upside down is borrowed laughter
That brightens gloomy air with cheerful sound.

Laughter is a universal language
That people everywhere can understand;
It stimulates a warmer bond of friendship,
Like reaching out to clasp an outstretched hand.

Laughter can uplift a sagging spirit,
Touch a heavy heart and boost morale;
There aren't many clouds on the horizon
That laughter cannot help us to dispel.

Laughter has no bounds or limitations,
It's a talent we were born to share,
And no matter why or when we choose to use it,
There always will be plenty left to spare.

Laughter is a source of inner power
That sends a magic message to our brain,
Encouraging fresh starts and new beginnings,
Like rainbows turn on sunshine after rain.

Lucille Pearson

Chacos Woman

She's living in the canyon, amidst the kiva stone.
Spirits watching, wandering, who has left their home.
She sits there in the morning, gazing at the sun.
Chacos woman's home again, never more to run.

Gentle fingers probe the stone looking for a trace
Of the people come and gone, searching for the race.
Chacos woman calls to them, the spirits hear her thoughts.
Through her eyes they see the changes tears of time have wrought.

Here she walked, her silken hair blowing in the breeze,
A shaman shook his rattle, she could hear it in her dreams.
Chanting echoed from the canyon walls, and someone took her hand,
Hawkish grin and twinkling eyes, she saw the indian lands.

Will the walls of stone be built where children once had life?
Where spirits roam amidst the stone, bear witness to the strife.
The time is dear, the feeling's sweet for two who walked as one.
But chacos woman's home at last, never more to run.

Robert C. Pollitz

Night On A Harbor

I feel like a lonesome boat
standing on a shore of a harbor
that harbors my shadows and
shades sunny smiles, lunar lights
enveloped in long days and sleeping nights.

I sail all day, on a life-long conveyor belt
that's drifting away in the silence
of changing seasons,
hauling luggage of lost dreams
piled high and buried deep.

On no-man's land with no ID,
I leave them unclaimed on the belt
now running in circles.
Suddenly, the harbor closes.
Smiles, lights, dreams - all
disappear with me in the night mist.
We bid goodbye to the night on harbor.

Varsha P. Shah

Mother, Mother

Mother, Mother standing so famous and trustful,
standing so firm and proud.
Courageous and protective
fought for her life and others, she fought for what was right.
Not a stealer, murderer, nor a criminal.
Achieved her goal in life and sized power to make peace.

Mother, Mother I wish I knew you, had your qualities and skills,
but all I know is the things I've heard.
Even though I have a new mother who is not as
exciting, interesting, gifted, and
talented like you, I wish I knew you.

Mother, Mother even though I didn't know you, I still love you,

through your portraits, stories, and memories. Even though you died at my birth, I realize you had to sacrifice your life for me, and I cherish the life you have given me. I am glad you didn't abort me, that is why I am so fond of you.

Mother, Mother, I wish I could tell you this,
but wait at those Golden Gates,
I will meet you soon up where there is paradise
and everlasting life.

Kimberly Renee' Fields

Dealing With The Impossible

They tell me I'm wrong, but I know I'm right,
Standing up for what I believe in.
They tease a boy because of his weight,
They laugh at her because she's "ugly,"
They kick him as they walk by because he's poor.

In their eyes, there are only imperfection.
When someone gets beaten up.
Do they stand by to watch or get help?
Are their friends true friends?
Or just people to help spread the gossip?

I don't fit with the "in" crowd,
Nor change my beliefs to suit theirs,
But I do know that I'm never going to be in their group,
If it means having to stoop that low,
How can anyone get pleasure from hurting others?

In the meantime, how do I cope with this nuisance?
I'm afraid I don't have a solution,
It's too big to ignore,
But I've decided to go on, for this is a part of life,
Careful to resist their characteristics of inhumanity.

Khemarey Nuth

Destiny

On a mountain by the sea
stands an oak tree tall and free
holding stories of glory
stories of strife
stories of this land's struggles for life

On a mountain by the sea
stands an oak tree for no man to see
all the great nations that once stood tall
now their ashes blowing over all

Man once ruled this vast land of ours
now it's empty and full of scars
time will heal and cover the land
with trees and greenery where man use to stand

The time is near mans destiny is clear if man
cannot change mans world will surely disappear

On a mountain by the sea
stands an oak tree tall and free

Kenneth Frank Buchanan

Shadow Lighted Freshman

On the hill of Gauley Bridge,
Stands the High School great and strong,
'Twas here we freshman received the talking,
of things we did that were wrong.

The faculty says we're dumb and ignorant
But these sayings we cannot mind,
We'll try to gain some knowledge.
And leave the ignorance behind.

Let us cross the river of darkness,
And step on the land of light,
We'll soon be in the sophomore year
There's where we'll shine very bright.

When the courses we have completed,
Of our favorite "Gauley Hi",
The joys of our clubs and ball games,
In our memory will never die.

We'll leave the school for the followers,
Whom we hope will be filled with pep,
So they may carry the spirit,
That we've just taken up.

Violet R. Ford

Walking Boston's Freedom Trail

A row of brick leads the way down Freedom Trail
Starting at the Commons and ending at the bay.
We marvel at the State House with its golden dome.
Then on to Banner's masterpiece with brimstone cornerstone.

Past the granary burying ground, King's Chapel - stark and cold.
Mather's famous school house, Franklin's statue - proud and bold.
Boston Massacre site where Patriot's stood firm
Against the Battling British the cry to kill and burn.

Paul Revere's House - what a thrill to stand where he has stood
His musket, bedstead stand and blackened chimney hood.
The old graveyard - a reminder that even heroes die,
The tombstones slowly sinking where patriots now lie,

Old Ironside's in the bay at rest, a mighty ship, a dauntless crew,
With whom our lands's been blest.
So much to see and admire in this great land of ours,
Oh may our youth aspire to climb the freedom towers.

Marian M. Siegler

Essence Of Love

Essence of love is the perfect existence known to man,
Stillness, but yet radiating the energy of passing moments.
No need for relying on others for serenity, only willingness
To connect to the one source that matters, love! Filling
our being with light and joy to transform the sorrow of
yesterday once more.
Forward we go to continue our journey, to the realm where
Only love can enter. Here and now we will encounter, should
We choose to accept our inheritance, the gift of love to
Encircle our hearts, just waiting for us to notice its
presence. Will we answer the call? Or will we once again
continue the cycle of uncertainty! No rationalization can
change the urgency of our foundation, only our conviction
can support us towards illumination. Search no more, for
we are here now to unlock the gate to our hidden treasure.

Katherine L. Bakerink

A Rainbow Tale

At the end of a rainbow, is a pot of gold, I'd heard this story, so often told.
So off I went to seek this quest, an endless journey, with little rest.
On and on, I trudged for years, no closer did I come, I feared, for as I moved, so did it too, so I knew this had to be the clue.
The friends I'd met along the way, seemed to brighten those dreary days,
their friendship meant so much to me, that my heart was saddened, when I had to leave.
And now I sit and think back when, I travelled far with all my friends,
it seems that gold is a worthless thing when compared to the wealth that friendship brings.
So at the end of the rainbow, now I know, your friends and memories will be your gold!

Paul N. Kloppenborg

Finale

As the sun rises from its shadowy slumber
Streaking reds and blues across the darkness
Like a careless child's masterpiece
I awake from my dream world's wonder
Into another dimension of existence
Out of my mind's control
A firebolt of reality's sunshine
Seems to laugh at me playfully
Knowing my dilemma
Suddenly life becomes the ticking of time
Slivering more out of my grasp
Growing louder and louder....

Sharon Trimble

"The Fantasy"

Together we look towards the distant horizon
Stretching our hands out for the setting sun

As we sit solemnly with our heads bowed
The bittersweet tears become our shroud

The Fantasy has finally fled beyond our grasp
It has forever disappeared from us at last

We chase the myths through rotten lands
With our eyes blinded searching with our hands

Soon we find there is nothing to be found
And we leave this place, this burning ground

And we realize

That the fantasy has finally fled beyond our grasp
And that it has forever disappeared from us at last

Philip Liu

The Symphony

Looking down upon me
Stroking my hair
His eyes so loving
Closing my eyes and playing the fantasy
Somehow lost in it
Feeling so intense
The silkiness of this rose
The strength of its nature
The fantasy is real
Being lifted upon this realness
The symphony plays on
Growing stronger at this point
My heart pounding with the drums
The senses crashing with the symbols and riding ooh
Riding on the waves of the music
and the last stroke of the violin has played
I collapse in the conductors arms

Lori-An Ryan

Everyday!

Everyday my love for you grows
strong but also weak.
And everyday I hear you and feel
happiness, joy, sadness, and pain.
Everyday I see you and fall to my
knee's and weep in pain.
Everyday my love grows deeper but
knows it shouldn't.
Everyday people tell me I'm wrong
when I know I'm right.
And everyday people say it can't come
true but I know in my heart I will meet you.
Everyday I dream that we'll be together
but I know we won't but sense I can dream we'll always be!

Monica Boudreau

Grass

It grow and it blows, its grass.
Tender young spring grass to chew on.
Sun rich summer grass to play on.
Ripe mature autumn grass to
build dreams on.
Vast oceans of rippling prairie
grass; pillows of soft mossy valley grass.
A single blade becomes a parade.
Get lost in it.
Stare up at the sky from within it.
Enjoy the grass while it last...

Mary L. Elges

Love

Love, hate, sex.
Stupidity.
Love is a fallacy.
A great lucid pearl,
black with emotion, void of all.
A great festering sore.
The gaping wound that is my love.
My heart stops. My brain implodes.
You come to me, a vision, a dream, a fantasy.
You are real. You are not real.
A torturous being of all men.
My hatred grows.
The hate for you, for all mankind.
My black soul sees your inner self.
I think I shall not go.
What? What do you want?
My death? My immortality? My inner sanctum.
You are not real. You are an inexplicable device.
I will not give in.
I will not die. You will not love.

Steve Byars

I Remember You

As the sun begins to set, I still remember you, the stillness that
surrounds me, reminds me that you gave me life, you gave me hope,
and you gave me unconditional love.
All silent but indeed noticeable. Mother you made me the strong
woman I am today.
Though you are no longer with me, I feel your warm gentle
tough and guidance from heaven up above.
The memories of you still linger deep in my heart and mind.
I love you mother, to me you'll never die. You will always be
beautiful to me, my dear precious mother.
Though you never asked for much, but gave your all, I will
be forever grateful for a mother as wonderful as you.
The years have past and gone, but today as time goes on, I sit
and watch the sun rise, I know I will some day be with you
again in paradise.....
Mother I will always remember you!

Wanda Edwards

Except It

Except the pain,
Swallow the pride,
Don't try to gain,
Or fight what's inside,
Think to yourself it's for the best,
Keep it in your head don't give it a rest,
Tell yourself this for me,
To bring out the best, the best that I can be,
Open your mind to a new level of learning,
Let it absorb and send you turning,
Breathe as if this were your last breath,
Exhale as if this were your way to death,
Don't try to stand pretty,
Just stand and take the pity.
Lead your mind, to find, the center brake,
Except your mistake.
Except it like you would a prize,
With all this you will rise,
Because you have taken a step many don't dare take,
You've swallowed your pride and excepted your mistake.

Sherry Yasay

"Here I'll Stay"

I'm not an Angel; I'm a woman;
Take my hand...
We laughed and played at first, like a game;
And then into my Heart you came...
Here I'll stay until it's time for me to go!

Yes, we've seen different worlds'
We're not always the same...
You could of stayed outside my Heart;
But, in you came...
Here I'll stay until it's time for me to go!

My love has no beginning;
My love has no end...
And tho I won't ask for forever;
I'll just ask your heart for now...
Here I'll stay until it's time for me to go!

The future is, just that;
How long we have is uncertain...
Even tho behind a curtain...
But Still;
Here I'll stay until it's time for me to go!

Pamela Hunnicutt

Untitled

Teach me to laugh, I know how to cry,
Teach me to sing, as the years pass me by.
Teach me joy and teach me now,
Teach me love, for I forgot how.
When you left me, I thought my world would end.
How do I go on, when pain is my only friend.
I look out the window.
I run to the door,
But you're not there,
and won't be any more.
I wish I could tell you what
your love meant to me.
Wish I could hold you like it used to be.
So please teach me to laugh,
even though we had to say goodbye.
Teach me to laugh, I know how to cry.

Willa F. Zellner

Tears Of Heaven

Tears of Heaven have fallen down upon me,
Tears of heaven have set me free,
Tears of God have touched my face,
helping me to find my place.
Tears of heaven are helping me to see,
just where God will lead and carry me.

He has now carried me for many long miles,
full of laughter, tears and smiles.
The will of mine is His very own,
helping me be prepared to be shown.

I put my faith in all that he will do,
helping me feel strong and secure too.
My trust in Him is like the sands,
falling down into his protective hands.
Reaching for the sky and calling up,
hearing you voice will allow His love to erupt.

Tears of heaven have filled my life,
taking away all of my sorrow, trouble and strife.
Tears of heaven are in my heart,
knowing in the end that we will never part.

Toni Marie Miller

My Prayer

I say a prayer for you tonight
Telling God, to make sure your alright

To keep you safe in your hours of need
To cuddle you with his sympathy

To tell you how much that you are loved
To show you the powers from up above

To forget about the pain and the tears
To remember the things that fill you with cheer

To show you how much that you are worth
To help you with your mission here on earth

To tell you to be kind and loving to man
To go out of your way to lend a hand

The light from this prayer is bright and clear
To let him know I am very sincere

As it shines straight up to the heavens above
It will fill all the angels with glory and love

The will come down and help you just as I asked
And try to lead you on the right path

Knowing my light will shine its way through
All my prayers shall be given to you

Sarah Grimm

Weeping Sky

I see flowers by the grave watered down by nature's tears, tears of sorrow, tears of pain, and the tears of torment!

As the earth is hurled around the sun, as the moon melts into the mountains the tears fall endlessly, filling a thirsty man's cup and cleaning a dirty man's hands, face, and feet reborn unto the world, the better image of a man, he has become.

And as the dove flies toward the heavens the sun and rain embrace. A rainbow is born.

Steve Siwek

"Destined"

From the moment we first
talked, I know you were the one to grow
old with. The year's we shared together,
became a test of our bond. For a moment,
we've almost given up, but, our hearts
told us better. I love you more than you'll
ever know, and will be with you, an eternity.

Monique Guerrero

Here's To Love

Here's to love,
I've travelled that road before,
Here's to love,
Intertwined our souls before.

Siamese twins,
With our emotions under siege,
Yes, I've been there before,
In the great commune of one,
And with every deed,
I vie something must be done
To gratify this need,
Oh-oh-oh-yes, here's to love,
Our conscious epitaph.
As down the road we go
Having known what only some have known.

While impassioned kisses obscure,
All that we deplore.
Yes, I've been that road before.

But, here's to love, in all its diversified varieties.
And no one can deplore, the heights to which we soar.

Eugenia C. Forée

Moon Light

The moon shines so bright in the sky
I sometimes wonder why we have to die

Someday our time will be near
Death will be the only thing to fear

We wonder why life will end
Only after the generation bend

I guess someday we will have to go
I think that is all that we need to know.

Jason George

Untitled

It is the nighttime that
I suppose I fear the most.
There is something forbidding
in the descending shadows
which compounds my trepidation
of another empty night.
I must preoccupy my mind
through the motion
of the passage of time.
In that,
I realize that although
the emptiness envelops me,
it is really me
beginning to know my heart.

Bobbi M. Schutz

Untitled

Did you ever feel love?
I think you seldom have

Will you ever say to me
I love you...

By that time, it will either be
to late
Or love will have gone

So when I say to you
I love you
It doesn't mean I know you
won't ever go

It will only mean, I wish you
didn't have to...

Judith Giacobbe Schmick

"A Better Place"

How great I felt, graduation was near,
I thought I'd burst with pride.
For me the goal was all too clear,
To continue in my chosen field.
The acting "bug" was well entrenched,
My lines were firm and full of strength.
Now on to greater things was next,
But first I'd have to change my "text."
So California here I come,
What dreams abound, I've yet to count.
The years go by with no regrets,
I ply my trade, my mind is set.
But soon my life will take its toll,
The final chapter to unfold!

James has left for a better place,
Where pain is not a thing to fear.
He flies with angels out in space,
We always know that he'll be near.
So rest in peace, we love you James,
And someday we shall meet again.

George P. Sposito

Hello

I went back home last week.
I thought I'd say hello to friends
That I'd lost track of —
The ones I used to know.

We joked and talked and laughed a lot.
We caught up right away.
It wasn't long before we searched
For something new to say.

As the awkward pauses lengthened,
I realized then just why.

I'd gone back home of say hello —
but I'd really said goodbye.

John Burnett

Life

It's a gift from God
I truly feel.
It creates situations
That I must deal.

It's the little things
That means a lot
It's the thoughts
That come from the heart.

It takes me here,
And takes me there.
Life is in bloom
Everywhere.

It's so precious
And so free.
That's why it's so
Special to me.

Barbara S. Popeleski

Only Me

I thought I could be like you.
I wanted to be like you.
I admired you.
Everything you did
inspired me so.
Absolutely perfect,
not a flaw to your name;
so difficult the task,
yet so hard I tried.
On a pedestal,
with dreams of being just like you.
It took a hard fall
off of that pedestal
to open my eyes,
and allow me to see
that the person I wanted to be
was not you,
only me.

Dawn Knight

The Reason

If I can make someone happy
If I can remember friends, far and near
Then I really know the reason
Why God sent me here.
I was made in His image, so I'm told
A miracle to behold
I must not forget
How very much I am in His debt.
So I hope to follow - close to His plan,
Loving, caring and helping
My fellow-man.

Elaine S. Motte

My Home Was Destroyed!

Will I ever go back?
(I was asked by a stranger)
Since there is no more war,
and a fear of danger.

I answered: no!
and it has nothing to do with my fears.
My home was destroyed,
and I have already shed my tears.

Although the land is still there,
my home was destroyed.
Iran was the name that was kept,
by the people they employed.

Forgive me for not caring.
Believe me I have tried.
To care about my home,
and my main source of pride.

Hirbod Rashidi

"The Dream"

I once had a mysterious dream,
I was in a room full of steam.
There was nothing I could see;
I was thinking where could I be.
I could hear someone start to sing,
But I could still see nothing.
Finally I saw some light,
It was not a beautiful sight.
I look down into the light
And I saw I was in a fight.
I was lying on the ground;
I wasn't making any sound.
I knew that I was dead;
There was nothing to be said.
At least I'm in a better place,
Where I'll spend the rest of my days.

Fernando Moran Jr.

Untitled

if i could hold on to You, My Dear,
i'd hold You till the end untold,
till canyon fall and mountain small,
till life had none to behold,
till sun is dry and lowly fly,
till war and peace are one,
till sky not blue and liar true,
and diamond back to coal.
for sun not there and You brush Your hair,
as You nestle closer to my breast,
for if i could hold on to You, My Dear,
i'd hold onto You forever.

Anthony Distinti

If I Only Could

If I only could
If I only could
I would, oh, I would
Go to the stars
Around Mars
And catch a few
Of those on view.
Or maybe a trove
Or the whole bunch
Just for you, my love!
(And all before lunch.)

Fernando Ramos

Life

The sky is bright the sun is out
If feels like everything is right
Then come the changes
Whether it's time or ages
We wonder why this has to be
Life is jolly
We come and we go
And in between we do as we please
Sometimes we have joy and laughter
And other times we have pain and disaster
When we are down
The sun will come out after
We will be up and about
To continue the between
So you see
That's what it is all about
So don't despair
The sun will be out
And there will be
Joy and laughter

Christa Rohrich

If He Came Back

I'd give anything to hold him again
If he's not with me my life's at end.
Without his love, I'm too far to be worth.
If he came back, I would be in his arms,
I would immerse.
I need a lot affection.
If he came back, I would say
I love you I thought I would mention.
My life is in distress.
My feelings are a mess.
If only I could say or write.

Jessica Fooks

Untitled

How can I grow
If loved ones won't let go
Don't they know
I am me anyway
on my own . . .

If they hold on to yesterday so tight
even yesterday cannot breathe
Then how will they begin to know
the "Me" I became to be . . .

Perhaps they simply choose to refuse
Not to see,
Especially if what they "Do" see
is "Not" what they expected me to be . . .

If they could,
Do "You" suppose
That those whom I appreciate
could then appreciate me?

Cynthia L. Dalton

School

School, school,
If you go you're not a fool
School, school,
You can use it as a tool,
For working your way into life,
Not into jail like a gun or a knife,
School, school,
If you don't go you won't succeed,
Unless you flip burgers at Mic-E-Dees,
School, school,
If you go you're not a fool!

Erik Chinery

"To My Sweet Jesus"

There is no one above you
I'll always put you first,
your kingdom and your righteousness
I'll pray to daily thirst.
My life I set before you
to use me for your will,
teach me your commandments
teach me to stand still.
Let the Holy Ghost by my guide
before unrighteous men,
let the light inside me shine
to convict them of their sin.
Purify my heart and mind
is my prayer to you each day,
that I may be a witness
to the ones you send my way.
Thank you for Amazing Grace
and for the love you have for me,
May I "always" show my gratitude
for the day you set me free!

Alicia Lofthouse

At Grand Ma's House

When I am up at "Grand Ma's House"
I'm always good as gold -
I try so hard to be polite,
'Cause GrandMa's awfully old!

She dishes out my favorite food-
I eat an awful lot,
'Cause if I don't she feels my head
To see if it is hot.

And when it's time to go back home,
I give "Grandma" a squeeze;
'Cause "Grandma's" need a lot of love-
That's why they aim to please!

I think of all the many times
She's said my good night prayer,
And know the world won't be the same
When "Grandma" isn't there!"

Elizabeth B. Dawson

Luminescent Love

I need the heat absorbed from light.
I'm feeling cold and I feel black.
And when I'm warm and I feel white,
I send the light reflecting back.

And sometimes in the still of night,
I'm freezing cold and all alone.
It seems that I can't take this blight.
But dawn always makes itself known.

Some days the light I do impart.
I feel so warm my soul will sweat.
And just before it floods my heart,
Is when the sun will start to set.

And on some nights I am on fire.
A kindled light when two souls tie.
The source of light is blazed desire.
The aura seems it cannot die.

In mid day I can feel the shroud.
The warming light seems to retreat.
When my life turns into the cloud,
That blocks out all the light and heat.

Brian Pass

I Am The Leaves

A cold fall day
In a deep and dark October
I am alone
Gazing from my window
To the field below
Watching the silent fall of leaves
I am the leaves

I've built so many walls
So deep and wide
That no one can get in
I have no need for people
Because they cause pain
I am the leaves

And don't speak those three words
I've heard them so many times before
I have my books
And my poetry to protect me
Hiding in my room
No one will hurt me anymore
For I am the leaves

Billie-Jean Robinson

"The Ocean's Winter"

The sun rises up over the Pacific,
In a distance from the snowy beach lies,
Blocks of ice,
They sparkle in the sun's gleam.
Few rocks there are on that white beach,
I have a special one,
I sit on it every day,
"The ocean is vast,
As is the sky"
I ponder this every day.
Today as I sit on my rock I also think,
"The ocean loves the winter,
The ocean loves the winter,
As a mother loves a son.
It strives to hold on,
But can't, for the winter must go.

Brian Schultz

Untitled

I am in a strange situation,
In a strange land.
I don't know who, and when to turn to,
Please Lord give a hand.

I am on the threshold.
Just about to take flight.
I'm fighting with my feelings
It's deep rooted inside.

I hear voices calling me,
Is that you mon? Did you say Angie?
What am I to do? Is there a plan?
This feeling is gently out of hand.

I've searched and searched the Universe.
The answer is there, right at hand.
I think I will take Jacob's ladder,
And view the promised land.

Angela Gibson

Someone Out There

For a child

Someone out there loves you
in a very special way
and though the years may pass us by
the love will never fade.

For am I that someone out there
hoping one day you'll hear
how much I truly love you
even though I am not there.

I will always wonder about you
and imagine where you might be
You are a VERY SPECIAL SOMEONE
who means the world to me.

You will be in my thoughts and prayers
as each day comes to an end
I hope someday you'll understand
and know you have a friend.

God Bless you and keep you safe.

Jo Ann M. Kirn

I Wanna Be Saved

I'm flat on my back
in darkness

My heart is pulled apart
by thoughts crashing inside
with sharp edges
severing feelings
impossible to sort.

I grope clumsily
in the blackest part of night
knocking over a lamp,
cutting my finger
making me bleed.

I leave stained walls behind
looking for the light
that will save my life.

I don't wanna die
I don't wanna die

I wanna be saved.

Janice W. Hodges

You've Heard It A Hundred Times

Enjoy yourself in college,
In life's adventure you'll forage,
Careful as you start,
But you must study hard.

Learn what is taught.
As well as what is not.
All things difficult can be
Made simple and free.

Ponder before you speak
May seem slow and meek,
But promises are kept
And your heart's content.

Worries and fears we all have,
The decision is to take which path?
With courage, do not stagnate,
Choose the one that creates.

As you grow a year wiser,
And a heart kinder.
Your birthday is really a stepping stone
To a beautiful life of your own.

David Louis

Memory

You, in my thoughts,
in my dreams
can't get rid of you

Realizations,
you were the one that I was waiting for
yet now we're apart

Please leave me!
Hell is this,
torture, pain

Either be with me in life or not at all
the dreams, the thoughts,
You're teasing me!

Stop!!
My tears show my pain
I can't live like this
Have mercy on me

You in my thoughts,
in my dreams,
the only memory of you still with me
Yet I wish it would leave.

Elizabeth Aguilar

Seasons

"Twas fall, as I was sitting,
In sorrow, 'neath a tree,
That I heard its shim'ring leaves
Whisper this to me."

"Winter comes to everyone,
My bright foliage does not stay.
'Tis sad, my branches will become,
Soon, as barren as your heart today."

"Spread your cares upon my boughs,
I will hold them winter long.
'Tis known that spring will come.
Hearken for the spring birds song."

'Twas summer, as I was sitting,
That I heard its shim'ring leaves
Whisper this to me.

"Tis odd, my winter friend,
Come in joy, draw near,
The burden you left with me,
It is no longer here."

Jean Kramer

Untitled

See that man setting all alone
In the big city alley that he calls home
He has no one to care for him-
No place to lay his head
He just goes wherever he can
and there he makes his bed.

How did this fate befall him?
Where is his family?
Doesn't he know someone-
Who knows his desperate need?

Gone is his carefree childhood ways
Where he used to laugh and play
Now is replaced with lonesome hours
And the burden of the day.

All he wants is a morsel
to sustain his appetite
To dull the pain he feels inside
Before the morning light.

Heidi A. Bruce

Rain Fall

My soul finds peace
In the falling of the rain,
Rolling thru the gutters,
And on the window's pane.

The thunder of it,
Upon the metal roof
Reminds me of wild horses
Galloping hoof by hoof.

Duane Martinez

Whimsical Expression

Fingernails, toes, waistline and such,
In the scheme of the Universe
really don't mean much.
But if I am to be
the Person God created me to be
I must paint my fingernails,
wiggle my toes,
and garnish my waistline
in colorful clothes.
For my Spirit requires
an expression, you see,
a demonstration, somehow,
of all I'm meant to be.
So bring on the polish,
the mud and the belts.
I am learning to live
to be truly MYSELF!

Connie Inkmann

Untitled

Nature, nature everywhere,
in the sky and in the air.
Flowers blooming in the spring,
little birdies out to sing.
Little fish in the waters,
kangaroos and their daughters.
Penguins waddle to and fro,
don't forget the annoying crow.
Lions roaring with all their might,
the crickets that you'll here tonight.
Also the beaver that dams the river,
the porcupine that seams to shiver.
Earthworms that enrich the soil,
snakes and lizards in their coils.
Polar bears white and fluffy,
panda bears that look quite stuffy.
Bunny rabbits hippity hop,
eagles sore to the top.
Monkeys swing from tree to tree,
their all unique like you and me.

Cory Hull

Precious Poems Of Love

People, people
In the street
Won't you move
Or do you weep
I try to move
I try to see
The most
Important
Part of me.

Annette M. Nixon

My Love

My heart seeks for you,
In this wide, polluted world.
Life can be longer.

Especially when,
You know love is in the heart,
And when one loves you.

With inside of you,
Your heart attacks the love,
In which I gave you.

Jenny Hofmeister

Untitled

The devil dances, his eyes aglow
Inert his partner lies below
The devil dances, he picks up his pace
He scans the crowd for a fresh new face

The music was wild, I danced each round
Without a care, nor honor bound
Me from my worldly chase
For fun and frolic, no act too base

Too late I learned the devil's way
Exacts a price that I must pay
The faster we whirled, the wicked master
Waltzed me down to ruin and disaster

Too late to repent, to kneel and pray
My fickle friend has danced away
In truth could I still join in his revel
I'd still be dancing with the devil

Edith Buehler

Regeneration

Relentless lightning
Inflicts fiery wrath
Upon unsuspecting trees.

Hungry tongues of flame,
Fed by undergrowth,
Pursue fleeing animals.

Destroyer passes,
Appetite fulfilled,
Devastation in its wake.

Tendrils of grey smoke
Rise from forest floor
Aftermath of searing flames.

Cool nurturing rains
Encourage seedlings
Emergence from blackened earth.

Green forest rebirth
Gives food and shelter
For fire surviving fauna.

Carl Wm. White

Bubbled

Trapped,
inside the bubble
of expectation,
ordained by society.

Jason Fleming

Leg Lust

Today, as you can plainly see,
Interests are above the knee.
Micro-mini skirts the thing
With all the intrigue that they bring.

Most males I know will glare with glee
At areas far above the knee,
At twin mounds that they love to check
Which leaves them such a total wreck.

But I'm the kind of gammy guy
That doesn't seem to know just why
That female legs are my true measure
And the way I get my pleasure.

"Yes" .. hose and heels are my real bag,
Cause I find naked legs a drag.
So .. if you think that heavens above,
Don't forget, there's legs to love!

Herb Walsh

My Wonderful Boss

Slowly slithering across the halls
into his office.
At a glance one would not notice
the delicate curved fangs hiding
behind his smile.
Never knowing when he'll strike
But within a matter of moments
all self control is lost with
the rattling of his tail
and slashing of his fangs.

Arlyne Escobar

Far Beyond

Reaching far beyond, deeper and deeper
  Into my thoughts,
Touching the untouchable, feeling
  The unfeelable,
Hoping and anticipating something will
  Come about it,
But realizing they're only thoughts
  Nothing more.
Stop! What idiocy to think and feel
  Thoughts so far beyond.
Stop... touch my mind, feel my
  Thoughts, talk to me in my dreams,
Go beyond reality and come into my mind.
See what I see, feel what I feel,
  But only for a moment.
Let the freeness of two minds come out.
Out into the world of dreams and mystery.

Jennifer Kaping

Patrice - A Teacher

The purity of her soul,
is a reflection of His infinite love,
from which all true beauty and goodness
usher forth.
To be seen in countless ways,
that touch and heal those with
whom she meets,
in an ordinary day,
made special by her grace.

George Wayne Hunt

Untitled

An abandoned auto pushed away,
Into sea coast rocks,
Battling into the foghorn's way,
Once taxi toot, and clocks
Laced in white
by sea gulls' droppings
Glasses dulled by misty sight
Conspicuous for their window stopping
Friendly crabs and a stolen tire
One wet faced reprobate for hire
Rims of iron
In a mud-filled hole
Looking for the cleansing ocean
As the whitening wind will blow
If I die gearing for the load
Where will I be dead?
In little efforts on the road
On settling into the rocky bed.

John R. Shaw

Untitled

When the days of happiness flee
  into the dark depths of despair,
Something inside dies,
    withers away like a beautiful
  flower without sunlight.
    But when the sun comes out and
      joy returns,
  The flower blooms once again.

Jaime Young

"A Nightmare's Reality"

Loving
Is almost harder
Than knowing
What to feel
When you are around.

When I hear your voice
My heart melts
It is the most beautiful thing
I have ever felt.

I was never
Given a choice
I had to love
Without knowing
I had to know
Without loving.

Barbra Brosman

The Road Of Life

The road of life
Is bumpy and long
With many potholes
And confusing detours
Paths may be crossed
Numerous times
Old friends and new
Through good times and bad
Remember
Every road leads back to home

Jennifer McKee

Ice Cream

I think the taste I like the best
is cold and smooth and sweet.

I find no other food around
that I would rather eat!

From childhood to my senior years
I love that creamy stuff,

I've yet to find at any time
to seem to get enough.

You may think I'm almost wacky
because I love it so,

Seconds I must always have
even thirds will sometimes go.

Ice cream, ice cream, ice cream
please fill my empty dish!

There's nothing short of heaven
that could fulfill my wish.

Eugene F. Finke

Ode To You

The knowledge you share
Is enlightening, never boring.
Your kindness, so rare today
Has given me new hope for tomorrow.
Your beautiful smile
Has put a song in my heart forever.
The time you spend with me
Has helped me to grow more each day.
The strength you've shown
Has made me secure in your love.
Your love, so wonderful
Has made me bloom
Like a million flowers in spring.
What do I give one so deserving
All my love; forever.

Heather P. Gill

"Children, God's Precious Gift"

One of the most beautiful sounds
Is hearing laughing children at play,
And to know that they have found
Joy and peace to fill each day.

I love to see a happy smile
As I meet their little eyes
And see into the heart of a child
Who's not hiding in disguise.

And feel the touch of a child's hand
As they reach out a hand to me
Knowing that together we can band
And a comfort to them I can be.

They are sweeter than any flower
More precious than any gem,
I could spend so many hours
Thanking God for all of them.

Children are a priceless gift
That only God can give,
They always give me such a lift
In a world without kids, I wouldn't want to live

Barbara Weaver

Reflections

FOCUS
(is it a dream?)

SHIMMER
(flutter, flutter, go the beats of time)

THE IMAGE BEGINS TO TAKE SHAPE
(who? what? why?)

SOFT BROWN HAIR
(soft caress)

HIGH FOREHEAD ABOVE
(strength)

TWINKLING MISCHIEVOUS BROWN
EYES
(fun, yet caring)

SENSUOUS SMILE
(love for all time)

WHO IS THAT LOOKING BACK AT
ME?
(you)

IT IS BUT THE MIRROR OF MY
HEART

Brenda J. Mathes

Weeping Willow

Weeping willow why do you cry
Is it because I want to die
Weeping willow why do you weep
Is it because I want to sleep
I'm not happy can't you see
So please don't weep for me
I'm to sad to come tonight
Maybe I should stay all night
Will the sky fall tonight
Maybe the world will end with light
Weeping willow why do you cry

Courtney McLaren

Time

To reflect and write!
Is not simple at all.

You create to struggle.
With all your ability,
To write at all.

Why is writing so difficult?
There is not enough talent in everyone,
Mediocrity, wins out in most.

So you sit and sit,
Without any hope
To write at all.
To express anything
Meaningful is your fall.

Oh why is it easy
To some.
To many the words
Just linger.

"And nothing at all!!
Come to the mediocrities!!"

Bill Wallach

Our World

To be, or not to be.
Is that how we see?
In a world with lots of color,
A world unlike any other.
Black and white, red and green,
Not as simple as it seems.
Many feelings, needs, and desires,
All too many we require.
Animals, people, flowers, trees,
To be, or not to be.

Jennifer Onofrio

Careless

Why is the world so cruel?
Is the end coming soon?
We were given this land,
to share and cherish,
to love and protect,
to clean and purify.
But what went wrong?
Everyone turned away.
Ignored everything,
but themselves

Anna Rabe

Our Love

To know the depth of our love
Is to know the unmeasurable sea...

To feel the warmth of our love
Is to feel the sun kissing me.

To set the length of our love
Is to stop infinity...

To see the beauty of our love
Is to see a glimpse of eternity...

Jerry Anderson

"A Wonderful Man"

A wonderful man
is what I asked for
Someone to hold,
love, and adore.

Someone to pick
me up when I'm down
and when I'm depressed
to turn my life around

A shoulder to cry on
someone to be true
that wonderful man,
my darling is you.

Anita R. Whetzel

Harmony

Time and again
It is momentous
For us to stop
All of life's
Pandemonium,
And listen to
The tranquility
Of our souls.

Carol Keenan Zawislak

"The Rain Forest"

As we destroy it,
It does become less and less.
It tries to fight back.

The rain falls upon the trees,
Our need kept destroying it.

The rain stops falling.
We become its enemy
As greed takes over.

The great forests of green trees
Is now a field of sadness.

As it grows smaller,
Our future cures are destroyed.
Never to be found.

We destroy our own future.
We are our own enemies.

What used to be green
Has now lost the fight of hope,
And it is now gone.

Our tears are the rain that falls
On the brown ashes we left.

Christine Hetzke,
Lindsey Von Boeckman,
Susan Riemer,
Nick Terrell

Beauty

Beauty is not a sin.
It is just something that
We have within.
Within our hearts, minds, and souls
If you use it right
It will never grow cold.

Patience, love, and understanding
Are a big part.
All of this is usually
Found in your heart.

Beauty on the inside
Will reflect on the outside.
Beauty is not a sin.
It is just something
That we have within.

Alonda Weaver

Love's Reward

Inclined to hear heavenly sounds,
It is on earth that I am bound.
For my salvation I must stay,
But this is what I wish today.

I take one flight upon the wing.
With angles only I may sing,
Of love, of joy; it shall arise.
Bring forth a hush to anguished cries.

My cries I wail to God afar.
Oh, how I wish to be a star!
That I might live and be a light
Of hope, of warmth within your sight.

Oh, how I pray to share my love.
Oh Holy Spirit from up above,
Send me the patience to endure,
The pain I feel; — and to find the cure....

Deborah L. Clayton

Respite

Do not disturb my reverie.
It is only in that time and place
That I am completely myself
Only better.

I do not slip away
Often enough for you to feel threatened.
I come back to you refreshed
And strong enough to continue
My journey at your side.

And I return with gifts
Made manifold
By discourse between spirit and mind,
Having been allowed privy
To distant wonders
And the iridescent glimmerings
Of ultimate peace and joy.

Do not disturb my reverie.
I bring back love.

Arlene Cohen

Time Isn't Going Anywhere

Why must we always hurry time?
It isn't going anywhere,
Why do we run here and there
To just put on foolish airs?

Why must we out do someone else
Just to show them that we can?
We know the Lord is working,
But we won't stop to see his hand.

And we know the Spirit whispers,
"Slow down and rest awhile,"
But we curtly tell him, "later,"
And go on with stressful smiles.

At times, those in authority
Seem to holler, scream, and fuss,
But who's authority is higher?
Where do we really put our trust?

Don't let those others hurt you,
And tell you things you shouldn't,
Remember, Christ will strengthen you
To do the things you couldn't.

Christy Cumbie

Fear

The silence stretches on
It seems like forever
What do you say
When the anger is gone?
Do you just walk away
Or stay and comfort?
  Silence can be deadly
  When that's all there is
  Help is there when you need it
  But is it really there or are you
  Just imagining it?
Love is there, you just can't see it
You feel it in the air
And when you reach out to
touch it, it disappears into thin air
  Faith, the need, and the want
  Is what you can really have
  And it will never disappear

Amanda McBride

Love Just Happens

Love just happens
It just don't go away
I'm afraid love will be around
For a long time to stay.

Some say it's in the head
Some say it's in the heart
But there's one way to test it
That's to try and stay apart.

It will tear you to pieces
It will tear you apart
If it don't hurt your head
it will surely tear up your heart

So if you ever fall in love
You'll know about it for sure.
You sure can't hide it.
For love is clean and pure

So don't let it hurt your head
Don't let it hurt your heart
Just do what mother nature said
Don't try to test it, by staying apart.

Bobbie J. Blose

This Old House

This old house, sure needs some fixing
It looks like it's falling down
I guess the folks have all been right,
When they said I stayed away to long.
But maybe, with a little fixing
I can make it look like new,
and bring back all the memory's,
And the love I have for you.

Francis Maples

Untitled

Dear Love
It seems that I've been waiting;
waiting for you forever.
You're always on my mind;
invading my dreams,
whether I'm awake or asleep.
I wonder what you look like;
how you dress and how you act.
I've always pictured you
a rugged, dark haired cowboy;
making a living on a ranch.
I would be so very happy if
I could just find you and
make my life complete.
Dear Love,
I'm still waiting.
Signed your love.

Denise Gronke

A Gun

Strong, proud and loaded
It sits alone on the table.
It lays there for 1,000 years
Of killing it isn't able.

But then a man picks it up,
And now the danger starts,
For only a man, not a gun alone
Can put a bullet in someone's heart.

Candi Vlcek-Pionessa

Anger

Pain screams.
It shrieks,
Loudly.
Hate gracefully slips its
Claws into flesh.
Tearing slowly.
People wail, feeling and
Seeing their flesh being
Severed.
It can not be ignored.
A sliver of severed skin
Slips silently to sleep on
The soft ground,
And then,
Explodes.
And it is over.
Only death allows rest.

Janae Kirkpatrick

Growing Old

Growing old isn't easy
It takes a lifetime to achieve
Filled with joy and sadness
And pleasure and great pain

Growing old is not a choice
That a person can freely choose
Rather a gift from God
That should be respected and appreciated

Growing old is not always pretty
Our bodies wear our years
Yet what makes us who we are
Forever remains the same

Growing old is a great teacher
From which the young can learn
If they take the time to listen
To the knowledge of the aged

Growing old is an honor
For the old begin anew
In every person that they touch
With the wisdom they've attained

Joanna Paladino

Yesterday

I wrote a little poem
It was short, not long
With the dots and comma's
Right where they belong.

I didn't win a prize
You can easily guess
Because in writing it
The words had no class.

A cloud passed over the sun
And I heard a loud thunder
Could that be my fault?
No, it was mother nature's blunder

Soon I saw a rainbow
The colors beautiful and bright
Later I went to bed
And slept all night.

Grace Britt Horner

A Life Long Wish

If I had but one wish to make
It would hands down have to be
That I never lose the sacred part
Of the child that's still inside of me.

I couldn't bear losing the wonder
And the innocence of days gone by
I want to keep the imagination
As seen from a child's eye

I never want to become so cynical
And lose all of my trusting ways
That I possessed so long ago
In my cherished childhood days.

Ann Marie Albright

Hidden Love

I seldom say I love you
  it's a word you long to hear
I have never ever told you
  of my deep internal fear
I loved a puppy
  we had to move away
I loved my happy school ground
  but I grew to old to play
I loved my buddy
  he was a bosom friend
I lost him to the water
  where the rapid river bends
I know the gods are watching
  love is theirs - they always say
If they knew how much I loved you
  they would spirit you away!

Henry Wenda

Northeast October 1994

This Autumn song,
Its desperate untenable tone,
No gentle breeze
Nor quiet fall of colored leaves
May escape
The icy imminent landscape

Borne of wild fusion,
Full artistry illusion,
Mind and soul still unfound
In heaving earth's breathing ground
Desires of moist passion
Arguably fashioned

Soon long aimless nights,
In bitter chill that bites.
The imp cannot hold
His moment cold
Song, reminding us again and again
What is, what has always been.

Douglas A. Brandt

Tears Of Wax

Your angry tears fall
Like hot wax dripping
Dripping from a burning candle
Melted by an angry flame
Relentlessly burning down
Down until it consumes
All that us around it
I wish I could lick my fingers
Lightly touch you
Cooling your angry flame
Then breathe your loving smoke

Donald S. Lord

"A Father's Teachings"

Dear Dad, this poem is only for you
It's for all the things
You taught me how to do

You taught me how to camp
And you taught me how to fight
And you taught me what was wrong
And you taught me what was right

You taught me how to fish
And you taught me how to hunt
All this since I was a little runt

You have taught me these lessons
That no one could of done
Because they are lessons
That a Father shows his son

Now that I'm older and I too have a son
I will tell him that his Grandfather was the one
That showed me these things
That I teach him how to do
For that Dad, I really do love you
Love your son,

Dave Myers

Silent Scream

While worrying about the world outside
It's happening in your house,
Then your strong out going child
Becomes a timid mouse.

Things can changes drastically
In a matter of years,
Just like the silent scream
No one seems to hear.

You warn your child "To just say no"
To booze and illegal drugs:
But who would think to "Just say no"
To a relatives secret hugs.

I beg you to pay attention
Don't pass it off as lies
Please hear the silent scream
When you look into their eyes.

The shattered trust and emotional pain,
Will take sometime to heal,
But by being aware of what's going on
Your able to stop the next secret feel.

Becky Church

Of Death

Be not deceived of such as death,
It's just another door;
There are no limits to your paths,
You choose to come and go.

Bring courage to your lonely heart,
Of trust and faith be yours;
From the divine mind you're not apart,
There's no such thing as loss.

The sea awaits your journey evermore,
Embrace the ship and sail;
Embark and leave an ancient shore,
And wisdom shall prevail.

Dennis Panagopoulos

"Last Time"

I stopped by your house last night
It's still the same dear place...
Rustic wood and curtain gay
Mid trees of woven lace
The sampler hung upon the wall
its verse in red and blue
the radio was playing a love song
meant for two.
I slowly turned and walked along
the path of yellow sand
while a thousand blinding
stars looked down
and cried "we understand!"

Jean B. Zurich

The Perfect Wish

Look! In the sky.
It's the first star of the night.
It must be a wishing star.
Stop! Listen!
It is saying something.
"You shall have one wish from me...
But make it a wise one.
You may just get what you ask for."
The star's wise words made me wonder.
Is there such a thing as a perfect wish?
I could wish for money
But along with money comes greed.
What about world peace?
No there's always one corrupt mind.
I could wish to never be alone.
But then I'd have no privacy.
That's it! I've got it!
The perfect wish was right in front of my
eyes.
But where had the star gone?
It was lost in the maze of the galaxy.

Angelique Sekerzicky

The Battle

The moon stands glowing in
its victory
Over the sun
Little does the moon know the
battle has just begun
The clouds stand in a circle as
if to place their mark
A beam shines through to bring
An end to the dark
Purple and Pink fill the sky
As the moon slowly dies
The moon puts up one more fight
To keep it's only right, the night
The sun is high and the night is over
As the sun laughs so long my brother

Heather Hinman

Time

Don't let it go, don't give it up,
it's yours so make it last.
Our time on earth is short enough.
Take time, don't let it pass.
For time is precious we all know;
for there is a time to come
and a time to go.
And as we look back
through our fleeting years,
we ask our self, "Was it worth
the time and the painful tear's

John S. Nardi

This Great Land

The will of the angels are singing.
Joy in my heart only God knows.
The whispering pines telling a story,
About things we do not know.

The words of wisdom are flowing.
Only a few understand.
Why this life is worth living.
The wealth of this great land.

Look onward, and think homeward.
That is what comes to my mind.
No matter how hard we work,
Still have mountains to climb.

All tension at ease, enjoy the
Peace and quiet the night brings.
Tomorrow is another day to pave
The way to greatness again.

Jeanette Stamper Huff

What Is Beauty?

Beauty is not always,
Just in the things we see,
Sometimes it is hidden,
Like inside of you and me.
Beauty can be in,
The things we do and say,
And it can be shown in,
Our lives day after day.
Beauty is in the sounds,
We so often hear,
Beauty is in shedding,
A loving tear.
Beauty is all around us,
Each day that we live,
We feel it in ourselves,
Whenever we give.

Elouise Collins Mason

Puppy Love

There was a frightened little puppy
Just sitting in the sun
He was dreaming of a meadow
Where he could play and run.

But he only felt hot concrete
On his little paws which burned
He was last in New York City
He hoped his family would return.

But wait - he just remembered
He was wearing his ID
And the little man at the hot dog stand
Might find his family.

So two days past and then at last
He saw his master grin
And scooped him up and kissed him
With mustard on his chin.

Hazel Marie Miles

Random Hearts

Love thoughts cascading
like
silent
music
over
the wearying soul

Donna Denman

Wish You Were Here

I wish you were here,
Just so I could hold you near.
But you're so far away.
Why can't you love me just for one day?
Whenever I see you all I can do is stare,
I love you so much, don't you even care?
When I gaze into your eyes,
All you tell me are stupid lies.
You tell me that you love me,
And that we were meant to be.
Then you tell everyone,
That I'll never be the one.
Why do I still love you?
I guess it's cause I have no clue.
Do you enjoy to see me in pain?
Because if you do, that's really vain!

Courtney Harchak

Two Months Ago

Two months ago I called you up
Just to see what was what
You told me that you wanted to flee
And I gave up and set you free
Why I did that I don't know
Because it caused me so much woe

Here it is the 17th of September
And I bet you don't even remember
Two months ago I called you up
Just to see what was what
You said for us it was the end
But you have decided to begin again

Now here I am, sitting alone
My heart has turned harder than stone
You don't care about me anymore
But I already know what's in store
Two months ago I called you up
Only to say goodbye to us

Amanda Kutch

There Was A Place That I Once Knew

There was a place that I once
knew. Where the grass was
green, and where the sky
was blue. We would go there
you and I where we could be
sneaky and sly I love that
place with all my heart, that
place where we do part. We
play there day and night that
place where we don't fight.
I hope to see you very soon,
and hopefully under the gray
full moon.

Jackie Davison

Looking Out

I look out at this vast sky
Looking at the sheer beauty
Of this vast expanse
Questioning where it goes and ends
What unimaginable creator gave
It to us to view.
For it brings our sight a thoughts
In true perspective
We are in relation nothing but a
Speck of sand.
But are mighty in vision and
Thought to be able to cherish its or

J. Tauber

Midnight Star

The light of the moon
lasts forever casting
shadows on my room
people dance and
children sing songs
the light of the moon
makes them go on
stars look over the world
and angels pray to the Lord
to ask for childish dreams
the light of the moon
comforts those of you
who die too soon
as children we laugh to play
as others we laugh to cry
the light of the moon
will fade just as a tune
from a song
and the stars
will help it carry on.

Jodi Elisabeth Visconti

Distance

With the shadows around me.
Life is but a dream.
We know not where we go,
Nor what it all could mean.

What do we do?
What do we know?

None of it will matter
When the time comes to go.

For parting is the true evil
That all men do;
But if our hearts are strong,
In the end we will be true.

You may shout all you wish,
You may cry all you please;
But when we are reunited,
Your sorrow I will ease.

For parting is the true evil,
But please do not fear.
When the parting time is over,
We will again be near.

Jonathan L. Fritz

Nineteen Hundred And Ninety-Four

Splintered rainbows, broken dreams;
Life's not always all it seems.
Haunted days and tortured nights,
Angry blacks and angry whites.
Sleeping children dying young,
Serial rapists being hung.
Frats include sex galore,
Boy's a stud. Girl's a whore.
Earthquake, fire, cyclone, flood,
Guns are firing mixing blood.
Movie lead's a super hunk,
Getting rich and getting drunk.
Starving children, feed them all;
Venus, Mars, we hear your call.
Cancer ravaged and in pain.
Wasted money down the drain.
Buddah, Allah, God, Jehovah,
Cults in flames amongst the clover.
Red and blue. Blue and red.
Drive-by shooting. Bang, you're dead!

Anne Iskra

Orca

Gliding through the wetness
Like a bird soaring above
Massive, yet graceful
More beautiful than a dove

A song in the night
Is a conservation among friends
In a language unknown
And a meaning of no ends

Black offset by white
An appealing creation
Different from all others
In a world beyond imagination

I stare in amazement
This mystical beast
Surpassed by no other
Not in the least.

Jessie Benet

Restlessness

Pacing the floor
like a black panther,
wanting out
of this cage, my house.
Hearing the storm,
the thunder booms,
I want to be out
there in the rain.
I meander about
from room to room
looking for something
to take my mind away.
Outside my window
the rain pelts down
the wind howls, fierce,
calling to me,
"Come out"

Belinda Joy King

Listen

I speak smoothly and soothe
like a breeze
you can't hear me
only concerned of your needs
but what I need from you
just love and respect due
for the one that will always be there
and guide your way through
a true friend is near
so lay down your gear
both troubles and sorrows
will be washed away clear
just rest assure and you'll find
in me, peace of mind
from the one they call chosen,
my named is Divine.

Andrew Smith III

Lucky Break

A bird
Looking for food
Stands at my window sill
With a cat on the other side
And chirps

Donna Florio

Wishful Thinking

The bright moon smiles
like a nonchalant child,
stars pose like twinkling eyes;
relentless happiness, a surrounding glow.
In moments of sorrow
we almost wish
For a delicately lit staircase
leading up to that golden smile.
There we could sit
surrounded by its warmth
to ponder our most vulnerable thoughts,
like morning dew
gathering on the petal of a rose.

Annette Comey

"Desperation Or Love"

Nightfall comes in
Like a shadow within an open field
The wind whisper's
Slowly through the night.

The feelings are just right
The women come's out as a bit of moon.
Her eye's twinkle like a star
Her hair flowing in the light.

Your mind become's dazed
With a deep state of confusion
You think it's love at first sight
But you know it's not right

In desperation, you just might take
What you really don't want.
But desperation is not love
It has a long lasting effect on your life.

Like a sharp edge blade
Stabbing away at your heart.

James Downs

"The Puppet"

Pain rushes through my bones,
Like the river over the stones,
He screams at the shell that was created,
Only a puppet and I hate it,

He pulls my strings and I dance,
Escape, not a chance,
My mind is a pile of clay,
For him to mold and play,

All his thoughts, none are mine,
I have to break free this time,
Now my future, I can see,
It is death, R. I. P......

Jennifer Law

Celestial Wedding

'Tis only a lonely star,
Lost in the azure of night;
Tell me, star, if a traveler you are;
Bearing a golden light.
Close by a lovely cloud
Seems lost and lonely too;
Tell me, cloud, are you a shroud
Or a bridal veil of dew?
The lonely travelers meet.
A happy golden light
Gleams through the mist
Of the cloud it kissed
Wearing bridal robes of white.

Elizabeth P. Clarkson

All Alone

Sometimes I feel all alone
Like their no one to turn to
So I must keep on going
As I'm going I see people together
And wish that was me.
But that's the way
life goes.
So I must believe in me
and continue my journey
I go through many trials
and tribulations.
But all I have to do is
read the book of revelations
As I roam the streets
and think about
What's going on.
I realized that everything is gone.
And I'm all alone!

Jessica Smith

First Born

Mother listen - can you hear me?
Listen with your heart, see my joy.
Mother look - can you see me?
Shining like a star.

Mother listen, mother see.
See your first born's happiness
See my loved one.
Rejoice for me for she loves me too.

My son - I listen, I hear, I see.
You have found love and
I feel your joy.
Your loves glow warms my heart.

In finding your love
Memories you arouse.
Past shadows vanish in loves glow.

I rejoice with you,
My first born.
You are now a man in love.

I rejoice with you.

Esperanza F. Rodriguez

Stranger

There is a stranger
living with me
who is tolerated
by everyone but me.

She can't be as old
as she appears to be but
why can't she skip
and run
up the stairs and down
without worry.

I can't evict her
that is the rule
set by nature
who can be cruel.
But to live with her
I must look
in the mirror
and lie
that the stranger
cannot be me.

Irene Moss

Alone

Despair,
Loneliness,
A dark corner where nobody looks
Anymore.
Black,
Dark,
He never see's the light of
Happiness.
Always,
Alone,
Waiting for time to pass him by.
Evil,
Night,
Dark shadows start to fold
Upon him.
And yet,
He still does not arise.

Diane Creelman

The Crucifix

Around the neck of some holy priest,
Look at the image upon it at least.
To look upon it for many to see
A broken man, it is he.
Beaten and torn and wearing rags,
Under its weight, his body sags.
Upon his head, a crown of thorns,
Beneath his eyes, he silently mourns.
Nails that are driven into his hands,
Upon the day darkness lands.
Nails that are driven into his feet,
Knowing that death he is about to meet.
Here yet still, a spear in his side
Blood rushing forth in death to confide.
Here yet attached to a piece of wood
One day on this earth, he once stood.
It was for us that he was slain.
Only in three days to rise again.

Christopher M. Wilson

Home, Lord

I looked at my own homeland
Looking for what I'd but find,
Yet all I could find, Lord now there
Were memories left behind.

For you see not one forgave there
Not even one would but pray,
So I turned to you for answers
I was taught to live for today.

For you see not I supported
The acts, nor the mistakes
Yet cried on my Lord's shoulder
For this precious one not to forsake.

Perhaps looking in your closets,
I bet you will but find
Many sins to be uncovered
Then forgiveness you will, but find.

Gloria Webster

Love

Love is a sweet thing,
Love is for everyone or everything.
Love is for you and me
I guess what I'm saying is I love thee
Hope you feel the same as me
Cause I really do love thee.

Denise Storm

Squirt Goes The Bottle

Something I like allota
Lots of bubbles
You can forget your troubles
It's secure and free
Like lil-ole-me.
Lots of gas
That will soon pass
Chorus:
Squirt goes the bottle
Something I like allota
Lots of bubbles
You can forget your troubles
It's secure and free
Like lil-ole-me.

Just one drink
I just don't think
I found harmony
It sets me free
It's my destiny

Barbara Stewart

Marriage

Sharing and caring,
love and joy,
good times and bad times,
happy times and sad times,
a life full of memories shared
together, two as one.
A lifetime shared together,
each as his own, but still
a part of the other.
Someone to talk to,
or just to be with,
the feeling of being together.
The love you hold so dear,
seems to grow from day to day.
A hug, a kiss, a touch,
it's the little things that mean so much.

Faye Roth

Love Is

Love is the gate that opens the heart
Love is the star that brightens the dark
Love is the life you give to me
Love is the gift to set me free

Carol Bylock

Common Plea With Conclusion

Know my being, know me really!
Love my littleness unique,
Lift the essence-hiding veil,
Find the genuine you seek.

I appreciate your person,
Unsure self, so very dear,
Strive no more to prove your power,
I can love the lack you fear.

How at peace could be our living,
If in mutual recognition,
Each saw the other's sad unwholeness,
And cherished it into fused fruition!

Irma Frey Stevens

Our Love

I know that our
love runs deep.
Can't believe how
high and steep.
I could climb a
mountain as long as your there.
I would do anything
to show you how much I care.
I could swim
across the sea
as long as it's
just you and me.
You make me feel like
no one else can.
Something special between
one woman and one man.
I know it was
meant to be.
Forever, just
you and me.

Jennifer Janetzke

"The Little Gray Mouse"

The little gray mouse.
Loves everyone's house.
He's only so tiny.
But he is mighty.
He is rather pretty.
Mice, may be country or city.
Oh, what a pity.
He loves a home.
Doesn't want to be alone.
He comes and takes a peek.
Just to hear the woman shriek.
They are cute and rather nice.
Even if they are mice.

Agnes Nacke

4 A.M.

The golden round moon is hung
low in the velvet sky
The hint of rain touches your
face
The smell is like a clean
fragrance to your nose

It is peaceful and quiet out - with
no exhaust from cars
My faithful friend (shush - he
doesn't know he's a dog) and I
Walk to the store in quiet
serenity,

Me with my thoughts, and he, trying
to wet everything in sight
We come back home and go to
bed with peace.

Jonnie Fryrear

Scarred For Life

I remember that night and I must confess,
Lying down full of distress,
I can't even explain how I feel,
But this is all truly for real,
All I feel is shame,
And I'll never be the same,
I wanted to be free,
Why did it have to be me?
I really tried to escape,
Now I am just a victim of rape.

Elaine Katsoudas

Love

How does love feel?
Magic
Love is a magical gift.
You can't live without it. You need it.
You'll cherish it.
Never use or abuse. Choose who to love
And when.
What is love?
Love is the gift of the heart
The heart is the gift of life.

Janet E. Brown

Melodic Sounds

The toys
Make noise
When no one's there to hear
And it must sound so dear.
Like the little children playing
Or the sound of soft snow dropping
It will bring love
To any dove
As it brings happiness
To those of worldliness.
To the hearts of
Your lady love.

Gretchen Schneider

An Unfinished Portrait

A life cut short before its time.
Makes no reason, sense, or rhyme.

Like a picture roughly sketched
Then set aside for painter's rest.

Only an outline without detail
No color or shadow forever pale.

Who knows what he might have become
Or what great deed he may have done.

The pain and loss must be endured
Memories precious you try to hoard.
Your previous life forever changed
The canvas altered and yet the same.

He journeys on from here alone
His destination yet unknown.

Guided by our Lord above
To a place of perfect love.

Jessica Meene

Good Heartkeeping

All day the dust of trouble
met my eye
And shadows dimmed the beauty
of my view
I failed to see my loved ones
standing by
To help me change those cloudy
skies to blue

So through this darkling glass
I viewed my day
But suddenly ashamed -
I found my way
I lifted up the corner
of a prayer
And under it swept every
grief and care

Dorothy Laing Shoop

The Child Of Love

People complain about a name.
Many complain about deadbeat fathers.
I acknowledge a father yet
He denies me.
To deny interpreted as to refuse
To accept or to refuse to give
Why does a man refuse to give
His child his name.
Mother says that I was
A child born out of love
She says I should not worry
About the name.
People complain about single mothers.
What about the father who is
Also to blame.
If you are a father please
Concede.
After all how can a father
Deny a child of knowing herself.
You see it's not just a name.

Esthela Miranda

Divorce Cinquain

Contracts
May be broken
By the slightest glance
In the direction of a tempting
Situation.

Gloria Giles McCain

Camille

So that I,
May forever remember
Your smile, your light
Warm voice, and
Your smooth touch;
I would like to hold
You in my mind,
forever.
All thoughts may cease,
As thinking of you
Is thought enough.

Jeffrey Paul Hommerding

"Seein' Things Differently May Help"

The light at the end of the tunnel,
May not be what you think.
Just like at the end of a rainbow,
You'll find no gold to keep.

Some things do not always get better,
When you look down the road.
And the only way you can find happiness,
Is to work for all your gold.

When things get bad, make them better,
Do it today, tomorrow may never come.
Take the rainbow for its beauty,
And let the light in the tunnel shine on.

Frank Carlin, Jr.

Untitled

An artist paints what he sees,
Maybe exaggerated
Maybe illusion
but in his eyes perfection.
He measure the picture,
then squints,
and see it glow,
Now content and satisfied.
He put it up for sale.

Joyce Wetstone-Holstein

Memories

I'll keep the lovely
memories, that we have shared
and cherished.
And hush the little secrets
until I too have perished.
I'll miss her so, each
passing day, but yet in comfort
know.
That in God's hands, she's
found her home, with him
upon the throne.

Dorothy M. Lahue

Barn Owls!

Saucer eyes, shining bright
Menacing glare pierces the night.

Little ears, swiveling head
Loud enough to wake the dead.

Feathers white and feathers brown
Wings look like a golden gown.

Flying silent through the night
To a mouse, a deadly sight.

Mystic, mysterious, beautiful, big
Sleeps all day among the pigs.

Talons sharp, gleaming bright
Swallows food in one big bite.

Ears that hear the slightest sound
Listening, listening all around.

Jessica M. Little

A Wife's Elegy

Mourn me just a little when I'm gone
Miss me in the mornings
When I'm no longer here
To say good-bye.

Mourn me with a passion
That is missing
While I'm here
Saying good-bye.

Talk to me in loving tones
I never hear these days
Tell me that you'll love me
When I'm no longer here.

Touch my picture gently
As once you touched my hair
And tell the painted lady
Of the ache you have for her
When she's no longer here.

Mourn me with a passion
When I'm no longer here
Howl out the words in grief - that now I
long to hear.

Christine E. Preston

Jon's Poem

I love you now
more than words can say.
I think of you morning, noon, and night
Every minute of every day.

You're more man just a pal to me,
and more than just a friend.
If I had it my way,
our love would never end.

I have never felt this way,
but there's nothing I can do.
The only reason I feel like this
is all because of you.

Emily Payne

A Soldier's Memory

The florist arrived early in the
morning, on decoration day.
In his hand was a blooming Rose
Brush needing to be set.
Underneath its limbs there hangs
a card, and the writing on it said,
"Today I send a memory for someone
that is gone.
Someone everyone loved as one
of God's great sons.
So please take this my memory
and plant it on Dad's grave, to
say that, I am thinking of him
though I am so far away."

Joseph W. Baker

Dead End

I am spider I am spider
Mother sister father brother
Clicking spinning always weaving
Web of intrigue web of mercy
Are you hungry? Are you thirsty?
I will shelter I will feed you
Soothe your ego calm your panic
I will take you, home forever
I am spider I am spider
Clicking spinning always weaving
Web of darkness web of deceit
Hunger burning always growing
Coming closer to my webbing
I am spider I am sickness
I am your self, come to me
Enter cobwebs I will heal you
Stifling netting come to seal you
Home with mother home with father
I am spider I am your self
Kiss me

Bruce Paolozzi

No Gas!

I'm on the road, it's late at night
My car just starts to whine
I realize in a moment
I did not fill that tank on time.

There's no money in my pockets
Walking is very hard you see
Then I think of Grandma and her money
Oh, I can call, there's help for me.

Love always,

Grandma Ellen

"Unfettered Flight"

I take unfettered flight at dawn
My bones they rest in yonder grave
At last my spirit soars upon
Creation's light. Goodbye I wave.

From earth and all I've known and been
From my true loves, my family fair
If law dictates I'll come again
Into a body new I'll wear.

Pick up my life and start once more
As try I shall to rise above
With those same ones I did adore
Unfettered flight for this one dove!

But if OBLIVION is my friend
I'm gone forever in the wind!

Constance Durkin

"It Feels Like Only Yesterday"

So precious, so small,
My bundle of joy had it all.

It was love at first sight,
I wanted to hold you so tight.

Like a vase without its flower,
I felt empty and had no power...

To keep you with me,
It just wasn't meant to be.

You are in my heart,
We will never really part.

My first born son,
Will be compared to none.

I've accepted it somehow,
You wear a halo now.

You are my little angel,
And although at times it's painful...

May God's "will" be done,
But I still miss you son.

Cheryl Swanson

Untitled

Loneliness is knocking at
my door
I'm lying alone in the darkness

Staring into my walls, looking
for some answers.

Thinking of the past, wondering
What I could have done
different

Watching the shadows
Haunting memories linger in
my mind.

The skeletons in my closet
stalk me

Nobody around to talk to
I'm stuck in the darkness
and...loneliness is
knocking at my door.

Joanne M. King

My Times Are In Thy Hands

My times are in thy hands oh Lord
My faith is captioned "Free"
They wonder why, I tell them why
My faith is all in Thee.

I stand at times upon the brink
Of chasms deep and wide
I listen close for Your clear call
I stop! For You do guide.

Create in me Oh Lord above
Those times of testing true
And let me know Thy gentle love
In everything I do.

Let me meet friend and foe alike
And to them Jesus bring
And speak to them as to a 'mike'
Of my Saviour, Lord and King.

Clara M. Crist

Give It To God

Amid all of life's trials
My friend there is one who cares
He can take care of our worries
He listens to our prayers
Give it to God

When we feel lost and despondent
We feel that there is no end
To our trials and confusions
God is there, he is our friend
Give it to God

At times we may feel joyful
We are at the top of the world
Then we say thank you Lord
I always knew you could
Give it to God.

Isra Prince-Sammy

A Blessing

Do I have a talent?
My friends tell me so,
But I see it as a gift
from God whom I know,
Gives me many blessings
to be thankful for each day,
Without his guiding hands, I'd have
nothing worthwhile to say;

If he wasn't in my heart
to make me have such loving thoughts,
I'd only be a body,
Full of hate and finding faults.

But as it stands I do my best
to go the faith filled way,
And pray that I'll still be writing poems
when it comes to Judgment Day.

Brenda W. Looney

The Perfect Rose

The perfect Rose there is not one
Oh wait,
I was wrong.
Where is it you say
It's inside
You.

Barbie Wilson

Old Age

My eyesight is poor
My hearing no more
My joints seem to creak
And my outlook is bleak
Whenever I think of living
And not being able of doing
All the things of interest
That to me are dearest.

But thank goodness for friends
Of many ages and kinds
Who keep in touch
And take me to lunch
Or send me a gift
That gives me a lift
And I think as I snore
Ninety really isn't a bore.

Florence H. Walker

Crescendo - Decrescendo

We met
My heart beat faster

We were young and in love
My heart sang with passion

We married and reached middle age
My heart hummed a soothing song

You are gone
My heart is silent

Catherine Wojcik

Avalon

On wings of cherubs my soul has soared.
My heart has opened for the grand
reward;

Of sunny days
And starry nights;
Of Avalon
And paradise.

Of kisses sweet
As morning dew;
Where every dream
Is filled with you.

Of special moments
Yet to share;
Of love so fresh
And, oh, so rare.

Of silent peace
And warm embraces,
Gentle talk
And loving graces.

For when I thought love had passed me by,
God granted me just one more try.

Cassandra Jones

Untitled

Safe is the small man
No thoughts on his mind
Just the herd instinct
To keep to his kind
Where are the great ones
With ideas that sprout?
Check in your garbage
They have been thrown out.

Joyce Kwasneski

Waiting Upon Thee

O' the strength of my wings faileth
My lofty ideals I seem not to achieve
The height for which I strive
Casts its weights upon me
Yet my level will I maintain
As I learn to wait upon thee.

By reason of faith and a picture of hope
A rock steadfast I see
There will I drop my anchor
And wait with patience for thee.

As trees bring forth their sweetness
The bees whose honey I see
Though hindered by my feeble meet
Yet I have strength in thee

Teach me not to glory in success
For storms shall greet the proud
But in my frailty shall I know
That to learn is to wait upon thee.

James Jacob Gray

The Night Is Long

The night is long without your touch
My love is gone and missed so much
The days all slowly pass us by
You enter my thoughts; inside I sigh.

The love we shared can be no more
I had never felt that way before
There is no blame we both took part
And now the time will heal my heart.

The distance that was always felt
Made me want to scream for help
But yet I felt that no one was near
I tried to talk, but no one would hear.

This will be my last attempt
To show you where together we went.
After this no more I'll try
I'll only remember and inside I'll die.

Erica Cain

"Gone"

Thoughts run through
my mind spreading
everywhere. It doesn't
stop no matter how hard I
try, it won't stop.

It's starting to hurt. Hurt
so much. But in no matter
of time it stop. Fades away
so far away.

No pain, the pain is gone
nothing left but a bit of
imagination.

It's not enough though. As
the rest slips away, I start
falling and I can't stop
until someone
catches me,

But their's no one there.
I'm gone, gone from everything,
and I can't come back.

Ginger Golonka

"Time Keeper"

Gray hair and wrinkled brow -
my precious mother clutched the
wooden spoon-made doll-to her
bosom and closed her eyes-and
then she got up and made a
little bow-and clutched the
Bible in her other hand-

The same loving arms-not so
many years ago-hugged me
tight-when things weren't
right-and reminded us to
read our bibles at night-

Hair like silver, her gait slowed
with time - -
thank God I still have this
precious mother of mine —-

Gennett Burton

I Cannot Cry Anymore

I cannot cry anymore
My tears are gone so far away -
I seek deep into my heart -
I wonder what will come this next day-
The laughter joy and happiness
Yes it use to be mine -
But now I'm content to let it be,
And let the days pass one in time-
Oh, life, did I ask to come or go, me
this child of woe, now I sit and take
each day, I'll be content come what may -
I cannot cry anymore -

Emily A. Mathies

Equus Dances

Diffused light
naked lovers flee
through a passage
to a mystic space
Ecstasy forms
dreams of passion captured

Twilight blue
as night descends
impulse to find absolution
sweet asylum from
fear gripping down

Equus dances
opaque soft and wet
hard held open
colors, kaleidoscope
memories
spread unrepentant flames
yesterday's fire.

Jeffrey R. Blake

Holding Back; Holding On

Not a word is said;
No one makes a sound.....
Something is misunderstood
And hearts begin to pound...
Days blend into nights
Time goes too fast
Something is always changing;
Yet the anger and love lasts
False smiles become a mask
For emotions we don't show...
I smile saying - goodbye;
Crying for another chance
to say hello.

Jay Alec Ruby

Untitled

Through a tunnel I roam
never reaching the end.
Alone, scared, and fatigue
I lay to rest upon a stone.
Looking for sunlight to reach the end.
I stare from the windows of life.
But sunlight like heaven
never calls to me.
Darkness surrounds me and
I reside alone.
Stillness takes over as leaves
crack under every step I take.
To the end I shall see my
way out of hell
Alone and despaired I
keep walking.

Jena L. Salmons

No Hope

I gaze at her smile
Night after night
And look to her eyes
As my guiding light
Thinking of her
Brings feelings to life
I can't ever express
Try as I like
All that I want
But can never be
A life with just her
Standing next to me
A dream that it is
And all it can be
Leaving false hope
And disparity

Billy Hitchcock

Frozen Bird

With the first frost he fell;
No long winter for him ahead;
No struggle to survive the snowfalls
and cold winds.
These foes reserved for his friends.

Born of late autumn.
Time was his greatest enemy,
For he could not develop the strength
Which some later day would have
sustained him.

Ah! fallen bird; doth thy blithe spirit
somehow survive
In a world of flying and singing,
Where thou art ever alive;
Free from frost, cold winds, and
the Grim Reaper!

Earl Geldmeier

Silent Hearing

O to my Commonwealth
Oaths told in secrecy
try to remember
what we teach
for our listeners
remember better than we

Ashley Clements

"Among The Stars"

Come let's fly away so high
No more pain - no more cry
A place where lovers meet
A place that makes life complete
We shall go together to a world
far beyond the stars
There we'll be happy just the way we are
I'll love you, you'll love me
Neither of us will ever leave
We'll stay up among the stars
Away from the world down here
Where all around death is near
We'll be free up among the stars
And forever we will soon.

Jeanne Pruett

The LightHouse

The sky was dark
No stars were in sight
The storm had awakened the sea

The ship was lost
And blown off her course
And no one could steer her free

The Captain and his trusty crew
Had just about given up hope
For they knew this old ship
Couldn't withstand much more

When suddenly, from out of nowhere
A LightHouse seemed to appear
Its light so clear, and shining so bright
Helped guide the ship safely to shore

Clara Reynolds

Alone

Lost
No where to be found
Hopefully someone will
Come and break down my wall
To save me
Save me from what you
Us them
No that's not it
To save me from my ownself
Inside
Where its deep, dark and lonely
listen to me
No
Never
Not you
You hear what you want to hear
Not what I do
How can you listen to me
When you don't even listen to yourself.

Jenny Grace

Untitled

I sit hear at night thinking
of your love listing to love
songs we shared remembering
your touch and wanting for
that day to come back again
that day when we can hold
each other in our arms feeling
your sweet lips against mine
and wanting all your love.

Brooke Clarke

Nowhere To Be Found

No where to be found
not even a trace,
There's now a room that's
a ghostly space.

Sadness and trauma
is all that's left,
it's like a Hollywood
drama, a tragedy left.

Was it drugs or because
no one spoke,
that is what led to the
slash of her throat.

People said she never
tried, and in results
everyone shall cry.

Out of her room was a
ghostly sound, that's
where his spirit was
no where to be found.

Christina Coffee

Think Of You

Sitting here alone.
Not knowing
What to do.
I still think of you.
Often wondering
could this be true
The fear in your eyes
Running through in my mind
til every breath be his last
Becoming a memory in the past.

Caroline Jean Valdez

Drowning

Ocean rhythmic
Ocean swaying
Gently rocking me
Gently rocking me
Soothing my fears and fantasies
Mesmerized by its beauty
Hypnotizing me
Hypnotizing me
Saying, "Come and relax with me."
"I am all the God's beauty in the
deep blue sea." "Come and trust me
and all the beauty you will see
in my deep blue sea."

Claudia Cannon

Untitled

Past memories of happiness -
of playing and laughing.
Golden moments of sunshine -
of dancing and singing.
Soon they fade from my mind.
I cannot capture the thoughts -
for they slip through my fingers.
The laughter fades.
The memories vanish,
as I sit beside myself -
Alone -
Alone with no memories -
to cherish.

Asheley Bice

In All Of The Shadows

Her eyes tell the tale
Of all that has passed
Always keeping her safe.

It is all so clear
That her heart beats
With caution and care.

She cries like a baby
Laughs like a child
Only physique shows her age.

She longs to be held
To be loved and adored
Thick walls within know more.

She crawls to the edge
Never taking a step
Shaking from the depths of her core.

But because of her fate
And the uneven ground
She fumbles and falls without sound.

She never gives up and never looks back
To the place that has taken her soul.

Diana K. Georgeou

Pounding Hooves

Listening to the sound,
of distant pounding hooves.
The beautiful sight
of the Stallions,
gliding over the green hill top.

Coming towards my window,
then suddenly
like a flash of lightning,
they've gone away.
Only to leave a trail of dust,
and the sound of
distant pounding hooves.

Catherine C. Meacham

Crazy Quilt

Life's journey with its patches
of every size and hue,
Traveling its highroads and
lanes of somber blue,
Webbed together like a
crazy quilt in jumbled disarray
A blend of joy and sorrow,
of foolishness and pride
Worth every living moment
of its winding ride.
My quilt is nearly finished,
It will never fall apart.
Held together with faith
in God and the Loved
ones in my heart.

Agnes E. Vercillo

Thunderstorm

Dark clouds blanket the horizon.
Rain pounds against the window glass.
Lightning flashes through the dark sky.
You hear a crackle of thunder.

The sky returns to its clear state.
Once again, the bright sun wakens.
The grass glistens in the sunlight.
The storm is over, you decide.

Billy Abdale

Retrospection

As day drew to the close
of her short life's span,
a sigh burst-from deep within;
in mood of melancholy
wondered she,
where has my time gone,
and how has it been spent;
have I been good or evil -
gain or loss,
is it a world better
or grown worse,
because I have been today?

Carmelita K. Railing

Gentle Virginia

Peek-a-boo glimpse of foothill farms,
Of sandbox days, of country charms,
Sees gentle Virginia now;
In the peak of Fall! Holly cow!
Rock-a-bye mountains of Blue Ridge.

Hours I played in sifted sand,
Making roads with plastic trucks in hand.
The box now full of iron earth red,
Is live with fun. ALIVE, I said!
Rock-a-bye mountains of Blue Ridge.

Leapfrog leaves blow up and over,
Pastures of plantation clover,
Right by beautiful toy horses,
Framed with picturebook resources.
Rock-a-bye mountains of Blue Ridge.

Still looking through Life Saver holes,
At candy colored naptime knolls,
Sweet dreams in groves with lemon leaves
Are mine in Virginia, if I please.
Rock-a-bye, rock-a-bye, bye-bye.

Geaugua

"Rosehill"

I took a stroll through the land
Of the quiet rest and was moved
By the peace and beauty with every step
The herons and gulls were flying
Free amongst the pillar stones beneath
The trees
I thought of those who went before
To find their heavenly place and
Think of days to come when I too
Will find God's grace
There are those who lay who fought
A bitter fight to win a noble cause
For freedom bright.
Each life had purpose no matter what
The case and a Peaceful home is
Honored no matter what's your race

Jane G. Landini

Big Bear Lake

Lazily lounging
on the deck,
the lake before me,
I look
at fishermen everywhere,
lolling in their boats,
lines lingering for fish
reluctant to latch
onto their last meal.

Hedy Bonder Johnson

"Within A Image"

Living within a image
of this body
all feelings inside out

Days turning into night
Where has the memories gone
can you tell me?

Spring has been and gone
cold winter makes his way in
snow so white and soft
melts by a single touch of ones hand

Leaves that have been left behind
dry up by the single touch
of the sun; they fall to the ground
just like ones tears

Wind blowing leaves around
just leaving them behind, as we found them
now could a person be so blind

Living within a image in this body
I am lost
one day I will live only with happy thoughts...

Geraldina Oquendo

Everything Will Continue

Pop, little mindless bubble,
Off the top of my beer bottle.
For I know you must exist,
Though for me to live, I must resist.

Keep rising, soul-less foam
Create an air filled dome
I know you cannot resign,
Even though I'm losing my mind.

Peel off, two-dimensional label,
Off the wet side glass.
I am living, therefore unable,
To cool my hand's consistent grasp.

Pop away, sweet bubbles,
Turn my beer flat.

I know these words took time.
I understand things will continue,
Though slowly, I decline
And only find you,
To relate what's inside.

Diana V. Spindler

To The Young

Dream of tomorrow
oh delicate one.
With your wings take flight
to brighter worlds.
With your mouth
taste the fruits of nature
and the grains of the earth.
With your legs
land in safe havens of content.
With your mind
Imagine the worlds of tomorrow.
You are the creator
of all that is to come
all that shall be.
The worn and weathered will
be in your graces. Be kind.
Peace and unity shall be
where you are.

Hannah Robert

"Love Is Only A Gamble"

I'm gonna take a chance
on a new romance

After all, love is only a gamble.

I'm gonna find someone new
who will say, he'll be true

And I know it will be a gamble.

If he plays the game with
an open mind

Than I'll know for certain
he is worth my time

I'm gonna find someone who
will play the game through

If I loose
Love is worth the gamble.

Dolores Poland

Wormwood

Dawn claims no bond
On beauty's seed
That seldom grows
Unless to bleed.

With thoughts in car
We drive to moon
Of beach, of stars,
Of hearts immune.

To hide the wounds
Within each breath
And lose the chance
To speak with death.

Nightingales sing,
While we dance
From the tremors
Of night's advance.

Craig Stone

Plastic Indian

Plastic Indian
on the dashboard—-
eyes never to close again
in sun or sorrow.
A tribute or a trophy?
Can't quite understand
what this means
to hold something sacred
and present it on display such
hopeless icon.
What would you think fierce warrior,
to see your naked face
on the dashboard gathering dust
under the baking sun,
never to taste the rain again?
Would you notice the glass
and think that it covered
all of our hearts—
And would you think that none of us
have ever tasted the rain?

Oriel Collins

Untitled

Wishing well
our dreams

Alan Pollard

Far-Down Deep-Tunnel

Do you hear some thing, far clapping
on the walls.
Ringing like bells, as they fall.

Ring, ring, ring, as your going at a
fast speed.
Coming faster, and faster through the
deep.

Going down the long,
Going down the wrong.
I am still strong
I say to my self in deep thought.

Where is this taking me?
FAR DOWN, DEEP TUNNEL LANE!

I don't know where right on, I just know
some what.
Hear the wind,
I hear the ringing bells on the wind.

FAR DOWN, DEEP TUNNEL LANE!

Brian Locke

Works Of Art

Sky is nature's canvas
On which she paints her scenes,
Trees and flowers, birds and clouds,
Deep oceans, shallow streams.

She uses many colors,
Some soft while others bright,
The colors that you see by day
Change radically by night.

If you admire works of art
Then may I suggest,
You look upon her works of art
You'll find they are the best.

I need no paintings on my walls
For all I have to do,
Is gaze outside my window
To view her masterpiece on blue.

Barbara Jean Enquist

From Me

We had it all
Once upon a time
Each other
Together
Whenever
Loved you more than myself
Yet, we were young
So we grew apart
I accepted being rejected
Learned to love you from a distance
But I wanted you with me
Had to have you near
I settled for less
Lowered my standards
No one compared to you
I respected you
Couldn't let go
Now I know
No matter what changes may happen in
our lives
I assure you, life means nothing, if you're
too far away

Dana Taylor

R.I.P.

Close down the dark house!
Once upon a time
It was bright,
And had a sense of humor.

Board up the windows!
The sun fails to smile
On their panes.

Shut the kitchen!
The cupboard is quite;
Tins of tea, oatmeal,
Sugar and cloves, stand still...
The tea kettle no longer whistles.
Lock the door!
People won't come calling any more.
Momma is dead.

Gertrude Ann Conte

Starting Over

Build the fragile walls once more;
Only to watch them crumble
Hoping this would be the last time;
you would be humbled
Alike a rainbow catching the fading rays;
to reflect once again;
Only to find what we seek has paled;
has nature beset man
Never truly knowing if Love is real;
or just a dream
Maybe, but who amongst us can Live;
or Love without Dreams.

Jeffry D. Stafford

Knowledge

Look at the book
Open it up
Look inside
Hush up

Engulf yourself
Read along
The tales of Wizards and Lizards
A rhyme and song

A whole new world
Waiting for you
The princess awaits
The detective finds clues

Read more, keep going
Get ready
A world of knowledge
Going on steady, steady, steady

Watch the arrow
Spin the top
Living in books
Knowledge won't stop!

Elizabeth Joy Brown

Spring's Cameo

I muse on Spring's winsome
petalled cameo,
Wild Cherokee roses clambering
high on
April garden's split-rail
wooden fence,
Sharing intimacy of a
sun-warmed afternoon,
Perfumed in unforgettable
loveliness.

June Allegra Elliott

Death

Is it the end?
Or a beginning?
It is the end of the life we know;
But it could also be the beginning
of something unknown.
Maybe another life,
But one of the soul, not of the body.
The freeing of our soul;
The development of feelings and
emotions to a much more spiritual
level.
Or maybe life is just another chapter
of an untitled book;
One of those where we can't tell
what's going to happen next.
Could death be more peaceful than
this life?
I wish I knew the answers;
For I find myself wondering quite
often.

Carla Tavares

Warning

Could I have stayed a timid violet
or a nothing, nothing?
Then, I became a bird of many colors,
or was it a volcano that
that erupted from America to Paris?

Loved ones said it would not last

BUT

Birds of paradise will not be less

AND

Volcanos will erupt again.

Dorothy Mallett

Gone

To never look upon the ocean,
or again up at the sky;
to never watch the sunrise,
or the coming of the night;
to never feel the wind blow,
or the wetness of the rain;
to never see a rainbow,
or my love again;
these are things that I would mourn,
if in death I could feel pain.

For a living thing to die,
is like the sun without its fire;
like a night without the stars,
like a love without desire;
like a flower without petals,
like a bell that cannot ring;
like a wingless angel,
or a songbird that can't sing;
I can find no consolation
knowing I wont feel a thing.

James R. Hightower

Untitled

Do you believe in love?
Or do you mean death?
Love is death
In our world of rich, ass-kissing,
My-diamonds-are-bigger-than-yours
Society
Of hypocrites and non-believers
Reaching out to nothing
For something
Causing pain and disillusions
In the beauty of life.
Imperiled by death
With the freedom of expression.

Aundrea Lagoda

What Is A Pig?

I thought a pig was something to eat
Or is it something to keep?
I don't know any more but I'll give
you the score.
If you believe "Life" and some big
City police a pig is smart, brave,
beautiful and a nice pet to keep.

Green acres has its talking pig
Arnold but I believe it's a sham.
To me Arnold looked like ham.
If you believe some would be
Comic's the paper quote, a pig is
the fuss, the fuss is a cop and
I'm copping out.

Ethel Claywell

Father Of The Land

My Pharaoh has fallen.
Or was he my King?
He was my pretty prince.
No, he was my father.
Yesterday, I had flowers.
My trees were green of leaves.
I was proud, strong, erect.
My sky was blue.
My sun was shinning.
Today, I have no flowers.
My trees are bare.
"Oh God", I am scared.
My sky is black.
I have no sun.
I am so alone.
My father is gone.
"Oh, November twenty second,
why did you have to happen".

Esther Bustamante Nungaray

Eternity

As dawn is lurking
past the heavens
and deep within the sea

I find myself trapped
in the hands
of all eternity

Around the twisting
turning truth
there is no way to see

For trapped within
eternity
is all I've ever be

Jenny Mersand

With Imagination

I seem to be a person,
ordinary and plain,
but I really am the flowers,
dotting a peaceful lane.

Of course I am a person,
but I can be so many things in my mind,
may it be a beach, or a bird,
or a melon rind.

I am a sea gull,
flying over the shore,
Seeing all I want,
of blue oceans galore.

No I am a horse,
galloping on the plain,
The strong wind blowing,
my chestnut mane.

Now, there you have it,
I cannot make up my mind,
but with imagination,
I can be any species of any kind.

Diane Angela Cohen

Downsizing

Downsizing fever has hit us.
Our costs will be cut.
Including employees-
Who'll be out on their butts!

The President's scrutinizing
His friends and his foes.
He ultimately decides
Who stays and who goes.

The Human Resources Manager,
Though now wide awake;
Took one nap too many.
What a costly mistake!

He has been severed -
Kicked out the same door,
Used by those who preceded.
Those he'd axed before!

Cost cutting and downsizing
Will it ever end?
Will we see job permanency
Ever again?

Dorothy Carmen Johnson

Lovebound

I'd like to crochet a star of
our love together intertwined
as a crystal sanctuary etched
in white ivory. A timepiece
of heavenly sentiments everlasting.
Its placement lies
within the universe.

The holy memory of this wishful
refrain entranced me
whisking me above the heavens
unto the great beyond; the
ultimate zone.

Denise Tapper

Root

Turquoise slips my mind
out of gear, wandering in
search of fine silt and peaches.

Nectar staining turquoise,
I dig for roots as any
pig snuffling for truffles.

Ahead, wolves fight tenaciously;
thrashing and clawing in
their approach to devour.

Upon me, she bites.
Her teeth on my teeth;
Her tongue pushing on my tongue.

David Shane Shelton

Peace To Brotherhood

Oh mother earth your battlefields
overflow with red
The scars of memory will remain.
Where your native sons have bled.
Grieving wives and mothers,
drop tears on your crust,
Lying silent in the dust.
A father comes to pay respects.
A mother kneels to pray.
Friends embrace with tear-filled eyes.
Some one leaves a flower spray.
And one person's vision finally
fulfilled.

Albert Deroose

Of Work Art And Act II

Flash me by, your light so beautiful
Pass me by, your colors and smell
Speak to me, your talk so meaningful
Scapes me the time that flashed by
Life passed by me
and all is left, are the same memories
Left behind like scars
Left to testify
of time that flashed by
Life passed by me
and all is left, is right here.

Harald Nilsson Lins

What's The Forecast?

Fluttering softly the little breeze,
passed through the branches of the trees.
It took a short cut laughingly,
as the leaves danced merrily.
Lovingly it curled around
little flowers on the ground.
Old Mr. Jones was walking home
his hat atop his shiny dome.
The little breeze came sweeping by
and blew his hat into the sky.
Suddenly the little breeze
heard his mother's whispered plea,
"quiet now and stop your rambling,
I think I hear your father coming."
Then all at once his father came
with lightning, thunder and sheets
of rain.
Your play is over little breeze.
Time for business if you please.

Claire Sandlin

Life's Lonesome Journey

Life...a bustling winter scene,
People continually coming and going,
No one really looking.
All with families...
All frozen...
Without feelings for others.
Not giving, not receiving.
Not trusting, not trusted.
Prejudice, ignorance
Blinding truth.
Living skeletons of the poor
Proud and pompous rich
All alone.
No one to turn to
No one believes
One alone in the crowd
Everyone's a like
Alone afraid.

Julie Anne Clark

Once In A Lifetime

Once in a lifetime,
people fought for justice.
At time they succeed,
and laws were passed.
Euphoric feeling of happiness
reigned among the people,
while these laws are enforced.

However enforcement soon disappeared,
anger and outrage replaced happiness,
And the struggle resumed.
The oppressed vowing to fight,
by any means necessary to the end.

Islande Maitre

My Love And I

My Love and I, will never die
People often wonder why
Why we survive life's stormy blast
Is a mystery of our past
That will continue, if time shall last
My love and I will not grow old
My love and I are very bold
We are made of steel, that's very real
We know exactly what we feel
Amidst our sorrows and our tears
There's room for laughter and for cheers
Room for smiles, that will last for miles
Room for giving and for taking
But never there be, room for breaking
My love and I, we won't hide
Together, we'll ride the wreathed tide
We shall land safely on the other side
My love and I, we can't go wrong
My love and I are very strong
We've been together far too long

Eulit McCallum-Miller

Autumn Woods

Deep in the autumn woods,
Rabbits hurry,
and chipmunks scurry.
But on the leaf covered paths,
the deer hustle,
and the leaves rustle,
Deep in the autumn woods.

Carrie Lynn Anderson

Dreams

I was born from passion
perfection is a joke
my bones aren't ashes yet.
My presence is my habitation.

I read life with my ears
I hear all
I hear myself
I get rid of the gods.

I am here now
prime time
state of mind
my time

Life is a miracle
youth is a gift from life
old age is a work of art
time and love is real art

Man is great in his dreams
please
please
don't wake me up.

Arturo A. Meuniot

Whose Hearts Rejoice

Whose hearts rejoice to Love's delight,
perhaps regrets unfound.
To soothe, caress, embrace one might
when Passion still abound.

Forget what may those shadows bring.
Captured by Lust, confined...
To what compares Affection's sting?
how if it should define.

A kiss, forever sentenced to more,
oblivious to all but Charm.
But soon with time all glances change, for
how strange sweet Joy does harm.

Sensuous voice, such Woe lingers on;
too harsh hear I such sounds
that once did ring enticing gone.
Passion no longer abounds.

Charlie Huynh

A Winter Day

There she sits
photo album on her knee,
memories floating through her mind
like floating leaves on an airy
autumn day.

She remembers happy times and
a smile plays at her lips but
slowly turns into a frown as
she realizes those times are gone,
gone along with the leaves that fell
from the trees in autumn.
There she sits
memories in her hand
and as she turns the page,
a tear falls down upon it,
just like a snowflake,
falling on the frozen ground.

Angela A. Buoscio

Divorce

Who will save me now?
Pick me up when I fall
Hold me during nightmare nights
Read the map
Count the change
Light the pilot on the range?

Who will save me?
Hold my hand in the scary parts
Change the oil
Know the way
Stay there when I have to wait?

Who will baby me
Surprise me
Humor me
Be strong for me
Comfort me
Love me...
Tell me please - who?
Who will save me from myself?

Cathy McLafferty

Baseball Strikes Out

In those good old days of yore
Pick up a paper
Read the score.

When players would play...
Those care-free times
And fans would cheer and stay.

Suddenly a rumble in the ranks
Empty ballparks
No profits in the banks.

Let's hear a cheer
But on an August day
No game to endear.

As the babe hits one out
No one in the stands...
To stand and shout.

James Kotula

Life As We Know It

Life as we know it,
Pictured from birth to death,
Death, though, is where life begins.

Weak minds fear death.
Strong minds look upon death,
And think of it as reward.

When the time is right,
That God has chosen,
Freedom to the soul,
A burden lightened.

He lived brave,
A man of his country,
With honesty in his heart,
Glory in His views.

The time had come,
And His soul was lifted,
Ever so high,
To heaven above,
Amen,
And may his soul rest in peace.

Dennis R. Willard

Let Me In

Let me in,
please!
I feel so alone out here,
by myself,
without a friend to talk to.

Let me in,
please!
I need to feel
you care, your touch.
It's so cold without you.

Let me in, please!
Who are you,
this man so scared?
Let me help you.

No door to come in,
no way around.
Can't find my way.
Oh well, no one home.
Guess I'll knock on someone else' door.

Let me in, please.

Donna Raditz

Writing

In my first light
pondering of day
it seems that writing
is a laying in the weeds
waiting for invisible winds
to shake loose seeds of thought.

And good writing is
then a further craft
of peeling the chaff from these
grinding them and rolling
the dough to make the loaf whole.

Yet great writing,
wholly other, happens
when there is will
to stand unblinking
at the wind-bare edge
of a hideous cliff
pen in hand.

Cynthia d'Este

Time To Live

My savings, none to brag of,
Preference to figure out my love,
I live a step above.
I refuse to limit myself
Because of wealth...
I have my health.
We will all die one day,
So I pack many memories away
Nothing to fade.
Squash what's considered right,
Shut the publics eye,
I am high.
Inhale the minutes - absorbing,
Neglect the thought of conforming,
Accept what your emotions bring.
Life is too short for dying,
I've spent too many days crying,
It's time to survive.

It's time to live!

Brian Cavalone

A Thing Of Beauty

The long flowing stem,
Proof of the long flowing friendship
we have come to know
The soft petals,
As they fall, they are my tears of
joy falling, to be so lucky to have
met someone as special as you
The thorns show strength,
They represent the pain we each have
suffered and grown from
The shapely leaves,
So perfectly designed by nature,
are we two, so fortunate that we
as one, may be the perfect love......

May you always carry a Rose in your heart

June Gay Carr

Introspection

I curl against the belly of the bear,
(pulled in close, pulled in deep).

Let me be just here,
Listening...breathing...
Listening to the outside crickets sing.

In caves I roam.
I am looking for my bear father,
My bear mother,
asking their permission to remain
inside...
lost in tunnels of ancient stone,
in warm and welcoming hallways,
then clambering back to the
furry soft underbelly of comfort;

My bear's mind,
my solitary soul.

Andrea Axtell

Love

Lonely lethargic hearts
quicken their beat,
in response to
Cupid's precordial thump!

Ostracized feeling of youth
return, with out hesitation,
to rejuvenate the sole.

Venus Viscous fluids flow
freely....ah-h-h...
my cup runneth over.

Eternity is mine...
with...love.

Becky J. Bolden

Peace Of The People

People against people
Race against race
Insults said to your own face
Can you read my thoughts
Speak my mind
If so than you know my kind
A race war is coming
Should we keep running
Reach into my heart pull out my love
Rip out my soul
Tear out everything I behold
Make me smile make me laugh
Can't we have human peace at last?

Alexis Nicole Harwood

Untitled

Black onyx was the night
rain fell heavily
The wind promised that
the boughs of the trees
would be crippled before dawn.

The sun burst forth
in magnificent rays
Scorched the ground where
rain had lain.

The wind held her breath
was almost still
Trees welcomed the first
clear shrill
of the mockingbird.

Eleanor D. Bell

Times Gone By

There was a time when the rivers ran free,

and the air was fresh and clean,

where animals hunted for their food
in the forests and the stream.

Where the nights were clear and
and the stars were bright

Where trees stood tall letting
in the moonlight,

When the only noise at night was heard

Was the howling of the wind or
the flight of a bird.

Where the land was new untouched by man,

Where ocean water washed on
white clean sand.

It is sad to think that none of us
this marvelous view to see,

Of golden fields and forest green
stretched out from sea to sea.

Joseph Gillenson

The Trees Of Autumn

The trees of autumn
Reach out
With gnarled limbs
Toward dreams
Unrealized

Dreams which at
Twigdom, they dared to conjure.
Their multicolored leaves
.... a reminder.
That there is still time

To fly
with the winds...
To other forests.

The twisted limbs
Reach out
To forbidden glades.

Claire S. McAuliffe

"The Dance"

The strains of music softly begin,
reflecting a passion deep within
their hearts, two as one.
Hoping the moon never sees the sun.
Alone on the crowded floor they stand,
soul to soul, hand in hand.
A hero in her eyes,
he may already realize
her love, respect; her best friend.
He hopes the night will never end.
She is all he ever dreams,
day and night, it always seems.
Those words he longs to speak,
heart to heart, cheek to cheek,
never need be spoken,
the moment can't be broken.
Their hearts speak for them,
he to her, she to him.
Brought together by fate, by chance.
They may not have each other but they
will always have "the dance".

Charlene A. Stackhouse

October Twentieth Second

The lovely flowers
return to the soil
The lovely words
return of the day
Many happy returns

At the sight of the Saturday night
today's Saturday of the 22nd of the
October Twentieth Second of October '94
Tenth Twentieth Second of the year

America was born in
Fourth July IV
MDCCCXXCVI
July Twentieth 1969
y X 2169

Video, Vie, View, Volley and VOIZ
AMIGA
Videodream, Videomind, Volley will and
VOICE MAGIC

I'm glad to see you... CAROL'
Happy Birthday CAROL........

Antonio Peralta

Night Vision

Glistening silver
Ripples in the water
Shining like a lonely star
In a silent evening sky
I watch in wonder
As mother nature shows
A beauty so rare
So full of radiance
I sit and think
And dream of life
I watch the waves
Passionate stillness
Comes later on,
For now,
The calm is gone.

Christine Gallant

My Beautiful Red Rose

Have you ever seen a red
rose unfold?
It is the most beautiful
sight ever told?
The color is red, not pink
or gold
It is completely understandable
as it is in its mold
The scene is really delightful
and bold.
So please always take hold!
And always love "My Beautiful Red
Rose"

Dorothy Jean Farmer

From A Little Squirrel To A Little Boy

Hello there little boy;
Running free full of joy.
Bet you wish you were like me;
Scamp 'ring over all this tree
Lots of nuts I've stored away;
Hid them for another day.
Free you are to run down there
While the wind blows through your hair
Way out on a limb I'll go;
Jump from branches to and fro.
Some time you'll come up pretty far.
But just now stay down where you are!

Helyne L. Helmer

Alone

Inner locked
Sad and stubborn
to admit need,
mistake, and
ignorance

Heavy and hidden
Pretend knowing
by quietness

The anger of the others frightens me
I stay incognito

Alone

Charlene Bramlett Martin

How We Became Shepherds

"I need different clothes."
Said Adam to little Eve.
"My leaves are always wrinkled
And fading you can't believe."

So quickly Eve spoke to God
For material for their apparel,
"We must keep Adam's image up
Or place him in a barrel."

Now God had a problem and his
Thoughts were very deep,
Ah! Thinking wool is the answer
He zapped up a pair of sheep.

Now this was the prime reason
Why wool was then produced,
And sheep being proficient
The Shepherd was introduced.

So God created man,
Then Eve completed the core,
The third was wooly sheep
And the shepherd was number four.

Adam Walter

Going Home

Going home where I should be,
Sailing across the quiet sea;

Climbing that stairway to the sky,
Having my Lord waiting by;

Sheading a tear before I go,
To all my family and friends below;

Missing you is what I'll do,
Laughing and talking to all of you;

Looking up to that bright light,
Seeing God's face come into sight;

Feeling as happy as I can be,
Knowing my body is so pain free;

Stepping through that pearly gate,
Knowing now, that I'm not late;

Walking down the streets of Gold,
Never again to feel the cold;

Seeing my new place to live,
Sharing all God has to give;

I will never be alone,
Knowing now, I'm going home.

Brenda Doran

Down In The Valley

Reach out and hear me
scarred by a wrack of pain
left out in the cold winter
night, looking for warmth.

Seeking only the sun through the
cracks of a cardboard box,
they scurry by so the faint
smell of the subway is only
left as an afterthought.

Men of blue who walk the midnight
hours with your steel toe boots,
let me sleep so I can forget I am
down in the valley.

Jacqueline V. Sargeant

Untitled

Memories of Childhood
screaming, cursing
standing in the hall
listening in darkness
scared, angry, frustrated
wanting to do something
knowing the answer
they wont listen
I'm just a kid
or am I
how would they know
I can see them
do they see me
can they
I don't care
I wish they could see themselves
then maybe they could see me

Daniel J. Cassidy Sr.

I Love You

I never thought I would
see the day,
When a family member so close
would pass away.
I guess it was meant to be
his time to go,
and all the time the family spent
together it never went by slow.
It is so hard not to cry when
someone passes on,
It's not until later that you realize
their gone.
It's so hard to say good-bye to
someone who dies,
especially when that someone was a
really great guy.
Before someone passes on
there is so much you should say and do,
but before they pass on everyone
should say... I Love You!!!

Jennifer Sedler

"The Dark Blue Sky"

Look up at the dark blue sky,
see the stars sparkle, the moon fly.
Look up at the man in the moon,
floating in the big sky.
Look up at the dark blue sky,
you will see me, who am I?

Deanna Edwards

To You

Observing others and the way they act,
Seeing both honesty and wit,
Making up for what you lacked
By following the path they lit.

Helping not, only observing
Another's fall or mistake,
Even though it's quite unnerving
Prevents those you might make.

Taking parts of another's personality,
Some intelligence, others humor,
Makes you not a reality,
Only a wise consumer.

Carina de la Torre

A Troubled Friend's Story

The sorrows of a girl come from
Seeing her friend slowly
Corrupt before her and see him
Gradually fading.

The pain she feels when she can't do
Anything but wait, and
Watch, him get farther apart from
Her and everything else.

The problems of his family
And friends get into his
Better judgment. It gets so bad
That he starts thinking wrong.

The only things she can do are
Be patient, be a good
Listener, and eventually
He might come back again.

Grace Kim

On Keeping Out

Prying into the soul of another
seems but a sin.
But in the end, the one prying
may be the one you offend.
Ah, but the reader should beware
Because they might be in for a scare
For the life we lead
and the way it's perceived
Can be two different things
as I suppose you will see.
So, be forewarned
should you proceed in haste
For my views of you
may not be to your taste.

Barbara L. Watts

Soft Wounds

The last trace of consciousness
seeped out through Soft Wounds
recharged by the pity
of a thousand deaf ears.

Your furthermost triumphs
extorted from Soft Wounds
and wantonly buried
with all your past fears.

Your natural beauty
reeling from Soft Wounds
yet masked by the keepers
of your undermined tears.

Distorted lucidity
fleeting through Soft Wounds
replaced by the longing
of your discontent stares.

Embellished reality
gaping your Soft Wounds
propelled by the notion
you can no longer care.

Jake Lowinger

"Have We Forgotten"

Guns echoing their mighty yell,
Sending a thousand souls to hell.
Men braving the storm of death,
Hardly a sound, scarcely a breath.
Their tired bodies racked with pain;
Friends and foe alike were slain.
Guns that screamed their endless cry,
Summoning men soon to die.
To pause without a reason;
In battle is considered treason.
Night after night men were killed,
Dying maimed against their will.
Then came the peace they longed to come,
Tears and laughter, sleeping some.
Bless those who have died in vain,
This must never come again.
Peace for men of every nation,
Peace for then of all creation.
Let us strive in peace to thrive,
So all mankind may thus survive.

Edward K. Harley

White Winter Snow

Winter snow falling slow
Sending echoes home I go.
follow my footsteps in so deep
keep me safe till I fall asleep.
Listen for day break to enter in
the sunlight rays of sparkled wind.
Winter snow slowly falling.
Gentle winds I'll keep him coming...

Florence K. Holland

Song Of The Wind Chimes

Twisting, turning with the wind,
sending melodious chants that bring
a whisper from a hidden, haunting cave
that once stood silent.
Now it gave
its own sweet peal of laughter
and, then after,
it caught a million echoes
resounding in the wind
and yet,
not echoes
but the harps,
perhaps,
of long lost angels
searching for a place
to sing.

Dorothy Berentsen

Shadow Dance

I look outside my window pane
Shadow dance deep in the rain

Always out of sight it seems
Outlines walk through wicked dreams

Thunder rumbles lightning flashes
Rain drops fall from lips to lashes

I look down but I am dry
Shadow dance then slink by

I break a twig and hear it crack
Shadow goes don't look back

Run for cover near a tree
Shadow dance to torment me

I reach out to grab it why
Not of substance just leak by

I know forever is no more
Shadow vanish through lights last door

I close my eyes in tightened strain
Ultimate sorrow fear and pain
Where I dance deep in the rain

Alison Jacobowitz

Burn

My name is a darkness
shadowing the mind's eye.
She sang to my heart,
siren not quite whole.
I climbed rocks
after the ship wrecked...
stranded.
Light draws a moth,
sirens call to man;
the desire,
driven to the writhing flamed,
do we not all
burn?

Jason Allen Baretsky

Untitled

I spoke with my angel
She called me by name
But when she took my hand
It just wasn't the same
The angel I knew and loved
Wasn't in my arms
She flew away to the heavens
Escaping her pain and harm
This life wasn't for her
This life wasn't good enough
So our Lord called her home
Like a candle, her life snuffed
Fly to the heavens
For you my love endures
Fly to the heavens
Without you my life so unsure
Beautiful broken body
Left on earth to die
The soul moves on
Leaving a shell over which we cry

John Ferlmann

Moon Light

Moon light on the island
shines bright
silver light

Cast shadows on the sand
two lovers walking
hand in hand

Warm breeze in the night
coco palms swaying
in delight

Waves lapping at the sand
love blossoms
in this tropic land

David Thompson

Song For Brittanie

Brittanie made a paper doll, not too
short, and not too tall - she drew
its eyes, nose and mouth and
shoes upon its feet.

She came to see me yesterday with
colored crayons and paper mache, pencils,
and ribbons in a box, scissors and
some glue

Come help me make the clothes for her -
Red or blue - color her shoes - cut them
out and paste them on my dollie that
I made

We played together, Brittanie and I
making the clothes, trying them on
we laughed, we hugged, we had
a good time with Brittanie's
paper doll.

Joyce Torri

Untitled

Every time I smell a flower, it
reminds me of someone very special to me

The woman I love that is more
beautiful than a rose blooming

And may the love we have live
longer than a blooming rose.

Jon Suko

Preceding The Storm

Crescent moon peering through
si
nk
ing
clouds
Brutal sky of morbid tone
Instinctive manners of such
boisterous motion
and
flirtatious greetings
Reminiscing pictures of old time
teasing blue silhouette
Delicate pillows of phantom gray
trifling about eternal sky
Dancing winds bouncing around
the singing heavens.

Isabel C. Engle

Dreams

When the stillness of the night,
Silently surrounds me,
Dreams of things that might,
Whisper all around me.

When all the stars above,
Are shining in the sky,
There is a feeling deep as love,
To be something more than I.

Yet so often dreams of night,
Creep not within my day,
The winds of life dim the light,
Then blows them all away.

Jack Lynn Schroyer

You're Just A Memory

You're just a memory
Since you started to roam
It's been so long dear
Since you left your home
You're just a memory
I'm trying to forget
But sometimes I wonder
If you're happy where you're at.

When you left me dear
I cried and cried
I couldn't forget you
Even though you lied
But that's all in the past
And I'll forget some how
Because you're getting to be
Just a memory now.

Gertrude B. Collins

Untitled

When you're with me it's
Plain to see it had to be
you and me in love thought.
Out eternity, our love
shines like the red, white
and blue of America as long
as we live our hole life
through and are here
with star and stripes in
our mind we can go to
heaven with a clear mind
throughout all time.

Aaron Cutts

Choices Made

If I could sing and
sing to my unborn,
I would use my voice
to raise a lullaby
sweet and smooth to
stars of diamonds and
your sapphire moon.
That I may wipe away
every tear you would
have cried
and hold you
to my aching, full breasts.

And like the early tide
reaching the shore,
you would hear the melody
and feel the hum
gently wash over
you in your haven.
Safe from those tears
you shall never meet.

Christina M. Simmons

"A Scarecrows Dream"

I'm a scarecrow
sitting in a wheat field all alone.
Stuffed with straw from head to toe,
a scarecrow's life is all I know.
Dressed in a farmer's old clothes,
hanging around scaring the crows
with arms stretched out wide
with little back buttons for eyes
listening to the crows' screeching cry.
At night I look so real
standing alone in a field.
I'm helpless as you can see.
A scarecrow's dream is
to be set free.

Christy Appel

"Sweet-Dreams"

As I laid myself to
sleep last night I recalled
my mother telling me "sweet dreams"
I recalled the sweet, innocent
kiss she laid on my forehead.
The way she so carefully, gently
and silently closed the door behind her.
Oh, if she only knew
What goes on in my mind - in my dreams.
That same horror
That long-lived nightmare my mind
wont' let me forget.
Sweet dreams is anything but what
I've had since that cold December night.
Suddenly, I wake up as the tears
roll down my face.
And I pray I don't dream it again
but as I lay back down,
the nightmare cycle begins again.

Gina Gurkoff

Reflections

As I watch the shadows of eventide,
Slowly creeping from the west;
I reflect on this day I'd been given,
Lord, did I do my best?

Did I try to ease a saddened heart,
With a kind word and a smile?
Did I help to cheer a lonely soul
Just to stop... and sit a while?

Did I really turn the other cheek?
Share my love with my fellow man?
Was I thankful for all of my blessings?
Did I do the best I can?

I tried to do these simple things,
And to live by you great plan;
I'll pass this way but once, Lord,
Help me to do the best I can.

Bettie Duda

Susan's Garden

Hug the earth!
Smell the aroma
of dark soil-moist
with spring rains.
Watch the crowning,
the birth of green
blades, stalks and leaflets.
These children will blossom
in a profusion of colors,
shapes and sizes,
reaching their potential,
fulfilling their promise.
As a well-planned family
each member in place and turn
enhances the design
so carefully laid out.

Jean Jamis

Prejudice

They built a cross out in my yard,
so bold and to the point.

They did it catching me off guard,
a chill in every joint.

An anger rose inside of me;
hatred swarmed with passion.

How can someone hate another
in such an unkind fashion.

It stood there seeming to talk to me;
I tried to look away.

But, a hole it burned within my mind.
acknowledging my dismay.

Once again I'll have to move;
my home is never still.

To live in a country supposedly mine,
yet not to have free will.

So sarcastically I bring me down
and give this earth a kiss.

For what would the land of the free be like
without such PREJUDICE.

Adam Feirstein

So Big

So big the sun,
so insignificant we -
yet one can hold a coin, a hand,
against the sun
and see
unblindingly.

Dee Whitmore Schick

Friend Of All Friends

You came out of nowhere
So sudden and true,
You helped me, you listened,
With questions but few.

You held me, you told me
not to worry so much,
No matter what happens
things will work out as such.

As time went by, oh friend
you were beside me.
I would have never made
it without you to guide me.

Gladys Syring

Life

I wonder why time passes by
So swiftly when you're old —
To reminisce, as you deeply sigh
Your dreams do turn to gold.

The life you've led
Can be fulfilling,
As you have fed,
Your thoughts so willing
To try to please each soul.

The greatest treasure
You can measure
Are grand children, of course,
A beautiful trophy
Awarded in life
As you reach your destined goal.

Eve Jacques

"Freedom"

"Our differences were given by God."
So why doesn't everyone
let down their guard?
The thing that makes you different
is not to be offended by.
If you're curious, just ask them why?
If you don't get an answer
it'll soon come.
Cause deep in their hearts they
know we're all one.
Unity is a word that can be expressed
in different ways.
Different opinions from Europe
to the Coastal Bays.
Dr. King tried to tell us
the meaning of the word.
But with most, it was barely heard.
We need to learn to work for each other.
I can't change your mind.
You can't change my color!

Dakarai M. Williams

Lift Up Your Spirit

Music plays in my ear
soft and soothing
just what I need to hear,

A mountain of rocks
makes several caves
kick off my socks
and listen to the ocean make waves,

Starts to get dark
as the sun begins to rest
here in the park
manmade peace at its best,

Church bells ring
aches and sorrow slip away
the choir starts to sing,
A beautiful way to start any day.

However it is you do it
lift up your spirit!

Gina M. Best

A Red Rose On Her Table

Her evening meal is scant,
  Some crackers, maybe cheese
A glass of lemonade
  A square of chocolate cake.
With every bite she pauses
  Regarding with delight—
The red rose on her table.
  She listens to the evening news—
The sports, the weather,
  The names of those who
Lead or follow,
  At home or far away.
Arises from her chair
  Strokes the velvet petals of
The red rose on her table.
  She smiles and is content.
To change her life she is not able.
  There is no need, while there is still—
A red rose for her table.

Dorothy L. Hunt

Living

Yes! I am living,
  Some may say very well;
So poverty stricken;
  That out of poverty I wanna bell.
Oh! My big fancy cars,
  That attracts unwelcome approaches:
With run down houses;
  Human being and cockroaches.
Living is living,
  Brother! Sometimes you do slump:
So petrified in life;
  Our nerves just jumps.
Living here wishing for a fortune,
  Hoping for some fame:
It just a big painted picture;
  Nothing but a Game.
Living is like a dream,
  Until you have awaken:
Reality sets up in your mine;
  So a struggling breath I've taken.

Arthur Harris

Dreams

Dreams,
some of them you wish could come true,
some others you wish you never had,
but for the first time,
I had one of my sweetest dream come true,
and that dream was you.
To look at you,
is to day dream of you;
to glance at you
is to freeze my body,
chills running through it all,
while my heart pumps blood faster
than it ever has before.
Dreams do come true love,
dreams really do come true,
and you are the only one I can think of,
day and night, night and day.
you are truly a dream that became
reality for me.

Hernan H. Quintanar

Talent Lost

What is a poem? I ask myself,
Some words upon some author's shelf
The paper; cheap. The mood is black.
Written perhaps in a poor man's shack.
Then someone sees it, and shows a friend.
They say it starts a brand new trend.

The public loves it and pays his price
The authors style is very nice.
He writes one more, and then another,
And soon the people read no other.

The author's fat, he turns to vice.
He cannot write, he can't suffice.
Back to his hovel without a cent,
The poor man goes, his fortune spent!
The work is back upon the shelf.
But, now poor man he's by himself.

Duke Wisper

Who Cares

Homicide or Suicide
Someone Died and No one cried.
  Wasn't it sad
  Could this be bad
Are we all stark raving mad?
  Lying dead
  No one cares
Does this seem slightly rare?
  Are we all heartless and two faced?
  After the life he paced
Someone please help this world!

Dawn Burns

Untitled

A little bit of love,
Someone threw away,
A little bit of joy,
She brings to me each day.
This little dog of mine
She is my special Valentine.

I like to hold her on my lap,
Of me she is a part,
And with her head beneath my chin.
She puts a kiss upon my heart.

Jean Britner

When It Looks Like I Have Failed

Are you trying to tell me something. For failure doesn't mean I'm a failure. It does mean I haven't yet succeeded. It does mean I have learned something. Failure doesn't mean I have been a fool. It does mean I had enough faith to experiment. Failure doesn't mean I've been disgraced. It does mean I'm not perfect. Failure doesn't mean I've wasted my life. It does mean I haven't failed. I have an excuse for me to start over again. Failure doesn't mean I should give-up. It does mean I'll never make it. It does mean I need more patience. Failure doesn't mean you have abandoned me. It does mean you have a better job for me Lord.

Frank Strength

"Keep Going"

When things go wrong as they
sometimes will
When the road you're trudging
seems all up hill
When the funds are low and debts
are high
And you want to smile, but you
have to sigh
When care is pressing you down
a bit
Take it all, but never quit.

Jay Lawrence

Lies

I've hurt you and within my
soul I cannot forgive me.
I've broken your heart and
cannot repair the damage to mine.
I've brought tears to those
weary eyes, and to my inner sanctum
you can't see;
Lies eat at my soul, not all
meant to damage you.
Lies build walls around my
true feelings, and yours very fragile.
Lies hide the very essence of
me, and make you vulnerable too.
I've misused your trust,
unintentional and inappropriately,
I've no excuse except to offer my
life to you as compensation.
I've paid the final price for a
love for which I cherish,
and hold with my heart very deeply.

Daniel Whitlock

Lonely

Loneliness, you don't want
that. You will feel depressed,
sad, and angry all at the same
time. It can be very stressful.

You may feel this way because
you have no friends, your parents
aren't there for you, or you just
feel lonely.

Carol Burger

Untitled

Fear is like a disease, it rips your
soul into oblivion, shatters all hope
and peace of mind.
Makes you lose touch with reality,
Turns happiness to hate, desire to
destruction; until you're crushed
into societies human pit of misery.
Full of dismay and displace.
you hide in the darkened shadows of
Life, always running from the unknown;
Deceiving all who cares.
With drawn from the world in a state
of misery we call fear.

Benjamin Napier

Untitled

"Lady of the wildwood
Sweet rose of loves domain
Woman of sweet mysteries
Daughter of the rain
Come with me, and we will sail
Upon a sea of stars
And all the love, that's to be had
forever, will be ours."

Don Wingate

Soft Flesh Bare

Fistless punches
Take a jab
Poke me
Stab me
Make me sad
Lost my armor
Soft flesh bare
Need my armor
Need it bad!

Bernice A. Wherry-Smith

For the Love of Mom

Memories of our home
Take me back into the past
Every time we talk on the phone
The time seems to go too fast
And again I'm alone
But there's no one to blame
Call me foolish or naive
Back then I thought I knew the game
Stubbornness pulled at my sleeve
Innocence hid the flame

In my head I left to
Show us both that I have grown
You can't deny how fast I grew
When I was young I was shown
Just what money can do
Sadness and happiness
Depending on a devil
I took my own independence
So finances would level
And you don't have to stress

David DesJardins

Precise

There are times, as in life,
take precise timing.
And knowing just when to
draw the line,
Losing a beat, and yet,
still chiming a rhyme,
Direct contact is considered
straight with a blow,
Left abandoned, as a lonely
soul's heart overflows.
Some words can get lost
in a conversation,
Not quite sure what the
meaning is.
As in life things are
precious timing,
or just live it,
as is.

Carolyn Attianese

Triple Play

Three girls the same,
Taking the route to fame.
Blonde hair,
Blue eyes,
They're not hard to recognize.
Welcome girls to Hollywood,
With fortunes bad and good.
Leave the look of awe behind,
And join the modelling business,
You've got the perfect face.
Just set the time and date,
We can give it a whirl.
Someday you'll be famous.
I hope I'll see the day,
When you'll be the perfect triple play.

Amy Avila

With Thee

With thee I breathe sweet breath of wine.
taste the love and dew divine.

With thee I feel myself I crawl,
With uttermost yells I call.

With thee my pain is Thou undone,
my life is like a poem's pun.

With thee my love is bittersweet,
eyes so pure I feel them meet.

With thee his calmness is an art,
emotions deep if we should part.

With thee so kind and free from harm,
his precious heart will not alarm.

With thee his love so full of hope,
and now with life I can now cope.

Alisha Giurlani

On The Serenity Path

Crossing through the serenity path,
tears run down from my eyes.
Long is the journey and also
is harsh.
Too many memories appear on my sight.
Time has finally come to rest
and relax.
It's no time to look back.
Never knew this everlasting calm.
As I end my journey, real
life for me will start.

Alba Ruiz

Emperor Of The Orient

Last fall I saw a Ginkgo tree,
That beauteous, Sino mystery,
Its leaves, in various tints of tan,
So reminiscent of a fan,
Were spread around
In golden circles on the ground;
And as I turned and went,
I knew my time had been well spent,
Admiring this emperor of the Orient.

Jad Davies

A Trip To The Donut Shop

Donut shops are bus stations
that collect
the frustration
of caffeinated job hunters
and the mumbling disenfranchised

What brings our bodies to seek
our own slow death
through white-flour promises
of maximum shelf-life
and instant pleasure?

Gurgling and tender as children
we are baited with sugar and tainted
by greasy history, molasses boiling,
the fried smell of too many lives gone.
Tell me, who picked the sugar cane?
who picks the cane now, sugar?

Donut shops - quick fixes,
our own slow death
too many mumbling frustrations and
excuses.

Abby Lynn Bogomolny

Cutting Corners

Dividers separate our classrooms
that have little chairs with no desk.
Thirty-eight voices sing loudly
while others study for a quiz at noon.
What... A ... Mess!

Maybe we will be politicians too,
if we had enclosed rooms with a desk.
They make decisions, they think are new,
More pupils, cut staff, cutting comers.
What... A ... Mess!

Bettye Watford

A Song

Farewell my knights: my lady fair.
That I may bless you with my love
My fingers linger: brush each cheek
And in return, I would that thou,
Within thyselves embrace me well
With memories ere we say adieu.
For I would go adventuring
To where the Promise lights the way
Beyond the mists: beyond the pale.
To where the gleaming mansions soar,
Against new skies; new spangled stars,
That light a land and set a'gleam,
For faded eyes a splendid dawn.

John Joseph Martyn

There's Something In My Heart

There's something in my heart
that I should share,
It's that to give love and to
always care.
God made me just the way he
wanted me to be,
Because I love him and he loves me.
He came down to see a nice
little world,
Just to see the lovely boys
and girls.
God love us from his heart,
Because he was the one
right from the start.
God loves us everyday,
He loves us in a special way.
Some people plant love like a seed,
But the love from God is what
you only need.

DeJoie Aaron

Upon Leaving For College (With Cookies)

Little did my Great-Grandmother know
That I would be taking her
Oatmeal cookies
With me
To meet the World of Knowledge
Freshly baked
By my mother's hand,
To protect me
From the timid fears of books
And the Unknown,
Fortifying me
With sugar and spice
In case an Unsuspecting Dragon
Crosses my path
Lest I be left
Alone,
Unprepared,
Defenseless,
But oh,
So willing.

Diane Kopylow

A Little Mixed Up

Just a line to say I'm living.
That I'm not among the dead.
Though I'm getting more forgetful
And "mixed-up" in the head.

For sometimes, I can't remember
When I stand at the foot of the stairs.
If I must go up for something
Or, I've just come down from there.

And before the refrigerator so often
My poor mind is filled with doubt
Have I just put food away, or
Have I come to take some out.

So, if it's my turn to write you
There's no need getting sore,
I may think that I have written
And don't want to be a bore.

So remember I do love you
And I wish that you were near
But now it's nearly mail time
So I must say "Goodby dear."

Imogene Beichner

Soon

He left so soon
That my eye could not follow him.
He left so soon.
I could not sigh for honeymoon.
Was I too slim or just too prim
Or just a talking, shapely limb?
He left so soon.

Frank A. Langer

Beauty From Inside

I look around and see,
That no one likes me
No one cares;
When I'm in doubt I close
my eyes and look deep inside;
Only then do I see the inner beauty
that I possess;
I open my eyes and hold my head
up high and realize,
That all true beauty comes from,
my heart deep inside.

Christin Drysdale

The Weary Traveler

I never saw his face.
That one who came to my rescue,
I never knew.

My heavy load had fallen,
And thrust me to the ground.
And no one was there to help me.

I felt a gentle hand upon my shoulder.
A reassuring whisper in my ear.
Of whom, I did not know.

He gathered up my fallen load,
And offered me his hand.
We walked down the road, together.

Though I never saw his face,
I knew him in my heart.
He's always there to guide me on my way.
He is my friend.

Jenny Deck

Sweetest Mother

She is a little old fashion
That precious mother of mine
There are many whose beauty
Will my mother out shine.

She is a little old fashion
As I plainly can see
But she is the sweetest
Mother to me.

She is a little old fashion
She grows sweeter each day
I adore her plain features
And her thin locks of gray.

There is a glory around her
God abide it may be
And she is forever the sweetest
Mother to me.

Iva Nell Stokes Shaw

Love And Life Ongoing

My pen pours out the words of feelings
that seem to not stop flowing...
An endless stream
slowly trickling or
gushing in.
Love begins as a reason for living.
It is one of many dreams,
As love fades
I find other strengths
to sustain me.
Along with endless emotions
that persist,
I find
myself.

Elyse Ottina

Untitled

It is the call of the wild
that warms my heart,
the unity of body and
soul may they never part.
The forest is my home the
sky is a dream.
Though the ears do hear it is
not always as it seems.
The eyes see the light your
heart feels the heat,
Though the eyes may go blind
your heart will forever beat.
In the end you will find pure bliss,
Things as they are you will
never miss. Remember your heart,
Remember the heat.

JoAnne Gannon

Untitled

"Oh why does it always seem to be
that what we seek and what we find
are different things entirely
and only prove life unkind?

Oh why is it that what we dream
is never close to what we find
and bitter does truth always seem
to only prove life unkind?"

Brian C. Otto

The Bells Of Death

Drink up, shoot in
That's how my day begins
My life is a hell
The bells of death are near
They are ringing in the distance
Once in a while for just an instance
I think I might live
The bells are growing louder
Shadows fall all around me
Whatever is letting me be-let me go!
I just can't stand it anymore!
They are ringing in my head so loud
All of sudden
Silence
Peace at last
I never knew what hell was till now
And I got there so fast.

Chalise Preasmyer

Christmas

Presents and presents more and more.
That's not what Christmas is for.
It's really for Jesus's birthday.
It's the day He was born.
He was born in Bethlehem.
On Christmas day.
In a manger was were He lay.

Amanda Fryman

My Mother

Ribbons and sunbeams
That's what you are.
Organdy fineness,
A glow from afar.
Goblets of silver,
The shine in your eyes,
Much laughter, much strength,
But never disguise.
The gifts that you bring
One cannot erase,
Like the touch of your hand
Or the look on your face.
You're comfort, you're joy
What a lovely surprise!
You're witty and thoughtful
And really quite wise.
You're spring and you're summer,
And sometimes you're fall.
You blossom all year
Bringing much love to all.

Adrienne M. Anbinder

The Beginning Of The End

The end of the beginning is closer
The beginning of the end is near
The more I look, the less I hear
The more I look, the more I fear
The beginning of the end is near

I cannot tell how it starts
I cannot tell how it ends
All I know is we all must die
Before the year 2005
The beginning of the end is near

The visions I see are not very clear
My life itself is not very dear
I now must venture to the depth
That I must go from my crypt
The beginning of the end is here.

Allen Carr

The Fear Within

How will I overcome the fear within.
The body is willing,
The mind clear and sharp.
Yet, I cannot act,
I cannot speak.
I am frozen in time,
Unable to feel life.

Allen Sorensen

A Child Of The Flowers

I began with a glorious cry of the petals
the birth of a woman seed
through a bed of rich brown soil
I was born among the flowers
crystal dew drops
shining on my bare bottom
jeweled tears
stemming from my cherubic face
a child of this flowering race
I have made love to angels
upon the petals of roses
their wings have fondled my carnations
my heavenly interlude blossoms
me into our universal garden
I sing of beautiful black lilies
thrown into an amber african sky
I am poetry, I am Africa, I am black lily
I am glorious cry
and in my garden
dandelions have become flowers

Chi-Chi Mgbako

America

Every fourth of July we celebrate
The birthday of our nation;
It's two hundred eighteen years ago.
Since its organization.

An unknown future lies ahead
Of this greatest of all nations;
We pray it will stay safe and strong
For future generations.

May America be a beacon light
With stars and stripes unfurled;
May freedom, peace and brotherhood
Prevail throughout the world.

Dear God, endow our leaders
With integrity and truth;
And instill a sense of confidence
Into our growing youth.

We pledge allegiance to our flag
May it never cease to be
To all the world a symbol.
That all men must be free.

Anne F. Doyle

The Waves

See and listen to the waves sounding,
The cresting, breaking, pounding,
A symphony of songs,
Amidst discords, wrongs.

Then hear the patter amongst us,
Enemies, lovers, youngsters,
The melodies of life,
Sad, gay, loud sounds, strife.

Waves, eternal, from a distant past,
Born anew like our life's cast,
With rise, fall, peaceful end,
And message they send.

Each wave doesn't last long in glory,
Like each life's living story,
To guide it always true,
To heaven when through

Joe Benedetto

Who Killed Kurt Cobian

The people say they know,
So you ask why, the people keep on playing,
The music starts to die.

Why did he do it,
He was on drugs the people say,
Don't ask me, I'm not him,
It was gonna happen someday.

Why are we all critics,
Do the people really care,
I know I didn't ask, is it really that fair?

You should of seen it coming,
The shots were heard all around,
But it's too late now,
The people buried Mr. Lithium in the ground.

He had everything going,
Maybe that was why, the people all knew him,
That's the reason why he had to die.

What can we do now, did we kill his myth?
I still like him, just continue what he left us with.

.......OH WELL, WHATEVER NEVERMIND,.....

Curt McGinnis

The Art Of War

As graceful as a fighter jet
soaring to great height
As rugged as a mighty tank
traveling through the night
The art of war is quite a chore
it is not a pretty sight
Stop the wars started by some
before mother earths blown to kingdom come
Stop the hate and ease the pain
for being at war has nothing to gain
Being at peace is like golden honey
cause being at war costs lots of money
Treat all races just like a brother
cause there's only one world and no other
If we treat everyone like family
we'll all live in peace and harmony
If your spirits free and there's love in your heart
then the art of war won't have to start.

Justin Mills

Joys Of Life

Life has many joys for remembering,
Some are seeing the beauty around us,
Some are as we travel on vacation trips,
Walking along the sea shore, watching the waves
Remembering the family outings and happy picnics,
Just visiting with family and children.
The greatest joy of all, beautiful grandchildren.
Grandmother's memory to fill her quiet hours.

Gloria Palasik Ingram

Holly

The sea is gray, white horses bounding about
some nipping the shore to gain a foothold.

Called by singing willows combed by the wind
taunting them into a rythmetic dance.

We string temporary footprints on the beach
while carelessly sifting the sand in glances.

For nature's secret treasures; sharks teeth,
beauteous shells and time spent with you.

John H. Voll

It's Good To Dream

Dreams come into my head every night.
Some are wrong and some are right.
You see right now I doing time.
Dreaming about meeting friends of mine.
As I sit here day and night.
My mind drifts off into the light.
Happy memories, bad ones too.
In my mind deep running through.
Dreams, oh dreams, I know what you are!
You bring my hopes from near or far.
You make my goals become reality.
You make the future seem what it's suppose to be.
So glad to dream. Yes, so very glad to dream,
Even though, sometimes, I don't know what they mean.
Drifting, drifting, outside myself.
Going to places alone, with nobody else.
Dreaming sets me free. Yeah, I'll never give it up.
It brings me good fortune and a whole lot of luck.
So if you sleep tonight and your lonely it seems,
Remember this poem and let your mind dream.

Joseph Hill

The Bridge Of Life

The bridge of life, each one must cross
some long, some short, some soon forgot.
A homeless trip for some to take.
A careless life, others will make.
To live or die at someone's hand
God please forgive that selfish man.

The bridge of life each one must drive
success, some fail, some chose to thrive
on weak or innocence, they feed
and hurting some because of greed.

The bridge of life is often hard
for most to cross, because they're barred
because of race, color or sex
religious views man's so complex.
Why can't we just be left alone
to chose our road, and not be wronged.

The bridge of life still offers hope
to those who strive and chose to cope
with damaged roads, weather, or pits.
A place in life, each one must fit

Duane Eddings

Things I've Lost

Of all the things I've loved and lost,
Some of them had absolutely no cost.
I've lost my temper a time or two
And some other things I'll name for you.
I've lost my patience in a fit of hate,
I've lost my hair; it couldn't wait.
I've lost the feeling in my foot;
It was a short nap it took
I've lost my nerve when I was afraid
Thinking of all the mistakes I've made.
I've lost my face, and I'm telling you
That's very bad, even when you have two.
One thing I haven't lost is my fat.
It's still with me and I'm sorry about that.
I've lost my heart a time or two
And you know that's not the thing to do.
I've lost my mind and that's a shame
Now I cannot remember my name.
I've lost a lot more than these, but then
I'm looking around and I've lost my pen!

Charles V. "Bo" Bean

Love

Some say love is great,
Some say it's just your fate,
Some say love is strong,
Some say it's wrong.

Some say love isn't for them,
Some say it's not for him,
Some say love is what life is about,
Some say it's something you can't live without.

Some say love is a need,
But I sat it makes your soul bleed,
Some say love tears you apart,
I say love breaks your heart.

Ada C. Perry

"Gardens Of Stone"

Aligned in even rows,
Some white as snow, others lost their glow.
Bearing names upon their faces,
Telling us who lay below.

Innocent children, loving mothers,
Even those of fame.
Makes no difference now;
For they all share the same

Frozen now by death,
Making no sound.
Tucked in humble lairs side by side,
Peacefully resting under hallow ground.

Remember those fallen,
When a garden you've passed.
For a lair awaits to hold you,
Beneath lush green grass.

Then loved ones may visit
Your new found home.
Another name etched forever,
Amidst the garden of stone.

Jim Dawson

The Best And The Worst Of Times

The Teen years, what can I say?
Some wish they could always stay,
Some wish they would go away.
The boyfriends, the love, the fighting, the hate.
The first time ever going on a date.
The friends, the secrets, the closeness you feel.
Abound that no one could ever steal.
Off to good each day, looking your best,
After cramming for that Algebra test,
What should I wear to be notices by that guy.
Sometimes I wish I wasn't so shy.
The ups, the downs, the hopes and the dreams,
To us it all is much more than it seems.
The good times the bad times, the tears and the fears.
It's all just apart of those wonderful teen years.

Brandy Kenimer

Life Passed Me By

I sit at a corner cafe
someone passes me by
he is handsome
another man passes with his girl
then another and another and another pass by
then I feel a sharp pain as another passes
a white light appears
as another and another young and old pass by
then I die
but people still pass by

Christina Bixler-Riley

Why Is It?

Searching for the last hope of light,
Someone who would help discourage a fight;
A sibling of the sun,
For I am just a lightning bug.

Though I have a mere speck of light of the moon,
I shine it proudly even to a loon;
To me I am the sun of the night,
But the moon wants to put out my light.

When it's day I fill the sky,
My rays reach to the mountain highs;
Then Mother Nature takes effect,
Cloudiness covers me from the rest.

Darkness I fear, it brings the moon,
if hours delay, he won't be here soon;
Yet my home is but a sphere,
Darkness brings my greatest fear.

Then I learned from the stars,
When I run from afar,
Night is brought when I leave,
Yet the moon still terrorizes thee!

Armando Bernardo Leon

Where Did I Go?

Where have the years gone?
Something is wrong.
Why can't I laugh till I cry,
Sing till I feel I could die,
Tease, play tricks, play a game,
Call someone a silly name?
Where has my other self gone?

The occasions are there, but does anyone care?
Nothing is funny anymore.
I feel like a dummy unable to smile
Even once in a while.

Am I alone, the only one
Who faces each day in the same old way?

What to eat, adjust the heat...
Wait for the mail, drink ginger ale...
Watch TV, but never see...
Always be, just me,
But not the me that used to be.

Where did I go?

Alice G. Dow

Untitled

I know sometimes you wonder, why I do these things
Sometimes I ask myself the same.
I just don't know what gets into me or why I cause you pain.
I really, really love you, I know that by actions you can't tell.
I want to get to heaven, yet I live my life in hell.
I only want a kiss, or a hug or two, the way you used to love me,
I miss that very much, you are beautiful, mommy.
I long for your tender touch.
Time is truly wasting and I am getting old
I am the one God sent for you to mold.
I will always appreciate and remember the
things you've taught and shown me.
I am trying, dear mommy, to be the best I can possibly be.
So please, love me, hold me, reach me, and teach me.
Because, all that I am, and ever hope to be
Depends a lot on who you are and what you've been to me.

Brenda Griggs

Every Bit A Lady

Sometimes I'm not at my best.
Sometimes I'm a little less.

Sometimes I may use language that is obscene.
Sometimes I may say things that I don't really mean.
But I'm every bit a lady
If I'm doing something positive all the time
does it add to my womanhood.
Just because an angel wears a halo does that
mean she's always good?

I may not respect everyone all the time, but I
always respect myself.
You can remove me from your mantel and
place me on your shelf.
 I'm Every Bit A Lady
No matter how I dress or what I wear about
myself I'll always care.
I've made mistakes before lined up they could
reach from here to Haiti. BUT
I'm Every Bit Yes I'll Admit
I'm Every Bit A Lady!!

Donna F. Worsley

Life's Journey

Life is like a ship at sea
Sometimes it's calm, as calm as can be
But then the waves begin to roll
Slowing us down - keeping us from our goal.
What do we do? Full steam ahead!
We push the throttle and we are sped
on through the waves to the other side
where peace and calm and accomplishment reside.
The way is clear now we sail safely through —
Christ, the navigator of life, tells us what to do
to weather each and every strife
As we travel on this journey through life.

Helen Cheresini

"Things Old"

Antiques to look at, to sit on, to use,
Songs of the past, rhythm and blues,
Grandpas, grandmas, old maiden aunts,
Old southern mansions, dwelt in by haunts.

Dusty old books, with interesting lore,
Handed down legends of days of yore,
The one-room school, where children could pray,
The coal-burning trains on a busy railway.

Mom's wood-burning range.
Daddy's one-horse plow,
some things old, vanished.
Yet some exist now.

Bonnie J. Johnson

I Am Not A Pioneer

There is no echo in your face sonny.
Speak like overgrown weeds and burnt trees.
The perfume river lies just a fingertip ahead
But the leather padding of my feet sting.
Another dandelion day makes it hard to see
Bones of earth writhing beneath me.
I could be enclosed in a room with little sun
"No! No! I hold promise," I say in vain.
Naked repeater I am, little sicker I am.
Scents pass through me as I fall to the grass.
I could try to lift my head and meet each blade
Soak me in dew and plunge my head
I tried, but I am not a pioneer.

Christena M. Vitkovich

Perfect

Joy all around me, love is abound, kindness has been sought out, faith has not tired. Goodness and righteousness has been preserved! The world is still going around - people are still living and everything seems almost the same. People get along, there's no anger, no hatred, no filth, no badness, no sickness, no death, and no selfishness. It is a world where all work together, all worship together, all are in paradise, all love and worship Jehovah. We have peace, All former woes have past. We are calm, discreet, perfect in every way. We live in a perfect world, where everything we do is not for ourselves but for Jehovah - no one is alienated from god! No one forgets Jehovah - people are at peace, we have a worldwide brotherhood, the animals are at peace with each other and mankind, we sing praises to God. We all have perfect and beautiful voices. Our prayers will be heard at all times by Jehovah. We will learn more on how to praise Jehovah - We will be perfect, in a perfect world serving Jehovah, the one who deserves all our praise!

Child

The Ancestral Tree

It sprang from a tiny seed
Sown by the "Lordly and tyrannous power"
Promising to trample it or devour.
When plucked by loving hands
It was removed to better lands
In Holland, there to stand.
Ten years it grew, lovely and stout-hearted
But in size it was thwarted.
So on to plymouth to the wilderness
Challenge, damage, a year hard spent
It almost died, but never bent.
It was nurtured and cherished
For a hundred years or more
When jolted by lightning from the Mother shore.
Then Continental Congress examine it,
Loved it, and look it o'er
Said they preserve it, document it,
Label it ours forevermore.
Pruned and trimmed so tall they stand
Thirteen trees...hallowed by every man.

Jo Josey Matzen

The Motorcyclist

Never felt anything so free.
Speeding down the road so gallantly.
This man made arrangement of sculptured steel
 built to run as a two wheel.
It instantly reacts to your command and feel.
It's amazing where it will go; it scares you so.
Down ditches and across streams,
 in your faded shirt and plain, old blue jeans.
You are flying or jumping dangerously.
It's risky as hell, but you are compelled;
For the feeling is greater than one can express
 in gestures or verbally tell.
Wind fingers running through your hair,
 with your loose shirt flapping, you are without care.
Up the steep bank, you dare, and over the top as the people stare.
"Crazy or wild," they think,
 but they haven't felt the hot machine
 with their body racing in sync.
It grabs your inner being, and down deep you're seeing
 a peace amid all this, and a part of life's sweet bliss.

Bill Mitchell

Feelings In Song

I was looking for love in all the wrong places,
Spending a lot of Wasted Time;
I ran to you with Open Arms
And you told me it was Time For Me To Fly-
Love Hurts...
I think back on our Hot Rod Hearts
I thoughts I had found the Stairway to Heaven,
Little did I know You'd Drop A Bomb On Me.
I reality I was in The Highway To Hell.
You came back and we were Re-United,
I can love you like Nobody can,
Baby, Come to Me,
You turn and walk out, oh well,
There Goes Another Love Song!
Again you return-Like Magnet to Steel-
You Whisper Promises In The Dark
Confusing me like Smoke On The Water,
I know it will never be, for you are a Freebird,
Never wanting to be tamed-
Yet, I love you, Truly.

Caroline M. Tasch

A Woman's Voice

Sitting here alone in the dark
Spinning around the dial on the radio
Looking for a girl singer
I need to hear a woman's voice in this lonely room
A soothing and cajoling voice, to take away this gloom

Don't know how I ended up this way
All I know is, it too quiet
I need to hear a woman's voice in this lonely room
A sweet and gentle voice, to take away this gloom

A voice that stirs my soul, a voice that makes me whole
A voice that comes and never goes

This darkness inside has no end
I'm just looking for something to shine a little light
Maybe a girl singer, talking about true love
I need to hear woman's voice in this lonely room
A caring and soulful voice, to take away this gloom

Just making the night move along
To keep the loneliness from crashing in
I need to hear a woman's voice in this lonely room
A strong and comforting voice, to take away this gloom

David Isgur

My Own

I sit here watching you
Standing tall as an oak tree
With roots that have crossed over into foreign soil
Gaining knowledge and experience for many eyes to see

Even though I am proud of you,
I still curtail your roots within my mind
And confine them to the perimeter of domestic soil

I never regret you growing up,
But from a father to a son
I miss you, seeing me growing old

Ervin M. Freeman

Rock Collecting

The sunset matches the colors in the stone
Swirled tones - pearly white, green and peach
Smooth from years of tumbling in the sea
Cool and solid
Tiny speckled fragments crushed into one
like the thin left over pieces of soap
my mother used to gather into one large bar

Allison Sekol

Far Away Love

Far away in a distant part,
Stands a soldier with a wounded heart.
Not wounded from the enemies guns,
But wounded from being away from his love.

He's in a place where the days are long,
And every night seems to drag on and on.
A place where you're taught to show no fear,
Yet reading her letters you shed a tear.

And just when the pressure really gets to you,
It's the thought of her love that gets you through.
So when you feel lonely and all alone,
Think about your love who awaits for you at home.

Andrew J. Nowack

June

Every day should be like June,
Starry nights all lit by moon,
Warm air caressed with breezes,
No snow, no ice, no sloppy sneezes

The beach does beckon to us all,
Ocean breezes sing their call,
Sea shells speckle the quiet shore,
Always there at the seas door

Forest and fields do sing their lullabies,
Sylvan songs below blue skies,
Flowers dance in the wind,
To and fro their stems bend

O what a world it'd be,
If nature thought like me,
Sylvan songs, ocean breezes, starry moon,
If every day could be like June

Joey Forte

The Black Panther

Walking with its glossy mud stained coat,
starving in the dead of winter, it found nothing to eat.
Stalking through the moonlit woods nearly invisible,
with only a slight glare of its evil eyes.
Crouched in the snow,
it observed a white slender hare.
As it watched, the hare felt fear creep upon it,
for it felt the panther's presence.
Suddenly bolting like lightning, the black ghost seized the scrawny
animal. Instantly killing the helpless hare from the sudden strike.

Using its keen claws it vigorously tore open the hare's stomach,
leaving its claws bathed in warm, red blood.
After doing so it nudged its head into the gap in the hare's belly,
pulling out the bloody entrails of the now red hare.
When finished devouring the animal, it left it there to decay,
shoving the flesh and bones away, as if no longer hungry.
Today the panther has fulfilled its hunger,
but tomorrow it must hunt again.

Josh Hicks

Yellow Roses

Amigo Mio, this morning, I saw you standing in Sacred Heart of Jesus
statue,
Amigo mio, your gentleness hands, had a bottle of water,
Amigo mio, you put water in the yellow roses,
Amigo mio, our Sacred Heart of Jesus smiled at you,
Amigo mio, yellow roses, are beautiful,
Amigo mio, yellow roses and you, are rejoices to me,
Amigo mio, Sacred Heart of Jesus, do not have thorns.
Amigo mio, your goodness, do not have thorns.
Amigo mio, yellow roses, are in your kindness,
Amigo mio, will you, give to me, yellow roses grove in your heart!
Beautiful and lovely are your yellow roses!

Dolores Maria Bolivar-Brauet

"Memories"

Though myriad of lands and oceans parts,
Still I think of you each day,
And remember each night and day;
  The moment you came
    and greeted me.

Blissful memories brim my mind when I'm alone,
With unfathomed joy to depths unknown
When in my life you came anon;
  And cast the dilemma of my
    life forlorn.

In words says not thy poetic heart,
The things it's longing to part,
But simply whispers my lonely heart;
  Its love for you
    will never part.

Though myriad of lands and oceans parts,
Still I think of you each day,
And remember each night and day;
  That moment you came
    and said yes to me.

Andrew B. Menrije

Although Our Paths Have Crossed

Although our path have crossed we are still very different, you like your things and I like mine.
Although our paths have crossed, we come and go and it seems like we never meet at the same place.
Although our paths have crossed, you go one way I go another.
Although our paths have crossed, there could never be another.
Although our paths have crossed, I know you love me with all your heart, I hope you know I love you the same.
Although our paths have crossed, your in my life now and always no matter what has changed.
Although our paths have crossed, I love you just the same.

Hannah E. Moore

My Home Place

The wind in the pines.
Still whispers secrets of an unknown spirit.
Be not afraid only a few will hear it.
When you go to glance no one will see you standing there.
For you can never go home.
Or walk along the same path.
For what once was, years have changed.
The smell of the wild flowers.
The blossom of apple trees are no longer to be found.
Where once a garden lived of fruitful things.
Now only grass lies upon the ground.
For where I once lived and walked.
It will remain forever in memory of a time and place
that I never want to erase.
People come and go and try to build their own dreams.
Where I grew up they can never change.
What I remember of what I call my home place.

Barbara Edgerly

Holiday Contentment

T'was the day after Christmas, the house was a mess, everyone was stirring even our cat Tess. All the stockings were missing but we didn't care, as St. Nicholas, old Santa, had already been there.

All the children were happy, they got what they asked for. Each was in their room behind their closed door.

The Christmas tree was droopy, all bare and dismantled; it was being ignored now and rudely handled. It was missing some bulbs and the star from the top, tinsel and tassel lay right where it dropped. Just wait until next year, I'll shine again bright; Happy New Year to you and to all a good night!

Down in the basement click, click, click, was the sound of the play train brought by St. Nick. That was for Timmy, a playhouse for Sue, she had her Barbie all dressed up in blue.
Mother was in the kitchen straightening all the pots and pans-
Father out in the garage working with his hands.

Old Blue was in the dog house chewing on his bone - Tom the cat was on the window sill perched on his throne.

Everyone and everything was happy and content, thankful they were blessed with a day well spent.

Janet P. Gay

Standing

A leathery, weathered face,
  ...stoic,
Immobile, work-hardened hands clasped behind the back,
  Weary from a day of toil,
    Preparing fields for planting.
Deepset eyes gazing,
  Sweeping the western sky,
    Trying to foretell the weather,
Face unrevealing of plans made for tomorrow's sowing.

Bearing in mind the whimsical and beguiling ways of nature.
  Plans are also made for checking of equipment,
    if the weather is unfit for sowing.

Standing...
  Face unreadable,
    Leaning, with a shoulder against a tree.

Daniel W. Manosh

Wall Of Tears

In tribulation I have built for me a Wailing Wall
Stone upon stone in union with clay wetted by my tears
Laid by trembling hands craving to build rather than wring

I cry the sad lament of the lonely there
My broken heart aches against its hard, immovable presence
And for my thirst, I drink the destitution of the empty

Even so, in the breath of troubled winds, my soul shivers
And I am enveloped in cold, foreboding darkness, I know
In Creation's vast "All-Knowing-Somewhere", LOVE HEARS

Adele C. Jacobs

A Friend In Heaven

Someone to think about; someone to love;
Someone to care about; who is way up above.
It's the times that we would talk, and laugh within.
Who would ever have thought I would never see you again.
When that tragic phone call came, and told me you were no longer here,
I laid in my bed that night and prayed, to let you know I was near.
I know you are in heaven, An angel with its wings.
A sweet and innocent young man with so many dreams.
Since I know you are in heaven, I don't worry as much.
And though your not here on earth, I still think of you a bunch.

Alissa D. Washington

Don't Blink

Striving to grasp my own soul, I held on to the stone walls, but I was slipping just the same. I belong to myself and myself belongs to me. Senses are far behind me now. Mortal is what I am and Immortal, what I would like to be. I can't pretend to be something I'm not. I am so close to God's home. Oh but wait,......senses are slowly coming back. I have a better grip now and I can hear the steady rhythm of my heartbeat playing a new song I've never heard before. One blink and I'm gone. Two blinks and people welcome me. A Third, I'd love to tell you.....but I'm dead.

Caroline Tavares

The Tree

There is a tree standing in a barren field, commanding respect and striking fear into the hearts of everyone.
It is a strange tree, with only one branch, jutting out like an arrow that has been shot into the trunk, deep and straight.

The children are afraid of the tree, because of ghost stories the adults tell them about the tree's spirits.
Adults respect the tree; it gives them some control in an unstable world.

The tree has but one leaf at a time, and leaves on this tree do not live very long. The leaves hang, one by one, from the single branch, heavy and lifeless, peering into the darkness.

Children are afraid of the tree, and of the ghost stories told to them about the tree's spirits. Adults use the tree; it lets them control the uncontrollable.

I see a leaf on the tree now, swinging in the wind.
The whole town is watching it swing.
The leaf looks familiar as it peers into the darkness,
She was my friend, who wasn't afraid.

The children are afraid of the tree, and of becoming one of the tree's spirits. The adults need the tree, to keep the children afraid.

Brian W. Odle

What's A Boy's Pocket For?

Deep: For frogs, baseballs, worms.
String, safety pins.
Dogs clipped toenails.
Unused neatly ironed hanky.
Odd stones (one shaped a bit like a horse.
Hunk of willow branch, one half shoelace.
1 green penny, tar chewing gum.
Golf ball (cover missing).
Comb full of hair, couple acorns.
Bird's egg (wrapped in holey sock).
Dead fly on a string, bird feather.
Squished peanut butter sandwich (sand included).
Old fish scales in a lump.
Heel that come off your shoe.
Piece of bird nest.

Joanne Bauer

Freedom

Take my anger, let me laugh again,
Take my hurt, let my soul run free again.
Let me hear your voice,
Let me caress your body.
To feel you warm, and lying close to me reminding me
There is life within a broken heart.
My tears shall not fall,
My heart shall only fly high with only the key that you hold.
As I soar with the clouds so far and so high,
And ever so bold.

Jennifer Opela

God's Grace

Many times God was there for me when I was
Struggling, needed help, and a friend to talk to,
And so God will never turn his back and ignore
a person, he will be there to help me and you.
We are created in the image of God and
through his word we are supposed to live a holy life,
But every time we do sinful things, we are
crucifying God's son with a knife.
God sent his only son to die for our sins,
Before the world comes to an end, would people get on
their knees and start to pray to God for his
forgiveness before the destruction begins.
God takes an alcoholic, drug addict, prostitute,
and gambler and cleans them up to serve him,
We can not survive without God's
Grace that's our water, sun, and soil
and that's the end.

Benjamin Hicks

Untitled

I spent a pleasant afternoon
Studying the stars
At U.W.M.'s planetarium
From the Seven Sisters, to the planet Mars.

A coed gave the lecture -
And with the help of a machine
She took us to the North Pole
And down to New Orleans.

When she was finished
She asked, "could some one say
Where did we get the planets
And galaxies and Milky Way?"
A small boy in the darkness
She didn't have to prod -
His simple answer stunned her
He simply said "From God"

Elsa Mintzlaff

Grandfather

He said we would cast off before
Sunrise. But the sun is just
Starting to inch over the
Flat opaque buildings on the shore,
Their colors still nondescript in the false light.
Soon the sun will burn off the blue-green
Mist and the sea and sky will
Separate, still hard to say whether we'll
Have clear skies or not.
The wood of the boat is hard and coarse,
Slippery with the morning dew on the deck
And pitted with barnacles at the water's edge.
I can see him sitting on the dock
Talking to the old man with the beret.
The boat is motionless in the water, sails still down,
Waiting for the sun to fill the deck again,
While he sits rigid between overcast and daybreak.

Joseph A. Fronda

Persevering

She mingles, interacts, climbing the ladder,
taking in new information,
studying, taking tests,
taking medication
Her focus is never clear, always being pulled
The treadmill she's on throws her
Her babies are begging her please stay
She's stretched
She never stops trying to blend the two
Her life, the life she shares with her loved ones

Johann DiSalvo

Diving

Sparkling, shiny, dizzy, beautiful,
Surrounded in full by life,
Dark, cold, scary, mystical,
Such confusion and strife,
Breathe each breath as if it were your last,
Looking and searching ahead
No time to look back to the past.
Bright colours and shiny surfaces everywhere,
Clanks and clinks sound all around.
All alone with no one to say "Hey there!"
Plants and animals waving and swimming all about;
Big ones, little ones, scary ones and friendly ones.
Lights and darks with no way out.
Up, down, left or right,
No sense of balance, struggling with water in a bout;
Slowly, you rise, saying, "Good-bye, my friends",
Reach the surface of the water with a surprise,
Louder, with many bird calls,
Then you wake up as the last wave falls,
And as you leave the ocean screams, and you leave your dream.

Chris Chapin

Grace Is Beauty

Today I wake up, with the sun in my face.
Surrounding me is the beauty, of God's great place.
I may be bogged down, with all the problems that surround.
A tear streams down my cheek,
For I feel in such defeat.
Inside there's a sweet gentle voice,
That seems to care.
It tells me there's more to life,
And a lot of love,
That people need to learn to share.
So as the day goes on,
And the moon begins to shine,
I will give a smile,
In hoping that it helped someone out there
In their hard times.
Grace is beauty
Beauty is Depth
Let us all show our beauty,
And dig deep within ourselves.

Joanie Everette

The High's At The Finish

I'm in my fifth mile and haven't got it yet
Sweat's running in my eyes and my shirt's all wet
But they say this is fun a veritable ball
When your lungs are burning and you're ready to fall.
With an ache in my knee and a pain in my side
I start to slow down and shorten my stride.
I'm in great shape and I've been running for years
A true runner's runner I'm called by my peers
But as I keep loping and plodding along
A kid of twelve passes me and I know this is wrong.
I'm now in my sixth and my shoes feel like lead
Damn, I wish I were home and still in my bed.
I've done repetitions and fartleks and more
So why am I tired and sweaty and sore
Or could it be a fib or in truth just a lie
That there's no such thing as a real runner's high.
But as I run all my aches disappear
And the truth about running becomes very clear
That I've reached my high and my pain has diminished
But yes friends it's true the high's at the finish.

Barrington W. Keist

My Shadow

Ready to go whenever I wake.
Tagging along with each step I take.
Half my size but manages fine.
To mock my moves in about perfect time.
When big hands are busy little hands are too.
He's doing his best to do what I do.
His outlook on life he sees here in me.
It determines so much of what he turns out to be.
For just like a shadow at the end of a day.
He's sure to get taller and stretch farther away.
But wherever life takes him to me we're still one.
And my feelings he'll know when his shadows have come

Jeff C. Henthorne

Yearning

Bear with me. Let me share my soul and open my heart to you. Take away the dark bleak shades of winter and bring forth the sweet fresh colors of spring.

Let me dance again to the rhythm of your heart and the music of your love. Crush not my spirit while the waves of the ocean crash down heavily upon me. Wake me from this slumber which buries not the sadness of a child once lost.

For it is your warmth that comforts me. It is your strength that carries me through the storm as the wind and rain tear through me and drench my weary body.

Look fondly toward me as once the innocence of youth's sweet love was upon us. Forget not the memories that bind us. Favor these your thoughts to linger through the beauty of the petals of a rose once cherished.

Drown not your sorrow for dreams of love echo through the cavern as in the darkness sleeps. Beneath, you wake. The sudden burst of morning sun embraces and sustains you as dreams fade no longer touched by the stillness of night but beckons you to recapture again the mystery of love.

Jo-Anne De Martino

As I Moondance

The cold hearted orb, rising in midnight,
Takes me back, takes back those years,
And the love I lost that once ago midnight,
Is it the same moon, the same tears?

The stars this night, winter dream,
Make my tears seem so insincere,
And yet they were real, lost dream
That never was, yet they were so sincere.

I sleepwalk in memory too long,
And find loneliness is my only lover;
God give me back the feeling for my song,
To be together again, sister, lover.

But cold hearted, like the ghost of my soul,
The pale reflection of the hot sun, no more,
The feeling slips away; it's only a role, I play,
Never to be again like before.

For now, now we are both wise and old,
Dream apart of the stars above;
Yet the flower of youth will forever unfold
As winter dream sings my song of love.

Frank L. Paulson

One Summer Day

I was walking through the woods that summer afternoon, and began taking pictures of whatever caught my eye: Wondering how creative one must be to make such greatness that I saw before me. The wind was blowing through the clear blue sky, and the birds were flying up above, so high. I sat down, relaxed, and took a deep breath. Trying to imagine how many times this land had seen death, whether it had been a deer or an opossum, or just that flower that never blossomed. It could have been an Indian or a soldier, or anybody. It could have been any number of things from A to Z. But I wonder if I'm really a part of this land that will one day die? I know for a fact that I do hurt and cry. I do have feelings and I do often lie. I do have a certain shape that is all my own. I do have a voice and I do have a mind. I guess that this land and I are one of a kind. But what is my place on this land where I sit? Shall I remain still and become one more death that lie here, or shall I move on and make use of my resources? If I choose not to, then I will die: But if I move on I will live to survive. So I will keep on taking my pictures and walking through these woods. Hoping to see what truly lies before me...

Charlie R. Trevino

Stranger

The stranger I met in the park, stood
tall and handsome, and walked with
pride, as to say that life has not got him down.
Some of life's path's, and hills has left
some trace of sadless, but with each new day,
and each new tomorrow, that he might
face, as a man, he can still stand tall
through it all.
As I sat watching him, I knew this
stranger, was full of love and tenderness, as
I got up to walk away, are eyes met at that
moment I new I was his new tomorrow.

Dorothy J. Stidham

"Joy In My Soul"

There's joy now in my soul from God above
Taught me more lessons on life and on love
Love your enemies as well as your friends
Don't cast stones for it may not mend
Be kind and gentle with all people, learned
That at the church with the steeple
Be gracious and generous of heart
For God's close to us, never far apart
God gave me joy, happiness, and peace
What power and majesty, what a release
From guilt and shame and awful pain
God caused me to come in out of the rain
I praise my Lord for his holy word
To teach me, to guide me, to give me a sword
Of righteousness, tolerance, unconditional love
It's not of this world, but really should be, it's from above
It's shouted out loud for people to see
Changing shattered lives, renewing God's vows
I will preach it and teach it starting right now.

Bob Conroy

Untitled

In the distant future, a cosmic scream
Tears across the universe,
And worlds cry out in fear, pain, but recover
As all life will, at someday, sometime,
For life is and does and always will be,
As it shall be when
In the distant future, a cosmic scream
Echoes off the stars
And life does prevail.

Jacqui Adams

Miracles All

Miracles
Tears of joy
Crisp icicles
A rain glazed day
Sunshine like melting lemon drops upon my face.

Puppy paws
A child's smile
Laughter wild and free
My friend's hand when I feel pain.

Strawberries
Root beer and buttered popcorn
A box of paints
The breath of my angel's wings on my back.

Warmth
Blessings so numerous
Mine is wealth beyond belief.

Elizabeth G. Alvarado

Untitled

Hey there little golden haired boy
Tell me what your eyes see,
It's not that heartache and pain
I've seen on all humanity.

You have the world in the pocket
Of your little pair of jeans,
Run and play, run and play
You've plenty of time for dreams!

Hey there little golden haired boy
Don't worry about a thing
The good things in life will come
Your way, and such a happiness it will bring!

A super heroes heart
Eyes of wonder,
You have everything to gain

My eyes fill with tears
At any thought of you
Ever feeling pain!

Byron Kevin Hammond

Purple Mantle

Tell me where you go when skies are gray
Tell me where you hide on a rainy day
Is it deep inside where there is no pain?
and what do you do on a lonely night
when thoughts keep spinning round your head
and there is no place to escape
If I could hold the keys of freedom
and smell the scent of love
If I could wait for just an instant
till dreams vacate my mind
I'll tell you where I hide
if you tell me where you go
beneath the purple mantle
of the prison of my mind

Gilberto Padron

Tears

Tears are the hurting and burning drops,
That express our feelings.
When the tears come down,
They're like a screaming river,
Trying to wash you away.
Try to lock up your tears,
Till another day when you really need them.

Christopher Beatty

"My Son"

My son, one and one is two. We combine as one. He means more to me than any-one. For me I love only my son. Nothing else matters. He is the greatest thing in my life.

For my son, I would do anything, I would give up my life for my sons. For he is my life.

Where ever I am, he is. Where ever he is, I am. For we combine together as one, because he is my son. His life, formed in mine for nine months.

As I felt him growing and kicking inside me, from the time I was two months along, and the rest of the way through, I knew he would be born a fighter. My son, has a lot of strength, and I have a lot of love and belief in only my son. No one or nothing could ever take the place of my son. For he is a part of me and always will be. My son, and I will always be together, for now, for always and forever. Here, there and everywhere. For my son there will always be a today and tomorrow, yet to come, for my son to see, for I brought him into this world, and I will keep him in this world. Our lives are as one. I gave my son his life, as he came to be my life. For he is my son, he is my life for always. For there are many todays and tomorrows yet to come for my darling son.

Joyce Reifsnyder

My Friend

I had a good friend in the year 52
That always was talking of things to come true.
He would look up at the moon, in his usual way
And speaking with authority, he would say,
A man will walk on the moon some day.

His time was marked and he could not stay,
To see a man walking on the moon this day.
At his bed side, before they took him away,
He barely could speak, but I could hear him say
A man will walk on the moon some day.

We buried him where he would be,
With the moon shinning brightly he could see.
As time passed on, a man would try,
To reach the moon up in the sky.

One day he made it and we watched with glee,
As he walked on the moon for all to see.
I know my friend, if he could say,
A man walked on the moon, this beautiful day.

Charles E. Welsh

Music

Notes go together to make music
that breathes soft, sweet sounds
filling the air with peace and tranquility,
encompassing all, leaving a feeling of marvel
and awe to all who come within her boundaries,
floating along on the waves of sound,
bringing her beauty and meaning to all who listen,
rising above all, spreading her mysterious melodies,
constantly kindling the flame in one's soul
for the love and beautiful meaning of music.

Debbie Collins

Peace That Surrounds Us

The peace that surrounds me, the serenity that embraces me, Lord give me another day to absorb this beauty and joyous wonderland which adds more love and wisdom in my heart.

The peace that surrounds us, the serenity that embraces us, Lord give us all this extra day to absorb the beauty and joy with all mankind, which will add more love and wisdom in our most needed hearts.

Connie Cisneros

Mother's Day

No poets phrase can fully praise
That cherished name of mother
No tongue on earth can tell her worth
that one whom we call Mother
In trouble, woe, to her we go
How she has helped us, we all know
On Mothers Day we tell her so
That trusted friend our mother
But Mothers Day is just one day
And scarce enough time then to say
Or do the things which may convey
The love we owe our mother
So let each day bring forth the praise
and let each one their voices raise
In tribute to our mother, for time will come,
As has to some, when we see her no more
So may she hear, while she is near
To us she is s gift most dear
And on each day throughout the year
We show love to our mother.

Dorothy L. Clark

My Precious Love

Every time I look at you
That dear, sweet little face
I know that soon, it won't be long
A little girl will take your place
As you grow, I'll grow with you
We'll change together some
But somehow bittersweet, I feel
A teenager you'll become
Just when those sneakers start to wear
Your graduation will come
And soon before me will stand
A beautiful young woman
The roots begin small and weak the trunk is straight and true
The leaves are frail, but grow somehow
Then I stop, and look at you
If God can make a little tree into a forest grow
Then I know He will give me the strength to one day let you go
But as I gaze into the night, the tree it starts to bloom
A smile, a tear my precious love
I'll always think of you

Elaina Marble

A Mountain To Climb

I have climbed the highest mountain
that God sent to me that day
with only a stop at the fountain to quench
my thirst along the way, I tried my best,
was put through the test of hope faith and love.
God was watching my every move
from the Heavens up above.

I heard Gods voice and listened to what He said
"My child your journey has only begun,
go ahead you'll see the setting sun,
for there is work that has to be done."

My faith is intact, I've followed the sun.
My work is almost done, it took a little while
and as I looked up to the heavens above,
I saw your face my God with a loving smile,
so thanking you my God, I shall only look ahead
and tell my little story, of the mountain I climbed,
I endured the pain, but at the top there was only "Glory."

Dolores Ulibarri

Only You

I give to you a part, of my soul and my heart.

To let you know how much I care,
that I am here for you
when life is unjust and unfair.

To know you have me any time you may need.
Just call my name I'll come and heed.

You are so special in my life
you'll never know just how.
I am here to love you; yesterday
tomorrow, forever and now.

To cover all periods of time
in presence, and in mind.
To be here in spirit when together time
can't allow us to find.

Know that I am always with you
though apart we may be
No one is so special as you are to me.

I have given to you
in my words a part,
my love, my soul and my heart.

Debra Dimando

Faith's Place

Help me find the peace within,
that I may find my peace throughout.
In all this world I have a place
just where that is - in thus lies doubt.

For I just wander day after day
from happiness to sorrow, dusk to dawn.
You just can't see what you can't find.
You move the knight, sacrifice your pawn.

I've come and gone, never left may mark.
By God's own hand, he chose my space,
Before, my birth, yet unknown to death
for he's written my role upon his face.

There is but a reason to set me free,
though it be secret, it's soul is me.
There's no true peace in wake or sleep,
until your soul's given to Jesus, to keep.

Denice Peters

Illusion

For everybody knows or should know
That I want to be alive and well
For I appear content as flakes of snow
But I'm alone in my private hell
They see what ever they want to see in me
I'm nothing but a lonely little stem
On a huge and full but empty tree
I am alone and unhappy my friend
Maybe as you say, I glitter like gold
I'm giving up .... it is close to the end
Don't let my appearance fool you please
Reach out and hold on to what's left of me

Christina E. Bonner

The Finest Art

I see aesthetic beauty in the clothes upon the line,
The graceful blowing towels and sheets and other things of mine.
They're drying for a purpose that's as personal as love,
As the line swings back and forth, with help from up above.

It's a line of art, the finest art, that all we folks can show,
In any yard, on any day, where all the winds do blow.
Why do I stand and watch with pride in their align?
I see aesthetic beauty in the clothes upon the line.

Helen M. Sandon

Gulls

I had never seen the gulls before,
  That is not really.
They were passing birds along the shore,
  Before.

Like each and every living thing,
  Their style is their's alone
A happy squeal, a dashing dart,
  They jet above the loam.

Above the loam, or out to sea, snow white birds so full of glee;
Float up and down, for all to see.

They have a look of sureness, though seemingly they flee;
Their landings are surprising, made in perfect harmony.

When sitting on a sandy beach, all face in one direction.
Into the wind, as though to say, our need is for perfection.

Ask any sailor, sailing, why gulls fall into form.
The answer will be very swift, like sunrise on a morn.

Every flying gull you see, cloths the spirit of
A dear departed faithful gob, whose soul has gone above.

So when they fly, and swoop and soar, salute in humble fare;
It is not just a gull you see, but freedom everywhere.

Grace B. Romoser

A Mother's Love

There's no love like a mother's love,
that is surely blessed from heaven above
to soothe and comfort me when things go wrong
to caress my spirit like a slow sweet song

There's no love like a mother love,
it is as if the Lord above
desired her to always be
the caring arm surrounding me

I can't explain this love she has
that will allow her to care so much
but through it all, I must say
that I am truly blessed the Lord sent
Mom my way

I can only pray that soon some day
her love and caring I can repay
for her love she's shown throughout the years
through dedicated prayers and heartfelt tears
has shown me what true love consist of
not money, not diamonds but a mother's love.....

Jodie D. Robinson

The Sadness Within Me

I have this sadness within me
that just won't go away.
It's apart of me I live with
each and everyday.
It's about not having anyone to care about
and no one to care about you.
About no one being close enough
When your feeling OH SO BLUE!
I always dream of someone
who will love me just for me.
Not what's on the outside
but what no one else seems to see.
Maybe someday I'll find that special person
who will fill my heart with love.
Someone very special
sent from up above.

Amy Watkins

Time

Each moment must tell its story at a glance.
That moment never gets a second chance.

We capture the history of time in its flight
In a book or a song or film it with delight.

Unlike the clock that makes no demands;
It cuddles eternity in its tiny hands.

We ask it to wait when getting dressed;
Running late, for time we're pressed.

We ask it to hurry as we stand in line,
Waiting for a table so we can dine.

But time won't change to suit our plot
Not faster, not slower, like it or not.

Ignored for the moment when pain is real,
We also know that time can heal.

With sorrow and joy we color today,
Tomorrow will soon be yesterday.

As time recedes before our eyes,
We leave our mark that never dies.

Our special print, the waves we make:
Immortal spirit in our wake.

Doris Hare

Time

What is time?
That precious commodity of yours and mine
There never seems to be enough
To finish all of our important stuff

Would we could make it multiply
That would really be an emotional high
But we all have the same amount
Some are just better at making it count

They say planning is the key
But we all know how hard that can be
Save it here to spend it there
Sometimes it's so overwhelming, who gives a care

So we all do the best we can
To make the most of our daily plan
But when each day is done
The real question is - did we have fun?

Bonnie R. Austin

Man From The Other Side

Consider the cocoon
That was but an unsightly creature,
Yet with privilege chance,
What can possess more beautiful features?

Even the serpent,
Mankind's eternal foe,
But with chance, he strikes his blow.

Man from the other side
Is equal by birth,
Oh, where is chance who won't honor his worth?

Hundreds of years chance never showed,
Mankind suffered tremendous woes.
Let's be kind to His creation,
No more myths, no false accusations.
Tell chance to appear and expand her mind,
The world can benefit through all mankind.
Man from the other side, man is strong and wise,
Invite him in, with chance he can win.

Edna Fenceroy

WHY?

Why is it that no one can see,
That which is so obvious to me.
Are they walking in darkness through the night,
Confused because they're blinded by fright.

Believe what you will, but I've seen it all before,
Cruelty, crime, immorality - all this and more.
However, all this could end, if only we dare,
Decide we're in control and show that we care.

We've studied the past and decided to improve the present - still we ask,
Why is it taking so long to understand the problem and shoulder the task?
Let us eliminate the clouds and let the sun shine down,
and, it will sanitize the environment and brighten the town.

Again I say, "It's so obvious to me,
Why oh why, can't the rest of you see?
The light that shines brightly in the night,
And eliminates the shadows, which cause all your fright - Why?"

Charles A. Zuppa

The Angels Are Calling

The angels are calling, the angels are calling,
the angels are calling, for me and you.

Can you hear them calling for you, can you hear them
calling for me. Tell me can you hear them, clearly talking
speaking to each other calling so softly our names.

Tender words of wisdom coming from above, saying
come a little closer, reach a little higher, soar a little
longer and see the beauty of God's creation.

The angels are calling each of our names, to tell us
how much God loves us so. That each day and night
He has them watching over you and me.

Can't you hear their voices speaking in the air? Singing
sweet melodies of praises to the most high. Telling of
God's goodness and what He has in store for those who
love Him.

Each day as you walk and talk with one another, don't
forget to look up toward heaven to listen and hear the
angels calling for you and me.

Andrew L. Price Jr.

Untitled

One night I had a dream, the dream was world peace,
The best kind of fantasy,
Where the violence would cease.
Everybody was treated equal,
No matter what color, shape or form,
Everybody had the same things,
And no one was considered poor.
There was no sound of gunfire, in my neighborhood,
There was no sound of crying, and everything was good.
There was no gang warfare, and no drive by's.
There was no killing or violence
Or people dying too young.
No hate in this world, the hate was melted down.
No fear in this world, all the fear was drowned.
No guns in this world, the guns were melted down.
No weapons in this world, no weapons to astound.
This illusion seemed so true, this fantasy world of luck,
My world was secure, and then I woke up.

Christina Huckins

The Last Night Of The Revival

Now, it was an all-white baptist church.
  The best that great grandma could recall.
The last night of revival ending.
  Not one, profession by faith at all.

Congregation, had started singing.
  On last toll of bell in church steeple-
In walked a black stranger from the night.
  He was ragged, cold, old and feeble.

He sat quietly, on a back pew.
  Only a few knew, that he was there.
His tired weary eyes told his story.
  His years of hard work, abuse and care.

All heads were bowed at close of sermon.
  'Twas deathly quiet, on every hand.
A feeble voice started singing low-
  "Oh Buelah land, my sweet Buelah land."

The voice grew faint, and faded away.
  We knew the angels, were all around.
His peaceful smile and his tired eyes closed.
  Home at last, his Buelah Land he'd found.

Idele Hillebrand

Home

A lonely wind blows across the cracked plain.
The black trees stand twisted,
Wrenched into silent agony,
But they live.
There is no sun,
Only a smudge of broken orange decorates the still sky.
The clouds hang motionless,
And no birds hover above to sing to the dry ground.
The old shack that has stood for fifty years still
Defies the gusts.
The windows are cloudy, and all inside is obscured,
A hazy blur of stasis.
But little matter,
Nothing inside the warped walls moves.
A well lies empty,
Devoid of all but sand.
But on the porch,
An old woman sits in her chair,
And rocks eternity away.

Adam Lishawa

Untitled

Who knows
the boundaries between worlds when we
to darkened earth descend?
Scale patterns and lizard skin rain
awake
drenched in white water.

Wine and water.

Red glass and clear glass on cafe table
Blood and rain water sluice scarab sidewalk
Priests blessing earth's white water and wine;

O, palest, shinning water
  of the Prophet's pool!
O, wine ineffable!

Cathryn F. Rice-Simmons

The First of the Battles

The moon is arising; it climbs over heads
The brave men are sleeping; but not in their beds
The next morn they shall wake and lift up their swords
To fight off the galloping, galloping hordes
Many shall fall and few shall return
And the corpse of the hordes shall be tortured and burned
And as night falls again, and the eagles shall scream
They shall sharpen their swords 'till they are keen
And many days later as the battle tide bends,
Good shall overcome, and the battle shall end.

But this is but the first of many battles that shall be
That not the wisest of the lore masters could possibly foresee
And many a man and foe shall die,
Before the winners are raised on high
And as the war is at end, and the hordes are cast down.
The Heir of Isildur shall once more be crowned

David J. M. Knazek

Illusions Of Love

Your love was an illusion,
the child of my fertile imagination,
a fantasy of unconditional devotion,
fiery, passionate, aroused, steadfast and faithful true love.

Your love was an illusion,
the birth of my melancholy, distrust and disbelief,
a total enthrallment into confusion and self-doubt,
forever longing, yearning for tenderness and compassion.

Your love was an illusion,
the weakened man tormented into brutality and cruelness by a wicked female, merciless and hardhearted, in a tangled maze of love-hate for womankind, torturous, ruthless, yet bedazzling and scintillating.

Your love was an illusion,
mangling, tearing the human heart,
showing the soul the depths of emotional deprivation,
excruciatingly painful, crippling and aloof.

Your love was an illusion,
leaving behind a desolate landscape of love forsaken,
a sullen mood, the hopeless longing for requited love,
the sight of your face and the wish for illusions to come true.

Ivonne L. Nagy

Looking Homeward

The years are swiftly passing
The clocks are ticking our time away,
We are young today and old tomorrow,
This is Gods plan.

Life is like a Merry-Go-Round,
We are flying around and around,
Happy and gay,
Enjoying life every day too busy to stop
And pray for the unfortunate.

We keep on going around and around,
Never realizing the hell on the ground,
Wars, terrorism, hunger, greed and hatred.

Little children lying on the hard wet streets,
Unwanted, forgotten, hungry, cold and sick,
Crying for love and help, this their only home.

So let's come down from our Merry-Go-Round,
And take a look around at what we see on the ground,
Let's look "Homeward" to God for help.
He is always near with arms out stretched,
Waiting to hear our Prayer for Help.

Ann L. Anderson

Untitled

I am the heat upon a performer, sweating beneath the lights;
The cold within a breeze about two lovers in the night;
The twinkle in a smile, of a child, that shines so right;
The sweetness in their eyes, without disguise, that is life.

I am the cramp in an artist's wrist, the pain that pushes on;
The lift in a dancer's step, that sings a silent song;
The writer at three a.m. who has just begun to start;
The musician that alone, with his trumpet, in the dark.

The blueness in the moon, as memories, touch with tender;
The fragrance of a letter, that makes you miss the sender;
I am the power that turns the brawn into the debonair,
And the hard-skinned to a poet, with a serenading flair.

I am all this and more, a substance in everything,
Always felt, never touched. Always said, never seen.

Beatrice A. Abercrumbie

The Rivers Of My Heart

The rivers of my heart
the currents that thrive
have made me wonder how hope just survived
thrashing and throwing, roaring and rumbling
the pain and the fear of my soul kept me searching

The rivers of my heart
the ripples that roll
gently over my bosom to answer my call
have formed a small pool, so warm yet so cool
the delicate touch made fear seem like a fool
They bathe my young soul with pure liquid gold
imparting sensations of fairy tales old
and glisten like sunrays above the far hills
but frighten with depth, sending quivers and chills
The rivers of my heart
flow into the sea
and glide through the barriers to set my soul free
going far and returning, gyrating and churning,
keeping passion alive and forever extending

To a world with no strife where the souls quench their yearning.

Charisse J. Baldoria

Wind

The tree tops dance to the drops; the wind lifts their limbs.
The dance stops. Rain slips off the end of each leaf.

The wind leaves just passes through
The moving mass has more dances to do. How far? I don't know?
In three minutes, it moves right through. I see another wind
picks up, branches starting to move.
Is this another mass? Or the same wind making another pass.
I don't know where does the first one really go?
Has the wind always been the same?
Does it ever stop or just keep circulating to a different spot?

I know the Jet Stream, a planetary wind.
Do other winds just die out and become hot and cold air again?
To heat and cool, to rise and fall, the air is having an on going ball

Wind is moving air; before the air was hot and cold.
Does that wind stop and become air that's old?
To start the process of wind, I was never told.

Does that moving air find despair, when it can't roam?
With boundaries at the earth's atmospheric dome
Where the air does not exist - the wind goes on to roam-the earth
is airs only home.
The air has always been the same from whence it originally came.
Do we breath the same air with ancient civilizations?
We share the same hot, cold moving air...

Christine Frances Hughes

An Illusion

I know I shouldn't have gone there.
The desire drew me like a magnet
like a butterfly; flying carefree
towards the candle's flame.
It is too late, too late.

There was sunshine in my life.
The bright orange, yellow, blue sunrise
shone my hours, my minutes, my existence.
All gone now, too late, too late.

The darkness has fallen all over my being-
the feeling is so heavy- a dark blanket from
end to end, I am so tired, so brutally robbed
of my God given treasure.
All gone now, too late, too late.

No more sunshine, no more the smell of red roses
no more the aroma of Jasmine; after the sunset.
No turning back, I shouldn't have gone there.
It is too late, too late.

Ellie Kondy

Woman

The sun is rising in your eyes.
The earth moves under your feet
Why have we not seen your beauty
Please hold your hand, just one, to feel
the softness, the kindness, yet there is
might in your arm's, help me, help me!
For I'm blind and can't see. For I've sloped
you when you give "love", I have killed the
very thing, person, the woman which
gave me life, bring me to my grave, for
all is lost, there is a storm coming,
She will once again stand tall, while I
look for help, she will walk strong. While
I stumble, she will hold out her hand,
with tear's in eye's, pain of heart, she will
love me, cloth me, feed me, she is woman
look you are blind, you do not hear
you do not feel, for, she will always
be, woman forever.

David McGee

My Little Girl

Her crying brings my relief,
The end of waiting, the beginning of nurturing.
She, so small yet overwhelming,
This instinctive feeling to protect?

Her smile, her giggle, her hugs,
Her eyes... often glad, sometimes sad but always true.
She crawls, she walks, now dances,
She mumbles, she talks, now sings.

As she grows, I grow,
As I teach, she learns
As she learns to grow, I grow to learn.

Her happiness is my pleasure
Her sadness becomes my dilemma...
Discipline or that giggle.

The words adore, amour, love...
They seem so unfit for such a feeling.
An eternal embrace.

Angelo V. Michilli

Born To The Wind

The silent weaning of seed from stem that signifies the beginning and the end. The miraculous essence of life that instantly bonds one to and from the other with a veracity that binds all things to and of the other. The bough that twists and bends, shaking leaf from limb in a fitful, tumultuous flight for this one and only time. The magic that releases its offspring in a cataclysmic free fall to make way for the emergence of another...as a buckeye bursts its entrapment without... as a firefly delights in hide and seek, too shy to light in the same place twice. That astonishing and final separation of seed from stem all day and all night... The reverse of day's imaging.

All dripping wet with the sweat of life, its life bearing seeds on their way at last. Airborne for a fleeting moment, then at rest in the very spot from which they will be re-born to the winds of time. Yet, only those with an eye of quick will see the ageless dance and flight (no one does, when at night) that leaves one more ring in the tree of life for counting's sake..time's keepsake..time keeping's sake. A timeless pillar from which all others came. The ark of mankind conceived of the water and wind and light, bearing fruit for all that is and would be. The fire and fiber of life, rooted deep in the soil to hold the earth and all things together...
For it is the way of Our Lord.

Chuz Alfred

The Fear Above All Fears

A knock at my front door, a ring of my phone,
the fear above all fears is feeling alone.
The silence is peaceful, the air so serene,
I find my thoughts drifting to some other scene.

A vision of someone there, back in my past,
an image of great love which surely will last.
To know is to love. Can it not be true?
A seed was first planted, then watered, and grew.

It grew out of caring, and sharing, and needs,
to sprout many branches and choke out the weeds.
Then storms came upon it with furry and wrath,
to weaken its splendor with chaos and chafe.

How stable its members, how firm is its root,
but many who praised it have now become mute.
Its brilliance now tarnished, its manner oblique,
they group it along with the frail and the weak.

The past an illusion, the future unsure,
the present, for now, a time to endure.
A time to reap all of the seeds that were sown.
The fear above all fears, is feeling alone.

David Daub

Pioneers

Pioneers, drifting along on the dusty road.
The feet of the oxen going tramp tramp as
they disappear from view...

Looking for a better life,
free from fear
free of strife

They did not know so long ago
their quest for freedom would hurt us so.

Now the earth is barren,
the air is not clean,
we can hardly find a clear stream.

As we struggle to breathe,
when there is no food to eat,
and the water is not fit to drink,

Will we only find freedom as we disappear
from view...............................?

Doris Charles

Celebrate

Just the thought of Summer brings a smile to my face
The fragrance of tulips and roses multicolored and bursting with
happiness
Being at the pool on a blazing hot day and
Watermelon juice dripping on my toes
Families cooking chicken and hotdogs at the park
Strawberry ice-cream on my face and pink lemonade for sale,
Roasting marshmallows over the flaring campfire
Watching the stars come out at sundown
A midnight baseball game played by the moon's light
And a light drizzle of rain on your windowpane
Everything so engaging and free
It's Summer time the best season of the year.

Jackie Wilwerding

The Lake

In Loving Memory of Lester Allen

Our favorite picnic table is in the same old spot
The geese are still here and the sun is bright and hot
The sky is blue and clear, a single cloud billows so brave
As I look across the lake and watch the water wave

So many of our summer days and nights were spent right here
Watching boats go by, and fish and occasionally a deer
We swam by day, slow danced by night under the evenings full moon
We thought that we'd found heaven in our private small lagoon

We sat and planned our future here and how we'd pass our days
Last year I didn't know, that you would pass away
That God had plans for you to leave in the month of May
And I would walk alone on our bright and summer day

When you went you took my heart and left an empty space
Now I sit alone and watch the sunset, with tears upon my face
And know the place that you're in now has wondrous sight to see
More beautiful and peaceful than the sights you saw with me

So you will live within my heart, the flame of love will wait
Until I meet you in the land you walk, there at heaven's gate
And you can show me all the things that you've been blessed to see
And we will be together again as it was meant to be

Bonnie Longo Roth

Palm Prints

I was down at the photocopy store taking pictures of my palms
The guy on the next machine kept checking me out,
glancing at my antics through the corners of suspicious eyes
Because I have this terrible need to explain my actions to people
I was tempted to rattle off my very logical explanation,
my reasons for going to so much trouble, taking palm prints—
placing my hand just so and holding the flap over it
while adjusting the controls with each new take, varying shades
like it was a document on which my future hinged

Narcissism to a disgusting degree he might have thought
Let him think
How more interesting life is without logical explanations
A reason would rob him of a colorful story...
"There was this crazy dude down at the photocopy place..."

How better to say, "Can't FAX a hand." Or say nothing at all
Reasons rip through vulnerability like a hand grenade
Explain why you're taking pictures of your palm
and dig a deeper hole
"Yeah, yeah, you crazy sucker."
More fun to let him wonder

Bobby Harwell

Souls

Upon death does a soul rise miraculously from the body and
ascend to the heavens?
Does a quintessential belief in one's soul determine the path of
one's life?
Is the soul the conscience base?

People with culpable consciences, do they have immoral souls?
Contemptible souls wait an eternity to be purged of their sins
And long to achieve the same distinction as virtuous souls.
But these tormented souls are inexorably denied deliverance to heaven.

Oh! How the souls in hell burn and aimlessly reach out for succor,
Only to be spurned for their misdeeds.
How does this differ from life?
These agonized beings scream to be delivered from hellfire and
damnation.

But who is it that passes judgment on these souls?
Would a merciful God condemn the most wretched of transgressors to
such wickedness?
Is God not all forgiving?
Perhaps judgment is passed by the Soul of Mankind.

Jeanne M. Humphrey

Life Consequence

No one tells you of the pain you will feel
The hole sunken in so deep, you fall in the endless pit of emptiness
The heart at one time beat for life now rings death
No one tells you of the haunting memories
Flashing in your mind all day long sounds of vacuum suction
Blood and limbs sucked out of my womb into the trash
I shake and a tear slides down my face
Choice, it was my choice
Oh yes, they smile with compassion, dressed in sterile white robes.
Monotonely speaking...
"You've made the right choice."
"Everything will work out for the best."
No one tells you of the fear which freezes your body
As your legs propped V-shape, the switch turned on
Suction deafening to my ears
She vacuums me 4 1/2, taking out every ounce of life
As if another daily routine, another robotic motion,
Another statistic, choice, it was my choice
It's over 1, 2, 3, paid in cash, I can go...
"Be sure to get some rest." "Everything will work out for the best."

Cheryl Ann Lawson

More Than Magic

Sometimes when we touch
The honesty is just too much
I have to stop and close my eyes
I want to hold you 'til I die

When you reach out for me
I feel a love that no one can see
I hear your voice so tender to me
I hope in all your dreams, I will be

Let me be your sunshine a while
And you'll be the reason I'll always smile

Some may say that I'm a dreamer
But you give me a love that will last forever
You can understand how I feel inside;
There is nothing from you that I wish to hide
When your fingers gently touch mine
I know I've never felt a love of this kind

It's amazing the love I feel in my heart
I hope that we will never part
I know that whenever we are together
It's more than magic that will last forever

Angela Burrow

As I Enter The Fields

As I enter the fields I think I know,
The house is in the village down below,
No one can see me exploring here,
As I watch the countryside fill up with snow.
The people in town may think I have fear,
But I'll show them as I walk away from here,
I'll go through the woods and frozen lake,
On the snowiest evening of the year.
As my fingers grow numb and I begin to shake,
A thought crosses my mind is this a mistake,
Then I look around and see the beautiful snow-covered land
Like a youngster I try to catch a single snowflake,
I have miles to travel before I sleep,
I know I can get there I have a promise to keep,
The lesson I'll learn when my snowy evening has ended,
Is the woods are beautiful but cold, dark and deep.

Christine DeBlasio

Insecurity

The tiny and fearful mouse
The huge and dreaded broom
Menacing
Insecurity arises
Tiny mouse, overcome your inferiority
You may be small, you may be unique
but sha-la-la-lalay-sha, sing the song
You are of same status as your fierce enemy
There is a soul in your broom as is in you
The same equal yet very different
When scanned the situation in symbolic
and philosophic angles and perspective
The insecurity sinks, and tiny mouse, you
are just as special in your own unique
way as any other living or non-living being
in this vast universe

Allysan Isaac

This Time

I am getting better at it Lord,
the hurt did not last
quiet so long this time.
I am learning to protect myself Lord,
I did not go into it so fast,
just a little slower this time.
I am going to be just fine Lord,
unlike other times past,
I kept you on my mind this time.
I am going to say a prayer at night Lord,
to say 'Thank you' it won't be the last.
I will just be careful after this time!

George Allen Gray

Start And Stop

To start is to stop, even for a minute. Uncertainly is for the insecure, even when death is supposedly the only certainly. But then death is a stop of what is called the routine for the fallecido.

For at least this one person, stops and starts have a different meaning for the young, another meaning for the middle-aged. another meaning for the old, and the same meaning for the wise. The wise-guy has no meaning, since start is better than stop.

It is now better to stop, and continue being happy, not sappy though a start is in subtle motion when there are stops to begin some start, even if some starts are thwarted.

David Guzman

It's Time

It's time to stop and wager... the price you're going to have to pay.
The keepers of your tomorrows, as well as your yesterday.

It's time to count your self-worth, whether good of bad.
Your trivialities, compassions, damages... oh so sad.
What worth, your love, peace, or happiness... have your values had.

As you wander through life... so tense, no time for grief or
sorrow, just caught up in a net. What happens today, shall
repeat tomorrow: so time is obviously set.

It's time to add the songs you've heard, hands you've held,
embraces you've gave, giving smiles to lift souls from
despair. Did you rock the Cradles, then turned your back,
in this world riddled with none to care

It's time to pay the piper, what fee shall he
charge... Sorry...he says the world is so wicked, no chance
of change...perhaps
Try again, another time, when more time has lapsed.

Arena Kimbrel

Christmas Poem

I wish to write a poem about Christmas cheer,
The kind that lasts throughout the year.
The cheerful, fun kind,
That would light the life of the blind.
The noisy, celebrating cheers,
That would be heard by deaf ears.
The kind that would make the lame walk,
And make the mute talk.
The kind that is heard throughout the skies
And would raise up those who are paralyzed.

But alas, no poem exists
To allow us to attack what needs to be fixed.
All we have are hopes and dreams;
That's what makes us cope, it seems.

And as long as we have the Christmas Story,
This miracle of hope and glory,
All things will be well in time.
All things will be well in time.

John Rankin

Winter

As the days grow close to winter,
The last of the leaves slowly fall.
Now that the colors of fall are gone,
That tells us that our winter is soon upon.
As winter would come through the night,
You will awake and find nothing but white.
You can feel the chill in the cold winter wind,
For the snow begins to fall on Thanksgiving weekend.
The shorts and tank tops will be put away
And jeans and jackets will be used on this
Christmas holiday.
As Christmas and the holidays pass,
Spring will soon bring us beautiful flowers and green grass.

Amanda Cockayne

So Long

I looked around, and then I closed my eyes
The next thing you know I was in paradise
I feel no sorrow that I left that place
Now is tomorrow I can finally gaze upon
My masters face
Don't get me wrong I loved all of you
In times of trouble you helped me through
Be not discouraged and do not cry,
For you'll all se me again in the sweet
Bye and bye.

Bernadine E. Benjamin

Oh, My, The Aspen

Have you ever taken the time to watch the aspen tree?
The leaves quake and dance like no other sight I have ever seen.
Each petal has its own movement,
One upon the other, dancing a symphony nothing else can lend to.
Then, the branches bestow their movement, too!
Some are curved, and reach toward the surrounding pines.
Others stand straight and tall, looking toward the sky!
I have never seen such grace and movement.

Oh, aspen tree, dance your dance for me.
Don't take a single moment to stop and see
How absolutely beautiful you can be.
With sunshine giving you such a glow,
Only one who truly sees can know!

Dorothy Mary Brisbois Miskol

Dear Lord

Open my eyes and let me see
The life has been waiting for me

Please forgive me of all my sins
KEEP SATAN OUT, and never back in

I am tired of my life and living this way
I have so many things I have to say

There is no one that will or could ever be
As forgiving and perfect as only he

I want to better myself as a mother and wife
It's you I need to have in my life

Please let me see the light and guide me through
It's eternal life I want forever with you

I truly believe you died for all of our sins
I am sorry it took so long for me to finally come in

Your the key that opened up the door
I am sorry I wouldn't see this before

I want to commit my life to you
And set a good example for my family too

Thank you Dear Father for watching over me
Having you in my life, I am better off than I will ever be

Jamie Schroeder

This Earth

Bit of green hanging from a star
The light spirals about me
Each color of jewel lights about my body
Red, green, blue in one spot, then another.
Snow flakes whirl, the night deepens,
and my body gleams lighter, lighter.
The mind has curled like a cat in the corner
as I awaken, awaken, like a fruit stored
in the deep earth
Hands come down and cover my eyes
My love, you have worked hard, suffered much,
grown in wisdom, and we would give
you again a glimpse of joy
And the hands parted to a kaleidoscope
of multi-colored stars, twirling and singing surprise

Beth Kelly

The Shadow Behind Her

I'm the shadow that's behind her, the whisper in the night,
The love she never wanted, and tried so hard to fight.

In words she tried to tell me, but the truth was in her eyes,
She said she didn't love me, but those words I knew were lies.

Everything I ever wanted was just a kiss away,
Her lips told me to leave her, but her eyes told me to stay.

The first time that I saw her was the last time that I slept,
And the last time that I saw her was the first time that I wept.

Sometimes in the evenings, along the outside walls,
I strain to catch a glimpse of her, before the gray night falls.

Her beauty takes my breath away, my sole is ripped and torn,
Thoughts of her flash through my mind, like raindrops in a storm.

So will I go on wanting her until she calls my name,
She will be my destiny and haunt me to my grave.

John W. Kirkpatrick

Ode To Our German Shepherd

O' Alfie, we miss you. We wish we could kiss you.
The love that you gave us is now far above us;
To shine on our lives now.

This house was your home, every room you did roam.
The two acres we bought you, the things we both taught you.
The peek-a-boo nightly, you gave to us brightly.

Your eyes they would sparkle, with joy they would shine;
O' how remarkable; time after time!

We showed you we loved you each day you were ours.
The ten years you gave us was a beautiful star;
That now reflects your love for us from afar.

So, what can we say now, the light has gone out;
But how dearly we miss you, of this there's no doubt.

So, sleep in your slumber, may peace be with you;
For you were our angel, a shepherd so true.

This house is now empty, a shell in its own;
For you, dear Alfie, are gone and irreplaceable;
Till the good Lord, our master shepherd, calls us both home.

Catherine Atkinson

Hidden Inside

The years were long
The months were long
The days were long
All because no one saw me,
Heard me or listen to me,
Because I was hidden inside

I was beaten, Abused physically, mentally
But no one understood
I was hidden inside
I fought, pulled down curtains,
Tore down lights
Because I was hidden inside.

I cried, yelled, pushed,
Because I was hidden inside.
Until one day I was discovered by a
machine and was released like a bird
locked up in a cage.
No more,
Hidden inside the body of an artistic lady.

Julie Bankston

Dejame Ser

I am in fire-but I laugh,
The moon is dying
I run to save her,
Cross the bridge of dreams
Turn into nature
Turn into a star-but I fall.
Fall to the ground of Tears.
Running Giraffes are burning
The hypocrite ant works
The naked eyes cried
My tears join hers
In the river of hope
In the river of thirst
Were the desert of man has been built
Sacrifices is my hunger, "Estoy en la busca del bien"
Let me free from your jail
I want to be my own wind in my flute
Want to be the peaceful eagle on my moon
I want to be
Just myself.

Esther Collinetti

Just Wondering?

I never did believe
The moon was made out of green cheese
It was hard to agree, the world was square to please
I looked at the stars, that seemed so far
There must be something slip there where you are
I've been to lots of mountain tops
Saw the most beautiful settings
And decided they were God's celestial's crops
The spring-time in the desert's
Are so beautiful to behold.
Then again I knew God owned them
I didn't have to be told
And in autumn he puts the plants to sleep
Covers them with crunchy leave so cozy to neat.
When the awakening with the trumpets sound
And the vision of the golden gate is torn down
Will we walk on air, find time to share?
Just wondering?

Alice L. Hartley

The Awkward Age Of Fifty

They say we go through an awkward age as children, but they think it's the most crucial for the young ones. But they don't know - the young ones how lucky they are to be young, go through the Awkward Age and still be young, but to reach the Awkward Age of Fifty, I think, that's the Awkward Age, all the while being young you are climbing to the beautiful age of Fifty. Then all of a sudden you reach the age of Fifty and you know it's climbing down, because we reached the half-way margin. Suddenly you realize that's the Awkward Age. The children go, one by one and then you realize, O suddenly you realize. It's here, the Awkward Age of frustrations, change of life, sudden flashes, you take a good look at yourself and there you are - these things are me at the Awkward Age. So Mothers and Fathers wherever you are, when you tell your children (In front of them) you're going through the Awkward Age, please don't, that's the best of their life, growing up.
It's us old Fifties, going through the Awkward Age. We have to adjust they don't because they are Young and Beautiful. But, Fifty is a difficult age so if anyone has to adjust, we have to adjust to the Awkward Age.

Josephine Cornett

A State Of Emergency

Sometimes I sit and tingle inside
The mourning death of California's pride.

The democratic system from A to Z is
hard to comprehend believe you me,

How can a state progress in harmony
with the races fighting politically.

Racial prejudice must hit the road, before our
melting pot explode.

Can someone give me an answer please,
I'm begging God on bending knees.

Yes we must get up in our conscious minds
for so long we've been wasting time.

Life is too short there's work to do, today for us,
tomorrow our children too.

Let's unite with hate aside, to save California
with all our might.

Charles E. Smith

A Performer Dies

Page one has the news and we're hoping they lied,
The nation's in mourning... a performer has died.

They touch our lives whether by screen or by song,
Their impact remains long after they're gone.

Pfeiffer and Cher, their beauty' immense,
Pacino and Hoffman, could they be more intense?

Music is heaven sent as an Enya can prove,
While also uplifting as you dance to the groove.

I listen to a song from now or the past,
I remember what happened and the memory is cast.

T.V. has its opponents while it robs you of your senses,
But people are losing when they miss Picket fences.

There's also the shows that release all your tension,
The Seinfelds' and Fraziers' need I even mention?

The oldies we missed when there was only the screen,
We can now rent or buy and they all can be seen.

So when we hear the news and we all have cried.
There's no doubt what has happened... a performer has died.

Frank R. Hendricks

"The World"

What is this world coming too? They say the day's are bright
and the nights are dark, but it is the other way around, the nights
are bright, and the days are dark. During the day it is quite it,
it's like everyone is a sleep, but as soon as the sun goes
down, all hell come alive. We have the parties, love inns,
aides, hatred and killings, but there is an answer, and the
answer is for all of us to find our God, the God who loves us all:
Peace my friend:

John S. Roblyer

The Mirror

She doesn't live here anymore,
The one I used to be.
The cold, the losses and the lack
Were more than she could take.
She left so quietly that no one knew she'd gone.
I still see her sometimes with her compassion
Showing and her silly smile and real laughter.
She doesn't stay too long and
I am left totally alone with my own
Sadness lines in the mirror.

Cynthia F. Traisi

Rainbows

Stretching into the horizon, to the east and west, at times to
the North and South, in a graceful arc,
the rainbow reaches into the heavens

Starting with the wrath of a blazing fire, the redness seems to
show the anger of the heavenly angels,

Blending into the anger with passion, the splendor of the
orange appears blending itself into the fury,
showing the gleams of despair

Merging into despair, the serenity of the yellow gives the
illusion of hope for the future.

Fusing slowly with hope, spirit of green envy, tries to break
through the serenity and hope

Drifting into the serenity, the painter from the angels,
instills some sense of compassion, as the
blue of despair, tries to impregnate my soul

The calming tranquility of the purple, closes the gap between
the colors, revealing the magnificence,
of the rainbow

Aurora Ann Kelsey

Ocean

Endless
The ocean is
eternal
For all time
Before I was
While I am
After I go
The ocean
is
Restless, soothing, angry, peaceful, turbulent, calm,
raging, joyous, stormy, soft, fearful, serene
Emotions of life
Everything I am
it is
But unlike life
The ocean is
Endless

Dorothy Saville

Grandchild

Like the leaves that are scattered on the ground
The one that I love is no longer around
She slipped away like a thief in the night
Never to return, at least not in my sight
I can barely get through the day
Without a memory coming out to play
In my mind of things out of the past
How much longer can the pain last
When I hear a bird I remember your voice
You had to go, you didn't have a choice
Though we were close little did I know
That you were not happy, you had to go
You can't remember all the good times that we had
Someone helps you to remember only the bad
Maybe some day through all the letters I write
You'll remember the love and that leaving wasn't right
That as sure as the rose will bloom in the spring
You will come back home to me and I will live again

Dianne McKinley

Escape

Verse is my vessel for speaking my mind.....
The page hears me cry when no one has time.

Alone with my pen I'm free to share all
My worries of not being caught if I fall....

My heart remains shy...alone in the dark....
Unsure of showing where pain left its mark.

My heart overflows and words come with ease
No one to hear me - they drift with the breeze.

I'm trying so hard to open the door
To take risks for love and trust people more.

When I compose I can't hide what I feel....
Creative expression has helped me to heal.

Each page is silent - just waiting to be
A part of my soul, my heart's poetry.

The pen writes of love and so many tears
Of dreams and ambitions and my deepest fears....

I speak of in verse the things that I keep....
What makes my soul laugh and makes my heart weep....

My love of rhyme is God's sweetest gift
My means of escape for as long as I live....

Janet L. McMurray

The Expressionist

how can I express with words
the pain behind my tears
how can I explain in seconds
a nostalgia that remembers ten thousand years
how can I show you
things that only I can see
so in desperation I run like the wind
a shadow trying to catch reality
I run for miles and then pause
on a frozen landscape of black and white
my feet touch cold stone and I long to be free
but I don't have wings to reach the moon's light
with a flash of emotion I take a deep breath
I'm a lone wolf howling in the night

Dan Uphoff

The Showers

It's terrible, to think of.
The people walking slowly,
slowly, into the showers.
The showers that kill,
the showers that are not showers,
but actually a sentence of death.
As they walk slowly into the showers,
you can see the terror on their faces,
for they know, deep down inside themselves,
that when they step inside this shower,
they won't step out again.
The door closes,
there is a long silence,
a deathly silence,
then the sound of the people,
beating against the walls,
helplessly with their fists,
and screaming in torture and pain.
The doors open, you see body upon body.
It's terrible.

Delena Lee

The Little Dove

Old Glory was flying, so proudly on high,
The planes roared o're her up in the sky.
The rockets were blasting, the guns going boom,
Then silence fell, like in a tomb.
The soldiers lifted their eyes toward the sky,
They all wondered, why everything got quiet,
They saw a rainbow, that seemed never to end,
And they shouted it's a good omen.
Then a lone White Dove, glided over the crew,
And ever so slowly, toward the ground she flew.
When she came to rest, they all drew near,
One young man knelt, closer to her.
There were no heart beats, no fluttering of wings.
The lone little Dove, would never more sing.
A bullet from a rifle had pierced her heart,
It was so powerful, it nearly tore her apart.
Yet, somehow she'd managed to reach friendly shores,
Where she'd be buried and remembered, forever more.

Juanita Chandler

The Sterile Window Sill

Beep, beep, the sound of the machine attached to your heart.
The rasping of oxygen because your own lungs refuse to start.
The drip of the I.V. in your arm, your silent sterile room.
What little hair left, there for someone else to groom.
Lying in your sterile bed,
Looking to the world as though you're dead.
Seeing your pain filled eyes gaze at a sterile wall,
As muffled sounds of others come from the sterile hall.
My father who used to be so big and proud,
The man of a thousand smiles, his voice so loud.
A shadow of who he used to be,
But still he meant so much to me.
All the sounds of your sterile room echo in my head.
And I'll never forget the sight of you in your sterile bed.
I wish I could paint your sterile walls,
I wish I could cheer your sterile halls,
I'd like to put color in your sterile bed,
And return the life to your eyes so you don't look so dead,
But then one day the sterile room lay still,
And now I cry, by the sterile window sill.

Chauntee Johnston

Pavane For Jackie O

Jackie O...Your passing closed the chapter of my youth.
The rebirth and hopes for spring of a whole nation....
They are gone...all gone....

Young Americans striving for justice and peace,
not asking what the country can do for them...
They are gone...all gone...

Freedom Riders to Mississippi, arm in arm, black and white.
The dreams of promised land just beyond the horizon,
They are gone...all gone...

New England towns where no one locked their doors.
Freeways one could travel unafraid after dark...
They are gone...all gone...

Movies where a kiss was just so exciting.
TV, where 'love' was the 'four letter word',
They are gone...all gone...

Jackie O-mysterious, strong and cool-
you will always be remembered!
You touched the depth of my heart
and the hearts of a whole generation.

Hanna Wojciechowski

Loneliness

This loneliness is deafening.
The roar of silence pursues the space of time.
Reality is bent, folded by intangible dimensions.
Fantasy is the ghost of compassion.
My mind splits and splinters into new beings,
Gladly sharing this loneliness.

Jerome L. Vond Sr.

I Think Of You

I think of you as the rain plays upon
The roof, beating out a calming rhythm,
Like a soft-tuned piano in a dim
"Casablanca" love scene, attention drawn
By the melody to unheard music—
Louder than the thund'rous roar of my heart;
Softer than dawn. To you, beauty is art:
You compose a suite with the gentle flick
Of your hair, then repaint the sky with your
Smile, endearing even the falling leaves
To your favoring glance. This with such ease
That I cannot but hunger, thirst, for more.
I think of you and smile softly inside
And hear your name in the wind and a sigh.

Alan R. Hendrickson

My Self Image

There is a girl sitting in the corner of a classroom, reading,
The room is well lit and cheerful,
She's reading because she wants to I guess,
But why?
Is she interested in the book?
She has to be to always read,
If you don't know where she is,
She's always in the corner reading,
I look more closely,
A book about a girl's life,
she looks so interested,
Days go by,
She's still reading
I walk over to her,
I sit next to her,
Suddenly I look straight forward at her face,
The class turned into a wall of mirrors,
And there I was sitting alone,
Reading

Bryar-Lyn Ciampo

From The Roots

Up from the roots,
the shackles of slavery heaved the boot.
Fredrick, Harriet, and Nat; leaders of anti-slavery
got commended for their bravery.
Next came the educators;
the true legislators.
Carter, Marcus, Thurgood, Elijah, and Booker T. taught a nation
with nothing but sheer determination.
Up came the leaders of yesterday-
the path they paved.
Through Malcolm, Martin, and Huey in the '60s,
Civil Rights became a reality.
Let us not forget about today,
the history makers that we can never repay.
All in all from the roots of the tree-
how one nation can bleed.

David P. Messer II

The Air Below

The air below felt as dreamy as my worst nightmare.
The shivering wind seemed to make me want to throw my limp body over the endless cliff.
My mind scattered thoughts, the best times and the worst.
My life flashed before my eyes as I seemed to fly into the air below.

Anjuli Arora

Why?

The wind blows softly through the trees, I hear the singing of birds, and the buzzing of bees.
As I look up into the cloudy sky, all I can do is wonder why?
Why the clouds look that way, what really causes night and day?
Why do crickets sound like they do, and why do cows only say moo?
Some of these things we will figure out as the years pass by, and some the only answer will be why?
Not everything has a reason to be, so leave it at that and just wonder like me.

Amy Hall

God's Hand

The sun is shining and the birds are singing,
The sky a brilliant blue and the grass a deep green,
The array of colors, through many different flowers, is everywhere,
And as I look about me, I can see God's hand in creation.

Spring, summer and fall are behind us now, and winter has appeared,
The colors and flowers have all died away.
The tress are dark and bare,
Snow, ice and frost abounds everywhere,
And as I survey that cold white quiet, I can still see God's hand in creation.

And while standing there among his works,
His mighty wonders around me,
A fleeting thought criss crosses my mind,
So, I close my eyes and smile appears as a picture of you comes to mind,
Because, I can see God's hand there too.

Carol A. Fox

The Only One To Be

One eternal day
the sky was pitch and dark
there wasn't a sound to be heard
nor voice to be met
this loneliness had crept upon the only one to be
the only one to be had thought the thought of life
He made a thousand bright crystal balls for which to support all life
He made this life to be like, the only one to be
In which to see himself in all good thought and deed
he was no longer, the only one to be
yet is today every thing we see

Jonathan Wye

A Season To Remember

A soft breeze is blowing through my hair,
The smell of fresh cut grass is still in the air;
Tree are changing colors all around,
As their leaves fall onto the ground;
Laughter of children is heard as they play,
Taking advantage of those days that just won't stay;
Jackets are being readied for their wear,
As we see birds flying south in a pair;
The warmth of wood will be there as it burns,
When that sudden chill begins to return;
Days grow shorter as the weeks go by,
We just can't stop them matter how hard we try;
Something special is about to happen around us all,
As we share this season we call FALL.

Darlene Schepers

Marriage Of The Snowflakes

They say no two snowflakes are alike, just like no two days are alike. The snow falls to the ground either slowly or quickly and can be blown around in a whirl by fierce winds.

At first, the snow is blinding white like a wedding gown sewn with pearls. Glittering prisms from frost and iridescent candle-light all aglow.

When the snow stops falling, it settles to the ground. All is still and calm. Marriage begins this way; so serene, peaceful and content.

But then comes the late nights out with the guys, the lies, and no reassuring phone call that he's alright. The snowplows with their heavy blades push the snow aside as others spread gravel along the way.

As the lonely nights compound one on top of the other, the happiness begins to fade. Cars keep passing by. Exhaust fumes and dirt turn the piled up snow to a dingy grey.

As days pass by, the piles of grey, dirty snow begin to diminish and melt away. What used to be my love, turns to disappointment and resentment.

I'm waiting for a change; hoping it comes and not wanting to give in to the thought that it won't. Where's that beautiful, blinding white snow? I want it to come again...

Becky S. Adams

Untitled

I sit alone and watch a wing-ed beauty soar above me
The snow-white puffy clouds, the orange and red sunset
And a tear rolls down my cheek

The beauty seen and felt is more than I deserve
Deeply humble am I, and deeply feel
In my moment of silent reverence

Peace fills my soul

Bill Gilstrap

A Lonely Song

Tonight I sing alone down the long path of life,
The song so flat and meaningless without you.
As I sing down this path of life I stumble over a
few rocks in discouragement.
Far in the distance I see you.
Your arms out-stretched coming toward me.
As you pick me up and carry me away,
Your lips touch mine, and we fly away together.

The song so beautiful.

Felice Sanchez

Nautical Mile From The Canal Side

Nautical Mile in Freeport Long Island, it's
the South Shore, it's Woodcleft Avenue parallel
to Guy Lombardo Avenue...

Nautical Mile is a special street and waterway
where we go to eat and play; to see and be;
to fish and wish; to stop for gifts and get a lift.

But, best of all Nautical Mile is reversible.
From the canal side as I cruise on "Miss
Freeport" I see Trawlers and Yachts, Speed boats,
Fishing boats, sailboats, and then the majestic
"Nautical Princess". I see slips and water-
decked out backyards, with yachts, yachts, and
boats, boats everywhere.

Nautical Mile is everywhere. When I am there
I am in Hilton Head, at Rehoboth Beach, at Nags
Head, at Hong Kong Beach, at St. Simon's Island.
I love Freeport'

Bettye J. Miller

The Creator

Let us give thanks to him who has created the heavens and earth,
The stars, moon and sun.
The Creator
Who has more wisdom than The Creator. Let him speak.
Before the earth was formed - The Creator made wisdom. Who
has knowledge and understanding let him speak. Can such a man
tell us the beginning of the heavens or the earth, how The
Creator drew a circle on the deep and established the heavens
and wisdom was there like a master workman.
Can such a man tell us how the foundation of the earth was laid.
Who determined its measurements or who laid its cornerstone,
when the morning stars sang together and all the sons of God
shouted for joy.
Where can you find such a man that knows The Creator like this.
The law of The Creator is perfect for reviving the soul.
Name a man that has mastered perfection.
Who could care for the small and great with such love and
understanding as The Creator.
Yet the God of Abraham is not known to this generation.

Dwight Nawls

Problems Of The World

Our society is just falling apart,
The subway walls are filled with graffiti art,
And dozens of countries are fighting in wars,
And teenagers with guns are out robbing stores,
And some don't wear condoms to avoid getting AIDs,
And then, they have to suffer through the horror and pain,
And people do drugs, like smoking the weed,
And major corporations are run mostly by greed,
And nobody wants to deal with the truth
About the problems of society's youth,
And children look to TV to find their role models,
But, instead, all they see is ads with beer bottles,
And everyone wants to come out number one,
And for less than half a day's salary, you can go buy a gun,
And men have affairs with other men's wives,
And psychos kill babies with the ends of their knives,
And there's never a day when nobody cries,
And I see all these troubles and I ask myself "Why?"
Some people say they kill others because they need to survive,
But, that cannot be true if we truly are civilized.

Dan Guyton

Vision

Dawning
The sun is rising
shooting forth brilliant rays
It is not a joyous celebration
nor offering any consoling heat
It is a dank illuminator
revealing, exposing the hiding places
safety, shelter and security - gone
Enemies now have a clear view
the prey is vivid;
capture is simplistic
No enveloping darkness
cool and surrounded by the intimate embrace
Instead there is stark light
plain and naked, open
to the predator
surrounded, under siege — cut off
With the climaxing of the sun
comes the creeping silence of
imminent death

Jael Henckel

Tonight I Watched The Sunset

Just before the day met the night -
The sun lingered a while with its warm light.
The sky was painted in tropic hues -
And I knew in a moment I would loose
This beautiful sight.
Because now the day has become the night.
It somehow reminds me of our time together
So beautiful, so warm, so light hearted and peaceful,
We linger awhile
We know it must end
But just as the sun will rise to meet a new day
We also will meet and will spend
Many more moments this wonderful way.

Catherine V. Holahan

The Ocean

The gentle breeze playing on the reeds
The swooshing and swishing of the foaming calm waves lapping on the shore
Just the faintest scent of the spring salty air
And the soft oozing sand squishing between my toes.
Then the dusk starts fading into the sparkling night
The cool wind rushes past my hair
The wild waves go crashing onto the shore
The heavy rain goes pounding on, washing away all life.
The lighting flashes from above
Thunder goes rolling and crashing on
The helpless reeds are washed away.
A sparkling light comes shinning through
The dawn is lighting up the shore
The wind isn't whistling anymore

Heather Pollack

Fates Plan

In the back roads of my mind,
Their are pleasant memories of a certain kind,
Unknown, unplanned we would meet,
In a parking lot, or along a busy street,
Throughout the years this kept happening,
It was uncanny, it was unplanned,
Through some strange stroke of fate,
Our lives are now entwined,
And fate has completed her plan,
To bring together two mortals
Who began meeting each other unplanned.

Hazel A. Thiel

Lost

Without feeling my soul hath grasped
The sword of peace cut my hurt in half

Down my arm the pain does run
Pouring out my veins

Tears of joy as the slices sting
who held back the rain?

Hidden passions are still to lie found
My water of life trickles to the ground
Holding in my arms lost hopes

A child wished for in my poisoned
womb does choke

Men with love, stab my heart
I promised my feelings would not part

My everlasting love is faithfully devoted
To a spirit unnoticed

Take me to your cave of warmth
Where the staff of life is not withheld

Jaime Lorraine

Innocent Thought

As I sit here and think I can still feel
the warmth of my bed where we laid,
My body becomes flushed as I remember
what I allowed to happen today.

My mind goes in circles from the words I have heard,
And I wonder if I should believe what words he said.

He touched my body in places forgotten
and it burns through to my soul,
His hands caressed my body firmly
and molded my every move.

As I lay here now my own hands begin to trace
where his once were,
And I can still feel my thighs trembling
with anticipation once more.

Oh God, don't let me fall too hard,
after all, maybe it's true what they say.

And I wonder, if little boys only grow tall.

Dana Diamond

You Don't Stop Caring Because It's Through

The night I met you no one could know,
The way I felt from head to toe.

My feelings I kept all bottled inside,
The way we were, just you and I.

It's different now, times have changed,
We don't know why, we can't explain.

You've gone your way and I've gone mine,
Our paths will cross some day in time.

I'm sure by then it will be too late,
For we will each have another mate.

You'll never know all the times I've cried,
And how many times inside I've died.

If only then I'd known what to do,
And how to show my feelings for you.

But, now as time goes passing by,
I can only sigh and wonder why.

With all my heart, I tell you true,
You don't stop caring because it's through.

Janna Trueblood

Like Me

I take up my brush and paint a picture,
The way I'd like things to be.
I paint in the beauty of a glorious day,
And not the dark and gloomy things I see.
I paint the picture of a beautiful young woman,
Full of bubbling life and pride.
Not a frail and graying old lady,
Who has already died.
Dead because there no dreams left,
Except those that are gone and past.
The fading dye of a fleeting life
Has already been cast!
I draw my picture sadly,
The way I'd like things to be.
I reach out a trembling hand,
And to my lips I raise a cup of Tea!!

Elizabeth O. Dobo

Light Of Life

The tallow nourishes,
The wick present to guide-
Sustains the ever-glowing taper,
In the journey of existence.

With a gleam that streams,
Through the darkness of the night,
The unique luminescence sparkles,
Shining with determination and warm intensity-
That endures with splendor and brilliance.

At times the wind threatens,
And the menacing water surges,
Trying to douse and destroy the spark-
By extinguishing the delicate symbol.

But even if the flame,
May flicker or die out,
The memories of this solitary figure,
Will always warm our hearts.

Julie Bellin

Look Over

In the moonlight I shall not fear
The wolves emerge from their lonely taverns
The cry out for out for help that I cannot give;

The moonlight shines in your eyes
Sparkle among them
Cross fire tortures;
Wind is my friend
Cold is all I know.

The darkness my companion

Look over the canyon
In the mountains covered
with snow;

Sit down my love
Join me in this pain
for misery does not want
company, but welcomes
it freely friend.

Jessica Harris

"Lord Touch Me"

Lord touch my eyes that I may see
The wondrous things you've done for me,
Lord touch my ears that I may hear
The sound of your voice both far and near.

Lord touch my hands, so I may share
The feeling of love you have placed there.
Lord touch my lips, so I may impart
The witness and proclamation
Of how great thou art.

Lord touch my feet that I might run
To tell the good news of Jesus, your son.
Lord touch my mind, that I might remember
All the good I have learned
And the evil to surrender.

Lord touch my heart
So the love may run free
And encompass all within range of me.

Lord touch me wholly, that I may understand
The shortcomings of myself and my fellow man.

Lord please hear my plea and incline thine ear to me. Amen.

Helen Shambley

Industrialization

When I was that very young boy
The woods were where I would play
The earth so green was my toy
The sky so blue like it is in May.

But he grew up, this boy so young
And moved away from the earth so green
The forest sounds in his ears, unsung
The sky so blue he never again has seen.

He moved to the city of concrete and steel
And lived in a downtown high-rise
His mind turned so numb he couldn't feel
He becomes old, decrepit, and dies.

So to find God, stay in the forest
Stay to find heaven and eternal rest.

Andrew Kendall

Breaking Up Is Hard To Do

As I lay down on the bed, wishing you were here
The word "breaking up" is tempting me
The only thing that would come in my mind besides
Making love to you is to torture my self, as I
Stared at those four ugly walls
Asking myself where did we go wrong
The answer seems to never be discovered.
Oh, baby I miss you so
WWWWWWWHHHHHHHYYYYYYYYYY?
Why can't we be together? Why can't this last forever?
These are the few questions I frequently ask myself
I wonder if you do the same.
I know and believe with all my heart that you love me so
And I also believe that we would stay together always,
Once again I was wrong
WWWWWWWWHHHHHHHHHYYYYYYYYY?
Why me? Why us? The only way we could answer those
question are
By listening to our hearts and pray to God.
Once again my lost soul, I'll always love you........
Nothing could ever change that. Promise........

Darlene D. Dieujuste

History Unhinged

When you're outside the world,
the word epidemic seems so exotic.
Where you're living inside the world,
the world curses with havoc.

Conjuring up images like Camus' The Plague,
melodramas set to fiction's stage.
Adding to AIDS is the "promiscuous gay plague",
but where is history's truth and the responsible rage?

Unhinge the history,
it is being written in interpreted ignorance.
Scratch and scrawl out the magical mystery,
let the living and dying know of society's play at chance.

Commemorate communities lost in this braving, crying,
and an unjustifying slaughter.
Memorialize them like we do war veterans dead in battle.
Symbolize their life's gifts like a sculpting clay potter.
Trivialize the value and AIDS is just poison,
ready to rise up, curl, and rattle.

Gary Allen Leinbach

My Child's Prayer

Tonight I heard my child in prayer.
The words weren't mine, but her's alone.
I know I felt God's presence there,
And I know her prayers reached to God's throne.

The thoughts were simple, yet sincere,
She prayed for sister, Dad and Mom.
And as she prayed, I felt a tear.
And my heart was moved by this little one.

It's such a task for a parent today,
To rear a child in a world of sin.
But, if one knows just how to pray,
God can help if we trust in Him.

My child has faith that God can hear,
And He will answer if she prays.
Lord, teach me through my little child,
To learn more fully all Thy ways.

Help me to lead as a father should,
To show my children Jesus' love.
Help them to give their lives to Thee,
And serve Thee 'till we meet above.

Jay Dargan

Dreamers

Dreamers come and go with time
Their ambitions for all to see
They don't need money for what they seek
for thought is completely free

They come in search of many things
such as money, love, and fame
But no matter how diverse their wants
all dreamers are the same

Some long for things impossible
others are easier to provide
Although most never get their wish
at least they know they've tried

Eternity spent in search of a dream
may seem to you time lost
But to those who yearn their long life through
forever is worth the cost

Dreamers come and dreamers go
never knowing good or bad
For the only reason for dreams at all
is to judge the life they've had

Billy Wayne Collett

A Good Friend

A good friend is something you should cherish
Their friendship lasts until you perish
A good friend thinks about you every day
And listen to everything you say
A good friend knows when you are sad
And they also know when you are feeling bad
A good friend will help you in every way they can
Ever since your friendship began
A good friend will let you cry on their shoulder
Especially as you get older
You call a good friend when your in trouble
And they are there on the double
I could go on and on about how a good friend could be
But alas I still haven't found a good friend for me
At sixty nine I hope there still is time to find a good friend
I could call mine

Finding a good friend isn't easy you see
If you do find one you are lucky as can be

Doris Frohl

Ruffled Feathers

If an eagle is what you want to be,
Then fly my darling;
But without me.
If being an eagle, will make you feel free.
Then fly my darling
But without me.
Soar there the clouds, fly there the winds
Pick your mate; but believe of your fate.
You'll burn your wings
And ruffle your tail, cause love is blind.
And soft rains are like hail.
You'll wet your feathers, and they'll weigh you down
Just to land on a perch.
With no-one-around.
King of the sky-way, with no place but down
And all you eagles will end on the ground.
So my darling, fly high-and fly wide.
Look for those you want to see and an image of you will come to be.
With all of you eagles perched on the ground
No one will be there. You'll never be found.

Antonette McColleen

"Thank You Jesus For Saving Me"

I was lost and knew not what to do...
Then Jesus renewed my mind and open my eye's..
and brought me through!!!!
Then God told me son keep your eye's on me.....
and I will guarantee you peace.

I've confessed my sin's and ask Jesus to be Lord of my life...So now the prison doors has open and if it's God's Will, I'll be blessed with a wife!!!!

There are these who aren't physically incarcerated, because they're not behind a bar....But they are spiritually incarcerated and you know who you are!!! You need to know that God loves you so much and that's why Jesus set us free...

Today, "Praise God Almighty "is why I'm able to understand how blessed we are and say...
Thank You Jesus For saving Me!!

Gerard Herriott

Ode To My Biker

First you find a bike,
Then make changes that you like;
Make it unique, your personal touch,
Finding parts that cost so-o-o much.

You give her a name,
It's all part of the game;
Hang out with a new crowd,
For recognition and fame...

You bathe her
Wax and buff her;
She's like your best friend;
The fun must not end.

Important things are put out of your mind.
Your family, the ol' lady; from them you hide;
Not really runnin'; you just want to ride,
Putting the rest of the real world aside.

Once in awhile when you hop on your putt,
You take your lady 'cause you'll miss her butt;
She has a way of fillin' the days,
Her warm body and gentle ways.

Denise A. S. Bassford

"True Friends"

True friends are dealt lies, and disappointments.
Then must face the truth.
In life, unlike fantasies, there are no cures,
such as medicines, gels, or ointments.

As we learn together to deal with the good and bad,
as well as the happy, and the sad.
It's said some will hurt more than others.
Always remember though, "Time heals all wounds."

To intentionally hurt a friend should not be in sight
A friendship means much more.
That feeling it's worth it to put up a fight.
The times that have been shared.
Along with the people for which been cared.
Should say something of friendship.

It should be saying that friendship is right.
To reopen the communications may help once again.
Joining in what becomes the "friendship fight."

Colleen L. Porter

Why

Although questions are asked,
then sought after,
some may never be able,
to be answered.

Yet as people,
we need something.
to keep us going.

Whether that something is,
love, money future, or past,
we keep going on
without a real realization of exactly why.

Sometimes it's a conglomerate,
of many things that we rationalize
to be the reason.

Will we ever really know why,
we go on with this,
this thing called life

We may never know until the day of final death
and only then is it to late,
to truly live for the ultimate goal.

James N. Kriesel

Two Years? Too Late

"Frank has two more years to go before my dear retires.
Then we will move to our other place
in sunny, warm Ft. Myers."
But life you see has other plans
To thwart our hearts' desires
Ill health steps in and has his say
And Frank will never see that day in sunny, warm Ft. Myers.
The best laid plans and dreams we have
Should not be put on hold
No, we should move at once, be bold, and surely not delay
We have to grasp the moment.
There may not be another day.
Think not that you'll be the exception
Ah, that my friend is the great deception.
So don't delay and procrastinate
Or you may find that it's too late.
Too late, too late to see the spires
From your sunny home in warm Ft. Myers.

Donald W. Moffat

Prelude To Love

Touching, soon to hold, awake this infidel in her nakedness.
Then, without torment, ignite the oils of life, sprinkled upon her.

Behold the internal combustion as it burns into the flesh,
torching the apathy, yet cooling the soul.

Gently touch the heart, start the beat, hear the beauty of
fulfillment as it races through her body.

Caressing tenderly, I explore to reach the peak. Then without
warning, exploding pleasure. Crystals shimmer in my veins,
yet I feel as a child, clean with purity.

Embracing the hand, raise her and whisper, "Come with me to be
one of two." We will share our knowledge of ecstasy, yet be
submissive to the other without thorns of deceit.

Let us reflect through the center of time, exploring the unknown
till the moon caresses the sun, knowing that in this eclipse it
shall not be a darkening but the joining of two bodies.

Evelyn Kratky

Someday In The Future

You came into my life so quietly at first.
Then you changed right over night.
And soon you went too fast and I begged you to slow down.
But you laughed away my fears at what might lie ahead
and you caught me by surprise for I fell in love with you.

And someday in the future, in a quiet Sunday place
at an hour during sunset, I can see there in my mind
as the father of my child and the keeper of my heart
together with the woods sounds, we'll reflect upon our pasts
and remember the day we met and the road that brought us here
to the storybook happy ending we deserve; it's ours at last.

Deborah Reading

The Voice Of The Wind

Since blooming of time
There's been a voice in the wind
Dry, crying, whispering, and howling
Slowing to move cloud's quietly on their way
Still, whirling, spinning, twisting, and turning
Haling of rain, making waves of water
Blowing by the plains, sand of dessert, and mountainous rock
Leaving marks solely, its toll on time
A voice of air in motion, as of chimes
Singing sojourn, to wind and more
The voice of the wind

Jack T. Armstrong

With This

With this I reaffirm my love for you
There has never been a love so strong and true
A love as good as if it were new, my days and
Nights are filled with thoughts of you, I am happy
When I think of what we can do, with this I reaffirm
My love for you.

A love that will last as time goes by
A love that without I would surely die
A love not to question one that is faithful
And true, one that means so much because I share
It with you, with this I reaffirm my love for you

You have a special place in my heart and soul it
Is with you I want to grow old, to share a life together
One with hope of things that we can do, to make each other
Happy as lovers often do, with these words I reaffirm my love
for you.

Bill Davis

Memories

In all of time
there has never been or ever will
be another you in our lives,
You were truly one-of-a-kind
You were an eternity happening,
A spirit that flew freely
Never to be duplicated.
A life that can never be repeated...
Each moment that we spent together is forever recorded
In our hearts and memories!
You were a part of history, never to be erased.
We have always loved you and always will
You're remembered in our hearts!
You have made our lives richer and more beautiful
Just because you were a part of it!
We are forever grateful and blessed because of you
Being in our lives to teach us!
But most of all
We thank you for all the time you spent with us,
For loving us, "UNCONDITIONALLY".

Donna Bidwell Falgout

The Heart Must Burn

To fully enjoy every aspect of life,
There is but one thing to learn,
In order to feel passions unfold,
The heart must burn.

Friendship is a commodity felt deep down,
And something that you earn,
One special feeling defines it to all,
The heart must burn.

Love is felt in the deepest soul,
Something for which we all yearn,
But love isn't truly felt until you know,
That the heart must burn.

Life can be felt as well as lived,
As long as you don't spurn,
That one thing that makes us feel this life:
The heart must burn.

Janci Krmpotich

Don't Shut The Door

Last night I had a dream there were people all reaching out to me.
There were crippled and blind, young and old, black and white
all reaching out to me.

They kept chanting and chanting these words in my ears,
"you left us alone, you left us alone, where did you go?",
but I couldn't hear.

Then my eyes were opened and I saw the rags on their backs,
and their thinning jaws.

A little boy cried out (please give me some crumbs),
I patted his head and said sorry I have none.

I shut the door and went back to my feast when I awoke I cried Lord
"no not me!"

He said, "no child, but you represent the world, tell them, please
tell them don't shut the door."

They keep chanting, and chanting these words in your ears,
"don't leave us alone, don't leave us alone."
Where can you go, that you can not hear.

Judith K. Turner

My Constant

To possess you, is to limit your space
Therefore, I cannot possess you.

To suspect you, is to move you away from me,
Therefore, I shall not suspect you.

To put you on a pedestal, is to say you are different from me,
Not what you were when I first saw you,
Not the dream that I would someday realize,
Therefore, I cannot put you on a pedestal.

To be jealous of you, is to invite the demon of separation into our
lives, to allow the dark wind of uncertainty to blow a
lifeless void into our hearts,
Therefore, I shall not let my jealousy prevail.

To hurt you, is to hurt I, for you are a healer of my most inner
wounds, the life blood of my soul runs through you into a
spring of constant rebirth. Therefore, I must not hurt you.
For you are I and we are...

To understand you, is but a lesson of life,
A book in time that I don't ever want to put down.
To know you I hope a lifetime is enough.
To possess you, I think not....

James Lake

Christmas Love

The signs of Christmas are everywhere
There's excitement in the air
The trees are trimmed with lights so bright
And the presents are wrapped with care.

It's the time of year for love and hope
And peace on earth to all
To count our blessings God has given
No matter how great or small.

For Christ was born on Christmas Day
The greatest gift of love
Sent down to every man and child
From our Heavenly Father above.

So let us take the time each year
In thankfulness and prayer
And spread God's love and peace on earth
And together our blessings share.

Carol K. Williams

Forever Bound

When I met you I remember seeing your eyes,
There's nothing more beautiful to me.
The color reflects the deep blue skies,
As far as the mind can see.
Your hair comes in rows of brown
That I feel with the tips of my fingers
And when you leave me to go home at night
The smell of you still lingers.
Believe me when I say to you
I love to squeeze you in my arms,
And whenever I may hurt that heart,
Trust, that I mean no harm
For you are my hopes and dreams,
that which every man wishes.
I cannot just forget your presence,
Or your passionate kisses.
So when I seem to make you sad,
And your world turns upside down.
Always remember that I love you,
And that we are forever bound.

Curtis McKinzie

These Hands

These hands, I know you see
These hands that never fret
Rugged and worn, swollen and battered, scared and wearied,
Depicted by years of destitute
These hands that pained and cried
These hands indeed never denied.

These hands that picked
These hands that sewed
Oh! These hands that forever glows
Struggles of despair, still could not quit.

Beaten by the cold, wind and rain
I know these hands; I love these hands
That kept me full of love and joy and freed me of my pain.

The fruit that fill the jars
Strong may the detergent be
Long may the daily wind that blows
The wash that swings from the line.

The long nights awaken from their sleep
Oh, these hands that gentle touched my feet
Surely! These hands are like that of gold, do you see?

Carrie L. Douglas

To Honey On Her Birthday

I love you, oh, so much
These words will express my feelings of such.

I think of you everyday,
The way your hair curls,
The way you're always happy and gay.

I think of how you wear your slippers in the car,
The way you make biscuits,
And how you walk far.

I think of how many books you've read,
The way you whistle
And how you tuck me in bed

I think of how you paint your fingernails clear
The way you smell,
When you come near,
Happy birthday, I love you best.

Jennifer Watson

My Grandmothers

My grandmothers are women; loving and kind.
They always seem to know what is on my mind.
They love me so dearly,
I see that so clearly.
Thank you, Oh God, for my grandmothers.

My grandmothers are people; good hearted and true.
They always cheer me up when I am blue.
They are not boring; but fun,
They have time for everyone.
Thank you, Oh Lord, For my grandmothers.

Charlene Bartolotta

The Pilgrims' New Life - 1620-1621

The Pilgrims landed in a new land,
They called it Plymouth, was it grand?
No, the first winter was terrible;
It was almost unbearable.

Then one spring morning things seemed to be good,
When the Pilgrims went out,
To where an Indian stood.
The Indian, his name was Samoset,
But he didn't really help them yet;
Until he introduced them to another Indian,
Who, this time, helped them again and again.

This Indian, his name was Squanto,
Taught them everything from how to fish to row.
The Pilgrims were some friends in need,
Squanto was a friend indeed.
Now with Squanto there,
There wasn't as much to bear.

Could you say the first Thanksgiving was the best,
Even though it wasn't like all the rest?

Jaime Thomas

Whales

Whales are big and black
They can see you even if there eyes sight is slack.

Their biggest wish is to eat fish
When they eat they don't need a dish.

Some whales act happy and silly
just like the whale on the movie "Free
Willy".

Most whales are endangered,
by people like us, the unkind strangers.
We all know that whales are good,
and the unkind stranger know they should,

NOT KILL WHALES!!

Ebonie Gray

Speak Not Kind Words

Speak not kind words to me.
They cannot change the past.
Shed not your tears for me.
They cannot wash away the pain.
Do not offer a helping hand.
This burden is mine alone to bear.

But please,
Present me with your precious jewels;
I'll need them as I travel through the storm.
Give me your smiles,
For they will be comfort.

Jennifer Dittmar

"They Were Left Standing Alone"

As they jump off the chopper, into the tall green grass.
They fight for freedom, they fight for honor.
In the rice patties of Nam, the blood flowed on.
As the bags are filled, with the young at skilled,
   Americans hatred for the war is on.
Politics rule, Marines just do,
   and do if so much better.
They rather die a defender,
   than give up and surrender.
Other wars were honorable, Nam, wasn't even tolerable.
As they die from bullets of communist guns,
   we hear the solute of the twenty one guns.
When the war was over, the glory was gone.
As the men come home, they're all alone,
For the glory was gone,
   and the bands were not on,
   the platform of honor.
   Marines,
   they were left standing alone.

Anthony Castro

"Red Alert"

All children in the world are precious.
They have so much to offer and give.
If given a chance and a little support.
We'll be astonished at the amazing results!
It will take care, love, and grace.
After carefully nurturing the child.
Be sure to have a little faith.
Then, when all this is applied to his or her life.
Don't forget to add "a little love and a little spice."
"After it's all said and done, both parent
and child will be elated of the victory Run!"
Parents! Lets get our act together before it's too late.
If we want our children to achieve their goals in life.
Instead of expressing so much anger and hate.

Erma Lee Sudds

Peace

Soft white clouds drift across an azure sky
they kiss as they pass ever so slowly and then goodbye.
Far below the grass is green and soft serenity and peace abide.
I touch the place where now he rests, and feel the serenity,
still comforting, still powerfully strong as if alive.
I lay a rose so gently down, my one and only love.

Betty Zack

My Geese Are Pets

Geese are loving, geese are sweet.
They love to walk and see people to meet.
There's big goose, little goose, goose goose
Lucy goose.
They are all gray as goose can be,
Then there's sugar and spice and puff and cream
They are all white pretty and clean.
They swim in the pool.
They duck and they dive.
They all look around when they hear a truck.
Then if it's my husband, they're in luck.
For they love to walk and see people to meet.
Geese are loving and geese are sweet.
My geese are for petting and not to eat.

Charlean Lindahl

"Puppets"

Useless thoughts, once seemed so amusing
They parade in our minds and take us for our soul
Now those sparks all seen so confusing
They turn us on, then we do what we're told.

Like little toys, we seem a bunch of puppets,
Dressed up in gowns and standing on a stage
We fight our wars and build our wealthy nations
Like plastic pieces playing on some board game

We kill and destroy for love, hate and money
Then say a prayer and justify it in the end
Sometimes I think we're all a bunch of dummies
Human nature wearing through and thin

If we could only stop the world and think it over
Try to find a good in hell and sin
Maybe change the world for all the children
Let them all be happy in the end.

Joshua Darby Warren

My Love

My love I met you when I was young wild and free.
They say those are the best years of our lives.
But I found out different, for the best years began
the day you came into my life.
Our bodies and souls became one, and those wild days
grew into the deepest love I've ever known.
You became my life and I yours.
Your name is carved in my heart for no other will have it again.
My best friend, my love stay with me always.
Now that I have tasted this sweet love, no other will do.
For ours is the greatest it has withstood the test of time.
We've climbed the highest mountains and pulled each other along
the way.
My love nothing will ever stand in our way.
Together always forever more, I've never told you but you
make me feel secure.
Keep me always by your side, for the thought of loosing you
brings tears to my eyes.
Thank God for you it was planned from the start,
that you and I will live in each others heart.

Betty Jean Kuter

The Two Trees

There're two trees near to me,
They see who I am, who I want to be.

They witness my joy, they witness my pain,
They're here in sunshine, here in rain.

They're here when I celebrate, here when I cry,
They're here when I question, when I sigh.

They're here when I have to let anger go
Every single secret, these trees know.

These two trees see every caper,
These trees are my pencil, and my paper.

Stephanie Edwards

Count The Words

These three words, I love you.
These four words, my love is true.
These five words, make me your loverman.
These six words, by your side I'll always stand.
These seven words, lets make love and have a baby.
These eight words, the touch of your just drives me crazy.
These nine words, these's just no way I can keep going on.
These ten words, just when it comes to it I'll go till dawn.

Brenda Smothers

Rocky Mountain Majesty

Rugged and beckoning
they silently plead with me
to leave this captive traitor of joy...
the icy winds and hidden crevices
promise nothing more
than the honesty it takes
to live amidst their awesome beauty...
the natural granite will somehow feel more soothing
than the endless concrete shoes
of the city...
even now the pine aroma
pierces my existence...
I hunger for the majesty to reclaim my soul...
I shiver in anticipation of once again
following my conscience to a ridge
high above memory, and while a chilling wind
warms my heart, thanking God
for this magnificent illusion
in a make believe world...

Joni Brown

Untitled

Remember the ones who died at the Alamo?
They took their stand and didn't go.
Remember Pearl Harbor-such a terrible cost
So many ships and precious lives lost.
Remember the Normandy Invasion?
What a Battle and what a War WON!!
Remember Viet Nam- all our killed and MIA'S?
They gave their all for us without a word to say.
America is beautiful, so mighty, powerful and strong;
How true The National Anthem - "Her" song.
All branches of service - so proud should they be
for they keep America, "The Home of the Free"!!!
If it weren't for those who gave of their lives
Left mothers, children and loving wives;
We couldn't hold our heads up high
When we see "Old Glory" passing by!
And for all of this tears fill my eyes
For it's because of ALL THEM -
We Have OUR "Fourth of July"!!!!

Chris O'Steen

A Lost Love

As the teardrops fall from my tear filled, weary eyes,
They touch the ground to rest for eternity.
No one will ever see them or feel them, but I know they will
always be lying in their own isolated grave.
The grave of my loneliness and longing for my lost cause of life.

Life can be unfair, but our wiser elders told us to deal with it.
I do not know what to do next, life is like a rock, you can never
break into the inner feelings until you have been stabbed through
the heart with your own selfish fears.
My first love I have lost, and I do not know how to face the grief.

I cannot explain my feelings and worries; it just seems too unfair.
The road of life may be easy for some people, but it holds too
many bumps and turns for me.
My grip I am losing and I cannot hold on much longer to the
essence and meaning of my so called precious life.

I miss my love so much that it cannot be understood by the
wisest men of the ancient world. The past held so much love and
beauty that it cannot be repeated in the present. I know I must
face that facts of the period of mourning, but I cannot go on.

I leave only two final words for you, good bye.

Eileen Everett

Please Listen

If tears could talk, what would they say?
They'd whisper "I'm so very sorry."
They'd cry out "I'm hurting."
Tears do talk, but they say too much
and reveal too much.
So they are hidden and wiped away.
They could have told you so much.
Like a grandmother, grandfather telling
a story about the good old days. Like a friend giving a hug.
They are like a novel - a thousand words. I wish you
would have tried to read my tears.

Donna Lynn Bishop

All Alone

They sit all alone, keeping to themselves....
They're younger days are over, they're just objects on a shelf,
Forgotten so after, there is pain in their eyes....
But when they see you they soften, and reminisce on old times,
You ask from them a favor, they agree with pleasure and joy....
They're glad to have you over, but to you, they're just a toy,
Then you leave them alone again, until you need or find a reason...
They're all alone in silence and pain,
You can't even try to please them.

One fall day, you get a call, they have passed away...
Suddenly inside your heart, a wall just breaks away,
You never really got to know them, but you always said, I will....
Now they've gone far far away, and you don't know them, still.
You leave to go back to your house, to your lonely, quiet home..
And now that they are really gone,
You are
all alone.

Deborah A. DuBois

The Lament Of The Ickator

From out the murky muck and mire
Thick with guck and gore —
Comes slipping - sliding - slickly gliding
The ancient Ickator.
Just once each year at summer's end —
And when the moon is bright —
It crawls out of its deep dark lair
And sings into the night.
The lament is a chilling one
Unearthly to the core —
Its eerie song goes on till dawn
And then it's heard no more.
It bows its head in silence —
Its one eye sheds a tear —
Then slowly back it slithers
Until another year.

Jane Rose Marie Ciucci

Change

The changes you've accomplished are some
thing unforgettable, for feelings inside
my heart are no longer invisible and
the pain you handed out was anything
but incredible, yet, the love I have for
you is always acceptable.

Change is something wonderful when
it deals with you, because, it's something
that occurs when involving
what's true, and, although aggravation
interferes with things that you do.
Always, try to be understanding
because I love you.

Hysin Chang

Untitled

Sometimes we may not realize that every
thing we do
Affects not only our own life but touches
other people too

It's when we've stopped to share a sorrow
and have given a helping hand
That joys return to us two fold when we
show we care and understand

For it's when we've learned in helping others
and have a thoughtful word
to give
That we might have helped in someone finding
beauty and realize this is a precious life
we live

And in this ever so busy world it's wonderful when
one still has the art
Of taking time in helping others and
giving from the heart

Irene Bortolot

The Mother

The mother is the most magnificent things God has created. A mother is everything to a child - a child can become so close to the mother that a bond forms, it forms so big and so large that nothing humanly possible can separate or so much as even break the power of love that forms between mother and child. The child is so important to the mother that it literally hurts the mother twice as much as it would the child, if that child were to be hurt. So remember that no matter who loves you, your mother will always love you more than anymore else in this whole-wide world. For a mother and a child are like a magnet and nail. So appreciate her; and if not for her, than for you. For she loves and cares for you.

Elizabeth Madden

Think Again

If you think you are lucky because you found me,
Think again

If you think you are lucky because I love you,
Think again

If you think you are lucky because I am your companion,
Think again

If you think you are lucky because I am your friend,
Think again

If you think you are lucky because I am your lover,
Think again

If you think you are lucky because I married you,
Think again, and think hard

I think I'm the lucky one, my love.

Fernando Rivera

In Loving Memory Of Theresa Boyle

As I sit here counting the tears falling down, it's hard to think you'll no longer be around.

I know where you are now; you're happy and safe, for heaven was reserving your place.

Always loving in your special way, sometimes you don't realize until it's too late.

Love can be deceiving; sometimes love can be blind, but to all of us Grandma, you were one of a kind.

The times you kept us laughing, the memories we all shared; just as the sun keeps rising every day, we'll love and remember you forever!

Christopher R. Baporis

She Sits Alone

She sits alone.
Thinking.
Thinking of the way people ignore her and talk of
her behind her back.
She sits alone.
Wondering.
Wondering if anyone cares.
She sits alone.
Staring.
Staring off into the faded blur of past images.
She sits alone.
Thinking,
Wondering,
and Staring.
But still,
She sits alone.

Bobbi Baker

Daddy's Only Son

This is to my Dad who I love more and more
This is to my Dad who I would give my life for

Drinking entered his life he hasn't been the same
Soon he'll realize that someday he'll have to change but until that
day will come I'll just have to love him for what he has done

When I was younger I couldn't understand
Why he thought drinking made him a man
He made promises he couldn't keep
When I needed him the most, he had to drink

Now I'm a man who still needs a Dad
The little boy inside who he had made sad

Now before you take that last drink I love you so
But until you stop drinking I'll just have to go

Now you're gone I never got the chance to say
I always needed you even though I couldn't stay

If you could hear me Dad where ever you are
I hope you understand that drinking didn't get you far

I know it was lonely I can feel your pain
But because of your drinking my life will never be the same
So please don't start just remember that drinking doesn't have a heart

Anthony E. Salazar

One Thought

Just how often do we allow
This life to pass us by?
We sit on the sidelines, afraid to move.
We only sit back and sigh.

We watch the few that make the moves,
And to their own selves be true.
When all that's required is a shift in thought.
And we could be there too.

Each of our lives is too short to waste
One moment in space and time.
Living each day as if it's our last
Would cause our world's to align.

So now it's time to make your move.
Step out, take a chance and give.
Pull it from deep within yourself,
And your heart's desires will live.

Dawn Robnolt

A Second Chance

Tonight for some reason, seems like the end
This night seemed the darkest of all nights
She lays in sand, looking up at the stars
Hoping in the morning, she won't wake up
She's tired of all the lies and the tears
She has shed during the years
She feels she's not valued by anyone
In this corrupt world
And if she's not valued by anyone
No one will miss her when she's gone
When morning came, she was still there
Laying on the sand looking up at the bright blue sky
Today for some reason, seems like the beginning
This morning seemed the brightest of all mornings
And she knows why
Because she is alive and there is someone that values her life
She does

Chantelle Melinda Jenkins

This Humble Man

He walked with saints and ate with thieves
This simple humble man
He carried a weight that no one knew
A burden no one can

He carried the cross to Calvary
Followed by the women of Galilee
For they knew the pain a mother would feel
To see a son climb up that hill

Even if you feel he is not God, just man
He has changed the world as no human can
For without him we would not know Christmas Peace
Or Easter Joy or a Communion Feast

And as he hung on the Cross between two thieves
A voice called out, in thee I am well pleased
So walk with saints and eat with thieves, as did this simple man
And to you one day a voice will say.

YOU HAVE DONE THE BEST YOU CAN.

Dorothy S. Zelenak

My Prayer

I would've never dared to think
This world was lost in sin
Until that wonderful and glorious day
The Lord, to my heart, came in
I never thought I was so bad
And to Hell I would go
If at first I didn't obey
And the Lord Jesus did know
But now I'm a new mother
With a little boy of my own
He will sin like his mother once did
And obey and know Jesus when he's grown
If there was just one small wish
That I could have to come true
It would be for people all over the world
To know the dear Lord as I do
So if you lie or cheat or steal
You should know you disobey
And without the Lord in your heart
To hell you'll go someday

Jennifer L. Mixon

Will You?

These young hands, soft and smooth with youth
This young face, so clear and unlined
These sparkling eyes, so full of life
I count down the days 'til I become your wife

But will you still love me
When I'm old and gray
Will you love me then
The way you do today

When these hands become withered
And this face starts to sag
When this hair grows gray
And beneath these eyes come bags

When these legs grow old
Will your patience dissipate
When I get too tired
Will you stop... and wait?

Now I am old and gray
And I've spent my life with you
I'd wondered if you'd love me
And now I know.... you do

Diane Supowit

Be Strong, Little Flower

Be strong, little flower
Those roots from which you first saw light
Want you to know that everything will be alright

Be strong, little flower
Your beautiful petals that have blossomed all these years
Are being weighed down by your sorrowful tears

Be strong, little flower
I know you are worried that he will go away for good
But if God wants to take him, he'll take care of him as you would

Be strong, little flower
Don't carry this load on your shoulders alone
You have so many prayers waiting for you at home

Be strong, little flower
We need your sunny smile; warm, fresh and glowing
To strengthen your own roots
To keep the garden growing

Brenda Bouyer-Windley

A Love Like Theirs

To find a love like my grandparents share "Till death do us part",
those words were not spared.
For they've loved beyond the hardships and strife,
creating together a beautiful life.
No burden too much that they both could not bear,
not only the joy but the pain they have shared.
Believing in one another they found their way,
to grow with each other through each passing day.
Trusting in more than just saying, "I do",
they looked to each other, to answer, "How to?"
Their children were raised with kind loving hands,
together facing the toughest demands.
Never turning away no matter the cost,
believing to them they'd never be lost.
Unconditional love they've shared through the years
regardless of the mistakes, or nights spent in tears.
From, remember when .... to, look at them now!
They've set the foundation for when, why and how.
No greater love could I have been shown;
to pray one day, I'll have for my own.

Dorothy M. Carr

Untitled

You gave me life with the words that you spoke
though death was upon your lips
And my ears did hear and soul understand
that the words were of a truth within me waiting to be heard
You've released my spirit and set my mind free
to be what I believe
To soar to new heights and escape the bonds of a limited reality
So I shall fly like a dove
to the farthest reaches of the earth
to seek the truths of this life
And I shall return to rest upon your shoulder
in the days that I grow old
and whisper in your ear the wisdom I have gained
And then shall life be upon your lips
to send me on my journey through death
always remembering the words that you spoke
And in the next life we shall be lovers
as we have been in all the others
And I shall greet you with a kiss
and the sweet taste of life upon my lips

Gary A. Cardell

With Every Stitch

With every stitch I sewed today,
thoughts of you passed my way,
I remembered how you used to say,
"set up the iron out of the way",
I remember how you toiled with care,
making us dresses that we would wear,
You would work all night to make us clothes,
so no one would ever turn up their nose,
With every stitch you took such care,
making them perfect so no one would stare,
You cut and threaded, stitched and picked,
threw a few fits when you felt licked,
With every stitch I sewed today,
I prayed I'd be as good as you some day.

Holly Hannie

Reminiscing My Memories

As I set here alone looking out
through my window at the starry sky
Reminiscing my memories of you of long ago
I can feel the cool breezes blowing through
my hair and touching my cheek likes a
gentle kiss.
I close my eyes for a moment
Taking in the sweet smell of the lilacs
As the cool winds blows I can here
You whisper my name and I know that
you are near.
My heart grows all soft inside me
As tears slide down my cheeks
They are tears of happiness my darling
Because I know you'll there close to me

Dorothy F. Henson

Tigress

As I watched, she moved with such supple grace;
Through the bush in search of their secret place.

There, she paused as the wind brought her my scent;
But no threat was I, so on she went.

As her young did leap and bound along;
Ever alert, she listened to their joyous song.

That man could deny such a wondrous thing;
I need ponder a new what tomorrow will bring.

They were created by God, so vibrant, alive;
We've no right to intrude so they cannot survive.

I would wake up tomorrow with no need to pray;
That a thing of such beauty not be taken away.

Debra A. Mecham

Follow Me

Flying high through the severed skies,
Through the land where men are wise,
Families of sunset rise, follow me to the home that dies.
Go on a journey only to find
The weakened thoughts of society's mind.
They tell us we're free, but we're slaves to the throne.
There's billions of us, and many alone.
As we grow, we become more spiteful,
Following the man who is unrightful.
Damaging what is not ours to destroy,
Using the Earth as our own little toy.
Modern kings and queens steal from us,
And yet, we still devote them all of our trust.
It makes no sense, this place where we die,
The world we survive, where everyone lies.
We must find a place we know nothing about,
Just follow me, we've no need for doubt.
Unite brothers and sisters, we'll flee this nightmare called
Reality, we can fly and be forever free, liberty for eternity.
Just follow me.

Jon Leavitt

Untitled

There is a cloud in my mind's eye
Through which no light can penetrate.
It is a cloud, not of weight, but of darkness.
As I reach toward the cloud,
To tear it from its place,
The cloud breaks apart, and falls
In shimmering, shattered fragments
Reflecting white light,
Incandescent heat,
Iridescent refractions,
Where once the cloud was.

Dorothy Shepherd

Spice And Sugar

The way my parents raised me was low
Thru poetry is how I know
Circumstances forced me to live with them again, a hard blow
Thank God I'm not under their control
It's like spice and sugar in the same bowl
Went to continue with poetry writing
Eventually found myself fighting
Situations making me lose sleep
They think I'm a creep
Trying to settle with talks
Ends up with me having strong desires for them to take the big walk
Still more meetings
Repeating, repeating
My poetry going out of sight
What do I write?
Lost a fight
Burns in my pit
But to think this is all fuel sooth's my pit
Sugar and spice oh! so nice!
Blessings in disguise.

Allan R. Picardy

Twice Will Kill Us

Wednesday, spice-memories or a kitten-eye illusion?
Thursday, we sprained our jugular vein.
Friday — over telephone wires I see your eyes-smile
that bruises. Remember those

5 a.m. dreams trifles? Tarsan and Alice in Foliageland.
Snapdragons puff out our twenty favorite friends.
We roast fresh-murder deer, love in clean sand.

I saw me beg you to borrow, steal, a coconut for
an infant's milk. You then lost our last sea-pearl
at the racetrack twenty two flowers built. We meet

and our minds cling but streak in an opposite direction,
Honey — sssh, the wind whispers our names.

Donna Memoly Koenig

Earth's Bountiful Gifts

Insatiate man entomb not thy duty.
thy duty lies far and wide!
Thou stands not alone!
Thou'as pleasur'd thyself on earth's
Bountiful gifts.
Thou'as nurtur'd on wonders of earth-
Giveth Thanks!
Glorify the forest, Glorify the fields,
Glorify the gardens that giveth-sustenance.
Glorify the waters spread so vast and wide!
Earths beauty should always be!
Mother earth has spread this abundantly out for we.
Oh, naked eye-naked eye canst thou see
to mend man's errors. Of air, land and sea?

As Jean M. Auel stated it so
respectfully in her novel "The Mammoth Hunters"
If we forget to respect or neglect our
Great Earth Mother, she will-
Withhold her blessing and no longer provide for us.
Which all should fear?

Elizabeth Tracy

Broken Dreams

Her love left her not long ago
Time seemed to linger and go so slow.
While he was gone she always cried
For him her broken heart had died.

Her soul was broken and filled with tears,
She had been afraid; so full of fear.
She laid there on the bed so cold
The choice was wrong, but oh so bold.

She took the razor and slit them wide
She crawled to the corner and began to cry.
It was over and there is no one here.
She died in peace,
But there's blood on the M-I-R-R-O-R.

Deanne Gail Workman

A Light Of Love

All alone, it's you and me,
Time to tell you just how I feel.
Babe to you I bare my heart,
A light of love, here in the dark.

I feel so secure when you hold me so tight,
There's nothing that could bring me down tonight
When I look into your eyes, I see a beautiful light,
That brightens my heart.

You always seem to know
The right words to say,
That bring a smile to my face
Each and every day.

The more we're together, the deeper I fall in
Love with you.

Allison A. Castellani

Untitled

Time,
Timeless in itself, melting away with each thought.
Spending time, but it doesn't work out...
A midnight deadline, ticking by...
Time bending away, no time to lose.
Time to read, a fountain of wisdom.
Dreams, coming and going.
Time is a pool of water slowly evaporating.
There is never any peace with time, always war.
An enemy of many, never a friend.

A clock hangs on a wall, ticking away.
It slowly smashes to the ground.
Glass scatters everywhere.
Only the small hand remains.

A tree stands all alone, in the middle of a deep, dark forest, ageing.
Time vanishes like the clouds in the blue,
Waiting for the bark to crackle.
Piece by piece,
It falls to the ground,
Only never to be seen again.

Elana Muchnik

Krismus

In the sheltering woodland
Times we walked in the winter dawn.
That knew her, stayed and watched that day
When she crossed the stream and was gone.

Now, I walk alone on the hill
And in the willows below.
This short, comely life alike
Her footsteps here in the melting snow.

George Grohowski

Sacrificial Harvest

They gathered in great numbers.
Tis' ritual, an event of every year.
They drink the wine of their fathers.
Prepared for them specially here.

Tradition of the ceremony, chooses among them one.
To come forth, in repayment, for those whose crops were none.

Filing slowly behind one another, expressionless faces.
No discussion, or awe.
Destiny distributed fairly.
Fate based upon the luck of the draw.

Cast out the victim pleads, the insanity of the incident to end.
When all of the sudden, the cry rings out for the stoning to begin.

Amy R. Fox

Untitled

My faith looks up through clouds of mist
To a mountain high that surely exists
Majestic it stands from where I am
In the darkest depths of the valley of man

Not many can see this mountain high
A plateau of life they remain till they die
To reach such heights, the depths they must go
Where rivers of thought constantly will flow.

These rivers are fed by springs of truth
Heart asking mind just reasons of proof
To go to such depth, you must do it alone
Let your heart hang loose and your mind will roam.

The mountain peak is a life time away
It's always ahead and one day I will say
My life was worth living clear to the peak
Send out my ashes for others to seek.

Joan C. Tyska

Sonnet To An Emerald Lady

Your dreams of the lady with the emerald eyes take you
To an enchanting shore of yore where time stands still.
Where the azure sky and breaking waves exude
A view of Erin's Emerald Isles where there will
Be time and place that's meant for only two.
The age is new, the time is new, her eyes behold!
A future that transmits itself beyond the words- "Can do".
Your love transcends every story of love that is ever to be told.
The time has come to release the shackles of before.
To start anew, to dream again, to exceed your grasp ere' you go.
Let you dream of the beautiful isles made by God in days of yore.
And then you'll know a future with her will have no woe.
A lady with a mystic smile whose eyes reveal the time
When all your dreams will forever come true with "Yes" from
Geraldine.

Burt Wiley

Without You

Dedicated to Brian Kevin Tate who will forever be loved and missed.

Today is not real. It is a hazy nightmare in which I long
to awaken to find that this pain in my heart can escape
and flee to never be known again.
I cannot sense any goodness, just the fog and numbness
in my soul that lightly throbs enough to let me know
that I am alive.
There was no yesterday, there is no tomorrow. There is
just now; no escape from myself. I am stripped of all hopes
and held captive in a single moment in time.

Brenda Kay Salisbury Matthews

A Mother's Prayer

Help me to be devoted and loving to the son entrusted to me.
Help me to be an example to him as You would have me be.
I ask for guidance, to teach my dear son, the way to Your
Heavenly abode- And pray that someday,
Your blessing You will - on my little boy bestow.

When I think of the trials along life's way and the tests' my son
must face. It break my heart to dwell on such things, knowing I
can't take his place Lead me dear Lord to say the right words
and to influence him in some way. That someday when grown,
he'll see what You've done and bless Your sweet name every day.

Help me be patient, when things he does seems to be a bother.
For I must be kind and show tenderness, - as that's the trait of a
Mother. Help me to smile when I could just cry, cause he's
broken my favorite vase For he's only a boy, and You know
boys are-lacking a wee bit in grace.

And so, dear Lord, I ask of You - teach me so I may teach him
For to set an example and live in it before him, is the only way
one can win. With love in my heart and tears in my eyes, I beg
you handle with care. Cause he is my son, my own little boy -
and was lent to me only through prayer.

Brenda S. Murray

Secure In Christ

Each morn when eyes are opened
To behold this wondrous world
Our bodies rebuke night's slumber
As dreams anew are unfurled
The gift of life is ours once more
With resources yet untouched
Beckoning both flesh and spirit
Toward mysteries still to be clutched
But morning merely breeds failure
For at dusk no challenge was met
There must be some reason for living
In an existence I'd sooner forget
As nightfall creeps up with it's stillness
And I focus my thoughts on this day
A surge of awareness engulfs me
With a message that prompts me to pray
When all at once a peace is felt
Which fuels my soul to sing
Nothing matters in this whole universe
For I am safe with Christ my King

John J. Leonard

Tear Drop

The mystic master has told to me,
To do the things that others might see.
When I was young and life was new
The sea was clear, the sky was blue,
But now I cannot see the sea nor sky
because of the teardrop within my eye.
But now that I have become a man
I will not bury my head within the
sand
I will live with my loved ones
through the coming years
And hope by autumn there will be no tears.
I shall fight till all are free,
I will be the master of my destiny
And whom the winter snow begin to blow.
I hope I am free and so is my soul.
And whom I meet the mystic
master on high,
I hope that my mommies never die.

Augustus V. Moseloy Sr.

My Elementary School Years

Kindergarten was our first from all the fun us little kids were about to burst.
Holiday Show The Eight Little Candles made our little hearts glow.
Thanksgiving Feast was definitely not one of the least.
We took our little bows together and moved up on to the next level.

Sleeping Beauty was worth the practice days.
Medieval Times was in our play.

Dinosaur, The Fruit Parade we got a good score
This was second grade.

Rain Forest, The Tundra too,
Multiplication took us straight through.
Our first debut was the Recorder Concert we all enjoyed that too.

Making the band, our first year of Chorus, The Indian Fair,
Climbing to the top of the stairs, Nature's Classroom was a blast.
It took us to the top real fast.

Holiday Hills was a thrill the Talent Show shows the school what we know.
Officer Marino has helped us throughout the year
He has taught us all about D.A.R.E. next comes the North American Fair.

There were Concerts, Halloween Parades, and Field Days too.
We definitely have to thank all of you, our parents too.
Saying good-bye will be hard to do; we will never forget any of you!

Jennifer Gavrich

Christmas

Christmas time is the season,
To buy toys for little girls and little boys.
Children sitting on the lap of santa clause,
With joy expressed in their smile,
Holding a toy list that's a mile.
In a low shy voice, telling santa what they need,
Having trouble telling him what the words read.

Going caroling with friends from house to house,
Snow falling on tree tops, which is as quiet as a mouse.
Driving to every town, going christmas shopping in every store.
Buying gifts, and a christmas tree,
To decorate on christmas eve.

Waking up christmas morning, with gifts under the tree,
Passing them out for the family.
Gathering together in a special way,
To give thanks and praise for the Lords birthday.

Helen Petrosevich

My Angels From Heaven

My Angels from Heaven were given to me
To cherish and treasure
Till they have to be set free
I look in their eyes and see hope and love
Knowing only that they were gifts from above
My Angels from Heaven are a boy and a girl
And no two finer Angers were sent to this world
I know in my heart till the day that I die
No matter where they will be, you will see
That my Angles from Heaven will always be free
The tears and joy that they give me so,
That God alone can only know
Their smiles and touch I see and feel
Can only be love, and it's real
My Angles from Heaven are gifts from God
That I can only say
I thank you God for another day
In which I spent with their love this way
And when I die and they are alone
May they have Angels from Heaven to call their own.

Benedict J. Sgro

"The Ache Of Pain"

I'm out of tears, I'm out of words,
to define, this beat up heart of mine.
Look at us then, look at what we've become
the angels cry, the wings of our love has broken.
Scattered thoughts, and shattered glass,
this is what fills my room, besides the haunted
memory of the very thought of you.
You were the sun that shone in my eyes.
you were the air that I breathed, but I fell in thin ice.
I've become cold like the autumns leaves.
Ever since that day, when the storms gathered.
the wind was calm, then it began to rain,
that's when the depth of my soul felt the ache of pain.

Angela Hale

Elegy On Sacred Ground

Foreign policy has evolved
to dominate our world,
yet you seem lost, and but forgotten
your war dismissed and all but solved.
"Farewell oh land of milk and honey,
Star of the middle eastern shore;
The olive tree has wept in mourning
for the mecca that is nevermore."

Many perished in this conflict
of seventeen years and score,
We must embrace the bitter carnage
and deliver peace through Diplomacy's door.
"Farewell oh land of milk and honey,
Star of the middle eastern shore;
The olive tree has wept in mourning
for the mecca that is nevermore."

The sorrow of torture that's consumed
a countries crippling fate,
has stripped the boughs of the olive branch
with man's indifference to the fury of hate.

Deborah M. Jamieson

Why?

Dedicated to Gerald Gallon

Why should I have to lie?
To express my feelings is hard.
If only all of my dreams came true.
I wouldn't have to put up my guard.

No one will ever seem to understand
The passionate love that I have for one man.
Although I know that God sent him to me
Why is my choice still made not to be.

When I think of how much I miss him,
And to think of how much I love him
I cry at night wondering why
Why do I have to lie?

I know that he's the one for me,
From him I've learned a lot.
At least, I know that the man I love.
Would give me his soul and heart!

Cindy Marie Bobe

Hearts Core

Some days, I'd go out of my way just to see him smile -
To feel sunlight's warmth within a blue-eyed sky.
Just enough to make it all seem worthwhile
So much more than "only getting by."

He would wave from his seat near the store window as I'd pass,
Detouring my stride, we'd talk and watch evening's arrival at last.
Once more, I'd lose myself inn his demeanor, so peaceful and calm,
My troubled soul finding solace and affection-a renewal so strong,
Gentle reassurance bereft of caution or alarm.

Of all the myriad of friends and associates at times around me,
They would quickly be forsaken for the pleasure of his company.
Now physically his presence is seen no more,
His spirit is ever nigh, still bestowing peace and love at heart's core.

Avis Marie Sandar

That Elusive Creature

A person may look their whole life through,
To find a creature as elusive as Yew.
What is this creature that evades us all,
The short the fat the slim the tall?
Some say this creature does not exist,
I say this creature most of us miss.
Most of us look for that perfect one,
We look and look and end up with none.
These creatures turn up in the strangest places,
And some may not have the best of faces.
But who is to say which creature is right,
And from the unknown, should we cover in fright?
Or which of these creatures is best for you,
When there are so many that come into view.
Forget about what people say should be,
For who knows the one for you, you'll see.
And once you recognize it to be a dove,
You'll know that creature's name is Love.

David P. Thomas

The Promise

I awoke to a golden light, and left behind the dark of night,
to find you waiting in the wing.

I realized that I'd been told, by someone who was very old,
that I am The Promise of spring.

I'll live, I'll love, I'll learn your ways,
to fill my everlasting days,
with a hope that the future will be mine,
for I am The Promise of spring.

Questions ponder on my mind, for answers of a lasting kind.
Do you know the reasons, for the changing or seasons?
Do you know the answer to the question of -

Who rakes the leaves in the forest?
Who picks the flowers in the park?
Who lights up the moon and gives a glow,
to see each other in the dark?

Who sifts the sand in the ocean,
and sprinkles the morning with dew?
No, it isn't me, now who can it be?
Tell me, can it be you?

Arlene P. Grymski

The Black Land

I have finally found my reason
To go back to the nocturnal land, where lies the Black Smoke.
To God this may be like treason,
Its substance so murderous; its solidness, my lungs do soak

Laughing and breathing the darkened air,
Dancing and falling on the lake of black poisoned ink.
When lied here its difference, the white light which I could not stare,
Was engulfed by the sky as if darkness was giving me a wink.

Blindly I fall upon the onyx lake
Feeling the liquid, so blood thirsty, grab onto my skin.
My pores drowning for oxygen; suicidally swallowing the ink as its intake;
My blood will never be red again.

I try to catch a glimpse of this obscure world only filling my eyes with lead;
My mind changing into a wonder.
The soul that light fed, now loving to be dead,
Frantically listening to the ring in my ear, that sounds like thunder.

It now creeps up to take my breathe
And manipulates my lungs to make me choke.
Happily and finally feeling the Blade of Death
Cremating my body and soul to join the others into the Black Smoke.

Jovan Hernandez

My Wedding Love

This woman of power softly speaks,
To have her way with all the beasts,
She knows you're there, before you are,
And makes you feel aware!

This woman of action slowly moves,
To take a position no one can improve,
She never wastes time with word or hand,
Yet let's us know softly where we stand!

This woman of power gently shows,
How to live and love; both meant to expose
True feelings! Yet to find even more
Honestly travels to every shore!

Power, Action, Love and Grace,
Of these four horseman, Love wins the race,
Love for her is a way of life,
My love for her has no strife.

From deep in my soul, this song rings true,
Please, come take my hand, Joy, for I love you!

Don H. Chapin

I'll Be There

Someone to share and shoulder your cross
To help you make it when the going is rough
Someone willing to share your every burden
When you seem to be weak and not strong enough
I'll be there

Someone who will not cease to pray
For the love of God Almighty to forever guide you
Someone who'll understand your sickness and pain
When you really seem not to know what to do
I'll be there

Someone's door to her heart wide open
To accept you now just the way you are
Someone to give you courage and strength
To forever be beside you until you cross the bar
I'll be there

Joyce Lee Johnson

No Mountains High Enough

There's no mountain high enough
To keep me in discord

There's no mountain high enough
To keep me from my Lord

There's no mountain high enough
To keep me on this side

There's no mountain high enough
To keep me from his side

Lord I'm coming, I'll find the bridge
That takes me to the very first ridge

I started climbing up the slope,
I slipped back, but knew I could cope

I looked up and prayed, Lord, tell that devil to go away
I'll be reaching the top of the mountain some day

That's why I feel so calm and humble this day

There's no mountain high enough to keep me from my Lord

Beverly Ann Clause

"Shadow Of Love"

I know I could be with you, through every lonely night
To lie there closes beside you, and wake my morning light
I cannot have the pleasure that I truly so desire!
To feel you're body soft and warm, liked Ember from a fire.

I cannot sit and talk with you the way I liked to do,
To have the time to learn about the uniqueness that is in you
I cannot walk with you at night and gaze at star filled skies,
To stop and hold you closer to me; while time goes softly by

Still my love is stronger than the day we first met,
And this is something I would liked you never to forget,
Because although we live apart, my love for you is true
And never will I love someone, the way that I love you

I cannot love you more, my dear! If every day we share,
For in the shadow of our love, there is no cold to despair,
You're love is all I need? How could I asked for more?
For you have touch me deeper, than anyone before!

And! So? My love for you will grow, liked flowers in the spring,
Because to me, you're my life, my world, my everything?
Through summer, Fall and winter, you're my only smile,
For in the shadow of your love? My soul can rest awhile!

Adriano A. Sanchez

"The Season's Of Life"

The season's come and go as darkness softly fades
to light.
Spring, summer, autumn, winter.
Birth, growth, harvest, sleep.
The cycle eternally to repeat.
The springtime of our life, is the day
that we are born.
The summer is our growth, hopefully yearning
To learn, and to be strong.
That autumn is our harvest, as we reflect
on wisdom gained.
The winter is our silent, Peaceful sleep
called death,
waiting for spring to return once again.

Joan Reego Gully

Time

I was born a streak in the sky.
To light the horizon so big planes can fly.
I don't ask questions and I don't know why.
I might be the hour that just passed you by.

I was born a whisper at night,
Enveloped in darkness, a secret of white,
Cool in the silent calm of the quiet,
A hope for the future, a stand for the right.

I was born with the first conscious mind.
I bleach out the heartaches emotions entwine
I live in a measure of any ole' kind.
My name is simple, just call me time.

Billie C. Moore

"Sunrise"

In the dark of night with chilling rain
To lonely Gethsemane I want in pain,
Carrying my burden and filled with fear
Knowing the hour of heart break was near.

Seeking to hold by the power of love
My dear one called home to heaven above,
I prayed, I pleaded, I sought relief
From traveling this road of sadness and grief.

But my Lord whispered low as I waited there
I know - I know, I hear your prayer"
And in words so tender He said to me
"Be not down-hearted, I'll walk with thee."

So I placed my hand in His nail torn palm
And lifted my eyes toward the Easter dawn,
I claimed His promise, I know it's true
By believing and trusting He'll see me thru.

To a brighter day with hope for tomorrow
By the cleansing blood of Calvary's sorrow
As the sun, and the rain draw flowers through the sod.
So peace comes to me from a loving God.

Clemmie Hall

Changed Man

He was there from morning till night
To love me and tuck me in tight
He helped with my school work
He tried all he could
To help me do better, I was sure I would
Until he suddenly started to change
And started acting so very strange
Then my life started down hill
With out any brakes or a steering wheel
He would come in later and go out earlier
He'd say he was at one place and be at another
He left us all alone to stay
For his girlfriend and her son that day
I was so angry and full of hate
Then I began thinking of it as fate
He was turning into a person I did not know
Instead of the person from so long ago

Brandi Hall

"The Moon"

The moon is a lovely sight, out here at sea.
Tonight it sends down its light, and shine its
light upon me.

For a few moments, at it I stare. Then, only then,
am I aware, of its bright glare. That it guides me.

And rids me of the darkness of the sea.

Darryl Daboo Washington

Tassie

To You.
To Me.
From You.
From Me.
What does it mean to die?
What gives someone the right to kill the young,
Or the middle age, or the elderly?
To take the right to pull a trigger, pull a plug, or
Empty a syringe into someone's body.
Nobody except God, but I wonder about Him,
The Almighty.
I thought you were supposed to
Have a long and fruitful life?
Then when everything is at
Its highest pinnacle of life,
Something has to go wrong, it's inevitable.
You're supposed to live without pain or suffering.
Please don't leave me, You're all I have.
Why did you have to go?
WHY?

Brett T. Ward

My Friends

A friend, what is a friend?
To me a friend is a someone who will be there
no matter what. Always be there.
Someone you can trust. Always trust.
A good friend is so much more.
Not a best friend, but someone who is true.
Always true to you. Someone who you can love
and will love you back, but still be a friend.
A best friend. Best friends mean the world to me.
I want to stay with them forever. Always. A best friend
is everything I said above, and more. A friend like this
is hard to leave. It is hard to think this might even happen.
But then boys come along. That's what tears us up.
Tears, tears of happiness, of sadness.
I know they will come. Maybe not often but they will.
Even when they leave us, they will probably come back one day.

Hope Krug

Hands Of Kindness

In stretching out an open hand,
To Moms and Dads and Babes we stand,
On solid ground within the realm,
Of those who are most overwhelmed,
By poverty and great despair,
Who do not e'er know pairs not there,
Have broken hearts and many babes,
To nurture until life just fades.
But then an outstretched hand is seen,
With help to bear up troubles deemed.
A comfort has come as it reaches out,
With sprinkles of love to stamp out a drought,
Of cold and careless doom each day,
That snatches the lives of our babes away.
But then an outstretched hand is seen.
And many by it are redeemed.
And given the faith and strength to know,
That in taking this hand it won't let go.
Hands of kindness, filled with love,
Reaching down to us from God above.

Joyce Frank-Ridgeway

Our Country

What has happened to this country of ours?
To most it seemed perfect, without any mars.
With all our many freedoms, as speech and prayers.
And many never hardly have a care.

The sun still shines, and goes down at night.
We still pledge to our flag, with all our might.
We know our country is the very best.
It has never failed in any test.

Then tell me why do we hate each other?
And shoot and kill, our friends and brothers.
Many of our youth, carry guns today.
Even in, the low school grades.

The parents will have to lead the way.
To show the children that drugs, gangs and liquor just don't pay.
We need love in the family, as in years before.
And stop the shooting and killing, and educate more.

Burga H. Vickers

What Kind Of A Woman Am I?

I drive down main street, and turn the corner
To park into the Hess's parking lot
My precious pale blue oldsmobile
I pull into the Handicap spot to shorten my distance
An old man walking by with a crutch
Yells at me!- I wince like Gizmo
Giving him control
Allowing him to hold me in the air with a skewer
I am a steak
He is suspending me in the air
He is slicing me with his unguals
As he speaks to me in nasty tone
Telling me what a rotten egg I am
His prehistoric mind grumbling angers me
I notice the pretty pinfion tree next to my car
That I am guarding like a vulture
Ready to pounce on any bystander one foot away
That old man will be ab offal if he trespasses
He is prehistoric, ready to place me in a pillory
He did not grow wise with age.

Erica Ackerman

She Passed Away At The Age Of Forty-One

The song says, "Let her go let, let her go;"
To peace, to rest, to God.
Loved ones have said their adieus.
But, then, they cry in the night;
And ask, why? Why? Why?

Why!
Because the sky is blue;
Because the wind sighs through the trees at night;
Because the snows come in winter;
And, because we are all voyagers through time.

Time to love, time to feel, time to be:
And, then, to know, through faith,
That time and God are one.

Jeanette B. Nicholas

One Side Of The P's And Q's Of Poetry

Perpetual purpose provides me a place
To pitter and patter along at a pace
That probably pleases the people's pretense
Proclaiming the poet a prominent prince.
The painting of poems or that of a pose
Are pretty perplexingly close I suppose.
The pencil and paper provide me a prop
To place all my poetry plainly on top
Of Pulitzer Prize winning poem publications
Pronouncing and printing my past inspirations.
Apparent appeal predicated by print
And popular previews procure and present
A profile depicting professional pride
By praising the products the poets provide.
So placid I perch on my pinnacle's peak
And practice perfecting my potent technique.

John Campbell

"Papa"

There are many thorns in this world which we live.
To reach the other side, we must walk among them.
We must endure the pain that they give.
Among the thorns, there are roses that
God gave to help along the way.
They brighten the journey and lighten the day.
There was a special seed God planted for me.
Its petals radiant, for the whole world to see.
God kept this rose sheltered by the pearly gate.
God knew its branches would be tall and straight.
The days passed by so quickly you see.
It didn't seem fair this rose was taken from me.
But there was a garden in heaven, that needed this radiant light.
The rose bent down gently one night.
It passed through the wall to the other side.
I'll always remember this rose with pride.
There are still thorns on my journey home.
But God left the sweet scent of that rose so I'm not alone.
The garden in heaven is now a much lovelier place.
The rose blooms there because of God's wonderful grace.

Dorothy Spencer

As We Speak...

The guard of justice is leaving to perform his trial,
To see his prisoner of war, who is chained to a fence of wire,
Who is child and is twelve years old -
Who is accused of being the daughter of a traitor and a liar
And that this is all her people's fault.

He is forcing himself upon her, performing his personal trial,
Like others performed it before and that he ends with as evil roar.

The sun is burning upon her and is crusting blood on her thigh.
It is burning her shaved head and is burning into her brain,
Eliminating the memory of her naked name.

He is grabbing the water bowl, that was placed in front of her,
That all day she tried to reach,
Longing to drink fresh and whole
- And that he is now slowly pouring into an arid ditch.

While she is gliding into the unconsciousness of her bare shame,
The guard of justice is returning to his quarters,
Where beneath a wall of his beheaded trophies,
He admires the visage of his game.

Inger Coopchik

Sorry

Sorry is really hard to say,
To some people that I hurt one day,
I didn't realize what was going through my mind,
I just wish I could turn back time.

I am locked up in this T.Y.C.
Just hoping my little brothers won't follow me.
I cry my self to sleep at night,
Because of all the things I did that weren't right.

Sorry is what I want to say,
But deep down inside it hurt me in another way.
I wish that I could tell you someday,
Exactly what I want to say.

Jeremie Sims

Reality

Reality is fact not fiction.
To some you dare to mention.

A dream world full of fantasy where they stand.
Hoping they wake up to reality one day.

Reality is true, it's never false.
The time you take is worth the cost.

Reality comes for some and it goes.
A thing impossible to hold.

Reality begins with a simple thought.
Already in your brain it can't be taught.

Reality is here and will never go away.
But if you're stuck in a fantasy world, it's a real price to pay.

So please just give in to reality, if you don't it's a crying shame,
Because in the long run my friend you will be the one to blame.

Yes a person can dream, sure that's ok.
But never let reality ever slip away.

My friends, reality is all over, we see everyday.
Some take it in, some let it get away.

So when reality sets in and you can't stand bare,
Get on your knees, take within prayer.

Frank P. Fields

Autumn Gossip

The wind whispers secrets
to the listening leaves,
spills summer gossip
so the willow, bending low,
may hear the latest news.
The maple, shedding red-gold leaves,
giggles when she discovers
her neighbor, the straight-laced oak,
lost her dignity one frosty night.
She chuckles at the tale of the dogwood
flirting with the lilac by her side.
The nosy wind has many secrets to tell
before the last leaf flutters to earth
and silence fills the air.
Then, with the first snow, tattle-tale wind
will blow across the barren hill
to sulk in sheltered crags
until spring arrives
with more news to share.

Jean Conder Soule

Rain On The Roof

I wake up in the night
To the steady beat of rain on the roof.
I think of the happiness of all the folk
Who's springs are low.
I think of thirsty plants
drinking up the rain.
Especially corn,
How fast it all will grow
When the sun comes out again.
As I listen to the steady beat
Of rain on the roof
I think of puddles in the morning.
Imagine little boys glee
As they stomp through those puddles merrily.
I think of dwindling ponds rapidly refilling
And swirling streams free flowing.
A cool breeze refreshing is blowing.
Clouds drift in the night across the August sky
I drift to sleep
To the steady beat of rain on the roof.

Joy Cenicola

One Ticket One Train

Today as I sat at home all alone, I hear the ringing of the phone. It took some time for me to rise, the words brought teardrops to my eyes.

There was this voice so strong, so bold. That said I am to do what I am told, or life this way will always remain, and he also refused to tell me his name.

The man that you love, the big drug guy, drop him today, or you'll surely die. Tell him you're leaving you're not in this game, and your life will be spared with one ticket, one train.

He hung up the phone, I fell to my knees. Oh what has he done, and God help me please. I heard this hard knocking upon my door, so I hide for protection, I can't stand no more.

It's I your lover and also your friend if you feel the same, you'll soon let me in. Your no friend of mine. I'm caught in your game, but I'll soon be free with one ticket one train.

I can't live in your world, it's all just a lie, and I promised today to tell you goodbye. I can't be your wife, and I won't take the blame. I don't need your drugs, just one ticket one train.

Donean King

Easter

The parched earth craves rain.
Totally desiccated, it attempts to bud,
But vainly the fallow ventures fertility,
It becomes a wild abandoned barren;
A void fancying a sterile future.

But the sky exposes the hope-sign,
A bright cloud hovering overhead.
The shadow of life covers the dry,
Raining promises of the pending outburst;
Adventing the sink of the quickening mist.

"Drop down dew, you heavens, from above,
And let the clouds rain the just one;
Let the earth be opened,
And bud forth a saviour."

Andy Czarny

From A Collection Of Love Thoughts

Your skin is golden brown
   Touched by Our Father's Sun.
Your dark brown eyes stare at me
   Like you're searching my body and soul.
It's absolutely Breathtaking the way
   You lay your head between my breasts.
And when you touch my bronze colored skin,
   Aaahhh, it's like the tender touch of a
Beautiful Peacock Feather.
   Your loving hands have awaken my dormant
Feelings of Intimacy.
   Your lips are soft, sweet, and delicate
As a ripe grape.
   I love the way your sweet moist
Tongue enters my mouth with much anticipation.
   Each moment with you is an exciting adventure;
I appreciate you for sharing a part of your life
   With me.

Ada M. Holmes

Untitled

I enter the room, darkness blinds me heat rushes towards my face and my body. Slowly the tribal beats surrounds me it engulfs me, my soul, my body, my mind. The flashing lights mesmerize me. I think, how could I ever leave. In a trance I sway, sway to the patterns of the lights and the rhythm of the music BAM, people pushing, thrashing, screaming. I fight back clawing my way to the front I look up I see all my anger. No longer is it haunting me or clouding my judgment. BAM, the beat is faster harder I push they push, hands all over me sweat dripping all over my face it feels good. BAM the music is louder harder my heart becomes the amp I know if it stops I stop. Faster I jump I can't stop, higher harder faster I reach out for my sanity it's gone. Silence. It's over I look around at the nameless faces. I silently walk to my car. Put in a tape and drive back to the dull, angry life that I have become accustomed to.

Claudia Kobrzynski

Untitled

Stressing the understanding of my blackness
Trying to find the door to my happiness
Hearing nothing but words but seeing all prejudice
To many people afraid of my kiss
I can't understand their common sense
To much for me to comprehence
I'm meant to be a equal but seen as a sequel, of what my ancestors were two-hundred years ago
I'm not sure they mean the things they say
There's to many of them for it to go away
One word said in class and attention is mine
They all stare at us, we're not hard to find
Just look at the students who are dying inside
From actions, laughter, from the glimpse of your eye
I'm totally against the things that they do
But who am I to speak, to them I might be one too.

Christine Alexander

Time After Time

Time after time, what I thought, was right
turns out wrong
Day after day, I wait for my dream love
out of some song.
Time after time I turn my life upside down.
For the true love I thought I had found.
Time after time how my heart breaks,
As I add another to my list of mistakes.
Day after day I sit and wonder why,
Love always seems to be a lie.
But day after day I continue to believe,
That one day true love I will receive,
Time after time I renew hope for my fate,
And day after day is one less day
I'll have to wait.

Bonnie L. Ely

Two Caring Souls

Sometimes, when reaching out to ones they love,
Two caring souls can lose their way, and fail
To find a common goal along life's trail;
But still, within their hearts, they care and love.

Although they go their separate ways,
A special love their hearts and souls will share,
Because, they are true friends who really care
About each other all their lasting days.

This is no less a love than passionate
Romance that flares so hot, then fades too soon;
True friends are as enduring as the moon,
And always loyal and compassionate.

How do we know that bond there is between
Us two; is it just friendship or is it
A deeper love that fuses our hearts to fit
The mould of mutual love and high esteem?

I know not what the answer is, sweetheart;
But, most assuredly, I know how much
I do love you, my sweetest one, with such
A strong emotion, deep inside my heart!

Eugene S. Browning

The Cowboy

She watched him over the rim of her cup of coffee
Under his pearl gray Stetson he was cowboy tanned and dusty
Quickly she looked away from him
Into the cup where many tears had begun to swim
She knew he was like all the rest
Who ran when their love was put to the test
She wasn't going to walk into what she'd just left
Not when she'd just gotten control of herself
But as she sat thinking of a long past day
The cowboy got up and headed her way
"You look like the world's just come to an end.
Maybe you could use a friend?" She looked up and smiled
And thought maybe they could just talk for a while
She knew what he'd say
When it came time for the cowboy to ride away, but to her surprise
They talked long into the night
And when it came time for the coffee shop to close
She discovered something that before she didn't know
The amazing gentleness in a calloused cowboy's hand
And the love of a good man

Gini M. Kenerly

Where Were You

All men have the ability to create a life, and become a father.
Unfortunately some men find this new life to be nothing but a bother.

Most feel blessed, and overjoyed to be a dad.
But for me, a dad, is something I never had.

Before I could walk or talk he has gone.
Never wanting to see this new life prosper and carry on.

With great love and affection.
My mother performed both roles with grace and perfection.

As I grew, I knew some part of me was missing.
And for many years, I did more than my share of wishing.

As I watched other kids with their fathers.
I prayed that mine would reconsider, and not see me as a bother.

Soon all of those dreams and wishes would come true.
As a teen-anger, I finally met the father I never knew.

But to my dismay, the hurt and pain in my heart didn't go away.
And once again, my father found it easier to leave than stay.

And know that I am grown, and out on my own.
There is still a void in my heart for the father I have never
truly known.

Although he will always have to live with the choice he made.
In time my loss and pain will slowly but surely fade.

David A. Garrett

Monumental Hill

On a hill so green and fertile, stood a brave Oak and Willow so gentle
United in their youth, their roots firmly stationed
Full of hope to fulfill their purpose of creation
The earth was warm and it was spring
Their beauty did grow and their hearts did sing
As the seasons did change the stronger they stood
Cold winters came, stormy winds did blow
They feared not, faith and courage you know
To their Creator they turned, the way He would show
Many a spring did come too, each more beautiful, each one new.
On warm winds their seeds did sow, so close their seedlings did grow
Gentle Willow and Oak so noble, how grand you stood in your trouble
Your seedlings were many as were their fears
Yet you braved the storms on that hill
Spread your bough wide and made the winds still
Seasons passed on and on, unflinching you were, ever so strong
Then thy Creator called on thee, come little Willow, come unto me
For all like you, who grow so stall, a heavenly garden beyond the wall
Brave Oak, so sad and lonely, a few more seasons for you only.

Alice Crupi

Unkind

All of my excitement was just drained from me;
unknowing,
unwilling.
Now I won't see you; only in my dreams,
I feel so isolated from your closeness
which is so far from me in a world asleep.
Depressions mother my weakened heart
as I slowly drift from you.
Why does this happen?
I can't find my happiness; I always thought it was in you.
Every word I have written fades away and so does my hopes.
I can only close my eyes and fall into my
infinite well of emotions that closes in
on me; suffocating me.
Why can't I touch you?
You're so far,
You're still moving,
You're feelings of apathy remain with me;
unwanted,
unkind...

Betsy Grey

The Gate Away To Freedom Is Peace

No man can say that he is free
unless there is peace in his heart
because with peace,
love is guaranteed,
and if each man love his neighbor
then they'll never drift apart.

I dream of the day
when every man is free
what ever his race or creed
when his heart is free
from hatred and prejudice,
and he sing a song of harmony.

Will that day ever come,
when men are able to love one another,
when the sky is filled with rainbows and dove,
and people of all races live together?

If you have ever dreamed of such a day
when we are free from violence and ridicule
listen to what I have to say
The gate away to freedom is peace.

Junet Jules

"Our Girls"

Life is dull here at the farm,
Until the lights and their charm walk in the door arm-in-arm.

The Girls lived with me from birth to one year
My heart was totally bought with them so near.
Their dark hair, dark eyes and curls,
Were to a mother of sons a directive from God
to do my best and not stand in the way,
Of a very young couple who were trying to stay
married to each other for the "sake of the kids".
When they were already in a dead skid.

Without a doubt five months of working six to five,
Made a man of a boy in such a short time.
Their love could not overcome the problems that arose,
Their marriage came to a difficult close.

Now their lives are separate as two can be,
Why oh why couldn't they see?

Our Girls come on Saturday.

Judy Moss

Deserted

I felt so alone
until you came along.

I had been deserted;
Deserted by the one who said he loved me

You made my days shine again;
You made my nights glow once more.

I felt the warmth when you were near,
And in your arms I felt no fear.

You whispered words of happiness in my ears
And kissed away all my tears.

I began to laugh again
You made my world turn once more;

But now that you've went away,
And left me all alone;

I have been deserted once again;
Deserted by the one who said he cared for me.

Emmy T. Parry

A Heart Once Shattered

My heart was once shattered
Unto a million prices
Now I realize it doesn't matter.
The pain that set in was hard.
I cried so many tears.
See my tears weren't dry.
I once loved him a lot
My life is at a still point no where to turn.
As hard as I tried.
All I do is cry from morning to night
I finally turned my life around and saw the light
My life will finally be alright.

Enid Borenstein

Of Age To Youth

Oh, brilliant light above, please shine
Upon my weathered face and still, cold body.
Bring life where life live not,
For I am all alone again.
Let your glow touch my heart with love,
And grow to bring me breath.
Oh, silent is the heart that has no blood.
Silent is the voice that has no ears.
When light did glow from me,
I knew not of what was there,
Bring to me the joys unknown of past,
And bring life to those all lost.

Amy Brown

Life

Life is what keeps us going. Sometimes it's what makes us stop.

But you have to keep on. Go at your own pace. It may take awhile, but stay in the race.

You have to be brave. Don't chicken out. You have to keep smiling. Even if there's nothing to smile about.

Don't say good-bye to the world that watched you grow. People care more than you may know.

Just take stride in your step. Walk with confidence. For life is precious. It just takes common sense.

Amy Jo Merrigan

"Through My Eyes And My Heart"

From the time you brought me into the world until God takes us to Heaven; you are the greatest Mother that anyone could be given.

Mother, through my eyes and my heart, you are the best friend a daughter could desire; and of your sweet and gentle attention, I will never tire.

Mother, through my eyes and my heart, God gave me the greatest teacher he could give. Since childhood and still today, you teach me how to live.

Mother, through my eyes and my heart, I have seen through yours, and when I have children of my own, I know how to love them no matter what their faults.

Mother, through my eyes and my heart, when God gave you to me, I received the greatest gift a person could receive, and though I could write a book of pages which would fill a great hall, I will end this poem by saying, you are the greatest Mother of them all.

Donna Parton

Plan

If a day is given you don't waste it
use it the best way you can.
Make it a little better than yesterday
this should be in your plan.
Yesterday is gone, now work on today
fill it with joy, love and caring,
tomorrow will take care of itself
if we think a little of sharing.
Perhaps just sit and think a bit
about some future plan
go in that direction and get there if you can.
Perhaps just talk to someone
it may brighten your day
as their thoughts are not your thoughts
but it may change your way.
Care about people they're just like you
wondering what's coming what will be new
follow your dreams whatever you do
it's worth it you see I did it too.

Helen Abbott

Tomorrow

Tomorrow: When peace shall spread like an epidemic over valley, over vales, over the hills, over this earth. When peace will flow like a mighty raging river angry, furious, lashing from shore to shore.

Tomorrow: When ideas for the elusive cures will pop up like the little seedlings in the spring, pushing up from the barren earth covering it with their foliage. When we will reach that mystic height and all will understand each other, even though we speak different languages.

Tomorrow: When class revolution will have been fought, the conclusion being: All classes are the same rich or poor except for one fact, outside appearances affect the status, inside we are the same: Pain, love, sadness, and happiness we feel with the same intensity. CAN YOU WAIT FOR TOMORROW?

Dorothea M. Crawford

A New Spring Day

As I looked over the hill
view brought to my eyes

Horizon golden and blue
light of the sunrise

A new day dawning
has come around
fresh morning dew drops
silently cover the ground

A new day's dawning
ready to begin
spring to life yawning
natures way again

Flowers burst open standing straight do blend
with dropping weeping willows blowing in the wind

Clouds like puffs of cotton filled the open sky
old dependable windmill turning by and by

Most beautiful yet serene this first spring morning in March
comes once every year with the singing of the lark

Charles Lattimore

Violence

What is violence you ask?
Violence is people who are timid and confused.
Why are they timid and confused you say?
They are timid....because they are confused....
because they have no meaning in life, or a
direction of what to do.
They are confused because they are afraid of the
difference between you and me....may it be
size, color, or race.
We are all flesh and blood!
You say this is life,
This is no life,
A life where hatred, cruelty, anger rule the world!

Danny McCredie

Casualties Of Death

Lives pretending to live,
Wandering aimlessly through the stages.
Complete absence of imagination,
Only mindless violence.
Illusions of a natural state,
Not knowing right from wrong.
Motions of emptiness dance in the shadows,
The truth hidden about our incompleteness.
The gruesome ritual of existence,
Embodies the very soul of consciousness.
Secrets encased in hollow shells,
Blinking to wash away the tears.
Casualties of a forgotten race,
Death pretends to be life.

Becky Thorson

Your Tears

My poems flow your tears...
Wandering reindeer flees in the loss,
Behind the autumn leaves swirl in the dust.
It's so sudden - so devastated
The cool breezes of September
The season of a beginning
The masterpieces of the poets.
It's so sudden, I caught
It's so sudden, I found a concept
On your face, your eyes.
That night the sky so immense, so traverse
Its echoes through the space
My poem reading...
The fragments of ragged fate
The tumbles of ephemeron
Its cruelty, frigidness of human
Freeze my mind, my body, my heart
I know I become a stillness - a death
Your tears warm me - warm me up
From a long long sleep of unexplored island.

Chau Ngoc Nguyen

When Love Hurts

These tears are for you as I sit alone
thinking of you the only love of my heart.
These tears are for you as I sit and
wonder why.
These tears are for you as I want
to keep loving you.
These tears are for you and all
the wrong thing's I said and done.
These tears are for you for all
the times I hurt you.
These tears are for you as I wish
you were still here with me.
These tears are for me and all
the pain I feel for you leaving me.

Alan Poupore

Hunter's Moon

I was rocked to sleep in the arms of the night-wind,
Warmed by the moon's white glow,
While the friendly ghosts from a time long past,
Whispered and sighed, soft and low.

Shadows and moonbeams played hide-and-seek,
Chased by the warm, restless wind.
A lovely, but sad, little lullaby
Kept weaving itself out and in.

Yearnings and fancies and things yet unseen
Sang to me all the night long.
Whispers and fragments of old, broken dreams
Rode on the strange, haunting song.

Lured from my sleep, I danced down the road,
Entranced by the music and light,
Then all of a sudden, I knew it was he,
The Pan-like God of the Night!

He winked and he smiled from beneath a cloud-cap,
And his song grew soft...and was gone.
Then his secret discovered, he floated away,
At the shimmery, faint touch of dawn.

Carol J. Ziegler

"A Tear"

A tear, a compact emotion, crystallized in its own beauty
warmth, and a way to get out everything that is wrong,
every pain that your feeling, and how bad the hurt is
imprinted into you, without saying a single word...

A tear, a singular small piece of you that drops and makes
its mark on the world, even though it doesn't seem to. It
is created by you and know one else can make a tear like
yours....

A tear, much like a snow flake, no two are the same,
each one is created around your every emotion. They can
be consisted of joy, sorrow from one who has past,
depression, from who you long for, or pain from a fight...

A tear is created for even the most shyest of all people
to let everyone know they exist and have feelings. A tear
is a very important thing in life, and should be expressed.
A tear represents who you are, and what you feel passionate
about; a tear describes you and holds all of your emotions
inside its clear crystal ball....

Jennifer M. Schwartzer

Pushed Off The Edge

One summer night she had realized that life
was a cliff and somehow she had fallen from it.
What could've pushed her, most will never know but
she would continue to fall, unless she chose to stop.

Depression, like a virus, had over time eaten away
any hope of happiness that her body tried to produce.
It controlled what she saw, so that she was blinded
from her family's faces, as she made her way up the
blackened neighborhood street that would end at the park.
There, she was surrounded by hills of freshly cut grass
and ominous bats that had awakened to claim the night.

Everyday she fallen farther and deeper but
no one cared, no one held their hand out to her, until now.
she approached the comforting figure of a tree with its
branches stretched towards her. It would hold her as she
closed her weary eyes and placed the gun to her temple.

Most are not yet aware that life is an edge
where some lose hope and fall, but instead
of pulling herself back up, she gave up
and let death catch her.........

Cynthia Carpenter

The Angel

One day I saw an angel that
was created far beyond mortal transition,
with eyes as lovely as the golden sun,
with lip sweet as honey, and soft
as a baby lamb. I just stood there
exposed to the radiance of her beauty.
Her sentimental aspect has captured my soul.
Then after we communicated that reinforced
my desire even more. If God can protect,
and keep his watchful eye on her,
if nature can reward itself by structuring
such a beautiful being, if time can give
her wisdom to know and understand
the principalities of life. Then I know
that there is still hope that one day my
longing for that little angel will come to be.

Delton Culpepper

Quiet Night

For Nick

The quietest night I remember
was going out deep-sea fishing.
Me and my little buddy were way out on a party boat fishing.
We caught a lot of blues.
Stars were shining bright
The ocean was pure tranquility
And the wind was calm and clear
As we were quiet
The fish were biting

David Barber

Lost Without You

I have tried to imagine my world without you:
Watching Geese soaring in formation, walking through the fields observing nature, the sparrows nesting each and every year on the porch, the beautiful deer grazing the fields at midnight, beneath the stars and moon so bright, the closeness of walking hand in hand along the beach, and know that none of it would be the same without you!

But most of all, I could never replace your smile,
your eyes when you look at me, your gentleness and giving, your loyalty and caring, the memories that we've made, the secrets that we've shared. The love that is always there despite time or distance.

So, today I celebrate your special birth,
Thanking my lucky stars that your life is my life, I give my deepest gratitude that of the millions of people and possibilities, Our lives were destined to be intertwined.

And as long as the ocean rushes to meet the shore, I want you to know,
clearly and forever, that my world would never be the same, without you!

Cathy A. Den Bleyker

Sad And Lonely Heart

I feel so sad and lonely, when you're not by my side,
To make me laugh, to make me smile, to make me warm inside.
I love your wonderful smile and your tear-stained, glassy, eyes,
When it comes to certain things I know you're very wise.

You may not be a genius, and I know you aren't dumb,
And, when I call your house you know who it's from.
You know what to say,
When I'm having a terrible day.

You know what to do,
When I'm sick or even have the flu.
I feel you are with me even though you aren't,
I guess you made a good impression, in my sad and lonely heart.

Jennifer L. Malone

Space

I calmly sit in an unknown space
Watching her fight against her mind
She's lost with no one she left behind
Snowy white clouds packed closely together
Like unforgettable thoughts
Tall willow trees tapering the cement below
Dying leafless trees falling to the ground
A mixture of colors surround your eyes
Your eyelashes shimmer from the sun above
Sweep your finger slowly across the sky
The beautiful birds are now crows
As they stop to rest on your finger tips
The web of a small brown spider is
clinging so tight
Take a deep breath and open your eyes
You're only dreaming of a place deep inside

Chelsey Richardson

I Will Always Remember

I will always remember ...
watching hot air balloons drifting in the sky.
I will always remember...
our hikes and bike rides.
I will always remember...
the otherside of the world.
I will always remember...
our long talks.
I will always remember...
his laughter at Christmas time.
I will always remember...
our picnic lunches.
I will always remember...
watching deer in the field through binoculars.
I will always remember...
his singing to me.
I will always remember...
how he is always there for me.
I will always remember him...
I will always remember my father —

Allison L. Brannen

Old Friends

I am sitting in my rocking chair
Watching the hummingbird hum
As I see Edward someone you might call a bum

I've known him since he was young
His father was almost hung for robbing a bank
They gave him a deadly spank
While little Eddie watched with his big brother Hank

Little Eddie cried that night
It gave me a fright
I'd never seen him act this way
So I thought I'd better go away
Ever since that day
We've all had a price to pay

For Edward is not the same
As I look out the window pane
I suddenly see the past
The future comes back fast

Little Eddie is now drink
And I'm sitting here
Watching the hummingbird hum

Jill Dryer

The Lonely Rose

She grew against a towering wall
Watered by the morning dew
Footsteps pass by each day
But yet no one never knew.
A tender touch she longed for
These petals of beauty she held
She kept blooming with a holding strength
Till one day, her petals fell.
Her life had been shaded to long
The loneliness slowly weaken her away
only the wall knew her anguish
With the dying of each day.
And now the wall stands alone
For once again, as once before
Death to soon whispered upon
Blooms for a little while and then no more.

Debra Millican

"The Coming Of Fall"

The long summer days quickly fade as fall pushes its
way. Overcast clouds some how darken the very day.
Cool brisk northern winds whistle softly through the
leaves, brilliant colors stand so bold and clear, this
is their time of the year. Darken dead grasses begin
to wilt as the landscape changes with snow soon felt.
Our water once so warm and clear, now very cool with
shadows of leaves rushing near. Nature, so sure and
bold, makes one last stand of beauty to prove its soul.
The mighty birds call as they fly south, the squirrels
hurry to gather nuts in their mouth. For this is
nature and seasons wrapped all in one. The coming of
fall has begun.

Julie Kay Lane

If I Could Tell You

If I could tell you
that I love but you
If I could tell you dear
It would be true.
If I could see you
what would you say?
If you said I love you too
what would I do?
If you should travel by my way,
what would I say?
If you should take my hand
and whisper words sublime,
what would I do?
If I should lift my eyes
To yours and see beyond
The lipped doors, what would you do?
If your arms should open wide and fold me safe
inside and hold me close while I cried, what would I do?
And if per chance your lips met mine I would
need no further sign, to know your love again is mine.

Velma Dahl

Blues Man

Down in the jail house he sings
the blues,
he wears the blues,
he has the blues.

With his slumped shoulders and baggy pants.
You'd never know he used to dance.

Oh what a guy he used to be,
everyone loved him, especially me.

Nancy M. McFarland

Oh My!

The last time I looked
I was thirty
Men were so friendly and
Flirty

If the next twenty's spent
Like the last twenty went
Aah time you are playing it
Dirty

Lillian Rappaport

Your Love

When my spirit was young
I was wild as the wind
Never to be tamed
I couldn't see 'round the bend

There were changes to come
And hardships and pain
Young love left me cold
I was crying in vain

Look into my eyes
Tell me what you see
I thought I was captive
but your love set me free

Where my heart had grown cold
Your touch made me warm again
Life had taken its toll
But you filled me with fire again

Rebekah Henry

The Ant

The ant,
I watched it as it
moved its food;
pushing, pulling
and stumbling over
a piece of bread,
clutching its prey
like a cat holding a mouse
it entered a tiny crevice
and rested.

And you my thought,
when will you
end your journey?
Tenaciously gripping
the idea
meandering over
the landscape of time,
a vast domain,
interminable
you wander on.

Vincent Samuels

The Matchmaker

Ah Po promised
I would be a person
when I married.
The mark of failure
slipped off
along with my red silk robe
of golden double-happiness.
Ma pain with silver
in a torn handkerchief.

Suzanne Tse

Found

I saw the matrix turning
I watched the matrix churning
turning, churning, burning
in my head

With inner eyes of wonder
I looked upon my blunder
as waves of sorrow thundered
through my head

I heard the silent choir
And watched as my empire
sank beneath the mire
in my head

I lost myself today
And would recall the way
but I think I'd rather stay
here in my head

Laura Lee Hill

The Other Side

As age besets upon me
I wonder how you are
How time has just flown by
Our souls are still so far

I feel like I've been cheated
Here in my twilight
The end is oh so near
It may take place tonight

We've spent with the others
The decades that have passed
I fought the bitterness fiercely
Hiding behind a mask

We gave our bodies away
Our hearts perished as well
But our souls are for each other
Time is yet to tell

In my heart I've always known
As I vanish with the tide
That soulmates always reunite
When they reach the other side

Louis Voiron Jr.

If I Had Wings

If only I had the wings of a dove
I would fly the world over
Searching, always searching
for the one that I love

I would fly to the mountains
I would fly to the sea
hoping, always hoping
that is where you would be

I would search hell with care
then on to heaven I would go
knowing, always knowing
that I would find you there

Then when I had found you
that is where I would stay
Rejoicing, always rejoicing
for that glad and happy day

Loraine Lee

Blessed Are The Poor

Sometimes I wish that I were rich
I'd really have a ball
To buy anything I wanted
As I walked throughout the mall

The things that I could have
if only I weren't poor
A house, a car, a diamond ring
clothes and shoes galore

But, blessed are the poor
At least that's what I'm told
So I guess I'm pretty lucky
hot to have that pot of gold

For everything I have in life
I thank the Lord above
He's given me the greatest gift
and that's the gift of love

So if you're poor, don't worry
don't waste your time and bitch
Just thank God that you are loved
and consider yourself rich

Karen Susanne Albers

Surroundings

Darkened by a whimsical smile,
If I ever knew its truth,
Fallen by my naive failures
of my painful youth.
Faulted by the ones that matter,
Lied to by the ones I hate,
I force a smile on my confusion,
Caught by my defense's bait.
Sitting on my pedestal
that I have built for me,
I tell them all to disappear,
and find what I must be.
Striving for my future's place,
With no good help from them.
On my pedestal I still sit
and wait for me to mend.

Tina Nicole Gregory

"Broken Promises"

What good is a promise
If it isn't kept true
You'll only end up
Feeling blue

When you give your word
It should be sincere
To all of us.
Who long to hear

Broken promises are
Known to be lies
They take away trust
And make others cry

So with a sign and
A wink of the eye
Let's make a promise
Never to lie

Rebecca J. Sands

The End

If smiles become frowns
If love becomes hate
if reality becomes fantasy
That'll be the end
If your words go unspoken
If I have to walk alone
by the sea
If I fail to help a friend
That'll be the end
If dreams become a dark emptiness
If your voice becomes
silent whispers
If the magic in your
tender kiss fades
That'll be the end
If the sparrow loses its wings
If a best friend tells a fatal lie
If I ever have to watch you go
the lights will dim
and I will surely die

Kett Khammanivong

Do You Need A Friend

Do you need a friend...
If so let it be me then.

When you are feeling sad and blue,
And you need someone to talk to,
Just call me, and I will be there,
No matter how far, no matter where.

If you need a shoulder to lean on,
You have my shoulders, from now on.

If you should happen to cry,
I shall be there to wipe your eyes dry.

If your heart is breaking in two,
I shall mend it for you.

If you feel that you cannot cope,
Just believe that there is hope.

When you feel that everything in your
Life has fallen apart,
I will be there to help you get a new start.

If you need a friend,
Please let it be me then.

Violet Csukardi

Speculation

I wonder what would happen
If the world were really flat?
Would we roll around like billiard balls
Upon a green felt mat?

I wonder what would happen
If we had no printing press?
Would the lack of news depress us
Or just make our troubles less?

I wonder what would happen
If we started changing laws?
Would we soon become more civilized
Or instigate more wars?

But what's the use in wondering
It's hard to speculate.
What the world would deem important
Would be open for debate.

So let's be optimistic
And with hope anticipate.
A progress more acceptable
Than this we've had to date.

Sybil Jason Drake

My Perfect Life

My life would be so perfect
If you were by my side
No cares, no worries in life to face
And nothing more to hide

I dream of waking up to you
In the morning with the sky so blue
To solely love and comfort you
And make your life so true

Your touch I long to feel
Your heart I long to hear
Your life I long to care for
Throughout out tender years

When will that day ever come
When will it finally be here
The day our souls come together
And wash away all our fears

Teresa Burdick

The Man In Black

The man in black waits patiently
"I'll wait forever for you."
The man in black listens quietly
"Tell me all your worries and fears."
The man in black whispers softly
"I'll change things if you let me."
The man in black weeps silently
"It's time to say good-bye."
The man in black laughs suddenly
"There's no turning back now."
The man in black turns quickly
"Remember, no regrets."
The man in black reaches out
"Give me your hand."
The man in black wickedly chants
"Your time has to end."

Kristie Johnson

Fast Lane

I better hurry (my friends await)
I'm going out to play.
I better hurry (I worked so hard)
It's graduation day.
I better hurry (to my new job)
I know I can't be late.
I better hurry (to meet my love)
This is my wedding date.
I better hurry (to catch my flight)
There's so much more to see.
I better hurry (my family waits)
They mean so much to me.
I better hurry (to say goodbye)
My time is up at last.
I better hurry (I wish that I)
Had "SLOWED UP" in the past.

Mrs. Ransom Smith

Lullaby

I'll whisper a lullaby
into your spirit
So quiet and gentle
you may not even hear it

Listen with your soul
not with your ears
And hear my lullaby
as nightfall nears.

Nancy Garcia

You Are The Reason

You are the reason
I'm here tonight
You are the reason
I open my eyes
You are the reason
I do the things I do

Melody in symphony,
I hear, when we kiss
Distant sounds of the sea
When we embrace
Electrifying, so electrifying.

You are the reason
I'm crying
You are the reason
I do the things I do
You are the reason
I'm a man tonight.

Lascelle A. Wright

Care Givers

I hope you will not shed a tear
I'm in your care while I'm here
I may look PALE and have FEAR(s)
I may cry and shed a few tears
When I awake from my sleep
I may hear voices and even count sheep.
In my bag there is a stuffed toy
It has no name, maybe I'll call it Joy
Good hands I will be
God will see to that for me
Enjoy this poem that I have written
I hope it strikes your heart like a kitten

Theodore Friedman

The Freest

I'm walking along the rim of heaven,
I'm looking down into the
depthless sea;
I'm as free as the freest
And I'm as wise as the wisest.
And I'm sure that I'm not going to die
Quite sure!
I talk with angels and
I laugh at devils
And I've made my comrade
The moon, the lune!
I'm free, I'm free!
All rhythm and harmony!
I have no problems and no worries
no cares or miseries!
I'm a completely privileged entity
You see, I have...no body!

Lorice F. Mulhern

Love

The only true test of love
Is how long you can withstand
The pain defy the fear and
Ignore the agony of an aching
Heart. The only way to know
One who cares is to know one
Who doesn't. To know what
It is not to have love so that
You recognize it when it is there
You know it is love not by how
Many times a person says it but by
How many times a person shows it
And when they show you over and
Over and over again you will be sure
That this is true love.

Katherine O'leary

No Drugs, No Joint

The days are passing, on and on,
I'm sober now, but for how long?
Emotions are on an even keel,
The scary part - I feel, I feel!

Chemicals tend to dull the soul.
To drop you into a deep dark blue.
The mind relates to things unseen
Reality - just a dream

Coming down is, oh, so new.
My hopes and dreams run askew.
My thoughts a tangled mass of strife,
As I learn this way of life.

Reality - to dream, to hope
To learn of life and how to cope.
Surely there's a leveling point.
I feel! I feel! No drug, no joint.

Susan Sims

Cloves & Black Light

Clouded misty eyes
In a sea of swirling pain
She shudders at the thought
Of Dark
And being alone in the rain
The sky escapes a cloud of
Light
Reflections of blue
And in the dark
She stands alone
Screaming whispers I love you
The tumbling rocks
And falling drops
A crimson faded hue
The summer sky the
Endless night
And countless dreams of you...

Kristine A. Gruninger

Night Haunts

Severed hands
In a tribal dance
Beneath the moonlit sky

A midnight orgy
Masquerade
Time for sacrifice

Like lemmings to the sea
They run
Their warnings go unheeded
And yet their God is
Angry still
More suicide is needed

Stephanie Phifer

Waiting

Solitary sea gulls
Keep the silence of the sky
The wings open
Penetrate vastness time
For each of them
I was waiting years
On the empty beach
But they were gone
Far, so far .....
With out caress me.

Nicole Pirvanescu

Untitled

Life seems to have placed me
in an endless charade
always hiding in shadows
a life like a masquerade.
My feelings run deep
in the caverns of my mind.
My emotions soar free
like a kite lost in the wind.
My face eternally hidden
through my painted emotions.
My actions forever sculpted
by society's desires.
As time passes
my mask will be lifted
piece by piece
as understanding sets in.
To you only the outside matters
all I ask
is wait until midnight
when all spells are broken.

Rachael Bigelow

To My Husband

Join me in life
In celebrating us
The joining of our souls
as one. You are my heart,
my breath, my spirit, my love.
You are now and forever my life.
I give you the greatest gift I can
me.
I see us - you, me for all
eternity in life and death
united as one.
My heart, your heart, one breath
Always,
US.

Maureen T. Wasikiewicz

Passages Of Time

He sits by the window
In his old favorite chair
Holding his pipe
Puffing smoke in the air

He stares back into time
Almost a century ago
To a forgotten place
We do not know

From boyhood days
To World War I
Through hard times and depression
Life's trials he has won

But now is the greatest test
His wife has been called
He says not a word
As a lonely tear falls

Now he waits quietly
As the clock ticks and chimes
But in his heart...his mind
Are the passages of time

Sherry Rupp

Block

Cramp
in index finger
and thumb
thumb digging into meat of index
while writing feverishly
and scrabble
pinky being chaffed by edge
of pages
holding pen.
Ache in grip
and possibly
not ink.
Look.
Bleeding.
Enough.

Manny A. Savopoulos

Tormented Heart

Oh the love that once was dear,
in my dreams she would now appear.
Passions stirred amid shared delights,
replaced by endless sleepless nights.

This tormented heart of mine,
seeking comfort in a glass of wine.
Gone joyous seasons of a love affair,
the emptiness of which I cannot bear.

Her bewitching eyes set my soul aflame,
Alas! Alas! it was all a game.
So tormented heart of mine,
have another glass of wine.

Ted V. Lebedew

"Ponder"

I ponder the questions
in search of the answers
that have always been hidden
in the lining of the one who knows all
and the knowledge partaken
by the children in waiting
seems to sprinkle upon
each and every soul like
raindrops on a clear summer night
and the echo of laughter
that thunders in the hollow
of the ears that won't hear
and the hearts that won't feel
as the light softly dims
casting shadows on your face
and all corners once hidden
are unveiled in the night
and the sight is so touching
so rich in its taste
as the questions are ending in a solemn
embrace

Kimberly A. Swift

Love Is Like A Butterfly

Love is like a butterfly
it goes from heart to heart
always knowing how to start
always sad to depart
but love will find another heart
and know exactly how to start
in hopes that someday
love might find a way
to forever stay

Misty Whitehead

I Believe

I believe
In the God above
Because he has given me
So much love

To me he his very
Nice and sweet
He made my hands, my arms,
My legs, and my feet

He made man
And woman, too
Just like he did
Me and you

I am blessed
With what I received
And that has caused me
To believe

Kira Lynn Dowdy Phillips

Untitled

The stars aren't just dots
in the sky
They're reminders of what we are
you and I
Looking at tiny lights,
lying on the earth
We realize how much
we are worth
For we are born
and then we die
But the stars still remain
in the sky.

Kelly A. Adams

Quiescence

Passing from awakeness to sleep
In the twinkle of an eye
Through a curtain that is not there
Or ever is: a mystery
Intractable in both darkness
And in light-time, transcendental.

So too in awaking we pass
In the blinking of the eye
Reclaimed from senseless slumber,
Pitch blankness, into second sight
Open to light and sun, day or night
Straightway from impotence to might.

Till comes that longer sleep for all
Instantaneous, sempiternal
God's call awakening to new life
All pass in His hands all knowing.

Morton S. Jaffe

I Am A Whale

I course through oceans dark and deep
In waters warm and cold I sleep
I am a Whale
I sing my song of ages past
Each note longer than the last
I am a Whale
Only plankton do I eat
So abundant and oh so sweet
I am a Whale
And though I'm Monarch of the Sea
Only one animal dares hunt me
And that is man
I am a Whale

William Delgado

California Windstorm #1

This morning a visit of wind blew
into town and undressed the trees.
Skipped rope with a clothesline.
Short-sheeted the Sunday paper.
Played kick-the-can. Flagged a
cap and rode it two streets
up and over.
Hugged a candy wrapper and two
used Kleenex. Fingered chopsticks
on my window. Rolled a tumbleweed
through a hoop of icy air. Whistled
a military tune. Sent an Airmail,
Special-Delivery letter to this
address, Sealed With a Kiss.
Blew smog rings out to sea and
watercolored the sky a breezy
bright blue. Then swept out of
town leaving no forwarding address.

Merrily Cummings Ford

A Tree

As I gaze upon a tree,
is it really thou I see.
How high you reach into
the sky, I can't believe
my eye.
What joy you bring in
the spring when with full
color thou awakens, and
in the fall thy changing
brilliance appears, telling
us the season's end is near.
Then silently you bow to
winters coat, and lie dormant
before the world.
To some it may seem odd,
but to me it's the hand of God.

Roland H. Stecker

"Thinking About Life"

What makes people so sad?
Is it something they saw that was bad?
Or something made them mad?
Something happened to their mom and dad?
Some people have some fun
But that's because they're with someone
Are they afraid to die?
To say good-bye?
To never be here?
To wonder if they still care
To talk with your friends
Who listens and understands
To feel you had to leave
To see what's it like to be free?
To have a dream
About wishing you were still a teen
To think about what's true?
A wish or you?

Marie Mak

Untitled

Cupid shot his arrow
It landed on my heart
We both gave it a chance
But our minds were far apart

I think about you often
I hope you do the same
You'll forever be remembered
For our love was no game

Korinn Scepka

The Mophead Down The Street

The mophead down the street
is really really dumb
his favorite veg a beet
his favorite fruit a plum

The mophead down the street
has a ugly pet toad
it just takes one little car
and that toad lies flat in the road

The mophead down the street
has long stringy red hair
he combs it very neat
but that is very rare

The mophead of down the street
moved away last week
now I really miss him....
NAH... JUST HIS SISTER KIM!

Shawn D. Bray

"Daydream Believer"

Daydream believer,
is that to much to ask?
To just look at the sky,
as I lie in the grass.

To hide from the world,
in my own little place.
To keep from the people,
to have my own space.

To be all alone,
is all that I want.
To escape all my fears,
and memories that haunt.

The lies the deception,
it's too much to bear.
Do they realize I'm gone?
I don't really care.

Daydream believer,
is that to much to ask?
To pretend I'm Ok.,
And forget my past.

Liz Hammett

Ruminations

As inevitable as our next breath,
is the certainty of our death.
Why not, therefore, enjoy this life
instead of filling it with strife.
Let peace and joy forever reign,
anathema to sadness, pessimism and pain.
With but one life to life,
let us not only take but give.
If a friend acts in a manner kyphotic,
why respond or act neurotic.
Never forget life is a precious gift,
permit it to give us a lift.
Take time to smell a flower,
or from the sea, experience its power.

Patrick N. Hart

Oh, Hi, Sweetheart

Your name came up
In conversation, again,
The other evening...
And when the laughter
Had subsided, we
Passed on to topics
Of more serious intent.

R. Tipton Biggs

Daily Beauty

The beauty in a day
isn't only for a while,
And if you see you may find
It may even make you smile,
For all God's creatures
He placed here on earth,
And commanded go forth and multiply,
They all give their birth.
The beauty of each new life
Starts fresh each dawning day
It's the world God created,
He wanted it that way.
So look into the sunrise
And always keep in mind
that what you see this morning
at sunset can still look fine.

William Robbins

Poetry

Poetry is another form of expression
It can go in any direction
But it has to have a start
Must come deep from the heart
It can show you have love
Given to us from heaven above
Or it can show deep sorrow
Like there is no tomorrow
Those of you that have that gift
Surely give many of us a lift
Poetry is like a fine song
It makes us feel like we belong
So poets, keep up the parade
And peace of mind is made
Look up to the stars and the moon
And a poetry phrase will come to you soon
True poems will never die
As long as there is a sky!

William Anderson

It's Got To Be Now

It's got to be now,
It cannot be then.
It's got to be you,
It cannot be them.
The youth of the future, the present;
Right Now!
Just look in the mirror
And like what you've found.
Drugs, Alcohol, Sex and Life.
There are choices to make
That you may not like.
They have to be made
They just can't wait.
It's got to be now.
Or you'll find it's too late!
Set your standards early.
Don't put it off.
It's got to be you.
It's got to be now!

Meghan Denson

Research Item

Roll over dear, let's make it fast
I've got the eight-fifteen to catch.
What do you mean, you can't erect
I gave you one long kiss, correct?
Performance is what I demand
Now do be quick about it else
To-morrow I shall have to find
Someone whose "gun" is set to fire.

Rita Carl

Soul

The Soul.
It don't matter the race.
It's the skull behind the face;
The frame to every picture,
And the rock from which I sit here.

The Soul.
It's the rock behind
The shrubbery,
It's our mind without the body.

Soulless, we are but shells
Washed up on the shore
Of the great e t e r n a l sea,
You and me.

Without the soul
We are dead
You see.

Neil S. Cox

My Red Ribbon

I have a ribbon it's red. I take
it everywhere I go, even to bed.

I use my Red Ribbon for everything
I do. If you had a Red Ribbon
you could too.

My Red Ribbon is shining bright.
It's like a star in the sky, my
Red Ribbon it's a beautiful sight.

My Red Ribbon is like a lucky
charm, when it's with me, I
feel no harm.

I know that my Red Ribbon
will be here, because I will
keep it forever near.

Kelly Jackson

The Prepared

I open my heart
It falls on lines
Nowhere else

They read it
With judging eyes
Eyes that cannot
Read me.
Still I'm scared
For they know me not.
Like on a stage
For the first time
They'll judge me by my work.

Mariza Snyder

Love Is Like A Seed

Love is like a seed.
It grows with time.
Provided there are no weeds.

Love is like a seed.
It blooms into a flower.
Its beauty lasts for all eternity.

Love is like a seed.
It grows from day to day, hour by hour.
It needs patience and care.
Just like the flower.

Love is like a seed.

Michelle Allison

Tree Of Life

Yet of little life
it hast,
it longs of memories
of the past.

How the fallen leaves and limbs
now mourn.
When once they could
wither the storm.

Now the trunk is
weak and hollow.
There are bound to be
less years to follow.

Kimberly Day Groom

In God "We" Trust

This man of faith, he walks with God.
It is a path that many trod.
He has no riches, owns no land.
He only heeds the Lord's command.

This man of riches walks with man.
Works at his job, earns all he can.
He buys his pleasures, likes to spend.
And very seldom helps his friend.

This Godly man will only ask
For strength and mind to do his task,
To help the poor and those in need
And ask for faith that they may heed.

That rich man's wants will never cease
His troubled mind cannot find peace.
Without his money, life's a bore
He wants a job that pays him more.

The Godly and the rich men met
They found a quiet place to set.
The rich man's troubles seem to cease.
They both departed and went in peace.

Lois M. Wellman

The Crow

There is a dark crow.
It is the crow which stands alone.
It flies alone,
It dreams alone,
It is alone, and has no home.

This crow's dream is long gone.
This crow's life dictates dawn,
And it has no hope.
It never knew hope.

Its lonely cry goes unheard
Its hollow soul goes unwatched

No one cares what happens to it,
No one cares what has happened to it.
If it were to die, no one would know.
It is all but dead, it is so alone.
The crow is not bitter,
It doesn't even bother anymore.
If flies with a bottomless emptiness,
It stands alone.

I am the crow.

Perlette Jura

"An Everyday Bum"

Orange and round
It rolls to the ground
He cuts off the peel
For this fruit is his meal

The snow is falling
Winter is calling
He has no home
He just seems to roam

As night fall will arrive
He will fight to stay alive
On a bench he will lay
Though, there he will not stay

Where next shall he go?
He'll never know
Feeding off liter
He awaits a long winter

Leann M. Rockford

My Love

When we're together
it seems like it will last forever;
but when we're apart,
how lonely my heart.

Because you are my love

I remember the first time we met,
I don't think I'll ever forget
the times we shared,
the more we cared.

Because you are my love

It's hard for me to say this,
but I'll leave you with a kiss.
Please don't forget me
for in the future you'll see
it was better this way—-

Because you are my love

Theresa Jensen

"The Last Game"

We make it to the last inning.
It seems like we are just beginning.
The fastest pitcher is on the mound,
but look at what I just found -
a hole in right field.
My confidence I must build.
I fouled it off twice.
That pitcher could for once be nice.
She pitched a ball -
My heart began to stall.
She pitched a strike,
Which I didn't like.
I knew I was out,
I lost the game,
but there's no reason to pout,
or to hide my name.
I won't put my head down,
I won't shed a tear,
I'll have another chance next year!

Lisa Kelly

The Seasons

Winter
It tests our patience.
It shows our vulnerability.
It humble us
Until we come to accept it.

Spring
It melts our hearts.
It is forgiving.
It heals.
It lifts our souls.
It gives life to all things.

Summer
It refreshes.
It is kind.
It allows all things to grow.
It brings us closer to life.

Autumn
It is generous.
It is giving and labors for all.
It quiets the spirit to prepare for rebirth.

Mary Ann Schaeffer

A Love Not Wanted

When I first heard your heavenly voice,
it was a sign to me.
I opened up my heart to you and
let my feelings free.
As I gazed into your loving eyes,
I hoped my dreams would be fulfilled.
Somehow I guess I always knew
your feelings were not as real.
Thus began my painful journey,
of learning to let you go.
But even to this day, the thought
of you still makes me glow.
Still I must continue in vain,
to let my feelings die.
Proceed to fool my heart and live
this temporary lie.
Yet the truth is something that's
hard to try and turn away.
Within my heart and soul, my love
for you will always stay.

Melody M. Kindt

The House By The River

The house by the river is my home,
It was there that I was born,
It was there that I met you,
By the river oh so blue,
The house by the river is my home.

I stood by the river on that day,
All the joy in my life had flown away,
But then you came alone,
Just like a pretty song,
Now the house by the river is our home.

We are so happy by the river in our home
And we live a merry life there alone,
We will never drift apart,
Cause I love you my sweetheart,
And the house by the river is our home.

Owen F. Luster

If Love Were

If love were a rainbow
It would last until the end
But rainbows fade away
And broken hearts don't mend.

If love were a butterfly
Its colors would glitter
But butterflies grow old
And angry words are still bitter.

If love were a book
The words would just flow
But the pages turn yellow
And sorrow's unknown.

If love were a color
It would be bright, bold and red
But colors fade away
And there are words left unsaid.

If love were a flower
Its petals would shine
But flowers wither away
I wish your were still mine.

Megan Rierson

Best Of Time

Those hot days have gone
it's cold now and all seem
happy that Summer is done

Then comes the Holidays
which is a happy occasion
in many ways

The Holiday Season is the
best time of the year for
most people receive that
special greeting

And the trimming, cooking
and going to parties makes
it the best of times along
with the tasty eating

During the Holiday Season
love relationships and other
relations seem to do well

It could be the sighting of
beautiful Holiday lights or
the sounding of a Xmas Bell.

Lazell Morgan

Raven

The Raven is my flag
Its cold sharp eyes
Its hated head
When love cannot exist
And hatred is all I have
When I'm not a being
When stiffness and cold
can only mean
Love
I am the Raven I soar
And then .... Pain
I fall ....
I am the raven cold, dark, and dead
For all the world to see
as cold as death can be
It only means happiness for me.

Lisa Dryer

Untitled

Rigid and scraggly exterior
Its demeanor coincides
The prestigious ivory emerges
Creating a prehistoric image.
How spectacular they are!

A thundering applause,
as they trample through their land,
not even knowing they are being pursued.
Innocent animals just trying to remain.
Glamorous, they are not, to some.
I understand this untamed creature,
their beauty and grace I distinguish.

Kimberly Pence

Free

Free is nothing on this earth.
It's just a word to fill up space.

If there was such a thing as free,
Then why would they have made money.

As the world goes around,
We stand still on the ground.
People are homeless and people are rich.

Neither helps the other out.
No one knows what the world's about.

Stacy L. Allen

My Heart

It's lonely here sometimes
It's never cold
But sometimes feels vacant

It has a voice sometimes
It speaks to me
When life seems misleading

It makes choices for me at times
When I'm confused or afraid
Or troubled with what lies ahead

It warms me sometimes
With the touch of a gentle hand
Or a simple smile

It shelters me at times
When dishonest words are spoken
And helps me see the truth

It hurts sometimes
But in time, it helps heal those wounds
And makes me strong again

Lisa J. Parker

A Dream Of Friendship

If I had a dream
Just one dream
But fortunate or dull
To hold on and pull
I'll still remain in Heaven's net
Which still remains as yet unmet
May this night end
And new day begin
Nobody loves you more than a friend
All day and all night
You hold your bear tight
And stare at a book
That has an awkward look
North, South, East, or West
Friendship is always the best.

Tamara Burnett

Not Me I See

I look in the mirror
It's not me that I see
someone else is there
with a different personality.
She's quiet
and keeps to herself
knowing nothing but her own
She doesn't see
the world around her
believing she lives alone.
Only flashbacks and memories
roam in her mind
no laughter nor cry
just a vision of people
a vision of my mimes
Call it depression
call it mood swing
Whatever it may be
I look in the mirror
And it's not me that I see.

Sara Leon-Guerrero

Summertime

Jesus saves
Ivana buys
The Pope tries
Presidents lie
Hungry children cry
Corruption
Deception
Limited perception
No protection
A little dab'll do ya
Harmful rays
Unemployed days
No more easy lays
Crowded bars
Crowded jails
Empty lakes...
...for Christ's sake
- the man does work in mysterious ways.

Paul Rusconi

A Baby's Prayer

My Mommy's up in heaven
Jesus paved the way

Daddy's gone to join her
I'll see them both someday

When life on earth is over
and time will be no more

I'll walk the road to Heaven
and knock upon the door

Wanda J. Branscum

Blind Silence

Hidden images never seen
laughter never heard of
tears that fall into a river
filled with broken dreams
let the river steal your soul
and count the endless waves
then find your hands ...
let them reach out
and search for the things most wanted
the things that will never be found.

Susan Shin

To Yourself And Others

May your thoughts be good
Just like some heavenly food.
Set goals of ambition -
Let that be your inspiration.

Speak words that are uplifting.
Through the day be they fitting.
As swords let your words be.
They are free and at no fee.

Do a good deed every day.
You will be happy all the way.
Let "Prepared" be your guide.
Good deeds will always abide.

May your omissions be few.
They will keep you true.
Do not let things be omitted.
By them you will be benefited.

Thaddeus Capek

Meaning Of Life

Some people say life is just living,
just living from day to day.
But it has to have a meaning
or time just fades away.

You have to have a goal
or you just live to take up space.
You have to have a meaning
to put a soul behind your face.

You need to know that you believe,
to put a reason in your mind
a reason to strive to go ahead
to never fall behind.

Your beliefs should be a foundation
holding your soul together,
for your body will die and rot away;
your soul will stay forever.

You may not understand,
why some people are forgiving.
They have found the secret.
The meaning of life is giving.

Scott Bland

Just Call On Jesus

When you are feeling down,
just look in the air and
call on Jesus, 'coz he is always there.

When I look to the sky, who is it I see?
It's Jesus, Jesus looking down on me.

When my tears start to fall, who
will wipe them away, and give
me his love forever and a day?

When I feel like I'm falling, who
puts me back on my feet and
gives me his love, so tender and sweet?

Together we will make it and at
the end we'll win,
'Coz if someone can help us honey,
It's Jesus, it's him.

Valerie Aguilar

Two People

Just one look feeds the flame.
Just one smile ignites the fire.
Two people hand and hand.
Two people make a stand.
One pair there so aware.
One pair it's their affair.
They take the time to realize.
They take the time it's no surprise.
Two people are happy now.
Two people are happy wow.
It was just one touch.
It was oh so much.
One kiss feeds the flame.
One kiss still remains.
In a sun lit day not much to say.
In a moon lit night they hold so tight.
Two people act as one.
Two people have so much fun.
Every day they live.
Every day they give.

Kevin Colgin

"Jack Frost"

Jack Frost came to my house
Just the other night.
He painted all the rooftops,
In a dazzling snowy white.
He painted lovely pictures
On all my window panes.
He painted hills and valleys,
with pine trees standing tall.
He also painted all those stars.
Above this lovely scene.
And I knew that he'll come
back again.
So I'll keep my windows clean.

Tina Weum

Robbery

What about the truth?
Justice obscured
Rape of my emotions
Mental gunshots in the night
Dark and light, live or die
Take it all back
Innocence lost
On a hard cold floor
Safety is a lie
It's Russian roulette
Reality fades to black
How do you face this?
A man playing God
Holds my life in his hands
This is a horrible knowledge
And I want to give it back
Voices rising and fading
Time standing still
Where did I go?
And where am I now?

Tracy Goellner

God Made Us

God made us to grow
like flowers,

With His good and
Holy powers

He is great, He is kind
He made us with His Holy mind

Tracy Power

The Door

It was so beautiful
Last night
So cold and clear
With so many stars
Lighting the heavens,
That there was no
Room for fear.

I cracked my door open
To take a peep outside,
And the glory took
My breath away,
So I opened the door wide

My heart had been so heavy.
And filled with such pain,
But the wonder of the night,
Gave me new hope again.

Whenever you are weary
depressed and uptight,
Just open up your door
And you will let in God's light.

Patricia Miller

Listen To My Cry

Reach out your hand and touch me,
Let me know you're there.
And that I'm not alone in this
Sadness and despair.
Open your mind and listen,
For I'm about to speak,
About a lonely dreamer
Whose words are growing weak.
Share with me your courage.
Help me to be strong.
I feel so very by myself
Show me that I'm wrong.
Let me deep into your heart
Teach me to be a friend,
Someone who is trustworthy.
On whom you can depend.

Stay by me forever,
Don't let me walk alone.
And your love is where I'll lay my roots,
And build myself a home.

Laura Linfoot

A Mother's Heart

Oh Mother's heart filled with sorrow,
let your heart be still.
Someday in the distant future,
you'll come to the top of the hill.
Should lightning strike in the
same place twice?
Who then with anger and pain
will pay such a costly price?
A rose signifying your separation,
you struggle in vain to hold on.
Between two friends, gently is
woven a loving bond.
The fear of losing all that you have,
is what makes you hold on tight.
But you know that given to God.
He'll make things turn out right.
Oh mother's heart rejoice and be glad,
because your child will never be sad.

Patricia L. Johnson

Moments Lost In Time

Come sit by me, he said
Let's listen to the mellow tunes;
Remembering all the times we danced
and daylight came too soon!

The laundry's piled high again
The children's clothes need mending.
There's just so many things to do
Was the answer she was sending.

As time went by, he'd ask again
Come sit by me, he pleaded.
And yet the same reply was heard
So much to do!.. her energy depleted.

And then one day - the music stopped -
With tear-stained eyes; in lonely gaze
I'll sit by you, she whispered softly.
I'll sit by you, and gently laid the flowers
on his grave.

Sandra M. Weiler

Black And Beautiful

The beauty of being black
Lies in the knowledge
of your blackness.
It is not the features
That mask the face
Nor the hue of the darkness.
It is the personality
That is projected
Through the level of your consciousness.
It is not your personal achievement
As a black man
But your positive contribution
To the black clan.
It is your ability
To deny society
The right to define black beauty.
It is not what is with out
But what is within,
That makes you
Black and beautiful.

Nia Gaskin

If This Is Life...

Love is fighting against hate,
Life is near to death.
Coldness is reaching,
Happiness is closer to desperation.

Peace is driven apart,
No smiles left, only tears falling.
No use to fight for justice,
The bad are making the rules.

If this is life, what is death?
If this is love, what is hate?
If this is right, what is wrong?
Tell me what is wrong...

Sermila Sposato

The Hunter

He slowly brought up his spear
Looking, stalking, everything's clear

The hunt, the chase, the end of the race
The hidden smile upon his face

The sky is blue, the birds grey
The hunter gaining the buffalo prey

The spear held high, head arched back
Buffalo meat on the Indian rack.

Nicole Converse

About Life?

Life is great.
Life is so beautiful.
Life is the most pressure thing
A person could have.

The world
The world would be a better.
Place to live.
If people would only think of
Peace on earth.
In steady of war.
God gave us a pressure gift
of life to live by peace
not war.

Shellie Patton

In Spite Of

faults that we have
life that we share
smiles that we fake
inside blind hate
dances in the night
prayers to the light
blows dealt in fear
looks resemble sneers
words that harsh speak
triumphs over meek
colors fight, so bright
sniffs of lady white
lovers multitude
our bad attitudes
because of... we love
in spite of He saves.

Oliver W. Wilson Jr.

Untitled

From the pits of hell you lifted me
like a giant beam of sunlight
you walk before me.
Following you, I can see myself now
casting the dark shadows behind
that follow me.
I shall not look back
for I see only the light of your love.
Ruby my love, my life
now and forever.

Regina Sonnenschein

Too Soon The Past

Why must the now come
like a hurricane
not to be slowed,
to become the then
gone so fast?

Damn the moment
gone too fast.
Slow the sunset,
make it last.
Enjoy the now

as it becomes
a yesterday.
Live it well,
the today that is
tomorrow's past.

Patricia J. Yankosky

Sherry

If I could fly above the hills
Like clouds upon the wind,
I'm sure I would see marvelous things
To make this old face grin.
If I could swim throughout the sea
Like a wandering ocean whale,
The things I could see could
Be written in a poetic tale.
But I am just an animal
That walks upon the earth,
And I will one day learn of death,
Like I have learned of birth.

Violet Christian

The Corridor Of Truth

Dreams are formed in our youth
Like comets colliding in space ..

Each flung searching for truth
in some far away place ..

Our dreams are like these stars
revolving like Venus and Mars ..

Sleep is the mother of dreams
as thoughts are gathered it seems ..

To recall while in deep slumber
the smiles of friends or endless numbers ..

The time of our youth is performed
in dreams once foretold ..

The dance of our dreams are adorned
with mud, diamonds and gold ..

Each person has a treasure box
where all their dreams are stored ..

Each dream is waiting there ..
to be opened and adored ..

For dreams are the corridors by which we
visit out youth..
But in reality - Dreams are the Corridor of
Truth

Lyle Edward Martinez

Cemetery

Tombstones sticking outward,
Like nails in the attic,
Icicles of the dirt.
To death's door
The key lies.
R.I.P. and do not
Wake their peace.
Leave the gates.
Light goes,
Dark comes.
Scared.

Vishal Kumar

Walking On Eggs

Bluest fractures
line
your ashen cheek
as silent
footsteps
leave
no
trace
in the hollow

Tracie H. Cobban

A Friend

You are a friend,
like no one else could be,
You laugh at almost
everything, and you know
exactly, how to have fun.
No one else, could ever
top you, never in a
lifetime, you will always,
be a friend, in any case
at all, I will always be
there, and, I will never
leave you, you are the
only friend, that could
ever be my best.

Rebekah Bruce

A Quiet Love

If I can't love you in public
Like other people do
Then I will have to settle for
The silence of me and you
I have you on my mind
In my thoughts, and in my heart
I've suffered quietly right
from the very start
I'll love you everyday
As if you were only mine
Until something in my heart
Says we've run out of time
And when you are gone.
And only memories remain
I can truly say I Loved You
And you loved me the same

Vincent Noschese

Myself

My hair is golden
Like the sun
My eyes are blue
Like the sky
My spirit is wild
Like the wind
My heart holds love
for everyone
I live in the land
Like a flower
I eat the seeds
Like a bird

Trina Monet Stafford

Her Guide

She sits,
listening,
waiting,
She hears him,
She knows he has come,
He kneels,
kisses her,
He guides her to his carriage,
gently,
carefully,
He lifts her to her seat,
Off they go,
To the life,
After her death.

Kelly L. Van Wagoner

This Lady

This lady, a person of two
Lives as one in my head
While I am in bed,
I think one of her is you.

It pains me to think of her this much
My head spins in a daze.
She has placed me in a maze
From the very first touch.

Logic burns in my desire
Fun far beyond sex and pleasure.
A mood...too vexed to measure.
Passionate glances kindle the fire.

In my heart, on a plaque,
Letters engraved on gold:
"YOU I LOVE", written so bold,
Stands in my mind from front to back.

So much love in heart and soul,
Please tell me what's enough.
This one cannot judge that stuff
My bodily cart might hold.

Keith A. Whittington

Trapped

Trapped inside
Living in a crust of porcelain shell
The inside torn and battered
Talk through
An open flowing gate
Where fears can not escape
Keeping inside
All the problems you try to hide
Talk
Nothing
Quiet
Nothing
Trapped...

Tonya Jamie Brewer

Halloween

The pumpkins go marching one by one
Long after the day is done
A silly grin, a fearsome scowl
A tiny squeak, a scary howl

So if you go out tonight
You might just get a fright
A black cat go's scooting by
A witch on her broom high in the sky

The pumpkins go marching one by one
Long after the day is done
A fearsome sight and one so scary
That even the gob-o-lins are wary

In the morning with the rising sun
Pumpkins are sleeping one by one
Among the corn, along the fence rail
And if you don't believe my tale

Go out tonight when the setting sun
Bids farewell, another day is done
So just sit back and watch the fun
And see the pumpkins march one by one!

Nancy Branam

A New Era - Fear Not

Look upward brave men, have faith.
Look upward, oh this shining hour.
Can you not feel its wondrous power?
Can you not see the miracle?

Men from the fields, hardened and true,
Look upward and see.
Why quiver, why flee
The storm which threatens you?
For it will pass, and in its wake
Will come the clear blue sky.
Look upward, don't ask why.
Look upward and see—HEAVEN!

Morton L. Divack

My Vision

Sitting in a park
Looking all around
Watching people
Act like clowns.

The sun shinning
Through off white clouds
Made me feel warm inside

Sitting in a park
Looking all around
There you were
Before my eyes

No words could I speak
My heart skipped a beat
Thinking to myself
How could this be.

Getting up to take a walk
Turned around and you were gone
My vision of you
Didn't last long

Rita L. Maurer

Love

Love is a best friend,
Love is a mom,
Love is a girl-friend,
Love is a prom,

Love is to meet,
Love is bring present,
Love is sweet
Love is giving a present,

Love is hearty,
Love is slow,
Love is a party,
Love makes you go,

Love is breakfast in bed,
Love is poodle's bark,
Love is a nicely combed head,
Love is walk in the park,

Love is love,
It's happy and gay,
Love is love, for all I can say.
LOVE

Mike Anthony Polizzi

Extreme Love

Love is here
Love is free
Love is here between you and me.

As we lay here tonight
All alone in the dark
I want to love you
With all my heart.

We would make love is that alright?
And not inside, but out in the moonlight.

So get here now before
I explode, and I won't
love you fast but I
would love you slow.

I would hold you close
And show you, you we're mine

Because I love you a lot
And glad you're by my side.

Veronica Hall

Love

Love is gentle,
Love is kind,
Love is forever,
Love you can't hide,
Love is easy,
If you can find it,
But for me I cannot succeed.

To fall in love,
To feel like a someone,
To reach the top of someone's heart,
To be locked in it forever,
To love the human,
To search a life,
Love-forever-until eternity ends.

Meagan Reeves

Love Is

Love is not wind blowing in your hair.
Love is not a person in your life.
Love is a feeling in your heart.

Love is not a gift from somebody.
Love is not a pleasant fragrance.
Love is something you find.

Love is not something you make.
Love is not words from somebody.
Love is something you have for somebody.

If you don't have any
of these things there' one
thing you'll always have.
and that is LOVE!

Lindsey Clark

Untitled

I see two children by a meadow
Laughing, prancing, dancing in spring
I see a bed of tulips in a garden
Laughing, prancing, dancing in spring
A purple kite flies high in the sky
Laughing, prancing, dancing in spring
Two butterflies flitter by
Laughing, prancing, dancing in spring
Spring is always a gay and joyous time
Where love is within
And beauty outside

Tanya Sinning

Our Love

Love is Happiness
Love is Tears
Love is Hope
Love is Fear

Love is Pleasure
Love is Pain
Love is Loss
Love is Gain

Love is Beginnings
Love is Ends
Love is Quarrels
Love is Amends

Love is Remembering
Love is Forgetting
Love is Separating
Love is Uniting

Love is YOU - and - Love is ME
Sharing - Caring - Living - Giving
Most of all - Love is Forgiving

Mary C. Ireland

Remember

I remember the days when
Loves glow was over me.
When your tender touch
made my heart quiver.
When your loving caress
was a dream come true.
When your beautiful smile
conveyed your message of
Love for me.
I remember your eyes that
said, I Love you.
I remember the days when...

Thomas Francis Drapac

Untitled

Tantaric thunder
Loves guiding hand
Oh! Gallant splendor
United bands

A violins brilliance
Forged by man
Your swinging motion
Time like sand

The eyes of a child
Your blessed demands
A light, a wilderness
Singing strands

Steven R. DeLuca

Walk The Green Valleys

I walk the green valleys,
Linked arm to arm with my Sally
With the blessing of Father O'Mallay.

I walk the burns and braes
In the smoky haze;
Like sheep, my thoughts graze.

I row my boat around the coves and bays,
As the sun on the water plays.
On my heart, love lightly weighs.

J. Pierritz

Why He Took You

You were so friendly and so
loving...
But God took you away all
for nothing...

I can't understand because you
were loved so much...
Doesn't he understand, how we were
all so touched...

Such a beautiful person gets taken
away...
It's really not fair, there's so much
I have to say...

I miss you, love you, and wish you
were here...
What can I do, but wipe away
my tear.

Lori A. Deluca

Kissed By The Sun

Feeling the warmth of the sun;
Lying, resting, warm and secure
There is nothing here, only me,
But I am not;
All the world slips away
And there is only the sun.
It becomes a part of me,
It wraps me with its warm blanket;
I slip away in dreamy thoughts;
I sleep with the kiss of the sun
Bathing me in its warm glow,
And as the day draws to an end
The sun loses its touch;
But the feeling remains, warm.

Merita Bodenheimer

Girl In A Classroom

Lonely eyes
make believe
happiness
come to me

Never you
never me
never hope
never see

Look at you
you look away
leave right now
not much to say

Another time
another place
some other face
she knows her place

Please just remember me.

Montgomery A. Lewis

Life Wage

Sittin' with mind a maze
lookin' at all the days
As you become of age
what paths of your life
will be the wage.

Look at all the turns you made
How many turns went the wrong way.
The paths were rough but
Followed them all the way.

Kathy Fisher

Untitled

Beautiful moon-lit nights and you
make everything feel right.
Warm winds blowing gently through the
air
being with you, I haven't a care.

Hold me gently, that's my wish,
Once again to feel your kiss.
To feel your strength from inside
a safe place sometimes for me to hide.

Pull me close so I will know
you really need me and won't let me go.
Let me feel your warm embrace
touch me gently on my face.

Stare down into my loving eyes
and maybe then you'll realize
that I love you more than I can say,
a love that's growing every day.

Patricia Hatfield

Snow Is Falling

Snow flakes are falling.
Making the ground turn white.
The wind in the tree's
Make the loose snow dance in the breeze
Snow is falling
Snow is falling
Making for a winter wonderland.
Children smile as snow falls
on there upturned face,
Snow is falling
Snow is falling
Making for our white snow
Covered winter wonderland.

Sharon Rutledge

Eyes In The Looking Glass

Eyes in the looking glass, so
many different kinds.
Eyes full of sorrow and woe from
sights in the past.
Children's eyes small and bright.
So full of mischief and curiosity.
Eyes blue, brown or green.
Eyes that are flirty, demanding
or strong.
Eyes that are piercing and make
you feel bad.
Sunken-in eyes from hunger and pain.
Huge round eyes of someone sad.
Eyes that think of life going by fast.
Many different kinds of eyes in
the looking glass.

Nancy R. Jones

The Brightness of Life

Morning the light on all things
Merry the sweet bird sings
Blue the skies purity brings
Fresh the air in mountain springs

Rolling winds sway the hill of trees
Roar the sounds of crashing seas
Calming the waves of life decrees
Happy are those in times like these

J. W. Van de Holst

Dear Jane,

I sit and try to remember,
Maybe it was late September,
All the leaves were turning brown,
As they begin to lay me down.

When I awoke in early dawn,
I saw that you were already gone.
Ten years now have gone by,
And still I wonder why.

I guess we knew it was wrong,
Thinking the night would be long.
I have been seeking high and low,
A love, which I can never know.

I have heard your life in verse,
I can not imagine anything worse.
Oh, that one crazy night of fun,
Now for us both, we are done.

I pray for the powers to be,
To release me from my HIV.
I pray to be, so very brave,
As they lower me to my grave. Giving
you my life, John

Roger D. Ashenfelter

Our Love

Our love has given
Me the strength to go on.
So now we have to figure
Out what went wrong.

Was it the love inside
The tears that said,
Hello and goodbye.

Was it a thing to cherish.
From our time past.
Could we have talked,
To make it last.

In our minds nothing
Could go wrong.
But now our love,
Is totally gone.

Kelly Robinson

Castles In The Sand

I took a walk through memories ruins
Met someone I thought was me
Chill winds start to blow
I just don't know
And another castle
Washes out to sea
I see the tide coming in
Washing away tears from years ago
Some castles I hid away
To save for that dreamers someday
They're the ones
That continue to grow
With foundations of love
Blue sky and rainbows above
All built with my own two hands
My dreams still alive
And I did survive
To keep on building
Castles in the sand

Kameron C. Miranda

Untitled

I have touched your soul
more than my own.
I have heard thoughts
you have not voiced.
I would have never expected
to have known you
in this lifetime.
I will tell you this now,
and carry it within my soul
forever.
I love you.
And even though these words
were made weak
with idle tongues,
my will is strong,
and a part of you
will be with me through
the incomprehensible time
we call eternity.....

Kathryn Storm

Never Alone

Man is not born into this world alone—
Mother has to be there.

Man need not live his life alone—
As long as love is there.

Man need not leave this life alone—
As long as God is there.

Mary E. Guyer

Untitled

What did you feel, Mary,
Mother of Christ,
As dying, he hung on the cross
Were you proud of his faith,
was there gain in your loss,
Did the pearl of his pain
shine out of the grief
Or were you all grief
for your man-child destroyed?
Could you know then
What is true for all men,
With so great a loss
How can there be gain?
Ah, the balance is there
like the sun and the rain:
The task is to find
the pearl in the pain.

Rita Gold

"Little Words With A Big Meaning"

Three little words can tell you so
much about the way I feel about you.

They can tell you how much I care
about you, and how I adore you.

They can tell you how considerate
you are, and how precious you are
to me.

These three little words are so
simple and small, but have a big
and special meaning.

I can tell you all of this and
more, but I love you says it all.

Tabitha Weatherford

"There Is A Reason"

For every pain that we
must bear,
For every burden, every care,
For every grief, that bows the
head,
For every tear-drop that
is shed,
There is a reason.
For every hurt,
For every plight,
For every lonely pain-racked
night,
There is a reason.
But if we trust God, as
we should,
It will work out for our good.
He knows the reason.

Katherine E. Richardson

The Train

"Come here peanut!"
my aunt's red hair
the way nana laughs
nana's pretty
hair things
"Come here peanut!"
my aunt's
gold bracelets
on the train
people around me
rocks and trees
"Come here peanut!"
nana's soft face
nana's midnight black hair
"come here peanut"
my aunt's nice face
the way my aunt laughs
"Come here peanut!"
it's time to go home

Krystal Geary

Sacred Moment

The sun not yet begun,
My dreams eclipsing
I rise to consciousness
and my child stirring.
As if without sight,
led by her sound, her scent
her skin beside
my womb still swollen,
I lift her to my open breast.
In that moment
of first touch,
her mouth to my breast,
I thank God.
And in that same moment
I know the dawn wherein
we, no longer
lie flesh beside flesh
yet linger,
grateful that the dawn of that sun
has not yet begun.

Rebecca Keogh

Homeless

My clothes are oh so ragged
My feet are but bare.
I come from a home with no meaning
I'm on the street alone going no where.

My life now has no purpose
I travel aimlessly about,
I go in search of food which someone
May feel bad and share.

I am but one of Gods creatures
who lost his place in life.
Some see and pity me and wonder
What I'm about.

But time will tell if I make it
As I wonder aimlessly about.

Wanda Horner

Untitled

Crashing waves
my getaway

Deep blue sea
green seaweed

An underground world of mine
the treasures it holds

As I walk on the sand
I feel the escape

The waves pull at my legs
like a friend wanting to play

The tide rolls in my thoughts
as I stand on the shore

The currents shift
and guide me to the bottom
to a dark pool of hope
where I see tomorrow

Kathryn Laughlin

Unsolved Meeting

As I lay down at night
My heart feels hurt paralyzed
Stunned by a blinding light.
I feel like I'm slowly dying.
Easing the pain is so hard
To do.
There's a wall in my way and
No matter how I try,
I can't break through.
So many dreams and hopes I pursue.
All on the other side of this wall.
If I could rise to the heavens
I would be able to see and
Feel all the love, hopes and dreams,
That for so many years
I could not see, but
Now that I have risen past the wall-
What should I do?

Sean Johnson

Stranger To Yourself

Walking down the street,
Millions of strangers.
Is one of them you?
Walking down the street,
One stranger left.

Monica Williams

Mother Of Pride

Congratulations!
My most precious gift
From God.

You've been your own man
Even as a child.

I'm full of motherly pride.

No matter how difficult,
You always tried.

As you graduate from
Senior high,

Look at the world with
Open eyes.

Follow your own conscience,

Let the Lord be your guide.

You're never alone,
He's always by your side.

And so am I, your mother of pride.

Renee Antoinette Harris

Courage

Whenever my heart is sinking low,
My smile must never let it show
Whenever the skies are dull and grey,
My laugh must be cheerful anyway
Whenever I think I'll lose all hope,
I must learn to live and cope with
everyday problems that may arise
that try to hide my smile
Or dim my skies. For each new day
invites me to try, to find the courage
needed to live by.

Regina Alexander

Beyond The Sky

Now that you have gone away,
my true, true love has past away.

Away beyond the big blue sky,
with white puffy clouds rolling
gently by and by.

I loved you then,
I love you now,
I shall love you always,
until I can't remember how.

So, the sky may thunder,
the sky may poor,
but only I will know the pain
I feel for my lost love I
shall always endure.

Renee Stanley

Untitled

Guilt haunts, like a hungry beast.
Nipping at my heels, I flee!

I find no escape, like a virus
destroying my mind.

Insanity around every corner,
I wake to face each day with
uncertainty.

Kelene Mabrey

Untitled

My thoughts sincere
My words misguided
I can't help
But twist reality
To be something it isn't
A safe haven
Is what I seek
but I can't find
My common sense
My reflexes quick
My actions clumsy
I can't help
But see myself
For who I am
A struggling individual
Inside
A self-conscious wanna-be
Outside

Natalia Dale

Positive

Being positive is important to one.
Negative only brings people down.
In life one must look forward
As one lives every day.
How else can one continue daily
Every moment within your life?
Life is lived in segments of time
So one needs to be productive
As one lived and breathes,
Life spent in a positive manner
Makes the moments interesting
And a challenge when trials are near.
Tell me, why would some one
Dwell on the bad moments of life
When it is more beneficial to smile
And sail throughout one's life.
Life lived in a good thoughtful attitude
Should be the purpose of one's life.

Margaret Rahn

Why

Why'd you do this?
Never again to see,
Kiss daughter or wife.
So much unfinished business
I can hardly bear to think of this
I'm sorry I couldn't feel your pain,
I couldn't understand
Maybe that's why
No one understood
No one seemed to care
We did
I did.
I guess you just couldn't see the light,
from the darkness.

Sierra Heck

Morning Dove

Morning birds chatter wildly
Mocking Bird, Dove, and Crow
Winging wire to wire to tree
For that reason I don't know
Sparrows chase their tiny prey
And Pigeons bill and coo
But the one that I love most of all
Is the Dove's sweet too-a-loo.

Michael Mitchell

Life

The day is long
never short.
The time drags on
never speeds up
As you sit along the
ocean thinking of,
tomorrow, the waves
crash on the jagged
rocks.
Tomorrow, the new day.
See friends and talk
laugh and giggle.
The life that has been
given to you, you greatly
enjoy.
Free as the waves,
birds and all
You are the ocean
waves and all.

Lisa Pouliot

Searching

As days become so painful
Nights are something I dread
And wishing for anything now
Is way out of my head

But life has so many questions
With no answers to me
Although I'm often told
That's how life's supposed to be

Fear is one thing that's
Been placed in my heart
And I know there's no guarantee
That it will ever depart

As I travel through this
What we call promises land
I realize that I will never
Find out who I really am

With yesterday never leaving
As for tomorrow I can't say
While it's becoming very difficult
Only dealing with today

Tana M. Brown

Dreamer

Have you ever thought...
No hope for things sought?
All work and no play,
Living day to day.
That's no way to go,
For this, I do know,
Be optimistic,
Not a lunatic,
There are others now,
Spouse, kids, pets we vow.
Be responsible,
No need to quibble!
Those days of the past,
Memories do last!
Everyday I dream,
For hours, it may seem.
House to call my own,
One without a loan.
Hearing their laughter,
Forever after!

Ronnie Tumbleson

Reflections Of A Retiree

No shrill alarm, no jangling phones,
No hungry mate, no child bemoans.
I waken now, do I arise
Or stay in bed and close my eyes,
To dredge up pictures of the past?
The bones are old, the movements slow
I have no plans, no place to go.
I've lived in peace, I've lived in joy
Survived a war, and even bore
Four lovely girls, a handsome boy.

It's nice to lie abed
Reliving moments good and bad
To daydream about old loves
And reminisce excitements had.
But I need my coffee, my stomach growls
The telephone rings, my pussycat howls.
So here I am, and here I'll stay
Till in God's own good time
I've lost my heart and soul
And will to make a rhyme.

Lois Sperling

Time And World

Time is life in the fast lane
No one stops, and pays attention
To what happens around them
We laugh once cry the other
I don't stop because I
Have no time in my life
To pay attention to see what's
Happening to us and to the world
We don't have time to see sunsets
We don't have time to watch snowfalls
We don't see the changes in the world
We don't watch the leaves fall in fall
We can't see changes in us
We don't barely make homemade meals
We just don't see the
changes in the world

Sarah Schermann

The Age of Aids

David had to fight Goliath
Noah had the ark to build
Mary had to do God's will
Moses had his ten commandments
Jesus had his cross to bear
But what purpose has Aids here?

Aids does not come from love
Aids is not born of hate
Aids does not discriminate
All genders and races are what it erases

It preys on the small and the weak
It even brings down the big and strong
Sometimes the disease progresses fast
Sometimes it is painfully long

Aids is not the latest fashion
With Aids we need compassion
There is no shame no one to blame
Aids can bring anyone to their knees
Aids is a deadly terminal disease

Nancy DeCarlo

The Hands Of Time

No matter where you're going
Nor the time that's showing
My love for you keeps growing
Until the end of time.

The hand of time are turning
While my heart is yearning
With my body burning
For your sweet love...

Silently, you lay sleeping
As dawn come slowly creeping
To find me quietly weeping
For the time we've lost....

The hands of time are sweeping
My heart, your love is keeping
Loves rewards are reaping
Through out eternity.....

Wanda Sue McGhee

Blue Air

Gregory Clark
Northwest woods baby,
born in a cedar shake house
built by Bob Kaufman,
whose room in the woods
close behind, your brother
led us up the trail to see.

Gregory Clark
Deadwood creek flows
in your bones, blackberry juice
runs wild in your veins.
Legs sturdy as Douglas fir
kicked their way to an early dawn.

Gregory Clark
you rest warm, light on my heart -
fawn hair, lips round as the
Ashley wood stove which will
heat your wet winters -.
Walk with vigilance this rugged valley,
travel easy in the blue air of my love.

Margaret Hoskins

Lonely

What does it mean?
Not having any friends,
Or not having happiness.
I don't seem to be lonely
I am always happy
Yet as I sit and wonder,
I wonder who I am
I look at myself,
Seeing my faults
As well as my good points.
It seems so funny
That others don't seem to worry.
Do they know?
Have they found the answer?
Do they know who they are?
I'm not sure who I am,
Or who I will be.
If you find the solution
Would you tell me please?

Mary Anne Greene

There Is No Life....

There is no life, no love, no sea....
Not once you've abandoned me....
There is no chance to start a new...
There is just no life dear, After you.

A long hard road that I must bear...
This heavy burden to find you there...
For I'm not willing to let you go.
Not with all that I now know.

There is no life, no love, no sea...
No way to call this being free...
There is no chance I'll start a new...
There's just no life dear, after you....

Rachel Armstrong

Paper Nail

Living my life like a paper nail.
Not strong at all. Weak.
But I'm easily driven.
I break under little pressure.

Fire rules my life.
Death fills my head.
Hatred feeds my heart.
But I don't care.

Soon I'll be worm food.
Forgotten by all.
Just wait. I'll return.
You'll regret what you did.

I'll be the most dreaded spirit.
You'll run from me.
Don't try to hide.
I'll find you, you'll see.

Soon this paper nail will turn to steel.
I'll be the strongest being ever.
But I will not be driven.
And won't break under anything.

Michelle Moses

Friendship

True friendships found deep in the heart,
not what the mind portrays.
It reaches out for every part
for the one in need today.

Your heart must be left open,
to hear the plea come through.
Your heart must be quite trusting.
To allow the pain of truth.

The heart be filled with honesty,
never to be unkind.
Never to break the promises.
That sharing has brought in time.

Don't break the bond of trusting,
for honesty turns to lies.
All that's left — is the fussing,
of a friendship that's suffered and died.

Be true to yourself and your friend,
never may you part.
Because of loose lip gossip,
of people who have NO heart

Tonya K. Garrett

Untitled

Take a Dream
Nurture it.
Believe in it.
Achieve it.
Life.

Lynton V. Harris

A Mother's Hope

When you were born, I had such dreams
Of all that you could be,
That thru your life, I could live
A little more of me.
I'd let you fly a little
To taste a bit of life,
Wanting more you struggled
Each step you had to fight.
With every goal exceeded
My heart beat fierce with pride,
And every disappointment
Tore me apart inside.
Our lives are ever changing
With joys and sorrows shared,
I only did what I thought best
Thru good and bad I cared.
Now that you are far away
Again, I'd like to try,
To let go the guilt and tears,
Sit back and watch you fly.

TerryAnn Moore Shannon

China Doll

What's this facade
Of charm and grace?
What lies behind
The smiling face?

While she laughs out loud,
Does she cry inside?
How many tears
Does her laughter hide?

All alone in her joy
No one is there.
All alone in her sorrow,
Does no one care?

Faster and faster she goes,
Living her life full of woes.
Never once letting go
Of the lies she has told.

'Round and round she'll spin
Just like a top.
Wanting to let go,
Unwilling to stop.

Kathleen M. Haselden

"Feelings Of Me"

I like to sit alone and think
of different ways I feel
For know one else can understand
Those feelings that are real!
Those feelings are so deep inside
that know one else can see
But when you put them
all together
Those feelings make me,
Me!

Lynda G. Smith

Life's Journey With A Friend

Time is only an invention
of man

Of life that he really doesn't
understand

One of the worlds greatest pleasures

Is to find a true friend and erase
that time measure

Though, it be just for a while

It's two hearts beating,
to share one little smile

Peter F. Acquaro

Mose Johns

Mose Johns was tired of tilling soil,
Of milking cows and reaping.
Said he, "Indeed, this is hard toil.
I'll leave this boresome keeping."

His parents wept and felt right sore,
And strong was their protestin'.
But not because of added chore
For Mose was mostly restin'.

He headed for a nearby town,
And there betook to drinkin'
He fell in love with a satin gown
Before he took to thinkin'.

He lost his job and self-support,
And still he kept on drinkin'.
And now I hear of late report,
Mose John is dead — and stinkin'.

Wilson Kuenzie

Untitled

Green is the color
of my loved one's eyes
Green waves crashing
under boundless skies.
Lush green grass
Waving gentle in the breeze,
Green leaves crowning
proud and stately trees.

Samantha Gooding

Ancient Rhyme

Searching for an ancient rhyme
of perfect love throughout all time
hidden well, by men so wise
before our eyes, just in disguise

Words that have so long been lost
words rich in hope, beyond all cost
is this a dream or just a myth
a hope, upon which, we subsist

It must exist, it must be true
I need these words to say to you
to tell you what is in my heart
and that without you, life is dark

I will seek, until I find
this wonderful, elusive rhyme
and share this secret found anew
with my greatest treasure, you.

Robert L. Mooney

The Hands Of My Mother

Hands full of blessings
of that mother of mine.
Hands full of blessings
of that mother whom I love.

Hands that now are rough
which at one time were
also perfumed as
white roses.

Many years have gone by,
more than seventy.
Those pure soft hands,
Life made them rough.

But now, as I contemplate
all I see in them,
is sweetness and softness
and forever this will be.

Olga Medina

The Opal Eye

You know not
of the beauty you hold
you just arrive
without being told
true and brilliant
you shine alone
as empty as time
like a hollow stone
sometimes here
and sometimes gone
but you will be back
as sure as the dawn
waiting for dark
you are never too soon
we have come to respect you
our beautiful moon

D. S. Davidson

Life Forever

He spoke
Of the mother's gift:
Of life to the child
Forever.

Such a gift!

She spoke
In a moment
Of frustration:
"I've given my life."

Such a gift!

Forever - eternal!
Always - unending!
Past: the now,
Glorious communion forever.

Ruth F. Gilman

The Wind

The wind so cold,
Not as pure as gold.
You can't see it,
You can't hold it,
But you can feel it go by.

The wind flies through
the trees,
Like a gentle breeze.
The wind...
...so cold.

Michelle Conroy

Forever In His Sight

As I lay in bed seeing the darkness
of the night,
My heart is full of fear,
wanting to see the light.

I have faith in the Lord,
even if it doesn't show.
I know he's going to be with me,
and to help me grow.

I stay awake everyday,
and every night.
Constantly asking God to keep me,
forever in His sight.

I read the bible,
and learn the Lord's way.
And he keeps me going,
as I pray from day to day.

Soon God will send
His only begotten son,
To come and say that,
THY WILL IS NOW DONE!

Phillip Martinez

It's Christmas!

Christmas Day's a week away!
Oh, me! Oh, my! Oh, yay! Hurray!
Let's hang up the stockings!
Cut down a tree!
Oh, my!, Oh yay! Hurray! Oh, me!
Now it's six days to Christmas Eve!
Gifts to give! Some to receive!
I'm glad all day long!
I'm glad in the night!
Don't make a mess!
Make the tree right!
I'm full of excitement!
All through the day!
You say it's November?
Thanksgiving! Oh, yay!

Rashi Rohatgi

December Mood

It was two below zero
on a cold December afternoon.
The trees were bare and the
cold December wind slowly tip-toed by,
but blew just enough to make the trees
shiver as to wish they hadn't shed
their leaves which could've kept them
warm for this dreadful winter. The
snowflakes fluttered to the ground, roof
tops, and on to the tops of children's
heads. Some of them opened their mouths
hoping to catch the snowflakes in their
mouths, but the wind pushed them right
over their heads, but other children
built snowmen while laughing and
talking. While I stood there watching
the snowflakes, children and the trees,
my hot cocoa which had once steamed up
into the frigid air was gone.

Patricia Huntsman

When The Moon Comes Up

When the moon comes up
On a cold winter night
It is buffeted by gray streaked clouds
It hears the cold north wind
Making a mournful noise as it circles
Around through cracks and crevices
Seeking to freeze the inhabitants
The moon so pale sees many things
From its perch on high
Where it reigns like a king
Majestically watching watching
There to sit all night long
With only the stars to talk to

Michael E. Hosch

To Sean

Seven months ago
On a plane ride for sights to see
A special question arose
From my sweetheart to me
It was finally The Day
As beautiful as it could be
If I'd marry him someday
Was the question he asked me
Now, it's Valentine's Day
And your gift won't come to mind
So, I thought that I could say
What you can easily find
Just hold onto my heart
And look into my eyes
My gift to you sweetheart
Is the love we share inside

Teri Snyder

Our World

As I swing in the hammock
On a warm summer's day
A slight wind blows
The birds fly away
A green leaf falls
And flutters to the grass
And up above me
The sky is clear as glass
As I drift off to sleep
Swaying softly in the breeze
The yellow sun warms me
I give a little sneeze
As I lay there I think
What a wonderful place
How could we be destroying
And sending it to waste?

Kristin Falls

An Artist's World

My world lies undefined
On chart or map,
It has no boundaries.
Its scenic shores
And fancied forests
Are but fleeting images,
Plucked like blossoms
Along the way of a
Wandering heart
In search beauty,
Reaching out to touch the infinite
And, for one brief moment,
Speak of love.

Kenneth Gunning

Lost Seasons

Mornings' frost
on fallen leaves
summer's lost
in autumns' breeze
natures host
til' winters' freeze

hurry and scurry
oh, little friend, make haste
food must be stored
for a long winters taste
the earth when barren
offers nothing to waste
dismal and bleak
its snow covered face
shelter and warmth
may thee the graced
til' spring blooms anew
winter's lost, without trace

Sallyanne Delgado

Rain falling gently
On field and forest
Bringing new life to the old.

Where did you come from
Wet, clear, refreshing
Provider of renewed life?

Atmospheric science?
Or a divine plan?
Or just nature's wonderworks?

Mary A. Fallon

Perfection

A perfect tiny snowflake fell,
On my coat sleeve, so it fell.
Then another and some more
perfect six points, as those before
Perfect! Perfect! as could be.
God sent them from heaven to me
To teach an unworthy soul like me.
That I should always perfect me.
An example for the world to see.
Thank you God for Remembering
An unworthy soul like me.
I shall do my very best for Thee
And keep ready for eternity!

Mark S. Russell

Dear Friend

I'm glad we met, dear friend
On that day so long ago
"By chance," we said and yet I think
That God had willed it so.

Your friendly way has brought me cheer.
The thoughtful things you do;
It means so much to have a friend
Who's always warm and true.

You are the one to whom I turn
When trouble comes my way;
You somehow help my heart to see
There'll come a brighter day.
My world's a brighter place
And I'd like you to know
It's because you are my friend
That helps to make it so.

Kim Christensen

A Winter Romance

Champagne kisses
on the cold Left Bank
send moist warmth
to parched, frozen lips.
Unrelenting embraces
fill them with ardour,
while tears of farewell
overflow into the Seine,
parting two lovers
with its icy waters
before spring can bloom.

Melisa Tebeau

Untitled

You should be skateboarding
on these walkways in the summer,
and cross country skiing
across these grounds in the winter.

In the breeze
I can hear the swoosh of skis
and the thud of wheels
crossing the cracks.

And your laughter,
forever silenced.

This place is too quiet.
If only you could disturb the peace
with the thunder of teenage activity.

But you're outnumbered by your elders
and stifled by death.

Kris Trout

"My Pen And Paper"

On this endless sea of life
on which that I live,
my feelings are my own to keep,
only on paper, do I give.

Trying only to stay afloat,
times I thought I'd drown,
my thoughts would come rapidly,
I must hurry to write them down.

Only on paper can I understand
this lonely life of mine.
My whole life is there before me,
written on every line.

My moods may vary from day-to-day,
only moments I shall share.
But only with pen and paper in hand,
my whole life do I bear.

The endless sea is constant,
waves of every kind.
And only with my pen and paper,
Can I ease what's on my mind.

Wendy L. Robinson

In The Depths

In the depths of
ones soul
behind all the meanness
past all the hatred
that keeps light away
there lies the gift
that people still want
the gift of love
that cannot be driven away.

Marcus Davis

A Precious Moment

It is the space in time that separates
one moment from all the rest;
It is the glow that brightens the
inner being I have become;
It is the magic note of sound to my
deaf ears of life in its infancy;
It is the brief interlude that unlocks
my soul and brings a smile;

It reveals to my eyes the hope of
dawn—and rouses my conscience;
It opens the doors to my secret
yearnings of life;
It is the seed from which a new
beginning will grow and blossom;
It is my spirit moving through the
skies of wonder and fulfillment;

It is the moment I realize I love you.

Sandra L. Gary

Oh Schizophrenia

Within my heart lies a secret person
One of peace and of gross perversion

Hidden away from the eyes of men
Seldom comes out but to hide again

There is great beauty within my heart
Never yet seen it's a secret art

One is a poet, with soul serene
Unlike all others as she does seem

The artist, the lover, she's often afraid
She would be seen if she were but brave

But there lies also a darker side
Oh dear self, if but she would hide

So cruel and uncaring to her prey
Twisted she hides from the light of day

Still further within is found the child
Her skin so fair and voice so mild

Not far beyond is found the toddler
Dependent on mother and not knowing father

As each year passes with silent resound
Another person is quickly found

Takouhie Ouzounian

Alone

I am mortal.
Only a long shadow,
on a September afternoon.

Only an empty shell,
on the endless beach,
that is life.

Awaiting the time,
the moment,
I meet you.

To listen to the echoes,
of the ocean.
To see the colors,
of the silhouette,
on the grass.

To fill the empty space,
in the palm of my hand.
I await you,
Love.

Robert J. Chace

Melt

The winter winds that chill the land
Only bring me joy
In remembering the day gone by
I lost my precious boy.

To find solace in this woeful thought
I am truly heaven blessed
To know the Good Lord grants us
Winter
So I may feel my angel rest.

Every time the iced wind sighs
I know my son is near:
The very season that took him away
brings him back to me each year.

I step into the howling storm
To drink its swirling hiss
For in every gust that touches me,
I feel my baby's kiss.

Kristin Feuer-Quintero

Friend

If you ever need a smile,
Or a friend to talk to,
Call me because I'll be here.

If you're ever feeling lonely,
And depressed,
All you see is blue,
I'll give you a hug,
To show that I care.

If someone breaks your heart,
Or your whole world falls apart,
The reason I don't care.
Just remember,
Need a friend, I'll be there.

Lorrene Hoven

Tribute To A Friend

Our paths they crossed too seldom
Our gratitude's run late
You're rising up to heaven
God's waiting at the gate

Your kind and gentle manner
The smile you always wore
The way you treated one and all
Opened to you God's front door

Your friends down here are grieving
Lost in a somber state
Our world is somehow lessened
By this twist of mortal fate

Your memory will be cherished
As a colleague and a friend
We know you're in for better days
But our hearts may never mend

A new world now approaches
Free of pain and free of hate
So fly with golden angels
God's waiting at the gate

Will E. Kennedy

Grumbling Joe 'Grumpa

Grumbling Joe 'grumpa let
out a sulphurous belch
and folded his magnificent
stomach like a table-cloth,
Sliding slowly into his
sponge cake sofa.

Kim Thompson

Adieu

When we remember those we love
Our love goes on a-living
And helps new loves to rise above
And love keeps on a-giving.

Loving memories are all we have
Our hopes to keep a-growing
And soothe our hurts like a salve,
When trouble comes a-sowing.

When we're sad and moan and our loss,
Or dread some sad, sad duty
And thinking only of the cost,
Instead of remembering beauty.

The sunset fades from summer skies
And pity comes, a thief,
To steal the beauty from our eyes
And gives to us its grief.

So I say farewell, adieu adieu
But not good-bye forever
In my heart, I'll remember you
As beautiful as ever.

Taylor E. Morrel

Wealth Of Time

Age is slowing down momentum
Our love is reaching deserts end
But you have been my lovely helpmate
You have been my friend.

You have been my inspiration
You have binded up my wounds
Given me inclination
I am slower in my telling.
Bear Thee, Charlot.

Once my eyes were sharp with vision
Clouded now and dim with age
But your comfort is the vision
I sometimes stumble at this stage.

All I have to offer you
Is now aging with the embers
What we capture today, you and I
Is what our heart remembers.
Bear Thee, Charlot.

Neta F. Bockover

Kittens At Play

Kittens of various colors and size;
Out on a sunny day to play.
Their eyes are full of mischief -
The dog better not get in their way.

They arch their backs and make a hiss;
Their fur is all a-fluff.
They do their little kitten pounce;
And try to look really tough.

They hide behind an old box
As their next victim, they spy.
They crouch down low and wiggle a little,
As the unsuspecting walks by.

They leap at another play-mate;
Who jumps with pretending fright.
They bat at each other with velvety paws,
Oh, what an entertaining sight!

At last the kittens are done playing;
And they snuggle in a small child's lap.
Time to rest and repeat it all later,
But first, take a kitten's nap.

Lori Gilbertson

Pre-Destination

All our dreams are ragged seams,
Our sentiments through windows screened,
Our formal feelings common themes,
And actions just a truncated means.

All we are are marionettes,
Our life cord simply nylon string
Held taut by one who hoards our faith.

As mimes pushed off the sidewalk curb,
We blindly fall to white concrete
And sand our wooden elbows smooth.

Our hollow hearts and burning brains
Are passive pitchers churning time,
Numbly awaiting the final chime.

As zoo-bound bears we pace our crate
Our hand shakes hinged to foreign bars,
Our gritted teeth a tainted tool.

Our painted smiles stiffen dry,
Until we're told we can not cry,
But if we're lucky, someday die.

All our dreams are ragged seams,
Our sentiments through windows screened,
Our formal feelings common themes
And actions just a truncated means.

Kelly Coveny

One September Morn

One early morn, not long ago
Our years of love began
Her blue eyes bright, a sunny smile
We welcomed Lori Anne
Sometimes we find, words cannot say
Most parents won't deny
We gladly gave our hearts away
With every day gone by
Our little girl is growing fast
Please let the years slow down
But we realize as time has passed
September will come round

Patricia Weiser

Unsaid Love

It flows over rocks,
Over all valleys, and over
The many miles
In my life.
Even if you don't say it
It flows over my face,
Through my body,
And then covers me like
A blanket.
Your love flows to me
With me now and forever.

Sarah Lewis

Unfulfilled Dreams

I have thoughts of many things,
Opportunities I've passed
Loves I've allowed to lapse
Several unfulfilled dreams.
When in truth, there's no such thing
As a dream to never be
I have faith in God and love
This is real this is life
This is me.

Sharon Moore

Untitled

We sew together every Tuesday
Over cake and coffee
In the sunny room, green with plants.
I bring my new things
And my torn things.
You do, too.
And the thread of conversation
Goes back and forth across the table
With gentle pulls.
And for an hour or so
We create
And mend.

Marilyn Blair

Untitled

The love and happiness
Passed by...
And with the rustling leaves
Flew to the sky...
The grass is covered with frost
Instead of dew...
And raindrops like a quiet ghost-
The saddest view...
Instead of warmth and light
The drizzling rain,
In solitude of darkest night
You wait in vain...
The memory of blissful spring is
Just a sigh...
And whisper in the autumn leaves:
"Goodbye...goodbye...".

Margaret Rainstein

Remember

The flags were waving
People gathered around
The parade had started

Today we remember our dead
The heroes of past and present
Long gone but not forgotten

Our friends and neighbors gather
To celebrate and reflect
Enjoying the day God gave us

Everyone needs to reflect
Remember what brotherhood means
What it's like to be an American

Men and boys fought bravely
They died to keep us free
We must remember them always

Some day there will be no war
No fighting in the streets
Everyone will know peace.

Patricia M. Blair

If It Only Snowed Gold!

If it only snowed gold,
people would be rich,
some people could buy meat
and some people could buy fish.

If that fish was good, good, good,
people would buy more than
they ever could.

I still wonder how gold
could fall from the sky,
I wonder if God would make
it in his spare time!

Krystal Panas

Thoughts

Jumbled full of memories,
Pictures of the past,
Feelings from the memories
That will always last.
Loves that have come
And gone with the wind,
Friendships of some
That would never end,
Books full of words
That have poured in here,
Some flew like birds;
Some I hold dear.
Being camouflaged with thoughts
Are soldiers of diversity
As they fight, being caught
In actions of adversity.

Lisa Catron

The Environment

Our earth's a wonderful
place to live, it's slowly dying
from thoughtless people

Woods are losing trees
for building houses. Animals
are becoming extinct when
people hunt them

Our oceans and waterways are being
polluted with raw sewage from
factories and industries,

Fish are being killed while
dolphins are caught in nets.

When God made man he wanted
humans to be protectors of the earth,
so we must save our earth

Life is precious

Marcia Whitfield

Chesapeake State Of Mind

Peaceful peach sky
playful sea gulls flying by
Chesapeake sea breeze kissing my face
a timeless road journey
melts my troubles away
I'm in love with the Chesapeake Tunnel
cruising along 60 m.p.h
John Denver's "Take Me Home" on the
radio
a rush of adrenaline overwhelms me
my heart collects the moments
My eyes collects the memories
The peach sky greets me hello and
goodbye.

Stacy Hawkins

Fly Away

Fly away oh precious one,
please fly away from me.
Can't you see how hard I've tried
to truly set you free?

God please make him listen,
he was never really mine.
He needs a higher mountain,
it's time for him to climb.

Nancy Dahlen

Untitled

He sees the master enter with
pride and dispense, as the crescendo
unfolds it leads to violence.
Whipped brutally then left
to bleed, punished for reflecting
the master's moral deeds.
He speaks he whispers
but no one will heed, the attention
he wants, the master he feeds.
Fooled by the master now
damaged for life, he cries, he
whimpers but puts up no strife.
Blood on his lip and
tears that won't halt, what the
master has done was all his fault.

Natalie Ann Bonanno

Rescued

Like a thief it creeps through the night,
Prowling into the mind.
Demanding a nagging attention,
As my peace it tries to bind.

This turmoil has many faces,
As power it tries to gain.
Guilt, grief, or worry,
But its companion is always pain.

Struggling to loose the ties,
That hold me in control,
I search for the deepest hope,
To rekindle joy within my soul.

For hope is my hero,
That rescues me from this thief,
With promises I can lean upon,
Filled with contentment and relief.

So as turmoils enter my life,
And I am challenged again to cope,
I will rest and not be disappointed,
For God has given me hope.

Susan M. Perry

Halloween Is Scary

Halloween is scary,
Pumpkins with faces.
Leaves changing color
All over the places.

Costumes are different,
There are all kinds;
Many with faces,
Some of them shine.

Black cats on fences,
Boiling pots with stew.
Wolves are howling.
It's a full moon.

Megan Long

What Are Clouds?

Are clouds but fleeting images
of forgotten dreams
vaporizing
ghost - like
into life - like caricatures?
...or
Could clouds be cotton puffs
brightly hued
cavorting
clown - like
across an endless sky?

Robert K. Walker

Salvation

In His own image
Pure and whole
He created me!

A life of sin
My penitent heart
He forgave me!

Began anew
And in His strength
He enabled me!

He'll come again
To claim His own
Praise God for saving me!

Marilyn Chadwick

Ghost Writer

I am the ghost writer
Putting words in your mouth,
Giving you all my secret
Desires and ambitions.
My precious loves
And bitter sorrows
Become your property.
Your public reads
With avid delight.
We pile confusion upon confusion
And still they read on,
Never suspecting that
I am the ghost writer
Controlling their minds.

Mable L. Dewey

Untitled

Light streaks thru the skies
Rainbows streaming down
Birds flying up high
Cool breezes come up from the ocean floor
Misty fog rolls in
Stars shining above the clouds
Thru the darkest of night
Fireflies pierce the thickness
A sparkle I encounter
Never to be matched
- the light in his eyes -

Regina Chase

A Father's Passing

Thoughts of his life before him,
Re-occurring in his mind.
His guidance meant to be wise and true,
Will stand the test of time.

Many branches from his tree have grown.
Some strong, some weak, some frail.
As long as they all grow together,
His life will not have failed.

His suffering now wished over,
Is destined but unknown,
To all his love has touched somehow,
His presence will always be known.

He'll be lovingly missed daily,
Once he's gone and far away.
His pain will finally be over,
When he passes on that day.

Sharon S. Voiles

The Voyage

The waters are my friend,
reflecting sunny beams.
The waves gently rocking,
'til I drift off in my dreams.
Leaving behind the worries,
of another endless age.
I enter the dreamers passage,
and turn another page.
Where happiness, like a blanket,
begins to unfold.
And sorrows suddenly vanish,
never again to be told.
So please my friend, don't wake me,
as hard as it may seem.
Instead, I beg come join me,
on the voyage of endless dreams.

Tommy M. Campbell

Untitled

Ember's smolder the blaze gone bye
Reflect's the glint in his eye's
Upon his face a wrinkled smile
Hear's the laughter of a child

Remembrance of stories
Treasures to my heart
To my son I tell his part
Life's Joy's

Heartaches and fun
Morning's watching the rising sun
All these things that have been done
Living Life

It's enough to be
And for my son, I hope he'll see
The love for him
And the part of me.

Preston Garrett

Purpose

The sand and the sea
Remind me of thee.
Ever changing, yet
A constant moving
Force. Unharnessed,
Destined to be free.

You instill within me
The power of the sea.
Without thee I am bare,
Unsheltered and cold.
Exposed forever to the wind.
Destined to careen.

Loretta Jividen

Rain

Rain is like a waterfall
Rushing to the ground
Making puddles everywhere
With a splish-splash sound.

Rain is like crystals
Crashing to the ground
Bringing water to our land
And freshness all around.

Rain falling gently
To the ground
Silently, softly
Without a sound.

Melissa Vettleson

"Love"

Your eyes, by the lake,
Roses smiling in the summer sky,
Wind whistling slowly,
The human heart,
How far will it go?
How much will it take?
Mountains lost in fog,
Lakes thrust in canyons,
Don't point at blood,
Magnolias flutter in the breeze,
She loved him,
He loved her,
The way they looked at each other,
This was no business agreement,
He would die for her,
She would die for him,
Paintings she would paint for him,
Gardens he would grow for her,
Hold each other like nothing mattered,
Like an eagle flying circles.

Radomir Luza Jr.

Remaining The Same

Flowers bloom,
Roses wilt.
Birds sing,
sparrows fly.
Friends laugh,
lovers cry.
People die,
skies fall.
Time stands still,
you moved on.
I cried,
you died.
Time has gone on,
I love again.
Now you're gone,
and I still remain the same.

Rachel Little

Sarah

(1975-1994)

Sarah, our butterfly
Sarah, our butterfly
A touch here
A touch there
A thing of beauty everywhere.

Butterfly
A beautiful, fragile bit of life
Follows nature's calling
Going from place to place
Leaving memories in a trail.

Oh Sarah, Sarah
Our butterfly
Left memories in her lilting trail
So beautiful
So graceful
So loving
So much a part of life
Even now in death.

Oh, Sarah, oh, Sarah
A legacy in a butterfly.

Marianne Ranson Giangreco

The Search

Life is searching. . .
Searching for the light in the darkness
Searching for the cure for the pain
Searching for the calm in the storm
Searching for the meaning of life

Sharon R. Yarrell

Being Of Sadness

Silently I sit,
secluded from life.
Alone I wait,
for the timeless.
My world is full of darkness,
No light to see the path,
The soul is buried underneath,
Sands of painful wrath.
A numbness of the heart,
Hardens the spirit of hope.
With a striped soul,
Your logic tries to cope.
My spirit has been murdered!
Blood flows beating from my heart.
The wings of joy torn from my mind,
All wisdom has fallen apart.
Loneliness consumes you,
Like a beast eating its prey.
He has won yet once again....
And now there is nothing more to say.

Lori Goodpaster

Love Is

Love is
sharing secrets and holding hands,
speaking the truth
and making plans.

Love is walking along
a moonlight beach
and being close
never out of reach.

Love is sharing the duties
and taking turns.
Love is lust and passion
but sometimes burns.

Love is confidence
and trust in what's right.
Love is hugging and kissing
after a fight.

Love is romantic
like dinner for two.
Love is
me and you!

R. Baker

"Forgotten Ones"

A young girl sits alone in her room,
She dreams of another life,
All believe she is nearly perfect,
She slowly sharpens the knife,

She over-compensates her stereotype,
By agreeing to all the "no's,"
Spirits enter to guide her back,
She sneers at their warning with "so?"

She's hooked on this fix,
Blood covers the knife,
The spirits now own her,
She's taken her life.

Shannon Simonds

"Other Self"

She saves my life
She helps me cry
She comforts without trying
In the madness of my world
She is an island

In her sweet, sane insanity
I can lose myself
Without a care

Even with her complexities
Perplexities of fault
I love her still

She sails the sea with me
When she can
We miss a lot
Catch what moments we can

We together are caught
In this life of woe and fear
Between the adolescent and adult
Going, we know not where
If not for her, I would be alone

Laura Lyn McCord

Man Of Purpose

Bare not true soul
shine nothing but
by were masked face
a gentle claw
under which world
kneel howingly
how same our shine

Thavisouk T. Inthasone

Like A Candle

You burn like a candle in the night,
shining on my path for me to see.
Just like a candle...
When the rain comes you head for shelter,
but never under my roof.
Just like a candle...
Part of you goes away,
whenever you feel the need for attention.
Just like a candle...
If I get to close to you,
I get burned.
Just like a candle...
Now my eager child will beg me,
to let her blow out the flame.
Just like a candle,
I'll light you up again.

Tara Smith

Her Love in His Hands

He came one day,
said his love must say good-bye.
She reached out and gave
her most fragile possession.
He looked at it.
Saw the imperfection,
then with a thought of sheer delight
and a tightened grip,
he brought it high.
With firm force it crashed to the floor.
A million pieces.
Hearts were made to be broken.

Michelle Caskey

Some Tomorrow

Slowly the housing called my body
Sighed deeply and ceased to be,
That which was me
Transformed into a free floating entity.
The galaxies are my stepping stones.

I use the moon as a ball
To play jacks with the stars.
I swirl with the vapors of the universe,
That cling around me from afar,
Like the perfumes of earth.

On clear days you have only
To look up to feel me.
I am all around you - don't you see?
Like once on Earth
I enter you each time you breathe.
Now I am forever!!!

Sheila A. Kelly

Little Bird

Song sparrow
singing a happy song
in the cool of the morning
and all day long.
She is saying
get up it's dawn
let's go look for seeds.

Later in the afternoon
a loud clap of thunder -
In come the dark heavy clouds
warning of a storm.
Rain falling in sheets -
the happy song is gone
Where did you go -
maybe to hide in a bush
or in a dense tree.

Storm over
song sparrow sings again,
Thanking the rain
with a bubbly song.

Melba Hollister

I Hear...

I hear the voices of the children,
Singing songs of peace and joy.
I hear the voices of the children,
Freedom for every girl and boy.

I hear the cheering of the women,
Praising God for freedom come.
I hear the cheering of the women,
Beating on their faithful drum.

I hear the shouting of the soldiers,
Finally dropping all their guns.
I hear the shouting of the soldiers,
Fighting for freedom for their sons.

I hear the whispers of the elders,
Praying for their children's love.
I hear the whispers of the elders,
Praising God in heaven above.

I hear the silence of the whole world,
Finally at peace and posterity.
I hear the silence of the whole world,
Forever peaceful the earth shall be.

Nicole Marie Bush

Remember

An old man
Sits on a chair
With tales of sorrow to be told.
With his hand shaking
And his mind racing
Words begin to flow.
With pain and ease his lips move
Of memories long gone.
He tells newcomers
so that the stories may live on.

Micki Rubenstein

Encounter

In her small chair, the rag mop doll
Sits queen-like and demure,
Her mouse-colored crinkly hair
Topped with a gold starred tiara,
She is resplendent
In lace and ribbons
And one big gold mesh bow.
Mitchell, age two,
Stops to ponder this small wonder;
I see the dark brown eyes
Grow soft... tender...
He does not touch
But respectfully
Moves on.
Who said the days of chivalry had gone?

Norma C. Rhodes

Down By The Sea

Once there was a young woman
Sitting by the sea
Gazing in the distance
Oh! so dreamily

Her skin was soft and tender
Her eyes blue as waters deep
Her hair like golden stalks
Of summer yellow wheat

I wish we had spoken
For just a little while
Then I would gaze upon her face
And see if she would smile

I took a pretty sea shell
Upon the golden sand
And placed it in her lovely folded hand

She didn't say a word
As she smiled up at me
I left her with her dreams
Down by the sea.

Teresa Miccio

As I Watch You Sleep

I wonder as I watch you sleep
so innocent and sweet
and kiss the angel face and hand
that's made my life complete,
Does every parent kiss their child
during silent, dream-filled slumber?
and does their heart explode with love
for this miracle and wonder
How life will treat their precious one
for whom their heart is beating?
And pray that God protects him
with a love that's undefeating.

Rosemarie Quinn

The Mystery

Tiny little lady bug
Sitting on a leaf
When your children fly away
Can you feel the grief?
Lovely graceful butterfly
Drinking from the flower
How do you stay warm and dry
Through a summer shower?
Funny little inch worm
Measuring hour after hour
Even though you have no legs
Do you ever tire?
Robin perched upon a limb
Singing in the tree
Your song is sweet and mellow
As you sing along with me.

Shelly Wilson

Untitled

Like a flower she wilts away,
slow but steady day by day.
Her petals shrivel up and die,
In her Hospital bed where she lies.
In a coma now she lays poor,
Little flower's going away.
Friends and family sit and cry,
for their flower soon shall die.
Sex and needles so they say.
Can she last another day?
AIDS is deadly, do you hear?
Pay attention, listen clear.
AIDS is something you must fear!
Now their flower has finally died.
And it's time to say goodbye.
Hear my warning!
Listen clear!
AIDS will kill you,
Do you hear?

Kathy Thomas

Fall Forest

I listen as the water
Slowly trickles by,
Then peacefully look up into
The beautiful amber sky.

The leaves turning orange now
And some are falling down,
I marvel at how silently
They float and hit the ground.

The sun has finished setting now
And the forest is fast asleep,
But now some little mice
Have started to move and creep.

My eyelids are getting heavy
And I'm slowly dozing away,
I think about going back home
But then tell myself, "I'll stay."

I hear the crickets softly chirping
Like a violinist fingering her strings,
And now I wait impatiently
For what the next day brings.

Rebeca Benitez

"All Aboard!"

He sleeps in shelter
- Smiling
Wrapped in warmth
The journey -
Long, lonely
Merged with that
of another

Surrounded by strength
Touched tenderly
With passion, pleasure
- Smiling
He sleeps in shelter

- In the distance
A train wails -

Kevin J. Mackey

Sneezes

Sneeze on Monday, sneeze for danger.
Sneeze on Tuesday, kiss a stranger.
Sneeze on Wednesday, sneeze for a letter.
Sneeze on Thursday, something better.
Sneeze on Friday, sneeze for sorrow.
Sneeze on Saturday, joy for tomorrow.
Sneeze on Sunday, miss a boy.

Melisa Sue George

Joe And Faye's Christmas

The gazebo holds a Christmas tree
so beautiful and so bright,
The azaleas that surround it
are now all snowy white

He strings the lights and garland
on top he puts a star
When night time finally comes around
you can see it from afar

She stands down by the old wood fence
he built so long ago
to remind her of a time gone by,
of things that she loves so

She looks up at the Christmas tree
and smiles with sheer delight,
Tonight they'll share a Christmas wish
and dine by candlelight

Wanda Taylor

Hope's And Dreams

You walked into my life
so long ago it seems
you gave me love and happiness
you gave me hopes and dreams
you took away my sorrow
I had felt for many years
you took away my loneliness
and wiped away my tears
I built my life around you
you were the joy of my days
I never knew I could be so happy
In so many different ways
you made my life world living
you gave me a reason to go on
The love you have giving me
is the greatest I have known

Mary Ledbetter

Joy Bells

I hear the joy bells ringing,
So long since I've heard them.
I hear the joy bells ringing,
It's happiness ahead.

I hear the joy bells ringing,
I thought they were broken.
I hear the joy bells ringing,
It's good music for my soul.

I hear the joy bells ringing,
It lets me know He's arrived.
I hear the joy bells ringing,
I know He heard my cry.

I hear the joy bells ringing,
He's answered my plea.
I hear the joy bells ringing,
I got to shout I am free!

Linda Lee Lane

"Forgive Me"

I've taken away so many lives,
So many small bundles of joy.
I'll always think back and wonder
If they might have been a boy or a girl.

I just can't find it in my heart
to ever think of being forgiven
For all those little hearts that
I've stopped from beating.

I've taken away countless ones
I don't know how long I can go on,
Living this cruel lie.
To think it was right,
for them to die.
This is the guilt that many bear.
And to think there are people
who just don't care.

Who gives us the right to say,
Who will live and who will die.

Mary Torres

To My Daughter

Your future is before you,
so many things to see,
The hopes, the dreams, the joy,
the woman you will be.
I've tried so hard to show you,
what the future may unfold,
With a gentle, loving touch,
not to place you in a mold.
The world won't always be gentle,
as you travel on your way,
I hope that I have shown you,
how to make the journey each day.
I love you now and always will,
I hope you know that's true,
I hope that you never forget,
the love I have for you.
Someday, you to will wonder,
if I have given all my love,
My only answer to that will be.
that it comes from God above.

Steven R. Schaefer

Lord, You Gave Me A Mountain To Climb

Lord, you gave me a mountain to climb
so many times I have said why,
Why have I walked this long lonely path.
I can't minster to your people
where in this lonely spot
Lord, take me where your people
are, awake people around the world
Now, I'm on top the mountain
surely Lord, the going down
on the other side will be easier.
Lord you gave me a mountain to climb.
Now take my hand and lead
me where I'm to go.

Virginia Johnston

A Better Place

So much pain,
So much anger and despair
In the world we live in,
Where not enough seem to care.

Each day's news we hear
Is worse than before
Brother fights Brother
Mother's are Mother's no more.

Children are abused
And their cries go unheard.
Crime and death fill the papers
With each and every word.

Where will it all end,
When will each of us see
That love and hope
Is what was meant to be.

What a beautiful place to live
In the land of the free
If we cared about each other
As much as each of us care about ME!!!

Sue Burge

Emotional Refugee

I am searching for my own true home
So my heart will not be alone
There the joy of singing love's song
Vibrates cavities to belong
The environment can surround
My emotions that seem so sound
But uncertainty, agony
Acceptance, rejection of me
Trying to become a part of
Communities and the hearts of
Those that will mask souls to fit in
Who, what am I, how can I win
The battle to test my courage
Pain from loss can well discourage
Discarding masks and finding me
Being, winning, for all to see
Living my own identity
Is by far the whole entity
I was searching for my own home
It's in my heart that is not alone.

Marcia Caspe

Death

Like a velvet blanket,
So soft, so warm, so deep,
With sounds of soulful music
From the beyond of earthly reach;
Death on wings of night birds,
With the speed of must and will,
Comes as an Angel of Mercy
His mission to fulfill.
And he who is tired and weary,
Whose journey has been hard,
Receives at last his merit—
His heav'nly calling card.
For Eternal rest now reaches
This weary, richly blessed,
As sleep brings rest to body and soul,
And slumber becomes — Death.

Marie A. Melaro

A Whisper

The touch was soft
So sweet in smell,
It made me upset
That one ever fell.

The pain we feel
Is something that stays forever,
A mind is boggled
This is something no one should endeavor.

We are all human
Always making mistakes,
Once we mess up
There are no more stakes.

How are we to learn
And make ourselves more bright,
When all we get is agony
Then we are filled with spite.

Martin Brandt

A Special Time

As the years come
So the years go
Some things are more precious,
This I'm sure you know.
So because it is your birthday
And because I love you so,
I'm giving you this little gift
Just to tell you so.
You will notice by its sparkle,
When you touch it to the light
It could hold far more than flowers,
It could hold just sheer delight,
And reflected in its beauty
There is something to be hold
For crystal like my little girl
Never will grow old.

Maggie Havens

Sometimes, God

Sometimes God sneaks into my life.
Something special happens.
I let go of everything. Even myself.
In a moment I am free. Glowing.
Absolutely shining. In the knowing.
So I ask, 'why'?
And it goes away. I wish to cry
But I can not. I am dead again.
Sometimes God sneaks into my life.

Rafael Stoneman

A Caring Soul

These little one's
so weak in body,

Yet not able to
understand the power
of their soul's

Yearning for the
closeness of loved one's

To help comfort them
in so many way's

Protect them from the
sadness and grief
of it all

By giving them your
smile and caring soul.

Susan Gann

My Soldier

I whispered it quietly
So you would not hear,
"Go with him, God,"
And held back a tear.

I whispered it silently
So you would not know,
"Take care of him Lord,
I shall miss him so!"

I whispered it numbly,
"Watch over my son,
Aloud all I said was,
"Write me-good-bye hon!"

Then you were gone—
The tears ran down free.
With you went my love
And a small part of me.

Mary L. Grasmick

Untitled

Stormy green eyes,
Soft brown hair,
One who never lies,
One who is truly fair.
My mother, my mother,
Oh how I love her!

Keela Mowles

If Only We

If only we could find
Some passage here through time,
To see all we have done.

To know the past
And experience the future,
To give and entwine as one.

Todd D. Nelson

Voices

Sometimes it does amaze me.
Some think I'm going crazy.
Voices, voices, in my head.

They say we will be friends
in time but I don't pay them any mind.
Voices, voices in my head.

Secretly they wish that I were dead.
I'd like to silence them with lead.
Voices, voices in my head.

Zodiak Wayne Paredes

Nightmare Dreams

I'm a dreamer. I like to dream.
Sometimes I feel like my dreams
are slipping through my fingers.
And how.
And how am I suppose to reach them
when I'm falling from my pedestal
to see someone else touch them.
And then I see my new nightmares
come down.
Come crashing down on my poor
still beating heart.
And how.
How can I stand in the night without
my arms.
Without my arms wrapped around you.
My dream.

Poet Jordan

Love Is A Battlefield

They say love is battlefield
Sometimes you win
Sometimes you lose
You'll have to keep looking
Till you find someone
Who pleases you
Someone who walks
Out of your dreams
And into your life
Right before your eyes
Not looking or planning
It just comes your way
Like bridges that join
And roads that meet
We were bound to cross
Each other path
Would you still
Have been a fantasy
Or would you have come
To be a reality

Stacey Leigh Fiorenzi

This Fragile Flesh

Will looking back
Sooth my hurt, ease my pain
Or trap me once again
In the turmoil of time
When life was painful
And emotion tossed?

Still, I feel pained
In lonely silence caged,
But am no longer tossed.
Looking back brings what gain?
All I see is loss
Of Self and of Pride.

In time bad things
Were buried, lost, forgot;
But in that burying
Was this fragile flesh marred?
Not flesh of body
But of mind and heart.

Paula Ault

Trees

I like to see a tree that's tall
Stretching upward leaves and all.
They seem to reach their branches high
As if they'd like to touch the sky.

Peter B. Eccles

Magic

When we met,
Sparks were in the air.
I swear I saw fireworks everywhere.
When we were together,
A fire burned bright.

But now,
Things don't feel so right.
All that's left is a smoky haze.
I wish we could go back
To the magical days.

Zoe Einbinder

John F. Kennedy

I dreamed I saw John Kennedy
Standing on the square,
I ran a mile in my bare feet
To see Him standing there.

Outside the town, I was where I found.
Him speaking to a crowd..
And as I drew near, His voice to hear,
When then so clear and loud.

John Kennedy, John Kennedy
It's a terrible shame,
You were taken away, from this great land
With you're famous name.

But God above with his great love,
In heaven away most high,
With take you in his arms there,
Where you no more will die

Michael Ward

Life After Death

As I tumbled through a tunnel.
Started as a funnel.
So narrow along the way.
So helpless there I lay.
My thoughts on death.
Seems I had no breath.
The voyage getting broad.
Thoughts of life unfolding
My hand you were holding
I see water darkness and gloom.
With despair, for me no room.
Brightness of light I see
No human eye could view.
I knew I was one of few.
The peace I found.
Surety I wasn't left behind.
Remembering a prayer.
A promise I made.
Let me live.
My life forever I give.

Myrtle Marcum

Black Woman

Strong black man
Strong black woman
He watches the sun
She watches the ground.

His eyes are toward the sky
But her eyes never wonders that high
Is it because he is better than she
Oh no! she is better
Because he comes from she.

Kira R. King

Mountain Stream

It's like a mountain stream
Starting slowly from melting snow
Growing bigger each day
Full of life
Unknowing
Forever changing
Flowing on
Getting yet bigger
Flowing on and on
Where ever It might Lead
Forever
Because growing inside me
are the feeling I feel for you
I love you
Forever

Steven A. Crabbs

Levitation???

What about I began to pray,
starting the day?
What was it I wanted to say,
along the way?...
How does our word get swept away
at the mere flight-
Of those aircraft over the hill,
well out of sight?

Why then our soul does feel
a thrill,
all mused away
by just a few sheer passing
wings
above the fray?

Is there something with most of us
that smiles and sings,
lifting our mind in universe
to far-off things???

Narcisse G. Malary

The Last Leaf

When the last colorful leaf
still hangs on its bough,
In contrast to our belief,
It says to us, "Life is now".

Then it flutters gently down
Its colors vividly furled,
And lies motionless on the ground
With its edges ruffled and curled.

Life makes us Father, or Mother,
And our blood in its blending
Makes us like no other,
But makes for US, Life unending.

If we are the last of our family,
Living beyond all others,
Let us know, that's to be;
And weep not for the others.

Weep not for the setting sun,
Rather, look back on your youth,
Cry not for the things undone,
But be a guardian of the truth.

Wilma Griffin Bradshaw

Not By Choice

Alone in a corner
Stripped of his rights,
He sits making no sound,
In the dim moonlight.

A prisoner of war
As if he had a choice.
In this world
No one has a voice.

Thinking about his family
While he sits and waits
For the war to finally end.
He silently counts the dates.

Wanting to make a call
To let them know he's well.
Of that there's no chance.
They don't have pay phones in Hell.

Alone in a corner
Stripped of his rights,
He sits making no sound,
In the dim moonlight.

Lisa Synhoff

Definition

It comes from within
strong and with might

Control ever cringing
with fury and fright

Never no harm meant
but now it's too late

The damage is well spent
decided by fate

To stop it before hand
the only true way

No matter the best plan
can falter and stray

Without a solution
the ultimate stage

Sadistic intrusion
known only as rage.

William C. Mauger, Jr.

Strong Black Woman

I am a strong black woman
Strong but sensitive
So don't try to take advantage of me
Just ask and I will give

I am a strong black woman
I've seen the struggles of my man
I've felt the pain he carries inside
because he's used his hand

I am a strong black woman
who's moved mountains to get by
I refuse to take the easy road
just so I will not cry

I am a strong black woman
I have a story you must hear
It's one of determination
A story where I persevere

I am a strong black woman
and I refuse to change that truth
Though troubles stare me in my face
I will always get through

C. R. Johnson

Merry Christmas Happy Birthday

With Goodwill, Peace, and Joy
Such a glorious time this is
The birth date of a precious baby boy
Who elected to arrive on Christmas

May the joy today surpass all others
Like glistening roses, sunshine and dew
For my special, wonderful big brother
Our world is nicer, thanks to you

So I wish you a Merry Christmas
A most Blessed, Happy Birthday too
A rapid recovery and all good wishes
To make your every dream come true

Lisa Hendricks

What Is Love?

What is love?
Such a small word,
that means so much.
Something for sure and forever.
To be in love,
is a strong feeling,
that I don't understand.
Love cannot be explained,
but only felt.
But what is love?
And when will I feel it?

Sherry Keene

...Misty Remembrances...

Skies that were blue
Suddenly turn to grey.
Clouds burst into tears
For they remember yesterdays.
As the heavens begin to clear
A mist can be seen near the panes metal,
Floating and tumbling onto a roses petal.
For a glimmering instant
A memory of you is born,
As the dew drops silently
Onto the thorn.

Kelly Lovett

Counterculture

Delusions of the truth
Sway a person right or wrong,
Since societies norms
Dictate a way of life.

A thought is not your own
It is theirs, since
They all want to judge you,
Determine if you are right or wrong.

Must break from their reign
Develop alternate methods
To express ideas,
Free to be a personality.

Travel the other side
A path seldom used,
Those who know it
Flourish in its abundance of diversity.

Free to live
Out of the publicity
Amongst "Outcasts"
Together you share a world of counterculture.

Ori Yacobi

Drive-By

Happy little child,
sweet and small and mild,
playing in your yard.
Feel a bullet hard
slam into your skull;
metal cold and dull
screaming though your brain.
Now you feel the pain.
Because of someone's fun
your young life is now done.
Because of someone's glee
you will no longer be
a happy little child,
sweet and small and mild.
Some junkies in a car
have killed one more so far.

Melissa A. Chamberlain

Riches-Of-His-Grace

I know nothing about
sweet- oil seeds.

That grow so precious fragrance be.
The smell
the touch- above human
hands. The anointed oil
from- God's hands.
Above the seed
Above the smell
Above its oils
That so swell
Above its drops- that
can be
From God hand
to you and me.

Moedon Singleton

On A Violin

I heard a violin sweetly singing
Sweetly singing through the night.

Singing through the dusty ages
Grecian plinths and persians dome
Glorie's fading, victors vanquished
Caesar dead, the fall of Rome;

Singing of the trees that wither
Singing of the fallen leaves
Singing of the reapers, binding
Corn among the yellow sheaves:

Singing of the Lord eternal
Changing darkness into light
I heard a violin sweetly singing
Sweetly singing through the night.

Rida Salant

Untitled

You were the night's mist,
that entices my craving.
You were the night's height,
calling love and passion eternally.
Our souls clashed, then parted.
Between the breathings, echoes
of our beating hearts, then silence.

We were the night mist,
fulfilling our craving.
We became the heighten nights,
called by love and passion eternally.
Two souls clashed and parted.
Breathing, echoes, silence.

Theodora Brown

Darkest Night

Darkness masks the dawn's reprieve
Swirling light; the shadows thieve
Fates rising threat towers blind
Journey past reality
Endless realm of fantasy
Forgotten moments alter time

Partially sheathed destiny
Hidden among faded dreams
Venture innocent into black
Falter as the night appears
Chilling breeze instilling fear
Follow closely - the charted path

Loosen the chains from your past
Grab onto the future fast
Confusion lurks behind the bend
Trembling alone in despair
Balancing these desperate prayers
Hold on tight 'til the journeys end

Sherry Marie Cook

To Be Beautiful

Bleed and tear
Take a razor to your skin,
Pluck and vanish
Such pain we all love,
Paint and cover
Pile on some weight,
Squeeze and squirt
Sweet smells of added stench,
Rub and blend
To erase those smudges,
Sharpen and color
To fancy those dull knives,
Stuff and push
Suck it in, size three?
Rake and tease
Spray it so it dare not move,
Ah, to be beautiful!

Shanon Conrad

Say Nine Syllables

I'll Pick a Pursuit and Perfect it!
Talents will prosper select it!
Let loose the juice direct it!
Dedicate to truth resurrect it!

I'll Pick a Pursuit and Perfect it!
Decide to be great and reflect it!
Dabble in dreams to deflect it!
Elevate demonstrate and elect it!

I'll Pick a Pursuit and Perfect it!
Bricks as the glue I'll erect it!
Die hards learn to protect it!
Casual care can complex it!

The stable ground to pound is moist,
The able wound in sound is choice!
Decide or glide must choose or loose,
Ride with pride choose one and cruise!

Sailing detailing hero's of thought,
Unstressed skill is will whose caught,
Hold of momentum triple P no slip,
Pickin' a Pursuit and Perfectin' it, sip!

Ken Flamer

Now

If you love me
Tell me now.
Do not wait until I am dead.
If you love me
Show me now.
Do not wait until I am dead.
If you love me
Hold me now.
Do not wait until I am dead.
If you wait
I may never hear,
Never see or feel.
Please do not put it off until tomorrow.
I need your love NOW!
I hurt NOW!
I am desperate NOW!
If you love me
NOW is the time.
Do not wait until I am dead!

Margie Kolter

Untitled

Tell me what you think
Tell me what you say
Tell me what goes on when I walk away.

Do you laugh
Do you cry
Do you have any emotions inside?

Who do you know
Who do you talk to
Who do you comfort when we're though?

Where's the anger
Where's the fear
Where's a man who can cry real tears?

What's love
What's hate
What's you and me, are we fate?

Is this the end
Is this the start
Is this what happens when you can't open
your heart?

Tracy Baker

Daily Trials

Bus Driver, Bus Driver,
Tell me where I am,
Tell me where I'm going
Tell me where I've been.

Numbers, numbers everywhere
Zip codes, area codes and more
Well, tell me, what is the fare?

I want to look at you
And you to look at me
I want to talk about the sea
And to know your point of view.

What? This is my stop?
There is ice and snow.
What should I do?
Where should I go?

Perhaps I'll cross the street
Catch the bus back to where I began
Start all over again.

Sally A. Hunt

Burned

In a blaze of glory
terror rose.
The lights out on
the ramshackle porch.
Quelled in flames a
malevolent phantom
was on the way.
Fire sirens screaming,
water scaling,
then silence in Maycomb.

Kellie Bave

Illusions

So many things in life we see
that are only an illusion.
It is difficult to actually know
when we are truly facing reality.
At times much of life is black
and white, although the colors can
change within the blink of an eye.
A pool of light which caresses our
body's filling us with warmth.
Suddenly the sensation is gone,
only to be replaced by a shadow
of dim hope.
Subconsciously we hold close to
our hearts what we wish to be true.
But only when it is too late
do we know that we were blinded
by what we thought we knew.

Stacie Singleton

Mists Of Life

There's a playful mist in morning,
That dances on the sun.
Mournful, teary patterns,
In a game that can't be won.

Shadows try to surround them,
Though they cast out only gray.
And as one's life would have it,
Most shadows fade away.

But though the sun is warm in Spring,
It sometimes burns too long.
And as you watch this dance go by,
It dries these mists in song.

Maggie Jones

Unconditional

You are my dad, and
that is true. For apart
of me is always with
you. I hold you close
and dear to my heart,
and always pray we
never part. Through
all the bad, and good
times too, you never
come up out of the blue.
And through, everything
you always knew that
no matter what I'll
always love you.

Tamra Matula

Teenage Suicide

You think everyone hates you
That no one cares.
You feel like you just
Don't belong anywhere.

So you just give up
You don't even try.
Why do you do it?
Please tell me why.

Life is so precious
Don't throw it away.
Tomorrows another
Beautiful day.

You may think that life
Is just too hard to cope
But please dear child
Don't ever give up hope.

There is just one more thing
That I want you to know
I love you, sweet child
Please don't let go.

Tammy Laskoski

Hurt Is Like The Ocean

Hurt is like the ocean
that runs so deep inside.

That tiny little tear drops
keep filling up in side.

How does the hurt go away,
When it's drowning deep inside.

And the hurt just keeps on
growing, when it's so hard
to confide.

Afraid to keep on going,
yet swallowing the tears.

So why doesn't the hurt
go away when there's nothing
else to fear.

Mary Louise Gardner

grandma died

A preternaturally long wick
that was ready to last out
its full century
but got cheated
by a couple of years

burned down
yesterday
leaving
soft white smoke
and the fragrance of hyacinth
in every room

Mary Winfrey Trautmann

Tell Me

To hear him say I Love You
That wearing on my breast,
Leaves much pain and sorrow.
Him, unsuspecting, wants to know my love,
But only the angels know the rest

To say I Love You
That fading from my breath
I, unsuspecting, feel for you
Yet hide all of my lovingness.

Kristal Myers

Fifty?!? Today!

Just writing you to let you know,
That what I've got I hope don't show,
On this very day - here and now
I'm half a century old, somehow!

I feel like stating it another way,
I'm twenty and thirty on this day,
Or maybe it's just five and ought
That really doesn't help a lot!

How silly! I'm just forty-nine plus,
Why should I make such a fuss,
Cause if you cut one hundred in half
My age would really be a laugh!

I guess - actually - what all this means,
And I'm sure - to everyone - it seems,
As though, I can not, will not, say
That Rosalie Whaley is p-p-p-pifty today!!

Rosalie Whaley

Fighting Our Destiny

I dream of a tomorrow
that will never come.
I fight against the
realization of the doom
that's impending. I fight
against the destruction
that is our destiny.
The fight is of no consequence
because by fighting destiny
we only bring it closer
but yet we fight
because of our instinct
to survive.

Rachel Castro

In My Mind

Would you like to tell me,
that you love me so?
Don't you know, we are the souls,
the spirits, living in flesh above all.

Come, come to your senses
and learn about self just more.
Become wise and comprehensive
and within yourself integrated.

I love you as you love me.
I understand your heart.
In my mind I stay "dispassionate"
to all that what moves and waves.

I resolves the dualities
of higher and lower in myself,
making "of twain one new man,"
of the true...I Am That I Am.

Zeno De La Mare Stachowicz

I Am Your Life

Wind that blows the trees,
That's me.
Air that fills your lungs,
The atmosphere around you.
I fill the space in your bubble
People run through me,
Never noticing,
That I am their lives,
And I am their purpose.

Lydia DiTirro

The Old Stone Church

Again, today, my God showed me
The beauty of His land
An old gray church He let me see;
The stone all cut by hand.
Upon the stoop I read the date,
Put there so long ago.
Two hundred fifty years have passed....
How could this church last so?
The stained-glass windows muted tones,
Still rich with colors rare,
Seemed so to cast a 'welcome mat'
To all who lingered there.
The winding paths that circled 'bout,
The lawn so soft and green
Gave me the thought that I had found
A 'jewel' no one had seen.
I'm sure God 'plants' these 'stepping stones'
In places I may see
To make me think of all He does
To prove His love for me.

rae hanlin

A Mirror New

Today I bought, a mirror new
The better I might see
But, alas sadly to say
The reflection wasn't me

It was surely a vision untrue
An aged face, ravished by time
Wispy hair, faded eyes of blue
Puffy lids and sagging chin
Not me, a reflection out of rhythm

My mental vision of beauty true
Frosted hair, like silk to frame
Skin soft, aglow eyes of blue
Taunting lips sweet as wine
Tis the real me that I claim

I tell myself inner beauties no jest
To achieve is to be sincerely blessed
What care I what the mirror proclaims
I'll see me, as I chose, it's my conquest.

Laura L. Lewis

Memories Never Fade

The babbling of the little brook,
The buzzing of the bees,
Sets your mind to wandering,
To days of memories.
Of setting on my daddy's lap,
And the stories he would tell,
Of the days when he was young,
Was just like fairy tales.
He'd tell the stories on and on,
Until sleep time took its toll.
He'd tuck us in so warm and tight,
To keep out all the cold.
And let sweet dreams come on in,
'till morning came around again.
No, matter what comes round in life,
This one thing I know,
Fond memories never fade with age,
As you are growing old.

Rosie B. Sneed

Freedom

Sometimes I fail to see
The darkness overcomes me
But the candle burns brightly
And I know you are there with me
I praise you Lord Almighty
Your truth has set me free

Alan Parker

Gone, But Not Forgotten

Sometimes I never think of you
The days are filled with things to do
Working, playing, life goes on
Loneliness seems almost gone.
Then night sets in, pushing, prodding
Memories come, begin uprooting
Happier times, before you were gone.
How sad it is to sleep alone!

Frances T. Cunningham

Within

Outside,
the earth receives a drink of
downy snow.
Inside,
a cheery heartside now is all
aglow.
Without,
the pressures of the world still
weigh one down.
Within,
the wondrous grace of God one's
soul doth crown.

Clara Thoren Rottmann

The Face Of The Forgotten Man

The face of Uncertainty.
The eyes bearing the weight of the world,
Striving to stay open, to see the future.
The lading of his brow,
burden heavily on his squint of hope.

The face of Hardship.
The lips pursed in a confined grimace,
unable to tell his story.
For the forgotten one
is not to be heard.

The face of Poverty.
The skin is coarse and calloused,
from a day of fruitless work.
The faded clothes are worn
with the air of worth.

The face of the Forgotten Man,
is the face of every man.
When will his turn come
to hear the voice of welcome?

Jenessa Johnson

Limerick

I once found a fossil on the ground
There it was very round
Filled with air
Tossed over there
The fossil I had found.

Eleanor Flynn

When Fairy Godmothers Appear

Greek mythology professes
The Fates controlled all destiny
Weaving great cables of fancy
Atropos, Clotho and Lachesis

I feel destiny is opened
When Fairy Godmother's appear
Granting favors of hope and cheer
With love that's far from imagined

A specific fay comes to mind
Cinderella has naught on me
Her heart is the noblest kind
Befriending my own destiny
Her presence is not hard to find
She's my own Godmother, Connie.

Jody Mathis

"The Prize"

The time is close
The finally draws near
His triumphant entry will
soon be revealed
So cast off darkness
to catch the dawn
There is but one road you
should be on
Make diligent your labor
delay not your calling
Do not continue your stumbling
and falling
Keep your eyes on the mark
your feet to the track
His glory you will see and your
reward will you receive.

Donyale Ahmed

The Future

A baby is born
The future has just begun
The sun shines
The moon glows
The stars are bright
to let you know,
God's love is sealed tight
A baby is born
and the future has just begun
a new day has dawned
and the sun shines on

Alister Coutain

Senario Of Life

Visions of eternity,
the gifts of human charity,
these emotions show with a clarity,
that surpasses all light.

Scenes of love,
peaceful as that of Noah's dove,
this hope I feel comes from above,
given to man by God.

Textures of land,
rough as that of sand,
created by holy hands,
made for man kind.

Sights of change,
the love overshadowed by pain,
there to teach the human brain,
the lessons of life.

Aaron Doubet

A Court/Ship

My dearest love; I have not known thee more
Than half a year; it's just last spring we met.
And yet I'll warrant no one could adore
Thee more than I, who never will forget.
Away from thee, I dream of times we spent
Alone; oh how we frolicked in the sun
And rain! It mattered not how far we went
In this impassioned courtship just begun.
And now I long to feel thee close again,
Alive and vibrant, eager for the flight
Across our world, the sea. No stinging rain
Nor blistering sun can lessen our delight.
Oh lovely lady, fleetest of the fleet,
I'll prove my love for thee when next we meet!

H. T. Davis

The Cowboy Rides No More

The dragon has become more intriguing
than the helpless damsel trapped in his lair,
and the Spanish Main has grown silent—
no more are pirates seen sailing there.
Merlin, magic, and the knights of the table round
can be found only in books of legend and lore;
and in the wild, golden West the cowboy rides no more.

These things I thought would save me
when I was young, my fancy free to roam around;
but now I see them as formless fantasies
since time has planted my feet firmly on the ground.
High adventure is of a time long past,
and there is no more monster behind the closet door,
the thrill in life is now getting the job done and the cowboy rides no more.

Such are the dreams that youth may hold,
it's sad to watch them pass away,
but we can not live for times gone by,
when we must worry only about today.
But someday, if we're lucky we can sit back and grin
and proudly say to the world "the cowboy rides again."

Michael Fuller

The Best Of Two Worlds

I have given love to the extent that it was spread to thin than when I thought all was lost, love was returned again, I have seen the best of two worlds as if I'm seeing it at the very beginning, I have seen the best of two worlds as if I'm seeing it during the end, some people may think that materialistic things is the best of everything, but I've learned that love and happiness is the best that one can gain, the best of two worlds one must maintain, never to get hung up in that social game, live life to its fullest, and breathe in every breath, because the best of two worlds will someday come to an end.

Marjean Ellis

Consolation

A poem? What does the ancient pundit say
That clarifies the words that come in play?
What rhythm, rhyme or reason do impart
A sense of season to the heart and ear
That hear its message crystal clear?
Those clarion words that say love still lives on
In hearts whose faltering beat, alas, has gone.
If you can comfort find in soundless song.
In words whose music silently plays on,
Then you define the poem's end to be
A grieving heart returned to sanity.

Lorraine A. Girard

My Awakening

Husband thank you,
Thank you my husband.
You're old. Don't depend on me for
your entertainment.

These statements, at the moment were
rude... unkind... even hurtful!

I thank you my husband,
I thank you for your startling words
that awakened choices.

Status quo? Remain in your shadow?
Possibilities?
Stretch...
Risk...
Grow!

Startled by your words,
My spirit awakened.
A new beginning, my empowerment!

V. Gast

Things That Belong To Me

Let me tell all you folks out there, it's no joke
That all the things that belong to me, can go up in smoke.
But, until they do, you see, they are
all mine, they are all free.
To begin: the bird that sings his songs
above my head
The squirrels that chase round and round
the tree bed.
The trains whistle in early morn that
sounds like the Ram's horn.
The clouds that skip like baby sheep,
that baa, baa but never sleep.
The mountains; the hills; the valleys and streams
Pure white snow as in a dream.
The flowers that bloom in spring,
the trees; the shrubs, these things.
All this, these priceless jewels
and snow white wool.
All that one can hear and see
are the "Things" that belong to me.

Peggy Williams Chatwin

Cold As Ice

Those ice blue eyes,
That cold as steel heart.

Blue can be as cold as ice cold water,
Blue can be as warm as the sunny blue sky.

Steel can be cold and hard,
Steel can be protective and smooth.

That hard and elusive exterior,
Is it real or just armor designed to scare away the weak?
Is it a mask designed to trick the many?
For only the few shall see past it.

The same hand that can be clinched to destroy,
Can be opened to soothe.

The same eyes that can give a colds stare,
Can also give a warm glare.

The path has been long and rough,
But things always get better,
Because tough times don't last.

The cold brings beautiful snow flakes,
Each unique and beautiful in its own way.

The cold brings quiet and peaceful serenity.

Paul Piciucco

Wings

A distant dreaming expression
That defines you to a hilt
A bird with wings always fluttering
Never takes time to land

No special moment can capture you
With no reflection in your eyes
A soft gentle breeze just passes through you
Couldn't carry you anyway
With the holes in your wings..

And your wings are always fluttering
So you're always in flight
Searching for a landing place
Where shapes and colors never change
Sometimes sinking low you push harder
To keep yourself adrift
Unaware the holes are getting bigger
Eventually you'll have to land
And find a resting place to heal...

Russell R. Van Heel

Searching

In youth a woman finds herself among the trials and tears
that face each person as they grow and wander through their years.
A woman stretches put her hands to grasp a lover's hand, he leads
her through the lonely nights to teach her loves commands.
Passing swiftly through these years of searching and of change,
she discovers love and craves it to remain.
Youth begins to fade a bit as years go swiftly by, it seems that
every now and then she has the need to cry. She longs for the
sweet moments with her lover and she beams, but memories of
what has been must sustain her as she dreams.
A woman's heart holds many things, the laughter and the tears,
but through it all comes hope which banishes her fears.
The years have passed, the children are all grown,
the house is empty, but, now and then you'll hear a silent moan.
The lovers are much older, the time is now at hand to try to
bring back memories of dreams and plans they had.
The woman started out alone, afraid of what might be, but found
a deep abiding faith and prays it will remain.

Marcella Morrison

Perpetrators

It was the lies, My Love,
that finally did us in,
jagged, charcoaled and cruel,

The lies that slither so coolly
from you to me
like snakes through summer's green.

Lies, frosty as your muddled indifference:
Two calm killers,
glacial and arrogant.

The bloodied victims, small and fragile:
Trust, Hope,
Joy, Love.

Katherine Newman

"Isolation"

How lonely is the mountain peak,
That rises thirteen thousand feet.
Caught in between the earthly crowds,
And mocking packs of cirrus clouds.
Let's nothing settle, nothing grow,
Nothing rest but new-fallen snow.
Viewed with majesty, come daylight;
Goes unnoticed in the night.
Until the next ice age it shall stand,
Where then it is crushed and returns to sand.

Matt Turnipseede

Doing What's Best (A Divorced Mother's Prayer)

Oh Lord I'll make just one request
That for my son I'll do what's best.
Not for me, but for his sake
So he won't pay for our mistake.
Though not with me he lives for now,
Let me make this sacred vow:

No one will ever love him more
Or miss his presence felt so before -
Nor will they ever share the bond,
That he and I have touched upon.
For no one else will ever know
How very much I love him so.

So please, dear Lord, guide him each day,
Watch over him at night I pray,
Keep his heart from being broken,
Hear his prayers when they are spoken.
Keep him always in thy care
Assure him when needed, I'll always be there.

Kim Ouellette

The Judlloron's Symbol

Refreshing are the breeze and cool water spray
That gently brush our faces this fine summer day.
We're cruising Old River in the Judlloron;
The blue fiberglass boat carries us from lake to pond.
We're always on the lookout for white perch and bream,
As a snake and an alligator near us swim.
Earlier, orange rays of the rising sun's beam
Combed smoky vapor from the crystal, rippling stream.
Silence brews reflections from the wonderful past:
Flashing images that fifty-three years have cast.

Our cozy home was blessed beyond any measures
When a daughter and two sons become our treasures.
The first three letters from their names birthed "Judlloron".
More than a boat, she stands for a close family bond.
Judy, Lloyd, and Ronnie are credited with the name.
It's up to their offspring to continue the game.
With divine torchlights, they will boost the family ties!
Welded with love, they will avow that the bond never dies!

Lloyd, Sr. and I are thankful to be very blest!
Retired and relaxed, we bask in beautiful rest.

Mary Alice Giglio Turner

Thoughts Of You

It seems as though it was yesterday...
that I had you on my mind...

Looking back over the memories in my life...
You had been there all the time...

Pleasant thoughts caress this soul... so warm and so bold
I dare not let the moment go... it's thought of you I hold

Somewhere... somehow our spirits will suddenly meet...
And knock us right off of our feet

Leaving us with wonderful dreams and everlasting tastes.
Of life... so sublime... so carefree... and so full of grace

I cry inside for joy and the happiness that surrounds...
You and I together... in love we are justly bound

There are clear sights of you... floating like little clouds...
When I think about you and whisper your name aloud...

Even though you are not near... but only a distance away...
I find myself praying to God... that in my life you'll stay

Mmmmm... there are those warm and tingling thoughts of you
my friend
I must lay them down for a moment... because...
They'll start all over again

Mary L. Harris

My Sermon To You

"I hold you in my heart" PHIL 1:verses 3,7,8,19
Our fellowship is different
that is plain to see,
it reaches all the way to God
just look at verse three.

There is nothing wrong with the way I feel
it's something the world can't ever sever
because I hold you in my heart
take a peek at verse seven.

Our fellowship God knows about
I simply tell it straight
it stands in heaven's court
just look at verse eight.

The news we receive many times
shatters our greatest dreams,
your prayers for me will see me through
just look at verse nineteen. Amen.

Paul E. Hendricks

Winter's Bountiful Beauty

The moon above gives off a light,
That looks upon a sea of white.
With all its snowflakes sparkling bright,
They illuminate the darkness and take away the night.

The air taste fresh and smells of pine,
Like sampling all the finest wines.
The trees stand tall and in a straight line,
The wind echoes through and whispers, "Everything is fine."

This beauty of nature brings on a smile,
That can be as long as the river Nile.
Even though everyone has their own style,
Winter can still bring folks together for miles.

Sandra M. Downing

Untitled

Despair, despair for all the confusion
That rains upon us like steel knives
Cutting into the muscle and turning
until the sinew tears and burns.
Scream, scream as the hypocrites taunt and prod you
Smile as they lead you on.
Watch them laugh as they knives.
Crawl, crawl into the corner and down
in your own blood as
the shackles bind your hands,
Die, die and believe that all was perfect.

Vanessa L. Fort

Gift Of Love

We have given each other a gift,
that very few can give;

It is the greatest gift that can be given.

There is no price tag on this gift,
for it is priceless;

It comes from within the hearth and soul.

God has granted us this gift,
to give to who we choose;

But this precious gift should be forever,
not taken for granted.
So, I know that is what we will be
.....forever

Patty J. Newton

Another Age Of Reason

This age is a handful of experience
That tastes like absolutes.
It leaves the honest quandaried,
Above board while bilges of truth
Wreak in reality.
This realm is a stagnant pool of potential
Blooming as ichor beneath
Bloodletting suns.
All that remains is promise
Uninvested; truth negotiated and
Of vague necessity,
Yawns in compromise.
Great knowledge creaks
Under the weight of eyes
Hollow and unnumbered;
Nor can it withstand the scrutiny
Of countless ghost-like souls.
Humanity is become
The shade of its wisdom,
And the myth this age denies.

Patrick Loudon

The Seasons Of Our Life

The first time they met, one glance and they knew
That they were meant for each other and would always be true.
They knew that their love was a beautiful thing
They started life together—this was their spring.

Then came the children, parents proud as could be,
Their life was full, work and play, you see
Ball games to play, a skinned knee to tend
A picnic to go on—this was their summer then.

Years passed swiftly by, the children were grown
Each one following a dream, having children of their own,
Each grand-child was special, they loved them all,
And they counted their blessings—this was their fall.

Now they sit and dream of days long gone
When joy and laughter filled their home,
And they share their memories—this husband and wife,
This is their winter—the seasons of their life.

Velma Persinger

Her

It is said for every man there is a woman,
That they will meet by things such as
  luck, fate, and omen.

Some say I'm lucky and that I have found my way
Because I have found my woman this very day.

Since I was born she has wanton for me,
It's taken many years but now I see.

My friend I guess, truly I hate to speak,
For her presence shall I never need seek.

Although I love her not she loves me,
She burdens my heart oh can't you see.

I reveal her now and now only,
She has a harsh name, her name is lonely.

Phillip B. Hughes, Jr.

The Sun

The sun is like a beam from God
That shines on me.
The light of the sun helps me see where to walk,
Without the sun the world would be
Cold and dark

LeAnne Ellis

The Spirit Within

There is a spirit raging within
That wants to erupt to conquer to win
God planted the seed at birth to begin
The road maybe treacherous, so we must have the yen

The journey begins with our family on loan
The travel permits our ability to become grown
The road is never carved in stone
We were given free will to set the tone

The mountain ahead is steep and unclear is the way
The search is difficult for that enlightened ray
The raging spirit within makes us begin again
at the break of each day
Knowledge abounding, the light will be seen some spring in May

Thus mountains climbed, adventures untold
Lead us on a journey so exciting, so bold
The energy of spirit nudges us on
To never seize the search for the enlightened down

M. Pat McCormick

Dear Mr. Bus Driver

Dear Mr. Bus Driver we want you to know,
That we appreciate you so!
We don't always put on a show,
But our love for you continues to grow!
You're always there in rain, sleet, and snow,
To make our bus go, go, go!
As you drive our bus to and from school,
We certainly know to follow the rules!
You're always there with a big caring smile,
Driving the bus safely mile after mile!
Again, Mr. Bus Driver we want you to know,
That we appreciate you so!

Mae Young

Is God Angry At The World

Is God so angry at the world
That we can't see him anywhere
We are living a life of fear
And nobody seems to really care
The world is upside down
Is God still looking down
We seem to be facing an eternal end
Because we cannot live an mutual friends

Is God angry, that I am scared of this world
There is so much uncertainty
We pray to see a peaceful day
We pray to see another way
We pray to save humanity
We pray to see the world set free.

Is God angry at the world
That man can't live in harmony
Must he take another's life
Must he struggle to survive
Must he race for better arms
To later destroy his fellow man.

Ricardo M. Baker

Broken Wing

The life and beauty of one girl's soul,
the honesty and truth that she once told,
has all of a sudden died away,
and she has too I'm sad to say.
Once so bright and so pure for so long,
has become so mean and jokingly strong.
Now like a character all she does is pretend,
This beautiful girl I once called my friend.

Marisa Syms

Patience Is A Virtue

Patience is a virtue
That you treasure and you keep
With it you can accomplish anything
Even the magic you seek
All the joys you have today
Has come to you in time
Even the ones you longed and searched for
Knowing you would never find
Patience is the key
To all your feelings and success
With it you strive toward all your goals
Never settling for anything but the best
Patience is a virtue for all life
And He carries you under his brass ring
So keep these thoughts close to your heart
And with it you can accomplish anything

Staci Triplett

Consciousness Of Man

What is it
That's happening to the hearts and minds of man
Who plants those seeds of hate and rage
Deep in their consciousness.

How come they think when they strike out
Their own anguish and hurt will be far less.

How long before they realize
The grim and evil things they do
Will never bring them happiness.

They have a choice tho' they know it not.
Is it too late - have they strayed too far
Forever trapped in the net they've wrought.

Yet, there is hope
If within the Consciousness of Man
A spark of light exists.

Phyllis Blanche Disney

"My Love Is Like A Red, Red Rose"

O, my love is like a red, red rose.
That's newly sprung in June.
O, my love is like the melody,
That's gently played in tune.

And fare thee well, my only love
And fare thee well a while!
And I will come again, my love,
Tho' it were ten thousand mile.
And my love will come again and never goes,
O, my love is like a red, red rose.

Lisa Simes

Untitled

Tears run down when we hear the news.
The children didn't have a chance
to choose whether to live or whether to die.
Someone choose it for them and no one knows why.

The sadness in the world rose. No more wiping their nose. Thousands of people come from all around as they put them in the ground. Six feet under they bury them deep as they rest in a deep deep sleep.

Good-bye to the boys who are no longer here.
Our hearts filled with wonder, worry, and fear.
We know your in Gods holy light, where He will take you in his arms and hold you tight.

Kay Englebert

"No Weight"

They say birds of a feather flock together
That's true in so many cases
But God only knows why humans judge each other
By the color of their faces

Why do the color of one's skin carry so much weight?
If this continues - Will anyone be allowed to enter heaven's gate

We suppose to be the most intelligent of all God's creatures
And from the standpoint of anatomy, we all possess the same features
We all laugh and cry, and if we cut, we all bleed
And for being loved, we all have this insatiable need

So why do the color of one's skin carry so much weight?
We could end all wars, if love and could take the place of hate

Rich man, poor man, black man, white man
We're all suppose to be brothers
No problems of the world would be too great
If we only supported and love one another

But why do the color of one's skin carry so much weight?
It's not supported and love one another

Cause come judgement day - The color of one's skin will carry "noweight"
And our definitive acts of benevolence may just determine our fate

Larry Washington

Amber

On the 12th day of October in 1989,
The air was warm and sun really shined.

That was unusual for this time of year.
So I knew this would be a great day of cheer.

I held in my arms the greatest gift in the world.
The most beautiful and delicate bright eyed little girl.

You brought with you joy and oh so much pride.
You filled in the emptiness I'd been feeling inside.
When you opened your eyes, I could only smile.
And you just stared at me for a really long while.

Your amber colored eyes and your dark brown hair.
I thought of your name, right then and there.

Amber, I said, there is no other name.
None to describe your eyes in that way.

I made a promise on that very day.
That I'd let no one hurt you or take you away.

And I'll keep that promise for as long as you like.
And remember I'll love you for the rest of my life.

Michelle Renee Fisher

Joy

Joy is a drop of dew on an orchid petal,
The arms of a child around my neck,
The giggles of a toddler that I try to catch,
Joy is the stroke of a cat on my naked legs,
The purr of a kitten to awaken me gently,
The dance of a white butterfly around my head.
Two hands on the skin of my back for an embrace,
Eyes that show me who I really am,
A voice and a song that lift my soul with emotion,
A tree that stands tall with no judgement,
A spring of water glittering with light.
Joys is what I can create with my hands.
Joy is witnessing a friend taking a freedom flight.
Joy is sharing bread, cheese and wine with friends.
Joy is walking barefoot in the ocean during a sunset.
Joy is knowing that I am worth loving.
Joy is sharing pearls of tears for enlightenment.
Joy is God letting me know that I am His Son.

Peter Sanderson

Looking For Rain

Cracked and dry the parched earth waits.
The barren land waits for the infinite grey sky to offer it the precious gift of rain. The rain doesn't come. It would be so easy to ask the sky for rain. It could grab hold of her and take the sweet liquid but, if the earth failed no cloud would ever offer a drink and the blue expanses would never forgive it. The earth continues to wait and it continues to die.
Die, crumbling to dust.
Dying, no more life.
Dead.
Sand shifts over the bones of the earth and waits.
The waste land lies dead waiting for the infinite grey sky to offer it the precious gift of rain. The rain doesn't come. It doesn't rain in the desert.

Seth Dorman

The High Flyer

It is ten o'clock the high flyer says.
The beautiful people look into the mirror,
people sashay across the old diamond floor.
Flowers bloom in utter magnificence.
It's the timely existence of the atom
that leaves all of the wonder out of it.
Dave is a little confused about things,
and he crouches deep into his corner,
his closet is shut the time is not now.
The beautiful people all laugh and play
and dance into the morning's early light.
People are sitting lonely on a park bench,
of all the things to happen, why this?
Questions fill up Mary and spill into Jenn.
Why do all of the things happen this way?
Is it time for bed, to rest in the dark?
How do they know how to do it that way?
Is that how things actually take place?
The powerful music fills all their heads.

Raymond T. Seeley

The Lonely Silence

They were just, symbols to me,
The beauty in them, I could not see.
You turned them to music, the sweetest loot,
You played with perfection, the magic flute.

The love of all ages, I never before heard,
The sound was compelling, it took me and lured
My emotions, now I can't be without
Your musical love, is what I'm about.

You've taken it afar, that magical sound,
I yearn to hear it, where can it be found?
It simply can't, it's gone away,
But the loneliness is here, with me, everyday.

Nathaniel Cooper

The Chair

It holds me now,
the chair.
It bore your weight, and now mine,
with resigned indifference.
It has no memory of you,
of your stilled limbs
dangling
below its broad arms;
of your twisted smile and
unfocused eyes staring into the face of
the neighbor,
Death.

Katherine Gongora

Correspondence

He sees me for the first time on a hot desert day;
The carrier hands me to him, and I feel the warmth of love
Lingering in his touch as he reads my sender's address;
He puts me in his pocket - goes about his work;
I wait as impatiently as he for a break in soldierly duty,
Knowing I bring him bright news and happiness;
When he finds a time for rest, he sits down in privacy -
Pulls me from his pocket; He looks down at me for a moment,
And I in turn study him....
His kindly face, dirty, dusty, quite serene;
He rips me open; it does not hurt, but fills me with life-
Short-lived though it may be- and anticipation;
I feel hot teardrops fall upon me, for my words make him happy;
My words bring his heart closer to his wife and children;
I begin to die as he refolds me,
But I feel gladness,
Knowing I shall soon be reborn-
And reborn once and again-
For I am a cherished part of his life now...
And I will be treated accordingly-

B. K. Kissane

My Own Back Yard

I've marveled at the beauty of
  the cherry trees in bloom
knelt to pick a wild flower in the meadow.
I've gazed at mountains washed
  by the moon.
Watched the wild and raging
river flow
Nothing I have seen or read upon a card.
Can surpass the fragrance of the
Locust trees - in my own back yard.

Rosalie A. Menalia

The Computer Room

The room is darkened now, and silent;
The clickety-clack of keyboards,
With their deep and important thoughts,
Are muted at last - and speechless.
The men and women who think these thoughts,
And put into endless code the nebulous dreams
Of dreamers, have gone away to other lives,
And the solitude is left to machines
Who sit there alone, screens alive
With the flickering patterns of screen saver light.
What thoughts, what vast uncharted thoughts,
Are racing through those electric brains -
Still waiting for that elusive clue of knowledge to be found.
Tomorrow the tasks will begin again,
And humans will resume their separate quests —
But for tonight, this is a world of dancing electrons.

Robert P. Studer

March Sky

The sky is like a person,
The clouds its moods portray;
An ever changing countenance
Looks down from day to day.

Sometimes the clouds have settled
Like a frown upon its face
And we sense a kind of struggle
In their slowly moving pace.

Then stealing through between the rifts
The rays of sunlight file,
To bathe them all in dazzling light
And triumph with a smile.

Rosamond O. Reau

I Must Be!

On a raft, at the edge of Midnights shore,
The cold wind of terror nips bitterly at me.
The freezing! It chills to the core!
Reluctantly, I push the skiff to sea.

Tattering the sail, I throw away the ore,
Wise to how this trip must appear to be.
Helpless. And, I, knowing what for.
How frightened am I of he!

But I must put my fright behind the door.
Cowardice of mine he must not see.
For tonight! In his heart a dagger will I bore!
Alas! Unlike other nights! Will I be free!

Waking dreamily. That must I be!
Clutching my dagger. I must be free!

Melissa Kelley

The Unwept Calls

The unwept calls of a forlorn mother
The compassionate words of an unspoken brother
Emotion understanding that few have truly to endeavor
Love that so many have fallen short of forever
Entanglements of love that hold together
Crumble within the realms of a self righteous heart
The taste of pure love sweet when first acquired
Becomes bitter when time to retire
Fatal attraction; ice made moth to fire
Time burned pains; wanted,
Remedy Required

Noah Christophersen

Flight Into Night

Drifting through the oceans of night
The eagle has landed, but now it must take flight
Soaring throughout the sky without a care
Life has just begun, the eagle accepts the dare

Living upon what is scarcely provided
The eagle is fearless for the trouble is sighted
Fighting against the evils of night
Sunrise has begun, the eagle seeks light

Inching closer and closer toward light
The eagle gains knowledge, overpowering night
Providing what night once demanded
Peace is once again, the eagle has landed

Tonya Marie Thatcher

Untitled

  Times gone by and things have changed,
The feeling in my heart seems to have been rearranged.
  Could it be I've had my last cry or
Maybe I've just heard the last lie.
  You see me moving away more everyday
It's just because I see this feeling cannot stay.
  I tried not to cry I tried to stay strong,
I just need you to tell me where I went wrong.
  There was a time I thought there was something I could do,
But now I just realize that we are through.
  I need you to mature and I need you to grow,
I need you to know the feelings I had for you will always show.
  But now there's a whole new me in store,
And the new me just can't say I love you anymore.

Stephanie Wadsworth

A Display Of Hatred

The show begins and I lay back in bed, behind closed doors
- the first firecracker sounds-
and it's so forceful it brings tears to my eyes.
To carry them away I close my eyes
And up floats a scene which drowns out the noise.
The tall weeds bend in the breeze as my little legs stretch to leap
My baby hand grasps a fistful of dandelions
I smile so wide I nearly crack
I giggle so much I nearly burst
and just as I am about to run into her arms
- a firecracker murders my memories
and I am drawn back to the show
I crack open the door and see her
But I no longer want to leap into her arms,
Now, I frown so much I have forgotten how to smile
I cry so much I don't remember how to laugh
I watch her unsmiling mouth scream without emotion,
her slits of eyes disappointed without reason
my ears ring and ache.
- I never want to see fireworks again

Kelsey Montague

Great Smoky Mountains

In smokies have nature and fresh air to breath.
The forests, perennial, streams, ephemeral flower give
everyone the great feeling to be there.
It's a place to be free as a bird.
When it rain, and smell wonderful from the forest.
You can sit, dreams for hours and hours.....
A place to understand what it's now and forever.
Wildlife is us and the animals, who
came through the Great Smoky Mountains.
The things you never forget what
you saw until it pass away.....

Kathleen Ingrassia

Love's So Fragile

Love's so fragile, handle with care
The fruit of life, taste if you dare
Love is tender don't bump or bruise
If you cherish it, there's more to use
Take what's given, expect no more
Take it for granted, it's out the door
It's always there for you if you choose
Why not try it there's nothing to lose
So bear in mind a heart you may break
if you try love you think's a mistake.
But if your bold and decide to taste it
and always are careful, never to waste it
love will return to you twenty fold
for love lasts forever, no matter how old.
But always, no matter when or where,
Love is fragile, handle with care.

Kurt Wilkens

The Mixed Up Poem

The birds sing, the bees make honey
The grass grows green, the corn grows tall
The cows in the corn, chickens in the feed
Cats fight the dog, the dog runs the cat
The dog runs the rabbit, the cat chases the rat
I like to dream, do you like to sing?
The cars run on gas, the horse runs on grass
Birds flap their wings, squirrels crack their nuts
I like to sing when it's going to rain
My brain isn't the same.

Ray Dicus

Love Song

I awoke in your arms without fear
The hurt had gone, trust replaced the tear.
The depth within your eyes, your soul burning bright
Shining a love song with the Immortals might.

Gather all the words to sing within your heart
Get it all together, let's have a brand new start.
Sweet, gentle teasing tells me that you care
Patterns of electric feeling whenever you are there.

So, sing sweet lullabies softly in my ear
Caress each memory as long as we are here
Hold me close, let the oceans roar
From sea to shining sea our love be evermore.

Lynn Marlowe

Respect

The lack of respect between a husband and wife or a parent and child
The lack of respect for life or another human being.
The lack of standards and morals
It does not matter what color your skin is or God you pray to.
Stop taking each other for granted and lead a loving healing hand.
Follow the traditions of the past,
blended together with the ways of the present.
First take a look inside to see where you yourself can change.
End the malice and pain
Don't judge each other
Accept each person for who they are
Let go of the bitterness, anger and hatred.
If you be rich or poor
Man or woman
Famous or common
You deserve respect and to be treated with dignity.
For no one is better than the next.
No one needs the hurtful words that are said or the violence that does occur.

Lori R. Mueller

Life's Changes

I don't feel I'm made of glass anymore and that
the least little wind would cause me to fall,
I don't hang my head down and look at the ground
I'm beginning to stand up straight and tall.
I hear the birds singing now-and it's such a pretty sound,
My eyes are opening and I can see the beauty
all around. I don't feel anymore... like an alien
from space, I do feel sad though for all the
waste. The waste of a life caught up in
incest, the loss of child dreams, But
I don't fall asleep anymore so scared that I
could scream. The world is beginning to welcome
me now as it seemed to elude me before,
I feel like I belong now, and I like this
feeling more and more. So I will take my
inner child everywhere I go, for she was
robbed but I will teach her how very much we
can grow. And we will be happy, her and I
because we both deserve it, will dance and sing
to our heart's content, because I know now that were going to make it

Rosemarie Olson Reid

Special

The night our eyes met, I knew you were special.
The day you said hello, I knew you were special.
The moment you touched me, I knew you were special.
The moment you kissed me, I knew you were special.
The night you said I was special, I knew I loved you.

Paula Daniels

Wedding Eve

As she wandered through the garden,..........she smiled;
the light crisp air trailed over her forehead as the
reflection of the moon stroked gently across her cheek.
The leaves rolled along the ground with graceful ease,
knowing the path well, as if traveled before and yet...
still feeling anew.
The night was black, yet alive with anticipation and wonderment,
and as her heart beat, the passion of life swept through her,
touching each and every nerve in her body.
It was a new beginning and she knew her life would change,
just as each new day abounds, and yet.....
as the night became morning, her eyes traveled up, up, up
to the sky above with a breathless delight.
As she waited for the sun to rise high above the hill,
she felt a small quiver.
A new light, a new day, a new life...
and she smiled.

Patricia Winegar

The Night

The night, the heat, the excitement.
The moment your lips found mine.
When our inhibitions fell victim
To the passion growing between us.
The sound of a dress falling to the floor.
The whispered words trying, failing,
To express what we felt.
We walked through the fire
Unscathed by the flames.
We shared each other's secrets without a word.
We unleashed one another's hidden desires.
When the morning sun shone in
We parted ways with promises to call
Mumbled through a cigarette haze.
Though I know we'll never meet again
Last night will live in my heart forever.

Mike Wever

In The Depths Of Your Eyes

In the depths of your eyes
The moon shines down on crystal blue waters
As two souls swim together
To a once-forgotten place.
Darkness.
Cries ring out into the star-filled sky
Passion fills the salty air
As their bodies mingle.
Their longing for each other
Comes alive.

Melissa Miller

Life

Life is what happens when you're not paying attention.
The mortgage needs to be paid, and the cars broken down again.
The water heater is leaking, the well is almost dry.
The kids need to be hauled from ball practice to music lesson.
Then.
There's an accident and everything stops.
There a sickness that isn't going away.
Suddenly,
I stop to look at clouds racing in the sky.
I notice the leaves softly tumbling to the ground.
Life
Fragile
Fleeting
pay attention.

Sandy Lankford

"Summer Magic"

Summer's ending.
The mystery and magic unravelling to reveal something
as harsh as birth; being ripped from the warmth and
security of a mother's womb.
During the height of the season she felt as if she was in
charge and in control of her feelings. She was in love, and
he loved her back, their time together seemed to never end.
But new as the season draws to a close, his feelings do too.
And the girl is left confused, and hurt, feeling small, and
insignificant; not wanted, or needed, or most of all, loved.
She knows (in her heart) that he'll regret leaving her someday,
when he looks back on the way things were. She knows
(in her heart) that he'll come back to her someday, and
then things will begin again right from where they were left off.
She knows (in her mind) that she should move on and not
wait for that day. She knows (in her mind) that she can
survive without him, and that he won't be the last; she'll love
again.
Maybe next summer when the mystery and magic sprout
up with the flowers, as they always do; she'll find
someone new, and maybe he'll be the right one.

Mollie Milward

My Friend

Do you want to know my Friend?
The one who said I will keep to the end.
Won't you try my friend and see?
That He will keep His promise to you, like He has to me.

How wonderful it is, to have such a Friend,
Who will keep His promise to the end.
I am no more alone, He is always by my side
He loves me and with me does abide.

If you will obey me, and hold me ever so dear,
You will triumph and know, that I am always near.
I won't promise you, that you will never shed a tear.
For this life you see, is only temporal here.

But in eternity you shall live with ME.
Now I am free, I am kept in His love.
I am waiting a home in heaven above.
Praise GOD, some day His face I will see.

Mrs. Edwin Retzloff

Moment Of Now

In the Moment of Now
the P/u/l/s/e of Pain pounded its dreary cadence
and smothered the Sound of Hope.

Miles from the Memory of Joy
- in the latitude of Fallen Stars -
Death awaited the coward's approach.

Stitched onto his skin,
a fleece of tangled myths.

Nailed to his feet,
dreams carved of stone.

Limbed, but lame,
Sensate, but numb,
Breathing, yet breathless, he pampered his crusted wounds and
cursed life's long winter.

Katherine Humphries

The Little Boy I Never Knew

His first and only touch, fit in mom and daddy's hand;
The pain it hurt so much, they just could not understand.
He really was to young, to leave their arms so soon;
He was there only son, leaving memories much too few.
Was there anything at all gained, other than drizzling tears;
Could he feel any of the pain, nearly as harsh as theirs?
Does he have his daddy's eyes, while sharing mommy's traits;
Does he hear their many cries, while in Heaven he now waits?
As I pray on knees, does he hear me too;
Is he watching over me, the little boy I never knew?
We all experience loss, yet are never quite prepared;
To ever count the cost, of a parent's worst nightmare.
Does he now own wings, and does he really fly;
Can he hear the angels sing, about the "sweet by and by?"
We have you would be proud, if here with us you'd be;
You'd feel the love around, all of your family.
Not one birthday passes, that we would ere forget,
We'll reunite at last, but our time's not come yet.
I know as for me, there still is work to do;
Until I finally meet, the little boy I never knew.

Tanya Erdman

Carolina Autumn

October is the loveliest of seasons —
the parade of red, the mystical glow of yellow,
the dazzling festival of nature's flames
engulfing the hills and enlightening the heart,
in a brief and beautiful captive moment,
like a flower flowing in the river of time.

Renato L. Dijamco

Home

What makes a house a home
The people that within it dwell
Their contributions are unique
For here lies the realization of every thing
The intimacy cannot be compared
Trifles and confusion add to the glamour
Not forgetting the voice of authority
That puts the house on an even keel
For all this is their sanctuary
Within these walls one is his true self
To dream and sometimes drift into fantasy
Forgetting worldly cares and relieving ones anxiety
For here we should acquire our inner sense of security

Theodore Clayton

The Great North Woods

There's a hundred lakes in the great north woods where the pines fringe the water's brink
Where at eventide, at the sunset hour, the deer come down to drink
There lurks the mighty "musky" and the black bass leaps and plays.
A land supreme where to fish and dream, through golden summer days.

There you will find, in this land sublime, a haven from worry and pain
Far from the strife that goes with this life in its greed for gold and gain
There oft on the breast of a moonlight lake 'neath starry canopied sky
Comes the wailing of the lonesome loon, the whip-poor-will's plaintive cry
The haunting rapture of the wild - a peace that fills the soul
There in the heart of the great north woods is the nature lover's goal.

H. C. Blair

"Building A Railroad"

Where the sky was blue and fields were green
the plowed ground as far as could be seen,
Railroad ballast top of rail, you could see no ties
The long long way you saw ran into miles.
And working one day, it come up a cloud,
so glad to see rain, I yelled out loud.
Got to the cross landing, there was the truck,
and before we got there, we nearly got stuck!
As my mate and I got into the truck we got tickled,
Because behind the seats was our slickers!
With wet heads and muddy feet,
We pressed down the dirt road to retreat.
After getting over the sticky road we gave a sigh,
Because we made to town where it was dry.
I'm here building railroad by all means,
And as my vacation instead of seeing New Orleans.
Looking over my shoulder across the plains,
Another blue cloud guess that means rain.
Guess I'll stop and gather things up,
Get ready again to run to the truck.

Marie Kerry

"Blue Steel"

Blue is the color that we all feel
The pride that we carry with the strength of steel.
It came as a surprise from no where at all
For fright ran straight through me when I got that call.
I thought it was a dream a nightmare at most
But I lay awake at night talking to his ghost.
My daddy is gone, it has happened so fast
For we can only look back as he is a memory of our past.
I tried to stay strong and stand so tall
For I know that my daddy would not let me fall.
My mommy needed me to be there by her side
For all I could do was hold her when she cry.
It is a time that has made us come closer together
For our family is something that we will have forever.
There were so many things that I wanted to say
For I can only do it now when I kneel and pray.
I love you daddy though you never really knew
Because daddys like you were one in a few.

Michael Piccinnini

February 17

Twas on this day I chose to die, this year of '94
The problems rose above my head, and I could bear no more.

I thought for quite a while, of whom to give my things.
My valuables virtually worthless, I owned no gold, no diamond rings.

I thought of death, this one way out, I thought of how to die.
I thought great thoughts of Heaven, of living in the sky.

And then I thought of Hell, this fiery pit below.
If I should take my life this way, is this where I would go?

And then I thought of Jesus Christ, and how H died for us.
I shrugged and thought of Hell again, and living was a must.

My next thoughts were of all my friends, and how I loved them dear.
And then I thought of all the times with them that I held near.

I tried to picture in my thoughts, my dreams that lay ahead.
I couldn't fill a single one, not one...If I were dead.

I sat and wept, for by myself, I knew not what to do.
And then I realized, life was grand, for I was loved by you.

Ray Hope

Untitled

No one seems to see the deepness of the Soul,
the richness of the Spirit.
Why do they hide from their purpose?
All that they know can be seen or heard or smelled or tasted or touched.
All that they desire is tangible and ordinary.
None of their everything matters;
Not looks, not lust, not money, not power.
Short-lived desires are only for this world.
Will they be empty when it is time to move on
beyond places and people and time?
They are only people;
nothing more than flesh and bones and blood with empty souls.
Always thinking
Never searching
Skimming across the surface of life
Afraid to go too deep
Fearful of answers they can't find here
They isolate themselves in humanity
Ignoring their Oneness of Spirit.

Kate Ryer Wilson

The Outer World

The ticking sounds going though my head,
the ringing sounds pounding in my mind,
and the breeze blowing through my ears.
As my eyes fill up with tears.

The sky a beautiful shade of violet,
the clouds as black as they can be,
and the moon seems so far away, but not to far
to see. No matter how dangerous the outer world may be
it is still the most wonderful thing to me.

The sound of silence at four a.m.,
or the loud sirens from the danger in the streets,
the sounds of the undergrounds when the water runs,
or maybe even the heat coming from the sun.
May be a tree, or a honey bee. It doesn't matter
what it is for it is all so wonderful to me.

Rachel Anderson

With Time

With time
the same hands
that pushed and struggled and clenched
so that I nearly bore holes in my palm
can hold another, can caress his skin.
The same hands that felt the lies
can rest peacefully
on the pillow while I sleep.

With time the same eyes
that glared in fear
and endured the darkness
can now see the light, can sparkle with joy.
The same eyes that could only see the past
can look upon the present with optimism.

With time the same heart
that broke and tore and dripped
with unjust sorrow can still love,
can thank the past for its teachings.
The same heart that longed to die
has learned to live again...to Love again.

Karyn M. Hamaguchi

The Creative Explosion

The Cosmos displays on a grandiose scale
the same symphony waiting to be played within.
A microcosm of the Creative Explosion.

A universe of dancing galaxies sing
in a visual chorus fitting kings.
Yet inside there awaits artistic things.

Infinitesimal speck of dust is man
yet from within creation can
Continue anew.

The Human displays on a smaller scale
the same symphony played with out.
A microcosm of the Creative Explosion.

From tiny man a symphony sprang
to mimic what nature drew.
Artistic Rivers, Mountains, Oceans.

Continue on, Creative Explosion,
Create again through Man.
Span both outer and inner spaces.
Fulfill the destined plan.

Lawrence Scott

Fleeting Thoughts

As swift as light from rays of sun, through darkness of ocean floors
The sands of time go on and on, as breezes on distant shores.

Fleeting moments pass in a blink, what seemingly is moving slow
Is actually passing swift and strange, and quiet as a winter's snow.

The measures of life takes its toll, living for great expectations
Searching for ways to make it last, with no feelings or reservations.

Seasons change and take new form, once cold and raw they turn
To heat and warm the summer nights,
as if time itself is trying to confirm.

A constant search for longer life, is a mystery beyond compare
To reach for more time and space, but finding there's none to share.

Waves will pound and winds will blow, forever 'till the end,
But that of time and of life, must never try to blend.

How long is time? How long is life? A mere twinkle of an eye
For when it's thought the secrets found, in truth, it's time to die.

Kenneth W. Johnson

La Isle De Formosa

Esta La Isle de Formosa! The Sparkling Jades,
The silver tides splash the pearls on your eyes.
The sky with floating cotton clouds wink,
The Sun casts the silent kisses on your cheek.
Ah!, Your Name: The Paradise. The Haven to the refugees

King Dragon stretches his bloody wings,
and throws down his fiery red tongues,
pouring down the furnace flames and masses
dusts upon the paradise, La Isle
Ah!, Your name obscures the sun. Formosa! no more

Fight the Devil dragons' destruction! We must restore!
see! human bloody melees spread on La Isle
The Righteous seed are sown and sprout again on La Isle
under the Sun, the dream come true, the hope on the Paradise
no more destruction! No more tears! Joys on the Island of Jades

The Lord shakes the mountains and seas,
O! my children, be strong and brave! wipe your tears!
You will be born again, the resurrection truly comes,
Esta La Isle! the Lord will restore sparkling Jades.
Again! Free! Dignity! be yours, the Island of the Beauties

Philip C. F. Hwang

A Gloomy Morning

It was a windy morning
The sky was streaked with gray,
It was a gloomy morning
The children stayed inside to play.

The rain-filled clouds were drifting
The sun was hidden in the sky,
Everyone seemed to be waiting
For soon heaven would start to cry.

Her tears would wet the meadows
Water all the plants and trees,
She would bathe and cleanse our precious land
And freshen the air we breathe.

Our hearts would be filled with thankfulness
For this blessing from above,
For we know this gloomy morning
Was sent to us with love.

W. Arletha Ball

One Day With Meals On Wheels

Don has the van all rived up to go
The sky's overcast, will it rain or snow?
Heave-ho the food chest, handle with care.
No spilled food is always our prayer.

As Captain of the ship sets Alta at the wheel,
"Come on helpers, let's deliver these meals"
Marie does the packing, hot food here, cold there,
Closing the lid with tender care.

Down alley's and streets we bounce on our way,
Marie's milk-crate seat is beginning to sway.
Karen does the running and she really must run,
Cold rain is falling, not very much fun.

Here and there we stop at a door,
Carrying our goodies and a happy "hello"
They meet us and greet us with smiles so sweet,
While Karen stands shivering in the rain in the street.

Neither rain or snow or gloom of night
Will keep these couriers from their flight.
Back to the Center we are on our way.
Happy and hungry on a cold rainy day.

Marie McCracken

"The Unknown"

A shriek from hell
The smell of souls burning
Tears of joy for life everlasting from heaven
The soft, satin wings on Angels.
Praying in the cold rain as tears
Fall from Heaven
A slow moving hearse walks towards its grave
Its dreams are now frozen and it has nowhere to hide
Heaven or Hell? Where he went
Is left to the unknown to decide
Is it an Angel raising up from a tomb?
Is it a demon peeling out of the dark?
Are his nightmares finally ending;
Or are they just beginning?
Was his judgement day full of blood and regret,
Or was it a lifetime experience he'll never forget?
Is he burning at the core,
Or living a dream?
All I can do is hope and pray this man
has been redeemed.

Kristy Jones

The Darker Face Of Twilight

I miss the cold winds that flowed from the corners.
The softened step of moist morning soil and wet leaf.
Seeping light rushing quietly into my subtle pupils.
On the brim of death we cherish the fair smile of life.
Living, we shield our mind's against death's knocking.
Only to find some neutral place to immortally exist.
Resting upon the darker face of twilight.

I miss the small cracks across lust tinged lips.
The sounds uttered for what sake of madness.
Shadows found beneath the attic window last midnight.
For whom stays your reflection upon spilled candle wax.
I sit legs bent up, hands pressed firm, head tight,
between shafts of flesh drawn bone.
Atop, above, ascending the darker face of twilight.

Miles, paths, vines along the fencing.
Hungry, needing, friend of emptiness walks
the strays of belief and hope.
Silent, dreaming, full of fantasy sleeps
the bold of heart. Within, what side,
what waits for us beyond the darker face of twilight.

Michael T. Smith

Remember When...

Remember when we first met?
The sparks, the excitement, the hidden secret.
Remember when we first spoke?
Being tongue-tied and words getting caught in the throat.
Remember when we first kissed?
The magic we felt was so hard to miss.
Remember when we first lay close?
Unspoken feelings stirring...
Love on the approach.
Understanding each other by mind and soul,
Difference, being our ultimate goal.
Little by little, our bodies entwined,
Feeling emotions, so deep in the mind.
Yet I sit here sometimes, looking above,
Trying to remember when...
We fell in love...

Noelle Busalacchi

My Grandmother

Old. Senior citizen. In the winter of her life,
The stories she could tell of her joys, her strife.
So strong, so vibrant, with energy to burn, the
Center of our family - Our guide to things to learn.

Well-known in the community especially for cakes and pies
Respected in the family for her strength and being wise.
Facing each new day as a challenge to defeat
Reflecting on days gone by - so solemn, so sweet,

My Grandmother! I watched the light in her eyes grow dim,
But never for a moment did I doubt that she knew Him.
She trusted in Him completely: Our Father up above.
And though she is now with Him, we will always remember
Her LOVE!

Sharon M. Tiggett

Moon Reflections

Reflections over a nearby pond.
The sky opens up with a full moon.

A soothing glow softening the very shape of things.
Calming the waters of troubled times.

Magical and romantic showing, who am I.
Erasing details overpowering, my mind.

Bouncing my ambitions hopes and plans.
Stepping into the moonlight, I dream my dreams.

Pat Bordner

In Heavenly Peace

Peaceful death and pretty flowers
The storm has passed its darkest hour.
Family and friends have mourned the end
Only memories of yesterday remain.

As we walk and cry to say good-bye,
As you rest in peace far away,
We'll miss you waking your tired eyes
And always remember you day by day.

Through this life you've climbed a wall
Sometimes it seemed no one cared at all.
You were loved and had a home
As you were climbing, you weren't alone.

We feel so empty that you're not around
So we look to the sky, the drifting clouds,
You are in our hearts, you are on our minds
Someday we will join you, when this life passes by.

Sleep... sleep...sleep...

(In Memory of Loved Ones Gone Safely Home)

Stephen L. Brown

Never Alone

As I walk down the sandy beech
The sun is just peaking over the water.
I think of you often,
for every step reminds me of our love.
The waves washing up on my feet give me the warm feeling of your touch
It's not cold, but shivers run up my spine and back down again,
Waiting for the next one.
The slowly rising sun suggests the way our relationship began.
Slow at first, but before you realize it
It is shining bright, burning into our hearts.
The course sand sticks to my wet feet.
I try to rub it off, but as with you in my heart
It cannot be removed.
The waves slam upon the rocks with tremendous force,
Cleansing them with every blow, like our love showers our faults.
I am alone, but looking out across the turquoise sea
I realize that I am not alone
For your love is all around me
And will be as long as this sea exists.

William Klei

Unfulfilled

I float on a fragile rainbow bubble,
the sunlight splitting my little-girl dreams
into a prism of white nights, silver-edged gardenias
and Ava Maria echoing among a field of damp, lace-edged hankies.
I have arrived late,
missing the early matinee of my life.
Instead I find rumpled sheets in a warmed bed,
unabashed belching at the kitchen table,
and high-pitched interruptions wrapping themselves
around tired, blue-veined legs.
I wait, looking out the water-spotted window
for the pot at the end of my rainbow.
Often, I hide inside my heart,
afraid of raising my voice,
fearing there will be hollow echoes to answer me.
With regret I bristle among the lint balls and rust-ringed toilets,
mumbling threats of doing what I want to do,
whatever that is.
I leave on an unfinished breath,
never fully understood.

Rosanne T. Burac

The Palette Of My Mind

Oh, empty palette of my mind, what shall I paint today?
The sweet blue sky with puffy clouds that slowly sail away,
The leafy boughs that flutter ever gently in the breeze,
The soaring flights of birds accomplished with apparent ease,
The chatter of the insects, the buzzing of the bees,
Even grass looks beautiful when viewed with such as these.
The flowers in my garden nodding gently on their stems
With brilliant colors swirling like a bowl of many gems.
My mind absorbs these pictures and I wonder at the love
That gives to us these treasures — these bounties from above.
But not too far from where I live the world is not so sweet.
The color that is mostly seen is blood upon the street.
And when I see the rain fall down that nourishes my ground
I sometimes think that God is weeping for the killing all around.
How long can things go on like this, when shall the slaughter end?
Will God one day say, "This is it, be gone, Earth, `bye, Amen!"

Marie Lee

Kiss

A kiss,
the touch of two lips
that is often soft as rose petals
gentle as a mother's cares
moving as an earthquake

Can be comforting,
friendly passionate

Can stir one's soul
or leave one cold

Can ignite a love that will last a lifetime
or extinguish a love with its icy chill

Can give one breath or
take it away

And
no matter how it's given
or received
effects both the participants

Forever....

Stephenie T. Baumann

"Mother Nature's Garden"

Laying in Mother Nature's garden, I can feel the warmth of the sunshine covering my body like a blanket.
The grass strokes my skin leaving a trail of shivers. A soft rain begins to fall, leaving its sweet drops kissing every inch of my body bringing a feeling I want to never end.
While the wind whispers my name as it softly blows. I spread my arms like the wings of a bird, I can feel myself fly higher and higher into the sky to a place filled with great love.
A feeling of joy over comes me as I become one with that which touches me.
I close my eyes and let myself slowly float down back to my place in Mother Natures garden, letting myself drift off to a peaceful sleep while the suns warmth covers me I softly smile.

Tammy Mauer

The Path

With His guidance and direction
The way for you, He'll surely show-
Just ask in prayer whatever you will;
And believe in His name, that he will give. (Mk. 11:24)

Petition wisdom and knowledge for your journey
To lighten your pathway-
Get understanding and hold fast to it;
Then speak HIS WORDS endowed by HIS SPIRIT. (Pr. 3:13)

He hath not given a spirit of fear
Nor that of anxiety-
He will supply your every need;
If you follow wherever He may lead. (Mt. 6:8)

Thank him above all that you have been chosen
Count it a blessing and a privilege;
Stand firm in his might when the tempter comes-
Keep leaning and depending on His everlasting arms. (1 Cor. 10:13)

And when as a pilgrim you've passed through this land
Your voice can no longer be heard;
He will bid you to enter that Heavenly Home-
And say to you, "Well Done My Servant, Well Done"!
(Mt.25:21)

Phyllis Drawhorne-Piece

Roses

Roses are made of petals so fine. The way that they sparkle,
The way that they shine. They move in the wind with each
little gust, and then they turn brown like the color of rust.
As the petals die and start to fall down,
They fall kind of slow and then reach the ground.
Eventually, a new bud will begin to sprout.
It will really get red and begin to spread out.
As it opens up and starts to get wider,
there in the middle sleeps a tiny spider.
The spider uses the rose for just one night,
then climbs down at the first sign of light.
As he climbs down, he lands on a thorn and when he jumped back
up the poor rose was torn.
The petals fell down as the rose was now dead, but the next one
will bloom so beautifully red.

Samantha Grannemann

Fly Away Home

Soaring high above the whispering waves,
The wind ruffles my feathers.
The sun warms my cold body
Bringing life and hope.
Home!
It is the only thought that filters through my mind.
Home, to someone who loves me.

My wings surge upward again,
Bringing me closer to home.
The sun reflects on the wide ocean,
Mirroring my sparkling hope.
Here, at this lofty height, I catch sight of my home.
The rolling hills stand out against
The ever darkening sky.
I welcome the tiny wisping waves,
As they lap against the shore.

As my feet touch the ground, my heart rejoices.
Now, my spirit takes wing.

Susan Emhardt

"Together In Time"

I remember when we first met
the words came so easy then
Now time has passed and things have changed,
but I don't know when.

I do know I still love you
maybe in a different way
Not any less than yesterday,
though a little more today.

I just don't tell you how much
as often as I should,
if I was able to let you inside
my soul, I would.

Let me tell you this:
"I long for only you",
Just look deep into my eyes
to see that this is true.

Time will keep us together
not tear us farther apart,
The words of love that we have spoken
are forever written in my heart.

Mary Beth Peterson

Poems

Poems are phrases that express one's thoughts.
The words of a poem can not be taught.
The thoughts of an author are expressed in lines,
the source of them comes from deep inside.
The words of an author are not always printed clear,
though a true poet holds his work very dear.
The words of a poem do more than form lines,
these special words do not even have to rhyme.
The real thing that separates a poem from mere lines,
are the thoughts and emotions from the author's inside...

Stacy Paul Kuyawa

"Mattingly At The Bat"

On the 8th of July only 8 years ago,
the Yankees' first baseman began a great show
He hit the ball hard and knew it was gone
and all the fans shouted "Way to go Don!"

He got in a groove that day in July,
and if you asked him about it, he'd tell you why-
He was seeing the ball well, in day and at night
And 5 days in a row, he hit the bleachers in right

And then '23', "The Hit Man" by name,
on July 16, had another great game
He hit a grand slam, his 4th of the year,
with 7 RBIs, a high in his career

Then once again, two days after that,
he tied an old record with the crack of his bat
He stepped from the dugout and up to the plate
and hit a homerun for the 8th day straight!

The record was set back in '56,
'til Donnie came up and got in his licks
Dale Long held the record for 31 years
But now he and Donnie can share all the cheers

Terri Kietur

God's Own Ice Show

The trees are bare
Their foliage is gone
Winter is upon us
And the snow flakes fall
Like diamonds upon the Earth below
Ice forms on the tree branches
A dance occurs - a tinkling sound is heard
When the branches sway to and frow
it's God's own ice show

Louise J. O'Connor

The World Of Fear

Little children no longer roam free,
Their spirits are chained to me.
I am their worst fear.
I suck their lives away.
Through their nostrils they breathe my poison.
Little do they know that I am near them.
I am all the destruction they face every day,
The death that reeks the air,
The tears that fall,
Every time mommy has to work late,
Just to get food on the table.
The disease that corrupts cities,
The acid rain, the polluted rivers,
The angry and mean faces they see every day.
The world full of fear of what is apt to happen.
The world that no longer has any love for them.
I feed off the fear, anger and hate,
I feed off all the little children who grow up afraid.

Rachelle Rivera

The Children Of Tomorrow

The Children of Tomorrow are growing up today.
Their values and their ethics are being learned at play.

"Don't hit your brother, Johnnie," and, "Mary, don't you lie."
While Daddy batters Mommy and Mommy's heard to cry.
She tells the cops she's guilty, she really is to blame.
And Daddy says that, "Yes, that's true," That she must bear the shame.

A teacher at the local school is found to have some dope.
He'd shared it with his students, and the children lost more hope.
Big brother's friend was wanted by every gang in town.
Until he finally he left them all, when someone gunned him down.

Scarlet graffiti adorns the walls of the Institute for the blind.
Though those inside can't see the marks, they're burned in each
child's mind.
Violence and rage roar out from the screen; the News shows life
at its worst.
And, the children listen and learn. They hear it now; they hear it
first.

The Children of Tomorrow are growing up today.
Their values and their ethics are being learned each day.

Marilynn Moran

This Is War Time

War is hard, war is pain, and after this war nothing will be the same.
Lord I wish this war didn't have to be but what it comes down
to we will have to wait and see.

Lord I don't know all about it some how I wish I did. I wish
I could make a different and make it right again, but what
can I do. I wish I knew because if I did it won't be no more war.

I am sitting here looking at the news with sorrow in my heart
it is so many families being torn apart
Mother and father, sister and brother, husband and wife all
are somebody's child, let us all PRAY and stand by there side
because GOD is all of our father and we are his child.

Susie Pearl Robinson

"Thus Way Of Love"

Thus honeysuckle vines - entwine
themselves along a fence to grow,
this is what makes them strong
whenever the winds begin to blow,
and by nature, this is meant to be,
just as thus love, I have for thee.

I know there is no place in my heart,
that I could ever feel good without you,
and that I want only to spend my life on earth with you,
and if I'm given a choice, I know this is what I will do,
for there is only one reason I live,
and Darling! that is to be with you.

Though thus love in my heart for you
is so pure, as only a newborn can be
it will outshine the sun and
reach from sea to sea,
so if I could only hold you, I know
I could make you feel,
that this love in my heart for you,
is really, really, REAL.

Mary Marie Still

Untitled

Misty shadows slip silently across the water,
then evening is upon us.
Look up into the galaxy, worlds beyond our shadows.
See the tiny heartbeats which light up the darkness.
Quiet, peaceful awareness of secrets untold are suddenly
bestowed upon our hearts, our souls.
Catch a shooting star and place it in your pocket for safe
keeping until the ocean meets the sky.
The sky touches Earth.
Gaze upon the cycles made up of melancholy memories and try
to find the answers to the questions they arouse.
Misty shadows slip silently across the Universe,
then destiny sweeps us away.

Pamela A. Kay

Senses Of Love

If love were taste,
then love to me would be one of your sweet kisses,

If vision were love,
then all I would see is you,

If touch were love,
then all I would feel is your hand in mine,

If smell were love,
then all I would smell is your sweet perfume,

If sound were love,
then all I would hear is your voice,

So, if you ask me what is love,
I have to say Love is you in every sense known to me.

Russell Ver Mulm

My World

In my world there is no crime
There are no drugs, no murders, no deaths.
In my world there are no Bills, no headaches, no worries.
Everyday happy everyday sunny.
In my world everyone is courteous, everyone polite
nobody gets angry and nobody has to fight.
In my world love is something beautiful and marriage is forever.
In my world everyone is equal and no one is left out in the cold.
But I only get to see my world when I close my eyes tight,
for I live in a dream world and I only get there at night.

Thomas Kelly

Glimpses

Glimpses of you have become as fleeting as clinches... and there-forth more memorable. Ceaselessly instilling a taste in me... leaving a hunger for you.

Starry-eyed and bedazzled... my rampant imaginable thoughts of you have managed to bring to the waking moments of the day the magic of the night's twilight. And set sailing the emotional thoughts which so much has me enslaved.

Festive be the pain I endure for the circle be of my own making. And a choice I make freely as well as frequently.

At times it's obvious the pleasure I draw from the pain of not ever being able to hold and cuddle in my arms one which so much occupies my mind. Constantly there... like a powerful stimuli. Exhilarating me to the edge of sanity,
pass the limits of my dreams.

Robert E. Dougherty Jr.

The Promise Of Tomorrow

The promise of tomorrow that's what we hold today
There is no backing down we have to lead the way
This may frighten us a little for we are the years to come
It makes no difference when or where we're coming from
We have to live our lives just to come to this
To be smart young men and women who will strive at any risk
Believe there's no need to beg believe there's no need to plead
We just have to try our best and believe we will succeed
There may be a little sadness there may be a little sorrow
But our pride of today brings about the promise of tomorrow
This may be a little hard not quite as easy as it seems
But to the fellow society believe we have a dream

LaCrista Dawson

"Change"

Things change as people live,
There is so much that we could give,
To this world so full of hate.
We could change our direction and our fate.

People who lost hope seek reasons to live,
And victims of hate find ways to forgive.
We can make our grim futures, look bright,
For those who have lost their will to fight.

Everyday, people die on the street,
Watching poverty is bitter not sweet.
If we change our ways we could defeat...
The end laughter that we're bound to meet.

We should look at ourselves, stop promising
miracles, and stop telling lies,
And instead heal broken promises and stop
children's silent cries,
For a decent world to live in, a world of
compromise.

Melissa Vazquez

Untitled

Seems like it was only yesterday,
they where all right here
They are gone, but they will still survive
in our memories
Lord knows why he's taken them away
Memories will be our comfort everyday
Taking little things for granted is the greatest sin of
all, because I found out that in one second it could
all be gone. It doesn't matter the how's or why's,
They are gone, and I didn't get to say my final
Goodbyes. I know now that life isn't a race
Because I've seen to many of my friends go on to be
in heaven a better place.

Tammy Johnson

Alone

In the jungle of the slums
There stands a boy, a poor boy.
On the corner of the street he stands
Waiting, just waiting,
People stare, small minds judge.
They do not understand,
Inside he is crying.

He wants, he craves, he struggles, he fights,
No one comes, no one helps,
He is alone.
He has never smiled, he does not know how.
He is afraid, afraid of himself,
Inside he is crying.

There is no God, there is only hate,
There is no love, there is only hurt.
His heart screams with pain.
Where is love? Where is hope?
He has searched, but could not find.
Inside he is dying.

D. Jones

Don't Hate

I had a terrible headache while traveling on the train.
There was a Black lady that felt my pain.
She consoled me and offered me a pill.
I believe it was her concern that cured my ill.
How can I hate because she is Black?
We are all equal, but different and I like it like that.
So don't hate me for stating the truth.
It is the only means for saving our youth.
God created all colors and nationales.
We are all God's children despite the rationales.
Stop the hate towards each other.
After all, we are both sister and brother.
There is only one land, one water, and one air.
One day, it will become crystal clear when we learn to care.
Please, let's help each other overcome the fear.
There is only one place for us to live and that is here.
We must live together in equality and peace.
There is no other shelter to go in search of relief.

Pal Imeri

I Jesus Have Been There Too

A church is not built without laboring pains,
there's much to go thru when you bear my name.
Did I not say bear the cross
to reach the world of sinner's lost.
I know the things that you've been thru,
For I myself have been there too.

Many came for fish and bread,
when the multitudes I fed.
But in my trial I stood along
not one friend to call my own,
yes, I suffered much upon the cross.
To bring salvation to the lost.
They pierced a spear right in my side
they even mocked me while I died.

I bore my cross to calvary's hill,
now you must bear it from there still.
My people need the love you show
the word you preach so they can grow.
I'm depending on you my Son
to do the work I have begun.

Lulia Hamm Hockman

The Riots

Hollywood is burning, what a sight to see.
There's people hurt on the streets of our hometown.
The neon signs are all turned off on the boulevard tonight.
People screaming, people crying, it's such a horrid thing.
Don't they feel any remorse, when they see such evil doings?
We can't go outside, we're being kept prisoners; punishment,
for a crime our family didn't commit!
Hollywood a flame, buildings burnt to the ground, time to start anew.
The stars are still shining, at least they didn't take that
virtue away!
Guards standing on corners, with their weapons drawn;
what a scary thing to see.
I don't understand, I refuse to try; this fighting doesn't
belong in our backyard!
Locals watch and laugh, as the destruction takes its toll!
Their taking our homes and our lives and tossing them aside!
Hollywood a flame, buildings burnt to the ground, time to start anew.
Hollywoods a flame, idiots are to blame!

Leslie Sowles

She Is Poetry

Poetry is the essence of these words unspoken.
They are many thoughts from my soul and scarred from my heart once broken.

Although some stay sweet, those words to soft to whisper.
The thoughts that I share, maybe the only way I can hear her.

It is hard to see passed all that makes her symbol of my integrity.
For she is more then what I want, and nothing I need her to be.

I see her in my thoughts and hear her in my dreams.
As real as I make her, she is only as relative as this poem seems.

I feel as if no one can comprehend my feelings, or even try to relate.
For some day I will meet her passed the door that is locked by fate.

As reality slips away in these words, I feel like I am left behind.
But not for long, because I can love her with my soul, and touch her with my mind.

Kevin M. Zschach

"My Game"

When the world is dark, no one will remember my name,
they never knew my game, and still things can never be the same.

If you understood my world, you would never say that about me.
Seems that when my life is bright,
that's when something falls down on me.

I understand no one, and no one understands me,
that's just the way it has to be.
When I look at you I see nothing, but I still hope for everything,
Why do I do this to myself?

Tonight is the night, so you thought. But it happened today,
and that's okay, I didn't want to anyway.
When everyone stares into the light, I am the only one
with 20/20 vision, although pain's sight isn't perfect,
because I know much more than pain.

Kyle Green

Togetherness

A tree told me, "Touch my strength."
The wind said, "Remove your hat and I'll play in your hair."
The earth spoke, "If you love me, dance."

The air whispered, "Remember, whenever you can, wear me."
The sun added, "Each time, I'll kiss you everywhere."
Later, in silence, the protected me.

And then, the night entered my pores, bringing a dream.

Victor R. Bull

Me And Mommy

Mommy they laughed at me today,
they said something about my clothes,
second hand clothes are just fine
to me mommy,
Mommy they laughed at me today,
they said something about not having a
daddy, I have a father in heaven, don't I?
Mommy they laughed at me today
they said our house is ugly, it is just old,
Grandma is old and I love her,
Mommy they laughed at me today,
they said we don't have a car,
I like walking with you mommy,
Mommy they laughed at me today,
they said we don't have nice things,
all I need is you mommy,
Mommy they laughed at me today.
Mommy please wake up from your
coma, "please mommy, don't die!"

Robert Douglas Palacios

The Popular Crowd

Strutting down the hall,
They think they rule us all.

"I'm better than you,"
They like to say.

We know that story,
But in a different way.

They make fun of you for a laugh,
Just once they should be on this half.

What I would like to see,
Is a popular person who is like me.

Someone who tries to be nice to all,
Who wants to help you when you fall.

Who always tries to do her best,
Not caring if she's different from the rest.

Sarah Elizabeth Livers

Snow Child

As the angels fly through the trees in the sky
They will be my friends forever
Rainbows in the snow, deer running free
Snow child must be a part of me.

Dear Rainbow...

You will come to me, when you grow down
To be a friend I will love forever
Now you have a friend
Hearts I will see
Angels flowing up to the sky
I love the wind
I love the rain
I love my mom and dad...

Reanna Michelle Rahn

Dusty Morning Rose

Oh Father, what have you given me?
This delicate, beautiful thing,
Morning mist hovering around,
With a cool hush,
The sun's soft light upon it,
All the earth's pale colors laugh,
For this is their time,
Their time to glow and be beautiful,
But none as beautiful as my Dusty Morning Rose.

Shannon L. Fowler

To My Grandbaby

Something's are very precious in this world of ours
They're God's blue skies and his shining stars
He's given us so many beautiful things
But they don't compare to what new birth brings
Those tiny hands and feet so small
I wonder, "Will you be short or tall?"
Will you be "fair" or "darker too?"
What ever you're like - you will be you
I don't know if you're a girl or a boy
But I know that you'll bring a special joy
I don't know the color of your eyes or hair
And to tell you the truth I really don't care
What ever you are will be fine with me
And to my heart you'll hold the key
I have so much love for you already
And I thank God for your mommy and daddy

Sherry Howe

Mothers

To have a mother is oh so neat,
They're kind, they're caring they're all so sweet

Mothers stay up so everything's right
To see that her children are taken care of at night

She's a homemaker, caretaker, a judge and a friend,
Mother's stay with you right up to the end

Mother's are to be cherished all of the time,
They're like the finest jewels and the very best wine

A mother doesn't have to be biological,
Just someone who cares, and who is lovable

Who ever you call a mother, that's great,
Just show her how much you appreciate

So go find your mother and give her a kiss.
And tell her how much she is really missed

Laura L. Scott

Persona

Strong people know how to win!
They're persona endorse
like the mighty mountains.

Strong people are kind, also hard.
Soft, hard
hard, soft
for the endeavors of a strange world.

Strong people, carry on, like great nations.
They know when to change and when
to stand "FIRM!"
Strong people can do,

Can youuuu?

Robert J. DiGennaro

Beauty And Passion

She is a dream come true.
This woman is a flower of many colors.

She is a sensitive rainbow, responding to
Many kinds of weather.

She is a person of intense feelings of
Passion and love and affection for
People she cares about.

My mother, a living beauty, a special
Meaning in my life, like a gentle raindrop
Hitting the ground.

Rebecca Shari Lewis

"Life"

When life starts getting really rough,
Think about the future and start to get tough;

When life seems to have no ups, all downs,
And all you wish for are your sorrows to drown;

Think about the future,
Forget about the past,

For if you keep yesterday close,
Tomorrow will never last;

If you've ever heard the sayings 'forgive and forget,'
sticking with that is your best bet;

So go out there and make yourself proud,
Don't keep yourself under the same dark cloud.

Just remember your dreams,
Let them last;
Forgive the future,
Forget the past...

Kristin Gill

A Zoo Story

I was just killing time at the zoo,
thinking of God knows what, or who,
when suddenly I saw a cage
swept of hope, but choked with rage.

I was stopped short, not entertained:
there stood a beast, like me, contained;
and so I spoke, and it replied,
much as the self and soul confide.

It drew me wilds where good things thrive —
a habitat where life's alive!
Whereon I said, to tell men's scene,
"Here, honey's *gold* and money green."

I pitied it, as it did me,
and each one wished the other free;
and but for the bars - they say defend —
I'd have leapt in to embrace my friend.

Thomas Borthistle

Is There Someone Else?

Is there someone else that you're
thinking of? Is there someone else who is
sharing your love? Is there someone else
who is holding you tight? Is there
someone else who sleeps with you at night?
Is there someone else who waits for you
in bed? Is there someone else to whom
those special words were said? Is there
someone else who is there when you're
sad? Is there someone else who will
stay with you through the good and
bad? Is there someone else whose love
to you is true? Is there someone else
who loves you more than I do?

Tricia Vander Veen

Feelings

My heart is full of light,
Though the sky is so black.
Full of darkness,
No where to run,
No where to hide,
I feel very lonely and very sad.
But, one day I know my feelings will change.

Victoria Stroinski

Life Without A Friend

My poem is dedicated solely to my husband and best friend, Gil. Love always, your Linny.

Life is not complete without a friend
This friend would be there
when you're feeling happy
She will feel hurt when
you're down in despair.
The both of you will
share ideas about life in general
You will talk on the phone for hours
just to update jokes of the day.
Friends are very rare to
come by-and when you do
Accept it and enjoy it -
Because life's too short
not to enjoy it without
your friend.

Linda Alvarez

Founder's Grove

Hush!
This is a sacred place.

The air is haunted by hundreds of years. Heavy with ancient rain, it breathes Time's secrets, eerie and all-knowing.

From the misty green distance, ferns hover over the dark earth,
Undulated by an unfelt leviathan wind.
Footfalls are soundless on the needle carpet.

A lone bird cry bounces along the living backdrop. Ricochets gently. Fades.

Two magpie women, their voices piercing the thick quiet, burst from around a fern-clothed stump and hasten on. The silence rushes at their heels, propelling them forward and away.

High overhead dappled treetops dance.
Escaping the clouds, a sunbeam spotlights a fallen log, its bark spongy with hidden life. The dull gold banana slug poses, a still life against the moist earth.

Softly, the ancient song swells, echoes, dissolves.
Continuance. Endurance. Renewal.

This is a sacred place.
Hush!

Susan K. Lowell

Vagaries

I think I can no longer bear
This loneliness breaking my heart....
Each time I search in vain for you,
Amidst a thousand pallid faces
For that one toss of head familiar
And one such loved smile,
That shall bespeak of you.

I hunger for that inward light
Of eyes, that glow with joyful cognizance,
A look so dearly eloquent
That suddenly will still the endless
Questioning of this unfeeling heart,
With just a gentle sigh
Or yet a tender smile.

So strangely strange
That we have never met,
And yet somewhere, this self-same search
Must plague you, who are destined to be
The only clue to my identity.

Lourdes P. Goco

To See You Again

Grandad,
This place where you are, is it as they say,
a place where it is always day?
Do you fly without wings? Can you see all things?
The streets of gold, are they pure or
are they old.
Tell me that there are animals everywhere,
and flowers that are more beautiful so that I won't despair.
Even though you are in a better place, it hurts so bad
to see your face inside my mind as I think of you,
knowing you want to be with me too.
Please let me know from where you are even though I know it's far
how to keep from hurting so bad
so I can keep from being sad.

Vanessa Horner

Ignorance Is Bliss?!

Ignorance is Bliss?! or so they say; but in what way and where did this statement originate? To what degree does it influence our fate? Let us consider the words, "ignorance" and bliss". And let us begin to speculate.

Does it mean that if one does not know (something) that they are better off not knowing or, if one does know (something)they are better off; therefore, for not knowing, what information is amiss? Again let us consider and define this word bliss?

Defined as, "extreme happiness; joy. Ecstasy of salvation; spiritual joy". But to what extreme does this employ? Now for the meaning of "ignorance", let us discuss: define as, "without knowledge or education; displaying lack of knowledge or education; unaware or uninformed. Synonymous with ignorant, illiterate, nescient, uneducated, unlearned, unschooled and untaught, with the core meaning of the single word, "oblivious".?

Out of the birth canal we are blind, deaf and dumb. With knowledge of the races deeply embedded through eons of time, indelibly imprinted on the DNA patters in our minds.

Without the taste of knowledge of some fruits is to be contents as a vegetable in the garden of Eden; therefore, to those nothing is amiss. Hmm-m-m, I wonder, does this mean that "ignorance is bliss?!

To be oblivious does mean that something is amiss:. But by whose standards comes this judgement? To be aware is to know and to have the knowledge of choice. To be able to evade the pain is bliss?! To not be informed of the choice is to be ignorant? To be able to evade the pain of choice is bliss?!

Partricia Nadiyah Spencer

"Best Friends"

Best friends forever until the day we die
Those are the words that were said as we
looked into each others eyes
And as we kept talking more and more
I started to realize that I loved you, now so
much more than I did before
And if you knew how much I needed you so
Then maybe just maybe you would stay and
never go
You would stay forever and never leave
Because it would be just us, only you and me
It would last forever until the day we die
And even then we would never even think
of saying goodbye
Because our love is so strong and goes so deep
That we live for the future and think of
our most special memories
And there is no time for us to grieve or sorrow
Because there is always the thought of there
being a better day for tomorrow.

Luzviminda Engle

Remembering Baseball

The crowds, the cheers, seem too dim to recall
Those August nights, when there was baseball

That unmistakable crack of the bat
How proud, so proud, we wore the home team's hat

Radios on the beach, hey what's the score?
It's 4 to 1, wait, they ain't playin' no more!

So much of our youth, tied fondly to a game
When a strike was a pitch, and no need for blame

Now that Brooklyn hat, covers hair that is thinning
With a longing to stand for that old 7th inning

Cap day and glove day and the old double play
How do you tell a child, there's no game today

The game was smiles and tears, and the game winning laugh
Now it's a player, being paid for an autograph

"No game," is a sadness, as when a friend moves away
Like "Joltin Joes" gray hair on oldtimer's day

The players wonder why their paychecks are late
Maybe, because no one's come through the gate

We'll buy some peanuts and cracker Jack
And maybe, just maybe, we won't be back

Marty Miller

Beginnings

Long for the summers of days gone by,
Those who gave reasons for me to try,
Listen to wisdom for it is no tale,
Gave me the courage when I seem to fail,
No one is perfect, nothing is sure,
The sake of a challenge helps us endure,
Face in the mirror, stares back at me,
The thrill of the chase breeds our destiny.

Beginnings are fragile, as is our first step,
The secrets we told were so sacredly kept,
As if yesterday cried out calling our names,
Beginnings still hold us, like fire and flame

The patterns we live by, blueprints of hope
Come to divide us when we can't cope,
Sands of a million, act all as one,
Light in the window, the darkness, the sun,
Children deliver the staples of youth,
Carries them forward, there's strength in the truth,
Time may escape us, drift far away,
As long as tomorrow, feels like today.

Thomas G. Grenda

My Prayer For Today

O God,
Thou hast said, "Lean on me. My yoke is easy. I will come into your soul," Now, O Father, help us to do thy bidding. Help us to trust solely upon Thee, and Thou will make us whole —
in body and spirit. O Lord, we beseech Thee to give
us Thy Holy Presence that we might believe
All that Thou has promised us. O God, were we
loyal to Thee - as we should be - we could not conceive
The depths of Thy love for us. Father, help us to remember
our yesterdays are history; our tomorrows are mysteries;
Only Today is ours - a gift from Thee, indeed, a present
Thou has given to us to use now and into eternity.
O God, we know the day dawns, it passes away; yet today
is our only hope of our destiny.
By leaning on Thee, we can use all of our todays in a purposeful
Manner, keeping our lives in harmony
With Thy teaching. Too, O God, we can serve Thee and our
fellowman more humbly and with a contrite heart,
Because Thou hast shown us that by being meek and lowly,
Thy word is bound within us, never to depart.

Wilma Copeland Cathey

Another Symbol Of Love

The dandelion's a precious flower
Though as a weed it's known.
God plants them with the wind and shower
And plentifully they're grown.

God grows them in earth's garden
More bountifully than others
So loving little children
Can pick them for their mothers.

The gift from the heart of a thoughtful child
Of the only bouquet that he can afford
Sparks in mother a heart-warming smile-
A lovingly fitting reward.

They don't have such a fragrant smell
As other flowers, it's true,
But the tale of love they tell
As sure as roses do.

Though some may be denyin'
What only a mother knows
The beauty of a dandelion
Defies the perfect rose.

Margaret Deming

Upon the Shore

I stood alone, upon the shore
Though I knew I was not alone
I watched the sky, as the sea gulls soared
And the ocean waves crashed and foamed
I pondered the beauty of the world we are in
And the possibility of the ones beyond
And I realized that we are on a trail
Within us, he lives for us to respond

Michael J. McQueen

The Kite

I a kite fly high above, in the sky like a mourning dove.
Though I soar high above, I will not fly like a mourning dove.
So when my master asks me to fly,
I will just sit there and cry, cry, cry.

Paul Kowalewski

Confused

Ask not why my mind is confused
though life is not worth living,
but ask me why my mind's not mine,
and lies I will not tell you.
When anguish and pain and fear prevails,
and as tired as I am,
the blood which pumps to my heart
causes me to eat no tarts,
and as love and hate will be a mate,
forever and ever in my mind,
and the arrogance and ignorance of people
will destroy and not create,
and jealousy and tales will destroy mankind,
and the image which took a lifetime to create,
will seem like an empire destroyed in a dream
of your own,
the thought that love can do no harm,
deceit and lies will lead you astray,
'cause love can be the only thing,
to be an image which prevails.

Michael G. Hardial

Driven From Reality

I have no life that I see,
through my eyes, my life is a dream.
Parents yelling and me being their slave
That's all I am, like being in a grave.
In that grave I'm locked in a box
Can't breathe or move, all I see is the dark.
I wish I could get out but I can't.
Locked in for eternity, locked out from the rest.
No one to talk to, no one to see,
No one to cry to, no one to be.
What should I do, that I don't know,
Can't find myself through the darkness below.

Snow White

Reasons To Love

You are the sunshine, breaking
through the clouds of my soul.

Your beams reach out touch me,
bringing me out of the dark.

You sweet smile breaks through
the ice around my heart and warms me.

One look from you loving blue eyes
and the wounds of my soul start to heal.

You deep voice calms me and lures
me from the depths of my despair.

Your kiss is sweet like wine, intoxicating
and always leaves me wanting for more.

Your gentle touch is like a warm caress,
smoothing down my rough edges.

You've changed my life and made it
better. Is it any wonder I love you?

Lorie Rich

The Brook

The brook that's wondering through the trees
Through the soft shadows and the clean breeze
Winds through the meadow down through the rocks
Makes the wonderful sounds that no bird can mock
It caresses its banks with ferns and moss.
And always gives at no ones great loss.
Its sweet nectar is precious to many.
The earth gives out and there is always plenty
A leaf rides along, it swirls and dips.
And circles around its falls and cliffs.
The small brook trout shimmers in the light.
And catches dragon flies while their in flight.
The sun now is setting, the shadows getting long.
Mist shrouds the brook, the whippoorwill sings its song.
The blanket of darkness moves through the trees.
But still heard is the rippling brook and the cool breeze.

Ronnie Brandon

The Feather Pen

I once was a feather, afloat in the wind;
Till I landed in liquid, now I'm a Pen.
Man's mind is my power, his hand is my tool;
On me he depends, to help get him through.
I'm the world's greatest lover;
I've been held by all hands;
I'm known the world over,
On paper carpets, I stand.
There isn't a library, a book, or a blurb,
That I haven't written, Pen... is the word.
I edit all knowledge, Grammar is my school;
When my work is completed, all praise goes to you!

Sandra Seamon

My Favorite Friend

We've been together through good and bad,
Through times that were joyful and times that were sad.
She's been there for me through and through;
We like each other like best friends do.
She's a wonderful kid, always happy and bright;
She's made up first when we had a fight.
We're almost like sisters the difference is small.
She's got my blanket, I've got her doll.
Sleep-overs with her are exciting and great;
We talk and eat and stay up real late.
She teases my dad and fights my brother.
She sits down and talks with my mother.
She's like a sister, always there for me.
She knows the alarm code, she has a key.
She is cool, and always has clothes to lend;
She is my favorite, my favorite friend.

Katie Quinn

Fire

Your love burns like an eternal flame,
Through your blinded eyes,
I could do no wrong.
But I have and will again.
I've lead you to believe I'm worth all your love.
I'm not.
The love I hold for you burns unsteadily
And the darkness is closing in.
Soon the flame will go out completely
Along with my love for you
You already know nothing lasts forever.
And either will this fairy tale we've created
It will die,
Suddenly.
Without us ever knowing when.
But what happens next?
We'll go on living,
Alone
Until that flame burns again.

Stacey Kozeol

"Dreams Will Come True"

I never thought my dreams would come true
'Til I met you
I didn't want none of this
'Til we finally kissed
It was just a friendship
Now it's an outstanding relationship
I don't know when, or where I'll go
But love is always what I'll show
You're the only one I deeply love
Other than God above
I never thought my family and friends would
see me cry
'Til I heard the boy of my dreams say
good-bye.
Now that I won't see you no more, I just
want to say
I hope to see you again another day.

Nanette Taylor

Shelter Of Her Heart

He came to her so late in life
to fight her pains and her sorrows
to claim a place in her tomorrows
Although, he'll always have a place
in the circle of her arms,
he will never know the shelter of her heart.

Lupe Bloch

Graduation Night

We counted down the last school days
Till we reached our graduation in a daze
We look at each other and remember when
All of our lives together we mostly did spend
Now we say goodbye to go forth to prepare our future
As doctors, lawyers, or anything else we picture
But before the final tear and our final so longs
Let us remember the fun, laughing while singing songs
Many events have taken place that changed our ideas and feelings
Things that we witnessed - the beginnings and the endings
With a tear in my eye and a loss in my heart
Looking at my classmates together now but soon we'll part
It has been a blast for the last four years
We grew up together from freshmen to seniors
From children we've grown to the adults before you
Ready to experience the world-we're graduating from high school!
So as each of you get into your cars and go your separate ways
Remember each other for in my heart you will be always.

Melody Presley

My Mother/My Friend

A mother who was always gentle and kind, my mother was one of a kind.

To have you gone is so un-real, I can't believe what I feel.

My day's are endless when she comes to mind which is always all the time.

I know someday we will be entwined. Your gone from me and I know
What it is to be a mother, because I came from you and no other.

To be near you once again because she was my friend, my troubles
she always knew she was there for me till the end.

Now I find that I'm on my own, I cry with loss of her. Why did
you leave me because I miss you so, I wish you were here to dry
my tears, because without you I do have fears.

But now I go on my way and pray to God never to stray. My love
for you will never end, because you are my mother and my friend.

So rest my mother and be at peace you are my greatest treasure.
I keep your memory in my embrace that no one can ever erase.

You know it's hard to end this poem, because words I feel could roam.

So I say once again I love you, now I came to the end to my
Mother and My Friend

Marie C. Tirella

Morning

Get up, my friend, the sun is rising.
Time for us to start a brand new day.
Get up, my friend, the sun is blazing.
Do not plan on sleeping your life away.

Get up and take a walk with me.
Let us listen to the bird's beautiful song.
Get up and take a stroll with me.
The morning music does not last long.

Get up my friend and smell the fresh air.
Feel the warmth as the sun rises in the sky.
Get up my friend, I beg you.
Do not let this beautiful morning pass you by.

Oh fine, just lie there and sleep away.
Don't take heed to my warning.
But when you wake up don't blame me
That you missed a gorgeous morning.

Tinney William

Because I Love You

I'm taken in by such deep feelings,
time is on my side. Words are nothing,
expression is everything, because
I love you. Yes, I think I love you.
Hold me now, don't speak of your emotions,
for soon enough your words will fade.
Though your arms will ever embrace me,
and your heart will forever know this love.
For eternity you will hold me,
not psychically, but in mind. I know not
how you love me, but how this will soon be over.
Our feelings never again lost, because together,
we've made them found. So don't talk, listen.
Listen to my fragile heart. So mislead by your promises,
yet so understanding of my fears.
Because I love you. Yes, I know I love you.

Nicky Spinelli

We Love You

A child is born, months go by
Time soon tells how quick to be
Moving so slow and searchingly.
This sweet little child upon its knees.

The hope, the joy, the parents see.
Their sweet little child upon its knees
Into everything it seems to be.
This sweet little child upon its knees.

Mom scurries from here to there
To keep her child off the chair.
Down on the floor it goes again
To find someplace...it's already been

The day is spent...soon is the night
Tucked in its crib with eyes closed tight.
With rest for tomorrow and dreams to be
This sweet little child upon its knees.

Mom and Dad with hands held tight.
Thank GOD for their child through out the night.
Tomorrow has—come—and time to see,
This sweet little child upon its knees.

William F. Winkelman

Bridges

Friends that were there yesterday are no longer around
Time transformed them, time transformed me
What happened to the years?
Within a blink of my eye, they've disappeared.
Yesterday I did finger painting, now research papers.
People I didn't know as a child, now knock at my door.
I never knew their kind before, they're not my friends,
But they've filled me with experiences - some I'd rather not remember
They changed me.
Taken me through that rite of passage
I prepare to cross a bridge that's not yet complete
And it won't be until the start of summer
Not until the one I see in the mirror is dressed-
In a ceremonial gown.
Gripping her life in her hands while tears fall softly
She stands before a new unfinished bridge.

Tam-E Linette Ellis

Your Gift Of Water

Jehovah God, I love your water blue to see, to drink,
To float upon, for swimming in, but not in which to sink!
A gift of beauty to the eyes and also health from you,
Without it for ourselves, the earth and all, what would we do?

Ruth H. O. Darragh

The Man Without A Face

How could it all have happened?
To a man of talent and such grace.
For a professor of the English art.
To be gone without a trace.

In a town as small as this. Seen only by one or two.
Wondering why so carefully. He kept this body from our view.

I lastly came to know one day.
What truly that had happened.
How it was his face became. So rigid yet decayed.

After being struck head on.
The car burst into flames.
It took away a child's life. And left his body maimed.

They put the fault upon him solely.
The people of the town.
He never taught a class again.
Because of a parent's frown.

He disappeared one day.
Disappeared without a trace.
Leaving only to be known by those.
As the man without a face.

Scott Young

At The End... Or The Beginning....

To lose you now I can't comprehend
to a son, a daughter or even a friend.
Our lives together we have spent as one
as per our vows we took when we were young.

Don't go, don't leave me I want to say
but I know in the end it won't happen that way.
I've given my all for you to this day
for I would not have it any other way.

As I sit here, oh my lovely one
showering you with kisses and love
I pray to our Lord, the heavenly son
to take care of your spirit when it arrives above.

Larry Baasch

For Keeps

Suddenly, I'm yielding
To an Autumn leaf in flight.
Her smile is ever redolent
Of old years with PB and Js, and puppets and things.
Her stream does indeed flow sharp, thunderous, and
purposeful.
Have I ever not chosen her
To play on my team?

Presently, the old Birch sways
As it creaks rhythmically
And unsparingly.
Today, tears will trace lips
That say she is Mary-
And she is all of beautiful.

Mike Teyral

Heart Attack

Never thought of my mom so much,
'Till I awoke one night, with a touch.
Her eyes, I'd never seen that big before,
Her heart was knocking on death's door.
I always thought of her as being so strong,
But in just one moment, she could be gone.
I punished myself with much guilt,
Instead of telling her, the love I felt.
I thank God she's walking this day,
It's rearranged my perspectives in an awesome way.

Scott A. Hackman

"Dare To Discover"

I dare each person to discover their true inner self,
To be judged from within rather than by looks or by wealth.

To look in your soul and find happiness from within,
Rather than looking for comfort in the praise from your friends.

I dare you to look at yourself and like what you see,
Not what others would like you to be.

To forgive yourself for the mistakes that you make,
For life is challenging and there will be chances you must take.

I dare you to search into your heart for the strength to
like yourself for who you are.

To go through life proud of the person you've been,
Reflecting from the outside, the person within.

Kim Dobey

Cancer: The Renaissance

The wind blows cold, wicked and long.
To be punished this way I must have done something terribly wrong
My fight for life approached an unfamiliar crossroad.
As the wind blows cold and long.

The man in white read me my limited medical options
Leaving my feelings inside a safe, my body went through the motions
Questions swarmed my mind. Will I see 30? Will I die?
As the wind blows cold and long.

A malignant evil overtook my mind, body and soul
My life as I knew it, began to unfold
The block of support I built around me began to disintegrate
As the wind blows cold and long

I started to be weighed down into a pit of darkness
Pulled down with the force of a lion's caress
I must take control! This is my life, I've got to participate!
As the wind blows cold and long

The true shoulders to lean and cry on, began to emerge
I then realized that I was not alone running this race
As the wind blows cold and long,
I am warmed by my blanket of special friends.

LaTrice Mack

Cabin By The Lake

I wish I had a cabin by the lake
To build a fire and to barbecue a steak.
To sit and watch the stars come into view
And to watch the moon come out on cue,
To feel the touch of a gentle breeze
And to smell the sweet flowers
That cause me to sneeze.
To hear the bullfrogs calling for a mate
Or maybe they're asking for a date.
The cabin is quiet and peaceful now
And with this we make a vow,
To be at Peace with the one above
And to live in the cabin where there is love.

Phillip L. Eslinger

Feelin' Natural

Sometimes when I'm feelin' natural I let my body sink back
to from which it came I let my tired feet go a few inches
just to remind my body of its beginnings I plant myself
into the soft hardness of the soil connecting my body to
its roots and sometimes when I'm feelin' natural and I can
relate to the starved dried-up sterile weeds I let the drops
cascade into my soul...drenching my mind anointing my
spirit I let the ocean envelope me with wings and resurrect
my moistness and best of all when I'm feelin' the
naturalness of bein' natural I let my body my spirit my soul grow

Mika Webb

Illuminating The Truth

The word, a powerful source; to tear down,
to build up, to heal and restore life. Speak
that word that illuminate the truth, the
reality of the saviour, Jesus Christ.
On the whole and in context, the word
has power. Swift and quick, it cuts to the
bone. Exposing the heart, laying bare the issues.
Examine your motives, beware; your souls
at stake. The word has power to cut through
the facade of any masquerade.
What is in the heart, the word will reveal.
Compassion and mercy, goodwill towards man, or
envy and strife the companions of fools. By the
word all are unsealed.
God won't lie, his word is truth. Jesus
Christ he sent to save me and you; to bear good fruit.
Meditate on the word illuminate the truth.

Mignette Humphrey

Enough

Is there ever enough time?
To enjoy enough sunshine with cloudless skies of blue?
Or spend enough winters with snowflakes and you?

To travel enough roads with my back to the wind?
Or send enough letters to a dear old friend?

To sit enough quiet mornings with my beloved dog at my side?
Or hear enough hours the crashing of the tide?

To hold enough seconds a loved and cherished one?
Or touch enough times the strong hand of my son?

To share enough smiles with this sweet daughter of mine?
Or climb enough hills to the fresh scent of pine?

To watch enough springs come and go by?
Or stroll enough paths while the autumn leaves fly?

Or feel enough feelings?
Or give enough love?
Or pray enough times to God above?

Or laugh enough laughs?
Or cry enough tears?
Or just be given enough precious years?

Lisa Jensen

"Read Between The Lines"

Was I too deaf, was I too dumb?
To hear, to understand
The message you were communicating to me.
So many times in so many ways
Trying to let me know of things to come.
Of how you could not stay
Of how much you cared for me
Oh, why couldn't I read between the lines?

And now that you are gone from this life,
I can hear your words.
Today the picture is so clear to me.
Now all that remain are echoes of your sweet utterances
Which still resound in my ears
Your presence which is still felt in my heart
And your countenance which is still etched in my mind.

And through losing you
You and Father God
Have thought me oh so well,
How to listen better, and how to better understand
The art of how to read between the lines.

Susy Wynne Thiele

One Moment In Time

The hospital room, so many things all doing their part
to keep you alive. One question stills lingers in my
mind, why did you do this?

We were partying and having a good time. I told you I
would see you tomorrow and kissed you good night. I
left that party not knowing I would see you like this today.

A call came early this morning. Your mom told me what
had happened. You had too much to drink and hit a tree
head on. Now you are here today making us wonder if you
will live.

Everyone all dressed in black, circled around the grave.
I know this is not what you wanted. As they lower your
casket into the grave, I wonder what I could have done differently.

One careless moment made people grieve over something
that could have been prevented. The next time my
friends and I are at a party, we will think twice about
drinking and driving.

Lori Phend

Desert Storm

We regret to inform you...

Those are words a mother most fears
To lose her son she held so dear.

She wants to be brave and tries not to cry
As the tears flow gently from her eyes.

She silently says good-bye my son
Why, oh why, did the cold war come.

You did your duty and paid the price
You were just doing what you thought was right.

They took your life, but not without a fight
Just to give us freedom one more night.

God I pray you keep him safe
And save for me by his side a place.

Tina Jacob

The Light

I'm searching for a light;
To make me warm, when I'm cold;
To make me bright, when I'm dark;
To give me joy, while I'm lonely.
I have a light in my dream.
But I need the melodic words of a spiritual song;
Provoking me, in a shared wisdom;
With the sharpness of knowledge;
To reach my dream.
I need a light, when the storm rises;
To give me the power;
To reach your hands, to feel your fingers
and to hold our arms together.
I need a light, a colored light;
With a lot of words, songs and joy;
To demolish the dark gap
between you and me.
I need the light, we need the light...

Neamat Nojumi

Untitled

Bring your rays
to meet my stars
Bring your light
to meet my dark
Bring your day
to meet my night
and no fists will clench
and no jaws will set
But hearts will open
and souls will pour
and out will come the hate of the past
and the masks of today
the clouds will unleash the dragon
that is to burn the past
for the children that live for the rainbow

Kristine Fisher

Back To A Time

I wish only to be small again
To only greet the table legs
And to take the melting, mixing hours
of day with me
Into faraway lands

Naive and unaware of the newspaper
lying on the doorstep
That would revive my insightful
and knowing mind
If only again I could be that sheltered
and free
all at once

To be carried back to a time
Where my world was one in itself
Where a day of pointless play
Fed and satisfied my soul
And created harmony
Instead of thoughts in my mind

I can only dream
That the daylight will find my wish granted

Molly Collord

The Timeless Ash

I watch the clock,
to realize he's not coming home.
His presence is what kept me tickling,
but without him I am ash-
from a dying flame,
which is now merely a spark.

It's been two years of thoughts,
put into three weeks of endless love,
to make me realize my presence is no longer welcomed.

I want to turn back time,
to realize what I have lost,
Or maybe who I lost.
Did I want this to happen?

My life is over as
I grasp my heart.
I feel my inside shatter.
My time is up.

Teresa Skrepenski

The Scarecrow

He was out there in the fields of corn,
To scare away the crows forlorn.
Filled with straw and clothes so torn,
He greets all those that he may warn.
If he could talk and have things to say,
Just walk away, not lose his way,
Filled with pain or choose to stay,
For all his views you hear someday.
The scarecrow laughs when he is alone,
All things to say are left unknown.
Filled with life, a friend is home,
In fields with no end for a world of his own.
HE was out there in the rain one night,
Somewhere around the broken light.
Filled with sound of spoken sight,
He waves goodbye to be polite.
The scarecrow did his job so well,
All the years he gave them hell.
He had to go, so I bade farewell,
Where he went I will never tell.

William A. Pennucci

Peace After The Storm

One day I decided to take a walk down to the sea
To see if I could find a resemblance to me
To my surprise the water was calm that day
And all the waves were going on their merry way
I said to myself why this can't be true
There's so much turmoil in me and you
We as humans do have a lot in common with the sea
We have the potential to move universally
We have the power to rage just like the storm
Break up the monotony and get rid of the norm
But to my astonishment what we lack unlike the sea
Is after all the fuss join back together peacefully

William J. Peden

Forgotten Warriors

The reasons are many, still only they knew,
to serve their country, to answer the call.
When put to the test, poured red, white and blue.
But then what happens when soldiers fall?

Lebanon, Somalia and Panama too
the peace time heroes who gave their all.
Those who remember, who care, too few.
For these fallen warriors no Vietnam wall.

The Veterans of world wars, Korea, Vietnam,
Their purpose was just, their honor supreme.
But those that died when the world was calm
Were their deaths real or just a bad dream?

In desert storm, victory, still blood ran red.
Are patriotic feelings now on the rise?
Still what does it take to honor the dead
of forgotten victories and hollow cries?

Stan Domin

Caged

The rain pours down its wing, but still the caged bird has to sing. There isn't much to live for - nope - but still the caged bird has some hope. Although sometimes it gets annoyed, somehow this is its time of joy. Behind the bars no human's touch, but how the caged bird needs so much. To live and die this it knew but all it could do was sweetly "coo." Oh how it longed to be loved and cared for, but the caged birds heart got nothing but ignore. So every day it sung its song, every day its whole life long.

Stephanie Scarbrough

My Rare Gem

A token from my heart,
To symbolize my love.

Through all of life, good and bad,
You are truly the one who makes my heart glad.

Through all the mess, more or less,
my heart will always confess,
You are the one to whom my heart will always belong.

Friends forever, lovers for life, even in the bitterest of strife,
I am proud to be your wife.

Here's looking ahead to a brighter tomorrow,
Closing the door on yesterday's sorrow.

Genuine love is a hard thing to find, but when I think of love of that kind...

You come to my mind.

Your gentle smile and warm embrace,
A rare gem that I could never replace.

Sandra Pitcher

"Yesterday's Mourn"

Let us come, let us listen
To the old ones as they glisten
Of tales of wonderment so near and far
Of journey's encountered but seldom marred
Of times and places and moonlight gazes
Those twinkling eyes and shining faces.

Tell me please of those glorious times
Yesterday's longing all in your minds.
With memories so vivid I know at last
The reason they talked so much of the past.
It was faith and endurance with continuing love
And surely their guidance all from above.

Oralee Wright

Memory in Old Age

God, did you give me only so many words
to use in a lifetime—-
Long, short, beautiful ugly ones?
Was I to allot them day by day
pearls to be counted and rolled on my tongue?

Was I wasteful?
Was I extravagant?
Did I exceed my quota?
Did I talk too fast
too foolishly?

Is this the finish?
The last page of my script?
No codicil?
No epilogue?
The conversation is over.
My lips are sealed.
Tell me what to do with my thoughts
when the words are on the tip of my tongue
and nothing comes out.

Sybil Gale Gruner

From Prisoner To President

Africa, how you longed to be free,
To vote and decide your destiny
Awakened from a bitter past,
Now you're free! Yes! Free at last!

From the shackles of prison,
You held to a vision, and never gave up the fight;
Obscured by a dark veil of oppression,
You struggled for the right.

They thought you were forever lost,
On the waves of Injustice, Tempest Tossed;
So proud and strong, your head held high,
For this Noble cause, many had to die.

The land where our forefathers trod,
Given to them by almighty God;
Chant the joyous freedom song,
Your fight for democracy, is finally won.

On the pages of history,
Let this moment be;
A tribute to Mandela,
A salute of victory.

Regina E. Richardson

Together, Until The End Of Time

You and I, until the end of time
Together now, we'll never say goodbye.
You are the only true love I ever found
Until the end of time, we'll always be around.

We met, at a bar in Key Largo,
And you held me tight, you'd never let me go.
And I can see when I look into your eyes
You'd never lie, until the end of time.

Remember the days our love was brand new
You needed me, all I could dream of was you.
And you see me through tender eyes of love
That would never cry, until the end of time.

We fought obstacles, to keep our loving strong.
We felt so right, nothing could make us wrong.
And no one could steal our love, no matter how hard they try
Our love won't die, until the end of time.

Thinking back, I'm trying to recall
What made us strong, and helped us through it all.
And made us laugh, when we should have cried
We will survive, until the end of time.

Matthew S. Hearn

Untitled

As they sit in solitude
Together pondering life
Unity is woven from each one's soul
As they conquer each painful strife

Sometimes silent, sometimes not
As animation seem sometimes drained
Some fall in love, and some in hate
Some grow happy, some go insane

The boggled and the mismanaged
Can find no other place
Because their hearts long for love
And to see a familiar face

Sometimes indignation between these souls
Shrouds allegiance with blackened doubt
They always wander to a lonely diner
And forget what their fights were about

Sascha Mabus-Vosper

One Day

One day is all they had...
Together they shared their past loves, joys and pain.
Two people, both struggling for direction
in a life more than half lived.

He came from the Big Apple...
A life of theaters, stars and fancy eating places.
She came from the farm
with hoedowns, small town folks and McDonalds.

Tears told tales of things they had missed in life.
Career had deprived him of family, children, wife.
He eased the guilt she carried for
insisting her "actor" husband remain a family man.

He dared to dream of his own dinner theater...
A deserted building he could bring to life with laughter.
She offered an address of an empty store
holding great potential and parking places.

They exchanged phone numbers; they day was over...
Their paths have never crossed again.
Every time she passes the empty store
she remembers the closeness they felt that one day.

LaVerne Stevens

A Traveler's Day

Grandmother, meet me in the mist of heaven for together we will travel to uncharted heavens and explore the nebula bubble.

We will drift among the universe to other starry skies and count the stars in Plelades as we go floating by.

We'll move along gracefully on cosmic current waves and roam the hazy nebulas seeking quasars massive rays.

Meet me in the mist of heaven of together we will see, the harmony of heavens, God's greatest majesty.

For time will have no measurement not minutes hours or days, because you and I will have forever to complete a traveler's day.

Rita Bartell

Yesterday

The days run together
Tomorrow is yesterday before it's tomorrow
Some how the days are long
full of tears
hate and love
No time to feel or understand why
in the end
you seem to want to cry
when you find time to try understanding
what your problems may be
You realize your day has gone bye
you did everything but accomplished nothing
And then tomorrow comes and
today will be here
you know now it's yesterday
you fear

Mindy Lou High

Cycles

Yesterday is yesterday.
Tomorrow is yet to come.
Life cycles have started away.
Death mask has come for some.

How will I be remembered?
Will it be for leading a lavish life?
A tattered web - a bitch thrice scorned -
Come now. Whom will throw the next rice?

Or will I stop to embrace a kind, loving face -
One of trust to endure
Save in loving arms -
Certain serenity lovingly secure.

Riddles... riddles... and more riddles-
Life is very complex!
If you are fortunate to be around a little longer.
There will be more yet.

Marvin T. Johnson

What Is This Thing, Mom?

I overheard a little girl ask her mother what a flower was. Her mom took her up in her arms and told her about how God gave a seed to the ground; and with the sun and the rain's help, it became a flower.

She then asked her mother another question that she was having a problem with. She said, "Mom, our daycare teacher read us a story about a baby in a manger a long time ago. Who was this baby and why did these three Kings call him a King? Then tell me about a star and how He died."

She said, "My darling little daughter, you were also a baby. You see, the story your teacher told you was the story of the birth of Jesus, the Son of God up in Heaven. God gave us life and this beautiful world; but, God was not pleased with how his people were living.

"You see, God loved His people and did not want them living this way. So God sent down His own Son to save His people. My darling, you see the baby in the manger is God's son, Jesus. You see, this was the first Christmas present ever given by our Heavenly Father to His children on earth.

"You too, my dear daughter, are a gift from God to your father and me, and we love God with all our hearts and soul." Now that I know the story I will give Jesus a present this year...my faith, hope and love, for now I know He died for me too.

Lila Mae Meyers

A Day In My Life

Is that which is final the ultimate? It is a long road we
travel some roads paved with gold,
Some with cobblestone, others with gravel.
My pockets are gaping exhibitions of lurid dismay
Turned inside out, it's funny in a certain way,
But also it is strange, for I cannot laugh again
Because I'm afraid my tears will fall forever like rain.

Jealous of the long empty hours spent in despise,
Spent starting and dreaming with such hungry eyes
Or greeting acquaintances with simple shrugged shoulders,
The gestures emanating my hate for the pain I feel as I grow older.

Eyes of the hopeful believing, wishing, dreaming
Eyes of the hopeless shouting, sweating, screaming
The eyes of the fearful and those of the sad...
The eyes of the exhausted and those of the mad
The eyes of the wounded, sodden in red...the eyes of the
dying, and those of the dead in a search for the answers, so
confusing and often endless we tend to lose our true selves,
becoming lonely, frightened, and friendless.

Robert James Lalor

Fall - Natures Magical Season

It must be the fall season, with trees a splendor
Trees that are now dressed, in magnificent color
Gaily moving, dancing, to breezes whistling
As if knowing this celebration of color is fleeting

Different hues beautifully blending
Bright red, yellow, blue, green and white
All signaling the close of another season ending
With trees radiantly adorned, in colors gloriously bright

As if by magic, trees large and small
From green leaves are turning
Brightly colored, naked, bare
The natural progression, of the season, fall

Once the home of birds flitting and chirping gay
Tending their young without the semblance of a care
Soon all is silent, as the trees stand bare
No leaves brightly colored, no songs of birds at play

Birds who once nested in those branches green
Have all departed, to grace some other scene
Once thicked leafy branches; now appear as twigs dry
Within whose skeletal forms, life still reside

Wintor Henderson Niles

Being Pensive

Work on, slave on, Sandburg would say,
True logic he easily displayed.
But the starting is to the finishing
As de Milo would be to fire lighting.
The man that makes himself.
Through education gaining his wealth,
Up life's ladder he doth climb, until,
Through lofty perches he views heaven sublime.
If through evil means he wished this throne
God rebellion seen,
Would have him from heaven thrown.

D. B. Dale

Sandybottom

Yo soy el estanque y
Tu le caillou me fais eruption

A pebble splits the calm darkwater of a backwoods pond
Sending sprays of excitement and bits of granite
Along with its quartz into an
Uncaring atmosphere

Sweet pebble sink soft and secure into your lover's silt embrace
Muddy bottom familiar to you both, and
Rest assured
The pond will ripple on until near eternity with
Love for you and a profound
Relief that you are safe in bottom's arms

For who is a pond to uphold a pebble?

S Lawson Searle

Untitled

Who are you?
To me, you are many smiles.
You overshadow my reality and
help me create for myself a fantasy.

With you I am a woman
after much time of being only a person.
Touch me tenderly and love me lingeringly.
Let me savor every delicious moment
for our time is fleeting and goodbyes are close at hand.

Sharie Stewart

Reality

In a dark alley where black rats creep,
Under a blanket lies a child asleep.
Foodless and poor she manages to survive
She dreams of finding enough change to keep her alive.

Up above the alley in a small apartment,
sleeps an ancient little man full of resentment.
He used to work, and led a moderate life.
But dreams of a peaceful world absent of strife.

In the dark mountains can be seen a glow,
of a recluses cottage buried under snow.
He spends his days with the native wildlife,
And dreams of understanding the language of mice.

At the base of the mountain is a grand estate,
Within its walls sits a man wide awake.
He spends his time worrying about his investments;
If he dreamed it would be of monetary improvements.

Each with their own niche in this world,
Struggles and dreams of improving their hold.
Paralleled dream with many similarities,
isolated, yet unified, tangent realities.

Nicole London

Bus Stops

I still remember lying with him
Under the warm summer sky
Feathering his fingers and feeling safe
As the light faded into dusk

The ocean rocks standing as powerful guardians
Of the secrets between men and women.

In the beginning we were so drunk
With the touch and scent of each other
Our vows were of understanding, friendship, and love.

But as the cold winds of other's opinions
And envy crept into our hearts
Our fear and anger coiled up and
We struck out at each other.

Why do the forces in modern life
Tear up love and anything tender
Like patterned silk in the mouth of a mongrel dog.

And why are we left alone
At our bus stops
With only the swirl of dirty wind
And garbage around us.

Kathleen Rampton

Fortunately

Fortunately, Shana is my friend.
Unfortunately, she is moving.

Fortunately, Jessica is my friend.
Unfortunately, her dad wants to go to England.

Fortunately, Jennifer A. is my friend.
Unfortunately, I only see her in the afternoon.

Fortunately, Jon is my friend.
FORTUNATELY, I see him every day!

Sara Lisa Davis

My Wonderful Dancing Doll

Petite.
Unique.
Celestially Exquisite.
The Very Sweetest Of The Most Sweet.

The brilliance of green eyes,
Disarming sweetness of bright, sunlit smiles,
The conquering enchantments of your always lovely moves,
Eternally caress my adoring, anxious moods.

So much energy and quiet pep.
Such an intensity of ginger,
That my pure love for you
Just has to linger.

Captivated by the intoxicating essence
Of your infinitely inviting presence.
If you will let me know that you do love me too,
What, then, shall I do?

Instantly will I surrender
My soul, my all,
To My Wonderful Dancing Doll!

Raymond Sutherland

Why You Should Believe

No, I can not tell you, why you should believe,
Unless I also show you, by the life I lead.
For how will you follow, sincere words alone,
Words can ring so hollow in an empty soul,
But...
If at first, I reach out, just as Jesus did,
fill your hurting heart with hope,
and show myself a friend,
intercede on your behalf,
and be there in the storm,
your hardened heart may start to melt,
and in this soil warm,
I'll once again tell of my Lord,
and of His love for you,
of how He died upon the cross,
to give you life anew,
and the seed which God has planted,
will soon begin to grow,
Until it one day blossoms,
and bears fruit of its own.

Laura Christine Mathwig

Untitled

Emergency! Do not enter!
Unless of course your dollars are good,
You've done all you should
Have an unmortgaged house and a legal spouse.
Perhaps you'll die...still
Answer your life away!
Everyone bleeds a little everyday.
Everyway!
Anyway!
Emergency, do not enter
Unless you can pay for care.
Just die...anyday
Anywhere!
America has people to spare...

Miriam E. Fisher

You Could Kill The Body, But You Can't Touch My Soul

How far can a human last
Until the earth subdues the soul
How can someone be so full of hate
That God tends to know
For there is a message for everyone to know
You could kill the body, but you can't touch my soul

God bless all of his people
Not to see them all in pain
For the world belongs to him
Just to fill your heart within
You could kill the body, but you can't touch my soul

Keeping the peace within your heart
To glorify the children to grow inside
To see the anger grow within our soul
For God knows his people are free
Until the earth has passed my rule
You could kill the body, but you can't touch my soul

Until then I shall promise my people
For life is what you make it
You could kill the body, but you can't touch my soul

Rodney Dennis

Life's Realities

Life's realities are amazing to me.
Upon awakening each morning,
Sometimes it's difficult to see,
That a new day is dawning.
Another chance, another day to find the way
Yet, life, each day we still take for granted.
We continue to strive for more success and power.
We let life slip by day by precious day.
Time is ticking away, could be there's just one more hour.
Life's reality is, to me—Are you ready?
Should this be the hour, should this be the day;
What have you done today, did you pray?
Did you say a kind word to a weary soul?
Did you reach out your hand, and say, friend grab a hold.
Grab a hold, my friend let's enjoy life's wonderful realities.
Before they all end.
And it's time to go, to join our greatest friend;
In the greatest reality there's ever been.

Sandra Earley

Midnight Lover

Midnight lover I await for you
Upon the nights' magical hour
Gentle kisses, sacred love
Heated passion to devour

Midnight lover alone I stand
Awaiting to hold your hand
Anticipating a love we can handle
Shadows flicker, in the light of a candle

Midnight lover sweep me in your arms
With all of your loving charms
Dance me off my feet
Our hearts together, become one beat

Midnight lover our lips passionately press
Your heavenly body I tenderly caress
For you, I long to hold
Shinning in my eyes, sparkles of gold

Midnight lover
In my dreams, my heart has spoken
Why did you not appear?
Your promise has left my heart broken upon my pillow lies a tear

William W. C. Long III

A Boys Life

Depressed, repressed, transgressed. All dressed, undressed, unrest.
Uremittant, unrepentant?

Always striving never arriving, always contriving, maybe always lying.

Jeers, fears and buckets of tears.
Hopeful, yet doubtful, never a cupful only a handful.

Offered, proffered but never coffered. Illusion, delusion,
CONFUSION!
Expected, corrected, rejected - dejected.
Contracted, protracted, exacted. Always indebted, never credited.
Wanted, taunted, created for joy. Only a failure at being a toy.
Grandmother/mother, grandfather/father.
Mother, father, father - sister,
Half-sister, half-sister, half-sister.
Can there be such a thing as a half-sister?
You're a mother, a father, a brother, a sister.
Being a half is not worth the bother. Wife, wife - so much strife.
You deserved a better life. Loved and known, but not matrimony.
Is she a wife? Is she a wife? Is she a wife?

Fatherhood tried, children died. Wife cried...And cinema lied.

Seemingly tame, Dialing for Dollars is the insidious family game.
What a darn shame.

Todd Sidwell

Crack And Cocaine

To all people of the world who
Use these drugs, I say no way stop
It today, it makes you lie and
cheat and steal, and it takes away
your will, so I am begging all you
people to leave it alone,
all it does is break up your home.
I know it messes up your life,
because of these drugs I divorced my wife.
Every night I beg God and pray,
somehow make this crack and cocaine go away.
I have family and friends who have gone astray.
Because of this crack and cocaine,
they are just wasting their lives away.
So God if you can hear my plea
set these people on crack and cocaine free,
and give my friends and family back to me.

Larry G. Johnson

Our Pine And Calico Club

Around the Pine table, six friends sit,
Waiting for the candles to be lit.
The coffee pot is singing, a merry little tune,
Blending with the tinkling of dishes and spoons.

It's a Tuesday night and for the last five years,
We have been together, these friends so sincere.
We were born one hundred years too late,
That's the reason we won't separate.

For we love antiques, blue dishes, pine and calico,
The way people worked and lived, many years ago,
And smells from wood fires, ticking of old clocks,
Sunsets, birds, and walls of gray rocks.
Faded red tablecloths, copper, pewter and brass,
The blue sky above us, the green of the grass,
Lilacs in spring, daisies nodding in the breeze.
How very lucky we are to appreciate all these.

So if you are blue, come linger with us,
Wear your old clothes because we never fuss
And I sincerely hope, that you will agree
The very best things in this world are free.

Sukey Patten

As Life Goes On

The world is so full of new things
waiting to be discovered
New challenges to face each day

When you rise from your bed each morning
this day will not be similar
to yesterday or tomorrow
for each day bears significance

Find your inspiration that helps
to face the obstacles
and look them right in the face
you are able

There is an inner strength that drives you
become familiar with it
embrace it and thank the power
from above

You are able, let determination be your guide
you will succeed, let no one trample over your goals
each day brings promise

The coming true of your dreams
will be the ultimate reward
and then let a bath of success
wash the worries of failure away

Sarita Chapman

"Communication"

On my road to salvation -
Walking around in this nation;
Don't want to head for starvation -
I'm always full of aberration.
I don't have no good explanation -
Just trying to reach a destination;
Stumbling over complications -
Hoping to survive in this population.
Wanting to further my education -
So I can find an occupation;
That will give me exultation.

Because of the violence in this generation -
People trying to keep up with my reputation;
Don't want to be bothered with hallucination -
Trying to avoid all this temptation;
I think it's time for variation.
We all are really just excavation -
People living their lives through usurpation -
But just for everyone's in formation.....
I think this world will soon be under extermination

Marie Hartley

Once Again

Waiting on a meal, not worried about who is flipping the bill.

No, it's not me, the one with the never ending
wallet it tis another, my friend.
so we can eat once again,
thank you my friend....

Now we can hit the streets again
looking for me, I was looking for u
we split up as we were looking for more
or should you call it our space.

All in all we're here to just have a ball

So, no matter how drunk you get or how hard you fall,
enjoy the winter that comes along, so you can spring back
into the summer months to watch the leaves fall

Come and see us
we love you all.

Michael C. Lewis

Sunset Of Love

Dance with me into the sunset of love
Waltz with a twilight star
To where the wild things are
Sail away to the edge of the world
Where moonbeams slice through life
And you fall right off
Into the sunset of love
Better to dance than stand still as stone
And always alone
Better to dance right onto a lance
So come dance with me into the sunset of love
Where the pathways gleam
Littered with broken dreams
Join the heaving breathing walls of people
Embrace the curling fingers of the sea
Come dance with me
Into the sunset of love.

Zheela Hameed

"A Teacher's Prayer"

I stand before them
Wanting to say Your Name
Wanting to tell them about You
Your holy birth, the angels, Mary
Your death on a cross, Calvary, hatred -
It's hatred that doesn't allow me to speak of You
Out of my want, my desire, my love
Comes a need to say Jesus
Jesus, mercy
Mercy on these children
Mercy on America
Mercy on a country founded on "God we trust"
But now, not allowed, not allowed
To say Your Name
A teacher in a Public school in America
Not allowed to wear a cross in view
Not allowed to bring these children to You
Except by example and prayer.

Theresa C. Beccatelli

Keeping The Secret Hidden Away So No One Can See This Part Of Me

When I talk to you I lose all control
Wanting to yell and scream why does this have to be me?
What did I do to deserve this?
Oh how I wish that this part of my life would simply go away
Telling you is easy, I can keep what I feel far away,
But eventually these feelings of rage and anger
Will come back to haunt me, slowing down, taking my time,
It all seems to be such a waste of time
I run away hoping to find a place where one no can see the
Secret that I hide deep within me
If I risk everything and tell you about my secret
Will you understand or walk away?
Stand by me, believe in me, I need you to see this part of me
Understand my need, can't you see that this is really hard for me
I need to feel that I am safe in sharing this secret
The time has come to share this with you
I need you to know who I am
I have searched high and low and it has been a long road
I have finally begun to see that there is someone
Special deep down inside of me.......

Kathleen Sue Hale

"Our Dog, Friskey"

His legs were short, only 1 inch long,
Was also fat, his stomach touched the ground.
One leg pointed North and the other pointed South,
Loved his goodies, always drooling at the mouth.
And when it came time for our "Goodbyes,"
He would look at me with his soulful eyes.
I'd say "stay" and he would stop completely,
I'd nod my head and he'd move slightly.
He died at the hospital, on 18th of March,
I still picture him, napping, on our couch.
It seems unreal and yet I know it's true,
Because I hugged him that last day,
And told him, "I LOVE YOU."

Terry Weatherbee (March 24, 1994)

Untitled

When Kennady died every ones heart
Was like a broken wing.
How could someone do this awful thing,
the whole world mourned his death,
and watched while he laid to rest,
HOW a person could do this act
with their own hand,
While history took place all over the land.
They took a life and widowed his
wife, and left his children behind.

Patricia Chiarenga

Sweet Kiss (Eileen)

The sweetest kiss I ever had
was the last I had from her
The kiss that said goodbye sweetheart
Until we meet again
The kiss that said, my dear, you must go on alone
The kiss that said It's OK, I'm finally going home
That kiss that said I love you
returned my love for her
Sweet kiss of reassurance
Sweet embrace of love
Last hug of love for lovers true
Just one goes on, one life is through

Lee Gray

The Promise

The greatest achievement of my wife and I
Was the recent birth of our baby girl
Who is as beautiful and perfect
As a Tiffany pearl.
Standing proud testament
To our conjugal creation
Mikhaela Shakti Singh
Is the epitome of world nation.
She is the proud miracle
Of an Australian mama and Indian papa
Who though settled in New York
Conceived her in the Bahamas.
Our daughter congresses families and friends
A magic bridge of peace and love
Bringing together all countries and ages
Radiating her force like the proverbial dove.
Our child is the loveliest gift
In the eyes of grandparents on both sides
We all rejoice in her significance
Fulfilling the promise of the groom and bride.

Karun K. Singh

A Basket Of Memories

The very first time you ever laid eyes on me,
was while installing officers in your auxiliary.
I began as a basket, flowers and ribbons bare,
all assembled by your State Grandmother, fair.
I followed you to the Convention in Pacific,
where we saw friends and had times terrific.
Clinton's 18th Anniversary was where next we met,
In a place of honor at the head table I did set.
At the Spring Conference again we would meet,
where friends and acquaintances we would greet.
Your auxiliary presents me as a gift to you,
from all your Sisters of years tried and true.
We shared lots of good times and through many a door,
the last being to your home, and I will travel no more.

K. R. Biles

"My First Love"

I remember my heart full of love,
watching the birds fly above.
Day by day, I think of him in every way.
The time I met him, seemed like a long time.
He was the most wonderful guy,
and the one pictured in my eye.
In a bright day, he was my guiding way.
In the night, he was my romantic
moonlight.
Time passed by, with love in my eye.
But the first thing I think of,
was that he will always be my
lighting way and my dreamy first love.

Zora Abernathy

Life's Simple Treasures

A child's joy on Christmas morn,
watching your first baby born.

The natural beauty of an opening rose,
wearing comfortable worn out clothes.

A flock of geese in formation flight,
or celebrating on a special night.

The warmth you feel from the sun's embrace,
the way a puppy licks your face.

A great big hug from a tiny child,
the many flowers that grow wild.

Snowflakes that silently drift from the sky,
enjoying a piece of your favorite pie.

Seeing an eagle soar high above
or spending time with those you love.

Watching the sunrise with a friend,
a sunset that never seems to end.

Sharing a laugh, having some fun,
hearing that your favorite team has won.

All these things that bring you pleasure
are indeed life's simple treasures.

Mary Cooksey Wilks

"The Best"

To know you is to love you
To have you means caring for you
To caress you means sharing with you
To be with you means eternal joy

To ease the fear is to think you're near
To build our love stronger means working together
To make the best means not creating a mess
For to know you is to love you
Because you deserve the best.

Maxwell H. Comma

Crimson Beach

The Ocean of Death murmurs its sweet song
Waves of Pain and Loneliness thrash against me and then back away,
as if begging me to follow
The Waves crash along the Beach of Reality, yet far away I see the
Calmness, and I long to reach that place
As I step into the Crashing Waves, they turn Crimson...
So Red.
I ride along towards the middle into the Calm
As the Crashing Waves leave me, I am free from all pain
No more crimson.
Now it is Calm, and I drift along
I look back, but there is Nothing
Have I hurt them?
No, only Myself
The Ocean of Death murmurs its sweet song
And I drift in the Sea of Pain and Loneliness.

Rhonda L. Lee

Untitled

Oh! Michael and Alex, where can you be?
We are looking for you but we can not really see.

For you aren't where we are hoping,
But we are all barely coping.

For your mother is the one,
That really knows your out-come.

Soon everyone's heart will ache
Because you both are at the bottom of the lake.

Oh! Michael and Alex, we are really sad,
To think of your mother, we get surely mad.

K. Fithen

Serenity

Life is becoming too complicated.
We are met with many challenges:
emotionally, economically, spiritually, ...
We need a spindle — to keep us focused.
Serenity is a key word for living a healthier life.
Serenity is a key word.
If one can function with serenity,
I suppose one can manage almost anything.
Finding serenity takes some work.
Finding peace of mind, accepting who we are,
how the world is,.....
It's a struggle.
Meeting these challenges with serenity would render
our life more productive.
So let serenity be our main task.

Patrizia Marrone

Life's Little Twists

I gaze upon your shadow and see my own reflection,
We are one in the same.
We carry a common future on this uphill quest for happiness,
searching for our destiny.
We stumble upon our leaders trail, a broken, muddled path,
not to perfect like we had dreamed.
Hidden beyond the rainbow is a life of raging rivers and towering
mountains,
All of which we must conquer.
We stand and heed our journey ahead,
and smile as we talk of reaching that final peak.
Off we go to conquer the holders of our destiny.
Along the way the rapids grasped at our ankles and I fled
But you, you were not strong enough,
and were engulfed by this wicked force,
And I wept as I watched my future wash away.

Tammy Jo Nye

To Heir Is To Pass It On

There are no color sides to the Human Race——
We are Successors of All Humanity.

Those human beings living in the World today must realize this fact of successorship and
"Pass it On".

Today's human beings are the Heirs of Mankind!

To H-E-I-R— is to PASS IT ON!
"To HEIR is to"
"PASS IT ON"

Some people say, "To Error is only Human".
Let's say, "To Heir is to pass it on!"

Larry W. Loud

The Line

As midnight appears, the conscious disappears
We begin to dream,
or maybe just wading through the
subconscious stream
Is it real or just a pill
You'll walk the line many a time
To find out what's really in the mind
Life's learning maze often can put you into a daze
There'll be times of grief and time for peace
They'll be no one to blame if you lose the game
Just pinch your cheek and be the one it wont beat
Temptation will call if you let yourself fall
Open your eyes and cleanse of any lies
We've all a journey, as we pass through life
walk strong and stand tall
Know who you are, or you'll drift without a sail
Be mentally strong and with the mind
There's no chance you won't walk the line.

Robert A. Penuel

Goodbyes

The time has come to say goodbye
We hadn't much choice, the time had come
The times we had good and bad,
Will be memories, that we'll always have
We know it was love and it will always be
But first love, isn't always meant to be.
Maybe we'll meet again.
but until, then we must try to maintain
Don't ever forget me for I will always
be in your heart and you'll forever always
be in mine.

Keri Neubarth

"Our Last Good-Bye"

Even tho our age was young,
We knew then our love had just begun,
My love for her will always be.
The day she said, good-bye to me.
The day her mommy took her away
I knew then our good-bye was to stay
Even now, so old and gray,
I'll never forget that good-bye day.
If tears were counted as stars in the sky,
there would be rivers to heaven -
Just because of our last good-bye.

Martin L. Grimord

Save The Children

In Memory to Michael and Alex Smith

Michael and Alex are laid to rest
We know for their souls, they're with the best
They were beautiful children we sure could see
They touched a lot of hearts, The world and me

We pray to the Lord for the help we need
Take care of these children, we all do plead

It's time we stop this evil and crime
Even if it takes a little bit of time
The world is rough, we sure do know
But don't hurt the children, they need to grow

When you feel like things are getting you down
Talk to a friend, your family or a clown

Some times we all need to get a way
But let the children stay out and play
Lets save the children from all the abuse.
Shall we all work together, and no-one refuse
Lets say goodnight to the children at play
And tomorrow will wake up to a beautiful day

Now Michael and Alex, we say goodbye
They held hands, while they went to the sky. Amen

Mona LaPage

Childhood Dreams

Tree houses, rusted bicycles, old toys and imagination, these things we leave behind for children of another generation turn our thoughts back to our childish days when we could be anyone at all; dreams of being ballerinas, presidents, astronauts, anything that answered fancy's call. We remember, too, those times when we were told we were too young to understand. Oh, and how upset we got when we were bad and still felt the sting of mother's hand. But, with time we grew and began to see. We finally had the chance to stand up for those things in which we believe. But with that new found freedom also came problems and opposition. Then we would turn to that faithful friend who was always there to listen. Of course we were often given advice from someone who seemed concerned. Sometimes we took it and sometimes not, but by every mistake we always learned.

And now we sit and ponder what happened to all that awe and wonder? We, of course, use those basic morals we were taught, but somehow we've lost that zest of youth — that beauty that can't be bought. The complexities of life have stolen that excitement for each new day, and disabled our imaginations we held so dear in childish play. Now, I say, reach out and relive—explore, and please never forget. No matter how old, with memories of childhood our dreams haven't been conquered yet.

Kimberly R. Underwood

Untitled

I want to die now
to forget that I am alive
to not know that all of this is hopeless
to cry, because my friend has died
not to question every little thing I do
to let go of every weight piled upon my back
to laugh from joy, not anger,
cynicism, resentment, or jealousy.
To look around and see life,
not to suspect conspiracy.
To not know that we are doomed
and there is nothing I can do,
except die.

Otto Esterle Jr.

"Let Go"

As the sun goes down each day,
we rarely recognize the true beauty it holds.
The power it has we sometimes over look.
It gives us strength that we may not know,
Not just yet any ways.
Soon enough as your wisdom increases,
You will know what the sun
is saying when no one else does:
"Each night when I go down,
give me a problem; give me your frown.
For when I awake us in the morning,
You shall see that your
problem no longer effects you or me.
It is lost somewhere in
time, where all problems should be
both yours and mine."
So when no one else listens,
when no one else cares, glance at the sky.
Stare at its beauty with
your magical eye and the sun will take your bad time.

Michele Juarez

Inward Love

We are all human beings, God gave us life
We should Love one another
Don't be judgmental on sight
Life is so beautiful, live as you see fit
We are all God's children,
Race has nothing to do with it.

Just close your eyes and walk for a while
And touch the one beside you
You would not know the color you touch
So, to hate is not good for you

Love is something we all should share
Give it daily because you care
No matter what color you were born with dear friend
Color remain color until the end.

When you see someone in trouble,
Please do what is right
You know it's a person,
You should know wrong from right
Because we are all human beings,
And God gave us life.

Urita Arthur

Diet Control

We are organic vegetarians from head to toe.
We will cook and eat anything we can grow.
His and her gardens are not just for show.
Okra for gumbo, beets from Harvard, Asparagus on toast.
Garbanzos and goobers and pumpkin for pies.
Zucchini and patty pan which ever you choose.
Red and green coleslaw and turnips of white, hot
or cold peppers are a delight.
Cauliflower, collards and broccoli with heads that are
great eggplant parmesan everyone knows.
Peas and carrots, bite size limas and corn on the cob.
Green beans and potatoes with sweet ones to bake.
Lettuce and tomatoes the best we can make.
Herbs and spices with garlic galore Forget-Me-Nots
and Daisies that give you a smile, these are
the things that make life worth while.
With hush puppies to fry, biscuits and corn bread to
bake we can stay busy for Heavens sake.
50 years of gardening with 50 to go but in Heaven,
we are not sure our gardens will grow.

Peggy Gonzalez

Isolation

Wind that sighs through mountain peaks
Web the spider had to leave
Drop that falls in a cave so deep
A solemn rock to make my seat
The mirrors of my mind reflect the thoughts
that make me weep

Norman P. Seman

Forever Embraced

There was a gift given to us on our
wedding night.
It is a statue of a man and a woman
embracing each other tight.

The statue reminds me so much of you,
he forever embraces the woman he loves too.

You've made me feel so secure in my life
first, our friendship, falling in love, and
now your wife.

You've made me feel forever embraced,
by your love, kindness, and patience
no matter the case.

Like the statue that sits on our T.V.
stand, I am forever embraced by
a wonderful man.

I just wanted to thank you for
loving me the way you do,
and let you know I will forever
love and embrace you.

Tina Marie Shelton

"Come Lay With Me"

Come lay with me in the white beach sand,
We'll stare up at the sky and get lost in ourselves,
Then night turns to day and the glow spreads over the land.

Come lay with me by the dark waters' edge,
We'll feel the cool waves wash and get lost in ourselves,
Then day turns to night and the dark creeps over the ledge.

So, come lay with me in the white beach sand,
And when it's time to move on we'll leave hand in hand...

M. K. Rutherford

Shut Down Who?

Seems like only yesterday the clouds
were gone the sky was never gray
And all around me I could hear
songs of angels humming in my ear
Tender laughter playful songs
Memories! The child has grown

Police the world! I don't give a damn
The future of all fellow man
Is at the point of self destruction
Pollution, wars, man made obstruction
I see it in the air I smell it in the sea.

I smell it in the air I see it in the sea.
Is it harming you? It's harming me
So what do we do shut down the factory's
Shut down that you shut down the me's

A. L. Fouch

The Dorchester's Heroes

The chaplains—Fox, Goode, Poling and Washington—
Were there;
When the Dorchester was attacked
By a sub, unaware.

This troop ship sank quickly,
In a mighty sweep;
But these four heroes saved two hundred,
Their souls to keep,
Before they were swallowed by the jaws of the deep.

They sacrificed all,
So that others might live;
What more is it possible,
for mere men to give.

Yet, while in the dark and briny deep they lay,
A voice of the "Master of the Sea" did say;
"You did it for those who are mine,
Thus you did it for Me;
Therefore, ye faithful, arise from the sea,
Your reward awaits you in Eternity."

Paul B. Renier

What If The World Were Black And White?

What if the world were black and white?
What a dull place it would be.
No skies of blue, no grass of green,
Not even the birds would want to sing.

What if the world were black and white?
How it could affect our appetite.
Can you imagine what an awful sight?
Why, nothing on the plate would even look right!
Black gravy, white steak and black milk to drink,
Something like this should really make us think:
How God must really love us,
For He colored our world and made us in living color!

Valerie Hill

If

If I could change the world to make the whole world see
what a little love and kindness would mean to you and me

If I could just erase the hate that lingers in the heart
Yes that would be a task I know, but that would be a start

If I could free the captive and send them on their way
If I could make the world at peace for just a single day

Yes that would be a mighty task, a mighty task for sure
but it's better to attempt to try than sit back and ignore

If I could feed the hungry and clothe the naked soul
If I could cure diseases before death takes its toll

If I could house the homeless, quince the thirst within a child
Who would say my efforts haven't been worthwhile

If one little thing I'd change would make this world all right
then I would surely give my life to end this worldly plight

Michele D. Fancher

Rebound

I threw a pebble in the lake,
What difference did it make?
The surface rings grew wide and disappeared.
The pebble gone, and as I feared,
No difference did my effort make.
Yet when I filled my cup with woe,
One bitter tear made it overflow.
So back to the lake to make it rise,
Though I cannot see it with my eyes.

Lucy De Santi

Can You Hear Me

I have discovered and I have uncovered
What a truly great marvel am I.
I'm a singular person, no better nor worse'n
But I shine like a flame in the sky.
My mind is elastic, my wit is fantastic;
I'm a treat for any good friend.
My articulate tongue stays incredibly young
Dripping pearl after pearl without end.
So, sit back and enjoy me, you can never annoy me
Sitting beside me in awe,
My wordage should sooth you and greatly amuse you
While you gape at the strength of my jaw.
It's no illusion and the real conclusion
As your guardian angel looks down
And sees you patiently listen she'll swiftly position
Another Gold Star in your crown.

Marion Fortier

A Walk With Jesus

We will walk with Jesus when we cross the other side
What a wonderful joy that will be
When we come to the golden stairs and Jesus says,
"Come, come unto me."
Then ever with Jesus we'll be.

When he takes me by my hand when my journey is o'er
And he says, "Come, come with me
I have a beautiful place just for thee."
Then ever with Jesus we'll be.

There are streets of gold where we'll walk hand in hand
What a beautiful place to behold
And Jesus will be there to walk with us then
And we'll forever be without sin
Then ever with Jesus we'll be.

We'll wear robes of white in this beautiful place
Made of precious stone
But most of all Jesus will be there
And we will never be alone.
Then ever with Jesus we'll be
Then ever with Jesus we'll be.

Zella Lee

The Woman Before You!

Look, don't you see her?
What, are you blind?
Why can't you see, the woman before?

Listen, don't you hear her?
What, are you deaf?
Why can't you hear, the woman before you?

Talk, can't you speak to her?
What, are you mute?
Why can't you speak, to the woman before you?

Oh! Never mind. I guess it's too late.
There's no need to look,
or to listen, or talk.
The woman has left, she's no longer there!

You can't see her or hear her
or tell her you're feelings.

She gave up on the silence.

She's moved on with her life.
Has she an important role, in you're life?

No, not really.
She was only your wife!

Rebecca Ann Rainey

Me

I step out of myself to view what others see,
What do they see in me.
Do I make them happy?
Do I make them cry?
Can I be all they want me to be.
My question is why.

Should I live alone again,
Where my best friend is my mind?
But if I become my only friend,
Will I give up on life and die?

Forever is eternity and eternity is just too long,
To live in a world where the other is always right,
And I am always wrong.

Maybe I just don't give a damn,
Or maybe I care too much.
For people who don't respect my dreams.
The people who can hurt me with the slightest touch.

I step back into myself to see what I may see.
The laughter, the happiness, the loving times,
The answer is I am me.

Audra Lynn

What Do You See?

When you look in the mirror...
What do you see?

Do you see yourself...
Or a image of someone you don't want to be?

When someone looks in your eyes...
What do they see?

Do they see sadness...
Or just a vision of someone they don't want to see?

When someone asks you...
"What's wrong?" do you answer or just respond?

Do you hear disgrace...
Or just a voice of someone you don't want to hear?

When someone gives you a hug...
Are you happy or does it make you sad?

Do you think of being yourself...
Or wanting to be someone else.

When you look in the mirror...
What do you see?
Do you see yourself...
Or a vision of the person you don't want to be?

Stacie Cheney

Alone...

One fist of money and my tired face, that's all I could offer,
What faults did I have, that they looked at me with hatred?

I do not love life, because I do not live it.
I do not believe in love, because I never experienced it.

I am weak, yet I hate weakness.
I am sad, yet I hate sadness.

I live for the moment,
Yet I die every day.

I hate myself and wish to stop the struggle within,
Yet I cannot do it.

God, I love you, yet I do not search for you.
God please forgive me, and my lack of gratitude.

Nicky Veltri

From Those Who Died....

No I say, leave us rot here:
What good do we hold in a land of virgin peace;
Our bodies have been dedicated to another world,
To a land fraught with fear, hate, insecurity.

Let us stay here;
We, the everlasting marks of man's livid wars,
Our white crosses will blazon the horrors of bloody conflict,
And from the halcyon graves our cries will rise.

Permit us rest over the seas, so you'll come to us and to these lands,
So you'll be tempted to solve the crass problems here,
So they won't have to send more white crosses over.

We'll stay here:
And we'll be your strategic bases in foreign lands.
We'll be your first line on defense against a repetition,
So that you'll watch over us, and mind the reason why we had to...

Yes, we must remain;
We'll lie here, seared in your hearts and brains,
So that you'll remember to keep our crosses white and fresh,
And come over to keep our rows and the land in which we lay
In order. Let us be.

Stephen Kantor

"Joy - Oil"

Where do I find joy?
  What is its measure?
Can joy be described?
  O! Such a treasure!

The world wants it for no cost.
  Those who do not have it-feel lost.
Trials and troubles seize its peace
  While causing much and varied dis-ease.

The Gospel is TRUTH and right teaching,
  And renders unto me joy unceasing.
By prayer and the WORD I can be sure
  My faith will be builded and thereby endure.

God is sovereign and in total control...
  His grace and liberty gives me...
    JOY-OIL.

Virginia L. Sharp

Will Or Desire

Why do you smoke
What is the desire that brings this craving about
Is it like the thirst for water
Or is it something like the hunger for food
Is it a thing of casual qualities
Or is it because you want to be in the grove
Do you drink because somebody else is thirsty
Do you eat because somebody else eats good
No! You smoke because you want to smoke
Your desire has overridden your better judgment
Your subconscience has taken over you and your conscience
Your will has been lessened by your desire
And more shameful than that yet!
Your will cannot beat that little cigarette
Which you so much inspire.

Luis R. Torres

All Praise The Name Of Angels

In all the angels of glory from the heavens above,
What lights do we see and feel inside their hearts of gold!
They bring together the shadows of colors and all that creates
The beauty and nature of the night.
On earth the stars of night shine on and on,
With the moon shining through the trees and beyond the rainbow
We dream of the bright white lights and say to the Angels
"Make bright the sky and let us see your beauty,
Come one and all, praise and see.
Angels bring love, support, guidance and truth,
Let no one take away our sense and abilities they give.
Praise to all the world, with pride in our hearts
To know what Christmas is all about.

Lisa Robbins

The Path

I wondered down a foggy path, unable to see.
What the path was made of, or where it would lead.

I walked this path of eggshells, stepping so carefully.
So as to please everyone, except of course, for me!

As I wondered down this path, that seemed so endlessly.
I tried to find my way around, so I could have peace.

Then one day I met a man along this path with such inner
peace. I had to stop and ask him, How can this be?

As if I were an open book, that he could simply read.
He leaned and whispered to me, oh so quietly.

"It's really very simple, once you can see. You simply
choose the path that leads you, to your own inner peace."

Maggie E. Martin

The Scare:

Be silent all:
What walks;
What lurks;
What roams around my room?
What malice hath wrought this terror to my night?
What goes behind, that door of mine,
Which terror all engulfs?
What thing, by who, made that noise downstairs,
Which made my blood run cold?
What, I must ask, makes all this be,
In the deepest darkness of the house,
that is misery?
There you shall find, the answer lies
In all the you's and me's.
What makes us scared isn't what's out there,
But what we think it be.

Rene David Rivero

Beyond The Stars

Haven't you ever wondered
What's beyond all the stars?
Could it be another world, similar to ours?
Maybe in this world, dreams always come true,
Maybe the oceans always stay blue,
Maybe a sun shines, without any harm,
Maybe there is no cause for concern or alarm,
Maybe there is no greed, money or power,
Maybe time is just one endless hour.
Maybe it's a place where the grass is kept green,
Maybe you can't hear even one child scream.
Maybe it's a place that learns from its past,
Maybe it's a place where forever can last.
Maybe there is no judgment by color or race,
Maybe "Paradise" is a good name for this place.
Or maybe it's just a world, completely different from ours,
Maybe it's just a place....
Beyond all the stars.

Kimberly D. LeRoy

"Mask"

Whenever you see him, you never know,
What's truly behind that face aglow.
That thing upon his face you see,
Has forever hidden his true identity.

The hurt and pain vivid in his eyes,
Could be covered up by no disguise.
Though people have been fooled time and again,
Only certain people see where he's been.

He masquerades as a jubilant boy,
But in reality, there is no joy.
He must live up to the expectations of glee,
But a happy young man he will seldom be.

No one to confide in when his heart is full,
And once again his heart strings will pull.
So far there's been none to hold this hand,
No one, not yet, to understand.

Melissa Kuipers

Christmas Eve Night

As I lay in my bed to await Christmas morn,
When all at the sudden, I heard at the door,
A loud rap, a tap, and then the sound died,
I ran to my bed for somewhere to hide.

What was he doing under the tree?
Stealing my presents, this I could see.

The courage in me built up deep inside,
I sprang from the bed and said: "I've
nothing to hide." I hit him, I punched
him, He cried out with a scream;

And I woke up to find, it was only a dream.

Morgan Penelope Jones

Thank You

Thank you for the times that you made me feel good
When everything else was so bad
And thank you for scolding me for silly thing that I did
I'm older now, I understand.

Thanks for the cooking, the cleaning
And such that you do in you own special way
Thanks for sister and brothers
And all the love that you give us each day.

Thank you Mom and Dad, for ME
For showing me good from bad
Thanks for believing in all my goals
You're the best parents a child could have.

Now that I'm, here away from home,
Your love is easily seen.
I realize now all the things that you do
Mean lots more that what they seem to be.

Words cannot say how thankful I am
To have a mother like you.
All I can say, though, is "I love you so much, Mom."
And thank you for all that you do.

Paul A. Cano

What Is Life?

We are born into the light.
What is life but a light,
What is life but a fight.
What is life .... knowledge,
And with much knowledge comes much sorrow.
What is death but a light,
What is death but another tomorrow.

Lamar A. Schlegel

"Blanket Of Colors"

It seems just like yesterday,
when everything was still fresh and green.
When the flowers were in full bloom.

I ask myself, where did the time go.
As I look out my window on this fall crisp day.
Most everything is covered with frost now.
Trying to remember, just where the flowers were
that I so much enjoyed.

The leaves that once belonged to the trees are now earth's blanket of colors.

The trees will wait patiently for their leaves to return.

As for me, I'll just enjoy the warm feeling from earth's blanket of colors.

Phyllis Kast

"Love From The Heart"

Tis that time of season when things are grand,
When folks are happy, it's a wonderland.
The air is crisp, the leaves are falling,
There is music in the air and our hearts are calling.
For peace on earth and good will towards men,
For love to abound all around us and then.
We can share in the birth and give praise on high,
All glory to God and his Son who did die.
To save our souls and be free from sin,
Put God in your heart and give love from within.

Melissa Sherry

A Boy And His Smile

Oh, what is so sweet as a little boy's smile
When he's praised for a task well done;
Or the grin on his face
At the end of the race
When he sees it is he who has won?

A boy without a smile is the day without sun,
Or the world without stars at night.
So never help to erase
That smile from his face
But e'er cheer him on in life's fight.

I think there could ne'er be a thing to compare
With a barefoot boy and his grin,
Unless 'twere the smiles
Of the angels "up there"
As they tenderly watch over him.

Rosie Etta Bondy

Love Fell From A Tree

I was having a picnic under a tree,
When I heard something rustle, I started to flee.
I looked up and there I saw
A dark figure and it started to fall.
I stepped back and tripped over a stump.
About that time, I heard a thump.
I looked to my right and what did I see;
Some gorgeous eyes staring at me!
"You're beautiful!" his voice said.
I tried to speak, but my voice had fled.
Later on we talked and held hands.
Next thing you know, we were walking in the sand.
That was a terrific day for me,
Because, Love fell from a tree.

Mary Lydia Finley

All I Have Left Of You

The other day I was going through some things
When I came upon all I have left of you
Is the memories
The watch
The pictures of you
The memories of you still stamped in my mind
Didn't fade away in time
For a moment you were trapped in time
The other day I was going through some things
When I came upon all I have left of you
Is the memories
The watch
The pictures of you
The memories of you still stamped in my mind
Until we meet again in another time
All I have left of you
Is the memories
The watch
The pictures of you
The memories of you still stamped in my mind

Nancy Barrett

Day And Night

When I look at the sky, I see birds fly high.
When I look all around, I see wonderful flowers from April showers.
When I look at the sky late at night, I can no longer see the birds in the sky fly high
and I can no longer see the flowers from April showers. But what I can see,
are the twinkling lights in the sky,
And the big yellow ball up high.
But then the next morning a certain sound wakes me up,
and what that sound is all the baby birds taking their first flight,
and colorful new flowers blooming.
Quite to my surprise, but right in front of my eyes was the sunrise.
But when I went outside parked right in front of me, was a child's dreams,
a truck full of ice cream. There was chocolate, butterscotch, and vanilla,
you know, that ice man he's quite a nice fella.
A few minutes later I finished my ice cream,
I'm very glad that it was not just a dream.
A few hours later as the sun light grew fainter,
it changed the colors of the flowers like being nature's painter.

Teresa Harp

Foreigner

It was the summer of '92
When I visited Prague.
It is a mystic city
Filled with relics and gypsies,
Resting upon the banks of the Danube.

Walking through the narrow cobblestone streets,
I passed store after store hidden in niches
Here and there displaying elegant crystal vases
And cheap T-shirts.

I stood upon an ancient stone bridge
Spanning the swollen river.
The soft tones and harmonies of a Czech choir floated out
Of a small church as I bathed in the warm
Golden sunlight and watched branches and debris sweep
Downstream in the river's muddy grip.

A few blocks from the river, in the middle of
A crowded city square, elves and princesses dance at the
Arrival of each hour, making the sunset with seven chimes.

It was the summer '92, when I left Prague.

Regan H. T. Yamasaki

A Mothers Grace

For all the times that you were there,
When I was certain no one else would care.

For every time that I lost hope,
Your example gave me strength to cope.

For the broken bones and the dirty knees,
For respecting my unreasonable pleas.

For everything you've sacrificed.
To make your children's future bright.

And even though the times were hard,
You made the best of what was ours.

If my thank you seems to slip away,
It's for lack of proper things to say.

And though I know it rarely shows,
My love for you forever grows.

Berger

The Light

What hypocritical truth revealed itself
When it suddenly saw the morning light
Bending down through broken beams
In the house of God?

An odor of life long past health,
Enlightenment oppressed and far from sight;
In their webs the spidery minions try to repair the seams
And the parasites tremble behind their cursed rod.

White-washed righteousness covered with wealth,
The true believer gone and long since contrite,
Such pews revealed themselves as tomb of dreams,
Faith buried seven feet under the sod.

M. D. Price

"Remembrance"

Well past midnight,
When it's dark,
When it's quiet,
When the loudest sound is the ticking of a clock
  or the turning of a key in a lock.
When every breath could easily be your last
  before you sleep.
That is when the memories come.
Some come quietly,
Softly as a tear slowly coursing down your check.
Some come swiftly,
Sharply stabbing little pains of regret.
And some come brightly with their tiny little smiles
That tug at the corners of your mouth,
And the corners of your soul,
And hurt the most of all
In their loss.

Michael H. Lucas

When It Hurts

When my heart is heavy and wrenching in pain
When I've lost; and I'm mourning once again
Words to describe the agony I feel
Don't come to mind, nothing seems real
While sobbing and grieving down on my knees
Jesus is felt kneeling next to me
He embraces my heart and says, "Feel my love;
I bring you comfort and strength from above
While your tears flow freely cleansing the stain
Look up and within my grace will remain
Rejoice and be thankful for memories of love
Find peace and acceptance by looking above."

Karen Belle

Sounds Of The Rainforest

There was a time not so long ago
  when leaves fell silently upon a dusty trail
The toucan sang a tune that only few would hear
A snake would slither silently, deep in the grass
  within the walls of nature.
Oh where have you gone, sweet friends of mine

Deep within the forest walls I hear a sound
  from the distance
The crackle of a fire brings to me
  the eerie sound of a cry for help
The falling of my friends bring painful
  memories of those who have gone before them
The death of a friendship that cannot
  be replaced or denied.
Oh the price we pay for the carelessness
  of the ignorant few
Justice reigns within the walls of this sanctuary
For when the rainforest shall disappear
  from this place, so shall we.

Shawn Salter

"Daughters And Sons"

How far doth drift the mind's bright eye
When musing barren spaces
How near doth draw the heart's true ties
When searching tiny faces

Through eyes undimmed by age despair
The wonders true unfold
To ears undimmed by mortal care
The precious tale is told

The strains of life are strummed, in time,
To rhythms of small voices
The cords of strife quick to unbind
Through soft-sung children's noises

No greater joy may fill the sky
Than unstained youthful graces
No purer love can cast life high
Than small and warm embraces

So treat with care the tiny ones
Whose lives are unspun gold
Go, Honor life and dare not shun
God's daughters and His sons.

Thomas Summers Hale

"Dedicated To Dionne"

A vibrant young woman's life was irrevocably shattered
when one night, she met up with a cruel twist of fate
She crossed paths with a drunk driver and was forever changed
for all that she has lost, nothing can compensate
This beautiful young woman's life hung in the balance
while her family sacrificed to remain by her side
And while she lay, barely alive, and suffering
those close to her prayed and they cried
A life interrupted and irreversibly altered
yet, today, she's still surviving and living on
Only she's not the girl she was once before
all of the dreams she once knew are now dead and gone
We try not to question the actions of the Lord
and yet we do wonder why this drunken driver still walks around
While the life of our beautiful Dionne is forever changed
and she remains disabled, without freedom, and wheelchair bound
Her inner beauty remains, though, as do our memories
and on all who knew her, this tragedy has left a scar
I'd just like to take this moment to tell her
Dionne, we love you just the way you are

Nicki Hardwick-White

A Grandfather's Thoughts

It was a snowy evening in the northwest sky,
When our newest little angel started to fly.
She landed here in Winter Park
Giving our lives a brand new spark.
For Julie the pain and Tim the worry,
Nothing could stop their moment of glory.
Her mother named her Emiley
What a beautiful baby had come to be.
Through the day and through the night
Her mother held her oh so tight.
On her father's face where pride and hope were shown
Could he love such a one, yet unknown?
Grandma acted with such perfect grace
You could feel the love fill each space.
And my, how soft and tenderly,
Gram would hold our Emiley.
Such blessings on you, Julie dear
As these words of praise you hear
May these thoughts of love find their way
To you now and each Mother's Day.

William J. Wilson

Flowing Path

Sometimes it seems, that life's a dream.
When suddenly we awake to find,
Our best times left behind.
But somehow we manage through,
The trials we face, the mistakes we do,
We always have those special times,
In our soul, heart, and mind.
And although it hurts, life must go on,
Just leaving you with memories from the past that is gone.
So cherish each moment as if it's your last,
For time can't go backward in the past.

Star Luffman

Decisions And Directions

The day will soon come
When we take the wrong road.
We'll go to the left
Instead of the right.
Going left is a hug
That never happened,
A decision that was made wrong,
Something that was hated instead of loved;
This is the left road.

Traveling on the right road is like
Making the correct decision,
Loving instead of hating,
Sharing and caring.

We'll all come to corners on whatever journey's made.
Some ways made the right way,
Most ways made the wrong.
But this is the way life is
You just have to be strong,
Even if the road taken is wrong.

Marnie Lynn Birdsall

Timeless Memories

Timeless memories and precious few moments are all that you left me.
When morning comes and daylight falls, my only prayer is,
Why not me?
Just when you think your almost there,
The tears begin like it was yesterday.
I know my place is with you and my purpose will be complete.
But until we meet, I will have timeless memories of you and me.

Linda Owens

So We Can Live

When will the rainfall be clean again?
When will the sky be blue?
Can you tell me when?
When will all of us learn to really trust?
Put our differences back.
There's so much to do.
Can't we see it through?
Can't we stay on the track?

So we can live a hundred years from now.
So we can live.
We'll teach our children how, to respect the earth,
and to know her worth, and to try to give what she needs.

When will the rivers be clean again?
When will the trees grow back?
Can you tell me when?

Is it no surprise?
Don't we realize?
Can't we see through the haze?

There's got to be, more from you and me.
Can't we see past today?

Sarah Fisk

Autumn

Autumn is a very beautiful time of year,
when you forget your troubles and jump with cheer.

The leaves change colors and fall from the tree,
as you look up to the sky and bend to your knees.

The clouds are a bright red and blue,
they seem to reach out and touch you.

The air smells so clean and fresh,
as the wind touches your breast.
The taste of fresh apple cider,
and the halloween spiders,
are all reminders of the fall
and the beauty of it all.

Linda E. Madron

"Sisters"

I love you my sister I'll tell you no lies
When you hurt like you do my heart truly cries

You are in my head and always in my heart
I am so hopeful and I pray a new life you will start

I used to sit and watch you asleep in your bed
You looked like a little angel with your bright face
And a curl atop your head

I always thought you were beautiful so what do you think of that?
I had so much fun playing with you no more dressing up the cat

And then we grew older and yes grew apart
Please forgive me for not knowing all the pain in your heart

I was trying to deal with the pain inside me
I wish I would have been wise enough
To know, to help, or to see

I love you my sister I want you to stay
You are a part of my life what more can I say

You are more precious than diamonds
And brighter than gold I want to plan on seeing you
Until we both grow old!

Mick Wempe

Sisters

If you're sick, I'll be there...
When your lonely, I'm always here...
If your depressed, you can count on me...
I have just one request, don't stop loving me.

There will be raging waters, at one point or another...
Don't ever forget, how we're able to soothe each other.
We have a lasting bond, no one can break...
Your the only one who understands, when my heart aches.

Children will leave you, at some point in life...
Husbands and lovers, they just might...
But not your sister, I'll always be here...
Don't ever doubt, the love that we share.

Laurie A. Carey

What Is A Mother

What is a mother, why does she care?
When you've disappointed her
Why is she always there?
When you need a helping hand,
Or just a kiss or two
Who's the one who comes thru with it,
Made especially just for you?
When your in trouble or just need bailed out,
Mother always comes through without a doubt.
When you're sick and up all night, she helps you to get well
Nevertheless she does it without a fight.
Who's the person who's your very best friend,
And always has an ear to lend.
Who's the one who has faith in you.
Regardless of the stupid things you do?
Who's the one who has the love so strong it came from up above,
A mother is life's greatest gift, but most of
All she's my best friend, and my love for her will never end.
A mother is someone who you can trust and she trusts you
She's someone who's proud of herself for what you have become!

Stacey Howie

Feelings

Nobody loves me, nobody cares
Whenever I cry every one just
sits and stares
They think I have no feelings at all
Then they are surprised when my tears start to fall.

I never do anything right
Even though I try with all my might
My dad doesn't understand how I feel,
He doesn't let my pain ever heal.

He doesn't think I love him, but I really do
I wish, just how much, he knew
When he fusses I know he's only
trying to help me
The fact that I understand this,
I have to make him see
Maybe one day I'll see the light
Find a way to stop all our fights
There's no telling when that day may come
Until then, to keep from hurting anymore,
I'll just keep my feelings numb.

Megan House

My Life As A New York Yankee

I'll take my stand in Yankee Stadium
where baseball became an art form and the players poetry
Where the Iron Man cried
and the Bambino tipped his hat to the crowd
and almost died from the cheers
and quiet little Bobby Richardson symbolized the purity of their legend
Where the clean blue lines of the pinstripes
demanded a form worthy of the timeless contrast

They eclipsed life...
touching the heavens from home plate
and stopping wars with a backhand stab down the third base line

Immortality
and line drives
were within reach
for moments at a time

They played a game
worth living...

those New York Yankees

Roger W. Barnes

Anonymously Yours, The Waiting Room: Idolization

Faulty bridges spurned a deep eye in/of unself awareness, valuation
Where, came the road, holding to your hearts' intent, idealization
Life's work, involving love and embracing eggs, incarnation
In this bartered system, of talk, repentance, interpretation
Forgetting or choosing not to be my round friend, civilization
Less-than ask's me, is there another room in the rain, donation
Tears are lonely, a fierce child, protecting hope, identification
History leaves a doorway up into this persona, spiritualization
Suffering, without bitterness, healing art forms us, symbolization

A morning double rainbow plays after bolt light, friction
Charged and chasing, dapple grey stallion, Nip, intervention
Winding the autumns mare's ripe to let go of the colt, conservation
Cool mountain air sets off patterns of instinct, migration
Down to borrow the burrowed land, re-searching, identification
Sharing mother earth's meager winter water wind field's, isolation
The coyote will often work with a badger for survival, compensation
Cock, canary, and crow, have what others crave, representation
Wait, wait, wait, watch, grass grow green, individualization
Wait now, for Indian summer, learning to walk on water, destination

Melody J. Swan LaRhette

Whose Realm?

When you die,
Where do you go?
Who do you see,
Who do you know?
Some say there is a tunnel with rays of streaming light,
Do you believe that? Or is it as black as night?
I believed in heaven, where the Angels soar with their wings,
Where Gods realm is, and the many wonderful things he brings.
But some say there is a hell,
Where the Devil is king.
Who could say this,
Who could say such a thing!
Where the fiery pits of hell blaze and glow,
I guess how well you lead your life determines where you go.
I hope you believe in heaven and its glory and grace,
Where the almighty Lord stands before you with a smile on his face.
With his arms open wide to take you in,
I hope you never committed any mortal sins.
But if you did, then I don't know,
To Whom's Realm you are sentenced to go.

Neil Carilli

Treachery

In the tiny island of LOVE
Where foolish simplicity reigned supreme
"Its" seeds were sown by foreign elements
Dormant they were, still Greed rained, and
The saplings sprouted under the brightness of
jealousy.
It thrived and blossomed and Trust was forgotten.
In its shade, characters plotted
As its roots sucked away the stream of Truth,
And Virtues choked and coughed
Till the ocean drowned LOVE.

Old order changeth to give place to new,
Love gives way to hate,
Trust vacates for treachery, and truth for
falsehood.
Thus, shall peace give way to Chaos.

K. Mondal

Velvet Black

I come from the black heart,
where I long to connect
to the roots I hold dear.
Arid skies tame windswept plains that rage,
a calming rage, that roars of
beige,
of brown, of black,
of flat veldt pushed forth by mountainous force.
And my people live this gentle,
oh so gentle land,
caressing it to life,
watching its beauty wax and wane.
My homeland
oh homeland
I do long to be with the black heart.

Veronica Nickel

Whispering Wind

Whispering wind.
Where is my love'd one tonight.
Whispering wind.
We just had a little fight.
I called her on the phone.
And she's not at home.
Now I'm so blue and I'm counting
on you.
Whispering wind
If you should blow into town.
Whispering wind.
And you should see her around.
Just whisper that I'm so lonely.
And I'm waiting for her only.
And forever I'll be grateful to you always
Forever I'll be grateful to you.

Lena Pepe

Remembering

Oh, God, if we might go to Palestine,
Where Mary was, long centuries ago;
If we might climb Judaean hills to find
The road to Bethlehem; if we might know

Which cobbled street led to His manger bed
(Since there was no room for them at the inn);
If we might watch the Star rise overhead
To show the Magi where their feet had been;

Or, God, if we might hear the angels sing
Their song of "Peace on earth, goodwill to men,"
Do you think we might pause, remembering,
And turn our wayward feet to Christ again?

Virginia S. Bursch

Home

When I say home I think of a place
Where the Lily flower blooms
I think about the starlit nights
And the glorious sun-filled days
I think of cowbells, goatskin drums and calypso beats
all merging into one
Home is a place where a carnival is the very best parade
Home is a place where the children play the games of long ago
Kick the can, Simon says and a hunting we will go
Home is a place where we played hide and go seek
And told stories late into the night
Home is a place where dreams are born
Struggles occur, tears are shed, prayers are said
And life goes on
Home is the place where love abides
And home is where my heart is forever bound.

Mack Dorothy

"Someone To Watch Over Me"

Who will watch over me?
Where's this earthen vessel with the blessed touch -
to sooth my back while I'm all curled up -
in flannel sheets with my bible laying next to me?
Oh, you've got Jesus did I hear you say? Yes,
but my God is not my man! So stop the funny looks
when you hear a sister say.
"Who will watch over me?" Our Father speaks
"It is not good for the man to live alone!"
Some precious brother is out there missing his
(rib bone). Bone of his bone flesh of his
flesh - no I'm not in a mess by what I confess.
I read it, God said it, this union is blessed.
So if when you're feeling alone and its color
is blue, don't act as if it isn't happening to you.
Just gird up your loins with the Spirit of Truth and look unto Jesus
to see you (safely) through. I wait patiently on God, he and me,
while I continue this journey - as God creates me to be
an equitable gift to present unto he who will jointly with
Father - watch over me.

Marcia L. Washington

Within....

There is a power, within me hides,
Which cries to be released.

I learn and do and try again,
Its pain will not be eased.

Its vindictiveness and hate-filled ways,
Consume my living soul.

I curl as though in my mother's womb,
It's ever on patrol.

It waits until my guard is weary,
Then lunges for the kill.

I protect the inner being that's me,
But, tired grows my will.

This monstrous thing, with teeth exposed,
Is slipping every day.

One step backwards, two steps forward,
It hasn't long to stay.

I thrust and parry with my sword,
And, strive to force it out.

This evil monster that lives within,
This thing that I call doubt.

Teresa Schell

Here Is The Peace

Walking alone down a narrow road which is the line of connection for these rich people and their grandeur houses, I take in a deep breath and then another of the fresh autumn air. My body begins to feel rejuvenated as the crisp freshness circulates through my being. As I look around me, I see God's splendor splashed on the trees of yellow, brown, and orange— and in the sky of icy-blue and fluffy-white. Although sadness and loneliness seem to have delved to the depths of my soul, their power has no bearing on me here, on this road, under this sky, and breathing this air. I am still alone, yet I am free, ecstatically free of the pain and sadness: I am one with all that surrounds me! For these few short minutes that pass as I stroll my leisurely pace, I am at peace. . .

Stacy Gilliland

Little One

The fragile lungs take that first sweet breath,
While calmly dismissing the presence of death.
With a cry the tiny soul is heard.
And within those who bear witness,
Only the most affectionate emotions are stirred.

The newest of voices pleads for much;
Yet easily soothed by another human touch.
So innocent and precious to hold that
With a mere hug, the story of love has been told.
And with a twitch of the pudgy little feet,
Newborn's cheek and mother's heart do meet.

Sean Gillespie

"The Beautiful Girl I Know."

Her whisper's like a summer breeze,
While flowing through the willow trees,
She makes up all my fantasies,
The beautiful girl I know.

When she comes near what do I do?
I want to confess my love to,
The maiden with the eyes of blue,
The beautiful girl I know.

She is a goddess one could say,
I want to tell her every day,
But there's no telling what she'd say,
The beautiful girl I know.

Soft complexion as a flower,
I wish I could woo and wow her,
With some strange and mystic power,
The beautiful girl I know.

"Tell her," you say, I wouldn't dare,
Such loveliness with soft blonde hair,
I'd tell her if I thought she'd care,
The beautiful girl I know.

Timothy Wade Wooten I

My Life

I sit in here alone and frighten'
While their out there fightin'
They go to court
For a certain case of a certain sort
It's about me
and who gets custody
The judge sends me to a different place
Tear roll down my tiny face
It's been years since I've seen my father
Why even bother?
I started to hate my mother
I'd rather have another
The judge gives me to my dad
It's not that bad
I've lived with my dad almost six years now
I love my mom and visit, wow!
At least I'm not in a foster home anymore
I have a lot of good things to look for!

Young H. Ekstrom

Ode To Quigley South (Preparatory Seminary)

What would have saved you, Quigley South,
While you stood as a lamb opened mouthed
As the first mortal blow was struck?
How we tried to stop the blood, from your side that flowed
Washing us clean from an illusion of church
And driving us into a deeper truer one within.

Who could have saved you, Quigley South
Amidst the protest of your children's cry?
When your own priests, whom you nursed in tender years,
Remained bound to a structure, fell in line, and saluted smartly.
But not all-a few brave sons stood by with the churches Long
Loyal Laity,
Who were most hurt and left alone with their hearts cry.
Betrayed, bewildered, but wiser for it!

Yes, what could have saved you from the bankers block
Smeared with cold bloody half truths,
And an unyielding cardinal's heart marching marching staunchly on.
Pruning here and slashing there this New Modern (catholic?) Church,
With little care who or what is left behind.

Kathleen Heenan

The Void

Lifeless hangs the barren space between the endless galaxies...
Whirling, swirling maze of stars and other sparkling things...
Quasars, quarks, and deep black holes...
Trinary systems and planets with rings...
In it all, so far away, glowing, growing, through endlessness
Is teeming life of variant groves, aliens in droves and droves,...
Magnetic forces and violent maelstroms, Nebulae and Larvae too.
And through it all, in ten times a million worlds of wonder,
Teems life in all its many forms...energy in churning storms...
And beauty far beyond the norms...multiforms, and thunderstorms...
And very ancient cuneiforms...
And planetary uniforms...mystical, lyrical unicorns...
And implausible creatures who travel in swarms...
And unlikely, improbable, strange lifeforms...
And love, and growing, and beauty and wonder...
And all around the lovely things...is the lifeless VOID.
Like the hole that was left in my soul when you left me.
A lifeless void, surrounding the very life it created...
I loved you, you know...

Mary Case

The Fawn

I have dreamt of her forever, the little fawn in the wood.
Who emerges quietly and shyly, afraid of man and of fire.
For, death is man to her.
Yet, I am one with the fawn.
One who is gentle as she.
Whose touch is a whisper in the wind,
Who will only protect and guard,
And love those frightened doe eyes.
My eyes, too, are afraid.
For, man cannot understand
This gentle, peaceful creature,
Who does no harm, only innocence.
Which so reflects, I.

I like to care for those, animals and people alike.
For, all are alive and feeling,
And have a heart to love.
The fawn, I dream, comes on soft hooves, she trods
Upon the leaves and snow onward to my trusting eyes,
My eyes and hands can cure and love
For, trust is all she needs.

Meghann Elizabeth Yaardrad

Yea, There Was A Man

Yea, there was a man,
Who fell at dusk in Tennessee.
Shot by a wretch whose skin was white
But, whose soul was black as sin in hell.
They carried him in an old farm cart
Beneath the dogwood blossoming.
Two mules, they drew his cold, still corpse
Behind the mass of sorrowing.
He stood upon the mountain top
And looked into the promised land.
He trod the streets for endless miles
And for seventeen times he was put in jail
That his people might be free.
He was laid to rest at Easter time
Beneath a cross of lilies white.
They buried him in the old grave yard
Nestled in among the slaves.
His skin was black but his soul was white
As the lilies under which he lay.
Yea, there was a man.

Martha Roberts Meyer

Be Strong

The prize is not given to the weak...
Who fold their arms and dare to think...
Tomorrow's another day they say...
"I'll motivate myself another day..."
"It's O.K."... I like the way you think..."
The devil says with a wink...

But life is precious and not very long...
It's so important to try to be strong...
Resist the thoughts that pull you down...
And look for words that are found...
In the Bible and with positive friends
That's the only way you can win

Life is a struggle for all of us...
But with the right thoughts, it's all a plus...
So don't give up...just sing this song...
My heart is fixed my mind's made up
And I know I must be strong.

Patricia Bradshaw

My Mother

She is the Rock of Gibraltar — my foundation of life
Who throughout her existence had so much strife,
Yet she never allowed tribulations and such
To dampen her spirits, or dispel her touch
Of coping with problems, and aiding us all,
When tragedies and heartaches did us befall.

I couldn't have survived, had she not been near
When I needed her touch and smile so dear.
She isn't famous — as fame is defined—-
She'll never be mentioned— her life won't be outlined,
As a poetess, authoress or scientist renowned—-
But in the book of my life— she's a queen on a throne.

She's dearly beloved by her grandchildren five,
For whom she labored— and of times strived;

To cater to their whims and demands so great.
In their estimation— she sure does rate.
She'll always be remembered— we'll never forget,
Her love overwhelming, and how she met
Each challenge with a face shine bright,
Causing clouds of gloom to quickly take flight.

Marguerite Miller

"A Smile Still Remains"

Every little raindrop leaves its mark upon the land.
While the manual chores we do leaves calluses
on the hands. Then, too, problems make troubles
for the brain. Tears fall down a cheek
to later leave their stain.
Though raindrops fall we need them all,
To quench the thirsty lands.
And men are proud to shout aloud
That they are glad to show callused hands.
Many troubles may make problems,
But they educate our brains.
And though each face in time
Some tears may stain; look closely,
A smile still remains.

Mabel Traeger Paquette

"You"

How far should a person give
When you have gave so much
that you may feel that you don't want to live
Everything that is around you you must observe
Only you know what you deserve
Sometimes you made have said
"I just want to stop thinking"
You may even wonder how it will feel
When you are no longer blinking
You may see and know how others go on
When someone dies at that moment
You'll say I can't believe he/she is gone
But you will wake up tomorrow
Not knowing what will follow.

Rosemary Folks

Where!

Where do I go when I have no one to talk to?
Where do I go when I have nothing to do?
Where do I go when my mother is no where to be found?
Where do I go when my father is not around?
Where do I look for that love and secure?
Where do I look when at times I'm not sure?
Who do I call when I'm lost and can't be found?
Who do I call when I'm feeling down?
I asked these question over and over again.
Til' I finally heard the Lord say "To me my friend."

Natasha R. Jones

Dhrangadhra

In reading the pages of my diary,
the images of unhappiness
float out like dead relatives from
the cracks of the palace walls.
The sweating palms,
the tightened stomach,
the tears of aloneness stain this moment.
They are rust on copper;
grey on black hair;
mosquitoes in pond water.
Like butterflies and grasshoppers,
I have metamorphosized out of
ugliness.
Happiness is to my inner self
like cotton to my body:
Breathable.
Lotus eater once again, I forget;
feeling only the sunshine,
the smiles on my lips,
my patria returned to me.

Angma Jhala

The Mystery Of Babes

Little children are tender and sweet
The instant they're born
Being so innocent and meek, many
times, they're left forlorn
Their complexion is something
to behold, their body is as
delicate as a fawn.

They're here to be nurtured and
cuddled, their gloss is as sleek
as a wet swan.

Babes are deft alert and cheery
Which keeps one from being gloomy
bleak, or dreary.

They're bright and sparkling
gleeful and merry, they're the
fruit of a new generation.
Like bananas, oranges, apples,
peaches, plums cherries and berries

George W. Gentry

Light Of My Life

You're the light of my life;
the island of my dreams,
A passion worth having;
so fiery a love it seems.

You can spark warmth
in a hungry heart;
like a fire about to start,
your love and mine entwines
like a lover's knot.

You're warm like the sun's rays'
and as gentle as a calm lake,
You're the fuel that burns
so hot within my heart.

Like a beautiful melody
played on a musician's fife;
you are my soul,
the light of my life.

Dhana Gunter

In The Night

Silent cries in my soul
The Lord above sets
the rules
I beg you please to
see through my eyes
A child is born and
then one dies
Alone to dwell in my
own hell
If only it were a fairytale
The pain takes a journey
Where I do not know
Only to fear tomorrow's sorrow
Crucify my being and set her free
Only to live life's tragedy
Another tear falls from
the sky
My baby has yet to understand why...

Dee Preijers

Happiness

I have often wondered
The meaning of the word Happiness
When two people are blended
Together there is no room for loneliness
God in all wisdom has meant
Our life to be heavenly sent
And filled with love
A love blessed from heaven above
Now here again is that word happiness
A word filled peaceful bliss
A word we search for to make our dreams
Come true and bring peace so it seems

Frank Myers

Mystery

I breathe
the mystery of night
with my friends,
the white trees,
misty in the purple sky.

Salty sea air
kisses silky waves
as wind blows
through my hair
whispering to me.

I want to fall
into nothingness
with silver leaves
shimmering
all around

And the autumn moon
gilding
slender tips
of branches reaching
high above.

Judith Lyn Sutton

An Acorn

Once an acorn oh so small.
Then an oak so big and tall.
The birds do nest among my bough.
I give the shade for many cow.
The wind is cold is cold and raw.
A man came down with a cross cut saw.
He fell me down upon the earth.
I lie in ashes on the hearth.

Betty T. Frederick

There are so many things I left undone

The endless race I never won
The only fear of leaving
Was to lose the love you gave
May the thoughts you have of me
Brighten your darkest days.
Life is the longest road
that winds through our hearts
each turn brings sorrow and despair
Happiness is merely a detour
to ease the pain we bear
May the road we travel
Have only signs of caution
to speed us on our way

George Catalano

Faithful Fans Sustain

Spring Training approaches,
The owners are being ferocious.

Some fans are complaining,
About the money the players are attaining.

Other fans are being fickle,
Turning their allegiance for a nickel.

But the faithful fans will remain,
Their allegiance will sustain.

When the first pitch is thrown.
Their excitement will have grown.

To them, the salary does not matter,
Only that there be a batter.

Earline Trlicek

Growing Up

I don't understand
The pain we're all going through
The crying we all suffer
The hurt we all fear
Where does it come from
It robs us of our emotions
Of our words and understanding
Where does it come from
What are the results
A broken heart of sorrow
A loss of someone close
It's all part of growing up

Danielle Jadin

"The Desert"

Sweltering heat -
The sun melting in the sky

Hot rays -
Beating down on the pavement,
As endless cars go by.

Parched land -
In need of a little rain.

Dry dust -
Floating by in swirling clouds.

Yet, even in this -
A beautiful cactus blooms.

Elizabeth H. Douglas

Burden Set Free

"Roll, roll!" the master yelled
the puppy getting tired
but obeyed without hesitance.

Then one mean day arose
the master wanting to be clever
forced the puppy to jump into the fire.

Needing to outdo others
he pushed the puppy everyday
training it to be the best.

The puppy wanted to stop
but did not have the courage
to stand up.

So the puppy became miserable
as each day passed
it increased.

Finally, when the master told the puppy to
jump into the hoop with fire
the puppy plunged its life to an end.

June Ohata

Paths

You are
the road
you walk on
gingerly or
rough
cockle shell
or softsand
we walk
on ourselves
our own path
leads us
nowhere
at the precipice
of faith
we hesitate
with fear
of one
wrong step

Elizabeth A. Frank

The Old Soddy

I can see the old soddy
The scene of my birth,
With its thick sturdy walls
Made of freshly turned earth.

Such a buffer were those walls
That in comfort we would meet
Both winters fierce storms
And summers blistering heat.

It was small, it was homely
It was squatty and well shod
With an overall layered roof
Made of the same virgin sod.

The house as a whole
Was a four room affair
For a family of ten
All quartered there.

Still never a stranger
Was turned from its door
If sheltered was needed
The soddy had room for more.

Ella Anderson

Rare Little Toad

You are a rare little toad
The sight of you halted
The construction of a new road!
The time is significant near and far
When men once bitter enemies at war
Signed peace treaties, shook hands
made front page news!

You also made bottom front page
news little toad
Which attests to man's concern
for all endangered species
Lives on and on in spite of
economic demands.

Little creature - halfdollar in size
To me today in mankind's race
You have won an enviable first place!
You prove to me man's respect
That in God's world
every creature has a place!

Etta Sharp

The Death Of A Sparrow

With one fell swoop
the sparrow did fall
She knew it was coming.
she could see it all.
It came down upon her
and shattered her dreams
This short life before us
what does it all mean?
The tone, not so pleasant,
the noise of her death
The sound reminiscent
of an angels breath.
As away go the dead,
for there is no cure,
for the broken hearted
that's one thing for sure.

Christine E. Carter

The Storm

The sky is eerie on a chilly night
The stars have vanished out of sight
The fog has begun to settle down
Quickly enveloping a tiny town
From above, the rain begins to pour
The wicked wind supports a roar
Throughout the sky lightning cracks
It flashed light, the clouds are black
The snap of thunder is heard from a far
The sky is dull, without a star
From behind the window glass I see
A storm so strong it broke to be free
It took the earth and washed it down
The wetness spilled and filled the ground
As the storm's force begins to die
There comes a brightness from the sky
For behind the rain on this stormy night
Awaits a new day of shining light.

Betty J. Reid

Threads

Threads weave the fabric of our lives
They tie up our loose ends
They mend the hurts that come to us
And bind together friends.

Joan Lauer

Seasons

The leaves fall,
The sun sets,
The moon rises,
Another autumn day is done.

The snow flies,
The sun disappears,
The moon has risen,
Another winter day is done.

The leaves unfold,
The sun rises,
The moon fades away,
A spring day has begun.

The flowers bloom,
The sun is hot,
The moon is gone,
A summer day has begun.

The leaves fall,
The sun sets,
The moon rises,
Autumn has began again.

Ann Soucie

One Day

One day I'll fly through
the thick clouds.
One day I'll make everyone
proud.

One day I'll have a wish
come to life.
One day there'll be only good
With everything in sight.

One day he will carry me off
to the stars.
One day all my problems will
seem so far.

With in my heart that's were
all the one days will start.

Deborah Bean

My Memory Of You

My life is so empty without you
the thought of you always come to mind
how you used to sit across from me
and smile with your eyes
how you whisper into my ears
saying, "I love you"
how you take care of me
when I was sick
when I was down
how you are there wiping my tears,
listening to me
telling me to be happy
I miss you so much, dear
when all the world is new
I know the day can bring no joy
because it brings not you.

Jeanette Lee

Untitled

To death I am not afraid
to life I am death is peace life is war
the war I can not fight the fear is
to great it is the peace I wish to find
to all I love to all I hate with fear
I love all and to all I wish that peace I
look for so to death I am not afraid

Johnny Raner

Nana

I knew it would come
The time for goodbye
Oh help me my Father
For I know not why

I don't understand
Why you took her from me
As I come home I wish
It was her I could see

To look at the pictures
The memories remain
To hope and to pray
I'll soon loose the pain

My life is so empty
I wish she were here.
She always could help me
To cope with my fear

But now that she's gone
It's all for the best
At least now I know
In peace she will rest.

Brandi Gordon

"Disease"

Clock hands are turning
The times are changing
Death stares me in the face

A new world is forming
A new song is dawning
I am a disgrace

People walking
Some are weeping
Seeking love in strife

Children dancing
Some are singing
Joyful for their life

Sun is swelling
Babes are fussing
Starving for their milk

Silence haunts us
Noise disrupts us
Do we see ourselves?

Erin Brockway

Untitled

Can you hear
The voices in the wind?
Calling you to them.
When a feeling of elation
Sweeps over you.
The animals become silent,
You can hear nothing but the wind.
Calling from the past and future,
The voices talk
Some in another language
Some in the language you know.
You can hear them crying,
You hear them laughing.
If you are lucky enough
One day you may catch a glimpse of them
Always fleeing before you can turn your head.

Faith Carlson

My Love

The sun is nothing without
the water below it to reflect
Its beauty. Rejoice my love for
I tardy. The night is upon me.
And so my touch is weak. My love
you should fear for your time
has come. My hope has no end.
Spring cometh late for you. Alas,
your cloud is not to high for
mortals as I.

Francisco Romero

Open Your Eyes

Open your eyes and see
the water, sky and mountains
See why we are beings

Open your eyes and see
your mother, father, sons
and daughters
Open your eyes and see
why we are beings

Open your eyes and see
the wonders of the world,
Open your eyes and see
why we are beings.

Delores Dascanio

Our Friend The Tree

What is a tree, just look and see
The ways you can recycle me.
I'm home to birds and squirrels to nest,
A table, chair and bed to rest.
My leaves are shade, then mulch to use
On compost piles and gardens too.
An artist's palette full of hues
Looks to me when Fall ensues.
The air you breathe concerns me too,
It's one more thing I do for you.
But best of all, the books you read
Are made of paper made from me.

Angela Landro

Worship

Can't keep my mind on shopwork.
The wood smells good
but I must go.

I call the dog
and off we run
down the lane to the woods.

Through the trees,
quietly, we walk,
listening to God's voice.

Like the isle
of a vast cathedral...
We aren't alone out here.

My dog explores
every thicket and stream,
and disturbs the rabbits.

And off she runs, excited at the chase,
though she doesn't know why.

We turn around
and head for the house.
Our worship is over for now.

Jeff Houseknecht

Lust

You turn my heart to ice
then melt it with smile
you break my heart in two
it mends after a while
you stir up some emotions
I never knew I had
I yearn for your body day and night,
I wander if that's bad
when I look into your eyes
I feel as if I'll burst
and suddenly I realize
it's your love I thirst
love and passion both
Oh, my heart's on fire
I feel as though I may explode
my body's a live wire
emotions are running in and out
like a morning's angry tide
I'm riding an emotional roller-coaster
but it's an incredible ride

Carrie Mayfield

Time

Little second, you passed me by,
Then the minutes flew on high.
The hours rolled on and soon were gone,
Then the day was done.

Weeks, months and years passed
When suddenly "where" I asked.
Gone and never to return
Like some old love spurned.

Once I wished time would pass
When a young, carefree lass.
But now as life ebbs, I pray
To recapture what has slipped away.

Dear ones gone and stories forgotten,
Acts of kindness and deeds undone.
I longed to love, create and build,
Now there is no time, only "will".

Jean Batchelder

"On the Meaning Of Life"

On the meaning of life
There could never be
An explanation so profound
To satisfy me.

I watch the Sun set,
I watch the Sun rise,
And I think to myself-
What a beautiful guise.

So much chaos and hatred,
A world so confused,
Surrounds each day with beauty-
I am truly bemused.

And what of the people-
Each and every race?
In such a rich land we suffer-
What a disgrace.

There are those who try to improve it
And those who try to destroy it.
But the children all around us,
They just try to enjoy it.

Deirdre K. Rogusky

You

You have always been
there for me when ever I'm
fallen; picking me up and
showing me the way, the
ways of life that is.

You! yes you have taught me
right from wrong. And I have
learned from my rights and
especially my wrongs.

You've also taught me that
it's better to forgive than to
forget; and to love than to
have never loved at all.

Mom! I love you.

Dekama S. McDonald

Somewhere In My Dreams

In a field so green
There is a crooked swing
A picnic basket
A blanket colored red
Initials are being carved on wood
Words of love are being said
It is a cool spring day
Not so far away
For friends who deeply care
We have made a special moment
A memory to share
As the day comes to an end
I turn to look at my friend
Tears of joy in my eyes he can see
His heart has been mine
If only for a short time
Somewhere in my dreams

Beverly Brantley

The Bounty Of Wildlife

Outside my window and door
There is more than a view.
There exists a bounty of wildlife
Creatures of every kind.
Large, medium, and small
Feather, fur, and shell.
They bring joy and peace
To my eyes, ears, and heart.
Deer, Skunk, Rabbit,
Raccoon, Possum, Squirrel;
Hawks, Blue-Jays, Cardinals,
Owls, Crows, Robins;
Beetle, Cricket, Dragon Fly,
Locust, Wasp, Butter Fly.

Fred L. Farnsworth

The Human Race

The human race, oh! My what a disgrace!
They like to kill baby seals,
pollute the air, lie and steal
for they no longer feel, not
for themselves nor for their
neighbor: Only the green back
called money makes them tick!
not the sky, not the birds
not the trees not even God.
Oh! how I wish I weren't
part of this thing called
the Human Race!

Anna Bowman

Leaving the Nest

There were a lot of heartaches,
There was a lot of pain.
I felt like a little girl
Standing lonely in the rain.
We did a lot of screaming
And many tears were shed.
Many nights I cursed your name
As I lay crying in my bed.
But now that I'm a woman
I can plainly see:
I wouldn't be where I am today
If you'd never yelled at me.
Now we do a lot of hugging,
Only tears of joy are shed.
Every night I thank God for you
Before I go to bed.

You listen to my problems,
My broken hearts you mend,
You will always be my mother,
But now you're my best friend.

Barbara Custer

Why

Why is it raining?
There's a cold darkness.
The sounds, his feelings
have been deadened.

Why is it raining?
Night — its darkness sheaded
brings about the sun
above in all brightness

There's warmth and splendor;
Yet, nothing is changing.
Still, I sit and ask —
Why is it raining?

Heather Whittaker

Gone

Since you've gone far away.
There's been no reason to play.
I miss you so.
Why did you go?
To torture me?
I cannot see
Don't you love, don't you need me?
Did you really want to leave me?
Don't you love me?
I love you.

Christine Makepeace

Friends

In any of the world
there's no friend truer than you,
your sweeter that candy
and prettier than any flower that grew,
no matter what evil lies in your path
you turn it to goodness
you'll be my friend forever
God bless

Carissa Vogt

Broken Vow

I had said good-bye
There's no turning back now,
He hurt me so bad
He had broken our vow.

He came home late at night
After being with her,
He had no idea
That I knew for sure.

After coming home from her
He would kiss me good-night,
I knew what I had to do
I had to get out of sight.

I lay awake in my bed
Thinking what had gone wrong,
Remembering our good times
And where our love had gone.

I knew what he had done
He had broken our vow,
I walked through the door
There's no turning back now.

Jennifer J. DeMara

Untitled

My glass is continually half empty,
These visions of my existence,
Seem distorted and deformed,
My views are based,
Not on reality,
But on the cruelty of my own mind,
The submission of the heart to the
maleficence in this world,
I cannot feel the virtues of society,
Nor enjoy the beauty it offers,
Knowing these are momentary,
Delusions one tries to hold on to,
Brief seconds of delight that in the end,
Always slip through your fingers,
Anger swarms all that I do,
Shadowing each emerging dawn with grief,
Having the recognition that life wasted on me,
And my ingratitude of this gift,
A gift that should have been given to a soul,
Whose glass is half full.

Heather Elaine Lehman

Hands

Today I have such little hands
They are so hard to control
When it comes to coloring and writing
It's not always neat I'm told.
But wait,
Someday I'll get better
Then I will write my parents
a nice long letter
To say thank you for all their help
in my youth
Just as they gave me help
when I lost my first tooth
For always being there
To tell them I really care
Someday when I grow big
But today
I'll live my life
Being a Little Kid.

Geri DiBartolo

"The Infantry"

Oh! The Infantry, oh, the Infantry,
They came from hell they say"
That's why we fight so hard,
'Cause we have a price to pay.

We're the back-bone for the Army,
We're the head for the Marine:
When the Country gets in trouble,
We;re the first ones on the scene.

We wrote our honor in the Flag,
Long may our banner wave:
It proves that we're the greatest,
When a Country must be save.

When "Tap's" is sound in Heaven,
All the Infantries will be there:
There will be no more fighting,
We'll be soldiers on the "Square."

Joseph H. Young

Untitled

How can they care?
They cannot,
For their eyes cannot
See past their demons—
Their chains.
How can one expect to swim
The depths of the ocean,
Not to be pulled down
By the weed of the seas?
Is it not profound to believe
That for one finite span
Of a breath, that lives
Could have been changed forever,
Simply because I didn't care?

Dale Allen

Growing Old

Flowers maintain life
They love life
They love life

I love
I hate

Where should I go
What should I do

I've loved
I've hated

I've created
Where should I go

Birds are created by God
not man

Man is created by man
not to be superficial

Angela Signorelli Ali

Whispers

Father eagle Sister sky
Upon the winds which
Will never die.

The trees that whisper
different names the flowers
beauty like the sky.

Dana Cardona

Ode To A Dandelion

So many people pass you by.
They never even see.
They look and find the blue of sky
And sparkling dew and me.

They hate you because you are a weed,
But who has called you this?
Like other plants, you spring from seed
And get the sunshine's kiss.

Like others, God created you
And all your golden glory.
The bees sure love you; I do, too,
And I shall write your story.

If orchids in a lawn should grow,
They, too, would seem amiss,
And all green-lawnites then would mow
To keep their grass in bliss.

Oh, far more happy is a lawn
With golden highlights shining,
A lawn reflecting back the dawn
Of Paradise's morning.

Diana Carolyn Ice

Where It All Begins

They say an eye for an eye,
They say a tooth for a tooth.
Whether to hate or love,
Whether the old or youth.

They say forgive and forget,
They say not to sin.
No one is perfect, but God,
Have faith, be born again.

To be so powerful and great,
To be like him who never hates,
To have love and peace,
All you need is to have faith.

He is here when needed,
He is forever you friend,
Open your heart, let him in,
Cause that's where it all begins.

Jennie Markovich

The Shoes Of A Lover

Slowly, stealthily,
They slide down the side
Of her cherry cheeks
As she stares through the pane
on which they also fall,
Sorrowfully, steadily,
until one by one they are
Pushed by the presence of still another
Drop of sadness from the sky.

Nature shares in her heaviness of heart
As she looks blurry-eyed out the
window whose face is also
Tear-stained.

But the pain and the passion
That pushes and pulls
As she longs for her lover,
Is something that Nature will never know.

Though Nature is often loved,
She has yet to step in to
the shoes of a lover.

Bonita Sasso Pistilli

Best Friend?

Upon the sand I wander
thinking of my old best friend.
I sit down and I wonder
what if broken hearts would mend?

And as I gaze into the sunset
and the glimmer which it sends.
Remembering the day we met,
and how we once were friends.

Silently I wonder as I walk upon the shore
when we both let friendship bend
into something so much more.
Was it then I lost my friend?

I hope from day to day
that if broken hearts would mend
I know for sure that some day
I'll have my old best friend.

Heather Van De Moortell

Twenty Years Ago

She was the first to embrace you
This night and evermore
Too many
Sparkley eyes
Crying breezes
Shiny shoes
Who's refuge
Looking through the leaves
Sleepless windows
Everlasting

Cheryl Royer

"Ladies First"

Since the age of chivalry
this slogan we have heard
"Ladies First" at every time.
Do we believe these words?
"Ladies First" at the table
gentlemen place their chairs
"Ladies First" in emergencies
of that we are aware.
Always consider the ladies
the best comes first to them
but when it comes to keep a date
who's first? Why ask the men!

Dorothy G. Kohler

Thank You

The hardest love has got to be
This type of love with you and me;
That can't be known
And can't be shown
Except in private moments.
But I'm grateful even then
For the special feeling that you bring
The joy and beauty I feel again.
And for the moments you are mine
However brief and fleeting
My spirit is high, my life worthwhile
Your loving fondness is the fuel
That stirs my heart to keep beating.
For all that you're brought me,
Thank you.

Lizabeth Schultz

When Will You Remember

When will you remember
Those nights we knew
When will you remember those
days before
When will you spend time
we spent anew
A lifetime passes quickly
The hours fly by each
moment is precious in
Our hearts and our minds
Let us go forward with a
quickened pace so we may
enjoy even more of our
lives as we pass by
each place.

David A. Riedel

"My Lovely Lady"

THOU ART a lovely lady might I say
Thou art not vain, nor proud, nor mean
And all thy true traits can be seen-
My Lovely Lady, lithe and gay,
Thou art a pure and kindly queen
Whom thy suitors worship if they may.
Thy hair is black as raven's wings
Thine eyes are blue as skies above.
Thy lovely lips true love songs sing,
Of beauty rare, of life, of love.
Oh lady let me be thy king
My lovely lady accept my love!!!

Dotty Lee Scott

The Trooper

He surely wanted to run,
Though
his march was rather slow
He was beat.

He was still a private
And had no Awards to show
He was glad to be home
It was sweet.

His woman stood suave
at the gate
with his son in her arms,

His older boy climbed
on the fence
His dog ran to meet him.

His mother came soon into view.

He was happy, but sighed
And he wept when they smiled,
He was home — it was sweet...

Annemarie Viglione

Untitled

Venture on yet again
To a place you were before
Not regression by any means
Just opening yet another door
A new chapter has begun
Saying good-bye to yesterday
To tears and to heartache
I'm saying good-bye to you
It's something I have to do
To rid me of my dismay
Just in time for me to wake
So I can live my life again.

Joseph R. Palumbo

Life's Statement

I want to be the King of Alabama
though I really don't know why
it's probably the only State
I think that I can BUY

KING ELMO of Alabama
it has a lovely sound
Congress would declare it
they'd think it so profound

I'd pay a fair price, of course
#5,000. Down, no more
with lots of long term paper
backed by land at rates of four

Oh—, to be the king of Alabama
what a marvelous LIFE'S STATEMENT
it will all come true of course
when I get the down payment.

Elmo Nosari

Field Of Dreams

I'd like to say thank you,
though I'm sure you don't know why.

Your kindness and sweetness too,
has never passed me by.

I always watch the things you do,
even though you'd never lie.

I always knew,
That it was true,
You would never leave my side.

I can't explain the way I feel,
when you grasp my heart so deep.

Your love and touch,
Will leave a seal,
That I will always keep.

Chari R. Malkin

Our Daughter Frankie

Your accomplishments are varied
Though your perspectives are not known
Still the potters wheel keeps turning
As the master builds his own.

In love and grace we each are moulded
Nothing on earth remains the same
The disciplines of burdens, sorrows
The promise of a new tomorrow.

Now a vessel of consecrated oneness
A strength of beauty, courage, peace
Born of healing, ready to hear
The master's call, his perfect will.

Edna Thurrott

Troubled Soul

Thoughts of horror
Thoughts of threat
Withheld from public eye
Locked inside without a key
Scared of what may be
A troubled soul
A troubled mind
The fear
The hate which lies inside
To die
Or not die is the question
When a troubled soul goes unrested.

Andy Bellamy

Alone Or Free?

As I gaze out of my window
Thoughts seize my mind.
As a loneliness comes over me,
A sadness I find.

For the children have grown
And soon will leave home.
Into adulthood they'll pass,
And I'll be alone.

I used to believe
It wouldn't matter to me.
For upon their departure,
I would be free.

But with this freedom
Comes loneliness,
A sadness that "will"
Weigh heavily!

Judy C. Morgan Austin

Rainy Days

Hovering clouds in the heavens
Through which I cannot see

Strong gusts of wind,
Carrying nature's debris

And rain falls heavily,
On valleys, mountains, and seas

Large muddy puddles cover the ground
Small water drops plummet from the leaves

And though many days have passed,
Rainy days will always come back.

Cynthia Perez

All Just To

I'd walk across the wilderness -
Thru' driving rain I'd pace.
No snow drift could ever stop me,
All just to see your face,
No music can you play for me,
No harps - no chimes of choice.
I'd trade the Philharmonic
All just to hear your voice.
I've roamed the whole world over
And saw the evening skies.
O, what I wouldn't give up
All just to see your eyes.
The wonder of the snowfall
The sight of an eclipse.
These joys I'd pass up gladly
All just to kiss your lips,
The need to speak my thoughts out
Too fast too slow — too much
I'd gladly keep my silence
All just to feel your touch.

Barbara O. Giemza

I Want To See You Smile

I know it's hard sometimes
to smile when your best
friend let's you down
But smile any way
It will fool your friends
and yourself
You will look and feel
better if you do
So how about just
a little one-

Janet A. Dowiat

Broken Promises

You said you'd never leave me,
'til the stars fall from the sky.
You said your gonna love me,
'til the end of time.

The stars are falling all around me
The end of time is near.
How do I get by on broken promises
and fear?
Please tell me what to do with
forever

The stars have stopped falling
The end of time has left with
your memory.
And my fear has gone away
Your broken promises are in the past.
The thing that remains is forever.
And that I know will cast.

Brenda Ann Wysinger

Time

I wish I had
Time
To make my dreams come true
And see the other side
Happiness and content
An illusion
Swirling in my mind
Stuccatoed in my memory
A thought
Stirs the embers
Of the dying flame
A dark-haired girl
To calm my soul
And share my kingdom
Will she come
And find the corners of my heart
Through the doors I've closed
And through the thorns
That time has grown

John C. David

My Love

Where do I begin
time and time again
seems with this sadness
there is no end
what have I done?
Where did I go wrong?
The will to live
just isn't as strong
as the time before
I try to ignore
the feeling of the past
how long will this last?
I've got to go on
with what lies up ahead
where I'd rather be instead
to share my dreams and my love
that comes from the heavens above
my life lays upon my hands
I will do the best
to ease the pain and be laid to rest.

Catherine Q. Perez

Time

Time is something special
Time can never be recaptured.
Time is valuable and should
be given to those special people.
Time is not everlasting
Time is nothing more than
a life passing through this world.
Time is something I need with you.
Because you are special and I want
to pass through this world with you,
then I would not have to worry about
re-capturing time that I could
never do.
Time is lost without you!

Dolores Lachciek

"Thanks Giving Of Yore"

I remember my childhood home
Time have past and gone
Mom stocking the old cook stove
with paper oil, wood and coal
the house smelling very nice
scents from flavors and spice.

Majorettes dressed in scanty attire
No matter how nippy the air
Marching in high school parade
Banners swaying what a craze,
The rest of the family
Off to church for a feast.

Dad stayed home all alone
Tending the fire while we were gone
Good friends, good food good eats,
Beautiful gathers oh! How sweet!!
There were always food for later snacks
How the years bring my memories back!!

Helen M. Reed

Loss of Purity

From time to time,
timid rays from the gold disk
pierce the usual gray fabric
of a wet spring;
and tears become crystal, here.
Over by you, I hear,
they are falling,
falling incessantly,
dripping silently
and streaming down your street
to lose their purity
as you wash your salty shoes.
I pity your white tears.

Jean Poincy

Friends

Friends are always there
To count on and to care
They're there to hang around
To laugh and be a clown
To tell your deepest thought
Friends cannot be bought
Through good times and bad
For friends you will be glad
Even when you're far away
In your heart a friend will stay
True friend never lie
A friend is a friend until you die

Amie Culbertson

Our Angel Friend

Once again he's opened heavens door
To a new face that's entering the land
By now she's an angel making new friends
Walking hand in hand.

We do not understand his reasons
For taking her so far away
But - we all will meet with her again
Someday yes, someday

It hurts so much to know she's gone
She left without any good-byes
But her days replay in our memories
As they will for the rest of our lives

And now that she's a part of Heaven
She'll watch over each one of us
Looking down with a heavenly smile
That lights our world with lots of love

Once again he's opened heavens door
To a face that is so new
Our angel friend - the memories we have
Seem right now too few....

Alisha Hall

Untitled

I'm waiting on a Saturday night
To do what's wrong, but feels so right
And afterwards I die of shame,
My heart explodes with all the pain.

I sit alone, here in the dark
In my hands I hold my heart
But you can't see, and you don't feel
And nothing that you say is real.

Please don't hurt me once again;
To return to you would be a sin
And I just can't seem to stay away.
Why do I always have to pay?

I love you, but you'll never know;
Those feelings I will never show.
I look for yours within your lies
And I receive a harsh reply.

Moving on is hard to do
But I know I must leave you,
Or hurt inside each time you lie
So with all that's dead for you— Goodbye.

Emily Steger

The Poem

There's nothing like a poem,
To keep your mind a growin.
They open up your eyes,
When life seems down otherwise.
Where would we be without them?
Our world would really be dim.
Imagination running wild,
Written words never denied.
So open up your thoughts,
Take pencil in your hand,
Jot down a few lines.
Spread joy throughout the lands.

Gary A. White

"The Years Gone By"

I asked in youth
To know the truth.

I saw in age
With angered rage.

I call in death
For wanted breath.

Juanita A. Grant

Dear Mother

Dear Mother, they have taken you from me
to land where there is no night.
But I will always remember you, Mother,
as my star that shone so bright.
You soothed my brow in fever.
You listened to all of my dreams.
You were always there when I needed you,
and you listened to all of my schemes.
You showed me the beauty of sunrise.
You lifted my spirits with prayer.
You've always been my inspiration,
and I'll meet you up yonder, somewhere.

Aileen R. Kunkel

To Someone Special

I never thought I'd have the mind
to let you think I'm dear.
When everything that's in my heart
would shake you up I fear.
I'd like to say I'm feeling fine —
and make just one thing clear.
There's not another in my life
that I could hold so dear!
If there's one thing that I might say
about my way of life,
It's that I doubt I'll ever change,
I'll keep you as my wife.
If there is anything you like,
announce it loud and clear.
For all to know — my loving you,
is my whole life's career!

Harlan Sidwell

Brown Baby

Holding brown baby
to my chest

Dreaming of dreams for you
But only wanting the best

Come my child I'll hold
you while you rest

The world will want to kill you.
They think you are a pest
I know better our history is true
I love you brown baby
They would too.

Janan Abdullah

Time Is:

Too slow for those who wait
Too fast for those who fear
Too long for those who grieve
Too short for those who rejoice
But for those who love
Time Is:
Eternity.

Anna Furtick

"Lady Blue Heron"

We were fishing for the fun of it
to pass the time of day,
When I met a lovely Heron
with feathers bluish gray.

I tossed a fish upon the bank
too small to be a keeper
Not knowing "Lady Blue" was waiting
just for me to feed her.

We caught an even dozen fish
to give to uncle Joe,
And six or seven little ones-
for "Lady Blue" - you know.

She caught each one and turned it 'round
then swallowed it head first
her neck stretched up and I could see
her neck would surely burst.

The way each fish just slithered down
was quite a sight to see,
But I'm just glad the neck was hers
and didn't belong to me-

Juanita Clarke

Uncertain

I think that now's the time,
to really let you know.
That I have feelings for you
that I can not let go.

You came into my life and
touched me in a special way.
It seems I need you more and more
each and every day.

When I'm with you I laugh
when I'm alone I cry.
I can't sort out these feelings
I have for you inside.

I don't know what you're thinking
and I don't know what to do.
But one thing is for certain,
I will always care about you.

Georgia Ann Luke

Poems

People who have a talent
to rhyme and write love
scenes in our heads.
Only the best can survive
in a world like ours.
Everyone must give it their
best effort, some win some
lose but you
always must try.
Men, women, kids and all
send in poems for money
to spend at the mall.
So now that you know
what poems mean to
me, I'm just an ordinary
kid writing this scheme!

Heather Willis

An Eagle's Wings

I opened my eyes
To see such a sight,
I just can't wait
For my very first flight.

I felt so majestic,
Flying so high,
Beyond all the forests,
Against the blue sky.

They took me to mountains,
And cliffs by the shore
Their eyes and their heart
Were hardened to the core.

They took me to a nest
Its young were fast asleep
It was very protective
It said nothing, not a peep.

The wings were very strong
And sometimes they were mean
Still, it flew so very graceful
I was treated like a queen.

Evita De La Parra

It Only Takes A Touch

It only takes a gentle touch,
to show how much you care,
to tell me that I'm special,
and you are always there.
It only takes a certain look,
to make me laugh out loud,
and point out that I'm someone great,
not just another face in the crowd.
It only takes one little hug,
to prove to me your love,
and state that here you will remain,
when push comes down to shove.
It only takes a simple touch,
to say all this and more,
so much we say is without words,
my friend forevermore.

Jennifer A. Gorgas

Winged Release

Where are the wings to take me up,
To soar at such great heights,
That I can break the earthly bonds,
To have a freer flight?

I want it so when I look below,
I'll see no human trace,
No walls or fences upon the land,
To mar the planet's face.

At such heights there is the hope,
Its beauty can be found,
One which all too well we know,
Looks different from the ground.

With wings I'll lift a sunken spirit,
And find my youth again,
Be free to glide within the currents,
And bathed by the wind.

Once above the sea of clouds,
I'll sail the open sky;
Let the others walk below,
I want to fly.

Jerry Capka

Professor, I Have A Question

As I sit here listening
To talk of bonding pairs,
I cannot help but wonder
If anybody cares.
It's good to know what atoms do,
At least that's what they say.
But what I truly want to know
Is "Will it ever pay?"
Another phrase they like to use,
"There's really nothing to it."
But let me ask one little thing,
Just "Will I ever use it?"
Well pardon me for asking
But I really want to know.
Unless the answers both be "Yes"
I might as well just go!

Andrew W. Applegarth

America ToDay—

"Heir" Of Freedom

Let us turn back the pages of time
To the day when a group of our peers
Documented a democratic way of life
That has reached over two hundred years,
Where in our expanding colonies
Were religions, races and creeds,
With free rein to explore all avenues
For acquiring vital needs,
Though in that long on-going process,
There were trials and tribulations,
Fierce loyalty to freedom's cause
Made us the leader of nations,
Technology has made the world closer
For travel and commercial ties,
It is high time to remove barriers
That still tend to polarize,
When man can live a whole life span
And havoc of wars will cease,
Our priceless freedoms, we will enjoy,
With love, harmony and peace.

Jack Wenof

Untitled

I looked from the mountain
 to the east
The sun is raising
I start each day this way

There is chill in the air
But immediately
 the sun is showing its color

I feel the warmth seep into my soul
And I know again
I can start fresh
this new day

Joyce C. Burris

Worlds Apart

Seems that we are worlds apart
Today, yesterday and tomorrow
How can we be friends, really good friends
Without our grief and sorrow

Fear not for what the future brings
Just be prepared to cope
Troubles come and go each day
Yet there's plenty of room for hope.

Georgia A. Jones

The Seas of Tomorrow

I go in my boat
To the seas of tomorrow,
Hoping to stay afloat
In the waters of sorrow.

The wind has a cry
That fills my sail,
It carries the sighs
Of all who have failed.

Someday I'll see
How cruel life can be,
And the black clouds will fill
And try to break my will.

We all have a boat
A boat of our own
We hope it will float
With love it is sown.

Amanda King

Untitled

We are challenged daily.
To walk in Jesus faith.
No matter the adversity,
We are hid in that secret place.

In the storms He states,
"Wait silently for me."
To express the fruits of His Kingdom
And show His glory.

We are challenged daily.
To walk in Jesus faith.
Look for Him in every circumstances.
He states "Trust me and obey."

As our Father He knows.
What truly lies ahead
Giving everyday direction,
To follow Him instead.

Our now faith takes care,
Of all our yesterdays
Because of that loving price,
The Son of God has paid.

Essie Brown

Limits

I can't make the sun rise
to warm my skin.
I can't take the chill
out of winter's wind.

I can't prevent waves
from crushing mountains into sand.
I can't halt time
by holding a clock by its hands.

I can't rid the Earth
of pestilence, famine and hate.
I can't bear the world's burdens,
though my heart feels the weight.

I can't make fallen stars
twinkle brightly again.
I can't return life
to where death has been.

Yes, I'm limited.
A lot of things I can't do.
But there is no limit
to my love for you.

Harold Banks

The Color Of Love

To you which hold all knowledge
To you the wisdom you hold
A question for your merry heart
 What is the color of love?

To you who spoil young children
with lies and gifts of money
Causing them forever shame
what is the color of love

To you who speak so softly
With your fancy clothes so rare
Seducing people with your treasures
 Do you know the color of love

The Lord's tears are falling
For his children you have maimed
If you missed the point, forgive me
For every color their is love.

May all the earth tremble
As he treads the mountain tops
As he wades across the oceans
 God is the color of love!

Chet Little

Sally

About a year ago they said six months,
Tonight she lay in a very deep sleep.
Calm and happy.
Relaxed, Amen.
Cancer she had,
A growth on her nose,
Ugly on the out,
but a heart like a rose.
I'll miss her I know,
It was for the better.
I must love her for what she was,
Not for what she is.
But deep in my heart,
I know so well,
My 13 year old dog,
was a puppy to me.
She was my very best friend,
She never told on me,
Why should she, she loved me!!

Beth Krieger

Jesus Is The Way

Life is such an ocean
 Tossing back and forth.
 Here one day—there another,
 Always moving through.
'Cause life so a troubling,
 We really need a way.
A way to toss.
 A way to move.
 A way to see us through.
When Jesus died upon that cross,
 He made the way for us.
 A way to calm our tossing lives,
 To move our lives on through.
He is the way,
 The only way,
 The only way for us.
When He gave His life for us,
 He made the way for us.
Jesus is the Way,
 THE ONLY WAY FOR US. Amen!

Barbara A. Shelton

Winter

I hear it coming down the road.
Trailing with it, the wind blows.
It spreads leaves all over the lawn.
It freezes up the near-by pond.

I see it coming down the road.
Stripping nature of its beauty.
It dyes the coloring of the grass.
From the rich green that it once had.

I smell it coming down the road.
It robs the air's sweet aroma.
Roses, daises, and marigolds.
It puts them all in a coma.

I feel it coming down the road.
It blocks the fresh sun rays.
And the warmth.
Of a full summer day.

I taste it coming down the road.
Wrapped in a blanket, sick with the flu.
My toes are cold.
I have chicken soup on the stove.

Brenda Mallory

The Deepness Of My Love

The deepness of my love
transcends time and space,
it was rooted in the depth's
of the deepest ocean, it reaches
into the outer galaxy, even
into the seventh heaven's, it was
formed in the heart of God and
eternity is its keeper.
The deepness of my love
is found in something as simple
as a spec of dust and yet made to
create everything that is.
The deepness of my love is
not merely for just anyone nor
any man it was predestinated
just for you.
The deepness of my love.

Deborah D. Frazier

Steep Climb

Life is like a mountain railroad,
Traveling through the years of time.
When at last we reach our destination.
And we've made that final climb.

There we'll greet our blessed Savior,
As we kneel before his throne.
Then all the works we did for Jesus,
Before the world will be made know.

Thou the road may be rough and rocky,
As we travel down here below;
Up there we'll have clear sailing,
When through the eastern gate we go.

Released at last from all our burdens,
That made our journey go so slow.
There we'll look upon the fire,
Where the chaff of life will glow.

Now down the streets of gold we'll travel,
Never more to cry or weep,
All of Glory we'll go exploring,
Then we'll kneel at Jesus' feet.

Harriet Plummer

Snowflake

A single flake of snow
Travels its long journey
Through the vast sheets of blue
Sparkling in the clear sunlight
It topples, turns, changes...
The flake, distinct in shape
Is easily distinguished
From its neighbors
When pointed out
Although it blends in quite nicely
When it is left alone

Jason Nickerson

Untitled

The blessings of war
Trees of flesh and streams of blood
On a land that lives off sin
A sky so black and full of things
And a city reduced to tin

Streets of bodies and allies of trash
Decorate the rubble of a store
All of these are man's creation
For these are the blessings of war!

Janisann Salas

One

Two people,
Two lives,
Two professions,
Two pasts,
Two personalities,
Two minds,
Two dreams,
Two hopes,
Two bodies,
Two hearts,
One beat,
One love,
One purpose,
One future—
Two people, in love,
together...

Julian J. Miller

Not To Be Taken Lightly

A Promise is a special bond
two people hold in trust
it's a solemn vow between them
to keep it is a must

A promise is kept
out of caring and concern
when you keep a promise
trust is what you earn

Sometimes outside forces
want our promise to dissolve
to be firm and keep it
should be our resolve

Never ever make one
due to just a whim
because to hurt someone
would really be a sin

Promises between two
should not be taken lightly
be sure to feel it in your heart
and hold it very tightly

Cindy Paddock

Loving You

Loving you is like a peaceful day
under a clear sky.
Only my love for you makes it worthwhile,
if it was not for the days,
that I share alone.
Loving you would not mean anything,
nor would the peaceful skies up above.
So I say to you, loving you
is like loving no other.
I truly love you, so here's to you.

Edwin McKinney

Earthlove

The
unexpected love
a flower has
for my eyes

Touches my mind
and heart
with surprise

Come closer,
talk softly,
so I can see
your voice

And
by the sweetness
of choice

Listen
to
the songs
in my soul...

Bernie Reading

"down"

i stagger into the fluorescent night
unnatural light glowing upon us
and nothing seems quite right

maybe I'm in the wrong place
maybe in a different time
the lives of age hardening my face

but I can't shake the feeling
that I'm in the wrong town
the foreignness sends me reeling

or maybe I'm just down

Chris Reynolds

Too Soon

Too soon I am old
Too late I am smart,

Too soon I go slow
Too late to make a mark,

Too soon I am silenced
Too late for kindly words,

Too soon I am alone
Too late to understand.

Evelyn R. Waters

"The Friendly Skies"

There are some points to ponder
Up in the wild blue yonder...
In this the age of space,
There are mysteries we face.

The skies are full of things
That are zipping to and fro,
While on earth our government says,
"That's not a UFO!!"

Airports are often crowded,
Even more if there's been snow...
And at the one in Denver,
Where did the baggage go?

Their computer tried so hard
To keep the luggage tracked;
As if that weren't enough,
Now they say the runway's cracked.

But still you can't get far,
Though you'd love to be alone;
It seems they towed the car
From the %#!@ white zone!!

Gary L. Travis

1947

Jackie, Jackie
up to bat.

Hitting
  little
    white
      balls,
with a big black bat.

Bradley S. Tice

Sweet Embrace

To feel the warmth
Upon your face.
A gentle touch,
A sweet embrace.

Inspired in me
Such passionate bliss.
To be held in your arms
Enchanted by a kiss.

David Rodriguez

Usually Love Begins With Strangers

Usually love begins with strangers,
Usually love has a start someplace.
Usually love takes a little time
And usually love has a stranger's face.

And after life has been unkind,
It's natural to be a little slower.
But we were never strangers.
Make no mistake,
What you know is true.
And I am here for you.

Usually love spends some time asking,
Wondering if it's really true.
Usually love is slightly awkward,
Rarely does it know just what to do.

But make no mistake,
What you know in your heart is true.
And the pains of love in the past
Were only so you'd know the pain was
  through.
And I am here for you.

Beau G. Randt

Untitled

Rose are red
Violets are blue
Which ever it
is it smells
Better than you!

Anna Chipman

Spring

Flowers bloom in an array of bright
vivid colors.
Birds begin to chant.
Streams and rivers
trickle
swoosh and
rush.
The wind echoes
Nature has arisen!

Ingrid D. Larson

Who He?

He ran with the wind;
walked on a log.
Crawled in a box
and slept with his dog.

He lay on his back
and communed with the sky.
Watching the birds,
he dreamed he could fly.

He swam in the creek
where he'd skated, too.
He captured fireflies,
then watched as they flew.

He sailed in a washtub;
drank from the spring.
He ate wild berries;
had to try everything.

He scaled the cliffs
just to see what he'd see.
He was happy and carefree.
He was young; he was me.

John E. Schwartz

To A Graduate

Sweet girl graduate
  Walking down the aisle
To an unknown fate
  you must reconcile.

Ply your earnest girlhood hope
  of your brief career
Into woman's larger scope
  of universal sphere.

Youthful courage can endure
  much that age forsakes,
But faith is investiture
  when womanhood awakes.

Zealously sustain the truth
  and ardently pursue
Dimensions of your eager youth
  that contributed to you.

Gladys Rhein

Hello Or Good-Bye

I used to believe stars told your destiny
Water told your past
My heart would lead the way
Now I believe you are one of many
Who believe love should be last
You will never have another chance
To say hello or good-bye.

Jennifer Nelson

Lake Michigan

Water blue,
Waves so high
often like they touch the sky.
Beautiful sight,
people think,
often deer pause to drink.
Sandy beaches,
miles and miles,
children swimming,
all smiles.
Jumping waves, diving too,
water crystal clear and blue.
Had a bad day, stop and look,
forget your troubles,
read a book, lay in the sand,
soak up the sun.
Run down the beach, isn't it fun?
It belongs to you - to me
Lake Michigan will always be.

Eirnella A. O'Neil

Etpos

We are many poets
We are ets
We are po

We are the poems
Of our parents
Written for time

Some of us complex
Some of us invisible

We are many poets
We are ets
We are po

Jose Luis Velazquez Cabret

Untitled

They said we are an endangered species
We change from boys to men quickly
And our families are broken to pieces
We are often misunderstood and blamed
For most of society's problems today
The world has the solution
But it seems not to come our way
We cry for help
And ask for guidance and lots more
We knock, we knock,
But no one answers the door
We treat our sisters
Bad and sometimes in a mean way
They fight back and strive even harder
Here today gone tomorrow
It's sad that way
I must truly say
We die fast and young
Let us pray.

Eugene Lee Watkins

Getting The Picture

We laugh, we play,
We cry, we rage,
Or maybe not
Suppressing what is real

Then we fully realize our situation
Trying to project all outcomes,
In this game call life.
Realizing what you had planned
Was only an idea
And what was realized
Was a priority from a HIGHER SOURCE.

Diana G. Corona

This Day And Forever

This Day and Forever,
We have planned so long.
The waiting and anxiety
will soon be gone.
Here this day we'll stand together,
before God and friends,
to form a bond of love and friendship
that will never end.

We thank God that He has blessed us
with each other,
and we pray that He will guide us
now and forever;
that our troubles and our burdens
may be few and small,
and that our true love for each other
will conquer all.

As we catch each other's glances, we'll
see joy and pride
and there may be some tears of happiness
that we can't hide.
But we both know that when all is said
and done,
This Day and Forever, we will be as one.

Charles R. Penberthy

Divorce

I'm alone now,
We parted long ago,
Each of us happy
To be going our separate ways,

He said I had grown old;
I knew he drank too much
And smoked,
And chased younger thighs.

I don't have the heartache
Any more.
My days are full of work,
Of friends and children,
And I sleep well.
But no one knows how much
I miss being in love!

Anne Hall

My Friend

My friend left me,
What did I do?
One day she said good-by.
Now my world is all blue.
I will think of her all my life,
All I know is, Kelly, I miss you.

Jennifer Timm

"How Could God Do This To Me?"

How could God do this to me?
We should have been together
for eternity.
Pure and innocent and named Ashley.
I'll never understand how this came to be.
Baby Charlie will never see his
twin sister, that bond will never be.
Part of him and part of me
will never be free for eternity.
How could God do this to me?

Jennifer Moerler

You And I

Yesterday
we were
together
So much
in love
with each other.
Today,
we're both
so far
away
Wanting
nothing
but...
yesterday.

Gilda Nanakorn

Autumn, A Picture In Words

The air is so pure
Well, as pure as can be
The colors a cure
By setting the mind free.

Winds serenade you
Like a soothing refrain
The birds Ballyhoo
In their Lofty domain.

The tempts, crisp and cool,
Awaken your senses
Ghosts, maybe a ghoul
Frolicking on fences.

Pumpkins and scarecrows
Embellish the landscape
The harvest moon glows
In its amber bright shape.

A joy to the eyes
This gift from the divine
One's soul does arise
At this marvel, design.

James D. Ryan

Love

Love
What is it
Where is it
how can we find it
can any one find it
is it even real
does any one know
But wait
I know where it is
we all do
it's in our hearts

Donna Hemlin

Tearful Attraction

If someone cries
what would you do
I'm crying now
because of you.

I would give
so you'd be glad
Then maybe I
would not be sad.

Romantic songs
play all around
I wait for the phone
but hear no sound.

When I watch
you looking at me
I always hope
you like what you see.

Carrie Ann McLain

What Is My Part?

What is the part you have for me?
What would you have me do?
I'll sit and wait until I hear,
You calling me to you.
Don't let me move until you move,
Or speak until you speak.
For you are Holy and you are strong.
I'm sinful and I'm weak.
To know your word, to speak it out,
To live it every day.
To die to self, and live to God,
To tread the narrow way
There is a way that's right to me,
a way that ends in woe.
Please help me find your way, dear Lord,
As on through life I go.
A humble heart, a steadfast love, a
commitment Lord to you.
What is the part you have for me?
What would you have me do?

Jeanette N. Ryan

The Night Of A Fight

I can remember the terrible night,
when everyone began to fight.

Bullets were flying in the air,
and nobody even seemed to care.

Children were scared in the street;
most of them in their bare feet.

There I stood with fear in my eye,
wondering if I was going to die.

I guess it doesn't matter now;
forget about it, but how?!?!

Nothing has ever worked out right,
all because of that terrible night.

Jacqueline Cecile Barronton

Loving

The world has a rosy hue
When I think of you
Shimmering moon makes me blue......
I think of you.

Josephine Pederson

God Is With Me

During the week
When everyone is gone,
I know in my heart
That I'm never alone.

For God is with me,
He's always here.
I know in his presence,
There's nothing to fear.

God makes birds fly,
Flowers bloom, and trees grow.
He makes the sun shine,
The rain and the snow.

God loves you,
God loves me,
And with us both
He'll always be.

Christine L. Brown

When The End Is Near

You shall know when the end is near
When God's call
Wakes us all from our eternal slumber
Alone we shall lay
Gone but not forgotten
Until that glorious day
When we all will awake and walk away
So my friend you will know
When the end is near.

Jeremy Spain

What Is Faith?

Faith is what's left,
when hope is all gone.
Faith is a prayer,
that life will go on.
Faith is a smile ,
when your heart is in tears.
Faith is courage,
when you shudder with fears.
Faith is trust,
when you've been betrayed.
Faith is patience,
when you've been delayed.
Faith is warmth,
when a hand clasp turns cold.
Faith is a spirit,
when the body grows old.
Faith is a rainbow,
when the sky is so black.
Faith is love,
calling you back.

Ellen Kelley

Assurance

Once upon a lifetime dreary,
When my heart was sore and weary,
Called I then upon my Lord,
Said, "I take you at your word"
And he healed me, made me strong,
Proved the evil one was wrong
When he thought to wreck my life
With heavy sorrow and with strife.
O Lord, what joy to know you're there
And always answer earnest prayer.

Anna Cottman Davis

My Entry:

There are times
when I wish
I lived in a tree house
high upon a hill
near the shore.
Where the grass
in its greenness
is higher than my knees.

And the winding path
consists of nothing
but the brownness of broken grass
that only my footsteps ever feel.

And, upon my door
a wreath of roses,
their color fading faster
as the new sun's warmth
wraps 'round their petals.

Janice L. Hillesheim

I Close My Heart

I close my heart
When others are near.
I close my heart
Because of fear.

I close my eyes
So I can't see
If they're really
Lying to me.

I close my mind
To their words
For fear that they'll
Fly away like the birds.

When I close my
Mind, heart, and eyes
With each passing moment,
A part of me dies.

No words of love
For me to hear
Till I open up
And find you here.

Anicia Bergeron

Mountain Echoes

Take me to that place,
Where eagles circle the sun;
And redwoods soar boundless to my eyes.

Where arrows of light
Pierce my soul,
And scatter leafs of gold.

Where the air is sweet
To my senses,
And the sky is of a true blue.

Where squirrels hurry,
And lizards bask
In the morning splendor.

Where the falls drop,
Crystal beads of amber hues.

Where leaves softly veil the earth;
And only the whispering winds are heard.

Cecilia Garcia Erickson

First Snow Of Season

'Twas mid December - last of year
When snow began to fall;
It stuck to windows - side and back
And several cars did fall.

I drove alone - my cat was home
Both dry and surly warm;
In coat of fur that closely fits;
Out window, saw the storm.

The snow continued coming down
To depth of six or more;
With shovel, cleaned the snow off drive
And wished that rain would pour.

The sun did melt the snow somewhat
Reveals uncut tall grass;
Perhaps the sun will warm the earth
I'll need to wear sun glass.

But showers fell for several days and
melted all the snow;
The Holidays have come and gone - no
balls of snow to throw.

But spring is still a distance off; I'm sure
we'll get more snow;
I love to view the winter scene - thru glass
of bungalow.

Emil J. Doubek

c'est la vie

that's what they say
when something goes
wrong.
an excuse.
for what?
for troubles we have?
for something we can't
do anything about?
c'est la vie.
why do we make
excuses?
why does it have to be this way?
c'est la vie.

Elizabeth A. Kreckow

Celestial love

I recall a most peaceful night
when the stars were thick and the
satellites rode the skies. There we
were, you and I in an endless
summer night.

The moonlight lit the world
around as bright as the love you
hold. Your skin so toned, the
moonbeams shown, hinting the same
colors of the Autumn that's coming.

A dream it seemed, to be in the
presence of two such precious things,
the purity and the beauty, like what
I see in you.

It's memories like these that one
can cherish forever, and hope it will
repeat again and again. For in a
love like ours, it surely will.

Jeffrey S. Dodd

Another Day

Colors stretch across the sky
When they're there I wonder why
The world is full of pain and hate
And how we can find Heaven's Gate
Living in this world of sin
Never caring why or when
Where children starve and madmen kill
Innocence dies and people will
Go to any length at all
To obtain a thing so small
This place where trees fall down and die
Pollution streaks across the sky
Wars rage on for years and years
Each night dreaming of the fears
Wondering how much we can stand
Sleeping and waking in this land
Living here among the pain
Thinking just of what we gain
The colors slowly fade away
And pain comes for another day

Jennifer Marie Judge

Our Daddy

Our Daddy left us
When we were young.
Growing up without him,
We'll it had to be done.
Mommy knew he was going
To be called that day.
Mommy knew he was passing away.
We didn't understand
When we saw her pray.
You and I wanted to know, WHY?
WHY? he couldn't stay.
Sometimes life throws you an Awful Curve,
So do the best that you can do.
We Love you and Miss you Dad,
And we hope, you always knew
That We'll always love and miss you daddy.
Even, with a broken heart too.

Dorothy P. Delaware

Can You See Into My Soul?

Can you see into my soul
When you gaze into my eyes?
Can you feel my trembling heart
As my hand within your lies?
Do you fear the same as I
What fate may hold in store?
Do you try to call out "STOP"
As your heart cries out for more?
Do you feel the rushing wind?
Does it take your breath away?
Do you feel the sun-kissed sand
As waves come in to play?
Beneath the hand of God we stand
Alone within the crowd,
Fearful...joyful...hopeful, too,
As we pledged our vows aloud.
Do you feel the kiss of angel wings?
Are we safe within the fold?
And as you gaze into my eyes
Can you see into my soul?

Carol Erhardt

Far Away

Far away, that's where you are
When you look at the sky
You see a twinkling star

You tell yourself how much we had
But, when you think of it
You're left quite sad

Far away, watching night skies glow
You think to yourself
How our hearts use to flow

I still want to thank you
For the times we had together
My memories of you
I'll cherish forever.

Elizabeth Ann K. Rodrigues

Died

All night long on my bed
Where dogs bark cats meow
The whistle of my mom calling
Calls and cries unendingly
Like some lost children
In tears and trouble
Hunting for my life
  Keep it together, I said
  Keep it together, Pa said
  Keep it together, Ma said
My life has died.

I see my parents
  What's wrong?
Their crying
What have I done?
  Ma I'm sorry!
  Pa I'm sorry!

Brandie McDonald

Left All Alone

Why have you left me?
Where have you gone?
I really do miss you,
But your memory lives on.
God, thought that it was meant to be
To take your heart away
From me.
I miss your kind words, and
Your sympathy.
Now there is no one left
To understand me,
You'll always have a place in my heart
Where I know we shall
Never be apart.
You will never be forgotten
But always missed,
Now to see you again would
Be my only wish.

Ann Lilienkamp

What Christmas Means To Me

I love to think of Christmas
With Santa and his elves
And decorated Christmas trees
and toys upon the shelves
But there's another meaning
To think of Christmas morn
That one bright night in Bethlehem
Christ our Lord was born

Barbara Lee Davidson

My Big Oak Tree

Under the oak tree
where the cows go
moo and the blue birds
flew I read a book about
captain hook and in that
book about captain hook
I read about a magic
boat that shook. The
boat shook because of
the mermaids under the
sea one was almost
as pretty as me but
nothing is as pretty
as my big oak tree.

Amy Carr

"The Grimm"

Where do you go when there's no
where to run?
Where do you go when there's no
where to hide?
You can try to run if you can but the
grimm somehow catches up with
you and reaches out his hand
for his hand is the hand of death,
that comes to take you on your
longest journey ever.
For the grimm love's nor does he hate
anyone, he is only the messenger of
death coming to take you on your
longest journey ever and to tell you
that your time is up.
The grim will lead you on a
road to heaven or hell.

Brandy Chatman

Rainbow

I stroll quietly on the shore.
Where waves rush to the bank and roar.
The obscure clouds take command.
White waves are defeated stand.
The thunder follows a bright light.
Confused sea birds lose their sight.
The house boat close by moves away.
I hear on it the victims pray.
Rain starts with full force.
Nature shakes within its course.
A vain hope rises to subdue.
Cry begins between me and you.
Ambiance is harsh and intense.
Rushing waves are tall and immense.
Nothing there looks divine.
Nasty lightening is the only shine.

Suddenly the storm stops the blow.
A crevice divides the sky for show.
Sudden light in the middle glow.
It is not the lightening, but the rainbow.

Ellie K. Belfiglio

Alone

Alone, all alone
With nothing to do
Or say. Why must we
Be all alone, and
Why must we hunger
For love? Why, why
Must we have to be
Alone?

Alison Hagedorn

"Conquering A New Day"

Thus A New Day has arrived
Which does have its differences,
As we surge forward armed
With life's past experiences.

Realizing that each bottle
has no guarantee we will win,
But soldiers of courage except
the challenges over and over again.

For each of our mistakes is
only a temporary stepping stone,
It increases our wisdom and gives
us stronger faith to journey on.

I may not accomplish all
the things I think I should,
But my soul will be content
knowing I did all I could.

And if the difference I make
is only in a small degree,
I shall gain comfort in trying,
for that's my victory.

Franklin Smith

Dreams

The music pours in
while life drains away —

The feeling is mutual;
and so starts the day —

With eyes close shut;
along with the mind —

I hunt for the peace
I'll eventually find —

The peace is broken by
a lone whispered word —

"Om" says the voice;
"I can see, for I heard" —

The mind was made for
more than just thinking;

I turn off the lights,
and again start the sinking —

I drift off and dream
that peace has been found;

I wake up and realize,
I'm still on the ground.

Annette Scotto

"My Mom"

There once was a child named Rose
Who didn't have stylish clothes.
She studied real hard
To gain some knowledge
But her parents couldn't afford
To send her to college.
She worked by day
And went to college at night
And tried so hard to do everything right.
No, she wasn't quite invincible
But now she's a school's
New vice principal.

Billy Givens

Untitled

To whom ever shall read this:
Who ever thought it would
last this long, long summer night's of
friendly conversation two lovers
keep apart by society. A kiss in
the darkness that will last for
eternity, but some how eternity
ended with out a warming a simple
good-bye was all that was said.
But how could it be over?
How could a love so deep get buried
in the sand? Well the waves
uncover the truth? Or will it
stay there burning itself
deeper, and deeper until the
memory itself is gone...

Jamie Pelley

A Birthday Wish

Happy birthday to my mother,
Who is like no other.

She takes the time to care,
She used to cut my hair.

She goes the extra mile,
And does it with a smile.

The hardest worker I know around,
Very intelligent, wise, and profound.

And though we span the miles,
I remember the good times and smiles.

Especially when we talk on the phone,
And she reminds me I'm missed at home.

I say to my friends -
I'll be happy when college ends.

Because I miss my mother
Who is better than any other.

She's the best above the rest,
And always tries her very best.

Eugene Forehand

A Squashing Tale

There once was a woman,
Who weighed 1,000 tons.
She was so very big,
She squashed her own sons.

The towns people were horrified.
She was charged with 1st degree murder.
So she squashed the jury and judge,
So no one could hurt her.

She squashed the whole town,
And the United States.
She squashed the whole world,
As flat as a plate.

No one could stop her,
There was nobody left.
Then all of a sudden she stumbled,
And squashed her own self.

Anna Duren

The Shepherd

He's the great Shepherd
Whom carries a staff
And leads all His sheep
Down the bright path

To the land we call Paradise,
Or Heaven above,
Where no evil dwells
Only those of us whom love.

Don't listen to Satan,
Whose words do entice,
For that path is of sin,
And you're caught in the vice.

Only the Lord can forgive
The things that we do.
For He has great mercy.
Grace and love too.

He is the Christ,
The Light in the dark.
Whose love is everlasting,
Which He proved with the ark.

Christopher Daniel Messer

What Is Life

What is life...what is it all about
Why are we here, upon this earth?
There must be a reason, without doubt,
Some deeper meaning to birth.
Do we live just for life's sake
I wonder if that could be true;
Perhaps we are part of something great
Just tiny atoms - me and you.
Could there be a puzzle of universal size
Of which we are pieces so small,
Too minute to even realize
The grandeur of it all?!

Erna Kaluza

Critical Mass

God of unbearable beauty,
Why must you
  Come and go...
  Come and go...
  Come and go...?

Is it because
  the only absolute
  is that there **are** no absolutes?

Or simply because you are so unbearable?

Alex Tolleson

Undeserving But Justified

What do I or anyone deserve
Who lives by God's creation?
Success by my work? - No!
Good health by my care? - Nay!
Happiness through our efforts? - Never!
Heaven itself by our merit? Impossible!
All this are gifts of God.

Therefore I stand undeserving
  With all creation,
Justified by that fact
  Of God's will. I am.

James Edward Roche

The Source Of My Reasoning

I long to search for reasons
Why, on earth, am I here?
If I do not find the answer
It will bother me, I fear.

So, I search through books,
And question the learned minds;
But from all these sources
No answers do I find.

Yet, the answer is so simple.
It comes from a source of old.
If we, but read through its pages,
All of our answers were foretold.

This source of my reference
Is a small yet simple book;
Yet throughout its pages,
The wisdom is there, you need but look.

This book is called the Bible,
Sent down from God above;
And if we follow the teachings
We will abide in God's unending love,

Frances Earnestine Turner

Dare To Discover Poetry

In the years that pass poetry
will last in the hearts of all who
listen to the loving words, the
heartbroken moments, and the
joyous sound of laughter.
With each minute it will send you
away where reality is forbidden.
The place you go no time will
last for it is not allowed; such
fast pace of the human race will
stay behind, while you float
with the sweet sound of poetry
composed by the author's mind.

Amy Loving

Dark Tinted Glass

A driver whose car has dark tinted glass
Will never get an "A" in my class.
I can't see the fool
Holding the tool
Known as a steering wheel.

Behind this arcade
Sits a person afraid
To face reality
With positive morality.
They'd rather hide.

Edward E. Powell

From The Ground Came A Tiny Seed

From the ground came a tiny seed,
Wind and water it will need.
The sun is a special glow,
It gives light to make it grow.
From the farm to the store,
We couldn't ask for anymore.
Grain and feed came from that seed.
Grace and love came from above.
Grace and grain fulfill our needs,
And from the ground came a tiny seed.

Cathy Gene Schultz

Morning Fair

The early light of morning fair,
Wind blowing off the calm sea.
Building up a warmth inside,
All is calm, no one's there.
Making you glad, just to be,
On His planet which we reside.
Light approaching, darkness recedes,
Half is light, the other dark.
Twinkling stars are left to die,
But the world sunlight needs.
Impressed by this I remark,
"Who's work is this by?"

Jason Turner

Lost

I think about her always
Wishing she could stay.
I think about her laugh
her humor and her kindness
toward others.
Although she has gone
to a better place,
I will always miss her.
I will always be lost
in a world of sorrow
without her.

Jamie Udelhofen

Where Is Justice In Death

Oh such a good man
With a heart of gold
Another man dies
Cause he's a little too old
Disease takes more
Than we can guess
Others are taken
by someone's quest
One persons hand
Can end it all
To them - it's an ending wall
There is no choice
Of color or creed
We'll leave life's bosom
With questionable deed
So on our last and final hour
The thought occurs that
No matter how we're destined to go
We feel no justice of death
Fast or slow

Delane Warzala

The Vanguard

The vanguard arrayed
  with armour
with staples high above
  the ground;
the arrested welding
unsolved, severs
the mechanics of bolts
where leverage is uncertain.
The shield protects the eyes
  from the rays
and denials control the
  prisoner
lined in alignment with
  the lathe
  with swishing sounds,
  always encumbered in heights,
  and tall with mounds.

Charles Lamar Nelson

Soft Feet

On soft feet she owns the Night.
With eyes aglow she treads light,
With tail awag she keeps watch
From the sill or the tall hutch.
Through the dark hours she keeps eye,
Whilst I in slumber's hold lie.
Ever she keeps vigil and peace,
Till morning comes and dreams cease.

Mice and other pests, beware!
She'll not allow you a dare,
Or the least foolish foray.
She'll take you in sport of play,
Then bring you straight to my bed,
And put you...right by my head!

James R. Poyner

Dis-Lilie-He-A

  To be in an ocean of paper
with no ability to make a wave
  Drifting in the defunctional
wind of fate
  My self embarrassed sewn together
by a raging ego of violence
  A life intoxicated by the
endless lines of not understanding
  Political sun using me as a
shade for profit.
  I am nothing more than pure
innocent,
  That never heard the bird
chirp with knowledge.
  With virtue that I do not
know how to use.
  Incapable of plagiarism
for I am stupid
  Thriving on common sense

Craig Coursen

Confusion

An ever quicker spin,
with no way to win,
unanswered questions,
with unlearned lessons,
what seems to be,
is not to be,
a multi-colored swirl,
caused by a girl,
a key that doesn't fit,
confusion does not quit.

Jeremy A. Guillemette

A Morbid Cry

Sitting alone in the dark,
with nothing to look at,
no one to talk to.
A dreadful fate passes over me,
I am dying.
No one can help me,
nothing can save me.
I am in desperate need of a friend,
a friend that I can talk to,
a friend that I can love.
If I cannot find this friend,
I will lose all hope,
and then,
and only then,
will I be damned in hell
FOREVER.

Sabia Ergot

The Ocean's Blue

The sun rises
with pink and orange hues,
melting with the ocean's
waves of blue.

The sun shines
brilliant all day through,
across the ocean's
body of blue.

The sun sets
streaking the sky anew,
meshing with the nighttime
shades of blue.

The moon shines
across the ocean too,
a bright, beaming light
dancing on blue.

Christine A. Sheehan

You And I!

Our future together, is finally here.
With you by my side, there is no fear.
I love you
I need you
I cherish our love.
I want you
to hold you
to captivate our love.
A simple touch, never questioned
A hidden fear, never mentioned
Our love is stronger,
than life itself.
When I look in your eyes,
My heart forever
M
E
L
T
S!

Jamie Mayer

The Same Sky

Little star so bright,
won't you fall down
and be my friend?
Little shine in the sky,
won't you be a friend
and fall on down?
Land down unto my ground,
so I can burn my feet
on the concrete while she speaks.
Do you realize your overwhelming heat?
Little star so bright,
You will soon say good bye.
You do every single night.
Then dreams take our sights.
A moon lingers in the same sky.
This man's shine
is devious,
but a dejected symbol takes time,
so I wish the sun was a friend of mine.

Christopher John Fabbri

Words

Words can be sharp
Words can be dull
Words can be sweet
Words can express love.

Words can be hurtful
Words can console
Words can be uplifting
Words can extol.

Words can make promises
Great if fulfilled
Words can cause pain
That takes time to heal.

Words can bring joy
Words can be fun
Words speak of our virtues
When our life is done.

There are words to live by
There are words we should heed
But words are only words
If not backed by our deeds.

Glen D. Parker

Rumors

Softly dropped are the
words we hear. From the
grape vine of yesteryear.
Secrets are told without
a singe thought. Words
that we have not forgot.

No regard for wrong or right.
True or false, words hold us tight.
Spoken poisons change our mind,
leaving common sense behind.

Jacob J. Payne

If

If I was a swan and you were a dove,
Would we still be in love?
If you were a dog and I was a cat,
Would it be just that?
If I was the ocean and you were the sea,
Would you still love me?
If you were never and I was forever,
Would we still be together?
If all these "If's" were true,
Would we be true?

Cindy Waters

"Dew Drop"

Roses are red, pink, white,
yellow, but only one of these
shows the true beauty of the
morning, the red. As the
sparkling dew drop slowly rolls
down the lightly fuzzed green
leaf, and only one destination.
To the soft moist morning soil
where it is absorbed by its soft
touch when it comes to a stop
and hits the soil at such an hour
of the morning.

Christi McCabe

A Baby

Baby why do you cry?
You are around your mother
most of the day. Do you miss
somebody? You probably have
a brother or sister.
Do you like to be a
boy or girl? If you are a boy
you probably like to be a boy.
If you are a girl you probably
like to be a girl. I just
wonder about that.
What do you say
when you talk baby talk?
When you say goo- goo- ga- ga-
You probably mean that you
are thirsty. Sometimes
when you laugh you laugh funny.
Are you in baby land?

Jennifer Amber Peich

"You Are"

You are my tender love.
You are my fear.
You are my happiness.
And my tears.

You are my sorrows.
You are my prayers.
You are my worries.
And my cares.

You are my thoughts,
You are my mind.
You are my future,
And I find...

That there is no-one
I'd rather be.
As long as you are
here with me.

Angela Marr

My Son

In this make believe world my son,
You can see what you want to see,
Like candy coated daisy's,
or a rainbow colored tree.

Just set yourself to thinking
and slowly turn around,
and what you've always wanted
is what you will have found.

There's a river flowing slowly
up a rolling hill,
the waters taste of lemonade
and you can drink your fill.

And you can see a sunrise
in the afternoon,
or ride a flying pony
to a picnic on the moon.

If you'd like to go there son,
just close your sleepy eyes,
and dream of cotton candy
in bright blue morning skies.

Diana Crim

Love

When love is in the air,
you can smell it.
When love has no fear,
you can tell it.
When love is forever,
you will know it.

From your heart,
you can see,
that your love is with me.
Love will be there, forever.

Heather Brown

Masterful Quality

It doesn't matter to what religion
you profess-

It doesn't matter how you choose
to dress-

It doesn't matter how much wealth
you possess-

It doesn't matter as to your intellectual
success-

Arms open wide conquers a feeling like
dross-

Mindfully, God formed us in the sign
of the cross.

Julia A. Pinkasewicz

Insanity

You're sitting there all alone.
You want to leave; want to go home.
You hear laughter, and crying too.
You realize-the crying is you.
You look around, you see no door.
You look up. You stand no more.
You pound and pound as you shout,
"Remove these walls! Let me out!"
No one answers to your cries.
The laughter heard was all lies.
You feel it strong; the pain - so true!
You weep again, as you always do.
Suicide you think about.
You feel it's the only way out.
You take the trip and land in hell.
You should've waited! Farewell, farewell!

Carla Morgan-Haase

Mother's Day Gift

Since the first day I opened my eyes
You were there for me.
As I took my first steps
You behind me I could see.
My first day of school,
How frightened, how scared.
But you took me by my hand
And I knew you really cared.
Now that I am all grown up,
I feel I need you more each day
To point me in the right direction,
To show me the right way.
So I say these words with all my heart
My love for you will never end.
Because you're more than just my mother.
You're my very best friend.

Jesse Vela

Wedding Night

I close my eyes and feel
your gentle kisses upon my face.
I reel from sweet emotions
in your loving warm embrace.

The sky is dark and dreamy
filled with bright and shiny stars,
And in the shimmering candlelight
the night sounds become ours.

Our beating hearts entwine as one
this night that we have wed,
And you've caressed my yearning soul
upon this feather bed.

When tousled hair and sleepy eyes
greet me in morning light,
I kiss you...yes, I truly know
I'm drenched in your delight!

My passion for you fills my mind
and never will it part.
My precious love, you have so sweetly
touched my tender heart.

Claudia Boden

Thundering

What happens when the fragments of
your life crumble and fall apart?
Are they scattered by the winds to the
four corners of the earth—
Do they remain where they fall, to be
pecked at by birds and predators-
Do the animals pause to sniff and
urinate on them?
Or does the good Lord see the fragments
and gently piece them together again?
Has life with all its struggles been
for naught?
Does anyone know—does anyone care?
Will we find happiness with the Lord
in his kingdom in heaven?
Do the good guys really wins?
Tell me— I want to know?

Grace H. Auman

To The One I Love

You have made my days happy one's
your thoughtful in every way
you're by my side when I need you
each and every day.

You can read my thoughts
and chase away my fears
You reach out and touch me
and kiss away my tears.

When I'm lonely
I close my eyes and see
The two of us together
the way it was meant to be.

Doris J. Jones

Magellan's Dream

Once, brave men went on a trip
Which was not for the fainthearted.
They took off for parts unknown,
And came back to where they started.

Carlos Montorfano

My First Love

You're my every breath I take.
You're my every heart beat.
You're the light in my day.
The shadow in every
step I take.
The love I have
for you will
always be true.
I know I'd be a
fool if I'd walk
away from you.
This love I have
inside, I'd take
it all and give it
all to you.
For you are at
last the love I have
longed for.

Barbara DeBottis

For Carol

I'm over here
You're over there
Write me a letter
If you care.

Send me a kerchief
That I can wear
Because I'm over here
And you're over there.

Mail me a ribbon
Untied from your hair
That will reach from me here
To you over there.

Send me your love
Which we will share
Though I'm over here
And you're over there.

Frank R. Tangherlini

Maybe...

Maybe the scream of her
who is doing away with herself
is so clear and coming from the heart.
Like a sob breaking to the air
and you can not look aside.
This sound pierces you like lightning.
Maybe the scream of her
who is doing away with herself
is such like this sound
which comes from inside me:
An infinite, painful scream
longing for love.

Eva Barati

My Friend And I

My friend and I, my friend and I
We cruise on through a friendly sky

I ask the moonbeams way up high
Do you remember my friend and I?

We often laugh, we even cry,
We often talk, my friend and I

We've traveled through some troubled times
We've had the best most other times

I ask the angels way up high
O please remember my friend and I.

Etta Kowalski

True Love

True love comes to us in our lifetime
we all will come face to face
with the one person in life
who would be our ideal mate
but for various reasons most never
get to actualize
the majesty of a true love's kiss
the wondrous fires that could burn deep inside
the magical tingling as true love
softly caresses the body and soul
or the firm yet gently sweet embrace
of a true loves hold
But I've been fortunate to recognize
the true love of my lifetime
no other love will I seek
no other love will I find
and whether or not my true love
ever chooses this love to be
I will always be grateful for the feeling
that this love has given me

Debora Mack

"A Crown Of Thorns"

They say there's no hope for the evils on earth.
We are taught this to death, from birth.
They hunger for food though they have none.
Those who want peace face the barrel of a gun.
The ones who stare upward will never be shunned.
For the one they pray to give us his son.

This son healed the sick and raised children from the dead.
He even fed thousands with only fish and bread.
He showed us the light; it was sinister they said.
Then he died on a cross with thorns on his head.
But don't be afraid if you're horrible or mean.
Read the book of John, chapter three, verse sixteen.

Jarod Munn

To My "Pen Pal"

"You" came into my life, a few short days ago.
We exchanged cards and letters- "you" found that I take
time to know!

Hearing from "you" now is an accepted thing
Each word from "You" is like a breath of spring.
Your cheering words always chase the blues and rain
It always seems that time stands still
Until "You" write again.

I wait anxiously for the mail, for beside your letters
The sun seems pale!
"You" are in my thoughts at different times of the day
And, interrupt my concentration in the various games
that I play!

Like all good things this ode must end
And so I say to "You"; "Stay sweet my friend!!
My days will be lonely - my nights will be blue
Until the mailman brings another letter from you!!

Arnold Smith

"My Grandchildren"

What a blessing to have them
What a blessing to love them
What a blessing to watch them grow
What a blessing to teach them
What a blessing to reach them
What a blessing to learn from them
What a blessing to be able to assist them

Dorothy M. Crowder

The Void

From nothing we are born into life
We gather experience of joy and strife

The sums of these experiences be
That which makes up you and me

For in the universe there can be only one
Unique are each of us under the sun

And if this be truth I speak above
Then is it not also in sadness and love
Just a game of chance played from above

With combinations of people in joy and strife
Who seek to find only the best in life

But if in all things one does not share
To risk, to give, to take the dare

Then who is to say what could have been
The best of one's destiny to lose or win
For from nothing is where we begin!

Christopher Stanley

Under Love

Together, under evergreen mountains
We sing as rain caresses our bodies
While we dance through orchards of love and despair
Our souls touch one another in the
Clouds of heaven as our eyes sleep in dreams of desire
Holding you, feeling the warmth of
Sunrise in the grasp of meeting passion
Let our lips touch above waterfalls so divine
While wind washes our tears of joy
into valleys of the rose

Honey flows over our hearts
As romance whispers in your ear
The stars gaze down upon us
as we drink thoughts of twilight
Your beauty shines forever,
As does my love for you.

Christopher David Grossnickle

Mothers Or Others

I know mothers are special because they did give us birth.
We weren't put here without a purpose on earth. Even before we were,
Jesus had a plan, and whatever it is, if we desire it, we can.
I believe we all know what we're suppose to do, and it's our Christian
duty to see it through. As long as Jesus is in it, it can not fail,
for God's ship will always sail.
Our mothers didn't bore us for no reason at all, and Jesus will
guide us if we'll remove that wall.
We must be willing to do what he has in store,
or else our Christian walk well be a bore.
My real mother I never knew, but I know she had to be special too.
God blessed me with a grand mother and she was grand.
I feel she was the best in land.
God gave her 92 years to live, yes her motherly love had plenty
of wisdom to give.
Today, she's in peace I know, because if we love Jesus it has to show.
Mothers can be our very best friend next to Jesus our Lord,
and our children are our blessing, and such a great reward.
So let's enjoy each other while we live each day, and don't forget
to thank Jesus for the ones he sent our way.

Betty Lou Davis

The Voice

I speak as a generation's disembodied voice.
We who when born were given very little choice.

The ozone is being depleted,
The Berlin Wall defeated.

The Arabs are making friends with the Jews.
Yet no one is safe from the evening news.

There is hunger, violence and war the world over.
Free sex is dead and everyone questions and fears their lover.

Political apathy runs rampant, unemployment is on the rise.
The hubble telescope becomes our eyes as we focus on the skies.

The world has indeed become a global village,
Gossip and scandal roar and spread like quicksilver,
world ecology effected by local spillage,
the voices of nature have become but a whisper.

We must decide to care. To look into the eyes as the thousand dies,
that's the dare. To not allow ourselves to become jaded,
To understand all that's been traded. To learn from the mistakes of
others, to become better fathers and mothers, sisters and brothers.
To understand that all is not lost.
But we are the generation that must begin to pay the cost.

Christine Dickson

The Highest Degree

When we reach the highest degree,
we will become experts in a field
that lacks common sense,
but it is intellectually sound...

How much can we bear
from work from the intellect
as we give whatever and whatfor
to every problem under the sun.

Complicating life can be easy
as long as a degree is required.
Courses upon courses of complete nonsense
in order to become experts in our field.

Sports, religion, and history
have been explained over and over
until it is running out of ears,
when we reach to our highest degree.

Gene Kaelin

What To Take On An Amazon Jungle Trek?

The guidebook says to take sunglasses, sunblock, insect repellent;
wear long pants, long sleeves, and hiking boots.

Under a cloudless sky we boated to the path in the jungle
some forty minutes away from the Ariau Tower.
There we trekked briefly observing the canopy overhead
and the dense floor of the forest.

As we emerged from the woods, the sky had changed its color,
and dark clouds dominated the horizon in the west;
we started going as fast as the little motor would take us
straight into the storm.

Before long, rain drops started to fall gently
until they changed to pelting rain stinging our skin;
we grabbed life jackets to shield our faces.

The loudest thunder that I ever heard,
the most brilliant lightning that I ever saw,
accompanied the downpour in a great display of sound and light.

Utterly drenched, we huddled on the floor of the little boat as
the temperature dropped markedly and we shivered in the midst of
Nature's show of grandeur.
What to take on a jungle trek? a raincoat.

Emma Leigh Goodwin

"Congratulations"

To that sister and brother in-law of mine on your golden
Wedding day
Not every-man can wake-up and say
Good morning to a bride of a fifty year marriage

A bride that has been his joy his pride!!
And by his -Side- of her own free will!,
Yes!! A wife that has helped him over the hill of -Life-,
for over fifty years!!

A wife still keeps house, cooks for -Him-,

Yet indeed thou cup is overflowing
With two daughters Vicky and Charlotte and three
Grand-sons may the Lord bless and guide you both all the
rest of your years.

Fred T. Boberg Sr.

I Have A Secret

I have a secret, I want to tell. But first I look in a deep dark
well. I love your kisses, the way you hold my hand.
I have a secret, I want to tell. But first I look in a deep dark
well. When we are together, I like the warmth you give me.
I have a secret, I want to tell. But first I look in a deep dark
well. You kiss my face, neck and breast, giving me fillings of
peace. I have a secret, I want to tell. But first I look in a deep
dark well. When you make love to me everything seems right.
I have a secret, I want to tell. But first I look in a deep dark
well. I watch as you slept, your body moving with dreams. I
have a secret, I want to tell. But first I look in a deep dark well.
The smell of body with your cologne wash over me. I have a
secret, I want to tell. But first I look in a deep dark well. The
words flow from me into the deep dark well.
"I love him can't you tell."

Dorothy A. Valdez

Snowfall

After a snowfall, all that I saw
were fields and trees covered with fluff, snow covered stuff.
The squirrels in their burrows, snug and warm,
the bees in their hive, all in a swarm.
Snowflakes slowly falling to the ground, making no sound.
Trees covered with snow, very pretty though.
I make a snowman nice and white, when the sun shines on it, it is
bright.
Snow is on top of all our roofs, tracks in the snow made of deer
hooves.
This must be a dream and I know it, nothing could be as
beautiful
as this! Snow is everywhere, and I am just sitting there, watching
this beautiful scene, the snow is so clean.
Sing this poem like a song, because pretty soon the snow will
be gone

Danielle Bradley

The Window

I look out the window.
What do I see paper people, houses,
and trees. If the sun turned to fire,
they would burn to ash. I would
watch them blow in the wind.
If the wind was music, what
would it play? Whispers of sweetness,
would send lonely leaves flying
in the wind. That makes the trees
dance to a sweet tone. And at the end
the wind will stop, silence will
cover the world. Music will play no more.
So I look out the window.
What do I see?

Cassandra Kapsos

Dreams

I dreamt that you and I
were under the moonlit sky.

You wrapped your arms around me so tight
I wished you could hold me all night.

We talked about nothing,
but oh, some feeling was there,
for when I looked into your eyes,
you had some special glare.

For a few moments we stare
making another move we do not dare.
Because this is one of those moments that is very rare.

I woke up from the dream
And rose out of bed.

Thinking in my head
are the thoughts and memories of the night
wishing they will happen
and oh, they just might.

Andrea Knoch

Despair

Oh Black Man, where ya gonna go?
What 'cha gonna do? Blood oozing,
drainin', losing the ones we love.

Making us feel things forgotten, but
not forgiven, rage, unrest, hurt, deep,
pain, makin' us weak, strength seepin' away.

Oh Black Man, just ebbing away, where you
gonna be? When it's time to stand up and
be counted who's gonna have yo' number?

Love's fading, runnin' cold on the streets,
helpless, hopeless, no dreams of being free.
Once a little boy, now just an echo of the
man you should be.

Where's the you, you always needed to be?
Oh Black Man where's your reality?

Belicia Simon

What's To Be Said 'Bout Death So Soon?

My friend is dying. I must go to her. She expects me soon.
What do I say?
Our eyes will meet, and in that moment of soul meeting soul,
We both will know that there be no pretenses, no dodging games,
Only stark reality of that which is. What do I say?
Do we start with the present? "How are you doing?"
Well, what is she doing, but dying soon?
What can she say? What can I say? What does one say?

Or do we examine that which dwells in the past?
The things that last. Our toddlers tricks. The teenagers kicks.
Where did the years go, oh, clock that ticks? What do I say?

Do we challenge tomorrows? Those seeking ways? Spoken of days?
Now where are those days which cease to be for her and not me?
What do I say?

She smiles and sighs. The look in her eyes says it's enough that
I realize:
There's no need to speak when two hearts seek each other in loving
goodbyes.

For what can she say? What do I say? We're grateful we have yet
today.

Jeanine Gordon

Across The Sea

Across the sea, the beautiful sea
What do I see? What do I see?
A ship with sails of purest white
On its way to England - a magnificent sight!

Across the sea the choppy sea,
What do I see? What do I see?
A castle high on moors of old
Truly a sight for the eye to behold.

Across the sea, the beckoning sea,
What do I see? What do I see?
A sailor with a maiden fair
with silken ribbons in her hair.
He holds her waist so firm secure
For they're in love in a different era.

Then I awake - twas but a dream-
the salty mysterious sea of green.

Chris Kulow

Twenty One

When a son grows up — sets out on his own
What does he take when he leaves home?
His clothes from the closet, his books from the self
His trophies, your money — is anything left?
His car with its dents, rattle and noise
The "busy" from the telephone, house full of boys
His place at the table, his step in the hall
His youthful exuberance and that's not all
The sounds he called music, wet towels on the floor
Midnight snacks, girls at the door
What he takes from the house is just a small part
A son, when he leaves, takes half of your heart.

Faye Trail Deaton

Untitled

I'm deeply sorry to hear about your mother.
What happened to her just wasn't right.
She had fought with that man so he wouldn't
hurt another.
He went a little further this time than just
a fist fight.

She tried to protect you against him.
She thought she could help him because she was his wife.
The next thing she saw was a light that appeared dim,
Rushing her to the hospital, she had lost her life.

Think of the memories that you two have shared.
All the great times and bad times,
And just know that she cared.
Words, alone, can't describe the feelings you're
having in these few lines.

Beth A. Rasche

How Will You Go Down In History?

Life, Joy, Pain, Sorrow,
what if you should die tomorrow?
Have you left your mark in the ages,
or are you just another book with blank pages?
Family, friends, lovers too,
would they still remember you?
Or, when you're chucked in the clay,
will you be forgotten that same day?
So, take a chance and you shall see
what this life has in store for thee.
Either do or don't, skip the maybe's,
'cause in the end your food for daisy's!

Brett A. Davis

"Good-Bye"

What happened to the love we use to share,
What happened to the special way we use to show how much we care.

We use to sit around and talk all day into the night,
laying in bed holding each other ever so tight.

Planning our future together and talking about all of our hopes and dreams, we were so close me and you together just like a team.

We laughed a lot together we cried together some to, and no one could break that special love shared between me and you.

Our problems grew greatly they got worse everyday, there was no more I'm sorry we started running away.

And now we are so angry and so bitter toward each other, we can no longer stay together, we are no longer good for each other.

We can no longer forgive or forget the pain we put each other through, it's time to move on it over we are through.

My love for you will never completely fade away or die,
but now my darling my dear it's time to say "Good-bye".

Jennifer Hughes

Dawn

What sunshine is to the day so radiant,
What sunrise is to the morning,

What sunrise is to the morning,
light the sky with brilliance
by smiling emitting waves of sunrays
that brightens all dazzled days
such gleam, as seen in a lustrous portrayal
of luxurious beauty
nonetheless breathtaking
an awe beyond compare

A soft glow of effervescent jubilation
piercing the darkness of the night,
maintaining the embodiment of strength
the delicacy of tenderness
The warmth of passion
Dawn is a universal visibility of
wisdom.

James C. Moore

This Thanksgiving Day

This thanksgiving day as we bow our heads to pray,
What will you thank God for?
Will you thank him for you health that you still have,
but for others it has left?
Will you thank him for always having a full pantry,
When for some, there's was always empty.
Will you thank him for that nice house that gives
you shelter from the cold.
While there are people that are homeless and dying all alone.
Will you thank God for family and friends that have gathered here
to share all that you have, but for some is so rare.
Will you remember other thanksgivings that you had,
and that they were all good and none were bad.
This thanksgiving day as we begin to part,
let's let God give us an attitude of thanksgiving
every day in our hearts?

Christine L. Gray

Let's Talk

Hey you, over there
what's wrong?
I sense something is the matter
will you tell me?

I am the one of whom
you can talk to
I am a very trusting person and confidential
at that
You won't be made a fool of
if you decide to talk back

You just don't understand, do you?
that if you talk to me, I might confide
in you
I need to be listened to, too!

Tell me what's wrong and I'll tell you
what's wrong
So that we both can feel good
You have a reason to speak and so do I...
Let's talk!!

Cynthia L. Belcher

Sad Goodbye

Your brother took one look and said, "You look terrible,
what's wrong?"
Eventually, you told him, "It's AIDS, but don't tell
Dad and Mom."
Eight months you bore the secret, as it ate at your
insides.
Till the gauntness and weight loss and skin sores
wouldn't let you hide.
You couldn't open the car door, to drive yourself
to the doc;
And the man on the bus said, "Don't sit here, boy!
You is ugly! Get lost!"
When the folks took you home, you fingered the past,
and the future that wasn't to be.
You gave them your anger, your pain, and your love;
they gave you back all three.

"Keep it simple and plain, as my life has been —
the white sweater will do just fine."
You said it succinctly before you withdrew,
"It was the living I feared — not the dying."

Dora Forden

Rejoice

There will come a time
when birds will sing not,
flowers will wilt,
seas will dry up.
Bells to peal not. Shades of black..
hues fiery with blistering regrets,
of the time I did not, was not, could not.
Depression sealing out the light
the sun that giveth life.
Drop my slump, I shall, I will, I can...
Enter back into the life of birds a flight,
of flowers bloomed
of rolling seas
of music sweet...that I lament, tis a shame.
I live on
free
I live!

Desiree Whitaker White

Garden Work

I've felt myself to be invisible
when eyes in a crowd turned away
as a lover can who looks with blinded sight
and cannot sense the change.

I've felt my voice grow soft then silent
when dry canyon walls avert their echo ears
As a partner who does not give reply
and sends back lonely solitude.

I've also felt my fingers numb
when dark clouds of private pain rolled in
and took away a mate to some other place and time
where I could never go and safely stay.

And life crept slowly on this measured way
stealing away my sight and voice
and adding callous by the layer to youthful fingertips
curling up together finally into fists.

When I had traveled far and long enough
I returned to the garden of my soul.
From there I saw a lily, a mirror to my heart
a soulmate seeking me.

Frank Frimodig

Soliloquy On A Winter Night

Who can forget those desperate weeks
When first I learn to cope with sorrow.
Guilt regret remorse never came to mind.
Only the agony the disbelief the loneliness.
You were my best friend, my haven
My protection, my joy even my serenity.
For next to my Almighty God I loved you.
But it was not always sunshine
Sometimes my Irish would erupt-
At the overcoat dumped on a chair
At the shirt left just lying there.
But oh for a hundred overcoats-
A thousand wrinkled shirts
Just to have you with me here
So many things to share.
And yet, I face a turning corner
A light I faintly see.
A kind of buoyancy returning.
Is it your gentle spirit,
Still guiding me?

Irene Brandt

Nostalgia

I lie resting and thinking of aimless things,
When from the distance a bell sounds its ring;
A breeze stirs in a nearby tree,
A bird wings away, and things seem to sing —-
And slowly, but surely, as if in a dream,
My childhood comes in, like waves on the sea,
And washes and washes over me.
I listen, and hear, and feel, and see
Those long-lost days
That used to be,
So sweet, so fragile, so fleetingly faint.
I grasp for them, but alas,
They're gone! They're gone!
Those bittersweet days,
Into the past and out of my reach,
Away and away
Till one would think
Them gone forevermore;
But no, I'll see them again,
I know, I know.

Beatrice Eagle Honeycutt

I Feel Life

Is there a name or word to explain?
When hours, days have passed and
Breasts are hard and body's aflame?

Tears and spilling.
It's pain, it's joy, it's heaven and it's hell.
Attention! It screams. Ecstasy swells.

Fire burn, emotions pour
The whole of it opens, closes, a crescendo!
There's rhythm, Melody tone, a private song.

All of the universe searches still
For tongue, hands, lips and more to feel.
Life! reality! Come again, again, again.

Juanita Marie Donahue

My Life Is A Mystery

My life is a mystery yet to unfold.
When I look back, I don't feel that old.
Thumbing thru pages of daily routines
I'm lost in confusion, too smart, it seems.
The more that I study, the less that I know.
Could I have started in front of before?
My child is far wiser, my parents are too.
Why, I can't even begin to keep up with the two.
Some say surrender, God's way is best.
Oh sure, I've tried that, in step with the rest.
Sounds simple, so tell me which line is shortest,
As usual, in all places, mine still is the slowest.
So harder I try, deeper I look,
But my life, as mystery, is still a closed book.

Indiana Watson

Mom's In The Rest Home

I went to visit mom in the rest home today.
When I started to leave, she asked me to stay.
I said, "Mom, I'm tired, I need to go on home".
She looked at me and asked, "Would you leave me here alone?"

I said, "No, Mom, I wouldn't do that to you"
I sat down beside her and thought, "What am I gonna do?"
"I'm not leaving now," I said, "I'm going to stay awhile."
I looked at her tired face. It was lit up with a smile,

After a few more minutes, I said to her again.
"Mom, I'm leaving soon". Then I told her when.
Her weary eyes looked up at me as though she seemed to know,
That I was getting tired and that I needed to go.

She stretched out her little hand and held mine very tight.
She whispered very softly, "Go on home tonight,"
I looked at her lying there and I started out the door,
I whirled around and said to mom, I'm staying 15 minutes more.

Then she said so softly, "That would be so sweet."
I looked down at her, she was sound asleep.
I bent down and kissed her and walked out the door,
Then I thought to myself, "I'm glad I stayed that 15 minutes more."

Eula Kirby

Winter

Winter is like a great white bird, settling on the land
Winter is when a soft snow covers all, like Gods protecting hand
Winter is when sparkling icicles glisten all around
Winter is the silent wilderness where you cannot hear a sound
Snowflakes softly fall and dance around the sky
Then the wind picks up, and through the air they fly
Winter is the cold air that chills your rosy face
What could be better than this wonderfully enchanting place?

Jennifer Casler

Ask Of My Children

When I'm old lonely, cheer me up
When my eyes are failing and I can't see, please see for me
When my skin is old and bruising, build a bubble around me
When I can't do for myself, do for me

If I become dependent on you, please find a place that will take care of me-
Like I took care of you

When you were babies, you kept me up nights and I didn't complain
When you fell down, I picked you up
When you needed me, I was always there
Now I need you to care for me, please be there

This is what I ask of thee because I love you and I know you love me
This is what I only ask of thee!

Crystal Sanchez

"That Night"

It was the eighth of April, 1994,
when my eyes met yours as I
walked in the door.
It must have been fate that
brought us together that night,
when the stars were shining and
the moon was bright.
As you held my hand and looked deep into my eyes,
I fell for you much harder than you realize.
When I think about you, my heart begins to ache,
You're the only habit that I can not break.
I'll never forgive myself for letting you go,
I regret it more than you will ever know.
I will try my best to forget about our fight,
But I can not forget what happened that night.

Bridget Premro

Will I Dream

Will I dream...
When paths unconnected converge into one?
When shades of the rainbow won't decide a man's fate?

Will I dream...
When people concur evil not them selves?
When no one envies the masses but their own?

When I wake...
Will all my fears be what I am, could it be I am what I'm afraid of?
Will the future ever stop turning into the present?

When I wake...
Will ignorance still be the standard to judge?
Will people stop claiming love and find out what it is?

David Furman

Infatuated

When she weeps the angels cry
When she laughs the angels fly
When she is mad the world is on fire
When she is in love I'm filled with desire
On top of the world in a sacred place
I look to the sky and I see her face
It illuminates through space and through time
Her image is engraved in the back of my mind
On a midnight beach the ocean whispers her name
When the wind blows it tells me the same
In this life she is all I hear, feel, and see
And for all the world she is my reality.

John Stanley

Summer's Gone

Where does summer go
When summer goes away.
I know I found today
It's hiding in the golden, crimson trees
The honey from the honey bees.
In the pumpkin, squash and corn
The brightness of an October morn
In the rippling waters of a stream
And frozen strawberries and peach ice cream
In all that's beautiful and bright
A warm and starry night
And in a blaze of glory it departs.
Leaving summer in our hearts.

Betty Benson Schrupp

Lucky Departure

If I'm lucky let me die after the sun goes down,
when the rose is dark, the birds are still and
gone from sight that far distant hill. The one
I promised I'd surely climb, someday, somehow,
sometime.
If I'm lucky let me go after the corn is tall
and what I planted in the Spring is not afraid of
Fall.
And if your lucky I won't say a thing when the cold
moon calls it fair, as he sends a beam to end my
dream and leaves you dreaming there.

Elizabeth Shelton

Heaven's A Better Place

When you watch them slip away,
When you can't believe your eyes,
When their death is very slow,
When they're in, horrible pain,
Heaven's a better place.
When you can no longer stand to see, that expressionless face,
Heaven's a better place.
When they're growing too old,
When that horrible disease is killing them, slow, and cold,
Heaven's a better place.
When they're dying and they know it,
Heaven's a better place.
When they've lived as long as they can live,
When they've done all that they can do,
When they're just lying in bed, waiting, to be dead,
Heaven's a better place.
When they know their life is done,
Heaven, is always, a better place.

Andrew M. Sniegowski

Stars Are Rare

When you feel abandoned or down
When you feel confused and an answer is needed to be found
When you feel lonely or sad
When you feel the world is doing deeds of bad
If you feel a tear rushing to your eye
Memories of time gone by
Think of those who feel the same
After all it's all in the name
The star I give to you is rare
It's to show you most of all I care
Of all you may feel
Look up at the sky
And think of the friendship that will never die

Amy Tal

"Too Young To Die"

A very close friend of mine is in the hospital, he is dying
whenever I try to talk about it, it always leaves me crying

People say I'm to old too cry
but he's to young too die

Why does God make you suffer in that kind of way
where you never get to tell a certain person what you want and need to say.

I might not get the chance to tell him I love him or even say good-bye,
I might not get the chance to tell him I care for him a lot and that's no lie.

Sometimes I think it's all my fault because I ran away
and Gods trying to get me back by taking his life away

I know that possibly can't be true,
but if it was I'm not sure what I would do

To many people love him please, please God don't let him die
because I know you're never ever too old to cry
but you're always too young to die.

Debbie Haynes

Questions

January 29, 1944... who am I? What am I?
Where am I? 50 years of living. Somedays
I am so weary of trying. Life, I try to live it.
Why do things get to jumbled in my head?
questions, questions, questions, always the questions.
Why do I want to know everything. I seek, to know!
not everything comes clear. What is my mission?
How will I know if it's complete? Do you die then?
what lies beyond death. Will I continue to seek knowledge?
Will I find the answers? How do we reflect on what is past?
How do we leave the past in past? I know that my past
affects me no matter how hard I try. It's part of me, it's what
makes me me. All those memories. Somedays it's so painful
just to remember the good times. I get an ache that goes
to the pit of my soul...the feelings go so deep that I weep just
from the sheer volume of what could have been...is this part of me?
who am I? what am I? where am I? does the life cycle change
every seven years? do I love? who do I love? where are all the
loves in my life? and what about happiness? is this something
that we all seek all the time? January 29, 1994 50 years later...

Donna N. Brown

Tears of the Past

Many tears have fallen
Where buildings now stand;
Ancestor's bones lie beneath
The hard concrete;
Their souls try to break away
To be reborn,
But the sidewalk holds them inside.

Their blood once ran free,
Stretching its fingers
Over the mountains
And through the woods,
Spreading their culture.

Now they lie in history books, and T.V.'s,
Portrayed as savages
Who killed for the joy of it.

Mistakes line the way
Through the new land.
Blood soaks the European's path.

Jenna Osburn

I Went Looking For God One Day

I went looking for God one day
Where do you think I found him?

I found him in the warm earth
  giving birth to a rose bush.

I found him in the treetops
  where birds were nesting their young.

I found him in the sun
  pouring out rays of warmth and light over the universe.

I found him in the air we breathe
  without which we could survive but a fleeting moment.

I found him in the blushing moon and twinkling stars.
I found him in the cooling winds and soothing raindrops.
I found him in the effervescent waves of the ocean.
I found him in the great words of the
  masters of literature and all the arts.
I found him in the gentle heart of noble men.
I found him in everything and everywhere.
If you truly seek him you will surely find him!!

Josef Morson

"Sleeping In The Rain"

Come inside- a stranger offered
Where it's warm and safe and dry
I couldn't see the face of the voice
That spoke to me - tears were in my eyes
Tonight I'm sleeping in the rain

I shook my head for words had left me
I just wanted to be alone
I pulled my collar, bowed my head
I walked the long way home
Tonight I'm sleeping in the rain

No need for shelter
Just a need to shed these tears
That flood in me
Tonight I'm sleeping in the rain
To wash away the pain
And maybe come morning
I'll walk beneath the sun

Arnita S. Sims

Fear Of Fear Unknown

When one's hovered in the valley of the shadow of death
Where life's held by a shallow breath.
When one's mind is troubled and all seems lost
And hope's faded into alarm.

When one's struggled in the depths of darkness
Wrest as a ship tossed in a violent storm
to have lived through one of these
One's known the fear of fear unknown

As one passes through the darkness into the light
A miracle's performed
through the grace of God when all seems lost
A new hope and faith rebomed.

As hope and faith entombed both mind and soul
the minds at ease, the soul's at peace
From deep with in the fear of fear unknown
through the mercy of God one has returned
the fear's now appeased and gone

Helen Miller

Trust

Will you meet me in the field
where right and wrong does not exist!
Where wholeness and love becomes real.
Will you take my hand and let me guide you to a place where only you and I can find the truth!
Where there are no distractions no games no masks?
Will you love me for who I am?
Will you forgive me for my idiosyncrasies?
Will you give only from you heart and soul; ignore outside influences which can persuade your feelings from past pain and insecurities?
Will you make love to not only my body but my being?
Will you share your deepest fears and joys?
Is this asking to much?
In return! the gift you will receive will empower you for a life time.
Will you meet me in that field without being afraid?

Cheryl Goldman

Bear Dog

We laid you to rest out alongside the hill
Where squirrels chatter and play at will;
And birds sing their songs all day,
Near the shady spot where you lay.

Your spirit follows us still along the way
As we take our rambling walks each day.
I glance over my shoulder expecting to see
You plodding slowly along behind me.

You'd sniff each tree you'd often sniffed before,
Tasting the special blades of grass once more.
Taking a side jaunt up a nearby lane,
Then running to catch up with us again.

You were not a puppy when you came to stay;
But an adolescent, still young enough to play.
So well trained and well behaved,
We grew to love you more each day.

Charlotte Costello

Marshmallow Heaven

Come to my chipper home
Where the doors are left wide open
With no worry come in
Your always welcome to roam

Everything is good, Everything is right
Man things around here are actually polite
Everything tastes good
'Cause the walls around me is my food for the night

Jump, leap, spring, bounce whatever you want
You're in my world now so come in my house

Come join me to look down we'll laugh together
At the miserable ones with the frown
Up here we're happy sitting on my puffy white cloud
Down there it's loud up here there's no sound

Come and impose I don't mind
Keep me company 'cause two is better than one
I'll share my splendid world if you promise to stay
And I'll promise it'll be a world of play

So hurry up jump, leap, spring, bounce
You're in my world now come in my house

Esperanza Cruz

"Let Me Dream A Sweet Dream For You"

Let me dream a sweet dream for you
Where the eagle soars in the sky
Where the roses have their sweetest scent
And the innocent don't have to die

Let me dream a sweet dream for you
Where the moon has a silvery glow
Where the robin sings its sweetest song
In a world with no sorrow or woe

Let me dream a sweet dream for you
Where you laugh and love and walk
Where pain has not made your body its home
And the shadow of death does not stalk

Let me dream a sweet dream for you
Where no snake coils its ugly head
Where your children's smiles and hopes and plans
Are in all of your dreams instead

Let me dream a sweet dream for you
Where God rests His gentle hand
Upon that tired and weary body
Where you've had more than a mortal can stand

Dixie E. Cureington

Life

On a cool, clear, December night,
Where the moon is full
and the stars are out,
I walk alone and wonder,
How life came about.

How did this world come to be,
Full of anger, hate, and hostility.
Who on this life has anything to gain,
By causing people misery and pain.
If we all stand together,
in a circle holding hands,
We can swallow our pride and make amends.

If we just stand tall,
and hold our heads high,
No one can bring us down,
or make us regret we have life.

Criselda Pena Ramirez

Tranquility

There is a place where I long to be
Where the sky is so blue it looks painted
Where the sun shines like a fluorescent light
Yet you can gaze into it
Where birds sing in unison
While they make their journey through the sky.
Where dreams will never die
Beneath it all is a glorious sea
Placid and calm, as the world should be
Colonies of fish forming chains and parades.
Love is made with the crashing of waves.
I ponder the thought of this land
And cry with the thought of human hand.
How could we tamper with such tranquility
This is gone in my own world.
But when I need to come here again,
I can get there through your eyes.

Ann Marie Stollmeyer

Pediment Guardians

Behind the shadows lies a land,
Where troubles are free from embarrassment.
All the judgements are seen above man,
Including the uttermost harassment.
Finding of a future so deep and cold,
To which no mortal could ever subscribe.
Punishing all those who dare to be bold,
Who unwillingly struggle just to survive.

The mirrors of land behind the shadows,
Reflect the fate of every mortal man.
Even the murky feeling falls and paddles,
To an unpromised, unfinished judgement hand.
Mortals' God was never in this place of judgement and mirrors;
Only those whose lives have become alive.
Grudges distinctly deflect some fears,
Yet the mirrors of the land hide the lie.

The land that lies behind the shadows grows,
And no one can stop such powered spirits.
For unless somebody steps in and knows,
Every mortal will live a life to fear it.

Holly Gunter

The Picture Dear To Me

There's a picture very dear to me
Which hangs upon my wall—-
It seems to smile down at me—-
I love it best of all.

Sometimes it seems as though 'twould speak
but it hangs in silence there,
and when I'm sad it seems
To say, "I'll your sorrows share."

I thank it o'er and o'er,
Even though it does not understand—-
And just wish and wish
I could hold the real one's hand.

With eyes of sympathy,
He seems to say,
"Never you mind, I'll come
Back to you some day."

So day by day
I live in hopes, you see
Of the blissful day
When he'll come back to me.

Esther Kerns Clary

I Wish ...

I wish there could be peace on earth,
which started at the moment of birth.

I wish there was no such thing as a gang,
that have guns and make them go bang.

I wish the earth was clean and nice,
don't litter, that's my advice.

I wish there was no such thing as hate,
hopefully things will change before it's too late.

I wish nobody knew the meaning of "race",
and people don't judge you by the color of your face.

I wish nobody would be sad,
if everything was like this, the earth would be rad.

Julie McDonald

Stroke

'Tis strange to see you lying there so still
While feeling and appearing like my hand.
With all your actions severed from the will
You're mine to contemplate but not command.
No matter what the force of my intent,
You have no power to strike to caress,
Or write what lines my fancy may invent
My deepest thoughts and feelings to express.
In all the years you served me like a slave
I took for granted every marvelous act,
But now that you're unable to behave,
I keenly feel the gratitude I've lacked.
Indeed, we can't appreciate the cost
Of giving up a blessing 'til it's lost.

James E. Kreisle

The Snorer's Dilemma

People that snore have problems for sure
While medical research focuses on a cure
Long a subject of comedy and domestic strife
I've had this problem most of my life

During scouting days when camping with boys
They would loudly protest my nocturnal noise
When I got married and all too soon
I found I had to sleep in another room.

I've tried every device for my wife's sake
Some help her but all keep me awake
From lumpy night shirts and gadgets by mail
What should I do when these things fail

Mouth sculpting procedures are not for me
Most are being evaluated with no guarantee
Since a cure-all may take many years
I'll try to convince my wife to plug her ears

In the meantime I'll be looking more and more
For any method or device proven anti-snore
Hope that day will come soon
So my wife will let me back in our own bedroom

Dewey I. Jones

"Doubts"

Is Gods teaching being taken in vain?
While the crimes in the world covers us with shame.
When we turn our backs on one in need.
And say we don't want to become involved "indeed!"

What will you say on judgement day,
When you face your master and hear Him say.
Hold out your hands and let me look
But they drip with blood and you are a crook.

Do you think he will take you into the fold,
And leave your story all untold?
Or point his finger at you and say,
You are just as guilty of the crime that day.

All men that Sin can atone,
He wasn't meant to Survive alone.
Or turn his back on his fellowman,
But help him all that his possibility can.

Turn your back on one in need,
And God most certainly records your deed.

Dorothy V. Hill

Bobby

In the classroom Bobby reads
While the prof spouts philosophical creeds
While Bobby sits and listens
Other's thoughts of beer are christened
While Bobby diligently writes
The rest of the class thinks, "This class bites"
Bobby stares with studious gazes
The rest of the class with drug induced hazes
While the class thinks that Bobby's habits must go
He's paid the price for his 4.0

Gregory Swigut

The Door

Beloved, do not call me back with tears;
Whisper my name! Speak out to me aloud!
Why cry in lonely torment when I'm here,
Sharing each day the love by which we're bound?

Don't be distraught that your warm, sleeping breast
Lies separated from my cold, still heart.
Our unity transcends the laws of flesh;
Believe me, we are just a breath apart.

I watch your eyes and long to soothe their hurt,
To tell you that mine, closed, see so much more.
Death is a mystery, but not a curse;
All is not lost, just changed, beyond its door.

Marie Raime

"A Remembered Dream"

Outside my window lies the snow, pure and
white,
Touched with love by the winter sun it
sparkles and glistens.
Bare are the trees-their autumn brilliance
gone - but nature is yet beautiful.

Inside my little house, one room sets apart,
warmed by the fire built of apple wood. We feel
a contentment.
The two of us talk-idly-as-friends do.
Slowly the fire turns to embers as dusk falls.
We are silent, sharing our companionship
Still sitting, half-asleep in the twilight,
comfortable with each other and our thoughts.

Eve Matthews

Untitled

Could someone help me discover
who I am. Could someone
help me over come my fears,
except my faults and strive
for excellence.

Could someone show me the way
To see what I can not and help
me understand what I can.
To be my compass when night
falls to keep me on the path to excellence.

Could someone help me to be
patient and take my time to not
lit my nervousness get the best of me

Could someone help me take interest far
burden in some way always sets in.

Julie Strassel

Who Is He?

Who is he? His eyes so blue.
Who is he? Is his heart true?
Who is he? I have to know. I know he's better
at being so - so he's very nice, he's very sweet he's
the kind of guy everyone wants to meet. I know who he
is and he knows me, but in the inside who
is he? On the outside he's cute as can
be, he's quite cunning to me. He's the
kind of guy other guys want to be. He's
got quiet a big heart anyone can see.
He's nicer than nice sweet as can be
smarter than smart, he's so cute to
me. He's perfect for me. His skin looks
so soft his eyes are so bright why
am I feeling like my wish has come
true for love that won't die that's the
right love for him and I. I know him
now by the sound of his voice, the scent
of him, the sound of his boots. I will
always love him and stick by his side.

Ashley Payne

Devotee To Mom

The love comes from one
Who knows how to give nothing but love.
She is now far gone
Her love now reaches us from above
She is with us each day
Her smile shines on the little one's face
In my heart she will stay,
Each corner of the house holds a trace
We were always well fed
She fed our bodies and our souls
Strangers in need she led
Food and love filled everyone's bowls
She taught us about God
His words and her faith kept her going
All three made a tripod
It supported her life ever showing
She has all the love now!
Cancer grew and took her from this life
So on my knees I bow,
I praise her as a great mom and wife.

Deborah A. Myers

Pride Before a Fall

There was once a very conceited toad
Who thought there was nothing as neat
As his expeditions, he'd go out on missions
In his little red Model T.

And how do you think his pride ended?
Well, the fall was very great.
And soon you will read about the toad
Who met his embarrassing fate.

He was taking his morning walk,
And holding his head up high.
When who should he spy, but an enemy nigh,
The silly queen and her maids.

Then suddenly without any warning,
His foot stumbled over a stone.
Then heels overhead, his heart filling with dread,
He flew into some mud with a groan.

His suit was now muddy with dirt,
And his leg, oh, how it did hurt!
So, with his head spinning, and the mocking queen grinning,
He slowly got out of the mud.

Dawn R. Weaver

The Dog And The Fat Cat

There once was a dog,
who went for a jog
down by the lake,
a stroll he did take
He was looking for something to eat,
something like meat
He looked down by his feet,
but didn't find a treat.
So he looks up real high,
to see something that could fly.
He sees something pass by
out of the corner of his eye.
It was a cat, and the cat was wearing a hat,
and the cat was real fat, and the dog really liked that.
The dog made a mat out of that cat,
And on it he sat, wearing that fat cats hat.

Christopher Alvin Swavely

Windfire (A Quodlibet)

The wind (It is fire's task to purify)
Whose vertigoed presence (- and fire's father, light -)
We cannot command, (to purge impressions of depravity,)
Winds us (Oh fire,)
Down the path of destiny, (from the human soul,)
Bathing the charred remains of choice (replacing them)
In its voluptuous breath, (with dignity and light.)
Purifying nothing, (Oh, to be bathed in the light)
Yet cleansing our memories (and nurtured there)
Of forgotten (as in the hands of)
Dreams. (A gentle mother.)

James A. John

A Friend

Am I supposed to feel this way or is it just me?
Why do I find a friend that's to good for me
And I don't see, see why there to good for me.
Or is it that I don't want to see that this friend
is too good for me.
A someone that's one step ahead of me in everything they do.
Some people tell me to stay with my own crew.
My friends say your gonna get hurt and I know that to.
But being me I still don't stop there,
Now I'm into deep and I actually care.
Care about a friend that I never thought I would.
I never thought I could care about what happens to someone who
I've only known such a short time.
But I do and now I can see,
See what friendship means to me.
Now all I can do is sit and wait,
And see that time brings my fate.
All I can do is hope and pray,
That good friends we will become and stay...
Forever!

Jen Shaak

Life

Everyone has worries
Which prayers let us face.
We'll each overcome them
Trying to live in God's grace.
Aiding people to help themselves
Is great to take some off their shelves.
For if they had from life retired,
Better use of time's admired.
One should never get discouraged.
Just look for loving every day.
While this takes a lot more courage
Our prayers can help us live this way.

Eileen R. Hallahan

I Wonder Why

When I am here I wonder why?
Why do I have to work until I cry
But then, I think for a moment
Then I wonder what if?
What if I couldn't be here
What would I be? How would I be? Where would I be?
Then! I hope, I am working until I die
Thank you Lord for letting me work until I cry.
Because I know where I am, how I am what I am.
And I'll know, forever, I'll know, until I die.
If you wonder where I am
Just look to the sky.
And you will see without a twinkling of an eye
That I am here working until I cry.
No more, will I wonder why!

Fannie White

The Rose And The Mask

My beautiful angel,
Why do you hide your face behind the mask?
Your voice enchants the angelic music that beckons to me as
I caress the rose.
Awaken my imagination.

The power of your voice,
The spirit of the dark music,
It holds me spellbound to your song.
The mask is but a shell,
To hide your beauty within,
Which is that of our rose.

As you turn from me who loves you in all ways,
The mask shatters, the rose wilts, and I die slowly from the
lack of love I was shown.

Candace Foster

Bye Grandmom

Grandmoms come and Grandmoms go
Why does your mother cloister you so?
Won't you ask her if you can come out to play
Before Grandmom goes away!

Joanne Borthwell

"Man Of Straw: Dreaming"

Withering away everyday
Why must it always be this way
I know I'm not the king - but I've always had a thing for you,
Never ending flame - it burns in me!
I can only see you in my dreams
Oceans away - someone's thinking of you
I know you hear the ring - it is me who turns you're chain around
Aspasia my queen - I love you
Riddle me a thought - unscramble it slowly
So that I may forever be inside your maze
Nights only way that we can play
So sleep my love
I will see you soon
I'll caress you're hair like you like me to
I will play with it
Until the night is through
I will never hold my breath for another my queen
My love is till the end -
For all seasons I shall serve,
I shall defend.

Jesse Caltzontzint III

Why Must They Die

Why must they die when they haven't yet lived?
Why must they die when they have so much to give?
Why are they taken from people who care?
Where do their souls go, do they rest in the air?
Why must family and friends mourn and weep?
And pray to God their souls to keep
Why must they die when they cared so much for life?
Why are they taken away in the stillness of the night?
Why can't we bring them back to say what has not been said?
Why are they taken away? Why are they dead?
We loved them so much and now it's too late to show
Did we express it enough? Did they really know?

We'll meet again in a place far away
And we shall live together again someday
Can we talk to them now if we look in the sky?
Can they hear our laughter and hear us cry?

So express your love before it's too late
And don't give in to anger and hate
For why they leave us we do not know
So tell them now, let it show!

Joni L. Jenkins

The Living Well

Have you been to the living waters?
Why not come there with me?
For it was there when I felt so thirsty, my Savior came to me.
"Dip your cup into the well dear child", this is what He said
"and drink as much as you can hold. And you will surely be fed."
So I dipped my cup down deeply as far down as it would go,
and suddenly I felt so full but why I didn't know.
Then I asked my Savior, "why do I feel this way?"
He put his arms around me and we began to pray.
"You were thirsty my child and this well is never dry.
And you wanted to drink so badly. That is the reason why."
And as we prayed together I felt so serene.
I know why others drink from the well. I know now what they mean.
Now I shall never be thirsty for to the well I'll go.
And I can just keep drinking and let my cup overflow.
So thank you, Heavenly Father, far the well that never runs dry.
I hope that others will stop and drink and never just pass by.
For water flows freely from it and here's the reason why,
The Savior wants to give you life.
I urge you now to try!

June M. Weber

The Queen Bee Of Windsor Castle Gardens Sayeth

"'To bee or not to be'
Why wrestle with the question of my be-ing,
When it is mind to command a perfume-splendored queendom?

It is for humans to philosophize, to live in houses and palaces,
But it is mine to live among the flowers - the garden, my bee'sphere;
For there, the lovely roses stand, neither vain nor foolish -
Their petals, velvet-wet with each morning mist's new dew,
Their thorns, my royal palace guard.

My honeycomb is my crown jewel-box, laden with treasure of celestial
nectars
Brought me by a royal procession, my loyal beeline of succession.
As I review my beescape, I exult in the honey-toiling of my species;
To sip from nature's spectrum is to engage the secret of the garden,
food among the flowers.

The garden is now just an ornamental landscape for humans;
'Twas not always so, when they lived in Eden.
O, pity the other Queen, the one of England.
Her stage is a cold ... old ... stone castle."

Janice Cox Jones

Heart's Garden

Within my heart a garden grows,
wild with violets and fragrant rose.
Bright daffodils line the narrow path,
my footsteps silent as I pass.
Sweet tulips nod their heads in rest;
I kneel in prayer to seek God's best

For 'round my garden a fence stands firm
to guard my heart so I can learn
who should enter, and who should wait
on the other side of my locked gate.
I clasp the key around my neck
and wonder if the time is yet.

If I unlocked the gate today,
would you come in? Or run away?

Angela Lucius

A Last Thought

A last thought before I go.
Will it be of myself? No-one will ever know.
A glimpse of my life, persons, places.
What will I see in those faces,
of so long ago, who could know?

Will I think only of life as ruthless,
or will I be thankful for all that I've been blessed?
In those last moments is the mind still filled with hate,
or from this petty course do our thoughts liberate?
Are we finally free from all the pain we see?
What will that last thought show, who could know?

In my past will I see all that I have loved,
or will I dwell on only what's above?
Might I not worry for those left behind,
as I wait to see what I will find?
Will I fight not to leave, will I feel bereaved?
Will I look forward or be sorry to go? Only I will know.

Eric D. Paton

Black Woman

Rankles in her face; a map of our time.
Wind and wind through the memories of past times.
Mind is sharp! A queen of our past.
Time has ticked on; for a member of a royal class.

Crevices are deep, teeth are all gone,
Been a life time singing "God take me home"
Time winding up! But, still the fight is left.
Doing it for other and not for herself.
A leader! Second to none, is what she will always be.
Holding a babe in her arms! Or bouncing one on he knee

Broad nose, piercing eyes, big lips are her only traits.
With a pure heart and a faith, she'll make the pearly gates.
South African, bush woman or modern American slave.
She demand! Respect; from the cradle to the grave.

Henry Boykins

I Have Been Where No Man Has Gone

I have been where no man has gone,
with only armor of flesh while sole and alone.

Some view me as fragile, born to be weak,
I say to them, I have reached the highest peak.

Blossom beauty unfolds like the most precious flower.
Courage hidden deep, fueled by God's own power.

I have been the portal of an immortal soul.
I was the destiny of fate, the ultimate goal.

An ordinary woman, no different from another,
Just an average female, chosen to be mother.

Arlene D. Jackson

Sky Dancer

Sky dancers of the afternoon.
Wings so worn they spiral downward.
Landing solidly like stone upon stairwells.
I watch them, wondering, if not for them,
then for who.

It is enough to know that I dream of them,
they of me, and us of others.

They try to move.
Spread wings, beat harder.
Push so strongly that the dust
at their feet stirs with the effort.

It is futile, their knowledge is lost.
I have angered them,
I cannot say why, but the feeling is mutual.

Gary Dyner

The Gloves

I have a little four year old
With a heart so big indeed.
A heart as pure as gold
Filled with appreciation for each small deed.

His brother, a pair of gloves, did need.
So off to the store we did tread
To purchase the gloves for brother big.
But two pair we bought, one pair blue, one pair red.

To big brother we gave the blue.
The little guy got the red.
His eyes popped open in complete surprise.
"For me?" in amazement he said.

His eyes bubbled over.
His voice all but trembled,
All day he clutched those treasured gloves.
That night he took them to bed!

So, to the store we went again.
In a cute nursery wastebasket came
His favorite snacks, but in it did not remain.
That night to bed the basket came!

June L. Wise

The Oyster And The Eagle

God gave the oyster an easy life
With a house and an ocean of food.
The oyster's head is muscle bound
With a hat like a stony hood.

God gave the eagle strong, wide wings
And the clearest hunting eye.
The Lord told the eagle, "Go build your nest
Where only the brave can fly."

The oyster lies on his ocean floor
With home and food near by.
The oyster lies with his head in the mud,
The eagles rules the sky.

But God, in His wisdom created nothing
Of no use in this world,
The oyster, from a grain of sand,
Creates a perfect pearl.

Doris Scott

Fall

Fall covers the hills and dales
with a magic quilt of ever changing colors
Fiery reds, deep rich browns, blazing orange,
and shimmering gold.
Gone are the fresh new days of spring
with all the promises that it brings
Young loves great expectations,
new life, new hopes, new dreams
Cool crisp mornings
Fog hanging like ghostly drapes
And the distant lonesome cry
of swallows winging south
Gone are the hot passionate days of summer
Moonlight picnics on a sandy beach
Swimming and dancing under starry skies
And dreams fulfilled in a lover's arms
As autumn leaves drift gently to and fro
putting on a dazzling show
It is time for reflection, and taking control
Before the long harsh days of winter takes its toll

Juanita Haskins

One Rose

An old friend came to me one day
with a smile upon his face.
And with a wink of his pensive eye,
I knew I was in the right place.

From his back he drew a dozen roses,
So exquisite in the precious sunlight.
Beside my friend I remained there in awe,
At these roses so fair yet so bright.

Each rose was flawless I could promptly tell
as he pointed each one out to me.
It was clear to me as I sat that day,
That these roses possessed more to see.

There was one rose that was distinctive; though,
For it was awfully modest to see.
To me he addressed this peculiar rose
and said, "This I Give Unto Thee."

He pulled me nigh and kindly said,
"I Pray That My Love You Take,"
For My Love Will Last 'Till These Die,"
And you see, the unique rose was fake.

Catherine Horton

Lost

My journey begins without a map or glasses
with each step, etching a trail.
I blissfully enjoy each moment that passes
knowing my heart need not fail.
Then shadows appear and darkness surrounds me.
I guess it's fear, my heart is pounding.
Onward I travel straining to see
and wandering further than my eyes perceive.
'til the light of dawn shines so bright
the darkness appears and shadows the night.
In the blindness I continue forever
remembering the warmth we had together.
Knowing my heart need endure the force
yet, hoping for nature to take its course.
Now the passage of my life, I plod on
wondering why the blissful moments are gone.
Just as I think I no longer know
I hear the leaves, my path
and follow the winds that blow.

Cyril P. Smith Jr.

St. Lisa Dressech

My lust has set the mirror's score to shame
With ev'ry surge of blood, my heart retreats
From when we two were but a lover's game;
Your chance to show, your care, I'm not to meet:
Within my brain resides a cancer foe;
Its food the sound of newly beating hearts,
As that in each of us begins to grow,
To stay would rear and cause your love a start.
Forgive my leave, my love for you is sent,
This sickness in my brain you cannot share;
I cannot know which way love's seed has went,
At least my poisoned heart is never there.
Resent the weakness I within maintain,
To choose without a choice presents my shame.

James P. Schuler

America America

America America oh what a wonderful place
With grace and dignity we have only God did create

America America this is the country to live
A prosperous land it is indeed
For all are wants and needs

America America sharing with other lands
Especially when there is poverty
We are there helping hands

America America where dreams do come true
For every boy and girl father mother too
You can venture into space until you reach the moon

America America a president as such
Should be honored in all his endeavors
For keeping each land in touch

America America love is cherished here
Reaching out to touch and listening to each ones fears

America America proud and tall we stand
Freedom and liberty is our beautiful land
Our motto represents why we are so strong
In God we trust our earth sings out with him we can't go wrong

Joyce Pahoski

A Given Life

An infant's love so small and sweet
With hands so tiny and tiny feet
A gentle touch of a baby's charm
falls to catch a mothers arms
A fathers smile with love and care
A given life only God could share
A love so small only God could give
Remembers this love throughout all its years
A cherished love you will always know
A baby's love will always grow.

Danny Glenn Drew

Isolation

Once in awhile someone else reaches into my cocoon
with love and laughter and warm hands;
Once in awhile someone else will light a smile
in my direction; true to form
I'll not believe wholly.
My self-cocoon has tough walls.
Words are my world, books and music
and midnight wandering on summer hills
introspective at stars.
I don't yet dare to look so closely to people.

This will have to change.
How can I be, failing to trust my own kind?

Esther Kramer

The Adirondack Chair

Someday I'll sit upon his adirondack chair
with memories flooding in...
the precision woodwork
the perfect cup of coffee
expert mechanic
household Mr. Fix-it
duck sounds of goodbye
Perry Mason and Barnaby Jones
trips out to the lake
lottery tickets
reading the newspaper
watching "Paint Your Wagon"
his ever-giving garden
and his love.
As the memories flood in, so does this love
and I let the strength of the wood support my thoughts.
And the warmth of the moment comforts me
as I sit upon Grandpa's adirondack chair
in the place of
his wonderful memory.

Amy Jean Kallenberger

"Feeling Free"

I'm happiest...when I'm feeling free...
with no walls confining me.
I love to breathe the cool fresh air...
feel the wind...blow thru my hair...

I love to climb the mountains high...
lay back and watch...the clouds float by.
To walk and walk to no destined place...
feel the sunshine...warm my face.

I want to hear...all nature's songs...
this is the music that I long.
The beauty that the woods abound...
is the greatest peace...I've ever found...
where there are no strings...
...to tie me down.

I want to live my life each day...
in just a simple...ordinary way.
To be thankful for what God above...
has given me...these things I love,
...and to be happy with...just being me...
Happiest...when I'm feeling...free.

Charlene A. Miner

"Mornings Full of Hate"

I arise to mornings full of hate,
With questions of life that test my faith.
Raindrops that tap on my face,
That rush along the ceiling as I pace.
Back and forth my direction goes,
As I ponder of my life woes.
To rise over the great person that I am to be,
Only to be put down with shots of my misery.
Braver than any man that walks the ground,
With love of the weight of the heaviest pound.
When the sun pulls me face away from the wet puddle in my palm,
I pursue the thoughts of life that would keep us tight and warm.
Allow me to perform for you the things that lovers do,
But do not join in because this belongs to only two.
Now that the moon has peered into the windows of the world,
Lets cover the act of love and darken the boy and girl.
Ways of yesterday are now out of date,
But they will repay us with only hate.
Wars that are raged in the heavens for entertainment,
Are closer to our heart than any material has meant.

Dennis A. Lindsey

The Journey

We come into this world with a wail and a cry,
With people who love us all standing by.
The doctors and nurses, family and friends,
Shedding joyous tears and shaking hands.

At this wondrous point our journey begins, how long it will be,
Where will it end.

The years of our childhood filled with so many things,
With learning and playing, wonderment, love, and care,
The part of our life that we remember with bliss and joy,
With the memories that linger forever in our hearts to be shared.

Adulthood comes along, with anticipation and great plans,
We're grown up now, our life is in our own hands.
We've waited so long for this time to approach, and each day,
The decisions we'll make will be with us
As this part of our journey moves along its way.

The career is successful and each day it expands,
It may take you to places across all these lands.

The family is grown and on their own and their journey
Will take on a life of its own.

And now as the journey is nearing its end,
What does this mean for my loving friend,
The Gods and the Fates are waiting in anticipation
For they have great plans for you in the next generation.

And together again in love and joy all of us will be
As new creatures on earth and another glorious journey.

Ginger Smith

"Once In A Lifetime"

Once in a lifetime, a good friend comes along, to joke with and laugh with - perhaps sing a song. To reminisce of old times and dream of days anew, because even the bad times we always get through.

Once in a lifetime, you meet a friend who is sincere. Someone to communicate with when no one else can hear. To listen to and be there for, because a friend offers so much more.

Once in a lifetime, you meet a friend who is true. A person to stand by your side when you're feeling blue. To lift your spirits when no one else can make you feel like a person again.

Once in a lifetime, you're lucky to meet a very special friend. It is a valued treat. Someone to tell your secrets to, especially when they bother you.

Once in a lifetime, you can give strength to someone else, by teaching her to have faith in herself. By pointing out where she is strong and showing where her patience is long.

Once in a lifetime, if you're as fortunate as me, maybe you'll meet someone as special as "Dee." A friend who is fair and a friend who is kind - I'm sure a friendship like this is -
Once In A Lifetime.

Holly A. DeRienzo

"You, My Friend"

So blue as the day's clear sky,
with the love in the tears that you cry;
in the warmth of new blood that you feel
should nature smile at one so deserved.

As seasons change and bring you hope anew,
your smile alone has told me that it's true;
I can't express the joy for you I feel:
an honest hint, my rarely smiling lips.

The sun will always rise another day,
my eyes from pain, my heart from grey;
and all the while I'll sit and wait
for autumn's fire, and you my friend.

Dan Vanderboom

Reflections

It's sad to watch the years drift by
With so many things undone,
So many words to be written yet,
So many songs to be sung.

What happened to the schemes of yesterday
To the dreams and hopes so high?
I was going to set the world afire
To pinnacles blithely fly.

But the years have gone, as they swiftly do
And each day that passes here,
Leaves all my dreams and all my plans
Just phantoms that never appear.

I've born a family and watched them grow
From childhood to their separate ways,
Kept a home and a job and loved a man
Can't say I've wasted my days.

But somehow my life is empty still
For the things I haven't done.
Does anyone ever accomplish all
And feel that they have won?

Beverly M. Hickok

Seven Angels IN The Snow

As dusk gently shades the sky from day into night
with spheres changing like guards of dark and light.
Whispering sounds pass an ear as winds blow,
through the drifts lie seven angels in the snow.
With heads planted firm and wings erect,
the trace of motion one can easily detect.
Feet spread wide to form a hem
with a symmetry encompassing all of them.
One could imagine these bodies so wee,
laughing and frisking for only God to see.
For words spoken softly are seldom heard,
now as the elder, memories only blurred.
When times were simple under tiny locks,
with cookies and milk and holly socks.
Sad or frightened we shed virgin tears,
a mere hug from Mom surrendered our fears.
You blink as life's parade has passed,
as the hope of tomorrow has come too fast.
Eras are like rainbows with their similar bend,
some with gold at the start, others at the end.
Beginning from the footprints which lead from this site,
the path to our future will not be as bright.
For age replaced the innocence we used to know,
when time faded away the seven angels in the snow.

Eric J. Weaver

Lies

I sit here watching the sunrise,
with the determination and hope in my eyes
when will I get a chance to see home
I'm hurt, I'm sad, and I'm all alone
Questions boggle in my head
is it better to be alive or better to be dead,
no one knows or evens finds out
And I'm not one to take that route
What is forgiveness and when does it come
should I face truth a should I run.
I am a criminal that did a lot of hurt
I robbed, I stole, and I never went to work
I depended on myself and no one else.
when trouble comes in rage
I'm a self-centered punk in a cage
I'm a menace to society
Theirs a lot of reasons why
I hurt, I robbed I stole
andofcourse——Ilied

Colin Haag Jr.

Untitled

I looked up to the shining moon,
With the stars gleaming at its side.
I sat on the grave of my Elizabeth,
And then I slowly cried.

I shed a tear for the time we lost,
I shed one for my heart.
I shed one for the love we had,
And for the pain that tears me apart.

I lay down on the grave of my Elizabeth,
Never wanting to leave her side,
And time went by as it always does,
And waited for me to die.

I looked up and saw my Elizabeth,
More beautiful than she had been,
And I held her for eternity,
For true love does not ever end.

Jamie R. Smith

Hunger

You come to me in the dead of night,
With whispers of love and passions so bright.
A thief, a rogue, a scoundrel, and beast,
Through your eyes I appear as a sumptuous feast.
You consume, and you gorge
and eat to your fill,
Then stare down at my body
lying lifeless and still.
It's happened before, it will
happen again,
You'll come to me soon
I just don't know when.

Angela L. Jones

One Summer's Night Dream

A walk on the beach
With you by my side
Would be everything to me
A moonlit night, stars fill the sky
Is where I want to be;

The sand so cold
The blanket warm
The music soft and slow
Here we are, the two of us
Until one will have to go;

Waves stay calm
The breeze so gentle
As boats in the water sail by
A moonlit reflection, the gleam on your face
Makes it harder to say goodbye;

I close my eyes
And smell ocean air
Only dreaming of you with me
But when they open, I look to my side......
All I find is me

Debra M. Del Mare

Dead Phone

Like a dead phone....
words do not reach my receiving ears no more.
Trying to understand a chaotic code that's too
set, well planned and unable to break.

Like a dead phone....
I too, am speechless.
Mimicking only sounds of silence.

Davied J. Peoples

Mother With Your Love

With your love, there is unconditional love.
With your love, you have taught me unconditional love.
With your love there is kindness.
With your love, you have taught me kindness.
With your love there is understanding.
With your love, you have taught me to be understanding.
With your love there is courage.
With your love, you have taught me to be courageous and
to overcome any obstacle.
With your love there is security.
With your love, you have taught me to be secure in myself
and my family.
With your love, I have been created.
With your love, I am here by your side.
With your love, I am me.
With your love, I am proud to be your daughter.
With your love, you should be proud and secure in knowing
that you are the best mother that any person could ever want.

Gina Webb

"Within As Without"

Within hurt there is pain.
Within pain there is sensation.
Within sensation there is feeling.
Within feeling there is experience.
Within experience there is contrast.
Within contrast there is life.
Within life there is love.
Within love there is peace.
Within peace there is contentment.
Within contentment there is happiness.
Within happiness there is God.
Within God there is meaning.
Without meaning you would not be here.....

Charles I. Bernold

Voice Of The Battered Child:
"Some Things I Would Like"

I would like to be wanted—
without having to ask
if it's ok
for someone to love me.

I would like to be loved—
and not be afraid
that somebody thinks
I'm full already.

I would like to be held—
in gentle arms
with strength
that merges beings.

I would like to be seen—
with loving full eyes
that aren't afraid
to know it's just me.

I would like to be wrapped—
by soft eyes and arms
into a tickly heart that says

"Hello there....You're real...and I love you."

Claire W. Noonan

A Soldier's Daydream

Strolling along down No Man's Lane
Wondering if 50 years from now it will be the same;
A cottage here, a cottage there,
And here and there a tree or two;
And there's Mrs. Murphy's flowers
That remind me so much of you.

The old stone bench where we sat and sang
Is still the same,
And once again the leaves have covered this beautiful
Old lane.
To some folks, it may not suit their modernistic air,
But then, they never shared the beauty
That you and I shared there.

The Surge broke in on my memories saying I had to go to bed,
I closed my eyes, but not to sleep,
I dreamed of your instead.
Once again we strolled, but this time it wasn't the same,
We turned in at our own little cottage,
And smiled back down upon No Man's Lane.

Collette Wells

"1994Sports"

The baseball season is over and done
Would you believe, no one won
It certainly has been a strange year
Many missed sports, they hold most dear
Hopefully football will go on as planned
Or will many players be canned
Basketball season is on the fence
Do you suppose they will strike, or be so dense
Maybe next year will be better
Lets all send them a letter
To tell them to change their ways
And get back to their "Sport-Minded" days!

Betty K. Cary

A Cup Of Tea

How nice to see you my dear,
Would you like a cup of tea?
Yesterday you say, I thought perhaps a year,
How nice of you to visit me.

Have you ever tried to plow?
Did you ever try to write only to...
What, was it I was saying now?
Oh dear, I must remember to...

As I was saying about the...
First though, would you like a cup of tea?
I believe I set it on the...
Say, did I offer you a cup of tea?

Oh, if only I could remember when...
I wasn't always this way you know,
There was a time when...
Would you like a cup of tea now,

Pardon me while I shut the window,
Well, would you believe, I have company,
I saw your car below,
Would you like a cup of tea?

Harvey N. Berg Jr.

Sea Turtle

Sea turtle, sea turtle, swimming the sea
with oceans so big, where might you be?
Warm waters, and so many plants and fishes to see,
next time ashore, won't you take me?

Amy L. Stevens

The Death Of A Friend

They carried him through the door
Wrapped in blue velvet, dead,
Lying on an elongated tea table
Like Mrs. Astor might have used
To entertain the Hoi Polloi Elite.
How sweet

Blue velvet and steaming crumpets
Sweet cakes and candy bits
Tears mixed with chinese tea
And lemon bitter taste of lemon drops
Don't drop him off, the girl cried, for he had died.

They staggered down the stairs and
All the dishes fell, pell mell
The sweet cakes and the candy bits
covered everything. The blue velvet
Stained with tea turned purple red on the table bed.

Down at last and slipped into the wagon
Wrapped, all the guests gone
Would Mrs. Astor have wished him well?
Who can tell....

Adrienne Fontana

I Cry Alone

I cry alone,
Yet not for me are the tears I shed,
They are for those whose hope has fled,
To be abandoned in life, in torment to fear
To be condemned for they do not Conform
To be abused, to have dreams forlorn.
To be deemed unfit for others tastes
Because they say we are not of the same Race,
To be left alone because there is Fear,
A fear so misplaced that it should not be there,
I long to embrace my brothers who call,
Who cry for Help or for Love
They who must die alone, suffer from life
or cannot go home.

John W. Lefflbine Jr.

We Were Adolescents And Put Off Love Till Tomorrow

At the time, the air resounded with the sounds of the city.
Yonder, the forest waited graciously to envelop us
with its green veil.
We felt that our first encounter called for quieter places
The sky was blue; no fog was in the offing.
It was noon. Yet, it seemed like dusk somehow!
We hadn't touched liquor, yet felt intoxicated.
How could we fathom the thirst for the unknown?
Or ignore the devouring looks of people...?
How could we trust the open spaces of the plains?
Or the eavesdropping of birds...?
Or the sly glances of the sunflowers?
Wasn't it a sin to make the leaves of the forest
yearn with longing when they looked upon us...?
What if the grass...where we frolicked...caught fire
From our torrid passion and burned up?
Hm? We were adolescents,
Which is why we put off love till tomorrow.

Gjeke Marinaj

Without You

I never thought you would say good-bye
you always told me that you
would never leave - it was all a lie
Now I'm sitting here broken hearted
and being hurt-very hurt.
I loved you with all I had inside.
I give you my heart, my love,
my body - and you tore them all into pieces.
I felt so guilty for the way
we ended, but now I realize that it was you.
I never hurt you - only loved you
and loving you sometimes hurt me
I'll never forget you - you loved me,
then you used me - how could I forget you?
I used to smile for you, laugh
for you, and even cry for you - but my crying is over.
I'm living a new life without you and I'm very happy.
Sure I miss you sometimes and wish the past was still
here, but the more I think about it - you're better off
without me — and I'm much better off without you!

Amanda Hisle

Winds Of Time

And so it goes...
You and I will be gone leaving imprints
on the winds of time.
The burst of life - the laughter, the joy, the sorrow;
The love, the caring, the painful partings;
The struggle, the triumphs, the rewards -
All these leave imprints on the winds of time.
New life, new generations will come...
as generations before us have come.
Endless.
Winds will unfold and reveal the imprints
of lives gone by -
Same moon, same stars, same sun, same
blue of the sky;
Same dusk and sunset, same sunrise...
all key witnesses to the unfolding times.
Endless.
Now.. your turn, making imprints on
the winds of time.

Aida A. Joshi

Love Is Forever

You whisper to me in the dead of night
You call my name to my heart's delight
Is it the rustle of the leaves I hear?
Or is it your voice that sounds so clear?
Is it true you've ceased to be
And no longer think of me?
Is it wrong for me to say
I love you more with each passing day?
My eyes have sunk back into my head
With all the tears that I have shed
My love, my love, be true to me
Let no other love come between you and me.

Jennis Mentone Gentile

"Baseball"

Baseball is the best of all.
You can play all year because we live here.
You play with mitts, bats and balls.
The umpire makes the calls.
When you get a hit it gets fielded in a mitt.
Baseball is the game I play - it always seems
to make my day.

Chris Starr

My Wish

I remember one day
You came along wanting to play
I was too busy to have fun and be with you
Now I wish I could tell you that my
love for you was true
Now you have gone far away
My only wish is that we could play
I wish I could be with you so much
And just touch you once, one single touch
If only I could say goodbye
But it's too late for that now
All I do is think about the
good memories we had and cry

Aretha Flucker

Meaningless Words

Words are meaningless when that is all you say.
You can take them back, but it will never be the same.
You can wish you never said the things you did in rage.
Perhaps one day I won't care even though they will forever
linger in my head.

You can take them away, but be careful of what you do.
Please don't expect me to be there to take care of you!
Be careful what you do, your words will now always protect you.
You may take them away but in your heart they will always
haunt you.

Words are meaningless when that's all you say.
You can take them back, but it well never be the same.

Arlene Treutle

Faceless

'Tis long over due that I should forgive
you; faceless soul whom I never knew. Here you are
not so I can accuse you. No fair, I say
no fair! to the skinless reaper whom has claimed you.

Angry I was and the reviews of your life
are but favorable to only a few and it is my choice
still to believe the stories I hear about
you. One with my blood has your face, I know not
which, however, if thine eyes and mind
had to know, then by faith will your face show.

Faceless, much I wish to say to you, yet
I know not how to start. Perhaps when the great
king comes with everlasting might, help
me he will with my heart.

Christopher L. Autmon

Sleeping

You have awakened the sleeping intricate part of my very being,
You have cleansed my inner-self and lifted my spirit to new highs
and spaces.
You have stolen my heart and soul, I am helpless, I cannot recover.
The breath of despair has clung firmly like frost on a naked tree
limb.
Its deadly silence creeps ever so slowly on my heels.
There appears a sparse light ahead, I try repeatedly to reach for
the faint illumination.
You appear, all despondency vanishes and retreats to its slumbering
depths.

Ann E. Bush

"Pile Of Leaves"

Both of us still feel the hurt
You know we need more time.
The ache for you will always be there
Your kiss to be dreamed about...treasured thousands of times.

Memories are not a patch of reality
No matter how hard we may try...
All the sensations, can't be conjured up
On lyin' shadows... making us cry...

Healing is a feeling, there's a cost we must pay
And is only received in time...
We all need to hear how important we are
When it comes to each other's lives...

She laughs with the dancing trees
She will cry with the whispering breeze..
Or I'll fly away with her heart... if I please,
And she can rake away love...like a pile of leaves...

Love piled high like the leaves
In the arms of a blustery breeze
I will fly to the tops of the trees
No longer I'll be... in a pile of leaves....

Anthony Jude Parisi

A Valentine For My "Mother-In-Law"

You love me like a daughter,
You love him like a son,
You're a mom to one of us,
But you'ld never know which one.

You never show partiality,
When things are going wrong.
We know it bothers you inside,
But still, you remain strong.

I love you, Mom, and always will,
From the bottom of my heart.
I hope I'll never loose you,
If your son and I must part.

You have taken the place of a mother I had,
And filled my heart with love,
Every night, I pray to God,
And thank the heavens above.

You're a "Mother-in-law" to one of us,
A "Mom" to the other.
To me, you're not my "mother-in-law,"
To me, you are my "Mother."

Grace Realbuto

Night Visitor

So many times I've seen you here,
You make it known when you are near.
But now there's something that's not right,
For usually, you come at night.

At night you come and dance for me,
You move within the blue night sea.
But here you are in full daylight.
The people say, you are a fright.

The mask you wear does hide your face,
But I think that you must leave this place.
Come back tonight, I'll look for you,
When the moon is high, and the grass is dew.

We'll watch each other across the lawn.
You'll pace and play and pose till dawn.
Then off you'll go to your secret place,
To fix the mask that hides your face.

Aletha Spencer

A.I.D.S.

Too sick and deplorable to acknowledge
You, might rape my mother, murder my father, torture my lover
Heedless and slovenly in method, you tactlessly thrive on
The excruciating torment of your self-made brutality
A monster, a snake
Your veins flow with the blood of crude venom
Those you encounter you ruthlessly attack
Then very
Very
Slowly
You poison with your ill contamination
But beware
You are not that empowering
Your strength runs in your filthy, grimy blood
That reeks a murderous odor
It may boil hot and deadly, but will one day be overcome
And curdle
Dry
And die.

Jennifer D. Foley

Child Of God Be Careful

You feel you have it all figured out... are you sure?
You mingle to mix with a crowd that is not right....
what dangerous lure.
Your pulled and tugged told not to trust anyone...
"Watch your own back," they say.
We are always wondering if your okay.

Child of God remember your upbringing.... never go astray.
Think of his goodness and how he has always been there in
the past.
Remember dear friend his love is meant to last.

Brandi S. Lee

Do As You're Told

Why don't you leave, just get out of my house
You never learn, all you do is live to burn
Your life's a mess, why dwindle in your past regrets
Please find the key, to release us from your misery

Do as I say, do as your told,
Do as I say, do as your told.

Get a job, it's time to find a life my boy
At least do something to give your parents a little joy.
They wait for days, to see if your brain is thumping
Oh, false alarm, it must have been a seizure, or something
Do as I say, do as your told
Do as I say, do as your told

Come on man, you can do it
Grab your life, there's nothing to it
Leave the nest, you should do it
You need your own life, that's all there is to it.
Do as I say, do as you're told
Do as I say, do as you're told

Joe Young

Love

We were sitting in a park, we were alone and it was dark. You put your arms around me, you whispered love so sincerely. It was cold on that dark night you pulled me close and held me tight. Two young lovers alone at last. We sat there and talked about the past, about the times good and bad, even times when we were sad. You told me that you loved me so, I told you that I loved you to and how I would always be true blue. Morning came fast that day, then we went our separate ways. One last night was all we had, one last night that had no bad.

Christine A. Saloma

The Poetaster

Thy unknown bard!
You never really tried that hard.
You never really had to...
Gods' gift as received by you,

Take, for instance, the color blue;
An interesting theme for a haiku...

Blue is a feeling,
When blue is not a color,
Yet, so much is blue.

Insecure even in your theme...
Someday you'd be there. One day!
The chips would fall your way,
Even if it meant living the dream.
Low on pride; short of self-esteem,
You meant to have the spot-light.
You dared to dream!

David Bluitt

I Used To Have A Friend

You said you would stick to the end.
You said you were my friend,
I guess you lied
They call that kind of death suicide.
Now your gone from my life.
What was so wrong,
that you couldn't find away to carry on?
I know you went through your problems alone.
Why couldn't you just pick up the phone?
That night nobody knew,
That you threw your life away.
I used to have a friend,
I thought he would stick to the end.

Amy Bickett

The Evolution Of Slavery (The Beast Speaks)

Through your eyes
You see only my vision
You are totally imprisoned
Trapped within my circumference
You have no light without me
You are my personal moon
And it didn't take long for me
To gain control of your soul
All I had to do - was to
Camouflage my sin - in a grin
And jus' like that - I was in
El Hajj Malik El Shabazz
Knew all to well
What you ignored
And tried to discard
He understand that the evolution of slavery
Would be a self imposed prison
In which the HUE-man being would be
Locked in - caged in
By mental bars

Carl Wharton

My Star

O star, my star, the biggest star in the sky
You shine so bright you black out the moonlight
The moonlight is at its fullest but yet your rays are still better than its
with your rays shining there fullest they put the moon to shame,
O star, my star, your rays can never be tamed.

Jade Rash

Running To Back-Track

I stared at you through the shiny glass.
You still looked same from where I stood.
Wow, so many memories filled my head at the sight of you - it was almost harsh reality.
I had worn that damned beret once while walking under the stars... holding your hand. (Sigh) and that smile was all too familiar... So many times it had been aimed at me and had made me smile through to my heart. I couldn't see your eyes but I knew they were that crystal blue and were probably dancing with mischief. I used to really enjoy the intensity of our conversations because I felt like you searched my soul with that stare.
Seeing you again flooded my mind with vivid pictures of moments we had shared. I had to shut my eyes to gain control again. When I opened them you were gone and I was left staring at my own face. The pain and emotion I felt was reflected in my eyes in the mirror of the glass. I felt so vulnerable, but the longer I stood there gazing at myself, the more I realized I was free to fly my own destiny. From then on I stopped running to back-track.
—and then I walked away

Amy Meininger

Untitled

In reality
You took your heart away from me
Or was it the other way around
I thought the love would last this time-again I was wrong
Sometimes I feel empty, other times I feel sick
There was always that little tension
That separated us and eventually took a piece of our heart
In reality
I loved you-and will always care
But everything is different now
The pain is always there-even so how can I leave you
When you were such an important part of my life
Good-byes are not always forever
I just feels that way in our heart
I never meant to hurt you
Why we went through so much pain-I will never know
I may never understand what has happened
All I know is I must let go.

Jennifer Lynn Young

Extreme

You made my day, when you smiled that way.
You touch my heart when you glance my way.
You may not touch me in any way, sometimes it's only what you say.
To be with you would be my dream even though it may be EXTREME.

This is fact, not a lie, when you walk by I want to die.
If you smile, or just say "Hi", sometimes I want to cry.
To be with you would be my dream, even though it may be EXTREME.

If only the day I have my way, to be near you and you near me.
I know that day is coming soon, and when it does you will see that it's not just me in love with you, it's you in love with me.
To be with you would be my dream even though it may sound EXTREME.

Today we meet on the stairs, you and I passing by.
How nice that sounds to my ears one day it will
sound to you the same way.
You smile whispers love, and to me it whispers sweet honesty.
I never hear harm in you, that I must say I love about you.
To be with you would be my dream, even though it may sound EXTREME.

You made my day when you smiled that way. This is fact, not a lie.
If only the day I have my way. Today we meet on the stairs.
To be with you would be my dream even though it may sound EXTREME.

Jessica M. Roumell

A Mother's Deepest Love

Tears of joy came to my eyes when I heard
you were on the way.
I counted every minute till that joyful day.
Love filled my heart when I first looked into your tiny face,
A little daughter to dress up in ribbon and lace.
I loved you and held you tight in my arms.
I wanted to protect you from all harm.
I tried to teach you right from wrong
And to fill your heart with song.
I watched you grow from a child to a woman
For you I did all I can.
I gave you my heart, my soul, my tears.
To me you'll always be dear.
For you my love will always be.
I just pray that you'll always love me.

Jada Hardin

Facets

I wasn't at all sure of you when we first met.
You were so stiff, so formal, so quiet, so serious, so
scared...so...
but that's another poem.

Your two smiles teased me to see you again.
How brightly they shone, even if only for an instant.
I saw a facet of you
that made me think maybe an elf lived behind that dour exterior.

As we saw each other more and more
Your changed expression insinuated myriad facets.
Your eyes twinkled, your face fairly cracked from the huge grin -
too big to really fit on your face-transforming you,
much as the sun breaking through a bank of leaden clouds,
causes a giddy, joyous metamorphosis throughout the earth below.

Like the sun, that smile was warming, open, caressing.
I still saw the serious side of you,
but also the elf, the eager child, the stubborn, immovable rock
and was enchanted by them all.

Judith E. Meyersberg

"Standing On the Corner"

I have never seen such a sight,
Young men, old men standing on the corners.

Some stay up all night long,
No money, no home, no shoes, no clothes and no hope.

Their conversation is always what I used to do.
The young men always talking about, how much money they used
to make and won't settle for anything less.
The old men talking about how long they had been on their
job before the layoff.

They sit around old abandoned houses, drinking, playing
cards, throwing dominos to pass the time away.
There was never enough money for the family, left behind,
though there is money for cigarettes, beer, cheap wine and
drugs — items very unnecessary.

How long will they continue to stand on the corners with that;
long, lost, lonely look of no hope.

Where there is no life, there is no hope.
Where there is life, there is hope.
How long will they continue to stand on the corner?
How long!!! How long!!!

Carolyn L. Houston

Black Man

Black man who are you, to kill
your brotherman. Stop your fear and
start to heal, for our slaves have, been set freed.

You steal and plead just
for your needs, why will you let your brother Bleed.

Black man who are you to say
that anger is may only friend.
We will stand tall, and break down
that wall. For the white man has captured me.

No more whips and chains, for
it's time to rearrange; go ahead and be
a man, for every man needs a strong woman!

Dollicia Williams

For Mom

Now the day has finally come,
your daughters will has now been done.
You let me go, walk down the isle,
but you've walked with me the other miles.
All my life, through the years,
you've dried my eyes and calmed my fears.
"Have faith and trust", you've always said,
which has prepared me for the task ahead.
Months of work and days gone past,
but brides and moms don't get to dance.
So this is to thank you for all that you do,
and for all to hear that I truly love you.

Jeannine Klos

Untitled

Tomorrow's child the world is growing up fast
Your future world will eliminate our past
And all are left are memories
Hold on to them tight for the future will steal them from you cleverly
Remember your friends, and remember me
What beholds in your future we will soon see
In your world we can never be sure
Nature can die out forever more
People not knowing that they've done wrong
Forever, regretfully, we'll sing a song
Nature's best is all a waste
To rebuild our world is made of haste
Tomorrow's child your future world will be our doom.
The world's destruction is coming too soon
Let's rebuild our world, our gift of earth,
And not destroy it with a sense of mirth
Pollution and hate shouldn't be part of the deal
For sadness might be what we'll forever feel
Let us attempt to clean up our world
So the hidden beauty can be unfurled

Benchaluck Brikshavana

Silence!

He looked at me and inquired,
Your smile is lovely quick and broad!
Why then do you're eyes stand cold?

Calling out to me it demanded silence!

Please help me to understand,
What faith in life do memories send?
Never speaking yet shouting out the desire for an end!

Calling out to me it demanded silence!

Looking at him it sank low,
Memories are sometimes better left forgotten.

Once again, my heart demanded silence!

Dina L. Jones

Knowing The Dream Is Mine To Keep

I reach for the face dancing above me,
Your ghost still haunts my nighttime memory.
Drifting in and out of consoling sleep,
Knowing the dream is mine to keep.

Fantasy rules the dark in tranquil ease,
My heart lifts as your laughter does tease.
The illusion carries me through the night's passing,
Embracing your touch, mine for the asking.

Your smile glories the dark and weary cast,
With hope's renewal like springtime, fast.
I grasp your image for comfort and aid,
Clinging to mercurial warmth as it fades.

My beautiful lover of bygone days,
You are no longer with me in the sunlight's haze.
So I wish to remain in slumber deep,
Knowing the dream is mine to keep.

Colleen Bartholomew

David's Devotee

Florentine Flashback:
Your hands they arrest me. I stand at allegiance to You in awe of such chiseled erection perfection.
Dos Angeles in the Flesh Flash Forward:

Falling water from the blackest hole wakes up two charmed souls of stone; spinal tap surges locking and unlocking damned up tales of cold. Insertion of puzzled pieces, desertion of muddled minds and fearful foes leaves our pasts too weak and meek to take hold.

TO BE PRESENT IN OUR PRESENCE IS ALL WE NOW KNOW.

Geralyn Motto

The Alien

Many people say that aliens don't exist, except in the back of your mind.
Well, friends, listen to this, about an alien of a different kind;
It's as close as a nearby city, as far as a foreign land.
It has grown quite rapidly, and it's getting out of hand;
For the alien in question here is knows as "prejudice";
and there's no place known to man where this monster can't exist.
For years we heard it mentioned amongst just blacks and whites;
but it has spread like an infection to those who neither read nor write.
It's affecting the blind, the deaf, and the lame;
Not a single handicap we find, gets by with its proper name.
Like garments from a factory, people are being labeled;
"Steer clear of these folks, they're either different or disabled".
The Lord made all of us, and died for all our sins;
Never questioning our abilities, or the color of our skin.
So, when you go out of your house today, keep these two things in mind;
Lock your doors and windows, but leave the alien behind.

Darcy Rosenberger

Hope

I wish I never met you or never heard
your name, things were so much better before
you ever came.
I was the one who loved you but she was the
one you saw, you said that we were just friends
and that hurt me most of all.
Whenever I found myself alone all I did was
cry, no one saw the tears I shed I wanted
to kiss my life goodbye.
All I did was lock it up and keep it deep inside
I was afraid to let it out at one point I thought I'd die.
I know someday the tears will stop
and I'll learn to cope, you see someone special
showed me this when I'd almost given up hope.

Brianne Lockwood

"I Miss You"

I miss you so much
your smile, your smell, your simple touch

The way we laughed, the way we cried
the way we made love, the feeling inside

A simple kiss or two or three
gave me feeling, a feeling so free

Free from the world and all its pain
so please close your eyes and kiss me again

These little things you need too
but please be patient and know
that I miss you....

Dominick Flaiban

Tissues In Your Pockets

I found tissues in your pockets and my kids' photos in your locket.
Your sweet tiny, grandma-shoes made me cry.
The old memories gave us tearful laughs,
And, those wonderful old photographs....
Did I ever get to tell you good-bye?

Worn lipsticks of vibrant red and years of stuff piled on your bed.
Your nighties and little socks made me sigh.
That gorgeous twinkly Christmas sweater,
You kept my girlish large-print letters....
Did I ever get to tell you good-bye?

Your signature scent "White Shoulders"
And cancelled checks jammed into folders.
Saved birthday cards and valentines neatly tied.
Jewelry boxes full of treasures; your love I could not measure....
Did I ever get to tell you good-bye?

Lillian G. McCausland
(January 28, 1904 - June 8, 1992)

Ode To A Hero

Dear friend
You're not standing alone where you are
For your heroic feat of bravery
On heaven's team you'll always be a shining star

The ocean splashed wild, ferocious waves
You departed abruptly, tragically
For the love of those behind
You sacrificed yours without a pause

Your voyage, friend has left us a void
Deep and wide as the ocean to fill
Yet we swell with pride
As you've given us your dream to fulfill

Our thoughts on you remain
On the day when kinship we'll regain
Now and always you are our HERO
A polished treasure of the triumph we feel within

The memories of you we celebrate
Your love and compassion we emulate
Kindness, joy and sensitivity
A proud legacy you left for us to share

Alton S. Dunbar

A Place Called Home

A far off roll of thunder
the coolness in the air.
I know the storm is coming,
soon the rain will be here.

The distant call of a whippoorwill,
the wind whistling through the pines.
And thoughts of you and me
keep drifting across my mind.

The gentle sound of a trickling brook
running through the trees.
And flowers blooming,
and their soft scents
floating on the breeze.

Sitting in the yard at night
a full moon glowing
large and bright.

A sky filled with stars
that form a shining dome,
over this place that I
call my home.

Vicky Marine

Grand Canyon

With one gigantic booming roar
The earth split open to its core,
To spawn a giant crevice where
Great cliffs rose endless in the air.
Enormous wide and jagged cut,
Tremendous, gaping monstrous rut,
Gargantua hugely magnified,
With layered colors on each side,
Where, far below, the shadows play,
As tumbling waters find their way
In seething froth and swirling flow
That wear the rocks and boulders low.
Immense and massive mark of age
By wind and rain made hoary sage —
May eagles high for eons more
Smile down upon you as they soar.

M. D. Haworth

"Family Thanksgiving"

Tonight when it's cold outside.
The elms trees are all cold and dead;
The family will eat.
  Turkey,
  Chat,
  Watch T.V.
I like to dance in the cold.
  though I'd not say so;
I like us all to dance out our troubles.
Let our minds wonder
through the cold;

My father says, "No"
Everyone agrees
Except for me;
I cry silently.

Maggie Coryell

Untitled

Little girls picking daisies and putting
them in their hair trying to look
their best for Easter so they know what
to wear

Sarah Lynn Kinney

Life

Life is like a burning candle
The flame the soul
The candle the body
Brightly it burns
Glowing with vibrance
Tranquil and controlled
Fragile and mortal
Yet potent and lethal in anger
Slowly it burns
Leaving its tiny indelible mark
With the passing time
The candle melts, the flame dims
and with a flicker
Silently passes
in a puff of smoke
on its invisible journey to the next world.

William M. Sutherland

January Thaw

Today I heard a blue jay cry,
The geese were also in the sky.

The hawk was circling way above,
I also heard the moan of the dove.

The cats are hunting in the field,
A fox was looking for a meal.

The water is running in the stream,
Rhyming with the lone hawks scream.

He's sweeping down to get his prey,
As if to say "you make my day".

The deer are eating and the frog crooks,
The horses grazing in the great oaks.

But this is January: it should be cold,
A day like this is just like gold.

Rudolph S. Belich

Graduation

Standing at the cross roads,
The goal, the dream at hand.
Four long, yet short years
Since it all began.

Here you are the "Graduate"
one step away from glory.
Pride, honor, and diploma in hand,
Ready to tell 'your' story.

Blood, sweat, and tears,
Dedication, frustration, and fears.
They've all played their part,
on the path to success thru these years.

Open the door,
To the world Brand new.
To take 'your' place,
And always believe in you.

Shonda Smith

Time Saving

Today was just another day in time
the hour went back and missed a
chime an hour more sleep I am blessed
I get to get my much needed rest
they say the day will be longer too
oh great now there will be more to do.
Backward or forward which is better
can you inform me and send a letter.

Robert M. Donald

Till Death Do Us Part

First comes
the gorgeous bridal gown
beautiful bride's maids
the ring bearer now enters
slowly politely presenting
the wedding band

Unity everlasting love
warmth direct from the heart
a wonderful life together as one
Till Death Do Us Part...

Little disagreements
turn to
innumerable battles
the anger wells up inside
then it bursts

The legal agreements
  endless documents
    custody battles cold glances
      in the pressuring courtroom
Till Death Do Us Part...

Kelly McNamee

Untitled

If I could dance,
  the grass would be my stage,
  the winds would be my music,
  the trees would be my audience.

I would not envy
  the birds for their wings,
  the deer for their grace,
  nor the swans for their beauty.

If I could dance,
  I would soar like the birds,
  with the grace of the deer.
My beauty would be within me.

If I could dance,
  I would not feel ugly.
If I could dance...
  would I really be happy?

Nanci Flett

For My Faraway Love

Somebody Misses You

Somebody misses your smile
The hugs and kisses you share
The warmth in your heart
The LOVE in your eyes
The way that you listen and care.
Somebody misses your laughter
Reassuring and kind and sincere
The touch of your hand
The sound of your voice
The comfort of knowing you're near.
Somebody misses the magic
Of the wonderful things that you do
The secrets you hold
The dreams you reveal
The way you make wishes come true.
Somebody waits for tomorrow
Another day closer to when
The hoping is ended
The wishing is over
And somebody holds you again.

K. Mowry

The Lady In The Chair

She was a beautiful lady,
The lady in the chair.
She played her mandolin as they danced,
A talent so very rare.

They gathered money while she played
And gave it to the poor.
She felt so humble...she could help
To open someone's door!

The rhythm that this lady had
Would make them look and stare.
She was my beautiful Mother —
The lady in the chair!

Sophie Sinigos

Life

The life I knew was never there
The life I know is very rare

For 1 out of 5 will feel like me
Suffering pain and agony

But those of us must stick together
Or this crime will last forever

I know the lord is by our side
He's taking the same journey-
He's taking the same ride

For the lord our god feels our fears
And comes down to wipe away our tears.

Lydia Martinez

Conversing Ebb

Crossed tongues, cheap shots,
The louder the better.
Limits cut, faint remembrances,
Boundaries become lines of illusion.

Whores of vocabulary,
Walls built quite high.
Basic instincts, backed to the bricks.
Can anyone understand?

Lost love, gender fears,
I can't make it out.
Heart break, and tears cascade,
Apocalypse is at hand.

Jaded affection, no cerebral colors.

E. Von Kreis

Restless Hearts

A soft crisp white evening
The moon afire
Stars kiss the sky
I lie pure in thought.

Stroking your soft curly brows
Touching your nectar lips
Pale clouds clip the moon
Tenderly I sculpt your existence,
ever so still.

Hearts longing.
I gently dust the sleep from your eyes.
Unconscious smiles.
I rest my worried hands and
Understand I'm holding in them
my life.

I awaken
Restless hearts.

Kena Lynn-Elkin Forbis

Jacuzzi Moonrise

Into the night sky,
the moon did rise.
Behind the clouds,
over the trees,
And through the mist
in front of me.
Rising, resurrected on
the curtain of night,
and casting shadows with
its eye of pale moonlight.
To a wandering eye
it does appear,
On this night and
in this sky so clear.
The ghost of the Sun
does haunt this night.
Only to return again with
its eye of pale moonlight.

Matthew J. Parmer

"Moondrops"

Maybe
The Moon means well
But believes
That in a constant universe
That in a constant consciousness
Things will never change

Yet
It cannot be denied
My eyes have wandered above me
Seeking this sphere
This pale Gray
Endeavor
Even while entertained
By a small circus of sunlight

And because of this
These same eyes
Drown
Under fathoms of tears
In tides
Only pulled by the Moon

Lynne Carretta

"The Misty Stair"

Seems air spirits gathered there,
- the mossy length of misty stair.
To reach the top in pensive thought,
the sight! I stop - in rapture caught.

And almost catch the spirit there,
seems almost speaks - on misty stair.
And almost guides - soft by the hand,
yes as in dreamy state I stand.

The stair of stone - in joy to climb,
so graceful flight invites the rhyme.
And spirits live to commune there,
- upon the height of misty stair.

Seems air spirits gathered there,
- the mossy length of misty air.
To reach the top in pensive thought,
the sight! I stop - in rapture caught.

Mark W. Haggerty

A Holiday Metaphor

Our Christmas tree has taken I'll.
The needles fall like rain.
Though cared for, oh so, faithful,
life within proceeds to drain.

The ornaments are breaking
and the flocking has grown old.
It used to be a work of art,
a beauty to behold.

And once it used to give our home
the fragrant scent of pine.
But, all that lingers for us now,
are memories in our minds.

I think it all a metaphor
regarding year gone past.
Just like our pretty Christmas tree,
It never seems to last,

Tami J. Healy

The Secret Of Love

The secret of love can conquer all
The negativity in today's society
From fat to thin, from short to tall
from drugs to crimes and from alcohol

The secret of love can't be brought
with various credit cards
The secret of love is within our hearts

The secret of love isn't impress
with beautiful homes and expensive cars
with fancy suits and with fancy dress

The secret of love applause a heart
that can't freely give,
that can unconditionally love,
is truly bless

The secret of love overlooks the colors
of black and white, of brown and yellow
The secret of love is a graceful path
that we should follow

The secret of love do believes that unity and
peace will positively establish today's society

Warnita Pleasant

Bank Burglars

I went to my bank last week
The one in the village on the right
As soon as I went inside
I saw an awful sight

There must have been a burglary
Yellow crime scene ribbons at the door
The dirty burglar scoundrels
Even took the rugs up from the floor

It looked like school vandals
Had done their dirty work that night
Why in one back room of the bank
They took everything in sight

They took the rug and walls
They even took the floor
I saw clean down to the dirt
They couldn't take away any more

I spoke to a bank official
About my observation
She said there was no burglar
They were having a renovation

Kenneth A. Benish

"Old Bear"

Remember our bear,
 the one that was gold?
A friend to each of us,
 and now he's so old.
He was patched and stuffed
 when his threads came unwound.
Once he wore out!
 So got a new coat of brown.
Lost an arm and an eye,
 but we loved him anyway.
Then we finally grew up
 and old-bear went away.
He went to bear heaven,
 my Mama told me.
But I know he's recycled
 to another family.
Kids make times happy,
 these things I am told.
Remember our bear?
 The one that was gold-

Sharon Norton

Do You Hear What I Hear?

Do you hear the cry of pain?
The pain that they endure;
Through war and hate and hunger,
And yet there is a cure.

Do you hear the cry of death?
The anger and horror of it all,
The torture that lies ahead,
The memories they recall.

Do you hear the cry of ignorance?
Do you see us gawk, and stare?
The world stands by and shakes its head,
But do we really care?

Do you hear the cry of hope?
The hope we give to others,
Let us not stand by and watch-
Under God we are all brothers.

Do you see the joy of life?
Their happy dreams fulfilled,
See the light back in their eyes,
The cup of life is filled.

Maria Surma

Abandon

LONELY
 The parched desert sand blows now.
LIFELESS
 The wind blows it fierce.
RECKLESS
 It rattles through termite range.
BROKEN
 Weather beaten in wind and tears.

Only a shell of abode remaining.
Grandfather ghost of lumber laid down.
Once gilded cage, twisted and worn.
This from where she was delivered.

She flew away, stark white and barren.
Dropping free flight feathers
In simple abandon and knowing.
The hinged door having fallen away.

Karen D. Tate

Missing You

I miss the hug this morning
The pat upon my head.
I know the tender "I love you"
Will never more be said.

"Gee, you sure look nice today,
I'm glad you are my wife."
Those words will echo in my mind
Thru joy and thru strife.

No valentine to buy this year
And not one to receive.
A single rose laid on your grave,
I'll hurt, and cry, and grieve.

No "how are you this morning"
No hugs, no pats, no smile,
For God took Donnie home with Him
To walk the final mile.

Mary Lou McCrary

Here Come The Storms

Here come the storms
The rain descends around me.
I can't endure the norms
They are as far as the eye can see.
Let the thunder cast down,
Let them leave me be.
They can be a striking sound
They can be hollow and grim,
They can be alone or in sets,
Like branches on a broken limb.
There should be no rendering of debts
Let the storms surround us.
We have to challenge their greatness
Can't you see we must.

Melissa McClure

"Love"

Love is like the ocean,
The sea is calm and blue.
Living life without you,
Would be too hard to do.

The love that's in my heart,
Tells me we can't be a part.
The faith that brought us together,
I wish would last forever.

Life is like a mountain,
People come and go.
Why they go away,
Nobody will ever know.

If you see a dove,
Flying through the air.
You will know it's filled with love,
For everyone to share.

Love is like the ocean,
The sea is calm and blue.
Living life without you,
I would die to have to do.

Shannon Platteter

Widower

Before -
The seeds are planted:

After the spring
the flowers of a Dogwood Tree,
the bloom of Cherry blossoms,
blush is painted on that day.

Baby's breath veils the face,
flowers are thrown
and petals to prick
are dropped-not blown
and are placed in baskets to dry.

Beware the thorns
that piece the wedding veil,
that takes away the blush,
the bride left pale.

Marc Edward Shelton

The Hour

Great prophets wrote us all
the signs are crystal clear,
the truth being re-told
but no one wants to hear-

Of the 'Old Rugged Cross'
or of the 'Promised Land',
we think ourselves righteous
but the hour is at hand.

The worry of money
and of possessions lost,
the words are not heeded
our souls are the cost.

As great light from the sky
approached far and near,
will you know who he is?
The hour is now here...

Lisa Witter

Night Shadows

Moon cast shadows stretch across
 the silent, silvery land,
their slender fingers part the grass
 and stroke the resting sand.

A tender, young evening breeze
 gently lifts each flower,
and softly weaves thru the trees
 mindless of the hour.

The slender branches shift and blow
 and set the shadows dancing,
while the leaves whisper soft and low
 about the moon's romancing.

Nancy Sanford

Love's Day

The sky was blue and high above,
The moon was new and so was love.
You came at last, love had its day,
that day has passed, you've gone away.

The sky is blue, the night is cold,
The moon is new but love is old.
And while I'm waiting here for you,
there's nothing else I'd rather do.
So why can't you open your eyes and see,
I'm praying for you to come back to me.

Thuy Nguyen

Memories Of Summer

The day is perfect.
The soft, blue sky mingles
with a few clouds.
The tide is out.
Waves break gently as if to
kiss the shoreline.
It must be early summer
For plants debris rests
along the coast.
The sand, a battlefield.
Once a place of action,
Now...ruins.
The two figures are happy.
They hold each other with
bonds of love
As a slight breeze blows against their back.
Their shadow reads just before noon.

Theresa Kramer

Untitled

I anticipate her with longing.
The soft words with which
I will caress her inner being
are forming inside me now.

I long to lie beside her form
as the morning light of day
lies softly on her skin;
a gentle breeze awakening her
to my touch.

Unspoken feelings, conveyed
by the tenderness of yielding lips
against her body,
are worn and unfolding within me.

Gently we're lost in the crystal waters
of each other's eyes;
letting the warm waves cover us, sharing
their rhythm,
tasting their saltiness, as they place us on
the warm
sand of trust.

Paula St. John

"Merry Christmas"

The snow is slowly falling
The stars are shining bright,
It's as if heaven is a diamond
On this Christmas night.

The silence is so peaceful
As the Christmas lights glow,
You can look out at the angels
The children made in the snow.

If only Christmas time
Could come more than once a year,
If only everyday
Was filled with so much cheer,

The children singing, laughing,
The few days go by so fast,
If only I were magic
I would make Christmas last.

Kimberley A. Weatherly

Rain

The animals are heading for shelter.
The storm is coming faster.
The rain, the thunder and lighting
is here.
Things are hectic Oh dear Oh dear!
I can hear the pitter pater of the rain.
The lightning sounds like a big bang.
The wind is blowing.
I wish it was snowing.
But since it isn't I will try to make
the rain more pleasant.

Kelly Dalluge

Unconditional Love

A love so pure
the strength to endure
provide shelter from the rain
comfort for the pain
no reason to fear
nothing to hide
no questions asked
nothing denied
fight for, breathe life for
never be cold
always a hand to hold
welcome with open arms
keep safe, keep warm
always a friend
from now till the end
can be put to the test
unlike all the rest
always accept
never reject
equal respect

Maureen Fulco

For Mother's Love

Cradled in Gravities warmth,
the Sun,
hushes through nurseries cycles,
her Son
While mystic breadth of evensong calls
the release from her care
as the breakdown of walls
For as safe as her orbit
keeps him today
this pull also pauses
Shared tenders way.

Thomas Perkins

Graduation

The day begins to wear away,
The sun is sinking low.
Suddenly Heaven is ablaze
With bursts of red and gold.

How like our Lord when life's day ends
To take his faithful home.
To take the hand who long has toiled
And claim him for his own.

Come Lord, Jesus, light the way
Of Heavens celestial door.
Bless this one who thou hast chosen
To live forevermore.

Come dwell with joy unspeakable,
Loved ones there to meet -
The last for which the first was made,
The unbroken circle complete.

Merle Barnett Jackson

Knight's Battle

Always waiting for the night.
The warmth it radiates, like love.
It knows it is the true existence.
Alone, it wanders through the day.
It waits for me to rise up and whisper,
O stay close to me, my knight!
Forlorn, I think on thee.
I wait, but he does not come.
The sun has erased him from my heart.
Jealous, the ardent attacker jumps.
And crushes my knight, who
Like a hawk, waits for the attack.
He pushes back the blade of light,
And rises, triumphant, with the stars.
Defiantly, he rests in my embrace.
Waiting the moment when he must again,
Come to battle.

Kara Underside

My Daughter, Barbie

I love you, darling, just
the way you are; when near
or when the distance in
between grows far; I love
your smile; the way you tease
your hair; your willingness
to go that extra mile,
regardless of for whom
or where. And deep within
your heart and agile mind,
there lies no hint of scorn
my dear, of any kind!

Sidney L. Shulters

Lost Youth

When I was a child
the whole world seems
so colorful and bright
the only thing missing
was freedom in my mind

Time has cut those ties which bound me
but freedom seems a bit trifle now
that I have it today
because autumn has come
and the colors of Spring
have faded away

Sebastian

The Sea

The sea is calm, the sky is blue,
The wind glides across the sea.
Under the sea it is different,
Dark, cold, frightfully haunting.
With great ships lying,
On the bottom of the sea.
It depends on how you see it,
The sea is very large.
Great reefs are laced with coral,
While iridescent fish race by.
There are fish you cannot see,
Because they are camouflaged.
There are creatures so small,
You can barely see them.
Then there are creatures,
That are bigger than boats.
In many ways the sea is quite mysterious,
It is a different world down there.

Wendy Jean Jock

Two Colors

They caress in each others arms;
Their lips combine slowly as one
He longs for her body,
As she searches his soul.

They felt the truth could never be,
Only a fantasy,
Than they embraced one another,
Kissing passionately.

He loved her like no one before,
Making her explode with passion,
Frightened she backs away,
Unsure of what to say.
They touch softly without hesitation,
She falls into his arms.
A fantasy becomes reality,
Not two colors but one.

Mary Ellen Caufield

Sonata In A Wahiawa Garden Oahu, Hawaii

In the heights of Wahiawa
There is a little garden glen,
Where rare botanical's flourish
In the playful pacific wind.

Lilting notes of a distant flute
On an outing when I was there,
Poured melody invisibly
Upon the benevolent air.

So pervasive was the music
And sympathetic to my ear,
It distracted from my thoughts
Exotic flora standing near.

Traveling palms clapped staccatos,
Hibiscus whispered tremolos,
An orchid on a banyan limb
Danced and swayed in the shaded grove.

The orchid conducted them all,
Blending the flute and its clear sound
With expressions from the flora
And raucous mynahs on the ground.

Lorraine Yearwood

My Family Tree

As I look at my family tree,
There's many people that I see,

Aunts and uncles, by the dozens,
Mothers, fathers, grandparents, cousins.

My brother, sister, and of course me
All right here in my family tree.

I love my family very much,
I always will, you see,

We'll all be together forever,
Here on my family tree.

Kristen Kuczenski

Sounds In My Head

The rustling of leaves
The still and silent sea
The sirens screams in the night
Sounds of gunshots in my head
These are confusing things....
but what would be of me
if there were none
of these things...

Salvatore Iacono

A Gift From God

Watching you Matt as you grow
there's nothing more fulfilling

From trikes to bikes,
through fears and tears,
there's always hugs and caring.

To hear your laughter
and watch you play
brings so much joy to me.

Your freckles, your smile
you're as cute as can be
I love you Matt, your a part of me.

I'm so proud of your achievements
and your eagerness to learn
just do your best that's all I ask
with that will come success.

Just be happy and always remember;
No matter what you do
I'll always love you Matt
for just being you.

Melissa West

Tear Drops

Sadness, pain, loneliness, hurt, tears.
These are my companions for the rest
of my years.

Sweet moments remembered,
They come to me at night
And vanish by the mornings light.

Oh! that they a were here again
In reality to stay
and didn't have to go away.
Cry!
Cry!
Cry!
Goodbye!

Miryah Robyn

The String Of Pearls

The Pearls?
They form slowly
and I string them one by one..
I'm careful where I lay them
that the string is not undone.

They have a glowing lustre
and a special inner shine..
they've developed from a rendering
made from the grit of time.

I hope that I can wear these pearls
and perhaps showing in my face..
the reflection coming from them
giving poise and quiet grace.

Close to my heart I'll wear them
of my life they are the sum..
my beautiful invisible string of pearls
the beads of acquired wisdom.

Kathleen Parker

"Puppy Talk"

She feeds me those teats
They give me the shits
I'm going to get me
Some kibbles and bits

Milton Yates

My Friends In The Sky

Sparkling lights in the night,
They glow so bright.
Like beautiful, tiny diamonds,
Oh, what a sight!

When I fell a little blue,
I long for the night to become due.
I talk to my little friends up there,
And my cares seem to disappear.

One night, joy was pouring out of my
heart.
So I rushed to tell my loved friends.
They shone ever so radiant,
Rejoicing at the happiness I found.

Brilliant stars, my true friends,
Are you as beautiful if you descend?
Will you be as caring
If I had you, in the palm of my hand?

Sarah Yap

Parents

They brought me into this beautiful land,
They held me with their strong hands,
They taught me how to love,
They gave me strength to rise above.
They taught me right from wrong,
They sang me a beautiful song.
They listened to me cry,
They listened to me shout,
They listened to me scream,
They listened to me pout.
They comforted my fears.
They held when I was in tears.
These beautiful people are my parents,
My father and my mother
And sometimes we don't bother
To tell them how much they mean
To you and me,
For these are the people
Who set us free.

Summer R. Chaudhari

Prayers

Prayers,
they help you out
Prayers,
you don't have to
shout'em out
Prayers, there really neat when
your worried

My prayer is-
When I pray
I pray so deep
I pray that
these prayers
will be keeps
who do I
pray to. I
pray to you
I pray that
my family will be
healthy and me too.

Stephanie Sheldon

Parents

When I come home late,
they say I'm bad.
When I'm full of hate,
they think that's sad.
When I make them wait,
it gets them mad.
Wouldn't it be great,
if they'd just be glad.

Kerrie Suzanne Hamilton

Untitled

Through drowning eyes
They see the glow
Then someone sighs
It's just not so...

In burning hearts
They feel the pain
The fire starts
They're all insane...

In tainted minds
They close the door
Then blackness blinds
Fear cry's for more...

Through breathless souls
They touch what's true
The faint bell tolls
My love for you

Louis Clifton Davies III

Dreams

In dreams I laugh, I cry, I see,
They seem to be a part of me.
Sometimes I'm travelling to and fro,
Always wondering, where I'll go.

Some dreams are strange,
Some dreams are fun,
Sometimes I walk, sometimes I run.

WILL I SWIM?
WILL I FLY?
AM I LIVING?
WILL I DIE?

If dreams aren't real, what could they be?
They seem to be a part of me.
Where did they come from?
Where will they go?
I'll just keep searching, until I know.

I sometimes awaken with a smile, or a
SCREAM!
But soon I remember, it was only a dream.
I try to remember, but find I forgot,
My dreams were just with me, but now
they are not.

Patricia Jane Hendzel

Plastic People

They love within their plastic walls;
They walk along their plastic halls;
They wear plastic smiles on plastic faces;
They care only for their plastic places.

They cannot see inside their souls;
They have, instead only holes.
They cannot look inside you or me;
They have plastic eyes, you see.

Katharine Heinrichs

Untitled

The walls are more secure now
This fortress of my heart
begging to be broken into
The walls had crumbled
The white knight entered
and slain all in sight
Now the doors are locked
The bridge drawn up
over the moat of tears
Inside the walls no one can see
The inner turmoil hidden
by smiling eyes and laughs
One citizen still begging
begging to be let out
The King Mind says no
For when one falls they all fall
there would be no fortress left

Marsha Ellen Melick

Dear Sully

Roses are red, violets are blue
This is the only way I can think of
to say I love you, I tried to find words
But it's hard for me, I'm much too shy
Than you are to me
I shouldn't have said
Those terrible words,
But you were getting
Right on my nerves
But I am truly sorry
As sorry as can be, so all I want
Is for you to forgive me
And even though,
Your name means dirt
You're the kind of girl
That I don't want to hurt
Before this poem ends
I have one thing to say
After all this stuff happened
I love you anyway

Robert Lee Flenoy V

Love

It fills the heart with happiness.
This thing they call love.
It can make your life very bright.
It makes your eyes sparkle,
like the stars in the night.
Everything feels so right.
This thing they call love.
It changes your way of life,
not knowing why.
One fine line about love, it can make
people cry and make people fight.
God never gave an answer as to why.
This thing they call love,
is a mystery in man's eyes.
We'll never know why,
it's only love.

Robert N. Madrid

Within

Few have a beauty that penetrates
to those depths beneath the skin,
but that beauty that you radiate
has a beginning deep within.

William L. Carroll III

A Glimpse Of Sunlight

I caught a glimpse of sunlight
Through a heavy mist;
Donning bright warm colors
And rays of tenderness.

I caught a glimpse of sunlight
Slithering through the trees;
A golden ray of sunlight
Swaying with the breeze.

I caught a glimpse of sunlight
As she went walking by;
I saw her quickly beam away
And nestle in the sky...

Ronald A. Lew

The Beckoning

Walk with me
through time
Our journey
is calling
The soul of eternity
begs us to follow
Clench my hand
with your heart
please
come with me
love with me
through life...

Kerry Hurley

Beauty Of Nature

Beauty so covered in a blanket of snow,
'Til the sun comes on the rise,
Melted away it them reveals,
Nature's true surprise.

Brown replaced by luscious green,
Rain replaces snow,
Vivid colored flowers,
Stand against the soft spring blow,

To Earth your known as Mother,
Father is that of time,
To nature your a blessing,
To human your peace of mind.

Victoria Rose Roberts

Family Reunion

Reunion time is again
Time to contact our family and friends
Hello will you be able to come
This year we plan to have big fun

We will try to do our best
To reach you and all the rest
As early as we possibly can
Tell all the others we have a plan

We come by bus and come by car
Sometime distance are so very far
We'll come by train and even plane
The joy of it all remain the same

To family and friend I'll say
Don't put off another day
To prepare to meet and greet them all
See how many faces you call recall

Hi mary, Jack and Sue
How's everything oh it's you
Oh I'm so glad that you could come
Family reunion is a Family bond

Margaret Miller

A Poet's Thought

Upon a bench I sit,
To capture a thought:
Watching searching the
things I feel:
Writing not drawing
a pictorial shot:
Awaking truths that
are so real:
This gives to me
Relaxing moments:
Feeling an unknown
goal to reach:
For "A Poet's thought"
is this special event:
In hopes of practicing
that what I preach.

Walter N. Parelius Jr.

Guardian Angels

They are the messengers of God
to do his work for him here,
to guide and protect us in this life
so we never have any fears.

A helping hand we'll always need
in most everything we do,
but sometimes things do go bad
then we pray our angel comes through.

They can't always change our lives
no matter how hard they try,
we just have to know they'll be there
and they will never say good-bye.

Most of us will never see them
and we most likely will never know,
that God has given each of us one
to guide us on the path we'll go.

So never forget God sent them
to help us with our fears,
live your life to the fullest
and give thanks your Guardian Angels near.

Sharon Theuerkauf

Tears Keep Falling

You left me here all alone
to grow up on my own
I wish you could have called
this doesn't seem like you
not at all
You left I said bye
I write you wrote
you called I received
but why so soon God
called you to leave
I miss you, oh how I do
I love you if only you knew
you left once, and then returned
you left again, but now
you're really gone

Nikkia Clark

Missing You

Making love to you
was, my way of showing
you my affection and
emotional love, for you

Kenneth Khrist Nebeker

Invitation

When I take your hand
to guide your eager touch,
When I cup your face
And drink passionfruit
from soft, wet lips,
I leave a lingering kiss
for you to taste
on even wetter lips

When you lay your smile
on the honey heat of me
watch me open
like the anemone, then
you are my butterfly
bringing hope to my flowers,
only then do I tremble
like the single petal
of a young rose
dancing beneath
the first early morning
rain of spring.

Kim-Monique Johnson

Thoughts

We give our souls
To Heaven's cries.
We open our mind
To Satan's lies.
We use our body's
For mans desire.
As we lend our life
To the final hour.

We see all that goes on around,
And hear each N-every sound.
To which we chose to watch and listen,
is of our own decision.

Michael J. Anderson

Tear Drops

Not to cry is easy to learn
To hold them in and let them burn
You always say "I have to be strong"
They'll rip you apart... it won't be long
Letting them out is hard to do
But if it has to be alone then do it... for you
Why is crying such a shame?
Did you ever wish those
Tear drops came?

Kathy Simmons

Dear Father

You have given me the strength
to make the transition, from being
a devil to a loving christian.
Your word I will preach both day
And night. I will serve you
faithfully with all my might.
My soul is whole and I owe
it all to you; you cleansed it
father and made it a new. Now
I must shine and be that
inspiration; to those who are
occupied by the devils temptation.
I will preach your word from
the mountain high, to the valley
low. I will preach your word
to both thy friend, and thy foe.

Willie D. Collins, Sr.

Doug Winnes

M.S. has slowed his body
to just this side of stopped.
He lives life—really lives it—
in bed or wheelchair propped.

He has a sense of humor,
he loved to smoke a pipe.
Accounting was his business
and he's the football type.

Best of all he prays for me;
a daily prayer I asked.
He promised for a year and,
then, fore'er took up the task.

Friends and family in their need
I often bring him, too.
Knowing he remembers them,
helps to get them through.

Blessings by the day and hour
have richly come to me.
I recommend to everyone
a partner such as he.

Sister Mary Timothy

It Hurts Me To My Heart

It hurts me to my heart
To know the people I love
Just die all of a sudden
Or choose to sell drugs

I've grown to love
Everyone that I know
Because you never know
Who's next to go

I admit there are
A few people I don't like
But you don't see me in their face
Trying to pick a fight

We should cling together
Like brothers and sisters
So destroy the drugs
And drop the pistols

Let's stop the hate
And show more love
Let's make Him proud
The One above

Tonja Milligan

Wild Heart

It was a time for me
to mend my heart
and search my soul
To look down lonely roads
and try to find myself
choosing to hold onto some memories
while letting others go
at times my heart raced with excitement
and others it ceased to beat
I stopped looking back
but instead looked forward
never looking down
only straight ahead
to where my wild heart
would race again...

Laura Elizabeth Evans

Little Acre Pond

Near the fence line,
To the edge of woods,
Was an acre pond
Mysterious and compelling.

Climb up a long incline of dirt and rock,
At the top,
Through pricker bushes,
needling.

There is the pond,
A few stones around,
some grass,
A corner where leaves and twigs
Have docked.

No ducks, or fish, just a gray cold pond,
With an old guardian maple tree,
Standing tall, bent, gnarled;

Keeps you lingering, looking.
Little acre pond, unspoiled
Beauty, mysterious, compelling.

Sally L. Henderson

Untitled

Fate has brought her
To where she lay.
Alone, cold, and wet from the rain.

An old sweatshirt,
Blanket or towel?
Too much to ask, anything at all?

My heart aches.
Tears fill my eyes.
I contemplate, wondering why.

Why is she there,
Living on the streets?
Asking for handouts, lost in defeat.

I look away.
Am I snob?
What differs us, me having a job?

I thank God above,
For a warm bed,
Food to eat, and a roof over my head.

Kym Lamb

My Feelings

I felt such an urgency
to write I felt pain,
At that very moment I
knew I would never be the same,

To say what you feel
and express it to others,
Is a spiritual feeling
that makes my heart flutter,

I cannot understand
what are these emotions I'm feeling,
perhaps it's God's way
Of showing me there is meaning,

To all that he has told us
from the beginning of time,
Like waking up in the morning
and seeing the sun shine,

All these things we take for granted
are not without cost,
But should we not have them would
surely feel lost

Theresa Brucculeri

Happy Birthday, My Love

Happy Birthday, my love.
Today is your day
To feel special and honored
In every way.

I love you, my dear
With all of my heart.
I cherish the day
That we got our start.

May we always be happy
Sharing joys and sorrows
With God and our families
In many tomorrows.

Robin Harvey

Alive Again

Bright sunshine, warm
tomorrows are here
Whispering to me are
the rays of sun peering
through the branches.
A glow of many colors
from mountains all around
Drenched by dew are the
leaves on each new tree
I see.
On a canyon the hills seem
level now
I can walk, better yet, I will
run till I reach the top.
It's not far, it was never
far at all.
I thank you God.

Laurie Myers

The Holocaust

In the camp, I only see
tons of bodies around me.
I'm unable to breathe because
of the smell that surrounds me.
Everyday is new to me.
No energy to move a knee.
No energy at all.
I'm hungry and tired.
So please remove me
from this place that doesn't need me.
The sight is unbearable to see.
It's no fair that they took me.
Oh, world don't you see me?

Rebecca McNulty

"Dreams In The Wind"

Dreams in the wind,
Too beautiful to be believed,
Dissipate like mist,
Leaving us bereaved.

Standing on a hilltop,
Watching as a bird flies,
Listening as our dreams are blown
To the great eternal skies.

Dreams in the wind,
Leaving us deceived,
Tempting our straining ears,
Leaving dreams to be conceived.

Lacey Wolforth

Autumn's Play

The trees sway,
touching the earth.

The leaves chant
their frightened song.

The winds of autumn
have come to play.

Bullying the trees
to bend as they say.

Hopefully soon the
play shall cease.

And once again
the trees shall be at peace.

Sabrina Watkins

The Moon

The moon lights
Traveling beams far and bright-
Light my darkness,
Fill my eyes,
Beautiful images
Take me high.
The moon searches
The desire, the need.
Shine on me,
Let me be
The one and only.
I'll light the darkness;
I'll fill the light
Through the journey of the night.

Monica M. Seefeldt

Ageing

Silently,
treading rolling waters,
keeping afloat
with fierce resolution.

Listening hard,
looking close,
seeking to maintain
a fragile equilibrium.

Things are different now.
new realities
flood
the caverns of my being.

I am different now —-
yet — more myself,
than ever I was before.

Willa M. Thompson

Untitled

Diamonds are forever: I often hear
them say, "My diamond found
A new love," and his is there
to stay. Now let me
ask you if I may. Is it
true a thousand words
a picture say? My baby's
picture said a word, which
was good-by today.

Ramiro Leal

Snowfall

The world is a snow globe
Turned upside down
When righted, soft snow flakes
Dance gracefully to the ground
Frosting the tree, the shrubs,
and the like
Transforming all nature to
Confectioned delights
Some dipped in sugar
Others whipped cream,
But none of it fattening
A sugar plum dream
Spoonfuls and sprinkles and dollops
of icing
Creates a dream world
Fresh and enticing
So forget your worries,
your heartaches and woes
Build snowmen and castles
Just have fun when it snows

Mary Jo Salfai

Days End

As the day slowly fades,
twilight settling in
tempers flare,
a sign of the days fatigue.
We sit across the room
from each other
staring.
Until we both laugh
realizing how petty our moods
must seem.
We move closer
together
holding each other
letting our tensions drain.
Together we lapse into
restful sleep.
At peace with each other
and the love that we
share.

Richard Swiontek

God's Gift

Three groups of rusty, rosy leaves,
Twin spirals rising from their midst
Exquisitely balanced
In a green glass vase;
This from my Smoke tree
On a day when I was ill
And house-bound.

From God's own hand
To brighten my day
As if an angel
Had stopped by my house
To leave this precious gift
That I might be uplifted
And smile.

Yet, what I did
Was snip it from the tree,
This priceless, loving gift
From God to me.

Ruby B. Rawlins

Thinking (River Run Wild)

My thoughts are like a river run wild,
Twisting and turning,
Endlessly flowing throughout my brain,
Entering and escaping;
In pools of emotions

Until they hit the falls,
Then the river freezes over,
All is still;
And all of time is gone

The only thing that remains
Is the melting of ice,
My thoughts; my feelings
Starting a new river run wild;
In someone else's mind, to come

Nicole Michelle Jameson

The Mysteries Of Life

The mysteries of life seems to be,
Unclear when I try to see
When times go by, tick-tock.
I look back, it's all quite a shock.
Moving on in a cautious glare,
Hoping in time I will still care,
What mysteries life holds for me,
Will God grant me time to see.
Can my mind still be strong.
Searching for right but accepting wrongs.
Standing firm on solid ground.
Pull myself up when life lets me down
Praying what God has planned for me
Will be fulfilled wholeheartedly.

Phyllis M. Brown

Strangely Beautiful

My dream's
unusual
and
bizarre
Some times wonderful
and strangely beautiful
Locked behind a door
that I want to open,
but I am scared
and I think
what I'm scared of
is.
Myself.

Kassandra Bentley

The Maple Woods

I remember the maple woods where we
used to seek freedom.
I remember running across the hazy
grass with confidence of you by my side.
I remember the eccentric touch of your
hand embalmed into mine.
I remember the flippant beat of my
heart when the drowning sun would get
caught in your eyes.
I remember the long nights, surrounded
by petals, as the breeze made my soul
shiver.
But most of all, I remember the maple
tree where our names use to be
intertwined with one another as if almost
one...

Sara Jawaid

The House Upon The Hill

The old white house sits regally
Upon her windswept hill
Windows looking out like "eyes"
On yesterdays gone by

She was built to weather out the storms
Of life's tempestuous "seas"
Her timbers braved the elements
A fortress in their might

She saw the changing of the seasons
"Her" children growing tall
She felt the warmth of family
Sheltered 'neath her massive walls

She heard the sounds of laughter
Children's feet upon her stairs
She saw the passing of the ages
As her daylight turned to night

Now no more the sounds of laughter
Or footsteps on her stairs
Only echoes of the past remain
In the House upon the Hill.

Leta Reimann

Time!

Every moment of time you reflect
upon those who guide, support
you in your Ideas

Every given day is time you
have chosen a new step in
your path of life to survive

Every week sums up who you
will become

Every month you have reaped
a new habit

Every year is a decade of
lost memories, and in those
you will find just"
"who you really are"

Kerima Salangsang

What Is An Idea?

An idea is...
very interesting
so amazing
quite serious
unbelievably creative
a lot of thinking
how mysterious!
The exaggerating gets bigger
very, very, exciting
quite spiritual
everything is carefree
so relaxed
all of the above are"
IDEAS!

Kathleen Ryan

The Note

A trembling hand produced this scrawl,
'Tis a short and simple query.
I beg, refrain from evasion or stall,
Did you love me much, or not very.

Now if without me you cannot abide,
Then, to my arms, return thee.
Else, toss this sodden note aside,
Without regard, seemingly as you did me.

Michael E. Gladstone Sr.

My Heart Belongs To You

We have only been together for a
Very short time.
But something inside me wants
you all the time.
I never knew what I was missing
till I met you.
Mark the happiness of loving you
is all I ever want.
My heart is yours forever so don't
let it go.
Keep it close to you and it will
always grow.

Verla Marlene Groomer

Painfully Apparent

Screams and sirens
Voices and whistles
Sounds that are not there
Is my mind playing games
Or is it acutely aware

It supposedly has the power
Capacities unlimited don't you know
Timeless and endless as space
The more stuff you add
The more room it makes

Vacant rooms and tasty cakes
They're good to have lying around
For unexpected company
No matter like or hate

That's the beauty of a poem like this
It's what you hear
And not what I say
Read it again or throw it away
My impression is made.
Late the - another day

Michael Macecsko

"The Dance"

In a crowded noisy room I sat
waiting for something I know not of
maybe for someone I know not
yet the clock still ticks
and the day waiting to end
oh moon-man will you dance with me?
And cast your magic rays upon me
send me a star so I may wish
for you to stay
but no the sun is fighting to come up
until night falls again
goodbye my moon-man

Tabitha Clark

Cowboys And Indians

Today
we played
cowboys and indians
can you imagine,
the two of us?

You locked me up
and promised
in the morning
I could be the Sheriff.

Another promise
from a man
who cannot shoot a gun.

Marisa J. Porto

Seabirds At Daytona

Wondrously versatile birds,
Walking, flying, swimming beings;
White down, grey and black
Wings and spiked sunny beaks.

Survivors of Spring Break,
Alka-Seltzer of stoned boys,
Shells and shovels of little brats,
Storms of wind and lightening bolts.

Graceful waifs, gulls of beauty,
Conquering waves, gathering booty
For nests of strident babies;
Taking care of God's business.

They are some of Creations best,
With strong little hearts beating
In innocent downy breasts.
God bless them; God bless.

Kathy Andrews

War

A war is a forgotten subject
War was time past,
Before time came
Like green pastures burn in,
In the wind like tanks
Rolling in over an open range,
Like a dog gone mad
Leaving destruction to and fro,
Like people who don't have
Anytime left to care.
Like outlaws shooting things up
Laws are bent,
Wars are like ships sinking in waters
While plane are plummeting.
From the blue flaming sky's.

Mathew A. Stout

Heavens Little Angel

Little Allan Whitledge
Was a special little boy,
Who always seemed to be
So full of joy.

His life was not easy.
He sometimes had it rough,
But he was strong
he was made tough.

Even when his illness
started to take its toll.
You'd never know by Allan,
He was always ready to roll.

And when the end came
And it was his time to go,
He reassured his Mommy
And let her know
That he would be in heaven
With God and his angels above.
And even though he was gone
She'd still have his love.

Rose Marie Whitledge

To Dad

My father was deaf and often I wondered,
where do words go that miss his ears,
to lands that never, never hear,

The same forbidding place I dread,
that go the words not ever said.

Martin F. Whalen

My Love

The love you feel for me inside,
was always there, it was never denied.
You care for me in a special way.
Loving me each and everyday.
Your love is like a ray of light
That shines down on me just right.
You mean so much to me,
Without you nothing would be
My life seems so complete now.
I'll love you forever-that's my vow.
You are my best friend.
And you will be to the end.
I believe in you and me.
I know our love will always be.
I'll love you till the end of time.
I love you so much
You'll always be mine!

Shelley M. Rentzheimer

The Lines Crossing Over

It was the silence that
was broken that I heard
in the night. The lines crossing
over from the dark to the light.
I closed my eyes the night before,
to awaken in a world where nothing
seemed real. People were everywhere,
most that I knew, places I had
been before, none were new.
Was it all a dream of lives gone
by? Would I awaken or had
I died. Line's crossing over
from the dark to the light.
Had I woke up this morning
or had I fallen asleep last
night.

Tena Lee-Bailey

The Rose

My love for you
was like a rose
nurtured with love
until it finally arose

With natures help
as it grew
my love for you
developed too

Now the rose and our love
is at its peak
but it looks as though
it's becoming weak

When the wind blows
it's gone forever
just like the love
we shared together.

Lori Rothermel

Untitled

About this time for many years
we welcomed Santa and his Reindeers.

He always comes so late at night,
but oh so jolly, fresh and bright.

He brings along a bag of toys,
for all the hid's, both girls and boys.

He knows the bad as well as good
but loves them all they knew he would.

Michael E. Shaffern

Dearest Friend

This poem my dearest friend
was written by me,
To compensate all the years
You have stood by me.

To let you know the care you shared
Helped to see me through
All those fiery trials and snares
That were to turn my spirit blue.

Whether I was right or wrong
You stood by me,
Like a beacon in the night
You showed your concerning love
Like your father on high.

May our father bless and keep you
For you are a pure delight,
In my father's eyes and as well in mine.

May our friendship grow in grace
And give us peace within
Until in heaven's portal gates
We both shall stand within.

Winona Hamm

Dee's days

What can we be?
We can be three!

Or five or six or seven
Next near to heaven.

Yep! Keep on goin'
Cause they be owen

Wow!
Not us
Havin' too much fun
Not
To get on the bus

We too
will see the sun

Many moons
Have past
This too
Will last

Linda K. Stanley

Healing Thoughts

Among our many blessings
We count our doctors' skills
And patient dedication
To caring for our ills

And when the grief of heart and soul
Exceeds our doctors' care
We have the Great Physician
Who meets with us in prayer

For grief does not just melt away
And broken hearts don't mend
But comfort comes, and healing,
From our Faithful Heavenly Friend.

Sally Vawter

Waking Smile

How do I find the words to say
What was so simple anyway.
Drawing you close, face to face,
Never wanting to leave this place.
Holding you that tender way
Was the perfect start of any day.

Peter M. Winscott

Out Of The Mist Of Our Dreams

Out of the mist of our dreams
We find happiness and memories
That lift our spirits high.

Oh, the joy and peace
That comes into our hearts,
And lets us drift into
The quiet time of life.

We can float on clouds
To majestic heights,
Or quietly find solitude.

We can dream about
When we were young,
Or let the hands of time slip by.

But most of all,
We can dream of love
That makes our life complete.

That's why, out of the mist
Of our dreams,
We can let our spirits soar
As we go down the span of life.

Ruth E. Mueller

So Be It

We have a mind that wants to know,
We have a soul that wants to show
Just what it is that we want so
To be.

To be what?...we often ask...
Could it be that if we'd cast
Aside the shackles of the past
We'd be free?

Being free, perhaps we'll know
The beauty that God's Will will show.
The butterfly has told us so...
So be it.

Russell Otto Mercer

Lazy Summer Days

As the sun slowly rises in the East
We roll over and close our eyes
Just a minute more of sleep
Before we have to give in and rise
We hurry to get breakfast over
While the cool breeze still lingers
Because in just a little while
The sun will be high in its splendor
There is a peace about these lazy days
When everything slows to a walk
Take a cold drink, sit in the shade
Without energy even to talk
A butterfly samples the nectar
Of fading Petunias and Marigolds
The cat lays stretching and panting
As the hot mid-day breezes blow
Even the birds are still
And the children are quiet
As they all impatiently wait
For another cool summer night

Marie Lea

Untitled

I remember You
when I see
what I've done
to Me

Marcella Morrison

But Daughter, Oh!

Outside were raging wind and snow -
We sat and watched the fire glow.
The flame was low, the ashes white -
He held my hand and pressed it tight!
My head was in its proper place -
His coat was rough against my face.
I watched him in the firelight;
His closeness was a sheer delight!
Then, suddenly, I heard a squeak!
I was so scared I couldn't speak!
I held my breath against my will -
He held my trembling fingers still.
There, in the doorway stood a man
Who awes me as no other can!
'Twas Santa Claus - just come to town!
And then my Daddy set me down.

LeVonne Davy Mulrooney

Untitled

The shape of a heart
were names of two
upon a oak tree
where love once grew

Young at age
young at heart
names were carved
sweetheart

Promises were made
always to keep
to love each other
thru-out eternity

No one know's who
those name's of two
if promises or dreams
were kept

But an old oak tree
where love once grew
stands tall all by
itself PAL poems about life

Ricky E. Cagle

Ocean

Waves washing upon the sand crystals,
wet against the rough surface.
Waves crashing and thundering,
leaving a white foam in return.
The sand awaiting the next sudden push,
against its spine.
All is peaceful and calm.
Sand castles being drenched,
by the upcoming tide.
Sea gulls being pushed by the sudden
bursts of wind
flying, flying to heaven above.
Again, all is peaceful and calm.

Kathryn Schuyler

Amtrak's Grand America

Stars of another kind were found
When we disembarked in Los Angeles -
Where we visited Universal Studios,
Disney Land Park and rode past
The Beverly Hills homes of
The rich and famous.
A wonderful, carefree way to see
Amtrak's Grand America

Velma J. Arey

Meant To Be

I spilled out to you
What I felt in my heart,
Only to find out that you
From my life would soon part.

I thought forever
You would be by my side,
Only to find out
It was all a lie.

For my well-being
You never cared at all.

I fell in love with you
For your love I needed.
Held wrapped in your arms
I felt I was needed.

To find out you lied
For I never meant anything,
Cause to you it was
Just another meaningless fling.

But now I can clearly see
It just wasn't meant to be.

Melynda Vining

Feelings

Love,
What is love?
Love, hate, fear, silence,
What are any of these?
Love turns to hate,
fear causes silence,
silence is violence.
Do you love the silence?
Or fear the hate?
Confusion,
you say that you love
but that's what you fear,
for your love is silenced,
by hate.
I love,
without fear
without silence,
without hate,
Is my love wrong?
feelings.

Krystal Livermore

Decreation

Are we so unreal that all is lost.
What is the cost?
The sky turns rust,
Like a ray of sun at dusk.

Our life was sweet,
Like a sugar treat.
As we drew aside,
The love which kept us alive.

We rule our lives,
As a strong retreat.
It cost us the love,
Of our God above.

He knows it all,
He sees what we do.
We've lost our love,
He knows this is true.

Now all is lost,
None to be found.
Our lives the cost,
Thus, this cold hard ground.

Lisa Hutton

Pastime Future

What time is it
What is time
Time is time
Within itself
every second is a minute
every minute is an hour
every hour is a day
everyday is a year
a year that you've had
to look at yourself
How do you see yourself
do you own a space
in time
or are you lost in time
do you live in the past
or will you make up for lost
time and look toward
the future before too
much time has passed?

Kevin D. Matthews

What If

If I was to say I loved you
What would you say to me?
If I was to say I need you
What would you say to me?
Would you look me in the eyes
or turn away and cry.
What would you say to me?
Would you tell me to walk away
or ask me to stay another day.
What would you say to me?
If I told you all these things

WHAT WOULD YOU THINK OF ME???

Keith Doherty

Oh My, God!

The winds are blowing down the trees!
What's going on, has God sneezed?

Here comes a bolt! Snap, crackle, pop!
Holy cow, God's blown his top!

Crash, boom, bang! A clap of thunder!
God's bowling pins have gone asunder!

Lots of water is flooding the mall!
God must have done a cannonball!

While God's having a vacation,
he's corrupting all creation!!!

Kendra T. Litvany

Beyond The Moon

Beyond the moon where lovers lie,
Where liars love and sinners die.
A deep blue sea holds time and fear.
There's much to lose, the end is here.

Beyond the moon, enchanted winds blow.
Destroying and loving unborn souls.
The liars, lovers, sinners and weak,
Create a bond. The truth they seek.
Beyond the moon...

Beyond the moon we are heard of no more.
Beyond the moon, I lock the door.

Sheri Pizzini

Tomboy

So I'm a tomboy,
What's wrong with that?
I just like taking chances,
That's just how I act.

I love playing soccer,
And livin' on the line.
I've been playin' Creek War,
Since I was nine.

People say I'm crazy,
For wanting to ride bulls.
I just say "Hey, it's my life,"
"I don't want it to be dull."

So what? I collect comics,
And play pogs for keeps.
And I'll get out of trouble,
Before I get in too deep.

I've told you my story,
Spilled out the facts.
So I hope you can understand,
About the way that I act.

Stacia Mumm

Untitled

In the middle of the night
when everyone is sleeping
If you listen quite close
you'll hear me weeping.
Life is a challenge
a challenge quite hard
Your life is a challenge
in which you starred.
Beat your challenge
face to face.
Take your time
it's not a race.
If you beat your challenge,
congratulations
I give you a standing
ovation.
Be proud
Take a bow
I shall go
beat my challenge now.

Liliana Rodrigues

I Remember

That long ago yesterday
When first I looked at you
While sharing a hymnal there
In an old church pew.

Our wedding day, our first home
High up on a hill,
The birth of sons, a tiny grave,
Are pictures vivid still.

We weathered many changes
Together through the years.
Many were the pleasant times
And moments full of tears.

I remember yesterday
The years did come and go
Now we're in life's evening
Our steps are growing slow.

I remember yesterday
But today is now and here,
Another day together
Perhaps another year.

Nova Felkins Bailey

Colored

When I'm born I'm black
When I grow up I'm black
When I go outside I'm black
When I get mad I'm black
When I die I'm black

But you............

When your born your pink
When you grow up your white
When you get mad your red
And when you die your pale......

And you call me colored.

Kalifa King

"Divinely Conquered"

There were times in my past,
when materials came first, from
the leather, to the drugs, with the
spirits came the worse.
The parties, the friends, seemed
to vanish through years, while
addiction steadfast, I quit looking
in mirrors.
Year's passed me by, this disease
was so strong, my illness so heinous,
praying death come along.
When time came to pass, the
feeling divine, came forth from a
realm, and I knew I'd be fine.
My prayer's were answered,
a celestial night, and I knew from
within, he had conquered my fight.

Katt McCray

No Wonder...

I love you because,
when we're together, the
rest of the world seems
to fade away! There's something
magical in every kiss we
share... and only you
can sweep me off my feet?
You're always willing to,
listen, even when I don't
have much to say, and
sometimes we don't need
any words at all to express
our feelings. A day spent
with you is a day full
of surprises... and every
day we're together has
a happy ending.

No wonder
I love you!
So much!

Teresa Harp

Time

Time.
When you are
Young
It is the snail.
When you are
Old
It is the eagle
Diving into a black canyon
Where he cannot take-off again.

Patria E. Danielson

On Getting Old

I guess that old is not so bad
When you have friends like these
Who brave the wildest winter storm
To meet and 'shoot the breeze'
With others, old and not so old,
Who say, "Remember when—?"

And look at snaps, and groan, "Oh, No!"
Did I look like that then?"
And friends who furnish food and drink,
And interesting fun,
And think there's nothing sacred
In what you've said and done,

And turn things into loving jokes,
Which cause unholy glee.
And friendly laughter fills the air
And fellowship flows free.
The flash bulbs flash, the cameras click,
And everyone says, "Cheese!"

No, getting old is not so bad
When you have friends like these.

Olive L. Kutz

Grandma's Gone

Grandma, it seems like only yesterday
when you were here with me.
You taught me how to love, to care
and in what I should believe.
You helped me understand my fears,
thoughts, and my dreams.
But now you're gone and I'm alone
I don't know what death means.
You left us all so very quick so
calm without no pain.
Before you left you said you love us
and we feel the same.
Our last goodbye's were oh so sad,
no words came out our mouths
When we arrived your soul was gone,
our cries were all so loud.
The point of this long poem is to
send you all my love.
I know I'll see you once again
in heaven up above.

Madelyn Rivera

One With You

My life is so fulfilled
When you're by my side
You fill my heart with love
So what you wish - I will abide

You have a special quality
No one else will ever succeed
To make me feel the way you do
And give me what I need.

You're a very special person
And so out - going
You touch my heart
Without even knowing.

I push away all my fears
And bad experiences too
So I start a new life
To be one with you.

Patricia Homan

Rendezvous

There is a meeting in the sky
where all things are revealed
to virgins of reality's denial
living lives of missionary style
trained years in traditional sin
bodies of only private-dutiful parts
purgatory is their cleansing place
a rendezvous where the dying wait

Times of letting go
branches shedding their leaves
sunset begets darkness
all are powerless, letting go
we and nature die to live
a process of continual becoming
reality is one day at a time
a rendezvous, rebirth- a setting free

Heaven is also found on earth where one
is made whole and alive
no boundaries or measured depths holy
and clean in passion's gift
caressing your thighs, I find my rest free
from the dying past
such moments are love's gift a rendezvous
of nocturnal bliss...

Peter M. Vesey

Soul To Soul

Hear the cry of my unknown soul.
Where are you kindred spirit?

To dance flesh to flesh,
touch to touch,
brings but fleeting joy.

Never to dance soul to soul,
spirit to spirit,
brings perpetual mourning.

A never ending quest it seems to be.
Where are you kindred spirit?

Such deep sorrow for the solitary heart.
To be unknown.
To be unknowing.

But recognition will end sorrow.
I will know you.
You will know me.

Then we shall dance,
soul to soul.

Lori Zimmerman-Shults

Dancing Apart

Dreaming of a time
When there was harmony
A single chord between us
My thoughts in your head
Your heart beating in my chest.

We danced to a tune
Which echoed our souls
In balance and peace
Lifting us above the world
Into a united spirit.

Then, we fell into discord
But still we danced
Dreaming it was the same
While the tempo carried us apart
Back into our separate worlds.

Patrick Mulvaney

Who Shall Rule? (The Unseen Ruler)

The one who speaks the loudest
Where everyone can hear,
Or the one who is the quietest
And no one seems to care.

Is it the one who is the strongest
Can move everything out the way,
Or the one who is the weakest
And don't forget to pray.

Is it the one who sees the farthest
And knows what is ahead,
Or the one who is the blindest
And feels he must be led.

Is it the one who moves the swiftest
And does things to suit his taste,
Or the one who is the slowest
So nothing will come to waste.

The unseen hand that guidest
And helps us pass the test,
And shows us there is nothing besidest
Is the one I like the best.

Wilhelmina R. Mendheim

What A Dream Is

A dream is a world within our mind,
Where everyone seems to be so kind,

A place where we are big and tall,
And we somehow leap, but do not fall,

Our hearts are forever joyous and gay,
And if we are lost we find the way,

There is no reason to ever do wrong,
And we are not weak, but very strong,

With our things we want to share,
And for others we truly care,

All of our wishes quickly come true,
And indeed we are never blue,

We can go back or ahead in time,
And we do not age beyond our prime,

We also are unusually wise,
And our goals are easily realized,

Everyday is sunny and bright,
And the climate is serene at night,

We can dance a waltz and sing,
Oh, we can do almost anything.

P. Sandra Oliver

"Thanksgiving"

Thanksgiving is a time of year
Which brings our friends and family near.

It truly is the time of year
To count our blessings that are so dear.

It is a time when all should care
And join together in a family prayer.

We have so much to be thankful for
But most of us want even more.

So on this Thanksgiving Day
Let's stop the clock and simply say,
"Thank you Lord for Thanksgiving Day".

Patricia A. MacKnew

Mrs. Peace

Mrs. Peace, Mrs. Peace,
Where have you gone?
Why did you flee?
I've been knocking on your door,
Wanting love, hate no more.
Many troubles on my mind,
Going backwards all the time.
But I can't take more of this,
So, please help me, Mrs. Peace.

Oh my friend, I'm glad you came,
Heard some people cry my name.
And here's what I got for you,
Simple things that all must do.
Learn to love, learn to give,
Don't give up, that's all you need.
Soon you'll find that it's not hard, if you open up your hearts.
But I beg you all the fighters, street night hustlers, lonely drivers.
Not too much time left for waste, do it now, it's getting late.
No my friend, I haven't gone, been here waiting for so long.
For you to come and see with me, how sweet life was meant to be.

Rene Otero Laborde

Untitled

In the infinity of life
where I am
All is perfect whole and complete.
Change is the natural law of life
and everyone should embrace it
and you will see that forgiving
Comes easier than you think.
It has a way of liberating the soul

It is with change that overwhelms the very existence
and one learns to appreciate life more.
The more resentment one releases
the more love can be expressed.
I've learned to make today and tomorrow
a more pleasurable experience
All is well in my world.

Steve Mathies

Where Sea Gulls Cry

I love a place where sea gulls cry,
where meets the glistening sea with sky,
where one can search for shells and such,
where one can feel the oceans touch!

To walk upon the whitened sand,
while clinging to a loved one's hand!
To sense the wonder of the place,
where marks of care are soon erased.

Although I know I can't be there,
I go on whispering wings of prayer,
to seashore with its splendorous view,
which soars my faith and strength renews.

Oh maker of the sand and sea,
May I return in memory,
to where I'll glimpse the oceans foam!
to where such treasured joys I've known.

Stefanie Dawson

Bon Voyage

I have seen the ships in bottles,
Where people take great pride
Not in what comes from the bottles,
But putting something back inside.

I've never tried to build a ship,
But damn, I've sunk a few.
If you're into ships in bottles,
Here's an empty one for you.

Every time I raise the bottle,
And pour another shot of gin,
I love the tide that's flowing out,
Not the ship that's coming in.

If you need bottles for your ships,
Just come and visit me.
I'll help you build the biggest fleet,
That ever sailed the sea.

Now another seal is broken,
As I start my daily trip.
Just hang around till I fall down.
Then build another ship.

Lee Rife

Please Hold My Hand Tenderly ...

For me you bring sunshine
Where there once was rain.
You have filled with happiness
Spaces once filled up with pain.
I do so enjoy your company
Especially your smile.
It gives me a warmth inside
I haven't had in quite a while.
I do not want to scare you
But, you I do not fear.
The feelings that you give to me
Every time that you are near.
I know that you are not alone
I to have been hurt before.
You have given new hope inside me
Opened up a brand new door.
Please hold my hand tenderly
I will handle yours with care.
Tomorrow it looks brighter
When you and I are there.....

Shelley R. Johnson

E-Z Street

E-Z street, how do I get to E-Z street?
Where's that beat, where happiness
Falls at your feet? I repeat, how do
I get to E-Z street... where life is
Sweet and everything's so neat, how
Do I get to E-Z street?

You have to cross rambling roads,
Hard and bitter scrambling roads,
Where the odds are gambling roads,
Before you reach that street!

Then you walk down the lane,
Passed the sign of "mock and pain,"
Near the drive marked "without - pride,"
On either side!

And, if you live all through this, then
You're on the road called "bliss," and,
Happiness, I guess, lies on the corner
Of "warm-caress"! There you'll find
That beat, right under your feet... but,
You have to suffer, to reach E-Z Street!

Maria Fehr

My Heart

You fell into my life,
Which surprised even me.
You captured my heart,
Which I was blind to see.
Your friendship was a blessing,
A blessing in disguise.
But the truth for which I was searching,
was right before my eyes.
It's taken me all these years,
to finally see the truth,
The truth to whom my heart belongs
Could only belong to you.

Mindy Kirk

Alone Again

Alone again, as with the sea
whispering by, as if unnoticed
I touch the light of day

And the swell returns
to push ahead
repeating its path
as if to conquer
Kissing the sky

Alone again
retreating silently
waves push back
softly caressing the shore
as the sea calls
the wave returns

The path will chance
with each passing swell
touching the shore
returning to the sea
alone again

Kate M. Lawrence

White

White is the color of a dove
White is the color of heaven above
White is a color you will know
When you see some falling snow
White is the color of a movie screen
White is a lily and a bean
White is the color of Santa's beard
It is the color of a wedding dress
It's what you think of when you rest
White is the color of teacher's chalk
White is the color of an athlete's socks
White is the color of very cold ice
White altogether is very nice
White is very very beautiful

And white is the color of Angels' wings
My heart sings because
White is the color that I see
When I think of God
With thee

This last stanza was written by Michael's mother after Michael's death.

Michael John Munson

Confusion

There once was a peach from Beruit,
Who was sure that he was a root,
He ran into a wall,
Saw his juice fall,
And found out that he was a fruit.

Mary Brunswick

The Haiku of Fences, Walls and Hedgerows

Sharp angled edges
Whitewashed and jutting upward
Stand at attention

Prize-winning hybrids
Thrust their green foliage through
Slatted barriers

Tall and big headed
Sunflowers look down over
White garden fences

Etched lichen symbols
Patterns of cycling seasons
Stone walls shaded face

Cemetery walls
Silent guardians of death
Cold rocks of ages

Rows of trees and shrubs
Broad windbreak leaning eastward
Sheltering farmsteads

Miriam Nesset Bill

Epitaph For W. A. Mozart

Here lives Mozart
Who believed in Something
It had no name
Nor was there a word for it,
He said it as music.
At his death
He was denied his own body -
They said it was unknown
And threw it into an unmarked grave.
We choose to believe
He was never buried never having died,
Listen.

Stymean Karlen

Jerks

Jerks are bosses
who don't care.
Jerks are bosses
who don't dare.
Jerks are bosses
who don't swear.
Jerks are bosses
who don't love, so there...

Linda Rappe

I Give My Heart To Thee

To all those men and women
who fought to keep us free
I give my heart to thee.
Some went as boys
and came back as men.
Some went as boys
and never came back again.
And those families left behind
Pray and pray each day till
One night they get a letter that says,
'Your son has passed away.'
Who could ever be so cruel
to let them die alone,
Where their souls could not rest in peace
because the fires never ceased.

Lisa Lopez

Teddy Bear

I have a teddy bear
Who is so kind,
He is so cuddly
And naturally nice.
We play together
All the time
During the day
And rest at night

But now I am older
And we don't play all the time,
But he is still so kind
And so cuddly
And naturally nice,
Waiting for another day to go by.

Kati Hageman

Victory Or Defeat

If you can sense the wonder of a child
Who is so pure and undefiled
And if your heart does so perceive
Your spirit will never, never grieve.

When you can see a rainbow
And the heart increases tempo
The spirit is sure to soar up high
And bring a peaceful, drawn out sigh.

When with understanding you can look
And see beyond the cover of a book
The heart has been the cause
And from the spirit will come applause.

So, in life, when all is said and done
And everything seems gone
—It isn't fame or fortune—
But the heart and spirit's feat
That determine life's victory or defeat.

Wendell E. Hauenstein

God's Message

Have you heard about the God of Heaven
Who sent his Son down to earth?
He gave up his life
With troubles and strife
So that we might all have a new birth.

That new birth is salvation
From the wrath of sin's dark way.
It gives man hope
And helps him to cope
And escape the flames of hell some day.

If you haven't heard the story,
Look into the word of God.
It's great to read
But better to heed
And have things settled before you die.

Wilda de la Cruz

The Flip Side

Youth, fun loving, when time between
winters seems forever.
Do you know that old age makes the
time between summers seem longest.

Day, when you have fun and sun.
Night, when you have fun and moon.

Tanya M. Schmidt

"Racism Hurts"

Racism hurts my people
Why?
What wrong have I done?
Racism hurts your people
Why?
What have you done to me?
Racism hurts "the people"
Why?
I still hear no answers
  But ... why?
Racism helps -?
Who?
You?
Me? Or them?
How?
Why?
When?
Racism hurts me... you... them
  ... But why?

Katasha Jackson

Why?

Why are there guns?
Why are there guns at all?
They land in so many places,
In the streets, in the halls.

People use them to rob,
Kids use them to be tall,
Police need for safety,
Gangbangers make others fall.

Anti-gun people,
Run into a wall,
While anxious parents,
Wait for the call

Kristin D. Zimmerman

"Hail To The Queen"

Who is the queen? Your mother,
wife, daughter, sister, sweetheart.
She's a girl, a lady, a woman.
She may be big, she may be small,
She may be tall, she may be short
  "She is the queen"
She has the miracle of birth
She may have a child or 2 or more
She love it with compassion, teach it
right from wrong.
She loves it through the trails and
tribulation of life
She is the queen - God save the queen
But God has called her, no matter
what age,
Hail to the Queen - for the
Queen is dead.

William L. Wye

"My Prayer"

"Dear Lord", grant me a home
with the sky for a roof
and the clouds for a floor
where my window stay open
and a rosebush at my door
where the birds sing all day
and the moon shines all night
where I'll join all my love ones
Whose memory, I treasure
Where i'd find peace of mind
And where living, is a pleasure.

Marie Pabon

My Special Rose

You stand as if the strongest
wind could never knock you down.
Standing straight as can be with
your roots firmly in the ground.
Every petal that you have is
a blossom of love you share.
Sharing your fragrance of happiness
for whom the people you care.
Every thorn on your stem
bears no pain to any heart.
Your just a bushel full of love
willing to share apart.
For my rose is very special to me.
A rose I can keep near.
A rose I hope to have forever.
That rose is you my dear.

Linda Acosta

Our Gift To Our Children

Swirling
winds.
Restless
leaves
Talking
squirrels.
Sunny
skies.
Cigarette butts.
Piling debris.
Dead bullets.
Discarded used condoms.
Our children's future playground.

Lira Kellerman

Seasons Change

Freezing air chilling my bones
Winter running rapid through me
Everything frozen, still as stones
But without winter, Spring cannot be.

Spring the explosion of life,
Winter being the slow nurturing sleep.
Summer to Spring a deep cutting knife,
Then fall comes in to weep.

This continuous process is all
When it ends so do we
Seasons come and go at natures call
So follow and appreciate what you see.

Marie Alice Frazier

Bits Of Beauty

Our world
With azure skies,
From sunrise to sunset
Bits of beauty each day unfold,
Behold!

Yoshiyuki Otoshi

Untitled

Ahhh youth
with its shimmering light of innocence
How I love thee so

If I could go back
through the passages of time
I would have long ago.

Kim Wilson

A Mother's Hurt

I sit alone in my dark room,
With my head bending down
For all the days I left you, son
And went to work downtown.

The nights are getting hard to bear,
I cry my poor heart out
I meditate on all our life
And how this came about.

I guess I never realized,
How much I'd hurt my little boy
'Twas Mother's time you craved inside
And not the latest toy.

But I was young and full of life,
I thought I'd bring you joy,
But all I did was break-
The heart of you, my little boy.

If there is found in your young heart,
A touch of sympathy,
I beg of you, my dearest son
Extend to me this blessed quality.

Ludi Chapa Hernandez

A Minute

Just a tiny little minute
With only 60 seconds in it

Time for thoughts to quickly rise
In a moment of surprise

Minute in quantity, rich within
Like the sharp point of a pin

Thoughts pour in and round about
Never seeking their whereabouts

Where they come from no one knows
Just to where the venture goes

Kingdoms rise and kingdoms fall
In a moment of recall

Their glory shared and glory lost
Disappeared like morning frost

If I could capture time in thought
A world of treasure could be caught

William Zoeller

Spring

Spring brings April showers
with rainbows
for all of us to fore.
Spring brings flowers
with bright colors
for all of us to share.
Spring brings rebirth
with love.
for all of us to care.

Nancy Massaro

My Dog

I have a medium-sized dog,
with the brain capacity of a frog.
I have no idea
why he loves me
or why he is such a hog.

Ramie Moran

My Fish

The fish was bright
With silver scales
And in the night
He played with whales

He wandered here
He wandered there
Not in fear
Not aware

I cast my line
Into the sea
He did not wait
He came towards me

The worm he sought
Upon the line
The hook he got
That fish was mine

I reeled him in
We had a fight
My fish swam off
Into the night

Stephanie Meyers

He Is The One

I am in love
With someone very dear
He holds me close
And wipes away my tears

He is the one
That really loves me
He will never let me go
Nor set me free

He is the one
I've always dreamed of
I never thought
That we would fall in love

He is the one
My better half
He makes me cry
But, still I laugh

He is the one
Who put the ring on my hand
He is someone
I call my husband

Melissa Overton

Island Magic

Once I went to an island,
with the smells of fish cooking,
and the sound of waves crashing.
I walked a bit,
and found a mirror.
I looked at myself,
I looked different.
I was very thin,
with straight red hair.
I walked on thinking,
"What happened to the real me?"
Then I looked in the sand,
and found a ruby ring.
I stared at it.
My reflection was, well me!
I dropped the ring,
and buried it in the sand.
I walked away thinking,
"What a great place"
Then I swam like a fish back home.

Lindsay James

Love

Here I lay on my bed
With thoughts of you
to fill my head.
Hair like silk, eyes so blue
Wonder this time if this
love is true.

When you're here my
eyes shine bright.
It's hard to say goodbye at night.
But you'll come tomorrow
then you'll see that
I missed you abundantly.

The time has come
for you to know
It's time to let
my feelings show
my love for you's like the
ever flowing streams
It's as fierce as the winds
and as hopeful as dreams.

Stephanie Davison

Going Home

I walked in the garden
with you today.
I walked, you talked
I said, "Please stay."
You said, "I'm not very
far away."
I walked in the garden
with you today.
I felt somehow I
had gone astray.
You said, "You'll be with
me soon one day."
I walked in the garden
with you today,
And this time
you took
my hand!

Lucille Nibbio

The Flower

I am blowing
without going
sitting...
Still
sadly
silently
waiting for a great wind
to make me twirl and bend
when can I go?
Why should I anyway?

Tandi Kilgore

Missing You

I thought I could live
without you.
But now I don't know what
to do,
Cause your important in my life,
So don't leave me boy think
twice,
Not only do you make me smile,
But make me feel so good inside,
And now I don't know what
to do, because I can't stop
missing you!

Sarah J. Arculeo

The Soul

Do we see eternally
without shape or form
You're eye's are closed
behind open doors
Can one become totally aware
of its surroundings
Through sight, touch or smell
can one be truly aware
through stages of consciousness
and unconsciousness
How far can one see
not fully understanding
without doubtfulness
Shall seek with in a presence
so unique, so intelligently known
as the inner soul.

Lori Sullens Smith

Days

Happy days, slide away
Without signs, without trace.

I try to remember the days
When crocuses raise their heads,
Snowdrops sway their bells,
and daffodils turn their faces.
When Robins patrol the lawns,
cardinals pursue their mates,
and Mockingbirds prepare their nests.
When the days are long,
the weather is warm,
and the trees are newly green.

Could you tell me how we spent the days
when they were so fair?
I could not recall any of those days,
only sweet feelings remains.

Lily Wong

Oh, Me, Woe...

Fits achin' all,
Wits flake 'n' fall!
Split, our love's lackin';
Hit, dour dove's crackin'!!
Yet, a paradigm:
Set, t' spare a dime —
Call baby, brayin',
Bawl, maybe, sayin'
Mus' hitch the tether,
Thus twitch t'gether,
Or trots out hope
Store got stout rope
For neck!!!

Your wreck,
Romeo

J. Cameron

A New Beginning

Treat each day as a new beginning
You can right the wrong of yesterday.
The sun rises, freshness fills the air.
The day is untouched ...
A challenge, a new beginning,
Today will be yesterdays memory ...
Make it the best memory, one to cherish.
Treat each day as a new beginning ...
Face it with hope, promise ...
A day of pride and accomplishment.

Sharon Hodge

Blue Bird

Blue bird up so high
Won't you come and sing to me
Fly so high to me
To me you will sing
A soft mellow song

A soft mellow song
Is like a bird in the wind
In the wind whistling
I can hardly hear

I can hardly hear
This blue bird singing so soft
Whistling so softly
So soft, so soft, so
I can hardly hear

Tiffany S. Dorey

Speak My Name

When you have a spare moment,
won't you speak my name?

I was with you for a few years,
I know it's not the same.

You were proud when I was born,
the name you gave to me.

When you share the memories of the past,
I hope you'll mention me.

Did I hear you say my name,
maybe a small tear you shed.

Please wipe your tear and make a smile,
and say my name instead.

My name you spoke and shared with thee,
and added it to our family tree.

Your still my family and my friends,
please speak of me beyond life's end.

Patricia M. Hyde

A Child!

I am a lost child in this
world trying to find a way.
A child trying to be heard
over the large world.
A child trying to live my
life the way I think it should be.
A child who is scared.
I am a child trying to grow.
A child trying to find
love, happiness.
A child trying to find
courage to be what I want to be.
So what do I want to be?
A child set FREE!

Olympia Castro

Exodus 20:12

Mandela
y
Coretta
S l
h i
Jackie
b
a
z
z

Sharon Wooten

Tribute To My Mother

I did not sleep at all last night, for
worrying about your journey and plight.
God has a mission for you to fulfill.
So he's sending you to a strange place
On this journey to full fill.
Your labor, and duties of love has
been done. Now it's time for you
to reap the harvest in return.
Someone to give you time and let
you rest, until he calls you home
to his land of the best. So make
your time peaceful and help all
you can, on your way to this
heavenly land.

Katie M. Parsons

"Larry"

Larry would dance, Larry
would sing, Larry loved
playing on swings.

Larry hoped, Larry feared,
wish, cared, loved and cried.

Larry wondered, dated, pondered,
and often times rebelled.

He never lied, nor bullied, Larry
studied, Larry tried, skated,
jumped and skipped.

He came, he went, he lived,
oh-oh so dear, until a pusher's
gun ended his young fifteen years!

Walter Wilson

Growing Old

The seasons come and go
Years of love flow away
As if foam on the tide
We think in wonder
At all we have come to know

Faces and places we remember fondly
Times together we have shared
Pain and sorrow, love and laughter
Through it all we have always had
You and I

Now as twilight fills our eyes
All our yesterdays are but a shadow
Our tomorrows never to come
And yet we will
Forever have today

Through this day I will be by you
Holding your hand as before
We will gather in our last memories
Realizing that we never had to fear
Growing old

Thomas E. Burgess II

Can't You Feel My Pain

How can you see me
yet look right through
Can't you feel my pain
can't you see I'm blue.
How can you hear me
yet my words, you ignore
Can't you feel my pain
can't you hear there's more.
How can you touch me
yet not feel what's wrong
Can't you feel my pain
can't you feel it's strong.
Seeing, hearing, touching me
yet not knowing I'm insane
Won't you pay attention
can't you feel my pain.

Kaleen Harfman

Untitled

A desire to know,
yet not, the will to see...
this glimpse is no glimpse,
my inner nakedness, this native me

my reason has paved,
a path to inherit...
the Pilgrim not I,
for deed is just merit

guest for thy answer,
though never unravel...
signs and missed signs,
of yesterday travel

spirits have knocked,
how hast thou listened?
as echoing thoughts thrall,
thou, are not christened
'till then

Michael James

The Coldness Of Lonely

Your touch was soft and loving.
Yet, now it burns me.
Your love made my heart glow.
Now, it makes my heart ache.
You used to send shivers through me,
Now, I shiver from the coldness
Of lonely.
You held me so tight,
And dropped me in disgust.
To know it was all a lie
Is the worst of all.
To know that I was nothing more
Than a mere thought;
Now a distant memory.
I'm gone from your mind now.
Your love warmed my heart.
Now, I shiver with the coldness of lonely.
And in the coldness of lonely,
I will find peace.

Stacy Brown

Written For Mr. Right

In a sky of blue
You are a shining star
On a road together
We will go far
In a cry for help
You are the wealth
In my darkest moment
You are the light
On the coldest night
You are the warmth
Stranded on a deserted island
You are hope
In this crazy world
You are my (ability) cope

Marie Antonette Serra

You

You are someone special
You are the one who fills my dreams
The thought of you makes me smile
When I see you, my heart races miles
You brighten my day with every word

I want to be yours
I need you to need me
You're all I can think about
You are my everything
You and only you are what I want

I think I am in love with you

Melissa Herod

The Face Beyond The Crowd!

Sudden chill,
You know it's there.
You look everywhere
You can't find it,
You hear a lot of noise,
but no one's around to make it,
All of a sudden,
You block out that noise,
and all you hear is your
heart, pumping.
You turn around,
then you wake.

Nicolle Quick

Early Morning Prayer

Lord, this day keep me from sin.
You know the temptations
That Satan will bring.
The hustle and bustle
That will be all around,
With decisions to make
It will surely abound.
I come to you, Lord,
To ask you for grace.
May your peace and your glory
Abide in this place.
Oh, lead me and guide me
That I may not fall
And bless me that I may
Be true through it all.

Amen!

Ruth Rose Flickinger

"I Can Not Deny It"

Since the first time I saw you
you made me flood my feelings
and damp my lips.

Now you are in every single living day;
Now I can not sleep
because I spend all night long
thinking of you.
(No matter how far you are)
you always are close to me
because you are all I ever wanted,
all I ever needed.

Sometimes I would like to be
a kite
and to fly until I reach your sky
or a sailor to navigate your whole
body
until I dry all your water, and I feel
that your wishes have died
because I killed them...with my caresses,
with my love.

William Rivera

Why

I loved the way
you played the piano
so gracefully and beautifully.

You had so much
to look forward to.
You were so great
at everything you did.

It's times like
this that make us
ask those questions
that only God
knows the answers to.

It makes us wonder
why God took the
life of such a great
person as you

Nicole Murr

Jamie

You're wild, untamed
you shine like a star,
so bright, so true
you're blinding.

Like poison, you slowly
make me numb.

Your bittersweet kisses
paralyze me.

I am so mesmerized by you,
I can not see past your
intense light.

You make me feel climactic, alive.

You are naturally pleasing
ever so innocently.

Sarah J. Olson

The Circle Of Life

Old forlorn friend,
You stand alone
on some forgotten hillside.

Timbers refusing to crumble
with the age felt in your bones.
You stand waiting
as you have through time.
Waiting like a faithful dog
listening for his master's footsteps.

Years have passed while you aged
listening to the rustle of vines
growing around your door.
You've been left alone
to crumble into dust and return
as the tree that made you.

Returning as a young maiden
in your new green gown.
No longer alone,
but full of the whispering wind
and morning sunlight.

Linda Hawley

I Love You

The first time I saw you
You took my sea of blue
And turned it into an ocean of Gold
You took the very worst thoughts
Out of my head and turned them into
Thoughts of love and affection for you
And you only.

My love is stronger than earths
Forces themselves and deeper than
The depths of any ocean
Say you love me say you will care
For me, till the end of man's time.

Tara Bird

At The Pond

Raindrops speckle the pond.
You used to cool your feet there
In the summer heat
The tiny minnows
Kissing at your ankles.
It was like a benediction
Watching you
The wrinkles of contentment
Around your eyes.

Peter Damm

Untitled

Awakened by the sound of
your beating heart
I stare at you through the
darkness as moonlight
shines in your eyes
They are all I see
The secrets of ones soul
are revealed through
these stars
Passion, hate, lust, fear
They pierce my chest
like daggers
The truth is in your gaze
Our love is not real

Larry Schwartz

Your My Wall

You are my lover.
Your my best friend.
Your the wall, which helps me
to stand.
What's mine is yours.
And yours is ours.
Your my strengths
Your my weakness.
Your the one who picks.
up the pieces.
Your the wall, that helps me
to stand.
Your my today.
Your my tomorrows.
Your the love of my life.
Your my wall, which helps me
to stand
And if ever asked, yes it has name.
Russell Decker because he is
all my strength.

Wendy Kadner

What You Mean To Me

You mean the world to me,
you're the air that I breathe.
Without you I'd be nothing,
So please don't ever leave.

I love everything about you,
In my eyes you can do no wrong.
You've surely been sent from heaven,
To love me all along.

By day you're a hidden rainbow,
At night my shining star.
I'll always stand beside you,
Go with you near or far.

If I could have but one wish,
Do you know what it would be?
I'd wish to spend the rest of my life,
with you eternally.

Patricia Dowell

Yesterday

Yesterday, I was happy,
youth was forever;
age tried to reach me,
catch me, it could never.

Yesterday, I was walking,
enjoying nature's trees;
wrinkles etched into my face,
like the falling, autumn leaves.

Yesterday, I was laughing,
life was free;
my voice trembled and broke,
time was stopping me.

Yesterday, I was sitting,
my hair had turned to gray;
Age had caught me,
but that was yesterday.

Phyllis Dickenson Salling

When The Season Is Ripe

We will not be gathered
We will not be plucked
We will not vanish from this earth
'Til the season is ripe.

Gather us, blessed earth
When the season is ripe,
When the earth calls us by our names.

But gather us, Mighty Lord
Not as forgotten, solitary harvests;
Not as forsaken slabs of earth;
Not as supplicants without a prayer.

Gather us, blessed sepulcher.

Gather us like sheaves of grains
Gathered by the Great Lord at dusk,
Before that blighted night
Which broods like an endless quarrel.

When darkness hovers like a perpetual companion;
When our loved ones are all gathered into thy bosom;
When the things we once cherished have lost lustre...

Then gather us, Great Lord, for the season is ripe.

Ochoro E. Otunnu

The Impotence Of Being Earnest!

Everyday you blaze a trail
with sense of anguish if you fail,
fall back in line with all the rest
it matters not you did your best.

Fly off here, and end up there,
'Cause you're type A, you do not care!
For what reason I always ask,
Do I shoulder this senseless task?

But come the weekend, at last retreat,
With friends and comrades we do meet.
Small talk, sports and families speak,
Renew our spirits for the coming week!

Michael E. Greenough

Envy

You've said to me so many times
You envy me my mirth.
I wish you knew me better—
I wish you knew the dearth
Of real contentment in my soul,
And how I, in my turn
Envy the tempered, lovely,
Balanced candle that you burn.
My happiness is but a front
I've built up through the years,
And all my laughter that you know
Is but a holiday from tears.

Pieter G. Kelder

It

When I was young and in my prime
Why I could do it all the time.

Now that I'm older and getting gray
I only do it once a day.

That's not quite right I confess
It comes up once a week I'm blessed

Oh yes I forgot to mention,
Now it almost never comes to attention!

Paul P. Porter

Father

For once there was a man who wore big shoes
Who worked so hard, he paid his dues
He stood as tall as a man can be
Which gave him a view of the world to see
For what he saw, from where he looked
Can not be taught, nor read in a book
The ultimate provider, he strives to be
Trying not to forget the forest for the tree
What gift to get for a wonderful father
Nothing would be too much of a bother
But no gift could show just how I feel
Of what is inside, of what is so real
I've known you from the very first day
And learned to do things in your special way
I wouldn't trade you, even for Einstein
Face it dad, you'll always be mine.

Todd Evan Katz

Love And War

All is fair in love and war?
Why are these two words compared?
Both are battles everyone likes to say they've won-but who really knows who the victor is?
The dumper? The dumpee? What if it's a mutual thing, then who is the victor?
Both can cause pain yet we would put ourselves on the battlefield with one beat of our heart.
the plan is all mapped out and you know the right route to take.
you won't get hurt if you do it right, but your heart leads you away from the plans you took time to make.

Both are great mysteries that no one knows the right answer to because there is no "one right answer."

Is all fair in love and way?
it is a mystery everyone must solve for themselves.

Rachelle Robinson

"True Love"

Your eyes were sparkling, when we first met.
Why did you do something, baby you would regret.
I gave you every thing a girl could ever dream.
You were on top like a princess it seemed.
Lets make love like we did before
You've got me wanting you even more.
We always talk about love every night
And kiss each other and turn out the lights.
The thrill was great, beyond something real.
Don't tell me this is some real Bad Deal.
Let's make love like we did before
You got me wanting you even more.
You know it's true love in every way.
We tried to make the most out of a day.
You fight the feeling with all your heart.
But you know I love you, I would never part
Your eyes were sparkling when we first met
Why did you do something you would regret.
Lets make love like we did before
You got me wanting you even more.

Sherry Jacobs

Old Phill

Once there was an old man named Phill,
who was walking up a hill.
The hill started to shake.
The old man started to break,
and you should have seen his hospital bill

Michelle Wright

Why?

Why did things have to be the way they were?
Why did you just ignore it?
Why did you tell lies to change the subject?
I always was true to you.
Until one day you just threw it all away.
So I said we were threw.

Why did it have to be this way?
All we did was fuss, fight, and play.
And I wasn't up for that.
Why was you so high tempered?
You acted as though it was my fault,
That you had problems.
All I did was try to help.
All you did was push me away.
I hated you for that.
But the question still stands why?

Why did you have to treat me that way?
I thought you would never leave me,
That you were here to stay, I guess it was all lies to.
Because I never did anything but try to LOVE YOU!

Shaunita Stephens

Grandma....

Why do people have to die? Why does life have to end?
Why do I feel like I just lost my best friend?

Unanswered questions run through my mind, while tears run down my face,
Devastated by the fact that you're in a different place.

I know that there is no pain and suffering in your everlasting light,
If this is true then why does my pain keep me up at night?

When I saw you last I held your hand and stroked your pepper gray hair,
From time to time I close my eyes and my thoughts can take me there.

I miss you more than words can say,
I can't seem to let go,
I guess it will take a while, but when it happens I'll know.

You are in my heart and always will be,
Please stay by my side to love and guide me.

I love you and I miss you, you were such a special friend,
Not good - bye, just farewell, until we meet again.

Kathleen J. Bulanda

Tears Of Love

When I was young and growing up, it always puzzled me;
Why old folks cried if they were sad, or were happy as could be.

I used to be ashamed of them and didn't know what to say.
Why do they always wipe their eyes, and have to act that way?

But now I feel quite different, for I am old, I fear
And things that mean the most to me are sure to bring a tear.

For I remember little boy's who gathered round my knees.
Who laughed and cried, who learned and played and were a part of me

I've cried when they succeeded and grieved if they were sad.
Sometimes we cried together cause I spanked if they were bad

It really takes a lot of tears, to polish up a stone.
To make your son's do better, or your home a real home.

I'm sure they feel ashamed of me, as I often wipe my eyes.
Cause I see them quickly turn their head and look up at the sky.
Tomorrow son, you'll understand, your eyes will have tears too;
And you'll remember long ago, when tears said, "I LOVE YOU".

Norma S. Franke

The Roads

Why is it that we shift so much in time
Why is there so much decision in our life
Why is it that we must decide

Decide
Decide

Why is it that there is only two roads
The one taken
The one mistaken

Why is it that we rather wallow in the mud of unhappiness
Roll in discordance and cling to execration

Why is it that we lose our sight endure to self reasoning

Why is it that we rather stay where feelings of
darkness, loneliness, death, pain, and despondency

But yet that's one road

Why do we remain
Why do we follow

Well why
Oh the other road
That's for you to decide

Rachelle Taluy

The Door

Aha - Who is this, that pounds at The Door?
Why it's knowledge and learning, and a surprise is in store!
She's wise and she's old,
And many's the tale that she has told.
So listen up you, who have minds that are bold!
With a book, she'll turn, page after page.
She's sharp, and a right jolly old sage.
She'll teach you to think,
And to write with black ink,
To spell and do sums,
And to probe globes with your thumbs -
Finding countries as quick as a wink!
Oh, it's fun to have learning,
And young minds are burning -
To be wise and to know all there is!
So don't be a fool, study hard in your school,
And you'll sit at the top of the world!
Don't be an old bore, or make it a chore,
And you'll find it is true before long,
'Twill be you who will pound at The Door!

Nancy E. Myers

Will Life Go On?

Life goes on as most say.
Why must it go on this way?
Why not the way that everyone else's does?
Is it just because?

All I want is to live free;
With everyone, I plea.
I wish to be helped, to make all go.
But to do this, I do not know.

Many say if I talk about it, it should make all go.
But let me say, I still don't know.

Please, just someone help me forget.
I know it is difficult, but I need to do it.
For me, that is all I want, to be free from all that haunts.

Tanya-Lee Holmes

"Our Sister"

The times we've been through seemed so tough,
why was our life always so rough?
Some were good and some were bad,
why did that cancer take our dad?
It took our mother then our brother,
now it seems to want another.
First there were ten now there is seven,
Soon we'll loose her only to heaven.
For she's too young and it's not her time,
it suddenly grabbed her right from behind.
We love our sister with all our heart,
why is this cancer tearing us apart?
The time will come for all goodbyes,
we'll brace and pray and always cry.
It won't be the same once she is gone,
deep down inside it seems to be wrong.
There's one thing we know, we sure will miss her,
as we all know she is our sister.

Lenny Zappa

"The Vision"

I envision a night, when a great beam of light,
Will blind some young brothers, while they fight.
This blindness will be temporary, and they will soon
regain their sight. The devices that go pop,pop,pop
at least for this night will stop. The corners that
are rough and mean, on this special night will be
calm and clean. Those that spread so wide, on this
night God will guide; while they do something productive
inside. These damn fools that always kill, should be
punished for all the graves they fill. All these parents
that keep themselves wild, just for one night hold and
love your child. I see all of this madness on the
streets I walk, to all troubled people I try to talk.
Maybe just for one day, this gloomy time will vanish
away. All this trouble and strife, I envision a new
way of life. I hope and pray this way will be,
and everyone can see the vision I see.

Terrance H. Drakes

Old House

There's a Lonely Old House by the side of the road. Its
windows now empty, its stories untold.
As I gaze at its beauty, now sadly disguised. It's seen so
much love in so many eyes.
In years passed I wonder what families lives there, with so
much love and such tender care.
I only hope someday someone else will see, this lonely Old House
and what it could be.
A family to share its beautiful grace, its windows full of light
will make such a lovely place.
So when you see it I hope you'll agree and make it your home,
I really wish it were me.

Martha Shaver

Gatekeeper

Gatekeeper:
Wipe my slate clean of jealously;
Wring my brow dry of sorrow.
Instead,
Give me a concrete conscience and
Inject some creative happiness into my parched veins.

Sharon B. Sookram

Freedom Reigns

As the sun falls rapidly to the darkening sky
Winds in a rage blood shed upon the ground
In a last light remains a last attempt
A cry rings out heard blatantly throughout the hearts around the world
It is an eagle soaring high in the rages of the wind
Crying out for freedom reign
As small flakes of snow fall endlessly to the ground
Blue water let drops out of order but as if tears were joined
From the black velvety clouds blood misted in array from wounds inflicted on each other
A man's soul drained from him suffering no more pain
It is free and crying out for freedom reign
The eagle's overwhelming shrieking attempt at freedom perched upon my ears
Standing in pride chest out head held high
Preparing for a battle of those crying out
If freedom was not worth drying for
For those who made it those that could not take it
And for those that lost their lives without them where would we be
Every day we should give thanks it is because of them we are free

Roger Lee Rowell

My Personal October

From season to season,
Winter to Spring, Spring to Summer,
But in the fall everything will die.
I will come around,
I am life.
Falling leaves and harrowing darkness,
The candle of a jack-o-lantern sacrifices its flame,
Giving up its shine, letting the darkness take control.
I will come around,
I am life.
But the bare tree limbs taunt you,
And the cold streets chill you,
And the early sunset follows your every move.
I will come around,
But everything must end.

Steve Hurd

The Fire Of Despair

Fire of despair, One life
Wisdom lost to individuality
Authority for acceptance
Fearless and unfeeling
False security and greatness
Aggression conquering inferiority
One standing alone, lost to nature

Ashes of grief, our struggle
Control with no direction
Given and taken, part of the whole
Insignificance destroying greatness
The awakening

Embers of faith, God's gift
Compassion, empathy, understanding and acceptance
One, part of the whole
Free will within the divine will
The significance of our insignificance
Our greatness, the embers of faith
Glowing from the fire of despair

Michael L. Sedlar

Dreams

A childhood dream that fascinates the boy blue.
Wishing on the stars that someday it'll come true.
Saying 'When I grow up that's what I'm gonna be.'
Still yet not doubting that it can't happen to me.
Even threw adolescence the thoughts remained.
But you never really think it can't be obtained.
Little things remind you of what you want to do.
Always hoping against hope that dreams can come true.
Finding things to do that keeps you close,
But not yet reaching the point to boast.
Then your idea is just a wondering thought,
For time slides by back again it can't be brought.
And then one day you're bite anew.
The tiny dream bug visits you.
You must find a way to grasp your dream,
Positive thinking in an extreme.
With the support of friends the journey begins.
Down the road of dreams your light never dims.
So don't you see, you've shown us too.
That even our dreams can come true.

Kimberly D. Davis

"Thoughts And Wishes"

I'm sitting all alone,
wishing you were here with me.
I picture you in my arms,
holding you tenderly.

I feel your heart beat next to mine,
but my heart is yet incomplete.
I see you with other girls,
girls with whom I can't compete.

I picture all these thoughts,
thoughts that may or may not come true
most of them are impossible,
but still, I love you!

I wish I could hold you,
hold you next to me,
though you're far away,
I still love you dearly!

Natalie Quebral

Faded Love

Shutting my eyes against the sun's rays I see your face
wishing you were still here with me,
your arms around me, keeping me close to you.

Just thinking about your glittering eyes and warm smile
my body gets a warm wave from head to toe.
My friends don't understand the love I have for you.
They say to give up and move on,
if it were only that easy.

The times we shared together are only a faded picture
But I hold that picture close to me for it shall be the last.
Although you have moved on and I am stuck in your shadow,
remember I will always be here for you,
maybe not as a lover but as a faithful and trusting friend.

Some day I shall laugh at my pain and sorrow,
However for now my heart has been torn in two.
Things can only get better now that we are apart.
Sounds crazy but God knew we weren't right for each other.
I can't make you love me but my love for you will never fade.
Although your love for me has faded and now joins me
in the dark shadows remember I always be here for you.

Nicole Nowak

The Journey Of Life

Life is but a journey on a train
With a face placed at every window pane
You walk the aisles searching for a seat
You nod your head to those you meet
As we ride along the track
Looking forward never looking back
We are engaged in sharing our future not our past
Our dreams, wishes and desires rushing by us so fast

As we ponder a place, we may sit here or maybe there
We listen carefully to the sounds that we can hear
Those sounds may be quiet to us or loud
Searching each one out of the crowd
I can only hope you'll sit, by my side
Let's enjoy it together, for it's such a short ride.

Lavernna L. Bayer

The Goodness And The Severity Of God

With a blink of an eye, there forms an eclipse.
With a flick of his finger, a mighty oak falls.
With a twinkle of his eye, a flower blooms in an instant.
With a sweep of his arm, the ocean pours into a tidal wave.
With a sway of his wings, the earth is clothed in warmth.
With a swing of his fist, a mountain crumbles to rocks.
With a caress of his hand, an injury is healed.
With a blast of his nostrils, a gale sweeps a field.
With the push of his body, the earth swings around the sun.
With the breath of his mouth, a thunderstorm rumbles across the land.

With the touch of his hand, a baby is born.
With a cough of his lungs, a sandstorm blows through a desert.
With a snap of his finger, a nation stands at attention.
With the clap of his hands, thunder roars through the sky.
With the swing of his arm, comets are flung across the universe.
With the gentleness of his voice, a storm calms and disappears.
With a stomp of his foot, an earthquake splits the ground.
With the smile of his lips, the earth glows in sunshine.
With the wind of his breath, a blizzard blankets a city.
With the fragility of his heart, a man dies.

Terry Jones

Lord Popcorn And Lady Liz

Lady Liz is a bookworm, her teachers confirm,
With a temperament mellow and sweet.
Lord Popcorn, our notion, is perpetual motion,
A terrestrial child of Mach speed.

We live in this house; she's just like a mouse,
His skateboard screeches the halls.
Both spend their days, in opposite ways,
With fights over telephone calls.

Lord Popcorn loves go-karts, body sounds, pop-art,
Baggy pants—crotch to the knees,
Videos, skis, music (oh, please!),
Guns to shoot balls or B-Bs.

Lady Liz adores dress-ups, kittens, toy pups,
Scones we have at high tea,
Make-up, shopping, dancing or hopping.
Writing stories about what could be.

Our pediatrician suggested our mission,
"Raise each like an only child."
This we have done, our daughter and son,
Artwork completely self-styled.

Renee Ritter Graham

Truly My Son

An old man stood, at the grocery stand
With a wrinkled brow, and a trembling hand
His poor old shoulders, were stooped and bent
As he counted his groceries, cent by cent.
His fingers were stiff, as he tried to pay
He dropped one of his pennies, and it rolled away.
Under the counter it rolled some more,
As he slowly bent himself to the floor
He tried, and tried, with the shaky hand
But he just couldn't get it from beneath the stand.
Men and women and teenagers too,
were impatiently waiting for him to get thru
Then a boy, stepped forward from the back of the line.
And I was filled with pride, because that boy was mine.
He stepped by the people, and up to the stand,
and handed the penny to the grateful old man.
"Thanks Son", said the man, as he went on his way
But his tiny smile told us he had brightened his day.
I was proud and contented, my work was well done.
He who helped the old man was truly my son!

Marjorie Pursley

Forever And Always

I loved you once
with all my heart I held you close to me...
I told myself, no other one
could ever really be -
I said you were the only one
I ever would adore.
However high the wishful waves
that washed away the shore,
And then the sun went down
and the stars were not the same...
And you became a memory
and just another name -
The fault was yours
as much as mine -
And maybe more your own
because you went away and left me all alone...
Now I know not what to say
I know not what to do...
But forever and always
I shall burn with love for you

Linda Paliska

Winter Song

Sleigh rides thru the snow, a rosy glow on cheeks, and noses bright with cold, the sight of old friends meeting; icicles agleam in beaming sunlight, faces bright in greeting. Steaming bowls of punch, the crunch of snow beneath your feet, the street athrong, a song in ev'rybody's heart, friends all catching up on times they've been apart. The sight of horses prancing, skaters dancing, sweethearts of all ages are romancing in the glow of winter's charms. Friendly arms are open wide in greeting, happy to be meeting friends of old. Hearts are all aglow and warm in winter's cold.

Children on their sleds are sliding, graceful skaters gliding o'er the ice, the nicest sight in winter; golden sunlight shining bright on snowcapped trees all white in winter. Icy fingers tingle in the cold, the sleighbells jingle, lovers hold each other closely as they go clip- clip-clopping, slip-slip-slopping thru the snow. The sounds of sleighbells ringing, voices singing all the songs we used to sing that bring back memories of days gone by. Spirits high we cry in joyful greeting, happy to be meeting friends of old. Hearts are all aglow and warm in winter's cold.

Vivian Durocher Hayter

Life

Life is like a two way street,
With different destinations.
It all depends on which one you choose
To bring success with determination,

Sometimes, if you follow your heart
You may end up on the right track.
Or, if you take the wrong path
You may have to counteract.

Positive thoughts and high ambition,
Go a long way, when you are on a mission.
Constructive criticism should be taken with good attitude
In order to reach great altitude.

Hard work and perseverance should exist initially,
It one wishes for success.
Persistence is important,
In looking for a goal eventually.

One must not forget honesty,
Which should never be left out.
It is one of the building blocks to happiness,
And a well cherished and meaningful success.

Olga Murray

Stop, Pray And Listen

I awake you in the wee hours of the morning to have supper with Me. A special invitation I'd given thee. Not now Lord, I just want to sleep. So, I close your eyes and watch you sleep. Late evenings when all are quiet, I've asked you to talk with Me. Not now Lord, I just want to watch this program on T.V. So again I wait to see if you will spend some time with Me. I've removed your mountains to make a straightway for thee. The credits are given to mankind, why not thank Me? I've carried you through the storms and rains, and even have delivered you through sickness and pains. Do you remember where I've brought you from unto where I have place you now? All thy blessings comes from Me. I have given and taken only to teach thee that I am your leaning tree and solid rock. I can bend and will not break. Use me Lord, I hear you pray. But first you must be tested and sincere. Pray and fast, have supper with Me. For the feast will be plentiful because you will be My special guest.

Shirley A. Hall

Elko

He had a gig in Elko
With miles yet to go
Down the mountain road;
When up ahead, a heavy load
Came to a screeching halt,
Long, dark tracks on the asphalt,
With no time to swerve,
Reacting with sheer nerve,
Lost a shipment of steer.
They scattered helter-skelter
Trying to seek shelter from the trauma,
But from it, came more drama,
Slipping in the diesel spill,
One trapped in the wreckage, till he ran to its defense,
Without thought of consequence.
Laid aside his own fear empowered by prayer, saved the steer.
Spattered with blood and diesel
Walked away with conscience peaceful.
Then he went along to sing his song.
He had a gig in Elko, with miles yet to go.

Patricia Ann Kerr

The Touch Of A Teacher's Hand

Sullen and silent, she sat there alone,
With neither a smile nor a frown.
She seemed unaware of all who passed by.
A fortress encircled her 'round.

Tossed to and fro like a ship in the wind,
With never an anchor to hold,
She'd bounced back and forth on waves of despair.
All warmth had long since turned cold.

I reached out my hand with heart full of love.
Her small hand reached right back to me.
My eyes said "I care and I am your friend."
Her walls tumbled down at my feet.

A journey began to an unknown shore,
But together we reached the land.
A life been changed, a course been set right,
By the touch of a teacher's hand.

Sue F. Martin

Ode To A Toad

What a life a toad must lead
With nothing to eat but a bug or a weed
Who never can speak with a chirp or a twitter
But must sadly croak like a sow with a litter.

Whose epidermis is covered with warts
And who cares not a whit for kings and courts.
No changes of clothing from spring to fall
In fact, he never wears clothes at all!

He sits and broods and contemplates
And doesn't know there are fifty states.
Should stocks go up or stocks go down
It's the same to a toad, he owns not a crown.

No wonder a toad always looks a bit vexed
I secretly think he's a shade undersexed.
From where he sits, life's not a joke
If I were a toad I think I'd croak.

Lamar Mulliner

The Make Believe Child

The little girl of three or four;
With parents well to do, liked to pretend
That she is poor then she's happy all day
through, her parents are busy with their
Friends and dance all night too:
When it's time to tuck her in she turns her face
To the wall, and pretend it's her mommy's
kiss, not the governess at all:

A little lad with dreams galore;
Will pretend his dad has money
He dreams of all the things he wants;
And forgets that he is poor:
The little girl from a broken home
pretends when school is out her Mom and Dad
Will pick her up, and she gives a great big
Shout:

When Dad left Mom, the little boy
would wonder about the house;
pretending dad would soon be home
And fill his heart with joy.

Mary Adair

Love

Once you flew like a bird free in the sky.
With passion in your heart and fire in your eyes.
You saw over the mountains and through the trees.
To what you knew you could achieve.
There was no stopping you alive and free.
Flying the blue sky skimming the trees.
The sun warmed you filled you with peace.
The wind touched you a warm summers breeze.

I thought I'd never see you give up the fight.
I thought I'd never see you drop out of sight.
No longer the wind under your wings.
No longer the fire gone the desire.
The sky you loved and knew so well erupted in red.
A silent hell.
I watched speech less with tears in my eyes.
My heart held heavy with one last cry.
The moon is full on the blue black sky.
One single star, your spirit can't die.
It will live, forever you see.
It will live forever in me.

Rachel I. Amado

Clouds Of Terror

A surprising whirl of quick accelerated wind
with roar of a freight train and funnels at two
hundred miles per hour speed of deadly maximum
powered force, splitting nature's forest and ripping
up the earth's soil. Mangling and mutilating anything
in sight. Reeking Havoc on human life, sparing no
one, causing major despair and devastation, leaving
empty shells of human souls, weakening the pride
of mankind with no warning to be known except
for the few seconds of rumbling impact. Tornados
are spirals of destruction which will be definitely
part of our future even more. Multibans of
twister disasters spawned from a much
higher source. The Almighty Mother Nature.

Wendy L. Randall

Morning Prayer

Dear Lord, please give me another fine day,
With warm sunshine to brighten all my way;
Fill my heart with joy, paint smiles on my lips
And lighten my burden in all my steps.

Let me see the little things I pass by -
Your handiwork under this azure sky,
To inspire me to do even lit'l things,
For all big deeds have humble beginnings.

Make me hear all Your sageful messages,
In whispers of breeze and swaying of trees,
In soft murmurs of distant waterfalls
And sweet music of the birds' mating calls.

Let my heart soften to all hapless ones -
Empathy my approach to everyone
And make my strong hands ready to extend -
The strength you give me to them shall I lend.

Let me live by Your commands all the time
And radiate soothing kindness to mankind,
That my footprints may glitter on the way,
To guide lonely souls who have gone astray. AMEN.

Teodulfo T. Yerro

Finally

The pictures of you my eyes can finally meet,
without any tears running down from my cheek.
The letters of promises I finally tore,
and I don't see you in my dreams anymore.
Thoughts of you are becoming less each day,
and the pain of memories has gone away.
I no longer want your arms around me.
Images of your face I no longer see.
I hear music without thinking of you.
I stopped thinking back on things we used to do.
I no longer miss the feel of your touch,
and your lips to mine, I don't care for that much.
I could now do the things that we once did,
without all of the tears, me having to rid.
Everything you gave me I put away,
and I stopped going through it everyday.
I will not be missing you annually,
because I have gotten over you, finally.

Kim Dufek

My True Love, First Love

A true love, the first love gone for good.
Wonderful feelings and memories go to waist.
Some things can never be replaced.
The sound of his mature loving voice calling me by night.
I know in my heart and mind he will never be there.
The feeling in my soul that no one else cares.
A first love, my true love gone to the heaven above.
Though I cry inside the pain is strong.
I have to survive and keep on.
Nobody will ever take this true love away from my heart.
I will always love him there is no doubt in my mind.
A first and true love like him I'll never find.
Missing him as I lay alone.
Loving him for bring unto me this precious gift.
His baby makes my spirits uplift.
A charming doll to hold and cradle.
His baby will grow and I will teach him his father's ways.
The love I have for both of them will always stay.

Maciel Ramirez

The Looking Glass

Every time we pass in halls,
words always seem to fail us.
Makes me think that never will
our relationship prevail us.

I pray that when you sleep at night
and when you awake, you'll think of me forever
and the memories well make.
Those memories will cling to us,
with picture books galore,
and long from now we'll look at them and
wish that there were more

Yes everyday we pass in halls, but
you always look right through me.
I hope that soon the day will come
when you start to look into me

Rachael Nightingale

The Field Of Nature

Over the mountains and hills of blue;
with orange and brown leaves covered in dew,
you'll find roses of pink, purple and red.
There's no place I'd want to be instead.
Whether rain or shine, day or night;
the field of nature is always bright.

Laura Michelle Berkowitz

Words

Words reflect an Individual.
Words should be uttered with Caution.
Words can penetrate and linger forever in the Heart.
Words can build our confidence or self esteem,
if spoken with encouragement.
Words are a long term investment to our children.
Words determine our intelligence or ignorance.
Words have an impact let's not forget.
Words are like a tidal wave, Cruel and Reckless.
Words have no way to turning Back.
Words whispered with love can bring a smile a century After.
Words are our responsibility; therefore should be Considered
carefully when spoken.
Words are powerful to the vocal cord, and should not Be
Underestimated
so be careful.
Words are stimulating to life.
Words inspired from above can lead our hearts to peace and love.
Words can be priceless, let's cherish them
Words are our tool to everyday life.
Words can build a friendship, or create an enemy.
Words can bring tears and laughter, joy and Happiness.
Words can build a destiny or destroy a Nation.
Words should flow flawlessly like a gently breeze that can be
Refreshing, Words are refreshing.

Mona Sewkumar

"Tired"

As is commonly said, "I'm very tired."
Working, mothering, following the clock.
Sometimes I feel like I must be wired.
My body's out of shape-it's going to pot.

There must be something else destined for me.
I feel like a person away from her kind.
It's there, I know it; but I just can't see.
I'll keep on looking, I know I'm not blind.

I have on sunglasses to dim the view.
It's scary out there all alone.
I'll need some help and encouragement, too.
To take them off and find my way home.

I'm out of my shell after all these years
Feeling and thinking what I really should be.
Sometimes I have this great big fear
That life won't go well, with regard to me.

My fan club is gone, never to return,
So what support should I enlist?
I'm on my own, do I need to learn
That I have to do more than barely exist?

Vickie Blasingim

I would If I could... But, God Can!

If I knew what to say, I would say it. If I knew what to do, I would do it. If I knew what path to take to help you get through it, I definitely would pursue it.

If I knew how to express the depth of my sympathy, I would appease by showing empathy. If I could free all your frustrations, phobias and fears, I would fill your life with joy where there are tears.

If I could just be a friend as God intend; and make you smile; it would make me feel worthwhile to know that together we can endure it. Or, If I had the ability to give you the necessary stability, I certainly would if I could... But, God can!

Stelline Hill

To Say The Words

To say the words would be unkind. To answer those words
would be to give my heart to your open arms -
to hold - to love again.
To say the words in kind could mean a heartbeat
from the silence - to love again.
Speak of love, speak of the memories, memories of a
love, not of a heart - to begin to love again.
Do I say the words, do I trust you with all that I am?
Your eyes speak of love, your touch tells of devotion,
but my heart remembers another's devotion - turned cold.
Now jaded, my own heart dreams of love but remembers
what it means "to say the words"...nothing.
Only from my lips do the words ever seem to echo
from a heart - my own.
To say the words holds no promises, but in your eyes
I will see, in your voice I will hear, in your arms
I will know what is true.
To say the words would be so cruel 'les I feel it from
your heart. Only then will my heart draw the courage
....to say the words - "I Love You."

Stephen Q. Roenneburg

Untitled

They say that time like cooling drops of summer rain,
would ease my grief and soothe my sick heart's pain.

False prophets they, strangers to dark despair,
how could they know that time makes scant repair,
but blurred as by a vail of fog, the wounds of years are denied.

And precious memories blown like leaves before an autumn wind,
yet, keen and piercing as wintry gale, my sorrow and
longing for you mother dear forever will prevail

Millie Goldenberg

If Tomorrow

If I could see beyond tomorrow
Would I tread softly on my way
Or backward step, to keep me safe
And never know the day
of strength, that hardship brings
to those while standing tall
Or would I rather stay secure
and never know at all
The challenge of another Spring,
to sing of joy or cry in Fall.

Today is mine to hold, to see
And yesterday's memories will always be
A source of strength, of love held dear
To guide me on my way, each day each year

And when tomorrow comes to light
with the rising of the sun.
My life will endure the yesterdays
My eternity has begun.

Rosalie Harrington

Cries Of War

To rot so rancid red and raw,
with chiselled features and porcelain jaw.
And beady eyes alone they glare,
so deeply sunk in dark despair.
To gloat in victory and goad them on,
young souls that bled, the hearts they won.
The poignant pain and pity past,
the first to die, but not the last.

Michelle McCarthy

Untitled

Our life was planned before we met so how were we to know that life would make us sisters with so much time to grow.

To grow into great friends, that's what we did you and I. It was very easy for us, we didn't even have to try.

For you are someone special and I think the world of you. We have so many memories, I'm so glad it was us two.

Remember when we had foil on our feet, wigs on our head, and playing with pantyhose while taking naps in grandma's bed. Or eating on the counter, taking naps together,or playing out in back. We've had so many great times, it's impossible to keep track.

We may be very different, but that didn't stop us from being close. For we have the same idea of what a sister is and that's what matters the most.

So when I say I have a sister, what I really mean to say, is if I could choose a friend for me, I'd have it no other way.

So walk along the path of life and save a spot, I will be there, for we have many more memories, we have so much more to share.

I love you little sister, we will be close until the end. For there is no better sister, there is no better friend!

Nicole Clifford

Poem For My Children

If I could write a song that the whole world would sing
would you listen?
Would you hear my words and the message I tried to bring?
Or would it fall on deaf ears because it came from me?

Would you learn from my example and remember how I continued
to try when everything was against me and times were so hard
for so long that it made my heart cry?

Would you straighten your back and make ready for a heavy load
directing your mind and efforts to win against the odds
and reach long awaited goals?

Would you simply think of reasons why the effort is too much
to struggle and achieve long felt wishes and desires
and distant dreams within your touch?

Would you delay taking action as pieces of your life quickly pass
by then perhaps just give up
with excuses, justification, resignation, and a sigh?

Would you some day in the future take time and think for a while
remembering our talks together
those past words of wisdom, and love
from a mother to her child?

Patricia Smalley

Gifts From The Past

We each are threads in a tapestry
Woven by our ancestry,
The future placed in younger hands,
Our hope, they'll use but golden strands.

The loom of hardship may reveal
An endurance strong as steel,
The strands, at times, may twist and break,
Still the picture is no fake.

Like uncut gems polished to jewels,
Genes are part of nature's tools
To weave with learned dexterity
A fabric beautiful to see.

Louise Carmack

My Poetry

Poetry dark ink
writing of poet
writing of all time
Poetry, poetry, bring joy bring fear.
bring my poet to a poetry back
When a poetry becomes a poet a two
come to two or one of one,
Poetry poetry dark ink I can use
my ink I con use my poet to
But my poetry rest poetry dark ink
dark ink poetry of
all poetry poetry a poet.
Come to a poet be gentle
Come to a poet see with his eyes.
Come to a poet live his way fateful
come to a poet you be level always.
poetry poetry send me your poem
come to my hand come to my
inch-a lots a inch is simple I
hold a pen called simple poet-

Marie Daigle

My Brotha

My brotha ya told me ya never do this, now ya back to this,
Ya keep breaking my heart, when will you ever stop
I doubt it, I had hope and belief in you, but cha' shot it
Do you want to live long?
You always taught me not to do wrong
I sit around worried, wondering why you're not home
You keep telling me the same old song
That you've been working and not out there doing wrong
But I know what's really going on
For me, please leave them drugs alone
For your kids, your wife, and everyone else
I can't make you stop
Ya gotta do it for yourself
I hope one day you'll wake
And realize your mistake
Ya can't rewind the things that happened in the past
But look ahead, I hope last night was your last
Ya only have one life to live
And when it's gone, it's gone
So sit back and think and leave them drugs alone.

Shana Dorsey

Marriage Over Divorce

My heart has no limit for your love
You are all!
My mind wonders when there is a conflict between us
I have never wanted another since I met you
You are all!
It is sometimes hard to show, but I try with all my heart
Our love is true, because we both truly care
You are all!
Sometimes I know it hurts to even accept me because you don't understand
We will never understand each other completely, but I still love you
We will fight and disagree many times
But we must work together to make us work
There will be times when we feel so far apart
But I still love you
We have come too far to let love go astray
Because I know my heart bleeds for you
My eyes shed tears for you
And my mind is not at ease when we aren't one
My heart and mind are yours, love me because I will always love you
You are all!

Kelvin G. Tarrance

On Becoming Parents

Two people in love, they marry and have a baby,
Years pass, they have two more, some say they are crazy.

They trade fine dining, theatre and vacations,
For diapers, late night feedings and other aggravations.

Whether Mom and Dad stay home or rely on day care,
They shoulder responsibility together, as much as they can share.

These little people grow so fast, whether girl or boy,
And develop their own personalities, down to their favorite toy.

Halloween costumes, Easter eggs, Christmas Eve decorating the tree.
What was two and a couple has become five and a family.

The years go by so fast, bunkbeds and desks replace the nursery,
Mom and Dad can't believe it is their 10th anniversary.

Life as parents is a challenge, it requires patience and perseverance.
Shuttling to school, the pediatrician, oh that daily schedule
adherence.

Scouts, t-ball and ballet, music lessons, training wheels,
Monthly budgets, discount shopping, searching for those special deals.

The time, the dedication and the sacrifices galore,
Are worth it just to watch grandkids with their grandparents at
the toy store.

Becoming parents is an adventure, raising children a labor of love,
Someday our children will say, "Thanks Mom and Dad, to you
and God above."

Lawrence J. Indiviglia

An Unknown Wonder

Whenever he moved his hand, he painted gold.
Yet never a painting had he sold.
In a subliminal world all his own,
all his works n' paintings were known.
The grandeur exhibited wi' the stroke of his hand.
left all bewildered, yet all understand.
For such beauty should be showered throughout the earth,
that the world might know the little man's worth.
But the little man desires no fortune and fame,
to him his art is no money game.
So quietly and patiently he sits in refrain,
an unknown wonder to the world he'll remain.

Tim Spetnagel

I Hear Your Smile

As I pick up the telephone to call you,
you answer
It is almost the way that it
used to be
My voice starts to quiver,
My heart starts to flutter,
I feel like a little girl again.

We talk about the past
Some moments bring laughter, some tears.

I call because the feelings for you
haven't left
As we continue to talk
I can hear your smile.

There are years between us now
as we both grow older
We see now what problems
we had then.

I only wish that we could have
worked them out.

I love you so!

Linda J. Kreimer

The Night Was Beautiful

I really enjoyed the time that we spent together last night.
You are a very beautiful woman with a wonderful personality
and I can find no words that can express all of the feelings
that I have whenever I am around you, it is like I have known
you all of my life and perhaps I have because I knew that
somewhere a woman existed like you someone that is not only
beautiful outside but a treasure inside you are all of that
and so much more that is why I feel so comfortable around
you it is because I can feel the goodness that comes from
within you and it is very special and unique. Last night as
we sat in front of the fire place it felt so good to be in
your arms listening to the music and feeling your soft touch.
I wish that the fire could have burned forever while you
looked into my eyes with your beautiful smile.

Murphy Edward Smith

Age Ten

When you are ten you are something in between
You are not a kid and you are not a teen
Santa has deserted you
The tooth fairy, too.
The Easter Bunnie has gone with the rest.
His disappearance I like the best.
I get to color and decorate Easter Eggs.
"Careful, don't spill," Mother begs.
I can join in the Easter Egg Hunt
I wish they'd have an eating contest with this stunt.
With salt and pepper I could eat a dozen.
It could be called the pie eating contest's cousin.

Lois Belcher

Social Immigrants

Don't cry you immigrants who come in peace.
You are not yet poor.
Your fathers were murdered by rulers of wealth
And your children carry a plague.
But, still it is time to rejoice
For the forgotten beliefs of your people
Have no known boundaries.

Fall into obscurity so that your true
Meaning will not be wounded when you fall
Away from the ship that stranded you abroad.
A time to believe is close at hand,
And the children all laugh at their
Shadows that dance in the halls.
Their only true hero's are the crying leaves
That tumble endlessly from their mother.
Don't cry forever... don't cry.

I don't believe that you fathom your wishes well.
For a pirate could only make you do his will
Without you embracing him, helplessly.
Forever sleep, social immigrants of peace.

Ted Millar

Your Shadow

You are the person I look up to
You are the meaning of me being here.
You are the one who brought me into the world
You're the one who showed me how to open doors to my life.
You are my Mother, my friend and my companion for life.
I am like your shadow wherever you are, I follow.
Everything you do, I do.
You are my Mother and I'm your daughter.

Tracey L. Bryant

The Rest Of Your Life Together

You are the one that makes me happy,
You are the one that makes me cry,
You are the one that brings joy to my heart,
when I deeply sigh,

When I first met you, something opened inside,
It was he, who telling me, to take it into stride.
When I first laid eyes on you, I knew for a fact,
That I be with you through eternity and back.
And, in closing, if I was granted three wishes,
The first one would be,
To make your life as happy as can be.
The second to be as rich as can,
So I could buy you that wedding ring.

Last, but not least the third wish I seek,
This is the best of them all, and this I can say.
I love you so dearly, it will have to be,
I'll say it again, WILL YOU MARRY ME!

Kevin Ivie

"My Friend"

You are my friend for life.
You are with me through all my strife.

I love you. You are my friend,
And I know you'll be there until the end.

When I need you, I know you're not far.
Always remember, I'll be there for you no matter where you are.

God made you to be my friend.
He knew I'd need someone who wouldn't pretend.

You always listen and seem to care.
You are so important just because you're there.

No one could take your place on this earth.
Only heaven itself could match your worth.

Miranda Joan Nobiling

Ode To Amanda

In one miraculous instant you breathed the breath of life
You became an embodied living soul spiraling to new heights
How delicate and fragile you seem to be!
How astoundingly beautiful and precious you are to me
My own mortality becomes bearable because of you
Holding you in the soft light of dawn I sense
You are an important instrument in life's symphony
In its ebb and flow you join in universal harmony
You'll find your worth and rightful part
As you open wide your mind and heart
You are loved simply because you are you
Not because of who you are or what you do
So make sweet music on life's way
Ensoul the beautiful love, laugh and pray
The knower deep within you knows
Just how each branch on the tree grows.

Pearl N. Sorrels

"Why?"

As I shared our tender dawn's soft joy with you
You grieved the absence of this one you never knew
This one you never met on earth yet knew his charm
And so as promised sun would warm to end all harm
Calm morning crimson cried your plight within my heart
I found no answer - I knew not where to start
You turned away to plead with our dream filled sky
Then turned to me - You kissed me asking why?

William Schaeffer

The Metamorphosis Of A Teenager's Parent

Once you have a teenager, life is never the same.
You begin to change.
You suddenly start speaking a different language;
One that teenagers can no longer understand.
Or, you become as mute as a nail.
You start to look odd and many times you even become invisible.
Your needs, wants and feelings take on a lesser value.
While theirs triple in importance.
Your possessions are no longer - just yours,
And may suddenly VANISH, never to be seen again.
The rules you once set with equal consideration
Are questioned, challenged or bent into various configurations.
Sometimes they are disregarded entirely.
You find your wallet emptying much more often
While your debts soar forever skyward.
And in their eyes, you take on the characteristics of an ogre.
Once you have a teenager in your life;
Your life is never the same.

Roseanne Koch

"Completely Yours"

If you ever lose your heart,
You can have mine.
I'll be yours forever,
Til' the end of time.
Constantly committed to you and you alone.
I'll bring you joy and happiness
Like you have never known.
The world would have such beauty
And simple harmony
As much as one desires,
Together you and me
We'll be lost in love eternally.
And this I know is true,
That I will not mind the wandering
As long as it's with you!

Wendy S. Onsted

Feeling Well

Feeling well,
You can tell,
When you can jump up and down,
Side to side and all around.

Feeling well with Christ in your life,
He removed all the strife out of your life.

You can go tell,
Others will listen
As you tell the joy of feeling well with Jesus.

Orville R. Brown

I Am Still Here Child

I am still here Child; I have not left thee.
You cannot see me with your natural eye.
But I am in each flower, and every living thing.
Have faith in my Word; it will prove I cannot lie.

I am still here Child; awaken to my call.
Reach out to me, while I'm reaching out to you.
Know my love and let it grow deep within your heart.
As the Spirit comes and fills your life anew.

I am still here Child; just waiting for you.
To come to me, Oh! precious little lamb.
So let me carry you, when deep hurt you feel.
I am the Christ who lives, "The Great I Am."

Marie Foster

Ode To My Breast Fed Babe

I nurse you - you suckle. I watch my heart buckles.
You drift off to sleep. You make not a peep.
It's peace at its best, it's time for a rest -
from the worries of the world; oh my beautiful girl...

Wake up to finish; the supply won't diminish.
Not my time nor my patience nor my love.

You continue to nurse, oh my heart bursts -
with caring beyond all control.

This is such an easy way, yet I'm here to say:
That this is the best choice for us.
No bottles to boil, no powders to toil,
no troubles, no worries, no fuss.

The best thing of all is that I know in my heart
that you get the best healthy start.
Immunities, vitamins, comfort and more;
I see it in your health, your body does soar...
So it's time to unlatch,
though my heart you did catch
while I nursed and fed you today.

Lori Walsh

Seek Your Bliss

Seek Your Bliss, no matter the cost
You got the dogged determination
To help it to succeed from the start!

Don't be afraid of any obstacles
That might stand in the way.
They can all be overcome if
You but take the time to
Think, Meditate, work hard and pray.

Seeking your bliss will not be easy to do,
Especially when society may seem to be against you!
But truly, it's what makes life worth living.
It's all part of the joy of self-sacrifice
And the Joy of Giving.

To seek your bliss means to fulfill
The greatest desires of your heart, soul and mind.
Yet these desires must be beneficial to all mankind.

So Seek, Seek, Seek with all your heart,
Never letting your dreams and goals depart!
No matter what others may say, think or do
YOU CAN ONLY SEEK AND FIND YOUR BLISS IF YOU
ARE WILLING TO BE YOU!!

Lissa Lee Loper

Take Your Time

All your life from when you were a child
You heard three little words from a voice soft and mild-
"Take your time" when you're learning to walk-
Learning to eat and learning to talk.
Then when it's time to go to school
To learn right and wrong and the golden rule-
"Take your time" from the teacher is heard
When learning your lesson and every new word.
When you became teenage and learn about life
And you're told "when it's time for a husband or wife"
"Take your time" and be sure it's someone you love
So your union will be healthy and blessed from above.
Now comes the family you've longed for so much
You've become parents with a golden touch-
"Take your time" to hear what they say
And respect will be yours each step of the way.
Now you have reached your autumn years
Your memories are filled with laughter and tears-
"Take your time" and reflect on your enchanted past-
For now it's your turn - "Take your time" - make it last.

Natalie D. Tovet

Tapping Into Ones' Emotions

When dealing with ones' emotions
you must be very gentle because
feelings are so very fragile.
Words chosen must be chosen
very wisely. Words used too harshly
may tend to lower ones' self esteem
leaving him or her to believe that
they're not worthy of all the good
things and people in which their
lives entwine. Someone who's self centered
wouldn't know anything about these
things called feelings because they're
so rapped up in themselves. Love yourself
by all means but also show a little
love for the one who loves you

Terrance Thornton

Genevieve

Oh Genevieve, my muse,
You of the "sweet" song and the crystal eyes-
You are dancing always in my heart.
You pirouette-
And look to see if I have seen.
Half asleep, you climb into my lap
And become 5 again.
Child-woman of the innocent smile,
Smile for me... and take me dancing!
I will put my arms around you,
Hold you close,
And lift you with my soul.

Livia Genise

"Very Good, Kimberly."

"Very good, Kimberly."
You say that without any tone, without any feeling.
"Very good, Kimberly."
What the hell is that supposed to mean?
Are you proud of me or not?
"Very good, Kimberly."
You've said it before, but you don't seem to mean it.
I have tried so hard, for so long to make you proud of me,
And all you say is, "Very good, Kimberly."
What does it take?
I don't need your approval,
I've learned to do without your love,
Can't you just be proud of me -
Just once?

Kimberly L. Mathews

Untitled

Everyone of us has a shadow
You take it with you wherever you go
Be it day or night dark or bright
It's there though it doesn't always show
Sometimes your shadow is in front of you
And you can see it stretched out on the ground
But it could easily sneak up from behind you
For your shadow never makes a sound
It will never tire or get out of step
You could not fool it even if you tried
For if it is not in front or behind you
Then it's surely standing off to one side
There are times when my shadow is very short
It can hardly be seen at all
And even though my height never changes
My shadow can grow very tall
Shadows care not if your rich or poor
Or if your color is black or white
For all you need do to see your shadow
Is simply step between it and a light

Leland Francis Corbett Jr.

A Mother's Love

When you were young and in your teens
You thought us not fair, but kind of mean.
But back then if you only knew
How much we did love you.

We learned to share our love with you
And God and that love brought us through.
Now that you're a mother too;
His love will also carry you through.

Now, it's not that we couldn't get you a card
But we wanted to give you something from the heart;
So reach out now child, and feel our embrace,
In our minds, hearts and prayers you will stay.

Praise your family with the love of God
And nothing, dear child, will be to hard.
Have peace and a happy day.

Leatha Augustus

A Prayer Just For My Son

Dear Jesus, I come to you asking
You to please help my son.

You know he got himself into some trouble,
And he is in need of your help.

He knows he was in the wrong,
But I am asking you please put your arms around him and just let him know you are by his side.

Jesus, please fill his heart with love and show
Him the right way to go.
Please don't let anything happen
To him while he is away.

Jesus, I love my son with all my heart
And I know if you are at his side he will be ok.
So please, dear Jesus, let my son come home to his Family as soon as you can.

Just let him know his family will be here for him
And let him know we love him with all our hearts.
Thank you, Jesus, for everything you have done
To help all of us.

In Jesus name, Amen.

Liz Swift

Balloon Fests, Past, Present, And Future

Past
You touched our lives with beauty and grace,
Put a smile upon so many a face.
The memories are so sweet and warm
Of you drifting slowly down onto our farm.

Present
We watch with excitement as you sail on through,
Hoping you'll touch us this year too.
Now, the winds didn't bless us as they did in the past,
But the August before this, in our hearts will ever last.

Future
We'll cross our finger at this time next year
And maybe you'll hear our voices in cheer:
"Come down oh so safely once again on our farm,
A hot air balloon with all of its charm!"

Nina Davis

My Love To Grow

It was almost Midnight when your Water broke.
You went into the delivery room with a smile,
even though you knew I lost my job and was broke.
You felt it was all worth while.

Eighteen hours went by, then he arrived
as a present full of surprise.
He has my nose, blue eyes, and smile;
now what more could a Dad surmise.

Thank you for not aborting Nicky Joe.
Mother of my child standing by me,
waiting all these years for my love to grow.

R. R. Wister

Mirror Image

I remember the day I met you
You were around two
I looked in your eyes
I knew you'd been abused
My heart it broke inside
So I held you and cried
Wanting to forever protect you
Lynn it's okay to cry
Lynn I'll be here by your side
Lynn you don't have to be afraid
Lynn it's okay to cry
Lynn I'll be here by your side
Lynn you don't have to run away
I remember the day I told you I wanted you
You looked in my eyes and hoped it would be true
I'll always be here for you
It doesn't matter what you do
Because it wasn't your fault
You were abused
Lynn. . .I'm the mirror image of you.

Stacy Lynn Harp

When Sleep Was So Alone

Dedicated to my loving wife, Lois.

Many years ago when sleep was so alone
You'd curl up and face the wall
Don't turn around
You dream I'm there

Then we were wed and we curled up and faced
The wall
You feel me laying beside you
Don't turn around
You know I'm there

When the time comes for you to sleep alone
Just curl up and face the wall
Don't turn around
You sense I'm there

Then when the time comes for your final sleep
Just curl up and face the wall
But fear not
For when you wake, turn around and I'll be there.

Len Morgan

Love Search

If you're looking for true, true, love,
you'll always look where you won't find it,
you won't see it, and you won't feel it,
in your quest to catch and bind it.

Love is quite the clever bandit,
it finds you, and when it does
you can hardly stand it!

It steals your choice,
you hear its voice,
and follow its savored sound,
and feel its penetrating warmth around
your racing heart and through your being,
and when you're truly feeling and seeing
the heat and beauty of its fire,
tasting its insatiable desire,

You either stay, or run away,
making you a victim, or a liar.

H. P. Bigham

To A Humming Bird

Oh, little bird with your long, slender beak,
You'll be gone in a day or, at most, a week.
The leaves grow golden and the air has a chill,
But through the summer you've given me a thrill.
We've had breakfast together through the summer,
With me watching you chasing another hummer.
What joy you've given me as I watched you so free,
As you sat on the branch of my chinaberry tree.
Once in a while I've glimpsed your ruby-red throat,
While you fed yourself until you'd almost bloat.
Hovering in the sun with your shimmering coat of green,
Surely you're the most beautiful bird I've ever seen!
Drinking the sugar-water colored a bright red,
Yes, you and your cousins have been very well fed.
As we've watched over you until dusk from daylight,
You've fed from my altheas of pink, purple, and white.
So, farewell today, and may God gently you keep,
May you find red flowers always waist deep.
And farewell to you as you go where you please,
And you will return next summer to your favorite nesting trees.

W. O. Holston

A Royal Address

In a dream at nineteen, my encounter endowed,
Your countenance appeared, a royal sculpture in clouds.

Blue heavens about you, your majesty so pure,
The face of time & authority & of knowledge is yours.

I stood there attentive, and then the silence soon broke,
You addressed the whole world, and commanding you spoke...

"I am Alpha & Omega, the beginning & the end,
Before me was nothing, I created all things.

I am the truth, and the way, and I am the light,
I am love, and I am great, and I am the life.

I send my word and my warning below,
Stop all of you who do break my law!

For the time is short, with heaven at hand,
Do right, be ready, I say to all man.

All things that are done, I'll account to light,
Do right, be ready, for Eternal Life!"

In tear & still gazing, silence came back in turn,
God's fair and is serious, I will wait his return.

Cause I know that for sure, he'll be back you see,
To restore all things beautiful, he's important to me!

Pedro J. Santana

Untitled

I see your dreams, your passions, quiet fantasies, stormy desires
Your feelings and emotions made of ice and fire...

Your powerful magnetic glance
Your eyes enslave, enrapture and enthrall
They cast a spell, they hold me in a trance,
They permeate into the depth of my entire soul...

My restless soul is searching for this force
One look from you has me entrapped in ecstasy
We lock our eyes, the power is beyond me
I'm helpless, frantic, the intensity is like the night-
With darkness it becomes me, consuming my entire self...

I turn away - I can't withstand the strength
My thoughts astray - I'm still possessed by this fanatic trance,
But in insatiable desire, I crave for more and more
Your glance sets me on fire, nowhere to run
I'm drawn to this magnet, I am petrified...

As I wake up from labyrinth of power,
Still wallowing in my perpetual sorrow,
And still so painfully drawn to your stare:
That awful dream - I thought I won't escape to see the end...

Yana Brayman

I Wish I Could Tell You

I wish you and I had been closer
Your laughter fills the air,
Today I long to know the
Kind of man you were

I wish I could tell you how I feel,
Now I realize your love for me wasn't real

In my eyes you were the reason for
living the promise of a better life to come

When God blessed me with you, you were
The most precious gift, I could ever receive
And no matter what else happens to me,
As long as you are here
I know life is worth living

You don't know how much I wanted you or missed you
I'm sure you knew or now know
I loved you but I never did say

Maybe I was to shy or just too scared but you never realized it
Now I can't tell you what's in my heart
it seems it's just too late to start they say all good things must
end someday if only I'd known it was going to be this way

Yvonne K. Kelley

Love's Light

My life is like a sailboat, at the mercy of the sea
Your love has been a beacon, shining out at me
you've filled my sails with winds of passion,
keeping me on course
Not even the mighty ocean can withstand
your compelling force

So, never let your light go out,
Or let my sails go slack
For without your love and passion
The ocean will drive me back

And if this should ever happen
Some fisherman may find my boat
But I will not be in it.
Instead this simple note.

"Never let your loves light
Get to far from thee
For if you do you'll be as I
Who's heart was lost at sea"

Leonidas G. Valsamis

A Poem Of Love To The Lord

Oh, Magnificent ONE who shows us
Your love in the flowers
And the trees
In the mountains and seas
In the birds and the honeybees;

You are ever singing out in colors too
Beautiful for words.
The winds blow strongly in praise of you
The sea breaks with your power.
Your love fills me every minute of every hour.

The babes smile with your smile to
This world full of worry;
A smile of LOVE and PEACE.
They laugh with your JOY also
Evident in nature everywhere
With your message for us not to despair;
Reminding us YOU WILL ALWAYS BE THERE.

Mere words could never thank you enough
For ALL YOUR BLESSINGS and ALL YOUR LOVE.

Laura Hunter

"An Ode To Beatrice"

To young ones in love:
Your minds turn to mush and your words to nonsense.
You giggle, you laugh and you play.
You act like the fools at whom you once rolled eyes.
You have lost all sense of objectivity, all dignity.
And before you get a chance to live your life,
you share it with some fool husband or wife.
You become poetry-writing sap-meisters
and you often take pity on the wiser.
You can't think straight and your thoughts are consumed with
matters of love, subjecting the mind to silliness.
But go to, fools! I'll no more want.
Some of us know the better.

'Tis not bitterness nor foolishness I utter.
'Tis one who still has her wits about her.
One who is free and spirited and can enjoy every stage of her life.

For men disrupt such lives.
They stomp on a broken heart and enslave a free spirit.
'Twas always thus.
'Twill never change.

Lori Jones

Happy Birthday Grandpa

We love you very much
You're not as young as you use to be
But you still have that loving touch
You work each day from 6 til 4
But Grandma is always there to greet you at the door
You know Grandpa we love you so
And I know you love us too
The smile when you're with us and all the things you do
I think the Lord must have sent us
To fill some happy dreams
For you and Grandma look so happy.
When you are watching our little teams
You take the patience with us to fix our bike and gun
With Indians wild and cowboys on the run
Just think as we grow older better pals we will be
We'll hunt the wild and fish the deep blue sea
Grandpa don't think of growing older
For that's not to be Ashamed
For young or old spring or summer
We'll love you just the same.

Thelma C. McMillan

Untitled

To look at you brings amazement to my eyes. The innocence of your youth shines from your face. You are a sweet creation of God. He has given you the most gentle smile, the softest lips and skin. The hair for some reason attracts my attention. It seems to radiate beauty. Nothing fancy, nothing special, just beautiful. But it's those eyes that are by far the most outstanding. They are so delicate, so optimistic, so young. Dear friend, let me warn you. Those eyes will see more than their share. Tears shall flow from them like water over some secluded falls. You are now filled with love, energy, and life. However, these treasures will soon be lost. It will not be a quick and simple parting. But rather a slow, grinding death. You see, event though you are now a beautiful creature, you will not always believe that. The love and pride that you have for yourself will perish. You will hate anything there might be about yourself. Your very being will be sold to false ideas. Slavery will take on a whole new meaning. The chains of self-disgust will bind you to your master. But take heart, you have the key to release the chains. How do I know this? Because you are me, and I am you. You'll make it, just hold tight and weather the storm. You can grow into a wonderful person. Just remember and repeat constantly, always be true to yourself.

Kevin Lyle Killingsworth

Lies And Betrayal

How could you have done that to your Mother, that which you did...
You've lied, betrayed her and isn't even keeping it hid.
You've hurt her so, also torn up her heart...
What terrible thing has she done to you, for you to have this start.
You don't see nor feel the pain that your lies have caused her
to have to cry...It hurt me so bad today, for she told me she
wanted to die. I can't even confront you, for she doesn't want
you to know...Yet she's suffering so much misery and pain,
protecting your feelings so that you want have to go. She's
Your mother, has always loved you with unconditional love....
Thanks to God our father which created her from up above.
Your betrayal and your lies that you are spreading is unfounded
also untrue...Your lack of knowledge from not knowing, you can't
even imagine what she's going through. I know what she's going
through, it hurts me so bad...Your lies, and betrayal, have
left her so very sad, have left me your-Aunt so very damn mad.

Wygenia Thompson

Second Coming

He has come to stay in our village for two farming seasons, amazing, he is tagged peace! His reason's to hunt for "Kurkunu" and roll them round match sticks, with this skills he eases the pain of the farmer from the scourge of this terrible kind of worm "the guinea worm".

For the cultural and traditional difference between us This U.S. peace boy didn't care. He sits on our own kind of chairs, our kind of wears he puts on look! he even eats our own kind of food and says "it is good". With such reasons, his teachings, searches and researches - effective.

Some railed, "he is a spy," he stayed calm, yet many would say we love and like him for his manners. "He is one among the many white men on a second coming to our land" my friend said. To me he has come to quest for and share knowledge among each other, black or white.

Ibrahim Kevin

A World At Dawn

I am a trailing web of interweaving mysteries,
of velvet moonlight across a path of silver
shadows, of skies the colour of rubies,
of a veil of lace removed of winter gloom,
where scented blooms send out sweet perfume,
such crimson among each grassy bed,
rainbow of colour in all their glory,
I am a meadow enriched with golden glow,
as sunlight plays a game of shadows,
I am a cloak of dark light that brings morn light,
I am a sky that lifts from grey to a day,
in a cluster of trees I am a confetti of leaves,
I am a blanket of mist sweeping over the sea,
I am a calm in the ocean a stir in the breeze,
I am a rock that wraps around a mountain,
in a future of beauty, Mother Nature,
preserve me..........

Paula E. O'Connor

You Too, My Mother Read My Rhymes

"You too, my mother
read my rhymes
for the love of fun,
forgotten times, and
you may chance to
hear once more,
the little feet,
along the floor."

Cassandra Roberts

Vampire's Night

From velvet night came forth black angels watching in eternal,
for time is only a dream and our mischief be infernal.
As the black angels watch ever neglecting
the living but not the undead.
Blessed are the hallowed and gracious.
For their blood shall keep us fed.
Head the electric thunder drawn like moths to a flame,
to a place of wicked wonder ... L.A. be thy name,
there in the night seven candles burn bright,
in the dead of night.
The full moon behind a veil.
The ocean crashing in my head.
My lips are red, my skin snow white, my eyes like fiery thunder,
turquoise dragons slip and slide into the night
in fright of the undead tonight.

Melanie Price

Untitled

Why do I feel so much pain
The pain I feel is real
Why must I endure this pain
Why must I endure it alone
When I feel this pain I know
I'm alive
But why must I endure this pain alone
I feel no one can hear my pain
So I continue to endure this pain alone
Cry out and cry out but no one
Still cannot hear my pain
So I endure this pain alone
Why must I endure this pain alone
I am alive still and will go
on still to endure my pain alone.

Alice Banks-Love

Evening

The evening entered
Soft and slow
As fragrance from
Flowers sweetly blowed
The heaven's were painted
Pale blue, with shadows
Of radiance, blended with
Hue, a bird on wing
Began to sing, so clear
An enchanting song I loved
To hear, the evening sun
Bowed real low, as gently
The clouds began to flow
Evening has such marvelous
Scenes as I wonder
And dream dreams.

Janice Murrell

'Teddy'

My teddy sits upon the shelf
and waits for tiny hands
to reach up high and pull him down
and tell him where he stands.

He does not understand this pause
in fun, and games and play.
He cannot see that I have grown
and changed from day to day.

Someday I'll take him down once more
to think of days gone by
Remembering the times we had
and how those years did fly.

Dara Tomlins

Promised And Signed

You said you were leaving
had to catch your dreams...
I knew this had to happen,
but I was still caught in love and pain.
Yet I feel we belong together and
that your heart will always be
mine, that our destiny was one
for each other, you and I.
So I promised and signed
as long as I live I will build
my life for you, so tell me
when you need me and I will
be right there.
This I promise and sign
I will wait for you no matter
how many years it takes or
how many dreams you catch, my
love for you will always be
here waiting.
This I promised and signed.

Carolina Limas

Love

Love is a bird
flying high in the sky,
Love is a chance
to get up and go, passing
you by
Love is my heart
pounding in my chest,
Love is the very,
very best.

Melissa Bennett

When You Look At Me

What do you see when you look at me?
Do you see only the things that others can see?
Or, when you look into my eyes can you see inside?
Do you see the things that I tend to hide?

Despite the obvious, what do you see,
As you are making passionate love to me?
Do you see the happiness that glows within?
Or, are you looking from the outside...afraid of looking in?

When you look at me, what do you see?
Do you see me as I am... or as someone you want me to be?
Do you see my sorrows? Can you feel my thoughts?
Do you see the good in me, or do you see only my faults?

What do you see when you look at me?
Are your visions through which only the eyes can see?
Or, can you see with your heart these things that I feel?
If you see me for what I am...you know my love for you is real.

Vickie Forrest Wiggs

Teacher

I was blind to the world of knowledge.
For stupidity is bound in the mind of a child,
So who am I to change history.
I wonder who would it be to help me through the years.
It was then you came along to show me the way.
You taught me how to read, write and spell,
How to multiply, divide, subtract and add.
You taught me something I never had.
If there is one thing that was meant to be,
It's you teacher, you were the one to help me.

As time went by I began to grow.
I knew that in the future you'll have to go.
You show me how to make it in this unjust world.
If there is one person who is special to me,
It's you teacher, you were the one that set me free.
You were helpful, thoughtful and understanding in many ways.
There will never be enough words to speak for you.
Don't ever change, or stop what you do.
You have inspiration and that's the truth.
This is my love and gratitude, I give to you.

John K. Boyce

I Know This Much Is True

A stroll through a park,
to hold you after dark.
A kiss of your lips,
as a tear from a rose pedal drips.
I'm lost in your eyes, how soft and blue,
I know this much is true!

A thought in my mind,
a picture of you is what I find.
A river of tears,
A box full of fears.
A soft whisper of "I Love You,"
I know this much is true.

A ton of years on my shoulders,
although I can't help but to grow older and older,
A lot of wasted years,
but when I have a problem who will be all ears?
Since early age my love for you just grew and grew,
I know this much is true!

Joaquin D. Lopez

Michael And Me

My son Michael is six years old.
He's very precious to me and usually does as he is told.
I never knew until I gave birth,
That having a child is one of the greatest joys on earth.

I've taken him to the Grand Canyon, to Disneyland, and to many
 other places.
He loves to laugh, to draw, and paint funny faces.
When Michael was two he asked, "Mommy, does Peter Pan have
 strings?"
I knew then that he would figure out a lot of things.

Michael loves to bicycle, to roller blade and to sing.
He has brought me the special happiness that only a child can bring.
Michael takes karate, he even practiced on me. Now he says he
 wants to take ice hockey.
I say, "Michael, we'll have to wait and see."

I'm teaching him to be a good citizen, to be resourceful,
 and to recycle.
I tell him he can do anything he wants except ride a motorcycle.
Michael, "It's you and me against the world," I say to him at times.
"Mommy, I love you and you're beautiful," is the sweetest things
 he's ever said.

I've had a lot of fun writing this poem that rhymes.
Though our poem has ended our adventures go on and on
Everyday until our prayers are said
And then Michael goes to bed.

Diane L. Onak

A Tribute To My Parents

Fifty years is golden
That's what we've all been told,
To share a life together
Is a treasure to behold.
I've been a part of most of those years
And am very happy to say,
I'm glad we have the opportunity
To honor you both today.
It's not always easy, as many couples know,
To look through the rain and see the flowers grow.
And when life threw the curves,
That we all must endure,
You summoned the strength to find the cure.
And so, Mom and Dad, thanks for giving to us
The chance of your lifetime to share,
May God bless you, love you and keep you
Forever in his care.

Kathy Traficante

My Kitty

My kitty sits
 on top of the fridge
Head tilted slightly
 watching my every move
Bright green eyes
 staring intensely, screaming out
"Feed me now
 or I'll rip your goddamned head off"

James A. Malumphy

"Impostor"

The warm, delicate breezes will never be the same.
Instead, the sky remains a toxic dusty-rose forever.
To be without the nourishing air that gives us fame
Is like a sin without a simple endeavor.
The Cheery Sun that gives us warmth, deserted us.
An impostor takes his place, "The Dictator has come," hear things say.
Yet, they are careless of the consequences, like dust.
Even though the innocent haven't seen they must pay
A trifle price for foolish consequences of stupidity.
A tainted life they live, their lives almost over.
Filled with grief and sorrow, until the mighty sun;
A hero, comes back triumphantly to regain his power.
With the champion in his place, the impostor tarnishes.
The warmth and happiness returns; the world flourishes.

Michelle Davis

"You Shake Me"

I feel my body begin to shake;
How much more of this can I take?
Baby; you know I can't pretend, that
I don't need you back again.
I hold your picture close to my heart,
And can feel my chest being torn apart.
You were my whisper in the night,
You were the love that felt so right.
Did you know, I hurt this bad?
Or were you just a dream I had?
I see your face in everything I do;
Sleepless nights, I think of you.
You said we'd always be together;
I should have known...
Love's not forever.

Thaedra T. Schneider

But!

But to believe in love where there is no love
But to show courage in the midst of defeat
But to bear fruit where there is no seed
But to have no fear when all seems lost
But to be anxious when all seems so slow
But to have no doubt in the midst of insecurity
But to be secure when all seems so fragile
But to have desire where there is none
But to make a lasting impression where there is no mark
But to succeed in the midst of failure
But to show mercy in the midst of torture
But to show signs of encouragement where there is absolute despair
But to read the unreadable
But to put effort where there is no strength
But to show compassion where there is no pity
But to have faith where is no hope
But to continue when everything stops.

Patrick Forte

Nightmares

Darkness, hovering,
Covering over me
Trying, can't get out
Can't even see

Scared, crying.
Shivering with fear
Visions of horror
With every tear

Hugging my pillow squeezing it,
holding on for dear life
With a pain in my chest
Being pierced by a knife

And even though my
body doesn't care
My mind wakes up screaming
From that horrible nightmare

Kristy Potter

Man Against Nature

A black bird, flying against a dark sky.
Soaring over the shadowed trees
Flying free. Into the whistling wind.
Not a care in the world. Free.

The man on the ground aims his gun,
at the black bird's head.
BANG.

He fires. He fires another
Then, still another

The once free bird falls to the cold
winter ground bleeding. His small
fragile heart slowly beating slower.
Until it beats no more.

The cruel man laughs and walks
away not realizing the giant
gun of God is pointed at his head.

Erin Lindenberg

Love

Love is like a shining star
That glows so bright inside,
Love is such an amazing thing
That many try to hide.

Love is meant for sharing
And you'll find that when you do,
When you share your love
It comes right back to you.

Love, a tender, special kind
The love that's meant to show,
A gentle, warm, spiritual love
That starts deep within your soul.

My love, I know, you are the one
That God did send to me,
I love you with all my heart and soul
A love that will always be.

The love I've found that's in my heart
Is as pure as the morning dew,
And now I know, that in my heart
My darling, I love you.

Brad Perry

Biographies of Poets

AARON, DE JOIE
[pen.] Joy, Dee-Dee or Dee.; [b.] August 22, 1980, Beaumont, TX; [p.] Mr. and Mrs. Leon and Shirley Aaron; [ed.] 9th Grade student at Central High School in Beaumont, Tx.; [memb.] Member of a Drama Club in my 8th Grade year. Member of the Greater Little Lion Baptist Church, and also a member of the usher board.; [hon.] I was an honor from the 3-9 grades in Reading, Math and History. Awards in acting, drawing, spelling and participating in other things such as swimming.; [oth. writ.] Reaching your Apex, My Two Valentines, This Black Man, A Beautiful Day, God's Children and Their Blessings.; [a.] Beaumont, TX

ABBOTT, CHRISTINA L.
[pen.] Christy Abbott; [b.] April 8, 1978, Kansas City, MO; [p.] Richard and Emilie Abbott; [occ.] Full time student; [hon.] National Honor Society, Who's Who Among American High School Students, An Honor Roll; [oth. writ.] Several poems yet to be published.; [pers.] I write about personal experiences and feelings. My influences have been family, friends, and one very special English teacher, Eva York.; [a.] Kansas City, MO

ABBOTT, CHRISTINA
[b.] November 2, 1978, Nepean; [p.] Kathleen and Stephen Abbott; [ed.] Grade 11, and currently attending North Grenville District High School; [occ.] Student at North Grenville District High; [memb.] Video Yearbook, Yearbook, Students Council, Music Club; [hon.] Awards in drafting, usual arts and mathematics. Honour roll for academic marks; [a.] Oxford Mills Ontario, Canada

ABIJAN, REMEDIOS NALUNDASAN
[pen.] Reecana; [b.] February 20, 1947, Philippines; [p.] Marciano and Zoila Nalundasan; [ch.] Sharon-sydney, Karl, Ma. Goretti; [ed.] 1. Bachelor of Science in Elem. Edu., 2. Master of Arts in College Teaching, 3. Doctoral Programme in Cultural Anthropology,; [occ.] Prof. of Humanities and Social Sciences, proprietor-private school; [memb.] 1. International Society of Poets (lifetime member), 2. Founder-Press Nature and Environment Study Club, 3. Chairman-Founder: Petals and Leaves Society of Poets, Mapua Institute of Technology, Manila, 4. Station Ideas for Writers, Founder; [hon.] 1. Graduated "cum laude" from college, 2. International Poet of Merit Awardee, ISP 1994, 3. Two times Editors Choice Awardee in Poetry, National Library of Poetry, MD USA, 4. Recipient of scholarship - University of the Philippines and Philippine Normal University; [oth. writ.] 1. "What is Peace" "Hope" "A Compact with the Wind" poems published by the NLP, US, 2. "A Process of Birth" Best Poems of 1995, NLP., 3. "In the Crimson Veld" read at the 1994 Intern'l Convention, WA, D.C., textbook writer for graders/hi-sch; [pers.] "I am so much awed by adventure in the inner space of man, I believe in making rainbows, and I admire the wind that carries its home and turns the world up or upside down. . ." "I abhor the ugliness of life painted by unknown schemes and the artless, I dwell my thoughts in the beauty of life.; [a.] Manila, Philippines

ABNER, AMELIA KATHERINE MAINES
[pen.] Kat Abner; [b.] March 3, 1931, Clark Co, KY; [p.] Ike and Belle Davis Maines; [m.] Lewis Abner (47 yrs.), April 19, 1947; [ch.] Brenda, Wanda, Linda, John, Randy; [ed.] Winchester Schools, various college classes—perpetual student Diploma from Children's Institute of Literature, attended Clear Creek Bible School/pastoral ministries; [occ.] Writer; [memb.] SS teacher New Hope Baptist, Associational clerk-Boones Creek Asso. VP programs-Winchester Writers; [hon.] Invited to New York, in 91 by World of Poetry, due to awards for poem Laughter; [oth. writ.] Rise Up and Weep, religious novel, Princess of the Springs, a legend both ready to publish - 8 published poems 1 short story/ 3 articles Winchester Sun. 5 church plays, 3 plays in progress for local theater, poetry published Sparrowgrass; [pers.] Each person I meet is a story. I love people. I read Ruskin and Merton, write as a victorian, blend the sacred and the profane, as does life. [a.] Winchester, KY

ACHOUKIAN, JOHN VASKEN
[b.] October 13, 1967, Detroit, MI; [p.] Setrag Achoukian, Eliza Bouladian Achoukian; [ed.] B.A. Political Science, Wayne State University.; [occ.] Graduate student; [memb.] St. John's Armenian Apostolic Church, Center for Peace and Conflict Study; [oth. writ.] For A Balkan Ghost, The Dream Comes To Life published in The Sun Diego Union Tribune; [pers.] Love more, hate less; [a.] Orchard Lake Village, MI

ACQUARO, PETER F.
[b.] February 28, 1948, Brooklyn, NY; [p.] Dominic P. and Lorraine V. Acquaro; [m.] Kathleen M. Acquaro, June 28, 1969; [ch.] Peter Jr., Philip, Paul, Kerrin; [ed.] A.A.S. - State Univ. of N.Y. and Farmingdale: - Aerospace Technology- B.S. - N.Y. Inst. of Tech. Old Westbury, Behavioral Science (Criminology) M.S. - L.I. Univ. C.W. Post Campus Greenville NY Education and counselling; [occ.] Airline Pilot for US Air, Inc.; [memb.] Airline Pilot Assoc. Air Force Association Lt. Col. in the U.S.A.F. Reserves.; [hon.] USAF - Vietnam Gallantry Cross Meritorious Service, N.Y.S. - Nassau Co. Police Dept.: - Meritorious Service Medal of Commendation; [pers.] It is very disturbing to hear and see the so called intellectually advanced individuals of our society perpetuating and fostering animosity among the masses; [a.] Selden, NY

ADAIR, MARY LEVONA
[pen.] Mary Levona Adair; [b.] November 26, 1916, Okleunion, TX; [p.] Richard and Lenora Armstrong; [m.] Francis Marion Adair, March 3, 1938; [ch.] Mary Frances, Jerry and Sandra; [ed.] Ninth Grade; [occ.] Retired; [memb.] A.A.R.P. and Senior Share and Care Club; [hon.] I have received silver and gold poet awards from world of poetry.; [oth. writ.] I have written many poems and songs, most are too long for publication; [pers.] I do not think of this as a talent it is natural in my family. I write by inspiration. I'm sure you don't hear from non college writers.; [a.] Duncanville, TX

ADAMS, APRIL NICOLE
[pen.] Tweetie; [b.] April 10, 1978, Newark; [p.] Norman and Trina Boone, Randall Hogan; [ed.] Jonathan Dayton High School 1996 Springfield N.J.; [memb.] NAACP Tri City Youth Council, Vice President Afro American Club - Jonathan Dayton, Antioch Baptist Church - Treasurer of the Junior Usher Board.; [hon.] National Sorority of Delta Pi Chapter Inc. Xinos Club, Delta Pi Chapter, Miss Debutante Ball 1994; [pers.] I write to lift up people's self-esteem body and soul to make them feel special.

ADAMS, DEBORAH KAY
[b.] March 12, 1957, Dallas, TX; [p.] O. T. and Nina Green; [m.] Fred William Adams, July 21, 1973; [ch.] Angela and Amanda; [ed.] Stonewall Jackson Elem. J. L. Long Jr. High, W. W. Wilson High School, Texas, College of Medical and Dental careers.; [occ.] Nurse Baylor Hosp.; [memb.] American Heart Association American Red Cross; [hon.] Most Congenial in Mrs. Texas International Pageant in 1990.; [oth. writ.] Poems published school newspaper.

ADAMS, RAMONA R.
[pen.] Mona Adams; [b.] September 24, 1952, Hinton, VA; [p.] James Barker, Margaret Barker; [m.] Garnett Adams, July 8, 1973; [ch.] James, Melenna, Kimberly, Karri, Bryan; [ed.] James Wood High, James Rumsey Tech. Institute, Sheppard College B.S.; [occ.] Mother, part-time operation manager at Summit Point Raceway a BSR Training School; [memb.] Ladies Auyli, V.F.W. PTA Townhawk Elem, Living Waters Ministries, past president local #425 ILWGU, AFLCIO 1970 - 1985; [hon.] Scholastic Achievement Award JRTI, Humanitarian Award LWM West VA. Workers Compensation Award; [oth. writ.] Labor studies, journals short stories, articles for the Martinsburg, the journal, newspaper, unpublished poems; [pers.] I wish to become a role model to others around me, to my children, to my friends, to have a dream come true - my writing in print to leave my children's children.; [a.] Hedgesville, WV

ADAMSON, RONDI
[ed.] I have a B.A. in Fine Arts.; [occ.] I have worked as an E.S.L. teacher in France, Turkey and Japan; [oth. writ.] I write in all genres and have had several nonfiction articles published but am currently focusing on poetry and short stories. I am the proud owner of two cats.; [a.] Ottawa, Canada

ADDIMANDO, LOU
[b.] May 27, 1943, New York City; [p.] Louis Sr. and Lillian Ross; [m.] Divorced; [ch.] Lou III and Michael; [ed.] Lincoln H.S. Yonkers, Swedish Institute for Massage, Real Estate School of N.Y., Creative Writing Westchester Community College; [occ.] Entrepreneur - Health Club Operator - Physical Trainer; [memb.] Lifetime Member "American Association for the Improvement of Boxing"; [oth. writ.] Many poems and short stories about real people's ups and downs in life; [pers.] "The poetry of life is written with the rough edges of rocks and stones picked up living life, smoothed and rounded by their bare knuckled application to survival: - Success is optional." "Lou Addimando"; [a.] Scarsdale, NY

ADELEYE, ERIC H.
[pen.] South Philly; [b.] May 7, 1972, Philadelphia, PA; [p.] Patrice Adeleye; [m.] Tawanda Adeleye, December 23, 1993; [ch.] Erica Holly Adeleye; [ed.] Community College of Philadelphia, United States Army Signal School, University of Maryland; [occ.] Satellite Communications Technician in the United States Army; [memb.] Christ Mission Church of the Apostolic Faith, Inc.; [hon.] Men with Hill SATCOM Soldier of the Month, 39th Signal Battalion Soldier of the Month.; [pers.] My poems are a direct reflection of the people, places, and experiences that have transpired in my life.; [a.] Philadelphia, PA

ADKINS, NATASHA RO'MELL
[pen.] Natasha Ro'Mell Adkins; [b.] September 26, 1977, Tyler, TX; [p.] Leon Adkins and Trenda Adkins; [ed.] A present student of the 11th grade at Plano East Senior High School; [occ.] Student; [memb.] Representative of the Student Council at Plano East Senior High, Member of Plano East Orchestra (violin); [hon.] Recognition of musical participation in solo/ensemble contest (93-94), achievement award received in Biology (94), recognition of Student representative in Junior High

School, Plano East Orchestra that I am a member of has been invited to perform at the Kennedy Center in Washington, D.C. in May, 1995.; [oth. writ.] Other writings are poems and short stories written in school and/or at home.; [pers.] Within the center of each poem comes a sense of everyday life I experience as well as others. Matters of the heart reflect throughout all my poems.; [a.] Plano, TX

ADKINS, STACY
[b.] August 9, 1972, Lexington, KY; [p.] Sue Burge and Johnny Burge; [m.] Kent Adkins, August 20, 1994; [occ.] Blue Grass Rural Electric Cooperation

AGBENYEGA, CHARLES AKWAFO
[b.] October 21, 1945, Acra Ghana, West Africa; [p.] Esther Adi and Solomon Agbenyega; [m.] 1976 (Divorced); [ch.] Charles Agbenyega Jr. and Charity Agbenyega; [ed.] Entered Aba Training College from 1965-1969 where I came out with Honors. I was an Administrator of a High School; [occ.] Housekeeper in one of the salons in New York; [hon.] I was honored to open primary and middle schools in one of the villages in Ghana, which became full grown schools; [oth. writ.] Wrote a lot of African stories which I have not published yet I also wrote few poems which I have not published yet.; [a.] Bronx, NY

AGOUDA, TAMIMOU OURO
[b.] January 1, 1964, Sotouboua, Togo; [p.] Bouraima Ouro-A, Alimatou Zakari; [ed.] Universite Du Benin (Lome - Togo), Institut National Des Sciences De L'Education (Lome - Togo), State University of New York at Purchase; [occ.] Postal clerk (casual), Yonkers General Post Office.; [oth. writ.] The Immortal (unpublished), No Need Worry (unpublished).; [a.] Yonkers, NY

AGUILAR, VALERIE
[b.] May 21, 1962, San Bernardino; [p.] Leonard Strong, Laura Strong; [m.] Pete Alaniz Sr., July 16, 1989; [ch.] Anthony Gomez, Richard Alaniz; [ed.] Montclair High School; [occ.] Housewife and Mother of two. I was a Nurse Aid.; [oth. writ.] Several poems, but not yet published. All good, but within with different kinds of feelings ranging from good, bad, happy or sad or just a poem to Jesus; [pers.] Jesus is love and when you have Jesus you are a never left alone. He will always be there and he has the power to change things. His love is real and we can trust him. He changed me.; [a.] Pomona, CA

AGUIRRE, MARIA DOLORES T.
[pen.] Mary Diane Austria; [b.] March 27, 1977, Manila, Philippines; [p.] Jesus Aguirre, Zenaida Aguirre; [ed.] Perpetual Help College of Rizal, Elizabeth Seton School, University of Santo Tomas; [occ.] Student (B. S. Pharmacy); [memb.] Junior Pharmaceutical Association (Gamma Chapter), Scholia Tutorial Club; [hon.] 7th Honorable Mention, 1st Place Poetry Writing Contest, 1st Place English Essay Writing Contest, 1st Place Religion Essay Writing Contest; [oth. writ.] Poems and articles published in the school paper and in the yearbook.; [pers.] I try to always include the existence of the Lord God in all my written works to send a message to those who will read them that without Him, we are nothing. I have been greatly influenced by my Catholic Faith.; [a.] Manila, Philippines

AKLE, BERNARD DIDIER
[b.] July 6, 1958, Los Angeles, CA; [p.] Wade Akle and Paulette Gibour; [ch.] Brandon and Dolores; [ed.] College of Redwoods, Travel and Trade Institute, "Leysin" American School of Switzerland; [occ.] Manager, International Airline Marketing, President, China Trade Americas; [memb.] Smithsonian Institute, National Amateur Astronomers, Int'l Air Transport Association; [hon.] Employee of the Year "1990", Korean Air Lines, Junior California Chess Championships - 3rd; [oth. writ.] Numerous poems of every subject.; [pers.] "Lost and failed love drives the emotions necessary for creating some of the worlds greatest poems."; [a.] Alhambra, CA

ALBERTS, JOHAN CHRISTIAAN
[b.] February 14, 1956, Dutch; [m.] Mary Jo Reed Alberts, December 25, 1985; [ch.] Christy, Alex, Allen; [ed.] 38 Yrs. of life; [occ.] Psychologically Disabled; [oth. writ.] The Phantom published "Journey of the Mind". As well as a many unpublished an unknown; [pers.] "Homelessness is a drag"; [a.] Cornersville, TN

ALBRIGHT, ANN
[pen.] Ann M. Albright; [b.] May 14, 1941, Mahanoy Plane, PA; [p.] John and Catherine Calpin; [m.] Harry J. Albright, January 20, 1962; [ch.] Ann Marie, Harry and (Jimmy, deceased); [ed.] Graduated from Little Flower Catholic High School for Girls, Philadelphia, PA. Currently enrolled in a writing course at children's Institute of Literature; [occ.] Certified Nursing Assistant; [memb.] Sacred Heart League Juvenile Diabetes Assoc. American Heart Assoc.; [hon.] Writing award presented to me by resident council of Randolph Hills nursing home, for newsletter features and poems, in Wheaton, Maryland.; [oth. writ.] Essays, Articles and poems for newsletters for nursing home! Also adult day care newsletter; [pers.] Having somebody else taking pleasure in reading something I wrote gives me immense pleasures, as any talent I may possess is given to me by my creator. Favorite poem - "Oh Captain, My Captain"; [a.] Silver Spring, MD

ALI, ANGELA SIGNORELLI
[b.] October 3, 1949, Cleveland, OH; [p.] Mario and Ramona Signorelli; [m.] Karim Nizar Ali, June 20, 1985; [ch.] Michael Angelo and Laura Angela; [ed.] Licensed Practical Nurse; [occ.] Owner and Angela Elderly Care.; [oth. writ.] Short stories for children.; [pers.] My thoughts reflect stages and productivity of life. Each life has meaning as it touches others.; [a.] Port Orange, FL

ALLEN, JULIET E.
[b.] February 20, 1966, Jamaica, West Indies; [p.] Patricia Morgan and E. G. Morgan; [ed.] Bell High School, Lasalle College, McGill Univ.; [occ.] Fund/admin. Assistant MD Management Assoc. with Can. Medical Association; [oth. writ.] Several short stories and poetry for school paper and personal diaries.; [pers.] "No one knows how for you will soar. Not even you till you give yourself the chance to spread your wings".; [a.] Carleton Place Ontario, Canada

ALLEN, MARCIA
[pen.] Marcia Allen; [b.] February 8, 1939, Saint John, New Brunswick, Canada; [p.] Clarence and Grace Allen; [m.] Nicholas Mihaluk, November 27, 1965; [ch.] Tara Tina, Joel Nicholas; [ed.] Saint John Vocational School, Graduate - Honor Student; [occ.] Piano Teacher; [hon.] Music Festival Award, May 1950 - Honor Award Certificates Grades 1 through 8, Silver Medal Award 1956 For Highest Grades in Grade 11 Classes.; [pers.] In other poems I have written, I have incorporated humour and a moral to the story of the poem, especially for the learning and entertainment of children.; [a.] Chamby Quebec, Canada

ALLEN, TERI L.
[pen.] Teri L. Allen; [b.] February 22, 1968, Jamestown, NY; [p.] Martin Allen and Linda Wood; [ch.] Zoe Winona Allen - May 20, 1994; [ed.] Hewes VoTech for Cosmetology, attended J.C.C. for Humanities in Jamestown, attended Art Institute of Seattle for Music and Video Business; [occ.] Full-time mother and possible child care for other people; [hon.] I've won spelling bees in middle school and won an award for the best essays and compositions.; [oth. writ.] I wrote two poems for this, Art and Manie Depression. That's as far as I went. I do have short stories. I dedicate my poem to my daughter, Zoe Winona.; [pers.] When I was depressed, I felt better when I had my feelings pored out on a paper instead of doing drugs. I listen to music also. I've written more things when I lived on the streets in Seattle. I learned a lot about life.; [a.] Jamestown, NY

ALLIGOOD, DANA
[pen.] D. Alligood; [b.] May 6, 1958, Houston, TX; [p.] Lester Cox, Caddie Cox; [m.] Rick Alligood, July 30, 1980; [ed.] New Caney High; [occ.] Homemaker; [hon.] Honor Graduate, Top Ten, Who's Who, National Honor Society; [oth. writ.] Poem published in "The Montana Caller"; [pers.] If one receives joy from my writing, it makes my heart sing ... for joy is a gift to bestow on one's heart.; [a.] Huntsville, TX

ALLISON, MICHELLE L.
[pen.] Rose Love; [b.] June 11, 1968, Harrisburg, PA; [p.] Elwood N. Carpenter and Mary V. Carpenter; [m.] Sgt. Dennis D. Allison, March 19, 1990; [ch.] Joseph Brian, Lukas, James Dean, and Jacob Neil; [ed.] Susquehanna Township High School Emergency Medical Training; [occ.] Homemaker; [memb.] American Heart Assoc., Boy Scouts of America, Baughman Memorial United Methodist Church, Wives of the Enlisted Army National Guard Support Group; [hon.] Honor Society, Gold Key Award in Art, Bowling Trophies, Signed certificate from Rep. Piccola (PA) for EMS Services, Mother of the Year Award, Most dedicated volunteer parent award.; [oth. writ.] I have written many poems which I keep in a private port-folio. Only a few have knowledge of them. This poems, (my first to be published) I hope touches everyone.; [pers.] I try to touch the hearts and souls of everyone in my writing. I am a romantic writer and have been greatly inspired by early romantic poets. Love lives in all. Find it.; [a.] New Cumberland, PA

ALSTON, BETTY R. JONES
[pen.] Ruth; [b.] September 14, Philadelphia, PA; [p.] Rev. J. F. Jones Sr., D. D. and Mrs. Maria Jones; [m.] Felton Alston, July 18, 1987; [ch.] Tiffany Nicole, Shanikka Antoinette Maria; [ed.] William Penn High School for Girls, Community College of Phila., and Business School.; [occ.] Disabled retirement; [memb.] Northshore Animal League, Second Pilgrim, Baptist Church Tutorial Program, Jones Gospel Chorus, Scholarship Committee and Youth Supervisor, Adult Choir, and a Volunteer.; [hon.] Service Awards - U.S. Postal Services, Student Government, U.S. Army Reserve Command Awards, Retirement Awards.; [oth. writ.] Heart to Heart, Today, Tomorrow and Always, Don't Worry About Me, Our Joe-Joe, If, Sometimes, Look Up, I forgot, etc. I sometimes write in remembrance of someone special for different families and friends.; [pers.] I write because I have been blessed with a wonderful gift from God. My sharing it is my way of saying, "THANK YOU" to God for my special gift and by helping to make someone smile.; [a.] Philadelphia, PA

ALTAIR, OCTAVIUS K.W.F.R.
[b.] October 30, 1969, Toronto, Ontario, Canada; [p.] Mr. and Mrs. R. Falloona; [ed.] Graduated from Sutton District High School. Then University of York to study briefly Psy/Soc., International Academy of Merchanding and Design - Studied Fashion Design (How to Conture); [occ.] Deal with Corporate Paid Accounts. For a supply company.; [memb.] N.A.M.B.L.A. (North American Man/Boy Love Assoc.), Project Truth; [oth. writ.] Have had other poems published by National Library of Poetry.; [pers.] An open mind is the sword against ignorance! My influences are Abu Nuwas, Allen Ginsberg and Irving Layton; [a.] Toronto Ontario, Canada

ALVAREZ, ALEXIS A.
[b.] September 2, 1972, Caracas, Venezuela; [ed.] Major: Business Administration, Minor: Theology Currently attending Chaffey Community College; [hon.] Spanish Literature Award, Caracas, English Literature Award, Caracas; [oth. writ.] "In my works, I strive to reflect the beauty and wisdom of Socratic logic, the Ten Commandments of Mount Sinai, the Five Pillars of Islam, the Eightfold Path to Buddha Enlightenment, and the Spanish Code of Chivalry."

ALVAREZ, LINDA
[b.] January 17, 1960, Yonkers, NY; [p.] Robert Gralicer and Barbara; [m.] Gilbert Alvarez Jr., August 21, 1988; [ed.] AA/Liberal Arts from Westchester Community College - Vahalla, NY. Minor in Deaf/Special Ed.; [occ.] Volunteering in a Nursing Home in Mamaroneck, NY (Clerical and Beauty Parlor Assistant).; [memb.] DAV/ Disabled American Veterans Commanders Club - Silver Leader); [hon.] 1984 - Honorary Theatre Member for teaching the play "Children of a Lesser God" in American Sign Language, as well as other plays. Dean's List from W.C.C.; [oth. writ.] Poetry, Prose, Created and Word Search Puzzles for the Sterling Reporter Newsletter from the Mental Health Association in White Plains, NY; [pers.] I wish to dedicate my poem of true friendship and love to my husband, Gil.; [a.] Yonkers, NY

ANAMTA, LAURETTA
[b.] November 20, 1956, Karachi, Pakistan; [p.] Christian H. Thompson, Gloria Thompson; [m.] Divorced; [ch.] Juanita, Amar, Sanam, Asad; [ed.] Studying for my B.A.; [occ.] Admin. Asst. BSC (hons) Program Lahore University of Management Sciences-Lhr; [oth. writ.] Poems (Not published)/A Diary showing my return from almost insanity caused by a dreadful marriage, and the strength it took to be whole again. Diaries for each of my kids (begun a few hours before they were born): amusing incidents, poems to them, and their touching thoughts.; [pers.] I believe that everyone can improve if they but focus on "One Step at a Time" - and never forgetting to give themselves a "Tap on the Back" instead of waiting for others to do it for them. There is goodness in each of us, though sometimes we have to strive a little bit harder to learn to trust ourselves.; [a.] Lahore, Pakistan

ANDERSON, CARRIE LYNN
[b.] May 18, 1982, McKeesport, PA; [p.] Kevin and Vicki Anderson; [ed.] Graduated sixth grade - 1994 South Allegheny High School starting September 1994 to the present; [hon.] High honors for grades in grade school; [a.] Port Vue, PA

ANDERSON, CHRISTINE LEE
[b.] June 22, 1978; [p.] Leroy and Rita Anderson; [ed.] Romeoville High School (Grade II).; [memb.] I don't have any memberships but, I play indoor soccer at a sports club.; [hon.] Second honor on the honor roll at my school

ANDERSON, ELLA
[b.] April 26, 1907, Dalton, NE; [p.] John and Pada Siefer; [m.] Elmer Westerhoff died 1963 - December 14, 1925, George Anderson, died 1986 - August 4, 1968.; [ch.] Karen Hippensteel, Roland Westerhoff; [ed.] Country School, Dalton High, Kearney and Chadron Teacher College. Taught all grades Country School 1924-25 Dist 19. Taught Lower grades consolidated 1966-1968.; [occ.] Home Caring; [memb.] Presby Church, SS teacher, Stephen Ministry, Extension Clubs. Writing Course years ago. Have worked in Lutheran Methodist as Volunteers at Hospitals Choirs.; [hon.] Pins for Volunteer Work where ever located; [oth. writ.] Just for programs family occasions. Never tried publishing before.; [pers.] Survived dirty thirties. Bank closings liked gardening and being a farm wife and mother. I try to bring a bit of sunshine to who ever and where ever. Moved near daughter, May 1994.; [a.] Laguna Hills, CA

ANDERSON, ERVA L.
[pen.] Erva Ande Anderson/Ande Anderson; [b.] June 5, 1912, Ephraim, UT; [p.] Roys/Ruth M. Anderson; [m.] J. Dwain Anderson (Deceased), August 4, 1930; [ch.] Connie, Carol, Fred; [ed.] High School Graduate with Honors; [occ.] Retired; [memb.] Honorary Charter for Outstanding Achievement (Int. Soc. of Poets); [hon.] Golden Poet Award Award of merit certificate for "Alas What To Do?" Award of Merit Certificate for "A True Story" Editors Choice Award by The National Library of Poetry; [oth. writ.] Stuck on The Desert Life's Ups and Downs Love is Fat-Free You Live and Learn Papa Taon Baja on The Rocks; [pers.] I cannot just sit down and write a poem, I have to be inspired. I got a late start, but am glad I got started.; [a.] Newport Beach, CA

ANDERSON, JANETTE
[b.] September 24, 1949, Savanah, GA; [p.] Leola Jackson; [m.] Lawrence Anderson, August 30, 1969; [ch.] Darren and Kevin Anderson; [ed.] Mercy College, B.A., Seminars - Elizabeth Seton College; [occ.] Principal Secretary to a Supreme Court Justice.; [memb.] Mt. Calvary Baptist Church Member of Adoption/Foster Care. Program of Westchester County. Member of the National Notary Association. Also member of National Authors Legistry.; [hon.] Editor's Choice Award for a poem. An Honorable Mention for a poem.; [oth. writ.] A novel, "Once Upon an Angry Girl." Several poems in Anthologies. Several poems being set to music.; [pers.] The things children say.; [a.] White Plains, NY

ANDERSON, MICHAEL J.
[b.] July 11, 1971, Long Beach, CA; [p.] Roland O. Anderson, Christina H. Anderson; [ed.] Central Kitsap High; [occ.] Dental Tech (USAF); [oth. writ.] A poem for you my love, jumping jellyfish, and many other unpublished works; [pers.] Life is but a dream, so you can always change it to make it better.; [a.] Silverdale, WA

ANDERSON, TRACY
[b.] January 8, 1980, Edmonton, Alberta, Canada; [p.] Allan and Janice Anderson; [ed.] Happy thought school (kindergarten to grade nine); [occ.] Student; [memb.] Sea cadets (RCSCC Daerwood) Red Cross (thru sea cadets); [oth. writ.] Poems for school, marriages and funeral (family); [pers.] I write poems to express my true inner feelings that I can't say in any other way. I just let my feelings pour out like ink in a pen. My main inspiration is my boyfriend Shaun De Boer.; [a.] East Selkirk Manitoba, Canada

ANDERSON, WILLIAM
[pen.] Bill; [b.] June 10, 1917, Chicago, IL; [p.] Norman and Gertrude Anderson; [m.] Margaret (Deceased), July 22, 1939; [ed.] 1 1/2 years High School and 2 years Trade School; [occ.] Retired; [memb.] Loyal or of moose U.P.W. Irving Park Lutheran Church; [oth. writ.] True Love, So Long For A While, A Tribute To A Loved One. I have many more; [pers.] People come to me for poems for all occasion. But they have to give me time. I only write then when they come to me. When I'm in bed or any time when they hit me.; [a.] Chicago, IL

ANDRADE, ALLISON
[b.] November 12, 1983, Berkeley, CA; [p.] Rod and Sue Andrade; [ed.] Lafayette Elementary School, Lafayette, CA; [occ.] Student; [memb.] Interests: Jazz dance, bike riding, roller blading, swimming and drama.; [oth. writ.] Poetry and short stories; [pers.] I like writing poetry because it expresses my feelings and thoughts; [a.] Lafayette, CA

ANDREW, ELLEN C.
[pen.] Ellen Gilfoyle Andrew; [b.] June 30, 1916, Ulster, PA; [p.] Timothy Gilfoyle, Catherine Gilfoyle; [m.] Robert L. Andrew, February 20, 1942; [ch.] Ellen McCloskey, Mary Evans, Robert Andrew Jr., Margaret Giragosian; [ed.] Mansfield High School, Pa, Mansfield State Teachers College BS degree, Duke University six summers, Peabody College one semester; [occ.] Housewife before retirement was Math and English teacher substitute many years; [memb.] Western Square Dance, Western Round Dance; [hon.] Fellowship to Peabody College 1942; [oth. writ.] Many poems - not published; [pers.] Personal My children and grandchildren are my main interests. Next comes Western round and square dancing.; [a.] Elmira, NY

ANDREWS, JEANNE
[b.] December 5, 1921, Sayre, PA; [m.] Widow, October 26, 1940; [ch.] 2 daughters; [occ.] Retired Secretary;

ANDREWS, KATHY
[b.] April 12, 1949, Chicago, IL; [ed.] AA, Anne Arundel Comm College, 1974, B.S. in Radiological Sciences, Univ. Central Fla. 1985, B.A. in English, UCF 1994; [occ.] Freelance writer; [memb.] Mensa Society; [hon.] Phi Kappa Phi, Golden Key National Honor Society, Sigma Tau Delta, Phi Theta Kappa; [oth. writ.] Several original recipes published in newspapers, articles in local Mensa newsletter and local newspaper; [pers.] I have a reverence for all life, whether it's the sea birds in Daytona, my dogs, or even my orchid collection and these are what I like to write about; [a.] Winter Springs, FL

ANDREWS, ROBERT C.
[b.] January 20, 1949, Boston, MA; [p.] Charles Andrews, Shirley Andrews; [m.] Elizabeth Andrews, November 25, 1972; [ch.] Charlene Thomas, Jeffrey, Laura, Matthew; [ed.] Beverly High, Stockbridge at U. Mass.; [memb.] Boy Scout Troop Committee; [pers.] I find writing relaxing and hope to bring enjoyment to others who read it.; [a.] Beverly, MA

ANDRUSYK, KRYSTAL
[pen.] "Diamond"; [b.] July 10, 1981, Welland, Ontario, Canada; [p.] John and Linda Andrusyk; [ed.] Presently finishing grade eight at Holy Name School; [occ.] Babysit part-time; [memb.] Previously - dancer, gymnast.; [hon.] Gold medal for gymnastics, Silver medal for gymnastics - many ribbons won. Bronze medal - cross country run.;

[oth. writ.] Likes to write stories poetry and letters.; [a.] Welland Ontario, Canada

ANGLIN, RICHARD
[b.] July 27, 1914, Smiley, TX; [p.] Richard W. and Josie Hughes Anglin; [m.] Luella Wilkie Anglin, March 10, 1957; [ed.] High School plus Business College; [occ.] Retired; [memb.] Methodist Church, Natl. Assn. of Ret. Fed. Employees, Natl. Assn. of Ret. Postal Inspectors, Amer. Assn. of retired persons.; [oth. writ.] Other Poems, Essays, Mostly Unpublished.; [pers.] I am proud to have among my good friends William D. Barney, A former poet Laureate of Texas, whose Poetry I have long - admired and who inspires me.; [a.] Richardson, TX

ANTAKI, ANTHONY AUGUST
[b.] March 29, 1968, Queens, NY; [p.] August and Dolores Antaki; [m.] Single as yet; [ed.] Hofstra University School of Law J.D. May 1993, Adelphi University B.A. May 1990 Major: Communications, Long Island Lutheran High School Graduated May 1986; [occ.] Lawyer, passed bar exam, but still unable to find job.; [hon.] Passed July 1994 New York Bar Examination, Student coordinator for ACCESS at Hofstra Law, Graduated Cum Laude from Adelphi University, National Honor Society - L.I. Lutheran High School; [oth. writ.] Poems and song lyrics, all unpublished as yet.; [pers.] Being born handicapped, unable to participate in favorite sport, i.e. ice hockey, gave me plenty of time to reflect. My disability is cerebral palsy. Most of my summers were earmarked and used for surgeries followed by intense physical therapy. My solid christian upbringing as well as loving determined parents taught me early on that where there is a will there certainly is a way, and keep the faith alive.; [a.] Hicksville, NY

ARAVANTINOS, ANASTASIA
[b.] July 23, 1979, Montreal, Quebec, Canada; [p.] Effy and Spiros; [ed.] High School will graduate in 1996; [occ.] Student of LeHoyne D'Iberville High School.; [pers.] Violence is not a solution it's a problem. This statement has always influenced me in my writings.; [a.] Brossard Quebec, Canada

ARCHER, ABBY
[pen.] Abigail Joy Archer; [b.] January 12, 1978, San Diego, CA; [p..] Jack Archer, Vicki Archer; [ed.] Rancho Bernardo High School; [occ.] Student studing to become a Equine Veterinarian; [oth. writ.] Publications and recognition in local magazines.; [pers.] Through all the hardships of life, there are two people that will be there to catch you when you fall ... your parents. I dedicate my poetry to Jack and Vicki Archer ... love always!; [a.] San Diego, CA

ARCHIBALD, FRANZ O. J.
[b.] February 1, 1972, Saint Christopher, West Indies; [p.] Wingrove O. Archibald, Jean E. Archibald; [ed.] Presently an Accounting and Finance major at Seneca College, North York, Ontario, Canada. Graduated the College of Further Education, June 1990, with the University of Cambridge General Certificate of Education.; [occ.] Business Entrepreneur/English Peer Tutor at Seneca College.; [hon.] President's Honour List/Recipient of the Certificate of Achievement for highest academic standing.; [oth. writ.] Author of book-in-progress called "Managing Self-Equity, The Winning Approach"; [pers.] My intent is to inspire a desire in the reader that has not yet been discovered. I truly admire dreamers and strongly respect achievers. Self-actualization is the key, positive reflection and constructive self-evaluation should be a way of life.; [a.] Markham Ontario, Canada

ARCHIE, ANGEL D.
[b.] January 29, 1975, La Grande, OR; [p.] Margaret and William Archie; [ed.] Elgin HS, Camp Johnson NC, Fort Huachuca, Arizona.; [occ.] Pioneer Engine Airframe Mechanical Technician United States Marine Corps; [pers.] Many loves grow and die but friendship remains strong; [a.] McAgee, CA

ARCUNI, JENNIFER M.
[b.] May 1, 1972, NYC; [ed.] Hamilton College '94; [occ.] Waitperson, Odd jobs; [memb.] Crow Canyon Archeological Center, BMG Music Service; [hon.] "Sound of Poetry" award for 'pumpkins' and 'Livin' Crazy in A Corner'.; [oth. writ.] 'Spotted Moonstones'. Red Weather (Magazine), 'Delinquent Angels' and 'Love Girl' hopefully to be published March '95, Treasure House Magazine; [pers.] I live in a riddle sit in the middle and watch the world shake in an uneven stillness; [a.] Santa Fe, NM

AREY, VELMA
[pen.] Velma Arey; [b.] January 3, 1910, Satin, TX; [p.] Thomas R. Jones, Nellie A. Campbell; [m.] Lonnie L. Arey (deceased), April 26, 1930; [ch.] One - deceased; [ed.] East Texas State University - Texas Commerce, Tx., taught in public school 2 years in Texas, received certificate in Fine Art from the famous artist's schools, three diplomas from writer's digest schools.; [occ.] Retired from life ins. business; [memb.] National authors registry, Charter lifetime member of the international society of poets. Teacher in World Bible School of the Church of Christ. Sequoia Dawn Club - Springville.; [hon.] The National Library of Poetry "Honorable Mention" in distinguished poets of America. The best poems of the '90s'. Iliad Press "Editor's Choice Award" in celebrations; [oth. writ.] "Odysseys" around the world. The "President's Award" in perceptions. "Honorable Mention" in remembrances. Sparrow grass poetry forum in poetic voices of America. Three books published, Novel pending.; [pers.] Family Tree Book. Psalms, positive thinking, writing, travel, health, loves people, stays active, play piano, organ, sing. Happy in Springville, CA.; [a.] Springville, CA

ARMSTRONG, JACK THOMAS
[pen.] Jack T. Armstrong; [b.] August 31, 1967, Detroit; [p.] Marion E. and Dolores L. Armstrong; [ed.] Attended Wayne County Community College; [memb.] North American Hunting Club 1994-1995; [hon.] I have received the editor's choice award's for Outstanding Achievement in Poetry presented by the National Library of Poetry in 1993 and 1994. Signed by (Editor) Cynthia Stevens and (Editor) Caroline Sullivan.; [oth. writ.] I'm published in dance on the horizon winter 1993-Poem Able. Also in at days end summer 1994-Poem Midnight Blue. And also on cassette, the Sound of Poetry. Musical Introduction by the English Chamber Orchestra. Readings by Nationally Regained Speaker Ira Westreich.; [pers.] I like the sound of the wind in spring and into the fall. It has a soul of its own. A happy note from a poet as I humbly reside in -.; [a.] Belleville, MI

ARMSTRONG, RACHEL
[b.] January 28, 1970, San Diego, CA; [p.] William and Joyce Armstrong; [m.] Paul Prochaska, December; [ch.] Brian Armstrong and Alexandra Prochaska; [ed.] MTI Western Business College.; [occ.] Homemaker/Secretary for a home business.; [oth. writ.] I've written hundreds of poems since 1981, a few published in Newsletters and small papers and 3 short novels unpublished.; [pers.] I have a dream to become a successful writer of poetry and fiction novels. Thanks to God my dream is beginning to awaken!

ARNOLD, KAREN
[b.] April 27, 1981, Philadelphia, PA; [p.] James Mitchell, Bonnie Mitchell; [hon.] Honor Roll at School each year. Several awards in sports.; [oth. writ.] Quite a few poem I have written, but never have been published. Writing my own songs.; [pers.] My poems are a feeling of self-expression. I've longed for this dream of being recognized and published. My poetry focuses on love and my inspiration is and other friends.; [a.] Philadelphia, PA

ARNOLD, SUSAN K.
[b.] June 30, 1953, Monroe, WI; [p.] Mr. and Mrs. Roger Coplien; [m.] Gregory L. Arnold, September 20, 1982; [ch.] Robin LeAnne, Jeffrey Lee; [ed.] Brodhead High, Fox Valley Technical College; [occ.] Data Entry Specialist, Quantum Health Care Innovations; [oth. writ.] Other poems to be compiled in my own treasury, two plays which were performed in Christmas programs, an Easter puppet show for children; [pers.] I hope to reflect the goodness of God's love toward mankind and to project words of hope to a turbulent world.; [a.] Oshkosh, WI

ARNOLDI, AMY
[pen.] Fountain of Life; [b.] November 19, 1962, St. Louis, MO; [p.] Gay Arnoldi; [ch.] Jeremy and Kia X; [ed.] Associate Arts Degree 1994; [occ.] Writer/Homemaker; [hon.] Dean's List outstanding Multicultural Student Award; [oth. writ.] "A Fountain of Life" - a collection of poetry currently being self-published, contributing lyricist for a local jazz musician's CD.; [pers.] "I am a warrior for universal justice, a spiritual truth-seeker and a fountain of life. My gift of writing dictates my path and my path directs my writing."; [a.] Minneapolis, MN

ARREOLA, MARY J.
[b.] January 20, 1971, Tampa, FL; [p.] Alphonsus B. and Janet L. Harding; [m.] Robbie Arreola, September 12, 1992; [ed.] Samuel Clemens High School - Diploma 1989, Southwest Texas State University - 1989 through 1991, USAF Basic Military Training, Technical School - 1994-95; [occ.] Airman, USAF, Communications Computer Systems Operator; [memb.] Texas Certified Nursery Person; [a.] Universal City, TX

ARRUDA, CHANTELLE MARIE
[pen.] Channy; [b.] February 18, 1977, Toronto, Canada; [p.] Victor and Lucy Arruda; [ed.] St. Joseph's College High School presently in Grade 12.; [occ.] Student; [oth. writ.] I have some other poems that I keep in a poetry book. Favorite quote: "If its worth having, it's worth fighting for." Author - Unknown.; [pers.] I only write what I feel. And I feel that writing is the best way to express how I feel. I am greatly influenced by historical romances and one day hope to become an author.; [a.] Toronto, Canada

ASUZU, EMEKA
[b.] March 8, 1961, Onitsha, Nigeria; [p.] Cecilia and Betrand Asuzu; [m.] Uche Asuzu (Nee Uwasomba), September 3, 1994; [ed.] B. A. (Honours) History/Archeology 1984 - University of Nigeria Nsurra, LL.B. 1988 University of Ibadan, Nigeria. BL 1989 Nigerian Law School Lagos; [occ.] Attorney-At-Law; [memb.] Nigerian Bar Association; [hon.] 1. Senate Scholarship Award, University of Nigeria 1980-1984. 2. Environmental Law Prize University of Ibadan 1988.; [oth. writ.] Several Unpublished Poems; [a.] Ikeja, Lagos

ATTIANESE, CAROLYN MARIE
[pen.] Cali; [b.] November 10, 1965, Brooklyn, NY; [p.] Adele and Salvatore Attianese; [ed.] P.S. 172, Dewey 136; [oth. writ.] Far Beyond, - Losing Childhood, - Children of St. Jude. - Tribute to Freddie Mercury. - Journey to Manhattan - Rush - Tuning to Poetry - Stirring - Coney Island; [pers.] I hope to have more of my work published one day. I have views and opinions on many topics and I express them through my poems. My favorite poets are E. Allan Poe, Jovan, Dorothy Parker; [a.] Brooklyn, NY

AUGELLO JR., LEONARD F.
[pen.] Lenny Augello Jr.; [b.] March 7, 1969, Rosedale, NY; [p.] Leonard Sr and Christina; [ed.] H. Frank Carey High School, St. John's University, St. Vincent's College; [occ.] CBS TV Network - Program and Facilities Manager; [oth. writ.] Cinema, Columnist in college paper "The Spectator," Several short stories with Jake Weber as recurring character - "A Walk in the Park", "A Voyage Beyond," "The Wrestler"; [pers.] "Getting a piece published is a dream come true - everyone go for their dreams"; [a.] Franklin Square, NY

AUGUSTUS, LEATHA
[b.] August 27, 1948, Waynesboro, GA; [p.] Elbert Drayton and Sadie Drayton; [m.] Damon Augustus, February 25, 1967; [ch.] Karen, Daniel, Damon Jr., Samuel, Diana and Henrietta; [ed.] Graduate of Gibbs High School St. Petersburg, FL.; [occ.] 'Cook Red River Army Depot'; [oth. writ.] I have written other poems, and short studies but nothing published; [pers.] I strive to encourage and enlighten young people that they can obtain their goals in life

AUSTIN, JUDY C.
[b.] May 13, 1948, Monette, AR; [ch.] Antony Ray Morgan, August 8, 1969, the late Joseph Karl Morgan, August 23, 1970/January 22, 1993; [ed.] Received secretarial training and G.E.D. while in job corp in Moses Lake, Washington 1967-68. Attended Purdue North Central in Westville, Ind. August '83 thru '86.; [occ.] Night receiver at Wal-Mart #1487, Michigan City, IN.; [oth. writ.] I have composed a number of poems into booklet form, with a title, which I someday hope to have published.; [pers.] I feel that I owe my enthusiasm, for writing my thoughts down on paper, to Dr. John J. Pappas, Valporaiso, IN. He was the director of the English Dept. and my English Professor the first two semesters that I attended Purdue North Central University.; [a.] Michigan City, IN

AXTELL, ANDREA
[b.] March 19, 1966, Berkeley, CA; [p.] Keith Axtell and Patricia Boster Axtell; [ed.] Sir Francis Drake High School, University of California, Santa Cruz; [occ.] Storyteller, Assistant Buyer at Educational Bookstore; [memb.] Save the Children sponsor, Amnesty International, "Story in Performance" Storytelling troupe, Northern California Children's Booksellers Association.; [oth. writ.] First poem published in October 1994, an untitled work, have begun writing all of my own material for my storytelling performances. Contributor to Marin Teachers' Store quarterly newsletter.; [pers.] Poetry is the greatest way I have to present my inner life to the world! Influences include Anne Sexton, Robert Bly, Rainer Maria Rilke and Richard Wilber.; [a.] San Rafael, CA

AYERS, KATHERINE
[pen.] Katherine Ayers; [b.] San Antonio, TX; [p.] Arthur and Dorothy Ayers; [ed.] Business and Psychology background; [memb.] Active Christian and Humanitarian; [oth. writ.] Poetry, songs; [pers.] I try to give an honest, objective approach to my writing.

BADEJO, DIEDRE L.
[b.] November 8, 1947, New York; [p.] David and Barbara Merritt; [m.] Divorced; [ch.] Kim Nelson, Ti Badejo, Bayo Badejo; [ed.] B.A. University of South California, M.A. University of California, Los Angeles Ph.D University of California, Los Angeles; [occ.] Professor, Univ. of Louisville Author, Speaker (African World Literature and Cultural Studies); [memb.] Kentucky Humanities Council Speakers Bureau, National Council for Black Studies, UCLA Alumni Association; [hon.] Fulbright Senior Research Scholar Award, Rockefeller Fellowship in the Humanities, Ford Foundation Scholarship, Outstanding Senior Recognition Award, V of South California; [oth. writ.] "Keepin' the Faith" in Newport Review, "Torunbo" in Black American Literature Forum, "Survival Motion", in Nelson Mandela Amandla, "Children of Rage" in Nelson Mandela Amandla, several articles in American and international journals and local newspapers.; [pers.] The world is truly a remarkable place, my literary goal is to infuse my writing with the voices, images, metaphors, perspectives, and stories of those who people our world. My work is influenced by african languages, asian philosophy, and american experiences.; [a.] Louisville, KY

BAILEY, ELLA LOUISE
[b.] January 10, 1944, Jackson, TN; [p.] Ophelia Clemons, Jake Clemons; [m.] Divorced; [ch.] Priscilla, Cheryl and Keshia; [ed.] MacKenzie High School (MacKenzie Tennessee), Rockland State School of Nursing, (Rockland, New York); [occ.] Radiologist Technician; [memb.] Columbia Presbyterian Medical Center 25 year club. - Urban League First Baptist Church - Jr Usher Board Advisor.; [hon.] Performance Award issue from the Neurological Institute; [pers.] This poem is dedicated to my handsome grandson Kyle Leslie, and my beautiful granddaughter Nicole Imani. I create poems about children and for children in hope to influence them positively, because the future is in their hands.; [a.] Englewood, NJ

BAILEY, JOYCE A.
[b.] January 31, 1950, Geridge, AR; [p.] Robert and Anna Bailey; [ch.] Antoinette, JaMesa, Jason; [ed.] Soldan High School, St. Louis, MO, 12th Grade Education; [occ.] Adv. Computer Attn. Southwestern Bell Telephone Co. 25 yrs. with SWBT.; [memb.] My church Rose Hill MB Church; [oth. writ.] I have written a total of over forty poems. Only one was submitted to Pro-life for their newspaper. "Unborn" was printed in their paper. I feel several poems that I have, are wonderful poems.; [pers.] I write from the heart and soul, and it shows in my poems.; [a.] Saint Louis, MO

BAILEY, NOVA IRENE FELKINS
[pen.] Nova Felkins Bailey; [b.] January 21, 1926, Ralston, OK; [p.] Henry F. Felkins, Annis C. Felkins; [m.] Robert W. Bailey, June 15, 1957; [ch.] Timothy John, David Jonathan; [ed.] Kiowa, CO High Rockmont College (now Colorado Christian University), Eastern Oregon College of Education (now Eastern Oregon State College); [occ.] Retired. Former elementary teacher in Colorado and Oregon; [memb.] Village Baptist Church American Assoc. of Retired Persons; [hon.] Sigma Alpha Chi. Honor Roll; [oth. writ.] Several poems published in high school and local newspapers, news articles in local newspapers, special occasion poems for family and friends, poems and articles contributed to books. (My Folks series, Capper Press).; [pers.] I consider my talent a gift to be used to enrich the lives of others.; [a.] Beaverton, OR

BAILEY, RHONDA
[b.] June 1, 1970, Calgary, Alberta, Canada; [p.] Dianna Mymko and Ken Jost; [m.] Dennis Bailey, August 12, 1989; [ch.] 2 young children; [ed.] Lindsay Thurber Comprehensive High School, Red Deer College Legal Assistant Program.; [occ.] Homemaker; [pers.] Since I was young, I have always written a poem to reflect my feelings rather than putting them in a diary. My poems reflect my life. This one was written for my mother.; [a.] Drayton Valley Alberta, Canada

BAIN, JULIEM L.
[pen.] Jules; [b.] July 25, 1967, Port of Spain; [p.] Lucia Bain; [ed.] Seneca College; [memb.] American Marketing Assoc.; [oth. writ.] Currently completing a book of poems; [pers.] When all that is desired seems out of reach, think not of the distance... consider the many ways of mending a bridge.; [a.] Toronto Ontario, Canada

BAIRD, HELEN E.
[pen.] Helen Haddix Baird; [b.] November 13, 1914, Western, NE; [p.] Harvey W. and Anna D. Haddix; [m.] Elmer W. Baird, January 5, 1932; [ch.] Joy, Pharaby, Robert, Duane; [ed.] Steele City High School, Art Instruction Commercial Art Course, Portraiture Lesel Saltzer, Artist, Teacher; [occ.] Home Maker, Retired; [memb.] World Wide Fellowship of New Testament Christians, Express of Aloha Terrace Coop. Six years Board Member.; [hon.] This is an Outstanding "Honor" "Award" unknown. My family four children, six grandchildren and "Twelve Great" are my fans; [oth. writ.] Book one, my autobiography "The Seventh Child" book two, continuation "Unnamed", contains many poems and hymns four with original tunes recorded; [pers.] As a student of the Bible over sixty years God's word has influenced my thinking and writing, my thankfulness for time and talents bestowed.; [a.] Seattle, WA

BAKER, EDITH M.
[b.] December 12, 1919, Greene Co, IN; [p.] Aaron and Opal Arthur; [m.] Raymond Baker, August 17, 1938 (Deceased); [ch.] Nine children; [ed.] 12th grade and some any tech.; [occ.] Retired in 1985 now part time teller; [oth. writ.] Many poems for many friends and family special occasions; [pers.] I enjoy my large family and my hobbies are gardening and writing.; [a.] Bloomfield, IN

BAKER, EVELYN L.
[pen.] Evelyn L. Baker; [b.] September 15, 1908, Malden, MA; [m.] Lt. Col. Theodore S. Baker, A.F. (Deceased), July 17, 1942.; [ch.] The Rev. Carole L. Baker, Theodore S. Baker, Jr.; [ed.] High School Growing up in the depression days precluded more formal education so I became a lover of books of everykind. They taught me.; [occ.] Retired; [memb.] Christ United Meth. Church, A.A.R.P., Mystery Guild, Crossings Reader's Digest; [hon.] God awarded me with two beautiful children, my husband honored me with 49 years of a faithful marriage.; [oth. writ.] Never submitted any previous works.; [pers.] As my life is winding down, I pray for a few more years to be mentally alert and to relish each passing day with family and books.; [a.] Malden, MA

BAKER, GEORGE R.
[b.] September 2, 1916, Sullivan, IL; [p.] John and Laura Baker; [m.] Harrietta Baker, January 23, 1937; [ch.] Darrell, Georgetta, Richard; [ed.] 8 grade, 4 high, 2 Bus. Col. 4 GI Bill of Rights Purdue, 4 Theo. Semn. Indianapolis; [occ.] Retired; [memb.] ECKANKAR, the SHARIYAT-KI SUGMAD.; [hon.] Masonic Lodge, the Honorable George Baker, Noble, the Principality of Hutt River Province, Western Australia, Doctorate, as a Metaphysician; [oth. writ.] "Ode to Oatmeal", The Flag, My Uncle was deaf, Why do I complain?, The Idyds of March, April; [pers.] Soon to be 79 borned 1916. Served in the Navy WWW2. Have been in Sales, for self and others. Have been Pres. and V.P. of three Oil Co. Have been unable to work, because of Heart and strokes, since 1977. Spend my time painting, and entertaining; [a.] Crawfordsville, IN

BAKER, MARY WAYE
[b.] May 24, 1925, Tallahassee, FL; [p.] Ernest and Lucy Waye; [ed.] Lincoln High, FAMU, Atlanta University; [occ.] Retired Educator Calhoun County; [memb.] Trustee and Financial Secretary of St. Paul AME Church Member of LVA; [hon.] Mother of the Year - 1992, St. Paul; [oth. writ.] Two novels: Don't Look Back and Llona: A Winthrup Woman; [pers.] I feel that poetry is the language of the soul. My novels reflect life in the South.; [a.] Blountstown, FL

BAKER, REBEKAH M.
[b.] March 16, 1976, Claremont, NH; [p.] Susan E. Baker, Gary L. Baker; [m.] Michael T. Metcalf, April 22, 1995; [ch.] Dylon M. Metcalf; [ed.] Graduated: Springfield High School, Springfield, VT; [occ.] Studying Physical and Occupational Therapy; [hon.] National Honor Society, German Exchange Trip.; [oth. writ.] Leisure poems; [pers.] Love is the most important gift. Without love there is no life.; [a.] Charlestown, NH

BAKER, RICARDO M.
[pen.] Ricardo M. Baker; [b.] October 30, 1955, Barbados, West Indies; [p.] Oneta Baker-Hunte, Ralph Walker; [m.] Bernadette Baker, July 3, 1993; [ch.] Corey, Randy and Eric; [ed.] Bachelor of Arts Urban Affairs and Sociology Queens College, New York; [occ.] Asst. Borough Commissioner NYC Department of Health; [memb.] Council of Barbarian Organizations, USA Eastern Zone Cricket Assoc. Community Board 18; [hon.] Advance person for Rev. Jesse Jackson - Sept.-Nov. 1992.; [oth. writ.] 1. Poor Bastard Child of Urban America. 2. Cold Winds of the Ghetto. 3. Tribute to David N. Dinkings. 4. All in the Night Fall. 5. One Love for Bob Marler.; [pers.] I am in sleeping giant now, but when I rise, I will rise to make changes - positive changes.; [a.] Brooklyn, NY

BAKER, SARAH
[pen.] Sarah Baker; [b.] December 8, 1922, Chicago, IL; [p.] Emory P., Louise W. Baker; [m.] Frank M. Bolek, December 29, 1945; [ch.] Ronald F. 47, Joanne L. 45, Benett 40, Leslie K. 37; [ed.] No degrees beyond high school but many credits in art, literature, Spanish language, etc.; [occ.] Working artist in San Antonio TX, painter, writer; [hon.] Participated in many art shows. Have had several one woman shows. Sold some have extensive body of work, paintings, drawings, etchings, silk screens.; [oth. writ.] Unpublished I consider myself first a painter. My writing is an auxiliary to my art work, titles, journals, letters.; [a.] San Antonio, TX

BAKER SR., JOSEPH W.
[pen.] J. W. Baker; [b.] May 10, 1934, Seymour, TN; [p.] Rev. Jason A. Baker, Sarrah Baker; [m.] Hazel J. Baker, July 24, 1964; [ch.] Joseph W. Jr., Richard A., Jeana L.; [ed.] Sevier County High, Harison Chilhowee Babtist Academy High, Alabama Christian College; [occ.] Barber-Retired; [oth. writ.] This is my first attempt to write any type of literature; [pers.] From deep feeling's within, I was inspired to write this poem in memory of my Dad and other service men's parents that died while they were away; [a.] Greenback, TN

BALDORIA, CHARISSE J.
[b.] January 3, 1976, Quezon City, Philippines; [p.] Eddie Baldoria, Riza Jose; [ed.] St. Theresa's College, Quezon City, University of the Philippines (U.P.); [occ.] Student; [memb.] U.P. Christ's Youth in action, U.P. Corps of Sponsors, U.P. College of Music Student Council; [hon.] Valedictorian (Grade School and High School), First prize: National Music Competition for Young Artists (Piano, 1985 and 1989, First prize: National Yamaha Electone Festival (1986, 1989), First Prize: 1992 U.P. College Piano Competition, currently a university scholar; [oth. writ.] Several unpublished poems and essays

BALDWIN, DANIEL ANTHONY
[b.] April 13, 1962, Cortland, NY; [ed.] Cortland High, USM; [occ.] Refiner of fine chocolate; [memb.] VFW; [hon.] Several Military Awards; [oth. writ.] Have several others of the West. Western Drifter, Cowboy's Ride, Country Girl, Dreamin', Etc.; [pers.] Horses are a part of my life the West as it once was I sure wish, and I dream. A true friendship shall last forever! Peace to all; [a.] Ottawa, KS

BALLING, WILLIAM R.
[pen.] R. Richard Beatty; [b.] April 28, 1935, Dayton, OH; [p.] Dorothy J. Balling; [ch.] Leilani Marie Bowman, Vicky K. Balling; [ed.] Fairborn High School, Glendale Community College, Capitol Radio Electronic Institute, National Aerounatic Space Administration Network Systems.; [occ.] Semi-Retired Manager of Apartment Complex.; [memb.] CREI-Alumni Association Lions Club; [hon.] Military - Korean Service Medal United Nations Service Medal, Good Conduct Medal, National Defense Medal; [oth. writ.] Numerous Poems Published in local newspaper "Cancun News" only English newspaper in Cancun Mexico. Collection of childrens stores under title of "Nature's Secret Paradise"; [pers.] Most of my poems we written by actual events in my life, during my 3 1/2 years in Cancun Mexico. This also influenced my writings of children's stories. I write about what I see, the average person may take for granted.; [a.] Tampa, FL

BANKS JR., HAROLD L.
[b.] October 3, 1958, Bridgeton, NJ; [ed.] Class of 77 Brockton High School, Brockton Mass Temple University and 4 years United States Marine; [occ.] Court Officer Probate and Family Court Brockton, MA; [oth. writ.] Currently composing a book of poetry with approximately 50 poems to date; [pers.] To express myself and beliefs through writing and to open as many hearts and minds as possible; [a.] Brockton, MA

BANKS-LOVE, ALICE LEE
[b.] April 24, 1959, Helen, AR; [m.] Jeffrey Orlando Love, July 24, 1989; [ch.] Eugene J.W., Dominick Darnell; [ed.] Hirsch High, Olive Harvey College Assoc. Degree, Chicago State University; [pers.] I write to reflect the moment and the feelings that are in my mind and heart for each poem; [a.] Chicago, IL.

BANKSTON, JULIE A.
[b.] February 28, 1960, Milwaukee, WI; [p.] Mr. and Mrs. John Bankston; [ch.] Bishara Dorre; [ed.] Bachelor's degree in Social Welfare a Master degree in Education; [occ.] OMRP - Qualified Mental Retardation Professional; [hon.] Former U.S. Peace Corps Volunteer - Tanzania East Africa; [pers.] The body is a temple to house the soul. My writings are healings for an individuals soul and temple; [a.] Milwaukee, WI

BARATI, EVA
[b.] May 13, 1966, Hungary; [ed.] Education; [oth. writ.] Several poems, short stories published in Hungary; [pers.] In my writing I strive to reflect the feelings of the human soul, the fairness and the ugliness of the everyday life.; [a.] Marina Del Rey, CA

BARBARA, BODFIELD
[b.] January 11, 1969, Lincoln, NE; [p.] John and Patricia Ballou, [m.] Scott Bodfield; [ch.] Derek Douglas and Branden Scott; [ed.] Northeast High - Lincoln Nebraska Southeast Comm. College - Lincoln; [occ.] Childcare Provider; [oth. writ.] A poem written to my son Derek on his first day of school August 29, 1994 and a poem written to my friend Gina who died October 16, 1994. We miss you Gina!; [pers.] I love to express my feelings in such a way that I can share it with others, they can read it and know just how I feel! I see their tears and I know I've succeeded! This one's for you Mom - Thank you for always being there for me! I love you!; [a.] Lincoln, NE

BARBER, CARRIE
[b.] February 7, 1979, Newark, AR; [p.] David O. and Deborah S.; [ed.] Sophomore at Lakewood High School, Graduate in 1997. Currently attending Barbizon Modelling School.; [occ.] Baby sitting jobs; [memb.] Spanish Club. Fine Arts Club. Was in Girl Scouts from 1st grade through 7th grade.; [hon.] In 9th grade I was acknowledge for my writing skills.; [oth. writ.] Submitted a short story - "Sweet Sixteen" to Seventeen Magazine.; [pers.] I have a deep love for animals. I was inspired to write this poem by the death of my Shetland Sheep dog.; [a.] Hebron, OH

BARETSKY, JASON ALLEN
[pen.] Raven Orpheus Blue; [b.] September 26, 1974, Rochester, NY; [occ.] Soldier in Army; [oth. writ.] Nothing that's been published as yet.; [pers.] Poetry is a weapon, with which we stab at the world with emotion.

BARGHOUTI, ASEM NAYEF AL
[b.] 1936, Jafa; [m.] Laila Attiyah, 1960; [ch.] Khalid, Samar, Sahar; [ed.] 1965 Masters Degree in Classical Archeology, Philadelphia 1974 Ph.d in Classical Archeology Chicago University.; [occ.] Staff Member at King Saud University, Riyadh; [pers.] During the past 17 years, I have been supervising several excavations held in both Jordan and Riyadh, during these periods have I been able to actually feel and live the past centuries, and the fascinating ancient empires, how the rose and fell, and against this background, I would like to add that archaeologists, in sharp contrast to what many may think, are not in human beings dealing with old stones and pots, but we are very much alive as we get to live and feel the evolution of the past while witnessing the present.; [a.] Amman-Jordan

BARLETTA, DANIEL P.
[b.] February 11, 1974, New Jersey; [p.] Guido and Trudy Barletta; [ed.] Only life; [occ.] Meaningless routine; [pers.] Never join the MACHINE; [a.] Rockaway, NJ

BARLIEB, BRANDON ROBERT
[pen.] Brandon Robert Barblie; [b.] February 20, 1975, Bethlehem, PA; [p.] Joan and Robert Barlieb; [ed.] Freedom High School, currently Kutztown University; [occ.] College student; [oth. writ.] Several unpublished short stories and poems; [a.] Bethlehem, PA

BARNETT, BARBARA A.
[pen.] Barbara Bridgers Barnett; [b.] May 24, 1937, Viola, AR; [p.] Drew Thomas and Alpha Bridgers, [m.] Gaston Ray Barnett, July 15, 1956; [ch.] Son Jeffery Ray Barnett; [ed.] Viola High, Kansas City Jr. College; [occ.] Retired Bookkeeper and Accountant 30 years in banking; [memb.] Charter Member of National Children's Home - Veteran Orphaned Children, Charter Member VFW past Auxiliary H9777.; [hon.] Special Alertness Award to Fraud in Banking; [oth. writ.] Several poems in the local newspaper.; [pers.] Poetry reflects deep feelings from the soul and is a special gift.; [a.] Salem, AR

BARNETT, LEE
[pen.] Mushki; [b.] February 18, 1941, Plainfield, NJ; [m.] J. Azavin Barnett, November 22, 1986; [ch.] Susan, Melissa and Craig; [occ.] Reg. Mgr. S.W. Ontario for The Canadian Diabetes Assoc.; [oth. writ.] Several poems published in womens periodicals. Writing children stories and poem tales. Contributions to a book currently in publication re' The Union of the Sexual and The Spiritual.; [pers.] I seek to open inquiry into the deeper nature of life, and explore as well, that which emerges from the creative - in whimsey and delight (especially for children).; [a.] Kingsville Ontario, Canada

BARR, MARIA
[b.] March 22, 1953, Yugoslavia; [p.] Toni and Darinka Ozbolt; [m.] Patrick, May 16, 1992; [ch.] 2 (Amy and Adam); [ed.] Mercy High School, Milwaukee; [occ.] Medical Secretary/Collection Manager-Cardiovascular Surgery Associates; [memb.] I am active in our church's variety show of singing, dancing, and acting; [oth. writ.] Several poems family and friends; [a.] Milwaukee, WI

BARRETT, CAITLIN ELLIS
[b.] August 13, 1981, Boston Brigham and Women's Hospital; [p.] Virginia Kime Shields, Edward C. Barrett; [ed.] Presently in 8th grade in the Chenery Middle School; [occ.] Student, Chenery Middle School, Belmont, MA; [hon.] A winner of the 1989 Charles River Watershed Association Poetry Contest; [oth. writ.] None published; [pers.] I love to write about the things that interest me, which are human emotions, the ocean, and mysterious places such as tombs or forests. In my poems, I try to make a statement about life or the beauty of nature. Right now I'm thirteen, I plan to be both a poet and an ichthyologist when I am an adult.; [a.] Cambridge, MA

BARRETT, CLINTON C.
[pen.] Chaz Bover; [b.] August 2, 1965, Jamaica, West Indies; [p.] Leonora McLaren, Vincent Barrett; [m.] Kathleen A. Hall; [ch.] Ajene, Shomari, Adam; [ed.] Dewitt Clinton H.S., City College of Cuny., (B.S. Degree); [occ.] Actor; [memb.] Arista Club, Honors Program, Scholarship Class; [hon.] Arista, Scholarship, Dean's List, Golden Circle Club; [oth. writ.] Several unpublished poems and songs. Currently writing a book to be published; [pers.] Negativity has its limits, but positivity is eternal.; [a.] Bronx, NY

BARRETT, NANCY E.
[b.] November 5, 1959, Brookline; [p.] James A. and Marguerite M. Barrett; [m.] Single; [ed.] New Bury College, 2 years school, 1989 Business Management and Marketing degrees.; [occ.] Assembler; [memb.] Crohn's and Colitrs Foundation; [oth. writ.] Had two poems set to music, recorded "Time Ticked Away" Loving every moment I have the only records 45 at home wrote at 16; [pers.] I write about life what comes from mepheart and what I feel. It seems to come naturally on any subject; [a.] Walpole, MA

BARRETT, ROBERT D.
[b.] June 22, 1959, New Braunfels, TX; [p.] Robert L. Barrett, Elizabeth Barrett; [ch.] Amber Marie, Trevor Ethan, Courtney Grace; [ed.] Balboa H.S., Canal Zone, Florida State University; [occ.] Factory worker, Amateur musician; [oth. writ.] Several non-published poems and song lyrics; [a.] Wappapello, MO

BARRETTE, LOUISE
[b.] July 15, 1967, Hawkesbery; [p.] Rolland and Rita Barrette (Marleau); [ch.] Michel Barrette; [ed.] Samuel-Genest, C.A.PP.A. Hair-Dresser, Bodybuilder, Trainer, 15 years of Piano, Royal Conservatory of Music, 15 years of Ballet, 3 years guitar, Modelling, Acting.....; [occ.] Writer, Mother, acting.; [hon.] Certificate from the Royal Conservatory of Music. (5); [oth. writ.] I am currently writing a book of my life story. Still writing poems with flair and movie script..; [pers.] I wish that my writing thy book of my life, I will be able to relax and leave the past behind. I get shivers in my hair when I look in the air, better be there for my next carriere.; [a.] Rockland Ontario, Canada

BARRONTON, JACQUELINE
[pen.] Stark Silver; [b.] November 19, 1976, Monroe, MI; [p.] Dolores and Donald Barronton; [ed.] Monroe/ Mason Alternative High School; [occ.] Student; [oth. writ.] There have been a few of my poems published in our school newspaper; [pers.] Poetry is the meaning of life!; [a.] Monroe, MI

BARTELL, PATRICE
[b.] April 13, 1979, Hornell, NY; [p.] John and Nancy Bartell; [ed.] Saint Ann's Grammar School, Hornell High (currently); [occ.] Student; [oth. writ.] first publication; [a.] Hornell, NY

BARTELL, STEPHEN MARK
[b.] February 5, 1949, Evanston, IL; [p.] Robert M. Bartell, Shirley Miller Bartell; [m.] Sherri Lynn Bartell, December 23, 1983; [ch.] Sophia Elizabeth Bartell; [ed.] B.A. Wilmington College, Ohio Graduate Work, Kent State University, Ohio Miami-Dade Community College, 4.0 avg 1972, also studied with James Lee Burke; [occ.] Asst. to Senior Vice President of Business Affairs, MGM/ UA Telecommunications Group; [hon.] 1st Place Florida Junior Colleges 1972; [oth. writ.] 15 screenplays, three novels couple dozen short stories, six one-hour teleplays, two songs, have optioned out several scripts and been hired to rewrite one.; [pers.] Poetry is incredibly disciplined. It requires intense hard work to convey the feelings clearly and with inspiration. I love being driven to capture just the right nuance and power.; [a.] Los Angeles, CA

BARTRAM, DONALD RAY
[b.] November 30, 1950, Louisa, KY; [p.] Deceased; [m.] Nanci Marie Bartram, February 12, 1992; [ch.] Katrina Elisha Marie Bartram; [ed.] 11th grace and G-E-D; [occ.] Parts Person; [hon.] 7th grade poet contest; [oth. writ.] various; [pers.] I would like to give my appreciation and respect to Frank Ciccio Manuli for making it possible for me to have his daughter for my wife, Nanci Marie Bartram whom inspired me to take this to the fullest, when with my daughter Katrina to make my dream come true; [a.] Toledo, OH

BASQUE, ANGELE
[b.] April 27, 1973, Windsor, Ontario, Canada; [p.] Claude and Marguerite Basque; [ed.] Study for 3 years at the University of Monczon, New Brunswick. Now I'm taking a correspondence course (ICS) in Journalism and short story writing.; [occ.] Work part-time at a grocery store; [a.] Lower-Neguarc New Brunswick, Canada

BASSFORD, DENISE A. SMITHART
[pen.] Hiawatha; [b.] April 15, 1960, Iowa City, IA; [p.] Richard Smithart, Doloris Denniston; [m.] Divorced, February, 1984; [ch.] Mother to three children; [ed.] Completed 11th grade and has completed a course in business management and is continuing her education.; [occ.] Dog groomer for over 6 years, plus cashier at a travel center; [memb.] Doberman Pincher Club of Greater Des Moines, PTA, has done volunteer work in local elementary schools, church nursery, taught pre-school day care ages 2-5, also trained my own show dog and won over 20 ribbons, 2 trophies. Holds a certificate; [hon.] In Business Management. Other talents include acrylic paintings, oils pastel, charcoal drawing, master violinist. She is of Indian Heritage and among her ancestors are John Lightfoot, Geronimo, sitting bull and Hiawatha.; [oth. writ.] Achieved college level English and grammar since 7th grade. Wrote for Institute of Children's Literature a short story about a little lost puppy, although it was not published to her credit. She was a minor.; [pers.] To find peace in oneself is to enjoy all that God has created. I am a true believer of finding some good in everyone.; [a.] Des Moines, IA

BATES, ROBERT WILLIAM
[b.] May 1, 1927, Hazel Park, MI; [p.] Mr. and Mrs. Frederick Bates; [ch.] Natasha Mary Bates; [ed.] B.A. Speech Wayne University (Detroit); [occ.] Retired; [memb.] Amnesty International Universalist Church; [oth. writ.] Essay: "Civil Disobedience In America" (Book) "Change-Over", Alan Swallow Press, Poems in magazines visions and revisions new scribes Detroit News; [pers.] I am interested in helping build a world in which conflicts are solved by negotiations, and by use of sanctions when necessary, economic pressure, etc. But one cannot expect morality from others unless nations and individuals are themselves moral.; [a.] Jersey City, NJ

BAUDAIS, KAREN
[b.] September 7, 1964; [p.] Dr. Jerome Schropp, Loretta Schropp; [ch.] Sarah Lynn; [ed.] Glenmary High, McKay College; [occ.] Medical Assistant; [memb.] Actively involved with Central Alberta Theatre.; [pers.] "THE OPEN DOOR" is dedicated to Hedley Blake, a talented photographer who's work inspired this piece.; [a.] Red Deer Alberta, Canada

BAUER, KAREN LYNN
[b.] June 20, 1953, Bremerton, WA; [p.] Royce M. and Christina A. Bacon; [m.] David Charles Bauer, Septem-

ber 7, 1975; [pers.] Words, sentences, poems and books make up who we were, and who we are and who we will be.; [a.] Baxter, MN

BAVE, KELLIE
[b.] October 16, 1976, Salt Lake City, UT; [p.] Peter and Robyn Bave; [ed.] West Jordan High Senior; [pers.] Some say poems come from the Heart, others say they come from Pain, a few say they come with age or with youth, some people say they come from experience ... well they're right! Poems can be found anywhere.; [a.] West Jordan, UT

BAXTER, GEORGE HENDERSON
[b.] December 4, 1968, Lanark, Scotland; [p.] David P. Baxter, Marion J. Baxter; [ed.] Larkhall Academy, Larkhall, Lanarkshire, Scotland; [occ.] Accountant; [oth. writ.] Poetry Now's "Connecting" Anthology (Satin Woman) Published in U.K., National Library Of Poetry: Best Poems Of 1995, A Moment In Time And Dance On The Horizon Anthologies.; [pers.] A Flower Gently Blossoms, Life, It Seems So Awesome, I Sit Here And I Wait, I Cannot Hesitate, To Love.; [a.] Bournemouth Dorset, United Kingdom

BAYER, JOHN
[b.] February 9, 1973, Sugarcreek, PA; [p.] Frank Bayer, Monika Bayer; [ch.] Crystal Bayer; [ed.] St. Gregory's High, Communication Arts student, Durham College; [memb.] Canadian Conservatory of Music, School writer's club; [oth. writ.] Poetry published with the "The Violet Circle" magazine, Music and lyrics for my own projects as well as some philosophical writing; [pers.] I occasionally reflect on my own opinions in my writing. But I usually strive to create a vast point of view.; [a.] Oshawa Ontario, Canada

BAYER, LAVERNNA L.
[pen.] 'Kitty'; [b.] September 4, 1927, Pittsburgh, PA; [p.] David George Logan, Celesta Logan; [m.] Joseph Leax Bayer, October 10, 1947, expired January 11, 1992, [ch.] James Lon, Karen Lianne, Vicki Lynne, Sheila Lane; [ed.] Turtle Creek High, T.C., PA., St. Francis School Nursing, Pgh, PA. Barry University Miami, FL; [occ.] Retired RN, BS, Staff Dev. Coordinator, Universal Medical Center, Plantation, FL; [memb.] South Florida Nurse Educators American Heart Association, American Diabetes Association, held offices and participated in fund raising.; [hon.] Florida Epsilon Chapter of Alpha-Chi, Employee of the Month 1987, Employee of the Year 1988, Graduated Magna Cum Laude, Barry University Miami, FL., June 1988; [oth. writ.] "Is Opportunity Knocking?", Patient Education Newsletter, Vol 8 No. 6 Dec. 1985; [pers.] I can only hope and strive to make a ripple in the ocean of life.; [a.] Sunrise, FL

BEAIRD, SARAH ELIZABETH
[b.] February 3, 1977, Columbia, MO; [p.] Elizabeth Beaird; [ed.] High School Senior Auto Body, Carpentry (Technical Career Center); [occ.] Student, U.S. Army - Software Analyst (Computers); [memb.] Vica (Vocational Industrial Clubs of America) Treasurer JROTC - Company CUR; [pers.] I do not create the poems. I am God's tool to release the secrets. I try to reflect the hopes and dreams and fears kept within, to show the true side of man; [a.] Poplar Bluff, MO

BEAL, KIMBERLY CARTER
[b.] July 21, 1969, Dayton, OH; [p.] Linda Rae Warrick Heis; [m.] Dwayne Anthony Beal, December 12, 1993; [ch.] Joshua Alexander Beal; [ed.] Miamisburg Sr. High School, Certified Dental Asst. Montgomery County Joint Vocational School, Attended Sinclair Community College; [occ.] Mother and wife; [hon.] Outstanding Youth Award City of Miamisburg; [pers.] My inspiration is devoted to my love for God and my precious family.; [a.] Cridersville, OH

BEATTY, CHRISTOPHER
[b.] July 24, 1982, Denville, NJ; [p.] George Beatty, Christine Beatty; [ed.] Currently in 7th Grade Hope Township School; [occ.] Student; [hon.] B Card Student, Honor Student; [pers.] If just one person and reads my poetry with feeling - that would make me happy.; [a.] Hope, NJ

BEAUDRY, JOHANNE
[b.] February 22, 1976, Hull, Quebec, Canada; [p.] Jean-Pierre and Constance Beaudry; [ed.] High School; [pers.] My dream's makes me the writer I am for creativity and fantasy is my chosen destiny.; [a.] Aylmer Quebec, Canada

BECK, DONNA
[pen.] Donna Murphy; [b.] June 15, 1940, Prairie Home, MO; [p.] Edward Cole and Audrey Page; [m.] September 1, 1959 (Died 1975); [ch.] Virginia (Beck) Merkley; [ed.] 1 year Nursing College LPN (MO) LVN (CA); [occ.] Nurse; [hon.] "Children's Institute" (Writing for Children's Books); [oth. writ.] "Is There A Christmas in Heaven", "One Year", "Jackie R.", "Stolen Moments", Tuesday Girl", "Broken Patches", "Just A Friend", Books: "The Throwaway Child" and "Beyond The Last Door"; [pers.] Most of my writings are about causes especially about drug addiction and child abuse.; [a.] Palmdale, CA

BECKSTEAD, JOHN J.
[b.] November 20, 1919, Fulton, County, Canton, IL; [p.] John J. Beckstead, Sr.; [m.] Clara L. Beckstead, August 14, 1937; [ch.] Judith Martin; [ed.] At Methodist Medical Center, Peoria, IL. My education 1 1/2 years. High School - A complete "college Preparatory" Course from a Chicago School - Then a "TV-Radio Course from ICS, Scranton, Penn. Repair/Servicing Course-June 2, 1970, I also took a drawing course-forgot the date, '82, I believe.; [occ.] Retired from International Harvester Co. - Now — Navistar; [oth. writ.] I wrote this poem in 1983 for a little church booklet, for each of our members. A favorite scripture, a poem, someone else's poem or writing that you liked, or praise to someone. My wife wanted me to write one. Only two days were left to write it. I wrote it in two days.; [pers.] A love for people who are honest and of good faith, as I believe that, "A Man Reaps What That He Sows." You don't reap corn by sowing wheat. As to poems, my favorite one was in my grade school book, "October's Bright Blue Weather."; [a.] Canton, IL

BEETHAM, JAMES W.
[pen.] Jimbo; [b.] October 28, 1924, Toronto, Ontario, Canada; [p.] James and Ione; [m.] Jude, October 7, 1979; [ch.] Janis, Marie, Chris, David; [ed.] Winchester Public, Jarvis Collegiate; [occ.] Retired (Toronto Hydro-Electric System Trouble Shooter); [memb.] Masonic Order, S.P.E.B.S.Q.S.A. Inc., Royal Canadian Legion; [hon.] Canadian Army W.W. II - 1939-45 Star, France/Germany Star, Canadian Volunteer Service Medal, Defense of Britain Medal, Victory Medal, Dominion Marksman (Gold), Barbershop International Chorus (Gold, Twice) (Silver, Twice); [oth. writ.] Forty-five poems on various subjects from 1943 up to date; [pers.] Writing poetry is my hobby. I write for my own enjoyment but my happiest times, in this life, are when others read my poems and enjoy them!; [a.] Baldwin Ontario, Canada

BEGGS, DOUG
[b.] December 1, 1945, Blytheville, AR; [p.] Roy and Christine Beggs; [m.] Judy A. Beggs, February 3, 1983 (Second marriage); [ch.] Anna Maria Smith and Robbin Rena Forrester; [ed.] High school diploma Special Wildlife Schools; [occ.] State Employee for the State of Ark.; [memb.] Masonic Lodge #198, Forrest City, AR.; [oth. writ.] I have written about 130 other poems, covering a lot of different subjects.; [pers.] Keep your face into the wind, never look back, the past can't be changed, the future can.; [a.] Hazen, AR

BEGUM, RUQYA
[pen.] Afshan; [b.] September 9, 1975, Hyderabad, India; [p.] Mohd Abdul Rahman, Ather Quraishi; [ed.] Till X in Kuwait, Intermediate from Villa Marie, presently in Shadan Degree College; [occ.] Student; [hon.] A prize for poetry writing contest in degree college.; [oth. writ.] 47 other poems all unpublished because I never tried to publish them.; [pers.] My poems portray feelings that one experiences in life both happy and sad. For this honour I'm indebted to my patents and the one who chose this poem for this contest - my inspiration; [a.] Hyderabad City Andhra Pradesh, India

BELCHER, CYNTHIA L.
[pen.] Cyn, Cynt, Cyndi and Eyes; [b.] January 9, 1961, Columbus, OH; [p.] Isaac L. Sr. and Bernice Belcher; [ed.] Franklin Heights High, Military Schools: (PLDC), (BSEP), 2 (AIT's: F1L1O and F2E10), and Basic Training; [occ.] Student at Columbus State Community College; [memb.] "Sister-Friends" and SOAR, organizations that belong to the college I'm presently attending.; [hon.] Numerous Military Awards and Recognition.; [oth. writ.] Several unpublished poems; [pers.] "No matter how rough the road may seem, keep on driving because it's bound to get smooth"... I'm still driving!"; [a.] Columbus, OH

BELFIGLIO, ELLIE K.
[b.] August 16, 1947, Tehran, Iran; [p.] Samad and Zari Kamran; [m.] Valentine J. Belfiglio, October 3, 1993; [ch.] Farokh and Soroush Navid; [ed.] MA in Persian and Russian Literature from the University of Tehran.; [occ.] Couturier; [memb.] Phi Cheta Kappa, Dallas, TX.; [hon.] Being an honor student during my college years enabled me to choose the school I wanted to teach in. I am also granted Phi Cheta Kappa on April 30, 1993 in Dallas, TX.; [oth. writ.] I am currently engaged in writing a novel about my experiences as an immigrant with Political Asylum. Two of my poems have been published in a book entitled Dusting Off Dreams in Texas. I have an upcoming poem which will be published by Quill books in early 1995. Many of my poems and short stories were published in the Persian language in Tehran, while I lived there. My first works a research about Iranian illiteracy. Published when I was seventeen years old.; [pers.] I feel that poetry is the nourishment of the soul.; [a.] Garland, TX

BELL, ELEANOR D.
[pen.] Eleanor D. Bell; [b.] 1917, Philadelphia, PA; [p.] Mr. and Mrs. George H. Saunders; [m.] Alfred D. Bell, January 27, 1937; [ch.] Three; [ed.] Polytechnic High; [occ.] Housewife; [memb.] V.F.W.; [oth. writ.] Small collection of poetry - tilled "Reflections of My Heart".

BELL, GLENNA PEARSON
[b.] October 6, 1970, Fort St. John, Britich Columbia, Canada; [p.] Chris Pearson and Angie Pearson; [m.] Dallas Bell, August 20, 1994; [ed.] North Peace Secondary High School, Fort St. John, BC, College Education in Edmonton, AB (Legal Secretarial); [occ.] Secretary; [hon.] Highest Grade Point Average Award in College, Perfect Attendance Award - College; [oth. writ.] Several poems written during overseas travels - generally about life, love, and friends.; [pers.] I strive to write all my poetry when completely driven by an event which helps the thoughts and words to flow - and always from my heart.; [a.] Valleyview Alberta, Canada

BENDER-BEAUMONT, IRENE G.
[b.] February 22, 1950, San Mateo, CA; [p.] John and Marjorie Negro; [m.] James E. Beaumont, August 22, 1992; [ch.] Colin, Demetria Bianca; [ed.] Sequoia High School, College of San Mateo; [occ.] Housewife; [memb.] International Society of Poetry, American Kennel Club, San Francisco Zoological Society Insider's Money Club; [oth. writ.] Poems published in "Treasured Poems of America", "Dusting Off Dreams", "After The Storm"; [pers.] I strive to let my emotions guide me into relaying my true feelings of the heart. I'm heavily inspired by the ocean, animals (especially mine), true romance and a child's honesty.; [a.] Redwood City, CA

BENDER, BETTY ANN
[pen.] Betty Bender; [b.] August 26, 1947, So Bend, IN; [p.] Mr. and Mrs. R. G. Koranda Sr.; [m.] Bill E. Bender, August 17, 1985 (Deceased); [ch.] Jamie Madeline Bender - 8 yrs.; [ed.] Montclair High, Pasadena City College; [occ.] Owner - small used Merchandise Store; [memb.] Board of Directors Girls and Boys Club, Girl Scout Uniform exchange person.; [pers.] I write about how I feel, what I see, and what I hear. Being a military's wife and living around military personal has influenced my writings.; [a.] Twentynine Palms, CA

BENGE, BEVERLY J.
[pen.] Beverly; [b.] April 15, 1941, Chilliwack, British Columbia, Canada; [p.] Archie and Amelia Cramer; [m.] John Noel Benge, October 8, 1960; [ch.] Deborah, John (Jr.), Ruby, Lola, Raewyn; [ed.] Graduate, Chilliwark, Sr. Sec. School, Univ. Entrance; [occ.] International Executive Secretary; [oth. writ.] Poem published in Canadian Anthology of verse, 1994.; [pers.] "Every good and perfect gift codes from Above", and I am thankful to God for this gift of writing poetry.; [a.] Clearbrook British Columbia, Canada

BENJAMIN, BERNADINE E.
[b.] February 17, 1941, Boston, MA; [p.] John and Azarine G. Abbott (Aunt and Uncle); [ed.] Commerce High School; [occ.] Senior Compensation Claims Clerk; [memb.] Choir St. James, 1. Episcopal Church, 2. Adult Awareness Club Church, 3. Former Glee Club Singer In School, 4. Olympia Sales Cards Order Rep., 5. Former Avon Representative in the President's Club; [hon.] Have honor and sales certificates a letter from my political party of appreciation for voting true to my party; [oth. writ.] Several songs all types with my arrangements only thing I cannot write notes I've been putting them on cassettes for possible getting notes and to be copy righted my attorney will negotiate a possible deal sound of a run away horse melody samples, walts, tango, country Spanish Cha Cha song rock mostly instrumental symphony violin music

BENLIEN, SANDA MAY
[pen.] Sanda Greenway Benlien; [b.] March 23, 1941, San Francisco CA; [p.] (deceased) Ted and Gertrude Greenway; [m.] David Benlien, June 26, 1959; [ch.] Rodney Benlien, Larry Benlien, Rocky Benlien; [ed.] I graduated from Leuzinger High School '59; [occ.] Private housekeeper for the "Wiles Family" in Millbrae, CA; [memb.] Pass membership Zoological Society. I plan to renew my membership; [hon.] Pass Honor's and Awards was in high school for one year "Drill Team" and two year "Flag Girl", "Cert Award and Medal" for drill team and flag girl; [oth. writ.] The Library of Congress, Washington. Has my manuscript on my life title "I was an abused child". I hope will be published in the future; [pers.] "A beautiful smile make's a happy heart"; [a.] Lawndale, CA

BENSON, TERRY
[b.] October 28, 1953, Weyburn, Saskatchewan, Canada; [p.] Arthur and Dorothy Hennie; [m.] Ross Benson, December 11, 1982; [ch.] Blair Adrienne; [ed.] Yellow Grass High - Grade 12 Academic Alberta Hospital Ponoka - Psychiatric Nursing Diploma; [occ.] Coordinator of Dementia Care Parkland Regional Care Centre, Melfort Saskatchewan, Canada; [memb.] Saskatchewan Psychiatric Nurses' Association, Saskatchewan Alzheimers' Association, Saskatchewan Dementia Care Resource Group; [oth. writ.] I have a personal collection of poems and song lyrics which I have written over the years. The Hired Hand is from this collection.; [pers.] Poetry, like music is a universal language I draw from life experience in my poetry and lyrics. My goal is to publish a collection of my work.; [a.] Melfort, Canada

BERENTSEN, DOROTHY
[pen.] Haryott Stevens; [occ.] Writer; [oth. writ.] "Sleeping Lady at Sunrise" A book of poetry published in New York, "Adoration" published in Mexico City (poetry); [pers.] I have traveled extensively to many countries. I am currently writing a book of short stories for children. If I can give pleasure in my writing, then it is well worth the time and effort.

BERG, LINDA
[pen.] Lynn; [b.] February 26, 1955, Glen Oaks, NY; [p.] Peter Berg, Barbara Berg; [ed.] Rosemary-Choate (H.S.) Skidmore College, NYU (B.A.) Gallatin Division, 20 credits toward M.A. Gallatin Division; [occ.] Actress, Artist, Music Student; [memb.] A.R.E., Recovery Project Return Players (Stigma Busters); [hon.] Art exhibitions at Tompkins Square, Fletcher Farm (Ludlow, Vermont), Torn Awning Gallery (New York City), Award for Faithful Volunteer work at Holy Apostles Church Chelsea Prize for Premier Performance for Project Return Players.; [oth. writ.] PTP Journal, A.R.E., Community Newsletter Project Return Newsletter; [pers.] My personal note really is a cliche, but I just wanted to write that people should be sensitive to each other, and as it written in the Bible "Treat Thy Neighbor as Thyself."; [a.] New York City, NY

BERGER, JEFFREY
[pen.] J. Berg; [b.] October 5, 1960, Milwaukee; [p.] Donald Berger, Charlotte Berger; [m.] Julie Anne, May 5, 1995; [ch.] Colton Blue; [ed.] Custer High School; [occ.] Diemaker/Drafts Person; [oth. writ.] Over fifty unpublished poems and lyric arrangements.; [pers.] As an aspiring lyricist, I find putting words to melody both natural and invigorating.; [a.] New Berlin, WI

BERLIN, DEAN EDWARD
[pen.] Tranx; [b.] January, 20, 1978, London, England; [p.] Heather Berlin and Everton Berlin; [ed.] King Edwards VI Grammar, Aston, Eng. Good Counsel High; [occ.] Student; [memb.] National Honor Society, School Forensics Team, School Newspaper Staff; [hon.] National Catholic Forensics League National Tournament Contestant MS 150K Bike Tour Completed; [oth. writ.] Several un-published poems one short story and novelette, a few have been published in the School Literary Magazine, Austringer; [pers.] We are alone in the world. Our curse is to give definite meaning to an ultimately futile and meaningless existence. In my poetry I try to reflect this sense of loneliness and despair, as if estranged in an ocean of darkness. I have been influenced by my friends, author Albert Comus and songwriter Robert Smith.; [a.] Silver Spring, MD

BERNSTEIN, NANCY G.
[b.] July 14, 1945, Detroit, MI; [p.] Sol C. Grossman M.D., Pauline F. Grossman MSW, BCD; [ch.] Julia Lynn, Stefannie Leigh; [ed.] Mumford High School (Detroit, Michigan), BA: University of Michigan Ann Arbor Michigan. MSW: University of Chicago, Chicago, Illinois School of Social Service Administration; [occ.] Psychiatric Social Worker, Northridge Hospital Medical Center and Private Practice; [memb.] 1. National Assoc. of Social workers, 2. Academy of certified Social Workers (ACSW), 3. Member: The Society for Clinician Social Work, 4. Board Certifies Diplomate in Clinical Social Work, 5. Life Secondary Teaching Credential, 6. Member: American Assoc. of Spinal Cord Injury Psychologists and Social Workers.; [hon.] 1. Phi Beta Kappa, 2. Pi Lambda Theta (National Education Honorary), 3. James B. Angell Scholar (University of Michigan), 4. Mortar Board (Senior Women's Honorary at University of Michigan).; [oth. writ.] Have not published anything I've written before.; [pers.] I was an English Major as an undergraduate and went into Social Work to help children with learning difficulties and family problems. My writing tries to reflect some insight into personal and family dynamics.; [a.] Tarzana, CA

BERRY, DONIELLE L.
[pen.] Dawn or Miss Dawn; [b.] June 6, 1982, Columbus, OH; [p.] Dorothea L. Bunch; [ed.] Clinton Middle School Grade 7; [pers.] I have been greatly influence by Maya Angelou; [a.] Columbus, OH

BICKETT, AMY MARIE
[b.] November 7, 1979, Gary, IN; [p.] Elizabeth Bickett, Chris Hollar; [occ.] School

BIERBAUM, JULIA ANNE
[b.] December 28, 1919, Corsicana, TX; [p.] Lola and Elbert Williams; [m.] Tibor Bierbaum, October 19, 1962; [ch.] Steve, Karan Sue; [ed.] Highland Park High School, Dallas Texas Graduated 1936, SMU Graduated 1940; [occ.] Housewife, Husband's secretary, Artist; [memb.] Sigma Kappa Sorority, Eastern Star, St. Peter's Lutheran Church, Humane Society; [oth. writ.] Several poems published in U.S. Army news papers while living in Germany.; [pers.] I support my husband's work at the high school where the teaches and is Commander of the JROTC.; [a.] Fort Wayne, IN

BIGGS, R. TIPTON
[pen.] R. Tipton Biggs; [b.] August 18, 1939, Arbela, MO; [p.] Robert E. and Martha A. Biggs; [m.] C. Maureen O'Brien, November 25, 1961; [ch.] Christopher, Adrienne, Erik; [ed.] B.S. of Ed. NE MO State Univ.

MA Univ of NE at Lincoln; [occ.] Professor Of Communication and Drama Iowa Western Comm. College - Council Bluffs, IA; [memb.] Willa Cather Pioneer Memorial, N.E.A, I.S.E.A., Several Genealogical Societies; [hon.] Acting and Directing and Designing Awards in Local Community Theatre groups.; [oth. writ.] Many poems, stories, essays, Three Musical plays; [pers.] Poetry is the high art of literature - the best we can get. It is language in its Sunday best. [a.] Omaha, NE

BIGHAM, H. P.
[pen.] Patrick Howard; [b.] November 15, 1948, Omaha, NE; [m.] Divorced; [ch.] Annette and Andrea; [ed.] BSE University of Nebraska at Omaha Major - English Minor - Humanities; [occ.] Executive Recruiter and Consultant; [memb.] American Heart Association, American Cancer Society; [oth. writ.] Published poems with sports themes and marketed them successfully; [pers.] I enjoy writing poetry on numerous subjects particularly loved and personal achievement I also enjoy writing song lyrics; [a.] Omaha, NE

BINET, JULIE
[b.] May 29, 1978, Three Hills, Alberta, Canada; [p.] John and Marla Binet; [ed.] I go to Prourie High School in Three Hills, AB. I'm in grade II.; [occ.] I work as a waitress part-time.; [oth. writ.] I've written some other poems, but I've never been published. I suppose it's just been a hobby. I didn't really think I had any talent.; [pers.] I'm a christian, I believe in Jesus Christ who died for my sins. I know I'm going to heaven. I have a wonderful, loving God who is always faithful.; [a.] Three Hills Alberta, Canada

BIONDE, MARY JANET
[pen.] M. J. Barclay; [b.] June 11, 1936, Selmer, TN; [p.] Boyol and Bertha Barclay; [ch.] Keith, Maria Lisa, Dionne Isadora; [ed.] Salisbury State College, Salisbury MD, California State University, Northridge, CA, University Southern California, Los Angeles, CA; [occ.] Program Coordinator; [memb.] Easter Seal Society; [pers.] Like my namesake, my grandmother, I have always written as an expression of feelings rather than for publication. Although, since childhood, an occasional piece has been published. My writing comes from the heart and is always a reflection of some fragment of my life.

BIRON, BRENDA
[b.] August 8, 1961, Ontario, Canada; [p.] Ken and Shirley Biron; [ed.] Webster University in Vienna, Austria. I received my Bachelor of Arts Degree in International Economy; [occ.] Director of Building Management; [memb.] 1. Writer's Federation of New Brunswick, 2. Romance Writers of America; [hon.] Howard Grimmar Prize, Honours: Dean's List, University of New Brunswick, Fredericton; [oth. writ.] Poems published in The Cormorant, Saint John's Literary Magazine; [pers.] The clearest path toward truth is honesty; [a.] Saint John New Brunswick, Canada

BISHOP, DONNA LYNN
[b.] October 11, 1966, Pittsburgh, PA; [p.] William and Nancy Jackson; [m.] William H. Bishop, December 31, 1992; [ch.] William H, Richard Allen, and Bobbi Jean; [ed.] Gateway High School, Boyce Campus and Western School of Business; [occ.] Nursing Assistant, Jacktown Manor.; [memb.] I am a social member for #3 Firchall of Monroeville.; [oth. writ.] I have written other poem but nothing printed.; [pers.] I have been writing any kind of poem since High School. And also I started writing more and more poems after I lost my best friend, my grandma, Jackson. This poem is for her!; [a.] Turtle Creek, PA

BITTARELLI, ANTONIO
[b.] February 16, 1941, Italy; [p.] Oreste, Rachelle Bittarelli; [m.] Milly, August 17, 1971; [ch.] Teddy, Damari

BLACK, ELVA P.
[pen.] Ellie B.; [b.] June 13, 1936, Bayhead, Nova Scotia, Canada; [p.] Archie C. MacDonald, Pearl B. (Pipes) MacDonald; [m.] Roy E. Black, January 17, 1959; [ch.] James R., Joel C., Janie E.; [ed.] Grade XI Rayhead Elementary School and Tatamagouche Rural High School Nova Scotia, Canada.; [occ.] General Worker Mt. Pleasant Lodge for elderly; [memb.] St. Andrews Presbyterian Church in Riverview N.S. Canada; [oth. writ.] Many songs and poems never submitted and some short stories; [pers.] I like to write about life and every day happenings - as I see it.; [a.] Port Howe Nova Scotia, Canada

BLACKHURST, REBECCA
[b.] October 10, 1972, Rochford, England; [p.] Phillip and Patricia Blackhurst; [ed.] Elmhurst Ballet School - England, English International College - Spain; [occ.] Secretary/Admin., BZW Securities Limited London; [memb.] The Poetry Library, Royal Festival Hall, South Bank Centre, London; [oth. writ.] Alot of poetry on many subjects and several short science fiction stories; [pers.] It's so important to believe in yourself no matter what others think - to listen to yourself and most importantly to trust yourself.; [a.] London, England

BLAIR, MARILYN
[b.] August 7, 1951, Charleston, WV; [p.] John C. McIntosh, Dorothy D. McIntosh; [m.] Howard W. Blair, June 29, 1974; [ch.] Deanna, Jesse; [ed.] University of North Carolina at Chapel Hill; [occ.] Computer Software development; [memb.] First Baptist Church Morganton, NC.; [hon.] National Conference of Christians and Jews - Distinguished Merit Citation.; [oth. writ.] Working on a Children's Book, poems published locally; [pers.] I'm still trying to figure out life - I do it better with a pen and paper handy. My music - piano, flute - help too. Faith helps the most. [a.] Valdese, NC

BLANFORD, PEGGY ANN
[b.] December 26, 1939, New Mexico; [p.] T.J. Edwards, Eiffie Edwards; [m.] Charles O'Blanford, February 18, 1968; [ch.] Juanita, James, Lawrence, Lance; [ed.] High School (12 yrs.); [occ.] Precision Optical Tech.; [oth. writ.] In memory of my mother, Eiffie Ola Edwards born January 28, 1905 died December 19, 1994. Eight children grand great grandchildren Homemaker - woman of the earth; [pers.] I always have other people's feelings and thoughts when I write, but you have to know yourself before you can feel for other people; [a.] Gleen Heights, TX

BLASINGINI, JULIA V.
[pen.] Jewel; [b.] March 15, 1944, Amarillo, TX; [p.] Daniel Townsend, Bette Townsend; [m.] John, November 15, 1974; [oth. writ.] Many other drafts of poems based on personal experiences, moods, and requests from others; [pers.] My poems and writings are based solely on my emotional state at the time I write them. Through the writings I can see, sometimes, who I really am, or what to be.; [a.] Houston, TX

BLIZZARD, F. ANDREA
[b.] February 03, 1926, Sciotoville, OH; [p.] John Rice, Catherine Rice; [m.] Franklin Blizzard, January 4, 1946 (Deceased); [ch.] Franklin Jr., Rosanna, Marlene and Retha; [ed.] Green Township Elem. and Grade 6, Junior High Franklin Furnace, Ohio, Adrian High 'Adult-Ed.' Adrian, Michigan; [occ.] Retired; [memb.] Adrian Church of Christ; [oth. writ.] Numerous of poems, song poems, and the beginning of my autobiography; [pers.] I strive with all of my being to show my love for my God and Creator my Lord and Savior Jesus Christ, my beloved family, friends, for all mankind and for my love of nature to shine through my poetry. That the world might know that there is but one God and without Him, my life would be empty and void. I have always loved poetry and have always admired such writers as Alfred, Lord Tennyson Robert, Louis Stevenson Elizabeth Barrett Browning; [a.] Manhou Beach, MI

BLOCH, LUPE
[b.] March 26, 1928, Madrid, NM; [m.] Louis Bloch (Deceased); [ed.] High School graduate; [occ.] Retired; [hon.] Honorable mention at writer's conference for poetry.; [oth. writ.] Children's stories which I have not yet submitted.; [pers.] We all need the healing power of humor ... and of beauty.; [a.] Thousand Oaks, CA

BLOSE, BOBBIE
[pen.] Sarge; [b.] September 2, 1938, Nowata, OK; [p.] Homer and Gertrude Blose; [m.] Diana L. Blose, May 28, 1993; [ch.] Bobbie Jr., Jerry, Anna; [ed.] 12 yrs. (GED) 2 yrs. Col U.S. Army Transportation School Ft Eustis, VA Traffic Management - Cargo Handler - Carpenter - Welding VO Tech - Post Master - Shipping and Receiving.; [occ.] Retired Army SSG; [memb.] 32nd Degree Mason Day Post #9 VFW 1320 In Sapulpa OK. BMI Nashville, Tenn.; [hon.] Letters of Commendations National Defense, Good Conduct (4th Award) Armed Forces Expeditionary Medal, Army Accommodation Medal (2nd Award) Vietnam Service - Vietnam Campaign - Vietnam Cross of Gallantry with Palm - Expert Rifle Badge - Master Paratroops Wings - President Unit Citation, Purple Heart; [oth. writ.] Let me talk to your heart, I knew from the beginning, she couldn't have loved us at all, never too late to forgive, loves like a water faucet.; [pers.] I just write as to what I feel in my heart and sometimes as to how I feel about my wife. I've always liked to write.; [a.] Sapulpa, OK

BLUM, ELLEN
[pen.] C. D. Roll; [b.] February 10, 1955, Chicago, IL; [p.] Ernest Kresen, Beatrice Kresen Smith; [m.] Steven Blum, January 20, 1984; [ch.] Lorri Lynn (Step-daughter); [ed.] Grace Lutheran Grade School Roosevelt High School; [occ.] On medical leave from position as manager in a convenience store.; [pers.] Most of my work reflects memories from my past and my perception of the hidden meanings in people's actions.; [a.] Baraboo, WI

BOBULA, SHARON LEE
[b.] July 6, 1949, Memphis, TN; [p.] Myrtle Marie McCarty, James Walter McCarty; [m.] Steven, December 7, 1985; [ed.] Roosevelt University; [occ.] Corporate Trainer, Quill Corporation; [hon.] Dean's List, 1st place City Wide Speech Contest; [oth. writ.] Many - none of which have been published. This is the first time I have shared any of my writings with anyone but family and friends.; [pers.] To share love, light and insight to every person and situation I may encounter along life's journey.; [a.] Buffalo Grove, IL

BODANZA, CHRISTOPHER L.
[b.] February 28, 1973, Quincy, FL; [p.] Ann C. Cox, John F. Bodanza; [ed.] Wildwood High School, Drexel University; [occ.] Graphic Artist; [memb.] Phi Kappa Sima National Fraternity; [oth. writ.] Several poems published in local journals; [pers.] Planning your entire life out ahead of you condemns you to a series of routines. Where you are now is just as important as where you are going to be.; [a.] Philadelphia, PA

BODEN, CLAUDIA JANE
[b.] July 16, 1955, San Bernardino, CA; [p.] Robert M. Shafor and Joyce E. Shafor; [ch.] Matthew Tyler Boden; [ed.] Katela High; [occ.] Administrative Assistant, Home Bank, Irvine, CA; [pers.] I dedicate my first publication to my family and friends for their unending love and support and I thank God for all of my blessings.; [a.] Irvine, CA

BODFISH, M.D. RALPH E.
[b.] January 24, 1922, Denver, CO; [p.] Thomas H. and Jessie L. Bodfish; [ch.] Todd McClellan and Timothy Scott Bodfish; [ed.] B.A. Duke Univ., 1949, MD., Emory Univ. Sch. of Medicine, 1954, Internship and Residency at Long Beach VA Med. Center, Flight Surgeon training, Sch. of Aerospace Med., San Antonio, 1970.; [occ.] Physician (Retired); [memb.] American College of Physicians (Fellow); [hon.] Who's Who in America, Who's Who in California, American Men and Women in Science, International Who's Who in Medicine.; [oth. writ.] Numerous publications in Medical journals on such topics as pituitary/thyroid function, radiation physics, renal assessment in spinal cord injury, treatment of thyroid cancer, alteration of metabolism in treating pulmonary insufficiency.; [pers.] Most of my experience with writing has been limited to a world of cells, enzymes and nuclear particles, without a hint of emotion. What a pleasure it is to explore a world which invites warmth of language in its description.; [a.] Los Alamitos, CA

BOGOMOLNY, ABBY LYNN
[b.] February 17, 1953, Brooklyn, NY; [p.] Frances Bogomolny and Sam Bogomolny; [ed.] B.A.: Brooklyn College, M.A.: San Francisco State University; [oth. writ.] Nauseous In Paradise: Poetry and Photographs from her books, Black of Moonlit Sea: Poetry from the Mist from WIM Publications, and People Who Do Not Exist from Burning Bush, PO Box 7361, Santa Cruz, CA 95061; [pers.] Writing of personal and planetary importance that celebrates multiple perspectives.; [a.] Santa Cruz, CA

BOLANOS, ROBERTA
[b.] February 14, 1954, Indio, CA; [p.] Henrietta Souice; [ch.] Samantha Bolanos [ed.] Oxnard High School California State - Northridge; [occ.] Receptionist - San Ysidro Mental Health Clinic, San Ysidro, CA; [pers.] Unfortunately, sensitivity, with life's experiences has turned me to write poems. I say unfortunately because not all experiences have a happy ending, only a happy beginning.; [a.] Chula Vista, CA

BOLDEN, BECKY J.
[pen.] BJ; [b.] September 8, 1944, Buffalo, NY; [p.] Thomas and Bessie Robinson; [m.] Curt, Divorced; [ch.] Tony, Scott and Phil; [ed.] 2 years College - Respiratory Cure Practitioner, Bennett High; [occ.] Respiratory Cure Practitioner; [memb.] MSRT, AARP, St. John United Methodist Church. American Heart Assoc.;[hon.] To be considered for the International Society of Poets (94-95) and to be a finalist in the last contest!; [oth. writ.] "Let the Sun Shine In" several songs and other poetry - short story.; [pers.] 1. Love is a necessity, just as the air we breath and the water we need. In the Climax of a loving act time seems to stand stall. 2. God is love and has not He promised us Eternity!??; [a.] Waterford, MI

BONANNO, NATALIE
[b.] July 3, 1981, Madison, WI; [p.] Sam and Connie Bonanno; [ed.] Kings Grant Elem., Hines Middle School; [occ.] Student; [memb.] Swim team, 1st chair viola player.; [hon.] School awards.; [oth. writ.] I've written many poems but this is the first one that I've entered in a contest.; [pers.] I admire the writings and books by Jack London and how he puts such simple things so elegantly.; [a.] Newport News, VA

BOONE, MELANIE R.
[pen.] Dietrich Scott Kuhlman; [b.] December 21, 1975, Macon, MO; [p.] Rhonda J. Mullins, Charles A. Boone; [ed.] Macon Sr. High; [hon.] 3rd Place in National Art Honor Society CCC District Contest in Computer Graphics, 3rd Place in VICA District Contest in Graphic Arts (written contest); [oth. writ.] I have written other poems although this is my first publication.; [pers.] I enjoy writing poems even though I have always wanted to become a photographer or something to do with Graphic Arts. I think people should pursue all of their talents instead of just one.; [a.] Macon, MO

BORDEN, CAROL A.
[b.] November 4, 1971, Cleveland OH; [p.] Sharon Rodriguez, Calvin Borden; [ch.] James Honaker Jr.; [ed.] M.T.I. Business College South High School; [occ.] Medical Assistant; [memb.] American Association of Medical Assistants; [hon.] Dean's List; [oth. writ.] Poetry published in the National Library of Poetry's book of anthologies, Journey of the Mind.; [pers.] My writings can take me to far away places, enable me to dream impossible dreams and feel emotions that ones heart only aches to feel.; [a.] Cleveland, OH

BORENSTEIN, ENID
[b.] September 21, 1951, Bronx, NY; [p.] Harold and Lilian Goodmar; [m.] Stanley Borenstein, March 28, 1976 (Separated); [ch.] Sherri Scott and Dawn; [ed.] Kindergarten to High School; [occ.] Clerk Typist and Tax Assistant for Bank of America; [oth. writ.] I helped my children with book reports and compositions for school.; [pers.] I want to thank my daughter Sherri for helping me understand I could write poetry, my daughter Sherri is also very good in poetry.; [a.] Bronx, NY

BORTOLOT, IRENE
[b.] August 21, 1923, New York; [p.] Antonio and Marianna Tognieri; [m.] Deceased, August 23, 1947; [ch.] 42 years old Precious Downs Syndrome; [ed.] Highs School, Medical Record Librarian, Nurse; [occ.] Recently Retired, Following a tenure of 52 yrs. in hospitals; [memb.] Senior Group, Alhambra Comm. Hosp., California, Porcelaine Artists Society, International Society of Poets, Whittier Art Association, Special Olympics; [hon.] Plaques issued in 1979- 1989-1991 with commendations for Hospital participation; [oth. writ.] Accumulation of over 250 poems written by me thru the years in hopes of future publication, creative designs in cards and calendars with my own poetic phrases sold and given thru the years. Paid my way thru NRSG. School selling close to 200 paintings (of which I have photo copies). Capping speech on graduating from NRSG School.; [pers.] My heritage and love of family and friends have given me the inspiration and courage to believe when a heart learns how to feel and care it has nourished the ability to reflect in my paintings and poems an appreciation for the beauty of nature and life.; [a.] Azusa, CA

BOSIRE, JANE N.*
[b.] 1961, Kissi; [p.] Rispur Mbone, Ezekiel Bosire; [ch.] Millicent Kerubo; [ed.] Nyanchwa Advertist Sec. School, Gusii Institute of Technology, Secretarial College; [occ.] Secretary; [pers.] It is a good idea always for one to be ambitious in writing.; [a.] Maseno, Kenya

BOSSE, JOAN
[pen.] Joan of Arc.; [b.] April 19, 1921, Spalding, Saskatchewan, Canada; [p.] F. Xavier Bouchard and Martine; [m.] Roland Bosse, October 27, 1942; [ch.] 4 children "adopted"; [ed.] Grade 7 when I had to quit school at 13 yrs. Took correspondence to grade 9 level in literature and English, that was in St. Front.; [occ.] Housewife, retired from librarian in Kelvington after 16 yrs. there.; [memb.] C.W.L. in Parish of Perigord. Library Board in Kelvington.; [hon.] Beautiful plaque from the Library Board upon my retirement in Kelvington.; [oth. writ.] I wrote some local news for newspapers for several years. When working as librarian I used to send an article in the paper every week, with review sketch on 3 books to encourage folks to borrow the books. Our children helped us celebrate our 50th W.A. with our friends and most of our relatives. It was very rewarding.; [a.] Kelvington Saskatchewan, Canada

BOSZ, SHASTA
[pen.] Shasta Lyn; [b.] April 12, 1982, Orange, CA; [p.] Vicki and Gary Bosz; [ed.] Santiago Hills Elementary, Sierra Vista Middle School; [memb.] National Charity League; [hon.] Honor Roll, (Santiago Hills Elementary and Sierra Vista Middle School); [oth. writ.] Several poems published in other anthologies.; [pers.] Animals and nature, I feel are very inspiring because they tend to show a side of life that humans don't often see.; [a.] Irvine CA

BOTTAZZO, ETTA
[pen.] Ruth Nick; [b.] August 8, 1911, Nutenburgh, PA; [p.] Clyde Nicodmus, Martha Bracken; [m.] John Bottazzo, June 27, 1931(Deceased); [ch.] Elizabeth Larue, Timothy John; [ed.] High School graduates Penticostal Church and Boces also F.H.L studied; [hon.] 1 poem submitted to Marinott Hotel won 1st place won $50.00 I have tried to equal my Lord.; [oth. writ.] I have written numerous poems and three stories I haven't had any experienced in public writing this is the second time I have mentioned I have written anything.; [a.] Honeoye, NY

BOYCE, CARRIE E.
[pen.] Ellen Carey; [b.] January 2, 1960, CA; [p.] Noreen and Charles; [occ.] Telecommunications Tech.; [oth. writ.] Personal poems and songs dating back to childhood.; [pers.] Loneliness is something one creates. Without it, we can get by. With it, our days and nights are long.; [a.] Albuquerque, NM

BOYCE, JOHN
[pen.] Kenny; [b.] October 12, 1962, Barbados, West Indies; [p.] Glevare and Audrey; [m.] Nola Boyce, August 20, 1994; [ch.] Neil, Ashron, Imani and Holly; [ed.] Modern High; [occ.] Maintenance (Painter) etc., Long Beach New York; [oth. writ.] Several unpublished poems; [pers.] Writing about nature and reality is the best way to send a message to people. Life is like a brick

wall, sometimes it crumbles at times it fall. Being creative is my influenced in life.; [a.] Brooklyn, NY

BOYD, IAN
[b.] May 26, 1967, St. Catharines, Ontario, Canada; [p.] Janis Webber, Robert Boyd; [ed.] B.A. - University of Western Ontario, B.L.S. and Teacher Certification, University of Maine at Presque Isle.; [occ.] Teacher of 8th Grade, Math, Science, Braille, and High School Special Education.; [oth. writ.] Essay for United Nations Conference in Ottawa - ON DEATH AND DYING, Lyrics performed by Jacquie Henderson - St Catharines Ontario; [pers.] That I may know Him and the power of His resurrection and the fellowship of His suffering.; [a.] L'Amable Ontario, Canada

BOYD, KIMBERLEY
[b.] February 10, 1974; [p.] Ken and Brenda Boyd; [occ.] Student; [hon.] 1. Who's Who Among American High School Students 1990/91 and 1991/92, 2. Certificate of Merit from Assembly of New York State at graduation, 3. N.Y.S. Regents Diploma, 4. High School Honor Award for maintaining honor grades in English, Music and Language.; [pers.] When life overwhelms you, as it often will, sometimes your only choice is to wrap up in the night and disappear.; [a.] Niagara Falls, NY

BOYD, MICHAEL
[pen.] Mike Boyd; [b.] September 14, 1978, Wyandanch, NY; [p.] Robert Boyd, Annebelle Graham; [ed.] Wyandanch High School; [memb.] Youth group, Faith Tabernacle Church; [pers.] I strive to be me. For the past is history and the future's a mystery, so just take each day for all you can. I was inspired by all the ladies who said they'll never find the right man.; [a.] Wyandanch, NY

BOYDEN, CHRISTOPHER W.
[pen.] Zeek, Zeke; [b.] January 4, 1952, Orange, CA; [ed.] Secondary, Phillips Andover Academy '70 (B.A.) Fairleigh Dickenson Univ. Madison, NJ '75, (J.D.) Sterum Hall Univ. School of Law '78; [occ.] Attorney at Law, North Palm Beach. FL.; [memb.] New Jersey Bar Assn., Florida Bar Assn., American Bar Assn., Palm Beach Country Bar Assn. (FL); [hon.] Fairleigh Dickenson Poetry Contest 1st Place 1974, Fairleigh Dickenson Univiversity "Magna Cum Laude" with University honors in Political Science (Dean's List 4 years), Seton Hall University School of Law "Cum Laude"; [oth. writ.] "The See-Saw of Life" (poem), "Why?" (poem), "Sunny and Warm" (poem), "Without You" (poem), "As You Sit There" (poem), "God Created Evolution, So Why All The Fuss?" (Article); [pers.] I seek to comprehend that certain grandeur, in this dimension of life, which maintains the ethereal balance with the many others, all in balance, arrayed across imanity.; [a.] North Palm Beach, FL

BOZYK, LISA BARBARA JORDANA
[pen.] Lisa De Bozy; [b.] Montreal, Quebec, Canada; [p.] Dr. Sana Bozyk Ph.D and Dr. Johannes Alexander Bozyk M.D.; [ed.] B.A. in French and M.A. Italian from Middlebury College, Vermont U.S.A. Professor of Modern Languages.; [occ.] Freelance painter and writer of poetry and prose.; [memb.] Friends of the Library, Blyth Theater, Gallery Stratford, London's Single's Gourmet Club.; [oth. writ.] "Peplexiity", "My Prodigal Muse", "Destination Nowhere", "Kaleidoscope", "Cahier De la Femme", American Poetry Anthology 1983 (p. 183); [pers.] "A young person expressing the daily perplexed sufferings of life, while searching continuously for the good in man."; [a.] Wingham Ontario, Canada

BRADLEY, JENNIFER
[b.] February 4, 1970, South County, RI; [p.] Ernesta Fragnito, James E. Bradley; [ed.] Attended Pennsylvania State Univ. for 1 year. Now taking classes part-time at Temple University.; [occ.] Receptionist, I also work part-time as a nail technician.; [memb.] International Thespian Society, Troupe #1154 of Springfield Twp. Senior High School, Montgomery County, PA.; [oth. writ.] I have written numerous poems, however none have ever been printed. I write a column for my company's newspaper.; [pers.] I mainly write for myself, whatever I am thinking for feeling at the time. I hope that my work reaches out to people and that they are able to fully understand it.; [a.] Oreland, PA

BRADSHAW, WILMA
[b.] October 16, 1917, Crosby Co., TX; [p.] Jack and Viva (Mc Daniel) Griffin; [m.] Joseph Kenton Bradshaw, December 24, 1954; [ch.] One son, two daughters; [ed.] High School 1936; [occ.] Retired Housewife; [memb.] First United Methodist Church, Order of Eastern Star, United Daughters of the Confederacy; [hon.] 1st, 2nd, third place in Amateur Oil Painting, 2nd, third, Honorable Mention in Fabric Painting; [oth. writ.] Family History; [pers.] If anyone else can accomplish anything, artistically, then if I strive hard enough, I can achieve a semblance of the same. We must use the talents we have for the benefit of others; [a.] Springtown, TX

BRANAM, NANCY J.
[b.] March 1, 1943, Salamanca, NY; [p.] Fred and Ruby Woodworth; [m.] Billy Ray Branam, March 24, 1984; [ed.] Salamanca Central Florida University-Division of continuing education; [occ.] Assistant Waste water Treatment Plant Operator; [memb.] Zion Evangelical Church-Creative Writers Group Of Salamanca; [hon.] Boces Graduate Creative Writing; [oth. writ.] Short Stories Published in local-papers-plus poems; [pers.] If I can help just one person laugh or step over a hurdle in their life, then I know my God given talent wasn't wasted; [a.] Salamanca, NY

BRANHAM, TERRI JO
[b.] January 5, 1962, CA; [p.] James B. Kimsey, Mary G. Kimsey; [m.] John E. Branham Jr., December 13, 1982; [ch.] Brittany, Javan, Emily; [ed.] Bonanza High School, Southern Nevada Vocational Technical Center; [occ.] Mommy and Wife, Cosmetologist; [a.] Prestonsburg, KY

BRATHWAITE, YVONNE CECILY
[pen.] Cecily; [b.] November 29, 1937, Barbados; [ch.] 1 son; [ed.] Lynch's Secondary School St Michael Barbados. Harrow Hospital, Harrow Middlesex England, Woking Maternity Hospital, Surrey England; [occ.] Health Sister R.N. St Michael, Polyclinic Barbados; [memb.] Women's Auxiliary St Michaels, Cathedral. AIDS Society of Barbados, Barbados Registered Nurses Association; [oth. writ.] Poem published in the public health nursing magazine several other poems not published; [pers.] I do the best that I can do and be the best that I can be always.

BRAY, SHAWN D.
[pen.] Shawn D. Bray; [b.] October 29, 1978, Merced, CA; [p.] Hershel and Shirley Bray; [ed.] High School on the sophomore level; [occ.] Student and food service; [memb.] Art club; [hon.] Every year Honor Roll and an Academic letter.; [pers.] Live while you are Living; [a.] Goodyear, AZ

BRIAN, BEVERLY JOAN
[pen.] Beverly Joan Brian; [b.] February 1, 1935, Portchester, NY; [p.] John and Mildred Kozik; [m.] Never married; [ed.] High School U.S., two years in London, England, went to Royal Academy of Music and Drama for one year. I hung out at museums and art galleries, went the old Vic once a month.; [occ.] I worked as an actress, singer, dancer for many years. At present I am still recovering from a very serious car crash in 1991.; [memb.] I'm not a joiner. I'm a passionate Individualist! [oth. writ.] Unfinished novel "The Wild Garden" I always have poems in progress. Fell deeply in love with Shakespeare.

BRIDGES, CARLTON
[pen.] The Bull; [b.] October 10, 1961, Gaffney, SC; [p.] Carl and Lois Bridges; [m.] Donna Ann Bridges, July 15, 1981; [ch.] Carlton Jr., Clayton, Christy; [ed.] Gaffney High School Spartanburg Technical College Professional Career Development Institute, Atlanta, GA; [occ.] Diesel Specialist Group leader Overnite Trans. Co.; [memb.] American Armwrestling Association, Concord Baptist Church; [hon.] Jefferson Award. Given by the National Institute of Public Service through WBTU Channel 3 in Charlotte, NC, Adopt A - Highway and Community Coordinator.; [oth. writ.] Health and Fitness Columnist once with the Gaffney Ledger now with the Cherokee Chronicle. Certified Personal Trainer and Nutritionist.; [pers.] If your mind can conceive it and your heart can believe it then you can achieve it, that's mind over matter; [a.] Gaffney, SC

BRIGGS, KRISTIE
[b.] September 30, 1979, Wilmington, DE; [p.] Larry and Mary Lou Briggs; [ed.] Avon Grove High School; [occ.] High school student; [memb.] Student Council; [hon.] Distinguished Honor Roll, Diretor's Award for Band, Principal's Award; [oth. writ.] Staff member for the high school newspaper.; [pers.] Life is not always what one wants it to be, but to make the best of it as it is, is the only way of being happy. J. Churchill; [a.] West Grove, PA

BRIGHTSTAR, QOESHEN RAINBOW
[pen.] Destiny, Qu, Zoel, Brightstar; [b.] April 23, 1949, Kamloops, British Columbia, Canada; [p.] Frank and Thelma Roberts; [m.] Divorced twice; [ch.] Melanie, Eric, Crystal, Emerald and Clint - all last name Morris; [ed.] Grade 11 J.L. Jackson High, Salmon Arm BC - Presently taking courses, in Metaphysical Science, from The International University of Metaphysics Study for Doctoral Degree And Masters.; [occ.] Homamaker, own small home business, Prince of Peace Enterprises; [memb.] Rosicrucian Order, AMORC, Urantta Foundation (Dues are Behind); [hon.] Received "Best In School" trophy for Art in Grade 10, Jackson High School; [oth. writ.] Have written over forty poems, many are of a spiritual nature, others family, pets, snow, farmers, etc., also world conditions. I also write non fictional. Informational papers, usually spiritual or religious in nature.; [pers.] I am inspired to write. When I enjoy nature, when I hear the news. I write about world conditions. I love the world and am filled will compassion for others and a desire to help any way I can. I wish to help as many as I can, out of poverty, while I am here.; [a.] Enderby British Columbia, Canada

BRITT, BRANDIE JEAN
[pen.] Evalina Louise; [b.] 15 yrs. old; [p.] Charles and Sheree Britt; [ed.] Currently a Sophomore in Heritage Christian School; [occ.] Student; [memb.] Year book

committee AWANA Clubs; [hon.] AWANA: Sprint Award - Excellence Award - Timothy Award - Meritorious Award - Church Camp Most Athletic Female - Academic Letter in High School - seven years of Soccer Trophies Baseball trophy.; [oth. writ.] Many short stories for school - book in progress - other poems - reports - essays etc.; [pers.] I try to live my life for the Lord. Hoping that my works will influence others in their walk. We have to remember to do our best at everything and "we can do all things through Christ who gives us strength."; [a.] San Diego, CA

BRITT, EDDIE
[b.] March 23, 1930, Glace Bay, Nova Scotia, Canada; [p.] Edward Britt, Ada Britt (Deceased); [m.] Barbara, September 10, 1958; [ch.] Edward Charles, Donald John; [ed.] New Aberdeen Public, I left school after grade nine to take machinist trade - which I worked at for 40 years to retirement.; [occ.] Retired; [memb.] Social action (helping seniors), Glace Bay Seniors Skating Club, Glace Bay Historical Society; [hon.] In recognition of contributions the therapeutic, recreational and social activities program of Seaview Manor, Glace Bay, Nova Scotia, April 21, 1994.; [oth. writ.] My poetry has appeared in the local newspaper (Coastal Courieu) for the past twelve years.; [pers.] I am a great fan of Poet Robert Burns. From reading his poetry I learned how to put some words together and write my own poetry.; [a.] Glace Bay Nova Scotia, Canada

BRITT, MICHAEL
[b.] September 28, 1976, Blackshear, GA; [p.] Born to Leisa Houston and Austin King (divorced) Adopted by Warren Britt until 12 years old; [ed.] A-B honor student through 6th grade at Grady Street and Memorial Drive Elem., in Blackshear dropped grades in 7th-8th, dropped out because of rebelliousness in 9th grade.; [occ.] not working; [oth. writ.] Many poems have been written, none other attempted to publish such as "Shooting Star"; [pers.] I like most other poets, can only speak for myself. I seek with much curiosity to find the source of dark human nature. I am greatly influenced by Edgar Allan Poe and James Morrison.; [a.] Blackshear, GA

BROADHEAD, MARY
[b.] England; [m.] Walter Cartwright; [ed.] RN; [occ.] Clinical Research; [memb.] Assoc. Clinical Pharmacology American Medical Writers Assoc.; [oth. writ.] Patient education literature, several poems in local publications, co-author of many scientific research papers.; [pers.] My poem reflects the love placed upon my soul, when as a new Christian, I encountered those lovely silently soldiers of Christ many of whom have no name - only a place in my heart

BRODEUR, PAUL C.
[b.] May 18, 1957, St. Boniface, Manitoba, Canada; [p.] Leo and Isabelle Brodeur; [ed.] 2 yrs. Science Diploma and 3 yrs. General B.A.; [occ.] Self-employed translator, editor and typesetter; [memb.] Associate Member of the Ass'n of Translators and Interpreters of Alberta (Canada) (for Italian into English); [pers.] I wish to see the Pope of Rome, obey the Mother of God by consecrating Russia to her exactly as she commanded him to do (cf. the 1929 sequel to her apparitions in Fatima, Portugal); [a.] Edmonton Alberta, Canada

BROOKS, JERRY L.
[pen.] Dredonyx; [b.] September 22, 1969, Port Arthur, TX; [p.] Carolyn Lyons, Kirklott; [m.] Karen Brooks, December 23, 1989; [ed.] Oynard Union High School - Tech Schools for my many jobs in the Navy; [occ.] U.S. Navy Naval Photographer Fleet Imaging Center Pacific; [oth. writ.] I have many poems and songs written but none of my work has ever been published; [pers.] My influences are the things I see in my every day world my mind is splintered and I am slowly pulling out those splinters; [a.] San Diego, CA

BROOKS, LORRIE L.
[b.] October 23, 1970, Toronto, Canada; [p.] Sandra Hall, Ken Hall; [m.] Kevin Brooks, October 20, 1990; [ch.] Erica Jane Brooks, Jenna Anne Brooks; [occ.] Full time mother of 2; [oth. writ.] Song writer, I am currently having two of my songs produced by Soundline Productions in Mississauga, Ontario.; [pers.] My writings either poetry or songs are a window to my heart.; [a.] Erin Ontario, Canada

BROUILLARD, LIONEL
[b.] August 29, 1974, Montreal, Quebec, Canada; [p.] Roger Brouillard and Edith Brouillard; [ed.] Pauline Johnson Collegiate - Vocational School, St John's College; [pers.] Everyone has inspirations, but not everyone can be an inspiration. Some of the most inspirations of a person while in this lifetime have long since given praise to their inspirations. Poetry allows one to express their deepest thoughts, fears, loves, and emotions. Hopefully someday, through my poetry, I can be an inspiration to some.; [a.] Brantford, Ontario Canada

BROWN, CHRISTINE L.
[b.] September 23, 1957, Glens Falls, NY; [p.] Harry and Cora LaBrum; [m.] William Brown, October 1, 1982; [ch.] Matthew Brown; [ed.] Milford Area Senior High, NH Vocational Technical Institute; [occ.] Homemaker; [memb.] Muscular Dystrophy Assoc. United Methodist Church; [pers.] To read my poems is to enter my heart.; [a.] Merrimach, NH

BROWN, DARLENE
[b.] October 21, 1976, Brantford, Ontario, Canada; [p.] Blair and Valerie Brown; [ed.] Brantford Collegiate Institute; [occ.] Salesperson; [oth. writ.] I have always wrote for my own, personal entertainment, but recently decided to try to get a few of my poems published. This is the first contest I have entered, and am grateful to be able to be a part of A Moment in Time.; [a.] Brantford Ontario, Canada

BROWN, ESSIE
[pen.] S. C. Brown; [b.] February 21, 1953, Greenville, SC; [p.] John and Nammie Brown; [ch.] Three; [ed.] 2 year college; [occ.] Aide; [memb.] Upper Room Tabernacle (Ministries)

BROWN, JENNIFER J.
[pen.] "Cookie" [b.] December 27, 1946, White Plains, NY; [p.] Rachel Brown Allen, Oliver Brown; [m.] James "Jimmy" Brown, June 22, 1985; [ch.] Teresa Angeline Bailen; [ed.] A.S. Business Administration, Middlesex Community College Middletown, CT 06457; [occ.] Human Resources Manager; [memb.] Society for Human Resources Management; [hon.] Equal Opportunity Award, Green Derby Award for hiring excellence.; [pers.] I strive to make what is anticipated as impossible, possible.

BROWN, JONI
[b.] February 19, 1946, Everett, WA; [p.] Daniel and Lucille Martin; [m.] Robert Brown, August 4, 1989; [ch.] Billy, Jeffrey, Thomas Sizemore...Jorja Green; [occ.] Free-lance writer; [memb.] Affiliated with BMI...Nashville, TN.; [hon.] One semi-finalist and six honorable mentions for song writing in the Billboard Song Writing Contest.; [oth. writ.] Two short stories... several poems published in M.O.C.S.A. anthology I've written two card lines...and copy...many songs...Country and country/blues...Currently working on a screen-play adapted from song written expressly for my husband.; [pers.] If I do but one good thing in this life....I hope it is for a child...It is my hope, that when I write-others, will feel and act upon those feelings.; [a.] Trenton, MO

BROWN, JUNE ARLENE
[pen.] J.B., Brownie; [b.] June 25, 1959, Kingston, Jamaica, West Indies; [p.] Olda Maud Williams; [ch.] Camille, Leonie, Marsha-K; [ed.] Balmagie Primary - Jamaica W.I., Penwood High - Jamaica, W.I.; [occ.] Pharmacy Technician, Rite - Aid Cooperation Newark, N.J.; [memb.] Affiliated to The Vailsburg Assembly of God Newark (N.J.), Wise Womens' Center, Essex City College, Newark N.J.; [oth. writ.] Presently compiling a selection of poems for possibly publication; [pers.] I know nothing, for a truly great person is the one that can say, "I know nothing, unless The Supreme One enables me to know."; [a.] Irvington, NJ

BROWN, M.S. JUDY ANN
[b.] December 7, 1949, Hamilton, OH; [ch.] John Mc. Brown; [ed.] Phoenix Union High School, 12 grade graduate Phoenix Ariz; [occ.] Reaching out to help others, through the words of poetry; [hon.] 2 Golden poet awards, 4 Honorable mention awards, 3 Editors choice awards; [oth. writ.] Santa's Coming Home, Daddy's Special Little Angel, Sunshine Rainbows and Rose's, Michigan Wonderland - America a Land of Beauty, Everlasting Love; [pers.] Poetry is lite an artist a beautiful work of art, it's a feeling that comes from within the heart; [a.] Engadine, MI

BROWN, ORVILLE ROY
[pen.] Villagesweets; [b.] June 11, 1970, New York; [p.] Caswall and Violet Brown; [ed.] Chisholm Trail Academy Keene, TX, Oakwood College Huntsville, AL; [occ.] Medical Service Specialist, USAF; [memb.] International Freelance Photographers Organization; [hon.] Honorable mention poem in Musings Illiad Press Summer '95; [oth. writ.] Poems published in church newsletter; [pers.] As we go about life's daily routine, life gives us experiences in which to write about. A lot of my poetry comes from simple experiences and also confrontations daily with other people.; [a.] Suffolk, England

BROWN-PAUL, SHIRLEY
[pen.] Shirley Gardner; [b.] January 2, 1942, Worcester, England; [m.] John R. Brown-Paul, December 23, 1994; [occ.] Physical Therapist; [oth. writ.] Several poems, only shown to family and friends; [pers.] All dimensions my writings are mainly on love, personal link with a spiritual awareness, which has benefited others as well as myself; [a.] Tully, NY

BROWN, PHYLLIS M.
[pen.] Susie Dry; [b.] September 4, 1956, Monroe, NC; [p.] Shirley and Sherman Dry; [ed.] South Rowan High School, China Grove, NC, Academy of Business Careers, Washington DC.; [occ.] Small business co-owner; [hon.] Honor roll student of The Academy of Business Careers, Certificate of Industrial Sewing; [oth. writ.] Obituaries, business slogans.; [pers.] While climbing the stairway to heaven, make each impression count.; [a.] Concord, NC

BROWN, SANFORD W.
[pen.] Sandy Brown; [b.] June 13, 1927, Asheville, NC; [p.] Frank Brown, Margaret Brown; [m.] Brenda J. Brown, August 17, 1990; [ch.] Randie, Lori, Stephanie, Sanford Jr., Roxanne Brown (Previous Spouse); [ed.] Sr. Snyder Continuation High School, University Of Washington (Seattle) BA Degree Psychology; [occ.] Retired - Quality Assurance Supervisor - Flighttest - The Boeing Co.; [memb.] Museum of Flight the Boeing Company; [hon.] "Share and care" a gift to those who need; [oth. writ.] Poems not published yet - "Beauty Brings Glory", "Old Green and Gold", "The Paper Home", "The Grand Old House", "A Rose That Will Always Bloom", "Christmas Day Walk"; [pers.] To bring myself and others to the ultimate feelings we desire in life.; [a.] Compton, AR

BROWN, STACY L.
[b.] February 2, 1979, Conyers, GA; [p.] Ann and Allan Brown; [ed.] Rockdale County High School; [occ.] Student at Rockdale County High; [oth. writ.] I am constantly writing everything from letters to poems to stories. Poems are my way to express my feelings and feelings of others.; [pers.] I admire anyone who tries their best, confusion is a deep state of mind that may trap you within its clutches!; [a.] Conyers, GA

BROWN, TANA
[pen.] Tee-Tee; [b.] August 5, 1956, Bronx, NY; [p.] Philip Weston, Mae Brown; [ch.] Christine, Crystal, Celeste, Tenasia; [ed.] Jane Adams VHS, Monroe College; [occ.] Cashier - Supermarket Generals; [hon.] Dean's List; [pers.] Communication - we must voice ourselves to the best of our ability. Influenced by the many poets and life's understanding; [a.] Bronx, NY

BROWNE, DOMINICK
[pen.] Dominick; [oth. writ.] Volume of Poetry published in book, in American magazine, in Irish magazine, United Kingdom Anthology, Short story in magazine, An essay critic on James Joyce's 'Exiles' commissioned in comburl hard back collection. Three stage plays produced in London, United Kingdom, one play produced in Belfast Northern Ireland, Play produced in Cork Republic of Ireland.; [pers.] I believe in the unity of the whole of mankind in diversity. And the unity of the whole world in diversity for Justice and peace.; [a.] London, United Kingdom

BROWNING, EUGENE S.
[b.] October 5, 1927, East Grand Rapids, MI; [p.] Dr. Eugene S. Browning, Gertrude Browning; [m.] Divorced; [ch.] Wun Sook, Shelley, Jean, Sara; [ed.] Ottawa Hills High, Davenport Business College, Aquinas College, Western Michigan University; [occ.] Retired Purchasing Agent, former Paratrooper and Korean War Combat Veteran; [oth. writ.] Poem published in local magazine, poem for a wedding program; [pers.] I strive to write rhymed verse in natural sounding language that flows smoothly and rhythmically, conveying clear images or messages with deep emotion. I believe the rhyme should be subtle, yet compliment and enhance the message and tone of the work.; [a.] Omaha, NE

BROXTON JR., TONY GENE
[b.] March 30, 1959; [ed.] Pace High School; [occ.] U.S. Postal Service; [memb.] Pace Vol. Fire Dept.; [pers.] Live life to the fullest, for it is your life you live, unless you let someone else tell you what to do, then its their life.; [a.] Pace, FL

BRUCE, PHYLLIS CAROLE
[pen.] Phyllis Carole Bruce; [b.] September 19, 1949, Brooklyn, NY; [p.] Rev. and Mrs. Eugene Peterkin; [m.] Widow/Charles S. Bruce, June 8, 1974; [ch.] Vaughn Christian Bruce; [ed.] Cornerstone Baptist Church Bible School, Wingate High, New York City University, Prince George Community College; [occ.] Early Childhood Educator, Sales Entrepreneur/Public Relations; [memb.] Saint Peters Spiritual Church, Queen, NY, National Assoc. Education for Young Children (NAEYC) Disabled Veterans Auxiliary (DAVA) Salesian Mission, American Heart Society, American Cancer Society Honorary Poetry Society, Jerry McAuley Mission, N.Y.; [hon.] Prince George Community Colleges Dean's List, Honorary Poetry Society, President Church Usher's Board; [oth. writ.] Received numerous honorary awards/Certificate/Honorary mention for poems from American Poetry Society, invite twice to participate at Nation Capital Washington, DC. Recitals for "Outstanding Poets (1991-92); [pers.] This poem is dedicated to my mentor the late Bishop Arlee Gilbert who always encouraged me to strive to succeed when I felt like giving up in my writing career.; [a.] Ken Gardens Hills, NY

BRUNEHU, ROBERT
[pen.] Robert Brunehu; [b.] February 8, 1950, Providence, RI; [p.] Gerard and Elizabeth; [ch.] Sarah and Cora; [ed.] Coventry High, Community College of Rhode Island, Charleston Southern University; [occ.] Unemployed; [memb.] Phi Theta Kappa, Alpha Chi; [hon.] Phi Theta Kappa, Alpha Chi, Dean's List; [oth. writ.] Poem selected for publication in Charleston Southern University Literary Magazine; [pers.] The fabric of our lives consists of every memory, happy and sad, and the true romantic is woven from the joy he finds in experiencing life.; [a.] Younge's Island, SC

BRUNEUA, MARSHA
[b.] October 2, 1978, Pine Falls, Manitoba, Canada; [p.] Edward Bruneau, Karen Bruneau; [ed.] Wanipigow School Grade II; [occ.] Student; [memb.] 3039 Hollow Water First Nation Cadet Corp.; [hon.] Athlete of the year, Top student in English, etc.; [oth. writ.] Other poems published in local newsletters, other writings published in "a collection of students writing Area III" Frontier School Division; [pers.] I believe all races of mankind should be treated equal. No one is better than anyone else. We are all equal.; [a.] Manigotogan Manitoba, Canada

BRYANT, SHIRLENE ALLEN
[pen.] Shirlene Bryant; [b.] Pittsburg, TX; [p.] Laymon and Pearl Allen; [m.] Claude Bryant, June 3, 1966; [ch.] Gregory and Michael; [ed.] Bachelor of Social Work from Texas Woman's University, Denton, Texas; [occ.] Substitute Teacher Dallas Independent School District; [memb.] National Association of Social Workers; [hon.] Alpha Delta Mu - National Social Work Honor Society, The National Dean's List, The National Register of Outstanding College Graduates; [oth. writ.] Other poems; [pers.] I try to express hope in my writings. I started writing poetry during my mothers illness and death. It's been therapy for me.; [a.] Dallas, TX

BRYLA, HELEN
[b.] December 8, 1933, Perth Amboy, NJ; [p.] Helen McLaughlin Boyer, Louis Boyer; [m.] Anthony Bryla, September 20, 1959 (Deceased); [ch.] Anthony Joseph, Christopher Scott; [ed.] Perth Amboy High School; [occ.] Library Clerk, Edison, NJ; [memb.] The Statue Of Liberty Foundation Special Olympics; [hon.] National Honor Society Of Journalists; [oth. writ.] Never sought to publish any.; [pers.] Hope to make a difference, however small, wherever I can.; [a.] Edison, NJ

BUCK JR., MRS. ADRIENNE DUGGER
[b.] August 15, 1932, Princeton, NJ; [p.] Caterior James L. Dugger, Hattie D; [m.] OB Gyn Specialist Abram H. Burk Jr., March 17, 1952; [ch.] Adrienne Marie-Alexis Frances, Aurora Teresa, Abram III, Autumn Ann, Ahmed C.; [ed.] Princeton High School, West Virginia State Teachers College; [occ.] Housewife, widow as of December 5, 1994; [memb.] Rosery Guild, St. Vincent De Paul Church, American Cancer Association, American Heart Association.; [hon.] Tidewater Award for Poetry, Norfolk, VA - Alpha Kappa - Alpha Pledge Club; [pers.] This was a first time try for poetry of this type usually Religious Poetry or warm sentiments for family members; [a.] Nashville, TN

BUCKHEIT, RACHEL
[b.] December 15, 1977, Long Island, NY; [p.] Margaret Papandrea, Daniel Buckheit; [ed.] East Islip High School; [occ.] Student (High School (11)) Junior; [memb.] East Islip Girls' Varsity Bowling Team, Foreign Language Honor Society (Spanish and American Sign Language); [hon.] Two time 1993-1994 winner of the Suffolk County Girls' singles Varsity Bowling Title, Scholar Athlete, High Honor Society, Volunteer Assistant Teacher at Suny Stony Brook for American Sign Language.; [oth. writ.] First publication; [pers.] Never turn your back on your family - sometimes they are all you've got; [a.] East Islip, NY

BUCKINGHAM, MARCIE
[pen.] Marcie Buckingham; [b.] October 17, 1978, Herrin, IL; [p.] Fred and Sharon Buckingham; [ed.] Zeigler - Royalton Elementary and Junior High, Herrin High School; [occ.] Student - Junior Year Herrin High School; [oth. writ.] I have wrote many other poems but none have been published.; [pers.] My favorite poet is Edgar Allen Poe. I also favor Langston Hughes. I use different emotions in my poetry. When people read my poems I want them to feel what I was feeling at that moment.; [a.] DeSoto, IL

BUDNEY, LISA
[b.] March 15, 1978, Edmonton, Alberta, Canada; [p.] Bernie and Darlene Budney; [ed.] Currently attending Ardrossan Jr., Sr. High School; [occ.] Student; [hon.] Academic Honour Awards throughout school, Various sports awards, Nominated for an Alberto Young Citizenship Award.; [pers.] Life's speedbumps are fewer if you follow your own roadmap and don't vary from the course you set. Always be proud to be different.; [a.] Ardrossan Alberta, Canada

BUGGS, ESTHER L.
[pen.] E. F. Buggs; [b.] January 6, 1947, Eldorado, AR; [p.] Sanders and Esther Ford; [m.] Deceased; [ch.] Tara Lynnee, Jacqueline, Kimberly; [ed.] Washington High, University of Arkansas and Pine Bluff, El Centro Jr. College, Richland Jr. College; [occ.] Retired Medical Research Technologist; [oth. writ.] None published, for personal pleasure; [pers.] One writes poetry reflecting experiences in life and methods of coping with difficulties with solutions that are beneficial.; [a.] Dallas, TX

BUKOVINA, WILHELM V. ANDRUK VON
[pen.] Vierel Berezowski, The Dragon; [b.] April 4, 1940, Cernauti, Romania; [p.] Theodore and Ana Andreiuc; [ed.] Institute of Economic Sciences - Bururesti-Roma-

nia, Foreign and domestic trade (Major), "E. Hurmuzachi" High School-Raduiti-Romania, Center for the Media Arts-New York, Television Arts and Cinematography; [occ.] Taxi driver, director' actor, stuntman, race car driver, politician; [memb.] The Eastern Orthodox Church Republican Party.; [hon.] The greatest Honor ever received along my existence is from The National Library of Poetry as of January 4, 1995 letter that enlighted my dire existence, sent by Howard Ely, it takes one to know one. Thank you.; [oth. writ.] Letters of goodwill and of non-involvement in the affairs of others foreign independent countries by the USA, addressed to US government, many unpublished essays and political calviews. Freelance diplomacy writings to head of states for peace.???; [pers.] I tried hard all along my existence, unsuccessfully, to eliminate Egotism, Violence, Ill, lie, and ignorance from my immediate, close surroundings, I'm for Universal, total equality and respect toward the fellow human being with intellect. Altruistic.; [a.] New York, NY

BURAC, ROSANNE T.
[b.] March 29, 1950, Milwaukee WI; [p.] Robert Campbel, Helen Campbell; [m.] James E. Burac, January 22, 1972; [ch.] Tara Nicole and Ryan Campbell; [ed.] Franklin High, Cardinal Stritch College; [occ.] Market Manager, Ameritech; [memb.] Who's Who Worldwide; [hon.] Dean's List - Magna Cum Laude; [pers.] The root of my poems and short stories is the expression of emotional honesty.; [a.] Franklin, WI

BURGE, SUE
[b.] December 26, 1950, Nicholasville, KY; [p.] Ruby Durham, Carl Durham; [m.] Johnny Burge, December 23, 1971; [ch.] Stacy Lynn; [occ.] Credit Manager at Rexroth Pneumatics; [pers.] I have loved writing poetry since I was in grade school. My daughter also writes poems, I choose to think she acquired her talent from her Mom! Poems are my way of expressing feelings and thoughts not always easily expressed.

BURGER, CAROL ELAINE
[b.] August 12, 1981, Las Vegas, NV; [p.] David and Florinda Burger; [ed.] Curundu Jr. High School; [memb.] Youth Center, Yearbook (School); [hon.] Honor Roll, D.A.R.E. program, School Patrol; [oth. writ.] School stories, poems in school.; [pers.] I'm glad that I've discovered a new talent. It makes me extremely proud about my writing! Thanks alot for making this possible; [a.] Apo, AA

BURGESS II, THOMAS E.
[b.] July 24, 1963, Mineral Wells, TX; [p.] Thomas and Sandie Burgess; [ed.] Payette High; [occ.] Retail Lawn and Garden Sales; [oth. writ.] Two poems published in other books, one honorable mention.; [pers.] I write from the heart, reflecting personal memories and feelings.; [a.] Yuba City, CA

BURK, AMANDA FAE
[b.] December 2, 1979; [p.] Jane Burk, Rick Burk; [ed.] 10th grade high school at Sparrows Point; [hon.] Honor Society, U.S. Achievement Academy 1994 National Awards; [oth. writ.] In musings: I love you a picture in my hand to my best friend.; [pers.] Inspired by Erin and Conor, my two best friends in Cockeysville; [a.] Baltimore, MD

BURKE, ERIN
[b.] June 3, 1982, Calgary, Alberta, Canada; [p.] Jessie and Mark Burke; [ed.] I attend Chestenmene Middle School, I'm a grade 7 student; [oth. writ.] Don't Cry (None published); [pers.] I really enjoy writing poetry, and I think that my poems reflect how I feel about issues in the world.; [a.] Calgary Alberta, Canada

BURNS, CARL W.
[pen.] Carl W. Burns; [b.] November 24, 1935, Mountain View, AR; [p.] Monroe and Mae Burns; [m.] Ruby, December 1, 1979; [ch.] Carla Lynn; [ed.] Formal; [occ.] Cabinet Maker; [oth. writ.] Children's poems some commercial writings for children, song writing, etc. material not published yet; [pers.] I have always been interested in what goes on in very young children's minds such as my poem describes. Also take interest in other writers work.; [a.] Cave City, AR

BURTON, GENNETT
[b.] January 18, 1945, Durant, OK; [p.] Mr. and Mrs. Lester Bowden; [m.] Joseph Robert Burton, August 26, 1988; [ch.] Carol, Larry, Joe, Steven, April and Patty; [ed.] G.E.D at 42 years Jr. College self achiever; [occ.] Writer; [memb.] First Assembly of God Onalaska Texas, Audibon, American Cancer Society, Anderson Network; [hon.] Cason article placed in vertical file at N.T.C.C., Cancer survivor; [oth. writ.] "The Rise and Fall of Cason Texas" Articles for various newspapers "Mother had the Upper Hand"; [pers.] Anything in life a person may want to accomplish in a lifetime is obtainable if he or she will find in themselves the desire to persevere!; [a.] Onalaska, TX

BUSALACCHI, NOELLE
[b.] August 28, 1973, Daly City, CA; [p.] Dwight and Sherry Busalacchi; [ed.] El Camino High School, Skyline College, Now attending San Diego State University; [occ.] Office Clerk at Associated Vitners Services; [memb.] Concert Choir at San Diego State, Snowboard Club; [hon.] San Francisco Italian Athletic Club Scholarship, Cal. Farm Insurance Scholarship.; [oth. writ.] I've written various poems, however most of them are for leisure.; [pers.] Most of what I write is influenced by my everyday life. I write about situations that affect me emotionally.; [a.] Daly City, CA

BUSBY, BRUCE
[b.] May 10, 1928, Trail, British Columbia, Canada; [p.] Arthur (Bill) Busby, Frances (Bobs) Busby; [m.] Martha, July, 14, 1948; [ch.] Five; [ed.] A bit of port secondary - mostly experiential, stage manager/actor, bush pilot, community press reporter, editor, publisher, restaurant/resort manager, etc; [occ.] Retired; [oth. writ.] As a weekly newspaper editor, many editorials and columns; [pers.] To be irreverent holding history only as a reference, never away of life.; [a.] Red Deer Alberta, Canada

BUTLER, DALLAS E.
[pen.] Riverboat Gambler; [b.] April 25, 1938, Ohio; [p.] Alfred and Katherine Butler; [m.] Barbara Butler, March 3, 1962; [ch.] Ashley, Rhett; [ed.] B.S. Aeronautics; [occ.] Pilot; [pers.] It is, indeed, unfortunate that most of us do not have more misfortune!; [a.] Honolulu, HI

BUTLER, SCOTT
[b.] February, 11, 1970, Granite City, IL; [p.] Cinda Butler and Richard Butler; [occ.] Student at University of Utah; [pers.] My philosophy: Life is just a tragedy a play for which we came but as we know of tragedies they all must end the same.; [a.] Tooele, UT

BYARS, STEVEN A.
[b.] November 20, 1966, Tripoli, Libya; [p.] Donald Byars, Sarah Butler; [ed.] East Rutherford High School, Mount Olive College, University of Maryland; [occ.] Tactical Aircraft Maintenance Specialist; [a.] Okinawa, Japan

BYLOCK, CAROL B.
[b.] January 18, 1924, Raymond, ME; [p.] J. Harrie and Anna Burdge; [m.] Abraham A. Bylock, November 28, 1968; [ch.] Colleen Anne and J. Russell Cook; [ed.] Raymond Grammar School Windham High School George Washington University; [occ.] Retired; [oth. writ.] Other poems; [pers.] I have always been a lover of poetry. My mother wrote many poems, I always use poetry for prize speaking.; [a.] Hallandale, FL

CABRET, JOSE
[pen.] Jose Cabret; [b.] September 27, 1956, Puerto Rico; [p.] Julio Valazquez, Rosa Maria Cabret; [ed.] Saint Peters College, N.J.; [occ.] Poet, Writer; [oth. writ.] Poems, Lyrics; [pers.] Seize the opportunity, command the moment!!!; [a.] New York City, NY

CADMAN, SARAH
[pen.] Sadi; [b.] October 17, 1978; [p.] Ann Cadman, Whit Cadman; [ed.] I am a student at North Allegheny High School; [memb.] I am a member of many animal protection groups, marching band and wind ensemble, and my youth group; [hon.] Allegheny valley honors band; [oth. writ.] Stories and poems published in school poetry magazines; [pers.] I write to express myself. I find it easier to write down my feelings than talk about them. It's easier to talk to paper - it doesn't talk back!; [a.] Pittsburgh, PA

CAGE, JOANNE RAMEY
[pen.] Joan Remy; [b.] December 27, 1934, Birmingham, AL; [p.] Gordon Ramey, Mary Elizabeth Ramey; [ch.] Virginia Anne, Jack, and James; [ed.] Leeds High School, University of Alabama.; [occ.] Data processing specialist; [memb.] Alabama State Poetry Society; [hon.] High school and college scholastic honor societies.; [oth. writ.] State and national poetry awards. Poems published in local newspapers and in a collection of Alabama poets' works. [A novel and a collection of poems currently submitted to publishers. I am writing a novel about Shakespeare.]; [pers.] My writing is most concerned with exploring the meaning of life and death and of the events, common to all, that so deeply influence our lives. [I try to express my wonder and gratitude for the consolations of nature and the small joys of everyday life.]; [a.] Birmingham, AL

CAHOJ, MARY
[b.] December 10, 1960, Chicago, IL; [p.] Donald and Lois Boox; [m.] Joseph Cahoj, June 23, 1984; [ed.] Notre Dame High School, DePaul University, Institute of Children's Literature; [occ.] Customer Service Rep. for General Cooperage Co.; [oth. writ] This is the first published piece in what I hope is a long line; [pers.] I love to travel and observe people. I hope this brings a vitality and worth to my writing. The 3 "R's" of my life are reading, writing, and roving!; [a.] Elmwood Park, IL

CAMMARATA, BARBARA
[b.] May 3, 1919, Port Jefferson, NY; [p.] Angela D'Imperio, Joseph D'Imperio; [m.] Thomas Cammarata, September 7, 1946; [ch.] Thomas Joseph, Denise Ann, Robert Paul; [ed.] Monroe High School; [occ.] Housewife; [memb.] Legion of Mary, Catholic Golden Age,

A.A.R.P.; [oth. writ.] Countless poems written to family and friends; [pers.] I believe that if all mankind were to love one another as God intended, there would be no discrimination or prejudice, no greed, and no wars.; [a.] Freeport, NY

CAMPBELL, DAHLIA E.
[p.] Deceased; [m.] Charles Campbell, June 3, 1968; [ed.] PH.D. Walden University, 1944; [occ.] Health Services; [memb.] President Head Injury Association, Durham Region, Vice President, Registered Nurses Association of Ontario, Executive, Canadian Federation University Women; [hon.] Doctoral Dissertation Award. Walden University 1994. Women of Distinction Award, 1994 Active Member of Orono United Church; [oth. writ.] Paper in "Health Beliefs, Health Behaviours and Quality of Life of Elderly, rural Women."; [pers.] My philosophy is to strive for excellence and never hesitate in taking the first step toward self-actualization.; [a.] Orono Ontario, Canada

CAMPBELL, EVELYN
[b.] September 23, 1933, Sampson Co., NC; [p.] Mr. and Mrs. James Cheek; [m.] Ralph Campbell, April 4, 1968; [ch.] Angela, Piper, Marty, and Wendy; [ed.] I finished High School and took a couple of College courses when I was fifty four years old; [occ.] Disabled; [hon.] Jesus Honors me every day, just by being savior; [oth. writ.] I have written or wrote other poems, but never sent them to be published; [pers.] My poems come when I am very happy. Jesus gives me the words. I have no one to lean on since my husband died, but Jesus. He takes care of me.; [a.] Forest City, NC

CAMPBELL, JACK C.
[pen.] Clay McKinley; [b.] May 3, 1928, Pittsburgh, PA; [p.] Unknown; [m.] Bonnie Doone, August 11, 1954; [ch.] 5 all grown Jack, Sandra, Bob, Bonnie, Bill; [ed.] High School Graduate (VIA GED) Albion High School Albion, PA.; [occ.] Retired; [memb.] V.F.W. American Legion American Bowling Congress; [hon.] Many Bowling awards and trophies for 16-years of bowling, started bowling when I was 50 years old for exercise to combate arthritis. Carry a 190-plus average.; [oth. writ.] Many stories and poems none published; [pers.] Enjoying writing, but wish I had been smart enough to have studied harder when I had the chance.; [a.] Hudson, FL

CAMPBELL, JENNIFER R.
[pen.] Sabrina Maria; [b.] September 14, 1979, Pittsburg, PA; [p.] Paul L. Campbell and Kathleen M. Kassanitsh Campbell; [m.] Unmarried; [ed.] Freshman at Hopewell Sr. High School; [oth. writ.] Many poems not yet submitted for publishing; [pers.] True poetry isn't an understanding, but a feeling from the heart. My greatest influenced are Edgar Allan Poe and K. Andreas Torrance; [a.] Aliquippa, PA

CANARY, NATALIE N.
[pen.] Natalie Canary; [b.] October 17, 1976, Norman, OK; [p.] Elmer and Dollic Canary; [ed.] I will graduate from Moore High School this year in May. I am planning to attend Cameron University in the fall. I will be working on a degree in Theatre.; [occ.] Full time student.; [memb.] I am a member of FHA, president of my local FHA Chapter, as well as FHA Sub-District Secretary. I am a member of Tri-L, my school's writing club. I am a member of the Speech/Debate club.; [hon.] I have been in Who's Who Among American High School Students, twice. Once my sophomore year, once my junior year.; [oth. writ.] I have written several other poems, as well as several short stories. I am currently working on a novel for for girls.; [pers.] I hope my poetry is a blessing to all who read it.; [a.] Moore, OK

CANNADY, MARK ANTHONY
[b.] August 4, 1972, Racine, WI; [p.] Gloria J. Cannady; [ed.] Quitman High School Quitman, MS; [occ.] U.S. Navy; [oth. writ.] I only write for enjoyment. This is my first published writings.; [pers.] I address different problems in the world through my writings. I also allow the romantic side of my personality to come out.; [a.] Quitman, MS

CAPISTRANT, GREGORY G.
[b.] June 2, 1950, Milwaukee; [p.] Dorothy Banner, Gerald Capistrant; [m.] Pamela A. Capistrant, June 12, 1971; [ch.] Richard, Gregory, Mathew, Nathan, Adam, Joshua; [ed.] South Division High Class of 1968; [occ.] Factory Worker; [oth. writ.] The Shaman - A novel unpublished, the seekers tree - a novel in progress; [a.] Milwaukee, WI

CAPOUANO, PEGGY CURTIS
[b.] August 9, 1946, Murphy, NC; [p.] Wayne H. and Edith L. Curtis; [m.] Albert D. Capouano, August 21, 1976; [ch.] Four (Stephanie, Bryan, David and Marcus); [ed.] Andrews High School, Andrews, N.C. Blanton's Business College, Rollins College - Accounting, Seminole Community College; [occ.] Wife, Mother, Part time Property Manager, Partime Poet/short stories; [memb.] Heathrow Women's Club, United States Tennis Assoc., General Federation of Women's clubs; [oth. writ.] Several Poems, Short Stories, People of Reliance - Famous Poets Society; [pers.] My poetry and short stories normally reflert life's observation and experiences some are humorous. Some are sad and other state opinion.; [a.] Longwood, FL

CAPTAIN, VELMA
[pen.] Vel Webb; [b.] May 5, 1945, Hallsville, TX; [p.] Elma and Cultis Webb; [ch.] Galilee High, El Centro College; [occ.] Funds Management Operations Accounting Clerk; [memb.] W. H. Atwell TA.; [hon.] Teacher Awards from Mountain View Church of Christ, AL Williams Fast Start Award, Appreciation Award from J. J. Rhoades School for Volunteer Service in School Award, for Teaching Divorced Mothers Class Perfect Attendance Awards from Nations Bank; [oth. writ.] I have many poems written by myself. That has never sent to any one to see if they are worth publishing and also written short skits and sayings.; [pers.] I am striving to have a positive attitude at all times - in my poem writings and other situations to make some one life more meaningful.

CARAFFA, ARQUELIO
[b.] August 20, 1926, Puerto Rico; [p.] Francisco and Mercedes Caraffa; [m.] Provi Caraffa, September 28, 1946; [ch.] Edith and Francisco A.; [ed.] Lincoln and Clearwater High; [occ.] Retired Ford Motor Co.; [memb.] Transfiguration Catholic Church; [oth. writ.] Pop and Gospel Songs.; [pers.] I reflect romanticism and the power and existence of our God the creator; [a.] Largo, FL

CARDENAS, JOSE J.
[b.] October 1, 1973, Mexicali, Mexico; [ed.] Mountain View High, DeVry Institute of Technology; [occ.] Design Engineer; [oth. writ.] Cogitatum De Exilium (Not yet published, constitutes of a collection of poems).; [pers.] I write to awaken the individual, for it is our nature to hide from shadows that lurk within, I wish you here for my thoughts not the agony, for only from the point of exile can one see the inner self.

CARDENAS, JOSE J.
[b.] October 1, 1973, Mexicali, Mexico; [ed.] DeVRY Institute of Technology; [occ.] Design Engineer; [oth. writ.] Cogitatum De Exilium, a collection of poems that I am worrying on their copyrights as well as their publishing.; [pers.] I write to awaken the individual, to let the subconscious overwhelm the fake reality we fail, I wish you here for my thoughts not my anguish.; [a.] CA

CARL, RITA
[ed.] BA-Adelphi College MA-Teachers College Columbia University; [memb.] PETA; [pers.] To find beauty and worth in all living things, is to enrich ones own life.; [a.] New York, NY

CARL, TIMI ANNE
[b.] October 5, 1965, Tacoma, WA; [ch.] Eric Joseph, Alexander Daniel and Brandon Wayde; [occ.] Nurse, Administrator Arcadia Health Cure, Sumner, WA.; [a.] Sumner, WA

CARLBERG, CHRISTOPHER H.
[b.] June 12, 1951, Richland, WA; [p.] Eileen, Hank; [m.] Linda R., July 10, 1976; [ch.] Joel Christian, Luke Christopher, Elizabeth Kristen; [ed.] Hoover H.S., des Moines, Iowa, B.A., English Creighton Univ. '73; [occ.] Self-employed, 15 years. Finish Carpenter; [a.] Omaha, NE

CARMICHAEL, DAVID F.
[b.] July 20, 1962, St James Barbados; [ed.] St. John Baptist Mixed School; [hon.] A certificate of award on Industrial Security, Award of merit certificate by world of poetry and A Golden Poet; [oth. writ.] "God is Love" on record album songs of Love - Songs of Life by Royal Master Records, Inc.; [pers.] Always try to be honest in whatever you do, and be discreet to persons whether bad or good.; [a.] Bridgetown, Barbados

CARR, AMY
[b.] March 15, 1983, Charleston, SC; [p.] Faith Carr Hibbard; [ed.] Student; [occ.] Student; [hon.] A student; [oth. writ.] School/English poems; [pers.] I enjoy writing about the earth and it's wonderful qualities. Writing poems came to me naturally, no classes.; [a.] Atlantic Beach, FL

CARR, DOROTHY M.
[b.] July 31, 1969, NH; [p.] Janet Locklin and Joseph Carr; [ed.] Tulare Union High, Fresno City College; [occ.] Strategic Marketing, People Soft Inc. Specialist; [pers.] If others are able to gain insight and find peace or hope through my poems, I have come one step closer to my dream.; [a.] Dublin, CA

CARRASCO, MAFALDA GRANDE
[b.] March 27, 1919, Farrell, PA; [p.] Catherine and John Grande; [m.] Michael Carrasco, January 2, 1992; [ed.] Farrell High, Macomb County Community College, Wayne State College, Peace Corps of Guatemala, Methodology EFL Teacher, Santo Domingo (Certificates for both foreign positions); [occ.] Retired (Army Emergency Relief); [hon.] Institute - Dominico-Americano, Department of the Army; [oth. writ.] News Writer, WBRB and WDET Radio Stations, Reporter for local (Beacon) Newspaper and Selfridge Air National Guard, Article Magazine Savoia - Milan Italy.; [pers.] I would like to reflect on a system of Philosophy - to express difficulties with calmness and composure.; [a.] Chicago, IL

CARSON, MAE BURNHAM
[b.] May 1, 1931, Pontiac, MI; [p.] Donald E. and Gladys P. Burnham (Deceased); [m.] Gerald (Jerry) W. Carson, December 6, 1987; [ch.] Five step-children (adults); [ed.] B.A. Mich. State U., MA U. of Mich., post-grad, various institutions.; [occ.] Retired teacher, Prepare docent/teacher material for enrichment; [memb.] Blue Ridge Arts Council, (VA) Charles Umlauf Sculpture Garden and Museum (Austin) Writer's Guild (VA), Newcomers (Georgetown, TA); [hon.] Back a while from a 4th grader (with great sincerity): "You're the 2nd best teacher I've ever had."; [oth. writ.] Recent: Poem on moving to Texas involving our cat-a "hairy cat tale", advice poem with tongue-in-cheek workbook on the "middle ages" intended for the baby-boomer and next older generations, other verses and thoughts for occasions, events through out my life, education related materials and topics.; [pers.] Too much adulation and monetary reward is given to societies "leaders," "CEO's," "stars," etc. The strivings and accomplishments of the earnest and sincere are of equal worth and should be acknowledged and valued, the difference in perceived worth is often gained by an over-active ego by the first mentioned, and is unwarranted. The unrecognized are hampered by the ingrained demand to be "humble," "to wait your turn, "and to "make do."; [a.] Georgetown, TX

CARTAR, TIMOTHY L.
[pen.] TLC; [b.] September 4, 1952, York, PA; [p.] Benjamin and Maetiwde Carter; [ch.] Jenelva-16, Shamona-14; [ed.] William Denn SUS - York, PA., York College of Pennsylvania - York. PA.; [occ.] Medical LAB Technologist - Texas Center for Infections Disease; [memb.] San Antonio Chess Club, American Medical Technologist, Texas Society for the American Medical Technologists.; [oth. writ.] 4 Copyrighted songs, two others a poems "Beauty Seem So You" "Cherish The Moment"; [pers.] "Give to life what life has given to you"; [a.] San Antonio, TX

CARTER, AUDREY F. FORREST
[b.] April 1, 1956, Greenwood, SC; [p.] Willie (deceased) and Ruth B. Forrest; [m.] Ewing Carter III, September 6, 1986; [ch.] Channing Kamille, Ewing IV; [ed.] Ninety-Six High, Bennett College, BA and BS, A and T State Univ, MA; Miami Univ of Ohio, Ph. D.; [occ.] English Professor, NCA and T State Univ. Greensboro, N.C.; [memb.] NCTE, CLA, PTA Board, General Green Elementary, Greensboro, NC; Partner, Cities in School, Greensboro, NC; [hon.] Who's who among Black Americans; [oth. writ.] Several Unpublished poems; [a.] Greensboro, NC

CARTER, CATHY
[b.] April 10, 1970, Burlington, Ontario; [p.] Frederick Carter, Constance Carter; [m.] Christos Ilias, May 13, 1995; [ed.] M. M. Robinson High, University of Waterloo, Institute of Childrens Literature; [occ.] Contract Technical Writer, Toronto, Ontario, Canada; [pers.] My writing helps me to explore myself and the wonderfully complex people around me. May it one day inspire another like so many writers have inspired me.; [a.] North York, Ontario

CARTER, CONNIE S.
[pen.] Connie Hubbell Carter; [b.] May 24, 1952, Chicago, IL; [p.] Vivian Hubbell Gries; [ch.] Nicole S. Carter; [ed.] West Central High School, Maynard, Iowa; [occ.] Marketing Research; [memb.] Cerebral Palsy Association; [hon.] National Honor Society; [pers.] Poetry simplifies the 'learning process' - it can inspire, encourage and guide you through every facet of life. My daughter's determination to prevail over her disability has been the motivation for many of my writings.; [a.] Omaha, NE

CARTER, IRENE L.
[pen.] Aries Production; [b.] March 23, 1955, Philadelphia, PA; [p.] John and Gertrude Mitchell; [m.] Divorced; [ch.] Shawnette and Tyesha Carter; [ed.] Olney High School, LaSalle College; [occ.] Team leader/Warehouser P&G Co. Hatboro, PA.; [memb.] Mt. Airy Church of God Staff member - Christian Day Care; [hon.] Poetry established in Arts and Craft Store - customers may purchase writings. A family affair - Abbington, PA., Straight A-Average student written over 150 poems - 3 gospel songs.; [oth. writ.] Poem published in the book of poems entitled motherhood poem published in company's newspaper entitled - Charity; [pers.] To God Be The Glory. I hope to bring happiness through words of encouragement and comfort. To be a vehicle in aiding our youth to build self esteem and awareness. To be a motivator and all that I can be.; [a.] Philadelphia, PA

CARTER, TIMOTHY L.
[pen.] T. L. C. aka T. C.; [b.] September 4, 1952, York, PA; [p.] Benjamin F. and Maetrude J. Carter; [m.] Divorced; [ch.] Jenelva Alena and Shamona Yvonne Carter; [ed.] William Penn SHS - York, PA, York College of Pennsylvania - York, PA; [occ.] Medical Technologist/ Supervisor Texas Center for Infectious Disease - San Antonio, TX; [memb.] American Medical Technologists, Texas Society for the American Medical Technologists, United States Chess Federation, San Antonio Chess Club; [hon.] President - York College Chess Club, Writer of Tomorrow Award - William Penn SHS; [oth. writ.] Poems - "Beauty Seems So You", "Cherish The Moment (New Year is Upon You)", Copyrighted Songs: "After the Rain", "Bless You", "Stand By My Side", "Midnight and You"; [pers.] Love of Life and and the Life You Love has to be One! MY EARLY PRAYER, This poem is dedicated to my York College English Professor who past on, Dr./Reverend H. G. Knight, who believed in my writing abilities. Also, to my mother, Maetrude J. Carter, who gave me courage and love.; [a.] San Antonio, TX

CARTHY, MARY M.
[pen.] Aries Woman; [b.] April 19, 1938, Beldit, WI; [p.] Mr. and Mrs. Mabel Ray Quigley; [m.] Divorced; [ch.] Tracy, Dena, Cindy and Tommy; [ed.] High school graduate 8 wk home management course to become a health aide; [occ.] Certified home health aide; [memb.] Central Christian Church Beldit - Wiso (But no longer go to church); [oth. writ.] Songs, other poems none published, 2 poem contest 1st place 3rd place 1972 and 1980; [pers.] I enjoy and love my children, writing songs and poetry, all music art, fishing, antiques, walking nature animals travel, watching people, listening to the elderly talk about love to fantasize about life and a better world, I have been influenced by author Thurmond Fleet "Rays of the Dawn". But most of all love - helping to raise my two grandsons, Steven 10, and Richie 5, believe in a higher power, and some good in all of us.; [a.] Beloit, WI

CARVER, CAROLYN
[b.] August 19, 1947, Stanley, ND; [p.] Bill and Grace Hadden; [m.] Phil Carver; [ch.] Peter, Amy and Jason Cardenas; [occ.] Sales Coordinator; [oth. writ.] Various poems, two children's stories, "Barney" and "Paper Angel".; [pers.] I try to write about life, and its ups and downs with compassion and a sense of humor.; [a.] Kerman, CA

CARY, BETTY K.
[pen.] Bard of Fremont"; [b.] April 15, 1925, Parker, SD; [p.] John and Mary Krager; [m.] Maurice I. Cary, November 9, 1946; [ed.] 8 years in country school houses 4 years high school - graduate of Parker Hi; [occ.] Retired - senior clerk; [memb.] United methodist women and president of auxiliary at walker health center; [hon.] My Award (reward) will be in heaven, I hope!; [oth. writ.] Poems only, written honoring relatives and friends; [pers.] My aim in life has always been to help others and be honest and upright in all situations; [a.] Minneapolis, MN

CASKEY, MICHELLE
[b.] October 30, 1961, Fresno, CA; [p.] Kenneth A. and Joan A. Bryers; [m.] Brian Caskey, August 8, 1987; [ch.] Michael and Cameron; [pers.] The piece submitted was written at the age of seventeen about a boy I was dating at the time.; [a.] Fresno, CA

CASLER, JENNIFER
[b.] June 13, 1981, New York, NY; [p.] Patricia C. Casler, Peter M. Casler; [ed.] I am currently in the 8th grade at Woodmere Middle School; [occ.] Student; [memb.] I am a member of many clubs at school, such as 8th grade Math Team, Yearbook Committee, Track Team, Orchestra, Chorus, Sabelotodo (the Spanish Team) and the school play. I am also the Features Editor of our school paper. I have been involved in Trivia Challenge, which is a fund raiser for United Cerebral Palsey (UCP) and in Math-A-Thon, which raises money for Saint Jude's Children's Research Hospital.; [hon.] Some awards that I have received include the Johns Hopkins CTY State award for scoring higher than an average college bound twelfth grader, on the SAT as a seventh grader. I have also received awards for participation in the New York State School Music Association (NYSSMD) festivals, for violin.; [oth. writ.] I have had my writings printed in the school newspaper and in the school literary magazine.; [pers.] I like to make writing interesting and fun. I have been influenced mostly by my teachers, parents, and friends.; [a.] Valley Stream, NY

CASTLETON, KIMBERLEY MARIE
[b.] August 22, 1981, Barstow, CA; [p.] Consuelo Castleton, Lon Castleton; [ed.] Severna Park Middle School, 8th grade; [memb.] Stingers (soccer team), Year Book Club; [hon.] Artist of the week; [oth. writ.] The Only One, A story untold (Neither one has ever been published because they were written for personal reasons only); [pers.] I would like to dedicate this poem to my sister, Jessica Castleton who has been my guardian angel through all the tough times that I have had since she has passed away. I love you sister and I love you God.; [a.] Severna Park, MD

CASTRO, OLYMPIA DEZEREA
[b.] May 3, 1978, Santa Maria, CA; [p.] Belly Riley, Rick Aquino; [ed.] Currently in High School; [occ.] Student; [memb.] Boys Girls Club of Santa Maria; [hon.] Reading; [oth. writ.] Been writing since 4th, one poem published in local newspaper.; [pers.] I don't think I would be the person I am today, if it wasn't for my 8th grade teacher, Miss Katie she always said that I can do it and she was right.; [a.] Santa Maria, CA

CASTRO, RACHEL
[b.] May 2, 1993, Long Beach; [p.] Melton (Castro)

Ophelia; [ed.] I started in Cerritas Elem. then in the second grade I transferred to Our Lady of the Rosary I graduated and attended and graduated from Paramount High; [occ.] I am full time student at Southwestern College; [memb.] I am currently an orange belt in Karate and Valentua in the Karate Class for the Boys and Girls Club of America.; [oth. writ.] Although I been writing for many years I never tried entering or publishing my poems; [pers.] I believe that we all go through life doing the best we can and that's all we can ask of one another.

CASWELL, LAUREN DEEANN
[b.] August 29, 1984, Long Beach, CA; [p.] Ronald Caswell, Delores Caswell; [ed.] A.E. Arnold Elementary; [occ.] 5th grade student; [memb.] Rad (Reading Aloud Daily) membership; [hon.] 5th grade class president, Blue Ribbon Science Fair Award Recipient, Arnold Reading Award, The Outstanding English Award; [oth. writ.] Several poems showcased in Little Lion Hall, Article published in the School Paper; [pers.] I write to reflect the thoughts in my mind. I picture people, objects, and things that I as a child may question. I write so that people will appreciate the beauty of reading.; [a.] Corona, CA

CATHEY, WILMA COPELAND
[b.] August 24, 1906, Collin County, TX; [p.] Mr. and Mrs. James C. Copeland; [m.] Thomas Brannon Cathey, June 27, 1937; [ed.] Master Degree - Standford University, Palo Alto, California, taught public school for 42 years; [occ.] Retired Teacher; [memb.] I was initiated into the Pi Lamb Theta - a National Honor and professional Association for women in Education - sponsored by Dr. H. Hanna Head of Stanford's Educational (for professional) department; [hon.] I've travel extensively - visiting all continents except Australia. I've been in all of the countries large cities. I've toured and studied in many European countries.; [oth. writ.] I've been writing since early childhood. Years spent writing "Thoughts for the Day" in prose last two years, I've written "Prayer for Today" in poetry, I'm planning on compiling a Daily Devotion with scripture and poem for calendar year.; [pers.] I am a widow of 25 years. I am the sole survival of a family of nine children. I'm 88 years old, badly crippled from Arthritis I live in a Retirement Center . I write for our new letter and spend my time reading and writing.

CATTON, DENNIS L.
[b.] December 15, 1963, Detroit, MI; [p.] Mildred and Sal; [ed.] BA in Communications from Central Michigan University; [occ.] Truck dispatcher; [memb.] PHI Beta Sigma a fraternity Inc.; [hon.] All were doing high school.; [oth. writ.] If I were dead, fear of the black man, came and love me, black mans relationship with the black women; [pers.] Why be serious when you don't have to. With out poetry, music or God is my life, I might have give up a long time ago. My poetry has always been serious and was reflected my experiences, thought, and reflections of life, love, loneliness etc. [a.] Detroit, MI

CAVALONE, BRIAN
[b.] October 3, 1974, Brooklyn, NY; [ed.] Monsignor Farrell High School; [occ.] Service Technician for Nynex (Telephone Company); [hon.] Personal pride; [oth. writ.] None published; [pers.] Sincerity, hence purity, nothing will ever divide me from myself!; [a.] New York, NY

CELOSIA, CARMEL B.
[pen.] Carjel Benturan; [b.] April 14, 1970, San Carlos City, Philippines; [p.] Cristituto Celosia, Marcelina Celosia; [ed.] Colegio De Santo Tomas-Recoletos, Southwestern University Doctor of Veterinary Medicine; [memb.] Southwestern University Alumni Association, Inc. and stop Trafficking of Pilipinos Foundation, Inc; [oth. writ.] Several articles published in WOMAN'S HOME COMPANION magazine, an, article in our College paper and a joke published in the same magazine; [pers.] Nothing is impossible if one has faith and courage in his inner self.; [a.] San Carlos City Negros Occidental, Philippines

CENICOLA, MERLE JOY AMITIN
[pen.] Joy Cenicola; [b.] April 5, 1936, Bronx, NY; [p.] Gladys Epstein Amitid and Ernest Amitin; [m.] Philip Cenicola, December 16, 1953; [ch.] Jessica Lynn, Louis Stephen, Philip A.; [ed.] Agriculture - art major in high school apprentice at surrey a barharbor maine playhouses theater arts, publicity and public relations.; [occ.] Kennel owner-operator breeder-canine trainer; [memb.] German Shepherd Dog club of America WDA, National Audobon SOC National Parks Assoc, International Wildlife Assoc.; [oth. writ.] Several honorable mentions in poetry contests. Published in a childrens magazine and two poetry anthologies. Articles in local newspapers, and editor of newsletter for NNJ Gifted child Assoc.; [pers.] My favorite poet Robert Frost - an early influence. I try to share my deep love and appreciation of nature through my poetry. My writing is an extension of my innermost being and beliefs, exposed and shared with all, wanting to see them! and willing to share them.; [a.] Brookfield, NY

CERAR, VIRGINIA
[pen.] Ginny; [b.] December 28, 1962, Bethpage, NY; [p.] Mr. and Mrs. Daniel Buckley; [m.] Jack Cerar, September 16, 1988; [ed.] Massapequa High School, Nassau Community College; [occ.] Electronic Sales for K.C. Electronics; [hon.] Published in after the storm and one moment in time.; [oth. writ.] Stranger Little Girl's Prayers, The Flight of a Bird, Thru The Eyes of a Child, Goodbye My Friend, Goodbye, The Caged Bird Flies; [pers.] This poem was written for a true friend she has loved me for me and has encouraged me to be who I am no more. No less just me. Gail Tessitore you are a special friend. I love you too.; [a.] Islip Terrace, NY

CERBERUS, DAMIEN RYAN
[pen.] DRC Ancient; [b.] April 19th, Si Gai San; [p.] Of the family tree; [m.] Of the breast cut, since destiny decided; [ch.] Ones lost within the day and left to the night time.; [ed.] Privately and individually tutored throughout life.; [occ.] Nocturnal writer and world traveler; [memb.] Brothers of the breast cut.; [hon.] To have experienced life and death. To be in love.; [oth. writ.] Book "Vampiric Verses" published by sunset publishing, ISBN 0-9642180-0-3. Various publications of the horror persuasion.; [pers.] Within birth comes life, within life comes death, within death comes immortality. Dream in technicolor; [a.] Si Gai San, DRC666

CHAKRABARTTY, SUJIT
[pen.] Sujit Chakrabartty; [b.] April 1, 1928, Rangpur, India; [p.] Upendra Chakrabartty, Kshirodbala Choudhury; [m.] Aruna Roychoudhury, April 23, 1959; [ch.] Avi, Shreela and Shomee; [ed.] University of Calculta, Brandies and Pittsburgh, Pa. Ph. D. in chemistry.; [occ.] Environmental consultant; [memb.] American Chemical Society Canadian Institute and Chemistry Chemical Society London, society of friends of Nepal. Hindu society of Alberta Ramakrishna mission and Malh india.; [hon.] Fellow, chemical institute of Canada. Energy Scholar National Science Foundation, U.S.A. Foreign Scholar: Japan MITI Award.; [oth. writ.] Technical Papers and communication on chemistry and fossil feels. Short stories and plays in Bengalee publications.; [pers.] Life-style and thought complex reflected in the teaching of 'Vedanta' philosophy are my beacon and guiding light. The life and writings of Romain Rolland have been my inspiration; [a.] Edmonton Alberta, Canada

CHALLIS, DOREEN
[pen.] Dorin or Ida Challis; [b.] June 13, 1931, Westminster, England; [p.] Theodore Haywood and Florence Haywood; [m.] Alfred Challis, December 26, 1952; [ch.] David and Madeline (Deceased), Grandchildren - Luke, Tomy, Wilson; [ed.] State Schools (England) (College Business) England Cheam UM; [occ.] Joint partner (family) Jocko's beach fishing resort; [memb.] Subud (UK) ISUL Group International (Ottawa Canada); [oth. writ.] Subud Journal Poems and Articles - poems I'm magazines 1958-1969.; [pers.] As a child I wrote Poetry constantly, which was regularly published in the school papers. Unfortunately this was all lost when our house was bombed in the 39/45 war. I believe my most imaginative work was done as a child, but have been unable to recall in detail only in theme this work. I am very interested in self growth through Meditative practises. My writing is usually concerned with injustice, as in war or famines, prejudices, and in spiritual growth, and reflective reverie.; [a.] Calabogie Ontario, Canada

CHAMBERS, FREEMAN GRANT
[pen.] Freeman G. Chambers; [b.] September 27, 1956, Pittsburgh, PA; [p.] Eugene F. Chambers and Helen Chambers; [ch.] Elisha A.V. Chambers; [ed.] Patterson Co-op high Univ. of Cincinnati; [occ.] Mechanical Designer, Designing Aircraft Lighting; [hon.] Employee of the year Kimstock Inc.; [oth. writ.] Other poems not published. Working on a novel at the time of this printing.; [pers.] 'My little gold mine' and written about a dear friend, teri maae. To know her, just read the poem. She is a joy to know and she is my little gold mine. Thank you my Lord Jesus for your love and all you have done for me.; [a.] Orange, CA

CHANDLER, RAQUAL
[b.] May 6, 1970, Fremont, CA; [p.] Dale Chandler, Patricia Chandler; [ed.] Esparto high, Esparto CA, Broward Community College, Penbroke Pines, FL; [occ.] Volunteer Receptionist, Middlesex Memorial Hospital Middletown, CT; [memb.] Juvenile Rheumatoid arthritis foundation, middlesex memorial hospital volunteer Services; [hon.] Third Place winner, Pan Ku poetry contest, pembroke pines, FL.; [oth. writ.] Several poems all unpublished at this time.; [pers.] As life gives tragedy, it also gives great beauty. Because I have rheumatoid arthritis and was in a wheelchair for the better part of fifteen years, my poems tend to show the beauty, hope, and peace one can find in life even when life is at it's most difficult.; [a.] Middletown, CT

CHANG, HYSIN T.
[pen.] Tinisia Marie Ortiz; [b.] March 24, 1956, Trenton, NJ; [p.] Mary M. Figueroa (Chang); [ed.] Wildwood High School, Glenwood Elementary School, Wildwood, NJ.; [occ.] Cashier; [hon.] Second Honors, Math Awards; [oth. writ.] Siblings, no turning back. Somewhere done for school articles and paper (The Warrior); [pers.] When I'm writing my poems its a reflection of my thoughts and feelings for myself and others.; [a.] Trenton, NJ

CHAPIN, DONALD H.
[b.] July 25, 1949, Wichita, KS; [p.] B. R. Chapin, Nan L. Chapin; [m.] Joy E. Chapin, May 28, 1994; [ch.] Hugh H., Evelyn A.; [ed.] B. Sc. in Mech. Eng., J.D.; [occ.] Total Quality Management Consultant; [memb.] American Society of Bakery Engineer Bema-Tech Committee, United States Dressage Federation, American Quarter Horse Assoc, Liberty Presbyterian Church.; [pers.] Passion defines greatness in anything we choose to do.; [a.] Everett, WA

CHAPMAN, CHRISTIE
[b.] September 3, 1978, Alexandria, VA; [p.] Barry and Teresa Chapman; [ed.] Currently attending Mount Vernon High; [oth. writ.] Short story published in school literary magazine, articles for school newspaper.; [pers.] "November" is about a real house. The style used was inspired by Richard Brautigan.; [a.] Alexandria, VA

CHAPMAN, PAUL T. N.
[b.] 1954, Baltimore, MD; [ed.] BA Psychology; [occ.] Director of Transitional Facility for Adults with Physical Disabilities; [oth. writ.] Unpublished Journey and Revelations; [a.] Philadelphia, PA

CHAPMAN, SARITA
[b.] August 18, 1975, Washington, DC; [p.] Mary E. Andoh; [ed.] Bancroft Elem. St. Augustine Catholic School, Lincoln Jr. High, McKinley Sr. High, Trinity College; [occ.] Office assistant (Dean of Students) - Trinity College; [memb.] Funds for the Community's future (FCF), Augustana Lutheran Church, Alpha Omega Sorority FBLA (Future Business Leaders of America); [hon.] Excellence in Spanish, A.S.M Memorial Reward for community work, Honor Roll, Citizenship, American Legion, Award for working at Xerox Corp. F.B.L.A. Award, Excellence Creative Writing, Dean's List; [oth. writ.] I am currently writing a book and have written various poems that have not been published.; [pers.] Always strive to be the best; [a.] Washington, DC

CHARLES, DORIS J.
[pen.] Doris J. Charles; [b.] Tulsa, OK; [p.] Cornelius and Louise Edwards; [m.] Joseph Charles, July 13, 1969; [ch.] L. Scott Charles, Charlton V. Charles; [ed.] B.S. Degree Psychology; [occ.] Staff Associate for Pacific Bell; [pers.] It is my belief that man must live in harmony with the environment, our lack of respect for the earth will eventually lead to our demise.; [a.] San Diego, CA

CHARLES, VIRGINIA
[b.] January 16, 1978, Dowagiac, MI; [p.] Joyce Charles; [ed.] Currently I am a high school student attending J.F. Kennedy Senior High (preciously attending south High, Minneapolis); [occ.] Student and daughter; [memb.] Big Brothers and Sisters (little) Boys and Girls Club; [hon.] Student of the Month, A-honor roll recognition, Community Service award (Boys and Girls Club), youth of the year nomination, 1st place 1994 big Brothers and sisters talent show; [oth. writ.] Short-Stories, plays, musical compositions, books (I've written 3) as well as many, many other poems 25.; [pers.] When writing my poetry I feel that I am putting a piece of myself on paper. My poems as well my other works, express my deep personal views about deep personal things. I hope those who read Sarah learn from it.; [a.] Bloomington, MN

CHAVEZ, LAURA M.
[b.] September 17. 1962, Albuquerque, NM; [m.] Frank A. Chavez, September 6, 1980; [ch.] Krystal Elaine, Ryan Adrian; [ed.] Graduated Bernalillo High School, attended TVI; [occ.] Homemaker; [oth. writ.] None Published; [pers.] Poetry allows you to experience life, in a few well chosen words; [a.] Bernalillo, NM

CHAVIS, RICKY G.
[b.] April 6, 1957, Hampton, VA; [p.] George W. Chavis and Mamie L. Everette; [m.] Marianne Chavis, October 23, 1994; [ch.] Tonya-D, Kosage-S, Ayunli-S, Kateri-D, Omaen-S, Kanawha-S; [ed.] High School Graduate; [occ.] Pipe Welder at Newport News Shipbuilding and Dry Dock Co.; [memb.] Haliwa-Saponi: Indian Tribe of Hollister N.C.; [oth. writ.] Warrior's Heart is my first poem which was written in November '91, since then I have written many other poems and also one article. With the exception of one poem, none of my writings have been published. This is the first time Warrior's Heart has been published.; [pers.] "A Moment In Time" Life's blessings far outweigh its tribulations, even in troubles, life's beauty was mine. I pondered its secrets and discovered its meaning, as I journeyed through a moment in time.; [a.] Como, NC

CHENEY, STACIE
[b.] April 13, 1980, Niagara, WI; [p.] Carol and Randy Cheney; [ed.] Currently enrolled in ninth grade after graduation I want to go to school to be a lawyer.; [occ.] Babbysitter, student; [memb.] Pepclub, SADD (students against drunk driving), Student Council, Youth futures, Tutor, Peer Helpers, Class Secretary, Volleyball, Forensics, Track; [hon.] Been on "High Honors" honor roll with a 3.98 grade point average for three and 1/2 years.; [oth. writ.] I have 125 poems that I have written but none have been published.; [pers.] Don't be afraid to put your feelings down on paper and send your poem in it. I write a lot of poems on sufferings in my life.; [a.] Niagara, WI

CHENEY, WINIFRED GREEN
[pen.] Winifred Green Cheney; [b.] February 14, 1913, Jackson, MS; [p.] Mr. and Mrs. Garner Wynn Green; [m.] Reynolds Smith Cheney, October 25, 1934; [ch.] Reynolds S. Cheney II, William Garner, Winifred Calhoan; [ed.] Graduated Magna Cum Laude, Millsaps College in 1933. Took special courses at University of Colorado; [occ.] Homemaker, writer; [memb.] Board of the Old Ladies Home, Chaplain of the Daughters of the King, St. Andrews Cathedral, Chairmen for the Blind Jackson Junior League of Jackson; [hon.] Miss Press Women named the Woman of Achievement in 1980, Phi Mu Sorority, Queen of Carnival Ball in 1934, "Singing His Song" honored by National Federation of Press Women; [oth. writ.] "Southern Hospitality Cookbook" and "Cooking for Company", "Singing His Song", "The Singing Heart," columnist for the National Observer, The Christian Science Monitor, Southern World, The Rotarian, and Southern Living; [pers.] My philosophy of life is "Sharing your love with each person you meet and trying to add joy to their lives."; [a.] West Point, VA

CHERESINI, HELEN M.
[b.] July 22, 1923, Lebanon, PA; [p.] Joseph and Sala Morinchin Cheresini; [ed.] Lebanon High School, Lebanon, PA 17042; [occ.] Retired from Federal Civil Service; [pers.] My favorite motto is "Just Do It."; [a.] Lebanon, PA

CHO, DAVID
[pen.] Barry Smith; [b.] September 30, 1984, Brooklyn, NY; [p.] Seung D. Cho, Kwang O. Cho; [ed.] Currently in the 5th grade at Claremont Ave. School, Colonia, NJ and P.E.G., program at Avenel Middle School, Avenel, NJ; [occ.] Student at Claremont Ave., School in Colonia, NJ; [memb.] Full Gospel, NY Church's Choir; [hon.] Township of Woodbridge Mayor's Resolution and Honor Roll Awards; [oth. writ.] Essay about The Barron Arts Center; [pers.] I always try to work hard and help other people become Christians.; [a.] Woodbridge, NJ

CHO, JEANNE CHRISTABELLE
[pen.] Kristian Emanuelle Taylor, or/and Celeste Deveraux Alastair; [b.] May 12, 1977, Seoul, Korea; [p.] Chun Il Cho and Sun Hee Cho; [ed.] LaGuardia High School of Music, Art, and Performing Arts; [oth. writ.] No poems published, but write poems as a hobby.; [pers.] Knowledge is like a temple of faith, it continues to grow stronger with each experience.; [a.] Brooklyn, NY

CHOPRA, NITI
[b.] April 28, 1964, Ahmedabad, India; [p.] Dr. Mrs. Madhu P. Desai and Dr. P. L. Desai; [m.] Mr. Asheesh Chopra, December 11, 1988; [ed.] Masters Degree in Development Communication. From Gujarat University Ahmedabad, India.; [occ.] Lecturer in Communication, Faculty of Journalism and Communication, M.S. University of Baroda, Baroda, Gujarat, India.; [memb.] Life Member: National Council for Development Communication. Varanasi, India. Member: Centre for Development Ccommunication Alumni, Gujarat University, Ahmedabad, India.; [hon.] Awarded Gold Medals at the under graduate and post graduate levels at the university.; [oth. writ.] Have written many scripts for television productions. Have written some articles for newspapers as a freelancer.; [pers.] I am in awe of the miracles of nature ——, and I believe in the simple joy of living — with an open mind. Good humor and a positive attitude.; [a.] Baroda Gujarat, India

CHORNOBRYWY, MARION
[pen.] "Chorno" [b.] January 7, 1933, Belfast; [p.] Bob and Maisie Agnew; [m.] 1961; [ch.] Dennis and Lynn; [ed.] DEC John Abbott College (Art), B.F.A. Concordia University (Art), M.A. Interior Design, Du, Montfort U. England; [occ.] Artist, Int. Design, Art Teaching for 30 years; [memb.] Lakeshore Assoc. of Artists Montreal.; [hon.] 1st Prize in with colours Toronto 1982-1983. Schneider School of Fine Arts, Honorable Mention for which News of the World England; [oth. writ.] Poetry published in Belfast N.I., England G.B., Vancouver Canada, Gazette Montreal Christmas story; [pers.] I love to express myself through - music, art, poems, stories, etc. helped by my travels to different countries and different cultures

CHORTOS, LES
[pen.] Les Chortos; [b.] December 21, 1956, Leamington; [p.] Joe and Elizabeth Chortos; [m.] Beverly Chortos, June 27, 1981; [ch.] Steven, Alex, Nathan; [ed.] Kingsville High St. Clair College.; [occ.] Manufacturing Engineer G.M. Canada; [memb.] United Church Ruthven; [hon.] Deans Honour Roll; [oth. writ.] Many other poems - based on personal experiences plan to writes childrens poems as my 3 boys like poetry.; [pers.] I write poetry because its artistic and a nice medium for artistic expression. It's fun and challenging. I would love to write songs for artists.; [a.] Ruthven Ontario, Canada

CHOUDHRY, GUL
[b.] July 1, 1980, Amsterdam, Holland; [p.] Ghulam Choudhry, Safia Choudhry; [ed.] St. Norbert Immersion School in Winnipeg, Manitoba, St. Joseph and St. Francis

School in Tilbury, presently attending Ecole secondaire de Pain Court.; [hon.] Trophy for English, Spelling Contest in 1990, Trophy for French Spelling Contest in 1990, Trophy for English Public Speaking Contest in 1990, Trophy for Cheer leading in 1993-1994, Gold Medal for Soccer in 1990, Gold Medal for Basketball Challenge Spirit Sportmanship in 1994, Plaque for Excellent Academic in History in 1993-1994, 2nd place winner for Quaid-I-Azam Speech in 1995.; [oth. writ.] French poem published in the 1992 school journal at St. Joseph school of Tilbury, french article about Christmas in my family published in the 1994 Windsor newspaper, Le Rempart.; [pers.] I am very proud that I am a semi-finalist in the 1994 poetry contest. I am very thankful to God to give me the opportunity to express myself.; [a.] Tilbury Ontario, Canada

CHRISTENSEN, JANE ELLEN
[pen.] Jane E. Bell, Jay-Chris, Ellen Bell, Jane E. Christensen; [b.] August 25, 1939, Welland, Ontario, Canada; [p.] Anne and Richard W. Bell; [m.] Widow [ch.] 4 children, Cynthia, Donald, Richard and Elizabeth; [ed.] Educated in Ontario, Studied Royal and Toronto Conservation of Music; under prof. James Ramsbottom; [occ.] Retired Law Clerk and Sheriff's Officer; [memb.] Member St. Paul's Choir, Northport Chorale, pride of Niagara chorus, harmony Incorporated Gold Medallist chorus, hospital chairman's circle, past Beta Sigma Phi, Lioness, Political groups, Business associations, Chamber of Commerce, and Numerous appointment to Boards and panels.; [oth. writ.] Partner in Van Ellen production, producing sing-a-long music programs for therapeutic use, items published in local publications, author of plays used in volunteer groups and classes taught children.; [pers.] Various personal writings given exclusively as gifts to family and close friends. I have a large portfolio of writings, some set to music in varying forms; [a.] Ridgeway Ontario, Canada

CHRISTENSON, CONNIE
[a.] Alberta, Canada

CHURCH, JENNIFER JEAN
[b.] March 20, 1977, Salt Lake City, UT; [p.] Richard Church, Linda Church; [ed.] Graduate of Skyline High School - Attending University of Utah; [occ.] Student and intern with Ogden Raptors Baseball; [memb.] Editor - Skyline High Yearbook, Key Club, Honor Roll; [hon.] Honored for Service for Salt Lake Co. Sheriff's office Search and Rescue - Winner "The Front" creative writing contest (SLC) - Outstanding employee - Ogden Raptors Baseball.; [oth. writ.] Essay for the Nat'l Inquirer - "Jack", "In the Shadows", and "Winter". Numerous novels and short stories.; [pers.] The world is coming at us and we have no choice but to step up to the plate and take a swing.; [a.] Kearns, UT

CISNEROS, CONNIE
[b.] December 3, 1949, Los Angeles, CA; [m.] Joe Cisneros Sr., May 28, 1961; [ch.] Carmen, Joe Jr., Deanna; [ed.] Jordan High; [occ.] Q.C. Inspector; [memb.] St. Peter and St. Paul Catholic Church Alta Loma CA.; [pers.] All good blessings upon everyone and better health to come

CIUCCARELLI, EILEEN B.
[b.] May 10, Mount Carmel, PA; [p.] Wm. F. Covaleskie and Anna Savitsky; [m.] Gae (Gaetano) Ciuccarelli, January 28, 1950; [ch.] 1 Daughter (Mt. Carmel); [ed.] Jr. and Sr. High, College of Art, Phila, Pa., Duquesne University, Pitts., PA., Hahnemann Medical College, Phila PA. - Medical Laboratory Technician.; [occ.] Poet and artist (freelance) and lyricist, songwriter Levittown artists; [memb.] Retired from to write and have time to pursue poetry. A member of "River Poets" of Newhope, PA. (An artist' community and tourist attraction); [hon.] Oh! I forgot World of Poetry, Sacramento, Calif., sent me a certificate of award. (Of honor) as a 1985 Golden Poet, and published my poem in an anthology other poets received the same kind of award, so it was not an "exclusive" award to me. [oth. writ.] Several poems published by forum publishing Inc Valley forges PA. (I was paid 75.00) what a feeling also, I am a lyricist and songwriter of Art songs, love songs, romantic and country Western.; [pers.] Perspective - in poetry, I found a voice, to say feeling, that everyday words do not say. I did not seek, I did not search? Ah, but I did. (In Philosophies and Poetics) it was given to me, a gift, but not for free, the price? Sufferings, in love and life and also joy and happiness, surprise. (And The gift, A Behooven Betoken Gift). Poetry, is an art form and artistry. I paint a picture, in words, and the canvas, to display it, is the white, white paper, and words, the picture and the gallery, not only my mind, of memory, but the Library of Books of Poetry, in our house, and the walls of time. Too, and the walls of time, eternity. And the haus of time, the years, that poetry lives, and the words, destructible and indestructible, the white paper, destructible and yet preserved, and the words become immortal and treasured. And of my Poetry, and the inspiration time, my life and experiences in love and life. And too, perhaps perchance, also my words, preserved, and saved. For "Time and Chance are Destiiny", for infinity and words too, and with me, the inspiration time, this time 4 A. M.; [a.] Langhorne, PA

CLAIR, SCOTT
[b.] October 28, 1971, Chicago; [ed.] Bachelor of Arts in Literature and Philosophy, 1994, Marquette University, Milwaukee, WI.; [memb.] Phi Beta Kappa, Sigma Tau Delta, Phi Kappa Tau: Honor Societies. Phi Delta Theta National Fraternity.; [oth. writ.] Published two original poems in Western reading services 1994 anthology, in other words, Denver, Colorado; [pers.] The aesthetic experience of poetry is, at this time, the main concern of my poems, with this, foremost in my reading and writing is the desire to express something new through and in the evolution of the poetic traditional.; [a.] Chicago, IL

CLAPS, ANDREW
[b.] March 16, 1967, New York, NY; [p.] Patricia Claps, Joseph Claps; [ed.] Archbishop Molloy H.S., C.W. Post College - Long Island University; [occ.] Proof Reader, Sterling Grace Capital Management, L.P., New York, NY; [memb.] Appalachian Mountain Club.; [hon.] Summa Cum Laude, News writing Merit Award, Freshman Honors Recipient, Dean's List.; [oth. writ.] Articles for college newspaper, poems published in school's literary journal, automobile-related pieces featured in several car magazines.; [pers.] My "Poetry" is aimed at the common nihilist in everyone. It usually speaks loudest to those who function better in the dark.; [a.] Queen Village, NY

CLARK, DOROTHY L.
[b.] December 16, 1991, Kenova, WV; [p.] Luther and Louise Davis; [m.] Widow, March 9, 1935; [ch.] Louise Drummond - Peggy Sheets; [ed.] High School-1929, Registered Nurse - 1932; [occ.] Retired R.N; [memb.] Members Pontius Methodist Church for 55 yrs; [hon.] Valedictorian 1929 Registered Nurse 1932; [oth. writ.] Numerous poems concerning family mostly.; [pers.] Most of my poetry was written for special occasions for school of church affairs; [a.] Columbia, OH

CLARK-GOLD, MELISHA RONA
[b.] April 6, 1955, NC; [p.] Helen Brooks and Daddy Brooks; [ch.] Emmanuel, Shantelle, Sylvia and Sharissa; [memb.] Parent Teacher Organization, New Shiloh Baptist Church; [hon.] Being selected as a semi-finalist in the 1994 North American open Poetry Contest and my poem published in A Moment in Time; [oth. writ.] My work is as intimate as me and as universal as you. These poems encompass many areas of life. I've written a book of poems. My greatest pleasure is experimenting with different literary forms of expression, and then discovering new exciting forms that represent me. I hope and pray that one day someone will publish my work and new life and meaning will be infused with each reading.; [pers.] I am a woman with great needs, very little means, and lots of faith." Therefore, "I believe that Jesus is the answer to everything!"

CLARK, GREEG
[b.] August 4, 1963, Mission British Columbia, Canada; [p.] Marion Clark, Bert Clark; [m.] Lisa Clark, July 2, 1988; [ch.] Ashley, Jordan; [ed.] Mission Senior Secondary; [occ.] Restaurant Manager; [pers.] This poem was originally given to my girlfriend, as a graduation gift, and was later used on our wedding invitations. It was also given on a scroll to each guest at our reception. All my poems have very special family ties.; [a.] Abbotsford British Columbia, Canada

CLARK, MRS. JOAN E.
[pen.] Evelyn Sefton; [b.] August 21, 1924, Liverpool, England; [p.] Frank and Olive Leeson; [m.] Anthony Clark; [ch.] David, Paul, Joanne and Lueinda; [ed.] Grammar School State Registered Nurse, Midwife and Health Visitor; [occ.] Retired; [oth. writ.] "The Brooch" Published by Minerva Press. 2nd Novel Almost complete; [pers.] It is never too late to start writing. Memories of the past become more meaningful as one gets older. Let the young read about them and make judgements.; [a.] Llanrhystud, Wales

CLARKE, BROOKE
[b.] January 10, 1977, Richmond; [p.] Frances and Lawrence Clarke; [ed.] Hermitage High 11th grade; [occ.] student; [memb.] FBLA, FHA Future Business Leaders of America, Future Homemakers of America; [pers.] My poetry is very personal it is through this I express my deepest thoughts and concerns. I hope other people can get enjoyment and pleasure out of something I enjoy; [a.] Richmond, VA

CLARKE, JUANITA DOTSON
[b.] September 16, 1921, Sumter, SC; [p.] Bessie Mae Evans Dotson and Oliver T. Dotson; [m.] Joseph Thomas Clarke, January 19, 1941; [ch.] Three sons, one daughter; [ed.] High School and 1 year post graduate Spokane, WA, where I grew up to adulthood; [occ.] Conservator and designer of Victorian fashions for Antique Dolls; [memb.] Les' Bebe' Doll Club. (Member UFDC) also member of the Camden N.J. Chapter of The Eastern Star - #35.; [oth. writ.] Many other poems through the years varied subjects. Some happy - sentimental - some sad, and more than these were my favorites about the lighter times I want to remember - 'My Roses in December'; [pers.] Tho my life has been through many painful periods, I've kept my head 'above water' by remembering the happiness times. These thoughts have sustained me. Much still is ahead for me.; [a.] Somerdale, NJ

CLARKE, LEONARD
[pen.] Leonard Clarke; [b.] Barbados, WI; [p.] Errol and Ismay Thornhill; [ch.] Rohand and Adrian; [ed.] Bay Primary Boys School, Barbados Community College; [occ.] Public Health Inspector (Associate Degree) (Diploma); [memb.] Ministry of Health Sports Club, United Athletic Club; [hon.] (Credit) National Independence, Festival of Creative Arts (1977); [pers.] God-given talents should be used to identify the minds of men, and also to express the love of God.

CLAYWELL, ETHEL
[pen.] Ethel Claywell; [b.] June 2, 1913, KY; [p.] Deceased; [m.] Deceased, October 7, 1933; [ch.] Two [ed.] High School; [hon.] I received many awards in art. The only writing I did was for the paper and for my own enjoyment.; [oth. writ.] I will buy the book of poems that my poem is in.; [pers.] I wrote for our local paper for years promoting an art group I had started. "An examples of my work enclosed."

CLEMENS, PATRICK S.
[b.] May 6, 1972, Columbia; [p.] B. William Clemens II, Barbara Bauer; [ed.] St. Marks Grammar School, St. Joseph's Collegiate Inst., S.U.N.Y. Geaeseo (2 years); [occ.] Line Cook, at Family Restaurant; [memb.] Phi Sigma Xi, Men's Soccer Club; [oth. writ.] Various unpublished poems some titled, "Run Little Child..." "A part of me" "The helping Cup" and various untitled poems; [pers.] I have loved poetry all my life both as an education subject and as a recreational hobbie. I am thankful to be able to share my work with you and am looking forward to reading your works as well. Success and happiness.; [a.] Buffalo, NY

CLEMENTS, MR. ASHLEY T.
[b.] June 19, 1973, Jacksonville, FL; [p.] Wellington I., Martha C. Clements; [pers.] "...Flee from such impeccable conviction thy creed is thy vow of animosity within our duration blasphemy prevails upon our existence"; [a.] Richmond, VA

CLEROUX, ROGER R.
[pen.] "Ted" [b.] September 12, 1936, Janier Ontario, Canada; [p.] Joseph-Cyprico and Ida Cleroux; [m.] Leola Irene Hannington; [ch.] Beverly and Patricia Hannington; [ed.] Completed secondary grade 12 High School. Theory of office management. Algebra and Geometry and Drafting.; [occ.] Shipping and Receiving Room - 12 years.; [memb.] Knight of Columbus in 1972, 5571 Eastview Branch.; [hon.] Mostly in sports. Bowling, LaCrosse and Broomball.; [oth. writ.] Sort of biographies of friends.; [a.] Janier Ontario, Canada

CLOKE, CHRIS
[b.] January 6, 1975, Colorado Springs, CO; [p.] William and Patricia Cloke; [ed.] Graduated from Washington High School in San Francisco, CA in 1993. Currently a sophomore at Central Washington University in the English Education Department.; [pers.] I am working towards my goal of becoming an English teacher for middle school children and to continue writing on the side.; [a.] Ellensburg, WA

CLONINGER, SYLVIA STORM
[b.] November 6, 1955, Redding, CA; [p.] June Storm Elfving and James P. Storm; [m.] Dr. Ashton Cloninger, November 3, 1984; [ed.] College of San Mateo; [occ.] Interior Designer and Art Dealer Along with Business Manager of Husbands Practice.; [memb.] Visual Aids, Project open hand, Stanford Childrens Circle; [oth. writ.] Several Poems Published locally and scholastically.; [pers.] Mrs. Storm - Cloninger endeavors to show the life experiences of woman, as child, teenager, and adult. She is greatly influenced by the writings of Sylvia Plath, Robert Frost, and Dyian Thomas; [a.] Belmont, CA

CLOWE, KATHLEEN JOSEPHINE
[pen.] Kate Thomson (Maiden Name) [b.] January 30, 1962, Priest Hill Glasgow, Scotland; [p.] Grace J. Thomson and Robert Chambers; [m.] Graham D. Hogg; [ch.] Tyrone V. Clowe; [ed.] Chilliwack High Chilliwack, B.C., Canada; [occ.] Packer for a moving company for past 10 yrs.; [hon.] My only awards received in my lifetime, have been for bowling (5 pin); [oth. writ.] Have been writing poetry since age 12, but, none have ever been published even though people have told me to send them in, after reading them, I just didn't have the confidence.; [pers.] All of my poetry is straight from my heart, and they usually revolve around present or past, circumstances in my life. I like to let my readers feel what I am feeling, whey I write my poems.; [a.] Chilliwack British Columbia, Canada

COE, BERNIECE
[pen.] Bee Coe; [b.] December 30, 1907, Valhalla, NY; [p.] Nellie and Edgar More; [m.] Henry Coe, November 20, 1965; [ed.] 2 1/2 yrs High School.; [occ.] Homemaker.; [memb.] Belford Methodist Church V.F.W. 2179 Nimble Fingers Community Service middletown Township Scheisure Group; [hon.] Nomurated nomanol year 1991 nominated Sr tennent of year. Certificate appreciation. 50 yrs. member church 44 yrs S.S. teacher. Clowiking for retarded children; [oth. writ.] Many poems my memories book. I can not purchase bable limited finances my brothers preston more meet by one.; [pers.] In 87 enjoy people active in organizations 14 years president of N.L.C.S. non profit org - making hand made bay clothes 1994 gone 1428 articles of clothing all how to local needy

COFFARO, MELANIE
[b.] June 24, 1975, Tampa, FL; [p.] Frederick Coffaro, Brenda Coffaro; [ed.] Gaither High School, Hillsborugh Community College; [occ.] Full-time student; [hon.] Phi Theta Kappa, Dean's List; [oth. writ.] Published letter in the commentary page of local newspaper.; [pers.] My endeavor is to utilize my writings as a tool in challenging others to realize the true treasures of our existence.; [a.] Tampa, FL

COFFEE, CHRISTINA
[pen.] Christina Coffee; [b.] November 12, 1978, Pico Rivera, CA; [p.] Patricia Coffee; [ed.] Junior in High School; [occ.] Student; [oth. writ.] Other poetry; [pers.] Poetry is my joy and is my life.; [a.] Whittier, CA

COGAN, SHEILA M.
[b.] November 26, 1971, Philadelphia, PA; [p.] Frank and Rita Cogan; [ed.] Little Flower Catholic H.S., Bloomsburg University, West Chester University; [occ.] Paralegal, Law Offices of Kevin C. Tierney, Phila, PA; [memb.] Phi Sigma Pi Nat'l Honor Fraternity; [oth. writ.] Several unpublished poems.; [pers.] My greatest literary influences: Absurdist drama and the poetry of John Donne and Emily Dickinson.; [a.] Philadelphia, PA

COHEN, ARLENE
[pen.] Arlene Botkelen or Arlene Botkelen Cohen; [b.] March 15, 1936, Brooklyn, NYC; [p.] Ben Batkelen and Rose Botkelen; [m.] Howard Cohen, August 1, 1977; [ed.] S.V. Tilden high, Brooklyn College; [occ.] Retired elementary school teacher, (artists poet as avocations); [memb.] National Assoc. of women artists (NAWA); [hon.] N.Y. Art student's league award Queensborough Community College Departmental Award for excellence in art; [pers.] Thoughout my life I have become increasingly aware of a spiritual force which consistenly and persistently moves us forward to ever higher levels of development. My poetry is a paean to this loving energy.; [a.] Long Island, NY

COHEN, DIANE ANGELA
[b.] April 28, 1981, Brooklyn, NY; [p.] Daniel and Paula Cohen; [ed.] P.S. 99 Sigma Program, Mark Twain Intermediate School for the Gifted and Talented; [occ.] Student; [memb.] Mark Twain Art Club, O.L.G. Basketball; [hon.] School Honor Roll; [oth. writ.] Poetry and articles published in school newspapers.; [pers.] I'd like to thank my family and friends for all their support.; [a.] Brooklyn, NY

COLBERT SR., ALBERT G.
[b.] December 27, 1951, Helena, AR; [p.] Louis and Clara Colbert; [m.] Reina M. Colbert, June 3, 1992; [ch.] Albert G. II, Brandy, Danielle, Derek Nathaniel; [ed.] Eliza Miller High (W. Helena, AR), United Electronics Institute (Louisville, KY), Southwest Missouri State University (Springfield, MD); [occ.] Contract Inspector City Utilities of Springfield, MD; [memb.] United States Naval Reserve; [hon.] 1990 New York Study Lift Award. (My Senior Year At Southwest Missouri State University); [oth. writ.] Two other poems, both of which won first place in two different local radio station contests.; [pers.] My writings bring forth my inner most feelings on any subject that I choose to write on.; [a.] Springfield, MO

COLGIN, KEVIN JOHN
[b.] May 22, 1957, Northridge, CA; [p.] Dr. Ruseel W. Colgin, Anne fourthoffer; [occ.] Customer service; [oth. writ.] Various; [pers.] Make the moment. Put a smile on your face. Have love in your heart. Respect yourself and life. Live to be the best you can be.; [a.] Woodland Hills, CA

COLLIER, CRYSTAL M.
[b.] March 6, 1978, Ohio; [p.] Donald and Gail Collier; [ed.] Junior withrow High School ISA (International Studies Academy) Cincinnati, Ohio; [occ.] Student; [memb.] Student council, girls scout, foreign language club, captain volleyball; [hon.] Selected for first honors, leadership award, perfect attendance, best all around, best defensive player, (Valleyball), Soccer; [oth. writ.] Freedom, the freedom, Mother knows best, the love in my eyes, everlasting freedom.; [pers.] I have been interest in writing poetry, since the sixth grade. I believe that it's good to write about personal experiences.; [a.] Cincinnati, OH

COLLINETTI, ESTHER
[b.] November 9, 1975, Nigeria, Lagos; [p.] Giovanni Collinetti, Christina Collinetti; [ed.] Nido De Aguilas (Chile) Colorado State University (U.S.A.); [occ.] Studying to be a future wild life veterinary; [hon.] I have won various diplomas for been champion in Chile for horse back riding (Dressage). Diplomas for been leader in High School! Honors for Artistic talent. [oth. writ.] I write for myself. It helps me think of what I feel in a special moment of the day.; [pers.] Bleeding tears may fall while your face is full of mud. But one must always find that internal nourishment to feed your dreams, goals, and accomplishments.; [a.] Fort Collins, CO

COLLINS, DELENE DEE
[b.] April 25, 1934, Los Angeles, CA; [p.] Martin and L. Inez Obermire; [m.] Kenneth L. Collins, October 21, 1951; [ch.] Kathy Jones, David and Karen Collins; [ed.] Bakersfield High, 1951 Fresno City College, A.S. Degree 1972 and Lic. Vocational Nurse; [occ.] Creative Housewife, Poet retired nurse; [hon.] Phi Beta Kappa, Dean's List; [oth. writ.] Several poems published in newspaper Geneology and Family Biography spaning 100 years near completion, Short story, childrens story. Montana De Oro travelog.; [pers.] In college at 36 to obtain a nursing degree, an interested Eng. teacher encouraged me to switch my major to writing. Seventeen years later I began to write. I love to express myself through written word. Will try my hand at greeting cards, lyrics, Hope to submit more of my work of publishers.; [a.] Oakhurst, CA

COLLINS, SHIRLEY ANN
[pen.] Bay; [b.] July 8, 1947, Brunswick, GA; [p.] Andrew and Alice Patterson; [ch.] Teresa, Lakesha and Kwame; [ed.] Risley High, Brunswick, GA, College Courses, at Community College, Philadelphia, PA; [occ.] Nurse Assistance Moss Reha Hospital; [oth. writ.] The man with white bags in his hand, I am I crazy, to be, and Mommy I want to cry. Can you come out to play; [a.] Philadelphia, PA

COMISKEY, MATT
[b.] December 29, 1969, Toronto, Ontario; [p.] Joseph Comiskey, Leitha Comiskey; [occ.] Soul searcher; [oth. writ.] "Hollow Man" - Amherst Society, Summer 1991. Some poems published in school newspapers, the rest clutter the floors of my apartment, waiting for life.; [pers.] Immensely inspired by the beat poets of the 1950's, Charles Bukowski and the writings of Jim Morrison. For me, writing is an instrument, A voice, crying out through obscured truths and false realities which have been force fed since - birth. To those who dare to write and dream: Cheers! [a.] St. Chatham Ontario, Canada

COMPTON, MICHAEL
[pen.] Mike Compton; [b.] May 24, 1958, Ashland, KY; [p.] Mary A. Compton and John H. Compton (Deceased); [ed.] Russell School System, Russell, KY, Ashland's Paul G. Blazer High School, Ashland, KY, Morehead State University, Morehead, KY; [occ.] Architectural Designer; [pers.] God gave us the gift to live on this earth, what we do after that creates our own destiny.; [a.] Lexington, KY

CONDRA, WILLIAM L.
[b.] January 29, 1949, Lexington, KY; [ch.] Lee and Thomas; [ed.] Lafayette High School; [occ.] Operations manager for Duncan Machinery Movers; [a.] Lexington, KY

CONNOLLY, MICHELLE
[b.] July 25, 1967, Toronto, Canada; [m.] Logan Connolly, February 20, 1993; [pers.] My insight will guide the path through my personal growth.; [a.] Hamilton, Canada

CONROY, ROBERT
[pen.] Bob Conroy; [b.] August 23, 1943, Denver, CO; [p.] Barbara Louise Laugdon, Robert L. Conroy; [m.] Divorced; [ch.] 4 Steven, Carrie, Robbin, Robert II; [ed.] High School graduated Santa Ana High School 1961 20 years in retail store management 5 1/2 years in custudial Janitorial work.; [occ.] Maintenance Janitor; [oth. writ.] I've written several christian poems and poems of love inspired by A love I once felt for a woman I met 8 months ago none have yet to be published till now.; [pers.] I have a deep a biding faith in Christianity and have come to know Jesus as my savior in 1983. It is my wish to serve God through christian poetry to reach out and touch other people. I have written for my love and many friends.; [a.] Yucaipa, CA

CONVERSE, NICOLE
[b.] May 29, 1978, Salem, OR; [p.] Bill and Ronna Shulz; [ed.] Douglas High School, 1701 Hamilton Street Douglas, Wyoming 82633; [occ.] McDonalds'; [memb.] Civil Air Patrol (Auxiliary of the Air force) Church Youth Group American Heart Association; [pers.] I love to write poems. Though sometimes I have to be in the mood. I like to express many feelings in them.; [a.] Douglas, WY

COOK, AMANDA
[b.] November 26, 1976, Hamilton, AL; [p.] Steve Cook, Becky Evans, [m.] Robert W. Tidwell, Jr., May 20, 1995; [ed.] Haleyville High School; [occ.] Hand sander, Unique Dinettes, Inc.; [oth. writ.] This is my first writing; [a.] Haleyville, AL

COOK, SHERRY MARIE
[pen.] Cheetah [b.] August 13, 1971, Bethlehem, PA; [p.] Russ Rader, Donna Simmons, Michael Simmons, Step-Father; [ed.] Nazareth high school; [occ.] Waitress, Bartender; [pers.] Writing lyrics and poems has always come naturally for me. I have written hundreds of lyrics. I have been greatly influenced by my mother and the rest of my family, who have always encouraged me.; have always encouraged me.; [a.] Nazareth, PA

COOKE, EDWARD ANDREW
[pen.] E. A. Cooke; [b.] November 6, 1964, Belfast, Northern Ireland; [p.] William and Ellen Cooke; [m.] Gillian Cooke, October 19, 1993; [ed.] Royal Belfast Academical Institution, The Queens University of Belfast; [occ.] Medical Doctor; [memb.] Fellow of Royal College of Surgeons in Ireland; [hon.] Irish Orthopaedic Association Prize, 1994 British Medical Association Bursary, 1994; [pers.] Quarere Verum - To seek the truth; [a.] Hillsborough, Northern Ireland

COOKE, HILARY
[pen.] Hilary Cooke; [b.] March 14, 1956, Stoutton-On-Tees; [ed.] State Education, Secondary Modern School.; [occ.] Company Director.; [oth. writ.] Several poems and song's about life as I see it.; [pers.] To be happy in this short life. You should give love and understanding to those you know and meet, but above all, love and understand yourself. So you can be complete.; [a.] Burham Rochester, England

COOPER, MARY ALICE
[pen.] M. Alice Cooper; [b.] May 23, 1926, Santa Barbara; [p.] Rayo and Victorina Hernandez; [m.] Samuel J. Cooper (Dec 1984), July 5, 1963; [ch.] 1 Step-Dau. Diane; [ed.] SB School System Graduated SBHS 1994. Studied French Adult Ed; [occ.] Retired; [memb.] RSVP (Retired senior volunteer program) taught spanish to seniors. Inactive member of native daughters golden west and sweet adelines. Also American diabetes Assoc.; [pers.] I love words, and foreign languages. I sponsor a Brazilian child for about 8-9 yrs. Tried learning portuguese, failed and put it on "Hold" for now. Love to travel; [a.] Santa Barbara, CA

COOPER, NATHANIEL
[b.] June 7, 1971, Long Island, NY; [p.] Ira Cooper, Rhona Cooper; [ed.] Queens College, Adelphi University; [memb.] American Political Science Association; [hon.] Dean's List, repeated mention; [oth. writ.] Several Poems awaiting publication, completing work on a novel.; [a.] Briarwood, NY

CORLETT, MARTHA
[b.] June 22, 1908, Big Patch, WI; [p.] William Douglas and Mary Alice Corlett; [m.] Old Maid!; [ed.] One year at Eastern State Teacher's College (1927-8) Summer Schools, Extension, correspondence, etc. - Received B.S. degree in Elementary Ed. in 1968, from Huron Colleges"; [occ.] Retired, Painting and writing poetry. (Grumbling!); [memb.] American Lutheran Church S.D. Retired Teachers.; [hon.] Nominated in 1993 for the "Spirit of Dakota" state award. Received local award.; [oth. writ.] "Creation of the flowers," "My Garden", "A Training for Peace" and "Black Hills" all in "Prairie Poets II," 1958 Edition, Many others in "Pasque Petals," S.D. Poetry Magazine.; [pers.] I taught 45 years, 29 in rural schools, 12 in Consolidated, 4 in DeSmet City School, retired in 1974. I Always tried to do 2 things, school should be fun, but we must do our work first, and I never made a promise I didn't intend to keep, and I expected the same from my pupils.; [a.] DeSmet, SD

CORONA, DIANA
[pen.] Natasha; [b.] March 20, 1958, Los Angeles; [p.] Gloria G. Ortiz; [m.] Victor Corona (artist), February 17, 1984; [ch.] Jennifer Nicole; [ed.] Sacred Heart of Jesus. High School, East. Los Angeles J.C., Calif. State University of Los Angeles; [occ.] Bookkeeper First National Funding Group; [oth. writ.] The leaf, 1975-76 National Book of Poetry (Natasha); [pers.] From my Heart Evolves my renditions of my poetry; [a.] El Monte, CA

CORONADO, SOFIA LAMB
[b.] August 12, 1949, Mexico City, DF; [p.] Thomas Lawerence, Alicia Sevilla Lamb; [m.] Divorced; [ch.] Ganelle D. Frizzell, Marcos A. Coronado; [ed.] Thomas Jefferson High, Ben Shaw Modeling Inst., Barbizon Modeling Inst.; [occ.] Completion of personal Chawking, for poetry chapbook 1995; [memb.] Lupus foundation, Christian Pro. Life, Club 12 A.A.; [hon.] Home-maker hand - maiden of God almighty; [oth. writ.] Bright lights, in the word, magazine assembly of God publication; [a.] TX

CORREA, JOHN DAVID
[b.] August 8, 1959, Chicago, IL; [p.] Joseph and Mary Correa; [m.] Maureen Lee Correa, July 4, 1990; [ch.] Damian Lee Correa; [ed.] Lewis University Northern Illinois University; [occ.] Broker for Collectibles International; [oth. writ.] Short stories, music lyrics; [pers.] Your mind, being your primary decision maker, should and can't be ignored but your heart and soul will give you so much more. Listen to all, and when you call, you'll find the right door.; [a.] Chicago, IL

CORTES, ALICIA
[b.] March 4, 1971, Rome, GA; [p.] Geof and Romi Colton; [ch.] Michael Antony and Amber Dawn; [ed.] Secretary; [hon.] Second place in Jr. High's country poetry contest and first prize in high school's country poetry contest.; [oth. writ.] I've been writing poetry since I was eight years old.; [a.] Miami, FL

CORYELL, PEGGY J.
[pen.] Maggie J. Coryell; [b.] May 22, 1955, Beeville,

TX; [p.] Cesario Trejo Jr., Mary Trejo; [m.] Larry G. Coryell, April 9, 1979; [ch.] Jason Robert, Anthony Lawrence; [ed.] Longmont Senior High School, Greeley Central High School, University of Northern Colorado, Colorado University; [occ.] Chef and Prep Cook.; [memb.] Spanish Baptist Church, North Shore Animal League, Evangelist Assoc. Billy Graham, Life Study Fellowship.; [hon.] Art IIIK Awards, Dean's List, Best Spanish Student.; [oth. writ.] Several poems, non-published as of now. Still hoping someday they will be like this one.; [pers.] I have greatly influenced by the will of God first of all. Then my family and friends. Especially my Mom who has always believe in my poems.; [a.] Greeley, CO

COSBY, TAMMY
[b.] June 26, 1964, Anniston, AL; [p.] James and Karvar Jenkins; [m.] Divorced; [ch.] LaDonna Brandy and Misti Reign; [occ.] Home maker; [hon.] This is the first honor, and its a big one for me, I've never submitted anything before so I can consider this my biggest accomplishment.; [oth. writ.] I've written 20 or 30 poems since I was 15 my writing's always are spontaneous and work to make me feel good inside and hopefully someone else too.; [pers.] Most of my writings stem from personal experience, or Just life in general. My inspiration has always been my children, and the goodness that inside us all.; [a.] Anniston, AL

COTE, DIANE
[pen.] Diane Cote; [b.] December 5, 1965, Rivere-Du-Loup, Quebec, Canada; [p.] Jean-Francois Cote and Rose-Anne Bealieu; [m.] Claude Vaillancourt; [ch.] Joanie and Pascale; [ed.] Universite De Montreal, College De Rimouski, C.E.G.P. De Riviere-Du-Loup, Languages: German and Spanish; [occ.] Human Resources Secretary; [pers.] The ink of my pen runs on from the blood in my veins.; [a.] Brigham Quebec, Canada

COTTON, LEWIS
[b.] November 24, 1949, Camella, GA; [p.] L. P. Cotton and Lillian V. Cotton; [m.] Kathryn B. Cotton, August 29, 1970; [ch.] Jennifer Cotton; [ed.] Manchester High School, The University of Alabama; [occ.] Lumber and Hardware Sales, Previous occupations: Psychiatric Social Work and Juvenile Probation Officer; [pers.] Precious moments can flow by in the blink of an eye, so don't cheat yourself by rushing past. Treasure your time spent with family and friends.; [a.] Tuscaloosa, AL

COURTNEY, ETHAN
[pen.] Ethan Courtney; [b.] New York City, NY; [p.] George Wiggs, Eloise Patrick Wiggs; [ed.] BA/American Religious History State Univ. of N.Y. Empire State College; [occ.] Actor/Writer; [memb.] Screen Actor's Guild, American Federation of TV and Radio Artists - Actor's Equity; [hon.] Have appeared in many feature films, TV films and soaps.; [oth. writ.] Film script in circulation about the second seminole war, and a jazz project currently on the market for the Times Square area of NYC.; [pers.] Know that God is the source of life.; [a.] New York, NY

COVENY, KELLY ANN
[b.] May 27, 1969, Manhattan; [p.] Richard and Linda Coveny; [m.] Stuart Brody; [ed.] Greenwich Academy and Northwestern University; [occ.] Freelance Copywriter-Chicago, IL; [pers.] Writing is about evolution. Of the self. And the work. About perception. And expression. Character. And experience. And each poem a milestone in life's ever-evolving journey.; [a.] Chicago, IL

COVERT, MEGAN
[b.] June 18, 1978, San Diego, CA; [p.] Thomas and Corrine Covert; [ed.] Student at Ranche Bernardo High School; [pers.] Always try your hardest and never give up, you until find that your key to success is already in your hand.; [a.] San Diego, CA

COX, GLORIA
[b.] March 6, 1929, Fresno, CA; [p.] Peggy and Alphonso Vergara; [m.] James Cox, March 23, 1969 (2nd marriage); [ch.] one daughter - living, one son and one daughter deceased; [ed.] Fresno Technical High School Graduated 1947; [occ.] Homemaker; [memb.] Baha'i Faith (Religion) A world religion focusing on Unity and oneness and man as a spiritual being.; [hon.] One poem published in "American Anthology of High School Poetry" - 1947; [oth. writ.] Several poems - unpublished. Personal journals kept over many years as keepsakes for my grandchildren so they will know who I am.; [pers.] I believe that poetry and music are languages of the soul. This language comes to the conscious mind out of our spiritual nature as we traverse the path of life.; [a.] Fresno, CA

COX, NEIL S.
[b.] June 16, 1977, Columbia MO; [p.] Dr. Curtis S. Cox and Mrs. Elise P. Cox; [ed.] Now Senior at Jefferson City High School.; [occ.] Student; [memb.] U.S.A. Hockey - Professional Association of Diving Instructors (PADI). - United States Tennis Association (USTA) - National Eagle Scout Association (pending). - Divers Alert Network. - Boy Scouts of America.; [hon.] Eagle Scout (pending, within a month).; [a.] Jefferson City, MO

COX, PAULA LYNN
[b.] May 14, 1968, Lexington, KY; [p.] Chester Blevins, Jessie Blevins; [m.] Clayton Grover Cox, December 31, 1993; [ch.] Dwayne, Danny Ray, Kasey, Christian; [pers.] I am truly inspired by the most precious gift on earth... my husband, and children.; [a.] Lexington, KY

CRABBS, STEVEN A.
[b.] January 13, 1962, Grand Rapids, MI; [p.] Don and Leona Crabbs; [ed.] High School Ed.; [occ.] Asst. Manager Ashland Oil Co.; [memb.] S.A.A. and U.F.O. 1 Club; [hon.] Golden Poet Award 1988, Silver Poet Award 1989 and 1990. Several Honorable Mentions.; [oth. writ.] My Little Nine, The Eagle, The Child Within and Conception; [pers.] Mountain stream is dedicated to all those in love. May you have the right words to tell that special someone how much you love them.; [a.] Grand Rapids, MI

CRAWFORD, EDWARD E.
[b.] July 31, 1929, Lawton, KY; [m.] Patricia (Dulin) Crowford, September 4, 1954; [ch.] Scott Edward and Susan Lynn; [ed.] Ph.D., The Catholic University of America.; [occ.] Licensed Psychologist (Md.) Private Practice; [memb.] American Psychological Association, Scottish Rite 32 degrees Mason, Shriner.; [hon.] Who's Who in the East, Who's Who in the World; [oth. writ.] Collection of poems.; [pers.] My poetry is always inspired, quickly drafted, and then later published. It is an attempt at expressing my own romantic views regarding coping in contemporary society.; [a.] Towson, MD

CREE, DONALD W.
[b.] January 7, 1965, Logansport Cass County, IN; [p.] Donald L. Cree, Hazel J. (Easter) Cree; [m.] Divorced; [ed.] Lewis Cass Jr./Sr. High School, Indiana University, Ball State University; [occ.] Engineering Tech. Howard County Soil and Water Conservation District, U.S.D.A. Kokomo, IN.; [memb.] Pechewa Longrifles.; [hon.] Dean's List, graduating with honors.; [oth. writ.] Published a few poems in high school paper, years ago, but the majority remain unpublished. My recent publications have been in the form of technical journals pertaining to archeology, my former career for some six years.; [pers.] Through my writing, I hope to make people more aware of their surroundings. Not only in the physical world around us, but within their own souls, and the lives of others.; [a.] Galveston, IN

CREHAN, ANNE
[b.] October 21, 1938, Dublin; [p.] James Patric Crehan, Esther Crehan; [ed.] Presentation convon boarding school Matloux Derbyshire, England; [occ.] Antique Trade, everydays Carer for brother Invaher; [memb.] Songwriters associate member Yorkshire poetry a motion came 16 one of 80 song tip contest and magazine publications; [hon.] Well published a magazines; [oth. writ.] Mostly songs Jingles adds poetry; [pers.] My name is Alice Jingles I am a Rhynist - yon see my mother before me so was aunty B. My grand father old D Sheehen Canon Sheehar; [a.] Gufted Pen

CRESWELL, ORLANDO
[pen.] Lando; [b.] June 2, 1963, San Francisco, CA; [p.] Louise Frisco, Reese Crewell; [ch.] Roshuna and Raheem Creswell (twins); [ed.] Incararated; [oth. writ.] Several poem that I'm trying to get published. Reflection, Daddy's Little Girl, Memories, Friends, Flying Colors, just to name a few.; [pers.] I try to mention God in most of my poems because He bless with the talent. I've been influenced by personal experience.; [a.] San Jose, CA

CROCKER, KEVIN MAXWELL
[pen.] Flaco; [b.] August 31, 1976, Redwood City, CA; [p.] Julian Doss Crocker and Donna Gilliss Crocker; [ed.] Senior in High School; [occ.] Student; [memb.] Amnesty International, American Field Service, California Scholarship Federation, Sierra Club; [hon.] 1st place, media category, 1993 San Luis Obispo County History Day Contest, 1993 San Luis Obispo Writing Contest-1st place, 1995 PTA Reflections Essay Contest-1st place, $550 American Field Service Scholarship and selection to be a foreign exchange student to Venezuela; [oth. writ.] Several articles of correspondence to the local newspaper from Venezuela, Two poems, "Never Have I Walked Happier" and "Music" published in local poetry magazine, "Death, Fear, and Magic" and "Sledding Dangerously", "A Kiss On The Cheek": personal experience essays; [pers.] Sometimes, I wish that writing would be as easy and as routine as brushing my teeth, but then I reflect on the unparalleled adrenaline rush I receive as I create a piece. The motivation to write lies in the mystery of not knowing what will be written until emotion is suddenly injected into the writer's body.; [a.] Templeton, CA

CRONE, EDNA ORR
[b.] December 9, 1918, Magnolia, MS; [p.] Charles Edwin Orr and Bertie Beatrice Orr; [m.] Marshall Eugene Crone, October 21, 1939; [ch.] One son, Marshall Eugene Crone Jr.; [ed.] Central High, Cozzens Secretarial and Business College; [occ.] Retired; [memb.] Order of the Eastern Star, National Association of retired federal employees; [oth. writ.] Many poems, one published in a local newspaper; [pers.] My writing are inspired by memories of treasured times, by my love for family and friends, and by my appreciation for other wonderful people who helped make my life better than it might otherwise have been.; [a.] Dalla, TX

CROUSE, C. KAY BROWNING
[pen.] C. C. Kay; [b.] January 18, 1942, Casper, WY; [p.] Leo C. and H. Marjorie Wagner; [m.] Billy D. Browning - April 3, 1958, Walter E. Crouse - December 22, 1969; [ch.] Billy D., Thos R., Judy K., V.J. Micker J. and Chas. L.; [ed.] Catholic Elementary, High School Graduate, 2 years Buss. College, Various Business Courses; [occ.] Aspiring writer and homemaker; [memb.] Crisis lines, various support groups; [hon.] Most achievement-dale carnegie crse; [oth. writ.] Prose, Poetry and short stories currently working on book re: Child's View; [pers.] Listen to and believe the children, our greatest teacher's our gift: Life's own experiences; [a.] Smyrna, TN

CRUZ, MELISSA DELA
[b.] September 7, 1971, Manila, Philippines; [p.] Alberto and Ching dela Cruz; [ed.] Convent of the Sacred Heart High School, San Francisco, CA, Columbia College, Columbia University BA 1993; [occ.] Computer consultant, Design-Options, Inc.; [hon.] Dean's List; [oth. writ.] First publication!; [pers.] Thank you to my family and MGV.; [a.] New York, NY

CRUZ, WILDA D. RUTH DELA
[b.] October 18, 1941, Wheelersburg, OH; [p.] Reginald and Sophia Ruth; [m.] Samuel de la Cruz, March 18, 1967; [ch.] Marcos and Becky de la Cruz; [ed.] H.S. - Princeton H.S. - Cincinnati, OH., B.S. - Anderson College (now Univ.) M.S. - TX. A and I Anderson, IN. (now A and M - Kingsville); [occ.] Sp./EM Bilingwood Elementary Teacher - also teach G.E.D - adult Educ. classes at Somerset Ind. Schol Dist.); [memb.]T.S.T.A. - Church Memership; [hon.] Merit Scholarships, Title VII sholarship for master's program for bilinguel, Bicultural Edec.; [oth. writ.] Poems and short stories for church or school use, including some devotional readings.; [pers.] My poem, "God's Message", tells mh philosophy and is a warning as well as a message of hope for a lost and dying world, our only hope for our nation and ourselves is God.; [a.] Somerset, TX

CSUKARDI, VIOLET I.
[b.] February 5, 1959, Perth Amboy, NJ; [p.] Zoltan Horvath, Anna Horvath; [m.] Joseph Csukardi, February 21, 1981; [ch.] Jason, Nicholas, Jonathan, Selina Csukardi; [ed.] Teaneck H.S., C.T.I, I.C.S.; [occ.] Self-employed; [hon.] C.T.I., I.C.S.; [pers.] I would like to dedicate this and all my poems, to my mother, my sisters, Anna Horvath and Maria Rosa. If it wasn't for them I would not be writing poems. So, I would like to thank them for their love, and patience.; [a.] Brooklyn, NY

CUETO, MARIA CIELO G.
[pen.] "Cielo", Shadow Stone; [b.] July 11, 1979, Manila, Philippines; [p.] Basilisa Gumapac and Romeo Cueto; [ed.] Third year High School in St. Theresa's College, Quezon City; [occ.] Student; [memb.] Corithians, Super Kids Club, Anchor Milk Club; [pers.] Always dare to be different; [a.] Quezon City, Philippines

CULPEPPER, DELTON
[b.] August 10, 1961, California; [p.] Dalton Sr. and Mary Culpepper; [m.] Single; [ch.] Paige Te'sha Culpepper; [ed.] Morningside High, El Carino J.C.; [occ.] US Postal service, Bus owner (#900 numbers) (print Lock Corp.) Manager.; [pers.] I have a speech impediment, and because of this impediment, singing and writing has became a part of me, because I'm able to express myself these 2 ways. Everyday I see Angel's, to me an angel was a pretty face, but then I notice. Their are angel's everywhere I looked, and it did not matter how they looked, or what color shape and size they were, it's what's on the inside that make them special angels.; [a.] Paramount, CA

CUMMINS, REIN
[pen.] Rein Cummins; [b.] April 19, 1977, Nairobi, Kenya; [p.] Brian and Mary Cummins; [ed.] Singapore American School, Cheffo School Malaysia, Faith Academy Philippines, Dover Court Singapore, K.C.S. Japan, Canadian Academy Japan.; [occ.] Student; [pers.] There are things in a life that matter, things in a past that can't be denied. Friends are luxuries not necessities so don't throw them away.; [a.] Ikoma-Shi Nara Ken, Japan

CURTIS, WAYNE WOODY
[b.] November 20, 1949, Andrews, NC; [p.] Wayne H. Curtis, Edith L. Curtis; [ch.] Matthew and Cassey; [occ.] Transportation Tech. N.C. Dept. of Transportation; [pers.] What I write is influenced only by life and what if for all of us the future is blurred vision and uncertainty—the past is clear as crystal and unchangeable; [a.] Andrews, NC

CUTTS, AARON
[pen.] Aaron Cutts; [b.] February 7, 1958, Saint Louis; [p.] Willa Dee Cutts; [ed.] 1 and 1/2 years of college; [occ.] SSI Resipreant; [oth. writ.] Some like the women of my desire; [pers.] When you write let it flow from the heart; [a.] Saint Louis, MO

CZARNY, ANDY
[pen.] Charles A. Czarny Jr.; [b.] October 20, 1947, Fort Worth, TX; [p.] Charles Czarny, Roma Czarny; [ed.] B. A.; [occ.] Bridge Teacher; [memb.] American Contract Bridge League. Johns Hopkins SAIS Rugby Football club. George Mason Rugby Football club.; [hon.] Too numerous to mention; [oth. writ.] None published; [pers.] Cogito Ergo Amo.; [a.] New Braunfels, TX

CZOLNO, MARY
[b.] May 5, 1922, Chicago, IL; [p.] Irene and Carl Willie; [m.] Deceased; [ch.] James, Roseann, Deborah; [ed.] One year of High School.; [occ.] Retired; [oth. writ.] Many - but this is my first one published.; [pers.] My poems are based on the feelings and troubles and praises of real person's such as "Toddles" for my son who passed away 4-91 for my daughters leaving home for the first time, for my other daughter when she was gone thru a difficult divorce; [a.] Napa, CA

DAHLKE, CYNTHIA
[pen.] Cynthia d'Este; [b.] September 12, 1943, Milwaukee, WI; [p.] Edward and Jacie Coffin; [m.] Albert (deceased); [ed.] UW - Milwaukee, Literature and Life Science 1968; [occ.] Career Consultant - Semi-Retirement Specialist; [oth. writ.] The Earth and Universe: An Oratorio - Departures - Tena Firma - Pale Sun - The Love Poems - The Most Beautiful Song in the Forest (some crap books - some set to music); [pers.] Nature and man - from the figuring point of beauty, one transcends one's life to a spiritual understanding of it.

DAIGLE, MARIA
[b.] March 10, 1959, Italy; [p.] Rosa and Alfonso; [m.] Lester Alan Lee Daigle; [ch.] Adam Lee, Maria, Christine; [ed.] Graduated 10; [occ.] Song writer ASO; [hon.] Awarded 1972 first prize; [pers.] There is so much to learn. So much to understand when we do is it too late or can we say it's never too late to begin.; [a.] Meriden, CT

DALE, DON B.
[pen.] Donado; [b.] April 24, 1942, Fort Collins, CO; [m.] Karen, December 28, 1965; [ch.] Lauren, Regan; [ed.] Garden City High, University of KS, (BA), Long Beach State Univ (MBA); [occ.] Owner: California Cornerstone Co./President-Intenat' Fishing Resorts, Inc.; [memb.] Metropolitan Club of S.D. Corporate Finance Council of S.D.; [hon.] Bronze Star, Co-Captain - 1964 Kurugby; [oth. writ.] Two books on "Future of Air Transportation in So. Calif." and "The Process of Going to Nuclear War", article on "Quick Look Analysis Approach for Finance Companies", "Do Tell - the Early Years", an autobiography; [pers.] One can only influence that which is in one's immediate sphere of control. All life is made simpler through the pleasure and joy of fishing.; [a.] San Diego, CA

DALE, NATALIA
[b.] November 16, 1977, Toronto, Ontario, Canada; [p.] Roman and Diana Dale; [ed.] Reitz Memorial H.S.; [memb.] Close-up, Key Club, CEF, ASHA; [hon.] Ribbons for Horseback riding; [pers.] Being a freak is a state of mind, not a way to dress.; [a.] Evansville, IN

DALIANA, GEORGIA
[pen.] Daliana; [b.] October 2, 1959, Athens, Greece; [p.] Antonios and Mrs. Eleftheria Statza; [m.] Mr. Evaggelos Daliana, November 01, 1982; [ch.] Miss Niki Daliana 7 years old; [ed.] Radio Officer; [occ.] Occasional publishing of articles and comments in a nautical newspaper.; [memb.] Literature Picaeus Rouse (Union of Picaeus Citizen Philologists); [hon.] 1. Award of Poetry "Nikos Kavadias" issued by the Ministry of the Merchantile Marine. (I am the unique woman poetess that has been honoured with the award of Nikos Kavadias), 2. Honorary distinction from the Panehellenic Union of Philologists at the Panehellem Poetry Competition, 3. Honorary diploma from the P.U. of Philologists during the Panehellenic Poetry contest at Delfous, 4. Medal Honorary distinction of Peace issued from the "Akropolis Appeal" and the "Presidentship of the National Metsovio Polytechnic" during the Poetry Competition at 1994 with subject (The Peace); [oth. writ.] In spite that I am occupied with the poetry almost 3 years I have not published a book yet. But a good number of my poems have been already published along with interviews in various magazines and newspapers.; [pers.] Concerning the style of my poetry since it is connected with the sea and the seafaces having a relationship almost erotic, it cannot be anything else but the other face of reality, a reality similar to a man slowly losing blood.

DALTON, CYNTHIA
[pen.] Cynthia Dalton; [b.] June 25, 1958, Upland, CA; [p.] Donald R. Carel, June W. Carel; [m.] Mitchell Dalton, December 6, 1986; [ch.] Jonathan, Benjamin, Adam, Christopher, Karen, Savannah; [ed.] Rim of the World High; [occ.] Domestic Engineer; [oth. writ.] Personalized greeting cards for friends and family.; [pers.] I enjoy writing about life's experiences, good and bad, and have found marriage and motherhood to be one of the most rewarding, sometimes painful lessons life can offer. I've learned along the way by listening and looking up to my parents, listening to my grandmother Carel tell stories of years of go, when life meant hard work and damn good eating, sharing myself with my husband and literary growing up with my children! I believe there is no greater education "in Life" than "Living Life" itself!; [a.] Palm Desert, CA

DALTON, GARRY L.
[b.] March 9, 1945, Clay County, IN; [p.] Virgil and Vernia Dalton; [m.] Bonita Dalton, March 21, 1970; [ch.] Sonya J. Dalton; [ed.] M.S. and B.S. from Indiana State Univ. in Secondary education; [occ.] Executive Director Clay County, Consolidated Farm Service Agency, USDA; [oth. writ.] Other numerous unpublished poems which express my interest and love for life.; [pers.] There's a sure test of a writer. Does his works say something the way you wish you had?; [a.] Clay City, IN

DAMASCO, IONE TARA
[b.] September 1, 1975, White Plains, NY; [p.] Honesto Damasco, Gloria Damasco; [ed.] Bishop Watterson High School, The Ohio State University; [hon.] Dean's List, Ohio State University Scholar, Minority Scholars Program, Battelle Scholar, High School valedictorian

DANIEL, JANET KAY
[b.] March 10, 1951, Kansas City, MO; [p.] Leonard and Patricia Chapman; [ed.] Cert. Nurses Assist., Cert. Medication Tech.; [occ.] Environmental Services at a Local Nursing Home. "Independence Health Care Center"; [pers.] Writing poetry gives me a chance to have quiet times and unwind from todays stressful life. To just stop and remember the good times.; [a.] Independence, MO

DANIELSON, RENAE L.
[b.] January 5, 1974, Olmsted, MN; [p.] Arnie and June Danileson; [ch.] Chelsea Danileson - Becker; [ed.] Gateway Technical College, Kenosha, Wisconsin; [occ.] Administrative Assistant at the Southeastern Wisconsin Labor - Management Council; [memb.] National Parks and Conservation Association, World Wildlife, Member of Quill Books and Five Star Music Masters of Boston, Tin Pan Alley, Inc., Cystic Fibrosis Foundation; [oth. writ.] Several poems published by Quill Books. Two songs composed by Five Star Music also Tin Pan Alley, Inc.; [a.] Kenosha, WI

DANZ, LYNETTE
[b.] February 27, 1970, Robbinsdale, MN; [p.] Phillip Danz, Yvonne Kern; [ed.] Edison High; [occ.] Receptionist, Haworth Group, Minnetonka, MN; [oth. writ.] Several poems that have yet to be published.; [pers.] Each of us were touched with a gift when we were born. If we all use our gifts to color the lives of the people around us, we will see those colors in our own as well.; [a.] Minneapolis, MN

DARGAN, JAY
[b.] April 15, 1941, Clarendon, Quebec, Canada; [p.] Rev. and Mrs. Robert E. Dargan; [m.] Margaret, December 21, 1962; [ch.] Sherilyn (McPherson), Deborah (Anderson); [ed.] B.A., M.R.E., M.A., M.Ed., Ph.D.; [occ.] Director of Development at Asbury Theological Seminary; [memb.] Assoc. of Institutional Development Officers, CASE (Council for Advancement and Support of Education), Christian Stewardship Association, National Society of Fund Raising Executives; [hon.] Elected to Outstanding Educator of American Commissional as Kentucky Colonel by Commonwealth of KY., Elected to Personalities of the South, Elected to International Who's Who in Education, Elected to Who's Who in the South and Southwest, Elected to Who's Who in American Education; [oth. writ.] Building Relationships in Development, Developing Successful Families, In My Kentucky Kitchen (a cookbook), Various Magazine articles); [pers.] All my gifts have come from God, and I want to give back to Him myself and my works. And, I want to give to others to inspire and encourage them as a part of my witness to my Lord.; [a.] Wilmore, KY

DARLINGTON, JOANNA
[b.] October 2, 1979, St. Ignatius, MT; [p.] Joe and Maggie Darlington; [ed.] Education continuing; [occ.] Student; [memb.] FFA, Cheerleading; [oth. writ.] Unpublished personal poetry.; [pers.] In my poetry the feeling of past, present, and a hopeful future come out easier than speaking them. I hope to someday write books and inspire others to do the same entertaining work.; [a.] Roman, MT

DARRAGH, RUTH H. O.
[b.] August 3, 1909, Chicago, IL; [p.] Dr. B. H. Orndoff and Bernice Harvey Orndoff; [m.] Alexander Leroy Hawkins Darragh, December 19, 1936, (Deceased); [ch.] Cynthia Hawkins Darragh Oatman, Alexander Hawkins Darragh, Deborah Harty Darragh Bercot Darragh; [ed.] Austin High School, Chicago, Northwestern University, Evanston, Ill., Class of 1930, Liberal Arts, Smith College, Northampton, Mass., (Graduate work in English) 1930-1931; [occ.] Witness of Jehovah; [memb.] (Resigned several) including N.S.D.A.R. (National Society Daughters of the American Revolution), N.S.D.C.W. (National Society Daughters of Colonial Wars), etcetera; [hon.] Phi Beta Kappa Mortar Board Final Emblem (3 Senior Women at Northwestern Univ.); [oth. writ.] Irrepressibly - More "Poems" serious, light, humorous...; [pers.] "...Out of the abundance of the heart the mouth speaks." Matthew 12:34b, (cf. Luke 6:45c;) New World Translation of the Holy Scriptures; [a.] Harrison, AR

DAUB, DAVID
[pen.] David Russell; [b.] April 30, Pottsville, PA; [p.] Russell Daub, Virginia Daub; [m.] Denise, 1979; [ch.] Kevin, Jessica, Lynn; [ed.] Pottsville High, Lincoln Technical Institute, Franklin Pierce College; [occ.] Mfg. Project Mgr. Digital Equipt. Corp.; [oth. writ.] This is my first attempt at publishing any of my writings; [pers.] I write poetry as a means to express the feelings, fears, and faith that we all deal with each day and sometimes just for fun; [a.] Salem, NH

DAVARE JR., DAVID
[pen.] Morrison; [b.] April 21, 1977, Pittsburgh, PA; [p.] Dr. David Davare, Mrs. Vondelle Davare; [ed.] Red Land High School; [occ.] Clerk at A-Z Video Superstore; [memb.] North American Fishing Club; [oth. writ.] Many poems and songs (most not published); [pers.] Live life day by day. Live life your own way. It works for me... Most of the time. Jim Morrison is my greatest influence. This is not the end.; [a.] Etters, PA

DAVID, JOHN C.
[b.] May 28, 1974, Milwaukee, WI; [p.] John V. David, Mary David; [ed.] Riverside High, University Wisconsin - Milwaukee; [hon.] Delta Epsilon Phi, Outstanding Student of German, AATG Speaking Contest Medalist 1989; [pers.] For the world to see, I give this poem to the woman who captures my love, should she dare. More importantly, I give the deepest thanks to my mother and father, whose memory I cherish.; [a.] Milwaukee, WI

DAVIDSON, BARBARA LEE
[pen.] Bobbie Davidson; [b.] September 30, 1943; [p.] Robert and Lillian Weber; [m.] Robert, October 29, 1960; [ch.] Robert Jr and Deborah, 1 grandson - B.J.; [ed.] Largo High, Clearwater High, St. Petersburg J. College; [occ.] Floral Designer; [oth. writ.] Other poems on occasion (when the spirit hits me!); [pers.] I write only what I feel is truly worthy. I like to try to encourage people to take time to think about the positive side of life.; [a.] Clearwater, FL

DAVIDSON, CHAD R.
[b.] September 2, 1974, Niagara Falls, NY; [p.] Christine and Jack Davidson; [ed.] High School, one year of College studying music. U.S. Army study of Radiology and Medical Specialist; [occ.] U.S. Army department of Medical Academy; [hon.] Music awards such as, jazz, leadership, most improved musician and many others. U.S. Army Physical Fitness award.; [oth. writ.] I currently have a collection of 60 writings that are unpublished.; [pers.] I dedicate this poem to my wonderful girlfriend Carla who inspired me and had faith in my poetry. The poems I write are a reflection of my feelings for her.; [a.] Niagara Falls, NY

DAVIES, AMANDA
[b.] July 12, 1972, Kermit, TX; [p.] Katheryne Brice, Jimmy Speed; [m.] Richard Davies, May 28, 1994; [ch.] Bethany Davies (July 13, 1994); [ed.] Monahans High, Class of 1991, Odessa Junior College; [occ.] Housewife and mother; [oth. writ.] Several poems and songs published in school newspapers; [pers.] I believe that all children are the miracles that hold our world together. If we love them enough today, they'll build us a future better than we ever thought possible.; [a.] Rocky River, OH

DAVIES, ANNIE GERTRUDE
[pen.] Ann; [b.] June 28, 1903, England; [p.] Robert and Mary Northcott; [m.] Thomas Davies, November 27, 1920; [ch.] Gwen, Glyn, Trevor; [ed.] Public School; [occ.] Retired Widow; [memb.] Baptist Church, I.F.A.W. - Bible Society; [oth. writ.] Many other poems I also have a melody in my mind for the poem which I sent you but cannot write the music for it.; [pers.] I am a retiring nature, living a secluded life in a Senior's apartment house. As I am handicapped I seldom go out and never alone. I have been in Canada 87 years.; [a.] Peterborough Ontario, Canada

DAVIS, ANNA L.
[pen.] Anna Cottman Davis; [b.] June 27, 1916, Indianapolis, IN; [p.] Howard Cottman - Myrle Cottman McNary; [m.] O. Charles Davis, Minister, February 26, 1938; [ch.] Gwen, Winifred, Cynthia, Jennie, Duane, Paula; [occ.] Writing Co-Chair Family Ministry; [memb.] PTA, Girl Scouts, Director Bible School, Choir Director; [oth. writ.] Inspirational Poems, Humorous and Children's Poems, Life stories, Travel diaries, Prayers, Greeting card verses; [pers.] I try to create, restore, or renew hope for the yearning spirit of mankind, and to bring joy and humor to the life of a child.; [a.] Rialto, CA

DAVIS, JANNIE
[b.] May 2, 1935, Bridgeport, TX; [p.] Aubrey Mattix, Elsie Mattix; [m.] Thomas Warren Davis, November 26, 1952; [ch.] Aubrey Warren, Michael Wayne, Sherri Lee, Beverly Denise; [ed.] Houston, TX - Jefferson Davis High; [occ.] Self employed — Awards Business; [oth. writ.] Several poems but none of them have been published.; [pers.] I write the feeling and thoughts that come into my heart.; [a.] Houston, TX

DAVIS, JESSICA
[b.] May 8, 1976, Hearne, TX; [p.] Jesse E. Davis Jr., Diane Carpenter; [ed.] Graduate of Will C. Wood High School (Vacaville Ca.) '94; [occ.] Restaurant Hostess and Delivery Driver; [pers.] If I wrote it and signed my

name to it, then at one time or another I felt at in my heart.; [a.] Vacaville, CA

DAVIS JR., ALLAN R.
[b.] April 12, 1911, Garland, TX; [p.] Mr. and Mrs. A. R. Davis Sr.; [m.] Mimi Olinger Davis, January 20, 1948; [ch.] M. R. Hayslip; [ed.] Garland High School - 1929, Southern Methodist University - 1933, S.M.L.-B.S.C.E. - 1936.; [occ.] Retired Engineer COE, 1969.; [memb.] Military Service 1942-1943 - CBI Theatre

DAVIS, KIMBERLY D.
[b.] April 30, 1964, Meadville, PA; [p.] Francis C. and Iva M. Malliard; [m.] Robert A. Davis, October 20, 1984; [ch.] Brenton D. and Nicholas D.; [ed.] Cochranton Jr.-Sr. High School; [occ.] Housewife and newspaper carrier; [pers.] My poems are very special to me because the words I write are always inspired by the ones I love. Each has their own story.; [a.] Cambridge Springs, PA

DAVIS, MARY L.
[b.] October 19, 1925, East Prairie, MO; [p.] William and Millie Kirks; [ch.] Robert A. Davis; [a.] Aurora, IL

DAVIS, NINA MAE
[b.] October 4, 1967, Breese, IL; [p.] Jack C. Schroeter and Marilyn M. Forehand; [m.] Bill E. Davis, March 13, 1986; [ch.] Trisha Mae, Kenny Edwin, Cory Joe; [ed.] Sandoval Community High School; [occ.] Homemaker and devoted mother; [memb.] Diamond Springs Baptist Church; [hon.] Graduated from high school with high honors.; [pers.] I would like to thank Wayne Woodall and the Centralia Chamber of Commerce for giving me the inspiration to write, my husband and children for their love and support, and my mom for her love and for giving me the talent.; [a.] Sandoval, IL

DAVIS SR., BILL
[b.] June 25, 1960, Livonia, MI; [p.] Linda L. Davis of Lincoln NE; [ch.] Billy Jr, (13), Lindsay Renee (10); [ed.] Assoc of Arts, University of Phoenix, Pursuing Degree at University of Nebraska, Lincoln; [occ.] Full time student, retired US Navy Ship serviceman 1st Class; [memb.] American Legion Post #3, Lincoln Nebraska (Worlds Largest); [hon.] Various military awards, retired from US Navy on 1 Oct., '94; [oth. writ.] Various poems and songs, this is my first publication.; [pers.] I strive to reflect Christ in all that I do or say, and leave a better world for my children and my Jane to enjoy. I am greatly influenced by my english girlfriend.; [a.] Lincoln, NE

DAWSON, ELIZABETH B.
[pen.] Elizabeth B. Dawson, Liz; [b.] January 29, 1928, Boston, MA; [p.] Dorothy and David A. Braytoon; [m.] John E. Dawson, August 18, 1956; [ch.] John Jr., Benjamin, Matthew and Samuel; [ed.] BS in Education, Wheebak College 1951, Alumn. Trustee and Corporator; [occ.] Retired Teacher, Administrator and Director of various organizations. You have this information on file as I am also the author of "At Grandma's House" which I submitted and which was accepted earlier this year; [memb.] Director of Frontier Nursing Service Wendover KY, Director of Faulkner Hospital Boston, Ma., Director of Animal Rasell League of Boston, Director of Fall River and Little Compton Historical Soc.; [hon.] 4 wonderful sons, 10 healthy grand children, 2 dedicated parents, 1 loving, loyal husband, many, many caring friends; [oth. writ.] Two self published and typed books of poem and 50, 1) Thoughts in Poetry, 2) Children's Poetry; [pers.] I believe we are here on Earth to make a difference to one another and to society as a whole. — "Faith, family and friends" are the strengths that sustain me and help me to make that difference. I try through poetry. Perhaps the greatest satisfaction in life is the opportunity to make a difference!"; [a.] Little Compton, RI

DE HAAN, JOANNA
[pen.] Joanne de Haan; [b.] January 19, 1972, Cape Town, South Africa; [p.] Dr. Hein de Haan, Anne Green de Haan; [ed.] Attending University of Toronto (Victoria College); [occ.] Student

DE JESUS, CHARLES
[pen.] Chase; [b.] December 29, 1970, Brooklyn, NY; [p.] Charles De Jesus Sr., Rita De Jesus; [ch.] Cha'nique Aurel De Jesus; [ed.] Paul Robeson High School, L.I.U. - Long Island University; [pers.] To find happiness and to solve the mysteries of the Universe, one must look within self and master self. As a master, one has the duty to teach man and mankind for the upliftment of the family human.; [a.] Brooklyn, NY

DE LOS SANTOS, KENIA
[b.] June 11, 1972, Dominican Republic; [p.] Dinora and Manuel De Los Santos; [ed.] George Washington High School, Borough of Manhattan Community College.; [occ.] Laboratory Technician, Columbia University (HHMI).; [memb.] Children International, Health Information Management.; [hon.] In High School for swimming and acting (drama). In swimming I got my awards in free style swimming, acting is several plays for the community and students of George Washington High School.; [oth. writ.] Several poems, but they have never been published for this is my first time trying to have it published.; [pers.] "In the middle of every difficulty lies an opportunity" - Albert Einstein. The day I wrote "Only Yesterday" I was going through a difficult time, my poem gave me the opportunity to enter this contest and here I am about to have it published for the love I have for A. M.; [a.] New York City, NY

DE MARZI, HARRY
[pen.] Harry De Marzi; [b.] July 3, 1924, New York City, NY; [occ.] Retired Musician/Composer; [oth. writ.] I have written 25 more animal poems, as well as various other topics which have not as yet been published.; [pers.] Along with becoming grandparent, I have been inspired to write humorous and up-lifting poems for children and for anyone who may enjoy them.; [a.] Montrose, CA

DEBOTTIS, BARBARA ANNE
[b.] April 16, 1978, Syracuse, NY; [p.] Diane B. DeBottis and John J. DeBottis; [ed.] Student at Marcellus Central School, Marcellus, New York. In grade 10; [occ.] Student at Marcellus Central School; [hon.] Certificate of Merit for concern for others; [pers.] I hope that one day people will realize that peace is the way to go, not hate and anger; [a.] Marcellus, NY

DECARLO, NANCY L.
[b.] July 1962, Syracuse, NY; [p.] Richard A. Tausend, Nancy R. (Nappa) Tausend; [m.] Michael J. DeCarlo; [ch.] Noah Daniel, Jessica Lynn; [ed.] North Syracuse Central High School, The Institute of Children's Literature; [oth. writ.] Several poems and articles published in local newspapers as well as numerous unpublished song poems/lyrics and children's short stories; [pers.] Like many riters most of my writing reflect my one personal feelings and experiences. It is my hope that what I write will somehow touch the lives of the people who read it. I believe that every writer writes with a certain "idea" in mind, but every reader interprets in their own way what was written. Poems can teach, touch and cause a variety of emotions in everyone.; [a.] Mattydale, NY

DEES, WHITNEY
[b.] May 27, 1982, Scotland Mem., Hosp.; [p.] Lewis Dees, Gwen Dees; [ed.] Presently in 7th grade at J.P. Knapp Jr. High.; [occ.] Student; [memb.] Knapp Majorette Squad, Currituck Soccer Team.; [hon.] 6th grade valedictorian, 2nd place Regional Science Fair Winner, Twice Lap program winner at Moyock Elem. 1994 Best Sportsmanship Award at Moyock Elem., 7th grade SAT participant, Environmental Essay Contest Winner; [oth. writ.] Environmental Essay, Martin Luther King Essay, and some small books and poems; [a.] Moyock, NC

DEEVERS, ROMAIN ANN
[pen.] Maine, Booges; [b.] February 19, 1954, Cleveland, OH; [p.] Russell J. and Elizabeth M. Kostelnik Sr.; [m.] LeRoy Dana Deevers, February 18, 1978; [ch.] Courtland James, Cameron Tyler, Caressa Dana; [ed.] Valley Forge H.S., Park College; [occ.] Training and Awards Coordinator for Defense Finance Accounting Services, Columbus Center, Accounting Directorate; [memb.] American Society of Military Comptrollers; [pers.] Living in today's world is a challenge. Above all things that we should share with other human beings is love. If I share love, the challenge of living in today's world is rewarding.; [a.] Columbus, OH

DEFOUW, MATTHEW
[b.] October 2, 1977, Kamloops, British Columbia, Canada; [p.] Bill and Mary Defouw; [ed.] Currently enrolled in Kamloops Senior Secondary School; [occ.] Student; [oth. writ.] Although my other writings are not published, I enjoy to write and have quite a portfolio emerging.; [pers.] In love there is life, just as in life there is poetry.; [a.] Savona British Columbia, Canada

DEIFER, RONALD J.
[b.] October 19, 1982, Lansdale, PA; [p.] Ronald A. and Susan D. Deifer; [ed.] Presently in the Sixth grade at Upper Perkiomen Middle School in E. Greenville, PA.; [oth. writ.] Continues to write poetry and lyrics to songs he hopes to write in the future.; [pers.] Ronald has suffered with attention - deficit disorder (ADD) since kindergarten. It wasn't till November 1993, that he was diagnosed with the disorder. After being placed on ritilan, Ronald has finally been able to control his thoughts and has since been able to express his feelings and frustrations in poetry.; [a.] East Greenville, PA

DELAWARE, DOROTHY PATRICIA JONES
[pen.] Marie Dela; [b.] April 13, 1945, City Hospital; [p.] Herman L. Jones and Mary R. Trice Jones; [m.] Roland Leon Delaware, October 2, 1964; [ch.] Guardian Of Wonda L., Pauline M., Aaron L., Tammy J. Brewton; [ed.] Paul Lawrance Dunbar Senior High School Graduation: June 8, 1964; [occ.] Poet, Artist, Entrepreneur; [memb.] Former Member of the Smithsonian Institution, International Society of Poets; [hon.] Associate Membership for accomplishment and a distinguished membership in the International society of poets as a member. I had the Editor's Choice Award Outstanding Achievement. The National Library of Poetry.; [oth. writ.] The poem Mom, Sea Party, Poem our Daddy.; [pers.] Respect love and believed in God and yourself. Take time to stop, look and listen around you. Ponder through what you see and hear. Learned from it. Move on don't stay there too long. To desire

and obtain more you must be willing to work and hard for it.; [a.] Baltimore, MD

DELONG, GREGORY A.
[b.] March 1, 1984, Kutztown, PA; [p.] Jeff and Bonnie DeLong; [ed.] Kutztown Elementary School; [occ.] Student; [pers.] This is my first poem. My fourth grade teacher, Mrs. Louise Roth, inspired me to write it as part of a language arts project on poetry.; [a.] Kutztown, PA

DEMARTINO, JO-ANNE P.
[b.] New York; [p.] Martha and Joseph De Martino; [ch.] one son John L. Reggio; [ed.] Bachelor of Social Welfare Adelphi University, Master of Social Work Adelphi University Certified Clinical Social Worker - N.Y. State; [occ.] Clinical Social Worker - Psychotherapist; [memb.] National Association of Social Workers, American Cancer Association; [hon.] Deans list, Magna Cum Laude; [oth. writ.] Several poems and essays.; [pers.] I like to paint pictures of emotions in my poetry. My father used to read poetry to me as a child. This influenced my love for poetry.; [a.] Floral Park, NY

DEMETER, GREGORY ALEXANDER
[pen.] J.A.D.E.; [b.] July 19, 1964, Pottstown, PA; [p.] Mr. and Mrs. John and Dolores Demeter; [m.] Jenny; [ch.] Julie, Tori, Beth, Jamie; [ed.] Norristown High School, self taught music, song and musician, writer...; [occ.] School for Law in Pennsylvania.; [memb.] St. Peter and Paul Church, A.S.C.A.P. Guild. Musicians friends.; [hon.] My honor is my beautiful fiancee Jenny and our beautiful daughters. Epic Records requested to hear my songs and I hope to make a C.D.; [oth. writ.] Songs presented and performed on T.V. Songs and poems written from life's experiences.; [pers.] Be true to yourself and what you believe in, to me, that is real happiness... God, faith and family... you can move mountains. Let your heart grow wings.; [a.] Bethlehem, PA

DEMING, MARGARET
[pen.] Emmy Dee, Peggy Silvers; [b.] February 4, 1946, Cols., OH; [p.] Pearl A. Stirling, Margaret Stirling; [m.] Calvin Collins (dec'd), Conway Deming, February 4, 1965, December 29, 1989; [ch.] Chuck Collins, Craig Collins, Calvin Collins Jr.; [ed.] St. Mary's Elementary School, South High - Cols., Oh, Some college may still be in the future. Possibly Columbus State or OSU; [occ.] 20 years bus operator for Central Ohio transit authority; [memb.] Calvary Temple Church transport workers union 208; [hon.] National Honor Society, PHILO (a high school sorority by invitation only) placed in several scholarship tests and represented my school in the finals; [oth. writ.] How the Canada goes got it's ring, how to write a poem, to hell for a kool and many other poems. Several have been published in church and work newsletters and bulletins; [pers.] When asked if I feel I'm talented, I often answer it's more like a mental illness. It's a compulsion to write and it's my way of dealing with many frustrations of life. I write what I feel. I can write "poems to order".; [a.] Columbus, OH

DENLEY, ALICIA M.
[b.] September 4, 1964, New Orleans, LA; [p.] Ursurle Duplessis, Wilkie Denley; [ed.] Regina Caeli High, Charity Hospital School of Surgical Technicians Santa Monica College School of Nursing; [occ.] Registered nurse, Orthopaedic Hospital, Los Angeles, Ca; [memb.] Association of Surgical Technicians, American Heart Association; [hon.] Dean's List; [pers.] Words which couldn't find a voice succumb to paper expressing the artist to the fullest. My only source of inspiration is whatever was transpiring in my life at the time.; [a.] Gardena, CA

DENMAN, DONNA
[pen.] Donna or the Farmers Wife; [b.] August 25, 1936, Monticello, NY; [p.] Wilfred and Georgina Smith De Voe; [m.] Raymond; [ch.] Christopher and Gene, grandchildren Lindsay and Coby; [ed.] Tri-Valley Central, Orange County Community College, Certified NYS Emergency Medical Technician; [occ.] Asst. Building Coordinator at County Museum, Office Manager for Sullivan County Farm Bureau, Home Based Desk Top Publishing Business (Sweetwater Publishing); [memb.] Grahamsville First Aid Squad, Captain, Sullivan County Historical Society, S.C. Farm Bureau, Neversink Agricultural Society, Craft Tent Coordinator, Catskill Toastmasters, Alchemy Club (Poetry Writing). I also sing at various churches and Christian Women's Club.; [hon.] Over 30 years service in volunteer pre-hospital emergency medicine.; [oth. writ.] Poems and essays published in local papers as well as the American Agriculturist, county woman and country folks.; [pers.] I write what I call "Volks" poetry (as in Volkswagen). Though some of my poetry may a have symbolic undertones it can be enjoyed for he obvious meaning alone. I want people to feel better for having read my work. There is enough violence and depravity in the real world. I feel no need to eulogize such events in prose and verse.; [a.] Grahamsville, NY

DER KACY, ANN AUSTIN
[pen.] Ann Austin Der Kacy; [b.] January 11, 1923, Australia; [p.] Arthur, John and Margaret Austin; [m.] Nicholas Der Kacy, June 9, 1947; [oth. writ.] Numerous poems, dozens of song compositions; [pers.] I dedicate this poem "Somewhere in the Darkness" to my ever loving husband of 47 years who departed this life on June 2, 1994 for the higher realm of life everlasting

DERIGER, SHANTY ROYCE
[b.] November 29, 1973, Ottawa, Ontario, Canada; [p.] Margo Royce, Pancho Deriger; [ed.] Nepean High School, Algonquin College; [occ.] Television Broadcasting; [hon.] CANPRO, first place national TV Ontario Telefest, second place both for long documentary; [oth. writ.] Many poems and short stories, but this is my first publication. Have written media releases and promotional information for corporate events.; [a.] Ottawa Ontario, Canada

DIAMA, BENJAMIN
[pen.] Ben Diama; [b.] September 23, 1933, Hilo, HI; [p.] Agapito Diama, Catalina Diama; [ed.] Hilo High School, School of the Art Institute of Chicago, Cincinnati Conservatory of Music, University of Hawaii; [occ.] Retired State of Hawaii Public School Teacher; [memb.] HSTA (Hawaii State Teachers Association), HEA (Hawaii Education Association), NEA (National Education Association), New York Academy of Sciences, ASCAP (American Society of Composers Authors and Publishers); [hon.] Hawaii State Foundation on Arts and Culture Painting - Purchase Award, National Library of Poetry Editor's Choice Award - Publication of Poem in the "Space Between" and recorded for presentation in "The Sound of Poetry", White House - President Bush Presidential Order of Merit; [oth. writ.] Author of "The Calendar Clock Theory of the Universe with Faith" (acknowledged by NASA in 1984), Author of "Beautiful Hawaii", a musical cassette of a musical play - story of Hawaii Immigration; [pers.] I believe all of mankind lives to inspire each other to believe and know our creator, whom I believe is our light for kindness, mercy, truth and love.; [a.] Kailua Kona, HI

DIAMOND, DANA B.
[b.] December 4, 1963, Burlington, VT; [m.] Michael W. Diamond, July 3, 1987; [occ.] Marine Corps. Wife; [pers.] Feelings, do we really have them, and if we do are they real, or the one's society tells us are acceptable. Life is just a highway, each by-pass is an experience. How we choose to interpret these experiences to others or to ourselves is only in our minds, for fear of non acceptance by mankind. Only the strong can transfer these experiences into feelings and write about them. The rest, well they're just unknown vehicles passing in the night, searching for their by-pass.; [a.] Havelock, NC

DIEUJUSTE, DARLENE
[pen.] Didi, DJ, Princess; [b.] October 19, 1976, Haiti; [p.] Jocelyne Dieujuste; [m.] Wilson Pierre; [ch.] Wilkerson B-Lee, Sharlyne; [ed.] Elizabeth High Newbury College; [occ.] Fashion Designer; [memb.] Black Student Union, The Pet Saver Foundation, Inc., The North shore Animal League, National Cancer Researcher Center; [hon.] Key Club, Honor Society, Principal Scholars, Math Wiz, Student of the month.; [a.] Boston, MA

DIMICHELE, AMANDA
[b.] October 26, 1978, Montreal, Quebec, Canada; [p.] Phil DiMichele, Connie DiMichele; [ed.] High School (James Lyng); [occ.] Student (Secondary V.); [memb.] Jame Lyng Newspaper (Co. Editor), James Lyng Yearbook Committee (Co. Editor).; [hon.] 1992-93 Newspaper (High school), 1993-94 Newspaper (High school); [oth. writ.] Short stories, poems, a novella. (None published); [pers.] My poems are born from the heart. They have been influenced by the many memorable people and moments brought into my life.; [a.] Montreal Quebec, Canada

DISNEY, PHYLLIS BLANCHE
[pen.] Phyllis Blanche Disney; [b.] July 4, Valley City, ND; [p.] Leslie Edward Disney, Blanche Cornelia Anderson; [ed.] Sheridan Montana High - Metropolitan Business College, Seattle - Drama - Ballroom Intrepretive Dance - French Reweaving - Tailoring - Clothing Design - Handcrafts - Health and Beauty; [occ.] Entrepreneur - Sales/Marketing - Minister - Counselor - Artist - Fashion Design - Teacher - Poet; [memb.] Toluca Lake Chamber of Commerce; [hon.] Montana Basketball Championship Team - Texas State Recognition: Girl Scout Day Camp Director - Girl Scout Established Camp Art Director - Festival of Arts, Laguna Beach - Recognition from various Companies for excelling in varied accomplishments. Above all, I am most grateful and appreciative of love and respect of all those who know me.; [oth. writ.] A book "On Butterfly Wings", a collection of poems. "The Beauty Of The Sea", "Come Laugh With Me", "Let Me Fly Free",... "An Eagle Rare". And my first two poems: "A Smile" - "A Tear" - 'twixt wake and sleep - written in the air for me.; [pers.] I have come to realize the greatest service I can render others is to encourage them back to the Living God within their Temple not built with living hands - too often the last place to seek their answers.; [a.] Toluca Lake, CA

DITTMAR, JENNIFER
[b.] January 18, 1977, Cleveland, OH; [p.] James and Donna Dittmar; [ed.] Buckeye High School; [occ.] Student; [memb.] National Honors Society; [hon.] Superior Rating, Ohio Music Educators Association Solo and

Ensemble Contest, Top Scholar Awards in Chemistry, English and Sociology; [pers.] We work to survive. We create to live.; [a.] Valley City, OH

DIVENUTI, PEGGY
[pen.] Peggy Warren; [b.] June 10, 1948, Boston, GA; [p.] Austin and Barbara (O'Malley); [m.] Warren Di Venuti, September 20, 1969; [ch.] (5) Paula Chase, Andrea Coyne, Janet, Billy and Linda Di Venuti; [occ.] Classified Advertising Boston Globe Newspaper Co.; [memb.] Nothing relative; [hon.] Nothing relative

DIXSON, DONNA
[b.] December 17, 1963, Munich, Germany; [occ.] Medical Paralegal for a major toxic tort litigation firm, former designer/model; [memb.] Dallas Opera Guild, Dala, National Trust for Historic Preservation, Earth Island Institute Whale Protection Program; [oth. writ.] Several poems and songs, currently compiling a collection of recent works; [pers.] I strive to capture the essence of simplicity and embrace the beauty of romance.; [a.] Dallas, TX

DO, HUAN
[pen.] Ho-di Nam (Vietnam Remembering); [b.] October 6, 1945, Vietnam; [p.] Linh Do and Tkang Nguyen; [m.] Hong Do, August 1970; [ch.] Long Do, Nina Do, Lan Do, Giao Do; [ed.] B.A. in Economics and Finance, M.A. in Public Administration (University of Public Adm. Vietnam), and some certificates in Laws and Letters and Music etc.; [occ.] Social Worker, Housing Specialist; [memb.] 1. University of Public Adm. Alumni Assoc., 2. Chu Van An High School Assoc., 3. Vietnamese Pen Club, 4. Vietnamese Press Club, 5. Quang Ngai Friendship Assoc.; [hon.] In Vietnam got some awards in Public Adm., Management, Poetry, etc., In U.S., got some awards in Teaching, Social Services, etc., Electronics and Computer Science; [oth. writ.] In U.S., Published 2 poem books: 1. Ngan Nam May Bay in 1992 (Flying Clouds) and 2. Ngay Do Ching Minh in 1993 (One day we're together). 3. Musical book Tam Tinh Ca Xa Xu 1, 4. 2 Musical Tapes: Tuiu Mong Mo and Mot Do i Rhuo Thuong etc...; [pers.] I'm loving poetry, writing books, newspapers, music... in Arts and Cultures, Architecture, Paintings, etc... and sports... Also I do like Philosophy, Sociology, Anthropology etc...; [a.] Garden Grove, CA

DODD, JEFFREY S.
[b.] May 3, 1967, Kansas City, MO; [p.] Nancy Dodd, Henry M. Dodd Jr.; [m.] Beth Jeanine Dodd, September 12, 1992; [ch.] Joshua Morgan Dodd; [ed.] Manzano High, Allen County Community College, Washburn University; [occ.] Engineering Technician, Kansas Department of Transportation; [memb.] St. Matthew's Parish; [oth. writ.] Many other poems, short stories, and song lyrics. Various publications; [pers.] My writings are inspired by my family, our surroundings, and our environment. - "Let your heart speak your mind."; [a.] Topeka, KS

DOETZEL, AUDREY
[b.] January 30, Saskatchewan, Canada; [p.] Jacob Doetzel, Justina Stang; [ed.] Saskatchewan Teachers College, B.A., B.Ed. - University of Saskatchewan Master of Divinity (M.Div.) - Toronto School of Theology University of Toronto, Doctor of Ministry (D. Min.) Toronto School of Theology University of Toronto; [occ.] Adult Educator, Education Consultant and Facilitator for Christian and Interfaith education.; [memb.] A member of the Congregation of Our Lady of Sion - an international Order or Roman Catholic Sisters. Co-ordinator of Relation and Encounter - which fasters mutual understanding between Christians and Jews.; [oth. writ.] I strive to bring the values of the Christian and Jewish faiths to work for a just peace through understanding, healing and reconciliation. I work to enable Christian-Jewish collaboration to combat, injustices which oppress and marginalize - especially those related to religion, race and ethnicity.; [pers.] Brooklyn, NY

DOHERTY, DARLENE
[pen.] Darlene Bunky Doherty; [b.] December 13, 1932, Vancouver, WA; [p.] Marion Wayne, Alina Wayne; [m.] Thomas J. Doherty, October 11, 1952; [ch.] Shelley Doherty, grandchildren: Doug Doherty - Darla Doherty; [ed.] Heppner High School; [occ.] Retired; [a.] Myrtle Point, OR

DOHERTY, KEITH
[b.] February 21, 1975, Boston, MA; [p.] Edward and Carol Doherty; [ed.] Johnson and Wales University of Culinary Arts, Providence, RI, Randolph High School, Randolph, MA.; [occ.] Student, Johnson and Wales University, Providence, RI; [hon.] Dean's List - Johnson's and Wales University two times

DOMINIQUE, SISTER MARY TIMOTHY
[pen.] Deborah Dominique; [b.] May 10, 1946, Fulton County, OH; [p.] Charles and Mary Jane Dominique; [ed.] Various grades schools in the U.S. and Germany (military career family), Hammond, H.S., Alexandria, VA, Sacred Heart Jr. Col., Belmont, NC; [occ.] Cloistered contemplative - Dominican Sisters of the Perpetual Rosary; [hon.] Dean's List, Assoc. in Arts, graduated with honors; [oth. writ.] Limited so far to poetry requested by members of our community; to extend thanks for gifts received, to commemorate special occasions; [pers.] With whatever talent God has given me, I would like to help my brothers and sisters to know him better, and so, love him more. Also, to help them realize that we are invited to become by grace (God sharing his life with us) what he is by nature.; [a.] Milwaukee, WI

DONAHUE, JUANITA MARIE
[b.] April 4, 1947, England, AR; [p.] Albert Crump and Eldora (Woodard) Crump; [m.] Theopalis Gene (Paul) Donahue, June 21, 1964; [ch.] Angela Marie Donahue, Suzanne Rochel Donahue and Bridgitte Denise Donahue; [ed.] Betton Gartrell Memorial High School - England, Ar., Capital City Business School - L. R. Ar., University of Arkansas at Little Rock - Ar., B.A. Liberal Arts and Med (Master's Education); [occ.] Disabled Teacher, Business Entrepreneur; [memb.] First Baptist Church, Highland Park. Kappa Delta Pi Education Honor Society, AETN Educational Television; [hon.] Kappa Delta Pi, Dean's List; [oth. writ.] Several articles printed in local newspaper. Poem "Transformation" selected by The National Library of Poetry for summer publication JOURNEY THROUGH THE MIND.; [pers.] As a novice poet, it is my goal to express the beauty and joy that is seemingly lost in the deep crevices of sorrow and despair and to inspire black women, men, boys, and girls to use all of life's experiences to create Juanita Marie (Crump) Donahue good.; [a.] Little Rock, AR

DONALDSON, MOYRA
[b.] March 8, 1956, Newtownards; [m.] John Liddle; [ch.] Claire (11), Jannah (4); [ed.] B.A. Honours Queen's University Belfast, Diploma in Social Work, University of Ulster, Certificate in Social Welfare Law, Queen's University Belfast; [occ.] Senior Social Worker in Education; [memb.] Ards Writers' Group. Festival Director for Ards all Ireland literary festival; [hon.] Winner of Belfast Telegraph short story competition. Shortlisted for 1995 Hennessy Cognac Literary Awards - Judging in Nov. 1995; [oth. writ.] Published in Various Literary Magazines Inc., honest Vlsterman, Gown Literary Supplement, Poetry Now etc., pamphlet coming out in Spring 1995, Published by Lapwing Publications. Public readings at Killybegs International festival, 'Aspects' festival of Irish writing, Queens University Festival Belfast; [a.] Newtownards Co Down, Northern Ireland

DOOLEY, JOSEPH P.
[pers.] On a pillow I am born. With past lives known I choose how I shall live I welcome night and expect to die to enter thee unknown; [a.] Melbourne, FL

DORMER, ELAINE KAY
[b.] January 20, 1970, Lincoln, NE; [p.] Larry and Sharon Schrader; [m.] Delmer L. Dormer, September 26, 1987; [ch.] 3 - Elizabeth, DJ, Auston; [oth. writ.] Several poems; [pers.] I strive to put my fears aside and achieve my goals. Only my deepest thoughts are in my writing, it helps me to get through rough situations.; [a.] Lincoln, NE

DOTSON, JEREMIAH
[b.] August 21, 1967, Bronx, NY; [p.] William Dotson, Celeste Dotson; [m.] Ericka Rivers, July 30, 1990; [ch.] Mark Dotson, Gregory Rivers; [ed.] Theodore Roosevelt HS, Paralegal Institute NY, NY; [occ.] Security Officer; [memb.] New York Road Runners Club; [pers.] It's not how much time you have that matters, it's what you do with the time that you are given.; [a.] Bronx, NY

DOTY, EARLEN
[pen.] Doty (Early Baby); [b.] February 14, 1942, Cruger, MS; [p.] Miller - Velma Doty; [m.] Single; [ed.] Froebel High - 1961, University of Illinois - 1973-4-76, University of IN. - 1984-85-86. Labor Law and History Labor Union studies; [occ.] Steel worker - Garywks 26 yrs title - Stocker Shipper; [memb.] NMCP - Operation Push - steel womens, Women of Steel Assoc., Local 1066 Member, Habit for Humanity Church of God in Christ. Small Business Assoc.; [hon.] Organized First Black Caucas at local 1066, Ran my own President in 1976. First Black Women on Safety and Civil Rights Committee for 10 years.; [oth. writ.] Looking for the Rainbow, So Be It. It's Over a Child's Face; [pers.] A person's true ability lies in his or her strengths and weakness. To see tomorrow is the thirst for more and more and the will ot yarn for more without drinking.; [a.] Gary, IN

DOUBET, AARON
[b.] March 16, 1977, Canton, IL; [p.] Jeannie and Andy Doubet; [oth. writ.] More than 100 poems and various short stories; [pers.] If with my writing, I touch one person's soul in the way other writers have touched mine, then I have done my job as an author.; [a.] Fairview, IL

DOUGHERTY JR., ROBERT E.
[pen.] Red, Crazee Bob, Doc.; [b.] June 30, 1952, Chester, PA; [p.] Alice and Robert Dougherty; [m.] Evelyn, July 19, 1980; [ch.] Wanda, Tanda, Mary, Tina; [ed.] Simon Gratz High, Bok Tech. for Photogrametry, Central Texas, College Europe for diesels and generators, self-taught building computers.; [occ.] U.S. Postal Service - Mail handler, tutor for Gateway Reading Program; [memb.] American Bible Society, Smithsonian Institute; [hon.] Army Achievement Medal, Army

Achievements Awards, Non Commioned Officer Academy Certificate.; [pers.] In a thought..., many lives are traveled and lived. And sometimes written. If I can help you I will. But if you won't help yourself, neither will I.; [a.] Philadelphia, PA

DOUGLAS, CARRIE L. HAYNES
[b.] July 24, 1939, Wrens, GA; [p.] Oliver Haynes, Hattie Haynes; [m.] Alton Douglas, August 22, 1962; [ch.] Craig, Rachel, and Tabatha Douglas; [ed.] Wrens High, Seton Hall University, Montclair State University, Edward Williams, NCR/IBM Computer and Programming School.; [occ.] County Government - Clerk Typist, Former Sr. Programmer System Analyst; [memb.] Peaceful Zion Church, Peaceful Zion Usher Board, Va., Day Committee, new member of Church Support Group, AAPP.; [hon.] Twice high school queen, "Miss Wrens High", high school second place, State Recital, Academic Achievement Award, Seton Hall University.; [oth. writ.] Have written several poems which I would like to have published soon. Also, I have nearly completed a rough draft of a book. Desire to have it published and to continue with other writings.; [pers.] Because of my upbringing, love, sincerity and concern for mankind, I am inspired to write. I am a creative person. Through my writing, I crane to express life in some meaningful way. Earlier and modern day poets immensely influence me.; [a.] Newark, NJ

DOUTHIT, SCHERRI L.
[b.] November 17, 1951, Anchorage, AK; [p.] Irma Lloyd, Bedford (Bud) Lloyd; [ch.] Aaron and Courtney; [ed.] Warsaw High, State Fair Comm. College; [occ.] Account Specialist, and Metal Processors, Inc.; [oth. writ.] Seven other poems (unsubmitted) and a book in the works; [pers.] I am passionate about revealing the inner beauty and qualities of people like my sin, Aaron. I want everyone to overcome their fear of things they don't understand and open their minds and hearts to those who are different; [a.] Sedalia, MO

DOW, ALICE
[ed.] B.S. Educ., M.A. English, Journalism - Milwaukee, B.A. Math, studied at Univ., of Rome, Slogo, Ireland, Foreign Amer Univ., Perugia, Italy, Niagara Univ., Carnegie Institute Technology; [occ.] Ohio State Fairgrounds as state of Ohio employee. Former "Director of the Writing Center" Ohio, Weslayon Univ., Delaware, Ohio; [oth. writ.] Articles on "Roaring Twenties", "Music of the Twenties", "The Depression of the Twenties and Thirties", Literary paper published in English Journal Recently completed a book of "Fantasy" for Juvenile Reading level. Short story contest entry. Judging Pending '95; [a.] Columbus, OH

DOWELL, PATRICIA
[b.] August 24, 1974, Burkesville, KY; [p.] James and Alice Dowell; [ed.] Clinton County High, North American Correspondence School; [occ.] Bank Teller, Standard Federal Bank, Bluffon, IN.; [a.] Bluffton, IN

DOWNING, SANDRA M.
[b.] December 25, 1953, Independence, IA; [p.] Shirley Downing, Robert Downing; [ed.] Jefferson High, Kirkwood Community College; [occ.] Computer Programmer; [pers.] A special thanks to Marsha York, for helping me believe in myself and forever dream.; [a.] Iowa City, IA

DRAGONETTE, JOAN A.
[pen.] Jade Long; [b.] October 3, 1936, Ballston Spa, NY; [p.] James H. Delong, Isabell Brackell Delong; [m.] Bernard Dragonette, January 13, 1957; [ch.] Angelo, Ann, Jeffery John; [ed.] 12 yrs High School (Ballston Spa); [occ.] Clerk at the State of New York Tax and Finance Dept.; [memb.] Assumption/St. Paul Church Choir, Catholic Daughters, Rosary Altar Society.; [oth. writ.] Several poems not printed yet.; [pers.] I love to write poetry, because it creates a wonderful door to the world of reality or fantizied's depending on how the mood of the poet chooses to present his or her works.; [a.] Mechanicville, NY

DRAKES, TERRANCE HENRY MARCUS JAMES
[pen.] Tee; [b.] May 28, 1975, Brooklyn, NY; [p.] Sylvia and Reginald Drakes; [ed.] South Shore High School, Morehouse College - 2nd year.; [occ.] Sophore Morehouse College - Atlanta Georgia; [memb.] Boy Scouts America Troop 263, Varsity Basketball and Track South Shore H.S., Vice President Senior Class Debating Team. Morehouse Youth Reading Enrichment Program. Mentor St. Philip Episcopal Church; [hon.] Dean Rask Elementary School. Flatbush YMCA. 1992 Player of the Year Flatbush YMCA. Highest Academic Average Varsity Team. 100 Blackmen Award for citizenship. MVP Basketball 1991. 1990 Camper of the year - Camp De Wolfe, Morehouse College Dean's List-Spring 1994.; [oth. writ.] For Valentines Day 1994 - I wrote seven poems for the seven women in my life - My mother, aunt, grandmother, godmothers, sister and girlfriend, "The Vision" was the first poem that I have ever written, I have some more that are also good; [pers.] This was my first poem that I wrote during my Senior year at High School. "If it is to be, then it's up to me."; [a.] Brooklyn, NY

DRESSLER, LIN
[b.] October 8, 1950, Edmonton, Alberta, Canada; [p.] Ken Nobbs, Lorraine Sowpal; [m.] Jacob Christopher Dressler, August 30, 1986; [ch.] Jodi, Michael, Kelly, Carolyn Cheryl; [ed.] Diploma - Social Service Worker; [occ.] Executive Director for Non Profit Agency - Assisting Battered Women and their children; [memb.] Post Pollio Society, Social Services Advisory Committee, Victims Services - RCMP.; [hon.] Nominated in 1994 for "Women who has made a difference in her community."; [oth. writ.] "A Fair Weather Friend" published February 1994. Canadian Poetry Institute in Anthology entitled "Island Sunsets"; [pers.] Poetry can be conceived through human suffering but it also begins the process of healing particularly when shared and understood by others who have difficulty expressing their emotions.; [a.] Vancouver British Columbia, Canada

DREW, DANNY GLENN
[b.] February 12, 1947, Longview, TX; [p.] W. L. and Ida Mae Drew; [m.] Ruthy A. Drew, December 11, 1965; [ch.] Rickey, Randy, Lana, Jennifer; [ed.] Longview High School, Kilgore College, Collin County Community College; [occ.] Management; [memb.] Plano Lodge #768; [pers.] I wrote this poetry in front of my wife in about 5 minute for we were in a hurry to get it to a baby shower. I pin this poem to a basket we were taking.; [a.] Dallas, TX

DRIVER, MICHAEL G.
[pen.] Michael Driver; [b.] March 29, 1942, Vallejo, CA; [p.] Orvil and Gretchen Driver; [ed.] George Washington High School, San Francisco State College; [occ.] English Teacher, Takachiho University and Oxford English School; [oth. writ.] "Driver's Tidbits On English Learning", a collection of my "The Daily Yomiuri" columns, published by World Communications., LTD; [pers.] On my wall is a chiaroscuro picture of Mr. Spock in deep meditation, and above his head I drew a balloon in which I wrote, "Everything isn't logical... That isn't logical." [a.] Ichihara City Chiba Prefecture, Japan

DRYER, JILL
[pen.] Jill Dryer; [b.] March 17, 1981, Indianapolis, IN; [p.] David Dryer, Vickie V. Dryer; [ed.] Plainfield Community Middle School; [hon.] One time National Champion Gymnastics 1986, honor roll; [pers.] I wouldn't call myself poet, I've only written 3 poems in my lifetime of 14 years. To tell the truth the only reason I wrote this one was for school. When I sent it in I didn't expect it to get this far. The funny thing about this poem was that I wrote in the dark and was also halfway asleep. Maybe that should be my philosophy for writing poems!; [a.] Plainfield, IN

DUHAIME, ROBERT
[b.] February 22, 1979, Pembroke, Ontario, Canada; [ed.] Queen Elizabeth High School; [occ.] Student, Writer; [memb.] Peer Support, National Author's Registry; [pers.] Where is the joy in writing unless you can hand a piece to a person and their response is, "You're crazy!" I get a kick out of that!; [a.] Edmonton Alberta, Canada

DULMAGE, DORIS R.
[pen.] Doris Daniells-Dulmage; [b.] April 7, 1919, Dorking, Ontario, Canada; [p.] Maurice and Lydia Daniells; [m.] Harry B. Dulmage, August 11, 1945; [ch.] Five boys, one girl (1 set of twins), nine grandchildren; [ed.] Writing for Children and Teeangers Institute of Children Literature; [occ.] Retired Business Executive; [memb.] Auxiliary of Gideon's International in Canada; [oth. writ.] Poems, children's stories, articles; [pers.] I like to show appreciation and wonder for God's marvellous creation.; [a.] Prescott Ontario, Canada

DULMAGE, HARRY B.
[pen.] Harry, "Slig"; [b.] December 4, 1923, Cherry Valley, Ontario, Canada; [p.] William Dulmage, Florence Dulmage; [m.] Doris Daniells Dulmage, August 11, 1919; [ch.] Ronald Blake, Donald Karl, David William, Daniel Paul, Graham Rae, Lois Ruth; [ed.] Prince Edward Collegiate, Radio College of Canada, Military Radio Communications WW II, BA Sc University of Toronto, MBA Queen's University at Kingston; [occ.] Retired Business Executive; [memb.] Life Member I.E.E.E., Gideons International in Canada, Institute of Environmental Science, National Association of Radio and Telecommunications Engineers Association of Ontario Professional Engineers.; [hon.] Gold Medal in Radio Communication WW II, Martha McGowan Scholarship in High School, David McLead Scholarship at Queen's University; [oth. writ.] Various economic commentaries published in local newspaper. Ghost writing senior cabinet minister. Author of several socio-economic studies, many technical reports; [pers.] I try to plan as though I will live forever and live like I will die tomorrow.; [a.] Prescott Ontario, Canada

DUMOND, CHERICE RANAE
[b.] November 1, 1960, Delhi, NY; [p.] Alvin L. Stewart, Margery K. Bouren; [m.] Andrew Steven DuMond, April 11, 1981; [ch.] Jeremiah Andrew, Joshua Paul, Jason Matthew; [ed.] K-3: Sidney, New York, 4-6: Unadilla Elementary, Unadilla, New York 7-12: Unatego Jr.-Sr. High School, between Welsbridge and Otego, New York,

graduated: 1978; [occ.] Housewife and Mother; [pers.] I give God the credit for each idea, and bringing together each word to tell meaningful stories, for I know I couldn't have done it on my own.

DURKIN, KEVIN T.
[b.] July 14, 1956, Evergreen Park, IL; [p.] Anthony F. Durkin Sr., Margaret Durkin; [m.] Bradley Carlson, November 23, 1991; [ed.] Brother Rice H.S. Columbia, University of Illinois, Chicago; [occ.] Retired Duntech Marketing Representative; [memb.] International Society of Poets, American Heritage Society, Smithsonian Institute.; [hon.] Editors Choice Award (Twice) and Marquis' Who's Who in America, Golden Falcon Award; [oth. writ.] Dusting off dreams darkside of the moon; [pers.] On December 29, 1994 Oak Park - Oak leaves did an article on me in the village section; [a.] Oak Park, IL

DUSHEK, BOZENA
[pen.] "Bo"; [b.] September 21, 1957, Kielce, Poland; [p.] Christina, Stefan Grzyb; [m.] Divorced, March 15, 1985; [ch.] Conrad - 6 years old.; [ed.] Slowacky High School, University of Kielce, Poland; [occ.] Psychologist; [oth. writ.] I wrote a book at age of 10.; [pers.] I believe in people, friendship and love. Thank you Mom and Dad. I love you Conrad.; [a.] Chicago, IL

EDDINGS, DUANE ALLEN
[pen.] Duane E.; [b.] February 4, 1960, San Francisco, CA; [p.] Oscar and Louise Eddings; [m.] Dena Villanueva, May 20, 1995; [ch.] Christian, Christina, Duane, Alexis, Shavonne, B.J.; [ed.] George Washington High, SFSU, Heald Business College, San Francisco; [occ.] Station Agent Bay Area Rapid Transit; [memb.] Jubilee Christian Center, SF Christian Center.; [oth. writ.] A Love So Rare, Yesterday, A Grandma's Love, Why?, How Could This Be? A Gift For You, To Paint A Picture, Forever Yours, My Children Not Seen.; [pers.] Humanity! Where are we headed. Jesus Christ is our only hope of salvation; [a.] San Jose, CA

EDWARDS, CHRIS
[b.] February 19, 1975, Leeds, England; [ed.] University of Bradford, England; [occ.] Business Studies Student; [a.] Colchester Essex, England

EDWARDS, LAUREN LEIGH
[b.] January 14, 1978, Attleboro, MA; [p.] Terry and Cynthia Edwards; [ed.] Currently a junior at Attleboro High School; [occ.] Student; [memb.] U.S.G.F. (United States Gymnastics Federation), Attleboro High School Gymnastics team.; [hon.] Honor Roll student in grades 5-11, Eastern Athletic Conference All-Star, (Gymnastics); [a.] Attleboro, MA

EDWARDS, THERESA L.
[b.] September 2, 1963, Chamersburg, PA; [m.] Rickey L. Edwards, May 1, 1982; [ch.] Tonya Jo Edwards, Derrick L. Edwards; [ed.] Graduate of Greencastle Senior High School, Nurses Aide Certificate Course, Career Development Center for 3 months, Electronic Typing Course; [occ.] Housewife, Babysitter, want to be a writer!; [memb.] Volunteer for Fundraisers - March of Dimes, Leukemia Society, Arthritis Foundation, Heart Lung Ass., Cancer Research; [hon.] Runner up for Father of the Year Contest Article; [oth. writ.] Father of the Year Contest in local paper and this poem are the only articles I have written thus far. So far I'm 2 for 2.; [pers.] The war against child abuse could be won if we begin from within! Feel only sorrow for those who think life is about material gain, for they are the poor!; [a.] Greencastle, PA

EDWARDS, WANDA D.
[b.] March 3, 1975, Staten Island, NY; [p.] Pauline J. Micleens and Clemme Jean Micleens; [ed.] Business Administration Major at Kingsborough Community College; [pers.] My mother and grandmother are my inspiration and guidance in my life. I owe them every thing. I thank God, for whom, I am here today. Thanks for everything with love.; [a.] Staten Island, NY

ELAM, JONNIE M.
[b.] May 13, 1949, Philadelphia, PA; [p.] John and Magdeline Dunmore; [m.] Leroy D. Elam; [ch.] Jason J. Elam; [ed.] Peirce Jr. College and Temple University; [occ.] Program Analyst, Social Security Administration; [memb.] Mizpah Inland Human Services and St. John Ame Zion Church; [hon.] Have received several awards for excellent performance as a Program Analyst for the Soc. Security Admin.; [oth. writ.] I have written several poems for special occasions or various events for church, work, community or personal reason; [pers.] I enjoy helping others and doing things to brighter their days. I try to express this in my poems. I am inspired by the famous poetress, Maya Angelou, and hope to meet her some day.; [a.] Mizpah, NJ

ELBERT, GARY R.
[b.] November 10, 1952, Fort Campbell, KY; [p.] Robert Davies Elbert, Angela Moonsuk Chang; [m.] Grace Elizabeth Hunter, May 14, 1994; [ed.] Walt Whitman Sr. High - Class of 1970, University of Maryland - 2 yrs, U.S. Naval Nuclear Power School - 1971, U.S. Naval Prototype - 1971, Watterson College - Paralegal Studies - Class of Dec. '87; [occ.] Paralegal, Taxi Cab Ariver; [oth. writ.] 90 poems, 3 novels in process; [pers.] I believe that God is! All things are only possible through Him. I am His son, and His employee. Each day is a new chance to glorify Him. All of us are of one family. His, so let's try to live like that.; [a.] Venice Beach, CA

ELGES, MARY LOUISE
[b.] November 3, 1966, Silver City, NM; [p.] Gerhart Elges; [m.] Maria Elges, 1963; [ed.] Presently Attending College; [occ.] Student; [memb.] National Off Rd. Biking Ass. (I race bikes); [hon.] Most of my achievements are athletic, because I had a learning disability my grammar suffered, so my early teachers did not encourage me, but my family did and the need to express myself kept me writing journals, stories and poetry; [pers.] In my writing I like to express what I know, and this being social and environmental issues.; [a.] San Antonio, TX

ELGIN, KELLY VOLLKOMMER
[b.] July 27, 1968, Kew Gardens Hosp.; [p.] William and Carol Vollkommer; [m.] Robert Elgin, February 2, 1990; [ch.] Jason and Spencer; [ed.] Richmond Hill High School, Half Hollow Hills, East Institute of Children's Literature, ICS Home Study Course - Childcare; [occ.] Housewife, Mom; [pers.] Life is like a roller coaster: It is full of ups and many downs. What is most important and I wish people would realize. Family should stay close and truly be "There for one another"

ELIAS, CAPTAIN BRYNLEY R.
[pen.] Philip David (John Elias); [b.] March 28, 1917, Wales; [p.] Elias Elias and Margaret; [m.] Annette M. Elias, February 14, 1949; [ch.] Penny Jayne; [ed.] Blaeng Wynfi Upaer School Green Street, High Wycombe Swindon College, Shrivenham Military College; [occ.] Retired (Hospital Administrator); [memb.] Fellow of the Chartered Institute of Secretaries. Fellow of the Institute of Hospital Administrators.; [oth. writ.] Several poems published in National Anthologies. Many articles in hospital magazines and journals. Created and edited "The Stag" a regimental newspaper.; [pers.] Initially wrote humorous personalized poetry - more latterly drawn to religious poems, poetry drawn from life studies and the beauty of nature and creation; [a.] Hailsham, East Sussex

ELLEDGE, HEATHER M.
[b.] January 13, 1980, Miami, AZ; [p.] Larry Elledge and Helena Thomas; [ed.] Freshman High School; [hon.] National Honor Society Student Council, Project Renaissance; [pers.] This poem Special Song was written because of my emotional dependency to relate my feelings with lyrics of songs. My mother also relates the same way. This poem was written for her.; [a.] Globe, AZ

ELLIOTT, HEATHER R.
[pen.] HRE; [b.] October 11, 1871, Texas; [p.] Storm and Shawn Bergin; [ed.] High School Graduate, Fort Campbell High 1989; [occ.] Pharmacy Technician, Decatur Memorial Hospital; [memb.] Volunteer for the Special Olympics.; [oth. writ.] I write a lot of poetry, but this is the first ever published.; [pers.] I would like to dedicate this poem to my cousin Joshua, who died at the age of nine from muscular dystrophy. He is my inspiration. I love you Josh.; [a.] Illiopolis, IL

ELLIOTT, JEFF
[b.] October 27, 1966, Fort Knox, KY; [p.] Silas and Patsy Elliott; [ed.] Shiloh High School, Hume IL; [occ.] Finisher for Vesuvius, Fisher IL; [memb.] National Rifle Association, Sidell Conservation Club; [hon.] Honorable Discharge U.S.A.F.; [pers.] I am influenced by my own experiences, I want you to feel as if you were there.; [a.] Metcalf, IL

ELLIS, BETTY MCADAMS
[pen.] BJ; [b.] June 15, 1946, Birmingham, AL; [p.] Lucy and Willie McAdams; [ch.] Rochelle Wallace and Tavarez Ellis; [ed.] Wenonah High School, Birmingham AL Southern College, Birmingham AL Port Huron Junior College, Pt. Huron Mich.; [occ.] CCS Specialist AT&T, Long d'st Opr. (20 yrs); [memb.] Matrons (Hopewell Bapt.) PTA, Daniel Payne Middle School; [oth. writ.] Poem, Treasures, Anthology Seasons to Come. Poem, American Poetry Anthology. Poem - My Pants are Falling, Remembrances, Anthology, Musings and several other anthologies.; [pers.] I thank God for any positive moments in my life. I know what it means to be thankful for sanity. Always reach for the stars, when you reach them... try for the moon; [a.] Birmingham, AL

ELLIS, EDWARD L.
[pen.] Staff Sergeant Ellis; [b.] February 21, 1949, Los Angeles, CA; [p.] Emma Jean Ellis, Arthur Nelson; [ed.] Jordan High School, Riis High School; [occ.] Retired Marine; [hon.] Six honorable discharges, several military related awards and commendations; [oth. writ.] None published; [pers.] I was utterly captured by reading the Holy Bible in its entirety, clearly the most fastenating book ever in print. I find particular pleasure in reading Psalms 35 and imagining the great congregation.; [a.] Compton, CA

ELLIS, LEANNE
[pen.] Leo; [b.] November 6, 1984, Cleveland, OH; [p.] Lucrecia Santiago, Lenoplis Ellis; [ed.] Blessed Sacrament Elementary School; [occ.] Student, 4th grade; [memb.] County Library, Boy and Girls Club, 4th grade Basketball Team.; [hon.] Principals Award for Student of the Year; [pers.] A 10 years old who loves school, playing basketball and helping others.; [a.] Cleveland, OH

ELLIS, MARJEAN
[pen.] Frenchic; [b.] May 7, 1957, Washington, DC; [p.] Royd and Myrtle Ellis; [occ.] Administrative Secretary; [pers.] When I write, I write from the heart. My poems reflect my joy, love, and sadness, but my poems show the strength and endurance through life's ups and downs.; [a.] Cheverly, MD

ELLIS, TAMMY
[pen.] Tam-E Ellis; [b.] May 26, 1977, Richmond, VA; [p.] Michael Ellis, Karen Ellis; [ed.] Lloyd C. Bird High School; [occ.] Assistant Dance Instructor, Encore Studio; [oth. writ.] Two poems published in church newspaper; [pers.] Never let the words of one man keep you from your dreams, always believe in yourself and you will succeed.; [a.] Richmond, VA

ELLISON, MARK STUART
[b.] January 11, 1961, Brooklyn, NY; [p.] Eli Ellison, Rita Ellison; [ed.] Columbia Grammar and Preparatory School, Franklin and Marshall College, Brooklyn College - Graduate Division, Pace University School of Law; [occ.] Trusts and Estates Attorney; [memb.] New York State Bar Association, Mosaic Outdoor Mountain Club of Greater New York; [hon.] Phi Beta Kappa, Pi Gamma Mu, Honor's List, Dean's List.; [oth. writ.] Piece on eating disorders commissioned by Mademoiselle, numerous articles published in high school, college, and law school newspapers.; [pers.] I try to create a blend of emotion, intellect and humanity in my writing.; [a.] Croton on Hudson, NY

EMERY, JENNIFER J.
[b.] September 15, 1971, Saint Paul, MN; [p.] Richard and Bonita Emery, Birth Father John Malachessen and Sandra Orellana Serrano; [m.] Sponser and Sayda Edith Guzman; [ed.] White Bear Lake Area High School, Minnesota Bible College, Rochester University Center, University of Minnesota.; [occ.] Student, Teacher, Translator, Waitress.; [oth. writ.] All together I have written over 200 poems in English, and Spanish, and some Italian, from which I'm in the process of compiling a book of my original poetry. However, this is my first published poem.; [pers.] Life is not fair, no easy, nor is any person perfect. However I believe we live in an ordered world created by a real and intimate God, thus I there to be special purpose and beauty in the living. I strive to look for and do good, to love and live fully. Via my writing I desire to express the depths of the human heart and soul in its entirety and the realities thereof to the best of my knowledge, observation and experience.; [a.] Vadnais Heights, MN

ENGEL, HELEN
[b.] August 3, 1923, Canada; [p.] John and Pauline Gdanski; [m.] Theodore Engel (Deceased), April 22, 1946; [ch.] Six; [ed.] High School and Business Academy; [occ.] Semi-retired; [memb.] International Association for New Science (IANS), Toast Masters International, International Crystallography Research Institute; [oth. writ.] Two articles in the Lapidary Journal; [pers.] I channel spiritual and scientific knowledge.; [a.] Selkirk Manitoba, Canada

ENGELEN, ELISABETH
[b.] December 28, 1954, Netherlands; [p.] Jacobus Engelen, Hennie Engelen Hersant; [m.] William Irwin; [ch.] 2 boys (Jacobus, Jeffery); [oth. writ.] Numerous letters published in local newspapers, Maclean's magazine.; [a.] Saint Catharines Ontario, Canada

ENGLE, ISABEL C.
[b.] April 18, 1976, Las Cruces, NM; [p.] Robert and Yong Ju Engle; [ed.] Mayfield High School, New Mexico State University.; [occ.] Full time college student.; [hon.] Earned Zia Scholarship at the University of New Mexico, earned cash award at White Sands Missle Range Defense Accounting Office; [oth. writ.] Many other poems including five minute audition graduation speech; [pers.] My inspiration comes from even the simplest of objects - a great "thank-you" to all who have supported me.; [a.] Las Cruces, NM

ENGLERT, DEBRAH
[pen.] Debrah Englert-Jackels; [b.] August 8, 1959, Wilmington, OH; [p.] Lamar Davis, Eleanor Davis; [m.] Rex T. Allen, July 8, 1995; [ch.] Thomas Dustin Englert; [ed.] Princeton High School, Great Oaks Vocational School of Cosmetology; [occ.] Cosmetologist - Master Hair Designer/Educator; [hon.] Educational Excellence, Outstanding Achievements, have many awards for hair styling; [oth. writ.] Several poems - currently none published, Book "In Search of Self", currently not published, Two Industry Related Manual, 1-Education, 1-Employee handbook; [pers.] "Believe in yourself and anything is possible", I have found only when I have had faith in myself have I experienced the joy I've sought in my life.; [a.] Cincinnati, OH

ENGLISH, ROBERT G.
[b.] September 12, 1945, Portland, OR; [p.] Mr. and Mrs. Samuel English; [ed.] 12 years High School, 2 years College, 4 years Army; [occ.] Poet, Author, Photographer; [memb.] Lifetime ISP, Stormbelt - Paris, France, National Museum of the American Indian; [oth. writ.] "Only Yours! Susanna My Rose", "Poetical Jest My Gestful World", "The Dream Catcher" - all by Carlton Press Inc.; [pers.] A moment in time. Our essence to sublime; [a.] Albuquerque, NM

ENQUIST, BARBARA J.
[pen.] Barbara Enquist; [b.] November 14, 1943, Chicago, IL; [p.] Roland and Betty Lazzeroni; [m.] Gary Enquist, October 2, 1976; [ch.] Mark, Michael, Mario, Gina, (Step children) Timothy and Todd; [occ.] Health and Beauty.; [hon.] Editors Choice Award - Nat'l Library of Poetry.; [oth. writ.] "Who, What or Where is God?" Published in the NLP anthology, "The Dark Side of the Moon."; [pers.] Although trying to understand God, Nature and Creation is difficult, writing about these is not.; [a.] Cicero, IL

EPPERSON, WILLIAM R.
[pen.] Bill Epperson; [b.] April 13, 1954, Casper, WY; [p.] Marvin and Vera Epperson; [m.] Evelyn Epperson, July 16, 1980; [ch.] Wendy 14, Kimmy 10, Marvin 2; [ed.] High School Diploma, Natrona Country High School, Casper, WY; [occ.] Metal cutter, Softouch Mfa., Monett MO; [hon.] Several awards writing for my High School paper. But my greatest honor is my mothers encouragement to keep writing.; [oth. writ.] Many, many more been writing since I was 10, but never till now shared with anyone.; [pers.] It is important to establish your priorities. For many years I have tried and failed, or my priorities change too quickly. Now I have put myself on top of my list and the rest falls in line by themselves... "I" must be the most important thing in your life.; [a.] Granby, CO

ERICKSON, MARY S.
[b.] August 29, 1934, North Conway, NH; [p.] Hugh and Elsie Mac Lean; [m.] Linwood Erickson; [ch.] Karen Holmes, Kirsten Huftalen, Paul Erickson; [occ.] Housewife; [memb.] Scott Lake Baptist Church; [oth. writ.] Poem in 1994 anthology by 'Poets on the Park' in Lakeland, FL; [pers.] My desire is to acknowledge and glorify God in all that I do. My life, observing mankind and all God's natural creation has been a great source of inspiration for writing poetry.; [a.] Lakeland, FL

ERICSON, RITA
[b.] March 1, 1981, Bossiere City, LA; [p.] Ronald A. Bowman, N. Rose Erickson; [ed.] O'Connell Middle School.; [occ.] Student; [memb.] Gee Science Fair, Shakespeare Festival '93, Arbor Day Homoree '88; [hon.] Citizenship Award, Presidential Academic Fitness Award; [oth. writ.] I wrote a poem in first grade for Arbor Day, I won a pine tree for it.; [pers.] How can you be happy if you're sad all of the time? So, don't worry be happy, brighten someone's day with a smile!; [a.] Lakewood, CO

ERWIN, STEVE
[pen.] Srerwin; [ed.] Five Arts Degree, Columbus College of Art and Design with supplemental studies at various other institutions.; [occ.] Artist/Writer; [memb.] Society of Communicating Arts Parapsychological Association International Youth Hostels; [oth. writ.] Articles, poetry, commentary and experimental works, both published and unpublished.; [pers.] My writing is a spontaneous expression of transient emotion, a sometimes explosive reaction to social environments we may feel limited power to escape. My influences come primarily from expatriate and beat writers of the second and third quarters of this century as well as from contemporary street poetry.; [a.] Columbus, OH

ESLINGER, PHILLIP L.
[pen.] Stinger Lee; [b.] May 29, 1935, Anthony, KS; [p.] Paul and Vineta Eslinger; [m.] Kathleen J. Eslinger, November 28, 1959; [ch.] Diana, Lori, Steven; [ed.] High School; [occ.] I work for Southwestern Bell Corp.; [oth. writ.] I have written 34 poems, beside the two that I entered. I also have been working on short stories. I am working on 5 now. I have written one religious song; [pers.] I have been blessed in the last few years. To be able to put down in words, and to express how I feel about life. Through my poems and short stories. For you see they have come from my mind, heart, and soul. Stinger Lee; [a.] Wichita, KS

ESWARAN, DR. KUMAR
[b.] May 11, 1947, Secunderabad; [p.] S.K.M. Umapathiswaran and Sundra; [m.] Suhasini Eswaran, May 26, 1973; [ch.] Akilesh (son), Deepthi (daughter); [ed.] M.S (I.I.T. Kanpur, 1968), Ph.D. (Madras Univ., 1973), Post-doctoral Fellow (Ohio State Univ. Columbus, Ohio, 1982); [occ.] Scientist, Research and Dev., Bharat Heavy Electricals Ltd., Vikasnagar, Hyderabad - 500593 India; [oth. writ.] Published many papers in International Journals (mostly technical). I am presently compiling all my poems so that they can make my first volume of poetry.; [pers.] My only aim is to be true to the spirit of poetry.; [a.] Secunderabad, India

EUGENE, JEAN ELIZABETH
[b.] March 11, 1967, England; [p.] George Eugene, Jacqueline Eugene; [ed.] To age 10 in England. To age 19 in Castries Comprehensive Secondary School and 'A' Level College in St. Lucia. Then University of Leeds England; [occ.] Civil Engineer, St. Lucia, West Indies; [memb.] Association of Professional Engineers, St. Lucia, West Indies.; [hon.] Student of the Year, Castries Comprehensive Secondary School, St. Lucia. Hold Bachelors of Engineering with Honours Degree in Civil Engineering with Architecture.; [oth. writ.] Songs in collaboration with a local St. Lucian Band.; [pers.] I have been fortunate to grow up and live in the beauty and history of England and the paradise of a tropical island that is St. Lucia, thanks to my parents.; [a.] Castries, Saint Lucia

EVANGELISTA, DARIO A.
[pen.] Darius ALC. Evangelista; [b.] November 18, 1953, San Pablo City, Philippines; [p.] Alfredo and Mercedes; [m.] Carmelita, January 21, 1987; [ch.] Darius Alexander and Carl Windsor Oliver; [ed.] Ateneo De Manila University, Pre Law Lacson College, BSC, Management and Accounting; [occ.] Entrepreneur, Free Lance Writer; [memb.] (Past) Waycees International Club, International Airlines Passengers Association; [hon.] Civic Leadership in Community Development and Social Services; [oth. writ.] Into the park (Saudi Inspired Published Pome). Canada's distinct multiculture heritage: A common approach (A Book in Writing). Various published articles; [pers.] Born as the 6th child from the 23rd pregnancy of my mother to one father and the 5th son among the 16th living children. Tears not in my sorrow. For there's a poem to lean on. When everyone mean it well. I wonder as a poet. While many perspired for a poem. Only few were inspired as a poet. Oh yea, great poet blooms. Once in a blue moon.; [a.] Etobicoke Ontario, Canada

EVANS, BERRINDA JEAN
[pen.] Tiny; [b.] November 10, 1951, Fayetteville, NC; [p.] Geraldine Sykes Evans, John Belton Evans; [m.] Single; [ed.] Poughkeepsie High School, Dutchess Community College; [occ.] Home Health Care, Hudson Valley Home Care, Wassaic Develop. Center, Developmental Asst.; [memb.] Trinity Temple Seventh Day Adventist Church, Speech Choir Director And Orator, Sabbath School Teacher, Adventist Youth Leader, Community Service Treasurer; [hon.] Several poems filed at copy right office. Short skits performed in Hudson Valley, NY; [oth. writ.] I have been inspired by our Lord and Savior Jesus Christ who has blessed me with this poetic talent. I endeavor to convey a unique message that will alert, influence, and occupy the minds of the reader for the times in which we live. I am influenced by James Weldon Johnson and Maya Angelo.; [pers.] Poughkeepsie, NY

EVANS, DOROTHY
[b.] June 19, 1936, Corpus Christi; [p.] Marlin and Viola Blundell; [m.] Jack Evans, April 1, 1994; [ch.] Butch, Linda, Mike, Matt; [ed.] NB Ray High, and Bee County College, Kingsville; [occ.] LVN for Manor Healthcare; [pers.] It is never too late for a new beginning. In 1994 I began a new career and new marriage at 58 and possibly, a new talent; [a.] San Antonio, TX

EVANS, TRACY ANGELINA
[b.] September 10, 1967, Asheville, NC; [ed.] James F. Byrnes High, Wofford College; [occ.] Product Analyst for BMG Music; [memb.] ASPCA, National Humane Education Society; [hon.] Beta Club, Dean's List, Honors in Art and Writing throughout school.; [oth. writ.] Currently working on a novel.; [pers.] I believe that music and poetry comprise the language of the soul and, in speaking and listening to that language, we as a species will learn to heal ourselves and Mother Earth. The compositions of Jeff Lynne taught me much about the soul's language and its infinite inspirations.; [a.] Duncan, SC

EVARISTO, LILIA L.
[b.] September 23, 1916, Mambusao, Capiz, Philippines; [p.] Roman Loyola and Salvacion Felisario; [m.] Johnny Evaristo Jr., (deceased), August 15, 1943; [ch.] Victor L. Evaristo; [ed.] Philippine Normal Univ. Graduate, Bachelor of Science in Educ. II, MA in English and Education; [occ.] Retired College English professor, just retired Dec. '94. Foster grand parent, Agnews Derpt/Center, San Jose, CA 95134; [memb.] YWCA, Altar Society (secretary) of the Holy Cross Church, San Jose. Treasurer of the Faculty Club, Univ. of San Agustin, Iloilo City, Philippines, Cursillos in Christianity.; [hon.] Elementary - valedictorian, High School - Salutatorian, Philippine Normal Sch. - honor roll, B.S. Education - cum laude, Foster - grandparents 10 yrs plaque for exemplary service, Jose, CA 6 yrs. Certificate Service Award from the Food Bank of San Jose, CA; [oth. writ.] Several poems, essays, and short stories in our college paper in the Philippines. Same in Agnews Derpt'l Centor Seniors' Newsletter San Jose, CA 95134, where I volunteer worked for 10 years; [pers.] As an Elementary, Hich School, and College English Teacher for none than 40 years. My motto has been service to humanity. Same when I did volunteer work as a Foster grandparent for 10 years; [a.] San Jose, CA

EVELSON, BORIS
[b.] February 13, 1959, Moscow, Russia; [p.] Anatoly and Tatiana Evelson; [m.] Divorced; [ed.] Nicholas, 3 yrs; [occ.] Banker; [memb.] IAFP (Int'l Association for Financial Planning); [oth. writ.] Misc. poems, Ballads in English and Russian; [pers.] The ultimate answer to life, universe and everything is 42.; [a.] New York, NY

EVERETT, EILEEN
[b.] August 27, 1978, Plainfield; [p.] Dr. William Everett, Margaret Everett; [ed.] Mt. St. Mary's Academy; [occ.] Student; [memb.] Saint Hubert's Giralda Zoo Crew, Spanish National Honor Society, Who's Who Among American High School Students, Pacific Whale Foundation, Peer Minister, J.E.T.S, Naturalist Club, Summit Symphony Orchestra; [hon.] North Jersey Regional Science Fair (Third Place, Zoology), Team Member of First Place Team of N.J. State J.E.T.S. Competition, Who's Who Among American High School Students, Third Place Earth Week Art Contest of A.T.&T.; [oth. writ.] Winner of Regional Daughters of the American Revolution writing contest; [pers.] I believe in expressing a connection between humans and animals in a creative way.; [a.] North Plainfield, NJ

EVERETT, MARION HORTENSE
[b.] May 13, 1925, Missouri; [p.] Gordon and Valena Hayes; [m.] Divorced; [ch.] Carol Lee Batsell; [ed.] North High, Cortez Peters Business College, Famous Writers School; [occ.] Retired Telephone Opr., Ex Entertainer and Model; [memb.] Lupus Foundation, Communications Workers of America; [hon.] Miss Personality, of Kansas City, Missouri, 1939, A vocalist contest.; [oth. writ.] Non published; [pers.] I was blessed, with a thirst for knowledge, of all cultures and peoples. I have the compelling desire, to share, by word and deed. It is defined as, pure love, of the human race.; [a.] Richfield, MN

EVERETT, RAYMEL
[pen.] Rev. Raymel Everett (Figgers); [b.] February 28, 1962, Waynesboro, MS; [p.] Melvin Figgers, Raynola Figgers; [m.] Loretta Everett, June 18, 1983; [ch.] Sheretta, Sharon Babin; [ed.] Beat Four High, Northwestern State Univ. of LA (US Army Military Police); [occ.] Pastor of the Bethel Baptist Church of Enterprise, MS; [memb.] New Light MB Church under the leadership of Rev. Ronnie Horne; [hon.] Honorable Discharge from US Army, Speech and Creative Writing; [oth. writ.] My Mother, When The World You Know, Today, Wisdom, and many more; [pers.] Live for today, plan for tomorrow and only remember the past for it will always remain untouchable.; [a.] Waynesboro, MS

EVERETTE, JOANIE
[b.] Pinetops, NC; [p.] Mr. and Mrs. John Cannon; [m.] Wayne; [ch.] Kenny, Timmy, and Stacey, (Grandchildren) Timothy, Mandy, and Nicole; [ed.] South Edgecombe High and Tech., Numerous Business Schools attended.; [occ.] Business Manager; [memb.] BMI and Songwriting Associations; [hon.] "100" Club Award, Star Achiever Award, National Winner in National Piano Playing Auditions, numerous Business Awards and Plaques; [oth. writ.] Poems, country, and christian songwriter. Songs - "Need a Friend" - "Show Me the Way", and many other songs.; [pers.] I feel my writings and songs are from a spiritual gift. I hope my writings will serve to be an inspiration, for all mankind to come.; [a.] Newport News, VA

EVERS, GENE
[pen.] Gene Alexander Evers; [b.] March 26, 1951, Manhattan; [p.] Lee Evers, Pauline Stein; [ed.] Graduated Pearl River and Hicksville H.S., Graduated with 4 yrs Liberal Arts from Stony Book U. and Nassau CC and State U at Old Westbury; [occ.] Songwriter, Scriptwriter; [memb.] Member of the INternational Society of Poets.; [hon.] Made the Deans List at Hicksville J.R.H.S.; [oth. writ.] Many other poems including 'Big Red Mountain' in the "Best Poets" 1995 of the National Library of Poetry. "Cindy Girl" the song, will be released nationally by Hilltop Records. Another lyric and movie script.; [pers.] Truth can be found in this world through the balanced harmony of passion and reason. Influenced by Wadsworth, Carlyle and Rosseau, amongst others.; [a.] Bethpage, NY

FABAC, TRACI
[b.] March 24, 1972, Kansas City, MO; [p.] Pat and Bill Nelson; [m.] Engaged to be married to David Harper; [ed.] White Station High School, Johnson County Community College and Maplewood Community College; [occ.] Work Temp. for different offices; [memb.] Deaf Club for the deaf; [hon.] Several awards for my drama in drama when I was in high school; [oth. writ.] Write poems on my spare time, sometimes write little stories but mostly poems.; [pers.] I write only about nature and love. To let my following readers know, I am deaf and very proud to be published for your book.; [a.] Kansas City, MO

FABBRI, CHRISTOPHER JOHN
[pen.] [b.] October 9, 1973, MA; [p.] Mr. and Mrs. Carl H. Fabbri; [ed.] St. Rose Elem., St Dominic Savio H.S., New England School of Art and Design; [occ.] Fine Artist; [hon.] Several works of art shown in Gallery 28 Newbury Street Boston, MA. Also First Expressions

gallery 81 Arlington St. Boston MA; [pers.] I strive to reflect the light of life in my art work. At a very young age I was taught the beauty of landscape painting by my grandfather Joseph Febo Fabbri. I'm a young artist who truly believes in tradition and art in our lives.; [a.] Chelsea, MA

FABRIAN, U. N.
[b.] April 19, 1953, Nigeria; [p.] Dominic and Regina; [ed.] MA University of Westminster London England; [occ.] Senior Administrative Officer, London Borough of Hackney London E8 1EA; [oth. writ.] The Missing (New), Dimensions of Heaven (book) published by Vantage Press in New York USA, The Future of Nigeria (book) published by P.A.P.A. London England UK; [pers.] Every man is a friend until he proves himself an enemy, one day, it will be my turn.

FAIRCHILD, BETTY
[b.] 1921, Niagara Falls, NY; [ch.] Elizabeth, Brian, Blaine, Barbara; [occ.] Retired...but not from life! I recently created an ongoing writing group: "Wide Vistas - Adventures in Writing for Women Over 60."; [oth. writ.] Co-author (with Nancy Hayward) of Now That You Know - publisher: Harcourt Brace Jovanovich - a guidebook for parents of lesbians and gay men. (Best Seller in its field since 1979.); [pers.] I believe the creative instinct dwells within each of us - and in a safe supportive and encouraging milieu, each of us can develop and express our creativity.; [a.] San Francisco, CA

FALGOUT, DONNA B.
[pen.] Donna Bidwell Falgout; [b.] November 2, 1960, Mobile, AL; [p.] Mr. and Mrs. Donald S. Bidwell; [m.] Stephen R. Falgout, March 23, 1983; [ed.] High School graduate; [occ.] Housewife; [hon.] I am honored because God gave me the talent to write, therefore giving me the gift to reach others through my writing.; [oth. writ.] Grey Lady - written for United States Navy: USS Vicksburg - published "Remember Yesterday" Golden Poet Award 1990. I have written 65 poems to date.; [pers.] Never give up on your dreams just reach for a star and you will never fail, unless you never try in the first place.; [a.] Theodore, AL

FALLAHI, BEHROUZ
[b.] October 14, 1965, Tehran; [pers.] Twenty-Nine was written a day after celebrating my 29th anniversary of getting old with one of the dearest persons of my life. She left for Montreal, leaving me in a state of emotional dubiosity which still persists. The poem is mainly the result of a hollowness that I felt while wishing her luck and bidding her good-by, although I tried to make the feeling meet the moment when every individual comes to miss every friend, and every foe - the consequence of lolling into an indefinite absence of time, that is, time as we perceive and define and depict it.; [a.] Gloucester Ontario, Canada

FARMER, MICHAEL W.
[b.] June 15, 1947; [ed.] Occidental College; [occ.] Management Consultant: Int'l. Mgmt. and Business Dev.; [memb.] American Chamber of Commerce in Belgium: Trade and Investment Committee, Seminars and Workshops Committee, Belgian Chamber of Commerce, British Chamber of Commerce in Belgium: Trade Promotion Committee, Executive Council (Board of Directors), Antwerp Committee, Management Centre Europe Faculty (International headquarters for American Management Association), American Common Market Club, American Belgian Association, European Unit Lawyers Antitrust Group, Middle East Management Centre Faculty; [oth. writ.] Books: "Business Writing for Results", 1995, Seminar Workbooks: "Selling and Marketing Through Distributors", 1985-1995, "Practical Sales Management for Results", 1986-1994, "Business Writing for Results", 1986-1995, "Communication Skills for Business Management", 1987, "Fundamentals of Marketing with Distributors", 1989-1995, "Fundamentals of Marketing Management", 1989-1994, "Fundamentals of Product Management", 1989, Magazine Articles: Business development articles: "Systems Selling" 1987 Grow Chemical, "Channel Conflict" 1986 Comdex, "Selling Software" 1986 Comdex, "Channel Conflicts and the Selection of Distribution Networks", 1991, "Selecting Your Business Partner - Marriage and Joint Venture", 1992, "The Case for Outside Services", 1986; [pers.] Poetry is how I express many of the personal feelings and emotions I have at spontaneous moments. It is a fun and expressive way to communicate.; [a.] Antwerp, Belgium

FARNSWORTH, FRED L.
[b.] May 13, 1953, Columbus, OH; [p.] John C. Farnsworth, Pauline F. Farnsworth; [ed.] Grove City High, Hocking College; [occ.] Have worked as: Fire Fighter/EMT, Land Surveyor, Inventory Analyst, Civil Engineering Site Inspector, Custodian, currently disable with CFIDS; [memb.] First Presbyterian Church, CFIDS Association of America, National Wildlife Federation, Boy Scouts of America, Firefighters Association, Lighthouse Society; [hon.] District Commissioner Boy Scouts of America, School Bell Award for service to community, not really important to me to receive honors/awards!; [oth. writ.] None published; [pers.] I strive to show love, express love in my writings. To encourage others in their walk of life, to reflect the beauty that surrounds us, and to give credit, honor, to the God that created all, the God and author of love.; [a.] Grove City, OH

FAWLEY, STACEY DAWN
[pen.] Stacey Fawley; [b.] March 15, 1976, Fairfield, CA; [p.] Steven Fawley and Yvonne Sherwood; [ed.] Various Nursing Courses, working through getting a G.E.D.; [occ.] Certified Nurses Assistant and Home Health Aide; [memb.] One of my favorite authors is Danielle Steel so I am a member of her fan club.; [hon.] I've received awards for my writing and poetry skills through school.; [oth. writ.] My Sunrise, I'm Letting You Go etc. Also I had an article about "Aids" printed in my High School paper.; [pers.] I have always been able to express myself through my writing. I feel you can really discover yourself through your thoughts.; [a.] Brisbane, CA

FEHR, MARIA
[pers.] I have maturity, charm, and wit. I do not like to be dated, or stereotyped, that goes against my artistic temperament! My background has been in publishing and communication, I'm interested in World Affairs.; [a.] Los Angeles, CA

FEIGENBAUM, LYLE A.
[b.] February 27, 1968, Indianapolis, IN; [ed.] B.S. Indiana University; [occ.] Actor; [oth. writ.] Creativity, Keychains from Within, The Changing of the Guard, Never Again; [pers.] For society to come together as a whole, we must first seek wholeness of our own individuality.; [a.] New York, NY

FELDMAN, KARI
[b.] May 10, 1973, Carle Place, NY; [p.] Douglas Feldman, Kathleen Feldman; [ed.] Carle Place High School, Hofstra University; [hon.] English Honor Society, Dean's List; [a.] Carle Place, NY

FENTON, PAULA JEANNE
[b.] December 15, 1971, Burlington, VT; [p.] Normand and Susan Lasnier; [m.] Richard O. Fenton, August 6, 1994; [ed.] Burlington High School, University of Vermont; [occ.] Teacher; [pers.] Try to write and live from your heart not from what society seems to be telling you.; [a.] Milton, VT

FEORE, JANE NEWBURY
[b.] February 7, 1947, Newport, RI; [p.] Helen T. Newbury; [ch.] Jennifer, Elizabeth, John; [ed.] Boston College; [occ.] Poet/Songwriter; [memb.] M.A.D.D., N.O.W., Habitat Partners Council, Holy Trinity Church; [oth. writ.] "The Vigil," which mirrors my work with the homeless, and my belief that we all have it within us, with God's help, to be Good Samaritans.; [pers.] I have always been drawn to the sea, especially early morning sunrises over the Atlantic. I see life there in all its beauty and goodness and power to heal. This becomes part of the landscape, part of me. I try to share this in my writing.; [a.] McLean, VA

FERER, HARVEY
[pen.] H. Sapot-Ferer; [b.] December 24, 1924, St. Louis, MO; [p.] Sidney Sapot, Hannah Cooper; [m.] Divorced, married April 1, 1959; [ch.] Aaron, Andrew, Ana; [ed.] 4 1/2 yrs. College (Completed at UCLA); [occ.] Aviation Consultant; [memb.] Institute of Navigation (ION); [a.] Marina Del Rey, CA

FERGUSON, STACY L.
[pen.] Stocha; [b.] November 9, 1966, Inglewood, CA; [p.] Joan and Robert Brewer; [ch.] Donna Louise, Valerie Renee, Rebecca Lynne, Allyssia Tiamaya and Victoria Rae; [ed.] Rim of the World High, San Bernardino Valley College; [occ.] Co-owner of "Another Baby Shower Game"; [oth. writ.] I have written for over 16 years, this is my first published piece, hopefully not my last one.; [pers.] I feel I have been able to take all the dirt that life has shoveled my way and turned it into a form of art. I can say proudly "Hold on to your Dreams."; [a.] Imperial Beach, CA

FEUER, RITA E.
[pers.] Shades of 1945; attended the United Nations Conference in San Francisco, California from the opening day of April 25, 1945, until the closing date of June 26, 1945. I held an "A" Press Card with no limitations as to attending sessions and news gatherings. This "A" card was issued by the U.S.A. State dept. This magazine publication was named Insignia and was sent to every country represented at the United Nations Conference with pictures from the first to the last day of the conference. Insignia Magazine was founded by Miss Toby Edison, Editor and Publisher and I was fortunate enough to hold the position of assistant editor.; [a.] Corpus Christi, TX

FIELD, JOYCE
[pen.] Joyce Field; [b.] October 24, 1913, Brooklyn, NY; [p.] Jack Stillman, Rebecca Stillman; [m.] Stanley Field, December 7, 1935; [ch.] Jeffrey Michael, Constance Elyse; [ed.] Alumnus of the Corcoran Gallery's School of Art, Washington DC, American University, Washington, DC; [occ.] Writer; [memb.] American Lung Association of San Diego, California, member of International Folk Art Museum, La Jolla California, San Diego Mu-

seum of Art; [hon.] The World of Poetry selected Joyce Field as Poet Laurette for 1991 and also gave her a Golden Poetry Award for 1991. Her poem, The Microscopic Germ of the Winter's Gems II book won cash award in 1994.; [oth. writ.] Award Winning and More Poems by Joyce Field, published by Windsor Associates at 4655 Cass St., #314 San Diego, CA 92109 in February 1995.; [pers.] Neither too glad nor saddened be, but accept life with equanimity. This is my personal credo.; [a.] San Diego, CA

FIELDS, CARALEE
[b.] February 26, 1980, Charleston, SC; [p.] Samuel Fields, Terri Fields, stepmother Brenda Fields; [ed.] 9th Grade Beaverton High School; [occ.] Student; [hon.] 4th place St. Marys Library Poetry Contest, Mary Lee Clark Middle School Donald Mitchell Award; [pers.] "Comes the day when life will end, so for now let's all be friends!"; [a.] Beaverton, OR

FIELDS, FRANK P.
[pen.] Positive Black Brother; [b.] January 2, 1968, Cook County Hospital; [p.] Cathrene Fields; [ch.] Glynis Cathriene Fields, Franklin Glen Fields; [ed.] High Park Career Academy; [memb.] The Wull Hall Park Advisory Council 73 Releadgen Ave.; [oth. writ.] I write lyrics to song mostly and poetry thanks to poetry writings I always have the millions in my mind; [pers.] I would like to thank my mother Cathriene for her love and support and my family believing in me. Also would like to thank the National Library of Poetry entering me and believing my poetry. For giving me God all mostly such pen gift.; [a.] Chicago, IL

FIENGANT, ERMIDA
[b.] October 19, 1978, Gonaive, Haiti; [p.] Ernest Fieneant, Bulette Fieneant; [oth. writ.] Many poems are waiting such as "Freedom", "Society", "Privacy", "My grandma is my Shepherd", "My Baby Boy", "Black is Beautiful" and etc...); [pers.] I am not only a dreamer but also a leader, so tomorrow I will always be the Italic of my name especially when my goal is very high above the sky.; [a.] Miami, FL

FIERROS, SALOME G.
[b.] May 8, 1949, Brownsville, TX; [p.] Carmen and Jesus Garza; [ch.] Jon - 22 yo, Steven - 16 yo; [ed.] San Benito High - San Benito Texas, Texas Southmost College - Brownsville Texas, St. Philips College - San Antonio Texas.; [occ.] Medical Lab Tech. - Texas Center for Infectious Disease; [memb.] St. Joan of Arc's Womens Council, Guadalupana's Society.; [hon.] High School Freshman English Award, Senior Economics - Civics Class Award, College Freshman - Dean's List, Highest Rank - 1971, A.S.C.P. - Certified Laboratory Assistant exam.; [pers.] The longer I live the more I began to appreciate how wondrously unique we are and what a grand adventure life can be.; [a.] San Antonio, TX

FIGEAC, LILLIAN L.
[pen.] Lil Figeac; [b.] August 16, 1947, Bakersfield, CA; [p.] Walter H. Clayton and Doris Peauler; [m.] Deceased; [ch.] Nanessa Lorraine Figeac; [ed.] Agnew Jr. High - Blackburn Business College, El Centro College; [occ.] Certified Dietary Manager, at Seago Manor Health Care, Seagoville TX; [memb.] DMA - Dietary Managers Ass.; [oth. writ.] I have been writing poems for almost 30 yrs. for family and friends.; [pers.] Poems are ways I keep in touch with my innermost feelings. How sometimes a special person may touch my heart, and how life sometimes can trip you up. Life is so incredible.; [a.] Seagoville, TX

FIGGS, EVETTE M.
[b.] January 25, 1966, Gary, IN; [p.] Diane and Herbert Amos; [m.] Reginald R. Figgs, November 8, 1992; [ch.] Christopher and Reginald III; [ed.] Roosevelt High, Pima College; [occ.] Staff Sergeant United States Air Force, (job) Material Facilities Specialist stationed at Davis-Monthan AFB, Tucson AZ; [memb.] (NCOA) Non Commissioned Officers Association; [hon.] (Air Force) 2 good conduct metals, Air Force Acommendation metal and 5 outstanding unit awards; [oth. writ.] Several poems published for school book.; [pers.] My poems portray real life on the streets today especially for the youths. Also I love to write about things to come. I am a great admirer of Maya Angelou she inspires me the most.; [a.] Tucson, AZ

FILONOV, JUDY
[b.] November 27, 1966, Ottawa, Ontario, Canada; [p.] Ken and Dorothy Reynolds; [m.] Deceased, July 6, 1989; [ch.] Ashley Savannah - Age 3 1/2 mos.; [ed.] High School Education, Honour Diploma; [occ.] New mother; [pers.] Since grade school, I have always has a passion for writing. I have enjoyed the art of creating characters and situations and spinning it into a story. Over the past decade however, my controversial and extreme lifestyles have allowed me to feed off of these experiences and share them with family and friends through short stories and most recently a non-fictional novel. I hope in the near future, through publication, will be able to share these works with others.; [a.] Ottawa Ontario, Canada

FINK, DENISE
[b.] January 24, 1963, Lehighton, PA; [p.] Lucille and Clinton Walck; [m.] Robert Fink, April 14, 1984; [ch.] Ryan Robert; [a.] Lehighton, PA

FINLEY, CHERLYN SUE
[pen.] Cheri Finley; [b.] December 12, 1960, Pocatello, ID; [p.] Max Artinger, Lily Artinger; [m.] Kevin Finley, November 28, 1992; [ch.] Nasreen Elizabeth, Dezante Orion; [ed.] Highland High School, Idaho State University; [occ.] Fabrication Operator, SGS Systems Microelectronics, Carrollton, TX; [oth. writ.] Personal poetry, songs, short stories not yet published.; [pers.] I wish for all of my writings to touch every individual's depth of existence.; [a.] Arlington, TX

FINLEY, MARY
[pen.] Mary Lydia Finley; [b.] June 26, 1969, Greenville, SC; [p.] Robert Finley, Martha Finley; [ed.] Parker High, Berea High, Enoree Vocational Center, Greenville Technical College; [occ.] Toddler Teacher, Saints Childcare Center; [memb.] Calvary Christian Fellowship; [hon.] Honor Roll (at Berea), Dean's List (GTC), Honors (at Enoree) in Tayloring; [oth. writ.] I have written a small book of love poems and others, two poems published in school newspaper at Parker, one in church bulletin, but never published by a publishing company.; [pers.] I started writing poetry when I was 15 yrs. old. I could, (and still can) look at almost anything, and it would inspire a poem. I write mostly love poems, but I also write on life.; [a.] Greenville, SC

FISHER, BARBARA GENE
[b.] December 6, 1922, Philadelphia, PA; [p.] Deceased; [ed.] PhD University of Pennsylvania; [occ.] Retired Librarian; [oth. writ.] 6 books of poetry [a.] Tallahassee, FL

FISHER, MICHELLE RENEE
[b.] November 1, 1969, Cincinnati, OH; [p.] John Fisher, Patricia, Fisher; [m.] Fiance Jeffrey Thomas, Engaged July 17, 1993; [ch.] Amber Lynn Frank; [ed.] Loveland High School Live Oaks, CDC and Southern Ohio College; [occ.] Secretary; [hon.] Typing Certificate, Certificate in Senior, Office Education; [oth. writ.] Several poems not published; [pers.] My poetry comes from the heart and usually tells a story about someone I know or my own experiences; [a.] Florence, KY

FIVIZZANI, LORETTA A.
[pen.] Lori Fizz; [b.] July 25, 1941, Kankakee, IL; [p.] Priscilla and Phillip Stebbins; [m.] Richard Dante Fivizzani, April 15, 1961; [ch.] Annette Harbeck, Patti Rogers, Maria Halleck; [ed.] 1944 to 1959 Maryville Academy (Grade School and High School), varied courses at Oakton Community College (Choir, Caligraphy); [occ.] Secretary at Oakton Community College; [memb.] Sunday School Staff, St. Isaac Jogues Church (5 yrs.) Assist. Girl Scout Leader 1969, St. Isaac Jogues Church Choir (5 yrs.); [hon.] Science Award 1957 at H.S. in Top Ten Best Employees at OCC 1994; [oth. writ.] Song "Fax Me Your Love" 1993 or "Telephonic Love" copyrighted; [pers.] I write from my heart and try to express true feelings. Raised in an orphanage, I missed the one-on-one relationship between parents and child. Our school had 800 children, 64 nuns and 5 priests. All children from orphanage have a common bond.; [a.] Morton Grove, IL

FLAIBAN, DOMINICK
[pen.] Duffy; [b.] June 29, 1971, Mineola; [p.] Americo and Dolores Flaiban; [ed.] St. John The Baptist D.H.S. Grumman Data Systems Institute Suny Farmingdale; [occ.] Draftsman; [memb.] Alcoholics Anonymous; [hon.] Voted "Best Dancer" class of '89. Most Valuable Goalie (Soccer) - Brentwood Invitational. 1985 K of C Roller Hockey Champs selected to the P.A.L. All Star Football team; [oth. writ.] Personal poems for inspiration; [pers.] I'd like to thank God for believing in me when I couldn't believe in myself. Without him, I would not be here today.; [a.] Deer Park, NY

FLANNERY, BRIDGET DACY
[pen.] Bree, Bird; [b.] August 1, 1969, CT; [p.] Betty Lavigne; [m.] Divorced; [ch.] Stefan Briatte; [ed.] Not that much, but enough, I'm happy; [occ.] Mother, writer, dreamer and worry machine; [hon.] Getting through life, remembering, who I am, being honest, being myself being a mother (ha he ha) and very important, being happy and being in love!; [oth. writ.] Many more poems trying to be published! This is the first! And still trying this is great!; [pers.] For my mother, who believes in me, and for Angel for putting up with me, and my son who drives me nuts all the time, and the rest of my family and even grandma!; [a.] Tarzana, CA

FLENOY V, ROBERT LEE
[b.] December 22, 1981, UCLA, Westwood, CA; [p.] Yvonne Caldera; [ed.] Student in 7th grade at South Middle School Downey CA; [hon.] Academic Achievement Award, 2nd place in a Geography Bee, Math field day, Principal's Honor Roll, Reading Award, Science Award, 2nd in 50 yd. dash, Language, Art and Spelling Awards, Social Studies all of these in 5th grade, Young Authors Contest in 1st grade (Fiction-Poetry-Non Fiction); [oth. writ.] 6th grade received at on two page story called The Bad Dream; [pers.] Poem written in the 6th grade before summer

FLETCHER, JOCELYNE
[pen.] Puss Cat; [b.] July 8, 1959, St. Lucia; [p.] Mr.

and Mrs. St. George Clarke; [m.] Wilfred Fletcher, October 12, 1983; [ch.] 3 Devonn, Ethan, Eddie; [ed.] S.D.A. Academy, (UWI) University of the West Indies; [occ.] Administration Officer - Govt. Statistics Dept.; [memb.] St. Lucia National Trust, St. Lucia Sickle Cell Association, Rotaract Club of St. Lucia; [hon.] Outstanding past Student Award.; [oth. writ.] Several poems published in local newspapers and magazines. Short story series for children.; [pers.] As long as I can live within my mind, I see a beautiful world and I am constantly happy. All I have to do is escape into my mind, then no worry lines, no sadness, I become rejuvenated, full of positiveness and optimisms.; [a.] Castries St. Lucia, West Indies

FLORES, JACQUELINE
[b.] August 30, 1966, Chicago, IL; [p.] Eleanor and Frank Flores; [ed.] Wenchell High School De Paul University; [occ.] Pre School Teacher - Mother Goose Pre School; [memb.] Bring Them Home, America Child Abduction and Abuse Prevention; [hon.] Won Best Story Award at small "Theater Pride" a local production company in 1990; [pers.] I've always enjoyed reading as a young child which leads me to write which I enjoy greatly and hope to do for a long time; [a.] Chicago, IL

FLORES, PAMELA K.
[b.] January 10, 1958, Clarksville, TN; [p.] Harold and Brigitte Trout; [m.] Alvaro E. Flores, July 3, 1982; [ch.] Benjamin, Alexander, Christopher [ed.] Spencer High - Columbus, Georgia, Enterprise State Jr. College - Enterprise, AL, (currently striving towards a Paralegal Degree); [occ.] Administrative Assistant; [memb.] PTA, United Methodist Church; [hon.] Principal's List, Dean's List, Management Training Scholarships, Career Development Scholarship; [oth. writ.] I have written several forms of poetry, but this is my first published poem.; [a.] Enterprise, AL

FLORES, ROSA
[pen.] Rosa Flores; [b.] September 19, 1979, Noyarit, Mexico; [p.] Andrea and Donauano Flores; [ed.] 6 yrs. Mexico, 2 1/2 years U.S., currently enrolled in the 9th grade at Murphy Middle School in Morgan Hill; [occ.] 9th grade Student; [hon.] I have received 2 Principal's awards. Which are known as very special awards. - 6 blue honor rolls (3.0-3.5 G.P.A.), 1 gold honor roll (3.5-4.0 G.P.A.); [oth. writ.] I have written several other poems in Spanish which I'm currently translating into English.; [pers.] All of my poems have been written by my hand but dictated by my heart I believe anyone can do anything they set their mind to.; [a.] Morgan Hill, CA

FLORIO, DONNA
[b.] February 21, 1964, Sandy Spring, MD; [p.] Leonard Dawson, Eloise Dawson; [m.] John Francis Florio, June 19, 1986; [ch.] Charles Francis; [ed.] Sherwood High, Florida Atlantic University, Palm Beach Atlantic College, Palm Beach Community College (Bachelor of Social Work) [occ.] Student; [memb.] National Association for Social Workers, Good Shepherd United Methodist Church Stephens Minister; [hon.] Cum Laude, Dean's List; [oth. writ.] Poem published in the American Collegiate of Poet's Anthology. High School year book, and in a collection of poems from high school; [pers.] Inspiration comes from the willingness to see what's going on around me - whatever moves me is worth writing; [a.] West Palm Beach, FL

FLOYD, CARL
[b.] July 23, 1971, New Orleans, LA; [occ.] Poet, vocalist, artist, photographer; [memb.] Douglas Coupland's fan club, if only he was given one!; [oth. writ.] A collection of Carl Floyd's poetry and selected artwork will be forthcoming.; [pers.] "Dusk 'til Forever" is about passing the point of withdrawing, and proceeding to explore the full spectrum of dark emotions harbored from the aftermath of great personal loss. The "Big Statement": My attitude is that everything in life can be seen as absurd! So it's okey to let your imagination entertain you.; [a.] River Ridge, LA

FLOYD, CARLIER
[b.] October 21, 1974, Newburgh, NY; [p.] Carlton and Gwendolyn Floyd; [ed.] North Junior High, Vails Gate School, Newburgh Free Academy; [occ.] Store Clerk and Hairstylist; [oth. writ.] Always wrote poems for friends and family members also for family forums; [pers.] I write based on my feelings and many persons have inspired me such as my Mom and Dad, teachers and close friends. One day I hope to publish a book or even give ideas for lyrics to song writers, you know you feel good when you can express yourself through poetry.

FLOYD, REV. BARBARA WRIGHT
[b.] March 5, TX; [p.] Ralph and Helen Wright; [m.] Melton Floyd; [ch.] 3 daughters Elizabeth, Cynthia and Deborah 1 grandson, Brandon Rutledge; [ed.] I am a Neonatal and Newborn Nurse previously at Methodist Hospital and am in the process of becoming a Clinical Hypnotherapist; [occ.] I am currently a Minister for The Congregational Church of Practical Theology. We hold classes on Meditation and Spiritual Healing. I have done this type service all my life. My paintings are also a reflection of spirituality.; [hon.] Outstanding Awards in College for Psychology. Received "Director of the year" while working at Mansfield College over 44 schools nationally. Award was due to my writings for others.; [oth. writ.] I write poetry with a message. Many of my poems have been published, nationally in The Daily Word for Unity Churches.; [pers.] My personal belief is that if each one of us can share our situations with others that brings upliftment, we are helping to give light and make this planet a better peace.; [a.] San Antonio, TX

FLUCKER, ARETHA
[b.] September 18, 1981, Secaucus, NJ; [p.] Mr. and Mrs. Robert Flucker; [memb.] West Coosa Junior Beta Club; [hon.] 6 Perfect Attendances, 2 Honor Roll Awards; [pers.] I have been influenced by writers such as Francine Pascal, R. L. Stine and Steven King. I have also been influenced by my English teacher Mrs. Ann Ezekial.; [a.] Goodwater, AL

FLYNN, ELEANOR R.
[b.] January 29, 1937, Worcester; [p.] John P. and Catherine O'Day Sullivan; [m.] John F. Flynn, February 20, 1960; [ch.] Five: Mary-Lee, John, Susan, Cara, James; [ed.] B.S.Ed, M.A.Ed., Post M.A. 49 cr., St Stephen's High School - 1958, Worcester State College BS 1958, M.A.Ed. Worc State 1960; [occ.] 4th grade Teacher - each year every student writes their own book of poems; [memb.] Faculty advisor for School Newspaper; [hon.] Recipient of two Horace Mann Awards; [oth. writ.] Published a book of Children's Creative Writing. I have written several short stories, several poems.; [pers.] Live life to its fullest, enjoy the world around you. Find the good in everyone and everything. Be creative, encourage creativity in others.; [a.] Leicester, MA

FOBI, NGWEBIFOR M.
[pen.] Mignon Fobi; [b.] August 5, 1977, Harbor City, CA; [p.] Dr. Mathias and Helen Fobi; [ed.] Freshman at Fisk University in Nashville, TN; [occ.] Student; [memb.] Community Missionary Baptist Church, Cameroon American Students Ass. at Los Angeles, Young Black Scholars, Youth Ministry; [hon.] Fisk University Academic Scholarship, Miss Ovalat Fisk; [oth. writ.] Several poems published in Fisk Herald; [pers.] "I believe the future belongs to those who can look at a challenge... and see an opportunity."; [a.] Nashville, TN

FOLKS, ROSEMARY
[b.] March 9, 1971, Brooklyn; [p.] Mrs. Annie and Mr. Lucious Folks; [ed.] Attended LaGuardia Community College; [occ.] Home Attendant; [oth. writ.] Several poems unpublished; [pers.] My poems are my most essential prize in life. I wish that all of God's children will allow themselves to recognize and appreciate all of the beautiful creations thy spirit have given us to see, smell, and hear. I thank you Maya Angelou (Poet) for all of your spiritual wisdom you have given me through your writings and your voice.; [a.] Long Island City, NY

FONTAINE, BERTRAM BILL
[b.] February 16, 1961, Pine Falls, Manitoba, Canada; [p.] Bert and Terry Fontaine; [m.] Darlene Fontaine, July 31,1993; [ch.] Aaron, Billy Jo and Tahni; [ed.] Sagkeeng Consolidate, F.H. Collins High, University of Manitoba; [occ.] Staying home looking after the children while Darlene attends college; [hon.] Graduate - Band and Northern Administration; [oth. writ.] Submitted poetry in the local newspaper "The Opasquia Times" The Pas, Canada.; [a.] The Pas Manitoba, Canada

FOOKS, JESSICA
[b.] July 12, 1982, Newcomb Hospital; [p.] Karen Powers, Bill Powers; [ed.] Jr. High; [hon.] Honor Roll; [oth. writ.] I have never tried to publish my work before.; [pers.] Writing is a way to express my feelings in a constructive way. When I'm upset or confused I write.; [a.] Pennsville, NJ

FORBIS, KENA LYNN ELKIN
[b.] May 29, 1954, Columbia, MO; [p.] Frank L. and Mildred Elkin; [m.] Curtis Forbis, September 2, 1972; [ch.] Jason, Julee and Casey Elizabeth; [ed.] Hallsville High, Stephens College, Columbia College; [occ.] Kindergarten teacher; [hon.] Graduate BA in Education, Summa Cum Laude; [pers.] My writing transposes from a place within that is much deeper than the soul. It reflects my truest passions for life, love and laughter.; [a.] Hallsville, MO

FORD, BOBBIE ANN
[b.] July 5, 1968, Liberal, KS; [p.] Robert Ford, Ann Sherman; [ch.] Maddelyn Ford, age 5; [ed.] Cody High School, Northwest College, National College of Technology; [hon.] Presidential Academic Fitness Award, Kiwanis Award of Merit for Business, Dean's List; [oth. writ.] I have written a great deal and have published an article in the HS newspaper.; [pers.] I have been greatly influenced by Sylvia Plath, Anne Sexton and Emily Dickinson.; [a.] Cody, WY

FORD, MERRILY CUMMINGS
[b.] March 16, 1921, Ecorse, MI; [p.] Mary Vincent and Lee Commings; [m.] Albert P. (Al) Ford; [occ.] Keeping on. Plowing Ahead. Finding out.; [oth. writ.] GLADvertising. Newspaper columns. Fast-print books of my poetry and travel letters. A plethora of ephemera for my Mail Art friends.; [pers.] I love words. I love my friends. I'm still around at 73 and holding!; [a.] Glendora, CA

FORD, VIOLET R.
[pen.] Violet R. Bennett; [b.] September 9, 1910, Poe, WV; [p.] Finley and Rouena Bennett; [m.] John W. Ford, March 1, 1930; [ch.] Robert W. Ford, Lois Johnson and Diana Kalinowski; [ed.] One year at Gauley Bridge High; [occ.] Home Maker; [memb.] SDA Church; [pers.] I have always liked poetry

FORDEN, DORA
[b.] December 9, 1935, Wintersville, OH; [p.] William Chappell, Viola Chappell; [m.] William Forden, January 15, 1982; [ch.] Kathryn Forden Sutera, Mark Anthony, Steven Anthony, Curt Anthony, Karen Miller; [ed.] Wintersville High School, Mt. Union College (Alliance, Ohio); [occ.] Retired Elementary Teacher, Lincoln Elem. School - Huntsville, AL; [pers.] Teaching children to think and write creatively was one of my greatest joys. It's wonderful to have the time now to pursue this interest more personally!; [a.] Huntsville, AL

FORNEY, MARY L.
[pen.] Mary L. Forney; [b.] January 27, 1949, Philadelphia, PA; [p.] Bill McKeown and Mary McKeown; [m.] William R. Forney, June 30, 1990; [ed.] Archbishop Prendergust HS, Community College 2 yrs. Nursing School at Roxborough Memorial Hospital; [occ.] Acme Markets Inc. for 5 years; [memb.] American Lung Assoc.; [hon.] None at present time. This was my first time in writing this poem about my Little Cat.; [oth. writ.] First writing as a poet.; [pers.] I strive to reflect the goodness in all my writings that I have done in the past years of my adult life, favorite poet is Robert Frost.; [a.] Philadelphia, PA

FORSYTH, REGAN LEE
[pen.] Veronica Martinez; [b.] March 14, 1974, Winnipeg, Manitoba, Canada; [p.] Glenn Forsyth and Susan Forsyth; [ed.] Westwood Collegiate - Winnipeg MB, University College of the Fraser Valley - Chilliwack BC; [occ.] College student/Nanny; [pers.] Out of the many poems, I have written "Heaven Awaits You" means the most to me. Paul Garner, was a dear friend who died tragically on August 4, 1993. He will always be remembered.; [a.] Chilliwack British Columbia, Canada

FORTE, JOEY
[b.] October 4, 1962, Staten Island, NY; [m.] Tami Forte, January 14, 1986; [ch.] Joseph; [a.] Staten Island, NY

FOSSELL, MICHAEL
[b.] April 12, 1954, Philadelphia, PA; [pers.] For Alice, my life, my love, my inspiration.; [a.] Glendora, NJ

FOSTER, DEITRA
[pen.] Deitra Dinkie Foster; [b.] April 30, 1971, Washington, DC; [p.] Harry and Helen Foster; [ed.] Bladenshure Senior High, Frostburg State University; [occ.] Self Employed; [memb.] Omega Psi Phi Sweetheart At Beta Kappa Chapter in Frostburg, Maryland.; [oth. writ.] Several other poems not yet in the light.; [pers.] If only someone could see Dinkie's rage.; [a.] Riverdale, MD

FOSTER, GABRIELLE
[pen.] Gabrielle Foster; [b.] January 4, 1957, Hollywood, CA; [p.] Howard and Marion Jarrett; [m.] Russell Foster, September 7, 1980; [ed.] Sheldon High School; [occ.] Order Filler, Coast to Coast Warehouse, Springfield, OR; [hon.] Theater Awards, High School; [oth. writ.] Unpublished poems; [pers.] I strive to express my most inner feelings in hopes of uplifting one's look on life.; [a.] Eugene, OR

FOSTER, JOHN M.
[b.] July 16, 1915, Kansas; [p.] Rose L. Foster, Francis M. Breen; [m.] Mary Ellen Smith Foster, July 11, 1939; [ed.] Colorado Springs High, University of Maryland; [occ.] Retired; [memb.] Lions International, The Retired Officers Assn.; [hon.] Air medal (WW II); [oth. writ.] USAF Manuals, other poetry for Organization News Letters. Article for Air Inspector General Magazine.; [a.] Hutchinson, KS

FOWLER, SHANNON LENORE
[b.] June 29, 1976, Conway, SC; [p.] Cecelia Johnson, Nicky Fowler; [ed.] South Columbus High, current freshman at University of North Carolina at Charlotte; [hon.] North Carolina Scholar, Academic Athlete Award; [oth. writ.] Several poems written; [pers.] I was greatly influenced by poets such as Edgar Allen Poe. I like to bring out the beauty of nature in my poems.; [a.] Monroe, NC

FOX, AMY R.
[pen.] Amy R. Fox; [b.] July 23, 1976, Parsons, KS; [p.] Tim Fox, Swana Fox; [ed.] Fredonia High School Labette Com. College; [occ.] Waitress - PJ's Diner, Altamont, KS; [memb.] Poets and Writers Inc., Labette Co. Orchestra, Music Clubs; [oth. writ.] A Silent Prayer, Motionless, Unchained etc. all have never been published.; [pers.] "There is a light waiting in this dark world, and the true believers will free themselves within its warm glow. They will suffer no more". "I hope my poetry will be used as a form of guidance"; [a.] Altamont, KS

FOX, CAROL A.
[pen.] C. A. Fox; [b.] January 24, 1950, Ashland, OH; [p.] Rex and Vesta Bowman; [m.] Daniel, September 21, 1990; [ch.] Tina Marie; [ed.] Ashland Senior High School, Ashland Ohio; [occ.] Secretary - Carriage Inn Home Health Care Agency; [memb.] Gold Wing Road Riders Association; [oth. writ.] Several poems; [pers.] I try to write about what I see, feel or hear. Sometimes, a word, a phrase, or even a person or place influence what I put on paper.; [a.] Salem, OH

FOX, PAULINE MOORE
[b.] April 30, 1910, Platner, CO; [p.] Walter Moore, Dorothy Heise Moore; [m.] Paul Jackson Fox, December 25, 1938; [ed.] Graduate High School June 16, 1927 South Denver, CO; [occ.] Alone - widow; [memb.] First Unitarian Church San Diego, CA; [oth. writ.] Other poems still writing started at age 12 or before; [a.] San Diego, CA

FRANCIS, J. MICHAEL
[b.] January 20, 1973, North Sidney; [p.] Lynn Stubbert, Michael Francis; [ed.] Graduated Memorial High School - Syndney Mines in top 10% June 1991, will graduate University College of Cape Breton in April 1995 with a BSC in Biology; [occ.] Student, Research Assistant, Clerk; [oth. writ.] None available at this time Scientific Publications in the works; [pers.] I believe life to be like an offer at McDonald's "For a Limited Time only - so you should enjoy it". I also think the perfect life is illustrated in a Disney movie. There is conflict between the good guys and the bad guys. However the good guys always win, get the beautiful princess and live happily ever after. - What more could you want?; [a.] Florence Nova Scotia, Canada

FRANCO, CRIVELLI
[b.] September 10, 1941, Pecetto (Al), Italy; [p.] Benvenuto and Bianca Crivelli; [m.] Julie Tan Crivelli, June 6, 1970; [ed.] Degree in Economics and Business, Bocconi University, Milan, Italy. MBA in Marketing, Baruch College, City University of NY; [occ.] International Accounts Mgr. Information Systems Business; [memb.] Italian Association for Cancer Research, American Chamber of Commerce in Italy.; [hon.] Fellowship at Baruch College, City University of New York.; [pers.] Only a man without nationalistic attitudes but with deep roots (I was born on the hills of Piedmont where a man's word is his own worth, filtered by the humanism of Emilia where a man is nothing but a man) can be a truly international man.; [a.] Segrate Milan, Italy

FRANCOIS, DAVID
[pen.] Davo; [b.] November 7, 1971, St. Croix; [p.] Augustin and Marie Francois; [ed.] High School, and presently college classes.; [occ.] Computer programmer and surveying, U.S. Army; [memb.] President of the Young People Department at the Central Nazarene Church in St. Croix, United States Virgin Island.; [hon.] Math, Poems; [pers.] I also love art, taking part in community activities, and working with young people, was also a member of the US National Guard and presently is a Paratrooper in the U.S. Army.; [a.] Fort Brad, NC

FRAZEE, FLORENCE IRENE
[pen.] F; [b.] December 22, 1922, Chicago, IL; [p.] Alfred Hansen Busk, Hannah Busk; [m.] Jarrell Amos Frazee, September 3, 1946; [ch.] Vernon Sharon, Carolyn, David, Yvonne, Beverly; [ed.] Mattawan High, Parson's Business College, Stetson (ECEd) Misc.; [memb.] First Church of God, Concerned Women of America; [hon.] Valedictorian (Scholarship), Asst. Publisher Alaska Hilights, (BD sent) missionary and related - years as early childhood teacher - also Secy, Bkpr, Mgr. Misc. (Daughter with fuller doctorate and PHD - Assoc Prof at Azuza), (In Israel this month!); [oth. writ.] Scales of poems and also unpublished - some stories for kids! (One of testimony - as a child (6) 6 mos in 3 different hospitals - spared to live (on 3 neg. 3 pos. yet today!) (Blood types, kept in balance!)) [pers.] I marvel at my maker's creativity and recreative powers, sustaining and sending us: "Wisdom and truth shall enter the very center of your being, filling your life with joy" Prov. 2:10; [a.] Lake Wales, FL

FRAZIER, DEBORAH
[pen.] Your Forever Love; [b.] May 18, 1956, Amityville, NY; [p.] William Johnson and Doris Allen; [ch.] Tamira, Kelvin, Immanuel and Daniel Frazier; [occ.] Nurse's Assistant, Mother, Pray Partner, Evangelist; [memb.] Bethel Tabernacle, A.M.E. 1630 Dean St. Brooklyn NY 11213 (Pastor A. Earl Jordon); [oth. writ.] Many unpublished; [pers.] A woman with God's gift of love and passion - this poem is dedicated first to God then to a special friend Rev. Kevin Jordon and my family.

FRAZIER, DIANA MARIE ROBINSON
[b.] February 4, 1954, Bronx, NY; [p.] Maude Ernestine; [m.] Aaron Maurice Frazier, November 23, 1984; [ed.] Ohio Wesleyan University Bay Ridge H.S.; [occ.] Asst. to VP of Marketing and Promotion Brooklyn Academy of Music; [oth. writ.] All other poems unpublished too many to be listed here; [pers.] I empathize with people in pain so they will know they are not alone; [a.] Brooklyn, NY

FREDERICK, BETTY
[pen.] Bette; [b.] August 18, 1911, Russellville, AL; [p.] George Todd, Eula Todd; [m.] Burnett Frederick, December 24, 1929; [ch.] Conrad Frederick, David Frederick; [ed.] Franklin High, 2 yrs. Alexandra Col-

lege; [occ.] Artist - my teacher Warree Le Braun; [memb.] Member of the First Presbyterian Church.; [oth. writ.] I have written poetry all my life but have never tried to have it published.; [a.] Sylacauga, AL

FREEMAN, ERVIN M.
[pen.] Brother Bones; [b.] March 2, 1966, Bradenton, FL; [p.] Winifred and Willie Lee Freeman; [m.] Tavis A. Freeman, June 18, 1987; [ch.] Kory and Shakara Freeman; [ed.] AA degree at Manatee Community College, Bradenton, FL; [occ.] Filing Clerk; [pers.] I believe no one should deny his or herself a better future. "Make a life, before creating a life." [a.] Palmetto, FL

FREEMAN, LALENA LEE
[pen.] Lalena Lee; [b.] May 15, 1971, Harrisburg, PA; [p.] Janet Pierich, Steve Freeman; [ed.] High School; [occ.] Exotic Dancer, Nursing Assistant; [oth. writ.] None published I have personal writings unyet published; [pers.] I write only what I feel would be necessary to tackle the minds, brain; [a.] York, PA

FRITZ, JONATHAN LAWRENCE
[b.] January 30, 1979, Omaha, NE; [p.] Dave and Becky Fritz; [ed.] Sophomore High School; [memb.] Speech Team, Quiz Bowl, Chorus, Band, Science Club, Spanish Club, Teens Against Drug and Alcohol, United Presbyterian Church; [oth. writ.] None this my first; [pers.] The only things you regret in life, are the risks you never took.; [a.] Laurel, NE

FROST, TONYA M.
[b.] October 13, 1967, Indianapolis, IN; [p.] Thomas Frost and Moneeca Frost; [pers.] A special thanks to my family for convincing me to share my writing with others.

FRYREAR, JONNIE
[pen.] Jonnie Fryrear; [b.] January 12, 1931, El Reno; [p.] John and Ollie Griffith; [m.] Divorced in 1976, married 1950; [ch.] 2 grown; [ed.] 60 hrs. college credits, since divorce most from Rose State in Midwest - 1 yr. at OV; [occ.] Retired; [memb.] Methodist Church; [oth. writ.] Some prose I published while at Rose State; [pers.] Have a cocker, and a toy poodle and their unconditional love constantly reminds me of how God's love is.; [a.] Norman, OK

FULKS, ALAINA M.
[pen.] Alaina M. Walker; [b.] November 19, 1963, Franklin, LA; [p.] Roy Walker, Enola Walker; [m.] Danny M. Fulks Sr., January 18, 1991; [ch.] Britany, Adrian Hixon, Dicie, Danny, Emma F.; [ed.] Centerville High School; [occ.] Housewife and mother of five.; [memb.] Sister of Christian Fellowship Church thanks to Louis and Pat Concienne.; [hon.] My poem has been a great honor for me and your publication my most precious award.; [pers.] Although we may not always understand the confusion of life, there are moments of relief, if we trust in the Lord. My poem was inspired by my family and above all, God Almighty and Jesus Christ my Savior.; [a.] Franklin, LA

FULLER, FORTUNATE T.
[b.] April 20, 1918, Haverhill, MA; [p.] Demenico and Catherine Spinelli; [m.] Edward L. Fuller, July 21, 1937; [ch.] 3 living - Edward, Beverly, Judy; [ed.] Haverhill High, smatterings at several colleges, castle tutoring several countries.; [occ.] Retired Artist, Volunteer Worker at dress shop; [memb.] RSVP; [hon.] Gamma Tau - bid - short story not as yet published in Modern Maturity Ribbon from Cuppertino Senior Center for poem "Prodigal Son."; [oth. writ.] Romantic novel not as yet published called "She Bent Over" or "Drop the Handkerchief". Poem entered Our Garden, Rhapsody with a Pilot; [pers.] I hope to rise above competition with more than one friend left, and also leave my impression on the world.; [a.] Palo Alto, CA

FUMMY, CRYSTAL
[pen.] Chris; [b.] December 12, 1981, Georgetown Hospital; [p.] Elaine Thompson Rickey; [ed.] Kindergarten, Grade School, High School; [occ.] Student 7th grade; [memb.] Holy Cross Faith Memorial Church; [hon.] If I win this it would be my first

FURMAN, DAVID
[b.] August 14, 1972, Philadelphia; [a.] Philadelphia, PA

FURTADO, STEPHANIE
[b.] April 23, 1976, Plymouth, MA; [p.] Michael and Elsie Furtado; [ed.] Plymouth North High School, currently attending New Hampshire College; [occ.] Full time college student; [memb.] Saint Peters Parish Center; [oth. writ.] This is my first publication and hope to have more publications in the future.; [pers.] My poems mean more to me than just words - they're thoughts and most importantly feelings which come from my heart.; [a.] Plymouth, MA

GACAYAN, TROY PHILLIP
[pen.] Sword Of The Spirit; [b.] August 31, 1971, Hawaii, HI; [p.] Gerald and Debbie Gacayan; [ed.] High School Diploma (Hawaii), Military Education (Air Force), University Anchorage Alaska, Pima Community College; [occ.] United States Air force Command and Control Specialist; [oth. writ.] Many others poems that I have shared with family and friends to encourage them to be stronger believers of God.; [pers.] All of my poems have been truly inspired by the holy spirit of the Lord Jesus Christ. I am not looking to make a name for myself, but hoping that thought me, the lord will be able to produce poems to touch the heart of people in this world.; [a.] Tuczon, AZ

GALTRESS, TANYA
[b.] October 1, 1969, Guelph, Ontario, Canada; [p.] Frances Galtress; [ed.] Ridgeway and Crystal Beach High School, McMaster University; [occ.] Fitness Instructor/ Personal Trainer; [memb.] Ontario Fitness Council, Canadian, Association of Fitness Professionals International Association of Fitness Professionals; [hon.] Ontario Scholar, Mcmaster Undergraduate Council Scholarship; [pers.] To me life can be summed up into the words of Rosita Perez: "You have a choice. Either lament the high notes you can't or won't hit, or leave them to Pavarotti and get on with the rest of your song."; [a.] Ridgeway Ontario, CANADA

GARCIA, NANCY
[b.] May 2, 1976, Cambridge, MA; [p.] Luis and Dolores Garcia; [ed.] Graduated from High School in 1994; [occ.] Receptionist for a small non-profit organization; [oth. writ.] Poems and short stories currently being revised for possible publishing.; [pers.] I write what I feel and I experiment with different styles. I strive to place myself with what I write. I hope the reader enjoys it too. I've been writing since the age of 12.; [a.] Stoneham, MA

GARDNER, VERONICA
[b.] November 11, 1945, Philadelphia, PA; [p.] Edward Stewart and Anna Marie Stewart; [m.] William A. Gardner, August 14, 1982; [ch.] Victoria Marie, Jennifer Ann; [ed.] St. Hubert's High School, School of Accounting and Finance and Business Administration; [occ.] Co-owner of Gardner's Automotive Diagnostic Repair Center, Phila, PA; [memb.] American Humane Society, American Heart Association, Nat'l Wildlife Fund; [hon.] Scholastic Honor Society; [oth. writ.] Currently compiling a book of my poetry reflecting my observations about life and nature article/observation Phila. Magazine; [pers.] Upon writing a poem, I've always found inspiration in retrospect of life's experiences and the exciting beauty and continuity in nature; [a.] Churchville, PA

GARRETT, TONYA K.
[pen.] T. K. Garrett; [b.] April 13, 1950, Pratt, KS; [p.] Bill and Cleo Hatzewbuehler; [ch.] Mishallee D. Garrett; [ed.] Adair High School, Adair, Okla. Rogers State College, Claremore Okla.; [occ.] Full time college student working for BA and Master in Psychology and sociology.; [hon.] Dean's list, certificate of achievement in quality service, connected with the Burlington Northern Rail Road. Honor roll in College Rogers state, claremore Okla.; [oth. writ.] Many poems written over 20 year, this is first I ever sent in for outside reading; [pers.] I strive for honestly within myself for a better life that maybe those around will receive a positive affect. Poems of struggle and triumphs have influenced me through my life.; [a.] Ketchum, OK

GARRISON, MATTHEW
[b.] February 24, 1970, Medicine Lodge, KS; [p.] Karen Dulac and Bernard Dulac; [ed.] Columbus College of Art and Design, Columbus State Community College; [occ.] Student; [oth. writ.] Several poems, play sketch, short story, diaries. [pers.] I desire an unwritten, objective projection of thought, though devoid of opinion and philosophy and only of movement, shape, clashing forms, colors, and emotional themes of spiritual conflict.; [a.] Westerville, OH

GARRITY, JUNE H.
[b.] June 15, 1929, Bingham Canyon, UT; [p.] John Werner and Helga Forsnes Holmes; [m.] William Denn Garrity (deceased), June 20, 1954; [ch.] John William Garrity; [ed.] BA, University of Nevada, Reno Certificate, Children's Institute of Literature, Major: Journalism, Minor in English; [occ.] Meeting Planner, Admin. Asst.; [memb.] Good Shepherd Lutheran Church, Past Matron and Grand Officer Order of Eastern Star, Gamma Phi Beta, International Assn. of Business Communicators, American Business Women's Assn. I'm proud of my religious heritage which dates back to the Vikings on both my father's and mother's side of the family.; [hon.] Utah Advertising Federation Gold Award, IABC Awards of Excellence, Society of Tech. Writers' Award of Excellence; [oth. writ.] Poem: An American Dream Children's Story, Billy's Friend Charlie, "Lucky Louie", "The Skier", and adult story: The Turning Point; [pers.] I want children to learn to become good readers, and my personal philosophy is that expressed by Auntie Mame, "Life is a banquet and most poor souls are starving to death!" I love to travel, ski, golf and looking forward to my next extensive trip which is to China with the University of Nevada Alumni Assn. March 15 - 29 1995.; [a.] Murray, UT

GARWOOD, LISA LEE
[pen.] Black Feather, Diamond Elliot; [b.] April 2, 1974, Marion, OH; [p.] Robert and Mary Garwood; [ed.]

Graduate of Bellefontaine High School; [occ.] Office worker for Kroger Company; [hon.] Honor Thespian; [oth. writ.] Black feather, who I am-by black feather a list of more than one hundred spiritual poems by black feather. The short stories the clutter of some ones mind and the love of a good man - By Diamond Elliot. Short stories that are either sci-fi or psychological thrillers. I have many of them.; [pers.] Long live the bards of today who love to entertain the people of Tymora with written word! [a.] Bellefontaine, OH

GASKIN, ARLEEN
[pen.] Nia Gaskin; [b.] February 23, 1963, Trinidad, WI; [p.] Eddison Salandy and Theresa Salandy; [m.] Atiba Gaskin, January 30, 1988; [ch.] Qalil Gibran Gaskin; [ed.] Diego Martin Governmen Secondary Modern Business School The Writing School Monrde Community College; [occ.] President U.A.I.A Productions; [memb.] Rochester black business committee; [oth. writ.] "Just watching your back" a column in Rochester Metro Challenger, Liner notes on the last five albums on "The Mighty Sparrow", "A Black Woman's Perspective; [pers.] My main objective is education if in the process I failed to educate, at least I would agitate. Nothing ventured nothing gained.; [a.] Rochester, NY

GASPER, JEAN ANGELA
[b.] November 3, 1942, Pittsburgh, PA; [p.] Rose Marie-Gualtieri and Joseph Gualtieri; [m.] Larry Ennis; [ch.] Michael Angelo, Cheryl Anne, Joseph Eugene and David Allen; [ed.] Lincoln High, Bucks County Tech.; [occ.] Secretary: Quality TV+VCR Serv. Center Consultant: (The Hairmakers Phila PA and Walnut St Theater); [memb.] St. Michaels, (C.C.D. Teacher) Church of Christ Benevolent Committee (Secretary Bristol Township Youth Aide Panel); [hon.] A Woman's Place (R/A) (For abuse woman and children); [oth. writ.] Local newspapers P/R. work poems pub. local newspaper; [pers.] My writing is my way of venting, thoughts of Christianity, music, my blessing, love, sharing, whether in labor or in thought. "Just pass it around." Truth and feelings express through good writings (of different types) is one of the best ways to reach humanity today! (one of my favorite (author's walter-rinder spectrum-of-love); [a.] Philadelphia, PA

GASTON, CAMERON
[pen.] Morbid Angel; [b.] January 11, 1974, Long Beach, CA; [p.] Pat and Robin Gaston; [m.] Megan Nicole Gaston, Jared Tyler Gaston, Nicholas Derele Gaston; [ed.] Western High, Cypress Community College, Cal St. Fullerton.; [occ.] Extended Day Care Center Asst. At Rossmoor Elem. School; [hon.] Golden St. Exam: High Honors in Algebra School Recognition in Chemistry; [oth. writ.] Many poems never published written to express my feelings.; [pers.] I'm back!!!! and this time I am her to stay.; [a.] Cypress, CA

GAUTHIER, JOANNE
[b.] July 24, 1979, Virden, Manitoba, Canada; [p.] Ray and Huguette Gauthier; [ch.] Yosep Woga (foster child); [ed.] Archbishop M.C. O'Neill High School.; [hon.] Grade 9 Honor roll; [oth. writ.] Creative with words Publ, Golden Taffy magazine; [a.] Regina Saskatchewan, Canada

GAVRICH, JENNIFER
[b.] September 27, 1983, Marlton, NJ; [p.] Jeff Gavrich and Deborah Gavrich; [ed.] Harrison Avenue School, Louis M. Klein Middle School Harrison, New York; [occ.] Student; [memb.] D.A.R.E. card, student body card, library card; [hon.] Presidential Academic Fitness, Outstanding Accomplishment, Journalism, D.A.R.E. medal and D.A.R.E award, Art honor at town offices, Honor's Roll, received highest grade on New York state writing test; [oth. writ.] Poem published in the Anthology of poetry by young Americans, title Thanksgiving Day.; [pers.] I enjoy writing poems and stories. I also enjoy drawing cartoon characters, mostly Disney. I'm in the art club at school and take figure skating lessons.; [a.] Harrison, NY

GEARY, KRYSTAL
[b.] April 17, 1984, CA; [p.] Mom (Kim) and Dad (Eddie); [ed.] In 5th Grade now; [oth. writ.] Poems, paper, clouds, our future, dreams, mothers day storeys: The lost forest, the boy who didn't know what a birthday was, running away, the cats; [pers.] Paper starts out white and blank but white and blank but if you put your mind to it, it can be come a legend.

GENNARO, ROBERT J. D. I.
[pen.] Bobby Di; [b.] February 14, 1952, Woodbury, NJ; [p.] Elizabeth Di Gennaro; [ed.] A.A. Liberal Arts G.C.C. working on Theatre Arts B.A. at Thomas Edison State College; [occ.] Substitute Teacher, Telemarketer Woodbury; [memb.] Lector - St. Patrick's church, Woodbury, NJ. Sketch club players - woodbury, N.J. Puttin' on the Ritz, Oaklyn, NJ.; [pers.] I look for the best in mankind, good always with over evil!!! In short "strung people know how to win!".; [a.] Woodbury, NJ

GENTRY, GEORGE W.
[b.] March 11, 1929, Okolona, AR; [p.] Ruby and Alberta Gentry; [m.] Ruth Gentry, December 15, 1956; [ed.] Elementary; [occ.] Retired from General Motors AC West Flint, MI; [oth. writ.] Books titled man of mystery some body tell me I want to know the deceivers and the deceived a nation that was, the climaxing of a man's reign americans last call, the rebels last yodel and eternal fall. The radical and the fool,; [pers.] Laconically I'm astoundedly adulated, I can't say enough for your being congenial and allowing me to share you reciprocity; [a.] Okolona, AR

GHOSH, RASHBEHARI
[b.] November 1, 1937, Bhagalpur; [p.] Late M. Ghost and Mrs. L. Ghosh; [m.] Professor Pratima Ghost, December 8, 1964; [ch.] (One) Dr. Arabindo Ghosh; [ed.] M.A. in English; [occ.] (Principal), University Professor of English, (V.B.U). Poet, Critic, Reviewer; [memb.] Lions International, Academic Council of the University, Senate-members of the university - Vinoba Bhave University, Hazaribag, Bihar.; [hon.] Man of the Year - ABI (U.S.A) International Man of the Year I.B.C. (U.K.), International Man of Achievement I.B.C. (UK). Distinguished Leadership Award (A.B.I) USA. Advisor to Research Board of Advisors. A.B.I. (USA). Biographies appear in at least 10 (ten) International Who's Who published by A.B.I. (USA) and I.B.C. Cambridge (U.K.); [oth. writ.] Published: 260 poems in reputed journals and anthologies;l published - my collections (poems) A Year Without -Gods, Hunger, Eves and ebbs, between you and me, despaired dreams, review on anthologies, published 20 literary articles - etc.; [pers.] If I live long, I shall pack and pile all men and women to a magic island and melt their elements to produce rich gems.; [a.] Dhanbad, Bihar India

GIBSON, FREEMAN G.
[pen.] Freeman Gibson; [b.] August 23, 1952, Roanoke Rapids, NC; [p.] W.F. Gibson and M.F. Gibson; [ed.] A.A.S Degree Business Adm. Criminal Justice Service Comm. Basic Nuclear Systems Graduate Roanoke Rapids High; [occ.] Nuclear Security Officer Surry Power Station, Surry, VA.; [memb.] Virginia Power CO/Worker Worldwide Church of God Society for prevention/Cruelty to animals. Professional Nuclear Institute; [hon.] Perfect Attendance Performance Award in Service. Design of Uniform Patch Insignia-Company uniform.; [oth. writ.] None published/a personal collection.; [pers.] The scepter of life is precious, so rejoice and life life to its' fullest!!" As a single man, I look and listen to the world, and learn from it's atrocities, and pleasures.; [a.] Smithfield, VA

GILBERT, JAMIE
[b.] August 5, 1981, Farmington, ME; [p.] Sharon L. Gilbert and James Gilbert; [ed.] 8th Grader; [hon.] High Honors Straight A student; [pers.] First serious poem I've ever written.; [a.] Farmington, ME

GILBERT, KENNETH E.
[pen.] Milk; [b.] October 10, 1973, Rock Island; [p.] Merle and Merrilee Gilbert; [m.] Donna Gilbert, March 20, 1993; [ch.] Jevon Anthony Gilbert; [ed.] High school grad, United Township High School, East Moline, IL, Military Police School, U.S. Army; [occ.] Rap artist in Hip-Hop group; [oth. writ.] A lot of original and unpublished writings; [pers.] No Jesus-no peace, know Jesus-know peace, racism is a deadly deteriorating mankind. Let's unite to find a cure; [a.] Fort Polk, LA

GILL, HEATHER P.
[b.] January 23, 1960, Barbados; [p.] Stanley Gill and Anita Stevenson; [ch.] Christopher Gill; [ed.] Modern High School, Montgomery College; [occ.] Sr. Library Assistant; [oth. writ.] Several poems I am in the process of writing a book.; [a.] Silver Spring, MD

GINGER, GOLONKA
[b.] October 17, 1981, Green Bay, WI; [p.] Ken and Shirley Golonka; [ed.] I go to Oconto, Washington Middle School. In the 7th grade.; [occ.] Student; [oth. writ.] I have never had this poem published. I am so pleased to have it published in a real book.; [pers.] Usually, when I had a hard day I go up in my room and think about things. To relive my stress I write a poem.; [a.] Oconto, WI

GIONET, VERNA A.
[b.] April 19, 1947, Halifax, NS; [p.] John and Beatrice Gerrior; [ch.] Vincent, Deanna; [ed.] Grade 12, Business Clerical Aduit Psychology (Highest Honors); [occ.] Section supervisor Sears Canada Inc.; [hon.] Customer Courtesy (Sears Canada Inc. Adult Psychology (Highest Hon.) Honors, awards, prizes solo, doo (sister Evelyn) Group (Son Vince, Evelyn, Myself); [oth. writ.] Song for brother Bill Gerrior, chairman for Intern. Family Reunion, letters to Editors (local papers) so it Anniversary poems and other inspirational writings.; [pers.] It was April 19, 1947 Halifax Nova Scotia when my parents John and Beatrice Gerrior gave me the gift of life and the gift of music. I have enjoyed recognition and many memorable events, sharing the bond of a talented family. Through my writing, poetry and music I give my greatest gift, the gift of "Love".; [a.] Halifax, NS

GIORGI, GINA MARIE
[b.] May 14, 1977, Mineola; [p.] Robert and Theresa Giorgi; [ed.] Earl L Vandermuelen High School, Starting Dowling College Fall 1995; [hon.] Poem writing award in 1989; [oth. writ.] May be next time... sadness

from the heart... days... broken heart... feeling.. sloving; [pers.] The time that I have alone is very special to me I get starry eyed and just start writing and can't stop I could cry, and put but I can only get this stare when I'm alone.; [a.] Port Jefferson, NY

GIRARD, LORRAINE ARATA
[b.] January 13, 1920, St Louis, MO; [p.] Frank E. Arata and Johanna K. Arata; [m.] John Emile Girard, May 24, 1947; [ch.] Frank E, John E., Charles P., Michael A., Daniel J., Paul A., Toni C., Vicki R., Johanna C., Barbara S. and Steven A.; [ed.] Marywood Academy, Grand Rapids, Michigan Aquinas College, Grand Rapids, Michigan; [occ.] Retired; [oth. writ.] Nothing recordable.; [pers.] "Consolation" was written to reflect my feelings at the lost of my son, Charles, in Vietnam, March 9, 1969.; [a.] Altadena, CA

GLENN, THOMAS
[pen.] Tom; [b.] December 18, 1924, Badin, NC; [p.] (Deceased) Lillie Mae Davis, (Glenn) Rev W.M.L. Glenn; [m.] Pearl Glenn, February 2, 1957; [ch.] David L. Glenn, Sherel; [ed.] Lynwood High - G.E.D Compton College and L.A. trade tech photography/ journalism/ printing were my main studies; [occ.] Retired christian sales man of christian literature 1960 - 1980; [memb.] AARP - Senior citizen senior citizen sport games holiday SPA; [hon.] Several sales awards for outstanding performance in Michigan conference of S.D.A lake region conference of S.D.A central conference of S.D.A southern conference of S.D.A retired here; [oth. writ.] Hundreds to be published this year under the title of: "King Solomon poetic pantry" being afro-american much is written to solve our problems.; [pers.] I write about all things God has created to reflect his character, and love. If I can inspire anyone to behold Gods love in giving us his son, his life, his blood, and his resurrection hope! great.; [a.] Lynwood, CA

GLIDEWELL, VERNIE
[b.] March 22, 1922, Green Co, MO; [p.] William D. Glidewell and Lavada Glidewell; [m.] Clara V. Glidewell, October 17, 1942; [ed.] 8th Grade Capernium Grade School Near Battlefield, MO; [occ.] Retired; [memb.] Wilson Creek Baptist Church, Ozark Anitque Auto Club; [hon.] First Class Chevrolet and Ford Mechanic; [oth. writ.] My hobby is restoring 1928 through 1931 model A. ford's my first poem. Eyes article in springfield magazine July 1987 springfield, MO; [pers.] Article I wrote in springfield magazine about my childhood days living on the cival-war battleground. Near wilson creek 7-1-1987 I was a small farmer the first 20 years of life. A auto mechanic the next 50 years all in MO state; [a.] Springfield, MO

GLUKLEV, HANNELORE M.
[pen.] Hannah; [b.] March 17, 1941, Germany; [p.] Luise and Wilhelm Bachmayer; [m.] Emil U. Gluklev, May 28, 1983; [ch.] Mike, Mark, Bianca, Trent, Denise, Garry; [ed.] Business education headed own business for 33 years; [occ.] Retired; [memb.] Various business Int. Society of poet; [hon.] (various) numerous business awards; [oth. writ.] Business own newsletter - business publications; [pers.] Enjoy every day of a life and pass it on to others. [a.] Mission British Columbia, Canada

GOCO, LOURDES PENA
[pen.] Sedroul Anep; [b.] Pampanga, Philippines; [p.] Felipe Y. Pena and Amalia S. Sison; [m.] Leonardo Santos Goco, July 16, 1960; [ch.] Bernadette P. Conley, Eliezar P. Goco, Rainerio, Norman and Alexis P. Goco.; [ed.] Torres High, University of the Philippines College of Pharmacy, Mapua Institute of Technology, Far Eastern University; [occ.] Regulatory Affairs, Sr. Specialist, IMS Limited, So. Elm CA.; [memb.] Regulatory Affairs Professional Phil. Pharm. Assn., Delta Lambda, Sigma Sorority; [oth. writ.] Poem titled "Rebirth" published in 1974 ed. of 'New Voices in American Poetry." Published several poems in company newsletters.; [pers.] All talent is God - given and should not languish in vain. It should inspire and lead others closer to the one who made all things possible. (I wrote from the heart, with no concern for rhyme or meter. My subconscious completes the poem in my mind before I am ready to write it down.); [a.] Covina, CA

GOESER, CHERYL
[b.] August 1, 1978, Houston, TX; [p.] Mike and Donna Goeser; [ed.] Junior in High School, at Mayde Creek High School in Houston, TX.; [occ.] Checker at Randall's in Houston, TX; [memb.] FBLA (Future Business Leaders of America).; [oth. writ.] I have also written 4 other poems titled: Lord, Christmas, A child, Grandma.; [pers.] My poems have come from my heart and are very special to me; [a.] Houston, TX

GOLD, RITA
[b.] May 26, 1917, New York City; [p.] Rose and Morris Weinstein; [m.] Herbert Z. Gold, July 4, 1941; [ch.] Son: Richard (deceased); [ed.] M.A. Teachers College, Columbia University (1962 - Education), M.A. Columbia University (1939 - English Lit.), B.A. Brooklyn College (1938 - Major: English, Minor: Education; [occ.] Music Teacher at Head Start; [hon.] 1988 - Citation: 7th Annual Human Rights Day Winner Nassau County, State of New York, Office of the Executive, 1988 - Rockville Centre Human Rights Commision Award, 1988 - Dr. Martin Luther King Award, 1981 - Testimonial Dinner given by the ABLE Alumni Association of Adlephi University: "More than any other teacher she gave us the true internatilization of knowledge."; [oth. writ.] "The Search" (Book of Poetry) "They chose a baby" (book for children about adoption); [a.] Hewlett, NY

GOLDBERG, ALI
[b.] October 25, 1983, West Chester, PA; [p.] Lawrence and Darcie Goldberg; [occ.] Student; [a.] West Chester, PA

GOLDENBERG, MILLIE
[b.] February 17, 1907, Berezovka, Russia; [p.] Pearl and Paul Kalalzowa; [m.] Aaron (Deceased), October 14, 1934; [ch.] Perry B. Goldenberg; [ed.] Public School; [occ.] Homemaker; [memb.] Sisterhood - Rossmoor; [hon.] Certificate of Participation 1980 Bronx Community College Senior Olympics; [oth. writ.] Miracle of Birth - A Rose and many others; [pers.] Honesty above all and the need for respect and Dignity

GOLDMAN, CHERYL
[p.] Renee Wenig and Norman Wenig; [ch.] Randi Goldman "My Inspiration"; [ed.] Emerson College 1) scarsdale High School 3) and studied art is the university of London.; [occ.] Real Estate Broker; [memb.] A member of long Island board of realtors, bachelor degree in Art; [pers.] I am inspired to write my emotional moments to reflect my inner feelings. I have been greatly influenced by the very special people in my life.; [a.] Woodbury, NY

GONGORA, KATHERINE
[b.] August 10, 1941; [ch.] Gregory, Gary; [oth. writ.] 1) Editor-David Copperfield published by Cethial Publications, in association with NBC Publications 2) Text Editor-Alexie Sundukov Art Book; [a.] Forest Hills, NY

GOODMAN, KENNETH GEORGE
[pen.] Ken Goodman; [b.] July 9, 1911, London, England; [m.] Kathleen Goodman, August 4, 1936; [ch.] Felicity (American) Michael Timothy (Australian); [ed.] Elementary; [occ.] Retired; [memb.] Buddengton Bowling Club.; [oth. writ.] Books - Images, This that and something else. Various single poems, Canberra times, Australian, Bobis. Outlook, Fremantle BA Press Galloping ON Willox (WA); [pers.] Having sung in three major Choir - Royal Livepool Choral, Huddesfield Choral University of Western Australia. My book of music means by poetry in rhythm is based on musical firms. Human philosophy in much of it's content; [a.] Port Western, Australia

GOODPASTER, LORI LYNN
[b.] November 3, 1972, Lincoln, IL; [p.] Robert Goodpaster and Vicki Hahn; [ch.] Chase Michael Wakeman; [sib.] Mt. Pulaski High School Class of 1990, graduated top ten with honors; [occ.] Mother; [oth. writ.] Written tons of poems, but this is the first one I let anyone read; [pers.] Feelings are an expression of a moment that reflects where you heart lies.; [a.] Mt. Pulaski, IL

GOODYEAR, CHRISTOPHER DAVID
[b.] May 18, 1971, Jersey; [ed.] Birkenhead College, Auckland Auckland University; [occ.] Student, but I also work a full-time week as a security guard; [memb.] None, but eventually I want to belong to something like ASCAP or BMI, and a music publisher such as Sony, MCA, Warner Bros, etc; [hon.] School Certificate, 6th Form Certificate, University Entrance, at end of 1995 I will also have a Bachelor of Arts degree (English major, also Philosophy, Political Studies, Linguistics) from the University of Auckland; [oth. writ.] Nothing published; [pers.] I would like to learn how to write AC ballad lyrics with the guidance from a respected music published because only in the written word do I feel comfortable communicating. I am pleased to share my idols and heroes with the rest of the world through the ballads I write for them.

GORMAN, MARILYN L.
[b.] July 19, 1932, Brockton, MA; [p.] Loyami and Rose Wedge; [ch.] Lynne, Kelley; [ed.] Brockton Schools - "Cake Decorating" Brockton High School 1952 - Taught Cake Decorating a Adult Education Classes; [occ.] Retired 1994 - Former Professional Cake Decorator and Retail Manager; [memb.] Former Treasure of Greater Brockton for Miss Scholarship Pageant: Ste. Colman's Player Group:; [hon.] Cake Decorating Awards: Retail Management Awards:; [oth. writ.] Several poems and I'm working on writing a children book. Also a novel - a true story: now that I'm retired and have the time.; [pers.] I'm hoping to leave behind something for my family and friends to remember me by: I've been influenced by: Joyce Kilmer's - Trees -; [a.] Brockton, MA

GORRECHT, WILLIAM T.
[pen.] Jed Moran; [b.] August 26, 1946, Columbia, PA; [p.] William W. Gorrecht and Anna L. Gorrecht; [m.] RuthAnn Gorrecht, February 17, 1979; [ch.] Christine, Thomas John and Leanna; [ed.] Columbia High School; [occ.] Macheenist Self Employed; [memb.] National Rifle Assn. Life Member Academy of Model Aeronau-

tics St. Johns Luthern Church; [oth. writ.] Personal documentation for future publications; [pers.] My goal to achieve an unbiased acclaim of my writings, for the thoughts and feelings felt by others; [a.] Columbia, PA

GOTTLIEB, PATRICIA A.
[pen.] Patsy Campion; [b.] August 27, 1944, New York City, NY; [p.] Francis T. Campion, Margaret Campion; [m.] Andrew J. Gottlieb, July 22, 1967; [ch.] Kristopher, Kevin (Twins), Kerri-Ann,; [ed.] Seton Hall H.S., Patchogue, NY, Mrs. Skinner's Business School, Garden City, NY; [occ.] Employed at Defense Investigate Service (DOD), Mineola, NY.; [memb.] Past - Editor of Twinsphere-Nassau County Mother's of Twins Club Editor of News N Views - Lynbrook PTA Editor of Lynbrook Athletic Assoc. Yearly Journals, Elected Member of St. Raymond's Parish Counsel, Teacher of Religious Education, St. Raymond's East Rockaway, NY. Member Ancient Order of Hibernians, Lynbrook, NY., 1st V.P. of Lynbrook Youth Athletic Association.; [hon.] Awarded Cash for Finalist in writer's Contest for National Publication's Short Story Contest, 1991. 1st Place Award, New York State as Editor of Twinsphere for two consecutive years. Merit Award, Lynbrook Art's Festival; [oth. writ.] "My Most Memorable Christmas", Our Sunday Visitor Publishing, Huntington, IN. 1991. Wrote Biographies for Lynbrook Youth Athletic Association Journals 1983-85. Lynbrook, NY. Wrote Articles for Twinsphere, 1973-75. Nassau County, NY; [pers.] "I write from my heart on personal experiences, discoveries and the growth of the human spirit. Composing unlocks the unconditional creative purity in all of us."; [a.] Lynbrook, NY

GOUDREAULT, TRACY
[b.] January 1, 1977, New-Liskeard ON, Canada; [ed.] Secondary School; [occ.] Student T.D.S.S.; [oth. writ.] One book Entitled "Tears of Ignorance" not published yet dedicated to some special people of the underground; [pers.] Into this life where society is judge mental. I expect things from myself, I go my way, and feel my own wisdom and thoughts blow into my hair knowing the truth, when society only master us with judgmental lies, thank you; [a.] New-Liskeard Ontario, Canada

GRACE, JENNY
[b.] September 25, 1977, Bossier, LA; [p.] Jimmy and Cathy Grace; [ed.] Finishing High School; [occ.] High School Student; [oth. writ.] I have many, but are unpublished.; [pers.] No matter how young or old, writing is a great way to express your feelings and for personal growth and enjoyment. Everybody should write, everybody can, it's just doing it.; [a.] Haughton, LA

GRADY, MARTIN DUANE
[b.] September 6, 1915, Minneapolis, MN; [p.] Vera and Martin J. Grady; [ch.] Brook, Shannon; [ed.] Architect Univ. of Minnesota; [memb.] Minneapolis Club American Institute of Architects; [oth. writ.] Short stories novel

GRAHAM, RENEE RITTER
[b.] February 7, 1951, Dallas TX; [p.] Herbert E. and Jane V. Ritter; [m.] Boyce L. Graham, March 24, 1979; [ch.] Boyce L. Graham IV and Elizabeth Jane Graham; [ed.] Charles Ellis School for Girls (H.S.) University of South Carolina, Columbia, Middle Tenn. State University, Murfreesboro, O'More of Design, Franklin, TN (B.A.); [occ.] Freelance: Set Designer/Photo Stylist (catalog advertising); [memb.] Society of Children's Writers and Illustrators, American Society of Interior Designers, Texas Board of Architectural Examiners, Board Member of my Two Children's Schools; [hon.] 3-Year visual art scholarship in high school ('66-'69), Catalog Assoc. of the month, J.C. Penney, Inc. (May '93). Personally: Creative honors in visual arts with numerous room designs published in books, shelter magazines, catalogs and 3 home furnishing videos.; [oth. writ.] A series of stories for children's books, several short stories and poems, and editor of two monthly newsletter for local schools.; [pers.] All children are the future. I find joy in creating stories to arouse humor and self-awareness so they may accept differences in the struggle to maintain personal and universal harmony.; [a.] Dallas, TX

GRATALES, DENISE
[b.] June 14, 1947, Jersey City, NJ; [p.] James Morano, Catherine Morano; [ed.] Memorial High, St Peter's College - B.A. in English Minor in Psychology; [occ.] Temporary Employment Specialist; [oth. writ.] Collection of poems, unpublished - entitled, "Madness, and other mishaps"; [pers.] My writing is a pure reflection of life itself as I have seen and experienced it, nothing more.; [a.] North Bergen, NJ

GRAY, CHRISTINE LYNN
[pen.] Chris L. Childers; [b.] December 27, 1962, Franklin, IN; [p.] Janice Jackson and Delmer Childers; [m.] Ernest Gray, March 26, 1988; [ch.] Sarah Lynn Gray; [ed.] Knox Central High; [occ.] Housewife; [oth. writ.] I have written several poems for my own enjoyment and I have sent one to "I deals magazine," but haven't had time to hear from them as of yet.; [pers.] When I sit down to write, it is an outlet for my deepest feelings and thoughts. I do hope that people who will read my poetry will be blessed by it.; [a.] Barbourville, KY

GRAY, DARREN
[b.] November 30, 1973, Bourbon County; [p.] Margie Gray and the late Marshall Gray; [ed.] Paris High School Degree in Mortuary Science from Mid-America College of Funeral Service; [occ.] Funeral Director Lusk-McFarland funeral Home; [memb.] Central Baptist Church Kiwanis Club, Football coach at Paris Independent Schools; [oth. writ.] Short stories and poems never published; [pers.] The price of life is only what you charge it. [a.] Paris, KY

GRAY, EBONIE DIANE
[pen.] Punk Rock; [b.] December 8, 1982, Greenville, NC; [p.] Allen Gray and Debra Gray; [ed.] Cum Eppes Middle School (Old Rose High); [memb.] Pep club, english chapel church choir, chorus, and bowling club.; [hon.] D.A.R.E. graduation, fitness diploma and super attendance program.; [oth. writ.] Writing tests, recent poem about what's was placed in the newspaper.; [pers.] I was influenced by myself, and I try to give a helpful to give a helpful message to help them.; [a.] Greenville, NC

GRAY, GEORGE ALLEN
[b.] October 30, 1940, Dallas, TX; [p.] Dora and Roy T. Gray; [ch.] Two sons, (One adopted, one blood); [ed.] 12 years public schooling at various grade and high schools-completing High School Sr. Year attending evening school - 1 year landscape architecture at L.S.U.; [occ.] Printer-Life Career; [memb.] Astronomical Society of Fort Worth, American Iris Society - Society of Horticulturist. International Printing Association.; [hon.] None Personal my awards have come through helping my son gain recognition through his achievement as he was growing up. Helping him with Pine wood derby and cub scout awaken baseball in the scouts, photographic awards in photography, wildlife,; [oth. writ.] Have written many philosophical items of personal nature. Many poems, abstract and real life. None have ever been published accept by me person personally for a select circle of personal friends and acquaintances.; [pers.] I love to express my views in writings of a personal, philosophical manner. Sometimes transferring these philosophies into poems. I find a need to express hunts of a personal nature into poems. I have learned to draw upon these poems for strength in moments of important decisions.; [a.] Irving, TX

GRECO, CECELIA H.
[b.] May 10, 1934, NY City; [p.] Joseph Hanley and Irene Hanley; [m.] Roland Robert Greco, July 2, 1962; [ch.] Roland Jr., Regina, Cecelia, Claire and Claudia; [ed.] College of New Rochelle, B.A., Hunter College Graduate School M.S. University College Dublin, Ireland; [occ.] Home Maker (former Teacher N.Y.C. Board of Education); [memb.] Parishioner of the Roman Catholic Community of St. Patrick in Armonk, New York; [hon.] Grand Mother ("Mima") of Roland III, Gabrielle, Elizabeth and Jack! #2 Mother of John and Christina; [oth. writ.] Poetry Short Stories for Children; [pers.] God, ("Abba") our Heavenly Father, as revealed to us by his divine son, Jesus christ, invites each of us to Holiness. Let us strive, by our love for one another, to accept his invitation; [a.] Armonk, NY

GREEN, ALPHONSO
[b.] September 19, 1965, Ft Pierce, FL; [p.] Barbara J. Green; [m.] Sonya M. Green, July 28, 1990; [ch.] DeVaughn M., Tyrell D., Shavontae T.; [ed.] Ft. Pierce Central High, Grambling State University; [occ.] HVAL specialist united state air force; [pers.] I strive to acknowledge Jesus Christ in my waiting so that others may know that Jesus is Lord.; [a.] Eglin AFB, FL

GREEN, CYNTHIA KAY
[pen.] Cindy Doyle; [b.] February 28, 1974, Anaheim, CA; [p.] Robert and Nancy Doyle; [m.] Paul Green, December 17, 1994; [ed.] Bethel Baptist High, 2 years of Teachers education, currently obtaining my paralegal degree.; [occ.] Secretary, Home maker; [memb.] Bethel Baptist Church, Bethel Baptist School Alumni,; [hon.] Dean's list, 4th place winner in National essay contest.; [oth. writ.] Essays on my view of green gables of Anne books by L.M. Montgomery.; [pers.] Writing has always been a way of life for me. I cannot exist without a pen in my hand and a paper to write upon. My goal in writing is to share my dream of how I perceive the world around us and how I dream that the world could be with God. [a.] Costa Mesa, CA

GREEN, JOANN DENISE
[pen.] Victoria Clark; [b.] April 30, 1972, Richmond, VA; [p.] Lillie Green and Samuel Green; [ch.] Jeremiah Green; [ed.] Huguenut High, Virginia Commonwealth University; [occ.] Data Entry Clerk, Full time student; [memb.] American Heart Association, YWCA, National Association of Female executives, NAACP; [oth. writ.] Several other short stories and poems; [pers.] I feel that people are influenced by what they read and they are more opted to be moved when what they read is poetry. I have been greatly influenced by Maya Angelou and Edgar Allen Poe; [a.] Richmond, VA

GREEN, ROBERT M.
[pen.] Robert Michael; [b.] June 30, 1940, Methuen; [p.]

Richard and Ontanina Green; [m.] Grace Marie Green, June 29, 1980; [oth. writ.] A few personal favorites are: "Awareness", "Choice", "A quiet dignity," "Welcomed Interruption," "A Gift," "Remembered moment," "Energy Applied."; [pers.] A completed poem brings me closer to my true inner self, with complete satisfaction in the fact that emotions and thoughts may be shared; [a.] Laurence, MA

GREEN, VALONDA L.
[pen.] Londa; [b.] September 28, 1982, San Francisco, CA; [p.] Gary L. Green; [m.] Thelicia T. Green; [ed.] 7th Grade; [occ.] Student; [memb.] New Birth Missionary Baptist Church, Decatur Georgie.; [hon.] 2 Time all star softball player; [pers.] Special thanks to my great grandparent, Rev. A.K. Williams and Celia Williams for their support, also my grandparents Harold and Sandra early and my Mom and Dad

GREENE, DENISE
[b.] July 8, 1978, Drumheller, AB; [p.] Diane Anhorn and Dennis Greene; [ed.] I am currently in grade ten in Morrin Alberta.; [hon.] Along with writing I play piano, I made it to finals last year in Music Festival.; [pers.] I like to reflect my life through writing, so that I might be able to use it to help some one else.; [a.] Drumheller, AB Canada

GREENOUCH, MICHAEL E.
[b.] July 25, 1950, Bolton, United Kingdom; [p.] William and Helen; [m.] Jean, June 4, 1977; [ch.] Samantha, Amanda; [ed.] Thornleigh College - England Caer Rhun Hall - Wales; [occ.] General Manager Geal Computers Inc; [memb.] Canadian Institute of Chartered Accountants; [oth. writ.] Various Poems; [pers.] I try to reflect my deepest thoughts in a manner that helps people understand we all face challenges; [a.] Colleyville, TX

GREGORY, TINA
[b.] August 16, 1977, Abington, PA; [p.] Arlene and Alan Gregory; [ed.] Palm Beach County School of Arts, Graduated from North Technical Education Center; [oth. writ.] I keep a collection of journals filled with poems of every emotion I've ever felt.; [pers.] Poetry is something that cannot be graded, it should be cherished for what it is.; [a.] Palm Beach Garden, FL

GREIG, MAYDELLE F.
[b.] August 20, 1959, St. Martinville, LA; [p.] Doreen B. Francois and Martin Francois; [m.] Captain Karl Anthony Greig, May 13, 1994; [ch.] John Patrick Mahon III; [ed.] St. Martinville Sr. High; [occ.] Homemaker and Mother; [pers.] Stop and listen to that small voice in your heart... we are never alone!!!

GRENDA, THOMAS G.
[pen.] Thomas George Grenda; [b.] August 22, 1964, Elizabeth, NJ; [p.] John and Elizabeth Grenda; [ed.] Woodbridge Senior High School; [occ.] Songwriter-lyricist/percussionist with music group decade; [hon.] Labeled as one of the top ten bands on the east coast-R.S.M. entertainment/with an organic and instinctive approach to their music, decade is winning audiences with their incendiary performances-rodell records.; [oth. writ.] Tom has also done several recording projects, most notably need your love tonight for R.S.M. entertainment's east coast revenge and rodell records release of I believe (love at first sight).; [pers.] My main purpose is to provide temporary escapism and to bring confidence and worth to all readers and listeners alike. I am greatly influenced by two of pop music's finest lyricist Bernie Taupin and Greg Lake; [a.] Woodbridge, NJ

GRIGGS, BRENDA
[b.] November 6, 1958, Elizabeth NJ; [p.] Phyllis and James Singley; [m.] Separated; [ch.] Natasha, Asia; [ed.] Thomas Edison High, Union County College; [occ.] Unit Secretary, Elizabeth General Medical Center, Elizabeth, NJ; [memb.] Volunteer visiting nurses, hospice services, Eliz. NJ; [oth. writ.] Essence Magazine, sheaf college quarterly, local newspaper; [pers.] I would like to share wonderful thoughts and experiences and to have the ability to put a smile on people's faces and hearts; [a.] Elizabeth, NJ

GRIMES JR., CHARLES AUSTIN
[b.] May 14, 1964, Pgh, PA; [p.] Charles A. Grimes Sr., Nadine Y. Grimes; [ed.] Central Catholic H.S. (Pgh PA) Clarion Univ of PA (B.S.), Chestnut Hill College (M.S.); [occ.] Individual family Psychotherapist,; [memb.] (IAAOC) Int'l Assoc., of addictions and offenders counselors, (AMHCA) American mental health counselors association (ASGW) Association for specialists in group work.; [oth. writ.] Several poems utilized for personal reflection; [pers.] I find myself being inspired by the natural beauty of sight, sound, and illumination. My Rx for healthy existence is self-awareness + self actualization resulting inner peace and serenity.; [a.] Bryn Maur, PA

GROOM, KIMBERLY D.
[b.] July 9, 1963, Leesburg, VA; [p.] Patricia and Russell Spiess; [m.] Kevin L. Groom, August 14, 1982; [ch.] Christopher, Joseph, Julianne; [ed.] Vista High School (Vista, CA), Calhoun Community College (Decatur, Al.); [occ.] Writer; [memb.] Madison Christian Church Board, Madison Jaycees, City of Madison Community Watch; [hon.] Respect for law award - 1989 (Madison, Ar.), Optimist Citizen of the year - 1989; [oth. writ.] Various Articles published in the Madison county record; [a.] Madison, AL

GROOMER, VERLA MARLENE
[pen.] Sue; [b.] May 5, 1962, Tampa, FL; [p.] Geraldine Allen and James Allen (step father); [m.] Mark S. Groomer, May 21, 1994; [ch.] Carrie Lynn Jones, August 24, 1985; [occ.] House wife; [oth. writ.] I have written several poems; [pers.] I write poems in my spare time. I really enjoy writing poems.; [a.] Indianapolis, IN

GROSSMAN, GWENDOLYN BRYANT
[b.] August 1, 1922, Milam County, TX; [p.] Raymond Gilbert Bryant, Minnie Bryant; [m.] Mitchell Mathew Grossman, June 3, 1942; [ch.] Charles Grossman Abraham; [ed.] Danbury High (Valedictorian) B.S. Degree Southern Methodist University (Dallas) Degrees: A.A., M. Ed., Ed. D. University of Houston Post Doctoral Work Laverne College, California, Leysin, Switzerland; [occ.] Retired after 48 years of teaching Elementary in Reading, Language Arts, Science San Pedro presbyterian Church; [memb.] Eastern Star Tomball Chapter Daughters of American Revolution Descendants of San Jacinto International Reading Association Alpha Delta Kappa Kappa Delta Pi Phi Delta Kappa American Childhood Education International; [hon.] Alpha Delta Kappa Scholarship Texas Chemical Council Fellowship Valley Forge Freedom's Foundation Classroom Teacher's Medal Who's Who: Childhood Professionals, World Women Prof Educators Outstanding Women of America America Educators Distinguished Americans, Texas Historical Commission Award; [oth. writ.] Articles for journals of the associations of which I am a member Summarized interpretations of Doctoral Dissertation in ERIC (Educ. Resources Information Center) July, 1968, and Kentucky Murray State Univ. Review Articles in: Texas Geography News, Texas Outlook, Instructor, Allyn - Bacon Newsletter, Texas Parents Teachers Ass.; [pers.] I strive to proclaim God's mighty acts and man's relationship to Him for His glory the following verse is an example of this He love his kids as fathers would Handsome, gentle, kind, good, He worked from dawn till midnight and save whatever he could. Sundays he prayed in church as spiritual Christians should God dwelt through his manhood.; [a.] San Antonio, TX

GROSSNICKLE, CHRISTOPHER DAVID
[pen.] Chris Grossnickle; [b.] August 20, 1976, South Bend, IN; [ed.] Graduate of Mishawaka High School, Mishawaka, IN [occ.] Attending the Art Institute of Pittsburgh; [hon.] In 6th grade I won a grand prize in the Campbell Soup National Writing Contest.; [pers.] I love to read and write poetry and will continue to write my form and style as long as I can. I hope others enjoy my work.; [a.] Pittsburgh, PA

GROSVENOR, EGBERT
[pen.] Sonny Grosvenor; [b.] January 22, 1921, Guyana, South Amercia; [p.] Gustavus Grosvenor and Estelle Grosvenor; [m.] Ellinor Grosvenor, July 3, 1972; [memb.] Bartica America Association Westminster Presbyterian Church

GRUNINGER, KRISTINE
[pen.] Voica Petrovich, Charlotte; [b.] September 15, 1970, Des Plaines, IL; [p.] Diane and Frederick Gruninger; [ch.] Brandon Lee; [occ.] Poet and Opportunist; [memb.] Art institute Chicago, museum of modern art S.F., poets for peace, Ireland's poetry on canvas.; [oth. writ.] Story of Alex, Voica, Pale Angel, untitled poems.; [pers.] One person's reality is another's fantasy, never misjudge how deep the water is before you swim in it, and if anything see it from another's viewpoint. You may like what you see. Or not...; [a.] San Leandro, CA

GRYMSKI, ARLENE P.
[p.] Edward Grymski, Pauline Grymski; [ed.] Harrison High Triton College, De Paul University; [occ.] Accountant; [oth. writ.] Short stories poems, and musical songs for children.; [pers.] I was inspired by the birth of my two grand-nieces, Katherine Dorothea and Deborah Anne Walters. My poem song reflects the moment of birth and the wonderment of a child.; [a.] Westchester, IL

GUERRERO, SARA LEON
[b.] June 18, 1974, Ft Polk, LA; [p.] Benito and Sun Cha Leon-Guerrero; [ed.] Challenger High School, Clover Park Technical College; [occ.] Dental Assistant, sales associate; [memb.] Future business leaders of America (FBLA); [pers.] My writings reflect my inner feelings and experiences which can only be expressed through poetry; [a.] Tacoma, WA

GUGEL, MATTHEW SYLVAN STIPEK
[b.] September 2, 1983, Montclair; [p.] George H. Gugel and Lorraine C. Gugel; [ed.] Student at Hope School, Hope, NJ; [memb.] 4 - H Warren County Junior Ranger; [pers.] Life goes on... as part of Nature's cycle... Forever; [a.] Hope, NJ

GUIN, DEBORAH L.
[b.] July 8, 1962, Hermosa Beach; [p.] Jack and Sharon Walker; [m.] Michael K. Guin, December 27, 1988; [ch.] Curtis Paul, Kailee Lauren, Kyle Michael, and Kory Michael; [occ.] Bookkeeper, Ralph's Market, Castaic,

Calif.; [memb.] First Christian Church of Palmdale; [pers.] Touching lives through my writings, I pray, I will bring joy and pleasure to those who read them. I thank God my achievements in this life!

GULLUSCI, MICHAEL JAMES
[pen.] Michael James; [b.] September 17, 1963, New Rochelle, NY; [p.] Joan and Dom Gullusci; [m.] Dawn Marie Gullusci, May 7, 1995; [ed.] Architectural Schooling at New York Institute of Technology, Musical Training at the Westchester Conservatory of Music.; [occ.] Truck Driver for a Building Supply Company.; [memb.] A member of the Parish of Christ the Redeemer, Episcopal Church; [hon.] Honored as "The New Man" in The Women's News Magazine for being unique as an individual.; [oth. writ.] Several other non-published titled and copywritten poems as well as prose.; [pers.] I hope to reach people's hearts with a possible new perspective. My writings translate the limitation man has created fro himself through fear, lack of self worth, etc. I feel life was created to exist in balance with all living things. I could go on eternally, thus the reason for my writing.; [a.] New Rochelle, NY

GUMM, SUSAN KATHLEEN
[b.] January 26, 1947, Seattle, WA; [p.] Norma Jean Nelson and Clarence L. Gumm; [ch.] April LeAnn, Joseph Daniel, Scott Anthony, Jacob Andrew, Amy Lyn; [ed.] Lake Washington H.S. Image School of Cosmetology; [occ.] Esthetician; [memb.] Member of the A.I.A.; [pers.] I would like to thank those who have been an encouragement to me. First to Jehovah my God who through his word and son has given me spiritual strength and to those who so lovingly have stood by me both in times of sorrow and times of laughter.; [a.] Lake Elsinore, CA

GUNNELLS, TONI L.
[b.] January 12, 1980, New Bern, NC; [p.] Sandra Dickinson; [ed.] West Craven High School; [hon.] All District Band, All County Band, National Honor Roll, Cheerleader, Marching Eagle, Natural Helper; [oth. writ.] A woman like that's why?; [pers.] There is a difference between thinking something and actually doing it. I personally thank God for all he has given to me.; [a.] New Bern, NC

GURKOFF, GINA
[pen.] Gina Gurkoff; [b.] September 25, 1976, Harrisburg, PA; [p.] Gloria and Jerry Gurkoff; [ed.] The Oakridge School Arlington, Texas; [occ.] Student; [memb.] Alcohol/drug awareness program. Equest- (Horseback riding academy for handicapped children and adults-volunteer - 3 years volunteer); [hon.] Most improve 11th grade english student. Accomplishments for community service hours.; [pers.] I write poetry because I love it - I love being able to write from my heart and later go back and read it and feel the same way I did as the day I wrote it.; [a.] Mansfield, TX

GURNEY, MITCH
[b.] April 1, 1953, Lynwood, CA; [p.] Martin and Dorylene Gurney; [oth. writ.] Numerous poems relating to life, love, spiritual matters. Philosophical, Spiritual thesis writings.; [pers.] I strive to reveal that the love and generosity and spirit of God is manifested through the honorable deeds and the hearts and soul of mankind in my writing. I have been greatly influenced my many romantic and mystic poets.; [a.] Lafayette, CA

GUSTAFSON, SEAN MICHAEL
[b.] January 3, 1981, Decatur, IL; [p.] Brad and Dalinda Gustafson; [ed.] Currently enrolled at Mt. Zion Junior High School. 8th Grade.; [memb.] First Church of God Lovington, Mt. Zion Jr. High Puppeteers and youth, co-editor Mt. Zion Jr. High Newspaper (smoke signal),; [hon.] President's award for outstanding community service, I led youth award for energy achievement award, Mt. Zion Jr. High High Honor student; [pers.] I believe life is a test. We each choose whether we pass or fail. Poetry is an art of feeling, and only a few can interrupt it,; [a.] Dalton City, IL

GUYER, MARY E.
[pen.] Mary E. Guyer; [b.] February 3, 1941, Boulder, CO; [p.] Rita and Anthony Colacci; [m.] Donald L. Guyer, January 30, 1990; [ch.] Michael, Kelly (sons); [ed.] Louisville High School Parks Jr. College University of Colorado; [occ.] Office Administration; [hon.] Honor Graduate of Louisville High and Parks Jr. College. Executive Club Secretary 1992-1993, Dean's list 1992 to 1993, Member the church of Jesus Christ latter day saints.; [oth. writ.] Fantasy planned head helps heart - both published in winds of the world various news papers.; [pers.] You have to be intelligent to be insulted! If our hands worked as fast as our mouths, think what we could accomplish!; [a.] Louisville, CO

GUYTON, DANIEL
[b.] July 21, 1977; [p.] David J. Smith and Deborah Guyton Smith; [ed.] Sachem South and Sachem North High School, just entering my senior year; [occ.] Student and Sachem North High School; [memb.] National Art Honor Society, MCCS (Middle Country Children's Soccer), referee, Italian, Club; [hon.] Four Honorable Mentions for three separate poems and a short story from school literary magazine; [oth. writ.] have had the majority of my poems accepted in the school's literary magazine, as well as some stories and even a play; [pers.] I have both a serious side and a humorous side in my writing. My works include everything from the poem you see here to a parody of MacBeth by William Shakespeare.; [a.] Farmingville, NY

HAAG, JR., COLIN
[b.] October 28, 1975, Langhorne, PA; [p.] Colin Haag Sr., Linda Bartle; [m.] Shannon Haag, October 21, 1994; [ed.] Catasauqua High, Buck County Community College; [occ.] Security Guard, Firm Security, Philadelphia, PA; [memb.] Black Belt Club, American Pastor Association Faith Baptist Church.; [hon.] Football Scholarships, 1st Degree Black Belt.; [oth. writ.] Several other poems not yet published.; [pers.] Each poem I right, actually took place in my life. I try too have my readers feel exactly how I feel. Have them be me for a brief period of time.; [a.] Levittown, PA

HAGOOD, CAROLINE
[b.] November 23, 1982, New York, NY; [p.] Louis and Patricia Hagood; [ed.] East Manhattan School for Bright and Gifted Children, Saint Ann's.; [occ.] Student.; [oth. writ.] Poem published in Creative Kids Magazine.; [pers.] Poetry is the pure pression of meaning.; [a.] Newyork, NY

HAIR, FLORD G.
[pen.] Floyd G. Hair; [b.] April 1, 1908, Fort Dodge, IA; [p.] Ira W. Hair and Susie; [m.] Pauline Lutz, November 24, 1929; [ch.] Floyd Leo, Max Alleh, Constance and Suzanne; [ed.] High School Grad, 2 years Study Univ. of Minn.; [occ.] Realtor-retired; [memb.] Santa Paula Methodist Ch., Santa Paula Rotary Club; [hon.] Citizen of the Year 1978, Distinguished Senior Award Ventura Country CA. 1992; [oth. writ.] Autobiography "Middle American" 1988, poem think not upon the things that are seen but the things that are unseen, publ. in the above.; [pers.] Don't just think about it. Do it!; [a.] Santa Paula, CA

HALE, KALYN
[pen.] Syn; [b.] February 25, 1981, North Bay, Ontario, Canada; [p.] Joan and Murray; [ed.] Laurentian Public School, Dr. Carruthers Public School; [occ.] Student; [hon.] Laurentian P.S. Vice-Principals Award 1992-93; [oth. writ.] From The Shadows, Lost Cause, Solitarium, For Shattering Silence and Jennifer's Body are poems I hope to publish in the future and I am currently working a novel titled 'Street Tag'; [pers.] Though I'm only 14 I hope that this will be my first piece published of many to come I have been influenced by Evelyn Lau and would like to thank Tara.; [a.] North Bay Ontario, Canada

HALL, BRANDI NICOLE
[b.] May 23, 1981, Athens Memorial Hosp.; [p.] Tanya Hall/Sister-Ashley; [ed.] Currently in 8th grade; [memb.] Cheerleader for the Benton Elem. Wildcats, Editor of the 8th grade School Paper, "The Benton Star," Plays softball for YMCA.; [hon.] Has won many awards for Baton twirling, dancing, singing, and modeling. Some include Tenn. All Star Talent, Wee Miss Folk County Little Miss Polk County and Little Miss Christmas Belle. I also made several commercials and appeared in Discovery TV. I also won a song writing contest in '92 in an environmental contest to protect the environment.; [oth. writ.] I have written other poems but have never submitted any until now. (Writing poems for me is away of releasing my emotions on paper); [pers.] Life is what you make of it. You must take control and guide it with patience and love and always strive to be the person you can be proud of.; [a.] Benton, TN

HALL, NALAVESHIA
[pen.] Magic Mind; [b.] May 15, 1980, Albany, GA; [p.] Agnes M. Johnson, and the late Willie C. Hall; [m.] (Boy friend) Fredrick L. Thomas; [ed.] Westover High School, as of now I'm in the 9th grade. But September of 1995 I'll be in the 10th grade.; [occ.] Student; [memb.] Debate Team, Literature Club and Student Council; [oth. writ.] Several poems, none of which have been published.; [pers.] The poem Misery was written to and about my mother, during her hard seven years of marriage. I also wrote it for other abused women, and hoping that I will never become one. I pray for every one; [a.] Albany, GA

HALL, SHIRLEY A.
[b.] November 14, 1956, Chicago, IL; [p.] Willie Henry, Sarah (Henry) Summers; [m.] Deceased, Alberta N. Hall, March 23, 1985; [ch.] 5 Foster Children, 6 mos. - 5 years old; [ed.] Austin High School, Cleveland Job Corp for Women's, Triton Community College; [occ.] Foster Parent, Formerly Mental Health Counselor - H.C.A. Riveredge Hosp.; [memb.] Kneeway Miracle Temple C.O.G.I.C.; [pers.] I give all thanks to the Lord for my writing ability.; [a.] Chicago, IL

HALLAHAN, EILEEN R.
[b.] May 19, 1993, Dorchester, MA; [p.] Helen Fitzgerald Hallahan, Zeremiah Joseph Hallahan; [ed.] Graduated from Boston Girls' High School, attend Boston Clerical, two years.; [occ.] Retired Stenographer. Former aid in Boston Public Schools.; [memb.] Roman Catholic

Church, Lifetime Member International Society of Poets; [hon.] Editor's Choice for Outstanding Achievement in Poetry presented by the National Library of Poetry in 1993 and again in 1994. Boston Seniority's Poet of the Month, October 1993.; [oth. writ.] Poem In The Desert Sun, Library of Congress, Cataloging in publication Data ISBN: 1-56167-047-2 (1994) Poem in A Far Off Place, ISBN 1-56167-254-8, many poem published in Boston Seniority, also Kit Clark News; [pers.] Let our Lord do the judging. Remember God loves each of us.; [a.] Dorchester, MA

HALVORSON, GREG
[b.] November 12, 1963, Los Angeles; [p.] Carol and Cliff Halvorson; [m.] Single; [ed.] BS Business Univ. of Oregon MPT Physical Therapy Univ. So. Cal.; [occ.] Grad Student in Physical Therapy (Univ of Southern California); [memb.] BOTT, APTA, SAS (Self Amusement Society); [oth. writ.] 10,000 pages of journal, 100's of poems, songs and several short stones I have only just begun to write!; [pers.] There are times in life that human beings feel the power of emotion but are hard pressed to explain. Writing helps me to capture such moments and presence then forever. I derive a sense of meaning in doing so and feel, somehow, I am contributing to the betterment of mankind.; [a.] Lake Oswego, OR

HAMAGUCHI, KARYN MICHELLE
[pen.] Karyn Michelle Hamaguchi; [b.] November 13, 1974, San Diego, CA; [p.] Douglas and Marjorie Hamaguchi; [ed.] San Diego State University (Fall 1992 - Spring 1994), California State University, Fullerton (Fall 1994 - Present)/Major English, Minor - Japanese; [occ.] Sales Representative, Receptionist/Secretary, Student (Full-time), Studying to be a teacher; [memb.] English Honor Society at CSUF, Horizon Christian Fellowship (San Diego).; [hon.] Academic Honors Student (1989-1992), Who's Who Among High School Students (1989-1992) Miss House of Japan (1990-1992), Outstanding Student of the Year, Japanese (1994), PTSA Reflections winner, Literature (1992); [oth. writ.] Self-written, self-published, autobiography titled: Journey to Salvation, written about my own experience and recovery with rape. [pers.] Through my writing, I strive to illuminate the complex yet universal plight of the human soul. If we look a little deeper, it is easy to see that we are all the same.; [a.] San Diego, CA

HAMEED, ZMEELA
[b.] April 29, 1974, London; [p.] Pervaiz Hameed, Aneesa Hameed; [ed.] BA English - Philosophy Chatham College PA.; [occ.] Student; [memb.] Amnesty International; [hon.] Sigma Tau Delta (English Honour Society).; [oth. writ.] Poems and short stories as yet unpublished; [pers.] I draw my inspiration from the struggle and strength of human emotions and the power and beauty of the natural world. The cosmos is great, but so is the human soul.; [a.] Karachi, Pakistan

HAMILTON, CYNTHIA
[b.] February 23, 1958, Carleton Place, Ontario, Canada; [p.] Arnold and Ada Hamilton; [ch.] Todd Joseph, Ashley Sarah, Bryan Daniel; [ed.] Gordon Graydon Secondary School; [pers.] My poetry has always been my soul's way of healing itself. Through it I have always been able to summon the strength to move forward.; [a.] Ridgeway Ontario, Canada

HAMMOND, CHRISTINE
[b.] August 24, 1976, Denver, CO; [p.] Deborah and Steven Hammond; [ed.] Sehome High, University of Washington; [occ.] Student; [a.] Seattle, WA

HANLIN, RACHEL
[pen.] Rae Hanlin; [b.] February 15, 1910, Johnstown, PA; [p.] John and Mary Berry; [m.] July 15, 1933; [ch.] Sara, Margaret, Katherine; [ed.] High School and 3 years Night School; [occ.] Receptionist at our Sr. Activities Center; [hon.] Over 15 years - many awards in Art and Poetry; [pers.] Everyone should have and hobby or the will to keep busy - I'm very happy that at age 85 I am still employed and loving my life; [a.] Johnstown, PA

HANNA, BRENDA KAY
[b.] March 3, 1960, Dickinson, ND; [p.] Irvin Kraus, Wendy Worthington; [m.] Randy Hanna, December 15, 1990; [ch.] 3 Girls, 1 boy; [ed.] I never finished High School, I started working at young age and looking back I don't think I would have wanted it any other way gain wisdom is by going out getting it.; [occ.] Manager, Assistant to Hanna Airlines, Solo Singer, writer.; [memb.] I devoted myself in free time to causes such as suffering to Animals hunger and abuse of children. And I devote thoughts to our position in the world in hopes that all of us may join together in peace.; [hon.] To be chosen from the National Library of Poetry to have my poem published; [oth. writ.] I have always been interested in being a journalist but I concentrate on writing to reflect my music of emotions.; [pers.] Poetry mixed with music can be the most powerful, with incredible results to those in spiritual need. Instead of silent prayer, sing it out and you will see exactly what I mean.; [a.] Ganges, British Columbia, Canada

HANWACKER, JESSICA
[b.] March 16, Summit, NJ; [p.] Patricia Ludwig, Jerry Hanwacker; [m.] Richard J. Seidman, October 7; [ed.] Millburn High School; [pers.] "Friends are the family we choose to be with" just want to say thank you to my family for always being there for me and helping me through the rough times! And a very special thanks to Richard Seidman the one I will always love; [a.] Millburn, NJ

HAPGOOD, DAVID L.
[pen.] Roderick Hapgood; [b.] June 28, 1970, New London, CT; [p.] Donald and Christine Hapgood; [ed.] Montville High, Huntington Institute, Mohegan Comm. College; [occ.] Struggling Actor/writer; [memb.] International Thespian Society; [hon.] Ct. State Choral Award, Southeast Ct. Writing Award, Toured Australia/New Zealand with U.S. National Choir and Band.; [oth. writ.] Many unpublished writings including poems, monologue, short stories, and one act plays. Appeared in New London Day (newspaper) before touring with National Choir.; [pers.] As we express ourselves through various mediums, we contribute a piece of the puzzle to an ideal and colorful world.; [a.] Burbank, CA

HARDEN, EDDIE J.
[pen.] Uncle Alfonzio; [b.] March 1, 1964, Hartford, CT; [p.] Mary E. O'Neal, Eddie Lee Harden; [ch.] Shante A. Harden; [ed.] Hampton High, Professional Career Institute.; [occ.] Independent Political Petitioner. Registrat of Voters.; [memb.] YMCA Teen Volunteer, Homeless Mentally Ill. Job Coach, and Influential Pen Pal For Disabled.; [hon.] Good Conduct Medal, Freelance Poet Award. Honorably Discharged Armed Forces.; [oth. writ.] Why fear me, summit of the mind, flight of a leaf.; [pers.] I write with sincere emotion, a word may express what not yet has come. To save a desperate soul, to heal someone's lonely pain, to pinch the skin of the young, to savour a serene moment.; [a.] San Diego, CA

HARDIAL, MICHAEL
[pen.] Teddy; [b.] December 14, 1955, Kingston Jamaica, WI; [p.] Harold and Deloris; [m.] Ana Damary Urena Hardial, May 22, 1981; [ch.] Monique, Philip, Michael II, Tabetha; [sib.] Newtown H.S., John Jay College of Criminal Justice; [ed.] Captain NYC Dept. of Correction, Trustee Elmont Board of Education.; [occ.] National School Board Assoc., NYS Masonic Lodge; [pers.] We must never fail to adequately educate our children, it is through them that we survive.; [a.] Elmont, NY

HARDIN, ZETTA E.
[b.] September 19, 1924, Slaughters; [p.] Omer McKinley Engels and Delia Hylanfoster Engels; [m.] Jasper Bailey Hardin, July 27, 1946; [ch.] Sherry L. Hardin, Lloyd Barry Allan Hardin; [ed.] High School, Some College; [occ.] Retired; [memb.] Faith Church Martinsville, In.; [hon.] A few first place ribbons for vegetables in local country fair.; [oth. writ.] One long poem written during World War II never published - several small poem's personalized for special occasions.; [pers.] Hobby - backing for special occasions at church. I've hand quiled 4 queen size quilts plus 4 quiled pillow shams in the last 2 years and working on another one now.

HARDING, AARON
[b.] July 21, 1976, Norfolk, VA; [p.] Sandra Daniels, Steve Harding; [ed.] Salem High School, Tidewater Community College; [occ.] Student; [memb.] Surfrider Foundation; [pers.] I write what comes from the inside.; [a.] VA Beach, VA

HARDY, BERNARD
[b.] November 24, 1941, Melbourne, Australia; [p.] Dr. L.A. Hardy, Mrs. K.A. Vaughan-Flood (Artist); [m.] Jill Hardy, July 23, 1969; [ch.] Bernard, Christopher, Rollo (3 sons); [ed.] Xavier College, Melbourne, University of Melbourne, Australia National University, B.A., Canberra Institute of the Arts, Dip. Fine Arts (Painting) A.N.U.; [occ.] Lecturer Painting, C.I.T.A Australia National Univ.; [oth. writ.] Poetry published in Prometheus, I, Public Works, Poetry Australia and Blast. Two books have been published: The Mobile Tower of Bable in 1971, and Veduta and other Poems published in 1991.; [pers.] It is my belief that if poetry is to be accessible, that is, to reveal clearly its various layers of meanings, its language should be cast to formulate its central truth, and be neither obscurantist nor capriciously inventive. Syntax and rhythm should assist to realize the poem's feeling tone in a firm way and words should be chosen for the way they most precisely reflect the poet's thought. Economy is an aspect of good writing, in that superfluous verbiage dissipates a poem's intensity.; [a.] Canberra, A.C.T., Australia

HARE, DORIS JOFFE
[b.] July 1, 1917, Meigs, OH; [p.] Guy Smith, Effie Smith; [m.] William T. Hare, November 14, 1977; [ch.] Michael Joffe, Steven Joffe; [ed.] High School, Arlington, VA.; [occ.] Retired, housewife, volunteer; [memb.] The Writer's Center, Bethesda Maryland; [hon.] Limerick, Published, Post Script, Saturday Evening Post.; [oth. writ.] My book (Along the Way) highlighting my life from age two through seventy-two (unpublished). Also, words and music to fifteen songs on my album (Yellow Rose), (Recorded but unpublished.); [pers.] I hope to maintain my appreciation of the little tings in life and contribute to the happiness of others.; [a.] Rockville, MD

HARLEY, EDWARD K.
[b.] February 5, 1926, New York City, NY; [p.] Eddie and Evelyn Harley; [m.] Elizabeth Harley, January 5, 1952; [ch.] Edward Jr., Ronald, Nathan, Diane, Kevin, Theresa and Evelyn; [ed.] Fayetteville State Teachers University, John Jay College of Criminal Justice and Fordham University and Bronx Community College; [occ.] Retired N.Y.C. Police Sergeant, N.Y.C. School Teacher, N.Y.C. pest Controller; [memb.] Y.M.C.A., Seton Fall Homeowners Association, A.R.M. C.N.Y.C. Retired Police Association) Convent Avenue Baptist Church (was a school teacher by the church in additional to my employment by the N.Y.C. Board of Education) P.B.S. - Channel 13; [hon.] Decorated by N.Y.C. Police for outstanding performance (3 Occasions) Promoted to the highest rank as a detective (1st Grade) Assigned to the Bx/Queens Commanding Officers' Investigative Unit and thereafter to Internal Affairs. Cited by the Federal Gov't (V.A.) monetarily for above average performance (Pest Controller); [oth. writ.] Have written more than 40 poems - some of which have been published in the "Voice", a college newspaper of which I was at the time Editor in Chief. Also poems were published in the Pittsburgh Courier; [pers.] I feel in love with the creativity of my mind and have been on a literary honeymoon ever since. Poetry is the offspring of that relationship.; [a.] New York, NY

HARNDEN, CHRISTY
[b.] June 25, 1960, Lincoln NE; [p.] LeRoy and Ruby Rogers; [m.] Grant Harnden, June 12, 1992; [ch.] Benjamin Michael, Jonathan, Amber Marie; [ed.] Southeast High, Southeast Community College; [occ.] Word Processing Specialist, University of Nebraska, Lincoln; [oth. writ.] This was my first poem which was inspired through the deep loss of my twin babies.; [pers.] Through the loss of my children I have discovered a hidden talent and hope to use it to help other grieving parents.; [a.] Lincoln, NE

HARRELL, LUCY YOLANDA
[b.] February 19, 1942, Roanoke Rapids, NC; [p.] Clearo and Carrie Johnston; [m.] January 6, 1959; [ch.] Lesli E. Brown, Anthony Brown, Rosaline Jones Ronald Brown and Sherell Brown; [ed.] Huntington High School, and Newport News General Hospital, Certified Nursing Assistant Program through Peninsula Area Health Education Center; [occ.] Disabled; [oth. writ.] Several poems and songs, but this is my first time entering a contest; [pers.] I've always loved reading poetry and buy a lot of books. Now that my children are all grown. I've had more free time and feel that I still have a lot to offer to the world.; [a.] Hampton, VA

HARRIS, ARTHUR
[pen.] Art; [b.] September 28, 1956, Itta Bena, MS; [p.] Ola Mae Farmer and John Edgar Harris; [m.] Unmarried; [ch.] 5, Natasha, John, Carl, Desmond, Sherrod Anderson; [ed.] High School Grad., Two Years of Vocational Schooling at Illinois School of Commerce, Certified in Business Studies; [occ.] Nurse Aide; [hon.] Super Striver Award from Illinois School of Commerce, Certificate of Award in Accounting Magum Cum Lotta in my class, Honor Roll Student two times in 1984, with A 5.94 average.; [oth. writ.] Just songs mostly R&B, Rap, and slow lyrics one some I had lead sheeted from Nashville Records.; [pers.] Living is to breath, to walk, to think, to talk and to achieve. If you come short of your success in life, then it's life you have deceived. Cause poetry from the heart sweet as I believe; [a.] Rock Island, IL

HARRIS, DELL
[pen.] Dell Harris; [b.] December 3, 1915, Cuba City, WI; [p.] Lillian Murphy, William Murphy; [m.] Marvin Harris, December 3, 1943; [ed.] Galena High School; [occ.] Retired; [oth. writ.] I composed 12 poems and sent to my husband in the U.S. Army, W.W. II. He passed away on our 50th wedding anniversary, Dec, 5, 1993. I found the poems among 2,500 letters we had sent to each other and saved for over 50 years.; [pers.] I am going to continue to compose poems and short stories about our 50 years of marriage. He wrote every day for four years while in the U.S. Army, so the letters are records of his life in the service.; [a.] Galena, IL

HARRIS, MARY L.
[pen.] Adeeba; [b.] Virginia; [p.] Charles W. Moody Sr., Jennie L. Moody (Deceased); [m.] Divorced; [ch.] Karen Harris, Larry B. Harris Jr.; [ed.] South Side High School, Delaware Valley College, Delaware Valley Community College (Credits Business Admin.) at Prudential Insurance Company, Fort Washington, PA 19034; [occ.] Quality Assurance Tester, Review, Test, and Analyze New Life and Health Policies prior to being introduced into todays market.; [memb.] Abyssinian Baptist Church - Newark (Women's Guild) New Jersey Chapter of Minority Interchange (Prudential Ins) N.A.A.C.P. of East Orange, Notary Public of New Jersey, Chamber of Commerce of East Orange, National Council of Negro Women Newark Section (Life Member/Chaplain), International Toastmaster New Jersey Charter (Prudential Ins. Co.), Weekly Personality WNJR Radio Show - Kitty Taylor's (Award Winning Living Legacy Program), O.E.S.P.H.A Bethlehem Chapter #41 (Officer); [hon.] Certified in Food Safety and Sanitation by the State of NJ, Dept. of Education (Child Care Nutrition), Numerous 'Quality Service Leadership Awards' from Prudential (Monthly/Quarterly), Resolutions from the City of Newark for the Living Legacy Program (1993 and 1994); [oth. writ.] Poetry displayed during Black History Month (1983). Main branch in Irvington, recital in Irvingtons Branch Library on 15th Ave. (1983), Poetry Readings at Library in Jersey City (1983). Jet Port Holiday Inn in Elizabeth (1992). Priory's Resturant in Elizabeth (1993). National Council of Negro Women Newark Section (Life Member/Chaplain) 1993, 1994. Prudential Ins. Co. 1991, 1992, 1993. St. Rose of Lima Catholic Church (1993), Paradise Baptist Church in Newark (1994), and Newark Library (Reading on Oct. 13 - Poem/Prose displayed during the month of October 13 through Nov. 13, 1994); [pers.] It is through my poetry that I want the world to know me. I am a person who feels the hurt, pain, and the joy of life. I am influenced by all poets and people. To develop my interpersonal skills in relationship to my career at prudential insurance company and be an outstanding leader in my community.; [a.] East Orange, NJ

HARRIS, NADA A.
[b.] 1917, Lancaster, TX; [p.] Richard and Amelia Willingham; [m.] Henry F. Harris, September 18, 1936; [ch.] 3 boys; [ed.] Graduate from Sunset High in 1934. Had scholarship for college but couldn't take it because 2 had to find work to help family; [occ.] Retired; [memb.] First Baptist Church of Forney; [hon.] National Honor Society Silver Pact Award 1986; [oth. writ.] Poetry, children's story, biography of my life (working on it). Funny incidents that happen to me on my first job, published in local paper; [pers.] I love poetry and have many that 2 have written but not published.; [a.] Forney, TX

HARRIS, NICK
[pen.] Harris Fishead Jesus; [b.] February 23, 1975, Bismarck, ND; [ed.] Graduate of what is affectionately knows as "Suicide High".; [occ.] Vagabond; [memb.] Leader of the Nursing Home Brigade, President of a small unnamed and unheard of sixth Scandinavian country from where I will conquer the earth.; [oth. writ.] A personal scrapbook, how to get bong water out of a persian cat (Bible and owner's manual), all kinds of poetry, stories, an senseless jabbering about absolutely nothing.; [pers.] The man next door has a sucking chest wound which won't stop bleeding but refuse to kill him, he sits on he roof all day screaming, "Shit happens! My butt is cold! And I have to use the bathroom!"; [a.] Huron, SD

HARRIS, RENEE ANTOINETTE
[pen.] The Messenger; [b.] February 16, 1955, Philadelphia, PA; [p.] Wilbert Harris, Alda Harris; [ch.] David LaMont B. Warner; [ed.] Camden High, Glassboro State College, Associated Business Careers Lyons Institute; [occ.] Retired from Sony Corporations (3-promotions); [memb.] Bethany Baptist Church under the Ministry of Reverent David G. Evans, Pastor; [hon.] National Honor Society Secretarial. Advance Formatter, Certified Medical Assistant Sales Coordinator, Audio Processor, Credit Adjustor; [oth. writ.] Memorials in poetry form for family and friends, delivered in a positive concept in hopes to uplift heavy hearts and troubled minds when life seems most unkind.; [pers.] My goal is to reach out to others who feel all alone, in reading my poetry find a comfort zone. It's a good feeling to help someone else along my heart goes out especially to the disabled, elderly and the young.; [a.] Lindenwold, NJ

HART, WILLIAM DOUGLAS
[b.] April 17, 1943, St. John's, Newfoundland, Canada; [p.] Douglas and Caterine Hart; [ed.] High School; [occ.] Unemployed; [pers.] This is my first attempt at poetry. Philosophy - Happiness is to love and be loved back. Unhappiness is to love and not be loved back. (Life is what other people make it.); [a.] St. Johns Newfoundland, Canada

HARTLEY, ALICE L.
[pen.] Ecila; [b.] June 15, 1907, Nebraska; [p.] Deceased; [m.] Deceased, August 31, 1936; [ed.] Three Summer's Teacher's Training, Major in Music-Dramatics 60 years Teaching Studio and Groups; [occ.] Retired; [memb.] Gov. Projects, Fatenal. Organizations Junior and Gem Teen Director, started commercially in 1935. Still entertain at senior function's have a seven year Pl in for later; [hon.] I have been blessed with accomplishment, my award was success, I have lots of material such as unpublish music poems and plays used in my work; [oth. writ.] My resitals were made up of my own plays, some original music and lyrics, I had a few poems in Women Mag. National, no commercial writings; [pers.] My poetry is strickly pleasure. Every dream starts with thought, to have a true meaning it must come from the heart and, experience. And, love of fellowship; [a.] Boise, ID

HARTLEY, MARIE
[pen.] Hott Chocolate; [b.] October 24, Louisiana; [p.] Dave and Henrietta Hartley; [ch.] Yalonda T. Hartley; [ed.] Edward Tilden High School; [occ.] L.S.M. Operator at So. Suburban Post Office Bedford Pk. Ill.; [memb.] Harvey Memorial Community Church; [hon.] Certificate of Appreciation from So. Suburban Post Office.; [oth. writ.] Many other poems not published.; [pers.] A special thank you goes out to my daughter, my sister Earnestine, and co-worker Yavonne for encouraging me

to enter my poem. As a thank you to National Library of Poetry. But most of all a thank you to my Mom and Dad and Almighty God for life.; [a.] Calumet Park, IL

HARTMAN, MS. HAZEL
[b.] April 8, 1947, Assiniloia, Saskatchewan, Canada; [p.] Stephen and Dorothy Galbraith; [m.] Divorced; [ch.] Patty, Graham and Paul, 4 Grandchildren; [ed.] Grade 12; [occ.] Special Needs Worker; [hon.] 1993 Schutzenfest Queen of the Army, Nava and Airforce Club Unit #5 Vernon, B.C. (Canada).; [oth. writ.] Have wrote other poems for some friends and family members.; [pers.] All my poems as based on personal experience with whom I am writing the poem for.; [a.] Vernon British Columbia, Canada

HARVEY, MS. LAVERNE
[b.] March 13, New York, NY; [ch.] Yannick Christophe; [ed.] Cuny-City College, Cum Laude BA English: Creative Writing Master's Candidate, English; [occ.] Substitute Teacher NYC (k-6); [memb.] Directors Guild of American; [hon.] Dean's List, The National Dean's List Alpha Sigma Lambda Honor Society, NEA/CBE Arts Education Fellowship, The City College Graduate Fellowship in English, The Council of Supervisors and Administrators of the city of New York Parent Leadership Award, The Goodman Fund TV and Film Award for screen writing, The Mayor's Scholarship, NYC; [oth. writ.] I've done several poetry readings and my poems have been published in several newsletters.; [pers.] In my writing I aim to develop a unique creative style that always echoes Truth, History and a love of mankind.; [a.] New York, NY

HARWELL, BOBBY R.
[pen.] Bobby Harwell; [b.] August 22, 1931, Nashville, AR; [p.] Leila M. Frey and J. Benjamin Morris Harwell; [ch.] Karen and Nancy Harwell; [ed.] B.S. University of Arkansas 1958 (Cum Laude); [occ.] Actor - Have appeared in Miami Vice and Picket Fences. Many National Commercials - Several Movies.; [memb.] Screen Actors Guild.; [hon.] Beta Gamma Sigma - (Honorary Business Graduate Fraternity); [oth. writ.] Two scripts for "Picket Fences", screen plays and short stories, travel article for Ft. Lauderdale Sun Sentinel.; [pers.] Served in U.S.A.F. in Korea 1952-1953. In my writings I try to manifest the diamond hard toughness of the human spirit. "We can overcome any set back".; [a.] North Hollywood, CA

HASKINS, ALMEDA JUANITA
[pen.] Juanita; [b.] June 3, 1935, Hull, York's, England; [p.] James and Ida Miranda; [m.] William C. Haskins, June 11, 1966; [ch.] John M. Erby Jr., Charles W. Haskins; [ed.] Central Girls High, York's England Augusta, Technical/Business, Augusta GA. Some, extended campus classes, Western Kentucky University; [occ.] Instructional Aide Green County Elementary School; [memb.] Green River Writers, Inc., Greensburg Methodist Church; [oth. writ.] Poems, Essays, Short Stories, presently working on an Autobiography. Nothing published yet.; [pers.] All of my writing has been from personal experiences. I find that writing is a way of expressing my feelings, and also a personal therapy in emotional times.; [a.] Greensburg, KY

HAUN, REGINA MAE
[pen.] Regina Haun; [b.] April 08, 1967, Dallas, TX; [p.] Martha and Norman Schroedter; [ed.] Skidmore-Tynan High, Bauder Fashion College; [occ.] Model; [memb.] National Honor Society Of High School Students, National Honor Society of College Students; [hon.] National Dean's List, Who's Who Among American High School Students Magna Cum Laude (College); [oth. writ.] Several poems, non-published; [pers.] This particular poem was written to my boyfriend, Charles H. McCovery.; [a.] Houston, TX

HAWKINS, STACY
[pen.] "The Hawk"; [b.] February 16, 1971, West, VA; [ed.] Williamstown High Communications Liberate Arts, Major WA, Minor in Speech at RCNJ; [occ.] Senior at Rowan College of NJ; [memb.] Avant, a Literary Magazine for Poets at the College, Campus Climate Committee an organization that helps resolves problems on campus; [hon.] NJ State Teen Arts Festival in 89, Astronomy Club, and Student Activities Board Member; [oth. writ.] At Teen Arts Festival I won State and County, poems published in Avant and I have taken poetry classes at Rowan.; [pers.] I'm blessed with a literary gift that utilizes the imagination, all of nature's splendor and the love of words.; [a.] Williamstown, NJ

HAYDEN, DONALD W.
[b.] December 28, 1938, Boston, MA; [p.] Horace Hayde, Helen Hayden; [ed.] Oceanside High, Oceanside College, Dick Groves School of Music [occ.] Calif. Retailer, Musician; [memb.] International Trumpet Guild; [hon.] Bank of America, Foreign Languages Award; [oth. writ.] Poetry readings at coffee houses, and book stores; [pers.] "The forces of good and evil are side by side interwomen in man-kind; [a.] Lake Hughes, CA

HAYES, MRS. NELLIE M.
[b.] January 5, 1939, Mississippi; [m.] Mr. Theodore Hayes, February 20, 1988; [ch.] Theresa Harris and Marilyn Thomas; [ed.] John Marshall High School; [occ.] Mail Carrier, Chicago Loop Post Office; [pers.] Hobbies are interior decorating, collecting old movies making quilts. Collecting Indian also Afro Merican dolls. My poems was inspired during one of my most negative moments by a true and most positive friend. A Ms. Barbara Turner.; [a.] Country Club Hills, IL

HAYNES, DEBBIE
[b.] April 23, 1978, Nashville, TN; [p.] Sandra and Jimmy Haynes; [ed.] Lavergne High, 10th grade; [occ.] Student; [a.] Lavergne, TN

HAYTER, VIVIAN DUROCHER
[b.] March 19. 1926, Seattle, WA; [p.] Madelaine and Phil Durocher; [m.] Robert M. Hayter, November 25, 1947; [ch.] Robin Hayter Downey; [ed.] 2 1/2 yrs. College, U of W; [occ.] Retired; [memb.] Formerly Dramatists Guild; [oth. writ.] Three Musical Plays (words, music and script): Once more with feeling, Nelly Bly, and (Co-written) Double Rainbow, plus many other songs.; [pers.] "Winter Song" is also a song, for which I wrote the music, and arranged for SATB chorus, with the only accompaniment the sound of sleighbells.; [a.] Port Ludlow, WA

HAZARD, CLAUDIA
[pen.] Hears Crow; [b.] May 7, 1951, Baltimore, MD; [m.] Big Toe; [ch.] Jack Hazard Hughes; [ed.] Thomas College, Waterville, ME; [occ.] Director, National Contracts Deloitte and Touche; [memb.] Children's Writer ICL, Connecticut Women's Circle; [oth. writ.] Current emphasis focuses on young adult short stories and the retelling of traditional Indigenous stories.; [pers.] "We are all related"; [a.] Norwalk, CT

HEARN, MATTHEW S.
[b.] July 07, 1974, Washington, DC; [p.] Kenneth S. Hearn, Joan Christine Scullen Hearn; [ed.] Kent County High School, Worton MD, Chesapeake College, Wye Mills MD, U.S. Navy Nuclear Academy, Orlando Fl; [occ.] U.S. Navy - Nuclear Academy, studying Nuclear Technology; [oth. writ.] Severals songs and poems similar to "You And I, Until The End Of Time".; [pers.] My poems and songs are written with the hope that one of my readers will be able to relate the words to their feelings. The poetry I write comes from the feelings I have for the people to whom I am closest; [a.] Kennedyville, MD

HEATON, DEBORAH
[b.] February 27, 1974, Brooklyn, NY; [p.] Ms. Carol Miller, Mr. Richard Heaton; [ed.] Haldane Central High School, Stenotype Academy; [occ.] Paralegal Student; [oth. writ.] Several poems published in High School Magazine called "Insight 1992". Also a poem published in my High School Yearbook.; [pers.] I am inspired by my inner feelings and how I can express them in my writings.; [a.] Cold Spring, NY

HEDGE, HEATHER
[b.] September 11, 1978, Paragould, AR; [p.] Darlene and Noble Hedge; [ed.] Currently in Pontotoc High School; [occ.] Student; [oth. writ.] Several poems in my own books at home.; [pers.] Everywhere has their own quota to make in their lives of loves to go bad to make you strong enough to handle the right one.; [a.] Tupelo, MS

HEENAN, KATHLEEN MACKIN
[b.] April 18, 1949, Chicago, IL; [p.] Joseph and Margaret Dwyer MacKin; [m.] William J. Heenan (deceased), June 27, 1971; [ch.] Michael 20, Catherine 18, Joseph 16, Mary 12; [ed.] B.S. of Ed. 3-8 and English 7-12 "Awakening Your Light Body" - Course; [occ.] Adult Education GED and English as a Second Language; [memb.] Circle of Light - St. Clare Holy Name Society and Arch Con - A.R.E. Association for Research and Enlightenment - Connecting Light Body.; [oth. writ.] Editorials - Circle of Light Articles - Children Stories, Dream Study - Play/Restore My Church; [pers.] "Be still, and know - I am God"; [a.] Chicago, IL

HEIDKAMP, SHERRY
[b.] May 16. 1980, Ft Lauderdale, FL; [p.] Cathy Heidkamp, Larry Bielski; [ed.] Currently a freshman at Ringgold High School; [memb.] Catoosa County Saddle Club; [pers.] I write an emotion and hopefully that emotion comes out in what I write.; [a.] Ringgold, CA

HEITMAN, INGEBORG
[b.] June 4, 1923, Germany; [ch.] Ingrid Dietlinde; [occ.] Writing [memb.] Lifetime Member in International Society of Poets, Member of a Literary Group.; [hon.] Editor's Choice Award from the National Library of Poetry 1993; [oth. writ.] "High Calling" - The first poem of 13 peace-poems is published in the Anthology "Dance On The Horizon, The National Library of Poetry 1994. Several poems published in Germany, among the prize-winning poems. True experiences written in the form of short stories.; [pers.] Poems are most inspiring and rewarding when they have that special innate quality - and are touched by the universal soul when they come through and received in a persons heart. This is a moment of joy! [a.] Tweed Heads New South Wales, Australia

HELLER, RAMONA "MONA"
[pen.] Ramona Heller; [b.] December 15, 1930, Cumberland, MD; [p.] Gearge and Hazel Shepherd; [m.] William F. Heller, April 16, 1983 2nd for both; [ch.] Rebecca Noelle Haven; [ed.] 12th Grade, Learned the computers at 60 yrs. old; [occ.] Retired from office manager position, also worked ten years in Diagnostic Chemicals; hobby is hot air ballooning.; [hon.] Was awarded the Governors Citatation when I took care of foster children in Maryland for several years.; [oth. writ.] I have been writing poems since I was 12 yrs old. One entitled "Criticism" and many others. Most of my poems are based on my own life experiences. I also do writings in our newspaper "A Slice Of Life"; [pers.] I have always liked all people, and regardless of their different views, I respect them. I try to see both sides, I sincerely believe in the "Golden Rule" I ask myself, how would I would like to be treated and proceed hence...; [a.] Winchester, VI

HENCKEL, JAEL
[pen.] Dominique Rand; [b.] January 13, 1975, Oklahoma City, OK; [p.] Robert and Sara Henckel; [ed.] Burlington High School - CO International Corresponding School CA - AA in Accounting; [occ.] Clerical Assistant; [memb.] Smithsonian Institution, National Honor Society; [hon.] FBLA Scholarship; [pers.] I have always admired Thoreau's idea of "sucking the marrow" out of life. Some of my poems seem morbid, but those works are simply my means to a peaceful and rather than a permanent mind set.; [a.] Barstow, CA

HENDERSON, SALLY
[b.] August 6, 1941, Brattleboro, VT; [p.] W. E. Henderson (deceased), Selma Henderson; [ed.] Grad. of Ewing High, Major in Business.; [occ.] Sales for medical supply for home care/uniform shop-for medical field.; [oth. writ.] Unpublished poems and short stories for children.; [pers.] To provide a calm and quiet area in one's life thru poem or story. I believe we all need to reflect on the heart as well as the mind for the good of all.; [a.] Fort Pierce, FL

HENDRICKS, REV. PAUL E.
[b.] June 17, 1917, Brown Co. Nasville, IN; [p.] Rev. James W. Hendricks, Blanche E. Hendricks; [m.] Edna Wynelle Hendricks, January 17, 1943; [ch.] Paula Gage, Shirley Hendricks, Barbara Whitsell; [ed.] Christiansburg Senior High School Univ. of Philippines, Florida State Univ. Univ. of MD, University of MD. Balt. CO, Correspondence courses - Moody Bible Just. S. Bapt. Theological Seminary, 120 Semester Hoves of College Work. USAF Retire - 30 yrs Ordained to Gospel Ministry 1965 Pastor -22 yrs; [occ.] Truck Chaplain, Allied Systems (Part time) Chaplain WW II Military Unit when needed. The unit de-activated after WW II; [memb.] Trinity Baptist Church 32d degree Masonic order Member Senior Citizens GP; [hon.] Several WW II military honors and unit stations. A plaque awarded by Freedoms Foundation at Valley Forge for article "What Is An American" dated 1971.; [oth. writ.] Several poetic sermons and other poems used in sermons. Other writings and various articles used in fellowship groups or get well and sympathy card writings; [pers.] I strive to help people all that I can particularly when called upon to visit, or preparation for death, supply preaching when needed and to minister to truck terminal personnel in a loving and position way.; [a.] Walderf, MD

HENNESSEY
[pen.] Tom; [b.] May 26, 1929, Dublin, Ireland; [m.] Edna May, September 22, 1957; [ch.] Colin, Paul, plus 4 grandchildren; [ed.] Grade 12; [occ.] Retired House Painter; [oth. writ.] Small Book s/p Shakespeare was an Irishman (Satire), many other stories under way.; [pers.] The Earth is but one country and mankind it's citizen's (bahaivilla)

HENOCH, ARDITH PAIGE
[pen.] Ardith Paige; [b.] November 27, 1973, Winnipeg, Manitoba, Canada; [p.] Lynn Henoch, Morris Henoch; [ed.] Joseph Wolinsky Collegiate, presently studying at Bar-Ilan University, Israel; [occ.] Full time student: B.A in English Lit. (Major), Jewish Art, (Minor) at: Bar Ilan University, Israel; [pers.] I write poetry to capture life's uncertainly, dance awhile with her wings, then set her free to fly.; [a.] Winnipeg Manitoba, Canada

HENSON, DORTHY F.
[b.] September 6, 1935, Berea, KY; [p.] William and Maggie Roberts; [m.] Raymond P. Henson, September 9, 1975; [ch.] 7 children, 4 boys and 3 girls also 3 step-child, 7th Grade, 1 little girl, I'm raising 8 years old. I've had her since she was 18 months. I have 29 grand children, 2 great grand child.; [occ.] Retired Nurse Aid and Cook; [memb.] Of Road to True Holiness Pentecostel Church for 32 years. [oth. writ.] I have written several poems and songs but don't have any published also short children stories; [pers.] I love God and my country.

HERNANDEZ, JOVAN L.
[b.] January 3, 1978, Texas City, TX; [p.] Jorge A. Hernandez, Sr., Irma V. Hernandez; [ed.] Texas City High School; [pers.] I live to write and play music to at least keep myself from going totally insane.; [a.] Texas City, TX

HERNANDEZ, ROBERT LOUIS
[pen.] Robert Louis; [b.] August 10, 1953, Charlotte, NC; [p.] Roberto, Lottie Hernandez; [m.] wife to be: Joanie Valek; [ch.] Manuela, Michael, Joseph; [ed.] John Fay H.S. (GED), Consortium College, and the American Bible Academy; [occ.] Director (founder) of the: Bay Ridge Anistian Basketball League; [hon.] In Baseball, Basketball, Paddle ball, and Bicycle Racing; [oth. writ.] Have appeared in the Consortium College Newspapers, and in the Bay Ridge United Church News Letters.; [pers.] Apart from Jesus. These is no hope in life!; [a.] Brooklyn, NY

HERRICK, CHRISTINE
[b.] July 20, 1955, Ft Worth, TX; [p.] James and Ruby Smith; [m.] James B. Herrick, March 9, 1990; [ch.] Jay Violet, Lesleigh Violet, Kyle Violet; [ed.] Van High School, Tyler Junior College, University Of Texas, Saddle Back College; [occ.] Volunteer for charity; [hon.] Deans List; [pers.] Writing my poems, express my feelings. I hope my poems will relate to someone else and let them know their not alone. I have been greatly influence by the early poets that expressed their feelings.; [a.] Mission Viejo, CA

HERZOG, REJANE
[b.] September 30, 1981, Prince Albert, Saskatchewan, Canada; [p.] Garth and Marie Anne Herzog; [ed.] Wild Rose Central for 8 years, then moved on the Wesmor High in Prince Albert, and I am still there.; [memb.] The Wesmor volleyball team, Wesmor choir.; [hon.] I won a first place medal in a singing competition. I also had the pleasure of writing a valedictorian speech for my grade 7 grad.; [oth. writ.] I have had my poetry published in the school paper quite a few times. I have a book of poetry which I work on every night.; [pers.] I find it hard to write when I'm not in the "mood". I need candle light or I have to be listening to my favorite CD in order to write good poetry. My parents and friends also influenced me a lot.; [a.] Mayview Saskatchewan, Canada

HESLIN, EVELYN M.
[pen.] Evelyn Hilpp Heslin; [b.] Louisville, KY; [p.] Julia and Adolph B. Hilpp Sr.; [m.] Thomas V. Heslin, October 4, 1947; [ch.] Gerry Olvey-Patricia L., Levi-Mary Naughton and Thomas G. Heslin, (Four children and three grandchildren), Grands: Jason, Jessica and Megan; [occ.] Homemaker (Executive Home Engineer); [memb.] AARP and Golden Age, American Heart Assoc., Assumption Catholic Church; [hon.] I have poems published in nine (9) Anthologies - several honorable mention awards - world of poetry. Several other publications, in booklets and newspapers.; [oth. writ.] Poems, A few articles and a Christmas story for my Hometown Newspaper, for seventeen years, consecutively. A few stories. Children's etc.; [pers.] I make an effort to write inspiring, original works, of good quality, but yet enhanced with a sparkle. "To be an author, it takes a heart of oak, and an unyielding determination."; [a.] Jacksonville, FL

HICKEN, JUDY
[pen.] Chris Murphy; [b.] May 5, 1948, Halifax, Nova Scotia, Canada; [p.] Leigh and Isabelle Murphy; [m.] Gary Hicken, June 2, 1979; [ch.] Elizabeth Hicken; [ed.] Duncan MacMillan High, 1 yr. Stenographic degree, St. Mary's Univ., qualified to teach Functional Illiterates. Various personal interest courses; [occ.] Family Manager, Library Volunteer; [memb.] The Greater Saint John Fibromyalgia Society; [oth. writ.] Several poems unpublished; [pers.] Be strong enough to stand up for the good in life, there are already too many on the other side.; [a.] Quispamsis New Brunswick, Canada

HICKMAN, HAZEL ALICE
[pen.] Hazel Alice Hickman; [b.] March 20, 1925, Pawnee Co., OK; [p.] Roy Skidgel, Elsie Skidgel; [m.] Marvin M. Hickman, January 1, 1941; [ch.] Five and thirteen grandchildren; [ed.] Schooloin in Pawnee Okla.; [occ.] Owner and manager of rental complex; [memb.] Bible Student, Teacher and Leader of the Church of Christ for 20 years; [oth. writ.] Articles and poems for the weekly church paper, "I Wish I Were An Angel" copyrighted with Sparrowgrass Poetry Inc. in "Treasured Poems Of America".; [pers.] At the age of ten, I was inspired to write by an encouraging school teacher, also by the poetry of the Bible, the love of nature, and the beauty of friends and family.; [a.] Stockton, CA

HICKS, VICTOR C.
[b.] May 17, 1927, Province of Quebec, Canada; [p.] Cy and Hilda Hicks; [m.] Divorced, December 30, 1986; [ed.] High School Graduate, Tech School Diploma, College 2 yrs, Adult Education Teacher Communications; [occ.] Retired; [memb.] Lions International President two yrs. Eagle Club Member, Elk and Moose; [hon.] Young Mens Christian Association for friendship and generous support. Lions International for Distinguished and Unselfish Support to their cause Actor's Guild Society for support of their cause; [pers.] To have reached the ear of this distinguished and well know association, the National Library of Poetry has undoubtedly encouraged me in writing poetry especially on the nature of personalities.; [a.] San Jacinto, CA

HIGGINS, ALYSE J.
[pen.] A. J. Voisinet [b.] July 26, 1914, Sacramento, CA; [p.] Alice and Julien Voisinet; [m.] Robert P. Higgins (Divorced), June 12, 1932; [ch.] Robert E., Alyse Maria; [ed.] High School Oakland, Calif. Reg. Electrologist Los Angeles, Calif.; [occ.] Retired; [pers.] I believe being an Electrologist for over 40 years gave me an opportunity to "get in touch" with inner feelings and hopes of other people and myself.; [a.] Lafeyette, CA

HIGHTOWER, JAMES RICHARD
[b.] January 26, 1960, Washington, DC; [p.] James H. Hightower, Wilma Jean Hightower; [ed.] Wheaton and Robert E. Peary High Schools, Wheaton MD, and Silver Springs MD, Indian River Community College, Ft. Pierce FL, Certified Master Gardener of FL.; [occ.] Student at Indian River Community College.; [memb.] FL Master Gardeners, Seed Savers Exchange, Flower and Herb Exchange, Dark Shadow Fan Club.; [hon.] Certificate of Completion: Intro to construction. Certified of completion: FL Master Gardener continued training. Montgomery county life skills diploma. College Diploma: A.S. in Agribusiness Technology, Majoring in Landscape, Florida Master Gardener Award.; [oth. writ.] A compilation of unpublished songs in my note book.; [pers.] Life is too short and should not be wasted on negativity.; [a.] Port St. Lucie, FL

HILL, JIM
[b.] September 21, 1940, Frontier, Saskatchewan, Canada; [p.] Van and Marie Hill; [m.] Carol; [ch.] Cheri; [ed.] High School; [occ.] Farming (hereford cattle and standardbred race horses.; [memb.] Canadian Trotting Association. United States Trotting Association.; [oth. writ.] First Book (1994) "Staying On Stride", column "Staying On Stride", column "Free Reining", book to be published in 1995 "Seasons In Verse"; [pers.] I write from the heart and shoot from the hip ... I am an optimist with realistic sensibilities.; [a.] Portage La Prairie Manitoba, Canada

HILL, VALERIE
[b.] February 2, 1955, Cleveland, OH; [p.] Mary (deceased) and Benjamin Hill; [m.] Rev. Charlie Hill Jr., May 10, 1975; [ch.] Erik, Andrea, Sondra, Tiffany, Charlie III; [ed.] Adult Education Center, Institute of Computer Management, Moody Bible Institute Extension School; [occ.] Homemaker, Minister wife, mother, and care giver; [memb.] Cornerstone Missionary Baptist Church; [oth. writ.] Inspirational writings, poems, and plays; [pers.] Stop looking gat the world through black and white lenses for we are a kaleidoscope of color, and we come in many shapes and sizes.; [a.] Cleveland, OH

HINES, ALLISON ELEASE
[b.] July 13, 1965, Birmingham, AL; [p.] Orsie Hines Sr., and Marry Hines; [ch.] Brandon Jamelle and Jamie Montrese; [ed.] West End High, Livingston University, Auburn University; [occ.] Manager; [oth. writ.] Currently writing a non-fiction book.; [pers.] Believe in yourself, your hopes, and your dreams.; [a.] Birmingham, AL

HINES, MITSIE
[b.] January 10, 1971, Jamaica, West Indies; [p.] Mr. L. Hines and Ms. L. Chrystie; [ed.] Jamaica and United State; [occ.] CNA

HINES, ROSE ANNA
[b.] March 25, 1947, Cairo, Egypt; [ed.] BA in Psychology and MS in Physical Therapy; [occ.] Physical Therapist, and Income Consultant, Success Coach; [hon.] Cum Laude Graduate, Toastmasters ATM, Area, Division A District Speech Contest Winner; [pers.] I am fascinated by human behaviour. My poems reflect the broad spectrum on the continuum of human experience feeling and responses. Because human experiences and behavior is diverse the subjects of my poems are diverse; [a.] Whittier, CA

HITCHCOCK, BILLY J.
[b.] July 18, 1965, Newark, OH; [p.] John and Dalma Hitchcock; [ed.] Newark Senior High School; [occ.] Commutator Finished Resinoid Engineering; [pers.] I write for myself, to help me come to terms with my feelings!; [a.] Newark, OH

HOBSON, LARRY BUDD
[pen.] Coin Hunter; [b.] February 28, 1947, Edna, TX; [p.] Mrs. L. H. Hobson; [ed.] Wharton Junior College and University of Houston Victoria Center; [occ.] House Painter; [memb.] Metal Detecting and Hobby Clubs of Texas; [pers.] In my writing I see the old cog train, from Durango to Silverton, Colorado, up in the clouds on its way to the station to pick up another load of people.; [a.] Edna, TX

HODGES, JANICE WILLIAMS
[m.] Thomas H. Hodges, Jr., May 24, 1986; [ch.] Marcus Eric and Danielle Nicole; [ed.] Johnson C. Smith University, English Major; [occ.] Pre-School Teacher; [memb.] National Honor Society; [hon.] Public Speaking Award; [oth. writ.] Poems published in other Anthologies and Writer's Showcase. Currently working on Children's Books and Book of Poetry for publication.; [pers.] I desire my work and touch the soul and heal aches, inspire the youth in all of us, yes....burn a hole through the soul and sizzle a brand deep within memory's folds. Admire words of Emily Dickinson, Maya Angelou; [a.] Raleigh, NC

HODOUS, SHANNON ALYCIA
[b.] July 16, 1978, Charlottesville, VA; [p.] Robert and Susan Hodous; [ed.] I am currently a junior at Charlottesville High School; [occ.] Student; [memb.] Spanish Club, Varsity Tennis Team, Drama Department and The United State Tennis Association (USTA).; [hon.] Honor Roll Student all semesters of High School and Most Outstanding Algebra 2A student. Most Valuable Volleyball Player and Most Improved Tennis Player.; [oth. writ.] Winter, Free Spirits, Hill of Hope, Out of Reach, The Sands Of Time, My Dream, Emptiness, The Rain and The Night (all poems); [pers.] Through my poetry I strive to reveal my emotions and thoughts. If you are true to yourself, you will be true to others. Honesty is a priceless gift.; [a.] Charlottesville, VA

HOFFMAN, JANE
[pen.] Jane Rose Hoffman [b.] Detroit, MI; [p.] Harold and Marguerite Williamson; [m.] Jack; [ch.] Susan; [ed.] Involved in a continuing educational course as a student of life and experience, learning through the reflection of nature, philosophy, and the arts. Ever turning for inspiration to the greatest philosopher, example, teacher of truth, and physician of mind and body, Jesus the Christ.; [occ.] Retired; [oth. writ.] Articles and poetry published in newspapers, magazines and anthologies. Also a self published book rhyme and reason; [pers.] Blessed to be a wife, mother, grandmother and friend where the delight and wonder of life is ever new, surprising and expanding. Living in a small Alpine community on the slope of Mt. Shasta where heaven and earth meet; [a.] Mt. Shasta, CA

HOGE, DOREEN MARIE
[b.] January 26, 1956, Cleveland, OH; [p.] Robert Henry and Dorothy Helen Newmann; [m.] Henry Eugene Hoge, August 23, 1980; [occ.] Piano Teacher - Self employed; [pers.] All the credit for this poem belongs to the Lord Jesus Christ. Accept His free in invitation repent, turn to Him, put your trust in Him, believe on Him - today. John 3:16-17, Romans 5:15-17, Romans' 6:23, John 3:3-7.; [a.] Willoughby Hills, OH

HOLAHAN, CATHERINE V.
[pen.] Catherine V. Holahan; [b.] Rochester, NY; [p.] Deceased; [m.] Deceased, September 24, 1946; [occ.] Retired; [pers.] I had to express my feelings - I wrote many poems 32 years ago after I met a very kind fellow who happened into my life when I really needed someone. I wrote them early in the morning when the sun was rising and later in the day at sunset.; [a.] Rochester, NY

HOLDEN, WHITNEY
[b.] January 15, 1982, Dallas, TX; [p.] Dwight and Sandra Haiden; [ed.] Cascia Hall Middle School; [hon.] Silver Honor Roll, Six Grade, Special Achievement; [oth. writ.] I've written stories on my own but never tried to publish them.; [pers.] I am honored that my poem has been chosen, and would like you to know that I am thrilled to have this opportunity. Thank you.; [a.] Tulsa, OK

HOLDMAN, JOAN F.
[pen.] Joan F. Holdman; [b.] December 26, 1939, Festus, MO; [p.] Harold Primo, Rachel Tangen; [m.] Leroy Holdman, April 15, 1988; [ch.] Lawrence, Kevin and Rick La Montagne Steven, David Holdman, Melissa Mobley; [ed.] Roosevelt High, Meramec Community College, St. Louis, MO.; [occ.] Author-writer; [oth. writ.] I have written several poems. I am now in the process of writing my first book. I will be searching for a publisher for it.; [pers.] While writing I draw on my emotions and experiences. This has developed me into a strong writer towards motivation and positive thinking.; [a.] Chesterfield, MO

HOLLAND, FLORENCE K.
[b.] January 4, 1962, NY; [p.] Laura and Rudolph; [ch.] Frank and Cesare, Delise and Rebecca; [ed.] Jane Addams VHS Orange County; [occ.] Customer Rep.; [pers.] Be yourself no matter what and always lone from deep inside

HOLLIMAN, NADINE
[b.] June 18, 1960, Philadelphia, PA; [p.] John Holliman, Mary Holliman; [ch.] Sherice N. Holliman; [ed.] William Penn High School, Community College of Phila.; [occ.] Homemaker, Community Assistant, Belmont Elementary School; [pers.] My poems reflects how I feel, what I feel and see in this upside down world. My words give me inspiration and strength.; [a.] Philadelphia, PA

HOLMES, TANYA LEE
[b.] January 23, 1977, Norristown, PA; [p.] Virginia Scalella; [ed.] Student - High School (12th); [occ.] United States Army Reserves, student; [hon.] Chemistry Award, Graduation from Combat Basic Training from the United States Army, Achievement Awards; [oth. writ.] "In Walk The Healers"; [pers.] Even though one may make it day by day, another may not.; [a.] King of Prussia, PA

HOMMERDING, JEFFREY PAUL
[b.] November 25, 1974, Santa Monica, CA; [p.] Debra

Jo Hommerding; [ed.] University of San Diego High School, currently attending, Humboldt State University; [occ.] Student; [memb.] Humboldt State University, Rowing Association; [oth. writ.] I keep a collection of my works.; [pers.] I have been greatly inspired by the works of Walt Whitman. I believe the closer one becomes to nature, the closer one begins to understand themselves, and their role in the grand scheme of the universe.; [a.] Arcata, CA

HONEYMAN, JAMI L.
[b.] December 20, 1977, Peoria; [p.] Harlan and Judy Honeyman; [ed.] Galesburg High; [hon.] Who's Who (academic), Who's Who (sports), Honor roll; [pers.] I take my inner most thoughts as the most precious thing. This is how I think every person should feel, it helps you feel good about your life.; [a.] Henderson, IL

HONG, EUGENE
[pen.] Scribe; [b.] May 15 1978, Seoul, Korea; [p.] Do Pyo Hong, Jing Ja Hong; [ed.] Still High School Student; [occ.] Student; [oth. writ.] My own poems not published, not yet....; [pers.] I just try to write good stuff, usually from a small inspiration at the spur of the moment, and it takes me a short time, I don't know if I'm doing it right, but that's how I do it. I've been most influenced by my brothers in C.O.G.; [a.] San Diego, CA

HONN, IOWA L.
[pen.] Mrs. Iowa [b.] April 1, 1910, Oxford, IA; [p.] William and Artie Floerehinger; [m.] Faye H. Honn, June 20, 1931; [ch.] Jonathan Jay, William Faye; [ed.] H.S., College (Iowa State Teachers, U.N.I. Kirkwood Com.); [occ.] Retired Elem., and Jr Hi Teacher; [memb.] Windham Missionary Anchor Bay Church; [oth. writ.] Many just filed away; [pers.] My greatest joy has been working with pre-teenagers. I tough many years and the children called me Mrs. Iowa (now I'm a great-grandma); [a.] Oxford, IA

HOOPER, WHITNEY ERIN
[b.] December 20, 1979, East Ridge, TN; [p.] Terry Hooper, Phyllis Wads worth; [ed.] LaFayette High, 9th Grade; [occ.] Student; [memb.] Fellowship of Christian Athletes (FCA), National Library of History.; [hon.] Best Poet Award, Piano Award, Honor Band, Honor Student, and Science Departmental Award.; [oth. writ.] The Tree, Heaven, Innocence, Peacefulness, and Regret.; [pers.] I write about peacefulness, and happiness, basically where I feel like being at the present time. I like to create feelings for others who read my work.; [a.] LaFayette, GA

HORN, DONNA MARIE
[pen.] Donna Marie E'Bell; [b.] July 4, 1936, Fresno, CA; [p.] Harry and Orpha E'Bell; [ch.] Mark D. and James E. Gane; [ed.] High School, Some College, self-improvement, personal interest classes.; [occ.] Secretary, City of Foundation Valley, Fountain Valley, CA; [oth. writ.] A few never-submitted, unpublished poems and two short stories.; [pers.] I find writing a wonderful form for self-expression and communicating one's impression of the world and the people around them.; [a.] Fountain Valley, CA

HORNBY, KIMBERLY ANNE MCKAY
[b.] January 23, 1960, Hamilton, Ontario, Canada; [p.] Carol L. Hornby, Brian Hornby; [m.] Divorced, Partner: Fred Thompson; [ch.] Amber Marie Van Ginkel; [ed.] Dundas District High School, Mohawk College; [occ.] Clerk, Health Records Hamilton General Hospital; [memb.] Canadian Society of Laboratory Technology; [hon.] Dean's List, final year of Med Lab Course; [oth. writ.] I enjoy writing poetry and short stories but lost soul is my first published poem.; [pers.] I am emotionally expressive and a romantic by nature. I love the classic poets and authors. My love for literature was bestowed on me by my mother. I especially enjoy anything regarding the King Arthur Legends. Thanks to my sister, Laura Hornby, for believing in my talent.; [a.] Dundas Ontario, Canada

HORNER, VANESSA NICOLE
[pen.] Nessa; [b.] August 13, 1979, Austin, TX; [p.] Gary J. and Pat A. Horner; [ed.] High School - Currently 10th Grade; [occ.] Student; [memb.] FFA - John Marshall High School; [hon.] Texas Alliance for Geographic Education and National Geographic Society "Green Hand" - FFA; [pers.] To be influenced is simply being open to share in others experiences and ideas.; [a.] San Antonio, TX

HORNER, WANDA
[pen.] Wanie; [b.] January 23, 1948, Scioto, County; [p.] Clyde and Alice Horner; [m.] Single; [ed.] High School Graduate Class of 67 Green Twp. High School; [occ.] Cook; [memb.] International Poet Society; [oth. writ.] Poem Eternal Spirits of the Chainless published in your book Journeys Of The Minds; [pers.] I love writing poetry. It helps me relax and get my mid off other things. I hope to publish my own book of poetry. Which I have almost finished writing.; [a.] Franklin Ice, OH

HORTON, PERRY
[b.] September 8, 1977, Sanford, NC; [p.] Paul and Candice Horton; [ed.] Lee County Senior High, University of North Carolina at Chapel Hill; [occ.] Student; [hon.] Josephine C. Gardner Creative Writing Award, North Carolina, English Teacher's Association Writing Contest, Regional Winner and 4th place in the State.; [oth. writ.] Several unpublished poetic manuscripts, locally published poems.; [pers.] Writing is not about money, nor recognition, but about the necessity of the soul to express itself in words. Writing is the purest form of art, because it comes directly from within.; [a.] Sanford, NC

HOSCH, MICHAEL E.
[b.] March 5, 1947, Santa Anna, TX; [p.] Mr. and Mrs. Pat Hosch; [ed.] Santa Anna High School; [occ.] Table Assembly Stempel Mfg Co.; [a.] Santa Anna, TX

HOUSE, MEGAN
[b.] November 9, 1980, Ft. Myers, FL; [p.] Thomas W. House, Christine White; [ed.] Baldwin County High School; [occ.] Student at BCHS; [memb.] Honor Society; [hon.] Honors Metal, Opportunity Key (From Honor Society); [oth. writ.] Several poems given to friends as gifts, and published in the school newspaper; [pers.] I try to put feeling into my poems to let others know how I feel.; [a.] Bay Minette, AL

HOUSEKNECHT, JEFFREY R.
[b.] February 26, 1953, Batavia, NY; [p.] Robert W. and Averyl Saunders Houseknecht; [m.] Cathy Houseknecht, May 28, 1978; [ch.] Danielle; [ed.] Pembroke Central High; [occ.] Custom Woodworking Shop and Studio Musician/Songwriter; [memb.] American Association of Christian Counselors (95-96); [hon.] Included in 1989 edition of Who's Who in American Christian Leadership cert. of part. Men's Leadership Prog. at North Darien Baptish Church; [oth. writ.] Montly articles in "Grapevine" and "Free, Indeed!" newsletters as well as poems in "Small Farmer's Journal" and others. Written songs currently being recorded.; [pers.] As a writer I try to influence all who read my work to the ways of Godliness and seeking the divine comfort of the Father and the saving grace of His Son, our Lord.; [a.] Darien Center, NY

HOWIE, STACEY RAE
[b.] December 10, 1968, Detroit, MI; [p.] Donald and Bonnie Knisley; [ch.] Brandon Bentley; [ed.] Royal Oak Dondero; [occ.] Secretary, Capital Carpet

HUDSON, DONNA
[b.] London, Ontario, Canada; [p.] Raymond and Dorothy (Deceased) McKenney; [m.] Brad Hudson; [ch.] Jennifer 13 and Matthew 8; [memb.] 'Hot Tonight for Manilow', based in Toronto, Ontario and the 'Barry Manilow International Fan Club', based in Los Angeles California.; [oth. writ.] Poem about Barry Manilow was printed in the Toronto-based newsletter.; [pers.] My mother wrote poetry almost everyday. After she was lost to us, I thought I would give it a try. Thanks Mom! This one is for you.; [a.] London Ontario, Canada

HUFF, JEANETTE STAMPER
[b.] May 2, 1934, Mayking, KY; [p.] Manda Caudill - William Stamper; [m.] William Huff, April 6, 1957; [ch.] 2 Kenneth and Tommy, 3 Grandchildren Mary Ann Kenny and Ryan; [ed.] Graduated from Whitesburgh High School 1953 Whitesburg, KY; [occ.] Disabled with cancer since August 1989. I felt I was near death when I informed my Dr. that I would die from the cancer. No more Kemo - therapy. That is when I begin writing. Inspired by my grandchildren because the first writing were about them.; [oth. writ.] Many other writings but none ever been published.; [pers.] My computer is the next best thing to my Dr. its my therapist its kept my sanity. I am not giving in to this cancer. I write and block it out of my mind live on transfusions and write.; [a.] Maple Hts, OH

HUGEL, THERESA ANN
[b.] August 16, 1964, Baltimore, MD; [p.] William and Janet Casey; [m.] Michael W. Hugel, 1985; [ch.] Michael W. Hugel, Jr.; [ed.] Archbishop Keough High, Anne Arundel Community College; [occ.] Operations Manager - Insurance Agency; [oth. writ.] I have a diversified collection of poems, many reflecting the human spirit's peaks and valleys.; [pers.] I try to be inspirational in my writings, but I also enjoy humorous writing. I hope that one would feel good after reading one of my poems.; [a.] Pasadena, MD

HUGHES, CHRISTINE
[b.] February 7, 1967, CT; [p.] Dr. and Mrs. W. F. Hughes; [m.] Gregory Gaudette, March 18, 1995; [ed.] Education Degree at Southern CT, State University Masters in Education - Loyola College MD; [occ.] Montessori Teacher at Beddow Montessori, School Ft. Washington, MD; [pers.] God has given me a gift to recognize and express the wonder and beauty in this world.

HUGHES, KAREN
[b.] June 14, 1953, Abington, PA; [p.] Ann and Russell Elvidge; [m.] Steven Hughes, October 11, 1980; [ch.] Sarah Lianne and Erin Nicole; [ed.] Hatboro-Horsham H.S., Penn State University (Fine Arts); [memb.] Two school PTO's, volunteer for Brownie Troop, Ford City Women's Pool League, National Weather Service Skywarn Observer; [hon.] Deans List; [pers.] My writing is a means of release, reflecting both the good and

evil, hate and love and the triumph and disillusionment in my world. Although my influences are wide and varied, I am largely driven by the lyrics of musician James Hetfield.; [a.] Adrian, PA

HUGHES, RICHARD BLAIR
[b.] September 12, 1951, Lindsay, Ontario, Canada; [p.] Earl and Lena Hughes; [m.] Glenda, August 9, 1985; [ch.] Philip Richard, Christian Blair; [ed.] Fenelon Falls Secondary School; [occ.] Guitar Player, Singer, Songwriter, House Husband; [memb.] Socan, Ascap; [oth. writ.] Catalogue of over 100 songs, 19 released on 2 albums, several poems published in local newspapers; [pers.] Writing, for me, is a necessity - a way to bring out an understanding of myself and my surroundings. Whether it be poetry or song, they are with me always.; [a.] Fenelon Fall Ontario, Canada

HUMPHREY, MIGNETTE
[pen.] MIG1 - Humphrey; [b.] May 19, 1956, Chicago, IL; [p.] Doris Jackson, Henry Lewis, deceased; [m.] Divorced; [ch.] Brent Humphrey, KimRose Humphrey; [ed.] High School Graduate; [occ.] Yeoman First Class, U.S. Coast Guard.; [memb.] New Testament Church Christ Holiness U.S.A. Los Angeles, CA, Our pastor teaches and we all believe salvation through Jesus Christ.; [hon.] To have you select this poem "Illuminating the Truth", as one of the semi-finalist is my first public honor. Thank you, but of course I thank God first.; [oth. writ.] Various poems have been published in the Church. "Journey Home", "Rosa Parks, Moving in the Shadows", "Flying High on Life" and "Peculiar Treasure".; [pers.] God is good isn't he? Everyone dreams of doing a particular something in life. That dream can become a reality when we finally recognize that all things are possible through Jesus Christ. In all things no matter how small acknowledge - God. He is sovereign.; [a.] Los Alamitos, CA

HUMPHRIES, KATHERINE
[b.] Gordon, GA; [p.] James Humphries, Katie Hawthorne; [m.] Divorced; [a.] New York, NY

HUNT, SALLY ANN
[b.] June 12, 1933, Washington, DC; [p.] Thomas G. and Agnes I. Hunt

HUNT, TIMOTHY A.
[b.] September 23, 1963, Sacramento, CA; [p.] Vern and Mary Hunt; [m.] Gloria, February 26, 1983; [ch.] Gerardette and Elijah Samson; [occ.] Police Officer; [oth. writ.] (Poems): "The forgotten soldiers", "Where have all the heroes gone?", "The second Christmas is coming" and a few others. (1 Book) "Weep not for me" all unpublished; [pers.] The original version of "The Vietnam Soldiers", called "The forgotten soldiers" and "Where have all the heroes gone?" were written in honor of my brother John, my father and all veterans to whom I owe my freedom.; [a.] Fremont, CA

HUNTER, CHRISTOPHER D.
[b.] October 6, 1973, Hazleton, PA; [p.] Donald (Jr.) and Debra Hunter; [ed.] Danville High School, Wilkes University, Delaware Community College; [occ.] Student; [hon.] Deans List; [pers.] My writing has helped me to express my grief and loss of a good friend - my dad, my mentor.; [a.] Danville, PA

HURDLE, LINDA FRANCES
[b.] February 25, Early 1950's, Los Angeles, CA; [p.] Sam and Nelma Hurdle; [m.] Never Married; [ch.] Lakeesha, Shawna and Crystal Page; [ed.] Manual Arts High School, Pruitt Business College, Southwest Junior College, Sacramento City College; [occ.] Day Care Teacher; [hon.] Editor's Choice Award from the National Library of Poetry.; [oth. writ.] I have numerous of writings submitted to the National Library to the Poetry and, many that haven't, and a book called Broken Dreams.; [pers.] Writing and Poetry is a part of my life. To me its like therapy; [a.] Sacramento, CA

HURST, DEBORA F.
[pen.] Auriel Masalone, L.D. (D); [b.] April 14, 1949, Xenia, OH; [p.] Marvin Eugene and Phyllis Theodore Faye Hurst; [ed.] Centrol State University B.S. Biology, University of Cincinnati Mis. Industrial Hygienist Certified Hypnotherapist - Ohio Academy of Hypnotherapy, Certified Hypno Anesthesia Therapist - Mid-West Training Institute of Hypnosis; [occ.] Industrial Hygienist, Ergonomics Program Manager, Wright Patterson Air Force Base; [memb.] Kettering Fellows, American Conference of Governmental Industrial Hygienist, National Association of Female Executives, Ohio Academy of Hypnotherapy Assoc., American Board of Hypnotherapy; [hon.] Beta Beta Biological Honor Society, Dean's List, Danforth Fellowship, 2 years. Graduate Studies in Biochemistry at University of Cincinnati; [oth. writ.] Masters thesis - Photosensitivity, In Grocery Store Workers, and other Technical writings.; [pers.] In my analytical world I use writing as a means of communication, expression, creating - self-discovery and development.; [a.] Xenia, OH

HURT, ELIZABETH E.
[b.] January 10, 1970, Phoenixville, PA; [p.] Ruth H. Morgan, H. Terrence Hurt; [ed.] Bachelor of Arts, English, University of Central Florida; [occ.] Network Management Coordinator, Aetna Health Plans; [hon.] Sigma Tau Delta, Intl., English Honor Society, Who's Who among students in American Universities and Colleges; [pers.] Poems published in literary anthologies including the cypress dome and brushing; [a.] Orlando, FL

HWANG, PHILIP CHYUAN-FUW
[pen.] Philip C.F. Hwang; [b.] February 18, 1933, Chia-Yi, Taiwan; [p.] Mo Hwang and Uhe-Che Kowa Hwang; [m.] Kwe Tzu Young, October 9, 1960; [ch.] Su-U Hwang and Phyllis Hwang; [ed.] Provincial Chiayi High School - 1952, Polytechnic University - 1969, National Taiwan University - 1957; [occ.] Licensed Professional Engineer (N.Y. State) Civil Engineering, The City of New York; [memb.] 1. Technical Guild, Local 375 DC37, AFSCME, AFL-CIO, 2. Licensed N.Y. State Professional Engineer, 3. Licensed Professional Engineer - Taiwan; [hon.] 1. Commissioner, Marilyn Gelber's Awards D.E.P., The City of New York, 2. Honors: "Who We Are:, 50 Anniversary Building A City, page 35; [oth. writ.] 1. Automating Engineering Audit Procedures, 2. Japanese version "City Tunnel No. 3 N.Y. City Water Supply System", 3. Few poems published in Taiwanese Weekly; [pers.] Well manage, appreciate and conserve the excellence of the Lord's gift - the planet.; [a.] Auburndale, NY

HYDE, PATRICIA M.
[pen.] Tracy T. Brady; [b.] March 25, 1944, Olean, NJ; [p.] Gertrude and Ronald Pierce; [m.] Donald Hyde, August 1, 1964; [ch.] Michelle, Michael, Tracia, Troy; [ed.] Scio High, Olean Business Institute; [occ.] Medical Secretary, James Barke M.D., Shinglehouse, PA; [memb.] St. Theresa Catholic Church; [pers.] This poem "Speak My Name" was inspired by God after the lost of our son. Only to hear his name mentioned and the pain softened, and to live on positively.; [a.] Shinglehouse, PA

IMERI, PAL
[pen.] P.I.; [b.] June 20, 1960, Albania; [p.] Mhill Imeri, Hana Imeri; [m.] Rusha Imeri, February 5, 1989; [ch.] Michael Imeri, Hana Imeri; [ed.] High School; [oth. writ.] Children magazine pioneer in Albenia.; [a.] Bronx, NY

INGRASSIA, KATHLEEN
[pen.] KathLeen Lopez Ingrassia; [b.] December 1, 1968, Patchogue Long Island, NY; [p.] Carlos and Eddia Lopez; [m.] Salvatore A. Ingrassia, June 4, 1987; [ch.] Christina Marie and Melissa Ann Ingrassia; [ed.] Bay Port/Blue Point H.S.; [occ.] Nurse Aide, Homemaker; [oth. writ.] This is the first of my poems to be published. I have many other writings which I hope to be published someday.; [pers.] I feel that everyone is gifted with a special talent. I hope that my poetry can inspire and give hope to all who read them. If my words can touch you're heart and soul then I've accomplish my goal and have used God's greatest gift to touch others peoples lives; [a.] Centereach Long Island, NY

INTHASONE, THAVISOUK
[b.] July 23, 1972, Savannakhet, Laos; [p.] Inthasone, Kosinh and Thipkaysone; [ed.] Graduated from Woodrow Wilson High School; [occ.] Unemployed; [pers.] I like to write about a real human characteristic, good or bad, not as an advocate or opposition to the function of it but as a rock-rigid idea or which the performer can full back to or any other person who are distracted by an unrealistic forces; [a.] Dallas, TX

IRELAND, MARY C.
[b.] September 17, 1969, Pomona, CA; [p.] John and Diane Ireland; [m.] Michael P. Kunze, October 11, 1994; [ed.] Etiwanda High School, California State Polytechnic University, Pomona; [occ.] Geoscientist at an Environmental Engineering Firm; [hon.] Cum Laude; [pers.] I write poetry for recreation. My inspiration is life and love. I am excited to share my poem with others.; [a.] Costa Mesa, CA

ISAACSON, IDA ARNOLD
[b.] December 17, 1907, Monroe, UT; [p.] Charles and Moud Arnold; [m.] Eddie Isaacson (deceased, September 21, 1990), December 23, 1927; [ch.] 1 Son Dr. E. D. Isaacson; [ed.] Grade School, High school, 2 yrs Snow College, Junior College and 2 yrs Mission with Eddie, husband, married almost 63 yrs.; [occ.] I am 88 yrs. at home; [memb.] Utah Poetry Society who put a star in place for me like the night of the nativity? Who has not made glad and helped another or his way has failed his noblest impulses His counsel to obey: There is no grandeur like the shape of kindness; [hon.] Many poems bought by Relief Womens Society of Church of Jesus Christ of Father Day Saints; [oth. writ.] I have a Book of Poetry many poems published love, my soul goes seeking Marian Anderson, this is my country, our country, our land; [pers.] The Russian writer Solitary said - God is my Desire; [a.] Salt Lake City, UT

ISBELL, ESTEENE JOHNSON
[pen.] "Roses In The Sand"; [b.] November 15, 1955, Birmingham, AL; [p.] Horace and Kathryn Johnson; [m.] Timothy Louis Isbell, September 5, 1992; [ch.] Jimmy, David, and Crystal; [pers.] This poem is dedicated to all the American Roses who sacrificed their own interests

and concerns for the sake of freedom. During Operation Desert Storm, which took place during 1990-1991. God bless each of them.; [a.] Columbiana, AL

ISKRA, ANNE
[b.] June 29, 1977, Geelong, Australia; [p.] Lydia Iskra; [ed.] Westville High School, In; [occ.] Student - Deakin University Australia.; [oth. writ.] None published as yet; [pers.] Written words are the greatest legacy any person can create. They are like an eternal flame, leaving in their wake, a thousand memories.; [a.] Geelong, Victoria, Australia

ISMET, SOEMARWENI
[pen.] Weni Ismet; [b.] June 9, 1926, Yogyakarta, Indonesia; [p.] Soeprapti Joedo, R. M. Gondhosoewirjo; [m.] Ismet, April 12, 1948; [ch.] Latifah Hanoem, Omar Faizal, Macmoud Hassan, Fauzia Meidina; [ed.] Senior High School, Teachers's Course; [occ.] Lecturer in Seminars, Courses, Women Circles.; [memb.] Subject: Etiquette and Personality. Helping people regain their health and self assurance.; [oth. writ.] Several poems published in local newspapers, foreign magazine. Personal poems for special events.; [pers.] Expressing my gratitude towards God's guidance by letting others understand the meaning of Life through duty, love and giving.; [a.] Sawangan, Indonesia

ISQUR, DAVID
[b.] September 17, 1957, Boston, MA; [p.] Irving Isqur, Arlene Noodell Isqur; [ed.] Framingham (MA) North High School Boston University; [occ.] Editor, The Hartford Business Journal; [memb.] Amnesty International, The Nature Conservancy, U.S. Holocaust Memorial Museum, and American Indian Relief Association; [hon.] New England Press Association awards for editorial and business writing; [oth. writ.] Several lyrics that have been performed by local musicians; [pers.] I write to tell the story of the emotions that we feel in being human. And I thank all the people who've supported me in the efforts to say these words.; [a.] West Hartford, CT

IVEY, COWANNA RAINES
[pen.] Cowanna Raines Ivey; [b.] December 17, 1944, Okla City, OK; [p.] Clarence and Davelene Raines; [m.] Donald Ivey, November 23, 1990; [ed.] G. E. D.; [occ.] Cashier; [memb.] Eastern Star; [pers.] Influenced by the love given to me thru out life. My desire is for the world to appreciate how precious, how powerful love and kidness, for it last beyond a life time. The greatest gift one can give to another; [a.] Shawnee, OK

IVIE, KEVIN F. M.
[b.] February 21, 1970, Metheum, MA; [p.] Kenneth and Jeanne Ivie; [m.] Andrea Ivie, August 20, 1994; [ed.] Palmdale High School; [occ.] Security Officer, Lancaster, CA; [pers.] The poems I write are the personal insights of the surroundings of our planet names earth. Love and life poetry are my greatest accomplishments.; [a.] Lancaster, CA

JACKSON, ARLENE D.
[b.] October 9, 1953, Saint Louis; [p.] Jimmie and Earline Franklin; [m.] Willie C. Jackson, April 22; [ch.] Lynnetta, Keithen, Ciarra and Michelle; [ed.] Associate Degrees - St. Louis Comm. College, Bachelor's Degree - Washington University; [occ.] Programmer, Analyst, Washington University; [memb.] Eugene B. Redmond Writers Club; [hon.] Phi Theta Kappa, Semi-finalist in National Library of Poetry contest; [oth. writ.] Several poems published in local magazines and in Limelight magazine.

JACKSON, DAPHNE
[b.] January 11, 1933, Bowen, Queens Land, Australia; [p.] Robert and Ada Selby-Hele; [m.] William George Jackson, August 23, 1952; [ch.] Peter, Christopher, Michael, Glenn and Lisa; [ed.] Yallourn High School, Camberwell High School; [occ.] Part time child-carer and home duties; [oth. writ.] Several poems and letters plus two childrens stories. Not yet presented for publication

JACKSON, DAWN
[b.] November 26, 1972, Waterbury; [p.] Mr. and Mrs. Jeffrey Dupre; [m.] Mr. Michael A. Jackson, December 27, 1992; [ed.] I attended Kaynor Tech. High School and took up fashion design.; [occ.] I'm attending M.E.T.C. in Waterbury for medical trans.; [memb.] V.I.C.A. for two years ; [hon.] I won a medal in a fashion design contest; [oth. writ.] I've had three poems for mother's day published in the local newspapers. [pers.] I know if I put my mind to anything I can do anything, To be strong is to never go wrong and to strive is to stay alive. I thank God for everything I can do!; [a.] Waterbury, CI

JACKSON, GERALD R.
[b.] October 30, 1957, Portland, OR; [p.] Clyde Jackson, Sandra Larson; [ch.] Shiela Marie Torkelson; [ed.] Jefferson High, Anoka Technical College; [occ.] Brazing, Thermo King Inc.; [oth. writ.] Other poems not yet published. Reminiscing, forever bonding love, searching no more.; [pers.] I enjoy putting true feelings into words for all to share and for whom may find difficult to express. Words not only from within myself, but from the hearts of many. I hope to share these feelings through greeting cards also.; [a.] Burnsville, MN

JACKSON, KATASHA
[pen.] Mouse; [b.] September 20, 1979, Winchester, VA; [p.] Pamela Roberts; [ed.] Presently in tenth grade, Hampshire High; [occ.] Student aspiring author; [pers.] People everywhere need to help put an end to racist cowards and try and be true to one another.; [a.] Romney, VA

JACOB, S. FRANCES
[p.] John B. and S. Cheatham Jacob; [ed.] M.A., Middlebury French School, Ph.D., Tulane University; [memb.] Eta Sigma Phi, Phi Sigma Iota, Delta Kappa Gamma; [hon.] A winning entry in Japanese haiku contest. Invitation to work with young dramatics in Theatre National Populaire of Paris; [oth. writ.] Several poems in magazines. "Joey", short story in Colorado Quarterly. Steel and Stars, self-published poems distinguishable from prose. Le Chasseur d'Etoiles, French play satirizing the history of mankind.; [pers.] The erasure of structural differences between prose and poetry may enrich the first but may improverish the second.; [a.] Staunton, VA

JACOBS, RICK
[b.] January 10, 1945, Akron OH; [p.] Otis/Judy Jacobs; [m.] Winnie Jacobs, July 25, 1981; [ch.] Richard, Debbie, Kim, Cathy, David, Tim, Kris, Ed; [ed.] High School - Green High Greenburg Ohio; [occ.] Store Manager Builders Square/Canton Ohio

JACQUES, EVE
[b.] April 21, 1921, Trinidad, CO; [p.] Luciano and Virginia Romero; [m.] Frank Jacques, April 21, 1949; [ch.] Juliette, Jeanette, Frank, Annette and Paulette; [ed.] University of New Mexico, Albuquerque - World War II Veteran (served in Asiatic-Pacific Theatre); [occ.] Retired from UC Berkeley (Administrative Asst to Director of Bancroft Library); [memb.] VFW; [hon.] Awarded 7 Military Medals; [oth. writ.] My String of Petals (1988); [pers.] Wisdom consists in knowing what to do with what you know; [a.] Pinole, CA

JACQUES, PENELOPE
[pen.] Penelope Portrait; [b.] London, England; [occ.] Journalist, Novelist, Fashion Consultant; [memb.] Anglo-American Press Association of Paris, The Fashion Group of Paris; [hon.] Medaille D'Argent de la Ville de Paris. (French Silver Medal of Paris in honor a book called "Patience Penelope") written in French.; [oth. writ.] "London Daily Mirror" Paris-based correspondent 10 yrs. Award winning novelist. "Patience Penelope". "A Pennyworth of Paris". Also "Gertrudes Gift" a novel now being considered for a film.

JAMES, IRMA D.
[pen.] Irma D. James; [p.] John and Daisy Dotson; [ed.] Monroe High School Albany State College, Alban, GA. University of Dayton, Dayton, Ohio; [occ.] Business/vocational teacher, Paul Laurence Dunbar High School - Dayton, Ohio; [memb.] Dayton Education Association, National Education Association, Vocational/Business Ed. Assn., Albany State College National Association, Inc.; [hon.] Dean's list National Honor Society Citizenship Award Certificate of Appreciation, Black College Tours, Inc.; [oth. writ.] Songs and Poems, poem accepted for publication by grand Recording Co., Quincy, MA; [pers.] I try to reflect the love and happiness that I feel in my heart in my writings, because I feel that love and happiness are special gifts from God.; [a.] Dayton, OH

JAMES, LINDSAY
[b.] January 30, 1983, Greenwich, CT; [p.] Debra James, William H. James; [ed.] 6th grade New Canaan Country School, New Canaan, CT; [occ.] Student; [a.] Stamford, CT

JAMIS, JEAN BOLENDER
[b.] St. Paul, MN; [p.] Harold Bolender, M.D, Hazel DuMez; [ch.] Lee Larson III, Dave Larson, Jeanelle La Walker, Kari Larson.; [ed.] 1. Webster University, St. Paul, MN, 2. Luther Seminary, St. Paul, MN, 1. BA. Music Education, 2. Master of Divinity; [occ.] Chaplaincy Intern at North Dakota State Hospital; [memb.] Coordinator of Volunteer Training, Prison Fellowship Minnesota and North Dakota; [oth. writ.] One poem published in local newspaper; [pers.] Poetry and music are paintings of the soul; [a.] Jamestown, ND

JANETZKE, JENNIFER
[b.] March 29, 1974, Oak Lawn, IL; [p.] Thomas and Monica Janetzke; [ed.] Queen of Peace High School, Moraine Valley Community College, Saint Xavier University; [occ.] Student at Saint Xavier University Major: Math, Minor: Education; [hon.] Award for academic excellence in Pre-Calculus, Dean's List; [pers.] I owe my inspirations to my first and only love, John, who has allowed me to see the beauty of life and love.; [a.] Hickory Hills, IL

JASKULSKY, LEANN M.
[pen.] Leann M. Jaskulsky; [b.] June 23, 1981, Torrance, CA; [p.] Richard Jr., Joyce Jaskulsky; [ed.] 8th grade (still in school) [occ.] Student; [memb.] CJSF (California Junior Scholarship Federation); [hon.] Presidential Academic Fitness Award, Student of the month, Ms. Junior America East Palmdale. [pers.] In poems I write it is

my true feelings. I have been influenced by my dear two neighbors Michael (most greatly) and Robert Campa.; [a.] Palmdale, CT

JENNY, BRET T.
[b.] April 18, 1976, Platteville, WI; [p.] Tom and Karen Jenny; [ed.] Belmont High College, Freshman - Edgewood College, Madison, WI; [occ.] Student [a.] Belmont, WI

JENSEN, TERRYL ESTHER
[pen.] Terry Esther Jensen; [b.] May 19, 1943, Hanover, NH; [p.] Orrin K. and Marjorie A. Chapin; [m.] S. Richard Jensen, October 9, 1982; [ch.] His 5, mine 2, our grandchildren 11; [ed.] Orford High School, Orford, N.H., Practical Estate School, Hartford, Vermont Famous Artist's School (Correspondence Course); [occ.] Tax Clerk-Mechanic falls, ME. Tutor-Gray-New Gloucester High School, Gray, ME.; [oth. writ.] Numerous poems 2 childrens' books; [pers.] Take time from your schedule to help people. It benefits you both.; [a.] Minot, ME

JERGOVIC, ZORICA
[b.] May 6, 1973, Croatia; [p.] Martin Jergovic, Milka Jergovic; [ch.] Never been married; [ed.] St. Raymonds Jr High (Ottawa) Highland Park High School (Ottawa) St. Catherin High (Hamilton); [hon.] Honor roll student of Highland Park H.S.; [oth. writ.] The sight of light. In memory of my father Martin Jergovic. (Unpublished) various poems writen.; [pers.] My inspiration on poetry has inspired other's as the influence and inspiration of Victor Hugo who I admire for his great writing, and poems. And to my sister Katie who encouraged me. Also Victor Hugo a dramatist, poet, and novelist. Best-known novel Les Miserables, was published in ten languages.; [a.] Ottawa Kanata, Canada

JHALA, ANGMA
[b.] April 26, 1978, Cambridge, MA; [p.] Tayasinhji and Rakhi Jhala; [ed.] Junior year at the Lawrenceville school Lawrenceville, New Jersey. Precious schools, the Shipley School, Princeton Day School and The Winsor School.; [occ.] High school student.; [hon.] First prize from the Rider College writing contest for fiction publication of my poem Italy in the under age magazine of Princeton. Dean's list. Silver Medal from the National Latin Association.; [oth. writ.] A novel entitled Sonna's Story written at the age of nine.; [pers.] I began writing at nine, when my parents were doing field work in India. Writing is a crucial part of my being, a way of portraying unspoken, hidden feelings. I am indebted to my parents, my loving sister, Mapu Chacha, Richard and Gran; [a.] Princeton, NJ

JOHNSON, CHERYL R.
[pen.] Rose Johnson; [b.] June 6, 1961, Winchester, VA; [p.] Curley Johnson, Mary Johnson; [m.] Divorced; [ch.] Erica Rose Liggins; [ed.] John Handley High School; [occ.] Technical Writer, American Woodmark Corporation; [memb.] St. Luke Baptist Church; [hon.] Received Honorable Mention in previous poetry contest.; [oth. writ.] Numerous poems written and recited at various community functions. Commentary written for and published by the local newspaper.; [pers.] Through God Almighty, all things are possible. "You also have the right to break the limits of the past and to build for yourself a brand new future for limits are made of glass." Rose Johnson; [a.] Winchester, VA

JOHNSON, DUANE F.
[b.] December 18, 1916, New Mexico; [m.] Jeanne E. Johnson, January 12, 1943; [ch.] Cynthia; [ed.] American U - One Year U of Cal - One Year U of Southern Cal - 3 Years; [occ.] Retired; [oth. writ.] Various poems; [pers.] Poetry is truly a universal language, since it expresses feelings which are human and universal.; [a.] Fullerton, CA

JOHNSON, JAMES ROBERT
[pen.] Robble Johnson; [b.] July 29, 1973, United Kingdom; [p.] Carol, James; [m.] Christina L. McCabe; [ed.] Bitburg High (Germany), Thomas Nelson Community College; [occ.] Pizza Delivery; [pers.] I dedicate my first publication to my granddad, "Jake the Fireman" let this be the first of many!; [a.] Hampton, VA

JOHNSON, KEN
[b.] October 1, 1948, Birmingham, AL; [p.] Mr. and Mrs. H. L. Johnson; [m.] Sherry, October 5, 1968; [ch.] Daryl 22, Dee Dee 15; [ed.] Woodlawn High School, Jefferson State Jr. Col., University of Alabama Birmingham, B.S. Degree Lang. Arts Secondary Edu.; [occ.] Teacher - Middle School Lang. Arts Eight Grade; [hon.] WBMG T.V. Golden Apple Award - education '91, Outstanding Reading Teacher Award Feb '93 from Law Firm of Balch and Bingham; [a.] Birmingham, AL

JOHNSON, KIU-MONIQUE
[b.] January 28, 1968, Wyandanch, NY; [p.] Alicia Johnson, James Johnson; [ed.] BA Psychology - Johns Hopkins University MSW, SUNY at Stony Brook; [occ.] HIV Program Coordinator; [memb.] National Association of Black Social Workers, Delta Sigma Theta Sorority, Inc.; [hon.] NAACP Youth Chapter Image Award, Dean's List JHU; [pers.] "To seek beauty in each day to celebrate the smile evoked by the simple things, and to share the blessings from the Creator, gives my life meaning and reason to write."; [a.] Amityville Long Island, NY

JOHNSON, KRISTIE
[b.] November 28, 1976, Broken Bow, NE; [p.] Marvin and Linda Johnson; [ed.] Senior at Broken Bow High School; [oth. writ.] Poem published by Reflections; [a.] Broken Bow, NE

JOHNSON, LARRY
[b.] January 24, 1950, Pascola, MO; [p.] Dester and Johnny Johnson; [m.] Divorced; [ch.] Melvin-Tasha Johnson; [ed.] High School Graduate; [occ.] Warehouseman; [pers.] I've been writing poems since the sixth grade, I'm living proof you can be good at whatever you set your goals to be.

JOHNSON, MARK
[b.] April 15, 1971, Saint Charles, MO; [p.] Roy and Beverly Johnson; [ed.] Bachelor of Arts in Music Merchandising Southern Illinois University at Edwardsville; [occ.] Music Teacher (Guitar and Music Theory); [hon.] Dean's List; [oth. writ.] Hundreds of poems/lyrics; [pers.] Visualization is the key to successful writing.....and is also the key to successful reading!; [a.] Glen Carbon, IL

JOHNSON, MARVIN THOMAS
[pen.] PJ; [b.] March 15, 1958, Montgomery, AL; [p.] Mr. and Mrs. Thomas Marvin Johnson; [ed.] William Burns Patterson-Elem. Franklin Elem. Jones Junior High Massillon Washington High - Alabama State University; [occ.] Health-Care Giver; [memb.] Massillon-NAACP PJ's Bar Essence Productions [founder]; [hon.] 8th grade city wide Wrestling Champion - Drama Club S.u.c.c.e.s.s Club Debate Team (Washington High) Akron Community Choir Member - Alabama State Choral Singer - Young Hearts Gospel Singer!; [oth. writ.] (Published poem - our words favorite poems [Who Am I] (Unpublished material) PJ Flair Vol. 1 and 2 /PJ's Chronicles Metamorphosis - butterfly to eagle! (etc.); [pers.] PJ's quotes from yond ashes I have arose to put together these mystical proses. Life is like a seed that is sowed nurtured by light and respect - beautifully bestowed!; [a.] Montgomery, AL

JOHNSON, PAMELA DANIELLE
[pen.] Johnson, Pamela; [b.] December 17, 1982, Detroit, MI; [p.] Josephine Evans, Vincent Johnson; [memb.] I am in middle school right now. 6th grade McClure Middle School; [hon.] Honor Roll, Mathematics Award, Perfect Attendance; [oth. writ.] My Dog Scorpi (story); [pers.] I am 12 years old. I was eleven when I wrote. I got this idea after having an argument when my friend did not believe me. Play the flute, have one younger brother and like cooking, participated in Southern Arizona Honor Band.; [a.] Seattle, WA

JOHNSON, PATRICIA LYNNE
[b.] January 30, 1965, Omaha, NE; [p.] Kyle D. and Carley J. Daugherty; [m.] Brent S. Johnson, September 14, 1985; [ch.] Katherine Christine, Clinton Tremain; [ed.] Peoria High School (Ariz.) Institute of children's literature; [occ.] Housewife; [pers.] I watch to see where a need is, and if I can, I meet it.; [a.] Corpus Christi, TX

JOHNSON, PETRA
[b.] May 21, 1977, San Fernando, Trinidad; [p.] Patricia and Carlton Johnson; [ed.] Sheepshead Bay High School; [pers.] One of my purpose in life is to help others. To inspire, to teach and to open blind eyes to the world's beauty in my writing. My inspirations came from God, my parents, famous writers and teachers.; [a.] Brooklyn, NY

JOHNSON, TOSHA
[pen.] Tee or TJ; [b.] October 16, 1975, Baltimore, MD; [p.] Sherry and William Johnson; [ed.] Northwestern Highland Fairmount Harford Institute; [occ.] Administrative Assistant; [memb.] Academic Champions of Excellence (ACE Program) Academic Boosters Club (ABC); [hon.] Honor and success roll; [oth. writ.] Several poems published in Complimentary newspapers.; [pers.] I sincerely wish the words of my poem positively inspire the lives of other individuals. I would also like to thank God for my rare and unique art. It has truly been a blessing.; [a.] Baltimore, MD

JOHNSON, WALTER L.
[b.] September 6, 1945, Missouri, KC; [p.] Bernice Johnson, Lawrence (deceased); [m.] Sara Raines (engaged); [ch.] Andre Johnson; [ed.] 1 yr. College; [occ.] Part time Skill Labor; [memb.] Church of Christ; [hon.] Couple are poem in past honorary merit awards and Bible coarse award, Merit Awards in USMC; [oth. writ.] Sara Raines; [pers.] I plan to continue writing poetry

JOHNSTON, VICTORIA
[b.] October 11, 1984, Ormstown, Quebec, Canada; [p.] Suzanne and William Johnston; [ed.] Grade 3 (1993-94), Ormstown Elementary School; [occ.] School/student; [hon.] Chateauguay Valley Young Writer's contest, 1991 kindergarden (English) prose 1992 grade 1 (French) prose; [oth. writ.] Budding student of nature, ardent admirer of nature in her serene and simplistic serenity. Joyous of life from the magnificent to the minute.; [a.] Howick Quebec, Canada.

JONES, ANGELA DAVIS
[b.] February 15, 1949, New York; [p.] Frank and Lillian Davis; [m.] Simon H. C. Jones, April 19, 1969; [ch.] Jason and Christopher; [ed.] Completed 12th grade, currently 2 G.E.D. student at Lehman College; [occ.] Homemaker

JONES, BILLY
[b.] January 16, 1979, Huntington, WV; [p.] Kristopher and Penny Jones; [ed.] 10th grade at Cabell Midland High School; [occ.] Computer aided designer for Hammers Industries, Inc.; [memb.] Boy Scout troop 790 of Barboursville, Lutheran Youth organization at Christ the King Lutheran Church; [hon.] 1st degree Black Belt in Champion Karate, 1994-1995 Hugh O'Brian Youth Leadership Participant National English Merit Award (NEMA) nominee.; [pers.] If poetry comes as natural as the leaves of a tree, it better not come at all.; [a.] Barboursville, WV

JONES, DINA C.
[b.] December 30, 1964, Tennessee; [p.] Ann Jones; [ed.] Completing Bachelor's; [occ.] Marketing Coordinator; [memb.] Skyline Wesleyan Church, Toast Master's International; [hon.] He demanded: Tell Me You Love Me, Desire's Cry, Why, Joyous Tomorrow; [oth. writ.] My poetry comes from my heart. As my life changes: the good times and the bad, I find it (i.e., life) a teacher. So, I write down both the joy's and the pains of my lessons.; [pers.] San Diego, CA

JONES, DORIS L.
[pen.] Louise; [b.] September 23, 1937, Broken Bow, OK; [p.] Jim Flowers, Ethel Flowers; [m.] David L. Jones, December 26, 1980; [ch.] Trent, Kevin, Michael Lucas; [ed.] High School, Klamath Union, Klamath Fan's, Oregon; [occ.] Housewife; [oth. writ.] Several poems unpublished, I have never entered my poems on the encouragement of my husband and mother I did enter "To The One I Love" you have made my days happy ones; [pers.] The poems that I have written have been inspired by my love of my family, and my eyes and heart that God has given to me to see and feel the beautiful world around me!; [a.] Citrus Heights, CA

JONES, GEORGIA ANN KNOWLES
[pen.] George; [b.] December 28, 1919, Alabama; [p.] Maude and Roscoe Knowles; [m.] Willis Jones Sr. (deceased), April 22, 1939; [ch.] Lanita, Mary, Amelia, Willis Jr., Maureen; [ed.] High School - 2 year Jr., College - 2 years night school, Home Eck., Dressmaking Arts and Crafts - Beauty culture.; [occ.] Retired-widowed, Cook; [memb.] Trinity United Church of Christ 532-400 West 95th St. Jeremiah A. Wright Jr, Pastor - also Carter Temple Jr - C.M.E., Church Trinity - 12 yrs, Carter Temple - 10 yrs, L.L. Barnes Pastor; [hon.] Woman of the Year from Carter Temple - 4000 members, Mother of Year Carter Temple, President - Senior group, 13 years awards, trophy's, 3 certificates, 5 plucks, 4 member active seniors - T.U.C.C.; [oth. writ.] For Church publications I wrote - Black Boy, "Free At Last". "The Traveler", all of my writings are purely inspirational, I love writing and reading poetry.; [pers.] Poems above was published only in Church wide study book of Trinity U.C.C. 1978-79. Favorite books are literature, poetry, Bible. I enjoy helping others. Doing art quilting. Other poems - Gods Paint Brush; [a.] Chicago, IL

JONES, GERALDINE MARTHA
[pen.] G. Martha Jones; [b.] October 10, 1920, Wenatchee, WA; [p.] Shedrick H. and Ellen Jane Jones; [ed.] Univ. of Washington, U.S.C., Los Angeles, U.S.I.U., San Diego; [occ.] Free-lance writer, church musician, retired teacher-administrator; [memb.] Alpha Kappa Alpha Sorority, writers way workshop, older women's league, United States International University Alumni; [hon.] Woman of distinction, San Diego women, incorporated; [oth. writ.] Letters to the editor, M. A. project on human relations in the classroom, Ph.D dissertation on comparative topical newspaper coverage; [pers.] Lord, may I pass on my life's gleanings via God-given talents of writing, musicianship, and complete love for all humanity; [a.] San Diego, CA

JONES, JANICE COX
[pen.] Janice Cox; [b.] November 4, 1937, Jackson, MS; [p.] Eugene Debs Cox, Thelma Beard Cox; [ch.] Allison Jones Sterling, Tamara Jones McKee; [ed.] Central High, Jackson, MS, Mississippi College, Clinton, MS, BS in El. Ed. University of Miami, Miami, FL, M. Ed. in El. Ed; [occ.] Elementary Teacher, Dale County Public Schools, Miami, Fl; [memb.] Tropical Audubon Society, Education Committee and Writer for Dade Heritage Trust, Fairchild Tropical Gardens, Miami Writer's Club, Florida Freelance Writers Association Miami Arts Exchange Council of International Visitors University Baptist Church of Coral Gables, FL; [hon.] Who's Who in American Colleges and Universities Who's Who in Education Profiled in newspaper and television locally, nationally, and internationally as mother and teacher while managing world wide modeling and acting career of young daughter Tamara Jones in late 70's and 80's, appearances on Merv Griffin TV, PM Magazine, etc.; [oth. writ.] "Romance of the Pineapple and the Rainbow", a poster of photography and poetry of Hawaii, Haiku series in Japan 4,3,2,1, Italy while in Italy, Geography Fun Facts: A Historical Trip in Poetry Across the USA - book that is presently in classroom testing in several states, "On Becoming a Model: The Photographs"; [pers.] I like to travel the world and look for insight on the meaning of life at each place. I reflect on it in poetry as I return home.; [a.] Miami, FL

JONES JR., CLARENCE E.
[b.] December 6, 1965, Washington, DC; [p.] Clarence E. Jones Sr., Ozabelle Jones; [ed.] University of the District of Columbia, Degree: Computer Science; [occ.] Computer Scientist, Department of Defense - Inspector General; [memb.] American Registry of Song-writers Association.; [hon.] Recently, I received Civilian of the Quarter, a prestigious career award, for outstanding job performance at the Department of Defense.; [pers.] All praise go out to God for making this possible! Special thanks go out to my mother and sister for inspiring and encouraging me to write and all of my extended family for their support. This poem is dedicated to my father, Clarence E. Jones Sr.; [a.] Washington, DC

JONES, KAREN
[b.] August 9, 1962, Rush Memorial Hospital, Rushville, IN; [p.] Edwin Mofield and Margaret Mofield; [m.] Dwayne Jones, August 11, 1979; [ch.] Michael D., Christopher J. and Amanda Nichole; [ed.] Rushville Consolidated High School; [occ.] Inspector at Ford Electronics and Refrigeration; [memb.] Garrison Creek Baptist Church, member of Hose Connection News Letter Team at Ford in Connersville; [oth. writ.] Several articles published in the Hose Connection, one of my stories was picked to be sent to the Library of Congress during my sophomore year in high school.; [pers.] I want to show all the people who don't have a formal education that with God they can be anything they want to be. I admire the writings of Helen Steiner Rice.; [a.] Rushville, IN

JONES, KENNETH R.
[b.] November 20, 1972, Tarboro, NC; [p.] Joseph Jones, Ethel Jones; [ed.] North Edgecombe High School, North Carolina Agricultural and Technical State University; [occ.] Full-time student; [memb.] Golden Key National Honor Society, Gamma Sigma Delta Honor Society, Agricultural Education Assn, Minorities in Agricultural and Natural Resource Related Sciences (MANRRS), peer advisor, Alpha Phi Alpha Fraternity, Inc.; [hon.] Chancellor's Scholar, who's who among colleges and universities, Dean's list (campus and national), North Carolina College Brother of the year AOA (1994-95); [oth. writ.] Several inspirational speeches for campus/community seminars and programs; [pers.] Poetry has to come from within. If I don't receive the "urge of expression" to inspire me, my poems are less effective in meaning. Most of my writing comes from true life experiences and my views on certain people, issues, etc. as you can tell in this poem of how I speak of..."my one true love.; [a.] Tarboro, NC

JONES, LLOYD
[pen.] Ken Jones; [b.] February 20, 1932, Trinidad and Tobago; [p.] Ewen and Victoria Jones; [m.] Cynthia Jones, September 16, 1962; [ch.] Kamella Sherman, Kary Anne Beddoe Grand Children. Jordane, Christopher Joshua Sherman: Corey and Sterra; [ed.] Queen's Royal College Trinidad and Tobago; [occ.] Semi retired; [oth. writ.] Former newspaper reporter in Trinidad and Tobago; [pers.] I thank God for giving me the gift of expressing my love for him and the concern of the children of the world in my writings.

JONES, LYNN
[b.] December 20, 1954, New York City; [p.] Dr. Vert and Ruth Mooney; [m.] Michael T. Jones, September 13, 1977; [ch.] Grace Lynn, Patrick Michael, Kenneth Vert, Adam Robert; [ed.] Downey Sr. High School, Westmont College, Cal State Fullerton (B.A. in English) 1978 secondary teacher's credential in English; [occ.] Home School parent, free-lance writer; [hon.] 1982, teacher of the Year Award at a private high school, 1972, talent winner for song and piano, fourth runner up for Miss Downey Contest, recipient of 3 certificates of completion from fundamentals of speaking, toastmaster classes; [oth. writ.] Essay, winner in grade school, article about men on the moon in local newspaper, currently I write for an Evangelistic newsletter "Images Through God's Eyes"; [pers.] As an Evangelical Christian, I endeavor to give God glory in all that I do and also strive for excellence. Helen Steiner Rice and Ann Kiemel Anderson are two Christian poets and authors who have inspired me.; [a.] Simi Valley, CA

JONES, MARJEL MARIE BARNES
[pen.] Marjel Jones; [b.] March 1, 1947, Richmond, CA; [p.] Howard C. and Maxine D. Barnes; [m.] John C. Jones, March 30, 1974; [ch.] 5 children J. Gabriel, Samuel Emily Isaac and Zachary (twins); [ed.] West Anchorage High, University of Alaska; [occ.] Homemaker; [pers.] "When I find something worthy to write about, I shall write." This I knew deep inside. Then on July 2, 1972, I met the Son of God. I found "He who is worthy." He gives me my philosophy, inspiration and purpose. I simply try to give back what He as so generously given me... worth.; [a.] Mount Pleasant, NC

JONES, MARK F.
[b.] January 15, 1966, Jamaica; [p.] Muriel Townsend, Hector Jones; [ed.] St. George's College University of the West Indies (Jamaica), Loyola University (Chicago,

IL); [occ.] Student at Jesuit School of Theology at Berkeley, CA; [oth. writ.] Several other poems for my own personal pleasure.; [pers.] I try to capture the human struggle that exists in the human heart. I believe in the victory of life and goodness.; [a.] Berkeley, CA

JONES, NATASHA RENEE
[pen.] Tasha; [b.] December 6, 1977, Jefferson, CO; [p.] Mr. and Mrs. Michael and Teresa Jones; [ed.] 10 Grade (Sophomore) Ensley Magnet High School; [memb.] JROTC, Metropolitan A.M.E. Zion Church Youth, Progressive, Mass Choir, Usher Board, and Vice President of the Youth Choir.; [hon.] The 1994 Keys to the Future Creative Writing Award.; [pers.] As a 17 year old being poetic is truly a gift from God. Poetry has always been my way of expressing my feelings. It's not all about putting words that sound alike together, it's more deep rooted, it's more like using your imagination to express your feelings. You should reconize your gift and strive to your upmost to do good and let nothing block your path. David in the book Psalms 125:1, said, "Those who trust in the Lord are like Mount Zion, which cannot be shaken but endures forever."; [a.] Birmingham, AL

JONES, PATRICIA
[pen.] P. J.; [b.] October 5, 1951, Detroit; [p.] Drexel and Louie Proctor; [ch.] Tyrone, Alesha, and Joey; [ed.] Working on Bachelors in communications; [occ.] Managing a gift shop; [memb.] Church - New Liberty Baptist Church; [oth. writ.] Author of "I Can't Let Go"; [pers.] All things work out in time.; [a.] Detroit, MI

JONES, SANDRA MOON
[b.] January 2, 1948, Washington; [p.] D. Julius Ellis and Evelyn Augusta (Best) Moon; [m.] M. Ronald Edwin Jones, December 14, 1985; [ch.] One son, Daniel; [ed.] BA, Fed. City Coll., 1975, MS, U.D.C., 1978, MA in Administer. and Supervision, 1992.; [occ.] Day Care Administrator, small business owner, D.C. Transp. Pub. Space Project, 1982-83 Vol. libr., Lorton (Va.) Reformatory Youth Ctr., 1979-80, co-founder Neighborhood Watch Program, Washington, 1981, community coord., 1987 V.P. of 6th district adv. council., 1982-83, historian for East Washington Park Citizens Assn., 1982-84, editor, 1982-83. Recipient of grass roots award from D.C. Fedn. Civic Assns., 1983. Mem. ALA, D.C. Libr. Assn., Prince Georges County Day Care Assn., Prince George County Day Care Resource Ctr.; [memb.] Administrv. Specialist Immigration and Naturalization Svc., Wash, 1975-79, Archivist Nat. Archives and Record Svc., Washington, 1980-82, libr. D.C. Pub. Schs., 1983-93, adminstr, parks/coop. play program Langston Pre-Sch., Washington, 1993-94 owner, dir. Evelyn-Ron Day Care, Clinton, MD., 1994; [hon.] Who's Who Among Students in American Universities and Colleges, 1992, Who's Who in the East, 1991-92, Who's Who in American Education, 1992-93. Democrat. Prebysterian.; [oth. writ.] From Dust to Dawn: A successful Literary Society - published 1977 by The Assac, for the Study of Afro-American Life and History's Negro History Bulletin; [pers.] One of my favorite quotation, "No star is ever lost we once have seen" - author unknown

JONES, SUSAN R.
[b.] March 27, 1940, Washington, DC; [m.] Divorced; [ch.] Andrea, James, Jr., Jon-Michael; [ed.] Gaithersburg High School, Gaithersburg, MD - 1958; [occ.] Retired from 27 years of Federal employ - 1994, as a Para-Legal and Executive Secretary; [memb.] National Association of Retired Federal Employees; [hon.] Department of Housing and Urban Development, U.S. Navy; [oth. writ.] "Ramblings of My Mind" copyrighted 1994 - a collection of poems and essays; [pers.] I desire to convey peace, joy and love in everything that I do and in doing so, to help make the world a better place.; [a.] Long Beach, CA

JONES, TERRY
[b.] November 1, 1970, Chicago, IL; [p.] Margaret Jones; [m.] (Future spouse) Tisha Johnson, September 1995; [ed.] Simeon Voc. High School; [occ.] Mail Processor, Kemper Financial Services; [memb.] Church of God Chicago IL, Illinois Youth Center-Warrenville Volunteer; [hon.] Outstanding volunteer service IYC-Warrenville; [oth. writ.] Several poems that were published; [pers.] The imagination of the mind can create anything it conjures up. In writing, building, or creating. It can take you as far as you want it to go.; [a.] Chicago, IL

JORDAN, DEBORAH L.
[b.] August 7, 1953, Allentown, PA; [p.] Costella and Edward Torrence; [m.] Phillip J. Jordan Jr., October 1, 1994; [ch.] Robert, Liayn, Daniel, Melissa, Aundrea; [ed.] Wm. Allen High, L.C.C. College; [occ.] Certified Nursing Assistant, and Operating Room Technician; [memb.] National Institute for the Certification of Health Care Processing and Distribution Personnel. Charlered Member of Penna A.C.O.A.; [hon.] 1st prize winner in Nursing Assistant's Magazine, New York, N.Y. 1983 essay on "What it take to make a good nursing asst."; [pers.] I find I am able to express myself, and my inner feelings through my poetry.; [a.] Allentown, PA

JORDAN, THEODORE LEO
[b.] October 2, 1969, Minneapolis, MN; [p.] Leo and Carol Jordan; [ed.] Wayzata Senior High, North Hennepin Technical College, Military Culinary School; [occ.] Chef; [hon.] Numerous Military awards; [oth. writ.] Rainbow Chasing; [pers.] Love who's around you and you'll never fear what's ahead of you.; [a.] Minnetonka, MN

JOSHI, AIDA A.
[b.] July 12, 1935, Daraga Albay, Philippines; [p.] Eufemia Imperial and Jose A. Alcala Sr. (both deceased); [m.] Sudhakar B. Joshi, August 18, 1971; [ed.] Ph. D. and M.A. in Educ., U.C. Berkeley, M. Ed., Univ. of the Philippines, B.S.Ed. St. Thomas Aquinas Univ., Legazpi City, Philippines.; [occ.] Professor of Education, Univ. of San Francisco, S.F., Calif.; [memb.] Professional Organizations in Educ.: ASCD, NCSS, ATE, NAME, World Affairs Council, Life Member, Univ. of California Alumni Assoc., Berkeley, Calif.; [hon.] Recipient of 2 graduate scholarship awards, U.C., Berkeley, awarded by the California Business and Professional Women's Clubs, Recipient of "Outstanding Educator" award by the Filipino Organization of No. Calif.; [oth. writ.] Educational articles in professional magazines i.e. The Social Studies, NAME's Multicultural Educ. Magazine, Textbook series in Social Studies, Elem. grades, Textbooks for Teaching English as a Second Language, Intermediate grades-published in Philippines.; [pers.] Humankind is one big family.; [a.] El Cerrito, CA

JOYCE III, JOHN E.
[b.] April 11, 1955, Morristown, NJ; [p.] John B. Joyce Jr., Lucy C. Joyce; [ch.] Alycia Ann 16, John E. IV 15; [ed.] Delbarton School; [pers.] Thank you God for the strength you give me and all the tools to help me see that if I want to be free sometimes, it will hurt to be...; [a.] Washington, NJ

JOYNER, STEPHANIE R.
[b.] July 20, 1965, Hampton, VA; [p.] Evelyn Colclough; [ch.] Brandi LaShe' Joyner; [ed.] Warwick High School, Several Community Colleges; [occ.] Pre-School teacher at Calvary Christian Academy; [memb.] Calvary Community Church; [oth. writ.] A Worthy Love, The Restoration, A Child Shall Lead Them, God Is Not Color Blind, A Dish Called Family Unity, God's Ten Percent, etc.; [pers.] I dedicate all my writings and poetry to the Lord because He directs my pen.; [a.] Newport News, VA

KACAJ, NDOC TOM
[pen.] "Uncle Tony"; [b.] June 5, 1940, Shkoder, Albania; [p.] Tom Luc Kacaj - Mrika Kacaj; [m.] Diana Gjelikacaj, December 15, 1994; [ch.] Alida (step daughter); [ed.] Drop out eight grade, self taught.; [occ.] Elevator operator at 590 Madison Ave. for 12 years (I.B.M); [memb.] 32 B.J. Union (AFL-CIO), American Conservative Union, Inspector of Board of Election for N.Y. City, a very centered democrat, I do vote for every Republican when they means good for "Uncle Sam"; [hon.] 1958 - Champion of Albanian Youth - Triple Jump Broad. 1961 - The Best Albanian Soldier in all Army Records. 1972 - Swimming the Buna River all dressed up, to the freedom in democracy, U.S.A.; [oth. writ.] A lot of writings but nothing published in Albanian language. Mostly patriotic poems, for Albanian Kosova.; [pers.] "The mother, the teacher, the media, love provide, protect!.." "The higher point of human character: Appreciation of (to) your benefactor!"; [a.] New York, NY

KAELIN, EUGENE J.
[b.] January 28, 1950, North Kingstown, RI; [p.] Fred Kaelin, Winifred Harris; [m.] Diane C. Kaelin, April 30, 1977; [ch.] Craig and Melissa; [ed.] 15 years; [occ.] Production Machinery Mechanic Work on a Naval Base Civil Service; [memb.] NADEA North Island Colorado, CA; [hon.] All League Football Player, Disabled American Veteran (Vietnam Era), Catholic Diocese Teacher, Employee of the Month, Beneficial Suggestion Award, 10 other work related awards, 3 united way eagles; [oth. writ.] Have about 500 different poems some religious and other non-religious. Have 15 works that were put to music.; [pers.] Our lives are governed when we think we are in control by another power which loves us dearly.; [a.] Spring Valley, CA

KANE, EMILY
[b.] June 10, 1978, Manassas, VA; [p.] Susan and Peter Kane; [ed.] So far - Osbourn High School; [occ.] Student; [memb.] National Honor Society, High School Newspaper Staff, Ass. Editor; [hon.] Honor Roll, Academic Letters, Athletic Letters; [oth. writ.] Some poems and short stories will be published in connections, a high school literary magazines; [pers.] I have been greatly influenced by rainy days, wandering minds, and rock and roll. I believe that anything not written from the heart is a waste of ink.; [a.] Manassas, VA

KANTOR, STEPHEN
[b.] June 5, 1925, Czechoslovakia; [p.] Emil and Elizabeth Kantor; [m.] Margie, July 31, 1979; [ch.] David, Elizabeth and Eugene; [ed.] Univ Calif. Berkeley AB 1948 USC 1953 M.D.; [occ.] General Surgeon; [memb.] AM. Medic Assoc, Orange country and calif Med Assoc, Orange count Surgical Assoc, Diplomate Amer. Board of Surgery 26th Yankee Division Vet. Assoc.; [hon.] Purple Heart, combat inf. badge.; [oth. writ.] Redich Articles; [pers.] The golden rule, as applied to every phase of life, without exceptions.; [a.] Laguna Beach, CA

KAPSOS, CASSANDRA MAY
[b.] August 24, 1980, Waukesha, WI; [p.] Timothy and Tina Kapsas; [ed.] High School at Lead Hill Arkansas, I'm a Freshman.; [hon.] Art and Music Awards for the highest grade in class. Solo 1st place Metals for Clarinet, I've played for 5 years.; [oth. writ.] I have many but I keep them personal area.; [pers.] Help the earth. It's the only we have, and the only one were getting like it. Poems come from the heart.; [a.] Lead Hill, AK

KASPEROVICH, ROSA L.
[pen.] Rose K; [b.] December 20, 1948, North Carolina; [p.] Maude K. Scott, Ezekiel Scott; [m.] John N. Kasperovich Jr.; [ch.] Sophia, Shelby, Charles, Dahlia; [ed.] Sunny Farmingdale, CW Post University; [occ.] Funeral Director; [memb.] BWE, NPWO; [hon.] Letter published in 1978 article: Civil Service leader-entitle "The Electric Pig" received best 6 her ideology award. 1992 inclusion in book 2000 notable womens. 1994 who's cooking what is America; [oth. writ.] Several poem enter in various contest.; [pers.] My motto "My service makes the difference" everything that I do, ever challenge I force. I try to make sure I do it different that the person before, so the results will be enhanced. I write what my best feel at that moment.; [a.] Brentwood, NY

KASSAM, RAHIMA
[b.] March 16, 1973, London, England; [p.] Hadi Kassam, Nargis Kassam; [ed.] Drayton Manor High, Hammersmith to West London College, College of Manchester Open Learning.; [occ.] Customer Service, Eaton Credit Co-orporation.; [hon.] Business Technology Certificate in Management Studies.; [pers.] I write as a means of expressing my thoughts, views and feelings, and feel this poem stresses the importance of love as being a relationship between mind, body and soul where mental satisfaction and emotional security are just as important as physical warmth to satisfaction.; [a.] North York Ontario, Canada

KATZMAREK, KARL
[pen.] K Katz; [b.] January 31, 1955, Chicago, IL; [p.] Carl and Geraldine Katzmarek; [m.] Genice Katzmarek, August 6, 1989; [ch.] Brittany, Rico, Brian; [ed.] Morgan Park High School. Moraine Valley Community College; [occ.] Mailhandler, US Post Office, Chicago; [memb.] African Wildlife Foundation, make a wish foundation.; [oth. writ.] Several other poems that have not been published.; [pers.] Always keep a positive attitude. Yesterday is gone, tomorrow is a dream, so make today count.; [a.] Chicago, IL

KAVANAGH, SEAN
[b.] October 8, 1953, Ireland; [p.] John and Kathleen; [ed.] Drimnagh Castle C.B.S., Clogher Road Technical College, Kevin St. College of Technology; [occ.] Technician; [pers.] Our time is so brief seize the moment and live each day; [a.] Dublin, Ireland

KEENE, SHERRY LYNN
[b.] August 7, 1979, Millington Naval Hospital; [p.] Wanda Keene, Thomas Keene; [ed.] Currently a freshman at Green Run High School; [occ.] Student; [memb.] NJROTC Navy Junior Reserve Officer Training Corps American Red Cross (I volunteer); [hon.] Honor roll, student of the month; [pers.] I believe that if you try and stay with whatever you do you will succeed. Eventhough I am a Freshman I do know because I have tried and frequently succeeded; [a.] Virginia Beach, VI

KEHOE, EDWARD
[b.] Dublin, Ireland; [occ.] Retired; [memb.] Member of the Jesuit Order (SJ) Christian Brothers; [oth. writ.] Niclaus Amatus, Fecit, 1671 Sunday. Tremendous Silence Low Tide, Ode to Autumn, Visitors, A Drama in seven scenes, Aran Villa, The Mother, Hopes Spring; [a.] Dublin, Ireland

KEISER, KIRSTEN
[pen.] Keek; [b.] February 28, 1980, Massapeous, NY; [p.] Regina Keiser, Douglas Keiser; [ed.] Berner Jr. High School; [hon.] A Silver-Medallist in the National talent competition. (Dancing); [oth. writ.] I write alot of other poems, which I plan on entering in the future.; [pers.] I think in order to live, you must love and in order to love you have to be able to either hold on to something or you have to be able to let go.; [a.] Massapeous, NY

KELDER, PIETER G.
[b.] July 16, 1917, Anna Arbor, MI; [p.] Catherine and Otto Kelder; [m.] 2 Marriages and 1 Divorce; [ed.] 2 years College; [occ.] Retired; [memb.] Los Angeles County Museum of Art, Los Angeles Conservancy, AARP, Los Angeles Library Foundation; [hon.] Awarded Chef's Cap and Apron by Sunset Magazine's Chefs of the West.; [oth. writ.] Book, Eye of Revelation (1930) Republished 1985 Ancient Secret of the Fountain of Youth, translated into both German and Dutch; [pers.] I try to live by the Golden Rule; [a.] West Hollywood, CA

KELLER, FAYE
[b.] October 18, 1949, Lacombe, Alberta, Canada; [p.] Lowell and Polly; [m.] Dieter Shoup Keller, March 20, 1976; [ed.] Grade 12 - High School Diploma; [occ.] Care Aide in Long-term Care Facility; [pers.] If I can find humour in bleak situations - so be it.; [a.] Enderby British Columbia, Canada

KELLERMAN, MISS. MARY
[pen.] Mary Kellerman; [b.] September 9, Lousville; [p.] Albert and Louise Kellerman; [m.] Divorced; [ed.] A.B. Psychology, University of Louisville, M.A. English - University of Louisville; [occ.] Investments - mostly real estate; [memb.] KY Humane Society - Audubon Soc.; [hon.] Poetry prize in graduate school, this was thrilling as two opponents were trying for Rhodes Scholarships which at that time I was not eligible, a tender memory; [oth. writ.] A novel being published next year - (Gothic Romance), a poem in an anthology called Retrospect (Rhone Valley and Barbarians); [pers.] I usually have no message in mind when writing - I try to make a lovely thing - as in the ballet; [a.] Louisville, KY

KELLY, BETH
[pen.] Aerin Towry; [b.] Miami, FL; [ed.] UCLA, BA in English; [occ.] Writer, artist; [oth. writ.] I've written for journals and newspapers such as Karmakaze, The Glendale News Press, and The Santa Monica News and Arts Publication. Essays, articles and poetry in newspapers and small prin. journals; [a.] Santa Monica Mountains

KELLY, LISA JUDITH
[b.] April 4, 1981, Macon, GA; [p.] Sam and Judith Kelly; [ed.] Saint Joseph's Catholic Grammar School - graduated June 1994 - (first honors), Jones County High School, freshman (currently); [occ.] Student; [memb.] Jones County High School Varsity Softball Team, Summer Reading Club - numerous years.; [hon.] 1. Little League All-Star Team - 2 years, 2. High School Freshman Honors Program, 3. Page in GA House of Representatives - 1993, 4. Mercer University Summer Scholars Program - 2 years, 5. Fire Marshall - 1992, 6. Placed 2nd in School Wide Geography Bee - 1993, 7. 1st Place in 4-H Fishing Tournament - 1991; [pers.] Responsibility is defined as self-discipline.; [a.] Macon, GA

KELLY, MARIANNE
[pen.] Marianne Kelly; [b.] October 9, 1966, Wesford, Ireland; [p.] James and Margaret Kelly; [ed.] Presentation Convent, Wesford Sacred Heart Convent, Waterford Mercy Convent, Waterford Technical College Waterford; [occ.] Retired from work caring for father and writing; [memb.] Winters news, England Waterford, Singers Oratorio Epouh, Star Frek Fan; [oth. writ.] Short Story for Star Folk Magazine called "Return to Yesterday" published also Star Folk Poems Published. Write Poetry.; [pers.] I try to reflect Gods great beauty and divinity in nature. Greatly influenced by Walter De La Mare and John Milton and the poets F. S. Cliot and Crashaw.; [a.] Waterford, Ireland

KELLY, PATRICIA
[pen.] P. Gubbins; [b.] October 28, 1952, Brooklyn, NY; [p.] Margaret Higgins, Joseph Higgins; [m.] Brian Kelly, June 30, 1993; [ch.] 2 stepchildren, Jessica and Maureen Kelly; [ed.] BA Summa Cum Laude Hofstrau 1988, MA Summa Cum Laude, Adelphi U-1990; [occ.] Teacher of english, at IS 93, Ridgewood, NY (where writing is encouraged); [memb.] ASCD Kappa Delta Phi - 1988-1992 (Have not gone to current meetings) was long time member of Long Island Poetry Society; [hon.] Recipient of Weimpah award in Fiction and poetry from hofstha University, 1987, 1988, co-recipient-grant for Global Education Curriculum with Ms Powis, Principal IS93, Recipient grant - "Save The World" 1991 - Teacher's consortium grant; [oth. writ.] Have published poetry in CW Post Journal of Poetry, and in Nassau Community College magazine editor of parent newsletter - IS93 Editor of Multicultural Magazine IS93-1992; [pers.] I think of writing as a third language, capable of constructing new meanings. I have been influenced by many poets, from yeats to adrienne Rich. However, my writing has been nourished, encouraged and influenced most by mother, whose life has been an inspiration to me.; [a.] New York, NY

KELLY, SAMANTHA LYNN
[b.] November 16, 1984, Washington Township; [p.] Debra Kelly; [ed.] Wrote poem in 4th grade Holly Glen School; [memb.] Student Council and in T.A.G. (Talented and Gifted Class); [hon.] Won second grade spelling bee; [a.] Williamstown, NJ

KELLY, SHEILA
[pen.] Tsechenake; [b.] June 12, 1956, Cleveland, OH; [p.] Paul Shortridge and Geraldine Harris; [ch.] Patrick, Steven, Nakya and George; [ed.] G.E.D., Lakeland Community College; [occ.] Hospice Aide and Social Worker Student; [memb.] Wolf Clan Teaching Lodge, Astara, American Indian Tribal Society; [hon.] Dean's List, National Honor Society, Phi Theta Kappa Honors Society Admission; [oth. writ.] Short Story in Playboy Magazine (1978), and "Goddess Within", Women's Magazine.; [pers.] Very close to my heart is the hospice movement. Much of my writings is centered around my patients and my experiences with them. Life is a full circle, (Good of the heart end at the beginning.); [a.] Painesville, OH

KELY, JOHN BARRY
[b.] February 9, 1952, Darby, PA; [p.] Joseph T., Helen R. Kelly; [ed.] St Andrew's Elementary Msgr. Bonner

H.S., University of Scranton; [occ.] Government Computer Operator at Maintenance Dept.; [memb.] Friendly Sons of St. Patrick Irish Terrier Club of America, Sons of Union Veterans of the Civil War; [hon.] Dean's List, Emery and Freight Educ., Fdn. Scholarship Recipient Award of Patriotism - Savings Special Achievement Award, Leadership Award - Combined Federal Campaign; [oth. writ.] Compiling Poems in Ledger. Article appeared in Boston Irish Echo: "Philadelphia's Irish Mariner, Commodore John Barry"; [pers.] Reenacts Revolutionary and Civil War History. A keen sense of history and a love of nature, books and place.

KENNEDY, JOANNA STEVES
[b.] April 10, 1964, Bronx, NY; [p.] Ernesto Steves, Cindy Steves; [m.] Brian Kennedy, October 13, 1985; [ch.] Brian Christopher and Nicholle Susan; [ed.] Immaculate Conception Elementary School and Saint Catherine Academy High School; [occ.] Administrative Assistant, Warburg, Pincus and Co.; [hon.] Miss T.E.E.N. New York 1981; [oth. writ.] Several personalized poems written and used for special occasions.; [pers.] The main inspiration for most of my writing is my family. The love I feel in my heart for them is brought out on paper.; [a.] Yonkers, NY

KENNEDY, WILL EDWIN
[b.] June 2, 1959, Murfreesboro, TN; [p.] George and Mary Kennedy; [m.] Lisa Kennedy, February 12th 1987; [ch.] Nicholas Jackson, Ashley Rea; [oth. writ.] Several poems published in local government and VA publications. (Alvin C. York times, Mainstream, the American Indian celebration pow pow); [pers.] I hope my poetry brings out an emotion in people hard to find. If so it has served its purpose. I would like to thank the national library of poetry for deeming my work worthy.; [a.] Murfreesboro, TN

KENNING, D.
[pen.] D. Kenning; [occ.] Assistant Professor of English; [memb.] English Literary Society of Japan, English Romantics Society of Japan, British Museum Society; [oth. writ.] Plays, historical and folkloric, Poetry, Articles on literature, culture, travel.; [a.] Fukuoka-ken, JAPAN

KERANS, LAINE A. MCINTOSH
[pen.] Elizabeth Oldham; [b.] September 27, 1956, South Weymouth, MA; [p.] Richard and Deborah McIntosh; [m.] Alan Kerans, November 30, 1985; [ch.] Alexandra (daughter); [ed.] Weymouth South High School, Aquinas Jr. College, University of Massachusetts; [occ.] Homemaker/Bridal Consultant, currently researching a cook book; [pers.] My writings are reflections of the people and ideals that have influenced and encouraged my artistic endeavors throughout my life.; [a.] Clinton Township, MI

KERBOW, DOTTIE CLANCY
[b.] March 9, 1922, Delta County, TX; [p.] Hubert J. Clancy and Mary Alma Cumming Clancy; [m.] Royce Kerbow, May 1, 1944; [ch.] Royce, Sandra, Stacie, Dottie and Denise; [ed.] Cooper High School and Durham Business College. She attended San Jacinto College and is presently enrolled in Writers Digest School. [occ.] Retired Real Estate Broker [memb.] International Society of Authors and Artist, the Poets Guild, and the National Authors Registry.; [hon.] Two certificates of Merit in the American Song Festival Lyric Composition Eight and has recently been published in several Poetry Anthologies.; [oth. writ.] Dottie-Jewel taught a monthly Relief Society homemaking lesson at her church and often wrote a four or five page poem to supplement the lesson. She writes poetry on any subject of interest and likes to communicate her ideas to others by letting the moral of her poetry speak for itself.; [pers.] [a.] Friendswood, TX

KERSE, ALAN C.
[b.] October 29, 1916, Masterton, NZ; [p.] W. J. Kerse and Portia Kerse; [ed.] Flockhouse Training, Farm Bulls, New Zealand, University of Manuwath at Masszy, Sheep Farming Diploma 1966; [occ.] Part time leading hard chance in Sydney, Australia.; [oth. writ.] Have written several (unpublished) novels. Also I've had two poems published one in the US, one in Australia.; [pers.] If one is wanting to be a writer then one has to write and construct a life to allow space to achieve this end.; [a.] Sydney New South Wales, Australia

KEY, JULIA E.
[b.] February 28, 1928, Grand Coteau, LA; [p.] Julie and George Eaglin; [m.] Francis Raymond Key (deceased), December 12, 1951; [ch.] 3 Daughters, Debra, Suzanne and Carla; [ed.] BA, from S.U. Baton Rounge, LA, farther studies at LSUE and USL, CNA from Lafayette, Retired Teacher Regional (Elem.); [occ.] Independent Private Nursing; [memb.] Ladies Auxiliary KPC, Mother Catherine Drexel Ladies of Grace American Legion Auxiliary Brook Richard Post 554 Sunset, LA, St. Charles Catholic Church, G.C. LA, Cheerful Volunteer Social Club, President; [hon.] Valedictorian of High School Class SPC High 1948, Retirement Plaques (teaching) from LTA, St. Landry Parish School St. LAE, many service awards from various organizations; [oth. writ.] History of family members (parents) Black History Poem, "Select Your Hero".; [pers.] I always encouraged writing to my students. I wrote speeches for family members; [a.] Grand Coteau, LA

KHOA, NGUYEN BADANG
[pen.] Badang; [b.] May 6, 1968, Saigon, Vietnam; [p.] Nguyen Ba Buong, Nguyen Thi Chi; [m.] Tran Ngoc Anh, June 16, 1991; [ch.] Stephanie, Andrea Nguyen; [ed.] Jasper Place High School, Carleton University; [occ.] Merchandiser at Shopper Drug Mart; [pers.] "Do whatever you think it is right for you to do." `Believe in faith'; [a.] Edmonton, Alberta

KIEFFER, NANCY
[b.] New York City; [p.] Robert and Thelma Kieffer; [ed.] B.A. Psychology, Syracuse University, Magna Cum Laude, M.A. Communications, Syracuse University; [occ.] President, Marketing Missions; [oth. writ.] Master's Thesis: Can the mass media cause stock price to increase or decrease?; [pers.] My poems are written to advance our knowledge of science.; [a.] New York, NY

KILGORE, AMBER TANDI
[b.] June 6, 1982, Lamesa, TX; [p.] Bob and Hope Kilgore; [ed.] Attends Jr. High at Klondike; [occ.] Student; [oth. writ.] All sorts of poems and some short stories. Nothing published before this.; [pers.] I love writing because its the best way to express my thoughts or feelings, my friends and my family have been my greatest influences.; [a.] Lamesa, TX

KIM, GRACE
[b.] September 4, 1979, Tillsonburg, Ontario, Canada; [p.] Joon Sik Kim, Jung Ae Kim; [ed.] Andress High School, Sophomore; [memb.] The National Authors Registry Press.; [pers.] Everything I write is from my heart, mind, and experience.; [a.] El Paso, TX

KIMBREL, ARENA BROWN
[b.] November 5, 1939; [ch.] Mother of four: Toye Ann Brown Mayberry, Wilbert Clifton, Lester Felix, Joye Anita Brown Beal. Grandmother of ten: Davina, Bobby Frank Jr., Marcus, Wilbert Clifton, Christina Mae, Lemaar, Carena, Marcell Champion, Tomica, Arena Beal; [ed.] Graduated: Northern High School - June, '57, Detroit, Michigan, Graduated: Medical field as a MED - Art Technician with Honor, Highland Park, Michigan, 1978, Highland Park Community College; [occ.] I tip-toe at writing

KING, CASSANDRA JUNEEN
[b.] May 22, 1971, St. Catharines, Ontario, Canada; [p.] Ron King, Kathinka King; [ch.] Christopher Daniel; [ed.] Grimsby High, Niagara College; [pers.] My greatest influences have been the love and patient teachings of my mother and the miracle that is my son. I value the well sought words of intelligent expression above the limited vocabulary of political correctness and conformist idealogy.; [a.] Vineland, Ontario, Canada

KING, DONEAN A.
[pen.] Pooh; [b.] June 16, 1969, Camden, NJ; [p.] Victoria Mae King; [ch.] Louis and Labrea King; [ed.] Lawnside Elementary School, Morgan Village Middle, Camden High School, Camden County College of Camden NJ; [occ.] Instructional Assistant at Morgan Village Middle School, Camden Board of Education; [oth. writ.] Kingdom of Dreams, Slave Girl, Not to Worry, etc.; [pers.] I write because there are places that I wish to go, there are places that I wish to have been. With pen in hand there are no limitations on where I can be. Inspiration Victoria (mother) Bevan Nelson (friend) Toylene Person (supervisor); [a.] Camden, NJ

KING-FARLOW, JOHN
[b.] July 9, 1932, London, OK; [p.] Denys King-Farlow MBE Hazel Guggelteny McKinley; [m.] Liz, May 16, 1992; [ed.] MA (Oxford AM (Duke) Ph.D. (Stanford); [occ.] Professor of Philosophy; [memb.] The Athenaeum (London); [hon.] Fellow, Royal Society of Canada. Past President, Chuadiau Philosophical Assn. Founding Editor, Canadian Journal of Philosophy, Past Doctoral Research Awards: Leverhome Foundation Pittsburgh, Etc.; [oth. writ.] "The Deadship" Adult books, London "Reason and Religion" Darton London "Faith and the life of reason" Reiden Holland "Self knowledge and social relatious" science history, New York.; [pers.] I love poetry but I love my God and my wife Liz, even more!!; [a.] Edmonton Alberta, Canada

KINGSBURY, PATRICIA
[b.] April 27, 1951, Providence, RI; [p.] Angelo Mascena, Rose Mary Mascena; [m.] Richard Kingsbury, September 11, 1971; [ch.] Shawn R., Wayne M., Megan M.; [pers.] This is my first published poem, I would like to dedicate it to my children, Shawn, Wayne and Megan with all my love.; [a.] Coventry, CT

KIRBY, EULA
[b.] April 24, 1935, Watauga County; [p.] Andrew and Ida Woodring; [m.] John Kirby, July 13, 1956; [ch.] Patricia and Lyndon; [ed.] Some college, was a teacher assistant for 29 years in the local elementary school until this fall; [occ.] Retired; [hon.] Poems published, one in local newspaper, one in the National Library of Poetry - "At Days End."; [pers.] My mother was a poet and song writer and had one poem copywriter and put to music. She had a great influence in my desire to write poetry. She could and would recite poetry till her death last summer at the age of 88.; [a.] Lenoir, NC

KIRKPATRICK, MAXWELL
[b.] October, 1914, Abilene, TX; [m.] Amabile (Calistri) Kirkpatrick, July 25, 1945; [ch.] Three; [ed.] Abilene, Texas H.S., 1931; [occ.] Retired; [oth. writ.] A few little memoirs; [pers.] I have seen and read much, learned little and remembered less. Sometimes when a scene returns to me sufficiently unblurred, I like to cast it about until something of accuracy and elegance can be presented.; [a.] De Soto, TX

KISSANE, B. K.
[m.] Roy Henrigues; [ch.] Anthony; [pers.] I am an instrument of God's illumination and take pride in my talent only in his name. If I were to be remembered by our fleeting world, I would wish it to be as an instrument of peace, of faith, and of hope. I am equal to all, superior to none, and I encourage "correspondence" with an ever-thirsty heart.

KIZZEE JR., LAWRENCE
[pen.] Kizzee; [b.] February 25, 1974, Huntsville, TX; [p.] Margaret Walker; [m.] Angela Byrd (soon); [ed.] The Art Institute of Houston, Major - Music and Video Business; [occ.] Weiners - Sales Associate; [memb.] Member of many performing groups, Presently the second half of a highly potential partnership (Partner - Laertes Davis); [hon.] 1988-1992 Several 1st and 2nd place talent shows, Top 25% of Freshman Class, 2nd Vice President of Varsity Choir, Nominated "Most Talented Male"; [oth. writ.] Combination of over 100 songs, and poems writer and and co-writer; [pers.] My life is a poem, my life is a song. So when I write, I'm writing my life and it's a blessing.; [a.] Huntsville, TX

KLANTE, MARY
[pen.] Mary Frances; [b.] October 31, 1965, Glendale, CA; [p.] John and Patricia Dinisi; [m.] Jeffrey G. Klante, January 15, 1984; [ed.] Northview High; [occ.] RDA; [oth. writ.] The bird, the whale's last hoorah, The beast, I feel like a drug, all writings unpublished; [pers.] Be kind to the mentally ill, my mother's A Paranoid Schizophrenic. I try to write in a manner that my words are not just thoughts but processed as feelings. I try to always speak truth influence. Edgar Allen Poe; [a.] Oceanside, CA

KLEI, WILLIAN
[b.] December 27, 1973; [p.] Charles Klei, Judith Klei; [ed.] Howell High School, Western MI Univ. Lake Superior State University; [occ.] Nursing Student; [oth. writ.] Several poems publishing in my high school publication; [a.] Sault Ste Marie, MI

KLEIN, KAILA
[pen.] Kaila C. Klein; [b.] September 9, 1980, Milwaukee, WI; [p.] Curt Klein, Sandi Klein; [ed.] Kennedy Elementary School, John Long Middle School, entering Grafton High School in 1995; [occ.] Student; [memb.] Girl Scouts of America, Dance Team of John Long Middle School, Children's International Fund; [hon.] Science Fair Honorable Mention, 1991; [oth. writ.] I have written a great deal of unpublished poems. My favorite is the one I entered in your contest, I am a fourteen year old girl who ...; [pers.] Most of this poem is about me being adopted and the feelings I have inside. They are not all bad feelings, but I think about them alot. Sometimes I wish I was not adopted, but most of the times I am glad I am understanding what my life would be like if I wasn't adopted. I have great expectation for myself in my life and would like to be able to achieve my goals; [a.] Grafton, WI

KLEIN, RACHEL
[pen.] Pamela; [b.] London, England; [p.] Annie and Joseph Stein; [m.] June 3, 1962; [ch.] Aviva Yedvav, Shuli Greitzer; [ed.] Dalston Grammar School, England, London University, England, City of London College, Hebrew University, Jerusalem, Israel.; [occ.] Family Social Worker, Group Counsellor, Local Spokeswoman; [memb.] National Association of Social Workers, "Voices", Israel Group of Poets in English, Israel Association of Zionist Hebrew Writers.; [hon.] B.A. Degree in Social Work, Diploma in Sociology; [oth. writ.] Several poems published in "Voices" Magazine, "Next Wave", Poets Magazine, Articles in Local Newspapers and Foreign Media (Jewish Chronicle, England, Jewish Press, U.S.A.).; [pers.] I believe that the land of Israel is the homeland of Israel is the homeland of the Jewish people. Only by believing in our heritage, and continuing it, can we achieve a true and lasting peace. This I try to reflect in my poetry.; [a.] Kiriat Arba-Heuron, Israel

KLOPPENBORG, PAUL NICHOLAS
[pen.] Paul Nicholas Kloppenborg; [b.] April 10, 1949, Davenport, IA; [p.] Nicholas T. Kloppenborg, Victoria R. Pfannenstiel; [m.] Melroy L. Kinney, May 3, 1981; [ch.] Brian K.; [ed.] Assumption High, Mesa Community College; [occ.] Communication Technician; [memb.] San Diego Aerospace Museum (Life member); [oth. writ.] "Artistic Journeys Presents: Early Times And Europe", "Artistic Journeys Presents: Journey of Agape", "Every Stamp Has a Story to Tell"; [pers.] You're born without a penny, and you die the same way too! This dash for money, in-between, has made this world a ZOO!; [a.] La Mesa, CA

KLOS, JEANNINE
[b.] June 5, 1970, Queens, NY; [p.] Mauro and Marie Guiffreda; [m.] David M. Klos, March 14, 1993; [ed.] Farmingdale H.S., Farmingdale College, Suffolk Community College; [occ.] Travel Marketing - Director of Membership Services; [pers.] Family values are an important inspiration in my life as well as in my writing.; [a.] Ronkonkoma, NY

KNAZEK, DAVID J. M.
[b.] June 8, 1979, Medford, NJ; [p.] Joseph S. Knazek, Susan A. Knazek; [ed.] Freshman Haddonfield, H.S., Haddonfield, N.J.; [occ.] Student; [memb.] Cathedral of the Woods Youth Group; [pers.] In love of the works of Professor Tolkien, I have written and submitted poems of certain events occurring in his stories. I have learned to love his works, and they have inspired me to write the poem.; [a.] Medford, NJ

KNIGHT, DAWN
[b.] December 9, 1975, Luray, VA; [p.] David and Marie Ponn, Glen Knight; [ed.] Luray High School, Lord Fairfax Community College; [occ.] Swing Shift manager; [hon.] Dean's list, president's list; [pers.] Thanks to my mother and family for their continual love and support.; [a.] Luray, VA

KNIGHT, JAN
[b.] March 16, 1946, Cherokee, IA; [p.] Lewis and Gayle Druyor Knight; [ed.] B.A., Univ. of Iowa, M.A., Miami University; [occ.] Elementary School Teacher and Teacher Trainer, Education Consultant; [memb.] Phi Delta Kappa, Association of Supervision and Curriculum Development, National Education Assoc., Calif., Teachers' Assoc. and many local math, reading, and science organizations; [hon.] Mentor Teacher Walnut Creek, School District for 4 years recipient of a variety of curriculum grants over past 20 years, Teacher of the Year, 1995, for Contra Costa County, California; [oth. writ.] Over 50 inspirational poems, several poems published in local newsletter and other bulletins; [pers.] My poetry is my gift to the world. My joy comes in knowing that thousands will read it and take time for reflection and introspection.; [a.] Pleasant Hill, CA

KOCUR, YASMIN S.
[b.] June 3, 1966, Wales, United Kingdom; [p.] Jeanette Sobhy, Yacout Sobhy; [m.] Robert J. Kocur, April 25, 1992; [ed.] University of Alexandria, Egypt - B.A. English Lit., MBA Student, University of Phoenix, Fountain Valley, CA., Phoenix, Fountain Valley, CA; [occ.] Admin. Asst., Translogic Corp., Laguna Hills, CA; [oth. writ.] Several short stories and poems (unpublished); [pers.] You can never get enough of your favorite book, each time you read it, you learn something new! My writings have been influenced by W. Blake, J. Keating, Shelley and many others.; [a.] San Clemente, CA

KOEHLER, CHRISTIE
[b.] September 1, 1966, Kitchener, Ontario, Canada; [ed.] Grand River CI, University of Gulph; [occ.] Veterinary Assistant; [memb.] Board of Directors - K-W Chamber Orchestra; [hon.] Art and English Awards throughout academic career; [oth. writ.] Many other poems and short stories, as yet unpublished; [pers.] Self impression has always been important to me - through both art work and writing. Greatest influences - Michaelangelo and Shakespeare; [a.] Kitchener Ontario, Canada

KOENIG, DONNA MCMOLY
[b.] April 3, 1952, Staten Island, NY; [p.] Raymond and Barbara Memoly; [ed.] Bachelor of Science in Nursing (BSN), Regents College, University of the State of NY, Albany, NY, Bachelor of Arts, Thomas Edison State College Trenton, NJ; [occ.] Registered Nurse; [memb.] American Association of Critical Care Nurses; [hon.] Best Didactic Instructress - Cardiovascular Technology School, Morristown Memorial Hospital in NJ, 1993; [oth. writ.] 12 Lead EKG Stat, A Light Heated Approach, CEU Access, Parsippany NJ, "What's Your Sign?" American Journal of Nursing 1/93; [a.] Parsippany, NJ

KOHLMEIER, SHARON L.
[pen.] Sharon; [b.] April 10, Wausau WI; [p.] Herbert and Lucille Hulke; [m.] Marvin, February 14, 1980; [ch.] Susan, Katherine, Kimberly, Christopher, Dianna, David, Rebecca; [ed.] Wausau High - East, Amateur Mycologist, currently studying Medicine; [occ.] Homemaker - mother; [memb.] Humane Society, Chequamegon Animal League; [hon.] Various Service Awards (Community Volunteer), Music (Singing) and Drama; [pers.] What regrets you have - destroy. What talents you have - employ. What blessings you have enjoy, for each of our lives are but a "Moment in time.; [a.] Park Falls, WI

KOLODZIK, SARA JANE
[pen.] Raven B. Payne; [b.] November 25, 1980, Oshawa, Ontario, Canada; [p.] Bonnie Kolodzik; [ed.] Grade 9, age 14, Doneva Public High School (Attending); [hon.] None at this point of time.; [oth. writ.] Many unpublished poems.; [pers.] I know the meaning of my work. But to the readers it's up to them to decide.; [a.] Oshawa Ontario, Canada

KONSTANTINOV, SVEHANA
[b.] November 25, 1968, Montreal, Quebec, Canada; [p.] Victor and Halina Konstantinov; [ed.] Rosemount High School, Dawson College: Field of study - Office

Systems Technology; [occ.] Receptionist, Int'l Aviation M.B.A. Programme, Concordia University, Montreal; [pers.] A poem in my point of view, is a poet's way of observing and expressing what surrounds his/her world. A poem should always send a positive message out to the reader, therefore, permitting the reader to absorb all the richness a poem has to offer.; [a.] Montreal Quebec, Canada

KOSAN, RICHARD
[pen.] RJ Kosan; [b.] April 19, 1974, Windsor, Ontario, Canada; [p.] Maria Slavik Kosan; [ed.] High School - Riverside Secondary School. Applied to University of Calgary.; [occ.] Student and Part time Bartender; [hon.] Committed to Canada, Social Academic, Musical Theatre Most Dedicated, Student Parliament Meritorious Contribution Award (Prime Minister); [oth. writ.] Poems - Burning Reminder, The Hole not yet published, Play - conscience not published; [pers.] No matter what they take from you don't let them have your mind. Greatest influence: Edgard Allen Poe; [a.] Windsor Ontario, Canada

KOTTAL, LENE
[b.] February 27, 1978, Odense, Denmark; [p.] Britta Kottal; [ed.] Skt. Klemensskolen in Odense, Denmark; [occ.] Student at Odense Katedralskole; [memb.] National Authors Registry; [hon.] Editor's Choice Award from the National Library of Poetry 1994.; [oth. writ.] The poem all alone published by the National Library of poetry in River of Dreams 1994.; [pers.] I've often tried to write down my feelings in prose but I've always found that poetry was the best solution. This time I'd like to dedicate my poem to my boyfriend, Soren Fink. Eternal love.; [a.] Odense, Denmark

KOUDY, ELLIE
[pen.] Ellie; [b.] August 18, 1930, Athens, Greece; [p.] Athena, Perikles; [ch.] 2 boys, 2 grandchidren; [ed.] High School (Athens/Greece) College (USA); [occ.] Fine Art Artist; [pers.] "Keep your mind and soul clear of evil thoughts and God will always be with you." Ellie; [a.] Floral Park, NY

KOWALEWSKI, PAUL
[b.] May 5, 1984, Philadelphia, PA; [p.] Joseph and Dianne Kowalewski; [occ.] Student, Maple Shade Elementary School; [memb.] 1. Korean Karate Academy, 2. Maple Shade Band and Chorus, 3. Yearbook Committee Member; [hon.] 1. Splitmasters Club, 2. School Honor Student; [a.] Croydon, PA

KOZIOL, STACY
[pen.] Stacy Koziol; [b.] January 16, 1981, Arlington Heights, IL; [p.] Patricia and Charles Koziol; [ed.] Elementary-Clearmont (EGV) Jr. High School (in Elk Grove) and I currently attend Elk Grove High School; [memb.] Honors writing, cheer leading, dance club, french; [hon.] Honor Roll, Presidents Award for Academical Fitness; [oth. writ.] I've only written poems that have never been publicly viewed, only a few close friends and family members have seen them; [pers.] "Hate, people say, is such a strong word. But, then again, so is love." I feel that there are two important people in your life, the one you hate and the one you love; [a.] Elk Grove Village, IL

KRACHE, TIFFANY
[b.] November 25, 1971, Pittsburgh, PA; [occ.] Waitress; [pers.] Poetry is a way of expressing everything and anything a person cannot put into words. It frees feelings I cannot show out loud; [a.] Parkville Baltimore, MD

KRALLMAN, COURTNEY CAROLINE
[pen.] "Courkie", Miss. O'Feelia Bust, and "Honey Bee"; [b.] October 23, 1980, Anderson, IN; [p.] Robert Krallman, S. Carrie White; [ed.] Jerry Thomas Elementary School, and Jupiter Middle School; [occ.] Student; [hon.] Presidential Academic fitness Award, many certificates of achievement, been on honor roll and grade busters many times.; [oth. writ.] A poem in the school paper, (images) and many others not published yet.; [pers.] Don't give up if you get a major case of "writers block," just set it aside and try again later. Reading books and poems inspire me and help with ideas.; [a.] Jupiter, FL

KRAMER, JEAN L.
[b.] March 14, 1934, Paullina, IA; [p.] Walter Warnke, Hilda Warnke Wester; [ch.] Sherry, Brenda, Scott, Karen.; [ed.] Paullina High, Paullina, IA; [occ.] Program Aide Green Thumb, Inc.; [memb.] AARP, Zion Lutheran Church; [oth. writ.] Several poems to be published in Sparrowgrass Poetry Forum's "Treasured Poems of America" in April, 1995; [pers.] My desire is to write poetry that all people who read it can understand, relate to, take into their hearts and make it their own.; [a.] Calumet, IA

KRAMER, MARK J.
[b.] July 9, 1955, Cambridge, NY; [p.] Ted and Barbara Kramer; [m.] Sallye M. Kramer, May 3, 1981; [ch.] Tara, Shannon and Jennifer Powers; [ed.] Heuvelton CHS, USAF; [occ.] Contractor; [oth. writ.] Various unpublished poems; [pers.] Poems are made by fools like me... but it's the fools of the world who plant the seed; [a.] Hoosick Falls, NY

KRATKY, EVELYN
[b.] April 19, 1939, Alva, OK; [p.] Austin and Ina Armstrong; [m.] Divorced; [ch.] Randy and Dennis Kessler; [ed.] High School; [occ.] Inspector Quality Control; [memb.] AARP; [oth. writ.] (Unpublished) "Where Has Love Gone", "Seekers of Hearts", "Shadows in my Mind", "Wings of Angels", "Mornings Blush"; [pers.] I would like to express to the people of the world the love and beauty around us if only for a moment. I was inspired to start writing by the loss of my son Dennis, who loved life.; [a.] Forth Worth, TX

KRELL, TIMOTHY SCOTT
[b.] July 25, 1967, West Bend, WI; [p.] Ellis Krell, Jean Krell; [ch.] Brodie Lovell Krell; [ed.] Associate Degree, Corrections Science MPTC Fond du Lac, WI, B.S. Criminal Justice Marian College Fond du Lac, WI; [occ.] Counselor/Program Coordinator Lutheran Social Services; [memb.] American Correctional Association/Wisconsin Correctional Association; [hon.] Who's Who in American Junior Colleges 1992-1993; [pers.] The secret to seeing another person's point of view lies not in the eyes, it resides in the mind; [a.] West Bend, WI

KRIESEL, JAMES N.
[b.] February 24, 1973, Appleton, WI; [p.] Frank and Nancy Kriesel; [ed.] High School Diploma. 1 1/2 year of Technical College; [occ.] Stocker at night in a grocery store. Official title Asst. Grocery Manager; [hon.] Many cooking awards. 1st place Regional Cooking contest 8th place state cooking contest.; [pers.] Dreams are worth going after. Your imagination takes you there, your abilities let you accomplish them.; [a.] Appleton, WI

KRISTJANSON, GABRIELLE FREEDOM
[b.] April 17, 1981, Leduc, Alberta, Canada; [p.] Mary-Jane Brown and Leo Steele; [ed.] I am now in the French Immersion Academic Program and am a certified touch for Health practitioner. I have had training in drama and singing at Rapide Fire Theator Camp and MUSICAMROSE.; [occ.] I am a student at Queen Elizabeth Junior High; [memb.] Friends of the Ukranian Village Society, Salvation Army, Choir, Drama Club, French Drama Club.; [hon.] Gold and silver medal in the French oratory contest and also bronze. I'm a junior soldier; [oth. writ.] My speaches for the oratory contest and several other poems for school.; [pers.] The poems and stories I write reflect the experiences of my life.; [a.] Wetaskiwin Alberta, Canada

KRYNAK, EDWARD M. J.
[pen.] Freddie M. Queen; [b.] January 4, 1974, Cleveland, OH; [p.] Sue and Jerry Krynak; [ed.] Two years at Baldwin Wallace College. Currently at Ohio State University; [occ.] Student; [pers.] Depression is like life, it goes the slowest when it's at its worst, and all you want is for it to end. Depression can mean the end of life, life can be the end of depression.; [a.] Columbus, OH

KUBASZAK, PAUL
[b.] April 10, 1950, Chicago; [p.] Josephine and the late Harry Kubaszak; [m.] Julie Kubaszak, April 24, 1970; [ch.] Christopher; [ed.] Thornton Fractional North H.S. in Calumet City, Ill. - 4 year (8000 hrs.) Pipefitter Apprenticeship; [occ.] Mechanical Foreman at Bethlehem Street, Burns Harbor Plant; [oth. writ.] I just started writing in Oct. of '94. I have written 9 poems based on personnel experiences, observations, and feelings; [pers.] To say at the end of the day, that you have honestly, within reasonable limits, did everything to accomplish your goals.; [a.] Portage IN

KUENZIE, WILSON
[b.] August 26, 1918, Monroe, WI; [p.] Samuel Kuenzie and Minnie Kuenzie; [m.] Monica Ann Kuenzie; [ch.] Kelly Ann, Thomas John, Fredrica Ann, Carol Ann, Lucy Jo; [ed.] Milwaukee State Teachers College (Now UWM) Marquette University; [occ.] Retired elementary school principal; [memb.] Schoolmaster Club of Wis. Admin. Supervisors council of Milwaukee Assn. of Wisconsin School Administrators; [hon.] Distinguished Service Award from Assn. of Wis. School Admin. Executive Secretary emeritis of School master's club of Wis.; [oth. writ.] A dozen or more unpublished poems.; [pers.] I try to portray a "slice of life" through observation and introspection.; [a.] Milwaukee, WI

KUIPERS, MELISSA L.
[b.] July 20, 1980, Ridgewood, NJ; [p.] Richard and Marilyn Kuipers; [ed.] Indian Rocks Christian School - Elementary and Middle School. Northside Christian High School; [occ.] Student; [memb.] National Junior Honor Society, Student Council, First Baptist Church of Indian Rocks - Solid Rock Drama Team.; [hon.] Student of the month - church youth group. Two softball trophies. Three basketball trophies. One volleyball trophy. Indian Rock Christian School's Journalism Award.; [oth. writ.] Grand prize winner in Favorite teacher essay contest. Published in 1994 Edition of anthology of poetry by young americans; [pers.] I can do all things through Christ who strengthens me. Philippians 4:13; [a.] Largo, FL

KUMAR, VISHAL
[b.] February 20, 1977, New Dehli, India; [p.] Veena

Olson, Timothy Olson; [ed.] Centreville High School, VA, Frankfurt International High School, Germany; [occ.] Student - will attend Lafayette College starting the fall of '95; [memb.] Student Council, Good Shepherd Lutheran Church, Easton, PA; [hon.] 1st round winner in Crowley Intuitional Poetry Book Tournament held in Centreville High School; [oth. writ.] Collection of poems called Drifts of Snow.; [pers.] Thank you to Todd Crowley, my 11th grade English teacher, for emphasizing poetry. Writing poetry allows you to escape from everyday, hectic life.; [a.] Easton, PA

KUMBATONIC, ROBERT
[b.] March 5, 1970, New York; [p.] Bogumil Kumbatonic, Nancy Kumbatonic; [ed.] BA New York University, JD Fordham Law School; [occ.] Attorney; [pers.] Today's Complacency Breeds Tomorrow's Regret; [a.] New York, US

KUTA, KEVIN IBRAHIM
[pen.] Pudre Boi Kevin; [b.] 29 years old; [p.] Mr. and mrs. Sergent Ibrahind Iliyasu Kuta; [pers.] O'Level (that is ordinary level); [occ.] Farming and music presentation on radio (F.M.); [oth. writ.] Moving picture script, book script (still trying to expose them to the public), love poems that go on the air each time I have a musical show on the radio; [pers.] There are more numbers of the ruled than the rulers; everyone needs what is good. [a.] Niger, Nigeria.

KUTZ, OLIVE
[b.] March 15, 1908, Jefferson, WI; [p.] Will F. and Elvira S. Kutz; [ed.] HSF HS BS, Whitewater T. College, WI; [occ.] Retired; [memb.] HARP, WREA, St. Pauls Lutheran Church, WWF, IWF, Nat. Audubon Soc., JCAREA, Friends - WHATV, Am. Can. Soc., BRW HS, American Lung Ass. Am Canch Soc., Am. Heart Assn.; [hon.] 2nd Place - Yarns of Yesteryear, Outstanding Elementary Teachers of America, 1972

KWASIBORSKI, LECH
[pen.] Andrew Francis; [b.] January 28, 1954, Montreal, Canada; [p.] Feliks Kwasiborski, Bronislawa Herba; [m.] Paula Pambianchi, April 29, 1990; [ed.] St. Pius X H.S., Control Data Institute, Vanier College; [occ.] Electronics Technician; [hon.] Canada's "Star of Courage" S.C., Canada's "Canadian Forces Decoration" C.D., Province of Quebec's "La Medaille du Civisme", United Nations Medal "U.N.E.F. II"; [oth. writ.] An unpublished short story titled "Legacy"; [pers.] "I learn by going where I have to go" Theodore Roe' ke; [a.] Pierrefonds Quebec, Canada

LACH, BARBARA JOYCE
[b.] February 29, 1940, Milwaukee, WI; [p.] Sherman and Grace Delker; [m.] Robert E. Lach, May 9, 1987; [ch.] Scott, Lyle, Sherman, Lance, Donald and Jennifer; [ed.] Completed High School and - Life itself; [occ.] Homemaker; [oth. writ.] Many other poems and "Causes, prognosis, diagnosis and cures for the ills of our world today" - nothing published; [pers.] I enjoy writing poems for myself, my children encouraged me to try to get them published. With all the beauty the Lord surrounded us with, it's hard not to write about it.; [a.] Franklin, WI

LACHCIEK, DOLORES
[pen.] Dee; [b.] April 9, 1944, Chicago, IL; [pers.] I only write what my heart truly feels. This makes my writings true and sincere.; [a.] Chicago, IL

LAGODA, AUNDREA K.
[b.] October 11, 1976, Lancaster, PA; [p.] Lenora and Greg Lagoda; [ed.] Blairsville High School; [occ.] Sales person, Spencer gifts - Indiana PA; [memb.] People for the Ethical treatment of animals, Greenpeace, National Wildlife Federation; [hon.] Who's who among American high school students, Arin Math Mentorship, Yearbook business editor, President of key club, Finalist Columbia College Presidential Scholarship Competition; [oth. writ.] Several poems published in local newspaper; [pers.] Smile, smile, smile and luv each other!!; [a.] Blairsville, PA

LAHUE, DOROTHY M.
[pen.] Dorothy M. Lahue; [b.] July 4, 1937, Iowa City, IA; [p.] Samuel W. and Dorothy N. Vargason; [m.] Divorced; [ch.] Timi, Misti, Dusti, Ketti Kelli; [ed.] 12th Grad HST Sr.; [occ.] Disabled - early retirement.; [pers.] Poem written in memory of Bertha Birch, (Grandmother)

LAKRITZ, SIMEON
[b.] September 23, 1954, Milwaukee, WI; [p.] Dr. Leo Lakritz, Esther Lakritz; [ed.] University of Wisconsin B.A. Cum Laude (History major/Chemistry minor), Western State University College of Law (Juris Doctor degree), Grossmont College (A.S. degree) (Accounting); [occ.] Attorney at Law; [memb.] State Bar of California, American Radio Relay League, Extra Class Hamrabid License, Third Class Commercial Radiotelegram License; [hon.] Dean's List at University of Wisconsin and Grossmont College, Phi Alpha Theta (History Honor Society, National Honor Society (High School); [oth. writ.] How Safe Is Your Safe Deposit Box? (published in Mature Living Magazine), Know Your Rights When You Fly (published in Mature Living), article on the Grand Jury System (published in a California journal for private investigators); [a.] Santee, CA

LALOR, ROBERT JAMES
[b.] September 7, 1974, New York City; [p.] Robert and Hilt Lalor; [ed.] Union High School, Seton Hall University, Syracuse University; [hon.] Delta Kappa Epsilon, poems published in collegiate publications.; [a.] Union, NJ

LAMBERT, AMANDA
[b.] July 2, 1980, Alberta, Canada; [p.] Dick and Holly Lambert; [oth. writ.] Several Poems, none of which have been published.; [pers.] My poems are centred around and dedicated to my father, who's tragic death in 1993 inspired my writing; [a.] Breynat Alberta, Canada

LAMBERT, DORIS
[b.] July 28, 1949, Perth Road, Ontario, Canada; [p.] William James Lambert, Mary Evelyn (Wilson); [ch.] Mary Magro, Effie Martin and January Martin; [ed.] Independent Learning Centre - Gr 12; [memb.] Canadian Cystic Fibrosis Foundation, American Civil War Historical Re-enactment Society; [hon.] Award of Merit (school), Honours List (school), Editor's Choice Award 1993 (National Library of Poetry); [oth. writ.] Short Stories; [pers.] Doris returned to the classroom in 1994 and has completed a course in Office Administration. Her writing is her way of keeping in touch with life and reality. She is also enjoying her time spent as a Living Historian at re-enactments; [a.] Guelph Ontario, Canada

LAMBERT, W. J.
[b.] December 24, 1919, Camden East, Ontario, Canada; [p.] The late Winnifred Holland and John Lambert; [m.] Evelyn Lambert, September 21, 1977; [ch.] Three daughters; [ed.] Very little, grade 8; [occ.] Propane operator; [memb.] War Amps Canada; [hon.] Entered in "Poetry Elite" a 1985 Anthology of Canadian Poetry "Nature's Bouquet" by William J. Lambert; [oth. writ.] I wrote for 2 years for a local newspaper (The Poets Corner) I have three books volume 1, 2 and 3 ("Treasured Thoughts"); [pers.] My inspirations are as swift as the waters, nature is my education, the best teacher of man, looks back on his boyhood days and all nature, around him, he started to put his thoughts into poem; [a.] Lyndhurst Ontario, Canada

LANDRO, ANGELA
[b.] November 14, 1926, Brooklyn, NY; [p.] Dominick and Marie Carlucci; [m.] Nicholas Landro, November 26, 1949; [ch.] Paula, Mark, Christine, Kathryn; [ed.] Graduated Glen Cove High School, Glen Cove, NY, 1944; [occ.] Wife, mother, grandmother; [pers.] A thought is wasted if not shared. Recently discovered amazing composer Yanni who said, "Anything great that has ever happened to humanity from the beginning, began with a single thought in someone's mind....." [a.] Sea Cliff, NY

LANDRUM, DAVID W.
[b.] February 10, 1962, New Haven, CT; [p.] Cecile S. Shure, Marquis C. Landrum; [ed.] Deerfield Academy, University of Oregon (2 yrs); [occ.] Reforestation, Trial construction and Forest Technician; [memb.] International Society of Arboriculture; [oth. writ.] Poetry for local readings, short stories and 1 article; [pers.] A wish to remain in touch with the elements; [a.] Port Townsend, WA

LANDRY, JUDITH ANN SLACK
[pen.] Judi Landry; [b.] October 30, 1942, Claremore, OK; [p.] Mr. and Mrs. LeRoy F. Slack; [m.] John D. Landry, November 20, 1964; [ch.] Molly Ann Landry Lively; [ed.] R.N. Graduate of Hotel Dieu School of Nursing class of 1964 Beaumont, TX; [occ.] Staff Nurse at Southeast Texas Hospice Orange, Texas 6 years; [oth. writ.] This will be my first published writing, most of my poems are personal feelings, I have put on paper.; [pers.] I mainly write for pleasure and to preserve my thoughts for my child and grandchildren; [a.] Port Neches, TX

LANE, LINDA LEE
[b.] December 25, 1952, Baton Rouge, LA.; [p.] Frank Lane Jr., Katie Mae Lane; [ed.] Scotlandville Sr. High School Southern University A and M College Southern University School of Law; [occ.] Temporary Employee, various temporary agencies in Atlanta.; [memb.] Ebenezer Baptist Church; [oth. writ.] Can't keep it to myself Pearls of Justus; [pers.] It is my desire to inspire all mankind to put God first in their lives, so they can spend eternity with Him.; [a.] Riverdale, GA

LANIEL, NORMANDO R.
[b.] July 31, 1970, Cornwall Ontario, Canada; [p.] Richard Laniel, Lucille Doucet; [ed.] Ottawa University - Honours in Spanish/Concentration Pol. Science.; [occ.] Student - Ottawa University; [hon.] Cum Laude in Spanish; [oth. writ.] A novela entitled the A.A.S.M. to be published in the next year.; [pers.] Writing poetry is the most sensible way for me to freely express my emotions and thoughts with spontaneity and to ensure their perpetuity.; [a.] Orleans Ontario, Canada

LANKFORD, SANDY
[b.] March 25, 1953, Kansas; [p.] Mr. and Mrs. T. J.

Ross; [m.] John, May 20, 1972; [ch.] Jeremy, Janna, Nathan; [ed.] Music Education, Ouachita Baptist University Ark., Elementary Ed. Certificate from USF Tampa. Working on masters.; [occ.] Teacher (elementary); [memb.] Pianist and Choir, Director at church. Teachers union, Music Educators Association; [hon.] Who's who in American Women, Dean's List.; [pers.] I wrote this poem after finding out I had fibromyalgia. (A debilitating medical syndrome). 6 months earlier, I'd had a stroke. I was incapicated for many long months, and had a long time to think about what is really important in life; [a.] Wauchula, FL

LAPAGE, MONA LISA
[b.] November 5, 1960, Huntingdon, Quebec, Canada; [p.] Nora and Leo LaPage; [ch.] Christopher Ball; [ed.] Salmon River Central and North Country Community College; [occ.] Correction Officer - Barehill Correctional Facility; [oth. writ.] Some of my poems been published in Malone Telegram and Plattsburgh Post Standard - local papers; [pers.] I like to write poems to help people stop and think, and to help do better in the world.; [a.] Malone, NY

LARSON, INGRID DANA
[pen.] September 30, 1965, Manchester, CT; [ed.] High school graduate/College graduate, East Bridgewater High School, Massasoit Community College - Associate Degree - Liberal Arts. Stonehill College - currently working on Bachelor's degree communications.; [occ.] Receptionist, Children's Author, and poet; [memb.] Society of Children Book Writers and Illustrators.; [hon.] Robin Cadell Memorial Award - awarded to me in high school for Creative Writing, Dean's List - high school and college; [oth. writ.] Children's stories - one currently in the works for publication.; [pers.] I want my writings to reflect upon the beauty of nature, the beauty of animals, and the goodness that lies within each and everyone of us.; [a.] East Bridgewater, MA

LASS, STACY MARIE ANNA
[b.] August 7, 1971, Saint Cloud, MN; [p.] Bernard L. Lass, Virginia S. Thelen; [ed.] Tech. High School, St. Cloud State University; [occ.] Councilor at Opportunity Manor Foster Home; [oth. writ.] One thousand writings yet to be heard.; [pers.] In my existence I stress the idea of living, and not merely breathing. The art of expression is a gift, and it is through poetry that I might communicate directly to your soul. Foot prints, I'll leave footprints here.; [a.] Saint Cloud, MN

LATOUCHE JR., GERALD J.
[b.] November 1, 1968, Dominica; [p.] Maynith and Gerald LaTouche; [ed.] Saint Mary's Academy and Clifton Dupigny Community College.; [occ.] Accounts and shipping clerk; [memb.] The Highlanders Club; [hon.] Certificate of achievement "The Caribbean Writers Institute Poetry Workshop" department of English University of Miami.; [oth. writ.] "The art of survival" published in anthology, all my tomorrows vol, VI, by Quill Books. The complete collection of 45 poems, "to catch a life", soon to be published, Janus publishing UK; [pers.] I go with my poetry deep into the psyche of life itself. If there is such a thing as a first love, I could safely say that poetry was my first love. She still is!; [a.] Roseau, Comm of Dominica

LATTIMORE, CHARLES A.
[pen.] Charles A. Lattimore; [b.] November 6, 1954, Medina, OH; [p.] Mary Ruth and Charles H. Lattimore; [ed.] Univ. of Akron; [occ.] Singer - Song writer; [memb.] Alpha Phi Alpha Fraternity, Fellowship Baptist Church; [hon.] WZAK Radio (Cleveland) has read poems of mine on their "For lovers only" show. My poems have also appeared in local newspaper. A few articles also.; [oth. writ.] I have written a personal collection of 2,000 poems. Have also written over 200 songs in my personal catalog.; [pers.] "Stay grounded but always reach for the stars". "I long to be, it writing or performing, add personal meaning in someone's life".

LAU, JASON MICHAEL
[b.] July 9, 1975, Toledo, OH; [p.]James Lau, Jill Roberts; [ed.] Lake High, University of Toledo, Toledo Art Museum, and Graphics Art Center; [occ.] Dynamic Visualist, Freelance, Millbury OH; [oth. writ.] Self published works only, Synthetic, Poetical collections, Trauma, Whispers in the wind, the graphic novel all gone black. Environment exhibition: Visades of heaven; [pers.] What is, is and all as shall be, to flow in the moment is to bring forth creation.; [a.] Millbury, OH

LAVIOLETTE, ALEXINA
[pen.] Alex Laviolette; [b.] April 28, 1910, Gravelbourg Saskatchewan, Canada; [p.] David and Josephine Gauthier (deceased); [m.] Gaetan Sr. Laviolette, May 20, 1933; [ch.] David, Marguerite, Gaetan Jr, Raymond, Marie.; [ed.] Part of High School, self educated, my husband passed away in 1977 Professor in Litterature, also Maths, Science, had a no. of degrees.; [occ.] Retired; [memb.] In 1970 published 11 poems in the Consumer's guide in Kapuskasing Ont Golden Age Club.; [hon.] The honorable Deinfenbaker received honors from the Queen in 1976 for being awarded "Companion of Honor"; [oth. writ.] One of the poems mentioned was published in Toronto evening star. In 1976 received a thank you letter from Balmoral Castle from the clerk, from Queen Elezibeth II. The same year a thank you letter from the Honorable J. G. Deinfenbaker Premier of Can. 1956.; [pers.] I have always read, studied about nature, I am of the sentimental type, the beauty in life, I have all the books of the great poets.

LAW, NICOLE C.
[b.] May 23, 1976, Pittsburgh, PA; [p.] Linda Law, Dwight Law Sr.; [ed.] Crescenta Valley High, University of Pittsburgh; [occ.] Student; [memb.] Some of God's Gospel choir; [hon.] Challenge grant to University of Pittsburgh for my essay on Dr. Martin Luther King, Jr.; [pers.] Throughout my life, poetry has been an inspiration to me. When I write my poems, I try and use all my heart and soul to express my feelings on my life.; [a.] Pittsburgh, PA

LAWRENCE, KATHLEEN MARIE
[b.] November 23, 1950, Santa Monica, CA; [p.] Kay M. Warren and John F. Gillespie; [ch.] Edward J. Hoffman and Dana M. Lawrence; [ed.] High School; [occ.] National Accounts Title Coordinator for First American Title Insurance Company; [oth. writ.] Many other poems for personal enjoyment.; [pers.] As with my poem, it seems to be with life - paths will change some bringing happiness while others may bring pain, yet in my journey, where one door closes another door opens.; [a.] Santa Ana, CA

LAWRENCE, MARY E.
[pen.] Molly; [b.] August 10, 1902, Vernonville Ontario, Canada; [ch.] One daughter - Elizabeth Campbell; [ed.] Teachers' College; [occ.] Retired teacher (includes teaching in one room rural school for several years); [memb.] Past and active horticultural society, Library board, Book club. Still an active member in all activities.; [oth. writ.] Poetry for schools, and other organizations wrote articles for local paper, and community care newsletter.; [pers.] Many hobbies - Gardening, painting, pets, love of nature and children still lives in own home but have many friends, and a family that I love. Life is full of interest each day. I read a great deal. And spend most of the time outdoors in summer.; [a.] Fenelon Falls Ontario, Canada

LAWS, MARGARET
[b.] February 8, 1939, Gateshead, England; [m.] May 11, 1955; [ch.] 4 (2 sons and 2 daughters); [ed.] Primary and High; [occ.] Shop Keeper; [oth. writ.] Poetry yesteryears the waiting years time of my own; [pers.] My aim is to try to make people see the hurt they cause others

LAWSON, CHERYL ANN
[b.] March 27, 1970, New York; [p.] Margo Lawson, Robert Lawson; [ed.] Martin Van Buren H.S., Hunter College; [pers.] Writing for me is reflective, I write to inspire and glorify God.; [a.] Cambria Heights, NY

LAXA, ETHELRIDA ZABALA
[pen.] Ethelrida; [b.] February 15, 1954, Leyte, Philippines; [p.] Ireneo N. Zabala, Flora C. Zabala; [m.] Divorced; [ch.] Ivan Raphael Zabala Laxa; [ed.] Bachelor of Science in Commerce major in Accounting (Certified Public Accountant-C.P.A.), Masters in Business Economics (University of Santo Tomas), Neurolinguistic Programming (NLP); [occ.] Auditor: Canadian Imperial Bank of Commerce (CIBC); [memb.] 1. Songwriters Association of Canada (SOCAN), 2. The Canadian Country Music Association (CCMA), 3. The Philippines Institute of Certified Public Accountants (PICPA), 4. The Moonrakers Band; [hon.] Represented the Central Bank of the Philippines (CBP) at the XVIIth International Commercial Banking Course in Pakistan with a citation for excellent performance, Dean's List, Honors, Top 5 Management Trainee (CBP).; [oth. writ.] Top 1000 Corporations (1974-75) Issues (Business Day Newspaper) with by line, Industry studies, poems, songs entered in composition (song writing) contest, monologues.; [pers.] "Life is God's precious gift to me and what I do with this life is my tribute to my God." I now open this gift and I share it to one and all. [a.] North York Ontario, Canada

LAYLON, LEEANN
[b.] August 2, 1977, Corvallis, OR; [p.] Lawrence Laylon, Della Laylon; [ed.] High School; [occ.] Senior at North Lake High School; [memb.] Cheer leading, 4-H, Christmas Valley Rodeo Assoc., Future Business Leaders of America; [hon.] Buckle for Queen of La Pine Rodeo, 91 - Buckle for Gymkana series, 90 - Trophy for Gymkana series, 92 - Trophy for Gymkana series, 94 - Buckle for Gymkana series 93-94 Lettered in Cheer leading; [a.] Christmas Valley, OR

LEA, JAMES MILTON
[pen.] James Milton Lea [b.] October 29, 1928, Grafton, WV; [p.] Virgil M. and Lucille D. Lea; [m.] (1st) Fawn L. Gattis May 19, 1951, (2nd) Maxine Dupont March 3, 1985; [ch.] Rhonda L., Phillip B., Charlotte Y.; [ed.] High School - Colton CA, 1947, Woodbury College, Los Angeles CA, 1957, B.B.A. Degree. Instrument Trainer and Instructor, Flight Simulator U.S.A.F. 1951 to 1954; [occ.] Retired Insurance Agency owner (21 yr.) San Fernando Valley and Westlake Village CA, 1964-1985; [memb.] Charter Pres. San Fernando Valley Club

Sertoma (West Valley); [hon.] Received outstanding sales award 3 years in row 1961-62-63 from Auto Club So. California worked for them 6 1/2 years 8/57 to 4/64, elected outstanding Airman S.A.C. Headquarters - Omaha, NE, 1954 - promoted to S/Sgt. for invention of a device used in simulators making cross country flights and training easier. I was featured in Link Aviation's 25th Anniversary magazine for this honor.; [oth. writ.] "The Vietnam Tragedy" 11/8/93 published in "The Writings on the Wall" Vietnam Vets. Assoc. Memorial, "D-Day" poem accepted by Normandy invasion Comm. forwarded to Achen France for use by researchers and scholars in the museum. "Air War Over Germany" accepted by the air museum in Britain to be published in their founding newsletter. Plus many more, poems of war and various subjects.; [pers.] I try to like everyone even tho' at times it seems impossible - hold no malice in your heart.; [a.] Rogers, AR

LEAL, RAMIRO
[b.] May 16, 1949, San Juan, TX; [p.] Samuel Leal, Consuelo Leal; [m.] Delia G. Leal, July 8, 1974; [ch.] 2; [a.] Wiley, CO

LEAVITT, JON
[b.] May 21, 1980, Eastlake, OH; [p.] William Pike, Sherry Pike; [oth. writ.] I write a lot but this will be my first published poem.; [pers.] I have been influenced by many philosophers such as Nietzche and also by Jim Morrison's poetry. I live life by what I know, not what I believe or want to believe and I try to show the truth in my work.; [a.] Eastlake, OH

LEDBETTER, MARY
[b.] January 2, 1970, Shelby; [p.] James Ledbetter, Mary Ledbetter; [ch.] Dustin Richard, Thomas Luther; [pers.] Writing has always been a way to express my feelings for others, I was greatly influenced by Susan Polis Schutz; [a.] Fallston, NC

LEDFORD, DEBORA G.
[b.] September 21, 1956, Detroit, MI; [p.] Kenneth and Lois Ledford; [ed.] B.B.A. Cleary College, M.S.A. Central Michigan Univ.; [occ.] Financial Analyst, General Motors Corp.; [hon.] Donald Silkworth Award; [a.] Ypsilanti, MI

LEDOUX, ELIZABETH FRAZIER
[b.] New York; [p.] George Arthur Frazier and Nancy Rossenbach; [m.] Richard Ledoux; [ch.] Matthew Thomas and Michael Arthur; [ed.] Holy Family Girls Academy, Glendale College, Moorpark College, Hawkeye Comm. College; [occ.] Student: Hawkeye Comm. College, Emergency Medical Tech. Program; [memb.] Suicide Prevention Hot Line Team; [oth. writ.] Celebration poetry for family and friends, short stories and personal essays.; [pers.] Much of my writing reflects the happiness of hopes of people everywhere. Most influenced by C. S. Lewis and D. H. Lawrence. Inspired by lighted windows at twilight: Orphaned in infancy and later adopted, those lighted windows represented the love and safety of family to a small, lonely child.; [a.] Waverly, IA

LEE, DELENA
[pen.] D. M. Lee [b.] March 10, 1978, Iowa City, IA; [p.] Lorita Welter, Hugh Elmond Lee Jr.; [ed.] Recently a student at Manson Northwest Webster High School; [hon.] I won a district Essay Contest on "Nursing Homes". I received a 1 rating at district for Individual Speech, Dramatic Acting.; [oth. writ.] Short stories: Vampire's Last Kiss, Lonesome Dove, The Jackknife Killer, What a Crisis, Wife Beating, Cherokee Rose, (not published), Poems: The Whys Through Life, What a Rainbow Means. (not published); [pers.] If you have a dream, don't let anyone tell you it's dumb or it will never happen. Ignore those statements and follow through with your dream. Take it all the way one day it will come true. Mine did!; [a.] Manson, IA

LEE, MARIE
[b.] June 9, 1920, Chicago, IL; [p.] Florence and Frank Riedl; [m.] Leonard Lee (deceased), October 18, 1947; [ch.] Elizabeth Sammit - James, Jeff and Robin Lee; [ed.] High School - Roosevelt Sr. High School, 3 Semesters of writing at Oakton Comm. College; [occ.] Retired; [oth. writ.] Several poems and essays published in church newsletters and in house organs at places of employment.; [pers.] I have been most creative in these latter years of my life. Raising my children seems to have been the most creative part of my earlier years; [a.] Glenview, IL

LEE, ZELLA MAE
[b.] June 28, 1928, Rogers, MN; [p.] Charlie and Sara Alice Bishop; [m.] Melvin Lee, December 12, 1950; [ch.] Myron Lee; [ed.] Roseau High School; [pers.] Zella and Melvin formed north of Badger until he died in 1990. Upon losing her eyesight she lived her remaining years at the Greenbush Nursing Home where she died February 19, 1993. Her Christian outlook on life is reflected in her poem - a walk with Jesus

LEFFLBINE JR., JOHN W.
[b.] July 2, 1971, Greenwich, CT; [p.] John Lefflbine, Rosemary Miles Lefflbine; [ed.] Masuk High, Western Connecticut State University; [pers.] I believe that poetry is an art by which emotions are given substance; [a.] Philadelphia, PA

LEGGE, SIMON ALEXANDER
[pers.] The glories of life and of being alive ought to be explored, celebrated, and expounded by and through arts magnificently crafted: Is not all life beautifully made? Inspiring our feelings and perceptions of existence, should art not then strive as well to be beautiful? Ought poesie especially, knowing as we do its powers, not strive to help all know and feel the glory we are part of? "Seeking for meanings and reasons we came, 'tis the work of the BARDS which sets all life before us plain." [a.] Ontario, Canada

LEHTI, MANUELA
[b.] February 28, 1960, Berlin, Germany; [m.] Richard A. Lehti; [ch.] Sven Airk Lehti; [ed.] Robert-Koch Gymnasium (Berlin), Lou Academy (Berlin); B.G.S. - English and History: UNO; [occ.] Freelance writer; [hon.] Phi Alpha Theta, Dean's List, graduated Magna Cum Laude; [oth. writ.] Comments published in local newspapers; [pers.] In my poetry and other works I try to show that everybody can do what he/she wants to do, no matter what limitations are put upon the person. To be positive is important for me; [a.] Bellevue, NE

LEIDY, SARAH ELIZABETH
[b.] September 26, 1983, Winston-Salem, NC; [p.] Tom and Marilyn Leidy; [ed.] Year 7 student at Queenwood Senior School in Sydney, Australia; [occ.] 10 year old student; [memb.] She is currently living in Australia while her father works for Sara Lee - Australia.

LEINBACH, GARY ALLEN
[pen.] Gary Allen Leinbach; [b.] June 5, 1963, Denver; [p.] Keith and Carol Leinbach; [ed.] Pace University - New York City; [occ.] AIDS (previously Account Executive for E! TV; [memb.] AIDS Project Los Angeles American Civil Liberties Union; [hon.] Phi Beta Sigma; [oth. writ.] Newspaper articles, Book of Poetry in a World of Aids.; [pers.] The earth is crammed with heaven. Find it.; [a.] Los Angeles, CA

LENNIGER, SISTER BARBARA ANN
[b.] December 27, 1932, Bronx, NY; [p.] Roland, Frances Lenniger; [ed.] BSED St. John's University, MA Hunter; [occ.] Executive Director of Thorpe Family Residence - a shelter for homeless families; [memb.] North Central Bronx Hospital, Citizens Advisory Board, Empire State Board for Homeless, Runaway Youth, Coordinator: Bronx Tier II Directors Steering Committee: N.Y.C. Tier II Directors; [hon.] "Woman Waging Peace Award" - from N.Y.C. Council of Women 1993, Honoree at Annual fund raiser by Aquinas Housing, BX, NY, 1993; [oth. writ.] Several poems, children's plays, skits for faculty parties or community festivities some of which are humorous and or satirical.; [pers.] I write to express deep feelings of injustices towards the poor, and to advocate for compassion towards the most powerless and vulnerable members of our society.; [a.] Bronx, NY

LEONARD, JOHN J.
[b.] July 3, 1935, Everett, MA; [p.] Denis Leonard, Margaret Leonard; [m.] Janice Leonard, April 27, 1963; [ch.] Judee, John Jr., Timothy, Jeanne, Michael; [ed.] Boston College High, Everett HGigh, Repeater and carrier school, Ft. Monmouth, NJ.; [occ.] Nynex Tech.; [memb.] Knights of Columbus, Telephone pioneers, St. Thevesa's choir; [pers.] My desire is for all mankind to be enhanced, through the majestic power of music and poetry, with a yearning for the holy spirit, igniting our love for Christ, whom God the Father gave for our peace and salvation.; [a.] North Reading, MA

LEQTERS, MARJORIE K.
[b.] Glendale, CA; [ed.] Attended Michigan State; [occ.] Retired from library; [memb.] Pilgrim Congregational Church; [a.] Claremont, CA

LEWINSKI, CHRISTI N.
[b.] August 16, 1978, Corpus Christi, TX; [p.] Richard Lewinski, Dahlia G. Lewinski; [ed.] Callalen High; [pers.] I'm still in high school and I notice my peers potential. An awesome number of them are never given a chance to excel because they are "average". I do believe these people will shine when they find the opportunity. This gives me infinite hope for my human family's future.; [a.] Corpus Christi, TX

LEWIS, ALWYN D.
[b.] October 18, 1934, New Zealand; [p.] Huia Georgia and Dorothy McIluride; [m.] Laurie, July 17, 1954; [ch.] Jeffrey and Martin; [ed.] Sacred Heart College, New Zealand; [occ.] Writer; [memb.] Jazz Action society of NSW, Fellowship of Australian writers; [oth. writ.] Interviews with U.S. jazz musicians in New York magazine cadence, articles in several publications, book of short stories, book of poetry, currently writing a novel.; [pers.] Through my writing I try to share my tiny perspective of the world in a way that will inform, hopefully, or in some way please, maybe even disturb, the reader, so that we establish a reciprocation of some kind.; [a.] Wingen Sydney, Australia

LEWIS, FRANCES
[b.] May 28, 1917, Columbus, OH; [p.] Elmer and

Glenna Bond; [m.] Edwin A. Lewis, April 17, 1970; [ch.] Glenda Schott, Allen Bergman, Dwight Bergman; [ed.] Westerville High, Ohio State U.; [occ.] Retired (formerly worked at Ohio State in office); [memb.] Inactive at present time. Formerly Cub and Girl Scout Leader, PTA Officer, Officer in Business Women of America, three year Volunteer for Illini Hospital and participated in many other organizations.; [a.] Mount Vernon, OH

LEWIS, SARAH A.
[b.] October 13, 1980, Morehead, KY; [p.] Ancil and Alice Lewis; [ed.] Currently in eighth grade at Verity Middle School, Ashland, KY; [occ.] Student; [memb.] Youth Group at the First Christian Church. Recently in school year book staff; [hon.] Tri-state Computer Show Graphics Contest Award 1993, Presidential Academic Fitness Award, Verity Middle School Honor Roll, Science Fair Awards; [pers.] I think that if you believe in something it can happen, even if others doubt; [a.] Ashland, KY

LILES, PATRICIA A.
[b.] February 6, 1960, Jourdanton, TX; [p.] Mr. and Mrs. Clinton and Elenora Montgomery; [m.] Michael C. Liles, July 11, 1981; [ed.] East Central I.S.D.; [occ.] Special Education - L.I.F.E. assistant, Alamo Heights I.S.D.; [memb.] Salem Sayers Baptist Church, The Humane Society of the United States; [oth. writ.] Poems in my personal library - "The unborn plea", "I dreamed of an old shack", "The pride of an Indian", and several others.; [pers.] I credit my ability to write to God. It is He, that has given me aopportunities and experiences in my life, that has allowed me to express it through my "inspirational" writings.; [a.] Converse, TX

LILIENKAMP, ANN
[pen.] Ann Lilienkamp; [b.] June 22, 1979, Kettering, OH; [p.] Darrell Lilienkamp and Kathy Lilienkamp; [ed.] Ascension School, Kettering Junior High School, Fairmont, High School; [occ.] Student; [memb.] Bowling League on Saturdays.; [hon.] School and bowling awards.; [oth. writ.] Several other poems for personal enjoyment.; [pers.] My writing comes straight from the heart. I dedicate this poem to my Grandmother who just recently passed away I still feel her presence in my heart and mind.; [a.] Kettering, OH

LILIENTHAL, LINDA K.
[b.] June 14, 1951, McCook, NE; [p.] Alfred and Maude Plourd; [m.] John A. Lilienthal, August 29, 1971; [ch.] Lisa Aleta, John Ace, Jacob Luke; [ed.] McCook Community College, Kearney State College, B.A., Univ. of Nebraska at Kearney, M.A.; [occ.] Kindergarten Teacher, Hayes Center Elementary School, Hayes Center, NE; [memb.] Kappa Delta Pi, Phi Alpha Theta, Hayes Center Education Asso.; [pers.] This poem is dedicated to the memory of Heidi Jo Lilienthal.; [a.] Culbertson, NE

LILLEY, DAWN M.
[b.] August 11, 1963, Woodbury NJ; [p.] George and Patricia Lilley; [m.] Gordon F. Berry III; [ch.] Jennifer L. Berry; [ed.] Deptford High; [oth. writ.] I have written several poems in the memoriam of family members in the obituaries in a local newspaper. I also write poems in my spare time as a hubby.; [pers.] The feelings I feel through others inspire me. It gives me the strength through them to express their inner most feelings. This poem is dedicated to the memory of Gordon F. Berry II; [a.] National Park, NJ

LINCOLN, CHRISTOPHER
[b.] April 6, 1974, Corydon, IN; [p.] Robert and Margaret Lincoln; [ed.] North Harrison High School; [occ.] Retail Sales; [memb.] Kentuckiana Blues Society; [hon.] National Merit Scholarship Semi-finalist; [oth. writ.] Many unpublished poems, short stories, and essays; [pers.] My poems deal with the struggle to stay sane in an insane world. My only influences are my own loneliness and depression.; [a.] Ramsey, IN

LINDSAY, PATRICIA
[b.] March 1, 1946, Sharon Hill, PA; [p.] James J. Leahy, Eleanor M. Leahy; [m.] James E. Lindsay, June 7, 1989; [ed.] Wildwood Catholic H.S., Glassboro State College (Limited Term); [occ.] Writer/author - book title "It Comes Down to Wanting Something", homemaker.; [memb.] International Society of Poets, Library of Congress - national member, Oxford Club, Concord Coalition, National Republican Party - sustaining member.; [hon.] Miss Cape May County, NJ-1964, Miss America Pageant Preliminary-NJ state level.; [oth. writ.] Formerly staff writer and recording artist - Jamie Records and Publishing Co. - Phila., PA. Formerly member of "BMI". Currently freelancing songwriter. [pers.] "If you are waiting for your ship to come in, be sure you have sent one out!" [a.] White Haven, PA

LINDSEY, DENNIS A.
[pen.] I-Ras; [b.] February 20, 1975, Wadesboro, NC; [p.] Juliet Lindsey; [ed.] Ellison High School; [occ.] Computer System/Software Analyst; [oth. writ.] Book of poems entitled "Babylon Chronicles."; [pers.] My work is the constant thought of love of being from life to death. Without my love for nature, human eras, and the longing to become one with myself, none of this would be possible. I would like to thank Heitco S., Choo P. and my mother
[a.] Killeen, TX

LINDSEY, WILLY
[pen.] Donovan Cortney; [b.] August 13, 1978, Great Falls, MT; [p.] Glora Wells, Bill Lindsey; [ed.] Currently Attending High School in the 10th Grade.; [occ.] Student; [hon.] Good Citizenship.; [oth. writ.] So far my only writings have been poetry.; [pers.] Life is to be valued. Through my poetry I value faults, strong points, defeats, victories, experiences, aspects, etc., and most important I value all forms of beauty, which beauty has no limits!; [a.] 29 Palms, CA

LINFOOT, LAURA
[b.] July 15, 1980, San Antonio, TX; [p.] Corky and Kathy Linfoot; [ed.] I'm currently enrolled in Grade 9; [occ.] Student; [hon.] I have 3 published poems.; [oth. writ.] I write children's stories in rhyme, and have many other poems.; [a.] Indio, CA

LIPPELT, JOHN W.
[b.] November 14, 1965, Coral Gables, FL; [p.] Eric E. Lippelt, Rose E. Lippelt; [m.] Maria A. Lippelt, September 23, 1994; [ch.] Steven William, Kevin Mathew; [ed.] Miami Sunset Sr. High; [occ.] Asst. Mgr., Home Depot; [oth. writ.] Poems written for family and friends.; [pers.] We all have seen the beauty of peace. We know the feeling of freedom it gives us. For those who wish to not seek it: allow those who do, to dwell in it freely.; [a.] Miami, FL

LISHAWA, ADAM
[b.] November 28, 1976, Gainesville, FL; [p.] C. Randal Lishawa, Debra Jackson; [ed.] New Hartford High, University of Florida; [occ.] Student; [memb.] Players of Utica, University of Florida Jazz Bands and Glee Club; [hon.] 1st place Poetry, 1991, New Hartford Central, Honorable Mention, Mohawk Valley Community College; [oth. writ.] Local publishing in newspaper, 73 page volume ready for publishing entitled "Twilight Dancer"; [pers.] Each poem is written for one person. Although I may never meet that person, I know they are out there, and they can read that poem and say, "This is me."; [a.] Gainesville, FL

LITTLE, JANA K.
[b.] March 26, 1964, Pasadena, TX; [p.] H. Doyle and Cindy Little/Wayne and Shirley Davis; [ed.] Tuloso-Midway High School, Corpus Christi, TX.; [memb.] National Multiple Sclerosis Society; [oth. writ.] Many other writings, never tried to be published.; [pers.] If people spoke as honestly as they wrote this world be a much better place to live; [a.] Greenville, TX

LIZANICH, NATALIE
[b.] February 4, 1930, Peckville, PA; [p.] Nicholas and Anita Kotch; [m.] Frank Lizanich, February 24, 1951; [ch.] Suzanne, Christine, Lawrence; [ed.] Olyphant High; [occ.] Homemaker; [memb.] Vice-pres. Scleroderma Support Group of Tampa Bay, Brandon Hospital Auxilliary, Volunteer the Village at Brandon Sunshine Apostolate of Nativity Church, RCIA Program Nativity Catholic Church, member of St. Francis Christian Community; [oth. writ.] Short story published by the Tampa Tribune; [pers.] By giving of myself to volunteer work in my community, my own life has been greatly enriched.; [a.] Brandon, FL

LIZARRAGA, CARLOS
[b.] April 16, 1951, Mexicali, Mexico; [p.] Francisco Lizarraga, Maria Franco; [ed.] Verdugo Hills High, Imperial Valley College; [occ.] Delivery Driver for PX Drugstore; [pers.] My writings are derived from the reflections of two cultural mirrors, Mexican and American. I can express myself in both the Spanish and English language; [a.] Tujunga, CA

LO PICCOLO, SAL M.
[b.] November 2, 1979, Farmingdale, Long Island, NY; [p.] Frank and Roseann Lo Piccolo; [ed.] Junior in Farmingdale High; [pers.] (To all writers) I would like to just say, when writing lets all your feelings come through, always write with heart and feeling, always keep your mind open, and your ideas will just follow from there. I would also like to just say: Grandpa may you rest in peace, and I'll always love you.; [a.] Farmingdale, NY

LOCKE, BRIAN
[b.] April 18, 1977, Weymouth; [p.] James W. Locke and Diana M. Locke; [ed.] A Junior at Whitman High.; [occ.] Student and Librarian; [oth. writ.] Every picture taken and a few others.; [pers.] "Do your best always, no matter how dim it looks"; [a.] Hanson, MA

LOERMANS, DAVID
[b.] July 4, 1970, Perth, Western Australia, Australia; [p.] Gerry Loermans, Julie Loermans; [m.] Allana, March 11, 1995; [ed.] Hedland Senior High School, Murdoch University (Computer Science); [occ.] Postman; [hon.] W.A. Naval Reserve Cadet of the Year 1988, 1990 Rotary Youth Leadership Awardee.; [oth. writ.] Large personal collection of poems, currently writing fantasy trilogy.; [pers.] I can think in words, but it takes a poem for me to explain just how I feel.; [a.] Perth Western Australia, Australia

LOFTHOUSE, ALICIA

[b.] July 3, 1956, Chicago, IL; [p.] Carlos and Carolin Smith; [ch.] Jody Lynn Lofthouse; [occ.] Live-in-caregiver for the elderly.; [memb.] I belong to "Faith Pentecostal Tabernacle"; [oth. writ.] Book called "Memories Of A Junkie" with 25 other poems of my past.; [pers.] God saved me from an addiction of drugs and alcohol after 22 years. My main goal is to reach others through my poems and let them know, there is a way of escape. And it's through Jesus Christ! "Heaven"

LOGAN, DERRICK

[b.] December 2, 1969, Halifax, Nova Scotia, Canada; [p.] Ralph, Nellie Logan; [ed.] Bachelor Arts major in English, Saint Mary's U. Halifax, NS, Canada; [occ.] Bartender; [oth. writ.] Short stories, articles, poetry and plays.; [a.] Halifax Nova Scotia, Canada

LOLLEY, DOROTHY J.

[pen.] Jean; [b.] August 3, 1939, Lake, MS; [p.] Mary Ellen and Charles H. Day; [m.] Travis Lolley, June 8, 1958; [ch.] Mike, Steve, Rich, Cindy, Sandy; [ed.] Went to Pascagoula High School in Pascagoula, MS, took GED in Thomasville, AL; [occ.] Housewife; [oth. writ.] I have two poems that was put to music and sung in church - I also have written 64 other poems of love.; [pers.] My poems are from my most inner feelings because of my love and convictions I have for God.; [a.] Faunsdale, AL

LOMONTE, SUSAN

[b.] June 24, 1967, Richmond Hill, Ontario, Canada; [p.] Lynne Morley, Jessie Spence; [ch.] Jessica, Sarah, Jonathon, Kayla; [ed.] Bayridge Secondary, Academy of Learning; [occ.] Mother/Student; [hon.] Diploma (Honours) MicroComputer Business Applications; [oth. writ.] Several poems that haven't been published, yet.; [pers.] Everything happens for a reason.; [a.] Kingston Ontario, Canada

LONARDO, WILLIAM

[pen.] Will Lonardo; [b.] September 5, 1943, Philadelphia, PA; [p.] Vito Lonardo, Della Lonardo; [m.] Kathy Lonardo, July 18, 1981; [ch.] Nikole, Michael; [ed.] Notre Dame High School, Girard College Philadelphia College of Art; [occ.] Promotional Writer and Designer; [memb.] Miller Memorial Blood Center, (Chairman), Hospital Central Services- (Director), Bethlehem Chamber of Commerce; [hon.] Numerous Graphic Awards: Neographics, case (College Publications) Paul Revere (Music Publications); [oth. writ.] Where have you been Billy Boy - (Novel), a time for hearts, souls and angels - (Novel), many (unpublished) poems; [pers.] Time represents the collective essence of many moments. Fill each one with faith and believe in the promise a new day brings. To idly watch a moment go by, is to waste the reason for being.; [a.] Hellertown, PA

LONG, CHRISTA G.

[pen.] Christa G. Long; [b.] November 13, 1935, Berlin, Germany; [p.] Roman and Hildegard Glowalla; [m.] Ralph Gerry Long, February 23, 1956; [ch.] Joffrey Long, 36, Dietrich Long, deceased; [ed.] German High School, Berlin, Germany Krakow Language School, Berlin, Germany Staatsoper Berlin Ballet School; [occ.] Real Estate Broker, Dance Instructor; [hon.] Taught dance at the School of American Ballet in 1969, at the personal invitation of Mr. George Balanchine.; [oth. writ.] Published articles in Dancemagazine, local newpapers, Orange County; [pers.] The performing and visual arts are of vital importance to any society for its very survival, we must, as a society, strive to pass a knowledge and passion for same onto our children and future generations. My favorite poet: Rainer Maria Rilke; [a.] Newport Beach, CA

LONGFOOT, DOROTHY D.

[b.] October 19, 1923, Alexandria, LA; [p.] Ahern Ashton Diagre and Alice C. Robbin; [m.] William C. Longfoot, April 4, 1943; [ed.] High School, Business College, National school of dress design, Alexandria Beauty College, (but most of what I know came from my elders, in traveling the USA, experience; [occ.] House keeper for my husband and this entails sewing, house painting, tiling, car repair, also built some furniture; [memb.] St. Francis Catholic Church, National humane education soc. and Louisiana sheriff's association (honoory member), belonged to a spiritualist church once.; [hon.] Award for volunteer in V.A. Medical Center, Alexandria LA, honor - a short story was published in "reminisce" mag. for their hard back book about world War II. "We pulled together... and won!" Was a contribution on my part. The honor was the publishing of said story for me.; [oth. writ.] Our daily town published every letter I wrote, from the early 1970's thru 1994 publishing my short Christmas story of a small child in 1980's. Tried out for our newspaper's summer time short story contest 3 times - (no win) but I am glad I tried. Always learn something.; [pers.] I try to write about the things I know about, events I or someone close to me has experienced. Sometimes I just use imagination upon hearing something funny and I extend it out into a little story, when I am `down' writing is a great `weight-lifter' for the mind.; [a.] Pineville, LA

LONGO, DOMENICO

[pen.] Emmanuele Primavera; [b.] December 4, 1966, Sicily, Italy; [p.] Giuseppe Longo, Maria Gacciatore; [ed.] Reseda High, Los Angeles Valley College; [occ.] Poet; [hon.] In recognition for Outstanding Performance in: Team Work, Staff of the Month.; [oth. writ.] I did publish a book of poetry on my own.; [pers.] I have so much love in my heart that I would like to share it with those who understand the art of love.; [a.] Palmdale, CA

LONNQUIST, JASON

[pen.] Jay Lonnquist; [b.] August 11, 1975, Vancouver, British Columbia, Canada; [p.] Bo Lonnquist - Brita Lonnquist; [pers.] Beast, bird, bud and bough. In all her fineless enfoldings Nature has ever been, and will remain, my greatest wellspring.; [a.] Vancouver, British Columbia, Canada

LOPER, LISSA LEE

[b.] February 6, 1964, Johnstown, PA; [p.] Teresa and John Juhas; [m.] John W. Loper, May 26, 1990; [ch.] Byriah John; [ed.] Central Cambria H.S., University of Pittsburg and Glassboro State College; [occ.] House parent/teacher/counselor; [hon.] Graduated Magna Cum Laude from undergrad and earned high honors from grad school; [pers.] A special thanks to my very best friend - my soulmate - husband who constantly encourages me as I encourage others to "seek their bliss"; [a.] Womelsdorf, PA

LOPEZ, JOAQUIN D.

[pen.] Matrix; [b.] April 6, 1978; [p.] Luz Lopez and David A. Schlicht; [ch.] Kaylyn Christina Cochran; [ed.] Costa Mesa High; [occ.] Student; [memb.] Nelles Chapel Deacon Congregation; [hon.] Several honor roll certificates, participation awards; [oth. writ.] I write many poems for my fiancee and a series of stories for my daughter; [pers.] "Winners never quit, quitters never win;" [a.] Costa Mesa, CA.

LOPEZ, LISA

[p.] Kathy Perkins and Tony Lopez; [hon.] This poem was selected for a Veteran's Day ceremony at Bandera Middle School; [a.] Bandera, TX

LOPEZ, OSCAR L.

[pen.] Latino Amante; [b.] August 28, 1972, La Paz, El Salvador; [p.] Maria E. Lopez and Jose M. Lopez; [ed.] Graduated from Catholic Central High School (CCH) including the Ontario Academic Credits.; [occ.] Student and Publisher of the JOVEN newsletter; [oth. writ.] A collection of unpublished poems written in English and Spanish.; [pers.] In my writings, I attempt to bring the feeling of the Latin American Soul into the English language. Writing, to me is like painting, and I try to portray the image of love in very simple pictures. However most of my writings project landscapes of solitude, it is only my style of expressing my thoughts. I have not been influenced by any poet, and I aim to make my own personal style. Nevertheless, there might be somebody else who writes in a similar style as I do, I am not a poet, I only write my thoughts on a piece of paper.; [a.] London Ontario, Canada

LOUD, LARRY W.

[pen.] LWL; [b.] August 14, 1950, Minneapolis, MN; [p.] Henrietta and Dayton Loud; [ch.] (One son) Leslie Tillman Loud; [ed.] University of Minnesota, Major in: Bus, Psy, Music composition. B.S. Degree Pending Dossier.; [occ.] Professional Musician-piano, voice, bass, brass, percussion; [memb.] Black music Educators of Minnesota. The musicians union; [hon.] Best stand-up singer award in 1970. Top salesman award selling keyboards at Schmitt Music Centers 1991; [oth. writ.] Several songs, to be released this year 1995, on CD and Video.; [pers.] I am constantly aiming to promote world peace through action. One of my goals is to truly develop my abundant personality mentality in the spirit of cooperation and interdependability.; [a.] Minneapolis, MN

LOUIS, DAVID

[b.] December 25, 1947, Hong Kong; [p.] Peter Louis, Janet Louis (deceased); [m.] Betty (deceased); [ch.] Justin Demetrius, Everett Lichen; [ed.] 1. Molecular Biology - SFSU, 2. Medical Doctor - College of Medicine and Dentistry of New Jersey; [occ.] Physician in Oakland, Consultant to Asian Health Services, Clinical Associate Professor UCSF, Clinical Instructor UCD, Clinical Instructor Stanford; [hon.] Best Medical Doctor in 1994 voted by readers of Alameda Group of Newspapers; [oth. writ.] "Tin", "She's Gone", "Heroes, "Betty", "Evolution"; [pers.] Poetry is a beautiful medium to express feelings; [a.] Oakland, CA

LOVE, RICHARD ANDERSON

[b.] Mount Pleasant, TN; [p.] Joseph Love and Altha Love; [m.] Janice (Sledge) Love; [ch.] Donna Regina and Angelia Dawn; [ed.] Hay Long High School, University of Maryland; [occ.] Management and Program Analyst; [memb.] American Federation of Musicians; [hon.] Bronze Star Medal (Vietnam) USAF, 2 Meritorious service medals, USAF, 3 Commendation medals, USAF; [oth. writ.] Touch me, a book of poems who I am, a book of poems designated lover, a country music album shadows of my mind, a country music album fly to the horizon, a novel portrait of a war, a short story numerous other songs and short stories; [pers.] All living things are brothers and sisters and earth is our mother. We should take care of our family.; [a.] Marion, TX

LOWERRE, SUSAN
[pen.] Sue; [b.] March 1, 1978, Bethpage, NY; [p.] Carol and Al Lowerre; [ed.] Massapequa High School on 9/5/95 I will be entering my senior year.; [occ.] Student; [memb.] U.S. Figure Skating Clubs, Certificate of award of M.H.S. for A Cappella; [oth. writ.] "Words" and "Seasons of Bliss" not published as yet.; [pers.] I've always had a gift since the 7th grade to put my thoughts in poems whether sad or happy. Mostly happy and sensitive words I have lived all my years in.; [a.] Massapequa, NY

LOWINGER, JAKE
[b.] April 9, 1976, Brooklyn, NY; [p.] Ronald Lowinger, Dr. Bonnie Lowinger; [ed.] Currently attending New York University; [occ.] Editor (part-time)

LUCAS, SHERYL
[b.] February 28, 1947, Toronto, Canada; [p.] Arthur Gordon, Gwenn Gordon; [ch.] Richard Edward, Dena Lee; [ed.] East High; [pers.] Writing holds the key to my world, my mother was my inspiration; [a.] Hemlock, NY

LUFFMAN, STAR SHAUNTA
[b.] March 15, 1980, Iredell Memorial; [p.] Myrtle Louise, Michael Foster; [ed.] 9th Grade; [hon.] Two trophies for basketball, one for bowling. Reward for best essay in D.A.R.E, got highest grade on writing test in elementary. Three class participation awards.; [oth. writ.] I have lots of other poems I have wrote. I wrote a book and hoping for its publication.; [pers.] Where your hearts lead you, follow it. That's what helps me follow my dreams. Whatever you want, you can have if you set your mind and heart to it. I thank all the support of my friends and family.; [a.] Statesville, NC

LUGO, ESTELA
[b.] June 27, 1980, Long Island, NY; [p.] Mike and Eneida Lugo; [ed.] Freshman at Farmingdale High School; [a.] Massapequa, NY

LUKE, GEORGIA
[b.] November 5, 1964, Galveston, TX; [p.] Walter and Shirley Gernand Jr.; [m.] David Luke, January 9, 1993; [ed.] Alvin High School, Alvin Community College, University of Houston at Clear Lake; [occ.] Associate Engineering Technician; [pers.] Poetry has allowed me to express my intermost feelings and emotions.; [a.] Friendswood, TX

LUONG, CRYSTAL-HANH
[b.] December 2, 1984, Vietnam; [p.] Sum Thanh Luong and My-Tien Le; [ed.] Hage Elementary School - 5th grade (now) in G.A.T.E. (Gifted and Talented Education) program student.; [occ.] Student; [hon.] Academic honor rolls, student of the month awards, in G.A.T.E. (gifted and talented education) program student, 24 game challenge semi-finalist.; [oth. writ.] Collection of unpublished poems: Freedom, Number one, the Great Idea, and more.; [pers.] I love to write poetry to express my ideas and feelings. This particular poem is written for my parents, my grandparents and my sister. I hope the reader of my poem will enjoy it as much as I have enjoyed writing it.; [a.] San Diego, CA

LUSTER, OWEN F.
[b.] February 24, 1936, Paris, TX; [p.] Mary C. Luster, Dewey Luster; [ed.] Paris High School, Paris Junior College; [occ.] Maintenance Dept. Paris Junior College; [oth. writ.] Several country and western songs. "Corner of twelth and vine" published in Paris Texas News; [pers.] I was influenced by Hank Williams - SR and my songs are written in his style.; [a.] Paris, TX

LYALL, RENATA WIRKNER
[b.] November 5, 1960, Karlovy Varyczech Republic; [ed.] German/Slavic/Scandinavian Studies (postgrad and research), English for special purposes, English/American Literature (grad postgrad); [occ.] Language Instructory/Translator/Language Consultant; [memb.] Steinbeck Foundation, CA, ACL (American Consultants' League) Canadian Institute of Strategic Studies, Canada Studies Ass., FMF (Association for Acquisition of Contemporary Foreign Languages, Germany), IATEFL (Int. Teachers' Ass. for English as Foreign/Second); [hon.] Delta Kappa Gamma; [oth. writ.] No publication of poetry, numerous writings since age 12, a large collection of writings in various languages upon mood and need of expression for myself.; [pers.] I have been searching to catch a feeling, a swing of mood, through reflection in verbal expression. My poems made it possible. With them I find in language the depth I was looking, or beyond the level of standard structures. Although every genre of poetry and literature undoubtedly left an impression behind. I was caught mostly by and caused to return to the writings of Ancient Greece and to the expressionist works of our century. To me poetry means the overflow of feelings pushing to the surface and finding their way into an everlasting world of silence.; [a.] Sandhausen, Germany

LYNCH, PEGGY
[b.] October 24, 1946, Murray, UT; [p.] Eugene and Arvilla Peterson; [m.] Scott Lynch, March 11, 1991; [ch.] Jeff, Brandi, Lainie; [ed.] Salt Lake Community College; [occ.] Account Executive, AT and T; [pers.] The reading and writing of poetry has provided me with many hours of enjoyment for many years.; [a.] Murray, UT

LYONS, CAROL
[b.] 1945, Vancouver, WA; [p.] H. Earl and Cleo Hutchison; [m.] Larry Lyons, 1987; [ch.] Donnie (stepson); [ed.] Graduated 1977 Clark College, Vancouver, WA; [occ.] Registered Nurse, Sacramento, CA; [hon.] 2nd place, Poetry Contest, High School Division, Archdiocese of Seattle, 1960. Semi-finalist, 1994 North American Open Poetry Contest.; [oth. writ.] Poem to be published in 1995 in Anthology, Songs on the Wind; [pers.] I have been writing off and on for approximately 35 years. Much of my poetry reflects my deep spiritual/christian beliefs. The poetry of Helen Steiner Rice has greatly inspired me.; [a.] Galt, CA

LYSACK, ALISSA
[b.] August 16, 1979, Swan River, Manitoba, Canada; [ed.] Currently studying at Swan Valley Regional Secondary School; [occ.] Student; [hon.] Language Arts and French Awards at grade nine graduation. Honor Roll throughout Junior High. Valedictorian at grade nine graduation.; [oth. writ.] Wrote poetry at a creative writing course during the summer of 1994 in Winnipeg, Manitoba with the Institute of Gifted Students; [pers.] I have always enjoyed the uniqueness that poetry gives to many people worldwide. I hope that in the future I will always be able to express my feelings in a way that people I care about will understand.; [a.] Swan River Manitoba, Canada

MABEY, AMANDA G.
[b.] December 21, 1980, Salt Lake City, UT; [p.] Gun S. Mabey and Edward M. Mabey; [ed.] Almost finished with grade school.; [occ.] Writer; [oth. writ.] I have several other poems which are better than "Memories" but couldn't enter them because of their length. None of my work has ever been published.; [pers.] I decided to become a writer 3 years ago. I'm 13 right now but extremely devoted. When I'm not writing, I'm not happy.; [a.] Scottsdale, AZ

MACDONALD, MARION
[pen.] Marion Clinton MacDonald; [b.] August 14, 1954, Souris P.E.I., Canada; [p.] Sally and Percy Clinton; [m.] T. Foch MacDonald November 24, 1973; [ch.] Brad - 20, Heather and Holly -18; [ed.] Grade Eleven; [occ.] Florist; [memb.] Church organizations, readers digest, Canadian Geographic, charitable organizations; [hon.] Your response felt like an award. My mother awards are loyal long term friendships.; [oth. writ.] I have other poetry but I've never tried to have anything published until this opportunity came up.; [pers.] There is nothing more important in life than people - be it family, friends or the stranger on the street. Poetry is an expression of one person's emotions.

MACDONALD, PAUL
[b.] February 18, 1976, Milton, Ontario, Canada; [p.] Phil and Betty MacDonald; [ed.] E.C. Drury High School, Lakehead University; [occ.] Advanced Waterski Instructor.; [memb.] Ontario Water Ski Association, Outdoor Recreation Student Society, Royal Life Saving Society of Canada; [pers.] My inspiration comes from Kimberlee. If I can show one person the beauty of life - I've done my job.; [a.] Milton Ontario, Canada

MACINTOSH, ROBERT
[b.] May 22, 1929, Newark, NJ; [p.] Alex and Florence MacIntosh; [ed.] Attended the school of fine and industrial arts in New Jersey. Served in the Korean conflict.; [occ.] Retired commercial artist spent some time as photo restorer; [memb.] Studied acting techniques under Gary Chases productions in Houston Texas; [hon.] I have done and sold many drawings using pastels. I specialize in scenes of Western and American Indian Culture, under the name "Cameron West."; [oth. writ.] I began writing three years ago. Short stories and a video film that was actually filmed, called "the holiday." I have compiled about 20 poems, some of which are still in process; [pers.] I believe that small everyday problems and joys of life can touch the hearts of people if they are highlighted properly. Memories of the past that are dusted off cleaned and polished; [a.] Houston, TX

MACK, DEBORA ALEXANDER
[hon.] Kappa Delta Phi, Honors in Education; [oth. writ.] Poems and Songs; [pers.] I thank God for his many blessings. Personal thanks to my mother. Dedication goes to my two children, and to all the children of the world. Special dedication to "Swisscheese."

MACKENZIE, MICHAEL
[b.] June 15, 1978, Abeliene, TX; [ed.] High-school student; [pers.] Even though I cannot play well (yet), I love guitar and find salvation in music publication in this edition and other's insistence has not convinced me of my ability to write. I maintain a depressed attitude and a pessimistic view of life. This message will self-destruct in five seconds. [a.] Cibolo, TX

MACKEY, KEVIN J.
[b.] March 20, 1955, Dubrin, Ireland; [p.] Larry, Peggy, Mackey; [ch.] Niamm, Brendan, Lisa; [occ.] Technology Consultant; [oth. writ.] I poem in "a far off place", book reviews; [pers.] We see ourselves reflected in others and others in ourselves

MACMILLAN, JILL ANN
[b.] March 12, 1974, Richmond, CA; [p.] James and Marcia Kay; [ed.] 2 years Laney College - Oakland, CA; [occ.] Student, still attending school, Major - Medicine; [memb.] World Wildlife Fund, National Parks and Conservation Assoc...Eastern Star, Northbrae Community Church; [hon.] None prevalent; [oth. writ.] Several Newspaper articles, book of poetry, as yet, unpublished.; [pers.] I was inspired by the early works of Shakespeare and Dickens. I believe that poetry is the purest expression of one's self.; [a.] Berkeley, CA

MACPHERSON, SELENA
[b.] May 19, 1978, Mareeba; [p.] Wayne MacPherson, Dianne MacPherson; [ed.] Saint Mary's College, Mount Carmel College; [occ.] Senior Student; [hon.] Academic awards of merit in years eight and ten; [oth. writ.] Recently one of my poems was chosen and published in an anthology for the International Year of the family.; [pers.] Everything, I guess influences me in some way. In everything there is always something to write about. There is never no limits until you stop thinking and using your imagination.; [a.] Charters Towers, Queensland

MADDOX, BARRIE P.
[pen.] Barrie Perdue-Maddox; [b.] March 4, 1940, Jacksonville, FL; [p.] Owens Perdue, Marguerite Perdue; [m.] Edward E. Maddox, July 27, 1955; [ch.] Sheryl Lynn, Terri Lynn, Edward E. Jr.; [ed.] State of Florida GED, St. Johns River Community College (Selective courses only, not a graduate) Institute of financial Education; [occ.] Bookkeeper - McCurdy - Walden, Inc.; [memb.] FJC - Advisory committee member on occupational education 1979-1981, Member of Audit Selection Committee for city of Green Cove Springs in 1978 and 1982, past chapter representative for the institute of financial education; [hon.] Phi Theta Kappa, Dean's List - 1992; [oth. writ.] Numerous unpublished poems; [pers.] My poems are inspirations from the heart, the first being written "To Dawn", my terminally ill niece, who departed this life at the young age of 32.; [a.] Orange Park, FL

MADRID, ROBERT NUNEZ
[b.] November 21, 1962, Vado, NM; [m.] Beatrice G. Madrid, August 5, 1995; [occ.] City Transit - Bus Driver; [hon.] Poetry - "Honorable Mention" 8th Grade; [pers.] Writing for me is the passage to my inner self. The world where I can be who I want to be, and it cost nothing. Beatrice is the key to my inspiration, my angel from heaven.

MADRIGAL, JULIE ANN
[b.] September 6, 1964, Torrance, CA; [p.] Ralph and Kay Madrigal; [ch.] Jaime Ralph, Natalie Rose, and Dennis Joseph; [ed.] High School Diploma; [occ.] Housewife; [oth. writ.] Several poems although none have ever been published.; [pers.] The poetry I write is deep feelings and alot for my beautiful children whom I love with all my heart. May they always be very proud of my accomplishments.; [a.] Huntington Park, CA

MAGNIN, FLORENCE
[b.] November 26, 1921, Darby, PA; [p.] Mary and Harry Drumm (D); [m.] Jules A. Magnin, June 27, 1942; [ch.] Barbara, Arthur, Elaine, Joyce; [ed.] Darby High School; [occ.] Home maker and foster grandmother at Melmark Home and School for retarded, handicapped children.; [memb.] Women's auxiliary of Sunday Breakfast Association, Inc. volunteer Foster Grandparent Program of Delaware Co. Pa. Folcroft Union Church, Folcroft, Pa.; [hon.] Office of United States Congressman, Curt Weldon Certificate of appreciation for successful participation in Delaware Co. F.P.G. and Honor certificate for significant service to the community as a foster grandparent by FGP of U.S.A.; [oth. writ.] Several poems published in the F.G.P. Newsletter. Numerous poems given to friends. Many poems put away to read now and then.; [pers.] I love to write poems for the children I care for. I am inspired by long fellow's poetry. I feel like Emily Dickerson, putting poems in my drawer of my chest and shoe boxes. Some of my friends are impressed.; [a.] Lansdowne, PA

MAININI, MICHAEL DAVID
[pen.] Mick Mainini; [b.] September 30, 1954, Oakland, CA; [p.] Mario and Louise Mainini; [ch.] Jared Mainini; [ed.] El Cerrito High School California Maritime Academy John F. Kennedy University; [occ.] Department Head of Facilities Scios Nova Inc.; [memb.] Parenteral Drug Assn. American Management Assn. International Society of Pharmaceutical Engineers; [oth. writ.] 35 poems since 1976 which have not been published.; [pers.] Sometimes inspiration for poems comes to me by the sight of special places. Other poems are inspired by persons I care about. This is for my son.; [a.] El Sobrante, CA

MAITRE, ISLANDE
[pen.] Baby Love; [b.] March 22, 1979, Port-au-Prince, Haiti; [p.] Laurence Bazard and Edward Maitre; [ed.] Mudwood High School; [occ.] Pediatrician

MAK, MARIE
[b.] November 12, 1980, Charlotte; [p.] Helen and King Him Mak; [ed.] Granard Jr. high; [pers.] I just like to write poems about how I feel about my emotions.; [a.] Gaffney, SC

MALARY, NARCISSE G.
[b.] July 31, 1933, Hinche, Haiti; [p.] Gesner and Lydia Malary; [ed.] Ecole Normale d'Institutions, Teachers College, Port-au-Prince; [occ.] Radio advertising; [memb.] Rosicrucian Order; [hon.] Speaker of the year award, 1983 (given within the Haitian diaspora in N.Y.); [oth. writ.] Unpublished poems in French and English; [pers.] My goal would be attained if, through the window of poetry, I could stand as an echo of my fellow men's graces, beauties, loftiness and frailties.; [a.] Queens Village, NY

MALECKI, THEODORE GEORGE
[pen.] Ted; [b.] December 14, 1914, Milwaukee, WI; [p.] Mr. and Mrs. Theodore and Mary Malecki; [m.] Evelyn Tillie Malecki, February 10, 1945; [ch.] Jean Mare Malecki; [ed.] Notre Dame High School Bryant Stratton Bus. College; [occ.] Retired heavy machine dynamic balancer; [memb.] UAW, St. Rita's, St. Florian W. Allis Senior Centre W. Milwaukee Senior; [hon.] Swimming and diving works for entertaining in various nursing homes, W. Allis Business College Awards for electronics for completion.; [oth. writ.] Compositions of other poetry. Compositions of songs and music; [pers.] My purpose for writing this poem is based on the motto "Don't try to fool a child." He don't forget. What's more he will love you for it.; [a.] West Allis, WI

MALLETT, DOROTHY
[pen.] Dam; [pers.] Wrote poetry in the early 70's. Had some published in small periodicals, then gave it up for family demands and getting a job. I am starting again with fresh blinds and having fun for the joy of writing.

MALLORY, BRENDA
[b.] February 17, 1964, Halifax County; [p.] Nannie Turner - Tana Blount; [m.] John Carry Mallory, March 25, 1981; [ch.] (3) Sophia Mallory - Jereme Mallory - Joan Shontel Mallory; [ed.] Weldon High School Halifax Community College; [occ.] Nursing Student at Halifax Community College; [pers.] Poetry gives me the opportunity to create things. I have an immense imagination. And I build my poetry on that. I love writing poetry. And I do best at night when every body and everything is quiet and still.; [a.] Roanoke Rapids, NC

MALVINA, GHITA
[pen.] Ghita M. Raci; [b.] September 20, 1920, Romania; [p.] Sander Szabo, Anna Szabo; [m.] Widow, 1946; [ch.] Hanna Ghieza; [ed.] High School - Petru Major Romania Philosophy courses.; [occ.] Retired; [memb.] Canadian Hungarian Community Services, Wagman Centre Art Section Barbara Frum Library (Hungarian Literature Circle) 60 Volunteer Friendship Assoc. Bernard Betel, Creative Living Centre Holocaust Institution; [hon.] Prized Volunteer - Mention in Painting and Ceramic; [oth. writ.] Several poems, articles and biography (Famous Woman in our time) published in local newspapers, Volunteer writer for the newspaper "Menora" Toronto; [pers.] Being influenced through real-life experiences, accepting the circumstances in our life! I try to express through my writings a view to mankind that Freedom, Love and Friendship are the most important things in our world.; [a.] Toronto Ontario, Canada

MANCLAW, RON
[pen.] Ron Manclaw; [b.] March 27, 1943, Little Falls, NY; [p.] Homer E and Verna E. Manclaw; [ed.] 1969 MBA - Marketing Syracuse University , 1967 BSIE (Production, Management), Syracuse University AAS - DeVry Technical Inst. - Chicago; [occ.] CEO - RM International Inc. (Recovery Management Inc), Business Manager Advance Insurance Inc., Lake Worth, Florida; [memb.] Waterfront Property, Owners Assn of Florida - Past Vice President.; [hon.] World Who's Who - top 5000 (Mar Quis), Travelers Insurance Humanitarian Award Acknowledgement Who's Who in Electronics Who's Who in Community Service; [oth. writ.] Stories and short articles of Human interest; [pers.] The glory and my life is dedicated to our Lord, Jesus Christ and especially the Great (Holy) spirit, my Angels and Demon's be out of here!; [a.] Fort Lauderdale, FL

MANCO, JUDITH ANN
[pen.] Judy Ann; [b.] August 6, 1947, Hoboken, NJ; [p.] Anna and Salvatore Congilose; [ch.] Rosario (Russell); [ed.] Associate in Science Associate in applied Science Ocean Country college, T.R. NJ.; [occ.] Registered Nurse, Certified MCOC, NJ; [oth. writ.] "The First Time I Cried" story written for the Nursing Spectrum magazine. Published Dec 27, 1994; [pers.] Through writing our thoughts we not only educate, but we touch the hearts and minds of all!; [a.] Toms River, NJ

MANECKE, ROBERT LESLIE
[pen.] Robert Leslie Manecke; [b.] November 17, 1961, Minneapolis, MN; [p.] R. Leslie Manecke, Vivian Manecke; [ed.] College of St. Thomas; [hon.] The National Collegiate Foreign Language Honor Society; [a.] Bemidji, MN

MANGANO, JOHN J.
[b.] February 12, 1936, Maryland; [m.] Jane Mangano; [ed.] Johns Hopkins General Motors Institute; [oth. writ.] Poetry Book- Speaking of Love (1994); [pers.] Each poem I write is an attempt to reach for deeper meanings in the trials and triumphs of everyday life.; [a.] Shorewood, WI

MANN, MEGAN
[pen.] Emily Starr; [b.] June 17, 1980, Morehead City, NC; [p.] Michael and Linda Mann; [ed.] Newport Elementary, Camp Glenn Elementary, Broad Creek Middle School, West Carteret High School; [occ.] Student/Poet; [memb.] Junior Beta Club; [hon.] 1st place in Morehead City Woman's Club lyrical poetry section; [oth. writ.] Queen of the Mountain, False Hopes, My Cat, Silence, In My Mind's Eye (all poems); [pers.] I always say I will succeed, therefore I always do.; [a.] Nwport, NC

MANNINO II, JOSEPH S.
[b.] November 11, 1972, Cortland, NY; [p.] Vito and Marilyn Mannino; [m.] Linda M. Mannino, November 12, 1994; [ed.] Clearwater High, Central Texas College, Dantes College; [occ.] US Marine; [memb.] Non-Commissioned Officers Association; [hon.] This is my first; [oth. writ.] Appeared in several local publications, the AJAX poetry letter; [pers.] I believe that within the heart of every human lies the ability and desire to create. Whether its a woman who longs to be a mother or a painter who longs to empty his soul on canvas the flame of inspiration burns brightly within each of us.; [a.] Clearwater, FL

MANOSH, DANIEL WILLIAM
[b.] July 27, 1922, Sheldon Springs, VT; [p.] Bernie and Ila Manosh; [m.] Barbara Crossett Manosh, December 12, 1958; [ch.] Daniel William Jr., and Peter John; [ed.] High School, Air Force Management Academy, A.F. Leadership Academy G.E. Shop Math Course G.E. Engineering courses 1 and 2, class A Machinist and Journeyman; [occ.] Retired; [memb.] American Legion; [hon.] Bronze Stars for Military Campaigns, Rome-Arno, Northern Appening, PO Valley, Southern France, Northern France, Rhineland, Maples-Forgia, Air Combat Balkays, Two Bronze Stars for 1st and 2nd winters Durwekoran war.; [oth. writ.] Memory of the mind, a tarn, a winter sunrise, the arctic; [pers.] I have read a lot on nature and am trying to put some of it into my own words.; [a.] East Fairfield, VT

MAPLES, FRANCIS C.
[pen.] Frank; [b.] October 25, 1924, Detroit, MI; [p.] Ira Margaret Maples; [m.] Shirley E. Maples, October 20, 1945; [ch.] Gary, Francis, Charlene; [ed.] 10th Gd; [occ.] Retired from Mental Health Dept. State of Michigan; [memb.] V.F.W.; [hon.] VET W.II. Purple Heart.; [pers.] I try to vision a story within a phone; [a.] Elgin, SC

MARCUM, MYRTLE B.
[pen.] Myrtle B. Marcum; [b.] July 20, 1924, Alabama, AL; [p.] R.L. and Sarah Burgess; [m.] Percy D. Marcum, March 21, 1942; [ch.] Five; [ed.] High School; [occ.] Retired from Exon Co.; [oth. writ.] I am semi invalid from seven back surgery, I have a very good life, many hobbies, a beautiful husband and children, writings poems is my love; [a.] Empire, AL

MARINAJ, GJEKE N.
[b.] May 26, 1967, Albania; [p.] Nik, File; [m.] Dusita, November 30, 1992; [ed.] Graduate of a technical institute (in Albania), with a major in journalism. Presently studying journalism at Richland College in Texas.; [occ.] Technician in the science of phlebotomy.; [hon.] In 1990 won First Prize in poetry, and Second Prize in prose in a literary contest held in Albania.; [oth. writ.] Began publishing articles, poems and short stories in Albania, at the age of 16. Due to be published soon are a volume of poetry and a novel.; [pers.] I find inspiration in the works of Pablo Neruda, Paul Eluard, and Rudolf Marku. In general, I like all styles of poetry, but prefer modern poetry above all.; [a.] Dallas, TX

MARINO, MARK V.
[b.] May 25, 1954, Staten Island, NY; [p.] Samuel C. and Grace Marino; [m.] Carleen Marino, May 4 1990; [ch.] Christine, David, Nicholas; [ed.] Msgr. Farrell H.S., Manhattan College, Wagner College, S.I. community College; [occ.] Retired 10/31/94 from N.Y.C. Police department detective 2nd grade; [hon.] Numerous awards while working for the N.Y. PD from both the job and from the community.; [oth. writ.] Numerous personal poems not yet seen of published. [pers.] "To be allowed to be creative and to share with others, who could ask for more"; [a.] Staten Island, NY

MARK, SHEILA DAPHNE JOAN
[pen.] Sheila Mark; [b.] December 1, 1945, Grenada, West Indies; [p.] Wellington Lalite, Theresa Lalite; [m.] September 10, 1964; [ch.] Evelyn Stephanie, Trudy Chantel Evlyn George; [ed.] New Jersey Medical School U.S.A., Mason University, Virginia, USA; City College, New York, U.S.A.; [occ.] Banker; [memb.] Life time member in the 2nd Battalion Airborne 505th Infantry, Panther Task Force - U.S. Military; [hon.] Cambridge Tutorial College, U.K. Dip. Office Management/Administration (Distinction) Dip. Personnel Management and Industrial Relations (Distinction), Skinner College of Business Studies Dip. Secretarial; [oth. writ.] Articles in local newspapers articles in staff newsletter (previous employment); [pers.] I strive to reflect God's love towards mankind. I am influenced by nature, the ineffable design of the Universe.; [a.] St. George's, Grenada, West Indies

MARKOVICH, JENNIE MARIE
[b.] March 16, 1974, Beech Grove, IN; [p.] Della M. Ault and John Markovich (Divorced); [ch.] Starletta Dawn and Angel Dawn; [ed.] Franklin High School in Indiana; [occ.] Mother for my children; [memb.] Rocklane Christian Church; [hon.] Citizenship Award in 9th grade while attending cedar key high in Florida; [oth. writ.] Several other poems not read by the public yet, but maybe someday will be published for everyone to enjoy.; [pers.] I'm influenced by my family and my children to write my poems to help tell people what I see in my family my children, and everybody life.; [a.] Chiefland, FL

MARLOW, VERN A.
[b.] October 24, 1923, Redfield, SD; [p.] Ben C., Rose M. (Keller) Marlon; [m.] Bonnie Laura (Hixon) Marlon, June 4, 1956; [ch.] Ben, Peri, and Tami; [ed.] Redfield High School; [occ.] Retired; [memb.] Good Sam Club, United Church of Christ Choir Member, Retired Fire Chief Org., Nat Bowling Congress; [hon.] National Honor Soc. Poen in County Record in Grade School in 1930's; [oth. writ.] Several poems in local news papers, this poem is Fireman Mag.; [pers.] I write about things in life that affect me most. I helped start a fire department and was chief for 32 years. I wrote poems about, mother, father, 50th school reunion, 30th Marlon family reunion; [a.] Redfield, SD

MARQUARD, TERI
[pen.] T. J. Marquard/little T; [b.] February 26, 1962, Wausau, WI; [p.] Tom and Mary Strehlow; [ed.] Oak Grove, High School San Jose, CA - 95123/A few business courses.; [occ.] Retail; [memb.] Aris Project - nonprofeit support to person(s) living with HIV/AIDS Virus; [oth. writ.] Published poem in "Dusting Off Dreams" Vol VII; [pers.] I've written poetry, and continue to write as a way of expressing my feelings. I started writing at the age of 14; [a.] San Jose, CA

MARROQUIN, IRMA B.
[b.] August 16, 1941, Germany; [p.] Hans Fichtbauer, Margaret Fichtbauer; [ch.] Jesse E., Diane J.; [ed.] Highschool/Trade School in Germany, St. Philips College TX. Immigrated to U.S.A. in 1962 naturalized in 1970; [occ.] Self Employed; [memb.] American Small Business Association; [hon.] Outstanding Scholastic Achievement; [oth. writ.] First writing; [pers.] By virtue of unfaltering determination one can overcome any obstacles in life and still find inner peace and happiness all around.; [a.] Universal City, TX

MARTELL, RALPH G.
[pen.] Ralph G. Martell; [b.] February 9, 1927, Mt. Clements, MI; [p.] Lawrence and Elizabeth; [m.] Alison, September 26, 1971; [ch.] Nevin Gabriel, Josephine; [ed.] 10th Grade; [occ.] Retired Restaurateur; [oth. writ.] Memories of the Mato Grosso, When Does the Fun Start, Fish Tales, To Get Hooked on Small Potatoes, and other stories; [pers.] Life is what you make of it so do your best and enjoy it.; [a.] Bouckville, NY

MARTIN, MAGGIE E.
[b.] May 11, 1962, Escondido, CA; [p.] Paul E. and Norma Jane McCollum; [m.] Jeffrey L. Martin, April 16, 1994; [ch.] Ryan James and Ashley Nicole; [ed.] Kofu High and Arizona Western College; [occ.] Licensed vocational Nurse for Lindom Medical Clinic's; [memb.] American Heart Association Los Angeles Zoological Society; [hon.] Employee of the month, Best of the Best 1993, 110% to 92; [pers.] I write my poems from the heart and my own experiences.; [a.] Fontuna, CA

MARTIN, ROBERT LANCE
[b.] December 11, 1973, Killean, TX; [p.] Bob and Deb Martin; [ed.] Washington Comm. H.S. Washington, IL Basic Training - Fort Jackson, SC; [occ.] Soldier; [memb.] Veterans of Foreign Wars; [hon.] Who's Who Among American High School Students, Armed Forces Expeditionary Medal, National Defense Medal, Army Commendation Medal (Impact); [oth. writ.] Several other poems, three songs that I hope get published someday; [pers.] After having seen the situation in Haiti through the eyes of a soldier, it has shown me that America is still a great country. Despite it's flaws, it is still the symbol of freedom for the entire world; [a.] Fort Drum, NY

MARTIN, SARA
[b.] December 2, 1980, Omaha, NE; [p.] Gary and Connie Martin; [ed.] Walt Disney elementary, Walnut Grove elementary, Pleasent Ridge elementary, Pioneer Trail Junior High; [occ.] Secretary for Swanson Gentleman Heart; [hon.] Principle's honor roll; [pers.] My poems come straight from my heart. It reflects personal things that have happened to me. Poetry is my way of letting things out, and I hope that someone can benefit from my poem; [a.] Overland Park, KS

MARTINEZ, DUANE M.
[pen.] William Shepeard; [b.] June 12, 1979, Sedro-

Wooley; [p.] Frank and Leona Martinez; [ed.] Eunice Academy (Home School); [occ.] I have no occupation, but I wish to be a poet.; [memb.] Hazel Dell Evangelical Free Church; [oth. writ.] The Iron Hand, She The Road; Anathema; The Gypsy Girl; Grace and Many Many More; [pers.] I wish to give thanks to Jesus Christ for bestowing upon me such a wonderful talent. A note to all other Christian poets, never compromise your beliefs in your writing for popularity; [a.] Vancouver, WA

MARTINEZ, LYLE EDWARD
[b.] March 12, 1944, Lawton, OK; [p.] Rose and Paul Martinez; [m.] Inez Martinez, May 17, 1969; [ch.] Lisa Diane, Thomas; [ed.] BA Degree - 1973 Central State University Edmond, Oklahoma; [occ.] Investigator; [memb.] VFW, American G.I Forum and Human race.; [hon.] Dean's Honor Roll, 1973 Vietnam service honors. 1967-68; [oth. writ.] Private poems written for private people; [pers.] Far out there on a solar wind we glide searching for a friend one to share our lifes warm flight and journey on into the night.; [a.] San Diego, CA

MARVEL, MRS. ROBERT - T. ANNE W.
[pen.] Meme [b.] June 20, 1931, Massachusetts; [p.] John Stanley Bower-deceased, Bertha Allen Bower-deceased; [m.] Robert Marvel, May 25, 1974; [ch.] Collin, Charles and Steven; [ed.] Only High School; [occ.] Fully retired, and loving every minute of it!; [memb.] New Hampshire General Court House of Representatives, 1970-74; [oth. writ.] Former reporter for Foster's Daily, Dover, NH; [pers.] "The Enchanted Flute" was written in 1969. Never give up hope.

MARVEN, KRISTA
[b.] July 11, 1974, Illinois; [p.] George and Pat Marven; [ed.] Naperville Central High School St. Petersburg Jr. College University of South Florida Hillsborough Community College; [occ.] Waitress at steak and ale; [pers.] Love inspires me to write poetry. This poem was inspired by Matt whom I will forever hold memories of him in my heart.; [a.] Tampa, FL

MASINO, MARLAILENE A.
[pen.] Ellis West; [b.] September 17, 1968, Philadelphia, PA; [p.] Anna Masino, Anthony Masino; [ed.] St. Maria Goretti, H. S. Moore College of Art and Design Fleischer Art School, Community college of Philadelphia; [occ.] Wedding consultant, Wedding bells bridal boutique; [hon.] Honorable mention award received at Immaculate College for Etchings in plexiglass and metal; [oth. writ.] Several poems and short story published in 2 consecutive issues of high school literary magazine "The Patroness" of which I was also the Art Editor in Junior and Senior year.; [pers.] My work has always been greatly affected by my strong emotional ties with the great Art Masters of both the renaissance and impressionism. Native American Culture and Art has been by greatest source of inspiration through out my life.; [a.] Philadelphia, PA

MASON, ELOUISE COLLINS
[pen.] Mary Louise McCoy; [b.] December 17, 1945, Pembroke, VA; [p.] Marrison and Hazel Collins (Deceased); [m.] Jerry David Mason, June 19, 1978; [ch.] Dennis W. Love and Laura A. Hilton; [ed.] Grad. Giles High School, New River Comm. College, Centertral VA. Phyic. Nurse Training; [occ.] Disabled; [memb.] Ephesus Free Will Baptist Church, Choir, And Ladies Aux.; [hon.] My honors and awards will be in Heaven. Here on earth it is an award when someone reads one of my poems, and enjoys it.; [oth. writ.] I have written many many poems all of spiritual nature. In this book there are two, I'm Not Alone and What is Beauty. I have written a book titled, "A Heart Full of Sunshine and Rainbows". It hasn't been published because of financially unable.; [pers.] If we can help lead another to the glory of God, then our lives will have meaning.; [a.] Blounts Creek, NC

MATHES, BRENDA J.
[b.] November 10, 1957, St Louis, MO; [p.] Lawrence and Betty Gerdes; [m.] Gerald Mathes, September 13, 1980; [ch.] Vanessa and Cyndi; [ed.] River Gardens Sr High School, St Charles County Community College, Lindenwood College; [occ.] Mo Air National Guard, Pay Entitlements Supervisor; [hon.] Dean's List; [pers.] Life is full of wonder and excitement. I try to always see this as through the eyes of a child so as not to lose out on life itself.; [a.] Harvester, MO

MATOVU, GERALD M. M.
[b.] October 16, 1947, Kijumba Village; [p.] Father dead, Mother alive; [m.] Nil; [ch.] One son; [ed.] Graduate of Makerere University - Northcote Hall - Uganda; [occ.] Lecturer of literature in English the institute of teacher education Kyambogo; [hon.] My name was at the head of those who, from Uganda, won prizes in the BBC Arts and Africa Poetry Awards in 1982.; [oth. writ.] 'Poor Timing' published by Heinemann, 'Achievements by Imagination' by Illumination, and 'Children Stories' published by Fountain Publishers Ltd.; [pers.] I would like to see modern poetry also beldming popular so that it is not a monopoly of ivory tower intellectuals; [a.] Kampala, Uganda

MATTHEWS, KEVIN DALTON
[b.] December 16, 1969, Winston-Salem, NC; [m.] Kathy Diane Mickey Matthews, February 14, 1992; [ch.] Amethyst Ashlyn Matthews; [ed.] High School G.E.D; [occ.] Landscaper and Musician (bass player); [oth. writ.] Other poems and song lyrics to the music I write; [pers.] Believe in yourself nothing is impossible follow your heart and be kind to your children; [a.] Winston-Salem, NC

MATTHEWS, PAUL
[b.] May 30, 1976, Ontario, Canada; [p.] Alan Matthews, Janet Matthews; [ed.] Rockland District High School Graduate of 1994; [occ.] Student; [hon.] Many awards for my achievements and success in sports; [oth. writ.] I have several more poetry writings that I keep in my personal book; [pers.] I try to express as many feelings as I can when I write. When love is in my heart, it is so easy to write. My poems reflect my life and how love affects me.; [a.] Rockland Ontario, Canada

MATZA, CHARLES A.
[b.] September 4, 1927, Manitowoc, Wis.; [p.] John and Mary (Deceased); [m.] Joyce, November 25, 1954; [ch.] Lisa, Hollis, Charles, Mitchel, Wendy and Jennifer.; [ed.] R.A. Waller High, College of DuPage; [occ.] Student; [memb.] VFW - PTK - Dead Readers Society, Phi Theta Kappa; [hon.] Phi Theta Kappa; [oth. writ.] Kafka - An Enigma, Macbeth - Shadow Ruler, Wife of Bath - The Court of Impossible Conclusion; [pers.] Whatever age in life, it is possible to dream.; [a.] Villa Park, IL

MATZEN, JO JOSEY
[pen.] Jo Josey Matzen; [b.] 1907, Hillsburg, KY; [p.] James and Martha Romack Matzen; [m.] Quentin Matzen; [ed.] Harrisburg High, Il, Mundelein College, Chicago, Northwestern U., Evanston, IL, Post Grad, Stanford, Berkeley, Claremont Grad., Claremont, CA.; [occ.] Retired 1972; [memb.] NEA, Calta, CAI Guidance Assn, U of Women's College Assn., Dicken's Fellowship, Christian Science Church.; [hon.] Who's Who of America, Women of Year, Personalities of West and Northwest, Ed. Awarded Project of 1 year length (Ch), 1.) Freedom's Foundation (8th grade teacher and class), 3rd in State of Cal. 1975, 2.) High school: Career Day, Palm Desert Chamber of Commerce, 3.) Children's Concerts (Tom Mancini Orchestera, Friends of Library, Palm Desert; [oth. writ.] Co-authored State (California) Ed. text in shorthand and transcript. Have children's book story in rough "A Tail of Love:, subject: a little "cockerpoo" black dog, smiling tongue, wagging tail of love.; [pers.] Influence by early romantic poets, Love life, Love achievement, Love People, Love all God's creations, literally, I Love America from its beginning.; [a.] Palm Desert, CA

MAUGER JR., WILLIAM C.
[pen.] Chuck; [b.] August 14, 1964, Magnolia, NJ; [p.] Mary and Bill Occhuzzo; [m.] Courtney Becker; [ch.] 3, Megan (9), Kristan (5) Nicholas (22 mos.); [ed.] Kingsway Regional High School Grad. Swedesboro, NJ; [occ.] Commercial and Residential Flooring; [oth. writ.] A poem, "Time Does Tell," published 1990, in a book titled, "Greatest poems of the Western Civilization" this was my only other writing besides "Definition" that I have previously submitted.; [pers.] Nothing is brain surgery, not even brain surgery.

MAY, MICHAEL CHARLES
[b.] October 14, 1960, Brooklyn, NY; [p.] Jean B. Tilghman; [ed.] Livermore High School; [hon.] U.S. Marine Corps Sergeant (At age 19) Numerous awards and certificates in High School basketball, football, and base ball.; [pers.] Writing has become a way for me to relax and reflect on the many events that have come to pass in my life time.; [a.] Tracy, CA

MCARTHUR, JENIFER L.
[b.] August 2, 1972, Warsaw, NY; [p.] Stephen and Donna McArthur; [ed.] Alexander Central School, Genesee Community College, AAS, Human Services; [pers.] In memory of my cousin Paul L. Fusco who may not always be spoken of, but is always remembered and loved.; [a.] Alexander, NY

MCAULIFFE, CLAIRE STEBBINS
[pen.] Valencia, California; [b.] Hartford, CT; [m.] Neil McAuliffe; [ch.] Neil McAuliffe III, Michael McAuliffe, Daniel McAuliffe, and Denise Bailey; [ed.] BFA and MFA - California Institute of the Arts; [occ.] Artist; [pers.] My mentor, poet - Richard Weakley, has helped me embark into and ultimate expression of my art.

MCCABE, TOM
[b.] December 5, 1976, New York City, N.Y.; [p.] Eugene McCabe, Linda McCabe; [ed.] St. Joseph's Grammar School, John, F. Kennedy Catholic High School; [memb.] S.A.D.D. Committee "Excalibur" literary Magazine Math League; [hon.] Captain of Cross Country and Track Team, Community Service Awards, business Awards; [oth. writ.] Mostly a couple of other poems. Once in a while articles for school newspaper.; [pers.] "Though friends move on and go their own ways, I know they will always be with me."; [a.] Mahopac, NY

MCCAIN, GLORIA GILES
[pen.] Gloria Giles McCain; [b.] November 22, 1944,

Omaha, NE; [p.] Betty Kenyon; [m.] Reece McCain, November 2, 1991; [ed.] English Literature, 1967, BA, Rollins College, Winter Park, FL, BS, Computer Science, 1971 Ohio Wesleyan - Orlando, Orlando, FL, Lee Edwards HS, Asheville, NC, Benson HS, Omaha, NE; [occ.] Self-Employed; [memb.] Mensa, Intertel; [hon.] Rollins College - Dean's List, President's List; [oth. writ.] Poems, Short Stories, Essays; [a.] Orlando, FL

MCCARTHY, MICHELLE
[b.] July 22, 1968, London; [ed.] St. Brigid's College, Cork, Ireland.; [occ.] R.N. Registered Nurse.; [hon.] I have only ever entered one poetry contest at home in Ireland when I was 12 and now first prize for my age category (i.e. 12-15 yrs old) but I have been writing poetry for many years.; [oth. writ.] Several poems.; [pers.] A lot of my poems have a religious influence and depict the beauty of this world and how we as people take it for granted and even contribute to destroying it. I believe in an after life which will be even more beautiful but only those who lead selfless lives will gain admission.; [a.] New York, NY

MCCAULEY, CHARLOS
[pen.] C. O. McCauley; [b.] July 19, 1940, Elkton, MD; [m.] Michelle McCauley; [ch.] Sean, Erin, Courtney, Brennan, Shane; [ed.] Univ of Maryland; [occ.] Retired Naval Aviator Vietnam Vet, Banking Executive; [oth. writ.] Sirens of the sun, word warrior (Both books are collections of my poetry); [a.] Martinez, CA

MCCLOUD, FRANCES D.
[b.] November 26, 1940, Caldwell County; [p.] William Kent and Marion C. Duncan (deceased); [m.] Maynard J. McCloud, June 25, 1961; [ch.] Sandra Gail McCloud Angel and Kimberly Beth McCloud Smith; [ed.] High school graduate from Granite Falls High School, Granite falls, N.C.; [occ.] My husband and I are self employed as operators of Auto Reconditioning and Pro of Granite Falls.; [hon.] High School Beta Club, letter for four-year an average in High school, Teacher of the year in church Sunday School.; [oth. writ.] Poem "As I Sit Thinking" was published in a church newspapers; two poems written by request for two class reunions, and others (both serious and humorous) written for fun that were not made public.; [pers.] Even though my poems can be serious or funny, I enjoy mixing seriousness and humor together at times. It seems to help me and others to laugh even when we feel it isn't possible to laugh.; [a.] Granite Falls, NC

MCCLURE, ANNIE L.
[b.] April 28, 1925, Navarro County, TX; [p.] Ida Rivers Williams and Jesse H. Rivers (deceased); [m.] E. Dean McClure (deceased), June 4, 1943; [ch.] Renee' Anne McClure; [ed.] Associates Degree (Arts and Sciences) Mountain View College Dallas, Texas; [occ.] Retired; [hon.] Dean's list. Outstanding Achievement Award.; [oth. writ.] Several Poems published; [pers.] Dedication to each endeavor. Words hold a special magic to stir the imagination and cleanse the soul.; [a.] Duncanville, TX

MCCLURG, SANDRA
[pen.] Sandy; [b.] February 2, 1979, Denver, CO; [p.] Terry and Coleen McClurg; [ed.] Arvada West High School; [occ.] Student; [hon.] I won a poetry contest in 8th grade. I got perfect attendance in 9th grade. I have many sports (soccer and softball) awards; [oth. writ.] I write many other poems, and I also write short stories.; [pers.] In my poems I let my true feelings of a situation show through because I think people should be able to express their feelings when they want and about what they want to.; [a.] Arvada, CO

MCCORMICK, CAMMI
[b.] May 3, 1979, Victoria, TX; [p.] Brian McCormick, Susan McCormick; [ed.] Calhoun High, currently enrolled in 10th grade; [memb.] CHS Women's and a capella choir, CHS choir council, whole adoption society; [hon.] Honor roll; [oth. writ.] 16 other original poems - none published, articles for school newspaper; [pers.] Writing poetry allows me to release inner feelings of anger and oppression while doing something constructive at the same time.; [a.] Port Lavaca, TX

MCCORMICK, KENZIE HEARD
[pen.] Kenzie Heard, Kenzie Paintings; [b.] February 5, 1949, Yazoo City, MO; [p.] Ollie Mae Hunter, Clarenee Heard; [ed.] Arsenal Technical High School, Indianapolis, Indiana Los Angeles Pierce College Woodland Hills, California; [occ.] Actor/Bouncer/Singer/House Painter - Canvas Abstract artist; [memb.] Family fitness, Neight or Hood Watch, Maxim Entertainment-West Hollywood. Club Mancinis-Canoga Park, CA; [hon.] As dorm chief in the air force, trained thirty-nine airmen with top honors in basic training in 1969. Received the targets stores Award of Excellence in Oct. 1921 in Canoga Park-West Hills California.; [oth. writ.] (Song) Tennessee Whiskey, (Book) The Oxie Moron, (Poem) The Mechanism; [pers.] The Oxie Moron is still in my briefcase in 500 pages of handwritten and printed script and has not been proofread or published yet. I believe that with faith, hope and love you will win.; [a.] Winnetka, CA

MCCORMICK, M. PAT
[pen.] Pat McCormick; [b.] May 20, 1934, Saint Louis, MO; [p.] Leona and Paul Guidry; [m.] John T. McCormick, August 5, 1961; [ch.] Michael, Steven, David and Mark; [ed.] Registered Nurse, Bachelor of Science of Nursing Arts.; [occ.] Nurse and Flight Attendant; [memb.] Kiwi (a philanthropy organization of flight attendants of American Airlines), W.O.W. (Woman of the World), St. Peter's Catholic Church; [hon.] Received awards from American Airlines twice called PFA (Professional Flight Attendant), Received an award from Northwest Community Hospital for ten years of service.; [oth. writ.] "Christmas Thoughts", "Angel, My Angel", "Graduation of a Nurse", "The Dove the Symbol of Love", "On this Day My Son", "A Tribute to Sister O Sanna", "A New Year", "My Sons Graduation"; [pers.] "Be alert". Be alert to all nature the earth, the sky, the wind, all winged and crawling creatures. Be alert to the wonders of everyday lifes. Be alert to our own power for good in this universe. Be alert to the omnipresence of almighty God.; [a.] Geneva, IL

MCCOY, SHIRLEY J. PARKER
[b.] August 8, 1936, Cleveland, OH; [p.] Frank Williams (Deceased) and Gussie Williams-Jones; [m.] Divorced, (November 1975), June 26, 1954; [ch.] James Parker Jr., Jessica Coleman, Dwayne Parker, Lawrence Parker, (Eleven Grandchildren); [ed.] High School Graduate - John Hay High Psychology Courses - Cuyahoga Comm. College Graduate - United States Postal Academy; [occ.] (Retired) Superintendent, United States Postal Serv.; [memb.] Arthritis Foundation St. Mark Baptist Church AARP, Retired Postal Employees Assoc.; [oth. writ.] Poems published in the following anthologies: Musings, American Poetry Anthology, Reflections, Best New Poems of 1994, American Poetry Annual, Poetic Voices of America, Voices of many Lands.; [pers.] The only things in life that are solely our own, are our thoughts, dreams and fantasies we truly give of ourselves, when we share our thoughts with others.; [a.] Maple Heights, OH

MCCRACKEN, MARIE REYNOLDS
[pen.] Marie Reynolds McCracken; [b.] August 5, 1911, Clark Co, AR; [p.] Robert and Henrietta Regnolds; [m.] George McCrackon, November 7, 1931; [ch.] Patsy-Peggy, Ronald; [ed.] Highs School, Licensed L.V.N., JOhn V. London School of Nursing, Groom Texas; [occ.] Retired-LVN.; [memb.] Martin first Baptist, Ladies Auxiliary to the V.F.W. #7782. Retired Senior's Volunteer, Program - Amarillo, TX; [oth. writ.] A Cowboy's Wife, Mother - L.V.N. for 25 years - At age 83 teaching my great grand son drivers aid.; [pers.] Be true to your God, your country and yourself.; [a.] Clarendon, TX

MCCRANIE, STARLA KAY
[b.] May 11, 1981, Montana; [p.] Terry McCranie, Teresa Johnston; [occ.] Student; [oth. writ.] Written many stories and poems for school events and other contests.; [pers.] Highly interested in writing poems based on death and hope. Philosophy on life is to take each day as it comes because there's no guarantee tomorrow will come.; [a.] Renton, WA

MCCRAY, KATHY ELLEN
[pen.] Katt; [b.] October 26, 1954, Spokan; [p.] Vern McCray, Marie McCray; [ed.] Sunset High; [occ.] Restaurant Cook; [oth. writ.] Many poems, unpublished; [pers.] I feel fortunate to be able to share what life has been, and can be, and not necessarily confined to this realm; [a.] Issaquah, WA

MCCUNE, FRANK
[pen.] Frank Macchione; [b.] August 22, 1972, Chicago, IL; [p.] Frank (Macchione) McCune, Ruby McCune; [m.] Evelyn (Rybnik) McCune, January 19, 1957; [ch.] Gregory Jay; [ed.] Loyola Univ., Arizona State University; [occ.] Retired History Teacher; [memb.] St. Joseph's Manna volunteer, P.O.A. of Lake Dalecarlia, Past member of IEA, N.E.A.; [oth. writ.] Exerpt of short story published in FRA Noi, an Italian-American Chicago Newspaper; [pers.] "No man is better than you and you are not better than anyone else." My father instilled this Philosophy in me at a very early age. I try not to judge other because of it.; [a.] Lowell, IN

MCCURDY, JOHN
[b.] August 29th, 1973, Burlington, Ontario; [ed.] Philosophy and Comparative Literature, McMaster University Hamilton, Ontario; [oth. writ.] I've been writing poetry and fiction since I was thirteen years old. I began writing fantasy stories, inspired by J.R.R. Tolkien and C.S. Lewis. I later developed a deep interest in James Joyce, William Faulkner and Virginia Woolf and my writing took a Modernist turn. At present, I am very excited by contemporary philosophy and literary criticism and hope to engage their themes and issues in both poetry and fiction and essays and criticism. [pers.] My experience with Cancer has both forced me and inspired me to examine the whole of my life and so I see what has happened to me as an opportunity or message to change and get closer to the essence of living. I am returning to University in the near future to continue my studies, though I not sure where they will lead me. I see myself someday as writing, teaching and being politically active. Life has become profoundly paradoxical to me, a stare of being inherently fraught with both joy and sorrow, where the human will unfolds yet also surrenders to the mystery within and without.; [a.] Burlington Ontario, Canada

MCDONALD, HOPE
[b.] December 10, 1978, Allentown, PA; [p.] Robert McDonald, Barbara McDonald; [ed.] Parkland High School; [occ.] Student; [memb.] National Honor Society, Latin Club, Who's who among American High School Students.; [a.] Coplay, PA

MCDONALD, ROBERT
[pen.] Robert McDonald; [b.] December 15, 1926, Brooklyn; [p.] Robert and Lillian McDonald; [m.] Divorced, 1948; [ch.] Robert, Billy, Keven, Tim, Jaynes, Barbara (6 children); [ed.] Graduate from public school short time at Woodrow Wilson High School joined the U.S. Navy 1944; [occ.] Retired from Dairy Barn Stores as day Manager after 27 years; [memb.] American Legion NY Post 0001 Veterans of Foreign Wars Post 6431; [hon.] Robert McDonald WWII Shipfitter Third class honorable discharge American theatre medal Asiatic-Pacific medal victory medal Philippine Liberation Ribbon Stationed in Philippine Island with the 10th and 42nd Naval Construction Battalions as A - "sea bee"; [oth. writ.] A Fall Fantasy. Time savings or about time, laughter, the companion, work out, pen pals; [pers.] I like to write short poem at the moment and time ranging from Funny Romantic to serious what I see feel or leave; [a.] Bay Shore, NY

MCFADDEN, MARGARET
[b.] September 2, 1944, Colorado Springs, CO; [p.] Barney and Dorothy Meents; [m.] Patrick McFadden, July 11, 1964; [ch.] Paul, Shannon and Patrick II; [ed.] Wasson H.S., Colo Spgs, Grinnell College, Grinnell, IA, Univ of Wisconsin - Milwaukee; [occ.] Insurance Intermediary for Prudential; [memb.] Wisc. Music Teachers Assoc. Symphony Board, United Way Board, Golda Meir Library-6W-M; [hon.] Phi Kappa Phi, Sigma Tau Delta; [oth. writ.] Personal musings and editorial comments on utilage life in Wisconsin for local newspapers; [pers.] My favorite Author is Willa Cather, and, although she was not a poet, I try to follow the same honesty and basic humanity she strived for in all my writing; [a.] Kewaskum, WI

MCGHEE, WANDA SUE
[b.] January 19, 1952, La Follette, TN; [p.] Preston and Lucille Kirby; [m.] Ricky McGhee, March 11, 1983; [ch.] Timothy Scott - James George and Jason Daniel; [ed.] Jacksboro High School, Tenn. Tech Voc- School, Roane State College; [occ.] Paint Lab Technician at American Metal Products, 17 yrs. employed.; [oth. writ.] I have written many poems since I was 17 yrs. old. But never had the nerve to submit them. I find peace and serenity when writing.; [pers.] No matter where your going, no the time that's showing, there is always time for love. My life style is hectic, it seems as if time flies by - yet I still have time to love everyone and I wish for peace upon the earth!; [a.] Caryville, TN

MCGOWAN, JAMES P.
[b.] March 24, 1957, Lackawanna; [p.] James McGowan, Audrey McGowan; [ch.] Jennifer Ann; [ed.] West Seneca High, Executive Protection Institute, Leilund College of Arts; [occ.] Martial Arts Instructor Personal Protection Specialist; [memb.] National college of Martial Arts.; [hon.] Hold 5 Black belts in various martial arts systems patent holder for invention featured on panther production video series; [oth. writ.] Infiltrators, Pincher uneathed, Rubber band treat, cellar dwellers, binds of prey. Defensive key holder basic training manual; [pers.] I hope after you have read, your deepest fears were fed.; [a.] Buffalo, NY

MCGUGAN, SUZANNE
[b.] February 16, 1948, Toronto, Ontario, Canada; [p.] Kelly Kidd, Ruby Kidd; [m.] Rodney McGugan, November 24, 1962; [ch.] Kevin, Diana, Deborah, Kelly; [ed.] Georgetown High School, Georgian College Barrie, Ont. Canada; [occ.] Secretary, Bookkeepper, P.G. Henderson Printing, Georgetown Ont.; [memb.] Ontario Real Estate Assc., Royal Canadian Legion; [hon.] Won a writing contest put on by a local newspaper for short story when I was 10.; [pers.] I have always wanted to write, but like anything the hardest part is getting started. I enjoy good love stories and murder mysteries.; [a.] Brampton Ontario, Canada

MCGUIRE, REV. RALPH M.
[b.] July 1, 1915, Maplewood, MO; [p.] Bert and Celestine McGuire; [m.] Loretta Louise McGuire, June 9, 1937; [ch.] 6; [occ.] Clergy - Retired; [hon.] Acknowledgment and appreciation from Hilliary Rodham Clinton at the "White House" on my poetry.; [oth. writ.] Poems have been published in newspapers, bulletins, Christian publications, also I am the author of a poem Book entitled "Spice Of Life Poetry"; [pers.] I strive to compose poetry on wide and varied subjects such as nature biblical and life. My theme is "poetry with a message".

MCINTIRE, MARY JO
[b.] December 9, 1961, Louisville, KY; [a.] Jonesville, SC

MCINTOSH, SIMON
[pen.] Haven Seen; [b.] October 19, 1974; [oth. writ.] Cryptic Bible; [pers.] Life is full of dull moments don't give up and it won't give up on you.

MCKAY, DARLENE
[pen.] Darlene McKay; [b.] February 11, 1958, Baldur, Manitoba, Canada; [p.] Alvin and Helen Delorme; [m.] Dale McKay, September 24, 1977; [ch.] Murray and Dwight McKay; [ed.] Just completed my High School through I.C.S. Correspondence school, will get my diploma soon.; [pers.] I like to believe there is goodness in everyone. Writing penpal was a labor of love, because my husband and my penpal were my influence and support.; [a.] Brandon Manitoba, Canada

MCKEEVER, PENELOPE J.
[b.] June 30, 1979, Pompton Plains, NJ; [p.] Katherine and Lawrence McKeever; [ed.] Troy High School, Troy, PA; [memb.] Girl Scouts, School Sports, S.A.D.D., Marching/Concert Band.; [pers.] In 1992 Julie Leaman was diagnosed with Leukemia. The day that she died in 1993 I was inspired to write this poem. She will be remembered by many of her friends and she'll always live in our hearts.; [a.] Gillett, PA

MCKENZIE, ARDELL SHALDON
[pen.] D'Kool; [b.] September 27, 1973, Belize, Central America; [p.] Mr. and Mrs. Geraldine and Lancelot McKenzie; [ed.] Los Angeles City College; [occ.] Secretarial - Kedren, Community Mental Center, L.A., CA.; [memb.] President - Young Adult Group; [oth. writ.] Several other unpublished poems some given to friends.; [pers.] I am influenced by life. I write what and how I feel.; [a.] Los Angeles, CA

MCKERLIE, MARIE E.
[pen.] Marie E. McKerlie; [b.] February 11, 1965, Tocoma, WA; [p.] Rita M. and George T. Houchens; [m.] Russell D. McKertie Sr., April 11, 1980; [ch.] Russell Dean Jr., Michael, Ashley; [ed.] GED, Comogoliogy School (the study of hair), currently Studies: High School Dimlopa, NRI Writing School, Par Legal School; [occ.] Hair stylist, Shear Performance, Phoenix, AZ; [memb.] Volunteer parents to help at schools (Avondale Elementary) to teach kids how to read. (In my daughters class); [hon.] 1st place awards in Fanasty Contents for hair. Several first and second places awards in Creamics, Severals Awards in hair stylist.; [oth. writ.] Write stories and skips for acting out in the salon's I work for, for competitions, and for fun.; [pers.] I travel the world, several times, I'm of Irish family, Dublin in home for me, most of my family still lives there on my mother side. Knowledge is power! To change the word. To me reading and writing are the greatest gift we have to give to our children and ourself. I live life to it's fullness, several hobbies of mind, are art's and crafts, reading writing; [a.] Avondale, AZ

MCKERNAN, JIM
[pen.] Jam; [oth. writ.] Copywrited song - "They Don't Mean A Thing" - PA 1-913-876; [a.] Farmingdale, NJ

MCKINLEY, JANA D.
[b.] April 11, 1968, California; [p.] Raelene Jurgella; [m.] William McKinley, October 25, 1988; [ch.] Amanda Noel, Zachary, William [ed.] Bonita High, Chaffey College; [occ.] Freelance Art Director; [oth. writ.] Self-published collection of poems entitled "A Tiny Glimpse of Light."; [pers.] In expanding our boundaries to include love and light we all succeed. Thank you.; [a.] Rancho Cucamonga, CA

MCKINZIE, CURTIS WAYNE
[b.] February 23, 1975, Lubbock, TX; [p.] James and Deborah McKinzie; [ed.] Honor High School Diploma, Currently attending Texas Tech University in Lubbock Texas; [hon.] High Honor Graduate, National Honors Society (High School) member. Being my parents son.; [oth. writ.] This poem was the first down to earth poem that I have ever written in my entire life.; [pers.] My father always told me while growing up to "Treat every person the same way that you would prefer yourself to be treated."; [a.] Lubbock, TX

MCKOWN, EMILY GUEST
[b.] September 23, 1927, Saint Louis, MO; [p.] Sames Ray Guest Sr, Nettie Bell Watson; [m.] June 12, 1948; [ch.] 6 (5 girls, - 1 boy); [ed.] Juilliard, UCHA, USC, TV School [occ.] Semi-retired [memb.] USGS Mother Nothing esentric, help to Van Kleinschmict USC Aided, US President since 1941. Mostly secret work. Still working. To do justice, the moment in time; [hon.] Most colleages and top secret gov't. Concert Mistress BH, 1st Grd Conductor Pres. TEC Bev H. Ca. Thrift clubs, Mother of six, God Mother civil service 1961, Drama Las Gatos Ca, Milliens Sweepstakes no money things things and cars. Mr. and Mrs. J. Roy Guest Sr. CLCB.; [oth. writ.] Daily writings and topings. "Bit a Nothing" Recipes by the Dozon. Personal poetries for friends, DJ's. Another Book Astred Psychology.; [pers.] Being first Fam. of USA and mom of first Fam. Va. I have had to very carefully tender philosophy and nurture it's repetitive cycles and re-attitude it's factual in tent; [a.] Santa Cruz, CA

MCMURRAY, JANET LOUISE
[b.] December 26, 1969, West Palm Beach, FL; [p.] Bruce McMurray, Louise McMurray; [ed.] Miami Killian Senior High; [occ.] Receptionist, Stephens, Lynn Klein and McNicholas, P.A., Miami, FL.; [pers.] Poetry is my means for others to feel my emotions and under-

stand my thoughts - to look within my heart and mind. All my love to Nikki for her support, Debbie - my fluffy friend - for that extra push and to Grandma, for her partiality!; [a.] Miami, FL

MCNAY, MARC
[b.] August 20, 1994, Smooth Rock Falls, Ontario, Canada; [p.] Anna and Lorne McNay; [ed.] Fort Frances High School - Grade Twelve Graduate Thunder Bay Confederation College - Welder/Fitter Course Graduate; [occ.] Courier Driver I am also self employed; [oth. writ.] I have had a poem published in the anthology a far off place as well as one published in the anthology best poems of 1995, this second book has not been released at the time I write this.; [pers.] Remember that even though we can not see them nor can we hear them, there is often someone somewhere "Thinking of you".; [a.] Oxdrift Ontario, Canada

MCNULTY, IAN MICHAEL
[b.] April 15, 1983, Wichita, KS; [p.] James McNulty, Marie McNulty; [ed.] 7th Grade student in the school of Calvert; [occ.] Student; [a.] Wichita, KS

MCWILLIAMS, LEONA
[pen.] Leona Gabriella; [b.] June 20, 1973, Derry, North Ireland; [p.] Leo and Bernadette McWilliams; [ed.] A Bachelors Degree in Education and Music. I am also a young soprano and I'm completing a Masters in Voice Production.; [memb.] I am a soloist in St. Fugenes Cathedral Choir Derry, and a member of the 'Irish Youth Choir.'; [hon.] Grade 8 award in both singing and piano. I have also win first place in a National Talent Competition; [pers.] I make every effort to capture beauty and tranquility and hope that I can somehow bring heaven and earth a little closer.; [a.] Waterside Derry, Ireland

MEACHAM, CATHERINE C.
[b.] March 2, 1966; [p.] Gordon Makinster; [ch.] Luke Henry and Shandi Marie; [ed.] Graduated from Beaverton High School 1984, North American Secretarial School 1989; [occ.] Mother [oth. writ.] Morning Dew - Quill Books. The Sleeping Rose; [pers.] I would like to thank Kimm Bohman for her constant friendship and confidence in me. To my Dad for his positive influence in my life.; [a.] Portland, OR

MEANS, YVETTE
[b.] August 4, 1967, Washington, DC; [p.] Catherine Means; [ch.] Herman Means; [ed.] Eastern High, Chamberlain Vocation School - Cosmetology; [occ.] None at present; [memb.] Washington Area lawyer of Arts.; [hon.] Volunteer Awards; [oth. writ.] Press On - Trigger Man - Sweet Dreams - My Tea Pot - I'm a bless tree. - Our flames never burning out. Several other poems.; [pers.] I desire to inspire people of all faces of races. It is my goal to inspire persons with Aids - cancer - other Illness.; [a.] Washington, DC

MEDVED, LARRY J.
[b.] June 10, 1958, McKeesport, PA; [p.] Matt Medved and Maryann Medved; [ed.] Elizabeth Forward High School; [occ.] Shipper/Receiver for McKeesport Candy Company; [memb.] Croation Fraternal Union, Teamsters Local 636; [hon.] 1975 - Showcase award for: screen printed Christmas card, in verse.; [oth. writ.] Many unpublished inspirational poems.; [pers.] "I am basically a new poet, my heart has been touched by our Lord, and my wish is to share my happiness. My Goal: To offer spiritual support and to spread the good news through my writings.; [a.] White Oak, PA

MEINTS, TONA
[b.] August 30, 1978, Bloomington, IL; [p.] Herschel and Donna Meints; [ed.] Prairie Central High School; [occ.] Student; [pers.] I get my information from what happens in daily life and what I feel deep in my heart.; [a.] Fairbury, IL

MELARO, MARIE A.
[b.] May 14, 1927, Oakmont, PA; [p.] John B. and Rose E. Melaro; [ed.] Oakmont H.S. - Hood College Duquesne Univ. - U of Pittsburgh - Pinkeaton Bus. Sch. -; [occ.] Retired H.S. Language teacher. (Pa. and Md. certification); [memb.] Democratic Party - Roman Catholic Church; [hon.] American Legion Medal award, honor society (2 yrs), Editor H.S. paper, literary editor H.S. Yr book, honor grad. (H.S.) - College: Dean's list, feature writer cool, newspaper and Frederick news (local paper), CH. U.N. interest group, hood delegate to U. N., State Ch.U.N Md and D.C Region, Ch. C.C.U.N. Ch. Twin Boros' beauty pageant (Verona and Oakmont), twin boros secretary, speaker on language instruction at PA. St. Ed. Assoc. Conference.; [oth. writ.] Publications in American Mercury, chaistias Science monitor progressive tchr, Family digest, today's Catholic Teacher; [pers.] Life is what we make of it, we shape our own destiny.; [a.] Silver Spring, MD

MELICK, MARSHA ELLEN
[b.] March 29, 1978, Columbus, OH; [p.] Bob Melick and Kathy Dakin; [ed.] Will graduate from Fairfield Senior High School in 1996.; [occ.] Register at McDonalds and IC Worker at investment research institute.; [oth. writ.] Many yet to be published; [pers.] Be yourself if that means different be accepting of the unusual in others; [a.] Fairfield, OH

MENDHEIM, WILHELMINA RILEY
[pen.] Willa or Mina; [b.] May 30, 1911, Jacksonville, FL; [p.] Bishop Riley, and Lula Riley; [m.] Roosevelt Mendheim, March 2, 1939; [ch.] Lerome - supervisor of a clinic, N.Y.C., Beverly-Ann was librarian, Univ. of Wash. (Author of Richard Valence) seattle, Wash.; [ed.] Florida, Michigan, Ohio, and N.Y.C. Finished high school in Mich, I received A.B Wilber force Univ., Ohio. Post graduate work in New York City.; [occ.] Retired; [memb.] St. Augustine R.C., Bronx, N.Y., and several Senior Citizen Organization Past - YWCA, and Girl Scouts (leader); [hon.] I taught seven years in Florida and received a life certificate. I taught twenty-six years in St. Augustine school, N.Y.C. I worked with federal and the N.Y. City organizations.; [oth. writ.] I wrote several poems (not published) I wrote a song, the comforter (copy wrighted) but not published.; [pers.] Certain things or happenings in the environment cause or inspire me to write.; [a.] Bronx, NY

MENDICKI, VIOLA
[pen.] Vi; [b.] February 1, 1919, Arma KS; [p.] Eva and Herbert De Voss; [m.] E. C. Mendicki, (deceased), January 4, 1939; [ch.] Carl, Marilynn, Gene; [ed.] Grad High School and a Pre College Course. Taught Pre School before I married.; [occ.] Retired from being a school bus driver 17 yrs quite an expression; [memb.] Henderson Hills Baptist church, A Christian Ladies club called Keep-in-touch. I'm a member of the Glory singers at church and a future member of heaven.; [hon.] No honors, but I am promised ETERNAL LIFE! John 3:16; [oth. writ.] Only the poems I have written for my own enjoyment and my family.; [pers.] I enjoy life and live it to the fullest. I love to laugh - even if its at myself. Laugh or leave - If you don't laugh - I'll leave. My motto. Life is too short to brood!

MENDOZA, DEANYA
[pen.] Deanya; [b.] January 14, 1962, Royal Oak, MI; [p.] David and Anne Cunningham; [m.] Jose Santos Aquirre; [ch.] Merranda, Reyna, Katie; [ed.] Highland High; [occ.] Bi-linguel Verifier; [memb.] Sluder Care Group, Family worship center.; [pers.] I know my poems are gifts from God. I thank Him for his blessings. I hope when someone reads my poems that it touches their hearts. My faith has been my strength and encourages me to do all I must.; [a.] Austin, TX

MENDOZA JR., TED F.
[b.] February 18, 1949, Santa Paula; [p.] Ted and Esthen Mendoza; [ed.] St. Bonaventura High School, Ventura Junior College, UCSB; [occ.] Warehouseman; [hon.] Scholarship Montalvo Womans Club, Honor Roll 1970, Deans List.; [oth. writ.] Several poems published in local papers around county, articles for home town newspaper; [pers.] I strive to write about all walks of life and do not limit myself to one subject I have written for subjects ranging from religion to sports; [a.] Ventura, CA

MENON JULIAN C.
[b.] May 18, 1976, India; [p.] Cinomie Blohm; [ed.] Norte Vista High School; [oth. writ.] A few personal poems; [pers.] "I hope and pray time will never lose me"; [a.] Riverside, CA

MESSER II, DAVID PHILLIP
[pen.] Da Maad Poet; [b.] November 28, 1973, Indianapolis, IN; [p.] Karen and Leo Odom; [ed.] Lawrence North High School, North Carolina Agricultural and Technical State University; [occ.] Student; [memb.] Midwest Aggie Club (MAC) Executive Board; [hon.] "Mr. Midwest '93"; [oth. writ.] Several poems printed in the local newspaper.; [pers.] My poetry reflects the reality of society. Too many poets cover the superficial aspects of society, not the real deal.; [a.] Greensboro, NC

MEUNIOT, ARTURO A.
[pen.] El Aguila; [b.] July 16, 1923, Michocan, Mexico; [p.] Miguel and Sara Meuniot; [m.] Suzy Cohen; [ch.] Gilbert Pancho Meuniot; [ed.] Business College Major, San Francisco State University; [occ.] Water Quality Control Engineer (Retired); [memb.] A lifetime advocate of Universal compassion to all living creatures.; [hon.] Honorable discharge, U.S. Army World War II. Bantamweight Champion U.S. Infantry U.S. Citizenship — May 17, 1944 in Superior Court, Salinas, Cal.; [oth. writ.] Humor: "For Stupidity No One Needs Experience" "Reality Is Nothing But A Collective Hunch" "All The Time Is Now, All The Place Is Here" "If You Drive Be Sure You Have A Car"; [pers.] Life is a miracle, youth is a gift of life. Love is time, a duration plus its possibility is poetry in action.; [a.] San Mateo, CA

MEYER, ELDON M.
[pen.] Marne Meyer; [b.] November 11, 1921, Forrest, IL; [p.] Albert Meyer, Mattie Meyer; [m.] Frances Meyer, January 24, 1948; [ch.] 3 daughters; [ed.] Ph.D Ed Leadership and Human Behavior MA - Ed Administration Supervision Bt - Education High school - Bay City Michigan; [occ.] Retired School Administrator.; [memb.] United Methodist Church, Natl Assn Elem Sch Adm. World Future Society, San Diego (organizer) 2nd Marine Division Assn; [hon.] Salutatorian at graduation Tehg and Adm. awards local San Diego Author award from WWII - People Heart; [oth. writ.] Future options unlimited both 1 and both 2 in house educational papers. Poems under title - "Give Me Your Hand"; [pers.]

I used to write poetry for myself. Using one of my poems in a church service led to sharing others. Now I am more willing to reveal my thoughts and inner self thru my poems and stories; [a.] Lemon Grove, CA

MEYER, MARTHA ROBERTS
[b.] September 21, 1911, Soddy, TN; [p.] James A. Roberts, Margaret M. Roberts; [m.] Samuel L. Meyer, April 6, 1935; [ch.] Samuel L. Meyer, James B. Meyer; [ed.] Hume Fogg High School, Nashville, Tenn., A.B., Vanderbilt University; M.S., Vanderbilt University; [occ.] Housewife; [memb.] Trinity Hill United Methodist Church, Alpha Omicron Pi, P.E.O.; [hon.] University Scholar, Vanderbilt University, General Education Board Scholar, University of Virginia, Phi Beta Kappa, Vanderbilt University; Mortar Board, Ohio Northern University; [oth. writ.] "Development of Neurofibrils in Chick Embryos," Bulletin of Vanderbilt University; [pers.] "I have always tried to have a positive attitude toward life."; [a.] Lexington, KY

MEYERS, THERESA E.
[pen.] Theresa Meyers; [b.] November 2, 1972, Fort Dix, NJ; [p.] Maj. Edward M. Meyers, Norma Meyers; [ed.] Lawrence North HS, Drew University Madison, NJ; [occ.] Lab Technician, Chemical; [memb.] Member American Chemical Society; [oth. writ.] I enjoy writing fiction as well as poetry. This is my first published work.; [pers.] In my writing I seek to inspire all who feel that the world has become devoid of hope and empty of meaning. I believe simple revelations exist in a person's every day life.

MICHEL, BAMBI ZEPHIR
[b.] October 18, 1980, New York; [p.] Flore Zephir and Edward Michel; [ed.] 9th grader West Junior High School; [occ.] Student; [hon.] Honor roll, American Association of teachers of French honor certificate for French National contest, student of the month award presidential academic fitness award.; [oth. writ.] A Hair published in 1993 in "Reflections." (Literary Journal of Columbia Catholic School; [pers.] I like animals and I wish to fight for their preservation. I would like to become a veterinarian.; [a.] Columbia, MO

MICHILLI, ANGELO
[b.] March 2, 1963, Bronx, NY; [p.] Guiseppe and Edda Michilli; [m.] Chiara, June 18 1988; [ch.] Adriana; [ed.] Pace University, Manhattan College; [occ.] President of Tectonix Inc. Design and Construction Co; [memb.] NYSPE; [oth. writ.] None published but have written several poems and short stories; [pers.] Seek to understand why instead of just accepting. First comes my family then everything else.; [a.] Bronx, NY

MIDDELVEEN, SHARON LOUISE
[pen.] Sharon Louise Scully; [b.] October 27, 1962, Ottawa, Canada; [p.] Dr. Edgar and Claire Scully; [m.] Thomas F. Middelveen, August 4, 1990; [ch.] 2 boys, Alexander and Robert Middelveen; [ed.] Attended French Schools from kindergarten to end of grade 13. Baccalaureate in Arts, Honors English, from University of Ottawa, October 1990; [occ.] Housewife; [oth. writ.] I am presently writing a book and also poems.; [pers.] Since graduating I have become a manic-depressive which both hinders and helps me to write. In my writings I seek to reach out to all readers yet I keep in mind those who are well educated in English Literature, French language, Philosophy as well as psychology. I have a great interest in learning about other cultures and customs.

MIDDLETON, JILLIAN
[b.] May 6, 1982, Sandpoint, ID; [p.] Christine and Randy Middleton; [ed.] 7th grade Antrim Elementry School, Pt Pleasant Bch. NJ 08742; [occ.] Student in 7th grade; [memb.] Cheer leeding and Art Club; [hon.] First honors writing Award 1991, Certificate of Drama Participation 1990 "A year of Poems", Certificate of Merit - Sanders Center for the Performing Arts.; [a.] Point Pleasant Beach, NJ

MILLER, BETTYE J. GLOVER
[b.] Bainbridge, GA; [p.] Allene Glover and Randolph Glover; [m.] Divorced; [ch.] Lori Jemil and James E. Miller; [ed.] Hampton Univ. - B.S., Hofstra University M.S., M.S., Ed. D. in Reading and language arts.; [occ.] Language Development Specialist and Reading Facilitator - Freeport Sch. Dist. Adjunct Professor of Reading - Nassau Comm. College; [memb.] Phi Delta Kappa, International Reading Assoc., Assoc. of Black Women in Higher Education, Doctorate Association of New York Educators.; [hon.] Phi Delta Kappa Around-The-World - Travel Scholar 1991, Outstanding Alumni Honoree, 1992, whose who of women in the world; [oth. writ.] Chapter in college textbook "Early Childhood Education", 1991, presentation at International Reading Conference Publishes in ERIC - Microfiche and hard copy 1983, synthesis of research in whole language; [a.] Freeport, NY

MILLER, CHRISTOPHER K.
[pen.] Chris, Sunshine; [b.] March 14, 1972; [p.] Karen A. Miller, Stephen P. Miller; [m.] Wendy M. Miller, May 24, 1993; [ch.] Alexis A. Miller; [ed.] Musselmen High, Naval Ordnance a school, Naval Aviation maintenance Admin a school.; [occ.] United States Navy, VF-143 Oceana virginia. Maintenance Administration.; [oth. writ.] Currently working on a book of poems containing most of my work since I was 14, titled Through My Eyes.; [pers.] I love to write and to be able to share my work with others.; [a.] Virginia Beach, VA

MILLER, EULIT
[pen.] Eulit McCallum-Miller; [b.] Clarendon, Jamaica, West Indies; [p.] Aston McCallum (deceased) Rubylin McCallum; [ch.] Michael and Raymond Hylton; [ed.] Educated in London, England; [occ.] Secretary New York City Board of Education; [oth. writ.] Several poems and songs, that have yet to be published.; [pers.] I enjoy very much writing romantic poetry and my objective is to reflect in my writing some of my personal romantic experiences.; [a.] Bronx, NY

MILLER, HELEN
[pen.] Helen Miller or Helen Carter Miller; [b.] February 7, 1915, Charlotte, NC; [p.] Luther T. and Susie Moyle Carter; [m.] Homer Lee Miller Sr., October 23, 1937; [ch.] H. Lee Miller Jr.; [ed.] Teck High, Central High and correspondence courses in religion; [occ.] Retired; [memb.] Heath memorial united methodist church, Richburg Chapter order of the Eastern Star; [oth. writ.] Fillers, thought for today, for the Charlotte observer, reporter Chester News Paper, Historian for Lando, S.C., and Heath memorial United methodist church. Poems and short stories for several papers.; [pers.] I live by the golden rule. A firm believer in prayer. I draw girl and boy figures with cats and dogs and write the verses for the all occasion cards I make. I had polio 1948 use crutches wheel chair; [a.] Tampa, FL

MILLER, KATT
[b.] November 29, 1977, Abington; [ed.] William Tennent SHS; [memb.] World Wildlife Foundation; [hon.] AAA Safety Award (1992), Math League (1991-1992), Theater Crew Award (1994); [oth. writ.] "To Those Brave Hearts" printed in Awaken To a Dream, The Kronikles Fanzine (editor-in-chief); [a.] Warminster, PA

MILLER, LANI
[b.] February 22, 1981, Smithers, British Columbia, Canada; [p.] Dave and Lorrie Miller; [ed.] Currently Attending Grade 8 at Summerland Secondary School; [occ.] Student; [memb.] Junior Girls Basketball Team, formerly a corporal in the Royal Canadian Air Cadet Squadron #902 Summerland.; [oth. writ.] Several poems written during elementary school years some of which were published in local anthologies.; [pers.] My favorite activities include going to Penticton Panther hockey games, playing all kinds of sports, and cuddling with my cat, 'Bud'.; [a.] Summerland British Columbia, Canada

MILLER, LORETTA JOAN
[b.] February 17, 1958, Turner Valley, Alberta, Canada; [p.] John Michael Miller, Nora Easter Miller; [m.] Cameron Fraser, July 2, 1981; [ch.] Nicholas Dominic Fraser, Nicole Amanda Fraser, Camela Lorreta Frazer, Tecla Gertrude Fraser, Jonathan Donovan Fraser, Dallas Chadwick Fraser, Justin Apollo Fraser, Sabrin De Voma Fraser, Delmar Aaron Fraser, Ryan Bailey Fraser; [hon.] I Loretta Fraser is honored to have my children influence me when I started to do poems of their personality when my children were months old I'm honored to have my husband Cameron Robert Fraser, our children be the inspiration of my poems becoming reality.; [oth. writ.] My children gave me inspiration of my dreams becoming true of doing poems; [pers.] To my best friend Dr. Paul Ewart Cameron who helped me to see I had talent then just being talented of raising children.; [a.] Kingston Ontario, Canada

MILLER, MARGUERITE
[pen.] Marguerite Miller; [b.] October 7, 1916, Hammond, IN; [p.] John and Anna Jasnowski; [m.] Raymond F. Miller (Deceased), July 31, 1939; [ch.] Jon, Theresa, Raymond, Bernard and Gerald; [ed.] Graduate of Ball State University and Indiana College of Mortuary Science; [occ.] Mortician Miller and Miller Colonial Chapel, Inc. Also taught school in Hammond, Ind.; [memb.] Mostly Social and Fraternal L.F.D.A. and N.F.D.A.; [oth. writ.] Several poems and my autobiography not only roots, but the whole tree; [pers.] These aren't the Golden Years - they are the lead years. At age 78, I find being a grief therapist, that life definite isn't a "bowl of chearers"; [a.] Evansville, IN

MILLER, MARTIN S.
[pen.] Marty Miller; [b.] December 27, 1936, Brooklyn, NY; [p.] Harry and Sylvia Miller; [m.] Marilyn Miller, November 3, 1962; [ch.] Beth Sammons, Cindy Miller, Grand Daughter Stephanie Sammons; [ed.] Tilden H.S., Brooklyn N.Y., 2 yrs - Brooklyn College; [occ.] Retired 28 yrs. as a yellow page salesman - Pacific Bell; [hon.] Numerous top ten sales awards over a period of 28 yrs., as a pacific bell yellow page advertising salesman.; [oth. writ.] Many comedic "Roasts" for various occasions, seemingly enjoyed by small and large audiences alike. (Written and performed) Many unpublished poems and songs.; [pers.] Appreciation and awareness of what one has, before it is lost or taken away. Life is just a series of hurdles and we should be judged my how each situation is handled, overcome and accepted.; [a.] Northridge, CA

MILLER, PATRICIA
[pen.] Patricia; [b.] October 7, 1931, Drumright, OK; [p.] Kenneth Gailey (deceased); [m.] Getty Miller (deceased), September 16, 1961; [ch.] Four - all grown and gone; [ed.] High School - Art school in Albany NY. (Painter); [occ.] private art teacher and artist leader of "The Hidden Life" prayer group; [oth. writ.] Just started writing poetry after husbands dead; [pers.] I have found much comfort in religious and it reflects in my writings and paintings I am Catholic - also write songs and sing Mass Music; [a.] Eunice, LA

MILLS, JUSTIN ANDREW
[pen.] JAM; [b.] March 2, 1980, Houston, TX; [p.] Gary and Doloras Mills; [ed.] Arnold Jr. High, Houston, TX, Cypress Fairbanks High School, Houston, TX; [occ.] Arnold Jr. High Regional Choir, Cypress Fairbanks Honor Choir; [pers.] My feelings of achieving peace and preserving life in all mankind are reflected in my writing; [a.] Houston, TX

MINER, CHARLENE A.
[b.] October 23, 1953, Brattleboro, VT; [p.] Charles and Arlene Slate; [m.] Kerry B. Miner, November 4, 1972; [ch.] Kara Leigh, Kyle Brennan; [ed.] Brattleboro Union High School; [occ.] Operator Service and Clerical Assistant - NYNEX; [memb.] IBEW Local 2324, Telephone Pioneers of America, American Legion auxiliary; [oth. writ.] Poems and Shorts stories, never had (or submitted) any for publication; [pers.] I love and appreciate all the beauty that nature has to offer.; [a.] Brattleboro, VT

MIR, AISHA
[b.] April 16, 1979, Pakistan; [p.] Bushra and Gunawar Mir; [ed.] Currently I am in my second year of high school, at David and Mary Thompson C.I.; [hon.] Honours in advance French in grade 9. Award in grade 8 for one of the Best Students in French.; [oth. writ.] Short stories and book report as an assignment from school.; [pers.] God is all truth and all love. If we are all true and loving this world will be a paradise therefore we must believe in God and must obey him too.; [a.] Toronto Ontario, Canada

MIRANDA, ESTHELA
[pen.] Esthela Miranda; [b.] May 30, 1941, New Mexico; [p.] Napoleon, Guadalupe; [m.] Inzuza Matt Miranda, February 11, 1967; [ch.] Yvonne, Michelle, Derek Miranda; [ed.] 8th Grade; [occ.] Homemaker; [hon.] Volunteer time with senior citizens; [oth. writ.] Several articles published in local newspaper. Like "Small Wonders Make This Season So Special"; [pers.] I have been greatly influenced, encouraged by my family.; [a.] Oxhard, CA

MISHLEY, W. SCOTT
[b.] January 24, 1970, Connecticut; [occ.] Expatriate in Spain as a television news anchorman and radio personality for US gov't.; [hon.] Received highest honors as 1st place entry in the "Thomas Jefferson Awards for Excellence in a Local Radio Radio Newscast" while working at a military radio station in Cuba in 1992. Four years of rehabilitation for improper civil displays of creativity as a youth.; [oth. writ.] 1,000's of poems, dozens of personal essays and many short stories.; [pers.] Influences range from Sophodes to Shakespere to Whitman to Cummings to Ginsberg to Burgio to waits and the same thing to influence each of them.

MITCHELL, MICHAEL W.
[b.] June 27, 1951, Salisbury, MD; [p.] Robert and Sara Mitchell; [m.] Trudy Mitchell, September 25, 1994; [ch.] Jennifer and Jeremiah; [ed.] Caesar Rodney H.S., Delaware Technical and Community College San Bernardino Valley College; [occ.] Assistant Director Salvation Army Homeless Shelter in San Bernardino; [oth. writ.] Several poems published in Phineas the San Bernardino Valley College annual literary publication; [pers.] Inspired by my mother Sara and my Godmother Susan Miller, occasionally any inner child enables we do share, in words, the wonder and beauty I see.; [a.] San Bernardino, CA

MIXON, JENNIFER LYNN
[b.] December 23, 1971, Shreveport, LA; [p.] Robert and Wanda Whisenhunt; [m.] Eric Mixon, September 7, 1991; [ch.] Brandon Mixon; [ed.] Fort Knox High School Marathon High School Florida Key Community College; [occ.] Teller at Nationsbank in Marathon, Florida; [memb.] Calvary Baptist Church Marathon, Florida; [oth. writ.] I wrote several poems in high school that were put in creative writing books, I also had a poem win a competition 7 years ago.; [pers.] My writing is a reflection of my faith in our Lord Jesus Christ. He is the one who gave me this wonderful talent so that others might come to know him.; [a.] Marathon, FL

MKRYAN, SONYA
[b.] March 1, 1935, Libanon; [p.] Vahram Faradjian and Mary Topalian; [m.] Karapet Mkryan, April 11, 1970; [ch.] Marine Mkryan, Anahit Mkryan, Lusine Mkryan; [ed.] PhD in Physics and Mathematics; [occ.] Eligiblity worker (DPSS); [hon.] Five 1st prize awards for my writings in Armenian Language, awarded by the "AAA" (Armenian Art Association); [oth. writ.] Few poems in English (unpublished). Several published poems in Armenian Language; [pers.] My deep admiration toward the amazing creation of the universe and mankind, with all it's glorious capabilities, uncomprehensible emotions and the complexities of his interworld, motivates me to share my love and pain through my writing.; [a.] Altadena, CA

MOBLEY, JOHN
[pen.] Gez; [b.] January 25, 1976, Springfield, MA; [p.] Yvonne Taranto - Joe Taranto; [ed.] Grady High School Brooklyn N.Y.; [occ.] Chief Assistant Actor and Song writer; [oth. writ.] Inside out the actor; [pers.] I strive to reflect the deep feelings of poetry the feelings of poetry the feeling that are embedded in people's hearts; [a.] Brooklyn, NY

MOFFAT, DONALD W.
[b.] September 15, 1922, Chicago IL; [p.] Henry T. and Mary Moffat; [m.] Janet Moffat; [ch.] Linda Mueller and Philip Moffat; [ed.] B.S. Speech Ed. M.F.A.; [occ.] Retired Secondary Teacher; [memb.] Promise keepers Shepherd Church of the Nazarene; [oth. writ.] Various newspaper and magazine articles; [pers.] My greatest joy is bringing joy to others; [a.] Columbus, OH

MOHIUDDIN, MOHAMMED KAMRAN
[pen.] Jigar; [b.] August 17, 1950, Hyderabad, India; [p.] Mohammed Quader Mohiuddin, Mrs. Lutufunnisa (late); [m.] Sajida Sultana Mohiuddin, July 27, 1978; [ch.] Nasiha, Furqan, Shahan, Naveen and Arsalan; [ed.] B.S. Mathematics, Osmania University India, B.S. civil engineering, Detroit, Mich. M.P.A Troy State University, Al; [occ.] Civil Engineer; [hon.] I am A U.S Airforce veteran with several military decorations and awards; [oth. writ.] Several poems and songs looking for a publisher; [pers.] Read between the lines, penetrate the facade, look under the carpet - our world could be better.; [a.] Santa Ana, CA

MONTELEONE, PATRICK
[b.] November 12, 1957, New York, NY; [p.] Pasquale and Corsignana Monteleone.; [m.] Heidi Aldin, June 14, 1980; [ch.] Ani Kristen, Caitlin Elizabeth.; [ed.] F. D. Roosevelt High School, Brooklyn, NY, School of Visual Arts, New York, NY.; [occ.] Freelance graphic designer/illustrator, jazz singer/ukulele instrumentalist.; [oth. writ.] Several as-yet unpublished children's books.; [pers.] "Humor confounds the need to say: `You don't bring me flowers...'"; [a.] Lahaska, PA

MONTGOMERY, LEWIS
[b.] January 20, 1972, Englewood, NJ; [p.] Greg and Roberta Lewis; [ed.] Graduate of Chatsworth H.S., attending Pierce College (Art major), Music student - plays both classical guitar and electric; [occ.] Student; [hon.] Dean's Honor Roll, Order of the Arrow (Boy Scouts with Amer.) [oth. writ.] A lot of things that no one has read; [pers.] Standards of beauty don't exist until they are invented by mad scientists, in tiny laboratories atop two-hundred mile high skyscrapers; [a.] Chatsworth, CA

MONTHONY SR., JOSEPH R.
[pen.] Rad Dad; [b.] May 14, 1957, Medina, NY; [p.] Clayton and Shirley Monthony; [m.] Cynthia Monthony, May 4, 1977; [ch.] Mae, Christina, Joseph Jr.; [ed.] High School, Army, Vocational two New York state Certifications through Comstock Michigan Fruit; [occ.] Maintenance and Production Supervisor; [memb.] North American Hunting Club; [oth. writ.] My own personal collection; [pers.] Don't get so caught up in life that you forget how to relax and enjoy yourself on occasion; [a.] Waterport, NY

MOONEY, ROBERT L.
[b.] January 8, 1947, San Antonio, TX; [p.] Joe and Adelle Mooney; [ed.] BA degree, Southwest Texas State Univ.; [occ.] Art sales executive; [a.] San Antonio, TX

MOORE, BRYAN
[b.] 1928, Wales; [m.] Gwendolyne Muriel, 1954; [ch.] 3; [memb.] The poetry Society (UK) International Soc of poets (USA) (Life Member) Chartered Assoc. of Certified Accountants; [oth. writ.] "Aunt Muriel's Little Folk Tales" (1993) (UK) "1995 Poets" (1994) (UK) and others (UK and USA); [pers.] I try to create "Reading Enjoyment" of poetry for children and adults - poetry should communicate between all - that is my aim; [a.] Chipstead Surrey, United Kingdom

MOORE, HANNAH ELIZABETH TREGASKES
[pen.] H.E.M. [b.] November 25, 1963, Weisboden, Germany; [p.] Sgt. Frederick J. Tregaskes, Arlene Tregaskes; [m.] Jeffrey D. Moore, June 3, 1982; [ch.] Jeffrey Frederick, Bradley Joseph, Steven Andrew, Hannah Aleaha; [ed.] Dayton High School; [occ.] Housewife; [memb.] NRA, Ladies Aux. Military Order of the Purple Heart; [pers.] I am inspired by my husband and children and I enjoy writing something people want to read.; [a.] Templeton, PA

MOORE, JOANNE L.
[pen.] Jo Moore; [b.] July 25, 1934, Detroit, MI; [p.] Gerald and Louise Redenbaugh; [m.] Keith A. Moore, October 20, 1956; [ch.] Stephen Blake, Scoh Kevin, Sean Patrick, Craig Eric, Keith Douglas, Kule Edward; [ed.]

A.S. in Bus. BA in English, History and Business Capital University, Cols. OH; [occ.] Retired on disability from Ross Laboratories; [memb.] Ascension Lutheran Church, Cum Christo of Columbus; [hon.] Dean's List, Award of Excellence in Productivity - Ross Labs; [pers.] In my poetry I strive to paint a picture of my own feelings and to stir the emotions of the reader; [a.] Columbus, OH

MOORE, LANA RACHELE
[b.] September 8, 1977, Olkahoma City, OK; [p.] Leland Moore, Lynda Freeze Moore; [ed.] In the 11th grade at Washington High School, Washington, OK.; [memb.] First Baptist Church of Washington, future homemakers of America, 4-H, Speech and Drama, Future, business leaders of America, Fellowship of christian Athletes, National Honors Society, Acteens; [hon.] Who's who among American High School Students. Academic Award in Pre-Algebra, Home economics. Track Award - Regional Finalist Discuss. Officer Service Award future Homemakers of America Historian.; [oth. writ.] I've wrote several other poems; [pers.] In this world today, living life is a challenge. I look to God for guidance and instruction. Philippians 4:13; [a.] Purcell, OK

MOORE, MR. JAMES C.
[b.] September 19, 1953, Washington, NC; [p.] James A. and Virginia D. Moore; [m.] Willa Jeanette Moore, December 23, 1983; [ch.] Joseph Omar, Tarua Terell, Latasha; [ed.] Aurora High School, Self Taught: Inquisitiveness, intellectual open mindedness and intellectual adaptability.; [occ.] Supply Chief/USMC; [memb.] NCOA; [hon.] 5th Award Good Conduct, 2 Navy achievement medals; [oth. writ.] Unpublished; [pers.] I endeavor to portray a perceived description of the subconscious yet psychosomatic associations between mankind and his universe. FUR 2 BSL, UCI, UBI, URI.; [a.] Oceanside, CA

MOORE, TERRENCE
[b.] September 25, 1969; [p.] Robert and Linda Moore; [m.] Sally Moore; [ed.] B.A. History and French, University of Western Ontario, B. Ed. Strathclyde University, Glasgow, Scotland.; [occ.] College Professor; [pers.] My poem was written for my wife, who made me realize that love can conquer all.; [a.] Island Lake Manitoba, Canada

MOOTS, IRA WILLIAM
[b.] May 4, 1943, Hurdland, MO; [p.] William and Carrie Moots; [m.] Betty, June 28, 1992; [ch.] James William Moots Cambria Dawn Moots Hunter Lecia Rachelle Hartsock; [ed.] Hurdland High School, Northeast MO University Olivet Nayerene University, A.B. English Nayerene theological seminary; [occ.] Substitute teacher; [memb.] United Methodist Church Brashear, MO; [hon.] Deans Honor list 1967-68 President Viking Male Chorus 1962-68 At Olivet Nayerene University.; [oth. writ.] God's timing published in Herald of Holiness 1980's Beyond the blue published in Dark sides of the moon-national library of poetry 1995.; [pers.] Nothing more valuable than a good friend - a good friend is a friend for life.; [a.] Queen City, MO

MORAN JR., FERNANDO
[b.] December 19, 1980, Chicago, IL; [p.] Fernando Moran Sr., Tina Moran; [ed.] Drexel School (Elementary); [occ.] School Student at Drexel School; [pers.] The poems I write are straight from the heart. My idol is Shakespeare and I try to learn more about him. He gives me my ideas and gives me an imagination about my poems.; [a.] Berwyn, IL

MORGAN, DAVID
[b.] June 27, 1945, Burry Port Waleb, UK; [p.] Edwin and Brenda; [m.] Helen, October 02, 1981; [ch.] Rheinallt; [ed.] Llanelli Technical College; [occ.] Area surveyor - local government; [memb.] Architects Institute, Certified Environment Inspector.; [oth. writ.] RA-Science Fiction Novel; [pers.] Why strive to colonize the moon before putting our own house in order; [a.] Carmarthen, UK

MORGAN, LAZELL
[pen.] Imala Nagrom; [b.] April 17, Coolidge, TX; [p.] Chrne Morgan; [ed.] As Degree English Literature Eastfield College, Mesquite, TX; [occ.] Retired and family counselor; [memb.] My membership in with my neighborhood and family members "No special name we are not looking for fame"; [hon.] I am honored as being the family counsel or now that's the greatest honor of all; [oth. writ.] Many poems and short stories. However, none has been published. My writings help me and family to have a better life.; [pers.] I put great effort into my poems, short stories and other writings. For example, I write to the common people. My writings are clear.; [a.] Dallas, TX

MORRIS, DONNA LEE
[pen.] Barbra Ammon; [b.] April 4, 1947, Manila, Philippines; [p.] Candida Magno, Ramon y'de Castro; [m.] Russel Leroy Morris, April 11, 1974; [ch.] Dennis and Jeffrey Morris; [ed.] La Concordia College, Manuel L. Quezon Institute, Far Eastern University, Manila, Phil, American Academy of Dramatic Arts, New York, University of California, Los Angeles; [occ.] Aesthetician (studies all the arts, from all countries and from all periods of history, in relation to their physical, social and cultural environments); [memb.] Screen Actors Guild; [hon.] Rode the Hollywood Christmas Lane Parade, 1977. Awarded for contributing to the Academy of Motion Picture Arts and Sciences.; [oth. writ.] Currently writing one book (untitled); [pers.] All we can do is to study and correlate with what wisdom and discretion may be ours, using the knowledge that may come for the good of those we seek to help, and recognizing that in the wise use of knowledge comes increased capacity to receive the hidden wisdom.; [a.] Granada Hills, CA

MORRISON, EDWARD
[b.] October 27, 1947, Middleboro, MA; [m.] Jo Anne Morrison, September 14, 1974; [ch.] Nicole, Jesse, Terri, Luke; [pers.] I find I can express myself more simply by writing in poetry form than speaking what I think; [a.] Somerville, MA

MORROW, JASON G.
[pen.] Maneno M. Utukufu; [b.] October 16, 1973, Brooklyn, NY; [p.] Janice Morrow, James Morrow II; [ed.] High School of Art and Design, Junior - year student at York College, Jamaica, NY; [occ.] English tutor, York College, Jamaica, New York; [hon.] Deans' List; [oth. writ.] Poems published in the Los Angeles sentinel, and school newspaper - Pandora's Box; [pers.] I have always thought of poetry as a garden. Where nurturing passion and creativity is the responsibility of all with literary talent. If more people used this form of expression, they would no longer take words for granted.; [a.] Baisley Park, NY

MOSELEY, AUGUSTUS V.
[pen.] Gus Moseley; [b.] August 19, 1931, Baltimore, MD; [p.] Robert Moseley; [m.] Regina A. Moseley, December 24, 1953; [occ.] Private Tutor; [memb.] AOA Frat; [a.] Sacramento, CA

MOSER JR., THOMAS EUGENE
[b.] July 21, 1967, Hagerstown, MD; [p.] Thomas Eugene Moser, Mary Lou Moser; [ch.] Kaitlyn Richelle Moser; [ed.] Smithsburg High school Hagerstown Junior College Shippensburg University; [occ.] Manager, Weis Markets, Inc.; [memb.] St. Marks Lutheran church American Legion; [oth. writ.] Several poems including David, Easter memory, conversation above, goodbye, six months and wake up America.; [pers.] My works are dedicated to the memory of my brother and best friend, David Wayne Moser. Without him, there would be no creativity.; [a.] Smithsburg, MD

MOSER, MEL
[b.] October 25, 1957, Regina, Saskatchewan, Canada; [p.] John and Melvina Moser; [m.] Jane Moser, October 17, 1981; [ed.] St. John Elementary, Campion High School, University of Regina (2 yrs) all located in Regina, Saskatchewan; [occ.] Owner/Manager, Professional Autobody Ltd.; [memb.] Regina Humane Society Knights of Columbus; [hon.] 2nd place, Regina SaskArt Competition 1989 - Abstract Art Category Knights of Columbus - Certificate of Appreciation 1993; [oth. writ.] To date I have written for my own personal enjoyment. This is the first poem I've had published.; [pers.] For the past 6 years I have battled clinical depression. Only recently have I been able to express in words my experiences of the past 6 years. I credit my family, friends and most of all my wife Jane for helping me make it through the "dark" times. Because of the strength and courage I gained, I write today what I could not yesterday; [a.] Regina Saskatchewan, Canada

MOSES, MICHELLE
[b.] April 17, 1978, Kingston, PA; [p.] Mike Moses, Marie Moses; [ed.] Pallas High School; [pers.] My main influence is Jim Morrison. Most of my poems are as park and depressing as his.; [a.] Shavertown, PA

MOSES, NOEL
[pen.] Noel Moses; [b.] December 25, 1952, Guyana; [p.] Mathilda Fresco; [ch.] Nyerere Moses, Kwame, Akini, Sharlene.; [ed.] B.S. Electrical Engineering MSC Computer and Education Advanced Degree in Educational Administration and Supervision; [occ.] Teacher of Engineering Brooklyn Technical High School; [memb.] National council of teachers of mathematics (NCTM); [oth. writ.] Expected publication of a book of poems.; [pers.] I believe in the principle of sharing and loving. I believe in the sanctity of time the sacred virtues of fear. I am committed to the principle of steadfast and exponential growth. I am first a universal man the only one that will ever be.; [a.] Brooklyn, NY

MOSES, VIVIAN
[pen.] Grannie Vee Moses; [b.] February 23, 1919, Windsor, OH; [ch.] Donald and James; [occ.] Retired; [memb.] Singing Grannies; [hon.] Scholarship to Cleveland School Music, 4 awards (trophies) for Ballroom Dancing.

MOSS, IRENE
[pen.] Irene Moss; [p.] Wolf Greenfield, Bella Greenfield; [m.] Nat Moss; [ch.] Robert Moss M.D., Ralph W. Moss, Ph.D.; [ed.] Washington Irving High, Brooklyn Museum Art School, School of Visual Arts, NYC, Private studies.; [occ.] Artist (Painter); [hon.] In collections of: Rose Art Museum (Brandies) Ma., New Britain Museum of Art, Ct., Norfolk Museum, Va, plus Commercial and Private Collections; [oth. writ.] Autobiography: "Divided Canvas, An Artist's Journey", Short Stories and

Poems, plus articles in art publications, paintings chosen to be reproduced on covers of college psychology and law textbooks.; [pers.] My writing and painting intermingle in my passion for self-expression. Each creates a climate of remembrance and imagination that feeds my soul.

MOSS, JUDY A.
[pen.] Anne Vincent; [b.] August 23, 1945, Ironton, MO; [p.] Claude E. Sencibaugh and Mary Givens; [m.] Thomas C. Moss, May 18, 1963; [ch.] Thomas G. and Martin L.; [ed.] BS in Business, Fontbonne College, Saint Louis, MBA Fontbonne College, St. Louis, Certified Economic Developer, American Econ. Dev. Council; [occ.] Business and Industry Specialist University of MO, University Extension; [memb.] Missouri Industrial Dev. Council, American Econ. Dev. Council, National Extension Assn., New Hartford Baptist Church; [hon.] Counselor for MO Industrial Dev. Council; [oth. writ.] None published under Judy A. Moss; [pers.] Having gone through humbling times personally, I strive to create a better economy for rural Americans. My motto is "Humility Creates Strength"; [a.] New Hartford, MO

MOULTON, JAYME
[b.] November 11, 1976, Potsdam, NY; [p.] Evaline Moulton; [m.] Scott Larson, July 22, 1995; [ed.] Union Elementary, Main Street. Middle School, Montpelier High School; [occ.] Dietary Aide, Mayo Nursing Home, Northfield, VT; [hon.] $100.00 cosmetology scholarship (Mary Elizabeth Redmond Memorial Scholarship); [pers.] "Follow your dreams, I did and finally I'm being recognized for something so special to me"; [a.] Northfield, VT

MOUSSEAU, DEBBIE
[pen.] Anna Dale; [b.] January 12, 1959, Red Deer, Alberta, Canada; [p.] Lois and Frank Yuhasz; [m.] Donald Mousseau, November 21, 1981; [ch.] Benjamin, Michael, Anna; [ed.] I am currently studying at the "University of Alberta" in the third year of B. Ed. Program.; [memb.] Calmar United Church: Member of the Evangelic Committee; [oth. writ.] "The Treasured Secrets" is a short story about a unique relationship that develops between a young child and her grandfather.; [pers.] Poetry by Theodore Roethke and George Barker have greatly influenced any prose or poetry that I have written. Like them, I am driven to write about relationships that reflect the kind of love that transcends what society believes a loving relationship ought to consist of.; [a.] Calmar Alberta, Canada

MUELLER, RUTH E.
[pen.] Sara [b.] September 25, 1916, Cincinnati, OH; [p.] Anselemt and Bertha Merritt; [m.] Deceased both husbands, 1st husbands Wm. M. Baker, 2nd Wm. L. Mueller, (1st) September 22, 1932, (2nd) February, 1972; [ch.] I only had children by only my first husband. 11 children both husbands and died of cancer, 7 boys and 4 girls; [ed.] St. Ursulas Academy, in Coldwell Ohio; [occ.] I am retired now. I only do my writing, poems, stories and lyrics for songs.; [memb.] I was in the Manfort Hts Council for many years, here in Cincinnati Ohio 45247, I was also on the Republican Party Task Force during President Ronald Reagan Terms; [hon.] I had my poems published by Standard Publishing Co., on Hamilton Ave in Cincinnati Ohio, and had poem published in the Gulf Port Miss., American Arts Association in the Western Press Newspaper here in Cincinnati, in white Oar Cincinnati, Ohio; [pers.] I only hope the gift of writing, buy my poems, songs and stories, that God has given me, can lift mankinds spirits or help him in same small way in humbly hope so.; [a.] Cincinnati, OH

MULCAHY, HAZEL C.
[b.] December 11, 1941, Ireland; [p.] William and Eileen Espey; [m.] Thomas D. Mulcahy, September 21, 1990; [ch.] Jonathan and Shane Garrett; [ed.] Collegiate College, Celbridge, Co Vildare, Ireland; [occ.] Artist [a.] Santa Ana, CA

MULLINER, LAMAR D.
[b.] February 22, 1906, Shamokin, PA; [p.] Edward and Anna Mulliner; [ed.] Shamokin High School Shamokin, Penna.; [occ.] Retired - former American consul - Gothenburg, Sweden and Cairo, Egypt; [memb.] United Church of Christ, Shamokin, Penna; [a.] New York, NY

MUNDEN, JONATHAN W.
[pen.] Jonathan; [b.] June 2, 1975, Kansas City, MO; [p.] Jack and JoAnn Munden; [ed.] Ruskin High, Longview Community College, University of Missouri Kansas city; [occ.] College Student; [hon.] All-American Scholar Award, Quill and Scroll Award of Honor; [oth. writ.] Poems published in the annual Longview College publication.; [pers.] I stand tall upon a mountain of dreams yet to dream, reaching for the heavens and grasping almost nothing, yet still I try.; [a.] Kansas City, MO

MUNSON, MICHAEL
[pen.] Michael Munson "Mike"; [b.] August 11, 1959, Minneapolis, MN; [p.] Gary and Catherine Munson; [ed.] Garden City Elementary School Brooklyn Ctr Mn; [memb.] St. Alphonsus Catholic Church Brooklyn Ctr Little League Baseball. Brooklyn Ctr Bowling League.; [pers.] Michael participated in his life, however brief with love and faith and courage. His poem touches on ever facet of his world as he knew it. It is in sharing his poetry that we continue to celebrate his life and the gift he was to us. This is Michaels "moment in time."

MURRAY, BRIAN J.
[b.] November 5, 1967, Piscataway, NJ; [p.] Barry and Judy Murray; [ed.] High School, some college at Community College of Phila.; [occ.] Disabled due to brain tumors since 2/92, on 10/30/94; [hon.] Won 1st prize in photo contest sponsored by the Philadelphia Zoo. The Camera Shop in 1982; [oth. writ.] Various unpublished poetry; [pers.] My poetry is inspired by the people I write about. Each person rings a different meaning to my life. One Immortal Soul was written for Ann Doyle.

MURRAY, JOHN J.
[b.] April 23, 1924, Plymouth, PA; [p.] James and Wraifred (Barret) Murray; [ed.] B.S. Univ. of Jeronton, M.A. catholic U. of America Phd New York University; [occ.] Retired from teaching at Duquesne U., Fona College, Seranton U.; [memb.] Modern Language Assoc; [oth. writ.] "Poetry Teaching Tools." J.G.E., "Four lines of Hamlet Disambiguated using symbolic logic," P.M.C.A, "Four sonnet, of Shakespeare Imitated," Scholia Satyvicon; [pers.] I believe in counter statement (see Kenneth Burge) to "Ars Poetical " (Mae Leish): For love? Nothing. The face of love is Dublin Dean - A poem should be but also mean.; [a.] Boynton Beach, FL

MURRAY, OLGA
[b.] April 12, 1950, Jamaica, West Indies; [p.] Violel James, Nathaniel Murray; [ch.] Andrea Doran, Barbara Doran, Effijeane Williams; [ed.] Attended Mannings High School and St Joseph's teacher college in Jamaica St Joseph's Teachers college in Jamaica W.I. currently pursuing bachelors degree in early childhood Ed. at Brooklyn College, Brooklyn NY; [occ.] Personal Care Aide; [hon.] Award of merit certificate presented for poem "Life". Presentation made by world of Poetry. Another award of merit certificate presented for poem "knowing who your friends are."; [oth. writ.] Several unpublished poems.; [pers.] Writing is one of my favorite passions. I reminisce many of my childhood and adult experiences and I realize that the older I get, the more I am better able to understand why many things happen the way they do. I express my innermost thoughts through poetry and I love it very much.; [a.] Brooklyn, NY

MYERS, DAVID W.
[pen.] David W. Myers; [b.] July 25, 1969, Cuba City, WI; [p.] Eugene and Barb Myers; [m.] Divorced; [ch.] Jeffery Todd Myers; [ed.] Iowa Grant High School, Welding School in North Carolina, Safety Instructor for Motorcycle riders; [occ.] Seeking a career as manager of progressive playground equipment.; [hon.] Served 4 years in the U.S. Marine Corp. I'm a Persian Gulf Vet.; [oth. writ.] I have many poems I have written, but have never sent any in before.; [pers.] When I write I try to let my emotions flow from my heart. I try to express my feelings as I see them.; [a.] Charlotte, NC

MYERS, LAURIE
[b.] August 3, 1958, Los Angeles, CA; [m.] Keith Myers, October 29, 1983; [ch.] Stephanie Erin, Derek Wade; [occ.] I am a homemaker; [oth. writ.] Various poems; [pers.] I am so grateful that God has some how taken the experiences of my life and turned them into blessings through poetry. I'm also deeply thankful for my family Keith, Stephanie and Derek.; [a.] Northridge, CA

MYERS, NANCY E.
[b.] September 4, 1929, Hammond, IN; [p.] Wm. D. and Nelle Miller; [m.] Allen D. Myers, June 24, 1950; [ch.] Timothy Myers and Bettina Christenson; [ed.] Attended public schools in Hammond, Indiana - was graduated from Moracco High School; [occ.] Retired - First and foremost a wife, mother and "Gommie"; [oth. writ.] Tapes and poems for grandchildren and children of friends; [pers.] Love children - therefore all stories and poems about and for children our seven grandchildren are the light of my life - miss them the months we winter in Fla. can't wait to "Be Back Home Again in Indiana."; [a.] Morocco, IN

NACE, ELIZABETH ADELE
[pen.] Elizabeth Adele Nace; [b.] January 15, 1973, Ohio; [p.] Roselyn and George Nace; [m.] Billy Joe Rector; [ch.] Sarah Beth, Tarah Lynn, Aleesha Rose, Billy Joe Jr.; [ed.] Boone City High School; [occ.] Housewife; [pers.] I am a housewife, and a mother of 4. This is my first poem to be published and written, but I hope to make more of this.; [a.] Union, KY

NASON, DIANA
[pen.] Diana Nason; [b.] July 27, 1961, Washington, DC; [p.] Ezio and Theresa Rebechi; [m.] Joseph T. Nason Jr., October 4, 1986; [ch.] Joseph Andrew and Evan Connor; [ed.] Meade Senior High and Baltimore City Community College; [occ.] Senior Clerk, Howard County Government, Bureau of Engineering; [pers.] My poem was inspired by my grandmother, Mary Eder. She passed away in June 1994 at the age of 86. My grandmother had a major impact on my life. I only hope to have such

an impact on my children's lives as she did on mine. While I tried to express my feelings about her in a short poem I feel that I could have written an entire book. She is greatly missed.; [a.] Baltimore, MD

NAVARRO, MAY JOAN
[b.] November 2, 1934, Suffern, NY; [p.] William and Jeanette Masker; [m.] Richard, September 28, 1952; [ch.] (7) 2 boys and 5 girls; [ed.] High School Graduate; [occ.] Housewife; [pers.] Always loved poetry, especially liked Louise May Alcott and Elizabeth Browning.

NAWLS, DWIGHT
[b.] November 4, 1968, Chicago, IL; [p.] Lillian Nawls; [ed.] Jean B.P. DuSable High, St. Ambrose University 1 1/2 yr.; [occ.] Bank Teller - Ashland State Bank - Chicago IL; [pers.] The ideology of men and the confusion amongst a world which was once in unity and love has created a very vain society deceived by the error of their ways. Let us return to the creator and away from idols created by the hidden one.; [a.] Chicago, IL

NAZIR, PHIROZIE
[b.] March 9, 1907, India; [ed.] Graduate Brooklands Aviation School, England (1931), Aeronautical research engineer, H.M. Government of India (1932), University of London, research on high lift devices (1933-37), lectured before Royal Aeronautical Society, discovered tip-stalling on tapered wings and developed new type lateral control useful as a high lift device.; [occ.] Pilot, Engineer, Researcher, Poet, Writer; [memb.] Institute of the Aeronautical Sciences, Institute of British Engineers, Associate Fellow Royal Aeronautical Society.; [hon.] (1944-1946) Joined United States Air Corps, at Wright Field, Dayton, Ohio. Assigned my B.L.C. Aircraft Patent No: 2700 516. to U.S. Govt. and is now adopted on most every flying aircraft! Without any compensation to me what-so-ever!; [oth. writ.] Published small book of poetry, entitled "Songs Of Shantee". Wrote many articles on a variety of subjects relating to life, and existence etc.; [pers.] (1946-1995) I have been able to receive divine gifts of God, in way of many spiritual writings, and innovations for the future benefit and upliftment of the consciousness of men! This indeed! Is the greatest blessing that cannot be spent away! I remain in the oneness of life forever!

NEAL, JANNETTE
[pen.] Sis Neal; [b.] March 20, 1929, Windsor, Ontario, Canada; [p.] Thomas and Rose Millben; [m.] Bennie Neal, February 4, 1966; [ed.] Patterson High School were in Windsor Ontario the other school indicated was in Detroit Michigan, Detroit Institute of Technology, Bulmer Business College High School and Business College; [occ.] Retired; [memb.] Ontario Chapel B.M.E. Church, Windsor Ontario; [pers.] God gives us all some type of gift. I have always believed mine was in writing, especially poetry. I stand to-day on solid ground, because of Him. May He, forever be praised.; [a.] Windsor Ontario, Canada

NEAL, VICKY L.
[pen.] Vicky L. Neal; [b.] October 5, 1962, Middletown, OH; [p.] Ancil and Mildred Downey; [m.] Robert Neal, August 28, 1988; [ch.] Christopher and Jessica; [ed.] High School Diploma major in English; [occ.] Self-employed in carpet cleaning business; [oth. writ.] Currently signed with a Hollywood agent for a science fiction script I wrote. Began writing stories at 16 and have about 25 unpublished full length stories to date.; [pers.] A true writer will never quit and eventually become successful; [a.] Middletown, OH

NEBEKER, KENNETH
[pen.] Kenneth Krist; [b.] October 14, 1968, Culver City; [oth. writ.] I also write songs and I'm studying to be a writer. And I had, recently another poem published in A Moment In Time, that I'm very glad about.; [pers.] This poem was written for a very special lady named Danette. She is so wonderful you wouldn't believe it if I told you. I love you, Danette (always); [a.] Yuba City, CA

NEBEKER, KENNETH
[pen.] Kenneth Khrist; [b.] October 14, 1968, Culver City, CA; [p.] Andrew and Linda Nebeker; [ed.] GED (Night School), Part-time college at Yuba Collge in Marysville CA; [oth. writ.] I also write songs and other poetry, such as ex-lovers, special friends and I love you like, which are also in "A Moment In Time"; [pers.] Yes, I would like to say something, I would like to say that a very special woman named Danette inspired me to write these poems and I would like to dedicate them to her too. Love you, Honey; [a.] Yuba City, CA

NEILSON, MARGARET FOSS
[b.] May 29, 1973, Buffalo, NY; [p.] Charles Foss, Vicki Duncan; [m.] Christopher Neilson, November 23, 1994; [ch.] Sara Madeline Foss Neilson; [ed.] New Bern Senior High (Advance Placement English and History); [occ.] Home maker, mother, occasional commercial cleaner; [oth. writ.] Poems, songs, short and children's stories, unfortunately still unpublished, an undiscovered; [pers.] I would love for someone professional to look at my songs, and perhaps someday complete a novel. I enjoy spending time with my daughter and living in the country.; [a.] New Bern, NC

NEISWENDER, CARYN
[b.] May 13, 1976, Escondido, CA; [p.] Dolly Cathrin Neiswender; [ed.] Currently at Mira Costa College, Capo Valley Christian School; [occ.] Sales Associate at Coast office Products, Tutor at Mira Costa; [memb.] Honor Student, Lifetime Member of CSF, Who's Who in American High School Students; [hon.] Printed in the Cera Foundation's The Poets And Anthology, Academic Athlete, Principal's List, Valedictorian, Honor Society, Professor Recommended Tutorialship, Bank of American Achievement Award, 2nd prize in Photography Exhibit; [oth. writ.] Many articles published in various newspapers, poem published in the Cera Foundation's The Poets An Anthology, CVCS writing honors.; [pers.] "The heavens declare the glory of God, the skies proclaim the work of His hands." Psalm 19:1; [a.] Carlsbad, CA

NELSON, SARAH
[b.] May 5, 1981, Appleton, WI; [p.] John and Joy Nelson; [occ.] Student; [memb.] National Junior Honor Society; [hon.] Duke University Talent Identification Program, National Junior Honor Society Member, Poetry published in district magazine, 3rd place winner - Mockingbird Chapter of Poetry Society of Texas; [oth. writ.] Poetry published in school and district magazines. 3rd place winner - Hockaday School Banner award; [pers.] I can be reached at E-Mail: Los Rios @aol.com; [a.] Plano, TX

NEWBERG, NICOLE
[pen.] Nicole Newberg; [b.] April 4, 1979, Springs, CO; [p.] Camille and Danny Newberg; [ed.] Bayport Bluepoint High School; [occ.] Student; [oth. writ.] 3 poems in the Spectrum Magazine; [pers.] I want to thank my mom for helping me out and for encouraging me to stick with my writing.; [a.] Bayport, NY

NEWMAN, MICHAEL JARED
[b.] July 10, 1979, Middletown, NY; [p.] March and Brenda Newman; [ed.] Valley Central High School; [memb.] Boy Scouts of America, National Eagle Scout Association, National Science Honor Society, National Brotherhood of the Order of the Arrow; [hon.] Eagle Scout Award ranked #1 in Sophomore Class (1994); [oth. writ.] Few poems written for school or to share with friends and relatives.; [pers.] The only answers one needs should come from within. I follow this statement in the life that I lead.; [a.] Walden, NY

NEWTON, PATTY J.
[b.] November 9, 1952, Shelbyville, IN; [p.] Wanetta and Bernard Sink; [m.] Richard Newton, November 29, 1989; [ch.] Ryan M. Berry, Greg A. Berry; [ed.] High School Graduate; [occ.] Home maker; [pers.] I express the feelings from my heart. Thru my writings of poetry and hope to comfort and inspire others.; [a.] Shelbyville, IN

NGUYEN, MS. CHAU NGOC
[pen.] Chau Ngoc; [b.] January 3, 1943, South of Vietnam; [p.] Ky Van Nguyen, Thin Thi Tran; [ch.] Alton, Vuton, Huyton, Thuyton; [occ.] International Gourmet Chef, Cooking and "Edible" Visual Art Teacher.; [oth. writ.] Several poems published in local newspapers in Vietnam, articles for "Hon-Viet" Magazine and Fresno Bee newspaper in California.; [pers.] I understand the mankind miseries and pains through my own. I want to interpret those unfortunates by my most true throbbing sounds of my own heart through my own pen the surrealistic and abstract artists influence a great deal in my thought.; [a.] Pasadena, CA

NICHOLAS, JEANETTE B.
[pen.] Jeanette B. Nicholas; [b.] October 15, 1922, Hartford, CT; [p.] Samuel Borg and Hildur Lysen Borg; [m.] Gordon Nicholas, December 22, 1945; [ch.] (6) Steven, Joan, Lana, Linda (twins) Vicky and Diane; [ed.] Amuerdson High School in Chicago, attended San Jose State College- California, B.A. from Western Montana College in Dillon, Montana; [occ.] Home maker; [memb.] First United Presbyterian Church, Browning Literary Club, formerly Amer. Assn. of University Women and Church Women United.; [hon.] High School National Honorary Society; [oth. writ.] Sentiments on sympathy cards; [pers.] Many interests - history, geography, philosophy, photography, genealogy, literature. Special interest - man's place in the universe.; [a.] Atlantic, IA

NICKERSON, JASON
[pen.] Jay Andrew; [b.] June 11, 1978, Portland, ME; [p.] Richard and Mary Nickerson; [ed.] Attending Scarborough High (Graduating Class of 1996); [occ.] Dreamer; [memb.] Campfire Board of Directors; [hon.] Student Ambassador to the Soviet Union, Student Representative in the U.S. Senate, Sophomore Class President; [oth. writ.] R.I.P (an original comedy for the stage), many short poems and human inquiries including Silence Within, The Glimmer, Devoured, and many others, comedy sketches, various monologs, and several screenplay concepts.; [pers.] My writing is inspired by only one thing, the essence of life. Life is an adventure, an adventure to explore the extreme depths of reality.; [a.] Scarborough, ME

NIEMAN, CAROLYN M.
[b.] January 14, 1973, Rochester, NY; [p.] Sharon and Douglas Nieman; [ed.] Central Columbia High School Bloomsburg University; [occ.] College Student; [memb.]

St. Lukes Lutheran Church, Hotline at Pregnancy Crisis Center, member of Psi Chi (Psychology National Honors Society), Psychology Association; [hon.] Dean's List; [pers.] I thank my Lord, Jesus Christ, for my life and all he has given me. Remember to always follow your dreams. There are no limits but the ones you set for yourself.; [a.] Bloomsburg, PA

NIV, DR. MOLLY
[pen.] Dr. Molly Niv; [b.] July 11, 1924, Vienna, Austria; [p.] Lisa and Victor Davidoff; [m.] Divorced [ch.] Nava and Gideon; [ed.] Notre Dame de Sion, Bulgaria University of London matriculation, Sorbonne, Paris Medical School, Hebrew University, New York Medical College; [occ.] Psychiatrist, formerly Assistant Professor of Psychiatry, course on Existential Psychiatry; [memb.] Medical societies, Animal protection agencies; [hon.] Merit Scholarship for Medical School, Fellow American Academy of Pediatrics; [oth. writ.] Many scientific publications in Pediatric and Psychiatric journals. Reason In Madness - currently in press this 500-pages book is a treatise on Existential psychiatry. Poems published in anthologies (e.g. American Poetry Anthology, 1989); [pers.] Do not forecefully strive to achieve happiness. Obey the dictates of your conscience and answer the call of your destiny. Happiness is incidental: the more you strive, struggle and push to achieve it, the further you close the door for the door to happiness opens from outside: From the side of Divine Providence. (S. Kierkegaard).; [a.] New York, NY

NOILES, BRENT
[pen.] Brent; [b.] January 11, 1979, Amherst, Nova Scotia, Canada; [p.] John and Connie Noiles; [ed.] Grade 10 at Amherst Regional High School; [oth. writ.] I have written many other poems. Some are: "The Right Cards", "Storm", "Truth", "Betrayal", "Dangerous Games". I have written many others.; [pers.] I credit my loving parents for all their support, and thank you very much Mrs. Boyd for all your time. "I hope that the words make you feel something deep inside." "Maybe even shed a tear if it's that good."; [a.] Amherst Nova Scotia, Canada

NOLAN, SHAWN T.
[pen.] Mumbly Snow; [b.] June 10, 1968, Cleveland, OH; [p.] Mike and Mary Nolan; [ed.] "Ohio University" Environmental Geography, Roger Bacon High "86"; [occ.] Commercial Fisherman/Landscape, Nursery "Yard Doctor" Juneau Alaska; [hon.] Spartan Spirit Award. Cincinatti Wrester of the Week, 86. Jim Newman Award.; [oth. writ.] Several poems and children's books - unpublished; [pers.] Man is just a trifull jest, on which the game dose play. To live and learn is everything, to not you fade away.; [a.] Juneau, AK

NORTHCUTT, BEATRICE
[b.] January 6, 1928, Castle, OK; [p.] Everett Wyrick and Henryetta Housewright; [m.] Billy D. Northcutt, February 17, 1945; [ch.] Thomas D., Garry D., Danny V.; [ed.] Okemah High School 1944, 2 yrs. at Independence, Kansas Jr. College; [occ.] Retired from Dodson's Nutritional Food Ctr.; [oth. writ.] Novel: "Tomorrow Will Be Better" and a sequel "What Time I Am Afraid" - unpublished several poems.; [pers.] It is my desire to inspire people to live better lives no matter their circumstances. My 92 yr. old mother has been the inspiration for my novels.; [a.] Noble, OK

NORTON, SHARON A.
[pen.] Sharon Norton; [b.] June 6, 1938, Lewiston, ID; [p.] William E. and Emily Hamilton; [m.] Allison Norton Jr., May 29, 1954; [ch.] (6) Wendy Kay, Delores June, Andrew W. Clay, James Scott, Linda Denielle, William Allison; [ed.] St. Maries High (ID), Art Instruction Inc. - Minneapolis, MN; [occ.] Retired from Safeway Stores Inc.; [memb.] Nazarene Church, A.A.R.P.; [oth. writ.] A Christmas poem (1994) in the local newspaper.; [pers.] Our large family is my source of inspiration. If I can give some happy thoughts to others, I feel I've given the gift of love. Whether it be nostalgic or exemplatory.; [a.] Yuma, AZ

NORTON, TAMEKA CHERIE
[pen.] Tameka Norton; [b.] December 13, 1978, Philadelphia, PA; [p.] Carrie and Charles Brown, William Norton; [ed.] George Washington High; [occ.] Full time Student; [memb.] SADD (Students against drunk driving), Dancer, Rising Juniors program; [pers.] Writing opens the doors to a world where you can be at peace with yourself. A world where you can be at peace. I wish I could write forever.; [a.] Philadelphia, PA

NORTON, TINA LOUISE
[pen.] Tina Louise Clark; [b.] September 9, 1962, Fort Bragg, CA; [p.] David and Hazel Clark; [m.] Jody Norton, October 18, 1986; [ch.] Katherine Valador, Daniel Norton, Austin Norton; [ed.] Fort Bragg High; [occ.] Active Journalist, Children's Author, Mother; [hon.] By you directly, thank you so much.; [oth. writ.] Children's Books, Oh Miss Judy, Living in the Love of Another. Many more to publish.; [pers.] May the love in my words reach the children of the world.; [a.] Fort Bragg, CA

NOSCHESE, VINCENT
[b.] February 22, 1952, New York; [p.] Michaelina and Joseph; [ch.] 1 daughter Kristina; [occ.] Disabled Banker; [hon.] Winner of many banking awards in my 23 years as a banker; [pers.] Solitude, aspires - feelings. Feelings of life and love, and oft times feelings we find in our hearts because of solitude

NOURSE, JOLIE
[b.] March 19, 1966, Hornell, NY; [p.] Vale Nourse, Mary Nourse; [ed.] Perry High, Washington High, Glendale Community College, Munson Williams School of Art; [occ.] Executive Secretary, Utica Corporation, Utica, NY; [oth. writ.] Several poems; [pers.] I'm inspired by the lessons of life. I write when I find it too painful to feel, and feel only after the last word is written.; [a.] Sylvan Beach, NY

NOWACK, ANDREW J.
[b.] March 1, 1974, Grand Rapids, MI; [p.] Randy and Laurie Falkowski, Jerry Nowack; [m.] Marci L. Nowack, June 25, 1993; [ed.] Wyoming Park High School; [occ.] United States Army; [memb.] The Way Ministry; [hon.] Army Achievement Medal, National Defense Medal, Australian Jump wings; [oth. writ.] Lonely and saying I love you written to my wife.; [pers.] My wife and God are my inspiration. Without them I could not overcome many of life's challenging goals. For that I thank God for making me the man I am and blessing me with my lovely wife.; [a.] Spring Lake, NC

NOWAK, NICOLE C.
[pen.] Nickel, Nikki Nowak; [b.] September 24, 1977, Milwaukee; [p.] Dr. Barbara J. Nowak; [ed.] Currently at Junior at Alief Hastings High School/Houston, TX, plan to go on to college and obtain a Master's degree in Journalism; [occ.] Student; [pers.] I focus my writings on those things that bring out strong emotions in me. Because those feelings are universal, they speak to many people.; [a.] Houston, TX

NYKAMP, RONALD
[pen.] Ron; [b.] June 13, 1930, Holland, MI; [m.] Elaine, August 11, 1950; [ch.] Lori, Steve, Dave; [ed.] Grade School, High School, one semester of Poetry at Hope College at age 58; [occ.] Retired; [memb.] Nature Groups, Fishing Clubs, Church Offices and work; [hon.] Written awards, letters and cards of thanks, gifts and acknowledgements; [oth. writ.] Many poems, A Children's Book, Poetry Book, at work on Book of Memories. Notes and cards for birthdays, for weddings etc.; [pers.] As my pen signature, I write from my heart. A gentle, caring, person and it comes through in the things I write.; [a.] Holland, MI

O'CONNELL, KEVIN B.
[b.] October 31, 1960, Long Island; [p.] Robert O'Connell and Josephine Ugo [ed.] Hafstra University - under Graduate, Stonybrook Univ Graduate; [occ.] Spanish Teacher, Baseball Coach/Instructor; [memb.] Faculty of William Floyd High School, LI, NY; [pers.] Death is but a physical passing the mind and spirit are universal and but pass from one corporeal entity to another, only conscious recognition separates man from immortality.; [a.] East Patthogue, NY

O'FARRELL, MARGARET
[b.] Concord, NH; [p.] Margaret Clark and Edward O'Farrell; [ed.] M.A. in English and Education from CCNY (City College Of New York) [occ.] Educator - Scarsdale Public Schools, Scarsdale, NY.; [memb.] Scarsdale Teachers Association, New York State Head Injury Association, Association of American Indian Affairs, National Museum of Women in the Arts United Federation of Teachers; [pers.] I have come to realize that you must have just enough sorrow in life in order to appreciate the joy.; [a.] Bronxville, NY

O'LOUGHLIN, JENNIFER P.
[b.] October 27, 1965, Passaic, NJ; [p.] Theresa Kaleta, Vincent Oddo; [m.] Joseph O'Loughlin, August 17, 1991; [ed.] New Jersey, H.S. Graduate, an Associates Degree in Accounting and BA Degree in speech Communication earned at IUP Indiana, PA and West Chester University, West Chester, PA.; [occ.] Organizational Accountant, Exton, PA.; [oth. writ.] Several poems however never pursued the publishing path before.; [pers.] Writing Poetry gives me inspiration to reflect on what touches my heart and then to express it through words.; [a.] Downingtown, PA

O'NEIL, EIRNELLA A.
[b.] July 28, 1943, Gould City, MI; [p.] Edmund W. Blanchard and Vivian M. (Hewitt) Blanchard; [m.] James R. O'Neil, July 22, 1961; [ch.] Jeannette Elsenheimer; [ed.] Graduated from Engadine High School June 1961.; [occ.] Assistant Manager, Bownan Gas Co., Gulliver, MI. Employed October 1, 1963; [pers.] This was my first attempt at actually submitting one of my poems for publication since High School. This certainly gives me the incentive to continue writing and with retirement looming in my future, I expect to spend a lot of my time forming new ideas.; [a.] Gould City, MI

O'NEIL, ELAINE M.
[pen.] Elayna; [b.] September 22, 1953, Winthrop, MA; [p.] Eugene and Marie Ricciardelli; [m.] William T. O'Neil, November 6, 1982; [ch.] Brandon O'Neil; [ed.]

Revere, High School, Solarl's School of Hair Design; [occ.] Hair Salon Owner and Manager. Sales Advisor for just America; [oth. writ.] Several poems for church and company meetings. Singles for business purposes.; [pers.] My desire is to make the world aware of how good God is and to bring hope to those that feel there isn't any. My inspiration has been my parents, family, and most of all the Holy Spirit.; [a.] Revere, MA

O'STEEN, CHRIS
[pen.] Chris O'Steen [b.] August 20, 1951, Poughkeepsie, NY; [p.] Mr. and Mrs. Thomas F. Christmas Sr.; [m.] Joseph L. O'Steen, February 14, 1987; [ch.] 4; [ed.] Graduate of Saint Augustine High School; [occ.] Lead Tech Librarian Grumman Saint Augustine; [memb.] National Geographic Assoc.; [oth. writ.] Writing poetry as a hobby and for friends; [pers.] I strive for each poem I write that it touches or inspires at least one person.; [a.] Saint Augustine, FL

O'TOOLE, DANNY
[b.] August 9, 1971, Norwood, MA; [p.] John and Helena O'Toole; [ed.] Boston University/Mathematics Degree; [occ.] Statistical Researcher/Technical Assistant; [oth. writ.] No published writings just an open and emotional journal and other poetry.; [pers.] Human Emotion is the ultimate form of poetry you've just got to take time to write it down.; [a.] Norwood, MA

OBERSCHMIDT, ERIC
[b.] February 25, 1978, San Diego, CA; [p.] Alec and Mary Oberschmidt; [ed.] High School Junior; [occ.] Student; [a.] Encinitas, CA

OCAMPO, MELODIE B.
[b.] September 27, 1965, Philippines; [p.] Ramon Bachiller, Faith Bachiller; [m.] Omar O. Ocampo; [ch.] Ohmeko, Mimiko; [ed.] Finished third year medicine, Philippines; [hon.] National Winner, Oratorical Contest Rotary Club Sponsed, Philippines 1982 Graduated cum laude, Medical Technology Amec Philippines; [pers.] The Memories of home and the persons, our family we shared it with are always closest and brings us the fondest of thoughts which we cherish in our heart of hearts and never forget in our lifetime. Hence have inspired me.; [a.] Alameda, CA

OHMAN, DANNY
[pen.] Danny Ohman; [b.] October 20, 1972, Albuquerque; [p.] Robert and Teresa Ohman; [ed.] La Cueva High, currently obtaining a degree in communications at University of New Mexico; [pers.] I draw my strengths from my family and friends. Without them, I would be alone. Life is too difficult to live, without having others to live it with.

OLIVEIRA, JOANIR FERREIRA DE
[pen.] Joanyr De Oliveira [b.] December 6, 1933, Aimores, Brazil; [m.] Nelcy G. Oliveira, March 21, 1959; [ed.] Universidade Do D. Federal (Lawyer), Journalist, Writer, Editor.; [occ.] Writer, (Retired Adviser House of Representative, Brasilia, DC.); [memb.] Member of Academia De Letras De Brasilia Academia Evangelica De Letres, (Do Brasil Crio), Academia De Letras Do Brasil (DF), Associacao Nacional De Escritores (DF), Sindicato Dos Escritores Do Distrito Federal; [hon.] "Grand Poeta De Brasilia." Won more of 20 prizes (poetry). Participate in Anthologies in Brazil, USA, Canada, Italy and India. Organized the first book published. In the new capital - poetry de Brasilia, 1962 and others poetry and short stories anthologies.; [oth. writ.] Author of Cantares, O Grito Submerso, Casulos Do Silencio, Luta A (R) Mada, Caminhos Do Amor and other books, several poems published in newspapers and magazins.; [a.] Brasilia DF, Brazil

OLOFSSON, YVONNE
[b.] October 19, 1956, New Orleans, LA; [p.] Ingmar and May-Britt Engdahl; [m.] Torgny Olofsson, July 31, 1981; [ch.] Jasmine, Kevin; [occ.] Mother - housewife; [oth. writ.] I have a collection of poems. Many which are over 20 lines that I have written I sent in two poems "Look Up To The Sky" and "Just Imagine" Just Imagine is the first to be published.; [pers.] Living is to love be kind to one another life is precious

OLVER, REBECCA
[b.] April 18, 1969, Zaire, Africa; [p.] Arnold and Shirley Olver; [m.] Warren Schatz (fiance), will be August 5, 1995; [ed.] B.R.E Prairie Bible College, MTSC Trinity Western Seminary; [occ.] Student/Coucelor; [oth. writ.] Wrote articles and poems for my high school newspaper, wrote occasional articles for the Central Alberta Adviser; [pers.] When I'm finding it difficult to express myself verbally, I put it on paper. Thus, my writing is an expression of my soul and of my relationship with God.; [a.] Langley, BC

ONSTED, WENDY S.
[pen.] Khadesha Sinclair; [b.] September 4, 1977, Andreus Air Force Base, MD; [p.] Stan and Kandy Onsted; [ed.] Grace Brethren Christian School Surrattsville Senior High School; [occ.] Student; [hon.] "Who's Who Among American High School Students"; [oth. writ.] Poems "Confessions of Love", "Coiled", "Tears of An Angel", "Finally Free", "The Last Goodbye", "Tribute to a Friend", "A Wilted Soul"; [pers.] I believe that it is the personal responsibility of every human being to allow themselves and others to live and think freely. Aaron Ungersma one said, "I am convinced that each human being is unique and that he has a right to be his own separate self." Believe in yourself!; [a.] Clinton, MD

ONUOHA, AUSTIN CHIAZOR
[pen.] Chiazonu; [b.] April 8, 1963, Lagos, Nigeria; [p.] Mr. and Mrs. Gabriel U. Onuoha; [m.] Mrs. Lynda Ngozi Onuoha, September 26, 1992; [ch.] Ihe Abunike Onuoha (Male); [ed.] Bachelor of Arts (History) University of IFE, ILE-IFE Nigeria; [occ.] Indirect Channel Manager (East); [memb.] Rotary Club of Eziukwu ABA, ABA Sports Club, Udokanma Age Grade Creme Club of Nigeria, Nigerian Institute of Marketing; [hon.] Best Salesman Rank Xerox (Nig) LTD Mar. 1993, Division One Leaguer for Salesman Managers 1993; [oth. writ.] Plays: In The Dark, The Peculiar Prince (Novel), Till You Fail (Drama), ...Before the Hangman's Noose (Drama), Behind the Mask (Drama), and Anonymous and other poems fall unpublished.; [pers.] Always live up to and do what you think you are. My writings manifest the pain of freedom and the freedom of pain as released from my experience of my environment; [a.] Aba, Abia

OOSTHUREN, MARELDA
[pen.] Mel/Indiana; [b.] September 26, 1973, Heidelberg, SA; [p.] Patric Oosthuren, Ans Oosthuren; [ed.] Verwoerdburg High; [occ.] Personnel Clerk; [oth. writ.] A few poems unpublished.; [pers.] I have been inspired by American Indians since I was a teenager. My dream is to one day meet an American Indian in person, in their territory.; [a.] Pretoria, South Africa

OREJOLA, WILMO C.
[b.] February 12, 1950, Basey, Samar, Philippines; [p.] Gregorio and Encarnacion Orejola; [m.] Crescencia Atillo Orejola, January 30, 1982; [ch.] Ingrid, Nadine, Cedric, Oliver; [ed.] Doctor of Medicine, Cebu Institute of Medicine, Philippines; [occ.] Physician-surgeon, researcher, inventor-entrepreneur; [memb.] American Society of Artificial Internal Organs; [hon.] Magna cum laude, Bachelor of Science, Excellence in the Study of Anatomy, Doctor of Medicine, awarded 6 U.S. Patents for inventions from toys to medical devices.; [oth. writ.] Poems, plays and essays of varied interests, some published in college papers, research studies published in scientific journals.; [pers.] In our search of Life's meaning, we tend to neglect one simple truth. Beating the odds to get here in the first place was tough enough. And before we could accomplish anything, we realize this existence is almost over. We must not squander even a moment of this precious time.; [a.] Pompton Plains, NJ

OREJOLA, WILMO C.
[pen.] Iwo; [b.] February 12, 1950, Basey, Samar, Philippines; [p.] Gregorio and Encarnacion Orejola; [m.] Cresencia Atillo Orejola, January 30, 1982; [ch.] Ingrid, Nadine, Cedric, Oliver; [ed.] Doctor of Medicine, Cebu Institute of Medicine, Philippines, 1974; [occ.] Physician-Surgeon, Researcher, Inventor-Entrepreneur; [memb.] American Society of Artificial Internal Organs; [hon.] Magna cum laude, Bachelor of Science, Excellence in the Study of Anatomy, Doctor of Medicine, awarded 6 U.S. Patents for inventions from toys to medical devices.; [oth. writ.] Poems, plays and essays of varied interests, some published in college papers, research studies published in scientific journals.; [pers.] In our search of meaning of this fleeting existence, we tend to neglect simple truths. Getting here in the first place was as tough as winning lottery jackpot. We should not squander even a moment of it.; [a.] Pompton Plains, NJ

ORMSBY, JOHN THEODORE
[pen.] Viper [b.] December 27, 1961, Sacramento, CA; [p.] William T., Helen M. Ormsby; [m.] Patricia Ann Ormsby, January 17, 1987; [ch.] Jessica Nichole, Amber Lynn; [ed.] Casa Roble High School, National Education Center, School of Hard Knocks; [occ.] Office Manager at Applied Technologies and Research Inc.; [memb.] Veterans of foreign wars post 3045, North American Fishing Club; [hon.] Military Honorable Discharge, Numerous letters of Accommodations.; [oth. writ.] Personal Meaningful poems published in the California Veterans, and in the cruise book for the Persian Gulf Cruise during my military career.; [pers.] I write from the heart, with as much feeling as the English Language allows.; [a.] Salem, SC

ORTH, CRYSTAL
[pen.] Orth, Crystal; [b.] October 21, 1979, Toledo, OH; [p.] Tammy Orth, Randy Orth; [ed.] Raymer Elementary, Northwood Middle School, Northwood High School.; [occ.] I am currently applying for jobs. I do baby sit.; [memb.] East Toledo Boys and Girls Club. Brownie. Girl Scout. Soccer, Basketball, and Cheerleading; [hon.] Soccer basketball, cheerleading. Air Hockey Tournament winner of the month a few times at East Toledo Boys and Girls Club. Swim Award at Boys and Girls Club. Qualified for the Miss Ohio Teen USA pageant of 1994.; [oth. writ.] I have also written 11 other poems.; [pers.] I believe in writing about what comes straight from my heart. I express my intermost, valued and true feelings of the past present and future of my life!; [a.] Northwood, OH

ORTIZ, JOSEPH A. NORIEGA
[p.] Martin Ortiz, Patria Noriega; [ed.] Morristown High, NJ., Country College of Morris, NJ.; [occ.] Purchasing/ Planner; [oth. writ.] Many of which none have been submitted for publication except this one.; [pers.] 'The Child' is the result of an epiphany. I thank my parents for the manner in which they had raised me, just as importantly I thank God for allowing me to enjoy the eternity that is consciousness. These are my influences.; [a.] Santa Ana, CA

OSAYIMWEN, ISE
[b.] June 10, 1966, Benin-City, Nigeria; [p.] Meke and Stella Osayimwen; [m.] Angela Osayimwen, March 21, 1993; [ed.] BA (Hons) Theatre Arts University of Port Harcourt Nigeria; [hon.] A merit certificate and honorable mention for poem "cries in the horn", by the world of poetry in Sacramento, California; [oth. writ.] Several articles and essays published in the Nigerian observer and essays published in the nigerian observer and the African concord magazine.; [pers.] My writings aim at portraying the existential condition of man and trusting that man's condition(s) can be improved in all spheres.; [a.] Boston, MA

OSBORN, SCOTT A.
[pen.] Scott A. Osborn; [b.] December 11, 1969, Stillwater, OK; [p.] Stanley Osborn, Carolyn Osborn; [ed.] Broken Arrow Senior High School, OK, Upper Merion High School, PA; [occ.] Industrial Raafer; [oth. writ.] "A Midthoughts Whim" Personal collection of poetry, short stories, and other assorted literary strands, of my doing.; [pers.] Life without life is worse than death...; [a.] King of Prussia, PA

OSBORNE, JIM
[b.] December 19, 1977, Galesburg, IL; [p.] Christina Allen and Walter Allen; [ed.] Abingdon High School, I plan to attend Northern Illinois University in the fall of 1996.; [occ.] I work for Gibbon's Masonry and Concrete during the summer break.; [hon.] The Presidential Academic Fitness Award, High Honor Roll; [pers.] I dedicated the poem to the late Gloria Tompkins. She was my aunt who passed away in November of 1994. She was very important to me, for I looked to her for wisdom.; [a.] Abingdon, IL

OSBURN, JENNA NOEL
[pen.] Jenna Osburn; [b.] December 17, 1979, Santa Monica, CA; [p.] John and Terry Osburn; [ed.] Wildwood School, Santa Monica, CA. Vieja Valley Elementary School, Santa Barbara, CA., Santa Barbara Middle School, Santa Barbara, Ca., Currently in 9th grade at Thacher.; [occ.] High School Student; [memb.] Music and Arts Conservatory of Santa Barbara; [hon.] Santa Barbara Fair and Expose 1991 - Four - First Place Ribbons - creative writing, 1992 - Three - First Place Ribbons - Creative Writing, 1993 - Three - First Place Ribbons - creative writing, December 6 and 7th Jenna's play "Trial and Error" which she wrote and directed-performed at the Granada Too Theater. 6th Grade - Student Body President 7th Grade - Goleta 4-H President.; [oth. writ.] School Year 1989-1990 Fourth Grade - Age 9, "The Story Of Neinland" Story, "I'm Just A Little Bit Too Big" Poem, "The Journey Of The Animals" Story, "The Seagull" Poem, "The Many Adventures Of The Miraculous Mouse Family" Story, "I Believe In" Poem, "The Magestic Treasure" Story, "The Courageous Adventure Of Nessy And Mallard" Story, School Year 1990-1991, Fifth Grade Age 10, "Camp Sunshine" Story, "Moon" Fable, "Trying To Solve Little Kid's Problems, Huh" Story, "The Courageous Adventures Of Rashaw And His Dog, Laybo" Story, "A Dream I Once Had" Poem, "Boy, It's Going To Be A Long Week" Story, "Rolly, Sally And The Weird Christmas" Story, "Would You Accept?" Poem, "Harry's Stupendous Adventure" Story, "Do You Believe?" Poem, School Year 1991-1992 Sixth Grade, Age 11. "The Truth Is" Poem, "Windy" Poem, "My River Flows" Essay, "I've Loved Flowers" Poem, "Blowing Wind" Story, "Tired" Poem, "Pay Attention" Poem, "Pompous, Pious Prissy" Story, "Rebirth" Poem, "Peace" Poem, "Love" Poem, "I Know" Poem, "My Tree" Poem, "What Is?" Poem, "Ticerella" Story, "Before Death" Poem, "Would You Dare?" Poem, "Falling Star" Poem, "Breath Of Life" Poem, "Strange" Poem, "To Be? Or Not To Be? That Is The Question" Story, "A Time Ago" Poem, "Reflection Of The Earth" Poem, "Gone" Poem, Sixth Grade, Age 11, Blooms Of Our Mother, Poem, The Sky At My Grasp, Poem Spring Calls, Winter Falls, Poem, Bored, Poem, Courage, Poem, I Am, Poem, Show Me Your Heart, Not Your Face, Poem, Jungle Dreams, Story, Not A Mistake, But A Catastrophe, Poem, Listen To Learn, Poem, Once In A Time, Poem, Follower, Poem, Hide, Poem, My Time, Poem, A Time When I Felt One, Poem, A Letter Home, Essay, Rise And Fall, Poem, The Dog, Essay, Everything Stops, Poem, Faces Shall Appear, Poem, It Came, Poem, Inside The Locked Door, Poem, Susan B. Anthony, Biography, My Heart, Poem, Silence, Poem, Horoscope, Poem, School Year - 1992-1993, Seventh Grade - Age 12, Forgotten Past, Poem, Simple Pleasure, Poem, Rough Edges, Poem, Trial And Error, Play, Shine, Poem, Pain, Joy, Fear, Poem, Between, Poem, One Day, Poem, A Bird Denied Flight, Poem; [pers.] The Worlds Chan GIN!! Makeup and perms for men, condoms for women, nude pictures in magazines, a democrat's in office. But people are still starving so obviously it hasn't changed enough!; [a.] Santa Barbara, CA

OSWALD, MICHELLE AMANDA
[b.] July 7, 1980, Matsqui BC; [p.] Ralph Oswald, Kim Oswald; [ed.] Shortreed Elementary (K-Gr 5) Betty Gilbert Elementary (Gr 6 and Gr 7) Aldergrove Community Secondary School (Gr 8 and Gr 9) (Abbreviation ACSS); [occ.] High school student; [memb.] SBAA Girls V-16 metro soccer team, girls V-14 and V-15 provincial soccer teams, ACSS grade nine basketball team and cross country team, Aldergrove Youth Soccer Association Referee.; [hon.] On the 'A' honor roll since grade one, academic excellence in grade six and seven, Patricia women's Institute Scholarship Award in grade eight, Athlete of the Year in Grade eight and MVP for basketball in grade eight.; [oth. writ.] Poems published in the local Aldergrove star paper and in the Winfield Calendar Newspaper. A poem read during her grandfather's funeral.; [pers.] I strive to be the best I can be and I've been influenced my grandfather.; [a.] Aldergrove, BC

OTEKPEN, BRENA
[pers.] I was influenced by the love and passion in the fifties when love was genuinely true. As a child I was deeply touched by the movie The Ten Commandments my gift was to write bible plays and it seem like destiny has been calling me that way I decided to answer my call

OTOSHI, YOSHIYUKI
[b.] July 23, 1920, Hiroshima, Japan; [p.] Asazo Otoshi, Tamano Otoshi; [m.] Betty Kiyoko Otoshi; [ch.] Grant Yukio and Beverly Yukino; [ed.] McKinley High School (Honolulu) American Institute of Banking (Standard Certificate); [occ.] Retired 1985 after 43 years working at First Hawaiian Bank as an accountant.; [memb.] Honolulu Japanese Chamber of Commerce Hawaii Economic Study Club Honpa Hongwanji Mission of Hawaii Japanese Cultural Center of Hawaii; [oth. writ.] My poem, "Of Tassels in the Wind" has been selected for printing in the anthology, Journey of the Mind, (Library of Congress ISBN 1-56167-263-7). My cinquain, "Bits of Beauty" has been chosen for printing in another anthology, "A Moment in Time," (Library of Congress ISBN 1-56167-266-1).; [pers.] I became a naturalized citizen of the United Sates of American on February 26, 1953 - it was a proud and happy moment of my life. To my Senior Class (1938) Core Studies teacher, Mrs. Mary Robey Harris, I am deeply grateful for first opening my eyes and mind into literature and poetry. With thoughs and deeds, however puny, I strive to make our world a bit more beautiful.; [a.] Honolulu, HI

OTOSHI, YOSHIYUKI
[b.] July 23, 1920, Hiroshima, Japan; [p.] Asazo Otoshi, Tamano Otoshi; [m.] Betty Kiyoko Otoshi; [ch.] Grant Yukio and Beverly Yukino; [ed.] McKinley High School (Honolulu), American Institute of Banking (Standard Certification); [occ.] Retired 1985 after 43 years working at First Hawaiian Bank as an accountant.; [memb.] Honolulu Japanese Chamber of Commerce, Hawaii Economic Study Club, Honpa Hongwanji Mission of Hawaii, Japanese Cultural Center of Hawaii; [oth. writ.] My poem, "Of Tassels in the Wind" has been selected for printing in the anthology, Journey Of The Wind, (Library of Congress ISBN 1-56167-263-7). My cinquain, "Bits of Beauty" has been chosen for printing in another anthology, "A Moment in Time," (Library of Congress ISBN 1-56167- 266-1).; [pers.] I became a naturalized citizen of the United States of America on February 26, 1953 it was a proud and happy moment of my life. To my Senior Class (1938) Core Studies teacher, Mrs. Mary Robey Harris, I am deeply grateful for first opening my eyes and mind into literature and poetry. With thoughts and deeds, however puny, I strive to make our world a bit more beautiful.; [a.] Honolulu, HI

OTTINA, ELYSE
[b.] May 8, 1957, New York, NY; [p.] Silverman [m.] Charles Ottina, August 7, 1983; [ch.] Charlie Dob [ed.] Masters in Social Work MSW, CSW on leave; [occ.] Doctor of Multiple Sclerosis; [memb.] NMSS Various disability agencies; [oth. writ.] Many various poems none submitted yet. Would like to.; [pers.] The slow deterioration of a body and a marriage has freed me to more fully express my thoughts and feelings about love, life and balance.

OTUNNU, OCHORO E.
[b.] October 24, 1963, Uganda; [p.] Yusto and Josphina Amato Otunnu; [ed.] BA, Government, Dartmouth Coll. BA, Politics, Philosophy, Economics (PPE), Oxford University JD Candidate, Columbia Law School; [occ.] Student; [memb.] 21st Century Trust; [oth. writ.] Several poems published in student's publications; [pers.] To me the works of the great poets are the truest affirmation of divine genius, without the necessary profession of faith. I can happily live without many things, but I need great poetry for my spiritual existence. Without it I would be lost!; [a.] New York, NY

OUTMAN, SUZANNE
[b.] December 23, 1981, Greenville, MI; [p.] Grant W. and Chong C. Outman; [ed.] 8th Grade; [occ.] Student; [hon.] Won 1st Place in Poetry Contest. Winner of Presidential Academic Fitness Award.; [oth. writ.] Poem titled: America; [a.] Fort Irwin, CA

OUZOUNIAN, TAKOUHIE ARAXIE
[pen.] Takouhie; [b.] March 1, 1977, New Port, CA; [p.] Meada and Moses Ouzounian; [ed.] I currently finishing High School. Will go on to higher forms of education; [memb.] The Church of Jesus Christ of Latter Day Saints; [hon.] Young Womanhood Medallon; [pers.] Life, as all things, is only what we make of it. C.T.R. and happiness will find you. There is truly a bit of the divine in all of us. Goals are always worth striving for. Life is good at 17.; [a.] Villa Park, CA

OVERTON, MELISSA RENEE WILLIAMS
[b.] March 21, 1975, Newton, MS; [p.] Robert Lee Williams and Barbara Lewis; [m.] Cary Max Overton Jr., December 5, 1992; [ed.] Newton City Elementary High School, Union High School until the last of 11th grade. I am working on getting my GED; [occ.] Housewife, In home baby sitter; [oth. writ.] I have written several poems and stories, but I have not tried to have them published.; [pers.] Poetry tells stories, usually about life.; [a.] Lawrence, MS

OWENS, ALISON E.
[b.] May 10, 1978, Canoga Park, CA; [p.] Susan and Merle Owens; [ed.] Currently in Junior year of high school; [hon.] Presidential Academic Fitness Award; [oth. writ.] I write short stories and poems but this is my first I've ever tried to publish.; [pers.] Writing is art, art is freedom, and total freedom is the imagination.; [a.] Simi Valley, CA

PACIS, FILOMENO L.
[b.] Baguio City, Philippines; [p.] Pascual Pacis and Celestina L. Pacis; [m.] Paz Ros Pacis, December 27, 1950; [ch.] Jorge, Olivia, Merie, Vilma, Isabel, Nilaflor, Victoria, Romulo, Adrian, Zenon, Andre; [ed.] Lawyer, 21 Law Seminars UP Law Center; [occ.] Lawyer-Poet; [memb.] Integrated Bar of the Philippines; [hon.] 1985 and 1986 Golden Poet Awards world of poetry Honorary Charter Member, International Society of Poets.; [oth. writ.] More poems; [pers.] Defend the Sacredness of Life for a better world.; [a.] Quezon City, Philippines

PAGAN, MELISSA ANN
[b.] July 9, 1977, Chicago; [p.] Jose and Maria Pagan; [ed.] St. Mark Grammar School, Notre Dame for girls high school; [occ.] Student; [memb.] I am a member of the Hispanic Club, French Club, Chamber Choir and I am a Senior Leader.; [hon.] In high school I have been on the Honor roll each year at least 3 times. I have also gotten awards in the past english courses I've taken.; [oth. writ.] I've never had any of my writings published in any books but I have written few other poems in my spare time.; [pers.] In my poems, I express my feelings for others and people in general. Experiences I've had with nature and all human kind influence my writing.; [a.] Chicago, IL

PALACIOS, ROBERT DOUGLAS
[b.] Fresno, CA; [m.] Irene Palacios; [ch.] Diana, Michelle, Nichole, Priscilla, Bobby

PALKA, MIKE B.
[pen.] Mike B. Palka; [b.] January 2, 1951, Yorkton, Saskatchewan, Canada; [p.] Steve and (Stella - Deceased 1985); [m.] Common-law Elona Payne; [ch.] 3; [ed.] Gr 12 High School (St Joseph's College) Secondary Technical Training Canadian Navy; [occ.] Sup Technician 911 Canadian Navy; [hon.] Canadian Decoration, Order of Military Merit; [oth. writ.] A Memorium to a United Nations Soldier published in local papers.; [pers.] I am usually inspired by emotional events or circumstances occurring around me. Many of my poems reflect a deep love of life and although I am a bit old fashioned I am a true romantic.; [a.] Victoria British Columbia, Canada

PALUMBO, JOSEPH R.
[b.] December 17, 1970, Staten Island, NY; [p.] Anthony and Barbara Palumbo; [ed.] Moore Catholic H.S., St. John's University; [occ.] Teacher (foreign languages) IS2, Staten Island, NY; [memb.] Gamma Kappa Alpha (Italian Honor Society), Staten Island Dart League, United Federation of Teachers; [hon.] Dean's List, President List, graduate Cum Laude; [oth. writ.] Several writings published in University Italian magazine; [pers.] Love one another, for the future is watching... [a.] Staten Island, NY.

PANAS, KRYSTAL
[pen.] Krystal Lee Panas; [b.] February 9, 1985, Milwaukee, WI; [p.] Grey and Lou Ann Panas; [ed.] Summit School, Attend 4th grade; [occ.] Student; [memb.] Hobbies, "Girl Scouts," "Pioneer Girls", Piano, Voice, Downhill sking, travel; [hon.] Interpretive reading competition - 1st place, Modeling opportunities, Modeling opportunities, Photo used in cruise brochure. [oth. writ.] Several poems and articles published in the "summit" school newspaper.; [pers.] I have been greatly influenced by my teachers to be creative thru poetry and short stories I would like to thank them for the knowledge and my mom and dad.; [a.] Oconomowoc, WI

PANZELLA, HEATHER
[b.] July 27, 1970, Pittsburgh, PA; [p.] Jane Panzella, Emmett Panzella; [ed.] Gateway Senior High, Penn State University; [occ.] Supervising Instructor, Orange county outdoor science school, Running Springs, CA; [pers.] Dedicated to my best friend Fabian J. Pugliano whose spirit will live within me forever.; [a.] Huntington Beach, CA

PAPIER, CHERI M.
[b.] August 31, 1946, Columbus, OH; [p.] Rose and William Papier; [m.] Gene Goldberg, April 6, 1978; [ch.] Allen and Roger Goldberg; [ed.] B.A - Biology Oberlin College, M.P.H. - Public Health University of North Caroline, M.S. - Epidemiology Harvard University; [occ.] Quit smoking counselor, Flutist, Writer; [memb.] American Public Health Assoc. (APHA), Ohio Public Health Assoc. (OPHA), Ohio Society of Public Health Educators (SOPHE), Doctor's ought to care (DOC), Americans for Nonsmoker's Rights (ANR), Action on Smoking and Health (ASH), Stop Teenage Addiction to Tobacco (STAT); [hon.] Recipient - U.S. Public Health Service Traineeship, Listed in world's who's who of women and community leaders of the world; [oth. writ.] Be a quitter. Quit smoking the way that works best for you, published poetry in 12 anthologies, Numerous articles in medical and public health journals; [pers.] Writing is for me the best way to express myself. "Sticks and stones can break one's bones, but words can set one free..." [a.] Columbus, OH

PAQUETTE, MRS. MABEL M.
[b.] August 7, 1928, New York, NY; [p.] Margaretha and Harry Traeger [m.] Roger J. Paquette, November 27, 1954; [ch.] 7 Children - 11 Grandchildren [ed.] Sharon Center School - 8th grade, Diploma - Equiv. diploma - Poughkeepsie High School, N.Y. Associate in Science - Therapeutic Recreation, In CT - Bachelor degree in Social Science - Social Welfare in CT Graduate Infant Care Tech. NY Foundling; [occ.] Retired (at present Hospital time PD).; [memb.] Member of the "Woman's Home League" at Salvation Army, Member of American Legion Post 186. I am a Catholic; [hon.] Mother's March of Dimes Drive - For Bethlehem, CT. (In a 19 Towns area) brought per Capita funds up from the previous year from the lowest per Capita Amt. to the highest per Capita amt. out of the 19 towns.; [oth. writ.] Have written 6 songs. Plus quite a few poems. Am concentrating (now that I am a widow) on writing short stories and getting them as well as my poems and songs sold.; [pers.] My poems, songs and stories reflect my feelings as well as my observance of life and how it has affected me and those I love; [a.] Spring Hill, FL

PARISI, ANTHONY JUDE
[pen.] Anthony Jude; [b.] February 13, 1959, Buffalo, NY; [p.] Rita Parisi-Nowak, Charles J. Parisi; [m.] Never been married; [ed.] 14 Holy Helpers Catholic - K-8 West Seneca East Sr. High 9-12 Eastman School of Music 77-81 D'Youville College 77-81 Graduated with BA Dean's List Honors; [occ.] Entrepreneur - singer songwriter and poet. Apparel Designer.; [memb.] St. Jude's Children Hospital; [hon.] Completed my 1st tape-album named: "Invulnerable Kid." Personally played all instruments, sang and wrote all the songs and produced this initial project. Sold over 30,000 units touring AZ, CO, CA, Nevada and Pacific West Venues. Participates in AZ Music Conference, South by Southwest, N.Y. Music Seminar etc.; [oth. writ.] Published in the National Library of Poetry, 1.) "Tears on a Cheek" - Dark Side of the Moon, 2.) "Has Time Passed Us By" - Songs on the wind, 3.) "Pile of Leaves" - A moment in time several poems published in AZ. Local newspapers as well as other newspapers out of state; [pers.] "Chance is the greatest voyage we may embark on in life so that we may experience life's grandest treasures and glories"; [a.] Chandler, AZ

PARKER, CEMILLE
[b.] February 3, 1949, Chester, PA; [p.] Wilbert and Helen Pritchett; [m.] Divorced; [ch.] Denise Nicole Parker, RN; [ed.] Chester High, Temple University, Neumann College, Technical Training Center in Norman, Oklahoma; [occ.] Vehicle maintenance facility clerk, U.S. Postal service; [memb.] Penn Street Civic Association, Chester Aids Coalition, American Postal workers union; [hon.] Pennsylvania Industrial Chemical Co. (PICCO) Scholarship, Dean's List at Neumann College; [oth. writ.] I've been inspired to greater heights of creativity by my 24 yr. daughter who in her spare time writes poetry and has had 2 articles on diet and health featured in prevention magazine.; [pers.] I've striven to live a life of dignity a life which wholly embraces the meaning of love and one that captures the true passion of creativity.; [a.] Chester, PA

PARKER, FRANCIS XAVIER
[pen.] Francis X. Parker; [b.] May 19, 1977, San Diego; [p.] William A. Parker, Jr., Maureen H. Parker; [ed.] El Capitan High School; [occ.] Thinker/Dreamer; [oth. writ.] Poems, short stories, essays for school and friends; [pers.] Be willing to die for the ones you love and love everyone.; [a.] El Cajon, CA

PARKER, GLENN ALAN
[b.] August 19, 1970, San Antonio, TX; [p.] Harold and Connie Parker; [ed.] Highlands high, The University of Texas at San Antonio,(Summer) Pre-Engineering program, Majoring in Information systems; [occ.] Technical support representative, Marcive, Inc. (Library Cata-

loging); [memb.] Cadence Cloggers; [hon.] Writing scholarship award, Folk dancing, Poetry reading, Dramatic presentations; [oth. writ.] First publication.; [pers.] Le the words speak to your heart; [a.] San Antonio, TX

PARKER, LISA J.
[pen.] Lee; [b.] July 19, 1965, Weymouth, MA; [p.] Phillip and Joyce Parker; [ed.] Bridgewater State College, Silver Lake High; [occ.] Legal Secretary, Brown and Stadfeld, Boston, MA; [hon.] Artist of Halifax, Ma Town Report (1982), Imperial of the Year, Horn Player of the year, 1983 Poetry contest - Silver Lake High School.; [pers.] The love and support of my family has been my inspiration to achieve my dreams,; [a.] Whitman, MA

PARKER, MARGARET M.
[b.] November 8, Chicago, IL; [p.] Rosa L. and Willie Parker Sr.; [ch.] Ronald L. McIntosh and Robin L. Parker; [ed.] Marshall High School - Chicago, Master of Science in Marketing Comm., Roosevelt Univ. - Chicago - Bachelor (Sociology and Psy.) Roosevelt University Chicago - AA with Honors, Loop Jr. College Chicago (Renamed Harold Washington); [occ.] Human Svc. Wkr (Case Manager) City of Chicago - Dept. of Human Services; [memb.] Pi Sigma Epsilon Mktg. Frat. Hon Mem. "United Negro Colleges", West Side Youth Booster and Civic Organization, American Mktg. Association - Westtown Political Education Committee; [hon.] Dean's List Asso. with Honors - Nominated for Inclusion in Who's Who Worldwide - Selected to tutor students in Roosevelt University "Writing Lab"; [oth. writ.] Written a minimum of 20 poems, several of which were published in Local newspaper and school papers; [pers.] Believing that romance will eventually contribute to world peace, I write mostly romantic poem from several aspects, IE happiness, sadness and questioning) I truly believe that "Love makes the world go around"; [a.] Chicago, IL

PARKS, PHILIP GUY
[b.] February 22, 1956, Tupelo, MS; [ed.] University of Wisconsin - Parkside; [occ.] Owner, The Eight Muse Art Gallery, West Hollywood, CA; [oth. writ.] The eight Muse Book of quotes, Muse-Ments; [pers.] I hope my work will always reflect the oneness of our experience while celebrating our diversity.; [a.] Northridge, CA

PARKS, THERESA J. BARNOUSKI
[b.] November 7, 1960, Christopher, IL; [p.] Frank Sr. and Mary Anne Barnouski; [m.] Daniel Kirk Parks, November 18, 1989; [ch.] Christopher Hampton, Sarah Hampton, Kevin Hampton, Andrew Hampton; [ed.] Christopher Community High School, Mt. Vernon Vocational High School, Rend Lake College, Southern Illinois University at Carbondale; [occ.] Wife, mother, Certified Nurses Assistant; [memb.] Founder and Facilitator of the Central Indiana Lyme Disease Group, I lost a child (ILAC); [hon.] Art Exhibition Award; [oth. writ.] Other unpublished poetry, articles published in the Lyme Disease Update; [pers.] My writings come from my heart and the experiences I have in my life.; [a.] Indianapolis, IN

PARR, JANIS LYNNE
[b.] March 18, 1951, Peterborough, Ontario, Canada; [p.] Lloyd McCurrie, Jean McCurrie; [m.] Larry E. Parr, August 25, 1973; [ch.] Matthew Gerald, Garry Edwin, Jennifer Erin; [ed.] Peterborough Collegiate and Vocational Institute, Peterborough Civic Hospital School of Nursing, SIR Sanford Fleming College in Peterborough; [occ.] Registered Nurse, Freelance writer - Children's Books; [memb.] College of Nurses of Ontario.; [hon.] Top honor grades in Coronary care I, Coronary care II, and emergency room certificate and Post diploma courses. Written commendations on three of my writings for children, from prominent publishers.; [oth. writ.] Newspaper article published on the safety of children at halloween. Several children's short stories not published yet.; [pers.] Very often in life, the plainer and more basic things rather than the lavish, although not always obvious, carry the greater meaning and value.; [a.] Campbellford Ontario, Canada

PARRA, EVITA DE LA
[b.] March 10, 1982, Beverly Hills, CA; [p.] Eva Cabello, Arturor De La Parra; [ed.] Attending Assumption of the Blessed Virgin Mary School; [occ.] Student; [hon.] Honor student, first place winner in the Catholic Daughters of the Americans Education Contest (Poetry Division), Received Knights of Columbus Annual Christian Living Award; [oth. writ.] One contest-winning poem published in the Pasadena Star News, several poems written and dedicated to close family and friends. Other poems: Who am I in God's eyes, angels, habits; [pers.] I write all my work with heart, mind, and soul. My poems are unique and come from a teenager's point of view and frame of mind. My talent is something that God has given me.; [a.] Pasadena, CA

PARROTT, FANNIE
[b.] June 7, 1973, Charlotte Court House, VA; [ch.] Shirleen, Calvin, Tom, Kay, Sylvia, Ann; [pers.] Read through the bible 99 times as of now. It's my road map to heaven and the will of my life. Read it to be wise and believe it to be saved. Follow it's teaching to make it in to heaven.; [a.] Carolina Beach, NC

PARTEE, MARIA CHANTELL
[pen.] Chantell Partee; [b.] April 15, 1970, Sacramento; [p.] Kathy and Earl Gellerman; [ed.] I'm in my third year of College as a Pre-med Student; [occ.] Full-time student; [memb.] I am a member of the Phi Beta Kappa honor society; [hon.] Being a member of the honors group, I'm also on the deans list and will graduate with honors; [pers.] My writing is my voice and soul; [a.] Reno, NV

PASSOS, BARBARA BATSON
[b.] June 8, 1962, Alexandria, VA; [p.] Paul and Linda Batson; [m.] Marcos A. Passos, October 29, 1988; [ed.] Roxbury High School, Succasunna, N.J. Joseph Paterno College of Beauty Culture, Dover, N.J. Both graduated from in 1980.; [occ.] Manager/stylist of pin-ups hair salon, Flanders, NJ.; [memb.] American Horse Show Association, International Arabian Horse Association, Arabian Horse Breeders Association of New Jersey.; [hon.] 2 Superior Achievement Awards from the N.J. Equine Advisory board, Regional Championships and a National Top Ten in the showing of Arabian Horses.; [a.] Newton, NJ

PASTIR, BETTY L.
[b.] March 7, 1956, Simcoe, Ontario, Canada; [p.] Clifford and Beatrice Pickard; [m.] Mark E. Pastir, July 17, 1976; [ch.] Michael Gordon, Marisa Tiffany; [ed.] Port, Dover Composite School; [occ.] Farmer/Electrical Contractor; [memb.] Ontario Federation of Agriculture, Ontario Electrical League.; [hon.] Honours Pin - 3 years at high school, President's Pin - 2 years - Ontario Electrical League.; [oth. writ.] Many poems not yet seen or published.; [pers.] I write from experiences and feelings which have shaped and directed my life.; [a.] Waterford Ontario, Canada

PATEL, BANSARI
[pen.] Bon, Bans; [b.] May 8, 1978, Baroda, India; [p.] Bharti Amin and Suryakant Patel; [ed.] A junior in high school (Lake Zurich High School); [occ.] Student, also work part-time at K-Mart.; [memb.] Prom Committee, Volunteer at Hospital (volunteer); [hon.] Honor roll, writing awards (for school) (young authors search, etc.); [oth. writ.] I've written a little book of poems, but I've never had the guts to send them all. I'm also writing a short story/novel, right now.; [pers.] Writing opens doors for verbal expressions and poetry is the beauty of language.; [a.] Howthorn Woods, IL

PATERSON, JOHN ROY
[pen.] J.R.P.; [b.] June 12, 1931, Brandford, Ontario, Canada; [p.] Roy and Laura Paterson; [ed.] Grade eight; [occ.] Poet; [memb.] Boy scouts of Canada, Leader. Handicapped action group. Roman Catholic church.; [hon.] Queens scout awards, award of recognition from the Handicapped action group.; [oth. writ.] The handicapped cop, a christmas kiss, the country church, the wild fire, a fishing brook, my first red ribbon, my first pony; [pers.] I want to start a publishing company for all the disabled. Being disabled myself, writing has given me the inspiration to want to work as a publisher, but I don't have the knowledge or money to start.; [a.] Thunder Bay Ontario, Canada

PATON, ERIC D.
[b.] November 20, 19065, Oceanside, NY; [p.] Henry and Isabel Paton; [ed.] B.S. Aeronautics/Aerospace Tech.; [occ.] State Employee.; [hon.] First Place-Adult Category-Essay 'Woman in History I most admire'.; [pers.] This can be found in another poem I wrote, but there's not enough space here. Maybe I'll find it to the next contest??? A favorite quote by I ask dinesen: "The Best Stories (poems) are a statement of our existence".; [a.] Oakdale, NY

PATRICK, BERT
[b.] April 5, 1912, Denver, CO; [p.] Bert and Mattie Patrick; [m.] Eugenia, 1940; [ch.] Reginald (Pro Photog.); [ed.] Willard-Lane Tech Chicago II Experience, Observation Dance Band Leader Postal Involvement; [occ.] Retired; [memb.] APWU (Postal Union); [hon.] Outstanding Achievement Awards U.S. Postal Service - Logistics Army Acclimation; [oth. writ.] There are several (It's just been a hobby I have no Ego. I'm New here. Oh yes, there's some newspaper articles.; [pers.] I'm not relegated to religion - however, I did borrow a chapter from the Bible (The 23 Psalms.); [a.] Lakeside, MI

PATTAVIHA, NORMA K.
[pen.] Norma Jain Deaux; [b.] July 31, 1952, Omaha, NE; [p.] William S. and Gladys Pattaviha; [ed.] Omaha Public Schools 12 years University of NE at Omaha 2 years.; [occ.] Restaurant Worker; [hon.] 3 Dicky Awards (Alternative awards for alternative behaviors in local theatrical productions.) 1978-Best Title (Arevedeci Turkey!) 1980-Worst Dressed. 1984 - The mirror cracked award for most unnatural enhancement to further career.; [oth. writ.] (l:b) The Pit of Lust (Revue) songs for Pit of Lust (Revue) 1978 (l:b) Bite My A— (Revue) songs for Bite My A—(Revue) Many poems - songs. Several teleplay skits for "Park Avenue Produce Presents" T.V. Show-local P.A.; [pers.] This is the promised land. Don't build things up in your mind unless

you can take them apart again or fit them into your ear. When you have finished your work you're out of a job. Thank you so much; [a.] Omaha, NE

PATTERSON, JUDITH E.
[b.] February 6, 1944, San Fernando, CA; [p.] Fred Patterson, Mary Patterson; [ch.] Wendy Rae, Jeffery Allen; [ed.] San Fernando High; [occ.] Electronic Supervisor; [oth. writ.] Freedom 1966 Recognition from President Johnson; [pers.] I enjoy writing about my inner most feelings; [a.] Oceano, CA

PATTON, SHELLIE M.
[pen.] Shell Patton; [b.] September 12, 1945, Laurel (Jones), MS; [p.] Mrs. Irene Griffin; [ch.] Alex 6, Rickey, Nathall, Jackie, Sarita, Derrick; [ed.] 11th grade but didn't complete 12th grade study for ged like two subjects.; [occ.] Hospice and Nurse Assistants.; [memb.] Arthritis and of the terminal IL PT. And love any kinds of Medical Ill work. And reach the books to.; [hon.] Honors in Nurse Assistants .04 Attends Awards, Achievement awards, Hospice Awards.; [oth. writ.] This my first poems I have send in. I write them all the time. But never had send one in until now; [pers.] I love to write, read, nurse assistants. Write poem. And listen, to what people have to say. I love judge movie. Law and Orden Movie. I am influenced on way people act and think.; [a.] Laurel, MS

PAULAUSKAS, GERARD J.
[pen.] J. J. Paul; [b.] March 24, 1958, New Haven, CT; [p.] Deceased; [m.] Myong K. Paulauskas, August 3, 1983; [ch.] David Lee and Thomas Anthony; [occ.] U.S. Postal Service Worker; [oth. writ.] "A Touch of April" published in the National Library of Poetry - At Day's End. "At Love's Bequest", published in the National Library of Poetry - Dance on the Horizon. "Untitled" [Re: Thoughts Inspired...] published in The National Library of Poetry - Tears of Fire. "Sleep's Far Shore", published in The National Library of Poetry - Best Poems of 1995.; [pers.] This poem [Re: Beyond the Wades O' Wandering Dire...] is dedicated to my sons David, age: 11 and Thomas, age: 8. Their good humor and good nature has rekindled my passion for writing and has inspired me to examine my youth.; [a.] Lancaster, CA

PAULHUS, STACEY ANN
[b.] March 21, 1979, Newport Beach, CA; [p.] Robert and Kathleen Paulhus; [ed.] Paularino Elementary School Costa Mesa High School; [occ.] Student; [memb.] Family Fitness Center; [hon.] Honor roll for three quarters 1993, Spiritleading Award 1993-1994, Outstanding Academic Achievement 1992-1993, Student Council Service Award 1993, Good Sportmanship Award 1991; [pers.] Writing is a way to express your feelings that at times you can't verbalize.; [a.] Costa Mesa, CA

PAULSON, FRANK L.
[pen.] Frank L. Paulson; [b.] April 17, 1947, White Oak, PA; [p.] Evert and Lillian Paulson; [ed.] BBA - Morchead State University, Morchead, Kentucky, MACC - Florida International University, Miami, Fl.; [occ.] Business Consulting and free-lance writing; [memb.] Unity church, Democratic National Committee, Amnesty International, Holocaust Museum, various others; [hon.] Eliga Watts Sells; [oth. writ.] Political tracts and essays, unpublished; [pers.] The journey through life should not be unmarked by some moment to these poems I have you.; [a.] Marco Island, FL

PAYNE, MONICA
[b.] April 12, 1963, Ecuador; [p.] Jose and America Narvaez; [ch.] Joisie and Kyle; [ed.] Homestead High; [occ.] Waitress; [oth. writ.] Several unpublished poems; [pers.] I write about my innermost feelings, thoughts. My poems are a reflection of me.; [a.] Leisure, FL

PEALOW, BARBARA ANNE
[pen.] Barbara Bruce-Pealow; [b.] July 17, 1934, Toronto, Ontario, Canada; [p.] David Bruce, Hilda Bruce; [m.] Lawrence Pealow, February 18, 1955; [ch.] Larry Jr., Sandra Lee, Barbara-Rose; [ed.] Kimberley School for the Deaf Toronto, Ontario; [occ.] Columnist; [memb.] Campbellford District Rural Transportation for the Disabled, More Abled Than Disabled Club, Independent Living, Kingston, Ontario. CMT International, CAD for the Deaf March of Dimes, Patients Right Ass.; [hon.] APSAO (The Adult Protective Services Association of Ontario) media award, Ontario March of Dimes; [oth. writ.] Weekly column "More Abled Than Disabled" for the local newspaper, Cembal Publication's Have written other stories and poems, but has never been published.; [pers.] In my writings I strive to reach out to disabled people and try to help them to become more independent in their lives and to learn to cope with everyday challenges. I myself am disabled and deaf; [a.] Campbellford Ontario, Canada

PEARCE, LORELEI ANN BARBARA
[b.] September 16, 1972, Philadelphia, PA; [ed.] St. Helena - Grade School Cardinal Daugherty - High School Pennsylvania State University - Administration of Justice Temple University - Criminal Justice Currently enrolled in the Pennsylvania State University's Paralegal Certificate Program; [occ.] Paralegal; [hon.] 1990 Mock Trial City Champions; [oth. writ.] Poem published in major city newspaper.; [pers.] Have an open mind - it maximize understanding and increases life's experiences.; [a.] Roslyn, PA

PECHOUS, KARI
[b.] May 4, 1975, Berwyn, IL; [p.] Vernon and Carole Pechous; [ed.] Morton High School, Morton College; [oth. writ.] My other writings include poems that have been included in school newspapers and literary magazines.; [pers.] My poems are based solely on inner emotions, in which I try to communicate to my readers.; [a.] Berwyn, IL

PEDDLESDEN, KATHY
[b.] November 15, 1958, Victoria, British Columbia, Canada; [p.] Brian, June Peddlesden; [ed.] Spectrum Community School, Vic., B.C., Bank St College of Art, Victoria BC; [occ.] Child care worker; [pers.] I live in a magical place, my home, Victoria, British Columbia, Canada, It's beauty is my inspiration for my epitaph ('Baker rises...).; [a.] Victoria British Columbia, Canada

PEDEN, WILLIAM JEROME
[pen.] Skee; [b.] March 19, 1965, Reading, PA; [p.] Erma Peden; [m.] Nikita Ann Bobo Peden August 15, 1992; [ch.] Elesha, Dominique, Chantal; [ed.] Academic High School at Trinity - Pawling College, Preparatory School (Pawling, NY), two years at Temple University - Communications Major; [occ.] Collection and Billing, Representative for Einstein Network; [memb.] Christianity is a way of life.; [hon.] English Honors (The Class of 1982); [oth. writ.] "Prisoner of Septa", published 4/11/90 by Phila. Daily News, "Cry for You and me", "Unified Progression", "Let the Truth be Known", "Like a Dove", "Cohen at Odds with Activists", caption published November 1989 Phila. Tribune; [pers.] There is nothing more powerful than words. The creator himself spoke His creation into existence. There is no other way to touch the very essence of the human soul.; [a.] Philadelphia, PA

PEEBLES, SUSAN
[b.] May 10, 1958, Calgary, Alberta, Canada; [p.] Wallace and June Hall; [m.] Scott Peebles, September 8, 1984; [ch.] Bryce Elliot, Lauren Michele; [ed.] Henry Wise Wood Sr. High; [occ.] Mother and Homemaker; [pers.] The love I have for my family spurs me to write that which is closest to my heart. My thoughts flow freely when I think of them.; [a.] Red Dier Alberta, Canada

PEICH, JENNIFER AMBER
[b.] November 14, 1984, Montclair, CA; [p.] Mr. and Mrs. George W. Peich; [m.] Christine Anne Grant, April 26, 1989; [ch.] (2) Jenny and Christopher; [ed.] Jenny student 5th grade Walnut Ele. Chino, CA, Christopher preschool; [occ.] Student; [memb.] Girl scouts, Burger King Kids Club; [hon.] Student of the Month 1st, 5th grade, 3 honor rolls (so far) "christmas" poems on show Magnolia Jr. High I citizenship award, attendance awards; [oth. writ.] Short story - "The very hungry bee", poem - "Christmas"; [pers.] I take pride in writing stories and poems, I enjoy it very much.; [a.] Chino, CA

PENCE, KIMBERLY D.
[b.] May 21, 1976; [p.] Dennis and Debbie Pence; [ed.] Ottumwa High School, Currently enrolled at Indian Hills Community College.; [memb.] Wildlife Conservation International; [pers.] I enjoy writing poetry that reflects my feelings on environmental issues of today.; [a.] Ottumwa, IA

PENNY JR., HARRY D.
[b.] September 14, 1938, Amarillo, TX; [p.] Harry Penny, Maxine Penny; [m.] Sharon Penny, August 11, 1990; [ch.] Kevin, Laura, Shalyn, Chad; [ed.] Van Nuys High School, L.A. Valley College, National University San Diego, Orange CO. Peace Officers Academy Los Angeles County Sheriff's Academy; [occ.] US Navy (Retired) and Law Enforcement; [hon.] Decorated Veteran: of the Vietnam War and Persian Gulf Cooperation Desert Shield/Desert Storm; [oth. writ.] Several articles and stories in local newspapers and magazines. (Varied subject matter) currently finishing first novel.; [pers.] To reach a goal the key elements are: Believe in yourself and put forth the effort. Both of these elements must be done. Each, alone, is not enough. You are only limited by the limits you put on yourself.; [a.] San Diego, CA

PENSABENE, FRANCINE
[b.] November 2, 1967, New York; [p.] Richard Pensabene, Angela Pensabene; [ed.] Lafayette H.S., BA Brooklyn College, Columbia University.; [occ.] Travel Reservationist; [pers.] Every man must strive towards his dreams. On his quest, he might lose track of friends and lovers. But, if he stays true to his heart and pure to his spirit, he will never lose track of himself.; [a.] Brooklyn, NY

PEOPLES, DAVIED J.
[b.] April 18, 1970, Bronx, NY; [p.] Bettye Peoples, Willie Jenkins; [ed.] J.F.K. High, Bronx Com. College and the City College of New York; [occ.] College Student; [hon.] Honor Roll; [oth. writ.] Other work published in Antrologies; [pers.] I live my life to the fulliest and try to be as diverse of a person as I possibly can.; [a.] Bronx, NY

PERALTA, ANTONIO
[pen.] Antonio Peralta; [b.] July 21, 1957, Ica, Peru; [p.] Narciso Peralta, Julia Lizarzaburu; [ed.] Ricardo Palma University, Miraflores, Peru (Psychology) Stony Brook University, Stony Brook New York (Psychology and Spanish); [occ.] "Unemployed", Actor, director, producer.; [hon.] The umbriafiction TV 1993 Festival in Perugia, Italy, the entire world audiovisual industry. Musical-Drama; [oth. writ.] Dramas, Musical-Videos; [pers.] Thank all poets gave me his/her time: Amiric Barack, June Jordan (Sweetheart), Toni Morrison, Octavio Paz, Eduardo Rada (My brother), Adrienne Rich, Sonia Sanchez and Mario Vargas Llosa.; [a.] Port Jefferson, NY

PEREIRA, BEATRIZ HELENA A.
[pen.] Beatriz Pereira; [b.] July 8, 1960, Sao Paulo, Brazil; [p.] Flavio A. Pereira, Maria Helena A. Pereira; [ed.] B.S. in Biology - University of Sao Paulo, Philosophy - University of Sao Paulo, Summer course "Composition" - Central Connecticut state University, admitted 1994 - master in Biology at central Connecticut state University; [occ.] Science Editor at "Nova Cultural Ltd. Publishing House"; [hon.] Rotary Award - 1977 Rotary Award - 1978 in the alternate list for the fellowship from AUUW.; [oth. writ.] Several articles on science published in local newspapers and magazines. As an editor, I signed several encyclopaedias and dictionaries in portuguese from Larousse Publishing House.; [pers.] A poem is the call of the soul.; [a.] Sao Paulo, Brazil

PEREZ, CATHERINE Q.
[pen.] Cat; [b.] April 21, 1960, San Antonio, TX; [p.] Anselmo and Celia Quintanilla; [m.] Ralph A. Perez, July 15, 1994; [ch.] David 17, Roxanne 15, Max 11; [ed.] George Ford Elem. - Detroit, MI, John F. Kennedy High - SA, TX. San Antonio College SA, TX.; [occ.] Dental Assistant with Dr. Benjamin P. Sanchez SA, TX.; [oth. writ.] Poems given to my husband and children as a gift of remembrance; [pers.] My inspiration comes from life experiences of the past, present, and hopes of the future.; [a.] San Antonio, TX

PEREZ, CYNTHIA J.
[b.] December 2, 1981, San Luis Obispo, CA; [p.] Juan Perez, Rosa Perez; [ed.] Bishop's Peak Elementary School, Laguna Middle School; [occ.] Student; [memb.] PETA, Woods Humane Society Inc.; [hon.] Presidential Academic Fitness Award; [pers.] For me, poetry is a way of expressing my ideas and feelings. I especially love writing about nature.; [a.] Sand Luis Obispo, CA

PERINO, KATHERINE
[b.] January 22, 1973, Brooklyn, NY; [p.] Joseph and Vincenza Perino; [ed.] Bishop Kearney High School; [occ.] College Assistant, Brooklyn College; [pers.] In loving memory of Dexter D. Rennie (1976-1992) and dedicated to Tara Lizzi, Tania Lopez, Jamil Griffith, Jelahn Griffith, Dion Curtis, Jerrmel Smoot and KDF.... All of which have given me the greatest gifts of all.; [a.] Brooklyn, NY

PERKINS, THOMAS
[pen.] Thomas; [b.] September 11, 1969, Brooklyn, NY; [p.] Sally and Tom Perkins; [ed.] Graduated Rutgers College 1992. Also studies one year in England at Exeter College. English History major; [occ.] English Teacher at Nakhon Sawan Teachers College in Thailand. Also was in the Peace Corps for 2 years in Thailand and India. While in India had the privilege to work with Mother Theresa.; [oth. writ.] Miscellaneous poems

PERKINS, WINTER
[pen.] Winter Perkins; [b.] December 11, 1980, Melrose Park; [p.] Diane Perkins and John W. Perkins Jr.; [m.] Single, not married never been; [ed.] 8th Grade; [hon.] Honor roll; [pers.] I put all the effort I can in writing poems. I enjoy writing poems for holidays. Like valentines, etc. I've been greatly influenced by my parent's John and Diane Love for me.; [a.] Bellwood, IL

PERRIN, GINA
[pen.] Gina Perrin; [b.] August 1, 1937, England; [p.] Philip and Doris Smith; [m.] Neville John Perrin, November 23, 1968; [ch.] Marcellina and Richard; [ed.] Leaving Certificate, Australia.; [occ.] Home Duties; [memb.] League and Bowling Clubs.; [hon.] Diploma of Freelance Journalism - January 2, 1989.; [oth. writ.] Story - A second chance - published by writers world, Queensland, Australia.; [pers.] Poetry to me is a way of expressing life as it exists today.; [a.] Lawson North South Wales, Australia

PERRY, CALVIN L.
[b.] October 15, 1953, Corpus Christi, TX; [p.] Flourastine Perry and Willie R. Lawrence; [ch.] (1) Brandon T. Perry; [ed.] High School (Graduate) Some College; [occ.] Air Frame Parts Repair Worker (CCAD); [oth. writ.] Poems of sympathy; [pers.] I feel that writing poems is my God gift to mankind.

PERRY, SUSAN
[b.] March 7, 1951, Marshfield, WI; [p.] Elmer and Burnetta Leichtnam; [m.] Jay Perry; [ch.] Daniel, Joshua, Jesse, Shane, Gretchen; [ed.] University of Wis., Green Bay, WI; [occ.] Registered Nurse, Manager of Obstetrics Dept.; [memb.] State and National Nursing Organizations; [oth. writ.] Personal portfolio of poetry, short stories; [pers.] Plain words on paper is shallow, but words from the heart is poetry.; [a.] Woodruff, WI

PETER, ALEXANDER E.
[b.] April 12, 1976, San Jose, CA; [p.] Nenette and Don Peter; [ed.] Gragvate Santa Teresa High School; [occ.] United States Marine; [hon.] National Defense Ribbon; [pers.] Life is just time between poems. Greatly influenced by Langston Hughes

PETERS, CONNIE SUE
[b.] January 23, 1962, Summitville, IN; [p.] Imogene and James Peters; [m.] Engage to... Tark I. Shelby; [ch.] Shawn Avery and Bryan Thomas; [ed.] MuHolland and Elwood High; [pers.] To my son's I leave my work of art, my words, as I see them in life influence's my pen. Love and peace be with you always love Mom; [a.] York Town, IN

PETERS, JOYCE L.
[b.] May 20, 1925, London, England; [p.] Ethel and William Lawrence; [m.] Charles H. Peters, November 8, 1947; [ch.] Janet and Glenn; [ed.] Parliament Hill High School, London, England City of London College, London, England, AOCLPN (Nursing School) Albany, N.Y.; [occ.] Retired; [memb.] Coxsackie Garden Club Licensed Practical Nurse; [oth. writ.] Write for my own pleasure and the pleasure of others. Published in the Local, district and State issues of the Federated Garden Clubs of NYS, Inc.; [pers.] Words are a reflection of the soul... poetry and music the ultimate vehicles. Poetry - a beautiful means of presenting a thought or conviction - an enjoyable challenge!; [a.] Hannacroix, NY

PETERS, RUTH E.
[b.] March 27, 1934, Akron, OH; [p.] Lester and Gertrude Wisard; [m.] Robert E. Peters, Sr, July 31, 1953; [ch.] Carol, Robert Jr., David and Linda; [ed.] 12 yrs., Cuyahoga Falls High School Grad.; 1 yr. only honors english, University of Akron; [occ.] Administrative Assist., Healthdyne Perinatal Services; [memb.] Fraternal Order of Police Auxiliary, Lady Elks, First United Methodist Church; [hon.] Semi-Finalist in the 1994 North American Open Poetry Contest resulting in the publication of my poem in an anthology Seasons to Come.; [oth. writ.] Poems and several essays, nothing published.; [pers.] Thanks to my uncle's gentle prodding, I was encouraged to submit my poem to the 1994 contest.

PETERSON, JANET MARIE
[b.] January 10, 1981, St. Thomas, Ontario, Canada; [p.] Cathy Marie Peterson, Daniel Albert Peterson; [ed.] Grade 9, South Huron District High School, Exeter, Ontario, Canada; [occ.] Student; [pers.] One way for me to express my feelings (happy or sad) is by writing poetry, when I start writing, I can't stop!; [a.] Exeter Ontario, Canada

PETERSON, MARY BETH
[b.] January 6, 1970, Syracuse, NY; [p.] Peterson Ann, Peterson Robert; [ed.] Baker High, Onondaga Community College; [occ.] SSAC (Solid State of the Arts Components - Production Line; [memb.] St. Mary's Catholic Church; [oth. writ.] Many poems written for family and friends on special occasion.; [pers.] The inspiration for my poetry comes from the feelings deep inside my heart. My family and friends help the words to flow freely.; [a.] Baldwinsville, NY

PETITO, JOSEPHINE CORNETT
[pen.] Joby Cornett; [b.] July 4, 1918, Brooklyn, NY; [p.] Albina and Giuseppi Gramegna; [m.] Jerome Cornett (deceased), September 9, 1944, Joseph Petito, September 30, 1989; [ch.] Barbara King, Richard Cornett, Bruce Cornett, Stephen Cornett; [ed.] Girls Industrial High School; [occ.] EKG Technician, Homemaker; [hon.] EKG Meritorious Completion Award; [oth. writ.] Other personal poems; [pers.] Respect each other and there will be peace and harmony individually and worldwide.; [a.] Howard Beach, NY

PHILLANDER, ANTHONY SHURLAND
[pen.] Aspire; [b.] June 16, 1950, Trinidad, West Indies; [p.] Molly and Carlton Phillander; [m.] Lystra, February 25, 1992; [ed.] Electronic Tech Diploma; [occ.] Electronics Technician Frisco Bay Industries of Canada; [oth. writ.] A poetic college of prose and poetry, a poetic cornucopia of prose and poetry, A poetic interlude of prose and poetry, a book of $100 sons titled A Love sons Song Book unpublished; [pers.] In daily life to aspire to make each new day better than the one which went before

PHILLIPS, JENNIFER
[pen.] J.P.; [b.] March 22, 1980, NC; [p.] Daniel and Debra Phillips; [ed.] Freshman in High School; [occ.] Student; [memb.] Band, Colorguard; [oth. writ.] Other poems I have wrote are Drifting to Another World, Goodbye, Your Pain, Carried Away and more.; [pers.] In my poetry I express pain and depression that comes everyday in my life. I hope that other people are able to relate to how I feel. I began writing because I need to get out my feelings.; [a.] Millsville, VA

PHILLIPS, JOSHUA CLAY
[b.] March 16. 1985, New York, NY; [p.] Mark and Patricia Phillips; [ed.] The Mirman School; [occ.] Student; [memb.] U.S. Chess Federation; [hon.] Gold Medal in Creative writing at Camp Hess Kramer; [oth. writ.] Poem published in "Anthology of Poetry by Young Americans" and in the "Communicator", The Journal of the California Association For the Gifted,; [pers.] I am very proud of my poetry and grateful to my teacher, Mrs. Julia Candace Corliss, for inspiring me to see the world through poetry.; [a.] Encino, CA

PHILLIPS, PATRICIA
[b.] October 2,, 1961, Philadelphia; [p.] Vivian Hodges and Daniel Best; [ch.] Clenet Terry, Larayne and Edward Phillips; [ed.] Philadelphia High School for girls; [occ.] Customer Service Rep. for PECO Energy Company; [pers.] It is because of God's grace and mercy that I am alive today. And all my praises and thanks are to Him.; [a.] Philadelphia, PA

PHILLIPS, PAUL G.
[ch.] Michaelene Kay, Shandley Keith; [ed.] BS Physical Science, Colorado State University, Fort Collins, Colorado; [occ.] Computer Illustrations and Animations for Childrens Books and CD-ROMS; [oth. writ.] "Some Happy Some Sad", "Love Poems of Paul G. Phillips" (unpublished) "Games for Youth", Introduction to Moral and Spiritual topics through games. (Unpublished); [pers.] American's Youth is a group of people who experience widespread discrimination. Regardless of Race, Faith, and Financial Status, the American teenager is expected to be trouble. The truth, as I see it, is that most teens are good people searching for a place to belong. The American Press seems to me to publish the bad news about young people without the proper balance of good news about good teens. I noticed more stories in 1994 than 1993 and I hope the trend continued. The American Teenager is part of the next generation of leaders. Respect is taught by example. If we adults have not shown respect to the next generation, how can we expect care in our old age. We must risk sharing what it was like to be young in our time and tell the stories of our love, our pain, our faith and our hope. Else the future for all is at risk.; [a.] San Diego, CA

PICARDY, ALLAN R.
[b.] August 9, 1972, Cleveland, OH; [m.] Single; [ed.] High School Grad. Olmsted Falls High; [occ.] Recently Discharged from U.S. Army (Honorable); [hon.] My poem being published in "A Moment In Time" was an honor; [oth. writ.] Working on my first book that will hopefully be published by June, 1994; [pers.] Just recently I've been seriously studying poetry and hope to make it a career. I write no specific style or about a specific subject just so I won't be self imposing any limits. I have a wide range of influences and try to look for their uniqueness in the art mainly.; [a.] Olmsted Township, OH

PIDHAYNY, WILMA
[b.] December 28, 1966, Ottawa, Ontario, Canada; [p.] Theodore and Irma Pidhayny; [ed.] Nepean High School, Ottawa, B.SC - University of Toronto, B. Ed. - Lakehead University, Thunder Bay, M.A. - University of Toronto; [occ.] Teacher; [pers.] I wrote "House of Cards" when I was 15 years old. I enjoy travel, competitive swimming, and animals.; [a.] Ottawa Ontario, Canada

PIDOR, MYKIE
[b.] September 6, 1983, Miami Beach, FL; [p.] Nolan and Emma Pidor; [ed.] in the 6th grade at St. Peter Academy River Edge, N.J.; [memb.] Student Council; [hon.] Recycling Contest Regional Winner, Honors: Honor Roll; [oth. writ.] 1 poem published in an anthology for kids; [pers.] 'I'm just a kid and I don't know what real poetry is, so I just write little imaginary poems.; [a.] Paramus, NJ

PIERRE, JEAN-MARIE
[pen.] Jean-Marie Pierre; [b.] February 3, 1948, Arcahaie, Haiti WI; [p.] Luc H. Pierre, C.P. Lise Marcellin; [m.] Anne-Marie L U. Pierre, October 22, 1977; [ch.] Mack-Evens, Adler, Jean-Marie R. Pierre; [ed.] Lycee Francois Duvalier (Arcahaie, Haiti), Lycee Toussant Louverture (Port-AU-Prince, Haiti), New York City Technical College. College of Staten Island.; [occ.] Medical Lab Technologist (Brooklyn Hospital Brooklyn, NY), Bilingual Assistant Teacher (Public School, Brooklyn); [memb.] R.A.U.S. (Social Club). Les Philadelphes #9 (Lodge) (Spiritual Group).; [hon.] Greatest Academic Progress in Medical Lab Program (New York City Tech College.; [oth. writ.] "Laube Sur Un Front" - Dawn of a Career" Poems' book (French poems) published in 1980 and few other manuscripts in preparation. From 1985 I've started writing in English. Several French poems have been written from 1964 to now.; [pers.] As a member of a United family, the universe, I believe that is a must, at a certain point, to commit myself to say loudly, via my poems, on behalf of the spiritual beloved ones or my presumed enemies, what others won't dare say during their existence.; [a.] Brooklyn, NY

PIESZCHALA, TERRY
[b.] November 18, 1948, Hammond, IN; [p.] Andrew Pieszchala, Maxine Craig; [ed.] Hillsborough High; [hon.] Award of Merit Certificate for the poem "Bicentennial Review", written in 1976, from World of Poetry 1990, Golden Poet 1991 from World of Poetry; [oth. writ.] The poem "Ancestors of Long Ago" (in the anthology "Edge of Twilight"). Also compiled two books "Lest They Be Forgotten", The Brinkerhoff-Bussart Genealogy and Custer's Last Stand.; [pers.] I like poems that are humorous that rhyme and also those that are uplifting to the spirit. Anyone can make a wonderful poem. All it takes is time and effort.; [a.] Tampa, FL

PIKE, BETTY R.
[b.] November 23, 1948, Longview, WA; [p.] Curtis R. Sr., (deceased) and Edrena J. Pike; [m.] Divorced; [ch.] William Eugene Peak, Curtis Richard Peak, Anthony Robert Peak; [ed.] Kelso High School, Western Business College; [occ.] Office Manager and Secretary; [oth. writ.] Poetry and Short stories; [pers.] My desire is to give readers as much pleasure as I find in writing poetry.; [a.] Toleda, WA

PILGRIM, AMANDA M.
[b.] December 22, 1978, Orangeville, Ontario, Canada; [p.] Bessie Pilgrim, Edmund Pilgrim; [ed.] Completing grade eleven in Mary Simms All Grade; [occ.] High School Student; [memb.] (S.A.D.D.) Students Against Drinking and Driving, Peer Tutoring, and Drama.; [hon.] Choices Counselor, Honor Role Student since Primary, won a writing (essay) contest, 2nd place in a Speech Contest, and four Science related Awards.; [pers.] I write simply for the fun and enjoyment of it. Poetry allows you to see the world in another view, different from any other. I receive much encouragement from my sister at heart, Christa.; [a.] Main Brook Newfoundland, Canada

PINTNER, CAROLINE BETH
[pen.] Carrie Pintner; [b.] March 19, 1982, Cleveland, OH; [p.] Elaine Pintner, Ron Pintner; [ed.] 7th grade at North Royalton Middle School; [occ.] Student; [memb.] Participates in North Royalton Summer Youth Theater, Summer Band, Softball, Cadette Girl Scouts, plays clarinet in North Royalton Middle School Band, sings in choir at North Royalton Middle School, Library helper at North Royalton Library, Youth Group at Calvary Lutheran Church.; [hon.] Outstanding R.T.A. Citizenship Award, Presidential Award at Albion School, G.C.C.T.M. (5th grade) - 1st place, trophy and ribbon, (6th grade) - 2nd place and T-shirt and ribbon, North Royalton Middle School Academic Achievement Award, Honor Roll - 4.0 average; [pers.] I love to read books and they influence me with my own writings.; [a.] North Royalton, OH

PINTNER, CAROLINE BETH
[pen.] Carrie Pintner; [b.] March 19, 1982, Cleveland, OH; [p.] Elaine Pintner, Ron Pintner; [ed.] 7th grade at North Royalton Middle School; [occ.] Student; [memb.] Participates in North Royalton Summer Youth Theater, Summer Band, Softball, Cadette Girl Scouts, plays clarinet in North Royalton Middle School Band, sings in choir at North Royalton Middle School, Library helper at North Royalton Library, Youth Group at Calvary Lutheran Church.; [hon.] Outstanding R.T.A. Citizenship Award, Presidential Award at Albion School, G.C.C.T.M. (5th grade) - 1st place, trophy and ribbon (6th grade) - 2nd place and T-shirt Honor roll - 4.0 average; [pers.] I love to read books and they influence me with my own writings.; [a.] North Royalton, OH

PIONESSA, CANDI VLCEK
[b.] February 17, 1947, Long Beach, CA; [p.] Charles and Carolyn Wilson; [m.] Raymond G. Pionessa Sr., July 9, 1994; [ch.] Jason Vlcek and Jimmy Vlcek; [ed.] Graduated Magna Cum Laude from Chapman University, Orange, CA in 1991 in Communications; [occ.] Employment Developer, Panhandle special needs, Inc.; [oth. writ.] Several feature stories published in local newspapers, and autobiography published in Chapman Class Catalog.; [pers.] I have always enjoyed writing especially about interesting people or causes I strongly believe in.; [a.] Moyie Springs, ID

PIRVANESCU, NICOLE
[b.] December 7, 1970, Resita, Romania; [p.] Victor and Margaret Pirvanescu; [ed.] High School, Matemotica - Fizica, Resita, Romania; [occ.] Student in Valley College of San Bernardino; [oth. writ.] I published some of my poems in the Newsletters for City of San Bernardino "The City Life". The poem "Love Game" published in The National Library of Poetry's.; [pers.] Believe in yourself and everything is possible.; [a.] San Bernardino, CA

PISTILLI, BONITA SASSO
[pen.] Bonnie Pistilli; [b.] Chicago, IL.; [p.] Henry and Jean Sasso; [m.] Larry Pistilli, May 17, 1986; [ed.] Loyola University, B.A. English, Governors State University, M.A., Communications Science, Hollywood Scriptwriting Institute, Certificate, UCLA Writer's Sequential Program, one course away from certificate in screenwriting, American Film Institute, screenwriting and related courses; [occ.] Technical Writer, Pacific Mutual Life Insurance Co.; [memb.] Ongoing screenwriting workshop; [hon.] W. Clement Stone Positive Mental Attitude Award; [oth. writ.] Poems in Nit and Wit Literary Arts magazine, Article in Success Magazine, Article

in Chicago Tribune, 7 original screenplays, Rainbow Records, Song, Hilltop Records; [a.] Fountain Valley, CA

PIZZOLANTE, CAROLE
[b.] Hamilton, Ontario, Canada; [p.] Ethel and John McKinlay; [m.] Paul; [ch.] Kimberley and John; [ed.] Honour Bachelor of Arts in French and German from McMaster University Hamilton, Ontario, Canada and Specialist's Teaching Certificate from University of Toronto; [occ.] Retired from teaching French and German; [memb.] Royal Ontario Museum and I sing with a 6 member group called "Praise Unlimited" and Teachers' Organizations; [hon.] Honourable mention in Stephen Leacock Limerick contest, 1992 - Albert Matthews Scholarship for languages and several prizes at University - Dean's Honour list all 4 years at University; [oth. writ.] Educational and textual material - short stories, - One novel; [pers.] Since retiring from teaching in June 1994, I have been heavily involved in charitable work, I have always been involved in music and playing piano, singing, dancing and choreography; [a.] Burlington Ontario, Canada

PLASKOFF, BART EZRA
[b.] November 1, 1968, Los Angeles, CA; [p.] Reuben G. Plaskoff, Claire F. Plaskoff; [m.] Cynthia L. Plaskoff, August 23, 1993; [ed.] Cal. State University at Northridge - B.A. in English Literature, 1991, Santa Monica High School, 1986.; [occ.] Insurance agent, Musician, Spiritualist, Traveler, Artist; [memb.] ASCAP, IIAA, Life; [hon.] Original band member - Schnee Bezen "Top 10 Hit - Live 105 - San Francisco "Highest Rated local band in KROQ History!" KROQ 106.7 - Los Angeles; [oth. writ.] Extensive library of unpublished poetry and short story. Extensive library of recorded and unrecorded music.; [pers.] "Perception ... my Aphrodisiac, Movement... Consummation (mine). Bart Ezra Plaskoff Bus stop Artist - 1991) my influences - British Literature and poetry with a tinge of American. Let's not forget Peter "Rael" Gabriel; [a.] Dayton, NV

PLAZEK JR., EDWARD L.
[b.] August 13, 1982, Bedford, OH; [p.] Jean and Edward Plazek; [ed.] Seventh grade education at Milkovich Middle School; [occ.] Student; [memb.] Maple Heights Boys League American Junior Bowling Assoc.; [hon.] All A's Award, Honors math student, Teacher- Mrs. Codney; [pers.] I enjoy school, Mrs. Allison Pfahl inspired my work. Special thanks to Mrs. Codney, Pfahl, and Parents. 4 time all-star catcher. Also thanks to Miss Jacy Larsen; [a.] Maple Hts, OH

PLEASANT, WARNITA
[b.] October 3, 1962, New Orleans; [p.] Warren Pleasant, Jeanette Pleasant; [ch.] Wenquetta Pleasant, Michael Pleasant; [ed.] Walter L. Cohen, Phillips Jr. College; [occ.] Youth Specialist; [memb.] Writer's Digest, Coordinator and Director of Covenant House Chorus; [oth. writ.] Several fictions and non-fiction - yet, unpublish. Also, a book of poetry, - yet unpublish. I write contemporary gospel and secelor songs; [pers.] Each of my writings are an expressions from the soul. With sincerity and personal desire, I hope that - you the readers will obtained positive personal growth and positive self excel. - regardless of conditions; [a.] New Orleans, LA

PLONKA, SKIP M.
[b.] October 1, 1952, Chicago, IL; [m.] Linda S. Plonka, November 3, 1973; [ch.] Michael, David, Jennifer and in memory Mandi.; [ed.] Downers Grove North High School, College of DuPage, Cleveland Institute of Electronics; [memb.] The American Group of Innovation and Technology. The National Air and Space Museum. The N.R.A.; [hon.] Honorable mention in the 1976 and 1978 American Song Festival, and by the Country Music Association in 1979.; [oth. writ.] Numerous unpublished Country and Pop songs.; [a.] Westmont, IL

PLOTTS, MARY LOU
[b.] April 23, 1952, Welch West, VA; [p.] Mr. and Mrs. Joe C. Hugerman; [m.] Gene Lerory Plotts, December 21, 1987; [ch.] Dawn Michelle, Summer, Terry; [ed.] High School 12th; [occ.] Certified Nurses Aide; [oth. writ.] I write children poems, Ghost poems, Christians poems, any kind of poem that a person can think up.; [pers.] I write my poems from my own personnel experience. I love to put my feelings into my poetry. I hope to become a very famous poetry writer.

PLYLER, CHERYL C.
[b.] April 25, 1953, Lancaster, SC; [p.] Nathan and Bette Hall; [m.] Ronnie D. Plyler, August 7, 1983; [ch.] Jana Layne Hough, Drewid Dyneane Plyler; [ed.] Buford High School, Lancaster, SC. Medical University of South Carolina, Charleston, SC.; [occ.] Multi-disciplinary Education Director - Catawha Wateree AHEC; [memb.] ARRT, ASRT, SCHA, Now Muse Alumni Association AHA; [hon.] Honors graduate muse elder - New Cat Presbyterian Church; [oth. writ.] Editorials to local paper research papers; [pers.] My reflections are statements of the simplicity of life. The more we grow and change - the more we realize "There is nothing new under the sea."; [a.] Lancaster, SC

POFF, RICHARD C.
[pen.] Dick Poff, Dick Curtis, Dick Richards; [b.] May 30, 1932, Charleston, WV; [p.] James M. and Alma V. Poff; [m.] Joanne Poff; [ch.] 5 by previous marriages; [ed.] Grades 1 thru 12 in D.C. BS Transportation - Southeastern University (D.C.); [occ.] Semi-Retired and Self Employed Delivery service and Handyman.; [oth. writ.] Country music songwriter many short stories and book length projects (none published) [pers.] I have been writing since childhood but never had the time or peace of mind to put time into it, now, at 62, I'd better hurry up! Need agency advice and guidance!!!; [a.] Elkton, MD

POGAN, FRANCIS J.
[b.] January 19, 1931, Jersey City, NJ; [p.] Deceased; [m.] Rita M. Pogan, July 19, 1958; [ch.] Three; [ed.] Henry Snyder High School Manual Arts Degree, Mercersburg Academy Gen. Tech. Coll. Prep. Degree, Princeton Univ. 2.5 yrs. Civil Eng'g., US Army Signal School Ft. Monmouth NJ, various Mgt. and Business related courses UCLA, USC, Kellog Sch. of Mgt. Pamonn CA; [occ.] Retired. Part time licensed Real Estate Loan Officer; [memb.] Hughes Aircraft Ret. Orgzn., Hughes Aircraft Management Club, Princeton Univ. Alumni Assoc. Mercersburg Acad. Alumni Assoc., St. Marks RC Church; [hon.] First poem written 7th grade, teacher said was published in American poetry magazine, in prep. school, won John N. Mountain Poetry prize 1950 and 1951.; [pers.] I am awed by the beauty of our earth and the indomnitability of man. My goal(s) is to be able to describe both, interwoven, with image provocation for the reader, hopefully putting them at the scene.; [a.] San Marcos, CA

POINDEXTER, CONSTANCE
[b.] January 23, 1947, Burbank, CA; [p.] Dorothy, Bradney, James Reed Poindexter; [m.] Anthony F. Durkin, November 18, 1985; [ch.] Christopher A. Durkin born February 13, 1987; [ed.] University of Life; [occ.] Staying alive.; [memb.] A member of the human race....otherwise, I"m Irish. I'm also Cherokee which puts me at great odds with myself from time to time.; [hon.] "Life" is the reward!; [oth. writ.] "Street Messiah" "Through the Valley", (Novels) and "Synapses" (Poetry), "An American In Ireland" - current project; [pers.] I don't believe in organized religion. It's too disorganized. I do believe in a higher force. Compared to man, any force is Higher.; [a.] Philadelphia, PA

POINTS, RACHEL
[pen.] Tanya Kracinski; [b.] August 30,1969, St. Charles, IL; [p.] Dave Peters and Rachel Grammer

POITIER, OLIVE CYNTHIA
[pen.] Poitier Olive Cynthia; [b.] Cat Island, Bahamas; [p.] Edgar and Glendena Poitier; [ed.] Knowle's Public School, Cat Island, Bahamas Western Senior School, College of The Bahamas, Uchee Pine Institute, Seal Alabama, USA.; [occ.] Payroll Officer; [memb.] Hillview Seventh-Day-Adventist, Pathfinder Club; [hon.] Dean's List, Ministry of Public Safety and Transport-Road Slogan Contest; [oth. writ.] (Slogan Contest) Road Traffic.; [pers.] The reality is, we are caught up in various storms:- Storms of depression, Storms of oppression, Storms of injustice and immoral, social and economic storms. I put myself in other people's place and feel their pain.; [a.] Nassau, Bahamas

POLLACK, HEATHER LEE
[b.] June 7, 1981, San Antonio, TX; [p.] Helene Pollack Partman and Howard Partman; [ed.] I am now in the Monticello Middle School 8th grade.; [memb.] Monticello Middle School Builders Club, Chorus, Band, Junior Honor Society.; [hon.] Presidential Academic Fitness Award, National Junior Honor Society.; [oth. writ.] School Magazine Article - "I hope I will have made a difference." Middle Wrinkle (Monticello Middle School Literary Magazine) 1994.; [pers.] I take great pleasure in studying the ocean and I hope to someday become a marine biologist.; [a.] Monticello, NY

POMELEO, THOMAS L.
[pen.] Giovanni Riccio; [b.] August 12, 1950, Rome, Italy; [p.] Thomas and Josephine Pomeleo Jr.; [ed.] Central High, Southern Colorado State College; [occ.] Central Office Technician US West Communications; [oth. writ.] Poetry, Lyrics, Music; [pers.] If you would be of one mind: One must never give up, misplace, nor lose, their sense of purpose, worth, and identity, but, in faith guided by love, reconcile— the wounded Heart in companionable silence.; [a.] Denver, CO

PONTICELLO, MAUDE JAMES
[pen.] "Maude" J.P; [b.] August 8, 1915, England; [p.] Charles and Mary Hark; [m.] Harold J. James, February 14, 1942, Salvatore Ponticello, December 07, 1968; [ch.] Walter, Eddy, Lawrence, Mary; [ed.] Cathedral High School, N.Y.C, N.Y. 2nd years Hunter College N.Y, N.Y, 1st year Assisium Inst. N.Y, N.Y; [occ.] Retired Postal Employee Hickville, N.Y; [memb.] Secular Order Franciscan 30 yr., Outreach - St. ELizabeth Ann Seton Palm Coast 5 yr FL., Eucharist Minister 5 yr. N.Y 8 yr FL.; [oth. writ.] Several poems published in Bulletin (Franciscan News Letter) and Catholic Digest.; [pers.] In life's journey I as true to reach out and know and help my fellow traveller on the journey to God.; [a.] Palm Coast, FL

PONZI, REGINA
[pen.] Gina Ponzi; [b.] July 5, 1969, Oswego, NY; [p.] Joe Ponzi, Kathy Ponzi; [ed.] Oswego High School, Suny Canton, Suny Oswego; [occ.] Copywriter, Gray Dominion Advertising; [memb.] Gymnastics Club, 1982, 1984, Oswego Soccer, 1984-1986, Oswego Softball, 1982-1993, Oswego Volleyball, 1982-1986, Oswego Figure Skating Club, 1981-1983; [hon.] Secretary, Freshman Class, President, Sophomore Class, Secretary, Alpha Chi Omicron, First Runner-up in Oswego County Story telling Contest, Suny Canton's Deans's List, Suny Oswego's Dean List and President List, Selected for all County Band; [oth. writ.] Received "Ancient Order of Bards in America's Poetic License"; [pers.] "Imagine where you'll be tomorrow, if you believe in yourself today"; [a.] Coral Springs, FL

POPELESKI, BARBARA S.
[pen.] Bunny; [b.] March 27, 1948, Rhode Island; [p.] Lou Stanzione and Elizabeth Crowley Stanzione; [m.] Mark Popeleski, July 24, 1971; [ch.] Lisa Marie, Mark Allyn, Kenneth Barry; [ed.] Bachelor BS from Easter Conn. State University. Masters from University of Connecticut School of Education.; [occ.] Grade 4 Teacher; [memb.] Phi Delta Kappa at Uconn. Honored by the Hartford Courant Special Edition for my accomplishments at home and at School on thanksgiving day 1994.; [hon.] Cooperating Mentor Teacher member. Phi Delta Kappa member with the University of Connecticut at Storrs, Ct.; [oth. writ.] I'm presently working on putting a children's book about epilepsy together.; [pers.] Writing is my way of relaxing and letting my thoughts flow freely. It's a way of expressing myself and my needs. It helps me to cope with stress.; [a.] Windham, CT

PORK, MATTIE F.
[b.] November 6, 1950, Heflin, LA; [p.] O. T. Smith, Catherine Smith; [m.] Raysylvan C. Pork, November 29, 1985; [ch.] Drike Smith; [ed.] Central High; [occ.] Texas Instrument Front End; [memb.] NWACP American Hearth Association

PORTA, MARIAH
[b.] July 26, 1984, Downey, CA; [p.] Linton and Nancy Porta; [ed.] Christian Chapel School 5th grade, Walnut, CA; [occ.] School; [hon.] Trophies, 1993 Miss Beauty, 1st place Beauty 1993, Age Group Princess 1993, Miss American Starlet, Best Smile 1993, Princess 1993, Reigning Beauty '93, Dance Silver Ribbons (2), 1995 Star Power Competition, National Talent, 1994 Czar 1st place (dance); [a.] Walnut, CA

POST, JAMES R.
[pen.] Jim Post; [b.] July 6, 1926, Brighton, MA; [p.] William M. and Laura H. Post; [m.] Divorced; [ch.] James M. Post, William Post, Patricia Vaughn; [ed.] High School Graduate Graduate Leland Powers School Of Radio and Theater on the Fenway Boston MA.; [occ.] Retired Realtor; [memb.] Board Of Realtors. Congregational Church.; [hon.] Salesman of the year, I was excited until I found it was like "Ed McMahon" No obligation but we'd love your to buy the books.; [oth. writ.] I've just written poems and short stories for personal satisfaction. This is my first venture for presenting my material for comment and criticism.; [pers.] My mother was a Third Grade Teacher, well-educated and intelligent. She did not enjoy poetry because it was not at all easy to understand my poetry is an easy to understand glimpse of life for the Layman.; [a.] Quincy, MA

POULSON, DOROTHEA
[b.] April 22, 1922, New York City, NY; [p.] (Deceased) Paul and Josephine Brown; [m.] Ralph Poulson (Deceased), December 31, 1943; [ch.] Ralph, Betty Anne, Joanne, Gary; [ed.] High School, I had intended to study Law, However WW II changed my desires!; [occ.] Retired (baby sit two of my grandsons ages 8 and 5; [memb.] Hale House, Red Cloud Indian School WNET (Channel 13); [oth. writ.] As a child I always wrote, stories and poetry. I would send them into the Brooklyn Eagle circa 1930's; [pers.] Reading has always been a marvelous experience to me. Not only is it relaxing I find it therapeutic, I instilled this in my family. Today I'm passing it on to my grands!; [a.] Brooklyn, NY

POWELL, LESLIE HARDING
[pen.] Leslie Harding Powell; [b.] May 24, 1958, Poplar Bluff, MO; [p.] Ephriam Powell, Dorothy Powell; [m.] Mary Ann Powell, July 27, 1981; [ed.] Poplar Bluff High School, Poplar Bluff, Missouri; [occ.] A.S.E. Parts Specialist Auto Tire and Parts; [hon.] A.S.E. Certified Machinist, A.S.E. Parts Specialist; [oth. writ.] Poems printed in "The Bulletin", a local Christian magazine.; [pers.] The inspiration for my poems comes from personal life experiences and feelings. I'm hoping that other people benefit from reading them.

POWELL, SHEILA
[b.] June 13, 1969, Kansas City, KS; [p.] Tom and Barbara Powell; [ch.] Beloved Niece - Ashton; [ed.] Humble High, N. Harris County College, Tarrant County, Univ. of Houston; [hon.] Dean's List; [oth. writ.] 3 other poems, this was my first.; [pers.] Poetry is therapy, it refreshes my mind.; [a.] Bethlehem, PA

POYNER, JAMES R.
[b.] February 14, 1950, Brockville, Ontario; [p.] Walter and Erma Jean Poyner; [ed.] Evanston Twp High School, Millikin University; [occ.] File Clerk, Elek-Tek, Skokie, IL; [memb.] Northwestern Society of Model rail roaders, Habit for Humanity volunteer, 4th presbyterian church of Chicago; [hon.] Dean's list; [oth. writ.] The sonnet "Beauty flows" in "Reflections of light", NLP., Several unpublished novels, to include "The travellers", A nine - book series.; [pers.] I always try to be honest, and to do the best I can, particularly whenever I pick up a pen or make a keystroke.; [a.] Chicago, IL

PRANZO, RACHELA
[b.] February 2, 1947, Brooklyn, NY; [m.] Peter J. Pranzo, July 27, 1969; [ch.] Anthony and Lorinda; [oth. writ.] Personal pieces symbolic of life, family, wonderment and deep thought.; [pers.] My inspiration includes spur of the moment, special occasion and reflection.; [a.] Smithtown, NY

PRATER, ANGELA DENISE
[b.] March 30, 1971, Memphis, TN; [p.] Artaree Braxton (Mom); [ed.] Television Production Major, will graduate May 1996 with 4 yr. degree; [oth. writ.] I write poetry as a hobby, although I have other writings this is the first one ever published.; [pers.] This poem reflects the end of a bad relationship and I think anyone can relate to it. That's why I wanted to share it with others by entering this contest.; [a.] Saginaw, MI

PRESLEY, MELODY
[pen.] Melody Dudziak; [b.] December 27, 1972, Gainesville, GA; [p.] Rev. William and Mrs. Shelby Presley; [m.] Engaged to Mark Dudziak; [ed.] Banks County High School; [occ.] Middle-Class Laborer working for the Future; [hon.] Honor roll, Spanish Certificate, yearbook awards, and College Prep. Gold seal on diploma; [oth. writ.] None published, but read by many and greatly praised; [pers.] Only through God's grace do I accept any recognition, for He is the one that blessed me with the talents that I have.; [a.] Maysville, GA

PRESTON, YVONNE
[b.] December 23, 1951, Toronto, Ontario, Canada; [p.] Gordon S. Woods, Patricia Woods; [m.] Robert Preston, August 1979; [ch.] Robert Elvis, Shane Preston, William Ashley Lance Preston; [ed.] Aurora High, Aurora Senior Public School; [occ.] Devoted Mother and Loving Wife; [oth. writ.] Short stories, songs, and other poems not entered for publication.; [pers.] From birth to death, we succumb to a smile, a loving touch or gesture. In that we are human, which makes us all the same. Yvonne Preston. January, 1995.; [a.] Aurora Ontario, Canada

PRICE, MARISA D.
[pen.] M. D. Price; [b.] December 20, 1973, California; [p.] Donald and Elaine Price; [ed.] Granada High School, Pacific Lutheran University, University of Oregon.; [occ.] Student at the University of Oregon.; [hon.] Special Award, 1993, American Collegiate Poets. Honorable mention, 1993, Saxifrage. Various Awards, 1990-1992, Pomegranate.; [pers.] Thank you, Walt Whitman and Maya Angelou, for inspiration, Mom and Dad, I could never have come this far without you.; [a.] Eugene, OR

PRINS, STEPHANIE
[pen.] Stephanie Prins; [b.] October 3, 1977, Burlington, Ontario, Canada; [p.] Bart and Jane Prins; [ed.] Presently, I am in grade 12 at Parkside High School in Dundas, Ontario, Canada.; [occ.] Customer Service Representative (teller) at the Royal Bank of Canada.; [memb.] National Geographic Society, Environment Club at Parkside High School.; [hon.] Robert Kirkland Kernighan Poetry Competition 1987-1988; [oth. writ.] I've only ever submitted two poems to any competitions or contents. Both poems won, but only one will be published.; [pers.] Emotions and a love of nature is usually what inspires me to write a poem; [a.] Dundas Ontario, Canada

PRISCILLA, PACHECO
[b.] August 13, 1980, Montreal; [p.] Antonio Pacheco, Linda Pacheco; [ed.] High School Laurier Macdonald; [hon.] Writing Awards, Ward for Iintelligence, involving writing; [oth. writ.] Lots of poetry, about different subjects, song writing and one music writing....; [pers.] I have a dream to fulfill, a dream to be a poet using my songs and poems to open the minds of humans, and with the melody of my voice. I walk towards a future of my God given talent...; [a.] Anjou Quebec, Canada

PROULX, DEBBIE THIBEAULT
[b.] March 21, 1959, Ottawa, Ontario, Canada; [p.] Romeo Thibeault, Beatrice Lebrun; [m.] John Proulx, September 8, 1984; [ch.] Jamie, Joey, Jimmy, Lyndsey Proulx; [ed.] St. Raymond Junior High Ottawa Ontario.; [occ.] Housewife and mother.; [oth. writ.] 13 others poems I song, called Is There A Christmas Up In Heaven, not published.; [pers.] I write the way I see thew world around me. I put myself in the other persons shoes to full I see what they do. And I write it in a poem.; [a.] Albert, Canada

PROWANT, ROSANA FISHER
[pen.] Rosanna Fisher; [b.] February 10, 1949, South-

ern, OH; [p.] Franklin Blizzard, Andrea Blizzard; [m.] Carl E. Prowant, April 28, 1993; [ch.] Sherry Andrea; [ed.] Adrian High School, Adrian College; [occ.] In home care Person and author; [memb.] Adrian Church of Christ I endorse: The National Arbor Day Foundation, American Heart Association, American Cancer Association, American Wild Life and Smithsonian Institution (Former Membership Foundations and Associations 1991-1993); [hon.] In 8th grade I won Ohio State Scholarship Award Nominated for Outstanding College Student of America Award while attending Adrian College; [oth. writ.] Numerous Poems/songs many short stories and the beginnings of 15 novels.; [pers.] The greatness of mankind is in the humility of man's heart unto one another and unto God. Also the beauties of nature lies in the reverence for the simple things in this life. "Both reflect the true greatness of God.; [a.] Maniton Beach, MI

PRUYNE, EILEEN
[b.] September 22, 1941, Dalton, PA; [p.] Richard Capwell, Ruth Capwell; [m.] Thomas E. Pruyne, August 18, 1962; [ch.] Randy Richard, David Wayne; [ed.] Falls-Overfield High Robert Packer Hospital School of Nursing; [occ.] Psychiatric Nursing Consultant Area Mental Health, Charlotte, N.C.; [memb.] Charlotte-Mecklenburg Coalition on Aging.; [hon.] Song writer of the year, Penn-York country Music Club. Sportsmanship Award-Patriots Bowling League.; [oth. writ.] Human interest stories for local newspapers, Original country music songs received radio play in P.A., N.Y. and Colorado, Life in these United States- Reader's Digest, Maintaining the Mentally Il Client in Community placement, (Professional).; [pers.] To answer life's questions talk with Senior Citizens.; [a.] Charlotte, NC

PUGH, MITCHELL D.
[pen.] Joseph Sterling; [b.] July 28, 1971, Allegan, MI; [p.] Kathey Dailey, Rodger D. Pugh; [ed.] Comstock High, Ambassador College, Gospel Echoes Team, Rhema Bible School, Marilyn Hickey Bible College, Family Radio School of the Bible; [occ.] Free-lance Writer, poet, and Musician; [memb.] Crossroads Institute, Urantia Foundation; [oth. writ.] Author of Corrupted by innocence, Publisher/Author of Razor wire, poetry published in the action resource guide; [pers.] If the continuance of time were to suddenly perish, as if an almighty wielded its potent hand, then the elapsing time that has taken its tole has grated me with good measure.; [a.] Fennville, MI

PUMMILL, JASON
[pen.] Hodgie; [b.] June 3, 1976, Bloomington, IL; [p.] David Pummill and Jolene Taylor; [ed.] Tri-Valley High School; [occ.] College Student; [oth. writ.] A few poems in a private collection entitled "Hodge Podge."; [pers.] I firmly believe that everyone's bound to get the shaft but it always gives me something to write about! All my works reflect pas experiences and feelings.; [a.] Plantation, FL

PURSER, MARGARET M. PAGE
[pen.] Margaret Page-Purser; [b.] Montreal, Canada; [m.] Ralph Bernard Purser (Eng.) of Ottawa, now of Beaconsfield; [ed.] University - Arts and The Logy - MTL.; [oth. writ.] Have Written numerous poems but seldom for publication.; [pers.] Music, art and the written word our truest expressions of reality; [a.] Beaconsfield Province of Quebec, Canada

PYFROM, PRISCILLA C.
[pen.] Priscilla Coe Pyfrom; [b.] December 13, 1896, Minneapolis, MN; [p.] Clarence S. and Lula Joy Coe; [m.] Harold Theadore Pyfrom, August 25, 1915; [ch.] Elizabeth Russell, Harold and Stanley Pyfrom; [ed.] Ruth Hargrove Institute, Key West, FL (Private Preparatory School for College); [occ.] Retired, State and Civil Service Employee; [memb.] United Methodist Church, Member Public Employee Retirees (State of California), Member of American Association of Retired People (AARP); [oth. writ.] Articles published locally, four books, Auto Biography (personal history of 20th Century Life in the United States.); [pers.] It was quite be accident that I started writing poetry. I always loved to write. I wrote many short story for my personal satisfaction. Then I began the Auto Biography experience. At present I am writing the fifth book entitled "Think of a Land." A granddaughter reading the introduction of this book remarked "This is Poetry."; [a.] Milton, FL

QUINN, ANNE
[b.] May 19, 1968, Newcastle, Australia; [p.] John Quinn, Patricia Quinn; [ed.] St Francis Xavier High School - Canberra, Copland College - Canberra, University of Canberra - Canberra; [occ.] Agency Coordinator, Crocodile Communications, Sydney, Australia; [hon.] Awarded 1st, 2nd and 3rd in several dramatic recitals at the 1993 New South Wales Eisteddfod.; [pers.] I have been influenced by authors who write with honesty and simplicity. "Louis" by Kathleen Stewart, an Australia author, creates situations with which readers can identify with. Her realistic approach appeals to me and it is this style that I strive to reflect in my writings.; [a.] Sydney New South Wales, Australia

QUINN, ELIZABETH
[b.] December 3, 1914, Carrickfergus NI; [p.] Harry and Alice Finlay; [m.] Samuel Quinn, April 9, 1939; [ch.] One Daughter Sandra Bradley; [ed.] Methodist College Belfast, Studied Music Associated Member of Trinity College London.; [occ.] Have just completed material for the Musical Calendar for the LISBURN BOROUGH COUNCIL. This includes "THE LAD FROM THE CREWE" (Poem you have selected. I own all rights); [memb.] Of Performing Right and Mechanical Rights. I am also a member of WAR ON WANT Northern Ireland. My work has been presented by Community Relations Units of Many Councils all over the province.; [hon.] Made an Honorary Georgia Citizen November 1988. Also Honoured by The Friendship Force (Atlanta) July 1992...I Participated in the Macon Cherry Blossom Festival; [oth. writ.] A STEP IN THE RIGHT DIRECTION, Wishing You Were Here, IRELAND'S CULTURAL HERITAGE IN WORDS AND MUSIC. The Music is Mine have been on Radio and Television many times. Have had many publications as well as publishing myself.; [pers.] My aim is to promote Peace Love and Understanding through my words and music. Have worked with 5,000 children over the past three years. Have been involved in Music teaching for over sixty years.

QUINN, ROSEMARIE
[b.] Brooklyn, NY; [p.] Edward and Dolores Somma; [m.] Kenneth Quinn, September 19, 1981; [ch.] John and Kenny; [occ.] Homemaker, P/T office worker; [oth. writ.] Waiting by God's Window published in the Tablet - 1975; [pers.] Enjoy writing about people and events close to my heart. I find it uplifting and rewarding. Admire the writings of Edna St. Vincent Millay and Helen Steiner Rice.; [a.] North Babylon, NY

QUINTERO, KRISTIN FEUER
[b.] July 11, 1978, Los Angeles; [p.] Linda and George Quintero; [ed.] Pinecrest Elementary, Sherman Oaks C.E.S., Cleveland High School Humanities Magnet Program; [occ.] High School Student; [memb.] Photo Editor of Cleveland's School paper, "Le Sabre"; [pers.] "When I consider the short duration of my life...I am frightened and am astonished at being here rather than there, why now rather than them" -Blaise Pascal; [a.] Chatsworth, CA

RADSICK, CARLA
[b.] August 5, 1980, Canton, OH; [p.] Rick Radsick, Lorett Badsick; [ed.] I am a freshman in High School. I'm 14 years of age.; [occ.] Take care of younger children.; [hon.] Have 3 awards for perfect attendance at school. Have a grade point average or 3.5. to a 4.0.; [oth. writ.] This poem has been written for Doughs McWilliams a sophomore in High School.; [a.] Canton, OH

RADZEVICIUS, AUDREY
[pen.] Audra Lynn; [b.] March 21, 1966, Evergreen Park, IL; [p.] Stanley Radzevicius, Minnie Etta Jones; [occ.] Legal Assistant Law Offices of Michelle Wong, Dallas, TX; [pers.] Explore the possibilities that lie within you. Special thanks to my mentor, Homer Chapa, for believing in me and to my kindred spirit, Kevin Badley, for enlightening me on the ways to be free. I miss you both.; [a.] Dallas, TX

RAFN, ELEANOR M.
[pen.] Eleonora D'Annunzio; [b.] September 18, 1932, Glens Falls, NY; [p.] Arturo (D'Annunzio) Morrissey, Anna Gennamore Morrissey; [m.] Robert Rafh (deceased), June 22, 1963; [ch.] Robert K. Rafh II; [ed.] Catholic Central High, Rensselaer Polytechnic Institute; [occ.] Senior Engineering writer/designer/illustrator and publications head for scanner Corp.; [memb.] Exec. Board Member - So. Calif. Motion Picture Council, Film Advisory board, HAVE (humanitarian Awards), Children's Committee on TV, Public Info. officer, Civil Air Patrol, member, writers' workshop, Asheville Chapter; [hon.] Semi-finalist, National repertory theatre, runner-up, Houston Playhouse competition, nominated for honorary doctorate for contribution to Space Sciences literature, lifetime membership, motion picture council for outstanding work in film industry promotion.; [oth. writ.] Poetry, articles published in various newspapers and magazines including "Westways" the AAA periodical, human interest column, gourmet cooking column, "Antelope Valley Newspapers", various promotional brochures, etc. for such organizations as L.A. County Museum of Art, L.A. Natural History Museum; [pers.] I find wonder and excitement in the sunrise of each new day and hope I always shall.; [a.] Asheville, NC

RAGSDALE, JON
[b.] June 20, 1955, Kerriville; [ed.] Sr. In College; [occ.] Disabled; [oth. writ.] An untitled poem in Journey of the Mind; [pers.] Coupd'e'tat was the first poem I wrote which I was satisfied with. Written in High School as I search for knowledge both then and still.; [a.] Kerrville, TX

RAHER, NATHAN RAY
[b.] August 5, 1983, San Diego, CA; [p.] Richard Ray, Robbi Louise; [ed.] Vail Ranch Middle School; [occ.] Student; [memb.] Calvary Chapel of Escondido; [hon.] 1st place cake design 1991 outstanding achievement, National PTA cultural arts program November 1994;

[pers.] "My poetry comes from the heart, and my ability from God."; [a.] Temecula, CA

RAINEY, KELLY ANN
[b.] September 5, 1981, Morristown, NJ; [p.] Paul William Rainey, Elizabeth Coogan-Rhodes; [occ.] Eight Grader-Student hope elementary Hope NJ; [oth. writ.] Mr. Lindon's Library, 1992 "Lidia," 1994; [a.] Hope, NJ

RAJKUMAR, KACHARLA
[pen.] Nil; [b.] June 1, 1966, Korotla, AP, India; [p.] K. Rajeshwar, K. Satyamma; [ed.] B.S.C., M.A. (Eng.), (Ph.D), Govt. City College, Hyd., People's College, Nanded (M.S.).; [occ.] Lecturer in English, College of Arts and Commerce, Purna 431511.; [memb.] 1. Life member, Indian Assciation for American Studies. 2. Life member, Indian, Society for Commonwealth Studies. 3. Indian Association for English studies. 4. African Studies of India.; [oth. writ.] A small collection of unpublished poems in English, as well as, in my mother tongue (Telegu).; [pers.] The idea that the human life is yet to achieve perfection, makes me restless and compels me to expose the found means in the society. I like Whitman's Poetry, not for its simplicity, but for its profound treatment with the issues, concerning humanity.; [a.] Nanded, Maharashtra

RAMIREZ, GABRIEL
[b.] April 8, 1965, Long Beach, CA; [p.] Arturo Ramirez, Felipa Ramirez; [m.] Single; [ch.] Carah Marie Ramirez; [occ.] PBX operator Mtel Corp (Fullerton CA.); [hon.] Apostolic Tabernacle (pentecostal church); [pers.] As I always said to my daughter: When you do good things, good things happen in your life, and when you do bad, bad things happen. It's the balance of life.; [a.] Angheim, CA

RAMON-FORTUNE', BARNABAS JOHN
[b.] November 6, 1917, Trinidad, West Indies; [p.] Desiderio and Eugenio Ramon-Fortune'; [m.] Barbara Allison Ramon-Fortune, September 19, 1942; [ch.] Twelve (12); [ed.] 1935: Oxford and Cambridge School Certificate.; [occ.] Public Servant (retired) Writes short stories, articles for further self-discovery and elucidation.; [hon.] Included in International Who's Who in poetry and poets Encyclopedia 7th Edition. (Biographical Centre, Cambridge, England.); [oth. writ.] Collections of Poetry: "Parian Currents" - 1948 "Black Aphrodire and poems of love and passion" - 1976. Various magazines and textbooks for school use. Novels: "The Understones of victory" - 1973. (First prize in the National Cultural of Trinidad and tobago literary competition. Two unpublished short novels. Short stories: "The Kite" British Broadcasting Corporation "Caribbean Voices" radio programme - sometime in the 1940's, Evans Brothers Ltd - England, 1976: English Literature Textbook, projection in literature: Scott, foresman and Company - 1967. "The Tallow Pole" ('Headway: A Thematic Reader): Holt, Rinehart and Winston, Inc., 1970, Other stories in various magazines and school anthologies. Considerable volume of unpublished poetic works.; [pers.] Cardinal Points of Reference for life: Faith, family and the discipline of writing. Theory of happiness: Sharing prudently everything one has with others.

RAMOS, FERNANDO
[b.] March 9, 1930, Rio De Janeiro; [p.] Joaquin Ramos, Maria Josefina Duarte Ramos; [m.] Barbara Ramos, November 3, 1980; [ch.] 6 from first marriage; [ed.] University of Coimbra, Portugal; [occ.] Actor, Writer; [memb.] Screen Actors Guild, Alexandre, Julio Cesar, Fernando Jorge, Maria de Lourdes, Elizio, Katia Isabella; [hon.] Nominated "Best Actor of 1985" in Rio de Janeiro, Brasil; [oth. writ.] "Anseio" collection of poems (Portuguese language), poems published in various newspapers in the fifties both in Brasil and Portugal. Screenplay "Of Orange Halves" both in Portuguese and English. Working on novel "The Fantastic Adventures of a Sparrow called Antonio."; [pers.] The Secret of Life: Its Purpose.; [a.] Los Angeles, CA

RAMPTON, KATHLEEN
[b.] September 14, 1948, Briaham City, UT; [m.] Single; [ed.] B.A. English, Sonoma State University, 3 courses short of a second B.A. in Business Management with an emphasis in Accounting.; [occ.] Accountant; [memb.] International Society of Poets; [hon.] Graduated with honors with my degree in English; [oth. writ.] National library of poetry is publishing three of my poems in their anthologies. Currently asking on a book entitled, dancing with the muses, that is more of an autobiographical statement but also contains some poetry.; [pers.] My current writing reflects my journey to reconnect more fully with the earth and her many lite forms. I am also interested in the healing movements currently on the rise in the U.S. and would like to make a literary contribution in that area.; [a.] Santa Rosa, CA

RANDALL, WENDY L.
[b.] April 13, 1964, Bronx, NY; [p.] Edna D. Cooper, Wade H. Cooper; [ch.] Shakina Randall, 12 years, Brittney Randall 4 years; [ed.] Florida School of Business Nursing Assistant (certified) Service Associate, future student of Johnson And Wales University, School of culinary arts major-executive chef; [occ.] Nursing Assistant, Service Associate; [oth. writ.] Several other poems, slogans and presentation for my automobile concept dream project for general motors and America.; [pers.] I am envisioned with messages from nurture for the future of this country. I believe we can all come together as one displaying a wonderland of love and Unity. We are all Gods children, different, but the same.; [a.] Princeton, FL

RANDO, ANNE H.
[pen.] Ahran; [b.] October 22, 1921, Lancaster Co., SC; [p.] George Washington Haire and Mary Elizabeth Caston Haire; [m.] Joseph Anthony Rando, December 11, 1946; [ch.] Jo Anne Rando-Moon; [ed.] BA (Fine Arts) University of New Orleans, East Jefferson High School (LA), Buford High School (S.C.); [occ.] Artist/Photographer/Writer; [memb.] Women for a better Louisiana, American Red Cross. East Jefferson Service Center, University of New Orleans Alumni Assoc.; [oth. writ.] Poems, currently researching and working with my husband on a book of his experiences in WW II. Published in WBL's Laureate; [pers.] I am sensitive to the beauty of Nature and accept the reality of it's cruelties. I cave when our water is fouled and our surroundings are littered and take action, thru proper channels, which these abuses are evident.; [a.] Metairie, LA

RAPPE, LINDA
[pen.] Jerks; [b.] April 4, 1957, Tampa, FL; [p.] Geraldine Boyetti; [m.] Carl Rappe, Jan 19, 1979; [ed.] Washington - Holmes Area Vocational Technical Center Chipley, FL. 32428, Concord Career Institute Tampa, FL 33609

RASCHE, BETH A.
[pen.] Shadow; [b.] July 8, 1977, Jasper, IN; [ed.] Jasper High School; [occ.] House Keeping at Holiday Inn in Jasper.; [oth. writ.] Some other poems published by the National Library of Poetry.; [pers.] I've been writing poems for 6 years, and I've never had any trouble finding a subject to write about. Look around, there's a poem in everything.; [a.] Jasper, IN

RASCON, DENISE
[b.] October 18, 1982, Fresno, CA; [p.] Mike and Mary Rascon; [ed.] (Mendota C.A.) Washington Kinder-grade 3 Elem. - (Kerman C.A.) Sun Empire Grade 3-6 Elem. - (Kerman C.A.) Kerman Middle School. Currently Grade 7.; [occ.] Full Time Student; [hon.] Honor roll, reading, writing, perfect attendance, westside cotton festival of oral interpretation, D.A.R.E., Physical fitness and Principals list. Straight "A" Student.; [oth. writ.] Various Poems Short Stories.; [pers.] I write my poems from my heart. I don't just put words down on a piece of paper. I write my poems based on what I feel and see. I am very thankful that God gave me this gift.; [a.] Kerman, CA

RASHEED, TAMARA
[b.] July 16, 1979, Detroit, MI; [p.] Bakkah Rasheed, Muhammad Rasheed; [ed.] Wayne County Community College; [occ.] Student; [memb.] United Nations Club, President Zora Neale Hurston Society WC3 Eastern Chapter; [hon.] Certificate of Merit, Certificate of Special recognition Zora Neale Hurston Society; [oth. writ.] Several poems published by the Main Detroit Public Library, also a poem and a story published in the Zora Neale Hurston Magazine. I have also written 34 short fiction stories.; [pers.] Mostly poems about feelings and thoughts that I have about myself and other people. I also write short fictitious stories.; [a.] Detroit, MI

RASMUSSEN II, ELMER A.
[pen.] Bud; [b.] February, 13, 1922, Racine, WI; [p.] Elmer A. Rasmussen, I and Gwendolyn L. Newman; [ch.] (7) children, (12) grandchildren and (6) great grandchildren.; [ed.] BSME, Marquette University and MBA, University of Wisconsin; [occ.] Retired Mechanical Engineer and Entrepreneur.; [memb.] American Legion Post #303, A.A.A.S., A.S.T.M.E., A.M.E., N.A.P.E., U.S.P.S., S.A.E., and N.R.A.; [hon.] Phi Beta Kappa, golden poet award 1989 and 1991, silver poet award 1988 and 1990, elected to hall of fame for living poets 1992, San Diego honor blood donor (38 gals); [oth. writ.] Currently in progress, three books of my own poetry and a novel and a separate manuscript of philosophy on communication of nature and humane beings.; [pers.] My inspirations come from my mermaid named holly. "Material things will never satisfy: Love, life or happiness. But, togetherness will. Bud; [a.] Santee, CA

RAVENSDALE, ANDREA
[b.] July 18, 1978, Guelph, Ontario, Canada; [p.] Jaqueline and Bruce Ravensdale; [ed.] Guelph Collegiate Vocational Institute; [occ.] Student-presently at the grade 11 level; [memb.] Y.M.C.A, Chicopee Ski club, Guelph figures skating club.; [hon.] Valedictorian, 3 public speaking speech finalist titles, 16 figure skating, medals, 11 baseball trophy's, honor roll 1993 chosen for young writer's conference 1989.; [oth. writ.] 2 poems published in local newsletters. Prize winning speeches.; [pers.] I try to reflect my personal feelings down on paper. I enjoy writing my deepest and innermost thoughts, it relieves a lot of tension and unhappiness; [a.] Guelph Ontario, Canada

RAYMOND, MELISSA
[b.] November 3, 1971, Staten Island, NY; [p.]

Rosemarie and Gerard Raymond; [m.] Joseph P. Meduri, May 23, 1996; [occ.] Still looking for my calling.; [oth. writ.] "Two paths of faith." I have books and books, this is my first time allowing anyone to read or judge my poetry. I hope you have found it to be a fun and inspiring reading; [pers.] The only way to be true happy is to embrace yourself, to except all your faults. Realize your a piece of art because there's only one of you on this massive planet. Your an original!; [a.] Staten Island, NY

REAL, ALFRED P.
[pen.] Klark-Karuston; [b.] December 6, 1960, Bridgeport, CT; [p.] Alfred Roje Kea; [ed.] 8 years Stoney Black Elementary school, 4 years Stratford High School; Stratford, CT.; [occ.] Chef; [memb.] U.S. Chess - writer's institutes.; [hon.] Music Award.; [oth. writ.] Have written poetry for poetry press in many anthologies.; [pers.] My life has been a failure. Filled with hope for a better time of my life.

REALBUTO, GRACE
[b.] October 12, 1953, New York; [p.] Grace and John Finnegan; [m.] James, September 5, 1976; [ch.] James and Lisa Realbuto; [ed.] Our Lady of Grace Elementary Aquinas High School; [occ.] Child Care Provider; [pers.] I would like to dedicate this poem to Eleanor, my other mom, who inspired me greatly. Also, special thanks to my family, for the warm, loving emotions I strive to reflect.; [a.] Mahopac, NY

REAMS, BRENDA SUE
[b.] April 30, 1949, Hazard, KY; [p.] Nancy and Marion Combs; [m.] February 19, 1972; [ch.] Nancy, Jamie and Eve; [ed.] 12th grade at Louisville Male High School, Louisville, KY; [occ.] Claims examiner for Pittman and Assocs.; [oth. writ.] Poems and articles not yet published; [pers.] I like to write articles and poems that are true and from the heart. My family are my main character.; [a.] Madison, TN

REARDON, SHARON O.
[b.] April 23, 1938, Waterbury, CT; [p.] Alice and Benjamin Ozaruff; [m.] Kevin Reardon - deceased; [ed.] B.S. Syracuse University M.A. Central Conn. State University; [occ.] Reading Consultant/Teacher Hartford, CT; [oth. writ.] Over 105 unpublished poems or grief and the recovery from grief.; [pers.] Writing poetry has been one of the key coping mechanisms I used after the death of my husband; [a.] Andover, CT

REAU, ROSAMOND O.
[b.] Toledo, OH; [p.] Gertrude and Thos E. Erim; [m.] Deceased; [ch.] Phyllis, Robert; [ed.] High School, Adult Ed. in Oil Painting, Sagre Aca. In Posmetology and cosmetologist 25 yrs.; [occ.] Retired; [hon.] "The Power of Creativity Poetry Contest" 1st place, miscellaneous Mary Whitlock Meadows, Trustee; [oth. writ.] It's been my pleasure to capture meaningful moments on canvas, but when oils are not fluid enough, too static, words fill the expression better!; [pers.] My High School Eng. Teacher said long ago, "Don't ever stop writing your poetry." Poems have presented them selves, needing to be put down as Sunday School skits, anniversaries, nature - life - enfolded.; [a.] Churchville, VA

REAVER, DANIEL
[b.] February 27, 1947, Columbus, OH; [p.] R.R. Reaver and Marcella Reaver; [m.] Linda Reaver, August 14, 1981; [ch.] 4; [ed.] Bishop watterson High School, St. Charles Borromeo College, Ohio State University; [occ.] Training Specialist; [memb.] Third Order of St. Dominic, National Society of Training and Development, Ohio and Columbus Right to Life; [oth. writ.] Although I've written poetry for over thirty years, this is the first time that I've submitted a poem for publication.; [pers.] I believe that the arts should aid us in the contemplation of truth. They should reflect the beauty found in nature and in people. They should help us to love God more.; [a.] Columbus, OH

REDDEN, PATRICIA L.
[pen.] Tish Redden; [b.] October 10, 1947, Lynn, MA; [p.] Donald K., Sabina A. Redden; [m.] Divorced; [ed.] Robert, Michael Webber; [occ.] T.R. Robinson High, Marian Court College, Kennesaw State College; [memb.] Administrative Assistant Kimberly-Clark Corporation Roswell, GA, Marian Court College Alumnae Association, Georgia Jaycee Congress; [hon.] Georgia Jaycee Congresswoman #126, Outstanding Young Woman in America; [oth. writ.] Today's Woman Essay sponsored by Georgia Jaycees, Write-up essay sponsored by Region Four Jaycees,; [a.] Roswell, GA

REED, EDITH
[b.] May 28, 1918, Portland, OR; [m.] Erling Reed, June 7, 1941; [ch.] Janice, Fredric and Richard; [ed.] Graduate of West Seattle High School; [occ.] Retired Real Estate Broker; [memb.] Write on Calligraphers; [oth. writ.] Being assembled for a collection.; [pers.] My objective is to bring a message is to bring a message, a tribute or an entertaining scenario in verse,; [a.] Seattle, WA

REED, HELEN
[pen.] Minnie Harvey; [b.] February 29, 1932, Saint Louis, MO; [p.] Minnie L. Jarmon, Stephanie Jarmon; [m.] James Reed, April 24, 1948; [ch.] Patricia A. Jones; [ed.] Vashon High, MVAS Watts Trade school, Ambassador College Waterson College; [occ.] Clerical-Retired; [memb.] Salesian Mission, Rescue mission, Northshore animal league, handicapped artist, disable veterans, cancer foundation.; [hon.] Certificates, watts, faith ambassador College, Waterson College, MVAS, Creative writings award.; [oth. writ.] Unpublished welcome address, shiloatt M.B. church.; [pers.] Youth when everything is young only rose colored glasses when you are grown.; [a.] Los Angeles, CA

REESE, NINA
[b.] Pampa, TX; [p.] Ruth Spearman and the Late John R. Spearman; [m.] Jay Rodney Reese; [ch.] Jay Reese Jr., Sharon Reese; [ed.] B.S. in Education Texas Tech. University graduate school - SMU; [occ.] Artist, decorator, writer; [memb.] Tri delta alumnae, mortar board alumnae, Dallas Museum Associates, Dallas Museum League, the shakespeare study club les femme dumonde committee; [hon.] Who's Who in American Colleges University, Who's Who on tech campus, outstanding woman student, all college recognition, the Nina Reese counseling center in Fortworth named in my honor.; [pers.] I seek truth honor and beauty in all things; [a.] Dallas, TX

REICH, LISELOTTE
[b.] January 12, 1920, Flensburg, Germany; [ch.] Son and daughter; [ed.] Public School and trade school in Germany I learned to become sales-lady, but still an apprentice, I was promoted to be also buyer for my department.; [occ.] Retired; [hon.] 1 award of price for poem about McIntosh apples (here) (while living in Canada) 1 award of price fr. German chocolate makers "Sarotti"; [oth. writ.] 1 Christmas Story and many christmas poems published in local newspapers (Lethbridge) have in my possession 1 book of poetry, several christmas. Poems for children (stories), and several fairy tales, all in poetry; [pers.] Always philosophical, I have loved poetry since early childhood and was proud of praises I've received about my own writings. I was published being 10 of age in my hometown newspapers. My love for the works of the great poets made me realize the value of the spoken word, the beauty of classic art.; [a.] Lethbridge Alberta, Canada

REID, BETTY J.
[b.] July 4, 1965, Cumberland, MD; [p.] Gene and Shirley Trenum; [m.] John R. Reid, August 3, 1985; [ch.] John Robert Reid; [ed.] Valley High School, Lonaconing, MD.; [occ.] Homemaker; [hon.] National Honor Society; [oth. writ.] Currently working on a collection of stories for children; [pers.] I love reading others thoughts as much as I love writing my own. Most people seem to "Hear" what they read, better, then they "hear" what you speak.; [a.] Ellicott City, MD

REID, JIM
[b.] December 4, 1921, Paisley, Scotland; [ed.] Graduate, Glascow University; [occ.] Retired, Head of English Newtonbook High school, North York, ON; [a.] Vineland, ON

REID, ROSEMARIE OLSON
[b.] July 5, 1937, Brooklyn, NY; [ch.] Jennifer, Jacqueline, Jeff; [ed.] St. Edmunds High School, Bklyn. NY; [occ.] Housewife; [memb.] To tell the truth (speaking out against sexual child abuse) I read 2 of my poems on October 1, 1994 at Florida's Speak out. This organization is now in 22 states; [hon.] It was an honor for me to speak before a large audience to recite my own poetry to over 400 people.; [oth. writ.] Other poems, but no others published yet.; [pers.] I am an incest survivor, and through my poetry and, perhaps book, would very much like to help stamp out childhood sexual abuse.; [a.] North Palm Beach, FL

RENDON JR., REGULO
[pen.] Reggie A.K.A Tint; [b.] August 23, 1959, Robstown, TX; [p.] Regulo SR and Eva Marquez; [ch.] 1 Child (Priscilla Rae Rendon); [ed.] High School, very little College, but every saturday I spent time on the Library. Very self educated.; [occ.] A warehouseman at a Corpus Christ Refinery.; [memb.] Only military; [hon.] Only military; [oth. writ.] I am now writing a fiction book its about pre-colombian America, I have written hundreds of poems; [pers.] Be adviced that I had never send any poems, besides to the library of poetry, I write hundreds of them lately I wrote two that I really like, but my writings are of everyday and past life.; [a.] Robstown, TX

RENIER, PAUL B.
[b.] April 13, 1936, Louisville, OH; [p.] Basil and Dorothy Renier; [m.] Mary D., July 18, 1970; [ch.] Elizabeth, Monica, and Geoffrey; [ed.] St Louis School, Louisville, Ohio Central Catholic High School, Canton, Ohio Athenaeum Univ. Youngstown, Ohio B.S. in ED. Xavier Univ. Cincinnati, Ohio M. Ed.; [occ.] I am presently a teacher of English at GlenOak High School in Canton, OH.; [memb.] Ohio Education Association National Education Association National Council of Teachers of English Knights of Columbus St. Barbara Church; [hon.] Knight of the Year Award for the year 1993. Puis X Award froam the Diocese of Youngstown 25 year Catechistical Ministry Award from the Diocese of Young-

stown in 1987.; [pers.] I am committed to staying as close to nature as possible. Almost all the food we eat is produced, grown, and prepared on our three acre city farm. I raise turkeys, chickens, ducks pheasants, rabbits as well as tend a large garden, a one hundred and ten tree orchard and a grove of 90 christmas trees.; [a.] Massillon, OH

RESOR, VALERIE
[b.] March 31, 1979, Hawaii; [p.] Howard, Faye Resor; [ed.] Sophomore at Caddo Hills High School; [memb.] Sr. Beta Club - reporter, S.A.D.D.; [hon.] Straight "A"s - two years. Top GPA-Art, Music, English III.; [pers.] Thanks to: Family, friends, Mrs. Barnes, and God - for giving me my life. Let God be your guide.; [a.] Norman, AR

RETTINGER, ALICIA
[pen.] Alicia or Alice or Ali; [b.] January 13, 1953, Mayaguez, PR; [p.] Alicia Aponte Gonzalez, Plinio Gonzalez; [m.] Eugene Rettinger, July 23, 1973; [ed.] Saint Gabriel High School; [oth. writ.] Sunny Days of you love of life and always loved.; [pers.] Brevity has nothing to do with courage, because brevity is truly an inspiration.; [a.] Bronx, NY

REYES, ELAINE RUTH S.
[pen.] Elaine Reyes; [b.] July 22, 1978; [p.] Proceso V. Reyes, Ruth S. Reyes; [ed.] University of Santo Tomas Pay High School (4th year HS); [pers.] I just love writings! I express what is inside my heart what ideas I have in mind.; [a.] Caloocan City, Philippines

REYNOLDS, CHRIS
[pen.] Yulian; [b.] November 8, 1978, Redwood City; [p.] Gene Reynolds, Susan Manning; [ed.] South San Francisco High School; [occ.] Student; [memb.] S.S.F.H.S. Drama Department; [oth. writ.] I publish an underground fanzine entitled Damn Purk and a book (if it can be called that) of my poetry entitled distorted Polaroids of bleeding tears. Neither of which are mass produced.; [pers.] I am influenced by the world around me and the words of Jim Morrison, Kort Cobin, and Trent Reznor. I'd like to thank my parents, Joseph Martinez, and Heather McQueen for their help and support.; [a.] South San Francisco, CA

REYNOLDS, CLARA
[ch.] Vincent and Lisa; [ed.] Franklin Klane High Sarah Brown Collegiate; [occ.] Asst. Court Analyst; [hon.] Court employees' art and crafts show; [pers.] My philosophy in life is to share my talent, and thereby help others along the way, without looking for rewards; [a.] New York, NY

REYNOLDS, PATRICIA L.
[pen.] Eloucia Rey-Lee; [b.] July 7, 1940, Santa Monica, CA; [p.] Amy Ruth King, Gerald E. Reynolds; [m.] Steven M. Lee, April 30, 1970; [ch.] Ronald Wayne Hanson; [ed.] A.A. B.A. masters, doctorate, ministerial MSCD., Metaphysics special Ed, Advanced Theosophy Astrology Numerology Cmp. Religion; [occ.] Research Hypnotherapist Healing and creative art consultant; [memb.] MAFA, MDMNH (Colo) A.A.U.M., (LA) Sierra Club (AM), AAR and R (Colo) founder "Jehn Zahr"; [hon.] A few; [oth. writ.] Essays documentaries research papers biographies poetry chronicles (newspapers etc.) charters, court data and arbitration, short stories and lyric philosophy.; [pers.] All the degrees, citations, licence, honors, trophies or awards collected to prove or privilege an ego are simply "dust-catchers" without integrity proved by performance ...which requires no degree!; [a.] Black Hawk, CO

RHODES, DARLENE DEARING
[b.] March 22, 1956, Chicago; [p.] Mr. Andrew Dearing, Mrs. Freddie Jean Daniels Dearing; [m.] Douglas Rhodes; [ch.] St. Lorenzo 7, Prince-Jerold and Prince-Jerell 4; [ed.] Birney Elem, Chicago's Westside graduate of Kewanee High School Kewanee IL; [occ.] Singer, writer, actress dancer and activist, song in many churches and clubs, written many articles but have never been paid had two leading roles in plays tambourines to Glory Langston Hughes and Sty of the blind pig, Phillip Dean Hayes, Won a Barney award for best supporting actress comedy-drama 1994 in Lansing MI at the Riverwalk Theatre have never been paid; [memb.] [hon.] L.S.C.O. Chairwoman at Belleveu Elem School in Detroit, I'm on state Welfare trying to find a place in America to get paid to do my best to help my country move forward, February 26, 1995, sang for United Black Artist USA Inc. in celebration of Black History Month here in Detroit MI, My son is an honor student at Bellewe; [pers.] I love children and teaching them to be whatever they were meant to be. I admire anyone in a teaching position that loves to do it and has truly committed their lives to our Future to make it better since we will all be in it together.

RHODES, GARY
[b.] March 8, 1943, Liberty, ME; [p.] Donald and Zelma Rhodes; [m.] Hrachik, October 8, 1964; [ch.] Wendy; [ed.] High School and Junior College; [occ.] Real estate loan agent; [hon.] A wife of 30 years; [oth. writ.] I have written many, many lyrics (songs) non yet published title such as "I've got you for Christmas" "You may not be everything" "I never caught your name" Etc...; [pers.] I write based on events I've seen, heard, or may wish to see. My country up bringing in Maine, the two room shack, the old yellow school house probably plays the major force in my writing. What I do know is that I write from the heart with feelings.; [a.] Thousand Oaks, CA

RHODES, WANDA
[b.] October 14, 1961, Washington, DC; [p.] William and Hattie Rhodes; [m.] Charles Martin Moody, June 1992; [ed.] BA Degree in Justice and Public Policy I am presently filling out applications for Law School.; [occ.] Administrative Secretary; [memb.] GAL - Guardian Ad-Litem Program Court Appointed Advocated to look out for the Welfare of Neglected and Abused Children.; [hon.] Its an Award just to be living.; [oth. writ.] I have been writing Poetry every since I was 15. A good friend of mine John W. Little convinced me to start seeing if I can get some published. Some of my works are I hear an Angel Calling for me, the day you die, Moma and me and lots more.; [pers.] I really didn't know I would be selected. Its a honor just for that. I want to give my thanks to John W. Little and God for helping me to write for so many years. I have over a hundred and some poems and it will be a honor to see them all ge published some day.; [a.] Durham, NC

RIAZ, KIRAN
[pen.] Kiran Riaz; [b.] August 8, 1981, Dera Ghazi Khan; [p.] Riaz Hussain/Nasreen Riaz; [ed.] Doing O, levels.; [occ.] Student; [pers.] I owe to my parents for encouraging me to write poetry. I have been very much influenced by John Keats and William Wordsworth.; [a.] Lahore, Pakistan

RICHARD, BRAD
[b.] August 19, 1956, Manhattan, KS; [p.] Juanita (Red) and Carlyn Johanningmeier; [ed.] M.F.L. High School, Monona Iowa; [occ.] Farmer - Truck Driver; [oth. writ.] This must be the end, is it too soon, ex memory and many others.; [pers.] Most of my works are my feelings relating to my painful separation and divorce. I'm currently trying to write country songs.; [a.] Luana, IA

RICHARDS, ELSBETH E. G.
[b.] Germany; [p.] Joachim Wohlfeil, Elsbeth A. Wohlfeil; [m.] John Richards; [ch.] Claudia Elsbeth; [ed.] Luneburg Leceum, Alqonquin and CEGEP College, Special Technician for Retardation; [occ.] Track and field Coach, Co-Ordinator Rhythmic Gymnastics' Special Olympics, Ontario; [memb.] Canadian Cancer Society, Eardley UCW, Federation of Gymnastics; [hon.] College Honor List, Coach of the Year, Minister of Canadian Heritage (Award of Merit); [oth. writ.] Articles for The Informer (Aylmer), Newswest (Ottawa); [pers.] I do not believe in the word handicapped, only in handicapable; [a.] Luskville, PQ

RICHARDS, JENNIFER E.
[b.] June 10, 1972, Kalamazoo, MI; [ed.] BS Secondary Education and English, from Ball State University; [pers.] Take from my poetry what it gives to you.; [a.] Indianapolis, IN

RICHARDSON, CHEBEY
[b.] April 16, 1980, Seattle, WA; [p.] Elizabeth Richardson, Frank Richardson; [ed.] Still in School nineth grade Junion high; [oth. writ.] Not published; [a.] Federal Way, WA

RICHARDSON, DONALD R.
[pen.] Donald R. Richardson; [b.] December 4, 1940, Dallas, TX; [p.] Maxine Tapscott, John Richardson; [m.] Divorced; [ch.] Donald R. Richardson II, Alesandro Richardson; [ed.] Phyllis Wheatly Sr. High, Texas Southern University, Preparing to take state licensure test for LCDC (Licensed Chemical Dependency Counselor); [occ.] Harris County Hospital District, Case Manager, Health Care for the Homeless Program.; [memb.] Board of Directors, Texas homeless network, Community based coalition, task Force, Texas education agency, Phi Beta Lambda.; [hon.] Chairperson, Mass Choir, first Shiloh baptist trustee, Youth/College Sunday teacher, other plaques and certificates for service to community, schools and churches.; [oth. writ.] The Tarzan Syndrome, old folks, Who Dat?, Young Folks, Where you at?, King, Times were... Changes, The Reversal Post, Black Folk, Then and Know.; [pers.] Lack of spirituality, greed and apathy is destroying us. We are running backwards. Lack of discipline in the home, the foundation of society and disregard for education, is at the root of our problems. Everything is either Democrat or Republican , black or white, we ignore history, Biblical and man, or The Rise and Fall of the Roman Empire.; [a.] Houston, TX

RICHMOND, BOBBIE JO
[pen.] Mari Jane Hunnington; [b.] September 22, 1980, Rapid City, SD; [p.] Vicki Tietgen and Robert Richmond; [ed.] I'm currently in 8th grade and I am an honor roll student.; [occ.] Student; [memb.] United Chung Do Kwan: Tae Kwon Do (Brown Belt); [hon.] I've been awarded with the Noon Optimist Award and the Dakota Nugget Award.; [oth. writ.] I've written many other poems but this was my first.; [pers.] My philosophy is "It doesn't matter where you come from but where you're going is very important."; [a.] Lake Havas City, AZ

RIDGEWAY, JOYCE FRANK
[pen.] Joy Eve Frankenridge; [b.] August 21, 1954, New Orleans, LA; [p.] Edward Frank, Joyce W. Frank (dec.); [m.] Leroy Ridgeway, November 09, 1976; [ch.] Edward Everidge, Eshiqita Everidge, (twins) Leiquisha Ridgeway; [ed.] John McDonogh Sr. High, Univ. of New Orleans, Greater, St. Stephen Full Gospel Baptist College and Theological Seminary; [occ.] Outreach Worker, Healthy Start- N.O., Minister (Licensed); [memb.] Gethsemane Prison Ministry, Charity Hospital Volunteer Chaplain, Women of Excellence (N.O. Chapter); [hon.] English Excellence Award, 1965 Quality Assurance Award of Excellence (for perfect record keeping), Volunteer of the year Mc of La. (Medical Center of LA); [oth. writ.] The rose of prose, (inspirational poetry) Articles for W.O.E. update, entering the spirit realm, and wisdom's cry.; [pers.] "Wisdom is the principle thing but in all thy getting, get understanding." The revenues of peace are better than silver and gold." Proverbs (KJV) Jesus is Lord of all.; [a.] New Orleans, LA

RIEDEL, DAVID A.
[pen.] David A. Riedel; [b.] October 31, 1929, Milwaukee, WI; [p.] Diseased; [m.] Dorothy, May 30, 1953; [ch.] David, Dorothy, Barbara, James, John and Russell; [occ.] Retired and Love it Travel, Travel.; [hon.] Military medals; [pers.] I believe in love and peace and if Government would work together maybe we would have any move work.; [a.] Milwaukee, WI

RIERSON, MEGAN
[b.] August 24, 1977, Owosso, MI; [p.] Ed and Debbie Rierson; [ed.] High School Senior, class of 1995. Plan on attending Central Michigan University for Education major.; [hon.] Various awards in band (as percussionist - 6 years) also awards in dance (jazz and modern ballet as well as pom-pon squad); [oth. writ.] Many short stories and poems unpublished, yet.; [pers.] I'd like to say thank you to Mrs. Johnson for all of her encouragement and the chance to do this.; [a.] Corunna, MI

RITCHEY, BETTY
[pen.] Betty J. Ritchey; [b.] September 15, 1938, Lubbock, TX; [p.] Juanita Fondy, Joe Fondy (deceased); [m.] Terry, November 3, 1984; [ch.] Lawauna Bullard, Donna Winslett, William Buford III, Alan Brown (previous marriages); [ed.] Slaton High School, Pan American University, Schriener College, San Antonio College, Valley Baptist School of Nursing-Diploma and Texas certification in 1976; [occ.] Retired licensed vocational nurse; [memb.] Alamo City Baptist Church, World Book Educational Products, Concerned Women for America, National right to life committee, AARP; [oth. writ.] I have just submitted a book entitled "Dare to be different" (non-fiction) for publication. I have also submitted two short children's in a contest with half-price books, if I am one of the winners, a book will be published from 17 finalists and 3 grand prize winners to help benefit literacy groups around the country.; [pers.] I have been influenced by many exceptional poets and writers during the romantic, victorian, 19th and 20th century. My own writing's tend to focus on the human compassion and suffering of mankind, as well our dedicated service to mankind. I feel that human suffering that endureth only makes us love even more.; [a.] Somerset, TX

RIVERA, DINA
[pen.] Lyzanna Paxton; [b.] January 29, 1979, Manhattan, NY; [p.] Joe and Miriam Rivera; [ed.] Tampa Bay Tech High School; [occ.] Student; [memb.] American Red Cross, National Vet Association, "Titan Thunder" - TBT School Newspaper; [hon.] Academic Excellence in Language Arts - Webb Jr. High - 1993; [oth. writ.] Where Devils Roam - not published; [pers.] With the love and support of my family and friends, I strive to make a difference in the world and make it a better place for my children and their children after them.; [a.] Tampa, FL

RIVERA, MADELYN
[b.] April 11, 1978; [p.] Carmen Rivera and Nelson Rivera; [ed.] Grace Dodge V.H.S; [pers.] I hope to accomplish the best for my future by expressing myself through poetry. I have my parents to thank for encouraging to do what makes me happy and proud.; [a.] Bronx, NY

RIVERO, RENE DAVID
[b.] July 1, 1978, Hanvana, Cuba; [p.] Alina and Rene Rivero; [ed.] I am only a Junior in Memorial High School; [occ.] Student; [oth. writ.] I have written several other plays, which have so far, gone unpublished.; [pers.] Writing is the only thing I can do best.; [a.] West New York, NJ

ROACH, SHONDEL
[b.] January 22, 1978, Guyana; [p.] Doris Smith; [ed.] Thomas Jefferson High School; [oth. writ.] A poem was published in the desert sun; [pers.] We should always remember who we are and where we come from and always thrive to make the most of life.; [a.] Brooklyn, NY

ROBBINS, LISA RENATA
[b.] September 18, 1967, NC; [p.] John, Cristina Robbins; [ed.] Community College 4 years Coronado H.S. Special Ed.; [occ.] Student; [memb.] Special Olympics YWCA Health Club church lector; [hon.] Silver Science Medal golden and silver, Special Olympic Medal bowling trophies; [oth. writ.] Newsletter poetry private poetry file composition on "Discrimination of the handicapped special occasion poetry"; [pers.] With higher standards of the handicapped become more athletic in their future dreams. My poetry writings include emotional bonds with friendship and unbroken family ties; [a.] El Paso, TX

ROBBINS, WILLIAM ALAN
[pen.] William A. Robbins; [b.] October 18, 1955, Killeen, TX; [p.] Fred House, Ann House; [ed.] Graduate Mesquite High School 1974; [occ.] Truck Driver; [oth. writ.] Nothing published I have quite a number of other poems written. Some lengthy poems including some Christmas poems. Also one or two written to be possibly country music songs.; [pers.] I try to put my feelings in my writings, and try doing to in such a way that it stirs the readers emotions as well I have been told some of my writings could be made into songs; [a.] Mesquite, TX

ROBERTS, JEANNE E.
[b.] November 4, 1927, Poplar Mont, US; [p.] Merle and Henry Callison; [m.] Garth Roberts, April 12, 1976; [ch.] Salli, Darrel, Ducane 4 step children, Doug, Sheila, Barry, Shelley; [ed.] Elementary School Teacher. U.B.C. U of V. U of Wn; [occ.] Retired; [hon.] B.C. Award for teaching Excellency.; [pers.] Life is what you make it. God is there to help us make decisions enjoy!!; [a.] Mission British Columbia, Canada

ROBERTS, JENI
[pen.] Jeni Roberts; [b.] April 8, 1973, Benton Harbor, MI; [ed.] Fox Senior High, Jefferson College Arnold, Missouri. Oklahoma Christian University Oklahoma.; [occ.] Permanent Student; [memb.] Thespians, Theatre, yearbook, student senate and youth Evangelical Team.; [hon.] Best Tech for costumes, head dresser in theatre. Member of International Thespian Society.; [oth. writ.] Articles in high school and college newspapers and yearbooks. Poems published in religions publications.; [pers.] I try to emphasize the simplicity and innocence of children in everything I do, and remember the kind words and encouragements of Krista, my mentor.

ROBERTSON, ANNE W.
[pen.] Anne W. Robertson; [b.] Scotland; [ch.] 2 Daughters Anne (Artist) Kathleen (Singer); [ed.] Grammar School; [occ.] Teacher of Effective speech and acting, private tuition; [memb.] ACTRA Verdun Operatic Socy Montreal; [hon.] Graduate of London College of music and London Academy of music and dramatic art, Gold Medal; [oth. writ.] As hostess of CBC Network program "Music on the Heather" wrote scripts prose and poetry for broadcasts also special T.V. and radio programs for CBC and C.T.V. T.V.; [pers.] I think poetry to be one of the highest forms of expression influenced by Shakespeare and the Scottish poet and humanitarian Robert Burns

ROBERTSON, NANCY TAYLOR
[b.] January 3, 1942, Holcomb, MO; [p.] Leslie and Emma Taylor; [m.] Divorced; [ch.] Leann, Marvin, Lesie, Robert and Benni-Carolyn.; [ed.] Jr. Coll. Richmond, VA.; [occ.] Owner and operator, Rainbow Inn Retirement home.; [hon.] Poems have been published in several newspapers.; [oth. writ.] I the summer of 95 my first book will be on the market titled (Heart and Mind); [pers.] While raising my children I often told them when they were grown I'd concentrate on my poetry. They are grown and I have!; [a.] Poplar Bluff, MO

ROBINSON, BILLIE JEAN
[b.] October 27, 1975, Canton, OH; [p.] William Robinson, Sharon Robinson; [ed.] Timken Senior High and First year of College; [occ.] Student cashier at Crystal Park Hardware; [memb.] Member of Central Babtist Church of Canton, OH; [hon.] National Honors Society, Canton Scholars, young authors, Who's Who among American High School Students; [pers.] You never know what you can do until you try. Thanks mom and dad!; [a.] Canton, OH

ROBINSON, JILL D.
[b.] October 13, 1976, Mannassas, VA; [m.] Single; [ed.] Saint Francis High School, University of California at Berkeley; [occ.] Full time student; [oth. writ.] I write when I can't breath.; [pers.] A poem should happen to you like/cold water or a kiss. Ntozake Shange; [a.] Cupertino, CA

ROBINSON, JODIE DWAYNE
[b.] September 27, 1954, Duncan, OK; [p.] Jodie and Letha M. Robinson; [m.] Cheryl Robinson, August 15, 1992; [ch.] Jamaal, Tarshish, Quanah, Treg; [ed.] Graduated Duncan High School attended Okla. State Tech and University of Albuquerque; [occ.] Assistant Director for an Information Technology Company; [pers.] A man lives with honor, when he is what he pretends to be.; [a.] Richardson, TX

ROBINSON, KELLY
[b.] September 28, 1980, Milwaukee, WI; [p.] John and Cynthia Robinson; [ed.] I am currently an 8th grade student at Garden Lakes Elementary School in Avondale,

AZ.; [memb.] National Junior Honor Society; [hon.] Student of the month several times, principal list, scholastic merit, science project, athletic awards; [oth. writ.] School published essays and production of magazines for a civics project, other poems (non-published); [pers.] I am mostly motivated by life and exposure to many personal experiences that help me to create the poetry and other writings. Although I'm not sure what my career destination will be, as I am only 14 years old, I like animal and human interests the most.; [a.] Avondale, AZ

ROBINSON, MARTHA E.
[pen.] Martha Petzold Robinson; [b.] March 17, 1923, Dresden, Germany; [p.] Willy Petzold, Elizabeth Petzold; [m.] Hubert F. Robinson, February 4, 1940; [ch.] Hubert Wm., Elizabeth, Kay and Justin; [ed.] LaPlata High School, Boyd School of Commerce, Seminars - Management, Business English, Famous Writers School, Institute of Children Writing; [occ.] Secretary - AAFB Credit Union (pt. time), Pres. DMR Robins, Inc. A home based Computerized Business Serv.; [memb.] Calvary United Methodist Church, Charles County Chamber of Commerce Better Business Bureau of Greater MD Foster Parent - 20 years with S. Services Society of Childrens Book Writers and Illustrators Other Voluntary work with handicapped children Organized Teen Hiking Club with American Teen Agers in Germany 51-53 sunday School Teacher, Union Methodist Church, Washington, DC - 1950-53.; [oth. writ.] Small Town Society Col. 1969-1970 - Md. Independent - "Waldorf Notes" Editor of BEAM, Company News Ltr. 65-67. Editor, John Hanson Briefs, Co. News ltr. 1979-85, also wrote articles. Story "Dusty" in Bits and Pieces Magazine 1979.; [pers.] It always gives me great pleasure to write poems/stories for and about little children because they are so honest and sincere in what they say and do.; [a.] Waldorf, MD

ROBINSON, SUSIE PEARL
[b.] July 15, 1934; [p.] Jack and Momie Lou Prosser; [ch.] 6; [ed.] 9th Grade; [occ.] Disability; [memb.] Baptist; [pers.] Yes I wrote the poem my self

ROBINSON, ULENA B.
[pen.] Blossom; [b.] August 20, 1952, Jacksonville, IL; [p.] Lee and Helen Baptist; [m.] David E. Robinson, August 17, 1978; [ch.] Dalena 14, Daniel 11, Douglas 7; [ed.] College Degree from Andrews University Berrien Spring, Michigan Major in Education and English minor; [occ.] Book Keeper and Housewife; [oth. writ.] Many poems while in the mission field (11 years in Taiwan) also short stories with lessons about life.; [pers.] Since God has given me life and the choice of life eternal, I desire to share his goodness with others.; [a.] Sutherlin, OR

ROBINSON, VICTORIA
[b.] July 8, 1970, Brooklyn NY; [p.] George and Bernice Robinson; [ed.] Currently a senior at Bowie State U. Graduate 1996, will receive B.S. Computer Sci. Attended High School - Franklin D. Roosevelt in Bensonhurst, Bklyn; [occ.] Clerk Typist/ Student National Institutes of Health - job; [memb.] ACM (American Computing Machinery) Club; [hon.] Miss Computer Science 91-92; [oth. writ.] Poem printed in "UJIMA" Title "VOID" UJIMA is a Black newsletter meaning collective work and responsibility; [pers.] I thank GOD for my mind, so I can share with others in kind; [a.] Upper Marlboro, MD

ROBINSON, WENDY L.
[pen.] W. Lee; [b.] August 9, 1961, Jonesport, ME; [p.] Philip and Frances Kilton; [ch.] Heath A. Urguhart; [ed.] High School Diploma Jonesport - Beals High; [occ.] Waitress; [memb.] National Arbor Day Foundation; [pers.] I write only what I feel. Poetry has been my great escape, ever since grade school. I am inspired to write usually at dawn.; [a.] Jonesport, ME

ROBLYER, JOHN SCOTT
[b.] September 23, 1959, Burlington, VT; [p.] Wallace L. and Barbara S.; [m.] Esther J. Roblyer, March 3, 1990; [ed.] G.E.D. Paralegal from Black Stone School of Law: 12-credits in community College Radio School of the Bible.; [occ.] Business man; [memb.] Bread for the world; [pers.] We have to all get along in life, so lets do it.; [a.] New York, PA

ROCCAPRIORE, CARLA MARIE
[b.] October 24, 1973, Jacksonville, FL; [p.] Robert A. and Nanette J. Roccapriore; [ed.] Mandrin High School (class of '91) I am currently attending Florida Atlantic University majoring in Education.; [occ.] Full-time student at Florida Atlantic University; [pers.] No matter who you are or where you come from, never let anybody tell you that you cannot be/do something. If you want to accomplish it or become it, believe in yourself and work toward it and more than likely, with time, you will achieve it. However, if you don't succeed, at least you will know that you did all you could to try and that is better than not trying at all. [a.] Boca Raton, FL

ROCKFORD, LEANN M.
[pen.] Leanne M. Rockford; [b.] February 18, 1978, Norwalk, OH; [p.] Alice N. James, Michael Rockford; [ed.] Indian Lake High School still attending; [occ.] Student at Indian Lake High School; [hon.] Art 1st prize 1993 comic strip, drawing in Lima; [oth. writ.] Life is a dream, battle lost, and several others; [pers.] Life is short live it well. Your worst enemy is yourself, you control your own future. Peace love and happiness; [a.] Lakeview, OH

RODEN, CATHY
[pen.] Catherine Roden; [b.] January 17, 1981, Birmingham, AL; [p.] Kenneth, Carol Roden; [ed.] I'm in the 8th grade and I attend Thompson Middle School; [memb.] National Junior, Student council and art club; [oth. writ.] Various other writings, such as books short stories, and poems.; [pers.] Poetry is like a passageway. It let's you enter your soul and put what you're feeling into words. One of the poets I admire is Edgar Alan Poe.; [a.] Alabaster, Al

RODRIGUES, ELIZABETH ANN
[pen.] Betty Ann, Liz; [b.] September 6, 1960, Honolulu, HI; [p.] (Dad deceased) (Mom-living, Darlyn K. Joanne); [ed.] Kapunahala Elem, King Inter., Castle High, Adult Educ.; [occ.] Used to work as a cook and pantry worker.; [pers.] I would like to thank God for giving me the opportunity and creative mind to wrote poetry, its a beginning for me. I would like to thank my mom for sticking up with me all this years. Also thanks to my sisters, brothers, Nephews and nieces. And also my very good friend Dorothy M. Brown. Love to all of you.; [a.] Aurora, CO

RODRIGUEZ, ESPERANZA F.
[b.] April 24, 1939, Milwank County; [p.] David and Felicitas Ralla; [m.] Alejandro Rodriguez, April 30, 1960; [ch.] Andres, Marta, Artemio, Catalina; [ed.] Lincoln High School; [occ.] Welder-Eaton Corp.; [pers.] My writings are inspired by loves and trials of my family.; [a.] Milwaukee, WI

ROEHRICK, ROSANNE
[pen.] Ann Marie; [b.] March 18, 1952, Minneapolis, MA; [p.] Nels, Irene Hoiland; [m.] James Roehrick, April 27, 1979; [ch.] Lucas James, Matthew Edwin; [occ.] Factory; [hon.] Girl Scouts, school science, A and B honor roll, school track.; [oth. writ.] Poems, song never published; [pers.] I like to write to express human emotion. Personal enjoyment.; [a.] Faribault, MN

ROHLF, JANET
[pen.] Janet Rohlf; [b.] March 15, 1950, Comanche, TX; [p.] The late Lester Burk and Nell Burk; [m.] Dennis Rohlf, May 25, 1974; [ch.] 1 Son - Shane Rohlf; [ed.] High School; [occ.] Independent beauty consultant for Mary Kay cosmetics; [hon.] In the early 1950's I auditioned and won a spot on a local television station for my recitation of "Somebody's Mother". Another local station heard me and asked my mother for permission to go on his show. I gave a recitation of viewers "In School days." By then the cards and letters were pouring into the first station to have me back again. I gave another recitation at the age of 4 years I began suffering severe migraine headaches. My mother decided the pressure of performing was causing my sickness. She ended my television career, but not my love of poetry.; [oth. writ.] I have a drawer full of poems and songs that I have never tried to get published. This one just touched my heart. I had to try for this one.; [pers.] I write about whatever I'm feeling at the time. It comes straight from my heart.; [a.] McQueeney, TX

ROHN, TONYA M.
[b.] September 27, 1976, Saginaw, MI; [p.] Bill, Deb Rohn; [ed.] I am a senior at Merrill High; [occ.] Student; [memb.] Future Homemakers of America, Yearbook, Student Council, School Improvement Team, Attendance target goal committee, and National honor Society.; [hon.] Principals Leadership Award, Honorable Mention All Conference - Softball, Honorable Mention All Area - Softball.; [pers.] I love sports and I plan to attend college to obtain in Accounting. [a.] Merrill, MI

ROHRICH, CHRISTA B.
[b.] December 7, 1939, Pforzheim, Germany; [p.] Walter Bechtle, Yene Bechtle; [m.] Robert R. Rohrich, July 23, 1977; [ed.] High School and Business school in Germany, further education at Mercy College and Pace University (NY) in computer science and finance.; [occ.] Artist; [oth. writ.] Unpublished "Life" was my first attempt of entering and to be published; [pers.] My other form of poetry is the artistry of "Pressed Flower Compositions" which have been exhibited in time arts and crafts shows and galleries. Most recently Dec. 94 solo exhibit at somers, NY Public Library (By Invitation); [a.] Putnam Valley, NY

ROLLINS, RITA
[b.] April 28, 1932, Montpelier, OH; [p.] Bill and Ella Lamont; [m.] Kenneth, May 11, 1962; [ch.] 3-Kyra Lynn, Brooks Walter, Brigelle; [ed.] Bryan High School, Bryan, OH; [occ.] Rehabilitation Technician; [memb.] First Luthern Church, American Heart Assoc. Loyal Order of Women of the moose; [hon.] Life Saving Award/CPR Hillsdale, MI.; [pers.] My poetry seems to evolve from the very deepest feelings that emerge particularly when I am at water's edge. Also love for my family motivates those deep feelings and the desire to share them.; [a.] Angola, IN

ROMEO, CYNTHIA
[pen.] Cindy Lou; [b.] April 7, 1956, Ilion, NY; [p.] Walter C. Burns, Lillie Pemberton; [m.] Louis A. Romeo, July 23, 1987; [ch.] Dominick Joseph Burns; [ed.] Ilion Central High, Herkimer County Community College, Reading Area Community College, Berks Technical Institute; [occ.] Certified Nursing Assistant; [memb.] Berks Technical Institute Student Council, Nursing Assistant Registry State of Pennslyvania; [hon.] Finished top 3 of my class at Berks Technical Institute; [oth. writ.] This way my first poem.; [pers.] My poem is a dedication to my sons involvement in baseball, and his love for the game and because he makes me feel like I am a part of it. Even though I only sit on the sidelines and just cheer himon.; [a.] Spring Hill, FL

ROMERO, FRANCISCO
[b.] Crystal City, TX; [ed.] B.A. Ca. St. Fullerton A.A. Yakima Valley Community College; [pers.] A poem from a collection of letters written for Diana. The heart of my words.

RONALDS, LEENA S.
[b.] March 17, 1969, Kuwait; [m.] Matthew Ronalds, August 8, 1993; [ed.] New English School (Kuwait) High School, American University of Cairo: 1985-88, Iowa State University: 1988-89 (B.A.); [occ.] English Teacher; [oth. writ.] Submitted poems to publishers in U.S.A., Canada and U.K. EG: "Herspectives magazine" (Canada) "first time poetry: National Hastings poetry competition" (U.K.). Poem "Curly and the dancing snowman" accepted for publication in New York.; [pers.] Writing poetry is not simply something you do: It's a way of life. My innermost sentiments and passions are moulded through the lines I write.; [a.] Bandar Seri Begawan, Brunei

ROSENBERGER, DARCY
[b.] May 15, 1956, Allentown, PA; [p.] Ernest and Nancy Neimeyer; [m.] William Rosenberger, May 7, 1977; [ch.] Kelly, Audrey and Raymond; [memb.] Grace Baptist Church Social director and staff member of "Grace Notes" newspaper for our church.; [oth. writ.] Several poems published in "Grace Notes" and often recited on "Grace for living" radio show.; [pers.] I not only enjoy writing poetry and songs but I enjoy reading other people's works as well. My ideas for my poems are all through Christ's inspiration in my life.; [a.] New Tripoli, PA

ROSS, ALICE E.
[pen.] Alice E. Ross; [b.] January 6, 1911, Council, ID; [p.] Thomas and Lucy Evans; [m.] Palmer H. Ross, December 3, 1929; [ch.] 3 Girls Linda, Betty, Mary 1 boy, Bruce; [ed.] Grade and High School at Parma, ID also studied piano and oil painting; [occ.] Retired housewife, poet and artist; [memb.] Wenatchee Nazarene church, my husband and I owned the little studio and gallery at Florence, OH. for 25 years. "The art-a-rie"; [hon.] In high school for essays, debates, sports, and oil paintings; [oth. writ.] Many poems (a book fall) other articles for a church magazine "the morning watch" and newspapers.; [pers.] My poems have all been put on paper when my Lord puts them in my mind and in my heart. Then I share as I feel "gifts" should shared! I have kept 30 poems and many other writings.; [a.] Wenatcher, WA

ROUKI, MAGGIE MARGARITA
[b.] May 8, 1068, Athens; [p.] Dimitris Roukis, Helen Riga-Dalla; [ed.] Sorbonne II in French, Cambridge Proficency in English, and a degree in English Literature (University of Athens).; [occ.] English teacher, and keyboard player of "Imago Dei"; [oth. writ.] Unpublished poems and songs. Some of my lyrics are to appear in two LP's in Greece by 1996.; [pers.] One's personal philosophy is a means to divert one-self when one's got the blues. Anything you do with love is an art. All arts are in the eyes of the beholder.; [a.] Loutraki, Greece

ROUSSETZKI, IVAN
[b.] June 10, 1956, Sofia, Bulgaria; [p.] Borislac Roussetzki and Ivanka Roussetzki; [m.] Ivanka Roussetzki, May 13, 1984; [ch.] Borislava Roussetzki, Pavel Roussetzki; [ed.] Sofia Government University, Philology; [occ.] Freelance writer; [oth. writ.] Many poems and short stories published in major magazines and newspapers in Bulgaria.; [pers.] The poetry is a mirror and window at the same time. Some poets see only themselves in its mirror. Others see the whole world through its open window. I prefer to be like the last ones; [a.] Brooklyn New York, NY

ROYER, BRANDI
[b.] September 15, 1975, Perris, CA; [p.] Sharon Doster, Manuel Rollins; [ed.] Perris Lake High School and Riverside City College; [occ.] Student; [memb.] Perris Community Theatre Guild; [oth. writ.] Several other poems not yet submitted to anyone.; [pers.] I found this poem deep in my soul, when the world lost A.I.D.S. actirist Pedro Zamora. He made me believe, we must never stop fighting for his dream.; [a.] Perris, CA

RUBIN, LARRY BRUCE
[b.] April 5, 1958, Chicago, IL; [p.] Helen and Phillip Rubin; [ed.] B.A., Roosevelt University Journalism; [occ.] Freelance-investigate-reporter; [memb.] "Pi Delta Epsilon," Journalism Fraternity; [hon.] In "Who's Who" books-8 times!; [oth. writ.] I wrote a book called: "The Silence of Success." I had written "numerous" poems.; [pers.] "People of all "types" must "break" the "silence" of "hatred," and "understand" each other's "needs," "desires," and "secrets."; [a.] Chicago, IL

RUBLETZ, CRAIG
[b.] July 10, 1969, Canora; [p.] Gerald and Iris Rubletz; [m.] Carrielyn Rubletz, July 9, 1988; [ch.] Alexander Rubletz; [ed.] Stargis Composite High, SIAST; [occ.] Farmer, Mechanic; [memb.] North American Hunting Association; [oth. writ.] Several poems; [pers.] I got my inspiration for writing this poem by being away from my wife and child for 5 months while I was commercial fishing on the Pacific Ocean.; [a.] Danbury Saskatchewan, Canada

RUDD, SUSAN DIANNE HALL
[b.] September 23, 1955, Columbus, CA; [p.] Quillian and Martha Sue Hall; [m.] Michael W. Rudd, Sr., August 26, 1978; [ch.] Jennifer, Michelle, Michael, Jr.; [ed.] Dougherty High School, Darton College Albany Tech Institute, Art Instruction School; [occ.] Executive Secretary, Corporate Information Mgt Office, Marine Corps Base, Albany, GA; [memb.] Byne Memorial Baptist Church and Choir and Mixed Ensemble Singers; [oth. writ.] Seasonal, holiday and commemorative poems which have been published in newsletters bulletins and church's 85th Anniversary and Historical Journal Song written: Mary's son.; [pers.] I pray that my poetry will touch hearts and lives for Christ and inspire people everywhere. Helen Steiner Rice's poems have inspired and influenced me greatly.; [a.] Albany, GA

RUDELBACH, JOSH
[b.] October 13, 1976, Santa Rosa, CA; [p.] Kurtis Rudelbach, Valerie Anderson; [ed.] Austin High School; [occ.] Clerk U.S. Forest Service, Austin, NV; [oth. writ.] Several poems published in statewide books.; [pers.] I hope my poetry can help heal tortured souls as I once was.; [a.] Austin, NV

RUEDA, MICHELLE
[b.] September 29, 1982, Queens, NY; [p.] Bertha Dippe Rueda, Jorge Rueda; [ed.] Kindergarten thru 5th grade P.S. 152 6th grade academy for the intellectually gifted. 7th grade, the brearley school, NY.; [occ.] 7th grade student at the brearley school in NY; [memb.] National honor society and junior arista, member of prep for prep (an organization to nurture a generation od leaders), choir member of the lady of fatima church, Queens, NY.; [hon.] Cum Laude excellence prep for prep, award for exceptional and extraordinary academic achievement, prep for prep.; [oth. writ.] Several poems and compositions published in the P.S. 152Q Newspaper, "The Courier", and in "Academia", the academy newspaper. Also, one of my last poems published in the brearley school literary magazine "The Beaver".; [pers.] The only thing that really inspires me to write something beautiful is a real life drama like the death of a person, and the most appropriate style to write this down is in a very profound piece of poetry.; [a.] East Elmhurst, NY

RUIZ, ROBERT
[pen.] Robert; [b.] December 23, 1949, Uvalde, TX; [p.] Steve and Esther Martinez; [ed.] Cradock H.S. Portsmouth, VA Univ Corpus Christi, TX; [occ.] Office Mer/ Paralegal; [a.] San Antonio, TX

RUIZ, SHELLEY LYNN
[pen.] Shelley Ruiz; [b.] August 27, 1997, Burnaby; [p.] Richard and Carol Ruiz; [hon.] Throughout Jr. High, I have been on the honor roll.; [oth. writ.] Published poems in year books; [pers.] With the encouragement from my father, I continue to strive to be the best I can. Even though I'm only 15 years old I believe improvements are on the way. Just let your imagination run wild; [a.] Surrey British Columbia, Canada

RUPP, SHERRY
[b.] November 3, 1949, Cherokee, IA; [p.] Garland Duvall, Pauline Duvall; [m.] Dennis Rupp, December 4, 1976; [ch.] Gary Paul; [ed.] Washington High School; [occ.] Housewife; [pers.] I have always had the yearning to write poetry. When I see someone or something that touches me inside, I would like to share this inspiration with others.; [a.] Quimby, IA

RUSSO-PITCHER, SANDRA
[pen.] Russo or Pitcher; [b.] September 20, 1962, Paterson, NJ; [p.] Jack and Joan Russo; [m.] Kevin Pitcher, June 30, 1985; [ch.] Alexis Corinne, Christianna Joy and Jaquelynn Rae; [ed.] Boonton High School County College of Morris Katharine Gibbs; [occ.] Administrative Assistant brotherhood of maintenance of way employees; [memb.] Grace Christian Fellowship weight watchers; [hon.] In High School I received a few awards for short stories that I wrote. Also, some of my poetry was printed in the school paper.; [oth. writ.] Over the years I have mostly written for enjoyment, as well as friends and family members. I wrote and recited a poem for other weight watcher members. (Poetry printed in school paper.); [pers.] Writing has always come naturally for me since the age of 13. It is the balance between my heart and mind. I especially enjoy writing for

others as a source of encouragement and to offer a different perspective. For me writing is a way to find the beauty in life and the lives of others.; [a.] Oxford, NJ

RYAN, DAVID P.
[b.] November 23, 1942, Port Arthur, TX; [p.] Sam and Geneva Provenzano; [m.] Suzanne, January 14, 1966; [ch.] Jennifer Katherine, Cullen David; [ed.] Lamar University, B.A. (Drama-English) 1965, University of Houston, J.D. 1972; [occ.] Attorney; [memb.] Various legal organizations and bar associations, Delta Theta Phi Law Fraternity, Alpha Psi Omega Drama Fraternity; [hon.] Theatre Patrons Award, Best Actor, Supporting Actor and Technical Theatre awards - Lamar University, Short Story Award - Lamar University, Various public education awards for legal representation of public entities.; [oth. writ.] Various poems and short stories in college literary publications.; [pers.] I try to live and love according to the lines I once wrote: "Great God! Let me feel, let me be true to all things and kneel to meet my rendezvous with you in time. But for now, let no love fall short to the rhyme of my heart and all its dizzy rhapsodies."

RYAN, KATIE
[pen.] Kathleen Ryan; [b.] April 16, 1985, Saint Louis, MO; [p.] Marian and Ronald; [m.] Single; [ed.] Mary, Queen of peace Catholic School; [occ.] Student, Mary Queen of peace, 3rd grade; [oth. writ.] Poems in newspapers and school newspaper; [a.] Saint Louis, MO

RYAN, LORI-AN
[pen.] Stage and Maden Van Winckle; [b.] September 24, 1962, Windsor, Ontario, Canada; [p.] William E. and Donna K. Van Winckle; [m.] Thomas Ryan, October 7, 1990; [ch.] Kathleen Marie Ryan, March 27, 1993; [ed.] Monarch SS Windsor, Ontario, Canada. Graduate June 29, 1980. Theatre of Arts six years one year Van Mar Ac. Motion picture and tel. act.; [occ.] Mommy, actress and singer, poet. I used to teach acting to children.; [memb.] Lake Manor Chapel Family Fitness.; [oth. writ.] Several poems published in the writers helper. Magazine by Lorraine Call. And stunt road newsletter.; [pers.] Let us share words and embrace in the wisdom, let your inner poet free itself, for all the world to see. Enclosed, release picture, actors resume, check, more poems. Thank you so much for publishing my work.; [a.] Costa Mesa, CA

SAAKE, BETTY JEAN
[pen.] Jean Saake; [b.] December 22, 1934, Pasadena, CA; [p.] Hazel and Laurance Largent; [m.] Carl Edward Saake, June 20, 1954; [ch.] Cheryl Ann And Patricia Lee; [ed.] Pasadena City College Wilson Jr. High, Pasadena; [occ.] Owner of Ceramic Business; [memb.] Daughters of American Revolution North Carolina Chapter; [hon.] Exhibited Ceramic work at the Hawaii Foundation for the Culture and the Arts. Exhibited college work at the Hawaii Public Library system continuing art exhibits.; [pers.] I have written poetry for myself since my marriage in 1954. The poems have been expressions of my feelings throughout these 40 years.; [a.] Asheville, NC

SADLER, PRISCILLA FRANCES
[b.] July 4, 1919, Swampscott, MS; [p.] J. Adams and Florence Ulman; [m.] Henry Allen Sadler Jr., November 21, 1937; [ch.] Three [ed.] 1-12 Swampscott High School, Swampscott Mass., Miss Pierce Secretarial School Boston, Mass.; [occ.] Housewife; [memb.] D.A.R. Mayflower Descendants, (National Society of) Old Plymouth Colony, Society of the Descendants of the Colonial Clergy. First Baptist Church of Lexington, Mass 02173.; [oth. writ.] I had a story of the "House Finch Nesting" in a local newspaper. (Arlington Advocate) Arlington, Massachusetts 02174; [pers.] I am very interested in things pertaining to nature. My poem is all true about our daily living, pattern. My (as a child) cousin and I held many funerals for `little birds that died'!; [a.] Lexington, MS

SAFFORD, MARTHA BLISS
[pen.] Bliss Safford; [b.] January 3, 1933, Cambridge, MA; [p.] Isabel Leighton Hall, Arthur C. Bliss; [m.] Nicholas H. Safford, April 10, 1965; [ch.] John Apthorp Safford, Jennie Anne Bliss Meyer; [ed.] Belmont High School, Cornell University B.A. Mills College Boston University M.A.; [occ.] Artist; [memb.] Rockport Art Association Kings Chapel, Boston; [oth. writ.] The Recchias Garden (poem) in "Poetry for Rockport 1995"; [pers.] I consider poems to be word paintings which can be carried around in the mind, enabling them to be remembered and shared more easily than most other art forms, as one would a song. Poetry encapsulates.; [a.] Rockport, MA

SAKOWSKI, ROBERT J.
[b.] July 8, 1942, Brooklyn, NY; [p.] Regina and Joseph; [ed.] AASBA Business Administration 4 yrs Electronics Training in U.S.N.; [occ.] Founder, Executive Director "Always Spring Foundation, Inc."; [memb.] Society of Logistics Engineers K of C, National Alliance to Rid Homelessness, People with AIDS Coalition, St. John the Evangelist Church Eucharistic Minister.; [hon.] Real Estate Executive Club, was asked to participate on the Federal Ryan Write Planning Council, published in The Marques Who's Who for accomplishments, former Art-Photographer Editor of "The Compass Suffoil Country" Community College.; [oth. writ.] Same not published; [pers.] "Just do it" and on a daily basis.; [a.] Manorville, NY

SALANGSANG, KERIMA LEE
[pen.] Lady Blue; [b.] January 18, 1954, Honolulu, HI; [p.] Matilda G. Wai, John Lee Wai; [ch.] Koreylene, Jaimie, Kimilee, Kerrilee; [ed.] Farrington High School; [occ.] Owner the Bodytalk Shop Consultant Personal Development Training Seminars; [memb.] PSI World Seminars, Women's Leadership Forum; [oth. writ.] Are done for Personal Development Training Workshops... Writings are done for individual affirmations and guidance.; [pers.] Your visions are real enough to pursue for they are the windows to your life's work. No one has the right to deny themselves this "precious present"; [a.] Honolulu, HI

SALAS, MARIA LAURA LANGE
[pen.] Jobey; [b.] February 24, 1981, Ecuador; [p.] Laura Lange, Joel A. Salas; [ed.] Franklin School Elementary in North Bergen; [occ.] Student; [a.] North Bergen, NY

SALAZAR, ANTHONY
[pen.] Tony; [b.] August 31, 1974, Bellflower, CA; [p.] Patricia Ward, and Edmund Salazar; [ed.] 2 years of automotive mechanical, graduation from valencia High School; [occ.] Ken-Mac metals Inc., warehouse man; [hon.] Southern Section champion, football, league champion.; [pers.] My first time writing a poem. I wrote it for my father with all my heart.; [a.] Fullerton, CA

SALISBURY, VERONICA
[b.] May 20, 1974, Amherst, OH; [p.] Robert and Mary Brown; [m.] Sammy Salisbury, February 8, 1994; [ch.] Sammy Lee Jr.; [ed.] Admiral King High School; [occ.] House wife - mother; [pers.] I am not an experienced writer, but I write what my heart tells me to, that is my advice to the world.; [a.] Lorain, OH

SALONGER, ALYSON
[pen.] Aly; [b.] June 21, 1986, White Plains, NY; [p.] Yvette Salonger, Mark Salonger; [ed.] George Washington Elementary School; [occ.] Student; [memb.] Soccer Traveling Team, School Chess Club, Girl Scouts-Browne, Ice Skating and Ballet.; [hon.] Awards: Read-A-Thon; [pers.] The world should be more peaceful and kids should not drink and drive. They should also not take drugs. I like to write fiction stories.; [a.] White Plains, NY

SALZIGER, ESTHER R.
[pen.] Cassi; [b.] September 15, 1968, Battle Creek, MI; [p.] Paul and Ruth Salziger; [ed.] Bladensberg High, Pierce College; [occ.] Assistant Plant Man. at Francosmetics Int'l.; [hon.] Several awards for art - this is my first poem ever to leave my journal.; [pers.] I would like to thank Errol Fiendel for inspiring me to write this poem, due to the broken heart he left me with.; [a.] Canoga Park, CA

SAMONS, NICOLE MASHEA
[b.] July 13, 1981, Pikeville, KY; [p.] Lowell Samons Jr., Evelyn Samons; [ed.] Prater Elementary; [memb.] The prestonsburg Church of Christ; [pers.] Keep on hoping and your dreams will come true. I am greatly influenced by my religious beliefs.; [a.] Banner, KY

SAMUELS, VINCENT
[pen.] Bill Simon; [b.] May 26, 1943, Jamaica, West Indies; [p.] Simeon And Margaret Samuels (Deceased); [m.] Caren Samuels, March 5, 1966; [ch.] Cecille, Karen, Michelle, Vincent Jr., Max; [ed.] Bronx Community College, Baruch College, The City University of New York; [occ.] Scholar, writer; [memb.] The Academy of American Poets, Thru-way Home Owners Association, Beersheba Old Students Association, Bronx Gospel Chapel; [hon.] Dean's List (5 times Bronx Community College), Phi Theta Kappa, Lambda Nu Chapter; [oth. writ.] Several poems published in Local Newspapers and Magazines including the literary magazine encounters published by Baruch College, The City University of New York.; [pers.] I am the voice of the homeless, the down trodden. As a philantropist, I strive to ventilate the views of these individuals and continue to make society aware of their plight.; [a.] Bronx, NY

SANCHEZ, ADRIANO A.
[b.] September 15, 1920, Sabana Grande, PR; [p.] Monserrate and Gabriel A.; [m.] Margarita A. Sanchez (deceased), October 28, 1945; [ch.] Esmeralda, Jose, Rosy-Liz-Ricky; [ed.] Graduate in P.R. at 8th grade the phillips secret service system "Pcl." Auto-Mechanic-vocational School in Puerto Rico Diplomas; [occ.] L.T.V. steel inspector steel mill "retired"; [memb.] Buckeye state-sheriffs' Association "Associate member" AARP Motoring Plan-Amoco-Motor Club, El Dorado Ranch-Estates Sacred heart church, Auxiliary yo-police department.; [hon.] 1988 Golden Poet-award world of poetry-award of merit certificate, for poem what's love November 11, 1987, and for poem title Thank You Another Merit.; [pers.] In moments of tranquilities my mind wonder in the real zone for loves poems words touch my innerself given me the inspiration and the flow of the nectar that made me moved my pen and wright whats in my heart; [a.] Youngstown, OH

SANCHEZ, CRYSTAL N. W.
[pen.] Crystal Sanchez; [b.] February 13, 1961, Tampa, FL; [p.] Mamie A. Watts; [m.] Divorced; [ch.] Amber and Angel Sanchez Jr.; [ed.] Jefferson High Bishop State College (Alabama) United electronics HCC; [occ.] Cosmetologist assistant manager first choice hair; [pers.] This poem I wrote in dedication to my mother. These are the words she could not say to express her feelings, due to a stroke which wiped her life away. This is the talent I truly inherited from her.; [a.] Tampa, FL

SANCHEZ, DANA MICHELLE
[pen.] Dana Michelle Sanchez; [b.] December 3, 1973, Mountainview, CA; [p.] Susan Hartle, William Sanchez; [ed.] Saint Francis High School; [occ.] U.S. Army Signal Corps; [memb.] Surfrider Foundation; [pers.] If you are not willing to take risks in life to achieve your goals, you'll never truly find happiness. Life is a lot of give and take, you have to give to receive.; [a.] Los Altos, CA

SANDAR, AVIS MARIE
[b.] September 17, 1950, Philadelphia, PA; [p.] Loretta Kathleen Bell, Gilmore Judge Chappell; [ed.] Cardinal Dougherty High School, Chapman College, Peace College, San Francisco Community College; [occ.] 1430 Transcriber Typist, Department of Social Services, SF, CA; [memb.] Consultant, Raffiki Project/Black Coalition on AIDS.; [hon.] Certificate of Recognition/Department of Social Services.; [oth. writ.] Several unpublished poems.; [pers.] My poetry is a reflection of deep, personal thoughts and feelings, as well as the quality and uniqueness of good relationships past and present.; [a.] San Francisco, CA

SANDERS, TINA M.
[b.] December 15, 1966, Gettysburg, PA; [p.] Wayne E. Sanders, Terry N. Sanders; [ch.] Damian Zen; [ed.] Catoctin High, Catonsville Community and Frederick Community Colleges, Computer Science.; [occ.] Student Service Coordinator, National Emergency Training Center, Emmitsburg, MD.; [memb.] Stronghold Metaphysical Retreat Center; [hon.] Catonsville CC - Deans List; [pers.] "Life's a Journey not a destination"; [a.] Emmitsburg, MD

SANDOVAL, CARMEN
[b.] October 25, 1971, Santa Fe, NM; [p.] Fidel Sandoval, Louise Sandoval Avila; [ed.] Santa Fe High School; [oth. writ.] Co-wrote an AIDS currently being acted out by Aztec Saint Theatre. Intitled "Till Death Do Us Part, Living with AIDS"; [pers.] Be true to your talent but more importantly be true to yourself.; [a.] Santa Fe, NM

SANDS, REBECCA J.
[b.] January 31, 1961, Fort Wayne, IN; [p.] M. Fred Brudi; [m.] Leo G. Sands, February 14, 1987; [ch.] Justin, Landon; [ed.] Elmhurst High School; [occ.] Retail Packaging; [hon.] General Business Assoc. Award; [oth. writ.] Several poems kept private; [pers.] I enjoy writing poetry as a hobby. I would like to pursue writing further; [a.] Huntington, IN

SANTI, LUCY DE
[pen.] Lucille Teddy; [b.] December 11, 1916, New York City; [p.] Silvester, Elena Marie; [m.] Victor, June 3, 1948; [ch.] Victor Jay; [ed.] PS 77 Bronx, PS 83 Queens, Newtown High, Brooklyn College 2 years; [occ.] Retired; [memb.] Arista; [hon.] The Old Lady doesn't show her medals but she has five from various scholarships and awards; [oth. writ.] A pile of scribbled poems beginning at age 14; [pers.] I write a poem to make a burden lighten or to understand a difficult situation and so set myself free to live and love again; [a.] Floral Park, NY

SANTINI, STEPHANIE AURORA
[b.] July 13, 1979, Fort Lauderdale, FL; [p.] Roberta A. Santini, MD; [ed.] Grade 10, Westminster Academy, Fort Lauderdale, FL; [occ.] High School Student; [hon.] Honor roll; [pers.] I love the arts and have been studying ballet, piano, flute, drama, and voice for many years. Life is precious for all. The welfare of children is in the hands of society and as part of it, we each can help in our own small way.; [a.] Fort Lauderdale, FL

SARAZIN, SHARI ANN
[b.] October 5, 1960, Tomah, WI; [p.] Margie, Ray Lowe; [m.] Randy Sarazin, April 11, 1981; [ch.] Michelle, Michael; [ed.] New Lisbon High School University of Wisconsin La Crosse, Private Piano, dance, voice; [occ.] Singer, Songwriter, Voice Teacher, Business Owner, Operator-Alaskan Motor Inn; [memb.] Songwriters of Wisconsin, ASCAP, Nashville Songwriters Association, International; [hon.] Dean's List; [oth. writ.] I have 8 other songs copywritten and recorded. Many of my poems songs are kept in a personal journal.; [pers.] My poems and songs are a reflection of the soul. My greatest joy is when I am able to share my talents with others. My passion for music and poetry consumes me and propels me into this beautiful God-given life.; [a.] Mauston, WI

SARNICOLA, MARIE ELENA
[pen.] Elena Nicol; [b.] July 24, 1941, Patterson, NJ; [p.] Mary and Pasquale Piccione; [m.] Andrew J. Sarnicola, Sr., June 3, 1962; [ch.] Regina Marie, Christine Ann, Andrew Joseph and Vincent Michael; [ed.] High School; [occ.] Sr. Executive Society, Hofstra University; [memb.] My Parish Church, Cursillo movement, Lupus Foundation; [oth. writ.] Several poems kept in journals, sent as gifts and published in church bulletins; [pers.] Some thoughts and experiences must be shared, written. Some never can be. They can only be held in your heart and touched in the air. I have been inspired by natures gift and "earthly" people.; [a.] Wantagh, NY

SAVAGE, BILLY WARD
[b.] May 24, 1955, Oakland, MD; [p.] Ward Savage and Geraldine Savage; [m.] Adelaide Lee Savage; [ed.] Northern High; [occ.] Truck driver - Caretaker Inc. Horse Trainer Marshy Meadow Farm; [memb.] USTRC, AQHA, WPRA, MTSC; [hon.] Represented MD in the United States Team Roping championships 1992 and 1993 Finals held in Guthrie, OK; [oth. writ.] Poems - The Leaning Oak, Gut Shot, Talking Truck and going to Kentucky; [pers.] Writes poems about the Cowboy lifestyle, real experiences from working with horses, and stories passed on to him by his father. Enjoys reading classic poetry by the 17th century poets.; [a.] McHenry, MD

SAVAGE, JOHN
[b.] July 7, 1970, Glasgow, Scotland; [p.] Jean and John McNair; [ed.] Penilee Secondary School Cardonald College/Stow College Cumbernauld College/Clydebank College; [occ.] Psychology Student; [oth. writ.] Articles on mental illness for small magazines, poems and short stories for Saccade magazine also drafted five novels and an auto-biography; [pers.] My work reflects the dark side of human nature, that part locked within and suppressed, also the pain experienced with loss, regret and loneliness.; [a.] Glasgow, Scotland

SAVOPOULOS, MANNY
[pen.] M. Savo; [b.] June 30, 1972, New York; [p.] Kalliope and Michael Milonakis; [ed.] Bronx High School of Science Currently attending John Jay College of Criminal Justice; [occ.] student/waiter; [oth. writ.] (not published) One Breathing (anthology of poems) "...by Deed" (short story-horror) "Then" (short story-crime) "Excursion", "Solitude", "Alone", "Barren" (short stories); [pers.] Language is a tool that divides and binds, to cleave the distance between writer and reader, that is my effort.; [a.] Valley Stream, NY

SAYRE, PENNY JANETTE
[b.] March 15, 1979, Grants Pass, OR; [p.] Penny and Chuck Sayre; [ed.] Sophomore in High School; [occ.] Student, Hidden Valley High School; [pers.] My heart flows through my pen, in words of truth, for others to see and know. The world of poetry is a beautiful place.; [a.] Grants Pass, OR

SCARBROUGH, STEPHANIE LEE
[b.] May 3, 1982, La Verne, CA; [p.] Cheryl and Terry Scarbrough; [ed.] I went to Maple Elementary School and I am currently going to Hesperia Jr. High in 7th grade; [occ.] Student; [memb.] Library; [hon.] Honor roll student for 6 years, and I have been in Softball - all stars for 3 years. I have gotten an award for a book I wrote in 2nd grade.; [oth. writ.] I had a book published in 2nd grade called the Horrible-Horrible Bad Fight of the Goblins. I have about 10 poems that I have written (but not published); [pers.] I am 12 years old I enjoy drawing-writing poems, baseball, basketball, football and hockey, I have written about 10 other poems. I keep them in a little book and have not yet published them. I also enjoy helping people.; [a.] Hesperia, CA

SCHAEFFER, WILLIAM
[pen.] Guyde Claussen; [b.] February 18, 1908, Chicago, IL; [p.] Sarah Paris Claussen, William Schaeffer; [m.] Peggy Roche, December 13, 1929; [ch.] Margaret and Susan; [ed.] Only foreigner attached to the State Theatre La Comedre franchise 2 years scenic designer for comedy francis 2 years actor singer stage manager all over England Wales England scotland Ben Greet Touring shakespeare company 2 years Director under madame Ouspenskayo; [occ.] Moscow Art Theatre 2 years wyc sole selfcreator and promotion of ATTA all-talk-to all history's only world wide; [memb.] Universal language for all also alone create and average of 4 poems per day now have 25,000 poems which were dedicated to over 500 affectionate persons only world wide world wide poetic cuterie also constantly creating literary genre attached sheet mentions these that I am now offering for publications created 20 years ago; [hon.] Honors None but yes two highly literate doughtiest hobbies 60 songs in 6 language ballroom dancer dedicated to lecturer rejuvenate longemty" skilled world traveler among which one 3 months around to world 1 yr residence in many foreign language countries; [oth. writ.] Also attached sheet drama erase she he said alone novel drama only one sin history 2 nights honeymoon Isle of Neebo rutabuto nut 2 nights conference of Kaulu kaulu Isle only stanza drama in all history 199 stanza 510 line search 2 hour drama universe; [pers.] A dramatic essay called "irrational transference" experience unique one man organize in 2 novels sequentially labor organizer and of the corporation executive this is see maquette I created now for comelie in francis columbia univ. NY museum of theatre signed Guy De Clavessa; [a.] Greensboro, NC

SCHELL, TERESA
[pen.] Terry; [b.] August 6, 1960, Los Angeles, CA; [m.] Matthew D. Schell, June 21, 1980; [ch.] Sandra, Dennis, Angela, Barbie, Heather; [ed.] Hamilton High Graduate; [occ.] Full time mother of five.; [oth. writ.] Many songs and poems, two of which are displayed at the local Y.W.C.A.; [pers.] I dedicate this, my first published poem, to my best friend and inspiration for this work, to Matthew. Without whose influence and patience it would not have been possible.; [a.] Missoula, MT

SCHENA, MICHAEL
[b.] April, 2, 1960, Chelsea, MA; [p.] Arthur and Tessie Schena; [m.] Yvonne Canuel (Girlfriend); [ed.] Tewksbury High School, Northern Essex Community College; [occ.] Quality Control Auditor; [memb.] Special Olympics, U.S.S.F. Soccer Official, Eastern MA Girls Soccer Coaches Association; [hon.] Graduated with honors at Northern Essex Community College.; [oth. writ.] Several Emotional poems written for my only true love, my girlfriend Yvonne Canuel.; [pers.] My writings are created from the love in my heart that have been brought out by a young woman that I loved from the start.; [a.] Tewksbury, MA

SCHERECK SR., WILLIAM J.
[pen.] William J. Ess; [b.] December 22, 1913, Chicago, IL; [p.] Frank and Adele (deceased); [m.] Flora George Schereck, May 19, 1943; [ch.] 7 Wm. Jr., Linda, Ralph, Florian; [ed.] B.S. (Sociology) University of Wisconsin Masters Candidate, Madison, 1952-54, Wofford College, SC 1948-51, Prairie du Chien, WI High School.; [occ.] Retired; [memb.] AARP, AM Legion, Retired Officers Association, Wisconsin Alumni Assoc., Wisconsin Memorial Union; [hon.] S. Carolina College Press Award (Poetry 1950), 1st Place Award 1955, Univ. Ohio State International Exhibition of Radio Programs, Bronze Star, Combat Infantry Badge, WW II.; [oth. writ.] Sounds of Heritage, (13 program radio series), Ghosts of the Battlefield, a collection of 23 poems written during WW II including a poem.; [pers.] The most eloquent speaker or reader may awe and dominate his audience into reverent or hypnotic silence, but once spoken, his words are gone. However, should we recast his praises into poetry they take on an eternal life of their own. The most successful way to live to old age is to just keep on breathing.; [a.] Harmony Grove, WI

SCHEUR, STEPHEN R.
[b.] April 7, 1954, Columbus, OH; [p.] William H. Schuer and Rita E. Schuer; [m.] Deborah E. Schuer, April 8, 1983; [ed.] Cambridge High, Cambridge Ohio and some college; [occ.] Retired I.C. Electrician first class - US Navy and now pinkerton security officer; [memb.] Nights of Columbus, life member of veterans of foreign wars and disabled American veterans; [oth. writ.] Several poems published in several navy cruise books.; [pers.] My poems were written because, GOD gave me something to say, something to share...; [a.] San Ysidro, CA

SCHMICK, JUDITH A. GIACOBBE
[pen.] J; [b.] July 27, 1946, Allentown, PA; [p.] Angelo and Helen Giacobbe; [m.] Charles Schmick, May 10, 1986; [ch.] Edward A. Julian, Vince E. Julian, 4 Grandchildren; [ed.] High School some non-credit courses; [occ.] Sales Correspondent, Stanley-Vidmar, Inc. 26 years; [oth. writ.] Several other poems non-published; [pers.] I always have been a romantic as heart, and I write what I'm feeling at the moment. I've read poetry, since I can remember also early English literature.

SCHMIDTKE, CLAUDETTE
[b.] January 25, 1967, Winnipeg, Manitoba, Canada; [p.] Joan and Lawrence Berard; [m.] Ed Schmidtke, August 11, 1984; [ch.] Rouchelle, John, Kathy, Adam; [ed.] Bonnyville Centralized High School; [occ.] House wife; [oth. writ.] Several poems published in church newsletter.; [pers.] My poems and songs portray things I have gone through and what I strive for in life. I've been writing since I was 15 years old.; [a.] Redwater Alberta, Canada

SCHMITT, JOHNNY E.
[pen.] Johnny E. Schmitt; [b.] October 21, 1971, Chicago, IL; [p.] Jerry and Marty Schmitt; [ed.] Graduated from Schaumburg H.S. (Schaumburg, IL); [occ.] U.S. Army; [oth. writ.] I have been writing biographical, environmental and inspirational poetry for several years now. This poem is the first poem that I have ever submitted for publication.; [pers.] I have been inspired by Frost and Poe and some modern day poets such as Melanie K. Wysocky. Through my expressions I hope to influence others in their guest for self-enlightenment, WORLD; [a.] Schaumburg, IL

SCHNEIDER, GEORGE
[b.] June 6, 1964, Buenos Aires, Argentina; [p.] Olga Rosell; [ed.] B.A. Physical Education, ex-tennis player, Post-Graduated Physiology studies.; [occ.] Head Tennis Professional at W.N.T.C. in California; [memb.] Poet's Guild, Amherst Society, Creative Arts and Sciences Enterprises, Argentina Professional Tennis Association; [hon.] Several as a tennis player, in poetry I just started to submit my work.; [oth. writ.] Several poems and essays for different anthologies.; [pers.] Day and night are two opposites which exist together in perfect harmony. We, the human kind, are one and we still don't seem to be capable of living, at least, in imperfect harmony.; [a.] San Gabriel, CA

SCHNEIDER, GRETCHEN C.
[pen.] Isabella d'Este; [b.] October 26, 1977, Fresno, CA; [p.] Sharon Schneider; [occ.] Student; [memb.] Sacramento Society for the Prevention of Cruelty to Animals (SPCA), Friends of the Library, People for the Ethical Treatment of Animals (PETA); [hon.] Who's Who of American High School Students (1992-1993, 1993-1994), Top 7 CATEEN 1st runner up Miss Carmichael Teen, USA. Veterans of Foreign Wars (VFW) Voice of Democracy Speech 1st place, 1st place Cold Reading Competition (SIMTC) Sunshine International Model and Talent Competition, CA Teen Leadership Program; [a.] Carmichael, CA

SCHNEIDER, THAEDRA TEHIRA
[pen.] "Terry" Powell; [b.] February 16, 1971, Lannsthul, West Germany; [p.] Linda and Gilbert Powell; [ch.] "Danny" Gene (Daniel) Powell; [ed.] Terrell Wells Jr. High, Pleasanton Jr. High and High School; [occ.[Manager of Restaurant; [hon.] District Art Awards and State Art Award (1st and 2nd places), Honor Art Award, and for creativity; [oth. writ.] Several poems in school newsletters; also, "You Shake Me" and many, many others; [pers.] Life is to be learned from, and my poems are really just times in my life written down on paper only to record as history. A sense of peace comes from each finished piece. [a.] San Antonio, TX.

SCHREYER, CYNTHIA A.
[b.] Phoenix, AZ; [ed.] Journalism Degree [oth. writ.] She enjoys writing short stories and poetry on life in the great southwest, and is inspired by Arizona towns from Sedona's rich, red rock beauty, to Tombstone's gun-slinging, wild west history.; [pers.] Attributing the beginning of her writing career to the faith of one life-long, childhood friend, Mary Catherine, she believes the secret to creative writing is to paint pictures with words like Norman Rockwell did on canvas.

SCHROEDER, JAMIE
[b.] June 14, 1963, San Gabriel, CA; [p.] Paul Garcia, Judith Garcia; [m.] Michael Schroeder, September 19, 1987; [ch.] Michael, Tamara, Brandi; [ed.] Bonita High; [occ.] Health and Beauty Consultant; [memb.] International Society of Poets.; [hon.] Editor's Choice Award from the National Library of Poetry 1994.; [oth. writ.] Several poems with the National Library of Poetry.; [pers.] My greatest influence has been our savior, Jesus Christ. Who has given me the gift of poetry.; [a.] Azusa, CA

SCHUELER, STEVEN
[b.] April 3, 1966, Kankakee, IL; [p.] John P. and Mary Louise; [ed.] Wayzata Senior High, Plymouth, MN, University of Wisconsin - Eau Claire, Eau Claire, WI, and Widener University, Chester, PA.; [occ.] Graduate Physical Therapy Student, Widener University, Chester, PA.; [oth. writ.] Several other unpublished poems.; [pers.] All of my poetry is inspired by personally emotional experience. It is my belief that such experiences, in some way, have touched many other people and my hope that those people will read, enjoy, and identify with my work.; [a.] Chester, PA

SCHULTZ, BRIAN
[b.] March 29, 1982, Fort Thomas, KY; [p.] Marvin Schultz, Mary Ann Schultz; [ed.] Taylor Mill Elementary Covington Latin High School; [occ.] student; [hon.] P.T.A. Reflections, Academic Team, Governor's Cup Awards: 1st Place Language Arts/2nd Place General Knowledge; [oth. writ.] Many poems I just write for myself some stories written. Never published.; [pers.] I try to talk about nature in my poems and the nature of humans. My greatest influence in my poems was my 4th grade teacher, Mrs. Richard son.; [a.] Taylor Mill, KY

SCHUMACHER, EVE C. DUNNIHOO
[b.] October 16, 1961, Seattle, WA; [p.] Dilys Abel; [m.] Duane R. Schumacher, May 18, 1991; [ch.] Stephanie, Corey, Ashley; [ed.] Shorecrest High School, Bellevue Community College; [occ.] Lead Cook, Kirkland, Roaster and Ale House; [a.] Kirkland, WA

SCHURE, KIMBERLY
[b.] May 23, 1976; [p.] Ralph and Ann Schure; [ed.] I will be graduating this June from high school and am currently applying to the University of Chicago; [occ.] Though I am a full-time student, I write on the side; [oth writ.] Recently of I completed have a model, it is an unusual cross between science fiction and fantasy. I have also written 54 short stories and twenty poems, most of which remain unpublished.; [pers.] Throughout my writing I try to be as daring and innovative as possible, breaking with past conventionalism, powerful imagery, ground breaking stories and excellence of prose as well as poetry I try to achieve. [a.] Darien, IL

SCHWARTZ, LARRY J.
[b.] May 25, 1970, Evanston, IL; [p.] Jerry and Judith Schwartz; [ed.] Libertyville High School, Southern Illinois University, Northwestern University; [oth. writ.] Poetry, screenplays, short stories, philosophy; [pers.]

Poetry is the result of ones state of mind when influenced by their heart and soul; [a.] Vernon Hills, IL

SCOTT, DORIS
[b.] December 22, 1921, Thailand

SCOTT, DOROTHY LEE
[pen.] Dotty Scott; [b.] May 13, 1917, Camden, NJ; [p.] Wilmer and Laura Garman; [m.] Charles Collins Scott, September 3, 1937; [ch.] three - one girl - two boys; [ed.] High School Graduate 3 years business school; [occ.] Retired private secretary now housewife ; [memb.] Past matron eastern star, Past pres. home and school association); [hon.] High School typing many original poems used by pastor in church work wrote greetings and poems for eastern star sisters wrote family poems for all occasions; [oth. writ.] Over our 57 years of marriage, our 2 sons and daughter, and also my wonderful husband and I have written poems and prose! We all love and appreciate poetry!; [pers.] Met my wonderful husband when I was 10 and be 11, married at 20 and 21 and love bad a most wonderful and successful life and 3 children can "quote the same" all are terribly happy!; [a.] Feasterville, PA

SCOTT, KIA
[pen.] Kia Scott; [b.] October 9, 1978, University of Pennsylvania; [p.] Joseph Scott III and Phyllis Scott; [ed.] 11th Grade, attend Dobbins/Randolph major in (HRT) Health Related Technology; [pers.] I try to encourage people to do the best they can by stressing the importans to strive for whatever it is in life that they would. In order to do that they have to be willing to go an extra mile.; [a.] Philadelphia, PA

SCOTT, PATRICIA HUGHES
[pen.] Cha Cha (for use in African fiction only; it means first-born in a tribal language); [b.] U.K.; [p.] Robert John Hughes, Ivy Webb; [m.] Divorced; [ch.] Robert Duncan Scott, Lain Campbell Scott, Francesca Hughes Scott; [ed.] Standard British education (fits one for anything!); [occ.] Last 2 years General Manager of a complex of self-contained cottages on the Kenyan Coast (which was to give me time to try to write novels); previously 9 years as an editor and foreign correspondent in Nairobi; [memb.] Past chairman, now honorary life member The Alpha Society (New Age), Toast Masters Intn'l, CTM Chairman, Kenya Volleyball Assoc., Beach Volley Commission; [hon.] Lady of the Year 1985 Nairobi; [oth. writ.] Many magazine articles over the last 12 years. I'm a lifetime poem writer (hardly ever shown to anybody!). I've written children's plays, some in verse. I've now submitted my first novel (fiction) for publication and also 'A Kenyan Beach Diary' (an account of my two years at the coast writing it). [pers.] Writing is my work, my hobby, my lifeblood. I was told by a psychic recently I came into this incarnation to write (although I've done a few other things too)! My personal philosophy is self development and awareness, and to know and help anyone I can whilst on my path. My first novel reflects my belief in reincarnation and the mysteries of life. [a.] Ukunda, Mambasa, Kenya, Africa.

SEAM, ARUN K.
[b.] April 13, 1950, Shimla, India; [p.] J. C. Seam, Krishna Seam; [m.] Neelam Seam, May 9, 1979; [ch.] Karan and Anant Seam; [ed.] Bachelor of Architecture, Panjab University, India.; [occ.] Architect, Himachal Pradesh University, Shimla 171005 (India); [memb.] Indian Institute of Architects, Bombay Executive member of local chapter of Indian Institute of Architects, Shimla. Registered Architect, Council of Architecture, New Delhi.; [hon.] NIL; [oth. writ.] Several articles and letters published in local dailies and journal mostly concerning on local issues of town.; [pers.] I am an ordinary man striving to leave a dot on the pages of time.; [a.] Shimla, India

SEAVER, ANITRA C.
[b.] May 17, 1951, Charleston, WV; [p.] Jason Conley, JoAnn Conley; [m.] George W. Seaver IV, January 8, 1972; [ch.] Amy Janelle, Susan Elizabeth; [ed.] George Washington High School, Concord College, Marshall University, MS. Ed.; [occ.] Second Grade Teacher Mercer Elementary School, Princeton, WV; [memb.] Delta Kappa Gamma Honorary Society, Mercer Co. Reading Council, WV Association for Young Children, Princeton Presbyterian Church.; [hon.] Governor's Blue Ribbon Commission, presenter for teachers in services, State Social Studies Fair, Rotary Club, RESA meetings, and various workshops.; [oth. writ.] Poems, working on several children's books.; [pers.] My writings are reflections of the past, present and future. Some are humorous, some sad, many are written for my classroom "through the eyes of a child."; [a.] Princeton, WV

SEBASTIAN, RACHEL ANNA
[pen.] Rachel Sebastian; [b.] October 29, 1955, Fort Worth, TX; [p.] Charles W. and Esther Robshaw; [m.] Robert Dwain Sebastian, February 28, 1987; [ch.] Bobby 13, Tim 12, April 10, Ashley 6, Jill 14; [ed.] High School grad. of Arlington Heights High School - 1974 (Fort Worth, TX); [occ.] Housewife, mother of 5; [oth. writ.] No others published at this time.; [pers.] I am a born again Christian. I love nature and the outdoors. I hope to someday publish some childrens books.; [a.] Fort Worth, TX

SEDLAR, MICHAEL L.
[b.] October 24, 1954, Marinette, WI; [occ.] Construction; [pers.] This poem represents an awakening, a coming of age, my 40th birthday. Reflections of past trials and their influence in present revelations; [a.] Milwaukee, WI

SEDLER, JENNIFER L.
[b.] January 25, 1978, Boynton Beach, FL; [p.] Debra Hendricks and Gary Hendricks; [ed.] Wellington Community High School; [pers.] This poem is dedicated in memory of my uncle, Robie C. Kirk, born June 6, 1924 and passed away December 17, 1991. He is remembered always; [a.] Loxahatchee, FL

SEEFELDT, MONICA M.
[b.] January 1975, Oakland, CA; [oth. writ.] Several poems published in other anthologies, most of which capture the passion and beauty of Spain.; [pers.] Whenever I approach a challenging feat, I take heed to the Spanish proverb, "El que no se atreve, no pasa el mar," which means, "He who does not dare to do, shall not pass over the sea."; [a.] Pleasanton, CA

SEIFERT, JAMES C.
[b.] April 9, 1959, Burnaby British Columbia, Canada; [p.] Peter Seifert, Fran Seifert; [m.] Joanne Seifert, August 18, 1990; [ch.] Nil; [ed.] Burnaby Central High; [occ.] Chief George Derby Hospital; [pers.] In the past two years I have attended a I Care program. (Its for people who are illiterate); [a.] New Westminster British Columbia, Canada

SELHORST, DORIS
[b.] March 19, 1948, Paintsville, KY; [p.] Marie Webb Ernest Hopson; [m.] Donald Selhorst, September 17, 1994; [ch.] Bill, Bob and Ben Curlis (step-children) Troy, Tonya and Yvonne; [ed.] State Certified geriatric and related disability activities doctor, 1986 Ohio state Lima Campus 1966 graduate Hardin Northern H.S. DA, OH; [occ.] Social Service Director admission the corinthian nursing home kenton Ohio; [memb.] Activity professionals of Ohio carriage to college M.C. Dunkirk, Ohio high street freewill baptist church - lima, Ohio Social Service Society Kenton, Ohio Community Concert Board - Kenton, Ohio; [hon.] Boards of education: Hardin northern high school Dola, OH, Vice Pres. Hardin County 1984 - 1987 Apollo career center lima, ohio 1986-1987 allen country past Pres, Area 3 Ohio Proffessional Activity Directors 1990 Geriatric Activity Director certification Instructor 1990 OHIO state Marion Branch; [oth. writ.] Children's short stories with a christian base my high school class poem.; [pers.] If we would have God our dreams fulfill - we must keep walking in His will.; [a.] Rushsylvania, OH

SEMCHUK, JOEL
[b.] July 21, 1976, Edmonton; [p.] Orest and Jennifer Semchuk; [ed.] First year student at the university of Alberta; [occ.] student; [hon.] Golden service aword for my grade 12 year; [oth. writ.] Various short stories, mainly for school; [pers.] Because poetry is an expression of your feelings there is no such thing as a bad poem.; [a.] Edmonton Alberta, Canada

SERNA, LINDA
[b.] March 15, 1958, Albuquerque, NM; [p.] Alex and Bertha Gurule; [m.] Robert Serna, July 29, 1977; [ch.] Susan Serna; [ed.] Graduate; [occ.] Bank teller; [oth. writ.] I don't think so I woke up today exercise is no demise; [pers.] Any poems I've ever written are mostly about my life it's always been easier to express my feelings on paper. It's also a good way of letting out my frustrations.; [a.] Albuquerque, NM

SEWELL, DOROTHY
[b.] July 14, 1932, Claresholm, Alberta, Canada; [p.] Vic and Mabel Davis; [m.] David Sewell, February 16, 1951; [ch.] James Philip, Marilyn Kaye; [occ.] Home maker and I farm with my husband; [pers.] This is my first attempt at sending a poem for possible publication! I'm thrilled! We have five grandchildren; [a.] Blackie Alberta, Canada

SEWELL, ELIZABETH GAIL
[pen.] Babe; [b.] January 27, 1949, Camden, AR; [p.] Eugene Ponder and Elizabeth Frances Harrison Ponder; [m.] Lonnie Clark Sewell, August 27, 1971; [ch.] Daymond Clark and Valeri Lynn Sewell; [ed.] Chidester High School, Southern Arkansas University, Southwestern A/G College, North East Texas Community College ; [occ.] Secretary; [memb.] Assembly of God Church; [oth. writ.] Poems and Music; [pers.] The poems and songs I write usually reflect teachings I have tried to give my children to become the adult with values they can pass to their children. My poems are inspired by the values my parents taught me as a child.; [a.] Woodbridge, VA

SEXTON, NANCY E.
[b.] July 2, 1958, Havre De Grace, MD; [p.] Robert Jones, Nora Jones; [m.] Charles C. Sexton Jr., January 28, 1991; [ch.] David Lee Green, Daniel Scott Green; [ed.] North East High; [occ.] Mail Clerk, Aberdeen MD,

Ordnance Center and School APG; [pers.] I want people to see the real, true incidents of what goes on in the world today and the effect it has on the person or persons involved, especially the ones we love. All my writings are true and experienced.; [a.] Colora, MD

SHAH, VARSHA P.
[b.] Gujarat, India; [p.] P. F. Saraiya, Sulochana Saraiya; [m.] Piyush C. Shah; [ch.] Pooja Amy, Raman, Nina; [ed.] M.B.A., C.P.A.; [occ.] Controller Warren Electric Co., Houston Texas; [pers.] Nature is everything. It includes us and our surroundings.; [a.] Houston, TX

SHANNON, JUDITH
[b.] September 19, 1940, Philadelphia, PA; [p.] John and Marie Van Fossen; [m.] David Shannon, May 7, 1960; [ch.] Donna, Marguerite, Mary Beth; [ed.] The Cecilian Academy, University of Baltimore, graduate studies at Loyola College and John Hopkins University; [occ.] English Teacher, Calvert Hall High School, Baltimore, MD; [memb.] Lawrence Durrell Society National Council of Teachers of English; [hon.] Sallie Mae Award for Outstanding First Year Teacher in MD., Edgar Allan Poe Award - University of Baltimore, Creative America Award - award given to the teacher of the first place winner in national creative writing contest.; [oth. writ.] Letters to Leopold - a one woman presentation based on Queen Victoria's writings presented in the Baltimore are, "On Magritte" - published in The Rectangle National Honor Society Collegiate magazine; [pers.] The essence of poetry is the emotional bond created between the writer and the reader.; [a.] Baltimore, MD

SHANNON, TERRY ANN
[pen.] Terry Ann Moore Shannon; [b.] May 7, 1957, Umatilla, OR; [p.] Wilmer and Mary Ann Moore; [m.] Robert Joseph Shannon, December 30, 1977; [ch.] Kimberlee Ann , Robert Jeremiah, Joseph Kevin; [ed.] Graduated High School 1975 went to Pendleton College Beauty graduated January 1977 licensed in Cosmetology, hairdressing, manicuring and barbering in the state of Oregon. Also took a year of secretarial courses at Blue Mountain Community College in Pendleton.; [occ.] Salesclerk, Mother and housewife.; [pers.] I love poetry and have been writing since I was 10 years old. It is the best way to express my feelings.; [a.] Umatilla, OR

SHARP, ETTA ROGERS
[b.] December 30, 1904, Clailoorne Co., TN; [p.] Campbell Cawood, Ann Christine Rogers; [m.] Dr. Luther Franklin Sharp (deceased), October 9, 1926; [ch.] Carolyn Sharp Hale, Frank Sharp; [ed.] B.S. Degree East Tenn. State College MA Degree E. Tenn. State University; [occ.] Retired Active in College Classes Art Writing; [memb.] Alpha Delta Kappa Sorority American Legion Aux. St. Thomas Episcopal Church Women's Group, Altar, Jr. Warden Book Club, Women's Club; [hon.] Assisted in writing family histories poetry published in smoky mountain manuscript club (1985) Address: Lee Sanders 1937 Maple wood drive Knayville Tenn. 37920; [oth. writ.] Two books of stories, articles written the past five yrs here Charlestown retirement center bound and now writing for 3'd book. (my life, family, travels fiction); [pers.] I have had a full life of hard work, adventure and a happy marriage (40 yrs) rearing two children, teaching school and many trips abroad. I write parts for our years little theater Arts.; [a.] Catonsville, MD

SHARP, VIRGINIA KANTACK
[pen.] "Ginny" Kantack; [b.] March 1, 1937, Glasgow, MT; [p.] George and Josephine Kantack; [m.] John Sharp, June 1, 1954; [ch.] Raymond, Fawneil, Glenda; [ed.] High School St. Teresa's Academy Boise, ID 1st Qtr College Spoken Falls Community College; [occ.] Quality Control in apples Wenatchee, WA; [memb.] Christian Writers Association (Chapter of Wanatchee, WA); [oth. writ.] Personal notations on life journaling, short stories, poems for the Lord and family; [pers.] I desire to proclaim God is very much alive, interested in all he created and present in our everyday. My Bible is essential to life.; [a.] Moses Lake, WA

SHAUNITA, STEPHENS
[pen.] Nita Stephens; [b.] April 30, 1979, Augusta, GA; [p.] Jennifer Ferrell and Lorenzo Ferrell; [ed.] Washington-Wilkes Comp. High School; [occ.] Student; [memb.] FHA Club; [oth. writ.] I am age 15. I am in the tenth grade. I enjoy writing and reading in my spare time. My poems have been in Obituaries and articles in school.; [pers.] I try to strive for the best and always try to do my best in what ever I don Because'the first impression is the best; [a.] Washington, GA

SHAW, JOHN R.
[b.] December 18, 40, San Francisco; [p.] John Evans, Mildred Helen; [m.] Andrea Shaw, February 14, 1989; [ch.] John, Andrew, Adam, Sarah; [ed.] 1958-1961 Ripon College, Ripon, Wisconsin, Bachelor of Arts Biology, 1961-1965 University of Wisconsin, Madison, Wisconsin Doctor of Medicine, 1965-1966 St. Luke's Hospital, San Francisco, California Medical Internship, 1966-1967 Harvard University, Cambridge, Massachusetts Psychiatry Fellowship, 1967-1968 United States Navey, Winter Harbor, Maine, 1968-Present Family Practice, Riverside, California Private Practice; [occ.] Family Physician; [memb.] 1972-Present Fellow of the American Academy of Family Practice recertification by the American Board of Family Practice in 1978, 1984 and 1990, due again in 1997 Member: American Medical Association, California Medical Association and the Riverside County Medical Association, 1974 Appointed Associate Professor of Family Practice at Loma Linda University, Loma linda, California, 1968-Present Family Practice Staff, Riverside Community Hospital, Riverside California, Publication: Journal of the American Medical Association "Diabetic Angiopathy and L-xylulose", November 7, 1966, Volume 198, Page 665, Office Hours: 7:30 a.m. to 5:30 p.m. Monday through Friday by appointment only, X-Ray, Pulmonary Function, E.K.G. and Lab work provided in office, Spanish spoken and interpreted in office, German understood, HMO and PRO provider, Taking new patients; [a.] Riverside, CA

SHAW, LEE F.
[pen.] Fanny Lee Baker Shaw; [b.] March 17, 1931, Binghamton, NY; [p.] Leah and Bernard Baker; [m.] Divorsed; [ch.] Gerald, Twins Danny and Donna; [ed.] Christopher Columbus, Binghamton North High School; [occ.] Retired; [memb.] American Diabetes Assoc.- AARP, Pres by Tarian Church Choir and Membership; [hon.] Honor Society Thru School; [oth. writ.] I Love You Mom, My Little Boy, Fall, Pops, I Did My Best, My Shadow, The Fifty Spring, Oh Mother.; [pers.] I like writing about people and things around me. Things that arouse my senses.; [a.] Syracuse, NY

SHEARS, GINA JANE
[pen.] "G"; [b.] May 10, 1975, Baltimore, MD; [p.] Ronald Shears Sr., Jeanette Shears; [ed.] Patapsco High, Southeastern School of Technology, Durdalk Community College; [memb.] Our Lady of Hope Parishioner; [hon.] Honor roll, Presidential Academic Award, Art Awards; [oth. writ.] Several other personal poems as gifts of dedication.; [pers.] Each poem that I write is specifically dedicated to one thing that has influenced my life emotionally.; [a.] Baltimore, MD

SHEETZ, TRACEY LEIGH
[b.] November 12, 1976, Fairfax, VA; [p.] Robert and Theresa Edwards; [ch.] April Renee; [ed.] Thomas A. Edison H.S., Bryant Alternative H.S.; [occ.] Rec, Aid, Ft. Belvoir NCO Club; [memb.] USMC delay; [oth. writ.] Poems published in H.S. paper and literary magazines; [pers.] Most of my writing comes from my heart and soul and reflects my life's experience; [a.] Alexandria, VA

SHELNUTT, ALEASHA ANN
[pen.] Aleasha Wales; [b.] December 23, 1974, Wichita Falls, TX; [p.] Floyd and Dianne Browning and the late ray Wales; [m.] Lee Shelnutt, January 1, 1994; [ed.] Rider High School, completed one semester at Oklahoma Christian University; [occ.] Housewife; [memb.] Key Club-Kiwanis, 6 years in National Piano Playing auditions; [hon.] Presidents Academic Scholarship to attend Okla. Christian University of Science and Arts. In 1989 earned District II medal for piano solo and ensemble contest, between years 1985 - 1990 earned 5 silver medals, 1 gold and 1 bronze medal for TMTA-SA whitlock Theory Awards in piano.; [oth. writ.] Several poems and several articles for Rider High School paper; [pers.] To dream is to wish for joy to love is to embrace it.; [a.] Wichita Falls, TX

SHELTON, DAVID
[b.] September 5, 1969, San Saba, TX; [p.] Allen Shelton, Jean Jamison; [ed.] Westwood High School, Southwest Texas S.U. - graduate May, 1995; [occ.] Student; [oth. writ.] Currently working in 1st book of poetry, 1st book of short stories (due in the next few years, hopefully).; [pers.] From the mechanical, acting form, in contrast with the animalistic, reacting form, I try to define our interplay with the surrounding environment.; [a.] Austin, TX

SHELTON, FREDERICK T.
[b.] September 9, 1976, Dallas, TX; [p.] James Shelton and Johnnye Shelton; [ed.] Skyline High School, Tuskegee University; [occ.] Full-time student; [memb.] Glendale Presbyterian Church; [oth. writ.] Several unpublished poems.; [pers.] I try to show reality through my poetry, whether it be reality of the past, present or future.; [a.] Dallas, TX

SHELTON, MARC EDWARD
[b.] November 11, 1970, Waterbury, CT; [p.] Lloyd E. Shelton, Shirley M. Shelton; [ed.] W.C. Bryant High School, The Harvey Milk High School; [occ.] Student: Lehman College Bronx, NY - Social Work Major, English Minor.; [memb.] Club: Christian Seekers Fellowship.; [hon.] The Michael Jeweler's Award, Teen Talent - for 2nd place male vocal soloist, excellence in scholarship award, letter N. Dinkins.; [oth. writ.] News articles: The Alpha and Omega newspaper, the community gospel church youth newsletter. Poems published: Grave Dodge Vocational H.S. Newspaper, AIDS Resource Center Newsletter.; [pers.] "To master the arts first one must be a slave to it....(M. Jackson); [a.] New York City Manhattan, NY

SHEPHERD, DOROTHY
[pen.] Dorothy Shepherd; [b.] September 1, 1933, Los Angeles, CA; [p.] Mr. and Mrs. W. J. Mankin; [m.] J. L. Shepherd, December 30, 1953; [ch.] Five girls, three boys; [ed.] M.A. - Clinical Art Therapy, B.A. - Biology; [occ.] Staff Art Therapist; [memb.] AATA, Scata; [oth. writ.] Clinical papers on psychology and art therapy; [pers.] All of the expensive arts, of which poetry is one, are vehicles to greater self awareness and understanding, and, as such, means to help others.; [a.] Sunland, CA

SHERRY, SHERRY
[pen.] Sherry Sherry; [b.] June 11, 1969, Ohio; [p.] Ray and Geneva Warden; [m.] Daniel Sherry; [ch.] Ashley, Adam, Andrea, and Angel; [ed.] 9th Grade only; [occ.] Child care, housewife; [memb.] Hillcrest Saturday night bowling mix; [hon.] High Handicap game, most improved bowler and 205 game trophies; [pers.] The poem I sent put together are actually one poem but I cut in half because 20 lines where what add called for I lost my brother at 17 years of age to a gun my only brother life can be taken away so easily and just when you think that can never happen to me.

SHIRAHADA, GILDA LOREDO
[b.] July 6, 1976, Manila, Philippines; [p.] Masashi Shirahada, Renilda Shirahada; [ed.] Our Lady of Grace Montessori, Immaculate Conception Academy; [memb.] National Author's Registry; [oth. writ.] 3 of my poems will be publish in Iliad Press' Voices anthology this summer.; [pers.] If you have a talent in writing, use it. Don't take it for granted. It's a way of expressing one's self through writing, what otherwise would have been so hard to say.; [a.] Saitama, Japan

SHIRLEY, LINDA M.
[pen.] Van Norren, Fraese, Scott, Heinrichs; [b.] May 6, 1954, Saskatoon, Canada; [p.] Leona Wilson; [m.] Scott Shirley, November 11, 1989; [ch.] Paul Van Norren, Jessica Van Norren; [ed.] Graduate Mount Royal Colligate Saskatoon, Saskatoon Canada; [occ.] Special Care Worker with adult mentally and physically challenged Armstrong Special Care Him.; [oth. writ.] Poems published in church bulletins, am currently working on more poetry, a novel and children's stories.; [pers.] I simply love to write, to convey thoughts in different form, and hopefully for the enjoyment of others.; [a.] Victoria British Columbia, Canada

SHUKLA, SHEFALEE
[b.] April 7, 1980, Saskatoon, Saskatchewan, Canada; [p.] Dr. K and Dr. S Shukla; [ed.] Attending Big Rive High School; [occ.] Student; [memb.] Volleyball, Badminton, High School Yearbook Editor, student representative council, piano; [hon.] First class Honors, proficiency award, track and field award, figure skating award, baseball award; [a.] Big River Saskatchewan, Canada

SIDEK KHAN, SARIFAH BIBI SARINA BT.
[pen.] Rina Khan; [b.] July 30, 1970, Kuala Lumpur; [p.] Sidek Khan and Aziah Ngah Abu Bakar; [m.] Jasmani Masran, May 1, 1992; [ch.] Natasha Annina and Alwi Ilyas; [occ.] Artist (Recording Singer) T.V. Show Host ("Pop Kuiz"); [oth. writ.] Several unpublished poems, unpublished short story, unpublished T.V. script.; [pers.] "Life is short, live to the fullest, don't leave any space in between."; [a.] Looview Selangor, Malaysia

SIDWELL, TODD
[b.] February 25, 1962, Ogden, UT; [ed.] Graduate of the University of Texas at Austin and Weber State University; [occ.] Writer/Director/Producer for Motion Pictures and Television; [memb.] NASE, Los Angeles Opera Guild, Smithsonian Associates, San Diego Zoological Society, Frank Lloyd Wright Association.; [oth. writ.] The Documentary "Pioneers in the Promised Land" for the Disney Channel. The Motion Picture Screenplay "Ruby and Jake" to lens in 1995. Numerous film treatments.; [pers.] If you're purpose in writing is not to get to the bottom of things the truth, if you will. What's the point?; [a.] Hermosa Beach, CA

SILBERGER, SARA
[pen.] Salem Mitchell; [b.] July 23, 1981, White Plains, NY; [p.] Monte and Patricia Silberger; [ed.] Currently in High School at Sleepy Hollow High; [occ.] Student; [oth. writ.] Many, none published at present; [pers.] When I write I like to think that it forms a bond between people. I hope it does, for the sake of the people.; [a.] Tarrytown, NY

SILKENSEN, CYNTHIA
[pen.] Gesso Cocteau [b.] May 23, 1954, California; [p.] George and Maryhelen, Babajian; [m.] Carl Brad Silkensen, April 11, 1974; [ed.] University of Hawaii, Hilo HI; [occ.] Sculptor and Owner of Digital Video Co 'Cocteau Communications'; [oth. writ.] 2 Poetry Books: 1) Dragonfly Lament, 2) The Balance; [pers.] Foreword-Gesso Cocteau is a rebel, a rebel with a rage to create. In the Zarathoustra Discourse, Nietzche described the three metamorphoses of the spirit, how the spirit becomes a camel, how the camel becomes a lion and how the the lion becomes a child. The camel represents the courage to shoulder a heavy task, the lion wants to win liberty and the child portrays innocence and forgetfulness. Gesso Cocteau illustrates attributes in her life as she writes and sculpts. She is a solitary figure who resents the idea of people trying to categorize her. She resides in a secluded desert of her own making and as believed, in the depths of a desert the spirit becomes a lion. Cocteau has the courage to attempt the impossible and make it a reality. Her instinct is to seek liberty, liberty from the rules that matter little to here, in order to break out of the normal expectations ascribed to artistic works. In her poetry, she finds her child, her innocence and forgetfulness that immortalizes a new beginning, a first movement, a sacred yes. What matters to her as she observes life is not what she actually sees, but what she perceives. Her feelings of a sexual intensity are expressed with a fresh naive vision and the effect of her work upon her can be compared to the effect of the Canato Fountain upon the goddess Juno who made a pilgrimage to the fountain each year to plunge into its cold water to gain back her virginity. Cocteau immerses herself in her words and in her descriptions of the most private indulgences of the soul, hers is an expression that transforms the most carnal experiences of life into a realm of beauty, innocence and purity. In the end, she gains back her virginity.; [a.] Indian Wells, CA

SIMES, LISA KAMILLIA
[pen.] Lee-Lee; [b.] April 15, 1978, Durham, NC; [p.] Mr. Pamela and Jasper Southerland; [ed.] Warren County High, I'm a sixteen year old Junior and plan to attend to Duke University, Durham, NC; [occ.] Volunteer, Coley Spring Community of Senior Citizens.; [memb.] Art Club, Homemakers of America and future teachers of America.; [hon.] Honor Roll and Dean's Lost; [oth. writ.] Several poems published in school newspapers; [pers.] I try to express my feelings in my writings, and also writing poems makes me relax and also it fun.; [a.] Norlina, NC

SIMMONS, CATHRYN RICE
[pen.] Cathy Rice, Cathryn Karinthe, C. Shipley; [b.] August 24, 1954, Seattle, WA; [p.] Leighton C. Rice, Marie Rice; [m.] Keith C. Simmons, December 20, 1986; [ed.] A.A. Tacoma Community College, B.A. University of Puget Sound, M.A. University of California, Sanha Barbara; [occ.] Institute Ventura, CH. Community College 4 yrs. part time; [memb.] Morton Bch. Ed 1986, Islamic Soc. of North America; [hon.] HS Debate town, Judge, UPS Honors in Communication and Theater Who's, Who among students in American Universities and College 1986; [oth. writ.] Poems published in local newspapers, small press and college magazines. Master's thesis.

SIMMONS, CHRISTINA
[pen.] C. Simmons; [b.] January 15, 1970, Alameda, CA; [p.] Wayne Simmons, Susan Simmons; [ed.] Analy High School Sebastopol, CA Pace University, NYC, NY; [oth. writ.] Various poems and short stories.; [pers.] I write to release emotions otherwise kept locked. Hopefully, the things I write of strike the reader as sincerely human, full and diverse with humor, pain, reflection and the relentless ability to evolve into something beautiful.; [a.] New York City, NY

SIMON, BELICIA
[b.] January 23, 1959; [p.] Carol Simon, Jimmy Gray; [ch.] Shakira, Candice, Edwin; [ed.] McGill-Toolen High School S.D. Bishop Junior College; [occ.] Business Student; [memb.] Apostolic Assemblies of Christ Sunday School Teacher and Member of Pastor's Aide of Christ Centered Apostolic Church, Inc.; [pers.] There is a God of Hope that is able to offer a way out of every dilemma. Mankind does not have to lost.; [a.] Columbus, OH

SIMONDS, SHANNON
[b.] August 29, 1974, Binghamton, NY; [p.] Paul and Donna Simonds; [occ.] Teacher's Aide for emotionally disturbed children.; [oth. writ.] Poems and Short Stories.; [pers.] I have never written for recognition nor have I had anything published. I lost my mother to Leukemia in 1993, and writing is simply my floatation device when I feel I'm drowning; [a.] Chenango Forks, NY

SIMONS, LORRAINE
[pen.] E; [b.] April 21, 1963, Paterson; [p.] Mary and Jerry Woodhouse; [m.] Pearl M. Simons Jr., July 13, 1984; [ch.] Shantrea Southerland; [ed.] Eastside High; [occ.] Secretary, mother; [memb.] Achor Ministry Group meetings, community church of love, Paterson, NJ 07514; [oth. writ.] Many different writings of every topic, 2nd one published by Nat'l Library of Poetry, song from Hollywood Artist; [pers.] I pray that society may relate to my personal poems and learn from many of them. I write from my heart as I experience such things; [a.] Paterson, NJ

SIMS, SUSAN
[b.] February 3, 1957, Charleston, SC; [p.] John and Margie Dorn; [m.] David Sims, September 1991; [ch.] Kevin Walton; [ed.] Respiratory Therapist - self taught computer guru; [occ.] Business Manager, Freelance writer; [oth. writ.] Articles for local newspaper, genealogy book self published for family poems to be published in several anthologies this year.; [pers.] Through my writing, I hope to express that the struggles we face in life

can be overcome, if only we maintain hope and faith.; [a.] Columbia, SC

SIMUNIV, NEVENKA
[pen.] Nevenka Simunic; [b.] August 11, 1950, Yugoslavia; [p.] Ivan Simunic, Maria Simunic; [ed.] Grade 12 Completed in Yugoslavia, 1969 Then Moved to Canada, 1980, Granton Institute, Hotel/Motel Management - Toronto Canada, 1983 Bank Teller Course - Calgary, Canada, "Karen Hall Careers" [occ.] Managing, Atlas Submarine Calgary's Restaurant - Also, worked previously for several hotels - As the Executive Housekeeper - In Calgary and Toronto; [hon.] Philosophical statement on love - "Love in life's precious treasured whose value is beyond measure" [oth. writ.] Several poems - published in Englands "First Time" poetry magazine.; [pers.] Words from my very first poem, "Like A Beautiful Bouquet" "Bouquet Of Feelings", Made wholly of flowers, Signifying Always That Tuneful Feeling, The Song With Rhythmic Words, Consists of real meanings a poem is then... A Bouquet Made Entirely Of Feeling." Mr. Howard. Thank you I'll carry with me, "A Moment in Time - until eternity.; [a.] Calgary, Canada

SINGADI, CHINNA DEVI
[pen.] Sheena, Hina; [b.] October 13, 1971, Guntakal Andhra Pradesh, India; [p.] Nettekallu Singadi, Lakshmi Devi Singadi; [ed.] Fatima School and Chowgule College, Margao, Goa, Doing M.A. (English), At S.K. University, Anantapur AP, India; [memb.] Hobbies Reading, Photography, Learning Languages (already conversant with seven Indian languages); [hon.] Adjudged best student in English at UG Level (1992-93), University first in first year M.A. Exams (1993-94); [oth. writ.] Songs and poems in Hindi, Lyrics and Gazals in a Mellifluous blend of Hindi and Urdu; [pers.] Through my writings, I seek to re-instil the hope of paradise (Bible Prophecy) in the weary hearts of mankind. I have been influenced by the Urdu Gazal tradition, especially its extensive use of imagery. I believe every man is born a man, but to die a man is positively an achievement; [a.] Anantapur Andhra Pradesh, India

SINGADI, CHINNA DEVI
[pen.] Sheena, Hine; [b.] October 13, 1971, Guntakal Andhra Pradesh, India; [p.] Nettekallu Singadi, Lakshmi Devi Singadi; [m.] Unmarried; [ed.] Fatima School and Chowgule College Margao, Gao: Doing M.A. (English) At S K University, Anantapur AP, India; [memb.] Hobbies reading, Photography, learning languages (already conversant with seven Indian Languages; [hon.] Adjudged best student in English at UG level (1992-93), University first in first year M.A. exams (1993-94); [oth. writ.] Songs and poems in Hindi, Lyrics and Gazals in a mellifluous blend of Hindi and Urdu; [pers.] Through my writings, I seek to re-instill the hope of paradise (bible prophecy) in the weary hearts of mankind. I have been influenced by the Urdu Gazal tradition, especially its extensive use of imagery. I believe every man is born a man, but to die a man is positively an achievement; [a.] Anantapur Andhra Pradesh, India

SINGH, KARUN KRISHA
[pen.] K-Singh; [b.] February 4, 1962, Bombay, India; [p.] Amar Singh, Sarah Singh; [m.] Moira Curtain, December 27, 1992; [ch.] Mikhaela Shakti Singh; [ed.] B.A. Englit B.A. Psychology, (Elphinstone College, India, 1983) (Earlham College, 1985, Indiana) M.S. Social Work (Columbia University School of Social Work, New York, 1987); [occ.] Ph.D. Student, Columbia University School of Social Work; [memb.] National Association of Social Workers, National Network for Social Work Managers, USA Table Tennis; [hon.] National Institute of Mental Health Scholarships (1993, 1994, 1995), The Duke of Edinburgh's Award Scheme Gold Award 1983, Silver Award 1977, Bronze Award 1976; [oth. writ.] Several poems published in College Magazines, public leaving testimony, notes on "The Force."; [pers.] New York, NY

SINGH, NARISHIA
[b.] May 15, 1978, Guyana; [p.] Prem/ Bebi Singh; [ed.] I am currently attending Brooklyn Technical High School.; [pers.] I wrote this poem to express the greatness that was found in Arthur Ashe. I enjoy reading the works of Byron, Whitman, and Frost, and poems by Alice Walker.; [a.] New York, NY

SINGLETON, MOEDON
[b.] February 3, SC; [p.] Stones; [occ.] Housewife; [a.] DeLand, FL

SINTIHAKIS, CHRISTINA NIKOLAI
[b.] November 22, 1976, Houston, TX; [pers.] My writing has always been a worn pathway towards getting acquainted more closely with myself. I feel that it reflects on fears and insecurities I have about life. My writing helps me release a burden of emotions and replaces it with an exquisite fulfilling.; [a.] Sugar Land, TX

SKILLINGS, TRAVIS C.
[b.] July 7, 1976, IL; [p.] Cathy F. Sapp, William L. Sapp; [oth. writ.] Poems, stories, manuscripts, and roleplaying games. (All unpublished); [pers.] I have learned to create meaning in all I discover.; [a.] VA

SKINNER, KAY F.
[b.] February 8, 1947, Sioux Falls, SD; [p.] Frank and Mildred Moerke; [m.] Peter R. Skinner, December 20, 1969; [ch.] Andrew Roy; [ed.] B. A. History, M. A. Education; [occ.] Homemaker and Mother; [oth. writ.] Various Poems; [pers.] I am motivated to write in learning to love and nurture my son. I believe children are great teachers.; [a.] Manhattan Beach, CA

SKIPPER, ALICIA DENISE
[b.] February 16, 1965, Chicago, IL; [p.] Sylvester and Dorothy Mae; [m.] Jeffery L. Skipper Sr., January 6, 1990; [ch.] Antwan, Jasmine Jeffery Jr., Eric; [ed.] International correspondence High School, Alfred D. Kohn Elementary; [occ.] Home Maker, aspiring writer.; [oth. writ.] 1993, Book Title, Bringing hope to a hopeless world, Boone wood Publication: Poem Title: Spirit, New Poets Generation, MOM and POP Publication, News paper sacramento California: Poem Title: Reminisce; [pers.] Writing is a spiritual thing for me. Maya Angelou once said, words can be measured. I find myself washing walls and dusting furniture to spiritually prepare my surroundings. I pray for the blessings of my fore mothers then I began to write.; [a.] Chicago, IL

SKORKA, NICOLE MARIA
[b.] August 7, 1974, Buffalo, NY; [p.] JoAnne I. Skorka, Nicholas P. Skorka; [ed.] Hutch Tech High School, St. Bonaventure University; [occ.] Full time student; [memb.] Member, Society of Professional Journalists, Member, St. Bonaventure University Concert Choir and Concert Band Disc Jockey, St. Bonaventure University Radio Station (WSBU 88.3 FM), member All-County Choir; [hon.] Dean's List; [oth. writ.] I have had stories and poetry published in a book entitled "Our Best," a book that is distributed throughout the Buffalo area.; [pers.] I put a lot of emphasis on human emotion when I write poetry. My poems reflect situations that I have dealt with and overcome in my life. Many are accolades of my family. I feel that it is easier to write what cannot often be said.; [a.] Buffalo, NY

SKOW, MARCIA
[b.] January 1, 1954, Yugoslavia; [p.] Milorad Rapaich, Milka Rapaich; [m.] John J. Skow, April 24, 1982; [ch.] Michael John, Steven Joseph; [ed.] South High, School in Europe; [occ.] Assembler at hydrolic plant in Amoha; [pers.] I have been influenced by friends who has read some of my other writings.

SLACK, KATHY TAYLOR
[pen.] Kathy Taylor; [b.] October 9, 1948, Perryville, MO; [p.] Floyd and Ella Taylor; [m.] Charles E. Slack, January 8, 1989; [ch.] Guy Lee Martin; [ed.] New College of U.S.F., Daytona Beach Community College; [occ.] Home Health Aide; [hon.] To be my parent's child and my child's parent; [pers.] Care, when we all care, we'll have no cares.; [a.] Ormond Beach, FL

SLASTEN, GUENNADI
[pen.] Slagen, Shakhrood Slagen; [b.] May 4, 1957, Kegichevka, Ukraine; [p.] Nikolai Slasten, Vera Boiko-Slasten; [ch.] Marina Slasten; [ed.] Schwerin Russian Secondary School (Germany), Kishinev State University (Moldavia), Moscow Institute of Information (Russia); [occ.] Philologist, teacher, translator, songwriter; [oth. writ.] A dozen poems in Russian (all published), twenty songs in Russians and in English; [pers.] My beloved readers, now is your time to create a common auxiliary language that will become the first one of its kind to be spoken by all and everyone. Interlinguistics can help a lot in establishing in the whole world.; [a.] Brooklyn, NY

SLAUGHTER, ANNA J.
[b.] September 12, 1948, SC; [p.] Barth and Pankie Jeter; [m.] Charles M. Slaughter Sr., June 1, 1968; [ch.] Charles Jr., Katrina and Tiffany; [occ.] Accounts Payable Coordinator, DVRPC; [memb.] Youth Aid Panel in Phila. 12 Dist. CFC Church Executive Board Member and Deaconess; [oth. writ.] Several poems and short stories and some have been published in my Jobs Social Club News Letters.; [a.] Philadelphia, PA

SLAVEN, ANNA W.
[b.] October 12, 1975, Tainan, Taiwan; [p.] Glen and Rosa Slaven; [ed.] Stevensville High School (Montana), United States Coast Guard Academy; [occ.] Cadet at U.S. Coast Guard Academy will be commissioned ensign upon graduation.; [memb.] Masonic order of Grand Cross, U.S. Tennis Association.; [hon.] Teen Community Serving Award, Tennis Most Valuable Player, American Legion Oratorical Contest, Girl's State Delegate.; [oth. writ.] Speeches in local newspapers.; [pers.] I live with the goal of always performing deeds with good intentions. The source through which I find my strength is nature. We all share a common bond, it is the bond of the fundamental qualities of the human spirit.; [a.] New London, CT

SLIFKA, CHERYL L.
[b.] May 11, 1973, Melrose Park, IL; [p.] Charles Slifka and Arlene Slifka; [m.] Single; [ed.] Glenbard East High School; [occ.] Secretary at coast to coast Hydraulics; [hon.] Young Authors Award (age 9); [oth. writ.] First

Time Published Piece.; [pers.] My writing reflects on my own personal experiences. I let my feelings and expressions flow through my pen. My talent and influence comes from the support of my entire family and for that I'm very grateful.; [a.] Lombard, IL

SMALL, VANESSA Y.
[pen.] Vee Vee Small; [b.] November 10, 1964, East Elmhurst, NY; [p.] Wheeler S. Small, Jr. and Mary Murchison-Gumbs; [m.] Ken Arrington; [ch.] Tatyana Arrington; [ed.] H.S. of Art and Design, and Hunter College; [occ.] Administrative Assistant, Chase Manhattan Bank.; [oth. writ.] I enjoy writing fiction short stories.; [pers.] I have been greatly influenced by poetess Maya Angelou and Author Terri McMillan

SMALLCOMB, TALESIA
[pen.] Tina; [b.] September 20, 1966, St. Frances, Lynwood; [p.] Willie and Annie Bryant; [m.] Raymond Smallcomb, February 27, 1993; [ed.] Cerritos College from 1984 to 1991; [occ.] CCW Supervisor for child abuse clients (New Alternatives); [pers.] Yes, a special thank you to my three brothers: Marium, LaFrance, and Eldrid Bryant for all your support and love we shared.

SMITH, BERNICE A. WHERRY
[pen.] Anna Bell [b.] March 28, 1960, Cleveland, OH; [p.] Bennie and Lela Wherry; [m.] Leigh R. Smith, December 3, 1982; [ch.] Jennifer, Clarissa, Brittany, [ed.] John Adams High, Bachelor of Science from Dyke College.; [occ.] Homemaker; [memb.] Central Elementary PTA, Bedford Heights, Ohio, Library of Congress Founding National Member Archives.; [hon.] 92-93 The National Dean's List, 92-93 Who's Who Among Students in American Universities and Colleges, Dyke College Dean's List.; [oth. writ.] Several unpublished poems 1989 Letter to the Editor, The Vindicator, Youngstown, OH.; [pers.] We cannot experience true happiness until we can understand our pain.; [a.] Bedford Heights, OH

SMITH, BONNIE
[b.] July, 1971, Alberta, Canada; [p.] Donna and Adolf Mantei; [m.] Ivor Smith, September, 1991; [ch.] Tyrell, Ebony and Dionn; [occ.] Homemaker; [pers.] I have always used my poetry as a get away or as part of a healing process. This was my first entry into any contest and I can't believe the results! A very special thanks to Mr. John Rollins and my loving family who supported me.; [a.] Calgary, Alberta, Canada

SMITH, CANDISE-LYNN LIORA
[pen.] Candise-lynn Smith; [b.] October 24, 1979, Pageton, WV; [p.] Caurline Smith and Kennith; [ed.] (Primary) Meron Bay (High School) Northlands Secondary (Still attending); [occ.] Student; [hon.] Honor badges and poetry awards, computer writing, science work and math; [oth. writ.] A poem was put in the news paper after winning a contest. And just writing for school; [pers.] I write to show my feelings and to express the way of life, I think it is much easier to write in poetry and its better to understand and I thank my mother and father for being their for me; [a.] Hamilton, Bermuda

SMITH, CHRISTINE M.
[pen.] Spoiled Bratt; [b.] Chicago, IL; [p.] Ann and Peter Flammang; [ch.] James A. Smith; [ed.] St. Michael Grade School, St. Michael Central High School; [occ.] Accounting Clerk; [pers.] I write poetry as a hobby, and for the enjoyment of family and friends. The poem in this book is dedicated to the life-long friendship between Agnes Koch, my sister and Jackie Kleich, her friend.; [a.] Chicago, IL

SMITH, EILEEN
[pen.] Vicki; [b.] March 28, 1957, Los Angeles, CA; [p.] Edmond and Jeanette Patenaude; [m.] John Smith, September 14, 1975; [ch.] Roxeen, Jayson and Jesse; [ed.] La Quita - Class of 1975; [oth. writ.] I have written others. But, I haven't had any published.; [pers.] Often during my life, I've felt oddly out of place, never knowing why, or where these feelings step from. Oddly, though a close brush with death caused information regarding someone - that up until then was totally unknown to me, even though I would not exist today if not for this person. I have to wonder - does this person feel like I do? Does this person believe in my existence and believe that I deserve the total knowledge surrounding the fact of my life, so that I might not feel oddly out of place?

SMITH, GREGORY ALEXANDER
[pen.] G. A. Smith; [b.] May 7, 1948, Victoria, British Columbia, Canada; [p.] Alex and Barbara Smith; [m.] Lynne Rosalie Smith (Nee) Povey, October 23, 1976; [ch.] Kent Alexander 17, Mark Scott 15; [ed.] O.D.H. Ontario Diploma in Horticulture from University of Guelph, Ontario, Canada; [occ.] Horticulturist, Former Golf Course Superintendent and R.C.M.P. Officer; [memb.] Life member of the University School old Boy's Association, Victoria British Columbia, Canada; [oth. writ.] Poem - to Qualicum with love - published in book - 'Qualicum Beach - a history of Vancouver Is. Best kept secret' by Brad Wylie. Poem - published in newspaper, 'The Passing Of The Flame'. (22 other poems, 24 short stories, 3 novels) (unpublished to date); [pers.] My poetry is influenced by the Flora and Fauna of Vancouver Is. And its surrounding waters. I am blessed to live in such a beautiful setting; [a.] Nanaimo British Columbia, Canada

SMITH, HENRIETTA
[b.] April 5, 1934, Brooklyn, NY; [ch.] Gary Smith and George E. Smith; [occ.] Retired; [oth. writ.] Short stories, speeches, sermonette.; [pers.] I wrote over fifty poems, and I tried to put myself in some, and to feel what others might.; [a.] Savannah, GA

SMITH, HERBERT H.
[pen.] Herbert H. Smith; [b.] February 15, 1928, Whitesburg, KY; [p.] Hewey and Leona Smith; [m.] Florence Ison Smith, February 5, 1949; [ed.] 2 years High School; [occ.] Retired; [memb.] 45 yrs Masonic Lodge, 29 yrs Shrine Club; [oth. writ.] Several other poems; [pers.] I worked in the coal mine for 30 yrs; [a.] Whitesburg, KY

SMITH III, ANDREW
[pen.] Drew; [b.] February 6, 1975, Brooklyn, NY; [p.] Andrew Smith Jr., Linda D. Smith; [ed.] Currently in Houghton College a Christian; [occ.] Loving my Lord ad Personal Savior Jesus Christ; [memb.] Basketball team, Spanish Club, Fellowship forum; [hon.] Numerous honors for basketball but I'm really looking for an award in the future for my writing so I can pass all the glory and honor over to my Lord.; [oth. writ.] Many other poems some published in school papers.; [pers.] I strive to open peoples eyes, by showing new in many different ways how my God speaks to us all.; [a.] Brooklyn, NY

SMITH III, GARLAND RAY
[pen.] B. J. Smith; [b.] December 20, 1982, Victoria, TX; [p.] Garland Ray Smith Jr., Dianna O'Quinn Mann; [ed.] Honor Student, Straight A-Student, Perfect Attendance Student, Patti Welder Jr. High School; [occ.] Student, Author; [memb.] Green peace, Topps Stadium Club, Christ The Victor Lutheran Church; [hon.] Presidential Award for Educational Excellence; [oth. writ.] Various other poems not published; [pers.] Life is short so pick it up and live with it as long as you can; [a.] Victoria, TX

SMITH, JOANNE
[b.] September 22, 1968, Clitheroe, England; [p.] Geoffrey Smith, Christine Horrocks; [ed.] St. Augustine's RC High (Billington), St Mary's 6th Form College (Blackburn), Blackburn College, Accrington College; [occ.] Secretary, UDU Operator, currently unemployed; [memb.] Clitheroe Singers, (community choir), Stephanie Powers Official Fan Club.; [oth. writ.] Short story published in anthology "New Fiction - Shorts from Lancashire", poem published in anthology "As Seen on Tu-Your Favorites" (all in UK), poem published in anthology "The Space Between (USA); [pers.] This poem is dedicated to Mr. Family and Mr. Friend Fiona Bannister (thank you for being my friend). Also to Robert Wagner and Stephanie Powers (may you always be `Hart to Hart'); [a.] Clitheroe Lancashire, England

SMITH, JOHNETTA DELORES
[pen.] Jai Dee Smith; [b.] December 27, 1942, Indianapolis, IN; [p.] Vera Mae Newby (mother); [ch.] Mother of four (adults); [ed.] GED; [occ.] Former Government Employee, Military Pay Techn.; [oth. writ.] Non published at present; [pers.] I desire to speak for those unheard, for the people with many untold feelings about life as we endured. And to reveal the deepest of our soul as we live in this world screaming unheard.; [a.] Indianapolis, IN

SMITH, LINDA
[pen.] Jessica Smith; [b.] September 24, 1968, Denver, CO; [m.] Ellis Smith, February 14, 1990; [ch.] Vincent Sean, Meagan Elisa, Jacob Keegan; [ed.] Huntington High, Control Data Institute; [occ.] Homemaker; [hon.] Mother of three (it is an honor, at least to me); [oth. writ.] Poems published in The Seedlings vol. XI 1980-81 and Poems place at Honorable Mention in the N.L.W.C. Poetry Contest September 1982. Haiku Poetry for A Japanese Celebration; [pers.] I am breaking the chains of generations of abuse. My goal is to raise children who know they are precious gifts from God. To nurture them the equip them to fill their place in Society and to find their Inner Excellence. In hopes they will shine like the stars they really are. Be an example of excellence to your children for their benefit and for our futures benefit.; [a.] Dallas, TX

SMITH, LORI
[pen.] Sissy; [b.] July 1, 1968, Belleville, IL; [p.] Bill, Sheila Sullens; [m.] Divorced; [ch.] Tessie, Mist; [ed.] Study in Paralegal; [occ.] Student; [hon.] Honorable Mentions World of Poetry; [oth. writ.] A Vision of Thought Tears; [pers.] I'd like to someday publish my poems and work for a writing firm; [a.] Scranton, PA

SMITH, MONICA E.
[b.] February 22, 1951, Cleveland, OH; [p.] Michael E. Stinich (deceased) and Olga Stinich (Nee Hritz); [m.] Scott F. Smith, December 28, 1975; [ch.] Jeremy Franklin, Aaron, Michael, Nathanael David, Veronica Marie; [ed.] Byzantine Catholic and Parma Senior high Schools, Kent State University; [occ.] Patient care assistant at Mt. Carmel Medical Center in Columbus, OH; [memb.] Amnesty International, Editor of "Peace Meal" (Catholic Worker Newsletter); [oth. writ.] Several poems published in "Peace Meal" and other religious and

peace justice newsletters. Poem accepted for publication in Creative Peace making in times of war (not yet published at this writing); [pers.] To love and be loved this, I feel, is the purpose of life. The many injustices of society have evoked in me a feeling of frustration. My poetry has become an out let, a vehicle through which I can express that frustration, question wrongs and teach God's truth, which is love. My life and poetry have been greatly influenced by Bob Dylan.; [a.] West Liberty, OH

SMITH, MURPHY EDWARD
[b.] September 13, 1962, Baltimore, MD; [p.] Ralph and Betty Peace; [ch.] Michael Wilcox; [ed.] Boston Technical High Catonsville Community College; [occ.] Film Librarian University Hospital, Baltimore, MD; [oth. writ.] Distinguished poets of America, in a different light, our world's favorite poems. Letters published in the Baltimore Sun Time Magazine, The Baltimore Chronicle; [pers.] Rosalind, thank you for being a good mother to our son and a beautiful person.; [a.] Baltimore, MD

SMITH, ROBERT LLOYD
[pen.] R. L. Smith; [b.] July 4, 1913, Nova Scotia, Canada; [p.] Greg Smith, Jemie E. Smith (Both deceased); [m.] Rite E. Smith, July 13, 1992; [ch.] Twin Peter and Pat Smith; [ed.] 2 yrs. University St. Joseph University NB; [occ.] Retired CM Machinest, Moncture NB; [memb.] Foresters Sect. Treas Mason United Church; [hon.] Retired Capt Hook and Ladder Ngi Moncton Volunteer Fire Dert St. John Ambulance.; [oth. writ.] The Atlantic Blackideper Diesel Dan Mayor of High St. Praiser Flower no Trees Nature Painy-Brush; [a.] Moncton New Brunswick, Canada

SMITH, SHONDA
[b.] December 18, 1970, Colorado Springs, CO; [p.] Arvel and Marie Smith; [m.] Single; [ed.] K-12, 3 yrs College, Central High School, Mesa State College; [occ.] E. K. G. Tech.; [memb.] American Diabetes Association, American Cancer Association, Health and Fitness Club, Emmanuel Baptist Church; [hon.] Senior Attendant (Home) coming letter in Band, Band Leadership, 2nd place in 8th Grade Art Contest Against Local High School and Colleges.; [oth. writ.] Many poems and short stories; [pers.] "You can't live in yesterday, because you don't know how many tomorrow you have! You can't worry about tomorrow, it may never come! Live today and be happy"; [a.] Grand Junction, CO

SMITH, TARA
[pen.] Tara Smith; [b.] June 26, 1979, Allentown, PA; [p.] Sandra and Robert Smith; [ed.] Boca Raton High School; [occ.] Student; [pers.] Through my poems I like to express the emotions many teens feel, while going through the hardships of this difficult decade.; [a.] Boca Raton, FL

SMITH, TODD
[b.] March 17, 1966, Dallas, TX; [ed.] BA degree in Journalism Baylor University, 1988; [occ.] Account Executive, Public Relations; [memb.] The Society of Professional Journalists; [oth. writ.] Various and collected poems (unpublished); [pers.] "Your reach should exceed your grasp... or what's a heaven for" Robert Browning; [a.] Nashville, TN

SMOTHERS, BRENDA F.
[pen.] Bren; [b.] January 12, 1954, LA; [p.] John and Mildred Tobin; [m.] John W. Smothers, April 20, 1986; [ch.] 1 Dellshone L. Wilson; [ed.] Finish High School In Los Angeles in 1971; [occ.] H/W; [memb.] Light House Church; [pers.] I strive to reflect my gift of God to many people.; [a.] Camp Lejeune, NC

SNIDER, THERESA ANN
[pen.] Terri; [b.] February 14, 1953, Zanesville, OH; [p.] Mr. and Mrs. Bernard Himmelspach; [m.] Douglas Richard Snider (ex-husband), May 18, 1974; [ch.] James Richard Snider 20, Marcus Allen Snider 10; [ed.] Grade school - 1 thru 8th St Nichoals School Jr. High, High school - 1 year and Rosecrans - 3 years, Maysville High School did not graduate in 1972, currently taking GED class 2 days a week.; [occ.] Homemaker mother, poem and songwriter.; [memb.] Eagles 302 Lady's Aux 1972, a member of National Library of Poetry for 1 year.; [hon.] Won Editor's Choice Award for the poem: The World is Far and Wide Within... which is published in at days end. Won Editor's Choice Award for poem called: When You're All Alone, Think Of... which is published in The Edge of Twilight.; [oth. writ.] How Can I Find My way to Who Do I... which will be published in spring of 1995. When You're All... which is a song which will be published in after the storm in summer of 1995. "Gone Are The Days of Harvest" which will be publish by sparrowgrass poetry forum in Sistersville, WV; [pers.] Take things the way they are, take each day as it is.; [a.] Zanesville, OH

SNOWDEN, DON JONES
[pen.] Don; [b.] March 7, 1978, Delaware; [p.] Gloria Snowden; [ed.] 11th grade; [occ.] Student; [memb.] Basketball Team, Soccer Team. Germantown Community Paper. Journalism Club.; [hon.] Honor Rolls 3 years; [oth. writ.] Don's Love Columns (Green Tree School); [pers.] I have been inspired by my Mom; [a.] Philadelphia, PA

SO, JENNIFER G.
[pen.] Jenny; [b.] September 17, 1979, Iloilo City, Philippines; [p.] Johnny So and Pacita So; [ed.] 3rd Year High School; [occ.] Student, Iloilo Central Commercial High School; [memb.] Managing Editor in School Publication, "The Chain"; [hon.] Honor Student, Class Best Debater, Class Best Speaker; [oth. writ.] Several Articles and Poems in school publications, "The Chain"; [pers.] The Essence of writing portrays, the inner soul of the writer. It is only in writing where you can be what you want to be.; [a.] Iloilo City, Philippines

SOBEL, DENISE MARIE
[b.] January 13, 1955, Bronx, NY; [p.] Alexander and Frances Lanzetta; [m.] Lenny Sobel, August 7, 1994; [ed.] Uniondale High; [occ.] Homemaker; [memb.] National Audubon Society, The CFIDS Assoc. of America, Inc., the Pittsburgh Center for Peace, Human Life International, Endometriosis Association.; [oth. writ.] "A Jasmine Song", "Ten Maple Trees Huddled Together", (2 poems unpublished); [pers.] My inspirations come from nature and my spirituality. "May we all grow in love and light, in respect for each other's beliefs and understandings about God, who is infinitely greater than our hearts, and yet who chooses to dwell in the depths of each of us."; [a.] Westbury, NY

SOLLECITO, CHRIS M.
[b.] October 28, 1974, Brooklyn; [ed.] Bernard Baruch College; [occ.] A full-time college student with a part-time job as a humble waiter earning less than $3 an hour with great dreams and aspirations of becoming an author.; [hon.] Medals for excelling in Science and Italian, certificate in recognition of outstanding Academic Achievement, Plaque commemorating acceptance into who's who American High School Students.; [oth. writ.] An, as of yet, unfinished and unpublished series of action-adventure, mystery books entitled Boys of Brooklyn, with tight continuity and lots of character development.; [pers.] The meaning of life is the pursuit of happiness. The keys of life are timing and patience. Love and pain go hand in hand. Sometimes you have to lose before you can win. Pace yourself and plan ahead. Life is a game in which there are no rules. Life goes on. Therefore, the game continues....; [a.] Brooklyn, NY

SONNENSCHEIN, REGINA C.
[b.] April 14, 1950, Germany; [m.] widowed; [ch.] Two Girls 9-12 years old [ed.] Electromechanic at High-School in Germany; [occ.] Housewife, writer in the making; [memb.] Former Soprano at Schwaebische Singer in N.J.; [oth. writ.] I am currently working on my first book, in which my poem, "Now and Forever" shall also be published. [pers.] Great human tragedies and triumphs long past, as well as experiences in my own personal life inspired me to write and there by express the inner most evil and beauty of the human spirit.; [a.] Hesperia, CA

SOOKRAM, SHARON
[pen.] Sharon Sookram; [b.] June 5, 1966, Guyana; [p.] D. and J. Sookram; [ed.] New Amsterdam Multilateral School (Guyana), Drake Business School (New York), Pace University (New York).; [occ.] Proofreader; [hon.] Dean's List, winner of Curtis Owens short fiction writing 1994 (Pace University); [oth. writ.] Short stories/ poems published in Aphros (Pace literary news magazine); [pers.] Love to explore that thin twisted line that separates good from evil!; [a.] Elmont, NY

SORENSEN, SIMON
[b.] June 1, 1976, Denmark; [p.] Hans Peter and Marie-Ann Sorensen; [ed.] Rocky Mountain Elementary and Elkford Secondary School; [occ.] Student at the University of Lethbrige, Alberta, Canada; [hon.] First place in two essay contests in the Elk Valley. English Excellency Awards.; [oth. writ.] None published however I have a major book project on the way.; [pers.] My writings come from the heart where I believe true poetry is born. This poem for instance was to my parents on my graduation day; [a.] Elkford British Columbia, Canada

SOUSA, HELEN NAOMI
[b.] February 27, 1912, Lincoln, RI; [p.] Mary and John Pierce; [m.] Joseph Soeira Sousa, 1946; [ch.] Johnathan Sousa, Jeff Sousa, Patti Lundsgren; [ed.] PatucKet High School RI.; [occ.] Retired, Worked - Nurses Aid, Ross Hospital Ross, CA. and Moren CO. Marin Generan Hosp.; [hon.] This is my first honor; [pers.] Never cease to believe because when you leased expect it, it will happen.; [a.] Rochlin, CA

SOUTHERN, TIFFANY
[b.] December 18, 1968, Illinois; [p.] Mollie and Don Langley and Rode and Mary Ann Southern; [occ.] Outdoor Rec. Asst. Patrick AFB, FL; [a.] Satellite Beach, FL

SOUTHWORTH, ELISHA
[b.] February 24, 1942, Vienna, Austria; [p.] Herta and Otto Kubitschek; [m.] Robert Southworth, July 13, 1992; [ed.] Teacher Training College Vienna, Austria, Registered Nurse in London, England, College of Psychotherapeutics in Kent, England; [occ.] Care-giver, gardener, counsellor; [memb.] Blanco Writer's Club, Quartus Foundation, Boerne, TX, Findhorn Foundation, Scotland, Creative Living, Israel, Harmonious Living,

Greece; [oth. writ.] Several articles in the Quartus Report; [pers.] I love seeing spirit express through all forms of life, moment by moment, and I greatly enjoy sharing this vision.; [a.] Blanco, TX

SPAETH, JONATHAN W.
[pen.] Riverhead [b.] December 31, 1973, Riverhead, NY; [p.] Joyce and Walter Spaeth; [ed.] Suffolk Community College, Long Island University, Southampton Campus; [occ.] Student; [memb.] Phi Theta Kappa, Pi Alpha Sigman; [pers.] I owe it all to Dr. Jeff Greenberger, my High School Latin teacher who helped me to "see".; [a.] Riverhead, NY

SPANGLER, MONICA ANN
[pen.] Monica Villa; [b.] March 3, 1978, Chicago, IL; [p.] Lera Villa, Antonio Villa Sr.; [ed.] West Point High School, 9th Grade, Attend Cullman Area Vocational School Subject Horticultural in FFA class; [occ.] Student in School; [hon.] FFA Honors; [oth. writ.] This was my first one that I've written others but never submitted them with now.; [pers.] I strive to try to make this a better world to live in. This is the time of the youth and it's up to us to try to change it with the help and Guidance of God our Father; [a.] Cullman, AL

SPARAGNA, JUDITH C.
[pen.] Judith Billings-Sparagna; [b.] Sacramento, CA; [p.] Mrs. Laura Toll Billings; [m.] John Sparagna, July 17, 1977; [ed.] 2 yrs College, Master's Equivalency in Computer Science (IBM Education); [occ.] Systems and Application Programmer; [memb.] Mensa Eligibility, Life time membership - CA. Scholarship Federation; [hon.] Grand Prize in the Robert Frost Chapter of Chaparal Poets (Circa 1977) Various other awards for poetry, Journalism Scholarship; [oth. writ.] Various poems/articles published in local publications, World of Poetry publication; [pers.] My work is dedicated to my mother who gave me faith, sprinkled with encouragement, and enfolded me with her ever present love.; [a.] Morgan Hill, CA

SPEER, CATHERINE EDWARDS
[b.] April 13, 1906, Dobbs, MD; [p.] Rev. Richard and Elsie Edwards; [m.] Hugh Speer, November 28, 1930; [ch.] Marcia Snook, Mary Lynn Shea; [occ.] Library of Congress, 1927-1930; [memb.] League of Women Voters Amer. Assoc. of University Women Wednesday Study Club; [oth. writ.] A Wooly Tale, Don't Take My Song Away, The Queen's in the Parlor, Susan Had a Little Lamb; [pers.] Service to mankind and appreciation of the universe.; [a.] Shawnee Mission, KS

SPELLS, SEIRGASTER L.
[pen.] S. Leigh Spells; [b.] November 16, 1948, Philadelphia, PA; [p.] Joseph Smith, Naomi Smith; [ch.] Stephanie Leigh, Marlena Seirgaster; [ed.] B.S. Marketing Management, Philadelphia College of Textiles and Science, M.S. Library Science, Drexel University; [occ.] Librarian, teacher Philadelphia Public School System, poet; [memb.] Philadelphia Coalition of Federated Women, American Heritage Society, Association of Philadelphia Librarians, American Library Association; [oth. writ.] Collection of poems and short stories; [pers.] I teach... I teach... I, too learn!; [a.] Philadelphia, PA

SPENCE, CHRISTINE ELY
[pen.] Christine Ely Jones or Spence; [b.] March 25, 1948, Dover, DE; [p.] Bettie Louise and Harry C. Ely; [m.] Richard Spence, April 29, 1994; [ch.] Melinda Wieber, David Jones; [ed.] Caesar Rodney High School - taught Fire Safety for Delaware State Fire School; [occ.] Administrative Assistant First State Coin Dover; [memb.] Past President and current honorary member Marydel Ladies Auxiliary; [oth. writ.] Poems in local newspaper, poems published in The Great Treasury of World Poems and The Family Treasury of Great Poems; [pers.] I'm influenced mainly by the romantic aspect of life and one of my dreams is to have one my poems set to music; [a.] Marydel, DE

SPENCER, GENEVA LAURA T.
[pen.] Geneva L. T. Spencer; [b.] June 23, 1925, Valparaiso, IN; [p.] Floyd L. and Edith L. Kinzie-Tucker; [m.] Wilbert Charles Spencer, September 9, 1944; [ch.] Wilberta, Joseph, Edward, Janet; [ed.] 1 Through 12; [occ.] Retired, Valparaiso community Schools; [memb.] Immanuel Luthern, Church President Immanuel Benefit Society Represent Immanuel Luthern Church for Church women united/life member of disabled American Veterans Ladies auxiliary chapter 6, South Bend, Ind.; [hon.] American Poetry Association Poet of Merit 1989 Santa Cruz, California Contributing Poet in best new poets of 1989 - American poetry Association Santa Cruz, California; [oth. writ.] As I stood silently alone sparrowgrass poetry poetic voices of America Sisteroville, WV - 1992; [pers.] I have a large collection and wish that someday publish all under one hardback book cover; [a.] Valparaiso, IN

SPERLING, LOIS PALMER E.
[b.] February 17, 1923, New London, WI; [p.] Charles and Nina Palmer; [ch.] Sharon, Jann, Linda, Richard, and Celeste.; [ed.] Attended Wisc. U., Indiana U., Rider College and Trenton State. No degrees.; [occ.] Retired Bookkeeper; [memb.] American Legion, Tues. AM, Bowling League, Mercer Co. Quilting Guild and various senior groups.; [hon.] Seven Gold, one Silver, and one Bronze Medal in the N.J. Senior Olympics.; [oth. writ.] Various articles in local publications. Children's Stories.; [pers.] So little time, so much to do. Love to bowl, golf, paint, write, travel, meet people, quilt and all sorts of crafts.; [a.] Trenton, NJ

SPETNAGEL, JOHN
[pen.] Tim Spetnagel; [b.] October 6, 1951, Chillicotte, OH; [p.] Joe and Shirley Spetnagel; [ed.] BA in psychology, pursuing advanced degree, California State University in Los Angeles (CSULA); [occ.] Career and Transition Counselor for high school students with disabilities.; [hon.] Dean's List, The National Dean's Honor List; [oth. writ.] Published several poems and a children's story "The Three Little Stars."; [pers.] I strive to paint a picture with the stroke of my pen on a canvas of paper.; [a.] Los Angeles, CA

SPINELLI, NICKY
[pen.] Nicky; [b.] February 5, 1980, Brockport, NY; [p.] Holly and Pat Spinelli; [ed.] Attending Byron-Bergen High School; [occ.] Student (9th grade at Byron-Bergen High School.; [hon.] Member of the National Honor Society. Member of JV Cheer leading squad. Member of 4-H Horse program. Completed successfully in both English style riding and driving, to the state level. In 1992, placed first at New York State fair, pleasure driving my horse.; [oth. writ.] Personal collection of various poems and writings.; [a.] Byron, NY

SPOSATO, SERMILA
[pen.] Sensi; [b.] May 2, 1971, Suriname; [p.] Soebhawarie and Kamta Gerhoe; [m.] Richie Sposato, May 19, 1993; [ch.] Nisha, Amber; [oth. writ.] Several poems and songs.; [pers.] Even though people won't interpret my poems with the exact same feelings. Hopefully they can relate to them in their own way; [a.] Liverpool, NY

STACKHOUSE, CHARLENE A.
[b.] April 16, 1964, Wilkes Barre, PA; [p.] Jo Ann and Charles Galinski; [m.] Duane S. Stackhouse, June 2, 1990; [ed.] Bishop Hoban High School Luzerne County Community College; [occ.] Registered Nurse, St. Lukes Hospital Operating Room, Bethlehem PA; [memb.] Association of Operating Room nurses; [hon.] Presidents Honor Roll; [pers.] I have been influenced by Elizabeth Barrett Browning and am a true Romantic heart and soul. I wish to thank Dr. Stephen Sinclair for encouraging my creativity and my husband Duane for his love and support.; [a.] Limeport, PA

STADLER, JUSTIN
[b.] July 25, 1981, Brooklyn, NY; [p.] Sherry Stadler, Herb Stadler; [ed.] Marine Park J.H.S., I.S. 34; [occ.] Student; [hon.] Certificate of Recognition, Certificate of Achievement, Certificate of promotion, Certificate of Service, Presidential Academic Fitness Award, Award of Merit, Drug Prevention Award, Math Team Award; [pers.] I have been supported by my parents, my grandmother Marilyn Helfman, and my brother Derek. You can do anything if you put your mind to it.; [a.] Staten Island, NY

STAFFORD, TRINA MONET
[b.] October 24, 1983, Baton Rouge, LA; [ed.] 5th Grade Student at Richland Elem, Quakertown, PA; [occ.] Student; [hon.] Honor Roll Student at School; [oth. writ.] I have a book of poems that I have written not published. I enjoy writing poems and will keep adding to my book.; [pers.] I enjoy writing also reading. I like to read about history and learn all the things I can about our country.; [a.] Quakertown, PA

STAMBAUGH, DEBORAH
[b.] April 10, 1966, Amarillo, TX; [ed.] BS Environmental Studies University of St. Thomas (junior year) Houston, TX; [occ.] Health, Safety and Environmental Affairs Data Analyst for Solvay America, Inc. Houston, TX; [memb.] Phi Sigma Tau Alpha Sigma Lambda, Houston World Affairs Cncl International Society of Poets; [oth. writ.] Poetry, Songs, short stories and three novels in the making; [a.] Houston, TX

STANAT, HEIDI MARIE
[pen.] Andelusia Isis; [b.] October 26, 1977, Rockville, CT; [p.] Sue and Kenneth Stanat; [ed.] East Windsor High; [memb.] FHA (Future Homemakers of America); [oth. writ.] Journals and many poems.; [pers.] It is my dream to be a poet of wondering wilderness. And it is my destiny to fill my dream with happiness (known or unknown).; [a.] Broad Brook, CT

STANLEY, CHRISTOPHER S.
[pen.] Chi; [b.] September 21, 1961, Washington, DC; [oth. writ.] Many other poems yet to be viewed by others who seek the truth.; [pers.] From the void within lives the one truth, the voice of the soul, the voice of God within us all!; [a.] Tucson, AZ

STANLEY, JOAN E.
[pen.] Elizabeth Martin Quigley; [b.] April 9, 1938, Chicago, IL; [p.] Charles H, Goggin, Mary Quigley Goggin; [m.] Divorced; [ch.] Laura, Christy, Michalene, Paula, Donna, Theresa, Frank, Brian; [ed.] Visitation

High, self taught in the art of poem, prose, song writing, lyrics.; [occ.] Executive Secretary, Big shoulders fund, archdiocese of Chicago.; [memb.] Lay Order of Carmel; [oth. writ.] Articles, poems, prose published in the vine newspaper, favorite writings are, "Michigan Avenue", Prose ("Edward", "Cup O' Tea", "Christmas Memories", 13 songs and lyrics; [pers.] My highest education was received in this Universe I live in, learning to open my mind and heart, and deepest part of my being to family, friends and people who cross my part and "being present to" All The Wonders on God's Green Earth.; [a.] Riverdale, IL

STANLEY, JOHN M.
[b.] August 22, 1972, Cincinnati, OH; [p.] Willard and Georgia Stanley; [ed.] Graduated North College Hill High Shool; [occ.] Musician, artist, singer, songwriter; [oth. writ.] Several published poems, and a wall mural; [pers.] We are all a spark in the flame of life. We all have the opportunity to shine, those who choose to do so, make the flame that much greater.; [a.] Cincinnati, OH

STANLEY, LINDA KAY
[b.] November 26, 1952, Modesto, CA; [p.] Dixie L. Santos; [m.] Richard A. Stanley, December 22, 1984; [ch.] Justin P. Kurdupski, Sonja L., Partain, Elaina R. Cowdell, Ronia Ann Stanley; [ed.] Modesto High School 1970; [occ.] Fernley Town - Park Maintenance; [memb.] Fernley Softball Ass. Bunko - Fernley Improvement Club - Volunteer for Lyons Club and Senior Citizens; [hon.] Yo Yo Contest in 4th grade. Best all around basketball player in 1966; [oth. writ.] Only a few for friends and family; [pers.] I feel my philosophy of life has been inspired from my grandfather, who was born in 1900 and moved from Kansas to California in the early 40's bought a bare piece of land and made a productive dairy farm our of it. A lot of my childhood was spent on the ranch helping my grandpa and learning his philosophy of life... To pour salt in the wound, hurts like hill, but kills all the infection and helps the wound to heal faster. At seventeen years of age I was the only one in the family who wanted the old windmill and the Ford tractor.; [a.] Fernley, NV

STARK, ANDREW PAUL
[b.] Buffalo, NY; [p.] Andrew and Helen E. Stark; [m.] Barbara A. Stark, August 13, 1977; [ch.] Jennifer, Andrea, Debra, Lisa, William; [ed.] University of Buffalo - B.A. History, Boston University Graduate School M.A. Studies in Communication Arts; [occ.] Vice President Communications, Mutual of America; [hon.] WGBH-TV (Boston) Scholarship - H.V. Kaltenborn Foundation Assistance Numerous Industry Awards; [oth. writ.] Unpublished: 6 Novels, 3 Volumes of poetry and numerous short stories. Published - all public relations work related.; [pers.] The light of discovery can come from conflict or love.; [a.] Edison, NJ

STEELE, ANGIE KAY
[pen.] A. K. Steele; [b.] December 8, 1959, Springfield, MO; [p.] Sarah Baier and Tim Tindle; [m.] Tom Steele, December 18, 1988; [ch.] Tim Nelson and Jandee Steele; [ed.] I went back to school in 1985, at the age of 25, and received my G.E.D. At Graff Extension Center in Springfield, MO; [occ.] Housewife and aspiring poetry and songwriter; [memb.] Top Records Songwriters Association and Ozarks Noteworthy Songwriter's Association; [oth. writ.] This is my 1st poem to be published, and I am very excited about accomplishing that.; [pers.] Every poem or song lyric that I write has been inspired by something I have seen or experienced. I always feel good about something I have written, knowing it has came from my heart for someone to enjoy; [a.] Springfield, MO

STEGER, EMILY
[b.] August 16, 1977, GA; [p.] David and Susan Steger; [ed.] Currently and senior at Riverton High School, Riverton, WY; [occ.] Student; [memb.] Riverton High School Swim Team, Riverton High School Speech Team, Riverton High School Drill Team-past member, Ducks Unlimited, Riverton Aquatic Team - past member; [hon.] 3rd place - Wyoming Writer's Guild Performance of Wyoming Cowboy Poetry Round up, performed in High School Play; [oth. writ.] Poems published in: Highlights for Children Riverton Ranger local newspaper

STELL, JOHN R.
[pen.] Jack; [b.] November 29, 1947, Toronto, Canada; [p.] "Jack" and "Ronnie" (Veronica); [occ.] Truck Driver; [memb.] "Can owners and pilots association." "Ontario bush plane heritage and forest fire educational centre" and member of the unpublished band of lucky people who have seen and felt the great expanses of the north from land, water, and air.; [oth. writ.] Poems for anniversaries of close friends and relatives and comical songs for certain situations.; [pers.] I've always been a bit interested in poetry and being a pilot and into photography, the world from those views is very poetic I was paid to explore our great countries and poetry like art, photography, etc. is limitless enjoyment of one's experiences of life that others don't get to see.; [a.] Mississuaga Ontario, Canada

STEPHENS, TARA
[pen.] T. Stephens; [b.] May 6, 1975, Surrey, British Columbia, Canada; [p.] Michael and Darlyn Stephens; [ed.] North Delta Senior Secondary School, Highschool Graduation 1993, CompuCollege School of Business, Travel and Tourism Diploma Program - 1994; [occ.] Food Service Clerk, New Westminster, British Columbia; [memb.] Lions Club International, Royal Leo's Club - Youth Program, Lions Youth Exchange Student - Australia 1993; [hon.] Citizenship Award - 1987-88 Elementary School, Leo of the Year Award 1992, Lions International; [oth. writ.] Several self written poems not published.; [pers.] I enjoy the freedom of personal expression and feeling in my writing. It is my freedom and personal enjoyment. I have been greatly influenced by the special people who are apart of my life and the precious memories that they have given me. Precious Memories is dedicated to the loving memory of my mom Darlyn Stephens, who passed away suddenly in December 1994; [a.] Surrey British Columbia, Canada

STEVENS, LAVERNE
[b.] March 12, 1936, Cleveland, OH; [p.] Emilie and Mike Evanko; [m.] Ted Stevens; [ch.] Gary Lee, Ellen, Leslie and Bonnie step children: Michael, Barry, Gayle, Eileen, Laura, and Tim; [ed.] Graduate: Berea High School and Writers Digest School; [occ.] Sole proprietor of BREAD AND BUTTER PRESS (independent publisher) part time: Public Information receptionist for Polk Co. Comm.; [memb.] National Assoc. Independent Florida Publisher's Group, Imperial Rose Society, Poets on the Park, Trinity United Methodist Church, Florida State Poetry Assoc.; [hon.] Award of Merit and Publication Anthology 93 for poem A WALK AROUND THE LAKE. Award of Merit and publication in Anthology 94 for poem CHICKEN COOP REFUGE. Letter of commendation from First Lady Nancy Reagan for newspaper features done on drugs in The News Journal 1983; [oth. writ.] Biographical novel titled: BREAD AND BUTTER DAYS book to prepare kindergarten students for vision screening process titled: LOOK AND SEE H O T V OR LETTER E numerous poems and newspaper features short piece in Down Memory Lane Magazine and Senior Times magazine.; [pers.] I leave a part of myself with mankind when I share my writing with those who choose to read it. I hope my readers will feel strong emotions that might make a difference in their lives after reading my work.; [a.] Lakeland, Fl

STEVENSON, ROBERTA L.
[b.] January 24, 1939, Orange, TX; [p.] Lillie Mae Myers and Henry Clayton Petry; [m.] Widow; [ed.] Lutcher Stark High School, Orange, TX AA Los Angels City College, Los Angeles, CA; [occ.] Legal secretary since 1965 having owned legal transcribing service as well as working for small and large law firms; [memb.] Beverly Hills, California Legal secretaries Association (past treasurer, secretary and president), First Baptist Church of Granada Hills, California former member of Finance Committee); [hon.] 1st Place Orange County, Texas girl's reading contest, 2nd and 3rd place Los Angeles County Fair (crafts); [pers.] I find great pleasure in and enjoy being able to do for other people. I do volunteer charitable work and am a patron of the arts - in particular the Hollywood Bowl and the Los Angeles Philharmonic.; [a.] Orange, TX

STEVENSON, TAMMY KAY
[b.] June 30, 1964, Hillside, MI; [p.] Robert and Elaine Stevenson/Charlene Mooney; [m.] Michael J. Jacobs; [ed.] Adrian High School Jackson Community College; [occ.] Receptions/Office Assistant; [memb.] Honor Society at Jackson Community College; [hon.] Phi Theta Kappa; [oth. writ.] I have a lot of poems and essays that I have written over the years.; [pers.] I strive to reveal that each individuals outlook on life has meaning and strive to reach that goal in my poetry; [a.] Adrian, MI

STEWART, BARBARA
[pen.] Barb; [b.] August 10, 1937, Passaic, NJ; [ed.] Attended St. Leo's School and Popepius High School in passaic, NJ; [pers.] I strive to accomplish for myself as, well as other people with, some with and humor for them to enjoy. Something that is badly need in this world of ours, if I could help anyone this is an accomplishment in itself; [a.] Newton, NJ

STEWART, PATRICIA AHRENS
[b.] July 15, 1921, Yokohama, Japan; [p.] Paul Downing Ahrens, Lily G. Wallbrook; [m.] Paul E. Stewart (deceased), R. G. Struthers, September 6, 1947; [ch.] Paula Bergstrom, Philip Stewart, Twins: Peter Stewart and Pamela Erekuff; [ed.] Canadian Academy, Kobe, Japan (7 yrs) Grinnell College, Grinnell, Iowa 1 1/2 yrs, Grossmont Jr. College (two years), San Diego State Univ. 1 1/2 yrs., Cambridge Univ. Philosophy and Divinity 1 year; [occ.] Retired; [hon.] None except some sports events; [oth. writ.] Essays, many essays, and many poems; [pers.] Having lived and travelled worldwide one has to be receptive to all mankind.; [a.] El Cajon, CA

STICHA, GARY
[b.] October 24, 1949, New Prague, MN; [p.] Joseph and Lillian Sticha; [ed.] B.S. Geog and History Education - Mankato State U., Mankato MN, M.A. Elementary School Admin., University of St. Thomas, St. Paul, MN; [occ.] Elementary/ Middle School Principal, Mpls. MN; [memb.] "MAP, Aliveness Project, Dignity, Basilica

of St. Mary, Annunciation School, NCEA, ASCD, KCS, St. Hubert School, Escola Maria Imaculada" (Past and present); [hon.] Volunteer and donor for every AIDS function and organization I can manage. Privileged to be evaluated in superior category as an openly gay catholic school principal.; [oth. writ.] "The Weekender" the weekly school publication. "Carnaval" - article on multicultural education appeared in "Momentum", nat'l. ed. journal for NCEA.; [pers.] I strive to take the "High Road" in every one of life's situations. Adventure, experience, and membership in the world family have taken the place of gaining material goods and prestige.; [a.] Minneapolis, MN

STIERS, MICHAEL NALON
[b.] July 20, 1977, Little Rock, AR; [ed.] High School Student Cabot High School

STILL, MARY MARIE
[b.] October 23, 1944, Sheridan, AR; [p.] Richard M. Clark, Ola G. Clark; [m.] Harold D. Still, March 29, 1975; [ch.] Diane, Kim, Karri, Kevan; [ed.] Arkadelphia Senior High, NACC; [occ.] Console Operator in Shipping. Millbrook Distribution Services - Harrison; [pers.] A friend, Rob Matthews, ask me to write a poem describing a person falling in love, so I got the inspiration to write this poem, when I remembered how I felt when I met my husband, Harold, My feelings go into what I write.; [a.] Harrison, AK

STILLWELL, MEGAN J.
[b.] December 4, 1979, Lebanon, IN; [p.] Rev. Ronald and Rowena Osborne; [ed.] Thorntown Elementary School (Indiana), Mann Middle School, Abilene High School Texas; [occ.] Student; [memb.] YWCA Teen Group, Central Baptist Church San Saba, TX R.O.T.C. - Color Guard Team, Rifle Drill Team, Saber Team; [hon.] Recognized for outstanding student performance in middle school and high school.; [oth. writ.] Young love, the night I met you (poems); [pers.] I want to thank my boyfriend for infinite caring and respect. He has inspired most all of my literary worker.; [a.] Abilene, TX

STOCKDALE, JAMIE LYNN
[b.] February 21, 1965, Flint, MI; [p.] Charles and Betty Powell; [m.] Richard Stockdale, November 19, 1986; [ch.] Danielle Lynn Stockdale; [ed.] Oceanside High, Mira Costa College; [occ.] Crafter; [a.] Oceanside, CA

STONE, JULIE M.
[b.] January 1, 1970, Davenport, IA; [p.] Bill and Mary Stonebraker [m.] Chad Stone, September 4, 1993; [ed.] Eldora-New Providence High School, University of Iowa, BA/English; [occ.] Membership Services Coordinator/ Alpha Phi International Fraternity; [memb.] Alpha Phi International Fraternity; [hon.] 1st Place Juries Selection Lucidity Poetry Journal; [oth. writ.] Short Stories and essays only other published work found in Lucidity; [pers.] I always try to create emotion in my writings, even in writing about things that are not necessarily emotional; [a.] Oak Park, IL

STONE, NIGEL IVAN
[b.] February 23, 1929, England; [p.] David and Evelyn Stone; [m.] Barbara A. Stone, June 25, 1955; [ch.] Jonathan D. Stone; [ed.] Castle Douglas High Scotland School, Kingston School or Art. England (Sculpture); [occ.] "Narrator" (Recitor); [memb.] "Britten On The Bay Inc.", "Literary Director", Grace performed Baptist. Church Amityville Long Island NY; [hon.] British T.V. BBC Commercials, Radio announcing, public reading, Madison SQ. Garden Manhatten.; [oth. writ.] Various prose and poems, Book readings on tape pilgrims progress, Jonathan Bishop J.C. Ryle, ET.C. Edwards A. Monod.; [pers.] I like to offer Christian comfort in my writings, and an influenced greatly by Calvinist doctrine, I came to saving faith in the Lord Jesus in 1978. ("A sorrowful yet always rejoices"); [a.] Amityville, NY

STONEMAN, RAFAEL
[pen.] Rafe Stoneman; [b.] September 11, 1971, Ambler, PA; [p.] Judy Glafand, William Stoneman; [m.] Raphaela Stoneman, September 18, 1993; [ch.] Sage Stoneman; [occ.] Being; [memb.] S.A.G.; [oth. writ.] Transformation, a diary. 'Melting The Ego' with Blessings of Devotion 'God Is Cool', (One Man Show); [pers.] Everything that is seen of the same seer. This one seer is the self supreme, the Immortal, Blissful consciousness, that is the source of (us) all.; [a.] Lambertville, NJ

STORHOFF, DIANA CARMACK
[pen.] Donya Soleil; [b.] September 10, 1946, Anderson, IN; [p.] Paul and Elsie Carmack; [ch.] Damon Anthony (25), James Justin (21); [ed.] Master of Science in Chemistry from Ball State University Madison Heights High School; [occ.] Research Scientist for Boehringer Mannheim Diagnostics; [memb.] American Chemical Society, Holy Trinity Lutheran Church, League of Women Voters of Muncie - Delaware County, East Central Indiana Audubon Society, National Authors Registry; [hon.] Sigma Zeta, Dean's List BSU, Honors Banquet Psychology - Indiana Univ., Outstanding Technical Achievement in 1991 Boehringer Mannheim, Community Service 1987 from East Central Indiana Audubon Society; [oth. writ.] "Live Again" an unpublished collection of poems. Paul's Dream, a poem I wrote after my father died on September 10, 1994, also unpublished; [pers.] I try to reflect the beauty of life, its everlasting qualities and how lucky we are for each day that we can give to make it better for others. I have been influenced by Robert Frost, Carl Sandburg, Edna St. Vincent Millay, Elizabeth Barrett Browning, Rachel Carson; [a.] Muncie, IN

STORM, DENISE R.
[b.] April 6, 1978, Columbus, IN; [p.] Lewis Storm, Teresa Storm; [ed.] Franklin Country High School; [memb.] German Club, Future Business Leaders of America; [oth. writ.] Several poems not yet published; [pers.] All of the feelings I have inside are expressed through my writing. I have been greatly influenced by my everyday life.; [a.] Laurel, IN

STOVALL, KRISTAL LYN
[pen.] Krislyn Brown; [b.] August 8, 1978, Harbor City, CA; [p.] Kaye Stovall, Larry Ellis; [ed.] Junior at MacArthur High School; [occ.] Student at MacArthur High School; [memb.] National Honor Society, Student Council, Academic Decathalon, School Newspaper, Art Club, and History Bawl; [pers.] My poems come from my heart and mind, that is what makes them truly mine.; [a.] Houston, TX

STRACHEN, CHAYNEEN
[b.] February 5, 1981, England; [p.] Maureen Cameron, Ren Strachen; [pers.] I try to write and express my feelings in a way that people can relate to.

STRASSEL, JULIE
[b.] August 26, 1970, Philadelphia, PA; [p.] Anna May Kampf; [ed.] Frankford High School, Community College of Phila. Association degree Accounting, Penn State.; [occ.] Personal Banker, Core States Bank, NA. Phila. PA.; [memb.] National Association for female Executives; [pers.] I will try to succeed in all that I set out to do. To be the best person I can possibly be. To excel to strive for excellence and to be as open minded and learn all I can about life.; [a.] Philadelphia, PA

STRAUSBAUGH, INGEBORG
[pen.] Andree Strausbaugh; [b.] January 13, 1939, Germany; [p.] Hermine Priester, Justus Aubel; [pers.] Remembrance of war - Remembrance of war

STRENGTH, FRANK
[b.] October 21, 1977, Texas; [p.] Carlton and Gay Strength; [ed.] Northeast High School; [occ.] Students 10th Grade; [memb.] Church; [hon.] D.A.R.E. Award; [pers.] I wrote my first poem at age 12 at my Grandmother's death; [a.] Meridian, MS

STROINSKI, VICTORIA
[pen.] Franklin; [b.] October 18, 1982, Phoenix; [p.] Scott and Mary; [ed.] St. Francis, St Thomas; [memb.] Wildlife Assc, The Random House Records, Wildlife Act File.; [hon.] For report cards, 2nd place in city basketball tournament 1st place city volleyball tournament.; [pers.] "Praise God", that is all I have to say.; [a.] Phoenix, AZ

STROMAN, OMAR
[b.] December 30, 1973, Trenton, NJ; [p.] Dorothy Stroman, Norris Stroman, Deseased; [ed.] Santaluces High School (Lantana, Fla); [oth. writ.] The Joker. In the midst of the root of despair. Peace, day and nite. Made your own fate. Choice. Mix. (Note, among other poems).; [pers.] I write to deal with life more better I live to understand life and people more better and to uncover thee's mysteries of the world. I focus on change and the root.; [a.] Lantana, FL

STRUPP, JANET K.
[pen.] Janet K. Strupp; [b.] April 19, 1954, Bryan, OH; [p.] Henry and Doris V. Strupp; [ch.] James, Erik, Jared; [ed.] BA - Sociology Psy D - clinical psychology; [occ.] Clinical Psychologist; [memb.] Various Psychological Groups, PETA, Green Peace National and International Wildlife, Local Animal Groups, World Wildlife Fund; [hon.] Scholarships, awards for writing; [oth. writ.] Other poems published in newspaper, dissertation published in "American Psychologist", working on a book presenting.; [pers.] "Real isn't how you are made," said the Skin Horse. "It's a thing that happens to you." "Does it hurt?" asked the Rabbit. "Sometimes," said the Skin Horse, for he was always truthful." When you are real, you don't mind being hurt. "Does it happen all at once or bit by bit?" asked the Rabbit "It doesn't happen all at once," said the Skin Horse. " You become. It takes a long time. Generally, by the time you are real, most of your hair has been loved off, and your eyes drop out and you get loose in the joints and very shabby. But these things don't matter at all, because once you are real you can't be ugly, except to people who don't understand."; [a.] Dayton, OH

STUDER, LOIS EZELL
[pen.] Lois Ezell Studer; [b.] December 30, 1916, St. Louis, MD; [p.] Charles A. Ezell; [m.] Leota Mariegoss, January 22, 1916; [ch.] Lois Evelyn Ezell; [ed.] Grade School and High School I worked in a gift shop for about 20 years. It was a wonderful job; [occ.] Retired now; [memb.] Unity Church Sedalia; [hon.] None that I can think of. I greatly enjoy the compliments I get from my

friends and relatives. They keep my "Ego" satisfied"; [oth. writ.] My poetry has been in our local paper - Almost once a week it has been accepted well by the readers.; [pers.] Much of my writing has been about "God" and our planet I walk two miles almost everyday if the weather is pleasant. I am very happy when I can be outside; [a.] Sedalia, MO

STYFUNYK, VIOLET
[b.] March 15, 1959, Ontario, Canada; [p.] Ralph and Sheila May Mortensen; [m.] Kerry Styfunyk; [ch.] Logan Kerry; [ed.] University of British Columbia; [occ.] Bookkeeper; [pers.] This poem is dedicated to my mother with love; [a.] Ladysmith British Columbia, Canada

STYPA, KAREN
[b.] May 3, 1964, Rochester, NY; [p.] Fernand and Luella Brunette; [m.] Eric Stypa, June 17, 1989; [ch.] Heather Marie and Shawna Mae; [ed.] Benjamin Franklin H.S. courses in Sign Language I and II; [occ.] Housewife, mother; [a.] Hamlin, NY

SUGITA, JANICE
[b.] February 23, 1960, Osaka, Japan; [p.] Lillian Sugita, Toyoji Sugita; [ed.] Alhambra High, Sound Masters Institute, Van Mar Academy.; [occ.] Mechanical Effects Technician, Lucasfilm, Ltd.; [memb.] American Film Institute, Aids Project Los Angeles, Hollywood Supports, I.A.T.S.E., The Center - GLCSC.; [a.] West Hollywood, CA

SULLIVAN, GAIL A.
[b.] March 20, 1960, Chicago; [p.] James and Anna Casey; [ed.] Oaklawn Community H.S. Moraine Valley Junior College; [occ.] Customer Representative, for COM-ED; [hon.] Slogan contest for Crusade of Mercy (3rd place), (1st place) for Division Slogan for the Western Region of COM-ED.; [pers.] My poetry is inspired by current events happening in our world today. Hopefully through my poetry, I will spark the humanity and humility, found in us all.; [a.] Lombard, IL

SULLIVAN, JENNIFER LYNNE
[b.] May 21, 1977, Lawrence, MA; [p.] William and Ellen Sullivan; [ed.] Nashua Senior High; [oth. writ.] Several poems, non published.; [pers.] In my writing I try to express the feelings and emotions that everyone tend to hide.; [a.] Nashua, NH

SULLIVAN, RICHARD
[pen.] ROB; [b.] June 25, 1966, Malden, MA; [p.] Dianne and Richard Alan Sr.; [occ.] Printer; [memb.] Weymouth Ski Club; [pers.] All Good Things, In all Good Time!; [a.] Andover, MA

SULLIVAN, ROBIN LEE
[b.] May 8, 1962, Saint Marie, MI; [p.] Vernon and Karen Sullivan; [ed.] Frankfurt American High School, West Germany, Bates Vocational Technical - Tacoma, WA; [occ.] Inventory Auditor, Nashville, TN.; [hon.] Certified Television Broadcast Technician; [pers.] The model is my first published poem. It was originally titled "Youth". The model was inspired by my own life experience and a news report on the early retirement age of models; [a.] Nashville, TN

SUPLEE, DIANA FABIANI
[pen.] Diana Fabiani; [b.] September 16, 1923, Springfield, MS; [p.] Frank and Katrine Brewster; [m.] Charles Suplee; [ch.] David Long, [ed.] Doctor of Musical Arts Degree B.S., W.C.U., PA., Juilliard, MA and DMA Combs College, PA.; [occ.] Composer and writer; [memb.] Cecilian Music Society, Tampa Bay Composer's Forum Sarasota Music Teacher Association.; [hon.] Sang opera with Phila Lyric Opera Co. and at Carnegie Hall, appeared on Mike Douglas Show and other TV spacious Produced musical programs in Phila.; [oth. writ.] Wrote book "7 Vocal Vitamins Techniques for better speaking and singing", composed volume of music "Music for Piano with options for instruments"; [pers.] The arts inter-relate with each other and every aspect of life. I am in constant wonder at the changing and intriguing perspectives one finds in life and human nature.; [a.] Sarasota, FL

SUPOWIT, DIANE
[b.] September 12, 1973, Princeton, NJ; [p.] H. Mildred and William Supowit; [m.] Leonard Manzie Jr., August 17, 1996; [ed.] Delaware Valley Regional High School; [memb.] ASPCA, People for Ethical Treatment of Animals (PETA), World Wildlife Fund, Best Friend's Animal Sanctuary, Greenpeace, American Lung Association, habitat for Humanity, Red Ribbon Foundation; [hon.] Achieved perfect score on writing section of the High School Proficiency Test (MSPT), Honor Roll; [oth. writ.] Editor of high school newspaper (responsible for coming up with new ideas for articles and writing my own as well).; [pers.] Writing about life, love and relationship, including the good and the bad, is what I find most pleasure in. I hope to touch people with my work and convey manages that most everyone can relate to, but will interpret in a different way. I have been profoundly influenced by the songwriting of Amy Grant.; [a.] Milford, NJ

SUTHERLAND, WILLIAM
[b.] September 17, 1965, New York City, NY; [p.] Irene J. Sutherland, grandmother; [ed.] Mamaroneck High School, Mamaroneck, NY, (1983), Iona College, New Rochelle, NY (1987); [memb.] U.S. National Holocaust Museum, American Red Cross, Covenant House, Parishioner Sts., John And Paul Church; [hon.] Who's Who in American Colleges and Universities (1987), Delta Epsilon Sigma, Summa Cum Laude; [oth. writ.] "Weep For Poccur", "The Presence" and various short-stories and poems.; [a.] Larchmont, NY

SUTULA, SUSAN J.
[b.] June 30, 1963; [p.] Rocco and Lois DeSisto; [m.] Frank Sutula, June 18, 1988; [ed.] Graduate of Randolph High School; [pers.] Susan's four (4) year battle with cancer inspired her to write this poem in an effort to help her family understand her inner thoughts and fears. Her courage throughout her illness was an inspiration to us all. She never gave up hope. We, her family, encouraged her to have her poems published in an effort to help other families who are facing the same tragedy. On November 14, 1994, Susan J. Sutula Passed away, just weeks prior to being notified that her poem was to be published.; [a.] Wharton, NJ

SWAN, MILDRED KING
[b.] July 3, 1919, Muskogee, OK; [p.] John Wm. and Scottie Rodgers King; [m.] Oscar Edward Swan Jr., September 14, 1940; [ch.] Oscar Swan III, Janet Hill; [ed.] Muskogee High School, Univ. of OK, A.B., Univ. of Colorado MA; [occ.] Retired; [memb.] Delta Delta Delta sorority, Chapter AD, PEO Sisterhood, Cheyenne, WY. PHI Beta Kappa honorary fraternity Presbyterian church, Hospital Guild Board, Lar. Co. Habitat for Humanity; [hon.] Special Ed. teacher in Colorado Public Schools, Speech, Communication and Audiology, life certified for K through 12 schools; [oth. writ.] Poetry in PEO "Record" family histories and stories local newspaper letters; [pers.] Writing lays the author bare. Only the courageous dare to put pen to paper.; [a.] Cheyenne, WY

SWANSON, CHERYL J.
[b.] February 10, 1951, McKeesport, PA; [p.] John Fragassi, Louise Fragassi; [m.] Victor L. Swanson, June 19 1971; [ch.] Victor L III, Amy Louise, and David James; [ed.] Thomas Jefferson High School; [occ.] Admin. Assistant, Addams Office Furniture, Comstock Park, MI; [memb.] National Tole Society; [pers.] My poem was written as a personal tribute to my first born son who passed away 26 hours after birth. My child's lifetime was only a few moments in time. May you treasure each day, no matter what comes your way...; [a.] Rockford, MI

SWARTZ, ROBERT J.
[pen.] Bob Swartz; [b.] May 19, 1946, Peterbourgh, NH; [p.] Alex Swartz and Elsie Swartz; [m.] Bonnie Swartz, June 15, 1968; [ch.] Michael Robert, Stephanie Ann; [sib.] [ed.] Millbrook High, Saint Clair College; [occ.] Labourer; [oth. writ.] Several poems written for friends and family, for book publication and poems to be put to music; [pers.] I strive to create love and self expression for all humanity so others may see the good in everyone poems inspired by people from all walks of life; [a.] Chatham Ontario, CA

SWIONTEK, RICHARD M.
[b.] September 14, 1957, Ada, MI; [p.] Richard F. Swiontek, Caroline Schaffer; [m.] Nancy Ann (Schindler) Swiontek, July 9, 1994; [ch.] Jason, Rebecca, Brian; [ed.] BreckenRidge High School, Moorhead Vo-Tech, Fergus Falls Community College.; [occ.] Concrete block machine operator, shift supervisor, Fergus Falls, MN.; [hon.] Omicron Omicron, Creative Writing Contest; [oth. writ.] Poems and articles published in local and regional newspapers, short stories published in "The Quill" Fergus Falls Community College; [pers.] My inspiration to write comes from the hope that others may improve their lives through my trials, errors, and insights, however slight they may be; [a.] Underwood, MN

SWITZER, LEX
[b.] September 9, 1925, New Zealand; [p.] Cyril and Isalyn Switzer; [m.] Shona, December 18, 1964; [ch.] Michael and Karl; [ed.] 3 years secondary school, 2 years University Diploma in Building Construction Management. NZ Institute Business Studies. Diploma Creative Writing.; [occ.] Retired; [memb.] New Zealand Freelance Writers Association; [oth. writ.] Poems and short stories being prepared for publishing. Book on Bone Carving ready for publish.; [a.] Whangarei

TAFT, KATRINA L.
[pen.] June 4, 1976, Colville, WA; [b.] Edward A. Taft, Kathleen W. Taft; [ed.] Selkirk High School; [oth. writ.] I have had a poem published in my school year book.; [pers.] My poetry comes from my own personal experiences and emotions; [a.] Ione, WA

TAFT, MARYELLEN
[pen.] Emmy; [b.] July 3, 1973, Jersey City, NJ; [p.] Joe and Jeanett Caulfield; [m.] Jose Castillo; [ch.] Patrick Joh; [ed.] Clifton High School Caldwell College, Bergun County Ems Training School; [occ.] Receptionist, Emergency Medical Technician; [memb.] Irvington Ruscue; [oth. writ.] Several poems and songs.; [pers.] I enjoy helping people through experiences. To help them find

ways to show their feelings as I found through poetry.; [a.] Clifton, NJ

TAKEN, LAURA BETH
[b.] February 25, 1978; [p.] Michael Taken, Maureen Taken; [ch.] Brea and Matt; [ed.] St. Francis Borgia Grade School, Divine Savior Holy Angels High School, one semester at Cedarburg High School; [occ.] High School student and Assistant teacher for dance; [pers.] With a combination of idealism and cynicism, I am a realist with hope.; [a.] Cedarburg, WI

TALBORT, DOROTHY
[b.] April 18, 1915, Wondsor, MO; [p.] Henry and Emma Miller; [m.] Deceased; [ch.] Louetta McKinnis and Fred Egbert; [ed.] Windsor, MO. Grade and High School 1 thru 12; [occ.] Retired; [memb.] MacPherson Presbyterian Church C.W.7, Fayetteville, First Christian (Disciples of Christ) Senior friendly singer, Faymont Baptist Church, Hope Mills Sunshine Center.; [hon.] Senior Queen, Ms. Cumberland County 1986, Senior Pageant Ms. District 2 Senior Citizen, Queen State Senior Pageant, Second Runner up. "1986", Several poems publishes in local newspapers, church papers "Nature, My Awesome Spirit" - Published in "Poetic Voices of America" 1985, Won 1sst, 2nd and 3rd in senior poetry comp.; [oth. writ.] "Now I Have A Mountain", "God Almighty", "Home". This was my first at fourteen years of age. "Our house", "My Trip Back Home", "Yes I Know Him", "I'd Like To Be A Cap On Old Santas Head.; [pers.] I strive to convey my innermost feelings of mind, heart and soul. Many of my poems just happen, they're there at all times, day and night and I write them down immediately. God is my help; [a.] Hope Mills, NC

TALLMAN, EVELYN
[b.] November 13, 1922, S. Westerlo, NY; [p.] Mrs. Hazel F. Mabie; [m.] Deceased, January 13, 1940; [ch.] Mr. Ralph R. Tallman; [ed.] Greenville High School National Baking School, 835 Diversey Parkway Chicago, IL; [occ.] Retired Cook and Baker; [memb.] Social Security Benefits Social Service by Albany County; [hon.] Golden Poetrygram - in 1989, World of Poetry; [oth. writ.] International Society Poets

TAMMI, SLIKER
[pen.] Dawn; [b.] January 27, 1975, Portsmouth, VA; [p.] Harold Sliker, Diana Balow; [ed.] Camden County High; [occ.] Order-filler at Distlefink Designs, Newton, NJ; [oth. writ.] Several other poems that have not yet been published, but I wish to try to get them done as well; [pers.] I write my poems from past occurrences in my life. Most of them are written for a friend of mine that passed away. All of my writings are for you Scott.; [a.] Newton, NJ

TANNER, GAY E.
[b.] June 13, 1944, Osmond, NE; [p.] Roy and Lois Koppelman; [m.] John E. Tanner; [ch.] Colin J. Tanner (Attorney), [ed.] BAE, MA; [occ.] English Teacher, High School; [oth. writ.] Wilory Farm Poetry Contest, 1978-1979; [pers.] For our first grandchild: "Nothing is at last sacred but the integrity of your own mind." (Emerson). We too were young once.; [a.] Upland, CA

TATE, MONICA LEACH
[pen.] Monica Leach Tate; [b.] December 08, 1967, Birmingham, AL; [p.] Willie Leach, Betty Leach; [m.] Reginald Tate, March 17, 1992; [ed.] Corner High School, Faulkner University, University of Alabama at Birmingham; [occ.] Teacher, Birmingham Public School System.; [memb.] Future Business Leaders of America, Student Support Services, Mu Alpha Theta, Sigma Epsilon Theta, National Trio Alumni.; [hon.] National Honors Society Merit Award, Appreciation Award American Federation of Teachers; [oth. writ.] Several poems published in newsletters at the American Federation of Teachers, Obituary writings, School publications at Faulkner University; [pers.] My favorite qoute was taken from a quadriplegic that appeared on the Oprah Winfrey show in 1992. "To have pain and suffering is inevitable, but choosing to be miserable is optional." Mine: Always live life to its fullest and never take even small things for granted; [a.] Birmingham, AL

TAUBER, JEFFREY
[b.] February 7, 1945, Southampton, UK; [p.] Mother; [m.] Divorced; [ch.] 2 Boy 17, Girl 14; [ed.] Grammer School education London England; [occ.] Sales in the electronic surplus industry; [hon.] Business award obtained at queens college NY 1972, after coming to the US in 1970; [oth. writ.] Lyrics for songs/music I have written in the past and of course other poetry works; [pers.] To express my feelings through words just as a painter or musician does through there works. Honest level headed expression is all that is needed; [a.] West Hempstead, NY

TAVARES, CARLA
[b.] June 20, 1978, Azores, Portugal; [p.] Filomena Tavares and Joao Tavares; [ed.] Junior in High School Westboro; [occ.] Work part time at a cleaners and at F.S.C.; [memb.] Volleyball WHS; [hon.] High honors in High School honor roll; [oth. writ.] My own private poems and stories.; [pers.] "No man should complete with nature, for he will lose." I am a nature lover, so I write a lot about love with nature.; [a.] Westboro, MA

TAVARES, CAROLINE
[b.] July 28, 1978, New York; [p.] Rafael and Silvia Tavares; [ed.] G. Holmes Braddock Senior High School; [occ.] Student; [pers.] Sometimes the most beautiful roses have the shapiest thorns.; [a.] Miami, FL

TAYLOR, DANA
[pen.] Diva, Movie Star; [b.] May 12, 1973, Los Angeles; [p.] Leotha and Robert Taylor; [ed.] Wharton School of business at University of Penn, Summer 1990, University of California at Berkeley; [occ.] Full-time student and English tutor; [memb.] Organization of African students, Eritrean student association, Peace studies student association, associated students of the University of California; [oth. writ.] Poems published in African Literary Magazine and in Poetry for the people at UC Berkeley; [pers.] I see myself as the sand on the Pacific coast, walked on neglected and abused. But I'm stronger than that, so I'm willing to assist you until I no longer can trust you. In strength and honor, sisters.; [a.] Berkeley, CA

TAYLOR, JOHN FULTON
[pen.] Fulton and Jack; [b.] June 27, 1923, Charlotte, NC; [p.] Canway and Laura Fulton Taylor; [m.] Anne Gerlach Taylor, November 14, 1947; [ch.] 2 sons (45 and 31) and 1 daughter (42); [ed.] PhD Univ. of Maryland 1971, M.A. Columbia Univ. 1950, B.A. Washington and Lee Univ. 1947, Student of Peabody conservatory of music Balthrone; [occ.] Retired formerly professor of english violist, maryland symphony); [memb.] Episcopal church, amnesty international; [hon.] Geo. A. Mahan Award in creative writing Washington and Lee; [oth. writ.] Many article, stories, etc. in newspaper, magazines etc. in Maryland and Florida "Hymn to the Christ Pinockhio" (poems innestree house - Baltimore); [pers.] My feeling is that the perils of the world are the product of universal greed, caused by human fear. My hope is that my artistry both as a musician and a writer, may offer solace.; [a.] Austin, TX

TAYLOR, ROWENA LORRAINE
[b.] August 24, 1979, Naples, FL; [p.] David Taylor, and Linda Taylor; [ed.] Home school since 2nd grade. Now attending Palatka High in Palatka, Fl, in 9th grade; [occ.] Student; [pers.] I'm 15 years old and I intend to pursue a career in writing. I believe that a person can do whatever he or she really wants to do in life if one is willing to go for it.; [a.] Palatka, FL

TEBEAU, MELISA
[b.] August 26, 1971, Miami, FL; [p.] Rollin and Mary Tebeau; [m.] Fiance, Timothy Haggerty; [ed.] Bachelor of Science Degree in Legal Studies, Nova Southeastern University; [occ.] Secretary, Nova Southeastern University; [memb.] Poetry Circle 1990-1992, Phi Alpha Delta Legal Fraternity 1989-1992; [hon.] Dean's List; [oth. writ.] Several unpublished poems and currently I am working on a novel; [pers.] I try to reflect my experiences in my writing so others will know that people do experience the same emotions. Writing poetry can bring something positive out of a negative feeling or situation.; [a.] Cooper City, FL

TECLAW, AMBER
[b.] January 1, 1977, Canada; [p.] Stan and Mary Teclaw; [ed.] Saint James the Apostle Elementary and currently attending bishop Ryan catholic secondary in Hamilton Ontario; [hon.] Proficiency in English award, leadership award: Class of 87 (received at Elementary School graduation 90-91) Sports Championship Certificate 1983 (Springboard Diving); [oth. writ.] Several poems and short stories, along with scripts.; [pers.] Listen to your heart. Don't even under estimate your talents. They may bring you fame and fortune one day. They did for me.; [a.] Stoney Creek Ontario, Canada

TEHONICA, MATT
[b.] August 16, 1980, Greenwood Hospital; [p.] Mike and Bonnie Garron; [ed.] 8th grade student at Hickory Tavern Elementary School; [hon.] National Junior Honor Society, citizenship award, choral leadership award; [oth. writ.] Other poems; [pers.] I work toward letting others know there is hope for tomorrow and to strive to reach their goals.; [a.] Waterloo, SC

TELFORD, HOLLY LYNN
[b.] November 28, 1958, Riverside, CA; [p.] Howard Telford (Deceased) and Joyce Worrell Telford; [m.] William Hargus, October 16, 1976; [ed.] Graduated "mid-term" Arlington High School, Riverside, CA.; [occ.] Mortgage Loan Processor; [memb.] Loyal order of the moose APM; [hon.] Graduated "mid-term" from Arlington High School 1976 also 1976 Riverside County Gymkhana Champion; [oth. writ.] High School Newspaper; [pers.] My writing comes from a reflection of current emotions and surroundings. I am constantly encouraged by my brother brad who is always there for me; [a.] Riverside, CA

TEMBERG, TARA L.
[b.] November 8, 1974, Muskegon, MI; [p.] Kathleen Temberg; [m.] Brandon Mahoney; [ed.] Graduated Montague High School, Montague MI in 1993 spent 2

years at a local Junior college; [occ.] General Merchandiser for Meijer Incin the N. Muskegon store; [oth. writ.] Numerous other poems and two unfinished short stories; [a.] Montague, MI

TESTER, ALICE
[pen.] Bibeau; [b.] August 24, 1913, Saltspring Island, British Columbia, Canada; [p.] Olive and Fred Bibeau; [m.] 1948; [ed.] Academic School Teacher - French then registered nurse from Montreal St. Luke Hospital; [occ.] I nursed in U.S.A. Canada, 41 yrs. in all mostly in operating room. I was the smallest but best looking french nurse, 4 foot 11 inches. Was no problem, retired 1979, I take piano lessons, I used computer, I still love to ride frisky horses. I am French Canadian from Montreal, Quebec, I left that province in 1942. Never returned as married English Canadian. I love music, good look I love to cook, widow now for since 1986 I was happy married 40 years; [pers.] Husband died Massive heart attack at 78 years old, I believed in God, I am true Christian, but I do not practice any religion, my motto "There is always a better tomorrow"

THEUERKAUF, SHARON
[b.] October 14, 1951, Menominee, MI; [p.] Ben and Alice Mikolas; [m.] Richard Marcin; [oth. writ.] Numerous other poems, my "Couples" poem which is being published in "Reflections of light." Book.; [pers.] For people to realize anything is possible no matter what your background is rich or poor, your dreams can come true and your prayers will be answered.; [a.] Menominee, MI

THIEL, HAZEL A.
[pen.] Hazel A. Thiel; [b.] October 10, 1916, Santa Cruz, CA; [p.] Sally Ann Amaya, James Dario Amaya; [m.] Deceased, May 21, 72 (2nd marriage); [ch.] Lance K. Bone; [ed.] Santa Cruz High School, class '35; [occ.] Retired; [memb.] Communications workers of America the Pacific telephone and Telegraphic Co. Telephone Pioneers of America (Pacific Chapter); [oth. writ.] This is my first attempt.; [pers.] In my writing I will strive to make aware to my readers the natural beauty that surrounds our daily lives. The ocean so angry with its waves of white foam crashing against the fog drenched cliffs. The mystery of the wind which is so powerful it can boss us and make us shiver or hug us and make us warm. This what I will write. Reality with fantasy.; [a.] Soquel, CA

THIELE, SUSY
[pen.] Susy Wynne Thiele; [b.] September 9, 1963, CA; [p.] Edward and Eleanor Thiele; [ed.] BA in English with emphasis in Literature from California State University, Northridge; [occ.] Recreation Assistant III, Coordinates recreation programs for persons with physical disabilities; [pers.] I believe that the Lord Jesus Christ gives every human being a special and unique talent which is to be used in reflecting His love and glory to one another.; [a.] Panorama City, CA

THOMAS, BROOKE
[pen.] Brooke Thomas; [b.] March 19, 1980, Silver Spring, MA; [p.] Bill and Barbara Thomas; [ed.] 9th grade student, Saint Vincent Pallotti High School, Laura Maryland; [occ.] Student; [oth. writ.] I've been writing since the 5th grade. I also wrote a child's book but I never had a chance to get it published; [pers.] This is a great honor; [a.] College Park, MD

THOMAS, CRYSTAL L.
[b.] March 30, 1959, Plattsburgh, NY; [p.] Morris Thomas, Pearlie Thomas; [ed.] Widefield High; [occ.] Retail merchandiser; [oth. writ.] For years I've written poems and verses, just for me. Like a hobby, but after showing them to friends, they wanted me to write poems for them.; [pers.] Most of my poems are about life experiences and the people who are close to me. Writing poems and verses, for me, is away to release my feelings. If I can bring a smile to someone, after reading writings that a plus.; [a.] Doraville, GA

THOMAS, HOLLY M.
[b.] October 19, 1973, Bremerhaven, Germany; [p.] Larry Thomas and Deborah Blair; [ed.] Graduated from South High School in Bakersfield, California; [occ.] Computer Specialist in the U.S. Army Letterkenny Army Depot; [hon.] Graduated Honor Roll, Honor Society for 3 years; [oth. writ.] Several poems, short stories, some poems published in local newspapers; [pers.] I believe in true love, soul mates. My writing reflects my belief that love conquers all.; [a.] Chambersburg, PA

THOMAS, JAIME LOUISE
[b.] June 30, 1980, Pottstown, PA; [p.] James Thomas, Karen Thomas; [ed.] Ninth grade home schooled student.; [oth. writ.] A short story that won 1st prize judged by a word of life author.; [pers.] When I find something of interest, sometimes I like to write about it.; [a.] Pottstown, PA

THOMAS, NICK A.
[b.] November 12, 1961, Chicago, IL; [p.] Louise De Cum and William A. Thomas; [ch.] Heidy Nicole Thomas, Joseph Nick Thomas; [ed.] High School Graduate of University High School Class of 1979; [occ.] United States Navy Chief; [pers.] Dedicated to Cynthia Kay Willand

THOMPSON, AMBER
[b.] May 12, 1981, Lansing General; [p.] Beth and Brad Thompson; [ed.] Currently attending charlotte junior high; [hon.] Christian wonch writing award (local award); [oth. writ.] I think of her spirit, her beauty, and grace the times she put a smile on my face. I think of the times we had before she went away. I love her dearly and only wish she'd be here right and now as a happy gift.; [a.] Charlotte, MI

THOMPSON, EARL CLAUDIOS
[pen.] E. C. Thommo; [b.] May 7, 1962, Jamaica, WI; [p.] Clifford and Calmina Thompson; [m.] Sheila Maud Thompson, March 31, 1992; [ch.] Sheena, Renee, Brian, Matthew, Tanika; [ed.] Clarendon College, Vere Tech; [occn] Security Guard; [oth. writ.] Only submission of writing to a correspondence course I did with I.C.S.; [pers.] I am greatly influenced by great Poets such as William Shakespear and a local Poet and goes by the name of Louise Bennett. I strive to bring out into the open what a lot of people are unable to put into words to their love ones; [a.] Oshawa, Canada

THOMPSON, JANE C.
[pen.] Kim Thompson; [b.] May 24th 1952, England; [p.] John and Simone Brunel-Cohen; [m.] Gary Thompson, February 3, 1980; [ch.] Sierra Kimberly 8; [ed.] British Public School, Priorsfield, and Cuckfield Park College; [occ.] Homemaker; [memb.] PTA School Site Council.; [hon.] Three Awards for Outstanding Service to the Children of Paso Robles.; [oth. writ.] Lots of other poems, just for fun!; [pers.] We live in the country with lots of animals, and good friends. I believe in children. They are magical. I believe in God, family, optimism and a sense of humor! Thanks!; [a.] Paso Robles, CA

THOMPSON, SAMUEL I.
[pen.] Ismail Abdus Shaheed; [b.] March 1, 1930, Philadelphia, PA; [p.] Philip Emannuel, Beatrice Thompson; [m.] Divorced, Shirley Griffin 1953-1970; [ch.] Michelle Vanessa Thompson and Peythia Lange Thompson Stubbs.; [ed.] Landreth, Hoffman, and Marth Washington Grammar Schools. Sulzberger Junior High School, and Ambler, Penna., High School, Murrell Dobbins Vocational-Technical School.; [occ.] Currently Retired from U.S. Gov't.; [memb.] Among other trainings, a graduate of Peirce School of Business Administration-Phila., PA.; [hon.] Honorably discharged disabled veteran.; [oth. writ.] Mainly because of my gift of writing on me from the very capable creator of our universe, I have successfully finished and copyrighted fourteen books of poetry, and associated other periodicals. It is my intention to write to the very end!; [pers.] It is my very earnest endeavor to influence any listening Human being qualified to put down the musing of their minds on paper, copyright said material (s), and therein share with the rest of the human family such gems; [a.] Philadelphia, PA

THOMPSON, SUE ANN
[pen.] Sue Ann Thompson; [b.] July 21, 1947, Columbus, GA; [p.] J. Elwood Hudson, Marianna Cote Hudson; [m.] Larry C. Thompson, November 21, 1975; [ch.] Anthony Ray (Tony) deceased, Tammy Lorraine; [ed.] Smith's Station High School (GED) Phenix City Arca Vocational/Technician Center accounting; [occ.] Retired from accounting; [oth. writ.] None published (Other than a couple of opinion articles in the local newspaper); [pers.] I've found that I'm most creative during those events in my life that cause strong emotions. This poem was inspired by the death of my son. I choose his resting place to be at the base of a pine tree.; [a.] Phenix City, AL

THOMSON, MRS. KAREN A. PHILLIPS
[pen.] "Rennie"; [b.] June 4, 1963, Kingston, Jamaica; [p.] Richard and Madge Phillips; [m.] Maurice C. Thomson, July 12, 1986; [ed.] Excelsior High School; [occ.] Sales marketing director for a variety of stationery and office and safe products.; [memb.] Friends of Bustamante children's Hospital and Woman Inc.; [oth. writ.] Various poetry writings within the last 10 years. Various post card on request.; [pers.] My writings reflect a mixture of my girlish enthusiasm my wildest dreams, damp memories and the experience of others as seen through my eyes. I have enjoyed poetry writing very much and I hope my writings will add love and laughter to all my readers.; [a.] Kingston Jamaica, West Indies

THORESSON, RONNIE
[b.] April 24, 1956, Johannesburg, SA; [p.] Norman Syoney and Emily Harhouse; [m.] Yvonne Thoresson, January 7, 1984; [ch.] Clinton, Chazron, Christon; [ed.] Mayfair High School, Traffic Police Training Academy, Airborne Helicopter Patrol.; [occ.] Factory manager previous 20 year traffic police; [hon.] Awards for bravery while in the traffic police. 20 concentrations for services above the normal call of duty.; [oth. writ.] Several poems yet unpublished with the object of having their publishes I strive to portray the uselessness of war, hate and murder, are the effect it has on mankind. The poems I have written are of personal experience and real weakenings in the world; [pers.] As a traffic policeman, I inferior horrors which are not witnessed by the man in the street, only a fellow policeman can understand this. The only escape I found was reflecting it in poetry.; [a.] Alberton Gauteny, Republic of South Africa

THORNTON, TERRANCE
[pen.] Sir Terrance; [b.] March 4, 1966, Memphis, TN; [p.] Constance Thornton; [m.] Kimberly Thornton, July 9, 1993; [ch.] Jameek Deaobry, Brandon Julian; [ed.] Murris High School; [occ.] Correction Officer; [oth. writ.] Songs for several rap artist; [pers.] Each one teach one; [a.] New York, NY

THRONES, HOLLY
[b.] November, 17, 1970, The Pas, Manitoba, Canada; [p.] Rolla and Linda Beecham; [m.] Gary Thrones, June 20, 1992; [ch.] Nichols John; [ed.] Margaret Barbour Collegiate (The Pas, Manitoba); [occ.] Homemaker; [oth. writ.] Children's stories and other poems.; [a.] Wanless Manitoba, Canada

THURROTT, EDUA BLANCHARD
[pen.] Edua Thurrott; [b.] August 28, 1921, McDuffie County Thompson, GA; [p.] James Wilson and Franbie, Paschal Blanchard; [m.] Richard Vauderburg Thurrott, October 25, 1942; [ch.] Frankie Diania, Richard V. Thurrott III, Trudy Lorraine Kephart; [ed.] Graduate of Thompson High School 1938, Thompson Georgia 30824, Attended Predmont College, Demorest Georgia and University of GA, Athens GA (Junior); [occ.] Presently retired to busy life in Sequim - active in; [memb.] Membership at faith Lutherem, Church member Life Time Int. Poets of No. America and in To Know Christ Is "Life" - Member Fraternal Aid to Lutheron Organization, Sequim Senior Citizens; [hon.] Honored to be mother of 3, wife of Dick, grandmother of 6 and a member of God family of believers born by God grace a worker in God vineyard that other many find God's love and peace.; [oth. writ.] Many poems some published, "Epitaph To Hector", discern to know one of a kind and grow with God in 93. "Mother Natures Power Display", "Day By Day With Jesus", "The Best Gift", "Our Daugther", Family Treasures", "Thoughts That Delight"; [pers.] I believe, I live move and have my being because of Gods creative power. By faith I trust in Jesus "Sermon on the mounts" I believe the 10 commandments were given to show us our sinful nature I accept by faith and God grace that I am a child of God.; [a.] Sequim, WA

TICE, BRADLEY S.
[b.] October 6, 1959, Palo Alto, CA; [p.] Lilburn T. Tice, Paula N. Tice; [ed.] Undergraduate degree history from San Jose State University.; [occ.] ESL Instructor; [memb.] JALT: The Japanese Association for Language Teaching.; [a.] Cupertino, CA

TIDABACK, KRISTIN LEA
[b.] June 6, 1984, Elkton, MD; [p.] Victoria Pryor, William H. Tidaback III; [ed.] 5th Grade Student Holly Hall School - Elkton Graduate of "Children Hour" Nursery School - Elkton.; [occ.] Student; [memb.] Cecil County Library; [hon.] Honor roll Student all through Elem. School straight a student second, third and forth grades, gifted and talented student, Odyssey of the mind student and currently the John Hopkins University Center in the John Hopkins of Academically talented youths program; [oth. writ.] None Published; [pers.] Enjoys readings, singing, making crafts, piano lessions writing poems, writing songs. Loves school is very concerned about the homeless and the environment.; [a.] Elkton, MD

TIGGETT, SHARON M.
[pen.] Marie Johns; [b.] June 27, 1952, Bridgeton, NJ; [p.] Willie B. Sr. and Leila M. Tiggett; [ch.] Shayne Micah Tiggett; [ed.] Dunedin High School, St. Petersburg Junior, University of South Florida, Nova University; [occ.] Elementary School teacher Ballast Point Elementary; [memb.] Alpha Kappa Alpha Sorority, Living water church; [hon.] Teacher of the year 1992-93 Ballast Point Elementary; [oth. writ.] None published. Recently accepted to the children's Institute of literature; [a.] Tampa, FL

TINNEY, WILLIAM EDWARD DENNIS
[b.] July 25, 1977, Fort Bragg, NC; [p.] Andrew and Robin Tinney; [ed.] 10th grade Madison H.S. San Antonio, TX; [occ.] Student; [memb.] National Forensic League Debate Team; [hon.] Voice of Democracy; [oth. writ.] "Tomorrow I'll Think About God" in Tidings, October 26, 1993; [a.] San Antonio, TX

TODD, JENNIFER
[b.] February 15, 1978, Nashville, TN; [p.] E. W. and Judy Todd; [ed.] Junior of High School graduating year '96; [hon.] Band Excellence Award; [pers.] I would like to thank "my sunshine" for all her help. I write to release captured emotions, thoughts, and feelings. It helps me become a better human being.; [a.] Kingston Springs, TN

TODD, WARREN KEITH
[b.] December 13, 1976, Tallahassee, FL; [p.] William V. Todd Jr. and Katherine R. Todd; [ed.] Senior attending Liberty County High School in Bristol, Florida.; [occ.] Part-time job at Food Lion grocery store.; [oth. writ.] Sports section for local newspaper.; [pers.] Poetry is more than mere self expression, it is an opportunity to present ideas and scenarios to readers in a way most have not imagined, therefore allowing as many personal interpretations as there are readers. In this manner, each individual can relate on some personal level of their own; [a.] Bristol, FL

TOLLESON, ALEXANDER L.
[pen.] Alex Tolleson; [b.] September 9, 1948, Austin, TX; [p.] Cecil L. and Sheila Tolleson; [ed.] The University of North Texas, Denton TX, B.A. in Advertising Art, 1970 also graduate of the asten center of natural therapeutics, Richardson, TX, 1994.; [occ.] Massage Therapist in the Dallas/Forth Worth area, also freelance writer and proofreader.; [memb.] American Massage Therapy Association (AMTA); [hon.] National Honor Society, Phi Theta Kappa; [oth. writ.] "The Rhythm and Resonance of the Human Body" thesis written at the Asten Center of Natural Therapeutics - publication pending), article entitled "Gender a question of essence?" in the quarterly newsletter engender.; [pers.] My purpose in writing is to act as a catalyst in order to open up new perceptions of reality.; [a.] Dallas, TX

TONYA, BREWER
[b.] October 8, 1974, New Brunswick, Canada; [p.] Don and Zena Brewer; [ed.] Tantramar Regional High School; [occ.] Teacher's Assistant, First Baptist Christian School, S. Weymouth MA; [pers.] 1 Corinthians 13:7 - Beareth all things, believeth all things, hopeth all things, endureth all things. I have been inspired by my Lord, my family with tender prodding from my precious mother. My own personal experiences greatly influence my poems.; [a.] South Weymouth, MA

TORRE, CARINA MARIA BIANCHI DE LA
[b.] August 13, 1979, Valparaiso, IN; [p.] Raul de la Torre, Blanca Bianchi De la Torre; [ed.] Our lady of Lourdes Academy, 10th grade (1994-95 school year); [occ.] Student; [memb.] Counselor, St. Thomas the Apostle Church, Youth Group and CCD Teacher and lector at St. Thomas the Apostle Church; [hon.] Lourdes Academy Honor Roll, featured in who's who among American High School student, 28th edition, scored in top 1% of college - bound sophomores taking the plan exam.; [oth. writ.] Unpublished poems and short stories; [pers.] "I did not wish to take a cabin passage, but rather to go before the most and on the deck of the world, for there I could best see the moonlight amid the mountains I do not wish to go below now."; [a.] Miami, FL

TORRES, L. R.
[b.] September 28, 1948, Puerto Rico; [p.] (Deceased) Julio Torres, Providencia Torres; [m.] Ines Torres, May 27, 1963; [ch.] Lucina, Natllely, Mark, Julio, Luis Jr.; [ed.] Washington High, Lee College; [occ.] Refrigiration Technician; [hon.] National Dean's List; [oth. writ.] New theory on gravity "The Theory of the Arm System" (not published) other poems: On UFO's, On Mountain Climbing, On Orderliness, On Crunch Love, (not published); [pers.] The purpose of life is to preserve life always towards a higher level of understanding, the Godly understanding; [a.] San Diego, CA

TORRES, MARY
[b.] September 15, 1957, Philadelphia; [p.] Edward Covar and Marie Covar; [m.] Kenneth Rensel, March 4, 1995; [ch.] Luis, Louiesa, Sophia, Laubrita, Patricia, and Angela.; [ed.] St. Patrick's School.; [occ.] Home Maker; [pers.] I believe in expressing my true feelings in my writing.; [a.] Philadelphia, PA

TRACY, ELIZABETH M.
[b.] October 9, 1909, Wisconsin; [p.] Fred Reinke, Ida Reinke; [m.] Emilio Sartori, Joseph Tracy, May 24, 1937, February 10, 1966; [ch.] Edward Joseph and Robert Richard Sartoci; [ed.] Elementary School; [occ.] Retired sales Clerk; [memb.] Legacy of St. Joseph Cardinal Cooke Guild Songwriters club of America; [hon.] For poetry, Tear Drops From Heaven, The Earths's Blood, The Addicted Soul, Magnificent Dream; [oth. writ.] A great number of songs without luck.; [a.] Yonkers, NY

TRAISI, CYNTHIA
[b.] July 20, 1949, Sheffield, AL; [p.] Dorotha and Louis Fisher; [m.] Chuck Traisi, November 22, 1978; [ed.] University of South Carolina B.A. Elementary Education M.A. Health Education; [occ.] Wildlife Rehabilitator co-manager of wildlife rehabilitation center; [oth. writ.] Recently completed book of short stories to be published in early 1996.; [a.] Ramona, CA

TRAUTMANN, MARY
[pen.] Mary Winfrey Trautmann; [b.] Des Moines, IA; [p.] Dr. and Mrs. F. D. Kershner; [m.] Paul R. Trautmann, 1950 (Deceased); [ch.] Three daughters, one deceased; [ed.] Butler University, University of Tennessee, University of Wisconsin. Two degrees, two years toward doctorate; [occ.] In California tutored English and German retired, taught composition and literature, U. of Wis. extension, Western Ill. Univ.; [memb.] Feminist Writers' Guild National Alliance for Mentally Ill Nature Conservancy; [hon.] The absence of the Dead Is Their Way of Appearing published 1984. Selections reprinted in parents' magazine, the volume Dying and Grieving (1989). Poems in anthology Cameos.; [oth. writ.] Poems and prose published in The Second Wave, Woman spirit, Crazy Quilt, Passager, Encodings, Ms. Magazine; [pers.] Writing is a lonely enterprise, like spelunking. Both have a high degree of difficulty. Somehow words

and images on paper never match exactly the visions that move the imagination in the first place. But you must try.; [a.] Whittier, CA

TRAVIS, GARY L.
[b.] April 10, 1956, Moorhead, MN; [ed.] Branham HS, San Jose, CA (1974) US Army NCO Academy (infantry) 1979-80); [occ.] 1995 - Most recently an emergency dispatcher-student: Computer repair; [memb.] National Forensic League (1974) American Legion (1988); [hon.] Amjin Scout Insignia for DMZ Service and Operation Paul Bunyan - Korea (1976); [oth. writ.] September 1986 - Haiku poem published in Japanese newspaper, Mainichi Daily News, Tokyo; [pers.] I have always been fascinated by people's reactions to events - amplified over the years by seeing in person people such as Jacques Cousteau, Moshe Dayan, Omar Bradley, Norman Schwarzkopf; [a.] Thousand Oaks, CA

TREADWELL, DAVE
[pen.] Dave Treadwell; [b.] March 23, 1961, Westover AFB, MA; [p.] Charles and Marilyn; [m.] Donna J., January 23, 1988; [ch.] Becky; [ed.] Armijo High Fairfield CAT Streets of life; [occ.] Transmission Mechanic; [memb.] Suisun American Firefighter Assoc. American Motorcycle Assoc. National Rifle Assoc.; [hon.] I feel that one shouldn't pat one's own back; [oth. writ.] Songs and Poetry but none submitted yet.; [pers.] Karma is a force that goes both directions, so I try to stay on her good side. With help from my grandmother Rita and Ruby; [a.] Suisun, CA

TREBILCO, ALISON
[b.] September 21, 1964, Wangaratta, Australia; [p.] John and Margaret McLean; [ed.] Rutherglen High School, Rutherglen Victoria Australia; [occ.] Outdoor Instructor/Bowen Therapist.; [memb.] Victorian Outdoor Education Association. Bowen Therapy Academy.; [oth. writ.] Instructional article published in Grass roots magazine.; [pers.] After the death of my husband, Wayne, in 1993, I began a search for self. While travelling throughout the USA in 1994, the experiences I had, and the people I met, inspired me to express my feelings in the form of several poems.; [a.] Chiltern, Victoria, Australia

TREGENZA, SHARON
[b.] June 14, 1951, Cornwall, England; [p.] William and Jean Rosewall; [m.] Alan Tregenza, February 14, 1975; [ch.] Ross, Natasha; [ed.] Normal British Education including College to Study English Literature; [occ.] Writer; [memb.] DUBAI Writers Group; [hon.] Several Certificates and prizes for short story writing and poetry; [oth. writ.] Many published stories and poetry in U.K. Middle East and U.S. Regular paid contributor to four magazines (Middle East and U.K.); [pers.] I like to play with prose, Pepper poems with whimsy humor touches more people than tears.; [a.] Dubai, United Arab Emirates

TRENHOLM, WESLEY ALEXANDER GORDON
[b.] May 22, 1977, Tatamagouche, Nova Scotia, Canada; [p.] Myrna and Peter Trenholm; [ed.] Grade 12, High School graduate; [occ.] Student; [memb.] Wallace River United Baptist Church; [oth. writ.] Many unpublished writings in my possession.; [pers.] In most of my poems I write from my heart, and try to put as much feeling into each of my poems. This poem is wrote to show faith in Jesus Christ, it was influenced by my faith in Christ.; [a.] Pugwash Nova Scotia, Canada

TRIGLETH, MAZINE
[b.] September 19, 1926, Flora, IL; [p.] Harry and Zula Tolbert; [m.] M. E. Trigleth, Jr., March 28, 1948; [ch.] Janice, Harry, Cheryl; [ed.] Attended Anderson, University, Anderson, Ind., LeTourneau, U Longview, Tx. Flora, High-school, Jenkins-grade school; [occ.] House-wife, former school teacher, speaker and soloist in Christian circles.; [memb.] Chairman of Music and Dept. in Conroe Church of God, Chrm. of C. E. Dept. in same church; [hon.] Recipient of the Golden Poet Award.; [oth. writ.] Writer of seven booklets of poems and sketches. Namely, A time to Remember, A Gift of Love, God's Big World, Gems Along My Path, The Odyssey, Reflections to Ponder, and A Potpourri of Thoughts.; [pers.] It is my desire to write with integrity; [a.] Montgomery, TX

TRINIDAD, SOCORRO CH. V.
[b.] June 27, 1918, Philippines; [p.] Deceased; [m.] Deceased; [ch.] Ten children; [ed.] College Level; [occ.] I am a senior, debut my time writing poem and short stories; [memb.] Religious and Social organization - active in missionary work helping the poor - the opprenned - bringing them back to normal life. Guidance and counseling is my work.; [hon.] I have gold medal at school - certificate of award in difficult sector where my work was honored. Still looking forward to help those who needed help - spiritually and normally.; [pers.] Whatever you do, do it the right way, for the reward is always on the way.; [a.] Brampton Ontario, Canada

TROUT, JUANITA
[b.] December 8, 1967, Windsor, MO; [p.] Alice Juanita Bunch; [m.] Patrick Wayne Trout, August 21, 1987; [ed.] Newport High School Newport, Arkansas; [pers.] I am deeply grateful and owe my love for writing to my high school English teacher: Mrs. Lynette Miller - Newport High School, Newport, Arkansas, 1985-1987; [a.] Waterloo-Columbia, IL

TROUT, KRIS
[b.] August 17, 1960, Great Falls, MT; [p.] Owen Kennedy and Carol Walker; [m.] John Trout, July 8, 1989; [ch.] Sam Trout; [ed.] B.A. English, University of Utah; [occ.] Business Consultant; [memb.] PETA; [hon.] Phi Beta Kappa, Phi Kappa Phi, Phi Eta Sigma; [pers.] This poem is dedicated to my younger brother Dylan Walker who committed suicide at the age. He was a handsome, athletic, kind hearted and brave kid.; [a.] Saltlake City, UT

TROYER, SHAWN
[pen.] Shawn Troyer; [b.] December 15, 1979, Saint Louis, MO; [p.] Lisa Troyer; [ed.] Simonsin, Jr, High; [memb.] Jefferson City Jays Football; [oth. writ.] Some none published collection of poems.; [pers.] I try to show life and feelings as people don't usually see them or want to.; [a.] Jefferson City, MO

TRUEBLOOD, JANNA
[pen.] Shannon Anderson; [b.] May 16, 1953, Dallas, TX; [p.] Bill and Jerry Cox; [m.] Gordon Trueblood; [ch.] Shannon and Michael; [occ.] Administrative Assistant; [hon.] Having this poem published in your newest book "A Moment In Time", with the National Library of Poetry.; [oth. writ.] Numerous poems currently writing a humorous novel. Wrote monthly free-lance articles for employer's news letters.; [pers.] Write what you feel and your readers will feel it too!; [a.] Mesquite, TX

TSE, SUZANNE
[b.] December 11, 1964, Hong Kong; [occ.] Third Grade Teacher, Marguerita Elem. School, Alhambra, CA; [pers.] To examine the small private choices that make a life and to render them honestly.; [a.] Rosemead, CA

TUMMILLO, MARY A.
[b.] January 16, 1928, New York City; [p.] Vito and Cecilia Tummillo; [ed.] B.S. Chemistry St. Joseph College SJC West HJD CT 1949, M.D. Medical College of Pennsylvania 1956; [occ.] Physician; [pers.] Lifetime of caring for the underprivileged with a holistic approach. 2. All activities done in honor of my God and parents; [a.] Windsor, CT

TUNLEY, EVELLE L.
[pen.] Evelle (Vell); [b.] May 29, 1973, Kansas City, MO; [p.] Karen E. Harrison and Maurice Wesson; [m.] Felicia Tunley, July 16, 1993; [ch.] Courtney Coleman and Jamell Tunley; [ed.] Lincoln College Prep. Academy National College (Business); [occ.] Presort Operator/Blockbuster cashier; [memb.] Third Street Baptist Church, YBAC (Young Blacks Achieving and Creating); [hon.] Winner: Local Talent show of K.C. 1990, winner: Yearly Juneteenth Rap Off" 1991. Concert at Sachel Paige Stadium for black charities.; [oth. writ.] Several poems and Raps about events in the community including: Blues Town, only living to die, Hypertone, my Suzuki, and the Nighttime is the right time; [pers.] What's the problem? Don't follow the leader, be a leader and let 'em follow you.; [a.] Kansas City, MO

TURCHANYI, GEORGE
[b.] March 14, 1977, Budapest, Hungary; [p.] Sandor and Eszter Turchany; [ed.] High School Student; [occ.] Swimming Instructor (part time); [memb.] Ontario Archery Assoc.; [oth. writ.] Poems; [pers.] My favorite poet is Edgar Allan Poe.; [a.] Etobicolce Ontario, Canada

TURNER, FRANCES EARNESTINE
[p.] Cloteal Saunders/Archie Scott Jr.; [m.] Freddy L. Turner, November 1, 1959; [ch.] Tremell F. Terrence E. Teion S.; [ed.] A.O. Sexton Elem., Englewood High School, Chicago state Univ. (BOFED) Northeastern Univ. (Masters of Urban Ed).; [occ.] Elementary Teacher at Thomas A. Scanlan School in Chicago Ill.; [memb.] Park Manor Christian Church; [hon.] Golden Poet 1991 world of poetry; [oth. writ.] Several poem in world of poetry anthology "91" illustration in children's workbook.; [pers.] My daily commitment is "for this is the day that the Lord hath made I will rejoice and be glad in it. "For greater is he that is in me then He is in the world."; [a.] Chicago, IL

TURNER, JASON
[b.] June 15, 1978, Orange Park, FL; [p.] Clayton Turner, Julia Turner; [ed.] Currently a junior in high school at satellite high school; [occ.] Student, Technician/Clerk at beach computers in Satellite Beach, FL; [oth. writ.] Several poems and essays that have not been published; [pers.] Thanks to my Lord and Savior Jesus Christ for the inspiration of my first published work, and to the love of my life, Sarah Joy Traphagen.; [a.] Satellite Beach, FL

TURNER, JOYCE W.
[b.] January 3, 1948, Trion, GA; [p.] Charles and Mabel Williams; [m.] Carl Jerry Turner, October 9, 1966; [ch.] Gayla, Frank, Tony; [ed.] Central High School; [occ.] Homemaker; [oth. writ.] Lots of poems - this is my first to be entered in a contest.; [pers.] I love my family - com-

ing from 18 children my love for mankind comes out in my poems being one of nine girls and a father named Charlie is where "Charlies Angels" come in.; [a.] Rossville, GA

TURNER, JULIE L.
[b.] December 10, 1957, Patrick AFB, FL; [p.] Charles David Turner and Phyllis Lindsey Turner Payne; [ed.] Associate Science Degree in Architectural and Construction Technology and continuing towards a Bachelor Degree.; [occ.] Engineering Technician III and Computer Aided Design. Manager; [memb.] Women's Basketball Coaching Association (Affiliated Member); [hon.] Tampa Port Authority employee of the year (1994); [oth. writ.] Marker in time is first published poem.; [pers.] I would like to dedicate the poem to my aunt, Miss Inette Lindsey who died in February 1994. Her death moved me to write the poem. I would like to thank my family and mentor, Pat Hend Summit, for helping me believe in myself; [a.] Tampa, FL

TURNER, MARY ALICE GIGLIO
[b.] November 28, 1920, Saint Joseph, LA; [p.] Sam and Amanda E. Giglio; [m.] Lloyd J. Turner, January 4, 1941; [ch.] 3 married, Judy, Lloyd Turner Jr. and Ronald Turner, 9 grandchildren and 8 great grandchildren; [ed.] Graduated Bunkie High School, 1938. B.A. degree education, USL (1971). M.A. Ed. (1975-USL), Specialist, French, (1979-LSU) and Doctorate (LSU), 1981 (EdD) comes in Business Machine (Over trade School), Diploma in Paralegal (DCS-1993); [occ.] Retired classroom teacher; [memb.] Kappa Delta Pi, Arta, LA. Retired teachers asso., St. Anthony Catholic Church, CDA, Amer. Leg. Aux.; [hon.] H.S. Valedictorian, entry in outstanding personalities of the South (1969), Auxiliare of the year for 8th District, Am Leg Aux., (1963), 3rd place S.W. writer's Library Contest (1964), nominated "Teacher of the year" (1983); [oth. writ.] A poem published in High School "The Trumpet" paper and in local paper (The Bunhie Record) local correspondent for several area newspapers for 10 years, a poem published in each of 3 poetry anthologies, 1. American Poetry (1990), 2. Nat'l Library Of Poetry, best poems of the '90's (1992) and 3. Arcadia Poetry, winner 1994; [pers.] I record my travels and holidays with many color, photos, and my feelings in poetry. Looking on the "length side in situations and in people keeps me optimistic and meaning the word through "rare-colony" glasses, still facing reality; [a.] Bunkie, LA

TURNER, VANESSA ANNE
[b.] December 29, 1980, San Francisco, CA; [p.] Diane Turner; [ed.] Brentwood Science Magnet Elementary, Palms Gifted Magnet Junior High School (so far) currently 8th grade (L.A.U.S.D.); [memb.] Yeshe Nyingpo, Thubten Dhargye Ling, both Tibetan Buddhist Centers in Los Angeles, California; [hon.] Determined as talented in the visual arts by L.A.U.S.D., attended conservatory of fine arts in Cal State, L.A. (California); [oth. writ.] Written many other poems including "Destiny", "impermanence", "shadow", "...and so did I", and more, none have been published before; [pers.] I wish to acknowledge His Holiness, The Dalai Lama, and all other lamas who've helped and benefited so many sentient beings.; [a.] Los Angeles, CA

TURNIPSEED, PAUL DOUGLAS
[b.] August 23, 1961, Clarksville, TN; [p.] Johnnie H. Turnipseed, Hattie M. Turnpseed; [m.] Millie Denise Dates Turnipseed, July 11, 1987; [ch.] Johnnie Terrell and Rakim Kareem Turnipseed; [ed.] Port Gibson, High School (4 years) United States Air Force; [occ.] (Computer Science) student, Hinds Junior College, Utica, Mississippi; [memb.] Church of God in Christ in the order of Melchizedek; [hon.] Outstanding Achievement Award, Longevity Award (U.S.A.F.) Employee of the Month Continental Cablevision Los Angeles; [oth. writ.] Unpublished poems inspired by a "Spiritual Awakening".; [pers.] "All of the answers to life's everyday trials and tribulations are found in the Bible" He who has an ear, let Him Hear. "You're not a 'Man' until you've accepted Christ "Success" is accomplishing the goals that "God" has set for "you".; [a.] Port Gibson, MS

TURNIPSEEDE, MATTHEW JAMES
[b.] July 22, 1973, East Chicago, IN; [p.] Jim Turnipseede, Diane Prettyman; [ed.] Currently in School; [occ.] Student; [oth. writ.] A personal collection of poetry.; [pers.] This morsel of success is dedicated to my sister Jennifer.; [a.] Dublin, OH

TURPIN, LATRICIA
[pen.] Lacey; [b.] February 2, 1960, Indianapolis, IN; [p.] Phyllis Riewer and Jon Turpin

TUSSING, CYNTHIA S.
[b.] January 12, 1959, Columbus, OH; [p.] Mary and Howard Baumann; [m.] Olan Tussing; [ch.] Nicole, Victor, Guy, and Justin; [ed.] South High, OSSC College, The Institute of Childrens Literature; [occ.] Homemaker and write in my spare time.; [memb.] Saint Leo Parish, Harmony Glee Club.; [pers.] Your never to old to learn, nor to young to teach. My writing comes from my heart and my dreams. I have been in spired by Helen Steiner Rico, Grace E. Easley, and my family.; [a.] Columbus, OH

TYSKA, JOAN C.
[b.] May 14, 1942, Norwalk Conn; [p.] Myrle and Elsie English; [m.] Dennis Tyska, December 31, 1983; [ch.] Susan and Cindy from previous marriage Sue, Sherry, John and Barbara Foster; [ed.] West Chester High School Pennyhall Jr. College - 1 year (both in Pennysylvania); [occ.] Head waitress Carving Board Restaurant, Calverton, NY; [oth. writ.] Many other personal poems that have never been published; [pers.] Writings of any kind is a key to unlocking the soul to communicating your love as a bond to spirituality between souls; [a.] Calverton, NY

WADE, JULIE ELIZABETH
[b.] July 17, 1979, Jamaica, West Indies; [p.] Heather and Lester Wade; [ed.] Student at Immaculate Conception High School for girls.; [occ.] Student; [memb.] Key Club, Junior Achievement, a counsellor in training at Moorlands Camps.; [hon.] Award of excellence in art, year: 1992, Award of excellence in Art, year: 1993-1994, Goo Award for Good Citizenship in School; [oth. writ.] Personal collection of stories, comics, and poems.; [pers.] A book full of thoughts and poems, is like a heart filled with life and love.; [a.] Jamaica, West Indies

WAGENS, ROBERT
[pen.] Bob; [b.] October 5, 1948, Hazel Green, WI; [ed.] 13 yrs; [occ.] Tire plant; [hon.] National Defense Service Medal, Vietnam Service Medal, Vietnam Campaign Medal, Army Commendation Medal

WAGONER, KELLY VAN P.
[b.] January 21, 1977, Ann Arbor; [p.] Tana and Dennis Van Wagoner; [ed.] High School Student, I will attend College in the fall of 1995.; [occ.] Student; [memb.] S.A.D.D., National Honor Society, Yearbook, Varsity Volleyball; [hon.] I've received awards in English, Government, History, French, and Various activities.; [oth. writ.] I've written a lot of other poems and a variety of short stories.; [pers.] Tomorrow may be another day, but today is an original.; [a.] Grass Lake, MI

WAHLSTROM, TAMITHA DAWN
[pen.] Tammy Guajardo; [b.] August 21, 1960, Levelland, TX; [p.] Mary Elizabeth Johnson Barsun, Stepfather Elliott Barsun; [ed.] El Paso Community College 1989 (AA Degree); [occ.] United States Army Chaplain Assistant; [hon.] 1 Army Service Ribbon, 2 Overseas Ribbons, 3 Army Good Conduct Ribbons, 2 NCO Professional Development Ribbons, 3 Army Commendation Medals, 1 Southwest Asia Service Medal, 1 National Defense Medal, 1 Saudi Kuwait Liberation Medal, 3 Campaign Service Stars; [oth. writ.] Children's Stories and Poems, faith, real winner, come with me, provide Hope, an angel on my shoulder.; [pers.] The most influential person of my life is my mother, she is my life model and best friend. She has given values that have guided my life: loyalty, generosity and love. Her belief in me, and her unconditional love has been my motivating force in life. I dedicate my literary works to her; [a.] San Antonio, TX

WAKAL, OLGA ZELEZ
[b.] February 25, 1923, Rochester, NY; [p.] Eva Murascko and Ivan Zelez; [m.] Joseph Wakal, June 8, 1946; [ch.] Russell Ivan, Eva Loretta, Wanda Louise; [ed.] Stroubenmuller High School; [occ.] Retired, formerly - Jowz Delicatessen.; [memb.] Sweet Adelines (retired), Service Guild (church), Director childrens choir (church), Choir (church); [pers.] "Creating" is the only thing man has over other species. Man can create food, clothing, shelter, destiny. In order to keep a balance, man then created religion.; [a.] Brooklyn, NY

WALDEN, SELENA
[pen.] Tilly Walden; [b.] August 22, 1968, Brooklyn, NY; [p.] Eloise Walden, Charles Williams; [ch.] Justin Shaguille, Walden-age 1; [ed.] High School - John Jay H.S. - Brooklyn Kingsborough C.C. - Brooklyn NY; [occ.] Active duty U.S. Air force since March, 1991; [pers.] Good, better, best, never let it rest, until good becomes better, and better becomes best.; [a.] Newport News, VA

WALKER, ARCHIE
[pen.] Uncle Bud; [b.] April 19, 1929, Memphis, TN; [p.] Wilson, Mary Walker; [m.] Bertha Walker, March 17, 1946; [ch.] Felicia, Archie Jr., Pat, Ella, Bonita; [ed.] High School Myrthe Hall High. Clarksdale Miss. U.S. Marines 3 yrs. 17 years at County Hospital Chicago, ECG, 13 years at Illinois Research; [occ.] Retired; [memb.] Writers Club at my church, poems and short stories. We number five persons.; [oth. writ.] 30 Books of poems, some good, some maybe not.; [pers.] I wish to pass on some of my work to good kids etc. I'd like to be on print.; [a.] Chicago, IL

WALKER, FLORENCE HARRIS
[b.] December 17, 1892, Harveyville, KS; [p.] Sarah (Thackrey) Harris, Samuel Murrell Harris (divorced); [ed.] B.S. in Home Ec. 1925, M.S. in Inst. Ec. 1929, Kansas State University; [occ.] Retired; [oth. writ.] 2 short articles in the Missouri Ruralist 194?, [many write-ups of club meetings - as a H.D.A. in Mo. 1939-1942]; [pers.] My father wrote "Rhymes" which were published in the home town proper. A sister won a prize for a poem.

As the youngest in the family, I copied my elders!; [a.] Manhattan, KS

WALKER, JOAN KATHLEEN
[b.] December 12, 1934, England; [p.] Gladys and Norman Young; [m.] Douglas Walker; [ch.] 6; [ed.] Technical College Maidstone - Kent. U.K.; [occ.] House Wife; [memb.] Australian Lace Guild; [oth. writ.] Poems, a few short stories never been published before; [pers.] Main Hobby - Bobbin Lace Making. Immigrated to Australia in 1970.

WALKER JR., WILLIAM CONWAY
[pen.] "Will"; [b.] April 19, 1955, Fortlee, VA; [p.] William (Bill) Walker Sr., Loretta Walker; [ed.] Matoaca High, J. Sargeant Reynolds Community Col. Gallandet University, Yorktown Business Inst. American Fraternity Church; [occ.] Disabled now, Former (last) IRS; [memb.] 700 Club (Virginia Beach VA), Life Study Fellowship American Fraternity, Horizon, Washington City for Hard of Hearing.; [hon.] Honoree in the poetry 1991-1992, Boys Scouts Achievement Awards (1968); [oth. writ.] Still writing book since fall 1991, Title of book is in seclusion, must find publisher. To direct this book into movie.; [pers.] Be good to nature, and nature can be good to you. To solve problem, you must seek truth that comes from within "Share it with me"; [a.] Washington, DC

WALKER, JULIE
[occ.] Transformational Counsellor, Writer, Artist; [pers.] I've always been inspired to create. Through my writing and art I am able to share and express the love, peace and joy I feel inside. It's my way of saying "Thank you".; [a.] Sault Ste Marie, Canada

WALLACE, NICHOLE
[b.] March 24, 1980, Augsburg, Germany; [p.] Bob Wallace and Victoria Wayman; [ed.] A freshman at Mt. View High School (Kingsley, Pennsylvania); [memb.] NJHS, Wrestling cheer leading, Band, Yearbook staff, Majorettes; [hon.] NJHS (National Junior Honor Society); [oth. writ.] Other poems, sections (articles) for the school yearbook; [pers.] When I write poems, I write about my own experiences and hope that others can relate to my feelings. I was influenced by my friends and family. Thank you for believing in me.; [a.] Nicholson, PA

WALLACH, BILL
[b.] January 18, 1929, Brooklyn, NY; [p.] Sidney Wallach, Estelle Wallach; [m.] Marilyn Wallach, January 13, 1963; [ch.] Tani Jayne, Seth Peter; [ed.] New Utrecht High, Brooklyn College; [occ.] Retired; [memb.] Noble Grand - ODD Fellows; [oth. writ.] Several unpublished poems ex: I Am Terrified As I Withdraw To Sleep... etc.; [pers.] In December 1979 I conquered a massive MI with cardiac arrest. Many setbacks effected longing to originate and declare my inner ideas by way of poetry and painting or through; [a.] West Palm Beach, FL

WALLS, MATT
[b.] April 25, 1960, Dallas, TX; [p.] Robert A. Walls Sr. and Vera Adams; [m.] Susan J. Walls, February 25, 1994; [ed.] B.S. in Geology - 1982 - Sul Ross State University; [memb.] Home and Apartment Builders Association, Sales and Marketing Council; [hon.] Regional Finalist in Extemporaneous Verbal Communications while member in Vocational Office Education. Numerous Production and Sales Awards in Home building.; [oth. writ.] Poems, Short Stories, and Novelettes.; [pers.] Inspirations come in all forms, the only mistakes we make are in not following those driving forces, no matter how foolish, or trite they may seem.

WALT, EILEEN
[b.] April 17, 1924, Calgary, Alberta, Canada; [p.] Sydney Jenkins, Helena Jenkins; [m.] (Divorced) August 8, 1946; [ch.] James, Lyann, Barbara and Lynda; [ed.] Grade 12, Western Canada High, Calgary Alberta School Canada.; [occ.] Retired Medical Secretary; [memb.] Beta Sigma Phi Sorority (Member at large), Golden Horizons (Senior's Group), Home Based Business (Arts and Crafts), "Studio Four" (Arts and Crafts), Pacific National Exhibition (Vancouver, B.C.), Graduate of Uniquely B.C. Trade Show Vancouver B.C.; [hon.] 1, 2, 3, Class Ribbons, many.; [oth. writ.] Many poetry writings and presentations at our local church.; [pers.] "Growing old can be fun if we choose to be POSITIVE!"; [a.] Oliver British Columbia, Canada

WARD, BRETT T.
[b.] October 7, 1968, Rome, Georgia; [ed.] B.A. Stephen F. Austin State Univ., Nacogdoches, TX; [occ.] Professional Photographer; [memb.] Sigma Chi Fraternity, Life Loyal Sig, Texas Professional Photographers Assoc., Southwestern Photographers Assoc., National Skeet Shooting Assoc., Life Member Stephen F. Austin State Univ. Alumni Assoc., Sigma Chi Fraternity Alumni Assoc. [San Antonio Chapter]; [pers.] Nothing Ventured, Nothing Gained.; [a.] San Antonio, TX

WARD, BRIAN DOUGLAS
[pen.] Brian Douglas Warb; [b.] January 26, 1953, Orangeville, Ontario, Canada; [p.] George Ward, Elva Ward; [m.] Tana Jewel Ward, August 27, 1983; [ch.] Bethany Rose, Katherine Eileen, Joshua William, Aaron David, Rebecca Jewel; [ed.] Orangeville District Secondary, George Brown College, Canadian Forces Air Traffic Control Training Unit; [occ.] Air Traffic Controller, 8 Wing, Trenton, Ontario, Canada; [oth. writ.] Poems published in hometown newspaper, numerous poems written as a young boy which were lost after relocation of our family.; [pers.] It is my hope to portray the awesome love and majesty of the 'Great Creator' in my literary works, a task far too demanding for pen or tongue!; [a.] Trenton Ontario, Canada

WARD, MICHAEL
[b.] April 30, 1933, County Leitrim, Ireland; [p.] Annie O'Rourke Ward, Michael Ward; [ed.] 8th grade Cornagow National School Co Leitrim Ireland, Ck-on-Shannon.; [occ.] Fifth Ave Night Security New York City; [oth. writ.] Musician and Singer entertains at City Institutions sings with choir group, 4 part harmony. Also with harmonic group, drama group, choir group, seasoned singers group 4 group.

WASHINGTON, DARRYL
[pen.] "Soda Boy Johnson"; [b.] June 27, 1965, Eudora, AR; [p.] Leola Washington; [m.] Mary Jones, May 27, 1995; [ch.] Domonique and Amanda; [ed.] High School Graduate U.S. Navy Honorable discharge 1983-1986; [occ.] Central Moloney Employee; [memb.] Buffalo Soldier's Club; [oth. writ.] Mirror image, springs summer, to be a kind, 80 Chevy, memories of momma Jehovah's child etc.; [pers.] We go through this world, searching for that certain success, that certain happiness, and among these are life, love, and the pursuit of blackness.; [a.] Pine Bluff, AR

WASHINGTON, MARCIA L.
[m.] Single parent; [ch.] Dovie and Kelvin; [memb.] As founder of Morning Time Ministries a Womens fellowship, Community involvement is a regular way of life.; [oth. writ.] Currently finishing a book of inspirational writings regarding the female experience.; [pers.] Marcia wishes to personally thank her mother, Dovie, Ann for encouraging her to follow her pen.; [a.] Ann Arbor, MI

WATERS, EVELYN R.
[b.] February 7, 1921, Cleveland, OH; [p.] Deceased; [m.] Harold (deceased), 1943; [ch.] 4 married, 10 grand, 2 great grand; [ed.] High school, business college, completed course with Long Ridge Writers Group; [occ.] Retired; [memb.] Florida Cooperative Extension Service; [hon.] Volunteer Service in Childrens Literacy; [oth. writ.] Just personal essays and unpublished short stories and poems.; [pers.] Can't be notebly prosperous? Be humbly greatful - be the best at whatever you are.; [a.] Orlando, FL

WATFORD, BETTYE V.
[pen.] Bettye Watford-Faison; [b.] January 16, 1947, Colerain, NC; [p.] Willie and Verlean Watford; [m.] Divorce; [ch.] Micah; [ed.] Erasmus Hall High, Audrey Cohon College, School of Human Services.; [occ.] Human Service Professional and Teacher at Carl Fenichel Community Services; [memb.] Greater Mt. Pleasant Baptist Church, Project Care, Director, Peoples United Group, (Multi-Cultural group) Theater for a Greater Peace; [hon.] Dean's List; [oth. writ.] Several articles published in office annual magazine.; [pers.] I aim to make the readers of my poems aware of life affecting situations with facts tinted with satire. Many great poets have influenced me but Langston Hugh stands out.; [a.] Brooklyn, NY

WATSON, JENNIFER
[b.] October 7, 1980, Clarksville, TN; [p.] Phillip Watson (father-deceased), Micky and Dianne Pope; [ed.] Currently attends the Martin Luther king, Jr. Magnet School for Arts and Science; [occ.] Student, softball player; [memb.] Civitan Softball, MLK, Jr. Softball Team, Honor Society; [hon.] President's Scholar award.

WATSON, LORIE A.
[b.] May 23, 1960, Sparta, TN; [p.] Tom Ward, Patti Gaston; [m.] Carey Watson, March 29, 1985; [ch.] Shawn, Joseph, Daniel, Russell; [ed.] White County High School; [occ.] Self-employed Trucking Company; [memb.] Maple Hill Church of Christ, Lebanon, TN; [oth. writ.] Several poems published in Church newsletter.; [pers.] I love showing my love for God in the words of my poems. The encouragement I get from my family and friends is my strength for my writing.; [a.] Lebanon, TN

WATTS, NASEEMA
[pen.] Luciene Azique; [b.] September 29, 1946, India; [p.] Rabia Patel; [ch.] Marcus and Jason; [ed.] Ilkeston Secondary Modern and Ilkeston College of Further Education.; [occ.] Secretary; [oth. writ.] Book Titled: "Meditation, Mysticism and The Mystery." Poems published in magazines and self-published an anthology of "Awakening, Beauty and Reality."; [pers.] "If one perceives God with a logical mind, one does not discover perception or understanding, but engaging the extraordinary sense and intuition, man is closer to God's reality and truth. It is a road I traversed to find God."; [a.] Leicester, England

WEAVER, ALONDA
[pen.] Alonda Weaver; [b.] March 25, 1980, Chicago, IL; [p.] Wendell and Frances Weaver; [ed.] Emmanuel Christian School (elementary) Lindbloom Technical Highschool; [occ.] student; [memb.] Saint James United Methodist Church; [a.] Chicago, IL

WEAVER, BARBARA
[pen.] Barbara Weaver; [b.] March 5, 1938, Vian, OK; [p.] W. Ward Douglas, Fay Douglas; [m.] Billy Douglas Weaver, March 21, 1974; [ch.] Joel Bryan Sherrill - 28 yrs. old his father deceased; [ed.] B.S. in Elementary Education; [occ.] Retired Teacher, Retired - May, 1991; [hon.] Distinguished teacher awards - 1966-1968 and 1980, 1966 and 1968 - Dalhart, TX, 1980 - Bristow, OK; [oth. writ.] I've written approximately 100 poems in "Honor Of" or dedicated to family members and many inspirational, spiritual poems. The one submitted is the first to be published by "Sparrow Grass Poetry Forum" and hopefully by your "National Library of Poetry" Writing is a wonderful outlet for me to express myself.; [a.] Bristow, OK

WEBB, CANDY
[b.] February 23, 1959, Pasadena, CA; [p.] Robert and Betty; [m.] My best friend, March 4; [ch.] Jacob, Nigel and Shayla; [ed.] La Puente High; [occ.] Waitress; [memb.] I attend Bella Vista Community Church; [hon.] I have been honored by the saving grace of the Lord God. Ephesians 2:8. He has awarded me with the gift of life and writing.; [oth. writ.] I'm blessed by God to write many other poems and songs to glorify Him. Matthew 5:16; [pers.] Thank you my Saviour Jesus Christ. Thanks to my wonderful husband and children. I love you. John 1:12,13; [a.] Cottonwood, CA

WEBB, EUGENIA
[pen.] Macie; [b.] June 3, 1978, Seneca, SC; [p.] Anna and Eugene Webb; [ed.] Ravenel Elementary, Seneca Middle School, Current Junior at Seneca High School; [memb.] Seneca High School, Volleyball (3 years), Basketball (4 years), Journalism Staff - Editorial Editor Student Government; [hon.] Top 10 outstanding students '93, '94, Basketball - all conference 1993, 1994, All - county '93, '94, Coach's award '93, Best defense '94; [oth. writ.] Several poems just to reflect my feelings, and many written for ceremonies, programs, and special occasions; [pers.] I write from my heart, personal experiences, and with special people in mind. Most of my writings are love related or deal with sorrow.; [a.] Seneca, SC

WEBB, GINA
[b.] January 27, 1968, Utica, NY; [p.] John Mehaffy, Kathryn Mehaffy; [m.] Gerald Webb, October 26, 1990; [ch.] Dog Zane Webb; [ed.] U.F.A. High School, U.S.C. Business College; [occ.] Legal Assistant; [hon.] Alumni Art Award, Sold a water color painting freshman year in high school; [oth. writ.] Personal poems and short stories for family and friends; [pers.] I enjoy creating poems and short stories from my own feelings and having others understand and visualize what I create.; [a.] Utica, NY

WEBB, MIKA
[pen.] Senabiya; [b.] November 16, 1974, Chicago, IL; [p.] Anita Webb; [ed.] Hyde Park Career Academy, Spelman College, Georgia State University; [occ.] Student at Georgia State University; [memb.] International Black Winters Association; [oth. writ.] Poems in several anthologies: Voices of Black Strength, River Crossings, Echoes from the Silence, Arcadia Poetry Anthology. Also YSB magazine and Spelman's College's Newspaper Spotlight; [pers.] I try to present experiences in such a way that people are in touch with the realities of the world, the love, the hate, the prejudice... the simple things like thoughts we take for granted daily.; [a.] Atlanta, GA

WEBER, JUNE
[b.] March 7, 1924 Detroit, MI; [ed.] Graduated from high school, then went to RBI where I took a Medical Secretary course; [occ.] US Navy (Waves) where I spent 2 wonderful yrs. working in Naval Hospital. When I finished the Navy took an x-ray course at Strong Memorial Hospital in Rochester, N.Y.; [memb.] Browncroft Community Church; [oth. writ.] Have written several poems but never submitted any for publication.; [pers.] I mostly write for enjoyment about friends and family. I loved Edgar Guest for this reason. As I'm now much older I enjoy writing about Spiritual things. I'm lucky I have 2 wonderful daughter and 6 lovely grand children. I was widowed 3 1/2 yrs. ago after a beautiful life of 45 yrs. with a wonderful Christian man.

WEBER, MELLISA
[pen.] Missy Weber; [b.] June 1, 1974, Bridgeton, NJ; [p.] Craig and Cindy Weber; [ed.] Cumberland Regional High School, Cumberland County College.; [occ.] Student; [oth. writ.] "Beauty" published in days of future's past, Vol. II.; [pers.] Believe in yourself and your poetry, and through the divine grace of God, you will succeed. Psalm 23; [a.] Bridgeton, NJ

WEDGE, JOHN K.
[pen.] JKW; [b.] November 22, 1963, Brockton, MA; [p.] Richard Wedge, Charlotte Wedge; [m.] Cecelia Wedge, July 11, 1987; [ch.] Danielle Kathleen; [ed.] Brockton High, Stonehill College continuing Education; [memb.] Sacred Heart Parish; [oth. writ.] Many unpublished poems and essays.; [pers.] Love yourself first or you cheat the world out of a friend.; [a.] Brockton, MA

WEISS, STYMEAN KARLEN
[pen.] Stymean Karlen; [b.] 20th Century, Philadelphia, PA; [m.] The writer, David Weiss, whose 11 novels have been published in the US, UK, and 25 countries.; [occ.] Full time Poet, Painter; [memb.] The World; [hon.] My personal papers, poems, portrait poems, other material relating to my work are in the Weiss-Karlen Special Collection of Temple University in Philadelphia.; [oth. writ.] Two books of my poetry, insights and observations were published by The Amber Beetle Press. Other poems are in poetry magazines such as The Yale Poetry Review, Accent, Interm, Voices, Westminster Review, Beloit Journal and the Los Angles Times.; [pers.] "Every other has another definition of poetry, but every poem has it's own" - Stymean Karlen; [a.] La Jolla, CA

WELBORN, BERTIE P.
[b.] February 9, 1905, Duson, LA; [p.] L. E. Patterson, Cora Moss Patterson; [m.] William B. Welborn Jr., Decease; [ch.] Barbara Lynn, Betty Janell (deceased), William Bryan (deceased); [ed.] Gueyden Hi, La. State Normal - 2 yrs., Cert. Degree at U.S.L., University of Southwestern La.; [occ.] Retired; [hon.] One book published, "Golden Streak" 1988. 1 poem to be published, "Our Seasons"; [oth. writ.] "The Eskimo Children." "The Mystery of the Missing Treasure", not published, but I am hoping they will be soon.; [pers.] I have a great love for children. It is reflected in every story I write.; [a.] Lafayette, LA

WELCH, BARBARA
[pen.] B. J. Hall; [b.] November 17, 1949; [m.] Basil Welch, October 29, 1977; [ch.] Marlon, Sharrelle, Nathaniel Welch; [ed.] St. Catherine's Academy, Cerritos Community College, Compton Community College, Cal. State Dominguez Hills; [occ.] Disabled Registered Nurse; [memb.] Our Lady of Victory Catholic Church, South California MS Society; [hon.] Honors Award of Academic Excellence; [oth. writ.] Excerpts two poems in M.S. Newsletter. Songs on the wind; [pers.] Writing motivates me to clarify my feelings and harness the power of my spirit to meet the challenges of living with a chronic, debilitating disease.; [a.] Compton, CA

WELCH, RAYMOND LEE
[pen.] Rockin Raymond Prod.; [b.] July 31, 1964, Hollywood; [p.] Robert and Linda Welch; [ed.] High School Grad/Auto painting in college, a self teaching natural in all fields of arts and industry; [occ.] Parking equipment service tech.; [oth. writ.] Sunset and Paper Boats, Longtime, Father Time, I Wanna Believe, Come On and Take Some, Living in a Dream, Unlucky Man, and many many other songs and poems; [pers.] To a very special girl (Pearl) who showed me that true vision, comes not from the eyes, but the heart, mind, soul. I love you! A world full of visions, some true, some clouded, some mine.; [a.] Huntington Beach, CA

WELLMAN, LOIS
[b.] October 7, 1926, Stanley, WI; [p.] Chris and Roszella Christensen; [m.] Stanley Wellman, June 16, 1951; [ch.] 4, 1 stepson and 1 deceased; [ed.] High School grad.; [occ.] Retired; [memb.] Ouk Savior Lutheran Church.; [oth. writ.] High School when in a senior; [pers.] Went 8 years to a one room school. Raised with 10 brothers and sisters on a farm. A life of many blessing, but of many hardships. Our youngest daughter killed by drunk driver at 18 years age in 1982.; [a.] Freeport, IL

WELLMEELA, MS. DONA SOMAWATHIE
[pen.] Dona Samson; [b.] September 18, 1953, Malaysia; [p.] Don David Samson Esq. (Deceased); [m.] Michael Miller Zappone, getting married in August, in Sydney (1995)!; [ch.] Leonard G. W. Black (12) yrs. old.; [ed.] General Cert Education, convent all girls school (Malaysia), Library Technician (Tafe) - Australia. Self taught to write; [occ.] Freelance writer. Work 1 day a week in an art gallery; [memb.] Australian Library Association, Women Writers Network, Associate Member of Jessie Street Womens Library, New South Wales Poets Union.; [hon.] Art prize - Best Handmade Craft Award, Best Political Essay, First short-story when I was in high school won $100 (in Malaysia).; [oth. writ.] Several prose/poems published in Sydney Morning Herald, Local Paper, Library Journal. Poem and short-story in Malaysia Post. Recent poem in an Anthology "CENTRELINES". Poem and Book Review in Multicultural Journal.; [pers.] To reach out to the general public with my poems, prose and play. There is no barrier in writing! Would like to write a best-selling play for 1995! I was greatly influenced by Hemingway, T.S. Eliot, J. Scott Fitzgerald; [a.] Sydney, New South Wales

WELLS, COLLETTE
[pen.] Collette; [p.] Deceased; [m.] Divorced (Deceased); [ch.] Mike Wells, Marlena and Rebecca Wells; [ed.] High school, F.B.I., Finger-Print Tech., Modeling and Fashion Design, Photography; [occ.] Modeling, Director and Owner "Collette High Fashion Modeling Agency"; [hon.] A trophy high achievement award - 5 awards for my photography, a trophy for "all over team of models",

world modeling competing.; [oth. writ.] Poetry; [pers.] Strive for your dreams - my son was with President Ford, Carter, Regan and Bush on Air Force once. Both daughter is models, actress, my oldest - artist too.; [a.] Salt Lake City, UT

WELLS, KENT
[b.] March 9, 1952, Tellamook, OR; [p.] Ted and Herdis Wells; [ed.] Tillamook H.S. Willamette University; [occ.] Disabled; [memb.] American Federation of Radio and television artists; [oth. writ.] Autobiographical short stories, Poem published in the New York times.; [pers.] My poetry reflects wilderness themes from my childhood on the North Coast of Oregon as well as present day perspectives on disability themes.; [a.] New York City, NY

WEMPE, MICK
[b.] March 16, 1951, Spalding, NE; [p.] George and Evangeline McManaman; [m.] Richard Wempe, May 5, 1984; [ch.] Jacob; [occ.] Computer Specialist; [oth. writ.] I have a small business out of my home so I write short poems for my newsletter and I write product poems. But I have never submitted any for publication; [a.] Omaha, NE

WENDA, HENRY
[b.] April 25, 1923, Saint Joseph, MO; [p.] Harry Wenda, Lillian Wenda; [m.] Marie Wenda, September 8, 1946; [ch.] Mary Ann, Kathleen and William David; [ed.] Benton High, Rio Hondo Community College, California State University at Fullerton; [occ.] Retired; [memb.] National Honor Society Degree: Bachelor in Arts in English; [oth. writ.] Published in American Poetry Anthology 1989; [pers.] I receive no joy from elitist poetry, if a poem must be explained, then the poet has failed the readers.; [a.] Incline Village, NV

WENOF, JACK
[b.] Philadelphia, NJ; [m.] Florence Wenof; [ch.] Michael; [occ.] Throughout his career, Wenof wore many hats. He has serve as Montgomery County School Dental Examiner, dental consultant for the Department of Public Assistance, chief of the dental staff at the Valley Forge Heart Hospital (now Medical Center), chief of the dental staff at Dufur (now Horsham) Mental Hospital, acting head of the dental staff at Montgomery Hospital, now emeritus, and has also served as a lecturer and inventor.; [memb.] In his community, Wenof has served as president of the Kiwanis Club, president of Brith Sholom, and chairman of the board of the Salvation Army; currently, he is president of B'nai Brith. He is a past member of the Pennsylvania Dental Society, the Montgomery-Bucks Dental Society, the Eastern Dental Society, and the Academy of General Dentistry. Member of the American Dental Association and Freemasonry.; [oth. writ.] Dr. Wenof maintains an interest in poetry, music, golf, tennis, and bridge.; [a.] Prussia, PA

WEST, MR. SID
[pen.] Mrs. E. M. Priestley; [b.] October 3, 1923, Lafana; [ed.] Marine Engineering and Navigator School in Feensburg.; [occ.] Engineer, Pensioner; [memb.] The Poetry Society in London, and: The International Society of Poets. Owing Mills, MD 21117; [hon.] Editors Choice Award, presented by The National Library of Poetry Award.; [oth. writ.] Yes, book of late poetry "Triumph". And daily, diary pages collection.; [pers.] Very disturbed been and am very sorry for mid-December Final. I do return my book, as sample book "Triumph" to stay for publicity.; [a.] Bedford, England

WEUM, CHRISTINA M.
[pen.] Tina Weum; [b.] March 21, 1914, Norman County; [p.] Christ and Mathilda Bly; [m.] Tilford A. Weum, November 20, 1938; [ch.] Charles, JoAnn, David, Maryle, Le Roy; [ed.] I had to quit school in 7th grade. On account of the great depression. Then sickness hit me so I never went back.; [occ.] Home maker and taking care of a very sick husband.; [memb.] Zion Luthern Church, National Wild Life Federation - Human Society.; [hon.] Senior Coalition, Poet of Merit, The American Poetry Association. Volunteering at the Senior Center.; [oth. writ.] Poems - "Down A Country Road", "Fall", "Mothers Love" in the American Poetry of Anthology.; [pers.] I try to show my love to all people. Race makes no difference. Also of all God's little creatures, and nature.; [a.] International Falls, MN

WHALEN JR., MARTIN F.
[b.] March 24, 1936, Philadelphia, PA; [p.] Martin and Petronella Whalen; [m.] Divorced; [ch.] Martin III, Margaret, Thomas, Maria, Donna, Patrice, Michael; [ed.] West Philadelphia Catholic High; [occ.] Inspector of Communications NRPC (AMTRAK) 39 years service with Railroad Industry.; [memb.] Catholic War Veterans Railroad Holy Name Soc.; [oth. writ.] Letters to the editor local newspaper on Social Issues. Unpublished poetry works on children and family and childrens stories; [pers.] My writing has been influenced by my children and family the simplicity of children and their ways has created the basis of my work.

WHETZEL, ANITA
[b.] January 15, 1970, Grant County, Petersburg; [p.] James Dolly, Mary L. Dolly; [m.] Kenneth J. Whetzel, February 28, 1992; [ch.] James Joseph, Cassey Renea, Kenneth Micheal; [ed.] Keyser High School, Keyser Middle School, Burlington Elementary School; [occ.] Housewife; [oth. writ.] Several poems I keep in my folder at home.; [a.] Burlington, WV

WHIPPLE, JAMES P.
[b.] November 9, 1942, Wash., D.C.; [p.] Mary and Charles Whipple; [ed.] G.E.D., years of college, University of Baltimore; [occ.] Retired, had my own Private Detective Business; [memb.] Chairman, Discovery, also have done a lot of acting; [hon.] Dean's List; [oth. writ.] Several poems published in various magazines, newspaper and church paper; [pers.] A lot of my work comes from my past. I have done a lot of traveling. I have seen life close up and I try to write about the people, places and feelings I have experienced.; [a.] Potomac, MD

WHITE, CARL WILLIAM
[pen.] Cully White; [b.] September 21, 1925, Rockford, IL; [p.] John and Theresa Schmidt White; [m.] Margaret Ann Kiernan White, January 14, 1949; [ch.] Kiernan, John, Theresa, James, Andrew, Matthew; [ed.] Attended Los Angeles City College and Butler University.; [occ.] Accountant (Retired); [memb.] Mensa; [hon.] My only honor was to be wedded to Margaret for 46 years. The only awards, the six great children she presented me.; [oth. writ.] 1. Poetic Puns, 2. Questions and No Answers Session; [pers.] Love and let love; [a.] Indianapolis, IN

WHITE, JANICE K.
[b.] June 23, 1948, Ionia, MI; [p.] Jack and Nadeane Font; [m.] John H. Dellinger, December 30, 1994; [ch.] April Star and Elizabeth Jean; [ed.] Iona High School; [occ.] Nail Technician; [oth. writ.] Published poems in newspaper during high school. Won 2nd place in contest in Green Valley. The contest was for Valentine day. The name of the poem was "For You"; [pers.] I have a great love of poetry. I especially love E.E. Cummings and Walt Whitman. I have been writing poetry since the age of 8 or 9.; [a.] Sahuarita, AZ

WHITE, JO ANN
[b.] July 6, 1940, Baton Rouge, LA; [p.] Louise Decuir White, Wilbert White Sr.; [ed.] McKinley High, Southern University of Baton Rouge, University of Maryland.; [occ.] Science Teacher, Math, Science and Technology Consultant; [memb.] Louisiana Science Teachers Association, Challenger Education Foundation Center, National Science Teachers Association, Benign Blepharospasm Foundation, Louisiana Environmental Educators Association, Founder and President of Sci-Tech Projects, Inc., of Louisiana; [hon.] St. Jude Hospital Bike-A-thon, American Red Cross, Outstanding Teacher 1989, Sacred Heart School of Baton Rouge, Nasa Space Ambassador 1989 - Stennis Space Center, Bay Saint Louis, Miss., Nasa-Newest Program.; [oth. writ.] Articles - Newspapers on Science, Math and Technology, articles for magazine: Science and Children and "Lift off for Education - Landing for the Future" Newspaper Article; [pers.] It's wonderful to be a role model for Today's Youth who are meeting the challenges of tomorrow. I was lucky to have parents, sisters and brothers supportive of my work in Technology. This is why I am so proud of my heritage and loving, caring family.; [a.] Baton Rouge, LA

WHITE, KYLA YVETTE
[b.] May 13, 1984, Joliet, IL; [p.] Kennetth and Yvette White; [ed.] 5th grade; [occ.] Student at Union School Joliet, Illinois; [memb.] "Joliet Sonic Track Club", qualified for 1994 Junior Olympics National meet in 400 meter relay at the University of Florida. Kyla's a member of the Dynamos Tumbling Team of Joliet, Ill.; [hon.] A and B honor student since 1st grade at Union School; [oth. writ.] Poem published in Anthology of poetry Inc. 1994 edition; [pers.] I like to express my feelings when I write. When I grow up, I would like to be a writer.; [a.] Joliet, IL

WHITEHEAD, SUSANN
[b.] October 8, 1976, Fort Stewart, GA; [p.] Col. Butch Whitehead and Susan Whitehead; [ed.] Graduated from Tampa Catholic High School and I'm new a freshman at University of West Florida, majoring in Marine Biology; [occ.] College Student at University of West Florida; [oth. writ.] In 1992 had a poem published in "Anthology of Poetry by Young Americans," in 1994 I had a poem published in my school magazine and a poem put on my school's ecology club shirts. And in 1994 I had two poems published by Illiad press in "Mussings."; [pers.] I write from my heart and how I feel. I strive to teach people about how important the Earth is and how hard life is also. Without feelings and imagination, I believe poetry would have never existed on Earth; [a.] Pensacola, FL

WHITFIELD, MARCIA
[b.] November 28, 1953, Chicago Heights, IL; [p.] Margaret and James Schober; [m.] Robert L. Whitfield, February 4, 1991; [ch.] Margaret, Robert Jr., Tania; [ed.] High School Graduate; [memb.] Our Lady of Mercy Church; [pers.] I want to write poems about our world; [a.] Chicago, IL

WHITLEDGE, ROSE MARIE
[b.] January 6, 1960, Springfield, KY; [p.] James and Geneva Osborne; [m.] Michael Allan Whitledge, Au-

gust 27, 1977; [ch.] Fredrick Allan, Jason, Joey; [ed.] Henderson County High; [occ.] Housewife; [pers.] Many of my poems are written from personal experiences such as the death of my son. I have written poems for church, family and friends. I enjoy patting my feelings into poetry.; [a.] Henderson, KY

WHITLEY, LUCILLE H.
[pen.] Ceil Whitley; [b.] January 24, Nacogdoches, TX; [p.] Robert Higgins and Lida Higgins; [m.] Deceased; [occ.] Retired; [memb.] Literary Guild, Denton Creative Writing, Denton, TX. In her earlier years she maintains membership in the American Society for Physical Research, the Texas Society for Psychical Research, Understanding Inc., Spiritual Frontiers Fellowship, and the International Platform Association.; [hon.] First place - 1994 Springfest Denton, TX; [oth. writ.] Poetry, Short Stories, Character Sketches - "The Bird Woman of Los Angeles" took first place in 1994 Springfest, Denton, TX; [a.] Denton, TX

WHITLEY, VERA NOVA
[pen.] Vera Nova; [b.] Europe; [ed.] Traditional Art, Education in Europe (Moscow, Amsterdam, Roma etc.); [occ.] Artist, Neuralist; [memb.] ASCAP, 1994 (As a musician); [oth. writ.] "Subconscious realism" published by Sunstorm five Arts. 1992 Lots of lyrics for my songs, and other poetry and prose. I am writing a book An Artistic Notes on humans and the Universe" (almost finished); [pers.] I believe that our artistic and aesthetic abilities are given to us for much greater reason than to simply create art. Creativity is life itself.; [a.] Valley Village, CA

WHITLOCK, DANIEL U.
[pen.] D. Rosa; [b.] March 12, 1956, Saint Louis, MO; [p.] Joyce J. Whitlock; [ed.] Comptone, Southwest Jr. College, Comptone Sr. High School Horace Mann Jr. High, Colosseum St. Elementary School.; [occ.] Truck Driver; [pers.] I want to be closer to "Christ" and my only best friend in the whole world "M.R." thanks to her my world has new meaning.; [a.] Loma Linda, CA

WHITTEN, TIFFANY A.
[b.] July 25, 1979, San Bernardino, CA; [p.] Sheri Houghton and William Whitten; [ed.] Currently a freshman at Lemoore High School, Lemoore, CA; [occ.] High School Student; [hon.] "A" and "B" Honor Roll in 8th Grade.; [oth. writ.] Poems published in school papers, and have entered writing contest at school.; [pers.] I have been thankful for my gift, my wonderful family and my hopes are for people to enjoy my writings. I have been greatly influenced by my wonderful 8th grade teacher Mrs. Karleen Good who always told me to follow my dreams. Thank you to everyone who made this dream possible.; [a.] Nas Lemoore, CA

WHITTINGTON, KEITH ANTHONY
[b.] January 9, 1958, Black Mountain, NC; [p.] George Winslow and Minnie Stepp Whittington; [m.] Emily Marie Elizabeth Whittington, May 28, 1994; [ed.] Charles D. Owen High School Benea College, Bevea, KY, U.N.C.-Asheville Arts, Literary, Humanities and Philosophy Dept's. Asheville-Buncombe Technical; [occ.] Park Ranger with City of Asheville Police Dept.; [memb.] Park Law Enforcement Assoc. Nature Conservancy, World Wildlife Foundation, National Parks and Conservation Assoc. Airbourn Law Enforcement Assoc.; [hon.] Numerous "at-a-boys" and even more "Thank-you's."; [oth. writ.] Many personal yet unpublished poems dating back to early 1970's and 1980's.; [pers.] Even I am prejudice: The two things that erk me most are ignorance and hatred....in this world no one should go uneducated and every one should love everybody. Even risible light with which we see is made of all colors in the spectrum.; [a.] Black Mountain, NC

WICK, JOHN
[b.] August 25, 1969, Nanaimo, British Columbia, Canada; [p.] Joan Panich, Larry Panich; [ed.] Bev Facey CHS and Salisbury CHS.; [occ.] Yard Manager Garden Central Soil Supplies Ltd.; [pers.] Live your life for the day for if tomorrow fades away the true victory of your stay lies in the game of life you play; [a.] Sherwood Park Alberta, Canada

WICKI, CLAUDIA
[pen.] Claudia Fenton, Claudia Wicki; [b.] March 8, 1951, Sacramento, CA; [p.] James A. and Bernadette J. Fenton; [m.] Rudi Wicki, February 25, 1994; [ed.] University of Arizona, Tucson BFA, University of Southern Calif. Certif.; [occ.] Marketing Consultant; [memb.] SAG - Screen Actor's Guild, AEA - Actor's Equity Assoc., AFTRA - Am. Fed. of TV and Radio Artists, The American Club of Zurich, The Prof. Women's Group, Intl. Business Network.; [hon.] Phi Kappa Phi, Univ. Honors Frat.; [oth. writ.] Writer and Editor of the American Club of Zurich's "club news" 6 annual editions. Published articles in the Los Angeles Business Journal, past contributor to the National Library of Poetry.; [pers.] With advanced telecommunications at our fingertips, fewer people are writing. Correspondence by letter is rapidly diminishing. We must each make an effort to get back to and value the beauty and endurance of the written word; [a.] Zurich, Switzerland

WICKI, CLAUDIA
[pen.] Claudia Fenton/Claudia Wicki; [b.] March 8, 1951, Sacramento, CA; [p.] James A. and Bernadette J. Fenton; [m.] Rudi Wicki, February 25, 1994; [ed.] University of Arizona, Tucson BFA University of Southern Calif.; [occ.] Marketing Consultant; [memb.] Screen Actor's Guild, Actor's Equity Assoc., Am. Fed. of TV and Radio Artists, The American Club of Zurich, The Prof. Women's Group, Intl. Business Network.; [hon.] Phi Kappa Phi, Univ. Honors Frat.; [oth. writ.] Writer and Editor of the American Club of Zurich's "club news" 6 annual editions. Published articles in the Los Angeles Business Journal, past contributor to the National Library of Poetry.; [pers.] With advanced telecommunications at our fingertips, fewer people are writing. Correspondence by letter is rapidly diminishing. We must each make an effort to get back to and value the beauty and endurance of the written work.; [a.] Zurich, Switzerland

WIENCKOWSKI, BRUCE D.
[b.] September 29, 1966, Philadelphia, PA; [p.] Richard and Patricia Wienckowski (Adopted); [m.] Diane L. Riggins (Fiance), October 7, 1995; [ed.] Drexel University Phila., PA, B.S. in Computer Science; [occ.] Programmer/Analyst at SmithKline Beecham Clinical Labs.; [oth. writ.] Sci Fi/Fantasy - Torminor's Quest (unpublished), working on "The Gypsy Rose" another Science Fiction/Fantasy novel also without a publisher.; [pers.] I don't know where this came from. I may have heard it or developed it from my experiences but it works for me... "Everything happens for a reason and you have to remember that it all seems to work out for the better."; [a.] Harleysville, PA

WIITALA, FAWN MARIE
[pen.] Fawn Wiitala; [b.] October 17, 1981, Gillette, WY; [p.] Phillis Lanctot, (mother) Chris Lanctot (Step father), Chet Wiitala (Step mother), (Father) Debbie Wiitala; [ed.] Currently attending Jeffers High School 7th grade; [occ.] Student; [hon.] Young Authors Award in Elementary School in WYO for the Poem "Up there" Numerous Schoolastic Awards; [oth. writ.] "Up There", "Grandparents"; [pers.] Fawn enjoys writing poems, is currently competing in "Teen Magazine" beauty contest. Sings in our church's programs. Makes a lot of various arts and crafts loves to make people laugh; [a.] Painesdale, MI

WILEY, BURT
[b.] September 24, 1923, Whitesboro, TX; [p.] Clarence and Sue Wiley; [m.] Bonnie Willey, 1950; [ch.] Steve Wiley; [ed.] B.S. Texas Weslean College "Institute of Childrens Literature" New Bedford, Conn. (graduate); [occ.] Retired; [memb.] Eagles, American Legion; [oth. writ.] Many childrens stores - none as yet published; [pers.] My favorite poet is Samuel Taylor Coolenage. Am influenced by Robert Browning - especially his Browsing through used book stores; [a.] Oxnard, CA

WILHELM, VALERIE
[pen.] Rie (Crie); [occ.] A host on this planet; [hon.] Being the mother of Tonia and daughter of Mary Ann; [pers.] When I find my purpose, as myself and know I am a piece of something glorious and beautiful I know peace...and exhilaration this is what I choose; [a.] Boulder Creek, CA

WILKINS, ANTHONY
[b.] September 20, 1963, San Francisco, CA; [p.] Jesse and Annie Mae Stribling (Adoptive Parents), Zelma and Solomon Wilkins; [ed.] Dunbar Voc./Truman College (Chgo.), coursework included marketing, journalism English Literature.; [occ.] Telemarketing Consultant; [hon.] Nominated for The Editors Preference Award and The Dickinson Award both for poetry.; [oth. writ.] Life In General (currently in pre-publication): A Gay Man's Diary also writing Poets Heart, a book of 100 love poems.; [pers.] I've always been inspired to write about the things in life that matter to me, children, love friendships, etc. I guess I just have a "Poets Heart".; [a.] San Francisco, CA

WILKINSON, MRS. ANNE
[b.] February 16, 1930, Manchester, CA; [p.] Thomas, Annie Brown; [m.] Clifford, May 9, 1953; [ch.] Debra, Carl, Paul (three children); [ed.] Elementary; [occ.] Hosewife; [oth. writ.] one story, 3 poems published by new fiction 4 Hythegate Werrington Peterborough. Anchor Books 1-2 Wainman Rd. Woodston Peterborough; [pers.] I have two beautiful granddaughters Kelly Louise and Lucy Jade, aged 10 and 5. My ambition to save as many animals as possible; [a.] Britain

WILLARD, DENNIS R.
[pen.] Dennis R. Willard; [b.] March 4, 1975, Portland, OR; [p.] Jack and Debbie Willard; [m.] Misty Salina Willard, July 7, 1994; [ed.] High School - Scappose High School. I also took several course the Navy has to offer.; [occ.] US Navy - Sea bees; [oth. writ.] I have several other writings, that I have yet to fly and [pers.] I enjoy writing and I would like to fly and do it for a living.; [a.] Oxnard, CA

WILLIAMS, CAROL GOFF
[b.] September 6, 1942, Franklin Co., IL; [p.] Mr. and Mrs. Kenneth Goff; [m.] Donald R. Williams, October 21, 1960; [ch.] Christopher and Roxann; [ed.] Benton Consolidated High School; [occ.] 12 yrs as Computer

Oper/Bookkeeper for Olympia School Dist. #16; [memb.] Minier Assembly of God Church.; [pers.] I have written each of my 3 grandchildren a poem and framed it for them. My inspiration for writing comes from personal memories and I try to reflect God's love in my writing.; [a.] Atlanta, IL

WILLIAMS, DAKARAI MICHAEL
[b.] January 10, 1979, East Baton Rouge Parish; [p.] Barbara A. Berry and Michael Williams; [ed.] 10th Grade; [memb.] Boy Scout troop 426, Junior Choir at Elm Grove Baptist Church, Capitol High School Track; [hon.] 3rd place in poetry contest in the 8th grace, 1st place in the seventh annual Martin Luther King Jr. Commemorative day celebration, 1st place from Elm Grove Baptist Church, Poem published in "Today's Great Poems."; [oth. writ.] I wrote a short story named "The Room", I've had two poems published in books, and I keep a journal full of my poems. Such as "Strong Race, Poor Race."; [pers.] When I'm writing, its usually because I have something on my mind that I wish to expressing way that others can understand and relate to it. I almost always tie God into whatever I'm writing about. I thank and love God, my best friend which is my mother and my eight grace english teacher.; [a.] Baton Rouge, LA

WILLIAMS, DEBORAH A. HARRIS
[b.] December 15, 1955, Newport News, VA; [p.] Mr. and Mrs. Augusta and MaeBelle Harris; [ch.] Henry C. Crosby and Destiny R. Williams; [ed.] Denbigh High, Kee Business College, GSH Real Estate, Insurance System; [occ.] Self-employed (Harris-Williams Tax Prep, Newport News, Va; [oth. writ.] Professional composer (writing on songs of America Album), song name: "Feeling Secure", "I Thank You" (in a finalist contest) to be choosing the winner this summer of "95".; [pers.] God is the way! Have love in your heart and peace in your soul, faith in yourself, to reach your goal. (Writing will come natural if you let yourself feel what you are writing about).; [a.] Newport News, VA

WILLIAMS, ELEANOR L.
[b.] May 13, 1919, Astoria, OR; [p.] Ora Woods and Hugh Long; [m.] Richard F. Williams (divorced), June 7, 1948; [ch.] John Richard and Henry Fairfax; [ed.] Tipton Grammer Sch., Portiville High and Junior College, Fresno State University; [occ.] Former Occupation: Elementary Teacher, Beardsley Sch., Bakersfield, CA., Curric. Materials Technician, Clovis School Dist., Retired; [oth. writ.] Curriculumn materials for C.U.S.D. included primary level illustrated reading suppliments. At present, I write ideals as they come to me.; [pers.] I am striving for the truth. I want to understand the real reason for my beliefs — where did they come from? Who first nurtured them?, Who do they serve? I know there is more to God than what we can glean from the Bible and other religious holy books. I want a glimpse of it.; [a.] Clovis, CA

WILLIAMS, GRACE
[b.] January 27, 1981, New Port Richey, FL; [p.] Janet and Mitchell Williams; [ed.] River Ridge Middle High School; [hon.] A, B Honor Roll, Basketball Awards, OM awards; [oth. writ.] Other poems that have not been discovered; [pers.] I try to base my poems on everyday surroundings, I've been greatly influenced by my mother who also writes poems, Janet Williams.; [a.] New Port Richey, FL

WILLIAMS, JACQUELINE
[pen.] Jack Diamond; [b.] July 02, 1963, Georgia; [p.] Charlis and Catherine Williams; [m.] Divorced; [ch.] Conchata, Michael Mayfield; [ed.] Audrey Cohen College Bachelor's Degree (Human Services); [occ.] Para/activity specialist; [hon.] Dean's List English Award; [oth. writ.] 50 or more written poems (unpublished at present); [pers.] I strive to reflect the goodness of hope, struggles of life and spiritual awareness.; [a.] Jamaica, NY

WILLIAMS, LACE MARIE
[b.] June 7, 1972, Coeur D'Alene, ID; [p.] Dennis K. Williams, Bonnie M. Williams; [ed.] North Idaho College Lutheran Bible Institute of Seattle; [occ.] Student; [hon.] Phi Theta Kappa Dean's List; [oth. writ.] Several other poems and quotes.; [pers.] If I have not fully let go of my yearning for the warmth of summer, how can I find the beauty in the cold of winter?; [a.] Issaquah, WA

WILLIAMS, RUBY DARLENE
[pen.] Ruby Williams; [b.] April 28, 1955, Madison, FL; [p.] Wilmer and Carlene Bell; [m.] Single; [ch.] Phillip Nicholas Williams; [ed.] Vero Beach Senior High, Vero Beach Fla.; [oth. writ.] Several poems published in a local newspaper, also several publications in books of poetry.; [pers.] I enjoy writing poetry for others to read. I write what I feel in my heart.; [a.] Winter Beach, FL

WILLIAMS SR., IRA L.
[b.] August 30, 1953, Jackson, MO; [p.] Ira Cooper Williams and Glena Rice; [m.] Shellee Williams, February 6, 1985; [ch.] Taylor Williams, Ira Williams Jr.; [ed.] Bartlett High School, Memphis, Tenn. Houston Community College (Ass. Aviation Science); [occ.] Disabled December 23, 1992 construction accident, now writing full time; [memb.] Y.M.C.A. coaching staff, neighborhood bicycle fixer-upper. (For all kids!); [hon.] Honorable discharge (Army 1973) T-ball coaches' honor.; [oth. writ.] Holding? Two manuscripts-poetry, fiction thriller. Published poetry, books magazines, and political letters to the editor, S.A. Express News.; [pers.] I must write to stay sane. So many words, so few captured, makes me wonder if I'll ever catch the one which will make me whole. To write, then read it, ease back content, that is my goal.; [a.] San Antonio, TX

WILLIS, DONALD D.
[b.] April 9, 1942, Jefferson Co., AL; [p.] Henry Willis, Lola Willis; [m.] Mary Willis, June 26, 1965; [ch.] Michelle, Renee; [ed.] Minor High School, University of Alabama, Birmingham, Bevill State Community College; [occ.] Coal Miner, Jim Water Resources #3 Mine, Adger, Al.; [memb.] United Mine Workers of America; [oth. writ.] Several poems and song lyrics (unpublished); [pers.] I would love to be known as a great poet, but more as a great song writer.; [a.] Adamsville, AL

WILSON, CHRISTOPHER M.
[b.] May 5, 1977, Fullerton, CA; [p.] Dorothy M. Wilson, Mary Silverman; [ed.] First Baptist Academy High School Dallas, Texas; [occ.] Student, First Baptist Academy; [memb.] National Honors Society, International Thespians Society, Fellowship of Christian Athletes, Teen Advisors, Aims for Success, Academic Decathalon, Cornerstone Yearbook Staff; [hon.] Youth Intern, Best Poem Writer, Public Service Award, Historian, Best Article and Spread in Scholastic Journalism Workship, Spiritual Leadership; [oth. writ.] Various Poems published in anthologies by the Amherst Society, Iliad Press, Arcadia Poetry Press, and Sparrow grass Poetry Forum, Inc.; [pers.] Poetry paints a picture capable of being painted on the canvas of the mind. Poetry must be understood by the mind, felt by the heart, and pondered upon so that it can be truly appreciated and treasured.; [a.] Dallas, TX

WILSON, DAVID H.
[pen.] D. Harlan Wilson; [b.] September 3, 1971, Grand Rapids, MI; [p.] Harlan Wilson, Beth Wilson; [ed.] Wittenberg University; [occ.] International Salesman, Harmony Int. Corp./Part-time model/Part-time English Graduate Student; [pers.] I enjoy writing about the macabre and fantastical rather than mere reality. Ironically, I am a practicing christian. My major influences include Anthony Burgess, Shakespeare, and Medieval literature.; [a.] Grand Rapids, MI

WILSON, FRANK
[b.] November 1, 1947, Inverness, Scotland; [p.] Frank - Marjorie Wilson; [ed.] Grade 12 - many business associated courses; [occ.] Counselor in A and D Recovery.; [memb.] International Lions. Past president of various sports clubs, Hockey, Snowmobile, Motorcycles, Billiards; [hon.] Highest award in liouson. Various sportsman awards.; [oth. writ.] Many poems - none published - my first offering to the public.; [pers.] "Be free"; [a.] Kamloops, British Columbia, Canada

WILSON, KATE
[b.] September 11, 1978, Doylestown, PA; [p.] Susan Wilson; [ed.] Archbishop Wood High School Class of '96; [memb.] Hugh O'Brien Youth Foundation, The Singer's Network All Catholic Chorus; [hon.] Jacques Normand Award; [a.] Hatboro, PA

WILSON, RALPH GABY
[b.] Kansas City, MO; [p.] Helen and Clifford Wilson; [m.] Susan Vance Wilson, June 4, 1966; [ed.] Bachelor of Science, University of Kansas; [occ.] Screenwriter - Film Producer; [memb.] Writers Guild of America; [hon.] Publisher's Auxillary's, Editor of the year for investigative reporting, numerous Hermes and Cleo awards for advertising, Writing and Art Direction.; [oth. writ.] Feature Films, TV movies, TV sit-coms, Newspaper and Magazine Features and News stories, Radio mysteries.; [a.] Hollywood, CA

WILSON, REV. FELICIA J. WALKER
[b.] November 25, 1933, Saint Angustine, FL; [p.] Mrs. Martha Milligan, Mr. Lorenzo Walker; [m.] Mr Herbert Wilson, September 25, 1950; [ch.] David Anthony, Michael Jonathan, Wendell Harlan; [ed.] Wadlieigh High School, College of New Rochelle, New York Theological Seminary; [occ.] Dept. of Labor - Employment Service Youth Minister - Christ Church U.C.C.; [memb.] Christ Church Bronx, NY, N.A.A.C.P.; [hon.] Dean's List, Citation from the City Council, City of New York; [pers.] In life one may be a thorn of anger or a rose of love, I have chosen to be a rose!; [a.] Bronx, NY

WILSON, SHELLY
[pen.] Shelly Harris Wilson; [b.] May 4, 1963, Newark, OH; [p.] Byron and Linda Harris; [m.] Barry Wilson, September 1, 1985; [ch.] Ashley Louise and Brooke Erica; [ed.] Lakewood High, North Light Art School; [occ.] Singer, Homemaker; [hon.] Certificate of achievement in "The Fine Arts of painting and drawing."; [oth. writ.] Several short stories and poems unpublished.; [pers.] I love the company of good friends, my family and good music. And giving a little of yourself is sure to help others.; [a.] Newark, OH

WILSON, WILLIAM J.
[b.] November 24, 1933, Sherrad, IL; [p.] John L. and Anna S. Wilson; [m.] Patricia, March 19, 1972; [ch.] Mark W., Steven V., Timothy T.; [ed.] Allman High School; [occ.] Carpenter; [pers.] A tribute to my parents and family.; [a.] Longwood, FL

WINDLEY, BRENDA BOUYER
[b.] February 9, 1963, Brooklyn, NY; [p.] Cora and AB Bouyer; [m.] Leander Windley, September 14, 1991; [ch.] Expecting in June (1st Child); [ed.] Bachelors Degree from Baruch College (English Major) Eli Whitney V.H.S.; [occ.] Underwriter for Insurance Company; [hon.] Dean's List; [oth. writ.] Poetry Anthology (Baruch College) Songs, Poems, Short Stories, Plays, etc.; [pers.] I use events in my own life as a basis for my writing. It is written from the heart.; [a.] Brooklyn, NY

WING, LLOYD E.
[b.] July 27, 1920, Owosso, MI; [p.] Robert and Hattie Wing; [m.] Dorothy Jean, February 27, 1947; [ch.] Susan, James, Russell; [ed.] K-12, 2 yrs Business School; [occ.] Retired June 1, 1986; [memb.] Trinity United Methodist Church, American Legion 3 1/2 years in U.S. Navy, WW II; [hon.] 60th year membership same church; [oth. writ.] Many poems, mostly for personal of family enjoyment. One published in "Dark side of the moon."; [pers.] "If you don't want to know what I believe or think - don't ask me!"; [a.] Owosso, MI

WINSLOW, CHARLES L.
[b.] February 3, 1938, North Carolina; [p.] Mr. and Mrs. Charles W. Winslow; [m.] Gloria Winslow; [ch.] Charles L. Winslow II, Lorenzo R. Winslow, Charles W. Winslow II, Gloria Royane Winslow; [ed.] Graduate from North Carolina Art State University Greenshurst NY Mafm Business Ed. 1962; [occ.] Labor Service Representative NY State Dept of Labor, Hicksville, NY; [memb.] Long Island Black Artist Assoc.

WIREMAN, TAMARA LYN HOLBROOK
[b.] April 8, 1960, Portsmouth, OH; [p.] James D. Holbrook and Guyneth Wells Holbrook; [m.] Douglas Eugene Wireman, December 26, 1977; [ch.] Tabatha, Matthew, Whitney, James; [ed.] Greenup County High School Greenup Area Vocational School; [occ.] Housewife/Mother, Writer; [memb.] New Bethlehem, United Methodist Church, Shriners for cripple children sponsor for United Methodist Children's Home, Lexington, Kentucky.; [hon.] FBLA President, Art Award, Honors, Class Leadership Award; [oth. writ.] Several poems published in Ash land Daily Independent and the Indepent Plus.; [pers.] I try to write good moral stories and poetry that even a child can understand, giving encouragement to both young and old to keep striving for a better future.; [a.] South Shore, KY

WISE, SISTER AUDREY M.
[p.] Matthew and Vera Wise; [ch.] Noel, Robyn, Desmond, Torrian; [ed.] Booker High, York College; [occ.] C.E.O. of To God be the Glory "New Beginning Inspirational Writing;" [memb.] Women Struggling Yet Striving Ahead, Women Strike for Peace; [hon.] From The National Library of Poetry, News Day in Education; [oth. writ.] New Beginning Inspirational Writings, 3 books in work, and plays in work; [pers.] Reach for the stars and never look back for yesterday's promise and today's dreams can be tomorrow's reality. [a.] Hempstead, NY.

WITTENMYER, HILLYARD ALLEN
[pen.] Hillyard Wittenmyer, HAW.; [b.] January 26, 1908, Carmi, IL; [p.] Albert and Mary Wittenmyer; [m.] Fern, November 30, 1930; [ch.] Gerald, Keith, Robert; [ed.] High School, Business College; [occ.] Retired; [memb.] Virginia Avenue Baptist Church, Bartlesville, OK., Quivira Road, Baptist Church, Mission, KS., Woodlands Parkway Baptist Church, The Woodlands, TX., Nall Ave, Baptist Church, Mission, KS; [hon.] Eight grade, OK. State certificate of excellence. High school, recognition and recitation of poem. Recognition, National Library of Poetry. Fiftieth anniversary, High school graduation, Bartlesville, OK, recognition and recitation of poem.; [oth. writ.] High School poet Laureate Poems for special occasions.; [pers.] I must have received what talent I have in this area, from my father who was church leader, (super tendentin those days) of a Methodist church. I remember he wrote a poem, "The Teriff Man From Texas", which was published in an IL paper.; [a.] The Woodlands, TX

WOLF, ANDREA
[b.] September 14, 1981, London, Ontario, Canada; [p.] Alexander and Elizabeth Wolf; [ed.] West Elgin Senior Elementary School-Grade 8; [occ.] Student, Grade 8; [memb.] Secretary and Vice President of Student Council; [hon.] Medals or prizes for: Speech contest, Piano Festivals, Spelling Bees, Soccer, Poster Contests, Track and Field, Bookmark Contest. Highest Academic Average.; [oth. writ.] Unpublished stories and poems for personal satisfaction and class assignments. Weekly school activities column in two local newspapers.; [a.] West Lorne, ON

WOOD, RENAE
[pen.] Renae Wood; [b.] February 12, Lansing, MI; [p.] Bill nd Shirley Wood; [ed.] So far, Childersburg High School; [occ.] Yet assistant; [hon.] Honor Roll Beta Club; [oth. writ.] I write poems and stories that have not been recognized, except for this exciting chance.; [pers.] I would like to thank my parents for their support. Music and poetry opens the door to your inner soul of thoughts.; [a.] Sylacauga, AL

WOODS, LEE-ANNE
[b.] April 1, 1976, Peace River, Alberta, Canada; [p.] Larry and Kathy Woods; [ed.] Manning Paul Rowe High; [pers.] My younger brother, John inspired me to write this special poem and therefore I would like to dedicate it to him. This poem is fictional.; [a.] Dixonville Alberta, Canada

WORKMAN, DEANNE
[b.] October 27, 1974, Cheyenne, WY; [p.] Jimmy and Carla Workman; [ed.] Communication Arts Major at Montana State University - Billings; [occ.] Student and part-time waitress; [hon.] Several athletic awards, Casey Guisti Award, Miner Award, Heisey Award, and Track Scholarship to Jamestown College North Dakota; [oth. writ.] Several unpublished writings; [pers.] Many people do not understand how deep feelings affect them and others around them. In my poetry I try to express these feelings in a way that others can understand. "Peace and Wildflowers" [a.] Billings, MT

WORSLEY, DONNA F.
[pen.] Baby Girl; [b.] December 12, 1969, Jamaica Queens; [p.] Eddie Lee and Brenda Elizabeth Worsley; [ed.] Hempstead High School, Nassau Community College; [occ.] Customer Service Rep Long Island Savings Bank; [oth. writ.] Several poems published in the essence magazine.; [pers.] I strive to make other people stop and search themselves.; [a.] Hempstead, NY

WRIGHT, LASCELLE
[pen.] Larchibald Wright; [b.] February 28, 1958, Jamaica, WI; [p.] Amutal Wright, Samuel Wright; [ed.] New York city Technical College, Major: Construction Technology; [oth. writ.] Several poems and song lyrics unpublished.; [pers.] Do what you can today, since tomorrow is not promised.; [a.] Brooklyn, NY

WRIGHT, MICHELLE
[pen.] Michelle; [b.] February 20, 1983, Altanta, GA; [p.] Michael and LaShaun Wright; [ed.] I'm now attending McNair Middle School; [occ.] I'm a honor roll student (6th grade) at McNair Middle School; [memb.] I'm a member of New Life Christian Center Church; [hon.] D.A.R.E. Certificate of Achievement, Amateur Athletic Union Award, Scholastic Award Seat Belt Safety Award, Certificate of Award, write now certificate, Reading Award, Certificate of Baptism, Attendance Award, Academic Award; [oth. writ.] My yummy poem, poem about God and a poems of Mother and Father day poem. Write now I working on a book called "How My Best Friend Turned Into My Worst Eneny."; [pers.] I thank God for this opportunity to be a semi-finalist and I thank my mom and my dad for encouraging me to write.; [a.] San Antonio, TX

WRIGHT, ORALEE
[b.] October 28, 1942, Palo Alto, CA; [p.] Phon Harley Jeffers, Roberta Perez; [ed.] Castlemont High-Oakland, CA, Columbia School of Broadcasting - Radio Announcing - Commercials for T.V. and Radio.; [occ.] Secretary - Bookkeeper at Canarsie Glass and Lock; [memb.] Library Ministry at Day Break Assembly of God.; [pers.] We are stars in a universe of reflections - let us shine beyond our imagination; [a.] Brooklyn, NY

WRIGHT, VANESSA THORBURN
[b.] October 23, 1977, Middletown, NY; [p.] David Wright, Linda Wright; [ed.] Pittsford Sutherland High School; [occ.] Student; [memb.] Knight-lites vocal group, model United Nations, School Community Partnership Council; [hon.] AP Scholar with Honor, National Merit Commended Student, Sylvan Leadership Scholar - PSHS, finalist' Notre Dame Club of Rochester Junior of the year, Red Cross "Star Attraction" award for community service, Outstanding Artiest Rayeh charity auction. Who's Who Among American High School Students.; [oth. writ.] The Magic Mirror, children's book, several poems, short stories, essays; [pers.] "Adventure is not in the guidebook, beauty is not on the map: Seek, and ye shall find."; [a.] Rochester, NY

WYE, WILLIAM L.
[b.] April 16, 1926, New York; [p.] Kay Bridgeford (Mother); [m.] Ruth (Deceased); [ch.] Robert, John, Scynitha; [ed.] Ged, 1 1/2 College; [occ.] Retired; [oth. writ.] Not yet finish; [pers.] Life is short, so live it up and enjoy every moment you can. Do the things you always wanted to do, then when you are age. You can say I did it God bless all; [a.] San Jacinto, CA

WYMAN, ZON
[pen.] Zon; [b.] August 6, 1942, San Diego, CA; [p.] Roy Wyman, Margaret Wyman; [m.] Maria Wyman, 1965; [ch.] Anastasia Lyons; [ed.] Franklin High; [occ.] Marine Carpenter; [oth. writ.] Children book astrology, astronomy, Tarot cards special book of memories to my granddaughter Sarah. Book of poetry.; [pers.] I wrote

my first poem at age 9. Still have it. Poetry is something that is hard to teach. Good poets like good musicians are born who observed there environment and nature. I want to thank my daughter Anastasia and granddaughter Sarah for there love and inspiration.

YACOBI, ORAN EPHRAIN
[pen.] Ori Yacobi; [b.] November 2, 1975, Buffalo, NY; [p.] Dr. Avraham and Diana Yacobi; [ed.] Clarkstown North High School currently a sophomore at Ramapo College; [occ.] Student and reading tutor at Ramapo College; [memb.] Volunteer for a Shelter for Battered Women and their Children - fall 93'; [hon.] Deans List Fall 93' and 94'; [oth. writ.] This is my first publication; [pers.] Writing is an expression of my thoughts and opinions and a reflection on society, life as I see it. I wrote this poem on my 19th birthday.; [a.] New City, NY

YAMASAKI, REGAN H. T.
[b.] March 22, 1976, Honolulu, HI; [p.] Harvey T. and Carol N. Yamasaki; [ed.] Iolani School (Prep) Honolulu, Hawaii; [occ.] Student at Claremont McKenna College Claremont, California; [memb.] National Geographic Society Claremont McKenna Symphony Orchestra (1st violin); [hon.] Headmasters' List (Iolani School) National Latin Honor Society Iolani School Concert Orchestra (first violin, student of 8 years) Numerous international first place competitions, including peformances at Sydney Opera House and Carnegie Hall-NYC.; [pers.] Everyone should have the pleasure of reading works of author, Robert James Waller.; [a.] Honolulu, HI

YASAY, SHERRY L.
[b.] January 6, 1981, Chandler, AZ; [p.] Vince and Winnie Yasay; [ed.] Currently in 8th Grade; [memb.] Student Council, Arizona Fighting Arts Federation Assistant Martial Arts Instructor, Cheer Leader Garden Lakes Elementary; [hon.] Honor Roll Garden Lakes Elementary, 1st Place Teens Fighting United Fighting Arts Federation (UFAF) Karate Tournament; [pers.] I have lots of dreams to fulfill and being a poet is one of them.; [a.] Avondale, AZ

YASPARRO, ROSEMARY MUNTZ
[b.] October 18, Cynthiana, KY; [p.] Florence and Dean Muntz; [m.] Joseph Yasparro, October 4, 1969; [ed.] Buena Vista High School and Georgetown College; [occ.] Retired; [hon.] Dean's List; [oth. writ.] Many other poems; [pers.] I was influenced by a Great Southern Poetess, Jeanette Shelley Heflin. Although she is no longer with us I had the honor of knowing her, she never became famous but her wonderful verses still sing to my heart.; [a.] Lynbrook, NY

YERRO, TEODULFO T.
[b.] September 16, 1913, Numancia, Aklan, Philippines; [p.] Prudencio Yerro - Antonina Taluyo; [m.] Serina Dorado Dadivas, November 29, 1935; [ch.] Teodulfo Jr.-LLB, Jose Manuel-BSA, BSC, Luvisminda-BSC, Vicenta, Emily-Fashion Designing, Florence-BSE, Josephine-BSE, Claire-Med. Tech., Lynn-BSN, Faith-BSC, and Gladys-Hope MD; [ed.] P.N.S. Grad., B.S.E. and M.A. Minus Thesis; [occ.] Retired; [memb.] International Society of Poets - Lifetime Member, Phil. Pub. School Tea. Association - Lifetime Member, Aklan Pub. Sch. Teachers Association - Lifetime Member; [hon.] Received a Plaque as Outstanding Aklanon in Arts (Poetry) - Philippines, Received Trophies as Golden Poet of the Year for seven consecutive years from 1986 to 1992 from the World of Poetry of California, Received 14 Certificates of Merit Award, Hon. Mention from the World of Poetry, Received 2 Plaques as International Poet of Merit from the National Library of Poetry, Maryland, Received 2 Editor's Choice Certificates from the National Library of Poetry, Made Honorary Member of the Advisory Panel of the International Society of Poets, Included in Who's Who in Poetry, Volumes II, III, and IV, Received a Certificate as Outstanding School Administrator, Aklan, Philippines.; [oth. writ.] 6 short stories for children, 2 articles, and a few poems both in English and Pilipino were published in Teacher's Professional Magazines, in the Philippines. Ran a column, "As I see It" in the weekly paper Aklan Reporter, in the Philippines that lasted for 2 years. "If Eyes, Then..." a poem published in Far Eastern Literary Journal, a college organ. This poem was also included in an anthology which was included in an anthology published in the Philippines before WW II. 5 poems in 5 books published by Quill Books of Texas. 7 poems are included in 7 anthologies that were published by the World of Poetry. 5 Poems are included in 5 anthologies of the International Library of Poetry of Maryland. 2 poems are in 2 anthologies of the Sparrow grass Poetry Forum, Inc. of WV.; [pers.] The sageful saying "If I have Not Shared, I Have Not Lived", seems to prod me every day to aspire to be healthy and live longer in order to continue to give meaning to this lovely saying. If life is prone to give a helping hand even in a most humble way, it's like sowing seeds hoping that those falling on fertile grounds may blossom and bear seeds that may also disperse kindness giving joy to mankind.; [a.] North Hollywood, CA

YILLA, AHMED K.
[b.] November 30, 1980, Brooklyn, NY; [p.] Aboul and Betty Yilla; [ed.] Canarsie High School 9th Grade; [occ.] Student; [memb.] Peter Weltbrook Foundation in Fencing, Canarsie High School Track Team; [hon.] Social Studies Awards in school academics; [pers.] The meaning of my poem is for people to understand how life is and try to change it for positive things.; [a.] Brooklyn, NY

YOUNG, BILLIE JO
[b.] November 24, 1976, Lewisburg, PA; [p.] William K. Young, Maxine M. Young; [a.] Watsontown, PA

YOUNG, GEORGE A.
[pen.] G. Allen; [b.] May 8, 1929, Chesterton, IN; [p.] Val Dair Young, Jenny Florence Young; [m.] Hannelore Margaret Martel Young, December 27, 1957; [ed.] Chesterton High School, Purdue University, School of Humanities; [occ.] Retired Advertising Rep. have worn several other hats; [memb.] Navy, Noval Reserve, Purdue Alumni, Assn., Church of God; [hon.] B.S. with Distinction, 1967; [oth. writ.] Several unpublished monographs and poems, private journals; [pers.] I seek for the larger truth which under lies mundane reality. I love the poetic discipline of the sonnet, and also blank verse. I usually write in prose, but on occasion, it wants to soar.; [a.] Valparaiso, IN

YOUNG, JOSEPH
[b.] March 30, 1968, San Luis Obispo; [p.] Dr. and Mrs. Joseph Young Chlitornia; [ed.] Pirad - San Luis Obispo High School, Pirad Musicians Institute Hollywood California, attends Golden West College, has attented Long Beach State, Coesta College; [occ.] Guitar Music Teacher, Medical Assistant and art store employee. Professional Musician; [memb.] Classic Car Association (Restoration and Social Membership), 3 Professional Rock Bands.; [hon.] High School and Junior College Art Awards San Luis Community Art - Honorable Mention. Junior Olympics (local) President Fitness Award. Perfect Attendance High School.; [oth. writ.] Song lyrics for and with punk many rock songs. Publicity work for 3 rock bands. Creative calling cards.; [pers.] Paco Remo (Drum Co. Owner) Remo Drums spoke at my graduation from music school. He said, this "Hold on to your dreams, and get a small job." This is what I do now.; [a.] San Luis Obispo, CA

YOUNG, MAE
[pen.] Fran Jasper; [b.] July 16, 1949, Houston, TX; [p.] Lou and Mac Jasper; [m.] Claudell Young; [ch.] Monica Young; [ed.] Phillis Wheatley Hi, Texas Southern Univ., University of Houston - Central, Prairie View A and M Univ.; [occ.] Elem. Counselor, Virgil "Gus" Grissom Elem. School Houston, Tx.; [memb.] Xi Chapter, Eta Phi Beta Sorority, Mental Health Association, NEA/TSTA/HEA, Houston Counseling Association, YWCA. 1st St. Mark Baptist Church Mission Society.; [hon.] "Shad Queen" (Shad Club #2 Houston), Honor Society -TSU/UH/PV, Employee of Month (1990 and 1991), School Bus Program Award, Civic Worker Award, 1st St Mark Bapt. Church Choir Award. Fashion Show Sponsor Awards (Jackson MD, School 1984-1987). Fashion Model Awards. Athletic Queen 2nd Runner-Up (TSU) AIDs Food Drive Award.; [oth. writ.] Poems "Be Kool - Stay In School", "Fashion A Way To Go", articles for school newspaper.; [pers.] I have always endeavored to convey a positive message to youth and young adults in my writing. I am a lover and ardent reader of poetry!; [a.] Houston, TX

YOUNG, SHAKIMBRA A.
[b.] February 8, 1980, Mobile; [p.] Kelly and Priscilla Young; [ed.] I attend Theodore High School as a freshman in honors classes.; [occ.] Going to school; [memb.] A Girl's group called "Unity". Junior Choir of Mt. Ararat (president of), foreign language club; [hon.] Several honor roll awards and citizenship awards; [oth. writ.] Several other poems, short stories and plays.; [pers.] As a teenager growing up in the 90's, I've had a lot of good friends that have been there for me but when I found myself alone, I've always had my poetry, the point is, kids, there is always another alternative to violence. The key; [a.] Theodore, AL

YOUNG, SHAUN A.
[pen.] Sebastian J. Beadle; [b.] February 22, 1977, Tracy, CA; [p.] Robert A. Young, Tori Lynn Dexter; [ed.] High School Graduation in June '95; [occ.] Student; [memb.] International Thesbian Society Locust Valley Jesters; [hon.] Vocal Soloist at Carnegie Hall, Vocal Soloist at Universal Studios, Florida; [oth. writ.] The Undying Brotherhood, The Successor, Circle of Macabre, Thrill Seeking Tony, several poems and short stories published in school literary magazine entitled Perspective.; [pers.] Love and hate often inspire me to write intense literary works. If you tap into your strongest emotions, a masterpiece will always emerge. Thanks to my "families" and my best friend for their love and encouragement.; [a.] Locust Valley, NY

YOUNGER, JANICE K.
[pen.] Janice Kaye; [b.] August 15, 1949, Tyler, TX; [p.] Lorene Younger, Cletus Younger, Father (deceased)

ZAREMBA, JASON
[pen.] Jaysunn; [b.] June 9, 1977, Hammond, IN; [p.] Anthony and Karen Zaremba; [ed.] High School Junior Wheeler High School Valparaiso, IN 46383; [occ.] Stu-

dent; [memb.] Bear eat beat (editorial Editor); [pers.] Just be who you want to be. Don't care what other think about you.; [a.] Valparaiso, IN

ZAWISLAK, CAROL KEENAN
[b.] August 21, 1959, Pennsylvania; [p.] Carl and Kathryn Keenan; [m.] Edward Zawislak, Jr.; [ed.] Graduated from Keystone Jr College, completed other credited Art, English and Legal Courses; [occ.] Graphic Designer at color my world signs, a company my husband and I own and operate in Hemline, Pennsylvania; [hon.] Cum Luade with a Associates Degree in Fine Art

ZELLNER, WILLA F.
[ch.] David Zellner and Susan Stewart; [oth. writ.] In loving memory of my husband William A. Zellner; [a.] Independence, MO

ZEUTZIUS, ANDREW JAMES
[b.] November 7, 1969, Green Bay, WI; [p.] Betty Hoffmen, Paul Hoffmen; [ed.] Green Bay East High, Colorado, Institute of Art, and Life; [occ.] Poet, Artist; [oth. writ.] I have a few poems published in a college newspaper, there titles are "Freakshow" and "I Recal".; [pers.] I am a simple men whose only wish. Is through the power of words that I may enlighten or open a few minds. There is so much in this world we take for granted and words is one of them. Remember "its the little things that get you in the end."; [a.] Green Bay, WI

ZIMMERMAN, KRISTIN D.
[b.] February 26, 1982, Evanston, IL; [p.] Alan and Barbara Zimmerman; [ed.] 7th Grade at Daniel Boone Elementary; [occ.] Student; [memb.] Assistant Editor on a school newspaper; [hon.] None outside of school awards; [oth. writ.] Poems and short stories; [pers.] I wrote this poem "why" because of all the violence in the world; [a.] Chicago, IL

ZIMMERMAN, MALIA M.
[b.] September 6, 1968, Hawaii; [p.] Suzanne and Dennis McLaughlin; [m.] Tom Zimmerman, August 15, 1992; [ch.] Michael David Kekoa Zimmerman; [ed.] Maryknoll Schools, Hon, Hawaii BA, Chaminade University of Honolulu Minors in Business and Drama major - Broad Cast Communications; [occ.] Director of Development (Furdraising, marketing) for Maryknoll Schools; [oth. writ.] Poems published in local papers and in "The Space Between".; [pers.] The reality of life is excitement to be alive, curiosity to see all, and drive to be all. Don't let anyone take that away from you.; [a.] Honolulu, HI

ZIZZO, DIANE JEAN
[b.] January 2, 1955, Brooklyn; [p.] Jean Brown and Louis Lista; [m.] Philip J. Zizzo, March 19, 1977; [ch.] Joseph age 14, Michael age 11; [ed.] Grover Cleveland H.S.; [occ.] Receptionist/Chemical Co.; [memb.] PTA, Parents Music Assoc.; [oth. writ.] Personalized poems for special occasions.; [pers.] In everything around you, and everything you see, is poetry waiting to be written.; [a.] Levittown, NY

ZWIKSTRA, SHAWN
[b.] January 22, 1969, Edmonton, Alberta, Canada; [ed.] Paul Kane High. Future plans in a Vetrinary or Literary Field.; [oth. writ.] Various poems of a wide variety.; [pers.] Although my poem "to Kurt" was one of my quickest written, it is also the one most heart felt by me. I would welcome correspondence from anyone who feels and understands the emotions I had while writing it and feels the same way.; [a.] Edmonton Alberta, Canada

Index of Poets

Index

A

B

E

I

J

N

X

Y

Z